# HORSES

## IN TRAINING 2015

125th YEAR OF PUBLICATION

Raceform

# INDEX TO GENERAL CONTENTS




**Editor** — Richard Lowther; Raceform Ltd., 27 Kingfisher Court, Hambridge Road, Newbury, RG14 5SJ
Fax: 01635 578101 E-mail: richard.lowther@racingpost.com

**Assistant Editor** — Simon Turner

**Production Editor** — Adrian Gowling; Bloodstock Services, Weatherbys

**Production Assistants** — Kerry D'Elia, Chris Hill, Alan Mosley, Jenni Graham and Chris Bennett

**Typesetting** — Maggie Elvie; Printing Services, Weatherbys, Sanders Road, Wellingborough, NN8 4BX.

**Orders** — Raceform Ltd., Sanders Road, Wellingborough, Northants NN8 4BX.
Tel: 01933 304858
www.racingpost.com/shop
E-mail: Shop@racingpost.com

**Advertisements** — Julian Brown; Raceform Ltd., 27 Kingfisher Court, Hambridge Road, Newbury, RG14 5SJ
Tel: 08444 879810 E-mail: julian.brown@racingpost.com

**ISBN** — 978-1-909471-86-3

Printed and bound by CPI GROUP (UK) Ltd, Croydon, CR0 4YY

# INDEX TO ADVERTISERS

# 2015

# RACING FIXTURES AND SALE DATES

(SUBJECT TO ALTERATION)

Flat fixtures are in **Black Type**; Jump in Light Type; Irish in *Italic;*
*asterisk (☆) indicates an evening or Twilight meeting;*
*† indicates an All Weather meeting. Sale dates are at foot of fixtures*

# MARCH

| Sun | Mon | Tues | Wed | Thur | Fri | Sat |
|---|---|---|---|---|---|---|
| **1**<br>Huntingdon<br>*Navan*<br>Sedgefield | **2**<br>Fakenham<br>Southwell<br>**Wolverhampton†** | **3**<br>Exeter<br>Newcastle<br>**Southwell†** | **4**<br>Catterick Bridge<br>*Downpatrick*<br>Fontwell Park<br>**Kempton Park†☆**<br>**Lingfield Park†**<br>Fasig-Tipton Sale | **5**<br>Carlisle<br>**Chelmsford City†☆**<br>*Clonmel*<br>**Southwell†**<br>Wincanton | **6**<br>Ayr<br>*Dundalk†☆*<br>Leicester<br>Sandown Park<br>**Wolverhampton†☆** | **7**<br>Ayr<br>Chepstow<br>*Gowran Park*<br>Sandown Park<br>**Wolverhampton†** |
| **8**<br>Market Rasen<br>*Naas*<br>Warwick | **9**<br>Plumpton<br>Stratford-on-Avon<br>Taunton | **10**<br>Cheltenham<br>Sedgefield<br>**Southwell†**<br>**Wolverhampton†☆** | **11**<br>Cheltenham<br>Huntingdon<br>**Kempton Park†☆**<br>**Southwell†** | **12**<br>**Chelmsford City†☆**<br>Cheltenham<br>Hexham<br>Towcester<br>Cheltenham Sale | **13**<br>Cheltenham<br>*Dundalk†☆*<br>Fakenham<br>**Lingfield Park†**<br>**Wolverhampton†☆** | **14**<br>Kempton Park<br>*Limerick*<br>**Lingfield Park†**<br>Newcastle<br>Uttoxeter<br>**Wolverhampton†☆** |
| **15**<br>Carlisle<br>Ffos Las<br>*Limerick*<br>*Navan* | **16**<br>**Chelmsford City†**<br>Southwell<br>Taunton | **17**<br>*Down Royal*<br>Exeter<br>**Southwell†**<br>Wetherby<br>*Wexford* | **18**<br>**Chelmsford City†**<br>Haydock Park<br>**Kempton Park†☆**<br>Warwick | **19**<br>**Chelmsford City†☆**<br>Chepstow<br>Ludlow<br>*Thurles*<br>**Wolverhampton†** | **20**<br>*Dundalk†☆*<br>**Lingfield Park†**<br>Newbury<br>Sedgefield<br>**Wolverhampton†☆** | **21**<br>Bangor-on-Dee<br>Fontwell Park<br>*Gowran Park*<br>Kelso<br>Newbury<br>Stratford-on-Avon |
| **22**<br>*Downpatrick*<br>Market Rasen<br>Wincanton | **23**<br>Taunton<br>Towcester<br>**Wolverhampton†** | **24**<br>Hexham<br>Southwell<br>**Wolverhampton†** | **25**<br>**Kempton Park†☆**<br>**Lingfield Park†**<br>Newton Abbot<br>**Southwell†** | **26**<br>**Chelmsford City†☆**<br>*Cork*<br>Ffos Las<br>Newbury<br>**Wolverhampton†** | **27**<br>*Dundalk†☆*<br>**Lingfield Park†**<br>Newcastle<br>Wetherby<br>**Wolverhampton†☆** | **28**<br>**Chelmsford City†**<br>**Doncaster**<br>**Kempton Park†**<br>*Navan*<br>Stratford-on-Avon<br>Uttoxeter |
| **29**<br>Ascot<br>*Curragh*<br>**Doncaster**<br>*Limerick* | **30**<br>Chepstow<br>Kempton Park<br>Warwick | **31**<br>Exeter<br>Huntingdon<br>**Southwell†**<br>Fasig-Tipton Sale | | | | |

# APRIL

| Sun | Mon | Tues | Wed | Thur | Fri | Sat |
|---|---|---|---|---|---|---|
| | | | **1**<br>**Chelmsford City†**<br>*Dundalk†☆*<br>**Kempton Park†☆**<br>Towcester<br>Wincanton<br>Ascot Sale | **2**<br>*Clonmel☆*<br>Ludlow<br>Taunton<br>**Wolverhampton†** | **3**<br>**Lingfield Park†**<br>**Musselburgh** | **4**<br>Carlisle<br>*Cork*<br>Haydock Park<br>**Kempton Park†**<br>Newton Abbot |
| **5**<br>*Cork*<br>*Fairyhouse*<br>**Musselburgh**<br>Plumpton<br>Sedgefield | **6**<br>Chepstow<br>*Cork*<br>*Fairyhouse*<br>Fakenham<br>Huntingdon<br>Market Rasen<br>Plumpton<br>**Redcar**<br>**Wolverhampton†** | **7**<br>**Chelmsford City†**<br>*Fairyhouse*<br>**Lingfield Park†**<br>**Pontefract** | **8**<br>**Catterick Bridge**<br>**Kempton Park†☆**<br>**Lingfield Park†**<br>**Nottingham** | **9**<br>Aintree<br>**Chelmsford City†☆**<br>**Southwell†**<br>Taunton<br>*Tipperary☆* | **10**<br>Aintree<br>Fontwell Park<br>**Leicester**<br>*Wexford☆*<br>**Wolverhampton†☆** | **11**<br>Aintree<br>Chepstow<br>*Gowran Park*<br>**Lingfield Park†**<br>**Newcastle**<br>**Wolverhampton†☆** |
| **12**<br>Ffos Las<br>*Leopardstown*<br>Market Rasen<br>*Tramore* | **13**<br>Kelso<br>**Redcar**<br>*Tramore☆*<br>**Windsor** | **14**<br>Carlisle<br>Exeter<br>**Southwell†**<br>Ascot Sale | **15**<br>**Beverley**<br>Cheltenham<br>**Kempton Park†☆**<br>*Leopardstown☆*<br>*Limerick*<br>**Newmarket**<br>Tattersalls Sale | **16**<br>**Chelmsford City†☆**<br>Cheltenham<br>*Limerick*<br>**Newmarket**<br>**Ripon**<br>Tattersalls Sale | **17**<br>Ayr<br>**Bath☆**<br>*Dundalk†☆*<br>Fontwell Park<br>**Newbury**<br>Southwell☆ | **18**<br>Ayr<br>Bangor-on-Dee<br>*Navan*<br>**Newbury**<br>**Nottingham☆**<br>**Thirsk**<br>**Wolverhampton†☆** |
| **19**<br>*Curragh*<br>Stratford-on-Avon<br>Wincanton | **20**<br>*Cork☆*<br>Hexham<br>Kempton Park<br>Newton Abbot☆<br>**Pontefract**<br>**Windsor☆** | **21**<br>**Brighton☆**<br>Exeter<br>**Kempton Park†**<br>Ludlow<br>**Wolverhampton†☆**<br>Doncaster Sale | **22**<br>**Catterick Bridge**<br>**Epsom Downs**<br>*Fairyhouse☆*<br>Ffos Las☆<br>Perth<br>Taunton☆<br>Doncaster Sale | **23**<br>**Bath☆**<br>**Beverley**<br>Perth<br>**Southwell†☆**<br>*Tipperary☆*<br>Warwick<br>Doncaster Sale | **24**<br>Chepstow☆<br>**Doncaster**<br>*Dundalk☆*<br>*Kilbeggan☆*<br>Perth<br>Plumpton☆<br>**Sandown Park**<br>Cheltenham Sale | **25**<br>**Doncaster☆**<br>**Haydock Park**<br>**Leicester**<br>*Limerick*<br>**Ripon**<br>Sandown Park<br>**Wolverhampton†☆** |
| **26**<br>**Chelmsford City†**<br>*Gowran Park*<br>**Wetherby** | **27**<br>**Ayr**<br>**Kempton Park†**<br>*Naas☆*<br>**Southwell†**<br>**Windsor☆**<br>**Wolverhampton†☆** | **28**<br>**Brighton**<br>**Chelmsford City†☆**<br>**Newcastle☆**<br>**Nottingham**<br>*Punchestown☆*<br>**Wolverhampton†**<br>Osarus Sale | **29**<br>**Ascot**<br>Cheltenham☆<br>**Lingfield Park†☆**<br>**Pontefract**<br>*Punchestown☆*<br>**Wolverhampton†** | **30**<br>**Lingfield Park†**<br>Newton Abbot☆<br>*Punchestown☆*<br>**Redcar**<br>Sedgefield<br>Towcester☆<br>Tattersalls Sale | | |

# MAY

| Sun | Mon | Tues | Wed | Thur | Fri | Sat |
|---|---|---|---|---|---|---|
| **31**<br>Fakenham<br>*Kilbeggan*<br>*Listowel*<br>**Nottingham** | | | | | **1**<br>Bangor-on-Dee☆<br>**Chepstow**<br>Fontwell Park☆<br>**Lingfield Park†**<br>**Musselburgh**<br>*Punchestown☆*<br>Tattersalls Sale | **2**<br>**Doncaster☆**<br>**Goodwood**<br>Hexham☆<br>**Newmarket**<br>*Punchestown*<br>**Thirsk**<br>Uttoxeter |
| **3**<br>**Hamilton Park**<br>**Newmarket**<br>**Salisbury**<br>*Sligo* | **4**<br>**Bath**<br>**Beverley**<br>*Curragh*<br>*Down Royal*<br>Kempton Park<br>Warwick<br>**Windsor** | **5**<br>*Ballinrobe☆*<br>**Brighton**<br>**Catterick Bridge☆**<br>Exeter☆<br>Fakenham<br>Sedgefield | **6**<br>**Brighton**<br>**Chelmsford City†☆**<br>**Chester**<br>Kelso<br>Uttoxeter☆ | **7**<br>Carlisle☆<br>**Chester**<br>*Clonmel☆*<br>Newton Abbot<br>Wincanton☆<br>Worcester | **8**<br>**Ascot☆**<br>**Chester**<br>*Cork☆*<br>*Downpatrick☆*<br>**Lingfield Park**<br>Market Rasen<br>**Nottingham☆**<br>**Ripon☆**<br>Arqana Sale | **9**<br>**Ascot**<br>**Haydock (Mixed)**<br>Hexham<br>**Lingfield Park**<br>**Nottingham**<br>**Thirsk☆**<br>Warwick☆<br>*Wexford*<br>Arqana Sale |
| **10**<br>*Killarney*<br>*Leopardstown*<br>Ludlow<br>Plumpton | **11**<br>**Doncaster**<br>*Killarney☆*<br>**Musselburgh**<br>Towcester☆<br>**Windsor☆**<br>**Wolverhampton†** | **12**<br>**Beverley**<br>**Chelmsford City†☆**<br>*Killarney☆*<br>Sedgefield<br>Southwell☆<br>Wincanton | **13**<br>**Bath☆**<br>Kempton Park<br>*Naas☆*<br>**Newcastle**<br>Perth☆<br>**York** | **14**<br>Fontwell Park☆<br>**Newmarket☆**<br>Perth<br>**Salisbury**<br>*Tipperary☆*<br>**York** | **15**<br>Aintree☆<br>*Dundalk†☆*<br>**Hamilton Park☆**<br>*Kilbeggan☆*<br>**Newbury**<br>**Newmarket**<br>**York** | **16**<br>Bangor-on-Dee<br>**Doncaster☆**<br>**Newbury**<br>**Newmarket**<br>*Punchestown*<br>**Thirsk**<br>Uttoxeter☆ |
| **17**<br>*Limerick*<br>Market Rasen<br>*Navan*<br>**Ripon**<br>Stratford-on-Avon | **18**<br>**Leicester☆**<br>**Redcar**<br>*Roscommon☆*<br>**Southwell†**<br>Towcester<br>**Windsor☆**<br>Doncaster Sale<br>Fasig-Tipton Sale | **19**<br>**Chelmsford City†☆**<br>**Chepstow**<br>*Dundalk†☆*<br>**Newcastle**<br>Newton Abbot☆<br>**Nottingham**<br>Doncaster Sale<br>Fasig-Tipton Sale | **20**<br>**Ayr**<br>**Kempton Park†☆**<br>**Lingfield Park**<br>*Sligo☆*<br>Southwell☆<br>Warwick<br>Doncaster Sale | **21**<br>**Ayr**<br>*Clonmel☆*<br>**Goodwood**<br>**Nottingham☆**<br>**Sandown Park☆**<br>Wetherby<br>Goresbridge Sale | **22**<br>**Bath**<br>*Cork☆*<br>**Goodwood**<br>**Haydock Park**<br>**Musselburgh☆**<br>**Pontefract☆**<br>Worcester☆<br>Goresbridge Sale | **23**<br>**Beverley**<br>**Catterick Bridge**<br>*Curragh*<br>Ffos Las☆<br>**Goodwood**<br>**Haydock Park**<br>**Salisbury☆** |
| **24**<br>*Curragh*<br>Fontwell Park<br>Kelso<br>Uttoxeter | **25**<br>*Ballinrobe☆*<br>**Carlisle**<br>Cartmel<br>**Leicester**<br>**Redcar**<br>**Windsor** | **26**<br>*Ballinrobe☆*<br>Hexham☆<br>Huntingdon☆<br>**Leicester**<br>**Lingfield Park†**<br>**Redcar** | **27**<br>Cartmel<br>*Gowran Park☆*<br>**Hamilton Park**<br>**Kempton Park†☆**<br>Newton Abbot☆<br>**Thirsk** | **28**<br>*Fairyhouse☆*<br>**Haydock Park**<br>**Lingfield Park†**<br>**Sandown Park☆**<br>Wetherby☆<br>Worcester<br>Cheltenham Sale | **29**<br>**Brighton**<br>**Catterick Bridge☆**<br>*Down Royal☆*<br>**Haydock Park☆**<br>**Newcastle**<br>**Newmarket**<br>Stratford-on-Avon☆<br>*Tramore☆* | **30**<br>**Chepstow☆**<br>**Chester**<br>**Haydock Park**<br>**Newmarket**<br>Stratford-on-Avon☆<br>*Tramore*<br>**York** |

# JUNE

| Sun | Mon | Tues | Wed | Thur | Fri | Sat |
|---|---|---|---|---|---|---|
| | **1**<br>**Carlisle**☆<br>**Leicester**<br>**Lingfield Park**†<br>*Listowel*<br>*Naas*<br>**Windsor**☆ | **2**<br>**Brighton**<br>**Ripon**<br>Southwell☆<br>**Wolverhampton**†☆<br><br>Ascot Sale | **3**<br>**Chelmsford City**†☆<br>Fontwell Park<br>**Nottingham**<br>*Punchestown*☆<br>**Ripon**☆<br>**Wolverhampton**† | **4**<br>Ffos Las☆<br>**Hamilton Park**<br>**Kempton Park**†☆<br>**Lingfield Park**<br>*Tipperary*☆<br>**Wolverhampton**† | **5**<br>**Bath**☆<br>**Catterick Bridge**<br>*Downpatrick*☆<br>**Epsom Downs**<br>**Goodwood**☆<br>*Leopardstown*☆<br>Market Rasen<br><br>Baden-Baden Sale | **6**<br>**Doncaster**<br>**Epsom Downs**<br>Hexham<br>*Limerick*☆<br>**Lingfield Park**☆<br>**Musselburgh**<br>**Newcastle**☆<br>Worcester |
| **7**<br>*Curragh*<br>**Goodwood**<br>Perth | **8**<br>**Ayr**<br>**Pontefract**☆<br>*Roscommon*☆<br>**Thirsk**<br>**Windsor**☆ | **9**<br>Fontwell Park<br>**Lingfield Park**☆<br>*Roscommon*☆<br>**Salisbury**<br>Southwell☆ | **10**<br>**Beverley**<br>**Brighton**<br>*Fairyhouse*☆<br>**Hamilton Park**☆<br>**Haydock Park**<br>**Kempton Park**†☆<br><br>Goffs Sale | **11**<br>**Haydock Park**☆<br>*Leopardstown*☆<br>**Newbury**<br>**Nottingham**<br>Uttoxeter☆<br>Worcester<br><br>Goffs Sale | **12**<br>Aintree☆<br>**Chepstow**☆<br>*Clonmel*☆<br>**Goodwood**☆<br>Newton Abbot<br>**Sandown Park**<br>**York** | **13**<br>**Bath**<br>**Chester**<br>Hexham<br>**Leicester**☆<br>**Lingfield Park**☆<br>**Musselburgh**<br>*Navan*<br>**Sandown Park**<br>**York** |
| **14**<br>*Cork*<br>**Doncaster**<br>*Downpatrick*<br>**Salisbury** | **15**<br>**Carlisle**<br>**Nottingham**☆<br>*Sligo*☆<br>Southwell<br>**Windsor**☆<br><br>Goffs Sale (London) | **16**<br>**Ascot**<br>**Beverley**☆<br>**Brighton**☆<br>Stratford-on-Avon<br>**Thirsk** | **17**<br>**Ascot**<br>**Chelmsford City**†☆<br>**Hamilton Park**<br>**Ripon**☆<br>Uttoxeter<br>*Wexford*☆ | **18**<br>**Ascot**<br>**Chelmsford City**†<br>Ffos Las☆<br>**Leicester**☆<br>*Leopardstown*☆<br>**Lingfield Park**†☆<br>**Ripon** | **19**<br>**Ascot**<br>*Down Royal*☆<br>**Goodwood**☆<br>*Limerick*☆<br>Market Rasen<br>**Newmarket**☆<br>**Redcar** | **20**<br>**Ascot**<br>**Ayr**<br>*Down Royal*<br>*Gowran Park*<br>**Haydock Park**☆<br>**Lingfield Park**☆<br>**Newmarket**<br>**Redcar** |
| **21**<br>*Gowran Park*<br>Hexham<br>**Pontefract**<br>Worcester | **22**<br>**Chepstow**<br>*Kilbeggan*☆<br>**Wetherby**☆<br>**Windsor**☆<br>**Wolverhampton**† | **23**<br>*Ballinrobe*☆<br>**Beverley**<br>**Brighton**<br>**Leicester**☆<br>Newton Abbot☆ | **24**<br>**Bath**☆<br>**Carlisle**<br>**Kempton Park**†☆<br>*Naas*☆<br>**Salisbury**<br>Worcester<br><br>Tattersalls (IRE) Sale | **25**<br>**Hamilton Park**☆<br>*Leopardstown*☆<br>**Newbury**☆<br>**Newcastle**<br>**Newmarket**<br>**Nottingham**<br><br>Tattersalls (IRE) Sale | **26**<br>Cartmel<br>**Chester**☆<br>*Curragh*☆<br>**Doncaster**<br>**Newcastle**☆<br>**Newmarket**☆<br>**Yarmouth** | **27**<br>**Chester**<br>*Curragh*<br>**Doncaster**☆<br>**Lingfield Park**☆<br>**Newcastle**<br>**Newmarket**<br>**Windsor** |
| **28**<br>Cartmel<br>*Curragh*<br>Uttoxeter<br>**Windsor** | **29**<br>**Musselburgh**☆<br>**Pontefract**<br>**Windsor**☆<br>**Wolverhampton**† | **30**<br>**Brighton**<br>**Chepstow**☆<br>*Gowran Park*☆<br>**Hamilton Park**<br>Stratford-on-Avon☆ | | | | |

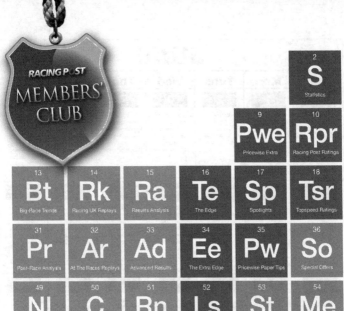

# JULY

| Sun | Mon | Tues | Wed | Thur | Fri | Sat |
|---|---|---|---|---|---|---|
| | | | **1**<br>**Bath☆**<br>*Fairyhouse☆*<br>**Kempton Park†☆**<br>Perth<br>**Thirsk**<br>Worcester<br>Arqana Sale | **2**<br>*Bellewstown☆*<br>**Epsom Downs☆**<br>**Haydock Park**<br>**Newbury☆**<br>Perth<br>*Tipperary☆*<br>**Yarmouth**<br>Arqana Sale | **3**<br>*Bellewstown☆*<br>**Beverley☆**<br>**Doncaster**<br>**Haydock Park☆**<br>Newton Abbot<br>**Sandown Park**<br>*Wexford☆* | **4**<br>*Bellewstown☆*<br>**Beverley**<br>**Carlisle☆**<br>**Haydock Park**<br>**Leicester**<br>**Nottingham☆**<br>**Sandown Park** |
| **5**<br>**Ayr**<br>*Fairyhouse*<br>*Limerick*<br>Market Rasen | **6**<br>**Ayr**<br>**Ripon☆**<br>*Roscommon☆*<br>**Windsor☆**<br>Worcester | **7**<br>**Brighton☆**<br>**Pontefract**<br>*Roscommon☆*<br>Uttoxeter☆<br>**Wolverhampton†**<br>Tattersalls Sale | **8**<br>**Bath☆**<br>**Catterick Bridge**<br>**Kempton Park†☆**<br>**Lingfield Park**<br>*Naas☆*<br>**Yarmouth**<br>Tattersalls Sale | **9**<br>**Carlisle**<br>**Doncaster**<br>**Epsom Downs☆**<br>*Leopardstown☆*<br>**Newbury☆**<br>**Newmarket**<br>Tattersalls Sale | **10**<br>**Ascot**<br>**Chepstow☆**<br>**Chester☆**<br>*Cork☆*<br>*Navan☆*<br>**Newmarket**<br>**York**<br>Tattersalls Sale | **11**<br>**Ascot**<br>**Chester**<br>**Hamilton Park☆**<br>**Newmarket**<br>**Salisbury☆**<br>*Tipperary*<br>**York** |
| **12**<br>*Dundalk*<br>Perth<br>*Sligo*<br>Southwell<br>Stratford-on-Avon | **13**<br>**Ayr**<br>*Downpatrick*<br>*Killarney☆*<br>**Wetherby**<br>**Windsor☆**<br>**Wolverhampton†☆** | **14**<br>**Bath**<br>**Beverley**<br>*Killarney☆*<br>**Thirsk☆**<br>**Yarmouth☆**<br>Ascot Sale | **15**<br>**Catterick Bridge**<br>*Killarney☆*<br>**Lingfield Park**<br>**Sandown Park☆**<br>Uttoxeter<br>Worcester☆ | **16**<br>**Chepstow**<br>**Doncaster☆**<br>**Epsom Downs☆**<br>**Hamilton Park**<br>*Killarney*<br>**Leicester**<br>*Leopardstown☆* | **17**<br>**Hamilton Park☆**<br>**Haydock Park**<br>*Kilbeggan☆*<br>**Newbury**<br>**Newmarket☆**<br>**Nottingham**<br>**Pontefract☆** | **18**<br>Cartmel<br>**Chester**<br>*Curragh*<br>**Haydock Park☆**<br>**Lingfield Park☆**<br>Market Rasen<br>**Newbury**<br>**Newmarket**<br>**Ripon** |
| **19**<br>*Curragh*<br>Newton Abbot<br>**Redcar**<br>Stratford-on-Avon<br>*Tipperary* | **20**<br>**Ayr**<br>*Ballinrobe☆*<br>**Beverley☆**<br>Cartmel<br>**Windsor☆** | **21**<br>*Ballinrobe☆*<br>**Chelmsford City†☆**<br>**Ffos Las**<br>**Musselburgh**<br>**Wetherby☆** | **22**<br>**Bath**<br>**Catterick Bridge**<br>**Leicester☆**<br>**Lingfield Park†**<br>*Naas☆*<br>**Sandown Park☆** | **23**<br>**Doncaster☆**<br>*Leopardstown☆*<br>*Limerick☆*<br>**Newbury☆**<br>**Sandown Park**<br>Worcester<br>**Yarmouth** | **24**<br>**Ascot**<br>**Chepstow☆**<br>*Down Royal☆*<br>**Newmarket☆**<br>**Thirsk**<br>Uttoxeter<br>*Wexford☆*<br>**York☆**<br>Goresbridge Sale | **25**<br>**Ascot**<br>**Lingfield Park☆**<br>**Newcastle**<br>**Newmarket**<br>**Salisbury☆**<br>*Wexford*<br>**York** |
| **26**<br>**Carlisle**<br>**Pontefract**<br>Uttoxeter | **27**<br>**Ayr**<br>*Galway☆*<br>Newton Abbot<br>**Southwell†☆**<br>**Windsor☆** | **28**<br>**Beverley**<br>*Galway☆*<br>**Goodwood**<br>Perth☆<br>Worcester☆<br>**Yarmouth** | **29**<br>*Galway☆*<br>**Goodwood**<br>**Leicester☆**<br>Perth<br>**Redcar**<br>**Sandown Park☆** | **30**<br>**Epsom Downs☆**<br>**Ffos Las☆**<br>*Galway*<br>**Goodwood**<br>**Nottingham**<br>Stratford-on-Avon | **31**<br>Bangor-on-Dee<br>**Bath☆**<br>*Galway☆*<br>**Goodwood**<br>**Musselburgh☆**<br>**Newmarket☆**<br>**Thirsk** | |

# AUGUST

| Sun | Mon | Tues | Wed | Thur | Fri | Sat |
|---|---|---|---|---|---|---|
| **30**<br>**Beverley**<br>*Cork*<br>*Curragh*<br>**Goodwood**<br>**Yarmouth** | **31**<br>Cartmel<br>**Chepstow**<br>**Epsom Downs**<br>Huntingdon<br>**Newcastle**<br>**Ripon**<br>*Roscommon☆* | | | | | **1**<br>**Doncaster**<br>*Galway*<br>**Goodwood**<br>**Hamilton Park☆**<br>**Lingfield Park☆**<br>**Newmarket**<br>**Thirsk** |
| **2**<br>**Chepstow**<br>**Chester**<br>*Galway*<br>Market Rasen | **3**<br>**Carlisle☆**<br>*Cork*<br>*Naas*<br>**Nottingham**<br>**Ripon**<br>**Windsor☆**<br>Fasig-Tipton Sale | **4**<br>**Catterick Bridge**<br>**Chelmsford City†☆**<br>*Cork☆*<br>**Ripon☆**<br>*Roscommon☆*<br>**Salisbury**<br>Fasig-Tipton Sale | **5**<br>**Brighton**<br>**Chepstow**<br>**Kempton Park†☆**<br>**Pontefract**<br>*Sligo☆*<br>**Yarmouth☆** | **6**<br>**Brighton**<br>**Haydock Park**<br>*Leopardstown☆*<br>**Newcastle☆**<br>**Sandown Park☆**<br>*Sligo☆*<br>**Southwell†☆**<br>**Yarmouth** | **7**<br>**Brighton**<br>**Haydock Park☆**<br>**Lingfield Park†**<br>**Musselburgh**<br>**Newmarket☆**<br>*Tipperary☆* | **8**<br>**Ascot**<br>**Ayr☆**<br>**Haydock Park**<br>*Kilbeggan☆*<br>**Lingfield Park☆**<br>**Newmarket**<br>**Redcar** |
| **9**<br>*Curragh*<br>*Downpatrick*<br>**Leicester**<br>**Windsor** | **10**<br>**Ayr**<br>*Ballinrobe☆*<br>**Thirsk☆**<br>**Windsor☆**<br>**Wolverhampton†** | **11**<br>**Carlisle**<br>**Ffos Las☆**<br>**Lingfield Park†**<br>**Nottingham☆**<br>Tattersalls (IRE) Sale | **12**<br>**Bath☆**<br>**Beverley**<br>*Gowran Park☆*<br>**Kempton Park†☆**<br>Newton Abbot<br>**Salisbury**<br>Tattersalls (IRE) Sale | **13**<br>**Beverley**<br>Fontwell Park<br>*Leopardstown☆*<br>**Lingfield Park☆**<br>**Salisbury**<br>*Tramore☆*<br>**Yarmouth☆** | **14**<br>**Catterick Bridge☆**<br>**Newbury**<br>**Newcastle**<br>**Newmarket☆**<br>**Nottingham**<br>*Tramore☆* | **15**<br>**Doncaster**<br>**Lingfield Park☆**<br>Market Rasen☆<br>**Newbury**<br>**Newmarket**<br>**Ripon**<br>*Tramore☆*<br>Arqana Sale |
| **16**<br>*Dundalk*<br>**Pontefract**<br>Southwell<br>*Tramore*<br>Arqana Sale | **17**<br>**Chelmsford City†☆**<br>**Kempton Park†**<br>*Roscommon☆*<br>**Thirsk**<br>**Windsor☆**<br>Arqana Sale | **18**<br>**Chelmsford City†☆**<br>**Kempton Park†**<br>**Leicester☆**<br>**Ripon**<br>*Sligo☆*<br>Arqana Sale<br>Ascot Sale | **19**<br>**Carlisle**<br>**Ffos Las**<br>**Kempton Park†☆**<br>*Killarney☆*<br>Worcester☆<br>**York** | **20**<br>**Chepstow**<br>**Hamilton Park☆**<br>*Killarney☆*<br>**Lingfield Park☆**<br>Stratford-on-Avon<br>**York** | **21**<br>Bangor-on-Dee<br>*Kilbeggan☆*<br>*Killarney☆*<br>**Salisbury☆**<br>**Sandown Park**<br>**Wolverhampton†☆**<br>**York** | **22**<br>**Bath☆**<br>**Chelmsford City†☆**<br>**Chester**<br>*Curragh*<br>*Killarney*<br>Newton Abbot<br>Perth<br>**Sandown Park**<br>**York** |
| **23**<br>**Brighton**<br>*Curragh*<br>Worcester | **24**<br>**Brighton**<br>**Carlisle☆**<br>*Downpatrick*<br>**Kempton Park†**<br>**Leicester☆** | **25**<br>*Ballinrobe☆*<br>**Brighton**<br>Fontwell Park☆<br>**Newbury☆**<br>**Yarmouth**<br>Doncaster Sale | **26**<br>**Bath☆**<br>*Bellewstown☆*<br>**Catterick Bridge**<br>**Kempton Park†☆**<br>**Lingfield Park**<br>**Musselburgh**<br>Doncaster Sale | **27**<br>*Bellewstown☆*<br>**Musselburgh**<br>Sedgefield☆<br>Southwell<br>Stratford-on-Avon<br>*Tipperary☆*<br>**Wolverhampton†☆**<br>Doncaster Sale | **28**<br>*Down Royal☆*<br>**Ffos Las (Mixed)**<br>**Goodwood☆**<br>**Hamilton Park☆**<br>**Newcastle☆**<br>**Newmarket**<br>**Thirsk** | **29**<br>**Beverley**<br>Cartmel<br>**Goodwood**<br>**Newmarket**<br>**Redcar☆**<br>*Wexford*<br>**Windsor☆** |

# SEPTEMBER

| Sun | Mon | Tues | Wed | Thur | Fri | Sat |
|---|---|---|---|---|---|---|
| | | **1**<br>**Epsom Downs**<br>**Goodwood**<br>**Hamilton Park**<br>Newton Abbot<br><br>Doncaster Sale | **2**<br>**Bath**<br>*Gowran Park☆*<br>**Lingfield Park**<br>Southwell<br>Worcester<br><br>Doncaster Sale | **3**<br>**Chelmsford City†☆**<br>*Clonmel☆*<br>**Haydock Park**<br>**Salisbury**<br>Sedgefield<br><br>Doncaster Sale<br>Baden-Baden Sale | **4**<br>**Ascot**<br>**Haydock Park**<br>**Kempton Park†☆**<br>*Kilbeggan☆*<br>**Musselburgh**<br>**Newcastle**<br><br>Baden-Baden Sale | **5**<br>**Ascot**<br>**Haydock Park**<br>**Kempton Park†**<br>*Navan*<br>Stratford-on-Avon<br>**Thirsk**<br>**Wolverhampton†☆** |
| **6**<br>*Dundalk*<br>Fontwell Park<br>**York** | **7**<br>**Brighton**<br>*Galway☆*<br>Perth<br>**Windsor** | **8**<br>*Galway☆*<br>**Leicester**<br>Perth<br>**Redcar**<br>Worcester | **9**<br>**Carlisle**<br>**Doncaster**<br>*Galway☆*<br>**Kempton Park†☆**<br>Uttoxeter | **10**<br>**Chelmsford City†☆**<br>**Chepstow**<br>**Doncaster**<br>**Epsom Downs**<br>*Laytown☆* | **11**<br>**Chester**<br>**Doncaster**<br>*Down Royal☆*<br>**Salisbury**<br>**Sandown Park** | **12**<br>**Bath**<br>**Chester**<br>**Doncaster**<br>*Leopardstown*<br>**Lingfield Park**<br>**Musselburgh**<br><br>Goffs Sale |
| **13**<br>**Bath**<br>*Curragh*<br>**Ffos Las**<br>*Listowel* | **14**<br>**Brighton**<br>*Listowel*<br>Stratford-on-Avon<br>**Wolverhampton†**<br><br>Keeneland Sale | **15**<br>**Carlisle**<br>**Catterick Bridge**<br>**Chepstow**<br>*Listowel*<br>**Yarmouth**<br><br>Osarus Sale<br>Keeneland Sale | **16**<br>**Beverley**<br>Kelso<br>*Listowel*<br>**Sandown Park**<br>**Yarmouth**<br><br>Osarus Sale<br>Keeneland Sale | **17**<br>**Ayr**<br>**Chelmsford City†☆**<br>*Listowel*<br>**Pontefract**<br>**Yarmouth**<br><br>Keeneland Sale | **18**<br>**Ayr**<br>Hexham<br>*Listowel*<br>**Newbury**<br>Newton Abbot<br><br>SGA Sale<br>Keeneland Sale | **19**<br>**Ayr**<br>**Catterick Bridge**<br>*Listowel*<br>**Newbury**<br>**Newmarket**<br>**Wolverhampton†☆**<br><br>SGA Sale<br>Keeneland Sale |
| **20**<br>**Hamilton Park**<br>*Gowran Park*<br>Plumpton<br>Uttoxeter<br><br>Keeneland Sale | **21**<br>**Hamilton Park**<br>**Kempton Park†**<br>**Leicester**<br><br>Keeneland Sale | **22**<br>*Ballinrobe*<br>**Beverley**<br>**Kempton Park†☆**<br>**Lingfield Park†**<br>Warwick<br><br>Keeneland Sale<br>Tattersalls (IRE) Sale | **23**<br>**Goodwood**<br>**Kempton Park†☆**<br>Perth<br>**Redcar**<br><br>Keeneland Sale<br>Tattersalls (IRE) Sale | **24**<br>**Chelmsford City†☆**<br>**Newmarket**<br>Perth<br>**Pontefract**<br><br>Keeneland Sale<br>Tattersalls (IRE) Sale | **25**<br>*Downpatrick*<br>*Dundalk†☆*<br>**Haydock Park**<br>**Newmarket**<br>**Wolverhampton†☆**<br>Worcester<br><br>Keeneland Sale | **26**<br>**Chelmsford City†☆**<br>**Chester**<br>**Haydock Park**<br>Market Rasen<br>*Navan*<br>**Newmarket**<br>**Ripon**<br><br>Keeneland Sale |
| **27**<br>*Curragh*<br>**Epsom Downs**<br>**Musselburgh** | **28**<br>**Bath**<br>**Hamilton Park**<br>Newton Abbot<br>*Roscommon* | **29**<br>**Ayr**<br>*Fairyhouse*<br>Sedgefield<br>Southwell<br>**Wolverhampton†☆**<br><br>Goffs Sale | **30**<br>Chepstow<br>**Kempton Park†☆**<br>**Nottingham**<br>**Salisbury**<br>*Sligo*<br><br>Goffs Sale | | | |

# OCTOBER

| Sun | Mon | Tues | Wed | Thur | Fri | Sat |
|---|---|---|---|---|---|---|
| | | | | **1**<br>Bangor-on-Dee<br>**Chelmsford City†☆**<br>*Clonmel*<br>**Newcastle**<br>Warwick<br>Goffs Sale | **2**<br>**Ascot**<br>*Dundalk†☆*<br>Fontwell Park<br>*Gowran Park*<br>Hexham<br>**Wolverhampton†☆**<br>Goffs Sale | **3**<br>**Ascot**<br>Fontwell Park<br>*Gowran Park*<br>**Newmarket**<br>**Redcar**<br>**Wolverhampton†☆**<br>Arqana Sale |
| **4**<br>Huntingdon<br>Kelso<br>*Tipperary*<br>Uttoxeter | **5**<br>Market Rasen<br>**Pontefract**<br>**Windsor** | **6**<br>**Brighton**<br>**Catterick Bridge**<br>**Kempton Park†☆**<br>**Leicester**<br>*Tipperary*<br>Ascot Sale<br>Tattersalls Sale | **7**<br>**Kempton Park†☆**<br>Ludlow<br>*Navan*<br>**Nottingham**<br>Towcester<br>Tattersalls Sale | **8**<br>**Ayr**<br>**Chelmsford City†☆**<br>Exeter<br>*Tramore*<br>Worcester<br>Tattersalls Sale | **9**<br>*Dundalk†☆*<br>Fakenham<br>Newton Abbot<br>**Wolverhampton†☆**<br>**York**<br>Tattersalls Sale | **10**<br>**Chelmsford City†☆**<br>Chepstow<br>*Fairyhouse*<br>Hexham<br>*Limerick*<br>**Newmarket**<br>**York** |
| **11**<br>Chepstow<br>*Curragh*<br>**Goodwood**<br>*Limerick*<br>Tattersalls Sale | **12**<br>**Salisbury**<br>Sedgefield<br>**Windsor**<br>Tattersalls Sale | **13**<br>Huntingdon<br>**Leicester**<br>**Newcastle**<br>**Wolverhampton†☆**<br>Tattersalls Sale | **14**<br>**Kempton Park†☆**<br>**Nottingham**<br>*Punchestown*<br>Wetherby<br>Worcester<br>Tattersalls Sale | **15**<br>**Brighton**<br>Carlisle<br>**Chelmsford City†☆**<br>*Punchestown*<br>Uttoxeter<br>Tattersalls Sale | **16**<br>*Downpatrick*<br>*Dundalk†☆*<br>**Haydock Park**<br>**Newmarket**<br>**Redcar**<br>Wincanton<br>**Wolverhampton†☆**<br>Tattersalls Sale<br>Baden-Baden Sale | **17**<br>**Ascot**<br>**Catterick Bridge**<br>*Cork*<br>Ffos Las<br>Market Rasen<br>Stratford-on-Avon<br>**Wolverhampton†☆**<br>Baden-Baden Sale |
| **18**<br>**Bath**<br>*Cork*<br>Kempton Park<br>*Naas* | **19**<br>Plumpton<br>**Pontefract**<br>**Windsor**<br>Arqana Sale<br>Fasig-Tipton Sale | **20**<br>Exeter<br>**Lingfield Park†**<br>**Wolverhampton†☆**<br>**Yarmouth**<br>Arqana Sale<br>Fasig-Tipton Sale | **21**<br>Fontwell Park<br>**Kempton Park†☆**<br>*Navan*<br>**Newmarket**<br>Worcester<br>Arqana Sale<br>Fasig-Tipton Sale | **22**<br>Carlisle<br>**Chelmsford City†☆**<br>Ludlow<br>Southwell<br>*Thurles*<br>Arqana Sale<br>Goffs Sale | **23**<br>Cheltenham<br>**Doncaster**<br>*Dundalk†☆*<br>**Newbury**<br>**Wolverhampton†☆** | **24**<br>**Chelmsford City†☆**<br>Cheltenham<br>**Doncaster**<br>Kelso<br>*Leopardstown*<br>**Newbury**<br>*Wexford* |
| **25**<br>Aintree<br>*Galway*<br>*Leopardstown*<br>Wincanton | **26**<br>Ayr<br>*Galway*<br>**Leicester**<br>**Redcar**<br>*Wexford*<br>Tattersalls Sale | **27**<br>Bangor-on-Dee<br>**Catterick Bridge**<br>*Punchestown*<br>**Wolverhampton†☆**<br>**Yarmouth**<br>Tattersalls Sale | **28**<br>**Chelmsford City†**<br>*Dundalk†☆*<br>Fakenham<br>**Kempton Park†☆**<br>**Nottingham**<br>Tattersalls Sale | **29**<br>**Chelmsford City†☆**<br>*Clonmel*<br>**Lingfield Park†**<br>Sedgefield<br>Stratford-on-Avon<br>Tattersalls Sale | **30**<br>*Down Royal*<br>*Dundalk†☆*<br>**Newmarket**<br>Uttoxeter<br>Wetherby<br>**Wolverhampton†☆**<br>Tattersalls Sale<br>Goresbridge Sale | **31**<br>Ascot<br>Ayr<br>*Down Royal*<br>**Newmarket**<br>Wetherby<br>**Wolverhampton†☆** |

# NOVEMBER

| Sun | Mon | Tues | Wed | Thur | Fri | Sat |
|---|---|---|---|---|---|---|
| **1**<br>Carlisle<br>*Cork*<br>Huntingdon<br>*Naas* | **2**<br>Kempton Park<br>Ludlow<br>Plumpton<br><br>Fasig-Tipton Sale | **3**<br>Exeter<br>**Redcar**<br>**Southwell†**<br>**Wolverhampton†☆**<br><br>Doncaster Sale<br>Keeneland Sale | **4**<br>Chepstow<br>*Fairyhouse*<br>**Kempton Park†☆**<br>**Nottingham**<br>Warwick<br><br>Doncaster Sale<br>Keeneland Sale | **5**<br>**Chelmsford City†☆**<br>Market Rasen<br>Musselburgh<br>*Thurles*<br>Towcester<br><br>Ascot Sale<br>Doncaster Sale<br>Keeneland Sale | **6**<br>**Chelmsford City†☆**<br>*Dundalk†☆*<br>Fontwell Park<br>Hexham<br>Musselburgh<br><br>Osarus Sale<br>Keeneland Sale | **7**<br>Aintree<br>**Chelmsford City†☆**<br>**Doncaster**<br>Kelso<br>*Naas*<br>Wincanton<br><br>Keeneland Sale |
| **8**<br>Ffos Las<br>*Limerick*<br>*Navan*<br>Sandown Park<br><br>Keeneland Sale<br>Tattersalls (IRE) Sale | **9**<br>Carlisle<br>**Kempton Park†**<br>Southwell<br><br>Keeneland Sale<br>Tattersalls (IRE) Sale | **10**<br>Huntingdon<br>Lingfield Park<br>Sedgefield<br>**Wolverhampton†☆**<br><br>Keeneland Sale<br>Tattersalls (IRE) Sale | **11**<br>Ayr<br>Bangor-on-Dee<br>*Dundalk†☆*<br>Exeter<br>**Kempton Park†☆**<br><br>Keeneland Sale<br>Tattersalls (IRE) Sale | **12**<br>**Chelmsford City†☆**<br>*Clonmel*<br>Ludlow<br>**Southwell†**<br>Taunton<br><br>Keeneland Sale<br>Tattersalls (IRE) Sale | **13**<br>Cheltenham<br>*Dundalk†☆*<br>**Lingfield Park†**<br>Newcastle<br>**Wolverhampton†☆**<br><br>Keeneland Sale<br>Tattersalls (IRE) Sale<br>Cheltenham Sale<br>SGA Sale | **14**<br>Cheltenham<br>**Lingfield Park†**<br>*Punchestown*<br>Uttoxeter<br>Wetherby<br>**Wolverhampton†☆**<br><br>Tattersalls (IRE) Sale<br>SGA Sale |
| **15**<br>Cheltenham<br>*Cork*<br>Fontwell Park<br>*Punchestown* | **16**<br>Leicester<br>Plumpton<br>**Wolverhampton†**<br><br>Goffs Sale<br>Arqana Sale | **17**<br>Fakenham<br>**Lingfield Park†**<br>Southwell<br>*Wexford*<br><br>Goffs Sale<br>Arqana Sale | **18**<br>Chepstow<br>*Fairyhouse*<br>Hexham<br>**Kempton Park†☆**<br>Warwick<br><br>Goffs Sale | **19**<br>**Chelmsford City†☆**<br>**Lingfield Park†**<br>Market Rasen<br>*Thurles*<br>Wincanton<br><br>Goffs Sale | **20**<br>Ascot<br>*Dundalk†☆*<br>Ffos Las<br>Haydock Park<br>**Wolverhampton†☆**<br><br>Goffs Sale | **21**<br>Ascot<br>*Gowran Park*<br>Haydock Park<br>Huntingdon<br>**Lingfield Park†**<br>**Wolverhampton†☆**<br><br>Goffs Sale |
| **22**<br>Exeter<br>*Navan*<br>Uttoxeter<br><br>Goffs Sale | **23**<br>**Chelmsford City†**<br>Kempton Park<br>Ludlow<br><br>Tattersalls Sale | **24**<br>Lingfield Park<br>Sedgefield<br>**Southwell†** | **25**<br>*Dundalk†☆*<br>Fontwell Park<br>**Kempton Park†☆**<br>**Lingfield Park†**<br>Wetherby<br><br>Tattersalls Sale | **26**<br>**Chelmsford City†☆**<br>Newbury<br>**Southwell†**<br>Taunton<br>*Thurles*<br><br>Tattersalls Sale | **27**<br>Doncaster<br>*Dundalk†☆*<br>Musselburgh<br>Newbury<br>**Wolverhampton†☆**<br><br>Tattersalls Sale | **28**<br>Bangor-on-Dee<br>Doncaster<br>*Fairyhouse*<br>Newbury<br>Newcastle<br>**Wolverhampton†☆**<br><br>Tattersalls Sale |
| **29**<br>Carlisle<br>*Fairyhouse*<br>Leicester | **30**<br>**Kempton Park†**<br>Plumpton<br>**Wolverhampton†**<br><br>Tattersalls Sale | | | | | |

# DECEMBER

| Sun | Mon | Tues | Wed | Thur | Fri | Sat |
|---|---|---|---|---|---|---|
| | | **1**<br>Lingfield Park<br>Southwell<br>**Wolverhampton†**<br>Tattersalls Sale | **2**<br>Catterick Bridge<br>**Kempton Park†☆**<br>**Lingfield Park†**<br>Ludlow<br>Tattersalls Sale | **3**<br>*Clonmel*<br>**Kempton Park†☆**<br>Leicester<br>Market Rasen<br>Wincanton<br>Tattersalls Sale | **4**<br>*Dundalk☆*<br>Exeter<br>Sandown Park<br>Sedgefield<br>**Wolverhampton†☆**<br>Tattersalls Sale | **5**<br>Aintree<br>Chepstow<br>*Navan*<br>Sandown Park<br>Wetherby<br>**Wolverhampton†☆**<br>Arqana Sale |
| **6**<br>*Cork*<br>Huntingdon<br>Kelso<br>*Punchestown*<br>Arqana Sale | **7**<br>**Chelmsford City†**<br>**Lingfield Park†**<br>Musselburgh<br>Ascot Sale<br>Arqana Sale | **8**<br>Fontwell Park<br>**Southwell†**<br>Uttoxeter | **9**<br>Hexham<br>**Kempton Park†☆**<br>Leicester<br>**Lingfield Park†**<br>Goffs Sale | **10**<br>**Chelmsford City†☆**<br>Newcastle<br>Taunton<br>Warwick<br>Goffs Sale | **11**<br>Bangor-on-Dee<br>Cheltenham<br>Doncaster<br>*Dundalk†☆*<br>**Wolverhampton†☆**<br>Cheltenham Sale | **12**<br>Cheltenham<br>Doncaster<br>Lingfield Park<br>**Southwell†**<br>*Tramore*<br>**Wolverhampton†☆** |
| **13**<br>Carlisle<br>*Navan*<br>Southwell | **14**<br>Ffos Las<br>Plumpton<br>**Wolverhampton†** | **15**<br>Catterick Bridge<br>**Kempton Park†**<br>**Southwell†**<br>Tattersalls (IRE) Sale | **16**<br>**Kempton Park†☆**<br>**Lingfield Park†**<br>Ludlow<br>Newbury | **17**<br>**Chelmsford City†☆**<br>Exeter<br>**Southwell†**<br>Towcester | **18**<br>Ascot<br>*Dundalk†☆*<br>**Southwell†**<br>Uttoxeter<br>**Wolverhampton†☆** | **19**<br>Ascot<br>*Fairyhouse*<br>Haydock Park<br>**Lingfield Park†**<br>Newcastle |
| **20**<br>Fakenham<br>**Lingfield Park†**<br>*Thurles* | **21**<br>Bangor-on-Dee<br>**Chelmsford City†**<br>Lingfield Park<br>**Wolverhampton†☆** | **22**<br>Ayr<br>**Southwell†**<br>**Wolverhampton†** | **23**<br>*No Racing* | **24**<br>*No Racing* | **25**<br>*No Racing* | **26**<br>Fontwell Park<br>Huntingdon<br>Kempton Park<br>*Leopardstown*<br>*Limerick*<br>Market Rasen<br>Sedgefield<br>Wetherby<br>Wincanton<br>**Wolverhampton†**<br>*Down Royal* |
| **27**<br>Chepstow<br>Kempton Park<br>*Leopardstown*<br>*Limerick*<br>**Southwell†**<br>Wetherby | **28**<br>Catterick Bridge<br>Leicester<br>*Leopardstown*<br>*Limerick*<br>**Lingfield Park†** | **29**<br>**Chelmsford City†☆**<br>Doncaster<br>Kelso<br>*Leopardstown*<br>*Limerick*<br>Newbury<br>**Southwell†** | **30**<br>Haydock Park<br>**Lingfield Park†**<br>Taunton | **31**<br>**Lingfield Park†**<br>*Punchestown*<br>Uttoxeter<br>Warwick | | |

# DATES OF PRINCIPAL RACES

(SUBJECT TO ALTERATION)

## JANUARY

Betbright Dipper Novice Chase (Cheltenham) ... 1st
Fairlawne Handicap Steeple Chase (Cheltenham) ... 1st
EBF "Junior" Standard Open NH Flat Race (Cheltenham) ... 1st
Holden Plant Wilf Dooly Steeple Chase (Tramore) ... 1st
32Red Tolworth Hurdle Race (A Novices' Hurdle Race) (Sandown Park) ... 3rd
32Red Mares Hurdle Race (Sandown Park) ... 3rd
32Red Handicap Steeplechase (Sandown Park) ... 3rd
Lawlor's Hotel Novice Hurdle (Naas) ... 4th
Native Upmanship Steeple Chase (Thurles) ... 5th
Neptune Investment Management Novices' Hurdle Race (Registered As Leamington Novices' Hurdle Race) (Warwick) ... 10th
Betfred Classic Steeple Chase (A Handicap) (Warwick) ... 10th
Moscow Flyer Novices' Hurdle (Punchestown) ... 10th
William Hill Lanzarote Hurdle (A Handicap) (Kempton Park) ... 10th
williamhill.com Steeple Chase (Class 1) (Kempton Park) ... 10th
Dan Moore Memorial Handicap Chase (Fairyhouse) ... 11th
Coolmore Anaglog's Daughter EBF Novice Steeple Chase (Thurles) ... 15th
Kinloch Brae Steeple Chase (Thurles) ... 15th
Sodexo Clarence House Steeple Chase (Ascot) ... 17th
Keltbray Holloway's Hurdle Race (A Limited Handicap) (Ascot) ... 17th
OLBG.com Mares' Hurdle Race (Ascot) ... 17th
Racing Post Celebrates 200,000 Social Followers Novices' Steeple Chase (Haydock Park) ... 17th
Peter Marsh Steeple Chase (A Limited Handicap) (Haydock Park) ... 17th
Stanjames.com Champion Hurdle Trial (Haydock Park) ... 17th
Sky Bet Supreme Trial Novices' Hurdle Race (Haydock Park) ... 17th
Limestone Lad Hurdle (Naas) ... 17th
Woodlands Park 100 Naas Novices' Steeple Chase (Naas) ... 17th
Leopardstown Chase (Leopardstown) ... 18th
Boylesports Handicap Hurdle (Leopardstown) ... 18th
Boylesports Killiney Novices' Chase (Leopardstown) ... 18th
Goffs Thyestes Handicap Chase (Gowran Park) ... 22nd
Galmoy Hurdle (Gowran Park) ... 22nd
Galliardhomes.com Cleeve Hurdle Race (Cheltenham) ... 24th
JCB Triumph Hurdle Trial (A Juvenile Hurdle Race) (Cheltenham) ... 24th
Argento Steeple Chase (Cheltenham) ... 24th
Neptune Investment Management Novices' Hurdle Race (Cheltenham) ... 24th
Freebets.com Trophy Steeple Chase (A Handicap) (Cheltenham) ... 24th
Racing Post Lightning Novices' Steeple Chase (Doncaster) ... 24th
Albert Bartlett Novices' Hurdle Race (Registered As River Don) (Doncaster) ... 24th
OLBG.com Mares' Hurdle Race (Doncaster) ... 24th
Sky Bet Chase (A Handicap) (Formerly The Great Yorkshire Chase) (Doncaster) ... 24th
BHP Irish Champion Hurdle (Leopardstown) ... 25th
Frank Ward Solicitors Arkle Novices' Steeple Chase (Leopardstown) ... 25th
Synergy Golden Cygnet Novices' Hurdle (Leopardstown) ... 25th
Betfred TV Scilly Isles Novices' Steeple Chase (Sandown Park) ... 31st
Betfred Mobile And Levy Board Heroes Handicap Hurdle Race (Sandown Park) ... 31st
Betfred 'Double Delight' Contenders Hurdle Race (Sandown Park) ... 31st
Totepool Towton Novices' Steeple Chase (Wetherby) ... 31st
Welsh Champion Hurdle (Limited Handicap) (Ffos Las) ... 31st
Solerina Mares' Novices' Hurdle (Fairyhouse) ... 31st

## FEBRUARY

INHSO Series EBF Novices' Hurdle (Punchestown) ... 1st
Tied Cottage Steeple Chase (Punchestown) ... 1st
Grand National Trial Handicap Steeple Chase (Punchestown) ... 1st
John Smith's Scottish County Hurdle (A Handicap Race) (Musselburgh) ... 1st
John Smith's Scottish Triumph Hurdle Trial (A Juvenile Hurdle Race) (Musselburgh) ... 1st
Powerstown Novices' Hurdle (Clonmel) ... 5th
Betfair Denman Steeple Chase (Newbury) ... 7th
Betfair Cash Out Steeple Chase (Registered As The Game Spirit Chase) (Newbury) ... 7th
Betfair Hurdle Race (Handicap) (Newbury) ... 7th
Betfair Commits £40 Million To British Racing Bumper Standard Open NH Flat Race (Newbury) ... 7th
Star Sports Kingmaker Novices' Steeple Chase (Warwick) ... 7th
Warwick Mares Hurdle Race (Warwick) ... 7th
Deloitte Novice Hurdle (Leopardstown) ... 8th
Dr P J Moriarty Novices' Steeple Chase (Leopardstown) ... 8th
Spring 4yo Hurdle (Leopardstown) ... 8th
Hennessy Gold Cup Steeple Chase (Leopardstown) ... 8th

Bathwick Tyres Plymouth Novices' Hurdle Race (Exeter) ........ 8th
Jane Seymour Mares' Novices Hurdle (Sandown Park) ........ 13th
Betfair Ascot Steeple Chase (Ascot) ........ 14th
RSA Trial Novices' Steeple Chase (Registered As Reynoldstown Novices' Steeple Chase) (Ascot) ........ 14th
Weatherbys Hamilton Insurance Steeple Chase (A Limited Handicap) (Ascot) ........ 14th
Albert Bartlett Novices' Hurdle Race (Haydock Park) ........ 14th
Betfred Mobile Hurdle Race (Registered As Rendlesham Hurdle Race) (Haydock Park) ........ 14th
Betfred Grand National Trial (A Handicap Steeple Chase) (Haydock Park) ........ 14th
Bathwick Tyres Kingwell Hurdle Race (Wincanton) ........ 14th
Red Mills Trial Hurdle (Gowran Park) ........ 14th
Red Mills Steeple Chase (Gowran Park) ........ 14th
Ladbrokes Boyne Hurdle (Navan) ........ 15th
Flying Bolt Novices' Steeple Chase (Navan) ........ 15th
Ten Up Novices' Steeple Chase (Navan) ........ 15th
Sidney Banks Memorial Novices' Hurdle (Huntingdon) ........ 19th
Betbright.com Adonis Juvenile Hurdle Race (Kempton Park) ........ 21st
Betbright Mobile Pendil Novices' Steeple Chase (Kempton Park) ........ 21st
Sky Bet Dovecote Novices' Hurdle Race (Kempton Park) ........ 21st
Betbright Steeple Chase (Handicap) (Kempton Park) ........ 21st
Compare Bookmakers at bookmakers.co.uk Cleves Stakes (Lingfield Park) ........ 21st
coral.co.uk Winter Derby Trial (Lingfield Park) ........ 21st
Winning Fair 4yo Juvenile Hurdle (Fairyhouse) ........ 21st
At The Races Bobbyjo Steeple Chase (Fairyhouse) ........ 21st
Totepool National Spirit Hurdle Race (Fontwell Park) ........ 22nd
Paddy Power Johnstown Novice Hurdle (Naas) ........ 22nd
Paddy Power Newlands Steeple Chase (Naas) ........ 22nd
Nas Na Riogh Novices' Handicap Steeple Chase (Naas) ........ 22nd
Michael Purcell Memorial Novices' Hurdle (Thurles) ........ 26th
£1.25 Million Scoop6 Premier Kelso Hurdle Race (Kelso) ........ 28th
totepool.com Premier Steeple Chase (Kelso) ........ 28th
Stanjames.com Supporting Greatwood Gold Cup Handicap Steeple Chase (Newbury) ........ 28th
William Hill - Bet On The Move Mares' Novices' Hurdle (Doncaster) ........ 28th
Carrickmines Handicap Steeple Chase (Leopardstown) ........ 28th

## MARCH

William Hill Imperial Cup Handicap Hurdle Race (Sandown Park) ........ 7th
European Breeders' Fund William Hill 'National Hunt' Novices' Hurdle Race (Sandown Park) ........ 7th
EBF Stallions / TBA Mares' Standard Open National Hunt Flat Race (Sandown Park) ........ 7th
Ladbrokes Lady Wulfruna Stakes (Wolverhampton) ........ 7th
Shamrock Handicap Steeple Chase (Gowran Park) ........ 7th
Irish Racing Writers Kingsfurze Novices' Hurdle (Naas) ........ 8th
Directors Plate Novices' Steeple Chase (Naas) ........ 8th
Leinster Grand National Handicap Steeple Chase (Naas) ........ 8th
Stan James Champion Hurdle Challenge Trophy (Cheltenham) ........ 10th
Racing Post Arkle Challenge Trophy Steeple Chase (Cheltenham) ........ 10th
Sky Bet Supreme Novices' Hurdle Race (Cheltenham) ........ 10th
OLBG David Nicholson Mares' Hurdle Race (Cheltenham) ........ 10th
Ultima Business Solutions Festival Handicap Steeple Chase (Cheltenham) ........ 10th
National Hunt Steeple Chase (Amateur Riders' Novices' Steeple Chase) (Cheltenham) ........ 10th
Rewards4Racing Novices' Handicap Steeple Chase (Cheltenham) ........ 10th
Betway Queen Mother Champion Steeple Chase (Cheltenham) ........ 11th
RSA Steeple Chase (Cheltenham) ........ 11th
Neptune Investment Management Novices' Hurdle Race (Registered As Baring Bingham Novices' Hurdle Race) (Cheltenham)... 11th
Weatherbys Champion Bumper (A Standard Open National Hunt Flat Race) (Cheltenham) ........ 11th
Coral Cup (A Handicap Hurdle Race) (Cheltenham) ........ 11th
Fred Winter Juvenile Handicap Hurdle Race (Cheltenham) ........ 11th
Ladbrokes World Hurdle Race (Cheltenham) ........ 12th
Ryanair Steeple Chase (Registered As Festival Trophy Steeple Chase) (Cheltenham) ........ 12th
JLT Novices' Steeple Chase (Registered As Golden Miller Novices' Chase) (Cheltenham) ........ 12th
Brown Advisory and Merriebelle Stable Plate (A Handicap Steeple Chase) (Cheltenham) ........ 12th
Pertemps Network Final (A Handicap Hurdle Race) (Cheltenham) ........ 12th
Betfred Cheltenham Gold Cup Steeple Chase (Cheltenham) ........ 13th
JCB Triumph Hurdle Race (Cheltenham) ........ 13th
Albert Bartlett Novices' Hurdle Race (Registered As Spa Novices' Hurdle Race) (Cheltenham) ........ 13th
Johnny Henderson Grand Annual Steeple Chase Challenge Cup (Handicap) (Cheltenham) ........ 13th
Foxhunter Steeple Chase (Cheltenham) ........ 13th
Vincent O'Brien County Handicap Hurdle Race (Cheltenham) ........ 13th
Coral.co.uk Winter Derby (Lingfield Park) ........ 14th
bookmakers.co.uk Hever Sprint Stakes (Lingfield Park) ........ 14th
32Red Spring Cup (Lingfield Park) ........ 14th
Betfred Midlands Grand National Steeple Chase (A Handicap) (Uttoxeter) ........ 14th
Dawn Run EBF Mares Only Novices' Steeple Chase (Limerick) ........ 15th
Shannon Spray EBF Mares Only Novices' Hurdle (Limerick) ........ 15th
EBF Novices' Chase Series Final Handicap Steeple Chase (Navan) ........ 15th
EBF Stallions & TBA Mares' 'National Hunt' Novices' Hurdle Race Finale (A Limited Handicap) (Newbury) ........ 21st

William Hill In The App Store Doncaster Mile Stakes (Doncaster) ... 28th
William Hill - Bet On The Move Cammidge Trophy (Doncaster) ... 28th
Spring Mile (Handicap) (Doncaster) ... 28th
Betway Lincoln (Handicap) (Doncaster) ... 28th
6 Places At Aintree At BetVictor Magnolia Stakes (Kempton Park) ... 28th
An Uaimh Steeple Chase (Navan) ... 28th
EBF Park Express Stakes (Curragh) ... 29th
Hugh McMahon Memorial Novices' Steeple Chase (Limerick) ... 29th
Kevin McManus Pro/Am 4yo Only Bumper (Limerick) ... 29th

# APRIL

Patton Stakes (Dundalk) ... 1st
Betfred Mobile Lotto Snowdrop Fillies' Stakes (Kempton Park) ... 4th
Power Gold Cup Novices' Steeple Chase (Fairyhouse) ... 5th
EBF Mares Novice Hurdle Final (Fairyhouse) ... 5th
Coolmore NH Sires Festival Novices' Hurdle (Fairyhouse) ... 5th
INHSO Final Novices' Handicap Hurdle (Fairyhouse) ... 5th
Imperial Call Steeple Chase (Cork) ... 5th
Easter Handicap Hurdle (Cork) ... 5th
Cork Sprint Stakes (Cork) ... 6th
Boylesports Irish Grand National Limited Handicap Steeple Chase (Fairyhouse) ... 6th
Rathbarry & Glenview Studs Hardy Eustace Novices' Hurdle (Fairyhouse) ... 6th
Ballybin Hurdle (Fairyhouse) ... 6th
Greenogue Novices' Handicap Steeple Chase (Fairyhouse) ... 6th
Keelings Hurdle (Fairyhouse) ... 6th
John & Chich Fowler Memorial EBF Mares Steeple Chase (Fairyhouse) ... 6th
thetote.ie Handicap Hurdle (Fairyhouse) ... 7th
Tayto 4yo Hurdle (Fairyhouse) ... 7th
Normans Grove Steeple Chase (Fairyhouse) ... 7th
totepool EBF Stallions Barry Hills Further Flight Stakes (Nottingham) ... 8th
Crabbie's Injured Jockeys Fund 50th Anniversary 4-Y-O Juvenile Hurdle Race (Aintree) ... 9th
Crabbie's Fox Hunters' Steeple Chase (Aintree) ... 9th
Betfred Bowl Steeple Chase (Aintree) ... 9th
Doom Bar Aintree Hurdle (Aintree) ... 9th
Crabbie's Manifesto Novices' Steeple Chase (Aintree) ... 9th
Crabbie's Handicap Hurdle Race (Aintree) ... 9th
Crabbie's Red Rum Handicap Steeple Chase (Aintree) ... 9th
Crabbie's Melling Steeple Chase (Aintree) ... 10th
Crabbie's Mildmay Novices' Steeple Chase (Aintree) ... 10th
Doom Bar Sefton Novices' Hurdle Race (Aintree) ... 10th
Crabbie's Top Novices' Hurdle Race (Aintree) ... 10th
Crabbie's Topham Steeple Chase (Handicap) (Aintree) ... 10th
Alder Hey Children's Charity Handicap Hurdle Race (Aintree) ... 10th
Crabbie's Mares' Standard Open National Hunt Flat Race (Aintree) ... 10th
Crabbie's Grand National Steeple Chase (Handicap) (Aintree) ... 11th
Silver Cross Stayers' Hurdle Race (Registered As The Liverpool Hurdle Race) (Aintree) ... 11th
Doom Bar Maghull Novices' Steeple Chase (Aintree) ... 11th
Pertemps Network Mersey Novices' Hurdle Race (Aintree) ... 11th
Crabbie's Handicap Steeple Chase (Aintree) ... 11th
Weatherbys Private Banking Champion Standard Open (Aintree) ... 11th
32Red International Trial Stakes (Lingfield Park) ... 11th
Leopardstown 1000 Guineas Trial (Leopardstown) ... 12th
Ballysax Stakes (Leopardstown) ... 12th
Leopardstown 2000 Guineas Trial (Leopardstown) ... 12th
Heritage Stakes (Leopardstown) ... 12th
Ceres Estates Silver Trophy Steeple Chase (A Limited Handicap) (Cheltenham) ... 15th
Lanwades Stud Nell Gwyn Stakes (Newmarket) ... 15th
CSP European Free Handicap (Newmarket) ... 15th
ebm-papst Feilden Stakes (Newmarket) ... 15th
Connaught Access Flooring Abernant Stakes (Newmarket) ... 16th
Weatherbys Hamilton Insurance Earl Of Sefton Stakes (Newmarket) ... 16th
Novae Bloodstock Insurance Craven Stakes (Newmarket) ... 16th
EBF / TBA Mares Novices' Steeple Chase Finale (A Handicap) (Cheltenham) ... 16th
OLBG.com Supports Mares Jump Racing Mares Handicap Hurdle (Cheltenham) ... 16th
TBA Mares' Novices' Hurdle (Cheltenham) ... 16th
Whitsbury Manor Stud & EBF Stallions Lansdown Fillies' Stakes (Bath) ... 17th
Hillhouse Quarry Handicap Steeple Chase (Ayr) ... 17th
QTS Scottish Champion Hurdle Race (A Limited Handicap) (Ayr) ... 18th
Arcadia Consulting William Dickie & Mary Robertson Future Champion Novices' Steeple Chase (Ayr) ... 18th
Coral Scottish Grand National Handicap Steeple Chase (Ayr) ... 18th
Scotty Brand Handicap Steeple Chase (Ayr) ... 18th
Dubai Duty Free Stakes (Newbury) ... 18th
Dubai Duty Free Finest Surprise Stakes (Newbury) ... 18th
Aon Greenham Stakes (Newbury) ... 18th
Salsabil Stakes (Navan) ... 18th

Gladness Stakes (Curragh) ........ 19th
Alleged Stakes (Curragh) ........ 19th
Bet365 Mile (Sandown Park) ........ 24th
Bet365 Gordon Richards Stakes (Sandown Park) ........ 24th
Bet365 Classic Trial (Sandown Park) ........ 24th
totepool EBF Stallions King Richard III Stakes (Leicester) ........ 25th
Bet365 Celebration Steeple Chase (Sandown Park) ........ 25th
Bet365 Gold Cup Steeple Chase (Handicap) (Sandown Park) ........ 25th
Bet365 Oaksey Steeple Chase (Sandown Park) ........ 25th
Bet365 Select Hurdle (Sandown Park) ........ 25th
Martin Molony Stakes (Limerick) ........ 25th
Victor McCalmont Stakes (Gowran Park) ........ 26th
Woodlands Sprint Stakes (Naas) ........ 27th
Evening Herald Champion Novice Hurdle (Punchestown) ........ 28th
Growise The Ellier Novice Steeple Chase (Punchestown) ........ 28th
Boylesports Drogheda Champion Steeple Chase (Punchestown) ........ 28th
Bragbet Handicap Hurdle (Punchestown) ........ 28th
Longines Sagaro Stakes (Ascot) ........ 29th
bet365 Paradise Stakes (Ascot) ........ 29th
Irish Daily Mirror War of Attrition Novices' Hurdle (Punchestown) ........ 29th
Attheraces Champion Bumper (Punchestown) ........ 29th
Bibby Financial Punchestown Gold Cup Steeple Chase (Punchestown) ........ 29th
Guinness Handicap Steeple Chase (Punchestown) ........ 29th
Ladbrokes World Series Hurdle (Punchestown) ........ 30th
Ryanair Colliers Novices' Steeple Chase (Punchestown) ........ 30th
Three.ie Black Hills Handicap Steeple Chase (Punchestown) ........ 30th

## MAY

Racing Post Punchestown Champion Hurdle, (Punchestown) ........ 1st
Tattersalls Ireland Champion Novice Hurdle (Punchestown) ........ 1st
Aon Limited Novice Handicap Chase (Punchestown) ........ 1st
EBF Glencarraig Lady Mares Only Handicap Steeple Chase (Punchestown) ........ 1st
Qipco 2000 Guineas Stakes (Newmarket) ........ 2nd
Qatar Bloodstock Jockey Club Stakes (Newmarket) ........ 2nd
Pearl Bloodstock Palace House Stakes (Newmarket) ........ 2nd
Makfi Newmarket Stakes (Newmarket) ........ 2nd
£5 Million Scoop6 Today Briytish Stallion Studs EBF Conqueror Stakes (Goodwood) ........ 2nd
Betfred £5 Million Scoop6 Today EBF Stallions Daisy Warwick Stakes (Goodwood) ........ 2nd
EBF Mares Champion Hurdle (Punchestown) ........ 2nd
Aes Champion 4yo Only Hurdle (Punchestown) ........ 2nd
Setanta Sport Handicap Hurdle (Punchestown) ........ 2nd
Palmerstown House Pat Taaffe Limited Handicap Steeple Chase (Punchestown) ........ 2nd
Qipco 1000 Guineas Stakes (Newmarket) ........ 3rd
Qatar Bloodstock Dahlia Stakes (Newmarket) ........ 3rd
Tweenhills Pretty Polly Stakes (Newmarket) ........ 3rd
Athasi Stakes, (Curragh) ........ 4th
Mooresbridge Stakes (Curragh) ........ 4th
Tetrarch Stakes (Curragh) ........ 4th
Betway Chester Cup (Heritage Handicap) (Chester) ........ 6th
Weatherbys Private Banking Cheshire Oaks (Chester) ........ 6th
Mbna Chester Vase (Chester) ........ 7th
Betfair Price Rush Huxley Stakes (Chester) ........ 7th
Boodles Diamond Ormonde Stakes (Chester) ........ 8th
Betfair Cash Out Dee Stakes (Chester) ........ 8th
Carey Group Buckhounds Stakes (Ascot) ........ 9th
£7.5 Million Totescoop6 Victoria Cup (Heritage Handicap) (Ascot) ........ 9th
Pertemps Network Spring Trophy Stakes (Haydock Park) ........ 9th
Pertemps Network Handicap Hurdle Race (Haydock Park) ........ 9th
Follow Scoop6 At Totepoolliveinfo.com Chartwell Fillies' Stakes (Lingfield Park) ........ 9th
betfred.com Derby Trial Stakes (Lingfield Park) ........ 9th
Betfred £7.5 Million Scoop6 Today Oaks Trial Stakes (Lingfield Park) ........ 9th
EBF Stallions Weatherbys Bloodstock Reports Kilvington Fillies' Stakes (Nottingham) ........ 9th
Derrinstown 1000 Guineas Trial Stakes (Leopardstown) ........ 10th
Derrinstown Derby Trial Stakes (Leopardstown) ........ 10th
Amethyst Stakes (Leopardstown) ........ 10th
Ladbrokes Handicap Hurdle (Killarney) ........ 10th
unibet.co.uk Royal Windsor Stakes (Windsor) ........ 11th
Duke Of York Clipper Logistics Stakes (York) ........ 13th
Tattersalls Musidora Stakes (York) ........ 13th
Blue Wind Stakes (Naas) ........ 13th
Betfred Dante Stakes (York) ........ 14th
Betfred Middleton Stakes (York) ........ 14th
Betfred Hambleton Stakes (York) ........ 14th
Betway Yorkshire Cup (York) ........ 15th
Ginger Grouse Braveheart Stakes (Hamilton Park) ........ 15th

Irish Champions Weekend Fillies' Stakes (York) 15th
Langleys Solicitors LLP EBF Stallions Marygate Stakes (York) 15th
Al Shaqab Carnarvon Stakes (Newbury) 16th
Al Shaqab Fillies' Trial Stakes (Newbury) 16th
Al Shaqab Lockinge Stakes (Newbury) 16th
Al Shaqab Aston Park Stakes (Newbury) 16th
Tamdown King Charles II Stakes (Newmarket) 16th
Tamdown Fairway Stakes (Newmarket) 16th
Vintage Crop Stakes (Navan) 17th
Bibendum Height Of Fashion Stakes (Goodwood) 21st
Casco EBF Stallions Cocked Hat Stakes (Goodwood) 22nd
Betfred.com Temple Stakes (Haydock Park) 23rd
Betfred Mind Blowing Scoop6 Today EBF Stallions Stakes (Haydock Park) 23rd
32Red Casino Stakes (Goodwood) 23rd
32Red Stakes (Goodwood) 23rd
Tattersalls Irish 2000 Guineas, (Curragh) 23rd
Weatherbys Greenlands Stakes (Curragh) 23rd
TRI Equestrian Ridgewood Pearl Stakes (Curragh) 23rd
Marble Hill Stakes (Curragh) 23rd
Etihad Airways Irish 1000 Guineas (Curragh) 24th
Tattersalls Gold Cup (Curragh) 24th
Airlie Gallinule Stakes (Curragh) 24th
Cantor Fitzgerald Henry II Stakes (Sandown Park) 28th
Cantor Fitzgerald Brigadier Gerard Stakes (Sandown Park) 28th
Cantor Fitzgerald Corporate Finance Heron Stakes (Sandown Park) 28th
Cantor Fitzgerald Equities National Stakes (Sandown Park) 28th
Timeform Jury Stakes (Haydock Park) 30th
Pinnacle Stakes (Haydock Park) 30th
Winning Express Achilles Stakes (Haydock Park) 30th
Stowe Family Law LLP Grand Cup (York) 30th

# JUNE

Weatherbys Private Banking Leisure Stakes (Windsor) 1st
Lacken Stakes (Naas) 1st
Coolmore Stud Juvenile Fillies Stakes (Naas) 1st
Rochestown Stakes (Naas) 1st
Whitehead Memorial Stakes (Naas) 1st
Investec Oaks (In Memory Of Sir Henry Cecil) (Epsom Downs) 5th
Investec Diomed Stakes (Epsom Downs) 5th
Princess Elizabeth Stakes (Epsom Downs) 5th
Investec Surrey Stakes (Epsom Downs) 5th
Seamus & Rosemary McGrath Memorial Savel Beg Stakes (Leopardstown) 5th
Nijinsky (For King George V Cup) Stakes (Leopardstown) 5th
Investec Derby (Epsom Downs) 6th
Investec Coronation Cup (Epsom Downs) 6th
Investec Specialist Bank 'Dash' (Heritage Handicap) (Epsom Downs) 6th
Investec Woodcote Stakes (Epsom Downs) 6th
Silver Stakes (Curragh) 7th
Ballyogan Stakes (Leopardstown) 7th
Lord Weinstock Memorial Stakes (Newbury) 11th
Glencaim Stakes (Leopardstown) 11th
Betfred 'Hat Trick Heaven' Scurry Stakes (Sandown Park) 13th
Ian and Kate Hall Macmillan Ganton Stakes (York) 13th
William Hill Scottish Sprint Cup (A Heritage Handicap) (Musselburgh) 13th
EBF Stallions Cathedral Stakes (Salisbury) 14th
Noblesse Stakes (Cork) 14th
Midsummer Sprint Stakes (Cork) 14th
Voute Sales Warwickshire Oaks Stakes (Nottingham) 15th
St James's Palace Stakes (Ascot) 16th
Queen Anne Stakes (Ascot) 16th
King's Stand Stakes (Ascot) 16th
Coventry Stakes (Ascot) 16th
Windsor Castle Stakes (Ascot) 16th
Prince Of Wales's Stakes (Ascot) 17th
Queen Mary Stakes (Ascot) 17th
Duke Of Cambridge Stakes (Ascot) 17th
Jersey Stakes (Ascot) 17th
Royal Hunt Cup (Heritage Handicap) (Ascot) 17th
Sandringham Handicap Stakes (Ascot) 17th
Gold Cup (Ascot) 18th
Ribblesdale Stakes (Ascot) 18th
Norfolk Stakes (Ascot) 18th
Tercentenary Stakes (Ascot) 18th
Britannia Stakes (Heritage Handicap) (Ascot) 18th
Ballycorus Stakes (Leopardstown) 18th

Coronation Stakes (Ascot) ........ 19th
Commonwealth Cup Sprint Stakes (Ascot) ........ 19th
King Edward VII Stakes (Ascot) ........ 19th
Albany Stakes (Ascot) ........ 19th
Queen's Vase (Ascot) ........ 19th
Wolferton Handicap Stakes (Ascot) ........ 19th
Diamond Jubilee Stakes (Ascot) ........ 20th
Hardwicke Stakes (Ascot) ........ 20th
Wokingham Stakes (Heritage Handicap) (Ascot) ........ 20th
Chesham Stakes (Ascot) ........ 20th
Scottish Sun / EBF Stallions Land O'Burns Fillies' Stakes (Ayr) ........ 20th
totepool Pontefract Castle Stakes (Pontefract) ........ 21st
Naas Oaks Trial Stakes (Naas) ........ 24th
EBF Stallions bet365 Eternal Stakes (Nottingham) ........ 25th
Betfred TV / EBF Stallions Hoppings Stakes (Newcastle) ........ 26th
International Stakes (Curragh) ........ 26th
Betfred Tv Chipchase Stakes (Newcastle) ........ 27th
John Smith's Northumberland Plate (Heritage Handicap) (Newcastle) ........ 27th
Bet365 Criterion Stakes (Newmarket) ........ 27th
bet365 Fred Archer Stakes (Newmarket) ........ 27th
bet365 Empress Stakes (Newmarket) ........ 27th
Unibet 'Road To Rio Challenge' Midsummer Stakes (Windsor) ........ 27th
Dubai Duty Free Irish Derby (Curragh) ........ 27th
Dubai Duty Free Railway Stakes (Curragh) ........ 27th
Dubai Duty Free Stakes (Curragh) ........ 27th
Dubai Duty Free Celebration Stakes (Curragh) ........ 27th
Belgrave Stakes (Curragh) ........ 27th
Pretty Polly Stakes (Curragh) ........ 28th
At The Races Curragh Cup (Curragh) ........ 28th
Grangecon Stud Balanchine Stakes (Curragh) ........ 28th

## JULY

Ambant Gala Stakes (Sandown Park) ........ 3rd
Dragon Stakes (Sandown Park) ........ 3rd
Bet365 Lancashire Oaks (Haydock Park) ........ 4th
Bet365 Old Newton Cup (Heritage Handicap) (Haydock Park) ........ 4th
Coral-Eclipse (Sandown Park) ........ 4th
Coral Charge (Sandown Park) ........ 4th
Coral Distaff (Sandown Park) ........ 4th
Coral Marathon (Sandown Park) ........ 4th
Brownstown Stakes (Fairyhouse) ........ 5th
Lenebane Stakes (Roscommon) ........ 6th
Weatherbys VAT Services Pipalong Stakes (Pontefract) ........ 7th
Princess Of Wales's Boylesports.com Stakes (Newmarket) ........ 9th
Portland Place Properties July Stakes (Newmarket) ........ 9th
Bahrain Trophy (Newmarket) ........ 9th
Hastings Direct Sir Henry Cecil Stakes (Newmarket) ........ 9th
Qipco Falmouth Stakes (Newmarket) ........ 10th
Duchess Of Cambridge Stakes (Sponsored By Qipco) (Newmarket) ........ 10th
Betfred Mobile Stakes (Heritage Handicap) (Newmarket) ........ 10th
Totepool Summer Stakes (York) ........ 10th
Fred Cowley Mbe Memorial Summer Mile Stakes (Ascot) ........ 11th
Totepool Heritage Handicap Stakes (Ascot) ........ 11th
Darley July Cup (Newmarket) ........ 11th
666Bet Superlative Stakes (Newmarket) ........ 11th
666Bet Bunbury Cup (Heritage Handicap) (Newmarket) ........ 11th
Bet With Corbett Sports City Plate (Chester) ........ 11th
John Smith's City Walls Stakes (York) ........ 11th
John Smith's Silver Cup Stakes (York) ........ 11th
55th John Smith's Cup (Heritage Handicap) (York) ........ 11th
Tipperary Stakes (Tipperary) ........ 11th
Grimes Hurdle (Tipperary) ........ 11th
Cairn Rouge Stakes (Killarney) ........ 13th
Bourn Vincent Memorial Handicap Steeple Chase (Killarney) ........ 14th
Challenge Stakes (Leopardstown) ........ 16th
Meld Stakes (Leopardstown) ........ 16th
EBF Stallions Glasgow Stakes (Hamilton Park) ........ 17th
The Rose Bowl Stakes - Sponsored by Compton Beauchamp Estates Ltd (Newbury) ........ 17th
Al Basti Equiworld Hackwood Stakes (Newbury) ........ 18th
Doom Bar Stakes (Newbury) ........ 18th
Newsells Park Stud Stakes (Newmarket) ........ 18th
Darley Irish Oaks (Curragh) ........ 18th
Jebel Ali Anglesey Stakes (Curragh) ........ 18th
Sapphire Stakes (Curragh) ........ 19th
Kilboy Estate Stakes (Curragh) ........ 19th

Minstrel Stakes (Curragh) ........ 19th
Sweet Mimosa Stakes (Naas) ........ 22nd
The British Stallion Studs EBF Chalice Stakes (Newbury) ........ 23rd
Irish Champions Weekend EBF Stallions Star Stakes (Sandown Park) ........ 23rd
Silver Flash Stakes (Leopardstown) ........ 23rd
Tyros Stakes (Leopardstown) ........ 23rd
Woodcote Stud EBF Stallions Valiant Stakes (Ascot) ........ 24th
The British Stallion Studs EBF Lyric Fillies' Stakes (York) ........ 24th
King George VI And Queen Elizabeth Stakes (Ascot) ........ 25th
Princess Margaret Juddmonte Stakes (Ascot) ........ 25th
Titanic Belfast Winkfield Stakes (Ascot) ........ 25th
Longines International Stakes (Heritage Handicap) (Ascot) ........ 25th
Skybet York Stakes (York) ........ 25th
Skybet Supporting The Yorkshire Racing Summer Festival Pomfret Stakes (Pontefract) ........ 26th
Qatar Lennox Stakes (Goodwood) ........ 28th
Bet365 Molecomb Stakes (Goodwood) ........ 28th
Qatar Sussex Stakes (Goodwood) ........ 29th
Qatar Vintage Stakes (Goodwood) ........ 29th
Neptune Investment Management Gordon Stakes (Goodwood) ........ 29th
thetote.com Galway Plate Handicap Chase (Galway) ........ 29th
Qatar Richmond Stakes (Goodwood) ........ 30th
Qatar Goodwood Cup (Goodwood) ........ 30th
Sterling Insurance Lillie Langtry Stakes (Goodwood) ........ 30th
Guinness Galway Handicap Hurdle (Galway) ........ 30th
Corrib EBF Fillies Stakes (Galway) ........ 30th
Qatar King George Stakes (Goodwood) ........ 31st
L'Ormarins Queens Plate Stakes (Goodwood) ........ 31st
Coutts Glorious Stakes (Goodwood) ........ 31st
Bonhams Thoroughbred Stakes (Goodwood) ........ 31st
Betfred Mile (Heritage Handicap) (Goodwood) ........ 31st

# AUGUST

Qatar Nassau Stakes (Goodwood) ........ 1st
Qatar Stewards' Cup (Heritage Handicap) (Goodwood) ........ 1st
Ladbrokes Mervue Handicap Hurdle (Galway) ........ 1st
MBNA Queensferry Stakes (Chester) ........ 2nd
Give Thanks Stakes (Cork) ........ 4th
Platinum Stakes (Cork) ........ 4th
Ballyroan Stakes (Leopardstown) ........ 6th
Abergwaun Stakes (Tipperary) ........ 7th
El Gran Senor Stakes (Tipperary) ........ 7th
Betfred Rose Of Lancaster Stakes (Haydock Park) ........ 8th
Betfred TV / EBF Stallions Dick Hern Fillies' Stakes (Haydock Park) ........ 8th
German-Thoroughbred.com Sweet Solera Stakes (Newmarket) ........ 8th
Phoenix Stakes (Curragh) ........ 9th
Patrick O'Leary Memorial Phoenix Sprint (Curragh) ........ 9th
EBF Stallions Upavon Fillies' Stakes (Salisbury) ........ 12th
Hurry Harriet Stakes (Gowran Park) ........ 12th
Totepool Sovereign Stakes (Salisbury) ........ 13th
Desmond Stakes (Leopardstown) ........ 13th
Bathwick Tyres St Hugh's Stakes (Newbury) ........ 14th
Betfred Hungerford Stakes (Newbury) ........ 15th
Betfred Tv Geoffrey Freer Stakes (Newbury) ........ 15th
Denford Stud Stakes (Newbury) ........ 15th
EBF Stallions Highfield Farm Flying Fillies' Stakes (Pontefract) ........ 16th
Juddmonte International Stakes (York) ........ 19th
Betway Great Voltigeur Stakes (York) ........ 19th
Tattersalls Acomb Stakes (York) ........ 19th
Ruby Stakes (Killarney) ........ 19th
Darley Yorkshire Oaks (York) ........ 20th
Pinsent Masons Lowther Stakes (York) ........ 20th
Sir Henry Cecil & EBF Galtres Stakes (York) ........ 20th
Coolmore Nunthorpe Stakes (York) ........ 20th
Weatherbys Hamilton Insurance Lonsdale Cup (York) ........ 21st
Sky Bet City Of York Stakes (York) ........ 21st
EBF Stallions Stonehenge Stakes (Salisbury) ........ 21st
Lough Leane Handicap Chase (Killarney) ........ 21st
European Wealth Solario Stakes (Sandown Park) ........ 21st
Thoroughbred Breeders' Association Atalanta Stakes (Sandown Park) ........ 22nd
Irish Thoroughbred Marketing Gimcrack Stakes (York) ........ 22nd
Betfred Play Today's £2Million+ Scoop6 Strensall Stakes (York) ........ 22nd
Betfred Ebor (Heritage Handicap) (York) ........ 22nd
Julia Graves Roses Stakes (York) ........ 22nd
Win £10,000,000 On Betdaq Colossus Chester Stakes (Chester) ........ 22nd
Renaissance Stakes (Curragh) ........ 22nd

Curragh Stakes (Curragh) ........ 22nd
Brandon Handicap Hurdle (Killarney) ........ 22nd
Debutante Stakes (Curragh) ........ 23rd
Galileo EBF Futurity Stakes (Curragh) ........ 23rd
Ballycullen Stakes (Curragh) ........ 23rd
Royal Whip Stakes (Curragh) ........ 23rd
Fairy Bridge Stakes (Tipperary) ........ 27th
Doom Bar Celebration Mile (Goodwood) ........ 29th
Whiteley Clinic Prestige Stakes (Goodwood) ........ 29th
Absolute Aesthetics March Stakes (Goodwood) ........ 29th
Betfred Beverley Bullet Sprint Stakes (Beverley) ........ 29th
Stobart Members Club Hopeful Stakes (Newmarket) ........ 29th
188Bet Winter Hill Stakes (Windsor) ........ 29th
118Bet August Stakes (Windsor) ........ 29th
Doom Bar Supreme Stakes (Goodwood) ........ 30th
Dance Design Stakes (Curragh) ........ 30th
Round Tower Stakes (Curragh) ........ 30th
Flame Of Tara Stakes (Curragh) ........ 30th
Irish Stallion Farms EBF Ripon Champion Two Years Old Trophy 2015 (Ripon) ........ 31st

# SEPTEMBER

Country Gentlemen's Association Dick Poole Fillies' Stakes (Salisbury) ........ 3rd
Winning Post Bookmakers Bristol Handicap Stakes (Heritage Handicap) (Ascot) ........ 5th
Betfred Sprint Cup (Haydock Park) ........ 5th
Betfred.com Superior Mile (Haydock Park) ........ 5th
Betfred Fun and Friendly Stakes (Haydock Park) ........ 5th
Totescoop6 September Stakes (Kempton Park) ........ 5th
Totescoop6 'Millionaire Maker' Sirenia Stakes (Kempton Park) ........ 5th
Betfred Garrowby Stakes (York) ........ 6th
Oyster Stakes (Galway) ........ 7th
Ballybrit Novices' Steeple Chase (Galway) ........ 8th
John Smith's Original Scarbrough Stakes (Doncaster) ........ 9th
DFS Park Hill Stakes (Doncaster) ........ 10th
Japan Racing Association Sceptre Stakes (Doncaster) ........ 10th
Socialites Electric Cigarettes Doncaster Cup (Doncaster) ........ 11th
John Smith's Extra Smooth May Hill Stakes (Doncaster) ........ 11th
Polypipe Flying Childers Stakes (Doncaster) ........ 11th
Weatherbys Stallion Book Flying Scotsman Stakes (Doncaster) ........ 11th
Ladbrokes St Leger Stakes (Doncaster) ........ 12th
OLBG Park Stakes (Doncaster) ........ 12th
At Races Champagne Stakes (Doncaster) ........ 12th
Feel The Rush At Betfair Stand Cup (Chester) ........ 12th
QIPCO Irish Champion Stakes (Leopardstown) ........ 12th
Coolmore Matron Stakes (Leopardstown) ........ 12th
Clipper Logistics Solonoway Stakes (Leopardstown) ........ 12th
Breeders Cup Trial Golden Fleece Stakes (Leopardstown) ........ 12th
KPMG Kilternan Stakes (Leopardstown) ........ 12th
Palmerstown House St Leger Stakes (Curragh) ........ 13th
Moyglare Stud Stakes (Curragh) ........ 13th
Goffs Vincent O'Brien National Stakes (Curragh) ........ 13th
Moyglare Stud Blandford Stakes (Curragh) ........ 13th
Derrinstown Stud Flying Five Stakes (Curragh) ........ 13th
Latrigue 4yo Handicap Hurdle (Listowel) ........ 15th
Nigel & Carolyn Elwes Fortune Stakes (Sandown Park) ........ 16th
EBF At The Races John Musker Fillies' Stakes (Yarmouth) ........ 16th
Guinness Kerry National Handicap Chase (Listowel) ........ 16th
Listowel Stakes (Listowel) ........ 16th
Ladbrokes Handicap Hurdle (Listowel) ........ 17th
EBF Stallions Harry Rosebery Stakes (Ayr) ........ 18th
Dubai Duty Free Cup (Newbury) ........ 18th
William Hill Firth Of Clyde Stakes (Ayr) ........ 19th
William Hill Ayr Gold Cup (Heritage Handicap) (Ayr) ........ 19th
William Hill 80th Anniversary Book Launch Doonside Cup (Ayr) ........ 19th
Dubai Duty Free Mill Reef Stakes (Newbury) ........ 19th
Dubai Duty Free Legacy Cup (Newbury) ........ 19th
Dubai International Airport World Trophy (Newbury) ........ 19th
Cordell Lavarack Stakes (Gowran Park) ........ 20th
R H Hall Foundation Stakes (Goodwood) ........ 23rd
Somerville Tattersall Stakes (Newmarket) ........ 24th
Jockey Club Rose Bowl (Newmarket) ........ 24th
Shadwell Joel Stakes (Newmarket) ........ 25th
Shadwell Rockfel Stakes (Newmarket) ........ 25th
Princess Royal EBF Sakhee Stakes (Newmarket) ........ 25th
Nayef Rosemary Stakes (Newmarket) ........ 25th
Mawatheeq Godolphin Stakes (Newmarket) ........ 25th

Connolly's Red Mills Cheveley Park Stakes (Newmarket) ... 26th
Vision.ae Middle Park Stakes (Newmarket) ... 26th
Juddmonte Royal Lodge Stakes (Newmarket) ... 26th
Betfred Cambridgeshire (Heritage Handicap) (Newmarket) ... 26th
Juddmonte Beresford Stakes (Curragh) ... 27th
CL & MF Weld Park Stakes (Curragh) ... 27th
Blenheim Stakes (Curragh) ... 27th
Loughbrown Stakes (Curragh) ... 27th
Kilbegnet Novices' Steeple Chase (Roscommon) ... 28th

# OCTOBER

Diamond Stakes (Dundalk) ... 2nd
Londonmetric Noel Murless Stakes (Ascot) ... 2nd
BMW Cumberland Lodge Stakes (Ascot) ... 3rd
John Guest Bengough Stakes (Ascot) ... 3rd
Totepool EBF Stallions October Stakes (Ascot) ... 3rd
Albert Bartlett Stakes (Ascot) ... 3rd
Totepool Challenge Cup (Heritage Handicap) (Ascot) ... 3rd
Kingdom Of Bahrain Sun Chariot Stakes (Newmarket) ... 3rd
Triconnex Oh So Sharp Stakes (Newmarket) ... 3rd
EBF Stallions National Stud Boadicea Fillies' Stakes (Newmarket) ... 3rd
totescoop6 EBF Guisborough Stakes (Redcar) ... 3rd
totepool Two-Year-Old Trophy (Redcar) ... 3rd
Gowran Champion Chase (Gowran Park) ... 3rd
Kilkenny Racing Festival Handicap Hurdle (Gowran Park) ... 3rd
Concorde Stakes (Tipperary) ... 4th
Tipperary Hurdle (Tipperary) ... 4th
Joe Mac Novices' Hurdle (Tipperary) ... 4th
Like A Butterfly Novices' Steeple Chase (Tipperary) ... 4th
Star Appeal Stakes (Dundalk) ... 9th
Betfred Goals Galore Autumn Stakes (Newmarket) ... 10th
Betfred Mobile Pride Stakes (Newmarket) ... 10th
Betfred Cesarewitch (Heritage Handicap) (Newmarket) ... 10th
Betfred TV Stakes (Heritage Handicap) (Newmarket) ... 10th
coral.co.uk Rockingham Stakes (York) ... 10th
Waterford Testimonial Stakes (Curragh) ... 11th
Finale Stakes (Curragh) ... 11th
Lanwades & Staffordstown Studs Silken Glider Stakes (Curragh) ... 11th
Totepool Persian War Novices' Hurdle Race (Chepstow) ... 11th
Totepoolliveinfo.com Silver Trophy Handicap Hurdle Race (Chepstow) ... 11th
Ladbrokes Munster National Handicap Chase (Limerick) ... 11th
Greenmount Park Novices' Hurdle (Limerick) ... 11th
Grabel Mares Hurdle (Punchestown) ... 15th
Carvills Hill Chase (Punchestown) ... 15th
Buck House Novices' Steeple Chase (Punchestown) ... 15th
Dubai Fillies' Mile (Newmarket) ... 16th
Dubai Dewhurst Stakes (Newmarket) ... 16th
Vision.ae Challenge Stakes (Newmarket) ... 16th
Dubai Cornwallis Stakes (Newmarket) ... 16th
Darley Stakes (Newmarket) ... 16th
Carlingford Stakes (Dundalk) ... 16th
Queen Elizabeth II Stakes Sponsored By Qipco (Ascot) ... 17th
Qipco Champion Stakes (Ascot) ... 17th
Qipco British Champions Fillies & Mares Stakes (Ascot) ... 17th
Qipco British Champions Sprint Stakes (Ascot) ... 17th
Qipco British Champions Long Distance Cup (Ascot) ... 17th
Navigation Stakes (Cork) ... 17th
Garnet Stakes (Naas) ... 18th
Kinsale Handicap Steeple Chase (Cork) ... 18th
totepool EBF Stallions Silver Tankard ... 19th
Mercury Stakes (Dundalk) ... 23rd
Racing Post Trophy (Doncaster) ... 24th
Scott Dobson Memorial Doncaster Stakes (Doncaster) ... 24th
Worthington's Whizz Kidz Stakes (Newbury) ... 24th
Worthington's Burlison Inns Stakes (Newbury) ... 24th
Al Basti Equiworld Celebration Stakes (Newbury) ... 24th
Killavullan Stakes (Leopardstown) ... 24th
Trigo Stakes (Leopardstown) ... 24th
Bettyville Steeple Chase (Wexford) ... 24th
Eyrefield Stakes (Leopardstown) ... 25th
Knockaire Stakes (Leopardstown) ... 25th
32Red / ebfstallions.com Fleur De Lys Fillies' Stakes (Lingfield Park) ... 29th
32Red.com / Choose EBF Nominated Stallions River Eden Fillies' Stakes (Lingfield Park) ... 29th
Irish Stallion Farms 'Bosra Sham' EBF Fillies' Stakes (Newmarket) ... 30th
WKD Hurdle (Down Royal) ... 30th

Hamptons EBF Mares Only Novices' Hurdle (Down Royal) .......... 30th
Cooley Stakes (Dundalk) .......... 30th
Agma Holdings James Seymour Stakes (Newmarket) .......... 31st
Ben Marshall Stakes (Newmarket) .......... 31st
EBF Stallions Montrose Fillies' Stakes (Newmarket) .......... 31st
United House Gold Cup Handicap Steeple Chase (Ascot) .......... 31st
Bet365 Charlie Hall Steeple Chase (Wetherby) .......... 31st
Bet365 Hurdle Race (Wetherby) .......... 31st
Jnwine Champion Chase (Down Royal) .......... 31st
Ladbrokes Skymas Steeple Chase (Down Royal) .......... 31st
Mac's Joy Handicap Hurdle (Down Royal) .......... 31st

# NOVEMBER

Paddy Power Novices' Hurdle (Cork) .......... 1st
Paddy Power EBF Novices' Steeple Chase (Cork) .......... 1st
Paddy Power Cork Grand National Handicap Steeple Chase (Cork) .......... 1st
Poplar Square Steeple Chase (Naas) .......... 1st
Brown Lad Handicap Hurdle (Naas) .......... 1st
Haldon Gold Cup Steeple Chase (A Limited Handicap) (Exeter) .......... 3rd
Betdaq 50% Commission Refund Floodlit Stakes (Kempton Park) .......... 4th
Thurles Chase (Thurles) .......... 5th
Betfred TV EBF Stallions Breeding Winners Gillies Fillies' Stakes (Doncaster) .......... 7th
Betfred 'Goals Galore' Wentworth Stakes (Doncaster) .......... 7th
Betfred Monet's Garden Old Roan Steeple Chase (Aintree) .......... 7th
Stanjames.com Elite Hurdle Race (Wincanton) .......... 7th
Rising Stars Novices' Steeple Chase (Wincanton) .......... 7th
Fishery Lane 4yo Hurdle (Naas) .......... 7th
Fortria Steeple Chase (Navan) .......... 8th
Lismullen Hurdle (Navan) .......... 8th
For Auction Novices' Hurdle (Navan) .......... 8th
Clonmel Oil Steeple Chase (Clonmel) .......... 12th
EBF T A Morris Memorial Mares' Only Steeple Chase (Clonmel) .......... 12th
Coral Churchill Stakes (Lingfield Park) .......... 14th
Unibet Golden Rose Stakes (Lingfield Park) .......... 14th
Neptune Investment Management Novices' Hurdle Race (Cheltenham) .......... 14th
JCB Triumph Hurdle Trial (Cheltenham) .......... 14th
Paddy Power Gold Cup Steeple Chase (A Handicap) (Cheltenham) .......... 14th
Murphy Group Handicap Steeple Chase (Cheltenham) .......... 14th
Racing Post Arkle Trophy Trial Novices' Steeple Chase (Cheltenham) .......... 15th
Sky Bet Supreme Trial Novices' Hurdle Race (Cheltenham) .......... 15th
Stanjames.com Greatwood Hurdle Race (A Handicap) (Cheltenham) .......... 15th
Stan James Morgiana Hurdle (Punchestown) .......... 15th
Florida Pearl Novices' Steeple Chase (Punchestown) .......... 15th
Craddockstown Novices' Steeplechase (Punchestown) .......... 15th
Blackwater Handicap Hurdle (Cork) .......... 15th
Cash Out On The Betdaq+ App / EBF Stallions Hyde Stakes .......... 18th
Coral Hurdle Race (Ascot) .......... 21st
Amlin 1965 Steeple Chase (Ascot) .......... 21st
Betfair Steeple Chase (Haydock Park) .......... 21st
Betfair Cash Out "Fixed Brush" Handicap Hurdle Race (Haydock Park) .......... 21st
Monksfield Novices' Hurdle (Navan) .......... 22nd
Ladbrokes Troytown Handicap Steeple Chase (Navan) .......... 22nd
ITBA Mares Bumper (Navan) .......... 22nd
Proudstown Handicap Hurdle (Navan) .......... 22nd
BetBright.com Wild Flower Stakes (Kempton Park) .......... 25th
Rsa Worcester Novices' Steeple Chase (Newbury) .......... 26th
Fuller's London Pride Novices' Steeple Chase (Newbury) .......... 27th
Bet365 Long Distance Hurdle Race (Newbury) .......... 28th
Hennessy Gold Cup Steeple Chase (Handicap) (Newbury) .......... 28th
Stanjames.com Fighting Fifth Hurdle Race (Newcastle) .......... 28th
Ballyhack Handicap Steeple Chase (Fairyhouse) .......... 28th
New Stand Handicap Hurdle (Fairyhouse) .......... 28th
Bar One Royal Bond Novice Hurdle (Fairyhouse) .......... 29th
Bar One Hattons Grace Hurdle (Fairyhouse) .......... 29th
Bar One Drinmore Novice Steeple Chase (Fairyhouse) .......... 29th
Winter Festival Juvenile Hurdle (Fairyhouse) .......... 29th
Porterstown Handicap Steeple Chase (Fairyhouse) .......... 29th

# DECEMBER

Neptune Investment Management Novices' Hurdle Race (Sandown Park) .......... 4th
Betfred Becher Handicap Steeple Chase (Aintree) .......... 5th
Tingle Creek Steeple Chase (Sandown Park) .......... 5th
Racing Post Henry VIII Novices' Steeple Chase (Sandown Park) .......... 5th
Peterborough Steeple Chase (Huntingdon) .......... 6th
John Durkan Memorial Chase (Punchestown) .......... 6th

Kerry Group Hilly Way Steeple Chase (Cork) ... 6th
Kerry Group Cork Stayers Novices' Hurdle (Cork) ... 6th
Lombardstown EBF Mares Only Novices' Steeple Chase (Cork) ... 6th
Majordomo Hospitality Handicap Steeple Chase (Cheltenham) ... 11th
Albert Bartlett Novices' Hurdle Race (Cheltenham) ... 12th
Stanjames.com International Hurdle Race (Cheltenham) ... 12th
Osborne House Relkeel Hurdle Race (Cheltenham) ... 12th
December Gold Cup (A Handicap Steeple Chase) (Cheltenham) ... 12th
Bet365 December Novices' Steeple Chase (Doncaster) ... 12th
Bet365 Summit Juvenile Hurdle Race (Doncaster) ... 12th
Navan Novices' Hurdle (Navan) ... 13th
Future Champions Bumper (Navan) ... 13th
Tara Handicap Hurdle (Navan) ... 13th
Foxrock Handicap Steeple Chase (Navan) ... 13th
Mitie Kennel Gate Novices' Hurdle Race (Ascot) ... 18th
Ascot Novices' Steeple Chase (Ascot) ... 18th
Coral App Download From The App Store Quebec Stakes (Lingfield Park) ... 19th
JLT Long Walk Hurdle Race (Ascot) ... 19th
Ladbroke (A Handicap Hurdle Race) (Ascot) ... 19th
Kauto Star Novices' Steeple Chase (Kempton Park) ... 26th
Williamhill.com Christmas Hurdle Race (Kempton Park) ... 26th
William Hill King George VI Steeple Chase (Kempton Park) ... 26th
William Hill Rowland Meyrick Handicap Steeple Chase (Wetherby) ... 26th
Racing Post Novice Chase (Leopardstown) ... 26th
Knight Frank Juvenile Hurdle (Leopardstown) ... 26th
Greenmount Park Novices' Steeple Chase (Limerick) ... 26th
Coral.co.uk Future Champions Finale Juvenile Hurdle Race (Chepstow) ... 27th
Coral Welsh Grand National (A Handicap Steeple Chase) (Chepstow) ... 27th
Williamhill.com Novices' Steeple Chase (Kempton Park) ... 27th
Williamhill.com Desert Orchid Steeple Chase (Kempton Park) ... 27th
Paddy Power Future Champions Novice Hurdle (Leopardstown) ... 27th
Paddy Power Dial A Bet Chase (Leopardstown) ... 27th
Paddy Power Handicap Steeple Chase (Leopardstown) ... 27th
Tim Duggan Memorial Handicap Steeple Chase (Limerick) ... 27th
Christmas Hurdle (Leopardstown) ... 28th
Lexus Steeple Chase (Leopardstown) ... 28th
Sporting Limerick 4yo Hurdle (Limerick) ... 28th
Betfred Goals Galore Challow Novices' Hurdle Race (Newbury) ... 29th
Ryanair December Hurdle (Leopardstown) ... 29th
Topaz Fort Leney Novice Chase (Leopardstown) ... 29th
EBF Mares Only Hurdle (Leopardstown) ... 29th
Dorans Pride Novices' Hurdle (Limerick) ... 29th

| | |
|---|---|
| **Front cover** - | Mark Johnston schooling horses at his Middleham gallops in North Yorkshire. |

# INDEX TO TRAINERS

**†denotes Permit to train under N.H. Rules only**

Name Team No.

BRADSTOCK, MR MARK 061
BRAVERY, MR GILES 062
BRENNAN, MR BARRY 063
BREWIS, MISS RHONA 064
BRIDGER, MR JOHN 065
BRIDGWATER, MR DAVID 066
BRISBOURNE, MR MARK 067
BRITTAIN, MR CLIVE 068
BRITTAIN, MR MEL 069
†BROOKE, LADY 070
BROTHERTON, MR ROY 071
BROWN, MR ALAN 072
BROWN, MR ANDI 073
BROWN, MR DAVID 074
†BRYANT, MISS MICHELLE 075
†BUCKETT, MRS KATE 076
BUCKLER, MR BOB 077
BURCHELL, MR DAI 078
BURGOYNE, MR PAUL 079
BURKE, MR K. R. 080
†BURNS, MR HUGH 081
BUTLER, MR JOHN 082
BUTLER, MR PADDY 083
†BUTTERWORTH, MRS BARBARA 084
BYCROFT, MR NEVILLE 085

## C

CAMACHO, MISS JULIE 086
CAMPION, MR MARK 087
CANDLISH, MS JENNIE 088
CANDY, MR HENRY 089
CANN, MR GRANT 090
CANTILLON, MR DON 091
CARR, MRS RUTH 092
CARROLL, MR DECLAN 093
CARROLL, MR TONY 094
CARSON, MR TONY 095
CARTER, MR LEE 096
CASE, MR BEN 097
CECIL, LADY JANE 098
CHAMINGS, MR PATRICK 099

Name Team No.

CHANNON, MR MICK 100
CHAPMAN, MR MICHAEL 101
CHAPPLE-HYAM, MS JANE 102
CHAPPLE-HYAM, MR PETER 103
CHARALAMBOUS, MR PETER 104
CHARLTON, MR GEORGE 105
CHARLTON, MR ROGER 106
CHISMAN, MR HARRY 107
†CLARK, MRS JANE 108
†CLARKE, MRS ANGELA 109
CLEMENT, MR NICOLAS 110
CLINTON, MR PATRICK 111
COAKLEY, MR DENIS J. 112
COLE, MR PAUL 113
COLTHERD, MR STUART 114
COOGAN, MR ALAN 115
COOMBE, MR JOHN 116
CORBETT, MRS SUSAN 117
CORCORAN, MR LIAM 118
†CORNWALL, MR JOHN 119
COWELL, MR ROBERT 120
COWLEY, MR PAUL 121
COX, MR CLIVE 122
COYLE, MR TONY 123
CRAGGS, MR RAY 124
CRATE, MR PETER 125
CRISFORD, MR SIMON 126
CROOK, MR ANDREW 127
CROWLEY, MISS JO 128
CUMANI, MR LUCA 129
CUNNINGHAM-BROWN, MR KEN 130
CURRAN, MR SEAN 131
CURTIS, MISS REBECCA 132
CUTHBERT, MR THOMAS 133

## D

D'ARCY, MR PAUL 134
DACE, MR LUKE 135
DALGLEISH, MR KEITH 136
DALY, MR HENRY 137
DARTNALL, MR VICTOR 138

| Name | Team No. |
|---|---|
| DASCOMBE, MR TOM | 139 |
| †DAVIDSON, MR TRISTAN | 140 |
| DAVIES, MR JOHN | 141 |
| †DAVIES, MR PAUL | 142 |
| DAVIES, MISS SARAH-JAYNE | 143 |
| DAVIS, MISS JOANNA | 144 |
| †DAVIS, MISS LOUISE | 145 |
| DAVISON, MISS ZOE | 146 |
| †DAY, MR ANTHONY | 147 |
| †DAY, MISS LISA | 148 |
| DE BEST-TURNER, MR WILLIAM | 149 |
| DE GILES, MR ED | 150 |
| DE HAAN, MR BEN | 151 |
| DEACON, MR GEOFFREY | 152 |
| DENNIS, MR DAVID | 153 |
| DICKIN, MR ROBIN | 154 |
| †DIXON, MR JOHN | 155 |
| DIXON, MR SCOTT | 156 |
| †DIXON, MR STEVEN | 157 |
| DOBBIN, MRS ROSE | 158 |
| †DODGSON, MR ASHLEY | 159 |
| DODS, MR MICHAEL | 160 |
| DONOVAN, MR DESMOND | 161 |
| DORE, MR CONOR | 162 |
| DOUMEN, MR FRANCOIS | 163 |
| DOW, MR SIMON | 164 |
| DOWN, MR CHRIS | 165 |
| †DRAKE, MR RICHARD | 166 |
| DREW, MR CLIVE | 167 |
| DU PLESSIS, MISS JACKIE | 168 |
| DUFFIELD, MRS ANN | 169 |
| DUKE, MR BRENDAN W. | 170 |
| DUNCAN, MR IAN | 171 |
| DUNLOP, MR ED | 172 |
| DUNLOP, MR HARRY | 173 |
| DUNN, MRS ALEXANDRA | 174 |
| DUNNETT, MRS CHRISTINE | 175 |
| DURACK, MR SEAMUS | 176 |
| DWYER, MR CHRIS | 177 |
| DYSON, MISS CLAIRE | 178 |

## E

| Name | Team No. |
|---|---|
| EARLE, MR SIMON | 179 |
| EASTERBY, MR MICHAEL | 180 |
| EASTERBY, MR TIM | 181 |
| †ECKLEY, MR BRIAN | 182 |
| EDDERY, MR PAT | 183 |
| EDDERY, MR ROBERT | 184 |
| EDMUNDS, MR STUART | 185 |
| †EDWARDS, MR GORDON | 186 |
| ELLIOTT, MR GORDON | 187 |
| ELLIS, MISS JOEY | 188 |
| ELLISON, MR BRIAN | 189 |
| ELSWORTH, MR DAVID | 190 |
| ENDER, MISS SARA | 191 |
| ETHERINGTON, MR TIM | 192 |
| EUSTACE, MR JAMES | 193 |
| EVANS, MR DAVID | 194 |
| †EVANS, MR HYWEL | 195 |
| EVANS, MR JAMES | 196 |
| †EVANS, MRS MARY | 197 |
| EVANS, MRS NIKKI | 198 |
| EWART, MR JAMES | 199 |
| EYRE, MR LES | 200 |

## F

| Name | Team No. |
|---|---|
| FAHEY, MR RICHARD | 201 |
| FAIRHURST, MR CHRIS | 202 |
| FANSHAWE, MR JAMES | 203 |
| FARRELLY, MR JOHNNY | 204 |
| FEILDEN, MISS JULIA | 205 |
| FELLOWES, MR CHARLIE | 206 |
| FERGUSON, MR JOHN | 207 |
| FFRENCH DAVIS, MR DOMINIC | 208 |
| FIERRO, MR GIUSEPPE | 209 |
| FIFE, MRS MARJORIE | 210 |
| FITZGERALD, MR TIM | 211 |
| FITZPATRICK, MR JEREMIAH | 212 |
| FITZSIMONS, MR PAUL | 213 |
| FLINT, MR JOHN | 214 |
| FLOOD, MR DAVID | 215 |
| FORBES, MR TONY | 216 |

| Name | Team No. |
|---|---|
| FORD, MRS PAM | 217 |
| FORD, MR RICHARD | 218 |
| †FORD, MRS RICHENDA | 219 |
| FORSEY, MR BRIAN | 220 |
| FOSTER, MISS JOANNE | 221 |
| FOWLER, MRS LORNA | 222 |
| FOX, MR JIMMY | 223 |
| FRANCE, MISS SUZZANNE | 224 |
| †FRANKLAND, MR DEREK | 225 |
| FROST, MR JAMES | 226 |
| FROST, MR KEVIN | 227 |
| FROUD, MR HUGO | 228 |
| FRY, MR HARRY | 229 |
| FRYER, MISS CAROLINE | 230 |

## G

| Name | Team No. |
|---|---|
| GALLAGHER, MR JOHN | 231 |
| GANSERA-LÉVÊQUE, MRS ILKA | 232 |
| GARDNER, MRS SUSAN | 233 |
| GASK, MR JEREMY | 234 |
| †GASSON, MRS ROSEMARY | 235 |
| †GATES, MR MICHAEL | 236 |
| GEAKE, MR JONATHAN | 237 |
| GEORGE, MR TOM | 238 |
| GIFFORD, MR NICK | 239 |
| GILLARD, MR MARK | 240 |
| GIVEN, MR JAMES | 241 |
| †GLEDSON, MR J. L. | 242 |
| †GOLDIE, MR JIM | 243 |
| †GOLDIE, MR ROBERT | 244 |
| GOLDSWORTHY, MR KEITH | 245 |
| GOLLINGS, MR STEVE | 246 |
| GORDON, MR CHRIS | 247 |
| GORMAN, MR J T | 248 |
| GOSDEN, MR JOHN | 249 |
| GRAHAM, MRS HARRIET | 250 |
| GRANT, MR CHRIS | 251 |
| GRASSICK, MR LIAM | 252 |
| GRASSICK, MR M. C. | 253 |
| GRAY, MR CARROLL | 254 |
| GRAYSON, MR PETER | 255 |
| GREATREX, MR WARREN | 256 |
| GREEN, MR PAUL | 257 |
| GRETTON, MR TOM | 258 |
| GRIFFITHS, MR DAVID C. | 259 |
| †GRIFFITHS, MR SIRRELL | 260 |
| GRISSELL, MRS DIANA | 261 |
| GUBBY, MR BRIAN | 262 |
| GUEST, MR RAE | 263 |
| GUEST, MR RICHARD | 264 |
| GUNDRY, MISS POLLY | 265 |

## H

| Name | Team No. |
|---|---|
| HAGGAS, MR WILLIAM | 266 |
| HALES, MR ALEX | 267 |
| HALFORD, MR MICHAEL | 268 |
| HALL, MISS SALLY | 269 |
| HAMBRO, MRS MARY | 270 |
| HAMER, MRS DEBRA | 271 |
| HAMILTON, MRS ALISON | 272 |
| †HAMILTON, MRS ANN | 273 |
| HAMMOND, MR MICKY | 274 |
| HAMMOND, MR MIKE | 275 |
| HANNON, MR RICHARD | 276 |
| HARKER, MR GEOFFREY | 277 |
| HARNEY, MR W. | 278 |
| †HARPER, MR RICHARD | 279 |
| HARRINGTON, MRS JESSICA | 280 |
| HARRIS, MISS GRACE | 281 |
| HARRIS, MR RONALD | 282 |
| HARRIS, MR SHAUN | 283 |
| HARRISON, MISS LISA | 284 |
| HASLAM, MR BEN | 285 |
| HAWES, MRS FLEUR | 286 |
| HAWKE, MR NIGEL | 287 |
| HAWKER, MR RICHARD | 288 |
| †HAYNES, MR JONATHAN | 289 |
| HAYNES, MR TED | 290 |
| HAYWOOD, MISS GAIL | 291 |
| HEAD-MAAREK, MRS C. | 292 |
| HEDGER, MR PETER | 293 |
| HENDERSON, MR NICKY | 294 |

| Name | Team No. |
|---|---|
| HENDERSON, MR PAUL | 295 |
| HERRINGTON, MR MICHAEL | 296 |
| HIATT, MR PETER | 297 |
| HIDE, MR PHILIP | 298 |
| HILL, MRS LAWNEY | 299 |
| HILL, MR MARTIN | 300 |
| HILLS, MR B. W. | 301 |
| HILLS, MR CHARLES | 302 |
| HOAD, MR MARK | 303 |
| HOBBS, MR PHILIP | 304 |
| HOBSON, MISS CLARE | 305 |
| HODGES, MR RON | 306 |
| HODGSON, MR SIMON | 307 |
| HOGAN, MR EAMONN | 308 |
| †HOGARTH, MR HENRY | 309 |
| HOLLINGSWORTH, MR ALAN | 310 |
| HOLLINSHEAD, MR ANDREW | 311 |
| HOLLINSHEAD, MRS STEPH | 312 |
| HOLMES, MR PATRICK | 313 |
| HOLT, MR JOHN | 314 |
| HONEYBALL, MR ANTHONY | 315 |
| HOWE, MR STUART | 316 |
| †HUGHES, MR JAMES | 317 |
| HUGHES, MRS JO | 318 |
| †HUGHES, MR STEPHEN | 319 |
| HUGO, MS N. M. | 320 |
| HUMPHREY, MRS SARAH | 321 |
| †HUNTER, MR KEVIN | 322 |
| †HURLEY, MISS LAURA | 323 |
| HUTCHINSON, MISS ALISON | 324 |

## I

| Name | Team No. |
|---|---|
| †IKIN, MRS CAROLE | 325 |
| INGRAM, MR ROGER | 326 |
| IVORY, MR DEAN | 327 |

## J

| Name | Team No. |
|---|---|
| JACKSON, MISS TINA | 328 |
| †JACKSON, MRS VALERIE | 329 |
| JAMES, MR LEE | 330 |
| JARDINE, MR IAIN | 331 |
| JARVIS, MR TIMOTHY | 332 |
| JARVIS, MR WILLIAM | 333 |
| JEFFERSON, MR MALCOLM | 334 |
| JENKINS, MR J. R. | 335 |
| †JESSOP, MR ALAN | 336 |
| JEWELL, MRS LINDA | 337 |
| JOHNSON, MR BRETT | 338 |
| JOHNSON HOUGHTON, MISS EVE | 339 |
| JOHNSON, MR ROBERT | 340 |
| †JOHNSON, MRS SUSAN | 341 |
| JOHNSTON, MR MARK | 342 |
| JONES, MR ALAN | 343 |
| JONES, MS LUCY | 344 |
| JONES, MR MALCOLM | 345 |
| JORDAN, MRS VIOLET M. | 346 |

## K

| Name | Team No. |
|---|---|
| KEEVIL, MRS CAROLINE | 347 |
| †KEHOE, MRS FIONA | 348 |
| KEIGHLEY, MR MARTIN | 349 |
| KELLETT, MR CHRISTOPHER | 350 |
| KELLEWAY, MISS GAY | 351 |
| †KENDALL, MISS LYNSEY | 352 |
| KENT, MR NICK | 353 |
| KING, MR ALAN | 354 |
| KING, MR NEIL | 355 |
| KINSEY, MR WILLIAM | 356 |
| KIRBY, MR PHILIP | 357 |
| KIRK, MR SYLVESTER | 358 |
| KITTOW, MR STUART | 359 |
| KNIGHT, MR WILLIAM | 360 |
| KUBLER, MR DANIEL | 361 |

## L

| Name | Team No. |
|---|---|
| LAFFON-PARIAS, MR CARLOS | 362 |
| LAMPARD, MR NICK | 363 |
| LANIGAN, MR DAVID | 364 |
| LAVELLE, MISS EMMA | 365 |
| LEAVY, MR BARRY | 366 |

| Name | Team No. |
|---|---|
| LEE, MR RICHARD | 367 |
| LEECH, MRS SOPHIE | 368 |
| LEWIS, MRS SHEILA | 369 |
| LINES, MR CLIFFORD | 370 |
| LITTMODEN, MR NICK | 371 |
| LLEWELLYN, MR BERNARD | 372 |
| LLOYD-BEAVIS, MISS NATALIE | 373 |
| LOCKWOOD, MR ALAN | 374 |
| LONG, MR JOHN E. | 375 |
| LONGSDON, MR CHARLIE | 376 |
| LOUGHNANE, MR DANIEL MARK | 377 |
| LYCETT, MR SHAUN | 378 |
| LYONS, MR GER | 379 |

## M

| Name | Team No. |
|---|---|
| MACKIE, MR JOHN | 380 |
| †MACTAGGART, MR ALAN | 381 |
| MACTAGGART, MR BRUCE | 382 |
| †MADDISON, MR PETER | 383 |
| MADGWICK, MR MICHAEL | 384 |
| MAIN, MRS HEATHER | 385 |
| †MAKIN, MRS JANE | 386 |
| MAKIN, MR PETER | 387 |
| MALZARD, MRS ALYSON | 388 |
| MANN, MR CHARLIE | 389 |
| MARGARSON, MR GEORGE | 390 |
| MARTIN, MR A. J. | 391 |
| †MARTIN, MR ANDREW J. | 392 |
| MASON, MR CHRISTOPHER | 393 |
| MASON, MRS JENNIFER | 394 |
| †MATHIAS, MISS JANE | 395 |
| †MAUNDRELL, MR G. C. | 396 |
| MCAULIFFE, MR KEVIN | 397 |
| MCBRIDE, MR PHILIP | 398 |
| MCCAIN, MR DONALD | 399 |
| MCCARTHY, MR TIM | 400 |
| MCCORMICK, MISS DANIELLE | 401 |
| MCENTEE, MR PHIL | 402 |
| MCGRATH, MR MURTY | 403 |
| MCGREGOR, MRS JEAN | 404 |
| MCLINTOCK, MS KAREN | 405 |
| MCMAHON, MR ED | 406 |
| MCPHERSON, MR GRAEME | 407 |
| MEADE, MR MARTYN | 408 |
| MEADE, MR NOEL | 409 |
| MEEHAN, MR BRIAN | 410 |
| MENUISIER, MR DAVID | 411 |
| MENZIES, MISS REBECCA | 412 |
| MIDDLETON, MR ANTHONY | 413 |
| †MIDDLETON, MR PHIL | 414 |
| MIDGLEY, MR PAUL | 415 |
| MILLMAN, MR ROD | 416 |
| MILLS, MR ROBERT | 417 |
| MITCHELL, MR NICK | 418 |
| MITCHELL, MR PHILIP | 419 |
| MITCHELL, MR RICHARD | 420 |
| MOFFATT, MR JAMES | 421 |
| MOHAMMED, MR ISMAIL | 422 |
| MONGAN, MRS LAURA | 423 |
| MOORE, MR ARTHUR | 424 |
| MOORE, MR GARY | 425 |
| MOORE, MR GEORGE | 426 |
| MOORE, MR J. S. | 427 |
| MORGAN, MR KEVIN | 428 |
| MORRIS, MR DAVE | 429 |
| MORRIS, MR M. F. | 430 |
| MORRIS, MR PATRICK | 431 |
| MORRISON, MR HUGHIE | 432 |
| MOSS, MR GARRY | 433 |
| MUIR, MR WILLIAM | 434 |
| MULHALL, MR CLIVE | 435 |
| MULHOLLAND, MR NEIL | 436 |
| MULLANEY, MR LAWRENCE | 437 |
| MULLINEAUX, MR MICHAEL | 438 |
| MULLINS, MR SEAMUS | 439 |
| MULLINS, MR WILLIAM P. | 440 |
| MURPHY, MRS ANABEL K. | 441 |
| MURPHY, MR COLM | 442 |
| MURPHY, MR MIKE | 443 |
| MURPHY, MR PAT | 444 |
| MURTAGH, MR BARRY | 445 |
| MUSSON, MR WILLIE | 446 |

| Name | Team No. |
|---|---|
| **N** | |
| NAYLOR, DR JEREMY | 447 |
| †NEEDHAM, MR JOHN | 448 |
| NELMES, MRS HELEN | 449 |
| †NENADICH, MR CHRIS | 450 |
| NEWCOMBE, MR TONY | 451 |
| NEWLAND, DR RICHARD | 452 |
| NEWTON-SMITH, MISS ANNA | 453 |
| NICHOLLS, MR DAVID | 454 |
| NICHOLLS, MR PAUL | 455 |
| NIVEN, MR PETER | 456 |
| †NIXON, MR RAYSON | 457 |
| NORMILE, MRS LUCY | 458 |
| NORTON, MR JOHN | 459 |
| NOSEDA, MR JEREMY | 460 |
| **O** | |
| O'BRIEN, MR A. P. | 461 |
| O'BRIEN, MR DANIEL | 462 |
| O'BRIEN, MR FERGAL | 463 |
| O'GRADY, MR EDWARD J. | 464 |
| O'KEEFFE, MR JEDD | 465 |
| O'MEARA, MR DAVID | 466 |
| †O'NEILL, MR JOHN | 467 |
| O'NEILL, MR JONJO | 468 |
| O'SHEA, MR JOHN | 469 |
| OLDROYD, MR GEOFFREY | 470 |
| OLIVER, MR HENRY | 471 |
| OSBORNE, MR JAMIE | 472 |
| **P** | |
| PALMER, MR HUGO | 473 |
| PANTALL, MR H. A. | 474 |
| PANVERT, MR JOHN | 475 |
| †PARROTT, MRS HILARY | 476 |
| PAULING, MR BEN | 477 |
| PEACOCK, MR RAY | 478 |
| PEARCE, MRS LYDIA | 479 |
| PEARS, MR OLLIE | 480 |
| †PEARSON, MR DAVID | 481 |

| Name | Team No. |
|---|---|
| PECKHAM, MR GEORGE | 482 |
| PERRATT, MISS LINDA | 483 |
| PERRETT, MRS AMANDA | 484 |
| PHELAN, MR PAT | 485 |
| PHILLIPS, MR ALAN | 486 |
| PHILLIPS, MR RICHARD | 487 |
| PICKARD, MISS IMOGEN | 488 |
| PIPE, MR DAVID | 489 |
| POGSON, MR CHARLES | 490 |
| POLLOCK, MR KEITH | 491 |
| POMFRET, MR NICHOLAS | 492 |
| PORTMAN, MR JONATHAN | 493 |
| POULTON, MR JAMIE | 494 |
| POWELL, MR BRENDAN | 495 |
| POWELL, MR TED | 496 |
| PRESCOTT BT, SIR MARK | 497 |
| PRICE, MR ANDREW | 498 |
| PRICE, MR RICHARD | 499 |
| PRITCHARD, MR PETER | 500 |
| PURDY, MR PETER | 501 |
| **Q** | |
| QUINLAN, MR NOEL | 502 |
| QUINN, MR DENIS | 503 |
| QUINN, MR JOHN | 504 |
| QUINN, MR MICK | 505 |
| **R** | |
| †REED, MR W. T. | 506 |
| †REED, MR WILLIAM | 507 |
| REES, MR DAVID | 508 |
| †REES, MRS HELEN | 509 |
| REGAN, MR SEAN | 510 |
| REID, MR ANDREW | 511 |
| †RETTER, MRS JACQUELINE | 512 |
| REVELEY, MR KEITH | 513 |
| †RICHARDS, MR DAVID | 514 |
| RICHARDS, MRS LYDIA | 515 |
| RICHARDS, MR NICKY | 516 |
| RICHES, MR JOHN DAVID | 517 |

| Name | Team No. |
| --- | --- |
| †RIGBY, MRS PATRICIA | 518 |
| RIMELL, MR MARK | 519 |
| †ROBERTS, MISS BETH | 520 |
| ROBERTS, MR DAVE | 521 |
| ROBERTS, MR MIKE | 522 |
| ROBINSON, MISS SARAH | 523 |
| ROBSON, MISS PAULINE | 524 |
| ROHAUT, MR FRANCOIS | 525 |
| ROPER, MR W. M. | 526 |
| ROTHWELL, MR BRIAN | 527 |
| ROWE, MR RICHARD | 528 |
| ROWLAND, MISS MANDY | 529 |
| ROYER-DUPRE, MR A. DE | 530 |
| RUSSELL, MS LUCINDA | 531 |
| RYALL, MR JOHN | 532 |
| RYAN, MR JOHN | 533 |
| RYAN, MR KEVIN | 534 |

## S

| Name | Team No. |
| --- | --- |
| SADIK, MR AYTACH | 535 |
| SANDERSON, MRS DEBORAH | 536 |
| †SANDERSON, MRS KATHLEEN | 537 |
| SANTOS, MR JOSE | 538 |
| SAUNDERS, MR MALCOLM | 539 |
| SAYER, MRS DIANNE | 540 |
| SCARGILL, DR JON | 541 |
| †SCOTT, MR DERRICK | 542 |
| SCOTT, MR JEREMY | 543 |
| †SCRIVEN, MR BERNARD | 544 |
| SCUDAMORE, MR MICHAEL | 545 |
| SEMPLE, MR IAN | 546 |
| SHAW, MR DEREK | 547 |
| †SHAW, MRS FIONA | 548 |
| †SHAW, MRS PATRICIA | 549 |
| SHEPPARD, MR MATT | 550 |
| SHERWOOD, MR OLIVER | 551 |
| †SHIELS, MR RAYMOND | 552 |
| SIDDALL, MISS LYNN | 553 |
| SIMCOCK, MR DAVID | 554 |
| SKELTON, MR DAN | 555 |
| †SLACK, MRS EVELYN | 556 |
| SLY, MRS PAM | 557 |
| SMAGA, MR DAVID | 558 |
| SMART, MR BRYAN | 559 |
| SMITH, MR CHARLES | 560 |
| SMITH, MR JULIAN | 561 |
| SMITH, MR MARTIN | 562 |
| SMITH, MR MICHAEL | 563 |
| SMITH, MR R. MIKE | 564 |
| SMITH, MR RALPH | 565 |
| SMITH, MRS SUE | 566 |
| SMITH, MISS SUZY | 567 |
| SMYLY, MR GILES | 568 |
| SNOWDEN, MR JAMIE | 569 |
| SOWERSBY, MR MIKE | 570 |
| SPEARING, MR JOHN | 571 |
| SQUANCE, MR MICHAEL | 572 |
| STACK, MR TOMMY | 573 |
| STANFORD, MR EUGENE | 574 |
| †STEELE, MR DANIEL | 575 |
| †STEPHEN, MRS JACKIE | 576 |
| STEPHENS, MR ROBERT | 577 |
| STEVENS, MR OLLY | 578 |
| STOKELL, MISS ANN | 579 |
| STONE, MR WILLIAM | 580 |
| STOREY, MR BRIAN | 581 |
| STOREY, MR WILF | 582 |
| STOUTE, SIR MICHAEL | 583 |
| STRONGE, MRS ALI | 584 |
| STUBBS, MISS KRISTIN | 585 |
| SUMMERS, MR ROB | 586 |
| SWINBANK, MR ALAN | 587 |
| SYMONDS, MR TOM | 588 |

## T

| Name | Team No. |
| --- | --- |
| TATE, MR JAMES | 589 |
| TATE, MR TOM | 590 |
| TEAGUE, MR COLIN | 591 |
| TEAL, MR ROGER | 592 |
| TETT, MR HENRY | 593 |
| THOMPSON, MR DAVID | 594 |
| †THOMPSON, MR VICTOR | 595 |

Name Team No.

THOMSON, MR SANDY 596
TINKLER, MR NIGEL 597
TIZZARD, MR COLIN 598
TODHUNTER, MR MARTIN 599
TOLLER, MR JAMES 600
TOMPKINS, MR MARK 601
TORK, MR KEVIN 602
TREGONING, MR MARCUS 603
TUER, MR EDWIN 604
TUITE, MR JOSEPH 605
TURNELL, MR ANDREW 606
TURNER, MR BILL 607
TURNER, MR JAMES 608
TUTTY, MRS KAREN 609
TWISTON-DAVIES, MR NIGEL 610

**U**

UNETT, MR JAMES 611
UPSON, MR JOHN 612
USHER, MR MARK 613

**V**

VARIAN, MR ROGER 614
VAUGHAN, MR ED 615
VAUGHAN, MR TIM 616
VON DER RECKE, MR CHRISTIAN 617

**W**

WADE, MR JOHN 618
WADHAM, MRS LUCY 619
WAGGOTT, MISS TRACY 620
WAINWRIGHT, MR JOHN 621
†WALEY-COHEN, MR ROBERT 622
WALFORD, MR MARK 623
WALFORD, MR ROBERT 624
WALKER, MR ED 625
WALL, MR CHRIS 626
†WALL, MRS SARAH 627
WALL, MR TREVOR 628
WALTON, MRS JANE 629
†WALTON, MR JASON 630
WALTON, MRS SHEENA 631
WARD, MR JASON 632
†WATKINS, MISS TRACEY 633
WATSON, MR FREDERICK 634
WATT, MRS SHARON 635
WAUGH, MR SIMON 636
WEAVER, MISS AMY 637
†WEBB-BOWEN, MR ROBERT 638
WEBBER, MR PAUL 639
WELD, MR D. K. 640
WEST, MISS SHEENA 641
WEST, MR SIMON 642
WESTON, MR DAVID 643
†WESTWOOD, MISS JESSICA 644
WEYMES, MR JOHN 645
WHEELER, MR ERIC 646
WHILLANS, MR ALISTAIR 647
WHILLANS, MR DONALD 648
WHITAKER, MR RICHARD 649
†WHITEHEAD, MR ARTHUR 650
†WHITING, MR ARTHUR 651
†WHITTAKER, MR CHARLES 652
WHITTINGTON, MR HARRY 653
WIGHAM, MR MICHAEL 654
WILESMITH, MR MARTIN 655
WILLIAMS, MR EVAN 656
WILLIAMS, MR IAN 657
WILLIAMS, MR NICK 658
WILLIAMS, MR NOEL 659
WILLIAMS, MR STUART 660
WILLIAMS, MISS VENETIA 661
WILLIAMSON, MRS LISA 662
†WILSON, MR ANDREW 663
WILSON, MR CHRISTOPHER 664
WILSON, MR JIM 665
WILSON, MR NOEL 666
WINGROVE, MR KEN 667
†WINKS, MR PETER 668
WINTLE, MR ADRIAN 669
WOODMAN, MR STEVE 670

Name Team No.

**WOODWARD, MR GARRY** ................ 671
**WOOLLACOTT, MR RICHARD** ........ 672

## Y

**YORK, MR RAYMOND** ........................ 673
**YOUNG, MRS LAURA** ........................ 674
†**YOUNG, MR WILLIAM** ...................... 675

## PROPERTY OF HER MAJESTY

# The Queen

Colours: Purple, gold braid, scarlet sleeves, black velvet cap with gold fringe

Trained by **Sir Michael Stoute**, Newmarket

### THREE-YEAR-OLDS

1 **CAPEL PATH (USA),** br c Street Cry (IRE)—Miss Lucifer (FR)
2 **CONFLICTING ADVICE (USA),** b c Iffraaj—Assertive Lass (AUS)
3 **DARTMOUTH,** b c Dubawi (IRE)—Galatee (FR)
4 **MUSTARD,** b c Motivator—Flash of Gold
5 **SURPRISE CALL,** ch c New Approach (IRE)—Calakanga

### TWO-YEAR-OLDS

6 **CLEAR EVIDENCE,** b c 5/4 Cape Cross (IRE)—Rainbow's Edge (Rainbow Quest (USA))
7 **DIPLOMA,** b f 26/4 Dubawi (IRE)—Enticement (Montjeu (IRE))
8 **HAMMER GUN (USA),** b br c 6/2 Smart Strike (CAN)—Caraboss (Cape Cross (IRE))
9 **LABYRINTH (IRE),** b f 27/2 Lawman (FR)—Kerry Gal (IRE) (Galileo (IRE)) (260000)

Trained by **Richard Hannon**, Marlborough

10 **MUSICAL COMEDY,** 4, b g Royal Applause—Spinning Top

### THREE-YEAR-OLDS

11 **GALLEY PROOF,** b c Galileo (IRE)—Fictitious
12 **PACK TOGETHER,** b f Paco Boy (IRE)—New Assembly (IRE)
13 **PEACOCK,** b c Paco Boy (IRE)—Rainbow's Edge

### TWO-YEAR-OLDS

14 **PATENT,** b c 4/5 Paco Boy (IRE)—Film Script (Unfuwain (USA))
15 **RING OF TRUTH,** b f 27/4 Royal Applause—Spinning Top (Alzao (USA))

Trained by **Roger Charlton**, Beckhampton

### THREE-YEAR-OLDS

16 **DEXTEROUS,** b f Mastercraftsman (IRE)—Daring Aim
17 **PITCH,** b f Montjeu (IRE)—Five Fields (USA)
18 **SAMPLE (FR),** b f Zamindar (USA)—Sanabyra (FR)

### TWO-YEAR-OLDS

19 **PURE FANTASY,** b f 30/3 Fastnet Rock (AUS)—Fictitious (Machiavellian (USA))

Trained by **Michael Bell**, Newmarket

### THREE-YEAR-OLDS

20 **ANANAS,** b f Nayef (USA)—Anasazi (IRE)
21 **FABRICATE,** b c Makfi—Flight of Fancy
22 **MOTION PICTURE,** b f Motivator—Starshine
23 **TOUCHLINE,** b f Exceed And Excel (AUS)—Trianon

### TWO-YEAR-OLDS

24 **BONHOMIE,** b f 23/4 Shamardal (USA)—Bonnie Doon (IRE) (Grand Lodge (USA))
25 **FORECASTER,** b f 31/1 Fastnet Rock (AUS)—Aurore (IRE) (Fasliyev (USA))
26 **LOUD APPLAUSE,** b f 6/3 Royal Applause—New Assembly (IRE) (Machiavellian (USA))
27 **MERRIMENT,** ch f 8/3 Makfi—Trianon (Nayef (USA))

## PROPERTY OF HER MAJESTY

# The Queen

Trained by **Andrew Balding**, Kingsclere

### THREE-YEAR-OLDS

**28 KINEMATIC,** b f Kyllachy—Spinning Top
**29 ORANGE WALK (USA),** b g Bernardini (USA)—Sally Forth

### TWO-YEAR-OLDS

**30 HUSBANDRY,** b c 7/2 Paco Boy (IRE)—Humdrum (Dr Fong (USA))
**31 MAKE FAST,** b f 10/3 Makfi—Raymi Coya (CAN) (Van Nistelrooy (USA))

Trained by **William Haggas**, Newmarket

**32 PRINCE'S TRUST,** 5, b g Invincible Spirit (IRE)—Lost In Wonder (USA)

### THREE-YEAR-OLDS

**33 AWESOME POWER,** b c Dubawi (IRE)—Fairy Godmother
**34 PICK YOUR CHOICE,** b c Elusive Quality (USA)—Enticement

### TWO-YEAR-OLDS

**35 DAPHNE,** b f 12/2 Duke of Marmalade (IRE)—Daring Aim (Daylami (IRE))
**36 LIGHT MUSIC,** b f 1/3 Elusive Quality (USA)—Medley (Danehill Dancer (IRE))
**37 ORIENTAL CROSS (IRE),** b f 19/3 Cape Cross (IRE)—Orion Girl (GER) (Law Society (USA)) (174603)
**38 RECORDER,** ch c 28/1 Galileo (IRE)—Memory (IRE) (Danehill Dancer (IRE))

Trained by **Mrs Gai Waterhouse**, Sydney, Australia

**39 BOLD SNIPER,** 5, b g New Approach (IRE)—Daring Aim

Trained by **Nicky Henderson**, Lambourn

**40 CLOSE TOUCH,** 7, ch g Generous (IRE)—Romantic Dream
**41 JACK FROST,** 5, ch g Midnight Legend—Bella Macrae
**42 KILLIECRANKIE,** 7, b g Kayf Tara—Bella Macrae
**43 OPEN HEARTED,** 8, b g Generous (IRE)—Romantic Dream
**44 SPECIAL AGENT,** 6, b g Invincible Spirit (IRE)—Flight of Fancy
**45 SUMMER STORM,** 5, b g Lucarno (USA)—Midsummer Magic
**46 WISHING WIND,** 5, b m Kayf Tara—Romantic Dream

To be allocated

### TWO-YEAR-OLDS

**47 FINAL CHOICE,** b c 1/5 Makfi—Anasazi (IRE) (Sadler's Wells (USA))
**48 FORTH BRIDGE,** b c 18/3 Bernardini (USA)—Sally Forth (Dubai Destination (USA))
**49 GUY FAWKES,** b c 4/3 Big Bad Bob (IRE)—Flight of Fancy (Sadler's Wells (USA))
**50 MAINSTREAM,** b c 4/5 Dansili—Golden Stream (IRE) (Sadler's Wells (USA))
**51 MOLTEN GOLD,** b c 29/3 New Approach (IRE)—Flash of Gold (Darshaan)
**52 WISHPOINT (USA),** b c 23/3 Street Cry (IRE)—Key Point (IRE) (Galileo (IRE))

**SOME TRAINERS' STRINGS ARE TAKEN FROM THE BHA RACING ADMINISTRATION WEBSITE AND INCLUDE HORSES LISTED ON THERE AS 'AT GRASS' OR 'RESTING'**

## 1 MR N. W. ALEXANDER, Kinneston

Postal: **Kinneston, Leslie, Glenrothes, Fife, KY6 3JJ**
Contacts: **PHONE (01592) 840774 MOBILE (07831) 488210**
**E-MAIL nicholasalexander@kinneston.com WEBSITE www.kinneston.com**

1 **AFTERCLASS (IRE),** 7, b g Stowaway—Afsana (IRE) **N. W. Alexander**
2 **ALWAYS TIPSY,** 6, b g Dushyantor (USA)—French Pick (USA) **JJ Cockburn AJ Wight P Home**
3 **ANOTHER MATTIE (IRE),** 8, b g Zagreb (USA)—Silver Tassie (FR) **Quandt & Cochrane**
4 **BACK ON THE ROAD (IRE),** 13, br g Broken Hearted—Special Trix (IRE) **J. F. Alexander**
5 **BENNY'S SECRET (IRE),** 5, br g Beneficial—Greenhall Rambler (IRE) **Mr B. C. Castle**
6 **BERTIE MILAN (IRE),** 10, b g Milan—Miss Bertaine (IRE) **Turcan Barber Douglas Miller Dunning**
7 **BRACING,** 6, ch m Alflora (IRE)—Sports Express **Bissett Racing**
8 **BUFFALO BALLET,** 9, b g Kayf Tara—Minora (IRE) **Mr HW Turcan & Sir Simon Dunning**
9 **CALIVIGNY (IRE),** 6, b g Gold Well—Summer Holiday (IRE) **A. H. B. Hodge**
10 **CEILIDH (IRE),** 7, b m Tamure (IRE)—Eyesabeatin (IRE) **J & S Dudgeon G & S Irwin W Alexander**
11 **CLAN CHIEF,** 6, ch g Generous (IRE)—Harrietfield **Clan Gathering**
12 **CLAN LEGEND,** 5, ch g Midnight Legend—Harrietfield **Clan Gathering**
13 **DUTCH CANYON (IRE),** 5, b g Craigsteel—Chitabe (IRE) **E Barlow, S Cochrane & A Parmiter**
14 **EL FONTAN (FR),** 10, gr g Verglas (IRE)—Valeriane (FR) **Kinneston Racing**
15 **FRANKIE'S PROMISE (IRE),** 7, ch g Fruits of Love (USA)—According To Molly (IRE) **Mr B. C. Castle**
16 **HEILAN REBEL (IRE),** 5, b g Where Or When (IRE)—Nordice Equity (IRE) **Unregistered Partnership**
17 **HERE'S TO HARRY,** 8, b g Helissio (FR)—Harrietfield **N. W. Alexander**
18 **ISLA PEARL FISHER,** 12, br g Supreme Sound—Salem Beach **Mrs P. M. Gammell**
19 **JANE'S FANTASY (IRE),** 5, br m Robin des Pres (FR)—Trendy Attire (IRE) **Turcan Barber Douglas Miller Dunning**
20 **JET MASTER (IRE),** 9, b g Brian Boru—Whats The Reason (IRE) **Mr HW Turcan & Sir Simon Dunning**
21 4, B f Dr Massini (IRE)—Lady du Bost (FR) **Mr M. R. D. Fleming**
22 **LANDECKER (IRE),** 7, br g Craigsteel—Winsome Breeze (IRE) **Mrs N. J. Hodge**
23 **LITTLE GLENSHEE (IRE),** 9, gr m Terimon—Harrietfield **Turcan Barber Douglas Miller Dunning 1**
24 **MARLEE MOURINHO (IRE),** 9, br g Pushkin (IRE)—Spur of The Moment **Kinneston Racing**
25 **MASTER BUTCHER (IRE),** 8, b g Court Cave (IRE)—Carleen Gold **N. W. Alexander**
26 **MCGINTY'S DREAM (IRE),** 4, br g Flemensfirth (USA)—Laboc **Mr B. C. Castle**
27 **NORTHERN ACRES,** 9, b g Mtoto—Bunting **C. Lysaght Media, Quandt & Cochrane**
28 **OR DE GRUGY (FR),** 13, b g April Night (FR)—Girlish (FR) **Lord Cochrane & Partners**
29 **PRESENTING ROSE (IRE),** 5, b m Presenting—Berkeley House (IRE) **Mr A. Cochrane**
30 **PRESENTLY TIPSY,** 6, b m Presenting—Great Jane (FR) **Mr M. R. D. Fleming**
31 **ROSSINI'S DANCER,** 10, b g Rossini (USA)—Bint Alhabib **Turcan Barber Fletcher Dunning**
32 **ROYAL CHATELIER (FR),** 10, b g Video Rock (FR)—Attualita (FR) **J. F. Alexander**
33 **SLANEY STAR (IRE),** 7, b g Cloudings (IRE)—Slaney Rose (IRE) **Darren Davies & Brian Castle**
34 **SPINNING AWAY,** 7, ch m Alflora (IRE)—Minora (IRE) **Horsindae Syndicate**
35 **STANDINTHEBAND (IRE),** 8, b g Old Vic—Superior Dawn (IRE) **Michelle And Dan Macdonald**
36 **THE FLAMING MATRON (IRE),** 9, b m Flemensfirth (USA)—The Mighty Matron (IRE) **The Ladies Who**
37 **THE ORANGE ROGUE (IRE),** 8, br g Alderbrook—Classic Enough **Mrs S. M. Irwin**
38 **TITIAN BOY (IRE),** 6, ch g Spadoun (FR)—Leodotcom (IRE) **Hardie & Robb**
39 **WHY BUT WHY (USA),** 7, b g Whywhywhy (USA)—Miss Orah **Kinneston Racing**
40 **WICKLOW LAD,** 11, gr g Silver Patriarch (IRE)—Marina Bird **Mr A. Cochrane**

**Other Owners:** Mrs S. R. Alexander, J. M. Barber, Miss E. M. Barlow, A. A. Bissett, Mrs J. Bissett, The Hon T. H. V. Cochrane, Lord Cochrane of Cults, Mr J. J. Cockburn, Mr D. J. Davies, Mrs J. Douglas Miller, J. G. Dudgeon, Mr A. W. B. Duncan, Sir Simon Dunning, Miss F. M. Fletcher, T. G. Hardie, C. Lysaght, Mrs M. Macdonald, Mr W. D. Macdonald, Miss S. Quandt, Mrs L. Robb, N. D. A. Stanistreet, H. W. Turcan, Mr A. J. Wight.

**Assistant Trainer:** Catriona Bissett

**Jockey (NH):** Lucy Alexander. **Conditional:** Blair Campbell, Stephen Mulqueen. **Apprentice:** Lucy Alexander. **Amateur:** Mr Kit Alexander.

## 2 MR CONRAD ALLEN, Newmarket

**Trainer did not wish details of his string to appear**

## 3 MR JIM ALLEN, Reigate

Postal: **Tin Tin Cottage, Littleton Manor, Littleton Lane, Reigate, Surrey, RH2 8LB**
Contacts: **MOBILE (07973) 243369**
**E-MAIL jallen@arenaracingcompany.co.uk**

1 **BEACH RHYTHM (USA),** 8, ch g Footstepsinthesand—Queen's Music (USA) **J. P. Allen**
2 **INCANTARE,** 5, gr m Proclamation (IRE)—Mythical Charm **J. P. Allen**

### THREE-YEAR-OLDS

3 **TWELFTH DAN,** ch c Proclamation (IRE)—Mythical Charm **J. P. Allen**

## 4 MR ERIC ALSTON, Preston

Postal: **Edges Farm Stables, Chapel Lane, Longton, Preston, Lancashire, PR4 5NA**
Contacts: **PHONE (01772) 612120 FAX (01772) 619600 MOBILE (07879) 641660**
**E-MAIL eric1943@supanet.com**

1 **BARKSTON ASH,** 7, b g Kyllachy—Ae Kae Ae (USA) **The Selebians**
2 **BLITHE SPIRIT,** 4, b f Byron—Damalis (IRE) **Liam & Tony Ferguson**
3 **CHESTER ARISTOCRAT,** 6, ch g Sakhee (USA)—New Light **Paul Buist & John Thompson**
4 **INVINCIBLE RIDGE (IRE),** 7, b g Invincible Spirit (IRE)—Dani Ridge (IRE) **Paul Buist & John Thompson**
5 **KING OF EDEN (IRE),** 9, b g Royal Applause—Moonlight Paradise (USA) **The Grumpy Old Geezers**
6 **KING OF PARADISE (IRE),** 6, b g Hurricane Run (IRE)—Silly Game (IRE) **P. G. Buist**
7 **LITTLE ELI,** 5, b g Green Desert (USA)—Princess Ellis **Whittle Racing Partnership**
8 **LORD FRANKLIN,** 6, ch g Iceman—Zell (IRE) **Whitehills Racing Syndicate**
9 **MIGUELA MCGUIRE,** 4, b f Sir Percy—Miss McGuire **Red Rose Partnership**
10 **RED BARON (IRE),** 6, b g Moss Vale (IRE)—Twinberry (IRE) **Edges Farm Racing Stables Ltd**
11 **RIDGE RANGER (IRE),** 4, b f Bushranger (IRE)—Dani Ridge (IRE) **C. F. Harrington**
12 **TENHOO,** 9, b g Reset (AUS)—Bella Bambina **Edges Farm Racing Stables Ltd**

### THREE-YEAR-OLDS

13 **CASTERBRIDGE,** b g Pastoral Pursuits—Damalis (IRE) **Liam & Tony Ferguson**
14 **NIQNAAQPAADIWAAQ,** b g Aqlaam—Aswaaq (IRE) **Paul Buist & John Thompson**
15 B g Medicean—Quiet Elegance **Mr & Mrs G. Middlebrook**

**Other Owners:** Mrs J. E. Buist, M. L. Ferguson, Mr C. A. Ferguson, J. E. Jackson, M. S. Kelly, G. Middlebrook, Mrs L. A. Middlebrook, Mr R. Ormisher, Mr A. J. Raven, M. M. Taylor, J. Thompson.

**Assistant Trainer:** Mrs Sue Alston

**Jockey (flat):** David Allan.

## 5 MR WILLIAM AMOS, Otterburn

Postal: **Rochester House Farm, Rochester, Newcastle upon Tyne, Northumberland, NE19 1RH**
Contacts: **PHONE (01450) 850323 MOBILE (07810) 738149**

1 5, B g Generous (IRE)—Border Mist (IRE) **W. M. Aitchison**
2 **DANTE'S FROLIC,** 7, b m Overbury (IRE)—Dusky Dante (IRE) **Aitchison Gauld**
3 **ISAACSTOWN LAD (IRE),** 8, b g Milan—Friends of Friends (IRE) **Mr I. A. Gauld**
4 7, B g Grape Tree Road—Little Blackie
5 **LOCHORE (IRE),** 9, b g Morozov (USA)—Fulgina (FR) **Mr I. A. Gauld**
6 **OIL BURNER,** 10, b g Sir Harry Lewis (USA)—Quick Quote **Mr J. W. Clark**
7 **PARKIE BOY,** 4, b g Central Park (IRE)—Parlour Game **Mr & Mrs D. S. Byers**
8 **REIVERS LAD,** 4, b g Alflora (IRE)—Reivers Moon **Mr J. M. Stenhouse**
9 **SILVA SAMOURAI,** 6, gr g Proclamation (IRE)—Ladykirk **Mr I. A. Gauld**

**Other Owners:** D. S. Byers, Mrs M. J. Byers.

## 6 MR CHARLIE APPLEBY, Newmarket

Postal: **Godolphin Management Co Ltd, Moulton Paddocks, Newmarket, Suffolk, CB8 7YE**
**WEBSITE www.godolphin.com**

1 **AHTOUG,** 7, b h Byron—Cherokee Rose (IRE)
2 **ANGLOPHILE,** 4, ch g Dubawi (IRE)—Anna Palariva (IRE)
3 **ARCTIC MOON (USA),** 4, b br f Raven's Pass (USA)—Golden Sphinx (USA)
4 **ARTIGIANO (USA),** 5, ch g Distorted Humor (USA)—Angel Craft (USA)
5 **BACCARAT (IRE),** 6, ch g Dutch Art—Zut Alors (IRE)
6 **BELLO (AUS),** 7, b g Exceed And Excel (AUS)—Cara Bella
7 **BILLINGSGATE (IRE),** 4, b g Exceed And Excel (AUS)—Island Babe (USA)
8 **BLUE RAMBLER,** 5, b g Monsun (GER)—La Nuit Rose (FR)
9 **BOW CREEK (IRE),** 4, b c Shamardal (USA)—Beneventa
10 **CAT O'MOUNTAIN (USA),** 5, b br g Street Cry (IRE)—Thunder Kitten (USA)
11 **DEVILMENT,** 4, b g Cape Cross (IRE)—Mischief Making (USA)
12 **DRAGON FALLS (IRE),** 6, b g Distorted Humor (USA)—Tizdubai (USA)
13 **DREAM CHILD (IRE),** 4, ch f Pivotal—Poseidon's Bride (USA)
14 **DULLINGHAM,** 4, b g Dubawi (IRE)—Dixey
15 **FENCING (USA),** 6, ch h Street Cry (IRE)—Latice (IRE)
16 **FIGURE OF SPEECH (IRE),** 4, b g Invincible Spirit (IRE)—Epic Similie
17 **FOOTBRIDGE (USA),** 5, b h Street Cry (IRE)—Thousand Islands
18 **FRANCIS OF ASSISI (IRE),** 5, b g Danehill Dancer (IRE)—Queen Cleopatra (IRE)
19 **FRENCH NAVY,** 7, b h Shamardal (USA)—First Fleet (USA)
20 **FULBRIGHT,** 6, b h Exceed And Excel (AUS)—Lindfield Belle (IRE)
21 **GOLD TRAIL (IRE),** 4, ch c Teofilo (IRE)—Goldthroat (IRE)
22 **GROUNDBREAKING,** 5, b g New Approach (IRE)—Ladeena (IRE)
23 **HISTORY BOOK (IRE),** 5, b m Raven's Pass (USA)—Pure Illusion (IRE)
24 **HOLIDAY MAGIC (IRE),** 4, gr g Dark Angel (IRE)—Win Cash (IRE)
25 **INTRIGO,** 5, b g Medicean—A Thousand Smiles (IRE)
26 **KHUBALA (IRE),** 6, b g Acclamation—Raghida (IRE)
27 **KIND INVITATION,** 4, b f New Approach (IRE)—French Bid (AUS)
28 **LONG JOHN (AUS),** 5, b g Street Cry (IRE)—Hosiery (AUS)
29 **MAJEYDA (USA),** 4, b br f Street Cry (IRE)—Alzerra (UAE)
30 **MUSIC THEORY (IRE),** 4, b g Acclamation—Key Girl (IRE)
31 **MYTHICAL MADNESS,** 4, b c Dubawi (IRE)—Miss Delila (USA)
32 **NEW YEAR'S NIGHT (IRE),** 4, ch g Raven's Pass (USA)—Nightime (IRE)
33 **OUTSTRIP,** 4, gr ro c Exceed And Excel (AUS)—Asi Siempre (USA)
34 **PAZOLINI (USA),** 5, b h Bernardini (USA)—Jolie Boutique (USA)
35 **PINZOLO,** 4, b g Monsun (GER)—Pongee
36 **PRETEND (IRE),** 4, b g Invincible Spirit (IRE)—Fafinta (IRE)
37 **RAZOR WIND (IRE),** 4, b c Dubawi (IRE)—Tender Is Thenight (IRE)
38 **RECKLESS ABANDON,** 5, b h Exchange Rate (USA)—Sant Elena
39 **SAFETY CHECK (IRE),** 4, ch c Dubawi (IRE)—Doors To Manual (USA)
40 **SAINT BAUDOLINO (IRE),** 6, b g Pivotal—Alessandria
41 **SIR FEVER (URU),** 4, b c Texas Fever (USA)—Sirina (ARG)
42 **SNOWBOARDER (USA),** 5, ch g Raven's Pass (USA)—Gaudete (USA)
43 **SOLIDARITY,** 4, b g Dubawi (IRE)—Assabiyya (IRE)
44 **SOUND REFLECTION (USA),** 4, b f Street Cry (IRE)—Echoes In Eternity (IRE)
45 **STEELER (IRE),** 5, ch h Raven's Pass (USA)—Discreet Brief (IRE)
46 **STRATEGICAL (USA),** 4, b g More Than Ready (USA)—Mary Ellise (USA)
47 **SUDDEN WONDER (IRE),** 4, ch c New Approach (IRE)—Dubai Surprise (IRE)
48 **TRYSTER (IRE),** 4, b g Shamardal (USA)—Min Alhawa (USA)
49 **URBAN DANCE (IRE),** 5, b g Street Cry (IRE)—Melikah (IRE)
50 **VANCOUVERITE,** 5, b g Dansili—Villarrica (USA)
51 **YARD LINE (USA),** 4, b c Discreet Cat (USA)—Perceive (USA)

### THREE-YEAR-OLDS

52 **AD DABARAN (GER),** b c Dubawi (IRE)—Allure (GER)
53 **ADELASIA (IRE),** ch f Iffraaj—Flaming Song (IRE)
54 **ANTIQUARIUM (IRE),** b c New Approach (IRE)—Antillia
55 **ARABIAN OASIS,** b c Oasis Dream—Love Divine
56 **AUSTIN FRIARS,** b g New Approach (IRE)—My Luigia (IRE)
57 **BARCHAN (USA),** b g War Front (USA)—Malamado (USA)
58 **BETA TAURI (USA),** b f Oasis Dream—Beta
59 **BITTER LAKE (USA),** b br f Halling (USA)—Suez

## MR CHARLIE APPLEBY - Continued

60 **BITTERN (IRE),** ch f New Approach (IRE)—Oiseau Rare (FR)
61 **BOW AND ARROW,** b c Iffraaj—Isobel Archer
62 **BUDDING ROSE (USA),** ch f New Approach (IRE)—White Rose (GER)
63 **CHARMING THOUGHT,** b c Oasis Dream—Annabelle's Charm (IRE)
64 **CHORUS OF LIES,** b c Teofilo (IRE)—Cherry Orchard (IRE)
65 **COIN A PHRASE,** b f Dubawi (IRE)—French Bid (AUS)
66 **COMEDY QUEEN (USA),** b br f Distorted Humor (USA)—Miss Caerleona (FR)
67 **DAZZLING TIMES (USA),** gr ro c Street Cry (IRE)—Blue Dress (USA)
68 **DEERFIELD,** b c New Approach (IRE)—Sandtime (IRE)
69 **DIRECTIONAL,** b g Raven's Pass (USA)—Rose Street (USA)
70 **EFFLORESCENCE (USA),** b f Exceed And Excel (AUS)—Floristry
71 **EMIRATES HOLIDAYS (USA),** b f Dubawi (IRE)—New Morning (IRE)
72 **EMIRATES REWARDS,** ch f Dubawi (IRE)—Asi Siempre (USA)
73 **EMIRATES SKYCARGO (IRE),** b c Iffraaj—Catchline (USA)
74 **EMIRATES SKYWARDS (IRE),** b c Dubawi (IRE)—Mont Etoile (IRE)
75 **ENDLESS TIME (IRE),** b f Sea The Stars (IRE)—Mamonta
76 **EVENING RAIN (USA),** ch f Raven's Pass (USA)—Danuta (USA)
77 **FESTIVE FARE,** b c Teofilo (IRE)—Al Joza
78 **FEY,** b f New Approach (IRE)—Persinette (USA)
79 **FLASH FIRE (IRE),** b c Shamardal (USA)—Flamelet (USA)
80 **FOLK SINGER,** b f Cape Cross (IRE)—Nadia
81 **FOREST MAIDEN (IRE),** b f Invincible Spirit (IRE)—Lady Marian (GER)
82 **FOUR SEASONS (IRE),** b c Dubawi (IRE)—Please Sing
83 **FREE STATE,** ch c New Approach (IRE)—Firenze
84 Ch f Dubawi (IRE)—Gacequita (URU)
85 **GAME SHOW,** b c Dubawi (IRE)—Dream Play (IRE)
86 **GOSSIPING,** b c Dubawi (IRE)—Gossamer
87 **HAWKESBURY,** gr g Shamardal (USA)—Nahoodh (IRE)
88 **HIGH VALLEY,** ch g New Approach (IRE)—Bathilde (IRE)
89 **HILLS AND DALES (IRE),** b g Acclamation—Soul Mountain (IRE)
90 **HOLLIE POINT,** b f Dubawi (IRE)—Camlet
91 **HONOURABLE ACTION (IRE),** b g Shamardal (USA)—Saoirse Abu (USA)
92 **JUNGLE CAT (IRE),** b c Iffraaj—Mike's Wildcat (USA)
93 **KING OF COUNTRY,** b c Dubawi (IRE)—Country Star (USA)
94 **LATHARNACH (USA),** b c Iffraaj—Firth of Lorne (IRE)
95 **LEGEND'S GATE (IRE),** b c New Approach (IRE)—Arthur's Girl
96 **LEGERITY (IRE),** b f Dubawi (IRE)—Much Faster (IRE)
97 **LEONCAVALLO (IRE),** b g Cape Cross (IRE)—Nafura
98 **MAGICAL EFFECT (IRE),** ch c New Approach (IRE)—Purple Glow (IRE)
99 **MERTON PLACE (USA),** b c Street Cry (IRE)—Lakabi (USA)
100 **MIDDLE ENGLAND (IRE),** b f Dubawi (IRE)—Mannington (AUS)
101 **MISTRUSTING (IRE),** b f Shamardal (USA)—Misheer
102 **MOJAWIZ,** b g Dubawi (IRE)—Zayn Zen
103 **MONEIN (USA),** ch c New Approach (IRE)—Spring Oak
104 **MOUNTAINSIDE,** ch g Dubawi (IRE)—Maids Causeway (IRE)
105 **MULZAMM (IRE),** b c Cape Cross (IRE)—Vine Street (IRE)
106 **NEW MUSIC (IRE),** ch f New Approach (IRE)—Musical Note
107 **NEWMARCH,** ch c New Approach (IRE)—Vallericca (USA)
108 **NEWSPEAK (IRE),** b c New Approach (IRE)—Horatia (IRE)
109 **NO DELUSION (USA),** b f Street Cry (IRE)—Dream Empress (USA)
110 **NORTH AMERICA,** b c Dubawi (IRE)—Northern Mischief (USA)
111 **OCEANOGRAPHER,** b c Sea The Stars (IRE)—Que Puntual (ARG)
112 **OUTLAW COUNTRY (IRE),** br c Teofilo (IRE)—Neverletme Go (IRE)
113 **PALLISTER,** b c Pivotal—Punctilious
114 **PATHWAY TO HONOUR,** ch c New Approach (IRE)—Cheerleader
115 **PERCHE,** ch c New Approach (IRE)—Persian Filly (IRE)
116 **PLAYMAKER (IRE),** b c Dubawi (IRE)—Playful Act (IRE)
117 **PORTAMENTO (IRE),** gr c Shamardal (USA)—Octave (USA)
118 **PRUSSIAN BLUE,** ch c New Approach (IRE)—Agata Laguna (IRE)
119 **PRYING,** ch f Dubawi (IRE)—Pryka (ARG)
120 **PULCINELLA (IRE),** b f Dubawi (IRE)—Petrushka (IRE)
121 **PUZZLER (IRE),** ch f New Approach (IRE)—Crystal Maze
122 **RARE RHYTHM,** b c Dubawi (IRE)—Demisemiquaver
123 **REGARDS (IRE),** ch c Shamardal (USA)—Truly Yours (IRE)
124 **REWRITTEN,** b g Dubawi (IRE)—Portrayal (USA)

## MR CHARLIE APPLEBY - Continued

**125 RISEN SUN,** b f Shamardal (USA)—Bright Morning
**126 ROSENBAUM,** b g Dubawi (IRE)—Rave Reviews (IRE)
**127 SAMITE (USA),** ch f Distorted Humor (USA)—Silk Blossom (IRE)
**128 SAMSONITE (IRE),** ch c Pivotal—Silca's Sister
**129 SATINSPAR,** b g Echo of Light—Siyasa (USA)
**130 SECOND WAVE (IRE),** b c New Approach (IRE)—Tessa Reef (IRE)
**131 SECRET BRIEF (IRE),** b c Shamardal (USA)—Discreet Brief (IRE)
**132 SERENE BEAUTY (USA),** b f Street Cry (IRE)—Divine Dixie (USA)
**133 SIMPLE ELEGANCE (USA),** b br f Street Cry (IRE)—Rutherienne (USA)
**134 SKY CAPE,** b c Cape Cross (IRE)—Green Swallow (FR)
**135 SKYWARDS MILES (IRE),** b f New Approach (IRE)—Park Twilight (IRE)
**136 SPACE AGE (IRE),** ch c New Approach (IRE)—Historian (IRE)
**137 SPANISH DOLL,** b f Dubawi (IRE)—Flame of Gibraltar (IRE)
**138 SPARRING (IRE),** b c Teofilo (IRE)—Henties Bay (IRE)
**139 SPERRIN (IRE),** b c Dubawi (IRE)—Speciosa (IRE)
**140 STAR CITIZEN,** b c New Approach (IRE)—Faslen (USA)
**141 STARLETINA (IRE),** b f Sea The Stars (IRE)—Favourable Terms
**142 STRONG CHEMISTRY,** b c Oasis Dream—Mambo Light (USA)
**143 SUBCONTINENT (IRE),** b c Dubawi (IRE)—Saree
**144 SYMBOLIC STAR (IRE),** b c New Approach (IRE)—Epitome (IRE)
**145 TRIESTE,** ch f Dubawi (IRE)—Porto Roca (AUS)
**146 TRUE COURSE,** b f Dubawi (IRE)—Sugar Free (IRE)
**147 TURNING TIMES (IRE),** ro f Pivotal—Antiquities
**148 VENTRILOQUIST,** ch g New Approach (IRE)—Illusion
**149 WANTING (IRE),** b f Acclamation—Bold Desire
**150 WENTWORTH FALLS,** gr g Dansili—Strawberry Morn (CAN)
**151 WHISTLER MOUNTAIN,** b c Oasis Dream—Canda (USA)
**152 WINSLOW (USA),** b g Distorted Humor (USA)—Justwhistledixie (USA)
**153 WINTER QUEEN,** ch f Dubawi (IRE)—Straight Lass (IRE)
**154 WORDCRAFT,** b f Shamardal (USA)—Forensics (AUS)
**155 YODELLING (USA),** b f Medaglia d'Oro (USA)—Echoes In Eternity (IRE)
**156 ZEPHUROS (IRE),** b g Invincible Spirit (IRE)—West Wind
**157 ZOELLA (USA),** b f Invincible Spirit (IRE)—Zaeema

## TWO-YEAR-OLDS

**158** B f 21/4 Distorted Humor (USA)—Abhisheka (IRE) (Sadler's Wells (USA))
**159** B c 13/2 Dubawi (IRE)—Anna Palariva (IRE) (Caerleon (USA))
**160** Ch c 15/2 Street Cry (IRE)—Arlette (IRE) (King of Kings (IRE))
**161** B f 17/4 Shamardal (USA)—Bal de La Rose (IRE) (Cadeaux Genereux) (119047)
**162** B c 22/2 Street Cry (IRE)—Blue Bunting (USA) (Dynaformer (USA))
**163** Ch c 25/3 Raven's Pass (USA)—Bold Desire (Cadeaux Genereux)
**164** B f 6/5 Dubawi (IRE)—Brattothecore (CAN) (Katahaula County (CAN))
**165** B c 13/2 Dubawi (IRE)—Cosmodrome (USA) (Bahri (USA)) (725000)
**166** B c 1/4 Dubawi (IRE)—Crystal Music (USA) (Nureyev (USA)) (1600000)
**167** B br c 6/2 Distorted Humor (USA)—Dear Bela (ARG) (Indygo Shiner (USA))
**168** B br f 8/3 Street Cry (IRE)—Divine Dixie (USA) (Dixieland Band (USA))
**169** B br f 8/4 Street Cry (IRE)—Fatefully (USA) (Private Account (USA))
**170** B c 23/1 Dubawi (IRE)—Flame of Gibraltar (IRE) (Rock of Gibraltar (IRE))
**171** B c 30/3 Dubawi (IRE)—Forensics (AUS) (Flying Spur (AUS))
**172** B c 9/4 Pivotal—Forgotten Dreams (IRE) (Olden Times) (220000)
**173** B br c 24/2 Bernardini (USA)—Gracefield (USA) (Storm Cat (USA))
**174** B c 8/2 Invincible Spirit (IRE)—Growling (IRE) (Celtic Swing)
**175** B c 10/2 Poet's Voice—Hi Dubai (Rahy (USA))
**176** B c 24/1 Shamardal (USA)—Hypnology (USA) (Gone West (USA)) (380000)
**177** B f 10/3 War Front (USA)—Icon Project (USA) (Empire Maker (USA)) (950000)
**178** B f 10/5 Invincible Spirit (IRE)—Ishitaki (ARG) (Interprete (ARG))
**179** B c 11/4 Exceed And Excel (AUS)—Jane Austen (IRE) (Galileo (IRE))
**180** B f 16/2 Shamardal (USA)—Lake Toya (USA) (Darshaan)
**181** B c 23/3 Invincible Spirit (IRE)—Mamonta (Fantastic Light (USA))
**182** B f 26/4 Bernardini (USA)—Marietta (USA) (Machiavellian (USA))
**183** B c 15/3 Street Cry (IRE)—Meeznah (USA) (Dynaformer (USA)) (1000000)
**184** Ch f 3/4 Dubawi (IRE)—Misheer (Oasis Dream) (750000)
**185** B br f 6/5 Street Cry (IRE)—Najoum (USA) (Giant's Causeway (USA))
**186** B c 31/3 Street Cry (IRE)—Northern Melody (IRE) (Singspiel (IRE))
**187** Ch c 31/3 New Approach (IRE)—Pictavia (IRE) (Sinndar (IRE))

## MR CHARLIE APPLEBY - Continued

**188** B c 12/2 Shamardal (USA)—Playful Act (IRE) (Sadler's Wells (USA))
**189** B c 13/2 Lonhro (AUS)—Puppet Queen (USA) (Kingmambo (USA))
**190** Ch c 25/2 Raven's Pass (USA)—Rare Tern (IRE) (Pivotal) (134920)
**191** B c 28/1 Street Cry (IRE)—Rosa Parks (Sadler's Wells (USA))
**192** B f 2/4 Street Cry (IRE)—Sander Camillo (USA) (Dixie Union (USA))
**193** B c 30/4 Oasis Dream—Seta (Pivotal) (425000)
**194** B f 20/4 Street Cry (IRE)—Suez (Green Desert (USA))
**195** B c 30/4 Lawman (FR)—Top Toss (IRE) (Linamix (FR)) (150793)
**196** B c 12/3 Shamardal (USA)—Unbridled Elaine (USA) (Unbridled's Song (USA))
**197** B c 24/2 New Approach (IRE)—Walk On Bye (IRE) (Danehill Dancer (IRE))
**198** B c 3/5 Street Cry (IRE)—Zaeema (Zafonic (USA))
**199** B c 17/2 Oasis Dream—Zee Zee Top (Zafonic (USA)) (625000)

---

## 7 MR MICHAEL APPLEBY, Newark

Postal: **Stubby Nook Lodge Bungalow, Danethorpe Lane, Danethorpe, Newark, Nottinghamshire, NG24 2PD**
Contacts: **MOBILE (07884) 366421**
**E-MAIL appleby477@aol.com WEBSITE www.mickapplebyracing.com**

1 **ADILI (IRE),** 6, ch g Dubai Destination (USA)—Adirika (IRE) **Dallas Racing**
2 **APOLLO ELEVEN (IRE),** 6, b g Manduro (GER)—Arlesienne (IRE) **F. McAleavy**
3 **ARABIAN FLIGHT,** 6, b m Exceed And Excel (AUS)—Emirates First (IRE) **Dallas Racing**
4 **ART SCHOLAR (IRE),** 8, b g Pyrus (USA)—Marigold (FR) **Mrs J. Scrivens**
5 **BANCNUANAHEIREANN (IRE),** 8, b g Chevalier (IRE)—Alamanta (IRE) **Dallas Racing**
6 **BE ROYALE,** 5, b m Byron—Sofia Royale **Mr Wayne Brackstone, Mr Steve Whitear**
7 **BEYEH (IRE),** 7, b m King's Best (USA)—Cradle Rock (IRE) **T. R. Pryke**
8 **BOGNOR (USA),** 4, b g Hard Spun (USA)—Ms Blue Blood (USA) **21C Telecom.co.uk**
9 **BRASSBOUND (USA),** 7, b g Redoute's Choice (AUS)—In A Bound (AUS) **Ferrybank Properties Limited**
10 **BRIGADOON,** 8, b g Compton Place—Briggsmaid **Castle Racing**
11 **CARLANDA (FR),** 5, ch m Lando (GER)—Carousel Girl (USA) **Mr C. Bacon**
12 **CLASSICAL DIVA,** 4, b f Amadeus Wolf—America Lontana (FR) **Classical Partnership**
13 **DAME LUCY (IRE),** 5, b m Refuse To Bend (IRE)—Sheer Glamour (IRE) **Mr P. A. Cafferty**
14 **DEWALA,** 6, b m Deportivo—Fuwala **Mr A. M. Wragg**
15 **ELECTRIC QATAR,** 6, b g Pastoral Pursuits—Valandraud (IRE) **Peter Smith P. C. Coaches**
16 **FALCON'S REIGN (FR),** 6, ch g Haafhd—Al Badeya (IRE) **Mr W. J. Sewell**
17 **FAVORITE GIRL (GER),** 7, b m Shirocco (GER)—Favorite (GER) **T. R. Pryke**
18 **FLASH TOMMIE (IRE),** 7, b g City Honours (USA)—African Keys (IRE) **Mr C. Bacon**
19 **GUISHAN,** 5, b m Ishiguru (USA)—Fareham **B. D. Cantle**
20 **HELL HATH NO FURY,** 6, b m Oratorio (IRE)—Sagamartha **Mr C. Bacon**
21 **HESKA (IRE),** 4, b g Rock of Gibraltar (IRE)—Sweet Sioux **Dennis & Andy Deacon**
22 **HIDDEN ASSET,** 5, ch g Sakhee's Secret—Petite Epaulette **T. R. Pryke**
23 **IT MUST BE FAITH,** 5, b g Mount Nelson—Purple Rain (IRE) **M. Appleby**
24 **JACOBS SON,** 7, ch g Refuse To Bend (IRE)—Woodwin (IRE) **The Rain Dancers**
25 **JOHN COFFEY (IRE),** 6, b g Acclamation—Appleblossom Pearl (IRE) **Mick Appleby Racing**
26 **KHAJAALY (IRE),** 8, b g Kheleyf (USA)—Joyfullness (USA) **New Kids On The Trot**
27 **LAUGHING ROCK (IRE),** 5, b m Rock of Gibraltar (IRE)—The Last Laugh **Mick Appleby Racing**
28 **LULU THE ZULU (IRE),** 7, ch m Danroad (AUS)—Timbervati (USA) **The Ab Kettlebys**
29 **LUV U WHATEVER,** 5, b g Needwood Blade—Lady Suesanne (IRE) **21C Telecom.co.uk**
30 **MAGGIE PINK,** 6, b m Beat All (USA)—Top Notch **Mr A. W. Bult**
31 **MARCIANO (IRE),** 5, b g Pivotal—Kitty Matcham (IRE) **Formulated Polymer Products Ltd**
32 **MAWAQEET (USA),** 6, b g Dynaformer (USA)—Lady Ilsley (USA) **F. McAleavy**
33 **MOPS ANGEL,** 4, b f Piccolo—Tanning **Sarnian Racing**
34 **MR RED CLUBS (IRE),** 6, b g Red Clubs (IRE)—Queen Cobra (IRE) **Ferrybank Properties Limited**
35 **NAVAJO DREAM,** 4, ch f Selkirk (USA)—Rubies From Burma (USA) **Ferrybank Properties Limited**
36 **PEARL NATION (USA),** 6, b g Speightstown (USA)—Happy Nation (USA) **Iddon, M & C Dixon, Taylor, Finn, O'Brien**
37 **PERCYS PRINCESS,** 4, b f Sir Percy—Enford Princess **Exors of the Late Mr N. A. Blyth**
38 **POYLE VINNIE,** 5, b g Piccolo—Poyle Dee Dee **Dallas Racing & C. L. Bacon**
39 **QUEEN OF SKIES (IRE),** 6, b m Shamardal (USA)—Attractive Crown (USA) **Ferrybank Properties Limited**
40 **REAL GLORY,** 4, b f Three Valleys (USA)—Group Force (IRE) **Mr R. Devereux**
41 **RI NA SI,** 5, b g Green Horizon—Luisa Miller (IRE) **Mr M. Park**
42 **ROYAL PECULIAR,** 7, b g Galileo (IRE)—Distinctive Look (IRE) **T. R. Pryke**
43 **ROYAL SIGNALLER,** 5, b g Dylan Thomas (IRE)—Whirly Bird **Mr Archibald Hargie & Mr Brian Hargie**

## MR MICHAEL APPLEBY - Continued

44 **SCARBOROUGH (IRE),** 4, ch f Dandy Man (IRE)—Alchimie (IRE) **M. C. Wainman**
45 **SELLINGALLTHETIME (IRE),** 4, ch g Tamayuz—Anthyllis (GER) **Mr R. Oliver**
46 **SERGEANT ABLETT (IRE),** 7, b g Danehill Dancer (IRE)—Dolydille (IRE) **M. Appleby**
47 **SIOUX CHIEFTAIN (IRE),** 5, b g Mount Nelson—Lady Gin (USA) **Ferrybank Properties Limited**
48 **SLEET (IRE),** 4, b g Amadeus Wolf—Secret Justice (USA) **M. Appleby**
49 **STARFIELD,** 6, b g Marju (IRE)—Sister Moonshine (FR) **Dallas Racing**
50 **STREET FORCE (USA),** 4, b c Street Cry (IRE)—Maskunah (IRE) **Mr T. Al Nisf**
51 **SYNONYM (ITY),** 4, ch f Haatef (USA)—Shatarah **Almond Appleby Harris Woodward**
52 **TARTAN TRIP,** 8, b g Selkirk (USA)—Marajuana **Mick Appleby Racing**
53 **TEAJAYBE (USA),** 7, b br g Street Cry (IRE)—Wild Heaven (IRE) **Mrs C. Sandall**
54 **THE LOCK MASTER (IRE),** 8, b g Key of Luck (USA)—Pitrizza (IRE) **Kenneth George Kitchen**
55 **THORPE BAY,** 6, b g Piccolo—My Valentina **Dallas Racing**
56 **WESTMINSTER (IRE),** 4, b g Exceed And Excel (AUS)—Pivka **Rod In Pickle Partnership**

### THREE-YEAR-OLDS

57 **APACHE STORM,** ch f Pivotal—Best Side (IRE) **Ferrybank Properties Limited**
58 **CELESTIAL DANCER (FR),** b br f Dr Fong (USA)—Rabeera **Kinder & Golding**
59 **GOLDEN HIGHWAY (USA),** ch c Elusive Quality (USA)—Awesome Chic (USA) **Mr T. Al Nisf**
60 **OLD FASHION,** b f Shirocco (GER)—Oriental Dance
61 **PERLE EXPRESS,** b f Rail Link—Perle d'or (IRE)
62 **TOBOUGGAN RUN,** b g Tobougg (IRE)—Justbetweenfriends (USA) **The Rain Dancers**

**Other Owners:** Mr Stephen Almond, Mr Michael Appleby, Mr C. L. Bacon, Mr Wayne Brackstone, Mr V. H. Coleman, Mrs N. Cooper, Mr Dennis Deacon, Mr Andy Deacon, Mr Christopher Dixon, Mr Martin R. Dixon, Mr Danny Fantom, Mr Dominic Finn, Mr D. R. Gardner, Mr Mark A. Glassett, Mr M. J. Golding, Mr Michael Gromett, Mr Alan Grummitt, Mr Archibald Hargie, Mr Brian Hargie, Mr Mick Harris, Mr Nick Hoare, Mr Richard Hoiles, Mr R. A. Hunt, Mrs Nicola Hunt, Mr Chris Iddon, Mrs Vivienne Kinder, Mr A. W. Le Page, Mr C. Le Page, Miss A. Muir, Mr Steven Nightingale, Mr Richard O'Brien, Mr J. O'Shaughnessy, Mr David Pick, Mr O. Robinson, Mr Matthew Taylor, Mr J. R. Theaker, Mr Stephen Wain, Mr Mark Ward, Mr S. J. Whitear, Mr Denis Woodward.

**Assistant Trainer:** Mr Jonathan Clayton **Head Lad:** Niall Nevin

**Jockey (flat):** Liam Jones, Luke Morris, Andrew Mullen, Hayley Turner. **Jockey (NH):** Richard Johnson, Charlie Poste. **Conditional:** Jonathan England. **Apprentice:** Jane Elliott, Ali Rawlinson, Ryan Tate. **Amateur:** Miss Serena Brotherton.

---

## 8 MR DAVID ARBUTHNOT, Beare Green

Postal: **Henfold House Cottage, Henfold Lane, Beare Green, Dorking, Surrey, RH5 4RW**
Contacts: **PHONE (01306) 631529 FAX (01306) 631529 MOBILE (07836) 276464**
**E-MAIL dwparbuthnot@hotmail.com WEBSITE www.henfoldracing.co.uk**

1 **BEDARRA BOY,** 9, ch g Needwood Blade—Roonah Quay (IRE) **Mr P. M. Claydon**
2 **DANGLYDONTASK,** 4, b g Lucky Story (USA)—Strat's Quest **P. Banfield**
3 **DARING DEPLOY (IRE),** 9, b g Deploy—Daring Perk (IRE) **The Daring Partnership**
4 **FILLE GOOD,** 4, br f Cape Cross (IRE)—Dolydille (IRE) **The Gryffyns Stud Partnership**
5 **FOLLOWMYBUTTONS (IRE),** 5, br g Kalanisi (IRE)—Clondalee (IRE) **Mr A T A Wates & Mrs S Wates**
6 **GANDALFE (FR),** 10, b br g Laveron—Goldville (FR) **A. T. A. Wates**
7 **MAX MILAN (IRE),** 6, b g Milan—Sunset Leader (IRE) **Mr P. M. Claydon**
8 4, B g Robin des Champs (FR)—Sarah Princess (IRE)
9 **SNOWBALL (IRE),** 8, gr g Alderbrook—Rosafi (IRE) **The Daring Partnership**
10 **STARLUCK (IRE),** 10, gr g Key of Luck (USA)—Sarifa (IRE) **A. T. A. Wates**
11 **STROLLAWAYNOW (IRE),** 8, b g Oscar (IRE)—Rose of Salome (IRE) **A. T. A. Wates**
12 **TINGO IN THE TALE (IRE),** 6, b g Oratorio (IRE)—Sunlit Skies **G. S. Thompson**
13 **TOPOLSKI (IRE),** 9, b g Peintre Celebre (USA)—Witching Hour (IRE) **Mr P. M. Claydon**
14 **URCALIN (FR),** 7, b g Network (GER)—Caline So (FR) **Mr A T A Wates & Mrs S Wates**
15 **WELLUPTOSCRATCH (FR),** 4, b br g Irish Wells (FR)—Aulne River (FR) **Mr A T A Wates & Mrs S Wates**
16 **WESTAWAY (IRE),** 8, b br g Westerner—I'llaway (IRE) **Mr P. M. Claydon**

**Other Owners:** A. A. W. Jackson, Mrs H. J. Ringrose, Mrs S. M. Wates, Mr K. Wiggert.

**Jockey (NH):** Tom Cannon, Daryl Jacob.

## 9 MR MICHAEL ATTWATER, Epsom

Postal: **Tattenham Corner Stables, Tattenham Corner Road, Epsom Downs, Surrey, KT18 5PP**
Contacts: **PHONE (01737) 360066 MOBILE (07725) 423633**
**E-MAIL Attwaterracing@hotmail.co.uk WEBSITE www.attwaterracing.com**

1 **ASK THE GURU,** 5, b g Ishiguru (USA)—Tharwa (IRE) **Canisbay Bloodstock**
2 **BRAVO ECHO,** 9, b g Oasis Dream—Bold Empress (USA) **Canisbay Bloodstock**
3 **BRONZE PRINCE,** 8, b g Oasis Dream—Sweet Pea **Canisbay Bloodstock**
4 **CUTHBERT (IRE),** 8, ch g Bertolini (USA)—Tequise (IRE) **Canisbay Bloodstock**
5 **EMBANKMENT,** 6, b g Zamindar (USA)—Esplanade **Canisbay Bloodstock**
6 **EMPIRE STORM (GER),** 8, b h Storming Home—Emy Coasting (USA) **The Attwater Partnership**
7 **FLEETWOOD BELLA,** 4, ch f Byron—Royal Ivy **Canisbay Bloodstock**
8 **HEAD SPACE (IRE),** 7, b g Invincible Spirit (IRE)—Danzelline **Mr J. M. Duggan & Mr T. P. Duggan**
9 **KICKING THE CAN (IRE),** 4, gr c Aussie Rules (USA)—Silk Meadow (IRE) **Mr J. Daniels**
10 **LADY PHILL,** 5, ch m Avonbridge—Lady Filly **Mrs M. S. Teversham**
11 **LET'S CONFER,** 6, ch m Doyen (IRE)—Vrennan **Canisbay Bloodstock**
12 **NOBLE DEED,** 5, ch g Kyllachy—Noble One **Canisbay Bloodstock**
13 **PLOVER,** 5, b m Oasis Dream—Short Dance (USA) **Canisbay Bloodstock**
14 **POLAR KITE (IRE),** 7, b g Marju (IRE)—Irina (IRE) **C. Main**
15 **PROFESSOR,** 5, ch h Byron—Jubilee **Canisbay Bloodstock**
16 **PURFORD GREEN,** 6, ch m Kyllachy—Mo Stopher **Canisbay Bloodstock**
17 **ROOKERY (IRE),** 4, b g Raven's Pass (USA)—Zacheta **C. Main**
18 **SALIENT,** 11, b g Fasliyev (USA)—Savannah Belle **Canisbay Bloodstock**
19 **SQUIRE,** 4, b g Teofilo (IRE)—Most Charming (FR) **The Attwater Partnership**
20 **SUNSHINE ALWAYS (IRE),** 9, b gr g Verglas (IRE)—Easy Sunshine (IRE) **Miss M. E. Stopher**
21 **TITAN TRIUMPH,** 11, b g Zamindar (USA)—Triple Green **Canisbay Bloodstock**

### THREE-YEAR-OLDS

22 **BLACKASYOURHAT (IRE),** b c Le Cadre Noir (IRE)—Mattrah (USA) **B. Neaves**
23 **FLEETWOOD POPPY,** br f Kheleyf (USA)—Steppin Out **Canisbay Bloodstock**
24 **KNIGHT MUSIC,** b c Sir Percy—Lyric Art (USA) **The Attwater Partnership**
25 **MAJOR FRANKO,** ch g Major Cadeaux—Royal Future (IRE) **The Attwater Partnership**
26 B c Kheleyf (USA)—Royal Ivy **Canisbay Bloodstock**
27 **THE NAB (USA),** ch c Lookin At Lucky (USA)—Moon's Tune (USA) **The Attwater Partnership**

**Other Owners:** Mr B. M. Attwater, Mr M. J. Attwater, Mr James Michael Duggan, Mr T. P. Duggan, Mr Allan Graham, Mr Paul Hancock, Mr R. F. Kilby, Miss Maureen Stopher.

**Assistant Trainer:** S. Sawyer

**Amateur:** Mr Edward Sibbick.

## 10 MR NICK AYLIFFE, Minehead

Postal: **Glebe Stables, Little Ham, Winsford, Minehead, Somerset, TA24 7JH**
Contacts: **PHONE (01643) 851265 MOBILE (07975) 657839**

1 **MIX N MATCH,** 11, b g Royal Applause—South Wind **Miss L. L. Griffin**
2 **SPARKLING HERO,** 7, gr g Arkadian Hero (USA)—Sparkling Lass **Mrs M. A. Barrett**
3 **VALONA STAR,** 7, b m Man Among Men (IRE)—Valona Valley (IRE) **Mrs M. A. Barrett**
4 **VIRGILE DE GENE (FR),** 6, b g Le Fou (IRE)—Dame de Gene (FR) **Mrs M. A. Barrett**

## 11 MR ALAN BAILEY, Newmarket

Postal: **Cavendish Stables, Hamilton Road, Newmarket, Suffolk, CB8 7JQ**
Contacts: **PHONE (01638) 664546 FAX (01638) 664546 MOBILE (07808) 734223**
**WEBSITE www.alanbaileyracing.co.uk**

1 **BADDILINI,** 5, b g Bertolini (USA)—Baddi Heights (FR) **Mrs M. Shone**
2 **COINCIDENTLY,** 5, b m Acclamation—Miss Chaussini (IRE) **Mr Tom Mohan & Allan McNamee**
3 **GO FAR,** 5, b g Dutch Art—Carranita (IRE) **Mr R. J. H. West**
4 **MASTERPAVER,** 4, gr g Mastercraftsman (IRE)—Most-Saucy **Mrs A. M. Riney**
5 **MEGALEKA,** 5, b m Misu Bond (IRE)—Peyto Princess **North Cheshire Trading & Storage Ltd**
6 **MIMI LUKE (USA),** 4, b f U S Ranger (USA)—Hard As Nails (USA) **Dr S. P. Hargreaves**
7 **PEARL RANSOM (IRE),** 5, b g Intikhab (USA)—Massada **T & Z Racing Club**

## MR ALAN BAILEY - Continued

8 **POPPY BOND,** 5, b m Misu Bond (IRE)—Matilda Peace **North Cheshire Trading & Storage Ltd**
9 **SAFFIRE SONG,** 4, ch f Firebreak—Saffwah (IRE) **Mrs A Shone & Mr P Baker**
10 **SIXTIES QUEEN,** 5, b m Sixties Icon—Lily of Tagula (IRE) **Tregarth Racing & Partner**
11 **VIVAT REX (IRE),** 4, b c Fastnet Rock (AUS)—Strawberry Roan (IRE) **Mr J. F. Stocker**

## THREE-YEAR-OLDS

12 **BEAUTIFULL MIND (IRE),** gr f Zebedee—Alexander Family (IRE) **Mr M. Lowther**
13 **COMMANDER PATTEN (IRE),** ro g Clodovil (IRE)—Idle Rich (USA) **Mr J. F. Stocker**
14 **FRANGARRY (IRE),** b c Lawman (FR)—Divert (IRE) **Dr S. P. Hargreaves**
15 **GLENBUCK LASS (IRE),** gr f Dandy Man (IRE)—Certainlei (IRE) **North Cheshire Trading & Storage Ltd**
16 **HIGH RAIL,** b c High Chaparral (IRE)—Cool Catena **Dr S. P. Hargreaves**
17 **HONEY REQUIRED,** b f Makfi—Tiger Mist (IRE) **Mrs A Shone & Mr P Baker**
18 **MRS EVE (IRE),** ch f Bahamian Bounty—Catbells (IRE) **Mr C. M. & Mrs S. A. Martin**
19 **SEAMUS THE PAVER (IRE),** ch g Fast Company (IRE)—Bent Al Fala (IRE) **Mrs A. M. Riney**
20 **THIS IS TOO (IRE),** b f Fast Company (IRE)—Suzi's A Smartlady (IRE) **A. J. McNamee**
21 **VIMY RIDGE,** ch c American Post—Fairy Shoes **Mr J. F. Stocker**
22 **WAROFINDEPENDENCE (USA),** b br g War Front (USA)—My Dear Annie (USA) **Mr J. F. Stocker**

## TWO-YEAR-OLDS

23 **FAST LAYNE,** gr c 8/5 Sakhee's Secret—Tiger's Gene (GER) (Perugino (USA)) (6500) **Mrs Dee Summers**

**Other Owners:** A. Bailey, Mr P. Baker, Mr H. Hall, C. M. Martin, Mrs S. A. Martin, Mr Allen McNamee, T. M. Mohan, Mrs A. Shone, Mr R. L. Williams.

**Assistant Trainer:** J. Parr

**Apprentice:** Tim Clark.

---

## 12 MRS CAROLINE BAILEY, Holdenby

Postal: **Holdenby North Lodge, Spratton, Northampton, Northamptonshire, NN6 8LG**
Contacts: **PHONE (01604) 883729 (Home) (01604) 770234 (Yard) FAX (01604) 770423 MOBILE (07831) 373340**
**E-MAIL caroline.bailey4@btinternet.com WEBSITE www.carolinebaileyracing.co.uk**

1 **BIG GENERATOR,** 9, ch g Generous (IRE)—Frizzball (IRE) **G. T. H. Bailey**
2 **BISHOPHILL JACK (IRE),** 9, b g Tikkanen (USA)—Kerrys Cross (IRE) **The On The Bridle Partnership**
3 **BRIGSTOCK SEABRA,** 7, b m Sea Freedom—Inbra **G. T. H. Bailey**
4 **CARLI KING (IRE),** 9, br g Witness Box (USA)—Abinitio Lady (IRE) **Varley, Lloyd & Bailey**
5 **CARLO ROCKS (IRE),** 5, b g Carlo Bank (IRE)—Rock Garden (IRE) **Mrs S. Tucker**
6 **CHASSE EN MER (FR),** 5, b m Protektor (GER)—Cybertina (FR) **Mrs S. Carsberg**
7 **DEALING RIVER,** 8, b g Avonbridge—Greensand **Exor of the late Mrs S. M. Richards**
8 **DENALI HIGHWAY (IRE),** 8, ch g Governor Brown (USA)—Amaretto Flame (IRE) **Ian Payne & Kim Franklin**
9 **GALWAY JACK (IRE),** 10, b g Witness Box (USA)—Cooldalus (IRE) **Mrs M. E. Moody**
10 **GLOBAL BONUS (IRE),** 6, b g Heron Island (IRE)—That's The Bonus (IRE) **Mrs S. Carsberg**
11 **GLOBAL DOMINATION,** 7, b g Alflora (IRE)—Lucia Forte **Mrs S. Carsberg**
12 **GLOBAL DREAM,** 5, ch g Lucarno (USA)—Global Girl **Mrs S. Carsberg**
13 **GOLD INGOT,** 8, ch g Best of The Bests (IRE)—Realms of Gold (USA) **Mr James E. Cowan**
14 **HIGH RON,** 10, b g Rainbow High—Sunny Heights **Mrs G. A. Burke**
15 **MALAPIE (IRE),** 7, b g Westerner—Victorian Lady **Mr & Mrs D. Bailey**
16 **NOBLE LEGEND,** 8, b g Midnight Legend—Elmside Katie **Mr P. Dixon Smith**
17 **NORMAN BATES,** 6, b g Norse Dancer (IRE)—Well Maid **Mr & Mrs R. Scott**
18 **PRINCE DES MARAIS (FR),** 12, b br g Network (GER)—Djeba Royale (FR) **C. W. Booth**
19 **QUEEN OLIVIA,** 7, b m King's Theatre (IRE)—Queen's Leader **Mr J. M. B. Strowbridge**
20 **SEA OF CORTEZ,** 5, b m Tobougg (IRE)—Cee Cee Rider **Mice and Men**
21 **SMARTMAX (FR),** 6, ch g Until Sundown (USA)—Quendora (FR) **C. Flinton**
22 **TRAPPER PEAK (IRE),** 6, b g Westerner—Banningham Blaze **R. & P. Scott & I. Payne & K. Franklin**

**Other Owners:** Mrs D. A. Bailey, Mr D. C. Bailey, G. F. Davies, Miss K. M. Franklin, A. P. Gregory, N. R. Jennings, Mr R. B. Lloyd, Mr I. T. Payne, R. Scott, Mrs P. M. Scott, Mr J. Torrington, Mr M. Varley.

**Jockey (NH):** Tom Messenger, Adam Pogson, Andrew Thornton. **Amateur:** Mr Jonathan Bailey.

## 13 MR KIM BAILEY, Cheltenham

Postal: **Thorndale Farm, Withington Road, Andoversford, Cheltenham, Gloucestershire, GL54 4LL**
Contacts: **PHONE (01242) 890241 FAX (01242) 890193 MOBILE (07831) 416859**
**E-MAIL info@kimbaileyracing.com WEBSITE www.kimbaileyracing.com**

1 **A SHADE OF BAY,** 7, b m Midnight Legend—Pulling Strings (IRE) **Have Fun Racing Partnership**
2 **ALLEZ ENCORE (IRE),** 6, b m Turtle Island (IRE)—Glebe Beauty (IRE) **GSTTKPA Charity Partnership**
3 4, B g Authorized (IRE)—Azalee (GER) **K. R. Ellis**
4 **AZURE AWARE (IRE),** 8, b g Milan—Luck Penni (IRE) **J. F. Perriss**
5 **BALLYKNOCK LAD (IRE),** 6, b g Bach (IRE)—Ballyknock Lass (IRE) **Mrs Julie Martin & David R. Martin**
6 **BAY MAX,** 6, b g Fair Mix (IRE)—Suilven **I. F. W. Buchan**
7 **BOOLAVARD KING (IRE),** 6, b g Winged Love (IRE)—Eastender **Kim Bailey Racing Partnership II**
8 **BRAW ANGUS,** 5, b g Alflora (IRE)—Suilven **I. F. W. Buchan**
9 **CHARINGWORTH (IRE),** 12, b g Supreme Leader—Quinnsboro Guest (IRE) **A & S Enterprises Ltd**
10 **CRAZY JACK (IRE),** 7, b g Royal Anthem (USA)—Cindy's Fancy (IRE) **May We Never Be Found Out Partnership 2**
11 **DARNA,** 9, b g Alflora (IRE)—Dutch Dyane **Mrs Julie Martin & David R. Martin**
12 **DERRINTOGHER BLISS (IRE),** 6, b g Arcadio (GER)—His Fair Lady (IRE) **The Irrational Group**
13 **FAERIE REEL (FR),** 5, b m Country Reel (USA)—Final Whistle (IRE) **Mrs E. A. Kellar**
14 **FIZZY DANCER,** 5, ch m Norse Dancer (IRE)—Mrs Fizziwig **A & R Racing Club Partnership**
15 **GAELIC MYTH,** 5, b g Midnight Legend—Shannon Native (IRE) **A. N. Solomons**
16 **GALLERY EXHIBITION (IRE),** 8, b g Portrait Gallery (IRE)—Good Hearted (IRE) **The GFH Partnership**
17 **GOLD MAN (IRE),** 6, ch g Presenting—Mama Jaffa (IRE) **Mr C. A. Washbourn**
18 **GRAND MARCH,** 6, b g Beat All (USA)—Bora Bora **Mme J. B. Baldanza**
19 **HARRY TOPPER,** 8, b g Sir Harry Lewis (USA)—Indeed To Goodness (IRE) **A. N. Solomons**
20 **KING SIMBA (IRE),** 4, b g Let The Lion Roar—Anaaween (USA) **GSTTKPA Charity Partnership**
21 **KNOCKANRAWLEY (IRE),** 7, gr g Portrait Gallery (IRE)—Hot Lips (IRE) **Kim Bailey Racing Partnership VIII**
22 **KNOCKLAYDE EXPRESS (IRE),** 6, b m Scorpion (IRE)—Aupora (IRE) **J. F. Perriss**
23 **LADY OF LLANARMON,** 4, b f Yeats (IRE)—One Gulp **R. J. McAlpine & Mrs David Johnson**
24 **MAGIC MONEY,** 7, b m Midnight Legend—Sticky Money **M. D. C. Jenks**
25 **MIDNIGHT OSCAR (IRE),** 8, br g Oscar (IRE)—Midnight Light (IRE) **The Oscar Partnership**
26 **MOLLY'S A DIVA,** 8, ch m Midnight Legend—Smokey Diva (IRE) **J. F. Perriss**
27 **MOR BROOK,** 7, b g Kayf Tara—Miss Quickly (IRE) **Mor Fun Partnership**
28 **MRS PEACHEY (IRE),** 8, b m Brian Boru—Maracana (IRE) **The Boom Syndicate**
29 **NAM HAI (IRE),** 4, b g Fastnet Rock (AUS)—Bowstring (IRE)
30 **NET WORK ROUGE (FR),** 6, b g Network (GER)—Lychee de La Roque (FR) **John Wills & David ReidScott Partnership**
31 **PREMIER PORTRAIT (IRE),** 8, b g Portrait Gallery (IRE)—Shesnotthelast (IRE) **Mrs P. A. Perriss**
32 **PULLING POWER,** 5, br m Erhaab (USA)—Pulling Strings (IRE) **The Real Partnership**
33 **RHIANNA,** 4, b f Robin des Champs (FR)—La Harde (FR) **Mr N. Carter**
34 **SUCH A LEGEND,** 7, ch g Midnight Legend—Mrs Fizziwig **The Real Partnership**
35 **SUNBLAZER (IRE),** 5, gr g Dark Angel (IRE)—Damask Rose (IRE) **Kim Bailey Racing Partnership X**
36 **TARA'S RAINBOW,** 5, b m Kayf Tara—Nile Cristale (FR) **Kim Bailey Racing Partnership**
37 **THE PLAYFUL PRIEST (IRE),** 8, ch g Presenting—First Strike (IRE) **Mr Peter Elliott**
38 **THE SCARLETT WOMAN,** 6, b m Kayf Tara—Double Red (IRE) **Mrs P. A. Perriss**
39 **THEDRINKYMEISTER (IRE),** 6, b g Heron Island (IRE)—Keel Row **J. F. Perriss**
40 **UN ACE (FR),** 7, b g Voix du Nord (FR)—First Ball (FR) **Ace In The Pack Partnership**
41 **UP FOR AN OSCAR (IRE),** 8, b g Oscar (IRE)—Queen of Harts (IRE) **The Hon Mrs A. M. Cookson**
42 4, B g Presenting—Water Rock **K. C. Bailey**
43 **WEST END (IRE),** 8, b g Westerner—Brown Bess (IRE) **D. A. Hall**

**Other Owners:** Mr K. C. Bailey, Mrs Kim Bailey, Mr James Barnett, Mr Oliver Bell, Mr Leon Caine, Mr Stephen Cannon, Mr Kevin T. Clancy, Mr Dermot M. Clancy, Mr Richard Connolly, Mr Gordon Farr, Lady Hatch, Mrs David Johnson, Mr P. S. Kerr, Mr D. J. Keyte, Mr Henry Kimbell, M. L. W. Bell Racing Ltd, Mrs Julie Martin, Mr David R. Martin, Mr R. J. McAlpine, Mr Paul Monger, Mr David Reid Scott, Mrs Sandra Steer-Fowler, Dr Martyn Steer-Fowler, Mr Chris Straghalis, Mr G. D. W. Swire, Mrs C. A. T. Swire, Mrs Nicky Van Dijk, Mr P. J. H. Wills, Mr S. J. Winter.

**Assistant Trainer:** Mathew Nicholls

**Jockey (NH):** Ed Cookson, Jason Maguire.

## 14 MRS TRACEY L. BAILEY, Hungerford

Postal: **Soley Farm Stud, Chilton Foliat, Hungerford, Berkshire, RG17 0TW**
Contacts: **PHONE (01488) 683321 MOBILE (07831) 300999**
**E-MAIL t413@btinternet.com**

1 **BROADWAY SYMPHONY (IRE),** 8, ch g Broadway Flyer (USA)—Flying Hooves (IRE) **N. R. A. Sutton**
2 **COUNT SALAZAR (IRE),** 10, b g Revoque (IRE)—Cherry Sent (IRE) **The Phoenix Partners**
3 **THE GOVERNOR (IRE),** 6, b g Dushyantor (USA)—Some News (IRE) **N. R. A. Sutton**

**Other Owners:** Mr N. Sutton, Mrs S. A. Sutton.

**Amateur:** Mr Dominic Sutton.

## 15 MISS EMMA BAKER, Cheltenham

Postal: **Brockhill, Naunton, Cheltenham, Gloucestershire, GL54 3BA**
Contacts: **FAX (01451) 850199 MOBILE (07887) 845970**
**E-MAIL emmajbakerracing@hotmail.co.uk WEBSITE www.emmabakerracing.com**

1 **BACK BY MIDNIGHT,** 6, ch g Midnight Legend—Roberta Back (IRE) **Mrs J. Arnold**
2 **BAJARDO (IRE),** 7, b g Jammaal—Bit of Peace (IRE) **Mrs J. Arnold**
3 **BOURDELLO,** 6, b m Milan—Haudello (FR) **Mrs J. Arnold**
4 **BRINESTINE (USA),** 6, b g Bernstein (USA)—Miss Zafonic (FR) **Brians Buddies**
5 **CHURCH HALL (IRE),** 7, b g Craigsteel—Island Religion (IRE) **Mrs J. Arnold**
6 **CRACKERJACK,** 8, ch g Lahib (USA)—Tidesong **Mrs J. Arnold**
7 **GLANCE BACK,** 4, b g Passing Glance—Roberta Back (IRE) **Mrs J. Arnold**
8 **GREY MESSENGER (IRE),** 6, gr g Heron Island (IRE)—Turlututu (FR) **Miss E. J. Baker**
9 **MASTER CARDOR VISA (IRE),** 10, br g Alderbrook—Princess Moodyshoe **Mrs J. Arnold**
10 **MIDNIGHT CHARMER,** 9, b g Midnight Legend—Dickies Girl **Mrs J. Arnold**
11 **PADDLEYOUROWNCANOE (IRE),** 14, b g Saddlers' Hall (IRE)—Little Paddle (IRE) **Miss E. J. Baker**
12 **SNOWELL (IRE),** 8, b g Well Chosen—Snow Water (IRE) **Miss E. J. Baker**
13 **SUBTLE APPROACH (IRE),** 10, b g Subtle Power (IRE)—Rotoruasprings (IRE) **Mrs J. Arnold**
14 **WATERLOO DOCK,** 10, b g Hunting Lion (IRE)—Scenic Air **Mr R. G. R. Spencer**

**Other Owners:** Mr Michael J. Arnold, Mr W. G. Cullen.

## 16 MR GEORGE BAKER, Manton

Postal: **Barton Yard, Manton House Estate, Marlborough, Wiltshire, SN8 4HB**
Contacts: **PHONE OFFICE: (01672) 515493 (01672) 516234 FAX (01672) 514938**
**MOBILE (07889) 514881**
**E-MAIL gbakerracing@gmail.com WEBSITE www.georgebakerracing.com**

1 **ANCIENT GREECE,** 8, b g Pivotal—Classicism (USA) **George Baker & Partners**
2 **AQUA ARDENS (GER),** 7, b g Nayef (USA)—Arduinna (GER) **Mrs C. E. S. Baker**
3 **BELGIAN BILL,** 7, b h Exceed And Excel (AUS)—Gay Romance **PJL, Byrne & Baker**
4 **BOOMSHACKERLACKER (IRE),** 5, gr g Dark Angel (IRE)—Allegrina (IRE) **PJL Racing**
5 **BOUNTYBEAMADAM,** 5, b m Bahamian Bounty—Madamoiselle Jones **Whitsbury Hopefuls**
6 **CASTORIENTA,** 4, ch f Orientor—The Lady Caster **Mr David Barrie**
7 **DAISY'S SECRET,** 4, ch f Sakhee's Secret—Darling Daisy **Mrs P. A. Scott-Dunn**
8 **DANA'S PRESENT,** 6, ch g Osorio (GER)—Euro Empire (USA) **Mrs C. E. S. Baker**
9 **DESTINY'S GOLD (IRE),** 5, b g Millenary—Knockhouse Rose (IRE) **Delancey & Mrs V Finegold**
10 **DOUBLE DASH,** 11, b g Sir Harry Lewis (USA)—Dashing Executive (IRE) **Mrs P. A. Scott-Dunn**
11 **ETON RAMBLER (USA),** 5, b br g Hard Spun (USA)—Brightbraveandgood (USA) **The Eton Ramblers**
12 **FIFTYSHADESFREED (IRE),** 4, gr g Verglas (IRE)—Vasilia **Team Fifty**
13 **FIFTYSHADESOFGREY (IRE),** 4, gr g Dark Angel (IRE)—Wohaida (IRE) **Team Fifty**
14 **FOUR NATIONS (USA),** 7, ch g Langfuhr (CAN)—Kiswahili **The Transatlantic USA Syndicate**
15 **GEORGE BAKER (IRE),** 8, b g Camacho—Petite Maxine **Mr G. Baker**
16 **GONE VIRAL (IRE),** 4, ch g Virtual—Dorinda Gray (IRE) **Mr G. Baker**
17 **HALLEY (FR),** 8, b g Loup Solitaire (USA)—Moon Glow (FR) **PJL Racing**
18 **HOPONANDSEE,** 4, b f Nomadic Way (USA)—Jago's Girl **Mr C. Giles**
19 **HUMIDOR (IRE),** 8, b g Camacho—Miss Indigo **Delancey Real Estate Asset Management Limited**
20 **I'M FRAAM GOVAN,** 7, ch g Fraam—Urban Dancer (IRE) **Sir Alex Ferguson**
21 **I'M HARRY,** 6, b g Haafhd—First Approval **Wickfield Stud & Hartshill Stud**
22 **INTIBAAH,** 5, b g Elnadim (USA)—Mawaared **Mr G. Baker**

## MR GEORGE BAKER - Continued

23 **ISHIAMBER,** 5, ch m Ishiguru (USA)—Black And Amber **Mrs P. A. Scott-Dunn**
24 **ISLA MAYFLY,** 4, b f Desideratum—Calandria (IRE) **George Baker & Partners**
25 **JACK'S REVENGE (IRE),** 7, br g Footstepsinthesand—Spirit of Age (IRE) **PJL Racing**
26 **JOEY'S DESTINY (IRE),** 5, ch g Kheleyf (USA)—
Maid of Ailsa (USA) **Delancey Real Estate Asset Management Limited**
27 **LAUGHING JACK,** 7, b g Beat Hollow—Bronzewing **Mr P. A. Downing**
28 **LOVING YOUR WORK,** 4, b g Royal Applause—Time Crystal (IRE) **The Loving Your Work Syndicate**
29 **MENDACIOUS HARPY (IRE),** 4, b f Dark Angel (IRE)—Idesia (IRE) **Mr R. Curry**
30 **MISTER MAYDAY (IRE),** 4, br g Kheleyf (USA)—Soxy Doxy (IRE) **Asprey, Kane & Thomas**
31 **MR ROCK (IRE),** 4, b c Galileo (IRE)—Kitza (IRE) **Sir Alex Ferguson**
32 **MRS WARREN,** 5, b m Kyllachy—Bold Bunny **Mr P. A. Russell**
33 **MUIR LODGE,** 4, ch g Exceed And Excel (AUS)—Miss Chaussini (IRE) **Pittam, Mather & Baker**
34 **NOVA CHAMP (IRE),** 4, ch g Intikhab (USA)—Baby Bunting **The Ratpack Partnership**
35 **PILGRIMS REST (IRE),** 6, ch g Rock of Gibraltar (IRE)—Holly Blue **Pittam, Mather & Baker**
36 **RED FOUR,** 5, ch m Singspiel (IRE)—Protectorate **Lady N. F. Cobham**
37 **REFRESHESTHEPARTS (USA),** 6, ch m Proud Citizen (USA)—St Francis Wood (USA) **Mr M. R. de Carvalho**
38 **RORING SAMSON (IRE),** 4, b g Art Connoisseur (IRE)—Marju Guest (IRE) **Mr G. Baker**
39 **SECULAR SOCIETY,** 5, b g Royal Applause—Fantastic Santanyi **Mrs S. C. Head**
40 **SINBAD THE SAILOR,** 10, b g Cape Cross (IRE)—Sinead (USA) **Baker, Coleman, Wand & Williams**
41 **UGANDA GLORY (USA),** 5, br m Hat Trick (JPN)—Febrile (USA) **George Baker & Partners**
42 **YUL FINEGOLD (IRE),** 5, b g Invincible Spirit (IRE)—Mascara **Mrs Virginia Finegold & PJL Racing**

## THREE-YEAR-OLDS

43 **BEAUSANT,** ch c Orientor—Hanella (IRE) **F. Brady**
44 **COMMODORE (IRE),** b c Kodiac—Deportment **Highclere Thoroughbred Racing - Trinity**
45 **DESTINY'S SHADOW (IRE),** b g Dark Angel (IRE)—
Lunar Love (IRE) **Delancey Real Estate Asset Management Limited**
46 **ELIJAH CREEK,** b g Avonbridge—Forest Girl (IRE) **Miss Cat Ilott**
47 **EVERYDAY (IRE),** b g Alfred Nobel (IRE)—Profound Emotion **George Baker & Partners**
48 **FLUTTERBEE,** b f Equiano (FR)—Dunya **PJL Racing**
49 **HARRY HURRICANE,** b c Kodiac—Eolith **PJL Racing**
50 **HERECOMESTHEBAND,** b c Bertolini (USA)—Green Supreme **Herecomestheband Partnership**
51 **LADY BEE (IRE),** b f Lawman (FR)—Rainbow Lyrics (IRE) **The Countess of Bathurst**
52 **ORLANDO ROGUE (IRE),** b c Bushranger (IRE)—Boston Ivy (USA) **Mr & Mrs J. Pittam**
53 **RED PERDITA (IRE),** b f Approve (IRE)—Bakewell Tart (IRE) **Mr A. Li**
54 **RUNNER RUNNER (IRE),** gr f Dark Angel (IRE)—Distant Piper (IRE) **PJL Racing 1**
55 **SPANISH DANSER (IRE),** ch f Lord Shanakill (USA)—
Highwater Dancer (IRE) **Fiona Stonehouse & Peter Skinner**
56 **WILL I FINEGOLD,** b f Aqlaam—Angel Song **Breton Partnership**
57 **ZUBAIDAH,** b f Exceed And Excel (AUS)—Bedouin Bride (USA) **Equi ex Incertis Partners**

## TWO-YEAR-OLDS

**58** Br c 26/3 Authorized (IRE)—Barley Bree (IRE) (Danehill Dancer (IRE)) (42000) **George Baker**
**59** Ch c 29/3 Monsieur Bond (IRE)—Birthday Belle (Lycius (USA)) (12000) **Seaton Partnership**
**60** B c 3/3 Assertive—Even Hotter (Desert Style (IRE)) **Lady Whent**
**61** Ch c 23/2 Monsieur Bond (IRE)—Formidable Girl (USA) (Roman Ruler (USA)) (1904) **Mr Mike McKeever**
**62 FUNNY OYSTER (IRE),** gr f 12/4 Dark Angel (IRE)—
Carpet Lover (IRE) (Fayruz) (30476) **Skinner, Baker & Partners**
**63** Ch f 22/3 Showcasing—Georgie The Fourth (IRE) (Cadeaux Genereux) (23809) **PJL Racing**
**64** B f 11/2 Tobougg (IRE)—High Tan (High Chaparral (IRE)) **Seaton Partnership**
**65** B c 20/3 Raven's Pass (USA)—Lukrecia (IRE) (Exceed And Excel (AUS)) (25000) **PJL & Nick & Linda Clark**
**66** B f 9/4 Duke of Marmalade (IRE)—Miss Estrada (IRE) (Noverre (USA)) (15079) **Mrs Renata Coleman**
**67** B c 5/2 Mount Nelson—Mrs Penny (AUS) (Planchet (AUS)) (48000) **PJL Racing**
**68** Ch c 28/1 Shamardal (USA)—Solar Midnight (USA) (Lemon Drop Kid (USA)) (65000) **PJL Racing**

**Other Owners:** Miss E. Asprey, Mrs C. E. S. Baker, Mr George Baker, Mr P. Bowden, Earl Of Brecknock, Mr Norton Brookes, Mr Justin Byrne, Mr A. Coleman, Mr Peter M. Crane, Delancey, Miss L. Egerton, Mrs Virginia Finegold, Mr Nicholas Finegold, Mr A. Flintoff, The Hon H. Herbert, Highclere Thoroughbred Racing Ltd, Miss L. Hurley, Mr David Jenks, Mrs Jonathan Leigh, Mr L. Lugg, Sir I. Magee, Mr Craig Mather, Mr Bobby McAlpine, Mr Frank McGrath, Mr J. Pittam, Mrs A. J. Pittam, Mrs Peter Robinson, Earl Spencer, Mr Toby Wand, Mrs P. H. Williams.

**Assistant Trainers:** Patrick Murphy, Valerie Murphy

**Jockey (flat):** Pat Cosgrave. **Jockey (NH):** Andrew Tinkler. **Apprentice:** Alfie Davies, Chris Meehan.

# 17 MR ANDREW BALDING, Kingsclere

Postal: **Park House Stables, Kingsclere, Newbury, Berkshire, RG20 5PY**
Contacts: **PHONE (01635) 298210 FAX (01635) 298305 MOBILE (07774) 633791**
**E-MAIL admin@kingsclere.com WEBSITE www.kingsclere.com**

1 **ABSOLUTELY SO (IRE),** 5, b g Acclamation—Week End **The George Smith Family Partnership**
2 **ANGELIC UPSTART (IRE),** 7, b g Singspiel (IRE)—Rada (IRE) **Mr B. Burdett**
3 **BREAKHEART (IRE),** 8, b g Sakhee (USA)—Exorcet (FR) **I. A. Balding**
4 **CAPE VICTORIA,** 4, b f Mount Nelson—Victoria Montoya **Kingsclere Racing Club**
5 **CHESIL BEACH,** 4, b f Phoenix Reach (IRE)—Seaflower Reef (IRE) **Kingsclere Racing Club**
6 **CHIBERTA KING,** 9, b g King's Best (USA)—Glam Rock **The Pink Hat Racing Partnership**
7 **COLLABORATION,** 4, b g Halling (USA)—Red Shareef **Another Bottle Racing 2**
8 **DANDY (GER),** 6, b g Nayef (USA)—Diacada (GER) **Mr R. E. Tillett**
9 **DESERT COMMAND,** 5, b g Oasis Dream—Speed Cop **J. C. Smith**
10 **DUNGANNON,** 8, b g Monsieur Bond (IRE)—May Light **Dr E. Harris**
11 **ELBERETH,** 4, b f Mount Nelson—Masandra (IRE) **D. Taylor**
12 **FIELD OF FAME,** 4, b g Champs Elysees—Aswaaq (IRE) **Thurloe Thoroughbreds XXXI**
13 **GRACE AND FAVOUR,** 4, b f Montjeu (IRE)—Gryada **N. M. H. Jones**
14 **HAINES,** 4, ch g Shirocco (GER)—Spring Dream (IRE) **Bow River Racing**
15 **HANNINGTON,** 4, ch g Firebreak—Manderina **I. A. Balding**
16 **HAVANA BEAT (IRE),** 5, b g Teofilo (IRE)—Sweet Home Alabama (IRE) **Mick and Janice Mariscotti**
17 **HERE COMES WHEN (IRE),** 5, b g Danehill Dancer (IRE)—Quad's Melody (IRE) **Mrs F. H. Hay**
18 **HIGHLAND COLORI (IRE),** 7, b g Le Vie Dei Colori—Emma's Star (ITY) **Mr E.M. Sutherland**
19 **INTRANSIGENT,** 6, b g Trans Island—Mara River **Kingsclere Racing Club**
20 **KOKOVOKO (IRE),** 4, br g Trans Island—Khazaria (FR) **Mrs T. L. Miller**
21 **MAN OF HARLECH,** 4, b c Dansili—Ffestiniog (IRE) **Elite Racing Club**
22 **MELVIN THE GRATE (IRE),** 5, b g Danehill Dancer (IRE)—Hawala (IRE) **Fromthestables.com & I. A. Balding**
23 **MERRY ME (IRE),** 4, b f Invincible Spirit (IRE)—Thought Is Free **Mrs F. H. Hay**
24 **MIME DANCE,** 4, b g Notnowcato—Encore My Love **D. E. Brownlow**
25 **MODERN TUTOR,** 6, b g Selkirk (USA)—Magical Romance (IRE) **D. E. Brownlow & Mr P. Fox**
26 **MONTALY,** 4, b g Yeats (IRE)—Le Badie (IRE) **The Farleigh Court Racing Partnership**
27 **MYMATECHRIS (IRE),** 4, br g High Chaparral (IRE)—Splendeur (FR) **D. E. Brownlow**
28 **NABATEAN (IRE),** 4, b g Rock of Gibraltar (IRE)—Landinium (ITY) **Lord J. Blyth**
29 **PERFECT LEGEND,** 4, b g Norse Dancer (IRE)—Flamjica (USA) **The Cadagan Partnership & D. H. Caslon**
30 **PERFECT MISSION,** 7, b g Bertolini (USA)—Sharp Secret (IRE) **Mildmay Racing**
31 **POOL HOUSE,** 4, b g Sakhee's Secret—Gitane (FR) **D. E. Brownlow**
32 **PRIORS BROOK,** 4, b g Champs Elysees—Dyanita **Mrs L. M. Alexander**
33 **PURCELL (IRE),** 5, b g Acclamation—Lyca Ballerina **Highclere Thoroughbred Racing-JohnPorter**
34 **QUEEN'S STAR,** 6, ch m With Approval (CAN)—Memsahib **Sir Gordon Brunton**
35 **RAWAKI (IRE),** 7, b g Phoenix Reach (IRE)—Averami **Kingsclere Racing Club**
36 **RIZAL PARK (IRE),** 4, b g Amadeus Wolf—Imelda (USA) **L. L. Register, Martin & Valerie Slade**
37 **ROYAL WARRANTY,** 4, ch f Sir Percy—Royal Patron **Sir Gordon Brunton**
38 **SCOTLAND (GER),** 4, b g Monsun (GER)—Sqillo (IRE) **Mrs F. H. Hay**
39 **SEA SOLDIER (IRE),** 7, b g Red Ransom (USA)—Placement **Mrs C. J. Wates**
40 **SECRET HINT,** 4, b f Oasis Dream—Teeky **G. Strawbridge**
41 **SIDE GLANCE,** 8, b br g Passing Glance—Averami **Pearl Bloodstock Limited**
42 **SMILING STRANGER (IRE),** 4, br g Nayef (USA)—Carraigoona (IRE) **N. M. Watts**
43 **SPECTATOR,** 4, br g Passing Glance—Averami **Kingsclere Racing Club**
44 **STORM FORCE TEN,** 4, b g Shirocco (GER)—Stravinsky Dance **R. B. Waley-Cohen**
45 **TULLIUS (IRE),** 7, ch g Le Vie Dei Colori—Whipped Queen (USA) **Kennet Valley Thoroughbreds VI**
46 **WHIPLASH WILLIE,** 7, ch g Phoenix Reach (IRE)—Santa Isobel **J. C. & S. R. Hitchins**
47 **ZAMPA MANOS (USA),** 4, b g Arch (USA)—Doryphar (USA) **N. M. Watts**
48 **ZANETTO,** 5, b g Medicean—Play Bouzouki **Mick and Janice Mariscotti**

## THREE-YEAR-OLDS

49 **ARABIAN ILLUSION (FR),** ch c Makfi—Arabian Spell (IRE) **Mrs F. H. Hay**
50 **ASKANCE,** b g Passing Glance—Seaflower Reef (IRE) **Kingsclere Racing Club**
51 **ASTRAL STORM,** br c High Chaparral (IRE)—Highland Shot **J. C. Smith**
52 **BALLYNANTY (IRE),** br c Yeats (IRE)—Reina Blanca **Mr R. J. C. Wilmot-Smith**
53 **BERKSHIRE BEAUTY,** b f Aqlaam—Salim Toto **Berkshire Parts & Panels Ltd**
54 **BLOND ME (IRE),** ch f Tamayuz—Holda (IRE) **Mr & Mrs R. M. Gorell**
55 **BRANDON CASTLE,** b g Dylan Thomas (IRE)—Chelsey Jayne (IRE) **R. P. B. Michaelson & Dr E. Harris**
56 **CAPE SPIRIT (IRE),** b f Cape Cross (IRE)—Fearless Spirit (USA) **G. Strawbridge**
57 **COSMIC RAY,** b g Phoenix Reach (IRE)—Beat Seven **Winterbeck Manor Stud Ltd**
58 **COUNTERMAND,** b g Authorized (IRE)—Answered Prayer **Ms K. Gough Mr R. Wilmot-Smith Mr K. Ghaly**

## MR ANDREW BALDING - Continued

59 **CRITICAL SPEED (IRE),** ch f Pivotal—Speed Cop **J. C. Smith**
60 **DANCE OF FIRE,** b c Norse Dancer (IRE)—Strictly Dancing (IRE) **J. C. Smith**
61 **DOCTOR BONG,** b g Sleeping Indian—Vax Rapide **The Pink Star Racing Partnership**
62 **DURETTO,** ch c Manduro (GER)—Landinium (ITY) **Lord J. Blyth**
63 **ELM PARK,** b c Phoenix Reach (IRE)—Lady Brora **Qatar Racing Limited**
64 **FARLETTI,** b f Royal Applause—Le Badie (IRE) **The Farleigh Court Racing Partnership**
65 **FAST APPROACH (IRE),** ch f New Approach (IRE)—Exorcet (FR) **J. C. Smith**
66 **GALEOTTI,** ch g Paco Boy (IRE)—Bella Lambada **Mick and Janice Mariscotti**
67 **GUIDING LIGHT (IRE),** b g Acclamation—Venus Rising **Thurloe Thoroughbreds XXXIV**
68 **HALA MADRID,** ch f Nayef (USA)—Ermine (IRE) **N. M. Watts**
69 **HAVISHAM,** b c Mount Nelson—Ile Deserte **D. E. Brownlow**
70 **HEARTLESS,** ch f New Approach (IRE)—Honorine (IRE) **Qatar Racing Limited**
71 **HIGH ADMIRAL,** ch c New Approach (IRE)—Wosaita **D. E. Brownlow**
72 **HIGHLAND BLAIZE,** ch g Dutch Art—Off Stage (IRE) **Mr E.M. Sutherland**
73 **HIT LIST (IRE),** ch g Makfi—Kassiopeia (IRE) **Another Bottle Racing 2**
74 **KIND OF HUSH (IRE),** b f Marju (IRE)—Affinity **Elite Racing Club**
75 **KINEMATIC,** b f Kyllachy—Spinning Top **Her Majesty The Queen**
76 **KINGSTON MIMOSA,** b g Kheleyf (USA)—Derartu (AUS) **Mr Richard Hains**
77 **KINGSTON SASSAFRAS,** b c Halling (USA)—Kingston Acacia **Mr Richard Hains**
78 **LADY PINNACLE,** b f Zamindar (USA)—Lady Donatella **Mrs C. J. Wates**
79 **LUNAR LOGIC,** b g Motivator—Moonmaiden **Martin & Valerie Slade & Partner**
80 **MAKE IT UP,** b c Halling (USA)—American Spirit (IRE) **G. Strawbridge**
81 **MAN LOOK,** b c Nayef (USA)—Charlecote (IRE) **C. C. Buckley**
82 **MASTER APPRENTICE (IRE),** gr c Mastercraftsman (IRE)—Lady Hawkfield (IRE) **Jadara Stables SL**
83 **MR QUICKSILVER,** gr c Dansili—Last Second (IRE) **J. L. C. Pearce**
84 **MS GRANDE CORNICHE,** ch f Pivotal—Miss Corniche **J. L. C. Pearce**
85 **MUNSTEAD PRIDE,** ch g Sir Percy—Memsahib **Sir Gordon Brunton**
86 **NADDER,** ch f Notnowcato—Tavy **Mrs A. Wigan**
87 **NORDIC BEAT,** ch g Norse Dancer (IRE)—Florida Heart **Kingsclere Racing Club**
88 **NORTRON (IRE),** b c Makfi—Nessa (FR) **Maldon Racing SL**
89 **OPERA LAD (IRE),** b c Teofilo (IRE)—Opera Glass **Mr J. C. Smith**
90 **OPTIMYSTIC (IRE),** ch f Exceed And Excel (AUS)—Psychic (IRE) **BA Racing**
91 **ORANGE WALK (USA),** b g Bernardini (USA)—Sally Forth **Her Majesty The Queen**
92 **PARADISE BIRD,** ch f Kyllachy—Amanjena **Mrs C. J. Wates**
93 **PRINCE OF CARDAMOM (IRE),** b g Nayef (USA)—Tiger Spice **Mr M. A. Burton**
94 **RATTLING JEWEL,** b c Royal Applause—Mutoon (IRE) **Mick and Janice Mariscotti**
95 **RED RUBLES (IRE),** b g Soviet Star (USA)—Shantalla Peak (IRE) **Mr P. Brend & Mr J. Dwyer**
96 **ROCKET PUNCH (IRE),** b c Makfi—Crystal Reef **Qatar Racing Limited**
97 **ROCKY RIDER,** b c Galileo (IRE)—Blue Symphony **Qatar Racing Limited**
98 **ROSE ABOVE,** b f Yeats (IRE)—Sabah **Sir Roger Buckley, Mr Gerald Oury**
99 **ROYAL NORMANDY,** b g Royal Applause—Border Minstral (IRE) **M. Payton**
100 **SCARLET MINSTREL,** b g Sir Percy—Sweet Mandolin **J. C., J. R & S. R. Hitchins**
101 **SCOTS FERN,** b f Selkirk (USA)—Ushindi (IRE) **Hot To Trot Racing Club & Mrs P. Veenbaas**
102 **SCOTTISH (IRE),** b g Teofilo (IRE)—Zeiting (IRE) **Mrs F. H. Hay**
103 **SHEER HONESTY,** b f Hellvelyn—Honesty Pays **Miss A. V. Hill**
104 **SNOOZING INDIAN,** ch g Sleeping Indian—Balnaha **G. Strawbridge**
105 **SONNOLENTO (IRE),** b c Rip Van Winkle (IRE)—Dreams Come True (FR) **Mick and Janice Mariscotti**
106 **ST SAVIOUR,** b c Danehill Dancer (IRE)—Titivation **Highclere Thoroughbred Racing (Jersey Lily)**
107 **STAR SYSTEM (USA),** b br g Whipper (USA)—Beiramar (IRE) **Mr L. L. Register**
108 **STEALING THE SHOW,** b c Makfi—Belle Reine **Qatar Racing Limited**
109 **STHENIC (FR),** b c Fastnet Rock (AUS)—Ela's Giant **Mr N. N. Botica**
110 **VICTORIA POLLARD,** b f Sir Percy—Victoria Montoya **Kingsclere Racing Club**
111 **WHITCHURCH,** b g Mawatheeq (USA)—Silvereine (FR) **I. A. Balding**

## TWO-YEAR-OLDS

**112** B f 3/2 Poet's Voice—Amallna (Green Desert (USA)) (146825) **Mrs F. H. Hay**
**113** B c 3/3 Champs Elysees—Amarullah (FR) (Daylami (IRE)) (30000) **Mr D. Powell**
**114** B c 11/4 Approve (IRE)—Annellis (UAE) (Diesis) (11904)
**115** B c 13/2 Champs Elysees—Averami (Averti (IRE)) **Kingsclere Racing Club**
**116** B c 2/2 Champs Elysees—Belladera (IRE) (Alzao (USA)) (65000) **Qatar Racing Limited**
**117** **BINGO GEORGE (IRE),** b c 9/2 Holy Roman Emperor (IRE)—Kalleidoscope (Pivotal) **The Smith Family**
**118** **BOTH SIDES,** b c 10/2 Lawman (FR)—Pearl Dance (USA) (Nureyev (USA)) **Mr G. Strawbridge**
**119** **BRIEF VISIT,** b f 5/2 Fastnet Rock (AUS)—Brevity (USA) (Street Cry (IRE)) **Mr P. Freedman**
**120** B c 11/2 Canford Cliffs (IRE)—
Camp Riverside (USA) (Forest Camp (USA)) (30000) **James/Michaelson/Greenwood**

## MR ANDREW BALDING - Continued

**121 CHARMY,** b f 22/3 Yeats (IRE)—Saturday Girl (Peintre Celebre (USA)) **Mr R. Wilmot-Smith**
**122** B f 1/3 Acclamation—Come What May (Selkirk (USA)) (31745)
**123** B f 26/3 Poet's Voice—Costa Brava (IRE) (Sadler's Wells (USA)) (67460) **Thurloe Thoroughbreds XXXVI**
**124** B f 24/3 Holy Roman Emperor (IRE)—Crystal Gaze (IRE) (Rainbow Quest (USA)) **Qatar Racing Limited**
**125** B c 6/5 Canford Cliffs (IRE)—
Danehill's Dream (IRE) (Danehill (USA)) (63491) **Happy Valley Racing & Breeding Limited**
**126** Br c 21/2 Acclamation—Dark Missile (Night Shift (USA)) **Mr J. C. Smith**
**127** Ch f 13/5 Showcasing—Darling Daisy (Komaite (USA)) **Mrs Scott-Dunn**
**128** Ch f 10/2 Manduro (GER)—Eastern Lily (USA) (Eastern Echo (USA)) **Qatar Racing Limited**
**129** B c 19/5 Dalghar (FR)—Ela's Giant (Giant's Causeway (USA)) **N. Botica**
**130** B f 22/4 Pour Moi (IRE)—Fast Flow (IRE) (Fasliyev (USA)) **Mr J. C. Smith**
**131** Br c 8/4 Passing Glance—Florida Heart (First Trump) **Kingsclere Racing Club**
**132 GALLEY BAY,** ch c 11/3 Bahamian Bounty—
Rosabee (IRE) (No Excuse Needed) (60000) **Mick and Janice Mariscotti**
**133 HUSBANDRY,** b c 7/2 Paco Boy (IRE)—Humdrum (Dr Fong (USA)) **Her Majesty The Queen**
**134 IAN FLEMING,** b c 29/4 Makfi—High Cross (IRE) (Cape Cross (IRE)) (50000) **Chelsea Thoroughbreds**
**135 IBERICA ROAD (USA),** b br c 5/2 Quality Road (USA)—
Field of Clover (CAN) (Bluegrass Cat (USA)) (51586) **The Mucho Men Racing Partnership**
**136** Ch c 7/2 Exceed And Excel (AUS)—Indian Love Bird (Efisio) (200000) **Salem Rashid**
**137** B c 23/3 Dashing Blade—Inhibition (Nayef (USA)) **Kingsclere Racing Club**
**138** B c 22/2 Rock of Gibraltar (IRE)—Izzy Lou (IRE) (Spinning World (USA)) (34126) **Kennet Valley Thoroughbreds**
**139** B c 25/4 Rip Van Winkle (IRE)—Jabroot (IRE) (Alhaarth (IRE)) (170000) **Mrs F. H. Hay**
**140** B f 2/5 Dream Ahead (USA)—Jessica's Dream (IRE) (Desert Style (IRE)) **Qatar Racing Limited**
**141** B c 31/3 Shirocco (GER)—Lady Brora (Dashing Blade) **Kingsclere Racing Club**
**142 LE TISSIER,** ch c 6/4 Sir Percy—
Incarnation (IRE) (Samum (GER)) (13491) **Mrs L. E. Ramsden & Mr R. Morecombe**
**143** Ch c 21/3 Sakhee's Secret—Lochangel (Night Shift (USA)) **Mr J. C. Smith**
**144 LORD ASLAN (IRE),** b c 13/2 Thewayyouare (USA)—
Lunar Lustre (IRE) (Desert Prince (IRE)) (85000) **D. E. Brownlow**
**145 LORD HUNTINGDON,** b c 12/1 Lord of England (GER)—Marajuana (Robellino (USA)) **Kingsclere Racing Club**
**146 LORELINA,** b f 9/5 Passing Glance—Diktalina (Diktat) **Mr A. Anderson**
**147** B f 1/3 Makfi—Loulou (USA) (El Prado (IRE)) (52000) **Qatar Racing Limited**
**148 MAKE FAST,** b f 10/3 Makfi—Raymi Coya (CAN) (Van Nistelrooy (USA)) **Her Majesty The Queen**
**149** B c 7/4 Oasis Dream—Miss Cap Ferrat (Darshaan) **Mr J. L. C. Pearce**
**150 MONTAGUE WAY (IRE),** b c 12/3 Rock of Gibraltar (IRE)—
Shanghai Lily (IRE) (King's Best (USA)) (16000) **Martin & Valerie Slade**
**151 MOON OVER MOBAY,** b f 24/3 Archipenko (USA)—Slew The Moon (ARG) (Kitwood (USA)) **Miss K. Rausing**
**152 MR ANDROS,** b c 27/1 Phoenix Reach (IRE)—Chocolada (Namid) (33333) **Winterbeck Manor Stud**
**153** B f 14/2 Siyouni (FR)—Once Over (Sakhee (USA)) **Kingsclere Racing Club**
**154** B f 21/3 Fastnet Rock (AUS)—Opera Glass (Barathea (IRE)) **Mr J. C. Smith**
**155** B c 28/2 Passing Glance—Orbital Orchid (Mujahid (USA)) **Mr J. S. Newton**
**156 ORMITO (GER),** b c 13/2 Mamool (IRE)—
Ormita (GER) (Acatenango (GER)) (19047) **Mrs L. E. Ramsden & Mr R. Morecombe**
**157** B f 13/3 Passing Glance—Perfect Act (Act One) **Mildmay Racing**
**158** B c 14/5 Lope de Vega (IRE)—Queen Bodicea (IRE) (Revoque (IRE)) (134920) **Mrs F. H. Hay**
**159** B br c 3/2 Cape Blanco (IRE)—Real Doll (USA) (Known Fact (USA)) (60000) **Mick and Janice Mariscotti**
**160 REHEARSE (IRE),** b c 3/3 Big Bad Bob (IRE)—
And Again (USA) (In The Wings) (134920) **Highclere Thoroughbred Racing (Disraeli)**
**161** B f 30/3 Cape Cross (IRE)—Sabria (USA) (Miswaki (USA)) **Walter R. Swinburn**
**162** B f 20/1 Pour Moi (IRE)—Saturn Girl (IRE) (Danehill Dancer (IRE)) **Mr M. Tabor**
**163** B f 9/3 Passing Glance—Seaflower Reef (IRE) (Robellino (USA)) **Kingsclere Racing Club**
**164 SHONGOLOLO (IRE),** b c 10/4 Manduro (GER)—
Nipping (IRE) (Night Shift (USA)) (23809) **Martin & Valerie Slade & Partner**
**165** B f 1/2 Arcano (IRE)—Siren's Gift (Cadeaux Genereux) **Mr J. C. Smith**
**166** B c 21/2 Iffraaj—Solva (Singspiel (IRE)) (120000) **Happy Valley Racing & Breeding Limited**
**167** B f 11/3 Exceed And Excel (AUS)—Soviet Terms (Soviet Star (USA)) **Sheikh Juma**
**168** B c 16/2 Lilbourne Lad (IRE)—Stoney Cove (IRE) (Needwood Blade) (18000) **B. McGuire**
**169** Gr c 27/3 Cacique (IRE)—Strawberry Morn (CAN) (Travelling Victor (CAN)) (105000) **Salem Rashid**
**170** B f 17/4 Aqlaam—Strictly Dancing (IRE) (Danehill Dancer (IRE)) **Mr J. C. Smith**
**171 SUNFLOWER,** ch f 24/2 Dutch Art—Swan Wings (Bahamian Bounty) **Coln Valley Stud**
**172** B f 15/3 Frozen Power (IRE)—Symbol of Peace (IRE) (Desert Sun) (33333) **Qatar Racing Limited**
**173 THE GRADUATE (IRE),** gr c 18/2 Mastercraftsman (IRE)—
Ballyvarra (IRE) (Sadler's Wells (USA)) (100000) **Mick and Janice Mariscotti**
**174** B f 9/2 Duke of Marmalade (IRE)—
Three Moons (IRE) (Montjeu (IRE)) (49205) **Happy Valley Racing & Breeding Limited**

## MR ANDREW BALDING - Continued

**175 TOUCHDOWN BANWELL (USA),** b br c 13/3 Fairbanks (USA)—
Friendly Thunder (USA) (Friends Lake (USA)) (11474) **Mr L. L. Register**
**176** Gr f 15/4 Aussie Rules (USA)—Victoria Montoya (High Chaparral (IRE)) **Kingsclere Racing Club**
**177 VISCOUNT BARFIELD,** b c 16/3 Raven's Pass (USA)—
Madonna Dell'orto (Montjeu (IRE)) (90000) **Mr D. Brownlow**
**178** B br f 17/2 Cape Blanco (IRE)—War Clan (USA) (War Front (USA)) **Mrs F. H. Hay**
**179** B c 6/3 Paco Boy (IRE)—Waypoint (Cadeaux Genereux) (9523) **Mr J. Dwyer & Mr P. Brend**
**180 WENSARA DREAM,** b f 29/4 Lilbourne Lad (IRE)—Emerald Fire (Pivotal) (14285) **Martin & Valerie Slade**
**181** Ch g 28/4 Dylan Thomas (IRE)—Wishing Chair (USA) (Giant's Causeway (USA)) (6190) **I. A. Balding**

**Other Owners:** Mr N. B. Attenborough, Mrs I. A. Balding, Mr I. A. Balding, Mr Paul Blaydon, Mr Peter Box, Mr P. A. Brend, Mr John Bridgman, Mr David Brownlow, Sir Roger Buckley, Mr D. H. Caslon, Mr Carl Conroy, Mr N. A. Coster, Mrs G. Cullen, Mr J. Da La Vega, Mr M. E. T. Davies, Dr Bridget Drew, Mr John Drew, Mr N. R. R. Drew, Miss G. B. Drew, Mr John Dwyer, Mr P. E. Felton, Mr Philip Fox, Mr S. G. Friend, Mr Karim Ghaly, Mr Jim Glasgow, Mr R. Gorell, Mrs W. Gorell, Ms Karen Gough, Mr S. Harding, Mr N. G. R. Harris, Dr E. Harris, Mr D. A. Hazell, Mr T. Henderson, The Hon H. Herbert, Highclere Thoroughbred Racing Ltd, Mr Tony Hill, Mr S. Hill, Mr J. C. Hitchins, Mr S. R. Hitchins, Mr J. Hitchins, Sir C. J. S. Hobhouse, Mr R. S. Hoskins, Mr G. R. Ireland, Mr Luke Lillingston, Mr Mick Mariscotti, Mrs Janice Mariscotti, Mr I. G. Martin, Mr C. McFadden, Mr R. P. B. Michaelson, Mr Richard Morecombe, Mr John A. Newman, Miss M. Noden, Mr S. O'Donnell, Mr O. J. W. Pawle, Miss J. Philip-Jones, Mrs L. E. Ramsden, Mr L. L. Register, Mr N. J. F. Robinson, Mr D. M. Slade, Mrs V. J. M. Slade, Mr M. Smith (Leicester), Mrs G. A. E. Smith, Mr G. A. E. Smith, Mr J. A. B. Stafford, Mr Bruce Swallow, Mr R. C. Thomas, Mr S. R. Thomas, Mr A. J. Thomas, Mrs P. I. Veenbaas, Mr Richard Wilmot-Smith.

**Assistant Trainer:** Chris Bonner

**Jockey (flat):** Liam Keniry, David Probert, Jimmy Fortune, Oisin Murphy. **Apprentice:** Thomas Brown, Ed Greatrex, Rob Hornby, Kieran Shoemark, Daniel Wright. **Amateur:** Mr Hugo Hunt.

---

## 18 MR JOHN BALDING, Doncaster

Postal: **Mayflower Stables, Saracens Lane, Scrooby, Doncaster, South Yorkshire, DN10 6AS**
Contacts: **HOME (01302) 710096 FAX (01302) 710096 MOBILE (07816) 612631**
**E-MAIL j.balding@btconnect.com**

1 **BEDLOE'S ISLAND (IRE),** 10, b g Statue of Liberty (USA)—Scenaria (IRE) **Mr A. C. Timms**
2 **FORTINBRASS (IRE),** 5, b g Baltic King—Greta d'argent (IRE) **Mr W. Herring**
3 **IMAGINARY WORLD (IRE),** 7, b m Exceed And Excel (AUS)—Plutonia **Hairy Gorrilaz**
4 **LUCKY MARK (IRE),** 6, b g Moss Vale (IRE)—Vracca **Mr C. Priestley**
5 **NAABEGHA,** 8, ch g Muhtathir—Hawafiz **Hairy Gorrilaz**
6 **POINT NORTH (IRE),** 8, b g Danehill Dancer (IRE)—Briolette (IRE) **Mr W. Herring**
7 **ROCKY HILL RIDGE,** 4, b g Auction House (USA)—Amwell Star (USA) **Miss H. P. Chellingworth**
8 **SHOWBOATING (IRE),** 7, b g Shamardal (USA)—Sadinga (IRE) **Mr M & Mrs L Cooke & Mr A McCabe**
9 **SILLY BILLY (IRE),** 7, b g Noverre (USA)—Rock Dove (IRE) **R. L. Crowe**
10 **SLEEPY BLUE OCEAN,** 9, b g Oasis Dream—Esteemed Lady (IRE) **Mr W. Herring**

### THREE-YEAR-OLDS

11 **LUNAR KNOT,** b f Stimulation (IRE)—Moon Bird **The Michaelmas Daisy Partnership**

**Other Owners:** Mr A. J. Sharp.

**Assistant Trainers:** Claire Edmunds, Jason Edmunds

---

## 19 MR RICHARD J. BANDEY, Tadley

Postal: **10 Plantation Farm Cottages, Wolverton, Tadley, Hampshire, RG26 5RP**

1 **ALSKAMATIC,** 9, b g Systematic—Alska (FR) **The Plantation Picnic Club**
2 **BRIDS CLASSIC (IRE),** 6, ch m Presenting—Classic Enough **Mr Mark Burton**
3 **HERBERT PERCY,** 8, b g Morpeth—Cold Feet **Mrs S. King**
4 **MISTER CHANCER (IRE),** 10, b g Craigsteel—Cluain Chaoin (IRE) **Mr R. J. Bandey**
5 **MOREBUTWHEN,** 8, b m Morpeth—Lady Noso **Mrs S. King**
6 **ROSSMORE LAD (IRE),** 10, b br g Beneficial—Celestial Rose (IRE) **Mr Mark Burton**

## 20 MR MICHAEL BANKS, Sandy

Postal: **Manor Farm, Manor Farm Road, Waresley, Sandy, Bedfordshire, SG19 3BX**
Contacts: **PHONE (01767) 650563 FAX (01767) 652988 MOBILE (07860) 627370**
**E-MAIL waresleyfarms@btconnect.com**

1 **CLERK'S CHOICE (IRE),** 9, b g Bachelor Duke (USA)—Credit Crunch (IRE) **M. C. Banks**
2 **JODIES JEM,** 5, br g Kheleyf (USA)—First Approval **Mrs R. L. Banks**
3 **LOMBARDY BOY (IRE),** 10, b g Milan—Horner Water (IRE) **M. C. Banks**
4 **MAX LAURIE (FR),** 10, bl g Ungaro (GER)—Laurie Mercurialle (FR) **Mrs R. L. Banks**
5 **ROGUE DANCER (FR),** 10, b g Dark Moondancer—Esperanza IV (FR) **M. C. Banks**

## 21 MRS TRACEY BARFOOT-SAUNT, Wotton-under-Edge

Postal: **Cosy Farm, Huntingford, Charfield, Wotton-under-Edge, Gloucestershire, GL12 8EY**
Contacts: **PHONE (01453) 520312 FAX (01453) 520312 MOBILE (07976) 360626**

1 **BRUSLINI (FR),** 10, gr g Linamix (FR)—Brusca (USA) **A Good Days Racing**
2 4, Gr g Daylami (IRE)—Fionnula's Rainbow (IRE) **Miss H. L. Taylor**
3 **LAUGHING MUSKETEER (IRE),** 4, b g Azamour (IRE)—Sweet Clover **A Good Days Racing**
4 **MASTER CYNK,** 8, ch g Diableneyev (USA)—Model View (USA) **A Good Days Racing**
5 **TAKE OF SHOC'S (IRE),** 11, ch g Beneficial—Dear Dunleer (IRE) **A Good Days Racing**

**Amateur:** Mr Geoff Barfoot-Saunt.

## 22 MR MAURICE BARNES, Brampton

Postal: **Tarnside, Farlam, Brampton, Cumbria, CA8 1LA**
Contacts: **PHONE/FAX (01697) 746675 MOBILE (07760) 433191**
**E-MAIL anne.barnes1@btinternet.com**

1 **APACHE PILOT,** 7, br g Indian Danehill (IRE)—Anniejo **M. A. Barnes**
2 **BOBS LADY TAMURE,** 8, b m Tamure (IRE)—Bob Back's Lady (IRE) **J. R. Wills**
3 **CARRIGDHOUN (IRE),** 10, gr g Goldmark (USA)—Pet Tomjammar (IRE) **M. A. Barnes**
4 **DEE BEES GIFT,** 4, gr g Firebreak—Josie May (USA) **Mr C. Davidson**
5 **DESERT ISLAND DUSK,** 4, b g Superior Premium—Desert Island Disc **Miss A. P. Lee**
6 **DYNAMIC DRIVE (IRE),** 8, b g Motivator—Biriyani (IRE) **Ring Of Fire**
7 **EVERREADYNEDDY,** 5, ch g Ad Valorem (USA)—Maugwenna **M. A. Barnes**
8 **FLYING JACK,** 5, b g Rob Roy (USA)—Milladella (FR) **M. D. Townson**
9 **HARRYS WHIM,** 10, b m Sir Harry Lewis (USA)—Whimbrel **Mr J. Wills**
10 **HEART O ANNANDALE (IRE),** 8, b g Winged Love (IRE)—She's All Heart **K. Milligan**
11 **INDIAN VOYAGE (IRE),** 7, b g Indian Haven—Voyage of Dreams (USA) **Mr D. Carr & Mr M. Carlyle**
12 **LOCKEDOUTAHEAVEN (IRE),** 4, ch g Rock of Gibraltar (IRE)—Second Burst (IRE) **M. A. Barnes**
13 **LOULOUMILLS,** 5, b m Rob Roy (USA)—Etching (USA) **M. D. Townson**
14 **MY IDEA,** 9, b g Golan (IRE)—Ghana (GER) **The Whisperers**
15 **OVERPRICED,** 9, b m Chocolat de Meguro (USA)—One Stop **M. A. Barnes**
16 **PASSAGE VENDOME (FR),** 9, b g Polish Summer—Herodiade (FR) **Edinburgh Woollen Mill Ltd**
17 **PERFECT PRINT (IRE),** 6, b g Kodiac—Naughtiness **Mr R. E. Wharton**
18 **QUICK BREW,** 7, b g Denounce—Darjeeling (IRE) **The Wizards**
19 **RED MYSTIQUE (IRE),** 6, b g Red Clubs (IRE)—Sacred Love (IRE) **Mr M. Barnes, Mr Scott Lowther**
20 **SIR TOMMY,** 6, ch g Sir Harry Lewis (USA)—Rose of Overbury **J. R. Wills**
21 **STORMONT BRIDGE,** 7, b g Avonbridge—Stormont Castle (USA) **M. A. Barnes**
22 **TOLEDO GOLD (IRE),** 9, ch g Needwood Blade—Eman's Joy **Mr M. Barnes, Mr Scott Lowther**
23 **TRANSLUSCENT (IRE),** 5, b g Trans Island—Little Miss Diva (IRE) **M. A. Barnes**
24 **WATCHMEGO,** 7, b m Supreme Sound—One Stop **M. A. Barnes**
25 **WILLIE WHISTLE,** 6, b g Supreme Sound—Zahara Joy **A. B. Graham**

**Other Owners:** Mr M. Barnes, Mr R. H. Briggs, Mr J. M. Carlyle, Mr David Carr, Mr J. H. Gibson, Mr J. G. Graham, Mr Keith Greenwell, Mr Stevan Houliston, Mr S. G. Johnston, Mr Scott Lowther, Mr Nigel North.

**Jockey (NH):** Michael McAlister. **Conditional:** Stephen Mulqueen.

## 23 MR BRIAN BARR, Sherborne

Postal: **Tall Trees Stud, Longburton, Sherborne, Dorset, DT9 5PH**
Contacts: **PHONE (01963) 210173 MOBILE (07826) 867881**
**WEBSITE www.brianbarrracing.co.uk**

1 **BALLYHEIGUE (IRE),** 6, b g High Chaparral (IRE)—Lypharden (IRE) **Mrs Elizabeth Heal**
2 **CASTLEMORRIS KING,** 7, br g And Beyond (IRE)—Brookshield Baby (IRE) **Miss D. Hitchins**
3 **FOLLOW THE TRACKS (IRE),** 7, br g Milan—Charming Mo (IRE) **Brian Barr Racing Club**
4 **GREEN DU CIEL (FR),** 10, gr g Smadoun (FR)—Sucre Blanc (FR) **Tim & Liz Heal**
5 **IN THE CROWD (IRE),** 6, ch g Haafhd—Eliza Gilbert **Brian Barr Racing Club**
6 **MADAM BE,** 5, b m Kayf Tara—Mrs Be (IRE) **Miss D. Hitchins**
7 **MARTY'S MAGIC (IRE),** 6, b g Tale of The Cat (USA)—Steno (USA) **Miss D. Hitchins**
8 **NORFOLK SKY,** 6, ch m Haafhd—Cayman Sound **Miss D. Hitchins**
9 **SHANANDOA,** 4, b f Shamardal (USA)—Divisa (GER) **Miss D. Hitchins**
10 **TUFFSTUFF,** 7, b g Generous (IRE)—Life Line **Miss D. Hitchins**
11 **UNDER REVIEW (IRE),** 9, b g Danetime (IRE)—Coloma (JPN) **Liz & Tim Heal**

### THREE-YEAR-OLDS

12 B c Piccolo—Ceilidh Band **Ms Mary Todd**

**Other Owners:** Mr T. Heal, Mrs Katrina Hitchins.

**Assistant Trainer:** Daisy Hitchins

**Jockey (NH):** Nick Scholfield, Gavin Sheehan. **Amateur:** Mr H. A. A. Bannister.

## 24 MR RON BARR, Middlesbrough

Postal: **Carr House Farm, Seamer, Stokesley, Middlesbrough, Cleveland, TS9 5LL**
Contacts: **PHONE (01642) 710687 MOBILE (07711) 895309**
**E-MAIL christinebarr1@aol.com**

1 **A J COOK (IRE),** 5, b g Mujadil (USA)—Undertone (IRE) **Mrs V. G. Davies**
2 **AL FURAT (USA),** 7, b g El Prado (IRE)—No Frills (IRE) **Mrs V. G. Davies**
3 **FOREIGN RHYTHM (IRE),** 10, ch m Distant Music (USA)—Happy Talk (IRE) **R. E. Barr**
4 **GRACEFUL ACT,** 7, b m Royal Applause—Minnina (IRE) **D. Thomson**
5 **MIDNIGHT WARRIOR,** 5, b g Teofilo (IRE)—Mauri Moon **Mr K. Trimble**
6 **MITCHUM,** 6, b g Elnadim (USA)—Maid To Matter **P. Cartmell**
7 4, B f Josr Algarhoud (IRE)—Pay Time

### THREE-YEAR-OLDS

8 **AROUSAL,** b f Stimulation (IRE)—Midnight Mover (IRE)
9 **PLAYBOY BAY,** b g Indesatchel (IRE)—Dim Ofan

**Other Owners:** Mrs R. E. Barr, J. O. Barr, B. Cunningham, Frank Mullins.

**Assistant Trainer:** Mrs C. Barr

**Amateur:** Miss V. Barr.

## 25 MR DAVID BARRON, Thirsk

Postal: **Maunby House, Maunby, Thirsk, North Yorkshire, YO7 4HD**
Contacts: **PHONE (01845) 587435 FAX (01845) 587331**
**E-MAIL david@harrowgate.wanadoo.co.uk**

1 **ART OBSESSION (IRE),** 4, b g Excellent Art—Ghana (IRE) **Mr D. Pryde & Mr J. Cringan**
2 **BERTIEWHITTLE,** 7, ch g Bahamian Bounty—Minette **Norton Common Farm Racing II&JKB Johnson**
3 **COLONEL MAK,** 8, br g Makbul—Colonel's Daughter **Norton Common Farm Racing,O'Kane,Murphy**
4 **DUKE COSIMO,** 5, ch g Pivotal—Nannina **Mrs S. C. Barron**
5 **DUTCH DESCENT (IRE),** 4, b g Royal Applause—Wagtail **Twinacre Nurseries Ltd**
6 **ESTEAMING,** 5, b g Sir Percy—Night Over Day **D. E. Cook**
7 **FAST TRACK,** 4, b g Rail Link—Silca Boo **R. C. Miquel**
8 **FIELDGUNNER KIRKUP (GER),** 7, b g Acclamation—Fire Finch **Harrowgate Bloodstock Ltd**
9 **FREE CODE (IRE),** 4, b g Kodiac—Gerobies Girl (USA) **Ron Hull & Laurence O'Kane**
10 **HITCHENS (IRE),** 10, b g Acclamation—Royal Fizz (IRE) **Mr Laurence O'Kane & Mr Paul Murphy**

## MR DAVID BARRON - Continued

11 **INDY (IRE),** 4, b c Indian Haven—Maddie's Pearl (IRE) **Hardisty Rolls II**
12 **JAMESBO'S GIRL,** 5, ch m Refuse To Bend (IRE)—Donna Anna **Hardisty Rolls**
13 **JOFRANKA,** 5, b m Paris House—Gypsy Fair **Mr M. R. Dalby**
14 **LAWYER (IRE),** 4, b g Acclamation—Charaig **Laurence O'Kane & Ron Hull**
15 **LONG AWAITED (IRE),** 7, b g Pivotal—Desertion (IRE) **Peter Jones**
16 **LUCY PARSONS (IRE),** 4, ch f Thousand Words—Consensus (IRE) **Norton Common Farm Racing Ltd**
17 **MAGICAL MACEY (USA),** 8, ch g Rossini (USA)—Spring's Glory (USA) **Harrowgate Bloodstock Ltd**
18 **MONEY TEAM (IRE),** 4, b g Kodiac—Coral Dawn (IRE) **Hardisty Rolls II**
19 **NEWSTEAD ABBEY,** 5, b g Byron—Oatcake **Let's Be Lucky Partnership**
20 **NORSE BLUES,** 7, ch g Norse Dancer (IRE)—Indiana Blues **The Vikings**
21 **PEARL SECRET,** 6, ch h Compton Place—Our Little Secret (IRE) **Qatar Racing Limited**
22 **ROBOT BOY (IRE),** 5, ch g Shamardal (USA)—Pivotal's Princess (IRE) **Mr Laurence O'Kane & Paul Murphy**
23 **SPES NOSTRA,** 7, b g Ad Valorem (USA)—Millagros (IRE) **Mr J. Cringan & Mr D. Pryde**
24 **TAROOQ (USA),** 9, b g War Chant (USA)—Rose of Zollern (IRE) **EPL Investments**
25 **TOM MANN (IRE),** 4, ch g Sir Percy—Fantasy Princess (USA) **Norton Common Farm Racing Ltd**
26 **TRES CORONAS (IRE),** 8, b g Key of Luck (USA)—Almansa (IRE) **Mr D. Pryde & Mr J. Cringan**
27 **TWIN APPEAL (IRE),** 4, b g Oratorio (IRE)—Velvet Appeal (IRE) **Twinacre Nurseries Ltd**
28 **VIVA VERGLAS (IRE),** 4, gr g Verglas (IRE)—Yellow Trumpet **R. C. Miquel**
29 **ZAC BROWN (IRE),** 4, b g Kodiac—Mildmay (USA) **Mr R. G. Toes**

## THREE-YEAR-OLDS

30 **BEAU EILE (IRE),** b f Arcano (IRE)—Mona Em (IRE) **Mr S W D McIlveen & Miss Aisling Byrne**
31 **BILLYOAKES (IRE),** b g Kodiac—Reality Check (IRE) **D. E. Cook**
32 **BRACKA LEGEND (IRE),** ch g Approve (IRE)—Glyndebourne (USA) **Mr D. Kelly**
33 **BUSHTIGER (IRE),** b g Bushranger (IRE)—Emma's Surprise **Billy & Debbie Glover**
34 **CAIGEMDAR (IRE),** b f Tagula (IRE)—Honey Feather (IRE) **Home Farm Racing Limited**
35 **CAIUS COLLEGE GIRL (IRE),** b f Royal Applause—Galeaza **Mr C. A. Washbourn**
36 **CHILWORTH BELLS,** ch g Sixties Icon—Five Bells (IRE) **Harrowgate Bloodstock Ltd**
37 **CIAO CIELO (GER),** br g Lord of England (GER)—Celebration Night (IRE) **Home Farm Racing Limited**
38 B g Bushranger (IRE)—Cloneden (IRE) **Ms Colette Twomey**
39 **HANDSOME DUDE,** b c Showcasing—Dee Dee Girl (IRE) **Mr W D & Mrs D A Glover**
40 **LANAI (IRE),** b f Camacho—Stately Princess **Mr R. Hull**
41 **LIKELY (GER),** ch f Exceed And Excel (AUS)—La Pilaya (GER) **Qatar Racing Limited**
42 **MIDTERM BREAK (IRE),** ch g Intense Focus (USA)—Kayak **L. G. O'Kane**
43 **MIGNOLINO (IRE),** b g Kodiac—Caterina di Cesi **Mr R. G. Toes**
44 B c Captain Rio—Over The Ridge (IRE) **Dr N. J. Barron**
45 **RED TYCOON (IRE),** b g Acclamation—Rugged Up (IRE) **Lets Be Lucky Racing 4**
46 Ch f Aqlaam—Red Zinnia **Twinacre Nurseries Ltd**
47 **SIR RUNS A LOT,** b g Sir Percy—Monjouet (IRE) **Qatar Racing Limited**
48 **SWIFT EMPEROR (IRE),** b g Holy Roman Emperor (IRE)—Big Swifty (IRE) **DC Racing Partnership**
49 **TIMMY TACTOR (IRE),** b g Hurricane Run (IRE)—Sapiranga (GER) **Dr N. J. Barron**

## TWO-YEAR-OLDS

50 **ANGEL GRACE (IRE),** gr f 11/3 Dark Angel (IRE)—Light Sea (IRE) (King's Best (USA)) (30000) **Mr C. A. Washbourn**
51 B c 18/4 Zebedee—Appletreemagic (IRE) (Indian Danehill (IRE)) (17142) **Twinacre Nurseries Ltd**
52 **ASPEN AGAIN (IRE),** b f 4/2 Intikhab (USA)—Deira Dubai (Green Desert (USA)) (15872) **Mr C. A. Washbourn**
53 Ch c 2/3 Mount Nelson—Bella Beguine (Komaite (USA)) (14000) **Twinacre Nurseries Ltd**
54 **BIGMOUTH STRIKES (IRE),** ch c 14/2 Raven's Pass (USA)—Chiosina (IRE) (Danehill Dancer (IRE)) (120000) **Mr C. A. Washbourn**
55 Ch c 13/2 Compton Place—Dance Away (Pivotal) (47619) **C & C Bloodstock Limited**
56 B f 17/3 Canford Cliffs (IRE)—Galeaza (Galileo (IRE)) (29523) **C & C Bloodstock Limited**
57 B c 22/4 Sakhee's Secret—Grandmas Dream (Kyllachy) (6666) **Harrowgate Bloodstock Ltd**
58 B c 5/2 Compton Place—La Gessa (Largesse) (22000) **Harrowgate Bloodstock Ltd**
59 **PARISIANNA,** b f 17/4 Champs Elysees—Simianna (Bluegrass Prince (IRE)) (5000) **Bearstone Stud Limited**
60 B c 31/1 Makfi—Present Danger (Cadeaux Genereux) (47619) **Qatar Racing Limited**
61 **RANTAN (IRE),** b c 25/2 Kodiac—Peace Talks (Pivotal) (61904) **Mr H. D. Atkinson**
62 B f 17/2 Kodiac—River Bounty (Bahamian Bounty) (28571) **Twinacre Nurseries Ltd**

**Other Owners:** T. D. Barron, Mr C. Blaymire, Miss A. Byrne, Mr H. P. T. Chamberlain, Mrs I. Chamberlain, J. A. Cringan, Mr D. B. Ellis, Mr W. D. Glover, Mrs D. A. Glover, Mr R. A. Gorrie, Mr S. T. Gorrie, Mrs S. J. Mason, S. W. D. McIlveen, Mr P. A. Murphy, D. G. Pryde, Mr P. Rolls, Mrs J. Rolls, Mr E. J. Snow.

**Assistant Trainer:** Nicola-Jo Barron

## 26 MR MICHAEL BARRY, Fermoy

Postal: **Mondaniel, Fermoy, Co. Cork, Ireland**
Contacts: **PHONE (00353) 25 31577 FAX (00353) 25 31792 MOBILE (00353) 87 2536815**

1 **ALL TO ONE SIDE (IRE),** 6, b g Brian Boru—Carrigmore Lass (IRE) **Michael Barry**
2 **BARE NECESSITIES (IRE),** 5, b g Sandmason—Marquante (IRE) **Michael Barry**
3 **COLLS CORNER (IRE),** 12, ch g Beneficial—Pandoras Hope (IRE) **Michael Barry**
4 **SWEET AS A NUT (IRE),** 5, b g Vinnie Roe (IRE)—Sarahall (IRE) **Michael Barry**

**Assistant Trainer:** Ronan Barry

## 27 MR P. BARY, Chantilly

Postal: **5 Chemin des Aigles, 60500 Chantilly, France**
Contacts: **PHONE (0033) 3445 71403 FAX (0033) 3446 72015 MOBILE (0033) 6075 80241**
**E-MAIL p-bary@wanadoo.fr**

1 **BILLABONG (MOR),** 6, ch h Gentlewave (IRE)—Lunattori **Jalobey Stud**
2 **FAUFILER (IRE),** 4, b f Galileo (IRE)—Six Perfections (FR) **Niarchos Family**
3 **MENARDAIS (FR),** 6, b g Canyon Creek (IRE)—Madeleine's Blush (USA) **G. Sandor**
4 **MISTERDAD (IRE),** 4, b c Cape Cross (IRE)—Flaming Cliffs (USA) **Niarchos Family**
5 **RUSSIAN MARIA STAR (USA),** 4, b f Medaglia d'Oro (USA)—Russian Empress (USA) **Luffield Venture Syndicate**
6 **SMOKING SUN (USA),** 6, b br h Smart Strike (CAN)—Burning Sunset **Niarchos Family**
7 **SPIRITJIM (FR),** 5, b h Galileo (IRE)—Hidden Silver **Hspirit**
8 **STEPHILL (FR),** 4, ch c Footstepsinthesand—Magic Hill (FR) **Laghi France**
9 **SUNSTREAM (FR),** 4, b f Falco (USA)—Suenna (GER) **Franklin Finance SA**
10 **TANTRIS (FR),** 5, ch h Turtle Bowl (IRE)—Tianshan (FR) **G. Sandor**
11 **TATOOINE (FR),** 4, ch c Galileo (IRE)—Three Mysteries (IRE) **Niarchos Family**
12 **TELETEXT (USA),** 4, b c Empire Maker (USA)—Conference Call **Prince Faisal Bin Khaled**
13 **THEME ASTRAL (FR),** 4, b c Cape Cross (IRE)—Lumiere Astrale (FR) **Haras du Mezeray**
14 **ZHIYI (USA),** 5, b g Henrythenavigator (USA)—Burning Sunset **Niarchos Family**

### THREE-YEAR-OLDS

15 **AMUSER (IRE),** ch f Galileo (IRE)—Six Perfections (FR) **Niarchos Family**
16 **BELPHEGORIA,** b f Teofilo (IRE)—Pietra Santa (FR) **Ecurie La Boetie**
17 **CINQ RUES (FR),** b c Mastercraftsman (IRE)—Coup d'eclat (IRE) **Saeed Nasser Al Romaithi**
18 **COLORADOJIM,** b c Iffraaj—Sandbar **Hspirit**
19 **COMPARATIVE,** b g Oasis Dream—Indication **K. Abdullah**
20 **ENDERS CAT (USA),** ch c Giant's Causeway (USA)—Ender's Valentine (USA) **Luffield Venture Syndicate**
21 **FIERE ALLURE (IRE),** b f Nayef (USA)—Fresh Laurels (IRE) **Ecurie des Monceaux**
22 **FRASQUE (IRE),** b f Iffraaj—Khassah **Emmeline de Waldner**
23 **FULL ATTIRE,** b f Champs Elysees—Buffering **K. Abdullah**
24 **GOLDEN FASTNET (FR),** b f Fastnet Rock (AUS)—Militante (IRE) **Sutong Pan**
25 **GOLDMETAL JACKET (IRE),** b c Acclamation—Twinspot (USA) **Sutong Pan**
26 **GREEN MISS (FR),** b f Air Chief Marshal (IRE)—Green Shadow (FR) **Emmeline de Waldner**
27 **HARVESTIDE (IRE),** b f Duke of Marmalade (IRE)—Herboriste **Mme R. G. Ehrnrooth**
28 **HELVETIA (USA),** b f Blame (USA)—Helstra (USA) **K. Abdullah**
29 **IF I DO (FR),** b f Iffraaj—Doriana (FR) **Sutong Pan**
30 **INORDINATE (USA),** b c Harlan's Holiday (USA)—Out of Reach **K. Abdullah**
31 **JULES ET JIM,** b c Teofilo (IRE)—Alsace **Hspirit**
32 **LAUNCHED (IRE),** b c Galileo (IRE)—Apsara (FR) **Niarchos Family**
33 **MAGNETICJIM (IRE),** br gr c Galileo (IRE)—Dibenoise (FR) **Hspirit**
34 **MAJVER (IRE),** b f Mastercraftsman (IRE)—Marie de Blois (IRE) **Laghi France**
35 **MITRE PEAK,** ch f Shamardal (USA)—Milford Sound **K. Abdullah**
36 **MOI MEME,** b f Teofilo (IRE)—Di Moi Oui **Scuderia Vittadini Srl**
37 **MOONLIGHT SWING (FR),** b f Palace Episode (USA)—Moonlight Sail (USA) **Galileo Racing**
38 **NIGHT OF LIGHT (IRE),** b f Sea The Stars (IRE)—Celestial Lagoon (JPN) **Niarchos Family**
39 **ORELLE,** ch f Three Valleys (USA)—Bouvardia **K. Abdullah**
40 **POUND STERLING,** b f Champs Elysees—Silver Yen (USA) **K. Abdullah**
41 **PYTHON,** b c Dansili—Imbabala **K. Abdullah**
42 **SAMIRE (FR),** ch c American Post—Semire (FR) **G. Sandor**
43 **SATED,** br f Manduro (GER)—Quenched **K. Abdullah**
44 **SEYFERT GALAXY,** b c Dalakhani (IRE)—Three Mysteries (IRE) **Niarchos Family**
45 **SHERLOCK (GER),** b c Areion (GER)—Sun Valley (GER)

## MR P. BARY - Continued

46 **SPREZZATURA,** b f Mount Nelson—She of The Moon (USA) **Niarchos Family**
47 **STARCHY LEITENONT (IRE),** b g Arcano (IRE)—Starchy **Luffield Venture Syndicate**
48 **TALE OF LIFE (JPN),** br c Deep Impact (JPN)—Second Happiness (USA) **Flaxman Stables Ireland**
49 **TANTIVY (USA),** ch f Giant's Causeway (USA)—Witching Hour (FR) **Flaxman Stables Ireland**
50 **THINDY (FR),** b c Footstepsinthesand—Windy (FR) **Laghi France**
51 **TRACT (IRE),** b c Fastnet Rock (AUS)—Sterope (FR) **Niarchos Family**
52 **TURKANA,** b f Sea The Stars (IRE)—Lion Forest (USA) **K. Abdullah**
53 **WEBSITE,** b c Oasis Dream—Homepage **K. Abdullah**
54 **WILMA (FR),** ch f Starspangledbanner (AUS)—Windya (FR) **G. Sandor**
55 **YOUNKOUNKOUN,** b g Elusive City (USA)—Arbalette (IRE) **Ecurie La Boetie**

## TWO-YEAR-OLDS

56 **AL LOPEZ (FR),** b c 21/3 Lope de Vega (IRE)—Almilea (GER) (Galileo (IRE)) (47619) **Ecurie J. L. Bouchard**
57 Ch gr f 18/3 Sea The Stars (IRE)—Alix Road (FR) (Linamix (FR)) (253968) **Ecurie des Charmes**
58 **ANGEL ERIA (IRE),** b f 18/3 Siyouni (FR)—Arcangela (Galileo (IRE)) (51587) **Ecurie J. L. Bouchard**
59 **BATLADY (FR),** gr f 1/1 Slickley—Belga Wood **G. Sandor**
60 **BEYOND APOLLO (FR),** b br c 4/4 Sea The Stars (IRE)—
Celestial Lagoon (JPN) (Sunday Silence (USA)) **Niarchos Family**
61 B f 1/1 Elusive City—Black Jack Lady **Hspirit**
62 B c 24/2 Afleet Alex (USA)—Brief Look (Sadler's Wells (USA)) **K. Abdullah**
63 B c 16/3 Rail Link—Buffering (Beat Hollow) **K. Abdullah**
64 **CARDARA (FR),** b f 1/1 Dylan Thomas—Cool Woman **Razza Dormello Olgiata**
65 B f 4/2 Oasis Dream—Concentric (Sadler's Wells (USA)) **K. Abdullah**
66 B c 30/3 Zamindar (USA)—Costa Rica (IRE) (Sadler's Wells (USA)) **K. Abdullah**
67 B c 13/1 Manduro (GER)—Dansilady (IRE) (Dansili) (75396) **Hspirit**
68 B f 10/2 Wootton Bassett—Elodie (Dansili) (103174) **Skymarc Farm Inc.**
69 **EMPIRIC,** b c 4/4 Holy Roman Emperor (IRE)—
Sierra Slew (Fantastic Light (USA)) (27777) **Emmeline de Waldner**
70 **FIDUX (FR),** b c 29/3 Fine Grain (JPN)—Folle Tempete (FR) (Fabulous Dancer (USA)) **Patrick Barbe**
71 **GOLD VIBE (IRE),** ch c 10/3 Dream Ahead (USA)—
Whisper Dance (USA) (Stravinsky (USA)) (300000) **Sutong Pan**
72 **GOLDEN TEMPO (IRE),** b f 10/4 Canford Cliffs (IRE)—Haute Volta (FR) (Grape Tree Road) (75396) **Sutong Pan**
73 **HIORT (IRE),** b f 12/4 Rip Van Winkle (IRE)—Gifts Galore (IRE) (Darshaan) (47619) **Laghi France**
74 B c 1/1 Equiano (FR)—Hometown (Storming Home) (107142) **Hspirit**
75 B f 26/1 First Defence (USA)—Ixora (USA) (Dynaformer (USA)) **K. Abdullah**
76 B c 1/4 Oasis Dream—Love The Rain (Rainbow Quest (USA)) **K. Abdullah**
77 B f 8/2 Country Reel (USA)—Maka (FR) (Slickly (FR)) (25396) **Franklin Finance SA**
78 **MAX'S SPIRIT (IRE),** b c 18/4 Invincible Spirit (IRE)—
My Uptown Girl (Dubai Destination (USA)) (87301) **Ecurie J. L. Bouchard**
79 **MOVING (USA),** b c 13/4 War Front (USA)—
Visions of Clarity (IRE) (Sadler's Wells (USA)) **Flaxman Stables Ireland**
80 **MYTHOLOGICAL (USA),** b f 8/3 Bernardini (USA)—
Witching Hour (FR) (Fairy King (USA)) **Flaxman Stables Ireland**
81 **NOMADIC (FR),** b f 18/2 Duke of Marmalade (IRE)—Teepee (JPN) (Deep Impact (JPN)) **Niarchos Family**
82 **OPEN MIND (FR),** b f 17/2 Orpen (USA)—Simple Act (USA) (Kingmambo (USA)) (30158) **Ecurie J. L. Bouchard**
83 B f 4/4 Oasis Dream—Orford Ness (Selkirk (USA)) **K. Abdullah**
84 B f 5/3 Northern Afleet (USA)—Out of Reach (Warning) **K. Abdullah**
85 **PHIDIAN (IRE),** b c 15/2 Galileo (IRE)—
Divine Proportions (USA) (Kingmambo (USA)) **Flaxman Stables Ireland Ltd**
86 B f 10/4 Dubawi (IRE)—Sandbar (Oasis Dream) **Lady O'Reilly**
87 B f 6/2 First Defence (USA)—Soothing Touch (USA) (Touch Gold (USA)) **K. Abdullah**
88 **SPRING MASTER,** b c 17/3 Mastercraftsman (IRE)—Cracovie (Caerleon (USA)) (59523) **Ecurie J. L. Bouchard**
89 **TUILERIES,** b f 22/2 Cape Cross (IRE)—Toi Et Moi (IRE) (Galileo (IRE)) **Grundy Bloodstock Ltd**
90 Ch f 23/1 Bahamian Bounty—Utmost (IRE) (Most Welcome) **Ecurie J. L. Bouchard**
91 **VITAL SUN (FR),** ch c 5/3 Pivotal—Burning Sunset (Caerleon (USA)) **Niarchos Family**
92 B c 6/3 Champs Elysees—Winter Solstice (Unfuwain (USA)) **K. Abdullah**
93 Gr f 1/1 Sea The Stars (IRE)—Ysoldina (FR) (Kendor (FR)) (476190) **Hspirit**
94 B f 9/2 Rip Van Winkle (IRE)—Zibeling (IRE) (Cape Cross (IRE)) (59523) **Ecurie J. L. Bouchard**
95 B c 26/1 Iffraaj—Zomorroda (IRE) (Chineur (FR)) **Ecurie J. L. Bouchard**

**Assistant Trainer:** Josephine Soudan

**Jockey (flat):** Stephane Pasquier, Christophe Soumillon. **Apprentice:** Pierre Bazire.

## 28 MISS REBECCA BASTIMAN, Wetherby

Postal: **Goosemoor Farm, War Field Lane, Cowthorpe, Wetherby, West Yorkshire, LS22 5EU**
Contacts: **PHONE (01423) 359783 MOBILE (07818) 181313**
**E-MAIL rebeccabastiman@hotmail.co.uk WEBSITE www.rbastimanracing.com**

1 **BORDERLESCOTT,** 13, b g Compton Place—Jeewan **James Edgar & William Donaldson**
2 **GONE WITH THE WIND (GER),** 4, b g Dutch Art—Gallivant **Mrs P. Bastiman**
3 **GREEN HOWARD,** 7, ch g Bahamian Bounty—Dash of Lime **Ms M. Austerfield**
4 **HELLOLINI,** 5, b m Bertolini (USA)—Smiddy Hill **I. B. Barker**
5 **JOHN CAESAR (IRE),** 4, b g Bushranger (IRE)—Polish Belle **Mrs P. Bastiman**
6 **KYLLACHYKOV (IRE),** 7, ch g Kyllachy—Dance On **Ms M. Austerfield**
7 **LIZZY'S DREAM,** 7, ch g Choisir (AUS)—Flyingit (USA) **Mrs P. Bastiman**
8 **NOVALIST,** 7, ch g Avonbridge—Malelane (IRE) **Mr E. N. Barber**
9 **SECRET CITY (IRE),** 9, b g City On A Hill (USA)—Secret Combe (IRE) **Ms M. Austerfield**
10 **SEE VERMONT,** 7, b g Kyllachy—Orange Lily **Mr J. Smith**
11 **SHIKARI,** 4, ch g Sakhee's Secret—Hickleton Lady (IRE) **Ms M. Austerfield**
12 **SINGEUR (IRE),** 8, b g Chineur (FR)—Singitta **Ms M. Austerfield**
13 4, B f Desideratum—Smiddy Hill **I. B. Barker**
14 **TROY BOY,** 5, b g Choisir (AUS)—Love Thing **Ms M. Austerfield**

### THREE-YEAR-OLDS

15 **BIG RED,** ch f Sakhee's Secret—Hickleton Lady (IRE) **Ms M. Austerfield**
16 **MADAM MAI TAI,** ch f Compton Place—Dash of Lime **Ms M. Austerfield**
17 **ROYAL ACCLAIM (IRE),** b g Acclamation—Top Row **Ms M. Austerfield**

### TWO-YEAR-OLDS

18 B c 3/3 Approve (IRE)—Kind Regards (IRE) (Unfuwain (USA)) (16666) **Mrs P. Bastiman**
19 B f 23/3 Monsieur Bond (IRE)—Smiddy Hill (Factual (USA)) (3809) **I. B. Barker**

**Other Owners:** Mrs P. Bastiman, Mr Robin Bastiman, Mr William Donaldson, Mr James Edgar.

**Assistant Trainer:** H. Bastiman

**Jockey (flat):** Robert Winston, Daniel Tudhope, Jason Hart. **Amateur:** Miss R. Bastiman.

## 29 MRS ALISON BATCHELOR, Petworth

Postal: **Down View Farm, Burton Park Road, Petworth, West Sussex, GU28 0JT**
Contacts: **PHONE (01798) 343090 FAX (01798) 343090**
**E-MAIL alison@alisonbatchelorracing.com WEBSITE www.alisonbatchelorracing.com**

1 **AMBRE DES MARAIS (FR),** 5, ch m Network (GER)—Fee des Marais (FR) **Mrs A. M. Batchelor**
2 **GRAPHICAL (IRE),** 6, b g High Chaparral (IRE)—Woopi Gold (IRE) **Mrs A. M. Batchelor**
3 **HIGHTOWN (IRE),** 8, b g King's Theatre (IRE)—Faucon **Mrs A. M. Batchelor**
4 **POLISHED ROCK (IRE),** 5, ch g Rock of Gibraltar (IRE)—Where We Left Off **Mrs A. M. Batchelor**
5 **TAGGIA (FR),** 8, b m Great Pretender (IRE)—Ecossaise II (FR) **Mrs A. M. Batchelor**
6 **TARA DOVE,** 7, gr m Kayf Tara—Kildee Lass **Mrs A. M. Batchelor**
7 **TRY CATCH ME (IRE),** 10, b g Commander Collins (IRE)—Misty River (IRE) **Mrs A. M. Batchelor**
8 **US ET GARRY (FR),** 6, b g Ballingarry (IRE)—Us Et Coutumes (FR) **Mrs A. M. Batchelor**
9 **YUR NEXT (IRE),** 7, br m Definite Article—Listen Up **Mrs A. M. Batchelor**

**Amateur:** Mr S. Hanson.

## 30 MR BRIAN BAUGH, Stoke-On-Trent

Postal: **Meadow Cottage, 47 Scot Hay Road, Alsagers Bank, Stoke-On-Trent, Staffordshire, ST7 8BW**
Contacts: **PHONE (01782) 706222 MOBILE (07771) 693666**
**E-MAIL bpjbaugh@aol.com**

1 **ART DZEKO,** 6, b g Acclamation—Delitme (IRE) **Richard and Nicola Hunt**
2 **BUY OUT BOY,** 4, gr g Medicean—Tiger's Gene (GER) **Richard and Nicola Hunt**
3 **CONSISTANT,** 7, b g Reel Buddy (USA)—Compact Disc (IRE) **Miss J. A. Price**
4 **DEAR BEN,** 6, b g Echo of Light—Miss Up N Go **Mr B. P. J. Baugh**
5 **ELITE FREEDOM (IRE),** 4, b f Acclamation—Jebel Musa (IRE) **Richard and Nicola Hunt**

## MR BRIAN BAUGH - Continued

6 **JOHN POTTS,** 10, b g Josr Algarhoud (IRE)—Crown City (USA) **Miss S. M. Potts**
7 **MASTER OF DISGUISE,** 9, b g Kyllachy—St James's Antigua (IRE) **Richard and Nicola Hunt**
8 **MEYDAN STYLE (USA),** 9, b g Essence of Dubai (USA)—Polish Ruby (USA) **Mr B. P. J. Baugh**
9 **PICCOLO EXPRESS,** 9, b g Piccolo—Ashfield **Mr G. B. Hignett**
10 **REFLECTION,** 4, ch f Major Cadeaux—River Song (USA) **Saddle Up Racing**
11 **SEPTENARIUS (USA),** 6, b g Empire Maker (USA)—Reams of Verse (USA) **Mr S. Holmes**

### THREE-YEAR-OLDS

12 **COMPTONSSECRET,** ch f Compton Place—Ashfield **Mr G. B. Hignett**

**Other Owners:** Mr R. A. Hunt, Mrs N. Hunt, Mr G. Ratcliffe, Mrs M. Robinson, Mr K. V. Robinson.

**Assistant Trainer:** S Potts

---

## 31 MR CHRIS BEALBY, Grantham

Postal: **North Lodge, Barrowby, Grantham, Lincolnshire, NG32 1DH**
Contacts: **OFFICE (01476) 564568 FAX (01476) 572391 MOBILE (07831) 538689**
**E-MAIL chris@northlodgeracing.co.uk WEBSITE www.northlodgeracing.co.uk**

1 **ANDREO BAMBALEO,** 11, ch g Silver Patriarch (IRE)—Time And A Place (IRE) **Miss F E Harper & Mr C W Litchfield**
2 **BENEVOLENT (IRE),** 8, ch g Beneficial—Bobs Lass (IRE) **Paul Read & Dave Cook**
3 **BLACK LILY (IRE),** 7, b m Quws—Sandaluna (IRE) **Triumph In Mind**
4 **BLACKBERRY WAY,** 6, b m Overbury (IRE)—Ardeal **C. C. Bealby**
5 **CHAC DU CADRAN (FR),** 9, b g Passing Sale (FR)—L'indienne (FR) **Bingley, Williams & Pepperdine**
6 **CUL DEALGA (IRE),** 6, b m Kalanisi (IRE)—Yes Boss (IRE) **The Rann Family**
7 **DIEGO SUAREZ (FR),** 5, b g Astarabad (USA)—Shabada (FR) **Mrs M. J. Pepperdine**
8 **DREAM MISTRESS,** 6, b m Doyen (IRE)—Arcady **C. C. Bealby**
9 **INTENT (IRE),** 6, b m Jeremy (USA)—Cant Hurry Love **The Rann Family**
10 **LEGENDARY HOP,** 9, b m Midnight Legend—Hopping Mad **Messrs Duke,Umpleby,Holmes & Bealby**
11 **LUNA NUOVA (IRE),** 5, b m Milan—Perfect Prospect (IRE) **The Rann Family**
12 **MY CAVE OR YOURS (IRE),** 5, ch g Fruits of Love (USA)—Primitive Annie **Mrs A. M. Williams**
13 **OVER THE WATER,** 6, b g Overbury (IRE)—Waterline Dancer (IRE) **C. C. Bealby**
14 **PRIMITIVE SAM,** 7, b g Samraan (USA)—Jeanann **Mr T. Evans**
15 **RUARAIDH HUGH (IRE),** 6, b g Craigsteel—Decent Shower **Paul Read & Dave Cook**
16 **SEND FOR KATIE (IRE),** 7, b m Kayf Tara—Katsura **J. H. Henderson**
17 **SIR LYNX (IRE),** 8, gr g Amilynx (FR)—Minilus (IRE) **Sir Lynx Partnership**
18 **THE PURCHASER (IRE),** 7, b g Definite Article—Cash Customer (IRE) **J. H. Henderson**
19 **VINTAGE RED,** 7, ch g Grape Tree Road—Simply Stunning **C. C. Bealby**
20 **WINGS ATTRACT (IRE),** 6, b g Winged Love (IRE)—Huncheon Siss (IRE) **The Rann Family**

### THREE-YEAR-OLDS

21 **PUSS MOTH,** b f Paco Boy (IRE)—Seeking Dubai **Miss F E Harper & Mr C W Litchfield**

**Other Owners:** Mrs E. A. Bingley, Mr D. M. Cook, B. G. Duke, Miss F. Harper, F. M. Holmes, R. A. Jenkinson, Mr C. W. Litchfield, Mr G. P. D. Rann, Mrs L. E. Rann, Mr P. L. Read, Mr P. Umpleby, Mr T. Wendels, R. F. Wright.

**Jockey (NH):** Tom Messenger, Noel Fehily, Adam Wedge.

---

## 32 MR RALPH BECKETT, Andover

Postal: **Kimpton Down Stables, Kimpton Down, Andover, Hampshire, SP11 8QQ**
Contacts: **PHONE (01264) 772278 FAX (01264) 771221 MOBILE (07802) 219022**
**E-MAIL trainer@rbeckett.com WEBSITE www.rbeckett.com**

1 **AIR PILOT,** 6, b g Zamindar (USA)—Countess Sybil (IRE) **Lady N. F. Cobham**
2 **AIR SQUADRON,** 5, b g Rail Link—Countess Sybil (IRE) **Lady N. F. Cobham**
3 **BELROG,** 4, ch g New Approach (IRE)—Millennium Dash **Qatar Racing Limited**
4 **CINNILLA,** 4, b f Authorized (IRE)—Caesarea (GER) **J. L. Rowsell**
5 **DINNERATMIDNIGHT,** 4, b g Kyllachy—The Terrier **The Rat Pack Partnership**
6 **EVITA PERON,** 4, ch f Pivotal—Entente Cordiale (IRE) **Newsells Park Stud Limited**
7 **FOXTROT JUBILEE (IRE),** 5, b g Captain Marvelous (IRE)—Cool Cousin (IRE) **Mrs I. M. Beckett**
8 **GREEN LIGHT,** 4, b g Authorized (IRE)—May Light **Sceptre**
9 **HAAF A SIXPENCE,** 6, b g Haafhd—Melody Maker **Melody Racing**

## MR RALPH BECKETT - Continued

10 **INKA SURPRISE (IRE),** 5, b g Intikhab (USA)—Sweet Surprise (IRE) **McDonagh Murphy & Nixon**
11 **MELROSE ABBEY (IRE),** 4, ch f Selkirk (USA)—Villa Carlotta **J. H. Richmond-Watson**
12 **MICK DUGGAN,** 5, ch g Pivotal—Poppy Carew (IRE) **Mr M. A. Muddiman**
13 **MOONRISE LANDING (IRE),** 4, gr f Dalakhani (IRE)—Celtic Slipper (IRE) **P. D. Savill**
14 **MR BOSSY BOOTS (IRE),** 4, b c Teofilo (IRE)—Zelding (IRE) **Merriebelle Irish Farm Limited**
15 **NICEOFYOUTOTELLME,** 6, b g Hernando (FR)—Swain's Gold (USA) **Mr R. J. Roberts**
16 **PERFECT ALCHEMY (IRE),** 4, b f Clodovil (IRE)—Desert Alchemy (IRE) **The Perfect Partnership & D H Caslon**
17 **POYLE SOPHIE,** 4, b f Teofilo (IRE)—Lost In Lucca **Cecil and Miss Alison Wiggins**
18 **POYLE THOMAS,** 6, b g Rail Link—Lost In Lucca **Cecil and Miss Alison Wiggins**
19 **POYLE TOBY (IRE),** 5, b g Bahamian Bounty—Lost In Lucca **Cecil and Miss Alison Wiggins**
20 **SEASIDE SIZZLER,** 8, ch g Rahy (USA)—Via Borghese (USA) **I. J. Heseltine**
21 **SECRET GESTURE,** 5, b m Galileo (IRE)—Shastye (IRE) **Qatar Racing Ltd & Newsells Park Stud**
22 **SIZZLER,** 5, ch g Hernando (FR)—Gino's Spirits **Heseltine, Henley & Jones**
23 **TAMASHA,** 4, ch f Sea The Stars (IRE)—Tamarind (IRE) **N. Bizakov**

## THREE-YEAR-OLDS

24 **ALBORETTA,** b f Hernando (FR)—Alvarita **Miss K. Rausing**
25 **AMBER MILE,** b f Rip Van Winkle (IRE)—Rose Street (IRE) **Dr Bridget Drew & The Redvers Family**
26 **ARC CARA (ITY),** b g Arcano (IRE)—Folcara (IRE) **Mr R. Ng**
27 **ARGUS (IRE),** b c Rip Van Winkle (IRE)—Steel Princess (IRE) **Qatar Racing Limited**
28 **AZURE AMOUR (IRE),** b f Azamour (IRE)—Al Euro (FR) **The Dirham Partnership**
29 **BELLAJEU,** b f Montjeu (IRE)—Arbella **QRL/Sheikh Suhaim Al Thani/M Al Kubaisi**
30 **BOLD APPEAL,** b g Nayef (USA)—Shy Appeal (IRE) **Wood Street Syndicate II**
31 **CAMAGUEYANA,** b f Archipenko (USA)—Caribana **Miss K. Rausing**
32 **CAPE CAY,** gr f Cape Cross (IRE)—White Cay **R. Barnett**
33 **CHEMICAL CHARGE (IRE),** ch c Sea The Stars (IRE)—Jakonda (USA) **Qatar Racing Limited**
34 **CRACKER,** b f Smart Strike (CAN)—Tottie **J. H. Richmond-Watson**
35 **DANEGA,** b f Galileo (IRE)—Danelissima (IRE) **N. Bizakov**
36 **ENCORE D'OR,** b c Oasis Dream—Entente Cordiale (IRE) **Newsells Park Stud Limited**
37 **ENGAGING SMILE,** b f Exceed And Excel (AUS)—Bronze Star **Qatar Racing Ltd & Mr N H Wrigley**
38 **FAIR'S FAIR (IRE),** b f Lawman (FR)—Winning Sequence (FR) **Larksborough Stud Limited**
39 **FORTE,** ch f New Approach (IRE)—Prowess (IRE) **Mr J L Rowsell & Mr M H Dixon**
40 **GOLD BUD,** b c Kyllachy—Fluttering Rose **Mr S. Pan**
41 **GOLD FLASH,** b g Kheleyf (USA)—My Golly **Mr S. Pan**
42 **GOLD WALTZ,** b f Acclamation—Corps de Ballet (IRE) **Mr S. Pan**
43 **GOLD WILL (IRE),** b c Invincible Spirit (IRE)—Ermine And Velvet **Mr S. Pan**
44 **GRAND CANYON (IRE),** b g High Chaparral (IRE)—Cleide da Silva (USA) **Sir R. Ogden C.B.E., LLD**
45 **GREAT GLEN,** b c High Chaparral (IRE)—Grand Opening (IRE) **J. H. Richmond-Watson**
46 **GREEN TORNADO (IRE),** b c Equiano (FR)—Loch Verdi **J. C. Smith**
47 B f Duke of Marmalade (IRE)—Guantanamera (IRE) **QRL/Sheikh Suhaim Al Thani/M Al Kubaisi**
48 **HARD TO HANDEL,** b g Stimulation (IRE)—Melody Maker **Melody Racing**
49 **HAWKIN (IRE),** b f Big Bad Bob (IRE)—Margaux Magique (IRE) **The Hawk Inn Syndicate 4**
50 **INEXORABLE TIDE (IRE),** gr g Verglas (IRE)—Atlas Silk **Mr R. J. Roberts**
51 **KING JERRY (IRE),** b g Intikhab (USA)—Lady Docker (IRE) **The SoCS**
52 **L'INGENUE,** b f New Approach (IRE)—Green Room (FR) **Aylesfield Farms Stud**
53 **LEAR'S ROCK (IRE),** b g Rock of Gibraltar (IRE)—Cordelia **The Outlaws**
54 **LOGORRHEIC,** b g Thewayyouare (USA)—Thousandkissesdeep (IRE) **Frewen & Ahkong**
55 **MAGIC CIRCLE (IRE),** b g Makfi—Minkova (IRE) **Mr & Mrs David Aykroyd**
56 **MAGIC DANCER,** b c Norse Dancer (IRE)—King's Siren (IRE) **J. C. Smith**
57 **MARMA'S BOY,** ch g Duke of Marmalade (IRE)—Graduation **Mr R. Ng**
58 **MASTER OF IRONY (IRE),** b g Makfi—Mother of Pearl (IRE) **Qatar Racing Limited**
59 **MAXWELL (IRE),** b g Big Bad Bob (IRE)—Gladiole (GER) **Kennet Valley Thoroughbreds IV**
60 **MIDNIGHT DANCE (IRE),** b f Danehill Dancer (IRE)—Dark Missile **J. C. Smith**
61 **MR CRIPPS,** b g Sir Percy—Pella **Mrs H. I. Slade**
62 Ch c Pivotal—Murrieta **Sceptre**
63 **PACIFY,** b g Paco Boy (IRE)—Supereva (IRE) **The Prince of Wales & The Duchess of Cornwall**
64 **PACKED HOUSE,** b f Azamour (IRE)—Riotous Applause **The Eclipse Partnership**
65 **PARNELL'S DREAM,** b f Oasis Dream—Kitty O'shea **Mr & Mrs David Aykroyd**
66 **PENSIONNAT (IRE),** b f Cape Cross (IRE)—Surval (IRE) **Mr R. Ng**
67 **PERRAULT (IRE),** b c Rip Van Winkle (IRE)—La Persiana **Lady G. De Walden**
68 **POYLE JESSICA,** b f Royal Applause—Poyle Caitlin (IRE) **Cecil and Miss Alison Wiggins**
69 **PURE LINE,** b f Zamindar (USA)—Pure Grain **R. Barnett**
70 **REDSTART,** b f Cockney Rebel (IRE)—Ecstasy **A. D. G. Oldrey**
71 **RIVERS RUN (IRE),** b f High Chaparral (IRE)—Quiet Waters (USA) **Ballymore Sterling Syndicate**
72 **SHAPE UP,** ch f Raven's Pass (USA)—Fashion Rocks (IRE) **Thurloe Thoroughbreds XXXIV**

## MR RALPH BECKETT - Continued

73 **SHE IS NO LADY,** b f Lope de Vega (IRE)—Capestar (IRE) **D & J Newell**
74 **SI NON OSCILLAS (IRE),** b f Fastnet Rock (AUS)—Playboy Mansion (IRE) **Mrs E. Kennedy**
75 **SILKEN OCEAN,** b f Dynaformer (USA)—Mambo Jambo (USA) **J. L. Rowsell**
76 **SINGULAR QUEST,** ch c Dalakhani (IRE)—Singuliere (IRE) **Ashbrittle Stud,Jameson,Carolan,Edwards**
77 **SOUTHERN STORM (IRE),** b f Cape Cross (IRE)—Stormy Blessing (USA) **Mr C. McHale**
78 **SWEET DREAM,** b f Oasis Dream—Sweet Stream (ITY) **Britannia Thoroughbreds**
79 **SYRDARYA,** ch f Galileo (IRE)—Rock Salt **N. Bizakov**
80 **TASSELLED,** b f Tobougg (IRE)—Roseum **Mr N H Wrigley & Qatar Racing Ltd**
81 **TODEGICA,** b f Giant's Causeway (USA)—Totally Devoted (USA) **N. Bizakov**
82 **WHAT ASHAM,** b c Pivotal—Coy (IRE) **What Asham Partnership**
83 **WHO'STHEDUDE (IRE),** b g Duke of Marmalade (IRE)—Island Dreams (USA) **Mr R. Ng**

## TWO-YEAR-OLDS

84 Ch f 14/2 Dutch Art—Agony And Ecstasy (Captain Rio) (109523) **Clipper Group Holdings Ltd**
85 Ch c 23/4 Kyllachy—Agony Aunt (Formidable (USA)) (26000) **The Pickford Hill Partnership**
86 **ALYSSA,** b f 28/1 Sir Percy—Almiranta (Galileo (IRE)) **Miss K. Rausing**
87 **ANOTHER BOY,** ch c 7/4 Paco Boy (IRE)—Kurtanella (Pastoral Pursuits) **Mrs Philip Snow & Partners**
88 B c 12/4 Kyllachy—Autumn Pearl (Orpen (USA)) **Mr K. Watts**
89 B f 10/2 Makfi—Bahamamia (Vettori (IRE)) **Qatar Racing Limited**
90 **CARNTOP,** b c 10/2 Dansili—Milford Sound (Barathea (IRE)) **The Prince of Wales & The Duchess of Cornwall**
91 B f 2/4 Pour Moi (IRE)—Diamond Light (USA) (Fantastic Light (USA)) **Pearl Bloodstock Limited**
92 B f 12/2 Bahamian Bounty—Echo Ridge (IRE) (Oratorio (IRE)) **J. C. Smith**
93 B f 19/5 Pastoral Pursuits—Ecstasy (Pursuit of Love) (3000) **Mr A. D. G. Oldrey & Partner**
94 Br f 8/4 New Approach (IRE)—
Ensemble (FR) (Iron Mask (USA)) (420000) **H.H. Sheikh Mohammed bin Khalifa Al-Thani**
95 B f 3/2 Montjeu (IRE)—Festoso (IRE) (Diesis) (105000) **Clipper Group Holdings Ltd**
96 B f 13/2 Speightstown (USA)—Forest Crown (Royal Applause) **The Eclipse Partnership**
97 B f 4/2 Sakhee's Secret—Funny Enough (Dansili) (20000) **Dr Bridget Drew & Mr R. A. Farmiloe**
98 **GO AHEAD (IRE),** ch c 6/3 Dream Ahead (USA)—Gladstone Street (IRE) (Waajib) (59523) **K. A. Dasmal**
99 **GOLD FAITH (IRE),** gr c 26/2 Dark Angel (IRE)—Livadream (IRE) (Dalakhani (IRE)) (200000) **Mr S. Pan**
100 **GOLDEN CHAPTER,** b f 26/1 Danehill Dancer (IRE)—Farfala (FR) (Linamix (FR)) (200000) **Mr S. Pan**
101 **GOLDEN STUNNER (IRE),** ch f 26/2 Dream Ahead (USA)—Pina Colada (Sabrehill (USA)) (91269) **Mr S. Pan**
102 B c 5/4 Acclamation—Greek Easter (IRE) (Namid) (70000) **Mr R. Ng**
103 B f 20/3 Rock of Gibraltar (IRE)—Green Room (FR) (In The Wings) **Aylesfield Farms Stud**
104 Ch c 14/4 Makfi—High Lite (Observatory (USA)) (33333) **Kennet Valley Thoroughbreds VII**
105 **HOLY ROMAN PRINCE (IRE),** b c 17/4 Holy Roman Emperor (IRE)—Princess Ellen (Tirol) **Five Horses Ltd**
106 **KALAMATA,** b f 27/1 Sir Percy—Kalamkas (USA) (Kingmambo (USA)) **N. Bizakov**
107 B c 4/2 Equiano (FR)—King's Siren (IRE) (King's Best (USA)) **J. C. Smith**
108 B f 30/3 Galileo (IRE)—Landmark (USA) (Arch (USA)) (420000) **Sheikh Khalifa, Sheikh Suhaim & QRL**
109 Ch f 11/2 Compton Place—Lavinia's Grace (USA) (Green Desert (USA)) (25000) **Mrs I. M. Beckett**
110 Ch f 5/4 Danehill Dancer (IRE)—Loch Verdi (Green Desert (USA)) **J. C. Smith**
111 **MATIDIA,** ch f 4/2 Manduro (GER)—Caesarea (GER) (Generous (IRE)) **J. L. Rowsell**
112 **NASSUVIAN PEARL,** br f 15/4 Bahamian Bounty—Melody Maker (Diktat) **Melody Racing**
113 B f 14/4 Kodiac—Pearly Brooks (Efisio) (40000) **Chelsea Thoroughbreds - Cap Ferrat**
114 **PILLAR,** b c 5/3 Rock of Gibraltar (IRE)—Ceilidh House (Selkirk (USA)) **J. H. Richmond-Watson**
115 **POINT OF WOODS,** b c 27/2 Showcasing—Romantic Myth (Mind Games) (110000) **Mr & Mrs David Aykroyd**
116 B f 20/3 Dutch Art—Pure Song (Singspiel (IRE)) (80000) **R. Barnett**
117 **RAIN IN THE FACE,** b c 26/4 Naaqoos—
Makaaseb (USA) (Pulpit (USA)) (11428) **P. K. Gardner T/A Springcombe Park Stud**
118 B c 12/4 Notnowcato—Red Blossom (Green Desert (USA)) (15872) **Mr R. J. Roberts**
119 **RED ENDEAVOUR (IRE),** ch c 13/4 Intikhab (USA)—
Crimson Lass (IRE) (Dubawi (IRE)) (22857) **The Pickford Hill Partnership**
120 B c 20/4 Kodiac—Right After Moyne (IRE) (Imperial Ballet (IRE)) (39681) **Mr R. Ng**
121 B f 25/1 Dutch Art—Roscoff (IRE) (Daylami (IRE)) **Merriebelle Irish Farm Limited**
122 **SACRAMENT (IRE),** b f 4/2 Acclamation—
Alstemeria (IRE) (Danehill (USA)) (75000) **Highclere Thoroughbred Racing (Disraeli)**
123 **SANDAHL (IRE),** b c 4/4 Footstepsinthesand—Little Scotland (Acclamation) (63491) **Mr & Mrs David Aykroyd**
124 Ch f 16/5 Exceed And Excel (AUS)—
Sensational Mover (USA) (Theatrical) **P. K. Gardner T/A Springcombe Park Stud**
125 B f 14/2 Shamardal (USA)—Shastye (IRE) (Danehill (USA)) **Newsells Park Stud Limited**
126 **SIGHTLINE,** b f 29/1 Rock of Gibraltar (IRE)—Look So (Efisio) **J. H. Richmond-Watson**
127 B f 27/2 Cape Cross (IRE)—Snoqualmie Star (Galileo (IRE)) **J. C. Smith**
128 **SPARRING QUEEN (USA),** b f 25/3 War Front (USA)—Spa Break (USA) (Giant's Causeway (USA))
129 B c 4/5 Big Bad Bob (IRE)—Special Cause (IRE) (Fasliyev (USA)) (34000) **Mr R Roberts & Partner**
130 **TANGBA,** b f 11/3 Dansili—Tamarind (IRE) (Sadler's Wells (USA)) **N. Bizakov**

## MR RALPH BECKETT - Continued

**131** B c 29/4 Zamindar (USA)—
Tender Morn (USA) (Dayjur (USA)) (158730) **H.H. Sheikh Mohammed bin Khalifa Al-Thani**
**132 TOUMAR,** ch f 4/3 Sea The Stars (IRE)—Tingling (USA) (Storm Cat (USA)) (100000) **N. Bizakov**
**133** B c 28/2 Dream Ahead (USA)—Tropical Treat (Bahamian Bounty) **J. C. Smith**
**134** B f 11/4 Intikhab (USA)—Vampire Blues (IRE) (Azamour (IRE)) (5238) **The Millennium Madness Partnership**

**Other Owners:** The Prince Of Wales, Duchess of Cornwall, Mr A. R. Adams, Mr B. Ahkong, Mr M. A. M. K. Al - Kubaisi, Sheikh S. A. K. H. Al Thani, Mrs L. M. Aykroyd, D. P. Aykroyd, Mr T. Bennett, J. J. Brummitt, Mr J. A. Byrne, Mrs D. Camacho, Mr D. E. Carolan, D. H. Caslon, Chelsea Thoroughbreds Ltd, D. W. Dennis, M. H. Dixon, Dr S. B. Drew, J. R. Drew, Mr P. F. Edwards, N. R. Elwes, Mrs C. P. Elwes, Mr R. A. Farmiloe, N. J. Forman Hardy, Mr R. J. Fowler, W. F. Frewen, A. J. J. Gompertz, Mr C. P. Gordon-Watson, Mrs M. R. Gregory, G. C. Hartigan, The Hon H. M. Herbert, Highclere Thoroughbred Racing Ltd, Mr J. Hillier, Mr R. S. Hoskins, Mr P. Jameson, Mr S. J. Kattau, Mr M. J. Kershaw, Mr R. P. Legh, Mr M. D. Moroney, Mrs K. J. Morton, Mr P. G. Murphy, D. J. M. Newell, Mrs J. Newell, S. F. Oldrey, Mr M. Patel, Mr N. Patsalides, O. J. W. Pawle, Mr T. J. Ramsden, Mrs M. U. B. Redvers, Mr D. Redvers, J. P. Repard, N. J. F. Robinson, A. H. Slone, Mrs H. L. Smyly, Mrs J. I. Snow, Miss B. A. Snow, Mr J. A. B. Stafford, Mr M. R. Stokes, L. G. Straszewski, The Hon Sir Mathew Thorpe, Mr R. Weston, C. Wiggins, Miss A. J. Wiggins, T. V. Wilkinson, N. H. T. Wrigley.

**Assistant Trainers:** Adam Kite, W. Jackson-Stops

---

## 33 MR MICHAEL BELL, Newmarket

Postal: **Fitzroy House, Newmarket, Suffolk, CB8 0JT**
Contacts: **PHONE (01638) 666567 FAX (01638) 668000 MOBILE (07802) 264514**
**E-MAIL office@fitzroyhouse.co.uk WEBSITE www.michaelbellracing.co.uk**

1 **ASTRAL WEEKS,** 4, b f Sea The Stars (IRE)—Miss Universe (IRE) **Mr C Wright & Lordship Stud**
2 **BIG ORANGE,** 4, b g Duke of Marmalade (IRE)—Miss Brown To You (IRE) **W. J. and T. O. C. Gredley**
3 **BORN TO REIGN,** 4, b g Sir Percy—Oat Cuisine **Mrs G. E. Rowland-Clark**
4 **FASHION LINE (IRE),** 5, b m Cape Cross (IRE)—Shadow Roll (IRE) **Sheikh Marwan Al Maktoum**
5 **GEORGE CINQ,** 5, b g Pastoral Pursuits—Fairnilee **Michael Morris & Keith Breen**
6 **HABESHIA,** 5, ch g Muhtathir—Lumiere Rouge (FR) **Mr Brian Goodyear**
7 **INSTANT KARMA (IRE),** 4, b g Peintre Celebre (USA)—Kotdiji **L. Caine & J. Barnett**
8 **JAYEFF HERRING (IRE),** 4, b g Excellent Art—Biasca **M. L. W. Bell Racing Ltd**
9 **KEY TO YOUR HEART,** 4, b f Sakhee (USA)—You Too **Wildcard Racing Syndicate**
10 **LEWAMY (IRE),** 5, b g Amadeus Wolf—Thai Dye (UAE) **Mr Brian Goodyear**
11 **SUGAR RUSH,** 4, ch g Pastoral Pursuits—Panic Stations **D. W. & L. Y. Payne**
12 **THATCHEREEN (IRE),** 4, ro f Mastercraftsman (IRE)—Roof Fiddle (USA) **Mr Tim Redman & Mr Peter Philipps**

### THREE-YEAR-OLDS

13 **ANANAS,** b f Nayef (USA)—Anasazi (IRE) **Her Majesty The Queen**
14 **AUSSIE BERRY (IRE),** gr g Aussie Rules (USA)—Berry Baby (IRE) **Mr Dermot Hanafin**
15 **BANDITRY (IRE),** b c Iffraaj—Badalona **Sheikh Marwan Al Maktoum**
16 **BANZARI,** b f Motivator—Bantu **Bell Broughton Deterding Headfort Stafford**
17 **BAREFOOT DANCER,** b c Dansili—Charlotte O Fraise (IRE) **Racing Fillies**
18 **BERLAND (IRE),** b c Cape Cross (IRE)—Ballantrae (IRE) **Sheikh Marwan Al Maktoum**
19 **BEYOND FASHION,** b f Motivator—Friendlier **W. J. and T. O. C. Gredley**
20 **BIPARTISAN (IRE),** b f Bahamian Bounty—Bijou A Moi **Mr Richard Frisby**
21 **CHASING RUBIES (IRE),** b f Tamayuz—Laureldean Lady (IRE) **Lordship Stud 4 & Mr Christopher Wright**
22 **COCONUT KREEK,** ch f Pivotal—Maycocks Bay **Lady Bamford**
23 **DOWN TO EARTH,** gr c Aussie Rules (USA)—May Fox **P. A. Philipps & C. E. L. Philipps**
24 **ELLA FITZ,** b f Pivotal—Under The Rainbow **W. J. and T. O. C. Gredley**
25 **FABRICATE,** b c Makfi—Flight of Fancy **Her Majesty The Queen**
26 **FRANKLIN D (USA),** b c Medaglia d'Oro (USA)—Kissed By A Star (USA) **W. J. and T. O. C. Gredley**
27 **GRACELAND (FR),** b br f Mastercraftsman (IRE)—Jeunesse Lulu (IRE) **The Chriselliam Partnership**
28 **HAVAIANAS (USA),** b f Elusive Quality (USA)—Flip Flop (FR) **Mrs Ben Sangster & Mrs Hugo Lascelles**
29 **INDEPENDENT ROSE,** ch f Mount Nelson—Red Roses Story (FR) **Chippenham Lodge Stud Limited**
30 **JARGON (FR),** b g Naaqoos—Cobblestone Road (USA) **The Royal Ascot Racing Club**
31 **LE ROUQUIN (FR),** ch g Siyouni (FR)—Tenue d'amour (FR) **Mr David Fish & Mr Edward Ware**
32 **MALVIA,** b c Exceed And Excel (AUS)—Always On My Mind **Karmaa Racing Limited**
33 **MIDAS HAZE,** ch f Pivotal—Eva's Request (IRE) **Lady Bamford**
34 **MOTION PICTURE,** b f Motivator—Starshine **Her Majesty The Queen**
35 **MY STRATEGY (IRE),** b g Strategic Prince—Mythie (FR) **Mr W. E. A. Fox**
36 **NEYMAR,** ch c New Approach (IRE)—Just Like A Woman **Mascalls Stud**
37 **NIBLAWI (IRE),** b c Vale of York (IRE)—Finnmark **Sultan Ali**

## MR MICHAEL BELL - Continued

38 **ON THE HUH,** b g Avonbridge—Red Sovereign **Mr Paddy Barrett**
39 **ONE MAN ARMY,** b c Mount Nelson—Hms Pinafore (IRE) **Mrs Lisa Garton**
40 **ORANGE BLOOM,** ch f New Approach (IRE)—Fleur de Lis **W. J. and T. O. C. Gredley**
41 **PENANG PAPARAJA (IRE),** b c Dansili—Penang Pearl (FR) **Mrs A. K. H. Ooi**
42 **PUNCHY LADY,** b f Invincible Spirit (IRE)—Finchley **The Duchess Of Roxburghe & Mrs Clare Rooney**
43 **ROCK OF MAX,** b c Royal Applause—Poldhu **Karmaa Racing Limited**
44 **SAMPERA (IRE),** b f Iffraaj—Al Cobra (IRE) **Saif Ali**
45 **SARITA,** b f Galileo (IRE)—Sariska **Lady Bamford**
46 **SAVOY SHOWGIRL (IRE),** ch f Kyllachy—The Strand **Miss Emily Asprey & Christopher Wright**
47 **STONE ROSES (IRE),** gr f Zebedee—Blanche Dubois **Michael Morris & Keith Breen**
48 **STORYTALE,** ch c Rip Van Winkle (IRE)—Night Haven **Mr Michael Tabor**
49 **STRAIT OF MAGELLAN (IRE),** ch g Captain Rio—Golden (FR) **Murt Khan X2**
50 **TAPER TANTRUM (IRE),** b c Azamour (IRE)—Maramba (USA) **Secular Stagnation**
51 **TARANDO,** b f Equiano (FR)—Christmas Tart (IRE) **Middleham Park Racing XCVIII & Partner**
52 **THEM AND US (IRE),** ch c Rock of Gibraltar (IRE)—Sagrada (GER) **W. J. and T. O. C. Gredley**
53 **THUNDER IN MYHEART (IRE),** gr f Mastercraftsman (IRE)—
Happy Land (IRE) **C. Wright, Mrs C. Forsyth and Miss H. Wright**
54 **TOUCHLINE,** b f Exceed And Excel (AUS)—Trianon **Her Majesty The Queen**

## TWO-YEAR-OLDS

55 **ACADEMY HOUSE (IRE),** b c 4/3 Kodiac—
Joyfullness (USA) (Dixieland Band (USA)) (57142) **W. J. and T. O. C. Gredley**
56 B f 22/2 Medicean—Agrippina (Timeless Times (USA)) (70000) **Mr Paddy Barrett**
57 B f 25/2 Kyllachy—Albavilla (Spectrum (IRE)) (105000) **Mr Michael & Mrs Michelle Morris**
58 B c 10/4 Clodovil (IRE)—Aldburgh (Bluebird (USA)) (41269) **Mr Michael Lowe**
59 Ch c 21/3 Teofilo (IRE)—Badalona (Cape Cross (IRE)) **Sheikh Marwan Al Maktoum**
60 **BOCKING END (IRE),** b f 1/3 Paco Boy (IRE)—Miss Wells (IRE) (Sadler's Wells (USA)) **W. J. and T. O. C. Gredley**
61 **BONHOMIE,** b f 23/4 Shamardal (USA)—Bonnie Doon (IRE) (Grand Lodge (USA)) **Her Majesty The Queen**
62 B f 24/3 Kyllachy—Coy (IRE) (Danehill (USA)) (28000) **Mr M. V. Magnier**
63 **DAVEY BOY,** ch c 27/3 Paco Boy (IRE)—
She's So Pretty (IRE) (Grand Lodge (USA)) (18000) **Mr David Lockwood & Mr Fred Lockwood**
64 **FORECASTER,** b f 31/1 Fastnet Rock (AUS)—Aurore (IRE) (Fasliyev (USA)) **Her Majesty The Queen**
65 **GENERAL HAZARD (IRE),** gr c 2/3 Cacique (IRE)—
In The Soup (USA) (Alphabet Soup (USA)) (32000) **Mr R. P. B. Michaelson**
66 **GOLDEN HELLO (IRE),** b c 28/4 Zebedee—Your Opinion (IRE) (Xaar) (35000) **W. J. and T. O. C. Gredley**
67 Ch c 15/3 Duke of Marmalade (IRE)—Incheni (IRE) (Nashwan (USA)) (32000) **Mr J. Barnett**
68 B f 24/2 Poet's Voice—Juniper Girl (IRE) (Revoque (IRE)) (35000) **Mr M. B. Hawtin**
69 B f 6/3 Lawman (FR)—Kyniska (IRE) (Choisir (AUS)) (87301) **Clipper Logistics**
70 Ch c 20/4 Cape Blanco (IRE)—Latte (USA) (Pleasant Tap (USA)) (114744) **Qatar Racing Limited**
71 B c 22/1 Authorized (IRE)—Local Spirit (USA) (Lion Cavern (USA)) **Sheikh Marwan Al Maktoum**
72 **LOUD APPLAUSE,** b f 6/3 Royal Applause—New Assembly (IRE) (Machiavellian (USA)) **Her Majesty The Queen**
73 **MERRIMENT,** ch f 8/3 Makfi—Trianon (Nayef (USA)) **Her Majesty The Queen**
74 B c 11/2 Acclamation—Mini Driver (Danehill (USA)) **Mr M. V. Magnier & Lady Carolyn Warren**
75 B c 11/2 Sir Percy—My First Romance (Danehill (USA)) (55000) **Secular Stagnation**
76 **ROSECOMB (IRE),** b f 19/3 Rip Van Winkle (IRE)—
Malyana (Mtoto) (39681) **Sir Thomas Pilkington, BT & Mr W E A Fox**
77 B f 7/4 Dream Ahead (USA)—Sister Sylvia (Fantastic Light (USA)) (45000)
78 **THE MAJOR,** b c 22/4 Major Cadeaux—Ballerina Suprema (IRE) (Sadler's Wells (USA)) (4500) **Lady Clare Law**
79 Ch f 22/3 Monsieur Bond (IRE)—Tibesti (Machiavellian (USA)) (16190) **Qatar Racing Limited**
80 **TOWERLANDS PARK (IRE),** b c 15/1 Danehill Dancer (IRE)—
Strategy (Machiavellian (USA)) (120000) **W. J. and T. O. C. Gredley**
81 Ch f 2/2 Dream Ahead (USA)—Wedding Gown (Dubai Destination (USA)) **Mr Christopher Wright**

**Assistant Trainer:** Edward Smyth-Osbourne

**Jockey (flat):** Tom Queally, Jamie Spencer. **Apprentice:** Michael Kenneally, Lulu Stanford, Louis Steward.

---

## 34 MR JAMES BENNETT, Wantage

Postal: **2 Filley Alley, Letcombe Bassett, Wantage, Oxfordshire, OX12 9LT**
Contacts: **PHONE (01235) 762163 MOBILE (07771) 523076**
**E-MAIL jabennett345@btinternet.com**

1 **IDOL DEPUTY (FR),** 9, gr g Silver Deputy (CAN)—Runaway Venus (USA) **Miss J. C. Blackwell**

**MR JAMES BENNETT - Continued**

2 **PRINCESSE KATIE (IRE),** 9, b m Presenting—Another Shot (IRE) **Miss J. C. Blackwell**
3 **STAR CLOUD,** 4, b g Nayef (USA)—Space Quest **Miss J. C. Blackwell**

**Assistant Trainer:** Miss J. Blackwell

**Jockey (flat):** Racheal Kneller.

## 35 MR ALAN BERRY, Cockerham

Postal: **Moss Side Racing Stables, Crimbles Lane, Cockerham, Lancashire, LA2 0ES**
Contacts: **PHONE (01524) 791179 FAX (01524) 791958 MOBILE (07880) 553515**
**E-MAIL mosssideracing@tiscali.co.uk WEBSITE www.alanberryracing.co.uk**

1 **AMIS REUNIS,** 6, b m Bahamian Bounty—Spring Clean (FR) **A. B. Parr**
2 **BIX (IRE),** 5, b g Holy Roman Emperor (IRE)—Belle Rebelle (IRE) **A. Berry**
3 **BUSY BIMBO (IRE),** 6, b m Red Clubs (IRE)—Unfortunate **A. Berry**
4 **DRUMMERS DRUMMING (USA),** 9, b g Stroll (USA)—Afleet Summer (USA) **A. Berry**
5 **ECONOMIC CRISIS (IRE),** 6, ch m Excellent Art—Try The Air (IRE) **Mr & Mrs T. Blane**
6 **GRETHEL (IRE),** 11, b m Fruits of Love (USA)—Stay Sharpe (USA) **Mr J. P. Smith**
7 **I'LL BE GOOD,** 6, b g Red Clubs (IRE)—Willisa **Do Well Racing**
8 **JORDAURA,** 9, br g Primo Valentino (IRE)—Christina's Dream **A. B. Parr**
9 **KAY GEE BE (IRE),** 11, b g Fasliyev (USA)—Pursuit of Truth (USA) **A. Berry**
10 **LICENCE TO TILL (USA),** 8, b g War Chant (USA)—With A Wink (USA) **A. Berry**
11 **MYSTIFIED (IRE),** 12, b g Raise A Grand (IRE)—Sunrise (IRE) **A. Willoughby**
12 **PARTNER'S GOLD (IRE),** 5, b h Red Clubs (IRE)—Unfortunate **Partner's Brewery**
13 **PLUNDER,** 5, ch g Zamindar (USA)—Reaching Ahead (USA) **A. Berry**
14 **RAISE A BILLION,** 4, b c Major Cadeaux—Romantic Destiny **T Blane, F Flynn, H Rocks & M Rocks**
15 **RARE COINCIDENCE,** 14, ch g Atraf—Green Seed (IRE) **A. Willoughby**
16 **RED FOREVER,** 4, ch g Major Cadeaux—Spindara (IRE) **Sporting Kings**
17 **SMILE FOR ME (IRE),** 4, br f Elnadim (USA)—Pershaan (IRE) **A. B. Parr**
18 **STRAIGHT GIN,** 4, b g Major Cadeaux—Nee Lemon Left **J Berry/ W Burns**
19 **WIZARDS DUST,** 13, gr g Environment Friend—Linoats **A. Berry**

**THREE-YEAR-OLDS**

20 **CATIES DO DAH,** b f Misu Bond (IRE)—Mitchelland **Mr R. R. Whitton**
21 **GOOD BOY ALEX,** gr c Arabian Gleam—Animal Cracker **Mr R. R. Whitton**
22 **ICANDI,** b f Indesatchel (IRE)—Some Diva **A. B. Parr**
23 **KEPPLE'S BEST (IRE),** b c Moss Vale (IRE)—Mrs Kepple **W. Burns**
24 **MACARTHURS PARK (IRE),** b f Equiano (FR)—La Tintoretta (IRE) **A. B. Parr**
25 **SHAMKHANI,** b c Mullionmileanhour (IRE)—Matilda Peace **Do Well Racing**

**Other Owners:** Mr S. J. Allen, J. Berry, T. W. Blane, Mrs S. Blane, Mr G. D. Brown, Mr F. G. Flynn, Mr I. Griffiths, Mr I. D. Johnson, Mr B. J. Maxted, Mr H. Rocks, Mr M. Rocks, Mr N. Sharp.

## 36 MR J. A. BERRY, Blackwater

Postal: **Ballyroe, Blackwater, Enniscorthy, Co. Wexford, Ireland**
Contacts: **PHONE (00353) 5391 27205 MOBILE (00353) 8625 57537**
**E-MAIL Johnaberry@eircom.net**

1 **ACRIVEEN (IRE),** 13, ch g Accordion—Raheen River (IRE) **J. A. Berry**
2 **BALLYROE RAMBLER (IRE),** 8, br g Lahib (USA)—Victoria's Rose (IRE) **Fire & Ice Syndicate**
3 **CATCH MY DRIFT (IRE),** 6, ch g Subtle Power (IRE)—Deliga Lady (IRE) **J. A. Berry**
4 **COOTAMUNDRA (IRE),** 12, ch g Broken Hearted—Sigginstown **Turbine Syndicate**
5 **CROGHILL TUPPENCE (IRE),** 10, gr g Great Palm (USA)—Shady's Rose (IRE) **Turbine Syndicate**
6 **DAY DAY (IRE),** 5, b m Hurricane Run (IRE)—Mem O'rees **J. P. McManus**
7 **DEEP INSPIRATION (IRE),** 7, b g Heron Island (IRE)—The Wrens Nest (IRE) **Mrs Joan Berry**
8 **FAMOUS BALLERINA (IRE),** 7, b m Golan (IRE)—World of Ballet (IRE) **J. A. Berry**
9 **MARIRA (IRE),** 7, b m Craigsteel—Vinnies Choice (IRE) **Turbine Syndicate**
10 **PENNYWELL (IRE),** 5, b m Gold Well—Boyne Bridge (IRE) **Not For Friend Syndicate**
11 **RABANO (IRE),** 6, b g Kalanisi (IRE)—Tarasandy (IRE) **Go For It Syndicate**
12 **RIGHTY RUE (IRE),** 5, b m Mountain High (IRE)—Last of Many (IRE) **Mrs A. Berry**
13 **TELL ME THIS,** 6, b g High-Rise (IRE)—Gallic Flame **Mrs A. Berry**

## MR J. A. BERRY - Continued

14 **TRY IT AGAIN (IRE),** 5, b m Flemensfirth (USA)—Mohboss **J. A. Berry**
15 **WHATS ON THE MENU (IRE),** 11, ch g Anshan—Leading Dream (IRE) **Mrs J. Berry**

**Assistant Trainer:** Blain Parnell

**Conditional:** A. F. O'Neill. **Amateur:** Mr B. Brooks.

---

## 37 MR JOHN BERRY, Newmarket

Postal: **Beverley House Stables, Exeter Road, Newmarket, Suffolk, CB8 8LR**
Contacts: **PHONE (01638) 660663**
**WEBSITE www.beverleyhousestables.com**

1 **FEN FLYER,** 6, ch g Piccolo—Maraffi (IRE) **Mr D. Tunmore**
2 **GRAND LIAISON,** 6, b m Sir Percy—Dancinginthedark (IRE) **Barrie Catchpole & Mike Meaney**
3 **INDIRA,** 4, ch f Sleeping Indian—Forever Loved **Severn Crossing Partnership**
4 **MAGIC ICE,** 5, b m Royal Applause—Winter Ice **J. C. De P. Berry**
5 **NEAR WILD HEAVEN,** 4, b f Robin des Champs (FR)—Love Supreme (IRE) **The Beverley Hillbillies**
6 **PLATINUM PROOF (USA),** 5, b br g Smart Strike (CAN)—Keeper Hill (USA) **J. C. De P. Berry**
7 **ROY ROCKET (FR),** 5, gr g Layman (USA)—Minnie's Mystery (FR) **McCarthy & Berry**
8 **RUSSIAN LINK,** 5, b m Rail Link—Zathonia **Mrs E. L. Berry**
9 **SENATOR MATT,** 5, b h Joe Bear (IRE)—Anytime Anywhere **Mrs M. Lethbridge-Brown**
10 **ZAROSA (IRE),** 6, b m Barathea (IRE)—Shantalla Peak (IRE) **Mr R. G. Vicarage**

### THREE-YEAR-OLDS

11 **FEN LADY,** b f Champs Elysees—Query (USA) **Mr D. Tunmore**
12 **GALETTE DES ROIS,** b f Joe Bear (IRE)—Peach Galette (USA) **Mr Stuart McPhee**
13 **SO MUCH WATER (FR),** gr f Le Havre (IRE)—Minnie's Mystery (FR) **J. C. De P. Berry**

### TWO-YEAR-OLDS

14 **HYMN FOR THE DUDES,** br c 5/4 Sakhee's Secret—Hermione's Dream (Oasis Dream) **Mr Charles Wentworth**
15 **SACRED ROCK (IRE),** b g 5/2 Rock of Gibraltar (IRE)—Snowpalm (Halling (USA)) (30158) **Raffles Thoroughbred Racing**
16 **SIRLI (FR),** b f 14/3 Carlotamix (FR)—Tailzie (Mtoto) (3968) **The Beverley House Stables Partnership**
17 **WHITE VALIANT (FR),** gr g 26/3 Youmzain (IRE)—Minnie's Mystery (FR) (Highest Honor (FR)) **J. C. De P. Berry**

**Other Owners:** Mr John Berry, Mrs Emma Berry, Mr Claude Berry, Mr A. Brannon, Mrs A. Brannon, Mr D. Collings, Mrs D. Collings, Mr K. Crofton, Dato Yap Kim San, Mr J. Dumas, Mr R. Fleck, Mr K. Gibbs, Mr B. Granahan, Mr J. Heggarty, Mr Richard Jones, Mr A. Mayne, Miss L. I. McCarthy, Mrs I. McCarthy, Mr S. McCormick, Mr A. McLeod, Mr T. O'Rourke, Mrs M. L. Parry, Mr A. Pike, Raffles Stud (NZ), Mr K. Reynolds, Mr B. M. Sherwin, Mr R. Sims, Mr P. Steele-Mortimer, Mr P. Stock, Mr Larry Stratton, Mr L. C. Wadey, Mr I. Walton, Mr S. Waterhouse, Mrs S. Waterhouse.

**Assistant Trainer:** Hugh Fraser

**Jockey (flat):** John Egan. **Jockey (NH):** Will Kennedy, Jack Quinlan. **Amateur:** Mr Richard Sims.

---

## 38 MR JIM BEST, Lewes

Postal: **Grandstand Stables, The Old Racecourse, Lewes, East Sussex, BN7 1UR**
Contacts: **PHONE (01435) 882073 (01273) 480249 FAX (01435) 882073 MOBILE (07968) 743272**
**E-MAIL jimandtombest@btinternet.com WEBSITE www.jimandtombestracing.co.uk**

1 **ARAMADYH,** 4, gr f Authorized (IRE)—Swift Dispersal **Mr & Mrs F. W. Golding**
2 **BORU'S BROOK (IRE),** 7, b g Brian Boru—Collybrook Lady (IRE) **Cheltenham Dreamers**
3 **BROTHER BENNETT (FR),** 5, gr g Martaline—La Gaminerie (FR) **The Best Elite Partnership**
4 **DORRY K (IRE),** 6, b m Ad Valorem (USA)—Ashtaroute (USA) **The K Team**
5 **FLASH CRASH,** 6, b g Val Royal (FR)—Tessara (GER) **Mr J. J. Callaghan**
6 **GENEROUS JACK (IRE),** 6, ch g Generous (IRE)—Yosna (FR) **Mr J. J. Callaghan**
7 **HEADING TO FIRST,** 8, b g Sulamani (IRE)—Bahirah **Homewoodgate Racing Club**
8 **INCH WING (IRE),** 7, b m Winged Love (IRE)—Incharder (IRE) **Mr & Mrs F. W. Golding**
9 **INTO THE WIND,** 8, ch m Piccolo—In The Stocks **Into The Wind Partnership**
10 **JAZZY LADY (IRE),** 4, b f Intikhab (USA)—Lock's Heath (CAN) **Mr J. J. Callaghan**
11 **KIAMA BAY (IRE),** 9, b g Fraam—La Panthere (USA) **Chris Dillon & Barry Reilly**
12 **LUCKY PRINCE,** 8, b g Lucky Owners (NZ)—Sun Bonnet **B. J. Eckley**
13 **LYSSIO (GER),** 8, b g Motivator—Lysuna (GER) **Mr J. J. Callaghan**

## MR JIM BEST - Continued

14 **MARIA'S CHOICE (IRE),** 6, b g Oratorio (IRE)—Amathusia **Billericay Racing Club**
15 **MISSILE MAN (IRE),** 6, b h Winged Love (IRE)—Miss Ondee (FR) **Jack Callaghan & Christopher Dillon**
16 **NEW STREET (IRE),** 4, gr c Acclamation—New Deal **Mr J. J. Best**
17 **OFFICER DRIVEL (IRE),** 4, b g Captain Rio—Spiritville (IRE) **M. J. Benton**
18 **OUTRATH (IRE),** 5, b g Captain Rio—Silver Grouse (IRE) **Mr J. J. Best**
19 **PADDOCKS LOUNGE (IRE),** 8, b g Oscar (IRE)—Sister Rosza (IRE) **Mrs R. Wenman**
20 **PLANETOID (IRE),** 7, b g Galileo (IRE)—Palmeraie (USA) **Planetoid Partnership**
21 **RAMONA CHASE,** 10, b g High Chaparral (IRE)—Audacieuse **Fruits Incorporated**
22 **RED ORATOR,** 6, ch g Osorio (GER)—Red Roses Story (FR) **Wishful Thinkers Partnership**
23 **SAINT HELENA (IRE),** 7, b m Holy Roman Emperor (IRE)—Tafseer (IRE) **Mr J. J. Best**
24 **SLOWFOOT (GER),** 7, b h Hernando (FR)—Simply Red (GER) **Mr J. J. Best**
25 **STAFF SERGEANT,** 8, b g Dubawi (IRE)—Miss Particular (IRE) **Mr M. Jackson**
26 **THATS MY RABBIT (IRE),** 6, b g Heron Island (IRE)—Minnie Turbo (IRE) **The Best Elite Partnership**
27 **THEHILL OFTHE ROCK (IRE),** 5, ch g Indian River (FR)—Ballyburn Lady (IRE) **Mr & Mrs F. W. Golding**

**Other Owners:** Mr A. Achilleous, Mr E. Barker, Mr M. Benton, Mr J. Best, Mr J. Callaghan, Mr M. Callow, Mr C. J. Dillon, Mr P. E. Gardener, Mr F. W. Golding, Mrs M. J. Golding, Mr T. J. Good, S. P. Graham, Mr J. Haste, Mr M. Jackson, Mrs E. Lucey-Butler, Mr B. Reilly, Mr C. W. Wilson.

**Assistant Trainer:** Mr Tom Best

**Jockey (flat):** William Twiston-Davies. **Jockey (NH):** Jason Maguire, A. P. McCoy.

---

## 39 MR JOHN BEST, Borden

Postal: **Eyehorn Farm, Munsgore Lane, Borden, Kent, ME9 8JU**
Contacts: **MOBILE (07889) 362154**
**E-MAIL john.best@johnbestracing.com WEBSITE www.johnbestracing.com**

1 **BERRAHRI (IRE),** 4, b g Bahri (USA)—Band of Colour (IRE) **Curtis, Malt & Wykes**
2 **BIG WHISKEY (IRE),** 5, ch g Ad Valorem (USA)—El Opera (IRE) **Mr N. Dyshaev**
3 **CHARLIES MATE,** 4, br g Myboycharlie (IRE)—Retainage (USA) **Mrs J. O. Jones**
4 **FEARLESS LAD (IRE),** 5, b g Excellent Art—Souffle **Mrs J. O. Jones**
5 **GUNG HO JACK,** 6, b g Moss Vale (IRE)—Bijan (IRE) **Mr J. R. Best**
6 **HIORNE TOWER (FR),** 4, b c Poliglote—Hierarchie (FR) **Mrs J. O. Jones**
7 **LUPO D'ORO (IRE),** 6, b g Amadeus Wolf—Vital Laser (USA) **Mr S. Malcolm, Mr M. Winwright & Mr P. Tindall**
8 **MOSSGO (IRE),** 5, b g Moss Vale (IRE)—Perovskia (USA) **Hucking Horses V**
9 **NINETY MINUTES (IRE),** 4, b g Oratorio (IRE)—Fleeting Mirage (USA) **Andy Carroll, Kevin Nolan & Mark Curtis**
10 **PRINCESS SPIRIT,** 6, b m Invincible Spirit (IRE)—Habariya (IRE) **Mr N. Dyshaev**
11 **SHEIKH THE REINS (IRE),** 6, b g Iffraaj—Wychwood Wanderer (IRE) **Curtis, Malt, Williams & Harris**
12 **STONE OF FOLCA,** 7, b g Kodiac—Soyalang (FR) **Rock Racing**

### THREE-YEAR-OLDS

13 **ADMIRAL'S GOLD (IRE),** ch c Mount Nelson—Lolita's Gold (USA) **Mr N. Dyshaev**
14 **BENJAMIN DISRAELI (IRE),** b c Champs Elysees—Strike Lightly **Mrs L. C. G. Malcolm**
15 **ETON NESS,** b c Mullionmileanhour (IRE)—Neissa (USA) **Multi Mullion Racing**
16 **FAST SPRITE (IRE),** b c Fast Company (IRE)—Salty Air (IRE) **Mr N. Dyshaev**
17 B f Mullionmileanhour (IRE)—Hucking Harmony (IRE) **Five In Harmony**
18 **JUST BECAUSE,** b g Mawatheeq (USA)—Muwakaba (USA) **Mr N. Dyshaev**
19 **MULLIONHEIR,** b g Mullionmileanhour (IRE)—Peyto Princess **Mr S. D. Malcolm**
20 **REVISION (FR),** b br g Vision d'etat (FR)—Karmibola (FR) **Curtis, Malt & Williams**
21 B c Mullionmileanhour (IRE)—Santiburi Girl **H. J. Jarvis**
22 **SARAFINA,** b f Mullionmileanhour (IRE)—Nala (USA) **Multi Mullion Racing**
23 **TEMPRANILLO,** b f Mullionmileanhour (IRE)—Numanthia (IRE) **Multi Mullion Racing**
24 **VALE OF IRON (IRE),** b c Vale of York (IRE)—Lady Van Gogh **Mr N. Dyshaev**

### TWO-YEAR-OLDS

25 B c 6/5 Mullionmileanhour (IRE)—Bollywood Style (Josr Algarhoud (IRE))
26 B f 8/5 Mullionmileanhour (IRE)—Cheap N Chic (Primo Valentino (IRE))
27 B f 22/3 Mullionmileanhour (IRE)—Daughters World (Agnes World (USA))
28 B c 26/2 Mullionmileanhour (IRE)—Dolly Parton (IRE) (Tagula (IRE))
29 B f 28/2 Mullionmileanhour (IRE)—Hannah's Dream (IRE) (King's Best (USA)) **Lingfield Park Owners Group**
30 B c 7/3 Mullionmileanhour (IRE)—Neissa (USA) (Three Wonders (USA))

## MR JOHN BEST - Continued

**31** Gr c 25/4 Arabian Gleam—Neptune's Girl (IRE) (Verglas (IRE)) (8571) **Mr M. B. Curtis**
**32** B c 21/2 Mullionmileanhour (IRE)—Numanthia (IRE) (Barathea (IRE))
**33** B c 23/2 Mullionmileanhour (IRE)—Phantom Ridge (IRE) (Indian Ridge)
**34** B c 16/2 Mullionmileanhour (IRE)—Retainage (USA) (Polish Numbers (USA)) (9523) **Mr M. B. Curtis**
**35** B f 21/3 Mullionmileanhour (IRE)—Santiburi Girl (Casteddu) **Mr J. R. Best**

**Other Owners:** Mr R. C. Malt, Miss H. J. Williams, Mr M. J. Winwright.

---

## 40 MISS HARRIET BETHELL, Arnold

Postal: **Arnold Manor, Black Tup Lane, Arnold, Hull, East Yorkshire, HU11 5JA**
Contacts: **PHONE (01964) 562996 MOBILE (07733) 424242**
**E-MAIL harrietbethell@hotmail.co.uk**

**1 FUJIN DANCER (FR),** 10, ch g Storming Home—Badaayer (USA) **W. A. Bethell**
**2 IMPERIAL VIC (IRE),** 10, b br g Old Vic—Satco Rose (IRE) **W. A. Bethell**
**3 NALIM (IRE),** 9, b g Milan—Hati Roy (IRE) **W. A. Bethell**
**4 TEDDY'S REFLECTION (IRE),** 12, b g Beneficial—Regal Pursuit (IRE) **W. A. Bethell**
**5 TRI NATIONS (UAE),** 10, ch g Halling (USA)—Six Nations (USA) **W. A. Bethell**

---

## 41 MR JAMES BETHELL, Middleham

Postal: **Thorngill, Coverham, Middleham, North Yorkshire, DL8 4TJ**
Contacts: **PHONE (01969) 640360 FAX (01969) 640360 MOBILE (07831) 683528**
**E-MAIL james@jamesbethell.co.uk WEBSITE www.jamesbethell.com**

**1 FAB LOLLY (IRE),** 5, b m Rock of Gibraltar (IRE)—Violet Ballerina (IRE) **Clarendon Thoroughbred Racing**
**2 GOTCHA,** 4, gr f Fair Mix (IRE)—Shazana **Mr R. F. Gibbons**
**3 HOUSEWIVES CHOICE,** 4, ch f Black Sam Bellamy (IRE)—Maid of Perth **Mr R. F. Gibbons**
**4 KIRKMAN (IRE),** 4, ch g Virtual—Validate **Mr M. Dawson**
**5 LAST SUPPER,** 6, b m Echo of Light—Scotland The Brave **Mr R. F. Gibbons**
**6 MISTER BOB (GER),** 6, ch g Black Sam Bellamy (IRE)—Mosquera (GER) **Mr R. F. Gibbons**
**7 PINTRADA,** 7, b g Tiger Hill (IRE)—Ballymore Celebre (IRE) **Scotyork Partnership I**
**8 RICH AGAIN (IRE),** 6, b g Amadeus Wolf—Fully Fashioned (IRE) **Clarendon Thoroughbred Racing**
**9 THANKYOU VERY MUCH,** 5, b m Lucky Story (USA)—Maid of Perth **Mr R. F. Gibbons**
**10 TRUE PLEASURE (IRE),** 8, b m Choisir (AUS)—Absolute Pleasure **Clarendon Thoroughbred Racing**

### THREE-YEAR-OLDS

**11 BRIARDALE (IRE),** b g Arcano (IRE)—Marine City (JPN) **Clarendon Thoroughbred Racing**
**12 BURNESTON,** br c Rock of Gibraltar (IRE)—Grain of Gold **Clarendon Thoroughbred Racing**
**13 COMIN UP ROSES,** b f Schiaparelli (GER)—Shazana **Mr R. F. Gibbons**
**14 GRAND DEPART,** b f Royal Applause—Path of Peace **Mrs L. Peacock**
**15 KELLY'S FINEST (IRE),** ch f Intense Focus (USA)—Priory Rock (IRE) **Mr J. S. Lambert**
**16 NOBBLY BOBBLY (IRE),** br c High Chaparral (IRE)—Rock Queen (IRE) **Mr J. S. Lambert**
**17 PRINCESS PEACHES,** ch f Notnowcato—Miss Apricot **Mr D. Kilburn**
**18 THE MUNSHI,** b g Multiplex—Maid of Perth **Mr R. F. Gibbons**

### TWO-YEAR-OLDS

**19** B f 12/2 Kheleyf (USA)—Annie Gee (Primo Valentino (IRE)) **Mr F. Brady**
**20** Ch c 17/4 Lord Shanakill (USA)—Boschendal (IRE) (Zamindar (USA)) (19000) **Clarendon Thoroughbred Racing**
**21** B c 23/3 Champs Elysees—Fly In Style (Hernando (FR)) (30000) **Clarendon Thoroughbred Racing**
**22 FRUIT SALAD,** ch f 7/5 Monsieur Bond (IRE)—
Miss Apricot (Indian Ridge) (2857) **Clarendon Thoroughbred Racing**
**23 HAPPY BIRTHDAY,** b f 27/3 Schiaparelli (GER)—Shazana (Key of Luck (USA)) **Mr R. F. Gibbons**
**24 HAZELY,** b f 1/5 Cape Cross (IRE)—Sentimental Value (USA) (Diesis) (15000) **Clarendon Thoroughbred Racing**
**25** B c 30/1 Rock of Gibraltar (IRE)—Ocean Talent (USA) (Aptitude (USA)) (25000) **Mr Buckingham**
**26 ON FIRE,** b c 14/3 Olden Times—La Notte (Factual (USA)) **Hon Mrs L. B. Holliday**
**27 RICH PURSUITS,** ch c 9/4 Pastoral Pursuits—Salvia (Pivotal) (38000) **R. T. Vickers**
**28** Gr ro f 6/4 Hard Spun (USA)—Silver Games (IRE) (Verglas (IRE)) **Mr C. Wright**
**29** B f 8/3 Canford Cliffs (IRE)—
Soul Mountain (IRE) (Rock of Gibraltar (IRE)) (42000) **Clarendon Thoroughbred Racing**

**MR JAMES BETHELL - Continued**

**30** B c 29/1 Henrythenavigator (USA)—Watchful (IRE) (Galileo (IRE)) (20634) **Mr Buckingham**
**31 WESTWARD HO (IRE),** b c 12/4 Fastnet Rock (AUS)—
Thought Is Free (Cadeaux Genereux) (35000) **Mr G. N. van Cutsem**

**Other Owners:** Mr G. A. Barnes, Mr J. D. Bethell, Mrs James Bethell, Mr Michael Gibson, Mr J. A. Tabet.

---

## 42 MR EDWARD BEVAN, Hereford

Postal: **Pullen Farm, Ullingswick, Herefordshire, HR1 3JQ**
Contacts: **PHONE/FAX (01432) 820370 MOBILE (07970) 650347**

**1 BOLD CROSS (IRE),** 12, b g Cape Cross (IRE)—Machikane Akaiito (IRE) **E. G. Bevan**
**2 BOLD DUKE,** 7, b g Sulamani (IRE)—Dominant Duchess **E. G. Bevan**
**3 BRON FAIR,** 6, b m Multiplex—Spectacular Hope **G. Williams**

### THREE-YEAR-OLDS

**4 BOLD GROVE,** b g Proclamation (IRE)—Trysting Grove (IRE) **E. G. Bevan**

**Assistant Trainer:** Michelle Byrom

---

## 43 MR GEORGE BEWLEY, Hawick

Postal: **South Dean Farm, Bonchester Bridge, Hawick, Roxburghshire, TD9 8TP**
Contacts: **PHONE (01450) 860651 MOBILE (07704) 924783**
**E-MAIL southdean.farm@btconnect.com**

**1 BRAE ON (IRE),** 7, ch g Presenting—Raphuca (IRE) **West Coast Racing Partnership**
**2** 4, B g Milan—Broken Gale (IRE) **G. T. Bewley**
**3 CARTERS REST,** 12, gr g Rock City—Yemaail (IRE) **Mrs D. Walton**
**4 CHICAGO OUTFIT (IRE),** 10, b g Old Vic—Lambourne Lace (IRE) **G. T. Bewley**
**5** 4, B g Westerner—Contessa Messina (IRE) **G. T. Bewley**
**6 CUMBRIAN FARMER,** 8, ch g Alflora (IRE)—Quark Top (FR) **Southdean Racing Club**
**7 DIAMOND D'AMOUR (IRE),** 9, gr g Danehill Dancer (IRE)—
Diamond Line (FR) **Mr J Hope,Mr K Twentyman & Mr J Gibson**
**8 HUNTERS BELT (IRE),** 11, b g Intikhab (USA)—Three Stars **Mr R. A. Fisher**
**9 INNIS SHANNON (IRE),** 5, br m Stowaway—Put On Hold (IRE) **Mrs Lesley Bewley & Mr John Gibson**
**10 MESSINA STRAIGHTS,** 7, br g Blueprint (IRE)—Calabria **G. T. Bewley**
**11** 4, B c Definite Article—Mrs Avery (IRE) **martingrayracing**
**12 OUR JOEY (IRE),** 7, b g Wareed (IRE)—Put On Hold (IRE) **John Gibson,Kevin Twentyman & Bewley**
**13 PICKLE AND TICKLE (IRE),** 5, ch g Shirocco (GER)—
Cream of Society (IRE) **Mr George Bewley & Mrs Sue Johnson**
**14 QUEST MAGIC (IRE),** 9, ch g Fantastic Quest (IRE)—Magic Sign (IRE) **West Coast Racing Partnership**
**15 REV UP RUBY,** 7, b m Revoque (IRE)—Kingennie **G. T. Bewley**
**16 ROMANY RYME,** 9, ch g Nomadic Way (USA)—Rakaposhi Ryme (IRE) **martingrayracing**
**17** 5, Gr m Mahler—Sika Trix (IRE) **G. T. Bewley**
**18 WHATS UP WOODY (IRE),** 10, b g Beneficial—Lady Noellel (IRE) **G. T. Bewley**

**Other Owners:** Mrs L. Bewley, Mr J. H. Gibson, Mr I. M. Gray, Mrs G. Gray, J. Hope, Mrs S. Johnson, Mr D. Kerr, Mr K. Twentyman, Mr A. L. Wilson.

**Jockey (NH):** Jonathon Bewley. **Amateur:** Miss Joanna Walton.

---

## 44 MR JOSEPH BEWLEY, Jedburgh

Postal: **Newhouse Cottage, Camptown, Jedburgh, Roxburghshire, TD8 6RW**
Contacts: **PHONE (01835) 840273 MOBILE (07758) 783910**
**E-MAIL bewley18@tiscali.co.uk**

**1 DARING EXIT,** 6, b g Exit To Nowhere (USA)—Aberdare **J. R. Bewley**
**2** 6, B g Overbury (IRE)—Evening Splash (IRE) **J. R. Bewley**
**3 MAJOR RIDGE (IRE),** 6, b g Indian Danehill (IRE)—Native Novel (IRE) **J. R. Bewley**

**Assistant Trainer:** Mrs K Bewley

**Conditional:** Callum Bewley.

## 45 MRS PIPPA BICKERTON, Almington

Postal: **Almington House, Pinfold Lane, Almington, Market Drayton, Shropshire, TF9 2QR**

1 **TROPICAL BACHELOR (IRE),** 9, b g Bachelor Duke (USA)—Tropical Coral (IRE) **Mrs P. F. Bickerton**
2 **TROPICAL SUNSHINE (IRE),** 7, b g Bachelor Duke (USA)—Tropical Coral (IRE) **Mrs P. F. Bickerton**

## 46 MR SAEED BIN SUROOR, Newmarket

Postal: **Godolphin Office, Snailwell Road, Newmarket, Suffolk, CB8 7YE**
Contacts: **PHONE (01638) 569956**
**WEBSITE www.godolphin.com**

1 **AFRICAN STORY,** 8, ch g Pivotal—Blixen (USA)
2 **AHZEEMAH (IRE),** 6, b g Dubawi (IRE)—Swiss Roll (IRE)
3 **BASEM,** 4, b c Pivotal—Gonbarda (GER)
4 **BE READY (IRE),** 4, ch c New Approach (IRE)—Call Later (USA)
5 **BRAVE BOY (IRE),** 4, b g Invincible Spirit (IRE)—Chan Tong (BRZ)
6 **CAVALRYMAN,** 9, b h Halling (USA)—Silversword (FR)
7 **CLON BRULEE (IRE),** 6, ch g Modigliani (USA)—Cloneden (IRE)
8 **DESERT SNOW,** 4, gr f Teofilo (IRE)—Requesting
9 **ELITE ARMY,** 4, b c Authorized (IRE)—White Rose (GER)
10 **EMIRATES FLYER,** 4, b g Acclamation—Galapagar (USA)
11 **EXCELLENT RESULT (IRE),** 5, b g Shamardal (USA)—Line Ahead (IRE)
12 **FAST DELIVERY,** 4, b g Authorized (IRE)—Rosenreihe (IRE)
13 **FIRST FLIGHT (IRE),** 4, b g Invincible Spirit (IRE)—First of Many
14 **FLAG WAR (GER),** 4, ch g Dubawi (IRE)—Fantastic Flame (IRE)
15 **FLIGHT OFFICER,** 4, b c New Approach (IRE)—Danuta (USA)
16 **FREE WHEELING (AUS),** 7, b g Ad Valorem (USA)—Miss Carefree (AUS)
17 **FUTURE REFERENCE (IRE),** 5, ch g Raven's Pass (USA)—Mike's Wildcat (USA)
18 **HAAFAGUINEA,** 5, ch g Haafhd—Ha'penny Beacon
19 **HIDDEN GOLD (IRE),** 4, b f Shamardal (USA)—Melikah (IRE)
20 **HUNTER'S LIGHT (IRE),** 7, ch h Dubawi (IRE)—Portmanteau
21 **MEMORIAL DAY (IRE),** 4, b c Cape Cross (IRE)—Reunite (IRE)
22 **MUSADDAS,** 5, b g Exceed And Excel (AUS)—Zuleika Dobson
23 **PRINCE BISHOP (IRE),** 8, ch g Dubawi (IRE)—North East Bay (USA)
24 **QUICK WIT,** 8, b g Oasis Dream—Roo
25 **ROYAL FLAG,** 5, b h New Approach (IRE)—Gonbarda (GER)
26 **ROYAL HISTORY,** 4, b c New Approach (IRE)—Tessa Reef (IRE)
27 **SAXO JACK (FR),** 5, b g King's Best (USA)—Gamma (FR)
28 **SECRET NUMBER,** 5, b h Raven's Pass (USA)—Mysterial (USA)
29 **SILENT BULLET (IRE),** 4, b g Exceed And Excel (AUS)—Veil of Silence (IRE)
30 **SKY HUNTER,** 5, b g Motivator—Pearl Kite (USA)
31 **SONGCRAFT (IRE),** 7, b g Singspiel (IRE)—Baya (USA)
32 **TAWHID,** 5, gr g Invincible Spirit (IRE)—Snowdrops
33 **THA'IR (IRE),** 5, b h New Approach (IRE)—Flashing Green
34 **TIJAN (IRE),** 4, b g Shamardal (USA)—Cherry Orchard (IRE)
35 **TRUE STORY,** 4, b br g Manduro (GER)—Tanzania (USA)
36 **VALIDUS,** 6, b g Zamindar (USA)—Victoire Finale
37 **WADI AL HATTAWI (IRE),** 5, b g Dalakhani (IRE)—Carisolo
38 **WILLING FOE (USA),** 8, b br g Dynaformer (USA)—Thunder Kitten (USA)
39 **WINDHOEK,** 5, b h Cape Cross (IRE)—Kahlua Kiss
40 **WINTER THUNDER,** 4, gr c New Approach (IRE)—Summer Sonnet

### THREE-YEAR-OLDS

41 **ALHANIA (USA),** b br f Medaglia d'Oro (USA)—Dessert (USA)
42 **ALWAYS SMILE (IRE),** b f Cape Cross (IRE)—Eastern Joy
43 **BEAUTIFUL ENDING,** ch f Exceed And Excel (AUS)—Pearl Kite (USA)
44 **BEAUTIFUL ROMANCE,** b f New Approach (IRE)—Mazuna (IRE)
45 **BEST EXAMPLE (USA),** ch g King's Best (USA)—Born Something (IRE)
46 **BEST OF TIMES,** b c Dubawi (IRE)—Nabati (USA)
47 **CLASSIC COLLECTION,** b c Cape Cross (IRE)—Local Spirit (USA)
48 **DREAM JOB,** b f Dubawi (IRE)—Coretta (IRE)

## MR SAEED BIN SUROOR - Continued

49 **ELITE GARDENS (USA),** ch f Speightstown (USA)—Flagrant (USA)
50 **EMIRATES AIRLINE,** b g Dubawi (IRE)—Moonlife (IRE)
51 **ERSHAADAAT (IRE),** b f Cape Cross (IRE)—Almansoora (USA)
52 **EXCELLENT TEAM,** b c Teofilo (IRE)—Seradim
53 **FINE VIEW (USA),** b f Arch (USA)—Nesselrode (USA)
54 **FLY WITH EMIRATES (IRE),** b c Lawman (FR)—Keriyka (IRE)
55 **FUTURE EMPIRE,** ch c New Approach (IRE)—Fann (USA)
56 **GLOBAL FORCE (IRE),** b g Shamardal (USA)—Pioneer Bride (USA)
57 **GOOD CONTACT (USA),** b c Teofilo (IRE)—Mayoress
58 **GOOD JUDGE (USA),** gr c Cape Cross (IRE)—Summer Fete (IRE)
59 **GOOD PLACE (USA),** ch f Street Cry (IRE)—Causeway Lass (AUS)
60 **GREAT JOB,** b f Makfi—Brattothecore (CAN)
61 **GREATEST JOURNEY,** ch g Raven's Pass (USA)—Sensationally
62 **HIGHEST LEVEL (IRE),** b g Invincible Spirit (IRE)—Halle Bop
63 **HIGHEST QUALITY (IRE),** b f Invincible Spirit (IRE)—Princess Taise (USA)
64 **HOLD TIGHT,** ch c Exceed And Excel (AUS)—Kangra Valley
65 **IJMAALY (IRE),** ch c Makfi—Wedding Gown
66 **IMPORTANT MESSAGE,** b br c New Approach (IRE)—Plaza (USA)
67 **IMPORTANT POINT (USA),** b br c Street Cry (IRE)—Zofzig (USA)
68 **INTERNATIONAL NAME,** ch g Iffraaj—Dove (IRE)
69 **KEEP IN LINE (GER),** b c Soldier Hollow—Kastila (GER)
70 **KEEP UP (GER),** b g Monsun (GER)—Katy Carr
71 **KEEPING QUIET (GER),** ch f Samum (GER)—Kapitol (GER)
72 **KHUSOOSY (USA),** b g Hard Spun (USA)—Elmaleeha
73 **LEADING DESIGN (IRE),** b f Dubawi (IRE)—Watership Crystal (IRE)
74 **LET'S GO (USA),** b br g Street Cry (IRE)—Lady Darshaan (IRE)
75 **LOCAL TIME,** b f Invincible Spirit (IRE)—Marie de Medici (USA)
76 **LOVELY MEMORY (IRE),** b f Shamardal (USA)—Folk Opera (IRE)
77 **MAFTOOL (USA),** b br c Hard Spun (USA)—With Intention (USA)
78 **MEDIA ROOM (USA),** b br f Street Cry (IRE)—Mialuna
79 **MOVIE SET (USA),** b br c Dubawi (IRE)—Short Skirt
80 **MUQARRED (USA),** b br g Speightstown (USA)—Bawaara (FR)
81 **MUZAKHREF (IRE),** b c Oasis Dream—Manayer (IRE)
82 **NEVER CHANGE (IRE),** b f New Approach (IRE)—Auspicious
83 **NEVER MISS,** b f Shamardal (USA)—Pictavia (IRE)
84 **NEW STRATEGY (IRE),** b g Lawman (FR)—Kate The Great
85 **NEW STYLE (USA),** b f Street Cry (IRE)—Land of Dreams
86 **RACING HISTORY (IRE),** b c Pivotal—Gonbarda (GER)
87 **STAY SILENT (IRE),** b f Cape Cross (IRE)—Veil of Silence (IRE)
88 **STAY STRONG (GER),** b c Monsun (GER)—Sasuela (GER)
89 **SUPER KID,** b c Exceed And Excel (AUS)—Crimson Year (USA)
90 **TAQWEEM (USA),** b br f Medaglia d'Oro (USA)—Hatheer (USA)
91 **THAWRAAT,** b f Cape Cross (IRE)—Raaya (USA)
92 **TIME CHECK (USA),** ch f Shamardal (USA)—Alizes (NZ)
93 **TRUE RESPECT (IRE),** b c Shamardal (USA)—Deveron (USA)
94 **VERY SPECIAL (IRE),** ch f Lope de Vega (IRE)—Danielli (IRE)
95 **WELL OFF (GER),** b c Monsun (GER)—Wells Present (GER)
96 **WILD STORM,** b f Dubawi (IRE)—The World
97 **WINTER HOUSE,** b g Cape Cross (IRE)—Villarrica (USA)
98 **WINTERS MOON (IRE),** ch f New Approach (IRE)—Summertime Legacy
99 **YAMLLIK,** b g King's Best (USA)—Anaamil (IRE)
100 **ZAMZAMA (IRE),** b f Shamardal (USA)—Zahrat Dubai

## TWO-YEAR-OLDS

101 **AFNAAN,** ch c 29/3 Raven's Pass (USA)—Almansoora (USA) (Bahri (USA))
102 **AHAZEEJ (IRE),** b f 6/4 Dubawi (IRE)—Albaraari (Green Desert (USA))
103 B br c 18/3 Hard Spun (USA)—Alzerra (UAE) (Pivotal)
104 B f 25/3 Street Cry (IRE)—Aryaamm (IRE) (Galileo (IRE))
105 Ch f 25/2 Dubawi (IRE)—Badminton (Zieten (USA))
106 B c 26/3 Hard Spun (USA)—Born Something (IRE) (Caerleon (USA))
107 B f 5/2 Poet's Voice—Cercle d'amour (USA) (Storm Cat (USA))
108 B c 8/4 Shamardal (USA)—Champagnelifestyle (Montjeu (IRE)) (111111)
109 Ch c 29/3 Poet's Voice—Classical Dancer (Dr Fong (USA)) (75000)
110 B c 23/2 Dubawi (IRE)—Comic (IRE) (Be My Chief (USA)) (1400000)

## MR SAEED BIN SUROOR - Continued

**111** B c 6/4 Dark Angel (IRE)—Cool Kitten (IRE) (One Cool Cat (USA))
**112** B c 7/4 Dansili—Counterclaim (Pivotal)
**113** B f 17/3 New Approach (IRE)—Danehill Dreamer (USA) (Danehill (USA)) (200000)
**114** Ch c 26/2 Dubawi (IRE)—Dash To The Front (Diktat) (800000)
**115** Ch f 28/1 Exceed And Excel (AUS)—Dove (IRE) (Sadler's Wells (USA))
**116 DUBAI FASHION (IRE),** b f 3/3 Dubawi (IRE)—Oriental Fashion (IRE) (Marju (IRE))
**117** B f 6/3 Dubawi (IRE)—Dubai Smile (USA) (Pivotal)
**118 EBTIHAAL (IRE),** ch c 4/2 Teofilo (IRE)—Dance Troupe (Rainbow Quest (USA))
**119** B c 20/2 Shamardal (USA)—Express Way (ARG) (Ahmad (ARG))
**120** Ch c 10/3 New Approach (IRE)—Garden City (FR) (Majorien) (158730)
**121** Ch c 7/3 Shamardal (USA)—Hometime (Dubai Destination (USA)) (253968)
**122** B f 28/1 Acclamation—Jeu de Plume (IRE) (Montjeu (IRE)) (142857)
**123 JUFN,** b c 2/2 Nayef (USA)—Deyaar (USA) (Storm Cat (USA))
**124** B c 6/5 Hard Spun (USA)—Laureldean Gale (USA) (Grand Slam (USA))
**125** B c 2/4 Dubawi (IRE)—Longing To Dance (Danehill Dancer (IRE)) (500000)
**126** B c 12/3 Sea The Stars (IRE)—Magic Tree (UAE) (Timber Country (USA))
**127** B c 1/3 Street Cry (IRE)—Measured Tempo (Sadler's Wells (USA))
**128** B br c 16/2 Distorted Humor (USA)—Michita (USA) (Dynaformer (USA))
**129** Ch c 20/4 Exceed And Excel (AUS)—Miss Brief (IRE) (Brief Truce (USA))
**130** Ch c 5/3 Dubawi (IRE)—Nadia (Nashwan (USA))
**131** B c 14/2 Teofilo (IRE)—Native Blue (Seeking The Gold (USA))
**132** B f 7/4 Street Cry (IRE)—Nawaiet (USA) (Zilzal (USA))
**133** B f 23/1 Exceed And Excel (AUS)—Nitya (FR) (Indian Ridge)
**134** B c 7/4 Dubawi (IRE)—Ocean Silk (USA) (Dynaformer (USA))
**135** B c 1/5 Shamardal (USA)—Perfidie (IRE) (Monsun (GER))
**136** B c 18/3 New Approach (IRE)—Pietra Santa (FR) (Acclamation) (134920)
**137** B f 26/1 Kodiac—Rekindled Cross (IRE) (Cape Cross (IRE)) (110000)
**138** B f 31/1 Teofilo (IRE)—Reunite (IRE) (Kingmambo (USA))
**139** B c 29/3 Sea The Stars (IRE)—Rhadegunda (Pivotal) (130000)
**140** B f 22/3 Invincible Spirit (IRE)—She Storm (IRE) (Rainbow Quest (USA))
**141** B f 11/2 Hard Spun (USA)—Storm Lily (USA) (Storm Cat (USA))
**142** Gr ro f 26/2 Street Cry (IRE)—Summer Fete (IRE) (Pivotal)
**143** Ch c 20/2 Iffraaj—Tadawul (USA) (Diesis) (95238)
**144** B c 3/4 New Approach (IRE)—Tanzania (USA) (Darshaan)
**145** B c 25/3 Shamardal (USA)—Time Honoured (Sadler's Wells (USA)) (206348)
**146** B c 14/3 New Approach (IRE)—Under The Rainbow (Fantastic Light (USA)) (160000)
**147** B br c 20/3 Poet's Voice—Vintage Gardenia (Selkirk (USA))
**148** Ch f 8/2 Pivotal—Zoowraa (Azamour (IRE))

---

## 47 MR KEVIN BISHOP, Bridgwater

Postal: **Barford Park Stables, Spaxton, Bridgwater, Somerset, TA5 1AF**
Contacts: **PHONE/FAX (01278) 671437 MOBILE (07816) 837610**
**E-MAIL hevbishop@hotmail.com**

**1 ALMAAS (USA),** 6, ch g Hard Spun (USA)—Summer Dream Girl (USA) **Miss H. P. Tate**
**2 CRUISE IN STYLE (IRE),** 9, b m Definite Article—Henrietta Street (IRE) **Mr S. G. Atkinson**
**3 FIELD FORCE,** 4, b g Champs Elysees—Fairy Steps **Miss H. P. Tate**
**4 INNOX PARK,** 5, b g Helissio (FR)—Redgrave Bay **W. Davies**
**5 JUST SPOT,** 8, ch m Baryshnikov (AUS)—Just Jasmine **K. Bishop**
**6 PRECIOUS GROUND,** 5, b g Helissio (FR)—Wild Ground (IRE) **Jim Kilduff & Ken Jones**
**7 SHADY GREY,** 5, gr m Helissio (FR)—Compton Amica (IRE) **Mr A. S. Meaden**
**8 SOMERSET JEM,** 6, b g Sir Harry Lewis (USA)—Monger Lane **Slabs & Lucan**
**9 TARA TAVEY (IRE),** 10, gr m Kayf Tara—Slieve League (IRE) **K. Bishop**
**10 UN DE CES JOURS (FR),** 7, b br g Robin des Champs (FR)—Sagarade (FR) **Miss H. P. Tate**
**11 WITHY MILLS,** 10, gr m Baryshnikov (AUS)—Gipsy Rose **Slabs & Lucan**

**Other Owners:** Mr Ken Jones, Mr K. J. Kilduff, Mr C. J. Macey, Mr C. H. Roberts.

**Assistant Trainer:** Heather Bishop

**Jockey (NH):** James Best. **Conditional:** Conor Smith.

## 48 MISS LINDA BLACKFORD, Tiverton

Postal: **Shortlane Stables, Rackenford, Tiverton, Devon, EX16 8EH**
Contacts: **PHONE (01884) 881589 MOBILE (07887) 947832**
**E-MAIL overthelast@talktalk.net WEBSITE www.overthelast.com**

1 **CHANCE ENCOUNTER (IRE),** 9, br g Anshan—Glittering Grit (IRE) **Over The Last Racing**
2 **LOUIS PHILLIPE (IRE),** 8, ch g Croco Rouge (IRE)—Presenting's Wager (IRE) **Over The Last Racing**
3 **MOUNTAIN OF MOURNE (IRE),** 6, ch g Mountain High (IRE)—Katies Native (IRE) **Over The Last Racing**
4 **SHADES OF AUTUMN (IRE),** 10, ch g Anshan—Be Right (IRE) **Mr M. P. Beer**
5 **THATS YER MAN (IRE),** 7, ch g Marignan (USA)—Glengarra Princess **Over The Last Racing**
6 **WOLFE MOUNTAIN (IRE),** 6, b g Mountain High (IRE)—Rachel's Choice (IRE) **Over The Last Racing**

**Other Owners:** Miss L. A. Blackford, Mr M. J. Vanstone.

**Assistant Trainer:** M. J. Vanstone

**Jockey (NH):** Nick Scholfield. **Conditional:** Micheal Nolan, Conor Smith. **Amateur:** Mr Joshua Guerriero, Mr S. Houlihan.

## 49 MR ALAN BLACKMORE, Hertford

Postal: **'Chasers', Stockings Lane, Little Berkhamsted, Hertford**
Contacts: **PHONE (01707) 875060 MOBILE (07803) 711453**

1 **COOL CHIEF,** 6, b g Sleeping Indian—Be Bop Aloha **A. G. Blackmore**
2 **MONROE PARK (IRE),** 10, b g Spectrum (IRE)—Paloma Bay (IRE) **A. G. Blackmore**
3 **OCCASIONALLY YOURS (IRE),** 11, b g Moscow Society (USA)—Kristina's Lady (IRE) **A. G. Blackmore**

**Assistant Trainer:** Mrs P. M. Blackmore

**Jockey (NH):** Marc Goldstein.

## 50 MR MICHAEL BLAKE, Trowbridge

Postal: **Staverton Farm, Trowbridge, Wiltshire, BA14 6PE**
Contacts: **PHONE (01225) 782327 MOBILE (07971) 675180**
**E-MAIL mblakestavertonfarm@btinternet.com**

1 **ABLE DASH,** 5, ch g Dutch Art—Evasive Quality (FR) **West Wilts Hockey Lads**
2 **AKSOUN (IRE),** 7, b g Red Ransom (USA)—Akdara (IRE) **The Moonlighters**
3 **CAPTAIN GEORGE (IRE),** 4, b g Bushranger (IRE)—High Society Girl (IRE) **Staverton Owners Group**
4 **CITY DREAMS (IRE),** 5, b m Rakti—Attymon Lill (IRE) **B Dunn & J Pierce**
5 **FLYING PHOENIX,** 7, b m Phoenix Reach (IRE)—Rasmalai **Mr F. Tieman**
6 **GRAPESHOT VERSE,** 6, ch m Grape Tree Road—Caballe (USA) **B. S. Hicks**
7 **LAMPS,** 8, b g Dynaformer (USA)—Conspiring (USA) **The Moonlighters**
8 **PICK A LITTLE,** 7, b g Piccolo—Little Caroline (IRE) **Mrs J. M. Haines**
9 **ROCKY REBEL,** 7, b g Norse Dancer (IRE)—Gulchina (USA) **Mrs J. M. Haines**
10 **STOW,** 10, ch g Selkirk (USA)—Spry **Mrs J. M. Haines**
11 **TYPICAL OSCAR (IRE),** 8, b g Oscar (IRE)—Kachina (IRE) **The Moonlighters**
12 **WELD ARAB (IRE),** 4, b g Shamardal (USA)—Itqaan (USA) **The Moonlighters**

**Other Owners:** M. J. Blake, Mrs S. E. Blake, Mrs V. A. Butcher, Mr R. C. Butcher, B. Dunn, Mr J. V. Pierce.

## 51 MR MICHAEL BLANSHARD, Upper Lambourn

Postal: **Lethornes Stables, Upper Lambourn, Hungerford, Berkshire, RG17 8QP**
Contacts: **PHONE (01488) 71091 FAX (01488) 73497 MOBILE (07785) 370093**
**E-MAIL blanshard.racing@btconnect.com WEBSITE www.michaelblanshard.co.uk**

1 **AMALFI DOUG (FR),** 5, gr g Network (GER)—Queissa (FR) **W. Garrett**
2 **CARRERA,** 5, b g Sixties Icon—Aileen's Gift (IRE) **D. Carroll**
3 **DISHY GURU,** 6, ch g Ishiguru (USA)—Pick A Nice Name **The Reignmakers**
4 **FAIR COMMENT,** 5, b m Tamayuz—Cliche (IRE) **Fair Comment Partnership**
5 **GALACTIC HALO,** 4, b f Rail Link—Star Cluster **Lady E. Mays-Smith**
6 **IVANHOE,** 5, b g Haafhd—Marysienka **The Lansdowners & N. Price**
7 **JUST DUCHESS,** 5, b m Avonbridge—Red Countess **Price, Poole, Williams**

## MR MICHAEL BLANSHARD - Continued

8 **JUST ISLA,** 5, ch m Halling (USA)—Island Rapture **D. A. Poole**
9 **JUST RUBIE,** 4, b f Refuse To Bend (IRE)—Island Rapture **D. A. Poole**
10 **MONASHKA BAY (IRE),** 4, b g Kodiac—River Style (IRE) **W. Murdoch**
11 **RED DRAGON (IRE),** 5, b g Acclamation—Delphie Queen (IRE) **Lady E. Mays-Smith**
12 **STELLARTA,** 4, b f Sakhee's Secret—Torgau (IRE) **Mr V. G. Ward**
13 **THE COMPOSER,** 13, b g Royal Applause—Superspring **A. D. Jones**
14 **TIGER STONE,** 4, b f Tiger Hill (IRE)—Lacandona (USA) **Ian Lewis & Partners 2**

### THREE-YEAR-OLDS

15 **GAVARNIE ENCORE,** b c Intikhab (USA)—Greeley Bright (USA) **Hill, Price & Williams**
16 **HAWKMEISTER (IRE),** gr g Mastercraftsman (IRE)—Lake Ladoga **Hawkmeister Partnership**
17 **REIGNING,** b f Sakhee's Secret—Raindrop **The Reignmakers**

### TWO-YEAR-OLDS

18 Ch f 30/4 Major Cadeaux—Cultural Role (Night Shift (USA))
19 **MAID OF MEDINA,** b f 6/4 Pastoral Pursuits—La Pantera (Captain Rio) (7000) **N. Price**
20 **PROMENARD,** b f 25/4 Champs Elysees—Coveted (Sinndar (IRE)) (4000) **The Reignmakers**
21 **PROSPERITEE,** b f 22/4 Paco Boy (IRE)—Goodie Twosues (Fraam) (7000) **J K Racing Club**
22 B f 1/2 Royal Applause—Snake's Head (Golden Snake (USA)) (3500) **The Reignmakers**
23 B f 28/4 Approve (IRE)—So Blissful (IRE) (Cape Cross (IRE)) (5000) **L. Hill & Partners**

**Other Owners:** Mr J. F. Baldwin, Mr M. Blanshard, Mr D. Cannings, Mr Lloyd Hill, Mr Ian Lewis, Mr Brian Mitchell, Mr Charles Phillips, Mr D. A. Poole, Mr M. J. Prescott, Mr Nick Price, Mrs Ginny Rusher, Mr R. T. Wilkins, Mr T. Williams.

---

**52**

## MR J. S. BOLGER, Carlow

Postal: **Glebe House, Coolcullen, Carlow, Ireland**
Contacts: **PHONE (00353) 56 4443150 (00353) 56 4443158 FAX (00353) 56 4443256**
**E-MAIL racing@jsb.ie**

1 **AERIALIST (IRE),** 4, ch c Sea The Stars (IRE)—Maoineach (USA) **Mrs J. S. Bolger**
2 **ALTESSE,** 4, ch f Hernando (FR)—Alvarita **Miss K. Rausing**
3 **CLUB WEXFORD (IRE),** 4, b c Lawman (FR)—Masnada (IRE) **Dave Bernie**
4 **INTENSICAL (IRE),** 4, b c Intense Focus (USA)—Christinas Letter (IRE) **Mrs J. S. Bolger**
5 **LIGHT HEAVY (IRE),** 6, ch h Teofilo (IRE)—Siamsa (USA) **Mrs J. S. Bolger**
6 **LOCH GARMAN (IRE),** 5, b h Teofilo (IRE)—Irish Question (IRE) **Mrs J. S. Bolger**
7 **NEWS AT SIX (IRE),** 5, ch h New Approach (IRE)—Dublin Six (USA) **Mrs J. S. Bolger**
8 **PARISH HALL (IRE),** 6, b h Teofilo (IRE)—Halla Siamsa (IRE) **Mrs J. S. Bolger**
9 **TOBANN (IRE),** 5, b m Teofilo (IRE)—Precipitous (IRE) **Mrs J. S. Bolger**

### THREE-YEAR-OLDS

10 **ABU SIMBEL,** b c Teofilo (IRE)—Hundred Year Flood (USA) **Godolphin**
11 **ALERTNESS (IRE),** b f Teofilo (IRE)—Napping (USA) **Mrs J. S. Bolger**
12 **ALGONQUIN,** gr c Archipenko (USA)—Alborada **Miss K. Rausing**
13 **ALTERNO (IRE),** b c Fastnet Rock (AUS)—Altarejos (IRE) **Mrs J. S. Bolger**
14 **ARDNOSACH (IRE),** b f Teofilo (IRE)—Ard Fheis (IRE) **Mrs J. S. Bolger**
15 **ARTSCAPE,** b c Iffraaj—Artisti **Godolphin**
16 **BOXING CLEVER (IRE),** b c Teofilo (IRE)—Sassy Gal (IRE) **Godolphin**
17 **CATCH WORD (IRE),** b c Raven's Pass (USA)—Cache Creek (IRE) **Godolphin**
18 **DEONTAS (IRE),** b f Teofilo (IRE)—Duaisbhanna (IRE) **Mrs J. S. Bolger**
19 **DUNQUIN (IRE),** b c Cape Cross (IRE)—Last Resort **Godolphin**
20 **EASTERN APPROACH (IRE),** ch c New Approach (IRE)—Key To Coolcullen (IRE) **Mrs J. S. Bolger**
21 **ELUSIVE APPROACH (IRE),** b f New Approach (IRE)—Soilse Na Cathrach (IRE) **Mrs J. S. Bolger**
22 **EMPEROR'S PALACE (IRE),** ch c Teofilo (IRE)—Lia (IRE) **Godolphin**
23 **FIELDS OF MAY (IRE),** ch f Intense Focus (USA)—Abigail's Aunt **Mrs June Judd**
24 **FLASHES OF THOUGHT (IRE),** b f Shamardal (USA)—Emirates Girl (USA) **Godolphin**
25 **GEORGIE HYDE,** b f Yeats (IRE)—Edabiya (IRE) **Mrs June Judd**
26 **GOLDEN INK (IRE),** ch c New Approach (IRE)—Solasai (USA) **Mrs J. S. Bolger**
27 **HALL OF FAME (IRE),** ch c Teofilo (IRE)—Halla Siamsa (IRE) **Mrs J. S. Bolger**
28 **INTENSE STYLE (IRE),** ch c Intense Focus (USA)—Style Queen (IRE) **Mrs J. S. Bolger**
29 **JALEO (GER),** ch c New Approach (IRE)—Jambalaya (GER) **Godolphin**
30 **KNOCKNAGREE (IRE),** b f Galileo (IRE)—Tyranny **Mrs Joan Brosnan**
31 **LEAFY APPROACH (IRE),** ch f New Approach (IRE)—Tiz The Whiz (USA) **Mrs J. S. Bolger**
32 **LETTER FOCUS (IRE),** b c Intense Focus (USA)—Christinas Letter (IRE) **Mrs J. S. Bolger**

## MR J. S. BOLGER - Continued

33 **LUCHT NA GAEILGE (IRE),** b f Teofilo (IRE)—Danemarque (AUS) **Mrs J. S. Bolger**
34 **LUCIDA (IRE),** b f Shamardal (USA)—Lura (USA) **Godolphin**
35 **MAINICIN (IRE),** b f Teofilo (IRE)—Luminaria (IRE) **Mrs J. S. Bolger**
36 **MCGUIGAN (IRE),** ch c Teofilo (IRE)—Scribonia (IRE) **Mrs J. S. Bolger**
37 **MESMERISM (USA),** b c Dubawi (IRE)—Bedazzle (USA) **Godolphin**
38 **MIDWIFERY (IRE),** b f Teofilo (IRE)—Night Visit **Godolphin**
39 **MORNING MIX (IRE),** b c Teofilo (IRE)—Fainne (IRE) **Mrs J. S. Bolger**
40 **NEW DIRECTION (IRE),** b c New Approach (IRE)—Gearanai (USA) **Mrs J. S. Bolger**
41 **NOVIS ADVENTUS (IRE),** b c New Approach (IRE)—Tiffed (USA) **Mrs J. S. Bolger**
42 **PARISH BOY,** gr c New Approach (IRE)—Requesting **Godolphin**
43 **PIROLO (IRE),** ch c Teofilo (IRE)—Zavaleta (IRE) **Mrs J. S. Bolger**
44 **PLEASCACH (IRE),** b f Teofilo (IRE)—Toirneach (USA) **Mrs J. S. Bolger**
45 **RING PRESENCE (IRE),** ch c Teofilo (IRE)—Maoineach (USA) **Mrs June Judd**
46 **ROBERTSTOWN (IRE),** b c Raven's Pass (USA)—Sogno Verde (IRE) **Godolphin**
47 **SALTHOUSE (IRE),** ch c Teofilo (IRE)—Sugarhoneybaby (IRE) **Godolphin**
48 **SELSKAR ABBEY (USA),** b c Street Sense (USA)—Saintly Hertfield (USA) **Mrs J. S. Bolger**
49 **SPIN POINT (IRE),** b c Pivotal—Daneleta (IRE) **Godolphin**
50 **STAIR AN DAMHSA (IRE),** ch f Teofilo (IRE)—National Swagger (IRE) **Mrs J. S. Bolger**
51 **STAR STREET (IRE),** b f Lawman (FR)—Manger Square (IRE) **Mrs J. S. Bolger**
52 **STEIP AMACH (IRE),** b f Vocalised (USA)—Ceist Eile (IRE) **Mrs J. S. Bolger**
53 **STELLAR GLOW (IRE),** b f Sea The Stars (IRE)—Glinting Desert (IRE) **Mrs Patricia Burns**
54 **STONEHART (IRE),** b c Shamardal (USA)—Loving Kindness (USA) **Godolphin**
55 **STOR MO CHROI (IRE),** b f Montjeu (IRE)—Landmark (USA) **Mrs Joan Brosnan**
56 **SUN FOCUS (IRE),** b c Intense Focus (USA)—Solas Na Greine (IRE) **Mrs J. S. Bolger**
57 **TAP FOCUS (IRE),** ch f Intense Focus (USA)—Gilded Butterfly (USA) **Mrs J. S. Bolger**
58 **TAPERING (USA),** gr c Invasor (ARG)—Unbridled Treasure (USA) **Mrs J. S. Bolger**
59 **VITALIZED (IRE),** b f Vocalised (USA)—Astralai (IRE) **Mrs J. S. Bolger**
60 **VOCAL NATION (IRE),** b f Vocalised (USA)—Six Nations (USA) **Mrs J. S. Bolger**
61 **VOCALISER (IRE),** b c Vocalised (USA)—Bring Back Matron (IRE) **Mrs J. S. Bolger**
62 **VOCIFEROUSLY (IRE),** b f Vocalised (USA)—Azra (IRE) **Mrs J. S. Bolger**
63 **VOICE OF CHOICE (IRE),** b c Holy Roman Emperor (IRE)—Dream On Buddy (IRE) **Mrs June Judd**

### TWO-YEAR-OLDS

64 **AN CAILIN ORGA (IRE),** ch f 19/3 Galileo (IRE)—Finsceal Beo (IRE) (Mr Greeley (USA)) **Mr M. D. Ryan**
65 **BALANCED APPROACH (IRE),** b c 4/4 New Approach (IRE)—
Soilse Na Cathrach (IRE) (Elusive City (USA)) **Mrs J. S. Bolger**
66 **BENIGNUS (IRE),** ch c 26/4 Galileo (IRE)—Saoire (Pivotal) **Mrs J. S. Bolger**
67 **BRONTIDE (IRE),** b c 10/3 Vocalised (USA)—Toirneach (USA) (Thunder Gulch (USA)) **Mrs J. S. Bolger**
68 **CAREER PATH (IRE),** b c 18/2 Lawman (FR)—Flea Cheoil (IRE) (Galileo (IRE)) **Mrs J. S. Bolger**
69 **CEOL AN GHRA (IRE),** b f 11/5 Teofilo (IRE)—Key To Coolcullen (IRE) (Royal Academy (USA)) **Mrs J. S. Bolger**
70 **CEOL NA NOG (IRE),** b f 29/3 Teofilo (IRE)—Ard Fheis (IRE) (Lil's Boy (USA)) **Mrs J. S. Bolger**
71 **CIRIN TOINNE (IRE),** ch f 8/6 Galileo (IRE)—Sister Angelina (USA) (Saint Ballado (CAN)) **Mrs J. S. Bolger**
72 **CLEAR CUT,** b c 1/3 Acclamation—Claiomh Solais (IRE) (Galileo (IRE)) (238095) **Mrs J. S. Bolger**
73 **CLINICAL APPROACH (IRE),** b c 29/1 New Approach (IRE)—
My Girl Sophie (USA) (Danzig (USA)) **Mrs J. S. Bolger**
74 **CONSTANCIO (IRE),** b c 29/5 Authorized (IRE)—Senora Galilei (IRE) (Galileo (IRE)) **Mrs J. S. Bolger**
75 B f 30/4 Dubawi (IRE)—Coretta (IRE) (Caerleon (USA)) **Godolphin**
76 **DYNAMIC FOCUS (IRE),** b f 27/3 Intense Focus (USA)—Super Hoofer (IRE) (Shamardal (USA)) **Mrs J. S. Bolger**
77 B c 4/3 Street Cry (IRE)—Firth of Lorne (IRE) (Danehill (USA)) **Godolphin**
78 **FIUNTACH (IRE),** ch f 23/2 Intense Focus (USA)—Ceist Eile (IRE) (Noverre (USA)) **Mrs J. S. Bolger**
79 **FOUNTAIN (IRE),** b c 1/3 Pour Moi (IRE)—Teolane (IRE) (Teofilo (IRE)) **Mrs J. S. Bolger**
80 **GEALAN (IRE),** b f 6/5 Intense Focus (USA)—Tintreach (CAN) (Vindication (USA)) **Mrs J. S. Bolger**
81 **GIRL OF THE HOUR,** b f 16/3 Makfi—American Spirit (IRE) (Rock of Gibraltar (IRE)) (90000) **Mrs June Judd**
82 **GLAMOROUS APPROACH (IRE),** ch f 7/2 New Approach (IRE)—
Maria Lee (IRE) (Rock of Gibraltar (IRE)) **Mrs J. S. Bolger**
83 B c 20/3 Teofilo (IRE)—Hall Hee (IRE) (Invincible Spirit (IRE)) **Godolphin**
84 B f 23/1 Invincible Spirit (IRE)—Her Own Kind (JPN) (Dubai Millennium) **Godolphin**
85 **HERALD THE DAWN (IRE),** b c 20/5 New Approach (IRE)—
Hymn of The Dawn (USA) (Phone Trick (USA)) **Mrs J. S. Bolger**
86 B f 27/4 Cape Cross (IRE)—Jealous Again (USA) (Trippi (USA)) **Godolphin**
87 B c 14/2 Sea The Stars (IRE)—Juno Marlowe (IRE) (Danehill (USA)) **Mrs June Judd**
88 B c 27/1 Street Cry (IRE)—Land of Dreams (Cadeaux Genereux) **Godolphin**
89 **LEAFY SHADE (IRE),** b f 5/3 New Approach (IRE)—Dublin Six (USA) (Kingmambo (USA)) **Mrs J. S. Bolger**
90 B c 25/4 Shamardal (USA)—Magna Graecia (IRE) (Warning) **Godolphin**
91 **MAOINEAS (IRE),** ch f 23/3 Teofilo (IRE)—Maoineach (USA) (Congaree (USA)) **Mrs J. S. Bolger**

## MR J. S. BOLGER - Continued

**92** B c 9/6 Teofilo (IRE)—Masnada (IRE) (Erins Isle) **Mrs J. S. Bolger**
**93** B c 24/3 Cape Cross (IRE)—Melikah (IRE) (Lammtarra (USA)) **Godolphin**
**94 OPEN HOUSE (IRE),** b c 11/3 Vocalised (USA)—Christinas Letter (IRE) (Galileo (IRE)) **Mrs J. S. Bolger**
**95 PARI PASU (IRE),** ch c 19/5 New Approach (IRE)—Tiz The Whiz (USA) (Tiznow (USA)) **Mrs J. S. Bolger**
**96 PARTY FOR EVER (IRE),** b f 2/5 Iffraaj—Miss Party Line (USA) (Phone Trick (USA)) (210000) **Mrs June Judd**
**97 RIOGA (IRE),** ch f 18/5 New Approach (IRE)—Groves Royal (USA) (Royal Academy (USA)) **Mrs J. S. Bolger**
**98 ROUND TWO (IRE),** b c 27/3 Teofilo (IRE)—Khazina (USA) (Kingmambo (USA)) **Mrs J. S. Bolger**
**99 RUNMHAR (IRE),** b f 12/4 Discreetly Mine (USA)—Excuse Me (USA) (Distorted Humor (USA)) **Mrs J. S. Bolger**
**100** Ch c 13/1 Distorted Humor (USA)—Sadler's Secretary (IRE) (Sadler's Wells (USA)) (258175) **Godolphin**
**101** B c 17/5 Henrythenavigator (USA)—Saintly Hertfield (USA) (Saint Ballado (CAN)) **Mrs J. S. Bolger**
**102 SANUS PER AQUAM (IRE),** b c 8/4 Teofilo (IRE)—Fainne (IRE) (Peintre Celebre (USA)) **Mrs J. S. Bolger**
**103** Ch c 7/3 Street Cry (IRE)—Say No Now (IRE) (Refuse To Bend (IRE)) (100000) **Godolphin**
**104 SIAMSAIOCHT (IRE),** b f 17/5 Teofilo (IRE)—Halla Siamsa (IRE) (Montjeu (IRE)) **Mrs J. S. Bolger**
**105 SPECIAL FOCUS (IRE),** b f 28/4 Intense Focus (USA)—Arjooch (IRE) (Marju (IRE)) **Mrs J. S. Bolger**
**106 SPLIT DECISION (IRE),** b f 1/4 Teofilo (IRE)—Night Visit (Sinndar (IRE)) (753967) **Mrs J. S. Bolger**
**107 TAISCE NAISIUNTA (IRE),** b f 3/2 Lawman (FR)—Ciste Naisiunta (IRE) (Galileo (IRE)) **Mrs J. S. Bolger**
**108** B c 3/3 Street Cry (IRE)—Tashelka (FR) (Mujahid (USA)) **Godolphin**
**109 THEODORICO (IRE),** b c 21/2 Teofilo (IRE)—Yes Oh Yes (USA) (Gone West (USA)) **Mrs J. S. Bolger**
**110** B c 11/4 Pivotal—Turmalin (IRE) (Dalakhani (IRE)) (150000) **Godolphin**
**111 TURRET ROCKS (IRE),** b f 8/4 Fastnet Rock (AUS)—Beyond Compare (IRE) (Galileo (IRE)) **Mrs J. S. Bolger**
**112 TWILIGHT PAYMENT (IRE),** b c 6/5 Teofilo (IRE)—Dream On Buddy (IRE) (Oasis Dream) **Mrs J. S. Bolger**
**113** B f 20/5 Dansili—Tyranny (Machiavellian (USA)) (700000) **Solis / Litt Bloodstock**
**114 VERBOSITY (IRE),** b f 25/1 Vocalised (USA)—Stitch Night (IRE) (Whipper (USA)) **Mrs J. S. Bolger**
**115 VOCAL ADVOCATE (IRE),** b c 20/1 Vocalised (USA)—
Matilda Moreland (IRE) (Invincible Spirit (IRE)) **Mrs J. S. Bolger**
**116 VOCAL CRITIC (IRE),** b c 13/4 Vocalised (USA)—Amhrasach (IRE) (Teofilo (IRE)) **Mrs J. S. Bolger**
**117 WAY OF THE SEA (IRE),** b c 1/4 Fastnet Rock (AUS)—Oiche Ghealai (IRE) (Galileo (IRE)) **Mrs J. S. Bolger**
**118 WEXFORD DREAMING (IRE),** b c 19/4 Dream Ahead (USA)—Saor Sinn (IRE) (Galileo (IRE)) **Mrs J. S. Bolger**
**119 WEXFORD VOICE (IRE),** b c 21/3 Vocalised (USA)—
Have A Heart (IRE) (Daggers Drawn (USA)) (15872) **Mrs J. S. Bolger**

**Other Owners:** Mr John Corcoran, Mrs John McCormack, Mr Tom McGurk, Mr Paddy Spain.

**Jockey (flat):** R. P. Cleary, Kevin Manning, R. P. Whelan. **Apprentice:** David Fitzpatrick, Daniel Redmond.

---

## 53 MRS MYRIAM BOLLACK-BADEL, Lamorlaye

Postal: **20 Rue Blanche, 60260 Lamorlaye, France**
Contacts: **(0033) 9774 89044 FAX (0033) 3442 13367 MOBILE (0033) 6108 09347**
**E-MAIL myriam.bollack@gmail.com WEBSITE www.myriam-bollack.com**

**1 COCKTAIL QUEEN (IRE),** 5, b m Motivator—Premier Prize **J. C. Smith**
**2 IRON SPIRIT (FR),** 5, b h Turtle Bowl (IRE)—Irish Vintage (FR) **M. Motschmann**
**3 NORSE KING (FR),** 6, ch g Norse Dancer (IRE)—Angel Wing **J. C. Smith**
**4 OUTBACK RACER (FR),** 4, b c Aussie Rules (USA)—Mary Linda **J. C. Smith**
**5 ROYAL PRIZE,** 5, ch g Nayef (USA)—Spot Prize (USA) **J. C. Smith**
**6 SLICE OF LIFE (FR),** 5, b m Nombre Premier—Cortiguera **P. Stein**
**7 ZIMRI (FR),** 11, b g Take Risks (FR)—Zayine (IRE) **Mme M. Bollack-Badel**
**8 ZYGMUNT (FR),** 4, ch c Vespone (IRE)—Zython (FR) **Ecurie Noel Forgeard**

### THREE-YEAR-OLDS

**9 ALBICOCCA (FR),** ch f Naaqoos—Ashley River **P. Fellous**
**10 BRONZINO (FR),** b c Creachadoir (IRE)—Berenice Pancrisia (FR) **Mme M. Bollack-Badel**
**11 EARTHRISE,** gr f Naaqoos—Divine Promesse (FR) **M. Motschmann**
**12 GALEOTTO (FR),** b c Naaqoos—Hay Amor (ARG) **Mme M. Bollack-Badel**
**13 HERACLEA (FR),** b f Panis (USA)—Hokey Pokey (FR) **M. Motschmann**
**14 KICK DOWN (IRE),** b f Arcano (IRE)—Star of Siligo (USA) **Mrs A. Michel**
**15 LADY JULIET,** b br f Authorized (IRE)—Lady Liesel **Mrs D. Swinburn**
**16 SAINTE ADELE (FR),** b f Naaqoos—Sambala (IRE) **Ecurie Noel Forgeard**
**17 VICTORY GARDEN,** ch f New Approach (IRE)—White House **Mrs D. Swinburn**
**18 VIKING RUNNER (FR),** b f Norse Dancer (IRE)—Speed of Sound **J. C. Smith**
**19 WAVE POWER (FR),** b c Motivator—Wave Goodbye (FR) **J. C. Smith**
**20 ZAHAB (FR),** b f Naaqoos—Zython (FR) **Ecurie Noel Forgeard**
**21 ZAMIYR (FR),** b f Naaqoos—Zayine (IRE) **A. Badel**

## MRS MYRIAM BOLLACK-BADEL - Continued

### TWO-YEAR-OLDS

22 **DESERT FORTUNE (FR),** b c 8/5 Kendargent (FR)—Saharienne (USA) (A P Indy (USA)) (25396) **J. C. Smith**
23 **DORSET DREAM (FR),** b f 6/5 Canford Cliffs (IRE)—Fontcia (FR) (Enrique) (27777) **J. C. Smith**
24 **ELUSIVE GIRL (FR),** b f 28/3 Elusive City—Wave Goodbye (Linamix) **J. C. Smith**
25 **GRAND VOILE (FR),** b f 2/5 Exceed And Excel (AUS)—Blue Sail (USA) (Kingmambo (USA)) (46031) **J. Dunne**
26 **INCITATOR (FR),** b c 4/4 Motivator—Summer Wave (IRE) (King's Best (USA)) **Ecurie Noel Forgeard**
27 **KORIANDRE (FR),** b f 10/4 Kouroun—Knout (Kendor) **Mrs G. de Chatelperron**
28 **SHAPOUR (FR),** b c 13/5 Siyouni (FR)—
Super Anna (FR) (Anabaa (USA)) (39682) **M. Motschmann / S. Oschmann**
29 **SIRINSKA (FR),** b c 1/1 Sir Percy—Rinskia (Bering) (27777) **J. C. Smith**

**Assistant Trainer:** Alain Badel

**Jockey (flat):** Alexis Badel.

---

## 54 MR MARTIN BOSLEY, Chalfont St Giles

Postal: **Bowstridge Farm, Bowstridge Lane, Chalfont St. Giles, Buckinghamshire, HP8 4RF**
Contacts: **PHONE (01494) 875533 FAX (01494) 875533 MOBILE (07778) 938040**
**E-MAIL martin@martinbosley.com WEBSITE www.martinbosleyracing.com**

1 **AIR OF GLORY (IRE),** 5, ch g Shamardal (USA)—Balloura (USA) **Walid & Paula Marzouk**
2 **ALFRESCO,** 11, b g Mtoto—Maureena (IRE) **Mrs A. M. Riney**
3 **BURNT CREAM,** 8, b m Exceed And Excel (AUS)—Basbousate Nadia **Mrs P. M. Brown**
4 **CAROBELLO (IRE),** 8, b g Luso—Vic's Queen (IRE) **Mr I. Herbert**
5 **COMPTON MAGIC,** 4, b g Compton Place—Phantasmagoria **Mr J. Patton**
6 **EXCEEDING POWER,** 4, b g Exceed And Excel (AUS)—Extreme Beauty (USA) **The Chalfonts**
7 **JOYFUL RISK (IRE),** 5, ch m Kheleyf (USA)—Joyfullness (USA) **Mrs B. M. Cuthbert**
8 **MISS BISCOTTI,** 7, ch m Emperor Fountain—Bellacaccia (IRE) **Mrs C. B. Herbert**
9 **TOPTHORN,** 9, gr g Silver Patriarch (IRE)—Miss Traxdata **Bosley - Vollaro - Clark**

### THREE-YEAR-OLDS

10 **NAMED ASSET,** b c Invincible Spirit (IRE)—Sabria (USA) **The Chalfonts**

### TWO-YEAR-OLDS

11 B c 29/1 Tagula (IRE)—Dualagi (Royal Applause) **Bayard Racing**

**Other Owners:** Mr M. R. Bosley, Mr G. F. Clark, Mr J. R. Hazeldine, Mr Walid Marzouk, Mrs Paula Marzouk, Ms L. Vollaro, Mrs K. Whitaker.

**Jockey (flat):** George Baker, Robert Havlin. **Amateur:** Mr Zac Baker.

---

## 55 MR MARCO BOTTI, Newmarket

Postal: **Prestige Place, Snailwell Road, Newmarket, Suffolk, CB8 7DP**
Contacts: **PHONE (01638) 662416 FAX (01638) 662417 MOBILE (07775) 803007**
**E-MAIL office@marcobotti.co.uk WEBSITE www.marcobotti.co.uk**

1 **AL THAKHIRA,** 4, b f Dubawi (IRE)—Dahama **Al Shaqab Racing UK Limited**
2 **CERUTTY (IRE),** 4, b c Shamardal (USA)—Mouriyana (IRE) **Mrs C. McStay**
3 **COUNTER RIDGE (SAF),** 6, b m Tiger Ridge (USA)—Counterpoise (SAF) **Australian Thoroughbred Bloodstock**
4 **DE RIGUEUR,** 7, b g Montjeu (IRE)—Exclusive **Mr N. A. Jackson**
5 **DRAGOON GUARD (IRE),** 4, b c Jeremy (USA)—Elouges (IRE) **K. A. Dasmal**
6 **EDU QUERIDO (BRZ),** 6, ch h Holzmeister (USA)—Kournikova (BRZ) **Mr S. Friborg**
7 **EMARATIYA ANA (IRE),** 4, b f Excellent Art—Tina Heights **A. Al Shaikh**
8 **ENERGIA DAVOS (BRZ),** 7, gr g Torrential (USA)—Star Brisingamen (USA) **Mr S. Friborg**
9 **ENERGIA FLAVIO (BRZ),** 5, gr h Agnes Gold (JPN)—Lira da Guanabara (BRZ) **Mr S. Friborg**
10 **ENERGIA FOX (BRZ),** 5, ch m Agnes Gold (JPN)—Super Eletric (BRZ) **Mr S. Friborg**
11 **ENERGIA FRIBBY (BRZ),** 5, b m Agnes Gold (JPN)—Karla Dora (BRZ) **Mr S. Friborg**
12 **EURO CHARLINE,** 4, b f Myboycharlie (IRE)—Eurolink Artemis **Team Valor LLC**
13 **FOXTROT ROMEO (IRE),** 6, b g Danehill Dancer (IRE)—Hawala (IRE) **Mr W. A. Tinkler**
14 **FRONT RUN (IRE),** 4, b c Amadeus Wolf—Prima Volta **Mr A. N. Mubarak**
15 **GOLDEN STEPS (FR),** 4, b g Footstepsinthesand—Kocooning (IRE) **Mr M. A. A. Al-Mannai**
16 **GRENDISAR (IRE),** 5, b h Invincible Spirit (IRE)—Remarkable Story **Mr M. A. M. Albousi Alghufli**

## MR MARCO BOTTI - Continued

17 **GREY MIRAGE,** 6, b g Oasis Dream—Grey Way (USA) **G. Manfredini**
18 **HASOPOP (IRE),** 5, b g Haatef (USA)—Convenience (IRE) **G. Manfredini**
19 **LACAN (IRE),** 4, b c New Approach (IRE)—Invincible Isle (IRE) **G. Manfredini**
20 **LADY DUTCH,** 4, b f Dutch Art—Monjouet (IRE) **Immobiliare Casa Paola SRL**
21 **LATIN CHARM (IRE),** 4, b g Cape Cross (IRE)—Di Moi Oui **Grundy Bloodstock Ltd**
22 **LINTON (AUS),** 9, gr g Galileo (IRE)—Heather (NZ) **Mr S. Friborg**
23 **MASAMAH (IRE),** 9, GR G Exceed And Excel (AUS)—Bethesda
24 **MIN ALEMARAT (IRE),** 4, ch g Galileo (IRE)—Baraka (IRE) **A. Al Shaikh**
25 **MOOHAARIB (IRE),** 4, b c Oasis Dream—Evita **Sheikh M. B. K. Al Maktoum**
26 **MOUNT ATHOS (IRE),** 8, B G Montjeu (IRE)—Ionian Sea
27 **NAADIRR (IRE),** 4, b c Oasis Dream—Beach Bunny (IRE) **Sheikh M. B. K. Al Maktoum**
28 **NORAB (GER),** 4, b g Galileo (IRE)—Night Woman (GER) **Mr M. Keller**
29 **PATENTAR (FR),** 4, b c Teofilo (IRE)—Poppets Sweetlove **Saleh Al Homaizi & Imad Al Sagar**
30 **QUIET WARRIOR (IRE),** 4, b g Kodiac—Pretty Woman (IRE) **Global First Racing & Bloodstock**
31 **SEISMOS (IRE),** 7, ch g Dalakhani (IRE)—Sasuela (GER) **Australian Thoroughbred Bloodstock**
32 **SOLAR DEITY (IRE),** 6, b h Exceed And Excel (AUS)—Dawn Raid (IRE) **Mr G Manfredini & Mr A Tinkler**
33 **SPIFER (IRE),** 7, gr g Motivator—Zarawa (IRE) **Mrs L. Botti**
34 **STONECUTTER (IRE),** 4, gr c Mastercraftsman (IRE)—
Sparkle of Stones (FR) **Mrs J Magnier, Mr D Smith & Mr M Tabor**
35 **TAC DE BOISTRON (FR),** 8, gr g Take Risks (FR)—Pondiki (FR) **Australian Thoroughbred Bloodstock**

## THREE-YEAR-OLDS

36 **AABIR (IRE),** b c Invincible Spirit (IRE)—Phillippa (IRE) **Sheikh M. B. K. Al Maktoum**
37 **ACCLAMATE (IRE),** b c Acclamation—Rouge Noir (USA) **Mr G Manfredini & Mr J Allison**
38 **AJMAL IHSAAS,** b f Acclamation—Secret History (USA) **Sheikh M. B. K. Al Maktoum**
39 **ALFAJER,** b f Mount Nelson—Sakhee's Song (IRE) **Saleh Al Homaizi & Imad Al Sagar**
40 **ASTRELLE (IRE),** br f Makfi—Miss Mariduff (USA) **Sheikh M. B. K. Al Maktoum**
41 **BALAYAGE (IRE),** b f Invincible Spirit (IRE)—Shamwari Lodge (IRE) **Mr M. Keller**
42 **BORAK (IRE),** b g Kodiac—Right After Moyne (IRE) **Saleh Al Homaizi & Imad Al Sagar**
43 **BRAVO ZOLO (IRE),** b c Rip Van Winkle (IRE)—Set Fire (IRE) **Mr M. A. M. Albousi Alghufli**
44 **CAPTAIN KOKO,** b g Selkirk (USA)—Lady Artemisia (IRE) **Mr J. Allison**
45 **CRYSTALIN (IRE),** b f Arcano (IRE)—Loose Julie (IRE) **Fabfive**
46 **DEIRA MIRACLE (IRE),** b f Duke of Marmalade (IRE)—Naval Affair (IRE) **Ahmad Abdulla Al Shaikh & Co**
47 **DREAM ON STAGE,** b g Aqlaam—Star On Stage **Mr Manfredini & Grundy Bloodstock**
48 **EMERALD (ITY),** b c High Chaparral (IRE)—Ekta **La Tesa SPA**
49 **FAITH MATTERS (IRE),** ch f Arcano (IRE)—Luanas Pearl (IRE) **Mr C. McHale**
50 **FANCIFUL ANGEL (IRE),** gr c Dark Angel (IRE)—Fanciful Dancer **Scuderia Blueberry SRL**
51 **GALILEANO (IRE),** ch f Galileo (IRE)—Flamingo Sea (USA) **Mr R. Ng**
52 **GENTLEMUSIC (FR),** b f Gentlewave (IRE)—Makhalina (IRE) **Mr U. M. Saini Fasanotti**
53 **GIANTOUCH (USA),** b g Giant's Causeway (USA)—Beauty O' Gwaun (IRE) **G. Manfredini**
54 **GIN SLING,** b c Shamardal (USA)—Gino's Spirits **Newsells Park Stud Limited**
55 **GO PACKING GO,** br g Equiano (FR)—Khubza **Mr M. B. Lee**
56 **HASSAH,** b f Halling (USA)—Regent's Park **Team Valor LLC**
57 **HAYBA,** b f Invincible Spirit (IRE)—Loch Jipp (USA) **Qatar Racing & Essafinaat**
58 **KASSBAAN,** br g Kodiac—Town And Gown **G. Manfredini**
59 **LADY ESTELLA (IRE),** b f Equiano (FR)—Lady Scarlett **Newsells Park Stud Limited**
60 **LEXI'S RED DEVIL (IRE),** b f Danehill Dancer (IRE)—Challow Hills (USA) **Dr M. B. Q. S. Koukash**
61 **LUNA MISSION (IRE),** b f Acclamation—Bowness **Mr J. Allison**
62 **MERHOOB (IRE),** b c Cape Cross (IRE)—Lady Slippers (IRE) **Sheikh M. B. K. Al Maktoum**
63 **MICAELA BASTIDAS,** ch f Rip Van Winkle (IRE)—Mime Artist (USA) **El Catorce**
64 **MUWAFFAK (FR),** b c Shamardal (USA)—Dancing Lady (FR) **Mr A. N. Mubarak**
65 **PLAISIR (IRE),** b f Elusive City (USA)—Sea Sex Sun **Mr U. M. Saini Fasanotti**
66 **PUISSANT (IRE),** b c Galileo (IRE)—Elletelle (IRE) **Puissant Stable**
67 **QATAR ROAD (FR),** ch c Footstepsinthesand—Amarinda (GER) **Mr A. N. Mubarak**
68 **SAMMY'S WARRIOR,** b c Myboycharlie (IRE)—Tahfeez (IRE) **Global First Racing & Bloodstock**
69 **SCIUSTREE,** b c Royal Applause—Tia Mia **Scuderia Rencati SRL**
70 **SHARP SAILOR (USA),** b c Henrythenavigator (USA)—Lady Ilsley (USA) **Mr R. Ng**
71 **SOLUBLE (GER),** b c Galileo (IRE)—So Squally (GER) **Mr M. Keller**
72 **TALAWAT,** b f Cape Cross (IRE)—Queen of Mean **Saleh Al Homaizi & Imad Al Sagar**
73 **VIVO PER LEI (IRE),** b f Mastercraftsman (IRE)—Sabancaya **Scuderia Effevi SRL**
74 **WAALEEF,** ch c Nayef (USA)—Ulfah (USA) **Sheikh M. B. K. Al Maktoum**
75 **WARM RECEPTION,** b f Acclamation—Feel **Scuderia Vittadini SRL**
76 **WINTER SERENADE (ITY),** b f Fastnet Rock (AUS)—Wickwing **La Tesa SPA**

## MR MARCO BOTTI - Continued

**77** **WOLF ALBARARI,** ch c Medicean—Pure Song **Mrs A. D. Fox**
**78** **YEENAAN (FR),** gr c Rip Van Winkle (IRE)—Japan (GER) **Sheikh M. B. K. Al Maktoum**

## TWO-YEAR-OLDS

**79** B f 3/3 Exceed And Excel (AUS)—Alamouna (IRE) (Indian Ridge) (52000) **Sheikh M. B. K. Al Maktoum**
**80** B c 29/4 Thewayyouare (USA)—Ann Kastan (Red Ransom (USA)) (13333) **H.E. S. Al-kaabi**
**81** **ANTIOCO (IRE),** b c 8/3 Motivator—Haraplata (GER) (Platini (GER)) (39000) **Mr M. Azzam**
**82** Ch c 7/5 Rip Van Winkle (IRE)—Apache Dream (IRE) (Indian Ridge) (85000)
**83** B f 27/2 Azamour (IRE)—Ares Flight (IRE) (Hernando (FR)) **Niarchos Family**
**84** Ch c 15/2 Zoffany (IRE)—Attalea (IRE) (Monsun (GER)) (34126)
**85** **BOHEMIAN SYMPHONY,** b f 19/2 Paco Boy (IRE)—Wish You Luck (Dubai Destination (USA)) (10476)
**86** **CANFORD THOMPSON,** b c 12/4 Canford Cliffs (IRE)—
Sadie Thompson (IRE) (King's Best (USA)) (16000) **Scuderia Blueberry SRL**
**87** B c 6/2 Canford Cliffs (IRE)—
Child Bride (USA) (Coronado's Quest (USA)) (133333) **Saleh Al Homaizi & Imad Al Sagar**
**88** **COUP DE MAIN (IRE),** b f 3/3 Oasis Dream—Termagant (IRE) (Powerscourt)
**89** B c 2/3 Champs Elysees—Dahama (Green Desert (USA)) (320000) **Al Shaqab Racing UK Limited**
**90** **DIVINE JOY,** b f 3/3 Rip Van Winkle (IRE)—Joyeaux (Mark of Esteem (IRE)) (28000) **Mr W. A. Tinkler**
**91** **DREAM FACTORY (IRE),** ch c 19/2 Manduro (GER)—Istishaara (USA) (Kingmambo (USA))
**92** **DREAM LORD (IRE),** ch c 10/2 Dream Ahead (USA)—
Silent Secret (IRE) (Dubai Destination (USA)) (60000) **K. A. Dasmal**
**93** B f 25/1 Zamindar (USA)—Dubai Media (CAN) (Songandaprayer (USA)) **A. Al Shaikh**
**94** Ch c 25/3 Archipenko (USA)—Empire Rose (ARG) (Sunray Spirit (USA)) **Sheikh M. B. K. Al Maktoum**
**95** **ENCORE MOI,** b f 15/4 Exceed And Excel (AUS)—Di Moi Oui (Warning) **Scuderia Vittadini SRL**
**96** **FEEL THIS MOMENT (IRE),** b c 14/3 Tamayuz—Rugged Up (IRE) (Marju (IRE)) (24761) **Mrs L. Botti**
**97** **FETCH,** b f 31/1 Arch (USA)—Fresnay (Rainbow Quest (USA)) **Scuderia Vittadini SRL**
**98** **FREESIA (IRE),** b f 8/5 Dansili—Field of Hope (IRE) (Selkirk (USA)) (160000) **Grundy Bloodstock Ltd**
**99** **GERRARD'S QUEST,** b c 23/4 Captain Gerrard (IRE)—
Ryan's Quest (IRE) (Mukaddamah (USA)) (13000) **Scuderia Blueberry SRL**
**100** Br f 9/4 Poet's Voice—Hear My Cry (USA) (Giant's Causeway (USA)) (37300) **Sheikh M. B. K. Al Maktoum**
**101** **IL SASSICAIA,** b c 7/3 Dick Turpin (IRE)—Step Fast (USA) (Giant's Causeway (USA))
**102** B c 9/1 Pour Moi (IRE)—
Island Dreams (USA) (Giant's Causeway (USA)) (135000) **Saleh Al Homaizi & Imad Al Sagar**
**103** **MILETAKETHEBALL (IRE),** b c 8/3 Vale of York (IRE)—Carrauntoohil (IRE) (Marju (IRE)) (9500) **Fabfive**
**104** **MISTY LORD (IRE),** b c 20/2 Lilbourne Lad (IRE)—Misty Night (IRE) (Galileo (IRE)) (51428) **Fabfive**
**105** **NAYEF DREAM,** b f 30/1 Nayef (USA)—Dream Belle (Oasis Dream) **Scuderia Blueberry SRL**
**106** B f 31/1 Shamardal (USA)—Nouriya (Danehill Dancer (IRE)) **Saleh Al Homaizi & Imad Al Sagar**
**107** **ONESIE (IRE),** b c 20/4 Dandy Man (IRE)—Easee On (IRE) (Hawk Wing (USA)) (38095) **Mr W. A. Tinkler**
**108** Ch c 18/2 Zoffany (IRE)—Opinionated (IRE) (Dubai Destination (USA)) (19047) **Sheikh M. B. K. Al Maktoum**
**109** **PACOMMAND,** b c 28/4 Paco Boy (IRE)—Indian Story (IRE) (Indian Ridge) (34126) **G. Manfredini**
**110** **PIACERE (IRE),** b f 10/2 New Approach (IRE)—
Aneedah (IRE) (Invincible Spirit (IRE)) (220000) **The Great Partnership**
**111** **PLENARY (USA),** ch c 6/1 Kitten's Joy (USA)—
Southern Alibi (USA) (Elusive Quality (USA)) (238095) **Mr M. Keller**
**112** B c 26/2 Fastnet Rock (AUS)—Qilaada (USA) (Bernardini (USA)) **Sheikh M. B. K. Al Maktoum**
**113** Br f 17/3 Cape Cross (IRE)—Raihana (AUS) (Elusive Quality (USA)) **Sheikh M. B. K. Al Maktoum**
**114** **RECONSIDER (IRE),** ch c 25/3 Approve (IRE)—Singora Lady (IRE) (Intikhab (USA)) (15872)
**115** B c 7/3 Fastnet Rock (AUS)—Reem (AUS) (Galileo (IRE)) **Sheikh M. B. K. Al Maktoum**
**116** **RIAL (IRE),** b f 31/1 Dark Angel (IRE)—Coin Box (Dubai Destination (USA)) (26190)
**117** **SAHALIN,** b f 15/1 Red Rocks (IRE)—Tamathea (IRE) (Barathea (IRE)) **Immobiliare Casa Paola SRL**
**118** **SISANIA (IRE),** ch f 4/2 Mastercraftsman (IRE)—Avril Rose (IRE) (Xaar) **Scuderia Rencati SRL**
**119** Ch f 9/3 Dutch Art—Strictly (USA) (Fusaichi Pegasus (USA)) (24000) **Sheikh M. B. K. Al Maktoum**
**120** **SURBETT (IRE),** b c 5/2 Rock of Gibraltar (IRE)—
Causeway Queen (IRE) (Giant's Causeway (USA)) (67460) **Scuderia Rencati SRL**
**121** **TRISHULI ROCK (IRE),** b f 18/4 Fastnet Rock (AUS)—Trishuli (Indian Ridge) (16000) **Scuderia Blueberry SRL**
**122** B f 21/3 Oasis Dream—Ulfah (USA) (Danzig (USA)) **Sheikh M. B. K. Al Maktoum**
**123** **VELVET REVOLUTION,** ch c 2/5 Pivotal—
Gino's Spirits (Perugino (USA)) (16000) **Heart Of The South Racing & Partner**

**Other Owners:** Mr A. A. Al Shaikh, I. J. Al-Sagar, Mrs Catherine Cashman, Mr D. P. Dance, Mr S. E. Duke, Mr S. C. Gereaux, Mr G. P. Gereaux, Mrs R. G. Hillen, Saleh Al Homaizi, Mr M. Johnston, R. M. Levitt, Mrs S. Magnier, A. Panetta, J. R. Penny, Miss E. Penny, Mr C. Pizarro, Mrs K. Pizarro, Mr T. N. Porter, Qatar Racing Limited, Mr A. Schutz, D. Smith, M. Tabor.

**Assistant Trainers:** Lucie Botti, Karen Paris

**Apprentice:** Toby Atkinson.

## 56 MR PETER BOWEN, Haverfordwest

Postal: **Yet-Y-Rhug, Letterston, Haverfordwest, Pembrokeshire, SA62 5TB**
Contacts: **PHONE (01348) 840486 FAX (01348) 840486 MOBILE (07811) 111234**
**E-MAIL info@peterbowenracing.com WEBSITE www.peterbowenracing.com**

1 **AL CO (FR),** 10, ch g Dom Alco (FR)—Carama (FR) **F. Lloyd**
2 **AWAYWITHTHEGREYS (IRE),** 8, gr g Whipper (USA)—Silver Sash (GER) **Karen Bowen, Saith O Ni & The Hedonists**
3 **BALLYBOUGH GORTA (IRE),** 8, b g Indian Danehill (IRE)—Eyelet (IRE) **Michael Bowen & Karen Bowen**
4 **BEREA VENTURE (IRE),** 7, b g Indian Danehill (IRE)—Ballinard Lady (IRE) **Mr A. J. R. Hart**
5 **BUACHAILL ALAINN (IRE),** 8, b g Oscar (IRE)—Bottle A Knock (IRE) **Roddy Owen & Paul Fullagar**
6 **CLOVER PARK,** 5, b g Norse Dancer (IRE)—Scottish Clover **Miss Jayne Brace & Mr Gwyn Brace**
7 **CRUISING BYE,** 9, b g Alflora (IRE)—Althrey Flame (IRE) **F. Lloyd**
8 **CURIOUS CARLOS,** 6, b g Overbury (IRE)—Classi Maureen **Mr C. W. Pyne**
9 **CYGNET,** 9, b g Dansili—Ballet Princess **Mrs K. Bowen**
10 **DARK GLACIER (IRE),** 10, b g Flemensfirth (USA)—Glacier Lilly (IRE) **G. J. Morris**
11 **DIPITY DOO DAH,** 11, b m Slip Anchor—Lyra **C. G. R. Booth**
12 **DOUBLE DOUBLE (FR),** 9, b g Sakhee (USA)—Queen Sceptre (IRE) **Roddy Owen & Paul Fullagar**
13 **DR ROBIN (IRE),** 5, b g Robin des Pres (FR)—Inter Alia (IRE) **David Robbins & Karen Bowen**
14 **EDMUND KEAN (IRE),** 8, b g Old Vic—Baliya (IRE) **Walters Plant Hire & James & Jean Potter**
15 **FLYING EAGLE (IRE),** 7, b g Oscar (IRE)—Fille d'argent (IRE) **West Coast Haulage Limited**
16 **G'DAI SYDNEY,** 7, b g Choisir (AUS)—Silly Mid-On **Mrs L. J. Williams**
17 **GHOST RIVER,** 5, ch g Flemensfirth (USA)—Cresswell Native (IRE) **Mr J. Andrews**
18 **GRAPE TREE FLAME,** 7, ch m Grape Tree Road—Althrey Flame (IRE) **F. Lloyd**
19 **HANDMAID,** 6, b m King's Theatre (IRE)—Hand Inn Glove **Property & Thoroughbred Services Ltd**
20 **HENLLAN HARRI (IRE),** 7, br g King's Theatre (IRE)—Told You So (IRE) **Mr W. E. V. Harries**
21 **HENRI PARRY MORGAN,** 7, b g Brian Boru—Queen of Thedaises **Ednyfed & Elizabeth Morgan**
22 **HOLLIES PEARL,** 5, b m Black Sam Bellamy (IRE)—Posh Pearl **R. D. J. Swinburne**
23 **I'MWAITINGFORYOU,** 6, ch m Needwood Blade—Elegant Lady **Mrs P. M. Morgan**
24 **KINARI (IRE),** 5, b g Captain Rio—Baraza (IRE) **Mr J. Andrews**
25 **KING OF ALL KINGS (IRE),** 5, b g Craigsteel—Back The Queen (IRE) **Mr M. B. Bowen**
26 **LAMBORO LAD (IRE),** 10, b g Milan—Orchard Spray (IRE) **Margaret and Raymond John**
27 **LAND OF VIC,** 7, b m Old Vic—Land of Glory **Mr W. G. A. Hill**
28 **LETBESO (IRE),** 7, ch g Vinnie Roe (IRE)—Go Hunting (IRE) **Roddy Owen & Paul Fullagar**
29 **MADE OF DIAMONDS,** 6, b m Alflora (IRE)—Posh Pearl **Mr M. B. Bowen**
30 **MISS EYELASH (IRE),** 5, b m Kayf Tara—Glacial Missile (IRE)
31 **PRINCESS TARA (IRE),** 5, b m Kayf Tara—Oscars Vision (IRE) **David Perkins & Kate Perkins**
32 **RED SIX (IRE),** 4, ch c Flemensfirth (USA)—Glacial Missile (IRE)
33 **REGAL DIAMOND (IRE),** 7, b h Vinnie Roe (IRE)—Paper Money (IRE) **Roddy Owen,Paul Fullagar & Karen Bowen**
34 **ROLLING MAUL (IRE),** 7, b g Oscar (IRE)—Water Sports (IRE) **Roddy Owen & Paul Fullagar**
35 **RONS DREAM,** 5, b m Kayf Tara—Empress of Light **Mrs T. S. P. Stepney**
36 **SANDYNOW (IRE),** 10, ch g Old Vic—Kasterlee (FR) **J Martin, C Morris, T Stepney, K Bowen**
37 **THE ROAD AHEAD,** 8, b m Grape Tree Road—Althrey Flame (IRE) **F. Lloyd**
38 **THUNDER AND RAIN (IRE),** 7, b g Craigsteel—Old Cup (IRE) **Roddy Owen & Paul Fullagar**
39 **UNFORGETTABLE (IRE),** 12, b g Norwich—Miss Lulu (IRE) **J. Rogers**
40 **VELATOR,** 8, b g Old Vic—Jupiter's Message **Steve & Jackie Fleetham**
41 **VIKING BLOND (FR),** 10, ch g Varese (FR)—Sweet Jaune (FR) **Mr W. E. V. Harries**
42 **WESTERN XPRESS (IRE),** 7, b g Westerner—Lockersleybay (IRE) **David Smith & Karen Bowen**

**Other Owners:** Mr B. G. Bowen, Miss M. J. Brace, D. G. Brace, P. J. Douglas, Mrs L. Douglas, Mr S. Fleetham, Mrs J. Fleetham, P. G. Fullagar, Mrs M. B. A. John, Mr R. D. John, Mrs J. E. Martin, Mr E. O. Morgan, Mrs E. Morgan, Mrs O. C. L. Morris, R. R. Owen, Mr D. J. Perkins, Mrs L. K. Perkins, B. S. Port, J. E. Potter, Mrs M. J. Potter, S. D. Reeve, D. J. Robbins, D. A. Smith, Walters Plant Hire Ltd, Mr P. R. Williams.

**Assistant Trainers:** Karen Bowen, Michael Bowen

**Jockey (NH):** Donal Devereux, Jamie Moore, Tom O'Brien. **Conditional:** Sean Bowen.

## 57 MR ROY BOWRING, Edwinstowe

Postal: **Fir Tree Farm, Edwinstowe, Mansfield, Nottinghamshire, NG21 9JG**
Contacts: **PHONE (01623) 822451 MOBILE (07973) 712942**
**E-MAIL bowrings@btconnect.com**

1 **ACE MASTER,** 7, ch g Ballet Master (USA)—Ace Maite **S. R. Bowring**
2 **CLUBLAND (IRE),** 6, b g Red Clubs (IRE)—Racjilanemm **Mr L. P. Keane**

## MR ROY BOWRING - Continued

3 **DANCING MAITE,** 10, ch g Ballet Master (USA)—Ace Maite **S. R. Bowring**
4 **DIVERTIMENTI (IRE),** 11, b g Green Desert (USA)—Ballet Shoes (IRE) **K. Nicholls**
5 **FLYING APPLAUSE,** 10, b g Royal Applause—Mrs Gray **K. Nicholls**
6 **FOOLAAD,** 4, ch g Exceed And Excel (AUS)—Zayn Zen **K. Nicholls**
7 **HICKSTER (IRE),** 4, br g Intense Focus (USA)—Surrender To Me (USA) **Mr L. P. Keane**
8 **LITTLE CHOOSEY,** 5, ch m Cadeaux Genereux—Little Nymph **K. Nicholls**
9 **MARINA BALLERINA,** 7, b br m Ballet Master (USA)—Marinaite **S. R. Bowring**
10 **MASTER OF SONG,** 8, ch g Ballet Master (USA)—Ocean Song **S. R. Bowring**
11 **MISU'S MAITE,** 4, b f Misu Bond (IRE)—Magical Flute **Charterhouse Holdings Plc**
12 **SOFIAS NUMBER ONE (USA),** 7, b br g Silver Deputy (CAN)—Storidawn (USA) **S. R. Bowring**
13 **SOLARMAITE,** 6, b m Needwood Blade—Marinaite **S. R. Bowring**
14 **THREE MMM'S,** 4, b f Milk It Mick—Marinaite **S. R. Bowring**
15 **WALTA (IRE),** 4, b g Tagula (IRE)—Hi Katriona (IRE) **S. R. Bowring**

### THREE-YEAR-OLDS

16 **COOL BEANS,** b g Kyllachy—Stellar Brilliant (USA) **Mr L. P. Keane**
17 Ch g First Trump—Exceedingly Good (IRE) **S. R. Bowring**
18 B g Resplendent Glory (IRE)—Marinaite **S. R. Bowring**
19 **REASSERT,** b g Assertive—Zonta Zitkala **Mr L. P. Keane**

---

## 58 MR JIM BOYLE, Epsom

Postal: **South Hatch Stables, Burgh Heath Road, Epsom, Surrey, KT17 4LX**
Contacts: **PHONE (01372) 748800 FAX (01372) 739410 MOBILE (07719) 554147**
**E-MAIL info@jamesboyle.co.uk & jimboylesec@hotmail.co.uk (Secretary)**
**WEBSITE www.jamesboyle.co.uk**

1 **ATLANTIS CROSSING (IRE),** 6, b g Elusive City (USA)—Back At de Front (IRE) **The "In Recovery" Partnership**
2 **CLEARING,** 5, br m Sleeping Indian—Spring Clean (FR) **The Paddock Space Partnership**
3 **DALAKI (IRE),** 4, b g Dalakhani (IRE)—Lunda (IRE) **The Paddock Space Partnership 2**
4 **GENTLEMAX (FR),** 5, b g Gentlewave (IRE)—Marcela Howard (IRE) **A. B. Pope**
5 **GIGAWATT,** 5, b g Piccolo—Concubine (IRE) **The "In Recovery" Partnership**
6 **LIBERTY JACK (IRE),** 5, b g Sakhee (USA)—Azeema (IRE) **Mr M. Fitzgerald**
7 **PERFECT PASTIME,** 7, ch g Pastoral Pursuits—Puritanical (IRE) **The Paddock Space Partnership 2**
8 **SONNETATION (IRE),** 5, b m Dylan Thomas (IRE)—Southern Migration (USA) **The "In Recovery" Partnership**
9 **WHAT A DANDY (IRE),** 4, b g Dandy Man (IRE)—Ibtihal (IRE) **Inside Track Racing Club**

### THREE-YEAR-OLDS

10 **ARTISTIC FLIGHT (IRE),** b c Art Connoisseur (IRE)—Robin **Inside Track Racing Club**
11 **GRAND PROPOSAL,** gr g Exceed And Excel (AUS)—Si Belle (IRE) **Epsom Equine Spa Partnership**
12 **INKE (IRE),** br f Intikhab (USA)—Chifney Rush (IRE) **Harrier Racing 2**
13 **ONORINA (IRE),** b f Arcano (IRE)—Miss Honorine (IRE) **Sir D. J. Prosser**
14 **PYROCLASTIC (IRE),** b c Tagula (IRE)—Gypsy Royal (IRE) **The "In Recovery" Partnership**
15 **RIPINTO (IRE),** ch c Rip Van Winkle (IRE)—For Evva Silca **The "In Recovery" Partnership**
16 **TO THE VICTOR (IRE),** b g Approve (IRE)—Wonders Gift **Harrier Racing 1**

### TWO-YEAR-OLDS

17 **BLACK BESS,** br f 21/1 Dick Turpin (IRE)—Spring Clean (FR) (Danehill (USA))
18 **EBBISHAM (IRE),** b c 9/3 Holy Roman Emperor (IRE)—
Balting Lass (IRE) (Orpen (USA)) (51586) **The "In Recovery" Partnership**
19 **MASTER OF HEAVEN,** b c 22/1 Makfi—
Maid In Heaven (IRE) (Clodovil (IRE)) (40000) **Maid In Heaven Partnership**
20 **NORTHMAN (IRE),** b c 10/4 Frozen Power (IRE)—
Chifney Rush (IRE) (Grand Lodge (USA)) (11904) **Harrier Racing 3**
21 B f 31/3 Lilbourne Lad (IRE)—Song To The Moon (IRE) (Oratorio (IRE)) (7936) **Epsom Ups & Downs Partnership**

**Other Owners:** Mr K. Booth, Mrs P. Boyle, J. R. Boyle, A. J. Chambers, Ms J. E. Harrison, Mr D. J. Hegarty, Mr J. Hillier, Ms T. Keane, Mr P. O. Mooney, Mr R. O'Dwyer, E. Sames, Mr R. Stanbridge, Mr P. A. Taylor.

**Apprentice:** Nathan Alison, Daniel Cremin.

## 59 MR DAVID BRACE, Bridgend

Postal: **Llanmihangel Farm, Pyle, Bridgend, Mid-Glamorgan, CF33 6RL**
Contacts: **PHONE (01656) 742313**

1 **BAJAN BLU,** 7, b g Generous (IRE)—Bajan Girl (FR) **D. Brace**
2 **BOB THE BUTCHER,** 6, b g Needle Gun (IRE)—Brydferth Ddu (IRE) **D. Brace**
3 **BRINGINTHEBRANSTON,** 7, ch g Generous (IRE)—Branston Lily **D. Brace**
4 **DBOBE,** 6, br g Needle Gun (IRE)—Braceys Girl (IRE) **The Brace Family**
5 **DONT TELL PA (IRE),** 8, b g Oscar (IRE)—Glacial Snowboard (IRE) **D. Brace**
6 **DUNRAVEN ROYAL,** 5, b g Black Sam Bellamy (IRE)—First Royal (GER) **D. Brace**
7 **FIREING PIN,** 6, b m Needle Gun (IRE)—Coolvawn Lady (IRE) **D. Brace**
8 **GERALDO THE SPARKY (IRE),** 5, ch g Araafa (IRE)—Little Firefly (IRE) **D. Brace**
9 **IT'S PICALILLY,** 5, b m Needle Gun (IRE)—Branston Lily **D. Brace**
10 **IT'S THE WOOLUFF,** 6, b m Needle Gun (IRE)—Branston Lily **D. Brace**
11 **IWANABEBOBBIESGIRL,** 5, b m Mahler—Bajan Girl (FR) **D. Brace**
12 **MIKE THE POACHER,** 6, b g Needle Gun (IRE)—Poacher's Paddy (IRE) **D. Brace**
13 **ONLY TIME'LL TELL (IRE),** 7, b g Gamut (IRE)—Rock Abbey (IRE) **D. Brace**
14 **SILVER TOKEN,** 10, gr g Silver Patriarch (IRE)—Commanche Token (IRE) **D. Brace**
15 **TOMMY THE TIGER,** 6, b g Needle Gun (IRE)—Lynoso **D. Brace**
16 **WAROFTHEGIANTS,** 7, b g Tikkanen (USA)—Lucylou (IRE) **D. Brace**

**Other Owners:** Mr A. Brace, Mr M. Brace.

**Assistant Trainer:** Robbie Llewellyn

## 60 MR MILTON BRADLEY, Chepstow

Postal: **Meads Farm, Sedbury Park, Chepstow, Gwent, NP16 7HN**
Contacts: **PHONE (01291) 622486 FAX (01291) 626939**

1 **COMPTON PRINCE,** 6, ch g Compton Place—Malelane (IRE) **E. A. Hayward**
2 **DIVINE CALL,** 8, b g Pivotal—Pious **E. A. Hayward**
3 **HAMIS AL BIN (IRE),** 6, b g Acclamation—Paimpolaise (IRE) **P. Banfield**
4 **INDIAN AFFAIR,** 5, b h Sleeping Indian—Rare Fling (USA) **J. M. Bradley**
5 **JAZRI,** 4, b g Myboycharlie (IRE)—Read Federica **J. M. Bradley**
6 **NEW DECADE,** 6, ch g Pivotal—Irresistible **Asterix Partnership**
7 **NOTNOW PENNY,** 4, ch f Notnowcato—Tuppenny **J. M. Bradley**
8 **PANDAR,** 6, b g Zamindar (USA)—Pagnottella (IRE) **Dab Hand Racing**
9 **SPIRIT OF GONDREE (IRE),** 7, b g Invincible Spirit (IRE)—Kristal's Paradise (IRE) **Paul & Ann de Weck & Partner**
10 **TEMPLE ROAD (IRE),** 7, b g Street Cry (IRE)—Sugarhoneybaby (IRE) **J. M. Bradley**
11 **TRIPLE DREAM,** 10, ch g Vision of Night—Triple Joy **J. M. Bradley**
12 **VOLCANIC DUST (IRE),** 7, b m Ivan Denisovich (IRE)—Top of The Form (IRE) **Miss D. Hill**
13 **ZAND MAN,** 5, b g Zahran (IRE)—Shellatana **D. Smith**

### THREE-YEAR-OLDS

14 **AMADEUS DREAM (IRE),** b c Amadeus Wolf—Spring Glory **E. A. Hayward**
15 **CHETAN,** b c Alfred Nobel (IRE)—Island Music (IRE) **Roger & Val Miles,Colin Miles,Tony Stamp**
16 **GLEAMING PRINCESS,** b f Arabian Gleam—Hansomis (IRE) **J. M. Bradley**
17 **INDIAN TIM,** b c Sleeping Indian—River City Moon (USA) **J. M. Bradley**

### TWO-YEAR-OLDS

18 Ch f 26/3 Assertive—By Definition (IRE) (Definite Article) **Paul de Weck**
19 B g 27/4 Sleeping Indian—Hiraeth (Petong) (3333) **E. A. Hayward**
20 B f 18/2 Piccolo—Talamahana (Kyllachy) **Paul de Weck**
21 B f 6/4 Bushranger (IRE)—Validate (Alhaarth (IRE)) (3333) **E. A. Hayward**

**Other Owners:** Mrs A. De Weck, C. M. Hunt, S. McAvoy, K. R. Miles, Mr C. R. Miles, Mrs V. Miles, D. Pearson, A. D. Pirie, Mr A. P. Stamp.

**Assistant Trainer:** Mrs Hayley Wallis

**Jockey (flat):** Richard Kingscote, Adam Kirby, Luke Morris. **Jockey (NH):** Chris Davies. **Apprentice:** Leroy Lynch.

## 61 MR MARK BRADSTOCK, Wantage

Postal: **The Old Manor Stables, Letcombe Bassett, Wantage, Oxfordshire, OX12 9LP**
Contacts: **PHONE (01235) 760780 MOBILE (07887) 686697**
**E-MAIL mark.bradstock@btconnect.com WEBSITE www.markbradstockracing.co.uk**

1 **CARMINO (IRE),** 6, ch g Stowaway—Fiddlers Pal (IRE) **North Star Partnership**
2 **CARRUTHERS,** 12, b g Kayf Tara—Plaid Maid (IRE) **The Oaksey Partnership**
3 **CONEYGREE,** 8, b g Karinga Bay—Plaid Maid (IRE) **The Max Partnership**
4 **DAMBY'S STAR (IRE),** 5, b g Kayf Tara—She Took A Tree (FR) **North Star Partnership**
5 **FLINTHAM,** 6, b g Kayf Tara—Plaid Maid (IRE) **The Rasher Partnership**
6 **LADY OVERMOON,** 6, b m Overbury (IRE)—Lady Fleur **The Lady Overmoon Partnership**
7 **LORD VALENTINE,** 7, b g Overbury (IRE)—Lady Fleur **The Lady Overmoon Partnership**
8 **RIGOUR BACK BOB (IRE),** 10, ch g Bob Back (USA)—Rigorous **D. Chapman-Jones, J. McIntyre, J. Carroll**
9 **ROBERT'S STAR (IRE),** 5, b g Oscar (IRE)—Halona **North Star Partnership**
10 **STAR RIDE,** 6, b g Kayf Tara—Star Diva (IRE) **Dorchester On Thames Syndicate**

**Other Owners:** M. F. Bradstock, Mr J. Carroll, Dr D. Chapman-Jones, R. C. Douglas, Lady Dundas, Mrs M. J. Kelsey Fry, D. King, Mr J. McIntyre, Lady Oaksey, Miss J. Seaman, M. S. Tamburro, Mr R. W. Tyrrell, C. A. Vernon, A. M. Waller.

**Assistant Trainer:** Sara Bradstock

## 62 MR GILES BRAVERY, Newmarket

Postal: **2 Charnwood Stables, Hamilton Road, Newmarket, Suffolk, CB8 7JQ**
Contacts: **PHONE (01638) 454044 MOBILE (07711) 112345**
**E-MAIL Braverygc@aol.com WEBSITE www.gilesbravery.com TWITTER: @GilesBravery**

1 **AMBER SPYGLASS,** 5, ch h Act One—Northern Bows **Hyphen Bloodstock**
2 **BISON GRASS,** 5, b g Halling (USA)—Secret Blend **Mr J. P. Carrington**
3 **PANOPTICON,** 4, ch f Lucky Story (USA)—Barnacla (IRE) **The TT Partnership**
4 **PUZZLE TIME,** 5, b m Araafa (IRE)—Puzzling **J. J. May**
5 **SPIRIT RIDER (USA),** 5, b g Candy Ride (ARG)—Teenage Queen (USA) **Mr J. F. Tew**
6 **SUBTLE KNIFE,** 6, ch m Needwood Blade—Northern Bows **D. B. Clark & Russel Grant**

### THREE-YEAR-OLDS

7 **DARRELL RIVERS,** b f Hellvelyn—First Term **The TT Partnership**
8 **MOORSTONE,** b f Manduro (GER)—Pan Galactic (USA) **Mrs L. A. Howe**
9 **MS ARSENAL,** b f Mount Nelson—Magical Dancer (IRE) **The TT Partnership**
10 B f Authorized (IRE)—Piedmont (UAE) **M. R. James**

### TWO-YEAR-OLDS

11 **LUCIA SCIARRA,** ch f 23/4 Monsieur Bond (IRE)—Oke Bay (Tobougg (IRE)) **D. B. Clark**

**Other Owners:** Mrs F. E. Bravery, Mr G. C. Bravery, Mr D. B. Clark, Mr R. C. Grant, Hyphen Bloodstock, Mr Mark James, Mr D. R. Tucker.

## 63 MR BARRY BRENNAN, Kingston Lisle

Postal: **Little Farm, Kingston Lisle, Wantage, Oxon OX12 9QH**
Contacts: **MOBILE (07907) 529780**
**E-MAIL barrybrennan2@hotmail.co.uk WEBSITE www.barrybrennanracing.co.uk**

1 **ALONGTHEWATCHTOWER (IRE),** 7, b g Heron Island (IRE)—Manesbil (IRE) **K. P. Brennan**
2 **BATHCOUNTY (IRE),** 8, ch g Tobougg (IRE)—Seasons Estates **Dr I. A. Cragg**
3 **BIN END,** 9, b g King's Best (USA)—Overboard (IRE) **D. R. T. Gibbons**
4 **BUNCLODY,** 10, b g Overbury (IRE)—Wahiba Reason (IRE) **F. J. Brennan**
5 **KALUCCI (IRE),** 6, b g Kalanisi (IRE)—Anno Luce **D. R. T. Gibbons**
6 **SWAMPFIRE (IRE),** 7, b g Anabaa (USA)—Moonfire **Mr D. J. Lewin**
7 **TETRALOGY (IRE),** 6, b g Old Vic—Quadrennial (IRE) **D. R. T. Gibbons**
8 **VICKY'S CHARM (IRE),** 6, b m Old Vic—Sweet Charm (IRE) **Dr I. A. Cragg**

## 64 MISS RHONA BREWIS, Belford

Postal: **Chester Hill, Belford, Northumberland, NE70 7EF**
Contacts: **PHONE (01668) 213239/213281**

1 **BURGUNDY BEAU,** 9, br g Grape Tree Road—Chantilly Rose **Miss R. G. Brewis**
2 **CLOVELLY,** 5, b m Midnight Legend—Chantilly Rose **Miss R. G. Brewis**

## 65 MR JOHN BRIDGER, Liphook

Postal: **Upper Hatch Farm, Liphook, Hampshire, GU30 7EL**
Contacts: **PHONE (01428) 722528 MOBILE (07785) 716614**
**E-MAIL jbridger@btconnect.com**

1 **BOOKMAKER,** 5, b g Byron—Cankara (IRE) **T Wallace & J J Bridger**
2 **BYRD IN HAND (IRE),** 8, b g Fasliyev (USA)—Military Tune (IRE) **Marshall Bridger**
3 **CHORAL FESTIVAL,** 9, b m Pivotal—Choirgirl **Mrs E. Gardner**
4 **FAIRY MIST (IRE),** 8, b g Oratorio (IRE)—Prealpina (IRE) **Mr J. J. Bridger**
5 **LILY EDGE,** 6, b m Byron—Flaming Spirt **Mr J. J. Bridger**
6 **LIVE DANGEROUSLY,** 5, b g Zamindar (USA)—Desert Lynx (IRE) **W. A. Wood**
7 **MEGALALA (IRE),** 14, b g Petardia—Avionne **Mr T. Wallace**
8 **MOVIE MAGIC,** 4, b f Multiplex—Alucica **Mr & Mrs K. Finch**
9 **PHAROH JAKE,** 7, ch g Piccolo—Rose Amber **The Hair & Haberdasher Partnership**
10 **SHIFTING STAR (IRE),** 10, ch g Night Shift (USA)—Ahshado **Night Shadow Syndicate**
11 **SILVEE,** 8, gr m Avonbridge—Silver Louie (IRE)
12 **STARDANSE,** 4, b f High Chaparral (IRE)—Danse Spectre (IRE) **Mr J. J. Bridger**
13 **STARWATCH,** 8, b g Observatory (USA)—Trinity Reef **Mr J. J. Bridger**
14 **WELSH INLET (IRE),** 7, br m Kheleyf (USA)—Ervedya (IRE) **Mr J. J. Bridger**

### THREE-YEAR-OLDS

15 **DISC PLAY,** b f Showcasing—Gitane (FR) **K. Finch**
16 **MOONSTONE LADY,** ch f Observatory (USA)—Force In The Wings (IRE) **K. Finch**
17 Ch f Avonbridge—Too Grand **Mr J. J. Bridger**

### TWO-YEAR-OLDS

18 **ARCTIC FLOWER (IRE),** gr f 29/4 Roderic O'Connor (IRE)—
Just In Love (FR) (Highest Honor (FR)) (8000) **Mr & Mrs K. Finch**
19 B f 17/2 Canford Cliffs (IRE)—Serafina's Flight (Fantastic Light (USA)) **J. Bridger**
20 B f 8/2 Sakhee's Secret—Sister Moonshine (Averti (IRE)) **J. Bridger**
21 **STORMFLOWER,** b f 11/4 Arcano (IRE)—
Someone's Angel (USA) (Runaway Groom (CAN)) (4200) **Mr & Mrs K. Finch**
22 B g 18/2 Piccolo—Turkish Delight (Prince Sabo) (3200) **J. Bridger**

**Other Owners:** Mrs D. Ellison, Mrs D. Finch, T. M. Jones, C. Marshall, Mr A. P. Prockter, Mrs J. M. Stamp, Mrs D. Stewart.

**Assistant Trainer:** Rachel Cook

## 66 MR DAVID BRIDGWATER, Stow-on-the-Wold

Postal: **Wyck Hill Farm, Wyck Hill, Stow-on-the-Wold, Cheltenham, Gloucestershire, GL54 1HT**
Contacts: **PHONE (01451) 830349 FAX (01451) 830349 MOBILE (07831) 635817**
**E-MAIL sales@bridgwaterracing.co.uk WEBSITE www.bridgwaterracing.co.uk**

1 **ACCORDING TO TREV (IRE),** 9, ch g Accordion—Autumn Sky (IRE) **Mr F. J. Mills & Mr W. Mills**
2 **BALLY SANDS (IRE),** 11, b g Luso—Sandwell Old Rose (IRE) **Mr R. Mathew**
3 **BAWDEN ROCKS,** 6, b g Anabaa (USA)—Late Night (GER) **Mr Simon Hunt**
4 **BELMONT PARK (FR),** 4, b br g Al Namix (FR)—Goldoulyssa (FR) **Terry & Sarah Amos**
5 **BIG TALK,** 8, b g Selkirk (USA)—Common Request (USA) **Deauville Daze Partnership**
6 **BILLERAGH MILAN (IRE),** 8, b br g Milan—Billeragh Thyne (IRE) **D. G. Bridgwater**
7 **BRAVO RIQUET (FR),** 9, gr g Laveron—Jeroline (FR) **Mr R. Mathew**
8 **BUBLE (IRE),** 6, b g Milan—
Glorious Moments (IRE) **Mrs Mary Bridgwater, Mrs J. A. Chenery, Mr R. J. Chenery**
9 **COLLODI (GER),** 6, b g Konigstiger (GER)—Codera (GER) **Stocky, Gunny and Chappy**
10 **CONDUCTING,** 7, b g Oratorio (IRE)—Aiming **B.A.A. Management Ltd**

## MR DAVID BRIDGWATER - Continued

11 **DANISA,** 6, b m Shamardal (USA)—Divisa (GER) **Nigel Holder, Peter Glanville**
12 **DONT DO MONDAYS (IRE),** 8, b g Rashar (USA)—Bit of A Chance **F. W. K. Griffin**
13 **EDGAR (GER),** 5, b g Big Shuffle (USA)—Estella (GER) **K. J. McCourt & Partners**
14 **ENGAI (GER),** 9, b g Noroit (GER)—Enigma (GER) **Building Bridgies**
15 **FERGAL MAEL DUIN,** 7, gr g Tikkanen (USA)—Fad Amach (IRE) **J. Messenger S. Kerwood J. Buob-Aldorf**
16 **GARNOCK (IRE),** 7, b m Craigsteel—Sister Stephanie (IRE) **Mrs M. Turner**
17 **GINO TRAIL (IRE),** 8, br g Perugino (USA)—Borough Trail (IRE) **Mrs J. Smith**
18 **GOLAN DANCER (IRE),** 7, b g Golan (IRE)—Seductive Dance **S. Hunt, R. Butler, D. Ward, S. Girardier**
19 **IFYOUSAYSO (IRE),** 8, ch g Definite Article—Rosato (IRE) **The Joaly Partnership**
20 **KILLSHANNON (IRE),** 6, ch g Royal Anthem (USA)—Fortune And Favour (IRE) **Mr P. A. Hodge**
21 **LAKESHORE LADY (IRE),** 5, b m Lakeshore Road (USA)—Chiminee Chime (IRE) **Simon & Liz Hunt**
22 **LORD NAVITS (IRE),** 7, b g Golan (IRE)—Nanavits (IRE) **Jobarry Partnership**
23 **MON PETIT ANGE (FR),** 4, b g Ultimately Lucky (IRE)—Line Tzigane (FR) **Terry & Sarah Amos**
24 **NO BUTS,** 7, b g Kayf Tara—Wontcostalotbut **Wontcostalot Partnership**
25 **NOMADIC STORM,** 9, b g Nomadic Way (USA)—Cateel Bay **Mrs V. Williams**
26 **OPECHEE (IRE),** 4, b g Robin des Champs (FR)—Falcons Gift (IRE) **Dean Bostock & Raymond Bostock**
27 **OSCAR HILL (IRE),** 9, b g Oscar (IRE)—Elizabeth Tudor (IRE) **K. W. Bradley**
28 **PLUM PUDDING (FR),** 12, b g Fado (FR)—Tale (FR) **Mr J. Messenger, Mrs S. Kerwood, Mr J. Buob-Aldorf**
29 **REGAL ONE (IRE),** 7, b g Antonius Pius (USA)—Regal Dancer (IRE) **Terry & Sarah Amos**
30 **RINGA BAY,** 10, ch g Karinga Bay—Redgrave Wolf **Malhi & Co.**
31 **ROCKMOUNT RIVER (IRE),** 6, b g Rock of Gibraltar (IRE)—Littlefeather (IRE) **Mr P. A. Hodge**
32 **RUSSIAN BOLERO (GER),** 4, ch g Tertullian (USA)—Russian Samba (IRE) **BAA Management Ltd**
33 **SAFFRON PRINCE,** 7, b g Kayf Tara—Jan's Dream (IRE) **Mrs J. A. Chenery**
34 **SAMUEL MAEL DUIN,** 5, gr g Black Sam Bellamy (IRE)—Fad Amach (IRE) **Mr J. Messenger, Mrs S. Kerwood, Mr J. Buob-Aldorf**
35 **SPEEDY BRUERE (FR),** 9, gr g Turgeon (USA)—Divine Bruere (FR) **Terry & Sarah Amos**
36 **TEMPURAN,** 6, b gr g Unbridled's Song (USA)—Tenderly (IRE) **D. J. Smith**
37 **THE GIANT BOLSTER,** 10, b g Black Sam Bellamy (IRE)—Divisa (GER) **Simon Hunt & Gary Lambton**
38 **VINNIESLITTLE LAMB (IRE),** 7, b m Vinnie Roe (IRE)—Polar Lamb (IRE) **D. A. Hunt**
39 **WYCK HILL (IRE),** 11, b g Pierre—Willow Rose (IRE) **J. P. McManus**

### THREE-YEAR-OLDS

40 **COCKLE TOWN BOY,** ch g Cockney Rebel (IRE)—Rare Cross (IRE) **Mr Wayne Hennessey**

**Other Owners:** Mr B. A. Adams, Mr T. P. Amos, Mrs S. P. Amos, Mrs Catherine Borghoff, Mr J. R. Bostock, Mr Dean Graham Bostock, Mr R. J. Brennan, Mrs Mary Bridgwater, Mr D. G. Bridgwater, Mr G. Bryan, Mr J. M. Buob-Aldorf, Mr S. Chapman, Mr R. J. Chenery, Mr A. A. Clifford, Mr R. L. Clifford, Mr Peter Glanville, Mr A. Gunn, Mr Wayne Hennessey, Mr M. Hills, Mr P. A. Hodge, Mr Nigel Holder, Mrs Liz Hunt, Mr Simon Hunt, Mrs S. Kerwood, Mr Gary Lambton, Mr C. D. Massey, Mrs J. Massey, Mr R. Mathew, Mr K. J. McCourt, Mr James Messenger, Mr F. J. Mills, Mr W. R. Mills, Mr Tim Payton, Mrs A. Sprowson, Mr P. Sprowson, Mr Stewart Stockdale, Mrs Anne Sumner, Mrs M. Turner, Mr David Ward, Mrs V. Williams.

**Assistant Trainer:** Mrs Lucy K. Bridgwater

**Jockey (NH):** Tom Scudamore. **Conditional:** Jake Hodson. **Amateur:** Miss Poppy Bridgwater, Mr Jake Launchbury.

---

## 67 MR MARK BRISBOURNE, Nesscliffe

Postal: **Ness Strange Stables, Great Ness, Shrewsbury, Shropshire, SY4 2LE**
Contacts: **PHONE (01743) 741536/741360 MOBILE (07803) 019651**

1 **DANCING PRIMO,** 9, b m Primo Valentino (IRE)—Tycoon's Last **L. R. Owen**
2 **ELLE REBELLE,** 5, b m Cockney Rebel (IRE)—Lille Ida **The Bourne Connection**
3 **HIGH ON THE HOG (IRE),** 7, b g Clodovil (IRE)—Maraami **Trevor Mennell & Kathie Gwilliam**
4 **MARKET PUZZLE (IRE),** 8, ch g Bahamian Bounty—Trempjane **W. M. Brisbourne**
5 **MYSTICAL MAZE,** 4, br f Multiplex—Musical Maze **Mark Brisbourne & Marshall Barnett**
6 **OMOTESANDO,** 5, b g Street Cry (IRE)—Punctilious **P. G. Evans**
7 **ROYAL TROOPER (IRE),** 9, b g Hawk Wing (USA)—Strawberry Roan (IRE) **W. M. Brisbourne**
8 **SAKHRA,** 4, b g Nayef (USA)—Noble Desert (FR) **P. R. Kirk**
9 **SARLAT,** 4, b f Champs Elysees—Midnight Sky **The Bourne Connection**
10 **STORM LIGHTNING,** 6, b g Exceed And Excel (AUS)—All For Laura **Law Abiding Citizens**
11 **TAHAF (IRE),** 5, b g Authorized (IRE)—Lady Zonda **Mr W. M. Clare**
12 **TARO TYWOD (IRE),** 6, br m Footstepsinthesand—Run To Jane (IRE) **Rasio Cymru Racing 1**
13 **TWO JABS,** 5, b g Teofilo (IRE)—Red Bravo (USA) **Mr Raymond Tooth**
14 **WHIPPHOUND,** 7, b g Whipper (USA)—Golden Symbol **Mr W. M. Clare**

## MR MARK BRISBOURNE - Continued

### THREE-YEAR-OLDS

15 Br f Captain Gerrard (IRE)—River Ensign **Mrs D. M. Brisbourne**

### TWO-YEAR-OLDS

16 B g 10/3 Captain Gerrard (IRE)—Ensign's Trick (Cayman Kai (IRE)) **Mrs D. M. Brisbourne**
17 **PIVOTAL DREAM (IRE),** br f 14/2 Excellent Art—Oasis Fire (IRE) (Oasis Dream) (4000) **The Bourne Connection**

**Other Owners:** Mr Alan Banton, Mr & Mrs Roy Broughton, Mr P. Clare, Mr Derek Dean, Mrs Marie Dean, Mrs C. M. Gibson, Mr Ray McNeil, Mr Peter Mort, Mr Mike Murnoy, Mrs C. A. Naylor, Mr John Owen, Mr Andy Pitt, Mr John Pugh.

**Assistant Trainer:** Antony Brisbourne

**Jockey (flat):** Graham Gibbons, Shane Kelly. **Jockey (NH):** Liam Treadwell. **Apprentice:** Becky Brisbourne, Cam Hardie.

---

## 68 MR CLIVE BRITTAIN, Newmarket

Postal: **'Carlburg', 49 Bury Road, Newmarket, Suffolk, CB8 7BY**
Contacts: **OFFICE (01638) 664347 HOME (01638) 663739 FAX (01638) 661744**
**MOBILE (07785) 302121**
**E-MAIL carlburgst@aol.com**

1 **ACCLIO (IRE),** 4, b f Acclamation—Hovering (IRE) **S. Manana**
2 **AFKAR (IRE),** 7, b g Invincible Spirit (IRE)—Indienne (IRE) **C. E. Brittain**
3 **AMTHAL (IRE),** 6, b m Dalakhani (IRE)—Al Ihtithar (IRE) **A. M. A. Al Shorafa**
4 **AQLAAM VISION,** 4, b f Aqlaam—Dream Vision (USA) **S. Manana**
5 **AUTOMATED,** 4, b g Authorized (IRE)—Red Blooded Woman (USA) **S. Manana**
6 **BAHAMIAN HEIGHTS,** 4, b g Bahamian Bounty—Tahirah **Sheikh J. D. Al Maktoum**
7 **BRAZOS (IRE),** 4, gr c Clodovil (IRE)—Shambodia (IRE) **S. Manana**
8 **CAPE CASTLE (IRE),** 4, b f Cape Cross (IRE)—Kaabari (USA) **S. Manana**
9 **CAPELENA,** 4, br f Cape Cross (IRE)—Roslea Lady (IRE) **S. Manana**
10 **CAPELITA,** 4, b f Cape Cross (IRE)—Zamhrear **S. Manana**
11 **DUBAI SKYLINE (USA),** 4, b f Medaglia d'Oro (USA)—Love of Dubai (USA) **Mr M. Al Shafar**
12 **FOUR CHEERS (IRE),** 4, b c Exceed And Excel (AUS)—O Fourlunda **S. Manana**
13 **GUARACHA,** 4, ch g Halling (USA)—Pachanga **C. E. Brittain**
14 **HATSAWAY (IRE),** 4, b c Dubawi (IRE)—Scotch Bonnet (IRE) **S. Manana**
15 **INTIMIDATOR (IRE),** 4, b c Intikhab (USA)—Zither **S. Manana**
16 **MANOMINE,** 6, b g Manduro (GER)—Fascinating Hill (FR) **Mrs C. E. Brittain**
17 **MEDICEAN QUEEN (IRE),** 4, b f Medicean—Qui Moi (CAN) **S. Manana**
18 **MUDHISH (IRE),** 10, b g Lujain (USA)—Silver Satire **C. E. Brittain**
19 **NEW STREAM (IRE),** 4, b c New Approach (IRE)—Shimna **S. Manana**
20 **RED AGGRESSOR (IRE),** 6, b g Red Clubs (IRE)—Snap Crackle Pop (IRE) **C. E. Brittain**
21 **RIZEENA (IRE),** 4, b f Iffraaj—Serena's Storm (IRE) **Sheikh R. D. Al Maktoum**
22 **STEALTH MISSILE (IRE),** 4, b f Invincible Spirit (IRE)—Wing Stealth (IRE) **S. Manana**
23 **SURETY (IRE),** 4, b c Cape Cross (IRE)—Guarantia **S. Manana**
24 **YUKON GIRL (IRE),** 4, b f Manduro (GER)—Yukon Hope (USA) **S. Manana**

### THREE-YEAR-OLDS

25 **AMAZING CHARM,** ch f King's Best (USA)—Bint Doyen **M. Al Nabouda**
26 B f Aqlaam—Beat As One **Saif Ali & Saeed H. Altayer**
27 B f Royal Applause—Chicane **S. Manana**
28 **CRACK SHOT (IRE),** ch c Lope de Vega (IRE)—Slap Shot (IRE) **S. Manana**
29 **DUBAI BREEZE (IRE),** b f Lope de Vega (IRE)—Expectation (IRE) **S. Manana**
30 **EBREEZ,** b c Dutch Art—Half Sister (IRE) **Sheikh R. D. Al Maktoum**
31 **FREE RUNNING (IRE),** b f Iffraaj—Street Star (USA) **Sheikh R. D. Al Maktoum**
32 **FURIOUSLY FAST (IRE),** b c Fast Company (IRE)—Agouti **Sheikh J. D. Al Maktoum**
33 **HAALAN,** b f Sir Percy—Fin **S. Manana**
34 B br f Invincible Spirit (IRE)—Mazaaya (USA) **S. Ali**
35 Gr f Alexandros—Miss Sazanica (FR) **S. Manana**
36 **MY MATE (IRE),** ch c Approve (IRE)—Date Mate (USA) **S. Manana**
37 **RAAS (USA),** b f Iffraaj—Sarmad (USA) **S. Manana**
38 **SECRET CONVOY,** b c Hellvelyn—Tee Cee **S. Manana**
39 **TEOFILO'S PRINCESS (IRE),** b f Teofilo (IRE)—Very Nice **S. Manana**
40 **TEOSROYAL (IRE),** br f Teofilo (IRE)—Fille de Joie (IRE) **Sheikh J. D. Al Maktoum**
41 **TEPELENI,** b f Teofilo (IRE)—Bronwen (IRE) **Mr A. S. Belhab**

## MR CLIVE BRITTAIN - Continued

42 **TEPUTINA,** ch f Teofilo (IRE)—West Lorne (USA) **S. Manana**
43 **VIA VIA (IRE),** b c Lope de Vega (IRE)—Atalina (FR) **S. Manana**

### TWO-YEAR-OLDS

44 B c 20/2 Dream Ahead (USA)—Anadolu (IRE) (Statue of Liberty (USA)) (40000) **S. Manana**
45 B f 16/4 Poet's Voice—Bezant (IRE) (Zamindar (USA)) (50000) **Sheikh J. D. Al Maktoum**
46 B f 8/4 Aqlaam—Bint Doyen (Doyen (IRE)) **M. Al Nabouda**
47 Ch c 19/3 Poet's Voice—Calakanga (Dalakhani (IRE)) (35000) **S. Manana**
48 B c 30/5 Kheleyf (USA)—Grecian Air (FR) (King's Best (USA)) (17000) **S. Manana**
49 B f 14/2 Aqlaam—Highland Jewel (IRE) (Azamour (IRE)) (10000) **S. Manana**
50 Br f 29/1 Makfi—Islandia (USA) (Johar (USA)) (20000) **S. Manana**
51 B c 8/4 Manduro (GER)—Krynica (USA) (Danzig (USA)) (24000) **Sheikh J. D. Al Maktoum**
52 B f 28/3 Approve (IRE)—Louve Sereine (FR) (Sadler's Wells (USA)) (20000) **S. Manana**
53 B f 20/2 Cape Cross (IRE)—Najam (Singspiel (IRE)) (10000) **S. Manana**
54 B c 23/3 Bahamian Bounty—Penny Ha'penny (Bishop of Cashel) (19000) **S. Manana**
55 Ch c 7/2 Kyllachy—Rhal (IRE) (Rahy (USA)) (27000) **S. Manana**
56 Ch c 6/2 Iffraaj—Soxy Doxy (IRE) (Hawk Wing (USA)) (25000) **S. Manana**
57 Ch c 19/4 Arcano (IRE)—Star Approval (IRE) (Hawk Wing (USA)) (50000) **Sheikh J. D. Al Maktoum**

**Other Owners:** S. H. Altayer.

**Assistant Trainer:** Mrs C. E. Brittain, Philip Robinson

---

## 69 MR MEL BRITTAIN, Warthill

Postal: **Northgate Lodge, Warthill, York, YO19 5XR**
Contacts: **PHONE (01759) 371472 FAX (01759) 372915**
**E-MAIL email@melbrittain.co.uk WEBSITE www.melbrittain.co.uk**

1 **BROCKFIELD,** 9, ch g Falbrav (IRE)—Irish Light (USA) **M. A. Brittain**
2 **CARRAGOLD,** 9, b g Diktat—Shadow Roll (IRE) **M. A. Brittain**
3 **COOL MUSIC (IRE),** 5, b m One Cool Cat (USA)—Musicology (USA) **M. A. Brittain**
4 **DIFFERENT SCENARIO,** 4, b f Araafa (IRE)—Racina **Northgate Orange**
5 **DREAM SCENARIO,** 5, b m Araafa (IRE)—Notjustaprettyface (USA) **Northgate Black**
6 **HARMONIC LADY,** 5, ch m Trade Fair—First Harmony **M. A. Brittain**
7 **HARMONICAL,** 4, ch f Desideratum—First Harmony **M. A. Brittain**
8 **HUSSAR BALLAD (USA),** 6, b g Hard Spun (USA)—Country Melody (USA) **M. A. Brittain**
9 **LUCKY LODGE,** 5, b g Lucky Story (USA)—Melandre **M. A. Brittain**
10 **LUCKY TIMES,** 4, b f Lucky Story (USA)—Paradise Eve **M. A. Brittain**
11 **MAYFIELD BOY,** 4, b c Authorized (IRE)—Big Pink (IRE) **M. A. Brittain**
12 **MAYFIELD GIRL (IRE),** 5, br m One Cool Cat (USA)—Rose of Mooncoin (IRE) **M. A. Brittain**
13 **MISTER MARCASITE,** 5, gr g Verglas (IRE)—No Rehearsal (FR) **S. J. Box**
14 **SOOQAAN,** 4, bl g Naaqoos—Dream Day (FR)
15 **STEEL STOCKHOLDER,** 9, b g Mark of Esteem (IRE)—Pompey Blue **M. A. Brittain**
16 **WHITE ROSE RUNNER,** 4, b f Virtual—Entrap (USA) **M. A. Brittain**

### THREE-YEAR-OLDS

17 **MISTER YORK,** b g Monsieur Bond (IRE)—Knavesmire (IRE) **M. A. Brittain**
18 **STANGHOW,** b c Monsieur Bond (IRE)—Melandre **M. A. Brittain**

### TWO-YEAR-OLDS

19 Ch f 2/5 Monsieur Bond (IRE)—Knavesmire (IRE) (One Cool Cat (USA)) (761)
20 B f 1/5 Monsieur Bond (IRE)—Melandre (Lujain (USA)) (3047)
21 Ch f 6/5 Monsieur Bond (IRE)—Mozayada (USA) (Street Cry (IRE)) (761)

**Other Owners:** Mr Mel Brittain, Mr Paul Chambers, Mr J. Jarvis, Mr Donald B. White.

**Head Lad:** Neil Jordan

**Apprentice:** Mathew Still.

## 70 LADY BROOKE, Llandrindod Wells

Postal: **Tyn-y-Berth Farm, Dolau, Llandrindod Wells, Powys, LD1 5TW**
Contacts: **PHONE (01597) 851190 MOBILE (07977) 114834**
**E-MAIL suebrooke@live.co.uk**

1 **AMERICAN WORLD (FR),** 11, b br g Lost World (IRE)—Rose Laura (FR) **Lady Brooke**
2 **FREE WORLD (FR),** 11, b g Lost World (IRE)—Fautine (FR) **Lady Brooke**
3 **RADUIS BLEU (FR),** 10, gr g Dadarissime (FR)—Regence Bleue (FR) **Lady Brooke**
4 **SATU (IRE),** 11, b g Marju (IRE)—Magic Touch **Lady Brooke**
5 **SPECIAL MATE,** 9, br g Generous (IRE)—Flying Iris (IRE) **Lady Brooke**

**Assistant Trainer:** Lorna Brooke (07786) 962911

**Amateur:** Miss Lorna Brooke.

## 71 MR ROY BROTHERTON, Pershore

Postal: **Mill End Racing Stables, Netherton Road, Elmley Castle, Pershore, Worcestershire, WR10 3JF**
Contacts: **PHONE/FAX (01386) 710772 MOBILE (07973) 877280**

1 **BASLE,** 8, b m Trade Fair—Gibaltarik (IRE) **Mr M. A. Geobey**
2 **KAABER (USA),** 4, b g Daaher (CAN)—Taseel (USA) **Mr J. Holt**
3 **LADYDOLLY,** 7, b m Kyllachy—Lady Pekan **Mr M. A. Geobey**
4 **LOUIS VEE (IRE),** 7, b br g Captain Rio—Mrs Evans (IRE) **Mrs P. A. Wallis**
5 **MAXDELAS (FR),** 9, ch g Sabrehill (USA)—Quendora (FR) **Mrs C. A. Newman**
6 **RENEWING,** 4, b g Halling (USA)—Electric Society (IRE) **Mr J. Holt**
7 **RUGGERO,** 5, b g Tiger Hill (IRE)—Bergamask (USA) **Mr J. Holt**
8 **SOEUR BLANCHE (IRE),** 9, b m Oscar (IRE)—Sunset Leader (IRE) **P. Drinkwater**
9 **UP YOUR GAME (IRE),** 7, b g Milan—Katie Snurge (IRE) **Millend Racing Club**
10 **WEST COAST DREAM,** 8, b g Oasis Dream—Californie (IRE) **Miss E. J. Byrd**

**Other Owners:** Mr Roy Brotherton, Mr T. L Martin.

**Assistant Trainer:** Justin Brotherton

**Jockey (flat):** Tom Eaves. **Conditional:** Ryan Hatch. **Amateur:** Mr Sam Drinkwater.

## 72 MR ALAN BROWN, Malton

Postal: **Lilac Farm, Yedingham, Malton, North Yorkshire, YO17 8SS**
Contacts: **PHONE (01944) 728090 FAX (01944) 728071 MOBILE (07970) 672845**
**E-MAIL ad.brownn@globaluk.net**

1 **BLUE SEA OF IBROX (IRE),** 7, gr m Subtle Power (IRE)—Jerpoint Rose (IRE) **Mr S. Brown**
2 **FAIR BUNNY,** 8, b m Trade Fair—Coney Hills **Mrs S. Johnson**
3 **HARRIS (IRE),** 8, b g Beneficial—Porter Tastes Nice (IRE) **Mr D. J. Sturdy**
4 **JASANI,** 7, b g Gentleman's Deal (IRE)—Bred For Pleasure **A. Brown**
5 **JEBEL TARA,** 10, b g Diktat—Chantilly (FR) **Miss E. Johnston**
6 **LADY IBROX,** 5, b m Ishiguru (USA)—Last Impression **Rangers Racing**
7 **LADY MARGAEUX (IRE),** 5, b m Redback—Storm Lady (IRE) **A. Brown**
8 **LAZARUS BELL,** 5, ch g Bahamian Bounty—Snake's Head **Mr F. E. Reay**
9 **MEANDMYSHADOW,** 7, ch m Tobougg (IRE)—Queen Jean **G. Morrill**
10 **MISS MOHAWK (IRE),** 6, ch m Hawk Wing (USA)—Karmafair (IRE) **Mrs M. A. Doherty**
11 **ONLY FOR YOU,** 5, b m Elusive City (USA)—Enlisted (IRE) **Mr S. Brown**
12 **RED SHADOW,** 6, b m Royal Applause—Just A Glimmer **S. E. Pedersen**
13 **REDALANI (IRE),** 5, b m Redback—Zafaraya (IRE) **S. E. Pedersen**
14 **RIQUET THE KING (FR),** 6, b g Laveron—Brave Chartreuse (FR) **Mr D. J. Sturdy**
15 **SAB LE BEAU (FR),** 6, b g Sabiango (GER)—La Peliniere (FR) **Mr D. J. Sturdy**

### THREE-YEAR-OLDS

16 **POPPY IN THE WIND,** b f Piccolo—Vintage Steps (IRE) **B Selective Partnership**

## MR ALAN BROWN - Continued

### TWO-YEAR-OLDS

17 **NEFETARI,** b f 15/2 Kodiac—Town And Gown (Oasis Dream) (30476) **Mr F. E. Reay**

**Other Owners:** Mrs W. A. D. Craven, Mr T. P. Curry, R. Hartley, Mr J. T. Winter.

---

## 73 MR ANDI BROWN, Newmarket

Postal: **Southfields Stables, Hamilton Road, Newmarket, Suffolk, CB8 7JQ**

1 **JERSEY CREAM (IRE),** 4, ch f Iffraaj—Unicamp **Faith Hope and Charity**
2 **KIRTLING,** 4, gr g Araafa (IRE)—Cape Maya **Faith Hope and Charity**
3 **RED SHUTTLE,** 8, b g Starcraft (NZ)—Red Azalea **Miss L. Knocker**

**Other Owners:** A. S. Brown.

---

## 74 MR DAVID BROWN, Averham

Postal: **The Old Stables, Averham Park, Newark, Nottinghamshire, NG23 5RU**
Contacts: **PHONE (01636) 613793 MOBILE (07889) 132931**
**E-MAIL david@davidbrownracing.com**

1 **CLUMBER STREET,** 4, ch g Compton Place—Tinnarinka **J. C. Fretwell**
2 **FLOW (USA),** 5, b br h Medaglia d'Oro (USA)—Enthused (USA) **J. C. Fretwell**
3 **JACQUOTTE DELAHAYE,** 4, ch f Kyllachy—Mary Read **Just For Girls Partnership**
4 **KATIE ELDER (FR),** 4, b f High Chaparral (IRE)—Cool And Composed (USA) **Mr D. H. Brown**
5 **MUNFALLET (IRE),** 4, b g Royal Applause—Princess Mood (GER) **J. C. Fretwell**
6 **SAMHAIN,** 4, b g Compton Place—Athboy Nights (IRE) **J. C. Fretwell**
7 **SCENE ONE,** 5, b g Act One—Gloriana
8 **SIR JACK LAYDEN,** 4, b g Sir Percy—Barawin (IRE) **Ron Hull, David Brown & Clive Watson**
9 **WIND FIRE (USA),** 4, b f Distorted Humor (USA)—A P Dream (USA) **Qatar Racing Limited**

### THREE-YEAR-OLDS

10 **ANCIENT GODDESS,** b f Kyllachy—Isis (USA) **Mr D. H. Brown**
11 **ARMISTICE DAY (IRE),** b f Azamour (IRE)—Announcing Peace **Premspace Ltd**
12 B g Acclamation—Benedicte (IRE) **J. C. Fretwell**
13 **BRIGHT FLASH,** ch f Dutch Art—Quadri **J. C. Fretwell**
14 **DOCTORS PAPERS,** ch g Stimulation (IRE)—Inya Lake **Mr D. H. Brown**
15 **DUTCH GARDEN,** b c Fastnet Rock (AUS)—Swan Wings **J. C. Fretwell**
16 **GRANOLA,** b f Makfi—Common Knowledge **Mrs F. Denniff**
17 **LADY ATLAS,** ch f Dutch Art—Paquerettza (FR) **Miss C. A. Carr**
18 **LAYERTHORPE (IRE),** b c Vale of York (IRE)—Strobinia (IRE) **J. C. Fretwell**
19 **LOOKING GOOD,** b f Makfi—Primo Heights **Qatar Racing Limited**
20 **MEDRANO,** b c Archipenko (USA)—Trick Or Treat **Peter Onslow & Mr & Mrs Gary Middlebrook**
21 **MUHAAFIZ (IRE),** br g Lord Shanakill (USA)—Yasmin Satine (IRE) **J. C. Fretwell**
22 **ON THE TILES,** gr c Royal Applause—Secret Night **J. C. Fretwell**
23 Ch c Mount Nelson—Pasithea (IRE)
24 **SECRETS SAFE (IRE),** b c Arcano (IRE)—Keritana (FR) **J. C. Fretwell**
25 **X RAISE (IRE),** gr f Aussie Rules (USA)—Raise (USA) **Onslow Hughlock Brooke & Brown**

### TWO-YEAR-OLDS

26 **ARIZE (IRE),** b f 31/3 Approve (IRE)—Raise (USA) (Seattle Slew (USA)) (12000) **P. Onslow**
27 B c 2/4 Showcasing—Be Decisive (Diesis) (39047) **J. C. Fretwell**
28 **BIT OF A LAD (IRE),** b c 5/1 Lilbourne Lad (IRE)—Sacred Love (IRE) (Barathea (IRE)) (16000) **Mr D. H. Brown**
29 B c 25/3 Bahamian Bounty—Celestial Welcome (Most Welcome) (32380) **J. C. Fretwell**
30 B c 9/2 Paco Boy (IRE)—Crown (IRE) (Royal Applause) (10476) **J. C. Fretwell**
31 B c 8/4 Showcasing—Garter Star (Mark of Esteem (IRE)) (42000) **J. C. Fretwell**
32 B f 5/5 Bernardini (USA)—Getaway Girl (USA) (Silver Deputy (CAN)) (57372) **Qatar Racing Limited**
33 **MIDNIGHT MACCHIATO (IRE),** b c 12/4 Dark Angel (IRE)—Lathaat (Dubai Destination (USA)) (19000) **D. A. West**
34 Ch c 18/2 Equiano (FR)—Millsini (Rossini (USA)) (33333) **J. C. Fretwell**
35 B f 21/3 Smart Strike (CAN)—More Hennessy (USA) (Hennessy (USA)) (200803) **Qatar Racing Limited**
36 B f 5/4 Compton Place—Never Lose (Diktat) (30476) **Qatar Racing Limited**
37 B f 8/4 Acclamation—New Deal (Rainbow Quest (USA)) (53174) **Qatar Racing Limited**

## MR DAVID BROWN - Continued

38 **PALPITATION (IRE),** b c 10/5 Fast Company (IRE)—Sensation (Soviet Star (USA)) (20000) **D. A. West**
39 Ch f 16/4 Medicean—Paquerettza (FR) (Dr Fong (USA)) **Miss C. A. Carr**
40 Gr ro c 15/2 Monsieur Bond (IRE)—Pendulum (Pursuit of Love) (38000) **J. C. Fretwell**
41 B f 15/2 Hellvelyn—Pizzarra (Shamardal (USA)) (10000) **Mr D. H. Brown**
42 B c 8/4 Strategic Prince—Primissima (GER) (Second Set (IRE)) (15238) **J. C. Fretwell**
43 Ch c 18/4 Medicean—Quadri (Polish Precedent (USA)) (571) **J. C. Fretwell**
44 Gr c 8/2 Paco Boy (IRE)—Rock Ace (IRE) (Verglas (IRE)) (13333) **J. C. Fretwell**
45 B c 2/4 Equiano (FR)—Tiana (Diktat) (22000) **Mrs F. Denniff**
46 **TIKTHEBOX (IRE),** b c 22/4 Approve (IRE)—Nicene (USA) (Pulpit (USA)) (12500) **Mr D. H. Brown**
47 **TIME AGAIN,** b f 12/3 Kyllachy—Record Time (Clantime) **P. Onslow**

**Other Owners:** Mr D. M. Brooke, Mr R. J. Hughlock, Mr R. Hull, G. Middlebrook, Mrs L. A. Middlebrook, Mr C. Watson, Mrs J. A. Youdan.

**Assistant Trainer:** Dushyant Dooyea

**Jockey (flat):** Harry Bentley, Philip Makin, Jamie Spencer, Robert Winston. **Apprentice:** Claire Murray.

---

## 75 MISS MICHELLE BRYANT, Lewes

Postal: **Bevern Bridge Farm Cottage, South Chailey, Lewes, East Sussex, BN8 4QH**
Contacts: **PHONE/FAX (01273) 400638 MOBILE (07976) 217542**

1 **HAWK GOLD (IRE),** 11, ch g Tendulkar (USA)—Heiress of Meath (IRE) **Miss M. P. Bryant**
2 **QUERIDO (GER),** 11, b g Acatenango (GER)—Quest of Fire (FR) **Homewoodgate Racing Club**

**Other Owners:** Mrs E. Lucey-Butler, C. W. Wilson.

**Amateur:** Miss M. P. Bryant.

---

## 76 MRS KATE BUCKETT, Bishops Waltham

Postal: **Woodlocks Down Farm, Upham, Bishops Waltham, Hampshire, SO32 1JN**
Contacts: **PHONE (01962) 777557**

1 **BOARDWALK EMPIRE (IRE),** 8, b g Overbury (IRE)—Mighty Mandy (IRE) **Mrs K. A. Buckett**
2 **JOIN THE NAVY,** 10, b g Sea Freedom—Join The Parade **Mrs K. A. Buckett**
3 **UPHAM ATOM,** 12, b g Silver Patriarch (IRE)—Upham Lady **Mrs K. A. Buckett**
4 **UPHAM RUNNING (IRE),** 7, b g Definite Article—Tara Brooch (IRE) **Mrs K. A. Buckett**

**Jockey (NH):** Mark Grant, Liam Treadwell. **Amateur:** Miss Chloe Boxall.

---

## 77 MR BOB BUCKLER, Bridgwater

Postal: **Gibb Hill, Courtway, Spaxton, Bridgewater, Somerset, TA5 1DR**
Contacts: **PHONE (01278) 671268 MOBILE (07785) 773957**
**E-MAIL rbuckler@btconnect.com WEBSITE www.robertbucklerracing.co.uk**

1 **BALLYEGAN (IRE),** 10, b g Saddlers' Hall (IRE)—Knapping Princess (IRE) **R. H. Buckler**
2 **DIGGER'S MATE,** 7, b g General Gambul—Miss Diskin (IRE) **M. J. Forrester**
3 **REDLYNCH ROCK (IRE),** 7, b g Brian Boru—College Ground (IRE) **R. H. Buckler**
4 **SAY MY NAME (IRE),** 4, ch g Fleetwood (IRE)—River Reine (IRE) **Mr T. S. MacDonald**
5 **SOMERSET LIAS (IRE),** 7, b g Golan (IRE)—Presenting Gayle (IRE) **D. R. Fear**
6 **THE HAPPY WARRIOR,** 7, b g Luso—Martomick **N. Elliott**
7 **TINKER TIME (IRE),** 7, b g Turtle Island (IRE)—Gypsys Girl (IRE) **Golden Cap**
8 **UGOLIN DE BEAUMONT (FR),** 7, b g Alberto Giacometti (IRE)—Okarina de Beaumont (FR) **A. J. Norman**

**Other Owners:** Mrs H. E. Shane.

**Head Lad:** Giles Scott (07774) 033246

**Jockey (NH):** Liam Heard, Sam Jones, Gerard Tumelty. **Conditional:** Giles Hawkins, Gary Derwin.

## 78 MR DAI BURCHELL, Ebbw Vale

Postal: **Drysiog Farm, Briery Hill, Ebbw Vale, Gwent, NP23 6BU**
Contacts: **PHONE (01495) 302551 MOBILE (07980) 482860**

1 **ACAPULCO BAY,** 11, b g Pursuit of Love—Lapu-Lapu **J. Parfitt**
2 **BACK BURNER (IRE),** 7, br g Big Bad Bob (IRE)—Marl **Mr R. Emmanuel**
3 **BLUE TOP,** 6, b g Millkom—Pompey Blue **B. M. G. Group**
4 **GUANCIALE,** 8, b g Exit To Nowhere (USA)—Thenford Lass (IRE) **The Beefeaters**
5 **MOOJANED (IRE),** 4, b g Raven's Pass (USA)—Mufradat (IRE) **Mr R. Emmanuel**
6 **NEWFORGE HOUSE (IRE),** 7, b g High-Rise (IRE)—Treasure Island **The Beefeaters**
7 **NIGHT'S WATCH,** 5, b h Authorized (IRE)—Nachtigall (GER) **Mr R. Emmanuel**
8 **ONE FOR THE BOSS (IRE),** 8, b g Garuda (IRE)—Tell Nothing (IRE) **J. E. Mutch**
9 **REBECCAS CHOICE (IRE),** 12, b g Religiously (USA)—Carolin Lass (IRE) **J. E. Mutch**
10 **SYMPHONY OF PEARLS,** 4, b f Lucarno (USA)—Echostar **T. R. Pearson**

### THREE-YEAR-OLDS

11 **SYMPHONY OF ANGELS,** b g Sulamani (IRE)—Flying Lion **T. R. Pearson**
12 **SYMPHONY OF HEAVEN,** b g Sulamani (IRE)—Echostar **T. R. Pearson**

**Other Owners:** Mr W. R. A. Davies, Mr A. J. Mutch, Mrs S. Mutch, Mr David Protheroe.

**Assistant Trainer:** Ruth Burchell

**Jockey (flat):** Sam Hitchcott. **Jockey (NH):** Robert Dunne. **Conditional:** Paul John, Robert Williams.
**Amateur:** Mr Nick Williams, Mr Frank Windsor Clive.

## 79 MR PAUL BURGOYNE, Wincanton

Postal: **Knowle Rock, Shepton Montague, Wincanton, Somerset, BA9 8JA**
Contacts: **PHONE (01963) 32138 MOBILE (07894) 081008**
**E-MAIL knowlerockracing@hotmail.co.uk**

1 **FIRE KING,** 9, b g Falbrav (IRE)—Dancing Fire (USA) **Knowle Rock Racing**
2 **ORPEN'ARRY (IRE),** 7, b g Orpen (USA)—Closing Time (IRE) **Knowle Rock Racing**
3 **QUADRIGA (IRE),** 5, b g Acclamation—Turning Light (GER) **Knowle Rock Racing**
4 **RUNAIOCHT (IRE),** 5, ch g Teofilo (IRE)—Julie Girl (USA) **Knowle Rock Racing**
5 **TEEN AGER (FR),** 11, b g Invincible Spirit (IRE)—Tarwiya (IRE) **Mrs C. Leigh-Turner**
6 **WEST LEAKE (IRE),** 9, b g Acclamation—Kilshanny **Mrs C. Leigh-Turner**

### THREE-YEAR-OLDS

7 B f Piccolo—Fizzy Lady **Mr A. J. Taylor**
8 **SAMMY'S CHOICE,** ch g Pastoral Pursuits—Diane's Choice **Mr A. J. Taylor**

### TWO-YEAR-OLDS

9 **BRIDGET KENNET,** b f 2/4 Kier Park (IRE)—Kathleen Kennet (Turtle Island (IRE))

**Other Owners:** Mr M. Burgoyne.

**Assistant Trainer:** Mrs C. Leigh-Turner

**Jockey (flat):** Liam Keniry, Jimmy Quinn. **Apprentice:** David Parkes.

## 80 MR K. R. BURKE, Leyburn

Postal: **Spigot Lodge, Middleham, Leyburn, North Yorkshire, DL8 4TL**
Contacts: **PHONE (01969) 625088 FAX (01969) 625099 MOBILE (07778) 458777**
**E-MAIL karl@karlburke.co.uk WEBSITE www.karlburke.co.uk**

1 **ANGUS OG,** 5, b g Pastoral Pursuits—Winter Moon **Mr D Simpson & Mrs E Burke**
2 **ARCAMANTE (ITY),** 4, b g High Chaparral (IRE)—Caractere (IRE) **Mr T. J. Dykes**
3 **BARON RUN,** 5, ch g Bertolini (USA)—Bhima **Mrs E. M. Burke**
4 **DALMARELLA DANCER (IRE),** 4, gr f Mastercraftsman (IRE)—Ting A Greeley **Dr M E Glaze & Mr I Mcinnes**
5 **DOYNOSAUR,** 8, b m Doyen (IRE)—Daring Destiny **Mrs E. M. Burke**
6 **EVA CLARE (IRE),** 4, b f Majestic Missile (IRE)—College of Arms **The Mount Racing Club & Mrs E Burke**
7 **FAIR LOCH,** 7, gr g Fair Mix (IRE)—Ardentinny **Mr B Fulton & Mrs E Burke**
8 **FLEMISH SCHOOL,** 5, ch m Dutch Art—Rosewood Belle (USA) **Mrs B. M. Keller**

## MR K. R. BURKE - Continued

9 **FRONTLINE PHANTOM (IRE),** 8, b g Noverre (USA)—Daisy Hill **Ontoawinner & Mrs E Burke**
10 **GEORGIAN BAY (IRE),** 5, b g Oratorio (IRE)—Jazzie (FR) **Market Avenue Racing Club & Mrs E Burke**
11 **HEAVENLY RIVER (FR),** 4, b f Stormy River (FR)—Aaliyah (GER) **Ontoawinner, M Hulin & E Burke**
12 **HOT RIGHT NOW,** 5, ch m Sleeping Indian—American Rouge (IRE) **Mrs E. M. Burke**
13 **INTENSE TANGO,** 4, b f Mastercraftsman (IRE)—Cover Look (SAF) **Cosy Seal Racing Limited**
14 **ISHIKAWA (IRE),** 7, b g Chineur (FR)—Nautical Light **Mr T. J. Dykes**
15 **JAY KAY,** 6, b g Librettist (USA)—Turn Back **Mr J. Kenny**
16 **MAGIC MUSIC MAN,** 4, b g Authorized (IRE)—Magic Music (IRE) **R. Bailey**
17 **MEDIA HYPE,** 8, b h Tiger Hill (IRE)—Hyperspectra **Mrs E. M. Burke**
18 **MIAMI GATOR (IRE),** 8, ch g Titus Livius (FR)—Lovere **Ontoawinner & Mrs E Burke**
19 **ODELIZ (IRE),** 5, ch m Falco (USA)—Acatama (USA) **Mrs B. M. Keller**
20 **REVE DE NUIT (USA),** 9, ch g Giant's Causeway (USA)—My Dream Castles (USA) **Mrs Z. Wentworth**
21 **RIVELLINO,** 5, b g Invincible Spirit (IRE)—Brazilian Bride (IRE) **Mrs M. Bryce**
22 **ROMANTIC BLISS (IRE),** 4, b f Holy Roman Emperor (IRE)—Thea di Bisanzio (IRE) **Mrs E. M. Burke**
23 **RONYA (IRE),** 4, b f Bushranger (IRE)—Beenablaw (IRE) **Mr H. J. Strecker**
24 **SKINNY LOVE,** 4, b f Holy Roman Emperor (IRE)—Lady Mickataine (USA) **Mr T. J. Dykes**
25 **STEPPING AHEAD (FR),** 5, ch g Footstepsinthesand—Zghorta (USA) **Mr Mark James & Mrs Elaine Burke**
26 **TRIXIE MALONE,** 5, b m Ishiguru (USA)—Lady-Love **Mrs E. M. Burke**
27 **WE'LL SHAKE HANDS (FR),** 4, b g Excellent Art—
Amou Daria (FR) **Market Avenue Racing Club & Mrs E Burke**
28 **YEEOOW (IRE),** 6, b g Holy Roman Emperor (IRE)—Taraya (IRE) **Mrs E. M. Burke**
29 **YOU'RE FIRED (IRE),** 4, b c Firebreak—My Sweet Georgia (IRE) **Market Avenue Racing Club & Tim Dykes**
30 **YOURARTISONFIRE,** 5, ch g Dutch Art—Queens Jubilee **Mr J O'Shea,Mr W Rooney & Ontoawinner**

## THREE-YEAR-OLDS

31 **ART CHARTER (FR),** b f Artiste Royal (IRE)—Lady Sylvester (USA) **Mr R Bailey & Mrs E Burke**
32 **CAPRIOR BERE (FR),** b g Peer Gynt (JPN)—Hush Hush (USA) **Mrs E. M. Burke**
33 **EXPLOSIVE LADY (IRE),** gr f Alfred Nobel (IRE)—
My Girl Lisa (USA) **Market Avenue Racing Club & Mrs E Burke**
34 **FELIX LEITER,** ch g Monsieur Bond (IRE)—Spiralling **Mr T Dykes & Mrs E Burke**
35 **FIDELMA MOON (IRE),** b f Dylan Thomas (IRE)—Ridiforza (FR) **The Mount Racing Club & Mrs E Burke**
36 B f Naaqoos—Fire Finch **Middleham Park Racing XXI & Mrs E Burke**
37 **GLENALMOND (IRE),** b c Iffraaj—Balladonia **Mrs M. Bryce**
38 **JOLIEVITESSE (FR),** b c Elusive City (USA)—Volvoreta **Owners For Owners: Jolievitesse**
39 **LIBERAL ANGEL (FR),** b f Librettist (USA)—Angel Voices (IRE) **Mr Mark Bates & Mr D McMahon**
40 **LITTLE LADY KATIE (IRE),** b f Lord Shanakill (USA)—Akarita (IRE) **Ontoawinner 5, M Hulin & Mrs E Burke**
41 **LORD BEN STACK (IRE),** b c Dylan Thomas (IRE)—Beringold **Owners For Owners: Lord Ben Stack**
42 **LOSTOCK HALL (IRE),** b c Lord Shanakill (USA)—Cannikin (IRE) **Mr D W Armstrong & Mrs E Burke**
43 **MALLYMKUN,** b f Kheleyf (USA)—Harriet's Girl **R. Bailey**
44 **MILLAR ROSE (IRE),** b f Vale of York (IRE)—Barbera (GER) **Ontoawinner 7, M Hulin, E Burke**
45 **MOTHERS FINEST (IRE),** ch f Tamayuz—Sheer Glamour (IRE) **Mr H. J. Strecker**
46 **MYSTIC AND ARTIST,** b f Excellent Art—Mystical Spirit (IRE) **Mr M Charge & Mrs E Burke**
47 **RITA'S BOY (IRE),** b c Captain Rio—The Oldladysays No (IRE) **Middleham Park Racing CVI & Mrs E Burke**
48 B g Soldier of Fortune (IRE)—Sandrella (IRE) **Burke & Partners**
49 **SIX CENTS (IRE),** b f Shirocco (GER)—Slawomira (GER) **Hunscote Stud**
50 **TECUMSEH (IRE),** br g Danehill Dancer (IRE)—Absolute Music (USA) **Mr S O'Sullivan & Mrs E Burke**
51 **THE LAMPO GENIE,** b g Champs Elysees—Samar Qand **Mr P Dean & Mrs E Burke**
52 **TIME SPACE (CAN),** b f Arch (USA)—Tiz My Time (USA) **Mr H. J. Strecker**
53 **TOOCOOLFORSCHOOL (IRE),** b g Showcasing—Spring Surprise **Ontoawinner 6, M Hulin, E Burke**
54 B f Azamour (IRE)—Whos Mindin Who (IRE) **Mrs E. M. Burke**

## TWO-YEAR-OLDS

55 Gr ro f 5/3 Paddy O'prado (USA)—Allegro Lady (USA) (Souvenir Copy (USA)) (20634)
56 **ANGEL OF THE NIGHT (IRE),** br f 23/4 Footstepsinthesand—
Princess Sabaah (IRE) (Desert King (IRE)) (2000) **Mr H. A. A. M. Al-Abdulmalik**
57 Ch c 31/3 Falco (USA)—Augusta Lucilla (USA) (Mr Greeley (USA)) (11111) **Mr T Dykes & Mrs E Burke**
58 B c 1/5 Fastnet Rock (AUS)—Balladonia (Primo Dominie) (35000)
59 **BANDIT BOB (IRE),** b c 10/4 Manduro (GER)—Neat Shilling (IRE) (Bob Back (USA)) (12000) **Mr T. J. Dykes**
60 **BE BOP TANGO (FR),** b c 29/4 Soul City (IRE)—Divine Poesie (FR) (Enrique) (6349) **M. R. Johnson & J. Kenny**
61 B c 28/4 Medicean—Bellona (IRE) (Bering) (31746) **Owners For Owners: Timeless Art**
62 **BONJOUR BABY,** ch f 14/3 Duke of Marmalade (IRE)—
Briery (IRE) (Salse (USA)) (22000) **Mr H. A. A. M. Al-Abdulmalik**
63 **DAISY BERE (FR),** b f 13/4 Peer Gynt (JPN)—Jackette (USA) (Mr Greeley (USA)) (8730) **Mrs E. M. Burke**
64 Ch f 3/4 New Approach (IRE)—Dance Lively (USA) (Kingmambo (USA)) (70000) **Mr H. J. Strecker**
65 B f 15/4 Kodiac—Dancing Steps (Zafonic (USA)) (15872)

## MR K. R. BURKE - Continued

**66** B c 25/2 New Approach (IRE)—Doctrine (Barathea (IRE)) (80000) **Mr H. J. Strecker**
**67 FALLEN ANGEL (FR),** ch f 28/2 Dalghar (FR)—Angel Voices (IRE) (Tagula (IRE)) **Mrs E. M. Burke**
**68** B f 23/4 Holy Roman Emperor (IRE)—Fame Game (IRE) (Fasliyev (USA)) (26666) **Mr H. J. Strecker**
**69** Ch c 12/2 Lord Shanakill (USA)—Four Poorer (IRE) (Oasis Dream) (18000)
**70** B c 22/4 Bushranger (IRE)—Golden Shine (Royal Applause) (12380)
**71** B f 1/3 Harlan's Holiday (USA)—Gypsy Monarch (USA) (Wavering Monarch (USA)) **Mr H. J. Strecker**
**72 HAUGHMOND,** b c 25/1 Kheleyf (USA)—Orapids (Oratorio (IRE))
**73** Gr ro c 11/4 Paddy O'prado (USA)—I Insist (USA) (Green Dancer (USA)) (8032) **Mrs E. M. Burke**
**74** Ch f 16/3 Notnowcato—Inaminute (IRE) (Spectrum (IRE)) **R. Bailey**
**75 KATIE'S DIAMOND (FR),** b f 21/2 Turtle Bowl (IRE)—
Aaliyah (GER) (Anabaa (USA)) (14285) **Ontoawinner 6, M Hulin, E Burke**
**76** B f 19/2 Excellent Art—Little Empress (IRE) (Holy Roman Emperor (IRE)) (15079) **Mr H. J. Strecker**
**77** B f 18/4 Exceed And Excel (AUS)—Magic Music (IRE) (Magic Ring (IRE)) **R. Bailey**
**78 MASTERFUL MAN (IRE),** gr c 21/4 Mastercraftsman (IRE)—
Lamanka Lass (USA) (Woodman (USA)) (45000) **Mr H. A. A. M. Al-Abdulmalik**
**79** Ch f 28/3 Kheleyf (USA)—
Musical Twist (USA) (Woodman (USA)) (12380) **Middleham Park Racing CVII & Mrs E Burke**
**80** Gr c 20/3 Alfred Nobel (IRE)—
My Girl Lisa (USA) (With Approval (CAN)) (37300) **Market Avenue Racing Club & Mr P Garvey**
**81** B c 8/4 Equiano (FR)—Mystical Spirit (IRE) (Xaar) (40000) **Palatinate Racing A Chandler L Westwood**
**82 OCEANELLA (IRE),** b f 18/3 Canford Cliffs (IRE)—
Mundus Novus (USA) (Unbridled's Song (USA)) (16190) **Ontoawinner 7, M Hulin, E Burke**
**83** B f 17/3 Nayef (USA)—Quiritis (Galileo (IRE)) (23809)
**84** B f 24/2 Bahamian Bounty—
Salonga (IRE) (Shinko Forest (IRE)) (9523) **Middleham Park Racing LXIV & Mrs E Burke**
**85** Ch f 26/3 Lope de Vega (IRE)—Salpiglossis (GER) (Monsun (GER)) (23809) **Mrs Z. Wentworth**
**86 SAUMUROIS (FR),** b br c 1/3 Doctor Dino (FR)—
Sabolienne (FR) (Marchand de Sable (USA)) (19841) **Unregistered Partnership**
**87 SCARLET WINGS,** ch f 2/2 Sir Percy—Wendylina (IRE) (In The Wings) (24000) **Mr T Dykes & Mrs G Buchanan**
**88** B f 25/3 Frozen Power (IRE)—Spring Surprise (Hector Protector (USA)) (44443) **Clipper Group Holdings Ltd**
**89** B c 1/3 Sir Percy—Star of Gibraltar (Rock of Gibraltar (IRE)) (10000)
**90** B f 18/4 Alfred Nobel (IRE)—
Startarette (USA) (Dixieland Band (USA)) (12698) **Middleham Park Racing XXXV & Mrs E Burke**
**91** Ch c 18/3 Strategic Prince—Swirling (IRE) (Galileo (IRE)) (23809) **Ontoawinner 14 & Mrs E. Burke**
**92** Br c 24/4 Alfred Nobel (IRE)—Tallassee (Indian Ridge) (22221) **Ontoawinner 9 & Mrs E Burke**
**93** B f 8/2 Arcano (IRE)—Tides (Bahamian Bounty) (10000)
**94** Ch c 7/4 Muhtathir—Troiecat (FR) (One Cool Cat (USA)) (13492) **Ontoawinner, Mr R Mckeown & E Burke**
**95** B f 20/2 Sir Percy—Wings of Fame (IRE) (Namid) (20634) **Mr M Nelmes-Crocker & Mrs E Burke**
**96 YOU N ME,** b f 16/2 Footstepsinthesand—
Centenerola (USA) (Century City (IRE)) (24000) **Mr H. A. A. M. Al-Abdulmalik**
**97** Ch c 8/5 Poet's Voice—Za Za Zoom (IRE) (Le Vie Dei Colori) (20000)

**Other Owners:** D. W. Armstrong, Mr D. C. Bacon, Mr M. Bates, Mr S. Bridge, Mrs G. Buchanan, J. Burley, Mr A. Chandler, Mr M. Charge, P. Dean, Mr A. N. Eaton, Dr C. I. Emmerson, Mr J. Fairrie, Mr K. Flanagan, B. N. Fulton, P. Garvey, Dr M. E. Glaze, Mr G. W. Holden, Mr E. J. Hughes, Mr M. A. S. Hulin, Mr M. J. James, M. R. Johnson, Market Avenue Racing Club Ltd, I. McInnes, Mrs S. J. McKeever, Mr R. C. McKeown, Mr D. S. McMahon, Mrs S. M. Morley, Mr P. Moroney, M. Nelmes-Crocker, Mr J. Nolan, N. J. O'Brien, Mr J. O'Shea, S. O'Sullivan, Palatinate Thoroughbred Racing Limited, T. S. Palin, M. Prince, Mr W. Rooney, D. Simpson, S. M. Smith, Mrs L. A. Smith, Mr L. J. Westwood.

**Assistant Trainer:** Mrs E. Burke

**Jockey (flat):** Martin Harley, Daniel Tudhope. **Apprentice:** Joey Haynes, Peter Sword, Jordan Vaughan.

---

## 81 MR HUGH BURNS, Alnwick

Postal: **Rose Cottage, Hedgeley Hall, Powburn, Alnwick, Northumberland, NE66 4HZ**
Contacts: **PHONE (01665) 578972 MOBILE (07914) 018987**
**E-MAIL hughburns123@hotmail.co.uk**

**1 ABOU BEN (IRE),** 13, b br g Beneficial—Sister Ruth (IRE) **Mr H. Burns**
**2 GARTH MOUNTAIN,** 8, b g Rock of Gibraltar (IRE)—One of The Family **Mr H. Burns**
**3 JABUS (IRE),** 9, b g Bob Back (USA)—Salsita (FR) **Mr H. Burns**
**4** 4, B f Duke of Marmalade (IRE)—Sabindra **Mr H. Burns**
**5 STAR WAR (IRE),** 10, b g Publisher (USA)—Betty Hand (IRE) **Mr H. Burns**

## 82 MR JOHN BUTLER, Newmarket

Postal: **The Bungalow, Charnwood Stables, Hamilton Road, Newmarket, Suffolk, CB8 7JQ**
Contacts: **MOBILE (07764) 999743**
**E-MAIL johnbutler1@btinternet.com**

1 **BEAU AMADEUS (IRE),** 6, b g Amadeus Wolf—Degree of Honor (FR) **Mr Ian Herbert**
2 **BLACKTHORN STICK (IRE),** 6, b g Elusive City (USA)—Hi Lyla (IRE) **Mr J. Butler**
3 **COME ON DAVE (IRE),** 6, b g Red Clubs (IRE)—Desert Sprite (IRE) **Wildcard Racing Syndicate**
4 **CONGAREE WARRIOR,** 5, ch g Congaree (USA)—Peace And Love (IRE) **K. Quinn/ C. Benham/ I. Saunders**
5 **DEADLY STING (IRE),** 6, b g Scorpion (IRE)—Gaza Strip (IRE) **Maxilead Limited**
6 **DIAMOND MINE,** 5, gr g Rock of Gibraltar (IRE)—Kassiyra (IRE) **Miss Amy Murphy**
7 **FINAL DRIVE (IRE),** 9, b g Viking Ruler (AUS)—Forest Delight (IRE) **Par 4 Racing**
8 **HALO MOON,** 7, br g Kayf Tara—Fragrant Rose **Level Par Racing**
9 **MOONDAY SUN (USA),** 6, gr h Mizzen Mast (USA)—Storm Dove (USA) **Mayfair Racing**
10 **NEZAR (IRE),** 4, ch g Mastercraftsman (IRE)—Teddy Bears Picnic **Maxilead Limited**
11 **NOVABRIDGE,** 7, ch g Avonbridge—Petrovna (IRE) **Mayfair Racing**
12 **OFFICER IN COMMAND (USA),** 9, b br g Officer (USA)—Luv to Stay n Chat (USA) **Mr J. Butler**
13 **ONE CHANCE (IRE),** 4, b f Invincible Spirit (IRE)—Towards (USA) **Recycled Products Limited**
14 **PARTY ROYAL,** 5, b g Royal Applause—Voliere **Mr Micheal Orlandi**
15 **TRENDSETTER (IRE),** 4, b g Mastercraftsman (IRE)—Fashion Trade **Maxilead Limited**

### THREE-YEAR-OLDS

16 **ANGELS ABOVE (IRE),** b c Dark Angel (IRE)—Fag End (IRE) **Maxilead Limited**
17 **GHAROOR,** b c Thewayyouare (USA)—Connessa (IRE) **Kingnee Bloodstock**
18 **IFITTAKESFOREVER (IRE),** b br g Kodiac—Bobby Jane **Recycled Products Limited**
19 B c Bahamian Bounty—Pressed For Time (IRE) **Mr P. A. Cafferty**
20 **SIR VEILLANCE,** b c Authorized (IRE)—Caught You Looking **Kingnee Bloodstock**
21 **THREE TIMES A LORD,** br gr c Three Valleys (USA)—Sesmen **Kingnee Bloodstock**

**Other Owners:** Mr Imad Al-Sagar, Mr Chris Benham, Mr Andy Bonarius, Mr N. J. Bonarius, Mr P. A. Cafferty, Mr M. J. Gavin, Mr Saleh Al Homaizi, Mr Kevin Quinn, Mr Ian Saunders, Mr Damian Tiernan.

**Assistant Trainer:** Alice Haynes (07585) 558717

## 83 MR PADDY BUTLER, Lewes

Postal: **Homewood Gate Racing Stables, Novington Lane, East Chiltington, Lewes, East Sussex, BN7 3AU**
Contacts: **PHONE/FAX (01273) 890124 MOBILE (07973) 873846**
**E-MAIL homewoodgate@aol.com**

1 **ALL OR NOTHIN (IRE),** 6, b g Majestic Missile (IRE)—Lady Peculiar (CAN) **Miss M P Bryant, David & Eileen Bryant**
2 **CATALYZE,** 7, b g Tumblebrutus (USA)—Clarita Dear (CHI) **Homewoodgate Racing Club**
3 **CORLOUGH MOUNTAIN,** 11, ch g Inchinor—Two Step **Miss M. P. Bryant**
4 **ESTIBDAAD (IRE),** 5, b g Haatef (USA)—Star of Siligo (USA) **Miss M. P. Bryant**
5 **MY SILVER CLOUD (IRE),** 8, gr g Cloudings (IRE)—Royal Patrol (IRE) **Homewoodgate Racing Club**
6 **PICCOLO TED,** 4, ch g Piccolo—Quality Street **Mr D. M. Whatmough**
7 **QUEEN OF NORWAY (IRE),** 4, b f Papal Bull—Fanacanta (IRE) **Homewoodgate Racing Club**
8 **SUTTON SID,** 5, ch g Dutch Art—Drastic Measure **Miss M. P. Bryant**
9 **SWEET PICCOLO,** 5, ch g Piccolo—Quality Street **Mr D. M. Whatmough**
10 **WHAT'S FOR TEA,** 10, b m Beat All (USA)—Come To Tea (IRE) **E Lucey-Butler,Chris Wilson,Anne Horrell**

**Other Owners:** Mr D. Bryant, Mrs E. Bryant, Mrs A. Horrell, Mrs E. Lucey-Butler, C. W. Wilson.

**Assistant Trainer:** Mrs E Lucey-Butler

**Amateur:** Miss M. Bryant.

## 84 MRS BARBARA BUTTERWORTH, Appleby

Postal: **Bolton Mill, Bolton, Appleby-in-Westmorland, Cumbria, CA16 6AL**
Contacts: **PHONE (01768) 361363 MOBILE (07778) 104118**

1 **AGE OF GLORY,** 6, b g Zamindar (USA)—Fleeting Moon **Miss E. Butterworth**

## MRS BARBARA BUTTERWORTH - Continued

2 **KNIGHT VALLIANT,** 12, gr g Dansili—Aristocratique **Mrs B. Butterworth**
3 **SNOWED IN (IRE),** 6, gr g Dark Angel (IRE)—Spinning Gold **Miss E. Butterworth**

**Assistant Trainer:** Miss Elizabeth Butterworth

**Jockey (NH):** Sean Quinlan. **Amateur:** Miss Elizabeth Butterworth.

---

## 85 MR NEVILLE BYCROFT, Malton

Postal: **Cotman Rise, Brandsby, York, YO61 4RN**
Contacts: **PHONE (01347) 888641 MOBILE (07802) 763227**

1 **ADIATOR,** 7, b m Needwood Blade—Retaliator **N. Bycroft**
2 **BYRONAISSANCE,** 6, ch g Byron—Renaissance Lady (IRE) **N. Bycroft**
3 **DUAL MAC,** 8, br g Paris House—Carol Again **Mrs C. M. Whatley**
4 **EIUM MAC,** 6, b g Presidium—Efipetite **Mrs J. Dickinson**
5 **FAMA MAC,** 8, b g Fraam—Umbrian Gold (IRE) **Mrs C. M. Whatley**
6 **GURU MAC,** 5, b m Ishiguru (USA)—Zacinta (USA) **N. Bycroft**
7 **HARPERS RUBY,** 5, b m Byron—La Belle Katherine (USA) **Mr S. P. Griffiths**
8 **MAYBEME,** 9, b m Lujain (USA)—Malvadilla (IRE) **Mrs J. Dickinson**
9 **MISU MAC,** 5, b m Misu Bond (IRE)—Umbrian Gold (IRE) **Mrs C. M. Whatley**
10 **WILLBEME,** 7, b m Kyllachy—Befriend (USA) **Mr P. D. Burrow**

### THREE-YEAR-OLDS

11 **EURO MAC,** ch f Sir Percy—Oomph **Mrs J. Dickinson**

**Other Owners:** Mr J. D. Martin.

**Assistant Trainer:** Seb Spencer

**Jockey (flat):** Jimmy Quinn, Franny Norton.

---

## 86 MISS JULIE CAMACHO, Malton

Postal: **Star Cottage, Welham Road, Norton, Malton, North Yorkshire, YO17 9QE**
Contacts: **PHONE (01653) 696205 FAX (01653) 696205 MOBILE (07779) 318135 / (07950) 356440**
**E-MAIL julie@jacracing.co.uk WEBSITE www.juliecamacho.com**

1 **DANDARRELL,** 8, b g Makbul—Dress Design (IRE) **Mr J. S. De W. Waller**
2 **DIESCENTRIC (USA),** 8, b g Diesis—Hawzah **Axom (XVIII)**
3 **DUBAI CELEBRATION,** 7, b g Dubai Destination (USA)—Pretty Poppy **Miss J. A. Camacho**
4 **FAR RANGING (USA),** 4, b f U S Ranger (USA)—Hutchinson (USA) **Axom XLVII**
5 **ILLUSTRIOUS PRINCE (IRE),** 8, b g Acclamation—
Sacred Love (IRE) **Lee Bolingbroke, Graeme Howard & Partners**
6 **MY SINGLE MALT (IRE),** 7, b g Danehill Dancer (IRE)—Slip Dance (IRE) **Mr N. Gravett**
7 **PLEASE LET ME GO,** 4, ch f Sleeping Indian—Elhida (IRE) **Mr N. Gravett**
8 **REX WHISTLER (IRE),** 5, b g Tamayuz—Dangle (IRE) **Axom XXXVIII**
9 **TOM SAWYER,** 7, b g Dansili—Cayman Sunset (IRE) **Bolingbroke J Howard FAO MerseyR & Ptns**
10 **WILDE INSPIRATION (IRE),** 4, ch g Dandy Man (IRE)—Wishing Chair (USA) **Judy & Richard Peck**

### THREE-YEAR-OLDS

11 **BURTONWOOD,** b g Acclamation—Green Poppy **Judy & Richard Peck & Julie Camacho**
12 **SWAHEEN,** b g Lawman (FR)—Whole Grain **Judy & Richard Peck**
13 **TWINKLE TWINKLE,** b f Exceed And Excel (AUS)—Kalinova (IRE) **Elite Racing Club**

**Other Owners:** Axom, Mr Lee Bolingbroke, Mr Tony Bruce, Mr S. Burrows, Miss Julie Camacho, Mr Dan Downie, Mr Nigel Gravett, Mr Brian Hankey, Mr Tony Hill, Mr Graeme Howard, Ms S. M. Jamieson, Miss M. Noden, Mrs Faith O'Connor, Mr J. E. Townend.

**Assistant Trainer:** Mr S. Brown

**Jockey (flat):** Tom Eaves, Barry McHugh.

## 87 MR MARK CAMPION, Malton

Postal: **Whitewell House Stables, Whitewall, Malton, North Yorkshire, YO17 9EH**
Contacts: **PHONE (01653) 692729 FAX (01653) 600066 MOBILE (07973) 178311**
**E-MAIL info@markcampion-racing.com WEBSITE www.markcampion-racing.com**

1 **CHARMING GRACE (IRE),** 9, b m Flemensfirth (USA)—Lady Laureate
2 **DESERT NOVA (IRE),** 13, ch g Desert King (IRE)—Assafiyah (IRE)
3 **MINKIE MOON (IRE),** 7, b g Danehill Dancer (IRE)—Minkova (IRE)
4 **SADDLERS' SECRET (IRE),** 10, b m Saddlers' Hall (IRE)—Birdless Bush (IRE)
5 4, Ch g Proclamation (IRE)—Tish Too

### THREE-YEAR-OLDS

6 **COSMIC BLUE (IRE),** b f Kalanisi (IRE)—Gift of Freedom (IRE)
7 Ch f Getaway (GER)—Founding Daughter (IRE)

**Owners:** Mr A. M. Campion, Faulkner West & Co, Pan's People, The Saddlers' Flyers, Whitewall Racing, Mr J. P. Whittaker.

**Assistant Trainer:** Mrs F. Campion

## 88 MS JENNIE CANDLISH, Leek

Postal: **Basford Grange Racing Stables, Basford, Leek, Staffordshire, ST13 7ET**
Contacts: **PHONE (07889) 413639 (07976) 825134 FAX (01538) 360324**
**E-MAIL jenniecandlish@yahoo.co.uk WEBSITE www.jenniecandlishracing.co.uk**

1 **ASTAROLAND (FR),** 5, b g Astarabad (USA)—Orlandaise (FR) **P. W. Beck**
2 **BARAFUNDLE (IRE),** 11, ch g Flemensfirth (USA)—Different Dee (IRE) **Mrs J. M. Ratcliff**
3 **BASFORD BEN,** 7, b g Trade Fair—Moly (FR) **The Best Club In The World**
4 **BEAUBOREEN (IRE),** 8, b g Revoque (IRE)—Roseboreen (IRE) **Mrs A. V. Hall**
5 **BOB'S WORLD,** 6, b g Multiplex—Vocation (IRE) **Mr R. J. Cant**
6 **BRYDEN BOY (IRE),** 5, b g Craigsteel—Cailin Vic Mo Cri (IRE) **Alan Baxter & Brian Hall**
7 **DECENT LORD (IRE),** 11, b g Lord of Appeal—Otorum (IRE) **Mrs J. M. Ratcliff**
8 **GRANDE ANTARCTIQUE (FR),** 5, b g Antarctique (IRE)—Puerta Grande (FR) **Mr P. & Mrs G. A. Clarke**
9 **GRANVILLE ISLAND (IRE),** 8, b g Flemensfirth (USA)—Fox Glen **Mr P. & Mrs G. A. Clarke**
10 **GRAPHENE,** 4, b g Nayef (USA)—Annapurna (IRE) **Mr D. T. Spratt**
11 **GROVE SILVER (IRE),** 6, gr g Gamut (IRE)—Cobbler's Well (IRE) **Alan Baxter Anthony Bloor Dave Cheetham**
12 **KILKENNY KIM (IRE),** 6, b m Beneficial—Benbradagh Vard (IRE) **Mr M. M. Allen**
13 **LUCKY LUKEY,** 9, gr g Cape Town (IRE)—Imprevue (IRE) **John Pointon & Sons**
14 **LUKEYS LUCK,** 9, b g Cape Town (IRE)—Vitelucy **John Pointon & Sons**
15 **MAOI CHINN TIRE (IRE),** 8, b g Mull of Kintyre (USA)—Primrose And Rose **The Best Club In The World**
16 **PARTY ROCK (IRE),** 8, b g Vinnie Roe (IRE)—Garryduff Eile (IRE) **Mrs P. M. Beardmore**
17 **RESTRAINT OF TRADE (IRE),** 5, br g Authorized (IRE)—Zivania (IRE) **A. J. Baxter**
18 4, Ch g Stowaway—Roseboreen (IRE) **Mrs A. V. Hall**
19 **ROUGH KING (IRE),** 6, b g King's Theatre (IRE)—Ringzar (IRE) **Mr P. & Mrs G. A. Clarke**
20 **SKAGHARDGANNON LAD (IRE),** 9, b g Flemensfirth (USA)—Lady Briarsfield (IRE) **Mrs P. M. Beardmore**
21 **SLEEPY HAVEN (IRE),** 5, b g Indian Haven—High Society Girl (IRE) **Alan Baxter Anthony Bloor Dave Cheetham**
22 **TIMEFORFIRTH (IRE),** 5, b m Flemensfirth (USA)—Don't Be Upset (IRE)
23 **WAKE YOUR DREAMS (IRE),** 7, b g Oscar (IRE)—Rose Karanja **Pam Beardmore & Alan Baxter**

### THREE-YEAR-OLDS

24 B c Lucarno (USA)—Basford Lady (IRE)
25 B f Presenting—Princess Rainbow (FR) **Mr P. & Mrs G. A. Clarke**

**Other Owners:** Mr H. A. E. Bloor, Ms J. Candlish, Mr D. A. Cheetham, Mr P. Clarke, Mrs G. A. Clarke, Mr B. J. Hall.

**Assistant Trainer:** Alan O'Keeffe

**Jockey (flat):** Joe Fanning, Paul Hanagan.

## 89 MR HENRY CANDY, Wantage

Postal: **Kingston Warren, Wantage, Oxfordshire, OX12 9QF**
Contacts: **PHONE (01367) 820276 / 820514 FAX (01367) 820500 MOBILE (07836) 211264**
**E-MAIL henrycandy@btconnect.com**

1 **ANYA,** 6, b m Monsieur Bond (IRE)—Dyanita **Mrs L. M. Alexander**
2 **CAPE PERON,** 5, b g Beat Hollow—Free Offer **The Earl Cadogan**
3 **CORNISH PATH,** 4, b f Champs Elysees—Quintrell **Major M. G. Wyatt**
4 **COSETTE (IRE),** 4, b f Champs Elysees—Luanas Pearl (IRE) **Mr P. A. Deal/Mr H. Candy**
5 **DINKUM DIAMOND (IRE),** 7, b h Aussie Rules (USA)—Moving Diamonds **The Eight Star Syndicate**
6 **GREENSIDE,** 4, b c Dubawi (IRE)—Katrina (IRE) **Clayton, Frost, Kebell & Turner**
7 **JETHOU ISLAND,** 4, ch f Virtual—Lihou Island **Mrs F A Veasey & Partners**
8 **MUSIC MASTER,** 5, b h Piccolo—Twilight Mistress **Mr Godfrey Wilson**
9 **PEDRO SERRANO (IRE),** 5, b g Footstepsinthesand—Shaiyadima (IRE) **Six Too Many**
10 **PENNINE PANTHER,** 4, b g Notnowcato—Kozmina (IRE) **Deal, Lowe, Silver, Woods**
11 **SCARLET SASH,** 4, b f Sir Percy—Scarlet Buttons (IRE) **Henry D. N. B. Candy**
12 **SPRING FLING,** 4, b f Assertive—Twilight Mistress **Six Too Many/T A Frost/ G Wilson**
13 **WHITE RUSSIAN,** 4, ch f Sir Percy—Danse Russe **Six Too Many**

### THREE-YEAR-OLDS

14 Ch f Kyllachy—Alenushka **Mrs Fiona Gordon**
15 **ALONSOA (IRE),** ch f Raven's Pass (USA)—Alasha (IRE) **Mrs Patricia J. Burns**
16 **CAPE XENIA,** b f Cape Cross (IRE)—Xaphania **Simms, Blackburn & Candy**
17 **CHAIN OF DAISIES,** b f Rail Link—Puya **Girsonfield Ltd**
18 **EXOPLANET BLUE,** b f Exceed And Excel (AUS)—Tut (IRE) **One Too Many Partners**
19 **FLASHY DIVA,** ch f Showcasing—Dazzling View (USA) **The Flashy Diva Partnership**
20 **GERALD,** b g Bahri (USA)—Gerardina **Henry D. N. B. Candy**
21 **GOLDCREST,** ch f Assertive—Level Pegging (IRE) **Lady Whent**
22 **HAROLD LLOYD,** b c Cape Cross (IRE)—Silent Act (USA) **Mr & Mrs R. Scott**
23 **ICONIC (IRE),** b f Kodiac—Christa Maria **First Of Many And Turner**
24 **LE TORRENT,** ch g Sir Percy—Cinnas Ransom **First Of Many And Turner**
25 **LIGHT OF LOVE,** b f Dylan Thomas (IRE)—May Light **Brightwalton Bloodstock Limited**
26 **LIMATO (IRE),** b g Tagula (IRE)—Come April **P. G. Jacobs**
27 **MARAUDER,** b g Thewayyouare (USA)—Louise d'arzens **Henry D. N. B. Candy**
28 **OAT COUTURE,** b f Kyllachy—Oat Cuisine **Mrs G. Rowland-Clark**
29 **PERCEIVED,** ch f Sir Percy—New Light **Candy, Pritchard & Thomas**
30 **PERESTROIKA,** b f Sir Percy—Lekka Ding (IRE) **Henry D. N. B. Candy**
31 **PERSICARIA,** br f Halling (USA)—Danae **Girsonfield Ltd**
32 **POSTBAG,** b f Three Valleys (USA)—Postage Stampe **Major M. G. Wyatt**
33 **SELDOM HEARD,** br g Bahri (USA)—Turtle Dove **Henry D. N. B. Candy**
34 **SELFRESPECT,** b f Thewayyouare (USA)—Self Esteem **Henry D. N. B. Candy**
35 **SKYMASTER,** gr g Aussie Rules (USA)—Last Slipper **D. B. Clark**
36 **SOME SHOW,** ch f Showcasing—Dancing Nelly **The Rumble Racing Club**
37 **SON OF AFRICA,** b g Equiano (FR)—Generously Gifted **One Too Many Partners**
38 **STOIC BOY,** ch g Paco Boy (IRE)—Dramatic Turn **Mrs David Blackburn & Mr M. Blackburn**
39 **TAP SHOES,** ch f Equiano (FR)—Ruff Shod (USA) **D. B. Clark**
40 **TREATY OF YORK (IRE),** b g Haatef (USA)—Pretty Woman (IRE) **One Too Many Partners**
41 **TUNNEL CREEK,** b g Tobougg (IRE)—Free Offer **The Earl Cadogan**
42 **TWILIGHT SON,** b c Kyllachy—Twilight Mistress **Mr Godfrey Wilson**
43 **UELE RIVER,** b f Refuse To Bend (IRE)—Baddi Heights (FR) **Mrs A. R. Ruggles**
44 **WOTNOT (IRE),** gr f Exceed And Excel (AUS)—Whatami **Mr & Mrs D. Brown**

### TWO-YEAR-OLDS

45 **BALTIC TIGER (IRE),** b c 11/4 Tagula (IRE)—Kamarita (IRE) (Octagonal (NZ)) (11110) **Simon Broke & Partners**
46 **BOUNCE,** b f 2/4 Bahamian Bounty—Black Belt Shopper (IRE) (Desert Prince (IRE)) (32000) **Landmark Racing Limited**
47 **CAPTON,** b c 15/5 Cape Cross (IRE)—Flavian (Catrail (USA)) **Mr W. Wyatt**
48 **DENHAM SOUND,** ch f 7/2 Champs Elysees—Presbyterian Nun (IRE) (Daylami (IRE)) **The Earl Cadogan**
49 **DREAMS ALLOWED,** b f 26/2 Authorized (IRE)—In Your Dreams (IRE) (Suave Dancer (USA)) **Mr K. Arrowsmith**
50 B f 2/3 Kyllachy—Floating (Oasis Dream) (19047) **Potensis Bloodstock Ltd**
51 **FREE PASSAGE,** ch c 1/3 Medicean—Free Offer (Generous (IRE)) **The Earl Cadogan**
52 Ch f 22/4 Dandy Man (IRE)—High Chart (Robellino (USA)) (19047) **Potensis Bloodstock Ltd**
53 **JACK NEVISON,** b c 27/4 Dick Turpin (IRE)—Creative Mind (IRE) (Danehill Dancer (IRE)) (9523) **Henry Candy & Partners**
54 **LIMONATA (IRE),** b f 28/1 Bushranger (IRE)—Come April (Singspiel (IRE)) (90000) **P. G. Jacobs**

## MR HENRY CANDY - Continued

**55** B f 16/2 Kodiac—Nassma (IRE) (Sadler's Wells (USA)) **Mrs Patricia J. Burns**
**56** B c 5/3 Compton Place—Neqaawi (Alhaarth (IRE)) **Mrs D. Blackburn**
**57** **PAST MASTER,** b c 26/4 Mastercraftsman (IRE)—
Millestan (IRE) (Invincible Spirit (IRE)) (40000) **Mr D. B. Clark, Mr A. R. Bentall, Mr H. Candy**
**58** B c 7/4 Medicean—Quintrell (Royal Applause) (25000) **One Too Many, N. Agran, M. Silver**
**59** **REGAL GAIT (IRE),** b c 2/5 Tagula (IRE)—Babylonian (Shamardal (USA)) (42857) **P. G. Jacobs**
**60** **ROSIE ROYCE,** b f 5/2 Acclamation—Rebecca Rolfe (Pivotal) **Hunscote Stud**
**61** Br f 2/4 Manduro (GER)—Sea of Galilee (Galileo (IRE)) **Mr Dominic Burke**
**62** B f 6/5 Art Connoisseur (IRE)—Shakeeba (IRE) (Sendawar (IRE)) (4500) **Candy, Pritchard & Thomas**
**63** **SHOWING OFF (IRE),** ch c 25/1 Notnowcato—
Walk On Water (Exceed And Excel (AUS)) **Dowager Duchess Of Bedford**
**64** **SQUIGGLEY,** b f 20/4 Sir Percy—Oat Cuisine (Mujahid (USA)) **Mrs G. Rowland-Clark**
**65** B f 4/2 Hellvelyn—Talampaya (USA) (Elusive Quality (USA)) (50000) **Qatar Racing Limited**
**66** **TIME TO EXCEED (IRE),** b f 24/4 Exceed And Excel (AUS)—In Your Time (Dalakhani (IRE)) **Hunscote Stud**
**67** **VIBRANT CHORDS,** b c 11/4 Poet's Voice—Lovely Thought (Dubai Destination (USA)) (71428) **P. G. Jacobs**

**Other Owners:** Mr Alexander Acloque, Mr N. Agran, Mr A. Bentall, Mrs David Blackburn, Mr S. Broke, Mr Henry Candy, Mr S. Clayton, Mr P. A. Deal, Mr A. Deal, Mrs A. Dixon, Mr D. J. Erwin, Mr Richard Farquhar, Mr Alexander Frost, Mr T. A. F. Frost, Mr N. E. Gosset, Mr T. Gould, Mr P. R. Greeves, Mr J. Inverdale, Mr J. Kebell, Mr T. J. Le Blanc-Smith, Mr G. Lowe, Mr D. Norris, Mr N. Patsalides, Mrs A. Pinder, Mrs C. Poland, Mr Roy Pritchard, Mr Robert Scott, Mrs P. M. Scott, Mr M. J. Silver, Mr John Simms, Mrs J. Snowball, Mr F. C. Taylor, Mr Gerry Thomas, Mrs F. A. Veasey, Mr Godfrey Wilson, Mr Richard Woods.

**Assistant Trainer:** David Pinder

---

## 90 MR GRANT CANN, Lower Hamswell

Postal: **Parkfield Farm, Hall Lane, Lower Hamswell, Bath, Gloucestershire, BA1 9DE**
Contacts: **PHONE (01225) 891674 MOBILE (07968) 271118**

**1** **ARCTIC WATCH,** 10, gr g Accondy (IRE)—Watcha (USA) **P. J. Cave**
**2** **CAILIN (IRE),** 7, b m Golan (IRE)—Castle Arms Cailin (IRE) **J. G. Cann**
**3** **I'M IN CHARGE,** 9, b g Rakaposhi King—Cloudy Pearl **J. G. Cann**
**4** **MASTER TODD (IRE),** 10, ch g Dream Well (FR)—Falika (FR) **The Borris Partnership**
**5** **MILLER'S MAVERICK,** 7, b g Millkom—Gables Girl **P. J. Cave**
**6** **WHAT A FRIEND,** 12, b g Alflora (IRE)—Friendly Lady **J. G. Cann**

**Other Owners:** Mr A. R. M. M. Kavanagh, Miss R. McMorrough Kavanagh.

---

## 91 MR DON CANTILLON, Newmarket

Postal: **10 Rous Road, Newmarket, Suffolk, CB8 8DL**
Contacts: **PHONE (01638) 668507 MOBILE (07709) 377601**

**1** **GREEN TO GOLD (IRE),** 10, gr g Daylami (IRE)—Alonsa (IRE) **Sir Alex Ferguson & Sotirios Hassiakos**
**2** **IT IS I (IRE),** 5, b g Presenting—Nivalf **D. E. Cantillon**
**3** **LA ESTRELLA (USA),** 12, b g Theatrical—Princess Ellen **D. E. Cantillon**
**4** **ODIN (IRE),** 7, b g Norse Dancer (IRE)—Dimelight **Mrs C. Reed**
**5** **SPEED CHECK (IRE),** 8, ch g Kris Kin (USA)—Zaola (IRE) **Mr D. McGrath**
**6** **THIS IS ME,** 7, b g Presenting—Shayzara (IRE) **D. E. Cantillon**
**7** **TRUCKERS DARLING (IRE),** 8, b m Flemensfirth (USA)—Nicat's Daughter (IRE) **Mrs C. Reed**
**8** **WESTERN WAY (IRE),** 6, b g Westerner—Faucon **D. E. Cantillon**

### TWO-YEAR-OLDS

**9** B f 26/4 Mastercraftsman (IRE)—Anamarka (Mark of Esteem (IRE)) (41269) **Mrs C. Reed**
**10** B f 3/3 Zoffany (IRE)—Trois Graces (USA) (Alysheba (USA)) (55555) **Mrs C. Reed**

## 92 MRS RUTH CARR, Stillington

Postal: **Mowbray House Farm, Easingwold Road, Stillington, York, North Yorkshire, YO61 1LT**
Contacts: **PHONE (01347) 823776 (home) (01347) 821683 (yard) MOBILE (07721) 926772**
**E-MAIL ruth@ruthcarrracing.co.uk WEBSITE www.ruthcarrracing.co.uk**

1 **ADVANCE (FR),** 4, b g Aqlaam—Rabeera **M.A.G Fire Group & Mrs R Carr**
2 **ALMUHALAB,** 4, b br g Dansili—Ghanaati (USA) **Michael Hill**
3 **AMAZING BLUE SKY,** 9, b g Barathea (IRE)—Azure Lake (USA) **G Scruton, D Williamson & R Carr**
4 **ASIAN TRADER,** 6, b g Acclamation—Tiger Waltz **Mrs R Carr & The Bottom Liners**
5 **BE PERFECT (USA),** 6, b g Street Cry (IRE)—Binya (GER) **The Beer Stalkers & Ruth Carr**
6 **BEN HALL (IRE),** 4, b g Bushranger (IRE)—Sassy Gal (IRE) **Miss V. A. Church**
7 **BIG STORM COMING,** 5, b g Indesatchel (IRE)—Amber Valley **Fishlake Commercial Motors Ltd**
8 **CONO ZUR (FR),** 8, b g Anabaa (USA)—Alaskan Idol (USA) **Ruth Carr Racing**
9 **COSMIC CHATTER,** 5, b g Paris House—Paradise Eve **Mrs R. A. Carr**
10 **DANISH DUKE (IRE),** 4, ch g Duke of Marmalade (IRE)—Bridge Note (USA) **Michael Hill**
11 **DREAM SIKA (IRE),** 4, b g Elnadim (USA)—Enchantment **Michael Hill**
12 **DUBAI DYNAMO,** 10, b g Kyllachy—Miss Mercy (IRE) **The Bottom Liners**
13 **ELLAAL,** 6, b g Oasis Dream—Capistrano Day (USA) **The Bottom Liners & Paul Saxton**
14 **EXOTIC GUEST,** 5, ch g Bahamian Bounty—Mamoura (IRE) **21st Century Racing,A Swinburne,R Carr**
15 **FAVOURITE TREAT (USA),** 5, b g Hard Spun (USA)—Truart (USA) **Paul Saxton & The Bottom Liners**
16 **FLASH CITY (ITY),** 7, b g Elusive City (USA)—Furnish **Mr S. R. Jackson**
17 **FROSTY THE SNOWMAN (IRE),** 4, gr g Mastercraftsman (IRE)—Sleeveless (USA) **Bruce Jamieson, Barbara Dean, Ruth Carr**
18 **FURAS (IRE),** 4, br g Shamardal (USA)—Albaraari **The Bottom Liners & Mrs R. Carr**
19 **GLADYS' GAL,** 7, b m Tobougg (IRE)—Charming Lotte **Fishlake Commercial Motors Ltd**
20 **HAB REEH,** 7, gr g Diktat—Asian Love **Grange Park Racing & Mrs B Taylor**
21 **KERBAAJ (USA),** 5, b g Dixie Union (USA)—Mabaahej (USA) **The Bottom Liners & Mrs R. Carr**
22 **LEXINGTON PLACE,** 5, ch g Compton Place—Elidore **Mrs M. Chapman**
23 **LIGHT THE CITY (IRE),** 8, b g Fantastic Light (USA)—Marine City (JPN) **Mrs R. A. Carr**
24 **MARCRET (ITY),** 8, b g Martino Alonso (IRE)—Love Secret (USA) **Northern Line Racing Ltd**
25 **MESHARDAL (GER),** 5, b g Shamardal (USA)—Melody Fair (IRE) **The Hollinbridge Partnership & Ruth Carr**
26 **MUTAFAAKIR (IRE),** 6, b g Oasis Dream—Moon's Whisper (USA) **Ms Helen Barbour & Mr Dario Neri**
27 **ORPSIE BOY (IRE),** 12, b g Orpen (USA)—Nordicolini (IRE) **Miss V. A. Church**
28 **QUASQAZAH,** 4, ch g Bahamian Bounty—Rock Lily **The Hollinbridge Partnership & Ruth Carr**
29 **RASSELAS (IRE),** 8, b g Danehill Dancer (IRE)—Regal Darcey (IRE) **Mr A. N. Gargan**
30 **RED CAPE (FR),** 12, b g Cape Cross (IRE)—Muirfield (FR) **Middleham Park Racing LVI**
31 **ROCHAMBEAU (IRE),** 4, b g Sir Percy—Tableau Vivant (IRE) **Michael Hill**
32 **SAN CASSIANO (IRE),** 8, b g Bertolini (USA)—Celtic Silhouette (FR) **Mr S Jackson, Mr L Shaw, Mrs R Carr**
33 **SLEMY (IRE),** 4, b g Raven's Pass (USA)—Wolf Cleugh (IRE) **J. A. Swinburne**
34 **TANAWAR (IRE),** 5, b g Elusive City (USA)—Parakopi (IRE) **G Scruton, D Williamson & R Carr**
35 **VALLARTA (IRE),** 5, b g Footstepsinthesand—Mexican Miss (IRE) **D. C. Renton**
36 **VICTOIRE DE LYPHAR (IRE),** 8, b g Bertolini (USA)—Victory Peak **The Beer Stalkers & Ruth Carr**
37 **ZAIN ZONE (IRE),** 4, ch g Pastoral Pursuits—Right After Moyne (IRE) **21St Century Racing & Mrs R Carr**

### THREE-YEAR-OLDS

38 **CHEECO,** ch g Shami—Mandarin Lady **Mrs A. Clark**
39 **FOXTROT KNIGHT,** b g Kyllachy—Rustam **The Double 'A' Partnership**
40 **MININGROCKS (FR),** b g Lawman (FR)—Fashion School **Miss B Houlston, Mrs M Chapman & Mrs R Carr**

### TWO-YEAR-OLDS

41 Ch g 20/4 Haafhd—Mandarin Lady (Timeless Times (USA)) **Mrs A. Clark**

**Other Owners:** Ms H. M. Barbour, T. J. E. Brereton, A. W. Catterall, Mrs B. Catterall, S. B. Clark, A. D. Crombie, Mrs B. I. Dean, Mr M. Gibbons, J. P. Hames, Miss B. J. Houlston, Mr A. B. Jamieson, Mr D. R. Kelly, Mr D. G. Neri, Mr P. Newell, T. S. Palin, R J H Limited, RHD Research Limited, P. A. Saxton, Mr G. Scruton, Mr L. D. Shaw, Mr E. Surr, Mrs B. Taylor, S. L. Walker, Mr D. J. Williamson, Mr R. W. Wilson.

**Jockey (flat):** P J McDonald, James Sullivan. **Jockey (NH):** Jake Greenall. **Amateur:** Miss Serena Brotherton.

## 93 MR DECLAN CARROLL, Malton

Postal: **Norton Grange Stables, Park Road, Malton, North Yorkshire, YO17 9EA**
Contacts: **PHONE (01653) 698517 FAX (01377) 236161 MOBILE (07801) 553779**
**E-MAIL declancarrollracing@gmail.com**

1 **BEAUTY'S FORTE (IRE),** 4, b g Kyllachy—Viking Fair **C. H. Stephenson & Partners**
2 **BOLD SPIRIT,** 4, b g Invincible Spirit (IRE)—Far Shores (USA) **Mrs S. A. Bryan**
3 **BOUSFIELD,** 4, b g Duke of Marmalade (IRE)—Exodia **Bousfield Boys**
4 **BUONARROTI (IRE),** 4, b g Galileo (IRE)—Beauty Is Truth (IRE) **D. Hardy**
5 **FARANG BER SONG,** 4, b g Selkirk (USA)—Dazzle **L. C. Ibbotson**
6 **GLASGON,** 5, gr g Verglas (IRE)—Miss St Tropez **Mr M. J. Rozenbroek**
7 **HAGREE (IRE),** 4, b g Haatef (USA)—Zuniga's Date (USA) **R. J. Flegg**
8 **LLEWELLYN,** 7, b g Shamardal (USA)—Ffestiniog (IRE) **Mrs S. A. Bryan**
9 **MY DESTINATION (IRE),** 6, b g Dubai Destination (USA)—Gossamer **Mrs S. A. Bryan**
10 **MYSTERIAL,** 5, b g Invincible Spirit (IRE)—Diamond Dilemma (IRE) **Mrs S. A. Bryan**
11 **PULL THE PLUG (IRE),** 4, b f Sleeping Indian—Babylonian **Mr C. J. Harding**
12 **SAVE THE BEES,** 7, b g Royal Applause—Rock Concert **Mr S. P. Ryan**
13 **SWIFTLY DONE (IRE),** 8, b g Whipper (USA)—Ziffany **Mr D Watts, Miss C King, J Syme & M Syme**
14 **TWEETY PIE (IRE),** 4, ch f Rock of Gibraltar (IRE)—Princesse Sonia (FR) **Mr J. G. Johnson**
15 **TWO PANCAKES,** 5, b g Compton Place—Fancy Rose (USA) **Mr K. McConnell**
16 **WHOZTHECAT (IRE),** 8, b g One Cool Cat (USA)—Intaglia (GER) **Mr S. R. Bean**

### THREE-YEAR-OLDS

17 **ELMER J,** b g Hellvelyn—Mis Chicaf (IRE) **Mr M. C. Saunders**
18 **FARANG JAI DEE (IRE),** b g Approve (IRE)—Fruit O'the Forest (IRE) **Kenny Mackay & Lee Ibbotson**
19 **FLORRIE (IRE),** b f Baltic King—Folk Kris (IRE) **Mr M. C. Saunders**
20 **LIGHTNING STEPS,** b g Champs Elysees—Fairy Steps **The Commissioning Team**
21 **MONSIEUR JIMMY,** ch g Monsieur Bond (IRE)—Artistic License (IRE) **Mr Ray Flegg & Mr H J Bousfield**
22 **MRS BIGGS,** ch f Paco Boy (IRE)—Hoh Chi Min **Mr K. Mackay**
23 **RUTLAND PANTHER,** b g Alhaarth (IRE)—Desert Lynx (IRE) **Mr G. Barot**
24 **STONEBOAT BILL,** ch g Virtual—Applauding (IRE) **Mr D. J. O'Reilly**
25 **UNFORGETTABLE YOU (IRE),** br f Captain Rio—The Gibson Girl (IRE) **Mr D. Tate**

**Other Owners:** Mr H. J. Bousfield, D. Carroll, Miss J. C. King, Mr A. Middlehurst, C. H. Stephenson, Mrs V. Stephenson, Mr M. W. Syme, D. Watts.

**Jockey (flat):** Jason Hart. **Apprentice:** Neil Farley, Luke Leadbitter. **Amateur:** Mr Kyle Walker.

## 94 MR TONY CARROLL, Cropthorne

Postal: **The Cropthorne Stud, Field Barn Lane, Cropthorne, Pershore, Worcestershire, WR10 3LY**
Contacts: **PHONE (01386) 861020 FAX (01386) 861628 MOBILE (07770) 472431**
**E-MAIL a.w.carroll@btconnect.com WEBSITE www.awcarroll.co.uk**

1 **ADMIRABLE ART (IRE),** 5, b g Excellent Art—Demi Voix **Mr D. S. G. Morgan**
2 **AMBITIOUS ROSIE,** 4, b f Striking Ambition—Cerulean Rose **Mr J. Loftus**
3 **ASSERTIVE AGENT,** 5, b m Assertive—Agent Kensington **Wedgewood Estates**
4 **BALTIC PRINCE (IRE),** 5, b g Baltic King—Brunswick **Mr A. Mills**
5 **BOOM THE GROOM (IRE),** 4, b c Kodiac—Ecco Mi (IRE) **Mr G. Attwood**
6 **BOSTON BLUE,** 8, b g Halling (USA)—City of Gold (IRE) **Mr B. J. Millen**
7 **BOUCLIER (IRE),** 5, ch h Zamindar (USA)—Bastet (IRE) **Mr M. Chung**
8 **BY RIGHTS,** 4, b f Byron—Legend House (FR) **Last Day Racing Partnership**
9 **CASPIAN PRINCE (IRE),** 6, ch g Dylan Thomas (IRE)—Crystal Gaze (IRE) **Mr S. Louch**
10 **CRAZY BOLD (GER),** 12, ch g Erminius (GER)—Crazy Love (GER) **Mrs S. R. Keable**
11 **DUKE OF DUNTON (IRE),** 4, b g Duke of Marmalade (IRE)—Southern Migration (USA) **Mr S. Louch**
12 **EASYDOESIT (IRE),** 7, b g Iffraaj—Fawaayid (USA) **T. R. Pearson**
13 **EVIDENT (IRE),** 5, b g Excellent Art—Vestavia (IRE) **Mr Morgan, Bright, Clarke & Parris**
14 **EXPANDING UNIVERSE (IRE),** 8, b g Galileo (IRE)—Uliana (USA) **A. W. Carroll**
15 **FIRST REBELLION,** 6, ch g Cockney Rebel (IRE)—First Dawn **Brian, Mark & Carolynn Day**
16 **FORCEFUL BEACON,** 5, ch g Assertive—Shore Light (USA) **A. W. Carroll**
17 **GREAT LINK,** 6, b g Rail Link—The Strand **Mr C. Hodgson**
18 **HEURTEVENT (FR),** 6, b br g Hold That Tiger (USA)—Sybilia (GER) **L. T. Cheshire**
19 **INNOKO (FR),** 5, gr g Carlotamix (FR)—Chalana **Mill House Racing Syndicate**

## MR TONY CARROLL - Continued

20 **KEYS (IRE),** 8, b g Doyen (IRE)—Freni (GER) **Seasons Holidays**
21 **KING OLAV (UAE),** 10, ch g Halling (USA)—Karamzin (USA) **Cover Point Racing**
22 **LARAGHCON BOY (IRE),** 6, ch g Stowaway—Hannah Mooney (IRE) **Mr M. S. Cooke**
23 **LE BACARDY (FR),** 9, b g Bahhare (USA)—La Balagna **Mr C. Hodgson**
24 **MALANOS (IRE),** 7, b br g Lord of England (GER)—Majorata (GER) **Mr B. J. Millen**
25 **MAYAN FLIGHT (IRE),** 7, b g Hawk Wing (USA)—Balimaya (IRE) **A. W. Carroll**
26 4, Bl gr g Dr Massini (IRE)—Miss Tehente (FR)
27 **MISSIONAIRE (USA),** 8, b br g El Corredor (USA)—Fapindy (USA) **Mr B. J. Millen**
28 **MR MAFIA (IRE),** 6, b g Zerpour (IRE)—Wizzy (IRE) **Three Counties Racing**
29 **NEW TARABELA,** 4, ch g New Approach (IRE)—Tarabela (CHI) **Mrs P. J. Clark**
30 **NOUVELLE ERE,** 4, b g Archipenko (USA)—Sinister Ruckus (USA) **Lady Jennifer Green & Martyn C Palmer**
31 **OCEAN LEGEND (IRE),** 10, b g Night Shift (USA)—Rose of Mooncoin (IRE) **Mr W. McLuskey**
32 **OEIL DE TIGRE (FR),** 4, b g Footstepsinthesand—Suerte **Miss C. A. Baines**
33 5, B m Double Trigger (IRE)—Oleana (IRE) **Seasons Holidays**
34 **PAHENTE,** 7, br gr g Silver Patriarch (IRE)—Miss Tehente (FR) **Mayden Stud**
35 **PAR THREE (IRE),** 4, b br g Azamour (IRE)—Little Whisper (IRE) **A. W. Carroll**
36 **POLYDAMOS,** 6, b g Nayef (USA)—Spotlight **Mrs S. R. Keable**
37 **POUR LA VICTOIRE (IRE),** 5, b g Antonius Pius (USA)—Lady Lucia (IRE) **Curry House Corner**
38 **PRAIRIE TOWN (IRE),** 4, b g High Chaparral (IRE)—Lake Baino **Cooke & Millen**
39 **PROMINNA,** 5, ch g Proclamation (IRE)—Minnina (IRE) **Mayden Stud**
40 **QUEEN AGGIE (IRE),** 5, b m Elnadim (USA)—Catfoot Lane **Shropshire Wolves 4**
41 **RANCHER (IRE),** 5, b g High Chaparral (IRE)—Shot of Redemption **Mr A. M. Cosnett**
42 **RIGHTWAY (IRE),** 4, b g Cockney Rebel (IRE)—Caeribland (IRE) **Mr B. J. Millen**
43 **ROSIE PROBERT,** 6, b m Dylan Thomas (IRE)—Corsican Sunset (USA) **Seasons Holidays**
44 **SAINT POIS (FR),** 4, b g Le Havre (IRE)—Our Dream Queen **Mr G. Attwood**
45 **SALVADO (IRE),** 5, b g Invincible Spirit (IRE)—Easter Fairy (USA) **Contubernium Racing Club**
46 **SAN QUENTIN (IRE),** 4, gr g Lawman (FR)—In The Soup (USA) **Mr S. Louch**
47 **SEAHAM HALL HOTEL,** 4, b f Tiger Hill (IRE)—Molly Mello (GER) **Seasons Holidays**
48 **SERENITY SPA,** 5, gr m Excellent Art—Molly Mello (GER) **Seasons Holidays**
49 **SHALAMBAR (IRE),** 9, gr g Dalakhani (IRE)—Shalama (IRE) **Mr B. J. Millen**
50 **SMART CATCH (IRE),** 9, b g Pivotal—Zafaraniya (IRE) **Cover Point Racing**
51 **SMOKY HILL (IRE),** 6, gr g Galileo (IRE)—Danaskaya (IRE) **Millen & Cooke**
52 **SPIRITOFTOMINTOUL,** 6, gr g Authorized (IRE)—Diamond Line (FR) **The Sunday Players**
53 **SPRAY TAN,** 5, b m Assertive—Even Hotter **Silks Racing Partnership**
54 **STAND TO REASON (IRE),** 7, ch g Danehill Dancer (IRE)—Ho Hi The Moon (IRE) **Seasons Holidays**
55 **SUPA SEEKER (USA),** 9, b br g Petionville (USA)—Supamova (USA) **A. W. Carroll**
56 **SYMPHONY OF KINGS,** 4, b g Lucarno (USA)—Flying Lion **T. R. Pearson**
57 **THE RIGHT TIME,** 7, b m Val Royal (FR)—Esligier (IRE) **A. W. Carroll**
58 **THE YANK,** 6, b g Trade Fair—Silver Gyre (IRE) **Mr G. Attwood**
59 **THINGER LICHT (FR),** 6, b g Clety (FR)—Family Saga (FR) **Mr C. Hodgson**
60 **TIME MEDICEAN,** 9, gr g Medicean—Ribbons And Bows (IRE) **A. W. Carroll**
61 **TIME SQUARE (FR),** 8, b g Westerner—Sainte Parfaite (FR) **Mr M. S. Cooke**
62 **VAGUELY SPANISH,** 4, b g Oratorio (IRE)—Spanish Quest **D. Boocock**
63 **VEDANI (IRE),** 6, b g Dalakhani (IRE)—Velandia (IRE) **Six Pack**
64 **VERTUEUX (FR),** 10, gr g Verglas (IRE)—Shahrazad (FR) **Mr J. Rutter**
65 **VIVACISSIMO (IRE),** 8, ch g Muhtathir—Valley Orchard (FR) **Mr C. Hodgson**
66 **VIZZY'S THUNDER,** 7, gr g Fair Mix (IRE)—Vizulize **Last Day Racing Partnership**
67 **WARM ORDER,** 4, b f Assertive—Even Hotter **Mrs V. C. Gilbert**
68 **WEDGEWOOD ESTATES,** 4, ch f Assertive—Heaven **Wedgewood Estates**
69 **WOWEE,** 4, b g Archipenko (USA)—Katya Kabanova **Wedgewood Estates**
70 **YOUM JAMIL (USA),** 8, gr g Mizzen Mast (USA)—Millie's Choice (IRE) **Montpellier Racing**

## THREE-YEAR-OLDS

71 **AGENT GIBBS,** ch c Bertolini (USA)—Armada Grove **A. W. Carroll**
72 **CITISONSMITH (IRE),** b g Amadeus Wolf—Ink Pot (USA) **Mr A. Mills**
73 **DUSTY BLUE,** ch f Medicean—Jazz Jam **A. W. Carroll**
74 **IRISH BELLE (IRE),** ch f Duke of Marmalade (IRE)—Flower of Kent (USA) **Mr & Mrs J. B. Bacciochi**
75 **MONSIEUR VALENTINE,** ch c Monsieur Bond (IRE)—Minnina (IRE) **Mayden Stud**
76 **OCEAN BENTLEY (IRE),** b g Amadeus Wolf—Bentley's Bush (IRE) **Mr W. McLuskey**
77 **TONI'S A STAR,** b f Avonbridge—Canina **A Star Recruitment Limited**
78 **ZANNAQLAAM (FR),** b f Aqlaam—Zanna (FR) **Miss C. A. Baines**

## MR TONY CARROLL - Continued

**Other Owners:** Mr J. Babb, J. T. Bacciochi, Mrs J. M. Bacciochi, Mr D. R. Blake, Mr A. D. Bright, N. A. Brimble, Mr R. Buckland, Mr C. E. Carroll, Mr M. B. Clarke, Mr J. R. Daniell, Miss C. J. Day, Mr M. S. Day, J. A. Dewhurst, Mrs D. S. Dewhurst, Lady J. Green, Ms K. A. Gwilliam, Mr J. Lawrence, D. J. Lowe, Mr T. R. Mennell, R. J. Millen, Mr M. Nichol, Mr W. G. Nixon, Mr M. C. Palmer, Mr K. J. Parris, Dr A. D. Rogers, N. Scanlan, D. T. Shorthouse, R. Simpson, Miss A. L. Statham, Mr J. A. Sullivan, Mr R. Ward, Mrs I. Whitehead.

**Jockey (NH):** Lee Edwards. **Conditional:** Josh Hamer. **Apprentice:** George Downing.

---

## 95 MR TONY CARSON, Newmarket

Postal: **5 Churchill Avenue, Newmarket, Suffolk, CB8 0BZ**
Contacts: **PHONE (01638) 660947 MOBILE (07837) 601867**
**E-MAIL topcatcarson@ymail.com**

1 **BARWAH (USA),** 4, b f Discreet Cat (USA)—Enfiraaj (USA) **Hugh & Mindi Byrne**
2 **MAY HAY,** 5, b m Dubai Destination (USA)—Trounce **W. F. H. Carson**
3 **MAY'S SISTER,** 4, b f Tiger Hill (IRE)—Trounce **W. F. H. Carson**
4 **PEACE SEEKER,** 7, b g Oasis Dream—Mina **Hugh & Mindi Byrne**
5 **SPIRITUAL STAR (IRE),** 6, b g Soviet Star (USA)—Million Spirits (IRE) **Hugh and Mindi Byrne & Macattack**

### THREE-YEAR-OLDS

6 **CORNTON ROAD,** b g Bertolini (USA)—Sister Rose (FR) **W. F. H. Carson**
7 **CRAZY QUEEN,** ch f Le Fou (IRE)—Queen of Norway (USA) **W. H. Carson**
8 **DEEP BLUE SEA,** b f Rip Van Winkle (IRE)—Semaphore **The Chriselliam Partnership**
9 **EQUILLINSKY,** ch f Equiano (FR)—Millinsky (USA) **The Chriselliam Partnership**
10 **MY MISTRESS (IRE),** ch f Mastercraftsman (IRE)—Majestic Eviction (IRE) **David J. Newman & Ross Bennett**
11 **SCENT OF POWER,** b f Authorized (IRE)—Aromatherapy **W. F. H. Carson**
12 **SHE'S NO BIMBO,** ch f Recharge (IRE)—Senorita Parkes **Mr G. P. Taylor**

### TWO-YEAR-OLDS

13 B f 31/3 Kyllachy—Aromatherapy (Oasis Dream) (1142)
14 Ch c 25/2 Pivotal—Celeste (Green Desert (USA)) (35000)
15 B f 26/2 Bertolini (USA)—Doric Lady (Kyllachy) (2285)
16 **ON BUDGET (IRE),** b g 25/4 Duke of Marmalade (IRE)—Henties Bay (IRE) (Cape Cross (IRE)) (23000)
17 **PLACEDELA CONCORDE,** b c 5/4 Champs Elysees—
Kasakiya (IRE) (Zafonic (USA)) (18000) **The Chriselliam Partnership**
18 B f 19/4 Royal Applause—Tee Cee (Lion Cavern (USA)) (9000)
19 **TULIP DRESS,** ch f 29/3 Dutch Art—White Dress (IRE) (Pivotal)

**Other Owners:** Miss E. Asprey, Mr R. Bennett, Mr Hugh Byrne, Mrs Mindi Byrne, Mr W. H. Carson, Mrs E. Carson, Mr T. J. McLoughlin, Mr D. J. Newman, Mr Christopher Wright.

**Assistant Trainer:** Graham Carson

**Jockey (flat):** William Carson. **Amateur:** Mr Graham Carson.

---

## 96 MR LEE CARTER, Epsom

Postal: **The Old Yard, Clear Height Stables, Epsom, Surrey, KT18 5LB**
Contacts: **PHONE (01372) 740878 FAX (01372) 740898 MOBILE (07539) 354819**
**E-MAIL leecarterracing@aol.co.uk WEBSITE www.leecarterracing.com**

1 **ANGEL FLORES (IRE),** 4, b f Art Connoisseur (IRE)—Emmas Princess (IRE) **Mr J. McTaggart**
2 **BENNELONG,** 9, b g Bahamian Bounty—Bundle Up (USA) **Mr J. J. Smith**
3 **CENSORIUS,** 4, b g Notnowcato—Meredith **Clear Racing**
4 **COPPERWOOD,** 10, ch g Bahamian Bounty—Sophielu **Mr J. J. Smith**
5 **DOC HAY (USA),** 8, b g Elusive Quality (USA)—Coherent (USA) **Mr J. J. Smith**
6 **HALF WAY,** 4, b g Haafhd—Amhooj **Mrs I. Marshall**
7 **INVESTISSEMENT,** 9, b g Singspiel (IRE)—Underwater (USA) **Mr J. J. Smith**
8 **MUNSARIM (IRE),** 8, b g Shamardal (USA)—Etizaaz (USA) **Wackey Racers Harefield**
9 **PERMITTED,** 4, b f Authorized (IRE)—Discerning **Clear Racing**
10 **PERSEPOLIS (IRE),** 5, gr g Dansili—La Persiana **Mr J. J. Smith**
11 **ROCK 'N' ROLL STAR,** 4, b g Cockney Rebel (IRE)—Sweet Afton (IRE) **Mr J. J. Smith**
12 **RUFFORD (IRE),** 4, b g Invincible Spirit (IRE)—Speedy Sonata (USA) **Mr R. Cooper**
13 **SEEK THE FAIR LAND,** 9, b g Noverre (USA)—Duchcov **Mr J. J. Smith**

## MR LEE CARTER - Continued

14 **TAKEITFROMALADY (IRE),** 6, b g Intikhab (USA)—Pinheiros (IRE) **Only One Bid Partnership**
15 **TIDAL BEAUTY,** 4, gr f Verglas (IRE)—Tidal **Mrs B. Quinn**
16 **TIDAL'S BABY,** 6, b g Dutch Art—Tidal **Mrs B. Quinn**

## THREE-YEAR-OLDS

17 **BLUE AMAZON (IRE),** b f Acclamation—Amazon Beauty (IRE) **Tattenham Corner Racing IV**
18 **COURIER,** b f Equiano (FR)—Pivotal Drive (IRE) **One More Bid Partnership**
19 **GEORGIA'S GAMBLE (IRE),** b g Strategic Prince—My Sweet Georgia (IRE) **The Shard Seven**
20 **PACT,** b f Paco Boy (IRE)—Jade Pet **Ewell Never Know**
21 **TABLA,** b f Rail Link—Questa Nova **Mr J. J. Smith**
22 B f Dutch Art—Tidal **Mrs B. Quinn**
23 **WALLY'S WISDOM,** b c Dutch Art—Faldal **Mr R. Cooper**

**Other Owners:** N. Boyce, Mr K. B. Brant, Mrs K. T. Carter, J. D. A. Gordon, Mrs M. M. Greening, B. J. Greening, Mr J. O'Hara, Mr J. Rowe, Mr D. Wood.

**Apprentice:** Paige Bolton.

---

## 97 MR BEN CASE, Banbury

Postal: **Wardington Gate Farm, Edgcote, Banbury, Oxfordshire, OX17 1AG**
Contacts: **PHONE (01295) 750959 FAX (01295) 758840 MOBILE (07808) 061223**
**E-MAIL info@bencaseracing.com WEBSITE www.bencaseracing.com**

1 **ALPANCHO,** 9, ch g Alflora (IRE)—Run Tiger (IRE) **Apple Pie Partnership**
2 **BALLAGH (IRE),** 6, b g Shantou (USA)—Go Along (IRE) **Mrs C. Kendrick**
3 **BEBINN (IRE),** 8, b m Brian Boru—Windmill Star (IRE) **The Polk Partnership**
4 **BRASS TAX (IRE),** 9, b g Morozov (USA)—Cry Before Dawn (IRE) **Mrs C. Kendrick**
5 **BREAKING THE BANK,** 6, ch g Medicean—Russian Dance (USA) **D. C. R. Allen**
6 4, B f Midnight Legend—Clover Green (IRE) **D. C. R. Allen**
7 **COCHINILLO (IRE),** 6, b g Shantou (USA)—Nut Touluze (IRE) **Goodman, Hemstock, Case & Case**
8 **CROCO BAY (IRE),** 8, b g Croco Rouge (IRE)—April Thistle (IRE) **Lady Jane Grosvenor**
9 **CROOKSTOWN (IRE),** 8, b g Rudimentary (USA)—Millview Lass (IRE) **Mrs C. Wallace**
10 **DEEP TROUBLE (IRE),** 8, b g Shantou (USA)—Out of Trouble (IRE) **Lady Jane Grosvenor**
11 **EASTERN MAGIC,** 8, b g Observatory (USA)—Inchtina **Mrs C. Stevenson**
12 **FREDDY FOX (IRE),** 5, ch g Shantou (USA)—Ballyquinn (IRE) **Mrs C. Kendrick**
13 **GAMAIN (IRE),** 6, b g Gamut (IRE)—Glass Curtain (IRE) **D. C. R. Allen**
14 **GINGER FIZZ,** 8, ch m Haafhd—Valagalore **Itchen Valley Stud**
15 **LILLY OF THE MOOR,** 7, b m Flemensfirth (USA)—Serenique **S. Hemstock**
16 **MAZURATI (IRE),** 6, b g Definite Article—Mazuma (IRE) **As If Partnership**
17 **MIDNIGHT JAZZ,** 5, b m Midnight Legend—Ring Back (IRE) **D. C. R. Allen**
18 5, B h Kayf Tara—Mille Et Une (FR) **Lady Jane Grosvenor**
19 **MOVIE LEGEND,** 5, b g Midnight Legend—Cyd Charisse **D. Hing & N. Langstaff**
20 **MR GREY (IRE),** 7, gr g Great Palm (USA)—Presenting Shares (IRE) **D. C. R. Allen**
21 **MY NOSY ROSY,** 7, b m Alflora (IRE)—Quiz Night **Case Racing Partnership**
22 **MY RENAISSANCE,** 5, b br g Medicean—Lebenstanz **N. S. Hutley**
23 **ORANGEADAY,** 8, b g Kayf Tara—One of Those Days **D. C. R. Allen**
24 **PETERPANOPIRATEMAN (IRE),** 6, b g Kalanisi (IRE)—Year'fthehorse (IRE) **Mrs C. Kendrick**
25 **PETROU (IRE),** 5, b g Mountain High (IRE)—Evnelu (IRE) **J. Wright**
26 **PHARE ISLE (IRE),** 10, b g Turtle Island (IRE)—Pharenna (IRE) **Nicholson Family Moore Moore & Kendrick**
27 **PRETTY ROSE (IRE),** 5, b m King's Theatre (IRE)—Rosies All The Way **Case Racing Partnership**
28 **PROFIT MONITOR (IRE),** 7, b g Court Cave (IRE)—Knock Abbey Castle (IRE) **Mrs C. Kendrick**
29 **ROLLO'S REFLECTION (IRE),** 5, b g Shantou (USA)—Lola's Reflection **T. W. Moore**
30 **SHANTOU RIVER (IRE),** 7, b g Shantou (USA)—River Mousa (IRE) **Mrs L. R. Lovell**
31 **SNOWY DAWN,** 5, gr g Notnowcato—Tereyna **Mrs C. A. Stevenson**
32 **TEMPEST RIVER (IRE),** 9, b m Old Vic—Dee-One-O-One **Fly Like The Wind Partnership**
33 **THEMANFROM MINELLA (IRE),** 6, b g Shantou (USA)—Bobomy (IRE) **Mrs C. Kendrick**
34 **THORESBY (IRE),** 9, b g Milan—I Remember It Well (IRE) **D. C. R. Allen**
35 **VESUVHILL (FR),** 6, ch g Sabrehill (USA)—L'orchidee (FR) **Case Racing Partnership**
36 **VINEGAR HILL,** 6, b g Kayf Tara—Broughton Melody **Swanee River Partnership**
37 **WESTON FLAME,** 5, b m Westerner—Rocheflamme (FR) **E. R. Hanbury**
38 **WISH IN A WELL (IRE),** 6, b g Gamut (IRE)—Lady Bellingham (IRE) **Case Racing Partnership**
39 **WITHER YENOT (IRE),** 8, b g Tikkanen (USA)—Acacia Bloom (IRE) **Mrs C. Kendrick**

**MR BEN CASE - Continued**

**TWO-YEAR-OLDS**

**40** B f 13/4 Kalanisi (IRE)—Dee Two O Two (IRE) (Rudimentary (USA)) **B. Case**

**Other Owners:** Mr D. Baines, Mr N. Biggs, Mr T. Boylan, Mr B. I. Case, Mrs S. Case, Mrs Robert Case, Mr A. Case, Mrs A. Charlton, Mr T. Childs, Mr C K Crossley Cooke, Mr J. Deeley, Mr O. Denny, Mr W. Duffin, Mr J. English, Mr D. Foulk, Mr A. R. Franklin, Mrs A. Gladden, Mr E. Gladden, Mr John Goodman, Mr A. Goodsir, Mr D. Green, Mrs J. Grindlay, Mr R. Hagen, Mr P. Hallett, Mr R. Harper, Mrs S. Harrison, Mr Steve Hemstock, Mrs M. Howlett, Mrs J. Hulse, Dr. C. Ilsley, Mrs B. Joice, Mrs Carolyn Kendrick, Mrs C. Lawrence, Mrs H. Loggin, Mr P. Lush, Miss A. Lush, Mr M. Marshall, Mr M. Matthews, Mrs Wendy Moore, Mr T. W. Moore, Mr D. Muffitt, Mrs P. Murray, Mr Grahame Nicholson, Mr C. Nixey, Mr J. Nowell-Smith, Mr R. Palmer, Mr & Mrs G. D. Payne, Mrs K. Perrem, Mrs C. Pestel, Mr John Polk, Mr James Polk, Mr J. Shaw, Mr David Smith, Mr J. Stephenson, Mr David Watson, Mr N. Wellington.

**Jockey (NH):** Daryl Jacob, Kielan Woods. **Amateur:** Mr M. J. P. Kendrick.

---

## 98 LADY JANE CECIL, Newmarket

**Trainer did not wish details of her string to appear**

---

## 99 MR PATRICK CHAMINGS, Basingstoke

Postal: **Inhurst Farm Stables, Baughurst, Tadley, Hampshire, RG26 5JS**
Contacts: **PHONE (01189) 814494 FAX (01189) 820454 MOBILE (07831) 360970**
**E-MAIL chamingsracing@talk21.com**

1 4, Ch g Iffraaj—Astuti (IRE) **F. T. Lee**
2 **BENTWORTH BOY,** 4, b g Archipenko (USA)—Maria di Scozia **Robinson, Wiggin, Hayward-Cole, Roberts**
3 **CHELWOOD GATE (IRE),** 5, b gr g Aussie Rules (USA)—Jusoor (USA) **K. W. Tyrrell**
4 **CHURCH LEAP (IRE),** 4, gr g High Chaparral (IRE)—Alambic **Robinson, Wiggin, Hayward-Cole, Roberts**
5 **DIRECTORSHIP,** 9, br g Diktat—Away To Me **Mrs R. Lyon**
6 **DOUBLE CZECH (IRE),** 4, b g Bushranger (IRE)—Night of Joy (IRE) **K. W. Tyrrell**
7 **FOXFORD,** 4, b f Clodovil (IRE)—Pulau Pinang (IRE) **The Foxford House Partnership**
8 **FOXHAVEN,** 13, ch g Unfuwain (USA)—Dancing Mirage (IRE) **The Foxford House Partnership**
9 **HIT THE LIGHTS (IRE),** 5, b g Lawman (FR)—Dawn Chorus (IRE) **The Select Racing Club Limited**
10 **PERFECT OUTCOME,** 4, b f Echo of Light—Cautiously (USA) **Mildmay Racing & D. H. Caslon**
11 **SCOTTISH GLEN,** 9, ch g Kyllachy—Dance For Fun **The Foxford House Partnership**
12 **TAKE A NOTE,** 6, b g Singspiel (IRE)—Ela Paparouna **The Foxford House Partnership**
13 4, Ch g Tobougg (IRE)—Tamise (USA)
14 **THE REEL WAY (GR),** 4, br f Reel Buddy (USA)—Nephetriti Way (IRE) **The Foxford House Partnership**
15 **THOMAS BLOSSOM (IRE),** 5, b g Dylan Thomas (IRE)—Woman Secret (IRE) **The Select Racing Club Limited**

**THREE-YEAR-OLDS**

16 **REGAL MISS,** b f Royal Applause—Pretty Miss **Mrs J. E. L. Wright**

**Other Owners:** D. H. Caslon, P. R. Chamings, Dr S. B. Drew, J. R. Drew, Mrs N. Hayward-Cole, Mr S. Hill, Mrs M. Roberts, Mr N. R. Robinson, Mr D. P. Wiggin.

**Assistant Trainer:** Phillippa Chamings

---

## 100 MR MICK CHANNON, West Ilsley

Postal: **West Ilsley Stables, West Ilsley, Newbury, Berkshire, RG20 7AE**
Contacts: **PHONE (01635) 281166 FAX (01635) 281177**
**E-MAIL mick@mick-channon.co.uk/susan@mick-channon.co.uk WEBSITE www.mickchannon.tv**

1 **AL MANAAL,** 5, b m Echo of Light—Mall Queen (USA) **M. R. Channon**
2 **AMAHORO,** 4, b f Sixties Icon—Evanesce **Dave & Gill Hedley**
3 **ARANTES,** 4, b g Sixties Icon—Black Opal **M. R. Channon**
4 **ARNOLD LANE (IRE),** 6, b h Footstepsinthesand—Capriole **Mr J. M. Mitchell**
5 **BALLYPATRICK (IRE),** 9, b br g Presenting—Jewell For A King (IRE) **Martin, Jocelyn & Steve Broughton**
6 **BRIDIE FFRENCH,** 4, b f Bahamian Bounty—Wansdyke Lass **M. R. Channon**
7 **CHILWORTH ICON,** 5, b g Sixties Icon—Tamara Moon (IRE) **Mr W. G. Parish**
8 **CRAZEE DIAMOND,** 4, b f Rock of Gibraltar (IRE)—Final Dynasty **Nick & Olga Dhandsa & John & Zoe Webster**

## MR MICK CHANNON - Continued

9 **CRUCK REALTA,** 5, b m Sixties Icon—Wansdyke Lass **Anne & Steve Fisher**
10 **DEEDS NOT WORDS (IRE),** 4, b g Royal Applause—Wars (IRE) **G. D. P. Materna**
11 **DING DING,** 4, ch f Winker Watson—Five Bells (IRE) **Dave & Gill Hedley**
12 **DIVINE (IRE),** 4, b f Dark Angel (IRE)—Carallia (IRE) **Mr M. Al-Qatami & Mr K. M. Al-Mudhaf**
13 **ELIDOR,** 5, br g Cape Cross (IRE)—Honorine (IRE) **Jon & Julia Aisbitt**
14 **FITZWILLY,** 5, b g Sixties Icon—Canadian Capers **P. Taplin**
15 **FOSTER'S ROAD,** 6, b g Imperial Dancer—Search Party **Dave & Gill Hedley**
16 **GOOD MORNING LADY,** 4, b f Compton Place—Baldemosa (FR) **M. R. Channon**
17 **GRATZIE,** 4, b f Three Valleys (USA)—La Gazzetta (IRE) **C Corbett, David Hudd, Chris Wright**
18 **GREVILLEA (IRE),** 4, b f Admiralofthefleet (USA)—Louve Heureuse (IRE) **N. J. Hitchins**
19 **HIGHLIFE DANCER,** 7, br g Imperial Dancer—Wrong Bride **The Highlife Racing Club**
20 **ISABELLA BIRD,** 4, b f Invincible Spirit (IRE)—Meetyouthere (IRE) **Jon & Julia Aisbitt**
21 **JAYWALKER (IRE),** 4, b g Footstepsinthesand—Nipping (IRE) **Insignia Racing (Crest)**
22 **JENNY SPARKS,** 4, b f Winker Watson—Stephanie's Mind **M. R. Channon**
23 **JERSEY BROWN (IRE),** 4, br f Marju (IRE)—Daniysha (IRE) **Lakedale**
24 **KAIULANI (IRE),** 4, b f Danehill Dancer (IRE)—Royal Shyness **Mrs T P Radford & Tails Partnership**
25 **KNOCK HOUSE (IRE),** 6, ch g Old Vic—Lady's Gesture (IRE) **Mrs C. M. Radford**
26 **LINCOLN (IRE),** 4, b c Clodovil (IRE)—Gilt Linked **Mr W. G. Parish**
27 **LOCH BA (IRE),** 9, b g Craigsteel—Lenmore Lisa (IRE) **Peter Taplin, Susan Bunney & Partners**
28 **LUNARIAN,** 4, ch f Bahamian Bounty—One Giant Leap (IRE) **Mrs A. C. Black**
29 **MICKS LAD (IRE),** 5, b g Beneficial—Floreen (IRE) **Mrs C. M. Radford**
30 **MISS CAPE (IRE),** 4, b f Cape Cross (IRE)—Miss Sally (IRE)
31 **MR KITE,** 4, b g Sixties Icon—Mar Blue (FR) **M. R. Channon**
32 **NAFA (IRE),** 7, br m Shamardal (USA)—Champs Elysees (USA) **Mrs T. Burns**
33 **NANCY FROM NAIROBI,** 4, b f Sixties Icon—Madame Hoi (IRE) **Norman Court Stud**
34 **NARBOROUGH,** 4, b g Winker Watson—Solmorin **M. R. Channon**
35 **NEEDLESS SHOUTING (IRE),** 4, b g Footstepsinthesand—Ring The Relatives **Lord Ilsley Racing (Russell Syndicate)**
36 **NUTBUSH,** 4, b f Sixties Icon—Hairy Night (IRE) **M. R. Channon**
37 **PALERMA,** 4, b f Shamardal (USA)—West Lorne (USA) **Jon & Julia Aisbitt**
38 **PARADISE VALLEY (IRE),** 6, b g Presenting—Native Wood (IRE) **Mrs C. M. Radford**
39 **ROUGH COURTE (IRE),** 4, b f Clodovil (IRE)—Straight Sets (IRE) **Mr W. G. Parish**
40 **SAONA ISLAND,** 5, b m Bahamian Bounty—Perfect Partner **M. R. Channon**
41 **SGT RECKLESS,** 8, b g Imperial Dancer—Lakaam **Mrs C. M. Radford**
42 **SHADOWS OFTHENIGHT (IRE),** 4, b f Fastnet Rock (AUS)—Madaen (USA) **Mr W. G. Parish**
43 **SHORE STEP (IRE),** 5, br g Footstepsinthesand—Chatham Islands (USA) **Jon & Julia Aisbitt**
44 **SOMERSBY (IRE),** 11, b g Second Empire (IRE)—Back To Roost (IRE) **Mrs C. M. Radford**
45 **STONEHAM,** 4, b f Sixties Icon—Cibenze **Insignia Racing Limited**
46 **TANOJIN (IRE),** 4, ch f Thousand Words—Indiannie Moon **Nick & Olga Dhandsa & John & Zoe Webster**
47 **THE HON MACKINLAY (IRE),** 6, ch g Bold Fact (USA)—Khadija **Miss C. A. B. Allsopp**
48 **THE LAST CAVALIER (IRE),** 5, br g Presenting—All Set (IRE) **Mrs C. M. Radford**
49 **THE POCKET DOT,** 4, ch f Lucky Story (USA)—Daisy Do (IRE) **M. R. Channon**
50 **VIVA STEVE (IRE),** 7, b g Flemensfirth (USA)—Eluna **Mrs C. M. Radford**
51 **WARDEN HILL (IRE),** 7, br g Presenting—Moon Storm (IRE) **Mrs C. M. Radford**
52 **WEE JEAN,** 4, b f Captain Gerrard (IRE)—Reeli Silli **Mr B. Robe**

### THREE-YEAR-OLDS

53 **ALPHA SPIRIT,** b f Sixties Icon—Queen of Narnia **M. R. Channon**
54 Ch f Piccolo—Blakeshall Rose **Mr R. W. Bastian**
55 **BOSSY GUEST (IRE),** b c Medicean—Ros The Boss (IRE) **John Guest Racing Ltd**
56 **CALTRA COLLEEN,** b f Sixties Icon—Mistic Magic (IRE) **Anne & Steve Fisher**
57 **CAMCHICA (IRE),** b f Camacho—Varnay **Jon & Julia Aisbitt**
58 **CLOCK OFF,** b c Showcasing—Ticki Tori (IRE) **M. R. Channon**
59 **CONSTABLE BUCKLEY,** b c Naaqoos—Naadrah **Nick & Olga Dhandsa & John & Zoe Webster**
60 **DIAMOND JOEL,** b c Youmzain (IRE)—Miss Lacroix **Mrs N. S. Harris**
61 **DOZEN (FR),** ch f Mastercraftsman (IRE)—She Is Zen (FR) **Mrs A. C. Black**
62 **DUTCH ROBIN (IRE),** b f Fast Company (IRE)—Autumn Star (IRE) **Mrs T. Burns**
63 **EL CHE,** gr f Winker Watson—Rose Cheval (USA) **Norman Court Stud**
64 **ESSAKA (IRE),** b c Equiano (FR)—Dream Vision (USA) **M. R. Channon**
65 **EUTHENIA,** b f Winker Watson—Funny Girl (IRE) **Norman Court Stud**
66 **EXENTRICITY,** b f Paco Boy (IRE)—Wansdyke Lass **Mr W. G. Parish**
67 **FINGAL'S CAVE (IRE),** ch c Fast Company (IRE)—Indiannie Moon **The Motley Cru I**
68 **FITZWILLIAM,** ch g Sixties Icon—Canadian Capers **Bargate**
69 **FOLLOW THE FAITH,** b f Piccolo—Keeping The Faith (IRE) **George Materna & Mark Barrett**
70 **HARLEQUIN STRIKER (IRE),** b g Bahamian Bounty—Air Maze **Harlequin Direct Ltd**

## MR MICK CHANNON - Continued

71 **IFICANIWILL (IRE),** b f Mastercraftsman (IRE)—Hollow Hill (IRE) **The Motley Cru I**
72 **JUST SILCA,** ch f Teofilo (IRE)—Silca Chiave **Aldridge Racing Partnership**
73 **JUVENTAS,** ch f Sixties Icon—The Screamer (IRE) **Norman Court Stud**
74 **KING CRIMSON,** ch c Captain Gerrard (IRE)—Elegant Lady **Wilde & Webster**
75 **KNIGHT OF THE AIR,** b c Bushranger (IRE)—Picolette **Insignia Racing (Crescent)**
76 **KRAZY PAVING,** b g Kyllachy—Critical Path (IRE) **Mr Aiden Murphy & The Hon. Mrs Foster**
77 **MALABAR,** b f Raven's Pass (USA)—Whirly Bird **Jon & Julia Aisbitt**
78 **MAY ONE,** b f Winker Watson—Excellent Day (IRE) **M. R. Channon**
79 **MBOTO GORGE,** b g Sixties Icon—Spring Bouquet (IRE) **M. R. Channon**
80 **MOBSTA (IRE),** b c Bushranger (IRE)—Sweet Nicole **Mr W. G. Parish**
81 **MOONRAKER,** ch c Starspangledbanner (AUS)—Licence To Thrill **Christopher Wright & Miss Emily Asprey**
82 **MOYDIN,** b c Motivator—Yding (IRE) **Mr & Mrs D. D. Clee**
83 **PENDLEBURY,** b c Showcasing—Trinny **Jon & Julia Aisbitt**
84 **PERSUN,** ch f Sir Percy—Sunley Shines **The Teeton Partnership**
85 **POPESWOOD (IRE),** b g Haatef (USA)—Binfield (IRE) **N. J. Hitchins**
86 **PORTASH,** b f Tobougg (IRE)—Circadian Rhythm **J. W. Haydon**
87 B f Captain Marvelous (IRE)—Purepleasureseeker (IRE)
88 **REBEL YELL,** b c Shamardal (USA)—Solaia (USA) **Chris Wright & The Hon Mrs J. M. Corbett**
89 **SKYLIGHT (IRE),** b f Acclamation—Swingsky (IRE) **Mrs T. Burns**
90 **STARRING GUEST (IRE),** b f Teofilo (IRE)—Queen of Stars (USA) **John Guest Racing Ltd**
91 **THE BLUE BOMBER,** b c Stimulation (IRE)—Mar Blue (FR) **M. R. Channon**
92 **TIDAL MOON,** b f Sea The Stars (IRE)—Miss Riviera Golf **Jon & Julia Aisbitt**
93 **VOLUNTEER POINT (IRE),** b f Footstepsinthesand—Piffling **Box 41**
94 **WAGSTAFF (IRE),** b g Rip Van Winkle (IRE)—Ride A Rainbow **G. D. P. Materna**
95 **WALRUS GUMBOOT,** b c Sixties Icon—Nedwa **M. R. Channon**
96 **ZIGGERT (IRE),** b c High Chaparral (IRE)—Billet (IRE) **Sheikh M. B. K. Al Maktoum**
97 **ZUZINIA (IRE),** b f Mujadil (USA)—Sinegronto (IRE) **Nick & Olga Dhandsa & John & Zoe Webster**

## TWO-YEAR-OLDS

**98** Ch c 9/3 Atlantic Sport (USA)—Aries (GER) (Big Shuffle (USA)) (2857)
**99** B f 26/3 Canford Cliffs (IRE)—Aurelia (Rainbow Quest (USA)) (32000) **Harlequin Direct Ltd**
**100** B f 18/1 Lilbourne Lad (IRE)—Bellacoola (GER) (Lomitas) (31428) **M. R. Channon**
**101** B c 25/2 Rock of Gibraltar (IRE)—Berry Baby (IRE) (Rainbow Quest (USA)) (35000)
**102** B c 3/5 Sakhee's Secret—Blakeshall Rose (Tobougg (IRE))
**103** Ch c 15/4 Sixties Icon—Cibenze (Owington)
**104** B f 6/2 Bahamian Bounty—Clodilla (IRE) (Clodovil (IRE))
**105** **CUPPATEE (IRE),** b f 21/3 Canford Cliffs (IRE)—Fanditha (IRE) (Danehill Dancer (IRE)) **Mrs T. Burns**
**106** B c 25/1 Shirocco (GER)—Cyber Star (King's Best (USA)) (85000) **Jon & Julia Aisbitt**
**107** B f 28/4 Motivator—Dawnus (IRE) (Night Shift (USA)) (30000)
**108** B f 4/5 Sixties Icon—Evanesce (Lujain (USA))
**109** B c 23/2 Sixties Icon—Excellent Day (IRE) (Invincible Spirit (IRE))
**110** B f 27/4 Sixties Icon—Fading Away (Fraam)
**111** B f 16/3 Sixties Icon—Fire Crystal (High Chaparral (IRE))
**112** B f 18/2 Sixties Icon—Fiumicino (Danehill Dancer (IRE))
**113** B f 22/3 Sixties Icon—Hairspray (Bahamian Bounty)
**114** B c 8/3 Notnowcato—Hope Island (IRE) (Titus Livius (FR)) (23809)
**115** Gr c 2/5 Lawman (FR)—Indian Dumaani (Indian Ridge) (20000)
**116** **JERSEY BREEZE (IRE),** gr f 20/1 Dark Angel (IRE)—
Sixfields Flyer (IRE) (Desert Style (IRE)) (83333) **Mrs S. G. Bunney**
**117** Ch f 18/3 King's Best (USA)—Jezebel (Owington) (20000) **Prince A. A. Faisal**
**118** Gr f 21/4 Clodovil (IRE)—Justice System (USA) (Criminal Type (USA)) (25396)
**119** Gr f 6/3 Dark Angel (IRE)—Kelsey Rose (Most Welcome) (155000) **John Guest Racing Ltd**
**120** B f 4/3 Sixties Icon—La Gifted (Fraam)
**121** Ch c 21/5 Sixties Icon—Lakaam (Danzero (AUS))
**122** Br c 1/4 Lawman (FR)—Lebenstanz (Singspiel (IRE)) (22000)
**123** Br c 31/1 Atlantic Sport (USA)—Linda Green (Victory Note (USA))
**124** **LORD TROTTER,** b c 6/3 Elusive City (USA)—
Abusive (Green Tune (USA)) **Allen,Porter,Firefly,Voute Partnership**
**125** B f 21/4 Raven's Pass (USA)—Lucky Norwegian (IRE) (Almutawakel) (75396)
**126** B c 28/2 Acclamation—Magic Eye (IRE) (Nayef (USA)) (60000) **Christopher Wright & Miss Emily Asprey**
**127** B f 20/2 Lilbourne Lad (IRE)—Margaux Magique (IRE) (Xaar) (13000)
**128** B f 11/2 Bushranger (IRE)—Miss Megs (IRE) (Croco Rouge (IRE)) (6348)
**129** Gr c 20/3 Medicean—Moon Empress (FR) (Rainbow Quest (USA)) (50000) **M. R. Channon**
**130** B f 27/4 Sixties Icon—Nadinska (Doyen (IRE))
**131** B f 7/3 Winker Watson—Nedwa (In The Wings)

## MR MICK CHANNON - Continued

**132** Br f 9/4 Showcasing—Oystermouth (Averti (IRE)) (32000) **Mr M. Al-Qatami & Mr K. M. Al-Mudhaf**
**133** B c 30/3 Baltic King—Regal Lustre (Averti (IRE)) (3174)
**134** B br f 7/4 Clodovil (IRE)—Ringarooma (Erhaab (USA)) (23000) **M. R. Channon**
**135** B f 12/3 Approve (IRE)—Riymaisa (IRE) (Traditionally (USA)) (19047)
**136** Ch f 17/3 Sixties Icon—Rose Cheval (USA) (Johannesburg (USA))
**137** B c 19/3 Intense Focus (USA)—Royal Esteem (Mark of Esteem (IRE)) (45714) **M. R. Channon**
**138** B f 30/4 Champs Elysees—Russian Empress (IRE) (Trans Island)
**139** Br f 20/3 Atlantic Sport (USA)—Search Party (Rainbow Quest (USA))
**140** Ch gr c 24/1 Aqlaam—Si Belle (IRE) (Dalakhani (IRE)) (8000)
**141** Gr f 3/3 Clodovil (IRE)—Special Lady (FR) (Kaldoun (FR)) (20000) **J. Abdullah**
**142** B f 27/4 Acclamation—Speedy Sonata (USA) (Stravinsky (USA)) (142857)
**143** B f 17/4 Sixties Icon—Summer Cry (USA) (Street Cry (IRE))
**144** B f 23/2 Sixties Icon—Sweet Pilgrim (Talkin Man (CAN))
**145** B f 22/3 Thousand Words—Texas Queen (Shamardal (USA)) (15872)
**146** B f 8/4 Sixties Icon—The Screamer (IRE) (Insan (USA))
**147** **TIGERWOLF (IRE),** br c 26/4 Dream Ahead (USA)—
Singing Field (IRE) (Singspiel (IRE)) (120000) **George Materna & Roger Badley**
**148** B f 25/1 Acclamation—Triton Dance (IRE) (Hector Protector (USA)) (80000)
**149** B c 23/4 Zamindar (USA)—Valoria (Hernando (FR)) (14000)
**150** B c 31/3 Baltic King—Vertigo On Course (IRE) (Anabaa (USA)) (30000) **J. Abdullah**
**151** B f 27/3 Sixties Icon—Vilnius (Imperial Dancer)
**152** B c 18/3 Medicean—Violet (IRE) (Mukaddamah (USA)) (55238) **J. Abdullah**
**153** B f 18/3 Thousand Words—Zarafa (Fraam) (1714)

**Other Owners:** J. R. Aisbitt, Mrs J. M. Aisbitt, K. M. Al-Mudhaf, Mohammed Jasem Al-Qatami, E. Aldridge, Miss C. T. Aldridge, Mr T. J. Allen, Miss E. Asprey, Mr R. Badley, M. Barrett, D. Bloy, Sir M. F. Broughton, S. W. Broughton, D. D. Clee, Mrs J. P. Clee, The Hon Mrs C. Corbett, Dr N. Dhandsa, Mr T. V. Drayton, Mr S. D. Fisher, Mrs A. P. Fisher, Hon S. Foster, Ms G. H. Hedley, Mr D. L. Hudd, Mrs A. M. Jones, Mike Channon Bloodstock Ltd, H. A. Murphy, Mrs J. M. Tice O.B.E., Mr P. Trant, Mrs T. G. Trant, Mrs G. Voute, Mr J. Webster, Mrs S. Wilde, J. A. Williams, C. N. Wright.

---

## 101 MR MICHAEL CHAPMAN, Market Rasen

Postal: **Woodlands Racing Stables, Woodlands Lane, Willingham Road, Market Rasen, Lincolnshire, LN8 3RE**
Contacts: **PHONE/FAX (01673) 843663 MOBILE (07971) 940087**
**E-MAIL woodlands.stables@btconnect.com WEBSITE www.woodlandsracingstables.co.uk**

1 **DONTUPSETTHERHYTHM (IRE),** 10, b br g Anshan—Whatalady (IRE) **J. M. Robinson**
2 **EPEE CELESTE (FR),** 9, ch m Spadoun (FR)—Juste Ciel (USA) **Exor of the late Mrs S. M. Richards**
3 **FEELING PECKISH (USA),** 11, ch g Point Given (USA)—Sunday Bazaar (USA) **J. E. Reed**
4 **FIGHT FOR YOU (IRE),** 8, b g Antonius Pius (USA)—Amiela (FR)
5 **JOYFUL MOTIVE,** 6, ch g Motivator—Triple Joy **C. Cheesman**
6 **KHESKIANTO (IRE),** 9, b m Kheleyf (USA)—Gently (IRE) **F. A. Dickinson**
7 **L'ES FREMANTLE (FR),** 4, b g Orpen (USA)—Grand Design **Quench Racing Partnership**
8 **MAZOVIAN (USA),** 7, b g E Dubai (USA)—Polish Style (USA) **Mrs M. M. Chapman**
9 **MONZINO (USA),** 7, b br g More Than Ready (USA)—Tasso's Magic Roo (USA) **Mrs M. M. Chapman**
10 **PEAK SEASONS (IRE),** 12, ch g Raise A Grand (IRE)—Teresian Girl (IRE) **J. E. Reed**
11 **SIMPLIFIED,** 12, b m Lend A Hand—Houston Heiress (USA) **R. A. Gadd**
12 **SOPHIE'S BEAU (USA),** 8, b g Stormy Atlantic (USA)—Lady Buttercup (USA) **Mrs M. M. Chapman**
13 **TAYARAT (IRE),** 10, b g Noverre (USA)—Sincere (IRE) **Mrs M. M. Chapman**
14 **THE SOCIETY MAN (IRE),** 8, ch g Moscow Society (USA)—Redruth (IRE) **A. Mann**
15 **TROPICAL SKY (IRE),** 7, b g Librettist (USA)—Tropical Breeze (IRE) **Mrs M. M. Chapman**
16 **VOGARTH,** 11, ch g Arkadian Hero (USA)—Skara Brae **Mrs M. M. Chapman**
17 **VOLCANIC JACK (IRE),** 7, b g Kodiac—Rosaria Panatta (IRE) **A. Mann**

### THREE-YEAR-OLDS

18 B c Bushranger (IRE)—Cayambe (IRE) **Mrs M. M. Chapman**

**Other Owners:** Mr B. Downard, Mr M. Preedy, Mr R. J. Smeaton.

**Assistant Trainer:** Mr S. Petch

**Conditional:** Joe Cornwall. **Amateur:** Miss Alice Mills.

## 102 MS JANE CHAPPLE-HYAM, Newmarket

Postal: **Rose Cottage, The Street, Dalham, Newmarket, Suffolk, CB8 8TF**
Contacts: **PHONE (01638) 500451 FAX (01638) 661335 MOBILE (07899) 000555**
**E-MAIL janechapplehyam@hotmail.co.uk**

1 **INJUN SANDS,** 4, b g Halling (USA)—Serriera (FR) **Mr H. H. Morriss**
2 **JUNGLE BAY,** 8, b g Oasis Dream—Dominica **Brewster, Harding & Essex Racing Club**
3 **LARA LIPTON (IRE),** 4, b f Excellent Art—Dyness (USA) **Lady Susan Renouf & Jane Chapple-Hyam**
4 **LEVEL CROSSING,** 6, b g Rail Link—Mirthful (USA) **Mr Matt Bartram**
5 **MOONFAARID,** 4, b g Dubawi (IRE)—Manoeuvre (IRE) **Jane Chapple-Hyam**
6 **MULL OF KILLOUGH (IRE),** 9, b g Mull of Kintyre (USA)—Sun Shower (IRE) **Invictus Racing**
7 **POWER UP,** 4, b f Rail Link—Melpomene **Ms D. Harding**
8 **SAHARA DESERT (IRE),** 4, b g Montjeu (IRE)—Festoso (IRE) **Mr Matt Bartram**
9 **SASKIA'S DREAM,** 7, b m Oasis Dream—Swynford Pleasure **Mr Peter Bottomley & Mrs Jane Chapple-Hyam**
10 **SECRET ASSET (IRE),** 10, gr g Clodovil (IRE)—Skerray **Mr & Mrs S Pierpoint/Dave & Wendy Hughes**
11 **TOMMY'S SECRET,** 5, gr g Sakhee's Secret—La Gessa **Mr John McGuire & Jane Chapple-Hyam**
12 **VALBCHEK (IRE),** 6, b g Acclamation—Spectacular Show (IRE) **Bryan Hirst Ltd**

### THREE-YEAR-OLDS

13 **AVENUE DES CHAMPS,** b g Champs Elysees—Penang Cry **The Tuesday Club**
14 **CAPTAIN FELIX,** b c Captain Gerrard (IRE)—Sweet Applause (IRE) **Mr Matt Bartram**
15 **GOOLAGONG GIRL (IRE),** b f Avonbridge—Lady Berta **Essex Racing Club & Jane Chapple-Hyam**
16 **GYNGER,** ch g Haafhd—Collect **Abington Stables Partnership**

### TWO-YEAR-OLDS

17 **BULLINGTON BEAR (FR),** b c 15/2 Youmzain (IRE)—
Maternelle (FR) (Machiavellian (USA)) (7142) **Bryan Hirst Limited**
18 **CLEVERCONVERSATION (IRE),** b f 18/4 Thewayyouare (USA)—
Monet's Lady (IRE) (Daylami (IRE)) (7936) **The Hon A. S. Peacock**
19 B c 30/3 Firebreak—Miss Elegance (Mind Games) (1200) **The Lord Taveners**
20 **ROYAL MIGHTY,** b f 11/4 Mighty—
Royal Hush (Royal Applause) (5047) **John & Marilyn McGuire & Jane Chapple-Hyam**

**Assistant Trainer:** Abigail Harrison

## 103 MR PETER CHAPPLE-HYAM, Newmarket

Postal: **St Gatien Stables, All Saints Road, Newmarket, Suffolk, CB8 8HJ**
Contacts: **PHONE (01638) 560827 FAX (01638) 561908 MOBILE (07770) 472774**
**E-MAIL pchapplehyam@yahoo.com WEBSITE www.peterchapplehyam.com**

1 **AROD (IRE),** 4, b c Teofilo (IRE)—My Personal Space (USA) **Qatar Racing Limited**
2 **BUCKSTAY (IRE),** 5, b g Lawman (FR)—Stella Del Mattino (USA) **Mrs Fitri Hay**
3 **DIRECT TIMES (IRE),** 4, b g Acclamation—Elegant Times (IRE) **Mr A. Belshaw**
4 **ETERNITYS GATE,** 4, b g Dutch Art—Regency Rose **Mrs Fitri Hay**
5 **FARQUHAR (IRE),** 4, ch c Archipenko (USA)—Pointed Arch (IRE) **Mr T Elliott & Mr P Cunningham**
6 **HYDROGEN,** 4, b c Galileo (IRE)—Funsie (FR) **Qatar Racing Limited**
7 **SHURIKEN (IRE),** 4, b f Hurricane Run (IRE)—Wurfklinge (GER) **Bright Bloodstock**
8 **VOICE OF A LEADER (IRE),** 4, b g Danehill Dancer (IRE)—
Thewaytosanjose (IRE) **Mrs Fitri Hay, Michael Tabor & Mrs John Magnier**

### THREE-YEAR-OLDS

9 **AHLAN EMARATI (IRE),** b c Holy Roman Emperor (IRE)—Indaba (IRE) **Ahmad Abdulla Al Shaikh**
10 **BANK OF GIBRALTAR,** ch g Rock of Gibraltar (IRE)—Banksia **Mr M. Beaumont**
11 **DAGHER,** b c New Approach (IRE)—Sakhya (IRE) **Ziad A. Galadari**
12 **GOATHLAND (IRE),** b c Teofilo (IRE)—Royals Special (IRE) **Mr M. Venus & Partner**
13 **MAKING SHAPES,** b c Makfi—Danceabout **Qatar Racing Limited**
14 **MALICE,** b f Makfi—Shemriyna (IRE) **Qatar Racing Limited**
15 **MISLEADING,** ch g Footstepsinthesand—Danny's Choice **Mrs Fitri Hay**
16 **MURGAN,** b c Galileo (IRE)—Approach **Qatar Racing Limited**
17 **RASEEL,** b f Aqlaam—Waafiah **Ziad A. Galadari**
18 **REETAJ,** b c Medicean—Bakhoor (IRE) **Ziad A. Galadari**
19 **SOCIOPATH (IRE),** b c Fastnet Rock (AUS)—Nancy Spain (IRE) **Mrs Fitri Hay**
20 **SOQOTRA,** b f King's Best (USA)—Yemen Desert (IRE) **Hintlesham Racing Ltd**

## MR PETER CHAPPLE-HYAM - Continued

### TWO-YEAR-OLDS

21 **AHRAAM (IRE),** b c 24/4 Roderic O'Connor (IRE)—Simla Sunset (IRE) (One Cool Cat (USA)) (23000) **Mr A. R. Elliott**
22 Ch c 14/4 Danehill Dancer (IRE)—Althea Rose (IRE) (Green Desert (USA)) (90000) **Mrs Fitri Hay**
23 B c 2/3 Lope de Vega (IRE)—Caravan of Dreams (IRE) (Anabaa (USA)) (75000) **Mrs Fitri Hay**
24 B c 3/3 Lawman (FR)—Corrozal (GER) (Cape Cross (IRE)) (35000) **Paul Hancock**
25 B f 30/3 Makfi—Danceabout (Shareef Dancer (USA)) **Qatar Racing Limited**
26 B f 9/2 Acclamation—Elvira Delight (IRE) (Desert Style (IRE)) **Saleh Al Homaizi & Imad Al Sagar**
27 **EMARATI MIN DUBAI,** b c 11/2 Royal Applause—Umseyat (USA) (Arch (USA)) (15872) **Khalifa Ahmad Al Shaikh Association**
28 B c 7/4 Cape Cross (IRE)—Faithful One (IRE) (Dubawi (IRE)) (103174) **Qatar Racing Limited**
29 **FNOON (IRE),** b f 8/2 High Chaparral (IRE)—Falling Rain (IRE) (Danehill Dancer (IRE)) (23809) **Hussain Alabbas Lootah**
30 **LOHALVAR (FR),** ch c 29/3 Le Havre (IRE)—Loup The Loup (FR) (Loup Solitaire (USA)) (59523) **Mrs Fitri Hay**
31 B c 25/3 Lawman (FR)—Mauresmo (IRE) (Marju (IRE)) (26000) **Paul Hancock**
32 B c 31/3 Lawman (FR)—Millay (Polish Precedent (USA)) (111110) **Qatar Racing Limited**
33 **MZYOON (IRE),** b f 11/4 Galileo (IRE)—High Society (IRE) (Key of Luck (USA)) (190476) **Hussain Alabbas Lootah**
34 B f 28/4 Makfi—Nouvelle Lune (Fantastic Light (USA)) (45000) **Woodcote Stud Limited**
35 **PARAFIN YOUNG,** ch c 11/3 Cape Blanco (IRE)—Hasty (IRE) (Invincible Spirit (IRE)) **Mrs Fitri Hay**
36 B c 3/5 Kyllachy—Regency Rose (Danehill (USA)) (220000) **Saleh Al Homaizi & Imad Al Sagar**
37 **SAYEDAATI SAADATI (IRE),** b c 7/2 Montjeu (IRE)—Guessing (USA) (Kingmambo (USA)) **Ahmad Abdulla Al Shaikh & Co**
38 B c 2/3 Zoffany (IRE)—Spinning Wings (IRE) (Spinning World (USA)) (20952) **Paul Hancock**
39 **TIMES LEGACY,** b c 28/3 Cape Cross (IRE)—Simply Times (USA) (Dodge (USA)) **Mr A. Belshaw**

---

## 104 MR PETER CHARALAMBOUS, Newmarket

Postal: **30 Newmarket Road, Cheveley, Newmarket, Suffolk, CB8 9EQ**
Contacts: **PHONE (01638) 730415 MOBILE (07921) 858421**
**E-MAIL info@pcracing.co.uk WEBSITE www.pcracing.co.uk**

1 **BOONGA ROOGETA,** 6, b m Tobougg (IRE)—Aberlady Bay (IRE) **pcracing.co.uk**
2 **COLINCA'S LAD (IRE),** 13, b g Lahib (USA)—Real Flame **pcracing.co.uk**
3 **ELA GOOG LA MOU,** 6, b m Tobougg (IRE)—Real Flame **pcracing.co.uk**
4 **KALON BRAMA (IRE),** 4, b f Kodiac—Gilded Truffle (IRE) **pcracing.co.uk**
5 **L GE R,** 4, b f Pastoral Pursuits—Cashbar **pcracing.co.uk**
6 **TRULEE SCRUMPTIOUS,** 6, b m Strategic Prince—Morning Rise (GER) **pcracing.co.uk**

### THREE-YEAR-OLDS

7 **THEYDON BOIS,** b f Three Valleys (USA)—Velvet Waters **pcracing.co.uk**
8 **THEYDON THUNDER,** b g Virtual—Lady Agnes **pcracing.co.uk**

### TWO-YEAR-OLDS

9 Gr c 18/1 Champs Elysees—Cheerfully (Sadler's Wells (USA)) (9000) **Mr E. Oriordan**
10 B f 21/4 Poet's Voice—Match Point (Unfuwain (USA)) **Mr E. Oriordan**
11 B c 3/4 Royal Applause—Velvet Waters (Unfuwain (USA)) (5238) **Mr E. Oriordan**

**Other Owners:** Mr P. Charalambous, Trudie Tideswell.

---

## 105 MR GEORGE CHARLTON, Stocksfield

Postal: **Mickley Grange Farm, Stocksfield, Northumberland, NE43 7TB**
Contacts: **PHONE (01661) 843247 MOBILE (07808) 955029**
**E-MAIL gcharlton@fsmail.net**

1 **BALLYVOQUE (IRE),** 9, b g Revoque (IRE)—Timissa (IRE) **J. I. A. Charlton**
2 **BOGSIDE (IRE),** 11, ch g Commander Collins (IRE)—Miss Henrietta (IRE) **Mrs S. M. Wood**
3 **KNOCKARA BEAU (IRE),** 12, b g Leading Counsel (USA)—Clairabell (IRE) **J. I. A. Charlton**
4 **VAULKIE,** 6, b g Revoque (IRE)—Cromarty **Northumbria Leisure Ltd**

**Assistant Trainer:** Mr J. I. A. Charlton

**Jockey (NH):** Lucy Alexander

# 106 MR ROGER CHARLTON, Beckhampton

Postal: **Beckhampton House, Marlborough, Wiltshire, SN8 1QR**
Contacts: **OFFICE (01672) 539533 HOME (01672) 539330 FAX (01672) 539456**
**MOBILE (07710) 784511**
**E-MAIL r.charlton@virgin.net WEBSITE www.rogercharlton.com**

1 **AL KAZEEM,** 7, b h Dubawi (IRE)—Kazeem **D. J. Deer**
2 **BE MY GAL,** 4, b f Galileo (IRE)—Longing To Dance **D. J. Deer**
3 **CAPTAIN CAT (IRE),** 6, b br g Dylan Thomas (IRE)—Mother of Pearl (IRE) **Seasons Holidays**
4 **CHAUVELIN,** 4, b g Sir Percy—Enforce (USA) **Mr Simon de Zoet & Partners**
5 **DAVID LIVINGSTON (IRE),** 6, b h Galileo (IRE)—Mora Bai (IRE) **Hugo Merry / Dr Cyrus Poonawalla**
6 **ELEMRAAN,** 4, b br g Shamardal (USA)—Tadris (USA) **Beckhampton Racing**
7 **ELITE FORCE (IRE),** 4, ch g Medicean—Amber Queen (IRE) **H.R.H. Sultan Ahmad Shah**
8 **EQUITY RISK (USA),** 5, b g Henrythenavigator (USA)—Moon's Tune (USA) **Mike Spence & Partners**
9 **GRANDEST,** 4, b g Dansili—Angara **Lady Rothschild**
10 **HUNTSMANS CLOSE,** 5, b g Elusive Quality (USA)—Badminton **Brook House**
11 **MAJOR JACK,** 4, b g Kheleyf (USA)—Azeema (IRE) **D. J. Deer**
12 **MARZANTE (USA),** 7, gr ro g Maria's Mon (USA)—Danzante (USA) **Beckhampton Stables Ltd**
13 **MATEKA,** 4, ch f Nayef (USA)—Marakabei **Mrs J. Poulter**
14 **MR GREENSPAN (USA),** 4, b g Mr Greeley (USA)—In Escrow (USA) **Axom XLII**
15 **QUEST FOR MORE (IRE),** 5, b g Teofilo (IRE)—No Quest (IRE) **H.R.H. Sultan Ahmad Shah**
16 **RANDOM SUCCESS (IRE),** 5, b m Shamardal (USA)—Foreplay (IRE) **Mr Paul Inglett / Beckhampton**
17 **TEMPTRESS (IRE),** 4, ch f Shirocco (GER)—Femme Fatale **The Pyoneers**

## THREE-YEAR-OLDS

18 **ACCRA BEACH (USA),** ch g Speightstown (USA)—Didina **K. Abdullah**
19 **ACOLYTE (IRE),** b g Acclamation—Obsara **Highclere Thoroughbred Racing (Coronation)**
20 **ALLEZ ALAIA (IRE),** ch f Pivotal—Cassandra Go (IRE) **Trevor Stewart**
21 **ALLUMAGE,** b f Montjeu (IRE)—Alaia (IRE) **M J Taylor & L A Taylor**
22 **ARROWTOWN,** b f Rail Link—Protectress **K. Abdullah**
23 **ATAMAN (IRE),** b c Sholokhov (IRE)—Diora (IRE) **M. Pescod**
24 **BOLD,** b c Oasis Dream—Minority **K. Abdullah**
25 **CAPTAIN MARMALADE (IRE),** gr g Duke of Marmalade (IRE)—Elisium **Seatrees, Doyle & Beckhampton**
26 **CHAMPAGNE CERI,** b f Montjeu (IRE)—Freni (GER) **Mrs Sharon Kinsella**
27 **CLOWANCE ONE,** b c Oasis Dream—Clowance **Seasons Holidays**
28 **DEVONSHIRE PLACE (IRE),** b f Rip Van Winkle (IRE)—Councilofconstance (IRE) **Mr Paul Inglett & Mr Paul Dean**
29 **DEXTEROUS,** b f Mastercraftsman (IRE)—Daring Aim **Her Majesty The Queen**
30 **FARENDOLE (USA),** b f First Defence (USA)—Quick To Please (USA) **K. Abdullah**
31 **HEART LOCKET,** b f Champs Elysees—Zante **K. Abdullah**
32 **INTIZARA,** b f Dansili—Landela **Mr Chris Humber**
33 **JUDICIAL (IRE),** b g Iffraaj—Marlinka **Elite Racing**
34 **JULIETA (IRE),** ch f Teofilo (IRE)—Home You Stroll (IRE) **Mr Chris Humber**
35 **JUXTAPOSED,** b f Three Valleys (USA)—Contiguous (USA) **K. Abdullah**
36 B f Shamardal (USA)—Lady Grace (IRE) **D. J. Deer**
37 **LIBBARD,** ch f Galileo (IRE)—Clouded Leopard (USA) **Lady Rothschild**
38 **MARMOT,** b c Champs Elysees—Winter Bloom (USA) **K. Abdullah**
39 **MASTER ZEPHYR,** b g Shirocco (GER)—Missy Dancer **Paul Inglett / Lady Tidbury**
40 **MCCREERY,** br c Big Bad Bob (IRE)—Dolma (FR) **Lady Rothschild**
41 **MELODICA,** b f Dansili—Maganda (IRE) **D. J. Deer**
42 B f Kheleyf (USA)—Morning After
43 **MOUNTAIN RESCUE (IRE),** b g High Chaparral (IRE)—Amber Queen (IRE) **Lady Richard Wellesley**
44 **OOTY HILL,** gr c Dubawi (IRE)—Mussoorie (FR) **A. E. Oppenheimer**
45 **ORIENTAL SPLENDOUR (IRE),** br c Strategic Prince—Asian Lady **H.R.H. Sultan Ahmad Shah**
46 **PETIT TRIANON,** b f Dansili—Jolie Etoile (USA) **K. Abdullah**
47 **PITCH,** b f Montjeu (IRE)—Five Fields (USA) **Her Majesty The Queen**
48 **ROYAL SILK,** b f Royal Applause—Silky Dawn (IRE) **D. J. Deer**
49 **SAMPLE (FR),** b f Zamindar (USA)—Sanabyra (FR) **Her Majesty The Queen**
50 **SCOONER (USA),** ch c Mizzen Mast (USA)—Palisade (USA) **K. Abdullah**
51 **SKATE,** gr g Verglas (IRE)—Strut **Lady Rothschild**
52 **STAR FIRE,** b f Dark Angel (IRE)—Bunditten (IRE) **Axom LIII**
53 **STARLIT NIGHT,** b f Nayef (USA)—Perfect Night **Mr S. Emmet & Miss S. Emmet**
54 **SUFFUSED,** ch f Champs Elysees—Scuffle **K. Abdullah**
55 **TIME TEST,** b c Dubawi (IRE)—Passage of Time **K. Abdullah**
56 **UNMATCHED,** ch f Champs Elysees—Singleton **K. Abdullah**

## MR ROGER CHARLTON - Continued

57 **WHEAT SHEAF,** b c Iffraaj—Harvest Queen (IRE) **Lady Rothschild**
58 **YULONG XIONGBA (IRE),** ch g Kodiac—Moon Legend (USA) **Owners Group**
59 **ZEB UN NISA,** b f Iffraaj—Tullynally **A. E. Oppenheimer**

## TWO-YEAR-OLDS

60 B c 1/3 Oasis Dream—Alaia (IRE) (Sinndar (IRE)) **M. J. & L. A. Taylor**
61 Ch f 20/5 Strategic Prince—Asian Lady (Kyllachy) **H.R.H. Sultan Ahmad Shah**
62 **BLUE BUTTERFLY,** b f 11/5 Kyllachy—Raysiza (IRE) (Alzao (USA)) **A. & S. Brudenell**
63 **CHINA BELLE,** b f 23/3 Makfi—China Tea (USA) (High Chaparral (IRE)) **Elite Racing**
64 B f 15/4 Dansili—Clowance (Montjeu (IRE)) **Seasons Holidays**
65 Ch c 19/4 Champs Elysees—Cross Your Fingers (USA) (Woodman (USA)) (36000) **Kessly Equine**
66 **EGLANTYNE DREAM,** b f 14/4 Oasis Dream—Bright Morning (USA) (Storm Cat (USA)) **Paul Hearson**
67 B c 22/4 Invincible Spirit (IRE)—Expressive (Falbrav (IRE)) (70000) **H.R.H. Sultan Ahmad Shah**
68 B c 21/3 Acclamation—Gay Mirage (GER) (Highest Honor (FR)) (140000) **H.R.H. Sultan Ahmad Shah**
69 **HIGH SHIELDS (IRE),** b c 11/5 Shamardal (USA)—Marine City (JPN) (Carnegie (IRE)) (100000) **M. Pescod**
70 **HORRAH,** b c 23/2 Royal Applause—Aegean Shadow (Sakhee (USA)) (26000) **Mrs H. T. Thomson Jones**
71 Gr f 24/4 Clodovil (IRE)—Indiannie Moon (Fraam) (25000) **Paul Inglett & Partners**
72 B f 2/5 Cacique (IRE)—Innocent Air (Galileo (IRE)) **K. Abdullah**
73 **IRREVOCABLE (IRE),** b f 18/3 Big Bad Bob (IRE)—Out of Time (IRE) (Anabaa (USA)) (35000) **The Pyoneers**
74 **KUMMIYA,** b br c 20/2 Dansili—Balisada (Kris) **A. E. Oppenheimer**
75 B f 24/4 Royal Applause—Olimpic Girl (IRE) (Darshaan) (8000) **Jane Allison**
76 **PACIFIC SALT (IRE),** gr c 23/1 Zebedee—Villa Nova (IRE) (Petardia) (210000) **Mr J. S. Kelly**
77 Gr c 4/5 Exchange Rate (USA)—Palisade (USA) (Gone West (USA)) **K. Abdullah**
78 Ch f 9/2 Dutch Art—Pearl Mountain (IRE) (Pearl of Love (IRE)) (25714) **De La Warr Racing**
79 **POPPYLAND,** b f 10/4 Equiano (FR)—Follow Flanders (Pursuit of Love) (18000) **Bole, Carter, Deal and Hambro**
80 B br f 17/1 Arch (USA)—Princess Kris (Kris) (200000) **Chris Humber & Steven Smith**
81 **PROJECTION,** b c 24/2 Acclamation—Spotlight (Dr Fong (USA)) (85714) **The Royal Ascot Racing Club**
82 **PURE FANTASY,** b f 30/3 Fastnet Rock (AUS)—Fictitious (Machiavellian (USA)) **Her Majesty The Queen**
83 **PURE VANITY,** b f 1/2 New Approach (IRE)—Miss Pinkerton (Danehill (USA)) **A. E. Oppenheimer**
84 **QUICK MARCH,** b f 31/3 Lawman (FR)—Strut (Danehill Dancer (IRE)) **Lady Rothschild**
85 B f 20/3 Showcasing—Rare Virtue (USA) (Empire Maker (USA)) **K. Abdullah**
86 **SALAD DAYS,** b f 26/1 Pivotal—Scarlet Runner (Night Shift (USA)) **N. M. H. Jones**
87 Gr b f 13/3 Dansili—Scuffle (Daylami (IRE)) **K. Abdullah**
88 B f 15/2 Danehill Dancer (IRE)—Shaleela (IRE) (Galileo (IRE)) **M J Taylor & L A Taylor**
89 **SNOBBERY (IRE),** b c 26/2 Duke of Marmalade (IRE)—Boast (Most Welcome) (26000) **Lady Rothschild**
90 B c 1/3 Cacique (IRE)—Star Cluster (Observatory (USA)) **K. Abdullah**
91 **TAMBOUR,** b c 13/4 Notnowcato—Tamso (USA) (Seeking The Gold (USA)) **Lady Rothschild**
92 B f 7/3 Oasis Dream—Wince (Selkirk (USA)) **K. Abdullah**

**Other Owners:** Axom, Mr A. A. Bamboye, D. Bauckham, Beckhampton Stables Ltd, Mr A. N. C. Bengough, Lady Bengough, Mr Simon de Zoete, Mr Paul Dean, Mr Dan Downie, Mr S. Emmet, Miss Rosalind Emmet, Mr Tony Hill, Miss M. Noden, Mrs Victoria Pakenham, Mr A. E. Pakenham, Mrs V. Seatree, R. Stephens, Mr M. J. Taylor, Mr L. Taylor, G. Webber.

**Assistant Trainer:** Harry Charlton

---

## 107 MR HARRY CHISMAN, Stow-on-the-Wold

Postal: **The Retreat Stables, Maugersbury, Stow-on-the-Wold, Gloucestershire, GL54 1HP**
Contacts: **PHONE (07787) 516723**
**WEBSITE www.harrychisman.co.uk**

1 **ALL RILED UP,** 7, b m Dr Massini (IRE)—Martha Reilly (IRE) **Goodall, Baker, Flint, Grabham, Wood, Welch**
2 **AUGHCARRA (IRE),** 10, b g High Chaparral (IRE)—Pearly Brooks
3 **CAPTAIN KENDALL (IRE),** 6, b g Clodovil (IRE)—
Queen's Lace (IRE) **S. Kirkland, D. Welch, P. Baker, M. Atherton**
4 **GAINSBOROUGH'S ART (IRE),** 10, ch g Desert Prince (IRE)—
Cathy Garcia (IRE) **D. Wood, S. Grabham, H. Byrne, V. Cooke**
5 4, Br f Presenting—One Swoop (IRE) **Mr R. Goodall**

**Other Owners:** Mr M. Atherton, Mr P. M. Baker, Mr Phillip Bueno De Mesquita, Mrs H. Byrne, Mr Harry Chisman, Mr V. R. Cooke, Mr Michael Flint, Mr Ray Goodall, Ms Shirley Grabham, Mr S. Kirkland, Mr D. Welch, Mr Duncan Wood.

**Jockey (NH):** Tom O'Brien, Sean Quinlan, Andrew Tinkler. **Conditional:** Daniel Hiskett.

## 108 MRS JANE CLARK, Kelso

Postal: **Over Roxburgh, Kelso, Roxburghshire, TD5 8LY**
Contacts: **PHONE (01573) 450275 FAX (01573) 450606 MOBILE (07977) 053634**
**E-MAIL janerox@tiscali.co.uk**

1 **FIDDLERS REEL,** 12, ch g Karinga Bay—Festival Fancy **Mrs M. J. Clark**

## 109 MRS ANGELA CLARKE, Llangadog

Postal: **Marlands, Llangadog, Dyfed, SA19 9EW**

1 **PANACHE,** 10, b g King's Best (USA)—Exclusive **Dr S. R. Clarke**
2 **WOODYWHISPER,** 6, b g Needle Gun (IRE)—Driving Miss Suzie **Dr S. R. Clarke**

## 110 MR NICOLAS CLEMENT, Chantilly

Postal: **37, Avenue de Joinville, 60500 Chantilly, France**
Contacts: **PHONE (0033) 3445 75960**
**E-MAIL clementoffice@wanadoo.fr**

1 **GABELLA (FR),** 5, gr m Archange d'or (IRE)—Premiere Chance (FR)
2 **LASEEN (IRE),** 4, b f Dylan Thomas (IRE)—La Seine (USA)
3 **MING ZHI COSMOS (FR),** 4, b f Duke of Marmalade (IRE)—The Wise Lady (FR)
4 **NOT GOLIATH (USA),** 4, b g Henrythenavigator (USA)—Miss Shegaas (USA)
5 **PRESTIGE VENDOME (FR),** 4, gr c Orpen (USA)—Place Vendome (FR)
6 **SEA FIGHT (USA),** 9, ch g Smart Strike (CAN)—Incredulous (FR)
7 **TUCANO (IRE),** 4, b c Monsun (GER)—Tenderly (IRE)

### THREE-YEAR-OLDS

8 **AL SHOSHALEA (IRE),** b f Oasis Dream—Quetsche (USA)
9 **ALAKEEL,** gr c Dalakhani (IRE)—Misk (FR)
10 **ATTRACTIVE LADY,** ch f Teofilo (IRE)—Lumiere Rouge (FR)
11 **CELESTIAL HOUSE,** b c Acclamation—Mystic Spirit (IRE)
12 **CHALMONT (IRE),** gr c Dalakhani (IRE)—Gadalka (USA)
13 **DUKE OF ELLINGTON (FR),** b g Duke of Marmalade (IRE)—Abime (USA)
14 **ELUSIVE DANCER (FR),** b g Elusive City (USA)—Snake Dancer (IRE)
15 **GAME THEORY (IRE),** b f Aussie Rules (USA)—Atullia (GER)
16 **GREY VENDOME (FR),** gr c Mr Sidney (USA)—Theoricienne (FR)
17 **INDIGO KING (IRE),** b c Danehill Dancer (IRE)—Mood Indigo (IRE)
18 **JAM SESSION (IRE),** ch c Duke of Marmalade (IRE)—Night Dhu
19 **JAWAHER (FR),** b f Fastnet Rock (AUS)—Chaibia (IRE)
20 **LESTER LAW (IRE),** b c Lawman (FR)—Lockup (IRE)
21 **LILY DES INDES (FR),** b f American Post—Fleur des Indes (FR)
22 **LUXE VENDOME (FR),** gr c Kendargent (FR)—Place Vendome (FR)
23 **MA CAGNOTTE (FR),** b f King's Best—Masaya (SWI)
24 **MALKO (IRE),** b c Giant's Causeway (USA)—Never Busy (USA)
25 **MELON,** ch g Medicean—Night Teeny
26 **MER ET JARDIN,** b f Lord Shanakill (USA)—Mirandola's Dream (FR)
27 **MINOTAUR (IRE),** b g Azamour (IRE)—Mycenae
28 **MORGENLICHT (GER),** b f Sholokhov (IRE)—Monbijou (GER)
29 **MOSTANEER (IRE),** ch c Dutch Art—King's Doll (IRE)
30 **MOTS CROISES,** b br f Cape Cross (IRE)—Epistoliere (IRE)
31 **NOM DE PLUME (FR),** b f Aussie Rules (USA)—Another Name (USA)
32 **NUIT AUX PLANCHES (FR),** b f Le Havre (IRE)—Interior (USA)
33 **OASIS (FR),** b f Desert Style (IRE)—Saulace (FR)
34 **PRINCESSE VENDOME (FR),** ch f Turtle Bowl (IRE)—Huroof (IRE)
35 **PROMISE ME (IRE),** b f Montjeu (IRE)—Hula Angel (USA)
36 **ROYAL SPRING (FR),** ch c Tamayuz—Main Spring
37 **SHIMMERING SANDS (FR),** b f Medicean—Royal Confidence
38 **TIDES RISE (USA),** b c Henrythenavigator (USA)—A Party For Two (CAN)
39 **VESKING (FR),** ch c Vespone—Shaking
40 **VESPUCIO (SWI),** b c Soldier of Fortune (IRE)—Vanishing Prairie (USA)

## MR NICOLAS CLEMENT - Continued

### TWO-YEAR-OLDS

**41** B c 10/5 Myboycharlie (IRE)—Age of Refinement (IRE) (Pivotal)
**42 ALASKA DANCER (FR),** b c 12/4 Elusive City (USA)—Aliyeska (IRE) (Fasliyev (USA)) (41269)
**43** Ch f 14/3 Beat Hollow—Atiza (IRE) (Singspiel (IRE)) (59523)
**44 BENGALI DREAM (IRE),** b f 1/2 Acclamation—Gems of Araby (Zafonic (USA)) (39681)
**45 BOYISSIME (FR),** b c 5/3 Exceed And Excel (AUS)—Caprarola (USA) (Rahy (USA))
**46 BRIX GAL (USA),** b f 7/4 Warrior's Reward (USA)—B Gene (USA) (Point Given (USA)) (4016)
**47 CLASSE VENDOME (FR),** b f 1/1 Kendargent (FR)—Place Vendome (FR) (Dr Fong (USA))
**48 DIVINISSIME (USA),** b c 1/2 Discreet Cat (USA)—Southern Letters (USA) (Capote (USA)) (37292)
**49** B f 7/2 Monsun (GER)—Dubai Rose (Dubai Destination (USA)) (515873)
**50** Ch f 8/5 Exceed And Excel (AUS)—Ela Merici (FR) (Beaudelaire (USA))
**51 EQUINOXE (FR),** b c 13/2 Equiano (FR)—Porza (FR) (Septieme Ciel (USA))
**52 FASTNET LIGHTNING (IRE),** b c 24/3 Fastnet Rock (AUS)—Arosa (IRE) (Sadler's Wells (USA))
**53 FLEUR D'IPANEMA (FR),** b f 10/3 Le Havre (IRE)—Anthropologie (IRE) (Okawango (USA)) (42063)
**54 GARRI LE ROI (FR),** ch c 18/3 Linngari (IRE)—Kikinda (FR) (Daliapour (IRE)) (49206)
**55 ILLUSTRISSIME (USA),** b c 29/1 Mizzen Mast (USA)—Ghost Friendly (USA) (Ghostzapper (USA)) (17211)
**56 KENSHABA (FR),** b f 20/3 Kendargent—Sabasha (Xaar)
**57** B f 19/2 King's Best (USA)—Lady of Akita (USA) (Fantastic Light (USA))
**58** B f 29/1 Siyouni (FR)—Lady Oriande (Makbul) (158730)
**59 LORD HENRI (FR),** b c 1/3 Lawman (FR)—Avola (FR) (Galileo (IRE)) (57142)
**60 MARCASSIN,** b c 17/4 Lawman (FR)—Mirina (FR) (Pursuit of Love) (126984)
**61 MERI DEVIE (FR),** b f 11/2 Spirit One (FR)—Folle Biche (FR) (Take Risks (FR)) (50000)
**62 OAKMONT (FR),** ch c 28/3 Turtle Bowl—Onega Lake (Peintre Celebre)
**63 PRINCESS GIBRALTAR (FR),** b f 20/1 Rock of Gibraltar (IRE)—
Princess Sofia (UAE) (Pennekamp (USA)) (158730)
**64 PRIVATE AFFAIR (FR),** b c 22/1 Pour Moi (IRE)—Private Eye (FR) (American Post) (79365)
**65 RIBOT DREAM (IRE),** b c 13/4 Dream Ahead (USA)—Halong Bay (FR) (Montjeu (IRE)) (47619)
**66 ROCK DARGENT (FR),** b br c 20/1 Kendargent (FR)—Melinda (FR) (Numerous (USA)) (54761)
**67 SAND GLORY (FR),** b f 21/2 Tamayuz—Ascot Glory (IRE) (Kheleyf (USA)) (31746)
**68** B f 5/2 Myboycharlie (IRE)—Sapfo (FR) (Peintre Celebre (USA)) (23809)
**69 STORMY DANCE (FR),** b br c 18/1 Stormy River (FR)—Danzigs Grandchild (USA) (Anabaa (USA)) (11111)
**70** B c 15/3 Lawman (FR)—The Wise Lady (FR) (Ganges (USA)) (12698)
**71 TRAFFIC JAM (IRE),** b f 8/3 Duke of Marmalade (IRE)—Place de L'etoile (IRE) (Sadler's Wells (USA)) (51586)
**72** Bl f 14/3 Kendargent (FR)—Vauville (IRE) (Invincible Spirit (IRE))
**73** Gr c 24/2 High Chaparral (IRE)—Viva Maria (FR) (Kendor (FR)) (134920)

---

## 111 MR PATRICK CLINTON, Doveridge

Postal: **Lordlea Farm, Marston Lane, Doveridge, Ashbourne, Derbyshire, DE6 5JS**
Contacts: **PHONE (01889) 566356 MOBILE (07815) 142642**

**1 BUSINESS BAY (USA),** 8, b br g Salt Lake (USA)—Jeweled Lady (USA) **In The Clear Racing**
**2 NEZAMI (IRE),** 10, b g Elnadim (USA)—Stands To Reason (USA) **In The Clear Racing**

**Other Owners:** P. L. Clinton, G. Worrall.

**Jockey (flat):** Russ Kennemore.

---

## 112 MR DENIS J. COAKLEY, West Ilsley

Postal: **Keeper's Stables, West Ilsley, Newbury, Berkshire, RG20 7AH**
Contacts: **PHONE (01635) 281622 MOBILE (07768) 658056**
**E-MAIL racing@deniscoakley.com WEBSITE www.deniscoakley.com**

**1 GABRIEL'S LAD (IRE),** 6, b g Dark Angel (IRE)—Catherine Wheel **Killoran Ennis Conway**
**2 GOLDANE (IRE),** 4, b gr f Clodovil (IRE)—Golden Ora (ITY) **Mrs B. Coakley**
**3 HARDY PLUME,** 6, ch g Manduro (GER)—Macleya (GER) **Mrs B. Coakley**
**4 KASTINI,** 5, b g Halling (USA)—Toucantini **West Ilsley Racing**
**5 KING CALYPSO,** 4, ch g Sir Percy—Rosa de Mi Corazon (USA) **Count Calypso Racing**
**6 KUALA QUEEN (IRE),** 4, b f Kodiac—See Nuala (IRE) **Keeper's 12**
**7 MISS MARJURIE (IRE),** 5, b m Marju (IRE)—Kazatzka **C. T. Van Hoorn**
**8 MON CIGAR (IRE),** 4, b g Bushranger (IRE)—Practicallyperfect (IRE) **Mrs B. Coakley**
**9 NEW IDENTITY (IRE),** 4, b g Rock of Gibraltar (IRE)—Zaafran **Mr T. A. Killoran**

## MR DENIS J. COAKLEY - Continued

10 **ROCKFELLA,** 9, ch g Rock of Gibraltar (IRE)—Afreeta (USA) **Mrs B. Coakley**
11 **STEPPE DAUGHTER (IRE),** 4, b f Steppe Dancer (IRE)—Carmencita **C. T. Van Hoorn**

### THREE-YEAR-OLDS

12 **AUNTIE MAY (IRE),** b f Steppe Dancer (IRE)—Auntie Mame **J. C. Kerr**
13 **CATAKANTA,** b g Notnowcato—Akanta (GER) **Catakanta Partnership**
14 **FANNY AGAIN,** b f Nayef (USA)—Sweet Wilhelmina **C. T. Van Hoorn**
15 **SAUMUR,** b f Mawatheeq (USA)—Sparkling Montjeu (IRE) **Sparkling Partners**

### TWO-YEAR-OLDS

16 B c 11/3 Pour Moi (IRE)—Anyuta (Singspiel (IRE)) (18000) **C. T. Van Hoorn**
17 B c 22/2 Frozen Power (IRE)—Bonny Rose (Zaha (CAN)) (16000) **Mrs B. Coakley**
18 B f 12/3 Rock of Gibraltar (IRE)—Gabriellina Klon (IRE) (Ashkalani (IRE)) (10000) **The Good Mixers**
19 **JUST FRED (IRE),** br c 26/4 Excellent Art—Consignia (IRE) (Definite Article) (18000) **Cargreen Racing**
20 B c 2/4 Footstepsinthesand—Mi Rubina (IRE) (Rock of Gibraltar (IRE)) (32000) **C. T. Van Hoorn**
21 B f 24/3 Paco Boy (IRE)—Speech (Red Ransom (USA)) (15000) **Sue Huntingdon & Partners**

**Other Owners:** Rupert Bentley, Mr A. P. Bloor, R. J. Bolam, Mrs M. Carmichael, Mr J. Carmichael, Mrs Barbara Coakley, John Conway, P. M. Emery, J. T. Ennis, David Harris, Lady S. M. G. Huntingdon, Mr A. Killoran, Countess of Lonsdale, David Malpas, Mr G. Oakley, J. G. Ross, Antony Scriven, Jonathan Whymark.

---

## 113 MR PAUL COLE, Whatcombe

Postal: **Whatcombe Estate, Whatcombe, Wantage, Oxfordshire, OX12 9NW**
Contacts: **PHONE (01488) 638433 FAX (01488) 638609**
**E-MAIL admin@paulcole.co.uk WEBSITE www.paulcole.co.uk**

1 **BERKSHIRE (IRE),** 4, b c Mount Nelson—Kinnaird (IRE) **H.R.H. Sultan Ahmad Shah**
2 **BLUEGRASS BLUES (IRE),** 5, gr g Dark Angel (IRE)—Dear Catch (IRE) **Mrs F. H. Hay**
3 **COMPLICIT (IRE),** 4, b c Captain Rio—Molomo **9.36 from Paddington Partnership**
4 **DARK DAYS,** 4, b c Black Sam Bellamy (IRE)—Darwinia (GER) **Mrs E. Bass**
5 **DUTCH ART DEALER,** 4, b g Dutch Art—Lawyers Choice **Mr R. Green**
6 **ELYSIAN PRINCE,** 4, b c Champs Elysees—Trinkila (USA) **Mr Dun Lee**
7 **KUBEBA (IRE),** 4, b g Kodiac—Brillano (FR) **Mr D. L. Hadley**
8 **LISAMOUR (IRE),** 4, b f Azamour (IRE)—Lisa de La Condra (IRE) **Mr F. Stella**
9 **MERITOCRACY (IRE),** 4, br g Kheleyf (USA)—Chiosina (IRE) **Blenheim**
10 **PENDO,** 4, b g Denounce—Abundant **Mr B. K. Hopson**
11 **SILVERHEELS (IRE),** 6, gr g Verglas (IRE)—Vasilia **P. F. I. Cole Ltd**
12 **STORMBOUND (IRE),** 6, b g Galileo (IRE)—A Footstep Away (USA) **P. F. I. Cole Ltd**
13 **STRATEGIC STRIKE (IRE),** 5, b g Strategic Prince—Puteri Wentworth **H.R.H. Sultan Ahmad Shah**

### THREE-YEAR-OLDS

14 **BRITISH ART,** b g Iffraaj—Bush Cat (USA) **Mr R. Green**
15 **DANCING ACES,** ch c Shamardal (USA)—Rainbow Dancing **Dato Fuad Ali**
16 **DANEGELD,** b c Danehill Dancer (IRE)—Kirkinola **Mr C. Shiacolas**
17 **FAST ROMANCE (USA),** b f Fastnet Rock (AUS)—Satulagi (USA) **Mrs F. H. Hay**
18 **FOXY BORIS (FR),** gr g Aussie Rules (USA)—Why Worry (FR) **Irina Korolitcki**
19 **GENERAL POTEMPKIN (IRE),** b c Rip Van Winkle (IRE)—Muskoka Dawn (USA) **Irina Korolitcki**
20 **IMPERIAL LINK,** b f Rail Link—Imperia (GER) **Mrs E. Bass**
21 **JASMINE BLUE (IRE),** b f Galileo (IRE)—Impressionist Art (USA) **Mrs F. H. Hay**
22 **KTCLOUSEAU (IRE),** b f Notnowcato—Prithee **Kevin McCarthy & P.F.I. Cole Ltd**
23 **LONDONIA,** gr c Paco Boy (IRE)—Snowdrops **H.R.H. Sultan Ahmad Shah**
24 **MOLTEN LAVA (IRE),** b c Rock of Gibraltar (IRE)—Skehana (IRE) **Red Run Racing**
25 **ROCKAROUNDTHECLOCK (IRE),** ch c Starspangledbanner (AUS)—Lulawin **Mr Chris Wright & P.F.I. Cole Ltd**
26 **ROTHERWICK (IRE),** ch c Starspangledbanner (AUS)—Pivotalia (IRE) **H.R.H. Sultan Ahmad Shah**
27 **SCIMITARRA,** gr f Motivator—Scrupulous **Mrs E. Bass**
28 **SECRET FANTASIES,** b f Fastnet Rock (AUS)—Trinkila (USA) **Mr Dun Lee**
29 **SIR HENRY RAEBURN (IRE),** b c Henrythenavigator (USA)—La Traviata (USA) **Mr R. Green**
30 **UPSTAGING,** b c Mount Nelson—Corndavon (USA) **H.R.H. Sultan Ahmad Shah**
31 **WEST SUSSEX (IRE),** b c Teofilo (IRE)—Quixotic **Mrs F. H. Hay**

## MR PAUL COLE - Continued

### TWO-YEAR-OLDS

32 Ch c 30/3 Cape Blanco (IRE)—A Mind of Her Own (IRE) (Danehill Dancer (IRE)) (40952)
33 **ARCHIMEDES (IRE),** b c 27/3 Invincible Spirit (IRE)—
Waveband (Exceed And Excel (AUS)) (190476) **Mrs F. H. Hay**
34 **BARON BOLT,** bl c 6/3 Kheleyf (USA)—
Scarlet Royal (Red Ransom (USA)) (48000) **Asprey, Wright, Meyrick, PJL Racing**
35 **BATTLE OF BOSWORTH (IRE),** b c 16/5 Duke of Marmalade (IRE)—
Muskoka Dawn (USA) (Miswaki (USA)) (45000) **Wright, Asprey, Meyrick, PJL Racing**
36 **BY THE RULES,** b f 20/5 Aussie Rules (USA)—Bay Tree (IRE) (Daylami (IRE)) **H.R.H. Prince Faisal Salman**
37 **CAITIE (IRE),** b f 3/3 Canford Cliffs (IRE)—The Shrew (Dansili) (40000) **Mr H. Robinson**
38 **CLIFFHANGER,** b f 11/2 Canford Cliffs (IRE)—Copy-Cat (Lion Cavern (USA)) (78000) **Mr F. Stella**
39 Ch f 26/2 Black Sam Bellamy (IRE)—Darcique (Cacique (IRE)) **Mrs E. Bass**
40 Ch f 18/4 Poet's Voice—Darwinia (GER) (Acatenango (GER)) **Mrs E. Bass**
41 **HONIARA,** b c 19/4 Rock of Gibraltar (IRE)—
Indian Maiden (IRE) (Indian Ridge) (47619) **Meyrick, Wright, Asprey, PJL Racing**
42 **HOUSE OF COMMONS (IRE),** b c 23/3 Sea The Stars (IRE)—Reality (FR) (Slickly (FR)) (150000) **Mrs F. H. Hay**
43 **JAZZ CAT (IRE),** ch f 10/4 Tamayuz—Chelsea Rose (IRE) (Desert King (IRE)) (277777) **Mrs F. H. Hay**
44 B c 26/4 Lilbourne Lad (IRE)—Montefino (IRE) (Shamardal (USA)) (58000) **Mr T. A. Rahman**
45 B c 21/4 Arch (USA)—Muneefa (USA) (Storm Cat (USA)) (30000) **PJL Racing, Wright, Asprey, Meyrick**
46 **PILOT HILL (IRE),** b f 29/3 Intikhab (USA)—
Song of Passion (IRE) (Orpen (USA)) (48000) **H.R.H. Prince Faisal Salman**
47 **PINK ANGEL (IRE),** gr f 10/3 Dark Angel (IRE)—Xarzee (IRE) (Xaar) (20952) **P. F. I. Cole Ltd**
48 **RECENT ACQUISITION (IRE),** b c 16/4 Approve (IRE)—Dear Catch (IRE) (Bluebird (USA)) (45000) **Mr R. Green**
49 Gr f 12/5 Black Sam Bellamy (IRE)—Scrupulous (Dansili) **Mrs E. Bass**
50 **SWEET DRAGON FLY,** b f 5/2 Oasis Dream—Sweet Cecily (IRE) (Kodiac) (140000) **Mrs F. H. Hay**

**Other Owners:** Mr G. Baker, Mr A. Chudasama, Mr R. Colfer, Mr P. Erochkine, Mrs J. Green, Mr D. A. Klein, Ms I. Korolitcki, Mr L. Lugg, K. P. McCarthy, Ms I. Molodtsov, Mr P. T. Mott, Mrs K. Rizayeva, Ms J. M. Smith, Mr N. Wilcock, C. N. Wright.

**Assistant Trainer:** Oliver Cole

---

## 114 MR STUART COLTHERD, Selkirk

Postal: **Clarilawmuir Farm, Selkirk, Selkirkshire, TD7 4QA**
Contacts: **PHONE (01750) 21251 FAX (01750) 21251 MOBILE (07801) 398199**
**E-MAIL wscoltherd@clarilawmuir.wanadoo.co.uk**

1 **AMETHYST ROSE (IRE),** 8, ch m Beneficial—Cap The Rose (IRE) **Coltherd Whyte Campbell Swinton Ruddy**
2 **AWEE DEOCH ANDORIS,** 6, b g Merit (IRE)—Whitemoss Leader (IRE) **Whitemoss Golf Syndicate**
3 **AYE WELL,** 10, b g Overbury (IRE)—Squeeze Box (IRE) **Exors of the Late Mr J. Hogg**
4 **CAPTAIN REDBEARD (IRE),** 6, ch g Bach (IRE)—Diesel Dancer (IRE) **W. S. Coltherd**
5 **DARSI DANCER (IRE),** 7, b g Darsi (FR)—Jaystara (IRE) **Coltherd Gillie**
6 **GUNNER LINDLEY (IRE),** 8, ch g Medicean—Lasso **Mr A. Gunning**
7 **HOTGROVE BOY,** 8, b g Tobougg (IRE)—Tanwir **Coltherd Cawkwell**
8 **HURRICANE RITA (FR),** 5, gr m Sagamix (FR)—Madonna da Rossi **Mr S. Shiel**
9 **LACHLAN MOR,** 6, b g Josr Algarhoud (IRE)—Miss Campanella **Harelaw Racing**
10 **LUCYDOLI,** 6, b m Endoli (USA)—Kariba Dream **W. S. Coltherd**
11 **NORFOLK SOUND,** 4, b f Pastoral Pursuits—Cayman Sound **Mr M. J. Hood**
12 **OXALIDO (FR),** 13, b g Brier Creek (USA)—Galene de Saisy (FR) **Coltherd, Jeffrey & Hall**
13 **RESOLUTE REFORMER (IRE),** 6, b g Arcadio (GER)—Booking Note (IRE) **D. Neale**
14 **SCOTSMAN,** 7, b g And Beyond (IRE)—Kariba Dream **W. S. Coltherd**
15 **SEVENTEEN BLACK (IRE),** 7, b g Subtle Power (IRE)—Snowbaby (IRE) **Mr A. G. Whyte**
16 **SHARNEY SIKE,** 9, ch g And Beyond (IRE)—Squeeze Box (IRE) **Exors of the Late Mr J. Hogg**
17 **SUPRISE VENDOR (IRE),** 9, ch g Fath (USA)—Dispol Jazz **Mr A. Gunning**
18 **TALKIN SENCE (IRE),** 10, b g Heron Island (IRE)—Catatonia (IRE) **Gunning, Conchar, Hancock**
19 **TEKTHELOT (IRE),** 9, b g Shantou (USA)—Bryna (IRE) **Mrs A. Trevaskis**

**Other Owners:** Mr G. Campbell, Mr S. F. Cawkwell, Mr T. Conchar, Mr R. M. Cox, Mr E. Gillie, Mr I. Hall, Mr N. Hancock, J. B. Jeffrey, Mr P. H. Pitchford, Mr J. E. Ruddy, Mr S. Swinton, R. V. Westwood, Mrs E. M. Westwood.

**Jockey (NH):** Richie McGrath, Henry Brooke, Brian Harding. **Apprentice:** Gary Rutherford.

## 115 MR ALAN COOGAN, Ely

Postal: **31 Hasse Road, Soham, Ely, Cambridgeshire, CB7 5UW**
Contacts: **PHONE (01353) 721673 FAX (01353) 721117**

1 **MAC'S SUPERSTAR (FR),** 5, b g Elusive City (USA)—Diamond Light (USA) **A. B. Coogan**
2 **SUNNY BANK,** 6, b g Notnowcato—Sweet Mandolin **A. B. Coogan**

### THREE-YEAR-OLDS

3 **RALPH MCTELL,** ch g Tobougg (IRE)—Alashaan **A. B. Coogan**
4 **SILVER DETAIL (IRE),** b f Youmzain (IRE)—Ayam Zainah **A. B. Coogan**

## 116 MR JOHN COOMBE, Weymouth

Postal: **Sea Barn Farm, Fleet, Weymouth, Dorset, DT3 4ED**
Contacts: **PHONE (01305) 761745 (0780) 3752831 FAX (01305) 775396 MOBILE (07796) 990760**
**E-MAIL wib@seabarnracing.com WEBSITE www.seabarnracing.com**

1 **CHESIL BEACH BOY,** 12, b g Commanche Run—Eatons **M. J. Coombe**
2 **DAIS RETURN (IRE),** 11, b g Lahib (USA)—Bayazida **J. D. Roberts**
3 **JUST WATCH OLLIE (IRE),** 9, b g Indian Danehill (IRE)—Westgate Run **M. J. Coombe**
4 **PROPOSABLE (FR),** 8, b g King's Best (USA)—Irika (USA) **M. J. Coombe**
5 **SAN MARINO (FR),** 12, ch g Bering—Sienne (FR) **M. J. Coombe**

**Assistant Trainer:** Mr John Roberts

**Amateur:** Mrs M. Roberts.

## 117 MRS SUSAN CORBETT, Otterburn

Postal: **Girsonfield, Otterburn, Newcastle upon Tyne, Tyne and Wear, NE19 1NT**
Contacts: **PHONE (01830) 520771 FAX (01830) 520771 MOBILE (07713) 651215**
**E-MAIL girsonfield@outlook.com WEBSITE www.girsonfield.co.uk**

1 **ALL THAT REMAINS (IRE),** 10, b g King's Theatre (IRE)—Morning Breeze (IRE) **Mr F. W. W. Chapman**
2 **BOB'S LEGEND (IRE),** 9, b g Bob's Return (IRE)—Pepsi Starlet (IRE) **The Winning Tipster**
3 **DUN TO PERFECTION,** 8, ch g Endoli (USA)—Dun To A Tern **Mr W. F. Corbett**
4 **GLEN LEA (IRE),** 6, b g Indian Danehill (IRE)—Masquerade Ball (IRE) **Mr F. W. W. Chapman**
5 **HARLEYS MAX,** 6, b g Winged Love (IRE)—Researcher **Mr W. F. Corbett**
6 **JUST MY LUKE,** 6, b g Ferrule (IRE)—Briar Rose (IRE) **Mr J. Goodfellow**
7 **MAGIC SHOES (IRE),** 4, b f Manduro (GER)—Ammo (IRE) **Mr J. Pearce**
8 **MISTER HENDRE,** 7, gr g Fair Mix (IRE)—Bonne Anniversaire **Mr G. Foley**
9 **RIPONIAN,** 5, ch g Trade Fair—Dispol Katie **Mr W. F. Corbett**
10 **SPARVILLE (IRE),** 9, ch g Docksider (USA)—Play The Queen (IRE) **Mr W. F. Corbett**
11 **SUPER COLLIDER,** 8, b g Montjeu (IRE)—Astorg (USA) **Mrs J. L. Corbett**
12 **VIRNON,** 4, b g Virtual—Freedom Song **Mr J. Pearce**

### THREE-YEAR-OLDS

13 **JOEY BLACK,** b g Kheleyf (USA)—Black Moma (IRE) **Mr J. Pearce**
14 **SPERANZA,** b f Bahri (USA)—Toarmandowithlove (IRE) **Ms R. Enright**

### TWO-YEAR-OLDS

15 **THE AULD KIRK,** b c 5/5 Millkom—Lady Counsellor (Turbo Speed) **Mr J. Nelson**

**Other Owners:** Mr B. Merritt.

**Assistant Trainer:** Mr W.F. Corbett

**Conditional:** James Corbett.

## 118 MR LIAM CORCORAN, Kingsbridge

Postal: **Pittaford Farm, Slapton, Kingsbridge, Devon, TQ7 2QG**
Contacts: **MOBILE (07789) 368234**
**E-MAIL corcoranracing@aol.co.uk**

1 **ARCAS (IRE),** 6, br g Shamardal (USA)—Callisto (IRE) **G. Doel**
2 **BARON'S BEST,** 5, gr g Lucky Story (USA)—Dispol Isle (IRE) **Mrs V. A. P. Antell**
3 **CUTE COURT (IRE),** 8, b g Court Cave (IRE)—Cute Play **Mrs V. A. P. Antell**
4 **FLASHY LAD (IRE),** 8, ch g Blueprint (IRE)—Flashy Pearl (IRE) **A. J. Norman**
5 **GAIR LEAT (IRE),** 11, ch g Oscar Schindler (IRE)—Valsdaughter (IRE) **Mr R. B. Antell**
6 **GIREVOLE,** 7, b g Tiger Hill (IRE)—Taranto **Mr R. B. Antell**
7 **MURCAR,** 10, ch g Medicean—In Luck **Mr R. B. Antell**
8 **SPENCER MOON (IRE),** 7, b g Dr Massini (IRE)—Nana Moon (IRE) **G. D. Building Ltd J. Parsons**
9 **WORTH A GO (IRE),** 8, gr g Hasten To Add (USA)—Love Or Porter (IRE) **G. Doel**

**Other Owners:** GD Building Ltd, Mr James Parsons.

## 119 MR JOHN CORNWALL, Melton Mowbray

Postal: **April Cottage, Pasture Lane, Hose, Melton Mowbray, Leicestershire, LE14 4LB**
Contacts: **PHONE (01664) 444453 FAX (01664) 444754 MOBILE (07939) 557091**
**E-MAIL johncornwall7@gmail.com**

1 **FLICHITY (IRE),** 10, br g Turtle Island (IRE)—Chancy Gal **J. R. Cornwall**
2 **PHOENIX DES MOTTES (FR),** 12, b g Useful (FR)—Camille des Mottes (FR) **J. R. Cornwall**
3 **THAT'S THE DEAL (IRE),** 11, b br g Turtle Island (IRE)—Sister Swing **J. R. Cornwall**
4 **THE JUGOPOLIST (IRE),** 8, b g Oscar (IRE)—Chance My Native (IRE) **J. R. Cornwall**

**Conditional:** Joe Cornwall.

## 120 MR ROBERT COWELL, Newmarket

Postal: **Bottisham Heath Stud, Six Mile Bottom, Newmarket, Suffolk, CB8 0TT**
Contacts: **PHONE (01638) 570330 MOBILE (07785) 512463**
**E-MAIL robert@robertcowellracing.co.uk WEBSITE www.robertcowellracing.co.uk**

1 **CARDINAL,** 10, ch h Pivotal—Fictitious **Mrs J. May**
2 **COPPER CAVALIER,** 4, ch g Haafhd—Elle Crystal **Mrs D. Rix, Mr J. Partridge & Partner**
3 **DARK DIAMOND (IRE),** 5, b g Dark Angel (IRE)—Moon Diamond **Mr Khalifa Dasmal & Bottisham Heath Stud**
4 **DORNOCH (USA),** 4, b br g Mizzen Mast (USA)—Gainful (USA) **Malih L. Al Basti**
5 **DUKE OF FIRENZE,** 6, ch g Pivotal—Nannina **Cheveley Park Stud Limited**
6 **FREE ZONE,** 6, b g Kyllachy—Aldora **Fromthestables.com Racing McBride McKay**
7 **GOLDREAM,** 6, br g Oasis Dream—Clizia (IRE) **Mr J. Sargeant & Mrs J. Morley**
8 **IFFRANESIA (FR),** 5, ch m Iffraaj—Farnesina (FR) **C. Humphris**
9 **INDIAN TINKER,** 6, b g Sleeping Indian—Breakfast Creek **Mr J. Sargeant**
10 **INTRINSIC,** 5, b h Oasis Dream—Infallible **Malih L. Al Basti**
11 **KINGSGATE NATIVE (IRE),** 10, b g Mujadil (USA)—Native Force (IRE) **Cheveley Park Stud Limited**
12 4, Ch c Teofilo (IRE)—Neat Shilling (IRE) **Malih L. Al Basti**
13 **NORMAL EQUILIBRIUM,** 5, b g Elnadim (USA)—Acicula (IRE) **T. W. Morley & Mrs J. Morley**
14 **PRINCE ALZAIN (USA),** 6, b h Street Sense (USA)—Monaassabaat (USA) **Mr A. Al Banwan**
15 **REPECHAGE (FR),** 4, ch f Gold Away (IRE)—Acola (FR) **C. Humphris**
16 **ROXY HART,** 4, ch f Halling (USA)—Possessive Artiste **The Roxy Hart Partnership**
17 **ROYAL ACQUISITION,** 5, b g Royal Applause—Flavian **Mr J. Sargeant**
18 **SECRETINTHEPARK,** 5, ch g Sakhee's Secret—Lark In The Park (IRE) **Mia Racing**
19 **SHINING EMERALD,** 4, gr g Clodovil (IRE)—Janayen (USA) **J. Abdullah**
20 **SPEED HAWK (USA),** 4, b br c Henny Hughes (USA)—Cosmic Wing (USA) **K. A. Dasmal**
21 **STUNNED,** 4, b c Shamardal (USA)—Amazed **Malih L. Al Basti**
22 **ZAIN EAGLE,** 5, b h Dylan Thomas (IRE)—Pearl City (USA) **Mr A. Al Banwan**
23 **ZAIN EMPIRE,** 4, b c Dubawi (IRE)—Just Like A Woman **Mr A. Al Banwan**

### THREE-YEAR-OLDS

24 **ARABIAN BRIDE (IRE),** ch f Raven's Pass (USA)—Rasana **Mr A. Jaber**
25 **CLASSIC ROSES,** b f Youmzain (IRE)—Masque Rose **Mr A. Jaber**
26 **ERNEST,** b g Showcasing—Excello **Bottisham Heath Stud**

## MR ROBERT COWELL - Continued

27 **EXCEEDINGLY,** b f Exceed And Excel (AUS)—Miss Rochester (IRE) **Cheveley Park Stud Limited**
28 **FAIRY DUCHESS (IRE),** b f Duke of Marmalade (IRE)—Fairybook (USA) **K. Quinn/ C. Benham/ I. Saunders**
29 **FALSIFY,** ch f Compton Place—Swindling **K. Quinn/ C. Benham/ I. Saunders & Partners**
30 **GRAND BEAUTY (IRE),** ch f Kheleyf (USA)—Grand Zafeen **J. Abdullah**
31 B f Pivotal—Hypnology (USA) **Mr A. Al Banwan**
32 **JUST US TWO (IRE),** b c Royal Applause—Sarah's First **Mr A. Al Mansoori**
33 **MASTER ZAIN (IRE),** b c Mastercraftsman (IRE)—Tafseer (IRE) **Mr A. Al Banwan**
34 **MOONLIGHT RUN,** ch c Pivotal—Moon Goddess **Cheveley Park Stud Limited**
35 **MORE SPICE (IRE),** b c Exceed And Excel (AUS)—High Spice (USA) **K. A. Dasmal**
36 **MOST TEMPTING,** ch f Showcasing—La Carot **The Family Of Gay Leader**
37 **ONE MOMENT,** ch f Notnowcato—Two Step **Bottisham Heath Stud**
38 **QUEEN ZAIN (IRE),** b f Lawman (FR)—Tropical Lady (IRE) **Mr A. Al Banwan**
39 **QUIET BEAUTY,** b f Acclamation—Upperville (IRE) **Mr A. Al Mansoori**
40 **QUITE SMART (IRE),** b f Arcano (IRE)—Lyca Ballerina **Mr A. Al Mansoori**
41 **RAHMAH (IRE),** b c Vale of York (IRE)—Sweet Home Alabama (IRE) **S. Ali**
42 **RAINBOW ORSE,** b c Zebedee—Khafayif (USA) **Mr G. M. C. Johnson**
43 **SAMSAMSAM,** b c Sakhee's Secret—Greenfly **Malih L. Al Basti**
44 B f Teofilo (IRE)—Sister Sylvia **Druid Racing**
45 **SUMMER LOVE,** ch f Cockney Rebel (IRE)—Tessara (GER) **Furlong Bloodstock**
46 **THE WISPE,** ch f Kyllachy—Twitch Hill **Manor Farm Stud & Miss S. Hoare**
47 **TWIN TURBO (IRE),** b g Dark Angel (IRE)—Scarlet O'hara (IRE) **J. Abdullah**
48 **USE YOUR FILBERT (IRE),** b c Acclamation—Wishing Chair (USA) **Mr G. M. C. Johnson**
49 **ZAIN COLLEEN (IRE),** br f Elnadim (USA)—Safqa **Mr A. Al Banwan**
50 **ZAIN GALILEO (IRE),** b c Galileo (IRE)—Nausicaa (USA) **Mr A. Al Banwan**
51 B f Excellent Art—Zigarra **Mr A. Al Banwan**

## TWO-YEAR-OLDS

52 B c 28/4 Royal Applause—Acicula (IRE) (Night Shift (USA)) (30000) **Mr M. Al Shafar**
53 B f 15/3 Kodiac—Aguilas Perla (IRE) (Indian Ridge) (100000) **Malih L. Al Basti**
54 B f 12/5 Aqlaam—Areyaam (USA) (Elusive Quality (USA)) **Mr A. Jaber**
55 B c 16/3 Lilbourne Lad (IRE)—Blondie's Esteem (IRE) (Mark of Esteem (IRE)) (40000) **Mr A. Al Mansoori**
56 B c 25/3 Munnings (USA)—Catch Me Later (USA) (Posse (USA)) (16064) **K. Quinn/ C. Benham/ I. Saunders**
57 B br f 18/3 Street Boss (USA)—Cosmic Wing (USA) (Halo (USA)) (17211) **K. A. Dasmal**
58 Ch c 18/4 Sakhee's Secret—Excello (Exceed And Excel (AUS)) **Bottisham Heath Stud**
59 **FINGERTIPS,** b f 15/4 Royal Applause—Hanging On (Spinning World (USA))
60 B c 28/2 Blame (USA)—Fiscal Policy (USA) (Wildcat Heir (USA)) (38439) **Malih L. Al Basti**
61 B c 5/2 Holy Roman Emperor (IRE)—Love Thirty (Mister Baileys) (71428) **Mr A. Al Banwan**
62 Ch c 23/2 Halling (USA)—Masaya (Dansili) (50000) **Mr A. Al Mansoori**
63 B c 21/3 Lilbourne Lad (IRE)—Next To The Top (Hurricane Run (IRE)) (10000) **S. Ali**
64 B f 30/4 Royal Applause—Pretty Majestic (IRE) (Invincible Spirit (IRE)) **Mr A. Jaber**
65 **ROSE ZAFONIC,** b f 29/3 Poet's Voice—With Distinction (Zafonic (USA)) (32000) **J. Abdullah**
66 Ch c 13/2 Le Havre (IRE)—Sainte Colombe (IRE) (Danehill Dancer (IRE)) **J. Abdullah**
67 B f 18/3 Danehill Dancer (IRE)—Shaanara (IRE) (Darshaan) (67460) **Mr A. Al Banwan**
68 B f 9/2 Elnadim (USA)—Startori (Vettori (IRE)) (22000) **Mr M. Al Shafar**
69 Ch c 28/2 Scat Daddy (USA)—Volver (IRE) (Danehill Dancer (IRE)) (65978) **K. A. Dasmal**

**Other Owners:** Mr Chris Benham, Bottisham Heath Stud, Mr N. A. Coster, Mr R. M. H. Cowell, Mr Khalifa Dasmal, Ms D. M. Deegan, Mr M. V. Deegan, Mrs M. Ferguson, Mr Robert J. Gough, Miss S. Hoare, Mr D. Laflin, Manor Farm Stud (Rutland), Mr I. G. Martin, Mr Myles McBride, Mr Glen McKay, Mrs J. Morley, Mr T. W. Morley, Mr J. Partridge, Mr Kevin Quinn, Mr F. Read, Mrs Diana Rix, Mr J. Sargeant, Mr Ian Saunders, Mrs Doreen M. Swinburn.

**Assistant Trainer:** Mr Ross Studholme

---

## 121 MR PAUL COWLEY, Banbury

Postal: **Lodge Farm, Culworth, Banbury, Oxfordshire, OX17 2HL**
Contacts: **PHONE (01295) 768998 MOBILE (07775) 943346**
**E-MAIL paulcowleyequine@yahoo.co.uk**

1 **BILL THE LAD (IRE),** 8, b g Classic Cliche (IRE)—Quilty's Rose Bud (IRE) **S. G. West**
2 **FIRST PAGE,** 5, b m Definite Article—Campannello **Mrs A. Cowley**
3 **GLENDERMOT (IRE),** 6, b g Portrait Gallery (IRE)—Native Bandit (IRE) **George Beyts & Stan West**
4 **GRAND ARTICLE (IRE),** 11, ch g Definite Article—Grand Morning (IRE) **S. G. West**
5 5, Ch g Acambaro (GER)—Miss Busy Lizzy (IRE) **The BMW's**
6 **SEAS OF GREEN,** 8, ch m Karinga Bay—Emerald Project (IRE) **CW Booth & The Grafton Hounds Choice Club**

## MR PAUL COWLEY - Continued

**Other Owners:** Mr R. Batchelor, Mr George Beyts, Mr C. W. Booth, Mr Paul E. Cowley, Mrs Alana Cowley, Mr Gulliver, Mr J. Leadbeater, Mrs M. Miller, Mrs P. Parsons, Mrs P. Richmond-Watson, Mrs S. Shepherd-Cross, Mrs F. Sinclair, Mrs J. Smyth-Osbourne, Mr W. Welton, Mr Stan West, Mrs T. White, Mr D. Wilson.

---

## 122 MR CLIVE COX, Hungerford

Postal: **Beechdown Farm, Sheepdrove Road, Lambourn, Hungerford, Berkshire, RG17 7UN**
Contacts: **OFFICE (01488) 73072 FAX (01488) 73500 MOBILE (07740) 630521**
**E-MAIL clive@clivecox.com WEBSITE www.clivecox.com**

1 **AFTER THE SUNSET,** 4, ch c Pivotal—Abandon (USA) **Qatar Racing Limited**
2 **BOWBERRY,** 4, b f Cockney Rebel (IRE)—Blaeberry **Lady Bland**
3 **BRIGHT CECILY (IRE),** 4, b f Excellent Art—Roman Love (IRE) **Old Peartree Stud**
4 **CAPE ICON,** 4, b g Mount Nelson—Cape Merino **Mondial Racing & Robert Haim**
5 **DUTCH S,** 4, ch f Dutch Art—Park Law (IRE) **Mondial Racing & Robert Haim**
6 **FEAR OR FAVOUR (IRE),** 4, b g Haatef (USA)—Insaaf **A. G. Craddock**
7 **HIGHLAND DUKE (IRE),** 6, b g Dansili—House In Wood (FR) **Highland Thoroughbred Ltd**
8 **JIMMY STYLES,** 11, ch g Inchinor—Inya Lake **P. N. Ridgers**
9 **LE MAITRE CHAT (USA),** 4, b g Tale of The Cat (USA)—Bedside Story **M. H. Watt**
10 **MILLY'S GIFT,** 5, b m Trade Fair—Milly's Lass **Ken Lock Racing**
11 **MUSICORA,** 4, b f Acclamation—Belladera (IRE)
12 **MY MAJOR (IRE),** 4, b g Holy Roman Emperor (IRE)—Greek Easter (IRE) **Mr P. W. Harris**
13 **PERFECT BLESSINGS (IRE),** 4, b f Kheleyf (USA)—Yxenery (IRE) **Mr John Drew & Mr Ian M Brown**
14 **PERFECT CRACKER,** 7, ch g Dubai Destination (USA)—Perfect Story (IRE) **Mildmay Racing**
15 **PERFECT MUSE,** 5, b m Oasis Dream—Perfect Echo **R. J. Vines**
16 **POET,** 10, b g Pivotal—Hyabella **Mrs T. L. Cox**
17 **SEEKING MAGIC,** 7, b g Haafhd—Atnab (USA) **The Seekers**
18 **SHADES OF GREY,** 8, gr m Dr Fong (USA)—Twosixtythreewest (FR) **Dr & Mrs John Merrington**
19 **SHANKLY,** 4, br g Monsun (GER)—Miracle Seeker **Qatar Racing Ltd & Mr D J Burke**
20 **STRATEGIC FORCE (IRE),** 4, b g Strategic Prince—Mooching Along (IRE) **P. N. Ridgers**
21 **TEARS OF THE SUN,** 4, b f Mastercraftsman (IRE)—Perfect Star **Mr John Drew**
22 **UNFORGIVING MINUTE,** 4, b c Cape Cross (IRE)—Ada River **Mr P. W. Harris**
23 **VOYAGEOFDISCOVERY (USA),** 4, b br g Henrythenavigator (USA)—Look Out Lorie (USA) **The Navigators**
24 **WESTERN BELLA,** 4, b f High Chaparral (IRE)—Sindarbella **Theakston Stud**
25 **WINTER SPICE (IRE),** 4, gr g Verglas (IRE)—Summer Spice (IRE) **Spice Traders**

### THREE-YEAR-OLDS

26 **BEAUTY PRINCE,** b g Arcano (IRE)—Singed **One Carat Partnership**
27 **BRAZEN SPIRIT,** gr g Zebedee—Never Say Deya **Mr T. H. S. Fox**
28 **CALLENDULA,** ch f Halling (USA)—Oatey **R. Haim**
29 **DUC DE SEVILLE (IRE),** b g Duke of Marmalade (IRE)—Splendid (IRE) **Dukes Of Beechdown**
30 **FRUITY (IRE),** b f Camacho—Belle of The Blues (IRE) **Qatar Racing Limited**
31 **HYPHAEMA (IRE),** b f Rock of Gibraltar (IRE)—Kotdiji **Mrs M. Phelan**
32 **ICE LORD (IRE),** gr c Verglas (IRE)—Special Lady (FR) **Hintlesham Racing Ltd**
33 **IMPERIAL MARCH (IRE),** b g Arch (USA)—Sneak Preview **Inner Circle Thoroughbred - Lavery**
34 **KODI BEAR (IRE),** br c Kodiac—Hawattef (IRE) **Mrs O. A. Shaw**
35 **LADY D'S ROCK (IRE),** gr f Aussie Rules (USA)—Za Za **Mrs A. M. Dawes**
36 **LAIDBACK ROMEO (IRE),** b c Kodiac—Belmora (USA) **Mr R. P. Craddock**
37 **LITTLE PALAVER,** b g Showcasing—Little Nymph **Mr T. H. S. Fox**
38 **LOAVES AND FISHES,** b f Oasis Dream—Miracle Seeker **D. J. Burke**
39 **LOUIE DE PALMA,** b c Pastoral Pursuits—Tahirah **P. N. Ridgers**
40 **MIKANDY (IRE),** b f Arcano (IRE)—Belle de Cadix (IRE) **The Mikandy Partnership**
41 **OUTBACK RULER (IRE),** gr c Aussie Rules (USA)—My American Beauty **The Rulers**
42 **PERFECT BOUNTY,** ch f Bahamian Bounty—Perfect Cover (IRE) **Mildmay Racing**
43 **PISTON (IRE),** b g Paco Boy (IRE)—Fairy Contessa (IRE) **A. J. Perkins**
44 **PRESSURE,** ch g Equiano (FR)—Classical Dancer **Mr A. D. Spence**
45 **PROFITABLE (IRE),** b c Invincible Spirit (IRE)—Dani Ridge (IRE) **Mr A. D. Spence**
46 **QUINTUS CERIALIS (IRE),** b c Vale of York (IRE)—Red Fox (IRE) **Brighthelm Racing**
47 **QUITE A STORY,** ch f Equiano (FR)—Perfect Story (IRE) **Mildmay Racing & D. H. Caslon**
48 **RAW IMPULSE,** b c Makfi—Marika **Qatar Racing Limited**
49 **RENKO,** b g Archipenko (USA)—Park Law (IRE) **Mondial Racing & Robert Haim**
50 **ROSALIE BONHEUR,** ch f Siyouni (FR)—Crozon **Mrs Hugh Maitland-Jones**
51 **SECRET SPIRIT,** b f Sakhee's Secret—Naayla (IRE) **Secret Agents**
52 **SHALIMAH (IRE),** br c Dark Angel (IRE)—Jemima's Art **Mrs C. A. Craddock**

## MR CLIVE COX - Continued

**53 ST GEORGES ROCK (IRE),** b c Camacho—Radio Wave **Mrs A. M. Dawes**
**54 TICKS THE BOXES (IRE),** ch c Fast Company (IRE)—Swan Sea (USA) **Miss J. Deadman & Mr S. Barrow**
**55 TRIKASANA,** ch f Leporello (IRE)—Baileys Honour **Mrs J. C. Ridgers**
**56 VICTORY MEGASTAR,** b c Medicean—Bourbon Ball (USA) **One Carat Partnership**
**57 WEETLES,** b f High Chaparral (IRE)—Millestan (IRE) **D. J. Burke**

## TWO-YEAR-OLDS

**58 ANGIE'S GIRL,** b f 8/3 Exceed And Excel (AUS)—
Expedience (USA) (With Approval (CAN)) (130000) **Mrs A. M. Dawes**
**59** B c 15/4 Zebedee—Artemis Culture (USA) (Smart Strike (CAN)) (20634) **New Syndicate**
**60 ATTITUDE ROCKS,** b c 12/5 Dansili—Dorelia (IRE) (Efisio) (140000) **Mrs Angie Dawes**
**61** B f 26/3 Makfi—Aunty Mary (Common Grounds) **Qatar Racing Limited**
**62** B c 25/2 Monsieur Bond (IRE)—Bidding Time (Rock of Gibraltar (IRE)) (28571) **New Syndicate**
**63 CARPE DIEM LADY (IRE),** b f 2/5 Acclamation—Greenisland (IRE) (Fasliyev (USA)) (85000) **Mrs A. M. Dawes**
**64 CHELSEA'S BOY (IRE),** br gr c 30/4 Rip Van Winkle (IRE)—
St Roch (IRE) (Danehill (USA)) (110000) **Mr D. J. Dawes**
**65 CORELLA (IRE),** b f 25/3 Dream Ahead (USA)—Nashira (Prince Sabo) **Old Peartree Stud**
**66 COVER CHARGE,** ch c 17/3 Kheleyf (USA)—Perfect Cover (IRE) (Royal Applause) (16190) **A. Butler**
**67** B c 25/2 Acclamation—Dani Ridge (IRE) (Indian Ridge) **Mr Con Harrington**
**68** B f 26/4 Elusive City (USA)—Fisadara (Nayef (USA)) (15000) **Wood Hall Stud Limited**
**69** B f 8/5 Kyllachy—Flamenco Dancer (Mark of Esteem (IRE)) (42000) **Mr M. Flitton**
**70 FLIRTY THIRTY (IRE),** b f 18/3 Big Bad Bob (IRE)—
Three Decades (IRE) (Invincible Spirit (IRE)) (33333) **M. P. & R. J. Coleman**
**71 FUTOON (IRE),** b f 8/1 Kodiac—Vermilliann (IRE) (Mujadil (USA)) (31745) **Ahmad Abdulla Al Shaikh & Co**
**72** B c 30/3 Kheleyf (USA)—Go Go Girl (Pivotal) **Mr & Mrs D. Cash & P. Turner**
**73** B c 28/4 Poet's Voice—Golden Nun (Bishop of Cashel) (75000) **Mr A. D. Spence**
**74** B c 24/3 Holy Roman Emperor (IRE)—High Reserve (Dr Fong (USA)) (25396) **Mr A. G. Craddock**
**75** Ch f 6/2 Sakhee's Secret—Ice Haven (IRE) (Verglas (IRE)) **Mrs O. A. Shaw**
**76 LIGHT UP LIFE (IRE),** b c 9/3 Acclamation—
Golden Destiny (IRE) (Captain Rio) (34285) **Miss J. Deadman & Mr Stephen W. Barrow**
**77 LITTLE SALAMANCA,** ch c 18/4 Sakhee's Secret—Little Nymph (Emperor Fountain) **Mr T. H. S. Fox**
**78** B c 11/2 Pastoral Pursuits—Littlemisssunshine (IRE) (Oasis Dream) (25000) **Kenneth MacPherson**
**79** B f 9/3 Exceed And Excel (AUS)—Molly Brown (Rudimentary (USA)) (70000) **Mr A. D. Spence**
**80** B c 12/3 Kyllachy—Night Premiere (IRE) (Night Shift (USA)) (80000) **Mrs O. A. Shaw**
**81 OUR JOY (IRE),** b f 2/2 Kodiac—Great Joy (IRE) (Grand Lodge (USA)) **Mr P. McCartan**
**82 PERFECT QUEST,** br f 12/2 Bushranger (IRE)—Love Quest (Pursuit of Love) **J. R. Drew**
**83 PRIME PURPOSE (IRE),** b c 22/4 Kodiac—
Open Verse (USA) (Black Minnaloushe (USA)) (38095) **Miss J. Deadman & Mr Stephen W. Barrow**
**84** B c 23/4 Pivotal—Regal Rose (Danehill (USA)) (12698) **Mr Peter Ridgers**
**85** Gr c 12/4 Hellvelyn—Rioliina (IRE) (Captain Rio) (12380) **Mr David Russell**
**86** B c 9/4 Pour Moi (IRE)—Sallanches (USA) (Gone West (USA)) (21428) **Mr Charles Wenworth**
**87** B f 26/2 Kheleyf (USA)—Sarah Park (IRE) (Redback) **Mr & Mrs D. Cash & P. Turner**
**88** Ch f 2/4 Zoffany (IRE)—Sky Red (Night Shift (USA)) (23809) **Hot To Trot Racing Club**
**89 STAUNCH,** b c 26/2 Pivotal—Striving (IRE) (Danehill Dancer (IRE)) (60000) **Cheveley Park Stud Limited**
**90 STRAWBERRY SORBET,** b f 27/3 Street Cry (IRE)—
Strawberrydaiquiri (Dansili) (125000) **Cheveley Park Stud Limited**
**91 THE SPECIAL ONE (IRE),** br f 29/3 Cape Cross (IRE)—
Capote West (USA) (Capote (USA)) (30000) **Mr Dave Dawes**
**92** B f 6/3 Sir Percy—Tintac (Intikhab (USA)) **Mr Martin A. Collins**
**93 TOUCH OF COLOR,** b f 17/2 Sixties Icon—Shesells Seashells (Tiger Hill (IRE)) **Mrs H. Fitzsimons**
**94** B c 13/3 Invincible Spirit (IRE)—Zanzibar (IRE) (In The Wings) (100000) **Mr Con Harrington**
**95 ZONDERLAND,** ch c 21/2 Dutch Art—Barynya (Pivotal) (70000) **Cheveley Park Stud Limited**

**Other Owners:** Miss Barbara Allen, Mr Stephen W. Barrow, Mr J. Bernstein, Mrs N. M. Booth, Mr Ian M. Brown, D. H. Caslon, Miss Julie Deadman, Mr Alastair Donald, Dr Bridget Drew, Mr G. W. Elphick, Mr T. Elphick, Miss C. A. Green, Mr R. Haim, Mrs R. J. Hargreaves, Mr P. K. Hargreaves, Mr John Hetherington, Mr Geoff Hill, Mr S. Hill, Ms Diane Jones, Mrs R. F. Lowe, Mr A. McIntyre, Miss C. McIntyre, Dr J. Merrington, Mrs U. Merrington, Mr J. G. Moore, Mr M. O'Brien, Mr R. C. Thomas, Miss Audrey F. Thompson, Mr A. Thompson, Mr Nigel Wagland.

**Assistant Trainer:** Jenny Ferguson

**Jockey (flat):** Adam Kirby. **Apprentice:** Megan Nicholls, Ryan Tate.

## 123 MR TONY COYLE, Norton

Postal: **Long Row Stables, Beverley Road, Norton, Malton, North Yorkshire, YO17 9PJ**
Contacts: **MOBILE (07976) 621425**
**E-MAIL tonycoyleracing@hotmail.co.uk**

1 **ANSAAB,** 7, b g Cape Cross (IRE)—Dawn Raid (IRE) **Mr C. Buckingham**
2 **BILLY CUCKOO (IRE),** 9, b g Alderbrook—First Battle (IRE) **Gary Dewhurst & Tony Coyle**
3 **BOB'S CALL (IRE),** 6, b g Scorpion (IRE)—Whizz **Noel Curtin & T Coyle**
4 **CHECKPOINT,** 6, ch g Zamindar (USA)—Kalima **Twenty Four Seven Recruitment Services Ltd**
5 **FLOWER POWER,** 4, br f Bollin Eric—Floral Rhapsody **Ms M. H. Matheson**
6 **FRIZZO (FR),** 8, ch g Ballingarry (IRE)—Floridene (FR) **Morecool Racing & Tony Coyle**
7 **ITALIAN,** 5, b g Pivotal—Taranto **Gap Personnel & Craig Buckingham**
8 **KEEP IT DARK,** 6, b g Invincible Spirit (IRE)—Tarneem (USA) **N. Hetherton**
9 **LANDMARQUE,** 6, b g Milan—M N L Lady **C. E. Whiteley**
10 **LENDAL BRIDGE,** 4, ch g Avonbridge—Dunloe (IRE) **Mrs V. C. Sugden**
11 **LIFT THE LID (IRE),** 5, b g Robin des Pres (FR)—Kindly Light (IRE)
12 **LUCKY LANDING (IRE),** 9, b br g Well Chosen—Melville Rose (IRE) **Gary Dewhurst & Tony Coyle**
13 **MY OH MOUNT BROWN (IRE),** 8, b g Millenary—My O Mio (IRE) **Mr C. Buckingham**
14 **NEWGATE QUEEN,** 4, gr f Phoenix Reach (IRE)—Arctic Queen **W. P. S. Johnson**
15 **PROBABLY SORRY,** 6, ch g Osorio (GER)—Twist The Facts (IRE) **Mr A. C. Coyle**
16 **RED PRIMO (IRE),** 4, b g Iffraaj—Testa Unica (ITY) **Mr C. Buckingham**
17 **SEA LION,** 4, ch g Sea The Stars (IRE)—Bourbonella **Mr B. Kerr**
18 **SENSOR (USA),** 6, b g Street Sense (USA)—Minister Wife (USA) **Mr A. C. Coyle**
19 **SHIROCCO PASSION,** 4, b f Shirocco (GER)—Pete's Passion **P. D. Smith Holdings Ltd**
20 **SILVER DRAGON,** 7, gr g Silver Patriarch (IRE)—Gotogeton **Twenty Four Seven Recruitment Services Ltd**
21 **THATCHERITE (IRE),** 7, gr g Verglas (IRE)—Damiana (IRE) **Mr B. Kerr**
22 5, B m High Chaparral (IRE)—Tribal Princess (IRE)
23 **TY'N Y WERN,** 6, b g Dylan Thomas (IRE)—Silk (IRE) **Mr A. C. Coyle**

### THREE-YEAR-OLDS

24 **ALASKAN WING (IRE),** br g Kodiac—Canary Bird (IRE) **Mr M. Beaumont**
25 **ALDERAAN (IRE),** gr f Zebedee—Rublevka Star (USA) **Middleham Park Racing XLII & Partner**
26 **CENTURY FIGHTER,** b g Shamardal (USA)—Bergamask (USA) **Mr B. Kerr**
27 **FLICKA'S BOY,** b g Paco Boy (IRE)—Selkirk Sky **Twenty Four Seven Recruitment Services Ltd**
28 **FLYBALL,** gr g Proclamation (IRE)—Bella Bertolini **Mr C. Buckingham**
29 **GONEINAMINUTE,** b f Bushranger (IRE)—Nevada Princess (IRE) **Mr A. C. Coyle**
30 **HORSFORTH,** b f Kyllachy—Lady McBeth (IRE) **Morecool Racing**
31 **MAGIC EMPRESS (IRE),** b f Baltic King—Red Trance (IRE) **Mr A. C. Coyle**
32 **MAUREB (IRE),** br f Excellent Art—Almost Blue (USA) **Gap Personnel & Craig Buckingham**
33 **MOLLY APPROVE (IRE),** b f Approve (IRE)—Kathleen Rafferty (IRE) **Kerr's Cronies**
34 **OUR KYLIE (IRE),** b f Jeremy (USA)—Prakara (IRE) **Morecool & Cool Racing**
35 **RED TOUCH (USA),** b br g Bluegrass Cat (USA)—Touchnow (CAN) **Mr C. Buckingham**
36 **ROMANTICISED (USA),** b g Street Sense (USA)—Delighted (IRE) **Mr C. Buckingham**
37 B f Multiplex—Romping Home (IRE) **Mr G. Dewhurst**
38 **SAMSONITE (IRE),** ch c Pivotal—Silca's Sister **C. R. Green**
39 **TAFFETTA,** ch f Paco Boy (IRE)—Tarneem (USA) **Mrs H. B. Raw**
40 **U THINK UR FUNNY (IRE),** b f Zebedee—Northern Tara (IRE) **Mr A. C. Coyle**

### TWO-YEAR-OLDS

41 B g 29/3 Clodovil (IRE)—Chelsea Morning (USA) (Giant's Causeway (USA)) (4761)
42 B f 22/2 Excellent Art—Gypsie Queen (IRE) (Xaar) (12380) **Mr C. J. Varley**
43 B g 5/5 Haafhd—Jenise (IRE) (Orpen (USA)) (761) **W. P. S. Johnson**
44 B f 26/4 Sir Percy—Lady Le Quesne (IRE) (Alhaarth (IRE)) (1904)
45 B c 23/1 Makfi—Santa Agata (FR) (Anabaa (USA)) (11428) **Mr A. C. Coyle**
46 B f 11/3 Paco Boy (IRE)—Spring Green (Bahamian Bounty) (10476)

**Other Owners:** Mr S. Bland, Mr J. J. Cosgrove, Mr N. J. Curtin, Gap Personnel Franchises Limited, Mr T. D. Nield, T. S. Palin, M. Prince, Mr M. Sykes, Mr A. Wilson.

**Assistant Trainer:** Jaimie Kerr

**Jockey (flat):** Stephen Craine, Barry McHugh. **Amateur:** Miss Harriet Dukes.

## 124 MR RAY CRAGGS, Sedgefield

Postal: **East Close Farm, Sedgefield, Stockton-On-Tees, Cleveland, TS21 3HW**
Contacts: **PHONE (01740) 620239 FAX (01740) 623476**

1 **DOWNTOWN BOY (IRE),** 7, br g Kheleyf (USA)—Uptown (IRE) **R. Craggs**
2 **FLEURTILLE,** 6, b m Tillerman—Miss Fleurie **R. Craggs**
3 **NEEDWOOD PARK,** 7, br g Needwood Blade—Waterpark **R. Craggs**
4 **PARK HOUSE,** 6, b g Tillerman—Rasin Luck **R. Craggs**
5 **TAKE A BREAK,** 4, b f Josr Algarhoud (IRE)—Waterpark **R. Craggs**

### THREE-YEAR-OLDS

6 **WELL I NEVER,** b g Josr Algarhoud (IRE)—Tour d'amour (IRE) **R. Craggs**

**Assistant Trainer:** Miss J N Craggs

## 125 MR PETER CRATE, Dorking

Postal: **Springfield Farm, Parkgate Road, Newdigate, Dorking, Surrey, RH5 5DZ**
Contacts: **MOBILE (07775) 821560**
**E-MAIL peterdcrate@jandjfranks.com**

1 **ELUSIVITY (IRE),** 7, b g Elusive City (USA)—Tough Chic (IRE) **P. D. Crate**
2 **LUJEANIE,** 9, br g Lujain (USA)—Ivory's Joy **Peter Crate & Gallagher Equine Ltd**
3 **PICANSORT,** 8, b g Piccolo—Running Glimpse (IRE) **P. D. Crate**
4 **SANDFRANKSKIPSGO,** 6, ch g Piccolo—Alhufoof (USA) **P. D. Crate**
5 **SMOOTHTALKINRASCAL (IRE),** 5, b g Kodiac—Cool Tarifa (IRE) **P. D. Crate & Gallagher Equine Ltd**
6 **TAAJUB (IRE),** 8, b g Exceed And Excel (AUS)—Purple Tiger (IRE) **P. D. Crate**
7 **TOP OFFER,** 6, b g Dansili—Zante **P. D. Crate**

### TWO-YEAR-OLDS

8 B g 14/4 Equiano (FR)—Alhufoof (USA) (Dayjur (USA)) (4761) **P. D. Crate**

**Other Owners:** Gallagher Equine Ltd.

**Jockey (flat):** George Baker, Shane Kelly. **Amateur:** Mr George Crate.

## 126 MR SIMON CRISFORD, Newmarket

Postal: **Crisford Racing Limited, Calne Stables, 49A Bury Road, Newmarket, Suffolk, CB8 7BY**
Contacts: **PHONE (01638) 662661**

1 **FAINTLY (USA),** 4, b c Kitten's Joy (USA)—Tinge (USA)
2 **GANG WARFARE,** 4, b g Medicean—Light Impact (IRE)
3 **HESBAAN (IRE),** 4, b g Acclamation—Celestial Dream (IRE)
4 **KNAVERY (USA),** 4, b br c Candy Ride (ARG)—Tight Spin (USA)
5 **MUSTADAAM (IRE),** 4, br g Dansili—Sundus (USA)
6 **MUTAWATHEA,** 4, b g Exceed And Excel (AUS)—Esteemed Lady (IRE)
7 **PERIL,** 4, ch g Pivotal—Portodora (USA)
8 **THE HOODED CLAW (IRE),** 4, ch g Dandy Man (IRE)—Changari (USA)

### THREE-YEAR-OLDS

9 **AL BANDAR (IRE),** b c Monsieur Bond (IRE)—Midnight Mystique (IRE)
10 **FORBIDDEN LOVE,** b f Dubawi (IRE)—Indian Love Bird
11 **PHYLLIS MAUD (IRE),** ch f Halling (USA)—Debonnaire

### TWO-YEAR-OLDS

12 B c 24/2 New Approach (IRE)—Airline (USA) (Woodman (USA)) (63492)
13 B c 3/4 Teofilo (IRE)—Antillia (Red Ransom (USA)) (50000)
14 B c 20/2 Raven's Pass (USA)—Bunting (Shaadi (USA))
15 **DAAFIK,** b c 2/2 Shamardal (USA)—Princess Danah (IRE) (Danehill (USA)) (220000)
16 **DAQEEQ (IRE),** b c 21/4 New Approach (IRE)—Asawer (IRE) (Darshaan)
17 B f 10/4 Elusive Quality (USA)—Delighted (IRE) (Danehill (USA))
18 B f 12/5 Poet's Voice—Demerger (USA) (Distant View (USA)) (80000)
19 **DONNERHALL (IRE),** b c 21/3 Kendargent (FR)—Daidoo (IRE) (Shamardal (USA)) (20634)

## MR SIMON CRISFORD - Continued

**20** **ESKANDARI (IRE),** b c 27/2 Kodiac—Alexander Icequeen (IRE) (Soviet Star (USA)) (60000)
**21** B c 12/3 Iffraaj—Flamenco Red (Warning) (72000)
**22** **FLOWER CUP,** b f 14/4 Acclamation—Amber Queen (IRE) (Cadeaux Genereux) (50000)
**23** Br f 29/4 Poet's Voice—Fragrancy (IRE) (Singspiel (IRE))
**24** B c 2/4 Rip Van Winkle (IRE)—Grecian Dancer (Dansili) (170634)
**25** **JAWAAYIZ,** b f 26/3 Kodiac—Silkenveil (IRE) (Indian Ridge) (64761)
**26** **KINDLY,** b f 7/2 Kyllachy—Touching (IRE) (Kheleyf (USA)) (75000)
**27** B f 21/1 Dubawi (IRE)—Lady Zonda (Lion Cavern (USA))
**28** B c 6/4 Dick Turpin (IRE)—Lawyers Choice (Namid) (15000)
**29** **LORD MARMADUKE,** ch c 14/3 Duke of Marmalade (IRE)—Maid To Treasure (IRE) (Rainbow Quest (USA))
**30** **LUCKY LOT,** b f 4/2 Exceed And Excel (AUS)—Sweetie Time (Invincible Spirit (IRE)) (130952)
**31** B c 2/4 High Chaparral (IRE)—Malayan Mist (IRE) (Dansili)
**32** B f 5/5 Shamardal (USA)—Miss Hepburn (USA) (Gone West (USA))
**33** B f 18/3 Intikhab (USA)—Mneme (FR) (Ocean of Wisdom (USA)) (70000)
**34** **NEW HAPPINESS (IRE),** br f 17/2 Teofilo (IRE)—Anyaas (IRE) (Green Desert (USA)) (21428)
**35** Ch c 3/4 Kyllachy—Polly Floyer (Halling (USA)) (38000)
**36** **PRIDE OF ANGELS,** gr f 1/2 Dark Angel (IRE)—Openness (Grand Lodge (USA)) (65000)
**37** **RAASHDY (IRE),** b c 23/5 Intikhab (USA)—Maghya (IRE) (Mujahid (USA))
**38** Ch c 5/5 Lope de Vega (IRE)—Rain Dancer (IRE) (Sadler's Wells (USA)) (47000)
**39** **TAFTEESH (IRE),** b c 12/4 Kodiac—Mudalalah (IRE) (Singspiel (IRE)) (95238)
**40** **TIME TO BLOSSOM,** b f 7/5 Cape Cross (IRE)—Time Over (Mark of Esteem (IRE)) (65000)
**41** Ch c 18/3 Approve (IRE)—Vintage Escape (IRE) (Cyrano de Bergerac) (28000)
**42** **WAFI STAR (IRE),** b c 8/3 Showcasing—Ophelia's Song (Halling (USA)) (79364)
**43** B f 17/3 Kheleyf (USA)—Weood (IRE) (Dubawi (IRE))
**44** B c 27/1 Pivotal—Wild Silk (Dansili) (80000)
**45** B c 10/3 Acclamation—Winged Harriet (IRE) (Hawk Wing (USA)) (55555)
**46** B c 18/5 Poet's Voice—With Fascination (USA) (Dayjur (USA)) (14000)
**47** **ZANJABEEL,** b c 31/3 Aussie Rules (USA)—Grain Only (Machiavellian (USA)) (210000)

---

## 127 MR ANDREW CROOK, Leyburn

Postal: **Ashgill Stables (Yard 2), Tupgill Park, Coverham, Middleham, North Yorkshire, DL8 4TJ**
Contacts: **PHONE (01969) 640303 MOBILE (07764) 158899**
**E-MAIL andycrookracing@fsmail.net WEBSITE www.andrewcrookracing.co.uk**

**1** **AGESILAS (FR),** 7, gr g Ultimately Lucky (IRE)—Aimessa du Berlais (FR) **R. P. E. Berry**
**2** **AIR CHIEF,** 10, ch g Dr Fong (USA)—Fly For Fame **Lucky Catch Partnership**
**3** **ALONG CAME THEO (IRE),** 5, b g Vertical Speed (FR)—Kachina (IRE) **Friends Of Theo & Select Racing**
**4** **CERTIFICATION (IRE),** 5, b g Authorized (IRE)—Most Charming (FR) **Mr W. Henderson**
**5** **EARLY BOY (FR),** 4, b g Early March—Eclat de Rose (FR) **R. P. E. Berry**
**6** 4, B f Alflora (IRE)—Fairlie
**7** **HE WHO DARES,** 4, gr g Act One—Who Goes There
**8** **JIMMIE BROWN (USA),** 7, b g Street Cry (IRE)—Vid Kid (CAN) **The 100 Club**
**9** **K O KENNY,** 4, b g Apple Tree (FR)—Cool Island (IRE)
**10** **LUCY MILAN (IRE),** 6, b m Milan—Katty Barry (IRE)
**11** **MUTANAWWER,** 6, br g Red Ransom (USA)—Nasheed (USA) **RA Syndicate**
**12** **NASHVILLE (IRE),** 6, b g Galileo (IRE)—Brown Eyes **Mr D. Carter**
**13** **ONE IN A ROW (IRE),** 8, ch g Saffron Walden (FR)—Rostarr (IRE) **Lucky Catch Partnership**
**14** **REMEDIO (IRE),** 5, b g Ramonti (FR)—Cant Hurry Love **Lucky Catch Partnership**
**15** **SHEILAS LADY,** 7, b m Tamure (IRE)—Ladies From Leeds **Mr T. E. England**
**16** **SOHCAHTOA (IRE),** 9, b g Val Royal (FR)—Stroke of Six (IRE) **John Sinclair (Haulage) Ltd**
**17** 4, B f Martaline—Tokahy (FR)
**18** **VENTUREPREDEMENTIA,** 4, b g Indian Danehill (IRE)—Sounds Familiar (IRE)
**19** **ZAZAMIX (FR),** 10, b g Sagamix (FR)—Ombre Bleue (FR) **Mrs C. Hopper**

### THREE-YEAR-OLDS

**20** **FOUR BUCKS,** b g Virtual—Jontys'lass

### TWO-YEAR-OLDS

**21** B c 3/5 Alfred Nobel (IRE)—Twinberry (IRE) (Tagula (IRE)) (6190)

**Other Owners:** Mr A. Crook, Mr G. Heap, Mr J. Saxby, www.Select-Racing-Club.co.uk.

**Jockey (NH):** John Kington. **Apprentice:** Neil Farley.

## 128 MISS JO CROWLEY, Whitcombe

Postal: **Whitcombe Moneymusk Racing Stables, Whitcombe, Dorchester, Dorset, DT2 8NY**
Contacts: **PHONE (01305) 265300 FAX (01305) 265499 MOBILE (07918) 735219**
**E-MAIL jocrowley61@hotmail.co.uk**

1 **CAPTAIN STARLIGHT (IRE),** 5, b g Captain Marvelous (IRE)—Jewell In The Sky (IRE) **Kilstone Ltd**
2 **COMADOIR (IRE),** 9, ch g Medecis—Hymn of The Dawn (USA) **Exors of the Late Mrs E. A. M. Nelson**
3 **DREAM RULER,** 4, b g Holy Roman Emperor (IRE)—
Whatcameoverme (USA) **Exors of the Late Mrs E. A. M. Nelson**
4 **MUSIC MAN (IRE),** 5, b g Oratorio (IRE)—Chanter **Kilstone Ltd**
5 **MYSTICAL SAPPHIRE,** 5, b m Sakhee's Secret—Nadyma (IRE) **Exors of the Late Mrs E. A. M. Nelson**
6 **PATAVIUM PRINCE (IRE),** 12, ch g Titus Livius (FR)—
Hoyland Common (IRE) **Exors of the Late Mrs E. A. M. Nelson**
7 7, Ch m Byron—Porcelana (IRE) **Mrs J. A. Cornwell**
8 6, B m Hurricane Run (IRE)—Regatta (USA) **Mrs J. A. Cornwell**
9 **ROSARINA,** 4, ch f Rock of Gibraltar (IRE)—Spring Fashion (IRE) **Exors of the Late Mrs E. A. M. Nelson**
10 **THE HOLYMAN (IRE),** 7, ch g Footstepsinthesand—Sunset (IRE) **Kilstone Ltd**
11 **THRASOS (IRE),** 6, b g Invincible Spirit (IRE)—Plymsole (USA) **Kilstone Ltd**
12 **WILFRED PICKLES (IRE),** 9, ch g Cadeaux Genereux—Living Daylights (IRE) **Kilstone Ltd**

### THREE-YEAR-OLDS

13 **OISHIN,** b g Paco Boy (IRE)—Roshina (IRE) **Kilstone Ltd**
14 **SEA FANTASY,** b f Paco Boy (IRE)—Takarna (IRE) **Mrs J. A. Cornwell**
15 **SHAVAUGHN,** b f Kheleyf (USA)—Shannon Falls (FR) **Exors of the Late Mrs E. A. M. Nelson**
16 **TANZINA,** b f Equiano (FR)—Pilcomayo (IRE) **Exors of the Late Mrs E. A. M. Nelson**
17 **YOU BE LUCKY (IRE),** b f Thewayyouare (USA)—Lovely Dream (IRE) **TMBS Solutions Ltd**

### TWO-YEAR-OLDS

18 Ch c 25/2 Roderic O'Connor (IRE)—Bianca Sforza (Anabaa (USA)) (19047) **Mrs J. A. Cornwell**
19 B c 9/3 Frozen Power (IRE)—Lady Golan (IRE) (Golan (IRE)) **Mrs J. A. Cornwell**
20 B f 19/2 Royal Applause—Merle (Selkirk (USA)) (8500) **Mrs J. A. Cornwell**
21 B f 26/3 Iffraaj—Speak Softly To Me (USA) (Ogygian (USA)) (18000) **Mrs J. A. Cornwell**
22 B f 11/4 Dick Turpin (IRE)—
Whatcameoverme (USA) (Aldebaran (USA)) (9000) **Exors of the Late Mrs E. A. M. Nelson**

**Assistant Trainer:** Anthony Clark

**Jockey (flat):** Dane O'Neill, Fergus Sweeney.

## 129 MR LUCA CUMANI, Newmarket

Postal: **Bedford House Stables, Bury Road, Newmarket, Suffolk, CB8 7BX**
Contacts: **PHONE (01638) 665432 FAX (01638) 667160 MOBILE (07801) 225300**
**E-MAIL luca@lucacumani.com WEBSITE www.lucacumani.com**

1 **AJMAN BRIDGE,** 5, ch g Dubawi (IRE)—Rice Mother (IRE) **Sheikh Mohammed Obaid Al Maktoum**
2 **AYAAR (IRE),** 5, b br h Rock of Gibraltar (IRE)—Teide Lady **Al Shaqab Racing UK Limited**
3 **BLUE WALTZ,** 4, b f Pivotal—Blue Symphony **Fittocks Stud & Andrew Bengough**
4 **COMEDY KING (IRE),** 4, b br g Dansili—Comic (IRE) **Sheikh Mohammed Obaid Al Maktoum**
5 **CONNECTICUT,** 4, b c New Approach (IRE)—Craigmill **Sheikh Mohammed Obaid Al Maktoum**
6 **CROSS COUNTRY (IRE),** 4, b c Cape Cross (IRE)—Altruiste (USA) **Sheikh Mohammed Obaid Al Maktoum**
7 **JORDAN PRINCESS,** 4, b f Cape Cross (IRE)—Princess Nada **Sheikh Mohammed Obaid Al Maktoum**
8 **KLEO (GR),** 4, b f Kavafi (IRE)—Selfish **Mrs M. Marinopoulos**
9 **LUNASEA (IRE),** 4, b c Sea The Stars (IRE)—Musical Treat (IRE) **Mr J. S. Kelly**
10 **MAKAFEH,** 5, br g Elusive Quality (USA)—Demisemiquaver **Sheikh Mohammed Obaid Al Maktoum**
11 **MISSION APPROVED,** 5, b g Dansili—Moon Search **Al Shaqab Racing UK Limited**
12 **MIZZOU (IRE),** 4, b c Galileo (IRE)—Moments of Joy **Mr J. S. Kelly**
13 **MOUNT LOGAN (IRE),** 4, ch c New Approach (IRE)—Vistaria (USA) **Sheikh Mohammed Obaid Al Maktoum**
14 **PENHILL,** 4, b g Mount Nelson—Serrenia (IRE) **Mr T. Bloom**
15 **PLEASANT VALLEY (IRE),** 4, b f Shamardal (USA)—Poughkeepsie (IRE) **Wildenstein Stables Limited**
16 **POSTPONED (IRE),** 4, b c Dubawi (IRE)—Ever Rigg **Sheikh Mohammed Obaid Al Maktoum**
17 **ROSEBURG (IRE),** 4, ch c Tamayuz—Raydaniya (IRE) **Sheikh Mohammed Obaid Al Maktoum**
18 **SAIGON CITY,** 5, b g Mount Nelson—Hoh Chi Min **Mr L. Marinopoulos**
19 **SECOND STEP (IRE),** 4, b g Dalakhani (IRE)—My Dark Rosaleen **Merry Fox Stud Limited**

## MR LUCA CUMANI - Continued

**20 SEUSSICAL (IRE),** 5, b br g Galileo (IRE)—Danehill Music (IRE) **O.T.I. Racing**
**21 WISTAR,** 4, b c Dubawi (IRE)—Vallota **Sheikh Mohammed Obaid Al Maktoum**

## THREE-YEAR-OLDS

**22 ADHBA,** b f New Approach (IRE)—Patacake Patacake (USA) **Al Shaqab Racing UK Limited**
**23 AL,** b c Halling (USA)—Incarnation (IRE) **Hunter, Moulton, Ramsden**
**24 ARANKA,** ch f Iffraaj—Vallota **Mrs M. Marinopoulos**
**25 BARSANTI (IRE),** b c Champs Elysees—Silver Star **Sheikh Mohammed Obaid Al Maktoum**
**26 BARTHOLOMEW FAIR,** b c Dansili—Rebecca Sharp **Sheikh Mohammed Obaid Al Maktoum**
**27 BERMONDSEY,** b c Galileo (IRE)—Barter **Fittocks Stud Ltd**
**28 BESS OF HARDWICK,** b f Dansili—Request **The Duke of Devonshire**
**29 DELAINE,** b f Beat Hollow—Rivara **Miss S. J. E. Leigh**
**30 DREAMLIKE,** b f Oasis Dream—So Silk **Fittocks Stud & Andrew Bengough**
**31 DUFFEL,** ch c Shamardal (USA)—Paisley **Fittocks Stud Ltd**
**32 FEI KUAI,** b f Paco Boy (IRE)—Goldrenched (IRE) **Bartisan Racing Ltd**
**33 FIBRE OPTIC,** b g Rip Van Winkle (IRE)—Wind Surf (USA) **Mr Nagy El Azar**
**34 FIESOLE,** b c Montjeu (IRE)—Forgotten Dreams (IRE) **Fittocks Stud Ltd**
**35 FRANCOPHILE (FR),** ch c Sea The Stars (IRE)—
Empress of France (USA) **Sheikh Mohammed Obaid Al Maktoum**
**36 FRENZIFIED,** b f Yeats (IRE)—Librettista (AUS) **Mr S. A. Stuckey**
**37 GRAND SPIRIT (IRE),** b c Lord Shanakill (USA)—Spirit Watch (IRE) **B. Corman**
**38 HANDBELL (IRE),** b f Acclamation—Dulcian (IRE) **Sheikh Mohammed Obaid Al Maktoum**
**39 IRISH HAWKE (IRE),** b c Montjeu (IRE)—Ahdaab (USA) **Mr J. S. Kelly**
**40 KIBENGA,** b f Oasis Dream—Kibara **Fittocks Stud Ltd**
**41 KING BOLETE (IRE),** b c Cape Cross (IRE)—Chanterelle (FR) **Sheikh Mohammed Obaid Al Maktoum**
**42 KOORA,** b f Pivotal—Kithanga (IRE) **Fittocks Stud Ltd**
**43 LA BOHEME (GER),** b f Montjeu (IRE)—La Reine Noir (GER) **Mr J. S. Kelly**
**44 LADY OF DUBAI,** b f Dubawi (IRE)—Lady of Everest (IRE) **Sheikh Mohammed Obaid Al Maktoum**
**45 LAURENCE,** b c Dubawi (IRE)—Victoire Celebre (USA) **Fittocks Stud & Andrew Bengough**
**46 LILIAN BAYLIS (IRE),** b f Shamardal (USA)—Kiyra Wells (IRE) **Sheikh Mohammed Obaid Al Maktoum**
**47 MONIQUE,** ch f Motivator—Basque Beauty **Countess R. Coventry**
**48 MONOTYPE (IRE),** b c Makfi—Mill Guineas (USA) **Sheikh Mohammed Obaid Al Maktoum**
**49 NORO LIM (IRE),** b g Thewayyouare (USA)—Rohain (IRE) **O.T.I. Racing**
**50 OPTIMA PETAMUS,** ch c Mastercraftsman (IRE)—In A Silent Way (IRE) **Dahab Racing**
**51 PAMONA (IRE),** b f Duke of Marmalade (IRE)—Palanca **Highclere Thoroughbred Racing (Albany)**
**52 RAGGETY ANN (IRE),** b f Galileo (IRE)—Sassenach (IRE) **Mr J. S. Kelly**
**53** Ch f Galileo (IRE)—Ramruma (USA) **Mrs J Magnier, Mr M Tabor & Mr D Smith**
**54 RICHARD OF YORKE,** b c Oasis Dream—Cascata (IRE) **Mr S. A. Stuckey**
**55 SHAKOPEE,** b c High Chaparral (IRE)—Tentpole (USA) **Mrs A. A. Lau Yap**
**56 SPINNER (IRE),** b c Pivotal—Zomaradah **Sheikh Mohammed Obaid Al Maktoum**
**57 SPIRITING (IRE),** b c Invincible Spirit (IRE)—Gold Bubbles (USA) **Sheikh Mohammed Obaid Al Maktoum**
**58 STARS AND STRIPES,** ch c Selkirk (USA)—Capannina **Sheikh Mohammed Obaid Al Maktoum**
**59 SUMMER NAME (IRE),** b c Duke of Marmalade (IRE)—Summer's Eve **Mrs L. E. Ramsden**
**60 WHITE LAKE,** b c Pivotal—White Palace **Sheikh Mohammed Obaid Al Maktoum**
**61 WINTERVAL,** b c Dubawi (IRE)—Festivale (IRE) **Sheikh Mohammed Obaid Al Maktoum**
**62 WREN CASTLE (IRE),** b c Acclamation—Dixie Eyes Blazing (USA) **Mr L. Marinopoulos**

## TWO-YEAR-OLDS

**63 AJMAN PRINCE (IRE),** b c 31/5 Manduro (GER)—
Jumaireyah (Fairy King (USA)) **Sheikh Mohammed Obaid Al Maktoum**
**64 AJMAN PRINCESS (IRE),** b f 17/2 Teofilo (IRE)—
Reem Three (Mark of Esteem (IRE)) **Sheikh Mohammed Obaid Al Maktoum**
**65** B c 6/3 Rock of Gibraltar (IRE)—Amaya (USA) (Kingmambo (USA)) (90000) **Mr Nagy El Azar**
**66** B c 30/4 Rip Van Winkle (IRE)—Anne Tudor (IRE) (Anabaa (USA)) (125000) **Al Shaqab Racing UK Limited**
**67 ARTICLE BLEU,** gr c 7/3 Dansili—Article Rare (USA) (El Prado (IRE)) (50000) **Mr L. Marinopoulos**
**68** B c 22/4 Kyllachy—Ashraakat (USA) (Danzig (USA)) (65000) **Mr L. Marinopoulos**
**69 BEAUTIFUL MORNING,** b f 15/3 Galileo (IRE)—
Date With Destiny (IRE) (George Washington (IRE)) (650000) **Mr J. S. Kelly**
**70** B f 6/4 Teofilo (IRE)—Blinking (Marju (IRE)) **The Duke of Devonshire & The Duke of Roxburghe**
**71** B f 22/2 Oasis Dream—Cascata (IRE) (Montjeu (IRE)) **Mr S. A. Stuckey**
**72** B c 22/4 Kodiac—Chiba (UAE) (Timber Country (USA)) (47000) **Emma Capon Bloodstock**
**73 CIENAGA (IRE),** b c 1/2 Oasis Dream—
Tupelo Honey (IRE) (Sadler's Wells (USA)) (220000) **Sheikh Mohammed Obaid Al Maktoum**
**74 CRYPTIC (IRE),** br c 28/4 Lord Shanakill (USA)—Privet (IRE) (Cape Cross (IRE)) (65000) **Mrs A. Silver**
**75 DAILY NEWS,** b c 11/3 Street Cry (IRE)—Zeeba (IRE) (Barathea (IRE)) **Sheikh Mohammed Obaid Al Maktoum**

## MR LUCA CUMANI - Continued

76 B f 15/3 Galileo (IRE)—Danedrop (IRE) (Danehill (USA)) **Coolmore**
77 B f 3/4 Dansili—Dash To The Top (Montjeu (IRE)) **Helena Springfield Ltd**
78 **EL VIP (IRE),** b c 10/4 Pivotal—Elle Danzig (GER) (Roi Danzig (USA)) (250000) **Al Shaqab Racing UK Limited**
79 **EX LOVER,** ch c 2/4 Monsun (GER)—
Tu Eres Mi Amore (IRE) (Sadler's Wells (USA)) (200000) **Sheikh Mohammed Obaid Al Maktoum**
80 **FASTNET MONSOON (IRE),** b c 2/2 Fastnet Rock (AUS)—
Mona Lisa (Giant's Causeway (USA)) **OTI Racing & Partners**
81 Ch f 27/4 Zoffany (IRE)—Guajira (FR) (Mtoto) (60000) **Mr C. Wright & Mr W. Asprey**
82 **HAGGLE,** ch f 29/3 Pivotal—Barter (Daylami (IRE)) **Fittocks Stud Ltd**
83 **KILIM,** b f 5/5 Dansili—Kibara (Sadler's Wells (USA)) **Fittocks Stud Ltd**
84 **KISS,** b f 2/3 Sir Percy—Kintyre (Selkirk (USA)) **Fittocks Stud Ltd**
85 B f 10/3 Oasis Dream—Lady of Everest (IRE) (Montjeu (IRE)) (500000) **Mr S. Al Homaizi & Mr I. Al Sagar**
86 **MATERIALISTIC,** b f 6/3 Oasis Dream—Pongee (Barathea (IRE)) (550000) **Fittocks Stud Ltd**
87 **MY FAVOURITE THING,** b f 21/3 Oasis Dream—
The Sound of Music (IRE) (Galileo (IRE)) **Sheikh Mohammed Obaid Al Maktoum**
88 **NADA,** b f 20/3 Teofilo (IRE)—Zomaradah (Deploy) **Sheikh Mohammed Obaid Al Maktoum**
89 **PINSTRIPE,** br c 25/5 Dansili—Paisley (Pivotal) **Fittocks Stud**
90 Gr c 3/4 Lawman (FR)—Pocket Watch (Pivotal) **Mr S. A. Stuckey**
91 **POINT OF VIEW (IRE),** b c 12/4 New Approach (IRE)—
Artisti (Cape Cross (IRE)) (400000) **Sheikh Mohammed Obaid Al Maktoum**
92 **RATTLE ON,** ch c 19/2 Pivotal—Sabreon (Caerleon (USA)) (300000) **Sheikh Mohammed Obaid Al Maktoum**
93 Ch f 26/3 Rock of Gibraltar (IRE)—Rivara (Red Ransom (USA)) **Miss S. J. E. Leigh**
94 **ROCK'N GOLD,** b c 17/4 Fastnet Rock (AUS)—La Concorde (FR) (Sadler's Wells (USA)) **Bartisan Racing Ltd**
95 **SHAHABAD,** b f 21/3 Shamardal (USA)—Gulbarg (Dubawi (IRE)) **Sheikh Mohammed Obaid Al Maktoum**
96 **SHARJA PRINCESS,** b f 19/1 Invincible Spirit (IRE)—
Khor Sheed (Dubawi (IRE)) **Sheikh Mohammed Obaid Al Maktoum**
97 **SHARJA QUEEN,** b f 6/2 Pivotal—
Dubai Queen (USA) (Kingmambo (USA)) **Sheikh Mohammed Obaid Al Maktoum**
98 **SILK SUIT (FR),** b c 14/3 Rip Van Winkle (IRE)—
Silk Gallery (USA) (Kingmambo (USA)) (65000) **Buxted Partnership**
99 B c 12/3 Lawman (FR)—Stars In Your Eyes (Galileo (IRE)) (14000) **Mr L. Marinopoulos**
100 **SUBOTAL (IRE),** ch c 3/4 Pivotal—
Suba (USA) (Seeking The Gold (USA)) **Sheikh Mohammed Obaid Al Maktoum**
101 **SUN LOVER,** b c 16/4 Oasis Dream—
Come Touch The Sun (IRE) (Fusaichi Pegasus (USA)) (360000) **Sheikh Mohammed Obaid Al Maktoum**
102 **TAKE SILK,** b c 30/4 Sea The Stars (IRE)—
So Silk (Rainbow Quest (USA)) **Fittocks Stud Ltd & Andrew Bengough**
103 B f 12/4 Duke of Marmalade (IRE)—Taking Liberties (IRE) (Royal Academy (USA)) (63491) **Mr M. Morris**
104 B c 2/5 Champs Elysees—Triomphale (USA) (Nureyev (USA)) (55000) **Mr L. Marinopoulos**
105 **UAE PRINCE (IRE),** b c 22/4 Sea The Stars (IRE)—
By Request (Giant's Causeway (USA)) (650000) **Sheikh Mohammed Obaid Al Maktoum**
106 B f 29/4 Canford Cliffs (IRE)—Vallota (Polish Precedent (USA)) **Mr M. Marinopoulos**
107 Ch f 6/4 Duke of Marmalade (IRE)—Victoire Finale (Peintre Celebre (USA)) **Mr S. Stukeley**
108 Ch c 1/3 New Approach (IRE)—Wadaat (Diktat) (150000) **Al Shaqab Racing UK Limited**
109 **YELLOW BAND (USA),** ch f 13/2 Dalakhani (IRE)—
My Dark Rosaleen (Sadler's Wells (USA)) **Merry Fox Stud Limited**
110 **ZABEEL PRINCE (IRE),** ch c 7/3 Lope de Vega (IRE)—
Princess Serena (USA) (Unbridled's Song (USA)) (325000) **Sheikh Mohammed Obaid Al Maktoum**
111 **ZABEEL PRINCESS,** b f 17/3 Dubawi (IRE)—
Mundana (IRE) (King's Best (USA)) **Sheikh Mohammed Obaid Al Maktoum**

**Assistant Trainer:** Amy Murphy

## 130 MR KEN CUNNINGHAM-BROWN, Stockbridge

Postal: **Danebury Place, Stockbridge, Hampshire, SO20 6JX**
Contacts: **PHONE (01264) 781061 FAX (01264) 781061 MOBILE (07802) 500059**
**E-MAIL kcb@danebury.co.uk**

1 **BULLETPROOF (IRE),** 9, b g Wareed (IRE)—Laura's Native (IRE) **Danebury Racing Stables**
2 **TAMUJIN (IRE),** 7, b g Elusive City (USA)—Arabian Princess **Danebury Racing Stables**

**MR KEN CUNNINGHAM-BROWN - Continued**

**THREE-YEAR-OLDS**

3 **INDIAN CHARLIE,** b f Compton Place—Emerald Fire **Danebury Racing Stables**
4 **MISS GERONIMO,** b f Hellvelyn—Churn Dat Butter (USA) **Danebury Racing Stables**
5 **SECRET STRIKER,** ch f Sakhee's Secret—Silver Purse **Danebury Racing Stables**

**Other Owners:** Mr K. Cunningham-Brown, Mrs V. E. Cunningham-Brown.

**Jockey (flat):** Chris Catlin, Dane O'Neill.

---

## 131 MR SEAN CURRAN, Upper Lambourn

Postal: **Sean Curran Racing Limited, Frenchmans Lodge Stables, Upper Lambourn, Hungerford, Berkshire, RG17 8QW**
Contacts: **PHONE (01488) 72095 FAX (01488) 72095 MOBILE (07774) 146169**
**E-MAIL seancurran99@hotmail.co.uk**

1 **ALDO,** 8, b g Lucky Owners (NZ)—Chaperone **Power Bloodstock Ltd**
2 **ANGLO PADDY (IRE),** 6, ch m Mountain High (IRE)—Hazel Sylph (IRE) **Janet Kirk, Michael Lowry & Keith Adams**
3 **BREEZY KIN (IRE),** 7, ch g Kris Kin (USA)—Presentbreeze (IRE) **Mr P. M. Mannion**
4 **DREAM N (IRE),** 7, b m Flemensfirth (USA)—Roses Niece (IRE) **Mr P. M. Mannion**
5 **INTERIM LODGE (IRE),** 6, b m King's Theatre (IRE)—Brownlow Castle (IRE) **Mr R. K. Adams**
6 **JAY BEE BLUE,** 6, b g Kyllachy—Czarna Roza **Scuderia Vita Bella**
7 **JUBILEE BRIG,** 5, b g Kheleyf (USA)—Voile (IRE) **Power Bloodstock Ltd**
8 **LACOCK,** 4, b g Compton Place—Puya **Ron Smith Recycling Ltd**
9 **ROCK ME ZIPPO (IRE),** 7, b g Millenary—Babylonia (IRE) **Scuderia Vita Bella**
10 **THE BOSS OF ME,** 4, ch g Bahamian Bounty—Orange Pip **Scuderia Vita Bella**
11 **UNCLE CHIZZA,** 6, b g Avonbridge—Sparkling Jewel **Scuderia Vita Bella**
12 **WEBBSWOOD (IRE),** 6, b g Catcher In The Rye (IRE)—Victory Run (IRE) **H. J. M. Webb**

**Other Owners:** Mr L. Graffato, Mrs J. Kirk, Mr M. J. Lowry, Mr J. Norman.

---

## 132 MISS REBECCA CURTIS, Newport

Postal: **Fforest Farm, Newport, Pembrokeshire, SA42 0UG**
Contacts: **PHONE (01348) 811489 MOBILE (07970) 710690**
**E-MAIL rebcurtis@hotmail.com**

1 **AMBER GAMBLER (GER),** 5, b g Doyen (IRE)—Auenglocke (GER) **G. Costelloe**
2 **ASHES HOUSE (IRE),** 9, b g Dushyantor (USA)—Cailinclover (IRE) **Diamond Racing Ltd**
3 **AT FISHERS CROSS (IRE),** 8, b g Oscar (IRE)—Fermoy Supreme (IRE) **J. P. McManus**
4 **AUDACIOUS PLAN (IRE),** 6, b g Old Vic—North Star Poly (IRE) **Mr A. McIver**
5 **AURILLAC (FR),** 5, gr g Martaline—Ombrelle (FR)
6 **BALLYHOLLOW,** 8, ch m Beat Hollow—Ballet-K **Diamond Racing Ltd**
7 **BEAST OF BURDEN (IRE),** 6, ch g Flemensfirth (USA)—Nuit des Chartreux (FR) **Mr C. S. Hinchy**
8 **BINGE DRINKER (IRE),** 6, b g Spadoun (FR)—Our Honey (IRE) **Corsellis, Stockdale & Seyfried**
9 **BOB FORD (IRE),** 8, b g Vinnie Roe (IRE)—Polar Lamb (IRE) **The Bob Ford Partnership**
10 **BOB KEOWN (IRE),** 7, b g Indian Danehill (IRE)—Arteea Princess (IRE) **C. R. Trembath**
11 **CAPTAIN MCGINLEY (IRE),** 5, bl g Robin des Pres (FR)—Rocella (GER) **G. Costelloe**
12 **CARNINGLI (IRE),** 6, b g Old Vic—Name For Fame (USA) **The Newport Partnership**
13 **CHAMPAGNE RIAN (IRE),** 7, b g Dr Massini (IRE)—Vul Gale **Mr C. S. Hinchy**
14 **CHURCHTOWN LOVE (IRE),** 7, b m Beneficial—Katie Murphy (IRE) **Mr A. J. Rhead**
15 **CLANCY'S CROSS (IRE),** 6, b g Oscar (IRE)—Murphy's Lady (IRE) **Mr C. S. Hinchy**
16 **DOING FINE (IRE),** 7, b g Presenting—Howaya Pet (IRE) **Mr C. S. Hinchy**
17 **DRUID'S FOLLY (IRE),** 5, b g Beneficial—Sweet Vale (IRE) **Mr D. J. Harden**
18 **EL MACCA (IRE),** 6, ch g Old Vic—Cluain-Ard (IRE) **J. P. McManus**
19 **FORYOURINFORMATION,** 6, b g Kayf Tara—Sleepless Eye **Mr C. S. Hinchy**
20 **GLENWOOD STAR (IRE),** 7, b g Oscar (IRE)—Shuil Ar Aghaidh **Mr M. A. Sherwood**
21 **GLOBALISATION (IRE),** 5, b g Tikkanen (USA)—On A Mission (IRE) **J. P. McManus**
22 **GOING FOR BROKE (IRE),** 5, b g Gold Well—Kokopelli Star **J. P. McManus**
23 **GUARD OF HONOUR (IRE),** 4, b g Galileo (IRE)—Queen of France (USA) **Mrs L. M. Sherwood**
24 **HOLY CROSS (IRE),** 4, b g Yeats (IRE)—Bleu Ciel Et Blanc (FR) **Mr N. D. Morris**
25 **HOW ABOUT IT (IRE),** 6, b g Kayf Tara—Midnight Gift (IRE) **Mr C. S. Hinchy**
26 **IMAGINE THE CHAT,** 6, b g Kayf Tara—Be My Bird **J. P. McManus**

## MISS REBECCA CURTIS - Continued

27 **IRISH CAVALIER (IRE),** 6, gr ro g Aussie Rules (USA)—Tracker **Mr A. McIver**
28 **JESSIE WEBSTER (IRE),** 6, b m Kayf Tara—Blueberry Bramble (IRE) **Miss R. Curtis**
29 **KNIGHT TO OPEN (IRE),** 5, b g Oscar (IRE)—Sunset View (IRE) **The Bruton Street Partnership**
30 **LOOKSLIKERAINTED (IRE),** 8, b g Milan—Kilcrea Gale (IRE) **Mr A. J. Rhead**
31 **MINELLA ON LINE (IRE),** 6, b g King's Theatre (IRE)—Bally Bolshoi (IRE) **AHB Racing Partnership**
32 **MONKEY KINGDOM,** 7, b g King's Theatre (IRE)—Blast Freeze (IRE) **Mr C. S. Hinchy**
33 **MURPHYS WAY (IRE),** 5, b g Oscar (IRE)—Festival Leader (IRE) **Mr N. D. Morris**
34 **O'FAOLAINS BOY (IRE),** 8, b g Oscar (IRE)—Lisa's Storm (IRE) **Trembath, Hyde, Outhart & Hill**
35 **OFF DUTY (IRE),** 5, b g Oscar (IRE)—Glen Dubh (IRE) **J. P. McManus**
36 **ONE TERM (IRE),** 8, b g Beneficial—One Edge (IRE) **Miss L Reid & Mr G Costelloe**
37 **PECKHAMECHO (IRE),** 9, b g Beneficial—Nolans Pride (IRE) **C. R. Trembath**
38 **POTTERS CROSS,** 8, b g Alflora (IRE)—Teeno Nell **Conyers, O'Reilly, Roddis, Zeffman**
39 **PRESELI ROCK (IRE),** 5, ch g Flemensfirth (USA)—Chantoue Royale (FR) **The Bruton Street Partnership**
40 **PRESELI STAR (IRE),** 5, b g Scorpion (IRE)—Horner Hill (IRE) **Mrs J. C. Corsellis**
41 **RED DEVIL LADS (IRE),** 6, b g Beneficial—Welsh Sitara (IRE) **Mr A. McIver**
42 **RELENTLESS DREAMER (IRE),** 6, br g Kayf Tara—Full of Elegance (FR) **Mr N. D. Morris**
43 **SCORPIANCER (IRE),** 6, b g Scorpion (IRE)—Janebailey **Bruton Street UK - II**
44 **TARA ROAD,** 7, b g Kayf Tara—Sparkling Jewel **Mr N. D. Morris**
45 **TEAFORTHREE (IRE),** 11, b g Oscar (IRE)—Ethel's Bay (IRE) **Conyers, O'Reilly, Roddis, Zeffman**
46 **THE CLONLISK BUG (IRE),** 5, b g Scorpion (IRE)—Apollo Lady **A. Longman**
47 **THE ROMFORD PELE (IRE),** 8, b g Accordion—Back And Fore (IRE) **Trembath & Outhart**
48 **VERIPEK (FR),** 6, ch g Robin des Champs (FR)—Attualita (FR) **J. P. McManus**
49 **VINTAGE VINNIE (IRE),** 6, b g Vinnie Roe (IRE)—Bobby's Jet (IRE) **Trembath, Hyde, Outhart & Hill**
50 **WILD ROVER (IRE),** 6, b g Scorpion (IRE)—Pandalute (IRE) **The Wild Rover Partnership**
51 **WINTER WALK (IRE),** 6, b g Blueprint (IRE)—Dubai Seven Stars **Diamond Racing Ltd**

**Other Owners:** Mr J. Conyers, Mr L. Fitzwilliams, Mr M. D. Hankin, Mr J. C. I. Heilbron, M. Hill, Mr R. Hyde, Marwyn Asset Management SPC, Merriebelle Irish Farm Limited, Mr J. P. O'Reilly, A. J. Outhart, Miss L. Reid, Mr D. A. Robinson, Mr N. M. Roddis, Mr E. J. N. Seyfried, Mr J. M. Stockdale, Mr G. B. Williams, D. C. Zeffman.

**Assistant Trainer:** Paul Sheldrake

---

## 133 MR THOMAS CUTHBERT, Brampton

Postal: **Woodlands, Cowranbridge, How Mill, Brampton, Cumbria, CA8 9LH**
Contacts: **PHONE (01228) 560822 FAX (01228) 560822 MOBILE (07747) 843344**
**E-MAIL cuthbertracing@fsmail.net**

1 **EDAS,** 13, b g Celtic Swing—Eden (IRE) **Mrs J. Cuthbert**
2 **LANDESHERR (GER),** 8, b g Black Sam Bellamy (IRE)—Lutte Marie (GER) **T. A. K. Cuthbert**

**Assistant Trainer:** Helen Cuthbert

**Amateur:** Miss H. Cuthbert.

---

## 134 MR PAUL D'ARCY, Newmarket

Postal: **Charnwood Stables, Hamilton Road, Newmarket, Suffolk, CB8 7JQ**
Contacts: **PHONE (01638) 662000 FAX (01638) 661100 MOBILE (07768) 807653**
**E-MAIL pauldarcy@fsmail.net WEBSITE www.pauldarcyracing.com**

1 **GLOBAL LEADER (IRE),** 5, b g Dark Angel (IRE)—Headborough Lass (IRE) **Dr J. S. Kinnear**
2 **RED INVADER (IRE),** 5, b g Red Clubs (IRE)—Tifariti (USA) **C. M. Wilson**
3 **TRUE SPIRIT,** 5, b g Shamardal (USA)—Petonellajill **P. W. D'Arcy**

### THREE-YEAR-OLDS

4 **ANASTAZIA,** br f Kyllachy—Meddle **Mr K. Snell**
5 Ch g Dutch Art—Barreda (IRE) **Champion Bloodstock Limited**
6 **MONEY PRINTER (IRE),** b g Intense Focus (USA)—Biasca **Champion Bloodstock Limited**
7 **SPRING LOADED (IRE),** gr g Zebedee—Nisriyna (IRE) **Rowley Racing**

### TWO-YEAR-OLDS

8 B c 22/2 Arcano (IRE)—Melanesia (IRE) (Chevalier (IRE)) (50000) **Champion Bloodstock Limited**
9 **ROCKLEY POINT,** b c 14/4 Canford Cliffs (IRE)—Statua (IRE) (Statoblest) (29523) **Rowley Racing**

## MR PAUL D'ARCY - Continued

**Other Owners:** Mrs S. I. D'Arcy, Mr W. P. Drew.

**Assistant Trainer:** Sue D'Arcy

**Apprentice:** Stacey Kidd. **Amateur:** Mrs Rachel Wilson.

---

## 135 MR LUKE DACE, Billingshurst

Postal: **Copped Hall Farm & Stud, Okehurst Lane, Billingshurst, West Sussex, RH14 9HR**
Contacts: **FAX (01403) 612176 MOBILE (07949) 401085**
**E-MAIL lukedace@yahoo.co.uk WEBSITE www.lukedace.co.uk**

1 **AMERICAN SPIN,** 11, ch g Groom Dancer (USA)—Sea Vixen **Mr G Collacott & Mr R Gadd**
2 **BOBBY BENTON (IRE),** 4, b g Invincible Spirit (IRE)—Remarkable Story **M. J. Benton**
3 **ECHO BRAVA,** 5, gr g Proclamation (IRE)—Snake Skin **M. J. Benton**
4 **GREELEYS LOVE (USA),** 5, ch g Mr Greeley (USA)—Aunt Winnie (IRE) **M. J. Benton**
5 **LORD ALDERVALE (IRE),** 8, br g Alderbrook—Monavale (IRE) **Mr D. N. Boxall**
6 **MY LORD,** 7, br g Ishiguru (USA)—Lady Smith **Robert E Lee Syndicate**
7 **SECRET MILLIONAIRE (IRE),** 8, b g Kyllachy—Mithl Al Hawa **Robert E Lee Syndicate**
8 **SHAMAHAN,** 6, b g Shamardal (USA)—Hanella (IRE) **Forever Hopeful**
9 **STATSMINISTER,** 4, b f Champs Elysees—Sailing Days **Mrs E. A. Cyzer**
10 **WESTERLY,** 4, b f Rail Link—Humility **Mrs E. A. Cyzer**

### THREE-YEAR-OLDS

11 **FOYLESIDEVIEW (IRE),** b g Dark Angel (IRE)—Showerproof **M. C. S. D. Racing Partnership**
12 **NOBLE CAUSE,** b f Showcasing—Noble Peregrine **Copped Hall Farm & Stud**

### TWO-YEAR-OLDS

13 **BELEAVE,** gr f 21/3 Avonbridge—Grezie (Mark of Esteem (IRE))
14 **STYLISTIK,** ch f 12/4 Sakhee's Secret—Passing Hour (USA) (Red Ransom (USA))

**Other Owners:** Mr Mark Benton, Mr G. Collacott, Mr Luke Dace, Mrs L. J. Dace, Mr R. A. Gadd, Mr Barry J. McClean, Mrs Maggie McClean, Dr L. Parks, Mrs Fiona Young.

**Assistant Trainer:** Mrs L Dace

**Amateur:** Mr J. Doe.

---

## 136 MR KEITH DALGLEISH, Carluke

Postal: **Belstane Racing Stables, Carluke, Lanarkshire, ML8 5HN**
Contacts: **PHONE (01555) 773335**

1 **ALL THE ACES (IRE),** 10, b g Spartacus (IRE)—Lili Cup (FR) **Straightline Construction Ltd**
2 **ARCHIE'S ADVICE,** 4, b g Archipenko (USA)—Flylowflylong (IRE) **G L S Partnership**
3 **ARGAKI (IRE),** 5, ch g Strategic Prince—Amathusia **D. G. Savala**
4 4, B g Westerner—Autumn Sky (IRE) **Equus Syndicate**
5 **BEAUTIFUL STRANGER (IRE),** 4, b g Iffraaj—Monarchy (IRE) **Weldspec Glasgow Limited**
6 **BERTIE MOON,** 5, b g Bertolini (USA)—Fleeting Moon **Straightline Construction Ltd**
7 **CHOOKIE ROYALE,** 7, ch g Monsieur Bond (IRE)—Lady of Windsor (IRE) **Raeburn Brick Limited**
8 **CHOOKIE'S LASS,** 4, ch f Compton Place—Lady of Windsor (IRE) **Raeburn Brick Limited**
9 **COACHIE BEAR,** 4, ch c Grape Tree Road—Gentle Approach **Prestige Thoroughbred Racing**
10 **CORTON LAD,** 5, b g Refuse To Bend (IRE)—Kelucia (IRE) **Mr J. J. Hutton**
11 **FARM SALE,** 4, ch g Piccolo—Bundle **Equus Syndicate**
12 **FRANKTHETANK (IRE),** 4, ch g Captain Gerrard (IRE)—Mi Amor (IRE) **R. McNeill**
13 **GINGER JACK,** 8, ch g Refuse To Bend (IRE)—Coretta (IRE) **C. H. McGhie**
14 **HANALEI BAY (IRE),** 5, b h Tamayuz—Genial Jenny (IRE) **Mrs F. E. Mitchell**
15 **INCURS FOUR FAULTS,** 4, b g Halling (USA)—Rapsgate (IRE) **J. S. Morrison**
16 **JACOB BLACK,** 4, b c Amadeus Wolf—First Eclipse (IRE) **Redgate Bloodstock & Charles Wentworth**
17 **MEET THE LEGEND,** 4, b g Midnight Legend—Combe Florey **Straightline Construction Ltd**
18 **MONTOYA'S SON (IRE),** 10, ch g Flemensfirth (USA)—Over The Grand (IRE) **Straightline Construction Ltd**
19 **NEXIUS (IRE),** 6, b g Catcher In The Rye (IRE)—Nicolaia (GER) **Straightline Construction Ltd**
20 **PRESSURE POINT,** 5, b g Oasis Dream—Arrive **Mrs J. M. MacPherson**
21 **REPOSER (IRE),** 7, br g Kheleyf (USA)—Tragic Point (IRE) **J. S. Morrison**
22 **SALVATORE FURY (IRE),** 5, b g Strategic Prince—Nocturnal (FR) **Prestige Thoroughbred Racing**

## MR KEITH DALGLEISH - Continued

**23 SANTEFISIO,** 9, b g Efisio—Impulsive Decision (IRE) **Weldspec Glasgow Limited**
**24 SCURR MIST (IRE),** 4, gr g Aussie Rules (USA)—Stratospheric **Lamont Racing**
**25 SEASIDE ROCK (IRE),** 5, b g Oratorio (IRE)—Miss Sacha (IRE) **Sharron & Robert Colvin**
**26 SEWN UP,** 5, ch h Compton Place—Broughton Bounty **Mr J. Kelly**
**27 SHOW ON THE ROAD,** 4, b g Flemensfirth (USA)—Roses of Picardy (IRE) **Equus Syndicate**
**28 SO IT'S WAR (FR),** 4, b g Orpen (USA)—Impulsive Decision (IRE) **Weldspec Glasgow Limited**
**29 SOUND ADVICE,** 6, b g Echo of Light—Flylowflylong (IRE) **G L S Partnership**
**30 SPARKY (GER),** 4, ch g Sholokhov (IRE)—Simply Red (GER) **Equus Syndicate**
**31 STONEFIELD FLYER,** 6, b g Kheleyf (USA)—Majestic Diva (IRE) **Mr G. R. Leckie**
**32 SURAJ,** 6, ch g Galileo (IRE)—Maid of Killeen (IRE) **Straightline Construction Ltd**
**33 TARA MAC,** 6, b m Kayf Tara—Macklette (IRE) **Straightline Construction Ltd**
**34 TARA MACTWO,** 5, b m Kayf Tara—Macklette (IRE) **Equus Syndicate**
**35 WAYWARD GLANCE,** 7, b g Sadler's Wells (USA)—Daring Aim **Straightline Construction Ltd**

### THREE-YEAR-OLDS

**36 CARRON VALLEY,** b c Royal Applause—Clear Impression (IRE) **Prestige Thoroughbred Racing**
**37 CHANCES ARE (IRE),** ch f Dandy Man (IRE)—Incendio **S. J. Macdonald**
**38 COMEBAKNASHWAN,** b g Arabian Gleam—Suka Ramai **Evergreen Racing**
**39 DISUSHE STAR,** ch g Kheleyf (USA)—Canis Star **R. C. Miquel**
**40 EDGAR BALTHAZAR,** b c Pastoral Pursuits—Assistacat (IRE) **Middleham Park Racing XXII**
**41** B f Mount Nelson—Manila Selection (USA) **Weldspec Glasgow Limited**
**42 PENELOPE PITSTOP,** b f Captain Gerrard (IRE)—Obsessive Secret (IRE) **Lamont Racing**
**43 SIR LANCELOTT,** b g Piccolo—Selkirk Rose (IRE) **Mr G. Brogan**
**44 TOMMY DOCC (IRE),** b c Thewayyouare (USA)—Liturgy (IRE) **Mr R. Docherty**

### TWO-YEAR-OLDS

**45** B f 16/3 Strategic Prince—Ardent Lady (Alhaarth (IRE)) (11428) **Middleham Park Racing XXIII**
**46** B c 7/2 Approve (IRE)—Beauty And Style (AUS) (King of Kings (IRE)) (20000) **Prestige Thoroughbred Racing**
**47** B f 2/4 Elnadim (USA)—Bijan (IRE) (Mukaddamah (USA)) (9523)
**48** Br gr g 9/4 Aussie Rules (USA)—Bolshaya (Cadeaux Genereux) (4761) **Equus Syndicate**
**49** B f 2/2 Bushranger (IRE)—Choice House (USA) (Chester House (USA)) (5714) **Equus Syndicate**
**50** B f 16/1 Zebedee—Derval (IRE) (One Cool Cat (USA)) (23809)
**51** B c 15/2 Bushranger (IRE)—Estimation (Mark of Esteem (IRE)) (5714) **Middleham Park Racing XXVII**
**52** B f 14/2 Dark Angel (IRE)—Jemima's Art (Fantastic Light (USA)) (34126)
**53** B f 14/4 Wootton Bassett—Killer Class (Kyllachy)
**54** B c 5/3 Approve (IRE)—Lady of Windsor (IRE) (Woods of Windsor (USA)) **Raeburn Brick Limited**
**55** B f 14/1 Fast Company (IRE)—Lucky Leigh (Piccolo) (52380) **Straightline Construction Ltd**
**56 MAIFALKI (FR),** b c 11/2 Falco (USA)—Makila (IRE) (Entrepreneur) (8730) **Lamont Racing**
**57** B c 18/1 Kheleyf (USA)—Majestic Diva (IRE) (Royal Applause) **Mr G. R. Leckie**
**58** B f 10/4 Roderic O'Connor (IRE)—
Maundays Bay (IRE) (Invincible Spirit (IRE)) (35714) **Weldspec Glasgow Limited**
**59** B c 26/1 Pastoral Pursuits—Oh So Saucy (Imperial Ballet (IRE)) (14285) **Prestige Thoroughbred Racing**
**60** B g 4/4 Sir Percy—Panna (Polish Precedent (USA)) (24761) **Straightline Construction Ltd**
**61** Ch f 14/2 Compton Place—Pink Delight (IRE) (Rock of Gibraltar (IRE)) (13333)
**62** B f 24/2 Kodiac—Sattelight (Fraam) (21904)
**63** B f 11/4 Frozen Power (IRE)—Silver Whale (FR) (Highest Honor (FR)) (12698)
**64** B c 2/5 Jeremy (USA)—Step With Style (USA) (Gulch (USA)) (55555) **Weldspec Glasgow Limited**
**65** B g 20/3 Arcano (IRE)—Third Dimension (FR) (Suave Dancer (USA)) (73015) **Straightline Construction Ltd**
**66** B f 23/2 Dark Angel (IRE)—Unicamp (Royal Academy (USA)) (25714) **Straightline Construction Ltd**
**67 WOLF ISLAND,** b f 6/3 Sleeping Indian—Newkeylets (Diktat) **Mr T. Young**
**68** B c 23/3 Zebedee—Zara's Girl (IRE) (Tillerman) (35714)

**Other Owners:** Mr S. J. Baird, Mr W. Burke, R. Colvin, Mrs S. Colvin, Mr D. C. Flynn, Miss E. Foley, A. R. M Galbraith, Mr R. P. Gilbert, Mrs E. McClymont, Mr D. McClymont, J. Millican, T. S. Palin, M. Prince, Mr S. C. Reay, C. V. Wentworth.

**Assistant Trainer:** Kevin Dalgleish

---

## 137 MR HENRY DALY, Ludlow

Postal: **Downton Hall Stables, Ludlow, Shropshire, SY8 3DX**
Contacts: **OFFICE (01584) 873688 FAX (01584) 873525 MOBILE (07720) 074544**
**E-MAIL henry@henrydaly.co.uk WEBSITE www.henrydaly.co.uk**

**1 ANOTHER COBBLER (FR),** 5, gr m Fragrant Mix (IRE)—Qualine du Maquis (FR) **Mrs A. W. Timpson**
**2 ARCTIC BEN (IRE),** 11, gr g Beneficial—Hurst Flyer **Mrs A. W. Timpson**

## MR HENRY DALY - Continued

3 **BANTAM (IRE),** 5, b m Teofilo (IRE)—Firecrest (IRE) **Brooke Kelly Partnership**
4 **BRAVE BUCK,** 7, b g Bollin Eric—Silken Pearls **P. E. Truscott**
5 **BRIERY BELLE,** 6, b m King's Theatre (IRE)—Briery Ann **Mrs H Plumbly, J Trafford, K Deane, S Holme**
6 **CALL ME KATE,** 5, b m Kalanisi (IRE)—Last of Her Line **T. F. F. Nixon**
7 **CASTLE CONFLICT (IRE),** 10, b g Close Conflict (USA)—Renty (IRE) **Strachan, Clarke, Gabb, Corbett & Salwey**
8 **CHICORIA (IRE),** 6, ch g Presenting—Coco Girl **T. J. Hemmings**
9 **CYRIEN STAR,** 8, b g Bollin Eric—Sainte Etoile (FR) **Puteus Profundus**
10 **DUNGEEL (IRE),** 9, b g Moscow Society (USA)—Mis Fortune (IRE) **Mr Martin Kemp**
11 **GO WEST YOUNG MAN (IRE),** 7, b g Westerner—Last of Her Line **T. F. F. Nixon**
12 **GOOHAR (IRE),** 6, b g Street Cry (IRE)—Reem Three **Rod Brereton & Kate Maxwell**
13 **GROVE PRIDE,** 10, b g Double Trigger (IRE)—Dara's Pride (IRE) **T. J. Hemmings**
14 **HARD TO SWALLOW (IRE),** 9, b g Snurge—Nicat's Daughter (IRE) **Mrs L. Jones**
15 **HERONSHAW (IRE),** 8, b g Heron Island (IRE)—Cool Merenda (IRE) **Strachan, Stoddart, Griffith, Barlow & Harf'd**
16 **KAYFLEUR,** 6, b m Kayf Tara—Combe Florey **B. G. Hellyer**
17 **KESHI PEARL,** 7, b m Kayf Tara—Pearly-B (IRE) **The Wadeley Partnership**
18 **KINGSMERE,** 10, b g King's Theatre (IRE)—Lady Emily **E. R. Hanbury**
19 **L STIG,** 5, b g Striking Ambition—Look Here's May **Strachan, Thompson, Inkin, Graham & Lewis**
20 **LORD GRANTHAM (IRE),** 8, b g Definite Article—Last of Her Line **T. F. F. Nixon**
21 **MICKIE,** 7, gr m Kayf Tara—Island Mist **Ludlow Racing Partnership**
22 **MIGHTY MINNIE,** 6, b m Sir Harry Lewis (USA)—Vanina II (FR) **E. R. Hanbury**
23 **NIGHTFLY,** 4, b f Midnight Legend—Whichway Girl **Mrs D. P. G. Flory**
24 **NIGHTLINE,** 5, b g Midnight Legend—Whichway Girl **Mrs D. P. G. Flory**
25 **NORDIC NYMPH,** 6, b m Norse Dancer (IRE)—Silken Pearls **P. E. Truscott**
26 **OYSTER SHELL,** 8, br g Bollin Eric—Pearly-B (IRE) **The Glazeley Partnership 2**
27 **PASKALIS,** 6, b g Kayf Tara—Easter Comet **Mr & Mrs S. C. Willes**
28 **PEARLYSTEPS,** 12, ch g Alflora (IRE)—Pearly-B (IRE) **The Glazeley Partnership**
29 4, Gr c Act One—Princess Angelique (FR) **Mr P. E. Truscott**
30 **QUEEN SPUD,** 6, b m Multiplex—Hurtebise (FR) **Barlow, Brindley, Hanley & Russell**
31 **QUENTIN COLLONGES (FR),** 11, gr g Dom Alco (FR)—Grace Collonges (FR) **Neville Statham & Family**
32 **ROCKITEER (IRE),** 12, b g Rudimentary (USA)—Party Woman (IRE) **Michael O'Flynn & John Nesbitt**
33 **SAFRAN DE COTTE (FR),** 9, gr g Dom Alco (FR)—Vanille de Cotte (FR) **Mrs A. W. Timpson**
34 **TARA MIST,** 6, gr m Kayf Tara—Island Mist **Strachan, Mangnall, Gabb, Griffith, Graham**
35 **THE ARTFUL COBBLER,** 4, gr g Saint des Saints (FR)—Serhaaphim **Mrs A. W. Timpson**
36 **THE LATE SHIFT,** 5, b g Midnight Legend—Ashnaya (FR) **R. J. Brereton**
37 **TOOT SWEET (IRE),** 8, b m Generous (IRE)—Cresswell Native (IRE) **A. J. Haden**
38 **TOP TOTTI,** 7, b m Sir Harry Lewis (USA)—Jannina (FR) **Hamer, Hawkes & Hellin**
39 **UPBEAT COBBLER (FR),** 7, gr m Brier Creek (USA)—Jade de Chalamont (FR) **Mrs A. W. Timpson**
40 **VICE ET VERTU (FR),** 6, b g Network (GER)—Duchesse du Cochet (FR) **Neville Statham & Family**
41 **WILL O'THE WEST (IRE),** 4, b g Westerner—Simply Divine (IRE) **Strachan, Stoddart, Salwey, Gabb & Griffith**

**Other Owners:** Sir John K. Barlow, Mr R. J. Brereton, Mr John Brindley, Sir Francis Brooke Bt., Mrs S. T. Clarke, Mrs P. Corbett, Mrs Henry Daly, Mr Henry Daly, Lord Daresbury, Mrs K. Deane, Mrs Roger Gabb, Mrs Douglas Graham, Mrs J. G. Griffith, Mr C. M. Hamer, Mr John Hanley, Mr M. Hawkes, Mrs Louise Hellin, Mrs S. Holme, Mr Peter Holt, Mr W. Jenks, Mr Diarmaid Kelly, Mrs Richard Mangnall, Mr Richard Mapp, Mrs Kate Maxwell, Mr John Nesbitt, Mr Michael O'Flynn, Mr Richard Pilkington, Sir Thomas Pilkington, Mrs Helen Plumbly, Mr Anthony Rogers, Mr R. Russell, Mr H. Salwey, Mr Neville Statham, Mrs P. Statham, Mr Michael Stoddart, Mrs Richard Strachan, Mrs Jane Trafford, Mr Simon Willes, Mrs S. C. Willes.

**Assistant Trainer:** Ed Barrett

**Jockey (NH):** Jake Greenall, Richard Johnson.

---

## 138 MR VICTOR DARTNALL, Barnstaple

Postal: **Higher Shutscombe Farm, Charles, Brayford, Barnstaple, Devon, EX32 7PU**
Contacts: **PHONE (01598) 710280 FAX (01598) 710708 MOBILE (07974) 374272**
**E-MAIL victordartnall@gmail.com WEBSITE www.victordartnallracing.com**

1 **ABYAAT (IRE),** 4, b g Halling (USA)—Why Dubai (USA) **V. R. A. Dartnall**
2 **ADMIRAL'S SECRET,** 4, b g Kayf Tara—Bobs Bay (IRE) **Mr G. Dartnall**
3 **AMBION LANE (IRE),** 5, b g Scorpion (IRE)—Thrilling Prospect (IRE) **Mr O. C. R. Wynne & Mrs S. J. Wynne**
4 **AMBION WOOD (IRE),** 9, b g Oscar (IRE)—Dorans Grove **Mr O. C. R. Wynne & Mrs S. J. Wynne**
5 **ASTRE ROSE (FR),** 5, b br g Al Namix (FR)—Quetcha d'isigny (FR) **Fine Wine & Bubbly**
6 **BELLE PARK,** 8, b m Hamairi (IRE)—Cape Siren **V. R. A. Dartnall**

## MR VICTOR DARTNALL - Continued

7 **BINDON MILL,** 6, b g Tamure (IRE)—Singing Cottage **Mrs E. S. Weld**
8 **DANCING SHADOW (IRE),** 6, br g Craigsteel—Be My Shadow (IRE) **The Dancing Shadows**
9 **DARLOA (IRE),** 6, br g Darsi (FR)—Lady Lola (IRE) **Mr S. W. Campbell**
10 **EXMOOR MIST,** 7, gr g Kayf Tara—Chita's Flora **Exmoor Mist Partnership**
11 **GOOD AUTHORITY (IRE),** 8, b g Chineur (FR)—Lady Alexander (IRE) **Mrs J. Scrivens**
12 **JEWELLERY (IRE),** 8, b br m King's Best (USA)—Eilean Shona **V. R. A. Dartnall**
13 **JEZZA,** 9, br g Pentire—Lara (GER) **Mrs J. Scrivens**
14 **KAYFAY ROYAL,** 5, b g Kayf Tara—Supreme Gem (IRE) **Mrs D. J. Fleming**
15 4, B g Stowaway—Kiniohio (FR) **Mrs C. M. Barber**
16 **MARY LE BOW,** 4, b f Sir Percy—Bermondsey Girl **Mrs J. Scrivens**
17 **MIDNIGHT SAPPHIRE,** 5, ch m Midnight Legend—Norton Sapphire **Mr R. Harding**
18 **MOTHER MELDRUM (IRE),** 6, b m Milan—Europet (IRE) **G. D. Hake**
19 **OUEST OCEAN (FR),** 4, b g Early March—Kalistina (FR)
20 **RICHARD'S SUNDANCE (IRE),** 13, b g Saddlers' Hall (IRE)—
Celestial Rose (IRE) **Mrs Lucy Barlow & Mrs Sara Vernon**
21 **RUGGED JACK (FR),** 8, b g Bonbon Rose (FR)—A Plus Ma Puce (FR) **V. R. A. Dartnall**
22 **SEEBRIGHT,** 8, b g Milan—Aranga (IRE) **Mrs D. J. Fleming**
23 **SHAMMICK BOY (IRE),** 10, b g Craigsteel—Dulcet Music (IRE) **First Brayford Partnership**
24 **SIDBURY FAIR,** 4, br f Fair Mix (IRE)—Manque Pas d'air (FR) **Mrs L. M. Northover**
25 **TOLKEINS TANGO (IRE),** 7, ch g Beneficial—Aule (FR) **Mrs S. M. Hall**
26 **TRESOR DE LA VIE (FR),** 8, gr g Epalo (GER)—Joie de La Vie (FR) **Edge Of Exmoor**
27 **UN BLEU A L'AAM (FR),** 7, b g Shaanmer (IRE)—Bleu Perle (FR) **F. R. Williamson**
28 **UNEFILLE DE GUYE (FR),** 7, b br m Voix du Nord (FR)—
Mascotte de Guye (FR) **The Second Brayford Partnership**
29 **UT MAJEUR AULMES (FR),** 7, ch g Northern Park (USA)—My Wish Aulmes (FR) **Mrs S. De Wilde**

**Other Owners:** Mrs L. Barlow, Mr Brian Dallyn, Mr V. R. A. Dartnall, Mrs Jean Dartnall, Mr G. A. Dartnall, Mr Jeffery Edelman, Mr I. F. Gosden, Mr N. P. Haley, Mrs Sonia M. Hall, Mr Colston Herbert, Mr G. Kennington, Mr Michael Nicholls, Mr M. W. Richards, Mrs T. M. Scott, Mr Lee Singleton, Mrs Sara Vernon, Mr R. Watts, Mr R. F. Willcocks, Mr David Willis, Mrs S. J. Wynne, Mr O. C. R. Wynne.

**Assistant Trainer:** G. A. Dartnall

**Jockey (NH):** Jack Doyle. **Conditional:** Giles Hawkins, Paul John. **Amateur:** Mr Matt Hampton.

---

## 139 MR TOM DASCOMBE, Malpas

Postal: **Manor House Stables, Malpas, Cheshire, SY14 8AD**
Contacts: **PHONE (01948) 820485 FAX (01948) 820495 MOBILE (07973) 511664**
**E-MAIL tom@manorhousestables.com WEBSITE www.manorhousestables.com**

1 **AL MUHEER (IRE),** 10, b g Diktat—Dominion Rose (USA) **T. G. Dascombe**
2 **BALLISTA (IRE),** 7, b g Majestic Missile (IRE)—Ancient Secret **Well Done Top Man Partnership**
3 **BARRACUDA BOY (IRE),** 5, b g Bahamian Bounty—Madame Boulangere **L. A. Bellman**
4 **BETTY THE THIEF (IRE),** 4, b f Teofilo (IRE)—Siphon Melody (USA) **Mr D. Ward**
5 **BROWN PANTHER,** 7, b br h Shirocco (GER)—Treble Heights (IRE) **Mr A. Black & Owen Promotions Limited**
6 **CAPO ROSSO (IRE),** 5, b g Red Clubs (IRE)—Satin Cape (IRE) **Deva Racing Red Clubs Partnership**
7 **CHOSEN CHARACTER (IRE),** 7, b g Choisir (AUS)—Out of Thanks (IRE) **Aykroyd & Sons Limited**
8 **CROWLEY'S LAW,** 4, b f Dubawi (IRE)—Logic **Paul Crowley & Co**
9 **DANA'S PRESENT,** 6, ch g Osorio (GER)—Euro Empire (USA) **Mr M. Wilson**
10 **DEAUVILLE PRINCE (FR),** 5, b g Holy Roman Emperor (IRE)—
Queen of Deauville (FR) **N & S Mather, C Ledigo, L Basran**
11 **DOUBLE DISCOUNT (IRE),** 5, b g Invincible Spirit (IRE)—Bryanstown Girl (IRE) **L. A. Bellman**
12 **ELOQUENCE,** 4, b f Oratorio (IRE)—Noble Plum (IRE) **South Wind Racing 3**
13 **GHOSTING (IRE),** 4, ro g Invincible Spirit (IRE)—Exclusive Approval (USA) **The United Rocks**
14 **JOLLY RED JEANZ (IRE),** 4, ch f Intense Focus (USA)—Sovienne (IRE) **MMIMM Racing**
15 **POLAR EYES,** 4, b f Dubawi (IRE)—Everlasting Love **The Illusionists**
16 **THATABOY (IRE),** 4, b g Green Desert (USA)—Hawas **David Lowe & Laurence Bellman**
17 **THE CHARACTER (IRE),** 4, b g Bushranger (IRE)—Operissimo **Aykroyd & Sons Limited**

### THREE-YEAR-OLDS

18 **ANGELIC LORD (IRE),** b c Dark Angel (IRE)—Divine Design (IRE) **The Mad March Hares**
19 **ARCHIE (IRE),** b c Fast Company (IRE)—Winnifred **Seamus Burns,Tom Flaherty,Sabina Kelly**
20 **BANGERS (IRE),** b g Alfred Nobel (IRE)—Sandbox Two (IRE) **The Big Easy Partnership**
21 **CAPTAIN REVELATION,** ch g Captain Rio—Agony Aunt **Cheshire Racing**

## MR TOM DASCOMBE - Continued

22 **CHAMPAGNE BOB,** gr g Big Bad Bob (IRE)—Exclusive Approval (USA) **Doak Garner Mather Owen**
23 **COCKER,** b g Shirocco (GER)—Treble Heights (IRE) **Owen Promotions Limited**
24 **CYMRO (IRE),** gr c Dark Angel (IRE)—Dictatrice (FR) **D. Passant & Hefin Williams**
25 **DAWN'S EARLY LIGHT (IRE),** gr g Starspangledbanner (AUS)—Sky Red **Empire State Racing Partnership**
26 **DIATOMIC (IRE),** b g Bushranger (IRE)—Gilded Truffle (IRE) **Mr J. D. Brown**
27 **ELLE DORADO,** ch f Paco Boy (IRE)—Clever Millie (USA) **Manor House Racing Club**
28 **EXCILLY,** br f Excellent Art—Afra Tsitsi (FR) **Bellman Lowe O'Halloran Trowbridge**
29 **JOSHUA POTMAN (IRE),** gr g Zebedee—Road To Reality (IRE) **The Mad March Hares**
30 **KOPTOON,** b g Rip Van Winkle (IRE)—Mania (IRE) **Lyn Rutherford, Mike O'Halloran & MHS**
31 **LONE STAR BOY (IRE),** b c Starspangledbanner (AUS)—Pascali **G. A. Mason**
32 **MARMALAD (IRE),** b g Duke of Marmalade (IRE)—Primissima (GER) **Caroline, Dave, Lol, Lyn & Nick**
33 **MARY'S SECRET,** b f Exceed And Excel (AUS)—Don't Tell Mary (IRE) **K. P. Trowbridge**
34 **NEUTRON BOMB (IRE),** ch f Lope de Vega (IRE)—Neutrina (IRE) **Manor House Racing Club**
35 **NEWERA,** ch c Makfi—Coming Home **Mr D. R. Passant**
36 **OPPORTUNA,** b f Rock Hard Ten (USA)—Veiled Beauty (USA) **Chasemore Farm LLP**
37 **PASSIONATE SPIRIT (IRE),** gr g Zebedee—El Morocco (USA) **The Passionate Partnership 2**
38 **REDHOTRAVEN,** ch f Raven's Pass (USA)—Blast Furnace (IRE) **Chasemore Farm LLP**
39 **ROUDEE,** b g Kodiac—Eau Rouge **Edwards Hughes Jenkins Roberts & Partner**
40 **SEVE,** ch g Exceed And Excel (AUS)—Flamenco Dancer **Mrs P. Good**
41 **SHAW TING,** b f Winker Watson—Shawhill **Chasemore Farm LLP**
42 **SNAP SHOTS (IRE),** b g Kodiac—Refuse To Give Up (IRE) **True Reds**
43 **WAR PAINT (IRE),** br f Excellent Art—Stairway To Glory (IRE) **Mr D. Ward**

## TWO-YEAR-OLDS

44 Ch c 5/3 Arcano (IRE)—Bond Deal (IRE) (Pivotal) (40000)
45 B f 1/2 Sea The Stars (IRE)—Bryanstown (IRE) (Galileo (IRE)) (70000)
46 **BULGE BRACKET,** b c 17/2 Great Journey (JPN)—Baldovina (Tale of The Cat (USA)) **Chasemore Farm LLP**
47 **CALDER PRINCE (IRE),** br c 22/5 Dark Angel (IRE)—
Flame of Ireland (IRE) (Fasliyev (USA)) (23809) **Calderprint Limited**
48 **CHESHAM ROSE (IRE),** gr f 24/4 Mastercraftsman (IRE)—
Rose's Destination (IRE) (Dubai Destination (USA)) (17460) **Chesham Rose Partnership**
49 B c 13/4 Iffraaj—Clever Day (USA) (Action This Day (USA)) (47619)
50 B c 5/3 Kyllachy—Dubai Bounty (Dubai Destination (USA)) (49523)
51 B c 15/4 Zoffany (IRE)—Enchantment (Compton Place) (17142) **Mrs Janet Lowe & Mr Tom Dascombe**
52 **FALCON ANNIE (IRE),** b f 16/3 Kodiac—Frosted (Dr Fong (USA)) (55555) **S Burns, M Smyth & D Studholme**
53 **FIRE DIAMOND,** b c 4/3 Firebreak—Diapason (IRE) (Mull of Kintyre (USA)) (2476) **Mr J. D. Brown**
54 **GAMBIT,** b c 22/1 New Approach (IRE)—Sospel (Kendor (FR)) (75000) **Laurence Bellman & Caroline Ingram**
55 **GAMESTERS BOY,** b c 4/4 Firebreak—Gamesters Lady (Almushtarak (IRE)) (2476) **Gamesters Partnership**
56 B f 14/3 Danehill Dancer (IRE)—Gilded Vanity (IRE) (Indian Ridge) (320000) **Chasemore Farm LLP**
57 B c 4/3 Bahamian Bounty—Goldamour (IRE) (Fasliyev (USA)) (51586) **L. A. Bellman**
58 B f 12/4 Exceed And Excel (AUS)—
Helena Molony (IRE) (Sadler's Wells (USA)) (83333) **Newsells Park Stud & Manor House Stables**
59 Ch c 27/4 Exceed And Excel (AUS)—Hill Welcome (Most Welcome) (80952)
60 **ICE DREAM (IRE),** b f 30/3 Frozen Power (IRE)—Mikes Baby (IRE) (Key of Luck (USA)) (22221) **Mr D. J. Lowe**
61 **IDEAL RECRUIT (IRE),** br c 16/3 Lord Shanakill (USA)—Gemma's Pearl (IRE) (Marju (IRE)) (17460) **Mr R. Jones**
62 B c 3/3 Captain Rio—Inourthoughts (IRE) (Desert Style (IRE)) (38095) **M Khan X2**
63 B f 1/3 Canford Cliffs (IRE)—Katy Nowaitee (Komaite (USA)) (50000) **Chasemore Farm LLP**
64 B c 3/4 Dandy Man (IRE)—La Bataille (USA) (Out of Place (USA)) (66666)
65 **LEMBIT AND BUTLER (IRE),** b c 7/4 Lilbourne Lad (IRE)—
Fathoming (USA) (Gulch (USA)) (55238) **The Amarone Partnership**
66 Ch f 19/2 Nayef (USA)—Lilac Moon (GER) (Dr Fong (USA)) **Chasemore Farm LLP & Owen Promotions Ltd**
67 **MONSIEUR GLORY,** ch c 15/4 Monsieur Bond (IRE)—Chushka (Pivotal) (38095) **Ms A A Yap & Mr F Ma**
68 B f 24/1 Fast Company (IRE)—Mrs Beeton (IRE) (Dansili) (10317)
69 B c 11/3 Bushranger (IRE)—Munaawashat (IRE) (Marju (IRE)) **J. A. Duffy**
70 **OUR ELTON (USA),** ch c 22/2 Speightstown (USA)—
Warsaw Ballet (CAN) (El Prado (IRE)) (63491) **D Studholme, M Smyth & S Burns**
71 **REFLEKTOR (IRE),** ch c 10/4 Bahamian Bounty—Baby Bunting (Wolfhound (USA)) (42857) **Mr D. J. Lowe**
72 B br c 25/2 Rock of Gibraltar (IRE)—Runaway Top (Rainbow Quest (USA)) (36190) **The Mad March Hares**
73 B c 11/4 Bushranger (IRE)—Satin Cape (IRE) (Cape Cross (IRE)) (17142) **Deva Racing Bushranger Partnership**
74 Ch c 20/3 Pivotal—Sharp Terms (Kris) (50000)
75 **SIMPLY ME,** b f 27/3 New Approach (IRE)—Ego (Green Desert (USA)) (90000) **L. A. Bellman**
76 **SPEY SECRET (IRE),** br c 18/3 Kyllachy—Chiarezza (AUS) (Fantastic Light (USA)) (71428)
77 **SPIRIT OF THE VALE (IRE),** b f 13/3 Royal Applause—
Nesmeh (USA) (More Than Ready (USA)) (25000) **Mr.D.B.Salmon,Mrs.L.Salmon&Mr.M.W.Salmon**

## MR TOM DASCOMBE - Continued

**78 SWANSWAY,** ch c 16/3 Showcasing—
Spring Stroll (USA) (Skywalker (USA)) (43650) **M Smyth S Burns D Studholme & T Flaherty**
**79** B c 4/2 Fast Company (IRE)—Temecula (IRE) (High Chaparral (IRE)) (55000)
**80** B f 28/3 Holy Roman Emperor (IRE)—Timeless Dream (Oasis Dream)
**81** B f 10/2 Zamindar (USA)—Veiled Beauty (USA) (Royal Academy (USA)) **Chasemore Farm LLP**
**82** B f 26/2 Rip Van Winkle (IRE)—Work Shy (Striking Ambition) **Chasemore Farm LLP & Owen Promotions Ltd**

**Other Owners:** Mr D. Athorn, N. B. Attenborough, A. M. Basing, Mr L. S. Basran MBE, A. W. Black, Mrs J. E. Black, Mr S. Burns, Mrs M. Coxon, B. Dascombe, Mr J. Doak, Mr M. Edwards, Sir A. Ferguson, Mr T. M. Flaherty, Mr I. R. Flanagan, M. D. Foster, Mrs J. Foster, Mrs J. Fuller, Mr N. R. Garner, Mr S. J. High, Mr M. O. Hough, Mr R. M. Hough, Mr N. J. Hughes, Mrs C. L. Ingram, Mr D. W. Jenkins, Mr T. D. Jones, Mrs S. Kelly, M. Khan, M. Khan, Mrs A. A. Lau Yap, Mr C. Ledigo, Mr C. Lindley, Mrs J. Lowe, Mr C. U. F. Ma, Mr N. P. Mather, Mrs S. E. Mather, Mr E. R. Mills, Mr S. N. Mound, Mrs A. C. Mound, Mr P. Naviede, Newsells Park Stud Limited, A. F. O'Callaghan, Mr M. O'Halloran, Mr M. Owen, Mrs B. M. Richmond, Mr A. Richmond, S. E. Roberts, L. M. Rutherford, Mr D. B. Salmon, Mr M. W. Salmon, Mrs Lynn Salmon, Mr G. Shepherd, Mr M. Smyth, Mr D. Studholme, Mr M. K. Williams, Mr H. Williams, Mr D. V. Williams.

**Assistant Trainer:** Colin Gorman

**Jockey (flat):** Richard Kingscote.

---

## 140 MR TRISTAN DAVIDSON, Carlisle

Postal: **Bellmount, Laversdale, Irthington, Carlisle, Cumbria, CA6 4PS**
Contacts: **MOBILE (07789) 684290**

**1 GREY AREA (IRE),** 10, gr g Portrait Gallery (IRE)—Queen's Run (IRE) **G. E. Davidson**
**2 LEANNA BAN,** 8, b g Alflora (IRE)—Gurleigh (IRE) **G. E. Davidson**
**3 NAILER (IRE),** 5, b g Coroner (IRE)—Celtic Serenade (IRE) **G. E. Davidson**
**4 ORCHARD ROAD (USA),** 8, b g Street Cry (IRE)—Aunt Mottz (USA) **G. E. Davidson**
**5 WILLIAM RUSSELL,** 7, b g With Approval (CAN)—Another Nightmare (IRE) **G. E. Davidson**

---

## 141 MR JOHN DAVIES, Darlington

Postal: **Denton Grange, Piercebridge, Darlington, Co. Durham, DL2 3TZ**
Contacts: **PHONE (01325) 374366 MOBILE (07746) 292782**
**E-MAIL johndavieshorses@live.co.uk WEBSITE www.johndaviesracing.com**

**1 IM DAPPER TOO,** 4, b g Dapper—Lonely One **Mr C. W. Davies**
**2 MILLKWOOD,** 5, b g Millkom—Wedgewood Star **Pipeline Precision Engineering Limited**
**3 QUEENS PARK (FR),** 4, b f King's Best (USA)—Anna Deesse (FR) **Mr & Mrs R. Scott**
**4 THE OSTEOPATH (IRE),** 12, ch g Danehill Dancer (IRE)—Miss Margate (IRE) **K. Kirkup**

### THREE-YEAR-OLDS

**5** B f Dapper—Bedtime Blues **Mr C. W. Davies**

### TWO-YEAR-OLDS

**6** Ch f 17/3 Zoffany (IRE)—Apple Brandy (USA) (Cox's Ridge (USA)) (9000) **J. J. Davies**
**7** B c 30/4 Sleeping Indian—Crimson Topaz (Hernando (FR)) **Mr P. Taylor**
**8** B g 10/3 Cacique (IRE)—Ommadawn (IRE) (Montjeu (IRE)) **Mr & Mrs R. Scott**
**9** B f 18/5 Ferrule (IRE)—Wedgewood Star (Bishop of Cashel) **K. Kirkup**

**Other Owners:** R. Scott, Mrs P. M. Scott.

**Jockey (flat):** P. J. McDonald.

---

## 142 MR PAUL DAVIES, Bromyard

Postal: **20 Hatton Park, Bromyard, Herefordshire, HR7 4EY**

**1 EMMA SODA,** 10, b m Milan—Ms Trude (IRE) **Mr P. S. Davies**
**2 MI MAN SAM (IRE),** 10, ch g Exit To Nowhere (USA)—Brinawa (IRE) **Mr P. S. Davies**

## 143 MISS SARAH-JAYNE DAVIES, Leominster

Postal: **The Upper Withers, Hundred Lane, Kimbolton, Leominster, Herefordshire, HR6 0HZ**
Contacts: **PHONE (01584) 711780 MOBILE (07779) 797079**
**E-MAIL sjdracing@live.co.uk**

1 **ACCESSALLAREAS (IRE),** 10, ch g Swift Gulliver (IRE)—Arushofgold (IRE) **Withers Winners**
2 **ANOTHER JOURNEY,** 6, b g Rail Link—Singasongosixpence **Miss S. J. Davies**
3 **CAPISCI (IRE),** 10, br g Tikkanen (USA)—Dolce Notte (IRE) **K. E. Stait**
4 **CHESTER ROSE,** 7, b m Grape Tree Road—Across The Water **G. H. Jones**
5 **DREAM'S PARK,** 5, b m Fictional—Monty's Dream VII **Mrs P. Vaughan**
6 **FOUR SHUCK MEN (IRE),** 7, b g Spartacus (IRE)—Shed **Good Evans Racing Partnership**
7 **HERR LARRY HEWIS,** 7, b g Sir Harry Lewis (USA)—Avenches (GER) **Mr R. A. Skidmore**
8 **KANDARI (FR),** 11, b g Kahyasi—Nee Brune (FR) **Mr A. J. Gough**
9 **MAGIC PRESENT,** 8, b g Presenting—Magic Bloom **Quadriga Racing**
10 **MAHAYOGIN (USA),** 7, b br g Dixie Union (USA)—Shiva (JPN) **Miss S. J. Davies**
11 **MISS DIMPLES (IRE),** 6, gr m Tikkanen (USA)—Scolboa House (IRE) **Pippin Bank Partnership**
12 **PASSING FIESTA,** 6, b m Passing Glance—Clarice Starling **Mr A. J. Gough**
13 **PEMBROKE HOUSE,** 8, gr g Terimon—Bon Coeur **Mr A. Mortimer**
14 **SPESSARTINE (IRE),** 5, b g Duke of Marmalade (IRE)—Lasting Chance (USA) **Miss S. J. Davies**
15 **SUPARI,** 6, b g Beat All (USA)—Susie Bury **Good Evans Racing Partnership**
16 **TWIN BARRELS,** 8, ch g Double Trigger (IRE)—Caballe (USA) **K. E. Stait**

**Other Owners:** Mr M. Evans, Mr J. H. M. Mahot, Mr K. J. Price, Mr D. Richardson, Mr J. F. Vincent.

**Assistant Trainer:** Jeremy Mahot

**Jockey (NH):** Will Kennedy, Liam Treadwell. **Amateur:** Miss Sarah-Jayne Davies, Mr Jeremy Mahot.

## 144 MISS JOANNA DAVIS, East Garston

Postal: **Parson Close Stables, School Lane, East Garston, Hungerford, Berkshire, RG17 7HR**
Contacts: **PHONE (01488) 649977 FAX (01488) 649977 MOBILE (07879) 811535**
**E-MAIL davisjo_007@hotmail.com WEBSITE www.jodavisracing.com**

1 **BOLD ARIAL,** 4, b f Authorized (IRE)—No Frills (IRE) **Dr P. J. Brown**
2 4, B f Rainbow High—Bright Spangle (IRE) **Jo Davis**
3 **CAPTAIN FLASH (IRE),** 6, br g Indian River (FR)—Westgate Run **Mr R. K. Allsop**
4 **DARK MUSIC,** 4, br f Misu Bond (IRE)—Tender Moments **Mrs P. M. Brown**
5 **DOCTOR OF MUSIC (IRE),** 9, ch g Dr Fong (USA)—Sublime Beauty (USA) **Mrs P. M. Brown**
6 **GALLIC DESTINY (IRE),** 4, b g Champs Elysees—Cross Your Fingers (USA) **Dr P. J. Brown**
7 **GRACIOUS LADY,** 4, b f Royal Applause—Succinct **Dr P. J. Brown**
8 **HEROES OR GHOSTS (IRE),** 6, br g Indian River (FR)—Awomansdream (IRE) **Tony Worth & Vic Bedley**
9 **INDIEFRONT,** 6, b m Indesatchel (IRE)—Jonchee (FR) **Mr R. K. Allsop**
10 **JOHN BISCUIT (IRE),** 7, ch g Hawk Wing (USA)—Princess Magdalena **Dr P. J. Brown**
11 **MR FITZROY (IRE),** 5, ch g Kyllachy—Reputable **Dr P. J. Brown**
12 **PASSATO (GER),** 11, br g Lando (GER)—Passata (FR) **Mr R. K. Allsop**
13 **POCKET WARRIOR,** 4, b g Tobougg (IRE)—Navene (IRE) **Mrs B. M. Cuthbert**
14 **PRAIRIE RANGER,** 5, b g Montjeu (IRE)—No Frills (IRE) **Dr P. J. Brown**
15 **ROSE OF THE WORLD (IRE),** 7, ch m Vinnie Roe (IRE)—Frankly Native (IRE) **Oakhedge Racing**
16 **WILLY BRENNAN (IRE),** 4, br g Bushranger (IRE)—Miss Assertive **Dr P. J. Brown**

### THREE-YEAR-OLDS

17 **RAHALLA,** br f New Approach (IRE)—No Frills (IRE) **Dr P. J. Brown**

**Other Owners:** Mr V. R. Bedley, Mr A. D. Hutchinson, Mrs J. P. Hutchinson, Mr Tony Worth.

**Jockey (NH):** Sam Jones.

## 145 MISS LOUISE DAVIS, Levedale

Postal: **The Stables, Hillcrest, Bradley Lane, Levedale, Stafford, ST18 9AH**
Contacts: **MOBILE (07426) 316685**
**E-MAIL vky1971@yahoo.co.uk WEBSITE www.louisedavisracing.co.uk**

1 **ESTOURAH (IRE),** 7, b g Dalakhani (IRE)—Canouan (IRE) **Miss L. V. Davis**
2 **HAMBLE,** 6, b g Librettist (USA)—Time For Tea (IRE) **Miss L. V. Davis**

## MISS LOUISE DAVIS - Continued

3 **MOUNT WELCOME (IRE),** 11, b g Bach (IRE)—Be My Vixen (IRE) **Miss L. V. Davis**
4 **NEVER PERFECT (IRE),** 6, b g Galileo (IRE)—Dapprima (GER) **Miss L. V. Davis**
5 **SAMAWI (IRE),** 5, b g Street Cry (IRE)—Hi Dubai **Miss L. V. Davis**
6 **SECOND BROOK (IRE),** 8, b g Celtic Swing—Mur Taasha (USA) **Miss L. V. Davis**

**Assistant Trainer:** Mr J. Freeman

---

## 146 MISS ZOE DAVISON, East Grinstead

Postal: **Shovelstrode Racing Stables, Shovelstrode Lane, Ashurstwood, East Grinstead, West Sussex, RH19 3PN**
Contacts: **FAX (01342) 323153 MOBILE (07970) 839357 & (07812) 007554**
**E-MAIL andy01031976@yahoo.co.uk WEBSITE www.shovelstroderacing.co.uk**

1 **AIREDALE LAD (IRE),** 14, b g Charnwood Forest (IRE)—Tamarsiya (USA) **Mrs S. E. Colville**
2 **ASKER (IRE),** 7, b g High Chaparral (IRE)—Pay The Bank **The Secret Circle**
3 **ATMANNA,** 6, br m Manduro (GER)—Samdaniya **A. J. Irvine**
4 **BOLD MAX,** 4, b g Assertive—Jane's Payoff (IRE) **Mr K. C. Bennett**
5 **BYRON'S GOLD,** 4, ch f Byron—Dance To The Blues (IRE) **Sussex Racing**
6 **CLOUDBUSTING,** 7, b m Midnight Legend—Minibelle **Miss A. Marshall**
7 **DERRYOGUE (IRE),** 10, b g Tikkanen (USA)—Snugville Sally **Sussex Racing**
8 **FRANK N FAIR,** 7, br m Trade Fair—Frankfurt (GER) **The Secret Circle**
9 **GEORGE NYMPTON (IRE),** 9, br g Alderbrook—Countess Camilla **Sussex Racing**
10 **GEORGIESHORE (IRE),** 7, b g Turtle Island (IRE)—Pride of St Gallen (IRE) **Sussex Racing**
11 **JOHN'S GEM,** 10, ch g Silver Patriarch (IRE)—Hollow Legs **Golfguard Limited**
12 **JUMEIRAH LIBERTY,** 7, ch g Proclamation (IRE)—Gleam of Light (IRE) **The Secret Circle**
13 **LINDSAY'S DREAM,** 9, b m Montjeu (IRE)—Lady Lindsay (IRE) **Mr S. P. O'Loughlin**
14 **MUT'AB (USA),** 10, b g Alhaarth (IRE)—Mistle Song **Miss A. Marshall**
15 **MYORAN OSCAR (IRE),** 7, b g Oscar (IRE)—Miss Bertaine (IRE) **Sussex Racing**
16 **NOIR GIRL,** 6, b m Beat All (USA)—Forever Shineing **Sussex Racing**
17 **NOZIC (FR),** 14, b g Port Lyautey (FR)—Grizilh (FR) **The Lump O'Clock Syndicate**
18 **PARADISE SPECTRE,** 8, b g Firebreak—Amber's Bluff **Sussex Racing**
19 **ROGER BEANTOWN (IRE),** 10, b g Indian Danehill (IRE)—Best Wait (IRE) **The Sophisticated Seven**
20 **SPARKLING ICE (IRE),** 4, gr f Verglas (IRE)—Sand Crystal (IRE) **Mr K. Corke**
21 **STANDING STRONG (IRE),** 7, b g Green Desert (USA)—Alexander Three D (IRE) **The Secret Circle**
22 **THELORDBEWITHYOU (IRE),** 11, b g Turtle Island (IRE)—Georgic **The Secret Circle**

**Other Owners:** S. J. Clare, Miss Z. C. Davison, Mr S. J. Moll, Mr W. Smith, A. N. Waters.

**Assistant Trainer:** A. Irvine

**Jockey (flat):** Sam Hitchcott. **Conditional:** Gemma Gracey-Davison.

---

## 147 MR ANTHONY DAY, Hinckley

Postal: **Wolvey Fields Farm, Coalpit Lane, Wolvey, Hinckley, Leicestershire, LE10 3HD**
Contacts: **PHONE (01455) 220225 MOBILE (07928) 835330**
**E-MAIL kathy197@btinternet.com**

1 **CHARMING LAD (IRE),** 10, b g Dushyantor (USA)—Glens Lady (IRE) **Mrs K. D. Day**
2 **COOL FUSION,** 6, b m Beat All (USA)—Fusion of Tunes **Mrs K. D. Day**
3 **POLLY LIGHTFOOT,** 6, b m Dalby Walks—Polly Live Wire **Mrs K. D. Day**
4 **SHESLIKETHEWIND,** 7, b m Central Park (IRE)—Velvet Leaf **Mrs K. D. Day**
5 **SOUND THE BUGLE,** 5, b g Overbury (IRE)—Fusion of Tunes **Mrs K. D. Day**

**Assistant Trainer:** Mrs K. D. Day (07546) 593485

**Amateur:** Mr Jon Day, Mr M. J. P. Kendrick.

---

## 148 MISS LISA DAY, Pontypool

Postal: **Well Cottage, Penyhroel, Pontypool, Gwent**

1 **FORCE TO SPEND,** 8, b m Reset (AUS)—Mon Petit Diamant **Miss L. Day**

## 149 MR WILLIAM DE BEST-TURNER, Calne

Postal: **8 North End, Calne, Wiltshire, SN11 9DQ**
Contacts: **PHONE (01249) 811944 HOME (01249) 813850 FAX (01249) 811955 MOBILE (07977) 910779**
**E-MAIL debestracing@hotmail.co.uk**

1 **CHICAGO SOCKS,** 5, b h Catcher In The Rye (IRE)—Sachiko **W. de Best-Turner**
2 **FOOLSANDORSES (IRE),** 7, b g Beneficial—All Honey (IRE) **De Best Racing**
3 **NELSON'S HILL,** 5, b g Mount Nelson—Regal Step **De Best Racing**

### THREE-YEAR-OLDS

4 **BOSTON RED,** ch g Schiaparelli (GER)—Maylan (IRE) **W. de Best-Turner**
5 **LORD YATESBURY,** b c Bertolini (USA)—Sachiko **W. de Best-Turner**

**Other Owners:** Miss S J Slade, Mr W. de Best-Turner.

**Assistant Trainer:** Mrs I. De Best

## 150 MR ED DE GILES, Ledbury

Postal: **Lilly Hall Farm, Little Marcle, Ledbury, Herefordshire, HR8 2LD**
Contacts: **PHONE (01531) 637369 MOBILE (07811) 388345**
**E-MAIL ed@eddegilesracing.com WEBSITE www.eddegilesracing.com**

1 **BAZOOKA (IRE),** 4, b g Camacho—Janadam (IRE) **T. Gould**
2 **CROQUEMBOUCHE (IRE),** 6, b g Acclamation—Wedding Cake (IRE) **Mr P. J. Manser**
3 **GO NANI GO,** 9, b g Kyllachy—Go Between **Mrs B. Smith**
4 **KINGSGATE CHOICE (IRE),** 8, b g Choisir (AUS)—Kenema (IRE) **Tight Lines Partnership**
5 **KOPENHAGEN (IRE),** 4, ch c Captain Rio—Quizzical Lady **Mrs B. Smith**
6 **MUHDIQ (USA),** 6, b g Hard Spun (USA)—Enfiraaj (USA) **T. Gould**
7 **NAPOLEONIC (USA),** 4, b g War Front (USA)—High Savannah
8 **PRINCE OF DREAMS,** 8, b g Sadler's Wells (USA)—Questina (FR) **Jennifer & Alex Viall**
9 **QUANTUM DOT (IRE),** 4, ch g Exceed And Excel (AUS)—Jeed (IRE) **Mrs Y. Fleet**
10 **QUINTA FEIRA (IRE),** 4, gr g Medicean—Bunditten (IRE) **Mr S. Treacher**
11 **SHINGLE,** 4, b g Oasis Dream—Orford Ness **T. Gould**
12 **SMIDGEN (IRE),** 4, b g Bahamian Bounty—Brazilian Style **Boardman, Golder, Sercombe & Viall**
13 **TIJUCA (IRE),** 6, b m Captain Rio—Some Forest (IRE) **Mrs B. Smith**
14 **TWENTY ONE CHOICE (IRE),** 6, ch g Choisir (AUS)—Midnight Lace **Penna Racing**
15 **ZUGZWANG (IRE),** 4, b g Kodiac—Kris's Bank **Mr S. Treacher**

### THREE-YEAR-OLDS

16 **AKAVIT (IRE),** b g Vale of York (IRE)—Along Came Molly **Mr S. Treacher**
17 Bl f Halling (USA)—Candle **E. B. de Giles**
18 **CAUGHT ON THE BID (IRE),** b c Footstepsinthesand—Peps (IRE) **2 1/2 - 3 1/2 Club**
19 B f Dylan Thomas (IRE)—Cloudchaser (IRE) **Mr P. R. Jarvis**
20 **PRENDERGAST HILL (IRE),** b c Raven's Pass (USA)—Daraliya (IRE) **Gwyn & Samantha Powell**
21 **WIND IN MY SAILS,** b c Footstepsinthesand—Dylanesque **Mr P. J. Manser**

### TWO-YEAR-OLDS

**22** B c 30/4 Kodiac—Awwal Malika (USA) (Kingmambo (USA)) (55000)
**23** B f 7/2 Holy Roman Emperor (IRE)—Be Amazing (IRE) (Refuse To Bend (IRE)) (52000)
**24** B c 28/4 Kodiac—Cabopino (IRE) (Captain Rio) (23809) **E. B. de Giles**
**25** B c 28/4 Lilbourne Lad (IRE)—Charaig (Rainbow Quest (USA)) (17460) **E. B. de Giles**
**26** B c 30/4 Bertolini (USA)—Cloudchaser (IRE) (Red Ransom (USA)) **E. B. de Giles**
**27** B c 2/3 Bahamian Bounty—Desert Location (Dubai Destination (USA)) (15238) **Clarke, King & Lewis**
**28** B c 8/4 Iffraaj—Engraving (Sadler's Wells (USA)) (70000)
**29** Ch c 28/3 Approve (IRE)—Felin Gruvy (IRE) (Tagula (IRE)) (19840) **Mrs C. R. Casdagli**
**30** B f 7/4 Shamardal (USA)—Gower Song (Singspiel (IRE)) (80000)
**31** B c 17/4 Kodiac—Mark One (Mark of Esteem (IRE)) (62000)
**32** **PETRONAS,** ch c 2/4 Pastoral Pursuits—Gilt Linked (Compton Place) (41904) **G. E. Powell**
**33** B c 12/5 Kodiac—Princess Atoosa (USA) (Gone West (USA)) (50000)
**34** B c 21/1 Mastercraftsman (IRE)—Wosaita (Generous (IRE)) (50000)
**35** **ZLATAN (IRE),** b c 18/4 Dark Angel (IRE)—Guard Hill (USA) (Rahy (USA)) (47619) **G. E. Powell**

## MR ED DE GILES - Continued

**Other Owners:** Mr R. J. Boardman, Mr D. Clarke, Mr M. J. Gibbons, Mr J. C. Golder, C. J. King, Mrs E. V. Lewis, Mr A. Mortazavi, Mr M. C. Penna, Mrs S. Powell, Mr P. R. Sercombe, Mrs S. Smith, A. J. Viall.

---

## 151 MR BEN DE HAAN, Lambourn

Postal: **Fair View, Long Hedge, Lambourn, Newbury, Berkshire, RG17 8NA**
Contacts: **PHONE (01488) 72163 FAX (01488) 71306 MOBILE (07831) 104574**
**E-MAIL bendehaanracing@aol.com WEBSITE www.bendehaanracing.com**

1 **DECIDING MOMENT (IRE),** 9, b g Zagreb (USA)—Fontaine Jewel (IRE) **W. A. Tyrer**
2 **NATIVE GALLERY (IRE),** 10, gr g Portrait Gallery (IRE)—Native Bev (IRE) **W. A. Tyrer**
3 **OCULIST,** 7, b g Dr Fong (USA)—Eyes Wide Open **Mrs C. Walwyn**

**Jockey (flat):** Adam Kirby. **Jockey (NH):** Noel Fehily, Daryl Jacob.

---

## 152 MR GEOFFREY DEACON, Compton

Postal: **Hamilton Stables, Hockham Road, Compton, Newbury, Berkshire, RG20 6QJ**
Contacts: **MOBILE (07967) 626757**
**E-MAIL geoffdeacon@aol.com WEBSITE www.geoffreydeacontraining.com**

1 **BANKS ROAD (IRE),** 10, b g Beneficial—Cecelia's Charm (IRE) **Mr C. W. Duckett**
2 4, B c Tiger Hill (IRE)—Circadian Rhythm **J. W. Haydon**
3 **DEWBERRY,** 4, br f Lucarno (USA)—Elderberry **Woodhall, Nicol, Gorringe-Smith & Co**
4 **ERIC,** 7, b g Delta Dancer—Bonita Bee **P. D. Cundell**
5 **ESEEJ (USA),** 10, ch g Aljabr (USA)—Jinaan (USA) **Miss S. J. Duckett**
6 **GLASTONBERRY,** 7, gr m Piccolo—Elderberry **Mr G. Deacon**
7 **IZZY PICCOLINA (IRE),** 7, b m Morozov (USA)—Chloara (IRE) **C. O. King**
8 **KOVOLINI,** 5, ch m Bertolini (USA)—Petrikov (IRE) **J. A. Dewhurst**
9 6, B g Overbury (IRE)—Maiden Aunt (IRE)
10 **MCDELTA,** 5, b g Delta Dancer—McNairobi **Jim Mellon & Partners**
11 **MOON TRIP,** 6, b g Cape Cross (IRE)—Fading Light **The Moon Trip Partnership**
12 **PICC OF BURGAU,** 5, b m Piccolo—Rosein **The Outta Lunch Partnership**
13 **PROPER VILLAN (IRE),** 10, b br g Naheez (USA)—Nativa Negra (IRE) **Business Moves Group Ltd**
14 **SPRINGHILL LAD,** 8, b g Kayf Tara—Anouska **J. Davies**
15 **WANNABE MAGIC,** 4, b f Authorized (IRE)—Wannabe Free **J. W. Haydon**
16 **YAIR HILL (IRE),** 7, b g Selkirk (USA)—Conspiracy **Mr G. Deacon**

### THREE-YEAR-OLDS

17 **LETTUCE SNOW (IRE),** b f Clodovil (IRE)—Lola Rosa (IRE) **The Stanford Dingleys**
18 **PICKET LINE,** b c Multiplex—Dockside Strike **Homegrown Partnership**

### TWO-YEAR-OLDS

19 B c 20/2 Tagula (IRE)—Copper Harbour (IRE) (Foxhound (USA)) (5158) **Mr G. Deacon**
20 Ch c 17/3 Monsieur Bond (IRE)—Minnina (IRE) (In The Wings) (17142) **J. A. Dewhurst**

**Other Owners:** Mr S. A. Cawkwell, Mrs S. M. Gorringe-Smith, Mr D. Greaney, Mr F. Hearty, R. Kent, Mr R. Lim, Mr J. Mellon, Mrs A. Nicol, Mr A. R. Pittman, D. M. Woodhall, Mrs H. C. L. Woodhall.

**Assistant Trainer:** Sally Duckett

---

## 153 MR DAVID DENNIS, Hanley Swan

Postal: **Tyre Hill Racing Stables, Hanley Swan, Worcester, Worcestershire, WR8 0EQ**
Contacts: **PHONE (01684) 565310 MOBILE 07867 974880**
**E-MAIL david@daviddennistrainer.co.uk WEBSITE www.ddracing.co.uk**

1 **A KEEN SENSE (GER),** 6, b g Sholokhov (IRE)—All Our Luck (GER) **Superdream Creative Limited**
2 **ANGINOLA (IRE),** 6, b m Kodiac—Lady Montekin **Help With Numbers**
3 **ANGUS GLENS,** 5, gr g Dalakhani (IRE)—Clara Bow (IRE) **Corbett Stud**
4 **ASK A BANK (IRE),** 5, b g Presenting—Highness Lady (GER) **Superdream Creative Limited**
5 **BALLYBOUGH PAT (IRE),** 8, b g Waky Nao—Princess Ruth (IRE) **Favourites Racing Ltd**
6 **CYCLOP (IRE),** 4, b g King's Theatre (IRE)—Tasmani (FR) **DD Racing & Professor L P Hardwick**

## MR DAVID DENNIS - Continued

7 **DOCTOR PHOENIX (IRE),** 7, br g Dr Massini (IRE)—Lowroad Cross (IRE) **Corbett Stud**
8 **FINAL NUDGE (IRE),** 6, b g Kayf Tara—Another Shot (IRE) **Corbett Stud**
9 **FOOTSTEPSINTHERAIN (IRE),** 5, b g Footstepsinthesand—Champagne Toni (IRE) **Favourites Racing Ltd**
10 **HAWDYERWHEESHT,** 7, b g Librettist (USA)—Rapsgate (IRE) **Favourites Racing Ltd**
11 **INDY FIVE (IRE),** 5, b g Vertical Speed (FR)—Beesplease (IRE)
12 **KEY TO THE WEST (IRE),** 8, b g Westerner—Monte Solaro (IRE) **Favourites Racing Ltd**
13 **KING'S SONG (FR),** 5, b g King's Theatre (IRE)—Chanson Indienne (FR) **Corbett Stud**
14 **LUCKY JIM,** 4, b g Lucky Story (USA)—Lateralle (IRE) **DD Racing & Professor L P Hardwick**
15 **MALLER TREE,** 8, b g Karinga Bay—Annaberg (IRE) **Favourites Racing Ltd**
16 **MARJU'S QUEST (IRE),** 5, b g Marju (IRE)—Queen's Quest **Favourites Racing Ltd**
17 **NORSE LIGHT,** 4, ch g Norse Dancer (IRE)—Dimelight **Corbett Stud**
18 **ROMAN FLIGHT (IRE),** 7, b g Antonius Pius (USA)—Flight Sequence **Favourites Racing Ltd**
19 **SET THE TREND,** 9, br g Reset (AUS)—Masrora (USA) **Corbett Stud**
20 **SILENT ALLIANCE (IRE),** 6, b g Desert King (IRE)—Lady de Loi (FR) **Favourites Racing Ltd**
21 **STEEL SUMMIT (IRE),** 6, b g Craigsteel—B Greenhill **Rose Farm Developments(UK) Ltd & Partner**
22 **THE ALAMO (IRE),** 4, b g High Chaparral (IRE)—Inner Strength (FR) **Favourites Racing Ltd**
23 **THE BIG DIPPER,** 6, b g Alflora (IRE)—Pougatcheva (FR) **The Lucky Seven**
24 **TYRE HILL (IRE),** 6, b g Catcher In The Rye (IRE)—Stay At Home (IRE) **DD Racing & Professor L P Hardwick**
25 **UN ANJOU (FR),** 7, b br g Panoramic—Idee d'estruval (FR) **Superdream Creative Limited**

### THREE-YEAR-OLDS

26 **DYLAN'S STORM (IRE),** b g Zebedee—Storm Lady (IRE) **Corbett Stud**
27 **MY MO (FR),** b g Silver Frost (IRE)—Anna Ivanovna (FR) **Corbett Stud**
28 **RETRO VALLEY (IRE),** b g Vale of York (IRE)—Retrato (USA) **Corbett Stud**
29 **VALE PARK,** b g Vale of York (IRE)—Sparkle Park **Corbett Stud**

**Other Owners:** Mr M. J. S. Cockburn, Mr J. M. Dyer, Prof L. P. Hardwick, C. D. Massey, Mrs J. Rees, Rose Farm Developments (UK) Ltd, Mr N. J. Witts-Hewinson.

---

## 154 MR ROBIN DICKIN, Alcester

Postal: **Hill Farm, Park Lane, Great Alne, Alcester, Warwickshire, B49 6HS**
Contacts: **PHONE (01789) 488148 (01789) 488249 MOBILE (07979) 518593 / (07979) 518594**
**E-MAIL robin@robindickinracing.org.uk WEBSITE www.robindickinracing.org.uk**

1 **ANTI COOL (IRE),** 6, b g Heron Island (IRE)—Youngborogal (IRE) **EPDS Racing Partnership 10**
2 **BADGERS COVE (IRE),** 11, b g Witness Box (USA)—Celestial Rose (IRE) **E. R. C. Beech & B. Wilkinson**
3 **BALLY LAGAN (IRE),** 7, gr g Kalanisi (IRE)—Rose Palma (FR) **Park Lane Partnership**
4 **BE MY WITNESS (IRE),** 6, b m Witness Box (USA)—Smokey Firth (IRE) **Mrs A. L. Merry & Mrs C. M. Dickin**
5 **CAPT LEN,** 11, ch g Executive Perk—Scallykit VII **P. W. Taylor**
6 **DAN'S QUEST,** 5, b g Kalanisi (IRE)—Piedmont (UAE) **Mr M. J. James**
7 **DANCE FOR LIVVY (IRE),** 7, br m Kodiac—Dancing Steps **Mr M. J. James**
8 **DONTMINDDBOYS (IRE),** 6, gr g Portrait Gallery (IRE)—Native Ocean (IRE) **EPDS Racing Partnership 7**
9 **GALACTIC POWER (IRE),** 5, ch g Gamut (IRE)—Celtic Peace (IRE) **EPDS Racing Partnership 10**
10 **GARRAHALISH (IRE),** 7, b g Presenting—Savu Sea (IRE) **Just 4 Fun**
11 **JACKFIELD,** 5, b g Norse Dancer (IRE)—Small Amount **Mrs C. M. Dickin**
12 **KAWA (FR),** 9, gr g Kouroun (FR)—Kulitch (FR) **Mrs C. M. Dickin, David Doolittle, Mark Burgess**
13 **KAYF TIGER,** 6, b g Kayf Tara—La Marette **The Jameson Partnership**
14 **KITEGEN (IRE),** 9, b g Milan—Keen Gale (IRE) **R. G. Whitehead**
15 **LETSFACETHEMUSIC,** 7, b g Witness Box (USA)—A Fine Romance (IRE)
16 **MERTESACKER (GER),** 6, b g Lord of England (GER)—Monalind (GER) **Nic Allen**
17 **MYROUNDORURS (IRE),** 5, b g Arakan (USA)—Six Bob (IRE) **John Nicholls Trading Ltd**
18 **PRESENTING PADDY (IRE),** 7, b g Presenting—Bula Beag (IRE) **The Bonnie Tyler Partnership**
19 **RESTLESS HARRY,** 11, b g Sir Harry Lewis (USA)—Restless Native (IRE) **R. G. Whitehead**
20 **ROUTINE PROCEDURE (IRE),** 5, b g Arcadio (GER)—Wayward Bride (IRE) **The More Of Us The Merrier**
21 **SPICY LADY,** 8, b m Fair Mix (IRE)—Icy Gunner **A. P. Rogers**
22 **SPURNED GIRL,** 5, b m Passing Glance—Highlight Girl **Mr Terry Hitchman**
23 **THE DE THAIX (FR),** 8, b g Polish Summer—Etoile de Thaix (FR) **J. Priday**
24 **THE LION MAN (IRE),** 5, b g Let The Lion Roar—Just Smart (IRE) **C. M. Dickin**
25 **THOMAS CRAPPER,** 8, b g Tamure (IRE)—Mollycarrs Gambul **Apis.uk.com**
26 **TIMON'S TARA,** 6, br m Kayf Tara—Princess Timon **Mr M. J. James**
27 **TROYAN (IRE),** 8, b g King's Theatre (IRE)—Talk The Talk **John Priday**
28 **UNDER THE PHONE (IRE),** 6, b g Heron Island (IRE)—Theo On The Bench (IRE) **The Tricksters**
29 **WILDMOOR BOY,** 4, b g Midnight Legend—Simple Glory (IRE) **E. R. C. Beech & B. Wilkinson**

## MR ROBIN DICKIN - Continued

30 **WINDY MILLER,** 4, ch g Sakhee's Secret—Oatcake **N. J. Allen**
31 **YOUNG LOU,** 6, b m Kadastrof (FR)—Wanna Shout **E. R. C. Beech & B. Wilkinson**

### THREE-YEAR-OLDS

32 **BLACK COUNTRY BOY,** b g Black Sam Bellamy (IRE)—Simple Glory (IRE) **E. R. C. Beech & B. Wilkinson**
33 **STORMING HARRY,** ch g Assertive—Miss Pebbles (IRE) **Mr N. K. Thick**

### TWO-YEAR-OLDS

34 B c 13/6 Black Sam Bellamy (IRE)—Simple Glory (IRE) (Simply Great (FR)) **E. R. C. Beech & B. Wilkinson**

**Other Owners:** Mr E. R. Clifford Beech, Mr Hugh Brown, Mr R. J. Burdett, Mr Brett Cahill, Mr R. A. Cockrell, Mrs M. A. Cooper, Mrs C. M. Dickin, Mr C. J. Dickin, Mr D. Hern, Mrs V. Jameson, Miss N. A. Jameson, Mr S. Kirby, Mr Michael Palmowski, Mr John Porter, Mr John Powell, Miss T. Sloan, Mrs Julia Venvell, Mr B. Wilkinson.

**Assistant Trainer:** Claire Dickin

**Jockey (flat):** Luke Morris. **Jockey (NH):** Charlie Poste. **Conditional:** Joseph Palmowski. **Amateur:** Miss Paige Jeffrey, Mr Toby Wheeler.

---

## 155 MR JOHN DIXON, Carlisle

Postal: **Moorend, Thursby, Carlisle, Cumbria, CA5 6QP**
Contacts: **PHONE (01228) 711019**

1 **CIRCUS STAR (USA),** 7, b g Borrego (USA)—Picadilly Circus (USA) **Mrs S. F. Dixon**
2 **CROFTON LANE,** 9, b g And Beyond (IRE)—Joyful Imp **Mrs S. F. Dixon**
3 **LITTLE JOYFUL,** 7, b m And Beyond (IRE)—Joyful Imp **Mrs E. M. Dixon**
4 **PISTOL (IRE),** 6, b g High Chaparral (IRE)—Alinea (USA) **Mrs S. F. Dixon**

**Amateur:** Mr J. J. Dixon.

---

## 156 MR SCOTT DIXON, Retford

Postal: **Haygarth House Stud, Haygarth House, Babworth, Retford, Nottinghamshire, DN22 8ES**
Contacts: **PHONE (01777) 869300 (01777) 869079/701818 FAX (01777) 869326**
**MOBILE (07976) 267019**
**E-MAIL scottdixon1987@hotmail.com / mrsyvettedixon@gmail.com**
**WEBSITE www.scottdixonracing.com**

1 **ABI SCARLET (IRE),** 6, b m Baltic King—Petarga **Ontoawinner 4 & Homecroft Wealth Racing**
2 **ARMELLE (FR),** 4, b f Milk It Mick—Park Ave Princess (IRE) **The Friday Follies**
3 **ASKAUD (IRE),** 7, b m Iffraaj—Tarabaya (IRE) **The Doncaster Racing Club**
4 **BEST TAMAYUZ,** 4, ch g Tamayuz—Pink Ivory **P. J. Dixon**
5 **BISCUITEER,** 4, ch f Byron—Ginger Cookie **P J Dixon & Partners**
6 **BURNHOPE,** 6, b g Choisir (AUS)—Isengard (USA) **P J Dixon & Partners**
7 **CADEAUX PEARL,** 7, b g Acclamation—Anneliina **P J Dixon & Partners**
8 **COISTE BODHAR (IRE),** 4, b g Camacho—Nortolixa (FR) **Miss Y. Lowe**
9 **DR RED EYE,** 7, ch g Dr Fong (USA)—Camp Fire (IRE) **The Red Eye Partnership**
10 **EVEN STEVENS,** 7, br g Ishiguru (USA)—Promised (IRE) **P. J. Dixon**
11 **FELICE (IRE),** 5, b m Papal Bull—Tarabaya (IRE) **Gen. Sir G Howlett Paul Nolan & Partners**
12 **INCOMPARABLE,** 10, ch g Compton Place—Indian Silk (IRE) **P J Dixon & Partners**
13 **LA PAIVA (FR),** 4, b f Milk It Mick—Cora Pearl (IRE) **The Achievers**
14 **LE LAITIER (FR),** 4, b g Milk It Mick—La Brigitte **Ms Yvonne Lowe, P J Dixon & Partners**
15 **MASKED DANCE (IRE),** 8, gr g Captain Rio—Brooks Masquerade **P J Dixon & Partners**
16 **MINISTER OF FUN,** 4, b g Pastoral Pursuits—Diane's Choice **P J Dixon & Partners**
17 **MORE MORE MORE,** 5, b g Milk It Mick—Snowmore **P J Dixon & Partners**
18 **PASTUREYES,** 5, ch m Milk It Mick—Veils of Salome **Paul J Dixon & Mrs Jayne Jackson**
19 **PEARL NOIR,** 5, b g Milk It Mick—Cora Pearl (IRE) **P J Dixon & Partners**
20 **PENNINE WARRIOR,** 4, b g Lucky Story (USA)—Discoed **Lease Terminated**
21 **PICENO (IRE),** 7, b g Camacho—Ascoli **Ontoawinner 4**
22 **SIR GEOFFREY (IRE),** 9, b g Captain Rio—Disarm (IRE) **General Sir G. H. W. Howlett**
23 **SIX WIVES,** 8, b m Kingsalsa (USA)—Regina **Sexy Six Partnership**
24 **SPOWARTICUS,** 6, ch g Shamardal (USA)—Helen Bradley (IRE) **P. J. Dixon**
25 **THREES GRAND,** 5, b m Milk It Mick—Ginger Cookie **Paul J Dixon & Mrs Jayne Jackson**
26 **WIMBOLDSLEY,** 4, ch g Milk It Mick—Chrystal Venture (IRE) **Paul J Dixon & The Chrystal Maze Ptn**

## MR SCOTT DIXON - Continued

### THREE-YEAR-OLDS

27 **CLOAK AND DEGAS (IRE),** b g Sakhee's Secret—Coup de Torchon (FR) **Homecroft Wealth Racing**
28 **COCK OF THE NORTH,** ch c Cockney Rebel (IRE)—Camp Fire (IRE) **Cope Dixon Kennerly**
29 **CROSSE FIRE,** b g Monsieur Bond (IRE)—Watersilk (IRE) **Chappell, Cope, Dixon**
30 **DUTCH DIVA,** b f Dutch Art—Hiddendale (IRE) **Mrs S. M. Roy**
31 **HAPPY DEAL (IRE),** b g Tagula (IRE)—Jeu Set Et Match (IRE) **Mr D Sharp and Partners**
32 **HIGH INTENSITY,** b c Sir Percy—Woodbeck **Andrea & Graham Wylie & Partner**
33 **HUGIE BOY (IRE),** ch c Art Connoisseur (IRE)—Piece Unique **Mr J. Radford**
34 **PEARLISE (FR),** b f Milk It Mick—Cora Pearl (IRE) **P. J. Dixon**
35 **PENNY DREADFUL,** b f Piccolo—Trina's Pet **Mr D Sharp and Partners**
36 **THUNDERBIRD,** b f Sakhee (USA)—Trustthunder **P. J. Dixon**

### TWO-YEAR-OLDS

37 **ALBERT BOY (IRE),** ch c 9/3 Falco (USA)—Trumbaka (IRE) (In The Wings) (20000) **Mr J. Radford**
38 **ALMOST SPANISH (IRE),** b f 6/2 Rock of Gibraltar (IRE)—
Spanish Quest (Rainbow Quest (USA)) (7000) **D. Boocock**
39 B c 24/4 Hellvelyn—Little Greenbird (Ardkinglass) (3809) **P. J. Dixon**
40 **RUPERT BOY (IRE),** ch c 20/4 Frozen Power (IRE)—
Curious Lashes (IRE) (Footstepsinthesand) (26000) **Mr J. Radford**

**Other Owners:** Mr A. D. Baker, Mr C. Bell, Mr S. E. Chappell, Mr A. I. Cope, Mrs Y. Dixon, Mrs J. Jackson, Mr R. Jackson, J. S. Kennerley, Mr D. R. Lucas, Mr P. Nolan, N. J. O'Brien, S. J. Piper, Mr N. Pogmore, Mr D. Sharp, Mr A. C. Timms, A. W. G. Wylie, Mrs A. Wylie.

**Assistant Trainer:** Mr K. Locking (07835 360125)

**Apprentice:** Matthew Hopkins. **Amateur:** Mr Kevin Locking.

---

## 157 MR STEVEN DIXON, Winterslow

Postal: **Apple Tree Barn, Livery Road, Winterslow, Nr Salisbury, Wiltshire, SP5 1RJ**
Contacts: **PHONE (01980) 862930 MOBILE (07771) 963011**
**E-MAIL sarahjdixon@hotmail.co.uk**

1 **RAGTIME LADY,** 7, b m General Gambul—Pink Lady **Mr S. D. Dixon**
2 **SUN QUEST,** 11, b g Groom Dancer (USA)—Icaressa **Mr S. D. Dixon**
3 **WARSAW PACT (IRE),** 12, b g Polish Precedent (USA)—Always Friendly **Mr S. D. Dixon**

**Assistant Trainer:** Mrs Sarah Dixon

**Jockey (NH):** Jamie Moore. **Amateur:** Mr Luke Kilgarriff, Mr James King.

---

## 158 MRS ROSE DOBBIN, Alnwick

Postal: **South Hazelrigg Farm, Chatton, Alnwick, Northumberland, NE66 5RZ**
Contacts: **PHONE (01668) 215395 (office) (01668) 215151 (house) FAX (01668) 215114 MOBILE (07969) 993563**
**E-MAIL hazelriggracing1@btconnect.com WEBSITE www.rosedobbinracing.co.uk**

1 **ANOTHER DIMENSION (IRE),** 9, b g Overbury (IRE)—Freshwater (IRE) **The Friday Lions**
2 **ATTENTION PLEASE (IRE),** 5, b g Kalanisi (IRE)—Dangerous Dolly (IRE) **Mr R. A. Jacobs**
3 **BENNYLICIOUS (IRE),** 6, b g Beneficial—Railstown Lady (IRE) **Mr & Mrs D Davidson & Miss J Matterson**
4 **BLYTH HARBOUR (IRE),** 6, gr g Turgeon (USA)—Snuff (FR) **D&D Armstrong Limited**
5 **CAERLAVEROCK (IRE),** 10, br g Statue of Liberty (USA)—Daziyra (IRE) **M S Borders Racing Club**
6 **CLASSIC STATEMENT,** 7, ch g Rashar (USA)—Bank On Inland **D&D Armstrong Limited**
7 **DOKTOR GLAZ (FR),** 5, b g Mount Nelson—Deviolina (IRE) **Mr & Mrs Duncan Davidson**
8 4, Ch f Beneficial—Drama Chick **Mr & Mrs D Davidson & Miss J Matterson**
9 **EVERYLASTING (IRE),** 8, b g Millenary—All French (IRE) **Miss C. L. Jones**
10 **FINAL FLING (IRE),** 4, b g Milan—Supreme Singer (IRE) **Unregistered Partnership**
11 **FLAWLESS FILLY (IRE),** 5, gr m Clodovil (IRE)—Min Asl Wafi (IRE) **Mr & Mrs Duncan Davidson**
12 **GOLANS CHOICE (IRE),** 6, b g Golan (IRE)—Sea Voyager (IRE) **Mr & Mrs Duncan Davidson**
13 **HONOURABLE GENT,** 7, b g Gentleman's Deal (IRE)—Gudasmum **Mr & Mrs Duncan Davidson**
14 **JURISDICTION,** 11, b g Goldmark (USA)—Juris Prudence (IRE) **Keswick, Jacobs & Dobbin**
15 **MARRAKECH TRADER (NZ),** 8, ch g Pentire—Eastern Bazzaar (IRE) **Mr T. P. Jenks**
16 **MONFASS (IRE),** 4, b g Trans Island—Ajo Green (IRE) **Mrs Dobbin & The Dimhorns**

**MRS ROSE DOBBIN - Continued**

17 **ON THE BUCKLE,** 7, b g Overbury (IRE)—Arctic Revel
18 **PEGASUS WALK (IRE),** 6, b g Beneficial—Porter Tastes Nice (IRE) **Mr A. G. Dobbin**
19 **POLITENESS (FR),** 6, b g Poliglote—Martiniquaise (FR) **Mr & Mrs Duncan Davidson**
20 **POTOMAC (IRE),** 7, b g Shamardal (USA)—Pippas Song **MS Borders Racing & Mr & Mrs Davidson**
21 **PROFESSOR PLUM (IRE),** 5, b g Kalanisi (IRE)—Miss Plum **Mr & Mrs Duncan Davidson**
22 **PROUD GAMBLE (IRE),** 6, b g Brian Boru—Sister Anna **Major-Gen C. A. Ramsay**
23 **PURCELL'S BRIDGE (FR),** 8, b g Trempolino (USA)—Theatrical Lady (USA) **Mr J. A. F. Filmer-Wilson**
24 **PYJAMA GAME (IRE),** 9, b g Hernando (FR)—Princess Claudia (IRE) **Mrs R. Dobbin**
25 **ROBIN'S COMMAND (IRE),** 8, gr g Tikkanen (USA)—Marian's Wish (IRE) **M Hunter, J Matterson & R Jacobs**
26 **SHADY SADIE (IRE),** 8, b m Dushyantor (USA)—Beltane Queen (IRE) **Mrs M. C. Coltman**
27 **SNOOKER (GER),** 9, ch g Acambaro (GER)—Sheraton (IRE) **Mrs R. Dobbin**
28 **SPITZ (FR),** 7, b g Enrique—Spezzia (FR) **Mr R. A. Jacobs**
29 **TRELIVER MANOR (IRE),** 7, b g Flemensfirth (USA)—Loch Lomond (IRE) **Mr & Mrs Duncan Davidson**
30 **TWEEDO PARADISO (NZ),** 8, br g Golan (IRE)—Buzz (NZ) **Mr J. L. Dickson**
31 **VINNY GAMBINI (IRE),** 8, b g Vinnie Roe (IRE)—Red Velvet **Mr & Mrs Duncan Davidson**
32 **WHERE'S MALACHY (IRE),** 7, ch g Muhtarram (USA)—County Classic **Mr & Mrs D. Davidson & Mr R. Jacobs**
33 4, B g Yeats (IRE)—Zalama (FR)

**Other Owners:** D. H. Davidson, Mrs S. K. Davidson, Mr L. Dimsdale, Mrs R. L. Elliot, Miss R. K. Hill, M. S. Hunter, J. R. Jeffreys, Sir Chippendale Keswick, Miss J. G. K. Matterson, Mr D. A. C. Spencer-Churchill.

**Assistant Trainer:** Tony Dobbin (07775) 680894

**Jockey (NH):** Wilson Renwick. **Conditional:** Shaun Dobbin. **Amateur:** Miss Holly Harper.

---

## 159 MR ASHLEY DODGSON, Thirsk

Postal: **Southerby House, Catton, Thirsk, North Yorkshire, YO7 4SQ**

1 **DICKY SHORE,** 7, b g Iktibas—Catton Lady **Mrs F. M. G. Dodgson**

---

## 160 MR MICHAEL DODS, Darlington

Postal: **Denton Hall Farm, Piercebridge, Darlington, Co. Durham, DL2 3TY**
Contacts: **PHONE (01325) 374270 FAX (01325) 374020**
**MOBILE (07860) 411590/ (07773) 290830 C Dods**
**E-MAIL dods@michaeldodsracing.co.uk WEBSITE www.michaeldodsracing.co.uk**

1 **BARNEY MCGREW (IRE),** 12, b g Mark of Esteem (IRE)—Success Story **N. A. Riddell**
2 **CARA'S REQUEST (AUS),** 10, gr g Urgent Request (IRE)—Carahill (AUS) **Denton Hall Racing Ltd**
3 **DESERT ACE (IRE),** 4, ch g Kheleyf (USA)—Champion Place **Mr & Mrs Paul Gaffney**
4 **ELTHEEB,** 8, gr g Red Ransom (USA)—Snowdrops **Mr & Mrs G. Turnbull**
5 **FINN CLASS (IRE),** 4, b g Exceed And Excel (AUS)—Finnmark **Pearson & Unique Sports Racing**
6 **GOWANHARRY (IRE),** 6, ch m Choisir (AUS)—Aahgowangowan (IRE) **L. Waugh**
7 **HALF A BILLION (IRE),** 6, b g Acclamation—Amankila (IRE) **I.Galletley, B.Stenson, S.Lowthian**
8 **KIWI BAY,** 10, b g Mujahid (USA)—Bay of Plenty (FR) **Kiwi Racing**
9 **KOMMANDER KIRKUP,** 4, ch g Assertive—Bikini **K. Kirkup**
10 **LE CHAT D'OR,** 7, b g One Cool Cat (USA)—Oh So Well (IRE) **Dr A. J. F. Gillespie**
11 **LOLA,** 5, b m Rob Roy (USA)—Seamill (IRE) **J. A. and M. A. Knox**
12 **MASH POTATO (IRE),** 5, b g Whipper (USA)—Salva **Bennett Potatoes & Banister**
13 **MASS RALLY (IRE),** 8, b g Kheleyf (USA)—Reunion (IRE) **Business Development Consultants Limited**
14 **MECCA'S ANGEL (IRE),** 4, gr f Dark Angel (IRE)—Folga **D. T. J. Metcalfe**
15 **MY NAME IS RIO (IRE),** 5, ch g Captain Rio—Walk In My Shadow (IRE) **Mr K Kirkup & Mrs T Galletley**
16 **ONE BOY (IRE),** 4, ch g Captain Gerrard (IRE)—Paris Song (IRE) **Sekura Trade Frames Ltd**
17 **ORBIT THE MOON (IRE),** 7, b g Oratorio (IRE)—Catch The Moon (IRE) **P Appleton and V Spinks**
18 **OSTEOPATHIC REMEDY (IRE),** 11, ch g Inchinor—Dolce Vita (IRE) **K. Kirkup**
19 **ROCKTHERUNWAY (IRE),** 6, ch g Nayef (USA)—Femme Fatale **Sedgewick,Dods,Sunley Racing Partnership**
20 **SLEEPING APACHE (IRE),** 5, ch g Sleeping Indian—Remedy **Mr & Mrs G. Turnbull**
21 **SPINATRIX,** 7, b m Diktat—Shrink **Mrs J. W. Hutchinson & Mrs P. A. Knox**
22 **TRINITY STAR (IRE),** 4, gr g Kheleyf (USA)—Zamiyla (IRE) **Trinity Racing**

## MR MICHAEL DODS - Continued

### THREE-YEAR-OLDS

23 **ALANS PRIDE (IRE),** ch g Footstepsinthesand—True Crystal (IRE) **Alan Henderson & Alan Bolton**
24 **APROVADO (IRE),** b g Approve (IRE)—Aldburgh **Hanson, McKiver, Percival**
25 **BLACKFOOT BRAVE (IRE),** ch g Iffraaj—Beatrix Potter (IRE) **D. R. Graham**
26 **BORROCO,** ch g Dutch Art—Straitjacket **Julie & Keith Hanson**
27 **BUCCANEERS VAULT (IRE),** gr g Aussie Rules (USA)—Heaven's Vault (IRE) **D. Neale**
28 **CADEAUX,** b g Major Cadeaux—Bikini **K. Kirkup**
29 **COLLOSIUM (IRE),** ch g Showcasing—Ragsta (IRE) **Business Development Consultants Limited**
30 **DENTON CARNIVAL (IRE),** ch g Captain Rio—Be My Lover **Denton Hall Racing Ltd**
31 **DENTON DAWN (IRE),** b f Fast Company (IRE)—Rectify (IRE) **Denton Hall Racing Ltd**
32 **DRAGON KING (IRE),** ch g Dylan Thomas (IRE)—Alexander Queen (IRE) **Cosy Seal Racing Limited**
33 **GET KNOTTED (IRE),** ch g Windsor Knot (IRE)—Genuinely (IRE) **D. Neale**
34 **HERNANDOSHIDEAWAY,** b c Hernando (FR)—Alba Stella **Mr D C Batey & Mr Foster Watson**
35 **LORD OF THE ROCK (IRE),** b c Rock of Gibraltar (IRE)—La Sylphide **Mr & Mrs G. Turnbull**
36 **NO NOT YET,** b f Notnowcato—True Vision (IRE) **T. K. Knox**
37 **OCEAN SHERIDAN (IRE),** b g Starspangledbanner (AUS)—Endless Night (GER) **Mr J Blackburn & Mr A Turton**
38 **POMME DE TERRE (IRE),** ch g Sakhee's Secret—Suzie Quw **Dunham Trading Ltd**
39 **PUNK ROCKER (IRE),** b f Fastnet Rock (AUS)—Cape Vintage (IRE) **Cosy Seal Racing Limited**
40 **SEA WOLF (IRE),** b g Amadeus Wolf—Rose de France (IRE) **Cosy Seal Racing Limited**
41 **SEKURAS GIRL (IRE),** b f Approve (IRE)—Alinda (IRE) **Sekura Trade Frames Ltd**
42 **STAR CRACKER (IRE),** ch g Starspangledbanner (AUS)—Champagne Cracker **Mr J. J. McLaren**
43 **TONTO'S SPIRIT,** b g Authorized (IRE)—Desert Royalty (IRE) **Mr M. J. Sedgewick**

### TWO-YEAR-OLDS

**44** **AMBRIEL (IRE),** gr f 7/3 Dark Angel (IRE)—Skehana (IRE) (Mukaddamah (USA)) (32000) **Mr W. A. Tinkler**
**45** Ch c 16/2 Thousand Words—Anazah (USA) (Diesis) (16666) **Sekura Trade Frames Ltd**
**46** Ch c 20/3 Captain Rio—Anklesocks (IRE) (Night Shift (USA)) (21428) **K. Kirkup**
**47** **BALTIC RAIDER (IRE),** b g 10/4 Baltic King—Frippet (IRE) (Ela-Mana-Mou) (21428) **Pearson & Lowthian**
**48** Ch c 15/3 Mount Nelson—Brave Mave (Daylami (IRE)) (20000) **M. J. K. Dods**
**49** B c 5/5 Lawman (FR)—Brazilian Bride (IRE) (Pivotal) (15872)
**50** B c 16/2 Jeremy (USA)—Coill Cri (IRE) (Shinko Forest (IRE)) (20634) **J A Wynn-Williams & D Neale**
**51** **CROFT RANGER (IRE),** b g 24/4 Bushranger (IRE)—
Alexander Duchess (IRE) (Desert Prince (IRE)) (7142) **Mr Ron Davison & Mr Hugh Linsley**
**52** **DARK COMMAND,** b g 25/2 Kheleyf (USA)—Desert Liaison (Dansili) (9000) **R. Davison**
**53** **DIAL A LOG,** b g 25/3 Mullionmileanhour (IRE)—Angelic Kitten (IRE) (One Cool Cat (USA)) **Mr J. Hamilton**
**54** B f 19/3 Holy Roman Emperor (IRE)—Fountain of Honour (IRE) (Sadler's Wells (USA)) (6348)
**55** B c 11/4 Excellent Art—Maybe Grace (IRE) (Hawk Wing (USA)) (30952) **The Better Together Partnership**
**56** **MEISTER (IRE),** b c 11/4 Mastercraftsman (IRE)—Dash Back (USA) (Sahm (USA)) (83333) **Mr W. A. Tinkler**
**57** Br g 2/4 Kheleyf (USA)—Naddwah (Pivotal) (10317) **M. J. K. Dods**
**58** Gr c 20/4 Mastercraftsman (IRE)—Paraphernalia (IRE) (Dalakhani (IRE)) (39681) **Cosy Seal Racing Limited**
**59** Ch c 12/2 Excellent Art—Party Feet (IRE) (Noverre (USA)) (13491) **Mr P. Appleton**
**60** Gr c 30/4 Clodovil (IRE)—Rahila (IRE) (Kalanisi (IRE)) (16000) **Mr A Wynn Williams & Mr D Graham**
**61** **REGAL RESPONSE (IRE),** b c 2/2 Acclamation—Qalahari (IRE) (Bahri (USA)) (83333) **Mr W. A. Tinkler**
**62** **RICHTER SCALE (IRE),** gr f 19/3 Lilbourne Lad (IRE)—
Danamight (IRE) (Danetime (IRE)) (39681) **Cosy Seal Racing Limited**
**63** **RISE UP SINGING,** b f 24/1 Showcasing—Sambarina (IRE) (Victory Note (USA)) (9523) **Mr J. Hamilton**
**64** B c 14/3 Majestic Missile (IRE)—Ron's Secret (Efisio) (18253) **M. J. K. Dods**
**65** B f 19/2 Lilbourne Lad (IRE)—Silk Dress (IRE) (Gulch (USA)) (10476) **D. T. J. Metcalfe**
**66** B c 16/2 Henrythenavigator (USA)—
Sunshine For Life (USA) (Giant's Causeway (USA)) (51586) **Cosy Seal Racing Limited**
**67** **WAYSIDE MAGIC,** b c 4/5 Thewayyouare (USA)—Poppy's Rose (Diktat) (9523) **Mrs C. M. Hewitson**

**Other Owners:** Mr C. Banister, D. C. Batey, Mr I. Bennett, Bennett Potatoes Ltd, J. N. Blackburn, Mr A. Bolton, Mr J. Cockcroft, Mr S. Cockcroft, Mr W. Cockcroft, Mr R. Cockcroft, Mrs C. E. Dods, Mr P. Gaffney, Mrs J. Gaffney, Mr I. Galletley, Mrs J. M. T. Galletley, Mr K. Hanson, Mrs J. Hanson, A. J. Henderson, Mrs J. W. Hutchinson, M. Hutchinson, Mrs M. A. Knox, Mr J. A. Knox, Mrs P. A. Knox, Mr H. M. Linsley, S. R. Lowthian, M. L. Mogg, Mr M. D. Pearson, N. Ridgway, Mr W. J. Salthouse, V. J. Spinks, J. W. Stenson, Mr G. C. Thompson, Mr G. Turnbull, Mrs S. E. Turnbull, Mr A. Turton, F. Watson, D. Watts, J. A. Wynn-Williams.

**Assistant Trainers:** C Dods, Steve Alderson (07533) 401887

**Jockey (flat):** Connor Beasley, Paul Mulrennan. **Apprentice:** Philip Dennis.

## 161 MR DESMOND DONOVAN, Newmarket

Postal: **The Beeches, London Road, Newmarket, Suffolk, CB8 0TR**
Contacts: **PHONE (01638) 578494 FAX (01638) 578494 MOBILE (07761) 841285**
**E-MAIL hareparkbloodstock@yahoo.co.uk WEBSITE www.desdonovan.co.uk**

1 **CHAMPAGNE CHARLEY,** 4, b f Myboycharlie (IRE)—Crossed Wire **River Racing (2)**
2 **ECLIPTIC SUNRISE,** 4, b f Compton Place—Winter Moon **Ms C. R. Sharp**
3 **GIANT SEQUOIA (USA),** 11, ch g Giant's Causeway (USA)—Beware of The Cat (USA) **River Racing**
4 **INDUS VALLEY (IRE),** 8, ch g Indian Ridge—Gloriously Bright (USA) **W. P. Flynn**
5 **IRONDALE EXPRESS,** 4, b f Myboycharlie (IRE)—Olindera (GER) **W. P. Flynn**
6 **MENELIK (IRE),** 6, b g Oasis Dream—Chica Roca (USA) **River Racing**
7 **STATE TROOPER (IRE),** 4, b g Lawman (FR)—Anthyllis (IRE) **W. P. Flynn**
8 **STEUBEN (GER),** 9, ch g Monsun (GER)—Schwarzach (GER) **Mr B. J. Lewis**
9 **TEVEZ,** 10, b g Sakhee (USA)—Sosumi **River Racing**

### THREE-YEAR-OLDS

10 Ch f Three Valleys (USA)—Crossed Wire **C. E. Giblett**
11 B g Sakhee (USA)—Olindera (GER) **W. P. Flynn**
12 **WEARDIDITALLGORONG,** b f Fast Company (IRE)—Little Oz (IRE) **The Wednesday Club**

**Other Owners:** Mr J. D. Donovan, Mr B. Drogman, P. P. Mclaughlin, Mr L. R. Pearce.

## 162 MR CONOR DORE, Frampton Fen

Postal: **Barford Farm, Swineshead Road, Frampton Fen, Boston, Lincolnshire, PE20 1SG**
Contacts: **PHONE (01775) 822747 MOBILE (07984) 609170**
**E-MAIL dores@supanet.com**

1 **A LITTLE BIT DUSTY,** 7, ch g Needwood Blade—Dusty Dazzler (IRE) **Mr David Baldwin & Mr Chris Marsh**
2 **AMENABLE (IRE),** 8, b g Bertolini (USA)—Graceful Air (IRE) **Mrs J. R. Marsh**
3 **ARCTIC LYNX (IRE),** 8, b g One Cool Cat (USA)—Baldemara (FR) **Mrs J. R. Marsh**
4 **CLOCKMAKER (IRE),** 9, b g Danetime (IRE)—Lady Ingabelle (IRE) **CHP Consulting Limited**
5 **DESERT STRIKE,** 9, b g Bertolini (USA)—Mary Jane **A. N. Page**
6 **GUD DAY (IRE),** 7, gr g Aussie Rules (USA)—Queen Al Andalous (IRE) **Mr C. R. Dore**
7 **HIGH OFFICE,** 9, b g High Chaparral (IRE)—White House **Boston Park Racing Club**
8 **JOHNNYS LEGACY (IRE),** 8, b g Ecton Park (USA)—Lexy May (USA) **Mr D. N. Baldwin**
9 **KUANYAO (IRE),** 9, b g American Post—Nullarbor **Mr M. Fitzsimons**
10 **RUN FAT LASS RUN,** 5, b m Sakhee (USA)—Feolin **Boston Park Racing Club**
11 **YASIR (USA),** 7, b g Dynaformer (USA)—Khazayin (USA) **Mrs L. J. Marsh**

### THREE-YEAR-OLDS

12 **EXCELLING OSCAR (IRE),** b g Excellent Art—Three Pennies **Mrs J. R. Marsh**

**Other Owners:** C. D. Marsh.

## 163 MR FRANCOIS DOUMEN, Bouce

Postal: **Le Gue, 61570 Bouce, France**
Contacts: **PHONE (0033) 2 33 67 11 59 FAX (0033) 2 33 67 82 37 MOBILE (0033) 6 07 42 33 58**
**E-MAIL doumenecouves@orange.fr WEBSITE www.francoisdoumenracing.com**

1 **BAMBOUZLE (FR),** 4, b f Forestier (FR)—Quibble (FR)
2 **CABARETUNE (FR),** 10, b g Green Tune (USA)—Cabaret Club (FR)
3 **DAUPHINE DOREE,** 4, b f Archange d'or (IRE)—Dauphine (SAF)
4 **GOLDIE JOLIE (FR),** 6, b m Gold Away (IRE)—Jolie Jim (FR)
5 **JOLIE NOCE (FR),** 7, b m Muhtathir—Jolie Jim (FR)
6 **NANIA (FR),** 4, b f Namid—Gigana (FR)
7 **PHIL MAN (IRE),** 6, b g Manduro (GER)—Fureau (GER)
8 **PRETZELLE (FR),** 4, b f Zamindar (USA)—Pretty As Can Be
9 **VAMOSALAPLAYA (FR),** 4, ch g Footstepsinthesand—Marital Bliss (FR)
10 **XPO UNIVERSEL (FR),** 6, b g Poliglote—Xanadu Bliss (FR)

## MR FRANCOIS DOUMEN - Continued

### THREE-YEAR-OLDS

11 **ARMADALE CASTLE,** b c Bahamian Bounty—Sign of Life
12 **BLISS IN THE CITY (FR),** b g Elusive City (USA)—Marital Bliss (FR)
13 **BRASS BELL (IRE),** gr g Footstepsinthesand—Cheyrac (FR)
14 **CAPITAL FLIGHT (FR),** ch f Motivator—Dauphine (SAF)
15 **DROIT D'AUTEUR (FR),** b c Authorized (IRE)—Margot Mine (IRE)
16 **ECHO MAKER (FR),** b c Siyouni (FR)—Heaven's Help (USA)
17 **JEWEL OF THE NILE (FR),** b f Authorized (IRE)—Diamond Dance (FR)
18 **KINGDOM COM (FR),** b f King's Best (USA)—Topka (FR)
19 **LINDIKHAYA (IRE),** b f Zamindar (USA)—Lidakiya (IRE)
20 **MAKWETI,** b f Makfi—Hometown
21 **PLUME D'OUTARDE,** b f Equiano (FR)—Azlaa
22 **REALLY TONIC (FR),** b f Country Reel (USA)—Hertzienne (FR)
23 **SILVER BULLET (FR),** gr f Silver Frost (IRE)—Folle Dingue (FR)
24 **SLEEKFONTEINE (FR),** b f Slickly (FR)—Turfontein (FR)
25 **SWING STATE (FR),** b g Siyouni (FR)—Fast Lane Lili
26 **THREE CARDS,** gr f Mastercraftsman (IRE)—Be My Lady (GER)
27 **XHALE (FR),** b g Halling (USA)—Xanadu Bliss (FR)

### TWO-YEAR-OLDS

28 **ACERBO (GER),** b c 10/4 Peintre Celebre (USA)—Acerba (GER) (Monsun (GER)) (23809)
29 **AIM TO PLEASE (FR),** b f 25/1 Excellent Art—Midnight Flash (IRE) (Anabaa Blue)
30 Ch c 8/4 Manduro (GER)—Anacapri (FR) (Anabaa (USA)) (28571)
31 **BIEN NOMMEE (FR),** b f 15/3 Whipper (USA)—Another Name (USA) (Giant's Causeway (USA))
32 **CONTE FLEURETTE (FR),** b f 30/3 Slickly—Pretty As Can Be (Giant's Causeway)
33 B f 14/3 Makfi—Eternal Beauty (USA) (Zafonic (USA))
34 **HIGH TOWER (FR),** b f 2/2 Dark Angel (IRE)—Heavenly Music (IRE) (Oratorio (IRE)) (75396)
35 **I'LL BE BACK (FR),** b f 30/1 Footstepsinthesand—Nude (Peintre Celebre)
36 **KOOK (FR),** ch g 23/4 Kheleyf—Folle Dingue (Golan)
37 **ROIDOR (FR),** b c 20/4 Creachadoir—Dauphine (SAF) (Rich Man's Gold)
38 B f 26/2 Rip Van Winkle (IRE)—Sea Sex Sun (Desert Prince (IRE)) (35714)
39 **VICTORY GARDEN,** b f 7/5 Monsieur Bond (IRE)—Madam President (Royal Applause) (40000)

**Owners:** Mr Dermot Cantillon, G R Baileys Ltd, Genesis Green Stud, Gold and Blue Ltd, Haras D'Ecouves, Marquise de Moratalla, Conte Henri de Pracomtal, Mr Eric Puerari, Mr Anthony Smurfit, Mr Michael Somerset-Leeke, Mrs Doreen Swinburn, Mr Joerg Vasicek, Mr Hans Peter Vogt.

**Jockey (flat):** Cristian Demuro.

---

## 164 MR SIMON DOW, Epsom

Postal: **Clear Height Stables (New Yard), Derby Stables Road, Epsom, Surrey, KT18 5LB**
Contacts: **PHONE (01372) 721490 FAX (01372) 748099 MOBILE (07860) 800109**
**E-MAIL simon@simondow.co.uk Office: mary@simondow.co.uk WEBSITE www.simondow.co.uk**
**Twitter: @SimonDowRacing**

1 **BROCKLEBANK (IRE),** 6, b g Diamond Green (FR)—La Stellina (IRE) **C. G. J. Chua**
2 **CLEAR PRAISE (USA),** 8, b g Songandaprayer (USA)—Pretty Clear (USA) **S. L. Dow**
3 **CROSSHARE,** 4, b g Crosspeace (IRE)—Perecapa (IRE) **Miss P. Stutchbury**
4 **DAWN ROCK,** 5, b m Rock of Gibraltar (IRE)—Ommadawn (IRE) **Malcolm & Alicia Aldis**
5 **DIAMOND CHARLIE (IRE),** 7, br g Diamond Green (FR)—Rosy Lydgate **David & Stanley Adams**
6 **FAIR VALUE (IRE),** 7, b m Compton Place—Intriguing Glimpse **Don & Val Churston**
7 **FIDUCIA,** 5, b m Lawman (FR)—Silca Key **P. G. Jacobs**
8 **FORCEFUL APPEAL (USA),** 7, b br g Successful Appeal (USA)—Kinetic Force (USA) **Mr S. A. Caunce**
9 **KAGAMI,** 4, ch g Teofilo (IRE)—Sky Wonder **S. L. Dow**
10 **KEEP KICKING (IRE),** 8, b g Tiger Hill (IRE)—Dalannda (IRE) **P. McCarthy**
11 **LITMUS (USA),** 6, ch m Latent Heat (USA)—Fairy Glade (USA) **T. G. Parker**
12 **MALAYSIAN BOLEH,** 5, ch g Compton Place—Orlena (USA) **JCG Chua & CK Ong**
13 **MARJONG,** 5, b m Mount Nelson—Vermilliann (IRE) **Mr J. L. Marsden**
14 **NONNO GIULIO (IRE),** 4, ch g Halling (USA)—Contrary (IRE) **Mr A. Li**
15 **PRESUMIDO (IRE),** 5, b g Iffraaj—Miss Megs (IRE) **R. Moss & J. Page**
16 **PROCUREMENT,** 4, b f Zamindar (USA)—Acquisition **T. G. Parker & Ken Butler**
17 **SIXTIES LOVE,** 4, b f Sixties Icon—Love Always **T. Staplehurst**
18 **SOUL INSTINCT,** 4, b g Myboycharlie (IRE)—However (IRE) **S. L. Dow**
19 **TOP SET (IRE),** 5, ch g Tamayuz—Pray (IRE) **Taylor, Meadows, Snell, Taylor & Wright**

## MR SIMON DOW - Continued

### THREE-YEAR-OLDS

20 **AUTUMN TONIC (IRE),** b c Approve (IRE)—Trempjane **K. F. Butler**
21 **EL CAMPEON,** b br g Multiplex—Villabella (FR) **Mr R. J. Moss**
22 **GALINTHIAS,** b g Sixties Icon—Tidie France (USA) **S. L. Dow**
23 **LADY BALLANTRAE (IRE),** b f Henrythenavigator (USA)—Marseille Express (USA) **Stoney's Bloodstock**
24 **LADY BRAMBLETYE (IRE),** b f Lawman (FR)—Steeple **Stoney's Bloodstock**
25 **SPARBROOK (IRE),** b f Kodiac—Summer Sunshine **Mr A. Li**
26 **TANGRAMM,** b br g Sakhee's Secret—Tripti (IRE) **Mr J. L. Marsden**
27 **WOOLSTONE ONE,** b f Authorized (IRE)—Saralea (FR) **P. G. Jacobs**

### TWO-YEAR-OLDS

28 **BUSTA NELLIE,** ch f 1/5 Pastoral Pursuits—Vezere (USA) (Point Given (USA)) (3500) **R. Moss & J. Page**
29 B f 20/4 Green Horizon—Calon Lan (Nayef (USA)) **Miss T. Walters**
30 **HOMBRE ROJO (IRE),** b c 27/4 Intikhab (USA)—Sidney Girl (Azamour (IRE)) (45000) **Mr R. J. Moss**
31 **HURRICANE ROCK,** ch c 8/3 Rock of Gibraltar (IRE)—Seasonal Cross (Cape Cross (IRE)) (9000) **Aldis & Hayes**

**Other Owners:** Mr M. A. Adams, Mr D. Adams, Mr S. J. Adams, Mrs A. Aldis, Mr M. S. Aldis, D. G. Churston, Mrs V. Churston, R. Gurney, Mr G. P. Hayes, Miss S. J. Hayes, Mrs S. P. Meadows, Mr F. Ong, Mr J. W. Page, Ms S. A. Snell, Miss J. E. Taylor, Mr W. J. Taylor, Mrs L. A. Wright.

**Assistant Trainer:** Daniel Hutchison

**Jockey (flat):** Tomas Harrigan.

---

## 165 MR CHRIS DOWN, Cullompton

Postal: **Upton, Cullompton, Devon, EX15 1RA**
Contacts: **PHONE (01884) 33097 FAX (01884) 33097 MOBILE (07828) 021232**
**E-MAIL cjdownracing@gmail.com**

1 **AROSEFOROSCAR,** 6, b m Oscar (IRE)—Made For A King **The Red White & Blue Partnership**
2 **BILLY DUTTON,** 9, ch g Sir Harry Lewis (USA)—Tinoforty (FR) **W. A. Bromley**
3 **BILLY MY BOY,** 6, b g Volochine (IRE)—Key West (FR) **Mr J. B. Radford**
4 **CRAIGANEE (IRE),** 8, b g Craigsteel—Hows She Going (IRE) **P Holland, JT Measures, MA Kerr, V Holland**
5 **CULM COUNSELLOR,** 6, ch g Erhaab (USA)—Miss Counsel **Culm Valley Racing**
6 **DRAGON'S DEN (IRE),** 8, b g Antonius Pius (USA)—Tallassee **G. R. Waterman**
7 **FROZEN OVER,** 7, b g Iceman—Pearly River **A G O'Neill, M Capps, M Di-Vincenzo, N Jones**
8 **HOT PEPPER,** 7, gr g Tikkanen (USA)—Copper Valley **Mrs G. H. Leeves**
9 **ICE TRES,** 6, br m Iceman—Tup Tim **Mrs W. Atkins**
10 **KEY TO MILAN,** 9, b g Milan—Key West (FR) **C. J. Down**
11 **LADIES DANCING,** 9, b g Royal Applause—Queen of Dance (IRE) **Upton Racing**
12 **LEGION D'HONNEUR (UAE),** 10, b g Halling (USA)—Renowned (IRE) **Mrs M. Trueman**
13 **LILY POTTS,** 6, gr m Proclamation (IRE)—Jucinda **C. J. Down**
14 **LOYAUTE (FR),** 8, ch m Green Tune (USA)—Iles Marquises (IRE) **Upton Racing 2**
15 **MISTER SNOWBALL (FR),** 8, ch g Ballingarry (IRE)—No Coincidence (IRE) **P Holland, JT Measures, MA Kerr, V Holland**
16 **ORDENSRITTER (GER),** 7, ch g Samum (GER)—Dramraire Mist **Red Baron Racing**
17 **RUSSIE WITH LOVE,** 9, b m Alflora (IRE)—Vieille Russie **Howzat Partnership**
18 **SARAS RUBY,** 6, ch m With The Flow (USA)—Sara Monica (IRE) **The Jack High Racing Partnership**
19 **TRIPLE CHIEF (IRE),** 4, b br g High Chaparral (IRE)—Trebles (IRE) **G. D. Thompson**
20 **UPTON WOOD,** 9, ch g Fleetwood (IRE)—Miss Counsel **C. J. Down & C. B. Stevens**

**Other Owners:** Mr A. Boylan, Mr M. G. Capps, Mrs S. J. Cork, Mr M. Di-Vincenzo, Dr M. J. Dixon, Mrs F. Down, Mrs J. Elliott, Mr N. D. Elliott, Mr A. D. Hill, P. D. Holland, Mrs V. Holland, Mr N. S. Jones, Ms M. A. Kerr, Mr J. T. Measures, Mrs S. E. Norman, Mr J. A. G. Norman, Mr A. G. O'Neill, Mr B. Stamp, Mr C. B. Stevens, K. W. Tyrrell.

**Jockey (flat):** Jemma Marshall. **Jockey (NH):** James Davies, Richard Johnson, Tom Scudamore.
**Conditional:** Giles Hawkins.

---

## 166 MR RICHARD DRAKE, Guiseley

Postal: **Manor Farm, Old Hollings Hill, Guiseley, Leeds, West Yorkshire, LS20 8EW**

1 **ANOTHER TIPPLE,** 5, b g Kayf Tara—Devon Peasant **Mrs J. E. Drake**

## MR RICHARD DRAKE - Continued

2 **RAKTIMAN (IRE),** 8, ch g Rakti—Wish List (IRE) **Mrs J. E. Drake**
3 **STUCKINTHEFENCE (IRE),** 8, b g Bienamado (USA)—Starshade (IRE) **Mrs J. E. Drake**
4 **WORK BOY,** 14, b g Nomadic Way (USA)—Swift Reward **Mrs J. E. Drake**

---

## 167 MR CLIVE DREW, Rampton

Postal: **Fox End Stables, 83 King Street, Rampton, Cambridgeshire, CB24 8QD**
Contacts: **PHONE/FAX (01954) 250772 MOBILE (07917) 718127**

1 **MAISON BRILLET (IRE),** 8, b g Pyrus (USA)—Stormchaser (IRE) **C. Drew**
2 **MONSIEUR ROYALE,** 5, ch g Monsieur Bond (IRE)—Bond Royale **C. Drew**

### THREE-YEAR-OLDS

3 Br f Halling (USA)—Maziona **C. Drew**
4 B br f Pastoral Pursuits—Nursling (IRE) **C. Drew**

**Assistant Trainer:** Miss Polly Drew

---

## 168 MISS JACKIE DU PLESSIS, Saltash

Postal: **Burell Farm, Longlands, Saltash, Cornwall, PL12 4QH**
Contacts: **PHONE (01752) 842362 MOBILE (07970) 871505**
**E-MAIL ziggerson@aol.com**

1 **ABSOLUTELY BYGONES (IRE),** 7, b g Alderbrook—Majella (IRE) **Miss J Du Plessis & Mr G Waterman**
2 **DIDDYPURPTOON,** 9, b m Lucky Story (USA)—Dafne **Miss J. M. du Plessis**
3 **DORIS DE SILVER,** 6, gr m Silver Patriarch (IRE)—Magic Valentine
4 **FEAR GLIC (IRE),** 9, b g Dr Massini (IRE)—Graineuaile (IRE) **Miss J Du Plessis & Mr G Waterman**
5 6, B m Blueprint (IRE)—Graineuaile (IRE) **Miss J. M. du Plessis**
6 6, B m Bandmaster (USA)—Halton Quay **Miss J. M. du Plessis**
7 6, Ch h With The Flow (USA)—Kingsmill Quay **Miss J. M. du Plessis**
8 **KIT HILL (IRE),** 10, b br g Turtle Island (IRE)—My Kit (IRE) **Miss J. M. du Plessis**
9 **LONG JOHN,** 8, gr g Silver Patriarch (IRE)—Magic Valentine **R. J. Reip, M. Stevenson**
10 **RAY DIAMOND,** 10, ch g Medicean—Musical Twist (USA) **Miss J. M. du Plessis**
11 **ST DOMINICK (IRE),** 8, b g Oscar (IRE)—Kilcrea Breeze (IRE) **Miss J. M. du Plessis**
12 **WINNING SPARK (USA),** 8, b g Theatrical—Spark Sept (FR) **Miss J. M. du Plessis**
13 **ZIGGERSON HILL,** 8, ch m Kadastrof (FR)—Tregale **Miss J. M. du Plessis**

**Other Owners:** Mr R. J. Reip, Mr M. F. Stevenson, G. R. Waterman.

---

## 169 MRS ANN DUFFIELD, Leyburn

Postal: **Sunhill Racing Ltd, Sunhill Farm, Constable Burton, Leyburn, North Yorkshire, DL8 5RL**
Contacts: **PHONE (01677) 450303 FAX (01677) 450993 MOBILE (07802) 496332**
**E-MAIL ann@annduffield.co.uk WEBSITE www.annduffield.co.uk**

1 **BEARSKIN (IRE),** 4, br g Kodiac—Dark Arts (USA) **The Duchess of Sutherland**
2 **CANTON MASSINI,** 4, b g Dr Massini (IRE)—Mandarin Star **Mr A. C. Cook**
3 **CHANT (IRE),** 5, b g Oratorio (IRE)—Akarita (IRE) **Mrs Ann Starkie & Mrs I. Starkie**
4 **IN VINO VERITAS (IRE),** 4, b g Art Connoisseur (IRE)—Robin **Mr J. A. Kay**
5 **LA HAVRESE (FR),** 4, ch f Le Havre (IRE)—La Buena (IRE) **Mr J. A. Kay**
6 **MASTER CLOCKMAKER (IRE),** 4, gr g Mastercraftsman (IRE)—Mairead Anne (USA) **Mrs J. D. M. Thompson**
7 **MISTER UNO (IRE),** 4, b c Tamayuz—Starlight Smile (USA) **Mr J. Gatenby**
8 **RED CHARMER (IRE),** 5, b g Red Clubs (IRE)—Golden Charm (IRE) **Mr I Farrington & Mr R Chapman**
9 **SONG OF NORWAY,** 4, b f Halling (USA)—Amarullah (FR) **RA Henley RP Marchant JP Carrington**

### THREE-YEAR-OLDS

10 **ASTROPHYSICS,** ch c Paco Boy (IRE)—Jodrell Bank (IRE) **Mr J. Dance**
11 **BARON SPIKEY (IRE),** ch g Lord Shanakill (USA)—
Sharp Diversion (USA) **Mr H & S Robson & Mr David K Barker**
12 **COLOMBIA (IRE),** b f Art Connoisseur (IRE)—Credibility **Easton Park Stud & Mr John Dance**
13 **COPIOUS KATIE,** ch f Notnowcato—Abundant **Mr A. C. Cook**
14 **DOPPLER EFFECT,** ch g Monsieur Bond (IRE)—Scarlet Oak **Mr L. Bond**

## MRS ANN DUFFIELD - Continued

15 **FAST CHARLIE (IRE),** b g Fast Company (IRE)—Where's Charlotte **Mr J. Dance**
16 **GEORGE DRYDEN (IRE),** gr c Zebedee—Key To Fortune (GER) **Mr S. Bradley**
17 **KAYO KOKO (IRE),** b f Zebedee—Negria (IRE) **Mr J. Dance**
18 **LA VIEN ZEN (IRE),** b f Dylan Thomas (IRE)—Se La Vie (FR) **Zen Racing**
19 **LANDING NIGHT (IRE),** b c Kodiac—Night Delight (IRE) **Mr J. Dance**
20 **MARSH PRIDE,** b f Stimulation (IRE)—Peneia (USA) **Mr J. Dance**
21 **MCLOVIN RIVERDANCE,** b g Lawman (FR)—Electric Dream **Mr J. Dance**
22 **MISTRESS MAKFI (IRE),** ch f Makfi—Rapid Ransom (USA) **Mrs S Bianco & Ms J Bianco**
23 **MR COOL CASH,** b g Firebreak—Cashleen (USA) **Mr I. Lawson**
24 **PASSIONATE APPEAL,** b g Lawman (FR)—Amaryllis (IRE) **The Strides Partnership**
25 **SHOW BOAT,** b c Showcasing—Bluegrass Gal (USA) **The Duchess of Sutherland**
26 **SPIRITUAL JOURNEY (IRE),** gr f Zebedee—Daneville (IRE) **Mr P Watson & Mr I Farrington**
27 **THE KURATOR (IRE),** ch g Art Connoisseur (IRE)—A L'aube (IRE) **J Pak, J Dance, J Kay & The Boys**
28 **TOBOGGAN'S GIFT,** b f Major Cadeaux—Toboggan Lady **Mr T. P. McMahon & Mr D. McMahon**

## TWO-YEAR-OLDS

29 B g 13/4 Bushranger (IRE)—Annus Iucundus (IRE) (Desert King (IRE)) (15000) **Mrs A. Duffield**
30 **ARCTIC ROYAL (IRE),** ch f 27/2 Frozen Power (IRE)—Bronze Queen (IRE) (Invincible Spirit (IRE)) (22221) **Mr J. Dance**
31 **BIG STUART (IRE),** b gr g 17/4 Bushranger (IRE)—El Morocco (USA) (El Prado (IRE)) (8729) **Mr J. A. Kay**
32 B c 14/4 Zebedee—Daneville (IRE) (Danetime (IRE)) (25000)
33 **DARK ILLUSTRATOR,** b f 19/3 Dutch Art—Xtrasensory (Royal Applause) (38095) **Mr Lee Bond & Mr John Dance**
34 B f 16/1 Compton Place—Deora De (Night Shift (USA)) (28571) **Qatar Racing Limited**
35 **ENCANTAR,** b f 6/4 Equiano (FR)—
Enrapture (USA) (Lear Fan (USA)) (11428) **Mr D J & Mrs S A Shewring & Partner**
36 **HEAVEN SCENT,** ch f 30/1 Phoenix Reach (IRE)—Hel's Angel (IRE) (Pyrus (USA)) **Mrs H. L. Baines**
37 **HILARY J,** b f 12/2 Mount Nelson—The Terrier (Foxhound (USA)) (38095) **E & R Stott**
38 B f 26/3 Zoffany (IRE)—Jamary (IRE) (Grand Reward (USA)) (28571) **Mr David Barker & Mr Douglas McMahon**
39 **LADY CHARA,** b f 16/1 Stimulation (IRE)—Noble Nova (Fraam) (17142) **The Duchess of Sutherland**
40 **LETBYGONESBEICONS,** b c 29/4 Sixties Icon—
Composing (IRE) (Noverre (USA)) (7619) **Birrafun Partnership & Partner**
41 **LOLAMOTION,** ch f 27/3 Equiano (FR)—
Ocean View (USA) (Gone West (USA)) (5714) **Mr L Bond & Mr & Mrs H Robson**
42 **LORD MCGUFFY (IRE),** b c 15/3 Frozen Power (IRE)—
La Herradura (Hernando (FR)) (15872) **Mr John Sagar & Mr Ian Hill**
43 **MARSH KING,** b c 10/4 Stimulation (IRE)—Peneia (USA) (Nureyev (USA)) (6000) **Mr J. Dance**
44 B f 21/1 Equiano (FR)—Midnight Fantasy (Oasis Dream) (48000) **Qatar Racing Limited**
45 **MISS MACCHIATO (IRE),** b f 15/5 Holy Roman Emperor (IRE)—
Cafe Lassere (USA) (Giant's Causeway (USA)) (12698) **Mr J. Dance**
46 **MR STRAVINSKY (IRE),** b c 29/3 Zebedee—
Galvano (IRE) (Galileo (IRE)) (26666) **Mrs Ann Starkie & Mr John Dance**
47 **MY AMIGO,** gr c 1/2 Stimulation (IRE)—Blue Crest (FR) (Verglas (IRE)) (36190) **Mr J. Dance**
48 **NINETTA (IRE),** b f 17/2 New Approach (IRE)—Pine Chip (USA) (Nureyev (USA)) (60000) **Ms J. F. Bianco**
49 **PASSIONATEPRINCESS (IRE),** b f 29/3 Elnadim (USA)—
Romany Princess (IRE) (Viking Ruler (AUS)) (13491) **The Passionate Partnership**
50 **PRAIRIE IMPULSE,** b f 26/3 Major Cadeaux—Prairie Sun (GER) (Law Society (USA))
51 **RISK ADJUSTED (IRE),** b c 8/5 Bushranger (IRE)—Silk Fan (IRE) (Unfuwain (USA)) (11904) **Mr J. Dance**
52 **SCRUFFY MCGUFFY,** b g 20/4 Firebreak—Eloquent Isle (IRE) (Mull of Kintyre (USA))
53 **SILHUETTE (IRE),** b f 24/3 Canford Cliffs (IRE)—Lisfannon (Bahamian Bounty) (17142) **Mr J. Dance**
54 **SILVER STREAK (IRE),** gr c 16/4 Dark Angel (IRE)—Happy Talk (IRE) (Hamas (IRE)) (35714) **Punchbowl Racing**
55 **SOUTHERN SEAS,** ch f 17/4 Archipenko (USA)—Sourire (Domedriver (IRE)) **Miss K. Rausing**
56 B c 11/3 Bushranger (IRE)—Suzie Quw (Bahamian Bounty) **Mr D. S. McMahon**
57 **TOBOGGAN'S FIRE,** b f 18/2 Firebreak—Toboggan Lady (Tobougg (IRE)) **Mr T. P. McMahon & Mr D. McMahon**
58 **WHISPERING SOUL (IRE),** b f 11/3 Majestic Missile (IRE)—
Belle of The Blues (IRE) (Blues Traveller (IRE)) (35714) **Mr John Dance & Mr John Gatenby**
59 **YOUNG WINDSOR (IRE),** ch c 11/3 Windsor Knot (IRE)—
Invincible Woman (IRE) (Invincible Spirit (IRE)) (12698) **Punchbowl Racing**

**Other Owners:** D. K. Barker, Mrs S. Bianco, Mr J. P. Carrington, Mr R. P. Chapman, Mr B. J. Connolly, J. Cullinan, Mr C. J. Edwards, Mr I. J. Farrington, R. A. Henley, Mr I. Hill, Mr R. P. Marchant, Mr D. McMahon, Mr T. P. McMahon, Mr J. Pak, Mrs B. M. Richmond, Mr A. Richmond, Mr C. H. Robson, Mrs S. J. Robson, Mr J. Sagar, Mr R. A. Sankey, Mr D. J. Shewring, Mrs S. A. Shewring, Mrs A. Starkie, Mrs I. L. A. Starkie, Miss R. Stott, Miss E. Stott, Mr M. C. P. Suddards, Mr C. P. Watson, Mr Peter Watson.

**Assistant Trainer:** George Duffield

**Jockey (flat):** P. J. McDonald. **Apprentice:** Rowan Scott.

## 170 MR BRENDAN W. DUKE, The Curragh

Postal: **Fenway House, Pollardstown, Curragh, Co. Kildare, Ireland**
Contacts: **PHONE (00353) 45 521104 FAX (00353) 45 521104 MOBILE (00353) 85 8189724**
**E-MAIL brendanwduke@hotmail.com**

1 **EMPRESS SCORPION (IRE),** 5, b m Scorpion (IRE)—Square Up (IRE) **Mr Joseph Duke**
2 **FENWAY TIGER (IRE),** 6, b g Tiger Hill (IRE)—Taca d'oli (FR) **Mrs Angela Duke**
3 **FOCAS MOR (IRE),** 4, ch f Intense Focus (USA)—Intriguing Humor (CAN) **Mrs Jackie Bolger**
4 **FOCUSSED (IRE),** 4, b g Intense Focus (USA)—Tus Maith (IRE) **Mrs Jackie Bolger**
5 **MUININ (IRE),** 4, ch f Teofilo (IRE)—Vasanta (IRE) **Mrs Jackie Bolger**
6 **OLD PHOBIE (IRE),** 8, b m Catcher In The Rye (IRE)—Blackchurch Mist (IRE) **Mr Patrick Brennan**
7 **PUNCH BAG (IRE),** 4, ch g Teofilo (IRE)—Heir Today (IRE) **Mr Martin Hayes & Mr Peter Slezak**
8 **QUI BONO (IRE),** 4, gr g Beneficial—Dream Witness (FR) **Mr Joseph Duke**
9 **TOBURG ISLAND (IRE),** 6, ch m Trans Island—Hayward's Heath **Mrs Angela Duke**
10 **WELSH NAYBER,** 6, ch g Nayef (USA)—Aberdovey **Mr Mark MacDonagh**

### THREE-YEAR-OLDS

11 **ALAINN (IRE),** b f Intense Focus (USA)—Aoibhneas (USA) **Mrs Jackie Bolger**
12 **FIONN'S LADY (IRE),** b f Cape Cross (IRE)—Fashion Trade **Mr Christopher Leonard**
13 **LAMH IN AIRDE (USA),** ch f Macho Uno (USA)—Fardus (IRE) **Mrs Jackie Bolger**
14 **RENEA (IRE),** ch f Fracas (IRE)—Rajani (IRE) **Mrs M. Joyce**
15 **UNO VOCE (IRE),** b g Vocalised (USA)—Derpat (IRE) **Mrs Jackie Bolger**
16 **VERBAL STILETTO (IRE),** b g Vocalised (USA)—Ceirseach (IRE) **Mrs Jackie Bolger**
17 **VOCAL ALERT (IRE),** b f Vocalised (USA)—Groves Royal (USA) **Mrs Jackie Bolger**
18 **VOCAL HEIR (IRE),** b f Vocalised (USA)—Heir Today (IRE) **Mrs Jackie Bolger**
19 **VOCAL VELOCITY (IRE),** b c Vocalised (USA)—Voronova (IRE) **Mrs Jackie Bolger**
20 **VOCAL WARM UP (IRE),** b f Vocalised (USA)—Faoileoir (USA) **Mrs Jackie Bolger**
21 **VOLT (IRE),** b f Vocalised (USA)—Sukeena (IRE) **Mrs Jackie Bolger**

### TWO-YEAR-OLDS

22 **ALLINONE (IRE),** b f 5/3 Bushranger (IRE)—Ambika (IRE) (Danehill Dancer (IRE)) (793) **Mr Patrick O'Donovan**
23 **ATHASACH (IRE),** b f 10/4 Manduro (GER)—Fashion Trade (Dansili) (10317) **Mrs Jackie Bolger**
24 **LEATH NA HOIBRE (IRE),** b c 15/5 Vocalised (USA)—Tus Maith (IRE) (Entrepreneur) **Mrs Jackie Bolger**
25 **THE MOUSE DOCTOR (IRE),** b c 25/2 Lord Shanakill (USA)—Afilla (Dansili) **Mr Joseph Duke**
26 **VOCAL DEFENSE (IRE),** br c 4/4 Vocalised (USA)—Redrightreturning (Diktat) (7936) **Mrs Jackie Bolger**

**Jockey (flat):** R. P. Cleary, K. J. Manning. **Jockey (NH):** David Crosse, M. P. Fogarty, Andrew Lynch. **Apprentice:** Killiam Hennessy, Daniel Redmond, Dillon Robinson. **Amateur:** Miss Jane Mangan.

## 171 MR IAN DUNCAN, Coylton

Postal: **Sandhill Farm, Coylton, Ayr, Ayrshire, KA6 6HE**
Contacts: **PHONE (01292) 571118 FAX (01292) 571118 MOBILE (07731) 473668**

1 **DEMETRIUS (IRE),** 7, gr g Antonius Pius (USA)—Innocentines (FR) **Dr S. Sinclair**
2 **FINAGHY AYR (IRE),** 7, ch g Lahib (USA)—Ali Ankah (IRE) **Mr A. J. R. Lilley**
3 **GOLDEN SPARKLE (IRE),** 9, ch m Samraan (USA)—Bye For Now **Miss H. A. Cross**
4 **MAURA LILY (IRE),** 6, br m Lahib (USA)—Ali Ankah (IRE) **Mr A. J. R. Lilley**
5 **MILBOROUGH (IRE),** 9, b g Milan—Fox Burrow (IRE) **Miss H. A. Cross**
6 **OLLISU LAD (IRE),** 6, b g Westerner—Nick's Jule (IRE) **Great Northern Partnership 2**
7 **PERSIAN FASHION (IRE),** 6, b m Lahib (USA)—Kiera's Gale (IRE) **I. A. Duncan**
8 **SPRING OVER (IRE),** 9, ch m Samraan (USA)—Superswap (IRE) **I. A. Duncan**

**Other Owners:** Mr A. L. Gregg, J. K. S. Law.

## 172 MR ED DUNLOP, Newmarket

Postal: **La Grange Stables, Fordham Road, Newmarket, Suffolk, CB8 7AA**
Contacts: **PHONE (01638) 661998 FAX (01638) 667394 MOBILE (07785) 328537**
**E-MAIL edunlop@eddunlopracing.co.uk WEBSITE www.edunlop.com**

1 **GOD WILLING,** 4, b c Arch (USA)—Bourbon Ball (USA) **Qatar Racing & Essafinaat**
2 **GWORN,** 5, b g Aussie Rules (USA)—Crochet (IRE) **Mr N. Martin**
3 **HANNO (USA),** 4, b g Henrythenavigator (USA)—Archstone (USA) **Mrs P. Moseley**

## MR ED DUNLOP - Continued

4 **ISLAND REMEDE,** 4, b f Medicean—Island Odyssey **Mrs J. M. Quy**
5 **MANNDAWI (FR),** 5, gr g Dalakhani (IRE)—Mintly Fresh (USA) **J M Haseler & OTI Racing**
6 **MUBARAZA (IRE),** 6, ch g Dalakhani (IRE)—Mokaraba **Hamdan Al Maktoum**
7 **OASIS FANTASY (IRE),** 4, br g Oasis Dream—Cara Fantasy (IRE) **Windflower Overseas & J L Dunlop OBE**
8 **QUENELLE,** 4, b f Nayef (USA)—Cruinn A Bhord **Miss J. Delves Broughton**
9 **RED AVENGER (USA),** 5, b br g War Front (USA)—Emotional Rescue (USA) **R. J. Arculli**
10 **RED CADEAUX,** 9, ch g Cadeaux Genereux—Artisia (IRE) **R. J. Arculli**
11 **RED GALILEO,** 4, b c Dubawi (IRE)—Ivory Gala (FR) **R. J. Arculli**
12 **TAQNEEN (IRE),** 4, b g Cape Cross (IRE)—Badee'a (IRE) **Hamdan Al Maktoum**
13 **TED'S SECRET,** 4, b g Sakhee's Secret—Sinduda **The Hon R. J. Arculli & Mr Robert Ng**
14 **TIMES UP,** 9, b g Olden Times—Princess Genista **Mrs I. H. Stewart-Brown & Mr M. J. Meacock**
15 **TRIP TO PARIS (IRE),** 4, b g Champs Elysees—La Grande Zoa (IRE) **La Grange Partnership**
16 **ZARWAAN,** 4, b g Dutch Art—Develyn **Hamdan Al Maktoum**

## THREE-YEAR-OLDS

17 **ALAN TURING (IRE),** b c Exceed And Excel (AUS)—Maggie Lou (IRE) **W. J. and T. C. O. Gredley**
18 **BIFF JOHNSON (IRE),** b g Dansili—Sagacious (IRE) **Mr G. B. Bolton**
19 **CLARENTINE,** b f Dalakhani (IRE)—Clarietta **Bluehills Racing Limited**
20 **DARK RED (IRE),** gr c Dark Angel (IRE)—Essexford (IRE) **R. J. Arculli**
21 Ch f Summer Bird (USA)—Dispute (USA) **Mrs S. M. Roy**
22 **DUTCH UNCLE,** b c Dutch Art—Evasive Quality (FR) **R. J. Arculli**
23 **EJBAAR,** br c Oasis Dream—Habaayib **Hamdan Al Maktoum**
24 **EUROPA (GER),** b f Arcano (IRE)—Easy Sunshine (IRE) **Hamdan Al Maktoum**
25 **FIELD OF LIGHT,** b g Pastoral Pursuits—Luminda (IRE) **P A Deal A L Deal David Sieff & ORS**
26 **FIELDSMAN (USA),** b c Hard Spun (USA)—
R Charlie's Angel (USA) **Highclere Thoroughbred Racing- Hard Spun**
27 B br g High Chaparral (IRE)—Final Legacy (USA) **Qatar Racing Limited**
28 **HARLESTONE HOPES,** b g Olden Times—Harlestone Lady **J. L. Dunlop**
29 **HEAVENS ABOVE (IRE),** b f Montjeu (IRE)—Sharplaw Star **Rathordan Partnership**
30 Ch c Lope de Vega (IRE)—Hold Off (IRE) **R. J. Arculli**
31 **IMVULA,** gr f Aqlaam—Reason To Dance **Mrs G. A. Rupert**
32 **JUSTICE FIRST,** b c Zebedee—Nelly's Glen **Mr R. Ng**
33 **KITTEN'S RED (USA),** ch c Kitten's Joy (USA)—Arbor (USA) **R. J. Arculli**
34 **LAMSA (IRE),** b f Invincible Spirit (IRE)—Golden Flyer (FR) **Hamdan Al Maktoum**
35 **MAHSOOBA (USA),** b f Hard Spun (USA)—Ishraak (USA) **Hamdan Al Maktoum**
36 **MULHAAM (IRE),** gr g Fast Company (IRE)—Park Approach (IRE) **M. Jaber**
37 **NAADY,** b br f Mawatheeq (USA)—Al Tamooh (IRE) **Hamdan Al Maktoum**
38 **NAIZAH (IRE),** b f Tamayuz—Etizaaz (USA) **Hamdan Al Maktoum**
39 **PRINCE GAGARIN (IRE),** b c Dubawi (IRE)—Cara Fantasy (IRE) **Windflower Overseas & J L Dunlop OBE**
40 **PYLA (IRE),** b f Footstepsinthesand—Beautiful Hill (IRE) **The Hoofmark Partnership**
41 **RAFEEQ (FR),** ch c Raven's Pass (USA)—Alzaroof (USA) **Hamdan Al Maktoum**
42 **ROCK LOBSTER,** ch g Bahamian Bounty—Reeling N' Rocking (IRE) **Lowe, Mitchell, Silver, Milmo & Allison**
43 **SAGACIOUSLY (IRE),** b f Lawman (FR)—Saga Celebre (FR) **The Sagacious Lot**
44 **SAMEEK (IRE),** b g Acclamation—Varenka (IRE) **Hamdan Al Maktoum**
45 **SCRUTINISE,** b g Intense Focus (USA)—Tetravella (IRE) **Thurloe Thoroughbreds XXXIV**
46 **SHURFAH (IRE),** ch f Sea The Stars (IRE)—Cap Coz (IRE) **Hamdan Al Maktoum**
47 **SOUK AL TAHAB (IRE),** b c Arcano (IRE)—Quiet Dream (USA) **M. Jaber**
48 **SPORTING PRINCE,** b g Pastoral Pursuits—Queen of Iceni **Mrs I. H. Stewart-Brown & Mr M. J. Meacock**
49 **TAJATHUB,** gr ro c Bahamian Bounty—Galapagar (USA) **Hamdan Al Maktoum**
50 **TARTOOR (GER),** br g Oasis Dream—Templerin (GER) **Hamdan Al Maktoum**
51 **THANAAYA (IRE),** b f Haatef (USA)—Mejala (IRE) **Hamdan Al Maktoum**
52 **TOCORORO (IRE),** b f Teofilo (IRE)—Firecrest (IRE) **Brooke Kelly Partnership**
53 **VERISMO,** b g Hurricane Run (IRE)—Cross Current **B. Andersson**

## TWO-YEAR-OLDS

54 **AHDAATH (IRE),** b f 25/3 Kodiac—Sonny Sunshine (Royal Applause) (114285) **Hamdan Al Maktoum**
55 **ALFAHAD (IRE),** b c 13/2 New Approach (IRE)—Al Tamooh (IRE) (Dalakhani (IRE)) **Hamdan Al Maktoum**
56 B f 3/4 Cape Cross (IRE)—Alleluia (Caerleon (USA)) (280000) **Mr Alec Leopold & Ms Leanne Norman**
57 **ALQUBBAH (IRE),** b f 25/2 Arcano (IRE)—Musharakaat (IRE) (Iffraaj) **Hamdan Al Maktoum**
58 Ch f 6/2 Rip Van Winkle (IRE)—
Always Attractive (IRE) (King's Best (USA)) (28000) **J. Strauss & Sir A. Page Wood**
59 B c 25/4 Teofilo (IRE)—Artisia (IRE) (Peintre Celebre (USA)) **R. J. Arculli**
60 **BIDAAYA (IRE),** b f 16/2 Naaqoos—Alzaroof (USA) (Kingmambo (USA)) **Hamdan Al Maktoum**
61 Ch c 25/3 Archipenko (USA)—Caribana (Hernando (FR)) (21000) **E. A. L. Dunlop**
62 B f 14/5 Cape Cross (IRE)—Cinerama (IRE) (Machiavellian (USA)) (42000) **Mr A. Jaber**

## MR ED DUNLOP - Continued

**63 COGENT,** b c 4/4 Paco Boy (IRE)—Logic (Slip Anchor) **W. J. and T. C. O. Gredley**
**64 GABRIELLE,** b f 3/2 Paco Boy (IRE)—Bounty Box (Bahamian Bounty) (31000) **The Belfour Partnership**
**65 GIRL WITH A PEARL (IRE),** ch f 31/3 Dutch Art—
Pointed Arch (IRE) (Rock of Gibraltar (IRE)) (120000) **Racing Fillies**
**66 GLORYETTE,** b f 27/4 Raven's Pass (USA)—
Cara Fantasy (IRE) (Sadler's Wells (USA)) **Windflower Overseas Holdings Inc**
**67** B f 18/4 Authorized (IRE)—Grand Lucre (Grand Slam (USA)) (6500)
**68 HAJEER (IRE),** b br f 22/1 Cape Cross (IRE)—Mejala (IRE) (Red Ransom (USA)) **Hamdan Al Maktoum**
**69 KAFOO,** br c 18/4 Dansili—Nidhaal (IRE) (Observatory (USA)) **Hamdan Al Maktoum**
**70 KHAFOUH (IRE),** ch c 23/3 Makfi—Kournikova (SAF) (Sportsworld (USA)) (39681) **M. Jaber**
**71** Ch c 25/2 Zoffany (IRE)—Lady Sadowa (Nayef (USA)) (13492) **The Octopus Partnership**
**72** B c 7/4 Bahamian Bounty—Little Annie (Compton Place) (27000) **Mr A. S. Al Naboodah**
**73 MANJAAM (IRE),** ch c 14/5 Tamayuz—Priory Rock (IRE) (Rock of Gibraltar (IRE)) (39681) **M. Jaber**
**74** B f 16/3 Rock of Gibraltar (IRE)—Manoeuvre (IRE) (Galileo (IRE))
**75 MICHAEL'S MOUNT,** ch c 14/4 Mount Nelson—Dumnoni (Titus Livius (FR)) (35000) **Miltil Consortium**
**76** B c 10/2 Pour Moi (IRE)—Miss Quality (USA) (Elusive Quality (USA))
**77 MUJAMALA (IRE),** b f 6/3 Exceed And Excel (AUS)—Habaayib (Royal Applause) **Hamdan Al Maktoum**
**78 OPPOSITION,** gr c 18/3 Dalakhani (IRE)—
Censored (Pivotal) (120000) **Highclere Thoroughbred Racing(Melbourne)**
**79 PALAVICINI'S GIRL (IRE),** b f 17/3 Palavicini (USA)—
Pairumani Princess (IRE) (Pairumani Star (IRE)) **Windflower Overseas Holdings Inc**
**80 PIMPERNELLA (IRE),** b f 5/2 Elusive Pimpernel (USA)—
Soviet Belle (IRE) (Soviet Star (USA)) **Windflower Overseas Holdings Inc**
**81** B f 5/5 Siyouni (FR)—Pink And Red (USA) (Red Ransom (USA)) (19841) **The Sagacious Lot**
**82 QEYAADAH (IRE),** b c 28/2 Acclamation—Effervesce (IRE) (Galileo (IRE)) (160000) **Hamdan Al Maktoum**
**83** Ch c 7/3 Sakhee (USA)—Queen of Iceni (Erhaab (USA))
**84 QUEENSBURY ODYSSEY,** ch c 21/4 Poet's Voice—
Russian Spirit (Falbrav (IRE)) (70000) **W. J. and T. C. O. Gredley**
**85 RAASMAAL,** b c 4/4 Poet's Voice—Luminda (IRE) (Danehill (USA)) (160000) **Hamdan Al Maktoum**
**86 RAS AL MAL (IRE),** ch c 6/3 Tamayuz—Midnight Glimmer (IRE) (Dr Devious (IRE)) (71428) **M. Jaber**
**87** B f 20/1 Fastnet Rock (AUS)—Red Fantasy (IRE) (High Chaparral (IRE)) **R. J. Arculli**
**88 ROCKERY (IRE),** b f 26/1 Fastnet Rock (AUS)—
Rain Flower (IRE) (Indian Ridge) (350000) **Sir Peter Vela & Hon Mrs Peter Stanley**
**89** B f 26/4 Frozen Power (IRE)—Saga Celebre (FR) (Peintre Celebre (USA)) (27777)
**90 SHAFAFYA,** b f 26/2 Shamardal (USA)—Tanaghum (Darshaan) **Hamdan Al Maktoum**
**91 SHARAAKAH (IRE),** b f 24/2 Roderic O'Connor (IRE)—Lanark Belle (Selkirk (USA)) (17460) **M. Jaber**
**92** B c 17/2 Champs Elysees—Skyrider (IRE) (Dalakhani (IRE)) (15000) **Bluehills Racing Limited**
**93 SNOW PIXIE (USA),** br f 5/5 Flower Alley (USA)—
Woodland Dream (IRE) (Charnwood Forest (IRE)) **Windflower Overseas Holdings Inc**
**94 SOCIAL MEDIA,** b f 30/3 New Approach (IRE)—
Mischief Making (USA) (Lemon Drop Kid (USA)) **Cliveden Stud Ltd**
**95 SWIFTEE (IRE),** ch c 16/4 Camacho—Algaira (USA) (Irish River (FR)) (25000) **Bluehills Racing Limited**
**96** B c 3/4 Lilbourne Lad (IRE)—There With Me (USA) (Distant View (USA)) (16190) **W. Cox**
**97 TOFFEE APPLE (IRE),** b f 23/4 Zoffany (IRE)—
Myrtle Beach (IRE) (Kenmare (FR)) (15500) **Bluehills Racing Limited**
**98 WEALTH TAX,** gr c 28/2 Canford Cliffs (IRE)—Firoza (FR) (King's Best (USA)) (19047) **W. J. and T. C. O. Gredley**

**Other Owners:** Sheikh M. B. K. Al Maktoum, S. A. Allison, Mr A. N. C. Bengough, Sir F. Brooke, Mrs G. M. Cotton, P. A. Deal, A. L. Deal, The Countess Of Derby, Mrs R. S. Dunlop, R. P. Foden, A. J. J. Gompertz, W. J. Gredley, T. C. O. Gredley, Mr J. M. Haseler, Mr M. Heffernan, B. G. Hellyer, Mr T. Henderson, The Hon H. M. Herbert, Highclere Thoroughbred Racing Ltd, Mr R. D. A. Kelly, Mr A. Leopold, G. A. Lowe, M. J. Meacock, P. H. Milmo, A. M. Mitchell, A. M. V. Nicoll, Ms L. C. Norman, Mr S. O'Donnell, Old Road Securities Plc, Sir Anthony Page-Wood, O. J. W. Pawle, Mr R. A. Pilkington, Sir Thomas Pilkington, Mr M. Quirke, A. P. Rogers, Mrs F. Schwarzenbach, Sir David Sieff, M. J. Silver, Mr J. A. B. Stafford, The Hon Mrs Frances Stanley, Mr N. J. Statham, Mrs J. Stewart-Brown, Mr J. E. A. Strauss, Sir P. J. Vela, Sir Reddy Watt.

---

## 173 MR HARRY DUNLOP, Lambourn

Postal: **Windsor House Stables, Crowle Road, Lambourn, Hungerford, Berkshire, RG17 8NR**
Contacts: **PHONE (01488) 73584 FAX (01488) 674172 MOBILE (07880) 791895**
**E-MAIL info@harrydunlopracing.com WEBSITE www.harrydunlopracing.com**

**1 CADMIUM,** 4, b f Major Cadeaux—Miss Mirasol **Susan Abbott Racing**
**2 EARLY MORNING (IRE),** 4, gr g New Approach (IRE)—Summer's Eve **Early Risers**
**3 FLAMBEUSE,** 4, b f Cape Cross (IRE)—Flamenba (USA) **Glanvilles Stud Partners**

## MR HARRY DUNLOP - Continued

4 **STAR ANISE (FR),** 4, b f Astronomer Royal (USA)—Sasicha (IRE) **The Astronomers 2**
5 **VIKING STORM,** 7, b g Hurricane Run (IRE)—Danehill's Dream (IRE) **Be Hopeful Partnership**

### THREE-YEAR-OLDS

6 **ANNA DOLCE (FR),** b f Areion (GER)—Anna Spectra (IRE) **Harry Dunlop Racing Partnership**
7 **BRITTLETON,** b g Aqlaam—Fairy Dance (IRE) **Sir Philip Wroughton & Mrs James Blyth Currie**
8 **CASIUS,** b c Teofilo (IRE)—Mary Pekan (IRE) **The Blue Bar Partnership**
9 **DON'T TARRY (IRE),** b c Elnadim (USA)—Bobbie Soxer (IRE) **Windflower Overseas Holdings Inc**
10 **ESTOURNEL,** b f Danehill Dancer (IRE)—Estephe (IRE) **Mr Patrick Milmo**
11 **LULANI (IRE),** b f Royal Applause—Louverissa (IRE) **Mr & Mrs James Blyth Currie**
12 **MARGOT ROSE,** b f Kheleyf (USA)—Sanjuna **Mrs C. D. Dunlop**
13 **MEMORIES GALORE (IRE),** b g Invincible Spirit (IRE)—
Persian Memories (IRE) **Windflower Overseas Holdings Inc**
14 **NONA BLU,** b g Diktat—Shivering **Mrs S. M. Roy**
15 **PACO'S DREAM,** b f Paco Boy (IRE)—Isle of Flame **Bermuda & Berrow Racing**
16 **PALOMA DANCER,** b f Refuse To Bend (IRE)—Anapola (GER) **The Quixote Quintet**
17 **RED TORNADO (FR),** ch g Dr Fong (USA)—Encircle (USA) **Blockley, Cross, Johnson, Whitaker, Woodley**
18 **RUM SWIZZLE,** b f Mawatheeq (USA)—Port Providence **Mr N. Pascall**
19 **SEEBEEDEE,** b f Multiplex—Border Ballet (IRE) **Glanvilles Stud Partners**
20 **SKYE MORNING,** b f Invincible Spirit (IRE)—Bright Morning (USA) **N. P. Hearson**
21 **STORM ROCK,** b c Rock of Gibraltar (IRE)—Seasonal Cross **Malcolm & Alicia Aldis**
22 **SUNDAY ROYAL (FR),** b g Sunday Break (JPN)—Princess d'orange (FR) **Mr & Mrs T. O'Donohoe**

### TWO-YEAR-OLDS

23 B f 28/2 Arcano (IRE)—All Began (IRE) (Fasliyev (USA)) (5000) **Windsor House Stables Partnership**
24 **BRETONCELLES (FR),** b f 22/2 Le Havre (IRE)—Carolles (FR) (Medicean) (15000) **D. MacAullife & Anoj Don**
25 Br c 5/3 Big Bad Bob (IRE)—
Causeway Charm (USA) (Giant's Causeway (USA)) (59523) **Weston Brook Farm, Bromfield & Whitaker**
26 **DYLANTELLE,** b f 18/2 Dylan Thomas (IRE)—Bay Swallow (IRE) (Daylami (IRE)) **Glanvilles Stud Partners**
27 B f 11/4 Poet's Voice—Fastback (IRE) (Singspiel (IRE)) **Brightwalton Bloodstock Limited**
28 **FINELCITY (GER),** b br c 19/3 Elusive City (USA)—Finity (USA) (Diesis) (7142) **Blue Bar Partnership**
29 Ch f 1/4 Sakhee's Secret—Gitane (FR) (Grand Lodge (USA)) (11904) **Gehring, Whitaker & Partners**
30 B c 8/3 Kheleyf (USA)—Glitz (IRE) (Hawk Wing (USA)) (8571) **Windsor House Stables Racing Partnership**
31 **GREAT COMPANY (IRE),** b c 5/3 Fast Company (IRE)—
Sunlit Silence (IRE) (Green Desert (USA)) (57142) **Khalifa Dasmal**
32 **INVIGORATE,** b c 9/2 Stimulation (IRE)—
Pesse (IRE) (Eagle Eyed (USA)) (8571) **Woodley, Gehring, Drake, Craig-Wood**
33 Gr f 7/5 Mastercraftsman (IRE)—Joyful (IRE) (Green Desert (USA)) (32539) **Glanvilles Stud Partners**
34 **LINGUIST (FR),** ch c 22/4 Linngari (IRE)—
Western Bowl (USA) (Gone West (USA)) (18253) **Janet Weston, Carolyn Whitaker, Sue Johnson**
35 **MEROULA (FR),** b f 16/4 Vision d'etat (FR)—
Laureldean Desert (Green Desert (USA)) (22222) **Mr & Mrs James Blyth Currie**
36 Br c 15/3 Dutch Art—Passing Stranger (IRE) (Dixie Union (USA)) **Mrs Susan Roy**
37 **POULICHE,** ch f 14/5 Monsieur Bond (IRE)—Tarneem (USA) (Zilzal (USA)) (4761) **Hot To Trot Racing Club**
38 **THREE BROTHERS (FR),** b br c 28/3 Slickly (FR)—Vivartic (FR) (Verglas (IRE)) (21428) **Mr Nicholas Pascall**
39 **TORQUAY,** b f 19/4 Aqlaam—Torcross (Vettori (IRE)) **Mr R. J. McCreery**
40 B c 25/3 Raven's Pass (USA)—Ultra Finesse (USA) (Rahy (USA)) (26000) **Crimbourne Stud**

**Other Owners:** Mr W. Douglas Procter, Dr G. W. Guy, Mrs Mary-Anne Parker, Mr Charles Parker.

**Apprentice:** Leah-Anne Avery.

---

## 174 MRS ALEXANDRA DUNN, Wellington

Postal: **The Gallops, West Buckland, Wellington, Somerset, TA21 9LE**
Contacts: **MOBILE (07738) 512924**
**WEBSITE www.alexandradunnracing.com**

1 **ANNAROE (IRE),** 6, b m Beneficial—Dun Belle Magic (IRE) **Mr W. A. Thomas**
2 **ARRAYAN,** 10, b g Catcher In The Rye (IRE)—Ganga (IRE) **Mr Dave Arthur & Dunn Racing**
3 **BLACK NARCISSUS (IRE),** 6, b m Westerner—Arcanum (IRE) **Team Dunn**
4 **BLU CAVALIER,** 5, b g Kayf Tara—Blue Ride (IRE) **Mrs A. Tincknell**
5 **BRAMBLE VODKA,** 7, b m Desideratum—Just Jay **Miss R. J. Smith-Maxwell**
6 **COME ON ANNIE,** 9, b m Karinga Bay—Irish Ferry **Mrs E. V. A. Trotman**
7 **DAVID JOHN,** 4, b g Overbury (IRE)—Molly's Secret **David J Llewellyn Toni P James**

## MRS ALEXANDRA DUNN - Continued

8 **ENTRY TO EVRYWHERE (IRE),** 7, b g Exit To Nowhere (USA)—Killowen Pam (IRE) **G Butler & T Dunn**
9 **HALFSIN (IRE),** 7, b g Haafhd—Firesteed (IRE) **Ms G. Butler**
10 **HELIUM (FR),** 10, b g Dream Well (FR)—Sure Harbour (SWI) **Dunn Racing**
11 **HOY HOY (IRE),** 4, b g Iffraaj—Luxie (IRE) **Mr T. H. Dunn**
12 **LAMUBAALY (IRE),** 4, b g Le Havre (IRE)—Seracina **Ms G. Butler**
13 **LION ON THE PROWL (IRE),** 11, b g Sadler's Wells (USA)—Ballerina (IRE) **Mrs K. R. Smith-Maxwell**
14 **PRINCE TOM,** 11, b g King's Theatre (IRE)—Cresswell Native (IRE) **Mrs Angela Tincknell & Mr W. Tincknell**
15 **ROYAL CHARM (FR),** 10, bl g Cadoudal (FR)—Victoria Royale (FR) **Tincknell & Dunn**
16 **SILK TRAIN,** 5, b m Rail Link—Monsoon Wedding **Mr R. Payne**
17 **STAY TUNED (IRE),** 7, ch m Saffron Walden (FR)—Just A Song (IRE) **Dunn Racing**
18 **TEACHMETOBOUGGIE,** 5, ch g Tobougg (IRE)—Teachmetotango **Mr T. H. Dunn**
19 **UGLY BUG,** 9, b g Runyon (IRE)—Mutual Decision (IRE) **Mrs T. P. James**
20 **WESTON SUPER MARE,** 5, br m Scorpion (IRE)—Proby Lady (IRE)
21 **WORLDOR (FR),** 9, b g Lost World (IRE)—Karenzed (FR) **Mr N. Berbillion**
22 **ZERO VISIBILITY (IRE),** 8, b g Classic Cliche (IRE)—Jessica's Pet (IRE) **D Fitzgerald & T Dunn**

**Other Owners:** Mr D. R. Arthur, Mr S. Cullum, Mr D. J. Fitzgerald, Mr D. J. Llewellyn, W. C. Tincknell, Trebles Holford Thoroughbreds.

---

## 175 MRS CHRISTINE DUNNETT, Norwich

Postal: **College Farm, Hingham, Norwich, Norfolk, NR9 4PP**
Contacts: **PHONE (01953) 850596 FAX (01953) 851364 MOBILE (07775) 793523**
**E-MAIL christine@christinedunnett.com WEBSITE www.christinedunnett.com**

1 4, Ch f Phoenix Reach (IRE)—Bongoali
2 **COLLEGE DOLL,** 6, ch m Piccolo—Southwarknewsflash **P D West, A S Machin & C A Dunnett**
3 **DANZOE (IRE),** 8, br g Kheleyf (USA)—Fiaba **One For All**
4 **ELLINGHAM (IRE),** 4, b f Bushranger (IRE)—No Way (IRE) **One For All**
5 **EMMESSESS (IRE),** 4, b g Desert Millennium (IRE)—Azira **Annwell Inn Syndicate**
6 **FLAMINGO BEAT,** 5, ch g Beat Hollow—Flamingo Flower (USA) **Mr P. D. West**
7 **GIVE IT A WHIRL,** 4, br f Pastoral Pursuits—Life's A Whirl **Mr A. Machin & Mrs C. Dunnett**
8 **GIVE US A BELLE (IRE),** 6, b g Kheleyf (USA)—Bajan Belle (IRE) **Mr F Butler & Mrs C Dunnett**
9 **HAPPYDOINGNOTHING,** 4, b g Avonbridge—Neferura **Mr P. D. West**
10 **HUMOUR (IRE),** 4, b g Invincible Spirit (IRE)—Hucking Hot **The Humourites**
11 **IRISH SWEETHEART (IRE),** 4, b f Desert Millennium (IRE)—
Run Sweetheart (USA) **Christine Dunnett Racing (Arryzona)**
12 **NORCROFT,** 13, b g Fasliyev (USA)—Norcroft Joy **Mrs C. A. Dunnett**
13 **PERSEVERENT PETE (USA),** 5, b br g Johannesburg (USA)—Indian Halloween (USA) **Mr P. D. West**
14 **SATIN WATERS,** 4, b f Halling (USA)—Velvet Waters **Ron Spore & P D West**

### TWO-YEAR-OLDS

15 B c 23/4 Mount Nelson—Djalalabad (FR) (King's Best (USA)) **Mr E. Sparkes & Mrs C. Dunnett**
16 **DUBAI WALK (ITY),** ch f 5/4 Vita Rosa (JPN)—Dubaila (Dubai Destination (USA)) (800) **Mr A. Machin**
17 **MARCMYWORDS (IRE),** ch c 26/3 Thousand Words—
Last Shaambles (IRE) (Shaamit (IRE)) **Mrs Mary Benjafield**
18 B g 2/1 Desert Millennium (IRE)—Run Sweetheart (USA) (Bold Run (FR)) **Mrs C. Dunnett**
19 B g 8/4 Sakhee's Secret—Rutland Water (IRE) (Hawk Wing (USA)) (2000) **Annwell Inn Syndicate**

**Other Owners:** Mrs Mary Benjafield, G. Bromley, Mr D. G. Burt, F. Butler, Mrs C. A. Dunnett, Mr A. S. Machin, Mr E. N. Sparkes, R. C. Spore, Mr P. D. West.

---

## 176 MR SEAMUS DURACK, Upper Lambourn

Postal: **The Croft Stables, Upper Lambourn, Hungerford, Berkshire, RG17 8QH**
Contacts: **PHONE (01488) 71941 MOBILE (07770) 537971**
**E-MAIL sd.111@btinternet.com**

1 **ALL TALK N NO DO (IRE),** 4, b c Kodiac—Woodren (USA) **Mrs A. Cowley**
2 **ALYASAN (IRE),** 4, ch c Sea The Stars (IRE)—Alaya (IRE) **The Alyasan Partnership**
3 **ARC LIGHTER (USA),** 6, b g Street Cry (IRE)—Flamelet (USA) **The Acorn Partnership & Ownaracehorse**
4 **BAY SLY (IRE),** 8, b g Stowaway—On A Mission (IRE) **Mr G. Tardi**
5 **CHUFFT,** 4, b f Sleeping Indian—Relkida **Deborah Collett & M. J. Watson**
6 **DEMOCRETES,** 6, ch g Cadeaux Genereux—Petite Epaulette **David Barrett & Dean Gregory**

## MR SEAMUS DURACK - Continued

7 **EN REVE,** 4, b f Shirocco (GER)—Night Symphonie **Hot To Trot Racing Club**
8 4, B g Gamut (IRE)—Financial Heiress (IRE)
9 **IFTIRAAQ (IRE),** 4, b c Muhtathir—Alzaroof (USA) **J. J. Hathorn**
10 **LINGUINE (FR),** 5, ch h Linngari (IRE)—Amerissage (USA) **Mrs A. Cowley**
11 **PAOLOZZI (IRE),** 6, b g Oscar (IRE)—Miss Eurolink **Mr C. A. Wilkinson**
12 **THE RECTIFIER (USA),** 8, b br g Langfuhr (CAN)—Western Vision (USA) **Mrs A. Cowley**
13 **TOUR DE VILLE (IRE),** 5, b g Beneficial—Galant Tour (IRE)
14 **TOURNAMENT,** 4, b c Oasis Dream—Concentric **S. P. Tucker**

### THREE-YEAR-OLDS

15 **ALFREDO (IRE),** ch c Arcano (IRE)—Western Sky **Mr Stephen Tucker & Mr Keith Mcintosh**
16 **CHAPEAU BLEU (IRE),** b f Haatef (USA)—La Petite Bleue (GER) **C. G. Mackenzie**
17 **GOODBY INHERITENCE,** b c Medicean—Chili Dip **Mrs A. Cowley**
18 **MOONWALKER (IRE),** b c Dark Angel (IRE)—Winesong (IRE) **Mr Stephen Tucker & Mr Keith Mcintosh**

### TWO-YEAR-OLDS

19 **HELLS BABE,** b f 23/4 Hellvelyn—Blues In Cee (IRE) (Sinndar (IRE)) **Mrs L. White**
20 B f 23/1 Tamayuz—Invincibile Stella (IRE) (Invincible Spirit (IRE)) (2777)

**Other Owners:** Mr D. Barrett, Miss D. Collett, Mr D. Gregory, Mrs F. K. Hathorn, Mr R. S. Hoskins, Mr R. Jones, L. Lillingston, Mr K. R. McIntosh, Ownaracehorse Ltd, M. J. Watson.

**Assistant Trainer:** Faye Bramley

**Jockey (flat):** George Baker, Micky Fenton. **Jockey (NH):** Conor O'Farrell.

---

**177**

## MR CHRIS DWYER, Newmarket

Postal: **Grooms Cottage, Brickfield Stud, Exning Road, Newmarket, Suffolk, CB8 7JH**
Contacts: **PHONE (01638) 570074 FAX (01638) 570074 MOBILE (07831) 579844**
**E-MAIL getadwyer@aol.com**

1 **BAILEYS EN PREMIER (FR),** 4, b g Exceed And Excel (AUS)—Numberonedance (USA) **G. R. Bailey Ltd (Baileys Horse Feeds)**
2 **BASIL BERRY,** 4, b g Tobougg (IRE)—Dolly Coughdrop (IRE) **Strawberry Fields Stud**
3 **BINT DANDY (IRE),** 4, b f Dandy Man (IRE)—Ceol Loch Aoidh (IRE) **M. M. Foulger**
4 **FOIE GRAS,** 5, b g Kyllachy—Bint Zamayem (IRE) **Mrs S. Dwyer**
5 **HANNAHS TURN,** 5, b m Dubai Destination (USA)—Fontaine House **Mrs I. L. Sneath**
6 **MIA'S BOY,** 11, b g Pivotal—Bint Zamayem (IRE) **Mrs S. Dwyer**
7 **NOGUCHI (IRE),** 10, ch g Pivotal—Tuscania (USA) **Mrs Fiona Shaw**
8 **PATRIOTIC (IRE),** 7, b g Pivotal—Pescara (IRE) **M. M. Foulger**
9 **SAVED MY BACON (IRE),** 4, b f Camacho—Sally Green (IRE) **Mrs J. Hughes & Mrs C. Kemp**
10 **TATTING,** 6, ch g Street Cry (IRE)—Needlecraft (IRE) **Mrs I. L. Sneath**

### THREE-YEAR-OLDS

11 **BRIDAL GOWN,** b f Arabian Gleam—Bridal White **Mr R. Devereux**
12 **DARK SIDE DREAM,** b g Equiano (FR)—Dream Day **M. M. Foulger**
13 **LADY ANTONIOS (IRE),** b f Bushranger (IRE)—Rahika Rose **Mr & Mrs H Nensey, Saif Nensey**

**Other Owners:** Mrs J. V. Hughes, Mrs C. J. Kemp, Mr H. S. A. Nensey, Mrs N. Nensey, Mr S. Nensey, G. F. L. Robinson, F. B. B. White.

**Assistant Trainer:** Shelley Dwyer (07949) 612256

**Apprentice:** Josh Crane.

---

## MISS CLAIRE DYSON, Evesham

Postal: **Froglands Stud Farm, Froglands Lane, Cleeve Prior, Evesham, Worcestershire, WR11 8LB**
Contacts: **PHONE (07803) 720183 (01789) 774000 FAX (01789) 774000**
**E-MAIL cdyson@live.co.uk WEBSITE www.clairedysonracing.co.uk**

1 **ADADREAM,** 6, b g Abzu—Madam Ross **Chris Green**
2 **BOOMTOWN,** 10, b g Fantastic Light (USA)—Ville d'amore (USA) **FSF Racing**

## MISS CLAIRE DYSON - Continued

3 **CHEAT THE CHEATER (IRE),** 8, b g Flemensfirth (USA)—Ballyclough Gale **Lisa Rogers, B. & S. Vaughan & Partner**
4 **CLASSIC TUNE,** 5, b g Scorpion (IRE)—Classic Fantasy **D. J. Dyson**
5 **CRESSWELL PRINCE (IRE),** 5, b g Bienamado (USA)—Faraday Lady (IRE) **B. & S. Vaughan**
6 **DR DREAMY (IRE),** 8, b g Dr Massini (IRE)—Proud Aldi (IRE) **Guy Sainsbury & Partner**
7 **ECHO FOXTROT,** 6, b g Echo of Light—April Lee (USA) **Mr K. Elvins**
8 **EL INDIO (IRE),** 8, b g Flemensfirth (USA)—Final Bond (IRE) **D. J. Pardy & D. J. Dyson**
9 **FORRESTERS FOLLY,** 9, b g Bollin Eric—Miss Wyandotte **FSF Racing**
10 **GIVEIMACHANCE (IRE),** 7, b g Exit To Nowhere (USA)—Native Lisa (IRE) **Miss R. J. Rowland**
11 **GIVEITACHANCE (IRE),** 8, b g Clerkenwell (USA)—Native Lisa (IRE) **Miss R. J. Rowland**
12 **GUS MACRAE (IRE),** 11, b g Accordion—Full of Surprises (IRE) **Not Told The Wife Yet**
13 **KHAZIUM (IRE),** 6, br g Kheleyf (USA)—Hazium (IRE) **Miss C. Dyson**
14 **LEAGUE OF HIS OWN (IRE),** 6, ch g Beneficial—Miss Eastwood (IRE) **D. J. Dyson**
15 **MANY MOONS (FR),** 6, b m Sleeping Car (FR)—Ishka Baha (IRE) **Mr G. E. P. Dudfield**
16 **MEMORY OF LIGHT (IRE),** 6, gr g Westerner—Be Thankfull (IRE) **Mr G. T. Sainsbury**
17 **MIDNIGHT OWLE,** 5, ch g Midnight Legend—Owlesbury Dream (IRE) **D. J. Dyson**
18 **MUSICAL WEDGE,** 11, ch g Sir Harry Lewis (USA)—Wedge Musical **D. J. Dyson**
19 **OVER MY HEAD,** 7, gr g Overbury (IRE)—Altesse de Sou (FR) **Ms I. Heritage**
20 **PEQENO DIABLO (IRE),** 10, br g Alexius (IRE)—Miss Huro (IRE) **FSF Racing**
21 **SISTER FABIAN (IRE),** 5, b m Turtle Island (IRE)—Dolly Lewis **D. J. Dyson**
22 **TARBAY,** 6, b m Kayf Tara—Pearly Bay **D. J. Dyson**
23 **TOAST AND JAM (IRE),** 6, b g Clerkenwell (USA)—Summittotalkabout (IRE) **Mrs D. E. Darragh**
24 **WHEELAVHER,** 9, br m Fair Mix (IRE)—True Rose (IRE) **Miss C. Dyson**
25 **WHEELAVIT (IRE),** 12, b g Elnadim (USA)—Storm River (USA) **FSF Racing**

**Other Owners:** Mr Dermot Corrigan, Miss C. Dyson, Mr D. J. Dyson, Mr D. J. Pardy, Mr Ian Pardy, Miss L. Rogers, Mr Guy Sainsbury, Mrs S. Vaughan, Mr B. Vaughan.

**Assistant Trainer:** Becky Rowland

**Jockey (NH):** Jamie Moore, Nick Scholfield. **Conditional:** Jake Hodson, Trevor Whelan. **Amateur:** Mr G. S. Quinn.

---

## 179 MR SIMON EARLE, Warminster

Postal: **Little Croft, Tytherington, Warminster, Wiltshire, BA12 7AD**
Contacts: **PHONE (01985) 840450 FAX (01985) 840450 MOBILE (07850) 350116**
**E-MAIL simon@simonearleracing.com WEBSITE www.simonearleracing.com**

1 **DALIANCE (IRE),** 6, ch g Dalakhani (IRE)—Everlasting Love **Mr John Powell**
2 **GET BACK TO ME (IRE),** 8, br g Presenting—My Name's Not Bin (IRE) **R. L. Dacombe**
3 **GUSTAV (IRE),** 5, b g Mahler—Pakaradyssa (FR) **The Plum Merchants**
4 **HEADLY'S BRIDGE (IRE),** 9, b g Tillerman—Brockton Flame **Mrs P. L. Bridel**
5 **KAVANAGHS CORNER (IRE),** 6, b g Coroner (IRE)—Annacarney (IRE) **Mrs Bridget O'Flynn**
6 4, B f Oscar (IRE)—Lala Nova (IRE)
7 **MONEY MAID (IRE),** 7, ch m Blueprint (IRE)—Maid of Music (IRE) **EPDS Racing Partnership 5**
8 **WATER RAIL,** 6, b g Manipulator (IRE)—Madame Mozaik (USA)
9 **ZAKATAL,** 9, gr g Kalanisi (IRE)—Zankara (FR) **David Furman & John Sugarman**

**Other Owners:** Mr A. C. Clift, Mr David Furman, Mr John Powell, Mr T. M. Santry, Miss T. Sloan, Mr John Sugarman.

**Jockey (flat):** George Baker. **Jockey (NH):** Paddy Brennan, Andrew Thornton. **Amateur:** Miss Alice Mills.

---

## 180 MR MICHAEL EASTERBY, Sheriff Hutton

Postal: **New House Farm, Sheriff Hutton, York, North Yorkshire, YO60 6TN**
Contacts: **PHONE (01347) 878368 FAX (01347) 878204 MOBILE (07831) 347481**
**E-MAIL enquiries@mickeasterby-racing.co.uk WEBSITE www.mickeasterby-racing.co.uk**

1 **AETNA,** 5, b m Indesatchel (IRE)—On The Brink **Mr B. Padgett**
2 **AMBLESIDE,** 5, b g Cape Cross (IRE)—Zarara (USA) **Hull Dewhirst Swales Blackburn & Turton**
3 **ANCIENT CROSS,** 11, b g Machiavellian (USA)—Magna Graecia (IRE) **P Bown, R Fiddes & S Hull**
4 **BAJAN REBEL,** 4, ch f Bahamian Bounty—Silca Key **Julian Rooney & Steve Hull**
5 **BARREN BROOK,** 8, b g Beat Hollow—Carinthia (IRE) **Mr D Scott, Mrs E Wright & Mr J Clark**
6 **BE LUCKY,** 5, ch m Kyllachy—Spritzeria **The Sangster Family & M W Easterby**
7 **BORIS GRIGORIEV (IRE),** 6, b br g Excellent Art—Strategy **Mrs L. M. Ward**
8 **BOSHAM,** 5, b g Shamardal (USA)—Awwal Malika (USA) **P. Easterby**

## MR MICHAEL EASTERBY - Continued

9 **CACTUS VALLEY (IRE),** 6, b g Lawman (FR)—Beech Gardens **D. Fielding, S. Holling & S. Hull**
10 **CAN YOU CONGA,** 5, b g Piccolo—Takes Two To Tango **M Cox, E Grant & S Hull**
11 **CAPTAIN JOE,** 4, ch g Captain Gerrard (IRE)—Bond Shakira **Mr D. A. Fielding**
12 **CITY GROUND (USA),** 8, b br g Orientate (USA)—Magnet (USA) **S. Hull**
13 **DAY OF THE EAGLE (IRE),** 9, b g Danehill Dancer (IRE)—Puck's Castle **S Hull, S Hollings & D Fielding**
14 **DAYLIGHT,** 5, ch g Firebreak—Dayville (USA) **Kennet Valley Thoroughbreds V**
15 **HANSEATIC,** 6, b g Galileo (IRE)—Insinuate (USA) **Blunt, Brook, Hull, Chandler & Westwood**
16 **HERNANDO TORRES,** 7, b g Iffraaj—Espana **M. W. Easterby**
17 **HOOF IT,** 8, b g Monsieur Bond (IRE)—Forever Bond **Mr A. Chandler & Mr L. Westwood**
18 **HOOFALONG,** 5, b g Pastoral Pursuits—Baymist **A Chandler, L Westwood, D & Y Blunt**
19 **HOT SPICE,** 7, b g Kodiac—Harlestone Lady **S Hull, D Swales, A Turton & J Blackburn**
20 **IGGY,** 5, ch g Lucarno (USA)—Fujakka (IRE)
21 **ITLAAQ,** 9, b g Alhaarth (IRE)—Hathrah (IRE) **WH & Mrs JA Tinning, M Cox, E Grant**
22 **KALK BAY (IRE),** 8, b g Hawk Wing (USA)—Politesse (USA) **Linda Folwell, Steve Hull & David Swales**
23 **LIGHTENING ROD,** 10, b g Storming Home—Bolero **N. W. A. Bannister**
24 **NARCISSIST (IRE),** 6, b g Dylan Thomas (IRE)—Gabare (FR) **The Friday Club**
25 **OIL STRIKE,** 8, b g Lucky Story (USA)—Willisa **Mr A. Saha**
26 **OLD MAN CLEGG,** 5, b g Pastoral Pursuits—Stolen Melody **Irkroy Racing & Steve Hull**
27 **PERFECT PASTURE,** 5, b g Pastoral Pursuits—Word Perfect **S Hull, S Hollings & D Swales**
28 **PIVOTMAN,** 7, ch g Pivotal—Grandalea **K. Wreglesworth**
29 **REAR ADMIRAL (IRE),** 9, b g Dushyantor (USA)—Ciaras Charm (IRE) **Mr S Hollings**
30 **SAINTS AND SINNERS (IRE),** 7, b g Gold Well—How Provincial (IRE) **Mr N Wrigley & Mrs J Lukas**
31 **SHADOWS LENGTHEN,** 9, b g Dansili—Bay Shade (USA) **T. A. F. Frost**
32 **SINGZAK,** 7, ch g Singspiel (IRE)—Zakuska **Clark Industrial Services Partnership**
33 **SLINGSBY,** 4, b g Dutch Art—Ballet Fame (USA) **Mr S Hull, Mr B Hoggarth & Mrs C Mason**
34 **SPACE WAR,** 8, b g Elusive City (USA)—Princess Luna (GER)
35 **STILL ACTING,** 4, gr f Act One—Karolina (FR) **Lord Daresbury & Mr Stuart Parkin**
36 **STRONG MAN,** 7, b g Gentleman's Deal (IRE)—Strong Hand **Mr S Hollings & Mr P Easterby**
37 **TAMAYUZ MAGIC (IRE),** 4, b g Tamayuz—Anne Tudor (IRE) **W. H. & Mrs J. A. Tinning**
38 **TAPIS LIBRE,** 7, b g Librettist (USA)—Stella Manuela (FR) **Mrs S. E. Mason**
39 **UP TEN DOWN TWO (IRE),** 6, b g Hurricane Run (IRE)—Darabela (IRE) **A Duke, B Delaney**
40 **VIVA STAR,** 4, gr f Verglas (IRE)—Jazan (IRE) **Lord Daresbury & Mr Stuart Parkin**
41 **WARLU WAY,** 8, b g Sakhee (USA)—Conspiracy **Mr B Hoggarth,Mr S Hollings & Mr S Hull**
42 **WE'LL DEAL AGAIN,** 8, b g Gentleman's Deal (IRE)—Emma Amour **K. Wreglesworth**
43 **WHO OWNS ME (IRE),** 9, b g Milan—Top Lassie (IRE) **Mr M. J. R. Bannister**

## THREE-YEAR-OLDS

44 **AMONG ANGELS,** b g Acclamation—Love Action (IRE) **E. Brook & A. Stott**
45 **ATREUS,** b g Indesatchel (IRE)—Devassa **Brian Padgett & Peter Hutchinson**
46 **BIONIC INDIAN,** b g Acclamation—Strawberry Moon (IRE) **Mr A. Saha**
47 **BOWSON FRED,** b c Monsieur Bond (IRE)—Bow Bridge **Mrs A. Jarvis**
48 **DEBT FREE DAME,** ch f Arcano (IRE)—Runkerry Point (USA) **A R Legal Collections & Sangster Family**
49 **FELIX DE VEGA (IRE),** b c Lope de Vega (IRE)—Lafite **A. Simpson, S. Hull**
50 **GRAZED KNEES (IRE),** b g Majestic Missile (IRE)—Carpet Lover (IRE) **J. Burton**
51 **HAFINA,** b f Multiplex—Danifah (IRE) **E. A. R. Morgans**
52 **LEAVE IT TO ARNO,** ch c Paco Boy (IRE)—Presto Vento **A R Legal Collections Limited**
53 **MOUNTAIN MAN,** b g Hellvelyn—Jane Jubilee (IRE) **Mr E Brook & Mr T Langley**
54 **PERFECT PEAK,** ch f Distant Peak (IRE)—Word Perfect **M. W. Easterby**
55 **PROCIDA,** b f Myboycharlie (IRE)—On The Brink **Mr B. Padgett**
56 **RECKLESS BLUE,** ch f Bahamian Bounty—Frambroise **S. Hull**
57 **SCOTTISH ISLES,** ch g Distant Peak (IRE)—Choral Singer **D. F. Spence**
58 **SHIP CANAL,** ch g Major Cadeaux—Smooth As Silk (IRE) **Mr B. Buckley**

## TWO-YEAR-OLDS

59 **ARREST WARRANT,** b c 6/3 Acclamation—Dream Day (Oasis Dream) **W. J. Gredley**
**60** B g 10/4 Monsieur Bond (IRE)—Ballet Fame (USA) (Quest For Fame) **Mrs C. Mason**
**61** B f 13/3 Monsieur Bond (IRE)—Bow Bridge (Bertolini (USA)) **Mrs A. Jarvis**
**62** Ch c 30/3 Monsieur Bond (IRE)—Chez Cherie (Wolfhound (USA)) (28571) **E. Brook, T. Langley & D. Scott**
**63** B f 16/3 Sakhee's Secret—Dancing Nelly (Shareef Dancer (USA)) (7619) **E. Brook & M. Hollingsworth**
**64** B c 25/4 Big Bad Bob (IRE)—Dazzling Dancer (Nashwan (USA)) (12000) **A R Legal Collections Limited**
**65** B f 28/2 Dutch Art—Grasshoppergreen (IRE) (Barathea (IRE)) (23000) **D. Spence & S. Hull**
**66** Br f 21/5 Monsieur Bond (IRE)—Ice Girl (Iceman) **Mr B. Padgett**
**67** B f 29/3 Monsieur Bond (IRE)—Ingleby Princess (Bold Edge) (2666) **D. Scott**
**68** Ch f 29/4 Monsieur Bond (IRE)—Janet's Pearl (IRE) (Refuse To Bend (IRE)) **T. Langley**
**69** B c 14/2 Piccolo—Lyndalee (IRE) (Fasliyev (USA)) **Mr B. Padgett**

## MR MICHAEL EASTERBY - Continued

**70** B c 13/2 Royal Applause—Maeander (FR) (Nashwan (USA)) (17142) **D. Spence & S. Hull**
**71** B br f 6/5 Medicean—Mistress Twister (Pivotal) (14285) **D. Scott**
**72** B f 4/5 Monsieur Bond (IRE)—Prices Lane (Gentleman's Deal (IRE)) **A. G. Black**
**73** Ch f 4/5 Monsieur Bond (IRE)—Royal Distant (USA) (Distant View (USA)) **T. Dewhirst**
**74** Ch c 1/4 Monsieur Bond (IRE)—Triple Tricks (IRE) (Royal Academy (USA)) (5714) **T. Langley**
**75** Ch f 10/4 Piccolo—Willisa (Polar Falcon (USA)) (9523) **Colts & Fillies Ltd**

**Other Owners:** A R Legal Collections Limited, Mr M. J. R. Bannister, Mr N. W. A. Bannister, Mrs A. Barker, Mr J. N. Blackburn, Mr David Blunt, Mrs Y. Blunt, Mr S. Bowett, Mr P. J. Bown, Mr E. A. Brook, Mr John Bryan, Mr Andrew Chandler, Mr S. Chappell, Mr Jim Clark, Mr A. W. Clark, Mr M. Cox, Lord Daresbury, Mr Bill Delaney, Mr T. C. Dewhirst, Mr A. Duke, Mr Peter Easterby, Mr Ritchie Fiddes, Mr Dean Fielding, Mrs L. S. Folwell, Mr E. Grant, Mr Bernard Hoggarth, Mr S. A. Hollings, Mr R. S. Hoskins, Mr Steve Hull, Mr Peter Hutchinson, Mr Terence Langley, Mrs Julia Lukas, Mrs C. E. Mason, Mr Mark W. Metcalfe, Mr J. R. Moore, Mr A. Morse, Mr B. Padgett, Mr Stuart Parkin, Mr N. J. F. Robinson, Mr Julian Rooney, Mr B. V. Sangster, Mr G. E. Sangster, Mr David Scott, Mr Nick Sharp, Mr Andrew Simpson, Stittenham Racing, Mr D. Swales, Mrs J. A. Tinning, Mr W. H. Tinning, Mr Andrew Turton, Mr Lee Westwood, Mrs E. Wright, Mr N. H. T. Wrigley.

**Assistant Trainer:** D. M. Easterby

**Jockey (flat):** Nathan Evans, Graham Gibbons, Paul Mulrennan, James Sullivan. **Conditional:** Jake Greenall. **Apprentice:** Danielle Mooney. **Amateur:** Mr H. Bannister, Miss S. Brotherton, Miss J. Coward, Miss Anna Hesketh, Miss Joanna Mason.

---

## 181 MR TIM EASTERBY, Malton

Postal: **Habton Grange, Great Habton, Malton, North Yorkshire, YO17 6TY**
Contacts: **PHONE (01653) 668566 FAX (01653) 668621**
**E-MAIL easterby@btconnect.co.uk WEBSITE www.timeasterby.co.uk**

1 **ANOTHER ROYAL,** 4, b f Byron—Royal Punch **C. H. Stevens**
2 **ARDLUI (IRE),** 7, b g Galileo (IRE)—Epping **C. H. Stevens**
3 **ATTENTION SEAKER,** 5, b m Bollin Eric—Pay Attention **Ryedale Partners No 6**
4 **AZAGAL (IRE),** 4, b f Azamour (IRE)—Brave Madam (IRE) **R. Sidebottom**
5 **BREAKABLE,** 4, ch f Firebreak—Magic Myth (IRE) **Ryedale Partners No 9**
6 **CAPTAIN DUNNE (IRE),** 10, b g Captain Rio—Queen Bodicea (IRE) **Middleham Park Racing XV & Partners**
7 **CHIVERS (IRE),** 4, b g Duke of Marmalade (IRE)—Thara (USA) **C. H. Stevens**
8 **COLOUR OF THE WIND,** 4, gr f Dylan Thomas (IRE)—Makhsusah (IRE) **S. A. Heley**
9 **DANCE KING,** 5, ch g Danehill Dancer (IRE)—One So Wonderful **A. R. Turnbull**
10 **DARK DUNE (IRE),** 7, b g Diamond Green (FR)—Panpipes (USA) **Ryedale Partners No 5**
11 **DEEPSAND (IRE),** 6, br g Footstepsinthesand—Sinamay (USA) **T. J. Hemmings**
12 **DUKE OF YORKSHIRE,** 5, b g Duke of Marmalade (IRE)—Dame Edith (FR) **Mr M. Stewart**
13 **DUTCH BREEZE,** 4, ch g Dutch Art—Oasis Breeze **Mr & Mrs J. D. Cotton**
14 5, B g Kayf Tara—Exclusive Davis (USA)
15 **FAST SHOT,** 7, b g Fasliyev (USA)—Final Pursuit **Ontoawinner 10 & Partner**
16 **FREDDY COOLE,** 5, b g Kayf Tara—Coole Presence (IRE)
17 **GETABUZZ,** 7, b g Beat Hollow—Ailincala (IRE) **Langham Hall Stud Three**
18 **GRAN CANARIA QUEEN,** 6, b br m Compton Place—Ex Mill Lady **Mr M. Gillies**
19 **GRISSOM (IRE),** 9, b g Desert Prince (IRE)—Misty Peak (IRE) **J. F. Bowers**
20 **HAWK HIGH (IRE),** 5, b g High Chaparral (IRE)—Septembers Hawk (IRE) **T. J. Hemmings**
21 **HEROIQUE (IRE),** 4, b f Acclamation—Gay Heroine **Mr K. Nicholson**
22 **JANAAB (IRE),** 5, ch g Nayef (USA)—Mood Indigo (IRE) **Numac Engineering Ltd**
23 **KENNY THE CAPTAIN (IRE),** 4, ch g Captain Rio—Kelso Magic (USA) **Reality Partnerships V**
24 **KING OF THE CELTS (IRE),** 7, b g Celtic Swing—Flamands (IRE) **Mrs B. Oughtred**
25 **MANHATTAN TRANSFER,** 5, b m Central Park (IRE)—Supreme Lady (IRE)
26 **MAPPIN TIME (IRE),** 7, b g Orientate (USA)—Different Story (USA) **P. Baillie**
27 **MAVEN,** 7, b m Doyen (IRE)—Bollin Jeannie **Mrs J. E. Pallister**
28 **MILLY BALOO,** 4, b f Desideratum—Tarabaloo **Mr R. W. Metcalfe**
29 **NO POPPY (IRE),** 7, b m Chineur (FR)—Capetown Girl **J. Musgrave**
30 **OFF ART,** 5, ch g Dutch Art—Off Camera **D. B. Lamplough**
31 **ONE WORD MORE (IRE),** 5, b g Thousand Words—Somoushe (IRE) **Mr M. J. Macleod**
32 **PENNY TARA (IRE),** 5, b m Kayf Tara—Penny Stall
33 **RELIGHT MY FIRE,** 5, ch g Firebreak—Making Music **J. Gill**
34 **RIBBLEHEAD (USA),** 4, b br c Arch (USA)—Moolakaya (FR) **Clipper Group Holdings Ltd**
35 **RIVER BOLLIN,** 5, b g Bollin Eric—Bollin Roberta **C. H. Stevens**
36 **ROYAL PRESERVE,** 4, ch g Duke of Marmalade (IRE)—Castaway Queen (IRE) **A. R. Turnbull**
37 **RUN RUCTIONS RUN (IRE),** 6, b m Westerner—Perfect Prospect (IRE) **T. E. Ford**
38 **SEE THE SUN,** 4, ch g Assertive—Cocabana **C. H. Stevens**

## MR TIM EASTERBY - Continued

**39 SILVERY MOON (IRE),** 8, gr g Verglas (IRE)—Starry Night **C. H. Stevens**
**40 SOUL BROTHER (IRE),** 4, b g Captain Rio—Goodwood March **C. H. Stevens**
**41 SURROUND SOUND,** 5, b g Multiplex—Tintera (IRE) **Mr C. Wilson**
**42 TARA THE TIGER,** 4, b f Kayf Tara—El Tigress (GER) **Reality Partnerships**
**43 TIMONEER (USA),** 5, b br g Elusive Quality (USA)—Gentle Gale (USA) **Mr D. Scott**
**44 TIPTOEAWAY (IRE),** 10, b g Insan (USA)—My Blackbird (IRE) **T. J. Hemmings**
**45 TRUSTAN TIMES (IRE),** 9, b g Heron Island (IRE)—Ballytrustan Maid (IRE) **P Armitage & I Armitage**
**46 WHITE FLAG,** 4, b f Sakhee's Secret—Rainbow Spectrum (FR)

## THREE-YEAR-OLDS

**47 ARRACOURT,** b g Multiplex—Retaliator **W. H. Ponsonby**
**48 BUSHRANGER BAY (IRE),** b g Bushranger (IRE)—Zafaraya (IRE) **Ryedale Partners No 8**
**49 CHOPPY WATER (IRE),** b g Zebedee—Brewing Storm (IRE) **Mr A Kerr & Partner**
**50 CISCO BOY,** b g Paco Boy (IRE)—Miss Wells (IRE) **Ryedale Partners No 7**
**51 DEW POND,** b g Motivator—Rutland Water (IRE)
**52 DON'T TELL ANNIE,** b f Royal Applause—Oasis Breeze **Dale & Ann Wilsdon & Partner**
**53 EYE GLASS (IRE),** b f Intense Focus (USA)—Petite Arvine (USA)
**54 FARRAH'S CHOICE,** b f Equiano (FR)—Esplanade **Middleham Park Racing CIV & Partner**
**55 FATHER BERTIE,** b g Firebreak—Magical Music **Mr J. R. Saville**
**56 HONEYSUCKLE LIL (IRE),** b f Alfred Nobel (IRE)—Twinberry (IRE) **A. R. Turnbull**
**57 LILAC VALE (IRE),** b f Moss Vale (IRE)—Lilac Mist
**58 LLYN,** ch f Dutch Art—Makara **Mr A. Gray**
**59 MATTMU,** b c Indesatchel (IRE)—Katie Boo (IRE) **J. F. Bowers**
**60 MIDNIGHT MOJITO,** b f Azamour (IRE)—Shaken And Stirred **D. A. West**
**61 MISS IVANOVIC (IRE),** br f Captain Rio—Goodwood March **Mrs A. G. Kavanagh**
**62 MOCKINGBIRD HILL,** b g Cockney Rebel (IRE)—Claws **N. A. Jackson**
**63 MULTELLIE,** b g Multiplex—Bollin Nellie **Mr D. Scott**
**64 MYSTIC MIRAAJ,** ch g Iffraaj—Salsa Brava (IRE) **R. Taylor & Mr P. Hebdon**
**65 PACNGO,** b f Paco Boy (IRE)—Orange Pip **D. B. Lamplough**
**66 PENNY ROYALE,** b f Monsieur Bond (IRE)—Royal Punch **C. H. Stevens**
**67 PIXEY PUNK,** gr f Mount Nelson—Mosquera (GER) **Mr J. R. Saville**
**68 RYEDALE MIST,** b f Equiano (FR)—Alhufoof (USA) **Reality Partnerships II**
**69 SAKHEE'S RETURN,** b g Sakhee's Secret—Sofia Royale **Ontoawinner, M Hulin & Partner**
**70 SIGN OF THE TIMES,** b f Medicean—Still Small Voice **J. Shack**
**71 SPECIAL VENTURE (IRE),** b c Azamour (IRE)—La Reine Mambo (USA) **David Scott & Co Ltd & Mr E A Brook**
**72 STORMIN TOM (IRE),** b g Dylan Thomas (IRE)—She Storm (IRE) **Three Jolly Farmers**
**73 UPWARD TREND (IRE),** b g Dark Angel (IRE)—Camassina (IRE) **Mr J. R. Beamson**
**74 WIGGLE,** ch f Dutch Art—Mookhlesa **Lovely Bubbly Racing**
**75 YOUCOULDNTMAKEITUP (IRE),** b f Captain Rio—Miss Donovan **Reality Partnerships III**

## TWO-YEAR-OLDS

**76** B g 11/2 Aussie Rules (USA)—Ailincala (IRE) (Pursuit of Love) **Langham Hall Stud**
**77** B f 24/3 Sakhee's Secret—Atnab (USA) (Riverman (USA)) (9523)
**78 BAZULA (IRE),** b c 18/4 Tagula (IRE)—Lilly Be (IRE) (Titus Livius (FR)) (24761) **G. Horsford**
**79 BEAUTIFUL FIRTH,** b f 15/3 Poet's Voice—Roslea Lady (IRE) (Alhaarth (IRE)) (17000) **R. Sidebottom**
**80** B f 4/4 Lilbourne Lad (IRE)—Beseech (IRE) (Danehill (USA)) (7936)
**81** B f 2/6 Multiplex—Bollin Annabel (King's Theatre (IRE))
**82** B f 7/2 Kheleyf (USA)—Buffy Boo (Agnes World (USA)) (2857)
**83** B f 15/4 Bushranger (IRE)—Cliche (IRE) (Diktat)
**84** B f 17/2 Monsieur Bond (IRE)—Cocabana (Captain Rio) (10000)
**85** B c 21/3 Duke of Marmalade (IRE)—Dayia (IRE) (Act One) (8000)
**86** Br f 14/2 Captain Rio—Delira (IRE) (Namid) (5714) **Rosemary's Racing**
**87** B f 15/3 Makfi—Estephe (IRE) (Sadler's Wells (USA)) (22000)
**88** B f 16/3 Big Bad Bob (IRE)—Express Logic (Air Express (IRE)) (12000)
**89** B c 19/4 Lawman (FR)—Feather Boa (IRE) (Sri Pekan (USA)) (7142)
**90 FIELD OFFICER,** ch c 11/2 Major Cadeaux—Its Another Gift (Primo Dominie) (17142) **Margaret's Partnership**
**91 FLYING PURSUIT,** ch c 6/4 Pastoral Pursuits—
Choisette (Choisir (AUS)) (20000) **Ontoawinner, M Hulin & Partner**
**92** B c 24/4 Captain Rio—Hallucination (IRE) (Last Tycoon) (11507) **Ryedale Partners**
**93** B f 12/2 Sakhee's Secret—Harryana To (Compton Place) (10000)
**94** B f 10/5 Royal Applause—Impetious (Inchinor) (13333)
**95** B f 24/3 Major Cadeaux—Katie Boo (IRE) (Namid) **Jim Bowers**
**96** Ch c 26/1 Sakhee's Secret—Kummel Excess (IRE) (Exceed And Excel (AUS)) (5714)
**97** B f 13/3 Sir Percy—Laverre (IRE) (Noverre (USA)) (2500)
**98** B c 20/3 Frozen Power (IRE)—Liscoa (IRE) (Foxhound (USA)) (25000)

## MR TIM EASTERBY - Continued

99 **MIDNIGHT MALIBU (IRE),** b f 5/3 Poet's Voice—Midnight Martini (Night Shift (USA)) (14285) **D. A. West**
100 B c 15/3 Sakhee's Secret—Montjeu's Melody (IRE) (Montjeu (IRE)) (15238)
101 **MOONLIGHT GIRL (IRE),** ch f 22/3 Arcano (IRE)—Moonlight Red (IRE) (Kheleyf (USA)) (18095) **P. C. J. Bourke**
102 B f 26/3 Approve (IRE)—Ms Cromby (IRE) (Arakan (USA)) (8729) **P. Taylor & Mr R. Hebdon**
103 Ch c 23/4 Assertive—Opopmil (IRE) (Pips Pride) (13333) **A. R. Turnbull**
104 B f 12/4 Bushranger (IRE)—Passi di Danza (IRE) (Bertolini (USA))
105 B f 7/4 Piccolo—Popocatepetl (FR) (Nashwan (USA)) **Jeremy Gompertz**
106 **POPSIES JOY (IRE),** b f 23/4 Alfred Nobel (IRE)—Senzate (Lujain (USA)) (3174) **Reality**
107 B c 25/1 Royal Applause—Poulaine Bleue (Bertolini (USA)) (11428)
108 Ch g 17/4 Pastoral Pursuits—Revue Princess (IRE) (Mull of Kintyre (USA)) (11428) **Alan Heley**
109 **ROCK ON (IRE),** ch c 27/3 Rock of Gibraltar (IRE)—
Spectacular Show (IRE) (Spectrum (IRE)) (40000) **Mrs J. E. Pallister**
110 Ch c 31/3 Approve (IRE)—Rockyriver Girl (IRE) (Rock of Gibraltar (IRE)) (9523)
111 B f 10/4 Piccolo—Rosein (Komaite (USA)) (20000) **Middleham Park Racing XII**
112 B f 21/3 Dutch Art—Royal Punch (Royal Applause) (60000)
113 B c 7/2 Monsieur Bond (IRE)—Sea Flower (IRE) (Acclamation)
114 **SEAPERLE,** b f 30/4 Firebreak—Ocean Grove (IRE) (Fairy King (USA)) (24000) **Bearstone Stud Limited**
115 Gr f 2/4 Sakhee's Secret—Silent Waters (Polish Precedent (USA)) (18000) **R. Taylor & Mr P. Hebdon**
116 **SILVER SANDS (IRE),** gr c 29/3 Zebedee—Eloquent Rose (IRE) (Elnadim (USA)) (28571) **C. H. Stevens**
117 **SILVER SNOW (IRE),** gr c 28/4 Zebedee—Sunrise (IRE) (Sri Pekan (USA)) (16190) **Miss B. C. Duxbury**
118 B c 8/3 Frozen Power (IRE)—Silvertine (IRE) (Alzao (USA)) (15872) **Ryedale no.10**
119 B f 9/2 Royal Applause—Sodashy (IRE) (Noverre (USA)) (3967)
120 **STILL KICKING (IRE),** b c 26/3 Bahamian Bounty—Sister Clement (IRE) (Oasis Dream) (9523) **Norman Jackson**
121 **TARNEND LASS,** b f 22/3 Equiano (FR)—Valjarv (IRE) (Bluebird (USA)) (15238) **Reality Racing**
122 B c 16/3 Art Connoisseur (IRE)—Tarziyma (IRE) (Kalanisi (IRE)) (4761)
123 B f 1/4 Lilbourne Lad (IRE)—Vanozza (FR) (Dylan Thomas (IRE)) (23809)
124 **WITCHKRAFT,** b f 25/4 Firebreak—Night Gypsy (Mind Games) (16000) **Bearstone Stud Limited**
125 **ZEEDA (IRE),** b f 4/3 Zebedee—Beau Petite (Kyllachy) (7142) **Mrs J. P. Connew**

**Other Owners:** Mr Ian Armitage, Mr Peter Armitage, Mr G. Barnard, Mr Peter Botham, Mr Simon Bridge, Mr E. A. Brook, Mrs J. Carnegie, Mr Les Clarke, Mr P. S. Cook, Mr J. D. Cotton, Mrs B. Cotton, Mr Alan D. Crombie, David Scott and Co (Pattern Makers) Ltd, Mr T. D. Easterby, Mr M. H. Easterby, Habton Farms, Mr Philip Hebdon, Mr Alastair Hodge, Mr Mark Hulin, Mr R. Jacobs, Mr Allan Kerr, Mr M. Key, Mr M. J. Lewendon, Mr Robert Lewis, Mrs Jessica Magnier, Mr N. McLaren, Mrs R. Morley, Mr P. E. Nodding, Mr R. Noy, Mr N. J. O'Brien, Mr N. O'Brien, Mr T. S. Palin, Mr A. Parker, Mr M. Pearson, Mr John Preston, Mr M. Prince, Ms M. G. Purkiss, Mr A. H. Raby, Mr A. Reid, Mr R. Riches, Mr E. Surr, Mr R. Taylor (York), Mr David Underwood, Mr D. Wilsdon, Mrs Ann Wilsdon.

**Apprentice:** Rachel Richardson. **Amateur:** Mr W. Easterby.

---

## 182 MR BRIAN ECKLEY, Brecon

Postal: **Closcedi Farm, Llanspyddid, Brecon, Powys, LD3 8NS**
Contacts: **PHONE (01874) 622422 MOBILE (07891) 445409**
**E-MAIL brian.eckley@live.co.uk**

1 **JAUNTY INFLIGHT,** 6, b g Busy Flight—Jaunty Walk **B. J. Eckley**
2 **JAUNTY THOR,** 5, b g Norse Dancer (IRE)—Jaunty Walk **B. J. Eckley**
3 4, B f Revoque (IRE)—Somethingaboutmary (IRE) **B. J. Eckley**
4 5, B m Desert King (IRE)—Sun Bonnet **B. J. Eckley**
5 **SUNSATIONAL GIRL,** 6, ch m Byron—Sun Bonnet **B. J. Eckley**

---

## 183 MR PAT EDDERY, Nether Winchendon

Postal: **Musk Hill Stud, Nether Winchendon, Aylesbury, Buckinghamshire, HP18 0EB**
Contacts: **RACING OFFICE: (01844) 296153 FAX (01844) 290282 MOBILE (07718) 984799**
**E-MAIL info@patedderyracing.com WEBSITE www.patedderyracing.com**

1 **BLACK WIDOW,** 4, b f Bertolini (USA)—Malvadilla (IRE) **P. J. J. Eddery**
2 **EZETIGER,** 5, b g Tiger Hill (IRE)—Guilty Secret (IRE) **Miss E L Owen & P. J. J. Eddery**
3 **GEORDIE MAN,** 5, b h Manduro (GER)—Opening Ceremony (USA) **Mr L. F. Daly**
4 **HINTON ADMIRAL,** 11, b g Spectrum (IRE)—Shawanni **P. J. J. Eddery**
5 **LUTINE CHARLIE (IRE),** 8, b g Kheleyf (USA)—Silvery Halo (USA) **Miss E. L. Owen**

## MR PAT EDDERY - Continued

6 **PASHAN GARH,** 6, b g Anabaa (USA)—Mimisel **Miss E. L. Owen**
7 **RAPID WATER,** 9, b g Anabaa (USA)—Lochsong **Miss E. L. Owen**
8 **STORM HAWK (IRE),** 8, b g Hawk Wing (USA)—Stormy Larissa (IRE) **P. J. J. Eddery**
9 **TWILIGHT ANGEL,** 7, ch m Compton Place—Leaping Flame (USA) **P. J. J. Eddery**
10 **WRENINGHAM,** 10, br g Diktat—Slave To The Rythm (IRE) **Miss E. L. Owen**

### THREE-YEAR-OLDS

11 **ALIDARA (IRE),** ch f Manduro (GER)—Artisia (IRE) **Mr L. F. Daly**
12 **ERTIDAAD (IRE),** b c Kodiac—Little Scotland **Miss E. L. Owen**
13 **ESCALATING,** ch c Three Valleys (USA)—Pure Joy **K. Abdullah**
14 **SUNNY MONDAY,** b c Manduro (GER)—Sunray Superstar **Mr L. F. Daly**

### TWO-YEAR-OLDS

15 B c 23/3 Canford Cliffs (IRE)—April (IRE) (Rock of Gibraltar (IRE)) (15000) **Mr L. F. Daly**
16 Ch c 8/4 Firebreak—La Sorrela (IRE) (Cadeaux Genereux) **P. J. J. Eddery**
17 B c 16/4 Firebreak—Leaping Flame (USA) (Trempolino (USA)) **P. J. J. Eddery**

**Assistant Trainer:** Miss Emma L. Owen (07718984799)

**Jockey (flat):** Stevie Donohoe, Joe Fanning, Tom Queally.

---

**184**

## MR ROBERT EDDERY, Newmarket

Postal: **Robert Eddery Racing, Heyward Place Stables, Hamilton Road, Newmarket, Suffolk, CB8 7JQ**
Contacts: **PHONE (01638) 428001 MOBILE (07938) 898455**
**E-MAIL info@robertedderyracing.com WEBSITE www.robbertedderyracing.com**

1 **BUSH WARRIOR (IRE),** 4, b g Bushranger (IRE)—Lady Corduff (IRE) **Mr I. Anderson & Mr J. Wright**
2 **CRAFTSMANSHIP (FR),** 4, ch c Mastercraftsman (IRE)—Jennie Jerome (IRE) **Trisha Keane & Julia Rayment**
3 **DONNCHA (IRE),** 4, br c Captain Marvelous (IRE)—Seasonal Style (IRE) **Mr D. Bannon**
4 **GRAYLYN RUBY (FR),** 10, b g Limnos (JPN)—Nandi (IRE) **Graham & Lynn Knight**
5 **ISABELLA LIBERTY (FR),** 4, b f Soldier of Fortune (IRE)—Samsa (FR) **Mr E Phillips & Mrs M Mathews**
6 **MISTER MUSIC,** 6, b g Singspiel (IRE)—Sierra **Longview Stud & Bloodstock Ltd**
7 **OLYMNIA,** 4, b f Teofilo (IRE)—Diotima **E. S. Phillips**
8 **RUDI FIVE ONE (FR),** 4, br g American Post—Dansia (GER) **Anderson, Mathews & Kerve**
9 **VASILY,** 7, b h Sadler's Wells (USA)—Red Bloom **Mr D. Bannon**

### THREE-YEAR-OLDS

10 B g Mullionmileanhour (IRE)—Alectrona (FR)
11 **BEACH WALKER,** b f Footstepsinthesand—Danemere (IRE) **Longview Stud & Bloodstock Ltd**
12 **CORNELIOUS (IRE),** b c Cape Cross (IRE)—Fantastic Spring (USA) **Mr D. Bannon**
13 **EAST COAST LADY (IRE),** b f Kodiac—Alexander Anapolis (IRE) **E. Phillips & O. Costello**
14 **FEELING EASY (IRE),** b f Bushranger (IRE)—Easy Feeling (IRE) **Mr E. Phillips & Mrs P. Aitken**
15 **SPORTING BOB,** b c Mawatheeq (USA)—Tanwir **Mrs Pamela Aitken & Mr John Wright**

### TWO-YEAR-OLDS

16 **ADMIRALS CHOICE,** b c 12/3 Mount Nelson—Admirable Spirit (Invincible Spirit (IRE)) **Longview Stud & Bloodstock Ltd**
17 **ARTISTICALLY,** b f 15/4 Holy Roman Emperor (IRE)—Artistry (Night Shift (USA)) **Longview Stud & Bloodstock Ltd**
18 **DIVINE TOUCH,** b f 26/2 Kheleyf (USA)—Easy To Love (USA) (Diesis) (10000) **Mr E. S. Phillips**
19 B f 29/3 Roderic O'Connor (IRE)—Korabushka (Selkirk (USA)) (3500) **Mr D. Bannon**
20 B c 29/3 Rail Link—Millistar (Galileo (IRE)) (17142) **Mr D. Bannon & Mr O. O'Brien**

**Other Owners:** Mrs Pam Aitken, Mr O. Costello, Ms Trisha Keane, Mr G. Knight, Mrs L. C. Knight, Mrs Millicent Mathews, Mr Edwin S. Phillips, Mrs Julia Rayment, Mr John Wright (Norwich).

**Jockey (flat):** Andrea Atzeni.

## 185 MR STUART EDMUNDS, Newport Pagnell

Postal: **Fences Farm, Tyringham, Newport Pagnell, Buckinghamshire, MK16 9EN**
Contacts: **PHONE (01908) 611406 FAX (01908) 611406 MOBILE (07778) 782591**
**E-MAIL Trishandstu@aol.com**

1 **BENEFIT CUT (IRE),** 9, b g Beneficial—I'm Maggy (NZ) **Asphalt Reinforcement Services Ltd**
2 **BONELLI'S WARBLER,** 5, ch m Notnowcato—Cetti's Warbler **Exors of the Late Mrs P. Robeson**
3 **CAROLINA WREN,** 6, b m Sir Harry Lewis (USA)—Wren Warbler **Exors of the Late Mrs P. Robeson**
4 **CLOONACOOL (IRE),** 6, b g Beneficial—Newhall (IRE) **Nick Brown Racing**
5 **DAWN COMMANDER (GER),** 8, gr g Mamool (IRE)—Dark Lady (GER) **Nick Brown Racing**
6 **EREYNA,** 6, gr m Erhaab (USA)—Tereyna **Exors of the Late Mrs P. Robeson**
7 **INCA DOVE,** 6, ch m Sleeping Indian—Stock Dove **Exors of the Late Mrs P. Robeson**
8 **KAYLA,** 5, b m Kayf Tara—Palila **Exors of the Late Mrs P. Robeson**
9 **MAYPOLE LASS,** 5, ch m Halling (USA)—Maigold Lass **Mr B. H. Turner**
10 **NATIVE PRINCESS,** 5, b m Tobougg (IRE)—Forest Pride (IRE) **The Oakley Partnership**
11 **PADDY THE DEEJAY (IRE),** 6, b g Fruits of Love (USA)—Sue Pickering (IRE) **KTDA Partnership**
12 **REYNO,** 7, b g Sleeping Indian—Tereyna **Exors of the Late Mrs P. Robeson**
13 **SAGE GROUSE,** 6, ch m Norse Dancer (IRE)—Hazel Grouse **Exors of the Late Mrs P. Robeson**
14 **SAN TELM (IRE),** 10, b g Oscar (IRE)—Magical Mist (IRE) **The Tyringham Partnership**
15 **SMART EXIT (IRE),** 8, b g Exit To Nowhere (USA)—Navaro (IRE) **The Ravenstone Partnership**

**Other Owners:** Mr D. J. Page, Mrs C. Page.

## 186 MR GORDON EDWARDS, Minehead

Postal: **Summering, Wheddon Cross, Minehead, Somerset, TA24 7AT**
Contacts: **PHONE (01643) 831549 FAX (01643) 831549 MOBILE (07970) 059297**
**E-MAIL angela@edwards3212.fsnet.co.uk**

1 **BRIEFCASE (IRE),** 10, b g Witness Box (USA)—Another Tycoon (IRE) **G. F. Edwards**
2 **SHANANN STAR (IRE),** 9, br m Anshan—Baile An Droichid (IRE) **G. F. Edwards**
3 **SUPREME DANEHILL (IRE),** 7, b g Indian Danehill (IRE)—Monte Rosa (IRE) **G. F. Edwards**

**Amateur:** Mr D. Edwards.

## 187 MR GORDON ELLIOTT, Co. Meath

Postal: **Cullentra House, Longwood, Co. Meath, Ireland**
Contacts: **PHONE (00353) 46 9555051 MOBILE (00353) 86 2495453**
**E-MAIL zoe@gordonelliottracing.com WEBSITE www.gordonelliottracing.com**

1 **ALTIEPIX (FR),** 5, ch g Fragrant Mix (IRE)—Naltiepy (FR) **Gigginstown House Stud**
2 **ANTILOPE DU SEUIL (FR),** 5, b m Alberto Giacometti (IRE)—Sweet Laly (FR) **Mr S. Munir & Mr I. Souede**
3 **ARZEMBOUY PREMIER (FR),** 5, b g Lavirco (GER)—Laurence (FR) **Mr S. Munir & Mr I. Souede**
4 **BALBIR DU MATHAN (FR),** 6, b br g Saint des Saints (FR)—Jeapano (FR) **Mr B. Connell**
5 **BALTAZAR D'ALLIER (FR),** 4, b br g Malinas (GER)—Kinoise d'allier (FR) **Mr Chris Donnelly**
6 **BE SEEING YOU,** 4, ch g Medicean—Oshiponga **Call It What You Like Syndicate**
7 **BONDAGE (IRE),** 8, b g Whipper (USA)—Shamah **Mr Tom O'Sullivan**
8 **CANOVA (IRE),** 4, ch g Art Connoisseur (IRE)—Rain Dancer (IRE) **Newcote Services Ltd**
9 **CAPE GLORY (IRE),** 5, b g Cape Cross (IRE)—Array of Stars (IRE) **Gigginstown House Stud**
10 **CAPTAIN VON TRAPPE (IRE),** 6, b g Germany (USA)—Culmore Native (IRE) **Gigginstown House Stud**
11 **CARRIG CATHAL,** 4, b g Fair Mix (IRE)—Blackwater Bay (IRE) **Mrs A. Roache**
12 **CAUSE OF CAUSES (USA),** 7, b g Dynaformer (USA)—Angel In My Heart (FR) **Mr John P. McManus**
13 **CHAMPIONE (IRE),** 5, b h Tikkanen (USA)—Star Trix (IRE) **Mollys Syndicate**
14 **CHATHAM HOUSE RULE,** 4, gr c Authorized (IRE)—Cozy Maria (USA) **Gigginstown House Stud**
15 **CLARCAM (FR),** 5, b g Califet (FR)—Rose Beryl (FR) **Gigginstown House Stud**
16 **CLINTON HILL (IRE),** 4, b g Flemensfirth (USA)—Smooching (IRE) **Mrs A. Roche**
17 **COGRYHILL (IRE),** 5, b g Presenting—Rare Gesture (IRE) **Gigginstown House Stud**
18 **CREDULOUS (IRE),** 4, ch g Jeremy (USA)—Moon Legend (USA) **Gigginstown House Stud**
19 **CURRENT EXCHANGE (IRE),** 10, ch g Beneficial—Musical Millie (IRE) **Kaniz Bloodstock Investments Ltd**
20 **DALLAS COWBOY (IRE),** 5, b g Beneficial—Watson River (IRE) **Gigginstown House Stud**
21 **DEFINITE ANSWER (IRE),** 7, b br g Definite Article—Wilderness Fox (IRE) **Mr P. Fleming**
22 **DELEGATE,** 5, ch g Robin des Champs (FR)—As You Leave (FR) **Gigginstown House Stud**
23 **DELVILLE WOOD (IRE),** 5, b g Winged Love (IRE)—Golden Alliance (IRE) **Mr R. Pugh**
24 **DERBYSHIRE (IRE),** 4, b g Green Tune (USA)—Statia (FR) **Gigginstown House Stud**

## MR GORDON ELLIOTT - Continued

25 **DESERTMORE STREAM (IRE),** 7, b g Celtic Swing—Another Cross (FR) **Gigginstown House Stud**
26 **DON COSSACK (GER),** 8, br g Sholokhov (IRE)—Depeche Toi (GER) **Gigginstown House Stud**
27 **DOUBLE IRISH (IRE),** 7, b g King's Theatre (IRE)—Palesa's Legacy (IRE) **Mr B. Connell**
28 **DUTCHESOFRATHMOLYN (IRE),** 6, b m Kutub (IRE)—Greenfieldflyer (IRE) **K. R. W. Douglas**
29 **EBONY ROC (IRE),** 5, br g Shirocco (GER)—Chia Laguna (IRE) **Mr G. Elliott**
30 **ESHTIAAL (USA),** 5, b g Dynaformer (USA)—Enfiraaj (USA) **Mr W. McKay & Mr W. Salthouse**
31 **FORT SMITH (IRE),** 6, b g Presenting—Land of Honour **Gigginstown House Stud**
32 **FREE EXPRESSION (IRE),** 6, b g Germany (USA)—Create A Storm (IRE) **Mr John P. McManus**
33 **FROM FROST,** 4, b g Nayef (USA)—Salutare (IRE) **Mr C. Donnelly**
34 **GENERAL PRINCIPLE (IRE),** 6, b g Gold Well—How Provincial (IRE) **Gigginstown House Stud**
35 **HALLING'S TREASURE,** 5, ch g Halling (USA)—Perfect Treasure (IRE) **Gigginstown House Stud**
36 **HARRY'S SUMMER (USA),** 4, b br g Roman Ruler (USA)—Magnificent Lady (USA) **Mr G. Elliott**
37 **HIGH EXPECTATIONS (FR),** 4, b g High Rock (IRE)—Tashifiya (FR) **Mr Martin Wasylocha**
38 **HOSTILE FIRE (IRE),** 4, b g Iffraaj—Royal Esteem **Mrs P. Sloan**
39 **IBSEN (IRE),** 6, b g Dubawi (IRE)—Really (IRE) **Miss A. F. J. Bowles**
40 **JETSTREAM JACK (IRE),** 5, b g Beneficial—Westgrove Berry (IRE) **Mrs Diana L. Whateley**
41 **JOHN MONASH,** 4, b g Kayf Tara—Miss Invincible **S. McGregor**
42 **JUST WILLIAM (IRE),** 7, b g Bandari (IRE)—Dark Horizon (IRE) **Mrs Jayne McConnell**
43 **LORD SCOUNDREL (IRE),** 6, b g Presenting—Noble Choice **Gigginstown House Stud**
44 **LUDDSDENENE (IRE),** 10, b g Beneficial—Kilcowan (IRE) **Mr Tom Howley**
45 **MALA BEACH (IRE),** 7, b g Beneficial—Peppardstown (IRE) **Mr Chris Jones**
46 **METAURUS (IRE),** 6, b g Catcher In The Rye (IRE)—Pepsi Starlet (IRE) **Gigginstown House Stud**
47 **MOONSHINE LAD (IRE),** 7, b g Milan—Parsons Term (IRE) **Mr Brendan Scully**
48 **MR LANDO,** 6, b g Shirocco (GER)—Capitana (GER) **Mr Oliver Murphy**
49 **MUSTADRIK (USA),** 4, b g Jazil (USA)—Uroobah (USA) **Mr Richard Gilbert**
50 **MYSTICAL DREAMER (IRE),** 6, ch g Flemensfirth (USA)—Voodoo Magic (GER) **Gigginstown House Stud**
51 **MYZTIQUE (IRE),** 5, b m High Chaparral (IRE)—Lady Rene (IRE) **Mr M. McNally**
52 **NATIONAL SERVICE (USA),** 4, b g War Chant (USA)—Cotton Club Ballet (USA) **Mr Tom Howley**
53 **NO MORE HEROES (IRE),** 6, br g Presenting—What A Breeze (IRE) **Gigginstown House Stud**
54 **NOBLE ENDEAVOR (IRE),** 6, b g Flemensfirth (USA)—Old Moon (IRE) **Mr Chris Jones**
55 **OFFICER CADET,** 6, b g Kayf Tara—Miss Invincible **Gigginstown House Stud**
56 **OSCAR BARTON (IRE),** 10, b g Oscar (IRE)—I Can Imagine (IRE) **Kaniz Bloodstock Investments Ltd**
57 **REALT MOR (IRE),** 10, b g Beneficial—Suez Canal (FR) **Mrs P. Sloan**
58 **RIVERSIDE CITY (IRE),** 6, ch g Presenting—Blazing Sky (IRE) **Mr John P. McManus**
59 **ROBIN THYME (IRE),** 5, b g Robin des Champs (FR)—
Boragh Thyme (IRE) **M. M. Sammon, M. A. Sammon, B. K. Fitzpatrick & R. Crean**
60 **ROCKY WEDNESDAY (IRE),** 8, b g Rock of Gibraltar (IRE)—Tuesday Morning **Gigginstown House Stud**
61 **ROI DU MEE (FR),** 10, b g Lavirco (GER)—British Nellerie (FR) **Gigginstown House Stud**
62 **ROLL IT OUT (IRE),** 6, b g Kayf Tara—Liss A Chroi (IRE) **Mr John P. McManus**
63 **ROMAN GOLD (IRE),** 5, ch g Beneficial—Another Burden **Gigginstown House Stud**
64 **ROMEU HAS (FR),** 4, b g Martaline—Royale Lombok (FR) **Gigginstown House Stud**
65 **RUSSIAN REGENT (IRE),** 11, b g Moscow Society (USA)—Micro Villa (IRE) **Mr James J. Reilly**
66 **SANDUSKY,** 7, b g Tiger Hill (IRE)—Red Carnation (IRE) **Mr W. McKay**
67 **SERGEANT BRODY,** 4, ch g Black Sam Bellamy (IRE)—Ardent Bride **Mr G. Elliott & Mr E. O'Leary**
68 **SHADOW CATCHER,** 7, ch g Haafhd—Unchain My Heart **Mrs P. Sloan**
69 **SKILLED,** 4, b g Mastercraftsman (IRE)—Treacle (USA) **Mrs A. Roche & Mr J. Power**
70 **SNOQUALMIE CHIEF,** 5, b g Montjeu (IRE)—Seattle Ribbon (USA) **Positively Syndicate**
71 **SOWEHEARD (IRE),** 8, ch g Accordion—Go Get Her (IRE) **Mr J. A. Fogarty**
72 **SPACE CADET (IRE),** 5, b g Flemensfirth (USA)—Shuil A Hocht (IRE) **Mr C. Jones**
73 **SPEED DEMON (IRE),** 6, b g Beneficial—Brierfield Lady (IRE) **Gigginstown House Stud**
74 **SWANTYKAY (IRE),** 6, b g Darsi (FR)—Glamorous Leader (IRE) **Mr Paul Holden**
75 **TAJSEER (USA),** 4, b br g Medaglia d'Oro (USA)—
Lear's Princess (USA) **J. Lynch, T. Howley, A. O'Ryan, G. Elliott**
76 **THE DRONE (IRE),** 4, b br g Mahler—Liberess (IRE) **Mr G. Elliott**
77 **THE SCOURGE (IRE),** 4, b g Whipper (USA)—House Rebel (IRE) **Barstool Prophets Syndicate**
78 **THE STORYTELLER (IRE),** 4, ch g Shantou (USA)—Bally Bolshoi (IRE) **Mrs P. Sloan**
79 **THUNDER ZONE,** 4, gr g Shamardal (USA)—Mussoorie (FR) **Gigginstown House Stud**
80 **TIGER ROLL (IRE),** 5, b g Authorized (IRE)—Swiss Roll (IRE) **Gigginstown House Stud**
81 **TIME FOR A PINT (IRE),** 7, b g Artan (IRE)—Bobazure (IRE) **Mr P. Beirne**
82 **TOMBSTONE (IRE),** 5, ch g Robin des Champs (FR)—Connaught Hall (IRE) **Gigginstown House Stud**
83 **TYCOON PRINCE (IRE),** 5, b g Trans Island—Downtown Train (IRE) **Gigginstown House Stud**
84 **UCELLO CONTI (FR),** 7, b g Martaline—Gazelle Lulu (FR) **Mr S. Munir**
85 **ULTIMATE HORSEMAN (IRE),** 5, b g Kalanisi (IRE)—Dawn's Double (IRE) **Gigginstown House Stud**
86 **UTMOST ZEAL (IRE),** 5, b g Big Bad Bob (IRE)—Dusseldorf (IRE) **Gigginstown House Stud**
87 **VALMY BAIE (FR),** 6, b g Crillon (FR)—Abondance (FR) **Mr B. Connell**

## MR GORDON ELLIOTT - Continued

88 **VASCO DU MEE (FR),** 6, b g Goldneyev (USA)—British Nellerie (FR) **Mr S. McAuley**
89 **VERCINGETORIX (IRE),** 4, b c Dylan Thomas (IRE)—Great Artist (FR) **Mr S. Munir & Mr I. Souede**
90 **WHISTLE DIXIE (IRE),** 5, b m Kayf Tara—Fairy Blaze (IRE) **Gigginstown House Stud**
91 **ZANOUSKA (USA),** 4, b f Bernardini (USA)—Zanoubia (USA) **Mr Chris Donnelly**

### THREE-YEAR-OLDS

92 **BOOTSANDCATS (IRE),** ch c Approve (IRE)—Aquiform **Mr G. Elliott**

**Assistant Trainer:** Oliver Murphy

**Jockey (NH):** Paul Carberry, Davy Condon. **Conditional:** Danny Benson, Luke Dempsey, Kevin Sexton, John Winston. **Amateur:** Mr Barry Browne, Miss Nina Carberry, Mr Stevie Clements, Mr Jamie Codd, Miss Lisa O'Neill.

---

## 188 MISS JOEY ELLIS, Newmarket

Postal: **Georgia House Stud, Bradley Road, Burrough Green, Newmarket, Suffolk, CB8 9NH**
Contacts: **PHONE (07827) 316360**
**E-MAIL georgiahousestud@live.co.uk WEBSITE www.joeyellisracing.co.uk**

1 **ERTIKAAN,** 8, b g Oasis Dream—Aunty Mary
2 **QUEEN'S ESTATE (GER),** 6, b g Hurricane Run (IRE)—Questabelle **Mrs A. B. Ellis**
3 **ROYAL CAPER,** 5, b g Royal Applause—Ukraine (IRE) **Mrs A. B. Ellis**
4 **SHAHRAZAD (IRE),** 6, b m Cape Cross (IRE)—Khulasah (IRE) **Mr L. J. Doolan**
5 **SILVER SECRET,** 4, gr g Moss Vale (IRE)—Alphilda **Mrs A. B. Ellis**

### THREE-YEAR-OLDS

6 **CELESTIAL VISION (USA),** b g Henrythenavigator (USA)—Damini (USA) **Mrs A. B. Ellis**

**Assistant Trainer:** Johnny Dekeyser

**Amateur:** Miss Joey Ellis.

---

## 189 MR BRIAN ELLISON, Malton

Postal: **Spring Cottage Stables, Langton Road, Norton, Malton, North Yorkshire, YO17 9PY**
Contacts: **OFFICE (01653) 690004 FAX (01653) 690008 MOBILE (07785) 747426**
**E-MAIL office@brianellisonracing.co.uk WEBSITE www.brianellisonracing.co.uk**

1 **ALASKAN BULLET (IRE),** 6, b g Kodiac—Czars Princess (IRE) **Racing Management & Training Ltd**
2 **ALMUHEET,** 4, b g Dansili—Arwaah (IRE) **Middleham Park Racing XXV & Partner**
3 **AMAZE,** 7, ch g Pivotal—Dazzle **A Farrell, A Williamson, H Lynn**
4 **ANNOUNCEMENT,** 4, ch f Proclamation (IRE)—Anapola (GER) **OC Racing Carrick Evans O'Shea & Rooney**
5 **APTERIX (FR),** 5, b g Day Flight—Ohe Les Aulmes (FR) **P. J. Martin**
6 **AUTUN (USA),** 5, b g Empire Maker (USA)—Sense of Joy **P. J. Martin**
7 **BALTY BOYS (IRE),** 6, b g Cape Cross (IRE)—Chatham Islands (USA) **Koo's Racing Club, Carr & Jacobs**
8 **BAR DE LIGNE (FR),** 9, b g Martaline—Treekle Toffee (FR) **P. J. Martin**
9 **BARAWEEZ (IRE),** 5, b g Cape Cross (IRE)—Aquarelle Bleue **A. R. Barnes**
10 **BEN CEE PEE M (IRE),** 10, ch g Beneficial—Supreme Magical **CPM Group Limited**
11 **BLUE BULLET (IRE),** 5, b g Red Clubs (IRE)—Blue Holly (IRE) **Mrs C. L. Ellison**
12 **BOTHY,** 9, ch g Pivotal—Villa Carlotta **Dan Gilbert & Jessica Bell**
13 **BUTHELEZI (USA),** 7, b g Dynaformer (USA)—Ntombi (USA) **Westbourne Racing Club 1 & Brian Ellison**
14 **CAPELLANUS (IRE),** 9, b g Montjeu (IRE)—Secret Dream (IRE) **Mrs C. L. Ellison**
15 **CARTHAGE (IRE),** 4, b g Mastercraftsman (IRE)—Pitrizzia **D Gilbert, M Lawrence, A Bruce**
16 **COME ON SUNSHINE,** 4, b g Authorized (IRE)—Tagula Sunrise (IRE) **Mr S Oldroyd & Brian Ellison**
17 **CONQUISTO,** 10, ch g Hernando (FR)—Seal Indigo (IRE) **P. J. Martin**
18 **DEBIT,** 4, b g Pivotal—Silver Kestrel (USA) **P Alderson, D Burke, M Francis**
19 **DEFINITLY RED (IRE),** 6, ch g Definite Article—The Red Wench (IRE) **P. J. Martin**
20 **DREAM WALKER (FR),** 6, gr g Gold Away (IRE)—Minnie's Mystery (FR) **Mr K. Brown**
21 **DUSKY BOB (IRE),** 10, br g Bob Back (USA)—Sunsets Girl (IRE) **Mr D. R. Gilbert**
22 **ECHO OF LIGHTNING,** 5, b g Echo of Light—Classic Lass **Victoria Greetham & Emily Beasley**
23 **EDGE OF SANITY (IRE),** 6, b h Invincible Spirit (IRE)—Saor Sinn (IRE) **Mr R. D. Rainey**
24 **EL MASSIVO (IRE),** 5, b g Authorized (IRE)—Umthoulah (IRE) **D Gilbert, M Lawrence, A Bruce**
25 **FILM DIRECTOR (IRE),** 7, b g Tiger Hill (IRE)—Stage Manner **P. J. Martin**
26 **FIVE IN A ROW (IRE),** 7, ch g Blueprint (IRE)—Ela Plaisir (IRE) **P. J. Martin**
27 **FLEET DAWN,** 9, b g Polish Precedent (USA)—Wychnor Dawn (IRE) **Prism Bloodstock**

## MR BRIAN ELLISON - Continued

28 **FULL DAY,** 4, ch f Champs Elysees—Capistrano Day (USA) **Mr D. R. Gilbert**
29 **GEORGE FERNBECK,** 7, ch g Java Gold (USA)—Burmese Days **Racing Management & Training Ltd**
30 **GONE FOREVER,** 5, b g Quest For Fame—Erudite **P. J. Martin**
31 **HARTFORD STARTS (IRE),** 5, b g Chineur (FR)—Desert Design **Mr K. Brown**
32 **HEAD OF THE CLASS (IRE),** 6, ch g Flemensfirth (USA)—Dinner At One (IRE) **Koo's Racing Club**
33 **HELLO BEAUTIFUL (IRE),** 4, ch f Captain Rio—Tekhania (IRE) **Mr N. Allenby**
34 **HERDSMAN (IRE),** 10, b g Flemensfirth (USA)—My Sunny South **D Gilbert, M Lawrence, A Bruce**
35 **HERE FOR GOOD (IRE),** 4, b g Aqlaam—North East Bay (USA) **Middleham Park Racing LXXII**
36 **ICE 'N' EASY (IRE),** 9, b g Dushyantor (USA)—Glacial Valley (IRE) **Koo's Racing Club**
37 **IT'S A MANS WORLD,** 9, b g Kyllachy—Exhibitor (USA) **David Foster & Brian Ellison**
38 **JAC THE LEGEND,** 6, b g Midnight Legend—Sky Burst **P. J. Martin**
39 **JIMMY CRACKLE (IRE),** 4, b g Intense Focus (USA)—Slieve **Mrs J. A. Martin**
40 **JOYFUL SOUND (IRE),** 7, b g Acclamation—Eman's Joy **Mr & Mrs E. J. Dolan-Abrahams**
41 **KNIGHTLY ESCAPADE,** 7, ch g Sakhee (USA)—Queen of Iceni **Mrs J. A. Martin**
42 **LAIKA,** 6, b m Rail Link—Space Quest **M Khan X 2 & Brian Ellison**
43 **LLANARMON LAD (IRE),** 6, b g Red Clubs (IRE)—Blue Crystal (IRE) **Middleham Park Racing XLIII & Partner**
44 **LUCKY CODY (IRE),** 6, b g Blueprint (IRE)—Ware Vic (IRE) **Mike & Eileen Newbould**
45 **MAGIC SKYLINE (IRE),** 5, b m Refuse To Bend (IRE)—Grecian Air (FR) **Mike & Eileen Newbould**
46 **MANHATTAN SWING (IRE),** 5, b g Invincible Spirit (IRE)—Bluebell Park (USA) **Mrs J. A. Martin**
47 **MARCH SEVENTEENTH (IRE),** 7, br g Flemensfirth (USA)—Palesa Accord (IRE) **Ms Z. Hatcher**
48 **MASHAARI (IRE),** 6, b g Monsun (GER)—Thakafaat (IRE) **P. J. Martin**
49 **MASIRANN (IRE),** 7, b g Tiger Hill (IRE)—Masilia (IRE) **Mike & Eileen Newbould**
50 **MAZURI COWBOY (IRE),** 10, b g Pilsudski (IRE)—Kabale (IRE) **Mr P. Holden**
51 **MIDNIGHT GAME,** 8, b g Montjeu (IRE)—Midnight Angel (GER) **Mrs J. A. Martin**
52 **MIXED MESSAGE (IRE),** 5, b m Kodiac—Berenica (IRE) **W. I. Bloomfield**
53 **MON BRAV,** 8, b g Sampower Star—Danehill Princess (IRE) **Koo's Racing Club**
54 **MONSEA (IRE),** 4, gr c Manduro (GER)—Sea Drift (FR) **Middleham Park Racing CVIII & B Ellison**
55 **MONTEFELTRO,** 7, ch g Medicean—Bustling **D Gilbert, M Lawrence, A Bruce**
56 **MOYODE WOOD,** 10, b g Overbury (IRE)—Country Choice (IRE) **Mr D. Foster**
57 **MUSICAL MOLLY (IRE),** 4, gr f Mastercraftsman (IRE)—Park Approach (IRE) **Mrs J. A. Martin**
58 **POLSKI MAX,** 5, b g Kyllachy—Quadrophenia **Market Avenue Racing & Tremousser**
59 **POWERFUL AMBITION (IRE),** 9, b g Bob Back (USA)—Native Shore (IRE) **Koo's Racing Club**
60 **POWERSTOWN DREAMS (IRE),** 6, b g Brian Boru—Our Idol (IRE) **P. J. Martin**
61 **PRESENTED (IRE),** 8, ch g Presenting—Rustic Court (IRE) **Miss C. A. Carr**
62 **RACING EUROPE (IRE),** 6, b g Kayf Tara—Titanic Quarter (IRE) **P. J. Martin**
63 **RED INCA,** 7, ch g Pivotal—Magicalmysterykate (USA) **D Gilbert, M Lawrence, A Bruce**
64 **RELIC ROCK (IRE),** 7, b g Bienamado (USA)—Nighty Bless (IRE) **P. J. Martin**
65 **SADDLERS DEAL (IRE),** 10, b g Saddlers' Hall (IRE)—Native Deal (IRE) **Ms Y Lowe & Brian Ellison**
66 **SAMTU (IRE),** 4, b c Teofilo (IRE)—Samdaniya **Mr C. Buckingham**
67 **SAND BLAST,** 4, b g Oasis Dream—New Orchid (USA) **D Standring, T Langley & WRS**
68 **SAPTAPADI (IRE),** 9, ch g Indian Ridge—Olympienne (IRE) **Koo's Racing Club**
69 **SEAMOUR (IRE),** 4, b g Azamour (IRE)—Chifney Rush (IRE) **P. J. Martin**
70 **SERENITY NOW (IRE),** 7, b g Key of Luck (USA)—Imdina (IRE) **Mr J. M. Basquill**
71 **SHRAPNEL (IRE),** 9, b br g Flemensfirth (USA)—Victoria Theatre (IRE) **Brian Ellison**
72 **SOUDAIN (FR),** 9, ch g Dom Alco (FR)—Ebene d'avril (FR) **P. J. Martin**
73 **SOUL INTENT (IRE),** 5, b h Galileo (IRE)—Flamingo Guitar (USA) **The Soul Intentions**
74 **STREETS OF NEWYORK,** 8, b g Dalakhani (IRE)—Minute Waltz **Koo's Racing Club**
75 **TEENAGE DREAM (IRE),** 7, b g Antonius Pius (USA)—Lucayan Star (IRE) **Market Avenue Racing Club Ltd**
76 **THE GREY TAYLOR (IRE),** 6, gr g Royal Anthem (USA)—Penny Tan (IRE) **P. J. Martin**
77 **TOP NOTCH TONTO (IRE),** 5, ch g Thousand Words—Elite Hope (USA) **Mr K. Brown**
78 **TOP OF THE GLAS (IRE),** 4, gr g Verglas (IRE)—Fury Dance (USA) **Market Avenue Racing Club Ltd**
79 **TOTALIZE,** 6, b g Authorized (IRE)—You Too **D Gilbert, M Lawrence, A Bruce**
80 **TWO MOONS,** 5, b g Echo of Light—Forever Loved **B. Dunn**
81 **TY GWR,** 6, b g Echo of Light—House Maiden (IRE) **Kevin Corcoran Aaron Pierce Chris Weare**
82 **ULTIMATE,** 9, b g Anabaa (USA)—Nirvana **Mr D. R. Gilbert**
83 **VIVA COLONIA (IRE),** 10, ch g Traditionally (USA)—Ansariya (USA) **Bolingbroke Racing, Mersey Racing**
84 **VODKA WELLS (FR),** 5, b g Irish Wells (FR)—Kahipiroska (FR) **Acorn Partners, Mike & Eileen Newbould**
85 **YORKIST (IRE),** 7, ch g Urban Ocean (FR)—Kilbarry Demon (IRE) **Mike & Eileen Newbould**
86 **ZAIDIYN (FR),** 5, b g Zamindar (USA)—Zainta (IRE) **P. J. Martin**
87 **ZAMRA (IRE),** 4, b f Azamour (IRE)—Deauville Vision (IRE) **Middleham Park Racing XXVI & Partner**
88 **ZELDINA,** 5, ch m Mount Nelson—Tetravella (IRE) **Mr S. L. Catchpole & Mr K. Hanson**

## THREE-YEAR-OLDS

89 **ACE OF MARMALADE (IRE),** b g Duke of Marmalade (IRE)—Pharapache (USA) **Mrs J. A. Martin**
90 **AMERICAN HUSTLE (IRE),** b f Jeremy (USA)—Love In May (IRE) **Market Avenue Racing Club Ltd**

## MR BRIAN ELLISON - Continued

91 **ART WORLD (IRE),** b g Art Connoisseur (IRE)—Human Touch **Brian Ellison**
92 **BOOLASS (IRE),** b f Bushranger (IRE)—Silent Secret (IRE) **Mrs J. A. Martin**
93 **CABELO (IRE),** b f Azamour (IRE)—Fringe **Julie & Keith Hanson**
94 **CANNY KOOL,** b g Kheleyf (USA)—Kool Acclaim **Market Avenue Racing Club Ltd**
95 **DOMINADA (IRE),** b c Mastercraftsman (IRE)—Red Blossom (USA) **Julie & Keith Hanson**
96 **EASTERN RACER (IRE),** b g Bushranger (IRE)—Queen Cobra (IRE) **Mrs J. A. Martin**
97 **GERRY THE GLOVER (IRE),** b g Approve (IRE)—Umlani (IRE) **Mrs J. A. Martin**
98 **INVINCIBLE WISH (IRE),** b g Vale of York (IRE)—Moonlight Wish (IRE) **Dan Gilbert & Kristian Strangeway**
99 **MAKE ON MADAM (IRE),** b f Captain Rio—Rye (IRE) **Mr K. Brown**
100 **MYBOYDANIEL,** b g Myboycharlie (IRE)—Priti Fabulous (IRE) **Miss Y. Lowe**
101 **NORTHGATE LAD (IRE),** gr g Dark Angel (IRE)—Canosa (IRE) **Mrs J. A. Martin**
102 **OFF THE SCALE (IRE),** b g Strategic Prince—Vanilla Delight (IRE) **J. Wade**
103 **PENNY BOO (IRE),** b f Acclamation—Daqtora **Mrs J. A. Martin**
104 **PERCY'S LASS,** gr f Sir Percy—Brave Mave **CPM Group Limited**
105 **SECRET OF DUBAI,** ch f Sakhee's Secret—Dubai Legend **D. & S. L. Tanker Transport Limited**
106 **SILVER GLAZE (IRE),** gr g Verglas (IRE)—Tullawadgeen (IRE) **Mrs J. A. Martin**
107 **SIR KELTIC BLUE,** b g Sir Percy—Bougainvilia (IRE) **Brian Dunn & Michael Beaumont**
108 **STAR ASCENDING (IRE),** ch g Thousand Words—Sakaka **Mr K. Brown**
109 **SWEET MISSI (IRE),** b f Thousand Words—Touch And Love (IRE) **Mr K. Brown**

### TWO-YEAR-OLDS

**110** Ch f 4/4 Haafhd—Ananda Kanda (USA) (Hero's Tribute (USA))
**111** B f 6/3 Approve (IRE)—Bokhara Silk (IRE) (Barathea (IRE)) (4761) **Andy Farrell & Brian Ellison**
**112** B c 16/4 Canford Cliffs (IRE)—Chatham Islands (USA) (Elusive Quality (USA)) (15872) **Koo's Racing Club**
**113** B g 20/4 Kheleyf (USA)—Crozon (Peintre Celebre (USA)) (26190) **A. R. Barnes**
**114** Ch f 11/2 Starspangledbanner (AUS)—Esuvia (IRE) (Whipper (USA)) (17460) **Brian Ellison**
**115** Gr f 22/4 Clodovil (IRE)—Fishy (Irish River (FR)) (10317) **Brian Ellison**
**116 G'DAY AUSSIE,** b c 1/5 Aussie Rules (USA)—Moi Aussi (USA) (Mt Livermore (USA)) (31745) **Mrs J. A. Martin**
**117 GENERAL ALEXANDER (IRE),** gr c 12/2 Zebedee—
Alexander Express (IRE) (Sri Pekan (USA)) (28571) **Mrs J. A. Martin**
**118** B c 21/3 Holy Roman Emperor (IRE)—Goslar (In The Wings) (14285) **Brian Ellison**
**119** B f 1/4 Lilbourne Lad (IRE)—Kiralik (Efisio) (9523) **Mr S. Laffan**
**120** Br f 15/3 Big Bad Bob (IRE)—Kristal Xenia (IRE) (Xaar) (20634) **M Khan X2**
**121** B f 11/2 Monsieur Bond (IRE)—Lily Lenor (IRE) (Bertolini (USA)) **Brian Ellison**
**122** Br f 22/4 Big Bad Bob (IRE)—Montbretia (Montjeu (IRE)) (31745) **M Khan X2**
**123 MR MORSE,** b ro c 19/5 Hellvelyn—Songsheet (Dominion) (32380) **Mrs J. A. Martin**
**124 ROMANTIC APPROACH (IRE),** ch c 7/5 New Approach (IRE)—
Park Romance (IRE) (Dr Fong (USA)) (23809) **Mrs J A Martin & Mrs C L Ellison**
**125** B c 3/5 Tagula (IRE)—Star Lodge (Grand Lodge (USA)) (7142) **Mr K. Brown**
**126** B g 6/5 Misu Bond (IRE)—Striking Cat (Striking Ambition) **Mrs C. L. Ellison**
**127 YORK ROSE,** b f 27/1 Vale of York (IRE)—Desertion (IRE) (Danehill (USA)) (16190) **Mrs J. A. Martin**
**128 ZEBEDAIOS (IRE),** b c 12/4 Zebedee—Refuse To Give Up (IRE) (Refuse To Bend (IRE)) (76190) **Mrs J. A. Martin**

**Other Owners:** P. S. Alderson, M. J. Beadle, Mrs E. Beasley, Mr M. Beaumont, Miss J. J. Bell, L. A. Bolingbroke, Mr A. J. Bonarius, Mr N. J. Bonarius, D. J. Burke, S. Cannon, A. Carr, Mr M. Carrick, Mr S. L. Catchpole, K. J. Corcoran, Mrs P. E. Dolan-Abrahams, E. J. Dolan-Abrahams, Mr J. G. Evans, Mr A. S. Farrell, Mr M. R. Francis, Mr N. Gravett, Miss V. Greetham, Mr D. P. Grundy, Mr D. J. Haddrell, Mr K. Hanson, Mrs J. Hanson, J. J. Hathorn, Mrs F. K. Hathorn, Mr W. D. Hawkes, Mrs M. C. Jacobs, R. H. Jennings, Mr M. Jones, M. Khan, M. Khan, Mr T. A. Langley, Mr M. Lawrence, Mr H. J. Lynn, J. M. Newbould, Mrs E. E. Newbould, Mr A. Nichol, Mr R. P. O'Donnell, Mr J. O'Shea, S. P. Oldroyd, T. S. Palin, Mr J. Parker, Mr A. T. Pierce, Mr J. V. Pierce, M. Prince, Mr W. Rooney, Mr D. M. Standring, Mr K. J. Strangeway, Mr M. R. Turner, Mrs J. Ward, Mr C. E. Weare, Westbourne Consultants Ltd, A. S. Williamson.

**Assistant Trainer:** Jessica Bell, Mobile (07939) 480860

**Jockey (flat):** Tom Eaves, Paul Pickard, Dale Swift. **Jockey (NH):** Danny Cook. **Conditional:** Craig Gallagher, Garry Lavery, Nathan Moscrop. **Apprentice:** Megan Carberry. **Amateur:** Mr John Willey, Miss Laura Wilson.

---

## 190 MR DAVID ELSWORTH, Newmarket

Postal: **Kings Yard, Egerton House Stables, Cambridge Road, Newmarket, Suffolk, CB8 0TH**
Contacts: **PHONE (01638) 665511 FAX (01638) 665310 MOBILE (07771) 804828**
**E-MAIL david.elsworth@virgin.net**

1 **BURNING THREAD (IRE),** 8, b g Captain Rio—Desert Rose **D. R. C. Elsworth**
2 **DASHING STAR,** 5, b g Teofilo (IRE)—Dashiba **J. C. Smith**

## MR DAVID ELSWORTH - Continued

3 **DERULO (IRE),** 4, ch g Arakan (USA)—Bratislava **G. W. Y. Li**
4 **FLASHYFRANK,** 6, b g Franklins Gardens—White Flash **D. R. C. Elsworth**
5 **HIGHLAND CASTLE,** 7, b g Halling (USA)—Reciprocal (IRE) **D. R. C. Elsworth**
6 **JUSTICE DAY (IRE),** 4, b c Acclamation—Rock Exhibition **Mr R. Ng**
7 **MASTER THE WORLD (IRE),** 4, gr g Mastercraftsman (IRE)—Zadalla **K. Quinn/ C. Benham/ I. Saunders**
8 **SLEEPY SIOUX,** 4, b f Sleeping Indian—Bella Chica (IRE) **Ten Green Bottles I**
9 **SPECULATIVE BID (IRE),** 4, b g Excellent Art—Barzah (IRE) **K. Quinn/ C. Benham/ I. Saunders**
10 **UPAVON,** 5, b g Avonbridge—Blaina **McPabb Racing**
11 **WATER DANCER (IRE),** 4, ch g Ad Valorem (USA)—River Patrol **J. C. Smith**

### THREE-YEAR-OLDS

12 **ARABIAN QUEEN (IRE),** b f Dubawi (IRE)—Barshiba (IRE) **J. C. Smith**
13 **BASTILLE DAY,** ch g Champs Elysees—Vivianna **Lordship Stud & David Elsworth**
14 **CANADIAN SUNRISE,** ch g Cockney Rebel (IRE)—Prairie Oyster **D. R. C. Elsworth**
15 **CASCADES (IRE),** b f Montjeu (IRE)—Seattle Ribbon (USA) **J. C. Smith**
16 **DANSILI DASH,** b c Dansili—Dashiba **J. C. Smith**
17 Ch f Paco Boy (IRE)—Haiyfoona **D. R. C. Elsworth**
18 **IVORS INVOLVEMENT (IRE),** b g Amadeus Wolf—Summer Spice (IRE) **W. I. M. Perry**
19 **IVORS REBEL,** b c Cockney Rebel (IRE)—Sopran Cross (ITY) **W. I. M. Perry**
20 **JUSTICE GOOD (IRE),** b c Acclamation—Qui Moi (CAN) **Mr R. Ng**
21 **JUSTICE WELL,** b c Halling (USA)—Porthcawl **Mr R. Ng**
22 **LA SUPERBA (IRE),** ch f Medicean—La Spezia (IRE) **Mr Mark Dixon & Luke Lillingston**
23 **MARK HOPKINS,** b g Mount Nelson—Halska **R. J. McCreery**
24 **MELODIOUS,** b f Cape Cross (IRE)—Gower Song **Mrs D. A. Tabor**
25 **MERDON CASTLE (IRE),** b c Acclamation—Siren's Gift **J. C. Smith**
26 **PISCES,** b f Halling (USA)—Optimistic **D. R. C. Elsworth**
27 **SPIRITED ACCLAIM (IRE),** b f Acclamation—Lafleur (IRE) **K. Quinn/ C. Benham/ I. Saunders**
28 **TITLED LADY,** ch f Sir Percy—May West **Elsworth & Nettlefold**
29 **YORKSHIRE DALES (IRE),** b g Vale of York (IRE)—Rock Exhibition **Mr R. Fell & Mr D. Elsworth**

### TWO-YEAR-OLDS

30 **AUSTRALIAN QUEEN,** b f 7/5 Fastnet Rock (AUS)—Barshiba (IRE) (Barathea (IRE)) **J. C. Smith**
**31** Br f 8/4 Dream Ahead (USA)—Celestial Dream (IRE) (Oasis Dream) (55000) **Mr R. Ng**
**32** Br gr c 16/5 Zebedee—Chantilly Beauty (FR) (Josr Algarhoud (IRE)) **Mr R. Ng**
33 **DASHING APPROACH,** ch f 15/2 New Approach (IRE)—Dashiba (Dashing Blade) **J. C. Smith**
**34** B f 11/2 Canford Cliffs (IRE)—Dibiya (IRE) (Caerleon (USA)) **Mr R. Ng**
**35** B f 24/3 Dream Ahead (USA)—Dorothy Dene (Red Ransom (USA)) (25000) **G B Partnership**
**36** B c 14/4 Acclamation—Fashion Rocks (IRE) (Rock of Gibraltar (IRE)) (75000) **Mr R. Ng**
**37** B br c 9/4 Scat Daddy (USA)—Lucky Be Me (CAN) (Peaks and Valleys (USA)) (47619) **Mr R. Ng**
**38** Gr f 22/4 Dark Angel (IRE)—Malaica (FR) (Roi Gironde (IRE)) **Mr R. Ng**
**39** B c 28/4 Intense Focus (USA)—Moon Shine (FR) (Groom Dancer (USA)) **Mr R. Ng**
40 **NORSE CASTLE,** b c 18/4 Norse Dancer (IRE)—Hursley Hope (IRE) (Barathea (IRE)) **J. C. Smith**
41 **SEA OF FLAMES,** ch c 30/3 Aqlaam—Hidden Fire (Alhaarth (IRE)) **J. C. Smith**
**42** B c 25/3 Dylan Thomas (IRE)—Shanghai Visit (IRE) (Peintre Celebre (USA)) **Mr R. Ng**
**43** B c 15/4 Kodiac—Spangle (Galileo (IRE)) (60000) **Mr R. Ng**
44 **THE NEW MASTER,** br c 26/4 New Approach (IRE)—Maziona (Dansili) (60000) **J. C. Smith**

**Other Owners:** Mr John Adams, Mr M. D. Elliott, Mr D. R. C. Elsworth, Mr R. G. Fell, Mr T. F. Harris, Mrs E. A. Harris, Mr D. Morgan, Mr Julian Nettlefold, Mr K. J. Parris.

**Assistant Trainer:** Mr Paul Holley

**Apprentice:** Ryan Holley.

---

## 191 MISS SARA ENDER, Malton

Postal: **57 Park Road, Norton, Malton, North Yorkshire, YO17 9EA**

1 **BOLD PRINCE RUPERT (IRE),** 5, br g Royal Anthem (USA)—Fortune And Favour (IRE) **N. P. Ender**
2 **CASTLEY LANE,** 9, b g Dapper—Holly **N. P. Ender**
3 **CLASSICAL CHLOE,** 7, b m Sleeping Indian—Mana Pools (IRE)
4 **GREY MONK (IRE),** 7, gr g Alderbrook—Thats The Bother (IRE) **N. P. Ender**
5 **ISLAND PUNCH (IRE),** 9, b g Turtle Island (IRE)—You're Poleaxed (IRE) **N. P. Ender**
6 **JUST TALKING (IRE),** 13, br g Windsor Castle—Fam-E Fam-E (IRE) **N. P. Ender**

## MISS SARA ENDER - Continued

7 **NEVER FORGET POPPY (IRE),** 10, b g Corrouge (USA)—Broadway Thorn (IRE) **N. P. Ender**
8 **SEDANO (FR),** 9, b br g Dark Moondancer—Kadalville (FR) **N. P. Ender**
9 **STITCHED IN TIME (IRE),** 8, b g Needle Gun (IRE)—Broken Pockets (IRE) **N. P. Ender**

---

## 192 MR TIM ETHERINGTON, Malton

Postal: **Wold House Stables, Langton Road, Norton, Malton, North Yorkshire, YO17 9QG**
Contacts: **OFFICE (01653) 692842 HOME (01653) 693049**

1 **PEPPERELLO,** 4, b g Lucky Story (USA)—Rhuby River (IRE) **P. G. Hepworth**

### THREE-YEAR-OLDS

2 **BECOME AWARE,** b g Sakhee (USA)—Sainte Gig (FR) **C. J. Clark**

**Other Owners:** T. J. Etherington.

---

## 193 MR JAMES EUSTACE, Newmarket

Postal: **Park Lodge Stables, Park Lane, Newmarket, Suffolk, CB8 8AX**
Contacts: **PHONE (01638) 664277 FAX (01638) 664156 MOBILE (07802) 243764**
**E-MAIL jameseustace@tiscali.co.uk WEBSITE www.jameseustace.com**

1 **AVIATOR (GER),** 7, br g Motivator—Amore (GER) **The MacDougall Two**
2 **BAINNE (IRE),** 5, b m Strategic Prince—Laemeen (IRE) **G. N. Carstairs**
3 **GIOS LAST (GER),** 5, gr g Paolini (GER)—Giovanella (IRE) **G. N. Carstairs**
4 **ICE SLICE (IRE),** 4, b g Dark Angel (IRE)—Ice Rock (IRE) **The MacDougall Two**
5 **IRON BUTTERFLY,** 6, b m Shirocco (GER)—Coh Sho No **H. D. Nass**
6 **MAJOR CRISPIES,** 4, b g Pastoral Pursuits—Nellie Melba **G. N. Carstairs**
7 **NIMBLE KIMBLE,** 4, ch f Kirkwall—Lovely Lyca **Mr I. L. Rushby**
8 **SANDY COVE,** 4, br g Oasis Dream—Maganda (IRE) **Blue Peter Racing 12**
9 **SCOTTISH STAR,** 7, gr g Kirkwall—Child Star (FR) **Mr I. L. Rushby**
10 **SPA'S DANCER (IRE),** 8, b g Danehill Dancer (IRE)—Spa **The MacDougall Two**
11 **TEA BLOSSOM,** 4, b f Rail Link—Snow Blossom **Major M. G. Wyatt**
12 **WILY FOX,** 8, ch g Observatory (USA)—Kamkova (USA) **Blue Peter Racing 10**

### THREE-YEAR-OLDS

13 **BLACK SHEBA,** b f Aqlaam—Duty Paid (IRE) **J. C. Smith**
14 **CHIEF SPIRIT,** b c Norse Dancer (IRE)—Indian Angel **J. C. Smith**
15 **NUFOOTH (IRE),** b f Elnadim (USA)—Sahaayeb (IRE) **The MacDougall Two**
16 **WIND PLACE AND SHO,** br g Shirocco (GER)—Coh Sho No **H. D. Nass**

### TWO-YEAR-OLDS

17 **APACHE MYTH,** ch f 5/3 Sakhee's Secret—Indian Angel (Indian Ridge) **J. C. Smith**
18 **GLITTERING,** ch f 10/3 Firebreak—Razzle (IRE) (Green Desert (USA)) (5714) **Sherin Lloyd and Friends**
19 B f 5/4 Makfi—Highland Shot (Selkirk (USA)) **J. C. Smith**
20 **LONG ISLAND,** b f 11/3 Firebreak—Fakhuur (Dansili) **R. J. McCreery**
21 **NEXT TRAIN'S GONE,** b g 16/3 Rail Link—Coh Sho No (Old Vic) **H. D. Nass**
22 **NORSE CUSTOM,** b f 10/2 Norse Dancer (IRE)—Accustomed (Motivator) **J. C. Smith**
23 **PENNERLEY,** b f 10/2 Aqlaam—Penelewey (Groom Dancer (USA)) **Major M. G. Wyatt**
24 **POCKET,** b f 14/2 Paco Boy (IRE)—Take The Plunge (Benny The Dip (USA)) (5000) **P. F. Charter**
25 Ch f 17/2 Champs Elysees—Rainbow Queen (FR) (Spectrum (IRE)) (10000) **Mr & Mrs R. Scott**
26 **THE NAME IS JAMES,** br c 14/2 Equiano (FR)—Miss Bond (IRE) (Danehill Dancer (IRE)) **J. C. Smith**

**Other Owners:** Mr R. P. Abel, Mr D. F. Ballheimer, T. H. Barma, Mrs B. J. Carter, Mr B. M. Cimmering, C. Z. Curtis, Mr T. E. Dyke, Mrs G. R. Eustace, Mr A. C. Frost, Mr R. J. Hagen, Mrs L. R. Lawson, Mrs K. A. McGladdery, Mrs K. J. Smith, Mr R. J. Uzupris.

## 194 MR DAVID EVANS, Abergavenny

Postal: **Ty Derlwyn Farm, Pandy, Abergavenny, Monmouthshire, NP7 8DR**
Contacts: **PHONE (01873) 890837 (07834) 834775 E. Evans FAX (01873) 890837 MOBILE (07860) 668499**
**E-MAIL info@pdevansracing.co.uk / pdevansracing@btinternet.com**
**WEBSITE www.pdevansracing.co.uk**

1 **AL'S MEMORY (IRE),** 6, b g Red Clubs (IRE)—Consensus (IRE) **Mrs R. L. Barnes**
2 **ANNALUNA (IRE),** 6, b m Whipper (USA)—Annaletta **N. Shutts**
3 **BATHWICK STREET,** 6, ch g Compton Place—Bahawir Pour (USA) **H. M. W. Clifford**
4 **BLACK DAVE (IRE),** 5, b g Excellent Art—Miss Latina (IRE) **Mrs E Evans & Mr J Smith**
5 **CABUCHON (GER),** 8, b g Fantastic Light (USA)—Catella (GER) **Mrs E. Evans**
6 **ESHTYAAQ,** 8, b g Mark of Esteem (IRE)—Fleet Hill (IRE) **T. H. Gallienne**
7 **HAADEETH,** 8, b g Oasis Dream—Musical Key **Mrs I. M. Folkes**
8 **JOHN REEL (FR),** 6, b g Country Reel (USA)—John Quatz (FR) **Walters Plant Hire Ltd**
9 **KHEE SOCIETY,** 4, b g Sakhee (USA)—Society Rose **H. M. W. Clifford**
10 **KNOW YOUR NAME,** 4, ch g Halling (USA)—Lady Agnes **Livvys Racing Group**
11 **KODAFINE (IRE),** 4, br f Kodiac—Zafine **Mrs E. Evans**
12 **LONE WARRIOR (IRE),** 4, b g Oratorio (IRE)—Warrior Wings **H. M. W. Clifford**
13 **SIR BILLY WRIGHT (IRE),** 4, b g High Chaparral (IRE)—Lure of The Moon (USA) **Shropshire Wolves**
14 **SWIFT CEDAR (IRE),** 5, ch g Excellent Art—Ravish **J. E. Abbey**
15 **TANGO SKY (IRE),** 6, b g Namid—Sky Galaxy (USA) **Mr J. A. Wilcox**
16 **TELEGRAPH (IRE),** 4, b g Bushranger (IRE)—Vampire Queen (IRE) **The Drink Pink Partnership**
17 **VERSE OF LOVE,** 6, b g Byron—Lovellian **H. M. W. Clifford**

### THREE-YEAR-OLDS

18 **ABBA ZABBA (IRE),** b g Bushranger (IRE)—Tipperary Boutique (IRE) **N. Shutts**
19 **ALBECQ,** b g Paco Boy (IRE)—Helen Sharp **T. H. Gallienne**
20 **ALFARAABY (IRE),** ch g Tamayuz—Aphorism **Mr W. Clifford, Mr D. Rolfe, Mr D. Price**
21 **ANONYMOUS JOHN (IRE),** gr g Baltic King—Helibel (IRE) **Mrs R. L. Barnes**
22 **BANNISTER BELL (IRE),** b c Holy Roman Emperor (IRE)—Bells of Ireland (UAE) **Livvys Racing Group**
23 **CHEERIO SWEETIE (IRE),** b f Captain Rio—Curve (IRE) **Walters Plant Hire Spiers & Hartwell**
24 **COME UPPENCE,** b g Captain Gerrard (IRE)—Waterline Twenty (IRE) **M. W. Lawrence**
25 **EDW GOLD (IRE),** ch g Fast Company (IRE)—Hams (USA) **Mrs E. Evans**
26 **FAST SCAT (USA),** ch f Scat Daddy (USA)—Furusato (USA) **Mr B Mould & Emma Evans**
27 **HILLGROVE ANGEL (IRE),** gr g Dark Angel (IRE)—Theben (GER) **Dukes Head Racing**
28 **JAGANORY (IRE),** b c Dylan Thomas (IRE)—Jacquelin Jag (IRE) **H. M. W. Clifford**
29 **JOSIE JOE,** ch f Stimulation (IRE)—Minette **T. Reffell**
30 **JUST MARION (IRE),** b f Bushranger (IRE)—Dolphin Stamp (IRE) **D. E. Edwards**
31 **LA ESTATUA,** b f Lope de Vega (IRE)—Statua (IRE) **Miss R. McMorrough Kavanagh**
32 **MISS MINUTY,** gr f Verglas (IRE)—Miss Provence **Mr J Abbey & Mr J Wilcox**
33 **MYWAYALWAYS (IRE),** b g Baltic King—Goose Island (IRE) **E. R. Griffiths**
34 **SMUGGLERS LANE (IRE),** b g Bushranger (IRE)—Finty (IRE) **Mr T Earle & Mr P D Evans**
35 **TAMARIN,** ch f Paco Boy (IRE)—Les Hurlants (IRE) **Mr B. J. Mould**
36 **YA HALLA (IRE),** gr f Dark Angel (IRE)—Stormy View (USA) **Mr R Kent & Mrs E Evans**

### TWO-YEAR-OLDS

**37** B f 25/3 Bushranger (IRE)—Alexander Confranc (IRE) (Magical Wonder (USA)) (12300) **Mr A. L. Al Zeer**
**38** B c 14/4 Aqlaam—Aswaaq (IRE) (Peintre Celebre (USA)) (15000) **Walters Plant Hire Ltd**
**39** B c 1/4 Arakan (USA)—Bayasiya (IRE) (Pennekamp (USA)) (4761)
**40** B f 22/1 Bushranger (IRE)—Beguiler (Refuse To Bend (IRE)) (2380) **Mrs E. Evans**
**41** Gr f 26/3 Zebedee—Charming Vista (Josr Algarhoud (IRE)) (6348) **Dukes Head Racing**
**42** B f 3/3 Bushranger (IRE)—Chica Whopa (IRE) (Oasis Dream) (872) **P. D. Evans**
**43 CLIVE CLIFTON (IRE),** b c 5/3 Wootton Bassett—Dearest Daisy (Forzando) (19840) **P. D. Evans**
**44** B c 7/4 Thewayyouare (USA)—Danjet (IRE) (Danehill Dancer (IRE)) **E. A. R. Morgans**
**45** B f 30/4 Approve (IRE)—Farthing (IRE) (Mujadil (USA)) (3174) **H. M. W. Clifford**
**46** B f 3/2 Myboycharlie (IRE)—Fortunately (Forzando)
**47** Gr f 29/4 Dark Angel (IRE)—Halliwell House (Selkirk (USA)) (28000) **Mrs E. Evans**
**48** Ch f 7/4 Intense Focus (USA)—Hurricane Havoc (IRE) (Hurricane Run (IRE)) (13000) **Mr A. L. Al Zeer**
**49** B f 30/4 Dylan Thomas (IRE)—Kindest (Cadeaux Genereux) **Mr N. I. O'Callaghan**
**50 KUMANAVSUMFUN,** b f 19/5 Captain Gerrard (IRE)—Samadilla (IRE) (Mujadil (USA)) **W. T. Whittle**
**51** B f 6/3 Baltic King—Lorena (IRE) (Bishop of Cashel) (4364) **Mrs E. Evans**
**52** B c 2/4 Strategic Prince—Miss Chamanda (IRE) (Choisir (AUS)) **E. A. R. Morgans**
**53** Ch c 3/3 Iffraaj—Moriches (IRE) (Alhaarth (IRE)) (23809)
**54** B f 22/2 Fast Company (IRE)—Queen of Fools (IRE) (Xaar) (6745) **Dukes Head Racing**

## MR DAVID EVANS - Continued

**55** Gr f 30/4 Thousand Words—Rectify (IRE) (Mujadil (USA)) (2777) **Mrs E. Evans**
**56** B f 11/4 Iffraaj—Road Harbour (USA) (Rodrigo de Triano (USA)) **Mrs T. Burns**
**57** B f 28/4 Approve (IRE)—Silca Boo (Efisio) (11110) **H. M. W. Clifford**
**58 SILVER WINGS (IRE),** gr c 24/3 Zebedee—Daisy Hill (Indian Ridge) (13491) **Mr Collins & Mr Reilly**
**59** B f 20/1 Approve (IRE)—Street Kitty (IRE) (Tiger Hill (IRE)) (4126) **P. D. Evans**
**60** B f 24/4 Kodiac—Thaisy (USA) (Tabasco Cat (USA)) (20634) **A. F. O'Callaghan**
**61** B f 14/3 Bushranger (IRE)—Ufallya (IRE) (Statue of Liberty (USA)) (3174) **Mrs E. Evans**
**62** B f 4/6 Virtual—Winsa (USA) (Riverman (USA)) (12380) **Mr A. L. Al Zeer**
**63 ZEEONEANDONLY (IRE),** b f 17/1 Zebedee—Subtle Shimmer (Danehill Dancer (IRE)) (19047) **E. R. Griffiths**

**Other Owners:** Mr J. Babb, J. L. Collins, Mr P. G. Dalton, Mr T. H. Earle, R. Kent, D. J. Lockwood, Mr F. M. Lockwood, Mr J. Lynch, Mr C. P. Lynch, Mr D. G. Price, Mr W. J. Reilly, Mr D. J. Rolfe, R. Simpson, Mr J. E. Smith, Spiers & Hartwell Ltd.

**Assistant Trainer:** Mrs Emma Evans

**Jockey (flat):** John Egan. **Apprentice:** Declan Bates, Harry Burns, Hollie Doyle. **Amateur:** Miss K. F. Begley.

---

## 195 MR HYWEL EVANS, Kidwelly

Postal: **Llwynpiod Farm, Llangyndeyrn, Kidwelly, Carmarthenshire, SA17 5HD**

**1 TOM BACH (IRE),** 11, ch g Bach (IRE)—Fiovefontaine (IRE) **Mr H. G. Evans**

---

## 196 MR JAMES EVANS, Broadwas on Teme

Postal: **Stone Farm, Broadwas, Worcester, Worcestershire, WR6 5NE**
Contacts: **MOBILE (07813) 166430**
**E-MAIL herbie_evans@hotmail.com WEBSITE www.hjamesevans.co.uk**

**1 BUCKONTUPENCE (IRE),** 7, b g Brian Boru—Miss Od (IRE) **The Prince Of Darkness Partnership**
**2 DESILVANO,** 6, b g Desideratum—Cruz Santa **International Plywood (Importers) Ltd**
**3 FRIENDSHIP BAY,** 11, b g Midnight Legend—Friendly Fairy **Mrs J. Evans**
**4 IT'S OSCAR (IRE),** 8, b g Oscar (IRE)—Lady Bramble (IRE) **Miss S. Troughton**
**5 JAMMY (IRE),** 6, b g Oscar (IRE)—Tabachines (FR) **Miss S. Troughton**
**6 LATERAL THINKING (IRE),** 5, b g Excellent Art—Sumingasefa **Mr B. W. Preece**
**7 LIGHTNING GLANCE,** 6, b m Passing Glance—Gentle Warning **M Fentiman W Bevans Matner Ant & Smith**
**8 MIDNIGHT BROWNIE,** 4, b c Midnight Legend—Friendly Fairy
**9 MINELLA BLISS (IRE),** 10, gr g Old Vic—Carraigrose (IRE) **Running Dragon Racing 2**
**10 MIXOLOGIST,** 8, gr g Fair Mix (IRE)—Matchboard Again (IRE) **Miss S. Troughton**
**11 PETRUS DE SORMAIN (FR),** 12, b g Milford Track (IRE)—Bialystok (FR) **Mrs J. Evans**
**12 PHOENIX FLIGHT (IRE),** 10, b g Hawk Wing (USA)—Firecrest (IRE) **Mrs J. Evans**
**13 RAGING BEAR (USA),** 5, b g Leroidesanimaux (BRZ)—Gliding Light (USA) **Mr P. Wright-Bevans**
**14 ROC DE GUYE (FR),** 10, b g Video Rock (FR)—Kasibelle de Guye (FR) **S. Crawley, T. Crawley**
**15 SHAKESPEARE DANCER,** 6, b m Norse Dancer (IRE)—Sharbasia (IRE) **James Evans Racing**
**16 TANNER HILL (IRE),** 7, b g Milan—Carlingford Leader (IRE) **P Wright Bevans S Matner P Smith & A Pidgeon**
**17 TRACKMATE,** 9, b g Muhtarram (USA)—Cruz Santa **Preece Hamilton Porter Deni**
**18 VENT NIVERNAIS (FR),** 6, ch g Shaanmer (IRE)—Lobella (FR) **Elegant Clutter Ltd**

### THREE-YEAR-OLDS

**19 REET PETITE (IRE),** b f Fast Company (IRE)—Damjanich (IRE) **Mrs J. Evans**
**20 SAPHIRA SILVER (IRE),** gr f Verglas (IRE)—Mean Lae (IRE) **Running Dragon Racing 2**
**21 SUNFYRE (IRE),** ch g Virtual—Dimensional **Running Dragon Racing 2**

**Other Owners:** Mrs S. Crawley, Mr T. P. M. Crawley, Mr James Evans, Mrs J. Evans, Mr M. S. Fentiman, Mr Martin Hamilton, Miss Deni Harper Adams, Mr Martin Llewelyn, Mrs Helen Llewelyn, Mr Steve Matner, Mr A. J. Pidgeon, Miss Tina Porter, Mr B. Preece, Mr Paul M. Smith, Mr Paul Wright-Bevans.

**Assistant Trainer:** Mrs Jane Evans

**Jockey (NH):** Mark Quinlan, Liam Treadwell.

## 197 MRS MARY EVANS, Haverfordwest

Postal: **Hengoed, Clarbeston Road, Haverfordwest, Pembrokeshire, SA63 4QL**
Contacts: **PHONE (01437) 731336**

1 **MAIZY MISSILE (IRE),** 13, b m Executive Perk—Landsker Missile **Mary & Billy Evans**
2 **MOUNTAIN OF ANGELS,** 6, b m Midnight Legend—Landsker Missile **Mary & Billy Evans**
3 **PRU,** 7, br m Weld—Floranz **Mary & Billy Evans**

**Other Owners:** Mrs M. Evans, W. J. Evans.

**Assistant Trainer:** W J Evans

## 198 MRS NIKKI EVANS, Abergavenny

Postal: **Penbiddle Farm, Penbidwal, Pandy, Abergavenny, Gwent, NP7 8EA**
Contacts: **(01873) 890957 FAX (01873) 890957 MOBILE (07977) 753437**
**E-MAIL nikki@penbiddle.fsnet.co.uk WEBSITE www.nikki-evans-racing.co.uk**

1 **AGREEMENT (IRE),** 5, b g Galileo (IRE)—Cozzene's Angel (USA) **N Bergourd, J Berry, S Hellens**
2 5, Ch g Dreams End—Atlantic Lady (GER) **Mrs N. S. Evans**
3 **BOGEY HOLE (IRE),** 6, gr m Aussie Rules (USA)—Sticky Green **Mr J. Berry**
4 **CYPRUSORMILAN,** 8, b g Milan—Persrolla **Hanford's Chemist Ltd**
5 **FOILED,** 5, b g Dutch Art—Isengard (USA) **Mr N. Bougourd**
6 **ILLEGALE (IRE),** 9, b m Poliglote—Pinkai (IRE) **Hanford's Chemist Ltd**
7 **JUST LEWIS,** 8, ch g Sir Harry Lewis (USA)—McMahon's River **Mrs N. S. Evans**
8 **MANDY THE NAG (USA),** 5, b br m Proud Citizen (USA)—Storm to Glory (USA) **Mrs M. E. Gittings-Watts**
9 **MARI ME OSCAR (IRE),** 5, b m Oscar (IRE)—Nostra (FR) **Hanford's Chemist Ltd**
10 **MY SON MAX,** 7, b g Avonbridge—Pendulum **Mrs M. E. Gittings-Watts**
11 **PREMIER JACK'S,** 4, b g Tobougg (IRE)—Arabellas Homer **Mr R. J. E. Evans**
12 **RYEDALE LASS,** 7, b m Val Royal (FR)—First Dawn **Nikki Evans Racing**
13 **SAKURAMACHI,** 4, b f Sixties Icon—Queen of Narnia **Hanford's Chemists Ltd/ John Berry**
14 **STEEL RAIN,** 7, b g Striking Ambition—Concentration (IRE) **Mr J. Berry**
15 **SWIFT ACT,** 6, b m Act One—Lasting Image **Welsh Connections Racing**
16 **THRTYPOINTSTOTHREE (IRE),** 4, b g Kodiac—Miss Taken (IRE) **Hanford's Chemists Ltd/ John Berry**
17 **TUNNEL VISION (IRE),** 8, b br g Craigsteel—Mill Top Lady (IRE) **Penbiddle Racing**

### THREE-YEAR-OLDS

18 **AS A DREAM (IRE),** b f Azamour (IRE)—Wedding Dream **Hanford's Chemists Ltd/ John Berry**
19 **STEEL BLAZE,** b f Striking Ambition—Ocean Blaze **Mr J. Berry**
20 **STEEL BREEZE (IRE),** b f Moss Vale (IRE)—Sail With The Wind **Mr J. Berry**
21 **WELSH REBEL,** ch g Cockney Rebel (IRE)—Lasting Image **Welsh Connections Racing**

**Other Owners:** P. T. Evans, Lady J. Hayward, Mr S. J. Hellens.

**Assistant Trainer:** Mr P. T. Evans

## 199 MR JAMES EWART, Langholm

Postal: **James Ewart Racing Limited, Craig Farm, Westerkirk, Langholm, Dumfriesshire, DG13 0NZ**
Contacts: **PHONE (01387) 370707 FAX (01387) 370733 MOBILE (07786) 995073**
**E-MAIL office@jeracing.co.uk WEBSITE www.jamesewartracing.com**

1 **ALANOS (IRE),** 6, b g Choisir (AUS)—Pickwick Papers **Mr N. J. Fortune**
2 **ANGE DES MALBERAUX (FR),** 5, b g Michel Georges—Petite Baie (FR) **Mrs Hugh Fraser**
3 **ARISTO DU PLESSIS (FR),** 5, b g Voix du Nord (FR)—J'aime (FR) **Mrs J. E. Dodd**
4 **ASSIREM (FR),** 5, b g Spirit One (FR)—Sweet Orientfawn (IRE) **Mr & Mrs Paul & Clare Rooney**
5 **AVIDITY,** 6, b g Passing Glance—Epicurean **Leeds Plywood & Doors Ltd**
6 **BALTIC PATHFINDER (IRE),** 11, b g Alflora (IRE)—Boro Bow (IRE) **Mrs E. M. Smith**
7 **BE MY PRESENT,** 8, b m Presenting—Simply Divine (IRE) **Graham Allen Carruthers Ancrum Panther**
8 **BENEFICIAL JOE (IRE),** 5, b br g Beneficial—Joleen (IRE) **Mr & Mrs Paul & Clare Rooney**
9 **BORN TO SUCCEED (IRE),** 5, b g Robin des Pres (FR)—Born To Win (IRE) **Mr & Mrs Paul & Clare Rooney**
10 **CA LE FERRA (FR),** 5, b g Turgeon (USA)—Branceilles (FR) **Southhayrigg, Friel, Wilson, Humbert**
11 **CALVA D'HONORE (FR),** 4, b g Khalkevi (IRE)—Elivette (FR) **Mr & Mrs Paul & Clare Rooney**
12 **CATCHING SHADOWS (IRE),** 6, b g Catcher In The Rye (IRE)—Castletown Girl **Sperling**
13 **COUSIN GUILLAUME (FR),** 6, b br g Kapgarde (FR)—Tante Zoe (FR) **Mr & Mrs Paul & Clare Rooney**

## MR JAMES EWART - Continued

14 **DREAMISI (IRE),** 6, b g Kalanisi (IRE)—Marvellous Dream (FR) **Mr & Mrs Paul & Clare Rooney**
15 **GILNOCKIE,** 7, b g Kayf Tara—Eloquent Lawyer **Ewart, Daresbury, Rocket & Stan Racing**
16 **HARRY THE LEMMON (IRE),** 9, br g Milan—Na Habair Tada (IRE) **Kay, Payne, Boyce, Panther, Wilson, Ancrum**
17 **HUEHUECOYTLE,** 5, br g Turgeon (USA)—Azturk (FR) **Mr & Mrs Paul & Clare Rooney**
18 **LEADING SCORE (IRE),** 5, b g Scorpion (IRE)—Leading Rank (IRE) **Ewart, Drew, Sperling**
19 **LIMOS (GER),** 5, br b g Sholokhov (IRE)—La Prima (GER)
20 **LORD WISHES (IRE),** 8, b g Milan—Strong Wishes (IRE) **Leeds Plywood & Doors Ltd**
21 **LYBOWLER,** 5, b g Lyphento (USA)—Bowling On **W. H. Whitley**
22 **MAGIC SHANTOU (IRE),** 5, b g Shantou (USA)—Magic Feeling (IRE) **Mr & Mrs Paul & Clare Rooney**
23 **MANKALA (IRE),** 5, b g Flemensfirth (USA)—Maracana (IRE) **Mr & Mrs Paul & Clare Rooney**
24 **MASTER OF THE GAME (IRE),** 9, ch g Bob's Return (IRE)—Lady Monilousha (IRE) **Mr & Mrs Paul & Clare Rooney**
25 **MIXBOY (FR),** 5, gr g Fragrant Mix (IRE)—Leston Girl (FR) **Mr & Mrs Paul & Clare Rooney**
26 **MY LITTLE CRACKER (IRE),** 5, b br m Scorpion (IRE)—Cailin Gruaig Dubh (IRE) **Mr & Mrs Paul & Clare Rooney**
27 **PADDY'S FIELD (IRE),** 5, b br g Flemensfirth (USA)—Kittys Oscar (IRE) **Mr & Mrs Paul & Clare Rooney**
28 **PREMIER GRAND CRU (FR),** 9, b g Kaldounevees (FR)—Last Harvest (FR) **Leeds Plywood & Doors Ltd**
29 **QUICUYO (GER),** 12, ch g Acatenango (GER)—Quila (IRE) **D. Coppola J. Ewart**
30 **ROC DE PRINCE,** 6, b g Shirocco (GER)—Louella (USA) **Ewart, Humbert, Kesson, Wilson**
31 **ROCKAWANGO (FR),** 9, b g Okawango (USA)—Janou La Belle (FR) **Mr S. A. Murrills**
32 **ROCKLIM (FR),** 5, b g Laverock (IRE)—Stille Baroque (FR) **Radford, Down, Ogilvie, Palmer**
33 **SA SUFFIT (FR),** 12, b g Dolpour—Branceilles (FR) **Friel, Humbert, Kesson, Wilson**
34 **SAINTE LADYLIME (FR),** 4, b f Saint des Saints (FR)—Lady Pauline (FR) **Mr & Mrs Paul & Clare Rooney**
35 **SCORPIONS STING (IRE),** 6, b g Scorpion (IRE)—Strong Wishes (IRE) **Dodd, Carruthers, Kesson, Murrills, Palmer**
36 **SKY FULL OF STARS (IRE),** 5, b g Mahler—Gold Flo (IRE)
37 **SLEEP IN FIRST (FR),** 9, b br g Sleeping Car (FR)—First Union (FR) **First Sleepers Union & Craig Syndicate**
38 **SNUKER,** 8, b g Snurge—Briar Rose (IRE) **Percy, Down, Boyd, Craig Farm Syndicate, Panther Racing**
39 **SONNEOFPRESENTING (IRE),** 5, b br g Presenting—Sonne Cinq (IRE) **Mr & Mrs Paul Rooney**
40 **SPACE WALKER (IRE),** 4, b g Astronomer Royal (USA)—Hot Property (USA) **Mr & Mrs Paul & Clare Rooney**
41 **TOUCH OF STEEL (IRE),** 6, b g Craigsteel—Tourmaline Girl (IRE) **Mrs Ann Fraser**
42 **UEUETEOTL (FR),** 7, gr g Tikkanen (USA)—Azturk (FR) **Going Grey**
43 **UN GUET APENS (FR),** 7, b g Enrique—Belisama (FR) **Drew, Sperling, Graham, Carruthers**
44 **UNEX CANALETTO,** 6, b g Motivator—Logic **The Craig Farm Syndicate**
45 **VERNI (FR),** 6, ch g Sabrehill (USA)—Nobless d'aron (FR) **Mr & Mrs Paul & Clare Rooney**
46 **WAKY HIGHLANDER (IRE),** 7, ch g Waky Nao—Highland May (IRE)
47 **WILDE PASTURES (IRE),** 10, gr g Oscar (IRE)—Kingsfield Clover **Border Pastures**
48 **ZARU (FR),** 9, b br g Laveron—Zianini (FR) **Mrs Humbert, Drew**

### THREE-YEAR-OLDS

49 B g Multiplex—Playful Lady

**Other Owners:** Mr James D. Allen, Mr Jason Boyce, Mr Robert Boyd, Mr R. Carruthers, Mr Dennis J. Coppola, Mr M. T. Cowen, Mrs J. M. Dodd, Mr D. Down, Mrs Lavinia Drew, Mr N. M. L. Ewart, Mr J. P. L. Ewart, Mrs E. M. Fairbairn, Mr Maurice Friel, Mrs Ann Graham, Mr David Graham, Mr W. Graham, Mrs J. U. Hales, Mr Mark Hood, Mrs A. G. Humbert, Mr Jimmy Kay, Dr Colin Kesson, Mr Steve Murrills, Mr Peter Ogilvie, Dr Roy Palmer, Panther Racing Ltd, Mr James Payne, Mrs J. D. Percy, Mr Graham Radford, Mr Dave Rolinson, Mr P. A. Rooney, Mrs C. Rooney, Mr Robert Smith, Mr N. A. Sperling, Mrs J. E. Sperling, Mr David Stanhope, Mr Iain Todd, Ms Heather K. Walker, Mr Kirk A. Wilson, Mr S. Wood.

**Assistant Trainer:** Briony Ewart

**Jockey (NH):** Lucy Alexander, Jason Maguire. **Conditional:** Daragh Bourke, Dale Irving. **Amateur:** Mr James Smith.

---

## 200 MR LES EYRE, Beverley

Postal: **Ivy House Stables, Main Street, Catwick, Beverley, North Humberside, HU17 5PJ**

1 **BOXING SHADOWS,** 5, b g Camacho—Prima Ballerina **Mr B. Parker**
2 **COMPTON PARK,** 8, ch h Compton Place—Corps de Ballet (IRE) **Mr B. Parker**
3 **DISCLOSURE,** 4, b g Indesatchel (IRE)—Gemini Gold (IRE) **Les Eyre Racing Partnership I**
4 **FAIRY POOLS,** 4, ch f Halling (USA)—Maritima **Mrs D. W. Davenport**
5 **FIRST COMMANDMENT,** 4, b g Major Cadeaux—Golden Nun **Mr T. G. Holdcroft**
6 **HELLO PRETTY LADYS,** 4, b g Revoque (IRE)—Staff Nurse (IRE) **S. W. Downes**

## MR LES EYRE - Continued

7 **MR MO JO,** 7, b g Danbird (AUS)—Nampara Bay **Sunpak Potatoes**
8 **QIBTEE (FR),** 5, b g Antonius Pius (USA)—Embers of Fame (IRE) **Mr N. C. White & Mrs C. E. White**
9 **REMEMBERANCE DAY,** 4, ch f Major Cadeaux—Today's The Day **Mr M. Moulds**
10 **ROSIE HALL (IRE),** 5, ch m Lion Heart (USA)—Baltic Dip (IRE) **R & E Hall & Son**

### THREE-YEAR-OLDS

11 **ASSERTIVEBYNATURE,** b f Assertive—Purely By Chance **GIB Bloodstock Limited**
12 **POOLSTOCK,** b c Equiano (FR)—Pure Speculation **Dunham Trading Ltd**

**Other Owners:** Mr T. S. Ely, Mr R. Hall, Mr R. C. Hall, Mr N. C. White, Mrs C. E. White, Mr A. Yates, Mrs S. J. Yates.

---

## 201 MR RICHARD FAHEY, Malton

Postal: **RF Racing Ltd, Mews House, Musley Bank, Malton, North Yorkshire, YO17 6TD**
Contacts: **PHONE (01653) 698915 FAX (01653) 699735 MOBILE (07713) 478079**
**E-MAIL enquiries@richardfahey.com WEBSITE www.richardfahey.com**

1 **ALBEN STAR (IRE),** 7, b g Clodovil (IRE)—Secret Circle **Mr J. K. Shannon & Mr M. A. Scaife**
2 **ARCTIC FEELING (IRE),** 7, ch g Camacho—Polar Lady **Percy / Green Racing 2**
3 **BAHAMIAN C,** 4, b g Bahamian Bounty—Amandian (IRE) **S & G Clayton**
4 **BAYAN KASIRGA (IRE),** 5, b m Aussie Rules (USA)—Gwyllion (USA) **Mr S. Humphreys**
5 **BOY IN THE BAR,** 4, ch g Dutch Art—Lipsia (IRE) **S. Rudolf**
6 **BRIAN NOBLE,** 4, b c Royal Applause—Little Greenbird **Dr M. B. Q. S. Koukash**
7 **BROOKE'S BOUNTY,** 5, ch g Bahamian Bounty—Choysia **Mr J. Gaffney**
8 **CANYARI (IRE),** 4, b g Dandy Man (IRE)—Morna's Fan (FR) **M. A. Leatham**
9 **CHISWICK BEY (IRE),** 7, b g Elusive City (USA)—Victoria Lodge (IRE) **Mr M. J. Macleod**
10 **COSMIC HALO,** 6, ch m Halling (USA)—Cosmic Case **The Cosmic Cases**
11 **DISCO DALE (IRE),** 4, gr g Verglas (IRE)—Artisia (IRE) **R. A. Fahey**
12 **DOCS LEGACY (IRE),** 6, b g Ad Valorem (USA)—Lunamixa (GER) **Mr D. A. Bardsley**
13 **DONE DREAMING (IRE),** 5, b g Diamond Green (FR)—Wishing Chair (USA) **Richard Fahey Ebor Racing Club Ltd**
14 **DUSKY QUEEN (IRE),** 5, b m Shamardal (USA)—Sanna Bay (IRE) **Mrs H. Steel**
15 **EASTERN IMPACT (IRE),** 4, b g Bahamian Bounty—Kate The Great **Exors of the Late Mr D. W. Barker**
16 **EL VIENTO (FR),** 7, ch g Compton Place—Blue Sirocco **John Nicholls Ltd/David Kilburn**
17 **EMERAHLDZ (IRE),** 4, b f Excellent Art—Sancia (IRE) **Mrs H. Steel**
18 **EXTRATERRESTRIAL,** 11, b g Mind Games—Expectation (IRE) **G. J. Paver**
19 **FARLOW (IRE),** 7, ch g Exceed And Excel (AUS)—Emly Express (IRE) **Red Sky Partnership 1**
20 **FLIGHTY CLARETS (IRE),** 5, ch m Bahamian Bounty—Flying Clarets (IRE) **The Matthewman One Partnership**
21 **GABRIAL (IRE),** 6, b g Dark Angel (IRE)—Guajira (FR) **Dr M. B. Q. S. Koukash**
22 **GABRIAL THE THUG (FR),** 5, b g Azamour (IRE)—Baliyna (USA) **Dr M. B. Q. S. Koukash**
23 **GABRIAL'S KAKA (IRE),** 5, b g Jeremy (USA)—Love In May (IRE) **Dr M. B. Q. S. Koukash**
24 **GABRIAL'S STAR,** 6, b g Hernando (FR)—Grain Only **Dr M. B. Q. S. Koukash**
25 **GLEESE THE DEVIL (IRE),** 4, br g Manduro (GER)—Causeway Song (USA) **Dr M. B. Q. S. Koukash**
26 **HEAVEN'S GUEST (IRE),** 5, b g Dark Angel (IRE)—Bakewell Tart (IRE) **Mr J. K. Shannon & Mr M. A. Scaife**
27 **HESKETH BANK,** 4, b g Aqlaam—Wendylina (IRE) **D. W. Armstrong**
28 **HI THERE (IRE),** 6, b g Dark Angel (IRE)—Ornellaia (IRE) **Market Avenue Racing Club Ltd**
29 **IMSHIVALLA (IRE),** 4, b f Acclamation—Subtle Affair (IRE) **Pow Partnership**
30 **INGLEBY SYMPHONY (IRE),** 5, b m Oratorio (IRE)—Alizaya (IRE) **Percy Green Racing 4 & Partner**
31 **INNOCENT TOUCH (IRE),** 4, bl g Intense Focus (USA)—Guajira (FR) **Nicholas Wrigley & Kevin Hart**
32 **IXELLES DIAMOND (IRE),** 4, br f Diamond Green (FR)—Silk Point (IRE) **Miss L. Tillett**
33 **JAN VAN HOOF (IRE),** 4, b g Dutch Art—Cosenza **M. A. Leatham**
34 **KHELMAN (IRE),** 5, b g Kheleyf (USA)—Mandolin (IRE) **S & G Clayton**
35 **LAS VERGLAS STAR (IRE),** 7, gr g Verglas (IRE)—Magnificent Bell (IRE) **CBWS Partnership**
36 **LATENIGHTREQUEST,** 4, b f Major Cadeaux—Love Quest **Middleham Park Racing XVI & Partner**
37 **LEXINGTON BAY (IRE),** 7, b g High Chaparral (IRE)—Schust Madame (IRE) **Mr Keith Denham & Mr Tony Denham**
38 **MAIDEN APPROACH,** 4, b f New Approach (IRE)—Ivowen (USA) **Middleham Park Racing LXVII**
39 **MAJESTIC MOON (IRE),** 5, b g Majestic Missile (IRE)—Gala Style (IRE) **Mr J. Gaffney**
40 **MCCARTHY MOR (IRE),** 4, b g Bushranger (IRE)—Alexander Anapolis (IRE) **M. A. Scaife**
41 **MENDELITA,** 4, ch f Archipenko (USA)—Dame de Noche **The G-Guck Group**
42 **MFIFTYTHREEDOTCOM (IRE),** 4, ch g Tamayuz—Pearl Trader (IRE) **M53 Motors Ltd T/A M53 Ford**
43 **MICA MIKA (IRE),** 7, ch g Needwood Blade—Happy Talk (IRE) **Mrs U. Towell**

## MR RICHARD FAHEY - Continued

44 **MISS LUCY JANE,** 4, ch f Aqlaam—Ocean View (USA) **Mr R. J. Bown**
45 **OAK BLUFFS (IRE),** 4, b g Royal Applause—Key Stage (IRE) **Mrs U. Towell**
46 **ORTAC ROCK (IRE),** 6, b g Aussie Rules (USA)—Fashion Guide (IRE) **Wildcard Racing Syndicate X2**
47 **OUR BOY JACK (IRE),** 6, b g Camacho—Jina (IRE) **Middleham Park Racing XXXVI**
48 **PERSONAL TOUCH,** 6, ch g Pivotal—Validate **The Richard Fahey Ebor Racing Club**
49 **PICCADILLY JIM (IRE),** 4, gr g Royal Applause—Silver Dip **Frank Lenny Financial Services Limited**
50 **QUEST OF COLOUR (IRE),** 4, b f Iffraaj—With Colour **Havelock Racing 2**
51 **ROYAL CONNOISSEUR (IRE),** 4, b g Art Connoisseur (IRE)—Valferno (IRE) **S & G Clayton, Mr A. Blower**
52 **SIMPLY SHINING (IRE),** 5, ch m Rock of Gibraltar (IRE)—Bright Smile (IRE) **Mrs H. Steel**
53 **SPIRIT OF THE LAW (IRE),** 6, b g Lawman (FR)—Passion Bleue **The Matthewman One Partnership**
54 **SUMMERINTHECITY (IRE),** 8, ch g Indian Ridge—Miss Assertive **Dr M. B. Q. S. Koukash**
55 **SUPPLICANT,** 4, b c Kyllachy—Pious **Cheveley Park Stud Limited**
56 **TATLISU (IRE),** 5, b g Red Clubs (IRE)—Zwadi (IRE) **Middleham Park Racing LIV**
57 **TIGER TWENTY TWO,** 4, b g Authorized (IRE)—Collette's Choice **P. D. Smith Holdings Ltd**
58 **TIME AND PLACE,** 5, ch g Compton Place—Forthefirstime **Mr Mel Roberts & Ms Nicola Meese 1**
59 **TWO SHADES OF GREY (IRE),** 4, gr g Oratorio (IRE)—Elitista (FR) **McCreary, Harrison, Astrop & Partner**
60 **VENTURA QUEST (USA),** 4, b g Henrythenavigator (USA)—Ing Ing (FR) **Middleham Park Racing LXIX**
61 **VERY GOOD DAY (FR),** 8, b g Sinndar (IRE)—Picture Princess **Dr M. B. Q. S. Koukash**
62 **WITHERNSEA (IRE),** 4, b g Dark Angel (IRE)—Charlene Lacy (IRE) **City Vaults Racing 1**
63 **WOODBRIDGE,** 4, ch g Exceed And Excel (AUS)—Kristal Bridge **R. A. Fahey**

## THREE-YEAR-OLDS

64 **ABBEY ANGEL (IRE),** b f Arcano (IRE)—Sanna Bay (IRE) **Mrs H. Steel**
65 **AKEED CHAMPION,** b c Dubawi (IRE)—Shy Lady (FR) **J. Abdullah**
66 **AL GOMRY,** b c Exceed And Excel (AUS)—Welsh Cake **Al Shaqab Racing UK Limited**
67 **ARCANO GOLD (IRE),** ch c Arcano (IRE)—Azia (IRE) **Middleham Park Racing XL & Partner**
68 **ARTIST CRY,** ch c Dutch Art—Twenty Seven (IRE) **Malih L. Al Basti**
69 **BAHAMIAN SUNRISE,** ch g Bahamian Bounty—Tagula Sunrise (IRE) **Mr Mel Roberts & Ms Nicola Meese**
70 **BALLYMORE CASTLE (IRE),** br g Invincible Spirit (IRE)—Ballymore Lady (USA) **Sheikh R. D. Al Maktoum**
71 **BAMBOCCIANTI,** ch c Dutch Art—Brooklyn's Sky **Al Shira'aa Stable**
72 **BEARDWOOD,** ch c Dutch Art—Valentina Guest (IRE) **D. W. Armstrong**
73 **BELLE TRAVERS,** ch f Bahamian Bounty—Forthefirstime **H. J. P. Farr**
74 **BILLY BOND,** b g Monsieur Bond (IRE)—Princess Cocoa (IRE) **Mr & Mrs P. Ashton**
75 **BIMBO,** b f Iffraaj—Birthday Suit (IRE) **The Countess of Halifax**
76 **BIRKDALE BOY (IRE),** br g Alfred Nobel (IRE)—Yaky Romani (IRE) **Middleham Park Racing LXXXII & C Tasker**
77 **BLETCHLEY PARK,** ch c Mastercraftsman (IRE)—Puzzling **R. A. Fahey**
78 **BLEU ASTRAL (FR),** b g Astronomer Royal (USA)—Passion Bleue **Mr J. Gaffney**
79 **BOND'S GIRL,** ch f Monsieur Bond (IRE)—Blades Girl **Crown Select**
80 **BONDS CHOICE,** ch f Monsieur Bond (IRE)—Collette's Choice **P. D. Smith Holdings Ltd**
81 **BROTHERLY COMPANY (IRE),** b c Fast Company (IRE)—Good Lady (IRE) **J. Abdullah**
82 **CADEAU MAGNIFIQUE,** b g Dutch Art—Cadeau Speciale **Mr M. J. Macleod**
83 **CHARACTER ONESIE (IRE),** b g Dark Angel (IRE)—Flame Keeper (IRE) **Aykroyd & Sons Limited**
84 **CHARLOTTE'S SECRET,** ch g Sakhee's Secret—Charlotte Point (USA) **Mr J. F. Doyle**
85 **CLOUDS REST,** b f Showcasing—Ahwahnee **Racegoers Club Owners Group**
86 **CODGER'S GIFT (IRE),** b f Footstepsinthesand—Moonbi Ridge (IRE) **Middleham Park Racing LXXXIX & Partner**
87 **COSMIC STATESMAN,** ch g Halling (USA)—Cosmic Case **Hazel Tattersall, Mr G. Hyde & Partner**
88 **DARRINGTON,** b g Archipenko (USA)—Rosablanca (IRE) **The G-Guck Group**
89 **DESIRE,** ch f Kyllachy—Colonel's Daughter **Mr P. J. Baldwin**
90 **DEVIOUS SPIRIT (IRE),** br g Intikhab (USA)—Unintentional **Percy/Green Racing**
91 **DON'T TOUCH,** b c Dutch Art—Expressive **Nicholas Wrigley & Kevin Hart**
92 **ELIZABETH ERNEST,** b f Exceed And Excel (AUS)—Elusive Sue (USA) **P. D. Smith Holdings Ltd**
93 **ELUSIVE EPONA (USA),** b f Elusive Quality (USA)—Genuine Charm (USA) **Middleham Park Racing XLVII & Partner**
94 **FARHAM (USA),** b c Smart Strike (CAN)—Diamondrella **Al Shaqab Racing UK Limited**
95 **FLASHY MEMORIES,** ch c Dubawi (IRE)—Flashy Wings **J. Abdullah**
96 **FROSTY FLYER (FR),** gr g Silver Frost (IRE)—Perruche Grise (FR) **Mr & Mrs J. D. Cotton**
97 **FULLON CLARETS,** ch g Equiano (FR)—Palinisa (FR) **The Matthewman Partnership**
98 **GABRIAL THE TIGER (IRE),** b g Kodiac—Invincible **Dr M. B. Q. S. Koukash**
99 **GEORGE BOWEN (IRE),** gr g Dark Angel (IRE)—Midnight Oasis **M. A. Scaife**
100 **GRANDAD'S WORLD (IRE),** b c Kodiac—Nose One's Way (IRE) **Mr D. Hardman & Mrs S. Hardman**
101 **GRUMPY ANGEL,** b f Exceed And Excel (AUS)—Eye To Eye **Richard Fahey Ebor Racing Club Ltd**
102 **HEAVEN'S SECRET (IRE),** gr g Clodovil (IRE)—Secret Circle **Mr J. K. Shannon & Mr M. A. Scaife**

## MR RICHARD FAHEY - Continued

103 **HOME CUMMINS (IRE),** b f Rip Van Winkle (IRE)—Alava (IRE) **Mrs H. Steel**
104 **INGLEBY SPRING (IRE),** br f Zebedee—Jouel (FR) **Percy Green Racing 3**
105 **INTIWIN (IRE),** b g Intikhab (USA)—Muluk (IRE) **Mrs H. Steel**
106 **JOHNNY B GOODE (IRE),** b g Approve (IRE)—Musica E Magia (IRE) **J. Gill**
107 **JUMEIRAH GLORY (IRE),** b g Fast Company (IRE)—Lady Dettoria (FR) **Sheikh R. D. Al Maktoum**
108 **KELLOURA (IRE),** ch f Mastercraftsman (IRE)—Ocean Talent (USA) **R. A. Fahey**
109 **LA DOROTEA (IRE),** ch f Lope de Vega (IRE)—Nawal (FR) **Richard Fahey Ebor Racing Club Ltd**
110 **LACING,** b f Equiano (FR)—Lacework **Cheveley Park Stud Limited**
111 **LIBERTY SKY (IRE),** b f Rip Van Winkle (IRE)—High Spot **Middleham Park Racing XCII & Partner**
112 **LOOM OF LIFE (IRE),** b g Rip Van Winkle (IRE)—
Feeling Wonderful (IRE) **Inner Circle Thoroughbreds - Munnings**
113 **LUIS VAZ DE TORRES (IRE),** b c Tagula (IRE)—Tekhania (IRE) **Lets Go Racing 1**
114 **MARSOOMAH,** b f Aqlaam—Bukhoor (IRE) **Sheikh J. D. Al Maktoum**
115 B f Footstepsinthesand—Mathuna (IRE) **Clipper Group Holdings Ltd**
116 **MIDNITE RIDE (IRE),** b f Footstepsinthesand—Takaliyda (IRE) **Middleham Park Racing I & Partner**
117 **MILADY EILEEN (IRE),** ch f Footstepsinthesand—Arazena (USA) **Mrs H. Steel**
118 **MISS VAN GOGH,** b f Dutch Art—Accede **Dyson Racing & Mr D Powell**
119 **MONTEFALCON (IRE),** b g Footstepsinthesand—Gwyllion (USA) **Mrs H. Steel**
120 **MUSTIQUE DANCER (IRE),** b f Rip Van Winkle (IRE)—Cilium (IRE) **Middleham Park Racing XCI & Partner**
121 **MY DAD SYD (USA),** b br c Acclamation—Weekend Fling (USA) **S. Rudolf**
122 **NEVER EASY (IRE),** gr c Zebedee—Silk Point (IRE) **The Clynes & Knaggs Partnership**
123 **NORMANDY KNIGHT,** b g Acclamation—Prayer (IRE) **Mrs H. Steel**
124 **PAMUSHANA (IRE),** b f Teofilo (IRE)—Singitta **East Layton Stud Ltd**
125 **PATRICK (IRE),** b c Acclamation—Red Liason (IRE) **Mrs A. M. Riney**
126 **PERARDUA,** ch f Cockney Rebel (IRE)—Quiquillo (USA) **Diamond Racing Ltd**
127 **PHOENIX STORM (IRE),** b c Zebedee—Dabtiyra (IRE) **Mrs H. Steel**
128 **PIN UP (IRE),** b f Lookin At Lucky (USA)—All My Loving (IRE) **R. A. Fahey**
129 **POSTULANT,** b f Kyllachy—Pious **Cheveley Park Stud Limited**
130 **QUILL ART,** b g Excellent Art—Featherweight (IRE) **P. S. Cresswell & Mrs P. A. Morrison**
131 **REALTRA (IRE),** gr f Dark Angel (IRE)—Devious Diva (IRE) **Middleham Park Racing XC**
132 **SACRED BOND,** ch f Exceed And Excel (AUS)—Gay Romance **R. A. Fahey**
133 **SANDGATE,** ch g Compton Place—Jump Ship **Havelock Racing & Partner**
134 **SARISTA (IRE),** b f Kodiac—Suffer Her (IRE) **S. Rudolf**
135 **SCARLET BOUNTY (IRE),** b f Bahamian Bounty—Red Kyte **Malih L. Al Basti**
136 **SHALABINA,** b f Nayef (USA)—Shibina (IRE) **Middleham Park Racing XCVI**
137 **SIGNORET (IRE),** ch f Naaqoos—Katelyns Kiss (USA) **Middleham Park Racing LXVIII & Partners**
138 **SPIRIT OF ZEB (IRE),** ch g Zebedee—Miss Glitters (IRE) **IMEJ Racing**
139 **SPRING OFFENSIVE (IRE),** b g Iffraaj—Night Sphere (IRE) **A. Rhodes Haulage & Mr P. Timmins**
140 **STAR OF THE STAGE,** b g Invincible Spirit (IRE)—Enact **Cheveley Park Stud Limited**
141 **STARDRIFTER,** b g Rock of Gibraltar (IRE)—Alchemilla **Mrs H. Steel**
142 **STELLA ETOILE (IRE),** b f Duke of Marmalade (IRE)—Sangita **S. Rudolf**
143 **SUPER QUICK (IRE),** b f Rip Van Winkle (IRE)—Public Ransom (IRE) **Mr & Mrs J. D. Cotton**
144 **TARLETON (IRE),** b c Invincible Spirit (IRE)—Aguinaga (IRE) **D. W. Armstrong**
145 **THERMAL COLUMN (IRE),** b c Vale of York (IRE)—Swiss Roll (IRE) **R. A. Fahey**
146 **THIRD TIME LUCKY (IRE),** gr g Clodovil (IRE)—Speckled Hen (IRE) **The Musley Bank Partnership & Partner**
147 **THORKHILL STAR (IRE),** b g Equiano (FR)—Reine de Romance (IRE) **Middleham Park Racing LXXV & Partner**
148 **TOWN COUNCIL (IRE),** gr g Mastercraftsman (IRE)—Catch The Blues (IRE) **Clipper Group Holdings Ltd**
149 **VAN WILDER (IRE),** b c Rip Van Winkle (IRE)—Zelding (IRE)
150 **WOOFIE (IRE),** b g Duke of Marmalade (IRE)—Violet Ballerina (IRE) **Mrs J. M. MacPherson**
151 **ZAZA ZEST (IRE),** ch f Approve (IRE)—Happy Talk (IRE) **Richard Fahey Ebor Racing Club Ltd**
152 **ZUHOOR BAYNOONA (IRE),** b f Elnadim (USA)—Spasha **J. Abdullah**

## TWO-YEAR-OLDS

Only the following two-year-olds were supplied by the trainer.

153 **BLACK MAGIC (IRE),** gr c 9/3 Poet's Voice—Centifolia (FR) (Kendor (FR)) (35714) **Mrs H. Steel**
154 **KIRI SUNRISE (IRE),** b f 15/3 Iffraaj—Lucky Flirt (USA) (Gulch (USA)) (87300) **Mrs H. Steel**
155 **LADY TURPIN (IRE),** gr f 18/5 Arakan (USA)—Proficiency (El Prado (IRE)) **UK Racing Syndicate**
156 **TURPIN STAR,** b c 26/1 Dick Turpin (IRE)—Classic Lass (Dr Fong (USA)) (22000) **CBWS Partnership**

## MR RICHARD FAHEY - Continued

**Other Owners:** A. Rhodes Haulage Ltd, Mr P. Ashton, Mrs P. Ashton, Mr Z. bin Hazza, Ms F. bint Hazza, Mr A. Blower, Mr Andy Bonarius, Mr M. Bradley, Mr Stuart Brown, Mr E. Bruce, Mr I. T. Buchanan, Mr J. P. Carr, Mr M. Channon, Mr A. Clark, Mr Steven Clayton, Mr James Clayton, Mrs G. A. Clayton, Mr N. Collins, Mr Arthur Collins, Mr A. E. Corbett, Mr S. C. Corbett, Mr J. D. Cotton, Mrs B. Cotton, Mr P. S. Cresswell, Mr K. A. Dean, Mr Keith Denham, Mrs K. A. Dyson, Mr R. A. Fahey, Mr Brian W. Goodall, Mr Jeff Goodall, Mr J. D. Gordon, Mr David A. Green, Mr Dean Hardman, Mrs Stella Hardman, Mr P. L. Harrison, Mr Martin Harrison, Mr Kevin Hart, Mr D. Holgate, Mr K. Hubery, Mr G. R. Hunnam, Mr G. Hyde, Inner Circle Thoroughbreds Limited, Mr D. R. John, John Nicholls (Trading) Ltd, Mr R. F. Johnson, Mr D. Kilburn, Mr D. M. Knaggs, Mrs Jackie Knaggs, Mrs J Malcolmson, Mr Robert McAlpine, Mr Daren McCreary, Mr Jim McGrath, Mr D. J. P. McWilliams, Mr T. M. McKain, Ms Nicola Meese, Mrs P. A. Morrison, Mrs Margaret Nelson, Mr John R. Owen, Mr T. S. Palin, Mr G. J. Paver, Mr David F. Powell, Mr M. Prince, Mr Mel Roberts, Mr Michael Ryan (Bradford), Mr M. A. Scaife, Mr J. K. Shannon, Mr D. W. E. Sowden, Mr Jim Struth, Mrs Doreen M. Swinburn, Lady Juliet Tadgell, Mr A. Tattersall, Mrs Hazel Tattersall, Mr D. M. Tempest, Mr Peter Timmins, Mr P. M. Watson, Mr G. Weaver, Mr John Wicks, Mr David Wild, Mr S. Wood, Mr Martin Wood, Mr N. H. T. Wrigley.

**Assistant Trainer:** Robin O'Ryan

**Jockey (flat):** Tony Hamilton, Paul Hanagan, George Chaloner. **Jockey (NH):** Brian Hughes. **Apprentice:** Samantha Bell, Jack Garritty. **Amateur:** Miss Alyson Deniel.

---

## 202 MR CHRIS FAIRHURST, Middleham

Postal: **Glasgow House, Middleham, Leyburn, North Yorkshire, DL8 4QG**
Contacts: **PHONE/FAX (01969) 622039 MOBILE (07889) 410840**
**E-MAIL cfairhurst@tiscali.co.uk WEBSITE www.chrisfairhurstracing.com**

1 **CROWN AND GLORY (IRE),** 8, b g Turtle Island (IRE)—Monteleena (IRE) **Mr & Mrs W. H. Woods**
2 **DISTRICT ATTORNEY (IRE),** 6, b g Lawman (FR)—Mood Indigo (IRE) **The PQD Partnership**
3 **GRAY WOLF RIVER,** 4, gr f Fair Mix (IRE)—Inkpen **Miss S. R. Robertson**
4 **HIGHFIELD LASS,** 4, b f Cayman Kai (IRE)—Jendorcet **Mrs P. J. Taylor-Garthwaite**
5 **MAGICAL MISCHIEF,** 5, b m Rob Roy (USA)—Magical Flute **Mrs C. Arnold**
6 **MOOTABAR (IRE),** 8, gr g Verglas (IRE)—Melanzane **Mrs A. M. Leggett**
7 **SHIRLS SON SAM,** 7, b g Rambling Bear—Shirl **Mrs C. Arnold**
8 **SPRUZZO,** 9, b g Emperor Fountain—Ryewater Dream **980 Racing**
9 **THACKERAY,** 8, b g Fasliyev (USA)—Chinon (IRE) **Mrs C. Arnold**
10 **TROUBLED WATERS,** 6, b m Kayf Tara—Air of Affection **Miss S. R. Robertson**
11 **WHO'S SHIRL,** 9, b m Shinko Forest (IRE)—Shirl **Mrs S. France**

### THREE-YEAR-OLDS

12 **DANZELLA,** b f Desideratum—Danzatrice **980 Racing**
13 **ELLERINA,** b f Stimulation (IRE)—Dream Quest **Mr Allan Davies**

### TWO-YEAR-OLDS

14 B c 3/4 Misu Bond (IRE)—Accamelia (Shinko Forest (IRE)) **Mrs C. Arnold**
15 B f 25/4 Haafhd—Danzatrice (Tamure (IRE)) **980 Racing**
16 **EMILIE BRONTE,** b f 9/3 Mullionmileanhour (IRE)—Yorke's Folly (USA) (Stravinsky (USA)) **Mrs A. M. Leggett**
17 **KAZOEY,** b f 7/2 Stimulation (IRE)—Dubawi's Spirit (IRE) (Dubawi (IRE)) (2000) **Mr Allan Davies**

**Other Owners:** Mr J. M. Tozer, Mr M. D. Tozer.

---

## 203 MR JAMES FANSHAWE, Newmarket

Postal: **Pegasus Stables, Snailwell Road, Newmarket, Suffolk, CB8 7DJ**
Contacts: **PHONE (01638) 664525 / 660153 FAX (01638) 664523**
**E-MAIL james@jamesfanshawe.com WEBSITE www.jamesfanshawe.com**

1 **CELESTIAL KNIGHT,** 4, b g Compton Place—Garter Star **Carivalis, Eady, Papworth & Swinburn**
2 **DON'T STARE,** 5, b g Zamindar (USA)—Joshua's Princess **Mr Guy A.A.C. Gredley**
3 **ELIZONA,** 4, b f Pastoral Pursuits—Morning After **Mrs Alice Cherry**
4 **ENCOUNTERING (IRE),** 4, b g Duke of Marmalade (IRE)—Naval Affair (IRE) **Mr James Fanshawe**
5 **FRESH KINGDOM (IRE),** 4, ch g Dubawi (IRE)—Polyquest (IRE) **Mr Cheng Wai Tao**
6 **GALE FORCE,** 4, b f Shirocco (GER)—Hannda (IRE) **Mr T. R. G. Vestey**
7 **HE'S MY BOY (IRE),** 4, gr g Dark Angel (IRE)—Rose of Battle **Mr P. S. Ryan**
8 **HIGH JINX (IRE),** 7, b g High Chaparral (IRE)—Leonara (GER) **Mr & Mrs W. J. Williams**
9 **HORS DE COMBAT,** 4, ch g Mount Nelson—Maid For Winning (USA) **Mr Chris van Hoorn**

## MR JAMES FANSHAWE - Continued

10 **KNIGHT OWL,** 5, b g Rock of Gibraltar (IRE)—Miss Ivanhoe (IRE) **Miss Annabelle Condon**
11 **MISSED CALL (IRE),** 5, b m Authorized (IRE)—Incoming Call (USA) **Mr Malcolm C. Denmark**
12 **NOVIRAK (IRE),** 7, gr g Noverre (USA)—Manchaca (FR) **Mr Norman Brunskill**
13 **RIBBONS,** 5, ch m Manduro (GER)—Sister Act **Elite Racing Club**
14 **SAAB ALMANAL,** 4, b c Dubawi (IRE)—Caribbean Pearl (USA) **Mr Mohamed Obaida**
15 **SHE'S GORGEOUS (IRE),** 4, b f Acclamation—Acquiesced (IRE) **Johnstone Partnership**
16 **SHINING GLITTER (IRE),** 4, b f Shamardal (USA)—Lune Rose **Dragon Gate**
17 **SPIRIT RAISER (IRE),** 4, b f Invincible Spirit (IRE)—Macadamia (IRE) **Lord Vestey**
18 **SWORDBEARER,** 4, ch g Selkirk (USA)—Isis (USA) **Dr Catherine Wills**

### THREE-YEAR-OLDS

19 **ACQUITTAL,** b f Lawman (FR)—Zamid (FR) **Cheveley Park Stud**
20 **ALMARED,** b c Makfi—Starstone **Mr Saeed bel Obaida**
21 **ALWAREED,** ch c Makfi—Sinduda **Mr Mohamed Obaida**
22 **ANGEL DELIGHT (IRE),** b f Dark Angel (IRE)—Roof Fiddle (USA) **Andrew & Julia Turner**
23 **ARTHENUS,** b c Dutch Art—Lady Hen **A. Coombs & J. W. Rowley**
24 **AUMERLE,** b g Authorized (IRE)—Succinct **Dr Catherine Wills**
25 **CELESTIAL FIRE,** b f Medicean—Celeste **Cheveley Park Stud**
26 **DROMCUS,** b c Teofilo (IRE)—Storming Sioux **Mr Mohamed Obaida**
27 **DUKE OF NORTH (IRE),** b g Danehill Dancer (IRE)—Althea Rose (IRE) **DABsters**
28 **ELGIN,** b g Duke of Marmalade (IRE)—China Tea (USA) **Elite Racing Club**
29 **ESTEEMABLE,** ch f Nayef (USA)—Ring of Esteem **Mrs C. R. Philipson**
30 **FLORISS,** b f Medicean—Joshua's Princess **Mrs K. M. Gredley**
31 **FULL OF SPEED (USA),** ch g Raven's Pass (USA)—Knock Twice (USA) **Tom Mohan & Michael Mcdonnell**
32 **GALLOPING ANGER,** b f Makfi—Whispering Blues (IRE) **Mr Mohamed Obaida**
33 Ch f Pastoral Pursuits—Hannda (IRE) **Mr T. R. G. Vestey**
34 **HIGHER POWER,** b c Rip Van Winkle (IRE)—Lady Stardust **Mrs Martin Armstrong**
35 **LANDWADE LAD,** b g Dansili—Sell Out **Mr Simon Gibson**
36 **LEONARDO (GER),** ch g Areion (GER)—Lolli Pop (GER) **Mr Malcolm C. Denmark**
37 **MAID OF KENT,** br f Halling (USA)—First Fantasy **Nigel & Carolyn Elwes**
38 **MIRO (IRE),** b c Rock of Gibraltar (IRE)—Mission Secrete (IRE) **Mrs A. M. Swinburn**
39 **MODERAH,** b f Makfi—Meetyouthere (IRE) **Mr Salem bel Obaida**
40 **MR PICKWICK,** b c Mount Nelson—Never Lose **Johnstone Partnership**
41 **OSIPOVA,** b f Makfi—Barynya **Cheveley Park Stud**
42 **PECKING ORDER (IRE),** b f Fastnet Rock (AUS)—Shemaya (IRE) **Merry Fox Stud Limited**
43 **PRESTO BOY,** b g Compton Place—Presto Levanter **Fred Archer Racing - Silvio**
44 **RETURN ACE,** b f Zamindar (USA)—Match Point **Helena Springfield Ltd**
45 **SPEEDY BOARDING,** b f Shamardal (USA)—Dash To The Front **Helena Springfield Ltd**
46 **STAR STORM (IRE),** b c Sea The Stars (IRE)—Sayyedati Storm (USA) **Mr Mohamed Obaida**
47 B c Azamour (IRE)—Teggiano (IRE) **Mr Malcolm C. Denmark**
48 **THAI NOON (IRE),** b f Dansili—Alsace Lorraine (IRE) **Merry Fox Stud Limited**
49 **THE TIN MAN,** b c Equiano (FR)—Persario **Fred Archer Racing - Ormonde**
50 **UP IN LIGHTS (IRE),** ch f Makfi—Spotlight **Mr Mohamed Obaida**

### TWO-YEAR-OLDS

51 **ALWAYS SUMMER,** b f 19/3 Flatter (USA)—Air Kiss (Red Ransom (USA)) **Dr Catherine Wills**
52 **ALZEBARH (IRE),** ch f 9/3 Poet's Voice—Dubai Pearl (IRE) (Refuse To Bend (IRE)) **Mr Mohamed Obaida**
53 B c 24/3 Archipenko (USA)—Armoise (Sadler's Wells (USA)) (65000) **Mr Chris van Hoorn**
54 **BATTAILES,** b c 29/1 Acclamation—Ada River (Dansili) (100000) **Mr Simon Gibson**
55 **BLUES SISTER,** b f 23/2 Compton Place—
Persario (Bishop of Cashel) (88000) **Mr & Mrs M Morris,Mr & Mrs P Hopper**
56 B c 1/2 Iffraaj—Classic Vision (Classic Cliche (IRE)) (95000) **Mr Joseph Chung**
57 **COLUMN,** b c 25/4 Mount Nelson—Tottie (Fantastic Light (USA)) **Mr J. H. Richmond-Watson**
58 B c 13/2 Dutch Art—Czarna Roza (Polish Precedent (USA)) (130000) **Mr Ben C. M. Wong**
59 **ENACTING (USA),** b c 3/5 Henrythenavigator (USA)—
Random Chance (USA) (Red Ransom (USA)) (135000) **Mr Ben C. M. Wong**
60 **ENMESHING,** ch c 28/2 Mastercraftsman (IRE)—
Yacht Club (USA) (Sea Hero (USA)) (110000) **Mr Ben C. M. Wong**
61 **FILUMENA,** ch f 27/1 Pivotal—Phillipina (Medicean) **Cheveley Park Stud**
62 **INDULGED,** b f 11/2 Teofilo (IRE)—Fondled (Selkirk (USA)) **Cheveley Park Stud**
63 **ISSUE,** ch f 12/5 Nayef (USA)—Isis (USA) (Royal Academy (USA)) **Dr Catherine Wills**
64 **KING OF NAPLES,** b c 4/2 Excellent Art—Avon Lady (Avonbridge) (16000) **Mr P. S. Ryan**
65 Gr c 22/2 Sir Percy—Mahima (FR) (Linamix (FR)) (19841) **Fred Archer Racing - Bend Or**
66 **MAZZINI,** ch c 26/2 Exceed And Excel (AUS)—Firenze (Efisio) **Mr & Mrs P Hopper,Mr & Mrs M Morris**
67 **NOBLE STAR (IRE),** b c 21/2 Acclamation—Wrong Answer (Verglas (IRE)) (130000) **Mr Tang Wai Bun Tony**

## MR JAMES FANSHAWE - Continued

68 **PERMISSION,** b f 25/2 Authorized (IRE)—
Continua (USA) (Elusive Quality (USA)) **Mrs Julia Scott, J. F. Dean & Lady Trenchard**
69 **POINTEL (FR),** b c 4/3 Le Havre (IRE)—Polysheba (FR) (Poliglote) (107142) **Mrs A. M. Swinburn**
70 B f 10/3 Fastnet Rock (AUS)—Quiet Protest (USA) (Kingmambo (USA)) (105000) **Mr John P. McManus**
71 **SILCA WINGS,** b f 29/4 Multiplex—Silca Destination (Dubai Destination (USA)) **Apple Tree Stud**
72 **SLEEPLESSINSEATTLE,** b f 10/2 Rip Van Winkle (IRE)—
Caught On Camera (Red Ransom (USA)) **Helena Springfield Ltd**
73 **STONEY BROKE,** b f 2/4 Dansili—Alvee (IRE) (Key of Luck (USA)) **Merry Fox Stud Limited**
74 **STYLISHLY,** ch f 13/5 Pivotal—Miswaki Belle (USA) (Miswaki (USA)) **Cheveley Park Stud**
75 **TEGARA,** ch f 14/3 Hard Spun (USA)—Damaniyat Girl (USA) (Elusive Quality (USA)) **Mr Mohamed Obaida**
76 B c 27/3 Dick Turpin (IRE)—Valiantly (Anabaa (USA)) (70000) **Mr Ngai**
77 **ZEST (IRE),** b f 24/1 Duke of Marmalade (IRE)—Affinity (Sadler's Wells (USA)) **Elite Racing Club**

**Other Owners:** Mr Geoffrey Baber, Mrs Denise Beetles, Mr Graham Beetles, Mr Isidore Carivalis, The Hon Mrs Penny Butler, Mr Roy Eady, Mrs Lilette Ebrahimkhan, Mr Rashid Ebrahimkhan, Mrs Libby Fanshawe, Mrs Georgie Fanshawe, Mr Brian Fanshawe, Mr Colin Gilbert, Mr Harry Johnstone, Mr John Johnstone, Mrs Zara Johnstone, Mrs Sarah King, Mr Arne Korsbakken, Mr Niall Lynch, Mr Gary Marney, Mrs Lorraine Marney, Mr Simon Massen, Miss Olivia Palmer, Mrs Pat Rowley, Mr David I. Russell, Mr William Russell, Mr Ulf Ryden, Ms Hermione Scrope, Mr Rob Stevens, Mrs Jan Trew-Smith.

---

**204**

## MR JOHNNY FARRELLY, Bridgwater

Postal: **Smocombe Racing Stables, Enmore, Bridgwater, Somerset, TA5 2EB**

1 **AMANTIUS,** 6, b g Multiplex—Ghana (GER) **H. M. W. Clifford**
2 **ASCENDANT,** 9, ch g Medicean—Ascendancy **F. A. Clegg**
3 **BATTLE GROUP,** 10, b g Beat Hollow—Cantanta **Jolly Boys Outing**
4 **BEDOUIN BAY,** 8, b g Dubai Destination (USA)—Sahara Sonnet (USA) **F. A. Clegg**
5 **COMTE D'ANJOU,** 6, b g Desert King (IRE)—Delayed (FR) **Mrs S. J. Faulks**
6 **DIMITAR (USA),** 6, b g Mizzen Mast (USA)—Peace And Love (IRE) **P. M. Tosh**
7 **FINISH THE STORY (IRE),** 9, b g Court Cave (IRE)—Lady of Grange (IRE) **Mr C. Howe**
8 **FORWARD MARCH,** 5, b g Beat Hollow—Cantanta **Third Time Lucky**
9 **HOLD THE FORT (IRE),** 8, b g Brian Boru—Go Katie **Hanford's Chemist Ltd**
10 **KAZLIAN (FR),** 7, b g Sinndar (IRE)—Quiet Splendor (USA) **Twelve Pipers Piping**
11 **MARKAMI (FR),** 5, ch g Medicean—Marque Royale **P. M. Tosh**
12 **MOLLY OSCAR (IRE),** 9, b m Oscar (IRE)—Bishop's Folly **J. Farrelly**
13 **MOVING WAVES (IRE),** 4, b f Intense Focus (USA)—Kimola (IRE) **Mrs Z. Wentworth**
14 **PENZFLO (IRE),** 9, b m Luso—Penzita (IRE) **P. M. Tosh**
15 **QULINTON (FR),** 11, b g Bulington (FR)—Klef du Bonheur (FR) **Mr R. M. Whitby**
16 **RODERICK RANDOM,** 5, b g Kayf Tara—Clotted Cream (USA) **Mrs S. J. Faulks**
17 **SPORTING BOY (IRE),** 7, b g Barathea (IRE)—Sportsticketing (IRE) **H. M. W. Clifford**
18 **TARABELA,** 12, b m Kayf Tara—Rocky Revival **G2 Recruitment Solutions Ltd**
19 **WAR SINGER (USA),** 8, b g War Chant (USA)—Sister Marilyn (USA) **The War Cabinet**

### THREE-YEAR-OLDS

20 **CHORLTON HOUSE,** ch g Compton Place—Really Ransom **Wildehall Bloodstock Limited**
21 **MINNIE (IRE),** b f Sakhee's Secret—Numerus Clausus (FR) **Mr P. E. Wildes**

**Other Owners:** Mr M. J. Fitzpatrick, Mr J. Gwyther, T. Neill, Palatinate Thoroughbred Racing Limited, Mr C. G. Paletta.

---

## MISS JULIA FEILDEN, Newmarket

Postal: **Harraton Stud, Laceys Lane, Exning, Newmarket, Suffolk, CB8 7HW**
Contacts: **PHONE (01638) 577470 FAX (01638) 578628 MOBILE (07974) 817694**
**E-MAIL juliafeilden@aol.com WEBSITE www.juliafeildenracing.com**

1 **ATTAIN,** 6, b g Dansili—Achieve **Newmarket Equine Tours Racing Club**
2 **AUTOMOTIVE,** 7, b g Beat Hollow—Bina Ridge **Stowstowquickquickstow Partnership**
3 **AVIDLY,** 5, b m Beat Hollow—Balmy **Mr & Mrs George Bhatti**
4 **BETHAN,** 6, b m Nayef (USA)—Elizabethan Age (FR) **Ms H. C. Ranner**
5 **BUSHY GLADE (IRE),** 4, b f Bushranger (IRE)—Cladantom (IRE) **R. J. Creese**
6 **CANDESTA (USA),** 5, b g First Defence (USA)—Wandesta **Mr & Mrs George Bhatti**
7 **DAKOTA CITY,** 4, b g Three Valleys (USA)—West Dakota (USA) **Good Company Partnership**

## MISS JULIA FEILDEN - Continued

8 **GUISING,** 6, ch g Manduro (GER)—Trick Or Treat **Mrs C. T. Bushnell**
9 **HANDHELD,** 8, ch g Observatory (USA)—Kid Gloves **Newmarket Equine Tours Racing Club**
10 **HONEYMOON EXPRESS (IRE),** 5, br m Mujadil (USA)—Royal Jelly **Miss J. D. Feilden**
11 **MEDDLING,** 5, ch m Halling (USA)—Piffling **Good Company Partnership**
12 **SABRE ROCK,** 5, b g Dubawi (IRE)—Retainage (USA) **Miss J. D. Feilden**
13 **SILVER ALLIANCE,** 7, gr g Proclamation (IRE)—Aimee Vibert **In It To Win Partnership**
14 **SKYE HIGH,** 4, b f Rainbow High—Celinda (FR) **A. R. Middleton**
15 **THE DUCKING STOOL,** 8, ch m Where Or When (IRE)—Dance Sequel **Newmarket Equine Tours Racing Club**
16 **TIGHT LIPPED (IRE),** 6, gr g Dark Angel (IRE)—Kayoko (IRE) **R. J. Creese**
17 **TOLLY MCGUINESS,** 4, ch c Araafa (IRE)—Golden Flyer (FR) **Newmarket Equine Tours Racing Club**
18 **VASTLY (USA),** 6, gr ro g Mizzen Mast (USA)—Valentine Band (USA) **The Sultans of Speed**
19 **VEERAYA,** 5, b g Rail Link—Follow Flanders **Mr A. R. Farook**

### THREE-YEAR-OLDS

20 **DUKE OF DIAMONDS,** gr g Duke of Marmalade (IRE)—Diamond Line (FR) **Carol Bushnell & Partners**
21 **MOMENT TO DREAM,** b f Halling (USA)—Pretty Majestic (IRE)
22 **PRUSSIA COVE (USA),** b f Afleet Alex (USA)—High Walden (USA) **Steve Clarke**

### TWO-YEAR-OLDS

23 **BIG BANG,** b c 9/3 Observatory (USA)—Bavarica (Dansili) **Miss J. D. Feilden**
24 **GO ON GAL (IRE),** b f 13/4 Approve (IRE)—Jeritza (Rainbow Quest (USA)) **Go On Gal Partnership**
25 **LITTLE ORCHID,** b f 7/3 Observatory (USA)—
Bushy Dell (IRE) (King Charlemagne (USA)) **R. J. Creese & Miss J. Feilden**
26 **SERENDIB'S GLORY (IRE),** b f 27/3 Holy Roman Emperor (IRE)—
Rose of Mooncoin (IRE) (Brief Truce (USA)) **Mr A. R. Farook**
27 Ch c 23/4 Archipenko (USA)—Sovereign Seal (Royal Applause)

**Other Owners:** Mr G. Bhatti, Mrs C. J. Bhatti, J. Birkett, Mr R. A. Birkett, C. M. Page, R. F. Wright.

**Assistant Trainer:** Ross Birkett

**Jockey (flat):** Adam Beschizza. **Apprentice:** Shelley Birkett, Ryan M. Moore. **Amateur:** Mr R. Birkett.

---

## 206 MR CHARLIE FELLOWES, Newmarket

Postal: **St. Gatien Cottage, Vicarage Road, Newmarket, Suffolk, CB8 8HP**
Contacts: **PHONE (01638) 666948 MOBILE (07968) 499596**
**E-MAIL charlie@charliefellowesracing.co.uk WEBSITE www.charliefellowesracing.co.uk**

1 **ACCESSION (IRE),** 6, b g Acclamation—Pivotal's Princess (IRE) **Lady De Ramsey**
2 **BARBARY (IRE),** 4, b g Rock of Gibraltar (IRE)—Silver Cache (USA) **Mr G. Mills**
3 **BUCKLAND (IRE),** 7, b g Oratorio (IRE)—Dollar Bird (IRE) **Mr P. S. McNally**
4 **BUCKLAND BEAU,** 4, b g Rock of Gibraltar (IRE)—Heavenly Whisper (IRE) **Mr P. S. McNally**
5 **LYCIDAS (GER),** 6, b g Zamindar (USA)—La Felicita **Mr G. Mills**
6 **ORDERS FROM ROME (IRE),** 6, b g Holy Roman Emperor (IRE)—
Fatat Alarab (USA) **The Dalmunzie Devils Partnership**
7 **PEARL ICE,** 7, b g Iffraaj—Jezebel **Lady De Ramsey**

### THREE-YEAR-OLDS

8 **BOARDING PARTY (USA),** ch g More Than Ready (USA)—Oceans Apart **Elite Racing Club**
9 **CAROLINAE,** ch f Makfi—You Too **Mr S. M. Bel Obaida**
10 **CLASSICAL ROSE,** b f Amadeus Wolf—Monaazalah (IRE) **Mr F. J. Perry**
11 Ch c Makfi—Dolydille (IRE) **M. Obaida**
12 **EXPIRY DATE,** ch c Makfi—Midnight Shift (IRE) **M. Obaida**
13 **LAHENT,** b c Makfi—Misty Waters (IRE) **Mr S. M. Bel Obaida**
14 **MINAHILL,** b f Observatory (USA)—Deceived **Newpinewood Stables Ltd**
15 **PERDURABLE,** br f Sakhee's Secret—Pain Perdu (IRE) **Barma / Harper / Dennis**
16 **POETIC POLLY,** ch f Lope de Vega (IRE)—Polly Floyer
17 B f Fastnet Rock (AUS)—Speak Softly To Me (USA)
18 **TEKFA (IRE),** b c Makfi—Night Club **Mr S. M. Bel Obaida**
19 **TOLAH,** ch f Mount Nelson—Tropical Barth (IRE) **Mr S. M. Bel Obaida**

## MR CHARLIE FELLOWES - Continued

20 **WET SAIL (USA),** b g Henrythenavigator (USA)—Aljawza (USA) **Qatar Racing Limited**
21 **ZOORAWAR,** b c Excellent Art—Sylvan Ride **Newpinewood Stables Ltd**

### TWO-YEAR-OLDS

22 B c 5/5 Champs Elysees—Eternity Ring (Alzao (USA)) (35000) **Saffron House Stables Partnership**
23 B f 12/3 Footstepsinthesand—Fillthegobletagain (IRE) (Byron) (20634)
24 B c 6/4 Lilbourne Lad (IRE)—Mooching Along (IRE) (Mujahid (USA)) (22221)
25 B c 28/2 Desert Party (USA)—Ras Shaikh (USA) (Sheikh Albadou) **M. Obaida**
26 **SALVO,** b f 6/3 Acclamation—Passe Passe (USA) (Lear Fan (USA)) **A. E. Oppenheimer**
27 Ch c 22/4 Poet's Voice—Shivaree (Rahy (USA)) (45000) **Emma Capon & Mrs Simon Marsh**
28 B c 23/4 Thousand Words—Sinegronto (IRE) (Kheleyf (USA)) (5952)
29 B c 28/3 Shirocco (GER)—Storming Sioux (Storming Home) **M. Obaida**
30 **TRODERO,** b f 30/3 Mastercraftsman (IRE)—Jules (IRE) (Danehill (USA)) (10000) **Newpinewood Stables Ltd**
31 **VINTAGE RUM (IRE),** b f 28/4 Rock of Gibraltar (IRE)—
Island Race (Common Grounds) (15000) **Newpinewood Stables Ltd**
32 B c 15/2 Footstepsinthesand—Zawariq (IRE) (Marju (IRE)) (22221)

**Other Owners:** T. H. Barma, Mr O. S. W. Bell, Mrs E. Capon, Mr R. Cooper, D. W. Dennis, Mr C. H. Fellowes, C. J. Harper, Mr A. J. Hill, Mrs J. F. Marsh, Miss M. Noden.

---

## 207 MR JOHN FERGUSON, Cowlinge

Postal: **Bloomfields, Cowlinge, Newmarket, Suffolk, CB8 9HN**
Contacts: **PHONE (01638) 500423 FAX (01638) 500387**

1 **AALIM,** 5, b g Nayef (USA)—Anna Palariva (IRE) **Bloomfields**
2 **AQALIM,** 5, b g Raven's Pass (USA)—Aviacion (BRZ) **Bloomfields**
3 **ARABIAN REVOLUTION,** 4, gr g Dalakhani (IRE)—Mont Etoile (IRE) **Bloomfields**
4 **ARABIC HISTORY (IRE),** 5, b g Teofilo (IRE)—Ruby Affair (IRE) **Bloomfields**
5 **BORDONI (USA),** 6, b g Bernardini (USA)—Argentina (IRE) **Bloomfields**
6 **BUCKWHEAT,** 5, b g Manduro (GER)—Russian Snows (IRE) **Bloomfields**
7 **CAYMAN ISLANDS,** 7, b g Shirocco (GER)—Barbuda **Bloomfields**
8 **CHESTERFIELD (IRE),** 5, ch g Pivotal—Antique (IRE) **Bloomfields**
9 **COMMISSIONED (IRE),** 5, b g Authorized (IRE)—Zelda (IRE) **Bloomfields**
10 **DEVILMENT,** 4, b g Cape Cross (IRE)—Mischief Making (USA) **Bloomfields**
11 **EARTH DREAM (IRE),** 12, b g Old Vic—Barbaras Mews (IRE) **Bloomfields**
12 **EL NAMOOSE,** 6, b g Authorized (IRE)—Hashimiya (USA) **Bloomfields**
13 **FATHER EDWARD (IRE),** 6, b g Flemensfirth (USA)—Native Side (IRE) **Bloomfields**
14 **HIGH BRIDGE,** 4, b g Monsun (GER)—Ameerat **Bloomfields**
15 **JALINGO (IRE),** 4, b g Cape Cross (IRE)—Just Special **Bloomfields**
16 **JOE FARRELL (IRE),** 6, b g Presenting—Luck of The Deise (IRE) **Bloomfields**
17 **LINCOLN COUNTY,** 4, b c Authorized (IRE)—Lane County (USA) **Bloomfields**
18 **MANTOU (IRE),** 4, ch g Teofilo (IRE)—Shadow Roll (IRE) **Bloomfields**
19 **MIJHAAR,** 7, b g Shirocco (GER)—Jathaabeh **Bloomfields**
20 **NABUCCO,** 6, b h Dansili—Cape Verdi (IRE) **Bloomfields**
21 **NEW YEAR'S EVE,** 7, b g Motivator—Midnight Angel (GER) **Bloomfields**
22 **PADDY MULLIGAN (IRE),** 6, b g Presenting—Laragh (IRE) **Bloomfields**
23 **PARLOUR GAMES,** 7, ch g Monsun (GER)—Petrushka (IRE) **Bloomfields**
24 **PINE CREEK,** 7, b g Doyen (IRE)—Valley of Gold (FR) **Bloomfields**
25 **PURPLE BAY (IRE),** 6, b g Dubawi (IRE)—Velvet Lady **Bloomfields**
26 **QEWY (IRE),** 5, b h Street Cry (IRE)—Princess Nada **Bloomfields**
27 **RED DEVIL BOYS (IRE),** 8, b g Oscar (IRE)—Lohort Castle (IRE) **Bloomfields**
28 **RUACANA,** 6, b g Cape Cross (IRE)—Farrfesheena (USA) **Bloomfields**
29 **SCARTEEN (IRE),** 5, b g Robin des Champs (FR)—Downsouth (IRE) **Bloomfields**
30 **SEA LORD (IRE),** 8, b g Cape Cross (IRE)—First Fleet (USA) **Bloomfields**
31 **SOUTHERN STRIFE,** 4, b g Dubawi (IRE)—Savannah Belle **Bloomfields**
32 **SWIVEL,** 4, ch c Shirocco (GER)—Pivotal Drive (IRE) **Bloomfields**
33 **THREE KINGDOMS (IRE),** 6, ch g Street Cry (IRE)—Chan Tong (BRZ) **Bloomfields**
34 **TOMMY O'DWYER (IRE),** 6, b g Milan—Always Present (IRE) **Bloomfields**
35 **ZIP TOP (IRE),** 6, b g Smart Strike (CAN)—Zofzig (USA) **Bloomfields**

**Other Owners:** Mr John P. Ferguson, Mrs John Ferguson.

## 208 MR DOMINIC FFRENCH DAVIS, Lambourn

Postal: **College House, 3 Oxford Street, Lambourn, Hungerford, Berkshire, RG17 8XP**
Contacts: **YARD (01488) 73675 Home (01488) 72342 FAX (01488) 73675 MOBILE (07831) 118764**
**E-MAIL ffrenchdavis@btinternet.com WEBSITE www.ffrenchdavis.com**

1 **APPROPRIATE (FR),** 5, b m Kapgarde (FR)—Oreli (FR) **J. B. Robinson**
2 **BRANDYWELL BOY (IRE),** 12, b g Danetime (IRE)—Alexander Eliott (IRE) **D. J. S. Ffrench Davis**
3 **CHILL IN THE WOOD,** 6, br m Desert King (IRE)—Zaffaranni (IRE) **Mr D. G. Cramm**
4 **IF I WERE A BOY (IRE),** 8, b m Invincible Spirit (IRE)—Attymon Lill (IRE) **Mr R. F. Haynes**
5 **PALADIN (IRE),** 6, b g Dubawi (IRE)—Palwina (FR) **D. J. S. Ffrench Davis**
6 **ROLLING DICE,** 4, b g Rail Link—Breathing Space (USA) **Miss Alison Jones**
7 **WHATTHEBUTLERSAW (IRE),** 6, br g Arcadio (GER)—Phar From Men (IRE) **D. J. S. Ffrench Davis**

### THREE-YEAR-OLDS

8 **JELLY MONGER (IRE),** b f Strategic Prince—Royal Jelly **Gary Black & Mark Duthie**

### TWO-YEAR-OLDS

9 B f 26/2 Lilbourne Lad (IRE)—Flash And Dazzle (IRE) (Bertolini (USA)) (26000)
10 B f 23/3 Duke of Marmalade (IRE)—Kekova (Montjeu (IRE)) (17000) **Mr R. F. Haynes**
11 Ch c 27/3 Strategic Prince—Support Fund (IRE) (Intikhab (USA)) (16000)
12 Ch c 3/4 Equiano (FR)—Swain's Gold (USA) (Swain (IRE)) (40000) **The Agincourt Partnership**

**Other Owners:** G. H. Black, Mr J. O. Chapman, M. Duthie, Mr T. G. Holroyd.

**Assistant Trainer:** Avery Ffrench Davis

**Jockey (flat):** James Doyle. **Jockey (NH):** Mark Grant.

## 209 MR GIUSEPPE FIERRO, Hednesford

Postal: **Bentley Brook House, Rawnsley Road, Hednesford, Cannock, Staffordshire, WS12 1RB**
Contacts: **HOME/YARD (01543) 879611 MOBILE (07976) 321468**

1 **FRANKIE FALCO,** 9, br h Bollin Eric—Marsh Marigold **G. Fierro**
2 **JUST LIKE BETH,** 7, b m Proclamation (IRE)—Just Beth **G. Fierro**
3 **LITTLE DOTTY,** 6, br m Erhaab (USA)—Marsh Marigold **G. Fierro**
4 **RED HOTT ROBBIE,** 6, b g Revoque (IRE)—Abbiejo (IRE) **G. Fierro**
5 **SUNDANCE BOY,** 6, gr g Proclamation (IRE)—Just Beth **G. Fierro**

**Assistant Trainer:** M Fierro

## 210 MRS MARJORIE FIFE, Stillington

Postal: **White Thorn Farm, Stillington, Easingwold, York, YO61 1LT**
Contacts: **PHONE (01347) 822012 MOBILE (07890) 075217**
**E-MAIL wfife10416@aol.com**

1 **AMTIRED,** 9, gr g Beauchamp King—Rising Talisker **Mr G. Smith**
2 **ASPIRANT,** 4, b g Rail Link—Affluent **Mr T. W. Fife**
3 **BEST TRIP (IRE),** 8, b g Whipper (USA)—Tereed Elhawa
4 **CAMEROONEY,** 12, b g Sugarfoot—Enkindle **Mrs J. Stapleton**
5 **JUST THE TONIC,** 8, ch m Medicean—Goodwood Blizzard **R. W. Fife**
6 **MANDALAY KING (IRE),** 10, b g King's Best (USA)—Mahamuni (IRE) **R. W. Fife**
7 **PAT'S LEGACY (USA),** 9, ch g Yankee Gentleman (USA)—Sugars for Nanny (USA) **J. P. McCarthy**
8 **PERFECT WORDS (IRE),** 5, ch g Thousand Words—Zilayah (USA) **Green Lane**
9 **RED TIDE (IRE),** 4, gr g Tamayuz—Rectify (IRE) **Mrs J. Mchugh**
10 **ROYAL HOLIDAY (IRE),** 8, ch g Captain Rio—Sunny Slope **Mrs M. Turner**
11 **SARTORI,** 4, b c Elnadim (USA)—Little Caroline (IRE) **Chris Tremewan, Mike Saini, Tom Fife**
12 **SHERMAN MCCOY,** 9, ch g Reset (AUS)—Naomi Wildman (USA) **Mr T. W. Fife**
13 **SIMMPLY SAM,** 8, b m Nomadic Way (USA)—Priceless Sam **Mrs S. M. Barker**
14 **SIRPERTAN,** 4, b g Sir Percy—Tanwir **Mr D. & Mr S. Woodall**
15 **THORNABY PRINCESS,** 4, b f Camacho—Ingleby Princess **The Fallen Angels**
16 **TIMBER KING,** 6, b g Desideratum—Chanteuse **P. Allison**
17 **YORKSTERS PRINCE (IRE),** 8, b g Beat Hollow—Odalisque (IRE) **Mrs M. Turner**

**MRS MARJORIE FIFE - Continued**

**THREE-YEAR-OLDS**

18 **ACCRA GIRL,** b f Captain Gerrard (IRE)—Ela d'argent (IRE) **Market Avenue Racing Club Ltd**
19 **POLITICO,** ch f Medicean—Tafawut **R. W. Fife**
20 **SAVANNAH BEAU,** b f Major Cadeaux—Mancunian Way **Market Avenue Racing Club Ltd**

**Other Owners:** Mr P. I. Baker, Mr C. R. Piercy, Mr M. Saini, Mr D. Scott, C. Tremewan, Mr D. Woodall, Mr S. Woodall.

---

## 211 MR TIM FITZGERALD, Malton

Postal: **Norton Grange, Norton, Malton, North Yorkshire, YO17 9EA**
Contacts: **OFFICE (01653) 692718 FAX (01653) 600214 MOBILE (07950) 356437**
**E-MAIL fitzgeraldracing@hotmail.com**

1 **ACRAI RUA (IRE),** 12, ch g Rock Hopper—Dontbelieveaword (IRE) **Grange Park Racing**
2 **CAPTAIN CHAOS (IRE),** 4, ch g Golan (IRE)—Times Have Changed (IRE) **T. J. Fitzgerald**
3 **COMERAGH KING,** 11, b g Kayf Tara—Velcro Girl (IRE)
4 **KASTELA STARI,** 8, b m Beat Hollow—Campaspe
5 **MR SYNTAX (IRE),** 11, b g King's Theatre (IRE)—Smile Awhile (USA) **Pinnacle N.H Partnership**
6 **RAINFORD GLORY (IRE),** 5, ch g Rock of Gibraltar (IRE)—My Dolly Madison **Dukes Racing 1**
7 **ROCK ON BOLLINSKI,** 5, b g Bollin Eric—Bred For Pleasure **Mr E. J. Worrell**
8 **WARFARE,** 6, b g Soviet Star (USA)—Fluffy **Dukes Racing 1**

**Other Owners:** A. D. Crombie, O. R. Dukes, Mrs K. Dukes, Ms S. V. Hattersley, B. Morton, Mr E. Surr.

---

## 212 MR JEREMIAH FITZPATRICK, Cork

Postal: **Deruna, Curragh, Kanturk, Co Cork, Ireland**
Contacts: **PHONE (00 353) 29 50175 MOBILE (00 353) 86 3101931**

1 **RORY ANNA (IRE),** 9, b m Viking Ruler (AUS)—Montana Miss (IRE) **Mrs W. M. Fitzpatrick**
2 **SYDLEY (IRE),** 5, ch g Wareed (IRE)—Hylady (IRE) **Mrs W. M. Fitzpatrick**

---

## 213 MR PAUL FITZSIMONS, Upper Lambourn

Postal: **Saxon Gate Stables, Malt Shovel Lane, Lambourn, Berkshire, RG17 8QH**
Contacts: **PHONE (01488) 72712 FAX (01488) 72716 MOBILE (07795) 566359**
**E-MAIL paulfitzsimons@saxon-gate.com WEBSITE www.saxon-gate.com**

1 **BANREENAHREENKAH (IRE),** 5, b m Steppe Dancer (IRE)—Carmencita **Saxon Gate Bloodstock**
2 **BEAUCHAMP MELBA,** 4, b f Compton Admiral—Ashford Castle (USA) **E. Penser**
3 **CLAPPERBOARD,** 4, b f Royal Applause—Roseum **Saxon Gate Bloodstock**
4 **COMPTON BIRD,** 6, b m Motivator—Noble Peregrine **E. Penser**
5 **COMPTON REX,** 4, br g Mount Nelson—Jane Austen (IRE) **E. Penser**
6 **TREE OF LIFE,** 5, ch m Medicean—Antebellum (FR) **Miss H. Moller**

**THREE-YEAR-OLDS**

7 **BEAUCHAMP ACE,** b g Compton Admiral—Aquarelle **E. Penser**
8 **BEAUCHAMP DIAMOND,** b f Compton Admiral—Orange Sunset (IRE) **E. Penser**
9 **BEAUCHAMP EAGLE,** ch g Compton Admiral—Ashford Castle (USA) **E. Penser**
10 **BEAUCHAMP RUBY,** b f Cockney Rebel (IRE)—Beauchamp Utopia **E. Penser**
11 **COMPTON VIKING (IRE),** ch c Equiano (FR)—Feather Boa (IRE) **E. Penser**
12 B f Bernstein (USA)—Euroslew (USA) **Eastwind Racing Ltd & Martha Trussell**
13 **WAR OF DESTINY (USA),** b g War Front (USA)—Dyna's Destiny (USA) **East Wind Racing Ltd**
14 **WAVE DANCER (IRE),** b c Montjeu (IRE)—Bonnie Byerly (USA) **Eastwind Racing Ltd & Martha Trussell**

**TWO-YEAR-OLDS**

15 **BEAUCHAMP AMARA,** b f 23/3 Aussie Rules (USA)—Baharah (USA) (Elusive Quality (USA)) (2095) **E. Penser**
16 **BEAUCHAMP DAME,** ch f 1/5 Archipenko (USA)—Beauchamp Utopia (Compton Admiral) (571) **E. Penser**
17 **BEAUCHAMP MONARK,** b c 16/4 Pastoral Pursuits—Orange Sunset (IRE) (Roanoke (USA)) (1428) **E. Penser**

## MR PAUL FITZSIMONS - Continued

18 **BEAUCHAMP PASHA,** b c 3/5 Pastoral Pursuits—Ashford Castle (USA) (Bates Motel (USA)) (5523) **E. Penser**
19 **BEAUCHAMP REBEL,** b c 29/3 Cockney Rebel (IRE)—Beauchamp Xiara (Compton Admiral) (1904) **E. Penser**
20 B f 5/4 Equiano (FR)—Stylish Dream (USA) (Elusive Quality (USA)) (16000) **Saxon Gate Bloodstock**

**Assistant Trainer:** Mikael Magnusson

---

## 214 MR JOHN FLINT, Bridgend

Postal: **Cherry Tree, 71 Woodlands Park, Kenfig Hill, Bridgend, Mid-Glamorgan, CF33 6EB**
Contacts: **PHONE (01656) 744347 FAX (01656) 744347 MOBILE (07581) 428173**
**E-MAIL john@johnflintracing.com WEBSITE www.johnflintracing.com**

1 **AMAZING STAR (IRE),** 10, b g Soviet Star (USA)—Sadika (IRE) **Mr W. G. Cleary**
2 **BERNISDALE,** 7, ch m Bertolini (USA)—Carradale **Mr R. M. James**
3 **BOB WILL (IRE),** 10, b g Bob's Return (IRE)—Mini Moo Min **Mr B. M. Jones**
4 **EDDIEMAURICE (IRE),** 4, ch g Captain Rio—Annals **Mr D. M. Mathias**
5 **KAYF MOSS,** 7, b g Kayf Tara—Madam Mosso **Mr L. H. & Mrs T. Evans**
6 **KOLIAKHOVA (FR),** 4, b f Literato (FR)—Lia Waltz (FR) **Mr D. M. Mathias**
7 **LAC SACRE (FR),** 6, b g Bering—Lady Glorieuse (FR) **Mr L. H. & Mrs T. Evans**
8 **RUN BOB RUN,** 4, b g Beat All (USA)—Rash-Gale (IRE) **Katchar Racing**
9 **TAROUM (IRE),** 8, b g Refuse To Bend (IRE)—Taraza (IRE) **J. L. Flint**
10 **TRAVIS BICKLE (IRE),** 4, b g Sky Mesa (USA)—Out of Woods (USA) **J. L. Flint**

**Other Owners:** Mr L. H. Evans, Mrs T. Evans, Mr S. A. Raymond, Mrs T. J. Raymond.

**Assistant Trainer:** Mrs Martine Louise Flint (07968) 044487

**Jockey (NH):** Rhys Flint.

---

## 215 MR DAVID FLOOD, Swindon

Postal: **15 High Street, Chiseldon, Swindon, Wiltshire, SN4 0NG**
Contacts: **PHONE (07919) 340619**
**E-MAIL davidflood1@hotmail.co.uk**

1 5, B g Lucarno (USA)—Kompete
2 **MISTER GREEN (FR),** 9, b g Green Desert (USA)—Summertime Legacy **Flood Family Racing Limited**
3 **PETIT ECUYER (FR),** 9, b g Equerry (USA)—Petite Majeste (FR) **Mr F. Michael**
4 **TRADER JACK,** 6, b g Trade Fair—Azeema (IRE) **Mr A. Lemon**

---

## 216 MR TONY FORBES, Uttoxeter

Postal: **Hill House Farm, Poppits Lane, Stramshall, Uttoxeter, Staffordshire, ST14 5EX**
Contacts: **PHONE (01889) 562722 MOBILE (07967) 246571**
**E-MAIL tony@thimble.net**

1 **HOLLINS,** 11, b g Lost Soldier (USA)—Cutting Reef (IRE) **Mr A. L. Forbes**
2 **MEDIEVAL BISHOP (IRE),** 6, b g Bachelor Duke (USA)—On The Backfoot (IRE) **Mr A. L. Forbes**
3 **NOLECCE,** 8, ch g Reset (AUS)—Ghassanah **Mr A. L. Forbes**

**Assistant Trainer:** Mr Tim Eley

---

## 217 MRS PAM FORD, Hereford

Postal: **Stone House Stables, Preston Wynne, Hereford, Herefordshire, HR1 3PB**
Contacts: **HOME/FAX (01432) 820604 MOBILE (07733) 152051**
**E-MAIL pam_ford@hotmail.co.uk**

1 **APACHE CHIEF,** 7, b g Tikkanen (USA)—Dara's Course (IRE) **K. R. Ford**
2 8, B m Erhaab (USA)—Candy Copper
3 **CAPTAIN OATS (IRE),** 12, b g Bahhare (USA)—Adarika **Miss V. A. M. Davies**
4 **FREDDIE BEAR,** 7, b g Grape Tree Road—Zajira (IRE) **Miss V. A. M. Davies**
5 **RUNNING SQUAW,** 7, ch m Denounce—Georgie McTaggart **K. R. Ford**

## MRS PAM FORD - Continued

**Assistant Trainer:** Mr K Ford

**Jockey (flat):** Hayley Turner, Royston Ffrench. **Jockey (NH):** James Davies.

---

## 218 MR RICHARD FORD, Garstang

Postal: **Lancashire Racing Stables, The Paddocks, Strickens Lane, Barnacre, Garstang, Lancashire, PR3 1UD**
Contacts: **PHONE (01995) 605790 (07802) 764094 MOBILE (07976) 522768**
**E-MAIL clarksonhorses@barnacre.fsbusiness.co.uk**
**WEBSITE www.lancashireracingstables.co.uk**

1 **DEBT TO SOCIETY (IRE),** 8, ch g Moscow Society (USA)—Nobody's Darling (IRE) **Mr & Mrs G. E. Pickering**
2 **DOESLESSTHANME (IRE),** 11, ch g Definite Article—Damemill (IRE) **R. J. Hewitt**
3 **DR BEAUJOLAIS (IRE),** 9, b g Dr Massini (IRE)—Satlin (IRE) **Winks Racing**
4 **ELLIES IMAGE,** 8, b m Lucky Story (USA)—Crown City (USA) **Mr J. H. Chrimes**
5 **EXKALIBER,** 6, b g Exceed And Excel (AUS)—Kalindi **Winks Racing**
6 5, B g Byron—Hasty Lady **Sports 360**
7 **INSOLENCEOFOFFICE (IRE),** 7, b g Kodiac—Sharp Diversion (USA) **CCCNLP**
8 **KYLE OF BUTE,** 9, ch g Kyllachy—Blinding Mission (IRE) **Mr J.H.Chrimes & Mr & Mrs G.W.Hannam**
9 **LATE FOR SUPPER (IRE),** 6, ch g Kahtan—Tillery (IRE) **The Coz Syndicate**
10 **MICK DUNDEE (IRE),** 5, b g Aussie Rules (USA)—Lucky Oakwood (USA) **Winks Racing**
11 **MISSESGEEJAY,** 5, br m Beat All (USA)—Riverbank Rainbow **Brandsby Racing**
12 4, B g Proclamation (IRE)—Monica Geller **The Most Wanted Partnership**
13 **MOONBI CREEK (IRE),** 8, b g Fasliyev (USA)—Moonbi Range (IRE) **Mrs S. E. Barclay**
14 **NOBLE JACK (IRE),** 9, b g Elusive City (USA)—Begine (IRE) **Mrs L. Buckley**
15 **POSTILLION (IRE),** 7, b h Sleeping Indian—Princess of Eden (GER) **Mr Andrew P. Whelan**
16 **RAINBOW BEAUTY,** 5, ch m Manduro (GER)—Just Like A Woman **Messrs Chrimes, Winn & Wilson**
17 5, B g Tiger Hill (IRE)—Rose Bounty **Mrs S. E. Barclay**
18 **STEADY PROGRESS (IRE),** 7, b g Flemensfirth (USA)—Creaking Step (IRE) **Helen Benwell & Stella Barclay**
19 **SWALEDALE LAD (IRE),** 8, b g Arakan (USA)—Tadjnama (USA) **Mr W. D. Challoner**
20 **SYRIAN,** 8, b g Hawk Wing (USA)—Lady Lahar **Mr S. Chaston**
21 **TROPENFEUER (FR),** 8, b m Banyumanik (IRE)—Tropensonne (GER) **Mr P. Bushell**
22 **UNIDEXTER (IRE),** 5, br g Footstepsinthesand—Run To Jane (IRE) **Winks Racing**

### THREE-YEAR-OLDS

23 **TOWN ORATOR,** gr g Proclamation (IRE)—Town House **Mr J. H. Chrimes**

**Other Owners:** Mr Leo Aspinall, Mr Alan Ayres, Mr John Ball, Mr Tony Ball, Mr Philip Bamford, Mr Dave Barlow, Mr David Benwell, Mr Ed Briscoe, Mr John Calderbank, Mr Andrew Calderbank, Mr Alec Cassie, Mrs Paula Chaston, Mr Paul Clarkson, Mr Martin James, Mr Paul Mann, Mr David Price, Mr John A. Raybone, Mr Paul Steadman, Mr Matt Watkinson, Mr Clive Wilson.

**Assistant Trainer:** Stella Barclay

**Jockey (flat):** Graham Lee. **Conditional:** Harry Challoner. **Apprentice:** Nikki Grundy.

---

## 219 MRS RICHENDA FORD, Dorchester

Postal: **Cross Farm, Brockhampton, Buckland Newton, Dorchester, Dorset, DT2 7DJ**

1 **BALL HOPPER (IRE),** 11, ch g Rock Hopper—Lady Vic (IRE) **K. B. Snook**
2 4, B f Pasternak—Coolers Quest
3 **DAYS AHEAD (IRE),** 8, ch g Kheleyf (USA)—Hushaby (IRE) **K. B. Snook**
4 **MADDOXTOWN (IRE),** 9, b g Luso—Augusta Victoria **K. B. Snook**
5 **SOMERBY (IRE),** 12, b g Sadler's Wells (USA)—Oriental Mystique **K. B. Snook**
6 **THE CAT'S AWAY (IRE),** 7, ch g Alderbrook—Mrs Jack Russell (IRE) **K. B. Snook**

## 220 MR BRIAN FORSEY, Taunton

Postal: **Three Oaks, Ash Priors, Taunton, Somerset, TA4 3NQ**
Contacts: **PHONE (01823) 433914 MOBILE (07747) 392760**
**E-MAIL forsey2001@yahoo.com**

1 **AUREATE,** 11, ch g Jade Robbery (USA)—Anne d'autriche (IRE) **B. Forsey**
2 **BARISTA (IRE),** 7, b g Titus Livius (FR)—Cappuccino (IRE) **Mr K. C. Jago**
3 **BOWMANS WELL (IRE),** 10, b m Cadeaux Genereux—Guignol (IRE) **P. D. Purdy**
4 **DROPZONE (USA),** 6, b g Smart Strike (CAN)—Dalisay (IRE) **Mr Alan Stevens & Mr Brian Forsey**
5 **FOLLOW THE MASTER,** 9, b g Alflora (IRE)—Daisy May **Mrs P. M. Bosley**
6 **VIVA VETTORI,** 11, ch g Vettori (IRE)—Cruinn A Bhord **B. Forsey**

### TWO-YEAR-OLDS

7 Ch f 6/3 Winker Watson—Quaker Parrot (Compton Place) **B. Forsey**

**Other Owners:** A. G. Stevens.

**Assistant Trainer:** Susan Forsey

## 221 MISS JOANNE FOSTER, Ilkley

Postal: **Brookleigh Farm, Burley Road, Menston, Ilkley, West Yorkshire, LS29 6NS**
Contacts: **PHONE (07980) 301808 MOBILE (07980) 301808**
**E-MAIL info@jofosterracing.co.uk WEBSITE www.jofosterracing.co.uk**

1 **ARD AGUS FADA (IRE),** 12, ch g Anshan—Whispering Dawn **J Batty & D Ellis**
2 **CARA COURT (IRE),** 9, b g Court Cave (IRE)—Tarasandy (IRE) **The Golden Syndicate**
3 **CRAIGDANCER (IRE),** 6, b g Craigsteel—Green Sea **Miss J. E. Foster**
4 **ESCAPE TO THE WEST,** 7, b g Westerner—Makeabreak (IRE)
5 **HOUNDSCOURT (IRE),** 8, b g Court Cave (IRE)—Broken Rein (IRE) **The Golden Syndicate**
6 **OUTTILALLHOURS (IRE),** 7, br g Dr Massini (IRE)—Cherry Vale (IRE) **Eshwin Racing & Partners**
7 **PINDAR (GER),** 11, b g Tertullian (USA)—Pierette (GER) **The Golden Syndicate**
8 **SICILIAN BAY (IRE),** 4, b f Jeremy (USA)—Taormina (IRE) **Mr J. Batty**
9 **URBAN GALE (IRE),** 10, b g City Honours (USA)—Margale (IRE) **Mr S. Currie**

**Other Owners:** Mr D. B. Ellis, P. Foster, Mr K. Quigley, Mr D. Taylor.

**Assistant Trainer:** P. Foster

**Conditional:** Sam Drake.

## 222 MRS LORNA FOWLER, Summerhill

Postal: **Rahinston, Summerhill, Co. Meath. Ireland**
Contacts: **MOBILE (00353) 87 126 7433**
**E-MAIL lorna.fowler@me.com WEBSITE www.rahinston.com**

1 **BENEFICIAL SOCIETY (IRE),** 5, ch m Beneficial—Renvyle Society (IRE) **Tom Bruton**
2 **GOOD EGG (IRE),** 12, b g Exit To Nowhere (USA)—Full of Surprises (IRE) **Mrs A. Frost**
3 **ROCK ON ROSIE (IRE),** 6, b m Gamut (IRE)—Macs Goose **Geraldine Devine**

## 223 MR JIMMY FOX, Marlborough

Postal: **Highlands Farm Stables, Herridge, Collingbourne Ducis, Marlborough, Wiltshire, SN8 3EG**
Contacts: **PHONE (01264) 850218 (07931) 724358 MOBILE (07702) 880010**
**E-MAIL jcfoxtrainer@aol.com**

1 **COPPER ERN,** 6, ch g Young Ern—Croeso Cynnes **Mrs S. J. Fox**
2 **DREAMING AGAIN,** 5, b g Young Ern—Maedance **The Dancing Partners**
3 **FRANKIE,** 4, gr g Firebreak—Winterbourne **R. E. Kavanagh**
4 **GRACIOUS GEORGE (IRE),** 5, b g Oratorio (IRE)—Little Miss Gracie **Mrs B. A. Fuller**
5 **HENRY GRACE (IRE),** 4, b c Oratorio (IRE)—Little Miss Gracie **Mrs B. A. Fuller**
6 **NEWTOWN CROSS (IRE),** 5, ch h Kheleyf (USA)—Sacred Pearl (IRE) **Mutton & Lamb**
7 **THE WEE CHIEF (IRE),** 9, ch g King Charlemagne (USA)—La Belle Clare (IRE) **R. E. Kavanagh**

## MR JIMMY FOX - Continued

### THREE-YEAR-OLDS

8 **BIRDIE MUST FLY,** ch f Major Cadeaux—Musical Day **Mrs S. J. Fox**

**Other Owners:** Mrs E. Estall, Mr D. S. Estall, Mr C. Fiford.

**Assistant Trainer:** Sarah-Jane Fox

**Jockey (flat):** Pat Dobbs.

---

## 224 MISS SUZZANNE FRANCE, Norton on Derwent

Postal: **Cheesecake Hill House, Highfield, Beverley Road, Norton on Derwent, North Yorkshire, YO17 9PJ**
Contacts: **PHONE (01653) 691947 FAX (01653) 691947 MOBILE (07904) 117531 E-MAIL suzzannemunchie@talk21.com**

1 **AD VITAM (IRE),** 7, ch g Ad Valorem (USA)—Love Sonnet **Arc Racing Yorkshire I**
2 **BOND BLADE,** 7, ch g Needwood Blade—Bond Cat (IRE) **Michael Marsh and Partners**
3 **DESTINY BLUE (IRE),** 8, b g Danehill Dancer (IRE)—Arpege (IRE) **Newstart Partnership**
4 **STAMP DUTY (IRE),** 7, b g Ad Valorem (USA)—Lothian Lass (IRE) **Newstart Partnership**

**Other Owners:** Mrs P. France, Mr P. R. France, Mr M. Marsh.

**Amateur:** Mr Aaron James.

---

## 225 MR DEREK FRANKLAND, Brackley

Postal: **Springfields, Mixbury, Brackley, Northamptonshire, NN13 5RR**
Contacts: **FAX (01280) 847334 MOBILE (07763) 020406 E-MAIL dsfrankland@aol.com**

1 **REBEL HIGH (IRE),** 11, ch g Hymns On High—Celia's Fountain (IRE) **D. S. Frankland & D. J. Trott**
2 **UNCLE ALBERT,** 14, gr g Gran Alba (USA)—Wotamona **D. S. Frankland & D. J. Trott**

**Other Owners:** D. S. Frankland, Mr D. J. Trott.

**Jockey (NH):** David Bass, Harry Skelton, Liam Treadwell.

---

## 226 MR JAMES FROST, Buckfastleigh

Postal: **Hawson Stables, Buckfastleigh, Devon, TQ11 0HP**
Contacts: **YARD (01364) 642267 HOME (01364) 642332 FAX (01364) 643182 MOBILE (07860) 220229**

1 **BOGOSS DU PERRET (FR),** 4, b br g Malinas (GER)—Lady Paques (FR) **N. W. Lake**
2 **FACE TO FACE,** 6, b g Kayf Tara—Monsignorita (IRE) **M. C. Denmark**
3 **GRISSOM (FR),** 7, ch g Sabrehill (USA)—Nuit de Chine (FR) **Mrs J. F. Bury & Mrs K. Morgan**
4 **HUNTSMANS LADY (IRE),** 5, b m Shantou (USA)—Falika (FR) **Frost Racing Club**
5 **ICE KONIG (FR),** 6, gr g Epalo (GER)—Isarwelle (GER) **Mr T. J. G. Martin**
6 **MILAN OF CRYSTAL (IRE),** 6, b m Milan—Native Crystal (IRE) **Mr T. Saye**
7 5, B m Morpeth—Miss Grace **Share My Dream**
8 **MISS SISKIN,** 6, b m Morpeth—Miss Grace **Mr T. G. Russell**
9 **PAPER LADY (IRE),** 7, b m Beneficial—Strong Craft **Mrs J. McCormack**
10 **PICCADILLY CIRCUS,** 6, b g King's Theatre (IRE)—Disallowed (IRE) **M. C. Denmark**
11 **RAILWAY VIC (IRE),** 8, b g Old Vic—Penny Apples (IRE) **Frost Racing Club**
12 **RUSTY NAIL (IRE),** 10, b g Tikkanen (USA)—Aoki (IRE) **Frost Racing Club**
13 **SANGRAM (IRE),** 8, b g Blueprint (IRE)—Margeno's Fountain (IRE) **Mr T. Saye**
14 **STRONG WIND (IRE),** 9, br g Anshan—Gale Eight (IRE) **Mr T. Saye**
15 **UNION SAINT (FR),** 7, b g Saint des Saints (FR)—Us Et Coutumes (FR) **P. M. Tosh**
16 **WELDUNDEE,** 6, b g Weld—Silcabee **Mr C. Unwin**

**Other Owners:** Exors of the Late Mr G. B. Balding, Mrs J. F. Bury, Mr J. D. Frost, Mr M. Kay, Mr Tony Maddison, Mrs K. Morgan.

**Assistant Trainer:** G. Frost

**Jockey (NH):** Hadden Frost. **Amateur:** Miss Bryony Frost.

## 227 MR KEVIN FROST, Alcester

Postal: **Red Hill Farmyard, Red Hill, Alcester, Warwickshire, B49 6NQ**
Contacts: **PHONE (07748) 873092 (07919) 370081**
**E-MAIL info@kevinfrostracing.co.uk WEBSITE www.kevinfrostracing.co.uk**

**1** 4, B f Lucarno (USA)—Avoine (IRE) **The Ferandlin Peaches**
**2 BEAUTIFUL WAR (IRE),** 5, b br m Presenting—Dunahall Queen (IRE) **The Ferandlin Peaches**
**3 BOROUGH ROAD,** 5, b g Stage Pass—Charlie Renne (IRE)
**4 BUS NAMED DESIRE,** 7, b m Alflora (IRE)—Arctic Ring **The Ferandlin Peaches**
**5** 4, B g Lucarno (USA)—Callitwhatyalike **The Ferandlin Peaches**
**6 CATCHING ZEDS,** 8, b m Lucky Story (USA)—Perfect Poppy **The Ferandlin Peaches**
**7 DOUBLE FIRST,** 4, ch f Avonbridge—Amicella **Smokey & The Bandits**
**8 FINE MOMENT,** 7, b m Pivotal—Evasive Quality (FR) **The Ferandlin Peaches**
**9 GLENGRA (IRE),** 6, gr g Beneficial—Zaraza (IRE)
**10 ILE DE RE (FR),** 9, gr g Linamix (FR)—Ile Mamou (IRE) **Mr D. Mead**
**11 NO CEILING (IRE),** 5, b g Turtle Island (IRE)—Pyrexie (FR) **The Ferandlin Peaches**
**12 OSORIOS TRIAL,** 8, ch g Osorio (GER)—Skytrial (USA) **Mr K. Frost**
**13 PIDDIE'S POWER,** 8, ch m Starcraft (NZ)—Telori **Mr D. Mead**
**14 RAISING CAIN,** 5, b g Beat All (USA)—Nouf
**15 SURF AND TURF (IRE),** 9, ch g Beneficial—Clear Top Waltz (IRE) **Mr K. Frost**
**16** 4, Ch g Sakhee (USA)—Taqreem (IRE)
**17 TOGA TIGER (IRE),** 8, b g Antonius Pius (USA)—Minerwa (GER) **Jan Mead Kelly Gould**
**18 WALKABOUT CREEK (IRE),** 8, b g Alderbrook—La Mouette (USA) **Mr K. Frost**
**19 YOUNGDOCGALLAGHER (IRE),** 6, b g Zagreb (USA)—Too Back (IRE) **Mr Denis Gallagher**

**Other Owners:** Mr P. V. Harris, Ms R. J. Harris, Mr Paul M. Harrison, Mr Russell Harrison, Mrs Jan Mead, Mr D. Mead, Mr S. D. Petty, Mr Julian D. S. J. Watson.

**Jockey (flat):** Stevie Donohoe. **Jockey (NH):** Brian Hughes. **Conditional:** Jake Hodson.

## 228 MR HUGO FROUD, Bruton

Postal: **Redlynch Farm, Redlynch, Bruton, Somerset, BA10 0NH**

**1 BEAUCHAMP VIKING,** 11, b g Compton Admiral—Beauchamp Jade **Mrs M. S. Emery**
**2 ETHERIDGE ANNIE,** 6, b m Leander—Lady Harriet **The Hugo Froud Racing Club**
**3 HONKYTONKTENNESSEE (IRE),** 6, b g Scorpion (IRE)—Polly Platinum (IRE) **Ms G. S. Langford**
**4 MACKEYS FORGE (IRE),** 11, b g Mr Combustible (IRE)—Lucy Walters (IRE) **The Gaudere Syndicate**
**5 MARKY BOB (IRE),** 10, b g Turtle Island (IRE)—Bobomy (IRE) **The Marky Bob Syndicate**
**6** 4, B c Tiger Hill (IRE)—Summer Lightning (IRE)
**7** 4, B f Kayf Tara—Top of The Dee **Ms G. S. Langford**
**8 WEST CHINNOCK,** 4, ch g With The Flow (USA)—Roaming West (IRE) **Ms G. S. Langford**

### TWO-YEAR-OLDS

**9** B c 8/5 Major Cadeaux—All The Nines (IRE) (Elusive City (USA))
**10** B c 9/2 Teofilo (IRE)—Piffling (Pivotal) (42000)

**Other Owners:** Mr A. C. Eveleigh, Mr H. C. Froud, Mr P. K. J. Langdown, Mr D. A. Mccormick, N. E. Sangster, Mr C. Vaughan-Fowler.

## 229 MR HARRY FRY, Seaborough

Postal: **Flat 1, Manor Farm, Seaborough, Beaminster, Dorset, DT8 3QY**
Contacts: **PHONE (01308) 868192 FAX (01308) 867512**
**E-MAIL info@harryfryracing.com WEBSITE www.harryfryracing.com**

**1 A COR ET A CRI (FR),** 5, b g Alberto Giacometti (IRE)—Millesimee (FR) **Potensis Bloodstock Limited**
**2 ACTIVIAL (FR),** 5, gr ro g Lord du Sud (FR)—Kissmirial (FR) **Potensis Bloodstock Limited**
**3 AIR HORSE ONE,** 4, b g Mountain High (IRE)—Whisky Rose (IRE)
**4 ASSAM BLACK (IRE),** 7, b g Oscar (IRE)—Contrasting Lady **The Tea Party Syndicate**
**5 AYALOR (FR),** 5, b g Khalkevi (IRE)—Physicienne (FR) **Mr Chris Giles & Potensis Bloodstock Ltd**
**6 BAGS GROOVE (IRE),** 4, b g Oscar (IRE)—Golden Moment (IRE) **M. Pescod**
**7 BILLY MERRIOTT (IRE),** 9, b g Dr Massini (IRE)—Hurricane Bella (IRE) **G. D. Taylor**
**8 BIM BAM BOUM (FR),** 4, b g Crossharbour—Quobalt (FR) **The Boomers**

## MR HARRY FRY - Continued

9 **BITOFAPUZZLE,** 7, b m Tamure (IRE)—Gaelic Gold (IRE) **Mr Chris Giles & Potensis Bloodstock Ltd**
10 **BLUE BUTTONS (IRE),** 7, b m King's Theatre (IRE)—Babet (IRE) **Harry Fry Racing Club**
11 **CAPTAIN PROBUS (IRE),** 5, ch g Trans Island—Recife (IRE) **Mr Richard Barber & Mrs S. J. Maltby**
12 **DANCING SOLO,** 6, ch m Loup Sauvage (USA)—Solo Dancer **Harry Fry Racing Club**
13 **DASHING OSCAR (IRE),** 5, b g Oscar (IRE)—Be My Leader (IRE) **Andy & Sharon Measham**
14 **DUNN'S RIVER (FR),** 4, gr g Mastercraftsman (IRE)—Prairie Moon **Harry Fry Racing Club**
15 **FLETCHERS FLYER (IRE),** 7, b g Winged Love (IRE)—Crystal Chord (IRE) **Masterson Holdings Limited**
16 **GARTON STAR (IRE),** 6, br g Presenting—Suir Decision (IRE) **Trailer Resources Ltd**
17 **GENERAL GINGER,** 5, ch g Generous (IRE)—Nuzzle **Hazard Chase Racing**
18 **HE'S A CHARMER (IRE),** 5, br g Mahler—Sunny South East (IRE) **Andy & Sharon Measham**
19 **HENRYVILLE,** 7, b g Generous (IRE)—Aquavita **R P B Michaelson & E M Thornton**
20 **HIGHLAND RETREAT,** 8, b m Exit To Nowhere (USA)—St Kilda **Harry Fry Racing Club**
21 **HOWABOUTAWIN (IRE),** 5, ch g Shantou (USA)—Sarah's Cottage (IRE) **Brannon Dick Hernon Matthewman**
22 **INSTINGTIVE (IRE),** 4, b g Scorpion (IRE)—Fully Focused (IRE) **Tom Taylor Racing**
23 **IVOR'S QUEEN (IRE),** 6, b m King's Theatre (IRE)—Sonnerschien (IRE) **Ivor Perry & Ashton Selway**
24 **JOLLY'S CRACKED IT (FR),** 6, b g Astarabad (USA)—Jolly Harbour **GDM Partnership**
25 **JOLLYALLAN,** 6, b g Rocamadour—Life Line **J. P. McManus**
26 **KARINGA DANCER,** 9, b g Karinga Bay—Miss Flora **H. B. Geddes**
27 **KNIGHT WATCHMAN (IRE),** 5, b g Brian Boru—Final Instalment (IRE) **Twelfth Man Partnership 2**
28 4, Br g Kayf Tara—Labelthou (FR)
29 **LADY OF LAMANVER,** 5, b m Lucarno (USA)—Lamanver Homerun **Dr D. Christensen**
30 **LITTLE ACORN,** 4, b f Presenting—Whiteoak (IRE) **Andy & Sharon Measham**
31 **MENDIP EXPRESS (IRE),** 9, b br g King's Theatre (IRE)—Mulberry (IRE) **The Mendip Syndicate**
32 **MERIBEL MILLIE,** 4, b f Kayf Tara—Ede'iff **Mr A. D. Polson**
33 **MICK JAZZ (FR),** 4, b g Blue Bresil (FR)—Mick Maya (FR) **Potensis Bloodstock Limited**
34 **NITROGEN (IRE),** 8, b g Old Vic—Katday (FR) **C. G. Roach**
35 **OPENING BATSMAN (IRE),** 9, b g Morozov (USA)—Jolly Signal (IRE) **The Twelfth Man Partnership**
36 **POLAMCO (IRE),** 6, b g Old Vic—Shanesia (IRE) **Mr A. D. Polson**
37 **POLLYOGAN (IRE),** 5, br m Oscar (IRE)—Marlogan (IRE) **R. A. Fry**
38 **POPULAR OPINION (IRE),** 5, b m Oscar (IRE)—Jeu de Dame **The Thatch Partnership**
39 **PRESENTING ARMS (IRE),** 8, b g Presenting—Banningham Blaze **Mr J. M. Dare**
40 **PURE OXYGEN (IRE),** 7, br g Presenting—Katday (FR) **C. G. Roach**
41 **QUEEN ODESSA (IRE),** 4, b f King's Theatre (IRE)—Ma Furie (FR)
42 **ROCK ON RUBY (IRE),** 10, b g Oscar (IRE)—Stony View (IRE) **The Festival Goers**
43 **RUBY YEATS,** 4, b f Yeats (IRE)—Newbay Lady **The Ruby Partnership**
44 **SHUIL ROYALE (IRE),** 10, b g King's Theatre (IRE)—Shuil Na Lee (IRE) **R. P. Fry**
45 **SIR IVAN,** 5, b g Midnight Legend—Tisho **The Eyre Family**
46 **SOLON GLORY (FR),** 4, b f Solon (GER)—Stille Baroque (FR)
47 **SPACE ODDITY (FR),** 4, b br g Al Namix (FR)—Schoune (FR)
48 **ST DENYS (IRE),** 6, br g Presenting—Diva Antonia (IRE) **C. G. Roach**
49 **SUMERIEN (FR),** 4, b g Califet (FR)—Suzuka (FR)
50 **TEMPLATE (IRE),** 4, ch g Iffraaj—Sagaing **Coral Champions Club**
51 4, Ch f Nickname (FR)—Tentsmuir
52 **THOMAS BROWN,** 6, b g Sir Harry Lewis (USA)—Tentsmuir **The Corse Lawners**
53 **TONGANUI (IRE),** 4, ch g Stowaway—Murrosie (IRE)
54 **TRIANGULAR (USA),** 10, b g Diesis—Salchow (USA) **GDM Partnership**
55 **VIVANT POEME (FR),** 6, b g Early March—Hasta Manana (FR) **Andy & Sharon Measham**
56 **VOIX D'EAU (FR),** 5, b g Voix du Nord (FR)—Eau de Chesne (FR) **Masterson Holdings Limited**
57 **VUKOVAR (FR),** 6, b g Voix du Nord (FR)—Noraland (FR) **GDM Partnership**
58 **ZULU OSCAR,** 6, b g Oscar (IRE)—Loxhill Lady **Caroline Fry & Susie Dilhorne**

### THREE-YEAR-OLDS

59 **CHALONNIAL (FR),** ch g Protektor (GER)—Kissmirial (FR)

**Other Owners:** J. R. Barber, P. K. Barber, Mrs S. Barber, R. Barber, P. H. Boss, Mr A. Brannon, G. Calder, Mrs J. Calder, G. Charlesworth, D. Charlesworth, S. J. Clare, Mr S. Cullum, Miss P. J. Dare, Mr A. D. Dick, Viscountess S. J. Dilhorne, E. J. Dolan-Abrahams, Mrs P. E. Dolan-Abrahams, Mr J. N. I. Edwards, Mrs C. A. Eyre, Mr H. Eyre, Miss R. E. Eyre, Mr C. G. S. Eyre, Mr D. E. Forster, Dr C. E. Fry, Mr C. M. Giles, Mr T. Hanrahan, Mrs F. Jackson, Mrs S. J. Maltby, Mr A. R. Measham, Mrs S. M. Measham, R. P. B. Michaelson, Miss C. O'Connor, W. I. M. Perry, Mr M. Powell, A. G. Selway, A. G. Sim, Mr M. Smith, Mrs S. J. Somner, Mr M. J. Taylor, Mr L. A. Taylor, E. M. Thornton, Mr J. P. G. Turner, P. M. Warren, Mr J. C. Whiting.

**Assistant Trainer:** Ciara O'Connor

**Jockey (NH):** Ryan Mahon, Noel Fehilly, Nick Scholfield. **Conditional:** Martin McIntyre, Gary Derwin. **Amateur:** Mr Will Biddick.

## 230 MISS CAROLINE FRYER, Wymondham

Postal: **Browick Hall Cottage, Browick Road, Wymondham, Norfolk, NR18 9RB**
Contacts: **PHONE (01953) 601257 MOBILE (07768) 056076**
**E-MAIL caroline@carolinefryerracing.co.uk WEBSITE www.carolinefryerracing.co.uk**

1 **BJORNLUCKY (IRE),** 5, b g Key of Luck (USA)—Super Trouper (FR) **Mr J. D. Ward**
2 **DOUGALSTAR (FR),** 6, b g Layman (USA)—Concert House (IRE) **A. J. White**
3 **IDE NO IDEA (IRE),** 11, b g Anshan—Gales Wager **Mrs S. Fryer**
4 **POLLY WIGGLE,** 6, ch m Generous (IRE)—Single Handed **Mr J. D. Ward**
5 **RIDDLESTOWN (IRE),** 8, b g Cloudings (IRE)—Gandi's Dream (IRE) **Mr J. D. Ward**
6 **SPECKLED DOOR,** 7, b g Brian Boru—Monte Mayor Golf (IRE) **Mr A. & Mrs P. Hurn**
7 **STORM TO PASS,** 7, b g Overbury (IRE)—Silver Peak (FR) **Miss C. Fryer**
8 **TINY HAVEN,** 6, b g Beat All (USA)—Flower Haven **A. J. White**
9 **TUCSON ARIZONA,** 4, b g High Chaparral (IRE)—Kasakiya (IRE) **Mr J. D. Ward**
10 **VOLCAN SURPRISE (FR),** 7, b g Dom Alco (FR)—Invitee Surprise (FR) **Mrs S. Fryer**
11 **ZELOS DIKTATOR,** 9, br g Diktat—Chanterelle (IRE) **A. J. White**

**Other Owners:** A. Hurn, The Hon Mrs A. Hurn.

## 231 MR JOHN GALLAGHER, Moreton-In-Marsh

Postal: **Grove Farm, Chastleton, Moreton-In-Marsh, Gloucestershire, GL56 0SZ**
Contacts: **PHONE/FAX (01608) 674492 MOBILE (07780) 972663**
**E-MAIL gallagherracing@phonecoop.coop WEBSITE www.gallagherracing.com**

1 **ADA LOVELACE,** 5, b m Byron—Satin Braid **Mr D. A. Clark**
2 **ALPHA DELTA WHISKY,** 7, ch g Intikhab (USA)—Chispa **The Juniper Racing Club Ltd**
3 **CELESTIAL ISLAND,** 8, gr m Silver Patriarch (IRE)—Celtic Island **Mr R. W. Brown**
4 **HEARTSONG (IRE),** 6, b m Kheleyf (USA)—Semiquaver (IRE) **C. Rashbrook**
5 **ISEEMIST (IRE),** 4, gr f Verglas (IRE)—Krasivaya (IRE) **K. Marsden**
6 **LADWEB,** 5, ch g Bertolini (USA)—Adweb **The Juniper Racing Club & Andrew Bell**
7 **LUNGARNO PALACE (USA),** 4, b g Henrythenavigator (USA)—Good Time Sally (USA) **Caveat Emptor Partnership**
8 **OSTRALEGUS,** 5, b g Choisir (AUS)—Midnight Pearl (USA) **The Oystercatcher Racing Syndicate**
9 **PORT LAIRGE,** 5, b g Pastoral Pursuits—Stylish Clare (IRE) **Quench Racing Partnership**
10 **SOUNDBYTE,** 10, b g Beat All (USA)—Gloaming **Mr O. M. Parsons**
11 **TOBAGO CAYS,** 4, b f Tobougg (IRE)—Cove Mountain (IRE) **J & L Wetherald - M & M Glover**

### THREE-YEAR-OLDS

12 **AMBER CRYSTAL,** b f Multiplex—Glitz (IRE) **R. Biggs**
13 **HARRISON STICKLE,** gr c Hellvelyn—Hollybell **Ms A. Clifford**
14 **MAJOR PUSEY,** ch c Major Cadeaux—Pusey Street Lady **C. R. Marks (Banbury)**
15 **MY BUBBA,** b g Dutch Art—Moyoko (IRE) **Mrs N. L. Young**
16 **ONE MORE PUSEY,** b f Hellvelyn—Pusey Street Girl
17 **VIRTUALISE,** ch g Virtual—Snake Skin **The Juniper Racing Club Ltd**

### TWO-YEAR-OLDS

18 **COCKNEY BOY,** ch c 24/3 Cockney Rebel (IRE)—Menha (Dubawi (IRE))
19 B g 10/4 Native Ruler—Dani (IRE) (Modigliani (USA))
20 Br gr f 22/3 Hellvelyn—Fayre Bella (Zafeen (FR)) (1523) **John Gallagher**
21 **PUSEY'S SECRET,** b f 2/5 Sakhee's Secret—Pusey Street Lady (Averti (IRE))

**Other Owners:** Mr D. Abraham, Mr A. Bell, Mr Arthur Brown, Mr B. Downard, M. P. Glover, Ms M. E. Glover, Mr M. W. Goodall, J. F. Long, Mrs B. A. Long, Mr M. Preedy, Mr P. P. Richou, Mr R. J. Smeaton, Mr J. A. Wetherald, Mrs L. T. Wetherald.

**Assistant Trainer:** Mrs R. Gallagher

**Jockey (flat):** Neil Callan, Jamie Spencer, Chris Catlin, Martin Lane.

## 232 MRS ILKA GANSERA-LÉVÊQUE, Newmarket

Postal: **Saffron House Stables, Hamilton Road, Newmarket, Suffolk, CB8 0NY**
Contacts: **PHONE (07981) 772715 MOBILE (07855) 532072**
**E-MAIL ilkagansera@gmail.com WEBSITE www.gansera-leveque.com**

1 **ANGEL ROSA,** 4, b f Multiplex—Rosi Quest **Mr G. Hynd**
2 **IMAN (GER),** 5, b g Dansili—Ioannina **Mr H. G. Wernicke**

### THREE-YEAR-OLDS

3 **DANCING LIGHT (CAN),** ch f North Light (IRE)—Dance Trick (USA) **M. J. Silver**
4 **IONIAN LIBRETTA (AUT),** b f Librettist (USA)—Ionia (IRE) **Mr T. Mueller**

### TWO-YEAR-OLDS

5 B f 2/3 Proclamation (IRE)—Anapola (GER) (Polish Precedent (USA)) (8000)
6 B br f 31/1 Naaqoos—Apulia (USA) (Street Cry (IRE)) (8730) **Lamont Racing**
7 **KATABATIK KATIE,** b f 2/5 Sir Percy—New Choice (IRE) (Barathea (IRE)) **Mrs P. A. Clark**
8 Gr f 2/3 Silver Frost (IRE)—Party Bag (Cadeaux Genereux) (15873) **Lamont Racing**
9 B f 19/3 Mawatheeq (USA)—Sanctum (Medicean)

**Other Owners:** Mrs E. McClymont, Mr D. McClymont.

**Assistant Trainer:** Stéphane Lévêque

**Jockey (flat):** Mickael Barzalona, Raul Da Silva, Lemos De Sousa. **Apprentice:** Tim Clark. **Amateur:** Mr Matt Johnson.

## 233 MRS SUSAN GARDNER, Longdown

Postal: **Woodhayes Farm, Longdown, Exeter, Devon, EX6 7SB**
Contacts: **PHONE/FAX (01392) 811213 MOBILE (07971) 097936**
**E-MAIL woodhayesstudfarm@btinternet.com**

1 **BACH ON TOW (IRE),** 8, b g Bach (IRE)—Handmade (IRE) **D. V. Gardner**
2 **BRAVE ENCOUNTER (IRE),** 7, br g Indian Danehill (IRE)—Dartmeet (IRE) **Mrs B. A. Russell**
3 **BREDON HILL LAD,** 8, ch g Kirkwall—Persian Clover **R. W. Mitchell**
4 **CLOUDS OF MIST,** 10, b m Cloudings (IRE)—Island Mist **G. N. Noye & P. A. Tylor**
5 **DOCTOR LOOK HERE (IRE),** 5, b g Dr Massini (IRE)—Eye Vision (IRE) **G. N. Noye**
6 **DUNNICKS SKIPPER,** 7, b g Pasternak—Dunnicks Chance **F. G. Tucker**
7 **FLYING AWARD (IRE),** 11, br g Oscar (IRE)—Kates Machine (IRE) **Mr & Mrs P George & Mrs B Russell**
8 **HERE'S HERBIE,** 7, b g Classic Cliche (IRE)—Tyre Hill Lilly **G. N. Noye**
9 **LOOK FOR LOVE,** 7, b g Pursuit of Love—Look Here's May **D. V. Gardner**
10 **MISS LAMORNA (IRE),** 6, br m Presenting—Paumafi (IRE) **G. N. Noye**
11 **RAFAFIE,** 7, b g Kayf Tara—Florie **D. V. Gardner**
12 **ROLL ON RODNEY,** 5, b g Relief Pitcher—State of Grace **Mr A. I. Leach**
13 **SIROP DE MENTHE (FR),** 5, ch g Discover d'auteuil (FR)—Jolie Menthe (FR) **Clear Racing & Partner**
14 **STORM ALERT,** 8, ch g Karinga Bay—Rash-Gale (IRE) **D. V. Gardner**
15 **TARA FOR LILLY,** 6, b m Kayf Tara—Tyre Hill Lilly **D. V. Gardner**
16 **TEA TIME FRED,** 6, b g Kayf Tara—Darjeeling (IRE) **The Farm To Plate Syndicate**

**Other Owners:** Mr P. George, Mrs A. M. George, Mrs M. M. Greening, B. J. Greening, P. A. Tylor.

**Assistant Trainer:** D. V. Gardner

**Jockey (NH):** Aidan Coleman, Lucy Gardner, Sam Thomas. **Conditional:** Micheal Nolan.

## 234 MR JEREMY GASK, Warminster

Postal: **The Beeches, Deverill Road, Sutton Veny, Warminster, Wiltshire, BA12 7BY**
Contacts: **PHONE (01985) 841166 FAX (01985) 840474 MOBILE (07507) 555303**
**E-MAIL info@horsesfirstracing.com WEBSITE www.horsesfirstracing.com**

1 **AL JAMAL,** 5, b m Authorized (IRE)—Kydd Gloves (USA) **Star Partners**
2 **CAMINEL (IRE),** 4, b f Kyllachy—Jalissa **Mr M. Allen**
3 **FLYING BEAR (IRE),** 4, b g Kodiac—Marinebird (IRE) **Flying Bear Partnership**
4 **GABBIANO,** 6, b g Zafeen (FR)—Hollybell **Mr A. G. Bloom**
5 **GOLLY MISS MOLLY,** 4, b f Exceed And Excel (AUS)—Amicable Terms **Amelco UK Ltd**
6 **KINGS CHAPEL (USA),** 4, b g Elusive Quality (USA)—Ladyecho (USA) **Jamie & Lucy Hart**

## MR JEREMY GASK - Continued

7 **KLAAZIA (FR),** 4, gr f Sinndar (IRE)—Kritzia **The Kathryn Stud Limited**
8 **LIGHT ROSE (IRE),** 5, b m Cape Cross (IRE)—Laureldean Lady (IRE) **Jamie & Lucy Hart**
9 **LUCKY ROYALE,** 7, b m Lucky Story (USA)—Bella Bertolini **Gracelands Stud Partnership**
10 **LUCKY SURPRISE,** 4, b f Lucky Story (USA)—Bella Bertolini **Gracelands Stud Partnership**
11 **MEDICEAN MAN,** 9, ch g Medicean—Kalindi **Mr Stuart Dobb & Miss Kate Dobb**
12 **NELSON QUAY (IRE),** 5, b g Holy Roman Emperor (IRE)—Frippet (IRE) **Brankin & Hawk Racing**
13 **NEW LEYF (IRE),** 9, b br g Kheleyf (USA)—Society Fair (FR) **Mr Guy Carstairs & Hawk Racing**
14 **SUTTON SIOUX,** 4, b f Sleeping Indian—Once Removed **The Sutton Veny Syndicate**
15 **TRENDING (IRE),** 6, gr g Dark Angel (IRE)—Call Later (USA) **The Twitterati**

### THREE-YEAR-OLDS

16 **ACOM,** ch c Compton Place—Pudding Lane (IRE) **Crowd Racing Partnership**
17 **FIRE AND PASSION,** b c Dutch Art—Mary Goodnight **Mr V. C. Y. Tan**
18 **TARRAGON,** b c Compton Place—Hennalaine (IRE) **Glebe Farm Stud**

### TWO-YEAR-OLDS

**19** B f 17/4 Elusive Pimpernel (USA)—Ebony Star (Desert Prince (IRE)) (9523) **Mr M. Eves**
**20** B f 1/3 Iffraaj—Emma Dora (IRE) (Medaglia d'Oro (USA)) (26666) **Mr M. Eves**
**21** B c 6/5 Mastercraftsman (IRE)—Fairest of All (IRE) (Sadler's Wells (USA)) (50000) **Anglo Australian Racing**
**22 FANDANGO (GER),** b c 8/2 Lord of England (GER)—
Fitness (IRE) (Monsun (GER)) (53174) **Anglo Australian Racing**
**23** Ch c 17/3 Manduro (GER)—Kesh Kumay (IRE) (Danehill (USA)) (14285) **Anglo Australian Racing**
**24** B c 9/4 Duke of Marmalade (IRE)—Miracolia (IRE) (Montjeu (IRE)) (45000) **Anglo Australian Racing**
**25 NOBLE MESSENGER (FR),** b c 26/1 King's Best (USA)—Nota Bene (GER) (Slickly (FR)) (25396)
**26** Ch c 22/2 Medicean—Panoptic (Dubawi (IRE)) (40000) **Mr M. Eves**
**27** Br c 30/1 Big Bad Bob (IRE)—Rejuvenation (IRE) (Singspiel (IRE)) (40000) **Anglo Australian Racing**
**28** B c 10/3 Key of Luck (USA)—Rumuz (IRE) (Marju (IRE)) (19047) **Mr M. Eves**
**29** B f 26/4 Fastnet Rock (AUS)—Square Pants (USA) (King of Kings (IRE)) (20000) **Horses First Racing Ltd**
**30** B c 22/3 Teofilo (IRE)—Whos Mindin Who (IRE) (Danehill Dancer (IRE)) (70000) **Anglo Australian Racing**
**31** Gr f 28/2 Zebedee—Why Now (Dansili) (30476) **Mr M. Eves**

**Other Owners:** Mr Denis Barry, Mrs Clare Barry, Mr Tony Bloom, Mr S. T. Brankin, Mr G. Carstairs, Miss K. M. Dobb, Mr Jamie Hart, Mrs Lucy Hart, Horses First Racing Limited, Mr J. A. Knight, Mr Eamonn Wilmott, Mrs Oriana Wilmott, Mr Bob Young, Mrs K. M. Young.

**Apprentice:** David Parkes.

---

## 235 MRS ROSEMARY GASSON, Banbury

Postal: **Alkerton Grounds, Balscote, Banbury, Oxfordshire, OX15 6JS**
Contacts: **PHONE (01295) 730248 MOBILE (07769) 798430**
**E-MAIL arb@aqf.myzen.co.uk**

1 **ADIOS ALONSO (IRE),** 9, b g Saffron Walden (FR)—Rosy Rockford (IRE) **Mrs R. Gasson**
2 **CROCO MISTER (IRE),** 8, ch g Croco Rouge (IRE)—Nimrods Dream (IRE) **Mrs R. Gasson**
3 **GENTLEMAN ANSHAN (IRE),** 11, b g Anshan—Second Violin (IRE) **Mrs R. Gasson**
4 **IRISH OCTAVE (IRE),** 5, b g Gamut (IRE)—Fairytaleofnewyork (IRE) **Mrs R. Gasson**
5 **JOLLY BOYS OUTING (IRE),** 12, b g Glacial Storm (USA)—St Carol (IRE) **Mrs R. Gasson**
6 **KILCASCAN,** 11, b g Alflora (IRE)—Peasedown Tofana **Mrs R. Gasson**
7 **MR MCGUINESS (IRE),** 5, b g Kalanisi (IRE)—Maig Mandy (IRE) **Mrs R. Gasson**
8 **SCARTARE (IRE),** 4, br g Trans Island—La Speziana (IRE) **Mrs R. Gasson**
9 **SCUTSISLAND (IRE),** 6, br g Heron Island (IRE)—Soviet Princess (IRE) **Mrs R. Gasson**

**Conditional:** Ben Poste.

---

## 236 MR MICHAEL GATES, Stratford-Upon-Avon

Postal: **Comfort Park Stud, Campden Road, Clifford Chambers, Stratford-Upon-Avon, CV37 8LW**
Contacts: **MOBILE (07581) 246070**
**E-MAIL comfortparkstud@hotmail.co.uk**

1 **CARN ROCK,** 7, b g Tamure (IRE)—Solent Sunbeam **M. Gates**
2 **FULL OV BEANS,** 11, ch g Midnight Legend—Scarlet Baroness **M. Gates**
3 **HANDSOME BUDDY (IRE),** 8, br g Presenting—Moya's Magic (IRE) **M. Gates**

## 237 MR JONATHAN GEAKE, Marlborough

Postal: **Harestone House, East Kennett, Marlborough, Wiltshire, SN8 4EY**
Contacts: **PHONE (01672) 861784 MOBILE (07768) 350738**
**E-MAIL jageake@yahoo.co.uk**

1 **A LASTING JOY,** 4, b f Refuse To Bend (IRE)—Sir Kyffin's Folly **Mrs A. Leftley**
2 **BEWARE CHALK PIT (IRE),** 11, b g Anshan—Rakiura (IRE) **Mrs A. Leftley**
3 **BONDI MIST (IRE),** 6, gr m Aussie Rules (USA)—Akoya (IRE) **Double Kings Partnership**
4 **GLENS WOBBLY,** 7, ch g Kier Park (IRE)—Wobbly **Mr R. G. Symes**
5 **LOUKHAAR (IRE),** 7, b g Westerner—Gold Air **Mrs A. Leftley**
6 **MICQUUS (IRE),** 6, b g High Chaparral (IRE)—My Potters (USA) **Mrs A. Leftley**
7 **SACRAMENTO KING (IRE),** 6, gr g Desert King (IRE)—Kindle Ball (FR) **Mrs P. D. Gulliver**
8 **SHOT IN THE DARK (IRE),** 6, ch g Dr Fong (USA)—Highland Shot **Mrs P. D. Gulliver**
9 **THEA'S DANCE,** 4, b f Delta Dancer—Tagula Song (IRE)
10 **TIPSY STAR,** 4, b f Tobougg (IRE)—Extremely Rare (IRE) **D Berry J Kovacs & Miss E Tanner**

### THREE-YEAR-OLDS

11 **FIDELITY,** b c Halling (USA)—Sir Kyffin's Folly **Mrs A. Leftley**

### TWO-YEAR-OLDS

12 **JUDE THE OBSCURE,** b c 13/5 Sakhee's Secret—Sir Kyffin's Folly (Dansili) **Mrs A. Leftley**

**Other Owners:** Mr D. Berry, Mrs S. A. Geake, Mrs M. R. Geake, Mr J. Kovacs, Miss E. Tanner.

**Assistant Trainer:** Mrs S. A. Geake **Pupil Assistant:** Mr Sam Geake

**Jockey (NH):** Mark Grant, Gerald Tumelty. **Apprentice:** Ryan Tate.

## 238 MR TOM GEORGE, Slad

Postal: **Down Farm, Slad, Stroud, Gloucestershire, GL6 7QE**
Contacts: **PHONE (01452) 814267 MOBILE (07850) 793483**
**E-MAIL tom@trgeorge.com WEBSITE www.tomgeorgeracing.co.uk**

1 **A GOOD SKIN (IRE),** 6, b g Presenting—Trixskin (IRE) **Power Panels Electrical Systems Ltd**
2 **AT YOUR PEARL (IRE),** 6, ch g Blueprint (IRE)—Normandy Girl (IRE) **Sharon C. Nelson & Dermot O'Donohoe**
3 **BABY KING (IRE),** 6, b g Ivan Denisovich (IRE)—Burn Baby Burn (IRE) **About Two Weeks**
4 **BALLINVARRIG (IRE),** 8, b g Beneficial—Leos Holiday (IRE) **Lady Hilda Clarke & Simon W. Clarke**
5 **BALLYALLIA MAN (IRE),** 10, b g Flemensfirth (USA)—
Hatch Away (IRE) **H. S. Smith, R. & M. Gabbertas P. Deal P. Gough**
6 **BARAZA (FR),** 4, gr g Smadoun (FR)—Gerbora (FR) **Mr S. W. Clarke**
7 **BENI LIGHT (FR),** 4, b g Crossharbour—Or Light (FR) **Crossed Fingers Partnership**
8 **BIG FELLA THANKS,** 13, b g Primitive Rising (USA)—Nunsdream **Crossed Fingers Partnership**
9 **BIG SOCIETY (IRE),** 9, b g Flemensfirth (USA)—Choice of Kings (IRE) **Simon Clarke & David Thorpe**
10 **CALL ME VIC (IRE),** 8, b g Old Vic—Call Me Dara (IRE) **C. B. Compton**
11 **CERNUNNOS (FR),** 5, b g Della Francesca (USA)—Jackette (USA) **J. P. McManus**
12 **CHARTREUX (FR),** 10, gr g Colonel Collins (USA)—Ruaha River (FR) **R. S. Brookhouse**
13 **COEUR DE FOU (FR),** 10, ch g Limnos (JPN)—Folly Lady (FR) **Lady H. J. Clarke**
14 **DANDY DUKE (IRE),** 4, b g Duke of Marmalade (IRE)—
Quest For Eternity (IRE) **Dermot O'Donohoe & Sharon C. Nelson**
15 **DARE TO ACHIEVE,** 5, b g Galileo (IRE)—Mussoorie (FR) **St Albans Bloodstock LLP**
16 **DARE TO ENDEAVOUR,** 8, b g Alflora (IRE)—Miss Chinchilla **J B Property Developments (Midlands) Ltd**
17 **DEFINITELY BETTER (IRE),** 7, ch m Definite Article—Chevet Girl (IRE) **Mrs E. A. Fletcher**
18 **DEXCITE (FR),** 4, b br g Authorized (IRE)—Belle Alicia (FR) **Crossed Fingers Partnership**
19 **DOUBLE RISK (FR),** 5, b g My Risk (FR)—Roots Sleeping (FR) **Crossed Fingers Partnership**
20 **DOUBLE SHUFFLE (IRE),** 5, b g Milan—Fiddlers Bar (IRE) **Crossed Fingers Partnership**
21 **DRILL BABY DRILL,** 4, b f Black Sam Bellamy (IRE)—Tulipa (POL) **Sharon C. Nelson & Dermot O'Donohoe**
22 **FIT THE BRIEF,** 5, b m Kayf Tara—Tulipa (POL) **Sharon C. Nelson & Dermot O'Donohoe**
23 **FORGOTTEN GOLD (IRE),** 9, b g Dr Massini (IRE)—Ardnataggle (IRE) **Mr & Mrs R. Cornock**
24 **FORMIDABLE (FR),** 5, b g Sageburg (IRE)—Forcat (FR) **McNeill Family Ltd**
25 **FROSTY STEEL (IRE),** 5, b g Craigsteel—Smiths Lady (IRE) **Dermot O'Donohoe & Sharon C. Nelson**
26 **GOD'S OWN (IRE),** 7, b g Oscar (IRE)—Dantes Term (IRE) **Crossed Fingers Partnership**
27 **GORSKY ISLAND,** 7, b g Turtle Island (IRE)—Belle Magello (FR) **Silkword Racing Partnership**
28 **GRAND ENTERPRISE,** 5, b g Fair Mix (IRE)—Miss Chinchilla **J B Property Developments (Midlands) Ltd**
29 **HARDROCK DAVIS (FR),** 4, b br g Saint des Saints (FR)—Trumpet Davis (FR) **Mr S. W. Clarke**
30 **HENRI DE BOISTRON (FR),** 5, b g Enrique—Highness Royale (FR) **H. Stephen Smith & The Gabbertas Family**

## MR TOM GEORGE - Continued

31 **JUST BEFORE DAWN (IRE),** 6, b g Millenary—Knocka Beauty (IRE) **Mr S. W. Clarke**
32 **KILBREE KID (IRE),** 8, b g Cloudings (IRE)—Bustingoutallover (USA) **Five Valleys Racing Partnership**
33 **MAJALA (FR),** 9, b g Lavirco (GER)—Majae (FR) **Sharon Nelson Jayne Taylor Darren Taylor**
34 **MODULE (FR),** 8, b g Panoramic—Before Royale (FR) **Mr S. W. Clarke**
35 **MOONLIGHT MAGGIE,** 8, b m Pasternak—Moyliscar **Capt & Mrs J. A. George**
36 **MOSS ON THE MILL,** 7, br g Overbury (IRE)—Mimis Bonnet (FR) **Mr & Mrs R. Cornock**
37 5, Ch m Midnight Legend—Moyliscar
38 **NO DUFFER,** 8, ch g Karinga Bay—Dolly Duff **Mr D. C. Robey**
39 **NOCHE DE REYES (FR),** 6, b br g Early March—Cochinchine (IRE) **Mr D. W. Fox**
40 **O MAONLAI (IRE),** 7, b g Oscar (IRE)—Another Gaye (IRE) **Power Panels Electrical Systems Ltd**
41 **OLOFI (FR),** 9, gr g Slickly (FR)—Dona Bella (FR) **McNeill Family Ltd**
42 **ON THE CASE,** 7, ch g Generous (IRE)—Tulipa (POL) **Sharon C. Nelson & Dermot O'Donohoe**
43 **PARSNIP PETE,** 9, b g Pasternak—Bella Coola **The Parsnips**
44 **RABUNDA (IRE),** 5, b g Milan—Cush Ramani (IRE) **Mr & Mrs M. C. Houghton**
45 **RISING BREEZE (FR),** 4, b g Shirocco (GER)—Moon Tree (FR) **Mr David Brookes**
46 **ROC D'APSIS (FR),** 6, gr g Apsis—Rocapina (FR) **Mr M. N. Khan**
47 **SAINT ARE (FR),** 9, b br g Network (GER)—Fortanea (FR) **Mr D. W. Fox**
48 **SEVEN NATION ARMY (IRE),** 6, gr g Rock of Gibraltar (IRE)—Crepe Ginger (IRE) **R. S. Brookhouse**
49 **SIR VALENTINO (FR),** 6, b g Early March—Valentine (FR) **Doone Hulse Susie Saunders & Lady Cobham**
50 **SMOKING JACKET (IRE),** 5, b g Beneficial—Unalaska (IRE) **Vicki Robinson & James Williams**
51 **SOME BUCKLE (IRE),** 6, b g Milan—Miss Moppit (IRE) **R. S. Brookhouse**
52 **SOME PLAN (IRE),** 7, b g Winged Love (IRE)—Lough Hyne **R. S. Brookhouse**
53 **SONG SAA,** 5, b m Midnight Legend—Mystere (IRE) **Sharon C. Nelson & Dermot O'Donohoe**
54 **STELLAR NOTION (IRE),** 7, b br g Presenting—Green Star (FR) **R. S. Brookhouse**
55 **STORMING STRUMPET,** 5, b m Kayf Tara—Rosita Bay **PJL Racing**
56 **THE OULD LAD (IRE),** 7, b g Heron Island (IRE)—Badger Hammel (IRE) **R. S. Brookhouse**
57 **TRUCKERS STEEL (IRE),** 7, b g Craigsteel—Frantesa **Crossed Fingers Partnership**
58 **UNTIL WINNING (FR),** 7, b g Kapgarde (FR)—Fripperie (FR) **Thoroughbred Ladies**
59 **VALSEUR DU GRANVAL (FR),** 6, b g Della Francesca (USA)—La Grande Vallee (FR) **Mr S. W. Clarke**
60 **VEYRANNO (FR),** 6, b br g Anzillero (GER)—Nheyranne (FR) **Miss J. A. Hoskins**
61 **WHATS HAPPENING (IRE),** 8, b g Lahib (USA)—
Rebeccas Star (IRE) **David Rea & Express Contract Drying Ltd**
62 **WILD WEST WIND (IRE),** 6, b g Westerner—Mhuire Na Gale (IRE) **Mr S. W. Clarke**
63 **WUFF (IRE),** 7, b g Beneficial—Dummy Run (IRE) **R. S. Brookhouse**

### THREE-YEAR-OLDS

64 **BOMBER COMMAND (FR),** gr g Al Namix (FR)—Ballade Nordique (FR) **Mr S. W. Clarke**

**Assistant Trainer:** Tjade Collier

**Jockey (NH):** Paddy Brennan, Alain Cawley, Rhys Flint.

---

## 239 MR NICK GIFFORD, Findon

Postal: **The Downs, Stable Lane, Findon, West Sussex, BN14 0RT**
Contacts: **OFFICE (01903) 872226 FAX (01903) 877232 MOBILE (07940) 518077**
**E-MAIL downs.stables@btconnect.com WEBSITE www.nickgiffordracing.co.uk**

1 **ARROYEAU (FR),** 5, ch g Nidor (FR)—Miss Lamour (FR) **P. H. Betts**
2 **CHRISTOPHER WREN (USA),** 8, ch g D'wildcat (USA)—Ashley's Coy (USA) **J. P. McManus**
3 **COVE (IRE),** 8, b m Westerner—Phillis Hill **Nick Gifford Racing Club**
4 **DEXTER BENJAMIN (IRE),** 6, b g Milan—Just Stunning (IRE) **D. G. Trangmar**
5 **DOLLAR BILL,** 6, ch g Medicean—Jardin **Ruth Gifford & Friends**
6 **FAIRY RATH (IRE),** 9, ch g Accordion—Killoughey Fairy (IRE) **Mrs C. L. Kyle**
7 **GENEROUS RANSOM (IRE),** 7, ch g Generous (IRE)—Penneyrose Bay **Sir Christopher & Lady Wates**
8 4, B g Dubai Destination (USA)—Gentle Caribou (IRE)
9 **KUILSRIVER (IRE),** 8, b g Cape Cross (IRE)—Ripple of Pride (IRE) **Mrs T. J. Stone-Brown**
10 **MAIZY,** 5, b m Presenting—Pairtree **S. L. Rodwell**
11 **MARKET COURT (IRE),** 4, b g Court Cave (IRE)—Piepowder **B. Noakes & Baroness S. Noakes**
12 4, B g Yeats (IRE)—Moray Firth (UAE) **J. P. McManus**
13 **NOTRE AMI (IRE),** 4, br g Kalanisi (IRE)—Shuilan (IRE) **The Morpheus Partnership**
14 **ON TREND (IRE),** 9, b g Jammaal—Comrun (IRE) **Ham Manor Farms Ltd**
15 4, B f Presenting—Peggies Run **Sir Christopher Wates**
16 **PROUTS PUB (IRE),** 6, b g Catcher In The Rye (IRE)—A Woman In Love **Nick Gifford Racing Club**
17 **SECRET STING (IRE),** 5, b g Scorpion (IRE)—Roxtown **B. Noakes & Baroness S. Noakes**

**MR NICK GIFFORD - Continued**

18 **SPECIALAGENT ALFIE,** 9, b g Alflora (IRE)—Oso Special **Mr M. K. O'Shea**
19 **STARS ROYALE (IRE),** 6, b g King's Best (USA)—Open Your Heart (IRE) **Jeremy Kyle & Friends**
20 **SURSPENDERS (FR),** 4, b c Whipper (USA)—Lanciana (IRE) **P. H. Betts**
21 **THEO'S CHARM (IRE),** 5, b g Presenting—Kates Charm (IRE) **Mr M. K. O'Shea**
22 **TOOHIGHFORME (IRE),** 6, b g Mountain High (IRE)—Summertime Girl (IRE) **Mrs R. E. Gifford**
23 **TULLAMORE DEW (IRE),** 13, ch g Pistolet Bleu (IRE)—Heather Point **Give Every Man His Due**
24 **VINNIE THE POOH (IRE),** 7, b g Vinnie Roe (IRE)—Ministerial Model (IRE) **Mrs R. E. Gifford**

**Other Owners:** Mr A. Bradley, Mr M. T. Forbes-Wood, Mr L. Horvath, Mr J. Kyle, Baroness S. Noakes, C. B. Noakes, Mr N. M. Roddis, Mr M. A. C. Rudd, Mr M. J. Tracey, Lady Wates.

**Jockey (NH):** Tom Cannon, Liam Treadwell.

---

## 240 MR MARK GILLARD, Sherborne

Postal: **Elm Tree Stud, Holwell, Sherborne, Dorset, DT9 5LL**
Contacts: **PHONE (01963) 23026 FAX (01963) 23297 MOBILE (07970) 700605**
**E-MAIL Mark@thegillards.co.uk WEBSITE markgillardracing.com**

1 **BYRON BLUE (IRE),** 6, br g Dylan Thomas (IRE)—High Society (IRE) **Ms T. Conner**
2 **CALL ME APRIL,** 7, b m Generous (IRE)—Anyhow (IRE) **Mrs J. V. Wilkinson**
3 **COMICAL RED,** 7, ch g Sulamani (IRE)—Sellette (IRE) **N. J. McMullan**
4 **DONT CALL ME OSCAR (IRE),** 8, b g Oscar (IRE)—Coolrua (IRE) **N. J. McMullan**
5 **ENCHANTING SMILE (FR),** 8, b m Rakti—A Thousand Smiles (IRE) **N. J. McMullan**
6 **KARL MARX (IRE),** 5, b g Red Clubs (IRE)—Brillano (FR) **Mr S. Bartlett**
7 **KAVACO (IRE),** 6, b g Choisir (AUS)—Nose One's Way (IRE) **Mrs P. M. R. Gillard**
8 **LAMB'S CROSS,** 9, b g Rainbow High—Angie Marinie **Out Of Bounds Racing Club**
9 **MAGIC MAGNOLIA (IRE),** 4, b f Azamour (IRE)—Royal Aly (USA) **Mr B. R. Rudman**
10 **MEDAL OF VALOUR (JPN),** 7, b g Medaglia d'Oro (USA)—Tres Tres Joli (USA) **Mr S. J. Garnett**
11 **NO NO CARDINAL (IRE),** 6, ch g Touch of Land (FR)—Four Moons (IRE) **T. J. C. Seegar**
12 **OFCOURSEWECAN (USA),** 5, b g Elusive Quality (USA)—Valid Warning (USA) **Mr Neil Budden & Mr Steven Hosie**
13 **PETITE FANTASIE,** 6, b m Flemensfirth (USA)—Rowlands Dream (IRE) **T. L. Morshead**
14 **REVAADER,** 7, b m Revoque (IRE)—Wave Rider **Miss Kay Russell**
15 **SPIN CAST,** 7, b g Marju (IRE)—Some Diva **Mr D. O. Winzer**
16 **SURPRISE US,** 8, b g Indian Ridge—Pingus **R. C. Hambleton**
17 **TENBY JEWEL (IRE),** 10, ch g Pilsudski (IRE)—Supreme Delight (IRE) **Out Of Bounds Racing Club**
18 **WICKLEWOOD,** 9, b g Mujahid (USA)—Pinini **Mr G. J. Singh & Mr Dil Singh Rathore**

**Other Owners:** Mr N. Budden, Mr M. E. Harris, Mr S. Hosie, Mr M. D. Kilsby, Mr G. J. Singh, Mr D. Singh Rathore.

**Assistant Trainer:** Pippa Grace

**Jockey (NH):** Tommy Phelan.

---

## 241 MR JAMES GIVEN, Willoughton

Postal: **Mount House Stables, Long Lane, Willoughton, Gainsborough, Lincolnshire, DN21 5SQ**
Contacts: **PHONE (01427) 667618 FAX (01427) 667734 MOBILE (07801) 100496**
**E-MAIL james@jamesgivenracing.com WEBSITE www.jamesgivenracing.com**

1 **ARTFUL PRINCE,** 5, ch g Dutch Art—Royal Nashkova **Ingram Racing**
2 **BUSHEL (USA),** 5, b g Street Cry (IRE)—Melhor Ainda (USA) **The Cool Silk Partnership**
3 **DISSENT (IRE),** 6, b g Dansili—Centifolia (FR) **The Cool Silk Partnership**
4 **GOLDMADCHEN (GER),** 7, b m Ivan Denisovich (IRE)—Goldkatze (GER) **Mr A. Clarke**
5 **KUNG HEI FAT CHOY (USA),** 6, b g Elusive Quality (USA)—Lady Succeed (JPN) **The Cool Silk Partnership**
6 **ODEON,** 4, b g Galileo (IRE)—Kite Mark **Mr A. Owen**
7 **ORIENTAL RELATION (IRE),** 4, gr g Tagula (IRE)—Rofan (USA) **The Cool Silk Partnership**
8 **RETURNTOBRECONGILL,** 5, ch g Pastoral Pursuits—Turn Back **The Cool Silk Partnership**
9 **ROYAL BAJAN (USA),** 7, gr ro g Speightstown (USA)—Crown You (USA) **The Cool Silk Partnership**
10 **SHADES OF SILK,** 4, b f Bahamian Bounty—Terentia **The Cool Silk Partnership**
11 **SNOWMANE (IRE),** 4, b g Galileo (IRE)—Tree Tops **The Cool Silk Partnership**
12 **THE DUKKERER (IRE),** 4, b br f Footstepsinthesand—Saffron Crocus **Mr A. Clarke**
13 **WILFUL MINX (FR),** 4, b f Le Havre (IRE)—Miskina **Mrs S. Oliver**

## MR JAMES GIVEN - Continued

### THREE-YEAR-OLDS

14 **BLUE MELODY GIRL (IRE),** b f Captain Rio—Salingers Star (IRE)
15 **DARK WAR (IRE),** b g Dark Angel (IRE)—Waroonga (IRE) **The Cool Silk Partnership**
16 **DARK WONDER (IRE),** b g Dark Angel (IRE)—Wondrous Story (USA) **The Cool Silk Partnership**
17 **GROSMONT,** br g Hellvelyn—Aimee's Delight **The Cool Silk Partnership**
18 **LA FRITILLAIRE,** b f Champs Elysees—Generous Diana **Ingram Racing**
19 **PASTORAL GIRL,** b f Pastoral Pursuits—Talampaya (USA) **The Cool Silk Partnership**
20 **PLAY NICELY,** ch c Naaqoos—Aalya (IRE) **Miss S. J. Ballinger**
21 **RUSSIAN PUNCH,** b f Archipenko (USA)—Punch Drunk **Lovely Bubbly Racing**
22 **SANDS CHORUS,** b g Footstepsinthesand—Wood Chorus **The Cool Silk Partnership**
23 **SHOW ME BAILEYS (FR),** b g Naaqoos—Exhibitor (USA) **G. R. Bailey Ltd (Baileys Horse Feeds)**
24 **YOU'RE COOL,** b g Exceed And Excel (AUS)—Ja One (IRE) **The Cool Silk Partnership**

### TWO-YEAR-OLDS

25 **CHARAMBA,** b f 8/4 Sir Percy—Rahcak (IRE) (Generous (IRE))
26 **COOL IT,** ch f 2/5 Medicean—Pantile (Pivotal) (4761) **The Cool Silk Partnership**
27 **COOL SILK BOY (IRE),** b c 18/3 Big Bad Bob (IRE)—
Kheleyf's Silver (IRE) (Kheleyf (USA)) (50000) **The Cool Silk Partnership**
28 **COOL SILK GIRL,** br f 12/5 Motivator—
Captain's Paradise (IRE) (Rock of Gibraltar (IRE)) (160000) **The Cool Silk Partnership**
29 **FEELIN DICKY,** b c 23/4 Dick Turpin (IRE)—Feelin Foxy (Foxhound (USA)) **The Cool Silk Partnership**
30 **GIRLS IN A BENTLEY,** b f 9/2 Acclamation—Laurelei (IRE) (Oratorio (IRE)) (57142) **The Cool Silk Partnership**
31 **SEARCH FOR ED,** b c 19/2 Monsieur Bond (IRE)—
Spontaneity (IRE) (Holy Roman Emperor (IRE)) (52380) **The Cool Silk Partnership**
32 **SIGN OF THE KODIAC (IRE),** b c 13/5 Kodiac—
Summer Magic (IRE) (Desert Sun) (47619) **The Cool Silk Partnership**
33 **SILK BOW,** b f 12/3 Elusive City (USA)—Ishraaqat (Singspiel (IRE)) (29523) **The Cool Silk Partnership**
34 **SIR DUDLEY (IRE),** b c 10/2 Arcano (IRE)—
Rosy Dudley (IRE) (Grand Lodge (USA)) (49523) **The Cool Silk Partnership**
35 **STONE QUERCUS (IRE),** b c 23/3 Rock of Gibraltar (IRE)—
Redglow (IRE) (Fasliyev (USA)) (47619) **The Cool Silk Partnership**
36 **STRANDS OF SILK (IRE),** b f 19/3 Kodiac—Saldenaera (GER) (Areion (GER)) (22857) **The Cool Silk Partnership**

**Other Owners:** Mr S. C. Appelbee, James Given, Mr P. A. Horton, Dr M. J. O'Brien, P. Swann, Mrs B. E. Wilkinson.

---

## 242 MR J. L. GLEDSON, Hexham

Postal: **Buteland Farm, Bellingham, Hexham, Northumberland, NE48 2EX**
Contacts: **PHONE (01434) 220911 MOBILE (07790) 977801**
**E-MAIL helengledson@yahoo.co.uk**

1 **CLONEA POWER (IRE),** 8, ch g Subtle Power (IRE)—Clonea Taipan (IRE) **J. L. Gledson**
2 **FAIRLEE GRACE,** 4, b f Fair Mix (IRE)—Halo Flora **J. L. Gledson**
3 **NEVILLE WOODS,** 8, b g Alflora (IRE)—Angie Marinie **J. L. Gledson**
4 **THEREVEREND CLOVER,** 6, b g Revoque (IRE)—Ring of Clover **J. L. Gledson**

**Assistant Trainers:** Mrs Helen Gledson, Mr Charles Carr

**Conditional:** John Dawson. **Apprentice:** Alistair Findlay. **Amateur:** Mr Charles Carr.

---

## 243 MR JIM GOLDIE, Glasgow

Postal: **Libo Hill Farm, Uplawmoor, Glasgow, Lanarkshire, G78 4BA**
Contacts: **PHONE (01505) 850212 MOBILE (07778) 241522**
**WEBSITE www.jimgoldieracing.com**

1 **A SOUTHSIDE BOY (GER),** 7, b g Samum (GER)—Anthurium (GER) **Mr G. Dunne**
2 4, B g Flemensfirth (USA)—Akayid
3 **ALEKSANDAR,** 6, ch g Medicean—Alexander Celebre (IRE) **Mrs M. Craig**
4 **ANOTHER FOR JOE,** 7, b g Lomitas—Anna Kalinka (GER) **Mr & Mrs Gordon Grant & J S Goldie**
5 **ARCTIC COURT (IRE),** 11, b g Arctic Lord—Polls Joy **Mr & Mrs Raymond Anderson Green**
6 **BLACK DOUGLAS,** 6, b g Kyllachy—Penmayne **Johnnie Delta Racing**
7 **BOOGIE LIFE,** 4, b f Tobougg (IRE)—Life Is Life (FR) **Mr & Mrs Raymond Anderson Green**
8 **BRAES OF LOCHALSH,** 4, b g Tiger Hill (IRE)—Gargoyle Girl **Johnnie Delta Racing**

## MR JIM GOLDIE - Continued

9 **CALEDONIA,** 8, b g Sulamani (IRE)—Vanessa Bell (IRE) **Johnnie Delta Racing**
10 **CALYPSO MUSIC,** 4, ch f Bahamian Bounty—Songsheet **Dr J. Walker**
11 **CLASSY ANNE,** 5, ch m Orientor—Class Wan **The Vital Sparks**
12 **COMPTON HEIGHTS,** 6, ch g Compton Place—Harrken Heights (IRE) **D. L. McKenzie**
13 **DHAULAR DHAR (IRE),** 13, b g Indian Ridge—Pescara (IRE) **Johnnie Delta Racing**
14 **FORREST FLYER (IRE),** 11, b g Daylami (IRE)—Gerante (USA) **Mrs V. C. Macdonald**
15 **FRAY,** 4, b f Champs Elysees—Short Dance (USA) **F. Brady**
16 **FUNDING DEFICIT (IRE),** 5, ch g Rakti—Bukat Timah **D. G. Pryde**
17 **GLENLINI,** 9, b m Bertolini (USA)—Glenhurich (IRE) **J. S. Goldie**
18 **GO GO GREEN (IRE),** 9, b g Acclamation—Preponderance (IRE) **Johnnie Delta Racing**
19 **GONINODAETHAT,** 7, b g Proclamation (IRE)—Big Mystery (IRE) **Mr G E Adams & Mr J S Goldie**
20 **GRAND DIAMOND (IRE),** 11, b g Grand Lodge (USA)—Winona (IRE) **Caledonia Racing**
21 **HAWKEYETHENOO (IRE),** 9, b g Hawk Wing (USA)—Stardance (USA) **Johnnie Delta Racing**
22 **HAYLEY,** 5, b m Halling (USA)—Gargoyle Girl **J. S. Goldie**
23 **HERO'S STORY,** 5, b g Mount Nelson—Red Roses Story (FR) **J. S. Morrison**
24 **HIGGS BOSON,** 10, b g Overbury (IRE)—Evening Splash (IRE) **The Vital Sparks**
25 **I GOT SUNSHINE,** 7, b g Grape Tree Road—I Got Rhythm **J. S. Goldie**
26 **ICON DREAM (IRE),** 8, b g Sadler's Wells (USA)—Silver Skates (IRE)
27 **IDYLLIC STAR (IRE),** 6, ch m Choisir (AUS)—Idolize **Mac Asphalt Ltd**
28 **JACK DEXTER,** 6, b br g Orientor—Glenhurich (IRE) **Johnnie Delta Racing**
29 **JONNY DELTA,** 8, ch g Sulamani (IRE)—Send Me An Angel (IRE) **Johnnie Delta Racing**
30 **JUMBO STEPS (IRE),** 8, b g Footstepsinthesand—Night Delight (IRE) **The Dregs Of Humanity**
31 **KARAKA JACK,** 8, ch g Pivotal—Mauri Moon **M. Mackay & J. Fyffe**
32 **LATIN REBEL (IRE),** 8, b g Spartacus (IRE)—Dance To The Beat **Mr R. W. C. McLachlan**
33 **LOCHNELL (IRE),** 6, b m Winged Love (IRE)—Nothing For Ever (IRE) **Alan & Barry Macdonald**
34 **LOS NADIS (GER),** 11, ch g Hernando (FR)—La Estrella (GER) **I. G. M. Dalgleish**
35 **MARGARET'S MISSION (IRE),** 4, b f Shamardal (USA)—
Wimple (USA) **Frank Brady, James Thom, Howard Slone**
36 **MERCHANT OF DUBAI,** 10, b g Dubai Destination (USA)—Chameleon **Highland Racing 2**
37 **MONEL,** 7, ch g Cadeaux Genereux—Kelucia (IRE) **Johnnie Delta Racing**
38 **MOWHOOB,** 5, b g Medicean—Pappas Ruby (USA) **Johnnie Delta Racing**
39 **NANTON (USA),** 13, gr ro g Spinning World (USA)—Grab The Green (USA) **Johnnie Delta Racing**
40 **NEVER FOREVER,** 6, ch g Sir Percy—Codename **Mr B. N. MacDonald**
41 **ORDER OF SERVICE,** 5, ch g Medicean—Choir Gallery **Whitestonecliffe Racing Partnership**
42 **ORIENTAL HEIGHTS,** 4, b f Orientor—Harrken Heights (IRE) **Johnnie Delta Racing**
43 **PIPER BILL,** 4, b g Halling (USA)—Murielle **Mrs J. M. MacPherson**
44 **PLUS JAMAIS (FR),** 8, b g Caballo Raptor (CAN)—Branceilles (FR) **Alba-Eire Syndicate**
45 **RASAMAN (IRE),** 11, b g Namid—Rasana **P. Moulton**
46 **RIOJA DAY (IRE),** 5, b g Red Clubs (IRE)—Dai E Dai (USA) **Ayrshire Racing & Partner**
47 **RONALD GEE (IRE),** 8, ch g Garuda (IRE)—Panache Lady (IRE) **J. S. Goldie**
48 **ROTHESAY CHANCER,** 7, ch g Monsieur Bond (IRE)—
Rhinefield Beauty (IRE) **The McMaster Springford Partnership**
49 **SILVER DUKE (IRE),** 4, gr g Papal Bull—Dumaani's Dream (USA) **Mac Asphalt Ltd**
50 **TESTA ROSSA (IRE),** 5, b g Oratorio (IRE)—Red Rita (IRE) **J. S. Morrison**
51 **THORNTOUN LADY (USA),** 5, b m Henrythenavigator (USA)—Valery Lady (ARG) **Mrs M. Craig**
52 **TIGER HEIGHTS,** 4, b g Tiger Hill (IRE)—Primo Heights **Johnnie Delta Racing**
53 **TIGER JIM,** 5, b g Tiger Hill (IRE)—Quintrell **J. S. Goldie**
54 **TITUS BOLT (IRE),** 6, b g Titus Livius (FR)—Megan's Bay **I. G. M. Dalgleish**
55 **TOO COOL TO FOOL (IRE),** 12, b g Bob Back (USA)—Mandysway (IRE) **Johnnie Delta Racing**
56 **TURTLE WATCH,** 7, b g Where Or When (IRE)—Cita Verda (FR) **Mr & Mrs Raymond Anderson Green**

### THREE-YEAR-OLDS

57 **CELTIC POWER,** b g Rail Link—Biloxi **Zen Racing & Mr J S Goldie**
58 **LADY CORDIE,** b f Monsieur Bond (IRE)—Lady Benjamin **Stuart & Emma Earley & Valerie Lampard**
59 **SEA OF GREEN,** b f Iffraaj—Sea of Leaves (USA) **Dr J. Walker**

**Other Owners:** Mr G. Adams, R. M. S. Allison, Mr E. N. Barber, Mr N. Boyle, Mr T. Cobain, Mr F. J. Connor, Mr G. Davidson, Mr J. Doherty, Mr S. D. Earley, Mrs E. Earley, Mr C. J. Edwards, Mr J. Frew, Mr M. Friel, Mr J. Fyffe, Mrs D. I. Goldie, Mrs L. Goldie, Mr G. R. Grant, Mrs C. H. Grant, R. A. Green, Mrs A. Green, A. G. Guthrie, P. Hampshire, Mrs V. A. Lampard, Mr A. G. MacDonald, M. F. Mackay, Mr A. Manson, Mr D. W. McIntyre, A. McManus, Mr T. B. McMaster, Mrs J. D. McMaster, W. A. Powrie, Mr R. A. Sankey, A. H. Slone, Mr N. Springford, Mrs D. Springford, J. G. Thom.

**Assistant Trainers:** James Goldie, George Goldie

**Jockey (flat):** Graham Lee. **Jockey (NH):** Lucy Alexander, Henry Brooke, Denis O'Regan.
**Amateur:** Mrs Carol Bartley, Mrs I. Goldie.

## 244 MR ROBERT GOLDIE, Kilmarnock

Postal: **Harpercroft, Old Loans Road, Dundonald, Kilmarnock, Ayrshire, KA2 9DD**
Contacts: **PHONE (01292) 317222 FAX (01292) 313585 MOBILE (07801) 922552**

1 **ALEXANDER OATS,** 12, b g Insan (USA)—Easter Oats **R. H. Goldie**
2 **ALFRED OATS,** 11, b g Alflora (IRE)—Easter Oats **R. H. Goldie**
3 **LAST OF THE OATS,** 7, b g Luso—Easter Oats **R. H. Goldie**
4 **VICTORIA OATS,** 9, b m Old Vic—Easter Oats **R. H. Goldie**

**Assistant Trainer:** Mrs R H Goldie

## 245 MR KEITH GOLDSWORTHY, Kilgetty

Postal: **Grumbly Bush Farm, Yerbeston, Kilgetty, Pembrokeshire, SA68 0NS**
Contacts: **PHONE/FAX (01834) 891343 MOBILE (07796) 497733**
**E-MAIL grumbly@supanet.com WEBSITE www.keithgoldsworthyracing.co.uk**

1 **CALDEY,** 6, b m Overbury (IRE)—Barfleur (IRE) **S. F. Barlow**
2 **HILLS OF ARAN,** 13, b g Sadler's Wells (USA)—Danefair
3 **WILLIAM HOGARTH,** 10, b g High Chaparral (IRE)—Mountain Holly **K. Goldsworthy**

### THREE-YEAR-OLDS

4 B c Dr Massini (IRE)—Prescelli (IRE) **S. F. Barlow**

**Assistant Trainer:** Mrs L. A. Goldsworthy

**Amateur:** Miss Charlotte Evans.

## 246 MR STEVE GOLLINGS, Louth

Postal: **Highfield House, Scamblesby, Louth, Lincolnshire, LN11 9XT**
Contacts: **YARD (01507) 343204 HOME/FAX (01507) 343213 MOBILE (07860) 218910**
**E-MAIL stevegollings@aol.com WEBSITE www.stevegollings.com**

1 **DEFICIT (IRE),** 5, gr g Dalakhani (IRE)—Venturi **I. S. Naylor**
2 **HANDIWORK,** 5, ch g Motivator—Spinning Top **Mr C. A. Johnstone**
3 **LOCAL HERO (GER),** 8, b g Lomitas—Lolli Pop (GER) **I. S. Naylor**
4 **MAKE ME A FORTUNE (IRE),** 7, b br g Heron Island (IRE)—Biora Queen (IRE) **Mr P W Baxter & Mr R C Key**
5 **RESPONSE,** 5, ch g New Approach (IRE)—Spotlight **I. S. Naylor**
6 **RUSSIAN GEORGE (IRE),** 9, ch g Sendawar (IRE)—Mannsara (IRE) **Mrs Jayne M. Gollings**
7 **SIR WALTER BENGAL,** 4, b g Tiger Hill (IRE)—Lady Darayna **Mr P. S. Walter**
8 **TROOPINGTHECOLOUR,** 9, b g Nayef (USA)—Hyperspectra **I. S. Naylor**
9 **ZAMOYSKI,** 5, ch g Dutch Art—Speech **I. S. Naylor**

**Other Owners:** Mr P. W. Baxter, Mr R. C. Key.

**Assistant Trainer:** Mrs J M Gollings

**Jockey (flat):** Jamie Spencer. **Jockey (NH):** Keith Mercer, Brian Hughes, A. P. McCoy, Tom Scudamore.
**Conditional:** Paul Bohan.

## 247 MR CHRIS GORDON, Winchester

Postal: **Morestead Farm Stables, Morestead, Winchester, Hampshire, SO21 1JD**
Contacts: **PHONE (01962) 712774 FAX (01962) 712774 MOBILE (07713) 082392**
**E-MAIL chrisgordon68@hotmail.co.uk WEBSITE www.chrisgordonracing.com**

1 **BALLYHEIGUE BAY (IRE),** 8, b g Rudimentary (USA)—Terinka (IRE) **E. J. Farrant**
2 **BLACK COW (IRE),** 7, br g Presenting—Back Market Lass (IRE) **Gordon Racing**
3 **BUTE STREET,** 10, b g Superior Premium—Hard To Follow **J. W. Mursell**
4 **COMEONGINGER (IRE),** 8, b g King's Theatre (IRE)—Miss Poutine (FR) **Mr & Mrs Michael Coates**
5 **DECIMUS MAXIMUS,** 4, b g Elnadim (USA)—Sempre Sorriso **P. J. & Mrs J. P. Haycock**
6 **FAIR RANGER,** 4, b g Bushranger (IRE)—Fairmont (IRE) **Mrs K. Digweed**
7 **FAMILY MOTTO,** 6, b g Tobougg (IRE)—Be My Mot (IRE) **Chris Gordon Racing Club**
8 **HERECOMESTHETRUTH (IRE),** 13, ch g Presenting—Beagan Rose (IRE) **C. E. Gordon**

## MR CHRIS GORDON - Continued

9 **JEBRIL (FR),** 5, b g Astronomer Royal (USA)—Happy Clapper **Mr D. F. Henery**
10 **KING UTHER,** 5, b g Master Blade—Cadbury Castle **C. E. Gordon**
11 **LADY A,** 5, ch m Apple Tree (FR)—Lady Kay **L. Gilbert**
12 **LIGHTENTERTAINMENT (IRE),** 7, b g King's Theatre (IRE)—
Dochas Supreme (IRE) **The Not Over Big Partnership**
13 **LOVES DESTINATION,** 4, b f Dubai Destination (USA)—Bijou Love (IRE) **C. E. Gordon**
14 **MORESTEAD SCREAMER,** 6, b m Imperial Dancer—The Screamer (IRE) **Chris Gordon Racing Club**
15 **NOBLE FRIEND (IRE),** 7, b g Presenting—Laragh (IRE) **Mrs K. Digweed**
16 **NORSE LEGEND,** 4, b g Norse Dancer (IRE)—Methodical **Woodhaven Racing Syndicate**
17 **ONWITHTHEPARTY,** 6, b g Sir Harry Lewis (USA)—Kentford Fern **C. E. Gordon**
18 **OSMOSIA (FR),** 10, b m Mansonnien (FR)—Osmose (FR) **Mr G. Sturt**
19 **PETTOCHSIDE,** 6, b g Refuse To Bend (IRE)—Clear Impression (IRE) **Mr D. F. Henery**
20 **POETIC JUSTICE,** 4, b g Byron—Toleration **Woodhaven Racing Syndicate**
21 **PROMISED WINGS (GER),** 8, ch g Monsun (GER)—Panagia (USA) **Chris Gordon Racing Club**
22 **REMILUC (FR),** 6, b g Mister Sacha (FR)—Markene de Durtal (FR) **L. Gilbert**
23 **SEA TIGER,** 5, b g Tiger Hill (IRE)—Possessive Artiste **Mrs K. Digweed**
24 **SEA WALL (FR),** 7, b g Turgeon (USA)—Si Parfaite (FR) **Draper Edmonds Draper**
25 **SEAS THE MOMENT (IRE),** 6, b m Westerner—Meursault (IRE) **Mr A. W. Spooner**
26 **STAR PRESENTER (IRE),** 7, b g Presenting—Star Councel (IRE) **C. E. Gordon**
27 **SWEET BOY VIC (IRE),** 7, b g Old Vic—Sweet Second (IRE) **Mr F. H. Ramsahoye**
28 **TARA BRIDGE,** 7, b g Kayf Tara—Annie Greenlaw **B. J. Champion**
29 **TIGRE D'ARON (FR),** 8, gr g Dom Alco (FR)—Fleche Noir II (FR) **Mr Roger Alwen Mrs Heather Alwen**
30 **VERY NOBLE (FR),** 6, b g Martaline—Isati's (FR) **A. C. Ward-Thomas**

### THREE-YEAR-OLDS

31 B f Indian Danehill (IRE)—Bijou Love (IRE) **C. E. Gordon**

**Other Owners:** Mr R. N. Alwen, Mrs H. J. Alwen, M. O. Coates, Mrs F. A. Coates, J. Draper, Mr M. J. Draper, T. W. Edmonds, Mrs J. L. Gordon, P. J. Haycock, Mrs J. P. Haycock, C. A. Leafe, Miss J. E. Reed, P. J. H. Rowe, R. M. Venn.

**Assistant Trainer:** Jenny Gordon

**Conditional:** Tom Cannon. **Amateur:** Miss M. R. Trainor.

---

## 248 MR J. T. GORMAN, Curragh

Postal: **Maddenstown Lodge Stables, Maddenstown, Curragh, Co. Kildare, Ireland**
Contacts: **PHONE (00353) 45 441404 FAX (00353) 45 441404 MOBILE (00353) 872 599603**
**E-MAIL jtgorman1@hotmail.com**

1 **A SMILE SAYS ALOT (IRE),** 5, b m Thousand Words—Masakira (IRE) **The Andrews Syndicate**
2 **GOLDEN SHOE (IRE),** 7, br g Footstepsinthesand—Goldilocks (IRE) **The Andrews Syndicate**
3 **PIERRE D'OR (IRE),** 6, ch g Rock of Gibraltar (IRE)—Gilded Edge **The Andrews Syndicate**
4 **SNAP CLICK (IRE),** 4, b g Kodiac—Happy Hour (GER) **P. Reilly**

### THREE-YEAR-OLDS

5 **ATHENRY BOY (IRE),** br c Excellent Art—Dancing With Stars (IRE) **P. Reilly**
6 **BUSY BUSH (IRE),** b f Bushranger (IRE)—Candela Bay (IRE) **Miss M. McWey**
7 **VICARAGE (IRE),** ch g Aristotle (IRE)—Breezit (USA) **The Andrews Syndicate**

### TWO-YEAR-OLDS

8 Br c 3/4 Bushranger (IRE)—Elitista (FR) (Linamix (FR)) (2380) **Miss M. McWey**
9 Gr f 5/5 Big Bad Bob (IRE)—Suailce (IRE) (Singspiel (IRE)) (2777) **Miss M. McWey**

**Jockey (flat):** Kevin Manning, C. D. Hayes, D. McDonagh. **Jockey (NH):** B. Dalton.

---

## 249 MR JOHN GOSDEN, Newmarket

Postal: **Clarehaven, Bury Road, Newmarket, Suffolk, CB8 7BY**
Contacts: **PHONE (01638) 565400 FAX (01638) 565401**
**E-MAIL jhmg@johngosden.com**

1 **BELLE D'OR (USA),** 4, b f Medaglia d'Oro (USA)—Glatisant
2 **CLOUDSCAPE (IRE),** 4, b c Dansili—Set The Scene (IRE)

## MR JOHN GOSDEN - Continued

3 **CORNROW,** 5, ch h New Approach (IRE)—Needlecraft (IRE)
4 **CRITERIA (IRE),** 4, b f Galileo (IRE)—Aleagueoftheirown (IRE)
5 **DEUCE AGAIN,** 4, b f Dubawi (IRE)—Match Point
6 **EAGLE TOP,** 4, ch c Pivotal—Gull Wing (IRE)
7 **FLYING OFFICER (USA),** 5, b g Dynaformer (USA)—Vignette (USA)
8 **FOREVER NOW,** 4, b c Galileo (IRE)—All's Forgotten (USA)
9 **GATEWOOD,** 7, b h Galileo (IRE)—Felicity (IRE)
10 **GM HOPKINS,** 4, b g Dubawi (IRE)—Varsity
11 **MADE WITH LOVE,** 4, b c Exceed And Excel (AUS)—Maid To Perfection
12 **MAHSOOB,** 4, b c Dansili—Mooakada (IRE)
13 **MARZOCCO (USA),** 4, b br g Kitten's Joy (USA)—Dynamia (USA)
14 **MUWAARY,** 4, b br c Oasis Dream—Wissal (USA)
15 **REMOTE,** 5, b h Dansili—Zenda
16 **ROMSDAL,** 4, ch c Halling (USA)—Pure Song
17 **SACRED ACT,** 4, b c Oasis Dream—Stage Presence (IRE)
18 **SOLAR MAGIC,** 4, ch f Pivotal—Moon Goddess
19 **STELLA BELLISSIMA (IRE),** 4, b f Sea The Stars (IRE)—Dolores
20 **WANNABE YOURS (IRE),** 4, b c Dubawi (IRE)—Wannabe Posh (IRE)
21 **WESTERN HYMN,** 4, b g High Chaparral (IRE)—Blue Rhapsody

## THREE-YEAR-OLDS

22 **AL RIFAI (IRE),** b c Galileo (IRE)—Lahaleeb (IRE)
23 **ALTHANIA (USA),** ch f Street Cry (IRE)—Gabriellina Giof
24 **BAQQA (IRE),** b f Shamardal (USA)—Love Excelling (FR)
25 **BLUE CHIP,** gr f Galileo (IRE)—Intrigued
26 **BOLLIHOPE,** ch c Medicean—Hazy Dancer
27 **CHRISTOPHERMARLOWE (USA),** b c Tapit (USA)—Dress Rehearsal (IRE)
28 **CILENTO (IRE),** gr c Raven's Pass (USA)—Kapria (FR)
29 **COUNTERPROOF (IRE),** br c Authorized (IRE)—Ellasha
30 **ENTERTAINMENT,** ch f Halling (USA)—Opera Comique (FR)
31 **FALLEN FOR A STAR,** b c Sea The Stars (IRE)—Fallen Star
32 **FALLING PETALS (IRE),** ch f Raven's Pass (USA)—Infinite Spirit (USA)
33 **FANNAAN (USA),** ch c Speightstown (USA)—Titian Time (USA)
34 **FAYDHAN (USA),** br c War Front (USA)—Agreeable Miss (USA)
35 **FIGMENT,** b f Acclamation—First Exhibit
36 **FRENCH DRESSING,** b f Sea The Stars (IRE)—Foodbroker Fancy (IRE)
37 **GENRES,** b c Champs Elysees—Musical Horizon (USA)
38 **GLOBALIST (GER),** b c Sea The Stars (IRE)—Global World (GER)
39 **GOLDEN HORN,** b c Cape Cross (IRE)—Fleche d'or
40 **GOLDEN LAUGHTER (USA),** b f Bernardini (USA)—Glatisant
41 **GREATEST HITS (USA),** b c Cape Cross (IRE)—Northern Melody (IRE)
42 **GREENWICH (IRE),** b g Acclamation—Champion Place
43 **GRETCHEN,** ch f Galileo (IRE)—Dolores
44 **I WANT TO FLY,** b c Lucarno (USA)—Las Flores (IRE)
45 **JACK HOBBS,** b c Halling (USA)—Swain's Gold (USA)
46 **JAZZI TOP,** b f Danehill Dancer (IRE)—Zee Zee Top
47 **JELLICLE BALL (IRE),** b f Invincible Spirit (IRE)—Dance Troupe
48 **JOHNNY BARNES (IRE),** b c Acclamation—Mahalia (IRE)
49 **JOURNEY,** b f Dubawi (IRE)—Montare (IRE)
50 **KASB (IRE),** ch g Arcano (IRE)—Cape Columbine
51 **KEBLE (IRE),** b c Teofilo (IRE)—Vadazing (FR)
52 **LA PETITE REINE,** ch f Galileo (IRE)—River Belle
53 **LADY CORRESPONDENT (USA),** b f War Front (USA)—Fanzine (USA)
54 **LAP OF LUXURY (IRE),** ch f Galileo (IRE)—Halland Park Lass (IRE)
55 **LASHKAAL,** b f Teofilo (IRE)—Mudaaraah
56 **LEMONCETTA (USA),** ch f Lemon Drop Kid (USA)—Excelente (IRE)
57 **LIBERALITY,** b f Shamardal (USA)—Charity Belle (USA)
58 **LOVING THINGS,** b f Pivotal—Fallen In Love
59 **MALAF (USA),** b c Elusive Quality (USA)—Holy Wish (USA)
60 **MARKSTEIN (IRE),** ch c Raven's Pass (USA)—Manerbe (USA)
61 **MARMION,** b c Cape Cross (IRE)—Margarula (IRE)
62 **MARTLET,** b f Dansili—Marywell
63 **MAWHEBA (IRE),** ch f Dubawi (IRE)—Qurrah (IRE)
64 **MELBOURNE SHUFFLE (USA),** b br f Street Cry (IRE)—Liffey Dancer (IRE)
65 **MILL SPRINGS,** b f Shirocco (GER)—Mezzogiorno

## MR JOHN GOSDEN - Continued

66 **MR SINGH,** b c High Chaparral (IRE)—Sundari (IRE)
67 **MULTILINGUAL,** b f Dansili—Zenda
68 **MUSTAQQIL (IRE),** b c Invincible Spirit (IRE)—Cast In Gold (USA)
69 **NEXT APPROACH,** ch c New Approach (IRE)—Carafe
70 **NIGEL,** b c New Approach (IRE)—Deirdre
71 **OCCULT,** b c Oasis Dream—Trojan Queen (USA)
72 **PERSIAN BREEZE,** b f Pivotal—Persian Jasmine
73 **PHOTOSPHERE,** b f Galileo (IRE)—Love The Rain
74 **RICHARD PANKHURST,** ch c Raven's Pass (USA)—Mainstay
75 **SCARLET GRAY (IRE),** b f Pivotal—Discerning
76 **SECATEUR,** b g Danehill Dancer (IRE)—Rose Cut (IRE)
77 **SIGNED SEALED (USA),** ch c Giant's Causeway (USA)—Latice (IRE)
78 **SNOANO,** b c Nayef (USA)—White Dress (IRE)
79 **SPERRY (IRE),** b f Shamardal (USA)—Badee'a (IRE)
80 **STAR OF SEVILLE,** b f Duke of Marmalade (IRE)—Stage Presence (IRE)
81 **STUBBINS,** b f Rip Van Winkle (IRE)—Skimmia
82 **SUGAR BOY (GER),** b c Areion (GER)—Sugar Baby Love (GER)
83 **SWISS AFFAIR,** b f Pivotal—Swiss Lake (USA)
84 **SWOT,** b c Exceed And Excel (AUS)—House Point
85 **TAYSH (USA),** b br c Bernstein (USA)—Normandy's Nell (USA)
86 **TEMPUS TEMPORIS (USA),** b c Dynaformer (USA)—Tempus Fugit (USA)
87 **TENDU,** b f Oasis Dream—Arabesque
88 **THE MIGHTY EAGLE,** ch c Shamardal (USA)—Gull Wing (IRE)
89 **TIMBA,** b f Oasis Dream—Teeky
90 **TIME FLIES,** b c Exceed And Excel (AUS)—Simply Times (USA)
91 **TUTTI FRUTTI,** b f Teofilo (IRE)—Soft Centre
92 **VIBE QUEEN (IRE),** b f Invincible Spirit (IRE)—Be My Queen (IRE)
93 **WAADY (IRE),** b c Approve (IRE)—Anne Bonney
94 **WALDNAH,** ch f New Approach (IRE)—Waldmark (GER)
95 **WANNABE SPECIAL,** b f Galileo (IRE)—Wannabe Posh (IRE)
96 **YASMEEN,** b f Sea The Stars (IRE)—Wissal (USA)
97 **YEATS MAGIC (IRE),** b c Yeats (IRE)—Orinoco (IRE)
98 **ZAMOURA,** b f Azamour (IRE)—Move

## TWO-YEAR-OLDS

**99** B c 8/3 New Approach (IRE)—Ahla Wasahl (Dubai Destination (USA)) (600000)
**100 AMANAAT (IRE),** b c 21/2 Exceed And Excel (AUS)—Pietra Dura (Cadeaux Genereux) (280000)
**101** B c 28/2 Dansili—Arabesque (Zafonic (USA))
**102** B f 19/2 Elusive Quality (USA)—Attractive (IRE) (Sadler's Wells (USA)) (90000)
**103 AUNTINET,** b f 7/3 Invincible Spirit (IRE)—Cozy Maria (USA) (Cozzene (USA))
**104** B f 7/4 Zebedee—Baileys Cream (Mister Baileys) (82000)
**105** B f 10/2 Dutch Art—Balatoma (IRE) (Mr Greeley (USA)) (35000)
**106** B f 22/4 Kodiac—Barracade (IRE) (Barathea (IRE)) (250000)
**107 BLUE GERANIUM (IRE),** b f 8/3 Dansili—Super Sleuth (IRE) (Selkirk (USA))
**108** B c 27/4 Fastnet Rock (AUS)—Bright Bank (IRE) (Sadler's Wells (USA))
**109** B c 26/2 Invincible Spirit (IRE)—Brusca (USA) (Grindstone (USA)) (680000)
**110 CAMPOSANTO,** b f 1/3 Pivotal—Field of Miracles (IRE) (Galileo (IRE))
**111 CASTLE HARBOUR,** b c 14/2 Kyllachy—Gypsy Carnival (Trade Fair) (200000)
**112** B f 27/2 Dubawi (IRE)—Casual Look (USA) (Red Ransom (USA)) (831899)
**113** Ch c 18/2 Footstepsinthesand—Celestial Girl (Dubai Destination (USA)) (70000)
**114** B c 27/4 Iffraaj—Cheal Rose (IRE) (Dr Devious (IRE)) (185000)
**115** B c 21/3 Rip Van Winkle (IRE)—Chehalis Sunset (Danehill Dancer (IRE)) (260000)
**116** B c 26/3 Iffraaj—City Dancer (IRE) (Elusive City (USA)) (55000)
**117** B c 3/2 War Front (USA)—City Sister (USA) (Carson City (USA))
**118** B f 13/4 Dubawi (IRE)—Claba di San Jore (IRE) (Barathea (IRE))
**119 COLONIAL CLASSIC (FR),** b f 9/4 Dansili—Flame of Hestia (IRE) (Giant's Causeway (USA))
**120** B c 19/2 Fastnet Rock (AUS)—Crystal Maze (Gone West (USA)) (80000)
**121** Ch f 8/2 Raven's Pass (USA)—Darmiana (USA) (Lemon Drop Kid (USA))
**122** B f 25/3 Oasis Dream—Dashing (IRE) (Sadler's Wells (USA)) (145000)
**123** B c 16/1 Lope de Vega (IRE)—Dazzle Dancer (IRE) (Montjeu (IRE)) (650000)
**124** B f 15/3 Invincible Spirit (IRE)—Design Perfection (USA) (Diesis)
**125 DHAROOS (IRE),** ch c 12/4 New Approach (IRE)—Cailiocht (USA) (Elusive Quality (USA))
**126** B f 8/2 Galileo (IRE)—Dialafara (FR) (Anabaa (USA)) (480000)
**127 EPSOM DAY (IRE),** b c 21/3 Teofilo (IRE)—Dubai Flower (Manduro (GER))
**128 EXIST,** b f 5/2 Exceed And Excel (AUS)—Harryana (Efisio) (180000)

## MR JOHN GOSDEN - Continued

**129 FALLEN FOR ANOTHER,** b c 19/3 Dansili—Fallen Star (Brief Truce (USA))
**130** B f 6/4 First Defence (USA)—Fanzine (USA) (Cozzene (USA))
**131** B f 22/2 Galileo (IRE)—Fleeting Spirit (IRE) (Invincible Spirit (IRE))
**132 FOUNDATION (IRE),** ch c 24/2 Zoffany (IRE)—Roystonea (Polish Precedent (USA)) (150793)
**133** B c 23/2 Invincible Spirit (IRE)—Ghurra (USA) (War Chant (USA)) (170000)
**134** B c 30/1 Pour Moi (IRE)—Glen Rosie (IRE) (Mujtahid (USA)) (67460)
**135** B f 5/4 Speightstown (USA)—Hidden Face (USA) (Empire Maker (USA))
**136** B c 7/2 Galileo (IRE)—Ice Mint (USA) (Awesome Again (CAN))
**137 INVESTITURE,** b f 28/1 Invincible Spirit (IRE)—Highest (Dynaformer (USA))
**138** B c 18/4 Galileo (IRE)—Jacqueline (IND) (King Charlemagne (USA))
**139** Gr f 25/1 Dark Angel (IRE)—Jasmine Flower (Kyllachy) (130000)
**140 KARAAMA,** b c 10/2 Oasis Dream—Eshaadeh (USA) (Storm Cat (USA))
**141** B c 25/2 Poet's Voice—Kelly Nicole (IRE) (Rainbow Quest (USA)) (200000)
**142** Ch c 26/2 Dutch Art—Kelowna (IRE) (Pivotal) (340000)
**143 KHASEEB,** ch f 20/2 Dutch Art—Kerry's Dream (Tobougg (IRE))
**144 KHAWANEEJ,** b c 19/3 Azamour (IRE)—Dance East (Shamardal (USA)) (105000)
**145** B c 7/3 Dansili—Kilo Alpha (King's Best (USA))
**146** B c 15/4 Dubawi (IRE)—Kiltubber (IRE) (Sadler's Wells (USA)) (120000)
**147** B br f 25/1 Iffraaj—Larceny (IRE) (Cape Cross (IRE)) (134920)
**148 LEE BAY,** b c 30/4 Cacique (IRE)—Bantu (Cape Cross (IRE)) (100000)
**149 LIGHTEN UP,** b f 1/5 Pivotal—Floodlit (Fantastic Light (USA))
**150** Ch f 17/3 Intikhab (USA)—Luanas Pearl (IRE) (Bahri (USA)) (27000)
**151** B c 19/2 Dansili—Lunar Phase (IRE) (Galileo (IRE))
**152** Br c 14/3 New Approach (IRE)—Mambo Halo (USA) (Southern Halo (USA)) (120000)
**153** B br c 30/1 War Front (USA)—Masseuse (USA) (Dynaformer (USA))
**154** B f 18/1 Galileo (IRE)—Miarixa (FR) (Linamix (FR))
**155 MIRAMONT,** b f 10/4 Iffraaj—Hasaiyda (IRE) (Hector Protector (USA)) (70000)
**156** B f 9/4 Dark Angel (IRE)—Miss Indigo (Indian Ridge) (360000)
**157** B c 19/2 Poet's Voice—Miss Lacey (IRE) (Diktat) (66666)
**158** B c 10/4 Shamardal (USA)—Multicolour Wave (IRE) (Rainbow Quest (USA)) (550000)
**159 NATHRA (IRE),** b f 25/3 Iffraaj—Rada (IRE) (Danehill (USA)) (270000)
**160** Ch c 7/3 Shamardal (USA)—Nightime (IRE) (Galileo (IRE)) (400000)
**161** Ch f 26/3 Dubawi (IRE)—Opera Comique (FR) (Singspiel (IRE))
**162 PALMERSTON,** b c 12/1 Oasis Dream—Marywell (Selkirk (USA))
**163** B c 18/3 Poet's Voice—Past The Post (USA) (Danzig (USA)) (475000)
**164 PERFECT VOICE,** b f 3/2 Poet's Voice—Perfect Spirit (IRE) (Invincible Spirit (IRE)) (700000)
**165 PERSUASIVE (IRE),** b f 16/3 Dark Angel (IRE)—Choose Me (IRE) (Choisir (AUS)) (142857)
**166 PRINCELY SUM (USA),** b f 24/1 Lemon Drop Kid (USA)—Honoria (IRE) (Sadler's Wells (USA)) (229489)
**167** B f 28/4 Sea The Stars (IRE)—Pursuit of Life (Pursuit of Love) (320000)
**168** B f 29/1 Dansili—Real Sense (IRE) (Galileo (IRE)) (186460)
**169 REMARKABLE,** b c 25/3 Pivotal—Irresistible (Cadeaux Genereux)
**170** B f 17/5 Sea The Stars (IRE)—Rosamixa (FR) (Linamix (FR))
**171** B f 17/2 Dansili—Selinka (Selkirk (USA)) (150000)
**172** B c 10/2 Oasis Dream—Sense of Pride (Sadler's Wells (USA))
**173** B f 18/1 Galileo (IRE)—Shadow Song (IRE) (Pennekamp (USA))
**174** B f 3/3 Zoffany (IRE)—Sioduil (IRE) (Oasis Dream) (260000)
**175 SOUTHERN STARS,** b f 9/2 Smart Strike (CAN)—Stacelita (FR) (Monsun (GER))
**176 STANLEY,** ch c 29/1 Sea The Stars (IRE)—Deirdre (Dubawi (IRE))
**177 SYMBOLIC,** b c 2/2 Shamardal (USA)—Resort (Oasis Dream)
**178 TAQAAREED (IRE),** ch f 3/2 Sea The Stars (IRE)—Ezima (IRE) (Sadler's Wells (USA))
**179 TAQDEER (IRE),** ch c 29/1 Fast Company (IRE)—Brigantia (Pivotal) (133333)
**180 TASHWEEQ (IRE),** b c 10/1 Big Bad Bob (IRE)—Dance Hall Girl (IRE) (Dansili) (142857)
**181** Ch c 23/2 Dubawi (IRE)—Teeky (Daylami (IRE))
**182** Ch c 7/4 Raven's Pass (USA)—Turkana Girl (Hernando (FR)) (55555)
**183** B c 15/1 Oasis Dream—Very Good News (USA) (Empire Maker (USA))
**184 WAJEEZ (IRE),** ch c 13/2 Lope de Vega (IRE)—Chanter (Lomitas) (190000)
**185 WANNABE FRIENDS,** ch c 15/2 Dubawi (IRE)—Wannabe Posh (IRE) (Grand Lodge (USA))
**186** B c 4/2 Oasis Dream—Warling (IRE) (Montjeu (IRE)) (550000)
**187 WESTERN PRINCE,** b c 12/3 Cape Cross (IRE)—Vigee Le Brun (USA) (Pulpit (USA)) (31746)
**188 WHITE HOT (IRE),** b f 27/2 Galileo (IRE)—Gwynn (IRE) (Darshaan) (1250000)

## 250 MRS HARRIET GRAHAM, Jedburgh

Postal: **Strip End, Jedburgh, Roxburghshire, TD8 6NE**
Contacts: **PHONE (01835) 840354 MOBILE (07843) 380401**
**E-MAIL hgrahamracing@aol.com**

1 **BE WISE (IRE),** 8, gr g Cloudings (IRE)—Crashtown Lucy **H G Racing**
2 **MACGILLYCUDDY,** 6, b g And Beyond (IRE)—Tofino Swell **Mr M. J. McGovern**
3 **MAGGIE BLUE (IRE),** 7, b m Beneficial—Top Ar Aghaidh (IRE) **Exors of the Late Mr R. S. Hamilton**
4 **SCOTSWELL,** 9, b g Endoli (USA)—Tofino Swell **H G Racing**
5 **SOUL MAGIC (IRE),** 13, b g Flemensfirth (USA)—Indian Legend (IRE) **H G Racing**

**Other Owners:** Mrs H. O. Graham, R. D. Graham.

**Assistant Trainer:** R D Graham

**Jockey (NH):** James Reveley.

## 251 MR CHRIS GRANT, Billingham

Postal: **Low Burntoft Farm, Wolviston, Billingham, Cleveland, TS22 5PD**
Contacts: **PHONE (01740) 644054 MOBILE (07860) 577998**
**E-MAIL chrisgrantracing@gmail.com WEBSITE www.chrisgrantracing.co.uk**

1 **ALLYCAT,** 5, b g Beat All (USA)—Alikat (IRE) **Mickley Stud & Derrick Mossop**
2 **AMOUR COLLONGES (FR),** 5, b g Lavirco (GER)—Kapucine Collonges (FR) **Elliott Brothers And Peacock**
3 **BACKWORTH SHANDY (IRE),** 7, b m Trans Island—Executive Ellie (IRE) **D&D Armstrong Limited**
4 **BALLALOUGH,** 5, b g Lucarno (USA)—Cerise Bleue (FR) **T. J. Hemmings**
5 **BARROW NOOK,** 5, b g Overbury (IRE)—Rippling Brook **M. R. Johnson**
6 **BEAU DANDY (IRE),** 10, b g Exit To Nowhere (USA)—Northern Dandy **D Lofthouse E Lofthouse Mrs M Nicholas**
7 **BEAUMONT'S PARTY (IRE),** 8, b g High Chaparral (IRE)—Miss Champagne (FR) **Elliott Brothers And Peacock**
8 **BROADWAY BELLE,** 5, b m Lucarno (USA)—Theatre Belle **Division Bell Partnership**
9 **BROKETHEGATE,** 10, b g Presenting—Briery Ann **C. Grant**
10 **CINNOMHOR,** 7, b m Grape Tree Road—Brass Buckle (IRE) **Miss A. P. Lee**
11 **DIMPLE (FR),** 4, gr g Montmartre (FR)—Dynella (FR) **D&D Armstrong Limited**
12 **DONNA'S DIAMOND (IRE),** 6, gr g Cloudings (IRE)—Inish Bofin (IRE) **D&D Armstrong Limited**
13 5, Gr g Tikkanen (USA)—Dusty Lane (IRE) **D&D Armstrong Limited**
14 **GENEROUS CHIEF (IRE),** 7, b g Generous (IRE)—Yosna (FR) **Mrs S. Sunter**
15 **HA'PENNY WOODS (IRE),** 5, b g Wareed (IRE)—Muriel's Pride (IRE) **D&D Armstrong Limited**
16 **HERECOMESTROUBLE,** 8, b g Gentleman's Deal (IRE)—Owenreagh (IRE) **J. H. Hewitt**
17 **HILLIER (IRE),** 5, b g Mahler—Buckland Filleigh (IRE) **T. J. Hemmings**
18 **JACKS LAST HOPE,** 6, b g King's Theatre (IRE)—Ninna Nanna (FR) **Mr J. Kenny**
19 **JEU DE ROSEAU (IRE),** 11, b g Montjeu (IRE)—Roseau **W. Raw**
20 **LITTLE WREN,** 6, b m Iktibas—Ouzel (IRE) **R. G. Bonson**
21 **LUCEMATIC,** 9, b m Systematic—Soldier's Song **Mrs P. C. Stirling**
22 **LUCKY BOOTS (IRE),** 7, b m Milan—Trench Hill Lass (IRE) **D&D Armstrong Limited**
23 **MOORAGH (IRE),** 5, b g Oscar (IRE)—Lisselton Lady (IRE) **T. J. Hemmings**
24 **MUWALLA,** 8, b g Bahri (USA)—Easy Sunshine (IRE) **Bell Bridge Racing**
25 **NOTONEBUTTWO (IRE),** 8, b g Dushyantor (USA)—Daiquiri (IRE) **D&D Armstrong Limited**
26 **OLLIE G,** 7, b g Denounce—Silver Rosa **D&D Armstrong Limited**
27 **OVERTOYOULOU,** 7, b m Overbury (IRE)—Champagne Lou Lou **D. Mossop**
28 **ROCK RELIEF (IRE),** 9, gr g Daylami (IRE)—Sheer Bliss (IRE) **D&D Armstrong Limited**
29 **SYDDAN ROSE (IRE),** 6, b m Desert King (IRE)—Goodonyou-Polly (IRE) **D&D Armstrong Limited**
30 **TEARS FROM HEAVEN (USA),** 9, b br g Street Cry (IRE)—Heavenly Aura (USA) **Mrs S. Sunter**
31 **THATILDEE (IRE),** 7, b g Heron Island (IRE)—Good Thyne Mary (IRE) **Peacock Boys Partnership**
32 **THEATRE ACT,** 4, ch f Act One—Theatre Belle **Division Bell Partnership**
33 **TOP CAT DJ (IRE),** 7, ch g St Jovite (USA)—Lady Coldunell **Miss A. P. Lee**
34 **TRAFORDS HERO,** 7, b g Parthian Springs—Be My Shuile (IRE) **D. Mossop**
35 **TRYNWYN,** 5, b m Grape Tree Road—Brass Buckle (IRE) **Miss A. P. Lee**
36 **WILLIAM MONEY (IRE),** 8, b g Cloudings (IRE)—All of A Kind (IRE) **D&D Armstrong Limited**
37 **WIZZARDS REALM,** 5, b g Prince Daniel (USA)—Micklow Magic **W. Raw**

**Other Owners:** T. Cunningham, J. M. Elliott, C. R. Elliott, Mr J. Henderson, R. Kent, Mr D. A. Lofthouse, A. Meale, Mrs L. Monkhouse, Mr J. H. Monkhouse, Mrs M. Nicholas, Mr R. Poole, A. D. Wright.

**Assistant Trainer:** Mrs S. Grant

**Jockey (NH):** Brian Hughes, Denis O'Regan. **Conditional:** Diarmuid O'Regan.

## 252 MR LIAM GRASSICK, Cheltenham

Postal: **Postlip Racing Stables, Winchcombe, Cheltenham, Gloucestershire, GL54 5AQ**
Contacts: **PHONE (01242) 603124 YARD (01242) 603919 MOBILE (07816) 930423**
**E-MAIL mark.grassick@btopenworld.com**

1 **CLEEVE CLOUD (IRE),** 9, b g Noverre (USA)—La Galeisa (IRE) **L. P. Grassick**
2 **KALLINA (IRE),** 7, b m Kalanisi (IRE)—Ballerina Babe (IRE) **S. J. Bryan**
3 **THE BANSHEE,** 9, b m Beat All (USA)—Miniture Melody (IRE) **C. M. Rutledge**
4 **WALTZING TORNADO (IRE),** 11, ch g Golden Tornado (IRE)—Lady Dante (IRE) **L. P. Grassick**

**Assistant Trainer:** Mark Grassick

## 253 MR M. C. GRASSICK, Curragh

Postal: **Fenpark House, Pollardstown, Curragh, Co. Kildare, Ireland**
Contacts: **PHONE (00353) 45 436956 MOBILE (00353) 86 3648829**
**E-MAIL mcgrassick@hotmail.com WEBSITE www.michaelcgrassick.com**

1 **BLUEBERRY GAL (IRE),** 4, b f Bushranger (IRE)—Mythie (FR) **Joe Keeling**
2 **ELUSIVE IN PARIS (IRE),** 6, b g Elusive City (USA)—Bradwell (IRE) **Joe Keeling**
3 **KING OF ARAN (IRE),** 8, b br g Val Royal (FR)—Innishmore (IRE) **Dont Tell The Missus Syndicate**
4 **LAUREL CREEK (IRE),** 10, b g Sakura Laurel (JPN)—Eastern Sky (AUS) **Mr Patrick McKeon**
5 **RO ALAINN (IRE),** 4, b f Westerner—Tordasia (IRE) **Roisin Walshe**
6 **TEXAS ROCK (IRE),** 4, b g Rock of Gibraltar (IRE)—Vestavia (IRE) **Joe Keeling**

### THREE-YEAR-OLDS

7 **MIZPAH (IRE),** b f Excellent Art—Philosophers Guest (IRE) **M. C. Grassick**
8 **RIVER INDIAN (IRE),** b g Sleeping Indian—River Pearl (GER) **Fenpark Syndicate**
9 **SCRIPTURIENT (IRE),** ch g Arakan (USA)—Kelso Magic (USA) **Fenpark Syndicate**
10 **TACENDA (IRE),** b f Flemensfirth (USA)—Tordasia (IRE) **Roisin Walshe**

### TWO-YEAR-OLDS

11 **TEXAS RADIO (IRE),** b c 20/4 Kyllachy—Miss Rochester (IRE) (Montjeu (IRE)) (31745) **Tadhg Geary**

**Assistant Trainer:** Dave Flynn

## 254 MR CARROLL GRAY, Bridgwater

Postal: **The Little Glen, Peartwater Road, Spaxton, Bridgwater, TA5 1DG**
Contacts: **MOBILE (07989) 768163**

1 **ALL BUT GREY,** 9, gr g Baryshnikov (AUS)—Butleigh Rose **Mr R. J. Napper and Mr N. P. Searle**
2 **BUSHWACKER (IRE),** 11, b g Top of The World—Tender Pearl **R. J. Hodges**
3 **CAUTIOUS KATE (IRE),** 8, b m Witness Box (USA)—Cautious Leader **Mr L. & Mrs J. Waring**
4 **INDIANA OSCAR,** 7, b g Oscar (IRE)—Indian Miss **optimumracing.co.uk**
5 **LAMBLORD (IRE),** 8, b g Brian Boru—Princess Symphony (IRE) **The Lamb Inn - Pethy**
6 **SAINT BREIZ (FR),** 9, b br g Saint des Saints (FR)—Balladina (FR) **Riverdance Consortium 2**

**Other Owners:** Mr M. J. Colenutt, Mr Richard Flenk, Mrs A. Johnson, Mr Andrew Lowrie, Mrs J. Lowrie, Mr R. Napper, Mr N. P. Searle, Mr R. L. Squire, Mr L. Waring, Mrs J. Waring.

**Assistant Trainer:** Mrs C. M. L. Gray

**Conditional:** Micheal Nolan. **Amateur:** Mr R. Hawker.

## 255 MR PETER GRAYSON, Formby

Postal: **Apartment 7, The Sandwarren, 21 Victoria Road, Formby**
Contacts: **PHONE (01704) 830668 FAX (01704) 830668**
**E-MAIL info@pgr.uk.com WEBSITE www.pgr.uk.com**

1 **AVONVALLEY,** 8, b m Avonbridge—Piper's Ash (USA) **R. S. Teatum**
2 **DINGAAN (IRE),** 12, b g Tagula (IRE)—Boughtbyphone **R. S. Teatum**
3 **FLOW CHART (IRE),** 8, b g Acclamation—Free Flow **Mr E. Grayson**
4 **RAJEH (IRE),** 12, b g Key of Luck (USA)—Saramacca (IRE) **R. S. Teatum**

## MR PETER GRAYSON - Continued

5 **RIGHTCAR,** 8, b g Bertolini (USA)—Loblolly Bay **R. S. Teatum**
6 **SENATOR BONG,** 5, ch g Dutch Art—Sunley Gift **Mr R Teatum & Mr E Grayson**
7 **STONEACRE OSKAR,** 6, b m Echo of Light—Keidas (FR) **R. S. Teatum**
8 **VHUJON (IRE),** 10, b g Mujadil (USA)—Livius Lady (IRE) **R. S. Teatum**

**Assistant Trainer:** Mrs S. Grayson

---

## 256 MR WARREN GREATREX, Upper Lambourn

Postal: **Uplands, Upper Lambourn, Berkshire, RG17 8QH**
Contacts: **PHONE (01488) 670279 FAX (01488) 72193 MOBILE (07920) 039114**
**E-MAIL info@wgreatrexracing.com WEBSITE www.wgreatrexracing.com**

1 **ACT OF SUPREMACY (IRE),** 5, b g Presenting—Supreme Touch (IRE) **Equis (B) Partnership**
2 **ALOOMOMO (FR),** 5, b g Tirwanako (FR)—Kayola (FR) **The Large G & T Partnership**
3 **ALPHABET BAY (IRE),** 5, b g Kalanisi (IRE)—A And Bs Gift (IRE) **J. P. McManus**
4 **ALWAYS MANAGING,** 6, b m Oscar (IRE)—Sunshine Rays **H. Redknapp**
5 **ALZAMMAAR (USA),** 4, b g Birdstone (USA)—Alma Mater **P. A. Deal & ROA Arkle**
6 **ANDI'AMU (FR),** 5, b g Walk In The Park (IRE)—Sainte Parfaite (FR) **The Pheasant Inn Racing Club**
7 **APRIL DUSK (IRE),** 6, b g Turtle Island (IRE)—Rabble Run (IRE) **R. C. Tooth**
8 **BABY MIX (FR),** 7, gr g Al Namix (FR)—Douchka (FR)
9 **BALLYCULLA (IRE),** 8, b g Westerner—Someone Told Me (IRE) **No Dramas Partnership**
10 **BARLOW (IRE),** 8, br g Beneficial—Carrigeen Kerria (IRE)
11 **BELLE DE LONDRES (IRE),** 5, b m King's Theatre (IRE)—J'y Reste (FR) **Wynnstay Wanderers**
12 **BELLS 'N' BANJOS (IRE),** 5, b g Indian River (FR)—Beechill Dancer (IRE) **The Maple Hurst Partnership**
13 **BERWICK BASSETT,** 6, b g Beat All (USA)—Hottentot **Mr J. F. F. White**
14 **BLUE ATLANTIC (USA),** 4, b g Stormy Atlantic (USA)—Bluemamba (USA) **R. S. Brookhouse**
15 **BOITE (IRE),** 5, b g Authorized (IRE)—Albiatra (USA) **Mrs T. J. Stone-Brown**
16 **BON ENFANT (FR),** 4, gr g Saint des Saints (FR)—Montanara Paris (FR) **Swanee River Partnership**
17 **BOUDRY (FR),** 4, b g Crossharbour—Lavande (FR) **Mr W. J. Greatrex**
18 **BRIAC (FR),** 4, b g Kapgarde (FR)—Jarwin Do (FR) **Mr Oliver Harris**
19 **BURLINGTON BERT (FR),** 4, b g Califet (FR)—Melhi Sun (FR) **M. St Quinton & Tim Syder**
20 **CAITYS JOY (GER),** 5, b m Malinas (GER)—Cassilera (GER) **Diamond Club**
21 **CAPELLINI,** 8, b g Cape Cross (IRE)—Red Stella (FR) **Bruce Pomford & Malcolm Frost**
22 **CEANN SIBHEAL (IRE),** 6, b g Flemensfirth (USA)—Imperial Award (IRE)
23 **CENTASIA,** 8, b m Presenting—Cent Prime **R. S. Brookhouse**
24 **CHASE THE WIND (IRE),** 6, ch g Spadoun (FR)—Asfreeasthewind (IRE) **Mrs Jill Eynon & Mr Robin Eynon**
25 **CHESTERTERN,** 8, ch g Karinga Bay—My Tern (IRE) **Mr P. C. Dutton**
26 **COLE HARDEN (IRE),** 6, b g Westerner—Nosie Betty (IRE) **Mrs Jill Eynon & Mr Robin Eynon**
27 4, Br f Robin des Pres (FR)—Dartmeet (IRE)
28 **DOLATULO (FR),** 8, ch g Le Fou (IRE)—La Perspective (FR) **Chasemore Farm LLP**
29 **EASY BEESY,** 7, b g Kalanisi (IRE)—Queen of The Bees (IRE) **Equis & Mrs Sandra Roe**
30 **GEE HI (IRE),** 9, b g Milan—Curzon Street **Equis**
31 **GLADSTONE (FR),** 4, b br g Mizzen Mast (USA)—Bahia Gold (USA) **In Vino Veritas**
32 **GOING FOR GOLD (FR),** 5, ch g Gold Away (IRE)—Sleeping Doll (FR) **GDM Partnership**
33 **GOOD OF LUCK,** 6, b g Authorized (IRE)—Oops Pettie **Mr & Mrs Bernard Panton**
34 **GROUNDUNDERREPAIR (IRE),** 4, b g Milan—Discerning Air **No Dramas Partnership 1**
35 **HANNAH'S PRINCESS (IRE),** 6, b m Kalanisi (IRE)—Donna's Princess (IRE) **Swanee River Partnership**
36 **HIGH KITE (IRE),** 9, b br g High-Rise (IRE)—Sister Rose (IRE)
37 **HORSTED VALLEY,** 5, gr g Fair Mix (IRE)—Kullu Valley **The Broadwell Fox Partnership**
38 **INTERIOR MINISTER,** 5, b g Nayef (USA)—Sister Maria (USA) **Charlie Austin**
39 **KAYSERSBERG (FR),** 8, b g Khalkevi (IRE)—Alliance Royale (FR) **Mrs Julien Turner & Mr Andrew Merriam**
40 **KING'S TEMPEST,** 6, b g Act One—Queen of Spades (IRE) **Mrs R. I. Vaughan**
41 **KNIGHT BACHELOR,** 5, ch g Midnight Legend—Fenney Spring **A. W. K. Merriam**
42 **LAKE BALATON (IRE),** 6, b g Brian Boru—Hilltop Belle (IRE) **Mr W. J. Greatrex**
43 **MA DU FOU (FR),** 5, b br g Le Fou (IRE)—Belle du Ma (FR) **Walters Plant Hire & James & Jean Potter**
44 **MADNESS LIGHT (FR),** 6, b g Satri (IRE)—Majestic Lady (FR) **Mrs T. J. Stone-Brown**
45 **MANSURI,** 4, ch g Piccolo—Antonia's Choice **Jack Doyle Partnership**
46 **MASQUERADE (IRE),** 6, b g Fruits of Love (USA)—Beechill Dancer (IRE) **Mrs S. Griffiths**
47 **MERCOEUR (FR),** 4, gr g Archange d'or (IRE)—Erivia (FR) **Urban Cookie Collective**
48 **MIGHTY MISSILE (IRE),** 4, ch g Majestic Missile (IRE)—
Magdalene (FR) **Bolingbroke, Howard, BJO, Duthie & Mercer**
49 **MILANESE QUEEN,** 4, b f Milan—Kaydee Queen (IRE) **Hockham Lodge Stud**
50 **MISS ESTELA (IRE),** 5, b m Tobougg (IRE)—Simply Divine (IRE) **R. S. Brookhouse**

## MR WARREN GREATREX - Continued

51 **MISS SOPHIEROSE (IRE),** 7, b m Flemensfirth (USA)—Gimme Peace (IRE) **P. Fisher W. Fisher C. Austin T. Clark**
52 **MISSED APPROACH (IRE),** 5, b g Golan (IRE)—Polly's Dream (IRE) **Alan & Andrew Turner**
53 **MR EDGE (USA),** 5, b g Added Edge (USA)—Beauty Times (USA) **Mr Goran Anderberg**
54 **NORTH GERMANY,** 6, b h Monsun (GER)—North America (GER) **Excel Racing**
55 **ONE TRACK MIND (IRE),** 5, b g Flemensfirth (USA)—Lady Petit (IRE) **Mr A. J. Weller**
56 **OSCAR PRAIRIE (IRE),** 10, b g Oscar (IRE)—Silver Prairie (IRE) **Mr W. J. Greatrex**
57 **PAINT THE CLOUDS,** 10, b g Muhtarram (USA)—Preening **Peter Deal & Jill & Robin Eynon**
58 **PENN LANE (IRE),** 4, b g Scorpion (IRE)—Belsalsa (FR) **Alan & Andrew Turner**
59 **RELENTLESS PURSUIT (IRE),** 4, b g Kodiac—Dancing Debut **Charlie Austin, Lee Bolingbroke & Paul Fisher**
60 **RITUAL OF SENSES (IRE),** 5, b g Milan—Nonnetia (FR) **Equis**
61 **ROYAL MOLL (IRE),** 8, b m King's Theatre (IRE)—Moll Bawn (IRE) **Let's Live Racing**
62 **SAVOY COURT (IRE),** 4, b g Robin des Champs (FR)—North Star Poly (IRE) **Mrs T. J. Stone-Brown**
63 **SEEDLING,** 6, b g Cockney Rebel (IRE)—Unseeded **Equis & Christopher Spence**
64 **SHAH OF PERSIA,** 8, b g Fair Mix (IRE)—Queen Soraya **Mrs M. M. Fox-Pitt**
65 **SHANTOU BOB (IRE),** 7, b g Shantou (USA)—Bobset Leader (IRE) **Fallon, Shipp & Bolingbroke**
66 **SIMPLE ASSIGNMENT (IRE),** 6, br g Westerner—Marlogan (IRE) **Bolingbroke, Howard, Hunnisett & Shipp**
67 **SKY WATCH (IRE),** 8, b g Flemensfirth (USA)—The Shining Force (IRE) **Bolingbroke, Lewis, Meggs & Horgan**
68 **TEOCHEW (IRE),** 7, b m Shantou (USA)—Papal Princess (IRE) **Hooch & Hooves Partnership**
69 **TOP DANCER (FR),** 8, b g Dark Moondancer—Latitude (FR) **The Lone Star Partnership**
70 **TRANQUIL SEA (IRE),** 13, b g Sea Raven (IRE)—Silver Valley (IRE) **Jean & Clemmie Shipp**
71 **TSAR ALEXANDRE (FR),** 8, b g Robin des Champs (FR)—Bertrange (FR) **The Pantechnicons III**
72 **VELVET COGNAC,** 7, b g Grape Tree Road—Scandalous Affair **Mr S. G. & Mrs C. O'Neill**
73 **VIA VOLUPTA,** 5, b m Kayf Tara—Via Ferrata (FR) **Equis**
74 **VIRTUOSE DU CHENET (FR),** 6, b g Irish Wells (FR)—Lili Bleue (FR) **Let's Live Racing**
75 **WARRANTOR (IRE),** 6, b g Turtle Island (IRE)—Pixie Dust (IRE) **Mrs S. M. Drysdale**
76 **WESTWARD POINT,** 8, ch g Karinga Bay—Hottentot **Mr J. F. F. White**
77 **WOJCIECH,** 5, b m Lucarno (USA)—Pondimari (FR) **Uplands Ladies**
78 **ZANDINO (FR),** 4, b g Doctor Dino (FR)—Belle des Champs **Mr W. J. Greatrex**

**Other Owners:** Mr R. K. Aston, Mr Charlie Austin, Mr M. Ball, Mr A. Black, Mrs J. E. Black, Mr Lee Bolingbroke, Mr T. Boylan, Mr A. R. Bromley, Mr J. Cavanagh, Mr Gregory Charlesworth, Mr Daniel Charlesworth, Mr Toby Clark, Mrs Wendy Coles, Mr C K Crossley Cooke, Mr P. A. Deal, Mr Charles Egerton, Mrs Judy England, Mr Duncan England, Mrs Sadie Evans, Mrs J. M. Eynon, Mr R. A. F. Eynon, Mrs Padraic Fallon, Mr P. Fisher, Mr S. Fisher, Mr William Fisher, Mr Rupert Fowler, Mr L. R. Frampton, Mrs D. S. Gillborn, Mr Warren Greatrex, Mr Steven Grubb, Mr R. Gurney, Ms Ginny Hambly, Mr John Horgan, Mr Graeme Howard, Mr R. S. Hunnisett, Mr Darren Johns, Mrs Michael Lambert, Mr Robert Levitt, Mr Christopher Lewis, Mr Charles Liverton, Mrs Anne Meggs, Mr A. W. K. Merriam, Mr S. Munir, Mrs Hugh Murphy, Mr E. R. Newnham, Mr S. G. O'Neill, Mrs C. O'Neill, Mr B. G. Pomford, Mr J. E. Potter, Mrs J. E. Potter, Mrs Sandra A. Roe, Mr Kieran P. Ryan, Mr S. W. Salkeld, Miss C. Shipp, Mr Michael Smith, Mr Isaac Souede, Mr Christopher Spence, Mr M. G. St Quinton, Mr Charles Sutton, Tim Syder, Mr Paul Syson, Ms Mary Taylor, Mrs Julien Turner, Mr J. S. E. Turner, Mr Alan R. Turner, Mr Andrew Turner, Walters Plant Hire Ltd, Major R. G. Wilson, Mrs R. M. Wilson.

**Assistant Trainer:** Trigger Plunkett **Head Lad:** Graham Baines, **Racing Secretary:** Oriana-Jane Young
**Assistant Racing Secretary:** Max Lindley

**Jockey (NH):** Dougie Costello, Gavin Sheehan. **Conditional:** Conor Walsh. **Amateur:** Mr Dominic Sutton.

---

## 257 MR PAUL GREEN, Lydiate

Postal: **Oak Lea, Southport Road, Lydiate, Liverpool, Merseyside, L31 4HH**
Contacts: **PHONE (0151) 526 0093 FAX (0151) 520 0299 MOBILE (07748) 630685**
**E-MAIL paulgreen@mitchell-james.com**

1 **BEAU MISTRAL (IRE),** 6, ch m Windsor Knot (IRE)—Carpet Lover (IRE) **The Winsor Not Group**
2 **DUBARA REEF (IRE),** 8, ch g Dubawi (IRE)—Mamara Reef **Oaklea Aces**
3 **FERDY (IRE),** 6, b h Antonius Pius (USA)—Trinity Fair **M. F. Nolan**
4 4, B f Myboycharlie (IRE)—Jilly Why (IRE)
5 **M J WOODWARD,** 6, b g Needwood Blade—Canina **P. Green**
6 **RUSTY ROCKET (IRE),** 6, ch h Majestic Missile (IRE)—Sweet Compliance **Seven Stars Racing**
7 **SUNI DANCER,** 4, b f Captain Gerrard (IRE)—Sunisa (IRE) **Mr I. Furlong**

## THREE-YEAR-OLDS

8 **ANNEANI (IRE),** b f Bushranger (IRE)—Hazium (IRE) **M. F. Nolan**
9 **BEATABOUT (IRE),** b c Bushranger (IRE)—Dress Up (IRE) **The Gift Horse Syndicate**

**MR PAUL GREEN - Continued**

10 **CUE THE MUSIC,** ch g Piccolo—Billiard **The Winsor Not Group 2**
11 **LYDIATE LADY,** b f Piccolo—Hiraeth **The Scotch Piper (Lydiate)**

**Other Owners:** Mr G. Barton, Mr C. J. Dingwall, I. P. Mason.

**Assistant Trainer:** Fiona Ford

---

## 258 MR TOM GRETTON, Inkberrow

Postal: **C/o Gretton & Co Ltd, Middle Bouts Farm, Bouts Lane, Inkberrow, Worcester, WR7 4HP**
Contacts: **PHONE (01386) 792240 FAX (01386) 792472 MOBILE (07866) 116928**
**E-MAIL tomgretton@hotmail.co.uk WEBSITE www.tomgrettonracing.com**

1 **ARMEDANDBEAUTIFUL,** 7, b m Oscar (IRE)—Grey Mistral **Not The Peloton Partnership**
2 **ARMEDANDDANGEROUS (IRE),** 10, b g Kris Kin (USA)—Lucky Fountain (IRE) **Not The Peloton Partnership**
3 **CLARA PEGGOTTY,** 8, b m Beat All (USA)—Clair Valley **Geoffrey Price & Edward Gretton**
4 **CRAZY JANE (IRE),** 6, br m Definite Article—Blue Romance (IRE) **T. R. Gretton**
5 **DOVER THE MOON (IRE),** 4, b g Bushranger (IRE)—Gold Script (FR) **G1 Racing Club Ltd**
6 5, B m Croco Rouge (IRE)—Emmasflora
7 **FINE JEWELLERY,** 6, b g Epalo (GER)—Lola Lolita (FR) **Ms A. S. Potze**
8 **JACKTHEJOURNEYMAN (IRE),** 6, b g Beneficial—Maslam (IRE) **The Delaynomore Group**
9 **KAUTO RIKO (FR),** 4, b g Ballingarry (IRE)—Kauto Relstar (FR)
10 **LITTLE JIMMY,** 8, br g Passing Glance—Sementina (USA) **Tom Gretton Racing & Ownaracehorse Ltd**
11 **PRIMO ROSSI,** 6, b g Primo Valentino (IRE)—Flaming Rose (IRE) **Ownaracehorse Ltd**
12 **RAINBOW LOLLIPOP,** 4, b f Dubawi (IRE)—Cross Section (USA) **T. R. Gretton**
13 **SWING STATE,** 10, b g Overbury (IRE)—Peg's Permission **G1 Racing Club Ltd**
14 **THATS BEN (IRE),** 10, b g Beneficial—Classy Dancer (IRE) **G1 Racing Club Ltd**

### THREE-YEAR-OLDS

15 **AULD FYFFEE (IRE),** b f Haatef (USA)—Lucky Fountain (IRE) **Mr J. R. Hynes**

**Other Owners:** Mrs L. Gretton, Mr E. P. Gretton, Mr G. H. E. Price.

**Assistant Trainer:** Laura Gretton (07789) 754806

**Jockey (NH):** Dougie Costello, Felix De Giles.

---

## 259 MR DAVID C. GRIFFITHS, Bawtry

Postal: **Martin Hall, Martin Common, Bawtry, Doncaster, South Yorkshire, DN10 6DA**
Contacts: **PHONE (01302) 714247 MOBILE (07816) 924621**
**E-MAIL davidgriffiths250@hotmail.com WEBSITE www.dcgracing.co.uk**

1 **BROTHER TIGER,** 6, b g Singspiel (IRE)—Three Secrets (IRE) **Norcroft Park Stud**
2 **CYFLYMDER (IRE),** 9, b g Mujadil (USA)—Nashwan Star (IRE) **Eros Bloodstock**
3 **DUTIFUL SON (IRE),** 5, b g Invincible Spirit (IRE)—Grecian Dancer **Salthouse, Chua, Griffiths**
4 **EXCELLENT JEM,** 6, b g Exceed And Excel (AUS)—Polar Jem **Norcroft Park Stud**
5 **MASTER WIZARD,** 5, b g Motivator—Enchanted **Norcroft Park Stud**
6 **ORINOCCO,** 6, b g Shirocco (GER)—Norcroft Joy **Norcroft Park Stud**
7 **ROCKWOOD,** 4, b g Rock of Gibraltar (IRE)—Hannah Frank (IRE) **Norcroft Park Stud**
8 **TAKE COVER,** 8, b g Singspiel (IRE)—Enchanted **Norcroft Park Stud**
9 **TASRIH (USA),** 6, b g Hard Spun (USA)—Rare Gift (USA) **Mr C. Buckingham**
10 **TIN PAN ALLEY,** 7, b g Singspiel (IRE)—Tazmeen **Jason Adlam & Eros Bloodstock**
11 **YUNGABURRA (IRE),** 11, b g Fath (USA)—Nordic Living (IRE) **Mrs S. Griffiths**

### THREE-YEAR-OLDS

12 **ANOTHER (IRE),** b f Lawman (FR)—Enchanting Muse (USA) **Eros Bloodstock**
13 **FREEZE THE SECRET (IRE),** b f Kodiac—Campiglia (IRE) **Dallas Racing, Owen Robinson & DCG**
14 **LOPITO DE VEGA (IRE),** ch g Lope de Vega (IRE)—Athenian Way (IRE) **Mr D Poulton & Mr N Hildred**
15 **PICKLE LILLY PEARL,** b f Captain Gerrard (IRE)—Branston Jewel (IRE) **Gee Gee Racing**
16 **RED UNICO (IRE),** b g Vale of York (IRE)—Testa Unica (ITY) **Mr C. Buckingham**
17 **WISTERIA,** br f Winker Watson—Begonia (IRE) **Daryl Clarke & Shaun Humphries**

## MR DAVID C. GRIFFITHS - Continued

### TWO-YEAR-OLDS

**18** Ch c 7/2 Equiano (FR)—Aberdovey (Mister Baileys) (20000) **Unregistered Partnership**
**19** B f 19/4 Fast Company (IRE)—Bonne (Namid) (3967) **Keeping Fast Company Partnership**
**20** B f 20/4 Multiplex—Gurteen Diamond (Kyllachy) (761) **Mrs S. Griffiths**
**21** Ch c 27/4 Art Connoisseur (IRE)—Ipanema Beach (Lion Cavern (USA)) (3174) **Mrs S. Griffiths**

**Other Owners:** Mr J. P. Adlam, C. G. J. Chua, Mr D. J. Clarke, A. D. Gee, Mr R. G. Gee, Mr M. A. Glassett, D. C. Griffiths, Mr N. R. Hildred, A. J. Hollis, Mr D. M. Hollis, Mr S. Humphries, R. P. B. Michaelson, Mr D. J. Poulton, Mr O. Robinson, Mr W. J. Salthouse.

**Assistant Trainer:** Mrs S. E. Griffiths

**Apprentice:** Ali Rawlinson.

---

## 260 MR SIRRELL GRIFFITHS, Carmarthen

Postal: **Rwyth Farm, Nantgaredig, Carmarthen, Dyfed, SA32 7LG**
Contacts: **PHONE (01267) 290321/290120**

**1 BRACKEN HILL,** 6, b g Darnay—Tirikumba **S. G. Griffiths**
**2 WELSH DESIGNE,** 7, ch g Midnight Legend—Barton Dante **S. G. Griffiths**
**3 Y O ME,** 8, ch m Alflora (IRE)—Yo Kiri-B **S. G. Griffiths**

**Assistant Trainer:** Martyn Roger Griffiths

---

## 261 MRS DIANA GRISSELL, Robertsbridge

Postal: **Brightling Park, Robertsbridge, East Sussex, TN32 5HH**
Contacts: **PHONE (01424) 838241 MOBILE (07950) 312610**
**E-MAIL digrissell@aol.com WEBSITE www.grissellracing.co.uk**

**1 ARBEO (IRE),** 9, b g Brian Boru—Don't Waste It (IRE) **Nigel & Barbara Collison**
**2 BISKY BAR,** 7, b m Nomadic Way (USA)—Deepritive **Ms C. A. Lacey**
**3 BLUE BEAR (IRE),** 6, b g Blueprint (IRE)—In For It (IRE) **Mrs D. M. Grissell**
**4 DOUBLE BUD,** 8, b m Double Trigger (IRE)—Little Bud **Mrs P. A. Wilkins**
**5 HOUSEPARTY,** 7, b g Invincible Spirit (IRE)—Amusing Time (IRE) **Ms G. P. C. Howell**
**6 NOMADIC WARRIOR,** 10, b g Nomadic Way (USA)—Jesmund **Ms C. A. Lacey**
**7 OSCAR BABY (IRE),** 9, b m Oscar (IRE)—Snowbaby (IRE) **Mr R. E. Halley**
**8 ROPARTA AVENUE,** 8, b g Nomadic Way (USA)—Miss Fizz **Mrs D. M. Grissell**
**9 SITTING BACK (IRE),** 11, b g Flying Legend (USA)—Double Pearl (IRE) **Ms G. P. C. Howell**
**10 TORERO,** 6, b g Hernando (FR)—After You **Mr E. S. Hicks**

**Other Owners:** Mr N. Collison, Mrs B. Collison.

**Jockey (NH):** Marc Goldstein, Sam Thomas.

---

## 262 MR BRIAN GUBBY, Bagshot

Postal: **Dukes Wood, Bracknell Road, Bagshot, Surrey, GU19 5HX**
Contacts: **OFFICE (01276) 850513 MOBILE (07768) 867368**

**1 DIAMONDS A DANCING,** 5, ch g Delta Dancer—Zing **B. Gubby**
**2 KINGLAMI,** 6, b g Kingsalsa (USA)—Red Japonica **B. Gubby**
**3 PAL OF THE CAT,** 5, ch g Choisir (AUS)—Evenstorm (USA) **B. Gubby**

**Assistant Trainer:** Larry Wilkins

## 263 MR RAE GUEST, Newmarket

Postal: **Chestnut Tree Stables, Hamilton Road, Newmarket, Suffolk, CB8 0NY**
Contacts: **PHONE (01638) 661508 FAX (01638) 667317 MOBILE (07711) 301095**
**E-MAIL raeguest@raeguest.com WEBSITE www.raeguest.com**

1 **APPARATCHIKA,** 4, b f Archipenko (USA)—Kesara **Ms K. Rausing**
2 **CALM ATTITUDE (IRE),** 5, ch m Dutch Art—Turban Heights (IRE) **The Calm Again Partnership**
3 **CAPE FACTOR (IRE),** 4, b f Oratorio (IRE)—Crossanza (IRE) **Mr Derek J. Willis**
4 **FIRST EXPERIENCE,** 4, b f Tamayuz—Lolla's Spirit (IRE) **Mr Guy Carstairs & Fit or Fat Racing**
5 **HEADLINE NEWS (IRE),** 6, ch m Peintre Celebre (USA)—Donnelly's Hollow (IRE) **Chestnuts**
6 **MEMORIA,** 4, b f Teofilo (IRE)—Midnight Shift (IRE) **Mr C. J. Mills**
7 **MINALISA,** 6, b m Oasis Dream—Mina **Mr C. J. Mills**
8 **MINISKIRT,** 4, b f Naaqoos—Minnola **Mr C. J. Mills**
9 **MIRZA,** 8, b g Oasis Dream—Millyant **Mr C. J. Mills**
10 **MOIETY,** 4, b f Myboycharlie (IRE)—Millinsky (USA) **Mr C. J. Mills**
11 **PHANTOM SPIRIT,** 4, b f Invincible Spirit (IRE)—Jackie's Opera (FR) **The Hightailers**
12 **ROSIE REBEL,** 5, ch m Cockney Rebel (IRE)—
Meandering Rose (USA) **Saunders, Guest & Exors of the Late O. Lury**
13 **STRIKE A LIGHT,** 4, gr f Dutch Art—Bridal Path **Mr Trevor Benton**

### THREE-YEAR-OLDS

14 Ch f Muhtathir—Anna of Russia (GER) **Ballymore Sterling Syndicate**
15 **BELLA BLUR,** ch f Showcasing—Ellablue **Ms C. Williams**
16 **CLASSIC IMAGE,** b f Exceed And Excel (AUS)—Reflected Image (IRE) **Mr Li Fung Lok**
17 **DALAMAR,** br f Montjeu (IRE)—Dalasyla (IRE) **Mr Andrew Tinkler**
18 **DREAM APPROACH (IRE),** b f New Approach (IRE)—Witch of Fife (USA) **Fishdance Ltd**
19 **DUCHESSOFMARMALADE,** b f Duke of Marmalade (IRE)—Helena Molony (IRE) **Fishdance Ltd**
20 **ELLA'S HONOUR,** b f Makfi—Danella (FR) **Mr Andrew Tinkler & Brook Stud**
21 **GLENEELY GIRL (IRE),** b f Intense Focus (USA)—Timber Tops (UAE) **Mr John Shannon & Rae Guest**
22 **GOODYEARFORROSES (IRE),** b f Azamour (IRE)—Guilia **The Hornets**
23 **IN PURSUIT,** b f Makfi—Entre Nous (IRE) **Mr Horace Cheng & Brook Stud**
24 **JANE'S MEMORY (IRE),** ch f Captain Rio—Dancing Jest (IRE) **Exors of the Late Mr Oliver Lury**
25 **MAY MIST,** b f Nayef (USA)—Midnight Mist (IRE) **Mr A. H. Bennett**
26 **MISS BUCKAROO (IRE),** b f Acclamation—Pearl Trader (IRE) **T Hirschfeld and The Buckhurst Chevaliers**
27 **MONT FEU (IRE),** b f Montjeu (IRE)—I'm In Love (USA) **Fishdance Ltd**
28 **SATIN AND LACE (IRE),** b f Mawatheeq (USA)—Katayeb (IRE) **Mr Derek J. Willis**
29 **SECRET PALACE,** ch f Pastoral Pursuits—Some Sunny Day **Sakal, Davies and Jennings**
30 **SILVERSMITH (IRE),** gr g Mastercraftsman (IRE)—Gleaming Silver (IRE) **Miss Emma O'Gorman**
31 **SPRING DIXIE (IRE),** gr f Zebedee—Dixie Jazz **Mr Barry Stewart**
32 **TELL ME ANOTHER,** b g Royal Applause—Silver Rhapsody (USA) **Mr Trevor Benton & Mr Rae Guest**
33 **THE DREAM FAST,** b c Sleeping Indian—Past 'n' Present **Miss Emma O'Gorman**
34 **VALE OF PARIS (IRE),** b f Vale of York (IRE)—Paris Glory (USA) **Miss Emma O'Gorman & Rae Guest**
35 **WHAT SAY YOU (IRE),** b f Galileo (IRE)—Alta Anna (FR) **Mr Huebert J. Strecker**

### TWO-YEAR-OLDS

36 **A LOVE STORY,** gr f 29/1 Archipenko (USA)—Albacocca (With Approval (CAN)) **Ms K. Rausing**
37 Ch f 2/4 Tamayuz—Allegrissimo (IRE) (Redback) (17000) **C. J. Murfitt**
38 B f 26/2 Vale of York (IRE)—
Barbera (GER) (Night Shift (USA)) (12698) **Guy Carstairs & Sakal, Davies & Jennings**
39 B f 22/3 Lilbourne Lad (IRE)—Christmas Tart (IRE) (Danetime (IRE)) **The Storm Again Syndicate**
40 B f 28/1 Elusive City (USA)—Distant Dreamer (USA) (Rahy (USA)) **Mrs Paula Smith**
41 **EARLY SUNSET (IRE),** gr f 15/3 Dark Angel (IRE)—
Dear Gracie (IRE) (In The Wings) (16000) **Mr Barry Stewart & Sakal, Davies & Jennings**
42 **GOMEZ,** b c 28/1 Multiplex—Elfine (IRE) (Invincible Spirit (IRE)) **Mr Derek J Willis**
43 Ch c 16/3 Duke of Marmalade (IRE)—Guilia (Galileo (IRE)) **The Hornets**
44 B c 2/3 Azamour (IRE)—Lastroseofsummer (IRE) (Haafhd) (38095) **The Boot Sarratt Racing Syndicate**
45 **MAYBERAIN (IRE),** b f 21/1 Acclamation—Luckbealadytonight (IRE) (Mr Greeley (USA)) **Mr Thomas Radley**
46 B f 25/2 Kyllachy—Noble Desert (FR) (Green Desert (USA)) **C. J. Murfitt**
47 Br f 1/1 Rock of Gibraltar—Takegawa (Giant's Causeway) **The Storm Again Syndicate**

**Assistant Trainer:** Nicholas McKee **Head Lad:** Steve Lodge

## 264 MR RICHARD GUEST, Ingmanthorpe

Postal: **Ingmanthorpe Racing Stables, Ingmanthorpe Grange Farm, Ingmanthorpe, Wetherby, West Yorkshire, LS22 5HL**
Contacts: **PHONE (01937) 587552 (07715) 516072 / (07715) 516073 FAX (01937) 587552 MOBILE (07715) 516071**
**E-MAIL enquiries@richardguestracing.co.uk WEBSITE www.richardguestracing.co.uk**

1 **BENIDORM,** 7, b g Bahamian Bounty—Famcred **Mrs A. L. Guest**
2 **CAPTAIN SCOOBY,** 9, b g Captain Rio—Scooby Dooby Do **Available For Sale Or Lease**
3 **HYDRANT,** 9, b g Haafhd—Spring **Mr C. Hatch**
4 **IT'S ALL A GAME,** 4, ch g Sleeping Indian—St Edith (IRE) **Viscount Environmental Ltd**
5 **LAST WISH (IRE),** 4, b g Raven's Pass (USA)—Quiet Dream (USA) **Mrs A. L. Guest**
6 **LAZY SIOUX,** 4, b f Sleeping Indian—Aimee's Delight **Mrs A. L. Guest**
7 **LORD BUFFHEAD,** 6, br g Iceman—Royal Pardon **Available For Sale Or Lease**
8 **MONTAFF,** 9, b g Montjeu (IRE)—Meshhed (USA) **The Sensible Drinks Company Limited**
9 **PABUSAR,** 7, b g Oasis Dream—Autumn Pearl **The Sensible Drinks Company Limited**
10 **POLAR FOREST,** 5, br g Kyllachy—Woodbeck **Maze Rattan Limited**
11 **PRECISION STRIKE,** 5, b g Multiplex—Dockside Strike **Resdev Ltd**
12 **ROAYH (USA),** 7, ch g Speightstown (USA)—Most Remarkable (USA) **Mrs A. L. Guest**
13 **RYLEE MOOCH,** 7, gr g Choisir (AUS)—Negligee **Katie Hughes, Sheila White, Julie Mccarlie**
14 **SAKHALIN STAR (IRE),** 4, ch g Footstepsinthesand—Quela (GER) **Bamboozelem**
15 **SPACE ARTIST (IRE),** 5, b g Captain Marvelous (IRE)—Dame Laura (IRE) **Mrs A. L. Guest**
16 **STRADATER (IRE),** 6, b g Catcher In The Rye (IRE)—Starring Role (IRE) **Mr D. A. Aarons**
17 **TORTOISE,** 4, b f Multiplex—Wonderful Island (GER) **Mrs A. L. Guest**

### THREE-YEAR-OLDS

18 **DAZZLING DISPLAY,** ch f Stimulation (IRE)—Dazzling Quintet **Team Guest Syndicate**
19 **PENALTY SCORER,** ch f Captain Gerrard (IRE)—Mindfulness **Ontoawinner & Guest**
20 **TED LARKIN (IRE),** b g Dandy Man (IRE)—Shewillifshewants (IRE) **Mrs A. L. Guest**
21 **WARAPITO,** b g Stimulation (IRE)—Shining Oasis (IRE) **The Sensible Drinks Company Limited**

### TWO-YEAR-OLDS

**22** B f 24/4 Compton Place—Beauty (IRE) (Alzao (USA)) (7000)
**23** Ch g 16/3 Major Cadeaux—Brogue Lanterns (IRE) (Dr Devious (IRE)) (5238) **Mrs A. L. Guest**
**24** Ch g 16/2 Assertive—Enclave (USA) (Woodman (USA)) (5714)
**25** B f 29/3 Sleeping Indian—Gentle Guru (Ishiguru (USA)) (4285)
**26** Ch g 9/4 Sakhee's Secret—Gib (IRE) (Rock of Gibraltar (IRE)) (2857) **Mrs A. L. Guest**
**27** B f 11/4 Pastoral Pursuits—Grin (Key of Luck (USA)) (3333)
**28** B g 13/2 Multiplex—Lady Duxyana (Most Welcome) (5238)
**29** Ch f 1/3 Equiano (FR)—Lady Natilda (First Trump) (21000)
**30** B g 21/2 Multiplex—Mi Amor (IRE) (Alzao (USA)) (16190) **The Sensible Drinks Company Limited**
**31** Ch f 2/3 Equiano (FR)—Peace And Love (IRE) (Fantastic Light (USA)) (3750)
**32** B g 5/5 Stimulation (IRE)—Shining Oasis (IRE) (Mujtahid (USA)) (2857)
**33** B g 2/4 Royal Applause—Sleek Gold (Dansili) (4000)
**34** B g 7/4 Windsor Knot (IRE)—Telltime (IRE) (Danetime (IRE)) (3809)
**35** B g 24/4 Bertolini (USA)—Tide of Love (Pursuit of Love) (3809) **Mrs A. L. Guest**

**Other Owners:** Mr R. C. Guest, M. J. Mahony, N. J. O'Brien, M. E. White, Mrs S. White.

**Jockey (flat):** Billy Cray, Robbie Fitzpatrick. **Jockey (NH):** Denis O'Regan, Jack Quinlan. **Apprentice:** Melissa Thompson. **Amateur:** Mr R. Asquith, Mr S. Bushby.

## 265 MISS POLLY GUNDRY, Ottery St Mary

Postal: **Holcombe Brook, Holcombe Lane, Ottery St. Mary, Devon, EX11 1PH**
Contacts: **PHONE (01404) 811181 MOBILE (07932) 780621**
**E-MAIL pollygundrytraining@live.co.uk**

1 **DAWSON CITY,** 6, b g Midnight Legend—Running For Annie **Ian Payne & Kim Franklin**
2 **EDEIFF'S LAD,** 8, ch g Loup Sauvage (USA)—Ede'iff **Hawks & Doves Racing Syndicate**
3 **HARRY'S FAREWELL,** 8, b g Sir Harry Lewis (USA)—Golden Mile (IRE) **Mr J. P. Selby**
4 **KAVESTORM,** 9, br m Kayf Tara—Tudor Gale (IRE) **G. P. Brown**
5 **SISTERBROOKE (IRE),** 6, ch m Trans Island—Cool Merenda (IRE) **J. F. Panvert**
6 **STUDFARMER,** 5, b g Multiplex—Samadilla (IRE) **Miss P. Gundry**

## MISS POLLY GUNDRY - Continued

7 **VERING (FR),** 9, b g Bering—Forcia (FR) **Michael & Will Potter**
8 **YOUNG CHEDDAR (IRE),** 8, b m Croco Rouge (IRE)—Sin Ceist Eile (IRE) **G. N. Carstairs**

**Other Owners:** Miss K. M. Franklin, Mr I. T. Payne, M. Potter, Mr W. E. Potter, J. P. Rawlins, J. L. Sunnucks.

**Assistant Trainer:** Edward Walker

**Jockey (flat):** Liam Keniry. **Jockey (NH):** James Best, Tom O'Brien. **Amateur:** Mr Robbie Henderson.

---

## 266 MR WILLIAM HAGGAS, Newmarket

Postal: **Somerville Lodge, Fordham Road, Newmarket, Suffolk, CB8 7AA**
Contacts: **PHONE (01638) 667013 FAX (01638) 660534 MOBILE (07860) 282281**
**E-MAIL william@somerville-lodge.co.uk WEBSITE www.somerville-lodge.co.uk**

1 **ARABIAN COMET (IRE),** 4, b f Dubawi (IRE)—Aviacion (BRZ) **Abdulla Al Mansoori**
2 **BATTALION (IRE),** 5, b g Authorized (IRE)—Zigarra **Sheikh Juma Dalmook Al Maktoum**
3 **CAPE CLASSIC (IRE),** 7, b g Cape Cross (IRE)—Politesse (USA) **Hamer, Hawkes & Hellin**
4 **DREAM SPIRIT (IRE),** 4, b g Invincible Spirit (IRE)—Dream Valley (IRE) **Roberts Green Whittall-Williams Savidge**
5 **GRAPHIC (IRE),** 6, ch g Excellent Art—Follow My Lead **The Royal Ascot Racing Club**
6 **HARRIS TWEED,** 8, b g Hernando (FR)—Frog **Mr B. Haggas**
7 **HOMAGE (IRE),** 5, b g Acclamation—Night Sphere (IRE) **Highclere Thoroughbred Racing**
8 **KARRAAR,** 4, b g Dubawi (IRE)—Maghya (IRE)
9 **MANGE ALL,** 4, b g Zamindar (USA)—Blancmange **Mr B. Haggas**
10 **MITRAAD (IRE),** 4, ch g Aqlaam—Badweia (USA) **Hamdan Al Maktoum**
11 **MUTAKAYYEF,** 4, ch c Sea The Stars (IRE)—Infallible **Hamdan Al Maktoum**
12 **MUTHMIR (IRE),** 5, b g Invincible Spirit (IRE)—Fairy of The Night (IRE) **Hamdan Al Maktoum**
13 **MY SPIRIT (IRE),** 4, b f Invincible Spirit (IRE)—My Renee (USA) **Miss Pat O'Kelly**
14 **OSARUVEETIL (IRE),** 4, b g Teofilo (IRE)—Caraiyma (IRE) **Sheikh Mohammed Bin Khalifa Al Maktoum**
15 **OUR CHANNEL (USA),** 4, ch c English Channel (USA)—Raw Gold (USA) **Abdulla Al Mansoori**
16 **PRINCE'S TRUST,** 5, b g Invincible Spirit (IRE)—Lost In Wonder (USA) **Her Majesty The Queen**
17 **QUEEN OF ICE,** 4, ch f Selkirk (USA)—Ice Palace **Cheveley Park Stud**
18 **SATELLITE (IRE),** 4, b g Danehill Dancer (IRE)—Perihelion (IRE) **Highclere Thoroughbred Racing - Distinction**
19 **SEAGULL STAR,** 4, b g Sea The Stars (IRE)—Dash To The Top **Mr A. G. Bloom**
20 **TELMEYD,** 4, b g Dutch Art—Blithe **Sheikh Ahmed Al Maktoum**
21 **WRANGLER,** 4, b g High Chaparral (IRE)—Tipsy Me **Highclere Thoroughbred Racing - Ashes**
22 **YUFTEN,** 4, b c Invincible Spirit (IRE)—Majestic Sakeena (IRE) **Saleh Al Homaizi & Imad Al Sagar**

### THREE-YEAR-OLDS

23 **ADAAY (IRE),** b c Kodiac—Lady Lucia (IRE) **Hamdan Al Maktoum**
24 **AFJAAN (IRE),** b c Henrythenavigator (USA)—Elusive Galaxy (IRE) **Al Shaqab Racing**
25 **ALAATA (USA),** ch f Smart Strike (CAN)—Alshadiyah (USA) **Hamdan Al Maktoum**
26 **ALASAAL (USA),** b br c War Front (USA)—A P Investment (USA) **Hamdan Al Maktoum**
27 **ALGHAAZ,** b c Dansili—Thakafaat (IRE) **Hamdan Al Maktoum**
28 **ASHDAQ (USA),** b g Distorted Humor (USA)—Sabooh (USA) **Hamdan Al Maktoum**
29 **AUSPICION,** b br c Dansili—Superstar Leo (IRE) **Lael Stable**
30 **AWESOME POWER,** b c Dubawi (IRE)—Fairy Godmother **Her Majesty The Queen**
31 **BELLA NOUF,** b f Dansili—Majestic Sakeena (IRE) **Saleh Al Homaizi & Imad Al Sagar**
32 **BLENHEIM WARRIOR,** br gr c Galileo (IRE)—Crystal Swan (IRE) **Saleh Al Homaizi & Imad Al Sagar**
33 **CHANTRY,** b f Galileo (IRE)—Winds of Time (IRE) **Mr & Mrs R. Scott**
34 **DIRECTOR (IRE),** b g Danehill Dancer (IRE)—Toolentidhaar (USA) **Highclere Thoroughbred Racing (Gold Cup)**
35 **DUFOOF (IRE),** b f Shamardal (USA)—Evensong (GER) **Hamdan Al Maktoum**
36 **DUTCH ROSEBUD,** b f Dutch Art—Regency Rose **Cheveley Park Stud**
37 **EASTERN ROMANCE,** b f Duke of Marmalade (IRE)—Dance East **Cheveley Park Stud**
38 **EFFUSIVE,** ch f Starspangledbanner (AUS)—Thrill **Cheveley Park Stud**
39 **FARSAKH (USA),** b f Smart Strike (CAN)—Ethaara **Hamdan Al Maktoum**
40 **FLYING FANTASY,** b g Oasis Dream—Disco Volante **Mr A. E. Oppenheimer**
41 **FLYING HAMMER,** b c Acclamation—Ruse **M S Bloodstock Ltd**
42 **FOREIGN DIPLOMAT,** b g Oasis Dream—Longing To Dance **Clipper Logistics**
43 **FOREVER POPULAR (USA),** b br f Dynaformer (USA)—Pussycat Doll (USA) **Lael Stable**
44 **HATHAL (USA),** ch c Speightstown (USA)—Sleepytime (IRE) **Al Shaqab Racing**
45 **HEARTBREAK HERO,** b c Exceed And Excel (AUS)—Artistic Blue (USA) **Mr J. C. Smith**
46 **INTRIGUE,** b f Fastnet Rock (AUS)—Riberac **Mr & Mrs G. Middlebrook**
47 **ITS GONNA BE ME (IRE),** b g Zebedee—Dorn Hill **Hamdan Al Maktoum**

## MR WILLIAM HAGGAS - Continued

48 **JAMM (IRE),** b f Duke of Marmalade (IRE)—Starship (IRE) **The Starship Partnership**
49 **JUNCART,** b c Dutch Art—Juncea **Mr Michael Beaumont**
50 **KARMADAL (IRE),** b f Shamardal (USA)—Karmifira (FR) **David & Yvonne Blunt**
51 **KHALAAS,** b g Iffraaj—Bahia Breeze **Hamdan Al Maktoum**
52 **MAJESTIC MANNER,** ch f Dubawi (IRE)—Majestic Roi (USA) **Jaber Abdullah**
53 **MANSION (IRE),** b g Invincible Spirit (IRE)—Manoeuvre (IRE) **St Albans Bloodstock LLP**
54 **MASTER CHOICE (IRE),** b g Mastercraftsman (IRE)—No Quest (IRE) **A. D. Spence**
55 **MAWJOOD,** b c Dubawi (IRE)—Gile Na Greine (IRE) **Hamdan Al Maktoum**
56 **MUBTAGHAA (IRE),** b c Acclamation—Mabalane (IRE) **Hamdan Al Maktoum**
57 **MUFFRI'HA (IRE),** b f Iffraaj—Grecian Dancer **Sheikh Juma Dalmook Al Maktoum**
58 **MUHTADIM (IRE),** b c Dubawi (IRE)—Dhelaal **Hamdan Al Maktoum**
59 **MY TREAS,** b f Dansili—Hidden Hope **Mr A. E. Oppenheimer**
60 **MYTHICAL MOMENT,** b f Authorized (IRE)—Dancing Fire (USA) **Sheikh Juma Dalmook Al Maktoum**
61 **NAZLI (IRE),** b f Invincible Spirit (IRE)—Lethal Quality (USA) **Saleh Al Homaizi & Imad Al Sagar**
62 **NOBLEST,** ch f Pivotal—Noble One **Cheveley Park Stud**
63 **PICK YOUR CHOICE,** b c Elusive Quality (USA)—Enticement **Her Majesty The Queen**
64 **PILLAR BOX (IRE),** ch g Sakhee's Secret—Red Red Rose **The Super Sprinters**
65 **PREDOMINANCE (IRE),** b c Danehill Dancer (IRE)—
Gilded Vanity (IRE) **Highclere Thoroughbred Racing (Queen Anne)**
66 **PROPERUS (IRE),** b c Lord Shanakill (USA)—Amistad (GER) **Mr Michael Beaumont**
67 **PYJAMA PARTY (IRE),** b c Rip Van Winkle (IRE)—Dancing Eclipse (IRE) **Mr D I Scott & Mr M Kerr-Dineen**
68 **QUAKE,** b f Dubawi (IRE)—Politesse (USA) **Mr B. Kantor**
69 **RIP N ROAR (IRE),** b g Rip Van Winkle (IRE)—Aine (IRE) **A. D. Spence**
70 **RIVE GAUCHE,** b f Fastnet Rock (AUS)—Raysiza (IRE) **Mr C. M. Humber**
71 **ROCK CAKE (IRE),** b f Fastnet Rock (AUS)—Queen's Pudding (IRE) **Mr & Mrs D Davidson & Mrs A Brudenell**
72 **ROOSSEY (IRE),** b c Acclamation—Tatiana Romanova (USA) **Sheikh Ahmed Al Maktoum**
73 **ROSE OF MIRACLES,** gr f Dalakhani (IRE)—Neartica (FR) **Saleh Al Homaizi & Imad Al Sagar**
74 **ROXY STAR (IRE),** b f Fastnet Rock (AUS)—Sweet Dreams Baby (IRE) **Mrs D. J. James**
75 **SARAHA,** b f Dansili—Kareemah (IRE) **Hamdan Al Maktoum**
76 **SCENT OF SUMMER (USA),** b br f Rock Hard Ten (USA)—
Wild Forest (USA) **Sheikh Rashid Dalmook Al Maktoum**
77 **SEALIFE (IRE),** b f Sea The Stars (IRE)—Bitooh **Sheikh Juma Dalmook Al Maktoum**
78 **SHARQEYIH,** br f Shamardal (USA)—Shabiba (USA) **Hamdan Al Maktoum**
79 **SQUATS (IRE),** b g Dandy Man (IRE)—Light Sea (IRE) **Sheikh Rashid Bin Dalmook Al Maktoum**
80 **STORM THE STARS (USA),** b c Sea The Stars (IRE)—Love Me Only (IRE) **Sheikh Juma Dalmook Al Maktoum**
81 **TADPOLE,** b f Sir Percy—Frog **Mr B. Haggas**
82 **TADQEEQ,** b g Makfi—Perfect Spirit (IRE) **Hamdan Al Maktoum**
83 **TALYANI,** ch g Halling (USA)—Italian Connection **Sheikh Ahmed Al Maktoum**
84 **TEMPTING,** ch f Pivotal—Entrap (USA) **Cheveley Park Stud**
85 **TERHAAL (IRE),** b g Raven's Pass (USA)—Silk Trail **Hamdan Al Maktoum**
86 **TOUJOURS L'AMOUR,** b f Authorized (IRE)—High Heel Sneakers **Mr Christopher Wright & Lordship Stud**
87 **VALLEY OF FIRE,** b c Firebreak—Charlie Girl **Sheikh Juma Dalmook Al Maktoum**
88 **WAR STRIKE (CAN),** b c Ghostzapper (USA)—Michillinda (CAN) **Mohamed Saeed Al Shahi**
89 **WEKEYLL,** b c Exceed And Excel (AUS)—Sensible **Sheikh Ahmed Al Maktoum**
90 **WONDER LAISH,** b c Halling (USA)—Wonder Why (GER) **Jaber Abdullah**
91 **ZAANEH (IRE),** br f Aqlaam—Intishaar (IRE) **Hamdan Al Maktoum**

## TWO-YEAR-OLDS

**92** B f 30/3 Poet's Voice—Annapurna (IRE) (Brief Truce (USA)) (70000) **Said Jaber**
**93** B c 9/2 Shamardal (USA)—Arthur's Girl (Hernando (FR)) (140000) **Sheikh Ahmed Al Maktoum**
**94** **BAAHY (IRE),** br c 13/2 Arcano (IRE)—Amjaad (Dansili) **Hamdan Al Maktoum**
**95** B f 10/2 Galileo (IRE)—Baraka (IRE) (Danehill (USA)) (238095) **Mr B. Kantor & Mr M. Jooste**
**96** **BEDROCK,** b c 1/2 Fastnet Rock (AUS)—
Gemstone (IRE) (Galileo (IRE)) (150000) **Highclere Thoroughbred Racing(Gladstone)**
**97** B c 26/2 Approve (IRE)—Blue Beacon (Fantastic Light (USA)) (70000) **Mr L. Sheridan**
**98** B c 2/2 Bahamian Bounty—Blue Lyric (Refuse To Bend (IRE)) (70000) **Sheikh Ahmed Al Maktoum**
**99** B f 23/4 Invincible Spirit (IRE)—Bratislava (Dr Fong (USA)) (238095) **Clipper Logistics**
**100** **BREDA CASTLE,** ch f 14/3 Dutch Art—Ice Palace (Polar Falcon (USA)) **Cheveley Park Stud**
**101** B f 6/5 Fastnet Rock (AUS)—Butterfly Blue (IRE) (Sadler's Wells (USA)) **Sir Peter Vela, D. Nagle, J. Magnier**
**102** B c 28/1 Kyllachy—Cardrona (Selkirk (USA)) (130000) **Sheikh Ahmed Al Maktoum**
**103** **CATOTONIC,** ch c 12/3 Notnowcato—Rumooz (Cape Cross (IRE)) **Mr & Mrs Ian Beard**
**104** B f 27/3 Galileo (IRE)—Crystal Valkyrie (IRE) (Danehill (USA)) (230000) **Al Shaqab Racing**
**105** Ch c 24/3 Champs Elysees—Dalvina (Grand Lodge (USA)) (110000) **St Albans Bloodstock LLP**
**106** **DAPHNE,** b f 12/2 Duke of Marmalade (IRE)—Daring Aim (Daylami (IRE)) **Her Majesty The Queen**
**107** B c 8/5 New Approach (IRE)—Davie's Lure (USA) (Lure (USA)) (150000) **Hamed Rashed Bin Ghadayer**

## MR WILLIAM HAGGAS - Continued

**108 DAWN HORIZONS,** ch f 5/3 New Approach (IRE)—Hidden Hope (Daylami (IRE)) **Mr A. E. Oppenheimer**
**109** B f 18/2 Kodiac—Dixieland Kiss (USA) (Dixie Union (USA)) (85000) **Sheikh Rashid Dalmook Al Maktoum**
**110 DREAM OF TARA (IRE),** b f 4/4 Invincible Spirit (IRE)—
Spirit of Tara (IRE) (Sadler's Wells (USA)) **Miss Pat O'Kelly**
**111 DUTCH DESTINY,** b f 8/3 Dutch Art—Danehill Destiny (Danehill Dancer (IRE)) **Cheveley Park Stud**
**112 DWIGHT D,** b c 27/4 Duke of Marmalade (IRE)—Perseida (IRE) (Galileo (IRE)) (30000) **Mr W. J. Gredley**
**113** B f 22/2 Dutch Art—Eastern Glow (Cape Cross (IRE)) (60000) **Said Jaber**
**114 ELECTRA VOICE,** b f 1/2 Poet's Voice—Electra Star (Shamardal (USA)) **Salem Bel Obaida**
**115 EMERALD BAY,** b f 5/2 Kyllachy—Bahia Emerald (IRE) (Bahamian Bounty) **Cheveley Park Stud**
**116 EMTIDAAD (IRE),** ch c 8/2 Kyllachy—Hana Dee (Cadeaux Genereux) (120000) **Ahmed Al Naboodah**
**117** B f 11/4 Sea The Stars (IRE)—Enticing (IRE) (Pivotal) **Lael Stable**
**118 FASHIONATA (IRE),** ch f 25/3 Fast Company (IRE)—Red Red Rose (Piccolo) (20634) **The Super Sprinters**
**119 FASTNET TEMPEST (IRE),** b c 26/1 Fastnet Rock (AUS)—
Dame Blanche (IRE) (Be My Guest (USA)) **OTI Racing, J. Magnier**
**120** B f 16/4 Dream Ahead (USA)—Flanders (IRE) (Common Grounds) (400000) **Lordship Stud**
**121** Ch f 31/3 Champs Elysees—Fleche d'or (Dubai Destination (USA)) (119047) **Clipper Logistics**
**122** Ch c 10/4 Poet's Voice—Ganga (IRE) (Generous (IRE)) (65000) **Mr Michael Morris**
**123** Br c 1/3 New Approach (IRE)—High Heel Sneakers (Dansili) (65000) **Sultan Ali**
**124** B c 4/3 Frozen Power (IRE)—Hollow Talk (Beat Hollow) (80000) **Sheikh Ahmed Al Maktoum**
**125 IJLAAL,** b c 21/3 Exceed And Excel (AUS)—
Special Dancer (Shareef Dancer (USA)) (317460) **Hamdan Al Maktoum**
**126** B c 24/3 Equiano (FR)—Impressible (Oasis Dream) (50000) **Saleh Bel Obaida**
**127 IN THE CITY,** ch c 3/4 Exceed And Excel (AUS)—Soft Morning (Pivotal) (100000) **Simon Munir & Isaac Souede**
**128** B c 28/2 Approve (IRE)—Incessant (IRE) (Elusive Quality (USA)) (60000) **Sheikh Juma Dalmook Al Maktoum**
**129** B f 12/2 Dream Ahead (USA)—Infamous Angel (Exceed And Excel (AUS)) **David & Yvonne Blunt**
**130** B f 8/1 Iffraaj—Kashoof (Green Desert (USA)) **Hamdan Al Maktoum**
**131** Ch c 12/2 Lope de Vega (IRE)—
Keep Dancing (IRE) (Distant Music (USA)) (95000) **Sheikh Rashid Dalmook Al Maktoum**
**132** B c 1/2 Fast Company (IRE)—Lady Xara (IRE) (Xaar) (66666) **Highclere Thoroughbred Racing (Walpole)**
**133** Ch f 22/4 Exceed And Excel (AUS)—Landela (Alhaarth (IRE)) (130952) **Sheikh Juma Dalmook Al Maktoum**
**134 LIGHT MUSIC,** b f 1/3 Elusive Quality (USA)—Medley (Danehill Dancer (IRE)) **Her Majesty The Queen**
**135** Ch f 4/2 Exceed And Excel (AUS)—Lochridge (Indian Ridge) **Mr J. C. Smith**
**136** Ch c 9/4 Pivotal—Mail The Desert (IRE) (Desert Prince (IRE)) (380000) **Al Shaqab Racing**
**137 MANSHOOD (IRE),** b c 27/2 Iffraaj—Thawrah (IRE) (Green Desert (USA)) (380000) **Hamdan Al Maktoum**
**138** B f 19/1 Acclamation—Map of Heaven (Pivotal) **Lael Stable**
**139** Ch f 15/4 Exceed And Excel (AUS)—Miss Honorine (IRE) (Highest Honor (FR)) (85000) **Abdulla Al Khalifa**
**140 MUSAANADA,** b f 7/3 Sea The Stars (IRE)—Gaze (Galileo (IRE)) **Hamdan Al Maktoum**
**141 MUTAYYAM,** ch c 21/4 Aqlaam—Sant Elena (Efisio) **Hamdan Al Maktoum**
**142 MUZDAWAJ,** b c 16/4 Dansili—Shabiba (USA) (Seeking The Gold (USA)) **Hamdan Al Maktoum**
**143 NAQDY,** b c 19/3 Aqlaam—Shuhra (IRE) (Marju (IRE)) **Hamdan Al Maktoum**
**144 NOBEL DUKE (IRE),** ch c 1/4 Duke of Marmalade (IRE)—
Dowager (Groom Dancer (USA)) (35714) **Roberts, Green, Savidge, Whittal-Williams**
**145 NOKHADA (IRE),** b c 20/3 Lilbourne Lad (IRE)—
Silverdreammachine (IRE) (Marju (IRE)) (70000) **Hamdan Al Maktoum**
**146** B f 24/2 Notnowcato—Nsx (Roi Danzig (USA)) (18000) **Scotney/Symonds/Fisher Partnership**
**147 ORIENTAL CROSS (IRE),** b f 19/3 Cape Cross (IRE)—
Orion Girl (GER) (Law Society (USA)) (174603) **Her Majesty The Queen**
**148 ORNATE,** b c 16/4 Bahamian Bounty—Adorn (Kyllachy) **Cheveley Park Stud**
**149** B f 25/2 Makfi—Our Little Secret (IRE) (Rossini (USA)) **Qatar Racing Ltd & Clipper Logistics**
**150 OUT AND ABOUT (IRE),** b c 25/3 Fastnet Rock (AUS)—Starship (IRE) (Galileo (IRE)) **The Starship Partnership**
**151** Ch f 19/3 Tamayuz—Peace Summit (Cape Cross (IRE)) (25000) **Sheikh Rashid Dalmook Al Maktoum**
**152** B c 20/2 Iffraaj—Quaich (Danehill (USA)) (110000) **Sheikh Ahmed Al Maktoum**
**153** B f 3/4 Oasis Dream—Quan Yin (IRE) (Sadler's Wells (USA)) (100000) **Sheikh Juma Dalmook Al Maktoum**
**154 RAHYAH,** b f 26/3 Acclamation—Kahlua Kiss (Mister Baileys) (75000) **Ahmed Al Naboodah**
**155 RAUCOUS,** b c 23/3 Dream Ahead (USA)—
Shyrl (Acclamation) (100000) **Highclere Thoroughbred Racing(Melbourne)**
**156 RECORDER,** ch c 28/1 Galileo (IRE)—Memory (IRE) (Danehill Dancer (IRE)) **Her Majesty The Queen**
**157 RELATIONSHIP,** ch f 18/2 Pivotal—Courting (Pursuit of Love) **Cheveley Park Stud**
**158** Ch f 14/2 Exceed And Excel (AUS)—Ronaldsay (Kirkwall) (80000) **Qatar Racing Limited**
**159 RUSSIAN FINALE,** b f 6/4 Dansili—Russian Rhythm (USA) (Kingmambo (USA)) **Cheveley Park Stud**
**160** B f 11/3 Iffraaj—Sahara Sky (IRE) (Danehill (USA)) **Mr Paul Makin**
**161 SAINTED,** ch f 8/3 Dutch Art—Blithe (Pivotal) **Cheveley Park Stud**
**162** B c 14/2 Bahamian Bounty—Skirrid (Halling (USA)) (80000) **Sheikh Juma Dalmook Al Maktoum**
**163** Ch f 27/2 Exceed And Excel (AUS)—Soodad (King's Best (USA)) (70000) **The Royal Ascot Racing Club**
**164** B f 5/3 Fastnet Rock (AUS)—Starfish (IRE) (Galileo (IRE)) (260000) **Al Shaqab Racing**

## MR WILLIAM HAGGAS - Continued

**165** B c 19/3 New Approach (IRE)—Superstar Leo (IRE) (College Chapel) **Lael Stable**
**166 TASLEET,** b c 19/3 Showcasing—Bird Key (Cadeaux Genereux) (49523) **Hamdan Al Maktoum**
**167** B f 21/4 Dubawi (IRE)—The World (Dubai Destination (USA)) **Abdulla Al Mansoori**
**168** B f 1/5 Holy Roman Emperor (IRE)—Theory of Law (Generous (IRE)) **Ahmad Alkhallafi**
**169** Ch c 9/3 Kyllachy—Thousandkissesdeep (IRE) (Night Shift (USA)) (60000) **Sheikh Juma Dalmook Al Maktoum**
**170** B gr f 26/3 Kyllachy—Vellena (Lucky Story (USA)) (50000) **Sheikh Rashid Dalmook Al Maktoum**
**171** B f 11/3 Pivotal—Whazzat (Daylami (IRE)) (200000) **Al Shaqab Racing**
**172 WRAPPED,** ch f 20/3 Iffraaj—Muffled (USA) (Mizaaya) (110000) **Cheveley Park Stud**

**Other Owners:** Mr Imad Al-Sagar, Mr Ian Beard, Mrs Christine Beard, Mrs T. Brudenell, Mr D. Davidson, The Hon H. Herbert, Highclere Thoroughbred Racing Ltd, Mr Saleh Al Homaizi, Mr R. Jackson, Mrs G. S. Jackson, L. K. Piggott Ltd, Mrs John Magnier, Mr G. Middlebrook, Mrs L. Middlebrook, Mr D. I. Scott, Mr Andrew Stone, Mrs M. F. Stone, Mr M. Tabor.

**Assistant Trainers:** Archie Watson, Jason Favell

**Apprentice:** Nathan Allison, Georgia Cox, Stephanie Joannides.

---

## 267 MR ALEX HALES, Edgecote

Postal: **Trafford Bridge Stables, Edgecote, Banbury**
Contacts: **PHONE (01295) 660131 FAX (01295) 660128 MOBILE (07771) 511652**
**E-MAIL alex@alexhalesracing.co.uk WEBSITE www.alexhalesracing.co.uk**

1 **ALLNECESSARYFORCE (FR),** 5, gr g Verglas (IRE)—Kosmic View (USA) **Mr S. Brown**
2 **BIG JIM,** 6, b g Revoque (IRE)—Chilly Squaw (IRE) **Gumbrills Racing Partnership**
3 **BRIGINDO,** 5, b m Kayf Tara—Lac Marmot (FR) **S. P. Bloodstock**
4 **COME ON HARRIET,** 6, b m Kayf Tara—Royal Musical **A. E. Frost**
5 **CRAFTY ROBERTO,** 7, ch g Intikhab (USA)—Mowazana (IRE) **S Brown H Steele D Fitzgerald**
6 **GILZEAN (IRE),** 9, b g Flemensfirth (USA)—Sheknowso **Edging Ahead**
7 **ISAAC BELL (IRE),** 7, b g Fruits of Love (USA)—Oso Well (IRE) **A. E. Frost**
8 **MAYBELL,** 4, b f Black Sam Bellamy (IRE)—Chilly Squaw (IRE) **Gumbrills Racing Partnership**
9 **MIDNIGHT CHORISTER,** 7, b g Midnight Legend—Royal Musical **The Choristers**
10 **MINELLAFORLEISURE (IRE),** 7, br g King's Theatre (IRE)—Dame Foraine (FR) **The Patient Partnership**
11 **OGARITMO,** 6, ch m Manduro (GER)—Querida **Edging Ahead**
12 **PERIQUEST,** 6, b g Overbury (IRE)—Rippling Brook **The Fortune Hunters**
13 **ROSENEATH (IRE),** 11, b g Saddlers' Hall (IRE)—Vital Approach (IRE) **The Strathclyders**
14 **ROYAL BARGE (IRE),** 5, b m Shirocco (GER)—Sahara Lady (IRE) **A. M. Hales**
15 **ROYAL SUPREME (IRE),** 5, br g Royal Anthem (USA)—Supreme Baloo (IRE) **The Patient Partnership**
16 **ROYAUME BLEU (FR),** 10, ch g Kapgarde (FR)—Dear Blue (FR) **The Royaume Bleu Racing Partnership**
17 **RUNNING WOLF (IRE),** 4, b g Amadeus Wolf—Monet's Lady (IRE) **The Wolfgangers**
18 **SALUT HONORE (FR),** 9, b g Lost World (IRE)—Kadalkote (FR) **The Hexagon Racing Partnership**
19 **SARANDO,** 10, b g Hernando (FR)—Dansara **Mrs D. W. James**
20 **SCOOTER BOY,** 6, b g Revoque (IRE)—Always Forgiving **The Scooter Boy Partnership**
21 **SHINOOKI (IRE),** 8, br g Blueprint (IRE)—Rapid Response (IRE) **D. C. R. Allen**
22 **STEPOVER,** 4, b f Midnight Legend—Ring Back (IRE) **D. C. R. Allen**
23 **TAKE TWO,** 6, b g Act One—Lac Marmot (FR) **S. P. Bloodstock**
24 **ULTIMATUM DU ROY (FR),** 7, b g Brier Creek (USA)—La Fleur du Roy (FR) **D. C. R. Allen**
25 **VAILLANT CREEK (FR),** 6, b g Brier Creek (USA)—Ker Marie (FR) **D. C. R. Allen**
26 **VAUBAN DU SEUIL (FR),** 6, b g Epalo (GER)—Parika du Seuil (FR) **A. M. Hales**

### THREE-YEAR-OLDS

27 **KNIGHT CRUSADER,** b c Sir Percy—Lac Marmot (FR) **The Of-Ten Racing Partnership**
28 **SEAMOOR SECRET,** b f Sakhee's Secret—Labaqa (USA) **Mr R. H. Harrison**

**Other Owners:** Mrs L. Barlow, Miss S. A. Baxter, Miss S. Burnell, Mr J. Cleary, J. S. C. Fry, Mrs K. A. Fry, R. E. Morris-Adams, Mr R. E. Partridge, Mrs H. Steele, Mrs C. Taylor, Mr S. T. Wallace, Mrs P. S. Wallace, Mrs J. Wood.

---

## 268 MR MICHAEL HALFORD, Kildare

Postal: **Copper Beech Stables, Doneaney, Kildangan Road, Kildare Town, Co. Kildare, Ireland**
Contacts: **PHONE (00 353) 45 526119 FAX (00 353) 45 526157 MOBILE (00 353) 87 2579204**
**E-MAIL info@michaelhalford.com**

1 **ALVAR (USA),** 7, ch g Forest Danger (USA)—Diameter (USA) **Mr Paul Rooney**

## MR MICHAEL HALFORD - Continued

2 **ASBURY BOSS (IRE),** 4, b br g Dalakhani (IRE)—Nick's Nikita (IRE) **Mr Nicky Hartery**
3 **BERMUDA BLISS (IRE),** 4, b f Balmont (USA)—Balmy Choice (IRE) **P. E. I. Newell**
4 **CASTLE GUEST (IRE),** 6, b g Rock of Gibraltar (IRE)—Castelletto **Mr Paul Rooney**
5 **CEBUANO,** 10, ch g Fraam—Ideal Figure **Mr Paul McMahon**
6 **CERTERACH (IRE),** 7, b g Halling (USA)—Chartres (IRE) **Mr Paul Rooney**
7 **DANCE AROUND (IRE),** 4, b f Bushranger (IRE)—Roundabout Girl (IRE) **P. E. I. Newell**
8 **DARK ALLIANCE (IRE),** 4, b g Dark Angel (IRE)—Alinda (IRE) **Mr Paul McMahon**
9 **EASTERN RULES (IRE),** 7, b g Golden Snake (USA)—Eastern Ember **Simon Hales**
10 **FAIRYCRAFT (IRE),** 4, gr f Mastercraftsman (IRE)—Fairybook (USA) **Mr John Connaughton**
11 **GLASSATURA (IRE),** 4, gr f Verglas (IRE)—Dunbrody (FR) **Mr Michael Enright**
12 **HASANOUR (USA),** 5, b g Giant's Causeway (USA)—Hasanka (IRE) **Mr R. McNally**
13 **KERNOFF (IRE),** 4, b g Excellent Art—Daganya (IRE) **J. D. Claque**
14 **KINGS RYKER (IRE),** 4, b c Bushranger (IRE)—Mia Mambo (USA) **Mr Eric Koh**
15 **LONAN (IRE),** 6, b g Dubawi (IRE)—Chartres (IRE) **Mrs M. Halford**
16 **LORD KENMARE (USA),** 9, b g Hold That Tiger (USA)—The Fur Flew (USA) **Mr B. Gallivan**
17 **PADDY THE CELEB (IRE),** 9, ch g Peintre Celebre (USA)—On The Razz (USA) **Mr Paul McMahon**
18 **POLITICAL POLICY (IRE),** 4, b g Bushranger (IRE)—Alexander Express (IRE) **F. Lynch**
19 **PRINCESS PEARLITA (IRE),** 4, b f Manduro (GER)—Pearlitas Passion (IRE) **Mr Michael Enright**
20 **REFUSETOLISTEN (IRE),** 4, b f Clodovil (IRE)—Smoken Rosa (USA) **Mr John Dewberry**
21 **RUMMAGING (IRE),** 7, ch g Chineur (FR)—Roundabout Girl (IRE) **Evan Newell**
22 **RUSSIAN SOUL (IRE),** 7, b g Invincible Spirit (IRE)—Russian Hill **Mrs A. Kavanagh**
23 **SEA THE LION (IRE),** 4, b g Sea The Stars (IRE)—Ramona **John Connaughton**
24 **SHADAGANN (IRE),** 5, b h Invincible Spirit (IRE)—Shamadara (IRE) **Mr Paul Rooney**
25 **SLIPPER ORCHID (IRE),** 6, b m Verglas (IRE)—Lahiba (IRE) **Mrs Caroline Roper**
26 **TEAM WORK,** 4, ch g Shamardal (USA)—Hi Dubai **P. Woods**
27 **TEMASEK STAR (IRE),** 4, b g Soviet Star (USA)—Crazy About You (IRE) **George Tay**
28 **VENEZIA (IRE),** 4, gr g Galileo (IRE)—St Roch (IRE) **Paul Hickman**
29 **VICTOR'S BEACH (IRE),** 5, b g Footstepsinthesand—Your Village (IRE) **Dr Keith Swanick**
30 **WON DIAMOND,** 5, b g Mount Nelson—Read Federica **Mr Paul Rooney**

## THREE-YEAR-OLDS

31 **ADARENNA (IRE),** b f Nayef (USA)—Adelfia (IRE) **HH Aga Khan**
32 **ALAMGIYR (IRE),** b c Desert Style (IRE)—Alaiyma (IRE) **HH Aga Khan**
33 **ANGEL'S GIFT (IRE),** b f Excellent Art—Meek Appeal (USA) **Mr Michael Enright**
34 **ARIF (IRE),** b c Nayef (USA)—Adjaliya (IRE) **HH Aga Khan**
35 **BELEZZA OSCURA (IRE),** br f Pastoral Pursuits—Flashing Blade **Mr George Tay**
36 **BLUE FRAGRANCE (IRE),** gr f Verglas (IRE)—Dazzling Day **Blessingndisguise Partnership**
37 **CELESTIAL LOVE (IRE),** b f Galileo (IRE)—Piste Noire (USA) **Mr Michael Enright**
38 **CHESTNUT FIRE,** ch g Showcasing—Music In Exile (USA) **Mrs R. Redmond**
39 **COPERNICUS (IRE),** ch c Teofilo (IRE)—Nick's Nikita (IRE) **Mr Nicky Hartery**
40 **DABIYLA (IRE),** b f Azamour (IRE)—Dabista (IRE) **HH Aga Khan**
41 **DEE MAJULAH (IRE),** gr g Zebedee—Alla Marcia (IRE) **Mr Eric Koh**
42 **DUCHESSOFFLORENCE,** b f Pivotal—Portal **Mr Michael Enright**
43 **EBAYYA (IRE),** b f Azamour (IRE)—Ebalista (IRE) **HH Aga Khan**
44 **FIVE CLAW (IRE),** b c Jeremy (USA)—Indus Ridge (IRE) **Dr Tan Kai Chah**
45 **GOLDEN RAVEN (IRE),** b br c Raven's Pass (USA)—Superfonic (FR) **Godolphin Management**
46 **HAT ALNASAR (IRE),** b c Moss Vale (IRE)—Dream State (IRE) **Mr Fathi Eqziama**
47 **IN THE DARK (IRE),** b f Fast Company (IRE)—Grand Oir (USA) **Mrs Caroline Roper**
48 **KIRKS RYKER,** b g Selkirk (USA)—Kesara **Mr Eric Koh**
49 **LEHBAB (IRE),** b g Fast Company (IRE)—Hi Katriona (IRE) **Nasser Mohamed Ahmad**
50 **LINET (IRE),** b f Oasis Dream—Molomo **Barouche Stud**
51 **MAIRA (IRE),** b f Zamindar (USA)—Masiyma (IRE) **HH Aga Khan**
52 **MAPLE HILL (GER),** b br c Rock of Gibraltar (IRE)—Manda Hill (GER) **George Tay**
53 **MAPLE NOBLE (IRE),** b g Lord Shanakill (USA)—Crossreadh (USA) **George Tay**
54 **MAPLE SPRING,** ch g Nayef (USA)—Rabshih (IRE) **George Tay**
55 **MONOLIGHT,** b c Iffraaj—Photo Flash (IRE) **Godolphin Management**
56 **PORTAGE (IRE),** b c Teofilo (IRE)—Galley **Godolphin Management**
57 **PROLOGUE (IRE),** b c Cape Cross (IRE)—Snippets (IRE) **Godolphin Management**
58 **RAYDARA (IRE),** b br f Rock of Gibraltar (IRE)—Raydiya (IRE) **HH Aga Khan**
59 **REDDOT EXPRESS,** ch c Iffraaj—Applauded (IRE) **George Tay**
60 **SHANNON SOUL (IRE),** b c Shamardal (USA)—Paimpolaise (IRE) **Mr Michael Enright**
61 **SIKANDAR (IRE),** ch c Medicean—Siniyya (IRE) **HH Aga Khan**
62 **SKERRAY RULES (IRE),** br f Aussie Rules (USA)—Skerray **Mr Michael Enright**
63 **TAILTEANN GAMES (USA),** ch c Hard Spun (USA)—Fine Jade (USA) **Michael Halford**
64 **TAMAZAN (USA),** ch c City Zip (USA)—Tawaria (FR) **HH Aga Khan**

## MR MICHAEL HALFORD - Continued

**65 TIDJANI (IRE),** b c Rock of Gibraltar (IRE)—Tilimsana (IRE) **HH Aga Khan**
**66 TOSCANINI (IRE),** b c Shamardal (USA)—Tuzla (FR) **Godolphin Management**
**67 VILMAN (IRE),** b c Mastercraftsman (IRE)—Velandia (IRE) **HH Aga Khan**
**68 WYCHWOOD WARRIOR (IRE),** b c Lope de Vega (IRE)—Pearlitas Passion (IRE) **Mr Michael Enright**
**69 ZUNERA (IRE),** b f Invincible Spirit (IRE)—Zalaiyma (FR) **HH Aga Khan**

## TWO-YEAR-OLDS

**70** Ch c 12/5 Iffraaj—Adelfia (IRE) (Sinndar (IRE)) **HH Aga Khan**
**71** B f 19/4 Shamardal (USA)—Anamato (AUS) (Redoute's Choice (AUS)) **Godolphin Management**
**72** B c 16/3 Fast Company (IRE)—Cappuccino (IRE) (Mujadil (USA)) (103174) **Godolphin Management**
**73 DALITARI (IRE),** gr c 23/4 Azamour (IRE)—Dalataya (IRE) (Sadler's Wells (USA)) **HH Aga Khan**
**74** Br f 14/3 Medicean—Daravika (IRE) (Soviet Star (USA)) **HH Aga Khan**
**75** B f 21/4 Footstepsinthesand—Deauville Vision (IRE) (Danehill Dancer (IRE)) **Mr Takaya Kimura**
**76** B c 10/4 Kodiac—Deportment (Barathea (IRE)) (160000) **Golphin Management**
**77** Ch c 6/5 Tamayuz—Ebalista (IRE) (Selkirk (USA)) **HH Aga Khan**
**78** Br c 15/2 Bushranger (IRE)—Fatwa (IRE) (Lahib (USA)) (4364) **Mrs M. Halford**
**79** B f 18/3 Pivotal—Fine Threads (Barathea (IRE)) (120000) **Godolphin Management**
**80** B f 22/3 Invincible Spirit (IRE)—Gonfilia (GER) (Big Shuffle (USA)) **Godolphin Management**
**81** B c 28/1 Acclamation—Hanakiyya (IRE) (Danehill Dancer (IRE)) **HH Aga Khan**
**82** Gr c 10/3 Manduro (GER)—Hazarafa (IRE) (Daylami (IRE)) **HH Aga Khan**
**83** Ch f 7/3 Pivotal—Hazarista (IRE) (Barathea (IRE)) **HH Aga Khan**
**84** Ch c 4/3 Dutch Art—Helen Glaz (IRE) (Giant's Causeway (USA)) (250000) **Godolphin Management**
**85** B c 16/5 Big Bad Bob (IRE)—Himiko (IRE) (Aussie Rules (USA)) **Mr Takaya Kimura**
**86** B c 4/4 Authorized (IRE)—Honky Tonk Sally (Dansili) (180000) **Godolphin Management**
**87** B f 1/3 Raven's Pass (USA)—Intapeace (IRE) (Intikhab (USA)) **Godolphin Management**
**88** B f 14/4 Holy Roman Emperor (IRE)—Kadayna (IRE) (Dalakhani (IRE)) **HH Aga Khan**
**89** B c 2/3 Holy Roman Emperor (IRE)—Kaladena (IRE) (Daylami (IRE)) **HH Aga Khan**
**90 KALASADI (IRE),** ch c 10/5 Exceed And Excel (AUS)—Kalidaha (IRE) (Cadeaux Genereux) **HH Aga Khan**
**91** B f 18/2 Invincible Spirit (IRE)—Lady Catherine (Bering) **Godolphin Management**
**92** B f 17/3 Holy Roman Emperor (IRE)—Mamacita (IRE) (High Chaparral (IRE)) **Mr Michael Enright**
**93** B c 1/4 Medicean—Natalisa (IRE) (Green Desert (USA)) (24000) **M. El Circy**
**94** B f 20/3 Teofilo (IRE)—Paimpolaise (IRE) (Priolo (USA)) **Mr Michael Enright**
**95** B f 17/4 Oasis Dream—Pearl Banks (Pivotal) **Mr Michael Enright**
**96** B f 1/5 Iffraaj—Pearlitas Passion (IRE) (High Chaparral (IRE)) **Mr Michael Enright**
**97** B f 16/2 Sea The Stars (IRE)—Pleasantry (Johannesburg (USA)) (200000) **Godolphin Management**
**98** B c 11/5 Shamardal (USA)—Queen of Denmark (USA) (Kingmambo (USA)) **Godolphin Management**
**99** Gr c 28/1 Iffraaj—Raisonable (USA) (El Prado (IRE)) (126984) **Godolphin Management**
**100** Br f 11/1 Holy Roman Emperor (IRE)—Rayka (IRE) (Selkirk (USA)) **HH Aga Khan**
**101** B c 2/3 Danehill Dancer (IRE)—Roselyn (Efisio) (49205) **George Tay**
**102** Ch f 10/3 Iffraaj—Shalama (IRE) (Kahyasi) **HH Aga Khan**
**103** B c 29/4 Multiplex—Skerries (IRE) (Dr Fong (USA)) (20634) **Mr George Tay**
**104** B f 2/2 Zoffany (IRE)—Smoken Rosa (USA) (Smoke Glacken (USA)) (9523) **Mr Nicky Hartery**
**105** B f 24/1 Dansili—Song (IRE) (Sadler's Wells (USA)) **Mr Michael Enright**
**106** B br c 12/4 Distorted Humor (USA)—
Stupendous Miss (USA) (Dynaformer (USA)) (79364) **Godolphin Management**
**107** B f 11/3 Raven's Pass (USA)—Vitoria (IRE) (Exceed And Excel (AUS)) **Godolphin Management**
**108** B f 26/3 Raven's Pass (USA)—Viz (IRE) (Darshaan) **Godolphin Management**
**109** B c 28/2 Holy Roman Emperor (IRE)—Zarebiya (IRE) (Galileo (IRE)) **HH Aga Khan**
**110** Br c 28/3 Holy Roman Emperor (IRE)—Zoumie (IRE) (Mark of Esteem (IRE)) (39681) **Mr George Tay**

**Assistant Trainer:** Garrett Cotter

**Jockey (flat):** Shane Foley. **Apprentice:** Conor Hoban, Sean Corby, Jamie Joyce, Shane B Kelly, Conor McGovern, Damien Melia. **Amateur:** Mr Evan Halford.

---

## 269 MISS SALLY HALL, Middleham

Postal: **Brecongill, Coverham, Leyburn, North Yorkshire, DL8 4TJ**
Contacts: **PHONE (01969) 640223 FAX (0800) 066 4274**
**E-MAIL sally@brecongill.co.uk**

**1 ALTHAROOS (IRE),** 5, br g Sakhee (USA)—Thamara (USA) **Colin Platts**
**2 MAGIC HAZE,** 9, b g Makbul—Turn Back **Miss S. E. Hall**
**3 ROCK A DOODLE DOO (IRE),** 8, b g Oratorio (IRE)—Nousaiyra (IRE) **Colin Platts**

**MISS SALLY HALL - Continued**

## THREE-YEAR-OLDS

4 Bl gr g Sulamani (IRE)—Charlotte Lamb **Miss S. E. Hall**
5 Ch f Monsieur Bond (IRE)—Pigment **Miss S. E. Hall**
6 B f Sakhee (USA)—Turn Back **Miss S. E. Hall**

## TWO-YEAR-OLDS

7 Ch g 17/4 Haafhd—Pigment (Zamindar (USA)) **Miss S. E. Hall**

**Assistant Trainer:** Colin Platts

**Jockey (NH):** Richard Johnson. **Amateur:** Mrs D.S. Wilkinson.

---

# 270 MRS MARY HAMBRO, Cheltenham

Postal: **Cotswold Stud, Sezincote, Moreton-In-Marsh, Gloucestershire, GL56 9TB**
Contacts: **PHONE (01386) 700700 FAX (01386) 700701 MOBILE (07860) 632990**
**E-MAIL maryhambro@mac.com**

1 **MATRAVERS,** 4, b c Oasis Dream—Maakrah **Mrs M. C. Hambro**

## THREE-YEAR-OLDS

2 **BADGER BANK,** gr g Zamindar (USA)—Rose Row **Mrs M. C. Hambro**
3 **TOAD CORNER,** b g Shirocco (GER)—Didbrook **Mrs M. C. Hambro**

---

# 271 MRS DEBRA HAMER, Carmarthen

Postal: **Bryngors Uchaf, Nantycaws, Carmarthen, Dyfed, SA32 8EY**
Contacts: **HOME (01267) 234585 MOBILE (07980) 665274**
**E-MAIL hamerracing@hotmail.co.uk**

1 **BRONWYDD,** 5, br m Needle Gun (IRE)—Talkingstick (IRE) **A. T. Bailey**
2 **CELTIC FELLA (IRE),** 8, gr b g Kahtan—Mens Business (IRE) **Mr T. M. Morse**
3 **LOOKS LIKE POWER (IRE),** 5, ch g Spadoun (FR)—Martovic (IRE) **Mr C. A. Hanbury**
4 **MAGICAL MAN,** 8, b br g Lahib (USA)—Majestic Di (IRE) **Mr C. A. Hanbury**
5 **PENNANT DANCER,** 8, b g Grape Tree Road—Pennant Princess **Mr P. J. Woolley**
6 **PENNANT LADY,** 5, b br m Black Sam Bellamy (IRE)—Pennant Princess **Mr P. J. Woolley**
7 **THESPIS OF ICARIA (IRE),** 9, b g Sadler's Wells (USA)—Hellenic **Miss L. Reid**
8 **WHO AM I,** 9, b br g Tamayaz (CAN)—Short Fuse (IRE) **W. J. Cole**

**Assistant Trainer:** Mr M P Hamer

---

# 272 MRS ALISON HAMILTON, Denholm

Postal: **The Dykes, Denholm, Roxburghshire, TD9 8TB**
Contacts: **PHONE (01450) 870323 MOBILE (07885) 477349**
**E-MAIL Alisonhamilton53@yahoo.com**

1 **CLONLENEY (IRE),** 9, ch g Broadway Flyer (USA)—Most Effective (IRE) **P Hegarty & Ms F Beirne**
2 **DANEHILLS WELL (IRE),** 7, b g Indian Danehill (IRE)—Collatrim Choice (IRE) **J. P. G. Hamilton**
3 **EMKAE (IRE),** 7, b g Milan—Hindi (FR) **J. P. G. Hamilton**
4 **GRANARUID (IRE),** 12, br g Alderbrook—Lady Lorraine (IRE) **J. P. G. Hamilton**
5 **LENEY COTTAGE (IRE),** 8, b g Witness Box (USA)—Fleur de Tal **P Hegarty & P Gaffney**
6 **PAINTERS LAD (IRE),** 4, b g Fruits of Love (USA)—Great Cullen (IRE) **J. P. G. Hamilton**
7 **SOME LAD (IRE),** 10, b g Beneficial—Some News (IRE) **J. P. G. Hamilton**
8 **TOWERBURN (IRE),** 6, b g Cloudings (IRE)—Lady Newmill (IRE) **J. P. G. Hamilton**
9 **WHAT A DREAM,** 9, ch g Supreme Sound—Ben Roseler (IRE) **R. J. Kyle, D. & J. Byers**

**Other Owners:** Ms F. Beirne, D. S. Byers, Mrs M. J. Byers, Mr P. M. J. Gaffney, Mr P. J. Hegarty, R. J. Kyle.

**Assistant Trainer:** Mr G. Hamilton

## 273 MRS ANN HAMILTON, Newcastle Upon Tyne

Postal: **Claywalls Farm, Capheaton, Newcastle Upon Tyne, NE19 2BP**
Contacts: **PHONE (01830) 530219 MOBILE (07704) 670704**
**E-MAIL annhamilton1952@hotmail.com**

1 **EDMUND (IRE),** 8, b g Indian River (FR)—Awomansdream (IRE) **I. Hamilton**
2 **KICKING LILY,** 5, b m Great Palm (USA)—Miss Royello **I. Hamilton**
3 4, Gr g Great Palm (USA)—Miss Royello **I. Hamilton**
4 **NINE ALTARS (IRE),** 6, b g Heron Island (IRE)—Tawny Owl (IRE) **I. Hamilton**
5 **RUNSWICK ROYAL (IRE),** 6, ch g Excellent Art—Renada **I. Hamilton**
6 **TRUST THOMAS,** 7, ch g Erhaab (USA)—Yota (FR) **I. Hamilton**
7 **WOODSTOCK (IRE),** 5, b g High Chaparral (IRE)—Woodwin (IRE) **I. Hamilton**

### TWO-YEAR-OLDS

8 B g 23/4 Great Palm (USA)—Miss Royello (Royal Fountain) **I. Hamilton**

**Assistant Trainer:** Ian Hamilton

## 274 MR MICKY HAMMOND, Middleham

Postal: **Oakwood Stables, East Witton Road, Middleham, Leyburn, North Yorkshire, DL8 4PT**
Contacts: **PHONE (01969) 625223 MOBILE (07808) 572777**
**E-MAIL mhracing1@hotmail.co.uk WEBSITE www.mickyhammondracing.co.uk**

1 **ALDERBROOK LAD (IRE),** 9, ch g Alderbrook—Alone Tabankulu (IRE) **Masters Of The Hall**
2 **AMIR PASHA (UAE),** 10, br g Halling (USA)—Clarinda (IRE) **M.H.O.G.**
3 **AULDTHUNDER (IRE),** 8, b g Oscar (IRE)—Jill's Girl (IRE) **The Rat Pack Racing Club**
4 **BEER GOGGLES (IRE),** 4, br g Oscar (IRE)—Tynelucy (IRE) **Straightline Construction Ltd**
5 **BIG FRANK (USA),** 6, b br g More Than Ready (USA)—Salchow (USA) **Give Every Man His Due**
6 **BLUE HUSSAR (IRE),** 4, b g Montjeu (IRE)—Metaphor (USA) **Mr R. M. Howard**
7 **CAPE WRATH,** 4, gr c Verglas (IRE)—Capades Dancer (USA) **Mr S. Paley**
8 **CARALINE (FR),** 4, b f Martaline—Vie Ta Vie (FR) **M. Hammond**
9 **CHOCOLATE DIAMOND (IRE),** 4, ch g Intense Focus (USA)—Sagemacca (IRE)
10 **CORREGGIO,** 5, ch g Bertolini (USA)—Arian Da **Forty Forty Twenty**
11 **DANCEINTOTHELIGHT,** 8, gr g Dansili—Kali **Maybe The Last Time**
12 **DARK CASTLE,** 6, b g Dark Angel (IRE)—True Magic **Mr J Cox & Mr E Tasker**
13 **DIDDY ERIC,** 5, b g Oratorio (IRE)—Amber Queen (IRE) **Mrs Rita Butler & Mrs Gemma Hogg**
14 **DRUNKEN COUNSEL (IRE),** 6, b g Scorpion (IRE)—Kilbarry Demon (IRE) **Racing Management & Training Ltd**
15 **ENDLESS CREDIT (IRE),** 5, b br g High Chaparral (IRE)—Pay The Bank **Mike & Eileen Newbould**
16 **EVERAARD (USA),** 9, ch g Lion Heart (USA)—Via Gras (USA) **Tennant, Sharp & Boston**
17 **FRANK THE SLINK,** 9, b g Central Park (IRE)—Kadari **M. D. Hammond**
18 **GONOW,** 7, b g Red Ransom (USA)—Isotta (GER) **Mike & Eileen Newbould**
19 **JUST CAMERON,** 8, b g Kayf Tara—Miss Fencote **Mr & Mrs Paul Chapman**
20 **KATHLATINO,** 8, b m Danbird (AUS)—Silver Rhythm **50/50 Racing Club**
21 **KHELAC,** 5, b g Kheleyf (USA)—Miss Lacey (IRE) **Half Cut Glass Partnership**
22 **LACERTA,** 4, b g Astronomer Royal (USA)—Rubber (IRE) **Mr R. A. Beattie**
23 **LARMOR (FR),** 4, bl g Green Tune (USA)—Mia's Baby (USA) **Straightline Construction Ltd**
24 **LIBBY MAE (IRE),** 5, b m High Chaparral (IRE)—Empty Pocket **Mr & Mrs Paul Chapman**
25 **LOWCARR MOTION,** 5, b g Rainbow High—Royalty (IRE) **Mr Irvin Lynch & Mr Barry Stead**
26 **MASTER OF THE HALL (IRE),** 11, b g Saddlers' Hall (IRE)—Frankly Native (IRE) **Masters Of The Hall**
27 **MAXWIL,** 10, b g Storming Home—Lady Donatella **M. Hammond**
28 **MERCHANT OF MEDICI,** 8, b g Medicean—Regal Rose **Mr J. F. Wilson**
29 **MINELLA HERO (IRE),** 7, b g Old Vic—Shannon Rose (IRE) **Ball & Lees**
30 **ONLY ORSENFOOLSIES,** 6, b g Trade Fair—Desert Gold (IRE) **Foolsies**
31 **PAY THE KING (IRE),** 8, b g King's Theatre (IRE)—Knocktartan (IRE) **Mr S. Paley**
32 **PERTUIS (IRE),** 9, gr g Verglas (IRE)—Lady Killeen (IRE) **M.H.O.G.**
33 **POLITBUREAU,** 8, b g Red Ransom (USA)—Tereshkova (USA) **Maybe The Last Time**
34 **RAYADOUR (IRE),** 6, b g Azamour (IRE)—Rayyana (IRE) **Jimmy Mac**
35 **ROSAIRLIE (IRE),** 7, ch m Halling (USA)—Mrs Mason (IRE) **The Late Night Drinkers & Wishful Thinkers**
36 **ROXYFET (FR),** 5, b g Califet (FR)—Roxalamour (FR) **Straightline Construction Ltd**
37 **RUSSIAN ROYALE,** 5, b m Royal Applause—Russian Ruby (FR) **Straightline Construction Ltd**
38 **SALAALEM (IRE),** 5, gr g Slickly (FR)—Macotte (FR) **TCH**
39 **SHERRY,** 4, b f Tobougg (IRE)—Vino **Guy Reed Racing**
40 **STICKLEBACK,** 6, ch m Manduro (GER)—The Stick **N. J. Rust**
41 **STRAIT RUN (IRE),** 4, ch g Rock of Gibraltar (IRE)—Gentlemen's Guest (USA) **M. Hammond**

## MR MICKY HAMMOND - Continued

42 **SUMMERLEA (IRE),** 9, ch g Alhaarth (IRE)—Verbania (IRE) **Maybe The Last Time**
43 **THE PEAKY BLINDER,** 5, b g Manduro (GER)—White Star (IRE) **The Dress Fine & Walk The Line Syndicate**
44 **THE RAMBLIN KID,** 7, b g Westerner—Disallowed (IRE) **J. Buzzeo**
45 **TYPHON (USA),** 5, b g Proud Citizen (USA)—Seven Moons (JPN) **D H Lees & Sons Limited**
46 **VECHEKA (IRE),** 4, b g Lawman (FR)—Lidanski (IRE) **Racing Management & Training Ltd**
47 **VERKO (FR),** 6, br g Lavirco (GER)—Lady Vernizy (FR) **Straightline Construction Ltd**
48 **WALK RIGHT BACK (IRE),** 4, b c Dandy Man (IRE)—Certainlei (IRE) **Masters Of The Hall**

### THREE-YEAR-OLDS

49 **APPLAUS (GER),** b g Tiger Hill (IRE)—All About Love (GER) **J. Buzzeo**
50 **BOLDBOB (IRE),** gr g Verglas (IRE)—Special Park (USA) **M.H.O.G. 2**
51 **LUVLYLYNNTHOMAS,** gr f Equiano (FR)—Dansa Queen **Bendery Properties Holdings Ltd**

**Other Owners:** Mr A. Bradley, Mr Justin Carthy, Mr J. W. Cox, Mr Richard Green, Mr M. D. Hammond, Mrs Gemma Hogg, Mr L. Horvath, Mr Mike Newbould, Mrs E. E. Newbould, Mr John Pettit, Mr Edward Price, Mr Nick Rust, Mr Angus Smith, Mr A. E. Tasker, Mr K. Ward, Mr O. R. Weeks, Mr P. Wyslych.

**Assistant Trainer:** Mrs. G. Hogg (07809) 428117

**Conditional:** Joe Colliver, Dylan McDonagh. **Amateur:** Miss R. Smith, Mr Joe Wright.

---

## 275 MR MIKE HAMMOND, Abberley

Postal: **Cherry Ash, Bank Lane, Abberley, Worcester, Worcestershire, WR6 6BQ**
Contacts: **PHONE (01299) 896057 MOBILE 07894 050183**
**E-MAIL mphatwellcottage@aol.com WEBSITE www.hammondracing.co.uk**

1 **PROVINCIAL PRIDE (IRE),** 8, b g Whitmore's Conn (USA)—Soraleda (IRE) **D Pain & Sons**

### THREE-YEAR-OLDS

2 B g Cockney Rebel (IRE)—Casablanca Minx (IRE) **Mr W. Hill**

**Other Owners:** Mr P. R. Pain, Mr A. Pain, Mrs S. Pain, Mrs P. R. Pain, Mrs A. S. Taylor.

**Assistant Trainer:** Zoe Hammond

---

## 276 MR RICHARD HANNON, Marlborough

Postal: **R. Hannon Limited, East Everleigh Stables, Everleigh, Marlborough, Wiltshire, SN8 3EY**
Contacts: **PHONE (01264) 850254 FAX (01264) 850076**
**E-MAIL richard.hannon@btinternet.com WEBSITE www.richardhannonracing.co.uk**

1 **BALTIC KNIGHT (IRE),** 5, b h Baltic King—Night of Joy (IRE) **Thurloe Thoroughbreds XXX**
2 **BEEDEE,** 5, b g Beat Hollow—Dawnus (IRE) **Mr & Mrs D. D. Clee**
3 **BUNKER (IRE),** 4, br g Hurricane Run (IRE)—Endure (IRE) **AlShaqabRacing Anderson Morecombe Hughes**
4 **COULSTY (IRE),** 4, b c Kodiac—Hazium (IRE) **Lord Vestey**
5 **CRICKLEWOOD GREEN (USA),** 4, ch g Bob And John (USA)—B Berry Brandy (USA) **Mr Chris Wright & Mr Andy Macdonald**
6 **EMELL,** 5, ch h Medicean—Londonnetdotcom (IRE) **Mr & Mrs D. D. Clee**
7 **FILOSOFO (IRE),** 4, b c Teofilo (IRE)—Think (FR) **Mr P. W. Reglar**
8 **LINDART (ITY),** 4, ch g Dutch Art—Linda Surena (ARG) **Mr R. Hannon**
9 **LORD OFTHE SHADOWS (IRE),** 6, ch g Kyllachy—Golden Shadow (IRE) **Richard Hitchcock Alan King**
10 **LUSTROUS,** 4, b f Champs Elysees—Tamzin **Mrs P. Good**
11 **MAGIC CITY (IRE),** 6, b g Elusive City (USA)—Annmarie's Magic (IRE) **Barker, Ferguson, Mason, Hassiakos, Done**
12 **NIGHT OF THUNDER (IRE),** 4, ch c Dubawi (IRE)—Forest Storm **S. Manana**
13 **NINJAGO,** 5, b h Mount Nelson—Fidelio's Miracle (USA) **Potensis Bloodstock Ltd & J Palmer Brown**
14 **PETHER'S MOON (IRE),** 5, b h Dylan Thomas (IRE)—Softly Tread (IRE) **J. D. Manley**
15 **SHAMSHON (IRE),** 4, b c Invincible Spirit (IRE)—Greenisland (IRE) **Al Shaqab Racing UK Limited**
16 **SHIFTING POWER,** 4, ch c Compton Place—Profit Alert (IRE) **Ms Elaine Chivers & Potensis B'stock Ltd**
17 **SHOWPIECE,** 4, b g Kyllachy—Striving (IRE) **Cheveley Park Stud Limited**
18 **TOORMORE (IRE),** 4, b c Arakan (USA)—Danetime Out (IRE) **Middleham Park Racing IX & James Pak**
19 **VIEWPOINT (IRE),** 6, b g Exceed And Excel (AUS)—Lady's View (USA) **The Heffer Syndicate**
20 **WINDSHEAR,** 4, b c Hurricane Run (IRE)—Portal **Mr M. Daniels**
21 **ZURIGHA (IRE),** 5, b m Cape Cross (IRE)—Noyelles (IRE) **S. H. Altayer**

## MR RICHARD HANNON - Continued

### THREE-YEAR-OLDS

22 **ABAQ,** b f Oasis Dream—Indian Ink (IRE) **Hamdan Al Maktoum**
23 **ACASTER MALBIS (FR),** ch c Arcano (IRE)—Acatama (USA) **Byerley Racing Limited**
24 **ALHAMAREER (IRE),** ch g Teofilo (IRE)—Ribot's Guest (IRE) **Al Shaqab Racing UK Limited**
25 **AVENUE DU MONDE (FR),** ch f Champs Elysees—Marla (GER) **S. Manana**
26 **BARREESH (IRE),** ch c Giant's Causeway (USA)—Astrologie (FR) **Al Shaqab Racing UK Limited**
27 **BASATEEN (IRE),** ch c Teofilo (IRE)—Tasha's Dream (USA) **Hamdan Al Maktoum**
28 **BLACK CHERRY,** b f Mount Nelson—Arctic Char **Mrs E. C. Roberts**
29 **BLUESBREAKER (IRE),** b c Fastnet Rock (AUS)—Jalisco (IRE) **M. Pescod**
30 **BNEDEL (IRE),** b c Teofilo (IRE)—Dance Club (IRE) **Al Shaqab Racing UK Limited**
31 **BURMA BRIDGE,** ro g Avonbridge—Mandalay Lady **C. I. C. Munro**
32 **BURNT SUGAR (IRE),** b c Lope de Vega (IRE)—
Lady Livius (IRE) **China Horse Club (HK) Investment Holdings Limited**
33 **CHEVALLIER,** b g Invincible Spirit (IRE)—Magical Romance (IRE) **Lady Rothschild**
34 **CHICAGO BERE (FR),** b c Peer Gynt (JPN)—Fitness Queen (USA) **Middleham Park Racing LXXXI**
35 **CLASSIC SENIORITY,** b c Kyllachy—Dramatic Solo **Middleham Park Racing LXIII & Mr R. Hannon**
36 **CULLODEN,** b c Kyllachy—Mamounia (IRE) **Ponsonby, Meredith, Maynard, Rice**
37 **DAME LIBERTY (IRE),** ch f Tamayuz—Elizabeth Swann **Mr Michael Cohen & Mr Adam Victor**
38 **DELUXE,** b c Acclamation—Ainia **Mrs J. Wood**
39 **DHARWA,** b f Equiano (FR)—Stoneacre Sarah **Hamdan Al Maktoum**
40 **DIVINE LAW,** ch c Major Cadeaux—Yanomami (USA) **Mrs A. Turner**
41 **ELYSIAN FLYER (IRE),** b c Majestic Missile (IRE)—Starisa (IRE) **The Low Flyers**
42 **EMPERORS WARRIOR (IRE),** ch g Thewayyouare (USA)—World Sprint (GER) **Shark Bay Racing Syndicate II**
43 **FLEETING STRIKE,** b c Acclamation—Cursory **Westward Bloodstock Limited**
44 **FORRES (IRE),** b f Fastnet Rock (AUS)—Slieve **Mrs A. Wigan**
45 **GAYATH (GER),** b c High Chaparral (IRE)—Gallivant **Al Shaqab Racing UK Limited**
46 **GIBEON (IRE),** b c Cape Cross (IRE)—Gravitation **Lady G. De Walden**
47 **HAIL CLODIUS (IRE),** gr c Clodovil (IRE)—Dhairkana (IRE) **Middleham Park Racing LXXXIV**
48 **HEIBA (IRE),** ch c Starspangledbanner (AUS)—Pina Colada **Saleh Al Homaizi & Imad Al Sagar**
49 **HOLLAND PARK,** b c More Than Ready (USA)—B Berry Brandy (USA) **Macdonald, Wright, Creed & Jiggins**
50 **I KNOW,** ch f Archipenko (USA)—I Do **Miss K. Rausing**
51 **IVAWOOD (IRE),** b c Zebedee—Keenes Royale **Westward Bloodstock Limited**
52 **JABEL OF QATAR (USA),** b c Medaglia d'Oro (USA)—
Gotta Have Her (USA) **H.H. Sheikh Mohammed bin Khalifa Al-Thani**
53 **JUPITER CUSTOS (FR),** b br c Le Havre (IRE)—Angel Rose (IRE) **M. Pescod**
54 **KING OF NORMANDY (FR),** ch c Soldier of Fortune (IRE)—Innocent Affair (IRE) **Carmichael Pryde**
55 **KING TO BE (IRE),** b c Myboycharlie (IRE)—Becuille (IRE) **J Palmer-Brown, Potensis Bloodstock, Mrs Ensor**
56 **KOOL KOMPANY (IRE),** br c Jeremy (USA)—Absolutely Cool (IRE) **Kool Kompany Partnership**
57 Ch c Compton Place—Lady Darayna **Mr M. S. Al Shahi**
58 **LAJJAH (IRE),** b f Invincible Spirit (IRE)—Idilic Calm (IRE) **Al Shaqab Racing UK Limited**
59 **LEXINGTON TIMES (IRE),** b c Paco Boy (IRE)—Fuaigh Mor (IRE) **Middleham Park Racing C**
60 **MAFTOON (IRE),** gr c Dark Angel (IRE)—Chincoteague (IRE) **Hamdan Al Maktoum**
61 **MARSH HAWK,** b f Invincible Spirit (IRE)—Asaawir **Rockcliffe Stud**
62 **MISTERIOSO (IRE),** b c Iffraaj—Roystonea **M. Pescod**
63 **MOHEET (IRE),** b c High Chaparral (IRE)—Abunai **Al Shaqab Racing UK Limited**
64 **MUNFARRID,** br g Showcasing—Thankful **Hamdan Al Maktoum**
65 **MUTASAYYID,** ch c Bahamian Bounty—Clear Voice (USA) **Hamdan Al Maktoum**
66 **NAYEL (IRE),** b c Acclamation—Soliza (IRE) **Capri M7**
67 **PEACOCK,** b c Paco Boy (IRE)—Rainbow's Edge **Her Majesty The Queen**
68 **PORT,** b c Hurricane Run (IRE)—Captain's Paradise (IRE) **Mrs J. Wood**
69 **PROPOSED,** b c Invincible Spirit (IRE)—On A Soapbox (USA) **Mrs J. Wood**
70 **REMBRANDT,** b c Dutch Art—Authoritative **Mrs J. Wood**
71 **SAWAAHEL,** b c Pastoral Pursuits—Sheer Indulgence (FR) **Hamdan Al Maktoum**
72 **SHADOW ROCK (IRE),** gr c Verglas (IRE)—Ice Rock (IRE) **Mr M. Daniels**
73 **SHAGAH (IRE),** b f Invincible Spirit (IRE)—Propaganda (IRE) **Al Shaqab Racing UK Limited**
74 **SILVER QUAY (IRE),** gr c Dark Angel (IRE)—She Runs (FR) **Mr H. R. Heffer**
75 **SIRHEED (IRE),** ch c Rip Van Winkle (IRE)—Rozella (IRE) **Al Shaqab Racing UK Limited**
76 **SKI SLOPE,** b f Three Valleys (USA)—Danehurst **Cheveley Park Stud Limited**
77 **SMAIH (GER),** b c Paco Boy (IRE)—Solola (GER) **Al Shaqab Racing UK Limited**
78 **SPICE BOAT,** ch c Shamardal (USA)—Frizzante **Lady Rothschild**
79 **SUITOR,** ch c Dutch Art—Entreat **Cheveley Park Stud Limited**
80 **TAKAHIRO,** b c Kyllachy—Marliana (IRE) **Mr A. A. Alkhallafi**
81 **TAWDEEA,** b c Intikhab (USA)—Sharedah (IRE) **Hamdan Al Maktoum**
82 **THAHAB (IRE),** ch c Dubawi (IRE)—Mise (IRE) **Al Shaqab Racing UK Limited**
83 **TIGGY WIGGY (IRE),** b f Kodiac—Kheleyf's Silver (IRE) **Potensis B'stock, C Giles & Merriebelle**

## MR RICHARD HANNON - Continued

84 **TOHFA (IRE),** ch f Dutch Art—The Fairies Did It (USA) **Saleh Al Homaizi & Imad Al Sagar**
85 **TOM HARK (FR),** ch c Makfi—Raisonable (USA) **J. D. Manley**
86 **TUPI (IRE),** b c Tamayuz—Carioca (IRE) **Michael Kerr-Dineen & Martin Hughes**
87 **VELOCITER (IRE),** ch g Zebedee—Polly Jones (USA) **Middleham Park Racing XCV**
88 **VESNINA,** b f Sea The Stars (IRE)—Safina **Cheveley Park Stud Limited**
89 **WAJEEH (IRE),** ch g Raven's Pass (USA)—Olympic Medal **Al Shaqab Racing UK Limited**
90 **WHO DARES WINS (IRE),** b c Jeremy (USA)—Savignano **W. H. Ponsonby**
91 **WILD TOBACCO,** br c More Than Ready (USA)—Princess Janie (USA) **Rockcliffe Stud**
92 **YA HADE YE DELIL,** br c Raven's Pass (USA)—Palatial **Al Shaqab Racing UK Limited**

## TWO-YEAR-OLDS

93 **AGE OF EMPIRE,** b c 17/2 Royal Applause—Age of Chivalry (IRE) (Invincible Spirit (IRE)) **Rockcliffe Stud**
94 **AGUEROOO (IRE),** b c 13/2 Monsieur Bond (IRE)—
Vision of Peace (IRE) (Invincible Spirit (IRE)) (70000) **Middleham Park Racing LXXXVI**
95 **AJA (IRE),** b f 5/2 Excellent Art—
La Vita E Bella (IRE) (Definite Article) (41000) **Mr Justin Dowley & Mr Michael Pescod**
96 B c 11/2 New Approach (IRE)—Al Joza (Dubawi (IRE)) (50000) **S. Manana**
97 B c 8/4 Authorized (IRE)—
Alamanni (USA) (Elusive Quality (USA)) (110000) **Michael Kerr-Dineen & Martin Hughes**
98 Gr c 9/4 Archipenko (USA)—Alba Stella (Nashwan (USA)) (30000) **Mr W. P. Drew**
99 B f 1/2 Invincible Spirit (IRE)—Albarouche (Sadler's Wells (USA)) **Mrs B. S. Facchino**
100 Gr c 21/3 Zebedee—Alexander Wonder (IRE) (Redback) (65000) **Sheikh J. D. Al Maktoum**
101 **ALSAADEN,** b f 13/2 Acclamation—Bahia Breeze (Mister Baileys) **Hamdan Al Maktoum**
102 B c 1/2 Sea The Stars (IRE)—Alshahbaa (IRE) (Alhaarth (IRE)) (240000) **Al Shaqab Racing UK Limited**
103 **ALTARSHEED (IRE),** b c 23/2 Lilbourne Lad (IRE)—
Lilakiya (IRE) (Dr Fong (USA)) (100000) **Hamdan Al Maktoum**
104 B c 30/3 Arakan (USA)—Ambonnay (Ashkalani (IRE)) (7619) **Mrs J. Wood**
105 B c 6/3 Rip Van Winkle (IRE)—Amhooj (Green Desert (USA)) (119047) **Al Shaqab Racing UK Limited**
106 **ATLANTIC SUN,** b c 15/2 Roderic O'Connor (IRE)—
Robema (Cadeaux Genereux) (49523) **Middleham Park Racing XLV**
107 B c 21/4 Canford Cliffs (IRE)—Attracted To You (IRE) (Hurricane Run (IRE)) **Mr M. S. Al Shahi**
108 **BAG OF DIAMONDS,** b c 8/3 Lilbourne Lad (IRE)—
Milnagavie (Tobougg (IRE)) (30000) **Stables Of The Burning Man**
109 B c 30/3 Dutch Art—Balalaika (Sadler's Wells (USA)) (75000) **Mr A. Jaber**
110 B c 25/3 Monsun (GER)—Baselga (GER) (Second Set (IRE)) (61111) **Unregistered Partnership**
111 B c 27/2 Canford Cliffs (IRE)—Before The Storm (Sadler's Wells (USA)) (60000) **M. Tabor**
112 B c 17/1 Dream Ahead (USA)—Belle Masquee (IRE) (Oratorio (IRE)) (67460) **M Hughes & M Kerr-Dineen**
113 B c 28/2 Dream Ahead (USA)—Blissful Beat (Beat Hollow) (198412) **Al Shaqab Racing UK Limited**
114 **BOYCIE,** b c 16/3 Paco Boy (IRE)—Eve (Rainbow Quest (USA)) (12000) **Mrs V Hubbard & Mr K T Ivory**
115 **BREAK FREE,** b f 22/1 Oasis Dream—Penny's Gift (Tobougg (IRE)) **Rockcliffe Stud**
116 B c 19/1 Canford Cliffs (IRE)—Bright Sapphire (IRE) (Galileo (IRE)) (270000) **Westward Bloodstock Limited**
117 **BURNINGFIVERS (IRE),** b c 4/4 Paco Boy (IRE)—
All Embracing (IRE) (Night Shift (USA)) (38095) **Mr M. F. Geoghegan**
118 **CANFORD CROSSING (IRE),** b c 10/1 Canford Cliffs (IRE)—Smartest (IRE) (Exceed And Excel (AUS)) (45000)
119 Ch c 9/3 Giant's Causeway (USA)—Canterbury Lace (USA) (Danehill (USA))
120 B c 29/3 Zoffany (IRE)—Chameleon (Green Desert (USA)) (114285) **Westward Bloodstock Limited**
121 **CHARLOTTE ROYALE (IRE),** gr f 21/1 Zoffany (IRE)—
Lady Gray (IRE) (High Chaparral (IRE)) (27777) **De La Warr Racing**
122 **CITY BY THE BAY,** b c 2/4 Myboycharlie (IRE)—
October Winds (USA) (Irish River (FR)) (21428) **Middleham Park Racing LXXVII & Mr R Hannon**
123 Ch c 15/3 Kyllachy—Clear Voice (USA) (Cryptoclearance (USA)) (70000) **Malih L. Al Basti**
124 Gr c 7/2 Exceed And Excel (AUS)—Comeback Queen (Nayef (USA)) (240000) **Al Shaqab Racing UK Limited**
125 **DALGARNO (FR),** b c 17/2 Sea The Stars (IRE)—
Jakonda (USA) (Kingmambo (USA)) (297619) **Westward Bloodstock Limited**
126 **DANEHILL KODIAC (IRE),** b c 6/4 Kodiac—Meadow (Green Desert (USA)) (28571) **R. Hannon**
127 B f 1/3 Arcano (IRE)—Danetime Out (IRE) (Danetime (IRE)) **Al Shaqab Racing UK Limited**
128 B f 9/1 Canford Cliffs (IRE)—Distant Skies (Tiger Hill (IRE)) (45000) **Coriolan Partnership**
129 **DUTCH TREATY,** ch f 15/3 Dutch Art—Entreat (Pivotal) **Cheveley Park Stud Limited**
130 **EFRON (IRE),** b c 29/1 Frozen Power (IRE)—Ribald (Alhaarth (IRE)) (24761) **Mr W. A. Tinkler**
131 **EJAAZAH (IRE),** b f 14/5 Acclamation—
English Ballet (IRE) (Danehill Dancer (IRE)) (91269) **Hamdan Al Maktoum**
132 B c 16/2 Elnadim (USA)—Eliza Doolittle (Royal Applause) (31745) **Mr M. S. Al Shahi**
133 B f 25/3 Canford Cliffs (IRE)—Elusive Galaxy (IRE) (Elusive City (USA)) (99206) **M. Tabor**
134 Ch f 21/4 Rip Van Winkle (IRE)—Faithful Duchess (IRE) (Bachelor Duke (USA)) **Mrs J. Wood**
135 B f 22/2 Holy Roman Emperor (IRE)—Folle Blanche (USA) (Elusive Quality (USA)) (63491) **Mrs F. H. Hay**

## MR RICHARD HANNON - Continued

**136** B gr f 6/4 Paco Boy (IRE)—Galapagar (USA) (Miswaki (USA)) (75000) **Sheikh J. D. Al Maktoum**
**137** B c 27/3 Oasis Dream—Generous Lady (Generous (IRE)) (185000) **Al Shaqab Racing UK Limited**
**138 GREAT PAGE (IRE),** b f 16/1 Roderic O'Connor (IRE)—
Areeda (IRE) (Refuse To Bend (IRE)) (27777) **Middleham Park Racing LXXVIII**
**139** B f 20/1 Kodiac—Greenflash (Green Desert (USA)) **Mrs J. Wood**
**140 GUAPO BAY,** b f 1/2 Showcasing—Cumana Bay (Dansili) **J. R. Shannon**
**141 HADLEY,** b c 29/4 Royal Applause—Brush Strokes (Cadeaux Genereux) (15238) **B. Bull**
**142** B c 21/4 Vale of York (IRE)—Handsome Anna (IRE) (Bigstone (IRE)) **Mrs J. Wood**
**143** B c 2/2 Lilbourne Lad (IRE)—Heavenly Quest (IRE) (Dubawi (IRE)) (71428)
**144 HERRIDGE (IRE),** ch f 29/4 Bahamian Bounty—
Quickstyx (Night Shift (USA)) (30000) **Norman Woodcock & Barry Bull**
**145** Ch c 23/2 Monsieur Bond (IRE)—Honesty Pays (Dr Fong (USA)) (16190) **Mrs J. K. Powell**
**146 HUMPHREY BOGART (IRE),** b c 4/4 Tagula (IRE)—
Hazarama (IRE) (Kahyasi) (31428) **Chelsea Thoroughbreds - Saint Tropez**
**147** B c 3/3 Monsieur Bond (IRE)—Icing (Polar Falcon (USA)) (36190) **Mr R. W. Tyrrell**
**148 ILLUMINATE (IRE),** b f 13/2 Zoffany (IRE)—
Queen of Stars (USA) (Green Desert (USA)) (90476) **Denford Stud Limited**
**149 IN THE RED (IRE),** b c 1/3 Elusive Pimpernel (USA)—Roses From Ridey (IRE) (Petorius) (34285)
**150** B c 10/3 Fastnet Rock (AUS)—Interlace (Pivotal) (42000) **Carmichael Pryde**
**151** B c 14/3 Champs Elysees—Island Vista (Montjeu (IRE)) (55000) **Macdonald, Wright, Creed, Jiggins & Miller**
**152** Ro c 28/4 Zebedee—Jalmira (IRE) (Danehill Dancer (IRE)) (62000) **R. Morecombe, D. Anderson, M. Hughes**
**153 KESSELRING,** ch c 22/4 New Approach (IRE)—Anna Oleanda (IRE) (Old Vic) (90000) **R. J. McCreery**
**154** B f 24/3 Lilbourne Lad (IRE)—Khatela (IRE) (Shernazar) (59523)
**155** B c 9/5 Zebedee—Kiva (Indian Ridge) (133333) **Westward Bloodstock Limited**
**156** B c 7/4 Canford Cliffs (IRE)—Lady Links (Bahamian Bounty) (55000)
**157 LEXINGTON LAW (IRE),** b c 25/2 Lawman (FR)—
Tus Nua (IRE) (Galileo (IRE)) (45000) **Unregistered Partnership**
**158 LIGHT INFANTRY (IRE),** ch c 7/3 Fast Company (IRE)—
Convidada (IRE) (Trans Island) (45238) **Mr Michael Pescod & Mr Justin Dowley**
**159** Ch c 29/3 Paco Boy (IRE)—Lilli Marlane (Sri Pekan (USA)) (65000) **S. Manana**
**160** B f 27/1 Iffraaj—Love Intrigue (IRE) (Marju (IRE)) (55000) **S. H. Altayer**
**161** Br f 19/4 Poet's Voice—Lucky Token (IRE) (Key of Luck (USA)) (115000) **Malih L. Al Basti**
**162** B c 2/4 Zebedee—Luvmedo (IRE) (One Cool Cat (USA)) **Mrs J. Wood**
**163** B f 9/4 Kodiac—Ma Vie En Rose (IRE) (Red Ransom (USA)) (7619) **Mrs J. Wood**
**164 MADRINHO (IRE),** ch c 24/2 Frozen Power (IRE)—
Perfectly Clear (USA) (Woodman (USA)) (52380) **Mr M. F. Geoghegan**
**165 MANAAFIDH (IRE),** b c 19/2 Zebedee—Starring (FR) (Ashkalani (IRE)) (261904) **Hamdan Al Maktoum**
**166 MANSOOB,** ch c 2/5 Paco Boy (IRE)—Descriptive (IRE) (Desert King (IRE)) (280000) **Hamdan Al Maktoum**
**167 MARENKO,** b f 7/3 Exceed And Excel (AUS)—Safina (Pivotal) **Cheveley Park Stud Limited**
**168** B c 17/3 Alfred Nobel (IRE)—Margaret's Dream (IRE) (Muhtarram (USA)) **Mrs J. Wood**
**169 MAWTHOOQ (IRE),** br c 13/3 Arcano (IRE)—Miss Corinne (Mark of Esteem (IRE)) **Hamdan Al Maktoum**
**170** B c 21/2 Air Chief Marshal (IRE)—Maya de La Luz (Selkirk (USA)) (11428) **Mrs J. K. Powell**
**171** B c 10/4 Rip Van Winkle (IRE)—Maybe I Will (IRE) (Hawk Wing (USA)) (10476) **Mrs J. Wood**
**172** B f 16/2 Fast Company (IRE)—Mean Lae (IRE) (Johannesburg (USA)) **Mrs J. Wood**
**173** B f 16/3 More Than Ready (USA)—
Medal Winner (USA) (Medaglia d'Oro (USA)) (45000) **Des Anderson & Ben Keswick**
**174** B f 15/3 Kodiac—Miss Chaumiere (Selkirk (USA)) (72000) **Mrs J. K. Powell**
**175** B c 24/2 Dream Ahead (USA)—Miss Chaussini (IRE) (Rossini (USA)) (42000) **Mr M. S. Al Shahi**
**176** B c 6/3 Dick Turpin (IRE)—Mookhlesa (Marju (IRE)) (70000) **Al Shaqab Racing UK Limited**
**177** B f 3/5 Cacique (IRE)—Moonlight Mystery (Pivotal) (160000)
**178** Ch c 27/2 Makfi—Mpumalanga (Observatory (USA)) (23000) **Mr D. P. N. Brown**
**179** Ch c 11/3 Sakhee's Secret—Nevada Princess (IRE) (Desert Prince (IRE)) (24761) **Merriebelle Irish Farm Limited**
**180 OH THIS IS US (IRE),** b c 12/3 Acclamation—Shamwari Lodge (IRE) (Hawk Wing (USA)) (87300) **Team Wallop**
**181** B c 7/1 Acclamation—Olympic Medal (Nayef (USA)) (80000) **Sheikh J. D. Al Maktoum**
**182** B c 7/4 Kyllachy—Orange Pip (Bold Edge) **Lady Whent**
**183 OUT OF THE DARK (IRE),** b f 20/2 Kyllachy—
Assumption (IRE) (Beckett (IRE)) (72000) **Mrs Boocock, Mrs Doyle, Mr Barry**
**184 OWER FLY,** b c 8/4 Pastoral Pursuits—Contrary Mary (Mujadil (USA)) (952) **A. Pitt**
**185** B f 5/3 Kodiac—Pale Light (USA) (Lemon Drop Kid (USA)) **Mrs J. Wood**
**186 PAPA LUIGI (IRE),** b c 18/4 Zoffany (IRE)—
Namaadhej (USA) (Swain (IRE)) (67460) **Middleham Park Racing XLVIII**
**187 PATENT,** b c 4/5 Paco Boy (IRE)—Film Script (Unfuwain (USA)) **Her Majesty The Queen**
**188** Ch f 19/4 Equiano (FR)—Path of Peace (Rock of Gibraltar (IRE)) (20000) **Miss I. Keogh**
**189 PERFORMER,** b f 23/3 New Approach (IRE)—Annalina (USA) (Cozzene (USA)) **Denford Stud Limited**

## MR RICHARD HANNON - Continued

**190 PHANTOM FLIPPER,** ch c 10/3 Bahamian Bounty—Artistic License (IRE) (Chevalier (IRE)) (43809) **Middleham Park Racing XCIII**
**191** B c 3/3 Sakhee's Secret—Phoenix Rising (Dr Fong (USA)) (10000) **Westward Bloodstock Limited**
**192** B c 28/2 Dream Ahead (USA)—Poppy Seed (Bold Edge) (123809) **Saleh Al Homaizi & Imad Al Sagar**
**193 PRESS GANG,** b c 5/2 Mount Nelson—Rutba (Act One) (57142) **M. Pescod**
**194** Gr c 10/4 Zebedee—Prime Time Girl (Primo Dominie) (80000) **Amanda Turner, Martin Clarke, Jim Jeffries**
**195** B f 9/3 Zoffany (IRE)—Promise of Love (Royal Applause) (95238) **R. Hannon**
**196 RACQUET,** b c 10/4 Pastoral Pursuits—Billie Jean (Bertolini (USA)) (12380) **Pall Mall Partners & Partner**
**197** B f 30/3 Acclamation—Raja (IRE) (Pivotal) **Al Shaqab Racing UK Limited**
**198** B f 27/4 Kodiac—Red Remanso (IRE) (Redback) (38095) **Mr M. A. A. Al-Mannai**
**199 RING OF TRUTH,** b f 27/4 Royal Applause—Spinning Top (Alzao (USA)) **Her Majesty The Queen**
**200 RISING SUNSHINE (IRE),** b c 26/3 Dark Angel (IRE)—Little Audio (IRE) (Shamardal (USA)) (95238) **Middleham Park Racing LXXXVIII**
**201 ROCOCOA (IRE),** b f 5/4 Zebedee—Nightbird (IRE) (Night Shift (USA)) (36190) **Elaine Chivers & Merlin Racing**
**202** B f 9/3 Dark Angel (IRE)—Rose of Battle (Averti (IRE)) (50000) **S. Manana**
**203** B c 5/3 Dandy Man (IRE)—Roskeen (IRE) (Grand Lodge (USA)) (57142) **Saleh Al Homaizi & Imad Al Sagar**
**204** B c 4/2 Paco Boy (IRE)—Royal Circles (Royal Applause) (19047) **Mrs J K Powell & Mr D. F. Powell**
**205** B c 14/3 Exceed And Excel (AUS)—Ruse (Diktat) (230000) **Al Shaqab Racing UK Limited**
**206** B c 8/2 Arcano (IRE)—Sally Wood (CAN) (Woodman (USA)) (41904) **Mr K. M. Al Attiyah**
**207** Gr f 26/3 Dark Angel (IRE)—Salt Rose (Sleeping Indian) (78000) **Sheikh J. D. Al Maktoum**
**208** Gr f 1/4 Dark Angel (IRE)—Screen Legend (IRE) (Invincible Spirit (IRE)) (31746)
**209** B c 12/4 Starspangledbanner (AUS)—Shaanbar (IRE) (Darshaan) (79364) **Al Shaqab Racing UK Limited**
**210 SHAWAAHID (IRE),** b c 20/4 Elnadim (USA)—Vexatious (IRE) (Shamardal (USA)) (100000) **Hamdan Al Maktoum**
**211 SHE'S ALL MINE,** b f 17/3 Sakhee's Secret—I'm All Yours (IRE) (High Chaparral (IRE)) **Mrs Caroline Cooper & Mr J Palmer-Brown**
**212 SIGNE (IRE),** b f 5/4 Sea The Stars (IRE)—Green Room (USA) (Theatrical) (873015) **Westward Bloodstock Limited**
**213** Br c 6/3 Dark Angel (IRE)—Sing Acapella (IRE) (Cape Cross (IRE)) (70000) **S. Suhail**
**214 SKY OF STARS (IRE),** b c 1/2 Frozen Power (IRE)—So So Lucky (IRE) (Danehill (USA)) (71428) **Elaine Chivers & Mr W P Drew**
**215** B c 28/3 High Chaparral (IRE)—Slow Sand (USA) (Dixieland Band (USA)) **Al Shaqab Racing UK Limited**
**216** B f 20/5 Lord Shanakill (USA)—So Sweet (IRE) (Cape Cross (IRE)) **Mrs J. Wood**
**217 SOMERS LAD (IRE),** b c 24/2 Lilbourne Lad (IRE)—Somaggia (IRE) (Desert King (IRE)) (55238) **Mrs A. Williams**
**218 SPATCHCOCK,** b c 26/4 Dutch Art—Lady Hen (Efisio) (78000) **M Hughes, D Anderson, R Morecombe**
**219** Ch f 22/1 Pivotal—Srda (USA) (Kingmambo (USA)) (50000) **S. Manana**
**220 STEEL OF MADRID (IRE),** b c 6/4 Lope de Vega (IRE)—Bibury (Royal Applause) (120000) **M. Pescod**
**221** B f 4/3 Acclamation—Street Style (IRE) (Rock of Gibraltar (IRE)) **Al Shaqab Racing UK Limited**
**222 SUQOOR,** b c 5/4 Equiano (FR)—Ukraine (IRE) (Cape Cross (IRE)) (49000) **Hamdan Al Maktoum**
**223** B c 31/1 Starspangledbanner (AUS)—Szabo (IRE) (Anabaa (USA)) (260000) **Al Shaqab Racing UK Limited**
**224 TABARRAK (IRE),** b c 22/1 Acclamation—Bahati (IRE) (Intikhab (USA)) (171428) **Hamdan Al Maktoum**
**225 TADAAWOL,** b c 13/4 Kyllachy—Bright Edge (Danehill Dancer (IRE)) (78095) **Hamdan Al Maktoum**
**226** B c 12/2 Paco Boy (IRE)—Tanwir (Unfuwain (USA)) **The Calvera Partnership No. 2**
**227 TAQWAA (IRE),** ch c 19/3 Iffraaj—Hallowed Park (IRE) (Barathea (IRE)) (140000) **Hamdan Al Maktoum**
**228 TARAABUT (IRE),** b c 31/3 Lilbourne Lad (IRE)—Cuilaphuca (IRE) (Danetime (IRE)) (123809) **Hamdan Al Maktoum**
**229 TASKEEN (IRE),** b c 21/2 Lilbourne Lad (IRE)—Lola Rosa (IRE) (Peintre Celebre (USA)) (140000) **Hamdan Al Maktoum**
**230 TERRAPLANE (IRE),** b f 13/3 Bushranger (IRE)—Sheer Glamour (IRE) (Peintre Celebre (USA)) (11904) **Mr Justin Dowley & Mr Michael Pescod**
**231** Br f 7/2 Dansili—Thai Haku (IRE) (Oasis Dream) (380952) **Al Shaqab Racing UK Limited**
**232** B c 2/2 Iffraaj—Through The Forest (USA) (Forestry (USA)) (120000) **S. Suhail**
**233** B f 29/1 Dark Angel (IRE)—Timbre (Dubai Destination (USA)) (35714)
**234 TOLEDO,** b c 21/3 Exceed And Excel (AUS)—Alovera (IRE) (King's Best (USA)) **Rockcliffe Stud**
**235 TONY CURTIS,** b c 23/3 Rock of Gibraltar (IRE)—Strawberry Lolly (Lomitas) (48000) **Chelsea Thoroughbreds - Saint Tropez**
**236 TORMENT,** bl gr c 9/3 Dark Angel (IRE)—Selkirk Sky (Selkirk (USA)) (160000) **Highclere T'Bred Racing (Palmerston)**
**237** B f 19/3 Dream Ahead (USA)—Traou Mad (IRE) (Barathea (IRE)) **Merriebelle Irish Farm Limited**
**238** B c 10/4 High Chaparral (IRE)—Ursula Minor (IRE) (Footstepsinthesand) (200000) **Al Shaqab Racing UK Limited**
**239** B c 20/3 Canford Cliffs (IRE)—Venetian Rhapsody (IRE) (Galileo (IRE)) (62000) **Mr H. R. Heffer**
**240 VENTURA FALCON (IRE),** b f 14/3 Excellent Art—Danish Gem (Danehill (USA)) (91269) **Middleham Park Racing LI**
**241 VIREN'S ARMY (IRE),** b c 17/1 Twirling Candy (USA)—Blue Angel (IRE) (Oratorio (IRE)) (91269)

## MR RICHARD HANNON - Continued

**242 WAR WHISPER (IRE),** b c 19/2 Royal Applause—Featherweight (IRE) (Fantastic Light (USA)) (91269) **Mr M. Daniels**
**243 WINDSWEPT,** b f 20/2 Kyllachy—Westerly Air (USA) (Gone West (USA)) **Cheveley Park Stud Limited**
**244 WISHSONG,** b f 9/3 Dansili—Princess Janie (USA) (Elusive Quality (USA)) **Rockcliffe Stud**
**245** B c 30/3 Elusive Pimpernel (USA)—Zeena (Unfuwain (USA)) (24761) **Mr W. P. Drew**

**Other Owners:** Ms H. Abdella, Princess M. Al Saud, I. J. Al-Sagar, Mr D. J. Anderson, Mr R. B. Antell, Exors of the Late Mr D. W. Barker, Mr D. Barrett, D. J. Barry, Mr R. A. Bevan, Mr D. Bickerton, Mr P. A. Bland, Mrs K. C. Boocock, Mr R. J. Bryan, Mr J. A. Bryan, Ms J. S. Butlin, Mrs F. J. Carmichael, Chelsea Thoroughbreds Ltd, Ms E. C. Chivers, Ms L. D. Chivers, Miss C. I. Chivers, Mr M. Clarke, D. D. Clee, Mrs J. P. Clee, Mr M. L. Cohen, Mrs C. A. Cooper, Mr A. J. Dann, Lord De La Warr, Countess De La Warr, Mr P. E. Done, Mr L. J. Dowley, Mrs A. M. Doyle, Mrs S. Ensor, Mr D. Fenn, Sir A. Ferguson, Mr S. J. Finch, Mr C. M. Giles, Mr P. M. Goldsmith, Mr J. S. Gutkin, R. V. Harding, S. Hassiakos, Mr R. P. Heffer, The Hon H. M. Herbert, P. Hickey, Highclere Thoroughbred Racing Ltd, R. G. Hitchcock, Saleh Al Homaizi, Mr T. G. Horley, Mrs V. Hubbard, Mr M. B. Hughes, K. T. Ivory, Mr J. Jeffries, Mr J. Jenner, M. Kerr-Dineen, Mr S. L. Keswick, Mr B. W. Keswick, A. S. Kilpatrick, A. E. King, Mr S. Leech, Mr A. T. Macdonald, Mr C. H. Madden, G. A. Mason, R. L. Maynard, Mrs M. F. Meredith, Mr I. D. Miller, R. H. W. Morecombe, Mr D. Murray, Mr G. O'Sullivan, Mr J. Pak, T. S. Palin, J. Palmer-Brown, O. J. W. Pawle, Mrs J. Plumptre, Potensis Bloodstock Limited, D. F. Powell, M. Prince, D. G. Pryde, Mrs G. E. Purkiss-Miles, Mr T. J. Ramsden, Mr W. A. Rice, R. A. Simmons, Mrs A. C. Simmons, Mr A. R. Skeites, Mr K. P. Skeites, Mr J. A. B. Stafford, Mr A. Victor, Mr M. K. Webb, Mr N. Werrett, Mr T. Withers, N. A. Woodcock, C. N. Wright.

**Jockey (flat):** Richard Hughes, Pat Dobbs, Sean Levey, Ryan Moore, Dane O'Neill, Kieran O'Neill.
**Apprentice:** Cam Hardie, Tom Marquand, Josh Quinn.

---

## 277 MR GEOFFREY HARKER, Thirsk

Postal: **Stockhill Green, York Rd, Thirkelby, Thirsk, North Yorkshire, YO7 3AS**
Contacts: **PHONE (01845) 501117 FAX (01845) 501614 MOBILE (07803) 116412/(07930) 125544 E-MAIL gandjhome@aol.com**

1 **BLING KING,** 6, b g Haafhd—Bling Bling (IRE) **P. I. Harker**
2 **BRANSTON JUBILEE,** 5, ch m Assertive—Branston Jewel (IRE) **G. A. Harker**
3 **CABAL,** 8, br m Kyllachy—Secret Flame **P. I. Harker**
4 **CONJOLA,** 8, b m Grape Tree Road—Conchita **Miss R. G. Brewis**
5 **COROLYNN,** 6, b m Grape Tree Road—Conchita **Miss R. G. Brewis**
6 **DABUKI (FR),** 5, b g Desert Style (IRE)—Semenova (FR) **Mr J Blackburn & Mr A Turton**
7 **JUDICIOUS,** 8, ch g Pivotal—Virtuous **Mr M. Reay**
8 **MISTY EYES,** 6, b m Byron—Wax Eloquent **Haven Stud Partnership**
9 **MOCCASIN (FR),** 6, b g Green Tune (USA)—Museum Piece **The Crazy Gang**
10 **QUITE SPARKY,** 8, b g Lucky Story (USA)—Imperialistic (IRE) **P. I. Harker**
11 **SHAMAHEART (IRE),** 5, b g Shamardal (USA)—Encouragement **A. S. Ward**
12 **TARTAN GIGHA (IRE),** 10, b g Green Desert (USA)—High Standard **A. S. Ward**
13 **WANNABE KING,** 9, b g King's Best (USA)—Wannabe Grand (IRE) **J. Binks**

**Other Owners:** J. N. Blackburn, Mr G. Burgess, Mrs P. L. Burgess, Mr N. Burns, Mr J. Clydesdale, Mr M. D. Fowler, Mr S. M. Taylor, Mr A. Turton.

**Assistant Trainer:** Jenny Harker

**Jockey (NH):** W. T. Kennedy. **Apprentice:** Jordan Nason.

---

## 278 MR W. HARNEY, Co. Tipperary

Postal: **Manna Cottage, Templemore, Co. Tipperary, Ireland**
Contacts: **PHONE (00353) 504 31534 FAX (00353) 504 31534 MOBILE (00353) 86 2498836 E-MAIL harneyvet@eircom.net**

1 4, Ch g Indian River (FR)—Ballyburn Lady (IRE) **Patrick Harney & Liam Breslin**
2 4, B g Tobougg (IRE)—First Katoune (FR) **Mrs W. Harney**
3 **FISCAL NOMAD (IRE),** 8, b g Flemensfirth (USA)—Tradaree (IRE) **Patrick Harney**
4 **GANDHI (IRE),** 5, b g Indian River (FR)—French Class **Mrs W. Harney**
5 **JOXER (IRE),** 8, b g Gold Well—Tender Return (IRE) **Mrs W. Harney**
6 **KILLTILANE ROSE (IRE),** 10, ch m Flemensfirth (USA)—Miss Rose (IRE) **Mrs W. Harney**
7 **ROBBINA (IRE),** 5, br m Robin des Champs (FR)—Sorrentina (IRE) **Mrs W. Harney**

## MR W. HARNEY - Continued

8 4, Br f Dubai Destination (USA)—Sorrentina (IRE) **Ms I. M. Fielding**
9 **THE CONKER CLUB (IRE),** 9, ch m Beneficial—Puff of Magic (IRE) **Old Port Syndicate**
10 4, B g Indian River (FR)—Wimbledonian **Patrick Harney & Liam Breslin**

**Assistant Trainer:** Rachel Harney

**Jockey (NH):** Bryan J. Cooper. **Conditional:** F. J. Hayes.

---

## 279 MR RICHARD HARPER, Banbury

Postal: **Home Farm, Kings Sutton, Banbury, Oxfordshire, OX17 3RS**
Contacts: **PHONE (01295) 810997 FAX (01295) 812787 MOBILE (07970) 223481**
**E-MAIL rharper@freeuk.com**

1 **CHAPEL HOUSE,** 12, b g Beneficial—My Moona **R. C. Harper**
2 **JUST SKITTLES,** 7, b g Storming Home—Miss Roberto (IRE) **R. C. Harper**
3 **TOP BENEFIT (IRE),** 13, gr g Beneficial—Cottage Lass (IRE) **R. C. Harper**

**Assistant Trainer:** C. Harper

---

## 280 MRS JESSICA HARRINGTON, Kildare

Postal: **Commonstown Stud, Moone, Co. Kildare, Ireland**
Contacts: **PHONE (00353) 5986 24153 FAX (00353) 5986 24292 MOBILE (00353) 8725 66129**
**E-MAIL jessica@jessicaharringtonracing.com WEBSITE www.jessicaharringtonracing.com**

1 **ANNIE OAKLEY (IRE),** 7, br b m Westerner—Gaye Artiste (IRE) **Mrs Gina Galvin**
2 **BELLE OF THE MOOR (IRE),** 6, b m King's Theatre (IRE)—Tempest Belle (IRE) **Mr Steve Hemstock**
3 **BLUE OWEN (IRE),** 6, b g Blueprint (IRE)—Princess Sheena (IRE) **Mr John Percy Griffin**
4 **BRIGHT TOMORROW (IRE),** 4, b g Robin des Pres (FR)—
Gweedara (IRE) **Mr Michael Buckley, Mr J. Carthy, Mr M. O'Neill**
5 **BURN AND TURN (IRE),** 9, b m Flemensfirth (USA)—Pescetto Lady (IRE) **Mr Joe O'Flaherty**
6 **CAILIN ANNAMH (IRE),** 7, b m Definite Article—Prairie Bell (IRE) **The Flyers Syndicate**
7 **CANDLESTICK (IRE),** 4, b g Scorpion (IRE)—Pescetto Lady (IRE) **Mr Brian Acheson**
8 **CELTIC NOBILITY (IRE),** 5, b g Celtic Swing—Noble Choice **Whole Of The Moone Syndicate**
9 **CHITTER CHATTER (IRE),** 5, b br m Robin des Pres (FR)—The Keane Edge (IRE) **Macs J Syndicate**
10 **DON'T TOUCH IT (IRE),** 5, b g Scorpion (IRE)—
Shandora (IRE) **David Reid Scott, Lynch Bages, Mr Justin Carthy & Partners**
11 **ETESIAN (IRE),** 5, b m Shirocco (GER)—True Crystal (IRE) **A Blessing In Disguise Partnership**
12 **FLAVIANA (IRE),** 5, b m Flemensfirth (USA)—Saddlers Green (IRE) **Mr Roberto Rea**
13 **GIMLI'S VOYAGE (IRE),** 5, b g Stowaway—Rathturtin Brief (IRE) **Mr Geoffrey Ruddock**
14 **GREEN ALLIGATOR (IRE),** 6, b g Diamond Green (FR)—In Denial (IRE) **Mr Jarlath Smyth**
15 **HIGH STRATOS,** 6, b g Montjeu (IRE)—Hyabella **Westerwood Global Ltd**
16 **HOLY WATER (IRE),** 4, b g Holy Roman Emperor (IRE)—Gambling Spirit **Port and Brandy Syndicate**
17 **HURRICANE RIDGE (IRE),** 6, b g Hurricane Run (IRE)—Warrior Wings **Lakeside Syndicate**
18 4, B g Fleetwood (IRE)—Inver Lady (IRE) **Commonstown Racing Stables Ltd**
19 4, B g Milan—Jade River (FR) **Lynch Bages, J. Carthy, Orpendale**
20 **JETSON (IRE),** 10, b g Oscar (IRE)—La Noire (IRE) **Mr Gerard McGrath**
21 **JETT (IRE),** 4, b g Flemensfirth (USA)—La Noire (IRE) **Mr Gerard McGrath**
22 **JEZKI (IRE),** 7, b g Milan—La Noire (IRE) **Mr J. P. McManus**
23 **KABJOY (IRE),** 4, b f Intikhab (USA)—Lunar Love (IRE) **Favourite Racing Ltd**
24 **KEPPOLS QUEEN (IRE),** 7, br m Indian River (FR)—Keppols Princess (IRE) **Mrs Mona O'Loughlin**
25 **LADY BRADLEY (IRE),** 5, b m Robin des Champs (FR)—Sweet Liss (IRE) **Mr Steve Hemstock**
26 **LOUGH LASS (IRE),** 6, b m Kayf Tara—Gazza's Girl (IRE) **Mr Arthur McCooey**
27 **MACNICHOLSON (IRE),** 6, b g Definite Article—Heroic Performer (IRE) **Mr Joe O'Flaherty**
28 **MADAME DES CHAMPS (IRE),** 5, ch m Robin des Champs (FR)—
Callherwhatulike (IRE) **Commonstown Racing Stables Ltd**
29 4, B g Milan—Majorite Bleue (FR) **Mr Brian Acheson**
30 **MODEM,** 5, b g Motivator—Alashaan **Mr Turlough Blessing**
31 **MR FIFTYONE (IRE),** 6, b g Jeremy (USA)—Maka (USA) **Mr David Bobbet**
32 **NEVERUSHACON (IRE),** 4, b g Echo of Light—Lily Beth (IRE) **Mr R. Galway**
33 4, B g Presenting—Northwood May **Favourite Racing Ltd**
34 **ODE TO PSYCHE (IRE),** 4, b f Dansili—Quan Yin (IRE) **Flaxman Stables Ireland Ltd**
35 **OSEZ JOSEPHINE (IRE),** 4, b f Let The Lion Roar—Line Grey (FR) **MD Bloodstock & Pegasus Farms Ltd**

## MRS JESSICA HARRINGTON - Continued

**36 PAINTED LADY (IRE),** 6, b m Presenting—Amathea (FR) **Mr Steve Hemstock & Commonstown Racing Stables Ltd**
**37 PHANTOM PRINCE (IRE),** 6, b g Jeremy (USA)—Phantom Waters **Mr Con Harrington**
**38 PRINCESS ALOOF (IRE),** 4, b f Big Bad Bob (IRE)—Little Miss Diva (IRE) **Commonstown Racing Stables Ltd**
**39 PROS 'N' CONS (IRE),** 5, br m Presenting—Cut 'n' Run (IRE) **Mr Elder Scouller**
**40 RAE'S CREEK,** 5, ch g New Approach (IRE)—All's Forgotten (USA) **Mr J. P. McManus**
**41 ROCK ON THE MOOR (IRE),** 7, b m Flemensfirth (USA)—Home At Last (IRE) **Mr Steve Hemstock**
**42 ROCK THE WORLD (IRE),** 7, b g Orpen (USA)—Sue N Win (IRE) **Mr Michael Buckley & Mr Justin Carthy**
**43 SADLER'SFLAURE (FR),** 9, b g Ballingarry (IRE)—Flaurella (FR) **Pegasus Farms Ltd**
**44 SANDYMOUNT DUKE (IRE),** 6, ch g Hernando (FR)—Joleah (IRE) **Mr Ron Wood**
**45** 4, B f Presenting—Seymourswift **Mr George Hartigan**
**46 SIN MIEDO (IRE),** 5, br g Intikhab (USA)—Xaviera (IRE) **Commonstown Racing Stables Ltd**
**47 SIXTEEN AGAIN (IRE),** 5, gr m Amadeus Wolf—Remiss (IRE) **Mr Geoffrey Ruddock**
**48 STEPS TO FREEDOM (IRE),** 9, b g Statue of Liberty (USA)—Dhakhirah (IRE) **Mrs Elizabeth Hussey**
**49 THERE YOU GO (IRE),** 4, b g Milan—Cuiloge Lady (IRE) **Mr J. P. McManus**
**50 TRI NA CEILE (IRE),** 5, ch m Galileo (IRE)—Pescia (IRE) **Mr J. P. McManus**
**51 TTEBBOB (IRE),** 6, b g Milan—Our Dream (IRE) **Mr David Bobbett**
**52 TWINKLETOES (IRE),** 4, gr f Daylami (IRE)—Cool N Calm **Commonstown Racing Stables Ltd**
**53 WALK TO FREEDOM (IRE),** 5, br g Arcadio (GER)—Carryonharriet (IRE) **Whole Of The Moone Syndicate**
**54 WOODLAND OPERA (IRE),** 5, br g Robin des Champs (FR)—Opera Hat (IRE) **Mrs Diana Cooper, Mrs Valerie Cooper & Mrs Carolyn Waters**

## THREE-YEAR-OLDS

**55 BARNACLE BILL (IRE),** gr c Big Bad Bob (IRE)—Katch Me Katie **Millhouse LLC**
**56 BOB'S THE BUSINESS (IRE),** b g Big Bad Bob (IRE)—Danzelline **Anamoine Ltd**
**57 BOCCA BACIATA (IRE),** b br f Big Bad Bob (IRE)—Sovana (IRE) **Flaxman Stables Ireland Ltd**
**58 BOLD BID (IRE),** b g Big Bad Bob (IRE)—Magpie (USA) **Commonstown Racing Stables Ltd**
**59 BOOM BOX (IRE),** b g Big Bad Bob (IRE)—Dona Alba (IRE) **Anamoine Ltd**
**60 BUYER BEWARE (IRE),** br g Big Bad Bob (IRE)—Adoring (IRE) **Anamoine Ltd**
**61 BUZZ OFF BARROSO (IRE),** b f Big Bad Bob (IRE)—Ulanova (IRE) **Anamoine Ltd**
**62** B f Rip Van Winkle (IRE)—Celeste (FR) **Commonstown Racing Stables Ltd**
**63 DANCING NORETTA (IRE),** b f Big Bad Bob (IRE)—Shaimaa (IRE) **Mrs Geraldine Kelly**
**64 I'LL FIND MY WAY,** b c Galileo (IRE)—Dhanyata (IRE) **Millhouse LLC**
**65 JACK BLUE (IRE),** b g Duke of Marmalade (IRE)—Key Secure (IRE) **Commonstown Racing Stables Ltd**
**66 JACK NAYLOR,** b f Champs Elysees—Fashionable **Mr Gerry Byrne**
**67 JEANNE GIRL (IRE),** b f Rip Van Winkle (IRE)—Sister Golightly **Mr R. Galway & Merriebelle Irish Farm Ltd**
**68 LAKE CHAMPLAIN (IRE),** b g Manduro (GER)—Fantasy Girl (IRE) **Anamoine Ltd**
**69 LIGHT THAT (IRE),** b g Echo of Light—Tucum (IRE) **Mr John Wholey**
**70 LOLA BEAUX,** b f Equiano (FR)—Polly Perkins (IRE) **Mr Brian Acheson & Hayley O'Connor**
**71 LOVE NEVER DIES (IRE),** b f Holy Roman Emperor (IRE)—Crazy About You (IRE) **Mrs Yvonne Nicoll & David Reid Scott**
**72 NEWBERRY NEW (IRE),** br g Kodiac—Sunblush (UAE) **Rathmoyle Exports**
**73 OUT OF CONTEXT (IRE),** b f Intikhab (USA)—Context **Mrs P. K. Cooper, Mr Bill Oppenheim & Mr Dermot Cantillon**
**74 PERIOD PIECE (IRE),** b f Intikhab (USA)—Babberina (IRE) **Mrs P. K. Cooper & Mr R. Galway**
**75 PRIVATE PARTY (IRE),** b g Big Bad Bob (IRE)—Meduse Bleu **Commonstown Racing Stables Ltd**
**76 UNYIELDING,** b c Oasis Dream—Victoria Cross (IRE) **Millhouse LLC**

## TWO-YEAR-OLDS

**77** B c 28/4 Pour Moi (IRE)—Bounce (FR) (Trempolino (USA)) (87300) **Favourite Racing Ltd**
**78 BRAVER THE BULL (IRE),** b c 18/3 Big Bad Bob (IRE)—Danzelline (Danzero (AUS)) **Anamoine Ltd**
**79 BRING THE BOTTLE (IRE),** b f 6/4 Big Bad Bob (IRE)—Sticky Green (Lion Cavern (USA)) **Commonstown Racing Stables Ltd**
**80** B f 30/3 Big Bad Bob (IRE)—Cabin Point (IRE) (Desert Story (IRE)) **Commonstown Racing Stables Ltd**
**81 CAMILE (IRE),** b f 23/4 Captain Rio—Heroic Performer (IRE) (Royal Applause) (13491) **Commonstown Racing Stables Ltd**
**82** B c 29/4 Big Bad Bob (IRE)—Chaperoned (IRE) (High Chaparral (IRE)) **Commonstown Racing Stables Ltd**
**83 EAGER TO PLEASE (IRE),** b f 16/3 Elusive Pimpernel (USA)—Toy Show (IRE) (Danehill (USA)) **Anamoine Ltd**
**84 ENGLISH PALE (IRE),** b c 24/2 Elusive Pimpernel (USA)—Terme Cay (USA) (Langfuhr (CAN)) **Anamoine Ltd**
**85** B f 24/3 Rip Van Winkle (IRE)—Ermena (Dalakhani (IRE)) (24000) **Commonstown Racing Stables Ltd**
**86 FINAL FRONTIER (IRE),** b c 31/3 Dream Ahead (USA)—Polly Perkins (IRE) (Pivotal) (29364) **Vimal Khosla & Mrs P. K. Cooper**
**87** B f 17/2 Arcano (IRE)—Follow My Lead (Night Shift (USA)) (30158) **Commonstown Racing Stables Ltd**
**88** B f 1/1 Excellent Art—Glamourous (GER) (Red Ransom) **Commonstown Racing Stables Ltd**
**89** Ch f 19/4 Duke of Marmalade (IRE)—Green Castle (IRE) (Indian Ridge) **Stonethorn Stud Farm Ltd**

## MRS JESSICA HARRINGTON - Continued

**90 HAMLEY (FR),** b f 19/3 Fastnet Rock (AUS)—Mary Arnold (IRE) (Hernando (FR)) **The Niarchos Family**
**91** B f 8/5 Fastnet Rock (AUS)—
Jazz Baby (IRE) (Fasliyev (USA)) (25396) **Miss Kate Harrington, Mrs Gina Galvin & Mrs Yvonne Nicoll**
**92 MISSGUIDED (IRE),** b f 15/3 Rip Van Winkle (IRE)—
Foolish Ambition (GER) (Danehill Dancer (IRE)) (17460) **Mr Gerry Byrne**
**93 MULLIGATAWNY (IRE),** b c 20/2 Lope de Vega (IRE)—
Wild Whim (IRE) (Whipper (USA)) (135000) **Millhouse LLC**
**94 PROUD MARIA (IRE),** ch f 6/2 Medicean—Foot of Pride (IRE) (Footstepsinthesand) **Mr Roland Alder**
**95** B f 12/1 Canford Cliffs (IRE)—Renashaan (FR) (Darshaan) (71428) **Sir Peter Vela**
**96** B ro f 26/4 Zebedee—
Shauna's Princess (IRE) (Soviet Star (USA)) (34126) **Mr J. Carthy, Mr M. O'Neill, Mr M. Buckley & Partners**
**97 STRIKING GOLD,** b c 16/3 Stimulation (IRE)—Dream Quest (Rainbow Quest (USA)) (3000) **Mrs Harriet Jellett**

**Assistant Trainers:** Mrs Emma Galway, Mr Eamonn Leigh

**Jockey (flat):** Fran Berry. **Jockey (NH):** Robert Power, Mark Bolger. **Conditional:** Paddy Kennedy. **Amateur:** Mr Mark Fahey, Miss Kate Harrington.

---

## 281 MISS GRACE HARRIS, Chepstow

Postal: **White House, Sirenewton, Chepstow, Gwent, NP16 6AQ**
Contacts: **PHONE (01291) 641542 MOBILE (07912) 359425**
**E-MAIL michellebusiness@btinternet.com**

**1 BOOGANGOO (IRE),** 4, b f Acclamation—Spice World (IRE) **Mr Ronald Davies & Mrs Candida Davies**
**2** 4, B c Phoenix Reach (IRE)—Cherry Plum
**3 LIVING LEADER,** 6, b g Oasis Dream—Royal Jade **Mrs M. Harris**
**4 PADDY THE OSCAR (IRE),** 12, b g Oscar (IRE)—Parsonage **Michelle Harris & Deberah Lawton**
**5 TEIDE PEAK (IRE),** 6, b g Cape Cross (IRE)—Teide Lady **Grace Harris Racing**
**6 THE BOGMAN'S BALL,** 9, gr g Silver Patriarch (IRE)—Monica's Story **Michelle Harris & James Colthart**

### THREE-YEAR-OLDS

**7 DIMINUTIVE (IRE),** ch f Fast Company (IRE)—Take It Easee (IRE) **Mrs M. Harris**
**8** B c Cape Cross (IRE)—La Concorde (FR) **Grace Harris Racing**

**Other Owners:** Mr J. Colthart, Mr R. I. D. Davies, Mrs C. M. Davies, Miss G. Harris, Mrs D. L. S. Lawton.

**Assistant Trainer:** Michelle Harris

---

## 282 MR RONALD HARRIS, Chepstow

Postal: **Ridge House Stables, Earlswood, Chepstow, Monmouthshire, NP16 6AN**
Contacts: **PHONE (01291) 641689 FAX (01291) 641258 MOBILE (07831) 770899**
**E-MAIL ridgehousestables.ltd@btinternet.com WEBSITE www.ronharrisracing.co.uk**

**1 ABOUT TURN,** 4, ch c Pivotal—Doctor's Glory (USA) **Mrs R. M. Serrell**
**2 AGERZAM,** 5, b g Holy Roman Emperor (IRE)—Epiphany **Mrs R. M. Serrell**
**3 ALHABAN (IRE),** 9, gr g Verglas (IRE)—Anne Tudor (IRE) **Ridge House Stables Ltd**
**4 CLASSIC PURSUIT,** 4, b c Pastoral Pursuits—Snake's Head **David & Gwyn Joseph**
**5 CORPORAL MADDOX,** 8, b g Royal Applause—Noble View (USA) **Robert & Nina Bailey**
**6 DANDYS PERIER (IRE),** 4, br g Dandy Man (IRE)—Casual Remark (IRE) **Ridge House Stables Ltd**
**7 DIAMOND VINE (IRE),** 7, b g Diamond Green (FR)—Glasnas Giant **Ridge House Stables Ltd**
**8 FANTASY JUSTIFIER (IRE),** 4, b g Arakan (USA)—Grandel **Farley, Fantasy Fellowship B & RHS**
**9 GOWER PRINCESS,** 4, ch f Footstepsinthesand—Hollow Quaill (IRE) **David & Gwyn Joseph**
**10 HILL FORT,** 5, ch g Pivotal—Cairns (UAE) **Mr J C G Chua & Ridge House Stables**
**11 ITALIAN TOM (IRE),** 8, b h Le Vie Dei Colori—Brave Cat (IRE) **S. & A. Mares**
**12 JUDGE 'N JURY,** 11, ch g Pivotal—Cyclone Connie **Robert & Nina Bailey**
**13 LADY MANGO (IRE),** 7, ch m Bahamian Bounty—Opera **Mr L. Scadding**
**14 LIGHT FROM MARS,** 10, gr g Fantastic Light (USA)—Hylandra (USA) **Mrs N. J. Macauley**
**15 MARGARET BAKER,** 5, b m Windsor Castle—Daisy Leigh **Exors of the Late T. G. Leigh**
**16 MR DANDY MAN (IRE),** 4, ch g Dandy Man (IRE)—Boudica (IRE) **S. & A. Mares**
**17 NIGHT TRADE (IRE),** 8, b m Trade Fair—Compton Girl **Ridge House Stables Ltd**
**18 NOCTURN,** 6, b g Oasis Dream—Pizzicato **Mrs R. M. Serrell**
**19 NOVERRE TO GO (IRE),** 9, ch g Noverre (USA)—Ukraine Venture **Robert & Nina Bailey**
**20 PENSAX LAD (IRE),** 4, gr g Verglas (IRE)—Betelgeuse **S. & A. Mares**

## MR RONALD HARRIS - Continued

21 **POWERFUL WIND (IRE),** 6, ch g Titus Livius (FR)—Queen of Fools (IRE) **Mr A. D. Cooke**
22 **SECRET WITNESS,** 9, ch g Pivotal—It's A Secret **Ridge House Stables Ltd**
23 **SPIC 'N SPAN,** 10, b g Piccolo—Sally Slade **P. Nurcombe**
24 **SUPERSTA,** 4, ch g Pivotal—Resort **Mrs Ruth Serrell & Ridge House Stables**
25 **TOP COP,** 6, b g Acclamation—Speed Cop **South Wales Argus & Chepstow Racing Club**
26 **TRIGGER PARK (IRE),** 4, ch g Tagula (IRE)—Raazi **Mr John & Margaret Hatherell & RHS Ltd**
27 **VINCENTTI (IRE),** 5, b g Invincible Spirit (IRE)—Bint Al Balad (IRE) **Robert & Nina Bailey**
28 **XCLUSIVE,** 5, b g Pivotal—Dance A Daydream **Monmouthshire Racing Club**

### THREE-YEAR-OLDS

29 **AIR OF YORK (IRE),** b c Vale of York (IRE)—State Secret **Anthony Cooke & Lynn Cullimore**
30 **ARCANMAN (IRE),** b c Arcano (IRE)—Rose Bourbon (USA) **S. & A. Mares**
31 **ARIZONA SNOW,** b g Phoenix Reach (IRE)—Calgary **Ridge House Stables Ltd**
32 **AUSSIE RULER (IRE),** br g Aussie Rules (USA)—Experiment (IRE) **S. & A. Mares**
33 **CASTANEA,** ch g Pivotal—Invitee **Ridge House Stables Ltd**
34 **INVINCIBLE ZEB (IRE),** gr g Zebedee—Cruise Line **David & Gwyn Joseph**
35 **KING'S BOND,** b c Monsieur Bond (IRE)—Oke Bay **David & Gwyn Joseph**
36 **MAJESTIC HERO (IRE),** b g Majestic Missile (IRE)—Xena (IRE) **Mrs Jackie Jarrett & Ridge House Stables**
37 **POWERFULSTORM,** b f Bertolini (USA)—Frisson **Mr A. D. Cooke**
38 **UNION ROSE,** b c Stimulation (IRE)—Dot Hill **Mr D. A. Evans**
39 **ZEBS LAD (IRE),** ro c Zebedee—Dubai Princess (IRE) **Mrs R. M. Serrell**

### TWO-YEAR-OLDS

40 **NORTHERN BEAU (IRE),** b f 10/4 Canford Cliffs (IRE)—View (IRE) (Galileo (IRE)) (7936) **Northern Marking Ltd**
41 **RIO GLAMOROUS,** b c 14/3 Aussie Rules (USA)—
Glamorous Spirit (IRE) (Invincible Spirit (IRE)) (7619) **Robert & Nina Bailey**
42 **TOPSOIL,** b c 30/4 Kheleyf (USA)—Edge of Gold (Choisir (AUS)) (7619) **R. M. Bailey**

**Other Owners:** Mrs J. H. Bailey, Mrs S. Bell, Mr P. Bell, A. M. Blewitt, C. G. J. Chua, P. Coll, Mr J. C. Colley, Mrs Lynn Cullimore, Mr I. Farley, Mr R. A. J. Hatherell, Mrs M. E. Hatherell, Mrs J. Jarrett, Mr D. M. Joseph, Mr D. G. Joseph, Mr S. Mares, Mrs A. Mares.

**Jockey (flat):** Liam Jones, Luke Morris, Robert Winston. **Apprentice:** Daryl Byrne, Abie Knowles.

---

## 283 MR SHAUN HARRIS, Worksop

Postal: **Pinewood Stables, Carburton, Worksop, Nottinghamshire, S80 3BT**
Contacts: **PHONE (01909) 470936 FAX (01909) 470936 MOBILE (07768) 950460**
**E-MAIL shaunharris.racing@hotmail.co.uk WEBSITE www.shaunharrisracing.co.uk**

1 **BEARING KISSES (IRE),** 4, gr f Clodovil (IRE)—Masakira (IRE) **Paul Birley & Wilf Hobson**
2 **BETTY BOO (IRE),** 5, ch m Thousand Words—Poker Dice **Mr A. K. Elton**
3 **BLUE CLUMBER,** 5, b m Sleeping Indian—Blue Nile (IRE) **Miss G. H. Ward**
4 **BOTANIST,** 8, b g Selkirk (USA)—Red Camellia **Nick Blencowe & Mark Lenton**
5 **BRIAN THE LION,** 4, b g Byron—Molly Pitcher (IRE) **Mr W. I. Jones**
6 **CHIEF EXECUTIVE (IRE),** 5, gr g Dalakhani (IRE)—Lucky (IRE) **Mr S. P. Giles**
7 **EL BRAVO,** 9, ch g Falbrav (IRE)—Alessandra **www.nottinghamshireracing.co.uk (2)**
8 **FATHOM FIVE (IRE),** 11, b g Fath (USA)—Ambria (ITY) **Nottinghamshire Racing**
9 **FUJIN,** 4, b g Oasis Dream—Phantom Wind (USA) **Mrs S. L. Robinson**
10 **HEAR THE CHIMES,** 6, b g Midnight Legend—Severn Air **Miss G. H. Ward**
11 **HELLBENDER (IRE),** 9, ch g Exceed And Excel (AUS)—Desert Rose **Southwell Racecourse Owners Group**
12 **HOLDERNESS,** 4, b f Indesatchel (IRE)—Zaville **J. Morris**
13 **IVY TRUMP,** 4, b f First Trump—Ivy Bridge (IRE) **Goldform Racing**
14 **LA DANZA,** 5, b m Country Reel (USA)—Freedom Song **All Weather Bloodstock**
15 **LORD FOX (IRE),** 8, b g Alflora (IRE)—Foxfire **Miss G. H. Ward**
16 **MAJOR MUSCARI (IRE),** 7, ch g Exceed And Excel (AUS)—Muscari **J. Morris**
17 **MEDAM,** 6, b m Medicean—Mamounia (IRE) **Burton Agnes Bloodstock**
18 **MUSIC HALL (FR),** 5, gr g Stormy River (FR)—Aaliyah (GER) **Vision Bloodstock**
19 **MYJESTIC MELODY (IRE),** 7, b m Majestic Missile (IRE)—Bucaramanga (IRE) **Mrs S. L. Robinson**
20 **NOTTS SO BLUE,** 4, b f Pastoral Pursuits—Blue Nile (IRE) **www.nottinghamshireracing.co.uk (2)**
21 **RAISED HOPE,** 4, b g Byron—Wax Eloquent **The Racing For Hope Partnership**
22 **REALITY SHOW (IRE),** 8, b g Cape Cross (IRE)—Really (IRE) **Miss G. H. Ward**
23 **RISE TO GLORY (IRE),** 7, b h King's Best (USA)—Lady At War **N Blencowe,J Sunderland,M Lenton,CHarris**
24 **ROCKWEILLER,** 8, b g Rock of Gibraltar (IRE)—Ballerina Suprema (IRE) **S. A. Harris**
25 **ROY'S LEGACY,** 6, b h Phoenix Reach (IRE)—Chocolada **P Birley, S Mohammed, S Rowley, S Harris**

## MR SHAUN HARRIS - Continued

26 **SLEEPER KING (IRE),** 4, b g Holy Roman Emperor (IRE)—Catherine Palace **Mrs J. Bownes**
27 **TACTICAL STRIKE,** 4, ch g Pivotal—Alvee (IRE) **Vision Bloodstock**
28 **THAT BE GRAND,** 4, b f Firebreak—Manila Selection (USA) **C A Harris & Peter Dawson**
29 **UNDERWRITTEN,** 6, b g Authorized (IRE)—Grain of Gold **Mr W. A. Robinson**
30 **VIKING WARRIOR (IRE),** 8, ch g Halling (USA)—Powder Paint **Nottinghamshire Racing**
31 **VODKA TIME (IRE),** 4, b c Indian Haven—Cappuccino (IRE) **S. A. Harris**
32 **WHATSUPJACK (IRE),** 8, b g Catcher In The Rye (IRE)—
Riverstown Girl (IRE) **Paula Ward & Shaun Harris Racing**
33 **ZACYNTHUS (IRE),** 7, ch g Iffraaj—Ziria (IRE) **Mrs J. Bownes**

### THREE-YEAR-OLDS

34 **AGADOO,** b f Multiplex—Agooda **J. E. Rose**
35 **FIRST SUMMER,** b g Cockney Rebel (IRE)—Silken Dalliance **Vision Bloodstock**
36 **KONNOS BAY,** b c Phoenix Reach (IRE)—Rasmalai **Winterbeck Manor Stud Ltd**
37 **PHOENIX PHIL,** ch g Phoenix Reach (IRE)—Pearl's Girl **Lime Tree Avenue Racing**
38 **YORKSHIRE (IRE),** b g Tagula (IRE)—Bun Penny **Mrs J. Bownes**
39 Ch g Bertolini (USA)—Zaville **J. Morris**

### TWO-YEAR-OLDS

40 B f 12/4 Multiplex—Agooda (Rainbow Quest (USA)) (2380) **J. E. Rose**
41 Ch f 19/2 Compton Place—Here To Me (Muhtarram (USA)) (1904) **Miss G. H. Ward**
42 **KYLLA,** b f 4/3 Kyllachy—Mamounia (IRE) (Green Desert (USA)) **Burton Agnes Bloodstock**

**Other Owners:** Mr P. Birley, Mr N. J. Blencowe, J. Branson, Mrs M. C. Coltman, The Hon Mrs E. S. Cunliffe-Lister, P. G. Dawson, Mr C. Harris, Mr R. Hawke, Mr S. R. Hillyer, Mrs E. F. H. Hillyer, Mr W. Hobson, Mr M. Lenton, Mr S. Mohammed, Mr S. Rowley, Mr R. J. Shearing, Mr J. Soiza, Mr J. J. Sunderland, Miss Paula Ward.

---

## 284 MISS LISA HARRISON, Wigton

Postal: **Cobble Hall, Aldoth, Nr Silloth, Cumbria, CA7 4NE**
Contacts: **PHONE (01697) 361753 FAX (01697) 342250 MOBILE (07725) 535554**
**E-MAIL lisa@daharrison.co.uk**

1 **ACROSS THE TWEED (IRE),** 9, b br g Alderbrook—Cash Chase (IRE) **Crone Graves Haughan & Gillespie**
2 **JOHNNY GO,** 5, b g Bollin Eric—Waverbeck (IRE) **Mr J. B. Harrison**
3 **LADY VIVONA,** 7, gr m Overbury (IRE)—Ladylliat (FR) **Mrs F. Crone & Mrs V. Birnie**
4 **SOLWAY BAY,** 13, b g Cloudings (IRE)—No Problem Jac **David A. Harrison**
5 **SOLWAY DANDY,** 8, b g Danroad (AUS)—Solway Rose **David A. Harrison**
6 **SOLWAY DORNAL,** 10, b g Alflora (IRE)—Solway Donal (IRE) **Abbadis Racing Club & Partner**
7 **SOLWAY LEGEND,** 8, ch g And Beyond (IRE)—Spicey Cut **Mr & Mrs Batey**
8 **SOLWAY PRINCE,** 6, ch g Double Trigger (IRE)—Solway Rose **David A. Harrison**
9 4, B f Overbury (IRE)—Solway Rose **David A. Harrison**
10 **SOLWAY SAM,** 12, b g Double Trigger (IRE)—Some Gale **David A. Harrison**
11 **SOLWAY SUMMER,** 6, b m Double Trigger (IRE)—Solway Donal (IRE) **David A. Harrison**
12 **SOLWAY TRIGGER,** 6, b g Double Trigger (IRE)—Double Flight **David A. Harrison**
13 **WILLIE HALL,** 11, b g Alflora (IRE)—G'ime A Buzz **R. H. Hall**

**Other Owners:** Mr K. D. Batey, Mrs A. E. Batey, Mrs V. A. Birnie, Mrs F. H. Crone, Mr D. Gillespie, Mr J. D. Graves, Mr N. Haughan, R. E. Jackson.

---

## 285 MR BEN HASLAM, Middleham

Postal: **Castle Hill Stables, Castle Hill, Middleham, Leyburn, North Yorkshire, DL8 4QW**
Contacts: **PHONE (01969) 624351 MOBILE (07764) 411660**
**E-MAIL office@benhaslamracing.com WEBSITE www.benhaslamracing.com**

1 **ABBOTSFIELD (IRE),** 5, ch m Sakhee's Secret—May Day Queen (IRE) **Middleham Park Racing I**
2 **CAMANCHE GREY (IRE),** 4, gr g Camacho—Sense of Greeting (IRE) **Mr L. Ashmore**
3 **DIAKTOROS (IRE),** 5, b g Red Clubs (IRE)—Rinneen (IRE) **Mr S Hassiakos & Sir Alex Ferguson**
4 **EASTERN DYNASTY,** 4, b g Exceed And Excel (AUS)—Agooda **Middleham Park Racing I**

## MR BEN HASLAM - Continued

5 **EVER SO MUCH (IRE),** 6, b g Westerner—Beautiful World (IRE) **J. P. McManus**
6 **HI CANDY (IRE),** 5, b m Diamond Green (FR)—Dancing Steps **Go Alfresco Racing**
7 **HI DANCER,** 12, b g Medicean—Sea Music **Mr R. Tocher**
8 **LILIARGH (IRE),** 6, b m Acclamation—Discover Roma (IRE) **Middleham Park Racing XXVII**
9 **MAD FOR ROAD (IRE),** 6, b g Galileo (IRE)—Potion **J. P. McManus**
10 **MOON OVER RIO (IRE),** 4, b f Captain Rio—Moonchild (GER) **Blue Lion Racing IX**
11 **OPERATEUR (IRE),** 7, b g Oratorio (IRE)—Kassariya (IRE) **Mrs C Barclay & M T Buckley**
12 **PINK CADILLAC (IRE),** 5, b m Clodovil (IRE)—Green Life **Go Alfresco Racing**
13 **PRINCE OF PIRATES (IRE),** 10, b g Milan—Call Kate (IRE) **J. P. McManus**
14 **SHESNOTFORTURNING (IRE),** 5, b m Refuse To Bend (IRE)—Diplomats Daughter **Mrs C. Barclay**
15 **TAUREAN BEAUTY,** 4, b f Firebreak—La Belle Katherine (USA) **Lauren Sanders**

### THREE-YEAR-OLDS

16 **BOUNTY'S SPIRIT,** b f Bahamian Bounty—Scarlet Buttons (IRE) **The Trojan Horse Partnership**
17 **CHARLIE'S APPROVAL (IRE),** b f Approve (IRE)—Authenticate **Mr L. Ashmore**
18 **DENWAY PARK,** b c Paco Boy (IRE)—Bolshaya **Middleham Park Racing XCVII**
19 **LADY LEKKI (IRE),** b f Champs Elysees—One Zero (USA) **Go Alfresco Racing**
20 **RIVERLYNX (IRE),** b f Holy Roman Emperor (IRE)—Banba (IRE) **Go Alfresco Racing**
21 **SPIRIT OF ARAKAN (IRE),** b f Arakan (USA)—Angel Rays **The Trojan Horse Partnership**

### TWO-YEAR-OLDS

**22** B f 25/4 Sleeping Indian—Esteraad (IRE) (Cadeaux Genereux) (7000) **Mrs C. Barclay**
**23** B f 17/5 Zoffany (IRE)—For Joy (Singspiel (IRE)) (30000) **Mrs C. Barclay**
**24** B c 15/4 Frozen Power (IRE)—Lady Bracknell (IRE) (Definite Article) (30000) **Mrs C. Barclay**
**25** B f 27/4 Kheleyf (USA)—Satin Braid (Diktat) (761) **The Trojan Horse Partnership**

**Other Owners:** Mrs C. Barclay, Mr M. T. Buckley, Miss Lynn Douglas, Sir Alex Ferguson, Mr B. M. R. Haslam, Mr S. Hassiakos, Mr T. S. Palin, Mr M. Prince, Miss Karen Theobald, Mr G. Walker, Mr R. Young.

**Jockey (flat):** Andrew Elliott.

---

## 286 MRS FLEUR HAWES, Diss

Postal: **Hill Farm Barn, High Rd, Bressingham, Diss, Norfolk, IP22 2AT**
Contacts: **MOBILE (07775) 795805**
**E-MAIL fleur@fleurhawesracingltd.co.uk WEBSITE www.fleurhawesracing.co.uk**

1 **ART HISTORY (IRE),** 7, gr g Dalakhani (IRE)—What A Picture (FR) **Mrs F. Hawes**
2 **FLAMING GORGE (IRE),** 10, ch g Alderbrook—Solmus (IRE) **A Fool & His Money**

**Other Owners:** Mrs E. Kenward.

---

## 287 MR NIGEL HAWKE, Tiverton

Postal: **Thorne Farm, Stoodleigh, Tiverton, Devon, EX16 9QG**
Contacts: **PHONE (01884) 881666 MOBILE (07769) 295839**
**E-MAIL nigel@thornefarmracingltd.co.uk WEBSITE www.nigelhawkethornefarmracing.co.uk**

1 **ACADIAN (FR),** 5, b g Sulamani (IRE)—Acarina (IRE) **Mead & Vowles**
2 **ANAY TURGE (FR),** 10, gr g Turgeon (USA)—Anayette (FR) **Mrs K. Hawke**
3 **ANIS DES MALBERAUX (FR),** 5, b g Reste Tranquille (FR)—Scavenger (FR) **Mrs K. Hawke**
4 **BELLINI DUBREAU (FR),** 4, ch g Anzillero (GER)—Lonita d'airy (FR) **Thorne Farm Racing Limited**
5 **BENIM,** 5, b m Authorized (IRE)—Princess Danah (IRE) **D. R. Mead**
6 **BERRY DE CARJAC (FR),** 4, ch g Epalo (GER)—Miria Galanda (FR) **Pearce Bros Partnership**
7 **CALIN DU BRIZAIS (FR),** 4, b g Loup Solitaire (USA)—Caline du Brizais (FR) **Pearce Bros Partnership**
8 **DECKERS DELIGHT,** 4, b f Tobougg (IRE)—Oleana (IRE) **Mr J. A. Vowles**
9 **DONT DO THAT,** 7, ch m Double Trigger (IRE)—Poles Pitch **Mr R. I. Clarke**
10 **FASHION ICON (FR),** 4, b f Arvico (FR)—Royale Sulawesie (FR) **The Why Not Partnership**
11 **FLORA AURORA,** 7, ch g Alflora (IRE)—Dawn Spinner **D. R. Mead**
12 **GREYBOUGG,** 6, gr g Tobougg (IRE)—Kildee Lass **Mead, Di-Vincenzo**
13 **KADALKIN (FR),** 9, b g Robin des Champs (FR)—Kadalma (FR) **D. R. Mead**
14 **LAFLAMMEDEGLORIE,** 9, b g Fair Mix (IRE)—Swazi Princess (IRE) **D. R. Mead**
15 **LOCH GARMAN (FR),** 4, gr g Maresca Sorrento (FR)—Ballade Nordique (FR) **D. R. Mead**
16 **MASTER NEO (FR),** 9, gr g Turgeon (USA)—Really Royale (FR) **Mr W. E. Donohue & Pearce Bros**

## MR NIGEL HAWKE - Continued

17 **MIDNIGHT REQUEST,** 6, b g Midnight Legend—Friendly Request **W. E. Donohue J. M. Donohue**
18 **MISS PROBUS,** 6, b m Erhaab (USA)—Probus Lady **Mr E. G. M. Beard**
19 **MISTER WISEMAN,** 13, gr g Bal Harbour—Genie Spirit **Mrs K. Hawke**
20 **PAGHAM BELLE,** 7, b m Brian Boru—Sambara (IRE) **N. J. McMullan & S. H. Bryant**
21 **PIRANS CAR,** 9, b g Sleeping Car (FR)—Karolina (FR) **R. J. & Mrs J. A. Peake**
22 **POINT N SHOOT (IRE),** 4, b g Broadway Flyer (USA)—Ali's Dipper (IRE) **Mead & Vowles**
23 **POMME,** 4, b f Observatory (USA)—Mirthful (USA) **Mrs K. Hawke**
24 **ROBBIE RABBIT (IRE),** 5, b g Flemensfirth (USA)—Leading Lady **Mr M. J. Phillips**
25 **SAMINGARRY (FR),** 8, ch g Ballingarry (IRE)—Samansonnienne (FR) **D. R. Mead**
26 **SEDGEMOOR EXPRESS (IRE),** 7, b br g Presenting—Pretty Native (IRE) **Pearce Bros 2**
27 **SKYBOURNE,** 6, b m With The Flow (USA)—Little Skylark **Exors of the Late Mr D. E. F. Bloomfield**
28 **SPEREDEK (FR),** 4, b br g Kapgarde (FR)—Sendamagic (FR) **Kapinhand & Partner**
29 **TAKE A BREAK (FR),** 4, b br g Sunday Break (JPN)—Popee (FR) **Pearce Bros Partnership**
30 **TELEX (USA),** 4, gr g Empire Maker (USA)—Kinetic Force (USA) **Thorne Farm Racing Limited**
31 **THEUNNAMEDSOLDIER,** 7, b g Revoque (IRE)—Miss Tango **D. R. Mead**
32 **TOKYO JAVILEX (FR),** 8, b g Sleeping Car (FR)—Etoile du Lion (FR) **D. R. Mead**
33 **WHIMSICAL NOTION,** 5, b g Midnight Legend—Friendly Request **W. E. Donohue**

### THREE-YEAR-OLDS

34 **BUFFALO SABRE (FR),** b g Turgeon (USA)—Kerry Rose (FR) **Mrs K. Hawke**
35 **CAMRON DE CHAILLAC (FR),** bl g Laverock (IRE)—Hadeel **Mrs K. Hawke**
36 **MY KING (FR),** b g Kingsalsa (USA)—My Belle (FR) **D. R. Mead**
37 **SPERONIMO (FR),** b g Diamond Green (FR)—Spepita (FR) **Pearce Bros Partnership**

**Other Owners:** Mrs Kate Brain, Mr Steve Bryant, Mr Richard Clarke, Mr Marcus Di-Vincenzo, Mr W. E. Donohue, Mrs J. M. Donohue, Mrs K. Hawke, Mr T. B. James, Mrs H. Jefferies, Mr N. J. McMullan, Mr D. R. Mead, Mr Dave Mitchell, Mr Russell J. Peake, Mrs J. A. Peake, Mr Steve Pearce, Mr David Pearce, Mr Mark Phillips, Mr William Simms, Thorne Farm Racing Ltd, Mr J. A. Vowles.

**Assistant Trainers:** Joe Tickle, Katherine Hawke

**Jockey (NH):** Dave Crosse, Tom Scudamore. **Conditional:** James Best. **Amateur:** Mr Lee Drowne.

---

## 288 MR RICHARD HAWKER, Frome

Postal: **Rode Farm, Rode, Bath, Somerset, BA11 6QQ**
Contacts: **PHONE (01373) 831479**

1 **BEAUJOLAIS BOB,** 7, bl gr g Grape Tree Road—Charliebob **R. G. B. Hawker**
2 **STORMIN EXIT (IRE),** 12, b g Exit To Nowhere (USA)—Stormin Norma (IRE) **Mrs G. Morgan**

---

## 289 MR JONATHAN HAYNES, Brampton

Postal: **Cleugh Head, Low Row, Brampton, Cumbria, CA8 2JB**
Contacts: **PHONE (01697) 746253 MOBILE (07771) 511471**

1 **BEYONDTEMPTATION,** 7, ch m And Beyond (IRE)—Tempted (IRE) **J. C. Haynes**
2 **FARMERS CROSS (IRE),** 11, b g Old Vic—Ace Conqueror (IRE) **J. C. Haynes**
3 **MRS GRASS,** 8, ch m And Beyond (IRE)—Tempted (IRE) **J. C. Haynes**

---

## 290 MR TED HAYNES, Highworth

Postal: **Red Down Farm, Highworth, Wiltshire, SN6 7SH**
Contacts: **PHONE/FAX (01793) 762437 FAX (01793) 762437 MOBILE (07704) 707728**
**E-MAIL reddownracing@aol.com**

1 **EBONY STORM,** 8, b g Zafeen (FR)—Stormworthy Miss (IRE) **Miss S. R. Haynes**
2 **MR TED,** 8, b g Kayf Tara—Fly Home **Miss S. R. Haynes**
3 6, B g Kier Park (IRE)—Rupert's Princess (IRE) **Miss S. R. Haynes**
4 **STANWELL,** 7, ch g Kier Park (IRE)—Magical Dancer (IRE) **The Reddown High Explosive Partnership**
5 **STORMWOOD,** 10, b g Fleetwood (IRE)—Stormworthy Miss (IRE) **Miss S. R. Haynes**
6 **THE NAMES HARRY,** 10, b g Sir Harry Lewis (USA)—Fly Home **Miss S. R. Haynes**

## MR TED HAYNES - Continued

### THREE-YEAR-OLDS

7 B c Crosspeace (IRE)—Fly Home **Miss S. R. Haynes**

### TWO-YEAR-OLDS

8 B c 22/5 Crosspeace (IRE)—Fly Home (Skyliner) **Miss S. R. Haynes**

**Other Owners:** Mr H. Edward Haynes, Mrs H. E. Haynes.

**Assistant Trainer:** Sally R. Haynes (07711) 488341

---

**291**

## MISS GAIL HAYWOOD, Newton Abbot

Postal: **Stacombe Farm, Doccombe, Moretonhampstead, Newton Abbot, Devon, TQ13 8SS**
Contacts: **PHONE (01647) 440826**
**E-MAIL gail@gghracing.com WEBSITE www.gghracing.com**

1 **HIJA,** 4, b f Avonbridge—Pantita **Haywood's Heroes**
2 **MAGNUS ROMEO,** 4, b g Manduro (GER)—Chili Dip **Miss G. G. Haywood**
3 **MILBURN,** 9, ch g First Trump—Baroness Rose **Mr R. E. Stuart-Jervis**
4 **QUEENSLAND BETTY,** 7, b m Kayf Tara—Ruby Star (IRE) **Miss G. G. Haywood**
5 **RICHARDOFDOCCOMBE (IRE),** 9, b g Heron Island (IRE)—Strike Again (IRE) **Mr R. E. Stuart-Jervis**
6 **RUSSIAN'S LEGACY,** 5, b m Kayf Tara—Ruby Star (IRE) **Mr I. F. Gosden**
7 **WEST HILL LEGEND,** 4, b f Midnight Legend—Bajan Blue **D. G. Staddon**

**Other Owners:** Mrs Suzie Haywood.

**Assistant Trainer:** W. G. McColl

**Conditional:** Lizzie Kelly. **Amateur:** Miss Alice Mills.

---

**292**

## MRS C. HEAD-MAAREK, Chantilly

Postal: **32 Avenue du General Leclerc, 60500 Chantilly, France**
Contacts: **PHONE (0033) 3445 70101 FAX (0033) 3445 85333 MOBILE (0033) 6073 10505**
**E-MAIL christiane.head@wanadoo.fr**

1 **ALTAIRA,** 4, b c Dubawi (IRE)—Peach Pearl
2 **ARTISTE LADY (FR),** 4, b f Artiste Royal (IRE)—Fantasy Lady (USA)
3 **GREENSTREET,** 4, b c Mr Sidney (USA)—Treasure Queen (USA)
4 7, B g Iron Mask (USA)—Padina (GER)
5 **SILVAPLANA (FR),** 4, b f Montmartre (FR)—Silvery Bay (FR)
6 **TREVE (FR),** 5, b m Motivator—Trevise (FR)
7 **VIVE JEANNE (FR),** 4, ch f Medicean—Victory Chant

### THREE-YEAR-OLDS

8 **ALPHA BRAVO,** b c Oasis Dream—Kilo Alpha
9 **AMERICAN BOY (FR),** b c Whipper (USA)—Queen America (FR)
10 **BE MY LADY,** b f Duke of Marmalade (IRE)—Za Za Zoom (IRE)
11 **CASPIAN BREEZE (USA),** b f Henrythenavigator (USA)—Light of Dubai (USA)
12 **CLARIDEN,** b c Zamindar (USA)—Winter Silence
13 **DEFINITION,** b f Dunkerque (FR)—Dives (FR)
14 **DENTELLE (FR),** b f Mr Sidney (USA)—Dalna (FR)
15 **DESTIN (FR),** b g Mr Sidney (USA)—Dissertation (FR)
16 **DIHNA (FR),** b f Fuisse (FR)—Dame Blanche (USA)
17 **DISSERTATION,** b f Champs Elysees—Reel Style
18 **EHTEYAT (FR),** b f Thewayyouare (USA)—Clara House
19 **EPICURIS,** b c Rail Link—Argumentative
20 **FONTANELICE (IRE),** b f Vale of York (IRE)—Choose Me Please (IRE)
21 **FORECAST,** ch c Observatory (USA)—New Orchid (USA)
22 **FULL (FR),** b c Mr Sidney (USA)—Funny Feerie (FR)
23 **FULL MAST (USA),** b c Mizzen Mast (USA)—Yashmak (USA)
24 **GALLICE (IRE),** b f Fuisse (FR)—Gout de Terroir (USA)
25 **GALLIUM (FR),** b c Mr Sidney (USA)—Golden Life (USA)
26 **GARANTIE (FR),** b f Motivator—Great News (FR)
27 **GHASHAAM (IRE),** b c Sea The Stars (IRE)—Out West (USA)

## MRS C. HEAD-MAAREK - Continued

28 **LONGROOM,** b c Oasis Dream—Phantom Wind (USA)
29 **MAGISTRATE (FR),** b f Motivator—Matanilla (FR)
30 **NIGWAH (FR),** b f Montjeu (IRE)—Sil Sila (IRE)
31 **QUEEN WINNER (FR),** b f Whipper (USA)—Queensalsa (FR)
32 **QUEST,** b f Mr Sidney (USA)—Treasure (FR)
33 **REALISATOR (FR),** b g Mr Sidney (USA)—Rouge (FR)
34 **REINETTE,** b f Dansili—Etoile Montante (USA)
35 **SAINTES (FR),** ch f Kentucky Dynamite (USA)—Soierie (FR)
36 **SALOME,** b f Fuisse (FR)—Silverqueen (FR)
37 **SALWA (IRE),** b f Galileo (IRE)—Photophore (IRE)
38 **SHORTFIN,** b f Exceed And Excel (AUS)—Bimini
39 **SOUTH BANK (USA),** gr ro f Tapit (USA)—Special Duty
40 **SOUVERAINE (FR),** b f Fuisse (FR)—Silvery Bay (FR)
41 **SPLASHING (FR),** ch g Fuisse (FR)—Spirale d'or (FR)
42 **TORIDE,** b f Fuisse (FR)—Trevise (FR)
43 **TROIS POINTS (FR),** b c Motivator—Trading
44 **VAGA (FR),** b f Gold Away (IRE)—Vassia (USA)
45 **VISTA (FR),** b f Mr Sidney (USA)—Villadolide (FR)

### TWO-YEAR-OLDS

46 B c 15/3 Zamindar (USA)—Acquisition (Dansili)
47 B c 1/4 Motivator—Argumentative (Observatory (USA))
48 B f 17/1 Oasis Dream—Arizona Jewel (Dansili)
49 B c 24/1 Medaglia d'Oro (USA)—Aviate (Dansili)
50 **CALINA (FR),** b f 27/4 Dunkerque (FR)—Cable Beach (USA) (Langfuhr (CAN)) (6349)
51 B f 1/1 Invincible Spirit—Candicans
52 B f 31/1 First Defence (USA)—Classy Touch (USA) (Maria's Mon (USA))
53 B f 14/2 Champs Elysees—Comment (Sadler's Wells (USA))
54 B f 11/3 Motivator—Contiguous (USA) (Danzig (USA))
55 **FERRANO (FR),** b c 1/1 Mr Sidney—Finella
56 **GARDENIA (FR),** b f 1/1 Galileo (IRE)—Gout de Terroir (USA) (Lemon Drop Kid (USA))
57 Ch f 12/2 Giant's Causeway (USA)—Gointobegone (USA) (Smart Strike (CAN))
58 B f 28/1 Dansili—Helleborine (Observatory (USA))
59 **HELLO MAJESTY (FR),** b c 30/3 King's Best (USA)—Hello Molly (FR) (Sillery (USA)) (31746)
60 B c 26/4 Oasis Dream—Kid Gloves (In The Wings)
61 **MAGELAN (FR),** b c 1/1 Fuisse—Mytographie
62 **MONDELINO (FR),** b c 1/1 Youmzain (IRE)—Mishina (FR) (Highest Honor (FR))
63 **PADOVA (FR),** b f 1/1 Gold Away—Pomonia
64 B f 1/3 Lawman (FR)—Perse (Rock of Gibraltar (IRE))
65 B c 4/5 Oasis Dream—Quest To Peak (USA) (Distant View (USA))
66 **SEMINI (FR),** b f 21/4 Fuisse—Spirale d'or (High Yield)
67 **SIR ALEC (FR),** b c 22/2 Mr Sidney (USA)—Rose Rose (USA) (Cozzene (USA)) (17460)
68 B f 31/3 Motivator—Spicebird (IRE) (Ela-Mana-Mou) (100000)
69 B f 10/3 Artie Schiller (USA)—Striking Example (USA) (Empire Maker (USA))
70 B c 14/3 Cacique (IRE)—Talkative (Oasis Dream)
71 **TOULOUSE (FR),** b f 1/1 Mr Sidney—Theoricienne
72 **TYRANA (FR),** b f 1/1 Motivator—Treasure (FR) (Anabaa (USA))
73 Ch c 1/1 Pivotal—Visualize (Medicean) (55555)

**Assistant Trainer:** Christopher Head

---

## 293 MR PETER HEDGER, Chichester

Postal: **Melcroft, Eastergate Lane, Eastergate, Chichester, West Sussex, PO20 3SJ**
Contacts: **PHONE (01243) 543863 FAX (01243) 543913 MOBILE (07860) 209448**
**E-MAIL hedgerlaura@hotmail.com**

1 **ARCHIBALD THORBURN (IRE),** 4, br g Duke of Marmalade (IRE)—Winged Harriet (IRE) **Mr R. Allcock**
2 **BARNMORE,** 7, b g Royal Applause—Veronica Franco **P C F Racing Ltd**
3 **BIG DUKE (IRE),** 5, b g Duke of Marmalade (IRE)—Liscune (IRE) **P C F Racing Ltd**
4 **BRIDGE BUILDER,** 5, b g Avonbridge—Amazing Dream (IRE) **P C F Racing Ltd**
5 **CLOWANCE KEYS,** 6, b g High Chaparral (IRE)—Seasons Parks **Mrs V. Keen**
6 **CONTINUUM,** 6, b br g Dansili—Clepsydra **P C F Racing Ltd**
7 **FRANCO'S SECRET,** 4, b g Sakhee's Secret—Veronica Franco **P C F Racing Ltd**

## MR PETER HEDGER - Continued

8 **ITS A DIZZY LIFE,** 5, b g Amber Life—Dizzy Massini **Mr A. C. B. Green**
9 **KAAFEL (IRE),** 6, b g Nayef (USA)—Tafaani (IRE) **P C F Racing Ltd**
10 **KITTY BEQUICK,** 4, ch f Piccolo—Cat Patrol **P. R. Hedger**
11 **LISAHANE BOG,** 8, b g Royal Applause—Veronica Franco **P C F Racing Ltd**
12 **LUCKY DI,** 5, br m Araafa (IRE)—Lucky Date (IRE) **P C F Racing Ltd**
13 **PUTMEINTHESWINDLE,** 5, ch g Monsieur Bond (IRE)—Birthday Belle **P C F Racing Ltd**
14 **RUZEIZ (USA),** 6, b g Muhtathir—Saraama (USA) **P C F Racing Ltd**
15 **SILVER DIXIE (USA),** 5, br g Dixie Union (USA)—More Silver (USA) **P C F Racing Ltd**
16 **SLIP SLIDING AWAY (IRE),** 8, b g Whipper (USA)—Sandy Lady (IRE) **Simon Holt, Mary Boylan, Wendy Mole**
17 **WHIPCRACKAWAY (IRE),** 6, b g Whipper (USA)—Former Drama (USA) **P. R. Hedger & P C F Racing Ltd**

**Other Owners:** Mrs M. J. Boylan, Mr S. R. Holt, Mrs W. A. Mole.

**Jockey (flat):** Charles Bishop. **Jockey (NH):** Leighton Aspell.

---

## 294 MR NICKY HENDERSON, Lambourn

Postal: **Seven Barrows, Lambourn, Hungerford, Berkshire, RG17 8UH**
Contacts: **PHONE (01488) 72259 FAX (01488) 72596 MOBILE (07774) 608168**
**E-MAIL nj.henderson@virgin.net**

1 **ACT ALONE,** 6, b g Act One—Figlette **S W Group Logistics Limited**
2 **ADMIRAL MILLER,** 5, b g Multiplex—Millers Action **W. H. Ponsonby**
3 **ALTIOR (IRE),** 5, b g High Chaparral (IRE)—Monte Solaro (IRE) **Mrs P. J. Pugh**
4 **AREA FIFTY ONE,** 7, b g Green Desert (USA)—Secret History (USA) **Middleham Park Racing III**
5 **BEAR'S AFFAIR (IRE),** 9, br g Presenting—Gladtogetit **G. B. Barlow**
6 **BEAT THAT (IRE),** 7, b g Milan—Knotted Midge (IRE) **M. A. C. Buckley**
7 **BELLATOR (FR),** 4, b c Network (GER)—Onysia (FR) **The Shillelagh Partnership**
8 **BERCE (FR),** 4, b g Peer Gynt (JPN)—Fauconnerie (FR) **Potensis Bloodstock Limited**
9 **BIG HANDS HARRY,** 6, b g Multiplex—Harristown Lady **A. D. Spence**
10 **BIRCH HILL (IRE),** 5, b g Kalanisi (IRE)—Miss Compliance (IRE) **R. A. Bartlett**
11 **BIVOUAC (FR),** 4, b g Califet (FR)—Pazadena (FR) **Potensis Bloodstock Ltd & Chris Giles**
12 **BLUE FASHION (IRE),** 6, b g Scorpion (IRE)—Moon Glow (FR) **Mr & Mrs J. D. Cotton**
13 **BLUE IS THE COLOUR (IRE),** 5, b g Dalakhani (IRE)—Coyote **A. D. Spence**
14 **BOBS WORTH (IRE),** 10, b g Bob Back (USA)—Fashionista (IRE) **The Not Afraid Partnership**
15 **BRIGADIER MILLER,** 8, gr g Act One—Tread Carefully **W. H. Ponsonby**
16 **BRINGITHOMEMINTY,** 6, gr g Presenting—Rosie Redman (IRE) **Walters Plant Hire Ltd**
17 **BROXBOURNE (IRE),** 6, b m Refuse To Bend (IRE)—Rafting (IRE) **The Gleneagles Partnership**
18 **BUVEUR D'AIR (FR),** 4, b g Crillon (FR)—History (FR) **Potensis Bloodstock Ltd & Chris Giles**
19 **CALL THE COPS (IRE),** 6, b g Presenting—Ballygill Heights (IRE) **Matt & Lauren Morgan**
20 **CAPTAIN CONAN (FR),** 8, b g Kingsalsa (USA)—Lavandou **Triermore Stud**
21 **CARACCI APACHE (IRE),** 5, b g High Chaparral (IRE)—Campanella (GER) **W. H. Ponsonby**
22 **CARDINAL WALTER (IRE),** 6, br b g Cape Cross (IRE)—Sheer Spirit (IRE) **Mrs F. H. Hay**
23 **CARNIVAL FLAG (FR),** 6, ch m Ballingarry (IRE)—Run For Laborie (FR) **The Perfect Day Partnership**
24 **CHAMPAGNE EXPRESS,** 5, b g Kalanisi (IRE)—Marvellous Dream (FR) **Owners Group 008**
25 **CHAPEL HALL (IRE),** 5, b g Arcadio (GER)—Auction Hall **R. M. Kirkland**
26 **CHOCCA WOCCA,** 5, b m Kayf Tara—Chomba Womba (IRE) **Mr & Mrs R. G. Kelvin-Hughes**
27 **CLEAN SHEET (IRE),** 6, b g Oscar (IRE)—High Park Lady (IRE) **J. P. McManus**
28 **CLEMENCY,** 4, b f Halling (USA)—China Tea (USA) **Elite Racing Club**
29 **CLONDAW BANKER (IRE),** 6, b g Court Cave (IRE)—Freya Alex **A. D. Spence**
30 **CLOSE TOUCH,** 7, ch g Generous (IRE)—Romantic Dream **Her Majesty The Queen**
31 **COCKTAILS AT DAWN,** 7, b g Fair Mix (IRE)—Fond Farewell (IRE) **R J H Geffen & Sir John Ritblat**
32 **COOL MACAVITY (IRE),** 7, b g One Cool Cat (USA)—Cause Celebre (IRE) **Triermore Stud**
33 **CULTIVATOR,** 4, b g Alflora (IRE)—Angie Marinie **Kimmins Family & Friends**
34 **CUP FINAL (IRE),** 6, ch g Presenting—Asian Maze (IRE) **J. P. McManus**
35 **DAWALAN (FR),** 5, gr g Azamour (IRE)—Daltawa (IRE) **Mr Simon Munir & Mr Isaac Souede**
36 **DAYS OF HEAVEN (FR),** 5, b br g Saint des Saints (FR)—Daramour (FR) **M. A. C. Buckley**
37 **DERKSEN (IRE),** 5, b g Robin des Champs (FR)—Anns Present (IRE) **T. J. Hemmings**
38 **DIFFERENT GRAVEY (IRE),** 5, b g High Chaparral (IRE)—Newtown Dancer (IRE) **Mr & Mrs R. G. Kelvin-Hughes**
39 **EARTH AMBER,** 6, ch m Hurricane Run (IRE)—Too Marvelous (FR) **Pump & Plant Services Ltd**
40 **ERICHT (IRE),** 9, b g Alderbrook—Lady Orla (IRE) **Mrs B. A. Hanbury**
41 **FAIRLEE GREY,** 6, gr g Fair Mix (IRE)—Halo Flora **J. L. Gledson**
42 **FELL RUNNER,** 4, b g High Chaparral (IRE)—Firoza (FR) **Anthony Speelman**
43 **FINIAN'S RAINBOW (IRE),** 12, b g Tiraaz (USA)—Trinity Gale (IRE) **M. A. C. Buckley**
44 **FOREVER FIELD (IRE),** 5, b g Beneficial—Sarahs Reprive (IRE) **R. M. Kirkland**

## MR NICKY HENDERSON - Continued

45 **FORGOTTEN VOICE (IRE),** 10, b g Danehill Dancer (IRE)—Asnieres (USA) **Mrs S. M. Roy**
46 **FRENCH OPERA,** 12, b g Bering—On Fair Stage (IRE) **Mrs Judy Wilson & Martin Landau**
47 **FULL SHIFT (FR),** 6, b g Ballingarry (IRE)—Dansia (GER) **J. P. McManus**
48 **GAITWAY,** 5, b g Medicean—Milliegait **Mrs J. K. Powell**
49 **GOLD PRESENT (IRE),** 5, br g Presenting—Ouro Preto **Mr & Mrs J. D. Cotton**
50 **GOLDEN HOOF (IRE),** 7, b g Oscar (IRE)—Nuovo Style (IRE) **The Hoof Partnership**
51 **GOOD IDEA (IRE),** 4, b g Arcadio (GER)—Aunt Annie (IRE) **Mrs F. H. Hay**
52 **GRANIT (IRE),** 5, b g Arcadio (GER)—Can't Stop (GER) **Mrs J. K. Powell**
53 **HADRIAN'S APPROACH (IRE),** 8, b g High Chaparral (IRE)—
Gifted Approach (IRE) **Mr & Mrs R. G. Kelvin-Hughes**
54 **HAMMERSLY LAKE (FR),** 7, b g Kapgarde (FR)—Loin de Moi (FR) **M. A. C. Buckley**
55 **HARGAM (FR),** 4, gr g Sinndar (IRE)—Horasana (FR) **J. P. McManus**
56 **HASSLE (IRE),** 6, b g Montjeu (IRE)—Canterbury Lace (USA) **A. D. Spence**
57 **HEL TARA,** 6, b m Kayf Tara—Heltornic (IRE) **Racegoers Club Owners Group**
58 **HERITAGE WAY,** 6, b g Tamayaz (CAN)—Morning Caller (IRE) **Million in Mind Partnership**
59 **HUNT BALL (IRE),** 10, b g Winged Love (IRE)—La Fandango (IRE) **Atlantic Equine**
60 **HUNTERS HOOF (IRE),** 6, b g Flemensfirth (USA)—Madgehil (IRE) **London Bridge Racing Partnership**
61 **HURRICANE HIGGINS (IRE),** 7, br g Hurricane Run (IRE)—Mare Aux Fees **A. D. Spence**
62 **IN FAIRNESS (IRE),** 6, b g Oscar (IRE)—Dix Huit Brumaire (FR) **Mr Simon Munir & Mr Isaac Souede**
63 **JACK FROST,** 5, ch g Midnight Legend—Bella Macrae **Her Majesty The Queen**
64 **JOSSES HILL (IRE),** 7, b g Winged Love (IRE)—Credora Storm (IRE) **A. D. Spence**
65 **JUST THE WAY IT IS,** 5, b m Presenting—Storm In Front (IRE) **Morecombe Sangster Sangster & Allison**
66 **KARAZHAN,** 7, b g Dr Fong (USA)—Karasta (IRE) **Pump & Plant Services Ltd**
67 **KILCREA VALE (IRE),** 5, b g Beneficial—Inflation (FR) **A. D. Spence**
68 **KILLIECRANKIE,** 7, b g Kayf Tara—Bella Macrae **Her Majesty The Queen**
69 **L'AMI SERGE (IRE),** 5, b g King's Theatre (IRE)—La Zingarella (IRE) **Mr Simon Munir & Mr Isaac Souede**
70 **LAUDATORY,** 9, b g Royal Applause—Copy-Cat **Mr E. R. Newnham**
71 **LAURIUM,** 5, ch g Gold Away (IRE)—Silver Peak (FR) **The Ten From Seven**
72 **LEADEROFTHEDANCE,** 6, b m Norse Dancer (IRE)—Glenda Lough (IRE) **T. J. Whitley**
73 **LESSONS IN MILAN (IRE),** 7, b g Milan—Lessons Lass (IRE) **T. J. Hemmings**
74 **LIEUTENANT MILLER,** 9, b g Beat All (USA)—Still Runs Deep **W. H. Ponsonby**
75 **LOLLI (IRE),** 5, b m High Chaparral (IRE)—Unicamp **Potensis Bloodstock Ltd & J Palmer Brown**
76 **LONG RUN (FR),** 10, b br g Cadoudal (FR)—Libertina (FR) **R. B. Waley-Cohen**
77 **LOUGH KENT,** 6, b g Barathea (IRE)—King's Doll (IRE) **Mrs C. M. Mould**
78 **LYVIUS,** 7, b g Paolini (GER)—Lysuna (GER) **T. J. Hemmings**
79 **MA FILLEULE (FR),** 7, gr m Turgeon (USA)—Kadaina (FR) **S. E. Munir**
80 **MAD ABOUT THE BOY,** 5, b g Robin des Pres (FR)—Dalamine (FR) **M. A. C. Buckley**
81 **MAESTRO ROYAL,** 6, b g Doyen (IRE)—Close Harmony **Mrs R. H. Brown**
82 **MAGIC BULLET (IRE),** 4, b g Flemensfirth (USA)—Some Bob Back (IRE) **C. N. Barnes**
83 **MAGNA CARTOR,** 5, b g Motivator—Hora **Mr & Mrs R. G. Kelvin-Hughes**
84 **MAGNIMITY (IRE),** 5, b g Generous (IRE)—Strawberry Fool (FR) **Sibbertoft Bloodstock Limited**
85 **MAYFAIR MUSIC (IRE),** 6, br m Presenting—Native Bid (IRE) **Mrs E. C. Roberts**
86 **MEDIEVAL CHAPEL (FR),** 7, gr g Ballingarry (IRE)—Best Ever (FR) **R. A. Bartlett**
87 **MEGALYPOS (FR),** 6, b br g Limnos (JPN)—Bourbonnaise (FR) **Mr Simon Munir & Mr Isaac Souede**
88 **MIGHT BITE (IRE),** 6, b g Scorpion (IRE)—Knotted Midge (IRE) **The Knot Again Partnership**
89 **MINSTREL ROYAL,** 5, b g Kayf Tara—Close Harmony **Mrs R. H. Brown**
90 **MISTER CHAIRMAN (IRE),** 7, b g Shantou (USA)—Out of Trouble (IRE) **Lady Tennant**
91 **MY WIGWAM OR YOURS (IRE),** 6, b g Beneficial—Midnight Pond (IRE) **The Happy Campers**
92 **NATIVE DISPLAY (IRE),** 5, b g Presenting—Native Shore (IRE) **Potensis Bloodstock Ltd & J Palmer Brown**
93 **NESTERENKO (GER),** 6, b g Doyen (IRE)—Nordwahl (GER) **Mr J. Meyer**
94 **NEW HORIZONS (IRE),** 5, b g Presenting—Namloc (IRE) **Lady Tennant**
95 **NEW MEMBER (IRE),** 4, b g Alhaarth (IRE)—Sincere (IRE) **Mrs F. H. Hay**
96 **NEW PROVIDENCE (FR),** 4, b br g Le Fou (IRE)—Bahamas (FR) **W. H. Ponsonby**
97 **NEWSWORTHY (IRE),** 5, br g Presenting—Cousin Jen (IRE) **Michael Buckley & Mrs Susannah Ricci**
98 **NICOLAS CHAUVIN (IRE),** 7, b g Saffron Walden (FR)—Kenzie (IRE) **The Gleneagles Partnership**
99 **O O SEVEN (IRE),** 5, b g Flemensfirth (USA)—Kestral Heights (IRE) **Triermore Stud**
100 **OK CORRAL (IRE),** 5, b g Mahler—Acoola (IRE) **Mrs S. Magnier**
101 **ONE FOR THE GUV'NR (IRE),** 6, b g Oscar (IRE)—Wintry Day (IRE) **Bradley Partnership**
102 **ONE LUCKY LADY,** 7, b m Lucky Story (USA)—One For Philip **S W Group Logistics Limited**
103 **ONLY FOR LOVE,** 4, br f Kalanisi (IRE)—Sardagna (FR) **W. H. Ponsonby**
104 **OPEN HEARTED,** 8, b g Generous (IRE)—Romantic Dream **Her Majesty The Queen**
105 **OSCAR HOOF (IRE),** 7, b g Oscar (IRE)—New Legislation (IRE) **The Hoof Partnership**
106 **OUT SAM,** 6, b g Multiplex—Tintera (IRE) **Mr & Mrs R. G. Kelvin-Hughes**
107 **PEACE AND CO (FR),** 4, b g Falco (USA)—Peace Lina (FR) **Mr Simon Munir & Mr Isaac Souede**
108 **PEGGY DO (IRE),** 7, b m Pierre—So Marvellous (IRE) **Mr Simon Munir & Mr Isaac Souede**

## MR NICKY HENDERSON - Continued

**109 PEPPAY LE PUGH (IRE),** 4, b g Arakan (USA)—Pinaflore (FR) **Potensis Bloodstock Limited**
**110 POLLY PEACHUM (IRE),** 7, b m Shantou (USA)—Miss Denman (IRE) **Lady Tennant**
**111 POUGNE BOBBI (FR),** 4, b br g Protektor (GER)—Amicus **Mr J. Meyer**
**112 PREMIER BOND,** 5, b g Kayf Tara—Celtic Native (IRE) **Middleham Park Racing XI**
**113 PRINCESS OMBU (IRE),** 4, gr f High Chaparral (IRE)—Cause Celebre (IRE) **Triermore Stud**
**114 PRIORY LAD (IRE),** 4, b g Arcadio (GER)—Auction Hall **R. M. Kirkland**
**115 QUIET CANDID (IRE),** 6, b m Beneficial—Lady of Appeal (IRE) **Middleham Park Racing XXXIV**
**116 RAJDHANI EXPRESS,** 8, br g Presenting—Violet Express (FR) **R. B. Waley-Cohen**
**117 RIVER MAIGUE (IRE),** 8, b g Zagreb (USA)—Minor Tantrum (IRE) **M. A. C. Buckley**
**118 ROBINS REEF (IRE),** 5, br m Robin des Champs (FR)—Tropical Ocean (IRE) **Kelvin-Hughes & Bartlett**
**119 ROLLING STAR (FR),** 6, b g Smadoun (FR)—Lyli Rose (FR) **Michael Buckley & The Vestey Family**
**120 ROYAL BOY (FR),** 8, b br g Lavirco (GER)—Quintanilla (FR) **M. A. C. Buckley**
**121 ROYAL IRISH HUSSAR (IRE),** 5, b g Galileo (IRE)—Adjalisa (IRE) **Triermore Stud**
**122 SAINT CHARLES (FR),** 5, b g Manduro (GER)—Tropical Barth (IRE) **J. P. McManus**
**123 SHAKALAKABOOMBOOM (IRE),** 11, b g Anshan—Tia Maria (IRE) **L. Breslin**
**124 SHERNANDO,** 8, b g Hernando (FR)—Shimmering Sea **Mr & Mrs Sandy Orr**
**125 SIGN OF A VICTORY (IRE),** 6, b g Kayf Tara—Irish Wedding (IRE) **Matt & Lauren Morgan**
**126 SILVERHOW (IRE),** 4, br g Yeats (IRE)—Monte Solaro (IRE) **Mrs P. J. Pugh**
**127 SIMONSIG,** 9, gr g Fair Mix (IRE)—Dusty Too **R. A. Bartlett**
**128 SNAKE EYES (IRE),** 7, b g Oscar (IRE)—Be My Belle (IRE) **J. P. McManus**
**129 SPARTAN ANGEL (IRE),** 7, b m Beneficial—Greek Melody (IRE) **Mrs Mary-Anne Parker & Crimbourne Stud**
**130 SPECIAL AGENT,** 6, b g Invincible Spirit (IRE)—Flight of Fancy **Her Majesty The Queen**
**131 SPEEDY TUNES (IRE),** 8, b g Heron Island (IRE)—Art Lover (IRE) **Jimmy Hack Racing Partners**
**132 SPRINTER SACRE (FR),** 9, b br g Network (GER)—Fatima III (FR) **Mrs C. M. Mould**
**133 SUGAR BARON (IRE),** 5, b g Presenting—Shuil Oilean (IRE) **Anthony Speelman**
**134 SUMMER STORM,** 5, b g Lucarno (USA)—Midsummer Magic **Her Majesty The Queen**
**135 SWEET DEAL (IRE),** 5, gr g Verglas (IRE)—Compromise (FR) **Mrs S. M. Roy**
**136 TANKS FOR THAT (IRE),** 12, br g Beneficial—Lady Jurado (IRE) **Mrs B. A. Hanbury**
**137 TAYLOR (IRE),** 6, b m Presenting—Britway Lady (IRE) **Mr Simon Munir & Mr Isaac Souede**
**138 THEINVAL (FR),** 5, b g Smadoun (FR)—Kinevees (FR) **Mr & Mrs Sandy Orr**
**139 TISTORY (FR),** 8, ch g Epalo (GER)—History (FR) **Mrs J. Wilson**
**140 TOP NOTCH (FR),** 4, b g Poliglote—Topira (FR) **Mr Simon Munir & Mr Isaac Souede**
**141 TOWERING (IRE),** 6, b g Catcher In The Rye (IRE)—Bobs Article (IRE) **Middleham Park Racing LIX**
**142 TRIOLO D'ALENE (FR),** 8, ch g Epalo (GER)—Joliette d'alene (FR) **Mr & Mrs Sandy Orr**
**143 VAILLANT NONANTAIS (FR),** 4, b g My Risk (FR)—Sweet Life (FR) **Mrs J. K. Powell**
**144 VANITEUX (FR),** 6, br g Voix du Nord (FR)—Expoville (FR) **Mr & Mrs R. G. Kelvin-Hughes**
**145 VASCO DU RONCERAY (FR),** 6, gr g Al Namix (FR)—
Landza de Ronceray (FR) **Mr Simon Munir & Mr Isaac Souede**
**146 VERYGOODVERYGOOD (FR),** 4, b g Yeats (IRE)—Rose d'or (IRE) **Walters Plant Hire Ltd**
**147** 4, B g Gamut (IRE)—Vivre Aimer Rire (FR) **Eventmasters Racing**
**148 VODKA 'N TONIC (IRE),** 6, b g Presenting—Ballagh Dawn (IRE) **Bradley Partnership**
**149 VOLNAY DE THAIX (FR),** 6, ch g Secret Singer (FR)—Mange de Thaix (FR) **Mrs J. Wilson**
**150 VYTA DU ROC (FR),** 6, gr g Lion Noir—Dolce Vyta (FR) **Mr Simon Munir & Mr Isaac Souede**
**151 WALT (IRE),** 4, b g King's Theatre (IRE)—Allee Sarthoise (FR) **Potensis Bloodstock Limited**
**152 WEST WIZARD (FR),** 6, b br g King's Theatre (IRE)—Queen's Diamond (GER) **Walters Plant Hire Ltd**
**153 WHAT A JEWEL (IRE),** 5, ch m Presenting—Borleagh Blonde (IRE) **Seven Barrows Limited**
**154 WHISPER (FR),** 7, b g Astarabad (USA)—Belle Yepa (FR) **Walters Plant Hire Ltd**
**155 WHOSHOTWHO (IRE),** 4, br g Beneficial—Inishbeg House (IRE) **The Blue Bar Partnership**
**156 WILLIAM DU BERLAIS (FR),** 4, b g Trempolino (USA)—King's Daughter (FR) **J. P. McManus**
**157 WILLIAM HENRY (IRE),** 5, b g King's Theatre (IRE)—Cincuenta (IRE) **Walters Plant Hire Ltd**
**158 WISHING WIND,** 5, b m Kayf Tara—Romantic Dream **Her Majesty The Queen**

## MR NICKY HENDERSON - Continued

**Other Owners:** Miss J. K. Allison, Mrs V. A. P. Antell, Mr R. B. Antell, Mrs D. E. Austin, Mrs F. Bartlett, Mrs S. M. Beckell, Mr M. J. Bell, Mr D. Bickerton, Mrs D. C. Broad, A. R. Bromley, B. G. Brown, Mr S. W. Buckley, Mr B. J. Bull, E. Burke, Mr M. J. Butt, Mr J. G. Camping, Mr N. J. Carter, Mr A. Chandler, Mr P. R. Clinton, Mrs J. F. Collins, Mrs L. Cooper, P. J. Cornell, Mr S. F. Coton, J. D. Cotton, Mrs B. Cotton, Mr J. P. Craft, J. M. Curtis, G. M. Davies, Mr D. Downie, Mrs G. J. Edwards, A. T. Eggleton, Mr T. K. Frame, Mr D. G. Fussey, Mr R. J. H. Geffen, Mr C. M. Giles, G. F. Goode, C. O. P. Hanbury, R. V. Harding, N. J. Henderson, Mr A. J. Hill, Mr B. M. Hillier, J. Hornsey, Mr E. J. Hughes, D. Humphreys, J. F. Jarvis, R. G. Kelvin-Hughes, Mrs E. A. Kelvin-Hughes, Mr M. B. J. Kimmins, Mr C. Kimmins, Mrs A. M. Kirk, Mrs S. D. Knipe, M. R. Landau, Mr R. Lewis, K. F. J. Loads, Mr J. Lomas, Mr R. Mackenzie, Miss N. Martin, Mr C. W. Matthews, Mr D. M. Menzies, Mr I. D. Miller, P. J. Mills, W. D. C. Minton, Mr J. Monaghan, R. H. W. Morecombe, M. Morgan, Mrs L. K. Morgan, Dr A. Morris, Mrs D. C. Nicholson, Miss M. Noden, Mr L. D. Nunn, Mrs C. R. Orr, Mr J. A. M. Orr, M. A. Osborne, T. S. Palin, J. Palmer-Brown, Mrs M. Parker, Mr C. M. Parker, S. R. C. Philip, S. I. Pollard, Brig C. K. Price, Mr S. P. Price, M. Prince, Mr R. J. Rexton, Mrs S. Ricci, Mr M. A. Richardson, Sir J. H. Ritblat, Paul Robson, Mr A. J. Romer, Miss P. A. Ross, Mr M. E. Sangster, Mr S. E. Sangster, U. E. Schwarzenbach, Mr H. S. Sharpstone, Mrs D. Sheasby, Mr G. A. Sheppard, Mr J. Simpson, Mr M. S. Smith, Mr I. Souede, D. F. Sumpter, Mrs N. J. G. Thorbek-Hooper, Mr D. Turner, Lord Vestey, The Hon W. G. Vestey, The Hon A. G. Vestey, Mr L. J. Westwood, Mr S. D. Whiting, Miss S. Wilde, Mr M. J. F. T. Wilson.

**Jockey (NH):** Barry Geraghty, A. P. McCoy, Andrew Tinkler, David Bass. **Conditional:** Jeremiah McGrath, Peter Carberry, Nico De Boinville, Freddie Mitchell.

---

**295**

## MR PAUL HENDERSON, Whitsbury

Postal: **1 Manor Farm Cottage, Whitsbury, Fordingbridge, Hampshire, SP6 3QP**
Contacts: **PHONE (01725) 518113 FAX (01725) 518113 MOBILE (07958) 482213**
**E-MAIL phendersonracing@gmail.com**

1 **ALRIGHT BENNY (IRE),** 12, ch g Beneficial—Flashey Thyne (IRE) **The Affordable (2) Partnership**
2 **ANOTHER LUSO (IRE),** 7, b h Luso—Itty Bitty Tear (IRE) **J. H. W. Finch**
3 **BACK IN JUNE,** 7, b g Bach (IRE)—Bathwick June (IRE) **Mrs D. H. Potter**
4 **CABALLO DE MARCUS (USA),** 8, b g Black Sam Bellamy (IRE)—Zizi Top **The Rockbourne Partnership**
5 **CALL ME WIN (IRE),** 6, gr g Fleetwood (IRE)—Betseale (IRE) **Mr R. B. Antell**
6 **CARHUE (IRE),** 8, b g Luso—Awtaar (USA)
7 **CHARGING INDIAN (IRE),** 9, b g Chevalier (IRE)—Kathy Tolfa (IRE) **Mr N. D. G. Brown**
8 **CHILL (IRE),** 7, b g Diamond Green (FR)—Time To Relax (IRE) **Mrs V. M. Brown**
9 **CNOC SEODA (IRE),** 10, b m Dr Massini (IRE)—Hill Diamond (IRE) **Mr R. B. Antell**
10 **DALLAS CLOUD (IRE),** 8, b g Cloudings (IRE)—Hardy Lamb (IRE) **Mr R. B. Antell**
11 **DANCING DIK,** 10, b g Diktat—Maureena (IRE) **The Rockbourne Partnership**
12 **FLASHY STAR,** 6, ch m Mr Greeley (USA)—Galileo's Star (IRE) **The Affordable (3) Partnership**
13 **GARDE FOU (FR),** 9, b g Kapgarde (FR)—Harpyes (FR) **Mr R. B. Antell**
14 **HENRY OLIVER (IRE),** 7, b g Hasten To Add (USA)—Lisnabrin (IRE) **The Affordable (3) Partnership**
15 **JOSIE JUMP,** 6, b m Crosspeace (IRE)—Chipewyas (FR) **D. V. Stevens**
16 **KATCHA KOPEK (IRE),** 7, b m Craigsteel—Moscow Money (IRE) **The Rockbourne Partnership**
17 **MARTIN CASH (IRE),** 9, b g Oscar (IRE)—Native Singer (IRE) **The Rockbourne Partnership**
18 **MISS OSCAROSE (IRE),** 8, b m Oscar (IRE)—Private Rose (IRE) **Sarah Habib & Ed Hawkings**
19 **MOUNT VESUVIUS (IRE),** 7, b g Spartacus (IRE)—Parker's Cove (USA) **Mr R. B. Antell**
20 **ONE MORE TUNE (IRE),** 7, b g Luso—Strong Gale Pigeon (IRE) **Mareildar Racing Part 1**
21 **PADDY THE STOUT (IRE),** 10, b g Oscar Schindler (IRE)—Misty Silks **The Pearly Kings Partnership**
22 **RIOR (IRE),** 8, b g King's Theatre (IRE)—Sara's Gold (IRE) **Mr R. B. Antell**
23 **SCHINDLERS ROCK (IRE),** 11, b g Oscar Schindler (IRE)—Smokey Lodge (IRE) **Mr R. G. Henderson**
24 **STARKIE,** 8, b g Putra Sandhurst (IRE)—Lysways **D. S. Dennis**
25 **WHERE'D YA HIDE IT (IRE),** 9, b g Old Vic—Stashedaway (IRE) **Mr R. G. Henderson**

**Other Owners:** Mr A. Butlin, Mr S. Clegg, Mr R. J. Galpin, Mrs S. J. Habib, Mr E. J. Hawkings, P. F. Henderson, Mr D. L. Lacey.

---

## MR MICHAEL HERRINGTON, Thirsk

Postal: **Garbutt Farm, Cold Kirby, Thirsk, North Yorkshire, YO7 2HJ**
Contacts: **PHONE (01845) 597793 MOBILE (07855) 396858 / (07554) 558217**
**E-MAIL info@michaelherringtonracing.co.uk WEBSITE www.michaelherringtonracing.co.uk**

1 **DAZEEN,** 8, b g Zafeen (FR)—Bond Finesse (IRE) **Mr & Mrs D. Yates**
2 **HADAJ,** 6, b g Green Desert (USA)—My Amalie (IRE) **Mr J. S. Herrington**
3 **INDASTAR,** 5, b g Indesatchel (IRE)—Charcoal **Mr K. Blackstone**

## MR MICHAEL HERRINGTON - Continued

4 **KINGSCROFT (IRE),** 7, b g Antonius Pius (USA)—Handsome Anna (IRE) **Mr G. Sheehy**
5 **MISHAAL (IRE),** 5, ch g Kheleyf (USA)—My Dubai (IRE) **Kelvyn Gracie & Lawrence McCaughey**
6 **PETER'S FRIEND,** 6, b g Gentleman's Deal (IRE)—Giffoine **Mr J. S. Herrington**
7 **SEVEN LUCKY SEVEN,** 4, b g Avonbridge—Moon Bird **Mr N. Galovics**
8 **STEELRIVER (IRE),** 5, b g Iffraaj—Numerus Clausus (FR) **Mr & Mrs D. Yates**
9 **TWIN POINT,** 4, br g Invincible Spirit (IRE)—Gemini Joan **Mr & Mrs D. Yates**
10 **WORCHARLIE'SLASS,** 4, b f Myboycharlie (IRE)—Angry Bark (USA) **H. M. Hurst**

### THREE-YEAR-OLDS

11 **PRYERS PRINCESS,** ch f Medicean—Opening Ceremony (USA) **H. M. Hurst**

### TWO-YEAR-OLDS

12 B f 5/5 Captain Gerrard (IRE)—Dazakhee (Sakhee (USA)) (1904) **Mr & Mrs D. Yates**
13 B c 31/3 Dutch Art—Miss Respect (Mark of Esteem (IRE)) **H. M. Hurst**
14 B c 19/4 Motivator—Opening Ceremony (USA) (Quest For Fame) (20952) **H. M. Hurst**

**Other Owners:** Mr Kelvyn Gracie, Mr Lawrence McCaughey, Mr D. Yates, Mrs Annaley Yates.

**Assistant Trainer:** Helen Lloyd-Herrington

---

## 297 MR PETER HIATT, Banbury

Postal: **Six Ash Farm, Hook Norton, Banbury, Oxfordshire, OX15 5DB**
Contacts: **PHONE (01608) 737255 FAX (01608) 730641 MOBILE (07973) 751115**

1 **COCONELL,** 5, b m Rock of Gibraltar (IRE)—Marula (IRE) **Mr C. Demczak**
2 **DESPERADO DANCER,** 4, b g Iffraaj—Madam Ninette **P. W. Hiatt**
3 **FLAG OF GLORY,** 8, b g Trade Fair—Rainbow Sky **N. D. Edden**
4 **GAME MASCOT,** 5, ch g Kheleyf (USA)—Tolzey (USA) **Robert E Lee Syndicate**
5 **GEEAITCH,** 6, ch g Cockney Rebel (IRE)—Grand Rebecca (IRE) **P. J. R. Gardner**
6 **LAMBERT PEN (USA),** 5, ch g Johannesburg (USA)—Whiletheiron'shot (USA) **P. W. Hiatt**
7 **MAZIJ,** 7, b m Haafhd—Salim Toto **P. Kelly**
8 **MEXICAN MICK,** 6, ch g Atraf—Artic Bliss **First Chance Racing**
9 **MONARCH MAID,** 4, b f Captain Gerrard (IRE)—Orange Lily **Mr C. Demczak**
10 **ROXY LANE,** 6, b m Byron—Comme Ca **Mr R G Robinson & Mr R D Robinson**
11 **THEWESTWALIAN (USA),** 7, b br g Stormy Atlantic (USA)—Skies Of Blue (USA) **P. W. Hiatt**
12 **WILDOMAR,** 6, b g Kyllachy—Murrieta **P. W. Hiatt**

**Other Owners:** M. J. Benton, Mrs S. V. Benton, Mr T. J. Boniface, Mr R. G. Robinson, Mr R. D. Robinson, Mr M. J. Savage.

**Assistant Trainer:** Mrs E. Hiatt

**Jockey (flat):** William Carson, Chris Catlin. **Apprentice:** Ryan Clark. **Amateur:** Miss M. Edden.

---

## 298 MR PHILIP HIDE, Findon

Postal: **Cissbury Stables, Findon, Worthing, West Sussex, BN14 0SR**
Contacts: **MOBILE (07768) 233324**

1 **BLACK CAESAR (IRE),** 4, b g Bushranger (IRE)—Evictress (IRE) **The Long Furlong**
2 **SILENT PURSUIT,** 4, br f Pastoral Pursuits—Lay A Whisper **Mr W. F. N. Davis**
3 **SNOW CONDITIONS,** 4, b f Aussie Rules (USA)—Snow Gonal (FR) **P. Turner, J. Davies & The Hides**
4 **URAMAZIN (IRE),** 9, ch g Danehill Dancer (IRE)—Uriah (GER) **S. P. C. Woods**
5 4, B g Yeats (IRE)—Western Skylark (IRE)
6 **ZAMBEASY,** 4, b g Zamindar (USA)—Hanella (IRE) **Heart Of The South Racing**

### THREE-YEAR-OLDS

7 **AYR OF ELEGANCE,** b f Motivator—Gaelic Swan (IRE) **Mr W. F. N. Davis**
8 **BALLROOM ANGEL,** gr f Dark Angel (IRE)—Ballroom Dancer (IRE) **Mr P. E. Hide**
9 **CLASSIC VILLAGER,** b g Authorized (IRE)—Sablonne (USA) **Mr F. L. Li**
10 Ch g Rock of Gibraltar (IRE)—Takegawa
11 **WINNING HUNTER,** b c Iffraaj—Miss Lacey (IRE) **Mr F. L. Li**

**MR PHILIP HIDE - Continued**

**TWO-YEAR-OLDS**

**12** B c 26/3 Fastnet Rock (AUS)—Cozzene's Angel (USA) (Cozzene (USA))
**13** B c 28/4 Fastnet Rock (AUS)—Dance Parade (USA) (Gone West (USA)) (60000)
**14** B c 29/4 Pivotal—Entre Nous (IRE) (Sadler's Wells (USA)) (45000)
**15** B c 3/5 Fastnet Rock (AUS)—Lasting Chance (USA) (American Chance (USA))
**16** B c 10/3 Archipenko (USA)—Native Nickel (IRE) (Be My Native (USA))
**17** Gr f 13/3 Hellvelyn—Soft Touch (IRE) (Petorius) **Heart Of The South Racing**

**Other Owners:** Exors of the Late Mr C. V. Cruden, J. Davies, Mr A. G. Hide, J. R. Penny, Miss E. Penny, Mr P. Turner.

---

## 299 MRS LAWNEY HILL, Aston Rowant

Postal: **Woodway Farm, Aston Rowant, Watlington, Oxford, OX49 5SJ**
Contacts: **PHONE (01844) 353051 FAX (01844) 354751 MOBILE (07769) 862648**
**E-MAIL lawney@lawneyhill.co.uk WEBSITE www.lawneyhill.co.uk**

1 **BILLY TWYFORD (IRE),** 8, b g Brian Boru—The Distaff Spy **Mr A. J. Weller**
2 **CARROWBEG (IRE),** 7, b g Cape Cross (IRE)—Love And Affection (USA) **A. Hill**
3 **CHANGEOFLUCK (IRE),** 7, b g Gold Well—Sotattie **For Fun Partnership**
4 **CHAPOLIMOSS (FR),** 11, ch g Trempolino (USA)—Chamoss (FR) **A Barr, J Basquill, A Hill, H Mullineux**
5 **COOLKING,** 8, b g King's Theatre (IRE)—Osocool **Sir Peter & Lady Forwood**
6 **DOUBLE HANDFUL (GER),** 9, bl g Pentire—Durania (GER) **Les Cross, Teresa Cross, Alan Hill**
7 **DOUBLE U DOT EDE'S,** 6, b g Rock of Gibraltar (IRE)—Reveuse de Jour (IRE) **The Sunday Night Partnership**
8 **EL TOREROS (USA),** 7, b g El Prado (IRE)—Soul Reason (USA) **Chasing Gold Limited**
9 **I HAVE DREAMED (IRE),** 13, b g Montjeu (IRE)—Diamond Field (USA) **G. Byard**
10 **MIGHTY MAMBO,** 8, b g Fantastic Light (USA)—Mambo's Melody **Fortnum Racing**
11 **OLIVER'S HILL (IRE),** 6, b g Shantou (USA)—River Rouge (IRE) **Mrs D. M. Caudwell**
12 **OSIRIS EMERY (FR),** 6, b g Equerry (USA)—Natashwan **Mr A. K. Phillips**
13 **RAVENS NEST,** 5, b g Piccolo—Emouna **Unregistered Partnership**
14 **ROYAL ETIQUETTE (IRE),** 8, b g Royal Applause—Alpine Gold (IRE) **A. Hill**
15 **RUDE AND CRUDE (IRE),** 6, b g Rudimentary (USA)—Sorry Sarah (IRE) **Sir Peter & Lady Forwood**
16 **SAFE INVESTMENT (USA),** 11, b g Gone West (USA)—Fully Invested (USA) **A. Hill**
17 **SHIMBA HILLS,** 4, b g Sixties Icon—Search Party **The Shimba Hills Partnership**
18 **SO OSCAR (IRE),** 7, b g Oscar (IRE)—So Proper (IRE) **Mrs K. G. Exall**
19 **TAKE A BOW,** 6, b g Norse Dancer (IRE)—Madame Illusion (FR) **Take A Bow Partnership**
20 **TORRAN SOUND,** 8, b g Tobougg (IRE)—Velvet Waters **Mrs D. Clark**
21 **VIEL GLUCK (IRE),** 12, b g Supreme Leader—Discerning Air **A. Hill**

**Other Owners:** Mr A. D. Barr, Mr J. M. Basquill, A. L. Cohen, Mr L. R. Cross, Mrs T. C. Cross, Sir P. N. Forwood, Lady H. R. Forwood, Ms G. H. Hedley, Mrs T. J. Hill, Mr B. L. Hiskey, Mr B. P. Jessup, Mrs H. C. Mullineux, D. F. Sumpter.

**Jockey (flat):** Dane O'Neill. **Jockey (NH):** David Bass, Aidan Coleman. **Amateur:** Mr Joe Hill.

---

## 300 MR MARTIN HILL, Totnes

Postal: **The Barn, Knaves Ash Stables, Nr Redpost, Littlehempston, Totnes, Devon, TQ9 6NG**
Contacts: **PHONE (01803) 813102 MOBILE (07980) 490220**
**E-MAIL info@martinhillracing.co.uk WEBSITE www.martinhillracing.co.uk**

1 **ABSOLUTLYFANTASTIC,** 8, b g Alhaarth (IRE)—Persian Walk (FR) **Fantastic Four**
2 **BUSINESSMONEY JUDI,** 9, ch m Kirkwall—Cloverjay **Business Money Promotions Limited**
3 **CARRE NOIR (FR),** 6, b br g Clety (FR)—Luella (FR) **The Pi Eyed Squared**
4 **DETROIT RED,** 9, b m Hamairi (IRE)—Kingston Black **The Detroit Reds**
5 **EASILY PLEASED (IRE),** 9, b g Beneficial—Bro Ella (IRE) **Roger Oliver & Claire Harding**
6 **ELLA'S PROMISE,** 6, ch m Doyen (IRE)—Sweet N' Twenty **M. E. Hill**
7 **FLAMENCO LAD,** 5, b g Tamure (IRE)—Monda **Kittymore Racing**
8 **GAELIC ICE,** 6, b m Iceman—Gaelic Lime **The Jack High Racing Partnership**
9 **LUCKY GAL,** 5, b m Overbury (IRE)—Lucky Arrow **The Village People**
10 **MIKEY MISS DAISY,** 4, ch f Champs Elysees—Savoy Street **Mr M. Leach**
11 **MIXELLE DAYS,** 4, gr f Sagamix (FR)—One of Those Days **Merv Leach & Jon Hearne**
12 **OCEAN VENTURE (IRE),** 7, ch g Urban Ocean (FR)—Starventure (IRE) **Mr R. G. Dennis**
13 **RYDON PYNES,** 7, b g Beat All (USA)—Persian Smoke **The Rydon Pynes Partnership**
14 **SHIVSINGH,** 6, b g Montjeu (IRE)—Vistaria (USA) **M. E. Hill**
15 **THE RATTLER OBRIEN (IRE),** 9, b g Beneficial—Clonea Lady (IRE) **Spirit Of Devon**

## MR MARTIN HILL - Continued

16 **TZORA,** 10, b g Sakhee (USA)—Lucky Arrow **Tzora Partners**
17 **WATCOMBE HEIGHTS (IRE),** 5, b g Scorpion (IRE)—Golden Bay **The R C Partnership**
18 **Y A BON (IRE),** 7, b g Black Sam Bellamy (IRE)—Tarte Fine (FR) **M. E. Hill**

**Other Owners:** Mr J. L. Coombs, Mrs J. Elliott, Mr N. D. Elliott, Mrs C. M. Harding, J. S. Hearne, Mrs A. L. A. Hutchings, Mr R. R. Lester, Mrs H. M. Luscombe, Mr D. Luscombe, Mr N. Matthews, Mrs E. J. Mogford, R. O. Oliver, Mr A. Palk, Mr K. Pook, Mr P. G. Serjeant, Mr R. Thomasson, Mrs C. D. Tibbetts, Mr D. R. Tribe, Mrs P. A. Wolfenden.

**Assistant Trainer:** Rachel Williams

**Jockey (flat):** Luke Morris. **Jockey (NH):** Hadden Frost. **Conditional:** Jeremiah McGrath. **Amateur:** Miss Alice Mills.

---

## 301 MR B. W. HILLS, Lambourn

Postal: **Kingwood House Stables, Lambourn, Hungerford, Berkshire, RG17 7RS**
Contacts: **PHONE (01488) 73144**
**E-MAIL rstanding@kingwoodhousestables.co.uk**

1 **ELKAAYED (USA),** 5, ch g Distorted Humor (USA)—Habibti (USA) **Hamdan Al Maktoum**
2 **MAWASEEL,** 4, ch g Sea The Stars (IRE)—Kareemah (IRE) **Hamdan Al Maktoum**
3 **MAZAAHER,** 5, b g Elnadim (USA)—Elutrah **Hamdan Al Maktoum**
4 **MEZEL,** 4, b g Tamayuz—Mumayeza **Hamdan Al Maktoum**

### THREE-YEAR-OLDS

5 **ALGAITH (USA),** b c Dubawi (IRE)—Atayeb (USA) **Hamdan Al Maktoum**
6 **BAYLAY (USA),** b g Blame (USA)—Rock Candy (USA) **Hamdan Al Maktoum**
7 **FADHAYYIL (IRE),** b f Tamayuz—Ziria (IRE) **Hamdan Al Maktoum**
8 **KAFAALA (IRE),** b f Shamardal (USA)—Hammiya (IRE) **Hamdan Al Maktoum**
9 **KIBAAR,** b c Pastoral Pursuits—Ashes (IRE) **Hamdan Al Maktoum**
10 **MARKAZ (IRE),** gr c Dark Angel (IRE)—Folga **Hamdan Al Maktoum**
11 **MOHATEM (USA),** ch c Distorted Humor (USA)—Soul Search (USA) **Hamdan Al Maktoum**
12 **MOONADEE (IRE),** gr g Haatef (USA)—Again Royale (IRE) **Hamdan Al Maktoum**
13 **MUFFARREH (USA),** b c First Samurai (USA)—Sarayir (USA) **Hamdan Al Maktoum**
14 **MUGHARRED (USA),** gr c Bernardini (USA)—Wid (USA) **Hamdan Al Maktoum**
15 **NAFAQA (IRE),** b c Sir Percy—Maghya (IRE) **Hamdan Al Maktoum**
16 **SAHAAFY (USA),** b br c Kitten's Joy (USA)—Queen's Causeway (USA) **Hamdan Al Maktoum**
17 **SARHAAN,** b g New Approach (IRE)—Coveted **Hamdan Al Maktoum**
18 **SIRDAAB (USA),** b c City Zip (USA)—Stormy Union (USA) **Hamdan Al Maktoum**
19 **TAFAHOM (IRE),** b c Acclamation—Dance Set **Hamdan Al Maktoum**
20 **TEDHKAAR (IRE),** b f Teofilo (IRE)—Merayaat (IRE) **Hamdan Al Maktoum**
21 **WARDAT DUBAI,** b f Mawatheeq (USA)—Efisio's Star **Mr K. Al Sayegh**

### TWO-YEAR-OLDS

22 **BASMA,** b f 9/3 Exceed And Excel (AUS)—Miss Chicane (Refuse To Bend (IRE)) (257936) **Hamdan Al Maktoum**
23 **BROADWAY MELODY,** b f 22/2 Arcano (IRE)—Oriental Melody (IRE) (Sakhee (USA)) **Hadi Al-Tajir**
24 **EHTIRAAS,** b c 24/3 Oasis Dream—Kareemah (IRE) (Peintre Celebre (USA)) **Hamdan Al Maktoum**
25 **FAWAAREQ (IRE),** b c 24/2 Invincible Spirit (IRE)—Ghandoorah (USA) (Forestry (USA)) **Hamdan Al Maktoum**
26 **JABBAAR,** ch c 7/4 Medicean—Echelon (Danehill (USA)) (400000) **Hamdan Al Maktoum**
27 **KHAMEELA,** b f 31/1 Equiano (FR)—Mina (Selkirk (USA)) (75000) **Hamdan Al Maktoum**
28 B f 11/3 Dream Ahead (USA)—Lady Livius (IRE) (Titus Livius (FR)) (210000) **Hamdan Al Maktoum**
29 **MAKANAH (IRE),** b c 19/1 New Approach (IRE)—Kitty Kiernan (Pivotal) **Hamdan Al Maktoum**
30 **MASARZAIN (IRE),** br c 29/3 Kodiac—Cache Creek (IRE) (Marju (IRE)) (220000) **Hamdan Al Maktoum**
31 **MASSAAT (IRE),** b c 20/2 Teofilo (IRE)—Madany (IRE) (Acclamation) **Hamdan Al Maktoum**
32 **MIDHMAAR,** b c 3/5 Iffraaj—Merayaat (IRE) (Darshaan) **Hamdan Al Maktoum**
33 **MITHQAAL (USA),** ch c 15/3 Speightstown (USA)—Bestowal (USA) (Unbridled's Song (USA)) **Hamdan Al Maktoum**
34 **MUBAJAL,** br c 19/2 Dubawi (IRE)—Jadhwah (Nayef (USA)) **Hamdan Al Maktoum**
35 **MUNTAZAH,** b c 2/2 Dubawi (IRE)—Rumoush (USA) (Rahy (USA)) **Hamdan Al Maktoum**
36 **MUSTAJEER,** b c 17/4 Medicean—Qelaan (USA) (Dynaformer (USA)) **Hamdan Al Maktoum**
37 **RAAQY (IRE),** gr f 30/3 Dubawi (IRE)—Natagora (FR) (Divine Light (JPN)) **Hamdan Al Maktoum**
38 **SIRDAAL (USA),** b c 16/3 Medaglia d'Oro (USA)—Sarayir (USA) (Mr Prospector (USA)) **Hamdan Al Maktoum**
39 **TANASOQ (IRE),** b c 7/2 Acclamation—
Alexander Youth (IRE) (Exceed And Excel (AUS)) (180000) **Hamdan Al Maktoum**

**Assistant Trainer:** Mr Owen Burrows. **Head Lad:** John Lake

**Jockey (flat):** Paul Hanagan, Dane O'Neill. **Apprentice:** Tommy O'Connor, Tyler Saunders.

## 302 MR CHARLES HILLS, Lambourn

Postal: **Wetherdown House, Lambourn, Hungerford, Berkshire, RG17 8UB**
Contacts: **PHONE (01488) 71548 FAX (01488) 72823**
**E-MAIL info@charleshills.co.uk WEBSITE www.charleshills.com**

1 **B FIFTY TWO (IRE),** 6, br g Dark Angel (IRE)—Petite Maxine **Gary and Linnet Woodward**
2 **BARBS PRINCESS,** 5, ch m Bahamian Bounty—Halland Park Girl (IRE) **Mrs Barbara James**
3 **BOOMERANG BOB (IRE),** 6, b h Aussie Rules (USA)—Cozzene's Pride (USA) **Mr R. J. Tufft**
4 **CABLE BAY (IRE),** 4, b c Invincible Spirit (IRE)—
Rose de France (IRE) **Julie Martin & David R. Martin & Partner**
5 **CAMBRIDGE,** 4, b f Rail Link—Alumni **Mr K. Abdullah**
6 **CAPTAIN BOB (IRE),** 4, b g Dark Angel (IRE)—Birthday Present **Mr A. L. R. Morton**
7 **FORGOTTEN HERO (IRE),** 6, b br g High Chaparral (IRE)—Sundown **Mrs Julie Martin and David R. Martin**
8 **GREEB,** 4, b g Oasis Dream—Shamtari (IRE) **Mr Hamdan Al Maktoum**
9 **JALLOTA,** 4, b g Rock of Gibraltar (IRE)—Lady Lahar **Mrs Fitri Hay**
10 **JUST THE JUDGE (IRE),** 5, b br m Lawman (FR)—
Faraday Light (IRE) **Qatar Racing Limited & China Horse Club**
11 **KIYOSHI,** 4, b f Dubawi (IRE)—Mocca (IRE) **Qatar Racing Limited**
12 **LUCKY BEGGAR (IRE),** 5, gr h Verglas (IRE)—Lucky Clio (IRE) **Hon Mrs Corbett, C. Wright, Mrs B. W. Hills**
13 **MOONTOWN,** 4, ch g Sea The Stars (IRE)—Eva's Request (IRE) **Mr B. W. Hills**
14 **OGBOURNE DOWNS,** 5, b g Royal Applause—Helen Sharp **S W Group Logistics Limited**
15 **PASSING STAR,** 4, b c Royal Applause—Passing Hour (USA) **Mr John C. Grant**
16 **QUEEN CATRINE (IRE),** 4, b f Acclamation—Kahira (IRE) **QRL/Sheikh Suhaim Al Thani/M. Al Kubaisi**
17 **TANZEEL (IRE),** 4, b g Elusive City (USA)—Royal Fizz (IRE) **Mr Hamdan Al Maktoum**
18 **XINBAMA (IRE),** 6, b h Baltic King—Persian Empress (IRE) **Tony Waspe Partnership**

### THREE-YEAR-OLDS

19 **ABHAJAT (IRE),** b f Lope de Vega (IRE)—Starry Messenger **Mr Hamdan Al Maktoum**
20 **ACES (IRE),** b c Dark Angel (IRE)—Cute Ass (IRE) **Qatar Racing & Essafinaat**
21 **ALJAAZYA (USA),** b f Speightstown (USA)—Matiya (IRE) **Mr Hamdan Al Maktoum**
22 **ALNASHAMA,** b c Dubawi (IRE)—Ghanaati (USA) **Mr Hamdan Al Maktoum**
23 **ANGELS WINGS (IRE),** b f Dark Angel (IRE)—Startarette (USA) **Lady Bamford**
24 **ARKANSAS SLIM (IRE),** b g Montjeu (IRE)—Janoubi **Mr B. W. Hills**
25 **ASIMA (IRE),** ch f Halling (USA)—Sospira **Sheikh Juma Dalmook Al Maktoum**
26 **ATAB (IRE),** b f New Approach (IRE)—Moon's Whisper (USA) **Mr Hamdan Al Maktoum**
27 **BEAT GOES ON,** gr c Piccolo—Cherrycombe-Row **Jim & Susan Hill**
28 **BLING RING (USA),** b br f Arch (USA)—Youcan'ttakeme (USA) **Sheikh Suhaim Al Thani/QRL/M. Al Kubaisi**
29 **CAELICA (IRE),** b f Sea The Stars (IRE)—Vital Statistics **Racegoers Club Owners Group**
30 **CALIMA BREEZE,** b f Oasis Dream—Paris Winds (IRE) **Mrs B. V. Sangster**
31 **CARPE VITA (IRE),** b f Montjeu (IRE)—Dance Parade (USA) **Sir Robert Ogden**
32 **CASTLE TALBOT (IRE),** b g Rock of Gibraltar (IRE)—Louve Sacree (USA) **Mr M. V. Magnier & Mrs Fitri Hay**
33 **COLORATION (USA),** b br f Rock Hard Ten (USA)—Tinge (USA) **Mr K. Abdullah**
34 **COMMEMORATIVE,** ch c Zamindar (USA)—Revered **Mr K. Abdullah**
35 **CORZETTI (FR),** ch g Linngari (IRE)—Green Maid (USA) **Linguine Partnership**
36 **COTAI GLORY,** ch c Exceed And Excel (AUS)—Continua (USA) **Ms A. A. Yap & Mr F. Ma**
37 **DANCETRACK (USA),** b c First Defence (USA)—Jazz Drummer (USA) **Mr K. Abdullah**
38 **DARK LIGHT (IRE),** b g Dark Angel (IRE)—Spring View **Jim & Susan Hill**
39 **DARK PROFIT (IRE),** gr c Dark Angel (IRE)—Goldthroat (IRE) **Mrs Fitri Hay**
40 **DOUBLY CLEVER (IRE),** ch g Iffraaj—Smartest (IRE) **Jim & Susan Hill**
41 **DUCHESS OF MARMITE (IRE),** b f Duke of Marmalade (IRE)—
Reprise **R. Morecombe, M. Gibbens, Des Anderson**
42 **DUTCH CONNECTION,** ch c Dutch Art—Endless Love (IRE) **Mrs Susan Roy**
43 **DYNAMO ACE,** b f Dansili—High Praise (USA) **Mr K. Abdullah**
44 **EARTH GODDESS,** b f Invincible Spirit (IRE)—Clara Bow (IRE) **Lady Bamford**
45 **EQUILICIOUS,** b f Equiano (FR)—Fabine **Mr D. M. James**
46 **FALCONIZE (IRE),** b f Henrythenavigator (USA)—Crystal Crossing (IRE) **Mrs Paul Shanahan & Mr A. V. Nicoll**
47 **FAST PICK (IRE),** b f Fastnet Rock (AUS)—Dream Time **Jim & Susan Hill**
48 **FINTON FRIEND (IRE),** b c Fast Company (IRE)—Right Ted (IRE) **Kennet Valley Thoroughbreds IX**
49 **FREE TO LOVE,** br f Equiano (FR)—All Quiet **Lady Whent**
50 **GIANT DANCER (USA),** ch f Giant's Causeway (USA)—A Mind of Her Own (IRE) **Jim & Susan Hill**
51 **GILDED LILI (IRE),** b f Big Bad Bob (IRE)—City Vaults Girl (IRE) **Mrs J. K. Powell**
52 **GRASS ROOTS,** gr g Pastoral Pursuits—Southern Psychic (USA) **Mrs J. K. Powell**
53 **HAKAM (USA),** b br c War Front (USA)—Lauren Byrd (USA) **Mr Hamdan Al Maktoum**
54 **HEATSTROKE (IRE),** b c Galileo (IRE)—Walklikeanegyptian (IRE) **Mrs Fitri Hay**
55 **HUNDI (IRE),** b f Fastnet Rock (AUS)—Hawala (IRE) **The Hon Mrs P. Stanley & Sir Peter Vela**

## MR CHARLES HILLS - Continued

56 **ILLUSIVE FORCE (IRE),** ch c Iffraaj—Geesala (IRE) **Sheikh Juma Dalmook Al Maktoum**
57 **INAUGURATION (IRE),** b f Acclamation—Carraigoona (IRE) **Mrs Fitri Hay**
58 B f Motivator—Israar **Sheikh Suhaim Al Thani/QRL/M Al Kubaisi**
59 **JUST CHING (IRE),** b f Fastnet Rock (AUS)—Adjalisa (IRE) **Triermore Stud**
60 **KHAREER (IRE),** b c Acclamation—Fantastic Account **Mr Hamdan Al Maktoum**
61 **KILL OR CURE (IRE),** b g Acclamation—Welsh Mist **Hillwood Racing**
62 **KIZINGO (IRE),** b f Oasis Dream—Enora (GER) **Mr K. Abdullah**
63 **KODIVA (IRE),** b f Kodiac—Operissimo **The Black Gold Partnership**
64 **KYLLARNEY,** b f Kyllachy—Hurricane Harriet **Mr D. M. James & Mr B. M. Gordon**
65 **LAMYAA,** ch f Arcano (IRE)—Divine Grace (IRE) **Mr Hamdan Al Maktoum**
66 **LEDBURY (IRE),** b c Lawman (FR)—Truly Magnificent (USA) **Qatar Racing Limited**
67 **LONGSIDE,** b c Oasis Dream—Hypoteneuse (IRE) **Mr K. Abdullah**
68 **MAGICAL MEMORY (IRE),** gr g Zebedee—Marasem **Kennet Valley Thoroughbreds I**
69 **MARY MCPHEE,** ch f Makfi—Aunty Mary **J. Gompertz, Sir Peter Vela, Qatar Racing**
70 **MILE HIGH,** b f Fastnet Rock (AUS)—Crinolette (IRE) **K. MacLennan, M. V. Magnier, Mrs P. Shanahan**
71 **MISS NEW ZEALAND (AUS),** b f Galileo (IRE)—Queen of Spain (IRE) **Jeffrey Hobby, Alex Frost, Mrs G. Galvin**
72 **MUHAARAR,** b c Oasis Dream—Tahrir (IRE) **Mr Hamdan Al Maktoum**
73 **MY REWARD,** b c Rail Link—Tarot Card **Mr K. Abdullah**
74 **NAWAASY (USA),** ch f Distorted Humor (USA)—Stormin Maggy (USA) **Mr Hamdan Al Maktoum**
75 **OPITO BAY (IRE),** ch f Bahamian Bounty—Reveuse de Jour (IRE) **Sir Peter Vela**
76 **PANDORA (IRE),** ch f Galileo (IRE)—Song of My Heart (IRE) **Sir Robert Ogden**
77 **PHARMACEUTICAL (IRE),** b c Invincible Spirit (IRE)—Pharmacist (IRE) **Mrs Fitri Hay**
78 **PURPLE ROCK (IRE),** b c Fastnet Rock (AUS)—Amethyst (IRE) **Morecombe, Anderson, Sangster, Farquhar**
79 **RATE,** b f Galileo (IRE)—Artful (IRE) **Qatar Racing Limited**
80 **RENAISSANCE RED,** ch g Medicean—Special Moment (IRE) **Mr & Mrs T. O'Donohoe**
81 **ROSSLARE (IRE),** b f Fastnet Rock (AUS)—Waterways (IRE) **Mrs E. Roberts**
82 **SAFE PLACE (USA),** b f Rock Hard Ten (USA)—Costume **Mr K. Abdullah**
83 **SAGUNA (FR),** b f Le Havre (IRE)—Sandy Winner (FR) **Mrs J. K. Powell**
84 **SALT ISLAND,** b c Exceed And Excel (AUS)—Tiana **Julie Martin & David R. Martin & Partner**
85 **SAVE THE DATE,** b c Zamindar (USA)—Daring Miss **Mr K. Abdullah**
86 **SILVER RAINBOW (IRE),** gr f Starspangledbanner (AUS)—Enchanting Way **Mr R. J. Tufft**
87 **STAR OF SPRING (IRE),** b f Iffraaj—Gift of Spring (USA) **The Chriselliam Partnership**
88 **STINKY SOCKS (IRE),** b f Footstepsinthesand—City of Cities (IRE) **Plantation Stud**
89 **STRATH BURN,** b c Equiano (FR)—Irish Light (USA) **Qatar Racing & Meikle Ben Stables Ltd**
90 **SYDNEY HEIGHTS (IRE),** ch c Lord Shanakill (USA)—Ashdali (IRE) **John C. Grant & Ray Harper**
91 **TAQNEYYA (IRE),** b f Raven's Pass (USA)—Misdaqeya **Mr Hamdan Al Maktoum**
92 **TEA WITH ELEANOR (IRE),** b f Duke of Marmalade (IRE)—Ms Sophie Eleanor (USA) **Jim & Susan Hill**
93 **THE TWISLER,** b g Motivator—Panna **Mr B. W. Hills**
94 **TWISTAWAY (IRE),** b f Teofilo (IRE)—River Mountain **Mr Rick Barnes**
95 **VALENTINE MIST (IRE),** b f Vale of York (IRE)—Silvertine (IRE) **The Valentine Mist Partnership**
96 **VIRGINIA CELESTE (IRE),** b f Galileo (IRE)—Crystal Valkyrie (IRE) **Triermore Stud**
97 **VIXEN HILL,** b f Acclamation—Heckle **Plantation Stud**
98 **WHERE'S SUE (IRE),** br f Dark Angel (IRE)—The Hermitage (IRE) **Jim & Susan Hill**
99 **WITH APPROVAL (IRE),** b c Approve (IRE)—Kelsey Rose **Mr K. T. Ivory**
100 **WOLF OF WINDLESHAM (IRE),** ch g Mastercraftsman (IRE)—Al Amlah (USA) **Gary and Linnet Woodward**
101 Ch f Compton Place—Zing **Lady Caffyn-Parsons**

## TWO-YEAR-OLDS

102 **A MOMENTOFMADNESS,** b c 19/3 Elnadim (USA)—Royal Blush (Royal Applause) (68571)
103 B c 25/2 Dutch Art—Akhira (Emperor Jones (USA)) (65000)
104 **ALBARAAHA (IRE),** b f 25/4 Iffraaj—Tolzey (USA) (Rahy (USA)) (104761)
105 **ALEEF (IRE),** b c 17/3 Kodiac—Okba (USA) (Diesis) (85000)
106 **AMAANY,** br f 13/3 Teofilo (IRE)—Almass (IRE) (Elnadim (USA))
107 **ANCIENT WORLD (USA),** ch c 19/4 Giant's Causeway (USA)—Satulagi (USA) (Officer (USA))
108 B c 23/3 Fast Company (IRE)—Ann's Annie (IRE) (Alzao (USA)) (80952)
109 **ARCAMIST,** gr f 22/2 Arcano (IRE)—Good Enough (FR) (Mukaddamah (USA)) (30000)
110 **ARITHMETIC (IRE),** b c 22/2 Invincible Spirit (IRE)—Multiplication (Marju (IRE)) (45000)
111 **ART STORY (IRE),** ch f 14/2 Galileo (IRE)—Impressionist Art (USA) (Giant's Causeway (USA))
112 B c 13/3 Canford Cliffs (IRE)—Basanti (USA) (Galileo (IRE)) (40000)
113 **BURMA ROAD,** b f 11/1 Poet's Voice—Strawberry Moon (IRE) (Alhaarth (IRE)) (16000)
114 B f 30/3 Iffraaj—Burren Rose (USA) (Storm Cat (USA)) (79364)
115 **CAPTAIN JOEY (IRE),** b c 1/3 Kodiac—Archetypal (IRE) (Cape Cross (IRE)) (70000)
116 Br c 15/4 Big Bad Bob (IRE)—Caro Mio (IRE) (Danehill Dancer (IRE)) (60000)
117 Ch f 3/2 Iffraaj—Chicane (Motivator) (65000)
118 B c 9/4 High Chaparral (IRE)—Civility Cat (USA) (Tale of The Cat (USA)) (91269)

## MR CHARLES HILLS - Continued

**119 CLOUDY GIRL (IRE),** gr f 11/2 Lawman (FR)—Vespetta (FR) (Vespone (IRE)) (38095)
**120** B c 27/4 Le Havre (IRE)—Como (USA) (Cozzene (USA)) (45000)
**121** B f 17/3 Shamardal (USA)—Dehbanu (IRE) (King's Best (USA)) (80000)
**122** Br c 23/3 Equiano (FR)—Delitme (IRE) (Val Royal (FR)) (20000)
**123** B f 27/2 Sakhee's Secret—Dimakya (USA) (Dayjur (USA))
**124 DR DREY (IRE),** ch c 28/3 Bahamian Bounty—Mount Lavinia (IRE) (Montjeu (IRE)) (35000)
**125 ELRONAQ,** b c 3/4 Invincible Spirit (IRE)—Cartimandua (Medicean)
**126** B f 11/4 Sixties Icon—Endless Love (IRE) (Dubai Destination (USA))
**127** B f 28/3 Scat Daddy (USA)—Excelente (IRE) (Exceed And Excel (AUS)) (126983)
**128** B c 31/3 Rip Van Winkle (IRE)—Faraday Light (IRE) (Rainbow Quest (USA))
**129** B f 14/2 Afleet Alex (USA)—Faraway Flower (USA) (Distant View (USA))
**130 GARTER (IRE),** b f 28/4 Fastnet Rock (AUS)—Princess Iris (IRE) (Desert Prince (IRE)) (87300)
**131** B c 13/4 Sir Percy—Half Sister (IRE) (Oratorio (IRE)) (28571)
**132 IBN MALIK (IRE),** ch c 23/2 Raven's Pass (USA)—Moon's Whisper (USA) (Storm Cat (USA))
**133** B br c 16/5 Congrats (USA)—Intercontinental (Danehill (USA))
**134 IONA ISLAND,** b f 9/3 Dutch Art—Still Small Voice (Polish Precedent (USA)) (100000)
**135 JADAAYIL,** b f 17/2 Oasis Dream—Muthabara (IRE) (Red Ransom (USA))
**136 JOULES,** b c 28/3 Oasis Dream—Frappe (IRE) (Inchinor) (215000)
**137 KAFOOR (IRE),** b c 20/3 Dubawi (IRE)—Tahrir (IRE) (Linamix (FR))
**138** Ch f 26/3 Dream Ahead (USA)—Khibraat (Alhaarth (IRE)) (55000)
**139** B c 8/4 Kodiac—Kilakey (IRE) (Key of Luck (USA)) (42000)
**140 KOMEDY (IRE),** b f 16/3 Kodiac—Dancing Jest (IRE) (Averti (IRE)) (55555)
**141** B f 26/4 Invincible Spirit (IRE)—Laywaan (USA) (Fantastic Light (USA)) (67000)
**142 LORD KELVIN (IRE),** b c 29/1 Iffraaj—Eastern Appeal (IRE) (Shinko Forest (IRE)) (120000)
**143 LORD TOPPER,** b c 23/4 Sir Percy—Fugnina (Hurricane Run (IRE)) (30000)
**144 MAHFOOZ (IRE),** b c 21/4 Teofilo (IRE)—Itqaan (USA) (Danzig (USA))
**145 MARBOOH (IRE),** b c 25/4 Dark Angel (IRE)—Muluk (IRE) (Rainbow Quest (USA)) (120000)
**146** B f 30/4 Champs Elysees—Marching West (USA) (Gone West (USA))
**147** B f 19/4 Roderic O'Connor (IRE)—Marigold (FR) (Marju (IRE)) (23809)
**148 MENAI (IRE),** b c 7/2 Dark Angel (IRE)—Glisten (Oasis Dream) (100000)
**149 MISHWAAR,** b c 7/2 Arcano (IRE)—Misdaqeya (Red Ransom (USA))
**150** B c 30/1 Kyllachy—Money Note (Librettist (USA)) (50000)
**151** B f 31/3 Clodovil (IRE)—Mrs Seek (Unfuwain (USA)) (60000)
**152 MUSTALLIB (IRE),** b c 27/3 Iffraaj—Rocking (Oasis Dream)
**153** Ch f 8/2 Exceed And Excel (AUS)—My Love Thomas (IRE) (Cadeaux Genereux) (90000)
**154** B c 20/4 Royal Applause—Never A Doubt (Night Shift (USA))
**155** B f 2/2 Makfi—Nimboo (USA) (Lemon Drop Kid (USA)) (31745)
**156** B c 12/4 Champs Elysees—Phantom Wind (USA) (Storm Cat (USA))
**157** Ch f 14/4 Teofilo (IRE)—Queen of Lyons (USA) (Dubai Destination (USA)) (65000)
**158** Ch c 4/4 Dubawi (IRE)—Revered (Oasis Dream)
**159** Ch f 21/2 Congrats (USA)—Rouwaki (USA) (Miswaki (USA))
**160 SAHREEJ (IRE),** b gr c 13/3 Zebedee—Petite Boulangere (IRE) (Namid) (160000)
**161** B f 17/4 Kodiac—Scarlet Empress (Second Empire (IRE)) (65000)
**162** B f 5/2 Dick Turpin (IRE)—Serial Sinner (IRE) (High Chaparral (IRE)) (23809)
**163 SERRADURA (IRE),** b f 14/2 Acclamation—Days of Summer (IRE) (Bachelor Duke (USA)) (79364)
**164 SHANGHAI GLORY (IRE),** ch c 7/3 Exceed And Excel (AUS)—Hecuba (Hector Protector (USA)) (91269)
**165** B c 19/5 Paco Boy (IRE)—Sheer Indulgence (FR) (Pivotal) (57142)
**166** B c 22/2 Champs Elysees—Short Dance (USA) (Hennessy (USA))
**167 SIR ROGER MOORE (IRE),** b c 1/4 Kodiac—Truly Magnificent (USA) (Elusive Quality (USA)) (79364)
**168** B f 2/3 Excellent Art—Summer Bliss (Green Desert (USA)) (37300)
**169 SWILLY SUNSET,** b c 8/2 Kyllachy—Spanish Springs (IRE) (Xaar) (63491)
**170 TAKATUL (USA),** b c 23/4 Smart Strike (CAN)—Torrestrella (IRE) (Orpen (USA))
**171** B f 27/2 Acclamation—Tesary (Danehill (USA)) (19047)
**172** B c 14/4 Dark Angel (IRE)—Toffee Vodka (IRE) (Danehill Dancer (IRE)) (19047)
**173** B f 21/3 Teofilo (IRE)—Towards (USA) (Fusaichi Pegasus (USA)) (55000)
**174 TURAATHY (IRE),** b f 5/3 Lilbourne Lad (IRE)—Key Girl (IRE) (Key of Luck (USA)) (61904)
**175** B f 18/5 Rip Van Winkle (IRE)—Windmill (Ezzoud (IRE)) (45000)
**176** B f 29/1 Canford Cliffs (IRE)—Winged Valkyrie (IRE) (Hawk Wing (USA)) (22000)
**177 ZAAKHIR (IRE),** b f 21/2 Raven's Pass (USA)—Zahoo (IRE) (Nayef (USA))
**178** B c 6/2 Elnadim (USA)—Zenella (Kyllachy) (35000)

**Other Owners:** Sheikh Rashid Dalmook Al Maktoum, Mr N. N. Browne, Mr Lee Tze Bunmarces, Cavendish Investing Ltd, Chelsea Thoroughbreds - Juan Les Pins, Crimbourne Stud, Mr Dan Hall, Highclere Thoroughbred Racing (Walpole), Mrs Clare Kelvin, Mrs John Magnier, Mick & Janice Mariscotti, Mr Paul McNamara, Mr George Popov, Mr A. M. Shead, Mr M. Tabor, Tony Wechsler & Ann Plummer.

**MR CHARLES HILLS - Continued**

**Assistant Trainers:** Kevin Mooney, Joe Herbert

**Apprentice:** George Blackwell.

---

## 303 MR MARK HOAD, Lewes

Postal: **Windmill Lodge Stables, Spital Road, Lewes, East Sussex, BN7 1LS**
Contacts: **PHONE (01273) 477124/(01273) 480691 FAX (01273) 477124 MOBILE (07742) 446168**
**E-MAIL markhoad@aol.com**

1 **AL GUWAIR (IRE),** 5, b g Shirocco (GER)—Katariya (IRE) **G. C. Brice**
2 **DOCTOR HILARY,** 13, b g Mujahid (USA)—Agony Aunt **J. Baden White**
3 **HIGHSALVIA COSMOS,** 4, b g High Chaparral (IRE)—Salvia **J. Baden White**
4 **ISHISOBA,** 5, ch m Ishiguru (USA)—Bundle Up (USA) **Mr M. M. Cox**
5 **RAGDOLLIANNA,** 11, b m Kayf Tara—Jupiters Princess **Mr D. M. & Mrs M. A. Newland**
6 **SANTADELACRUZE,** 6, b g Pastoral Pursuits—Jupiters Princess **Mr D. M. & Mrs M. A. Newland**
7 **SEBS SENSEI (IRE),** 4, ch g Art Connoisseur (IRE)—Capetown Girl **Mr M. J. Huxley**
8 **STAGE GIRL,** 4, b f Tiger Hill (IRE)—Primavera **Mrs I. L. Sneath**

### THREE-YEAR-OLDS

**9** B f Cockney Rebel (IRE)—Xandra (IRE)

**Other Owners:** D. M. Newland, Mrs M. A. Newland.

---

## 304 MR PHILIP HOBBS, Minehead

Postal: **Sandhill, Bilbrook, Minehead, Somerset, TA24 6HA**
Contacts: **PHONE (01984) 640366 FAX (01984) 641124 MOBILE (07860) 729795**
**E-MAIL pjhobbs@pjhobbs.com WEBSITE www.pjhobbs.com**

1 **ACCORDING TO SARAH (IRE),** 7, ch m Golan (IRE)—Miss Accordion (IRE) **P. J. Hobbs**
2 4, B g King's Theatre (IRE)—Afdala (IRE) **J. P. McManus**
3 **AL ALFA,** 8, ch g Alflora (IRE)—Two For Joy (IRE) **The Hon J. R. Drummond**
4 **ALISIER D'IRLANDE (FR),** 5, b br g Kapgarde (FR)—Isati's (FR) **R. S. Brookhouse**
5 **ALLTHEKINGSHORSES (IRE),** 9, b g King's Theatre (IRE)—Penny Brae (IRE) **Allthekingsmen**
6 **ASTON CANTLOW,** 7, b g Hurricane Run (IRE)—Princess Caraboo (IRE) **J. C. Murphy**
7 **AVEL VOR (IRE),** 4, ch c Green Tune (USA)—High Perfection (IRE) **Govier & Brown**
8 **BACCHANEL (FR),** 4, b g Vendangeur (IRE)—Pardielle (FR) **Gold & Blue Limited**
9 **BALLYGARVEY (FR),** 9, b g Laveron—Vollore (FR) **The Dark Horse Syndicate**
10 **BALTHAZAR KING (IRE),** 11, b g King's Theatre (IRE)—Afdala (IRE) **The Brushmakers**
11 **BERTIE BORU (IRE),** 8, b g Brian Boru—Sleeven Lady **Unity Farm Holiday Centre Ltd**
12 **BIG EASY (GER),** 8, b g Ransom O'war (USA)—Basilea Gold (GER) **J. T. Warner**
13 **BIG TOUCH (FR),** 4, br b g Network (GER)—Etoile d'or II (FR) **Walters Plant Hire Ltd**
14 **BILBROOK BLAZE,** 5, b g Kayf Tara—Za Beau (IRE) **Owners For Owners: Bilbrook Blaze**
15 **BINCOMBE,** 7, gr g Indian Danehill (IRE)—Siroyalta (FR) **M. Short**
16 **BOLD HENRY,** 9, b g Kayf Tara—Madam Min **J. P. McManus**
17 **BOOTED EAGLE (IRE),** 5, b g Oscar (IRE)—Warmley's Gem (IRE) **Mrs C. Skan**
18 **BROTHER TEDD,** 6, gr g Kayf Tara—Neltina **Scrase Farms**
19 **CARA CARLOTTA,** 6, br m Presenting—Dara's Pride (IRE) **T. D. J. Syder**
20 **CARRIGMORNA KING (IRE),** 9, b g King's Theatre (IRE)—Carrigmorna Flyer (IRE) **R. & Mrs J. E. Gibbs**
21 **CATHERINES WELL,** 6, b m Kayf Tara—Dudeen (IRE) **Mr M. Pendarves**
22 **CHAMPAGNE WEST (IRE),** 7, b g Westerner—Wyndham Sweetmarie (IRE) **R. S. Brookhouse**
23 **CHANCE DU ROY (FR),** 11, ch g Morespeed—La Chance Au Roy (FR) **Miss I. D. Du Pre**
24 **CHELTENIAN (FR),** 9, b g Astarabad (USA)—Salamaite (FR) **R. S. Brookhouse**
25 **CLOUD CREEPER (IRE),** 8, b g Cloudings (IRE)—First of April (IRE) **Mick Fitzgerald Racing Club**
26 **COLOUR SQUADRON (IRE),** 9, b g Old Vic—That's The Goose (IRE) **J. P. McManus**
27 **COPPER KAY,** 5, b m Kayf Tara—Presenting Copper (IRE) **Aiden Murphy & Alan Peterson**
28 **DALIA POUR MOI (FR),** 6, gr g Daliapour (IRE)—Khariyada (FR) **Highclere Thoroughbred Racing - Dalia**
29 **DANANDY (IRE),** 8, b g Cloudings (IRE)—Tower Princess (IRE) **P. J. Hobbs**
30 **DRUMLEE SUNSET (IRE),** 5, br g Royal Anthem (USA)—Be My Sunset (IRE) **R. S. Brookhouse**
31 **DRY OL'PARTY,** 5, ch m Tobougg (IRE)—Emergence (FR) **Woodmore Racing**
32 **DUKE DES CHAMPS (IRE),** 5, b g Robin des Champs (FR)—Ballycowan Lady (IRE) **Diana Whateley & Tim Syder**
33 **DUNRAVEN STORM (IRE),** 10, br g Presenting—Foxfire **Mrs K. V. Vann**

## MR PHILIP HOBBS - Continued

34 **FAYRE ENOUGH (IRE),** 5, ch g Whitmore's Conn (USA)—Fairy Tango (FR) **N Turner, C Schicht & A Merriam**
35 **FILBERT (IRE),** 9, b g Oscar (IRE)—Coca's Well (IRE) **R Triple H**
36 **FINGAL BAY (IRE),** 9, b g King's Theatre (IRE)—Lady Marguerrite **Mrs C. Skan**
37 **FREE OF CHARGE (IRE),** 6, ch g Stowaway—Sweetasanu (IRE) **A. P. Staple**
38 5, Br g King's Theatre (IRE)—Full of Birds (FR) **Mrs D. L. Whateley**
39 **GARDE LA VICTOIRE (FR),** 6, b g Kapgarde (FR)—Next Victory (FR) **Mrs D. L. Whateley**
40 **GAS LINE BOY (IRE),** 9, b g Blueprint (IRE)—Jervia **Mick Fitzgerald Racing Club**
41 **GEORGIE LAD (IRE),** 7, b g Gold Well—Top Step (IRE) **D R Peppiatt & Partners (Georgie Lad)**
42 4, B g Scorpion (IRE)—Glory Queen (IRE) **Mrs D. L. Whateley**
43 **GOLDEN DOYEN (GER),** 4, b g Doyen (IRE)—Goldsamt (GER) **Merry Old Souls**
44 4, B g Milan—Green Star (FR) **Mrs D. L. Whateley**
45 **HANDSOME HORACE (IRE),** 5, b g Presenting—Paumafi (IRE) **Mr Tim Syder & Mr M St Quinton**
46 **HE'S A BULLY (IRE),** 6, b g Westerner—Kitty Maher (IRE) **Owners For Owners: He's A Bully**
47 **HELLO GEORGE (IRE),** 6, b g Westerner—Top Ar Aghaidh (IRE) **M. St Quinton/ C. Hellyer/ M. Strong**
48 **HORIZONTAL SPEED (IRE),** 7, b g Vertical Speed (FR)—Rockababy (IRE) **Favourites Racing Ltd**
49 **ICONIC STAR,** 5, b m Sixties Icon—Cullen Bay (IRE) **R Bothway & R Boyce**
50 **IF IN DOUBT (IRE),** 7, b g Heron Island (IRE)—Catchers Day (IRE) **J. P. McManus**
51 **IMPERIAL CIRCUS (IRE),** 9, b g Beneficial—Aunty Dawn (IRE) **R. A. S. Offer**
52 **INK MASTER (IRE),** 5, b g Whitmore's Conn (USA)—Welsh Connection (IRE) **A. E. Peterson**
53 **IRISH BUCCANEER (IRE),** 8, b g Milan—Supreme Serenade (IRE) **J. P. McManus**
54 **JAYANDBEE (IRE),** 8, b g Presenting—Christines Gale (IRE) **J & B Gibbs & Sons Ltd**
55 **KAYF WILLOW,** 6, b m Kayf Tara—Mrs Philip **Mrs S. Hobbs**
56 **KUBLAI (FR),** 5, b g Laveron—Java Dawn (IRE) **Mr D. W. Hill**
57 **LA PYLE (FR),** 4, b f Le Havre (IRE)—Lidana (IRE) **Devlin, Knox & Wells, Monroe**
58 4, B f Oscar (IRE)—Lala Nova (IRE) **Dr V. M. G. Ferguson**
59 **LAMB OR COD (IRE),** 8, ch g Old Vic—Princess Lizzie (IRE) **J. T. Warner**
60 **MEETMEATTHEMOON (IRE),** 6, gr m Flemensfirth (USA)—Valleya (FR) **Mrs C. J. Walsh**
61 **MENORAH (IRE),** 10, b g King's Theatre (IRE)—Maid For Adventure (IRE) **Mrs D. L. Whateley**
62 **MIDNIGHT VELVET,** 5, b m Midnight Legend—Tamergale (IRE) **Mrs Caren Walsh & Mrs Lesley Field**
63 **MILES TO MILAN (IRE),** 5, b g Milan—Princesse Rooney (FR) **Mrs Lesley Field & Mrs Caren Walsh**
64 **MILOSAM (IRE),** 8, b g Milan—Lady Sam (IRE) **R. J. Croker**
65 **MISTER BIG (IRE),** 4, b g Scorpion (IRE)—Back To Roost (IRE) **The Spoofers**
66 **MOUNTAIN KING,** 6, b g Definite Article—Belle Magello (FR) **Mrs D. L. Whateley**
67 4, B c Kayf Tara—My Adventure (IRE) **Mrs K. V. Vann**
68 **NECK OR NOTHING (GER),** 6, b g Intikhab (USA)—Nova (GER) **R. S. Brookhouse**
69 **NEVILLE,** 7, b g Revoque (IRE)—Dudeen (IRE) **Mr M. Pendarves**
70 **ONEFITZALL (IRE),** 5, b g Indian Danehill (IRE)—Company Credit (IRE) **Mick Fitzgerald Racing Club**
71 **ONENIGHTINVIENNA (IRE),** 6, b g Oscar (IRE)—Be My Granny **Mrs J. A. S. Luff**
72 **ORABORA,** 9, b g Alflora (IRE)—Magic Orb **Dr V. M. G. Ferguson**
73 **OUT NOW (IRE),** 11, br g Muroto—Raven Night (IRE) **D. Maxwell**
74 **OZZIE THE OSCAR (IRE),** 4, b g Oscar (IRE)—Private Official (IRE) **Bradley Partnership**
75 **PERFORM (IRE),** 6, b g King's Theatre (IRE)—Famous Lady (IRE) **Merry Old Souls**
76 **PERSIAN SNOW (IRE),** 9, b g Anshan—Alpine Message **D. R. Peppiatt**
77 **POWERFUL ACTION (IRE),** 7, b g Tau Ceti—Abbey The Leader (IRE) **Miss I. D. Du Pre**
78 **PRINCELY PLAYER (IRE),** 8, b g King's Theatre (IRE)—Temptation (FR) **Thurloe 52**
79 4, B br g Scorpion (IRE)—Princess Supreme (IRE) **The Brushmakers**
80 **PULL THE CHORD (IRE),** 5, b g St Jovite (USA)—Gold Chord (IRE) **Brocade Racing**
81 **QUICK DECISSON (IRE),** 7, b g Azamour (IRE)—Fleet River (USA) **Owners For Owners: Quick Decisson**
82 **RETURN SPRING (IRE),** 8, b g Vinnie Roe (IRE)—Bettys Daughter (IRE) **D. J. Jones**
83 **RISK A FINE (IRE),** 6, ch g Saffron Walden (FR)—Portanob (IRE) **Mrs D. L. Whateley**
84 **RIVER DEEP (IRE),** 6, ch g Mountain High (IRE)—Testaway (IRE) **Merry Old Souls**
85 **ROALCO DE FARGES (FR),** 10, gr g Dom Alco (FR)—Vonaria (FR) **The Brushmakers**
86 **ROCK THE KASBAH (IRE),** 5, ch g Shirocco (GER)—Impudent (IRE) **Mrs D. L. Whateley**
87 **ROLL THE DICE (IRE),** 9, b g Oscar (IRE)—Sallowglen Gale (IRE) **The Kingpins**
88 **ROYAL PLAYER,** 6, b g King's Theatre (IRE)—Kaydee Queen (IRE) **Mrs D. L. Whateley**
89 **ROYAL REGATTA (IRE),** 7, b g King's Theatre (IRE)—Friendly Craic (IRE) **Mr J C Murphy & Mrs L Field**
90 **SADDLERS ENCORE (IRE),** 6, br g Presenting—Saddlers Leader (IRE) **R. & Mrs J. E. Gibbs**
91 **SANDYGATE (IRE),** 5, b g Golan (IRE)—Wet And Windy **T. J. Hemmings**
92 **SAUSALITO SUNRISE (IRE),** 7, b g Gold Well—Villaflor (IRE) **Mrs D. L. Whateley**
93 **SCOOP THE POT (IRE),** 5, b g Mahler—Miss Brecknell (IRE) **J. P. McManus**
94 **SILVER COMMANDER,** 8, gr g Silver Patriarch (IRE)—New Dawn **Exe Valley Racing**
95 **SIOUX ON THE RUN,** 5, ch g With The Flow (USA)—Wotabout Sioux **Mr S T R & Mrs C V Stevens**
96 **SMADYNIUM (FR),** 7, gr g Smadoun (FR)—Sea Music (FR) **The Vacuum Pouch Company Limited**
97 **STERNRUBIN (GER),** 4, b g Authorized (IRE)—Sworn Mum (GER) **J. T. Warner**
98 **STILLETTO (IRE),** 6, b g Westerner—Eastertide (IRE) **R. S. Brookhouse**

## MR PHILIP HOBBS - Continued

99 **SYKES (IRE),** 6, b g Mountain High (IRE)—Our Trick (IRE) **Bradley Partnership**
100 **TANERKO EMERY (FR),** 9, b g Lavirco (GER)—Frequence (FR) **Walters Plant Hire Ltd Egan Waste Ltd**
101 4, Br g Presenting—Tatanka (IRE) **Mrs D. L. Whateley**
102 **TEN SIXTY (IRE),** 5, br g Presenting—Senora Snoopy (IRE) **A. L. Cohen**
103 **THE DOOM BAR (IRE),** 6, ch g Beneficial—The Sceardeen (IRE) **The Test Valley Partnership**
104 **THE SKYFARMER,** 7, br g Presenting—Koral Bay (FR) **Mrs J. J. Peppiatt**
105 **THOMAS WILD,** 10, ch g Muhtarram (USA)—Bisque **C L T**
106 **TONY STAR (FR),** 8, b g Lone Bid (FR)—Effet de Star (FR) **Thurloe 51**
107 **TOOWOOMBA (IRE),** 7, b g Milan—Lillies Bordello (IRE) **Taylormaid**
108 **TRICKAWAY (IRE),** 7, b g Stowaway—Rosie's Trix (IRE) **The Mount Fawcus Partnership**
109 **UNCLE JIMMY (IRE),** 8, b br g Alderbrook—Carrabawn **Mr A. R. E. Ash**
110 **VAL D'ARC (FR),** 6, b g Le Balafre (FR)—Lextrienne (FR) **Thurloe 54**
111 **VIEUX LILLE (IRE),** 5, b g Robin des Champs (FR)—Park Athlete (IRE) **Louisville Syndicate III**
112 **VILLAGE VIC (IRE),** 8, b g Old Vic—Etoile Margot (FR) **A. E. Peterson**
113 **WAIT FOR ME (FR),** 5, b g Saint des Saints (FR)—Aulne River (FR) **A. L. Cohen**
114 **WAR SOUND,** 6, b g Kayf Tara—Come The Dawn **The Englands and Heywoods**
115 **WESTERN JO (IRE),** 7, b g Westerner—Jenny's Jewel (IRE) **T. J. Hemmings**
116 **WISHFULL DREAMING,** 4, ch g Alflora (IRE)—Poussetiere Deux (FR) **Mrs D. L. Whateley**
117 **WISHFULL THINKING,** 12, ch g Alflora (IRE)—Poussetiere Deux (FR) **Mrs D. L. Whateley**
118 **WOODFORD COUNTY,** 8, b g Sonus (IRE)—Moylena **The Englands and Heywoods**
119 5, B g King's Theatre (IRE)—Wyndham Sweetmarie (IRE) **Diana Whateley & Tim Syder**

**Other Owners:** Mr R. B. Antell, Mr D. J. Baker, Mr J. A. Barnes, Mr M. Blackmore, Mrs P. M. Bosley, Mr C. H. Bothway, Mr R. Boyce, Mr G. R. Broom, Mrs A. E. M. Broom, G. S. Brown, C. J. Butler, Mr A. J. Chapman, R. W. Devlin, Mr T. J. Dykes, Egan Waste Services Ltd, Mr A. D. England, Mrs E. England, Mr D. V. Erskine Crum, Mrs M. W. Fawcus, Mr D. S. Fawcus, Mrs L. H. Field, H. R. Gibbs, Mrs J. E. Gibbs, Mrs C. F. Godsall, Mr P. Govier, Mr P. F. Govier, Mr R. H. M. Grant, B. J. Greening, Mr T. M. Hailstone, J. R. Hall, S. R. Harman, C. G. Hellyer, The Hon H. M. Herbert, Mr A. H. Heywood, Mr A. S. Heywood, Highclere Thoroughbred Racing Ltd, Mr J. R. Holmes, Mr E. J. Hughes, Mr B. R. Ingram, Mr J. Johnson, Knox & Wells Limited, Mr D. Lockwood, Mr A. P. Maddox, Miss N. J. Manning, Mr T. M. Manning, Miss N. Martin, Mrs R. Mason, A. W. K. Merriam, Mr J. R. Monroe, H. A. Murphy, Mr I. A. Nunn, Mr T. E. Olver, O. J. W. Pawle, B. K. Peppiatt, N. D. Peppiatt, Mr A. C. Phillips, Miss J. Pimblett, Mr R. Poole, D. A. Rees, M. J. Rowe, Mr M. C. Sargent, Miss C. Schicht, Mrs J. E. Scrase, Mr N. D. Scrase, Mr J. M. Scrase, Mr H. J. Shapter, Mr A. Signy, Mr J. Simpson, M. G. St Quinton, Mr J. A. B. Stafford, S. T. R. Stevens, Mrs C. V. Stevens, M. C. Stoddart, M. A. Strong, M. A. Swift, Mrs Ann Taylor, Mrs N. C. Turner, T. C. Wheeler, Mrs T. S. Wheeler, Mr R. M. E. Wright.

**Assistant Trainer:** Richard White

**Jockey (NH):** James Best, Richard Johnson, Tom O'Brien. **Conditional:** Tom Cheesman, Chris Davies, Micheal Nolan, Conor Smith. **Amateur:** Mr Ciaran Gethings, Mr Sean Houlihan.

---

## 305 MISS CLARE HOBSON, Royston

Postal: **The Woolpack, London Road, Reed, Royston, Hertfordshire, SG8 8BB**

1 **HOBSON'S CHOICE (IRE),** 6, b m Milan—Monica's Story **Mr H. R. Hobson**
2 **HUSTLE (IRE),** 10, ch g Choisir (AUS)—Granny Kelly (USA) **Mr H. R. Hobson**
3 **IRISH REBEL (IRE),** 11, b g Tel Quel (FR)—Never On Sunday (IRE) **Mrs R. E. Hobson**
4 **ISHUSHARELLA,** 6, b m Doyen (IRE)—Emily-Mou (IRE) **Mr H. R. Hobson**
5 **LOTTA SCARES,** 7, b g Primitive Proposal—Scare McClare **Mr H. R. Hobson**
6 **RANDS HILL,** 5, b m Fair Mix (IRE)—Proper Posh **Mrs R. E. Hobson**

---

## 306 MR RON HODGES, Somerton

Postal: **Bull Brook Stables, West Charlton, Charlton Mackrell, Somerton, Somerset, TA11 7AL**
Contacts: **PHONE (01458) 223922 FAX (01458) 223969 MOBILE (07770) 625846**
**E-MAIL mandyhodges@btconnect.com**

1 **ACTONETAKETWO,** 5, b m Act One—Temple Dancer **The Gardens Entertainments Ltd**
2 **DON'T PANIC (IRE),** 11, ch g Fath (USA)—Torrmana (IRE) **Mr A. B. S. Webb**
3 **DREAMS OF GLORY,** 7, ch h Resplendent Glory (IRE)—Pip's Dream **P. E. Axon**
4 **MISS TENACIOUS,** 8, b m Refuse To Bend (IRE)—Very Speed (USA) **John Frampton & Paul Frampton**
5 **MISTER MUSICMASTER,** 6, b g Amadeus Wolf—Misty Eyed (IRE) **Mrs L. Sharpe & Mrs S. G. Clapp**
6 **ONE LAST DREAM,** 6, ch g Resplendent Glory (IRE)—Pip's Dream **Mrs L. Sharpe & Mrs S. G. Clapp**

**MR RON HODGES - Continued**

**TWO-YEAR-OLDS**

7 B f 29/4 Hellvelyn—There's Two (IRE) (Ashkalani (IRE)) **K. Corcoran**

**Other Owners:** Mrs S. G. Clapp, Mr R. J. Hodges, Mrs L. Sharpe.

---

## 307 MR SIMON HODGSON, Yeovil

Postal: **28 The Glebe, Queen Camel, Yeovil, Somerset, BA22 7PR**
Contacts: **PHONE (01935) 851152**

1 **ASTRA HALL,** 6, ch m Halling (USA)—Star Precision **The Villains**
2 **CHAMBRAY DANCER (IRE),** 7, b m Darsi (FR)—Cotton Gale **Simon Hodgson Racing Partnership 1**
3 **DOME PATROL,** 9, b g Domedriver (IRE)—Tahoe (IRE) **Mrs L. M. Clarke**
4 **NORPHIN,** 5, b g Norse Dancer (IRE)—Orphina (IRE) **Mr J. A. Mould**
5 **ON DEMAND,** 4, ch f Teofilo (IRE)—Mimisel **Mrs L. M. Clarke**
6 **PENNY'S BOY,** 4, ch g Firebreak—Sunderland Echo (IRE) **Simon Hodgson Racing Partnership 1**
7 **QUALITY ART (USA),** 7, b g Elusive Quality (USA)—Katherine Seymour **Mrs L. M. Clarke**
8 **QUEEN CEE,** 4, b f Royal Applause—Tee Cee **Simon Hodgson Racing Partnership 1**
9 6, Gr m Act One—Spindle's **Mrs L. M. Clarke**
10 **STAN NINETEEN (IRE),** 4, b g Kodiac—Redwood Forest (IRE) **The Villains**
11 **STRONG CONVICTION,** 5, ch g Piccolo—Keeping The Faith (IRE) **George Materna & Mark Barrett**

**THREE-YEAR-OLDS**

12 **BROTHER NORPHIN,** b c Norse Dancer (IRE)—Orphina (IRE) **Mr J. A. Mould**
13 **KYLIES WILD CARD,** b f Aussie Rules (USA)—Jemiliah **N. J. Stafford**
14 **MILDMAY ARMS,** b g Kheleyf (USA)—Akathea **Simon Hodgson Racing Partnership 1**

**Other Owners:** M. Barrett, G. D. P. Materna, Mr M. A. Muddiman, Mr S. A. J. Penny, L. R. Turland.

---

## 308 MR EAMONN M. HOGAN, Roscam

Postal: **Rosshill, Roscam, Galway, Co. Galway, Ireland**
Contacts: **PHONE (00353) 91756899 MOBILE (00353) 879175175**
**E-MAIL rosshillfarm@eircom.net WEBSITE www.rosshillfarm.com**

1 **ASTEROID BELT (IRE),** 6, ch g Heliostatic (IRE)—Affaire Royale (IRE) **BIMA Partnership**
2 5, Br m Kalanisi (IRE)—Easter Day (IRE) **P. Greally**
3 4, B f Brian Boru—Gaelic Leader (IRE) **Mary Theresa Hogan**
4 5, Ch g Subtle Power (IRE)—Miss Liz (IRE) **Brigid Hogan**
5 5, Ch m Definite Article—Norwood Cross (IRE) **Deirdre Greally**
6 **ROSSHILL BOY (IRE),** 5, b g Oscar (IRE)—Back To Bavaria (IRE) **E. M. Hogan**
7 5, Gr g Pilsudski (IRE)—Slieve League (IRE) **E. M. Hogan**

**TWO-YEAR-OLDS**

8 B g 18/5 Winged Love (IRE)—Bibi's Pearl (IRE) (Posidonas) **Brigid Hogan**

---

## 309 MR HENRY HOGARTH, Stillington

Postal: **New Grange Farm, Stillington, York, YO61 1LR**
Contacts: **PHONE (01347) 811168 FAX (01347) 811168 MOBILE (07788) 777044**
**E-MAIL harryhogarth@ymail.com**

1 **DENY,** 7, ch g Mr Greeley (USA)—Sulk (IRE) **Hogarth Racing**
2 **DUNDEE BLUE (IRE),** 7, gr g Cloudings (IRE)—Eurolucy (IRE) **Hogarth Racing**
3 **FIGHTING BACK,** 4, b g Galileo (IRE)—Maroochydore (IRE) **Hogarth Racing**
4 **HATTONS HILL (IRE),** 6, b g Pierre—Cluain Chaoin (IRE) **Hogarth Racing**
5 **LAKEFIELD REBEL (IRE),** 9, b br g Presenting—River Mousa (IRE) **Hogarth Racing**
6 **OVER AND ABOVE (IRE),** 9, b g Overbury (IRE)—Rose Gold (IRE) **Hogarth Racing**
7 **PAMAK D'AIRY (FR),** 12, b g Cadoubel (FR)—Gamaska d'airy (FR) **Hogarth Racing**
8 **ROJO VIVO,** 9, b g Deploy—Shareef Walk **Hogarth Racing**

**Other Owners:** Mr H. P. Hogarth, Mr P. H. Hogarth, Mr J. Hogarth, Mr J. L. Hogarth.

## MR HENRY HOGARTH - Continued

**Assistant Trainer:** Claire Nelson

**Conditional:** Tony Kelly.

---

## 310 MR ALAN HOLLINGSWORTH, Feckenham

Postal: **Lanket House, Crofts Lane, Feckenham, Redditch, Worcestershire, B96 6PU**
Contacts: **PHONE (01527) 68644/892054 FAX (01527) 60310 MOBILE (07775) 670644**
**E-MAIL kombined@btconnect.com**

1 **AGITATION,** 11, b g Cloudings (IRE)—Shadowgraff **Kombined Motor Services Ltd**
2 **BEAU BROOK,** 6, b m Kayf Tara—An Bothar Dubh **Kombined Motor Services Ltd**
3 **CHECKETS,** 7, b m Alflora (IRE)—Emmabella **Kombined Motor Services Ltd**
4 **CLEETONS TURN,** 8, b g Alflora (IRE)—Indyana Run **Kombined Motor Services Ltd**
5 **I CANCAN,** 7, b g Alflora (IRE)—Shadowgraff **Kombined Motor Services Ltd**

**Assistant Trainer:** Sharon Smith

**Jockey (NH):** James Davies, Nick Scholfield.

---

## 311 MR ANDREW HOLLINSHEAD, Lamorlaye

Postal: **6 Ancien 12 Rue Charles Pratt, 60260 Lamorlaye, France**
Contacts: **MOBILE (07968) 733080**
**E-MAIL hollinsheadracing@gmail.com WEBSITE www.hollinsheadracing.co.uk**

1 **ESSANAR,** 4, br g Notnowcato—Spirito Libro (USA) **Mr Paul Shaw & Mr Mark Round**
2 **FINAL ATTACK (IRE),** 4, b g Cape Cross (IRE)—Northern Melody (IRE) **N. Chapman /A. Hollinshead**
3 **FLYING CAPE (IRE),** 4, b g Cape Cross (IRE)—Reine Zao (FR) **J. L. Marriott**
4 **TREE OF GRACE (FR),** 4, ch g Gold Away (IRE)—Three Times (SWE) **N. Chapman /A. Hollinshead**
5 **WHITBY HIGH LIGHT,** 4, b g Halling (USA)—Ballroom Dancer (IRE) **N. Chapman**

### THREE-YEAR-OLDS

6 **DOESYOURDOGBITE (IRE),** b g Notnowcato—Gilah (IRE) **J. L. Marriott /A. Hollinshead**
7 **RICTRUDE (FR),** b f Zamindar (USA)—Park Acclaim (IRE) **Mr J. P. Evitt**

**Assistant Trainer:** Debbie Hollinshead (07977) 934638

---

## 312 MRS STEPH HOLLINSHEAD, Rugeley

Postal: **Deva House, Bardy Lane, Longdon, Rugeley, Staffordshire, WS15 4LJ**
Contacts: **PHONE (01543) 493656 MOBILE (07791) 385335**
**E-MAIL steph_hollinshead@hotmail.co.uk WEBSITE www.stephhollinsheadracing.com**

1 **MIDNIGHT MEMORIES,** 5, ch m Midnight Legend—Bajan Blue **Mrs S. C. Hawkins**
2 4, B f Indian Danehill (IRE)—Miss Holly **Mrs L. A. Hollinshead**
3 **MOHAIR,** 6, b m Motivator—Cashmere **Mrs V. C. Gilbert**

### THREE-YEAR-OLDS

4 **BEAU SPARKLE (IRE),** b f Baltic King—Cabopino (IRE) **Beaudesert Racing**
5 **CAHAR FAD (IRE),** b g Bushranger (IRE)—Tarbiyah **A Day, D Hodson, K Meredith & N Sweeney**
6 **CERISE FIRTH,** b f Pastoral Pursuits—Vermilion Creek **Mr M. Johnson & Mrs L. A. Hollinshead**
7 **FRANK THE BARBER (IRE),** gr g Zebedee—Red Rosanna **Mrs D. A. Hodson**
8 **HAZEL'S SONG,** b f Orpen (USA)—Songbook **Hazeldine Partnership**
9 **MISSANDEI,** b f Red Rocks (IRE)—Onda Chiara (ITY) **Mrs S. C. Hawkins**
10 **MISTRAL,** b f Multiplex—Song of The Desert **D. Sutherland**
11 **SPIRIT OF ROSANNA,** gr f Hellvelyn—Tharwa (IRE) **Mrs D. A. Hodson**

### TWO-YEAR-OLDS

12 **BELLEDESERT,** b f 1/4 Pastoral Pursuits—Ocean Blaze (Polar Prince (IRE)) **Beaudesert Racing**
13 B f 10/4 Equiano (FR)—Goldeva (Makbul) (2500) **Mrs D. A. Hodson**
14 B f 23/2 Piccolo—Maarees (Groom Dancer (USA)) **Beaudesert Racing**

## MRS STEPH HOLLINSHEAD - Continued

**Other Owners:** Exors of the Late A. P. Day, Mr A. J. Highfield, Mr D. Hodson, M. A. N. Johnson, K. S. Meredith, Mrs J. A. Naccache, Mrs C. A. Stevenson, Mr N. S. Sweeney.

**Assistant Trainer:** Adam Hawkins

---

## 313 MR PATRICK HOLMES, Middleham

Postal: **Little Spigot, Coverham, Middleham, Leyburn, North Yorkshire, DL8 4TL**
Contacts: **PHONE (01969) 624880 MOBILE (07740) 589857**
**E-MAIL patrick@foulriceparkracing.com WEBSITE www.foulriceparkracing.com**

1 **BEAR ISLAND FLINT,** 7, br g Overbury (IRE)—Chippewa (FR) **Mrs C M Clarke, Foulrice Park Racing Ltd**
2 **BOGARDUS (IRE),** 4, b g Dalakhani (IRE)—Sugar Mint (IRE)
3 **BOW FIDDLE (IRE),** 9, br m Anshan—Elite Racing **Mrs A. M. Stirling**
4 **COAX,** 7, b g Red Ransom (USA)—True Glory (IRE) **Foulrice Park Racing Limited**
5 **COOKIE RING (IRE),** 4, b g Moss Vale (IRE)—Talah **Mrs A. M. Stirling**
6 **FILLYDELPHIA (IRE),** 4, b f Strategic Prince—Lady Fonic **Miss D. Midwinter**
7 **FOOT THE BILL,** 10, b g Generous (IRE)—Proudfoot (IRE) **Mr C. R. Stirling**
8 **IMPERATOR AUGUSTUS (IRE),** 7, b g Holy Roman Emperor (IRE)—Coralita (IRE) **Foulrice Park Racing Limited**
9 **LIL SOPHELLA (IRE),** 6, ch m Indian Haven—Discotheque (USA) **Lease Terminated**
10 **MARINERS MOON (IRE),** 4, ch g Mount Nelson—Dusty Moon
11 **MUNJALLY,** 4, b g Acclamation—Parabola **Foulrice Park Racing Limited**
12 **PATRON OF EXPLORES (USA),** 4, b g Henrythenavigator (USA)—India Halo (ARG) **FPR Syndicate 3**
13 **PROSTATE AWARENESS (IRE),** 4, b g Camacho—Genuinely (IRE) **Mr C. Peach**
14 **SWISS LAIT,** 4, b f Milk It Mick—Matilda Peace **Hodge & Elsworth**
15 **TIME OF MY LIFE (IRE),** 6, b g Galileo (IRE)—In My Life (IRE) **Mrs C M Clarke, Foulrice Park Racing Ltd**
16 **VOICE FROM ABOVE (IRE),** 6, b m Strategic Prince—Basin Street Blues (IRE) **Foulrice Park Racing Limited**
17 **YOURHOLIDAYISOVER (IRE),** 8, ch g Sulamani (IRE)—Whitehaven **Mrs C M Clarke, Foulrice Park Racing Ltd**

### THREE-YEAR-OLDS

18 **FRAMLEY GARTH (IRE),** b g Clodovil (IRE)—Two Marks (USA) **D. R. C. Elsworth**
19 **GRENADE,** b g Paco Boy (IRE)—Amira **Mrs J. K. Powell**
20 **LIFE KNOWLEDGE (IRE),** ch g Thewayyouare (USA)—Rosa Bellini (IRE) **Foulrice Park Racing Limited**
21 **LORD OF WORDS (IRE),** b g Thousand Words—Dame Laura (IRE) **D Foster P Mawston A Crawford K Punton**
22 **MAPLE STIRRUP (IRE),** b f Duke of Marmalade (IRE)—Street Shaana (FR) **FPR Syndicate 4**
23 **ZUBOON (IRE),** b g Dansili—Tabassum (IRE)

**Other Owners:** Mrs C. M. Clarke, Mr A. A. Crawford, Brian Ellison, Mr D. Foster, D. A. Hodge, Mr P. Mawston, Mrs K. Punton.

**Assistant Trainer:** Russ Garritty

**Jockey (NH):** John Kington.

---

## 314 MR JOHN HOLT, Peckleton

Postal: **Hall Farm, Church Road, Peckleton, Leicester**
Contacts: **PHONE/FAX (01455) 821972 MOBILE (07850) 321059**
**E-MAIL hallfarmracing@btconnect.com WEBSITE www.hallfarmracing.co.uk**

1 **BOSSTIME (IRE),** 5, b g Clodovil (IRE)—Smoken Rosa (USA) **Planters (Leicester) Limited**
2 **FLAMING STAR,** 4, b f Firebreak—Day Star **J. R. Holt**
3 **FOXTROT PEARL (IRE),** 4, b f Bahamian Bounty—Nina Blini **J. R. Holt**
4 **GOADBY,** 4, gr f Kodiac—Gone Sailing **Cleartherm Glass Sealed Units Ltd**
5 **GRAPE,** 5, b g Grape Tree Road—Never Red (IRE) **Mr T. M. Dorman**
6 **MARY'S PRAYER,** 4, b f Champs Elysees—Phi Phi (IRE) **Get Fresh Investments Ltd**
7 **MINI'S DESTINATION,** 7, b m Dubai Destination (USA)—Heather Mix **J. R. Holt**
8 **NUMBER THEORY,** 7, b g Halling (USA)—Numanthia (IRE) **Mr M. S. Fonseka**
9 **SHARABOSKY,** 11, ch m Shahrastani (USA)—Bosky **Mr T. M. Dorman**
10 **SWEET SUMMER,** 4, ch f Sakhee (USA)—Sweet Reply **Mrs P. Y. Page**

### THREE-YEAR-OLDS

11 **SWEET MIDNIGHT,** b f Mawatheeq (USA)—Sweet Reply **Mrs P. Y. Page**

## MR JOHN HOLT - Continued

### TWO-YEAR-OLDS

**12** B f 16/3 Stimulation (IRE)—Laser Crystal (IRE) (King's Theatre (IRE)) (2000)
**13** B g 18/3 Stimulation (IRE)—Seren Teg (Timeless Times (USA)) (3809)
**14** Ch f 13/3 Captain Gerrard (IRE)—Summertime Parkes (Silver Patriarch (IRE)) (3333)

**Assistant Trainer:** Jessica Holt

---

## 315 MR ANTHONY HONEYBALL, Beaminster

Postal: **Potwell Farm, Mosterton, Beaminster, Dorset, DT8 3HG**
Contacts: **PHONE (01308) 867452 MOBILE (07815) 898569**
**E-MAIL a.honeyballracing@btinternet.com WEBSITE www.ajhoneyballracing.co.uk**

1 **ACT NOW,** 6, br m Act One—Lady Turk (FR) **Barrow Hill**
2 **AMBER ALERT,** 5, b m Vitus—Imperial Amber **A. Honeyball**
3 **ANDA DE GRISSAY (FR),** 5, b m Network (GER)—Karima II (FR) **The Deauville Connection**
4 **AS DE FER (FR),** 9, b g Passing Sale (FR)—Miss Hollywood (FR) **Midd Shire Racing**
5 **BIEN FAIRE (IRE),** 5, ch g Bienamado (USA)—Fairpark (IRE) **A. Honeyball**
6 **CHANTARA ROSE,** 6, br m Kayf Tara—Fragrant Rose **Steve & Jackie Fleetham**
7 **CHILL FACTOR (IRE),** 6, b g Oscar (IRE)—Glacial Princess (IRE) **Potwell Partners**
8 **CITY SUPREME (IRE),** 5, b g Milan—Run Supreme (IRE) **San Siro Six**
9 **CRESSWELL BREEZE,** 5, b m Midnight Legend—Cresswell Willow (IRE) **Bright N Breezy**
10 **DAN'S WEE MAN,** 6, b g Kayf Tara—Hazel Bank Lass (IRE) **Mrs F.Murphy, Mr R.Banks And Mr A.Smith**
11 **DREAM AND SEARCH (GER),** 4, b c Raven's Pass (USA)—
Diamond Eyes (GER) **Anthony Honeyball Racing Club Ltd**
12 **FOUNTAINS BLOSSOM,** 6, b m Passing Glance—Fountain Crumble **Mrs M. H. Bowden**
13 **HORACE HAZEL,** 6, b g Sir Harry Lewis (USA)—Kaream **T. C. Frost**
14 **JACKIES SOLITAIRE,** 7, ch m Generous (IRE)—Bond Solitaire **Steve & Jackie Fleetham**
15 **JULLY LES BUXY,** 5, b m Black Sam Bellamy (IRE)—Jadidh **Mr A. F. G. Brimble**
16 **LADY ASH (IRE),** 5, gr m Scorpion (IRE)—La Fiamma (FR) **J. P. Romans & R. Selway**
17 **LAMANVER ALCHEMY,** 4, b f Lucarno (USA)—Lamanver Homerun **Dr D. Christensen**
18 **LILY WAUGH (IRE),** 8, b m King's Theatre (IRE)—Killultagh Dawn (IRE) **Go To War**
19 **MAN OF LEISURE,** 11, b g Karinga Bay—Girl of Pleasure (IRE) **Anthony Honeyball Racing Club Ltd**
20 **MARIE DES ANGES (FR),** 7, b m Ballingarry (IRE)—No Coincidence (IRE) **Atlantic Racing & R. W. Huggins**
21 **OSCARTEEA (IRE),** 6, b g Oscar (IRE)—Miss Arteea (IRE) **Steve & Jackie Fleetham**
22 **PRINCE OF THIEVES (IRE),** 5, b g Robin des Pres (FR)—Sly Empress (IRE) **Sherwood Rangers**
23 **PURE VISION (IRE),** 4, b g Milan—Distillery Lane (IRE) **A. Honeyball**
24 **REGAL ENCORE (IRE),** 7, b g King's Theatre (IRE)—Go On Eileen (IRE) **J. P. McManus**
25 **ROUQUINE SAUVAGE,** 7, ch m Loup Sauvage (USA)—No Need For Alarm **J. P. McManus**
26 **ROYAL NATIVE (IRE),** 7, b g King's Theatre (IRE)—Hollygrove Native (IRE) **Michael & Angela Bone**
27 **ROYAL SALUTE,** 5, br g Flemensfirth (USA)—Loxhill Lady **Distillery Stud**
28 **SOLSTICE SON,** 6, b g Haafhd—Karasta (IRE) **The Summer Solstice**
29 **TARADREWE,** 8, b m Kayf Tara—Kaream **Frosties Friends II**
30 **THE GEEGEEZ GEEGEE (IRE),** 6, b g Beneficial—Shanann Lady (IRE) **Geegeez.co.uk PA**
31 **VICTORS SERENADE (IRE),** 10, b g Old Vic—Dantes Serenade (IRE) **Michael & Angela Bone**
32 **WILDE OAK (IRE),** 5, b g Oscar (IRE)—Tree Oaks (IRE) **Owners For Owners: Wilde Oak**

**Other Owners:** Atlantic Racing Limited, Mr R. Banks, Mr M. Bisogno, Mrs A. P. Bone, Mr Michael Bone, Mr. Adam Bott, Mr David Briers, Mr James Burley, Mr Jim Cannon, Mr Graham Craig, Mr Ian Dickson, Mr Tim Dykes, Mrs George Eyre, Mr J. P. Fairrie, Mr Steve Fleetham, Mrs Jacqueline Fleetham, Mr T. C. Frost, Mr M. S. Green, Mr A. Honeyball, Mr R. W. Huggins, Mr Jon Hughes, Mr Barry Jagger, Mr Max Jenkins, Mr F. McGuinness, Mr N. J. McMullan, Mr B. G. Middleton, Mrs Finola Murphy, Mr A. C. Pickford, Mr Robert Robinson, Mrs Margaret Robinson, Mr J. P. Romans, Mr M. Rowe, Mr R. Selway, Mr A. J. Shire, Mr Andy Smith, Mrs Sarah Tizzard, Mr R. G. Tizzard, Mr Chris Vowles, Mr N. D. Whitham.

**Assistant Trainer:** Rachael Green (07813) 984418

**Jockey (NH):** Aidan Coleman, Rachael Green, Ryan Mahon.

---

## 316 MR STUART HOWE, Tiverton

Postal: **Ringstone Stables, Oakford, Tiverton, Devon, EX16 9EU**
Contacts: **PHONE (01398) 351224 MOBILE (07802) 506344**
**E-MAIL hshowe@stuarthoweracing.co.uk**

1 **ASHKALARA,** 8, b m Footstepsinthesand—Asheyana (IRE) **C R Hollands Cutting Tools Company Ltd**

## MR STUART HOWE - Continued

2 6, Br m Lahib (USA)—Clifton Mist
3 **ETOILE DE VIE,** 5, ch m Lucarno (USA)—Spark of Life
4 **KAYF CHARMER,** 5, b m Kayf Tara—Silver Charmer **Mrs V. W. Jones**
5 **MY LEGAL LADY,** 10, b m Sir Harry Lewis (USA)—Clifton Mist **H. S. Howe**
6 **PARTY PALACE,** 11, b m Auction House (USA)—Lady-Love **B. P. Jones**
7 **TOUIG,** 4, ch f Tobougg (IRE)—Uig **B. P. Jones**

**Jockey (NH):** Tom Scudamore. **Conditional:** Giles Hawkins.

---

## 317 MR JAMES HUGHES, Tonypandy

Postal: **4 Pontrhondda Road, Tonypandy, Mid-Glamorgan, CF40 2SZ**

1 **MAGGIE ARON,** 9, gr m Generous (IRE)—Pems Gift **J. S. Hughes**

---

## 318 MRS JO HUGHES, Lambourn

Postal: **Hill House Stables, Folly Road, Lambourn, Hungerford, Berkshire, RG17 8QE**
Contacts: **PHONE (01488) 71444 FAX (01488) 71103 MOBILE (07900) 680189**
**E-MAIL johughes3@aol.co.uk WEBSITE www.johughesracing.co.uk**

1 **ANWYL HOUSE,** 5, gr g Auction House (USA)—Amwell Star (USA) **Chester Racing Club Ltd**
2 **CALEDONIA LAIRD,** 4, b g Firebreak—Granuaile O'malley (IRE) **Isla & Colin Cage**
3 **CALEDONIA PRINCE,** 7, b g Needwood Blade—Granuaile O'malley (IRE)
4 **CITY OF ANGKOR WAT (IRE),** 5, b g Elusive City (USA)—Kathleen Rafferty (IRE) **Mrs J. F. Hughes**
5 **COMPANY SECRETARY (USA),** 4, gr g Awesome Again (CAN)—Maria Elena (USA) **Mrs C. C. Regalado-Gonzalez**
6 **HANNAH JUST HANNAH,** 6, gr m Proclamation (IRE)—Evaporate **The New Kennet Connection**
7 **HEAVENS EYES (IRE),** 4, b f Oasis Dream—Snowtime (IRE) **Mrs C. C. Regalado-Gonzalez**
8 **JOSIE'S DREAM (IRE),** 7, b g Tau Ceti—Gallery Breeze **J. Smith**
9 **PARISIAN PYRAMID (IRE),** 9, gr g Verglas (IRE)—Sharadja (IRE) **Top Of The Hill Racing Club**
10 **PICKS PINTA,** 4, b g Piccolo—Past 'n' Present **Chester Racing Club Ltd**

### THREE-YEAR-OLDS

11 **AMADEITY (IRE),** b g Amadeus Wolf—Magadar (USA) **Chester Racing & Jo Hughes**
12 **ANGEL OF LIGHT (IRE),** b f Dark Angel (IRE)—Riymaisa (IRE)
13 **ANTONIO JOLI (IRE),** b c Arcano (IRE)—Snowtime (IRE) **Mrs C. C. Regalado-Gonzalez**
14 **ART LOOKER (IRE),** b g Excellent Art—Looker **Joseph Hearne & Jo Hughes**
15 **BITING BULLETS (USA),** b c Bluegrass Cat (USA)—Mary Ellise (USA) **Merriebelle Irish Farm Limited**
16 **CHERRY EMPRESS (IRE),** b f Holy Roman Emperor (IRE)—Cherry Creek (IRE) **James Henderson & Pat Hanly**
17 **CHESTER BOUND,** gr f Equiano (FR)—Varanasi **Chester Racing & Jo Hughes**
18 **FROSTMAN (FR),** gr g Silver Frost (IRE)—Santa Marina (FR) **Chester Racing & Jo Hughes**
19 **LADY CHARLIE,** b f Myboycharlie (IRE)—Fancy Rose (USA) **Miss L Ormsby & J Hughes**
20 **LADY GEMINI,** b f Myboycharlie (IRE)—Gemini Gold (IRE) **James Henderson & Pat Hanly**
21 **LOCOMMOTION,** gr g Proclamation (IRE)—Miss Madame (IRE) **Don Bird & James Hearne**
22 **MAGIC BUCKS (IRE),** ch c Zebedee—Bon Expresso (IRE) **James Henderson & Jo Hughes**
23 **MARILYN MON,** b f Multiplex—Future Regime (IRE) **Chester Racing Club Ltd**
24 **MONSART (IRE),** b g Echo of Light—Monet's Lady (IRE) **Chester Racing & Jo Hughes**
25 **MULTI QUEST,** b f Multiplex—Ryan's Quest (IRE) **James Hearne & Jo Hughes**
26 **SCULPTURED (FR),** b f Archipenko (USA)—Kelang **James Henderson,Hugh Downs,Jo Hughes**
27 **SHOW ME THE BAR,** b g Showcasing—Barboukh **L Ormsby, M West & J Hughes**
28 **STRAIGHT BAR,** b g Notnowcato—Tashkiyla (FR)
29 **STRIKING STONE,** ch g Archipenko (USA)—Lady Le Quesne (IRE) **Mrs J Kersey & Mrs Joanna Hughes**
30 Ch f Stimulation (IRE)—Summertime Parkes

**Other Owners:** D. G. Bird, Mrs I. Cage, C. J. Cage, B. H. Downs, Mr J. M. Duncan, Mr P. J. Hanly, Mr J. M. H. Hearne, Mr J. Hearne, Mr J. Henderson, Mrs J. Kersey, Miss L. Ormsby, Miss A. E. A. Solomon, Mr M. West.

**Assistant Trainer:** Paul Blockley (07778 318295)

**Jockey (flat):** Paul Hanagan. **Jockey (NH):** Mark Grant. **Apprentice:** Harry Burns, Josephine Gordon.
**Amateur:** Mr James Hughes.

## 319 MR STEPHEN HUGHES, Gilfach Goch

Postal: **Dusty Forge, 2 Oak Street, Gilfach Goch, Porth, Mid-Glamorgan, CF39 8UG**
Contacts: **PHONE (07823) 334300 (07943) 396083 FAX (01443) 672110 MOBILE (07823) 334282**
**E-MAIL maggiekidner2@gmail.com**

1 **BEYOND DREAMS (IRE),** 11, ch m Bob's Return (IRE)—You'll Never Know (IRE) **S. A. Hughes**
2 **FORTIFICATION (USA),** 12, gr g With Approval (CAN)—Palisade (USA) **S. A. Hughes**
3 **NOT YET HARTLEY,** 9, b g Relief Pitcher—Beinn Mohr **S. A. Hughes**
4 **TAQAAT (USA),** 7, b g Forestry (USA)—Alrayihah (IRE) **S. A. Hughes**

**Assistant Trainer:** Maggie Kidner Hughes

## 320 MS N. M. HUGO, Newmarket

Postal: **36 King George Avenue, Exning, Newmarket, Suffolk, CB8 7ES**
Contacts: **MOBILE (07736) 360550**
**E-MAIL nickyhugo1@gmail.com**

1 6, B m Fruits of Love (USA)—Mill Thyme **Ms N. M. Hugo**
2 **SIGNORE MOMENTO (IRE),** 9, b g Captain Rio—Gitchee Gumee Rose (IRE)
3 **SILENT CLICHE (IRE),** 11, b g Classic Cliche (IRE)—Mini Moo Min **K. Rowlands**

## 321 MRS SARAH HUMPHREY, West Wratting

Postal: **Yen Hall Farm, West Wratting, Cambridge, Cambridgeshire, CB21 5LP**
Contacts: **PHONE (01223) 291445 FAX (01223) 291451 MOBILE (07798) 702484**
**E-MAIL sarah@yenhallfarm.com WEBSITE www.sarahhumphrey.co.uk**

1 **BIG MIKE (IRE),** 7, b g Flemensfirth (USA)—Minoras Return (IRE) **Mrs S. Humphrey**
2 **CALL HIM SOMETHING (IRE),** 7, b g Heron Island (IRE)—
Stoned Imaculate (IRE) **A. Whyte, D. Nott & J. Custerson**
3 **CHENDIYR (FR),** 6, gr g Red Ransom (USA)—Cherryxma (FR) **Mrs S. Humphrey**
4 **EASTWARD HO,** 7, ch g Resplendent Glory (IRE)—Mofeyda (IRE) **Miss V. Pratt**
5 **FLEMI TWO TOES (IRE),** 9, b g Flemensfirth (USA)—Silva Venture (IRE) **Entente Cordiale**
6 **GLADSOME,** 7, b m Resplendent Glory (IRE)—Christening (IRE) **Miss V. Pratt**
7 **I'M A JOKER,** 6, ch g Erhaab (USA)—Yota (FR) **Come Up Trumps**
8 **INDIAN DAUDAIE (FR),** 8, ch g Nicobar—Aldounia (FR) **Entente Cordiale**
9 **JOHNEY FOLEY (IRE),** 11, ch g Quws—Fancy Me Not (IRE) **R. N. Fuller**
10 **KUWAIT STAR,** 6, ch g Resplendent Glory (IRE)—Mofeyda (IRE) **Miss V. Pratt**
11 **LANGHAM LILY (USA),** 6, b br m Badge of Silver (USA)—Silver Frau (USA) **Mr M. Howard**
12 **LARTETA (FR),** 6, b g Enrique—Ariel (IRE) **Yen Hall Farm Racing**
13 **MAHLERS SPIRIT (IRE),** 5, ch g Mahler—Belle Dame (IRE) **Mrs S. Humphrey**
14 4, B g Kalanisi (IRE)—Miss Compliance (IRE)
15 **MORNA'S GLORY,** 6, b m Resplendent Glory (IRE)—Tipsy Cake **Miss V. Pratt**
16 **RED SEVENTY,** 6, b g Sakhee (USA)—Dimakya (USA) **Mrs S. Humphrey**
17 5, Ch g Insatiable (IRE)—Rose Gallery (FR)
18 **STORM ON BY (IRE),** 5, b g September Storm (GER)—Ithastobesaid (IRE) **Mrs S. Humphrey**
19 **TOP MAN MARTY (IRE),** 6, b g Westerner—Tribal Princess (IRE) **Dr R. C. Britton**

### THREE-YEAR-OLDS

20 Ch g Resplendent Glory (IRE)—Heather Valley **Miss V. Pratt**
21 Ch g Resplendent Glory (IRE)—Mofeyda (IRE) **Miss V. Pratt**
22 Ch f Resplendent Glory (IRE)—Tipsy Cake **Miss V. Pratt**

**Other Owners:** Miss J. M. Custerson, Mrs S. J. Humphrey, Mr A. R. Humphrey, Mr D. F. Nott, Mr A. A. Whyte.

**Assistant Trainer:** Mr O. Williams

**Jockey (flat):** Mikey Ennis. **Jockey (NH):** James Banks, Mikey Ennis, Jack Quinlan. **Apprentice:** Shelley Birkett.

## 322 MR KEVIN HUNTER, Natland

Postal: **Larkrigg, Natland, Cumbria, LA9 7QS**
Contacts: **PHONE (01539) 560245**

1 **ALLIED ANSWER,** 7, gr g Danehill Dancer (IRE)—Hotelgenie Dot Com **J. K. Hunter**
2 **CLOGGY POWELL (IRE),** 8, ch g Classic Cliche (IRE)—Ann's Delight (IRE) **J. K. Hunter**
3 **GLENWOOD PRINCE (IRE),** 9, b g King's Theatre (IRE)—Moll Bawn (IRE) **J. K. Hunter**
4 **MILAN ROYALE,** 10, b g Milan—Siroyalta (FR) **J. K. Hunter**

## 323 MISS LAURA HURLEY, Kineton

Postal: **Kineton Grange Farm, Kineton, Warwick, Warwickshire, CV35 0EE**
Contacts: **PHONE (01926) 640380**

1 **BOOK'EM DANNO (IRE),** 9, ch g Moscow Society (USA)—Rifada **Mrs R. Hurley**
2 **CATCHIN TIME (IRE),** 7, b g Chineur (FR)—Lady Dane (IRE) **Mrs R. Hurley**
3 **GWILI SPAR,** 7, ch g Generosity—Lady of Mine **Mrs R. Hurley**

## 324 MISS ALISON HUTCHINSON, Exning

Postal: **116 Parkers Walk, Studlands, Newmarket, Suffolk, CB8 7AP**
Contacts: **PHONE (01638) 482180 MOBILE (07960) 630204**
**E-MAIL alison.hutchinson1@hotmail.co.uk**
**WEBSITE www.alisonhutchinsonhorseracing.weebly.com**

1 **BAY STREET BELLE,** 4, ch f Bahamian Bounty—Donna Anna **Miss A. L. Hutchinson**
2 **CASCADIA (IRE),** 4, br f Mujadil (USA)—Tucum (IRE) **Miss A. L. Hutchinson**
3 **DUKE OF HANOVER,** 4, b g Duke of Marmalade (IRE)—Caro George (USA) **Four Winds Racing Partnership**
4 **LADY HEIDI,** 4, b f High Chaparral (IRE)—Water Feature **Hardisty Rolls II**
5 **MARGUERITE ST JUST,** 5, b m Sir Percy—Ships Watch (IRE) **Miss O. Maylam**
6 **ROYAL MARSKELL,** 6, b g Multiplex—Socialise **Miss C. Y. Wootten**
7 **VODKA CHASER (IRE),** 4, b f Baltic King—Suffer Her (IRE) **Miss A. L. Hutchinson**

**Other Owners:** Mr S. J. Mear, Mrs E. A. Mear.

**Jockey (flat):** Tom Eaves, Robert Havlin, Oisin Murphy, James Sullivan. **Jockey (NH):** Dougie Costello. **Amateur:** Miss A. L. Hutchinson.

## 325 MRS CAROLE IKIN, Sutton In The Elms

Postal: **Walton Lodge Farm, Sutton In The Elms, Leicestershire, LE9 6RB**
Contacts: **PHONE (01455) 282321 MOBILE (07850) 278491**
**E-MAIL nevagree@yahoo.co.uk WEBSITE www.equinespa.co.uk**

1 **RIME AVEC GENTIL (FR),** 10, b g Kapgarde (FR)—Quenice (FR) **Mrs C. J. Ikin**

**Assistant Trainer:** Mr P. J. Ikin

## 326 MR ROGER INGRAM, Epsom

Postal: **Wendover Stables, Burgh Heath Road, Epsom, Surrey, KT17 4LX**
Contacts: **PHONE (01372) 748505 or (01372) 749157 FAX (01372) 748505**
**MOBILE (0777) 3665980**
**E-MAIL roger.ingram.racing@virgin.net WEBSITE www.rogeringramracing.com**

1 **ARU CHA CHA,** 4, b g Myboycharlie (IRE)—Royal Arruhan
2 **AWESOME ROCK (IRE),** 6, ch g Rock of Gibraltar (IRE)—Dangerous Diva (IRE) **Mr M. F. Cruse**
3 **BRIDGE THAT GAP,** 7, b h Avonbridge—Figura **Mr R. Ingram**
4 **BUXTON,** 11, b g Auction House (USA)—Dam Certain (IRE) **Mr P. J. Burton**
5 **DOLPHIN VILLAGE (IRE),** 5, b g Cape Cross (IRE)—Reform Act (USA) **Miss J. E. Webster**
6 **DUKES MEADOW,** 4, b g Pastoral Pursuits—Figura **The Stargazers**
7 **ENCAPSULATED,** 5, b g Zamindar (USA)—Star Cluster **Mrs E. N. Nield**
8 **NELSON'S PRIDE,** 4, b f Mount Nelson—Bandanna **Mrs C. E. Hallam**

## MR ROGER INGRAM - Continued

9 **ROSIE PROSPECTS,** 4, b f Byron—Sea Jade (IRE) **T. H. Barma**
10 **TRIPLE CHOCOLATE,** 5, b g Danehill Dancer (IRE)—Enticing (IRE) **Mr F. Al Dabbous**

### THREE-YEAR-OLDS

11 **BICKERSHAW,** b g Equiano (FR)—Ring of Love **Mr R. Ingram**
12 **PRINCE OF PARIS,** b c Champs Elysees—Cool Kitten (IRE) **Mr G. E. Ley**

**Other Owners:** D. W. Armstrong, Cheveley Park Stud Limited, M. W. Joy, Mr D. Ross-Watt.

**Assistant Trainer:** Sharon Ingram

**Apprentice:** Rhiain Ingram.

---

## 327 MR DEAN IVORY, Radlett

Postal: **Harper Lodge Farm, Harper Lane, Radlett, Hertfordshire, WD7 7HU**
Contacts: **PHONE (01923) 855337 FAX (01923) 852470 MOBILE (07785) 118658**
**E-MAIL dean.ivory@virgin.net WEBSITE www.deanivoryracing.co.uk**

1 **AYE AYE SKIPPER (IRE),** 5, b g Captain Marvelous (IRE)—Queenfisher **Heather Yarrow & Lesley Ivory**
2 **CRYSTALIZED (IRE),** 4, ch f Rock of Gibraltar (IRE)—Magnificent Bell (IRE) **Mr T. Glynn**
3 **DUCHESS OF GAZELEY (IRE),** 5, ch m Halling (USA)—Flying Finish (FR) **Heather & Michael Yarrow**
4 **FIRMDECISIONS (IRE),** 5, b g Captain Rio—Luna Crescente (IRE) **White Bear Racing**
5 **FOSSA,** 5, b g Dubai Destination (USA)—Gayanula (USA) **Mr G. M. Copp**
6 **GOLDEN AMBER (IRE),** 4, b f Holy Roman Emperor (IRE)—Time of Gold (USA) **Heather & Michael Yarrow**
7 **GOLDEN BIRD (IRE),** 4, b g Sinndar (IRE)—Khamsin (USA) **Mr K B Taylor & Radlett Racing**
8 **GREY ODYSSEY,** 4, gr g Verglas (IRE)—Reading Habit (USA) **Miss N. I. Yarrow**
9 **HILL OF DREAMS (IRE),** 6, b m Indian Danehill (IRE)—Shaunas Vision (IRE) **Mr I Gethin & Mr R Gethin**
10 **LANCELOT DU LAC (ITY),** 5, b g Shamardal (USA)—Dodie Mae (USA) **Mr M. J. Yarrow**
11 **LINKS DRIVE LADY,** 7, br m Striking Ambition—Miskina **It's Your Lucky Day**
12 **MALICHO,** 6, ch g Manduro (GER)—Shane (GER) **Mr K. B. Taylor**
13 **NOWDORO,** 6, ch g Notnowcato—Salydora (FR) **Wentdale Limited**
14 **RUSSIAN ICE,** 7, ch m Iceman—Dark Eyed Lady (IRE) **Mr R. Beadle**
15 **SHANTI,** 5, b g Dansili—Maycocks Bay
16 **SHAUNAS SPIRIT (IRE),** 7, b m Antonius Pius (USA)—Shaunas Vision (IRE) **Cynthia Smith & Dean Ivory**
17 **SIRIUS PROSPECT (USA),** 7, b br g Gone West (USA)—Stella Blue (FR) **Miss N. I. Yarrow**
18 **SOARING SPIRITS (IRE),** 5, ch g Tamayuz—Follow My Lead **Mrs D. A. Carter**
19 **SPEED THE PLOUGH,** 4, b g Kyllachy—Danceatdusk **John Waterfall & K T Ivory**
20 **TAGULA NIGHT (IRE),** 9, ch g Tagula (IRE)—Carpet Lady (IRE) **Gordon Papworth & John Fishpool**
21 **TOP SHOW,** 6, b g Sakhee (USA)—Rose Show **Mr R. Beadle**
22 **TROPICS (USA),** 7, ch g Speightstown (USA)—Taj Aire (USA) **D. K. Ivory**
23 **VALID REASON,** 8, b g Observatory (USA)—Real Trust (USA) **John B Waterfall & Radlett Racing**
24 **VARSOVIAN,** 5, ch g Refuse To Bend (IRE)—Queen of Poland **Geoff Copp & Radlett Racing**
25 **ZAEEM,** 6, b g Echo of Light—Across (ARG) **Richard Lewis & Steve Farmer**

### THREE-YEAR-OLDS

26 **BRIDEY'S LETTUCE (IRE),** b g Iffraaj—Its On The Air (IRE) **Mr G. M. Copp**
27 **CATHARINA,** ch f Dutch Art—Lambadora **K. T. Ivory**
28 **CHANSON DE MARINS (FR),** b f Le Havre (IRE)—Easy To Sing **M. Bass & R. Smith**
29 **GOLDSLINGER (FR),** b g Gold Away (IRE)—Singaporette (FR) **Heather & Michael Yarrow**
30 **KING'S CONCERTO (IRE),** ch g Thewayyouare (USA)—Major Minor (IRE) **Solario Racing (Radlett)**
31 **O DEE,** ch g Iffraaj—Queen's Grace **Mr G. M. Copp**
32 **ROSIE'S PREMIERE (IRE),** b f Showcasing—Golden Rosie (IRE) **Mrs H. Yarrow**
33 **STAKE ACCLAIM (IRE),** b c Acclamation—Golden Legacy (IRE) **Mr M. J. Yarrow**

### TWO-YEAR-OLDS

34 **ARCTIC ANGEL (IRE),** b c 11/2 Dark Angel (IRE)—
Charlene Lacy (IRE) (Pips Pride) (47619) **The Macaroni Beach Society**
35 B c 6/4 Canford Cliffs (IRE)—Gilded (IRE) (Redback) (11000)
36 **JUSTICE (IRE),** b f 23/2 Lawman (FR)—Sheboygan (IRE) (Grand Lodge (USA)) (21000) **K. T. Ivory**
37 B f 5/3 Lawman (FR)—Law of Chance (Pennekamp (USA)) (30000) **Mrs D. A. Carter**
38 **R BAR OPEN (FR),** b br c 6/5 Orpen (USA)—
Bahama Love (USA) (Hennessy (USA)) (11904) **The Macaroni Beach Society**
39 **TWIN SAILS,** b c 25/3 Sir Percy—Atwirl (Pivotal) (25000) **Mr H. R. Heffer**

**MR DEAN IVORY - Continued**

**Other Owners:** M. P. Bass, Mr S. T. J. Broderick, Dean Ivory Racing Ltd, Mr S. K. I. Double, Mr S. Farmer, J. E. Fishpool, Mr J. Foley, Mr I. R. Gethin, Mr R. Gethin, Miss N. J. Hood, Mrs L. A. Ivory, Mr R. A. Lewis, Miss E. Morgan, D. Morgan, Mr J. R. Neville, G. Papworth, Mr D. Rota, Mrs C. Smith, Mr K. W. Smith, Mr R. L. Smith, Mr J. B. Waterfall.

**Assistant Trainer:** Chris Scally

**Apprentice:** Paul Booth.

## 328 MISS TINA JACKSON, Loftus

Postal: **Tick Hill Farm, Liverton, Loftus, Saltburn, Cleveland, TS13 4TG**
Contacts: **PHONE (01287) 644952 MOBILE (07774) 106906**

1 **ARDESIA (IRE),** 11, b g Red Sunset—Lowtown **A. Jackson**
2 **FLEDERMAUS (IRE),** 5, br g Jeremy (USA)—Khayrat (IRE) **H. L. Thompson**
3 **JOSEPH MERCER (IRE),** 8, b g Court Cave (IRE)—Vikki's Dream (IRE) **Tina Jackson Racing**
4 **KING'S REALM (IRE),** 8, ch g King's Best (USA)—Sweet Home Alabama (IRE) **Tina Jackson Racing**
5 **PURPLE HARRY,** 7, gr g Sir Harry Lewis (USA)—Ellfiedick **H. L. Thompson**
6 **SIR POSEALOT,** 8, gr g Clerkenwell (USA)—Ellfiedick **H. L. Thompson**
7 **SORY,** 8, b g Sakhee (USA)—Rule Britannia **H. L. Thompson**
8 **WILLIAM WILD,** 7, b g Bollin Eric—Winnie Wild **H. L. Thompson**

**Other Owners:** Miss Tina Jackson, Mr H. L. Thompson.

## 329 MRS VALERIE JACKSON, Newcastle Upon Tyne

Postal: **Edge House, Belsay, Newcastle Upon Tyne, Tyne and Wear, NE20 0HH**
Contacts: **PHONE (01830) 530218 MOBILE (07808) 812213**

1 **CAST IRON CASEY (IRE),** 13, ch g Carroll House—Ashie's Friend (IRE) **Mrs V. S. Jackson**

## 330 MR LEE JAMES, Malton

Postal: **4 Wayfaring Close, Norton, Malton, North Yorkshire, YO17 9DW**
Contacts: **PHONE (01653) 699466 FAX (01653) 699581 MOBILE (07732) 556322**

1 5, B h Echo of Light—Alisdanza **L. R. James**
2 **EXCELLENT ADDITION (IRE),** 5, ch g Excellent Art—Race The Wild Wind (USA) **Mrs C. Lloyd James**
3 **FREEDOM FLYING,** 12, b m Kalanisi (IRE)—Free Spirit (IRE) **L. R. James**
4 5, B m Dubai Destination (USA)—Palisandra (USA) **Mrs C. Lloyd James**
5 **SHADOW OF THE DAY,** 8, b g Sugarfoot—She Who Dares Wins **Mrs C. Lloyd James**
6 **STRIKEMASTER (IRE),** 9, b g Xaar—Mas A Fuera (IRE) **Mrs C. Lloyd James**

**Assistant Trainer:** Carol James

**Jockey (NH):** Kyle James. **Amateur:** Mr Aaron James.

## 331 MR IAIN JARDINE, Hawick

Postal: **Paradise Cottage, Gatehousecote, Bonchester Bridge, Hawick, Roxburghshire, TD9 8JD**
Contacts: **PHONE (01450) 860718 MOBILE (07738) 351232**
**E-MAIL iainjardineracing@hotmail.co.uk**

1 **ARCHIPELIGO,** 4, b g Archipenko (USA)—Red Slew **Tapas Partnership**
2 **DOUBLE WHAMMY,** 9, b g Systematic—Honor Rouge (IRE) **Alex & Janet Card**
3 **GALLEONS WAY,** 6, gr g Generous (IRE)—Yemaail (IRE) **Mr A. Dawson & Mrs K. Campbell**
4 **L'INGANNO FELICE (FR),** 5, br g Librettist (USA)—Final Overture (FR) **Mr A. Dawson & Mrs K. Campbell**
5 **LA BACOUETTEUSE (FR),** 10, b g Miesque's Son (USA)—Toryka **Miss S. A. Booth**
6 **LUCARNO DANCER,** 5, b m Lucarno (USA)—Sing And Dance **Mr M. P. Wares**
7 **NAKEETA,** 4, b g Sixties Icon—Easy Red (IRE) **Alex & Janet Card**
8 **PUSH ME (IRE),** 8, gr m Verglas (IRE)—Gilda Lilly (USA) **Alex & Janet Card**
9 **QUEEN OF MILAN (IRE),** 7, b br m Milan—Bacard Beauty (IRE) **The Dregs Of Humanity**
10 **ROB'S BURN,** 7, ch g And Beyond (IRE)—Sharburn **Mr J. C. Thomson**
11 **VEINARD (FR),** 6, ch g Shaanmer (IRE)—Ombline (FR) **Mrs P. M. Shirley-Beavan**

## MR IAIN JARDINE - Continued

**Other Owners:** R. M. S. Allison, Mrs K. Campbell, Mr A. M. Card, Mrs J. A. Card, A. Dawson, A. G. Guthrie, Mr A. T. Murphy, A. Walmsley.

**Jockey (flat):** David Allan. **Jockey (NH):** Adrian Lane.

---

## 332 MR TIMOTHY JARVIS, Buckingham

Postal: **Old Granary, Mill Lane, Twyford, Buckingham, Buckinghamshire, MK18 4HA**

1 **ABOVE THE REST (IRE),** 4, b c Excellent Art—Aspasias Tizzy (USA) **Cedars Two**
2 **ALBONNY (IRE),** 6, b g Aussie Rules (USA)—Silk Law (IRE) **Mohamed Alhameli & Partners**
3 **ALWAYS RESOLUTE,** 4, b g Refuse To Bend (IRE)—Mad Annie (USA) **Market Avenue Racing Club & Partners**
4 **ANOTHER TRY (IRE),** 10, b g Spinning World (USA)—Mad Annie (USA) **The Twyford Partnership**
5 **BAARS CAUSEWAY (IRE),** 4, ch f Intense Focus (USA)—Barbera (GER) **Brian Goldswain & Jarvis Associates**
6 **CALRISSIAN (IRE),** 4, ch g Lando (GER)—Dallaah **Cedars Two**
7 **I AM NOT HERE (IRE),** 4, b c Amadeus Wolf—Newgate Lodge (IRE) **Jarvis Associates**
8 **LADY GIBRALTAR,** 6, b m Rock of Gibraltar (IRE)—Lady Adnil (IRE) **Buckingham Flooring**
9 **LAVENDAR FIELDS (IRE),** 4, b f High Chaparral (IRE)—Rose Parade **Cedars Two**
10 **NAVAJO CHIEF,** 8, b g King's Best (USA)—Navajo Rainbow **Mr G. S. Bishop**
11 **OETZI,** 7, ch g Iceman—Mad Annie (USA) **Allen B. Pope & Jarvis Associates**
12 **PRINCE REGAL,** 5, ch g Cockney Rebel (IRE)—Wachiwi (IRE) **T&J Partnership**
13 **ROGUE WAVE (IRE),** 4, b c Iffraaj—Lady Naomi (USA) **Market Avenue Racing Club & Partners**
14 **SAVANNA SPRING (IRE),** 4, b f Bushranger (IRE)—Brogan's Well (IRE) **Jarvis Associates**
15 **STAR OF MAYFAIR (USA),** 5, ch g Tale of The Cat (USA)—Kinsale Lass (USA) **Cedars Partnership**
16 **SUBSTANTIVO (IRE),** 5, b g Duke of Marmalade (IRE)—Damson (IRE) **Jarvis Associates**

### THREE-YEAR-OLDS

17 **AZZIR (IRE),** gr c Echo of Light—Lady Georgina **Mohamed Alhameli & Partners**
18 **ITALIAN BEAUTY (IRE),** b f Thewayyouare (USA)—Edelfa (IRE) **Mrs S. E. Simmons**
19 **SABHA (IRE),** b f Thewayyouare (USA)—Genipabu (IRE) **Mohamed Alhameli & Partners**
20 **STRAIGHT ARROW,** b g Refuse To Bend (IRE)—Spring Goddess (IRE) **Grant & Bowman Limited**

**Other Owners:** B. H. Goldswain, Mr T. O. Jarvis, Market Avenue Racing Club Ltd, A. B. Pope, Mr G. J. Reboul, Mrs H. Reboul.

---

## 333 MR WILLIAM JARVIS, Newmarket

Postal: **Phantom House, Fordham Road, Newmarket, Suffolk, CB8 7AA**
Contacts: **OFFICE (01638) 669873 HOME (01638) 662677 FAX (01638) 667328**
**E-MAIL mail@williamjarvis.com WEBSITE www.williamjarvis.com**

1 **CLERK'S CHOICE (IRE),** 9, b g Bachelor Duke (USA)—Credit Crunch (IRE) **M. C. Banks**
2 **DIXIE'S DREAM (IRE),** 6, b g Hawk Wing (USA)—Hams (USA) **The Dream Team Partnership**
3 **JODIES JEM,** 5, br g Kheleyf (USA)—First Approval **Mrs M. C. Banks**
4 **RASKOVA (USA),** 5, b m Henrythenavigator (USA)—Diamond Necklace (USA) **Mr K. J. Hickman**

### THREE-YEAR-OLDS

5 **BEAU KNIGHT,** b c Sir Percy—Nicola Bella (IRE) **Dr J. Walker**
6 **DANCETHENIGHTAWAY (IRE),** b f Holy Roman Emperor (IRE)—Dolce Dovo **Rathordan Partnership**
7 **DONETSK,** b g Medicean—Seasonal Blossom (IRE) **A. Foster**
8 **HENLEY,** b c Royal Applause—Making Waves (IRE) **The Marine Team**
9 **LACKADAY,** gr c Kyllachy—Day Creek **Ms E. L. Banks**
10 **LIPSTICKANDPOWDER (IRE),** gr f Mastercraftsman (IRE)—Raphimix (FR) **Mrs Melba Bryce**
11 **MISS OLIVE (IRE),** b f Rip Van Winkle (IRE)—Desert Darling **Mr K. J. Hickman**
12 **MUST HAVE (FR),** ch g Le Havre (IRE)—Belle Et Brave (FR) **Dr J. Walker**
13 **NUNO TRISTAN (USA),** b c Henrythenavigator (USA)—Saintly Speech (USA) **Mr C. A. Washbourn**
14 B g Azamour (IRE)—Sadie Thompson (IRE) **G B Turnbull Ltd & Partners**
15 **SILK KNIGHT,** ch c Sir Percy—Tussah **Dr J. Walker**
16 **SINEMA,** gr ro c Compton Place—Dictatrix **The Sinema Partnership**
17 **SOLSTALLA,** b f Halling (USA)—Solstice **G B Turnbull Ltd**
18 **TAVENER,** b c Exceed And Excel (AUS)—Sea Chorus **Mr C. A. Washbourn**
19 **YAT DING YAU (FR),** b f Air Chief Marshal (IRE)—The Jostler **Dr J. Walker**
20 **ZEBEAD (IRE),** gr c Zebedee—Sinead (USA) **The Zebead Partnership**

## MR WILLIAM JARVIS - Continued

### TWO-YEAR-OLDS

21 **HIGHWAY DREAM,** b f 19/2 Dick Turpin (IRE)—Just Dreams (Salse (USA)) (10000) **G B Turnbull Ltd**
22 B br f 16/1 Le Havre (IRE)—
La Chapelle (IRE) (Holy Roman Emperor (IRE)) (24000) **G B Turnbull Ltd & Mrs Susan Davis**
23 **LADY LLOYD,** b f 5/2 Paco Boy (IRE)—Carafe (Selkirk (USA)) (10000) **Robert Lloyd & Partners**
24 **MONTFORD (FR),** ch g 5/4 Air Chief Marshal (IRE)—Belle Et Brave (FR) (Falbrav (IRE)) (5555) **Dr J. Walker**
25 **ONWARDSANDUPWARDS,** b g 21/4 Multiplex—Turn Back (Pivotal) (11428) **A Partnership**
26 **ORGAN SCHOLAR,** b c 12/3 Nayef (USA)—Palatial (Green Desert (USA)) (50000) **Mr C. A. Washbourn**
27 **PORT PARADISE,** b gr g 10/3 Paco Boy (IRE)—Yacht Woman (USA) (Mizzen Mast (USA)) (32000) **A. N. Verrier**
28 B c 9/2 Dick Turpin (IRE)—Right Rave (IRE) (Soviet Star (USA)) **Rent Right**
29 B c 2/3 Elusive City (USA)—Sea Paint (IRE) (Peintre Celebre (USA)) (30000) **Wee Hui Hui**
30 **TIBIBIT,** br f 4/3 Kyllachy—Cat Hunter (One Cool Cat (USA)) **Mr David Cohen**
31 B g 4/3 Kheleyf (USA)—Weqaar (USA) (Red Ransom (USA)) (5000) **M. C. Banks**
32 **WIMPOLE HALL,** b c 17/4 Canford Cliffs (IRE)—
Sparkling Eyes (Lujain (USA)) (65000) **Mr C. A. Washbourn & Nigel Gadsby**

**Other Owners:** Mr James Bowditch, Mr N. T. Collins, Susan Davis, Matthew Farrell, Mr Anthony Foster, Mr Nigel Gadsby, Miss M. Greenwood, Miss S. E. Hall, Mr M. Heffernan, Mr William Jarvis, Mr Mark King, Mr A. M. Mitchell, Mr A. E. Pakenham, Mrs Victoria Pakenham, Mr A. S. A. Pamplin, Mr R. G. Percival, Mr Simon Porter, Mr M. Quirke, Mr E. Randall, Mr Nigel Rich, Mr Neil Warnock, Mr Clive Washbourn.

---

## 334 MR MALCOLM JEFFERSON, Malton

Postal: **Newstead Cottage Stables, Norton, Malton, North Yorkshire, YO17 9PJ**
Contacts: **PHONE (01653) 697225 MOBILE (07710) 502044**
**E-MAIL newsteadracing@btconnect.com WEBSITE www.malcolmjefferson.co.uk**

1 **ANNE'S VALENTINO,** 5, b m Primo Valentino (IRE)—Annie's Gift (IRE) **The Magic Circle**
2 **ATTAGLANCE,** 9, b g Passing Glance—Our Ethel **Mrs H Young, G Eifert, R Snyder**
3 4, B g Touch of Land (FR)—Ballybeg Katie (IRE) **Mrs K. M. Richardson**
4 **BISHOPS GATE (IRE),** 9, br g Bishop of Cashel—
Lischelle Star (IRE) **Mrs T. H. Barclay/Mrs F. D. McInnes Skinner**
5 **BOLLIN BEAUTY,** 6, br m Bollin Eric—Miss Danbys **D. T. Todd**
6 **BOY NAMED SIOUX,** 4, b g Indian Danehill (IRE)—Annie's Gift (IRE) **The Corse Lawners**
7 **CAPE TRIBULATION,** 11, b g Hernando (FR)—Gay Fantastic **J. D. Abell**
8 **CAPE YORK,** 7, ch g Revoque (IRE)—Altogether Now (IRE) **J. D. Abell**
9 **CARD GAME (IRE),** 6, b m Scorpion (IRE)—Cardona **Messrs Hales Dodd Wood & Dickinson**
10 **CHILLY MISS,** 6, b m Iceman—Fairlie **Racegoers Club Owners Group**
11 **CLOUDY DREAM (IRE),** 5, b g Cloudings (IRE)—Run Away Dream (IRE) **T. J. Hemmings**
12 **COOZAN GEORGE,** 6, b g Bollin Eric—Pasja (IRE) **A. N. Barrett**
13 **CYRUS DARIUS,** 6, b g Overbury (IRE)—Barton Belle **Mr & Mrs G Calder & Mr P M Warren**
14 **DANBY'S LEGEND,** 8, b g Midnight Legend—Miss Danbys **D. T. Todd**
15 **DANTE'S WAY (IRE),** 6, b g Scorpion (IRE)—Benedicta Rose (IRE) **T. J. Hemmings**
16 **DIAMANTE,** 4, br g Indian Danehill (IRE)—Our Ethel **G Eifert & R Snyder**
17 **DOUBLE W'S (IRE),** 5, ch g Fruits of Love (USA)—Zaffre (IRE) **Wharton & Wilson**
18 **DUBAI ANGEL (IRE),** 4, b g Dubai Destination (USA)—Just Another Penny (IRE) **Mrs D. W. Davenport**
19 **ENCHANTED GARDEN,** 7, ch g Sulamani (IRE)—Calachuchi **Mrs D. W. Davenport**
20 **ETHELWYN,** 5, ch m Alflora (IRE)—Our Ethel **Mrs T. H. Barclay/Mrs F. D. McInnes Skinner**
21 **FIRTH OF BAVARD,** 8, b g Flemensfirth (USA)—Ice Bavard **R. H. Goldie**
22 **FIRTH OF THE CLYDE,** 10, b g Flemensfirth (USA)—Miss Nel **R. H. Goldie**
23 **GREY LIFE,** 9, gr g Terimon—More To Life **D. T. Todd**
24 **HELMSLEY LAD,** 4, gr g Fair Mix (IRE)—Wuchowsen (IRE) **Derek Gennard & Gillian Gennard**
25 **HI GEORGE,** 7, b g Doyen (IRE)—Our Ethel **Forever Young Racing Partnership**
26 **HIGH HOPPER (IRE),** 5, b g Mountain High (IRE)—Stormy Moment (IRE) **Mr M. C. Thuey**
27 **JURBY,** 5, b g Motivator—Darariyna (IRE) **T. J. Hemmings**
28 **KING OF THE WOLDS (IRE),** 8, b g Presenting—Azaban (IRE) **Mr & Mrs G. Calder**
29 **KRASNODAR (IRE),** 5, gr g Medaaly—Azyouare (IRE) **Miss N. R. Jefferson**
30 **KWO NESHE (IRE),** 5, b br g Fruits of Love (USA)—Bonny River (IRE) **Dean Bostock & Raymond Bostock**
31 **LA DAMA DE HIERRO,** 5, gr m Proclamation (IRE)—Altogether Now (IRE) **J. M. Jefferson**
32 **LEMON JACK (IRE),** 6, ch g Fleetwood (IRE)—Polleroo (IRE) **Countess V. C. Cathcart**
33 **MAJOR IVAN (IRE),** 6, b g Fruits of Love (USA)—Martinstown Queen (IRE) **Mrs I C Straker & Steven Key**
34 **NAUTICAL TWILIGHT,** 5, gr m Proclamation (IRE)—Anabranch **Capt M. S. Bagley**
35 **OSCAR ROCK (IRE),** 7, b g Oscar (IRE)—Cash And New (IRE) **Mr & Mrs G. Calder**
36 **OUR BOY BEN,** 6, b g Revoque (IRE)—Magic Bloom **P. Nelson**

## MR MALCOLM JEFFERSON - Continued

37 **PAIR OF JACKS (IRE),** 7, ch g Presenting—Halona **Mrs R. Williams**
38 **PETAPENKO,** 4, b g Archipenko (USA)—Tricoteuse **R. Collins**
39 **QUITE THE MAN (IRE),** 10, b g Zagreb (USA)—Ballinard Lizzie (IRE) **Boundary Garage (Bury) Limited**
40 **RETRIEVE THE STICK,** 6, b m Revoque (IRE)—Anabranch **Newstead Racing Partnership**
41 **ROBINSON COLLONGES (FR),** 10, gr g Dom Alco (FR)—Grace Collonges (FR) **Mr & Mrs G. Calder**
42 **RYEDALE RACER,** 4, b g Indian Danehill (IRE)—Jontys'lass **Derek Gennard & Gillian Gennard**
43 **SECRETE STREAM (IRE),** 6, ch g Fruits of Love (USA)—Bonny River (IRE) **Mrs M. E. Dixon**
44 5, B g Kayf Tara—Shuildante (IRE) **Mrs K S Gaffney & Mrs Alix Stevenson**
45 **STOUT CORTEZ,** 4, b g Hernando (FR)—Zooming (IRE) **J. D. Abell**
46 **SUN CLOUD (IRE),** 8, b g Cloudings (IRE)—Miss Melrose **Boundary Garage (Bury) Limited**
47 **THE PANAMA KID (IRE),** 11, b g Presenting—Mrs Jodi **Mrs D. W. Davenport**
48 **UPPINGHAM,** 6, ch g Doyen (IRE)—Karakul (IRE) **J. D. Abell**
49 **URBAN HYMN (FR),** 7, b g Robin des Champs (FR)—Betty Brune (FR) **Mr & Mrs G. Calder**

**Other Owners:** Mrs T. H. Barclay, Mr J. R. Bostock, Mr Dean Graham Bostock, Mr G. Calder, Mrs J. Calder, Mr E. J. Dolan-Abrahams, Mrs E. J. Dolan-Abrahams, Mr Gary Douglas, Mr G. Eifert, Mrs K. S. Gaffney, Mr Derek Gennard, Mrs Gillian Gennard, Mrs S. Jefferson, Mr S. Key, Mrs F. D. McInnes Skinner, Mr R. Synder Jnr, Mr T. A. Stephenson, Mrs Alix Stevenson, Mrs I. C. Straker, Mr N. J. Taylor, Mr P. M. Warren, Mr R. Wharton, Mr J. H. Wilson, Mrs E. A. Young.

**Assistant Trainer:** Ruth Jefferson

**Jockey (NH):** Brian Hughes. **Conditional:** Jack Jordan, Finian O'Toole.

---

## 335 MR J. R. JENKINS, Royston

Postal: **Kings Ride, Baldock Road, Royston, Hertfordshire, SG8 9NN**
Contacts: **PHONE (01763) 241141 HOME (01763) 246611 FAX (01763) 248223**
**MOBILE Car: (07802) 750855**
**E-MAIL john@johnjenkinsracing.co.uk WEBSITE www.johnjenkinsracing.co.uk**

1 **AMOSITE,** 9, b m Central Park (IRE)—Waterline Dancer (IRE) **Mrs C. Goddard**
2 **AUDEN (USA),** 7, b g Librettist (USA)—Moyesii (USA) **Miss Caroline A. Jenkins**
3 **BILLY RED,** 11, ch g Dr Fong (USA)—Liberty Bound **Mrs I. C. Hampson**
4 **BLADEWOOD GIRL,** 7, b m Needwood Blade—Willmar (IRE) **Byron Boys**
5 **BOW BELLE,** 5, ch m Cockney Rebel (IRE)—Miss Ippolita **D. J. P. Bryans**
6 **BRAVE TOBY (IRE),** 4, b g Jeremy (USA)—Certainly Brave **Ms A. Juskaite**
7 **BUBBLY BAILEY,** 5, b g Byron—Night Gypsy **Mrs S. Bowmer**
8 **CARRABAMABABE,** 4, b f Beat All (USA)—Carranita (IRE) **Mr M. Turner**
9 **CLOSEST FRIEND,** 6, b g Kayf Tara—Princess of War **Lottie Parsons & Sue Raymond**
10 **DORKAS,** 6, b m Doyen (IRE)—Jawwala (USA) **P. J. Kirkpatrick**
11 **FINE 'N DANDY (IRE),** 4, ch g Dandy Man (IRE)—Pearly Brooks **Ms A. Juskaite**
12 **GALUPPI,** 4, b g Galileo (IRE)—La Leuze (IRE) **Miss A. Finn**
13 **GREAT EXPECTATIONS,** 7, b g Storming Home—Fresh Fruit Daily **The Great Expectations Partnership**
14 **HI TIDE (IRE),** 11, br g Idris (IRE)—High Glider **Mrs W. A. Jenkins**
15 **KARAM ALBAARI (IRE),** 7, b h King's Best (USA)—Lilakiya (IRE) **Mr M. D. Goldstein**
16 **LITTLE INDIAN,** 5, b g Sleeping Indian—Once Removed **Two Little Indians**
17 **MEEBO (IRE),** 4, b f Captain Rio—Abbeyleix Lady (IRE) **Mr B. L. Polkey**
18 **MISHRIF (USA),** 9, b br g Arch (USA)—Peppy Priscilla (USA) **Mrs W. A. Jenkins**
19 **MONSIEUR JAMIE,** 7, b g Monsieur Bond (IRE)—Primula Bairn **Mr M. D. Goldstein**
20 **MYBOYALFIE (USA),** 8, b g Johannesburg (USA)—Scotchbonnetpepper (USA) **R. Bradbury**
21 **ONLY TEN PER CENT (IRE),** 7, b g Kheleyf (USA)—Cory Everson (IRE) **B. Silkman**
22 **OSCARS JOURNEY,** 5, ch g Dubai Destination (USA)—Fruit of Glory **Mr Peter Watson**
23 **PERSPICACITY,** 4, ch f Sir Percy—Sakhacity **Mrs W. A. Jenkins**
24 **PRETTY BUBBLES,** 6, b m Sleeping Indian—Willmar (IRE) **Mr M. D. Goldstein & Mrs W. Jenkins**
25 **PURPLE SPECTRUM,** 4, gr g Verglas (IRE)—Rainbow's Edge **Roldvale Ltd G Pascoe Barry Silkman**
26 **QATAR PRINCESS (IRE),** 4, b f Marju (IRE)—Bridal Dance (IRE) **Mr Peter Watson**
27 **RAMBO WILL,** 7, b g Danbird (AUS)—Opera Belle **Mrs S. Bambridge**
28 **RUBY LOOKER,** 4, b c Bertolini (USA)—Ellcon (IRE) **Mr M. Turner**
29 **SAKASH,** 5, b h Sakhee (USA)—Ashwell Rose **Mr & Mrs C. Schwick**
30 **SAWWALA,** 5, b m Sakhee (USA)—Jawwala (USA) **P. J. Kirkpatrick**
31 **SILVER MOUNTAIN,** 4, gr g Sir Percy—Pearl Bright (FR) **Ms A. Juskaite**
32 **SPITFIRE,** 10, b g Mujahid (USA)—Fresh Fruit Daily **Mrs W. A. Jenkins**
33 **TIRADIA (FR),** 8, b br g Without Connexion (IRE)—Jimanji (FR) **B. S. P. Dowling**
34 **VA BENNY,** 4, b g Byron—Apple of My Eye **Mr R. Stevens**
35 **WHALEWEIGH STATION,** 4, b g Zamindar (USA)—Looby Loo **B. Silkman**

## MR J. R. JENKINS - Continued

### THREE-YEAR-OLDS

**36** B g What A Caper (IRE)—Barlin Bay **Vinnie Cooke & Sara Cooke**
**37** B f Archipenko (USA)—Bookiesindex Girl (IRE) **Mrs W. Jenkins**
**38** Ch f Champs Elysees—Cavallo da Corsa **Bookmakers Index Ltd**
**39 COME UP AND SEE ME,** b g Cockney Rebel (IRE)—Sakhacity **Robin Stevens & David Tattersall**
**40 GET PRANCER,** ch g Archipenko (USA)—Clever Omneya (USA) **Mrs I. C. Hampson**
**41** Ch g Notnowcato—Isabella d'este (IRE) **Michael Ng**
**42 LOLITA,** ch f Sir Percy—Miss Ippolita **Robert Ellis & Guy Montgomery**
**43** B c Hellvelyn—Once Removed **D. R. Tucker**
**44** Br g Kheleyf (USA)—Tilsworth Charlie **Michael Ng**

### TWO-YEAR-OLDS

**45** B f 14/4 Archipenko (USA)—Clever Omneya (USA) (Toccet (USA))
**46** B c 15/2 Mount Nelson—Ellcon (IRE) (Royal Applause) (1000) **Mr M. Turner**
**47** B f 8/4 Cockney Rebel (IRE)—Sakhacity (Sakhee (USA)) **Philippa Casey**
**48** B f 28/2 Mullionmileanhour (IRE)—United Passion (Emarati (USA)) (5000)

**Other Owners:** Mr David Abrey, Sheikh Ahmad Yousuf Al Sabah, Mrs S. Bambridge, Mrs S. Bowmer, Mr Roger Bradbury, Mr Stephen Bullock, Mr G. J. Burchell, Mr I. J. Callaway, Miss P. Casey, Mr Paul Cousins, B. S. P. Dowling, Mr Robert M. Ellis, Miss A. Finn, Mrs C. Goddard, Mr M. D. Goldstein, Mrs Irene Hampson, Mrs Wendy Jenkins, Ms A. Juskaite, P. J. Kirkpatrick, Mr Guy Montgomery, Michael Ng, Mrs Lottie Parsons, Mr G. J. Pascoe, Mr B. L. Polkey, Mrs Sue Raymond, Roldvale Limited, Mr C. Schwick, Mrs C. Schwick, Mr B. Silkman, Mr Robin Stevens, Mr D. J. Tattersall, Mr P. J. Trotter, Mr M. Turner, Mr Peter Watson.

---

## 336 MR ALAN JESSOP, Chelmsford

Postal: **Flemings Farm, Warren Road, South Hanningfield, Chelmsford, Essex, CM3 8HU**
Contacts: **PHONE (01268) 710210 MOBILE (07718) 736482**

**1 BLAZING GLEN (IRE),** 7, ch g Beneficial—Kofiyah's Rose (IRE) **Mrs G. Jessop**
**2 CHORAL BEE,** 6, b m Oratorio (IRE)—Chief Bee **Mrs G. Jessop**
**3 MAX MILANO (IRE),** 10, b g Milan—Stellissima (IRE) **Mrs G. Jessop**
**4 STICKERS,** 8, b g Generous (IRE)—Dunsfold Duchess (IRE) **Mrs G. Jessop**

---

## 337 MRS LINDA JEWELL, Maidstone

Postal: **Southfield Stables, South Lane, Sutton Valence, Maidstone, Kent, ME17 3AZ**
Contacts: **PHONE (01622) 842788 FAX (01622) 842943 MOBILE (07856) 686657**
**E-MAIL lindajewell@hotmail.com WEBSITE www.lindajewellracing.co.uk**

**1 BORN TO BE FREE,** 6, b m Phoenix Reach (IRE)—Charlie's Angel **C. Cheesman**
**2 CLONUSKER (IRE),** 7, b g Fasliyev (USA)—Tamburello (IRE) **Mr D. N. Yeadon**
**3 FINE TUNE (IRE),** 4, b g Medicean—Phillippa (IRE) **Mrs R. V. Watson**
**4 FLEETING INDIAN (IRE),** 6, b g Sleeping Indian—Glebe Garden **Mr M. J. Boutcher**
**5** 5, Ch g Resplendent Glory (IRE)—Heather Valley
**6 I'M LUCY (IRE),** 4, b f Papal Bull—Melaaya (USA) **Mrs R. V. Watson**
**7 ITOLDYOU (IRE),** 9, ch g Salford Express (IRE)—Adisadel (IRE) **Valence Racing Too**
**8 KAFEEL (USA),** 4, b g First Samurai (USA)—Ishraak (USA) **K. Johnson, K. Jessup**
**9 KAYFLIN (FR),** 7, b m Kayf Tara—Flinders **Leith Hill Chasers**
**10 KINGSCOMBE (USA),** 6, gr ro g Mizzen Mast (USA)—Gombeen (USA) **P. A. Oppenheimer**
**11 MACCABEES,** 6, b g Motivator—Takarna (IRE) **Mrs F. J. Dean**
**12 PRAISE N GLORY,** 4, ch f Resplendent Glory (IRE)—Tapsalteerie **Dick Churcher, Rev'd Canon C F Arvidsson**
**13 PRIORS DOOR (IRE),** 7, b g Subtle Power (IRE)—Lady Leila (IRE) **Valence Racing**
**14 RED ANCHOR (IRE),** 11, ch g Snurge—Clonartic (IRE) **Mrs S. M. Stanier**
**15 ROWE PARK,** 12, b g Dancing Spree (USA)—Magic Legs **Mrs L. C. Jewell**
**16 STRATEGIC ACTION (IRE),** 6, ch g Strategic Prince—Ruby Cairo (IRE) **Mr M. J. Boutcher**
**17 YES I WILL,** 6, b g Kahyasi—Flinders **Leith Hill Chasers**

**Other Owners:** Reverend C. F. Arvidsson, Mr R. Churcher, Mr K. P. Jessup, Mr K. W. Johnson, Mrs J. Maltby, Mr N. F. Maltby, Mrs A. May, R. I. B. Young.

**Assistant Trainer:** Karen Jewell

**Jockey (flat):** Steve Drowne, Robert Havlin, Liam Keniry. **Jockey (NH):** Andrew Thornton, Gerard Tumelty. **Apprentice:** Daniel Cremin. **Amateur:** Mr F. Mitchell.

## 338 MR BRETT JOHNSON, Epsom

Postal: **The Durdans Stables, Chalk Lane, Epsom, Surrey, KT18 7AX**
Contacts: **MOBILE (07768) 697141**
**E-MAIL thedurdansstables@googlemail.com WEBSITE www.brjohnsonracing.co.uk**

1 **ASSIST,** 5, b g Zamindar (USA)—Cochin (USA) **Tann Racing**
2 **CAYUGA,** 6, b g Montjeu (IRE)—Ithaca (USA) **B. R. Johnson**
3 **JELLY FISH,** 4, ch g Observatory (USA)—Grand Coral **J. Daniels**
4 **OAKBANK (USA),** 4, b g Empire Maker (USA)—Summer Shower **Mr C. Westley**
5 **SATCHVILLE FLYER,** 4, ch g Compton Place—Palinisa (FR) **Mr N Jarvis, Mr T Broke-Smith, Mr G Tann**
6 4, B c Oratorio (IRE)—Whassup (FR) **Mrs A. M. Upsdell**

### THREE-YEAR-OLDS

7 **SENOR FIRECRACKER (IRE),** b g Acclamation—Miss Eze **Tann Racing**

**Other Owners:** Mr T. W. Broke-Smith, Mr N. A. Jarvis, G. Tann, Mrs E. Tann.

**Assistant Trainer:** Vanessa Johnson

## 339 MISS EVE JOHNSON HOUGHTON, Blewbury

Postal: **Woodway, Blewbury, Didcot, Oxfordshire, OX11 9EZ**
Contacts: **PHONE (01235) 850480 (01235) 850500 (Home) FAX (01235) 851045**
**MOBILE (07721) 622700**
**E-MAIL Eve@JohnsonHoughton.com WEBSITE www.JohnsonHoughton.com**

1 **AJIG,** 4, ch f Bahamian Bounty—Atwirl **Eden Racing Club**
2 **AMULET,** 5, gr m Ishiguru (USA)—Loveofmylife **Mrs V. D. Neale**
3 **CHARLIE WELLS (IRE),** 4, b g High Chaparral (IRE)—Numbers Game **Eden Racing**
4 **COOL BAHAMIAN (IRE),** 4, b g Bahamian Bounty—Keritana (FR) **Mr L R Godfrey & Mr R F Johnson Houghton**
5 **DRIVE ON (IRE),** 4, b g Tagula (IRE)—Thelma Louise (IRE) **J. H. Widdows**
6 **FINDELN,** 6, b m Dubai Destination (USA)—Alpenrot (IRE) **Mrs V. D. Neale**
7 **KHUTZE (GER),** 4, b g Duke of Marmalade (IRE)—Kalahari Dancer **The Picnic Partnership**
8 **NEW RICH,** 5, b g Bahamian Bounty—Bling Bling (IRE) **Eden Racing Club**
9 **PANTHER PATROL (IRE),** 5, b g Tagula (IRE)—Quivala (USA) **G. C. Stevens**
10 **PINK DIAMOND,** 4, b f Champs Elysees—Fairy Dance (IRE) **Dr A. J. F. Gillespie**
11 **STARLIGHT SYMPHONY (IRE),** 5, b m Oratorio (IRE)—Phillippa (IRE) **Brian & Liam McNamee, Les & Ian Dawson**
12 **STARLIT CANTATA,** 4, b f Oratorio (IRE)—Starlit Sky **Mrs H. B. Raw**
13 **WHAT ABOUT CARLO (FR),** 4, b g Creachadoir (IRE)—Boccatenera (GER) **A. J. Pye-Jeary**

### THREE-YEAR-OLDS

14 **AEVALON,** b f Avonbridge—Blaina **Mill House Partnership**
15 **BEEKY,** ch g Haafhd—Vive La Chasse (IRE) **R. F. Johnson Houghton**
16 **BRITISH EMBASSY (IRE),** b g Clodovil (IRE)—Embassy Belle (IRE) **Eden Racing IV**
17 **GOLDEN WEDDING (IRE),** b g Archipenko (USA)—Peace Lily **Mrs F. M. Johnson Houghton**
18 **GORING (GER),** b c Areion (GER)—Globuli (GER) **G. C. Stevens**
19 **MISS INGA SOCK (IRE),** ch f Tagula (IRE)—Support Fund (IRE) **The Ascot Colts & Fillies Club**
20 **MISTAMEL (IRE),** b g Rip Van Winkle (IRE)—Without Precedent (FR) **A. J. Pye-Jeary**
21 **MUSCADELLE,** b f Azamour (IRE)—Sauterne **Mr P Wollaston & Mr R F Johnson Houghton**
22 **PLYMOUTH SOUND,** b g Fastnet Rock (AUS)—Shardette (IRE) **T Keane, M Page, D Smith & R Whichelow**
23 **POMME DE GUERRE (IRE),** b g Kodiac—Lucky Apple (IRE) **Mr L. R. A. Godfrey**
24 **ROOM KEY,** ch c Mount Nelson—Saturday Girl **The Picnic Partnership**
25 **SILENCE IN COURT (IRE),** b c Invincible Spirit (IRE)—Hammrah **G. C. Stevens**
26 **STARCROSSED,** b g Cape Cross (IRE)—Gretna **The Picnic Partnership**
27 **STEP ON IT (IRE),** b g Footstepsinthesand—Woodyousmileforme (USA) **B. Dunn**
28 **THE DAPPER TAPPER (IRE),** b g Dandy Man (IRE)—Sound Tap (IRE) **C Whichelow, D Smith & I Mavroleon**

### TWO-YEAR-OLDS

29 **CANFORD LILLI (IRE),** b f 20/2 Canford Cliffs (IRE)—Aine (IRE) (Danehill Dancer (IRE)) (17460) **Peter Wollaston & Peter Johnson**
30 B f 16/3 Lawman (FR)—Chervil (Dansili) (6000)
31 **COARSE CUT (IRE),** b c 2/3 Duke of Marmalade (IRE)—Keladora (USA) (Crafty Prospector (USA)) (16000) **Equi ex Incertis Partners**
32 B c 23/1 Mount Nelson—Fascination Street (IRE) (Mujadil (USA)) (8000)

## MISS EVE JOHNSON HOUGHTON - Continued

**33** Gr c 12/5 Clodovil (IRE)—Hasty Katie (IRE) (Whipper (USA)) (12698)
**34** B c 22/5 Frozen Power (IRE)—Incendio (Siberian Express (USA)) (21000) **Eden Racing III**
**35 LADY KATHERINE,** b f 3/2 Dick Turpin (IRE)—Vax Star (Petong) (8000) **R. F. Johnson Houghton**
**36** B c 3/2 Sabiango (GER)—Mattinata (Tiger Hill (IRE)) (26000) **A. J. Pye-Jeary**
**37** B f 10/3 Poet's Voice—Penang (IRE) (Xaar) (21428)
**38 SCARLET DRAGON,** b c 1/3 Sir Percy—Welsh Angel (Dubai Destination (USA)) (32000) **W. H. Ponsonby**
**39** B f 10/4 Roderic O'Connor (IRE)—Scottendale (Zilzal (USA)) (11904)
**40** B f 3/2 Zoffany (IRE)—Shenkara (IRE) (Night Shift (USA)) (20634) **Swanee River Partnership**
**41** B c 19/3 Manduro (GER)—Short Affair (Singspiel (IRE)) (12000) **The Pantechnicons V**
**42** B f 2/5 Holy Roman Emperor (IRE)—True Crystal (IRE) (Sadler's Wells (USA)) (14000) **Mrs V. D. Neale**

**Other Owners:** Mr N. B. Bentley, Mr P. Bowden, Mr T. E. Boylan, Mr C. K. Crossley Cooke, Mr L. W. Dawson, Mr I. W. Dawson, Mr P. J. Johnson, Miss E. A. Johnson Houghton, Ms T. Keane, Mr C. O. A. Liverton, Sir I. Magee, Mr I. G. Mavroleon, B. P. McNamee, Mr L. P. McNamee, Mrs J. A. McWilliam, Mr M. E. Page, D. M. Smith, J. R. Wallis, Major-Gen G. H. Watkins, Mr R. Whichelow, Mrs C. Whichelow, Mr F. Wintle, Mr P. R. Wollaston.

**Assistant Trainer:** R. F. Johnson Houghton

---

## 340 MR ROBERT JOHNSON, Newcastle Upon Tyne

Postal: **Johnson Racing Ltd, Grange Farm, Newburn, Newcastle Upon Tyne**
Contacts: **PHONE (01912) 674464 FAX (01912) 674464 MOBILE (07774) 131133**
**E-MAIL rjohnsonracing@talktalk.net WEBSITE www.rwjohnsonracing.co.uk**

1 **AZRUR (IRE),** 5, b g Sir Percy—Tiger Spice **Mr D. C. Moat**
2 **CAPTAIN SHARPE,** 7, ch g Tobougg (IRE)—Helen Sharp **J. L. Armstrong**
3 **CASH IS KING,** 5, b g Bahamian Bounty—Age of Chivalry (IRE) **Miss N. Morris**
4 **COOLANURE (IRE),** 6, b m Portrait Gallery (IRE)—Aiguille (IRE) **Sprayclad UK & CSS Group**
5 **LORD BRENDY,** 7, gr g Portrait Gallery (IRE)—Hervey Bay **T L A & R A Robson**
6 **MOYACOMB (IRE),** 7, b m Darsi (FR)—Matt Wood (IRE) **Mr A. V. W. Kidd**
7 **NOWREYNA,** 4, gr f Notnowcato—Kryena **Robert C Whitelock R Johnson**
8 **POLITELYSED,** 9, ch m Courteous—Allegedly Red **Mr Robert Johnson & Mr J. Lund**
9 **ROSQUERO (FR),** 10, ch g Blushing Flame (USA)—Kingsgirl (FR) **Alan Kidd Dave Bamlet Racing R Johnson**
10 **SUNRISE DANCE,** 6, ch m Monsieur Bond (IRE)—Wachiwi (IRE)
11 **VALNAMIXE DU MEE (FR),** 6, b g Al Namix (FR)—Kateline du Mee (FR) **TLA & RA Robson & Mrs L Gander**
12 **VODKA RED (IRE),** 7, b g Ivan Denisovich (IRE)—Begine (IRE) **Ontoawinner,R Johnson,Carter Thomson**
13 **YUKON DELTA (IRE),** 8, ch g Old Vic—Red Fern (IRE) **Magpie Racing**

**Other Owners:** Mr L. G. Aldsworth, Mr D. Bamlet, Mr I. M. Blacklock, Mr A. Carter, Mr A. L. Ellison, Mrs L. R. Gander, Mr N. N. Kane, Mr J. Lund, N. J. O'Brien, T. L. A. Robson, Mrs R. A. Robson, Mr M. Saunders, Mr S. Thompson, R. C. Whitelock.

**Jockey (NH):** Kenny Johnson. **Amateur:** Mr P. Johnson, Mr T. Speke.

---

## 341 MRS SUSAN JOHNSON, Madley

Postal: **Carwardine Farm, Madley, Hereford**
Contacts: **PHONE (01981) 250214 FAX (01981) 251538**

1 **BROOME LANE,** 6, b m Kayf Tara—Aranga (IRE) **I. K. Johnson**
2 **PEMBRIDGE,** 6, b m Kayf Tara—Supreme Gem (IRE) **I. K. Johnson**
3 **THE LAST BRIDGE,** 8, b g Milan—Celtic Bridge **I. K. Johnson**

**Jockey (NH):** Richard Johnson.

---

## 342 MR MARK JOHNSTON, Middleham

Postal: **Kingsley House Racing Stables, Middleham, Leyburn, North Yorkshire, DL8 4PH**
Contacts: **PHONE (01969) 622237 FAX (01969) 622484**
**E-MAIL mark@markjohnstonracing.com WEBSITE www.markjohnstonracing.com**

1 **ALPINE STORM (IRE),** 4, b f Raven's Pass (USA)—Lurina (IRE) **Sheikh Hamdan Bin Mohammed Al Maktoum**
2 **ATLANTIC AFFAIR (IRE),** 4, gr f Clodovil (IRE)—Adultress (IRE) **Kingsley Park 1 - Ready To Run Partnership**
3 **BLUE WAVE (IRE),** 5, b g Raven's Pass (USA)—
Million Waves (IRE) **Sheikh Hamdan Bin Mohammed Al Maktoum**

## MR MARK JOHNSTON - Continued

4 **BUREAU (IRE),** 4, ch f Halling (USA)—Embassy **Sheikh Hamdan Bin Mohammed Al Maktoum**
5 **FIRE FIGHTING (IRE),** 4, b g Soldier of Fortune (IRE)—Savoie (FR) **A. D. Spence**
6 **IFWECAN,** 4, b g Exceed And Excel (AUS)—Kirk **D. C. Livingston**
7 **KOSIKA (USA),** 5, b m Hard Spun (USA)—Song of Africa (USA) **Sheikh Hamdan Bin Mohammed Al Maktoum**
8 **LADY FRANCES,** 4, b f Exceed And Excel (AUS)—Lady Catherine **Sheikh Hamdan Bin Mohammed Al Maktoum**
9 **LEADERENE,** 4, b f Selkirk (USA)—La Felicita **Miss K. Rausing**
10 **LITTLE SHAMBLES,** 4, ch f Shamardal (USA)—Meiosis (USA) **Sheikh Hamdan Bin Mohammed Al Maktoum**
11 **LYN VALLEY,** 4, b g Shamardal (USA)—Demisemiquaver **Mr J. A. Barson**
12 **MAID IN RIO (IRE),** 4, ch f Captain Rio—Silver Whale (FR) **The New Fairyhouse Partnership**
13 **MAMBO RHYTHM,** 4, b f Authorized (IRE)—Mambo Halo (USA) **Around The World Partnership**
14 **MASTER OF FINANCE (IRE),** 4, ch g Mastercraftsman (IRE)—Cheal Rose (IRE) **J. D. Abell**
15 **MEDIATE,** 4, ch c New Approach (IRE)—Miss Prim **Sheikh Hamdan Bin Mohammed Al Maktoum**
16 **NOTARISED,** 4, b g Authorized (IRE)—Caribbean Dancer (USA) **Hugh Hart**
17 **ORIENTAL FOX (GER),** 7, ch g Lomitas—Oriental Pearl (GER) **Markus Graff**
18 **PIRATE COVE (IRE),** 5, b m Lawman (FR)—Uncharted Haven **Ballylinch Stud**
19 **POTENT EMBRACE (USA),** 4, b br f Street Cry (IRE)—
Karen's Caper (USA) **Sheikh Hamdan Bin Mohammed Al Maktoum**
20 **QUICKASWECAN,** 4, b g Shamardal (USA)—Arctic Air **D. C. Livingston**
21 **SEA THE SKIES,** 4, b c Sea The Stars (IRE)—Model Queen (USA) **A. D. Spence**
22 **SENNOCKIAN STAR,** 5, ch g Rock of Gibraltar (IRE)—Chorist **The Vine Accord Partnership**
23 **STETCHWORTH (IRE),** 4, ch c New Approach (IRE)—
Hallowed Park (IRE) **Sheikh Hamdan Bin Mohammed Al Maktoum**
24 **TIZLOVE REGARDLESS (USA),** 4, b c Tiznow (USA)—Dianehill (IRE) **Mick Doyle**
25 **WATERSMEET,** 4, gr g Dansili—Under The Rainbow **Mr J. A. Barson**

## THREE-YEAR-OLDS

26 **ADELE (GER),** b f Intikhab (USA)—Adalawa (IRE) **Conquer The World Partnership**
27 **ASSAULT ON ROME (IRE),** b f Holy Roman Emperor (IRE)—Naomh Geileis (USA) **Mrs C. E. Budden**
28 **BIZZARIO,** b g Raven's Pass (USA)—All's Forgotten (USA) **David & Jane Newett**
29 **BLACK N BLUE,** ch c Galileo (IRE)—Coyote **A. D. Spence**
30 **BLAME LOVE (USA),** b c Blame (USA)—Twisted Tale (USA) **Mick Doyle**
31 **BOSTON TWO STEP,** b c Pivotal—Danse Arabe (IRE) **Sheikh Hamdan Bin Mohammed Al Maktoum**
32 **CAPE LION (IRE),** b c Kodiac—Cheal Rose (IRE) **Markus Graff**
33 B f Halling (USA)—Caribbean Dancer (USA) **Hugh Hart**
34 **CASILA (IRE),** b f High Chaparral (IRE)—Miletrian (IRE) **M. Wormald**
35 **CASSANDANE (IRE),** br f Jeremy (USA)—Princess Atoosa (USA) **Kingsley Park 1 - Ready To Run Partnership**
36 **CHADIC,** b c Echo of Light—Hawsa (USA) **Sheikh Hamdan Bin Mohammed Al Maktoum**
37 **CHAMPAGNE RANSOM (FR),** b f Mastercraftsman (IRE)—Linorova (USA) **A. D. Spence**
38 **CRUSADING (USA),** b c Street Cry (IRE)—Danelagh (AUS) **Sheikh Hamdan Bin Mohammed Al Maktoum**
39 **DEEBAJ (IRE),** b c Authorized (IRE)—Athreyaa **Hamdan Al Maktoum**
40 **DENZILLE LANE (IRE),** ch g Iffraaj—Alexander Youth (IRE) **Sheikh Hamdan Bin Mohammed Al Maktoum**
41 **DISAVOW,** b f Shamardal (USA)—Dunnes River (USA) **Sheikh Hamdan Bin Mohammed Al Maktoum**
42 **DONNA GRACIOSA (GER),** br f Samum (GER)—Donna Alicia (GER) **Abdulla Al Mansoori**
43 **ENLACE,** b f Shamardal (USA)—Crossover **Sheikh Hamdan Bin Mohammed Al Maktoum**
44 **FAISEUR DE MIRACLE,** b c Makfi—Flawly **Newsells Park Stud Limited**
45 **FINAL,** b g Arabian Gleam—Caysue **C. H. Greensit**
46 **FREIGHT TRAIN (IRE),** b c Manduro (GER)—Sigonella (IRE) **A. D. Spence**
47 **GRIGOLO,** b c Shamardal (USA)—Dubai Opera (USA) **Sheikh Hamdan Bin Mohammed Al Maktoum**
48 **HINT OF PINK (IRE),** ch f Teofilo (IRE)—Fragrancy (IRE) **A. D. Spence**
49 **INDESCRIBABLE (IRE),** b g Invincible Spirit (IRE)—
Subtle Charm **Sheikh Hamdan Bin Mohammed Al Maktoum**
50 **JESTER,** b c Jalil (USA)—Laughsome **Sheikh Hamdan Bin Mohammed Al Maktoum**
51 **MACSHEESH (IRE),** b g Azamour (IRE)—Princess Roseburg (USA) **M. C. MacKenzie**
52 **MALIMBI (IRE),** b c Cape Cross (IRE)—Mirina (FR) **Sheikh Hamdan Bin Mohammed Al Maktoum**
53 **MAMBO PARADISE,** b f Makfi—Mambo Halo (USA) **Around The World Partnership**
54 **MANSHAA (IRE),** ch c Dubawi (IRE)—Ghizlaan (USA) **Hamdan Al Maktoum**
55 **MIDLANDER (IRE),** b c Shamardal (USA)—Mille **Sheikh Hamdan Bin Mohammed Al Maktoum**
56 **MISS EXCELLENCE,** b f Exceed And Excel (AUS)—Hunter's Fortune (USA) **Greenland Park Stud**
57 **MISSISIPI BAILEYS (FR),** b f Aqlaam—Missisipi Star (IRE) **Paul Venner**
58 **MISTER ROCKANDROLL,** b g Rock of Gibraltar (IRE)—Cruel Sea (USA) **The Originals**
59 **MISTER UNIVERSE,** br c Cape Cross (IRE)—Miss Ivanhoe (IRE) **Abdulla Al Mansoori**
60 **MONT D'ARGENT,** gr c Montjeu (IRE)—Ayla (IRE) **David & Jane Newett**
61 **MUKHMAL (IRE),** ch g Bahamian Bounty—May Day Queen (IRE) **Hamdan Al Maktoum**
62 **MURAAQABA,** br f Dubawi (IRE)—Nufoos **Hamdan Al Maktoum**
63 **MUSTAQBAL (IRE),** b c Invincible Spirit (IRE)—Alshamatry (USA) **Hamdan Al Maktoum**

## MR MARK JOHNSTON - Continued

**64 MYTHICAL CITY (IRE),** b f Rock of Gibraltar (IRE)—Rainbow City (IRE) **The Chriselliam Partnership**
**65 OREGON GIFT,** b c Major Cadeaux—Dayville (USA) **N Browne, M Bradford, Mrs Frosell, S Richards**
**66 POLARISATION,** b g Echo of Light—Concordia **Sheikh Hamdan Bin Mohammed Al Maktoum**
**67 PRECARIOUS (IRE),** b c Iffraaj—Screen Star (IRE) **Sheikh Hamdan Bin Mohammed Al Maktoum**
**68 PRINCE OF TIME,** ch g Bahamian Bounty—Touching (IRE) **Abdulla Al Mansoori**
**69 PUBLILIA,** b f Makfi—Terentia **Abdulla Al Mansoori**
**70 REGAL WAYS (IRE),** b f Royal Applause—Step This Way (USA) **S. R. Counsell**
**71 RESONANT (IRE),** b c Cape Cross (IRE)—Last Rhapsody (IRE) **Sheikh Hamdan Bin Mohammed Al Maktoum**
**72 REVOLUTIONIST (IRE),** b c Pivotal—Mysterial (USA) **Sheikh Hamdan Bin Mohammed Al Maktoum**
**73 SALIERIS MASS,** b c Mount Nelson—Sunley Gift **Newsells Park Stud Limited**
**74 SEA SILK,** b c Shamardal (USA)—Ocean Silk (USA) **Sheikh Hamdan Bin Mohammed Al Maktoum**
**75 SHIPWRIGHT (IRE),** b c Shamardal (USA)—Shinko Hermes (IRE) **Sheikh Hamdan Bin Mohammed Al Maktoum**
**76 SHOWSTOPPA,** ch f Showcasing—Harryana **Hot To Trot Racing Club & Whitsbury Manor Stud**
**77 SUBVERSIVE (IRE),** b g Invincible Spirit (IRE)—
Persian Secret (FR) **Sheikh Hamdan Bin Mohammed Al Maktoum**
**78 SUREWECAN,** b c Royal Applause—Edge of Light **D. C. Livingston**
**79 TADARROK,** ch c Elusive Quality (USA)—Don't Forget Faith (USA) **Hamdan Al Maktoum**
**80 THE SPECIAL HOUSE (IRE),** ro g Dalakhani (IRE)—Noble Galileo (IRE) **Mr C. Stockill**
**81 THINK SNOW (USA),** ch f Giant's Causeway (USA)—Snow Forest (USA) **Mr Christopher Wright & Vicky Snook**
**82 THREE MERRY LADS,** b c Danehill Dancer (IRE)—Obsessive (USA) **David & Jane Newett**
**83 TOGETHERWECAN (IRE),** b f Danehill Dancer (IRE)—Crystal Bull (USA) **D. C. Livingston**
**84 TRIPLE DIP (IRE),** ch f Three Valleys (USA)—Melpomene **Mrs C. E. Budden**
**85 VIVE MA FILLE (GER),** b f Doyen (IRE)—Vive Madame (GER) **R W Huggins & Atlantic Racing**
**86 WATER THIEF (USA),** b c Bellamy Road (USA)—Sometime (IRE) **Sheikh Majid Bin Mohammed Al Maktoum**
**87 YORKIDDING,** b f Dalakhani (IRE)—Claxon **Mr P. R. York**
**88 YORKINDRED SPIRIT,** b f Sea The Stars (IRE)—Paracel (USA) **Mr P. R. York**

## TWO-YEAR-OLDS

**89 ABAREEQ,** ch c 9/4 Haatef (USA)—Hafawa (IRE) (Intikhab (USA)) **Hamdan Al Maktoum**
**90** Ch c 26/2 Roderic O'Connor (IRE)—
Acushladear (IRE) (Tagula (IRE)) (7142) **Salem Rashid & Abdulla Al Mansoori**
**91** B c 17/4 Cape Cross (IRE)—Aguinaga (IRE) (Machiavellian (USA)) (25396) **Browne & Richards**
**92** B f 13/4 Manduro (GER)—Ailette (Second Set (IRE)) (22222) **J. D. Abell**
**93** B f 20/3 Pour Moi (IRE)—Alta Lena (FR) (Alzao (USA)) (23809) **Greenfield Stud Ltd**
**94 ANABEL,** ch f 27/1 Lord of England (GER)—Adalawa (IRE) (Barathea (IRE)) (19047) **Markus Graff**
**95** B f 1/3 Medaglia d'Oro (USA)—
Anna Wi'yaak (JPN) (Dubai Millennium) **Sheikh Hamdan Bin Mohammed Al Maktoum**
**96** B c 15/1 Cape Cross (IRE)—At A Great Rate (USA) (Arch (USA)) (47000) **Kingsley Park 3 - The Originals**
**97** B c 29/3 Dubawi (IRE)—Avongrove (Tiger Hill (IRE)) **Sheikh Hamdan Bin Mohammed Al Maktoum**
**98** B c 19/2 Cape Cross (IRE)—Await So (Sadler's Wells (USA)) **Sheikh Hamdan Bin Mohammed Al Maktoum**
**99 BAILEYS ESQUIRE,** b c 8/3 Halling (USA)—Silversword (FR) (Highest Honor (FR)) **Paul Venner**
**100** B c 2/4 Bernardini (USA)—Balanchine (USA) (Storm Bird (CAN)) **Sheikh Hamdan Bin Mohammed Al Maktoum**
**101** Ch f 4/2 Street Cry (IRE)—
Belenkaya (USA) (Giant's Causeway (USA)) **Sheikh Hamdan Bin Mohammed Al Maktoum**
**102** Br c 22/2 Cape Cross (IRE)—
Bella Monica (GER) (Big Shuffle (USA)) (119047) **Sheikh Hamdan Bin Mohammed Al Maktoum**
**103** B f 1/3 Cape Cross (IRE)—Belle Josephine (Dubawi (IRE)) **Sheikh Hamdan Bin Mohammed Al Maktoum**
**104** Ch c 1/3 Exceed And Excel (AUS)—
Bergamask (USA) (Kingmambo (USA)) **Sheikh Hamdan Bin Mohammed Al Maktoum**
**105** B c 21/3 Cape Cross (IRE)—
Bint Almatar (USA) (Kingmambo (USA)) **Sheikh Hamdan Bin Mohammed Al Maktoum**
**106** B c 17/1 Cape Cross (IRE)—
Blaugrana (IRE) (Exceed And Excel (AUS)) **Sheikh Hamdan Bin Mohammed Al Maktoum**
**107** B f 10/3 Medaglia d'Oro (USA)—
Blue Duster (USA) (Danzig (USA)) **Sheikh Hamdan Bin Mohammed Al Maktoum**
**108** Ch c 25/3 Bahamian Bounty—Breathless Kiss (USA) (Roman Ruler (USA)) (15238) **J. D. Abell**
**109** B f 14/3 Exceed And Excel (AUS)—
Bright Morning (Dubai Millennium) **Sheikh Hamdan Bin Mohammed Al Maktoum**
**110** B c 20/2 Authorized (IRE)—Broken Peace (USA) (Devil's Bag (USA)) (31746) **R. S. Brookhouse**
**111 BYRES ROAD,** ch c 12/4 Pivotal—Croeso Cariad (Most Welcome) (16000) **Dr R. Holleyhead**
**112** B c 30/4 Bahamian Bounty—Caribbean Dancer (USA) (Theatrical) **Hugh Hart**
**113** Ch f 16/2 Mastercraftsman (IRE)—Chaibia (IRE) (Peintre Celebre (USA)) (31746) **Bobby Flay**
**114** B br c 9/4 Discreet Cat (USA)—
Chilukki's Song (USA) (Elusive Quality (USA)) **Sheikh Hamdan Bin Mohammed Al Maktoum**
**115** B c 22/3 Cape Cross (IRE)—Chiquita Linda (IRE) (Mujadil (USA)) **Sheikh Hamdan Bin Mohammed Al Maktoum**

## MR MARK JOHNSTON - Continued

**116** Ch c 26/2 Tobougg (IRE)—City of Angels (Woodman (USA)) **R. S. Brookhouse**
**117** B c 12/2 Zamindar (USA)—Cochin (USA) (Swain (IRE)) (9523) **Michael Watt**
**118** **DALEELAK (IRE),** b c 29/5 Arcano (IRE)—Alshamatry (USA) (Seeking The Gold (USA)) **Hamdan Al Maktoum**
**119** **DAWAA,** ch f 24/4 Tamayuz—Athreyaa (Singspiel (IRE)) **Hamdan Al Maktoum**
**120** **DESSERTOFLIFE (IRE),** gr f 24/2 Mastercraftsman (IRE)—
Cranky Spanky (IRE) (Spectrum (IRE)) (42000) **Ted Brierley**
**121** B f 25/2 Exceed And Excel (AUS)—
Dubai Opera (USA) (Dubai Millennium) **Sheikh Hamdan Bin Mohammed Al Maktoum**
**122** B c 15/2 Cape Cross (IRE)—Eaton Street (Discreet Cat (USA)) **Sheikh Hamdan Bin Mohammed Al Maktoum**
**123** B c 20/2 King's Best (USA)—Embassy (Cadeaux Genereux) **Sheikh Hamdan Bin Mohammed Al Maktoum**
**124** **EQLEEM,** b c 25/3 Acclamation—Blessing (Dubai Millennium) **Hamdan Al Maktoum**
**125** Ch c 24/3 Poet's Voice—Ever Love (BRZ) (Nedawi) **Sheikh Hamdan Bin Mohammed Al Maktoum**
**126** B f 9/4 Royal Applause—Excellerator (IRE) (Exceed And Excel (AUS)) (30476) **Abdulla Al Mansoori**
**127** B f 26/3 Teofilo (IRE)—Fading Light (King's Best (USA)) **Sheikh Hamdan Bin Mohammed Al Maktoum**
**128** B br c 23/4 Street Cry (IRE)—Fifth Avenue Doll (USA) (Marquetry (USA)) (34423) **Sultan Ali**
**129** B c 22/2 Street Cry (IRE)—First Blush (IRE) (Pivotal) **Sheikh Hamdan Bin Mohammed Al Maktoum**
**130** Br c 19/3 Poet's Voice—Flying Flag (IRE) (Entrepreneur) **Sheikh Hamdan Bin Mohammed Al Maktoum**
**131** B c 9/3 Acclamation—Gold Bubbles (USA) (Street Cry (IRE)) (55555) **Kai Fai Leung**
**132** B c 3/3 Teofilo (IRE)—Green Swallow (FR) (Green Tune (USA)) (40000) **Newsells Park Stud Limited**
**133** Gr f 24/2 Mastercraftsman (IRE)—
Greta d'argent (IRE) (Great Commotion (USA)) (29364) **Compas Equine Columbus**
**134** Ch f 4/5 Dream Ahead (USA)—Hallie's Comet (IRE) (One Cool Cat (USA)) (23809) **Abdulla Al Mansoori**
**135** B r 3/5 Danehill Dancer (IRE)—Heavenly Bay (USA) (Rahy (USA)) (11000) **Greenfield Stud Ltd**
**136** B c 15/2 Shamardal (USA)—Herboriste (Hernando (FR)) (142857) **Sheikh Hamdan Bin Mohammed Al Maktoum**
**137** B f 18/2 Dream Ahead (USA)—In A Silent Way (IRE) (Desert Prince (IRE)) (3000) **Ali Saeed**
**138** Ch c 28/4 Shamardal (USA)—
Infinite Spirit (USA) (Maria's Mon (USA)) **Sheikh Hamdan Bin Mohammed Al Maktoum**
**139** B c 25/4 Raven's Pass (USA)—Innclassic (IRE) (Stravinsky (USA)) **Sheikh Hamdan Bin Mohammed Al Maktoum**
**140** B c 13/4 Exceed And Excel (AUS)—
Inner Secret (USA) (Singspiel (IRE)) **Sheikh Hamdan Bin Mohammed Al Maktoum**
**141** B c 8/5 Poet's Voice—Ivory Gala (FR) (Galileo (IRE)) (72500) **Sheikh Hamdan Bin Mohammed Al Maktoum**
**142** B f 14/2 Dark Angel (IRE)—Jo Bo Bo (IRE) (Whipper (USA)) (45714) **Lady Lonsdale**
**143** B f 3/5 Lonhro (AUS)—Journalist (IRE) (Night Shift (USA)) **Sheikh Hamdan Bin Mohammed Al Maktoum**
**144** Ch c 23/3 Giant's Causeway (USA)—Junia Tepzia (IRE) (Rock of Gibraltar (IRE)) (25000) **Mr A. R. Harrison**
**145** B c 27/4 Elusive City (USA)—Kosmic View (USA) (Distant View (USA)) (23809) **Paul Venner**
**146** Ch c 24/3 Exceed And Excel (AUS)—
Lane County (USA) (Rahy (USA)) **Sheikh Hamdan Bin Mohammed Al Maktoum**
**147** B f 10/2 Bernardini (USA)—
Late Romance (USA) (Storm Cat (USA)) **Sheikh Hamdan Bin Mohammed Al Maktoum**
**148** B c 24/1 Vale of York (IRE)—Livadiya (IRE) (Shernazar) (25396) **Kingsley Park 2 - Fairyhouse**
**149** B c 4/3 Shamardal (USA)—
Looking Glass (USA) (Seeking The Gold (USA)) **Sheikh Hamdan Bin Mohammed Al Maktoum**
**150** **LOUVENCOURT (FR),** br c 1/1 Halling (USA)—Lungwa (IRE) (One Cool Cat (USA)) (31746) **Abdulla Al Mansoori**
**151** B c 14/4 Bernardini (USA)—
Love Dancing (ARG) (Salt Lake (USA)) **Sheikh Hamdan Bin Mohammed Al Maktoum**
**152** Ch f 23/3 Shamardal (USA)—Lurina (IRE) (Lure (USA)) **Sheikh Hamdan Bin Mohammed Al Maktoum**
**153** B c 9/2 Sir Percy—Marakabei (Hernando (FR)) (31000) **Kingsley Park 3 - The Originals**
**154** B c 8/2 Cape Cross (IRE)—Margarita (IRE) (Marju (IRE)) **Sheikh Hamdan Bin Mohammed Al Maktoum**
**155** **MARIEE,** b f 16/4 Archipenko (USA)—Maria di Scozia (Selkirk (USA)) **Miss K. Rausing**
**156** Ch c 24/4 Fast Company (IRE)—Melpomene (Peintre Celebre (USA)) **Mrs C. E. Budden**
**157** B c 22/2 Kitten's Joy (USA)—Menekineko (USA) (Kingmambo (USA)) (57372) **Abdulla Al Mansoori**
**158** B c 28/3 Shamardal (USA)—Mille (Dubai Millennium) **Sheikh Hamdan Bin Mohammed Al Maktoum**
**159** B f 28/2 Cape Cross (IRE)—Million Waves (IRE) (Mull of Kintyre (USA)) (57000) **P. Dean**
**160** B c 16/2 Iffraaj—Miss Gibraltar (Rock of Gibraltar (IRE)) (75000) **Hamdan Al Maktoum**
**161** **MISTYMOISTYMORNING (IRE),** gr f 17/3 Alhaarth (IRE)—
Bermuxa (FR) (Linamix (FR)) (11110) **Mr Christopher Wright & Mrs Catherine Corbett**
**162** B c 13/4 Cape Cross (IRE)—
Monnavanna (IRE) (Machiavellian (USA)) (70000) **Sheikh Hamdan Bin Mohammed Al Maktoum**
**163** Ch c 24/2 Zamindar (USA)—Mosqueras Romance (Rock of Gibraltar (IRE)) (7936) **Markus Graff**
**164** **MUATADEL,** b c 21/2 Exceed And Excel (AUS)—
Rose Blossom (Pastoral Pursuits) (170000) **Hamdan Al Maktoum**
**165** B c 1/3 Dubawi (IRE)—Nahoodh (IRE) (Clodovil (IRE)) **Sheikh Hamdan Bin Mohammed Al Maktoum**
**166** B c 14/3 Azamour (IRE)—On A Soapbox (USA) (Mi Cielo (USA)) (55555) **Frank Bird**
**167** B c 30/3 Pivotal—Persinette (USA) (Kingmambo (USA)) **Sheikh Hamdan Bin Mohammed Al Maktoum**
**168** B f 16/4 Roderic O'Connor (IRE)—Pleasure Place (IRE) (Compton Place) (19047) **Abdulla Al Mansoori**

## MR MARK JOHNSTON - Continued

**169** B f 8/2 Oasis Dream—Prima Luce (IRE) (Galileo (IRE)) (31745) **Abdulla Al Mansoori**
**170** B f 18/3 Lonhro (AUS)—Rahiyah (USA) (Rahy (USA)) **Sheikh Hamdan Bin Mohammed Al Maktoum**
**171 RAINBOW REBEL (IRE),** b c 25/4 Acclamation—
Imperial Quest (Rainbow Quest (USA)) (22500) **Owners Group 004**
**172** Br c 12/2 Dalakhani (IRE)—Rappel (Royal Applause) (12000) **J. D. Abell**
**173** Ch f 13/4 Rock of Gibraltar (IRE)—Real Cat (USA) (Storm Cat (USA)) (7936) **Kingsley Park 2 - Fairyhouse**
**174** B c 25/1 Raven's Pass (USA)—
Red Intrigue (IRE) (Selkirk (USA)) (130000) **Sheikh Hamdan Bin Mohammed Al Maktoum**
**175 REGAL MONARCH,** b g 31/1 Notnowcato—Regal Fairy (IRE) (Desert King (IRE)) (10000) **East Layton Stud**
**176 RENFREW STREET,** b f 23/3 Iffraaj—
Malpas Missile (IRE) (Elusive City (USA)) (38000) **D. C. Livingston & Mark Johnston Racing**
**177** B c 16/3 Soldier of Fortune (IRE)—Ripley (GER) (Platini (GER)) (31746) **A. D. Spence**
**178** B c 4/5 Bernardini (USA)—River Street (Machiavellian (USA)) **Sheikh Hamdan Bin Mohammed Al Maktoum**
**179 ROAD TO THE STARS (IRE),** b c 16/2 Sea The Stars (IRE)—
Silk Trail (Dubai Destination (USA)) (31745) **R. W. Huggins**
**180** B c 15/2 Invincible Spirit (IRE)—
Rosia (IRE) (Mr Prospector (USA)) **Sheikh Hamdan Bin Mohammed Al Maktoum**
**181** B f 2/2 Intikhab (USA)—Salamanque (FR) (Medicean) (17460) **Abdulla Al Mansoori**
**182 SAMAAWY,** b c 25/3 Alhaarth (IRE)—Tasheyaat (Sakhee (USA)) **Hamdan Al Maktoum**
**183** B c 4/4 Soldier of Fortune (IRE)—Sanada (IRE) (Priolo (USA)) (7936) **Mr B. Yeardley**
**184** B c 7/4 Poet's Voice—Santolina (USA) (Boundary (USA)) **Sheikh Hamdan Bin Mohammed Al Maktoum**
**185** B c 10/3 Invincible Spirit (IRE)—
Save Me The Waltz (FR) (Halling (USA)) (111111) **Sheikh Hamdan Bin Mohammed Al Maktoum**
**186** B f 29/3 Alhaarth (IRE)—Sea of Time (USA) (Gilded Time (USA)) (11904) **Yong Nam Seng**
**187 SENNOCKIAN SONG,** ch c 24/4 New Approach (IRE)—Chorist (Pivotal) (52000) **The Vine Accord Partnership**
**188** B f 15/2 Exceed And Excel (AUS)—Shane (GER) (Kornado) **Sheikh Hamdan Bin Mohammed Al Maktoum**
**189** B c 20/3 Tobougg (IRE)—She's The Lady (Unfuwain (USA)) **R. S. Brookhouse**
**190** B c 28/2 Cape Cross (IRE)—Sherifa (GER) (Monsun (GER)) **Sheikh Hamdan Bin Mohammed Al Maktoum**
**191** Ch c 23/4 Shamardal (USA)—
Shinko Hermes (IRE) (Sadler's Wells (USA)) **Sheikh Hamdan Bin Mohammed Al Maktoum**
**192** B f 13/3 Danehill Dancer (IRE)—Showbiz (IRE) (Sadler's Wells (USA)) (26000) **Kingsley Park 3 - The Originals**
**193** B c 2/2 Lonhro (AUS)—Silk Blossom (IRE) (Barathea (IRE)) **Sheikh Hamdan Bin Mohammed Al Maktoum**
**194** B c 13/1 Fastnet Rock (AUS)—Slieve Mish (IRE) (Cape Cross (IRE)) (33333) **Kai Fai Leung**
**195 SPACE MOUNTAIN,** b c 29/1 Sea The Stars (IRE)—Ripples Maid (Dansili) (52380) **J. M. Brown**
**196** B br f 4/5 Intense Focus (USA)—Star of Siligo (USA) (Saratoga Six (USA)) (12698) **Kingsley Park 2 - Fairyhouse**
**197** B c 5/3 Pour Moi (IRE)—
Steam Cuisine (Mark of Esteem (IRE)) (27000) **White, Ross, Holleyhead & Mark Johnston Racing**
**198** B c 26/2 Eskendereya (USA)—Step Softly (Golan (IRE)) (5000) **Abdulla Al Mansoori**
**199** B br c 22/5 Poet's Voice—Sundrop (JPN) (Sunday Silence (USA)) **Sheikh Hamdan Bin Mohammed Al Maktoum**
**200** B f 13/3 Exceed And Excel (AUS)—
Sweet Folly (IRE) (Singspiel (IRE)) **Sheikh Hamdan Bin Mohammed Al Maktoum**
**201 TAWAKKOL,** b c 15/2 Firebreak—Dayville (USA) (Dayjur (USA)) (66666) **R. W. Huggins**
**202 TEMPLIER (IRE),** b c 6/5 Mastercraftsman (IRE)—Tigertail (FR) (Priolo (USA)) (39682) **Mr Gerry Ryan**
**203** B c 2/5 Cape Cross (IRE)—
Tessa Reef (IRE) (Mark of Esteem (IRE)) **Sheikh Hamdan Bin Mohammed Al Maktoum**
**204** B c 29/1 Bernardini (USA)—Tizdubai (USA) (Cee's Tizzy (USA)) **Sheikh Hamdan Bin Mohammed Al Maktoum**
**205** B gr c 27/2 Cape Cross (IRE)—
Vanishing Grey (IRE) (Verglas (IRE)) (125000) **Sheikh Hamdan Bin Mohammed Al Maktoum**
**206 WAHQA,** b g 24/2 Intikhab (USA)—Max One Two Three (IRE) (Princely Heir (IRE)) (33333) **Hamdan Al Maktoum**
**207** Ch f 30/4 Shamardal (USA)—
What A Picture (FR) (Peintre Celebre (USA)) **Sheikh Hamdan Bin Mohammed Al Maktoum**
**208** B f 4/3 Invincible Spirit (IRE)—White And Red (IRE) (Orpen (USA)) (85000) **A. D. Spence**
**209 YORKEE MO SABEE (IRE),** ch c 8/2 Teofilo (IRE)—Pivotal's Princess (IRE) (Pivotal) (70000) **Mr P. R. York**
**210** B f 1/5 Lonhro (AUS)—Zelanda (IRE) (Night Shift (USA)) **Sheikh Hamdan Bin Mohammed Al Maktoum**

**Assistant Trainers:** Deirdre Johnston, Jock Bennett

---

## 343 MR ALAN JONES, Minehead

Postal: **East Harwood Farm, Timberscombe, Minehead, Somerset, TA24 7UE**
Contacts: **FAX 01633 680232 MOBILE (07901) 505064**
**E-MAIL heritageracing@btconnect.com WEBSITE www.alanjonesracing.co.uk**

**1 BOBBITS WAY,** 10, b g Overbury (IRE)—Bit of A Chick **Mr T. S. M. S. Riley-Smith**
**2 BROGEEN BOY (IRE),** 7, br g Golan (IRE)—Brogeen Lady (IRE) **Mr T. S. M. S. Riley-Smith**

## MR ALAN JONES - Continued

3 **HUMBEL BEN (IRE),** 12, br g Humbel (USA)—Donegans Daughter **Burnham Plastering & Drylining Ltd**
4 **LETS GET CRACKING (FR),** 11, gr g Anabaa Blue—Queenhood (FR) **Mr T. S. M. S. Riley-Smith**
5 **MA'IRE RUA (IRE),** 8, ch g Presenting—Long Acre **Mr T. S. M. S. Riley-Smith**
6 **MOSS STREET,** 5, b g Moss Vale (IRE)—Street Style (IRE) **Burnham Plastering & Drylining Ltd**
7 **QUINCY DES PICTONS (FR),** 11, b g Kadalko (FR)—Izabel des Pictons (FR) **Burnham Plastering & Drylining Ltd**
8 **REST AND BE (IRE),** 8, b br m Vinnie Roe (IRE)—Bobs Star (IRE) **Mr T. S. M. S. Riley-Smith**
9 **SECRET DANCER (IRE),** 10, b g Sadler's Wells (USA)—Discreet Brief (IRE) **Burnham Plastering & Drylining Ltd**
10 **STAND BY ME (FR),** 5, b g Dream Well (FR)—In Love New (FR) **Mr T. S. M. S. Riley-Smith**
11 **SUPERNOVERRE (IRE),** 9, b g Noverre (USA)—Caviare **Mr T. S. M. S. Riley-Smith**
12 **TIQUER (FR),** 7, b g Equerry (USA)—Tirenna (FR) **Burnham Plastering & Drylining Ltd**

**Assistant Trainer:** Miss A. Bartelink

**Jockey (NH):** Richard Johnson, Paddy Brennan, Tom O' Brien. **Amateur:** Mr O. Greenall.

---

## 344 MS LUCY JONES, Kilgetty

Postal: **Stable Yard, Lawrenny, Kilgetty, Pembrokeshire, SA68 0PW**
Contacts: **MOBILE (07973) 689040**
**E-MAIL info@cleddauracing.co.uk WEBSITE www.cleddauracing.co.uk**

1 **CLEDDAU KING,** 4, b g Indian Danehill (IRE)—Dancing Credit
2 **HONEY'N'SPICE,** 6, b m Silver Patriarch (IRE)—Honey's Gift **Mr R. Evans**
3 **IFYOUTHINKSO,** 8, b g Hernando (FR)—Evriza (IRE) **Mrs J. M. Edmonds**
4 **LLANGWM LAD (IRE),** 6, b g Milan—Socialite Girl
5 **PRINCE PIPPIN (IRE),** 9, b g King Charlemagne (USA)—Staploy **Mr H. D. R. Harrison-Allen**
6 **SUPREME BOB (IRE),** 9, b g Bob's Return (IRE)—Suprememernories (IRE) **Mrs J. M. Edmonds**
7 **TOBEFAIR,** 5, b g Central Park (IRE)—Nan **Down The Quay Club**
8 **TOE TO TOE (IRE),** 7, br g Presenting—Tavildara (IRE) **Palms Landscaping Limited**

### THREE-YEAR-OLDS

**9** B g Sulamani (IRE)—Dancing Credit

### TWO-YEAR-OLDS

**10** B f 17/4 Sulamani (IRE)—Fruitfull Citizen (IRE) (Anshan)

**Other Owners:** Mr M. J. Cole, Mr A. G. Pannell.

**Amateur:** Ms Lucy Jones.

---

## 345 MR MALCOLM JONES, Treharris

Postal: **Pant-Y-Ffynnon House, Bedlinog, Treharris, Mid Glamorgan, CF46 6UH**

1 **ASHTOWN (IRE),** 8, b g Westerner—Christmas River (IRE) **M. G. Jones**
2 **GLENKEAL (IRE),** 9, ch g Marignan (USA)—Conna Dodger (IRE) **M. G. Jones**
3 **TA HA (IRE),** 7, br g Posidonas—Euro Dancer (IRE) **M. G. Jones**
4 **VALLEYOFTHEFOX,** 5, b g Petrovich (USA)—Ruby Dante (IRE) **M. G. Jones**
5 **WITNESS APPEAL (IRE),** 9, b g Witness Box (USA)—Dangerous Dolly (IRE)

---

## 346 MRS VIOLET M. JORDAN, Moreton Morrell

Postal: **Sanbrook Farm, Back Lane, Shrewley, Warwick, Warwickshire, CV35 7BD**
Contacts: **MOBILE (07831) 101632**
**E-MAIL jordyracer29@hotmail.co.uk**

1 **ALL THE FASHION (IRE),** 11, br m Alflora (IRE)—Fashion Day **Mrs Violet M. Jordan**
2 **BEE BUMBLE,** 10, b g Alflora (IRE)—Shadowgraff **Mr D. W. Tompkins**
3 **BOOKTHEBAND (IRE),** 5, ch g Dubawi (IRE)—Songbook **Farmers & Cricketers Partnership**
4 **KILLFINNAN CASTLE (IRE),** 12, br g Arctic Lord—Golden Seekers **Farmers & Cricketers Partnership**
5 **KNIGHT WOODSMAN,** 11, ch g Sir Harry Lewis (USA)—Jowoody **Mrs Violet M. Jordan**

## MRS VIOLET M. JORDAN - Continued

6 **MEESON,** 4, gr g Fair Mix (IRE)—Premiere Foulee (FR) **Mrs Violet M. Jordan**
7 **PROFILE STAR (IRE),** 6, b g Kodiac—Fingal Nights (IRE) **Mr F. A. Bishop**
8 **WOLF HALL (IRE),** 8, br g Presenting—Water Rock **Mr Dan & Mrs Heidi Haggerty**
9 **ZAT BE ZAT,** 8, b g Sampower Star—Blakeshall Girl **Mr F. A. Bishop**

**Other Owners:** Mr D. Haggerty, Mrs H. Haggerty, Mr D. J. Pearson, D. M. Thornton.

**Assistant Trainer:** Gaye Williams

---

## 347 MRS CAROLINE KEEVIL, Motcombe

Postal: **Larkinglass Farm, Motcombe, Shaftesbury, Dorset, SP7 9HY**
Contacts: **PHONE (01747) 854141 FAX (01747) 854141 MOBILE (07768) 867424**
**E-MAIL keevilracing@gmail.com WEBSITE www.keevilracing.com**

1 **A BITTER AFFAIR (IRE),** 6, b g Fruits of Love (USA)—Rosie Gold (IRE) **P. M. Bryant**
2 **BALLY LEGEND,** 10, b g Midnight Legend—Bally Lira **B. A. Derrick**
3 **BUCKSKIDBRUVVER (IRE),** 4, ch g Albano (IRE)—Green Sea **B. A. Derrick**
4 **CANARBINO GIRL,** 8, b m Beat All (USA)—Peasedown Tofana **Lady Sutton**
5 **CLOUDY LADY,** 7, gr m Alflora (IRE)—Cirrious **P. L. Hart**
6 **DARKESTBEFOREDAWN (IRE),** 8, br g Dr Massini (IRE)—Camden Dolphin (IRE) **The Jago Family Partnership**
7 **HAVERSTOCK,** 5, b g New Approach (IRE)—Endorsement **The Deep Pockets Partnership**
8 **JACK BY THE HEDGE,** 6, b g Overbury (IRE)—Bluebell Path **Mrs Sara Biggins & Mrs Celia Djivanovic**
9 **JUDGE DAVIS,** 8, b g Alflora (IRE)—Minimum **Gale Force Three**
10 **KNIGHT OFTHE REALM,** 6, b g Kayf Tara—Flow **Mrs H. R. Dunn**
11 **LA MADONNINA (IRE),** 7, b m Milan—Supreme Nova **Mrs H. R. Dunn**
12 **MATAKO (FR),** 12, b g Nikos—Verabatim (FR) **P. M. Bryant**
13 **MIDNIGHT LIRA,** 8, ch m Midnight Legend—Bally Lira **B. A. Derrick**
14 **MRS JORDAN (IRE),** 7, b m King's Theatre (IRE)—Regents Dancer (IRE) **The Hon J. R. Drummond**
15 **PALMARIA,** 5, b m Kayf Tara—Ollejess **Lady Sutton**
16 **POSH MILLIE (IRE),** 5, b m Relief Pitcher—Rainbow Nation **A. M. Midgley**
17 **QUARRYMAN,** 4, ch g Act One—Bluebell Path **P. L. Hart**
18 **REGAL FLOW,** 8, b g Erhaab (USA)—Flow **Mrs H. R. Dunn**
19 **STRAWBERRY HILL (IRE),** 9, b g Winged Love (IRE)—Icydora (FR) **K S B Bloodstock**
20 **SYLVAN LEGEND,** 7, b g Midnight Legend—Sylvan Warbler (USA) **B. A. Derrick**
21 **TAMBALONG,** 7, b m Tamure (IRE)—Baie d'along (FR) **Mrs D. R. Whigham**
22 4, B g Midnight Legend—Tilla **Mrs C. Keevil**
23 **WHAT LARKS (IRE),** 7, b g Pierre—Bint Rosie **Mrs C. Keevil**

**Other Owners:** Mrs S. J. Biggins, Mr K. W. Biggins, Mr W. R. Bougourd, Mrs S. S. Cole, Mrs C. J. Djivanovic, Mr A. P. Gale, R. J. Hodges, Mr P. J. A. Jago, Mrs J. L. Jago, Miss M. L. A. Jago, Mr F. C. A. Jago, Mrs M. E. Stirratt.

**Jockey (NH):** James Best, Tom O'Brien, Ian Popham. **Conditional:** Will Featherstone. **Amateur:** Mr Lee Drowne.

---

## 348 MRS FIONA KEHOE, Leighton Buzzard

Postal: **The Croft Farm, Wing Road, Stewkley, Leighton Buzzard, Bedfordshire, LU7 0JB**
Contacts: **PHONE (01525) 240749 FAX (01525) 240749 MOBILE (07795) 096908**
**E-MAIL f.kehoe@btinternet.com**

1 **VISION DU COEUR (FR),** 6, b g Saint des Saints (FR)—Jamais de La Vie (FR) **M. Kehoe**

---

## 349 MR MARTIN KEIGHLEY, Cheltenham

Postal: **Condicote Stables, Luckley, Moreton-In-Marsh, Gloucestershire, GL56 0RD**
Contacts: **MOBILE (07767) 472547**
**E-MAIL info@martinkeighleyracing.com WEBSITE www.martinkeighleyracing.com**

1 **ALTESSE DE GUYE (FR),** 5, ch m Dom Alco (FR)—Mascotte de Guye (FR) **Daydream Believers**
2 **ALWAYS BOLD (IRE),** 10, ch g King's Best (USA)—Tarakana (USA) **Mrs B. J. Keighley**
3 **ANNACOTTY (IRE),** 7, b g Beneficial—Mini Moo Min **Mrs E. A. Prowting**
4 **ANY CURRENCY (IRE),** 12, b g Moscow Society (USA)—Native Bavard (IRE) **Cash Is King**
5 **BENBANE HEAD (USA),** 11, ch g Giant's Causeway (USA)—Prospectress (USA) **Mrs L. Jones**

## MR MARTIN KEIGHLEY - Continued

6 **BOBBLE EMERALD (IRE),** 7, ch g Rudimentary (USA)—Aunt Emeralds (IRE) **D Bishop,C Bowkley,M Parker,D Thorpe**
7 **BRAVO BRAVO,** 8, b g Sadler's Wells (USA)—Top Table **Davies & Price**
8 **CASTLE CHEETAH (IRE),** 7, br g Presenting—Castle Crystal (IRE) **Mr B. Eccles**
9 **CHAMPION COURT (IRE),** 10, b g Court Cave (IRE)—Mooneys Hill (IRE) **M. Boothright**
10 **CLASSIC COLORI (IRE),** 8, b g Le Vie Dei Colori—Beryl **Mrs L. Ponting**
11 **COYABA,** 5, b g Midnight Legend—Peel Me A Grape **Mrs E. A. Prowting**
12 **CREEPY (IRE),** 7, b g Westerner—Prowler (IRE) **M. Boothright, T. Hanlon, S. Harman**
13 **DARNITNEV,** 5, b g Darnay—Lavender Della (IRE) **Mrs R. E. Nelmes**
14 **DUELING BANJOS,** 5, b gr g Proclamation (IRE)—Kayf Lady **R. Davies**
15 **EPIC STORM (IRE),** 7, b g Montjeu (IRE)—Jaya (USA) **Mr T. J. F. Exell**
16 **FLEMENTIME (IRE),** 7, ch m Flemensfirth (USA)—Funny Times **Figjam II**
17 **GEORGIAN KING,** 12, b g Overbury (IRE)—Roslin **R. Allsop**
18 **KYLES FAITH (IRE),** 7, b g Court Cave (IRE)—Littleton Liberty **Martin Keighley Racing Partnership**
19 **LAUGHINGALLTHEWAY,** 4, b g Darnay—Smilingatstrangers **Mrs Sarah Hamilton & Mr M Jenkins**
20 **MARLEY JOE (IRE),** 4, b g Arcadio (GER)—Tuscarora (IRE) **Mr O. F. Ryan**
21 **MERLIN'S WISH,** 10, gr g Terimon—Sendai **Miss R. Toppin**
22 **MONTY'S REVENGE (IRE),** 10, b g Bob's Return (IRE)—Native Bavard (IRE) **The Red Socks & Mrs Belinda Keighley**
23 **MORNING HERALD,** 4, br f Lucky Story (USA)—Wakeful **Mr C. G. M. Lloyd-Baker**
24 **MORTLESTOWN (IRE),** 7, b g Milan—Pima (IRE) **M. Boothright**
25 **PRIMO CAPITANO (IRE),** 7, b g Milan—Miss Mayberry (IRE) **Owners For Owners: Primo Capitano**
26 7, Br m Zagreb (USA)—Quel Bleu (IRE)
27 **REAL GONE KID,** 4, b g Kalanisi (IRE)—Karmest **Mr R Davies & Mr S Baikie**
28 **SEYMOUR STAR,** 7, b g Alflora (IRE)—Seymour Chance **Mrs C J Black & Mrs Sue Briscoe**
29 **SOLSTICE STAR,** 5, b g Kayf Tara—Clover Green (IRE) **Mrs L. Ponting**
30 **SPANISH ARCH (IRE),** 8, b g Westerner—Piepowder **James Hayman-Joyce & HJ Racing**
31 **SUTTON MAC,** 7, gr g Pursuit of Love—Filliemou (IRE) **Mrs Anne Izamis**
32 **THE KVILLEKEN,** 7, b g Fair Mix (IRE)—Wannaplantatree **M. Boothright**
33 **THE WEXFORDIAN (IRE),** 6, b g Shantou (USA)—Going My Way **M Boothright, T Hanlon & G Duncan**

**Other Owners:** P. R. Armour, Mr S. Baikie, D. Bishop, Mrs C. J. Black, Mr C. Bowkley, Mrs S. Briscoe, R. A. Davies, Mr P. K. Davis, G. K. Duncan, Mr T. J. Dykes, Mr G. Ellis, Mrs S. Hamilton, Mr T. Hanlon, S. R. Harman, Mr J. L. Hayman-Joyce, Mrs C. A. M. Hayman-Joyce, Mr E. J. Hughes, M. N. Jenkins, M. H. Keighley, Dr M. M. Ogilvy, Mr M. D. Parker, Mr A. G. Price, Mr P. R. Thomas, G. M. Thornton, D. A. Thorpe, Mr P. H. Watts.

**Assistant Trainer:** Mrs Belinda Keighley

**Jockey (NH):** Alain Cawley, Ian Popham. **Conditional:** Daniel Hiskett.

---

## 350 MR CHRISTOPHER KELLETT, Swadlincote

Postal: **Jubilee Racing Stables, Snarestone Road, Appleby Magna, Swadlincote, Derbyshire, DE12 7AJ**
Contacts: **PHONE (01530) 515395 FAX (01530) 515395 MOBILE (07966) 097989**
**E-MAIL christopherkellett@btinternet.com WEBSITE www.chriskellettracing.co.uk**

1 **A SWELL LYE,** 4, ch g Resplendent Glory (IRE)—Bahhmirage (IRE) **Miss S. L. Walley**
2 **BRYTER LAYTER,** 5, b g Deportivo—Bahhmirage (IRE) **Miss S. L. Walley**
3 **CASH IN HAND (IRE),** 15, b g Charente River (IRE)—Fern Fields (IRE) **Miss S. L. Bailey**
4 **DOUNYA'S BOY,** 6, ch g Sakhee (USA)—Dounya (USA) **Miss S. L. Bailey**
5 **GIFTED ROSE,** 4, b f Presenting—Santia **D. H. Muir & Exors of the Late Mrs R. E. Muir**
6 **HER RED DEVIL (IRE),** 4, b f Jeremy (USA)—All Began (IRE) **The Edwardsons**
7 **MARINA BAY,** 10, b m Karinga Bay—Marina Bird **Mr K. & Mr A. K. Smith**
8 **MR SQUIRREL (IRE),** 8, gr g Great Palm (USA)—Patsy Donnellan (IRE) **D. H. Muir & Exors of the Late Mrs R. E. Muir**
9 **PRAVDA STREET,** 10, ch g Soviet Star (USA)—Sari **The Edwardsons**
10 **SHINING MOMENT,** 5, b m Needwood Blade—Shaymee's Girl
11 **SIR LUKE ARNO,** 4, b g Lucarno (USA)—Never Lost **J. E. Titley**
12 **SMART MUSIC,** 8, ch g Band On The Run—Smart Rhythm **T. E. Wardall**
13 4, B f Dr Massini (IRE)—Tuckers Bay
14 **UPPER LAMBOURN (IRE),** 7, b g Exceed And Excel (AUS)—In The Fashion (IRE) **Miss S. L. Bailey**

### THREE-YEAR-OLDS

15 B f Rainbow High—Never Lost **J. E. Titley**

## MR CHRISTOPHER KELLETT - Continued

**Other Owners:** Mr K. W. Edwardson, Mrs J. L. Edwardson, D. H. Muir, Exors of the Late Mrs R. E. Muir, Mr K. Smith, A. K. Smith.

---

## 351 MISS GAY KELLEWAY, Newmarket

Postal: **Queen Alexandra Stables, 2 Chapel Street, Exning, Newmarket, Suffolk, CB8 7HA**
Contacts: **PHONE (01638) 577778 MOBILE (07974) 948768**
**E-MAIL gaykellewayracing@hotmail.co.uk WEBSITE www.gaykellewayracing.com**

1 **DOMINANDROS (FR),** 4, b g Teofilo (IRE)—Afya **Winterbeck Manor Stud & Partners**
2 **LAYLINE (IRE),** 8, b g King's Best (USA)—Belle Reine **Kelleway, Smith, Scandrett & Hart**
3 **ROYAL ALCOR (IRE),** 8, b g Chevalier (IRE)—Arundhati (IRE) **G. Kelleway, P. Kerridge & Panther Racing**
4 **SEALED (USA),** 4, b br g Speightstown (USA)—Sinister Sister (USA) **Mr R. Ng**
5 **SHOWTIME STAR,** 5, b g Byron—Piddies Pride (IRE) **Gay Kelleway**
6 **STOSUR (IRE),** 4, b f Mount Nelson—Jules (IRE) **B. C. Oakley**
7 **SWING ALONE (IRE),** 6, b g Celtic Swing—Groupetime (USA) **Crook, Kelleway, Stanbrook, Brown**
8 **UPHOLD,** 8, b g Oasis Dream—Allegro Viva (USA) **Miss G. M. Kelleway**
9 **YOJOJO (IRE),** 6, ch m Windsor Knot (IRE)—Belle of The Blues (IRE) **Winterbeck Manor Stud Ltd**

### THREE-YEAR-OLDS

10 **BLACK ART,** ch g Black Sam Bellamy (IRE)—Art Series **Fairfield Racing**
11 **ELSIE HAY (IRE),** b f Excellent Art—Magic Sister **LCA Lights Camera Action Ltd**
12 **JE T'AIME ENCORE,** b c Acclamation—Mimisel **Fairfield Racing**
13 **LIGHTSCAMERACTION (IRE),** ch c Pastoral Pursuits—Silca Boo **LCA Lights Camera Action Ltd**
14 **MARIGOT BAY,** b f Paco Boy (IRE)—Mamma Morton (IRE) **Rioja Racing**
15 **NEW ABBEY DANCER (IRE),** b f Thewayyouare (USA)—Brave Cat (IRE) **Mr A. G. MacLennan**
16 **OAKLEY STAR,** b f Multiplex—Star Welcome **B. C. Oakley**
17 **PLAY THE FIELD (IRE),** ch g Fast Company (IRE)—Tarakana (USA) **Fairfield Racing**
18 **WHAT A PARTY (IRE),** ch f Windsor Knot (IRE)—Tarziyma (IRE) **M. M. Foulger**
19 **ZAC COURAGEOUS (IRE),** b g Mastercraftsman (IRE)—Thats Your Opinion **Mr Y. C. Wong**
20 **ZAC TRUTH (USA),** ch c Lookin At Lucky (USA)—Rose of Zollern (IRE) **Mr Y. C. Wong**

### TWO-YEAR-OLDS

21 Gr f 3/4 Dark Angel (IRE)—Amistad (GER) (Winged Love (IRE)) (20634) **LCA Lights Camera Action Ltd**
22 **FULL AT LAST (DEN),** b c 21/5 Academy Award (IRE)—Aube d'irlande (FR) (Selkirk (USA)) (7945) **Gay Kelleway**
23 **IRVINE LADY (IRE),** ch f 28/3 Footstepsinthesand—Ascot Lady (IRE) (Spinning World (USA)) (15872) **Valerie Kerr**
24 **NEW ABBEY ANGEL (IRE),** gr c 10/3 Dark Angel (IRE)—Alinda (IRE) (Revoque (IRE)) (14285) **Alistair Maclennan**
25 **PHOENIX BEAT,** b f 28/3 Phoenix Reach (IRE)—Beat Seven (Beat Hollow) (66666) **Winterbeck Manor Stud**
26 Ch c 28/2 Phoenix Reach (IRE)—Pink Supreme (Night Shift (USA)) (18095) **Graham Kerr & Partners**
27 **RIVERBOAT LADY (IRE),** gr f 15/4 Zebedee—Tomanivi (Caerleon (USA)) (6745) **Nigel Scandrett & Partners**
28 **SAKHEE'S JEM,** ch f 22/1 Sakhee's Secret—Amandian (IRE) (Indian Ridge) (5000) **M. M. Foulger**
29 **SISU CAT (SWE),** b f 23/4 Helsinki (USA)—Primecat (Catrail (USA)) (1589) **Ben Parish**
30 **YEAH BABY YEAH (IRE),** b f 28/3 Art Connoisseur (IRE)—Royal Interlude (IRE) (King's Theatre (IRE)) (5555) **David Evans**

**Other Owners:** Mr D. A. Brown, Mr Ivor Collier, Mrs Debbie Collier, Miss Patricia Crook, Mr N. J. Hart, Mr Gary Hodson, Miss Gay Kelleway, Mr P. B. Kerridge, Mr N. J. O'Brien, Panther Racing Ltd, Mr A. B. Parr, Mr Nigel S. Scandrett, Mr Bob W. Smith, Mrs Lynne Stanbrook, Mr Paul Tyler, Winterbeck Manor Stud.

**Assistant Trainer:** Anne-Sophie Crombez **Head Girl:** Liz Mullin

**Jockey (NH):** Jamie Moore. **Apprentice:** Lauren Hunter.

---

## 352 MISS LYNSEY KENDALL, Carlisle

Postal: **The Stables, Lambley Bank, Scotby, Carlisle, Cumbria, CA4 8BX**
Contacts: **PHONE (01228) 513069 MOBILE (07818) 487227**
**E-MAIL lynseykendall@hotmail.co.uk**

1 **GRIMWITH,** 8, b g Doyen (IRE)—Poyle Caitlin (IRE) **Mr & Mrs R. S. Kendall**

**Other Owners:** Mr R. S. Kendall, Mrs M. E. Kendall.

## 353 MR NICK KENT, Brigg

Postal: **Newstead House, Newstead Priory, Cadney Road, Brigg, Lincolnshire, DN20 9HP**
Contacts: **PHONE (01652) 650628 MOBILE (07710) 644428**
**E-MAIL nick@nickkent.co.uk WEBSITE www.nickkent.co.uk**

1 **AROUND A POUND (IRE),** 10, b g Old Vic—Mary Ellen Best (IRE) **Nick Kent Racing Club**
2 **BALINDERRY (IRE),** 8, b g Flemensfirth (USA)—Erins Love (IRE) **BDS Pointers**
3 **BOWIE (IRE),** 8, br g Pelder (IRE)—La Fenice (IRE) **Cynthia Commons,Marina Kent,Nick Kent**
4 **CELTIC SIXPENCE (IRE),** 7, b m Celtic Swing—Penny Ha'penny **Cynthia Commons, Nick Kent**
5 **COMBUSTIBLE KATE (IRE),** 9, b m Mr Combustible (IRE)—Aussie Hope **Nick Kent Racing Club II**
6 **DJ GERRY,** 4, b g Cockney Rebel (IRE)—Lady Trish **J. N. Kent**
7 **ELLUSIVANCE (IRE),** 5, b g Elusive Quality (USA)—Germance (USA) **Mr W. H. Eastwood**
8 5, Ch m Primo Valentino (IRE)—Farmer's Pet
9 **HILLVIEW LAD (IRE),** 7, b g Vinnie Roe (IRE)—Kabale (IRE)
10 **IVANS BACK (IRE),** 10, b g Soviet Star (USA)—Better Back Off (IRE) **Ms V. M. Cottingham**
11 **LOST IN NEWYORK (IRE),** 8, b g Arakan (USA)—Lace Flower **Timbercare Racing Partnership**
12 4, B gr f Great Palm (USA)—Millquista d'or **Mrs Liz Horn**
13 **SKYFIRE,** 8, ch g Storm Cat (USA)—Sunray Superstar **Cynthia Commons, Nick Kent**
14 **THE WHITE DUKE (IRE),** 6, ch r Pelder (IRE)—Concinna (FR) **Cynthia Commons,Marina Kent,Nick Kent**

### TWO-YEAR-OLDS

15 B c 4/6 Captain Gerrard (IRE)—Yabint El Sham (Sizzling Melody) (761)

**Other Owners:** Mr R. F. Boot, Mr K. R. Boot, Mr R. A. Carter, Miss C. Commons, Mrs S. A. Daubney, Mr D. M. Evans, Mrs M. Kent, Ms V. Mitchell, Mrs W. M. Wesley.

**Assistant Trainer:** Mrs Jane Kent

**Jockey (NH):** Adam Wedge. **Conditional:** Charlie Deutsch. **Amateur:** Mr Tom Broughton, Miss Alice Mills.

## 354 MR ALAN KING, Barbury Castle

Postal: **Barbury Castle Stables, Wroughton, Wiltshire, SN4 0QZ**
Contacts: **PHONE (01793) 815009 FAX (01793) 845080 MOBILE (07973) 461233**
**E-MAIL alanking.racing@virgin.net WEBSITE www.alankingracing.co.uk**

1 **ANGEL FACE,** 4, b f Kayf Tara—Safari Run (IRE) **Walters Plant Hire Ltd**
2 **ARALDUR (FR),** 11, ch g Spadoun (FR)—Aimessa (FR) **Mr D. J. S. Sewell**
3 **AVISPA,** 6, b m Kayf Tara—Ladylliat (FR) **The Wasp Partnership**
4 **AWESOME ROSIE,** 4, b f Midnight Legend—Awesome Aunt (IRE) **Mrs Gwen Meacham, A King & Withyslade**
5 **BALDER SUCCES (FR),** 7, b g Goldneyev (USA)—Frija Eria (FR) **Masterson Holdings Limited**
6 **BALLOCHMYLE (IRE),** 5, b g Milan—Not So Green (IRE) **T. Barr**
7 **BAR A MINE (FR),** 6, b g Martaline—Treekle Toffee (FR) **Walters Plant Hire Ltd**
8 **BASTIEN (FR),** 4, b br g Panoramic—Que du Charmil (FR) **Alan King**
9 **BETTATOGETHER,** 6, b g Fair Mix (IRE)—Ella Falls (IRE) **R. Bailey**
10 **BIG CHIEF BENNY (IRE),** 4, ch g Beneficial—Be Airlie (IRE) **Oitavos Partnership**
11 **BILLY BISCUIT (IRE),** 7, b g Presenting—Native Novel (IRE) **Miss J. M. Bodycote**
12 **BOARD OF TRADE,** 4, ch g Black Sam Bellamy (IRE)—Realms of Gold (USA) **Ian Payne & Kim Franklin**
13 **BULFIN ISLAND (IRE),** 6, b g Milan—Tournore Court (IRE) **T. Barr**
14 **BULL AND BUSH (IRE),** 6, br m Presenting—Sound of The Crowd (IRE) **W. A. Harrison-Allan**
15 **CARRAIG MOR (IRE),** 7, b g Old Vic—Lynrick Lady (IRE) **Masterson Holdings Limited**
16 **CHATEZ (IRE),** 4, b g Dandy Man (IRE)—Glory Days (GER) **Mrs P. Andrews**
17 **CHOCALA (IRE),** 5, b g Rock of Gibraltar (IRE)—Arbella **High 5**
18 **CHOSEN WELL (IRE),** 6, b g Well Chosen—Killmaleary Cross (IRE) **Keirle, Love, Sullivan & King**
19 **CRIQ ROCK (FR),** 4, ch g Kap Rock (FR)—Criquetot (FR) **The Trouble Partnership**
20 **DALAVAR (IRE),** 7, b g Dalakhani (IRE)—Giant's Way (IRE) **N. S. G. Bunter**
21 **DARDANELLA,** 8, b m Alflora (IRE)—Ella Falls (IRE) **R. Bailey**
22 **DAYDREAMER,** 4, b g Duke of Marmalade (IRE)—Storyland (USA) **Mr & Mrs R. Scott**
23 **DESERT JOE (IRE),** 9, b g Anshan—Wide Country (IRE) **Mrs E. A. Prowting**
24 **DESERT ROBE,** 7, b g Desert King (IRE)—Hot 'n Saucy **A. P. Racing**
25 **DEVIL TO PAY,** 9, b g Red Ransom (USA)—My Way (IRE) **Horace 5**
26 **DUNDEE,** 7, ch g Definite Article—Gardana (FR) **T. J. Hemmings**
27 **DUSKY LEGEND,** 5, b m Midnight Legend—Tinagoodnight (FR) **Mr & Mrs R. G. Kelvin-Hughes**
28 **ELKSTONE,** 4, b g Midnight Legend—Samandara (FR) **Miss J M Bodycote & Alan King**
29 **FIGHTER JET,** 7, b g Oasis Dream—Totality **Ladas**
30 **FINE WORDS,** 7, b g Alflora (IRE)—Gospel (IRE) **Mrs S. C. Welch**

## MR ALAN KING - Continued

31 **FIRE FIGHTER (IRE),** 7, b g Tiger Hill (IRE)—Firecrest (IRE) **Masterson Holdings Limited**
32 **FIRST MOHICAN,** 7, ch g Tobougg (IRE)—Mohican Girl **W. H. Ponsonby**
33 **FRED LE MACON (FR),** 6, b g Passing Sale (FR)—Princess Leyla **Alan King & Niall Farrell**
34 **GABRIELLA ROSE,** 5, b m Kayf Tara—Elaine Tully (IRE) **The Godparents**
35 **GENSTONE TRAIL,** 9, b m Generous (IRE)—Stoney Path
36 **GIMME FIVE,** 4, b g Champs Elysees—Waitingonacloud **McNeill Family Ltd**
37 **GODSMEJUDGE (IRE),** 9, b g Witness Box (USA)—Eliza Everett (IRE) **Favourites Racing Ltd**
38 **GONE TOO FAR,** 7, b g Kayf Tara—Major Hoolihan **J. P. McManus**
39 **GRUMETI,** 7, b g Sakhee (USA)—Tetravella (IRE) **McNeill Family Ltd**
40 **HANDAZAN (IRE),** 6, b g Nayef (USA)—Handaza (IRE) **McNeill Family Ltd**
41 **HINDON ROAD (IRE),** 8, b g Antonius Pius (USA)—Filoli Gardens **A. J. Viall**
42 **HOLLOW PENNY,** 7, b g Beat Hollow—Lomapamar **Mr D. J. S. Sewell**
43 **HOWWRONGCANYOUBE,** 6, b g Kayf Tara—Diva **Mr C Fenton, Mr B Winfield & A King**
44 **HURRICANE VIC,** 5, b g Mount Nelson—Fountains Abbey (USA) **The Trouble Partnership**
45 **INNER DRIVE (IRE),** 7, b g Heron Island (IRE)—Hingis (IRE) **McNeill Family Ltd**
46 **KAREZAK (IRE),** 4, b g Azamour (IRE)—Karawana (IRE) **McNeill Family Ltd**
47 4, B f Kayf Tara—Katess (IRE) **Mrs M. C. Sweeney**
48 **KATIE TOO (IRE),** 4, b f King's Theatre (IRE)—Shivermetimber (IRE) **Mr & Mrs C. Harris**
49 **KERROW (IRE),** 5, b g Mahler—Olives Hall (IRE) **T. J. Hemmings**
50 **KING LOUIS,** 4, ch g Champs Elysees—Starparty (USA) **Mr & Mrs R. Scott**
51 **KINGS BAYONET,** 8, ch g Needwood Blade—Retaliator **W. H. Ponsonby**
52 **KUDA HURAA (IRE),** 7, b g Montjeu (IRE)—Healing Music (FR) **Thurloe 53**
53 **L'AMIRAL DAVID (FR),** 5, b g My Risk (FR)—Mme La Vicomtesse (FR) **Mr D. J. S. Sewell**
54 **L'UNIQUE (FR),** 6, b m Reefscape—Sans Tune (FR) **D. J. Barry**
55 **LADY PERSEPHONE (FR),** 4, br f Sir Percy—Acenanga (GER) **All The Kings Ladies**
56 **LASER BLAZER,** 7, b g Zafeen (FR)—Sashay **Calne Engineering Ltd**
57 **LETSBY AVENUE,** 7, b g Tikkanen (USA)—Peel Me A Grape **Mrs E. A. Prowting**
58 **MALAK DES MOTTES (FR),** 5, gr g Ange Gabriel (FR)—Anareta des Mottes (FR) **J. P. McManus**
59 **MALDIVIAN REEF (IRE),** 7, ch g Reefscape—Spirited Soul (IRE) **Alan King**
60 **MANYRIVERSTOCROSS (IRE),** 10, b g Cape Cross (IRE)—Alexandra S (IRE) **Mrs M. C. Sweeney**
61 **MARTHA MCCANDLES,** 4, b f Tobougg (IRE)—Tabulate **A. P. Racing**
62 **MCCABE CREEK (IRE),** 5, b g Robin des Pres (FR)—Kick And Run (IRE) **Ian Payne & Kim Franklin**
63 **MEDINAS (FR),** 8, b br g Malinas (GER)—Medicis (FR) **Mr & Mrs F. D. Bell**
64 **MEISTER ECKHART (IRE),** 9, b br g Flemensfirth (USA)—Carrabawn **Atlantic Equine**
65 **MIDNIGHT APPEAL,** 10, b g Midnight Legend—Lac Marmot (FR) **Mr D. J. S. Sewell**
66 **MIDNIGHT CATARIA,** 6, b m Midnight Legend—Calamintha **Mrs K. Holmes**
67 **MIDNIGHT COWBOY,** 4, gr g Midnight Legend—Kali
68 **MIDNIGHT LUCA,** 4, b g Midnight Legend—Diva **C.Fenton,J.Wright,R.Preston,B.Winfield**
69 **MIDNIGHT PRAYER,** 10, b g Midnight Legend—Onawing Andaprayer **The Legends Partnership**
70 **MIGHTY TIGRESS,** 4, b f Kayf Tara—Tiger Moss **S. M. Smith**
71 **MILES TO MEMPHIS (IRE),** 6, b g Old Vic—Phillis Hill **Mrs Lesley Field & Mr Jules Sigler**
72 **MIRKAT,** 5, b g Kalanisi (IRE)—Miracle **Bellamy, Burke, Hannigan & Harding**
73 **MISS CRICK,** 4, b f Midnight Legend—Kwaheri **Mr D. J. S. Sewell**
74 **MISS MINX,** 4, b f Tobougg (IRE)—Victory Flip (IRE) **Mr E. T. D. Leadbeater**
75 **MONEY FOR NOTHING,** 6, b g Kayf Tara—Top of The Dee **Mrs M. C. Sweeney**
76 **MONKSGOLD (IRE),** 7, b g Gold Well—Opium **The Dreamers**
77 **MONTBAZON (FR),** 8, b br g Alberto Giacometti (IRE)—Duchesse Pierji (FR) **Mr D. J. S. Sewell**
78 **MYSTERY DRAMA,** 5, b m Hernando (FR)—Mystery Lot (IRE) **Incipe Partnership**
79 **NED STARK (IRE),** 7, b g Wolfe Tone (IRE)—Last Moon (IRE) **The Dunkley & Reilly Partnership**
80 **NYANZA (GER),** 4, b f Dai Jin—Nouvelle Fortune (IRE) **Hunscote Stud**
81 **ORDO AB CHAO (IRE),** 6, b g Heron Island (IRE)—Houldyurwhist (IRE) **Mr A. R. W. Marsh**
82 **OUR PHYLLI VERA (IRE),** 6, b m Motivator—With Colour **Let's Live Racing**
83 **PAIN AU CHOCOLAT (FR),** 4, b g Enrique—Clair Chene (FR) **Million in Mind Partnership**
84 **PANTXOA (FR),** 8, b g Daliapour (IRE)—Palmeria (FR) **Mrs J. A. Watts**
85 **PIRATES CAY,** 8, b g Black Sam Bellamy (IRE)—Mistic World **Mr D. J. S. Sewell**
86 **PRECISION FIVE,** 6, b m Proclamation (IRE)—Sashay **Calne Engineering Ltd**
87 **PRESENTING LISA (IRE),** 6, b m Presenting—Miss Esther (GER) **Mrs E. A. Prowting**
88 **PRETTYASAPICTURE,** 6, b m King's Theatre (IRE)—Fortune's Girl **Let's Live Racing**
89 **PRIDE IN BATTLE (IRE),** 10, b g Chevalier (IRE)—Afasara (IRE) **Mrs E. Pearce**
90 **RAYA HOPE (IRE),** 4, b f Robin des Champs (FR)—Garden City (IRE) **Mr Simon Munir & Mr Isaac Souede**
91 **RIDGEWAY STORM (IRE),** 5, b g Hurricane Run (IRE)—Hesperia **W. H. Ponsonby**
92 **ROBERTO PEGASUS (USA),** 9, b br g Fusaichi Pegasus (USA)—
Louju (USA) **Mrs P Andrews, I Payne & Ms K Franklin**
93 **RONALDINHO (IRE),** 5, b g Jeremy (USA)—Spring Glory **The Ronaldinho Partnership**
94 **SALMANAZAR,** 7, b g Classic Cliche (IRE)—Leroy's Sister (FR) **Top Brass Partnership**

## MR ALAN KING - Continued

95 **SAY WHEN,** 7, b g Fair Mix (IRE)—Miss Wyandotte **Alan King**
96 **SEGO SUCCESS (IRE),** 7, b g Beneficial—The West Road (IRE) **Mr E. T. D. Leadbeater**
97 **SHADARPOUR (IRE),** 6, b g Dr Fong (USA)—Shamadara (IRE) **ARC Racing Syndicates**
98 **SIMPLY A LEGEND,** 6, b g Midnight Legend—Disco Danehill (IRE) **Mrs E. A. Prowting**
99 **SMAD PLACE (FR),** 8, gr g Smadoun (FR)—Bienna Star (FR) **Mrs P. Andrews**
100 **SMART MOTIVE,** 5, b g Motivator—Santana Lady (IRE) **Mrs C. Skan**
101 **SPELLBOUND,** 6, b m Doyen (IRE)—Kasamba **Withyslade**
102 **SPRINGBOKS (IRE),** 5, b g Flemensfirth (USA)—Roaming (IRE) **Mr & Mrs R. G. Kelvin-Hughes**
103 **STONEY'S TREASURE,** 11, ch g Silver Patriarch (IRE)—Stoney Path **Mrs S. C. Welch**
104 **TED'S LAD,** 5, b g Kayf Tara—Stravsea **Mr E. T. D. Leadbeater**
105 4, B f Kayf Tara—Temptation (FR) **D. J. Barry**
106 **THE BARBURY QUEEN (IRE),** 5, br m Milan—Royal Shares (IRE) **W. H. Ponsonby**
107 **THE MUMPER (IRE),** 8, br g Craigsteel—Na Moilltear (IRE) **The Weighed In Partnership**
108 **THE PIRATE'S QUEEN (IRE),** 6, b m King's Theatre (IRE)—
Shivermetimber (IRE) **The Dunkley & Reilly Partnership**
109 **THE TOURARD MAN (IRE),** 9, b g Shantou (USA)—Small Iron **Mr & Mrs F Bell,N Farrell, A Marsh**
110 **THE UNIT (IRE),** 4, b g Gold Well—Sovana (FR) **International Plywood (Importers) Ltd**
111 **THOMAS SHELBY (IRE),** 4, b g Witness Box (USA)—Deemiss (IRE) **McNeill Family & A King**
112 **TICKITY BLEUE,** 7, gr m Tikkanen (USA)—Cerise Bleue (FR) **Let's Live Racing**
113 **TIGER FEAT,** 5, b g Tiger Hill (IRE)—Hannah's Dream (IRE) **ROA Racing Partnership V**
114 **TOMOCHICHI (IRE),** 5, b g Indian River (FR)—Polar Lamb (IRE) **Mr D. J. S. Sewell**
115 **TOO FAR GONE (IRE),** 4, br g Jeremy (USA)—Rockahoolababy (IRE) **N. S. G. Bunter**
116 **TURN OVER SIVOLA (FR),** 8, b g Assessor (IRE)—Notting Hill (FR) **International Plywood (Importers) Ltd**
117 **ULZANA'S RAID (IRE),** 6, ch g Bach (IRE)—Peace Time Beauty (IRE) **T. Barr**
118 **URIAH HEEP (FR),** 6, b g Danehill Dancer (IRE)—Canasita **G Keirle, J Holmes, R Levitt & A King**
119 **UXIZANDRE (FR),** 7, ch g Fragrant Mix (IRE)—Jolisandre (FR) **J. P. McManus**
120 **VALDEZ,** 8, ch g Doyen (IRE)—Skew **Riverdee Stable**
121 **VENDOR (FR),** 7, gr g Kendor (FR)—Village Rainbow (FR) **Thurloe 52**
122 **WEST END ROCKER (IRE),** 13, b br g Grand Plaisir (IRE)—
Slyguff Lord (IRE) **Mr Barry Winfield & Mr Tim Leadbeater**
123 **WILDE BLUE YONDER (IRE),** 6, b g Oscar (IRE)—Blue Gallery (IRE) **Maybe Only Fools Have Horses**
124 **WILLIAM H BONNEY,** 4, b g Midnight Legend—Calamintha **Mrs K Holmes & Alan King**
125 **WINNER MASSAGOT (FR),** 4, ch g Muhaymin (USA)—Winnor (FR) **Masterson Holdings Limited**
126 **WISHING AND HOPING (IRE),** 5, b g Beneficial—Desperately Hoping (IRE) **Mrs P. Andrews**
127 **YANWORTH,** 5, ch g Norse Dancer (IRE)—Yota (FR) **J. P. McManus**
128 **ZIGA BOY (FR),** 6, gr g Califet (FR)—Our Ziga (FR) **Axom LI**

## THREE-YEAR-OLDS

129 **CAHILL (IRE),** b g Lawman (FR)—Malaspina (IRE) **McNeill Family Ltd**
130 B c Mawatheeq (USA)—Cosmea **Barbury Castle Stud**
131 **DUKE OF SONNING,** ch g Duke of Marmalade (IRE)—Moonshadow **McNeill Family Ltd**
132 **GILD MASTER,** b c Excellent Art—Nirvana **McNeill Family Ltd**
133 **MYSTERY CODE,** b f Tobougg (IRE)—Mystery Lot (IRE) **Barbury Castle Stud**
134 **OCEANE (FR),** b g Kentucky Dynamite (USA)—Zahrana (FR) **McNeill Family Ltd**
135 **PADDYS RUNNER,** gr g Sir Percy—Frosty Welcome (USA) **Masterson Holdings Limited**
136 Ch c Black Sam Bellamy (IRE)—Realms of Gold (USA) **Mrs Sue Welch & Alan King**

## TWO-YEAR-OLDS

137 **HARDINGTON,** b c 28/3 Fastnet Rock (AUS)—La Cucina (IRE) (Last Tycoon) (20000) **The Fastnet Partnership**
138 **TYRELL (IRE),** b c 3/2 Teofilo (IRE)—Sleeveless (USA) (Fusaichi Pegasus (USA)) (70000) **Apple Tree Stud**

**Other Owners:** Mr D. J. Anderson, Mrs V. A. P. Antell, Mr R. B. Antell, Axom Ltd, Ms C. A. Bailey Tait, M. Ball, Mrs H. L. Bell, Mr F. D. Bell, D. Bellamy, Mr R. J. Benton, Mrs A. Blackwell, Mr David Bond, A. R. Bromley, D. J. Burke, Mr R. J. Caddick, Ms C. L. Calver, Mr N. J. Carter, Mrs D. C. Casey-McCarthy, Mr M. L. Cheesmer, Mr J. H. Chester, Mr S. Clancy, J. L. Clarke, Mr N. Clyne, Mr J. B. Cohen, Mr P. G. Cooke, Mr J. A. Cover, J. R. Creed, R. Cressey, Mr D. Downie, P. J. Dunkley, Mrs D. Dunkley, A. T. Eggleton, Mrs S. Evans, N. Farrell, Mr C. F. Fenton, Mrs L. H. Field, L. R. Frampton, R. B. Francis, Miss K. M. Franklin, S. G. Friend, G. F. Goode, Mr M. Grier, Mr R. W. Guy, Mr A. J. Hannigan, P. R. Harding, Mr C. I. K. Harris, Mrs C. A. Harris, Mr D. A. Heffer, Mr R. Hellaby, Mr A. J. Hill, D. F. Hill, J. Holmes, Mr A. Horne, Mr A. Humphreys, D. Humphreys, Mr R. A. Jacobs, Mr J. Johnson, G. F. Keirle, Mr A. B. Kelly, R. G. Kelvin-Hughes, Mrs E. A. Kelvin-Hughes, Mrs R. J. King, Miss E. A. Lake, Mr W. P. Ledward, R. M. Levitt, S. Love, Mr A. T. Macdonald, Mrs S. M. Maine, Mr G. T. Mann, Mrs G. Meacham, W. D. C. Minton, Mr C. Mullin, Mrs M. T. Mullin, S. E. Munir, Mr J. J. Murray, Mrs D. C. Nicholson, Mr P. J. O'Neill, Mr P. Patel, O. J. W. Pawle, Mr I. T. Payne, Miss H. Pease, R. J. Preston, Mr S. P. Price, Mrs J. Prince, D. F. Reilly, J. P. L. Reynolds, R. Scott, Mrs P. M. Scott, J. Sigler, Prof D. B. A. Silk, Mrs L. A. Smith, Mr I. Souede, Mr J. A. B. Stafford, Mrs K. Stephens, Mr R. T. Sullivan, Mr J. A. Tabet, Mrs M. G. Thomas, A. J. Thompson, Mrs C. Townroe, Mr J. Turner, Mr D. Underwood, Mr B. Wallis, Mr T. N. White, B. Winfield, Mr T. Withers, J. Wright.

**MR ALAN KING - Continued**

**Assistant Trainers:** Oliver Wardle, Dan Horsford

**Jockey (NH):** Wayne Hutchinson, Robert Thornton. **Conditional:** Tom Bellamy, Jamie Insole. **Amateur:** Mr Danny Burton, Mr Lewis Ferguson, Mr Harry Teal.

---

## 355 MR NEIL KING, Wroughton

Postal: **Ridgeway Racing Ltd, Upperherdswick Farm, Wroughton, Swindon, Wiltshire, SN4 0QH**
Contacts: **PHONE (01793) 845011 FAX (01793) 845011 MOBILE (07880) 702325**
**E-MAIL neil@neil-king.co.uk WEBSITE www.neil-king.co.uk**

1 **BALLYVONEEN (IRE),** 10, b g Stowaway—Miss Ira Zarad (IRE) **The Ridgeway Racing For Fun Partnership**
2 **BRASS MONKEY (IRE),** 8, b g Craigsteel—Saltee Great (IRE) **The Ridgeway Racing For Fun Partnership**
3 **CICERON (IRE),** 9, b g Pivotal—Aiglonne (USA) **Mr M. Secretan**
4 **CONSERVE (IRE),** 5, b m Duke of Marmalade (IRE)—Minor Point **The Conserve Partnership**
5 **DELGANY DEMON,** 7, b g Kayf Tara—Little Twig (IRE) **C. M. Wilson**
6 **DIRE STRAITS (IRE),** 4, b g Teofilo (IRE)—Kalagold (IRE) **Mr D. S. Lee**
7 **HAZZAAT (IRE),** 5, ch g Iffraaj—Hurricane Irene (IRE) **JeeVeePee**
8 **INFINITYANDBEYOND (IRE),** 4, gr g Medaaly—Ten Dollar Bill (IRE) **Mrs H. M. Buckle**
9 **LIL ROCKERFELLER (USA),** 4, ch g Hard Spun (USA)—Layounne (USA) **Davies Smith Govier & Brown**
10 **LITTLE WINDMILL (IRE),** 5, ch g Mahler—Ennismore Queen (IRE) **Barry Williams & Donald Caldwell**
11 **LOOKS LIKE MAGIC,** 6, gr g Fair Mix (IRE)—Cirrious **Mark & Tracy Harrod**
12 **MASTER RAJEEM (USA),** 6, b br g Street Cry (IRE)—Rajeem **Barry Williams & Donald Caldwell**
13 **MERCERS COURT (IRE),** 7, b g Court Cave (IRE)—Vikki's Dream (IRE) **David Nott, Ken Lawrence, Tim Messom**
14 **MILANSBAR (IRE),** 8, b g Milan—Ardenbar **Mr R. N. Bothway**
15 **MINNIE MILAN (IRE),** 6, b m Milan—Shiminnie (IRE) **Mark & Tracy Harrod,P Branigan,T Messom**
16 **MOSS VALLEY WAY (IRE),** 4, b f Moss Vale (IRE)—Attymon Lill (IRE) **The Ridgeway Racing For Fun Partnership**
17 5, B m Multiplex—Mrs Oh (IRE) **N. King**
18 **OH LAND ABLOOM (IRE),** 5, b g King's Theatre (IRE)—Talinas Rose (IRE) **Reefer Distribution Services Ltd**
19 **PRINCETON ROYALE (IRE),** 6, br g Royal Anthem (USA)—Shelikesitstraight (IRE) **D Nott, P Beadles, R Clarke**
20 **QUINCY MAGOO (IRE),** 6, ch g Mountain High (IRE)—Vicky's Lodge (IRE) **Mark & Tracy Harrod**
21 **REGULATION (IRE),** 6, br g Danehill Dancer (IRE)—Source of Life (IRE) **Amber Road Partnership**
22 **ROCK OF AGES,** 6, ch g Pivotal—Magic Peak (IRE) **R. W. Smith**
23 **ROJA DOVE (IRE),** 6, b m Jeremy (USA)—Knight's Place (IRE) **Barry Williams & Donald Caldwell**
24 **SAFFRON WELLS (IRE),** 7, b g Saffron Walden (FR)—Angel's Folly **Mark Harrod & Peter Beadles**
25 **SINGAPORE STORY (FR),** 6, b g Sagacity (FR)—Vettorina (FR) **Mark Harrod & Peter Beadles**
26 **SOUTHWAY STAR,** 10, b m Morpeth—Nearly A Score **The Ridgeway Racing For Fun Partnership**
27 **THE BOSS'S DREAM (IRE),** 7, b g Luso—Mrs Kick (IRE) **SLIS Ltd, Mr M Gibbons & Mr D Nott**
28 **TOWN MOUSE,** 5, ch g Sakhee (USA)—Megdale (IRE) **Mr Brian Bell & Mr John Smith**
29 **UNBUCKLED (IRE),** 5, b m Presenting—Una Kasala (GER) **Mrs H. M. Buckle**
30 **VANDROSS (IRE),** 5, b g Iffraaj—Mrs Kanning **Mr D. S. Lee**
31 **WITCH FROM ROME,** 4, b g Holy Roman Emperor (IRE)—Spangle **Mr B. M. V. Williams**
32 **YOU'VE BEEN MOWED,** 9, ch m Ishiguru (USA)—Sandblaster **Barry Williams & Donald Caldwell**
33 **ZEROESHADESOFGREY (IRE),** 6, gr g Portrait Gallery (IRE)—Hazy Rose (IRE) **Mrs H. M. Buckle**

**Other Owners:** Mr P. M. H. Beadles, Mr B. Bell, Mr P. A. Branigan, G. S. Brown, Mr D. R. Caldwell, Mr N. J. Catterwell, Mr R. Clarke, J. Davies, Mr M. H. Gibbons, Mr P. Govier, Mr P. F. Govier, Mr M. Harrod, Mrs T. Harrod, Mr D. Jee, Mr K. Lawrence, Mr G. Loughlin, Mr T. J. Messom, D. F. Nott, Mr J. W. Preuninger, Mr J. H. Smith, Mr A. J. Smith, Stephen Lower Insurance Services Limited, Mr J. C. Webb.

**Assistant Trainer:** Charlotte Horsley **Head Girl:** Claire Law

**Jockey (flat):** Martin Lane, Liam Jones, Adam Kirby, Tom Queally, Hayley Turner. **Jockey (NH):** Leighton Aspell, Mark Grant, Richard Johnson, Jamie Moore, Trevor Whelan. **Conditional:** Trevor Whelan. **Amateur:** Miss Bridgett Andrews, Mr Ben Jay.

---

## 356 MR WILLIAM KINSEY, Ashton

Postal: **R Kinsey Partnership, Peel Hall, Gongar Lane, Ashton, Chester**
Contacts: **PHONE (01829) 751230 MOBILE (07803) 753719**
**E-MAIL will@kinseyracing.co.uk WEBSITE www.kinseyracing.co.uk**

1 **ALLBARNONE,** 7, b g Alflora (IRE)—What A Gem **Girls Are Loud**

## MR WILLIAM KINSEY - Continued

2 **ALPHA VICTOR (IRE),** 10, b g Old Vic—Harvest View (IRE) **Denton,Kinsey,Osborne Hse,Wesley-Yates**
3 **DUNCOMPLAINING (IRE),** 6, b g Milan—Notcomplainingbut (IRE) **D. Wesley-Yates**
4 **GENTLEMAN BOB,** 7, b g Gentleman's Deal (IRE)—Miss Odd Sox **Mr C. G. Lloyd**
5 **GWLADYS STREET (IRE),** 8, b g Portrait Gallery (IRE)—Native Ocean (IRE) **The Missing Link**
6 **PREMIER SAGAS (FR),** 11, b g Sagacity (FR)—Estampe (FR) **Mrs T R Kinsey & Mr P Jones**
7 **SHOULDAVBOUGHTGOLD (IRE),** 8, b g Classic Cliche (IRE)—Sancta Miria (IRE) **The Missing Link**
8 **STRIKE FAST (IRE),** 10, gr g Portrait Gallery (IRE)—Street Rose (IRE) **The Gentlemen Farmers**

**Other Owners:** Mr C. B. Denton, Mr T. B. Denton, Mr P. A. Jones, Mrs J. Kinsey, Mr W. R. Kinsey, Osborne House Ltd.

---

## 357 MR PHILIP KIRBY, Saltburn-By-The-Sea

Postal: **Groundhill Farm, Lingdale, Saltburn-By-The-Sea, Cleveland, TS12 3HD**
Contacts: **MOBILE (07984) 403558**
**E-MAIL wakingned1@hotmail.com WEBSITE www.philipkirbyracing.co.uk**

1 **AGGLESTONE ROCK,** 10, b g Josr Algarhoud (IRE)—Royalty (IRE) **Geoff Kirby & Pam Kirby & Brian Cobbett**
2 **AMAZING KING (IRE),** 11, b g King Charlemagne (USA)—Kraemer (USA) **Mrs Philippa Kirby**
3 **ANIKNAM (FR),** 5, b g Nickname (FR)—Kelle Home (FR) **Nojab Limited**
4 **BACK BABY PARIS (IRE),** 4, b f Flemensfirth (USA)—Babygotback (IRE) **Mr Keith Foster**
5 **BEDALE LANE (IRE),** 6, b m Kayf Tara—Misleain (IRE) **Mr R. N. Ellerbeck**
6 **BIRTHDAY GUEST (GER),** 6, ch g Areion (GER)—Birthday Spectrum (GER) **Nojab Limited**
7 **CALL IT ON (IRE),** 9, ch g Raise A Grand (IRE)—Birthday Present **Mrs Philippa Kirby**
8 **CAN'TBELIEVEIT,** 7, b g Tikkanen (USA)—Noreasonatall **The Philip Kirby Racing Partnership**
9 **CATHEDRAL,** 6, b g Invincible Spirit (IRE)—Capades Dancer (USA) **T & Z Racing Club**
10 **CAVALIERI (IRE),** 5, b g Oratorio (IRE)—Always Attractive (IRE) **The Cavalieri Partnership**
11 **CELTIC AGENT,** 7, b g Kayf Tara—Poor Celt **Mrs S. Johnson**
12 **CLEVE COTTAGE,** 7, ch g Presenting—Reverse Swing **Mr D. J. Phillips**
13 **COURTOWN OSCAR (IRE),** 6, b g Oscar (IRE)—Courtown Bowe VII **Nojab, Dolan & Sadler**
14 **DIBBLE BRIDGE,** 4, ch g Spirit One (FR)—Willows World **Mr C. Fletcher**
15 **DR IRV,** 6, ch g Dr Fong (USA)—Grateful **I. M. Lynch**
16 **DUE EAST,** 5, b m Bollin Eric—Poor Celt **Mrs S. Johnson**
17 **EMBSAY CRAG,** 9, b g Elmaamul (USA)—Wigman Lady (IRE) **Grange Park Racing IV & Partner**
18 **ENZAAL (USA),** 5, b g Invasor (ARG)—Ekleel (IRE) **C B Construction (Cleveland) Limited**
19 **EPISODE,** 4, b br g Lucky Story (USA)—Epicurean **Ontoawinner & Friends 1**
20 **EVERAARD (USA),** 9, ch g Lion Heart (USA)—Via Gras (USA) **Tennant, Sharpe & Boston**
21 **FACTOR FIFTY (IRE),** 6, b g Definite Article—Sun Screen **The Topspec Partnership**
22 **FULL SPEED (GER),** 10, b g Sholokhov (IRE)—Flagny (FR) **L & D Racing**
23 **GEORDAN MURPHY,** 4, b g Firebreak—Sukuma (IRE) **Mr Geoff Kirby**
24 **GIVE HIM A GLANCE,** 4, bl gr g Passing Glance—Giving **Mrs K. Holmes**
25 **GOLDAN JESS (IRE),** 11, b g Golan (IRE)—Bendis (GER) **The Jessies,Colin Fletcher,Brian Cobbett**
26 **HAIL THE BRAVE (IRE),** 6, ch g Lahib (USA)—Parverb (IRE) **Junco P'Tners Ontoawinner Foster Bocking**
27 **IFTIKAAR (IRE),** 5, b g Cape Cross (IRE)—Anbella (FR) **C B Construction (Cleveland) Limited**
28 **IMPROVED (IRE),** 5, ch g Rainwatch—Show Potential (IRE) **Mrs Philippa Kirby**
29 **ISTIMRAAR (IRE),** 4, b g Dansili—Manayer (IRE) **Mr C. M. Grech**
30 **JESSIE PINKMAN,** 4, b g Duke of Marmalade (IRE)—My Dream Castles (USA) **M. J. Ward**
31 **KAYF'S HONOR,** 4, b f Kayf Tara—Prophets Honor (FR) **Mrs Gareth Fawcett**
32 **KIWAYU,** 6, b g Medicean—Kibara **Mrs J. Sivills**
33 **LADY BUTTONS,** 5, b m Beneficial—Lady Chapp (IRE) **Mrs J. Sivills**
34 **MAN IN BLACK (FR),** 6, gr g Turgeon (USA)—Mimosa de Wasa (FR) **Nojab Limited**
35 **MOSCOW PRESENTS (IRE),** 7, b g Presenting—Moscow Madame (IRE) **Nojab & Tony Sadler**
36 **NABATEO,** 4, ch g Sea The Stars (IRE)—Rosa Del Dubai (IRE) **RedHotGardogs**
37 **NEXT EDITION (IRE),** 7, b g Antonius Pius (USA)—Starfish (IRE) **The Dibble Bridge Partnership**
38 **OLY'ROCCS (IRE),** 4, b g Tagula (IRE)—Orpendonna (IRE) **Mr C. M. Grech**
39 **OSCAR O'SCAR (IRE),** 7, b g Oscar (IRE)—Shining Lights (IRE) **Newroc 1**
40 **PASS MUSTER,** 8, b g Theatrical—Morning Pride (IRE) **C B Construction (Cleveland) Limited**
41 **PERENNIAL,** 6, ch g Motivator—Arum Lily (USA) **Ace Bloodstock & The Gathered**
42 **PLATINUM (IRE),** 8, b g Azamour (IRE)—Dazzling Park (IRE) **Mrs Philippa Kirby**
43 **ROCKY TWO (IRE),** 5, ch g Rock of Gibraltar (IRE)—Toorah Laura La (USA) **Mr Andrew S. Taylor**
44 **RUMBLE OF THUNDER (IRE),** 9, b g Fath (USA)—Honey Storm (IRE) **The Well Oiled Partnership**
45 **SAKHEE'S CITY (FR),** 4, b c Sakhee (USA)—A Lulu Ofa Menifee (USA) **C B Construction (Cleveland) Limited**
46 **SOEUR DE ROIS (IRE),** 5, br m King's Theatre (IRE)—Soeur Ti (FR) **Birtles, Bradshaw & Mahon**
47 **STOPPED OUT,** 10, gr g Montjoy (USA)—Kiomi **The Well Oiled Partnership**
48 **STORMY MORNING,** 9, ch g Nayef (USA)—Sokoa (USA) **Ownaracehorse Ltd**
49 **TRANSIENT BAY (IRE),** 5, b g Trans Island—Boarding Pass (IRE) **The Waking Ned Partnership**

## MR PHILIP KIRBY - Continued

50 **TRIPLE EIGHT (IRE),** 7, b g Royal Applause—Hidden Charm (IRE) **RedHotGardogs**
51 **UP THE BEES,** 5, b g Kayf Tara—West River (USA) **Mr C. L. W. German**
52 **VIC'S LAST STAND (IRE),** 5, b m Old Vic—Misleain (IRE) **Mr Robin Ellerbeck**
53 **WOODPOLE ACADEMY (IRE),** 8, b g Beneficial—Midday Caller (IRE) **Nojab Limited**

### THREE-YEAR-OLDS

54 **LADY WESTERNER,** b f Westerner—Lady Chapp (IRE) **C B Construction (Cleveland) Limited**
55 **SPLASH OF VERVE (IRE),** b g Fast Company (IRE)—Ellistown Lady (IRE) **The Splash Of Verve Partnership**

### TWO-YEAR-OLDS

56 **ICE GALLEY (IRE),** b c 29/1 Galileo (IRE)—Ice Queen (IRE) (Danehill Dancer (IRE)) (105000) **Mrs Jayne Sivills**

**Other Owners:** Mr T. Alderson, Mr Shaun Beach, Mr J. Bell, Mr John Birtles, Mr Steve Bocking, Mr Andrew Bradshaw, Mr Brian Cobbett, Mr Alan Davies, Mr Bernard Dolan, Miss Zora Fakirmohamed, Mr C. Fletcher, Mr K. Foster, Mr J. A. Glover, Mr R. Hamilton, Mr Stephen Harrison, Mr W. Hayler, Mr P. Kirby, Mrs P. S. Kirby, Mr Mick Mahon, Mr David Marshall, Mr Graeme Newton, Mr A. Norrington, Mr N. J. O'Brien, Mr G. R. Orchard, Mr Andrew J. Roberts, Mr Tony Sadler, Mr N. D. Skinner, Mr R. Standring, Mr J. Stent, Mr Terrence White, Mr Simon J. Wyatt.

**Assistant Trainer:** Simon Olley

**Jockey (NH):** James Reveley. **Conditional:** Adam Nicol. **Amateur:** Mr Ross Turner.

---

## 358 MR SYLVESTER KIRK, Upper Lambourn

Postal: **Cedar Lodge Stables, Upper Lambourn, Hungerford, Berkshire, RG17 8QT**
Contacts: **PHONE (01488) 73215 FAX (01488) 670012 MOBILE (07768) 855261**
**E-MAIL info@sylvesterkirkracing.co.uk WEBSITE www.sylvesterkirkracing.co.uk**

1 **BERWIN (IRE),** 6, b m Lawman (FR)—Topiary (IRE) **S. A. Kirk**
2 **CELESTIAL BAY,** 6, b m Septieme Ciel (USA)—Snowy Mantle **Homebred Racing**
3 **CHARLES CAMOIN (IRE),** 7, b g Peintre Celebre (USA)—Birthday (IRE) **Mr C. Wright & The Hon Mrs J.M.Corbett**
4 **DELAGOA BAY (IRE),** 7, b m Encosta de Lago (AUS)—Amory (GER) **Homebred Racing**
5 **DUKES DEN,** 4, b g Duke of Marmalade (IRE)—Green Room (FR) **Mr E Sharp, Mr T Pearson & Mr S Kirk**
6 **GREY GEM (IRE),** 4, gr g Danehill Dancer (IRE)—Tiffany Diamond (IRE) **J. C. Smith**
7 **GROUNDWORKER (IRE),** 4, b g Tagula (IRE)—Notepad **Deauville Daze Partnership**
8 **HEINRICH (USA),** 4, gr g Henrythenavigator (USA)—C'est La Cat (USA) **Verano Quartet**
9 **INSPECTOR NORSE,** 4, b g Norse Dancer (IRE)—Indiana Blues **J. C. Smith**
10 **LAST MINUTE LISA (IRE),** 5, b m Strategic Prince—Bradwell (IRE) **Mr G. Dolan**
11 **LEAD A MERRY DANCE,** 4, b f Bertolini (USA)—Green Supreme **Miss A. J. Rawding**
12 **MAYMYO (IRE),** 4, b c Invincible Spirit (IRE)—Lady Windermere (IRE) **Mr H. Balasuriya**
13 **MY ANCHOR,** 4, b g Mount Nelson—War Shanty **R. Hannon**
14 **NAKUTI (IRE),** 4, b f Mastercraftsman (IRE)—Sheba Five (USA) **Mr N. Hayes**
15 **ORCRAIG,** 5, b g Royal Applause—Our Faye **J. B. J. Richards**
16 **SCARIFF HORNET (IRE),** 4, b f Tagula (IRE)—Housa Dancer (FR) **Denis, Kieran & Andy Bugler**
17 **SEE AND BE SEEN,** 5, b g Sakhee's Secret—Anthea **T. K. Pearson & Partner**

### THREE-YEAR-OLDS

18 **BLUES DANCER,** b g Norse Dancer (IRE)—Indiana Blues **J. C. Smith**
19 **CARRY ON DERYCK,** b c Halling (USA)—Mullein **Walters Plant Hire Spiers & Hartwell**
20 **DIAMOND SAM,** ch c Compton Place—Kurtanella **Mrs Philip Snow**
21 **GALAGO (IRE),** b g Bushranger (IRE)—She's A Softie (IRE) **Thurloe Thoroughbreds XX**
22 **GOLD PRINCE (IRE),** b c Nayef (USA)—Premier Prize **J. C. Smith**
23 **JOLIE DE VIVRE (IRE),** b g Thewayyouare (USA)—Jolie Clara (FR) **Dr Barbara Matalon & Mr Ian Wight**
24 **KINNARA,** b f Kyllachy—Tinnarinka **Walters Plant,S & H Ltd,J Moody,R Hannon**
25 **MAGICAL DAZE,** b f Showcasing—Poulaine Bleue **Mr Timothy Pearson**
26 **MORE DRAMA (IRE),** b f Thewayyouare (USA)—Our Drama Queen (IRE) **Ms C. Cleary**
27 **MOUNTAIN MUSIC,** b f Three Valleys (USA)—Meadow Floss **D. J. Huelin**
28 **NOBLE MASTER,** b g Sir Percy—Eurolinka (IRE) **R. A. Gander**
29 **OAKLING,** b f High Chaparral (IRE)—Lambroza (IRE) **D O'Loughlin & Partner**
30 **ONELASTFLING,** b f Paco Boy (IRE)—Goodie Twosues **S. A. Kirk**
31 **PACOLITA (IRE),** ch f Paco Boy (IRE)—Clara (IRE) **The Calvera Partnership No. 2**
32 **PERCY VEER,** ch g Sir Percy—Fandangerina **Mr M Crow**
33 **PINK RIBBON (IRE),** b c Dark Angel (IRE)—My Funny Valentine (IRE) **Mrs M. Cousins**
34 **SIMONE ON TIME (IRE),** b f Lord Shanakill (USA)—Kathy Sun (IRE) **Mr N. Simpson**

## MR SYLVESTER KIRK - Continued

35 **SLEEPY DUST (IRE),** b f Rip Van Winkle (IRE)—Knockatotaun **Malih L. Al Basti**
36 **WESTERN PLAYBOY (IRE),** b g Kodiac—Dreamalot **Mr Des Kavanagh & Mr Derrick Murphy**

### TWO-YEAR-OLDS

37 **CALYPSO CHOIR,** ch f 22/2 Bahamian Bounty—Heavenly Song (IRE) (Oratorio (IRE)) **J. C. Smith**
38 B f 12/4 Fast Company (IRE)—Consensus (IRE) (Common Grounds) (15238) **M. M. Nicolson & Mr A. Wilson**
39 Ch f 5/5 Frozen Power (IRE)—Cristalita (IRE) (Entrepreneur) (4364) **S. A. Kirk**
40 Gr c 9/3 Medicean—Crocus Rose (Royal Applause) (20000) **S. A. Kirk**
41 Ch c 1/4 Dubai Destination (USA)—Full of Nature (Monsieur Bond (IRE)) **Ms C. Cleary**
42 **GAWDAWPALIN (IRE),** b c 17/4 Holy Roman Emperor (IRE)—Dirtybirdie (Diktat) (100000) **Mr H. Balasuriya**
43 **HEREWARD THE WAKE,** gr c 14/2 Fastnet Rock (AUS)—
Miss Universe (IRE) (Warning) (45000) **Mr C. Wright & The Hon Mrs J.M.Corbett**
44 **INDIE MUSIC,** ch f 8/3 Sakhee's Secret—Indiana Blues (Indian Ridge) **J. C. Smith**
45 B br c 2/4 Alfred Nobel (IRE)—Lahu Lady (Red Ransom (USA)) (12000) **Mr C. Conroy & Partner**
46 B c 16/4 Excellent Art—Meek Appeal (USA) (Woodman (USA)) (23809) **Mr E. McCay**
47 B c 25/1 Showcasing—Never Let You Down (IRE) (Barathea (IRE)) (100000) **Malih L. Al Basti**
48 **NORSE MAGIC,** b f 18/2 Norse Dancer (IRE)—Gift of Love (IRE) (Azamour (IRE)) **J. C. Smith**
49 B c 31/3 Equiano (FR)—Opera Dancer (Norse Dancer (IRE)) **J. C. Smith**
50 B c 20/4 Fastnet Rock (AUS)—Phrase (Royal Anthem (USA)) (16000) **N. Pickett**
51 B f 1/4 Acclamation—Sterope (FR) (Hernando (FR)) (7142) **Mr N. Simpson**
52 B c 13/2 Kyllachy—Welsh Anthem (Singspiel (IRE)) (55000) **Malih L. Al Basti**
53 **WINGED DANCER,** b c 21/2 Norse Dancer (IRE)—Winged Diva (IRE) (Hawk Wing (USA)) **J. C. Smith**

**Other Owners:** Mr Denis Bugler, Mr Andy Bugler, Mr Kieran Bugler, The Hon Mrs J. M. Corbett, Ms Gill Doran, Mr R. Hannon, Mr P. Hickey, Mr Sylvester Kirk, Mr D. A. Lucie-Smith, Dr Barbara A. Matalon, Mrs June Moody, Mr David P. Moss, Mr M. Nicholson, Mr D. O'Loughlin, Mr Timothy Pearson, Mrs Paul Shanahan, Mr E. K. W. Sharp, Spiers & Hartwell Ltd, Mr J. A. B. Stafford, Mr J. S. Threadwell, Mr Chris Wall, Mrs Sarah Wall, Walters Plant Hire Ltd, I. A. N. Wight, Mr Alastair Wilson, Mr Christopher Wright.

**Assistant Trainer:** Fanny Kirk

**Jockey (flat):** James Doyle, Liam Keniry. **Apprentice:** Jack Dinsmore.

---

## 359 MR STUART KITTOW, Cullompton

Postal: **Haynefield Farm, Blackborough, Cullompton, Devon, EX15 2JD**
Contacts: **HOME (01823) 680183 FAX (01823) 680601 MOBILE (07714) 218921**
**E-MAIL stuartkittowracing@hotmail.com WEBSITE stuartkittowracing.com**

1 **DAGHASH,** 6, b g Tiger Hill (IRE)—Zibet **Mrs P. E. Hawkings**
2 **DILGURA,** 5, b m Ishiguru (USA)—Dilys **R Ingham, S Kittow & R Perry**
3 **DUELLING DRAGON (USA),** 4, b g Henrythenavigator (USA)—Ometsz (IRE) **Chris & David Stam**
4 **FLIPPING,** 8, br g Kheleyf (USA)—Felona **R. S. E. Gifford**
5 **KALIFI (USA),** 4, b br f First Defence (USA)—Out of Reach **The Racing Guild**
6 **KLEITOMACHOS (IRE),** 7, b g Barathea (IRE)—Theben (GER) **E. J. S. Gadsden**
7 **MACDILLON,** 9, b g Acclamation—Dilys **Boswell,Pillans,Harris,Urquhart & Kittow**
8 **MAD ENDEAVOUR,** 4, b g Muhtathir—Capefly **R. S. E. Gifford**
9 **MAY BE SOME TIME,** 7, ch g Iceman—Let Alone **Dr G. S. Plastow**
10 **MIDNIGHT GYPSY,** 5, b m Midnight Legend—Romany Dream **Andrew Bull**
11 **OUR FOLLY,** 7, b g Sakhee (USA)—Regent's Folly (IRE) **Midd Shire Racing**
12 **PENGO'S BOY,** 6, gr g Proclamation (IRE)—Homeoftheclassics **Mrs P. J. Pengelly**
13 **PLAUSEABELLA,** 4, b f Royal Applause—Ellablue **Midd Shire Racing**
14 **PTOLEMY,** 6, b g Royal Applause—Rydal Mount (IRE) **R. S. E. Gifford**
15 **TOBOUGGALOO,** 4, ch f Tobougg (IRE)—Let Alone **Dr G. S. Plastow**

### THREE-YEAR-OLDS

16 **CARTMELL CLEAVE,** br g Pastoral Pursuits—There's Two (IRE) **Mr G. D. C. Jewell**
17 **DIZZEY HEIGHTS (IRE),** b f Halling (USA)—Extreme Pleasure (IRE) **Black Type Partnership IV**
18 **UPPISH,** ch g Compton Place—Uplifting **H. A. Cushing**
19 **VICTORINA,** ch f Kyllachy—Enrapture (USA) **P. A. & M. J. Reditt**

### TWO-YEAR-OLDS

20 Ch f 8/4 Compton Place—Dancing Storm (Trans Island) **M. E. Harris**
21 B f 5/4 Intikhab (USA)—Delta Diva (USA) (Victory Gallop (CAN)) **Andrew Bull**
22 B g 11/3 Compton Place—Dilys (Efisio)

## MR STUART KITTOW - Continued

23 **DORA'S FIELD (IRE),** b f 4/3 Rip Van Winkle (IRE)—Rydal Mount (IRE) (Cape Cross (IRE)) **R. S. E. Gifford**
24 **GUILDED ROCK,** gr c 30/4 Hellvelyn—Once Removed (Distant Relative) (9523) **The Racing Guild**
25 B c 16/4 Makfi—Super Motiva (Motivator) (11111) **Qatar Racing Limited**

**Other Owners:** Mrs S. G. Arnesen, D. W. Arnesen, John Boswell, Mrs A. Bull, Mr A. R. Ingham, W. S. Kittow, B. G. Middleton, The Hon Mrs R. Pease, Mrs R. J. M. Perry, Mr M. D. Pillans, Mrs P. A. Reditt, M. J. Reditt, A. J. Shire, Mr D. B. Stam, Dr C. Stam, Ms W. A. Stoker, R. A. Stoker, Mr J. R. Urquhart.

**Assistant Trainer:** Mrs Judy Kittow

**Jockey (flat):** Fergus Sweeney. **Jockey (NH):** Tom Scudamore.

---

## 360 MR WILLIAM KNIGHT, Angmering

Postal: **Lower Coombe Racing Stables, Angmering Park, Littlehampton, West Sussex, BN16 4EX**
Contacts: **PHONE (01903) 871188 FAX (01903) 871184 MOBILE (07770) 720828**
**E-MAIL william@wknightracing.co.uk WEBSITE www.wknightracing.co.uk**

1 **AUSSIE REIGNS (IRE),** 5, b g Aussie Rules (USA)—Rohain (IRE) **The Old Brokers**
2 **BEACH BAR (IRE),** 4, b g Azamour (IRE)—Toasted Special (USA) **P. Winkworth & Mrs Bex Seabrook**
3 **BLOODSWEATANDTEARS,** 7, b g Barathea (IRE)—Celestial Princess **Canisbay Bloodstock**
4 **DEINONYCHUS,** 4, b c Authorized (IRE)—Sharp Dresser (USA) **I. R. Hatton**
5 **EXALTED (IRE),** 4, b g Acclamation—Eman's Joy **The Old Brokers**
6 **FIRE SHIP,** 6, b g Firebreak—Mays Dream **IGP Partnership & P. Winkworth**
7 **GAVLAR,** 4, b g Gentlewave (IRE)—Shawhill **Chasemore Farm LLP**
8 **JACOB CATS,** 6, b g Dutch Art—Ballet **Canisbay Bloodstock**
9 **NOBLE GIFT,** 5, ch g Cadeaux Genereux—Noble Penny **Canisbay Bloodstock**
10 **PALACE MOON,** 10, b g Fantastic Light (USA)—Palace Street (USA) **Canisbay Bloodstock**
11 **ROWAN RIDGE,** 7, ch g Compton Place—Lemon Tree (USA) **Mr & Mrs N. Welby**
12 **SAOI (USA),** 8, ch g Wiseman's Ferry (USA)—Careyes (IRE) **Mr D. A. Docherty**
13 **SECRET ART (IRE),** 5, ch g Excellent Art—Ivy Queen (IRE) **Circuit Racing**
14 **SWEET MARTONI,** 5, b m Dubawi (IRE)—Sweetness Herself **Lavell Willis**
15 **SWEETHEART ABBEY,** 4, b f Dancing Spree (USA)—Hinton Pearl **Miss S. Bannatyne**
16 **TULLIA (IRE),** 4, b f Footstepsinthesand—Whipped Queen (USA) **Hot To Trot Racing Club & Mr P. Winkworth**

### THREE-YEAR-OLDS

17 **ALLEGRA ROYALE,** b f Royal Applause—Rapsgate (IRE) **Mrs S. M. Mitchell**
18 **ARTESANA,** ch f Mastercraftsman (IRE)—Koniya (IRE) **Mr T. G. Roddick**
19 **ASHAPURNA (IRE),** ch f Tamayuz—Bond Deal (IRE) **Jon & Julia Aisbitt**
20 B g Duke of Marmalade (IRE)—Bintalreef (USA) **W. J. Knight**
21 **CLOTILDE,** br f Dubawi (IRE)—Mary Boleyn (IRE) **Chasemore Farm LLP**
22 **COLORADA,** ch f Lope de Vega (IRE)—Isabella Glyn (IRE) **Mr T. G. Roddick**
23 B f Azamour (IRE)—Esclarmonde (IRE) **Mr & Mrs N. Welby**
24 **GOODWOOD MOONLIGHT,** gr g Azamour (IRE)—Corrine (IRE) **Goodwood Racehorse Owners Group (21) Ltd**
25 **ROYAL PARTY,** b f Royal Applause—Foxtrot Alpha (IRE) **P. L. Winkworth**
26 Ch f Aqlaam—Sharp Dresser (USA) **I. R. Hatton**
27 **SKY ROSE,** b f Sakhee (USA)—Intersky High (USA) **Jane Keir & Christine Sandall**
28 **SOLAR FLAIR,** b c Equiano (FR)—Air Biscuit (IRE) **Circuit Racing & The Kimber Family**

### TWO-YEAR-OLDS

29 **ARTISANDRA (FR),** ch f 27/1 Mastercraftsman (IRE)—Kezia (FR) (Spectrum (IRE)) (47619) **Wardley Bloodstock**
30 **AUTHOR'S DREAM,** b gr c 16/3 Authorized (IRE)—
Spring Dream (IRE) (Kalanisi (IRE)) (32000) **Heseltine & Conroy**
31 B c 4/2 Champs Elysees—Blast Furnace (IRE) (Sadler's Wells (USA)) **Chasemore Farm LLP**
32 B f 7/2 Equiano (FR)—Brazilian Style (Exit To Nowhere (USA)) (6666) **Fromthestables.com Racing V**
33 **COLONEL BOSSINGTON (IRE),** b c 27/3 Azamour (IRE)—
Ros The Boss (IRE) (Danehill (USA)) (50000) **The Expendables**
34 B c 22/4 Zebedee—Czars Princess (IRE) (Soviet Star (USA)) (32539)
35 B f 10/3 Champs Elysees—Dark Quest (Rainbow Quest (USA)) (8000) **Robert Barnett**
36 B c 23/4 Lilbourne Lad (IRE)—Elizabelle (IRE) (Westerner) (34000)
37 **GOODWOOD ZODIAC (IRE),** b c 28/1 Kodiac—Insieme (IRE) (Barathea (IRE)) (40000)
38 Br c 24/3 Sir Percy—Jardin (Sinndar (IRE)) (22000) **Angmering Park Thoroughbreds II**
39 **KIRINGA,** ch f 16/5 Kyllachy—Good Health (Magic Ring (IRE)) (28000) **Jon & Julia Aisbitt**
40 B c 6/4 Canford Cliffs (IRE)—Mackenzie's Friend (Selkirk (USA)) (23809) **Angmering Park Thoroughbreds I**
41 **NICEONECENTURION,** ch c 27/4 Teofilo (IRE)—Turn of A Century (Halling (USA)) (11000) **The Expendables**

## MR WILLIAM KNIGHT - Continued

**42** B c 11/2 Equiano (FR)—Point Perfect (Dansili) (9000) **Angmering Park Thoroughbreds III**
**43 ROBANNE,** b f 29/4 Paco Boy (IRE)—Arctic Song (Charnwood Forest (IRE)) (37000) **Mrs E. C. Roberts**
**44 SWEET SWAGGER,** ch f 13/2 Showcasing—Strawberry Leaf (Unfuwain (USA)) (40000) **The Oil Men Partnership**
**45 THE JUGGLER,** b c 30/1 Archipenko (USA)—
Oblige (Robellino (USA)) (8000) **Mrs Susie Hartley & The Kimber Family**

**Other Owners:** Mr Jon Aisbitt, Mrs Julia Aisbitt, Mr A. Black, Mrs J. E. Black, Mr G. J. Burchell, Mr I. J. Callaway, Mr Carl Conroy, Mr N. A. Coster, Mr P. J. Gregg, Mr Rupert Gregson-Williams, Mrs E. Gregson-Williams, Mrs Susie Hartley, Mr I. J. Heseltine, Mr R. S. Hoskins, Miss K. J. Keir, Mr R. F. Kilby, Mrs Carol Kimber, Dr Scott Kimber, Mr W. J. Knight, Mrs Emily Knight, Mrs Margaret Lavell, Mr Luke Lillingston, Mr I. G. Martin, Mr Nick Peacock, Mr N. J. Roach, Mr Mike Rudd, Mrs Christine Sandall, Mr J. Seabrook, Miss Maureen Stopher, Mr Mark Tracey, Mr N. Welby, Mrs N. Welby, Mr B. Willis, Mrs D. A. Willis, Mr P. Winkworth.

**Assistant Trainer:** Matthew Darling

**Apprentice:** Callum Shepherd.

---

**361**

## MR DANIEL KUBLER, Lambourn

Postal: **High View Stables, Folly Road, Lambourn, Hungerford, Berkshire, RG17 8QE**
Contacts: **MOBILE (07984) 287254**
**E-MAIL daniel@kublerracing.com WEBSITE www.kublerracing.com**

**1 BAILIWICK,** 4, b g Oratorio (IRE)—Imperial Bailiwick (IRE) **Mr & Mrs G. Middlebrook**
**2 CRUCIBLE,** 4, b g Danehill Dancer (IRE)—Baize **Mr & Mrs G. Middlebrook**
**3 FIREBACK,** 8, b g Firebreak—So Discreet **Kubler Racing Ltd**
**4 MARMANDE (IRE),** 4, ch f Duke of Marmalade (IRE)—Roselyn **Mr & Mrs G. Middlebrook**
**5 SHAMIANA,** 5, b br m Manduro (GER)—Camp Riverside (USA) **Mrs F. Denniff**
**6 TRIMOULET,** 6, b g Teofilo (IRE)—Riberac **Mr & Mrs G. Middlebrook**
**7 TWO SMART (IRE),** 4, b f Cape Cross (IRE)—Smartest (IRE) **David & Yvonne Blunt**

### THREE-YEAR-OLDS

**8 AFFILEO,** b f Teofilo (IRE)—Asinara (GER) **Capture The Moment**
**9 CHICA RAPIDA,** ch f Paco Boy (IRE)—Tora Bora **Who Dares Wins**
**10 COVENANT,** b c Raven's Pass (USA)—Love Everlasting **Mr & Mrs G. Middlebrook**
**11** B c Lawman (FR)—Kazinoki (UAE) **Keep Racing**
**12 LA DONACELLA,** b f Sir Percy—Tessie **Ms V. O'Sullivan**
**13 MANDRIA (IRE),** b f Duke of Marmalade (IRE)—Albertine Rose **Mr & Mrs G. Middlebrook**
**14 OUTRAGE,** ch c Exceed And Excel (AUS)—Ludynosa (USA) **D. Blunt & G. Middlebrook**
**15 PAZZO,** b g Paco Boy (IRE)—Clizia (IRE) **Bartisans Racing Ltd**
**16 WHO'STHEDADDY,** br g Avonbridge—Lisathedaddy **Mr & Mrs C. Wilson**

### TWO-YEAR-OLDS

**17 ALASKAN PHANTOM (IRE),** b f 2/3 Kodiac—Alexander Phantom (IRE) (Soviet Star (USA)) (30000) **J-P Lim**
**18 CHUPAROSA (IRE),** ch f 26/4 Approve (IRE)—Balamiyda (IRE) (Ashkalani (IRE)) **Mr P. J. H. Whitten**
**19** B f 10/3 Sky Mesa (USA)—Distinctive (Tobougg (IRE)) **Mr & Mrs G. Middlebrook**
**20 HILLTOP RANGER (IRE),** b f 29/1 Bushranger (IRE)—
Beatrix Potter (IRE) (Cadeaux Genereux) (12380) **Diskovery Partnership III**
**21** B f 7/4 Vale of York (IRE)—Irish Fountain (USA) (Irish River (FR)) **Mr M. Wichser**
**22** B f 12/3 Virtual—Petong's Pet (Petong) (2400) **Denarius Consulting Ltd**
**23 SILHOUETTE (IRE),** ch c 19/2 Frozen Power (IRE)—Missalonghi (IRE) (In The Wings) (13491) **Titan Assets Ltd**

**Other Owners:** Mr David Blunt, Mrs Y. Blunt, Mr Christopher Greenall, Kubler Racing Ltd, Mr G. Middlebrook, Mrs L. Middlebrook.

**Assistant Trainer:** Claire Kubler

---

## MR CARLOS LAFFON-PARIAS, Chantilly

Postal: **38, Avenue du General Leclerc, 60500 Chantilly, France**
**E-MAIL ecuries.laffon.parias@wanadoo.fr**

**1 ESLES (FR),** 7, b g Motivator—Resquilleuse (USA) **Bering S. L.**
**2 LYKASTOS (IRE),** 5, b g Holy Roman Emperor (IRE)—Granadilla **Stilvi Compania Financiera**
**3 PLANETAIRE,** 4, b c Galileo (IRE)—Occupandiste (IRE) **Wertheimer Et Frere**

## MR CARLOS LAFFON-PARIAS - Continued

4 **SHOTGUN WEDDING,** 4, b f Champs Elysees—Ransomed Bride **W. McAlpin**
5 **SPIRITUEUX (IRE),** 4, b c Invincible Spirit (IRE)—Stormina (USA) **Wertheimer Et Frere**

## THREE-YEAR-OLDS

6 **ABRAXAS STONE (FR),** b g Motivator—Katika (FR) **Stilvi Compania Financiera**
7 **ALCAUCIN (FR),** b c Siyouni (FR)—Trylko (USA) **Sarl Darpat France**
8 **ANASTER (FR),** b g Footstepsinthesand—Arikaria (IRE) **Stilvi Compania Financiera**
9 **ANDARIST (IRE),** ch g Halling (USA)—Alfreda **Stilvi Compania Financiera**
10 **ARCENFETE (IRE),** b c Arch (USA)—Soft Pleasure (USA) **Wertheimer Et Frere**
11 **ARTIFICIER (USA),** ch c Lemon Drop Kid (USA)—Quiet Royal (USA) **Wertheimer Et Frere**
12 **ARVIOS,** ch c Medicean—Akrivi (IRE) **Stilvi Compania Financiera**
13 **BACK SLANG (IRE),** b c Mastercraftsman (IRE)—Galaktea (IRE) **Stilvi Compania Financiera**
14 **BILISSIE,** b f Dansili—Balladeuse (FR) **Wertheimer Et Frere**
15 **CLARMINA (IRE),** b f Cape Cross (IRE)—Stormina (USA) **Wertheimer Et Frere**
16 **COLDSTONE (FR),** ch g Gold Away (IRE)—Vraona **Stilvi Compania Financiera**
17 **DAHOUM (FR),** b c Cape Cross (IRE)—Dubai (IRE) **Wertheimer Et Frere**
18 **DAUGHTER DAWN (IRE),** ch f New Approach (IRE)—Light Quest (USA) **Stilvi Compania Financiera**
19 **DIALECTIC (IRE),** b c Monsun (GER)—Wandering Spirit (GER) **Wertheimer Et Frere**
20 **GIBRALFARO (IRE),** b c Dalakhani (IRE)—Ronda **Sarl Darpat France**
21 **IMPASSABLE (IRE),** b f Invincible Spirit (IRE)—Gwenseb (FR) **Wertheimer Et Frere**
22 **JETON (IRE),** b c Montjeu (IRE)—Red Stella (FR) **Wertheimer Et Frere**
23 **LAFRIA (FR),** f Zamindar (USA)—Alyzea (IRE) **Stilvi Compania Financiera**
24 **LANASSA,** b f Duke of Marmalade (IRE)—Frynia (USA) **Stilvi Compania Financiera**
25 **MYRLA (FR),** b f Elusive City (USA)—Agiel (FR) **Stilvi Compania Financiera**
26 **OLANTHIA (IRE),** b f Zamindar (USA)—Olvia (IRE) **Stilvi Compania Financiera**
27 **ONYX (FR),** b f Orpen (USA)—Okalea (IRE) **Stilvi Compania Financiera**
28 **OOGLI,** b f Fastnet Rock (AUS)—Cross Section (USA) **W. McAlpin**
29 **PALE PEARL (IRE),** ch f King's Best (USA)—Pearl Earrine (FR) **Stilvi Compania Financiera**
30 **PICKAWAY (IRE),** b f Pivotal—Danzigaway (USA) **Wertheimer Et Frere**
31 **PITAMORE (USA),** b f More Than Ready (USA)—Pitamakan (USA) **Wertheimer Et Frere**
32 **PRIME SPOT (IRE),** gr c High Chaparral (IRE)—High Maintenance (FR) **Wertheimer Et Frere**
33 **PRIMLY (FR),** b f King's Best (USA)—Eriza **Stilvi Compania Financiera**
34 **QATARI ELEGANCE (USA),** ch f Giant's Causeway (USA)—Magnificent Honour (USA) **Al Shahania Stable**
35 **RIVEN LIGHT (IRE),** b g Raven's Pass (USA)—Vivacity **Stilvi Compania Financiera**
36 **SEASONAL (IRE),** ch g Samum (GER)—Never Green (IRE) **Wertheimer Et Frere**
37 **SERENDY (USA),** ch f Pleasantly Perfect (USA)—Ydillique (IRE) **Wertheimer Et Frere**
38 **SPIRIT OF QATAR (FR),** b c Monsun (GER)—Sandy Girl (FR) **Al Shahania Stable**
39 **SQUARE SET (FR),** b c Country Reel (USA)—Delfinia (FR) **Stilvi Compania Financiera**
40 **SYNDROMOS (FR),** b c Muhtathir—Dexandra (GR) **Stilvi Compania Financiera**
41 **TOLOX (FR),** ch c Zamindar (USA)—Briviesca **Sarl Darpat France**
42 **VOYELLE (USA),** ch f Broken Vow (USA)—Corrazona (USA) **Wertheimer Et Frere**

## TWO-YEAR-OLDS

43 **AERIE,** b f 27/2 High Chaparral (IRE)—Wingspan (USA) (Silver Hawk (USA)) **Wertheimer Et Frere**
44 **AKTORIA (FR),** b f 29/1 Canford Cliffs (IRE)—Granadilla (Zafonic (USA)) **Stilvi Compania Financiera**
45 B c 30/1 Whipper (USA)—Benalmadena (FR) (Nashwan (USA)) **Sarl Darpat France**
46 **BIENTEVEO (IRE),** b c 13/3 Pivotal—Kirkinola (Selkirk (USA)) **Felipe Hinojosa**
47 **BIG SUR (FR),** b c 29/1 Cape Cross (IRE)—Kylia (USA) (Mr Greeley (USA)) **Wertheimer Et Frere**
48 B f 2/2 Dalakhani (IRE)—Campanillas (IRE) (Montjeu (IRE)) **Sarl Darpat France**
49 B g 26/4 Mr Sidney (USA)—Casabermeja (USA) (Elusive Quality (USA)) (1587) **Lomba**
50 **DISTINGO (IRE),** b c 3/4 Smart Strike (CAN)—Distinctive Look (IRE) (Danehill (USA)) **Wertheimer Et Frere**
51 **EMOTICON (FR),** b c 18/1 Dansili—Flash Dance (IRE) (Zamindar (USA)) **Wertheimer Et Frere**
52 **ENJOY THE SILENCE (FR),** b c 18/4 Elusive City (USA)—
Cerita (IRE) (Wolfhound (USA)) **Stilvi Compania Financiera**
53 B c 28/3 Holy Roman Emperor (IRE)—Galaktea (IRE) (Statue of Liberty (USA)) **Stilvi Compania Financiera**
54 **IONI (FR),** b f 17/3 Ialysos (GR)—Mazea (IRE) (Montjeu (IRE)) **Stilvi Compania Financiera**
55 **KALVOS (FR),** ch c 13/2 Dutch Art—Loxandra (Last Tycoon) **Stilvi Compania Financiera**
56 **KARYNIA (FR),** ch f 1/2 Footstepsinthesand—Keisha (FR) (Green Tune (USA)) **Stilvi Compania Financiera**
57 B f 19/3 Mr Sidney (USA)—Kresna (FR) (Distant Relative) **Stilvi Compania Financiera**
58 **LEFT HAND,** ch f 17/3 Dubawi (IRE)—Balladeuse (FR) (Singspiel (IRE)) **Wertheimer Et Frere**
59 B c 21/5 Galileo (IRE)—Light Quest (USA) (Quest For Fame) **Stilvi Compania Financiera**
60 **NIMPHEAS (USA),** b f 6/3 Smart Strike (CAN)—Underwater (USA) (Theatrical) **Wertheimer Et Frere**
61 **NOT READY (USA),** gr ro f 21/2 More Than Ready (USA)—Zaftig (USA) (Gone West (USA)) **Wertheimer Et Frere**
62 **OKANA,** b f 16/4 Zamindar (USA)—Oceanique (USA) (Forest Wildcat (USA)) **Wertheimer Et Frere**
63 **PETUNIA (IRE),** b f 18/2 Pivotal—Esneh (IRE) (Sadler's Wells (USA)) **Wertheimer Et Frere**

## MR CARLOS LAFFON-PARIAS - Continued

64 **READY TO SMILE (USA),** b f 22/3 Distorted Humor (USA)—
Buster's Ready (USA) (More Than Ready (USA)) **Wertheimer Et Frere**
65 **REDCOLD (FR),** b f 10/3 Nayef (USA)—Russiana (IRE) (Red Ransom (USA)) **Wertheimer Et Frere**
66 **SASPARELLA (FR),** b f 9/4 Shamardal (USA)—Desertiste (Green Desert (USA)) **Wertheimer Et Frere**
67 **SINABOY (FR),** b c 26/3 Evasive—Sina (GER) (Trans Island) (20634) **C. Laffon Parias**
68 **TAX HEAVEN (IRE),** b f 3/2 Rock of Gibraltar (IRE)—
Futurista (USA) (Awesome Again (CAN)) **Wertheimer Et Frere**
69 **TOLOMEO (IRE),** b c 8/2 Dalakhani (IRE)—Tiyi (FR) (Fairy King (USA)) **Wertheimer Et Frere**
70 B c 6/5 Orpen (USA)—Trylko (USA) (Diesis) **Sarl Darpat France**

---

## 363 MR NICK LAMPARD, Marlborough

Postal: **South Cottage, 2 The Crossroads, Clatford, Marlborough, Wiltshire, SN8 4EA**
Contacts: **PHONE (01672) 861420**

1 **GOOCHYPOOCHYPRADER,** 8, ch m Karinga Bay—Mrs Ritchie **The Outside Chance Racing Club**
2 **JUST SATISFACTION,** 6, b m Trade Fair—Bathwick Fancy (IRE) **The Outside Chance Racing Club**
3 **SADMA,** 6, gr g Street Cry (IRE)—Blue Dress (USA) **Just A Bit Of Fun**

**Other Owners:** Ms C. J. Gaisford, Miss C. D. Roberts, Miss A. E. A. Solomon, Mr H. Spooner.

---

## 364 MR DAVID LANIGAN, Upper Lambourn

Postal: **Kingsdown Stables, Upper Lambourn, Hungerford, Berkshire, RG17 8QX**
Contacts: **PHONE (01488) 71786 FAX (01488) 674148 MOBILE (07803) 257864**
**E-MAIL david@laniganracing.co.uk WEBSITE www.laniganracing.co.uk**

1 **ALIGHIERI (IRE),** 4, b g Sea The Stars (IRE)—Ange Bleu (USA)
2 **BIOGRAPHER,** 6, b g Montjeu (IRE)—Reflective (USA)
3 **BOLD LASS (IRE),** 4, b f Sea The Stars (IRE)—My Branch
4 **DAWN SKY,** 11, b g Fantastic Light (USA)—Zacheta
5 **FOR WHAT (USA),** 7, ch h Mingun (USA)—Cuanto Es (USA)
6 4, B g Bushranger (IRE)—Fuerta Ventura (IRE)
7 **ILE FLOTTANTE,** 4, b f Duke of Marmalade (IRE)—Aqaarid (USA)
8 **INTERCEPTION (IRE),** 5, ch m Raven's Pass (USA)—Badee'a (IRE)
9 **LEONARD THOMAS,** 5, b g Singspiel (IRE)—Monawara (IRE)
10 **PLUTOCRACY (IRE),** 5, b g Dansili—Private Life (FR)
11 **POLYBIUS,** 4, b g Oasis Dream—Freedonia
12 **REMBRANDT VAN RIJN (IRE),** 4, b g Peintre Celebre (USA)—Private Life (FR)
13 **SALMON SUSHI,** 4, ch g Dalakhani (IRE)—Salsa Steps (USA)
14 **SEQUESTER,** 4, ch f Selkirk (USA)—Al Theraab (USA)
15 **WARRIOR OF LIGHT (IRE),** 4, b g High Chaparral (IRE)—Strawberry Fledge (USA)

### THREE-YEAR-OLDS

16 **ALMODOVAR (IRE),** b c Sea The Stars (IRE)—Melodramatic (IRE)
17 **ANZHELIKA (IRE),** ch f Galileo (IRE)—Ange Bleu (USA)
18 **COLDWATER CANYON,** b c Zamindar (USA)—Femme de Fer
19 **FAERY SONG (IRE),** b f Lawman (FR)—Chervil
20 **HELIOSPHERE (USA),** b f Medaglia d'Oro (USA)—Flying Passage (USA)
21 **HUMAN (USA),** b f Blame (USA)—Angel In My Heart (FR)
22 **INTROSPECTIVE,** b f Dynaformer (USA)—Reflective (USA)
23 B f Halling (USA)—Kisses
24 **MITCHUM SWAGGER,** b g Paco Boy (IRE)—Dont Dili Dali
25 **PALIMONY (IRE),** b f Oasis Dream—Palmeraie (USA)
26 **PIETRANGELO (IRE),** b c Galileo (IRE)—Alexander Goldrun (IRE)
27 **REAL SMART (USA),** gr f Smart Strike (CAN)—Rose Diamond (IRE)
28 **SNEAKING BUDGE,** b c Nayef (USA)—Ikat (IRE)
29 **SOVEREIGN TREATY,** b c Mawatheeq (USA)—Katya Kabanova
30 **SWEET DANCER (IRE),** ch c Danehill Dancer (IRE)—Thinking Positive
31 **SYNODIC (USA),** br c Henrythenavigator (USA)—Seven Moons (JPN)
32 **TERSE,** b f Dansili—Cut Short (USA)
33 **TETRATINA (USA),** b f Medaglia d'Oro (USA)—Trepidation (USA)
34 **TREVISANI (IRE),** b c Dubawi (IRE)—Geminiani (IRE)

## MR DAVID LANIGAN - Continued

## TWO-YEAR-OLDS

**35** B c 25/4 Arakan (USA)—Alexander Divine (Halling (USA)) (25000)
**36** B c 20/3 Sir Percy—Aqaarid (USA) (Nashwan (USA))
**37** B f 6/2 Fastnet Rock (AUS)—Arabian Mirage (Oasis Dream) (50000)
**38** B c 27/1 Raven's Pass (USA)—Cape Rocker (Cape Cross (IRE)) (42000)
**39** B c 5/3 Duke of Marmalade (IRE)—Course de Diamante (IRE) (Galileo (IRE))
**40** B c 11/3 Holy Roman Emperor (IRE)—Dahlia's Krissy (USA) (Kris S (USA)) (170000)
**41** **DREAM FREE,** b c 27/5 Oasis Dream—Freedonia (Selkirk (USA))
**42** B c 4/5 Smart Strike (CAN)—Exciting Times (FR) (Jeune Homme (USA)) (90000)
**43** B f 8/5 Shamardal (USA)—Geminiani (IRE) (King of Kings (IRE))
**44** B c 2/4 Shamardal (USA)—Gradara (Montjeu (IRE)) (79365)
**45** Br f 10/5 Dansili—Hoity Toity (Darshaan)
**46** B c 3/5 Dansili—Ikat (IRE) (Pivotal)
**47** Gr c 28/2 Kodiac—Krasotka (IRE) (Soviet Star (USA)) (40000)
**48** **MIND SHIFT (USA),** b c 15/2 Arch (USA)—Light Blow (USA) (Kingmambo (USA)) (229489)
**49** B c 6/3 Galileo (IRE)—My Branch (Distant Relative)
**50** B f 19/2 Gold Away (IRE)—Ourika (IRE) (Danehill Dancer (IRE)) (9000)
**51** B f 18/4 Sea The Stars (IRE)—Palmeraie (USA) (Lear Fan (USA))
**52** B c 8/3 Royal Applause—Queen of Heaven (USA) (Mr Greeley (USA)) (22000)
**53** B f 27/4 Acclamation—Rebelline (IRE) (Robellino (USA)) (230000)
**54** Gr c 8/5 Kendargent (FR)—San Sicharia (IRE) (Daggers Drawn (USA)) (103174)
**55** **THRILLED (IRE),** b f 19/3 Kodiac—Fuerta Ventura (IRE) (Desert Sun) (460000)
**56** B f 24/3 Kodiac—Wind Surf (USA) (Lil's Lad (USA)) (42000)

**Owners:** David & Elaine Ahearn, Mr Ben Arbib, Sir Martyn Arbib, Mr Oli Bell, Mrs Emma Capon, Mr John Connellan, Mr Paul Dean, Flaxman Stables Ireland Limited, Liza Judd, Jane Keir, Mrs David R. Lanigan, D. R. Lanigan, Mr & Mrs Bob Lanigan, Lord & Lady Lloyd-Webber, Mr H. K. Ma, Mrs John Magnier, Mrs Jane Marsh, Mr Stephen Martus, Mr Cameron McMillan, The Niarchos Family, Mr Bjorn Nielsen, Mr M. Tabor, Wedgewood Estates, Woodford Racing Limited.

---

## 365 MISS EMMA LAVELLE, Andover

Postal: **Cottage Stables, Hatherden, Andover, Hampshire, SP11 0HY**
Contacts: **PHONE (01264) 735509 OFFICE (01264) 735412 FAX (01264) 735529 MOBILE (07774) 993998**
**E-MAIL emma@elavelle.freeserve.co.uk WEBSITE www.emmalavelle.com**

1 **ABITOFBOB,** 6, b g Enrique—My World (FR) **Mrs N. Turner, Mrs P. Tozer & Miss C. Schicht**
2 **AKA DOUN (FR),** 4, b g Smadoun (FR)—Akar Baby **Mr A. Gemmell**
3 **ALBERT BRIDGE,** 7, gr g Hernando (FR)—Alvarita **The Cheyne Walkers**
4 **ANDY KELLY (IRE),** 6, ch g Flemensfirth (USA)—Fae Taylor (IRE) **The Optimists**
5 **BLOWN COVER,** 6, b g Kayf Tara—Cullen Bay (IRE) **Roger Hetherington & Colin Bothway**
6 **BRANTINGHAM BREEZE,** 7, gr m Tamure (IRE)—Absalom's Lady **Cottage Stables Racing Club**
7 **BRITANNIA,** 5, b m Notnowcato—Rule Britannia **Lady Bland**
8 4, B g Trans Island—Carnagh Girl (IRE)
9 **CASINO MARKETS (IRE),** 7, br g Fruits of Love (USA)—Vals Dream (IRE) **Mighty Acorn Stables**
10 **CAULFIELDS VENTURE (IRE),** 9, b g Catcher In The Rye (IRE)—Saddlers' Venture (IRE) **C. F. Colquhoun**
11 **CHAPEL GARDEN (IRE),** 6, br g Heron Island (IRE)—Grape Love (FR) **Tim Syder & N. Mustoe**
12 **CHARMING CHARLIE (IRE),** 5, b g Beneficial—Baile An Droichid (IRE) **Mrs Sarah Prior and Tim Syder**
13 **CHELSEA FLYER (IRE),** 4, b g Westerner—Aktress (IRE) **Mrs Rosemary Luck & Mrs Deirdre Walker**
14 **CLARET CLOAK (IRE),** 8, b g Vinnie Roe (IRE)—Bewildered (IRE) **Hawksmoor Partnership**
15 **CLOSING CEREMONY (IRE),** 6, b g Flemensfirth (USA)—Supreme Von Pres (IRE) **The High Altitude Partnership**
16 **COURT BY SURPRISE (IRE),** 10, b g Beneficial—Garryduff Princess (IRE) **N. Mustoe**
17 **COURT IN MOTION (IRE),** 10, br g Fruits of Love (USA)—Peace Time Girl (IRE) **N. Mustoe**
18 **CRACK AWAY JACK,** 11, ch g Gold Away (IRE)—Jolly Harbour **GDM Partnership**
19 **DAYMAR BAY (IRE),** 9, b g Oscar (IRE)—Sunset View (IRE) **The Hawk Inn Syndicate 2**
20 **DEMOGRAPHIC (USA),** 6, b g Aptitude (USA)—Private Line (USA) **Mrs A. C. Lavelle**
21 **EDGARDO SOL (FR),** 8, ch g Kapgarde (FR)—Tikiti Dancer (FR) **Axom XXXII**
22 **FIX IT RIGHT (IRE),** 7, br g Vinnie Roe (IRE)—Rock Cottage Lady (IRE) **The Hawk Inn Syndicate**
23 **FORTUNATE GEORGE (IRE),** 5, b g Oscar (IRE)—Fine Fortune (IRE) **The George Inn Racing Syndicate**
24 **FOX APPEAL (IRE),** 8, b g Brian Boru—Lady Appeal (IRE) **The Hawk Inn Syndicate 3**
25 **GULLINBURSTI (IRE),** 9, b g Milan—D'ygrande (IRE) **N. Mustoe**
26 **HATTON BANK,** 6, ch m Flemensfirth (USA)—Persian Walk (FR) **Mr G. P. MacIntosh**
27 **HIGHLAND LODGE (IRE),** 9, b g Flemensfirth (USA)—Supreme Von Pres (IRE) **The Unusual Suspects**

## MISS EMMA LAVELLE - Continued

28 **HOPE'S WISHES,** 5, b m Kayf Tara—Otarie (FR) **Mr E. J. M. Spurrier**
29 **JAVERT (IRE),** 6, b g Kayf Tara—Royalrova (FR) **Axom LII**
30 **JUNCTION FOURTEEN (IRE),** 6, b g King's Theatre (IRE)—Chevet Girl (IRE) **M. St Quinton & Tim Syder**
31 **KING BORU (IRE),** 7, b g Brian Boru—Final Instalment (IRE) **Lavelle Wallis Farrington**
32 **LADY MARKBY (IRE),** 4, b f Oscar (IRE)—Leitrim Bridge (IRE) **Mrs S. Metcalfe**
33 **LE BEC (FR),** 7, ch g Smadoun (FR)—La Pelode (FR) **T. D. J. Syder**
34 **LETS HOPE SO,** 5, b m Generous (IRE)—Baily Mist (IRE) **Swanbridge Bloodstock Limited**
35 **LITTLE MIX,** 4, gr g Sagamix (FR)—Folie Dancer **J. R. Lavelle & Dr Mark Scott**
36 4, Ch f Gold Away (IRE)—Maisie Daisie (FR) **GDM Partnership**
37 **MOSSPARK (IRE),** 7, b g Flemensfirth (USA)—Patio Rose **N. Mustoe & Tim Syder**
38 **MR MOUNTAIN (IRE),** 5, b g Mountain High (IRE)—Not Mine (IRE) **N. Mustoe**
39 **MRSROBIN (IRE),** 5, b m Robin des Pres (FR)—Regents Dancer (IRE) **T. D. J. Syder**
40 **OFF THE GROUND (IRE),** 9, b g Oscar (IRE)—Kaysel (IRE) **Axom (XXVI)**
41 **ONDERUN (IRE),** 6, b g Flemensfirth (USA)—Warts And All (IRE) **Lavelle Foster Metcalfe Copland**
42 **OUT OF THE MIST (IRE),** 6, b m Flemensfirth (USA)—Mistinguett (IRE) **Swanbridge Bloodstock Limited**
43 **PADRE TITO (IRE),** 7, b g Milan—Augusta Brook (IRE) **T. D. J. Syder**
44 **PARISH BUSINESS (IRE),** 7, b br g Fruits of Love (USA)—Parkality (IRE) **N. Mustoe**
45 **PAWN STAR (IRE),** 5, b g Beneficial—Missindependence (IRE) **Hawk Inn Syndicate 5**
46 **PENNY MAX (IRE),** 9, b g Flemensfirth (USA)—
Ballymartin Trix (IRE) **Highclere Thoroughbred Racing - Penny Max**
47 **PRIVATE MALONE (IRE),** 6, b g Darsi (FR)—Native Artist (IRE) **Mrs S. V. M. Stevens**
48 **SEE THE WORLD,** 5, b g Kayf Tara—My World (FR) **Mrs N. Turner, Mrs P. Tozer & Miss C. Schicht**
49 **SET LIST (IRE),** 6, b g Heron Island (IRE)—Copper Magic (IRE) **T. D. J. Syder**
50 **SHOTGUN PADDY (IRE),** 8, b g Brian Boru—Awesome Miracle (IRE) **Axom (XXXVI)**
51 **STARLIGHT SONATA,** 5, b m Tagula (IRE)—Starlight Express (FR) **D. M. Bell**
52 **SWALLOWSHIDE,** 6, b g Hernando (FR)—Kentford Grebe **D. I. Bare**
53 **TARA'S HONOUR,** 5, b m Kayf Tara—Prophets Honor (FR) **N. Mustoe**
54 **THE LAST EURO (IRE),** 5, b g Scorpion (IRE)—Nitelite **Highclere T'Bred Racing - The Last Euro**
55 **TIME IS MONEY,** 6, b m Presenting—No More Money **Cottage Stables Racing Club**
56 **ULLSWATER (IRE),** 7, b g Singspiel (IRE)—Uluwatu (IRE) **The Jumping Stars**
57 **VAGRANT EMPEROR (IRE),** 12, b g Oscar (IRE)—Dragonmist (IRE) **Mrs A. C. Lavelle**
58 **VENDREDI TROIS (FR),** 6, b g Shaanmer (IRE)—Legende Sacree (FR) **Awdry, Gemmell, Pomford & Williams**
59 **WATER WAGTAIL,** 8, b g Kahyasi—Kentford Grebe **D. I. Bare**
60 **WELL REGARDED (IRE),** 10, b g Dr Massini (IRE)—Glenelly Valley (IRE) **The Unusual Suspects**
61 **WELL REWARDED (IRE),** 5, b g Beneficial—Lady Fancy (IRE) **Andy & The Frisky Fillies**
62 **WOODLAND WALK,** 7, ch m Generous (IRE)—Duchess of Kinsale (IRE) **Cottage Stables Racing Club**
63 **YABADABADOO,** 7, b g Doyen (IRE)—Kabayil **Elite Racing Club**

**Other Owners:** Mr C. V. Awdry, Axom Ltd, Mr C. H. Bothway, G. Charlesworth, D. Charlesworth, Mrs J. Copland, Mr D. Downie, Mr L. P. Dunne, Mrs A. M. Dunne, Mr W. T. Farrington, Mr C. N. H. Foster, Mr R. J. Fowler, Mrs N. J. Haigh, Mr S. Halpern, Mrs C. D. Halpern, The Hon H. M. Herbert, Mr R. R. Hetherington, Highclere Thoroughbred Racing Ltd, Mr A. J. Hill, J. R. Hulme, Mr L. G. Kimber, J. R. Lavelle, R. J. Lavelle, Mrs R. A. Luck, Mr J. J. P. McNeile, Mr S. T. Merry, Mrs D. J. Merry, P. B. Mitford-Slade, Mrs C. A. Moysey, Mr P. Nicholls, Miss M. Noden, B. G. Pomford, G. R. Pooley, Mrs S. K. Prior, Mr J. W. Randall, Miss C. Schicht, Dr M. J. Scott, Mr M. Smith, M. G. St Quinton, Mrs K. M. Taylor, Mrs M. R. Taylor, Mrs P. Tozer, Mr J. W. Turner, Mrs N. C. Turner, Mrs J. C. Verity, Mrs D. Walker, J. R. Wallis, Mr P. R. Weston, Mr A. G. Weston, Mrs P. H. Williams.

**Assistant Trainer:** Barry Fenton

---

## 366 MR BARRY LEAVY, Stoke-on-Trent

Postal: **Cash Heath Farm, Cash Heath, Forsbrook, Stoke-on-Trent, ST11 9DE**
Contacts: **HOME/FAX (01782) 398591 MOBILE (07540) 806915**
**E-MAIL lauraleavy@hotmail.co.uk WEBSITE www.leavyracing.co.uk**

1 **DANCING DUDE (IRE),** 8, ch g Danehill Dancer (IRE)—Wadud **Cops & Robbers**
2 **DI KAPRIO (FR),** 9, b g Kapgarde (FR)—Miss Nousha (FR) **Cops & Robbers**
3 **FLOBURY,** 7, b m Overbury (IRE)—Miss Flora **Mr J. K. S. Cresswell**
4 **KING ZEAL (IRE),** 11, b g King's Best (USA)—Manureva (USA) **Deborah Hart & Alan Jackson**
5 **KORNGOLD,** 7, b g Dansili—Eve **N. Heath**
6 **LEAN BURN (USA),** 9, b g Johannesburg (USA)—Anthelion (USA) **N. Heath**
7 **MINISTEROFINTERIOR,** 10, b g Nayef (USA)—Maureen's Hope (USA) **Mrs Laura Leavy**
8 **MOHI RAHRERE (IRE),** 12, b g New Frontier (IRE)—
Collinstown Lady (IRE) **Mrs S. D. Ashford & Mr J. G. Williams**
9 **ON THE RIGHT PATH,** 8, b g Pursuit of Love—Glen Falls **Deborah Hart**

## MR BARRY LEAVY - Continued

10 **PHASE SHIFT,** 7, b m Iceman—Silent Waters **B. Leavy**
11 **ROOMIE,** 4, b f Pastoral Pursuits—Pomponette (USA) **Mrs A. Holmes**
12 **SOLIDAGO (IRE),** 8, b g Vinnie Roe (IRE)—Native Belle (IRE) **Mrs S. D. Ashford**
13 **TOM WADE (IRE),** 8, b g Rakti—Plutonia **Mr P. Tonks**

**Other Owners:** Mr Frank Dronzek, Mrs Deborah Hart, Mr Alan Jackson, Mr Barry Leavy, Mr Chris Nightingale, Mr D. Rowlinson, Mr J. G. Williams, Mrs S. D. Williams.

**Assistant Trainer:** Mrs L Leavy

**Conditional:** Harry Challoner. **Apprentice:** Ryan Holmes.

---

## 367 MR RICHARD LEE, Presteigne

Postal: **The Bell House, Byton, Presteigne, LD8 2HS**
Contacts: **PHONE (01544) 267672 FAX (01544) 260247 MOBILE (07836) 537145**
**E-MAIL rleeracing@btinternet.com WEBSITE www.rleeracing.com**

1 **ACES OVER EIGHTS (IRE),** 6, b m Old Vic—Conjure Up (IRE) **Mr S. Thorp**
2 **BARNEY RUBBLE,** 6, b g Medicean—Jade Chequer **J. D. Cound**
3 **DEFINITE FUTURE (IRE),** 6, b g Definite Article—Miss Marilyn (IRE) **Mr R. L Baker**
4 **GASSIN GOLF,** 6, b g Montjeu (IRE)—Miss Riviera Golf **W. Roseff**
5 **GOODTOKNOW,** 7, b g Presenting—Atlantic Jane **Burling Daresbury MacEchern Nolan Potter**
6 **GREY GOLD (IRE),** 10, gr g Strategic Choice (USA)—Grouse-N-Heather **Mrs M. A. Boden**
7 **HAPPY DIVA (IRE),** 4, b f King's Theatre (IRE)—Megans Joy (IRE) **W. Roseff**
8 **HIGHWAY CODE (USA),** 9, b g Street Cry (IRE)—Fairy Heights (IRE) **D. E. Edwards**
9 **INCENTIVISE (IRE),** 12, ch g Snurge—Festive Isle (IRE) **R Bartlett J Hulston & Mrs B M Ayres**
10 **KNOCK A HAND (IRE),** 10, br g Lend A Hand—Knockcross (IRE) **D. A. Halsall**
11 **KRIS SPIN (IRE),** 7, br g Kris Kin (USA)—Auditing Empress (IRE) **Six To Five Against**
12 **KYLEMORE LOUGH,** 6, b g Revoque (IRE)—One of The Last **Mr M. J. McMahon**
13 **MOLLY CAT,** 5, ch m Dylan Thomas (IRE)—Pentatonic **Mrs D. Jeromson**
14 **MOUNTAINOUS (IRE),** 10, b g Milan—Mullaghcloga (IRE) **Walters Plant Hire & James & Jean Potter**
15 **MR BACHSTER (IRE),** 10, b g Bach (IRE)—Warrior Princess (IRE) **R. A. Lee**
16 **RAVENS BROOK (IRE),** 9, br g Alderbrook—Triple Triumph (IRE) **R. A. Lee**
17 **RUSSE BLANC (FR),** 8, wh g Machiavellian Tsar (FR)—Fleur de Mad (FR) **Mr M. R. H. Jackson**
18 **SCALES (IRE),** 9, b g Bob Back (USA)—Mrs Avery (IRE) **A Beard B Beard S Ripley**
19 **SIMPLY WINGS (IRE),** 11, b g Winged Love (IRE)—Simply Deep (IRE) **Mr S. Thorp**
20 **THE CHAZER (IRE),** 10, gr g Witness Box (USA)—Saffron Holly (IRE) **Mr & Mrs C. R. Elliott**
21 **TOP GAMBLE (IRE),** 7, ch g Presenting—Zeferina (IRE) **Walters Plant Hire & James & Jean Potter**
22 **TRESOR DE BONTEE (FR),** 8, b g Grand Seigneur (FR)—Bontee (FR) **Glass Half Full**
23 **VICTORY GUNNER (IRE),** 17, ch g Old Vic—Gunner B Sharp **Mr R Bartlett & Mrs B M Ayres**

**Other Owners:** Mrs B. M. Ayres, R. Bartlett, A. C. Beard, B. M. Beard, Mr P. R. Burling, Mrs R. L. Burling, Lord Daresbury, C. R. Elliott, Mrs J. A. Elliott, Mr G. T. Gilbert, R. L. C. Hartley, J. P. Hulston, Mrs C. J. Lee, G. M. MacEchern, Mr P. Nolan, J. E. Potter, Mrs M. J. Potter, Lady H. S. Ripley, Walters Plant Hire Ltd.

**Assistant Trainer:** Kerry Lee

**Jockey (NH):** Richard Johnson, Charlie Poste. **Conditional:** Micheal Nolan.

---

## 368 MRS SOPHIE LEECH, Westbury-on-Severn

Postal: **T/A Leech Racing Limited, Tudor Racing Stables, Elton Road, Elton, Newnham, Gloucestershire, GL14 1JN**
Contacts: **PHONE (01452) 760691 MOBILE (07775) 874630**
**E-MAIL info@leechracing.co.uk WEBSITE www.leechracing.co.uk**

1 **ANTEROS (IRE),** 7, b g Milan—Sovereign Star (IRE) **K. W. Bell**
2 **BOHER LAD (IRE),** 8, b g Gold Well—Shindeesharnick (IRE) **C. J. Leech**
3 **COINAGE (IRE),** 6, b g Westerner—Sovereign Star (IRE) **K. W. Bell**
4 **DUN SCAITH (IRE),** 7, b g Vinnie Roe (IRE)—Scathach (IRE) **G Doel, RS Liddington & C J Leech**
5 **HIMALAYAN PEAK,** 5, b g Tiger Hill (IRE)—Rosy Outlook (USA) **C. J. Leech**
6 **KAPRICORNE (FR),** 8, b g Kapgarde (FR)—Colombe Royale (FR) **Cheltenham Racing Club**
7 **KASSIODOR (GER),** 8, b g Tiger Hill (IRE)—Kitcat (GER) **C. J. Leech**
8 **LE GRAND CHENE (FR),** 9, b g Turgeon (USA)—Faitiche d'aubry (FR) **T. Westmacott & C. J. Leech**
9 **LOVCEN (GER),** 10, b g Tiger Hill (IRE)—Lady Hawk (GER) **J. O'Brien & C. J. Leech**

## MRS SOPHIE LEECH - Continued

10 **MAN OF PLENTY,** 6, ch g Manduro (GER)—Credit-A-Plenty **G. D. Thompson**
11 **MART LANE (IRE),** 10, br g Stowaway—Western Whisper (IRE) **G. D. Thompson**
12 **NICENE CREED,** 10, b g Hernando (FR)—First Fantasy **French, Mitchell, Frame, Lawton, O'Brien**
13 **OLD MAGIC (IRE),** 10, b g Old Vic—Maeve's Magic (IRE)
14 **OLYMPIAN BOY (IRE),** 11, b g Flemensfirth (USA)—Notanissue (IRE) **J. Cocks & C. J. Leech**
15 **OWEN GLENDOWER (IRE),** 10, br g Anshan—Native Success (IRE) **C. J. Leech**
16 **RADMORES REVENGE,** 12, b g Overbury (IRE)—Harvey's Sister **CJ Leech & RS Liddington**
17 **RECWAY LASS,** 7, ch m Doyen (IRE)—Zarma (FR) **M E & A D I Harris & Out Of Bounds Racing**
18 **RIVER D'OR (FR),** 10, b g Saint Preuil (FR)—Une Pomme d'or (FR) **Frame,Lawton,Mitchell,O'Brien & Leech**
19 **ROCKY ELSOM (USA),** 8, b g Rock of Gibraltar (IRE)—Bowstring (IRE) **The Montpellier Friends**
20 **ROLLING DOUGH (IRE),** 7, b m Indian Danehill (IRE)—High Dough (IRE) **C J Leech & M E & A D I Harris**
21 **RUPERRA TOM,** 7, b g Kayf Tara—Cathy's Dream (IRE) **Mr T. J. Rees**
22 **SEASIDE SHUFFLE (IRE),** 10, b br g Wizard King—Leaden Sky (IRE) **Cheltenham Racing Club**
23 **SEVEN SUMMITS (IRE),** 8, b g Danehill Dancer (IRE)—Mandavilla (IRE) **C. J. Leech**
24 **SILMI,** 11, gr g Daylami (IRE)—Intimaa (IRE) **J. O'Brien & C. J. Leech**
25 **SPANISH TREASURE (GER),** 9, b g Black Sam Bellamy (IRE)—Santa Zinaada (GER) **Mr C. R. Leech**
26 **TAMARILLO GROVE (IRE),** 8, b g Cape Cross (IRE)—Tamarillo **G Doel, RS Liddington & C J Leech**
27 **WAYWARD FROLIC,** 9, br g Fair Mix (IRE)—Mighty Frolic **G. Doel & C. J. Leech**
28 **WINSTON CHURCHILL (IRE),** 9, b g Presenting—Star Councel (IRE) **G. D. Thompson**

**Other Owners:** Mr J. J. Cocks, G. Doel, Mr K. A. Frame, Mr A. I. French, Mr E. O. Haddock, Mr M. E. Harris, A. D. I. Harris, Mr C J Hodgson, Mr M. D. Kilsby, Mr D. W. Lawton, Mr R. S. Liddington, Mr D. Mitchell, J. O'Brien, Mr C. Parkin, Mr T. Westmacott, Mr B. Woodward.

**Assistant Trainer:** Christian Leech (07880) 788464

**Jockey (NH):** Paul Moloney.

---

## 369 MRS SHEILA LEWIS, Brecon

Postal: **Mill Cottage, Three Cocks, Brecon, Powys, LD3 OSL**
Contacts: **PHONE (01497) 847081 MOBILE (07890) 905089**
**E-MAIL millservices@btinternet.com**

1 **INTERPLEADER,** 10, b g Luso—Braceys Girl (IRE) **W. B. R. Davies**
2 **TRY IT SOMETIME (IRE),** 7, b g Milan—Lead'er Inn (IRE) **W. B. R. Davies**

---

## 370 MR CLIFFORD LINES, Exning

Postal: **Hethersett House, Church House, Exning, Newmarket, Suffolk, CB8 7EH**
Contacts: **PHONE (01638) 608016 FAX (01638) 608016 MOBILE (07980) 120157**
**E-MAIL hethersetthouse@gmail.com**

1 **AARANYOW (IRE),** 7, ch g Compton Place—Cutpurse Moll **Prima Racing Partnership**
2 **PRINCE BALLYGOWEN,** 4, b g Prince Arch (USA)—Ball Gown **Prima Racing Partnership**

**Other Owners:** Ms S. Cawthorn, C. V. Lines.

---

## 371 MR NICK LITTMODEN, Newmarket

Postal: **Cadland Cottage Stables, Moulton Road, Newmarket, Suffolk, CB8 8DU**
Contacts: **MOBILE (07770) 964865**
**E-MAIL nicklittmoden@btinternet.com WEBSITE www.nicklittmoden.com**

1 **ENRICHING (USA),** 7, ch g Lemon Drop Kid (USA)—Popozinha (USA) **Franconson Partners**
2 **KINDLELIGHT STORM (USA),** 5, b g Stormy Atlantic (USA)—Rose of Zollern (IRE) **Kindlelight Ltd, N. Shields & N. Littmoden**
3 **MAGNUS MAXIMUS,** 4, b c Holy Roman Emperor (IRE)—Chanrossa (IRE) **Franconson Partners & Nick Littmoden**
4 **POETIC CHOICE,** 4, b f Byron—Ennobling **A. A. Goodman, L. Stratton, N. Littmoden**
5 **SIR NOTE (FR),** 5, gr g Victory Note (USA)—Niangara (FR) **G. F. Chesneaux**
6 **SPREADABLE (IRE),** 4, br g Duke of Marmalade (IRE)—Spring View **G. F. Chesneaux**

## MR NICK LITTMODEN - Continued

### THREE-YEAR-OLDS

7 **AMAZE ME,** ch f Aqlaam—Princess Miletrian (IRE) **Franconson Partners**
8 **BAKER,** b g Teofilo (IRE)—Meydan Princess (IRE) **Franconson Partners**
9 **BETHNAL GREEN,** ch f Cockney Rebel (IRE)—Exodia **Franconson Partners**
10 **CLOSING,** ch f Compton Place—Rosewood Belle (USA) **Franconson Partners**
11 **DIRACAN (IRE),** br f Alfred Nobel (IRE)—Ikan (IRE) **Mrs Linda Francis**
12 **LITTLE MISS MIGHTY,** b f Mighty—Spia (USA) **Franconson Partners**
13 **ONE LIFE LIVE IT,** b c Holy Roman Emperor (IRE)—Lacandona (USA) **Franconson Partners**
14 **THE LAST MELON,** ch g Sir Percy—Step Fast (USA) **Franconson Partners**
15 **TONGUE TWISTA,** b f Stimulation (IRE)—Lady-Love **Franconson Partners & Nick Littmoden**

### TWO-YEAR-OLDS

16 B c 4/4 Hellvelyn—Amelie Pouliche (FR) (Desert Prince (IRE)) (22857)
17 Ch f 8/3 Kheleyf (USA)—Baddi Heights (FR) (Shirley Heights) (5000) **Franconson Partners**
18 B g 3/4 Kheleyf (USA)—Bella Chica (IRE) (Bigstone (IRE)) (1500) **Franconson Partners**
19 B c 8/2 Aqlaam—Blaenavon (Cadeaux Genereux) (21000) **Unregistered**
20 **BLAZING MIGHTY,** ch f 11/4 Mighty—Exodia (Dr Fong (USA)) (1500) **Franconson Partners**
21 Ch c 11/5 Aqlaam—Ermine (IRE) (Cadeaux Genereux) (22000) **Franconson Partners**
22 B f 10/4 Kheleyf (USA)—Last Romance (IRE) (Last Tycoon) (2000) **Franconson Partners**
23 **LEMONADE MONEY,** b f 13/3 Mighty—Stormy Weather (Nashwan (USA)) (1800) **Franconson Partners**
24 B f 21/1 High Chaparral (IRE)—Marcellinas Angel (Anabaa (USA)) (8000) **Franconson Partners**
25 Ch f 27/3 Bahamian Bounty—Medicea Sidera (Medicean) (20952)
26 **MIGHTY LADY,** ch f 2/2 Mighty—Spia (USA) (Diesis) (800) **Franconson Partners**
27 **MIGHTY MIX,** b g 2/3 Mighty—Heather Mix (Linamix (FR)) **Franconson Partners**
28 B f 8/5 Bahamian Bounty—Naayla (IRE) (Invincible Spirit (IRE)) (11000) **Unregistered**
29 B f 29/4 Nayef (USA)—Pale Blue Eyes (IRE) (Peintre Celebre (USA)) **Franconson Partners**
30 B f 26/2 Paco Boy (IRE)—Phantasmagoria (Fraam) (5000)
31 B c 26/2 Kodiac—Queen Althea (IRE) (Bach (IRE)) (23809)
32 B f 3/2 Aqlaam—Raggiante (IRE) (Rock of Gibraltar (IRE)) (14000) **Franconson Partners**
33 B f 19/3 Aqlaam—West Lorne (USA) (Gone West (USA)) (15000)

**Other Owners:** Mrs D. Curran, Mr D. Curran, Mr Paul Deavin, Mr A. Highfield, Kindlelight Ltd, Mr Nick Littmoden, Mr Nigel Shields.

---

## 372 MR BERNARD LLEWELLYN, Bargoed

Postal: **Ffynonau Duon Farm, Pentwyn, Fochriw, Bargoed, Mid-Glamorgan, CF81 9NP**
Contacts: **PHONE (01685) 841259 FAX (01685) 843838 MOBILE (07971) 233473/(07960) 151083**
**E-MAIL bernard.llewellyn@btopenworld.com**

1 **AAMAN (IRE),** 9, gr g Dubai Destination (USA)—Amellnaa (IRE) **Mr A. James**
2 **ARTY CAMPBELL (IRE),** 5, b g Dylan Thomas (IRE)—Kincob (USA) **Mr A. James**
3 **BOBBY DOVE,** 8, b g Fraam—Flakey Dove **Ms S. A. Howell**
4 **DRUMMOND,** 6, b g Zamindar (USA)—Alrisha (IRE) **Mr D. G. Jones**
5 **EDGE (IRE),** 4, b c Acclamation—Chanter **B. J. Llewellyn**
6 **FILATORE (IRE),** 6, ch g Teofilo (IRE)—Dragnet (IRE) **B. J. Llewellyn**
7 **FLANAGANS FIELD (IRE),** 7, b g Araafa (IRE)—Zvezda (USA) **Mrs E. A. Llewellyn**
8 **FUZZY LOGIC (IRE),** 6, b g Dylan Thomas (IRE)—Gates of Eden (USA) **G. Mills**
9 **GLOBAL THRILL,** 6, b g Big Shuffle (USA)—Goonda **Mr A. James**
10 **GOING NOWHERE FAST (IRE),** 10, b g Exit To Nowhere (USA)—Sister Gabrielle (IRE) **A. J. Williams**
11 **HAMILTON HILL,** 8, b g Groom Dancer (USA)—Loriner's Lass **T. G. Price**
12 **HANSUPFORDETROIT (IRE),** 10, b g Zagreb (USA)—Golden Needle (IRE) **Mr A. James**
13 **JAMES POLLARD (IRE),** 10, ch g Indian Ridge—Manuetti (IRE) **B. J. Llewellyn**
14 **KASHGAR,** 6, b g Hernando (FR)—Miss Katmandu (IRE) **Mr A. James**
15 **KING'S MASQUE,** 9, b g Noverre (USA)—Top Flight Queen **B. J. Llewellyn**
16 **KOZMINA BAY,** 6, b m Notnowcato—Kozmina (IRE) **Mr G. Anstee**
17 **L FRANK BAUM (IRE),** 8, b g Sinndar (IRE)—Rainbow City (IRE) **B. J. Llewellyn**
18 **LET ME IN (IRE),** 5, ch g Pivotal—I Hearyou Knocking (IRE) **B. J. Llewellyn**
19 **LIGHTS OF BROADWAY (IRE),** 9, b m Broadway Flyer (USA)—Supreme Call (IRE) **B. W. Parren**
20 **PANDORICA,** 7, b m Indesatchel (IRE)—Hope Chest **B. J. Llewellyn**
21 **PETRIFY,** 5, b g Rock of Gibraltar (IRE)—Frigid **Wesbry Racing**
22 **SCRIPTURIST,** 6, b g Oratorio (IRE)—Lambroza (IRE) **B. J. Llewellyn**
23 **SHADOW'S BOY,** 6, gr g Norse Dancer (IRE)—Inspired Role VII **G. Mills**
24 **STAG HILL (IRE),** 6, ch g Redback—Counting Blessings **Mr D. P. Maddocks**

## MR BERNARD LLEWELLYN - Continued

25 **SWEET WORLD,** 11, b g Agnes World (USA)—Douce Maison (IRE) **B. J. Llewellyn**
26 **TASTE THE WINE (IRE),** 9, gr g Verglas (IRE)—Azia (IRE) **A. J. Williams**
27 **TIJORI (IRE),** 7, b g Kyllachy—Polish Belle **B. J. Llewellyn**
28 **TORETTO (IRE),** 7, ch g Peintre Celebre (USA)—Petite-D-Argent **B. J. Llewellyn**

**Other Owners:** Mr R. Jasper.

**Assistant Trainer:** J L Llewellyn

**Jockey (flat):** David Probert. **Jockey (NH):** Mark Quinlan. **Conditional:** Robert Williams. **Apprentice:** Robert Williams. **Amateur:** Mr Jordan Williams.

---

## 373 MISS NATALIE LLOYD-BEAVIS, East Garston

Postal: **Parsonage Racing Stables, Newbury Road, East Garston, Hungerford, Berkshire, RG17 7ER**
Contacts: **PHONE (01488) 648347 MOBILE (07768) 117656**
**E-MAIL nlbracing@gmail.com**

1 **DEFTERA FANTUTTE (IRE),** 4, b f Amadeus Wolf—Carranza (IRE) **Mr Y. Mustafa**
2 **EDWARD ELGAR,** 4, ch g Avonbridge—Scooby Dooby Do **R. Eagle**
3 **FARMSHOP BOY,** 4, b g Sagamix (FR)—Littleton Zephir (USA) **M. J. Hills**
4 **FISHERMAN FRANK,** 4, b g Rail Link—Ribbons And Bows (IRE) **Mr T. Suttle**
5 **LEYLAND (IRE),** 6, b g Peintre Celebre (USA)—Lasting Chance (USA) **Mr Y. Mustafa**
6 7, B m Quick Move—Lost Keys (IRE) **Miss N. A. Lloyd-Beavis**
7 **MEYREM ANA,** 5, b m Beat All (USA)—Champagne Lou Lou **Mr S. Lloyd-Beavis**
8 **MUNICH (IRE),** 11, b g Noverre (USA)—Mayara (IRE) **Miss N. A. Lloyd-Beavis**
9 **ROLY TRICKS,** 4, b f Pastoral Pursuits—Freya Tricks **R. Eagle**
10 **UNTIL THE MAN (IRE),** 8, b g Tillerman—Canoe Cove (IRE) **M. J. Hills**
11 **WICKED TARA,** 5, b m Assertive—Tara King **Mr K. Walters**

### TWO-YEAR-OLDS

12 B f 2/5 Sixties Icon—Ishibee (IRE) (Ishiguru (USA)) (1500) **Mr G. B. Watts**
13 B c 3/3 Compton Place—Polar Dawn (Polar Falcon (USA)) (3000) **Mr T. Suttle**

**Jockey (NH):** David Bass. **Apprentice:** Charlie Bennett.

---

## 374 MR ALAN LOCKWOOD, Malton

Postal: **Fleet Cross Farm, Brawby, Malton, North Yorkshire, YO17 6QA**
Contacts: **PHONE (01751) 431796 MOBILE (07747) 002535**

1 **BELLE PEINTURE (FR),** 4, ch f Peintre Celebre (USA)—Grosgrain (USA) **Highgreen Partnership**
2 **PORT VIEW (IRE),** 9, b g Classic Cliche (IRE)—Francie's Treble **A. J. Lockwood**
3 **SAXBY (IRE),** 8, ch g Pastoral Pursuits—Madam Waajib (IRE) **A. J. Lockwood**

**Other Owners:** Mr T. Crawford, Mr J. Richardson, Mr J. Stubbs, Mr Derek Wilson.

---

## 375 MR JOHN E. LONG, Royston

Postal: **Lower Yard, Kings Ride Stables, Baldock Road, Royston, Hertfordshire, SG8 9NN**
Contacts: **MOBILE (07958) 296945/(07815) 186085**
**E-MAIL winalot@aol.com**

1 **BERMACHA,** 10, ch m Bertolini (USA)—Machaera **M. J. Gibbs**
2 **CATIVO CAVALLINO,** 12, ch g Bertolini (USA)—Sea Isle **M. J. Gibbs**
3 **CHANDRAYAAN,** 8, ch g Bertolini (USA)—Muffled (USA) **R. D. John**
4 **CHIPENKO,** 4, gr g Archipenko (USA)—Grey Pearl **Mr R. Favarulo**
5 **GRACEFUL WILLOW,** 5, b m Phoenix Reach (IRE)—Opera Belle **Mrs S. Bambridge**
6 **ICE APPLE,** 7, b m Iceman—Star Apple **Mr & Mrs K. G. Newland**
7 **MICROLIGHT,** 7, b g Sleeping Indian—Skytrial (USA) **R. D. John**
8 **SAIL HOME,** 8, b m Mizzen Mast (USA)—Bristol Channel **Mr P. Foster**
9 **SHEILA'S HEART,** 5, ch g Dubai Destination (USA)—Sefemm **Mr P. Foster**
10 **TRUST ME BOY,** 7, gr g Avonbridge—Eastern Lyric **R. Pearson & J. Pearson**

## MR JOHN E. LONG - Continued

### THREE-YEAR-OLDS

11 **GOLD LEAF,** ch f Kheleyf (USA)—Lefty's Dollbaby (USA) **Downlands Racing**
12 **WILLOW JUBILEE,** b f Champs Elysees—Opera Belle **Mrs S. Bambridge**

**Other Owners:** Mr K. G. Newland, Mrs J. E. Newland, Mr R. J. Pearson, Miss J. L. Pearson, Mrs A. M. Sturges, Mr R. W. Sturges.

**Assistant Trainer:** Miss S Cassidy

---

## 376 MR CHARLIE LONGSDON, Chipping Norton

Postal: **Hull Farm Stables, Stratford Road, Chipping Norton, Oxfordshire, OX7 5QF**
Contacts: **PHONE (08450) 525264 FAX (08450) 525265 MOBILE (07775) 993263**
**E-MAIL charlie@charlielongsdonracing.com WEBSITE www.charlielongsdonracing.com**

1 **A VOS GARDES (FR),** 5, br g Kapgarde (FR)—Miscia Nera (FR) **The Rollright Stones**
2 **APPLE OF OUR EYE,** 5, b g Passing Glance—Apple Anthem **The Tweed Clad Fossils**
3 **ARGOT,** 4, b g Three Valleys (USA)—Tarot Card **C. Longsdon**
4 **ATLANTIC GOLD (IRE),** 5, b br g Robin des Pres (FR)—Marys Isle (IRE) **C. W. Booth & Mark E. Smith**
5 **AZURE FLY (IRE),** 7, br g Blueprint (IRE)—Lady Delight (IRE) **Girls Allowed**
6 **BATTLE BORN,** 6, b g Kayf Tara—Realms of Gold (USA) **D. A. Halsall**
7 **BESTWORK (FR),** 4, bl g Network (GER)—Harmony (FR) **CLS Bloodstock**
8 **CADOUDOFF (FR),** 5, gr g Davidoff (GER)—Hera du Berlais (FR) **The Four Kings**
9 **COOLOGUE (IRE),** 6, b g Helissio (FR)—Scolboa (IRE) **The New Club Partnership**
10 **CRACK OF THUNDER (IRE),** 6, b g September Storm (GER)—Keep Hunting (IRE) **Crack Of Thunder Partnership**
11 **CRAZY PENGUIN (IRE),** 4, b g Milan—Lady Appeal (IRE) **Swanee River Partnership**
12 **DEADLY MOVE (IRE),** 6, b g Scorpion (IRE)—Sounds Attractive (IRE) **R. D. J. Swinburne**
13 **DONT TAKE ME ALIVE,** 6, b g Araafa (IRE)—Up At Dawn **Biddestone Racing Partnership III**
14 **DROP OUT JOE,** 7, ch g Generous (IRE)—La Feuillarde (FR) **The Jesters**
15 **ELY BROWN (IRE),** 10, b g Sunshine Street (USA)—Browneyed Daughter (IRE) **Countrywide Vehicle Rentals Limited**
16 **FRAMPTON (IRE),** 6, b g Presenting—Drumavish Lass (IRE) **Mr R. D. H. Brindle**
17 **GERMANY CALLING (IRE),** 6, b g Germany (USA)—Markir (IRE) **Mr T. Hanlon**
18 **GRANDADS HORSE,** 9, b br g Bollin Eric—Solid Land (FR) **Whites of Coventry Limited**
19 **GREEN BANK (IRE),** 9, b g Morozov (USA)—Queen Polly (IRE) **Mr R. J. Aplin**
20 **GREENLAW,** 9, b g Helissio (FR)—Juris Prudence (IRE) **Mr & Mrs Simon and June Cadzow**
21 **HARRISTOWN,** 5, ch g Bering—New Abbey **Kyuna Memories**
22 **HEATED DEBATE (IRE),** 5, b g Kayf Tara—Liss A Chroi (IRE) **The Jesters**
23 **IN THE GATE (IRE),** 7, b g King's Theatre (IRE)—The Distaff Spy **OE Racing NH Partnership**
24 **JAVA ROSE,** 6, b m Ishiguru (USA)—Mighty Splash **Mildmay Racing & Mark E. Smith**
25 **KALANE (IRE),** 6, b m Kalanisi (IRE)—Fairy Lane (IRE) **P. Murphy**
26 **KILCOOLEY (IRE),** 6, b g Stowaway—Bealaha Essie (IRE) **J. H. & S. M. Wall**
27 **KILFINICHEN BAY (IRE),** 7, b g Westerner—Cailin Deas (IRE) **Cracker Syndicate**
28 **KILLALA QUAY,** 8, b g Karinga Bay—Madam Bijou **Mr Richard & Mrs Susan Perkins**
29 **KITENEY WOOD (IRE),** 5, ch g Layman (USA)—She Runs (FR) **Swanee River Partnership**
30 **LEITH HILL LEGASI,** 6, b m Kahyasi—Leith Hill Star **Mr & Mrs N. F. Maltby**
31 **LONG LUNCH,** 6, b g Kayf Tara—Royal Keel **Battersby, Birchall, Halsall & Vestey**
32 **LONG WAVE (IRE),** 8, b g Milan—Mrs Avery (IRE) **Neysauteur Partnership**
33 **LOOSE CHIPS,** 9, b g Sir Harry Lewis (USA)—Worlaby Rose **Barrels Of Courage**
34 **MAGIC MUSTARD (IRE),** 4, ch g Stowaway—Honey Mustard (IRE) **Magic Mustard Partnership**
35 **MASTERPLAN (IRE),** 5, b g Spadoun (FR)—Eurolucy (IRE) **G. M. MacEchern**
36 **MIDNIGHT SHOT,** 5, b g Midnight Legend—Suave Shot **D. A. Halsall**
37 **NO NO MAC (IRE),** 6, b g Oscar (IRE)—Whatdoyouthinkmac (IRE) **R. Jenner & J. Green**
38 **NO NO MANOLITO (IRE),** 5, b g High Chaparral (IRE)—Dawn Bid (IRE) **R. Jenner & J. Green**
39 **ORANGE NASSAU (FR),** 9, gr g Martaline—Vilaya (FR) **The Ferandlin Peaches**
40 **ORBY'S MAN (IRE),** 6, b g Arcadio (GER)—Gleann Oisin (IRE) **Mr T. Hanlon**
41 **OSTLAND (GER),** 10, b g Lando (GER)—Ost Tycoon (GER) **Mr Richard & Mrs Susan Perkins**
42 **OUR KAEMPFER (IRE),** 6, b g Oscar (IRE)—Gra-Bri (IRE) **Swanee River Partnership**
43 **PENDRA (IRE),** 7, ch g Old Vic—Mariah Rollins (IRE) **J. P. McManus**
44 **PIED DU ROI (IRE),** 5, b g Robin des Pres (FR)—Long Acre **The Pantechnicons II**
45 **PRESENT TREND (IRE),** 6, br m Presenting—Trendy Attire (IRE) **Foxtrot NH Racing Partnership IV**
46 **PROMANCO,** 6, b m Kayf Tara—Shelayly (IRE) **Mrs S. I. Tainton**
47 **PURE STYLE (IRE),** 7, b g Desert Style (IRE)—Pure Fiction **Mr P. J. Curtin**
48 **READY TOKEN (IRE),** 7, gr g Flemensfirth (USA)—Ceol Tire (IRE) **Mr C. S. Horton**
49 **SACROBLEU (FR),** 5, gr g Sacro Saint (FR)—Harpyes (FR) **E. M. G. Roberts**

## MR CHARLIE LONGSDON - Continued

50 **SASSANOVA (FR),** 5, b m Sassanian (USA)—Anglaise (IRE) **Hopeful Half Dozen**
51 **SERGEANT MATTIE (IRE),** 7, b g Naheez (USA)—Glyde Lady (IRE) **Swanee River Partnership**
52 **SHANTOU MAGIC (IRE),** 8, b g Shantou (USA)—Supreme Magical **Owners For Owners: Shantou Magic**
53 **SHEAR ROCK (IRE),** 5, b g Spadoun (FR)—Sleeping Diva (FR) **Jones, Smith & Walsh**
54 **SIMPLY THE WEST (IRE),** 6, b g Westerner—Back To Stay (IRE) **Biddestone Racing Partnership XI**
55 **SPIRIT OF SHANKLY,** 7, ch g Sulamani (IRE)—Lago d'oro **D. A. Halsall**
56 **ST JOHNS POINT (IRE),** 7, b g Darsi (FR)—Dunsford Belle (IRE) **No Boys Allowed**
57 **SUPERIOR FIRE (IRE),** 5, b g Arcadio (GER)—Take Aim **The Stewkley Shindiggers Partnership**
58 **THE APPLEBOBBER,** 5, b g Passing Glance—Miss Crabapple **The Tweed Clad Fossils**
59 **THE FUGITIVE (IRE),** 4, b g Flemensfirth (USA)—Alleygrove Lass (IRE) **Owners For Owners: The Fugitive**
60 **THE OPPIDAN (IRE),** 5, b g Morozov (USA)—Pretty Flamingo (IRE) **OE Racing NH Partnership**
61 **TIDAL WAY (IRE),** 6, gr g Red Clubs (IRE)—Taatof (IRE) **Harold Peachey & Saddleworth Players**
62 **UP TO SOMETHING (FR),** 7, b g Brier Creek (USA)—Evane (FR) **E. M. G. Roberts**
63 **VIVE LE ROI (IRE),** 4, b g Robin des Pres (FR)—Cappard View (IRE) **Mr T. Richens**
64 **WELLS DE LUNE (FR),** 4, b c Irish Wells (FR)—Pepite de Lune (FR) **Swanee River Partnership**
65 **WESTERN MILLER (IRE),** 4, b g Westerner—Definite Miller (IRE) **The Pantechnicons IV**
66 **WILBERDRAGON,** 5, b g Kayf Tara—Swaythe (USA) **R. Jenner & J. Green**
67 **ZARA HOPE (IRE),** 4, b f Stowaway—Agua Caliente (IRE) **Mr M. E. Smith**
68 **ZARAWI (IRE),** 4, b g Marju (IRE)—Zarwala (IRE) **Catchusifyoucan Partnership**

**Other Owners:** Mr D. Abraham, Mr Tareq Al-Mazeedi, Mr Robert Aplin, Mr Hugh Arthur, Mr S. Aspinall, Mr George Bailey, Mr J. G. Bell, Mr Nigel Birch, Mr C. W. Booth, Mr Tim Bostwick, Mr T. Boylan, Mr Richard Brindle, Mr Ian M. Brown, Mr J. Burke, Mr James Burley, Mr R. Byron-Scott, Mr S. Cadzow, Mrs J. Cadzow, Mr John Cantrill, Mr Steve Corcoran, Mr C. K. Crossley Cooke, Mrs R. Doel, Dr Bridget Drew, Mr John Drew, Mrs Cax du Pon, Mr Ian Dunbar, Mr Tim Dykes, Mr H. Fentum, Mr Nicholas Finegold, Mr Ivan Howard Goldsmith, Mr Mark Goodall, Mrs J. Green, Mr Robert Greenhill, Mr J. N. Greenley, Mr M. W. Gregory, Mr Jonathan Halsall, Mr B. R. Halsall, Mr P. V. Harris, Ms R. J. Harris, Mr R. D. Hawkins, Mr W. John Henderson, Mr S. Hill, Mr Dev Hill, Mrs H. J. Hoffman, Mr Jon Hughes, Ms R. Jenner, Mr R. S. Johnson, Mr Colin Jones, Mrs Louise King, Mrs Sarah Jane Lavan, Mr O. Lee, Mr Charles Liverton, Mr J. K. Llewellyn, Mr Charlie Longsdon, Mrs S. Longsdon, Mrs N. F. Maltby, Mr N. F. Maltby, Mr C. Marriott, Mr David Mason, Mrs Sue Morley, Mr R. D. Nicholas, Dr M. M. Ogilvy, Mrs H. Pauling, Mr H. Peachey, Mr N. Pearse, Mr R. A. H. Perkins, Mrs R. S. Perkins, Mrs Penny Perriss, Mr B. P. Roberts, Mr John Roddan, Mr Hugh Shapter, Mr W. G. Shaw, Mr Mark E. Smith, Mr S. Spencer-Jones, Mrs S. Spencer-Jones, Mrs John Steel, Mr Paul Tuson, Mr J. H. Wall, Mrs S. M. Wall, Mrs Caren Walsh, Mr Richard Wilkin, Mr F. Wintle.

**Assistant Trainer:** David John Jeffreys

**Jockey (NH):** Noel Fehily. **Conditional:** Charlie Deutsch. **Amateur:** Miss Claire Hart.

---

## 377 MR DANIEL MARK LOUGHNANE, Butterton

Postal: **Butterton Racing Stables, Park Road, Butterton, Newcastle, Staffordshire, ST5 4DZ**
Contacts: **MOBILE (07805) 531021**

1 **APACHE GLORY (USA),** 7, b br m Cherokee Run (USA)—Jumeirah Glory (USA) **J. Stimpson**
2 **CANDY HOUSE GIRL (USA),** 5, b m Hard Spun (USA)—Princess Mitterand (USA) **J. Stimpson**
3 **CANTANKEROUS,** 4, b g Myboycharlie (IRE)—Akhira **Ian O'Connor & Clare Loughnane**
4 **COILLTE CAILIN (IRE),** 5, b m Oratorio (IRE)—Forest Walk (IRE) **Mr P. Moran**
5 **DILETTA TOMMASA (IRE),** 5, ch m Dylan Thomas (IRE)—Chronicle **J. Stimpson**
6 **DISCO DAVE (IRE),** 7, ch g Dalakhani (IRE)—Amoureux (USA) **Over The Moon Racing IV**
7 **FOR SHIA AND LULA (IRE),** 6, b g Majestic Missile (IRE)—Jack-N-Jilly (IRE) **Over The Moon Racing IV**
8 **GOLDEN SANDSTORM (IRE),** 6, ch g Golden Tornado (IRE)—Killoughey Fairy (IRE) **Mr R. M. Brilley**
9 **JUMBO PRADO (USA),** 6, gr ro g El Prado (IRE)—Sant Elena **J. Stimpson**
10 **LES GAR GAN (IRE),** 4, b f Iffraaj—Story **Mr J. P. Evitt**
11 **LOGANS LAD (IRE),** 5, b g Baltic King—Lulu Island **Mr Ian O'Connor**
12 **MATRAASH (USA),** 9, b h Elusive Quality (USA)—Min Alhawa (USA) **Over The Moon Racing**
13 **POLVERE D'ORO,** 5, b g Revoque (IRE)—Dusty Anne (IRE) **Mr P. R. D'Amato**
14 **PRIME EXHIBIT,** 10, b g Selkirk (USA)—First Exhibit **Mr R. M. Brilley**
15 **ROAD MAP (IRE),** 4, b g Saville Road—Lauren Eria **Mrs C. M. Loughnane**
16 **SENOR GEORGE (IRE),** 8, b g Traditionally (USA)—Mrs St George (IRE) **The Batham Boys**
17 **STANLOW,** 5, b g Invincible Spirit (IRE)—Ghazal (USA) **Mrs C. M. Loughnane**
18 **THE FIRM (IRE),** 6, b g Acclamation—Aspen Falls (IRE) **Mr D. S. Allan**
19 **UTMOST REGARDS,** 4, b c Green Desert (USA)—Utmost (IRE) **Ms A. Quinn**
20 **VERUS DELICIA (IRE),** 6, b m Chineur (FR)—Ribbon Glade (UAE) **Mr R. M. Brilley**
21 **YOURINTHEWILL (USA),** 7, ch g Aragorn (IRE)—Lenarue (USA) **Over The Moon Racing II**
22 **ZED CANDY (FR),** 12, b g Medicean—Intrum Morshaan (IRE) **J. Stimpson**
23 **ZED CANDY GIRL,** 5, ch m Sakhee's Secret—Musical Twist (USA) **J. Stimpson**

## MR DANIEL MARK LOUGHNANE - Continued

### THREE-YEAR-OLDS

24 **BINKY BLUE (IRE),** b f Approve (IRE)—Sabander Bay (USA) **The Batham Boys**
25 Ch g Monsieur Bond (IRE)—Floods of Tears **B. Kirby**
26 **ON A WHIM,** b f Tamayuz—Love Me Tender **Mr R. M. Brilley**
27 **STARLIGHT BANNER (IRE),** b f Starspangledbanner (AUS)—Dromod Mour (IRE) **Mr J. J. McGarry**
28 **TREASURY NOTES (IRE),** b c Lope de Vega (IRE)—Elegant As Well (IRE) **Ms A. Quinn**

### TWO-YEAR-OLDS

29 **ALWAYS ENDEAVOUR,** b f 7/4 Amadeus Wolf—Anaya (Tobougg (IRE)) (761) **Mr Ian O'Connor**
30 B f 19/4 Multiplex—Dockside Strike (Docksider (USA)) (8095) **Mr D. S. Allan**
31 **ORMANUMPS (IRE),** b c 16/2 Elnadim (USA)—Tawjeeh (Haafhd) **Mr R. M. Brilley**
32 B c 7/4 Thousand Words—Sombreffe (Polish Precedent (USA)) (9523) **Live In Hope Partnership**
33 **SOMEPINK (IRE),** b f 22/4 Lilbourne Lad (IRE)—Cloonkeary (In The Wings) (3174) **Mr R. M. Brilley**

**Other Owners:** K. J. Corcoran, B. Dunn, S. P. Hackney, Mr M. O. Hough, Mr A. T. Pierce, Mr C. E. Weare.

---

## 378 MR SHAUN LYCETT, Cheltenham

Postal: **Church Farm, Little Rissington, Cheltenham, Gloucestershire, GL54 2ND**
Contacts: **PHONE (01451) 824143 MOBILE (07788) 100894**
**E-MAIL trainer@bourtonhillracing.co.uk WEBSITE www.bourtonhillracing.co.uk**

1 **ALL THE WINDS (GER),** 10, ch g Samum (GER)—All Our Luck (GER) **Nicholls Family**
2 **ARTISAN,** 7, ch g Medicean—Artisia (IRE) **S. Lycett**
3 **DARROUN (IRE),** 7, gr g Dalakhani (IRE)—Darayka (FR) **Exors of the Late Mr P. Grocott**
4 **EXCELLENT PUCK (IRE),** 5, b g Excellent Art—Puck's Castle **Exors of the Late Mr P. Grocott**
5 **FADE TO GREY (IRE),** 11, gr g Aljabr (USA)—Aly McBear (USA) **Worcester Racing Club**
6 **GOODACRES GARDEN (IRE),** 8, b g Oscar (IRE)—Living A Dream (IRE) **D Gilbert, G Wills**
7 **HARVEST MIST (IRE),** 7, ch m Captain Rio—Thaw **Mr C. C. Buckingham**
8 **KALAMILL (IRE),** 8, b g Kalanisi (IRE)—Desert Pageant (IRE) **L & M Atkins**
9 **NUTCRACKER PRINCE,** 4, b g Rail Link—Plum Fairy **D Gilbert, M Lawrence, A Bruce**
10 **OUR GOLDEN GIRL,** 5, ch m Dutch Art—Nemorosa **The Golden Boys Partnership**
11 **OVERRIDER,** 5, b g Cockney Rebel (IRE)—Fustaan (IRE) **L & M Atkins**
12 **PENSNETT BAY,** 10, ch g Karinga Bay—Balmoral Princess **Mr H. S. Maan**
13 **SCOTSBROOK LEGEND,** 7, b m Midnight Legend—Scots Brook Terror **Mr P. E. T. Price**
14 6, Br g Alflora (IRE)—Tia Marnie **S. Lycett**
15 **TRAM EXPRESS (FR),** 11, ch g Trempolino (USA)—Molly Dance (FR) **Mr J. Wailes**
16 **WINDY WRITER (IRE),** 5, b br g Rudimentary (USA)—Hardabout (IRE) **Worcester Racing Club**

### THREE-YEAR-OLDS

17 B g Rainbow High—Scots Brook Terror
18 **VICARAGE GOLD,** b f Kheleyf (USA)—Kyleene **The Golden Boys Partnership**

**Other Owners:** Mr L. Atkins, Mrs M. Atkins, Mr D. R. Gilbert, M. P. Hill, Mr M. Lawrence, Mr M. Lovett, Mr R. Nicholls, Mrs E. Nicholls, Mr M. White, Mr G. Wills.

---

## 379 MR GER LYONS, Dunsany

Postal: **Glenburnie Stables, Kiltale, Dunsany, Co. Meath, Ireland**
Contacts: **PHONE (00353) 46 9025666 FAX (00353) 46 9025666**
**E-MAIL office@gerlyons.ie WEBSITE www.gerlyons.ie**

1 **ANGEL OF JOY (IRE),** 4, gr g Dark Angel (IRE)—Moy Joy (IRE) **Moyville Racing Syndicate**
2 **BRENDAN BRACKAN (IRE),** 6, b g Big Bad Bob (IRE)—Abeyr **Qatar Racing Limited**
3 **BURN THE BOATS (IRE),** 6, br g Big Bad Bob (IRE)—Forever Phoenix **Mr D. T. Spratt & L. Lyons**
4 **CHAPTER SEVEN,** 6, ch g Excellent Art—My First Romance **Qatar Racing Limited**
5 **CHOPIN (GER),** 5, b h Santiago (GER)—Caucasienne (FR) **Qatar Racing Limited**
6 **CRAFTED MASTERY (IRE),** 4, b f Mastercraftsman (IRE)—Pelican Waters (IRE) **Miceal Sammon**
7 **FOG OF WAR,** 4, b c Azamour (IRE)—Cut Short (USA) **Qatar Racing Limited**
8 **GREEK CANYON (IRE),** 6, gr g Moss Vale (IRE)—Lazaretta (IRE) **S. Jones**
9 **LAT HAWILL (IRE),** 4, b c Invincible Spirit (IRE)—Arbella **Qatar Racing Limited**
10 **PHANTOM NAVIGATOR (USA),** 4, gr g Henrythenavigator (USA)—Minicolony (USA) **S. Jones**
11 **PIRI WANGO (IRE),** 6, ch g Choisir (AUS)—Zoldan **Mr D. T. Spratt**

## MR GER LYONS - Continued

**12 PRAIRIE ROSE (GER),** 4, b f Exceed And Excel (AUS)—Prairie Lilli (GER) **Pearl Bloodstock Limited**
**13 ROHERYN (IRE),** 4, b f Galileo (IRE)—La Chunga (USA) **Qatar Racing Limited**
**14 TENNESSEE WILDCAT (IRE),** 5, b g Kheleyf (USA)—Windbeneathmywings (IRE) **S. Jones**
**15 THIRD DIMENSION,** 4, b g Dubawi (IRE)—Round The Cape **S. Jones**
**16 THIRTEEN DIAMONDS (IRE),** 4, b g Diamond Green (FR)—Latin Lace **Mr Declan Landy**
**17 TOCCATA BLUE (IRE),** 5, gr g Verglas (IRE)—Jinxy Jill **D. Nolan & L. Lyons**
**18 TRINITY FORCE (IRE),** 4, ch g Iffraaj—Nasharaat (IRE) **S. Jones**
**19 UNREQUITED (IRE),** 4, b c Authorized (IRE)—Superfonic (FR) **Tess Mahon**
**20 UNSINKABLE (IRE),** 5, gr g Verglas (IRE)—Heart's Desire (IRE) **Spratt / Lyons**

## THREE-YEAR-OLDS

**21 AINIPPE (IRE),** b f Captain Rio—Imitation **Qatar Racing Limited**
**22 ARCTIC LIGHT,** b g Iffraaj—Dance of Light (USA) **S. Jones**
**23 ARDHOOMEY (IRE),** b c Dark Angel (IRE)—Moy Joy (IRE) **Moyville Racing Syndicate**
**24 AZZURI,** b g Azamour (IRE)—Folly Lodge **Mr Sean Jones & Mr David Spratt**
**25 BACKSTAIRS BOUNDER (IRE),** b g Big Bad Bob (IRE)—Ski For Me (IRE) **Anamoine Limited**
**26 BAIRNS AT BAY (IRE),** b f Big Bad Bob (IRE)—Convent Girl (IRE) **Anamoine Limited**
**27 BEHIND BARS (IRE),** b g Big Bad Bob (IRE)—Daliyra (IRE) **Anamoine Limited**
**28 BERTIE LE BELGE (IRE),** b g Big Bad Bob (IRE)—Ski For Gold **Anamoine Limited**
**29 BROWN BEE (IRE),** b f Camacho—Amber Tide (IRE) **Qatar Racing Limited**
**30 BUENOS Y BOBOS (IRE),** b g Big Bad Bob (IRE)—Spanish Lady (IRE) **Anamoine Limited**
**31 CAPE AQRAAN,** b c Cape Cross (IRE)—Aqraan **S. Jones**
**32 CAPE WOLFE,** b g Piccolo—Cape Wood **S. Jones**
**33 CAPPELLA SANSEVERO,** b c Showcasing—Madam President **Qatar Racing Limited**
**34 CHENEGA BAY,** b c Kodiac—Risk A Look **S. Jones**
**35 CONVERGENCE (IRE),** b c Cape Cross (IRE)—Zahoo (IRE) **Mr Vincent Gaul**
**36 CREVASSE (IRE),** b g Clodovil (IRE)—Abysse **S. Jones**
**37 DANDYLEEKIE (IRE),** b c Dandy Man (IRE)—Cockaleekie (USA) **S. Jones**
**38 DEEP CHALLENGER (IRE),** b c Galileo (IRE)—Healing Music (FR) **Qatar Racing Limited**
**39 DOCALI (IRE),** b c Dark Angel (IRE)—Housekeeping **Spratt / Holland / McCarthy / McDowell**
**40 ENDLESS DRAMA (IRE),** b c Lope de Vega (IRE)—Desert Drama (IRE) **Qatar Racing Limited**
**41 GAME SET DASH (USA),** b c Arch (USA)—Proudeyes (GER) **Qatar Racing Limited**
**42 INTISARI (IRE),** b g Intikhab (USA)—Golden Rose (GER) **S. Jones**
**43** B g Makfi—Jalousie (IRE) **Qatar Racing Limited**
**44** B c Rip Van Winkle (IRE)—Lake Windermere (IRE) **S. Jones**
**45 MERRYN MOO (IRE),** b f Dark Angel (IRE)—Hemasree (IRE) **Mrs Lynne Lyons**
**46 METHODOLOGY (FR),** gr g Silver Frost (IRE)—Desert Nights (IRE) **Mr Vincent Gaul**
**47** B f Approve (IRE)—Miss Corinne **Qatar Racing Limited**
**48 NINGXAI (IRE),** b g Fast Company (IRE)—Valluga (IRE) **Mr Sean Jones & Mr David Spratt**
**49 PLUS CA CHANGE (IRE),** b f Invincible Spirit (IRE)—Allannah Abu **Airlie & Ennistown Studs**
**50 REALT EILE (IRE),** b f Dark Angel (IRE)—Line Ahead (IRE) **Mrs Clodagh Mitchell**
**51 SACRIFICIAL (IRE),** ch c Showcasing—Armanda (GER) **Qatar Racing Limited**
**52 SEA OF TREASURE (IRE),** b c Iffraaj—Go Lovely Rose (IRE) **Qatar Racing Limited**
**53 SLOPESTYLE (IRE),** gr g Dark Angel (IRE)—Kayoko (IRE) **S. Jones**
**54 SNOW BLITZ (IRE),** b g Approve (IRE)—Headborough Lass (IRE) **S. Jones**
**55 THE ICE MEISTER (IRE),** gr g Dark Angel (IRE)—Cape Cod (IRE) **S. Jones**
**56 TIGER MOON (IRE),** b c Iffraaj—Elutrah **S. Jones**
**57 URBESTCHANCE (IRE),** b f Zebedee—Blusienka (IRE) **RMS Syndicate**
**58 VALE DO SOL (IRE),** b c Vale of York (IRE)—Condilessa (IRE) **S. Jones**
**59 ZUBERI (IRE),** b br g Zebedee—Double Precedent **S. Jones**

## TWO-YEAR-OLDS

**60** B c 20/3 Kodiac—Becuille (IRE) (Redback) (55555) **S. Jones**
**61** B c 23/4 Zebedee—Bobby Jane (Diktat) (21428) **S. Jones**
**62** B c 12/3 Showcasing—Carsulae (IRE) (Marju (IRE)) (66666) **S. Jones**
**63** B c 24/2 Equiano (FR)—First Eclipse (IRE) (Fayruz) (26666) **S. Jones**
**64** B f 9/2 Elusive Quality (USA)—Fleeting Memory (Danehill (USA)) **Qatar Racing Limited**
**65** Ch c 15/2 Zoffany (IRE)—Frabjous (Pivotal) (47619) **Jones / Spratt**
**66** B c 10/3 Lord Shanakill (USA)—Goodwood March (Foxhound (USA)) (40000) **Qatar Racing Limited**
**67** B c 5/5 Rip Van Winkle (IRE)—I Hearyou Knocking (IRE) (Danehill Dancer (IRE)) (104761) **Qatar Racing Limited**
**68** B c 29/4 Equiano (FR)—Langs Lash (IRE) (Noverre (USA)) (55000) **S. Jones**
**69** Ch c 20/4 Danehill Dancer (IRE)—Madaen (USA) (Nureyev (USA)) (38000) **S. Jones**
**70** B c 11/2 Holy Roman Emperor (IRE)—Mango Groove (IRE) (Unfuwain (USA)) **Mr Jim McDonald**
**71** B c 18/5 Poet's Voice—Martha (IRE) (Alhaarth (IRE)) (15000) **S. Jones**
**72** B c 7/4 Lilbourne Lad (IRE)—Nisriyna (IRE) (Intikhab (USA)) (59523) **S. Jones**

## MR GER LYONS - Continued

**73** B c 7/3 Jeremy (USA)—Poulkovo (IRE) (Sadler's Wells (USA)) (40000) **S. Jones**
**74** B c 16/5 Zebedee—Primo Supremo (IRE) (Primo Dominie) (36507) **S. Jones**
**75** B c 10/4 Showcasing—Romantic Destiny (Dubai Destination (USA)) (26000) **S. Jones**
**76** B c 1/4 Azamour (IRE)—Sceal Nua (IRE) (Iffraaj) **Mrs Clodagh Mitchell**
**77** B c 18/2 Zebedee—Southern Barfly (USA) (Southern Halo (USA)) (55000) **S. Jones**
**78** B c 15/3 Vale of York (IRE)—Special Touch (IRE) (Spinning World (USA)) (28571) **S. Jones**
**79** Ch c 12/2 Lope de Vega (IRE)—Super Supreme (IND) (Zafonic (USA)) (59523) **Jones / Spratt**
**80** B c 14/1 Kodiac—Supreme Seductress (IRE) (Montjeu (IRE)) (59523) **Qatar Racing Limited**
**81** Ch c 15/2 Roderic O'Connor (IRE)—Tea Chest (IRE) (In The Wings) (33000) **S. Jones**
**82** Gr f 4/3 Dark Angel (IRE)—That's Hot (IRE) (Namid) **Mr John Burke**
**83** B f 27/3 Showcasing—Trinny (Rainbow Quest (USA)) (38095) **Qatar Racing Limited**
**84** B c 20/3 Big Bad Bob (IRE)—Undercover Glamour (USA) (Kingmambo (USA)) (20634) **S. Jones**
**85** B c 12/4 Approve (IRE)—Violet Flame (IRE) (Kalanisi (IRE)) (15872) **S. Jones**
**86** Ch c 30/3 Zoffany (IRE)—Yaky Romani (IRE) (Victory Note (USA)) (51586) **S. Jones**

**Assistant Trainers:** Shane Lyons, Andrew Duff

**Jockey (flat):** Gary Carroll, Colin Keane.

---

## 380 MR JOHN MACKIE, Church Broughton

Postal: **The Bungalow, Barton Blount, Church Broughton, Derby, Derbyshire, DE65 5AN**
Contacts: **PHONE (01283) 585604/585603 FAX (01283) 585603 MOBILE (07799) 145283**
**E-MAIL jmackie@bartonblount.freeserve.co.uk WEBSITE www.johnmackieracing.co.uk**

1 **ARIZONA JOHN (IRE),** 10, b g Rahy (USA)—Preseli (IRE) **Derbyshire Racing**
2 **AVAILABLE (IRE),** 6, b m Moss Vale (IRE)—Divert (IRE) **Derbyshire Racing V**
3 **BARTON BLOUNT,** 6, br g Beat All (USA)—Katie Savage **Mrs E. M. Mackie**
4 **CAPTAIN SWIFT (IRE),** 4, br g Captain Rio—Grannys Reluctance (IRE) **Mrs S. P. Adams**
5 **HALLSTATT (IRE),** 9, ch g Halling (USA)—Last Resort **NSU Leisure & Mrs Carolyn Seymour**
6 **HURRY HOME POPPA (IRE),** 5, b g Holy Roman Emperor (IRE)—My Renee (USA) **Mr D. Ward**
7 **ILLUSTRIOUS FOREST,** 7, ch g Shinko Forest (IRE)—Illustre Inconnue (USA) **Derbyshire Racing VII**
8 **IMPECCABILITY,** 5, b m Lucky Story (USA)—Impeccable Guest (IRE) **Derbyshire Racing IV**
9 **KANTARA CASTLE (IRE),** 4, b g Baltic King—Arbitration (IRE) **Derbyshire Racing III**
10 **KEEP CALM,** 5, b g War Chant (USA)—Mayaar (USA) **Derbyshire Racing VI**
11 **KNIGHT IN PURPLE,** 11, b g Sir Harry Lewis (USA)—Cerise Bleue (FR) **A J Wall, G Hicks & N Hooper**
12 **MARMAS,** 6, ch g Sir Percy—Kitabaat (IRE) **Mr G. R. Shelton**
13 **OFF THE PULSE,** 5, b g Araafa (IRE)—Off By Heart **G. B. Maher**
14 **RIVER PURPLE,** 8, b g Bollin Eric—Cerise Bleue (FR) **Sotby Farming Company Limited**
15 **ROCK SONG,** 6, b g Rock of Gibraltar (IRE)—Jackie's Opera (FR) **Sotby Farming Company Limited**
16 **SAINT THOMAS (IRE),** 8, b g Alhaarth (IRE)—Aguilas Perla (IRE) **P. Riley**
17 **STREAM OF LIGHT,** 4, b f Multiplex—Flawspar **R. Kent**

### THREE-YEAR-OLDS

18 **INFLEXIBALL,** b f Refuse To Bend (IRE)—Sphere (IRE) **Derbyshire Racing II**
19 **ROBBEN,** b g Dutch Art—Little Greenbird **Sotby Farming Company Limited**
20 **SECOND GUEST,** b f Refuse To Bend (IRE)—Impeccable Guest (IRE) **Derbyshire Racing VIII**

**Other Owners:** S. P. Adams, Mr G. B. Hicks, Mr N. P. Hooper, NSU Leisure Ltd, Mr D. R. Penman, Mrs C. Seymour, A. J. Wall.

---

## 381 MR ALAN MACTAGGART, Hawick

Postal: **Wells, Denholm, Hawick, Roxburghshire, TD9 8TD**
Contacts: **PHONE (01450) 870060 MOBILE (07711) 200445 / (07907) 924602**
**E-MAIL alan@mac060.plus.com**

1 **ROYAL MACKINTOSH,** 14, b g Sovereign Water (FR)—Quick Quote **Mrs A. H. Mactaggart**

**Assistant Trainer:** Mrs M. A. Mactaggart

## 382 MR BRUCE MACTAGGART, Hawick

Postal: **Greendale, Hawick, Roxburghshire, TD9 7LH**
Contacts: **PHONE/FAX (01450) 372086 MOBILE (07764) 159852/(07718) 920072**
**E-MAIL brucemact@btinternet.com**

1 **QUEENS REGATTA (IRE),** 6, b m King's Theatre (IRE)—Friendly Craic (IRE) **Greendale Racing Syndicate**
2 **RED TANBER (IRE),** 12, ch g Karinga Bay—Dreamy Desire **Hugh T. Redhead**
3 5, B m Flemensfirth (USA)—Water Stratford (IRE) **Greendale Racing Syndicate**

### THREE-YEAR-OLDS

4 B f Robin des Champs (FR)—Buffy **K. Rennie**
5 B f King's Theatre (IRE)—Daisies Adventure (IRE) **D. MacTaggart**
6 B f King's Theatre (IRE)—Water Stratford (IRE) **Hugh T. Redhead**

**Other Owners:** Mrs Frances Godson, Mrs Hilary Mactaggart, Mr Hugh T. Redhead.

**Assistant Trainer:** Mrs H. Mactaggart

---

## 383 MR PETER MADDISON, Skewsby

Postal: **5 West End Cottages, Skewsby, York, YO61 4SG**
Contacts: **PHONE (01347) 888385**

1 **BATTLEDANCER,** 9, b g Baryshnikov (AUS)—Cede Nullis **P. Maddison**
2 **MINDEN DAWN,** 9, gr m Baryshnikov (AUS)—Minden Rose **P. Maddison**
3 **SGT BULL BERRY,** 8, b g Alflora (IRE)—Cede Nullis **P. Maddison**

---

## 384 MR MICHAEL MADGWICK, Denmead

Postal: **Forest Farm, Forest Road, Denmead, Waterlooville, Hampshire, PO7 6UA**
Contacts: **PHONE/FAX (02392) 258313 MOBILE (07835) 964969**

1 **COMEDY HOUSE,** 7, b g Auction House (USA)—Kyle Akin **Los Leader**
2 **DARK TSARINA (IRE),** 4, b f Soviet Star (USA)—Dark Raider (IRE) **Recycled Products Limited**
3 **MACK'S SISTER,** 8, ch m Pastoral Pursuits—Linda's Schoolgirl (IRE) **Recycled Products Limited**
4 **MANHATTAN MEAD,** 5, ch g Central Park (IRE)—Honey Nut **Mrs L. N. Harmes, K. McCormack & M. Madgwick**
5 **MULTITASK,** 5, b g Multiplex—Attlongglast **Mrs L. N. Harmes**
6 **SHANTOU BREEZE (IRE),** 8, b m Shantou (USA)—Homersmare (IRE) **M. J. Madgwick**
7 **WARBOND,** 7, ch g Monsieur Bond (IRE)—Pick A Nice Name **M. J. Madgwick**

### THREE-YEAR-OLDS

8 **JERSEY BULL (IRE),** b g Clodovil (IRE)—Chaguaramas (IRE) **Mrs S. G. Bunney**
9 **TOMMYS GEAL,** b f Halling (USA)—Steel Free (IRE) **Recycled Products Limited**
10 **TOP POCKET,** b g Royal Applause—Movie Mogul **Recycled Products Limited**

### TWO-YEAR-OLDS

11 B g 7/4 Champs Elysees—Glorious Dreams (USA) (Honour And Glory (USA)) (4000) **Mr J. O'Donnell**
12 B g 10/6 Alkaased (USA)—Leading Star (Motivator) **Recycled Products Limited**
13 Ch f 27/3 Sixties Icon—Leleyf (IRE) (Kheleyf (USA)) **Mr P. Taplin**
14 **MULTIGIFTED,** b f 2/4 Multiplex—Attlongglast (Groom Dancer (USA)) **Mrs L. N. Harmes**
15 Ch g 13/3 Sakhee's Secret—Nom de La Rosa (IRE) (Oratorio (IRE)) **Saloop Ltd**

**Other Owners:** Mrs L. N. Harmes, Mr M. Madgwick, Mr K. McCormack, Mr Robert Oliver, Mr T. Smith, Mr Peter Taplin.

**Assistant Trainer:** David Madgwick

**Jockey (flat):** George Baker, Adam Kirby. **Jockey (NH):** Marc Goldstein.

## 385 MRS HEATHER MAIN, Wantage

Postal: **Kingston Common Farm, Kingston Lisle, Wantage, Oxfordshire, OX12 9QT**
Contacts: **PHONE (01367) 820124 FAX (01367) 820125**
**E-MAIL heather.main@hotmail.com WEBSITE www.heathermainracing.com**

1 **CHILDESPLAY,** 4, ch f Byron—Parting Gift **Wetumpka Racing & Andrew Knott**
2 **HECTOR'S CHANCE,** 6, ch g Byron—Fleur A Lay (USA) **Mr M. Scott Russell**
3 **TICINESE,** 5, b g Lucarno (USA)—Maidwell **R P Foden & Colin Waugh**

### TWO-YEAR-OLDS

4 **ARAGON KNIGHT,** b c 23/2 Kheleyf (USA)—Midnight Allure (Aragon) (16000) **Mr & Mrs D. R. Guest**
5 Ch f 1/4 Mount Nelson—Follow My Dream (Kyllachy) (1500)

**Other Owners:** R. P. Foden, Mr D. R. Guest, Mr A. Knott, Mrs H. S. Main, J. P. M. Main, Mr C. M. Waugh.

---

## 386 MRS JANE MAKIN, Lumby

Postal: **Fryston Lodge Farm, Off A63, South Milford, Leeds, North Yorkshire, LS25 5JE**

1 **OOJAR,** 11, b g Kayf Tara—Madame La Claire **Mr R. G. Makin**

**Assistant Trainer:** Mr R. G. Makin

---

## 387 MR PETER MAKIN, Marlborough

Postal: **Bonita Racing Stables, Ogbourne Maisey, Marlborough, Wiltshire, SN8 1RY**
Contacts: **PHONE (01672) 512973 FAX (01672) 514166 MOBILE (07836) 217825**
**E-MAIL hq@petermakin-racing.com WEBSITE www.petermakin-racing.com**

1 **CAPTAIN RYAN,** 4, b g Captain Gerrard (IRE)—Ryan's Quest (IRE) **Og Partnership**
2 **DARK PHANTOM (IRE),** 4, b g Dark Angel (IRE)—Stoneware **Mrs J. I. Simpson**
3 **DREAM IMPOSSIBLE (IRE),** 4, b f Iffraaj—Romea **Mrs J. N. Humphreys**
4 **FINDHORN MAGIC,** 4, b f Kyllachy—Enchanted Princess **Mr R. P. Marchant**
5 **KNAVE OF CLUBS (IRE),** 6, b g Red Clubs (IRE)—Royal Bounty (IRE) **Mr J. P. Carrington**
6 **KOHARU,** 5, b gr m Ishiguru (USA)—Vellena **Keith & Brian Brackpool**
7 **LUNAR LIMELIGHT,** 10, b g Royal Applause—Moon Magic **Mrs P. J. Makin**
8 **MORACHE MUSIC,** 7, b g Sleeping Indian—Enchanted Princess **R P Marchant D M Ahier Mrs E Lee**
9 **SIR TYTO (IRE),** 7, b g Fruits of Love (USA)—Sophie May **Mr WH & Mrs Jennifer Simpson**
10 **SPIDER LILY,** 4, b f Sleeping Indian—Scarlett Ribbon **Thoroughbred Racing Syndicate VI**
11 **SUITSUS,** 4, b g Virtual—Point Perfect **Suitsus Partnership**
12 **UNISON (IRE),** 5, b g Jeremy (USA)—Easter Song (USA) **Mr J. P. Carrington**
13 **WORDISMYBOND,** 6, b g Monsieur Bond (IRE)—La Gessa **T. W. Wellard & Partners**

### THREE-YEAR-OLDS

14 B f Fast Company (IRE)—Akariyda (IRE) **P. J. Makin**
15 **DRUOT,** b c Champs Elysees—Trick of Ace (USA) **R. P. Marchant & Paul Lee**
16 **ENTENTE,** b g Mawatheeq (USA)—Amarullah (FR) **Gerald Moss & Partners**
17 **JOHN JOINER,** b g Captain Gerrard (IRE)—Nigella **WH Simpson A Lomax & Partners**
18 **LUCY THE PAINTER (IRE),** b f Excellent Art—Royal Bounty (IRE) **Mr J. P. Carrington**
19 **MILLY ROYALE,** b f Royal Applause—Milly Fleur **Gerald Moss & Mrs P. J. Makin**
20 **MISS MITTENS,** b f Shirocco (GER)—River of Silence (IRE) **Mrs J. I. Simpson**
21 Ch f Assertive—Shustraya

### TWO-YEAR-OLDS

22 **SILVER GHOST (IRE),** br gr c 15/4 Dark Angel (IRE)—
Aqualina (IRE) (King's Theatre (IRE)) (26000) **Mr W. H. Simpson**

**Other Owners:** D. M. Ahier, B. A. W. Brackpool, K. Brackpool, Mr K. A. Carter, H. J. W. Davies, M. H. Holland, R. Kent, Mr P. A. Lee, Mr A. R. A. Lomax, The Countess Of Lonsdale, Mrs S. C. Lynch, Mr S. Marchant, Mr B. Mortimer, Mr G. Moss, Thoroughbred Racing Limited, T. W. Wellard.

**Jockey (flat):** Steve Drowne, Seb Sanders.

## 388 MRS ALYSON MALZARD, Jersey

Postal: **Les Etabl'yes, Grosnez Farm, St Ouen, Jersey, JE3 2AD**
Contacts: **PHONE (01534) 483773 MOBILE (07797) 738128**
**E-MAIL malzardracing@gmail.com**

1 **COUNTRY BLUE (FR),** 6, bl g Country Reel (USA)—Exica (FR) **Tony Taylor**
2 **FOURNI (IRE),** 6, ch m Rakti—Eckbeag (USA) **Joan Lowery**
3 **JACKPOT,** 5, b m Avonbridge—Strat's Quest **Phil Banfield & John Hackett**
4 **KERSIVAY,** 9, b g Royal Applause—Lochmaddy **Fast & Furious Racing**
5 **ORMER,** 4, b f Kyllachy—Authoritative **Pat & Trevor Gallienne**
6 **PAS D'ACTION,** 7, ch g Noverre (USA)—Bright Vision **Jim Jamouneau**
7 **PASSIONATE AFFAIR (IRE),** 4, ch g Broken Vow (USA)—Charmgoer (USA) **Tony Taylor**
8 **REACH OUT,** 7, ch g Phoenix Reach (IRE)—Cocorica (IRE) **Malzard Racing**
9 **ROSSETTI,** 7, gr g Dansili—Snowdrops **Sheikh A Leg Racing**
10 **SPANISH BOUNTY,** 10, b g Bahamian Bounty—Spanish Gold **Malzard Racing**
11 **SPEEDY WRITER,** 5, b g Byron—Merch Rhyd-Y-Grug **La Vallette Ltd**

### THREE-YEAR-OLDS

12 **BROWN VELVET,** b f Kodiac—Silkenveil (IRE) **La Vallette Ltd**

**Jockey (flat):** Jemma Marshall. **Jockey (NH):** Mattie Batchelor, Craig Walker. **Conditional:** Tom Garner.

## 389 MR CHARLIE MANN, Upper Lambourn

Postal: **Neardown, Upper Lambourn, Hungerford, Berkshire, RG17 8QP**
Contacts: **PHONE (01488) 71717 / 73118 FAX (01488) 73223 MOBILE (07721) 888333**
**E-MAIL charlie@charliemann.info WEBSITE www.charliemannracing.com**

1 **AIRPUR DESBOIS (FR),** 5, b g Canyon Creek (IRE)—Hero's Dancer (FR) **Power Panels Electrical Systems Ltd**
2 **ALWAYS SMILING (IRE),** 8, b m Dushyantor (USA)—Aherlabeag (IRE) **Mrs Julia Bannister**
3 **AREA ACCESS (IRE),** 7, b g Oscar (IRE)—Lady Bramble (IRE) **Edwyn Good & Bryan Beacham**
4 **ATTIMO (GER),** 6, ch g Nayef (USA)—Alanda (GER) **The Neardown VI**
5 **BIG JER,** 8, b g Flemensfirth (USA)—Roses of Picardy (IRE) **Mrs J. M. Mayo**
6 **BRIDAL SUITE (IRE),** 6, b g Craigsteel—Selinda Spectrum (IRE) **Mr P. T. Mott**
7 **CEDRE BLEU (FR),** 8, b g Le Fou (IRE)—Arvoire (IRE) **Tangledupinblue**
8 **CHAMPAGNE N CAVIAR (IRE),** 7, b g Tiger Hill (IRE)—Leukippids (IRE) **N. W. A. Bannister**
9 **CODY WYOMING,** 9, b g Passing Glance—Tenderfoot **Charlie Mann Racing Club**
10 **ELMORE BACK (IRE),** 6, b g Wareed (IRE)—Katie Buckers (IRE) **Mr A. Stone, Mr B. Brindle & Mrs C. Hill**
11 **EXPEDITE (IRE),** 4, b g Brian Boru—Angelica Garnett **Mr S. Kimber**
12 **FINE PARCHMENT (IRE),** 12, b g Presenting—Run For Cover (IRE) **Mr N. W. A. Bannister**
13 **GOWANAUTHAT (IRE),** 7, ch g Golan (IRE)—Coolrua (IRE) **Bryan Beacham & C. J. Mann**
14 **LAMBRO (IRE),** 10, b g Milan—Beautiful Tune (FR) **Put It To The Vote Partnership**
15 **LATELO,** 7, b g Shirocco (GER)—Laurencia **C. J. Mann**
16 **LIBECCIO (FR),** 4, b g Shirocco (GER)—Francais **Mr J. Heron**
17 **LORD OF HOUSE (GER),** 7, ch g Lord of England (GER)—Lake House (IRE) **Good Lord Partnership**
18 **MILLER OF GLANMIRE (IRE),** 7, b g Oscar (IRE)—Instant Queen (IRE) **The Millers**
19 **MURRAY MOUNT (IRE),** 5, b g Trans Island—Ash **Mr M. S. Hitchcroft**
20 **NATIVE EXPLORER,** 6, b m Kayf Tara—Explorer **R. J. Tompkins**
21 **NIMBUS GALE (IRE),** 6, b g Cloudings (IRE)—Barton Gale (IRE) **Amity Finance Ltd & Mr A. Pountney**
22 **NO BAD NEWS,** 5, b g Beat All (USA)—Emma's Dream **Mr M. S. Hitchcroft**
23 **PLUM STONE,** 6, b m Loup Sauvage (USA)—Stoney Path **The Neardown Racing Partnership**
24 **PORTMONARCH (IRE),** 5, b g Galileo (IRE)—Egyptian Queen (USA) **Mr J. Heron**
25 **ROYAL REDEMPTION (IRE),** 6, b g Milan—Royale Laguna (FR) **L. Kimber, J. Thorneloe & T. Swerling**
26 **RUN TO THE RHYTHM,** 5, gr g Erhaab (USA)—Grace Dieu **A. W. Stapleton**
27 **SANDS COVE (IRE),** 8, b g Flemensfirth (USA)—
Lillies Bordello (IRE) **Stapleton,Walsh,Thorneloe & Windsor-Clive**
28 **SEVENTH SKY (GER),** 8, b g King's Best (USA)—Sacarina **Mr J. Heron**
29 **SUPERB STORY (IRE),** 4, b g Duke of Marmalade (IRE)—
Yes My Love (FR) **A. Holt, J. Robinson, A. Taylor & S. Miller**
30 **SURENESS (IRE),** 5, ch m Hurricane Run (IRE)—Silk Dress (IRE) **Mr P. T. Mott**
31 **VERANO (GER),** 6, ch g Lord of England (GER)—Vive La Vie (GER) **The Hennessy Five**
32 **VICTOR LEUDORUM (IRE),** 8, b g Wareed (IRE)—Rock Garden (IRE) **C. J. Mann**
33 **WESTERN KING (IRE),** 8, b g Definite Article—Western Road (GER) **The Western King Partnership**

## MR CHARLIE MANN - Continued

**Other Owners:** Amity Finance Ltd, Mr David Batten, Mr Bryan Beacham, Mrs A. J. Boswell, Mr W. Brindle, Ms Sarah Cutcliffe, Mr Andrew Durham, Mrs A. Fitzgerald-O'Connor, Mr Robert Frosell, Mr Edwyn Good, Mr John Heron, Mrs C. Hill, Mr M. S. Hitchcroft, Mr A. Holt, Mrs Caroline Hunter, Mr N. J. Kempner, Mr L. G. Kimber, Mr S. Kimber, Mr David Klein, Mr Ian Macnabb, Mr Charlie Mann, Mrs Judy Maynard, Mr R. Michaelson, Mr S. Miller, Mr P. Mott, Mr C. R. Nugent, Mr David Obree, Mr A. Pountney, Mr J. Robinson, Mr T. Simmons, Mrs Gill Simmons, Mr Tony Stapleton, Mr Andy Stone, Mr T. A. Swerling, Mr A. Taylor, Mrs L. C. Taylor, Major J. G. Thorneloe, R. J. Tompkin, Mr C. R. Trembath, Mr N. Trott, Mrs P. J. Walsh, The Hon D. J. Windsor-Clive.

**Assistant Trainer:** Matthew Fox **Secretary:** Rose Osborn

**Jockey (NH):** Noel Fehily. **Conditional:** Thomas Dowling.

---

## 390 MR GEORGE MARGARSON, Newmarket

Postal: **Graham Lodge, Birdcage Walk, Newmarket, Suffolk, CB8 0NE**
Contacts: **HOME/FAX (01638) 668043 MOBILE (07860) 198303**
**E-MAIL george@georgemargarson.co.uk WEBSITE www.georgemargason.co.uk**

1 **ELHAAM (IRE),** 4, b f Shamardal (USA)—Loulwa (IRE) **Saleh Al Homaizi & Imad Al Sagar**
2 **ELUSIVE GUEST (FR),** 4, b g Elusive City (USA)—Mansoura (IRE) **John Guest Racing Ltd**
3 **EXCELLENT AIM,** 8, b g Exceed And Excel (AUS)—Snugfit Annie **Graham Lodge Partnership II**
4 **EXCELLENT GUEST,** 8, b g Exceed And Excel (AUS)—Princess Speedfit (FR) **John Guest Racing Ltd**
5 **IMAGINARY DIVA,** 9, b m Lend A Hand—Distant Diva **Graham Lodge Partnership II**
6 **JAMMY GUEST (IRE),** 5, b g Duke of Marmalade (IRE)—Ardbrae Lady **John Guest Racing Ltd**
7 **LUCKY KRISTALE,** 4, b f Lucky Story (USA)—Pikaboo **Graham Lodge Partnership**
8 **MAGICAL SPEEDFIT (IRE),** 10, ch g Bold Fact (USA)—Magical Peace (IRE) **Graham Lodge Partnership II**
9 **REBELLIOUS GUEST,** 6, b g Cockney Rebel (IRE)—Marisa (GER) **John Guest Racing Ltd**
10 **SHYRON,** 4, b g Byron—Coconut Shy **F. Butler**
11 **STORM RUNNER (IRE),** 7, b g Rakti—Saibhreas (IRE) **Graham Lodge Partnership II**
12 **TAMAYUZ STAR (IRE),** 5, ch g Tamayuz—Magical Peace (IRE) **Graham Lodge Partnership II**
13 **WOOLFALL SOVEREIGN (IRE),** 9, b g Noverre (USA)—Mandragore (USA) **Graham Lodge Partnership II**
14 **YOUNG JACKIE,** 7, b m Doyen (IRE)—Just Warning **Graham Lodge Partnership II**
15 **YOUNG MICK,** 13, br g King's Theatre (IRE)—Just Warning **G. G. Margarson**

### THREE-YEAR-OLDS

16 **LADY KYLLAR,** b f Kyllachy—Miss Otis **Mangiacapra, Hill, Hook Partnership**
17 **MY JUDGE,** b c Nayef (USA)—Full Steam **Saleh Al Homaizi & Imad Al Sagar**
18 **PRINCESS GUEST (IRE),** b f Iffraaj—Princess Speedfit (FR) **John Guest Racing Ltd**
19 **RED WORDS (IRE),** b f Intikhab (USA)—Literacy (USA) **Mr A. Al Mansoori**
20 **SNAPPY GUEST,** b g Kodiac—Golden Shadow (IRE) **John Guest Racing Ltd**
21 **STOLEN STORY (IRE),** b c Kodiac—Mirwara (IRE) **Mr A. Al Mansoori**

### TWO-YEAR-OLDS

22 Ch c 11/3 Poet's Voice—Diamond Run (Hurricane Run (IRE)) (80000) **John Guest Racing Ltd**
23 B f 19/2 Kodiac—Lady Avenger (IRE) (Namid) (40000) **Saleh Al Homaizi & Imad Al Sagar**
24 B c 12/3 Zoffany (IRE)—Princess Speedfit (FR) (Desert Prince (IRE)) (45000) **John Guest Racing Ltd**
25 B f 4/5 Monsun (GER)—Sasuela (GER) (Dashing Blade) (952380) **Saleh Al Homaizi & Imad Al Sagar**
26 **SHYPEN,** b f 6/2 Archipenko (USA)—Coconut Shy (Bahamian Bounty) **F. Butler**

**Other Owners:** I. J. Al-Sagar, Mr S. Hill, Saleh Al Homaizi, Mrs E. L. Hook, Mr J. G. Mangiacapra, Mrs C. D. Taylor.

**Assistant Trainer:** Katie Margarson

---

## 391 MR A. J. MARTIN, Summerhill

Postal: **Arodstown, Moynalvey, Summerhill, Co. Meath, Ireland**
Contacts: **PHONE (00353) 46 955 8633 FAX (00353) 46 955 8632 MOBILE (00353) 86 276 0835**
**E-MAIL arodstown@eircom.net**

1 **ANIBALE FLY (FR),** 5, b g Assessor (IRE)—Nouba Fly (FR) **Independent Syndicate**
2 **ANNER QUEEN (IRE),** 5, b m Invincible Spirit (IRE)—Market Hill (IRE) **Newtown Anner Stud Farms Ltd**
3 **BEAU ET SUBLIME (FR),** 5, b g Saddler Maker (IRE)—Jolie Jouvencelle (FR) **Gigginstown House Stud**
4 **BLACKMAIL (FR),** 7, b g Black Sam Bellamy (IRE)—Same To You (FR) **John Breslin**
5 **BLACKWATER BRIDGE (IRE),** 5, b g Westerner—Gale Johnston (IRE) **Out All Night Syndicate**
6 **BLAIR PERRONE (IRE),** 6, b g Rudimentary (USA)—Stonehallqueen (IRE) **John Breslin**

## MR A. J. MARTIN - Continued

7 **BOG WARRIOR (IRE),** 11, b g Strategic Choice (USA)—Kilmac Princess (IRE) **Gigginstown House Stud**
8 **BOUBAFLY (FR),** 4, b br g Le Balafre (FR)—Nouba Fly (FR) **Danny Houlihan**
9 **BUDDY BOLERO (IRE),** 9, b g Accordion—Quinnsboro Ice (IRE) **M. C. Denmark**
10 **BUSTED TYCOON (IRE),** 6, b m Marju (IRE)—Khatela (IRE) **John Breslin**
11 **CASSELLS ROCK (IRE),** 5, br g Rock of Gibraltar (IRE)—Se La Vie (FR) **Donal Houlihan**
12 **COBBLERS HILL (IRE),** 7, b g Oscar (IRE)—Klipperstreet (IRE) **Mr I. J. Barratt**
13 **DARA TANGO (FR),** 8, b g Lando (GER)—Dara Dancer **A Shiels/Niall Reilly**
14 **DARK CRUSADER (IRE),** 5, b m Cape Cross (IRE)—Monty's Girl (IRE) **Newtown Anner Stud Farms Ltd**
15 **DEDIGOUT (IRE),** 9, b g Bob Back (USA)—Dainty Daisy (IRE) **Gigginstown House Stud**
16 **DELVIN ROAD (IRE),** 7, b br g Beneficial—Susans Glory **Lily Lawlor**
17 **DOLLAR AND A DREAM (IRE),** 6, b g Fruits of Love (USA)—Gorgeous Georgina (IRE) **A Shiels/Niall Reilly**
18 **EDEYMI (IRE),** 7, b g Barathea (IRE)—Edabiya (IRE) **Gigginstown House Stud**
19 **ELISHPOUR (IRE),** 5, b g Oasis Dream—Elbasana (IRE) **Barry Connell**
20 **FILL YOUR HANDS (IRE),** 6, b g Milan—Cailin's Perk (IRE) **Gigginstown House Stud**
21 **FIVE O'CLOCK TEA (FR),** 8, b g Martillo (GER)—Sally's Cry (FR) **City Gunners Syndicate**
22 **FLEMENSTAR (IRE),** 10, b g Flemensfirth (USA)—Different Dee (IRE) **S. Curran**
23 **GALLANT OSCAR (IRE),** 9, b g Oscar (IRE)—Park Wave (IRE) **Mr G. Kelly**
24 **GLADIATOR KING (IRE),** 6, b g Dylan Thomas (IRE)—Sheer Bliss (IRE) **John P. McManus**
25 **GOLANTILLA (IRE),** 7, br g Golan (IRE)—Scintilla **Barry Connell**
26 **GREATNESS (IRE),** 5, gr g Dalakhani (IRE)—Dancing Diva (FR) **Newtown Anner Stud Farms Ltd**
27 **HEARTBREAK CITY (FR),** 5, b g Lando (GER)—Moscow Nights (FR) **Mr G. Swan**
28 **HEATHFIELD (IRE),** 8, ch g Definite Article—Famous Lady (IRE) **P. J. McGee / Jos Kirwan**
29 **JEREMY'S JET (IRE),** 4, b g Jeremy (USA)—Double Vie (IRE) **P. Reilly**
30 **KINNITTY CASTLE (IRE),** 5, b g Beneficial—Jendam (IRE) **A Shiels/Niall Reilly**
31 **LIFT THE LATCH (IRE),** 5, b g Beneficial—Queen Astrid (IRE) **John P. McManus**
32 **LIP SERVICE (IRE),** 6, ch g Presenting—Top Her Up (IRE) **M. C. Denmark**
33 **LIVING NEXT DOOR (IRE),** 9, b g Beneficial—Except Alice (IRE) **John Breslin**
34 **MANUKA (IRE),** 6, ch g Galileo (IRE)—Honey Gold (IRE) **Mr S. D. Fitzpatrick**
35 **MARBLE STATUETTE (USA),** 5, gr m Mizzen Mast (USA)—Offbeat Fashion (IRE) **Glen Devlin**
36 **MARINERO (IRE),** 6, b g Presenting—Peggy Maddock (IRE) **Gigginstown House Stud**
37 **MYDOR (FR),** 5, ch g Stormy River (FR)—Fabulousday (USA) **Mulvany's Bar Syndicate**
38 **NO DICE (IRE),** 6, ch g Presenting—Roxbury **M. C. Denmark**
39 **NOBLE EMPEROR (IRE),** 7, b g Spadoun (FR)—Cherry Tops (IRE) **John P. McManus**
40 **OKOTOKS (IRE),** 5, b g Gamut (IRE)—Whats Another One (IRE) **M. C. Denmark**
41 **OUR SOX (IRE),** 6, b g September Storm (GER)—Winning Sally (IRE) **Reddans Bar Syndicate**
42 **PETIT CHEF (FR),** 4, br g Sunday Break (JPN)—Luarca **Adrian Collins**
43 **PIRES,** 11, br g Generous (IRE)—Kaydee Queen (IRE) **Lily Lawlor**
44 **PYROMANIAC (IRE),** 5, b g Invincible Spirit (IRE)—Silly Goose (IRE) **Newtown Anner Stud Farms Ltd**
45 **QUICK JACK (IRE),** 6, ch g Footstepsinthesand—Miss Polaris **John Breslin**
46 **RIVAGE D'OR (FR),** 10, b g Visionary (FR)—Deesse d'allier (FR) **Gigginstown House Stud**
47 **SARWISTAN (IRE),** 5, b g Nayef (USA)—Seraya (FR) **John Breslin / Tony Martin**
48 **SAVELLO (IRE),** 9, ch g Anshan—Fontaine Frances (IRE) **Gigginstown House Stud**
49 **SHEMSHAL (FR),** 7, b g Dalakhani (IRE)—Shemala (IRE) **Dermot Kilmurray**
50 **SPACIOUS SKY (USA),** 6, b g North Light (IRE)—Ratings (USA) **P. Reilly**
51 **SRAID PADRAIG (IRE),** 9, b g Revoque (IRE)—Loughaneala (IRE) **Barry Connell**
52 **TED VEALE (IRE),** 8, b g Revoque (IRE)—Rose Tanner (IRE) **John Breslin**
53 **THOMAS EDISON (IRE),** 8, b g Danehill Dancer (IRE)—Bright Bank (IRE) **John P. McManus**
54 **TWENTY FOUR YEARS (IRE),** 8, br m Definite Article—Except Alice (IRE) **T. Steele**
55 **VALGOR DU RONCERAY (FR),** 6, gr g Al Namix (FR)—Malta de Ronceray (FR) **Gigginstown House Stud**
56 **VELVET MAKER (FR),** 6, b g Policy Maker (IRE)—Evasion de L'orne (FR) **Barry Connell**
57 **VIVE LA FRANCE (FR),** 6, b br g Westerner—Millesimee (FR) **Barry Connell**
58 **VOICES OF SPRING (IRE),** 5, b g Arcadio (GER)—Fatfrogsauce (IRE) **Sheila Moffett**
59 **WHEREUNOW (IRE),** 6, b m Let The Lion Roar—Mitsubishi Trium (IRE) **Robert Donaldson**
60 **WRONG TURN (IRE),** 9, b g Well Chosen—Friendly Spirit **John Breslin**

## THREE-YEAR-OLDS

61 **CLONARD STREET,** b c Archipenko (USA)—Moi Aussi (USA) **John P. McManus**

---

## 392 MR ANDREW J. MARTIN, Chipping Norton

Postal: **Yew Tree Barn, Hook Norton Road, Swerford, Chipping Norton, Oxfordshire, OX7 4BF**
Contacts: **PHONE (01608) 737288**

1 **MIDNIGHT MUSTANG,** 8, b g Midnight Legend—Mustang Molly **A. J. Martin**

**MR ANDREW J. MARTIN - Continued**

2 **MIGHTY MUSTANG,** 5, b g Passing Glance—Mustang Molly
3 **ORANGER (FR),** 13, b g Antarctique (IRE)—True Beauty **A. J. Martin**
4 **SONIC WELD,** 6, b m Zafeen (FR)—Jamadast Roma **A. J. Martin**
5 **SUNNY LEDGEND,** 10, b g Midnight Legend—Swordella **A. J. Martin**

## 393 MR CHRISTOPHER MASON, Caerwent

Postal: **Whitehall Barn, Five Lanes, Caerwent, Monmouthshire**
Contacts: **PHONE (01291) 422172 FAX (01633) 666690 MOBILE (07767) 808082**
**E-MAIL cjmason@tiscali.co.uk**

1 **EDGED OUT,** 5, b m Piccolo—Edge of Light **Mr & Mrs C. J. Mason**

**THREE-YEAR-OLDS**

2 Ch f Compton Place—Edge of Gold

**Other Owners:** C. J. Mason, Mrs A. L. Mason.

**Assistant Trainer:** Annabelle Mason

## 394 MRS JENNIFER MASON, Cirencester

Postal: **Manor Farm, Ablington, Bibury, Cirencester, Gloucestershire, GL7 5NY**
Contacts: **PHONE (01285) 740445 MOBILE (07974) 262438**
**E-MAIL pwmason2002@yahoo.co.uk WEBSITE www.jennifermasonracing.com**

1 **CATCHAROSE (IRE),** 5, b m Catcher In The Rye (IRE)—Persian Flower **The If At First Partnership**
2 **SHY JOHN,** 9, b g Kier Park (IRE)—Shy Lizzie **Shy John Partnership**

**Other Owners:** Mrs S. J. Ash, Mrs R. D. Greenwood, P. W. Mason, Mrs M. E. Slocock.

**Assistant Trainer:** Mr Peter W. Mason

**Jockey (NH):** Felix De Giles. **Amateur:** Mr Peter Mason.

## 395 MISS JANE MATHIAS, Llancarfan

Postal: **Crosstown, Llancarfan, Vale of Glamorgan, CF62 3AD**

1 **DEFINATELY VINNIE,** 5, ch g Vinnie Roe (IRE)—Sohapara **Mrs S. E. Mathias**
2 **SOVINNIE (IRE),** 6, ch g Vinnie Roe (IRE)—Sohapara **Mrs S. E. Mathias**

## 396 MR G. C. MAUNDRELL, Marlborough

Postal: **Ogbourne Down, Ogbourne St Andrew, Marlborough, Wiltshire**
Contacts: **PHONE (01672) 841202**

1 **DELINEATE (IRE),** 6, b m Definite Article—New Line (IRE) **G. C. Maundrell**
2 **MINOR CHORD,** 9, b m Alflora (IRE)—Minimum **G. C. Maundrell**
3 **TAMBURA,** 5, b m Tamure (IRE)—Singing Cottage **G. C. Maundrell**

**Amateur:** Mr Z. Baker.

## 397 MR KEVIN MCAULIFFE, Faringdon

Postal: **Fernham Farm, Fernham, Faringdon, Oxfordshire, SN7 7NX**
Contacts: **PHONE (01367) 820236 FAX (01367) 820110**
**E-MAIL kevin@fernhamfarm.com**

1 4, Ch c Pastoral Pursuits—Lady Le Quesne (IRE) **Mrs J. Kersey**
2 **RIBBON ROYALE,** 5, b m Royal Applause—Ribbonwood (USA)

## 398 MR PHILIP MCBRIDE, Newmarket

Postal: **Exeter House Stables, 33 Exeter Road, Newmarket, Suffolk, CB8 0NY**
Contacts: **PHONE/FAX (01638) 667841 MOBILE (07929) 265711**

1 **BRIGLIADORO (IRE),** 4, ch g Excellent Art—Milady's Pride **Mr S. Agodino**
2 **BUSH BEAUTY (IRE),** 4, b f Bushranger (IRE)—Scottendale **P. J. McBride**
3 **CHOICE OF DESTINY,** 4, ch f Haafhd—Lumpini Park **Four Winds Racing Partnership**
4 **DREAM AND HOPE,** 4, b f Royal Applause—Senta's Dream **P. J. McBride**
5 **OLD TOWN BOY,** 4, b c Myboycharlie (IRE)—Native Ring (FR) **Mr R. Wilson**
6 **RITE TO REIGN,** 4, b g Tiger Hill (IRE)—Magical Cliche (USA) **Maelor Racing**

### THREE-YEAR-OLDS

7 **ANARCHISTE,** ch f Archipenko (USA)—Hermanita **Miss K. Rausing**
8 **COCKNEY ISLAND,** b f Cockney Rebel (IRE)—Island Rhapsody **Mr P. H. Wagstaffe**
9 **GREY'S ANGEL,** gr f Notnowcato—Kryena **Mr I. J. Pattle**
10 **MR SHEKELLS,** b g Three Valleys (USA)—Quip **Mr Nigel Davies & Mr P. J. McBride**
11 **SKY STEPS (IRE),** ch g Strategic Prince—Best Dancing (GER) **Mr P. H. Wagstaffe**
12 **TINKERS KISS (IRE),** b f Intikhab (USA)—Edmondstown Lass (IRE) **P. F. Charter**
13 **VIRTUAL REALITY,** b g Virtual—Regal Riband **Pmracing (Uk) Ltd**

**Other Owners:** C. M. Budgett, N. L. Davies, Miss A. M. Farrier, Mr D. L. Jackson, S. J. Mear, Mrs E. A. Mear.

## 399 MR DONALD MCCAIN, Cholmondeley

Postal: **D McCain Racing Ltd, Bankhouse, Cholmondeley, Malpas, Cheshire, SY14 8AL**
Contacts: **PHONE (01829) 720352/720351 FAX (01829) 720475 MOBILE (07903) 066194**
**E-MAIL info@donaldmccain.co.uk WEBSITE www.donaldmccain.co.uk**

1 **ABBEY STORM (IRE),** 9, br g Presenting—Bobbies Storm (IRE) **Paul & Clare Rooney**
2 **ABRICOT DE L'OASIS (FR),** 5, b g Al Namix (FR)—La Normandie (FR) **Mr F. McAleavy**
3 **ACROSS THE BAY (IRE),** 11, b g Bob's Return (IRE)—The Southern (IRE) **Scotch Piper Syndicate**
4 **AL MUSHEER (FR),** 4, gr c Verglas (IRE)—Canzonetta (FR) **T W Johnson & G Maxwell**
5 **ALWAYS ON THE RUN (IRE),** 5, b g Robin des Pres (FR)—Kerrys Cottage (IRE) **Straightline Construction Ltd**
6 **AMIRLI (IRE),** 4, ch g Medicean—Amenapinga (FR) **Paul & Clare Rooney**
7 **AMYS CHOICE (IRE),** 5, b m Craigsteel—Tanya Thyne (IRE) **Paul & Clare Rooney**
8 **APPLES AND TREES (IRE),** 6, b g Oscar (IRE)—Native Bramble (IRE) **Penketh & Sankey Jech Racing Club 1**
9 **ARGENT KNIGHT,** 5, gr g Sir Percy—Tussah **Straightline Construction Ltd**
10 **ASKAMORE DARSI (IRE),** 6, b g Darsi (FR)—Galamear **Deva Racing Darsi Partnership**
11 **ASTRUM,** 5, gr g Haafhd—Vax Star **Sarah & Wayne Dale**
12 **BALLYBOKER BREEZE (IRE),** 7, b g Gold Well—Ballyboker Lady (IRE) **Paul & Clare Rooney**
13 **BEATU (IRE),** 6, b g Beat All (USA)—Auntie Bob **T. G. Leslie**
14 **BEEVES (IRE),** 8, b g Portrait Gallery (IRE)—Camas North (IRE) **Paul & Clare Rooney**
15 **BENEFICIAL JOE (IRE),** 5, b br g Beneficial—Joleen (IRE) **Paul & Clare Rooney**
16 **BENZANNO (IRE),** 6, b g Refuse To Bend (IRE)—Crossanza (IRE) **T. G. Leslie**
17 **BESPOKE LADY (IRE),** 6, ch m Presenting—Coole Alainn (IRE) **Paul & Clare Rooney**
18 **BIG BAD DUDE (IRE),** 6, ch g Blueprint (IRE)—Cathedral Ave (IRE) **Paul & Clare Rooney**
19 **BILLFROMTHEBAR (IRE),** 8, b g Morozov (USA)—Eden Breeze (IRE) **Mr M. W. Sanders**
20 **BILLY BUFF,** 5, b g Multiplex—Shanxi Girl **Paul & Clare Rooney**
21 **BLACK JACK ROVER (IRE),** 6, b g Vinnie Roe (IRE)—Kilgefin Tina (IRE) **Deva Racing Black Jack Partnership**
22 **BLACKWATER KING (IRE),** 7, b br g Beneficial—Accordian Lady (IRE) **Paul & Clare Rooney**
23 **BLEU ET OR (FR),** 4, b g Maresca Sorrento (FR)—Panoplie (FR) **Owners Group 002**
24 **BLURRED LINES (IRE),** 6, ch m Shantou (USA)—Balda Girl (IRE) **Deva Racing Bloodstock Partnership**
25 **BOURNE,** 9, gr g Linamix (FR)—L'affaire Monique **M. J. Taylor**
26 **CARRIGEEN LANTANA (IRE),** 6, b m Beneficial—Carrigeen Lily (IRE) **Paul & Clare Rooney**
27 **CINDERS AND ASHES,** 8, b g Beat Hollow—Moon Search **Dermot Hanafin & Phil Cunningham**
28 **CLONDAW DRAFT (IRE),** 7, b g Shantou (USA)—Glen Ten (IRE) **T. G. Leslie**
29 **CLONDAW KAEMPFER (IRE),** 7, b g Oscar (IRE)—Gra-Bri (IRE) **T Leslie & D Gorton**
30 **CLOUDY JOKER (IRE),** 7, gr g Cloudings (IRE)—Rosa View (IRE) **On Cloud Eight**
31 **CORRIN WOOD (IRE),** 8, gr g Garuda (IRE)—Allstar Rose (IRE) **Dermot Hanafin Robert Rose Ian Whitfield**
32 **COURT DISMISSED (IRE),** 5, b g Court Cave (IRE)—Carramanagh Lady (IRE) **Special Piping Materials Ltd**
33 **COURT OF LAW (IRE),** 7, b g Court Cave (IRE)—Divine Dancer (IRE) **D. R. McCain**
34 **COUSIN GUILLAUME (FR),** 6, b br g Kapgarde (FR)—Tante Zoe (FR) **Paul & Clare Rooney**
35 **CRACKED REAR VIEW (IRE),** 5, gr g Portrait Gallery (IRE)—Trip To Knock **Paul & Clare Rooney**
36 **DEBDEBDEB,** 5, b m Teofilo (IRE)—Windmill **The Sea Breeze Partnership**
37 **DEGOOCH (IRE),** 6, ch g Gamut (IRE)—Blonde Ambition (IRE) **Paul & Clare Rooney**

## MR DONALD MCCAIN - Continued

38 **DEISE DYNAMO (IRE),** 7, br g Zagreb (USA)—Magical Mist (IRE) **Mr D. Hanafin**
39 **DESERT CRY (IRE),** 9, b br g Desert Prince (IRE)—Hataana (USA) **N.Y.P.D Racing**
40 **DESOTO COUNTY,** 6, gr g Hernando (FR)—Kaldounya **Paul & Clare Rooney**
41 **DIAMOND KING (IRE),** 7, b g King's Theatre (IRE)—Georgia On My Mind (FR) **Mrs D. L. Whateley**
42 **DIOCLES (IRE),** 9, b g Bob Back (USA)—Ardrina **L. G. M. Racing**
43 **DISPOUR (IRE),** 5, ch g Monsun (GER)—Dalataya (IRE) **Paul & Clare Rooney**
44 **DOYLY CARTE,** 7, b m Doyen (IRE)—Generous Diana **Elite Racing Club**
45 **DR DALWHINNY,** 6, ch g Dr Fong (USA)—Snow Polina (USA) **Dalwhinnie Racing**
46 **DREAMS OF MILAN (IRE),** 7, b g Milan—Joe's Dream Catch (IRE) **Axom XXXVII**
47 **DRY YOUR EYES (IRE),** 4, b f Shamardal (USA)—Kindling **G. Mercer**
48 **DUKE ARCADIO (IRE),** 6, b g Arcadio (GER)—Kildowney Duchess (IRE) **Paul & Clare Rooney**
49 **DUNOWEN POINT (IRE),** 9, b g Old Vic—Esbeggi **T. G. Leslie**
50 **FAIR MONEY,** 6, gr g Fair Mix (IRE)—Mrs Moneypenny **Deva Racing Fair Mix Partnership**
51 **FEARLESS TUNES (IRE),** 7, b g Shantou (USA)—Miss Snapdragon (IRE) **Paul & Clare Rooney**
52 **FEATHER LANE (IRE),** 5, b g Court Cave (IRE)—Laffan's Bridge (IRE) **T. G. Leslie**
53 **FINAL PASS (IRE),** 7, b g Gamut (IRE)—Final Peace (IRE) **Paul & Clare Rooney**
54 **FIVE FOR FIFTEEN (IRE),** 6, b g Craigsteel—Gentle Eyre (IRE) **Let's Live Racing**
55 **FRANCISCAN,** 7, b g Medicean—Frangy **T. G. Leslie**
56 **FREDERIC,** 4, b g Zamindar (USA)—Frangy **Paul & Clare Rooney**
57 **FROMDUSKTILLDAWN (IRE),** 5, ch g Mahler—Lady Transcend (IRE) **Paul & Clare Rooney**
58 **GABRIAL THE GREAT (IRE),** 6, b g Montjeu (IRE)—Bayourida (USA) **Paul & Clare Rooney**
59 **GINGILI,** 5, b g Beat All (USA)—Gentian **Paul & Clare Rooney**
60 **GO CONQUER (IRE),** 6, b g Arcadio (GER)—Ballinamona Wish (IRE) **Paul & Clare Rooney**
61 6, B m Beneficial—Good Foundation (IRE) **D. R. McCain**
62 **GREENSALT (IRE),** 7, b g Milan—Garden City (IRE) **T. J. Hemmings**
63 **GROUSE LODGE (IRE),** 9, b g Well Chosen—Arctic Jane (IRE) **Mr F. McAleavy**
64 **HELLORBOSTON (IRE),** 7, b g Court Cave (IRE)—Helorhiwater (IRE) **D. R. McCain**
65 **HESTER FLEMEN (IRE),** 7, ch m Flemensfirth (USA)—Hester Hall (IRE) **Paul & Clare Rooney**
66 **HILLS OF DUBAI (IRE),** 6, ch g Dubai Destination (USA)—Mowazana (IRE) **T. G. Leslie**
67 **I NEED GOLD (IRE),** 7, b g Gold Well—Coola Cross (IRE) **Deva Racing Golden Partnership**
68 **I'M A ROCKER (IRE),** 6, b g Gold Well—Over Slyguff (IRE) **The Generals Men Racing Club I**
69 **ITCHYMEI'MSCRATCH (IRE),** 7, ch g Definite Article—Royal Molly (IRE) **Straightline Construction Ltd**
70 **JELLIED EEL JACK (IRE),** 6, b g Scorpion (IRE)—Melodic Tune (IRE) **A. J. Perkins**
71 **JONNY EAGER (IRE),** 6, b g Craigsteel—Dishy (IRE) **Paul & Clare Rooney**
72 **KALANISI GLEN (IRE),** 5, br g Kalanisi (IRE)—Glen Ten (IRE) **Paul & Clare Rooney**
73 **KASHMIRI SUNSET,** 4, b g Tiger Hill (IRE)—Sagamartha **Paul & Clare Rooney**
74 **KATACHENKO (IRE),** 6, b g Kutub (IRE)—Karalee (IRE) **T. J. Hemmings**
75 **KEENELAND (IRE),** 8, b g Westerner—Delphinium (IRE) **Paul & Clare Rooney**
76 **KIE (IRE),** 7, b g Old Vic—Asura (GER) **A. Stennett**
77 **KINGS BANDIT (IRE),** 7, b g King's Theatre (IRE)—Gentle Lady (IRE) **Mrs D. L. Whateley**
78 **KITCHAPOLY (FR),** 5, b g Poliglote—Kotkicha (FR) **Paul & Clare Rooney**
79 **KONIG DAX (GER),** 5, b g Saddex—Konigin Shuttle (GER) **Paul & Clare Rooney**
80 **KOUP DE KANON (FR),** 9, b g Robin des Pres (FR)—Coup de Sabre (FR) **M. J. Taylor**
81 **KRUZHLININ (GER),** 8, ch g Sholokhov (IRE)—Karuma (GER) **Paul & Clare Rooney**
82 **LAIRD OF MONKSFORD (IRE),** 6, b g Shantou (USA)—Back Log (IRE) **Paul & Clare Rooney**
83 **LEXI'S BOY (IRE),** 7, gr g Verglas (IRE)—Jazan (IRE) **T. G. Leslie**
84 **LIFE AND SOUL (IRE),** 8, b g Azamour (IRE)—Way For Life (GER) **M. J. Taylor**
85 **LIVELY BARON (IRE),** 10, b g Presenting—Greavesfind **T. J. Hemmings**
86 **LOUGH DERG WALK (IRE),** 6, b g Turtle Island (IRE)—Whispers In Moscow (IRE) **T. G. Leslie**
87 **LOVELY JOB (IRE),** 5, ch g Touch of Land (FR)—Wyckoff Queen (IRE) **Paul & Clare Rooney**
88 **LUCCOMBE DOWN,** 5, b g Primo Valentino (IRE)—Flaming Rose (IRE) **Paul & Clare Rooney**
89 **LYRIC STREET (IRE),** 7, b g Hurricane Run (IRE)—Elle Danzig (GER) **M. J. Taylor**
90 **MAHLER AND ME (IRE),** 5, ch g Mahler—Tisindabreedin (IRE) **Paul & Clare Rooney**
91 **MAHLER LAD (IRE),** 5, b g Mahler—Sister Merenda (IRE) **T. G. Leslie**
92 **MANKALA (IRE),** 5, b g Flemensfirth (USA)—Maracana (IRE) **Paul & Clare Rooney**
93 **MANSONIEN L'AS (FR),** 9, b g Mansonnien (FR)—Star des As (FR) **Let's Live Racing**
94 **MASTER DEE (IRE),** 6, b g King's Theatre (IRE)—Miss Lauren Dee (IRE) **Paul & Clare Rooney**
95 **MASTER OF THE GAME (IRE),** 9, ch g Bob's Return (IRE)—Lady Monilousha (IRE) **Paul & Clare Rooney**
96 **MASTER RED (IRE),** 6, b g Red Clubs (IRE)—Glory Days (GER) **Paul & Clare Rooney**
97 **MINMORE LODGE (IRE),** 5, b g Flemensfirth (USA)—Supreme Von Pres (IRE)
98 4, B f Kalanisi (IRE)—Miss Fara (FR) **Mr B. Richardson**
99 **MIXBOY (FR),** 5, gr g Fragrant Mix (IRE)—Leston Girl (FR) **Paul & Clare Rooney**
100 **MONBEG DOLLY (IRE),** 5, ch m Flemensfirth (USA)—Laughing Lesa (IRE) **Paul & Clare Rooney**
101 **MR BURGEES (IRE),** 6, b g Westerner—My Kinda Girl (IRE) **Paul & Clare Rooney**
102 **MR HOPEFUL (IRE),** 6, b g Helissio (FR)—Lisadian Lady (IRE) **Essential Racing 3**

## MR DONALD MCCAIN - Continued

103 **MUTDULA (IRE),** 5, b g Gamut (IRE)—Calendula **Paul & Clare Rooney**
104 **MY LITTLE CRACKER (IRE),** 5, b br m Scorpion (IRE)—Cailin Gruaig Dubh (IRE) **Paul & Clare Rooney**
105 **NAFAATH (IRE),** 9, ch g Nayef (USA)—Alshakr **Sarah & Wayne Dale**
106 **NEFYN BAY,** 6, b g Overbury (IRE)—So Cloudy **Tim & Miranda Johnson**
107 **NEVER NEVER (IRE),** 5, b g Jeremy (USA)—Argus Gal (IRE) **Paul & Clare Rooney**
108 **OFF THE CUFF,** 4, b c Zamindar (USA)—Comment **D. R. McCain**
109 **OPERATING (IRE),** 8, b g Milan—Seymourswift **Paul & Clare Rooney**
110 **OSCATARA (IRE),** 8, b br g Oscar (IRE)—Nethertara **T. G. Leslie**
111 **OUR MICK,** 9, gr g Karinga Bay—Dawn's Della **K. Benson & Mrs E. Benson**
112 **OUR ROBIN (IRE),** 5, b g Robin des Champs (FR)—Palm Lake (IRE) **Paul & Clare Rooney**
113 **OVERTURN (IRE),** 11, b g Barathea (IRE)—Kristal Bridge **T. G. Leslie**
114 **OVILIA (IRE),** 6, gr m Clodovil (IRE)—Five of Wands **David Lockwood & Fred Lockwood Partners**
115 **PALERMO DON,** 5, b g Beat Hollow—Kristal Bridge **T. G. Leslie**
116 **PERFECT POISON (IRE),** 7, b g Vinnie Roe (IRE)—Noddys Confusion (IRE) **D. R. McCain**
117 **PLAN AGAIN (IRE),** 8, b g Gamut (IRE)—Niamh's Leader (IRE) **Paul & Clare Rooney**
118 **PRINCE KHURRAM,** 5, b g Nayef (USA)—Saree **T. G. Leslie**
119 **RAISE A SPARK,** 5, b g Multiplex—Reem Two **Mr R Pattison & Mr R Kent**
120 **RED MERLIN (IRE),** 10, ch g Soviet Star (USA)—Truly Bewitched (USA) **M. J. Taylor**
121 **RED SPINNER (IRE),** 5, b g Redback—Massalia (IRE) **Paul & Clare Rooney**
122 **RIGHT TO RULE (IRE),** 6, b g Rock of Gibraltar (IRE)—Epistoliere (IRE) **D. R. McCain**
123 **ROCKY STONE (IRE),** 7, b g Cloudings (IRE)—Crandon Park **Penketh & Sankey Jech Racing Club**
124 **ROSERROW,** 6, ch g Beat Hollow—Sabah **Straightline Construction Ltd**
125 **ROSKILLY (IRE),** 4, ch g Hurricane Run (IRE)—Party Feet (IRE) **Straightline Construction Ltd**
126 **SACRED SQUARE (GER),** 5, ch g Peintre Celebre (USA)—Square The Circle **Mr A. G. Bloom**
127 **SAINTE LADYLIME (FR),** 4, b f Saint des Saints (FR)—Lady Pauline (FR) **Paul & Clare Rooney**
128 **SALTO CHISCO (IRE),** 7, b g Presenting—Dato Fairy (IRE) **Mrs D. L. Whateley**
129 **SEALOUS SCOUT (IRE),** 7, b g Old Vic—Hirayna **T. G. Leslie**
130 **SHANTOU TIGER (IRE),** 6, b g Shantou (USA)—Opus One **Deva Racing Shantou Partnership**
131 **SHARP,** 6, b g Haafhd—Brightest **D. R. McCain**
132 **SHORT TAKES (USA),** 7, ch g Lemon Drop Kid (USA)—Gabriellina Giof **Mr T. P. McMahon & Mr D. McMahon**
133 **SHOTOFWINE,** 6, b g Grape Tree Road—Icy Gunner **Paul & Clare Rooney**
134 **SIGN MANUAL,** 6, b g Motivator—New Assembly (IRE) **Graham & Carole Worsley**
135 **SILVER GENT (IRE),** 7, gr g Milan—All's Rosey (IRE) **Deva Racing Milan Partnership**
136 **SINDARBAN (IRE),** 4, ch g Teofilo (IRE)—Sinndiya (IRE) **Paul & Clare Rooney**
137 **SIR MANGAN (IRE),** 7, b g Darsi (FR)—Lady Pep (IRE) **Mr F. McAleavy**
138 **SONNEOFPRESENTING (IRE),** 5, b br g Presenting—Sonne Cinq (IRE) **Paul & Clare Rooney**
139 **STANLEY (GER),** 4, bl g Pivotal—Sky Dancing (IRE) **Paul & Clare Rooney**
140 **STARCHITECT (IRE),** 4, b g Sea The Stars (IRE)—Humilis (IRE) **Paul & Clare Rooney**
141 **STONEBROOK (IRE),** 7, b g Flemensfirth (USA)—Boberelle (IRE) **J. P. McManus**
142 **STYLE SETTER,** 5, b m Beat Hollow—Wooden Doll (USA) **R. Kent**
143 **SUBTLE GREY (IRE),** 6, gr g Subtle Power (IRE)—Milltown Rose (IRE) **Deva Racing Subtle Grey Partnership**
144 **SUPERFECTION (IRE),** 6, b m Shantou (USA)—Sarah's Cottage (IRE) **Chasing Gold Limited**
145 **SUPREME ASSET (IRE),** 7, b g Beneficial—Hollygrove Supreme (IRE) **Lucky Bin Racing**
146 **SWATOW TYPHOON (IRE),** 8, b g Shantou (USA)—Oscar Leader (IRE) **Mr G. Fitzpatrick**
147 **SWIFT ARROW (IRE),** 9, b g Overbury (IRE)—Clover Run (IRE) **Mrs A. E. Strang Steel**
148 **SYDNEY PAGET (IRE),** 8, b g Flemensfirth (USA)—Shuil Aoibhinn (IRE) **Roger O'Byrne**
149 **TAKE THE CASH (IRE),** 6, b g Cloudings (IRE)—Taking My Time (IRE) **T. J. Hemmings**
150 **THE BACKUP PLAN (IRE),** 6, ch g Presenting—Jay Lo (IRE) **N.Y.P.D Racing**
151 **THE BANTOWN LANE,** 5, b g Mahler—Flushtown Vale (IRE) **Mr D. Owens**
152 **THE LAST SAMURI (IRE),** 7, ch g Flemensfirth (USA)—Howaboutthis (IRE) **Paul & Clare Rooney**
153 **THEATRICAL STYLE (IRE),** 6, b g Alhaarth (IRE)—Little Theatre (IRE) **Deva Racing Palladium Partnership**
154 **THEREORTHEREABOUTS (IRE),** 7, b m Kalanisi (IRE)—The Vicars Lady (IRE) **Paul & Clare Rooney**
155 **THREE FACES WEST (IRE),** 7, b g Dr Massini (IRE)—Ardnataggle (IRE) **Paul & Clare Rooney**
156 **TONVADOSA,** 7, b m Flemensfirth (USA)—Sleepless Eye **T Meehan & D J Burke**
157 **TOUR D'ARGENT (FR),** 8, b g Martaline—Keep Well (FR) **Paul & Clare Rooney**
158 **TREND IS MY FRIEND (USA),** 6, b br g Lemon Drop Kid (USA)—Silva (FR) **T Leslie & D Gorton**
159 **UBALTIQUE (FR),** 7, b g Balko (FR)—Ode Antique (FR) **T. G. Leslie**
160 **UNCLE MONTY (IRE),** 6, b g Milan—She's A Gamble (IRE) **Clwydian International**
161 **UP AND GO (FR),** 7, ch g Martaline—Santoria (FR) **T. G. Leslie**
162 **UPPERCUT DE L'ORNE (FR),** 7, ch g Kapgarde (FR)—Murcie (FR) **Paul & Clare Rooney**
163 **VASCO PIERJI (FR),** 6, b g Sleeping Car (FR)—Angelina (FR) **Tim Johnson & Donald McCain**
164 **VENUE,** 5, b g Beat Hollow—Shirley Valentine **Straightline Construction Ltd**
165 **VERNI (FR),** 6, ch g Sabrehill (USA)—Nobless d'aron (FR) **Paul & Clare Rooney**
166 **VINSTAR (FR),** 6, b g Charming Groom (FR)—Kali Star (FR) **T. G. Leslie**
167 **VITAL EVIDENCE (USA),** 5, b g Empire Maker (USA)—Promising Lead **Paul & Clare Rooney**

## MR DONALD MCCAIN - Continued

**168 VOLCANIC (FR),** 6, b g Al Namix (FR)—Queen of Rock (FR) **Elite Racing Club**
**169 WELSH BARD (IRE),** 6, ch g Dylan Thomas (IRE)—Delphinium (IRE) **George Tobitt & Richard Gurney**
**170 WESTEND STAR (IRE),** 6, b g Old Vic—Camlin Rose (IRE) **Paul & Clare Rooney**
**171 WHATDOESTHEFOXSAY (IRE),** 6, ch m Vinnie Roe (IRE)—
She's The One (IRE) **Mrs Sarah Leslie & D McCain Jnr**
**172 WHISKEY CHASER (IRE),** 7, br g Flemensfirth (USA)—
Cregane Lass (IRE) **Deva Racing Flemensfirth Partnership**
**173 WHITSUNDAYS (IRE),** 6, b g Kutub (IRE)—Urdite's Vic (IRE) **Deva Racing Whitsundays Partnership**
**174 WILCOS MO CHARA (IRE),** 7, b g Oscar (IRE)—She's A Venture (IRE) **A&K Ecofilm Ltd**
**175 WITNESS IN COURT (IRE),** 8, b g Witness Box (USA)—Inter Alia (IRE) **T. G. Leslie**
**176 ZIP WIRE (IRE),** 6, b g Oratorio (IRE)—Jaya (USA) **M. J. Taylor**

### THREE-YEAR-OLDS

**177 FORTUNA GLAS (IRE),** gr c Verglas (IRE)—Fortuna Limit **Paul & Clare Rooney**
**178 MONKSFORD LADY,** b f Lope de Vega (IRE)—Viennese Whirl **Paul & Clare Rooney**
**179 MY DREAM BOAT (IRE),** b c Lord Shanakill (USA)—Betty Burke **Paul & Clare Rooney**
**180 SMOKE RING (USA),** gr ro c Smoke Glacken (USA)—With This Ring (USA) **Paul & Clare Rooney**
**181 YOU'RE MY CRACKER,** ch f Captain Gerrard (IRE)—Dalmunzie (IRE) **Paul & Clare Rooney**

### TWO-YEAR-OLDS

**182** B c 10/5 Captain Gerrard (IRE)—Dragon Flyer (IRE) (Tagula (IRE)) (19047) **Paul & Clare Rooney**
**183 HE'S MY CRACKER,** ch c 4/2 Captain Gerrard (IRE)—Dalmunzie (IRE) (Choisir (AUS)) **Paul & Clare Rooney**
**184** B f 24/3 Medicean—Piranha (IRE) (Exceed And Excel (AUS)) (21904) **Paul & Clare Rooney**

**Other Owners:** Axom Ltd, M. Ball, K. Benson, Mrs E. Benson, D. J. Burke, Mr N. Caddy, G. Caine, Mr M. J. Campbell, Mr A. P. Coyne, Mr K. Coyne, P. M. Cunningham, Mrs S. J. Dale, Mr W. R. Dale, Dalwhinny Bloodstock, Deva Racing, Mr W. A. Eastup, Elite Racing Club, J. C. Evans, M. D. Foster, Mrs J. Foster, L. R. Frampton, Generals Men Racing, Mr R. G. Griffiths, R. Gurney, Mr D. Hanafin, Mr A. J. Hill, Mr B. M. Hillier, Mr T. Johnson, Mrs M. Johnson, Mr G. L. Joynson, Mrs K. F. Kent, Mr S. Kent, Mr P. Landrum, Mr W. Lazar, Mrs S. C. Leslie, D. J. Lockwood, Mr F. M. Lockwood, Mr G. Maxwell, Mr I. McAleavy, Mr D. McMahon, Mr T. P. McMahon, Mr A. E. Meehan, Mr D. Moyes, Miss M. Noden, R. Pattison, D. P. Reilly, Mrs C. J. Reilly, Mr B. Richardson, Mr B. Robbins, Paul & Clare Rooney, Mrs C. Rooney, Mr R. Rose, Sea Breeze Partnership, Mr A. Steedman, Straightline Construction, Ms L. Stuart, G. M. Thomson, G. E. Tobitt, Mr E. C. Watson, Mr N. Watt, Mr I. Whitfield, Mr G. W. Worsley, Mrs C. P. Worsley.

**Assistant Trainer:** Adrian Lane

**Jockey (NH):** Jason Maguire, Adrian Lane, Wilson Renwick. **Conditional:** James Cowley, Nick Slatter.
**Amateur:** Mr Harry Stock.

---

**400**

## MR TIM MCCARTHY, Godstone

Postal: **Nags Hall Farm, Oxted Road, Godstone, Surrey, RH9 8DB**
Contacts: **PHONE (01883) 740379 FAX (01883) 740381 MOBILE (07887) 763062**

**1 CAVALRY GUARD (USA),** 11, ch g Officer (USA)—Leeward City (USA) **Surrey Racing Club**
**2 DUTCHARTCOLLECTOR,** 4, b g Dutch Art—Censored
**3 GHOST TRAIN (IRE),** 6, b g Holy Roman Emperor (IRE)—
Adrastea (IRE) **Homecroft Wealth Racing & T D McCarthy**
**4 JIMMY RYAN (IRE),** 14, b g Orpen (USA)—Kaysama (FR) **Mrs C. V. McCarthy**
**5 RUN FOR HOME,** 4, bl g Kheleyf (USA)—Dodona **A. D. Spence**
**6 UNDERSTORY (USA),** 8, b g Forestry (USA)—Sha Tha (USA) **Homecroft Wealth Racing & T D McCarthy**

**Other Owners:** T. D. McCarthy, S. J. Piper, Mr N. Pogmore.

**Assistant Trainer:** Mrs C.V. McCarthy

---

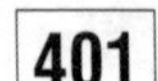


## MISS DANIELLE MCCORMICK, Lathom

Postal: **Blythe Hall, Blythe Lane, Lathom, Ormskirk, Lancashire, L40 5TY**
Contacts: **PHONE (01695) 572358 MOBILE (07590) 513752**
**E-MAIL danielle-mccormick@hotmail.co.uk**

**1 ECHO SPRINGS,** 5, b g Kayf Tara—Mrs Malt (IRE) **Blythe Stables LLP**
**2 MOXEY,** 4, ch g Nayef (USA)—Emily Blake (IRE) **Blythe Stables LLP**

## MISS DANIELLE MCCORMICK - Continued

### THREE-YEAR-OLDS

3 **BLYTHE PRINCE,** b c Dutch Art—Arculinge **Blythe Stables LLP**
4 **BLYTHE STAR (IRE),** b g Thewayyouare (USA)—Run To Jane (IRE) **Blythe Stables LLP**

**Other Owners:** Mrs Tracey Bell, Mr Andy Bell.

**Amateur:** Miss A. McCormick.

---

## 402 MR PHIL MCENTEE, Newmarket

Postal: **Racefield Stables, Carriageway, Hamilton Road, Newmarket, Suffolk, CB8 7JQ**
Contacts: **PHONE (01638) 662092 FAX (01638) 662092 MOBILE (07802) 663256**

1 **BIG CITY BOY (IRE),** 7, b g Tamarisk (IRE)—Cuddles (IRE) **Miss R. B. McEntee**
2 **EXPENSIVE TASTE (IRE),** 4, b g Moss Vale (IRE)—Priceoflove (IRE) **Mrs R. L. Baker**
3 **FLYING AUTHOR (IRE),** 4, b g Authorized (IRE)—Fly Free **Mr S. Jakes**
4 **HONITON LACE,** 4, ch f Tobougg (IRE)—Mellifluous (IRE) **Eventmaker Racehorses**
5 **JONNIE SKULL (IRE),** 9, b g Pyrus (USA)—Sovereign Touch (IRE) **R McEntee & The Guernsey Boys**
6 **NIFTY KIER,** 6, b g Kier Park (IRE)—Yeldham Lady **Mrs R. L. McEntee**
7 **PUTIN (IRE),** 7, b g Fasliyev (USA)—Consignia (IRE) **Mr S. Jakes**
8 **RAYMOND'S DREAM,** 5, br m Lightning Lad—Spirit of Song (IRE) **Miss C. McPhillips-Witt**
9 **SUMMERLING (IRE),** 4, br f Excellent Art—Sun Seasons (IRE) **Mr R. W. Carson**
10 **SWISS CROSS,** 8, b g Cape Cross (IRE)—Swiss Lake (USA) **Mr S. Jakes**
11 **TASAABOQ,** 4, b g Aqlaam—Seldemosa **Mrs R. L. McEntee**
12 **THE BLUE DOG (IRE),** 8, b m High Chaparral (IRE)—Jules (IRE) **Mr R. W. Carson**
13 **TORNADO BATTLE,** 5, b g War Chant (USA)—Child Bride (USA) **Mr S. Jakes**
14 **TOYMAKER,** 8, b g Starcraft (NZ)—Eurolink Raindance (IRE) **Eventmaker Racehorses**
15 **TWO NO BIDS (IRE),** 5, b br g Footstepsinthesand—Milwaukee (FR) **Eventmaker Racehorses**

### THREE-YEAR-OLDS

16 **LITTLE DANIELLE (IRE),** b f Dansant—Sacha Wild **Mrs C. Mackay**
17 **MARY ANN BUGG (IRE),** b f Bushranger (IRE)—Shobobb **Mr S. Jakes**
18 **MY MISTRESS (IRE),** ch f Mastercraftsman (IRE)—Majestic Eviction (IRE) **Mr H. R. Nothhaft**
19 **SUNSHINE BAND,** ch f Compton Place—Precedence (IRE) **Mr R. W. Carson**

**Other Owners:** Mr M. A. Humphris, T. D. Johnson, Mr M. D. Queripel.

---

## 403 MR MURTY MCGRATH, Maidstone

Postal: **Spicketts House, Kiln Barn Road, East Malling, Kent, ME19 6BG**
Contacts: **PHONE (01732) 840173 MOBILE (07818) 098073**
**E-MAIL mjmcgrath@hotmail.com**

1 **FREEMASON,** 4, b g Cape Cross (IRE)—Candy Mountain **Gallagher Equine Ltd**
2 **KENT RAGSTONE (USA),** 6, ch g Stonesider (USA)—Sweet Charity (USA) **Gallagher Equine Ltd**
3 **LEITRIM PASS (USA),** 5, ch g Raven's Pass (USA)—Santolina (USA) **Gallagher Equine Ltd**
4 **REZWAAN,** 8, b g Alhaarth (IRE)—Nasij (USA) **Gallagher Equine Ltd**
5 **SALAM ALAYKUM (IRE),** 7, b g Galileo (IRE)—Alicia (IRE) **Gallagher Equine Ltd**

**Assistant Trainer:** Heidi McGrath (07795) 178178

**Jockey (flat):** Shane Kelly.

---

## 404 MRS JEAN MCGREGOR, Milnathort

Postal: **Tillyrie House, Milnathort, Kinross, KY13 0RW**
Contacts: **PHONE (01577) 861792 MOBILE (07764) 464299**
**E-MAIL purebred68@hotmail.co.uk**

1 **BEST BEAR,** 7, b g Rambling Bear—Lingham Bridesmaid **Mrs D. Thomson**
2 6, B g Desideratum—Blue Morning **J. Thomson**
3 **JACKOFHEARTS,** 7, b g Beat Hollow—Boutique **Mr S. Taylor**
4 **NELSON DU RONCERAY (FR),** 14, b g Lute Antique (FR)—Trieste (FR) **Miss A. L. McGregor**
5 **SNOOZE N YOU LOSE,** 10, b g Helissio (FR)—Utmost (IRE) **The Good To Soft Firm**

**MRS JEAN MCGREGOR - Continued**

6 **THEHOODLUM,** 8, b g Fraam—Trilby **Tillyrie Racing Club**
7 **WATERSKI,** 14, b g Petoski—Celtic Waters **Mrs D. Thomson**

**Other Owners:** Mr J. A. S. Burnett, Mrs J. C. McGregor.

**Jockey (flat):** Andrew Mullen. **Jockey (NH):** Adrian Lane. **Conditional:** Jonathan England, John Kington. **Amateur:** Miss A.L. McGregor.

---

## 405 MS KAREN MCLINTOCK, Newcastle-Upon-Tyne

Postal: **The Byerley Stud, Ingoe, Newcastle-Upon-Tyne, NE20 0SZ**
Contacts: **PHONE (01661) 886356 MOBILE (07966) 776710**
**E-MAIL karen.mclintock@equiname.co.uk WEBSITE www.karenmclintock.co.uk**

1 **A GOOD CATCH (IRE),** 7, b g Catcher In The Rye (IRE)—Indian Squaw (IRE) **Mr A. C. Lamont**
2 **ANOTHER BYGONES (IRE),** 6, b g High-Rise (IRE)—Little Chartridge **Mr A. C. Lamont**
3 **AUSTRALASIA (IRE),** 5, b g Zerpour (IRE)—Leachestown (IRE) **06 Zoo Ltd**
4 **BYGONES OF BRID (IRE),** 12, b g Alderbrook—Glenadore **J. R. Callow**
5 **CARLITO BRIGANTE (IRE),** 9, b g Haafhd—Desert Magic (IRE) **06 Zoo Ltd**
6 **DERRYDOON,** 5, b g Multiplex—Wahiba Reason (IRE) **Mrs A. M. O'Sullivan**
7 **DEVENISH ISLAND,** 6, b g Multiplex—Wahiba Reason (IRE) **Mrs A. M. O'Sullivan**
8 **DUKEOFCHESTERWOOD,** 13, ch g Missed Flight—Gale Storm **Mrs C. J. Todd**
9 **EMPEROR SAKHEE,** 5, ch g Sakhee (USA)—Pochard **06 Zoo Ltd**
10 **GURKHA BRAVE (IRE),** 7, b g Old Vic—Honeyed (IRE) **Mr A. C. Lamont**
11 **MASON HINDMARSH,** 8, ch g Dr Fong (USA)—Sierra Virgen (USA) **B. Chicken**
12 **NORTHERN EXECUTIVE (IRE),** 7, b g Milan—Letterwoman (IRE) **Mr A. C. Lamont**
13 **THE LAST LEG (IRE),** 6, b g Old Vic—Raphuca (IRE) **06 Zoo Ltd**
14 **ULTIEP (FR),** 7, gr g Ragmar (FR)—Naltiepy (FR) **Mr A. C. Lamont**

### THREE-YEAR-OLDS

15 **GURKHA FRIEND,** b c Showcasing—Parabola **Equiname Ltd**
16 **TAOPIX,** b br c Rip Van Winkle (IRE)—Sinister Ruckus (USA) **Mr G. R. Stockdale**

### TWO-YEAR-OLDS

17 B c 25/2 Makfi—Clifton Dancer (Fraam) (60000)

**Other Owners:** Mr D. Eddy.

**Assistant Trainer:** Donald Eddy

---

## 406 MR ED MCMAHON, Lichfield

Postal: **Horsley Brook Farm, Tamworth Road, Lichfield, Staffordshire, WS14 9PT**
Contacts: **PHONE (01543) 481224 FAX (01543) 651100 MOBILE (07787) 951630**
**E-MAIL comeracing@horsleybrook.fsnet.co.uk WEBSITE www.edmcmahonracing.co.uk**

1 **ANGELITO,** 6, ch g Primo Valentino (IRE)—Supreme Angel **Least Moved Partners**
2 **COLOUR MY WORLD,** 5, gr g With Approval (CAN)—Nadeszhda **Mr P. A. Wilkins**
3 **EMJAYEM,** 5, ch g Needwood Blade—Distant Stars (IRE) **Mrs J. McMahon**
4 **EXPRESS HIMSELF (IRE),** 4, b g Dylan Thomas (IRE)—Lightwood Lady (IRE) **Milton Express Limited**
5 **GOLD CLUB,** 4, b g Multiplex—Oceana Blue **The C H F Partnership**
6 **MULTI BENE,** 6, b g Multiplex—Attlongglast **Mrs Richards & Mrs Brazier**
7 **NOBLE STORM (USA),** 9, b g Yankee Gentleman (USA)—Changed Tune (USA) **E. S. A. McMahon**
8 **ROCKET RONNIE (IRE),** 5, b g Antonius Pius (USA)—Ctesiphon (USA) **Mr C A Mills,Mr A Fallon,Mr G Purchase**
9 **SAKHEE'S ROSE,** 5, b m Sakhee's Secret—Isobel Rose (IRE) **Mr J. R. Dwyer**
10 **SECRET LOOK,** 5, ch g Sakhee's Secret—Look Here's Carol (IRE) **S. L. Edwards**
11 **VENUTIUS,** 8, b g Doyen (IRE)—Boadicea's Chariot **Mrs F. S. Williams**
12 **WHERE THE BOYS ARE (IRE),** 4, b f Dylan Thomas (IRE)—Promise of Love **Mr P. A. Wilkins**

### THREE-YEAR-OLDS

13 **LADY FOXLEY,** b f Bertolini (USA)—Muara **Mr W. R. Arblaster**
14 **LET RIGHT BE DONE,** gr g Lawman (FR)—Cheerfully **The LAM Partnership**
15 **PISTYLL RHAEADR,** ch f Mount Nelson—Sukuma (IRE)

## MR ED MCMAHON - Continued

16 **ROCKMOUNT,** b c Major Cadeaux—Fisher Island (IRE) **The C H F Partnership**
17 **SECRET GLANCE,** b g Sakhee's Secret—Look Here's Dee **S. L. Edwards**

### TWO-YEAR-OLDS

18 **ANDALUSITE,** br f 18/3 Equiano (FR)—Kammaan (Diktat) (8500) **The LAM Partnership**
19 Gr f 19/4 Dark Angel (IRE)—Gooseberry Pie (Green Desert (USA)) (20000) **The W.H.O. Society**
20 B f 26/3 Cacique (IRE)—Largo (IRE) (Selkirk (USA)) **S. L. Edwards**
21 **MYSTERIOUS LOOK,** ch f 3/2 Sakhee's Secret—Look Here's Carol (IRE) (Safawan) **S. L. Edwards**
22 B gr f 19/4 Aussie Rules (USA)—Oceana Blue (Reel Buddy (USA)) **The C H F Partnership**
23 **PURPLE REIGN (IRE),** b c 6/4 Duke of Marmalade (IRE)—Slieve (Selkirk (USA)) (50000) **Mr P. A. Wilkins**
24 **RENEGE,** ch f 14/2 Firebreak—Today's The Day (Alhaarth (IRE)) (4761)

**Other Owners:** Mrs S. M. Brazier, Mr A. Fallon, K. H. Fischer, C. H. Fischer, Dr M. F. Ford, Mr M. McGuinness, Mr C. Mills, Ms L. M. Mulcahy, F. G. Poingdestre, Mr G. Purchase, Mrs A. E. Richards, Mr D. Thomas.

**Assistant Trainer:** Bryan Arthur McMahon

---

## 407 MR GRAEME MCPHERSON, Stow-On-The-Wold

Postal: **Martins Hill, Bledington Road, Stow-on-the-Wold, Gloucestershire, GL54 1JH**
Contacts: **PHONE (01451) 830769 MOBILE (07815) 887360**
**WEBSITE www.mcphersonracing.co.uk**

1 **ACHIMOTA (IRE),** 9, b g Double Eclipse (IRE)—Tullyfoyle (IRE) **W. J. Odell**
2 **AMI DESBOIS (FR),** 5, b br g Dream Well (FR)—Baroya (FR) **EPDS Racing Partnership 11**
3 4, B g Double Eclipse (IRE)—Belle d'anjou (FR)
4 **BONIFACE (FR),** 4, b g Kapgarde (FR)—Kadjara (FR) **G. McPherson**
5 **BRACKEN HOUSE (IRE),** 8, ch g Great Palm (USA)—Carraig Aille (IRE) **Ms S. A. Howell**
6 4, B g Fair Mix (IRE)—Cadourova (FR) **Mr H. Burdett**
7 **CHARLIE COOK (IRE),** 6, b g Royal Anthem (USA)—Supreme Baloo (IRE) **Graham & Carole Worsley**
8 **CHERRY TIGER,** 5, b g Tiger Hill (IRE)—Lolla's Spirit (IRE) **Mrs S. M. McPherson**
9 **CITRUS MARK,** 10, b g Mark of Esteem (IRE)—Lemon's Mill (USA) **Miss A. L. Powell**
10 **CLARION CALL,** 7, b g Beat Hollow—Fanfare **The Maugersbury Racegoers**
11 **DARING INDIAN,** 7, ch g Zamindar (USA)—Anasazi (IRE) **Denarius Consulting Ltd**
12 **DO BE DASHING,** 7, b m Doyen (IRE)—Be Brave (FR) **Mrs C. J. Peake**
13 **DOLLY DIAMOND,** 6, b m Erhaab (USA)—Solid Land (FR) **Miss A. L. Powell**
14 **EVERVESCENT (IRE),** 6, b g Elnadim (USA)—Purepleasureseeker (IRE) **Ever Equine**
15 **EXIT TO NORA (IRE),** 6, b m Exit To Nowhere (USA)—Sweet Empire (IRE) **Arion Racing**
16 **EXTREME IMPACT,** 9, b g Rock of Gibraltar (IRE)—Soviet Moon (IRE) **Extreme Racing Fans**
17 **FLYING LIGHT (IRE),** 9, b g Chevalier (IRE)—Light-Flight (IRE) **The McPherson Racing Partnership**
18 **GREAT VALUE (IRE),** 10, b g Revoque (IRE)—Dame de L'oise (USA) **The McPherson Racing Partnership**
19 **HARRY HUNT,** 8, b g Bertolini (USA)—Qasirah (IRE) **Arion Racing**
20 4, B f Oscar (IRE)—Hazel Grove (IRE) **Mrs L. Day**
21 **HOLLYWOOD ALL STAR (IRE),** 6, b g Kheleyf (USA)—Camassina (IRE) **G. McPherson**
22 **IKORODU ROAD,** 12, b g Double Trigger (IRE)—Cerisier (IRE) **W. J. Odell**
23 **KAYF BLANCO,** 6, b g Kayf Tara—Land of Glory **Mrs L.Day, Mr H.Burdett & Mr G.McPherson**
24 5, Ch m Apple Tree (FR)—Lady Blade (IRE) **Ms S. A. Howell**
25 4, B g Dubai Destination (USA)—Maggie Howard (IRE) **The Ladies Of Martins Hill**
26 **MIDNIGHT GEM,** 5, b m Midnight Legend—Barton Flower **Ms G. E. Morgan**
27 **NEWORLD (FR),** 6, gr g Lost World (IRE)—Crusch Alva (FR) **Mr R. H. Hobson**
28 **OUR MAIMIE (IRE),** 9, b m Luso—Cormac Lady (IRE) **Ever Equine**
29 **PANDY WELLS,** 6, b m Kayf Tara—Alina Rheinberg (GER) **Mike & Linda Paul**
30 **PYRSHAN (IRE),** 6, b g Pyrus (USA)—Runshangale (IRE) **Mr K. J. N. Meek**
31 **RED ADMIRABLE (IRE),** 9, b g Shantou (USA)—Eimears Pet (IRE) **Wildcat Syndicate**
32 **SAMBULANDO (FR),** 12, gr g Kouroun (FR)—Somnambula (IRE) **Mr R. H. Hobson**
33 **SHADY GLEN (IRE),** 6, br g Dr Massini (IRE)—Poppins (IRE) **G. McPherson**
34 **SOCIETY SHARES (IRE),** 10, ch g Moscow Society (USA)—Presenting Shares (IRE) **Arion Racing**
35 **THE WINKING PRAWN (IRE),** 8, b g Beneficial—Rocamadoura **GJ Daly, A Davis & G McPherson**
36 **TICKATACK (IRE),** 10, gr g Tikkanen (USA)—Theflyingcannister (IRE) **Andy Weller & The Drummers**
37 **TITANS APPROACH (IRE),** 6, b g High Chaparral (IRE)—Armelles Approach (IRE) **Four Lawyers and a Banker**
38 **TRAFFICKER (IRE),** 8, b g Flemensfirth (USA)—Sulawesi (IRE) **Mr R. D. Potter**
39 **TRILLERIN MINELLA (IRE),** 7, b g King's Theatre (IRE)—Eva Fay (IRE) **Mrs L. Day**
40 **UJAGAR (IRE),** 4, gr g Dalakhani (IRE)—No Secrets (USA) **Denarius Consulting Ltd**
41 **WERENEARLYOUTOFIT (IRE),** 7, b g Asian Heights—Ballerina Laura (IRE) **The Ladies Of Martins Hill**

## MR GRAEME MCPHERSON - Continued

**Other Owners:** Mr S. Barnes, Mrs M. E. Barton, G. J. Daly, Mr A. D. Davis, K. R. Elliott, Mr R. J. P. Gilmore, Mr I. J. B. Gray, Mrs F. J. U. Ledger, Mr M. R. Paul, Mrs L. C. Paul, Mr J. R. Powell, Miss T. Sloan, Mr G. J. Styles, Mr A. J. Wadey, Mr A. J. Weller, Mr G. W. Worsley, Mrs C. P. Worsley.

**Assistant Trainers:** Mick Finn, Jodie Mogford

**Jockey (NH):** Wayne Hutchinson. **Conditional:** Ollie Garner, Killian Moore.

---

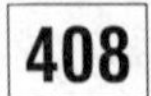

## MR MARTYN MEADE, Newmarket

Postal: **Sefton Lodge, Bury Road, Newmarket, Suffolk, CB8 7BT**
Contacts: **PHONE (01638) 666100 MOBILE (07879) 891811**
**E-MAIL lburgoyne@martynmeaderacing.com WEBSITE www.martynmeaderacing.com**

1 **ALDERLEY,** 4, b f Three Valleys (USA)—Doctor's Note
2 **DAMBUSTER (IRE),** 5, b g Dalakhani (IRE)—Threefold (USA)
3 **END OF LINE,** 4, b g Pastoral Pursuits—Just Devine (IRE)
4 **GLEN MOSS (IRE),** 6, b h Moss Vale (IRE)—Sail With The Wind
5 **SOLO HUNTER,** 4, b g Sleeping Indian—Night Owl

### THREE-YEAR-OLDS

6 **ASHFORD (IRE),** br f Yeats (IRE)—Little Empress (IRE)
7 B c Henrythenavigator (USA)—Ball Gown (USA)
8 B c Fastnet Rock (AUS)—Butterfly Blue (IRE)
9 **CITY OF NIGHT (IRE),** b c Elusive City (USA)—Testama (FR)
10 **CLERGYMAN,** b c Pastoral Pursuits—Doctor's Note
11 **DARMA (IRE),** b f Acclamation—Dark Dancer (FR)
12 **EXPLAIN,** ch c Kyllachy—Descriptive (IRE)
13 **FLIGAZ (FR),** ch f Panis (USA)—Fligane (FR)
14 **GREAT PARK (IRE),** b br c Vale of York (IRE)—Telesina (ITY)
15 **IRISH ROOKIE (IRE),** b f Azamour (IRE)—Bold Assumption
16 Ch g Kyllachy—Lady Broughton (IRE)
17 **LADY MAESMOR,** b f Kyllachy—Pulsate
18 **LEIGHTERTON,** ch c Halling (USA)—Dawnus (IRE)
19 **LOUMARIN (IRE),** b f Bushranger (IRE)—Masela (IRE)
20 B c Makfi—Lure of The Moon (USA)
21 **MAYBE DEFINITELY,** ch g Bahamian Bounty—Celestial Princess
22 **MISS JONH (FR),** ch f Deportivo—Flower
23 B br f Astronomer Royal (USA)—Miss Possibility (USA)
24 **MYSTERIOUS STAR (FR),** b c Iron Mask (USA)—Red Star (IRE)
25 **MYSTICAL SPIRIT (FR),** ch c Spirit One (FR)—Miss Maguilove (FR)
26 **NAVIGATE (IRE),** b c Iffraaj—Dorothy Dene
27 **SCALZO,** ch c Paco Boy (IRE)—Cruinn A Bhord
28 **SHUJAHA (AUS),** b f New Approach (IRE)—Umoya
29 B g Le Cadre Noir (IRE)—Social Upheaval (USA)
30 B g Le Cadre Noir (IRE)—Tarrifa (IRE)

### TWO-YEAR-OLDS

31 B f 2/5 Oasis Dream—Acts of Grace (USA) (Bahri (USA)) (51586)
32 B c 18/4 Iffraaj—Alexander Queen (IRE) (King's Best (USA)) (55000)
33 Ch f 12/3 Dutch Art—Angus Newz (Compton Place)
34 B c 8/2 Acclamation—Aris (IRE) (Danroad (AUS)) (103174)
35 B c 10/3 Arcano (IRE)—Ava's World (IRE) (Desert Prince (IRE))
36 Gr f 18/3 Kheleyf (USA)—Bunditten (IRE) (Soviet Star (USA))
37 B c 15/4 Tamayuz—Cannikin (IRE) (Lahib (USA)) (24602)
38 Ch f 4/3 Major Cadeaux—Cashleen (USA) (Lemon Drop Kid (USA)) (11000)
39 Ch c 28/4 Sea The Stars (IRE)—Chinese White (IRE) (Dalakhani (IRE)) (40000)
40 B c 12/2 Bushranger (IRE)—Cosenza (Bahri (USA)) (7142)
41 B f 22/4 Zebedee—Dazzling View (USA) (Distant View (USA)) (12000)
42 Ch c 16/3 Kyllachy—Doctor's Note (Pursuit of Love)
43 B c 1/4 Dream Ahead (USA)—Elegant Pride (Beat Hollow)
44 B f 12/3 Della Francesca (USA)—Loupana (FR) (Loup Solitaire (USA)) (9523)
45 B f 8/5 Canford Cliffs (IRE)—Mill Guineas (USA) (Salse (USA))
46 B f 2/4 Azamour (IRE)—Natural Flair (USA) (Giant's Causeway (USA)) (14000)
47 B c 12/3 Thewayyouare (USA)—Nellie Nolan (USA) (Storm Cat (USA)) (15238)

## MR MARTYN MEADE - Continued

**48** Ch c 16/5 Haatef (USA)—Non Ultra (USA) (Peintre Celebre (USA))
**49** B f 27/2 Vale of York (IRE)—Picture of Lily (Medicean) (5500)
**50** B f 10/5 Royal Applause—Pink Stone (FR) (Bigstone (IRE)) (14285)
**51** Ch f 14/4 Champs Elysees—Port Providence (Red Ransom (USA))
**52** B f 28/3 Bertolini (USA)—Primrose Queen (Lear Fan (USA))
**53** B c 28/1 Cape Cross (IRE)—Privalova (IRE) (Alhaarth (IRE)) (19841)
**54** B c 1/4 Motivator—Quip (Green Desert (USA)) (13000)
**55** Br c 28/2 Invincible Spirit (IRE)—Rakiza (IRE) (Elnadim (USA)) (35000)
**56** B f 17/2 Thousand Words—Red Empress (Nashwan (USA))
**57** B c 2/4 Clodovil (IRE)—Sakaka (Tobougg (IRE))
**58** B f 20/3 Sea The Stars (IRE)—Scarlet And Gold (IRE) (Peintre Celebre (USA)) (22000)
**59** B f 28/1 Equiano (FR)—Sceilin (IRE) (Lil's Boy (USA)) (5238)
**60** **SHEER INTENSITY (IRE),** ch f 25/4 Dutch Art—Sheer Elegance (IRE) (Pivotal)
**61** B c 11/2 Tamayuz—Soul Custody (CAN) (Perfect Soul (IRE)) (23809)
**62** B f 5/4 Sir Percy—Steady Rain (Zafonic (USA)) (9000)
**63** B f 6/4 Royal Applause—Three Ducks (Diktat) (11000)
**64** B c 6/4 Kheleyf (USA)—Tilly's Dream (Arkadian Hero (USA))
**65** B f 8/3 Zoffany (IRE)—Tropical Lake (IRE) (Lomond (USA)) (39681)
**66** Ch f 9/4 Dandy Man (IRE)—Viasta (IRE) (Soviet Star (USA))
**67** B f 20/3 Roderic O'Connor (IRE)—Viscoumtess Brave (IRE) (Law Society (USA))
**68** B f 8/2 Canford Cliffs (IRE)—What's Up Pussycat (IRE) (Danehill Dancer (IRE))
**69** B f 25/2 Hellvelyn—Willmar (IRE) (Zafonic (USA))
**70** B c 21/2 Clodovil (IRE)—Yali (IRE) (Orpen (USA)) (10000)

**Owners:** Mr Khalfan Al Suwaidi, Mr Rick Barnes, The Below Reeve Partnership, Mr David Caddy, Calypso Bloodstock And Partners, Mr J. C. G. Chua, Mrs L. Coffey, Mr D. Farrington, Mr P. Fitzsimons, Mr A. Hine, Dr Graham Jackson, Ladyswood Stud, Mr H. Link, Mr F. M. Meade, Mr Richard Morecombe, Mr Barry O'Connor, Mr W. Routledge, Mr W. J. Salthouse, Mr Adam Sangster, Mr H. Sherbourne, Mr Vartan Vartanov, Mr R. Withers.

**Assistant Trainer:** Freddie Meade

**Jockey (flat):** Fergus Sweeney.

---

## 409 MR NOEL MEADE, Navan

Postal: **Tu Va Stables, Castletown-Kilpatrick, Navan, Co. Meath, Ireland**
Contacts: **PHONE (00 353) 46 905 4197 FAX (00 353) 46 905 4459 MOBILE (00 353) 87 256 6039 WEBSITE www.noelmeade.com**

**1** **AENGUS (IRE),** 5, b g Robin des Champs (FR)—Which Thistle (IRE)
**2** **ANGE BALAFRE (FR),** 6, b g Ange Gabriel (FR)—Balafre Rose (FR)
**3** **ANOTHER PALM (IRE),** 10, gr g Great Palm (USA)—Park Rose (IRE)
**4** **APACHE STRONGHOLD (IRE),** 7, b g Milan—First Battle (IRE)
**5** **AVIDIUS CASSIUS (IRE),** 7, b g Flemensfirth (USA)—Rixdale (FR)
**6** **BAROSSA PEARL (IRE),** 5, b m Milan—What An Answer (IRE)
**7** **BENEMEADE (IRE),** 7, b g Beneficial—Millicent Bridge (IRE)
**8** **BONNY KATE (IRE),** 5, ch m Beneficial—Peppardstown (IRE)
**9** **BOSE IKARD (IRE),** 7, b g Brian Boru—Dolldyedee (IRE)
**10** **BRONCO BILL (IRE),** 5, b g Kalanisi (IRE)—Mill Lady (IRE)
**11** **BUSTY BROWN (IRE),** 9, b g Mr Combustible (IRE)—Misty Brown (IRE)
**12** **CHAMPOLEON (FR),** 5, gr g Turtle Bowl (IRE)—Trasimene
**13** **CHRISSIE MC (IRE),** 6, b m Oscar (IRE)—They Call Me Molly (CAN)
**14** 4, B g Primary (USA)—Cockpit Lady (IRE)
**15** **CORSKEAGH EXPRESS (IRE),** 4, gr g Daylami (IRE)—Zara's Victory (IRE)
**16** **COULEUR FRANCE (IRE),** 7, b g Flemensfirth (USA)—Gaye Mercy
**17** **CROSS APPEAL (IRE),** 9, b g Cape Cross (IRE)—Hadeb
**18** **CURLEY BILL (IRE),** 7, b g Heron Island (IRE)—In Excelsis (GER)
**19** 4, B g Robin des Champs (FR)—Daizinni
**20** **DAN BOGAN (IRE),** 6, b g Windsor Knot (IRE)—Housekeeping
**21** **DARING DECOY (IRE),** 7, gr g Great Palm (USA)—Blue Pool
**22** **DISKO (FR),** 4, gr g Martaline—Nikos Royale (FR)
**23** **DOWN ACE (IRE),** 8, ch m Generous (IRE)—Full of Birds (FR)
**24** **FESTIVE FELON (IRE),** 8, b g Gold Well—Takara (IRE)
**25** **FISHER BRIDGE (IRE),** 12, ch g Singspiel (IRE)—Kristal Bridge
**26** **FLINDERS RIVER (IRE),** 7, ch g Traditionally (USA)—Silver Tassie (FR)
**27** **GETTYSBURG ADDRESS (IRE),** 4, b g Milan—Cat Burglar (IRE)

## MR NOEL MEADE - Continued

28 **GLEESONSFORONE (IRE),** 4, b g Scorpion (IRE)—Kilmington Breeze (IRE)
29 **GLENMOREANGIE (IRE),** 6, b g Scorpion (IRE)—Sister Swing
30 **GRECO ROMAIN (FR),** 4, b g Martaline—De Haute Lutte (USA)
31 **HARVEY LOGAN (IRE),** 6, b g Saffron Walden (FR)—Baie Barbara (IRE)
32 **HECK THOMAS (IRE),** 7, b g Oscar (IRE)—Good Heighway (IRE)
33 **HOODOO BROWN,** 4, ch g Refuse To Bend (IRE)—Paradise Dancer (IRE)
34 **ICE COLD SOUL (IRE),** 5, b g Stowaway—Western Whisper (IRE)
35 **IKE CLANTON (IRE),** 6, b g Heron Island (IRE)—Shbrook (IRE)
36 **IPSOS DU BERLAIS (FR),** 9, gr g Poliglote—Isis Du Berlais (FR)
37 **JACK SLADE (IRE),** 5, ch g Stowaway—Sharps Express (IRE)
38 **JOHANNISBERGER (IRE),** 8, b g Arakan (USA)—Housekeeping
39 **JOSEPHINE MARCUS (IRE),** 5, b m Flemensfirth (USA)—Tart of Tipp (IRE)
40 **KILLER MILLER (IRE),** 6, b g Flemensfirth (USA)—Miss Brandywell (IRE)
41 **LA SCALA DIVA (IRE),** 5, b m Milan—Shaping
42 **LEOPARDS LEAP (IRE),** 5, br m Arcadio (GER)—Talk of Rain (FR)
43 **LETTRE DE CACHET,** 4, gr f Authorized (IRE)—Regrette Rien (USA)
44 **LONDON BRIDGE,** 9, br g Beat Hollow—Cantanta
45 **MONKSLAND (IRE),** 8, b g Beneficial—Cush Jewel (IRE)
46 **MULLAGHANOE RIVER (IRE),** 7, b g Beneficial—Wahiba Hall (IRE)
47 **NED BUNTLINE,** 7, b g Refuse To Bend (IRE)—Intrum Morshaan (IRE)
48 **NORTH STAR LAD (IRE),** 8, b g Stardan (IRE)—Forever Silver (IRE)
49 **OFFICIEUX (FR),** 4, ch g Discover d'auteuil (FR)—Souri des Champs (FR)
50 **OWEN MC (IRE),** 7, b g Oscar (IRE)—They Call Me Molly (CAN)
51 **PAT GARRETT (IRE),** 8, b g Fruits of Love (USA)—Junga Connection
52 4, B g Flemensfirth (USA)—Phardester (IRE)
53 **PROTARAS (USA),** 8, b br g Lemon Drop Kid (USA)—Seven Moons (JPN)
54 **RATHNURE REBEL (IRE),** 5, b g Beneficial—Euro Magic (IRE)
55 **RED GIANT (IRE),** 4, ch g Beneficial—Barrack Star (IRE)
56 **RICH COAST,** 7, b g King's Best (USA)—Costa Rica (IRE)
57 **ROAD TO RICHES (IRE),** 8, b g Gamut (IRE)—Bellora (IRE)
58 **ROCK OF GLENSTAL,** 5, b g Mount Nelson—Amandian (IRE)
59 **RUBE BURROW (IRE),** 6, b g Presenting—Sarah Massini (IRE)
60 **RUSSIAN BILL (IRE),** 5, b g Kalanisi (IRE)—Littleton Liberty
61 **SILVER TASSIE (IRE),** 7, b g Shantou (USA)—Silver Castor (IRE)
62 **SILVER TURTLE (FR),** 4, gr g Turtle Bowl (IRE)—Trasimene
63 4, B g Scorpion (IRE)—Silvestre (ITY)
64 **SIX STONE NED (IRE),** 9, gr g Great Palm (USA)—Ashfield Rosie (IRE)
65 **SNOW FALCON (IRE),** 5, b g Presenting—Flocon de Neige (IRE)
66 **SUCKER PUNCH (IRE),** 6, b g Scorpion (IRE)—Lemonfield Lady (IRE)
67 **SUNRAE SHADOW,** 6, b g Echo of Light—Please
68 4, B g Winged Love (IRE)—Swap Shop (IRE)
69 **TEXAS FOREVER (IRE),** 6, b g Heron Island (IRE)—Gravinis (FR)
70 **TEXAS JACK (IRE),** 9, b g Curtain Time (IRE)—Sailors Run (IRE)
71 **THE CONTENDER (IRE),** 6, b g Scorpion (IRE)—Welsh Rhapsody (IRE)
72 **THE HERDS GARDEN,** 6, b g Multiplex—Eternal Legacy (IRE)
73 **THOMOND (IRE),** 7, b g Definite Article—Hushaby (IRE)
74 **TICONDEROGA (IRE),** 4, b g Robin des Champs (FR)—Wayward Star (IRE)
75 **TIGER SAM (IRE),** 5, ch g Beneficial—Colleen Donn
76 **TOM HORN (IRE),** 9, ch g Beneficial—Lady Shackleton (IRE)
77 **TULSA JACK (IRE),** 6, b g Urban Ocean (FR)—Jessica's Pet (IRE)
78 **TURFMANS DAUGHTER (IRE),** 5, b m Flemensfirth (USA)—Atomic Winner (IRE)
79 **UNE LAVANDIERE (FR),** 4, b br f Laveron—Nouvelle Donne (FR)
80 **VERY WOOD (FR),** 6, b g Martaline—Ball of Wood (FR)
81 **VIRTUOSO ROUGE (FR),** 6, b g Laveron—Prompt
82 **WAXIES DARGLE,** 6, b g Sakhee (USA)—Cup of Love (USA)
83 **WES HARDIN (IRE),** 6, b g Beneficial—Luas Luso (IRE)
84 **WESTHAVEN (IRE),** 7, b g Alhaarth (IRE)—Dashiba
85 **WILDEBEEST (IRE),** 6, b g Oscar (IRE)—Cailin's Princess (IRE)
86 **WOUNDED WARRIOR (IRE),** 6, b g Shantou (USA)—Sparkling Sword
87 4, B g Central Park (IRE)—Zamyatina (IRE)
88 **ZIGGER ZAGGER (IRE),** 6, b g Mountain High (IRE)—Main Suspect (IRE)
89 **ZIP WYATT (IRE),** 6, ch g Flemensfirth (USA)—Tricky Present (IRE)

## MR NOEL MEADE - Continued

### THREE-YEAR-OLDS

**90** B c Jeremy (USA)—Cant Hurry Love
**91 WEIGHTFORDAVE (IRE),** b c Dark Angel (IRE)—Moon Diamond

### TWO-YEAR-OLDS

**92** B c 26/3 Roderic O'Connor (IRE)—Happy Flight (IRE) (Titus Livius (FR)) (14285)
**93** B f 24/3 Lend A Hand—Lush Sister (IRE) (Indian Danehill (IRE))

**Assistant Trainer:** Damien McGillick

**Jockey (NH):** Davy Condon, Paul Carberry. **Conditional:** Ger Fox. **Amateur:** Miss Nina Carberry.

---

## 410 MR BRIAN MEEHAN, Manton

**Trainer did not wish details of his string to appear**

---

## 411 MR DAVID MENUISIER, Pulborough

Postal: **To Agori House, Coombelands Lane, Pulborough, West Sussex, RH20 1BP**
Contacts: **MOBILE (07876) 674095**
**E-MAIL david@dmhorseracing.com WEBSITE www.dmhorseracing.com**

1 **MERCURY MAGIC,** 4, b g Oratorio (IRE)—Lochridge **Mr D. Rogers**
2 **SLUNOVRAT (FR),** 4, b br g Astronomer Royal (USA)—Slewmamba (FR) **Shinco Racing Ltd**
3 **TOM HALL,** 5, b g Pastoral Pursuits—Villarosi (IRE) **Hunter Racing**

### THREE-YEAR-OLDS

4 **HAVRE DE PAIX (FR),** b br f Le Havre (IRE)—Bridge of Peace **Mr C. A. Washbourn**
5 **HIER ENCORE (FR),** ch g Kentucky Dynamite (USA)—Hierarchie (FR) **Shinco Racing Ltd**
6 **SPECULATOR,** gr c Bahamian Bounty—Swift Dispersal **Gail Brown Racing (VI)**

### TWO-YEAR-OLDS

7 **CORPUS CHORISTER (FR),** b f 22/4 Soldier of Fortune (IRE)—
Bridge of Peace (Anabaa (USA)) **Mr C. A. Washbourn**
8 **NAZIBA (IRE),** gr f 19/4 Zebedee—Nashaat (Redoute's Choice (AUS)) (11000) **Skinfaxi Racing (I)**
9 **RODERIC'S SECRET (IRE),** ch c 20/3 Roderic O'Connor (IRE)—
Midris (IRE) (Namid) (12000) **Clive Washbourn & Robert Wasey**

**Other Owners:** Mrs H. G. Clinch, Shinco Racing Ltd.

---

## 412 MISS REBECCA MENZIES, Brandsby

Postal: **Rebecca Menzies Racing, Foulrice Farm, Brandsby, York, North Yorkshire, YO61 4SB**
Contacts: **PHONE (01347) 889652 MOBILE (07843) 169217**
**E-MAIL rebecca@rebeccamenzies.com WEBSITE www.rebeccamenzies.com**

1 **AQUILEGIA,** 7, b m Alflora (IRE)—Artemesia **Miss R. E. A. Menzies**
2 **ASUNCION (FR),** 5, b m Antarctique (IRE)—Liesse de Marbeuf (FR) **EPDS Racing Partnership 6**
3 **BALDING BANKER (IRE),** 9, b g Accordion—What A Breeze (IRE) **Club Racing Banker Partnership**
4 **BISHOP LIGHTFOOT (IRE),** 6, b g Helissio (FR)—Dawn Bid (IRE) **EPDS Racing Partnership 9**
5 **CAPTAIN MOWBRAY,** 4, ch c Shami—Some Like It Hot
6 **CELTIC ARTISAN (IRE),** 4, ch g Dylan Thomas (IRE)—Perfectly Clear (USA) **EPDS Racing Partnership 4**
7 **CHAVOY (FR),** 10, br g Saint des Saints (FR)—Dictania (FR) **Mr Masoud Khadem & Mr I Shaw**
8 **HALCYON DAYS,** 6, b g Generous (IRE)—Indian Empress **Club Racing Halcyon Partnership**
9 **IM TOO GENEROUS,** 5, ch g Generous (IRE)—Something Major (IRE) **John Dance & Partner**
10 **NORTHERN CHAMP (IRE),** 9, b g Mull of Kintyre (USA)—Comprehension (USA) **Mr J. W. Howley**
11 **PISTOL BASC (FR),** 11, ch g Maille Pistol (FR)—Moldane (FR) **Panther Racing Limited**
12 **POPPIES MILAN (IRE),** 6, b g Milan—Second Best (IRE) **Poppies Europe Limited**
13 **REVOLUTIONARY ROAD,** 7, b g Shirocco (GER)—Emilion **Yarm Racing Partnership & Partner**
14 **ROYAL MACNAB (IRE),** 7, b g Beneficial—Tina McBride (IRE) **The Extra Time Partnership**

## MISS REBECCA MENZIES - Continued

15 **SAMSON COLLONGES (FR),** 9, gr g Fragrant Mix (IRE)—Idole Collonges (FR) **Premier Racing Partnerships**
16 **SPOT THE PRO (IRE),** 6, b g Barathea (IRE)—Truly Precious (IRE) **Mr M. Khadem**
17 **THE BANASTOIR (IRE),** 6, b br g Presenting—Kimouna (FR) **Mr J. Dance**
18 **UNCLE BRIT,** 9, b g Efisio—Tarneem (USA) **Panther Racing Limited**
19 **VUVUZELA,** 9, ch g Sir Harry Lewis (USA)—Clair Valley **Premier Racing Partnerships**
20 **WATER GARDEN (FR),** 9, gr g Turgeon (USA)—Queenstown (FR) **Love To Race Partnership**

**Other Owners:** J. Berry, R. A. Brown, Mrs M. Feely, Ms D. Fields, J. H. Madden, Mr G. W. Peacock, Mr J. R. Powell, Mr I. Shaw, Miss T. Sloan, Major P. H. K. Steveney.

**Assistant Trainer:** Carly Dixon

---

## 413 MR ANTHONY MIDDLETON, Banbury

Postal: **Culworth Grounds Stables, Culworth, Banbury, Oxfordshire, OX17 2ND**
Contacts: **PHONE (01844) 292463 FAX (01844) 292463 MOBILE (07894) 909542**
**E-MAIL tony@granboroughracing.com WEBSITE www.granboroughracing.co.uk**

1 **AL DESTOOR,** 5, ch g Teofilo (IRE)—In A Silent Way (IRE) **Glen's Fools 2**
2 **AMERICAN LIFE (FR),** 8, b br g American Post—Poplife (FR) **Mr J. T. Watts**
3 **BALLINALACKEN (IRE),** 7, b g Fruits of Love (USA)—Miss Daisy **Chrissy's Passion Racing**
4 **CAFE AU LAIT (GER),** 5, b g Nicaron (GER)—Cariera (GER) **Nojab Limited**
5 **CARNAROSS,** 6, b g Norse Dancer (IRE)—Miss Lewis **Chrissy's Passion Racing & Nojab Ltd**
6 **CULWORTH BOY (IRE),** 5, b g Tajraasi (USA)—Cadre Idris (IRE) **Mrs D. Dewbery**
7 **FUTURE SECURITY (IRE),** 6, ch g Dalakhani (IRE)—Schust Madame (IRE) **Nojab & John Naylor**
8 **GRANDE VITESSE (IRE),** 5, b m Dr Massini (IRE)—Presenting Shares (IRE) **Phantom Filly Partnership**
9 **LOVE TANGLE (IRE),** 4, b g Azamour (IRE)—Dragnet (IRE) **Chrissy's Passion Racing**
10 5, B g Oscar (IRE)—Mandyslady (IRE) **Mrs D. Dewbery**
11 5, B g Erhaab (USA)—Miss Lewis **The Porchester Lads**
12 **PILGRIMS LANE (IRE),** 11, b g Dr Massini (IRE)—Miss Mylette (IRE) **Mrs S. E. Brown**
13 **SHOCK N FREANEY (IRE),** 8, ch g Clouseau (DEN)—Iliner (IRE) **Mrs D. Dewbery**
14 **SWANAGE BAY (IRE),** 8, b g Dilshaan—Special Mention (IRE) **Dr J. D. Dalton**
15 **THE BOOGEYMAN (IRE),** 9, br g King's Theatre (IRE)—Market Lass (IRE) **Mrs D. Dewbery**
16 5, Ch g Tajraasi (USA)—Turnpike Junction
17 **VA'VITE (IRE),** 8, b m Vinnie Roe (IRE)—Presenting Shares (IRE) **Ms B Woodcock & Mrs D Dewbery**

**Other Owners:** Mr R. J. Borsley, Mr B. H. Dolan, Mr T. M. Foster, Mr K. J. Mulville, Mr J.P Naylor, Mr A. Sadler, Ms B. Woodcock.

**Jockey (NH):** James Banks, Paul Moloney.

---

## 414 MR PHIL MIDDLETON, Aylesbury

Postal: **Dorton Place, Dorton Park Farm, Dorton, Aylesbury, Buckinghamshire, HP18 9NR**
Contacts: **PHONE (01844) 237503 FAX (01844) 237503 MOBILE (07860) 426607**

1 **EXITAS (IRE),** 7, b g Exit To Nowhere (USA)—Suntas (IRE) **Mr P. W. Middleton**
2 **TALES OF MILAN (IRE),** 8, b g Milan—The Millers Tale (IRE) **Mr P. W. Middleton**
3 **TANGOLAN (IRE),** 7, ch g Golan (IRE)—Classic Note (IRE) **Mr P. W. Middleton**

**Assistant Trainer:** Helen Day

---

## 415 MR PAUL MIDGLEY, Westow

Postal: **Sandfield Farm, Westow, York, YO60 7LS**
Contacts: **Office (01653) 658790 FAX (01653) 658790 MOBILE (07976) 965220**
**E-MAIL ptmidgley@aol.com WEBSITE www.ptmidgley.com**

1 **FUEL INJECTION,** 4, gr g Pastoral Pursuits—Smart Hostess **Mrs M. Verity**
2 **LINE OF REASON (IRE),** 5, br g Kheleyf (USA)—Miss Party Line (USA) **Taylor's Bloodstock Ltd**
3 **MONSIEUR JOE (IRE),** 8, b g Choisir (AUS)—Pascali **Taylor's Bloodstock Ltd**

**Assistant Trainer:** Mrs W. E. Midgley

## 416 MR ROD MILLMAN, Cullompton

Postal: **The Paddocks, Kentisbeare, Cullompton, Devon, EX15 2DX**
Contacts: **PHONE/FAX (01884) 266620 MOBILE (07885) 168447**
**E-MAIL rod.millman@ic24.net**

1 **BIOTIC,** 4, b g Aqlaam—Bramaputra (IRE) **Mrs B. Sumner**
2 **COTTON CLUB (IRE),** 4, b g Amadeus Wolf—Slow Jazz (USA) **The Links Partnership**
3 **DANCE,** 6, b m Erhaab (USA)—Shi Shi **Mrs C. Knowles**
4 **DOVIL'S DUEL (IRE),** 4, b g Clodovil (IRE)—Duelling **Always Hopeful Partnership**
5 **EUGENIC,** 4, br g Piccolo—Craic Sa Ceili (IRE) **B. C. Scott**
6 **GLADIATRIX,** 6, b m Compton Place—Lady Dominatrix (IRE) **Harry Dutfield & Partners**
7 **ICEBUSTER,** 7, ch g Iceman—Radiate **The Links Partnership**
8 **ISIS BLUE,** 5, b g Cockney Rebel (IRE)—Bramaputra (IRE) **Cantay Racing**
9 **MASAI MOON,** 11, b g Lujain (USA)—Easy To Imagine (USA) **B. R. Millman**
10 **MASTER CARPENTER (IRE),** 4, ch c Mastercraftsman (IRE)—Fringe **The Links Partnership/Cheveley Park Stud**
11 **MIDNIGHT RIDER (IRE),** 7, b g Red Ransom (USA)—Foreplay (IRE) **B. R. Millman**
12 **NORA BATTY,** 4, b f Zamindar (USA)—Soolaimon (IRE) **Five Horses Ltd**
13 **PRINCESS ANNABELLE,** 6, ch m Sworn In (USA)—Marybelle **B. R. Millman**
14 **SHAVANSKY,** 11, b g Rock of Gibraltar (IRE)—Limelighting (USA) **The Links Partnership**
15 **TAWS,** 4, b f Hernando (FR)—Reaf **K. Arrowsmith**

### THREE-YEAR-OLDS

16 **BONNIE GREY,** gr f Hellvelyn—Crofters Ceilidh **Howard Barton Stud**
17 **CAERLEON KATE,** ch f Medicean—Towaahi (IRE) **Five Horses Ltd**
18 **DEVONIAN,** b g Hellvelyn—Overcome **Mustajed Partnership**
19 **GO AMBER GO,** ch f Compton Place—Lady Chef
20 B c Sir Percy—Great Quest (IRE) **Seasons Holidays**
21 **HAWRIDGE DANCER,** b g Danehill Dancer (IRE)—Thermopylae **E. J. S. Gadsden**
22 **LORELEI,** b f Excellent Art—Light Dreams **The Links Partnership**
23 **LOTI,** ch f Monsieur Bond (IRE)—Bond Platinum Club **B. R. Millman**
24 B c Champs Elysees—Maramba **Five Horses Ltd**
25 **MARCANO (IRE),** b c Arcano (IRE)—Aquatint **The Links Partnership**
26 **NELSONS TRICK,** b f Mount Nelson—Mild Deception (IRE) **K. Arrowsmith**
27 **SEVEN COLOURS (IRE),** b f Thewayyouare (USA)—Stamatina **R. S. Solomon**
28 **ZEBELLA,** b f Paco Boy (IRE)—Delitme (IRE) **The Links Partnership**

### TWO-YEAR-OLDS

29 **BUKLE (IRE),** b c 26/2 Approve (IRE)—Rumline (Royal Applause) (20952) **Mr C. H. Saunders**
30 **CONCUR (IRE),** ch c 20/4 Approve (IRE)—Tradmagic (IRE) (Traditionally (USA)) (22857) **Miss G. J. Abbey**
31 B c 4/4 Hellvelyn—Crofters Ceilidh (Scottish Reel) (16190) **Mustajed Partnership**
32 **DANCE TUNE,** b f 29/3 Dutch Art—Russian Dance (USA) (Nureyev (USA)) **Cheveley Park Stud Limited**
33 B c 9/3 Aqlaam—Diam Queen (GER) (Lando (GER)) (6000)
34 B c 9/3 Hellvelyn—Emma Peel (Emarati (USA)) (15238) **G. D. Thompson**
35 **HANDYTALK (IRE),** b c 14/4 Lilbourne Lad (IRE)—Dancing With Stars (IRE) (Where Or When (IRE)) (30476) **Cantay Racing**
36 **METTE,** b f 22/3 Virtual—Regal Gallery (IRE) (Royal Academy (USA)) **Mrs B. Sumner**
37 B f 23/1 Compton Place—Nina Fontenail (FR) (Kaldounevees (FR)) **The Links Partnership**
38 **O'CONNOR (IRE),** ch c 16/4 Roderic O'Connor (IRE)—Fly By Magic (IRE) (Indian Rocket) (23809) **The Links Partnership**
39 **PUSHY LADY,** b f 9/1 Piccolo—Jane's Payoff (IRE) (Danetime (IRE)) (8000) **K. L. Dare**
40 B c 16/4 Showcasing—Showery (Rainbow Quest (USA)) (20000)
41 **SIR RODERIC (IRE),** b c 21/4 Roderic O'Connor (IRE)—Begin The Beguine (IRE) (Peintre Celebre (USA)) (47619) **The Links Partnership**
42 B c 27/2 Hellvelyn—Welcome Home (Most Welcome) (6666)

**Other Owners:** P. Bartlam, Mr H. Dutfield, Mr R. D. Gamlin, Mr M. Leach, V. B. Lewer, D. A. Little, Mr A. M. Nolan, Mrs M. O'Sullivan, Ms P. D. O'Sullivan, G. G. Payne, S. M. Perry, Mr T. Tompkins.

**Assistant Trainer:** Louise Millman

**Jockey (flat):** Andrea Atzeni. **Apprentice:** Pat Millman.

## 417 MR ROBERT MILLS, Epsom

Postal: **Loretta Lodge Racing Stables, Tilley Lane, Headley, Surrey, KT18 6EP**
Contacts: **PHONE (01372) 377209 FAX (01372) 386578**
**E-MAIL lorettalodge@aol.com**

1 **CHARLTON,** 12, b g Inchinor—Sabina **Mrs B. B. Mills**
2 **CLUB HOUSE (IRE),** 5, b g Marju (IRE)—Idesia (IRE) **Mrs B B Mills Mr A Foreman**
3 **LITTLE BUXTED (USA),** 5, b br g Mr Greeley (USA)—Mo Cheoil Thu (IRE) **Buxted Partnership**
4 **RYDAN (IRE),** 4, ch c Intense Focus (USA)—Lough Mewin (IRE) **Jacobs Construction (Holdings) Limited**
5 **SWING EASY,** 5, b h Zamindar (USA)—Shahmina (IRE) **Mrs B. B. Mills**
6 **TURNBURY,** 4, b g Azamour (IRE)—Scottish Heights (IRE) **Mrs B B Mills, T Jacobs, A Foreman**

### THREE-YEAR-OLDS

7 **ART OF SWING (IRE),** b g Excellent Art—Shahmina (IRE) **Mrs B B Mills, Mr J Harley, Mr T Jacobs**
8 **BEACH PLAZA (IRE),** b f Moss Vale (IRE)—Uhud (IRE) **Mrs B. B. Mills**
9 **DREAM OF YOU (IRE),** gr f Art Connoisseur (IRE)—Ms Sasha Malia (IRE) **Mrs B. B. Mills**
10 **ST LAWRENCE GAP (IRE),** ch c Tagula (IRE)—Kannon **R. A. Mills**

**Other Owners:** Mr A. Foreman, Mr Jim Hanifin, Mr J. E. Harley, Mr T. Jacobs, Jacobs Construction (Holdings) Limited, Mrs B. B. Mills, Mrs J. Ruthven.

**Assistant Trainer:** Vincenzo Cook

## 418 MR NICK MITCHELL, Dorchester

Postal: **1 Racklands, Piddletrenthide, Dorchester, Dorset, DT2 7QP**
Contacts: **PHONE (01300) 348049 MOBILE (07770) 892085**
**E-MAIL nick.mitch@btinernet.com WEBSITE www.nickmitchellracing.com**

1 **BAND OF THUNDER,** 7, ch g Shirocco (GER)—Black Opal **J. R. Boughey**
2 **CHETNOLE,** 5, ch m Apple Tree (FR)—Seemarye **Glanvilles Stud Partners**
3 **DANCE FLOOR KING (IRE),** 8, b g Generous (IRE)—Strawberry Fool (FR) **N. Elliott**
4 **PHONE HOME (IRE),** 8, b br g Heron Island (IRE)—Ancestral Voices (IRE) **Mr & Mrs Andrew May & Nick Elliott**
5 5, B g Sixties Icon—Summer Shades **Mr E. P. Swaffield**

**Other Owners:** Dr G. W. Guy, Mrs S. H. May, A. J. May, Mr W. D. Procter.

**Jockey (NH):** Daryl Jacob. **Amateur:** Mr R. G. Henderson.

## 419 MR PHILIP MITCHELL, Kingston Lisle

Postal: **Blowing Stone Stables, Kingston Lisle, Wantage, Oxfordshire, OX12 9QH**
Contacts: **PHONE (01367) 820299 FAX (01367) 820299 MOBILE (07836) 231462**
**E-MAIL philipmitchell48@gmail.com**

1 **AL QATARI (USA),** 6, b br g Dynaformer (USA)—Where's The Church (USA) **Mrs P. A. Mitchell**
2 **ROBIN HOOD (IRE),** 7, b g Galileo (IRE)—Banquise (IRE) **Amelco UK Ltd**

### THREE-YEAR-OLDS

3 Ch f Peintre Celebre (USA)—Virginias Best **Amelco UK Ltd**
4 **WYATT (IRE),** b g Lawman (FR)—Umlilo

**Jockey (flat):** Jack Mitchell. **Conditional:** Freddie Mitchell.

## 420 MR RICHARD MITCHELL, Dorchester

Postal: **East Hill Stables, Piddletrenthide, Dorchester, Dorset, DT2 7QY**
Contacts: **PHONE/FAX (01300) 348739 MOBILE (07775) 843136**

1 **BEDIBYES,** 7, b m Sleeping Indian—Aunt Sadie **J. R. Boughey**
2 **BENBECULA,** 6, b g Motivator—Isle of Flame **Mr & Mrs Andrew May**
3 **THUNDERING HOME,** 8, gr g Storming Home—Citrine Spirit (IRE) **Mrs K. M. Boughey**

**Other Owners:** Mrs S. H. May, A. J. May.

**Assistant Trainer:** Mrs E. Mitchell

## 421 MR JAMES MOFFATT, Grange-Over-Sands

Postal: **Pit Farm Racing Stables, Cartmel, Grange-Over-Sands, Cumbria, LA11 6PJ**
Contacts: **PHONE (01539) 536689 FAX (01539) 536236 MOBILE (07767) 367282**
**E-MAIL jamesmoffatt@hotmail.co.uk WEBSITE www.jamesmoffatt.co.uk**

1 **ALTRUISM (IRE),** 5, b g Authorized (IRE)—Bold Assumption **Mr V R Vyner-Brooks, Mr K Bowron**
2 **BORDER TALE,** 15, b g Selkirk (USA)—Likely Story (IRE) **D. J. Moffatt**
3 **CAPE ROSA,** 5, b m Sir Percy—Cashema (IRE) **Exors of the Late Mr M. W. Chapman**
4 **CAPTAIN BROWN,** 7, b g Lomitas—Nicola Bella (IRE) **K. Bowron**
5 **CAPTAIN RHYRIC,** 6, ch g Dylan Thomas (IRE)—Nuts In May (USA) **Bowes Lodge Stables**
6 **DOLLAR MICK (IRE),** 10, b g Presenting—Bula Beag (IRE) **Exors of the Late Mr M. W. Chapman**
7 **DUMBARTON (IRE),** 7, br h Danehill Dancer (IRE)—Scottish Stage (IRE) **K. Bowron**
8 **FANTASY KING,** 9, b g Acclamation—Fantasy Ridge **Mr V. R. Vyner-Brooks**
9 **FORSTER STREET (IRE),** 6, b g Acclamation—Easy To Thrill **K. Bowron**
10 **MAY'S BOY,** 7, gr h Proclamation (IRE)—Sweet Portia (IRE) **K. Bowron**
11 **MAYBE I WONT,** 10, b g Kyllachy—Surprise Surprise **The Sheroot Partnership**
12 **MOHAWK RIDGE,** 9, b g Storming Home—Ipsa Loquitur **K. Bowron**
13 **MORNING ROYALTY (IRE),** 8, b g King's Theatre (IRE)—Portryan Native (IRE) **Mrs E. M. Milligan**
14 **PENNINE JOSIE,** 6, b m Josr Algarhoud (IRE)—Pennine Star (IRE) **Exors of the Late Mr M. W. Chapman**
15 **QUEL ELITE (FR),** 11, b g Subotica (FR)—Jeenly (FR) **Hadwin, Hall, Moffatt, Chamberlain Bros.**
16 **REDPENDER (IRE),** 9, gr g Great Palm (USA)—Josie Murphy (IRE) **K. Bowron**
17 **RISK RUNNER (IRE),** 12, b g Mull of Kintyre (USA)—Fizzygig
18 **SAM LORD,** 11, ch g Observatory (USA)—My Mariam **Bowes Lodge Stables**
19 **SMART RULER (IRE),** 9, ch g Viking Ruler (AUS)—Celebrated Smile (IRE) **The Vilprano Partnership**
20 **TOKYO BROWN (USA),** 6, b g Marquetry (USA)—Miasma (USA) **K. Bowron**
21 **ZUILEKA,** 6, b m Observatory (USA)—Cashema (IRE) **Exors of the Late Mr M. W. Chapman**

### THREE-YEAR-OLDS

22 **DANNY O'RUAIRC (IRE),** b c Fast Company (IRE)—Tawoos (FR) **Bowes Lodge Stables**

**Other Owners:** Mr K. Hadwin, A. R. Mills, Mr S. Wilson, Mrs J. C. Wilson.

**Assistant Trainer:** Nadine Jameson

**Jockey (NH):** Brian Hughes. **Amateur:** Miss Alexander Wilson.

## 422 MR ISMAIL MOHAMMED, Newmarket

Postal: **Revida Place Stables, Hamilton Road, Newmarket, Suffolk, CB8 7JQ**
Contacts: **PHONE (01638) 669074 MOBILE (07771) 777121**
**E-MAIL justina.stone@dubairacingclub.com**

1 **ANA SHABABIYA (IRE),** 5, ch m Teofilo (IRE)—Call Later (USA) **A. Al Shaikh**
2 **APPROACHING STAR (FR),** 4, ch f New Approach (IRE)—Madame Arcati (IRE) **Sheikh J. D. Al Maktoum**
3 **EDUCATE,** 6, b g Echo of Light—Pasithea (IRE) **S. Ali**
4 **JAILAWI (IRE),** 4, b g Iffraaj—Tortue (IRE) **S. H. Altayer**
5 **LAWMANS THUNDER,** 5, b g Lawman (FR)—Rhapsodize **Sheikh J. D. Al Maktoum**
6 **MUBTADI,** 7, b g Dr Fong (USA)—Noble Peregrine **Mr A. Al Mansoori**
7 **NEW STORY,** 4, b c New Approach (IRE)—Al Hasnaa **S. Ali**
8 **RED WARRIOR (IRE),** 5, ch h Iffraaj—Wiolante (GER) **Mr I. Mohammed**
9 **RHOMBUS (IRE),** 5, b g Authorized (IRE)—Mathool (IRE) **Sheikh R. D. Al Maktoum**
10 **SIGHORA (IRE),** 4, b f Royal Applause—Singitta **Sheikh R. D. Al Maktoum**
11 **TOWER POWER,** 4, b c Nayef (USA)—Voile (IRE) **Mr A. Al Mansoori**

### THREE-YEAR-OLDS

12 **AMAZOUR (IRE),** b c Azamour (IRE)—Choose Me (IRE) **Sheikh J. D. Al Maktoum**
13 **GOLD CHIEF (IRE),** b c Acclamation—Easter Heroine (IRE) **Mr A. Al Mansoori**
14 **KAYSAR (IRE),** b c Iffraaj—Pivotal's Princess (IRE) **S. Ali**
15 **KEEN MOVE,** b g Aussie Rules (USA)—Kekova **S. Manana**
16 **KERRYMERRY (IRE),** b c Vale of York (IRE)—Reasonably Devout (CAN) **S. Ali**
17 **LOVELY SURPRISE (IRE),** ch f Shamardal (USA)—Dubai Surprise (IRE) **Dr A. Ridha**
18 **MUTAMID,** b c Medicean—Inchberry **S. Manana**
19 Ch f Compton Place—Profit Alert (IRE) **Sheikh J. D. Al Maktoum**
20 **SHAKSHUKA (IRE),** b f Dark Angel (IRE)—Tropical Moment (IRE) **Mr A. Al Mansoori**
21 **SPEEDY MOVE (IRE),** b c Iffraaj—Beautiful Filly **Dr A. Ridha**
22 **THE WAY YOU DANCE (IRE),** b g Thewayyouare (USA)—Beautiful Dancer (IRE) **Mr I. Mohammed**

## MR ISMAIL MOHAMMED - Continued

23 **VETLANA (IRE),** b f Vale of York (IRE)—Ahla Wasahl **S. Ali**
24 **YORK EXPRESS,** b f Vale of York (IRE)—Star Express **Dr A. Ridha**
25 **ZAHENDA,** b f Exceed And Excel (AUS)—Impetious **S. Manana**

### TWO-YEAR-OLDS

26 Ch f 13/3 Poet's Voice—Beat As One (Medicean) **Saif Ali & Saeed H. Altayer**
27 Ch f 30/1 New Approach (IRE)—Blue Rocket (IRE) (Rock of Gibraltar (IRE)) (80000) **Sheikh R. D. Al Maktoum**
28 B f 3/5 Lilbourne Lad (IRE)—Carbonia (IRE) (Alhaarth (IRE)) (42000) **Sheikh J. D. Al Maktoum**
29 Br f 2/3 Poet's Voice—Cheerleader (Singspiel (IRE)) **S. H. Altayer**
30 Ch c 3/5 Poet's Voice—Extreme Beauty (USA) (Rahy (USA)) (32000) **Dr A. Ridha**
31 B c 8/4 Big Bad Bob (IRE)—Interchange (IRE) (Montjeu (IRE)) (42000) **Mr I. Mohammed**
32 B c 3/5 Showcasing—Kathy's Rocket (USA) (Gold Legend (USA)) (55000) **Mr I. Mohammed**
33 B c 8/5 Compton Place—Lalectra (King Charlemagne (USA)) (75000) **Mr I. Mohammed**
34 B c 28/1 Street Sense (USA)—Love of Dubai (USA) (More Than Ready (USA)) **Mr M. Al Shafar**
35 B c 27/3 Authorized (IRE)—Moon Sister (IRE) (Cadeaux Genereux) **Mr A. S. Belhab**
36 B c 11/2 Shirocco (GER)—Pasithea (IRE) (Celtic Swing) **S. Ali**
37 B c 18/3 Big Bad Bob (IRE)—Red Shareef (Marju (IRE)) (58000) **Mr I. Mohammed**
38 B c 11/2 Kyllachy—Red Tiara (USA) (Mr Prospector (USA)) (57000) **Mr I. Mohammed**
39 B f 8/4 Iffraaj—Seminole Lass (USA) (Indian Charlie (USA)) (85000) **Mr I. Mohammed**
40 B f 7/4 Teofilo (IRE)—She Wolf (Medicean) (75000) **Dr A. Ridha**
41 B c 15/3 Iffraaj—Spiritual Healing (IRE) (Invincible Spirit (IRE)) (42000) **Mr I. Mohammed**
42 B f 9/4 Authorized (IRE)—Tegwen (USA) (Nijinsky (CAN)) **Mr A. S. Belhab**

**Other Owners:** S. Ali.

**Assistant Trainer:** Niall Collum

---

**423**

## MRS LAURA MONGAN, Epsom

Postal: **Condover Stables, Langley Vale Road, Epsom, Surrey, KT18 6AP**
Contacts: **PHONE (01372) 271494 FAX (01372) 271494 MOBILE (07788) 122942**
**E-MAIL ljmongan@hotmail.co.uk WEBSITE www.lauramongan.co.uk**

1 **ALSADAA (USA),** 12, b g Kingmambo (USA)—Aljawza (USA) **Mrs P. J. Sheen**
2 **CINEMATIQUE (IRE),** 7, br g King's Theatre (IRE)—Chantoue Royale (FR) **Mrs P. J. Sheen**
3 **DIVINE RULE (IRE),** 7, br g Cacique (IRE)—Island Destiny **Mrs L. J. Mongan**
4 **FIRST AVENUE,** 10, b g Montjeu (IRE)—Marciala (IRE) **Mrs L. J. Mongan**
5 **HIPZ (IRE),** 4, br f Intense Focus (USA)—Radha **Aberdour Racing Club**
6 **KEPPEL ISLE (IRE),** 6, b g Heron Island (IRE)—Wadi Khaled (FR) **Mrs P. J. Sheen**
7 **KING'S REQUEST (IRE),** 5, ch g New Approach (IRE)—Palace Weekend (USA) **Mrs P. J. Sheen**
8 **LEITH HILL (IRE),** 5, b g Mountain High (IRE)—Ballinacariga Rose (IRE) **Mrs P. J. Sheen**
9 **MADAME DE GUISE (FR),** 6, b m Le Balafre (FR)—Paradana (FR) **Mrs P. J. Sheen**
10 **MONTJESS (IRE),** 5, b m Montjeu (IRE)—Wing Stealth (IRE) **Mrs P. J. Sheen**
11 **MORGAN'S BAY,** 10, b g Karinga Bay—Dubai Dolly (IRE) **Mrs L. J. Mongan**
12 **NOOR AL HAYA (IRE),** 5, b m Tamayuz—Hariya (IRE) **Condover Racing**
13 **ORSM,** 8, b g Erhaab (USA)—Royal Roulette **Mrs P. J. Sheen**
14 **PEPITO COLLONGES (FR),** 12, b g Brier Creek (USA)—Berceuse Collonges (FR) **Mrs P. J. Sheen**
15 **RIVERMOUTH,** 10, ch g Karinga Bay—Rippling Brook **Mrs P. J. Sheen**
16 **SEA CADET,** 13, gr g Slip Anchor—Stormy Gal (IRE) **Mrs P. J. Sheen**
17 **SHINE IN TIME (IRE),** 7, b m Definite Article—Time To Shine **Mrs P. J. Sheen**
18 **SKIDBY MILL (IRE),** 5, b m Ramonti (FR)—Glasnas Giant **Charlie's Starrs**
19 **STAY IN MY HEART (IRE),** 6, ch m Medicean—Christmas Cracker (FR) **Make Way Partnership**
20 **TUSCAN GOLD,** 8, ch g Medicean—Louella (USA) **Mrs P. J. Sheen**
21 **WILLSHEBETRYING,** 4, b f Act One—Precedence (IRE) **SN Racing VII**

### THREE-YEAR-OLDS

22 **CHARLIE'S STAR,** b f Hellvelyn—Sweet Sorrow (IRE) **Charlie's Starrs & Laura Mongan**

**Other Owners:** Mr S. W. Bain, Mr A. W. Bain, Miss N. F. Davey, Miss F. Madel, S. Nunn.

**Assistant Trainer:** Ian Mongan

**Jockey (flat):** Liam Jones. **Jockey (NH):** Tom Cannon.

## 424 MR ARTHUR MOORE, Naas

Postal: **Dereens, Naas, Co. Kildare, Ireland**
Contacts: **PHONE (00353) 4587 6292 FAX (00353) 4589 9247 MOBILE (00353) 8725 52535**
**E-MAIL arthurlmoore@eircom.net**

1 **ARQUEBUSIER (FR),** 5, bl g Discover d'auteuil (FR)—Djurjura (FR) **Mrs A. L. T. Moore**
2 **BACK OFF MATE (IRE),** 7, b g Old Vic—Flyhalf (IRE) **M. Beresford**
3 **BALLYCAHANE (IRE),** 6, b g Flemensfirth (USA)—Laughing Lesa (IRE) **Ballycahane Syndicate**
4 **DAN'S ROLLS (IRE),** 7, b g Croco Rouge (IRE)—Angelas Choice (IRE) **Mrs Emer O'Brien**
5 **DANDRIDGE,** 6, ch g Doyen (IRE)—Arantxa **R. Bartlett**
6 **EL SORO (FR),** 7, b g Malinas (GER)—La Esplendida (FR) **P. McCarthy**
7 **FEVER PITCH (IRE),** 9, b g Dushyantor (USA)—Stormey Tune (IRE) **Mr J. P. McManus**
8 **GENTLEMAN DUKE (IRE),** 7, b g Bachelor Duke (USA)—Housekeeping **Mr J. P. McManus**
9 **HANNAH'S MAGIC (IRE),** 4, ch f Lomitas—Cool Storm (IRE) **Mrs A. L. T. Moore**
10 **HOP IN (IRE),** 8, b g Flemensfirth (USA)—Prowler (IRE) **C. Hanbury**
11 **MITEBEALL FORLUCK,** 7, b g Westerner—Iborga (FR) **C. Hanbury**
12 **ONTOPOFTHEWORLD (IRE),** 6, ch g Desert King (IRE)—Zaffre (IRE) **Mrs A. L. T. Moore**
13 **PASS THE HAT,** 8, ch g Karinga Bay—Moor Spring **M. Beresford**
14 **SEA BEAT,** 5, ch g Beat Hollow—Maritima **C. Jones**
15 **TALBOT ROAD (IRE),** 7, b g Old Vic—Over The Glen (IRE) **J. P. Byrne**
16 **THE TRACTOR MAN (IRE),** 5, ch g Flemensfirth (USA)—Sadie's Pet (IRE) **Mrs J. Magnier**
17 **TREAT YOURSELF (IRE),** 8, b g Beat Hollow—Cartesian **L. Breslin**

### THREE-YEAR-OLDS

18 **ONE COOL POET (IRE),** b g Urban Poet (USA)—Oasis Star (IRE) **Oliver Bernard Ryan**
19 **SANDY TIMES (IRE),** b f Footstepsinthesand—Lassie's Gold (USA) **Mrs A. L. T. Moore**
20 **WHATS THE PLOT (IRE),** b c Alfred Nobel (IRE)—Hazarama (IRE) **Mrs A. L. T. Moore**

### TWO-YEAR-OLDS

21 B c 10/5 Kalanisi (IRE)—Peratus (IRE) (Mujadil (USA)) (11904) **Mrs A. L. T. Moore**
22 Ch c 25/3 Windsor Knot (IRE)—Radio Wave (Dalakhani (IRE)) (17460) **Mrs A. L. T. Moore**

**Assistant Trainer:** M. O'Sullivan

## 425 MR GARY MOORE, Horsham

Postal: **Cisswood Racing Stables, Sandygate Lane, Lower Beeding, Horsham, West Sussex, RH13 6LR**
Contacts: **HOME (01403) 891997 YARD (01403) 891912 FAX (01403) 891924**
**MOBILE (07753) 863123**
**E-MAIL garyjayne.moore@virgin.net WEBSITE www.garymooreracing.com**

1 **ABUELO (FR),** 5, bl g Califet (FR)—Quolcevyta (FR) **Mr A. E. Dean**
2 **AGINCOURT REEF (IRE),** 6, b g Gold Well—Hillside Native (IRE) **Ashley Head, Richard Lockwood & Malcolm Burne**
3 **AHIO (FR),** 4, b g Chichi Creasy (FR)—Amalhouna (FR) **R. E. Anderson**
4 **ALKETIOS (GR),** 4, b g Kavafi (IRE)—Mazea (IRE) **G. A. Jackman**
5 **ANTONY (FR),** 5, b g Walk In The Park (IRE)—Melanie du Chenet (FR) **The Winning Hand**
6 **AR MAD (FR),** 5, b g Tiger Groom—Omelia (FR) **Mr G. L. Moore**
7 **ARLECCHINO (IRE),** 5, b g Hernando (FR)—Trullitti (IRE)
8 **ART LIBRE (FR),** 4, b g Librettist (USA)—Peinture Parfaite (FR) **G. L. Moore**
9 **AULD STHOCK (IRE),** 7, ch g Definite Article—Native Archive (IRE) **Mark Albon & Chris Stedman**
10 **BARON ALCO (FR),** 4, ch g Dom Alco (FR)—Paula (FR) **Mr J. K. Stone**
11 **BE ALL MAN (IRE),** 8, b g Dubawi (IRE)—Belle Allemande (CAN) **Mr A. Head, Mr R. Lockwood & Mr M. Burne**
12 **BEAUFORT BOY (IRE),** 6, b g Heron Island (IRE)—What A Mewsment (IRE) **Mrs A. Gloag**
13 **BIRDIE QUEEN,** 5, b m Pastoral Pursuits—Silver Miss (FR) **The Golf Partnership**
14 **BLACK SWAN KAUTO (FR),** 4, ch g Byzantium (FR)—Kauto Lorette (FR) **Mrs A. Gloag**
15 **BLUE SIRE (FR),** 4, b br g Day Flight—Hirlish (FR) **The Preston Family & Friends Ltd**
16 **BRAVE VIC (IRE),** 7, b g Old Vic—Baliya (IRE) **R. Henderson**
17 **BROCKWELL,** 6, b g Singspiel (IRE)—Noble Plum (IRE) **South Wind Racing 3**
18 **BUSTER BROWN (IRE),** 6, ch g Singspiel (IRE)—Gold Dodger (USA) **B. Siddle & B. D. Haynes**
19 **CABIMAS,** 8, b g King's Best (USA)—Casanga (IRE) **Mr A. D. Bradmore**
20 **CHANCEUSE,** 4, b f Lucky Story (USA)—Miss Madame (IRE) **Mr B. M. Parish**
21 **CHRIS PEA GREEN,** 6, b g Proclamation (IRE)—Another Secret **C Green & Galloping On The South Downs Partnership**

## MR GARY MOORE - Continued

22 **CIVIL WAR (IRE),** 6, b g Scorpion (IRE)—Silvestre (ITY) **Mr A. J. Head**
23 **CLAYTON,** 6, b g Peintre Celebre (USA)—Blossom **Mr A. J. Head**
24 **CRY FURY,** 7, b g Beat Hollow—Cantanta **Mr A. E. Dean**
25 **DABADIYAN (IRE),** 5, b g Zamindar (USA)—Dabista (IRE) **Mark Albon, Chris Stedman & G L Moore**
26 **DAIDAIDAI (FR),** 5, b g Lando (GER)—Noble World (GER) **Mrs S. M. Russell**
27 **DANCING SAL (IRE),** 4, b f Azamour (IRE)—Miss Tango Hotel **P. Naughton**
28 **DAZZA,** 4, ch f Bertolini (USA)—Another Secret **Galloping on the South Downs Partnership**
29 **DE BLACKSMITH (IRE),** 7, b g Brian Boru—Gift of The Gab (IRE) **Mrs E. A. Kiernan**
30 **DEAR LOTTIE (FR),** 4, b f Nickname (FR)—Vuelta Al Ruedo (FR) **Mr Jerry Hinds**
31 **DRACO'S CODE,** 4, b g Galileo (IRE)—Lady Karr **The Golf Partnership**
32 **DUBAWI LIGHT,** 4, b g Dubawi (IRE)—Shesadelight
33 **DUTCH MASTERPIECE,** 5, b g Dutch Art—The Terrier **R. Green**
34 **DYNAMIC IDOL (USA),** 8, b br g Dynaformer (USA)—El Nafis (USA) **Heart Of The South Racing**
35 **DYNAMIC RANGER (USA),** 4, b g U S Ranger (USA)—Dynamous (USA) **Mr M. L. Albon**
36 **ELSIE BAY,** 6, b m Sakhee (USA)—Mary Sea (FR) **Mrs J. A. Gawthorpe**
37 **EMPTY MARMALADES (FR),** 4, b g Poliglote—Arvicaya **Westbourne Racing Club**
38 **FENNANN,** 4, b g Dutch Art—Embraced **Mr M. R. Baldry**
39 **FLASHMAN,** 6, ch g Doyen (IRE)—Si Si Si **Mr A. D. Bradmore**
40 **FLUTE BOWL,** 5, b m Black Sam Bellamy (IRE)—Queen's Dancer **C. E. Stedman**
41 **FREDDY WITH A Y (IRE),** 5, b g Amadeus Wolf—Mataji (IRE) **double-r-racing.com & Mrs M J George**
42 **FREEMASON,** 4, b g Cape Cross (IRE)—Candy Mountain **Gallagher Equine Limited**
43 **FRUITY O'ROONEY,** 12, b g Kahyasi—Recipe **Heart Of The South Racing**
44 **GAELIC SILVER (FR),** 9, b g Lando (GER)—Galatza (FR) **The Winning Hand**
45 **GENEROUS HELPINGS (IRE),** 6, ch g Generous (IRE)—
Saffron Pride (IRE) **Galloping On The South Downs Partnership**
46 **GOLANOVA,** 7, b g Golan (IRE)—Larkbarrow **Galloping On The South Downs Partnership**
47 **GOLD CARROT,** 7, b g Beat All (USA)—Emma-Lyne **Mr Tony Head**
48 **GOOD LUCK CHARM,** 6, b g Doyen (IRE)—Lucky Dice **Heart of the South Racing**
49 **GORES ISLAND (IRE),** 9, b g Beneficial—Just Leader (IRE) **Collins, Horsfall, Michael & O'Sullivan**
50 **GRABTHEGLORY (IRE),** 9, b g Accordion—Full of Surprises (IRE) **Mr S. J. Cohen**
51 **GUARDS CHAPEL,** 7, b g Motivator—Intaaj (IRE) **Mr A. D. Bradmore**
52 **GUN SHY (IRE),** 7, b g Norwich—Debbies Scud (IRE) **P. R. Chapman**
53 **HALLING'S WISH,** 5, br g Halling (USA)—Fair View (GER) **WBC Partnership**
54 **HOIST THE COLOURS (IRE),** 4, b g Sea The Stars (IRE)—Multicolour Wave (IRE) **M. K. George**
55 **ILEWIN FOR HANNAH,** 8, b g Generous (IRE)—Ilewin Janine (IRE) **T. J. Segrue**
56 **ILEWIN GEEZ,** 5, ch g Generous (IRE)—Ilewin Janine (IRE) **T. J. Segrue**
57 **ILEWIN KIM,** 9, b g Grape Tree Road—Bridepark Rose (IRE) **T. J. Segrue**
58 **ILEWINDELILAH,** 7, b m Grape Tree Road—Bridepark Rose (IRE) **T. J. Segrue**
59 **INIESTA (IRE),** 4, b c Galileo (IRE)—Red Evie (IRE)
60 **JAY ARE (IRE),** 6, b g Heron Island (IRE)—Vulpalm (IRE) **G. L. Moore**
61 **JUPITER STORM,** 6, ch g Galileo (IRE)—Exciting Times (FR) **Heart of the South Racing**
62 **JUSTIFICATION,** 7, b g Montjeu (IRE)—Colorspin (FR) **Mrs E. A. Kiernan**
63 **KAMBIS,** 7, b g Tobougg (IRE)—Queen Tomyra (IRE) **Mr & Mrs Leslie Vine**
64 **KINGDOM (IRE),** 5, b g Montjeu (IRE)—Shadow Song (IRE) **Chris Stedman & Mark Albon**
65 **KNIGHT OF PLEASURE,** 6, ch g Exit To Nowhere (USA)—Kim Fontenail (FR) **The Knights Of Pleasure**
66 **KNOCKYOURSOCKSOFF (IRE),** 5, b g Tikkanen (USA)—
Didn't You Know (FR) **Westbourne Racing Club & G L Moore**
67 **KYLLACHY SPIRIT,** 7, b g Kyllachy—Cartuccia (IRE) **Mrs J R Jenrick & Mr R D Jenrick**
68 **LADY MARL,** 4, b f Duke of Marmalade (IRE)—Empress Anna (IRE) **Crimbourne Stud**
69 **LE CAPRICIEUX (FR),** 4, b g Alberto Giacometti (IRE)—Eria Flore (FR) **G. L. Moore**
70 **LEO LUNA,** 6, b g Galileo (IRE)—Eva Luna (USA) **Mr P. B. Moorhead**
71 **LIGHT WELL (IRE),** 7, b g Sadler's Wells (USA)—L'ancresse (IRE) **B. Siddle & B. D. Haynes**
72 **MAJESTIC SUN (IRE),** 4, b g King's Best (USA)—Shining Vale (USA) **The Horse Players Two**
73 **MAJOR MARTIN (IRE),** 6, b g Flemensfirth (USA)—Miss Emer (IRE) **Mr A. E. Dean**
74 **MARMALADY (IRE),** 5, ch m Duke of Marmalade (IRE)—Grecian Glory (IRE) **Heart of the South Racing**
75 **MOUNT SHAMSAN,** 5, b g Danehill Dancer (IRE)—Shamaiel (IRE) **Mr G. L. Moore**
76 **MR FICKLE (IRE),** 6, b g Jeremy (USA)—Mamara Reef **Mr G. L. Moore**
77 **NEBULA STORM (IRE),** 8, b g Galileo (IRE)—Epping **Mr R. H. MacNabb**
78 **NETHERBY,** 9, b g Fair Mix (IRE)—Lissadell (IRE) **Mr R. A. Green**
79 **NEW CODE,** 8, ch g Reset (AUS)—Illeana (GER) **Mrs E. A. Kiernan**
80 **OH SO FRUITY,** 5, b g Midnight Legend—Recipe **Heart Of The South Racing**
81 **OSGOOD,** 8, b g Danehill Dancer (IRE)—Sabreon **G. L. Moore**
82 **PROXIMATE,** 5, b g Nayef (USA)—Contiguous (USA) **Mr P. B. Moorhead**
83 **PUISQUE TU PARS (FR),** 5, b g Walk In The Park (IRE)—Pierre Azuree (FR) **Dedman Properties Limited**
84 **RAIN GOD (USA),** 5, b g Henrythenavigator (USA)—Lotta Dancing (USA) **Chris Stedman & Mark Albon**

## MR GARY MOORE - Continued

85 **REBLIS (FR),** 10, b g Assessor (IRE)—Silbere (FR) **Kingsley, Avery, Farr, Glover, Humphreys**
86 **REMIND ME LATER (IRE),** 6, b g Zerpour (IRE)—Two T'three Weeks **Mrs M. Devine**
87 **ROSSETTI,** 7, gr g Dansili—Snowdrops **Sheikh A'Leg Racing**
88 **ROYAL CLASSIC (FR),** 5, b g Anabaa Blue—Rapid Lomita (GER) **C. E. Stedman**
89 **RYDAN (IRE),** 4, ch c Intense Focus (USA)—Lough Mewin (IRE) **Jacobs Construction (Holdings) Ltd**
90 **RYEOLLIEAN,** 4, ch g Haafhd—Brave Mave **Mr B. Fry**
91 **SECRET MISSILE,** 5, b g Sakhee's Secret—Malelane (IRE) **Ms C. L. Salmon**
92 **SEVEN WOODS (IRE),** 9, b g Milan—Charlotte's Moss **M. K. George**
93 **SHALIANZI (IRE),** 5, b g Azamour (IRE)—Shalama (IRE) **Mr A. J. Head**
94 **SIRE DE GRUGY (FR),** 9, ch g My Risk (FR)—Hirlish (FR) **The Preston Family & Friends Ltd**
95 **SONG AND DANCE MAN,** 5, b g Danehill Dancer (IRE)—Song (IRE) **Ms A. R. Gross**
96 **STONEGATE,** 5, b g Kayf Tara—Megalex **Galloping On The South Downs Partnership**
97 **SUDDEN LIGHT (IRE),** 9, b m Presenting—Coolshamrock (IRE) **M&R Refurbishments Ltd**
98 **SUDDEN WISH (IRE),** 6, b m Jeremy (USA)—Fun Time **M&R Refurbishments Ltd**
99 6, Gr g Fair Mix (IRE)—Sunley Shines
100 **TAX REFORM (IRE),** 5, b g Namid—Happy Flight (IRE) **Mr M. R. Baldry**
101 **THE GAME IS A FOOT (IRE),** 8, b g Oscar (IRE)—Cooksgrove Rosie (IRE) **Mrs V Akehurst**
102 **THE GREEN OGRE,** 5, b g Dubai Destination (USA)—Takegawa **Leydens Farm Stud**
103 **THIRD STRIKE,** 4, b g Tertullian (USA)—Shaabra (IRE) **Mr C. E. Stedman & A. R. Blaxland**
104 **TOP DIKTAT,** 7, b g Diktat—Top Romance (IRE) **Miss T. R. Hale**
105 **TOTHEMOONANDBACK (IRE),** 7, gr g Dr Massini (IRE)—
Mrs Jones (FR) **Jane & Exors of the late David George**
106 **TRAFFIC FLUIDE (FR),** 5, b g Astarabad (USA)—
Petale Rouge (FR) **Galloping On The South Downs Partnership**
107 **TRIUMPHANT (IRE),** 6, b g Danehill Dancer (IRE)—Meek Appeal (USA) **Mark Albon & Chris Stedman**
108 **UBAK (FR),** 7, b g Kapgarde (FR)—Gesse Parade (FR) **Mr N. J. Peacock**
109 **UPTENDOWNONE (IRE),** 6, b g Oscar (IRE)—Lady Meribel **Mr J. K. Stone**
110 **VIA SUNDOWN (FR),** 7, ch g Until Sundown (USA)—Via Fratina (FR) **The Old Brokers**
111 **VIKEKHAL (FR),** 6, b g Khalkevi (IRE)—Gesse Parade (FR) **The Old Brokers**
112 **VINO GRIEGO (FR),** 10, b g Kahyasi—Vie de Reine (FR) **C. E. Stedman**
113 **VIOLET DANCER,** 5, b g Bertolini (USA)—
Another Secret **D Bessell & Galloping On The South Downs Partnership**
114 **VISION DES CHAMPS (FR),** 6, b g Saint des Saints (FR)—Manita Des Champs (FR) **Polo Racing & Friends**
115 **WHILE YOU WAIT (IRE),** 6, b g Whipper (USA)—Azra (IRE) **Galloping On The South Downs Partnership**
116 **WHINGING WILLIE (IRE),** 6, b g Cape Cross (IRE)—Pacific Grove **Mr P. B. Moorhead**

## THREE-YEAR-OLDS

117 **ART OF SWING (IRE),** b g Excellent Art—Shahmina (IRE) **Jacobs Construction (Holdings) Ltd**
118 **DAREBIN (GER),** ch g It's Gino (GER)—Delightful Sofie (GER)
119 **DUTCH FREDIE G,** ch f Dutch Art—Flawless Diamond (IRE) **Mr J. Griffin**
120 **DUTCH GOLDEN AGE (IRE),** b c Kodiac—Magic Melody **R. Green**
121 **EL FENIX (IRE),** b c Lope de Vega (IRE)—Woodmaven (USA) **Patterson Hinds & Curwen**
122 **GRAND FACILE,** b c Henrythenavigator (USA)—Santolina (USA) **Patterson Hinds & Curwen**
123 **GUNNER MOYNE,** b c Excellent Art—Maramkova (IRE) **Mr Danny O'Neil**
124 **LUCKY LEYF,** b f Kheleyf (USA)—Lucky Dice **Heart of the South Racing**
125 **MILKY WAY (IRE),** b c Galileo (IRE)—Beauty Bright (IRE) **Patterson Hinds & Curwen**
126 **ROCKFAST,** b g Fastnet Rock (AUS)—Empress Anna (IRE) **Crimbourne Stud**
127 **SEA SERPENT (FR),** b g Great Journey (JPN)—Serpolette (FR) **Mr Jerry Hinds**
128 **STEEVO (IRE),** b c Dark Angel (IRE)—Moriches (IRE) **Mr S. Curwen**
129 **SWEET PERSUASION,** ch f Motivator—Sweet Lemon (IRE) **Heart Of The South Racing**
130 **TOXARIS (IRE),** ch f Teofilo (IRE)—Right Key (IRE) **Chegwidden Systems Ltd**

## TWO-YEAR-OLDS

131 B c 21/4 Pour Moi (IRE)—Breathe (FR) (Ocean of Wisdom (USA)) (22000) **Mr Patrick Moorhead**
132 B c 26/3 Bahamian Bounty—
Carina Ari (IRE) (Imperial Ballet (IRE)) (25000) **Galloping on the South Downs Partnership**
133 **DEGAS BRONZE,** b f 19/2 Showcasing—Local Fancy (Bahamian Bounty) (45714) **Mr R. A. Green**
134 B f 16/2 Poet's Voice—Dignify (IRE) (Rainbow Quest (USA)) (29000) **Galloping on the South Downs Partnership**
135 **HEPWORTH MARBLE (IRE),** b f 15/3 Lilbourne Lad (IRE)—
Angel Nights (IRE) (Night Shift (USA)) (19047) **Mr R. A. Green**
136 **MODELLO (IRE),** b f 1/4 Intikhab (USA)—Precious Citizen (USA) (Proud Citizen (USA)) (51586) **Mr R. A. Green**
137 **PERSAVERANCE,** b c 28/1 Sir Percy—Marliana (IRE) (Mtoto) (38000) **Mr G. L. Moore**
138 B f 25/3 Notnowcato—Three Wrens (IRE) (Second Empire (IRE)) (6000) **Mr G. L. Moore**

## MR GARY MOORE - Continued

**Other Owners:** Mrs V. K. Akehurst, Mrs E. H. Avery, A. M. Basing, L. A. Bellman, Mr D. J. Bessell, A. Blaxland, Mr R. Bonney, Mrs H. M. Bonney, Mr A. R. Brightwell, R. L. Brown, Rev L. M. Brown, Mr M. Burne, A. Carr, Mr M. J. Coles, Mr J. A. Collins, Mrs P. Curlewis, Mr M. Curlewis, Mr S. Curwen, Double-R-Racing, Mr G. G. Fenlon, Mr J. K. Fletcher, Mrs M. J. George, Mrs J. George, Exors of the Late D. W. George, I. Goldsmith, Mrs M. R. Goldsmith, Mr M. Goodrum, Mr A. Graham, Mr C. Green, Mr P. Hancock, B. D. Haynes, Mr P. A. Herbert, Mrs J. R. Jenrick, Mr R. D. Jenrick, Mr W. Jupp, Mr P. M. Kingsley, Mr R. A. Lockwood, Mr S. A. Michael, Newco 1111 Ltd, Mr C. M. Parker, Mrs M. Parker, J. R. Penny, Miss E. Penny, Mr N. J. Roach, M. G. Rogers, R. M. Siddle, Mr L. R. Vine, Mrs S. J. Vine, Mr M. C. Waddingham, Mr M. K. Webb, Westbourne Consultants Ltd, Mr S. Wishart.

**Assistant Trainers:** David Wilson, Andrew Glassonbury

**Jockey (flat):** George Baker, Ryan Moore, Fergus Sweeney. **Jockey (NH):** Jamie Moore, Joshua Moore. **Conditional:** George Gorman, Jason Nuttall. **Apprentice:** Hector Crouch, Jason Nuttall. **Amateur:** Miss Hayley Moore.

---

## 426 MR GEORGE MOORE, Middleham

Postal: **Warwick Lodge Stables, Middleham, Leyburn, North Yorkshire, DL8 4PB**
Contacts: **PHONE (01969) 623823 FAX (01969) 623823 MOBILE (07711) 321117**
**E-MAIL georgeandcarolmoore@hotmail.co.uk WEBSITE www.george-moore-racing.co.uk**

1 **ASEELA (IRE),** 5, b m Teofilo (IRE)—Valse Mystique (IRE) **Mrs S. C. Moore**
2 **BENTONS LAD,** 4, br g Bollin Eric—Spirit of Ecstacy **Mr A. G. Benton**
3 **CHARLES DE MILLE,** 7, b g Tiger Hill (IRE)—Apple Town **Mrs Liz Ingham**
4 **COLONIAL STYLE (IRE),** 5, b g Gamut (IRE)—The Dukes Pert (IRE) **Mr T. S. Ingham**
5 **COWSLIP,** 6, b m Tobougg (IRE)—Forsythia **Mrs I. I. Plumb**
6 **ERICA STARPRINCESS,** 5, b m Bollin Eric—Presidium Star **Richard J. Phizacklea**
7 **EXCLUSIVE DANCER,** 6, gr m Notnowcato—Exclusive Approval (USA) **D. Parker**
8 **HIGHWAY PURSUIT,** 4, b g Pastoral Pursuits—Extreme Pleasure (IRE) **Mrs G. Kendall & Mrs Susan Moore**
9 **JACK THE GENT (IRE),** 11, b g Anshan—Asidewager (IRE) **J. B. Wallwin**
10 **JUST FABULOUS,** 6, b m Sakhee (USA)—Tipsy Me **Mr S. P. Graham**
11 **LADY BUSANDA,** 5, b m Fair Mix (IRE)—Spirit of Ecstacy **Sarah Pearson, J Tennant & J B Stead**
12 **LADY LIZ,** 4, b f Byron—Sister Rose (FR) **Mrs M. E. Ingham**
13 **LADY POPPY,** 5, b m Kyllachy—Poppets Sweetlove **Ingham Racing Syndicate**
14 **LADY YEATS,** 4, b f Yeats (IRE)—Oblique (IRE) **A Crute & Partners**
15 **MEDICINE HAT,** 4, b g Multiplex—Blushing Heart **Mrs S. M. Pearson**
16 **MORE PLAY,** 4, b f Multiplex—For More (FR) **Four At Play**
17 **ROKEBY,** 4, b g Byron—Scarlet Royal **Mrs M. E. Ingham**
18 **STORMBAY BOMBER (IRE),** 6, b g September Storm (GER)—Top Tottie (IRE) **J. B. Wallwin**
19 **TICKENWOLF (IRE),** 5, gr g Tikkanen (USA)—Emma's Choice (IRE) **G. R. Orchard**
20 **TOMORROW'S LEGEND,** 5, b g Midnight Legend—Colvada **Mrs M. Hatfield & Mrs S. Kramer**
21 **TOOLA BOOLA,** 5, b m Tobougg (IRE)—Forsythia **Ingham Racing Syndicate**
22 **WAR LORD (IRE),** 5, b g Aussie Rules (USA)—Carn Lady (IRE) **Mr & Mrs G. Turnbull**
23 **WOLF SHIELD (IRE),** 8, b g King's Theatre (IRE)—Garlucy (IRE) **Mrs J. M. Gray**
24 **WOLF SWORD (IRE),** 6, b g Flemensfirth (USA)—Dame O'neill (IRE) **G. R. Orchard**

### THREE-YEAR-OLDS

25 **BOND STARPRINCESS,** ch f Monsieur Bond (IRE)—Presidium Star **Richard J. Phizacklea**
26 **EGMONT,** b c Notnowcato—Salutare (IRE) **Mr T. S. Ingham**

### TWO-YEAR-OLDS

27 B c 22/2 Yeats (IRE)—Bogside Theatre (IRE) (Fruits of Love (USA)) **Geoff & Sandra Turnbull**
28 **RUBBER STAMP (IRE),** b f 7/3 Approve (IRE)—Cloud Break (Dansili) **A Crute & Partners**
29 **TARPORLEY,** b c 30/3 Bushranger (IRE)—Labisa (IRE) (High Chaparral (IRE)) **A Crute & Partners**

**Other Owners:** Mr T. S. Ingham, Mr Steve Boam, Mr D. G. Colledge, Mr A. Crute, Mrs C. A. Crute, Mrs Kate Davies, Mrs J. M. Gray, Mrs Mary Hatfield, Mrs Susan Kramer, Mrs Susan Moore, Mr G. R. Orchard, Mr M. D. Parker, Mrs Sarah Pearson, Mr J. B. Stead, Mr J. Tennant, Mr Geoffrey Turnbull, Mrs S. E. Turnbull.

**Assistant Trainer:** Mrs Susan Moore

**Jockey (flat):** Andrew Elliott, P. J. McDonald, Andrew Mullen. **Apprentice:** Keiran Schofield.

## 427 MR J. S. MOORE, Upper Lambourn

Postal: **Berkeley House Stables, Upper Lambourn, Hungerford, Berkshire, RG17 8QP**
Contacts: **PHONE (01488) 73887 FAX (01488) 73997 MOBILE (07860) 811127 / (07900) 402856**
**E-MAIL jsmoore.racing@btopenworld.com WEBSITE www.stanmooreracing.co.uk**

1 **DANGEROUS AGE,** 5, br m Sleeping Indian—Rye (IRE) **Mr D. Klein & J. S. Moore**
2 **SHEILA'S BUDDY,** 6, ch g Reel Buddy (USA)—Loreto Rose **R. J. Styles**
3 **TABLEFORTEN,** 4, ch g Pastoral Pursuits—Twitch Hill **Eventmasters Racing**
4 **TALKSALOT (IRE),** 4, b g Thousand Words—Lady Piste (IRE) **Mr J Bond-Smith & J S Moore**
5 **TEOLAGI (IRE),** 5, ch g Teofilo (IRE)—Satulagi (USA) **Mrs F. H. Hay**

### THREE-YEAR-OLDS

6 **CASCADING STARS (IRE),** b f Tagula (IRE)—Subtle Affair (IRE) **S. & A. Mares**
7 **CEIBHFHIONN (IRE),** b f Rip Van Winkle (IRE)—Antinea **J. S. Moore & Partner**
8 **CHARLTON HEIGHTS (IRE),** b g Strategic Prince—Personal Design (IRE) **Mr Kieron Badger & J S Moore**
9 **CHEFCHAOUEN (IRE),** b f Dylan Thomas (IRE)—Love Thirty **The Well Fleeced Partnership**
10 **EVER PHEASANT (IRE),** b g Alfred Nobel (IRE)—Indian Bounty **Ever Equine & J. S. Moore**
11 **HELMSMAN (IRE),** b g Alhaarth (IRE)—La Cuvee **J. S. Moore**
12 **INVINCIBLE DIAMOND (IRE),** ch g Arakan (USA)—Invincible Woman (IRE) **R. J. Styles**
13 **JIMMY'S HALL,** b g Kyllachy—Up At Dawn **J. S. Moore & Partner**
14 **OBSIDIAN ROCK (USA),** b br g More Than Ready (USA)—Balletomaine (IRE) **Mrs F. H. Hay**
15 B g Rock of Gibraltar (IRE)—Reine Violette (FR) **Mr G V March & J S Moore**
16 **SEA OF RED,** b g Duke of Marmalade (IRE)—Abandon (USA) **Mr D Kerr & J S Moore**
17 **SHAMROCK SHEILA (IRE),** ch f Fast Company (IRE)—Green Vision (IRE) **Mrs T Burns & J S Moore**
18 **SHEILA'S STEPS (IRE),** b g Excellent Art—Positive Step (IRE) **Mr Ray Styles & J. S. Moore**
19 **SOMEDAYSRDIAMONDS,** b f Equiano (FR)—Good Health **Mr G V March & J S Moore**

### TWO-YEAR-OLDS

20 B br f 13/2 Lilbourne Lad (IRE)—
Babberina (IRE) (Danehill Dancer (IRE)) (1745) **S Mares, E Tidmarsh & J S Moore**
21 B f 31/1 Bushranger (IRE)—Coastal Waters (Halling (USA)) (4761)
22 B f 1/4 Kodiac—Courte Paille (IRE) (Common Grounds) (6348) **The Swan Partnership**
23 **DARK REDEEMER,** b c 13/4 Dark Angel (IRE)—Lush (IRE) (Fasliyev (USA)) **Pineapple Stud & J S Moore**
24 B f 12/3 Thousand Words—Doting Amy (IRE) (Mujadil (USA)) (793)
25 Ch f 24/3 Lord Shanakill (USA)—Feet of Flame (USA) (Theatrical) (9523) **The Moore The Merrier**
26 B g 11/1 Indesatchel (IRE)—Find The Answer (Vital Equine (IRE)) (3967) **Mrs T Burns & J S Moore**
27 **FLEECED AGAIN (IRE),** b g 29/4 Bushranger (IRE)—
Sightseer (USA) (Distant View (USA)) (3809) **The Well Fleeced Partnership**
28 **FRENCH ENCORE,** b g 27/2 Showcasing—
French Connexion (IRE) (Chineur (FR)) (1904) **Mrs Evelyn Yates Mr T Yates and J S Moore**
29 **HIGH SAVANNAH (IRE),** b f 14/3 High Chaparral (IRE)—
Serengeti Day (USA) (Alleged (USA)) (25396) **Mr Donald Kerr & J S Moore**
30 B f 22/4 Fast Company (IRE)—Lovere (St Jovite (USA)) (2380) **The Petticoat Government**
31 B g 13/3 Dark Angel (IRE)—Manuka Magic (IRE) (Key of Luck (USA)) (1523) **J. S. Moore & Partner**
32 **MARY PARMENTER (IRE),** b br f 22/1 Dick Turpin (IRE)—Umniya (IRE) (Bluebird (USA)) **Mrs S. J. Moore**
33 B g 7/4 Art Connoisseur (IRE)—Novel Fun (IRE) (Noverre (USA)) (1428)
34 Gr f 15/4 Clodovil (IRE)—Rainbow Above You (IRE) (Mujadil (USA)) (1586)
35 **REBECCA'S SPIRIT,** b f 7/4 Equiano (FR)—
Sahariri (IRE) (Red Ransom (USA)) (3200) **Robert Tyrrell & J S Moore**
36 **REPEAT OFFENDER (IRE),** b c 4/4 Thewayyouare (USA)—
Dame Rochelle (IRE) (Danehill Dancer (IRE)) (14285) **D. M. Kerr**
37 Ch g 1/5 Intense Focus (USA)—Silesian (IRE) (Singspiel (IRE)) (1904)
38 **SKY FERRY,** br g 10/3 Captain Gerrard (IRE)—
Ellovamul (Elmaamul (USA)) (1983) **Caroline Instone & J S Moore**
39 **SKY ISLAND (IRE),** b f 2/5 High Chaparral (IRE)—
Nasanice (IRE) (Nashwan (USA)) (50000) **Mr Donald Kerr & J S Moore**
40 **WHERE IT BEGAN (IRE),** ch f 15/3 Strategic Prince—
Easy Going (Hamas (IRE)) (4364) **Mr Kieron Badger & J S Moore**
41 **WIOLETTA,** b f 12/4 Polish Power (GER)—Wizby (Wizard King) (1800) **The Petticoat Government**

**Other Owners:** Mrs R. Ablett, Mr M. J. Ablett, Mr Kieron Badger, Mr John Bond-Smith, Mr Kevin Elliott, Mr Ian J. Gray, Mr P. Grimes, Mr Donald M. Kerr, Mr G. V. March, Mr S. Mares, Mrs A. Mares, Mrs Sara Moore, Mr J. S. Moore, Mr R. J. Rexton, Mrs Denise Sheasby, Mr P. V. Smyth, Mr Ray Styles, Mr M. Winter, Mr T. Yates, Mrs Evelyn Yates.

**Assistant Trainer:** Mrs S. Moore

**Jockey (flat):** Liam Jones. **Apprentice:** Josephine Gordon.

## 428 MR KEVIN MORGAN, Newmarket

Postal: **Gazeley Park Stables, 13-15 Moulton Road, Gazeley, Newmarket, Suffolk, CB8 8RA**
Contacts: **PHONE (01638) 454830 FAX (01638) 551888 MOBILE (07768) 996103**
**E-MAIL kandcracing@hotmail.com**

1 **ANAN,** 9, br g Cape Cross (IRE)—Hawafiz **Roemex Ltd**
2 **BAIHAS,** 5, b g Nayef (USA)—Allegretto (IRE) **Richard Ward Romex Ltd**
3 **EZDIYAAD (IRE),** 11, b g Galileo (IRE)—Wijdan (USA) **Roemex Ltd**
4 **GHAAWY,** 4, b g Teofilo (IRE)—Asawer (IRE) **Richard Ward Roemex Ltd**
5 **GO RUBY GO,** 11, b m Karinga Bay—Nessfield **Mr J. Duckworth**
6 **HAAMES (IRE),** 8, b g Kheleyf (USA)—Jumilla (USA) **Roemex Ltd**
7 **ISDAAL,** 8, ch m Dubawi (IRE)—Faydah (USA) **Roemex Ltd**
8 **KALASKADESEMILLEY,** 4, b g Myboycharlie (IRE)—Congressional (IRE) **Mrs C. E. Peck**
9 **MAKHFAR (IRE),** 4, b g Bushranger (IRE)—Let Me Shine (USA) **Richard Ward Roemex Ltd**
10 **MAREEF (IRE),** 5, b g Oasis Dream—Katayeb (IRE) **Roemex Ltd**
11 **MEZMAAR,** 6, b g Teofilo (IRE)—Bay Tree (IRE) **Roemex Ltd**
12 **MUZAAHIM (IRE),** 4, ch g Tamayuz—Elizabeth Swann **Mrs C. E. Peck**
13 **MY FARMER GIRL,** 9, b m Karinga Bay—See My Girl **Mr J. Duckworth**
14 **RAAMZ (IRE),** 8, ch m Haafhd—Tarbiyah **Roemex Ltd**
15 5, Gr g Fair Mix (IRE)—See My Girl **Mr J. Duckworth**
16 **TAARESH (IRE),** 10, b g Sakhee (USA)—Tanaghum **Roemex Ltd**

**Head Lad:** Catherine Peck

## 429 MR DAVE MORRIS, Newmarket

Postal: **Mokefield, Baxters Green, Wickhambrook, Newmarket, Suffolk, CB8 8UY**
Contacts: **PHONE (01284) 850248 FAX (01284) 850248 MOBILE (07711) 010268**

1 **CHEZ VRONY,** 9, b g Lujain (USA)—Polish Abbey **Stag & Huntsman**
2 **WATER FOR LIFE,** 4, ch f Mount Nelson—Echo River (USA) **D. P. Fremel**

**Other Owners:** Ms C. C. Fagerstrom, Lord Hambleden.

**Jockey (flat):** Franny Norton.

## 430 MR M. F. MORRIS, Fethard

Postal: **Everardsgrange, Fethard, Co. Tipperary, Ireland**
Contacts: **PHONE (00353) 52 6131474 (00353) 52 6131654 FAX (00353) 52 6131654**
**E-MAIL mouse@eircom.net WEBSITE www.mousemorris.com**

1 **ALAMEIN (IRE),** 5, b g Beneficial—Lady of Appeal (IRE) **Gigginstown House Stud**
2 **ALLIED VICTORY (IRE),** 6, b g Old Vic—Echo Creek (IRE) **Gigginstown House Stud**
3 **ALPHA DES OBEAUX (FR),** 5, b g Saddler Maker (IRE)—Omega des Obeaux (FR) **Gigginstown House Stud**
4 **BAILY BAY (IRE),** 5, b g Robin des Pres (FR)—Native Sylph (IRE) **Mr R. A. Scott**
5 **BAILY CLOUD (IRE),** 5, ch g Touch of Land (FR)—Cap The Rose (IRE) **Mr R. A. Scott**
6 **BAILY GREEN (IRE),** 9, b g King's Theatre (IRE)—Dream On Boys (IRE) **Mr R. A. Scott**
7 **BAILY MOON (IRE),** 4, b g Milan—Givehertime (IRE) **Mr R. A. Scott**
8 **BAILY SMILE (IRE),** 4, b g Coroner (IRE)—Supertime (IRE) **Mr R. A. Scott**
9 **BAILY SUNSET (IRE),** 4, ch g Presenting—Kon Tiky (FR) **Mr R. A. Scott**
10 **BAND OF BLOOD (IRE),** 7, b g King's Theatre (IRE)—Cherry Falls (IRE) **Gigginstown House Stud**
11 **BELUSHED (IRE),** 6, ch g Beneficial—Nicajac (IRE) **E. Jordan, T. Kilduff**
12 **BRUFF (IRE),** 8, b g Presenting—Aniston (IRE) **Mr J. P. McManus**
13 **CALL ROG (IRE),** 7, b g Beneficial—Lady Fancy (IRE) **Mr J. P. McManus**
14 **CAROLE ROSE (IRE),** 5, ch m Mahler—Going For Home (IRE) **Mr S. O'Driscoll**
15 **DROMNEA (IRE),** 8, b br g Presenting—Fifth Imp (IRE) **Mrs A. Daly**
16 **EASTER HUNT (IRE),** 6, br g Kalanisi (IRE)—Easter Day (IRE) **Gigginstown House Stud**
17 **FIRST LIEUTENANT (IRE),** 10, ch g Presenting—Fourstargale (IRE) **Gigginstown House Stud**
18 **GORGEOUSREACH (IRE),** 7, b m Turtle Island (IRE)—Fifth Imp (IRE) **Mrs A. Daly**
19 **HORENDUS HULABALOO (IRE),** 6, b g Beneficial—Renvyle Society (IRE) **Gigginstown House Stud**
20 **JUST CAUSE (IRE),** 5, b g Court Cave (IRE)—Secret Can't Say (IRE) **Gigginstown House Stud**
21 **LET'S CELEBRATE (IRE),** 7, b g Oscar (IRE)—Blooming Quick (IRE) **Mr J. P. McManus**
22 **MIRADANE,** 8, b g Kayf Tara—Coolvawn Lady (IRE) **Mr B. Maloney**
23 **MOVING TARGET (IRE),** 4, ch g Flemensfirth (USA)—Hazel Sylph (IRE) **Mrs J. Magnier**

## MR M. F. MORRIS - Continued

24 **ORYX FALCON (IRE),** 6, ch g Presenting—Park Athlete (IRE) **Mr B. Maloney**
25 **RATHLIN,** 10, b g Kayf Tara—Princess Timon **Gigginstown House Stud**
26 **RAVISHED (IRE),** 7, b g Oscar (IRE)—Fair Present (IRE) **Gigginstown House Stud**
27 **REAL STEEL (IRE),** 7, br b g Old Vic—Grangeclare Dancer (IRE) **Gigginstown House Stud**
28 **ROGUE ANGEL (IRE),** 7, b g Presenting—Carrigeen Kohleria (IRE) **Gigginstown House Stud**
29 **RULE THE WORLD,** 8, b g Sulamani (IRE)—Elaine Tully (IRE) **Gigginstown House Stud**
30 **SCAMALL DUBH (IRE),** 5, b g Oscar (IRE)—Inchagreine (IRE) **Mr J. Morrissey**
31 **THE DOORMAN (IRE),** 6, b g King's Theatre (IRE)—Amber Light (IRE) **Mr J. P. McManus**
32 **TINAKELLYLAD (IRE),** 11, b g Witness Box (USA)—Iora (IRE) **Mrs B. Twomey**
33 **TROUBLESHOT (IRE),** 5, b g Stowaway—Beneficial Lady (IRE) **Gigginstown House Stud**
34 **TURNANDGO (IRE),** 7, b g Morozov (USA)—Crazy Alice (IRE) **Gigginstown House Stud**

---

## 431 MR PATRICK MORRIS, Prescot

Postal: **Avenue House, George Hale Avenue, Knowsley Park, Prescot, Merseyside, L34 4AJ**
Contacts: **MOBILE (07545) 425235**
**E-MAIL info@patmorrisracing.co.uk WEBSITE www.patmorrisracing.co.uk**

1 **ANGEL GABRIAL (IRE),** 6, b g Hurricane Run (IRE)—Causeway Song (USA) **Dr M. B. Q. S. Koukash**
2 **APOSTLE (IRE),** 6, gr g Dark Angel (IRE)—Rosy Dudley (IRE) **Dr M. B. Q. S. Koukash**
3 **BALLESTEROS,** 6, ch g Tomba—Flamenco Dancer **Dr M. B. Q. S. Koukash**
4 **CRUISE TOTHELIMIT (IRE),** 7, b g Le Vie Dei Colori—Kiva **Mr B. M. McLoughlin**
5 **DUKE OF CLARENCE (IRE),** 6, gr g Verglas (IRE)—Special Lady (FR) **Dr M. B. Q. S. Koukash**
6 **ENGLISH SUMMER,** 8, b g Montjeu (IRE)—Hunt The Sun **Dr M. B. Q. S. Koukash**
7 **GABRIAL THE HERO (USA),** 6, b g War Front (USA)—Ball Gown (USA) **Dr M. B. Q. S. Koukash**
8 **GABRIAL'S KING (IRE),** 6, b g Hurricane Run (IRE)—Danella (IRE) **Dr M. B. Q. S. Koukash**
9 **GATEPOST (IRE),** 6, br g Footstepsinthesand—Mandama (IRE) **Dr M. B. Q. S. Koukash**
10 **GRAMERCY (IRE),** 8, b g Whipper (USA)—Topiary (IRE) **Dr M. B. Q. S. Koukash**
11 **KYLLACHY STAR,** 9, b g Kyllachy—Jaljuli **Dr M. B. Q. S. Koukash**
12 **LAYLA'S RED DEVIL (IRE),** 4, b f Dalakhani (IRE)—Brazilian Samba (IRE) **Dr M. B. Q. S. Koukash**
13 **LEXI'S HERO (IRE),** 7, b g Invincible Spirit (IRE)—Christel Flame **Dr M. B. Q. S. Koukash**
14 **MASAMAH (IRE),** 9, gr g Exceed And Excel (AUS)—Bethesda **Dr M. B. Q. S. Koukash**
15 **MEHDI (IRE),** 6, b g Holy Roman Emperor (IRE)—College Fund Girl (IRE) **Dr M. B. Q. S. Koukash**
16 **MODERNISM,** 6, b g Monsun (GER)—La Nuit Rose (FR) **Dr M. B. Q. S. Koukash**
17 **MOUNT ATHOS (IRE),** 8, b g Montjeu (IRE)—Ionian Sea **Dr M. B. Q. S. Koukash**
18 **OUR GABRIAL (IRE),** 4, b g Rock of Gibraltar (IRE)—Jojeema **Dr M. B. Q. S. Koukash**
19 **POSTSCRIPT (IRE),** 7, ch g Pivotal—Persian Secret (FR) **Dr M. B. Q. S. Koukash**
20 **PUSHKIN MUSEUM (IRE),** 4, gr g Soviet Star (USA)—Chaste **Dr M. B. Q. S. Koukash**
21 **RENE MATHIS (GER),** 5, ch g Monsieur Bond (IRE)—Remina (GER) **Dr M. B. Q. S. Koukash**
22 **SEE THE STORM,** 7, b br g Statue of Liberty (USA)—Khafayif (USA) **Keating Bradley Fold Limited**
23 **SUEGIOO (FR),** 6, ch g Manduro (GER)—Mantesera (IRE) **Dr M. B. Q. S. Koukash**

### THREE-YEAR-OLDS

24 **BAHANGO (IRE),** b g Bahamian Bounty—Last Tango (IRE) **Chester Racing Club Ltd**
25 **BILLY SLATER,** br c Pastoral Pursuits—Procession **Dr M. B. Q. S. Koukash**
26 **GABRIAL THE VIKING (IRE),** b g Approve (IRE)—Xarzee (IRE) **Dr M. B. Q. S. Koukash**
27 **STEVE PRESCOTT,** gr ro g Dutch Art—Toy Top (USA) **Dr M. B. Q. S. Koukash**

**Other Owners:** M. R. Channon.

---

## 432 MR HUGHIE MORRISON, East Ilsley

Postal: **Summerdown, East Ilsley, Newbury, Berkshire, RG20 7LB**
Contacts: **PHONE (01635) 281678 FAX (01635) 281746 MOBILE (07836) 687799**
**E-MAIL hughie@hughiemorrison.co.uk WEBSITE www.hughiemorrison.co.uk**

1 **ARAB DAWN,** 4, gr g Dalakhani (IRE)—Victoire Celebre (USA) **Eason,Kerr-Dineen,Hughes,Edwards-Jones**
2 **BALTIC BRAVE (IRE),** 4, b g Baltic King—Negria (IRE) **The Brave Partnership**
3 **BROTHER BRIAN (IRE),** 7, b g Millenary—Miner Detail (IRE) **L. A. Garfield**
4 **BROTHER KHEE,** 4, ch g Sakhee's Secret—Cugina **Mr Raymond Tooth**
5 **CHANTECLER,** 4, b g Authorized (IRE)—Snow Goose **Sir Thomas Pilkington**
6 **CHIL THE KITE,** 6, b g Notnowcato—Copy-Cat **Mr Graham Doyle & Miss Hazel Lawrence**
7 **COUSIN KHEE,** 8, b g Sakhee (USA)—Cugina **Mr Raymond Tooth**

## MR HUGHIE MORRISON - Continued

8 **FELIX FABULLA,** 5, b g Lucky Story (USA)—Laser Crystal (IRE) **Mrs Isabel Eavis**
9 **FRUIT PASTILLE,** 4, b f Pastoral Pursuits—Classic Millennium **The Caledonian Racing Society**
10 **FUN MAC (GER),** 4, ch g Shirocco (GER)—Favorite (GER) **Mrs Angela McAlpine & Partners**
11 **MARSH DAISY,** 4, ch f Pivotal—Bella Lambada **Sir Thomas Pilkington & Mrs S. Rogers**
12 **MAX THE MINISTER,** 5, bl g Pastoral Pursuits—Franciscaine (FR) **Mrs M. D. W. Morrison**
13 **MOSHE (IRE),** 4, b g Dansili—Rosinka (IRE) **Exors of the Late Capt J. Macdonald-Buchanan**
14 **NEARLY CAUGHT (IRE),** 5, b g New Approach (IRE)—Katch Me Katie **Mr A. N. Solomons**
15 **PASTORAL PLAYER,** 8, b g Pastoral Pursuits—Copy-Cat **The Pursuits Partnership**
16 **SAMSON,** 4, ch c Black Sam Bellamy (IRE)—Riverine **Pangfield Racing IV**
17 **SISTER SIBYL (IRE),** 4, b f King's Theatre (IRE)—Rose of The Erne (IRE) **The Hill Stud**
18 **SWEEPING UP,** 4, b f Sea The Stars (IRE)—Farfala (FR) **Ben & Sir Martyn Arbib**
19 **THE POODLE FAKER,** 4, b g Pastoral Pursuits—Flirtatious **Mrs M. D. W. Morrison**
20 **THUNDER PASS (IRE),** 4, b g High Chaparral (IRE)—Hadarama (IRE) **Thurloe Thoroughbreds XXXIII**
21 **TRIGGER POINT,** 5, ch m Double Trigger (IRE)—Flirtatious **Mrs M. D. W. Morrison**
22 **TRIPLE STAR,** 4, b f Royal Applause—Triple Sharp **Lady Hardy**
23 **VENT DE FORCE,** 4, b c Hurricane Run (IRE)—Capriolla **The Fairy Story Partnership**

## THREE-YEAR-OLDS

24 **ACTIVATION,** b g Stimulation (IRE)—Patteresa Girl **Mr H. Morrison**
25 **ATALAN,** b c Azamour (IRE)—Capriolla **The Fairy Story Partnership**
26 **BLACK KEY,** b g Authorized (IRE)—
Pentatonic **Mr M. Hughes, Mr M. Kerr-Dineen, Mr S. Malcolm & Miss Annika Murjahn**
27 **CANOODLE,** b f Stimulation (IRE)—Flirtatious **Mrs M. D. W. Morrison**
28 **COMPTON MILL,** b c Compton Place—
Classic Millennium **Mr M. Bevan, Mrs R. Luard & Mrs M. D. W. Morrison**
29 **DUTCH LAW,** b c Dutch Art—Lawyers Choice **Mr Raymond Tooth**
30 **FERN OWL,** ch c Nayef (USA)—Snow Goose **Sir Thomas Pilkington bt**
31 **FIELD GAME,** b c Pastoral Pursuits—Tarqua (IRE) **Earl of Carnarvon**
32 **ICE BOAT (IRE),** b br c Verglas (IRE)—Yawl **Mr M. Dixon**
33 **KISSY SUZUKI,** b f Sakhee's Secret—Yonder **Mrs M. D. W. Morrison**
34 **LITTLE PRAIRIE,** ch f Exceed And Excel (AUS)—
Chetwynd (IRE) **Lord Margadale,Mrs Belinda Scott,Mr M. Kerr-Dineen, Mr H. Scott-Barrett**
35 **MAJOR MAC,** ch g Shirocco (GER)—
Spring Fashion (IRE) **Mr A. McAlpine, Mr P. Brocklehurst, Mrs Carolyn Whitaker & Mrs Rowena Luard**
36 **MANOLITO,** b g High Chaparral (IRE)—
Break Time **Mr Simon Malcolm, Mr & Mrs G. Hamilton-Fairley, Mrs A. Plummer & Mr T. Wechsler**
37 **NOT SO SLEEPY,** ch g Beat Hollow—Papillon de Bronze (IRE) **Lady Blyth**
38 **PAROLE (IRE),** ch c Mastercraftsman (IRE)—Leniency (IRE) **Mr M. Hughes & Mr M. Kerr-Dineen**
39 **PERCELLA,** b f Sir Percy—
Temple of Thebes (IRE) **Mrs A. Gabb, Mr S. De Zoete, Mr T. Pickford & Mrs Annika Murjahn**
40 **RESPECTABILITY,** b f Echo of Light—Respectfilly **The Fairy Story Partnership**
41 **ROCK HEROINE,** gr f Rock of Gibraltar (IRE)—Kinetix **Helena Springfield Ltd**
42 B f Duke of Marmalade (IRE)—Rosinka (IRE) **Exors of the Late Capt J. Macdonald-Buchanan**
43 **SARSTED,** b c Paco Boy (IRE)—Red Blooded Woman (USA)
**Miss Annika Murjahn, The Hon Miss M. Morrison, Mr S. De Zoete & Mr A. J. Struthers**
44 **SECRET JOURNEY (IRE),** ch g Sakhee's Secret—
Hinokia (IRE) **Mr S. De Zoete, Mrs A. Gabb, Mr T. Pickford & Miss Annika Murjahn**
45 **SHIFTING MOON,** b f Kheleyf (USA)—Fleeting Moon **Mr M. E. Wates**
46 **SLEEP EASY,** b c Rip Van Winkle (IRE)—
Strictly Lambada **Mr W. Eason, Mr M. Hughes, Mr M. Kerr-Dineen & Mr D. Malpas**
47 **STAR RIDER,** br gr f Cape Cross (IRE)—Starfala **Ben & Sir Martyn Arbib**
48 **SWEET SELECTION,** b f Stimulation (IRE)—Sweet Coincidence **Mr Paul Brockelhurst & Ms Magdalena Gut**

## TWO-YEAR-OLDS

49 **ADMIRAL'S SUNSET,** b f 18/4 Mount Nelson—Early Evening (Daylami (IRE)) (8500) **Mr A. N. Solomons**
50 **AMBUSCADE,** b f 6/3 Dick Turpin (IRE)—Tarqua (IRE) (King Charlemagne (USA)) **Earl of Carnarvon**
51 **AURORA GRAY,** gr f 11/5 Rip Van Winkle (IRE)—Summer's Eve (Singspiel (IRE)) **Wardley Bloodstock**
52 **BAHAMIAN BOY,** ch c 18/4 Paco Boy (IRE)—
Bahamian Babe (Bahamian Bounty) (22000) **Mr Paul Brockelhurst, Mr Hugh Scott-Barrett & Mr T. Pickford**
53 **CATALAN (IRE),** b f 7/3 Duke of Marmalade (IRE)—
Twice The Ease (Green Desert (USA)) (120000) **Mrs Sonia Rogers & Sir Thomas Pilkington**
54 **CHALCOT (IRE),** b f 14/2 High Chaparral (IRE)—
Law of The Jungle (IRE) (Catcher In The Rye (IRE)) (46031) **Mrs Carolyn Whitaker**
55 Ch c 18/4 Pastoral Pursuits—
Clarice Orsini (Common Grounds) (40000) **Mr A. McAlpine, Mr H. Scott-Barrett & Mr A. J. Struthers**

## MR HUGHIE MORRISON - Continued

**56 DESIRABLE,** b f 18/3 Stimulation (IRE)—Hot Pursuits (Pastoral Pursuits) (571) **Mrs Isabel Eavis**
**57** B f 22/4 Acclamation—
Divine Authority (IRE) (Holy Roman Emperor (IRE)) (55555) **Mr M. Hughes & Mr M. Kerr-Dineen**
**58 EXCELLENT SOUNDS,** b f 4/5 Exceed And Excel (AUS)—
Siren Sound (Singspiel (IRE)) (60000) **Helena Springfield Ltd**
**59** B f 12/2 Acclamation—Forgotten Me (IRE) (Holy Roman Emperor (IRE)) (55000) **Thurloe Thoroughbreds**
**60 HELFIRE,** b f 12/2 Archipenko (USA)—Relkida (Bertolini (USA)) **Mr M. Watson & Miss D. Collett**
**61 MARMELO,** b c 22/3 Duke of Marmalade (IRE)—Capriolla (In The Wings) **The Fairy Story Partnership**
**62** Ch f 19/4 Pivotal—Passiflora (Night Shift (USA)) (40000) **The End-R-Ways Partnership**
**63 PASTORAL MUSIC,** b c 5/3 Pastoral Pursuits—Jasmeno (Catcher In The Rye (IRE)) (857) **MNC Racing**
**64 PASTORAL STAR,** ch f 3/2 Pastoral Pursuits—
Movie Star (IRE) (Barathea (IRE)) (18095) **Mr G. Swire, Mr & Mrs R. Lloyd, Mr Richard Wright**
**65 RAVENS QUEST,** ch c 13/3 Raven's Pass (USA)—
Seradim (Elnadim (USA)) (150000) **The Fairy Story Partnership**
**66 ROSA DANICA (IRE),** b f 31/3 Danehill Dancer (IRE)—
Rose of Petra (IRE) (Golan (IRE)) (39681) **Yarborough, Stanley, Pilkington & Brooke**
**67** B f 11/3 Invincible Spirit (IRE)—Salsa Steps (USA) (Giant's Causeway (USA)) **Ben & Sir Martyn Arbib**
**68 SCARLET PIMPERNEL,** b f 1/3 Sir Percy—Sweet Pea (Persian Bold) **Mr Nicholas Jones**
**69** B c 4/4 Sir Percy—Sensationally (Montjeu (IRE)) **Castle Down Racing**
**70** B c 20/3 Sakhee (USA)—Some Sunny Day (Where Or When (IRE)) (40000) **The Black Gold Partnership**
**71 STEELY ROCK,** gr c 31/3 Rock of Gibraltar (IRE)—
La Gandilie (FR) (Highest Honor (FR)) (26000) **Mr M. Bevan & Mr S. Malcolm**
**72** Ch f 9/2 Aqlaam—Strictly Lambada (Red Ransom (USA)) **Helena Springfield Ltd**
**73 SUNSCAPE (IRE),** ch f 12/2 Roderic O'Connor (IRE)—
Opatja (Nashwan (USA)) (14000) **Fiona Trenchard, The Hon Miss M Morrison & Declan Morrison**
**74** B f 20/3 Stimulation (IRE)—Sweet Coincidence (Mujahid (USA))
**75** B f 28/1 Lilbourne Lad (IRE)—The Fairies Did It (USA) (Elusive Quality (USA)) (49205)
**Mr M. Kerr-Dineen, Mr M. Hughes, Mr W. Eason & Mr G. Rothwell**
**76** B c 13/2 Lawman (FR)—Tree Tops (Grand Lodge (USA)) (80000) **Mr Michael Kerr-Dineen & Mr Martin Hughes**
**77** B c 21/3 Roderic O'Connor (IRE)—
Union City Blues (IRE) (Encosta de Lago (AUS)) (44000) **Mr A. McAlpine, Mr S. De Zoete, Mr C. Hill**
**78 VAN DYKE,** b c 15/4 Excellent Art—Respectfilly (Mark of Esteem (IRE)) **The Fairy Story Partnership**
**79** B f 20/4 Sakhee's Secret—Yonder (And Beyond (IRE)) **Mrs M. D. W. Morrison**

**Other Owners:** Mr Ben Arbib, Sir Martyn Arbib, Mrs M. T. Bevan, Mr T. J. Billington, Mrs P. G. Billington, Mr T. M. Bird, Mr Paul Brocklehurst, Sir F. Brooke, Mr Simon de Zoete, Mr G. J. Doyle, Mr William Eason, Mr Marcus Edwards-Jones, Mrs H. S. Ellingsen, Mrs Roger Gabb, Mr M. Gibbens, Mr E. R. Goodwin, Miss Magdalena Gut, Mouse Hamilton-Fairley, Mr Martin Hughes, Mr Michael Kerr-Dineen, Miss H. M. Lawrence, Mr D. S. Little, Mr & Mrs R. Lloyd, Mrs Roly Luard, Mr Simon Malcolm, Mr David Malpas, Lord Margadale, Mrs Angela McAlpine, Mr Adrian McAlpine, Miss Annika Murjahn, Mr A. E. Pakenham, Mrs Victoria Pakenham, Mr O. J. W. Pawle, Mr R. A. Pilkington, Mrs Richard Plummer, Mrs S. M. Rogers, Mrs Belinda Scott, Miss C. S. Scott-Balls, Mr Hugh Scott-Barrett, Mr J. A. B. Stafford, P. H. C. Stanley, Mr A. Stone, G. D. W. Swire, Mr M. Taylor, Mr Raymond Tooth, Viscountess Trenchard, Mr G. Waylen, Mr J. A. Wechsler, Mr M. Weinfeld, Mr A. W. Wood, Mr R. Wright, The Earl Of Yarborough.

**Apprentice:** Charlie Bennett. **Amateur:** Mr Robert Pooles.

---

## 433 MR GARRY MOSS, Tickhill

Postal: **Ron Hull Group, PO BOX 590, Rotherham, South Yorkshire, S62 6WT**
Contacts: **PHONE (01302) 746456 (07872) 993519 MOBILE (07791) 888129**

**1 ARROWZONE,** 4, b g Iffraaj—Donna Giovanna **Mr R. Hull**
**2 FREDRICKA,** 4, ch f Assertive—Vintage Steps (IRE) **Mr R. Hull**
**3 HULCOLT (IRE),** 4, b g Acclamation—Fusili (IRE) **Mr R. Hull**
**4 READY (IRE),** 5, ch g Elnadim (USA)—Fusili (IRE) **Mr R. Hull**
**5 SLINKY MCVELVET,** 4, ch f Refuse To Bend (IRE)—Rania (GER) **Mr R. Hull**

### THREE-YEAR-OLDS

**6 BREAD,** b g Alfred Nobel (IRE)—Sweet Power **Mr R. Hull**
**7 WISETON (IRE),** b g Majestic Missile (IRE)—Laylati (IRE) **Mr R. Hull**

### TWO-YEAR-OLDS

**8** Ch f 13/3 Monsieur Bond (IRE)—Moorhouse Girl (Makbul) (571) **Mr R. Hull**
**9** B c 10/2 Lilbourne Lad (IRE)—Vintage Allure (IRE) (Barathea (IRE)) (30000) **Mr R. Hull**

## 434 MR WILLIAM MUIR, Lambourn

Postal: **Linkslade, Wantage Road, Lambourn, Hungerford, Berkshire, RG17 8UG**
Contacts: **OFFICE (01488) 73098 HOME (01488) 73748 FAX (01488) 73490**
**MOBILE (07831) 457074**
**E-MAIL william@williammuir.com WEBSITE www.williammuir.com**

1 **AVOCADEAU (IRE),** 4, b g Lawman (FR)—Christmas Cracker (FR) **Mr John O'Mulloy**
2 **BIG BAZ (IRE),** 5, b g Pivotal—Gracefully (IRE) **The Big Baz Partnership**
3 **FLECKERL (IRE),** 5, b g Danehill Dancer (IRE)—Spinola (FR) **Mr F. Hope**
4 **GULLAND ROCK,** 4, b g Exceed And Excel (AUS)—Sacre Coeur **Mr C. L. A. Edginton & Mr K. Mercer**
5 **IMPROVIZED,** 4, b f Authorized (IRE)—Rhapsodize **Foursome Thoroughbreds**
6 **LADY HORATIA,** 4, gr f Mount Nelson—Lady Xara (IRE) **Muir Racing Partnership - Ascot**
7 **LOVE SPICE,** 4, b f Cape Cross (IRE)—Zanzibar (IRE) **Usk Valley Stud**
8 **MAGIC SECRET,** 7, b g Trade Fair—Just Devine (IRE) **Carmel Stud**
9 **OPHIR,** 4, b g Nayef (USA)—Ermine (IRE) **Mr John O'Mulloy**
10 **ORACLE BOY,** 4, b g Mount Nelson—Snow Princess (IRE) **The Epicureans**
11 **PINK AND BLACK (IRE),** 4, b f Yeats (IRE)—Raysiza (IRE) **Mrs D. L. Edginton**
12 **ROYAL BRAVE (IRE),** 4, b g Acclamation—Daqtora **Muir Racing Partnership - Ascot**
13 **SIOUXPERHERO (IRE),** 6, b g Sleeping Indian—Tintern **Muir Racing Partnership - Bath**
14 **SO NOBLE,** 4, ch g Pivotal—Noble One **Muir Racing Partnership - Windsor**
15 **STEPPER POINT,** 6, b g Kyllachy—Sacre Coeur **Mr C. L. A. Edginton**
16 **STRAWBERRY MARTINI,** 4, ch f Mount Nelson—Strawberry Lolly **Newsells Park Stud Limited**
17 **TRUTH OR DARE,** 4, b g Invincible Spirit (IRE)—Unreachable Star **Carmel Stud**

### THREE-YEAR-OLDS

18 **ALWAYS WILL,** b g Sleeping Indian—China Beads **Muir Racing Partnership - Beverley**
19 **BEST ENDEAVOUR,** b c Medicean—Striving (IRE) **C L A Edginton & D G Clarke**
20 **BURAUQ,** b c Kyllachy—Riccoche (IRE) **Mr Syed Pervez Hussain**
21 **CODE RED,** ch c Bahamian Bounty—Just Devine (IRE) **Mrs M. E. Morgan**
22 **CROWN COMMAND (IRE),** ch c Lope de Vega (IRE)—Pivotal Role **Mr J. P. Kok**
23 **DON'T TELL LOUISE,** b f Medicean—Lyra's Daemon **R. W. Devlin**
24 **DUTCH FALCON,** ch g Pivotal—Luminance (IRE) **C Edginton, G Berkeley, R Haim**
25 **EAGER BEAVER,** b f Duke of Marmalade (IRE)—Kahlua Kiss **M. J. Caddy**
26 **EASY TIGER,** b g Refuse To Bend (IRE)—Extremely Rare (IRE) **Miss E. Tanner**
27 **EQUALLY FAST,** b c Equiano (FR)—Fabulously Fast (USA) **Muir Racing Partnership - Haydock**
28 **FINE JUDGMENT,** b f Compton Place—Blue Lyric **Muir Racing Partnership - Goodwood**
29 **HONOUR PROMISE (IRE),** b f Jeremy (USA)—Karenaragon **Heppelthwaite, Jones & Quaintance**
30 **INNISCASTLE LAD,** b c Kyllachy—Glencal **The Lavelle Family**
31 Ch c Pivotal—Irresistible **Mr S. P. Hussain**
32 **JET MATE (IRE),** ch g Fast Company (IRE)—Anazah (USA) **Mr M. P. Graham**
33 **NEATH ABBEY,** ch f Notnowcato—Ewenny **Usk Valley Stud**
34 **RESTORER,** gr c Mastercraftsman (IRE)—Moon Empress (FR) **Mr C. L. A. Edginton**
35 **ROBIN HILL,** b f Misu Bond (IRE)—Enchanting Eve **Mr J. M. O'Mulloy**

### TWO-YEAR-OLDS

36 **ARGYLE (IRE),** gr c 4/2 Lawman (FR)—All Hallows (IRE) (Dalakhani (IRE)) (71428) **C. L. A. Edginton**
37 **CALVADOS SPIRIT,** b c 5/2 Invincible Spirit (IRE)—
Putois Peace (Pivotal) (174603) **Muir Racing Partnership - Deauville**
38 B c 24/2 Dark Angel (IRE)—Dawn Chorus (IRE) (Mukaddamah (USA)) (60000) **Mr S. P. Hussain**
39 **ENTERTAINING BEN,** b c 14/4 Equiano (FR)—Fatal Attraction (Oasis Dream) (36000) **Berkeley, Edginton, Niven**
40 B c 10/2 Royal Applause—Good Girl (IRE) (College Chapel) (42000)
41 B f 5/4 Fastnet Rock (AUS)—Highwater Dancer (IRE) (Sadler's Wells (USA)) (30000)
42 B c 27/2 Kodiac—Jazzie (FR) (Zilzal (USA)) (48000)
43 B c 2/4 Kyllachy—Just Devine (IRE) (Montjeu (IRE)) (280000) **Muir Racing Partnership - Longchamp**
44 B c 18/4 Poet's Voice—Khubza (Green Desert (USA)) (45000) **Mr J. P. Kok**
45 **KITTY FOR ME,** b f 26/2 Pour Moi (IRE)—Purring (USA) (Mountain Cat (USA)) **Edginton, Morgan, Jeffery, Muir**
46 B c 20/4 Duke of Marmalade (IRE)—
Lady Hawkfield (IRE) (Hawk Wing (USA)) (30000) **Muir Racing Partnership - Chester**
47 B c 28/2 Makfi—Likeable (Dalakhani (IRE)) (10000) **Mr S. P. Hussain**
48 B c 6/5 Equiano (FR)—Mary Pekan (IRE) (Sri Pekan (USA)) (10000)
49 Ch c 19/4 Kyllachy—Miss Smilla (Red Ransom (USA)) (68571)
50 B f 22/3 Exceed And Excel (AUS)—Nantyglo (Mark of Esteem (IRE)) (65000) **Usk Valley Stud**
51 B c 28/4 Manduro (GER)—Ornellaia (IRE) (Mujadil (USA))
52 B f 29/3 Equiano (FR)—Polish Belle (Polish Precedent (USA)) (14000) **Newsells Park Stud Limited**
53 B c 5/3 Makfi—Rakata (USA) (Quiet American (USA)) (14000)

## MR WILLIAM MUIR - Continued

**54** B c 1/4 Pivotal—Regina (Green Desert (USA)) (30000)
**55** B f 17/4 Mount Nelson—Sassari (IRE) (Darshaan) (18000) **Mr J. M. O'Mulloy**
**56** Ch c 10/3 Rip Van Winkle (IRE)—Starbound (IRE) (Captain Rio) (55000)
**57** B c 20/2 Vale of York (IRE)—Tintern (Diktat) (24000)

**Other Owners:** Mr Glyn Charles, Mr D. G. Clarke, Mrs D. Cunningham-Reid, Mr C. L. A. Edginton, Mr Reuben P. F. Heppelthwaite, Mr Ken Jeffery, Mr Stewart Jones, Mr D. P. Knox, Mr S. Lamb, Mrs Judith Land, Mr Barry McCabe, Mr K. J. Mercer, Mrs S. Mercer, Mr Peter Morgan, Mrs Michelle Morgan, Mr W. R. Muir, Mr John O'Mulloy, Mr P. D. Quaintance, Mr D. L. Quaintance, Mr Graham Stacey, Mr M. Weinfeld, Mr P. J. Wheatley.

**Assistant Trainer:** Patrick MacEwan

**Jockey (flat):** Martin Dwyer.

---

## 435 MR CLIVE MULHALL, Scarcroft

Postal: **Scarcroft Hall Farm, Thorner Lane, Scarcroft, Leeds, LS14 3AQ**
Contacts: **PHONE (0113) 2893095 FAX (0113) 2893095 MOBILE (07979) 527675**
**E-MAIL clive@scarcrofthallracing.co.uk WEBSITE www.clivemulhallracing.co.uk**

1 **ANEEDH,** 5, b g Lucky Story (USA)—Seed Al Maha (USA) **Carl Chapman & Mrs Martina Mulhall**
2 **IFONLYWECUD (IRE),** 6, b g Celtic Swing—Mrs Dalloway (IRE) **Carl Chapman & Mrs Martina Mulhall**
3 **LADY LISA JAYNE,** 5, b m Moss Vale (IRE)—Mimic
4 **SHARADIYN,** 12, b g Generous (IRE)—Sharadiya (IRE) **Simon Ballance & Mrs C. M. Mulhall**
5 **THINK,** 8, ch g Sulamani (IRE)—Natalie Jay **Mrs C. M. Mulhall & Carl Chapman**
6 **TUKITINYASOK (IRE),** 8, b g Fath (USA)—Mevlana (IRE) **Carl Chapman & Mrs Martina Mulhall**
7 **WAR POET,** 8, b g Singspiel (IRE)—Summer Sonnet **Carl Chapman & Mrs Martina Mulhall**

### THREE-YEAR-OLDS

8 **CHEEKY CHAPMAN,** ch g Stimulation (IRE)—Athboy Auction **Carl Chapman & Mrs Martina Mulhall**
9 **LORD SERENDIPITY (IRE),** gr g Lord Shanakill (USA)—Elitista (FR)

### TWO-YEAR-OLDS

**10** B f 13/3 Frozen Power (IRE)—
Petticoat Hill (UAE) (Timber Country (USA)) (3333) **Carl Chapman & Mrs Martina Mulhall**
**11** B f 31/3 Fast Company (IRE)—Sugar Mountain (IRE) (Lomitas) (3333) **Carl Chapman & Mrs Martina Mulhall**

**Other Owners:** Mr Simon Ballance, Mr Carl Chapman, Mrs C. M. Mulhall.

**Assistant Trainer:** Mrs Martina Mulhall

---

## 436 MR NEIL MULHOLLAND, Limpley Stoke

Postal: **Conkwell Grange Stables, Conkwell, Limpley Stoke, Bath, Avon, BA2 7FD**
Contacts: **MOBILE (07739) 258607**
**E-MAIL neil@neilmulhollandracing.com WEBSITE www.neilmulhollandracing.com**

1 **AGAPANTHUS (GER),** 10, b g Tiger Hill (IRE)—Astilbe (GER) **Mr S. K. Brown**
2 **APPLE POPS,** 5, b m Apple Tree (FR)—Rio Pops **Mrs J. M. Abbott**
3 **ASHCOTT BOY,** 7, ch g Lahib (USA)—Last Ambition (IRE) **Mr J. Hobbs**
4 **AUCKLAND DE RE (FR),** 5, b br g Network (GER)—Osee de Re (FR) **Mrs D. C. Webb**
5 **BALLYDAGUE LADY (IRE),** 8, b m Luso—Cottstown Belle (IRE) **Neil Mulholland Racing Club**
6 **BAROQUE MAN,** 8, b g Revoque (IRE)—Barton May **Mr P. G. Gray & Mrs J. M. Abbott**
7 **BARTON ANTIX,** 6, b g Fair Mix (IRE)—Barton Dante **Lady H. J. Clarke**
8 **BARTON HEATHER,** 6, b m Midnight Legend—Home From The Hill (IRE) **Lady H. J. Clarke**
9 **BARTON ROSE,** 6, b m Midnight Legend—Barton Flower **Lady H. J. Clarke**
10 **BUCK MAGIC (IRE),** 9, b g Albano (IRE)—Green Sea **B. A. Derrick**
11 **CAROLE'S DESTRIER,** 7, b g Kayf Tara—Barton May **Mrs C. Skipworth**
12 **CAROLE'S VIGILANTE (IRE),** 4, ch g Flemensfirth (USA)—Gotta Goa (IRE) **Mrs C. Skipworth**
13 **CHICKSGROVE SPRITE (IRE),** 4, b f Scorpion (IRE)—Homebird (IRE) **Mrs A. R. Hart**
14 **COMMITMENT,** 6, b g Motivator—Courting **Mrs H. R. Cross**
15 **EARLS FORT (IRE),** 5, b g Kalanisi (IRE)—Lillando (IRE) **J. J. Maguire**
16 **EARTH LEGEND,** 4, b g Helissio (FR)—Maori Legend

## MR NEIL MULHOLLAND - Continued

17 **EBONY EMPRESS (IRE),** 6, br m Kris Kin (USA)—Auditing Empress (IRE) **Wincanton Race Club**
18 **FAST EXIT (IRE),** 8, b g Exit To Nowhere (USA)—Gift Token **Wellcroomed Ltd**
19 **GENERAL MONTGOMERY (IRE),** 6, b g Desert King (IRE)—
Supreme Course (IRE) **Mrs H R Cross & Mrs S A Keys**
20 **GREEK ISLANDS (IRE),** 7, b g Oasis Dream—Serisia (FR) **Mr P. Dewey**
21 **INDIAN BRAVE (IRE),** 4, b g Definite Article—Fridays Folly (IRE) **D. J. Bridger**
22 **ISTHEREADIFFERENCE (IRE),** 8, gr g Amilynx (FR)—Jennys Grove (IRE) **Colony Stable Llc**
23 **JOHNS LUCK (IRE),** 6, b g Turtle Island (IRE)—Jemima Yorke **Mr J. Hobbs**
24 **KING'S PROCESSION (IRE),** 4, ch g Teofilo (IRE)—Sateen **Neil Mulholland Racing Ltd**
25 **KRISTAL HART,** 6, b m Lucky Story (USA)—Moly (FR) **The White Hart Racing Syndicate**
26 **LADY HELISSIO,** 5, b m Helissio (FR)—Barton Dante **David H. Smith**
27 **LANGARVE LADY (IRE),** 7, b m Oscar (IRE)—Fashions Monty (IRE) **Mr B. F. Mulholland**
28 **LANGARVE LASS (IRE),** 6, b m Oscar (IRE)—Fashions Monty (IRE) **Mr B. F. Mulholland**
29 **LEAVE IT BE (IRE),** 8, gr g High-Rise (IRE)—Farh Quest (IRE) **Hanham Boys Racing Partnership**
30 **LIFETIME (IRE),** 7, b g Shamardal (USA)—La Vita E Bella (IRE) **Mr S. Noyce**
31 **LILY MARS (IRE),** 8, br m Presenting—Tiffany Jazz (IRE) **Mrs H. Dale-Staples**
32 **LIONS CHARGE (USA),** 8, ch g Lion Heart (USA)—Fellwaati (USA) **Neil Mulholland Racing Ltd**
33 **MAID OF TUSCANY (IRE),** 4, b f Manduro (GER)—Tuscania (USA) **Qdos Racing**
34 **MARSHGATE LANE (USA),** 6, b h Medaglia d'Oro (USA)—Louvain (IRE) **Neil Mulholland Racing Ltd**
35 **MASTER BURBIDGE,** 4, b g Pasternak—Silver Sequel **Dajam Ltd**
36 **MATROW'S LADY (IRE),** 8, b m Cloudings (IRE)—I'm Maggy (NZ) **Matrow Properties Limited**
37 **MIDNIGHT SEQUEL,** 6, b m Midnight Legend—Silver Sequel **Strictly Come Racing**
38 **MINELLA DEFINITELY (IRE),** 8, br g Definite Article—West Along **Wellcroomed Ltd**
39 **MINELLA PRESENT (IRE),** 6, b g Presenting—Dabaya (IRE) **Lady H. J. Clarke**
40 **MORRIS THE MINER,** 5, b g Apple Tree (FR)—Miner Yours **Mrs D. C. Webb**
41 **MR BURBIDGE,** 7, b g Midnight Legend—Twin Time **Dajam Ltd**
42 **MRS BURBIDGE,** 5, b m Pasternak—Twin Time **Dajam Ltd**
43 **NI SIN E MO AINM (IRE),** 7, b g Balakheri (IRE)—Bramslam (IRE) **N Webb & P J Proudley**
44 **PASS THE TIME,** 6, b m Passing Glance—Twin Time **Dajam Ltd**
45 **PERFECT TIMING,** 7, b g Shantou (USA)—Winnetka Gal (IRE) **Hanham Boys Racing Partnership**
46 4, B f Scorpion (IRE)—Perspex Queen (IRE) **Mrs D. C. Webb**
47 **PINK LIPS,** 7, b m Noverre (USA)—Primrose Queen **Sweet Sugar Racing Club**
48 **PROOFREADER,** 6, b g Authorized (IRE)—Blixen (USA) **Neil Mulholland Racing Ltd**
49 **PURE POTEEN (IRE),** 7, ch g Flemensfirth (USA)—Taking My Time (IRE) **Mr N. C. Robinson**
50 **PURSUITOFHAPPINESS (IRE),** 7, b g Classic Cliche (IRE)—Lake Tour (IRE) **B. A. Derrick**
51 **REALTA MO CROI (IRE),** 7, b m Westerner—Solar Quest (IRE) **Neil Mulholland Racing Ltd**
52 **ROUGH FIGHTER (USA),** 6, b g Mizzen Mast (USA)—Louis d'or (USA) **Maori Partnership**
53 **SHANTOU VILLAGE (IRE),** 5, b g Shantou (USA)—Village Queen (IRE) **Mrs J. Gerard-Pearse**
54 **SHARP SWORD (IRE),** 4, ch g King's Best (USA)—Pictavia (IRE) **Mrs H. Dale-Staples**
55 **SIRRAH STAR (IRE),** 7, gr m Great Palm (USA)—Simply Deep (IRE) **Wellcroomed Ltd**
56 **SOUTHFIELD ROYALE,** 5, b g Presenting—Chamoss Royale (FR) **Mrs A. B. Yeoman**
57 **SPECIAL REPORT (IRE),** 5, b g Mujadil (USA)—Ellistown Lady (IRE) **Six Shades Of Grey**
58 **STRICTLY THE ONE (IRE),** 5, b g Robin des Pres (FR)—Rita's Charm (IRE) **Strictly Come Racing**
59 **THE BAY BANDIT,** 8, b g Highest Honor (FR)—Pescara (IRE) **Neil Mulholland Racing Club**
60 **THE DRUIDS NEPHEW (IRE),** 8, b g King's Theatre (IRE)—Gifted **The Stonehenge Druids**
61 **THE YOUNG MASTER,** 6, b g Echo of Light—Fine Frenzy (IRE) **Dajam Ltd**
62 4, B g Helissio (FR)—Twin Time **Mr S. K. Brown**
63 **VEXILLUM (IRE),** 6, br g Mujadil (USA)—Common Cause **J. Heaney**
64 **WADSWICK COURT (IRE),** 7, b g Court Cave (IRE)—Tarasandy (IRE) **The Chosen Few**
65 **WHATS LEFT (IRE),** 7, b g Darsi (FR)—Dynamic Venture (IRE) **Mrs A. R. Hart**
66 **YESYOUCAN (IRE),** 10, b g Beneficial—Except Alice (IRE) **Prism Bloodstock**

## THREE-YEAR-OLDS

67 **HARLEY REBEL,** br g Cockney Rebel (IRE)—Al Kahina **Mrs G. P. Seymour**
68 **I'M ASKING (IRE),** ch f Ask—I'm Maggy (NZ) **Mrs H. R. Cross**

**Other Owners:** D. Abrey, Mrs J. A. V. Allen, Mrs L. S. Atwell, Mr G. J. R. Barry, Mrs M. A. Clark, Mrs A. C. Crofts, Mr S. J. Dew, Mr D. R. Gilbert, Mr P. Gray, Mr R. T. Greenhill, Mr S. Harbour, M. P. Hill, Mrs W. A. Jenkins, Mrs S. A. Keys, Mr P. H. King, Mrs C. Lewis, B. D. Makepeace, Mr J. G. Mogg, Mr N. P. Mulholland, R. D. Nicholas, Mr P. J. Proudley, Mr K. J. Strangeway, Mrs D. J. Symes, Mr J. N. Trueman, Mr G. J. Villis, N. E. Webb, Mr P. Webb.

**Conditional:** Andrias Guerin.

## 437 MR LAWRENCE MULLANEY, Malton

Postal: **Raikes Farm, Great Habton, Malton, North Yorkshire, YO17 6RX**
Contacts: **PHONE (01653) 668208 MOBILE (07899) 902565**

1 **DENISON FLYER,** 8, b g Tobougg (IRE)—Bollin Victoria **L. A. Mullaney**
2 **FIRST SARGEANT,** 5, gr g Dutch Art—Princess Raya **Rothmere Racing Limited**
3 **GALA CASINO STAR (IRE),** 10, ch g Dr Fong (USA)—Abir **G.B Racing Club**
4 **JACK LUEY,** 8, b g Danbird (AUS)—Icenaslice (IRE) **The Jack Partnership & Mr S Rimmer**
5 **KARA TARA,** 5, b m Kayf Tara—Matilda Too (IRE) **C. D. Carr**
6 **NOBLE REACH,** 4, b f Phoenix Reach (IRE)—Comtesse Noire (CAN) **G.B Racing Club**
7 **UNIQUE ROSE,** 5, b m Byron—Peachy Pear **Mr A. C. Fry**

### THREE-YEAR-OLDS

8 **EDIE WHITE,** b f Bahamian Bounty—Croeso Bach **Ian Buckley**

### TWO-YEAR-OLDS

9 **ARCANE DANCER (IRE),** b f 6/4 Arcano (IRE)—
La Reine Mambo (USA) (High Yield (USA)) (11110) **Mr S. J. Rimmer**

**Other Owners:** Mrs J. Copley, Mr K. Drysdale, Mrs T. Nason, Mr W. Nason, Mr A. P. Reed, Mrs H. L. Russell.

## 438 MR MICHAEL MULLINEAUX, Tarporley

Postal: **Southley Farm, Alpraham, Tarporley, Cheshire, CW6 9JD**
Contacts: **PHONE (01829) 261440 FAX (01829) 261440 MOBILE (07753) 650263**
**E-MAIL southlearacing@btinternet.com WEBSITE www.southleyfarm.co.uk**

1 **ANTON DOLIN (IRE),** 7, ch g Danehill Dancer (IRE)—Ski For Gold **C. R. Nugent**
2 **BRICBRACSMATE,** 7, b g Revoque (IRE)—Blissphilly **P. J. Lawton**
3 **FEISTY GIRL,** 5, ch m Erhaab (USA)—Dolly Duff **The Weaver Group**
4 **GABRIAL THE BOSS (USA),** 5, ch g Street Boss (USA)—Bacinella (USA) **H. Clewlow**
5 5, B g Starcraft (NZ)—Jig Time **S. A. Pritchard**
6 **JULIE'S LAD,** 5, ch g Primo Valentino (IRE)—Sunny Parkes **S. A. Pritchard**
7 **LORD OF THE DANCE (IRE),** 9, ch g Indian Haven—Maine Lobster (USA) **H. Clewlow**
8 **METHAALY (IRE),** 12, b g Red Ransom (USA)—Santorini (USA) **S. A. Pritchard**
9 **MINTY JONES,** 6, b h Primo Valentino (IRE)—Reveur **P. Clacher**
10 **MOLKO JACK (FR),** 11, b br g Lavirco (GER)—Line As (FR) **D. Ashbrook**
11 **MY TIME,** 6, b g Mind Games—Tick Tock **Mr M. Kilner**
12 **ORPEN BID (IRE),** 10, b m Orpen (USA)—Glorious Bid (IRE) **Miss L. S. Young**
13 **POOR DUKE (IRE),** 5, b g Bachelor Duke (USA)—Graze On Too (IRE) **Crewe & Nantwich Racing Club**
14 **ROMANN ANGEL,** 6, b m Sir Harry Lewis (USA)—Roman Gospel **M. Mullineaux**
15 **ROYAL SEA (IRE),** 6, b g Refuse To Bend (IRE)—Janayen (USA) **M. Mullineaux**
16 **SIR BOSS (IRE),** 10, b g Tagula (IRE)—Good Thought (IRE)
17 **SMIRFY'S SILVER,** 11, b g Desert Prince (IRE)—Goodwood Blizzard **Mrs D. Plant**
18 **SMIRFYS BLACKCAT (IRE),** 6, b m One Cool Cat (USA)—Smirfys Dance Hall (IRE) **Mrs D. Plant**
19 **STURDY DAWN,** 5, br m Striking Ambition—Lucky Find (IRE) **Mr K. Jones**
20 **TRACKSIDE FLYER,** 6, b g Revoque (IRE)—Montevelle (IRE) **Mr M. Davies**
21 **TWO TURTLE DOVES (IRE),** 9, b m Night Shift (USA)—Purple Rain (IRE) **Mr G. Cornes**
22 **VERY FIRST BLADE,** 6, b g Needwood Blade—Dispol Verity **Ogwen Valley Racing**
23 **WYMESWOLD,** 8, b m Alflora (IRE)—Dominie Breeze **The Hon Mrs S. Pakenham**

### THREE-YEAR-OLDS

24 **JACKSONFIRE,** ch c Firebreak—Fitolini **Mr O. D. Knight**
25 **OUTLAW KATE (IRE),** b f Bushranger (IRE)—Diosper (USA) **Mr & Mrs S Ashbrooke & J P Daly**

**Other Owners:** Mrs M. Ashbrooke, Mr S. Ashbrooke, Mr J. P. Daly, Mr G. Jones, Miss M. Mullineaux, Mr P. Murray, Mr N. Murray-Williams, Mr J. D. Ranson, M. G. West.

**Assistant Trainers:** Stuart Ross, Susan Mullineaux

**Amateur:** Miss M. J. L. Mullineaux.

## 439 MR SEAMUS MULLINS, Amesbury

Postal: **Wilsford Stables, Wilsford-Cum-Lake, Amesbury, Salisbury, Wiltshire, SP4 7BL**
Contacts: **PHONE/FAX (01980) 626344 MOBILE (07702) 559634**
**E-MAIL info@jwmullins.co.uk WEBSITE www.seamusmullins.co.uk**

1 **ADRENALIN FLIGHT (IRE),** 9, b g Dr Massini (IRE)—Chapel Queen (IRE) **Mr M. Adams**
2 **AL REESHA (IRE),** 4, b f Kayf Tara—Simply Kitty (IRE) **Mr N. J. G. Allsop**
3 **ALDER MAIRI (IRE),** 8, ch m Alderbrook—Amari Queen **F. G. Matthews**
4 **BAHRI SUGAR (IRE),** 7, b m Bahri (USA)—Church House Lady (IRE) **Mrs J. C. Scorgie**
5 **BAHUMBUG,** 5, b g Bahamian Bounty—Stan's Smarty Girl (USA) **Woodford Valley Racing**
6 **BONDS CONQUEST,** 6, ch g Monsieur Bond (IRE)—Another Conquest **F. G. Matthews**
7 **BOSS IN BOOTS (IRE),** 7, gr g King's Theatre (IRE)—Grey Mo (IRE) **Mr M. Adams**
8 **BRUNETTE'SONLY (IRE),** 10, ch m Flemensfirth (USA)—Pride of St Gallen (IRE) **Mrs M. M. Rayner**
9 **COMBUSTIBLE LADY (IRE),** 10, b m Mr Combustible (IRE)—Ladyogan (IRE) **J. W. Mullins**
10 **DANCING CONQUEST,** 5, b m Imperial Dancer—Another Conquest **F. G. Matthews**
11 **DOUNEEDAHAND,** 4, b f Royal Applause—Our Sheila **Caloona Racing**
12 **FERGALL (IRE),** 8, br g Norwich—Gaybrook Girl (IRE) **Andrew Cocks & Tara Johnson**
13 **FLUGZEUG,** 7, gr g Silver Patriarch (IRE)—Telmar Flyer **New Forest Racing Partnership**
14 **GIVEAGIRLACHANCE (IRE),** 6, b m Iffraaj—Farewell To Love (IRE) **The Five Plus One Partnership**
15 **GIZZIT (IRE),** 9, b g Son of Sharp Shot (IRE)—Suez Canal (FR) **J. W. Mullins**
16 **GLENARIFF,** 6, b m Kayf Tara—Lady Racquet (IRE) **The Up The Glens Partnership & D J Erwin**
17 **GLENARM,** 6, b m Kayf Tara—Rumbled **The Up The Glens Partnership**
18 **GRANDMASTER GEORGE (IRE),** 6, ch g Generous (IRE)—
Merewood Lodge (IRE) **Andrew Cocks & Tara Johnson**
19 **GREENGAGE SUMMER,** 4, b f Sixties Icon—Linda Green **J. W. Mullins**
20 **HEAD SPIN (IRE),** 7, b g Beneficial—Who Tells Jan **Mr M. Adams**
21 **HILL FORTS GYPSE (IRE),** 4, b g Bienamado (USA)—Whistling Gypse (IRE) **Mrs J. C. Scorgie**
22 **INDIAN JACK (IRE),** 7, ch g Indian Haven—Almaviva (IRE) **Mr M. Adams**
23 **JARLATH,** 4, b g Norse Dancer (IRE)—Blue Lullaby (IRE) **Phoenix Bloodstock**
24 **KASTANI BEACH (IRE),** 9, br g Alderbrook—Atomic View (IRE) **S Mullins Racing Club & Philippa Downing**
25 **KENTFORD HEIRESS,** 5, b m Midnight Legend—Kentford Duchess **D. I. Bare**
26 **KENTFORD MYTH,** 5, b m Midnight Legend—Quistaquay **D. I. Bare**
27 **LEXINGTON BLUE,** 5, b g Bertolini (USA)—Jasmine Breeze **Church Racing Partnership**
28 **MARMALADE MAN,** 9, ch g Karinga Bay—Kentford Duchess **D. I. Bare**
29 **MIGHTY MOBB (IRE),** 8, b g Accordion—Dusty Lane (IRE) **Mrs M. M. Rayner**
30 **MISS SASSYPANTS,** 6, ch m Hernando (FR)—Serraval (FR) **J. T. Brown**
31 **MOGESTIC (IRE),** 6, b g Morozov (USA)—Crosschild (IRE) **Andrew Cocks & Tara Johnson**
32 **NORMANTON (IRE),** 5, b br g Norwich—Fly Like A Bird **J. W. Mullins**
33 **OVERDO,** 4, br f Overbury (IRE)—Shuil Do (IRE) **Mrs F. J. B. Woodd**
34 **ROMEO AMERICO (IRE),** 8, b g Lord Americo—Crazy Falcon (IRE) **Mr M. Adams**
35 **RUBY SUSIE,** 4, b f Victory Note (USA)—Ruby Too **Dr R. Jowett**
36 **SIDBURY HILL,** 7, ch g Midnight Legend—Flora Macdonald **Mr S. J. Rawlins**
37 **SOMCHINE,** 7, b g Volochine (IRE)—Seem of Gold **Mr C. R. Dunning**
38 **SONG LIGHT,** 5, b g Echo of Light—Blue Lullaby (IRE) **D & C Bloodstock & Mr Albert Goodman**
39 **SPORTSREPORT (IRE),** 7, b g Coroner (IRE)—Goforthetape (IRE) **Mr C. J. Baldwin**
40 **STEEL CITY,** 7, gr g Act One—Serraval (FR) **J. T. Brown**
41 **THE INFORMANT,** 9, gr g Central Park (IRE)—Belle Rose (IRE) **Dr & Mrs John Millar**
42 **TIME TO THINK,** 10, b m Alflora (IRE)—Shuil Do (IRE) **Mrs V. F. Hewett**
43 **ULTIMATE ACT,** 4, ro g Act One—Ruffie (IRE) **Phoenix Bloodstock**
44 **WILDE AND WILLING (IRE),** 7, b g Oscar (IRE)—Turtlena (IRE) **Dr & Mrs John Millar**
45 **WILLY BE LUCKY (IRE),** 9, b g Classic Cliche (IRE)—Hadaani **Mrs M. M. Rayner**

### THREE-YEAR-OLDS

46 **MYTHICAL MAID (IRE),** ch f Arakan (USA)—Bonne **Caloona Racing**
47 **TRICKY ISSUE (IRE),** b f Manduro (GER)—Tricky Situation **Caloona Racing**

**Other Owners:** P. R. Attwater, Mr H. R. Attwater, J. E. Bone, Mr A. P. Cocks, Mr J. Collins, Mr P. Collins, Miss P. M. Downing, D. J. Erwin, A. A. Goodman, Mr A. K. Horsman, Miss T. Johnson, J. Kavanagh, Dr J. W. Millar, Mrs J. D. Millar, Mr R. J. Stammers, D. Sutherland, Miss R. Toppin, C. Wilson.

**Assistant Trainer:** Paul Attwater

**Jockey (NH):** Kevin Jones, Wayne Kavanagh, Ryan Mahon, Andrew Thornton. **Apprentice:** Lamorna Bardwell. **Amateur:** Mr Daniel Sansom.

## 440 MR WILLIAM P. MULLINS, Carlow

Postal: **Closutton, Bagenalstown, Co. Carlow, Ireland**
Contacts: **PHONE (00353) 5997 21786 FAX (00353) 5997 22709 MOBILE (00353) 8725 64940**
**E-MAIL wpmullins@eircom.net WEBSITE www.wpmullins.com**

1 **ABBEY LANE (IRE),** 10, b g Flemensfirth (USA)—Hazel Sylph (IRE) **Martin Lynch**
2 **ABBYSSIAL (IRE),** 5, ch g Beneficial—Mega d'estruval (FR) **Mrs Violet O'Leary**
3 **ADRIANA DES MOTTES (FR),** 5, b br m Network (GER)—Daisy des Mottes (FR) **Mrs S. Ricci**
4 **AINSI VA LA VIE (FR),** 5, gr m Lavirco (GER)—Joie de La Vie (FR) **Supreme Horse Racing Club**
5 **AIRLIE BEACH (IRE),** 5, b m Shantou (USA)—Screaming Witness (IRE) **Supreme Horse Racing Club**
6 **AKLAN (IRE),** 6, gr h Dalakhani (IRE)—Akdara (IRE) **Coach Partnership**
7 **AL WUKIR (IRE),** 5, b g Jeremy (USA)—Collada (IRE) **Mr A. N. Mubarak**
8 **ALELCHI INOIS (FR),** 7, b g Night Tango (GER)—Witness Gama (FR) **Mrs M. McMahon**
9 **ALONSO (SPA),** 6, ch g Green Tune (USA)—Lady Cree (IRE) **Andrea & Graham Wylie**
10 **ALVISIO VILLE (FR),** 5, gr g Visionary (FR)—Murphy Ville (FR) **J. P. McManus**
11 **AMINABAD (FR),** 5, b g Singspiel (IRE)—Amenapinga (FR) **Gigginstown House Stud**
12 **AN DEARG MOR (IRE),** 5, ch g Robin des Champs (FR)—Johnston's Flyer (IRE) **C.C.R. Racing Syndicate**
13 **ANALIFET (FR),** 5, b m Califet (FR)—Viana (FR) **Gigginstown House Stud**
14 **ANNIE O (IRE),** 6, b m Oscar (IRE)—Rocking Annie (IRE) **B. Fitzpatrick**
15 **ANNIE POWER (IRE),** 7, ch m Shirocco (GER)—Anno Luce **Mrs S. Ricci**
16 **ARBOR RUN (IRE),** 5, ch g Flemensfirth (USA)—Maghanns Pride (IRE) **F. N. Doyle Partnership**
17 **ARBRE DE VIE (FR),** 5, b g Antarctique (IRE)—Nouvelle Recrue (FR) **Mrs S. Ricci**
18 **ARCTIC FIRE (GER),** 6, b g Soldier Hollow—Adelma (GER) **Wicklow Bloodstock Limited**
19 **ARE YA RIGHT CHIEF (IRE),** 10, b g Flemensfirth (USA)—River Clyde (IRE) **Mrs M. McMahon**
20 **ARGENTINO (FR),** 5, br g Sinndar (IRE)—Syssiss (FR) **Gigginstown House Stud**
21 **ARKWRISHT (FR),** 5, b g Lavirco (GER)—Latitude (FR) **Gigginstown House Stud**
22 **AS DE FERBET (FR),** 5, gr g Dom Alco (FR)—Intrigue Deferbet (FR) **Gigginstown House Stud**
23 **AU QUART DE TOUR (FR),** 5, b g Robin des Champs (FR)—Qualite Controlee (FR) **Mrs S. Ricci**
24 **AUGUSTIN (FR),** 5, gr g Martaline—Lili Bleue (FR) **Mrs M. McMahon**
25 **AVANT TOUT (FR),** 5, ch g Agent Bleu (FR)—Quiwfty (FR) **Supreme Horse Racing Club**
26 **AVENIR D'UNE VIE (FR),** 5, gr g Lavirco (GER)—Par Bonheur (FR) **Gigginstown House Stud**
27 **BABYLONE DES MOTTE (FR),** 4, b br f Blue Bresil (FR)—Nellyssa Bleu (FR) **Mrs S. Ricci**
28 **BACHASSON (FR),** 4, gr g Voix du Nord (FR)—Belledonne (FR) **Edward O'Connell**
29 **BACK IN FOCUS (IRE),** 10, ch g Bob Back (USA)—Dun Belle (IRE) **Andrea & Graham Wylie**
30 **BALKO DES FLOS (FR),** 4, ch g Balko (FR)—Royale Marie (FR) **Gigginstown House Stud**
31 **BALLYCASEY (IRE),** 8, gr g Presenting—Pink Mist (IRE) **Mrs S. Ricci**
32 **BALNASLOW (IRE),** 8, b g Presenting—Noble Choice **Gigginstown House Stud**
33 **BEAU MOME (FR),** 4, b g Racinger (FR)—Lamoune (FR) **Mrs S. Ricci**
34 **BELLSHILL (IRE),** 5, b g King's Theatre (IRE)—Fairy Native (IRE) **Andrea & Graham Wylie**
35 **BELUCKYAGAIN (IRE),** 7, b m Old Vic—Whizz **Supreme Horse Racing Club**
36 **BLACK HERCULES (IRE),** 6, b g Heron Island (IRE)—Annalecky (IRE) **Andrea Wylie**
37 **BLOOD COTIL (FR),** 6, b g Enrique—Move Along (FR) **Mrs S. Ricci**
38 **BONBON AU MIEL (FR),** 4, b g Khalkevi (IRE)—Friandise II (FR) **Andrea & Graham Wylie**
39 **BORDINI (FR),** 5, b g Martaline—Didinas (FR) **Mrs S. Ricci**
40 **BOSMAN RULE (IRE),** 7, ch g Gamut (IRE)—Fairy Blaze (IRE) **Philip J. Reynolds**
41 **BOSTON BOB (IRE),** 10, b g Bob Back (USA)—Bavaway **Andrea & Graham Wylie**
42 **BRIAR HILL (IRE),** 7, b g Shantou (USA)—Backaway (IRE) **Andrea & Graham Wylie**
43 **BUISENESS SIVOLA (FR),** 4, b g Archange d'or (IRE)—Louve Orientale **Mr Simon Munir & Mr Isaac Souede**
44 **CHAMPAGNE FEVER (IRE),** 8, gr g Stowaway—Forever Bubbles (IRE) **Mrs S. Ricci**
45 **CHILDRENS LIST (IRE),** 5, b g Presenting—Snipe Hunt (IRE) **Mrs S. Ricci**
46 **CITY SLICKER (IRE),** 7, b g King's Theatre (IRE)—Donna's Princess (IRE) **J. P. McManus**
47 **CLONDAW COURT (IRE),** 8, br g Court Cave (IRE)—Secret Can't Say (IRE) **Mrs S. Ricci**
48 **CLONDAW WARRIOR (IRE),** 8, br g Overbury (IRE)—Thespian (IRE) **Act D Wagg Syndicate**
49 **DANEKING,** 6, b g Dylan Thomas (IRE)—Sadie Thompson (IRE) **Mrs S. Ricci**
50 **DEVILS BRIDE (IRE),** 8, b g Helissio (FR)—Rigorous **Gigginstown House Stud**
51 **DIAKALI (FR),** 6, gr g Sinndar (IRE)—Diasilixa (FR) **Wicklow Bloodstock Limited**
52 **DICOSIMO (FR),** 4, b g Laveron—Coralisse Royale (FR) **Mrs S. Ricci**
53 **DIGEANTA (IRE),** 8, b g Helissio (FR)—
Scolboa Gold (IRE) **Dr I. M. P. Moran, Colland Sand & Gravel Syndicate**
54 **DJAKADAM (FR),** 6, b g Saint des Saints (FR)—Rainbow Crest (FR) **Mrs S. Ricci**
55 **DOGORA (FR),** 6, gr g Robin des Pres (FR)—Garde de Nuit (FR) **Mrs S. Ricci**
56 **DON POLI (IRE),** 6, b g Poliglote—Dalamine (FR) **Gigginstown House Stud**
57 **DOUVAN (FR),** 5, b g Walk In The Park (IRE)—Star Face (FR) **Mrs S. Ricci**
58 **DRIVE TIME (USA),** 10, b g King Cugat (USA)—Arbusha (USA) **Andrea & Graham Wylie**
59 **EASY STREET (FR),** 6, b m Sassanian (USA)—Royale Sulawesie (FR) **Mrs John Magnier**
60 **FAUGHEEN (IRE),** 7, b g Germany (USA)—Miss Pickering (IRE) **Mrs S. Ricci**

## MR WILLIAM P. MULLINS - Continued

61 **FELIX YONGER (IRE),** 9, b g Oscar (IRE)—Marble Sound (IRE) **Andrea & Graham Wylie**
62 **FLASH OF GENIUS,** 9, b g Definite Article—Fortune's Girl **Gigginstown House Stud**
63 **FLORISHWELLS D'ETE (FR),** 5, b m Irish Wells (FR)—Florilla (GER) **J. P. McManus**
64 **FUGI MOUNTAIN (IRE),** 5, b g Diamond Green (FR)—Sixhills (FR) **Mrs J. M. Mullins**
65 **GITANE DU BERLAIS (FR),** 5, b m Balko (FR)—Boheme du Berlais (FR) **Mr Simon Munir**
66 **GLENS MELODY (IRE),** 7, b m King's Theatre (IRE)—Glens Music (IRE) **Ms Fiona McStay**
67 **GOOD THYNE TARA,** 5, b br m Kayf Tara—Good Thyne Mary (IRE) **N. G. King**
68 **GORGEOUS SIXTY (FR),** 7, b m Touch of The Blues (FR)—Sixty Six (IRE) **Mrs S. Ricci**
69 **GRANGECLARE PEARL (IRE),** 8, b m Old Vic—Grangeclare Rose (IRE) **Ethel Flanagan**
70 **HONEYS JOY,** 6, b m Kayf Tara—Two For Joy (IRE) **C.C.R. Racing Syndicate**
71 **HOT ON HER HEELS (IRE),** 5, b m Stowaway—Orinocco Blue (IRE) **Supreme Horse Racing Club**
72 **HURRICANE FLY (IRE),** 11, b g Montjeu (IRE)—Scandisk (IRE) **George Creighton**
73 **INISH ISLAND (IRE),** 9, ch g Trans Island—Ish (IRE) **Susan Flanagan**
74 **IVAN GROZNY (FR),** 5, b g Turtle Bowl (IRE)—Behnesa (IRE) **Andrea & Graham Wylie**
75 **JARRY D'HONNEUR (FR),** 6, b br g Baroud d'honneur (FR)—True Lovely (FR) **J. P. McManus**
76 **KALKIR (FR),** 4, b g Montmartre (FR)—Kakira (FR) **Mrs S. Ricci**
77 **KALMANN (FR),** 6, ch g Reste Tranquille (FR)—Sahmat (FR) **Mrs S. Ricci**
78 **KARALEE (FR),** 4, gr f Martaline—Change Partner (FR) **Mrs S. Ricci**
79 **KATE APPLEBY SHOES (IRE),** 6, b m Flemensfirth (USA)—Gotta Goa (IRE) **Leo McArdle**
80 **KILLER CROW (IRE),** 6, ch g Presenting—Rivervail (IRE) **Gigginstown House Stud**
81 **KILLULTAGH VIC (IRE),** 6, b g Old Vic—Killultagh Dawn (IRE) **Mrs Rose Boyd**
82 **LIMINI (IRE),** 4, ch f Peintre Celebre (USA)—Her Grace (IRE) **Mrs S. Ricci**
83 **LISTEN DEAR (IRE),** 5, b m Robin des Champs (FR)—Crescendor (FR) **Supreme Horse Racing Club**
84 **LIVELOVELAUGH (IRE),** 5, b g Beneficial—Another Evening (IRE) **Mrs S. Ricci**
85 **LOCKSTOCKANDBARREL (IRE),** 6, b g Flemensfirth (USA)—Omas Lady (IRE) **Mrs John Magnier**
86 **LUCKY BRIDLE (IRE),** 6, b h Dylan Thomas (IRE)—Auction Room (USA) **Andrea & Graham Wylie**
87 **LYRICAL THEATRE (IRE),** 6, b m King's Theatre (IRE)—Shuil Dorcha (IRE) **The Hibo Syndicate**
88 **MADE IN GERMANY (IRE),** 7, ch g Germany (USA)—Black Dot Com (IRE) **Gigginstown House Stud**
89 **MARASONNIEN (FR),** 9, b g Mansonnien (FR)—Maracay (FR) **Mrs S. Ricci**
90 **MASTER OF VERSE (IRE),** 6, b g Milan—Bacchonthebottle (IRE) **Gigginstown House Stud**
91 **MAX DYNAMITE (FR),** 5, b h Great Journey (JPN)—Mascara (GER) **Mrs S. Ricci**
92 **MCKINLEY,** 5, b g Kheleyf (USA)—Priera Menta (IRE) **Gigginstown House Stud**
93 **MEASUREOFMYDREAMS (IRE),** 7, b g Shantou (USA)—Le Bavellen **Gigginstown House Stud**
94 **MERRY NIGHT (IRE),** 5, b g Presenting—Our Prima Donna (IRE) **Mrs Violet O'Leary**
95 **MIDNIGHT GAME,** 8, b g Montjeu (IRE)—Midnight Angel (GER) **Gigginstown House Stud**
96 **MILSEAN (IRE),** 6, b g Milan—Boro Supreme (IRE) **Gigginstown House Stud**
97 **MORNING RUN (IRE),** 6, b m King's Theatre (IRE)—Portryan Native (IRE) **Mr H. Murphy**
98 **MOYLE PARK (IRE),** 7, ch g Flemensfirth (USA)—Lovely Present (IRE) **Mrs S. Ricci**
99 **MOZOLTOV,** 9, b g Kayf Tara—Fairmead Princess **Gigginstown House Stud**
100 **NET D'ECOSSE (FR),** 5, ch g Network (GER)—Ecossette (FR) **Gigginstown House Stud**
101 **NICHOLS CANYON,** 5, b g Authorized (IRE)—Zam Zoom (IRE) **Andrea & Graham Wylie**
102 **NICKNAME EXIT (FR),** 5, b g Nickname (FR)—Exit To Fire (FR) **Gigginstown House Stud**
103 **NOBLE INN (FR),** 5, b g Sinndar (IRE)—Nataliana **M. J. Mulvaney**
104 **ON HIS OWN (IRE),** 11, b g Presenting—Shuil Na Mhuire (IRE) **Andrea & Graham Wylie**
105 **OPEN EAGLE (IRE),** 6, b g Montjeu (IRE)—Princesse de Viane (FR) **Supreme Horse Racing Club**
106 **OUTLANDER (IRE),** 7, b g Stowaway—Western Whisper (IRE) **Gigginstown House Stud**
107 **PATANNE (IRE),** 7, b g Golan (IRE)—Best Wait (IRE) **Shanakiel Racing Syndicate**
108 **PERFECT GENTLEMAN (IRE),** 10, b g King's Theatre (IRE)—Millennium Lilly (IRE) **Mrs J. M. Mullins**
109 **PETITE PARISIENNE,** 4, b f Montmartre (FR)—Ejina (FR) **Gigginstown House Stud**
110 **PIQUE SOUS (FR),** 8, gr g Martaline—Six Fois Sept (FR) **Not Just Any Racing Club**
111 **POKER GOLD (FR),** 4, b c Gold Away (IRE)—Becquarette (FR) **Eamonn A. Dunne**
112 **PONT ALEXANDRE (GER),** 7, b g Dai Jin—Panzella (FR) **Mrs S. Ricci**
113 **POTTERS POINT (IRE),** 5, b g Robin des Champs (FR)—Tango Lady (IRE) **Gigginstown House Stud**
114 **PRIMROSEANDBLUE (IRE),** 11, b g Shernazar—Karlybelle (FR) **Mrs J. M. Mullins**
115 **PRINCE D'AUBRELLE (FR),** 5, ch g Malinas (GER)—La Star (FR) **Allan McLuckie**
116 **PRINCE DE BEAUCHENE (FR),** 12, b g French Glory—Chipie d'angron (FR) **Prince & Paupers Syndicate**
117 **PYLONTHEPRESSURE (IRE),** 5, b g Darsi (FR)—Minnie O'grady (IRE) **Mrs S. Ricci**
118 **RAISE HELL (IRE),** 8, b g Presenting—Markiza (IRE) **Gigginstown House Stud**
119 **RATHVINDEN (IRE),** 7, b g Heron Island (IRE)—Peggy Cullen (IRE) **R. A. Bartlett**
120 **RENNETI (FR),** 6, b g Irish Wells (FR)—Caprice Meill (FR) **Mrs S. Ricci**
121 **RETOUR EN FRANCE (IRE),** 5, b m Robin des Champs (FR)—Rayane (FR) **Mrs S. Ricci**
122 **RIO TREASURE (IRE),** 5, b m Captain Rio—Killiney Treasure (IRE) **Mrs M. McMahon**
123 **ROCKYABOYA (IRE),** 11, ch g Rock Hopper—Motility **P. W. Mullins**
124 **ROI DES FRANCS (FR),** 6, b g Poliglote—Grande Souveraine (FR) **Gigginstown House Stud**
125 **ROLLY BABY (FR),** 10, b g Funny Baby (FR)—Vancia (FR) **Teahon Consulting**

## MR WILLIAM P. MULLINS - Continued

126 **ROUGH JUSTICE (IRE),** 7, b g Beneficial—Ringzar (IRE) **Gigginstown House Stud**
127 **ROUMANIAN (FR),** 9, b g Kapgarde (FR)—La Grive (FR) **P. W. Mullins**
128 **ROYAL CAVIAR (IRE),** 7, b g Vinnie Roe (IRE)—Blackwater Babe (IRE) **Mrs S. Ricci**
129 **RUBI BALL (FR),** 10, ch g Network (GER)—Hygie (FR) **Sc Ecurie Madame Patrick Papot**
130 **RUPERT LAMB,** 9, gr g Central Park (IRE)—Charlotte Lamb **Mrs M. McMahon**
131 **SAMBREMONT (FR),** 5, b g Saint des Saints (FR)—Rainbow Crest (FR) **Shanakiel Racing Syndicate**
132 **SECURITY BREACH (IRE),** 6, b g Red Clubs (IRE)—Lear's Crown (USA) **Gigginstown House Stud**
133 **SEMPRE MEDICI (FR),** 5, b h Medicean—Sambala (IRE) **Mrs S. Ricci**
134 **SHAMSIKHAN (IRE),** 6, ch g Dr Fong (USA)—Shamdala (IRE) **Mrs Audrey Turley**
135 **SHANESHILL (IRE),** 6, b g King's Theatre (IRE)—Darabaka (IRE) **Andrea & Graham Wylie**
136 **SIC ET NON (FR),** 5, b g Forestier (FR)—Limaranta (FR) **Gigginstown House Stud**
137 **SIMENON (IRE),** 8, b g Marju (IRE)—Epistoliere (IRE) **Wicklow Bloodstock Ltd**
138 **SIMPLY GOOCH (IRE),** 7, b g Desert King (IRE)—Good Foundation (IRE) **Supreme Horse Racing Club**
139 **SIR DES CHAMPS (FR),** 9, b br g Robin des Champs (FR)—Liste En Tete (FR) **Gigginstown House Stud**
140 **SO YOUNG (FR),** 9, b g Lavirco (GER)—Honey (FR) **Mrs M. McMahon**
141 **STONE HARD (IRE),** 5, b g Robin des Champs (FR)—Amber Light (IRE) **Gigginstown House Stud**
142 **SUNTIEP (FR),** 9, b g Ungaro (GER)—Galostiepy (FR) **J. T. Ennis**
143 **SURE REEF (IRE),** 6, ch g Choisir (AUS)—Cutting Reef (IRE) **Andrea & Graham Wylie**
144 **TARABIYN (IRE),** 4, gr g Sinndar (IRE)—Timabiyra (IRE) **Supreme Horse Racing Club**
145 **TARARE (FR),** 6, b g Astarabad (USA)—Targerine (FR) **Mrs S. Ricci**
146 **TASIDANA (IRE),** 6, b m Presenting—Keeps Sake (IRE) **C.C.R. Racing Syndicate**
147 **TELL US MORE (IRE),** 6, b g Scorpion (IRE)—Zara's Victory (IRE) **Gigginstown House Stud**
148 **TENNIS CAP (FR),** 8, b g Snow Cap (FR)—Jijie (FR) **Mrs Violet O'Leary**
149 **TERESA DI VICENZO (IRE),** 5, b m Robin des Champs (FR)—Lusty Beg (IRE) **P. W. Mullins**
150 **TERMINAL (FR),** 8, b g Passing Sale (FR)—Durendal (FR) **Favourites Racing Syndicate**
151 **THE BOSSES COUSIN (IRE),** 10, b g King's Theatre (IRE)—Seductive Dance **Mrs J. M. Mullins**
152 **THE PAPARRAZI KID (IRE),** 8, b g Milan—Banbury Cross (IRE) **Byerley Thoroughbred Racing**
153 **THOUSAND STARS (FR),** 11, gr g Grey Risk (FR)—Livaniana (FR) **Hammer & Trowel Syndicate**
154 **TOTALLY DOMINANT (USA),** 6, b g War Chant (USA)—Miss Kilroy (USA) **Mrs S. Ricci**
155 **TURBAN (FR),** 8, b g Dom Alco (FR)—Indianabelle (FR) **Edward O'Connell**
156 **TURCAGUA (FR),** 5, gr g Turgeon (USA)—Acancagua (FR) **Mrs S. Ricci**
157 **TWINLIGHT (FR),** 8, b g Muhtathir—Fairlight (GER) **M L Bloodstock Limited**
158 **UN ATOUT (FR),** 7, b g Robin des Champs (FR)—Badrapette (FR) **Gigginstown House Stud**
159 **UN BEAU ROMAN (FR),** 7, bl g Roman Saddle (IRE)—Koukie (FR) **Aiden Devaney**
160 **UN DE SCEAUX (FR),** 7, b g Denham Red (FR)—Hotesse de Sceaux (FR) **E. O'Connell**
161 **UNCLE JUNIOR (IRE),** 14, b g Saddlers' Hall (IRE)—Caslain Nua **Mrs M. McMahon**
162 **UNIKA LA RECONCE (FR),** 7, b m Robin des Champs (FR)—First Wool (FR) **Mrs S. Ricci**
163 **UNION DUES (FR),** 7, b br g Malinas (GER)—Royale Dorothy (FR) **Allan McLuckie**
164 **UP FOR REVIEW (IRE),** 6, br g Presenting—Coolsilver (IRE) **Andrea & Graham Wylie**
165 **UPAZO (FR),** 7, b g Enrique—Honey (FR) **Philip J. Reynolds**
166 **UPSIE (FR),** 7, b m Le Balafre (FR)—Medjie (FR) **J. P. McManus**
167 **URADEL (GER),** 4, b g Kallisto (GER)—Unavita (GER) **Mrs M. McMahon**
168 **URANNA (FR),** 7, gr m Panoramic—Irresistible Anna (FR) **Supreme Horse Racing Club**
169 **URANO (FR),** 7, b g Enrique—Neiland (FR) **Mrs M. Mahon**
170 **VAL DE FERBET (FR),** 6, b g Voix du Nord (FR)—Intrigue Deferbet (FR) **Andrew Heffernan**
171 **VALERIAN BRIDGE (IRE),** 6, b g Heron Island (IRE)—Screaming Witness (IRE) **Gigginstown House Stud**
172 **VALSEUR LIDO (FR),** 6, b g Anzillero (GER)—Libido Rock (FR) **Gigginstown House Stud**
173 **VALYSSA MONTERG (FR),** 6, b br m Network (GER)—Mellyssa (FR) **Mrs S. Ricci**
174 **VAUTOUR (FR),** 6, b g Robin des Champs (FR)—Gazelle de Mai (FR) **Mrs S. Ricci**
175 **VEDETTARIAT (FR),** 6, bl g Lavirco (GER)—Platine (FR) **Mrs S. Ricci**
176 **VERAWAL (IRE),** 4, br g Sinndar (IRE)—Virana (IRE) **Supreme Horse Racing Club**
177 **VERY MUCH SO (IRE),** 5, b g Scorpion (IRE)—Lady Apprentice (IRE) **Supreme Horse Racing Club**
178 **VESPER BELL (IRE),** 9, b g Beneficial—Fair Choice (IRE) **Mrs S. Ricci**
179 **VICKY DE L'OASIS (FR),** 6, b m Ultimately Lucky (IRE)—Japonaise III (FR) **Wicklow Bloodstock Limited**
180 **VIVEGA (FR),** 6, ch g Robin des Champs (FR)—Vega IV (FR) **Mrs S. Ricci**
181 **VROUM VROUM MAG (FR),** 6, b m Voix du Nord (FR)—Naiade Mag (FR) **Mrs S. Ricci**
182 **WESTERNER LADY (IRE),** 5, b m Westerner—Cloghoge Lady (IRE) **Anthony P. Butler**
183 **WHITEOUT (GER),** 4, b f Samum (GER)—Wassiliki (IRE) **D. Lawlor**
184 **WICKLOW BRAVE,** 6, b g Beat Hollow—Moraine **Wicklow Bloodstock Limited**
185 **WOOD BREIZH (FR),** 5, gr g Stormy River (FR)—Polynevees (FR) **Supreme Horse Racing Club**
186 **ZAIDPOUR (FR),** 9, b g Red Ransom (USA)—Zainta (IRE) **Mrs S. Ricci**

## 441 MRS ANABEL K. MURPHY, Stratford-upon-Avon

Postal: **Warren Chase, Billesley Road, Wilmcote, Stratford-upon-Avon, Warwickshire, CV37 9XG**
Contacts: **OFFICE (01789) 205087 HOME (01789) 298346 FAX (01789) 263260**
**MOBILE (07774) 117777**
**E-MAIL anabelking.racing@virgin.net WEBSITE www.anabelkmurphy.co.uk**

1 **CAPTAIN BOCELLI (IRE),** 6, b g Kayf Tara—Beautiful Tune (FR) **Mrs D. L. Whateley**
2 **CROUCHING HARRY (IRE),** 6, b g Tiger Hill (IRE)—Catwalk Dreamer (IRE) **Ridgeway Racing Club & Partner**
3 **DORMOUSE,** 10, b g Medicean—Black Fighter (USA) **H. A. Murphy**
4 **INDIAN SCOUT,** 7, b g Indesatchel (IRE)—Manderina **Ridgeway Racing Club & Partner**
5 **KAKAPUKA,** 8, br g Shinko Forest (IRE)—No Rehearsal (FR) **Aiden Murphy & All The Kings Horses**
6 **KING'S ROAD,** 10, ch g King's Best (USA)—Saphire **Mrs A. L. M. Murphy**
7 **REAL MILAN (IRE),** 10, b g Milan—The Real Athlete (IRE) **Mrs D. L. Whateley**
8 **RIGOLLETO (IRE),** 7, b g Ad Valorem (USA)—Jallaissine (IRE) **All The Kings Horses**
9 **TODD,** 5, b g Gentlewave (IRE)—Voice **Touchwood Racing**
10 **VOLITO,** 9, ch g Bertolini (USA)—Vax Rapide **Mrs A. L. M. Murphy**
11 **WALTER DE LA MARE (IRE),** 8, b g Barathea (IRE)—Banutan (IRE) **Ridgeway Racing Club**

**Assistant Trainer:** Aiden Murphy

**Amateur:** Mr O. J. Murphy.

## 442 MR COLM MURPHY, Gorey

Postal: **Ballinadrummin, Killena, Gorey, Co. Wexford, Ireland**
Contacts: **PHONE (00353) 53 9482690 FAX (00353) 53 9482690 MOBILE (00353) 862 629538**
**E-MAIL murphyacolm@hotmail.com WEBSITE www.colmmurphyracing.ie**

1 **BLACK ZAMBEZI (IRE),** 6, br g Kalanisi (IRE)—Juresse (IRE) **Winning Ways Iontach Syndicate**
2 **CATALAUNIAN FIELDS (IRE),** 6, b g Fair Mix (IRE)—Leading Lady **Gigginstown House Stud**
3 **EMPIRE OF DIRT (IRE),** 8, b g Westerner—Rose of Inchiquin (IRE) **Gigginstown House Stud**
4 **KILLINEY COURT (IRE),** 6, b g King's Theatre (IRE)—Thimble Royale (IRE) **Mr Martin Bambrick**
5 **MERRY WESTERNER (IRE),** 6, b g Westerner—Merry Bar Lady (IRE) **Mr Thomas Friel**
6 **MISTER HOTELIER (IRE),** 8, b g Beneficial—Accordian Lady (IRE) **Mr Mark McDonagh**
7 **RYANSBROOK (IRE),** 7, b g Alderbrook—Lost Link (IRE) **Mr Thomas Friel**
8 **RYE MARTINI (IRE),** 8, b g Catcher In The Rye (IRE)—Nocturne In March (IRE) **Gigginstown House Stud**
9 **THE WESTENER BOY (IRE),** 8, b g Westerner—Designer Lady (IRE) **Mr J. P. McManus**
10 **TOP SPIN (IRE),** 8, b br g Cape Cross (IRE)—Beguine (USA) **Mr J. P. McManus**
11 **TRIPLE ISLAND (IRE),** 6, b g Turtle Island (IRE)—Rixdale (FR) **Mrs Teresa Murphy**

**Other Owners:** Patrick G. Walsh, S. Delaney.

**Assistant Trainer:** Patrick Murphy

## 443 MR MIKE MURPHY, Westoning

Postal: **Broadlands, Manor Park Stud, Westoning, Bedfordshire, MK45 5LA**
Contacts: **PHONE (01525) 717305 FAX (01525) 717305 MOBILE (07770) 496103**
**E-MAIL mmurphy@globalnet.co.uk WEBSITE www.mikemurphyracing.co.uk**

1 **AMERICAN HOPE (USA),** 4, b c Lemon Drop Kid (USA)—Cedrat (FR) **The Magnificent Seven**
2 **ANGEL WAY (IRE),** 6, br m Trans Island—Zilayah (USA) **Mr D. J. Ellis**
3 **BENANDONNER (USA),** 12, ch g Giant's Causeway (USA)—Cape Verdi (IRE) **M. Murphy**
4 **CHAPTER AND VERSE (IRE),** 9, gr g One Cool Cat (USA)—Beautiful Hill (IRE) **Mr D. J. Ellis**
5 **DANEGLOW (IRE),** 5, ch m Thousand Words—Valluga (IRE) **Mrs J. Thompson**
6 **DISCUSSIONTOFOLLOW (IRE),** 5, b g Elusive City (USA)—Tranquil Sky **Mr D. T. Spratt**
7 **GINUWINEFIZZ,** 4, gr g Lucarno (USA)—Desert Pearl **Foureights**
8 **GOLDEN EMERALD,** 4, b g Peintre Celebre (USA)—Flying Finish (FR) **Ms A. D. Tibbett**
9 **KAKATOSI,** 8, br g Pastoral Pursuits—Ladywell Blaise (IRE) **Mr R. E. Tillett**
10 **ROCK ANTHEM (IRE),** 11, ch g Rock of Gibraltar (IRE)—Regal Portrait (IRE) **R. Bright**
11 **SWEET CHARLIE,** 4, b f Myboycharlie (IRE)—Play Around (IRE) **Charlie's Angels**

### THREE-YEAR-OLDS

12 **CONJURING (IRE),** b f Showcasing—Trick (IRE) **The Hocus-Pocus Partnership**
13 **RIO RONALDO (IRE),** b g Footstepsinthesand—Flanders (IRE) **The Castaways**

## MR MIKE MURPHY - Continued

**14 ROYAL OCCASSION,** b c Royal Applause—Stagecoach Jade (IRE) **Mrs J. Thompson**
**15 SCARLET BLAKENEY (IRE),** ch f Sir Percy—Birdsong (IRE)
**16 SOULSAVER,** ch c Recharge (IRE)—Lapina (IRE) **R. J. Matthews**
**17 TITAN GODDESS,** b f Equiano (FR)—Phoebe Woodstock (IRE) **Phoebe's Friends**
**18** Ch c Excellent Art—Via Aurelia (IRE)
**19 WELSH GEM,** b f Dylan Thomas (IRE)—Gemini Joan **Mr R. E. Tillett**
**20 ZAMPERINI (IRE),** ch c Fast Company (IRE)—Lucky Date (IRE) **Mr R. E. Tillett**

### TWO-YEAR-OLDS

**21** Ch c 1/4 Sir Percy—Meredith (Medicean)
**22** B f 24/5 Multiplex—Nut (IRE) (Fasliyev (USA)) (4000)
**23** B f 7/3 Bahamian Bounty—Regal Asset (USA) (Regal Classic (CAN)) (6500)
**24** B f 13/2 Roderic O'Connor (IRE)—Tartufo Dolce (IRE) (Key of Luck (USA)) (26983)
**25** Br c 17/5 Big Bad Bob (IRE)—Trick (IRE) (Shirley Heights)

**Other Owners:** Mrs M. Bright, Mrs L. Buckton, B. E. Holland, Mr B. Rogerson, Mr P. Wise.

**Assistant Trainer:** J.P. Cullinan

---

## 444 MR PAT MURPHY, Hungerford

Postal: **Glebe House Stables, School Lane, East Garston, Nr Hungerford, Berkshire, RG17 7HR**
Contacts: **OFFICE (01488) 648473 MOBILE (07831) 410409**
**E-MAIL pat@mabberleys.freeserve.co.uk WEBSITE www.patmurphyracing.com**

**1 CATALINAS DIAMOND (IRE),** 7, b m One Cool Cat (USA)—Diamondiferous (USA) **Briton International**
**2** 4, Gr g Acambaro (GER)—Charannah (IRE) **P. G. Murphy**
**3 CLOUDY BOB (IRE),** 8, gr g Cloudings (IRE)—Keen Supreme (IRE) **Men Of Stone**
**4 EAGLES ROAD,** 5, br m Grape Tree Road—Look of Eagles
**5 ISLAND CRUISE (IRE),** 7, b g Turtle Island (IRE)—Chuckawalla (IRE) **Quintin Friends & Family**
**6** 4, B g Dylan Thomas (IRE)—Renowned (IRE) **Deangrange Limited**

**Other Owners:** B. H. Goldswain, Exors of the Late Mrs J. B. H. Goldswain, Mr R. Guest, Mr P. D. Lloyd, Mr S. N. Mound, Mrs A. C. Mound, Mrs L. Quintin, Mr R. L. Reynolds.

**Assistant Trainer:** Mrs Dianne Murphy

**Jockey (flat):** Steve Drowne. **Jockey (NH):** Leighton Aspell.

---

## 445 MR BARRY MURTAGH, Carlisle

Postal: **Hurst Farm, Ivegill, Carlisle, Cumbria, CA4 0NL**
Contacts: **PHONE (01768) 484649 FAX (01768) 484744 MOBILE (07714) 026741**
**E-MAIL sue@suemurtagh.wanadoo.co.uk**

**1 AUTHINGER (IRE),** 7, b g Sadler's Wells (USA)—Ange Bleu (USA) **Quattro Products Ltd**
**2 BARABOY (IRE),** 5, b g Barathea (IRE)—Irina (IRE) **A. R. White**
**3 CAPE ARROW,** 4, b g Cape Cross (IRE)—Aiming **Mr & Mrs A. Trinder**
**4 CAVITE ETA (IRE),** 8, br g Spadoun (FR)—Samarinnda (IRE) **Don't Tell Henry**
**5 DALSTONTOSILOTH (IRE),** 7, b g Gamut (IRE)—The Boss's Dance (USA) **Mr G. Vipond**
**6 FORESTSIDE (IRE),** 10, br g Zagreb (USA)—Silver Sunset **Mr James Callow**
**7** 6, B m Overbury (IRE)—Globe Dream (IRE) **G. & P. Barker Ltd**
**8 JEBULANI,** 5, b g Jelani (IRE)—Susan's Dowry **Mr G. Fell**
**9 KING'S CHORISTER,** 9, ch g King's Best (USA)—Chorist **Woodgate Partnership**
**10 PRINCE BLACKTHORN (IRE),** 9, b g Desert Prince (IRE)—Notable Dear (ITY) **Famous Five Racing**
**11 SPREAD BOY (IRE),** 8, b g Tagula (IRE)—Marinka **A. R. White**
**12 STANLEY BRIDGE,** 8, b g Avonbridge—Antonia's Folly **M. A. Proudfoot**
**13 TROUBLE IN PARIS (IRE),** 8, ch g Great Palm (USA)—Ten Dollar Bill (IRE) **Hurst Farm Racing**
**14 UNEX PICASSO,** 7, b g Galileo (IRE)—Ruff Shod (USA) **Mrs S. Murtagh**

**Other Owners:** Mr Robert Carter, Mrs F. K. Carter, Mrs M. Hutt, Mr James Murtagh, Mr F. P. Murtagh, Mr A. Trinder, Mrs A. Trinder, Mr Thomas Uprichard, Mr Derek Wilson.

**Assistant Trainer:** S A Murtagh

## 446 MR WILLIE MUSSON, Newmarket

Postal: **Saville House, St Mary's Square, Newmarket, Suffolk, CB8 0HZ**
Contacts: **PHONE (01638) 663371 FAX (01638) 667979**
**E-MAIL willie@williemusson.co.uk WEBSITE www.williemusson.co.uk**

1 **BOLD ADVENTURE,** 11, ch g Arkadian Hero (USA)—Impatiente (USA) **W. J. Musson**
2 **BROUGHTONS BANDIT,** 8, b g Kyllachy—Broughton Bounty **Broughton Thermal Insulations**
3 **BROUGHTONS BERRY (IRE),** 4, b f Bushranger (IRE)—Larrocha (IRE) **Broughton Thermal Insulations**
4 **BROUGHTONS RHYTHM,** 6, b g Araafa (IRE)—Broughton Singer (IRE) **Broughton Thermal Insulations**
5 **CANDYMAN CAN (IRE),** 5, b g Holy Roman Emperor (IRE)—Palwina (FR) **Miss A. Jones**
6 **COMMON TOUCH (IRE),** 7, ch g Compton Place—Flying Finish (FR) **Broughton Thermal Insulations**
7 **CROWN PLEASURE (IRE),** 4, b f Royal Applause—Tarbiyah **W. J. Musson**
8 **DONT HAVE IT THEN,** 4, b g Myboycharlie (IRE)—Mondovi **Mr L. J. Mann**
9 **MAC'S POWER (IRE),** 9, b g Exceed And Excel (AUS)—Easter Girl **Broughton Thermal Insulations**
10 **MADAME ALLSORTS,** 10, b m Double Trigger (IRE)—Always A Pleasure **R. D. Musson**
11 **MOUNTAIN RANGE (IRE),** 7, b g High Chaparral (IRE)—Tuscany Lady (IRE) **The Climbers**
12 **MUSICAL THEME,** 4, b f Mount Nelson—Motif **W. J. Musson**
13 **ROCKET ROB (IRE),** 9, b g Danetime (IRE)—Queen of Fibres (IRE) **Mr J. R. Searchfield**

### THREE-YEAR-OLDS

14 **BROUGHTONS HARMONY,** ch f Nayef (USA)—Park Melody (IRE) **Broughton Thermal Insulations**
15 **DEACON'S LADY,** b f Compton Place—Mistress Cooper **Mrs Rita Brown**
16 **SIR ERNIE,** b g Azamour (IRE)—Catherine Palace **Mr L. J. Mann**
17 **SNAPPY MANN,** ch g Sleeping Indian—Laminka **Mr L. J. Mann**

### TWO-YEAR-OLDS

18 B c 3/4 Indesatchel (IRE)—Artistic (IRE) (Noverre (USA)) (5500)
19 B f 3/3 Sakhee's Secret—Enchanted Princess (Royal Applause) (16000) **Broughton Thermal Insulations**
20 **HORATIA THE FLEET,** ch f 20/1 Bahamian Bounty—Countermarch (Selkirk (USA)) **Jim Mellon & Partners**
21 B f 4/3 Equiano (FR)—Juncea (Elnadim (USA)) (12500)
22 B f 12/2 Pastoral Pursuits—Lifetime Romance (IRE) (Mozart (IRE)) (8571) **Broughton Thermal Insulations**
23 B c 30/4 Kheleyf (USA)—Read Federica (Fusaichi Pegasus (USA)) (8000) **Broughton Thermal Insulations**
24 B f 21/3 Royal Applause—Reeling N' Rocking (IRE) (Mr Greeley (USA)) (1000) **Broughton Thermal Insulations**

**Other Owners:** Broughton Thermal Insulations, Mr I. Johnson, Mr Laurence Mann, Mr W. J. Musson, Mr Patrick Thompson.

## 447 DR JEREMY NAYLOR, Shrewton

Postal: **The Cleeve, Elston Lane, Shrewton, Wiltshire, SP3 4HL**
Contacts: **PHONE (01980) 620804 MOBILE (07771) 740126**
**E-MAIL info@jeremynaylor.com WEBSITE www.jeremynaylor.com**

1 **ACOSTA,** 11, b g Foxhound (USA)—Dancing Heights (IRE) **The Acosta Partnership**
2 **PADOVA,** 9, b g Shahrastani (USA)—My Song of Songs **The Acosta Partnership**
3 4, B f Striking Ambition—Sweet Request **Mrs S. P. Elphick**
4 **TOO TRIGGER HAPPY,** 6, b m Double Trigger (IRE)—Hilarious (IRE) **The Acosta Partnership**

**Jockey (NH):** Wayne Kavanagh.

## 448 MR JOHN NEEDHAM, Ludlow

Postal: **Gorsty Farm, Mary Knoll, Ludlow, Shropshire, SY8 2HD**
Contacts: **PHONE (01584) 872112/874826 FAX (01584) 873256 MOBILE (07811) 451137**

1 **BRINGEWOOD BELLE,** 12, b m Kayf Tara—Carlingford Belle **J. L. Needham**
2 **ELTON FOX,** 10, br g Bob Back (USA)—Leinthall Fox **Miss J. C. L. Needham**
3 **MAIN REASON (IRE),** 7, b m Golan (IRE)—Regents Dream **J. L. Needham**
4 **MORTIMERS CROSS,** 14, b g Cloudings (IRE)—Leinthall Doe **J. L. Needham**

**Assistant Trainer:** P. Hanly

**Jockey (NH):** Richard Johnson, Paul Moloney. **Amateur:** Mr R Jarrett.

## 449 MRS HELEN NELMES, Dorchester

Postal: **Warmwell Stables, 2 Church Cottages, Warmwell, Dorchester, Dorset, DT2 8HQ**
Contacts: **PHONE/FAX (01305) 852254 MOBILE (07977) 510318**
**E-MAIL warmwellstud@tiscali.co.uk WEBSITE www.warmwellracing.co.uk**

1 **ITSABOUTIME (IRE),** 5, gr g Whitmore's Conn (USA)—Blazing Love (IRE) **K. A. Nelmes**
2 **KALMBEFORETHESTORM,** 7, ch g Storming Home—Miss Honeypenny (IRE) **Warmwellcome Partnership**
3 **LLAMADAS,** 13, b g Josr Algarhoud (IRE)—Primulette **Mr K. Tyre**
4 **MR TOY BOY,** 5, b g Phoenix Reach (IRE)—Toy Girl (IRE) **All Sorts Dorset Partnership**
5 **NORSE DA,** 5, b g Norse Dancer (IRE)—End of An Error **K. A. Nelmes**
6 **ORVITA (FR),** 13, b g Lute Antique (FR)—Ulvita (FR) **K. A. Nelmes**
7 **THE CLYDA ROVER (IRE),** 11, ch g Moonax (IRE)—Pampered Molly (IRE) **K. A. Nelmes**
8 **THE FINGER POST (IRE),** 8, b g Zagreb (USA)—Mystic Madam (IRE) **K. A. Nelmes**
9 **UNOWHATIMEANHARRY,** 7, b g Sir Harry Lewis (USA)—Red Nose Lady **Miss S. J. Hartley**
10 **WITCHESINTUNE,** 8, b m Beat Hollow—Music Park (IRE) **Miss S. J. Hartley**
11 **ZULU PRINCIPLE,** 8, b g Tiger Hill (IRE)—Tu Eres Mi Amore (IRE) **T M W Partnership**

**Other Owners:** Mrs S. Cobb, Miss V. O. Kardas, Mr M. Miller, Mr C. E. Mundy, Ms A. M. Neville, Mr D. Price.

**Assistant Trainer:** K Nelmes

## 450 MR CHRIS NENADICH, Sutton

Postal: **Lakes Farm, Sutton, Herefordshire, HR1 3NS**
Contacts: **PHONE (01432) 880278 MOBILE (07860) 484400**

1 **BOLLIN JUDITH,** 9, br m Bollin Eric—Bollin Nellie **Chris & Nick Nenadich**
2 **OSCARS WAY (IRE),** 7, br g Oscar (IRE)—Derrigra Sublime (IRE) **Chris & Nick Nenadich**

**Assistant Trainer:** Marion Collins

## 451 MR TONY NEWCOMBE, Barnstaple

Postal: **Lower Delworthy, Yarnscombe, Barnstaple, Devon, EX31 3LT**
Contacts: **PHONE/FAX (01271) 858554 MOBILE (07785) 297210**
**E-MAIL huntshawequineforest@talktalk.net**

1 7, B g Storming Home—Bogus Penny (IRE) **Mrs S. Wetter**
2 **CAI SHEN (IRE),** 7, ch g Iffraaj—Collada (IRE) **Mr R. C. Williams**
3 **KAY SERA,** 7, b g Kayf Tara—Inflation **N. P. Hardy**
4 **LISA SAYS NO,** 5, b m Dubai Destination (USA)—Zuloago (USA) **N. P. Hardy**
5 **MAMBO SPIRIT (IRE),** 11, b g Invincible Spirit (IRE)—Mambodorga (USA) **N. P. Hardy**
6 **MY METEOR,** 8, b g Bahamian Bounty—Emerald Peace (IRE) **A. G. Newcombe**
7 **PATAVINUS,** 6, ch g Titus Livius (FR)—Bogus Penny (IRE) **George Fourth Partners**
8 **SPELLMAKER,** 6, b g Kheleyf (USA)—Midnight Spell **Joli Racing**

### THREE-YEAR-OLDS

9 **ALMOQATEL (IRE),** b c Clodovil (IRE)—Majestic Night (IRE) **A. G. Newcombe**

### TWO-YEAR-OLDS

10 B f 14/4 Alfred Nobel (IRE)—Shantina's Dream (USA) (Smoke Glacken (USA)) **Joli Racing**

**Other Owners:** Mr Chris J. Buckerfield, Mr Graham Craig, Mr R. Eagle, Mrs Stephanie Wetter.

**Assistant Trainer:** John Lovejoy

**Jockey (flat):** Dane O'Neill, Fergus Sweeney, Tom Queally. **Jockey (NH):** Liam Treadwell, Andrew Thornton.

## 452 DR RICHARD NEWLAND, Claines

Postal: **Newland Associates Ltd, Linacres Farm, Egg Lane, Claines, Worcester, WR3 7SB**
Contacts: **PHONE (07956) 196535**
**E-MAIL richard.newland1@btopenworld.com**

1 **AFICIONADO,** 5, ch g Halling (USA)—Prithee **G. N. Carstairs**

## DR RICHARD NEWLAND - Continued

2 **ARDKILLY WITNESS (IRE),** 9, b g Witness Box (USA)—Ardkilly Angel (IRE) **C E Stedman & Dr R D P Newland**
3 **BOBOWEN (IRE),** 9, b g Bob Back (USA)—Opus One **Dr R. D. P. Newland**
4 **BOMBADERO (IRE),** 8, b g Sadler's Wells (USA)—Fantasy Girl (IRE) **The Berrow Hill Partnership**
5 **BOONDOOMA (IRE),** 8, b g Westerner—Kissantell (IRE) **P Jenkins & C E Stedman**
6 **CELTIC FASHION (IRE),** 8, b g Celtic Swing—Happy Bay (ARG) **ValueRacingClub.co.uk**
7 **CORNISH BEAU (IRE),** 8, ch g Pearl of Love (IRE)—Marimar (IRE) **The London Foot & Ankle Centre**
8 **CUT THE CORNER (IRE),** 7, br g Vinnie Roe (IRE)—Snipe Victory (IRE) **Mr P. Drinkwater**
9 **DISCAY,** 6, b g Distant Music (USA)—Caysue **Foxtrot NH Racing Partnership VIII**
10 **EBONY EXPRESS,** 6, bl g Superior Premium—Coffee Ice **ValueRacingClub.co.uk**
11 **EXPRESS DU BERLAIS (FR),** 6, b g Saint des Saints (FR)—Euil Eagle (FR)
12 **GIOIA DI VITA,** 5, b g Sakhee (USA)—Dhuyoof (IRE) **Mark Albon & Chris Stedman**
13 **GRAN MAESTRO (USA),** 6, ch g Medicean—Red Slippers (USA) **ValueRacingClub.co.uk**
14 **JAYO TIME (IRE),** 6, b g Morozov (USA)—Billythefilly (IRE) **Mr P. Jenkins**
15 **JAZZ MAN (IRE),** 8, ch g Beneficial—Slaney Jazz **J. A. Provan**
16 **LYSINO (GER),** 6, ch g Medicean—Lysuna (GER) **Mrs M L Trow, Barwell & Newland**
17 **MASTEROFDECEPTION (IRE),** 7, b g Darsi (FR)—Sherberry (IRE) **The Berrow Hill Partnership**
18 **MURTYS DELIGHT (IRE),** 8, b g Bach (IRE)—Valley Supreme (IRE) **Mr P. C. W. Green**
19 **NEVEROWNUP (IRE),** 10, b g Quws—Cobble (IRE) **Dr R. D. P. Newland**
20 **PINEAU DE RE (FR),** 12, b g Maresca Sorrento (FR)—Elfe du Perche (FR) **J. A. Provan**
21 **ROCK GONE (IRE),** 7, b g Winged Love (IRE)—Guillem (USA) **Chris Stedman & Mark Albon**
22 **ROYALE KNIGHT,** 9, b g King's Theatre (IRE)—Gardana (FR) **C. E. Stedman & R. J. Corsan**
23 **SIGNIFICANT MOVE,** 8, b g Motivator—Strike Lightly **The Five Nations Partnership**
24 **SLIM PICKENS (IRE),** 7, b g Craigsteel—Couleurs D'automne (FR) **Mr P. C. W. Green**
25 **TOP CAT HENRY (IRE),** 7, b g Dr Massini (IRE)—Bells Chance (IRE) **Off The Clock Partners & Dr RDP Newland**
26 **VOSNE ROMANEE,** 4, ch g Arakan (USA)—Vento Del Oreno (FR) **Foxtrot NH Racing Partnership VI**

**Other Owners:** Mr D. Abraham, Mrs J. Abraham, Mr M. L. Albon, Mr M. P. Ansell, A. P. Barwell, Mr J. R. Couldwell, Mr P. D. Couldwell, Mr M. S. Davies, Mr J. M. O. Evans, Mrs L. J. Newland, C. E. Stedman, S. R. Trow, Mrs M. L. Trow.

**Assistant Trainer:** S. R. Trow

**Amateur:** Mr T. Weston.

---

## 453 MISS ANNA NEWTON-SMITH, Polegate

Postal: **Bull Pen Cottage, Jevington, Polegate, East Sussex, BN26 5QB**
Contacts: **PHONE (01323) 488354 FAX (01323) 488354 MOBILE (07970) 914124**
**E-MAIL anna_newtonsmith@o2.co.uk WEBSITE www.annanewtonsmith.co.uk**

1 **ALBATROS DE GUYE (FR),** 5, ch g Maille Pistol (FR)—Balibirds (FR) **Mr G. E. Goring**
2 **BURGESS DREAM (IRE),** 6, b g Spadoun (FR)—Ennel Lady (IRE) **Mr P. Worley**
3 **DUDE ALERT (IRE),** 5, b g Windsor Knot (IRE)—Policy **Mr M. R. Baldry**
4 **GORING ONE (IRE),** 10, b g Broadway Flyer (USA)—Brigette's Secret **Mr G. E. Goring**
5 **HERMOSA VAQUERA (IRE),** 5, b m High Chaparral (IRE)—Sundown **Mr M. R. Baldry**
6 **LITTLE ROXY (IRE),** 10, b m Dilshaan—Brunswick **The Ash Tree Inn Racing Club**
7 **THE CHILD (IRE),** 6, b g Vertical Speed (FR)—Chancy Hall (IRE) **Mr P. Worley**
8 **WALK OF GLEAMS,** 6, b m Gleaming (IRE)—Harlequin Walk (IRE) **Mrs J. Brightling**

**Other Owners:** Mr A. K. Walker.

**Assistant Trainer:** Nicola Worley

**Jockey (NH):** Marc Goldstein, Andrew Thornton, Adam Wedge. **Amateur:** Miss Megan Spencer.

---

## 454 MR DAVID NICHOLLS, Thirsk

Postal: **Tall Trees Racing Ltd, Tall Trees, Sessay, Thirsk, North Yorkshire, YO7 3ND**
Contacts: **PHONE (01845) 501470 FAX (01845) 501666 MOBILE (07971) 555105**
**E-MAIL david.nicholls@btconnect.com WEBSITE www.davidnichollsracing.com**

1 **APRICOT SKY,** 5, ch g Pastoral Pursuits—Miss Apricot **Mr G. D. Taylor**
2 **BAJAN BEAR,** 7, ch g Compton Place—Bajan Rose **C. McKenna**
3 **BARNET FAIR,** 7, br g Iceman—Pavement Gates **Mr D. Wheatley**
4 **CAHAL (IRE),** 4, b g Bushranger (IRE)—Cabopino (IRE) **D. Nicholls**
5 **COMPTON,** 6, ch g Compton Place—Look So
6 **DON'T CALL ME (IRE),** 8, ch g Haafhd—Just Call Me (NZ) **Matt & Lauren Morgan**

## MR DAVID NICHOLLS - Continued

7 **GREENHEAD HIGH,** 7, b g Statue of Liberty (USA)—Artistry **D. Nicholls**
8 **IMPERIAL LEGEND (IRE),** 6, b g Mujadil (USA)—Titian Saga (IRE) **Gaga Syndicate**
9 **INDEGO BLUES,** 6, b g Indesatchel (IRE)—Yanomami (USA) **Gaga Syndicate**
10 **INDIAN CHIEF (IRE),** 5, b g Montjeu (IRE)—Buck Aspen (USA) **Castle Construction (North East) Ltd**
11 **INXILE (IRE),** 10, b g Fayruz—Grandel **Mr D. Nicholls & Mrs J. Love**
12 **JOHNNO,** 6, br g Excellent Art—Vert Val (USA) **Mr A. H. L. Zheng**
13 **KIMBERELLA,** 5, b g Kyllachy—Gleam of Light (IRE) **Mr C. J. Titcomb**
14 **LAYLA'S HERO (IRE),** 8, b g One Cool Cat (USA)—Capua (USA) **D. Nicholls**
15 **MAJESTIC MANANNAN (IRE),** 6, b g Majestic Missile (IRE)—Miraculous (IRE) **Dubelem (Racing) Limited**
16 **MANATEE BAY,** 5, b g Royal Applause—Dash of Lime **Mrs A. A. Nicholls**
17 **MARMARUS,** 4, b g Duke of Marmalade (IRE)—Polly Perkins (IRE) **Bernard, Mark & Scott Robertson**
18 **MORE BEAU (USA),** 4, b br c More Than Ready (USA)—Frontier Beauty (USA) **Mr R. Ng**
19 **MUJAZIF (IRE),** 5, br g Shamardal (USA)—Red Bandanna (IRE) **Mr G. D. Taylor**
20 **NEXT STOP,** 4, b f Rail Link—Reaching Ahead (USA) **S. E. Hussey**
21 **ORION'S BOW,** 4, ch c Pivotal—Heavenly Ray (USA) **Cheveley Park Stud Limited**
22 **PEA SHOOTER,** 6, b g Piccolo—Sparkling Eyes **Mr A. H. L. Zheng**
23 **PEARL ACCLAIM (IRE),** 5, b g Acclamation—With Colour **M. A. Scaife**
24 **SECRET RECIPE,** 5, ch g Sakhee's Secret—Fudge **Mr J. A. Law**
25 **SOVEREIGN DEBT (IRE),** 6, gr g Dark Angel (IRE)—Kelsey Rose **Lady C. J. O'Reilly**
26 **SPRING BIRD,** 6, b m Danbird (AUS)—Dolphin Dancer **D. G. Clayton**
27 **STORM RIDER (IRE),** 4, b c Fastnet Rock (AUS)—On The Nile (IRE)
28 **STORM TROOPER (IRE),** 4, b c Acclamation—Maid To Order (IRE)
29 **STREET ARTIST (IRE),** 5, ch g Street Cry (IRE)—Portrayal (USA) **J. A. Rattigan**

### THREE-YEAR-OLDS

30 **KYRENIA CASTLE (GER),** b c Dashing Blade—Key To Win (FR) **Middleham Park Racing LXXXV**
31 **MAGH MEALL,** b f Monsieur Bond (IRE)—Tibesti **Dubelem (Racing) Limited**

**Other Owners:** Mrs J. I. Love, M. Morgan, Mrs L. K. Morgan, T. S. Palin, M. Prince, Mr M. A. Robertson, Mr B. A. Robertson, Mr S. B. Robertson, Mrs S. Thomson.

**Assistant Trainer:** Ben Beasley

**Jockey (flat):** Adrian Nicholls, Paul Quinn. **Apprentice:** Anna Hesketh. **Amateur:** Mrs Adele Mulrennan.

---

## 455 MR PAUL NICHOLLS, Ditcheat

Postal: **Manor Farm Stables, Ditcheat, Shepton Mallet, Somerset, BA4 6RD**
Contacts: **PHONE (01749) 860656 FAX (01749) 860523 MOBILE (07977) 270706**
**E-MAIL info@paulnichollsracing.com WEBSITE www.paulnichollsracing.com**

1 **ABIDJAN (FR),** 5, b g Alberto Giacometti (IRE)—Kundera (FR) **Axom L**
2 **AL FEROF (FR),** 10, gr g Dom Alco (FR)—Maralta (FR) **Mr J. R. Hales**
3 **ALBAHAR (FR),** 4, gr g Dark Angel (IRE)—Downland (USA) **Mrs S. De La Hey**
4 **ALCALA (FR),** 5, gr g Turgeon (USA)—Pail Mel (FR) **Andrea & Graham Wylie**
5 **ALISTAIR (IRE),** 7, b g Turtle Island (IRE)—Woodfield Lady (IRE) **A. E. Frost**
6 **ALL SET TO GO (IRE),** 4, gr g Verglas (IRE)—Firecrest (IRE) **C. G. Roach**
7 **ALL YOURS (FR),** 4, ch g Halling (USA)—Fontaine Riant (FR) **Potensis Limited**
8 **ALTO DES MOTTES (FR),** 5, b g Dream Well (FR)—Omance (FR) **Giles, Hogarth & Webb**
9 **AMANTO (GER),** 5, b g Medicean—Amore (GER) **Fogg, Kyle & Webb**
10 **ANATOL (FR),** 5, b g Apsis—Teresa Moriniere (FR) **Mrs S. De La Hey**
11 **ANNALULU (IRE),** 4, b f Hurricane Run (IRE)—Louve de Saron (FR) **Highclere Thoroughbred Racing -Anna Lulu**
12 **ANTARTICA DE THAIX (FR),** 5, gr m Dom Alco (FR)—Nouca de Thaix (FR) **I.Fogg, R.Webb, D.Macdonald & C.Barber**
13 **ARPEGE D'ALENE (FR),** 5, gr g Dom Alco (FR)—Joliette d'alene (FR) **Potensis Limited**
14 **ART MAURESQUE (FR),** 5, b g Policy Maker (IRE)—Modeva (FR) **Mrs S. De La Hey**
15 **AS DE MEE (FR),** 5, b br g Kapgarde (FR)—Koeur de Mee (FR) **The Stewart Family & Judi Dench**
16 **ATLANTIC ROLLER (IRE),** 8, b g Old Vic—Tourist Attraction (IRE) **C. G. Roach**
17 **AUX PTITS SOINS (FR),** 5, gr g Saint des Saints (FR)—Reflexion Faite (FR) **Mr J. R. Hales**
18 **BALLYCOE,** 6, b g Norse Dancer (IRE)—Lizzy Lamb **Potensis Limited & Mr Chris Giles**
19 **BE DARING (FR),** 4, gr g Dom Alco (FR)—Quinine (FR) **Mr J. R. Hales**
20 **BENVOLIO (IRE),** 8, b g Beneficial—Coumeenoole Lady **Dobson, Sutton & Woodhouse**
21 **BLACK RIVER (FR),** 6, b g Secret Singer (FR)—Love River (FR) **Andrea & Graham Wylie**
22 **BLACK THUNDER (FR),** 8, bl g Malinas (GER)—Blackmika (FR) **Donlon, MacDonald, Fulton & Webb**

## MR PAUL NICHOLLS - Continued

23 4, B br g Milan—Bonnie Parker (IRE)
24 **BOUVREUIL (FR),** 4, b g Saddler Maker (IRE)—Madame Lys (FR)
25 **BRIO CONTI (FR),** 4, gr g Dom Alco (FR)—Cadoulie Wood (FR) **The Gi Gi Syndicate**
26 **BUCK'S BOND (FR),** 9, gr g Turgeon (USA)—Buck's Beauty (FR) **Mrs C. E. Penny**
27 **BURY PARADE (IRE),** 9, br g Overbury (IRE)—
Alexandra Parade (IRE) **HighclereThoroughbredRacing- Bury Parade**
28 **CAID DU BERLAIS (FR),** 6, b g Westerner—Kenza du Berlais (FR) **Donlon, Doyle, MacDonald & C. Barber**
29 **CALIPTO (FR),** 5, b g Califet (FR)—Peutiot (FR) **Mr Chris Giles & Mr Ian Fogg**
30 **CEASAR MILAN (IRE),** 7, br g Milan—Standfast (IRE) **The Stewart & Wylie Families**
31 **CELESTINO (FR),** 4, b g Leeds (IRE)—Evamoon (FR) **Million in Mind Partnership**
32 **CHARTBREAKER (FR),** 4, b g Shirocco (GER)—Caucasienne (FR) **Mrs S. De La Hey**
33 **COWARDS CLOSE (IRE),** 8, br g Presenting—Parsee (IRE) **Mr Paul K Barber & Mr Barry Fulton**
34 **DO WE LIKE HIM (IRE),** 5, b g Beneficial—Pattern Queen (IRE) **The Kyle & Stewart Families**
35 **DODGING BULLETS,** 7, b g Dubawi (IRE)—Nova Cyngi (USA) **Martin Broughton & Friends**
36 **DORMELLO MO (FR),** 5, b g Conillon (GER)—Neogel (USA) **The Kyle & Stewart Families**
37 **DRUCILLA,** 6, b m Scorpion (IRE)—Priscilla **H. T. Cole**
38 **EARTHMOVES (FR),** 5, b g Antarctique (IRE)—Red Rym (FR) **R. M. Penny**
39 **EASTER DAY (FR),** 7, b g Malinas (GER)—Sainte Lea (FR) **B. Fulton, Broughton Thermal Insulation**
40 **EMERGING TALENT (IRE),** 6, b g Golan (IRE)—Elviria (IRE) **Mr & Mrs Paul Barber**
41 **FAGO (FR),** 7, b br g Balko (FR)—Merciki (FR) **Andrea & Graham Wylie**
42 **FAR WEST (FR),** 6, b g Poliglote—Far Away Girl (FR) **Axom XXXIX**
43 **FIRSTY (IRE),** 4, b g Flemensfirth (USA)—Loughaderra Dame (IRE) **Mrs K. A. Stuart**
44 4, Br g Presenting—Forgotten Star (IRE) **P. F. Nicholls**
45 **FULL BLAST (FR),** 4, b g Khalkevi (IRE)—La Troussardiere (FR) **Martin Broughton & Friends**
46 **GREAT TRY (IRE),** 6, b g Scorpion (IRE)—Cherry Pie (FR) **T. J. Hemmings**
47 **HAWKES POINT,** 10, b g Kayf Tara—Mandys Native (IRE) **C. G. Roach**
48 **HINTERLAND (FR),** 7, b g Poliglote—Queen Place (FR) **Mr C. M. Giles**
49 **HOWLONGISAFOOT (IRE),** 6, b g Beneficial—Miss Vic (IRE) **P. J. Vogt**
50 **IBIS DU RHEU (FR),** 4, b g Blue Bresil (FR)—Dona du Rheu (FR) **Mr J. R. Hales**
51 **IRISH SAINT (FR),** 6, b br g Saint des Saints (FR)—Minirose (FR) **Mrs S. De La Hey**
52 **IRVING,** 7, b g Singspiel (IRE)—Indigo Girl (GER) **Axom XLIX**
53 **IT'S A CLOSE CALL (IRE),** 6, br g Scorpion (IRE)—Sherin (GER) **C. G. Roach**
54 **JUST A PAR (IRE),** 8, b g Island House (IRE)—Thebrownhen (IRE) **Paul K. Barber & C. G. Roach**
55 **KATGARY (FR),** 5, b g Ballingarry (IRE)—Kotkira (FR) **Andrea & Graham Wylie**
56 **KELTUS (FR),** 5, gr g Keltos (FR)—Regina d'orthe (FR) **Donlon & MacDonald**
57 **KEPPOLS HILL (IRE),** 9, b g Indian Danehill (IRE)—
Keppols Princess (IRE) **Mr Paul Barber & Mr & Mrs Mark Woodhouse**
58 **LAC FONTANA (FR),** 6, b g Shirocco (GER)—Fontaine Riant (FR) **Potensis Limited**
59 **LAC LEMAN (GER),** 4, b g Doyen (IRE)—Learned Lady (JPN) **Andrea & Graham Wylie**
60 **LE MERCUREY (FR),** 5, b g Nickname (FR)—Feroe (FR) **Chris Giles & Colm Donlon**
61 **LIFEBOAT MONA,** 5, b m Kayf Tara—Astar Love (FR) **Axom LV**
62 **LUMPYS GOLD,** 7, b g Tikkanen (USA)—Elegant Accord (IRE) **Elite Racing Club**
63 **MARRACUDJA (FR),** 4, b g Martaline—Memorial (FR) **Potensis Limited**
64 **MCLLHATTON (IRE),** 7, b g Fruits of Love (USA)—Penny Haven (IRE) **Giles, Donlon & Macdonald**
65 **MINELLAHALFCENTURY (IRE),** 7, b g Westerner—Shanakill River (IRE) **Mr Jeffrey Hordle & Mr Peter Hart**
66 **MISTRESS MOLE (IRE),** 6, br m Definite Article—Emmylou du Berlais (FR) **The Significant Others**
67 **MON PARRAIN (FR),** 9, b g Trempolino (USA)—Kadaina (FR) **Mr & Mrs J. D. Cotton**
68 **MORE BUCK'S (IRE),** 5, ch g Presenting—Buck's Blue (FR) **The Stewart Family**
69 **MORITO DU BERLAIS (FR),** 6, b g Turgeon (USA)—Chica du Berlais (FR) **C. G. Roach**
70 **MR DINOSAUR (IRE),** 5, ch g Robin des Champs (FR)—Miss Generosity **Andrea & Graham Wylie**
71 **MR MIX (FR),** 4, gr g Al Namix (FR)—Royale Surabaya (FR) **Potensis Limited**
72 **MR MOLE (IRE),** 7, br g Great Pretender (IRE)—Emmylou du Berlais (FR) **J. P. McManus**
73 **OLD GUARD,** 4, b g Notnowcato—Dolma (FR) **The Brooks, Kyle & Stewart Families**
74 **ONWITHTHEPARTY,** 6, b g Sir Harry Lewis (USA)—Kentford Fern **A. A. Hayward**
75 **PEARL SWAN (FR),** 7, b g Gentlewave (IRE)—Swanson (USA) **Mr R. J. H. Geffen**
76 **PERSIAN DELIGHT,** 5, br g Lucarno (USA)—Persian Walk (FR) **Hypnotised**
77 **POLISKY (FR),** 8, b g Poliglote—Dusky Royale (FR) **Mrs S. De La Hey**
78 **PORT MELON (IRE),** 7, br g Presenting—Omyn Supreme (IRE) **C. G. Roach**
79 **PRESENT MAN (IRE),** 5, b g Presenting—Glen's Gale (IRE) **Mr Paul K Barber & The Stewart Family**
80 **PRESSIES GIRL (IRE),** 7, b m Presenting—Leader's Hall (IRE) **Sparkes & Gibson**
81 **PROVO (IRE),** 8, br g Presenting—Pairtree **Hilton & Lyn Ramseyer**
82 **PTIT ZIG (FR),** 6, b g Great Pretender (IRE)—Red Rym (FR) **Chris Giles,Barry Fulton & Richard Webb**
83 **QUALANDO (FR),** 4, b g Lando (GER)—Qualite Controlee (FR) **Mrs K. A. Stuart**
84 **RAINY CITY (IRE),** 5, b g Kalanisi (IRE)—Erintante (IRE) **Sir A Ferguson,G Mason,R Wood & P Done**

## MR PAUL NICHOLLS - Continued

85 **REBEL REBELLION (IRE),** 10, b g Lord Americo—Tourmaline Girl (IRE) **Mr & Mrs Woodhouse, Sutton & Dobson**
86 **ROB ROBIN (IRE),** 5, b g Robin des Champs (FR)—Ashwell Lady (IRE) **Mr J. R. Hales**
87 **ROCK ON OSCAR (IRE),** 5, b g Oscar (IRE)—Brogeen Lady (IRE) **P. F. Nicholls**
88 **ROCKY CREEK (IRE),** 9, b g Dr Massini (IRE)—Kissantell (IRE) **The Johnson & Stewart Families**
89 **ROLLING ACES (IRE),** 9, b g Whitmore's Conn (USA)—Pay Roll (IRE) **David Martin, Paul Barber & Ian Fogg**
90 **ROTHMAN (FR),** 5, b g Michel Georges—Bravecentadj (FR) **Mrs J. Hitchings**
91 **ROUGE DEVILS (IRE),** 4, b g Scorpion (IRE)—Penny's Dream (IRE) **Sir A Ferguson,G Mason,R Wood & P Done**
92 **SAINT ROQUE (FR),** 9, b g Lavirco (GER)—Moody Cloud (FR) **Mr Ian Fogg & Mr Chris Giles**
93 **SALUBRIOUS (IRE),** 8, b g Beneficial—Who Tells Jan **The Johnson & Stewart Families**
94 **SAM WINNER (FR),** 8, b g Okawango (USA)—Noche (IRE) **Mrs A. B. Yeoman**
95 **SAN BENEDETO (FR),** 4, ch g Layman (USA)—Cinco Baidy (FR) **P. J. Vogt**
96 **SAPHIR DU RHEU (FR),** 6, gr g Al Namix (FR)—Dona du Rheu (FR) **The Stewart Family**
97 **SELFCONTROL (FR),** 4, b br g Al Namix (FR)—L'ascension (FR) **The Kyle & Stewart Families**
98 **SHE'S DA ONE (IRE),** 6, b m Presenting—Leader's Hall (IRE) **The Kyle & Stewart Families**
99 **SILSOL (GER),** 6, b g Soldier Hollow—Silveria (GER) **Michelle And Dan Macdonald**
100 **SILVINIACO CONTI (FR),** 9, ch g Dom Alco (FR)—Gazelle Lulu (FR) **Mr Chris Giles & Potensis Limited**
101 **SIMON SQUIRREL (IRE),** 5, b g Robin des Champs (FR)—Misty Heather (IRE) **Andrea & Graham Wylie**
102 **SIN BIN (IRE),** 9, b g Presenting—Navaro (IRE) **T. J. Hemmings**
103 **SIRABAD (FR),** 5, b g Astarabad (USA)—Maille Sissi (FR) **Brooks, Kyle, Stewart & Webb**
104 **SIRE COLLONGES (FR),** 9, gr g Dom Alco (FR)—Idylle Collonges (FR) **Mrs Angela Tincknell & Mr W. Tincknell**
105 **SOLAR IMPULSE (FR),** 5, b g Westerner—Moon Glow (FR) **Andrea & Graham Wylie**
106 **SOUND INVESTMENT (IRE),** 7, b g Dr Massini (IRE)—Drumcay Polly (IRE) **Owners Group 001**
107 **SOUTHFIELD THEATRE (IRE),** 7, b g King's Theatre (IRE)—Chamoss Royale (FR) **Mrs A. B. Yeoman**
108 **SOUTHFIELD VIC (IRE),** 6, ch g Old Vic—Chamoss Royale (FR) **Mrs A. B. Yeoman**
109 **TAGRITA (IRE),** 7, b m King's Theatre (IRE)—Double Dream (IRE) **Axom XLVIII**
110 **TARA POINT,** 6, gr m Kayf Tara—Poppet **Mr R. J. H. Geffen**
111 **THE BROCK AGAIN,** 5, ch g Muhtathir—Half Past Twelve (USA) **Axom LIV**
112 **THE CHUCKMEISTER (IRE),** 6, b g Germany (USA)—Lady Florian
113 **THE EAGLEHASLANDED (IRE),** 5, b g Milan—Vallee Doree (FR) **Mrs Angela Tincknell & Mr W. Tincknell**
114 **THE OUTLAW (IRE),** 5, b g Presenting—Bonnie Parker (IRE) **Donlon, MacDonald, Giles & Webb**
115 **THERE'S NO PANIC (IRE),** 10, ch g Presenting—Out Ranking (FR) **The Stewart Family**
116 **ULCK DU LIN (FR),** 7, b g Sassanian (USA)—Miss Fast (FR) **Mrs S. De La Hey**
117 **UNIONISTE (FR),** 7, gr g Dom Alco (FR)—Gleep Will (FR) **Mr J. R. Hales**
118 **URUBU D'IRLANDE (FR),** 7, b g Sleeping Car (FR)—Noceane (FR) **Andrea & Graham Wylie**
119 **V NECK (IRE),** 6, b g Sir Harry Lewis (USA)—Swift Settlement **J. P. McManus**
120 **VAGO COLLONGES (FR),** 6, b g Voix du Nord (FR)—Kapucine Collonges (FR) **Andrea & Graham Wylie**
121 **VALCO DE TOUZAINE (FR),** 6, gr g Dom Alco (FR)—Narcisse de Touzaine (FR) **The Gi Gi Syndicate**
122 **VESPERAL DREAM (FR),** 6, bl g Network (GER)—Pampanilla (FR) **The Loving Insurance Partnership**
123 **VIBRATO VALTAT (FR),** 6, gr g Voix du Nord (FR)—La Tosca Valtat (FR) **Axom XLIII**
124 **VICENTE (FR),** 6, b g Dom Alco (FR)—Ireland (FR) **Mr John Hales & Mr Ian Fogg**
125 **VIDE CAVE (FR),** 6, b g Secret Singer (FR)—Kenna (FR) **Mr Jordan Lund & Mr Brian Taylor**
126 **VIRAK (FR),** 6, b g Bernebeau (FR)—Nosika d'airy (FR) **Hills of Ledbury Ltd**
127 **VIVALDI COLLONGES (FR),** 6, b g Dom Alco (FR)—Diane Collonges (FR) **The Gi Gi Syndicate**
128 **WIFFY CHATSBY (IRE),** 8, br g Presenting—Star Child (GER) **Inch Bloodstock**
129 **WILTON MILAN (IRE),** 7, b g Milan—Biondo (IRE) **J. T. Warner**
130 **WONDERFUL CHARM (FR),** 7, b g Poliglote—Victoria Royale (FR) **Mr R. J. H. Geffen**
131 **ZARKANDAR (IRE),** 8, b g Azamour (IRE)—Zarkasha (IRE) **Mr Chris Giles & Potensis Limited**

**Other Owners:** Axom Ltd, Mr C. L. Barber, P. K. Barber, Mrs M. G. Barber, Mrs M. C. Bolton, Mr M. Bower-Dyke, A. R. Bromley, Mr G. F. Brooks, S. W. Broughton, Sir M. F. Broughton, Broughton Thermal Insulations, Mr A. P. Brown, D. J. Coles, Mr M. H. Colquhoun, J. D. Cotton, Mrs B. Cotton, Dame J. O. Dench, Miss R. J. Dobson, Mr I. J. Donaldson, Mr P. E. Done, Mr C. A. Donlon, Mrs K. Donlon, Mr D. Downie, Mr A. Doyle, Mrs L. A. Farquhar, Sir A. Ferguson, Mr I. J. Fogg, Mrs W. Fogg, B. N. Fulton, Mrs M. J. K. Gibson, G. F. Goode, Miss L. J. Hales, P. L. Hart, The Hon H. M. Herbert, Highclere Thoroughbred Racing Ltd, Mr A. J. Hill, Mr B. M. Hillier, P. H. Hogarth, Mr M. J. Holman, J. G. Hordle, Mr P. J. Inch, Mrs L. Inch, Mrs D. A. Johnson, Mr S. D. Johnson, Mr C. L. Keey, Mrs C. L. Kyle, Mr J. E. Lund, Mrs M. Macdonald, Mr W. D. Macdonald, Mrs C. Mant, Mr D. J. Martin, G. A. Mason, Mr B. J. McManus, W. D. C. Minton, Mrs M. E. Moody, Mrs G. Nicholls, Mrs D. C. Nicholson, Miss M. Noden, Mr M. J. O'Shaughnessy, Mr H. Ramseyer, Mrs L. Ramseyer, Mrs L. Scott-MacDonald, Miss Claire Simmonds, Mrs K. M. Sparkes, Mrs C. E. M. Staddon, Mr D. D. Stevenson, Mr A. Stewart, Mrs J. A. Stewart, Ms C. Sutton, Mr B. Taylor, Mrs A. Tincknell, W. C. Tincknell, Mr R. A. Webb, Mr R. J. Wood, M. J. M. Woodhouse, Mrs T. A. Woodhouse, A. W. G. Wylie, Mrs A. Wylie.

**Assistant Trainers:** Tom Jonason, Andrew Doyle

**Apprentice:** Megan Nicholls, **Jockey (NH):** Ryan Mahon, Nick Scholfield, Sam Twiston-Davies.
**Conditional:** Sean Bowen, Jack Sherwood. **Amateur:** Mr Will Biddick, Mr James King, Mr Stan Sheppard.

## 456 MR PETER NIVEN, Malton

Postal: **Clovafield, Barton-Le-Street, Malton, North Yorkshire, YO17 6PN**
Contacts: **PHONE (01653) 628176 FAX (01653) 627295 MOBILE (07860) 260999**
**E-MAIL pruniven@btinternet.com**

1 **AREGRA (FR),** 5, gr g Fragrant Mix (IRE)—Elisa de Mai (FR) **Mr G. Wragg**
2 **ATOMIX (GER),** 4, b g Doyen (IRE)—Aloe (GER) **Mr G. Wragg**
3 **BEAT THE SHOWER,** 9, b g Beat Hollow—Crimson Shower **Mrs K. J. Young**
4 **BLADES LAD,** 6, ch g Haafhd—Blades Girl **Crown Select**
5 **CLEVER COOKIE,** 7, b g Primo Valentino (IRE)—Mystic Memory **Francis Green Racing Ltd**
6 **CONCENTRATE,** 4, b f Zamindar (USA)—Intense **Keep The Faith Partnership**
7 **ENGROSSING,** 6, b g Tiger Hill (IRE)—Pan Galactic (USA) **Mrs Browns's Boys 2**
8 **HARRY HUSSAR,** 5, b g Primo Valentino (IRE)—Jessie May (IRE) **Francis Green Racing Ltd**
9 **LITTLE POSH (IRE),** 6, br m Winged Love (IRE)—Lady Oakwell (IRE) **David Bamber**
10 **LUKIE,** 7, ch g Revoque (IRE)—Subtle Blush **Vanessa Frith & Stuart Barker**
11 **NORTH COUNTRY BOY,** 6, b g Revoque (IRE)—She Likes To Boogy (IRE) **Mrs P. A. Cowey**
12 **PINOTAGE,** 7, br g Danbird (AUS)—Keen Melody (USA) **S. J. Bowett**
13 **PIXIEPOT,** 5, b m Alflora (IRE)—Folly Foster **The Rumpole Partnership**
14 **REVANNA,** 6, b m Revoque (IRE)—Kingennie **Mrs J. A. Niven**
15 **ROBIN DAY (IRE),** 4, br g Robin des Pres (FR)—Omyn Supreme (IRE) **David Bamber**
16 **SIMPLY ROUGE,** 5, b m Croco Rouge (IRE)—Simply Mystic **Mrs J A Niven & Sandy Lodge Racing Club**
17 **SIR SAFIR,** 5, b g Croco Rouge (IRE)—Angela's Ashes **Francis Green Racing Ltd**
18 **SUGAR TOWN,** 5, b m Elusive City (USA)—Sweetsformysweet (USA) **S. V. Barker**
19 **UNDULATE,** 4, b f Three Valleys (USA)—Singleton **Mr G. Wragg**

### TWO-YEAR-OLDS

20 **MR LUCAS (IRE),** b c 11/5 Le Cadre Noir (IRE)—Maripova (IRE) (Marju (IRE)) (5238) **Mrs Muriel Ward**

**Other Owners:** Mr C. Ayris, Mrs J. Brown, M. J. Feneron, Miss C. Foster, Miss V. C. Frith, D. Holgate, Mr A. Needham, Mrs J. M. Newitt, P. D. Niven, M. A. Scaife, J. M. Swinglehurst, Mrs G. M. Swinglehurst.

## 457 MR RAYSON NIXON, Selkirk

Postal: **Oakwood Farm, Ettrickbridge, Selkirk, Selkirkshire, TD7 5HJ**
Contacts: **PHONE (01750) 52245 FAX (01750) 52313**

1 **JUST BEE (IRE),** 6, b m Zerpour (IRE)—Miss Jamielou (IRE) **Rayson & Susan Nixon**

**Assistant Trainer:** Mrs S. Nixon

**Jockey (NH):** Fearghal Davis.

## 458 MRS LUCY NORMILE, Glenfarg

Postal: **Duncrievie, Glenfarg, Perthshire, PH2 9PD**
Contacts: **PHONE (01577) 830330 FAX (01577) 830658 MOBILE (07721) 454818**
**E-MAIL lucy@normileracing.co.uk WEBSITE www.normileracing.co.uk**

1 **AGRICULTURAL,** 9, b g Daylami (IRE)—Rustic (IRE) **Mrs J. Carnaby**
2 **BADGED,** 6, b g High Chaparral (IRE)—Meshhed (USA) **The Explorers**
3 **BALLYCARBERY,** 9, b g Bollin Eric—Carbery Spirit (IRE) **Mrs F. M. Whitaker**
4 **BERKSHIRE DOWNS,** 5, b m Tiger Hill (IRE)—Cut Corn **Riverside Racing**
5 **CADORE (IRE),** 7, b g Hurricane Run (IRE)—Mansiya **L B N Racing Club**
6 **CRUACHAN (IRE),** 6, b g Authorized (IRE)—Calico Moon (USA) **P Carnaby & B Thomson**
7 **DR PADDY (IRE),** 8, b g Dr Massini (IRE)—Tina Torus (IRE) **Mrs P. Sinclair**
8 **HAIDEES REFLECTION,** 5, b m Byron—Exchanging Glances **Mr A. Doig**
9 **JUST ANNIE,** 7, b m Revoque (IRE)—Carbery Spirit (IRE) **Mrs F. M. Whitaker**
10 **KARINGO,** 8, ch g Karinga Bay—Wild Happening (GER) **Douglas Black,P A Carnaby,P J Carnaby**
11 **LORD REDSGIRTH (IRE),** 10, ch g Flemensfirth (USA)—Wisebuy (IRE) **L B N Racing Club**
12 **MISS DEEFIANT,** 9, b m Muhtarram (USA)—Hiding Place **Mrs L. B. Normile**
13 **MR MANSSON (IRE),** 8, b g Millenary—Supreme Dare (IRE) **Mr K. N. R. MacNicol**
14 **NEW YOUMZAIN (FR),** 6, b g Sinndar (IRE)—Luna Sacra (FR) **The Fiddlers**
15 **REMEMBER ROCKY,** 6, ch g Haafhd—Flower Market **Byrne Racing**
16 **RINNAGREE ROSIE,** 9, gr m Silver Patriarch (IRE)—Gretton **The Silver Tops**
17 **ROYAL DUCHESS,** 5, b m Dutch Art—Royal Citadel (IRE) **Mr S. W. Dick**

## MRS LUCY NORMILE - Continued

18 **SILVERTON,** 8, gr m Silver Patriarch (IRE)—Gretton **Twentys Plenty**
19 **SON OF FEYAN (IRE),** 4, ch g Nayef (USA)—Miss Penton **Mr K. N. R. MacNicol**
20 **STROBE,** 11, ch g Fantastic Light (USA)—Sadaka (USA) **Miss P. A. & Mr P. J. Carnaby**
21 **WOLF HEART (IRE),** 7, b g Dalakhani (IRE)—Lisieux Orchid (IRE) **Twentys Plenty**

### THREE-YEAR-OLDS

22 **ROYAL REGENT,** b g Urgent Request (IRE)—Royal Citadel (IRE) **Mr S. W. Dick**

**Other Owners:** Mr D. M. Black, P. Byrne, Miss P. A. Carnaby, Mr P. J. Carnaby, Mr P. Carnaby, Miss F. M. Fletcher, Mr A. C. Rodger, B. Thomson, D. A. Whitaker.

**Assistant Trainer:** Libby Brodie (07947) 592438

**Jockey (NH):** Lucy Alexander, Dougie Costello. **Conditional:** Alexander Voy. **Amateur:** Mr R. Wilson.

---

## 459 MR JOHN NORTON, Barnsley

Postal: **Globe Farm, High Hoyland, Barnsley, South Yorkshire, S75 4BE**
Contacts: **PHONE/FAX (01226) 387633 MOBILE (07970) 212707**
**E-MAIL johnrnorton@hotmail.com WEBSITE www.johnrnortonracehorsetrainer.co.uk**

1 **CAPTIVE MOMENT,** 9, b m Almaty (IRE)—Captive Heart **J. Norton**
2 **DEPORTATION,** 8, b g Deportivo—Kyle Rhea **Alfa Site Services Ltd**
3 **FIDDLER'S FLIGHT (IRE),** 9, b g Convinced—Carole's Dove **Fellowship Of The Rose Partnership**
4 **FLYING POWER,** 7, b g Dubai Destination (USA)—Rah Wa (USA) **Jaffa Racing Syndicate**
5 **GOREY LANE (IRE),** 9, b g Oscar (IRE)—Supremely Deep (IRE) **Jaffa Racing Syndicate**
6 **KINGSWINFORD (IRE),** 9, b g Noverre (USA)—Berenica (IRE) **Razor Ruddock Racing Club Limited**
7 **PHOTO OPPORTUNITY,** 8, b g Zamindar (USA)—Fame At Last (USA) **Razor Ruddock Racing Club Limited**
8 **SAMTOMJONES (IRE),** 7, ch g Presenting—She's All That (IRE) **J. R. Norton Ltd**

### THREE-YEAR-OLDS

9 **ANNIVERSARIE,** ch f Major Cadeaux—Razzle (IRE) **A. R. Middleton**

**Other Owners:** Mr R. M. Firth, Mr P. J. Marshall, Mr P. Woodcock-Jones.

**Amateur:** Mr P. Hardy.

---

## 460 MR JEREMY NOSEDA, Newmarket

Postal: **Shalfleet, 17 Bury Road, Newmarket, Suffolk, CB8 7BX**
Contacts: **PHONE (01638) 664010 FAX (01638) 664100 MOBILE (07710) 294093**
**E-MAIL jeremy@jeremynoseda.com WEBSITE www.jeremynoseda.com**

1 **AUSSIE ANDRE,** 4, b g High Chaparral (IRE)—Hana Dee
2 **GRANDEUR (IRE),** 6, gr ro g Verglas (IRE)—Misskinta (IRE)
3 **IAN'S MEMORY (USA),** 4, b br c Smart Strike (CAN)—Rite Moment (USA)
4 **MESSILA STAR,** 5, ch h Pivotal—Jamboretta (IRE)
5 **MIA SAN TRIPLE,** 4, b f Invincible Spirit (IRE)—Atlantide (USA)
6 **NIGEL'S DESTINY (USA),** 4, b c Giant's Causeway (USA)—Ticket to Seattle (USA)
7 **OUTBACK TRAVELLER (IRE),** 4, b c Bushranger (IRE)—Blue Holly (IRE)
8 **SLOANE AVENUE (USA),** 4, ch c Candy Ride (ARG)—Apt (USA)
9 **SMARTIE ARTIE (IRE),** 4, b c Smart Strike (CAN)—Green Room (USA)
10 **WAKEA (USA),** 4, b br c Cape Cross (IRE)—Imiloa (USA)
11 **YEAGER (USA),** 5, b br g Medaglia d'Oro (USA)—Lucky Flyer (USA)
12 **ZESHOV (IRE),** 4, b g Acclamation—Fathoming (USA)

### THREE-YEAR-OLDS

13 **BECKINSALE (IRE),** b f Fastnet Rock (AUS)—Winged Harriet (IRE)
14 **BUONAROTTI BOY (IRE),** b c Galileo (IRE)—Funsie (FR)
15 **CABLE STREET (USA),** gr c Street Cry (IRE)—Cable (USA)
16 **CERTAIN SMILE (IRE),** b c Lope de Vega (IRE)—Irish Flower (IRE)
17 **DANCE AWHILE (IRE),** b f Kodiac—Special Dancer
18 **DELPHYNE,** ch f Mount Nelson—Darmiana (USA)
19 **DEPTH CHARGE (IRE),** b c Fastnet Rock (AUS)—Myrtle
20 **DESAFINADO (IRE),** ch f Dutch Art—Sweetsformysweet (USA)

## MR JEREMY NOSEDA - Continued

21 **DUET,** ch f Pivotal—Miswaki Belle (USA)
22 Ch g Giant's Causeway (USA)—Element of Truth (USA)
23 **EYE CATCHING,** ch f Exceed And Excel (AUS)—Rainbow Queen (FR)
24 **FIRMAMENT,** b c Cape Cross (IRE)—Heaven Sent
25 **FREE ONE (IRE),** b c Fast Company (IRE)—Tatamagouche (IRE)
26 **HOPE AND FAITH (IRE),** gr f Zebedee—Fuerta Ventura (IRE)
27 **KEYSTROKE,** b c Pivotal—Fondled
28 **LIBRISA BREEZE,** gr c Mount Nelson—Bruxcalina (FR)
29 **LUNA MOON,** b f Equiano (FR)—Luanshya
30 **MISTER BRIGHTSIDE (IRE),** b c Lord Shanakill (USA)—Lamh Eile (IRE)
31 **OVERHEARD (IRE),** b f Lope de Vega (IRE)—Gutter Press (IRE)
32 **RAIN WIND AND FIRE (USA),** ch c Eskendereya (USA)—Call Mariah (USA)
33 **RENOUNCE (IRE),** b c Elnadim (USA)—Relinquished
34 **SAVVY (IRE),** gr f Verglas (IRE)—Alikhlas
35 Ch c Astronomer Royal (USA)—Sentimental Union (USA)
36 **STARLIKE (USA),** b f Eskendereya (USA)—Mysterieuse Etoile (USA)
37 **SUMEIDA (USA),** b br c Street Sense (USA)—Camargue (USA)
38 **UP TEMPO,** b f Pivotal—Light Hearted
39 **WICKEDLY SMART (USA),** gr f Smart Strike (CAN)—Wickedly Wise (USA)

### TWO-YEAR-OLDS

40 **BROADWAY ICON,** b c 29/1 Sixties Icon—Funny Girl (IRE) (Darshaan)
41 B c 12/4 Giant's Causeway (USA)—Cassis (USA) (Red Ransom (USA))
42 B c 29/3 Lilbourne Lad (IRE)—Donnelly's Hollow (IRE) (Docksider (USA)) (80000)
43 **DUTCH DREAM,** ch f 18/3 Dutch Art—Starry Sky (Oasis Dream) (45000)
44 **ELECTRIFY (IRE),** b f 29/4 Invincible Spirit (IRE)—Elopa (GER) (Tiger Hill (IRE)) (41269)
45 **ESCALATE (IRE),** b f 12/4 Fast Company (IRE)—Nova Tor (IRE) (Trans Island) (38095)
46 **FASTLADY (IRE),** ch f 25/1 Fast Company (IRE)—Brave Madam (IRE) (Invincible Spirit (IRE)) (9523)
47 B f 5/3 Lilbourne Lad (IRE)—Genuine Charm (IRE) (Sadler's Wells (USA)) (130000)
48 B c 14/2 Sixties Icon—Gift Dancer (Imperial Dancer) (80000)
49 **HEARTY (IRE),** b c 15/3 Big Bad Bob (IRE)—Ulanova (IRE) (Noverre (USA)) (59523)
50 B c 24/1 Kodiac—Pearl Magic (USA) (Speightstown (USA)) (70000)
51 B f 26/3 Canford Cliffs (IRE)—Sentimental (IRE) (Galileo (IRE))
52 B c 3/2 Eskendereya (USA)—Street Talk (USA) (Street Cry (IRE)) (97532)
53 B c 29/4 Canford Cliffs (IRE)—Western Sky (Barathea (IRE))

**Assistant Trainer:** Dave Bradley

---

## 461 MR A. P. O'BRIEN, Ballydoyle

Postal: **Ballydoyle Stables, Cashel, Co. Tipperary, Ireland**

The following list has not been supplied by the trainer and has been compiled from information in the public domain.

1 **ADELAIDE (IRE),** 4, b c Galileo (IRE)—Elletelle (IRE)
2 **ANGEL CHORUS (IRE),** 6, b m Dylan Thomas (IRE)—Fayre (IRE)
3 **BEACH OF FALESA (IRE),** 6, b m Dylan Thomas (IRE)—Leonia (IRE)
4 **CARRIGANOG (IRE),** 6, ch g Shantou (USA)—Penny Fiction (IRE)
5 **COUGAR MOUNTAIN (IRE),** 4, b c Fastnet Rock (AUS)—Descant (USA)
6 **DRACO,** 6, ch g Hernando (FR)—Easibrook Jane
7 **DRISHTI (IRE),** 4, b g Fastnet Rock (AUS)—American Queen (FR)
8 **DUE DILIGENCE (USA),** 4, b br c War Front (USA)—Bema (USA)
9 **EGYPTIAN WARRIOR (IRE),** 6, b br g Galileo (IRE)—Beltisaal (FR)
10 **GEOFFREY CHAUCER (USA),** 4, b c Montjeu (IRE)—Helsinki
11 **GREAT EXPLORER (IRE),** 5, b g Galileo (IRE)—Starchy
12 **HORSEGUARDSPARADE,** 4, b c Montjeu (IRE)—Honorlina (FR)
13 **KALOPSIA (IRE),** 4, b f Flemensfirth (USA)—Lunar Beauty (IRE)
14 **KILCLISPEEN (IRE),** 5, br g Definite Article—She's A Venture (IRE)
15 **KING LEON (IRE),** 6, b g Mountain High (IRE)—None The Wiser (IRE)
16 **KINGFISHER (IRE),** 4, b c Galileo (IRE)—Mystical Lady (IRE)
17 **LONE STAR (IRE),** 4, b g Sea The Stars (IRE)—Foolish Act (IRE)
18 **MACBRIDE (IRE),** 6, b g Oscar (IRE)—Carioca Dream (USA)
19 **MARCHESE MARCONI (IRE),** 6, b h Galileo (IRE)—Charroux (IRE)

## MR A. P. O'BRIEN - Continued

20 **MENTOR (IRE),** 5, ch g Vertical Speed (FR)—Pure Beautiful (IRE)
21 **NOAH WEBSTER (IRE),** 6, b g Galileo (IRE)—Matikanehanafubuki (IRE)
22 **OKLAHOMA CITY,** 4, b g Oasis Dream—Galaxy Highflyer
23 **PLINTH (IRE),** 5, b g Montjeu (IRE)—Crazy Volume (IRE)
24 **SHIELD (IRE),** 6, b g Dylan Thomas (IRE)—American Queen (FR)
25 **TAPESTRY (IRE),** 4, b f Galileo (IRE)—Rumplestiltskin (IRE)
26 **THE ISLANDER (IRE),** 4, b c Fastnet Rock (AUS)—Blue Cloud (IRE)
27 **WAVER (IRE),** 5, ch g Galileo (IRE)—Nell Gwyn (IRE)

## THREE-YEAR-OLDS

28 **ABSORBING (IRE),** ch f Duke of Marmalade (IRE)—Sanctify (IRE)
29 **ALOFT (IRE),** b c Galileo (IRE)—Dietrich (USA)
30 **ALONG THE SHORE (IRE),** b f Dylan Thomas (IRE)—Golden Dancer (IRE)
31 **ARCHANGEL RAPHAEL (IRE),** b c Montjeu (IRE)—La Sylvia (IRE)
32 **ASK ME NICELY (IRE),** b f Fastnet Rock (AUS)—Queen Titi (IRE)
33 **BANTRY BAY (IRE),** ch c Galileo (IRE)—Play Misty For Me (IRE)
34 **BATTLE OF MARATHON (USA),** b c War Front (USA)—Sayedah (IRE)
35 **BELONG (IRE),** b f Fastnet Rock (AUS)—Leonia (IRE)
36 **BEST KEPT SECRET (IRE),** b g Duke of Marmalade (IRE)—Rawabi
37 **BONDI BEACH (IRE),** b c Galileo (IRE)—One Moment In Time (IRE)
38 **CAPE CLEAR ISLAND (IRE),** b c Fastnet Rock (AUS)—Kushnarenkovo
39 **CENOTAPH (USA),** b c War Front (USA)—Sanserif (IRE)
40 **COCOON (IRE),** b f Galileo (IRE)—Mystical Lady (IRE)
41 **CRADLE MOUNTAIN (IRE),** b c Mastercraftsman (IRE)—Sea Picture (IRE)
42 **DIAMOND BANGLE (IRE),** b f Galileo (IRE)—Looking Back (IRE)
43 **DIAMONDSANDRUBIES (IRE),** b f Fastnet Rock (AUS)—Quarter Moon (IRE)
44 **DICK WHITTINGTON (IRE),** b c Rip Van Winkle (IRE)—Sahara Sky (IRE)
45 **EAST INDIA,** ch c Galileo (IRE)—Field of Hope (IRE)
46 **EASTER (IRE),** b f Galileo (IRE)—Missvinski (USA)
47 **ECHOES OF MY MIND (IRE),** b f Fastnet Rock (AUS)—In My Dreams (IRE)
48 **EISENHOWER (USA),** b br c War Front (USA)—Volga (IRE)
49 **FACADE (IRE),** b f Galileo (IRE)—Charlotte Bronte
50 **FATHER CHRISTMAS (IRE),** b c Bernardini (USA)—Christmas Kid (USA)
51 **FATHER FROST (IRE),** b c Rip Van Winkle (IRE)—Yaria (IRE)
52 **FIELDS OF ATHENRY (IRE),** b c Galileo (IRE)—Last Love (IRE)
53 **FLUFF (IRE),** b f Galileo (IRE)—Sumora (IRE)
54 **FOUND (IRE),** b f Galileo (IRE)—Red Evie (IRE)
55 **GIANT REDWOOD (IRE),** b c Galileo (IRE)—Gwynn (IRE)
56 **GIOVANNI CANALETTO (IRE),** ch c Galileo (IRE)—Love Me True (USA)
57 **GLENEAGLES (IRE),** b c Galileo (IRE)—You'resothrilling (USA)
58 **GOODWILL (IRE),** b c Montjeu (IRE)—Mora Bai (IRE)
59 **GRAN PARADISO (IRE),** ch c Galileo (IRE)—Looking Lovely (IRE)
60 **HALLMARK (IRE),** b c Montjeu (IRE)—Starlight Night (USA)
61 **HANOVER STREET (IRE),** ch c Galileo (IRE)—Halfway To Heaven (IRE)
62 **HANS HOLBEIN,** b c Montjeu (IRE)—Llia
63 **HIGHLAND REEL (IRE),** b c Galileo (IRE)—Hveger (AUS)
64 **HOBART (IRE),** ch c Galileo (IRE)—Mythical Echo (USA)
65 **HOMELAND (IRE),** b c Galileo (IRE)—Withorwithoutyou (IRE)
66 **I'LL FLY AWAY (IRE),** b f Galileo (IRE)—Twyla (AUS)
67 **ICE KINGDOM (IRE),** b c Quality Road (USA)—Weekend Strike (USA)
68 **IMPERIAL PALACE (IRE),** b c Montjeu (IRE)—First Breeze (USA)
69 **IVANOVICH GORBATOV (IRE),** b c Montjeu (IRE)—Northern Gulch (USA)
70 **JACOBEAN (IRE),** b c High Chaparral (IRE)—Civility Cat (USA)
71 **JAMAICA (IRE),** gr c Galileo (IRE)—Dialafara (FR)
72 **JINSHA LAKE (IRE),** b c Galileo (IRE)—Al Ihsas (IRE)
73 **JOHN F KENNEDY (IRE),** b c Galileo (IRE)—Rumplestiltskin (IRE)
74 **KILIMANJARO (IRE),** gr c High Chaparral (IRE)—Middle Persia
75 **KING OF ARAGON (IRE),** b c Montjeu (IRE)—Crazy Volume (IRE)
76 **KISSED BY ANGELS (IRE),** b f Galileo (IRE)—Lillie Langtry (IRE)
77 **LATIN QUARTER (IRE),** b c Montjeu (IRE)—Ecoutila (USA)
78 **LOS BARBADOS (IRE),** b c Galileo (IRE)—Milanova (AUS)
79 **LOVED (IRE),** b f Galileo (IRE)—Anna Karenina (IRE)
80 **OFTEN (IRE),** b f Galileo (IRE)—Mariah's Storm (USA)
81 **OL' MAN RIVER (IRE),** b c Montjeu (IRE)—Finsceal Beo (IRE)
82 **ON A PEDESTAL (IRE),** b f Montjeu (IRE)—Blue Cloud (IRE)

## MR A. P. O'BRIEN - Continued

83 **ORDER OF ST GEORGE (IRE),** b c Galileo (IRE)—Another Storm (USA)
84 **OUTSTANDING (IRE),** b f Galileo (IRE)—Absolutelyfabulous (IRE)
85 **PATHWAY (IRE),** b c Duke of Marmalade (IRE)—Beltisaal (FR)
86 **PINK LAVENDER (IRE),** ch f Duke of Marmalade (IRE)—Delphinium (IRE)
87 **PROSPECTOR (USA),** gr c Galileo (IRE)—Starlight Dreams (USA)
88 **QUALIFY (IRE),** b f Fastnet Rock (AUS)—Perihelion (IRE)
89 **RED CARDINAL (IRE),** b c Montjeu (IRE)—Notable
90 **ROYAL NAVY SHIP (USA),** b c War Front (USA)—Indy Punch (USA)
91 **SANDRO BOTTICELLI (IRE),** b c Galileo (IRE)—Ask For The Moon (FR)
92 **SEA OF BLUE (IRE),** b f Fastnet Rock (AUS)—Song of The Sea
93 **SHARK ISLAND (IRE),** b c Fastnet Rock (AUS)—Lady Lupus (IRE)
94 **SHERLOCK HOLMES (IRE),** ch c Galileo (IRE)—Golden Ballet (USA)
95 **SIEGE OF ORLEANS (USA),** b c War Front (USA)—Watch (USA)
96 **SIR ISAAC NEWTON,** b c Galileo (IRE)—Shastye (IRE)
97 **SMUGGLER'S COVE (IRE),** b c Fastnet Rock (AUS)—Chenchikova (IRE)
98 **SONG OF LOVE (IRE),** b g Fastnet Rock (AUS)—Delicate Charm (IRE)
99 **ST PATRICK'S DAY (IRE),** b c Fastnet Rock (AUS)—Race For The Stars (USA)
100 **TERRACOTTA (IRE),** b f Fastnet Rock (AUS)—Sacrosanct (IRE)
101 **THE CREWMASTER (IRE),** b c Mastercraftsman (IRE)—Pertinence (IRE)
102 **THE HAPPY PRINCE (IRE),** b c Rip Van Winkle (IRE)—Maid To Dream
103 **THE WARRIOR (IRE),** b c Exceed And Excel (AUS)—Aymara
104 **TIMBUKTU (IRE),** b f Fastnet Rock (AUS)—Flashing Green
105 **TOGETHER FOREVER (IRE),** b f Galileo (IRE)—Green Room (USA)
106 **TOOGOODTOBETRUE (IRE),** b f Oasis Dream—All For Glory (USA)
107 **TORREY PINES (IRE),** b c Galileo (IRE)—Beauty Is Truth (IRE)
108 **TRUTH (IRE),** b f Galileo (IRE)—Prudenzia (IRE)
109 **U S NAVY SEAL (USA),** b br c War Front (USA)—Questress (USA)
110 **WANDERING (IRE),** b f Fastnet Rock (AUS)—Piping (IRE)
111 **WAR ENVOY (USA),** b c War Front (USA)—La Conseillante (USA)
112 **WEDDING VOW (IRE),** b f Galileo (IRE)—Remember When (IRE)
113 **WORDS (IRE),** b f Dansili—Moonstone

## TWO-YEAR-OLDS

**114** B c 11/2 Galileo (IRE)—A Z Warrior (USA) (Bernardini (USA))
**115** B c 8/4 Galileo (IRE)—Airwave (Air Express (IRE))
**116** B c 22/1 Oasis Dream—All For Glory (USA) (Giant's Causeway (USA))
**117** **ALTISSIMO (FR),** b c 24/4 Galileo (IRE)—Altana (USA) (Mountain Cat (USA))
**118** Ch c 18/4 Galileo (IRE)—Another Storm (USA) (Gone West (USA)) (875000)
**119** B c 13/2 Montjeu (IRE)—Apticanti (USA) (Aptitude (USA))
**120** B c 25/4 Galileo (IRE)—Artistique (IRE) (Linamix (FR))
**121** Ch c 22/3 Galileo (IRE)—Ask For The Moon (FR) (Dr Fong (USA))
**122** B c 29/1 Galileo (IRE)—Banquise (IRE) (Last Tycoon)
**123** B c 16/3 Galileo (IRE)—Bonheur (IRE) (Royal Academy (USA))
**124** B c 23/3 Fastnet Rock (AUS)—Cherry Hinton (Green Desert (USA))
**125** B c 31/3 Galileo (IRE)—Chintz (IRE) (Danehill Dancer (IRE))
**126** B c 6/5 Galileo (IRE)—Christmas Kid (USA) (Lemon Drop Kid (USA))
**127** B c 8/5 Galileo (IRE)—Circle of Life (USA) (Belong To Me (USA))
**128** B c 16/3 Galileo (IRE)—Dame Again (AUS) (Danehill (USA))
**129** B c 22/5 Galileo (IRE)—Dance For Fun (Anabaa (USA))
**130** B c 28/2 Galileo (IRE)—Devoted To You (IRE) (Danehill Dancer (IRE))
**131** Gr c 5/5 Galileo (IRE)—Ecology (USA) (Unbridled's Song (USA))
**132** B gr c 16/1 Galileo (IRE)—Famous (IRE) (Danehill Dancer (IRE)) (600000)
**133** B c 1/3 Galileo (IRE)—Flirtation (Pursuit of Love) (750000)
**134** B c 6/2 War Front (USA)—Gold Vault (USA) (Arch (USA)) (1262191)
**135** B c 19/3 Fastnet Rock (AUS)—Golden Dancer (IRE) (Sadler's Wells (USA))
**136** Ch c 10/4 Galileo (IRE)—Halland Park Lass (IRE) (Spectrum (IRE))
**137** B c 19/2 Montjeu (IRE)—Honorlina (FR) (Linamix (FR)) (675000)
**138** B c 14/3 Galileo (IRE)—Hveger (AUS) (Danehill (USA)) (750000)
**139** B c 10/3 Oasis Dream—Ideal (Galileo (IRE))
**140** B c 19/3 War Front (USA)—Imagine (IRE) (Sadler's Wells (USA))
**141** B c 20/4 Galileo (IRE)—Inca Princess (IRE) (Holy Roman Emperor (IRE)) (238095)
**142** B c 1/2 Galileo (IRE)—Lady Icarus (Rainbow Quest (USA)) (400000)
**143** B c 23/1 Fastnet Rock (AUS)—Lady Lupus (IRE) (High Chaparral (IRE))
**144** B c 15/3 Galileo (IRE)—Lahinch (IRE) (Danehill Dancer (IRE))
**145** B c 31/1 War Front (USA)—Lasting Code (USA) (Lost Code (USA))

## MR A. P. O'BRIEN - Continued

**146** B c 5/5 Fastnet Rock (AUS)—Leonia (IRE) (Sadler's Wells (USA))
**147** B c 20/2 War Front (USA)—Liscanna (IRE) (Sadler's Wells (USA))
**148** B c 20/3 Pour Moi (IRE)—Marjalina (IRE) (Marju (IRE)) (210000)
**149** B c 30/3 Fastnet Rock (AUS)—Monevassia (USA) (Mr Prospector (USA))
**150** B c 28/2 Galileo (IRE)—Moonstone (Dalakhani (IRE))
**151** B c 25/1 Montjeu (IRE)—Moving Diamonds (Lomitas)
**152** B c 10/3 Galileo (IRE)—Mubkera (IRE) (Nashwan (USA))
**153** B c 27/4 Galileo (IRE)—Mythical Echo (USA) (Stravinsky (USA))
**154** B c 27/3 Galileo (IRE)—One Moment In Time (IRE) (Danehill (USA))
**155** B c 9/3 Galileo (IRE)—Penang Pearl (FR) (Bering) (2600000)
**156** B c 27/1 High Chaparral (IRE)—Penny Post (IRE) (Green Desert (USA))
**157** B c 28/4 Fastnet Rock (AUS)—Perihelion (IRE) (Galileo (IRE)) (317460)
**158** Ch c 16/2 Galileo (IRE)—Pipalong (IRE) (Pips Pride)
**159** B c 17/3 Fastnet Rock (AUS)—Prowess (IRE) (Peintre Celebre (USA))
**160** B c 24/4 Galileo (IRE)—Rags To Riches (USA) (A P Indy (USA))
**161** Ch c 18/2 Galileo (IRE)—Remember When (IRE) (Danehill Dancer (IRE))
**162** B c 17/2 Galileo (IRE)—Rimth (Oasis Dream)
**163** B c 17/2 Galileo (IRE)—Rumplestiltskin (IRE) (Danehill (USA))
**164** B c 17/5 War Front (USA)—Score (USA) (A P Indy (USA)) (745840)
**165** B c 17/5 Galileo (IRE)—Scribonia (IRE) (Danehill (USA)) (1190476)
**166** B c 9/2 Montjeu (IRE)—Seatone (USA) (Mizzen Mast (USA))
**167** B c 8/5 Galileo (IRE)—Secret Garden (IRE) (Danehill (USA))
**168** Ch c 19/5 Galileo (IRE)—Sharp Lisa (USA) (Dixieland Band (USA))
**169** B c 28/4 Galileo (IRE)—Sumora (IRE) (Danehill (USA))
**170** B c 2/2 War Front (USA)—Treasure Trail (USA) (Pulpit (USA))
**171** B c 2/5 Fastnet Rock (AUS)—Tree Chopper (USA) (Woodman (USA))
**172** B c 2/3 High Chaparral (IRE)—Walkamia (FR) (Linamix (FR)) (240000)
**173** B c 2/3 Galileo (IRE)—Walklikeanegyptian (IRE) (Danehill (USA))
**174** B c 25/3 Galileo (IRE)—Walzerkoenigin (USA) (Kingmambo (USA))
**175** B c 14/1 Oasis Dream—Wonder of Wonders (USA) (Kingmambo (USA))
**176** B c 5/4 High Chaparral (IRE)—Wurfklinge (GER) (Acatenango (GER)) (260000)

---

## 462 MR DANIEL O'BRIEN, Tonbridge

Postal: **Knowles Bank, Capel, Tonbridge, Kent, TN11 0PU**
Contacts: **PHONE (01892) 824072**

1 **ACHIEVED,** 12, b g Lahib (USA)—Equity's Darling (IRE) **D. C. O'Brien**
2 **BOSTIN (IRE),** 7, ch g Busy Flight—Bustingoutallover (USA) **D. C. O'Brien**
3 **GOLDEN GAMES (IRE),** 9, b m Montjeu (IRE)—Ski For Gold **Mrs V. O'Brien**
4 **INTHEJUNGLE (IRE),** 12, ch g Bob Back (USA)—Whizz **D. C. O'Brien**
5 **MINORITY INTEREST,** 6, ch g Galileo (IRE)—Minority **D. C. O'Brien**
6 **NOUAILHAS,** 9, b g Mark of Esteem (IRE)—Barachois Princess (USA) **D. C. O'Brien**
7 **QUARRY TOWN (IRE),** 13, b g Pistolet Bleu (IRE)—Dano Doo (IRE) **J. Pearce**
8 **SPARTILLA,** 6, b h Teofilo (IRE)—Wunders Dream (IRE) **D. C. O'Brien**
9 **STAGE KING,** 9, b g King's Theatre (IRE)—Blue Dante (IRE) **D. C. O'Brien**

**Assistant Trainer:** Christopher O'Bryan

**Jockey (NH):** Mattie Batchelor, Sam Twiston-Davies.

---

## 463 MR FERGAL O'BRIEN, Cheltenham

Postal: **Cilldara Stud, Coln St. Dennis, Cheltenham, Gloucestershire, GL54 3AR**
Contacts: **PHONE (01285) 721150 MOBILE (07771) 702829**
**E-MAIL fergaljelly@aol.com**

1 **ALLERTON (IRE),** 8, b g Flemensfirth (USA)—Bonny Hall (IRE) **T. M. Evans**
2 **ALVARADO (IRE),** 10, ch g Goldmark (USA)—Mrs Jones (IRE) **Mr & Mrs William Rucker**
3 **AN POC AR BUILE (IRE),** 6, ch g Mountain High (IRE)—Miniconjou (IRE) **The Yes No Wait Sorries**
4 **ARTHUR MC BRIDE (IRE),** 6, b br g Royal Anthem (USA)—Lucky Diverse (IRE) **John Gaughan & Rob Rexton**
5 **BRUCE ALMIGHTY (IRE),** 4, b g Yeats (IRE)—Lady Rolfe (IRE) **Mr A. D. Bradshaw**
6 **CHASE THE SPUD,** 7, b g Alflora (IRE)—Trial Trip **Mrs C. J. Banks**
7 **CREEVYTENNANT (IRE),** 11, b g Bob's Return (IRE)—Northwood May **Mrs P. Duncan**

## MR FERGAL O'BRIEN - Continued

8 **DIAMOND GESTURE (IRE),** 7, ch m Presenting—Rare Gesture (IRE) **M. Fahy**
9 **DOUBLE SILVER,** 8, gr m Silver Patriarch (IRE)—Shadows of Silver **Mr R. C. Mayall**
10 **FARMER MATT (IRE),** 9, b br g Zagreb (USA)—Ashville Native (IRE) **S. D. Hemstock**
11 **FLYING BANDIT (IRE),** 6, b g Bandari (IRE)—Pegus Love (IRE) **C. J. Bennett**
12 **GRAND INTRODUCTION (IRE),** 5, b g Robin des Pres (FR)—What A Breeze (IRE) **Geoffrey & Donna Keeys**
13 **GUNNER FIFTEEN (IRE),** 7, b g Westerner—Grandy Hall (IRE) **Masterson Holdings Limited**
14 **IORA GLAS (IRE),** 6, gr g Court Cave (IRE)—Crossdrumrosie (IRE) **Imperial Racing Partnership**
15 **ISLA FERNANDOS (IRE),** 5, ch m Flemensfirth (USA)—Kon Tiky (FR) **Graham & Alison Jelley**
16 **JENNYS SURPRISE (IRE),** 7, b m Hawk Wing (USA)—
Winning Jenny (IRE) **Yes No Wait Sorries & G & P Barker Ltd**
17 **LORD LANDEN (IRE),** 10, br g Beneficial—Agua Caliente (IRE) **The B Lucky Partnership**
18 **MANBALLANDALL (IRE),** 7, b g Flemensfirth (USA)—Omas Lady (IRE) **Mr G. Kennedy**
19 **NATIVE MOUNTAIN (IRE),** 6, b g Mountain High (IRE)—Blue Gale (IRE) **The General Asphalte Company Ltd**
20 **NERVOUS NINETIES,** 6, gr g Proclamation (IRE)—Born To Dream (IRE) **The Gud Times Partnership**
21 **OUR CAT (IRE),** 7, b m Royal Anthem (USA)—Run Cat (IRE) **The General Asphalte Company Ltd**
22 **OWEN NA VIEW (IRE),** 7, b br g Presenting—Lady Zephyr (IRE) **The Yes No Wait Sorries**
23 **PERFECT CANDIDATE (IRE),** 8, b g Winged Love (IRE)—Dansana (IRE) **ISL Recruitment**
24 **PITTER PATTER,** 5, b m Nayef (USA)—Pixie Ring **N. M. H. Jones**
25 **RIO MILAN (IRE),** 9, b g Milan—Lady Medina (IRE) **Mrs J. Cumiskey Mr T. Joyce**
26 **ROBERTS FORT (IRE),** 8, b g Milan—Clonboy Girl (IRE) **The Yes No Wait Sorries**
27 **ROCKCHASEBULLETT (IRE),** 7, b g Catcher In The Rye (IRE)—Last Chance Lady (IRE) **The Yes No Wait Sorries**
28 **SHAKE DEVANEY (IRE),** 5, b g Rakti—Ediyrna (IRE) **Mr T. Conway & Mrs Conway**
29 **SILVER ROQUE (FR),** 9, b g Laveron—Bible Gun (FR) **Lord Vestey**
30 **SON OF SUZIE,** 7, gr g Midnight Legend—Suzie Cream Cheese (IRE) **Mrs P. Duncan**
31 **SPY IN THE SKY,** 6, b m Generous (IRE)—Lady Deploy **Mrs L. Hall**
32 5, B m Kayf Tara—Sweet Stormy (IRE) **Mr F. M. O'Brien**
33 **THE GOVANESS,** 6, b m Kayf Tara—Just Kate **C. B. Brookes**
34 **TINELYRA (IRE),** 9, b g Mr Combustible (IRE)—Ladyogan (IRE) **Mr F. M. O'Brien**
35 **TRESPASSERS WILL (IRE),** 4, b g Scorpion (IRE)—Drum Majorette **Geoffrey & Donna Keeys**
36 **TROIKA STEPPES,** 7, b g Pasternak—Killerton Clover **Mr W. Williamson**
37 **WAR ON THE ROCKS (IRE),** 6, b g Wareed (IRE)—Rock Garden (IRE) **Shorey Fancutt Tucker**
38 **WILD AT MIDNIGHT,** 6, b m Midnight Legend—Wild Dream **Mr R. J. Rainbow**

**Other Owners:** M. A. Blackford, Mr S. W. Bowers, C. S. J. Coley, T. Conway, Mrs M. Conway, Mrs K. T. Cumiskey, Mr G. S. Fancutt, G. & P. Barker Ltd, Mr J. Gaughan, D. M. Hussey, G. S. Jelley, Mrs A. D. Jelley, T. F. Joyce, G. F. Keeys, Mrs C. M. Keeys, Mrs M. M. Kennedy, B. M. Mathieson, Mr P. Nurden, Mr R. J. Rexton, I. Robinson, Mrs G. C. Robinson, W. J. Rucker, Mrs A. Rucker, D. J. Shorey, M. Tucker.

---

## 464 MR EDWARD J. O'GRADY, Thurles

Postal: **Killeens, Ballynonty, Thurles, Co. Tipperary, Ireland**
Contacts: **PHONE (00353) 529 156 156 FAX (00353) 529 156 466 MOBILE (00353) 86 2590764**
**E-MAIL edward@edwardogrady.com**

1 **ALL DAY LONG (IRE),** 7, b g Sadler's Wells (USA)—Aunt Aggie (IRE) **John P. McManus**
2 4, B g Oscar (IRE)—Azaban (IRE) **John Power**
3 **BANANA FLAMBE (IRE),** 7, b g Darsi (FR)—Roupolino (IRE) **Mrs E. J. O'Grady**
4 **CAPBRETON (FR),** 5, b g Linda's Lad—Noblesse de Robe (FR) **Glebeland Farm Partnership**
5 **FLAMING DAWN (IRE),** 7, ch g Flemensfirth (USA)—Saddlers Dawn (IRE) **John P. McManus**
6 **GALLANT TIPP (IRE),** 7, b g Definite Article—Noble Delight (IRE) **John P. McManus**
7 **GETTING LATE (IRE),** 5, b g Milan—On The Hour (IRE) **John P. McManus**
8 **GREAT KHAN (IRE),** 4, b g Kalanisi (IRE)—Can't Stop (GER) **Jonathan O'Grady**
9 **HELL CAT MAGGIE (IRE),** 6, ch m Flemensfirth (USA)—Special Trix (IRE) **Kieran D. Cotter**
10 **ITSNOTHINGPERSONAL (IRE),** 5, b g Beneficial—Savu Sea (IRE) **John P. McManus**
11 4, B g Kalanisi (IRE)—Jemima Jay (IRE) **Simon J. H. Davis**
12 **JUMPTOCONCLUSIONS (IRE),** 6, b g Scorpion (IRE)—Can't Stop (GER) **John P. McManus**
13 **KITTEN ROCK (FR),** 5, b g Laverock (IRE)—The Cat Eater (FR) **John P. McManus**
14 **LORD OF LORDS (IRE),** 8, b g Flemensfirth (USA)—Abinitio Lady (IRE) **Mrs E. J. O'Grady**
15 4, B g Milan—Mrs Marples (IRE) **Mrs E. J. O'Grady, H. Tylor**
16 4, B f Scorpion (IRE)—Muckin About (IRE) **John P. McManus**
17 **MY MATADOR (IRE),** 4, b c Kandahar Run—My Special (IRE) **J. S. Gutkin**
18 **NERANO (IRE),** 4, b g Milan—Derriana (IRE) **Louise Fitzgerald (Loumar Partnership)**
19 **ORCHESTRAL RUN (IRE),** 4, b g Mahler—Baunfaun Run (IRE) **Mrs E. J. O'Grady (Loumar)**
20 **PRICKLY (IRE),** 5, ch g Definite Article—Connemara Rose (IRE) **Simon J. H. Davis**
21 **PRINCE KUP (IRE),** 4, ch c High Rock (IRE)—Lockup (IRE) **Louise Fitzgerald (Loumar Partnership)**

## MR EDWARD J. O'GRADY - Continued

22 4, B g Yeats (IRE)—Quadrennial (IRE) **Paul Holden**
23 **REFLET AMBRE (FR),** 5, b g Smadoun (FR)—Glinka Des Aigles (FR) **Ms Louise Fitzgerald**
24 **ROCONGA (IRE),** 5, b g Rakti—Nafzira (IRE) **Robert Byrne**
25 **SAILORS WARN (IRE),** 8, b g Redback—Coral Dawn (IRE) **P. Wilmott**
26 **SHOT FROM THE HIP (GER),** 11, b g Monsun (GER)—Sopran Biro (IRE) **John P. McManus**
27 **SLIEVEARDAGH (IRE),** 11, b g King's Theatre (IRE)—Gayephar **Simon J. H. Davis**
28 **SLIPPERY SERPENT (IRE),** 4, b g Scorpion (IRE)—Tres Chic (IRE) **Mrs E. J. O'Grady**
29 **SWIZZLER (IRE),** 6, b g Scorpion (IRE)—Arch Hall Lady (IRE) **Mrs E. J. O'Grady**
30 **THE WEST'S AWAKE (IRE),** 4, b g Yeats (IRE)—Bilboa (FR) **Mrs John Magnier**
31 **TIME FOR MABEL (FR),** 4, ch c Soldier of Fortune (IRE)—Athens Two O Four (USA) **Mrs E. J. O'Grady**

---

## 465 MR JEDD O'KEEFFE, Leyburn

Postal: **Highbeck, Brecongill, Coverham, Leyburn, North Yorkshire, DL8 4TJ**
Contacts: **PHONE (01969) 640330 FAX (01969) 640397 MOBILE (07710) 476705**
**E-MAIL jedd@jeddokeefferacing.co.uk WEBSITE www.jeddokeefferacing.co.uk**

1 **DARK OCEAN (IRE),** 5, b g Dylan Thomas (IRE)—Neutral **The Fatalists**
2 **INSTANT ATTRACTION (IRE),** 4, b g Tagula (IRE)—Coup de Coeur (IRE) **United We Stand**
3 **JACOB'S PILLOW,** 4, b g Oasis Dream—Enticing (IRE) **Limegrove Racing**
4 **NEW BIDDER,** 4, b br g Auction House (USA)—Noble Nova **Highbeck Racing**
5 **SATANIC BEAT (IRE),** 6, br g Dark Angel (IRE)—Slow Jazz (USA) **Caron & Paul Chapman**
6 **SHARED EQUITY,** 4, b g Elnadim (USA)—Pelican Key (IRE) **Caron & Paul Chapman**
7 **VASCO D'YCY (FR),** 6, b g Equerry (USA)—Ingrid des Mottes (FR) **Caron & Paul Chapman**
8 **WATERCLOCK (IRE),** 6, ch g Notnowcato—Waterfall One **Caron & Paul Chapman**
9 **WHERE'S TIGER,** 4, b g Tiger Hill (IRE)—Where's Broughton **Highbeck Racing**

### THREE-YEAR-OLDS

10 **DANOT (IRE),** ch g Zebedee—Hapipi **United We Stand**
11 B f Azamour (IRE)—Mischief Making (USA) **Caron & Paul Chapman**
12 **SOVEREIGN BOUNTY,** ch g Bahamian Bounty—Sovereign Abbey (IRE) **Caron & Paul Chapman**
13 **STRUCTURED NOTE (IRE),** b c Acclamation—Saik (USA) **Caron & Paul Chapman**

### TWO-YEAR-OLDS

14 B f 4/4 Bahamian Bounty—Anatase (Danehill (USA)) (16000) **Caron & Paul Chapman**
15 B c 20/3 Kheleyf (USA)—Desert Royalty (IRE) (Alhaarth (IRE)) (15000) **Highbeck Racing**
16 **INJAM (IRE),** b c 29/3 Pour Moi (IRE)—Sniffle (IRE) (Shernazar) (59523) **Miss Sharon Long**
17 B c 24/4 Kheleyf (USA)—Mint Royale (IRE) (Cadeaux Genereux) (6000) **Highbeck Racing**
18 B f 7/2 Dick Turpin (IRE)—Protectress (Hector Protector (USA)) **Caron & Paul Chapman**
19 Br c 20/2 Dream Ahead (USA)—Vasilia (Dansili) **Paul & Dale Chapman**

**Assistant Trainer:** Miss Leanne Kershaw

**Jockey (NH):** Brian Harding.

---

## 466 MR DAVID O'MEARA, Nawton

Postal: **Arthington Barn, Highfield Lane, Nawton, York, North Yorkshire, YO62 7TU**
Contacts: **PHONE (01439) 771400 MOBILE (07747) 825418**
**E-MAIL helmsleyhorseracing@gmail.com WEBSITE www.davidomeara.co.uk**

1 **AFONSO DE SOUSA (USA),** 5, br h Henrythenavigator (USA)—Mien (USA)
2 **AFTER TONIIGHT (FR),** 5, b g Lando (GER)—Affair (FR) **R. Collins**
3 **AL KHAN (IRE),** 6, b g Elnadim (USA)—Popolo (IRE) **R. Walker**
4 **ALEJANDRO (IRE),** 6, b g Dark Angel (IRE)—Carallia (IRE) **Lydonford Ltd**
5 **ALGAR LAD,** 5, ch g Kheleyf (USA)—Winding (USA) **Great Northern Partnership**
6 **BERLUSCA (IRE),** 6, b g Holy Roman Emperor (IRE)—Shemanikha (FR) **Mr P. Ball**
7 **BIRDMAN (IRE),** 5, b g Danehill Dancer (IRE)—Gilded Vanity (IRE) **Ebor Racing Club IV**
8 **BOP IT,** 6, b g Misu Bond (IRE)—Forever Bond **A. Turton, J. Blackburn & R. Bond**
9 **CUSTOM CUT (IRE),** 6, b g Notnowcato—Polished Gem (IRE) **Mr Gary Douglas & Mr Pat Breslin**
10 **DANSILI DUTCH (IRE),** 6, gr m Dutch Art—Joyful Leap **Direct Racing**
11 **EARTH DRUMMER (IRE),** 5, b g Dylan Thomas (IRE)—In Dubai (USA) **Middleham Park Racing LXV & Partner**
12 **ECCLESTON,** 4, b g Acclamation—Miss Meggy **D. W. Armstrong**
13 **EMRYS,** 4, ch g Shirocco (GER)—Movie Star (IRE) **R. Walker**

## MR DAVID O'MEARA - Continued

14 **FATTSOTA,** 7, b g Oasis Dream—Gift of The Night (USA) **Middleham Park Racing XXVIII & Partner**
15 **FIRST SITTING,** 4, b g Dansili—Aspiring Diva (USA)
16 **FRONTIER FIGHTER,** 7, b g Invincible Spirit (IRE)—Rawabi **Walker Nicholson**
17 **G FORCE (IRE),** 4, b c Tamayuz—Flanders (IRE) **Middleham Park Racing XVIII & Partner**
18 **HARWOODS VOLANTE (IRE),** 4, ch g Kheleyf (USA)—Semiquaver (IRE) **Great Northern Partnership**
19 **HE'S NO SAINT,** 4, b g Dutch Art—Stellar Brilliant (USA) **Mr D. Lavelle**
20 **HIGHLAND ACCLAIM (IRE),** 4, b g Acclamation—Emma's Star (ITY) **Mr E.M. Sutherland**
21 **HIT THE JACKPOT (IRE),** 6, ch g Pivotal—Token Gesture (IRE) **Hambleton Racing Ltd XXX**
22 **IFANDBUTWHYNOT (IRE),** 9, b g Raise A Grand (IRE)—Cockney Ground (IRE) **Claire Hollowood & Henry Dean**
23 **INGLEBY ANGEL (IRE),** 6, br g Dark Angel (IRE)—Mistress Twister **Mr D. Scott**
24 **INTISAAB,** 4, b g Elnadim (USA)—Katoom (IRE) **Mr S. Graham**
25 **KALANI'S DIAMOND,** 5, ch m Kalani Bay (IRE)—Cryptonite Diamond (USA) **The Armstrong Family**
26 **KING TORUS (IRE),** 7, b g Oratorio (IRE)—Dipterous (IRE) **Sprint Thoroughbred Racing Ltd**
27 **LASTUCE (FR),** 5, b m Orpen (USA)—Labamba (FR)
28 **LESSON IN LIFE,** 4, b f Duke of Marmalade (IRE)—Vanity (IRE) **Middleham Park Racing LXXVI & Partner**
29 **LOUIS THE PIOUS,** 7, b br g Holy Roman Emperor (IRE)—Whole Grain **F. Gillespie**
30 **MAGNIFIED,** 5, b g Passing Glance—Scrutinize (IRE) **The Maroon Stud**
31 **MARKET SHARE,** 5, b g Zamindar (USA)—Winter Solstice
32 **MASTER BOND,** 6, b g Misu Bond (IRE)—Bond Royale **Bonded Twentyten Partnership**
33 **MILLY'S SECRET (IRE),** 4, ch f Sakhee's Secret—Swan Sea (USA) **Nicholson Walker**
34 **MONDIALISTE (IRE),** 5, b h Galileo (IRE)—Occupandiste (IRE) **Mr & Mrs G. Turnbull**
35 **MONT RAS (IRE),** 8, ch g Indian Ridge—Khayrat (IRE) **Colne Valley Racing**
36 **MOVE IN TIME,** 7, ch g Monsieur Bond (IRE)—Tibesti **A. Turton, J. Blackburn & R. Bond**
37 **NEVER TO BE (USA),** 4, b g Thewayyouare (USA)—Kitty Foille (USA) **M Khan x2**
38 **NONCHALANT,** 4, gr g Oasis Dream—Comeback Queen **Mr E.M. Sutherland**
39 **OMANOME (IRE),** 4, b f Acclamation—Dance Set **Mr J. P. Halton**
40 **OUT DO,** 6, ch g Exceed And Excel (AUS)—Ludynosa (USA) **Mr E.M. Sutherland**
41 **PIM STREET (USA),** 5, b m Street Sense (USA)—Crown of Jewels (USA) **Dundalk Racing Club**
42 4, B c Passing Glance—Porcelain (IRE) **The Maroon Stud**
43 **POWERFUL PRESENCE (IRE),** 9, ch g Refuse To Bend (IRE)—
Miss a Note (USA) **The Lawton Bamforth Partnership**
44 **PROVIDENT SPIRIT,** 4, b g Invincible Spirit (IRE)—Port Providence
45 **REGAL DAN (IRE),** 5, b g Dark Angel (IRE)—Charlene Lacy (IRE) **One For The Road & Partner**
46 **RISK 'N' REWARD (IRE),** 4, ch g Dandy Man (IRE)—Sharp Diversion (USA) **Mr P. A. Cafferty**
47 **ROBERT THE PAINTER (IRE),** 7, b g Whipper (USA)—Lidanna **Mr S. Humphreys**
48 **ROSE OF THE MOON (IRE),** 10, gr g Moonax (IRE)—
Little Rose (IRE) **Middleham Park Racing XXXIII & Partners**
49 **RURAL CELEBRATION,** 4, b f Pastoral Pursuits—Queens Jubilee **Hambleton Racing Ltd - Two Chances**
50 **SALUTAMASORETA (USA),** 4, b f U S Ranger (USA)—My Little Dragon (USA) **Speedlic Racing**
51 **SAVED BY THE BELL (IRE),** 5, b g Teofilo (IRE)—Eyrecourt (IRE) **Mr J Blackburn & Mr A Turton**
52 **SCORELINE,** 4, b g Captain Gerrard (IRE)—Waterline Twenty (IRE) **Mr K Nicholson & Partners**
53 **SCRUTINY,** 4, b g Aqlaam—Aunty Mary **Direct Racing**
54 **SHAHDAROBA (IRE),** 5, b g Haatef (USA)—Gold Script (FR) **Barlow Racing Partnership**
55 **SHERIFF OF NAWTON (IRE),** 4, b g Lawman (FR)—Pivotal Role **Direct Racing**
56 **SIMPLY BLACK (IRE),** 4, br f Kheleyf (USA)—Tashyra (IRE) **Sterling Racing**
57 **SOPHISTICATED HEIR (IRE),** 5, b g New Approach (IRE)—My Girl Sophie (USA) **Colne Valley Racing**
58 **STEEL TRAIN (FR),** 4, b c Zafeen (FR)—Silent Sunday (IRE)
59 **TOTO SKYLLACHY,** 10, b g Kyllachy—Little Tramp **R. Walker**
60 **TWO FOR TWO (IRE),** 7, b g Danehill Dancer (IRE)—D'articleshore (IRE) **High Hopes Partnership & Partner**

### THREE-YEAR-OLDS

61 **BAHAMIAN DESERT,** b g Bahamian Bounty—Noble Desert (FR) **Direct Racing 1**
62 **BEACH ACTION (FR),** b br g Footstepsinthesand—Shagadellic (USA)
63 **CLEVER LOVE (FR),** gr g Silver Frost (IRE)—Sharp's Love (IRE) **Sterling Racing**
64 **COOL STRUTTER (IRE),** b c Kodiac—Cassava (IRE) **Qatar Racing Limited**
65 Ch c Flashy Bull (USA)—Da River Hoss (USA) **Mr G. Quintale**
66 B g Siyouni (FR)—Diamond Light (USA)
67 B g Royal Applause—Floating
68 **GOLDEN SPUN (USA),** b c Hard Spun (USA)—Scarlet's Tara (USA)
69 **HAIL THE HERO (IRE),** b c Galileo (IRE)—Mauralakana (FR) **Middleham Park Racing XXIX & Partner**
70 **HIGHTIME HERO,** b g Pivotal—Hightime Heroine (IRE) **Cheveley Park Stud Limited**
71 **JEBEDIAH SHINE,** ch f Kyllachy—Ardessie **Sterling Racing**
72 **JILLANAR (IRE),** b f Lawman (FR)—Lunduv (IRE) **Mr S. Rashid**
73 B f Paco Boy (IRE)—Pompey Girl **Mrs F. Denniff**
74 **SALLABEH,** b f Showcasing—Clincher Club **Mr S. Rashid**

## MR DAVID O'MEARA - Continued

75 **SALMA GONDIS (IRE),** b f Kodiac—Rainbowskia (FR) **Dr W. O'Brien**
76 **SECOND CUT (IRE),** b g Acclamation—Morality **Mr Gary Douglas & Mr Pat Breslin**
77 **SIGNORINA ROSEINA,** b f Captain Gerrard (IRE)—Rosein **Lancashire Lads Partnership**
78 **SNOW CLOUD (IRE),** b f Kodiac—Thistlestar (USA) **Middleham Park Racing L & Partner**
79 **SPRYT (IRE),** b g Invincible Spirit (IRE)—Out of Thanks (IRE)
80 **STATE OF THE UNION (IRE),** ch c Approve (IRE)—First Lady (IRE) **Middleham Park Racing XXXVIII**
81 **TAKAFOL (IRE),** b g Fast Company (IRE)—Jamary (IRE) **Nawton Racing Partnership**
82 **TBASHER (USA),** ch g Giant's Causeway (USA)—Pull Dancer (USA) **Mr N. Al Sabah**
83 **THANKSTOMONTY,** b g Dylan Thomas (IRE)—Beldarian (IRE) **Colne Valley Racing**
84 **WHISKY MARMALADE (IRE),** b f Duke of Marmalade (IRE)—
Nashatara (USA) **Middleham Park Racing LXX & Partner**

### TWO-YEAR-OLDS

85 B c 4/4 Kodiac—Albeed (Tiger Hill (IRE)) (15872)
86 **BOND BOMBSHELL,** ch f 20/4 Monsieur Bond (IRE)—
Fashion Icon (USA) (Van Nistelrooy (USA)) (1142) **Trendy Ladies**
87 B f 20/3 Galileo (IRE)—Clodora (FR) (Linamix (FR))
88 **FIRST BOMBARDMENT,** b c 26/4 Pastoral Pursuits—Magic Myth (IRE) (Revoque (IRE)) (17142)
89 B c 25/1 Lilbourne Lad (IRE)—Hawk Dance (IRE) (Hawk Wing (USA)) (26000)
90 Ch f 15/3 Pivotal—Hightime Heroine (IRE) (Danetime (IRE)) (4000)
91 B c 7/3 Wootton Bassett—Misty Heights (Fasliyev (USA)) (77000) **Mr S. Rashid**
92 **MON BEAU VISAGE (IRE),** br c 27/3 Footstepsinthesand—Hurricane Lily (IRE) (Ali-Royal (IRE)) (32539)
93 B c 18/1 Lawman (FR)—Moynsha Lady (IRE) (Namid) (25000)
94 Ch f 20/4 Frozen Power (IRE)—Pivotal Role (Pivotal) (1586)
95 **POPLAR CLOSE (IRE),** b f 6/5 Canford Cliffs (IRE)—Magena (USA) (Kingmambo (USA)) (13491)
96 Ch f 17/1 Tagula (IRE)—Santacus (IRE) (Spartacus (IRE)) (7936)
97 Ch c 16/3 Speightstown (USA)—Specific Dream (Danehill Dancer (IRE)) (60000)
98 B c 7/3 Kheleyf (USA)—Takarna (IRE) (Mark of Esteem (IRE)) (10476) **Hambleton Racing Ltd XXXIX**

**Other Owners:** Mr K. M. Al-Mudhaf, Mr M. J. Al-Qatami, Mr Neil Armstrong, Mr Ronny Armstrong, Mrs Penelope Avison, Mr Richard Baker, Mr S. H. Bamforth, Mr Federico Barberini, Mr Andrew G. Bell, Mr J. N. Blackburn, Mr R. C. Bond, Mr C. S. Bond, Mr Pat Breslin, Mr S. Chappell, Mr Lester Christie, Lord Daresbury, Mr H. T. H. Dean, Mr David Dennis, Mr Andrew Dickman, Mr L. L. Dickman, Mr Gary Douglas, Favourites Racing, Mr R. G. Fell, Mr Tony Fell, Mr Ritchie Fiddes, Mr Arnie Flower, Mr M. P. Glass, Mr A. L. Gregg, Hambleton Racing Ltd, Mr B. K. Haughey, Helmsley Bloodstock, Mr Gary Hensby, Mrs Claire Hollowood, Mr M. Keating, Mr Jason Kelly, Mr Tony Kelvin, Mr R. Kent, Mr Muhammad Nadeem Khan, Mrs Yasmin Reana Nadeem Khan, Mr Philip Laidler, Mr M. F. Lawton, Mr C. J. Murfitt, Mr K. Nicholson, Mr Trevor Noble, Dr W. O'Brien, Mr D. O'Meara, Mr Garreth O'Shea, Mr T. S. Palin, Mr D. J. Pentney, Mr M. Prince, Mr Peppe Quintale, Mr John Simpson, Mr P. Sutherland, Mr Michael Taylor, Mr Geoffrey Turnbull, Mrs S. E. Turnbull, Mr S. R. H. Turner, Mr Andrew Turton, Mrs Gaynor Voute, Mr Robert Watson, Capt J. H. Wilson, Miss Margaret Wood.

**Jockey (flat):** Sam James, Daniel Tudhope. **Apprentice:** Josh Doyle. **Amateur:** Miss J. Gillam, Miss R. Heptonstall, Mr S. Murray.

---

## 467 MR JOHN O'NEILL, Bicester

Postal: **Hall Farm, Stratton Audley, Nr Bicester, Oxfordshire, OX27 9BT**
Contacts: **PHONE (01869) 277202 MOBILE (07785) 394128**
**E-MAIL jgoneill4@gmail.com**

1 **CABARET GIRL,** 8, ch m Karinga Bay—Little Miss Prim **Ms D. Keane**
2 **GAIETY STAR,** 6, b m Zafeen (FR)—Little Miss Prim **J. G. O'Neill**
3 **ONURBIKE,** 7, b g Exit To Nowhere (USA)—Lay It Off (IRE) **J. G. O'Neill**
4 **SAMIZDAT (FR),** 12, b g Soviet Star (USA)—Secret Account (FR) **J. G. O'Neill**
5 **SHOWBIZ FLOOZY,** 6, b m Beat All (USA)—Laced Up (IRE) **J. G. O'Neill**

---

## 468 MR JONJO O'NEILL, Cheltenham

Postal: **Jackdaws Castle, Temple Guiting, Cheltenham, Gloucestershire, GL54 5XU**
Contacts: **PHONE (01386) 584209 FAX (01386) 584219**
**E-MAIL reception@jonjooneillracing.com WEBSITE www.jonjooneillracing.com**

1 **ADAM DU BRETEAU (FR),** 5, ch g Network (GER)—Odelie de Fric (FR) **Mrs Gay Smith**
2 **ALAIVAN (IRE),** 9, b g Kalanisi (IRE)—Alaya (IRE) **Mr J. P. McManus**
3 **ALLOW DALLOW (IRE),** 8, b g Gold Well—Russland (GER) **Regulatory Finance Solutions Limited**

## MR JONJO O'NEILL - Continued

4 4, Br g Kalanisi (IRE)—Anshabella (IRE) **Mr E. A. Brook**
5 **AT RECEPTION (IRE),** 8, b g Gamut (IRE)—Receptionist **Mrs R. D. Hodgson & G & P Barker Ltd**
6 **AUVERGNAT (FR),** 5, b g Della Francesca (USA)—Hesmeralda (FR) **Mr J. P. McManus**
7 **BANDIT COUNTRY (IRE),** 6, b g Flemensfirth (USA)—
Calomeria **Mrs John Magnier, Mr D. Smith & Mr M. Tabor**
8 **BEG TO DIFFER (IRE),** 5, ch g Flemensfirth (USA)—Blossom Trix (IRE) **Mrs Jonjo O'Neill**
9 **BEGGARS CROSS (IRE),** 5, b g Presenting—Ballygill Heights (IRE) **Mr T. J. Hemmings**
10 **BLACKTHORN PRINCE,** 5, b g Black Sam Bellamy (IRE)—Quark Top (FR) **Mr J. P. McManus**
11 **BOX OFFICE (FR),** 4, b g Great Pretender (IRE)—Quelle Mome (FR) **Mr J. P. McManus**
12 **BRONCO BILLY (IRE),** 5, b g Flemensfirth (USA)—
La Fisarmonica (IRE) **Mrs John Magnier, Mr D. Smith & Mr M. Tabor**
13 **BURTON PORT (IRE),** 11, b g Bob Back (USA)—Despute (IRE) **Mr T. J. Hemmings**
14 **CAPARD KING (IRE),** 6, b g Beneficial—Capard Lady (IRE) **Mr J. B. Gilruth & G & P Barker Ltd**
15 **CAPOTE (IRE),** 7, b g Oscar (IRE)—Kinsellas Rose (IRE) **Mr T. J. Hemmings**
16 **CATCHING ON (IRE),** 7, b g Milan—Miracle Lady **Mrs Gay Smith**
17 **CHAMPAGNE AT TARA,** 6, gr g Kayf Tara—Champagne Lil **Mr J. P. McManus**
18 **CHAMPAGNE PRESENT (IRE),** 5, br g Presenting—My Name's Not Bin (IRE) **Mrs Gay Smith**
19 **CLOUDY COPPER (IRE),** 8, gr g Cloudings (IRE)—Copper Supreme (IRE) **Mrs Gay Smith**
20 **COMMUNICATOR,** 7, b g Motivator—Goodie Twosues **Lady Davis**
21 **DON PADEJA,** 5, br g Dansili—La Leuze (IRE) **G & P Barker Ltd & Yes No Wait Sorries**
22 **EASTLAKE (IRE),** 9, b g Beneficial—Guigone (FR) **Mr J. P. McManus**
23 **FAUVE (IRE),** 4, b c Montjeu (IRE)—Simaat (USA) **Mrs John Magnier, Mr D. Smith & Mr M. Tabor**
24 **FINDING YOUR FEET (IRE),** 7, b br g Heron Island (IRE)—Silvretta (IRE) **Mr J. P. McManus**
25 **FLINSTONE (IRE),** 6, b g Presenting—Sweet Liss (IRE) **Jackdaws Castle Crew**
26 **FOR INSTANCE (IRE),** 5, b g Milan—Justamemory (IRE) **Mrs Peter Bond**
27 **FORT WORTH (IRE),** 6, b g Presenting—Victorine (IRE) **Mrs John Magnier, Mr D. Smith & Mr M. Tabor**
28 **FORTHEFUNOFIT (IRE),** 6, b g Flemensfirth (USA)—Sommer Sonnet (IRE) **Mr J. P. McManus**
29 **FOUNDATION MAN (IRE),** 8, b g Presenting—Function Dream (IRE) **Mr P. Hickey**
30 **GET ME OUT OF HERE (IRE),** 11, b g Accordion—Home At Last (IRE) **Mr J. P. McManus**
31 **GOODWOOD MIRAGE (IRE),** 5, b g Jeremy (USA)—Phantom Waters **Lady Bamford & Alice Bamford**
32 **GRAY HESSION (IRE),** 8, b g Vinnie Roe (IRE)—Little Paddle (IRE) **Alan G. Gray**
33 **HAWAII FIVE NIL (IRE),** 7, b g Gold Well—Polish Rhythm (IRE) **Regulatory Finance Solutions Limited**
34 **HEDLEY LAMARR (IRE),** 5, b g Gold Well—Donna's Tarquin (IRE) **J. C. & S. R. Hitchins**
35 **HINTON FAIRGROUND,** 8, b g Fair Mix (IRE)—Hinton Luciana **N. Moores & N. Sercombe**
36 **HOLYWELL (IRE),** 8, b g Gold Well—Hillcrest (IRE) **Mrs Gay Smith**
37 **HURRICANE'S GIRL,** 6, b m Hurricane Run (IRE)—Wise Little Girl **Phil Tufnell Racing Club**
38 **IVY GATE (IRE),** 7, b g Westerner—Key Partner **Jeremy & Germaine Hitchins**
39 **JOHNS SPIRIT (IRE),** 8, b g Gold Well—Gilt Ridden (IRE) **Mr Christopher W. T. Johnston**
40 **JOIN THE CLAN (IRE),** 6, b g Milan—Millicent Bridge (IRE) **Mr J. P. McManus**
41 **KAMOOL (GER),** 5, ch g Mamool (IRE)—Kiss Me Lips (GER) **Lets Live Racing**
42 **KELVINGROVE (IRE),** 5, b g Hurricane Run (IRE)—Silversword (FR) **The All In Syndicate**
43 **LAST SHADOW,** 6, b g Notnowcato—Fairy Queen (IRE) **Mr J. P. McManus**
44 **LOST LEGEND (IRE),** 8, b g Winged Love (IRE)—Well Orchestrated (IRE) **Mrs Gay Smith**
45 **MACKERYE END (IRE),** 6, b g Milan—Great Outlook (IRE) **Valda Burke & Diana L. Whateley**
46 **MAD JACK MYTTON (IRE),** 5, b g Arcadio (GER)—Gilt Ridden (IRE) **J. C. & S. R. Hitchins**
47 **MAGHERAL EXPRESS (IRE),** 6, b g Gold Well—Patzanni (IRE) **Mr Christopher W. T. Johnston**
48 **MATORICO (IRE),** 4, gr g Mastercraftsman (IRE)—Hashbrown (GER) **Mr J. P. McManus**
49 **MAXIE T,** 4, b g Dalakhani (IRE)—Ballet Ballon (USA) **Mr Christopher W. T. Johnston**
50 **MERRY KING (IRE),** 8, ch g Old Vic—Merry Queen (IRE) **Frank Gillespie**
51 **MILAN BOUND (IRE),** 7, b g Milan—Bonnie And Bright (IRE) **Mr J. P. McManus**
52 **MINELLA ROCCO (IRE),** 5, b g Shirocco (GER)—Petralona (USA) **Mr J. P. McManus**
53 **MONBEG GOLD (IRE),** 5, b g Gold Well—Little Hand (IRE) **Martin Broughton Racing Partners 2**
54 **MONT ROYALE,** 7, b g Hurricane Run (IRE)—Wild Academy (IRE) **Phil Tufnell Racing Club**
55 **MONTDRAGON (FR),** 5, b g Turtle Bowl (IRE)—Bonne Gargotte (FR) **Mr J. P. McManus**
56 **MORE OF THAT (IRE),** 7, b g Beneficial—Guigone (FR) **Mr J. P. McManus**
57 **MR SHANTU (IRE),** 6, b g Shantou (USA)—Close To Shore (IRE) **Local Parking Security Limited**
58 **ONTHEWESTERNFRONT (IRE),** 5, b g Robin des Champs (FR)—
Asian Maze (IRE) **Mrs John Magnier, Mr D. Smith & Mr M. Tabor**
59 **OPTIMISTIC BIAS (IRE),** 6, b g Sayarshan (FR)—Dashers Folly (IRE) **Optimistic Four**
60 **OSCAR FORTUNE (IRE),** 7, b g Oscar (IRE)—Platin Run (IRE) **The Jackdaws Strangers**
61 **PETROVIC (IRE),** 6, b m Old Vic—Petralona (USA) **Jonjo O'Neill Racing Club**
62 **PLAYING THE FIELD (IRE),** 10, b g Deploy—Gaelic Buccaneer (IRE) **Mrs Sarah Hall-Tinker**
63 **PRESENCE FELT (IRE),** 7, br g Heron Island (IRE)—Faeroe Isle (IRE) **Mrs Peter Bond**
64 **RAINMAN (IRE),** 5, b g Craigsteel—Trolly Dolly (IRE) **Mr Gerry McManus**
65 **RAYAK (IRE),** 5, b g Invincible Spirit (IRE)—Rayyana (IRE) **Mrs Nan Hickey & Bensaranat Club**

## MR JONJO O'NEILL - Continued

66 **ROCK DES CHAMPS (IRE),** 5, b g Robin des Champs (FR)—Zaffaran Blends (IRE) **Michael & John O'Flynn**
67 **ROCK N RHYTHM (IRE),** 5, b g Rock of Gibraltar (IRE)—Dark Rosaleen (IRE) **Chanelle Medical Group U.K.**
68 **ROSE REVIVED,** 4, b f Midnight Legend—Miniature Rose **Jones Broughtons Wilson Weaver**
69 **RUM AND BUTTER (IRE),** 7, b g Milan—Silent Valley **Mr J. P. McManus**
70 **SAINT LUCY,** 4, b f Selkirk (USA)—Sister Maria (USA) **Lady Bamford**
71 **SEBASTIAN BEACH (IRE),** 4, b g Yeats (IRE)—Night Club **The Megsons**
72 **SHE'S LATE,** 5, ch g Pivotal—Courting **Mrs Diane Carr**
73 **SHUTTHEFRONTDOOR (IRE),** 8, b br g Accordion—Hurricane Girl (IRE) **Mr J. P. McManus**
74 **SINGININTHEVALLEYS,** 6, b m Kayf Tara—Con's Nurse (IRE) **Phil Tufnell Racing Club**
75 **SPOIL ME (IRE),** 8, b g Presenting—Akayid **Mrs Peter Bond**
76 **SPOOKYDOOKY (IRE),** 7, b g Winged Love (IRE)—Kiora Lady (IRE) **The Piranha Partnership**
77 **STAND ASIDE (IRE),** 5, b g Golan (IRE)—Lady Accord (IRE) **Mr Mark Dunphy**
78 **STEPS AND STAIRS (IRE),** 5, b g Robin des Pres (FR)—Be Mine Tonight (IRE) **Mr Mark Dunphy**
79 **SUNNYHILLBOY (IRE),** 12, b g Old Vic—Sizzle **Mr J. P. McManus**
80 **TAQUIN DU SEUIL (FR),** 8, b br g Voix du Nord (FR)—Sweet Laly (FR) **Martin Broughton & Friends 1**
81 **THE NEPHEW (IRE),** 7, b g Indian River (FR)—Charlottine (IRE) **Geoff & Peter Bond**
82 **THE SAINT JAMES (FR),** 4, b g Saint des Saints (FR)—Aimela (FR) **Mr J. P. McManus**
83 **THERE IS NO POINT (IRE),** 6, b m Galileo (IRE)—Akilana (IRE) **Mr J. P. McManus**
84 **TITCHWOOD (IRE),** 7, b g Flemensfirth (USA)—Aker Wood **Mrs Gay Smith**
85 **TODAY PLEASE (IRE),** 5, b g Westerner—Casiana (GER) **Mr Mark Dunphy**
86 **TOM LAMB,** 5, ch g Central Park (IRE)—Lucinda Lamb **The Four Bosses**
87 **TOMINATOR,** 8, gr g Generous (IRE)—Jucinda **Exors of the Late Mr P. A. Byrne**
88 **TULSA (IRE),** 5, b g Scorpion (IRE)—Native Sparkle (IRE) **Mrs John Magnier, Mr D. Smith & Mr M. Tabor**
89 **TWIRLING MAGNET (IRE),** 9, b g Imperial Ballet (IRE)—Molly Maguire (IRE) **Mrs Gay Smith**
90 **UPSWING (IRE),** 7, b g Beneficial—Native Country (IRE) **Mr J. P. McManus**
91 **USTICA (IRE),** 5, b g Trans Island—Shady's Wish (IRE) **Deep Sea Partnership**
92 **VUJIYAMA (FR),** 6, br g Voix du Nord (FR)—Ili Dancer (FR) **Mr J. P. McManus**
93 **WAIT A SECOND (IRE),** 5, b g Scorpion (IRE)—Fast Time (IRE) **Mr J. P. McManus**
94 **WALKAMI (FR),** 4, b g Walk In The Park (IRE)—Ominneha (FR) **Babbit Racing**
95 **WHISTLING SENATOR (IRE),** 8, b g Presenting—Merry Batim (IRE) **Mr J. P. McManus**
96 **WILD GINGER,** 4, ch g Presenting—Diamant Noir **Mrs Valda Burke**
97 **WORTHY AWARD (IRE),** 7, b g Presenting—Take Ine (FR) **Mr J. P. McManus**

### THREE-YEAR-OLDS

98 **QUARENTA (FR),** b br g Voix du Nord (FR)—Negresse de Cuta (FR) **Martin, Jocelyn & Steve Broughton**
99 **SAPPHIRE BLUE,** b g Dansili—Precious Gem (IRE) **Lady Bamford**

---

## 469 MR JOHN O'SHEA, Newnham-on-Severn

Postal: **The Stables, Bell House, Lumbars Lane, Newnham, Gloucestershire, GL14 1LH**
Contacts: **(01452) 760835 FAX (01452) 760233 MOBILE (07917) 124717**
**WEBSITE www.johnoshearacing.co.uk**

1 **CLEMENT (IRE),** 5, b g Clodovil (IRE)—Winnifred **K. W. Bell**
2 **COUP DE VENT,** 4, b f Tobougg (IRE)—Pigment **TR Racing Partnership**
3 **DESCARO (USA),** 9, gr g Dr Fong (USA)—Miarixa (FR) **The Sandcroft Partnership**
4 **DOUCHKIRK (FR),** 8, b g Prince Kirk (FR)—Douchka (FR) **The Cross Racing Club**
5 **LITTLEDEAN JIMMY (IRE),** 10, br g Indian Danehill (IRE)—Gold Stamp **K. W. Bell**
6 **NICKY NUTJOB (GER),** 9, b g Fasliyev (USA)—Natalie Too (USA) **Quality Pipe Supports (Q.P.S.) Ltd**
7 **NINEPOINTSIXTHREE,** 5, b g Bertolini (USA)—Armada Grove **The Cross Racing Club**
8 **PEAK STORM,** 6, b g Sleeping Indian—Jitterbug (IRE) **Cross Racing Club & Pete Smith Car Sales**
9 **PORT AND WARD (IRE),** 6, ch m Captain Rio—Gold Stamp **Mr M. G. Wooldridge**
10 **RADMORES EXPRESS,** 6, b g Primo Valentino (IRE)—Emma Lilley (USA) **J. R. Salter**
11 **RED SKIPPER (IRE),** 10, ch g Captain Rio—Speed To Lead (IRE) **K. W. Bell**
12 **RING EYE (IRE),** 7, b g Definite Article—Erins Lass (IRE) **Mr G. C. Roberts**
13 **STAFFORD CHARLIE,** 9, ch g Silver Patriarch (IRE)—Miss Roberto (IRE) **N. G. H. Ayliffe**
14 **STAFFORD JO,** 6, ch g Silver Patriarch (IRE)—Miss Roberto (IRE) **N. G. H. Ayliffe**
15 **SWENDAB (IRE),** 7, b g Trans Island—Lavish Spirit (USA) **The Cross Racing Club & Patrick Brady**
16 **TRIBAL DANCE (IRE),** 9, br g Flemensfirth (USA)—Native Sparkle (IRE) **Quality Pipe Supports (Q.P.S.) Ltd**
17 **WHEN IN ROAM (IRE),** 6, b m Flemensfirth (USA)—Roaming (IRE) **J. R. Salter**

### THREE-YEAR-OLDS

18 B c Major Cadeaux—Under My Spell **J. R. Salter**

## MR JOHN O'SHEA - Continued

**Other Owners:** P. Brady, Ms J. M. Brooks, C. L. Dubois, Mr S. P. Jenkins, Mr V. P. Nolan, P. Smith, Mrs S. Smith, Miss S. F. Willis.

**Jockey (flat):** Robert Havlin, Luke Morris, Fergus Sweeney. **Amateur:** Miss S. Randell.

---

## 470 MR GEOFFREY OLDROYD, Malton

Postal: **Flint Hall Farm, Morr Lane, Brawby, Malton, North Yorkshire, YO17 6PZ**
Contacts: **PHONE (01653) 668279 MOBILE (07730) 642620**

1 **ALFRED HUTCHINSON,** 7, ch g Monsieur Bond (IRE)—Chez Cherie **R. C. Bond**
2 **BOND ARTIST (IRE),** 6, b m Excellent Art—Pitrizza (IRE) **R. C. Bond**
3 **BOND EMPIRE,** 5, b g Misu Bond (IRE)—At Amal (IRE) **R. C. Bond**
4 **BOND FASTRAC,** 8, b g Monsieur Bond (IRE)—Kanisfluh **R. C. Bond**
5 **BOND IN RIO,** 4, ch f Captain Gerrard (IRE)—Kanisfluh **R. C. Bond**
6 **BOND'S GIFT,** 5, ch m Monsieur Bond (IRE)—Bond Shakira **South Yorkshire Racing**
7 **CROSSLEY,** 6, ch g Monsieur Bond (IRE)—Dispol Diamond **Mr G. R. Oldroyd**
8 **ETERNAL BOND,** 4, ch g Monsieur Bond (IRE)—Bond Babe **R. C. Bond**
9 **JAMAICAN BOLT (IRE),** 7, b g Pivotal—Chiming (IRE) **R. C. Bond**
10 **MAGICAL BOND,** 4, ch f Monsieur Bond (IRE)—Triple Tricks (IRE) **R. C. Bond**
11 **PRINCESS KHELEYF,** 6, b m Kheleyf (USA)—Jugendliebe (IRE) **Mr G. R. Oldroyd**
12 **REGAL BOND,** 4, b c Misu Bond (IRE)—Bond Royale **R. C. Bond**
13 **REGGIE BOND,** 5, ch g Monsieur Bond (IRE)—Triple Tricks (IRE) **R. C. Bond**

### THREE-YEAR-OLDS

14 B c Monsieur Bond (IRE)—Forever Bond **R. C. Bond**
15 **JUBILEE SPIRIT,** b g Misu Bond (IRE)—Bond Babe **Moneypenny Racing**
16 **WHAT USAIN,** b g Misu Bond (IRE)—Bond Shakira **R. C. Bond**

### TWO-YEAR-OLDS

17 B c 10/4 Big Bad Bob (IRE)—Jinxy Jill (Royal Applause) (14285)
18 B c 14/3 Monsieur Bond (IRE)—Lady Paris (IRE) (Invincible Spirit (IRE)) **R. C. Bond**
19 **MAJESTIC BOND,** b f 22/1 Misu Bond (IRE)—Bond Royale (Piccolo) (19047) **Casino Royale Racing**

**Other Owners:** Mr R. C. Bond, Mr C. S. Bond, Mr E. Dupont, Mr W. Standeven.

**Assistant Trainer:** Craig Lidster

---

## 471 MR HENRY OLIVER, Abberley

Postal: **Stable End, Worsley Racing Stables, Bank Lane, Abberley, Worcester, Worcestershire, WR6 6BQ**
Contacts: **PHONE (01299) 890143 MOBILE (07701) 068759**
**E-MAIL henryoliverracing@hotmail.co.uk WEBSITE www.henryoliverracing.co.uk**

1 **BEATABOUT THE BUSH (IRE),** 4, b br g Bushranger (IRE)—Queen of Fibres (IRE) **Ms S. Howell**
2 6, B g Craigsteel—Coolharbour Lady (IRE) **Mrs H. M. Oliver**
3 **CRESCENT BEACH (IRE),** 8, b g Presenting—Angelas Choice (IRE) **R. G. Whitehead**
4 **DAZINSKI,** 9, ch g Sulamani (IRE)—Shuheb **Mr D. M. J. Lloyd**
5 **DESERT RECLUSE (IRE),** 8, ch g Redback—Desert Design **Mr D. M. J. Lloyd**
6 **DIAMOND ROCK,** 4, b g Kayf Tara—Crystal Princess (IRE) **R. G. Whitehead**
7 **DRESDEN (IRE),** 7, b g Diamond Green (FR)—So Precious (IRE) **Mr D. M. J. Lloyd**
8 **GRIMLEY GIRL,** 9, b m Sir Harry Lewis (USA)—Grimley Gale (IRE) **R. M. Phillips**
9 **KEEL HAUL (IRE),** 7, br g Classic Cliche (IRE)—Tara Hall **R. G. Whitehead**
10 **MINELLAFORLUNCH (IRE),** 8, b g King's Theatre (IRE)—Loughaderra (IRE) **R. G. Whitehead**
11 **MONDERON (FR),** 8, b br g Laveron—Lomonde (FR) **Mr A. Lane**
12 **MOSCOW ME (IRE),** 8, b g Moscow Society (USA)—Just Trust Me (IRE) **Mrs H. M. Oliver**
13 **OZZY THOMAS (IRE),** 5, b g Gold Well—Bramble Leader (IRE) **Mrs H. M. Oliver**
14 **REVERSE THE ODDS,** 5, ch m Lucarno (USA)—Run Tiger (IRE) **Ms S. A. Howell**
15 **SIGNED REQUEST (IRE),** 8, b g Fantastic Quest (IRE)—Magic Sign (IRE) **Mrs H. M. Oliver**
16 **TAKE THE CROWN,** 6, gr g Fair Mix (IRE)—Miss Wizadora **R. G. Whitehead**
17 **THEREGOESTHETRUTH (IRE),** 7, b m Flemensfirth (USA)—Beagan Rose (IRE) **Mr Pius Collins**
18 **WHISPERING HARRY,** 6, b g Sir Harry Lewis (USA)—Welsh Whisper **R. G. Whitehead**
19 **WITHOUTDEFAVOURITE (IRE),** 7, b g Oscar (IRE)—Camden Confusion (IRE) **R. G. Whitehead**

**Assistant Trainer:** Heather Oliver

## 472 MR JAMIE OSBORNE, Upper Lambourn

Postal: **The Old Malthouse, Upper Lambourn, Hungerford, Berkshire, RG17 8RG**
Contacts: **PHONE (01488) 73139 FAX (01488) 73084 MOBILE (07860) 533422**
**E-MAIL info@jamieosborne.com WEBSITE www.jamieosborne.com**

1 **ANOTHER PARTY (FR),** 4, ch c Pomellato (GER)—Jummana (FR) **Michael Buckley & Merriebelle Irish Farm**
2 **FIELD OF DREAM,** 8, b g Oasis Dream—Field of Hope (IRE) **Middleham Park Racing**
3 **HARDY BLACK (IRE),** 4, b g Pastoral Pursuits—Wondrous Story (USA) **Patrick Gage & Tony Taylor**
4 **LORAINE,** 5, b m Sir Percy—Emirates First (IRE) **Mrs F Walwyn Lady Aitken Mr A Taylor**
5 **MONSIEUR CHABAL,** 4, b g Avonbridge—Coup de Torchon (FR) **Homecroft Wealth Racing**
6 **MONSIEUR CHEVALIER (IRE),** 8, b g Chevalier (IRE)—Blue Holly (IRE) **Mr D. Ferguson**
7 **ORATORIO'S JOY (IRE),** 5, b m Oratorio (IRE)—Seeking The Fun (USA) **Mr A. F. Tait**
8 **OUTER SPACE,** 4, b g Acclamation—Venoge (IRE) **Tony Taylor & Patrick Gage**
9 **SUMMERSAULT (IRE),** 4, b g Footstepsinthesand—Sumingasefa **Mrs F Walwyn Mr A Taylor Mr D Christian**
10 **THE DANDY YANK (IRE),** 4, b g Dandy Man (IRE)—Bronze Queen (IRE) **Chris Watkins & David N. Reynolds**
11 **TOAST OF NEW YORK (USA),** 4, b c Thewayyouare (USA)—Claire Soleil (USA) **Al Shaqab Racing**

### THREE-YEAR-OLDS

12 **ABSOLUTE CHAMPION (USA),** b g Henrythenavigator (USA)—Alegendinmyownmind **Mr M. C. E. Wong**
13 **BORN TO BE BAD (IRE),** b g Arcano (IRE)—Lady of Kildare (IRE) **M Buckley J Chambers S Collins A Rowland**
14 **CAMDORA (IRE),** b f Arcano (IRE)—Crimphill (IRE) **Lady Blyth**
15 **DARK AVENGER (USA),** b br c Scat Daddy (USA)—Luxaholic (USA) **M. A. C. Buckley**
16 **DECLAN,** ch c Dylan Thomas (IRE)—Fleurissimo **Normandie Stud Ltd**
17 **FENG SHUI,** b g Iffraaj—Whazzis **Mr & Mrs R. G. Kelvin-Hughes**
18 **FROZEN PRINCESS,** b f Showcasing—Super Midge **Barratt & Johnsons**
19 **HEART OF THE SEA (IRE),** b f Rip Van Winkle (IRE)—
Langoustine (AUS) **D. Graham, Michael Buckley & Mrs P. Shanahan**
20 **HOUDINI,** b c Pivotal—Regina **Mr & Mrs R. G. Kelvin-Hughes**
21 **JOLLY JUICESTER (IRE),** b f Jeremy (USA)—Derval (IRE) **Mr D. G. Christian**
22 **KODIAC KROSSING,** b f Kodiac—Special Destiny **A&T Racing Club**
23 **LA CUESTA (IRE),** b f Showcasing—Dowager **Mr & Mrs R. G. Kelvin-Hughes**
24 **LIFE LESS ORDINARY (IRE),** b g Thewayyouare (USA)—
Dont Cross Tina (IRE) **Mr Michael Buckley & Mrs Karima Burman**
25 **LITTLE,** b f Paco Boy (IRE)—Wafeira **Mr A. F. Tait**
26 **MAJENSKI (IRE),** b g Camacho—D'addario (IRE) **Fromthestables.com & Partner**
27 **RIALTO MAGIC,** b f Monsieur Bond (IRE)—Discover Roma (IRE) **Fromthestables.com & Partner**
28 **SLEIGHT OF HAND (IRE),** b c Galileo (IRE)—Queen of France (USA) **M. A. C. Buckley**
29 **TOAST OF NEWBURY (IRE),** ch c Captain Rio—Pearl of The Sea (IRE) **Barratt, Devlin, Mulvey & Stronge**
30 **TUCO (IRE),** ch g Exceed And Excel (AUS)—Life Rely (USA) **Mrs G. Widdowson & Mrs R. Kelvin-Hughes**

### TWO-YEAR-OLDS

31 B f 1/3 Oasis Dream—Applauded (IRE) (Royal Applause) (150000) **Mrs P Shanahan Mrs H Lascelles Mr T Hyde**
32 B f 27/4 Dark Angel (IRE)—Border Minstral (IRE) (Sri Pekan (USA)) **Charlie Nelson & Partners**
33 **CANFORD CHIMES (IRE),** b c 4/4 Canford Cliffs (IRE)—
Appleblossom Pearl (IRE) (Peintre Celebre (USA)) (60000) **Apple Tree Stud**
34 B c 21/3 Holy Roman Emperor (IRE)—Ceoil An Aith (IRE) (Accordion) (45000) **Edmond Lee & Mr Fra Ma**
35 **DALAVAND (IRE),** ch c 29/3 Tamayuz—Kirunavaara (IRE) (Galileo (IRE)) **Apple Tree Stud**
36 Ch f 6/4 Cape Blanco (IRE)—Down The Well (IRE) (Mujadil (USA)) (11474) **Mr Danny Durkan**
37 **DREAM DANA (IRE),** b f 2/2 Dream Ahead (USA)—Lidanna (Nicholas (USA)) (100000) **Apple Tree Stud**
38 B f 5/2 Clodovil (IRE)—Elouges (IRE) (Dalakhani (IRE)) (21904) **Bo Derek's 10**
39 B f 2/2 Kodiac—Good Shot Noreen (IRE) (Sleeping Indian) (11428) **Homecroft Wealth Racing**
40 **HUNGARIAN RHAPSODY,** b c 13/2 Showcasing—
Rockburst (Xaar) (85000) **M. Buckley, Mrs S. Ricci & Mrs P. Shanahan**
41 **INHERENT VICE (IRE),** b c 27/4 Kodiac—
Ting A Greeley (Mr Greeley (USA)) (43650) **Mrs S. Ricci, M. Buckley, Mrs P. Shanahan**
42 B f 27/4 Zoffany (IRE)—Intimate Secret (IRE) (Invincible Spirit (IRE)) (5555) **Bo Derek's 10**
43 B c 9/2 Frozen Power (IRE)—Karaliyfa (IRE) (Kahyasi) (38095)
44 B f 19/3 Lawman (FR)—Kayak (Singspiel (IRE)) (14000) **Mr & Mrs I Barratt**
45 B c 21/1 Thewayyouare (USA)—Korresia (IRE) (Elnadim (USA)) (11904) **Fromthestables.com Racing**
46 Ch c 19/4 Roderic O'Connor (IRE)—
La Grande Zoa (IRE) (Fantastic Light (USA)) (18000) **Dunkley, Gumienny & Signy**
47 **LONG JOHN SILVER (IRE),** b c 14/4 Canford Cliffs (IRE)—
Billet (IRE) (Danehill (USA)) (83333) **M. Buckley, Mrs S. Ricci, Mrs P. Shanahan**
48 B f 17/4 Lawman (FR)—Mamela (GER) (Protektor (GER)) (19840) **Bo Derek's 10**
49 B c 4/4 Thewayyouare (USA)—Margaux Dancer (IRE) (Danehill Dancer (IRE)) (19840) **Michael Buckley**

## MR JAMIE OSBORNE - Continued

**50** B f 27/3 Lilbourne Lad (IRE)—Mary Spring Rice (IRE) (Saffron Walden (FR)) (23000)
**51** Ch f 4/3 Compton Place—Miss Rimex (IRE) (Ezzoud (IRE)) (7619) **Heads You Win Partnership**
**52** B c 5/4 Bahamian Bounty—Miss Villefranche (Danehill Dancer (IRE)) (48000)
**53** B f 14/1 Dream Ahead (USA)—
Moonlit Garden (IRE) (Exceed And Excel (AUS)) (33333) **Ian Barratt, Stephen Short & Adam Signy**
**54 PACKING (IRE),** b c 25/3 Lilbourne Lad (IRE)—Elegant Ridge (IRE) (Indian Ridge) (32000) **Mr & Mrs I Barratt**
**55** B f 27/3 Kyllachy—Poetical (IRE) (Croco Rouge (IRE)) (79364) **Mr & Mrs R. Kelvin-Hughes**
**56** B c 24/3 Henrythenavigator (USA)—
Purple (USA) (Royal Academy (USA)) (20000) **Chris Watkins & David N. Reynolds**
**57 RUE RIVOLI (IRE),** b c 6/4 Champs Elysees—
Rondo Alla Turca (IRE) (Noverre (USA)) (120000) **Mrs S. Ricci, M. Buckley & Mrs P. Shanahan**
**58** Ch f 13/5 Excellent Art—Savignano (Polish Precedent (USA))
**59** B f 14/4 Danehill Dancer (IRE)—Souter's Sister (IRE) (Desert Style (IRE)) **Mr Deron Pearson**
**60** B f 7/2 High Chaparral (IRE)—Summerhill Parkes (Zafonic (USA)) (20000) **Bo Derek's 10**
**61 WAYFARING STRANGER (IRE),** b c 28/2 Lope de Vega (IRE)—
Portelet (Night Shift (USA)) (71428) **M. Buckley & M. Watt**
**62** B f 16/3 Dream Ahead (USA)—Zeiting (IRE) (Zieten (USA)) (174602) **Mr & Mrs R. Kelvin-Hughes**

**Assistant Trainer:** Jimmy McCarthy

**Apprentice:** Lucy Barry, Kirsten Smith.

---

## 473 MR HUGO PALMER, Newmarket

Postal: **Kremlin Cottage Stables, Snailwell Road, Newmarket, Suffolk, CB8 7DP**
Contacts: **PHONE (01638) 669880 FAX (01638) 666383 MOBILE (07824) 887886**
**E-MAIL info@hugopalmer.com WEBSITE www.hugopalmer.com**

**1 ASCRIPTION (IRE),** 6, b g Dansili—Lady Elgar (IRE) **Mr V. I. Araci**
**2 EXTREMITY (IRE),** 4, ch g Exceed And Excel (AUS)—Chanterelle (IRE) **Kremlin Cottage II**
**3 FREMONT (IRE),** 8, b g Marju (IRE)—Snow Peak **Mr H. Palmer**
**4 LOBSTER POT,** 4, b f Dylan Thomas (IRE)—Classical Flair **Anglia Bloodstock Syndicate II**
**5 ROYAL MEMORY,** 4, b f Invincible Spirit (IRE)—Entre Nous (IRE) **Mr V. I. Araci**
**6 SHE'S MINE (IRE),** 4, b f Sea The Stars (IRE)—Scribonia (IRE) **Mr V. I. Araci**
**7 SHORT SQUEEZE (IRE),** 5, b g Cape Cross (IRE)—Sunsetter (USA) **W Duff Gordon, R Smith, B Mathieson**

### THREE-YEAR-OLDS

**8 AIR OF ASTANA (IRE),** b g Equiano (FR)—Fairnilee **Air Of Astana Partnership**
**9 AKTABANTAY,** b c Oasis Dream—Splashdown **Mr V. I. Araci**
**10 BELLA NOSTALGIA (IRE),** ch f Raven's Pass (USA)—Fafinta (IRE) **Mr V. I. Araci**
**11 COVERT LOVE (IRE),** b f Azamour (IRE)—Wing Stealth (IRE) **FOMO Syndicate**
**12 FALCON OF MALTA,** b g Sir Percy—Fizzy Treat **Ballymore Sterling Syndicate**
**13 HOME OF THE BRAVE (IRE),** ch c Starspangledbanner (AUS)—
Blissful Beat **Flemington Bloodstock Partnership**
**14 MILLEFIORI (IRE),** ch f Mastercraftsman (IRE)—La Lunete **Chris Humber & Amanda Brudenell**
**15 NEW PROVIDENCE,** ch f Bahamian Bounty—Bayja (IRE) **Mr C. M. Humber**
**16 NOT NEVER,** ch g Notnowcato—Watchoverme **Mrs D. M. Haynes**
**17 ONLY JOKING,** b f Aussie Rules (USA)—Cliche (IRE) **Anglia Bloodstock Syndicate V**
**18 PEACE PRIZE (IRE),** b f Alfred Nobel (IRE)—Applaud (USA) **Kremlin Cottage VII**
**19 PERSIFLAGE,** b f Sir Percy—Emirates First (IRE) **Kremlin Cottage V**
**20 SILVERY BLUE,** b f Paco Boy (IRE)—Blue Echo **Mrs Mary Taylor & Mr James Taylor**
**21 SPANISH SQUEEZE (IRE),** ch c Lope de Vega (IRE)—Appetina **W Duff Gordon, J Bond, Rascals Racing**
**22 SPIRIT OF SOUND (FR),** b f Invincible Spirit (IRE)—Sound of Summer (USA) **Mr V. I. Araci**
**23 STRONG STEPS,** br c Aqlaam—Wunders Dream (IRE) **Mr V. I. Araci**
**24 TWITCH (IRE),** b f Azamour (IRE)—Blinking **The Duke of Roxburghe & The Duke of Devonshire**
**25 ZIGGURAT (IRE),** gr c Tagula (IRE)—Visual Element (USA) **Mr C. M. Humber**

### TWO-YEAR-OLDS

**26** B c 25/3 Dutch Art—Bay of Pearls (IRE) (Rock of Gibraltar (IRE)) (40000)
**27** B c 15/2 Champs Elysees—Belgooree (Haafhd) (20000) **Mr A. Al Mansoori**
**28** B f 14/3 Azamour (IRE)—Bridal Dance (IRE) (Danehill Dancer (IRE)) (63491) **Mr C. M. Humber**
**29** B f 23/2 Zoffany (IRE)—Brigayev (ITY) (Fasliyev (USA)) (24761) **Mr C. M. Humber**
**30** B f 20/2 Mastercraftsman (IRE)—Dama'a (IRE) (Green Desert (USA)) (35000)
**31** B c 18/2 Lope de Vega (IRE)—Danielli (IRE) (Danehill (USA)) (150000) **Mr V. I. Araci**
**32** Ch f 12/3 Raven's Pass (USA)—Dubai Moon (USA) (Malibu Moon (USA)) (20000) **S. Manana**

## MR HUGO PALMER - Continued

**33** B c 11/4 Teofilo (IRE)—Eclaircie (IRE) (Thunder Gulch (USA)) **Sheikh J. D. Al Maktoum**
**34** Br f 30/3 Dark Angel (IRE)—Embassy Pearl (IRE) (Invincible Spirit (IRE)) (20000) **Mr H. Palmer**
**35** B f 23/1 Elusive Quality (USA)—Fashion Insider (USA) (Indian Charlie (USA)) (86058) **Sheikh J. D. Al Maktoum**
**36** Ch f 13/5 Mount Nelson—Fidelio's Miracle (USA) (Mountain Cat (USA)) (31745)
**37 FIFTYSHADESOFPINK (IRE),** b f 18/3 Pour Moi (IRE)—
Maakrah (Dubai Destination (USA)) (68000) **Mrs M. Bryce**
**38** Br c 19/3 Big Bad Bob (IRE)—Fire Up (Motivator) (69047) **Westward Bloodstock Limited**
**39** Ch c 31/1 Paco Boy (IRE)—Galicuix (Galileo (IRE)) (26190)
**40 INDIA,** ch f 24/3 Paco Boy (IRE)—Friendlier (Zafonic (USA)) **W. J. and T. C. O. Gredley**
**41** Ch c 11/3 Pivotal—Invitee (Medicean) (51587)
**42** Ch c 26/4 Mastercraftsman (IRE)—Jacquelin Jag (IRE) (Fayruz) (15000)
**43** B f 20/2 Fastnet Rock (AUS)—
Jewel In The Sand (IRE) (Bluebird (USA)) (70000) **Mr M V Magnier & Partners/ T Hyde**
**44** B c 16/3 Raven's Pass (USA)—Lady Elgar (IRE) (Sadler's Wells (USA)) (87301) **Mr V. I. Araci**
**45** B c 5/3 Oasis Dream—Lion Forest (USA) (Forestry (USA)) **Mr V. I. Araci**
**46 MAGICAL PATH (IRE),** b gr f 26/4 Zebedee—
Road To Reality (IRE) (Indian Danehill (IRE)) (15872) **Anglia Bloodstock Syndicate VI**
**47** Ch c 22/1 Arcano (IRE)—Manuelita Rose (ITY) (Desert Style (IRE)) (37000)
**48** B f 1/5 Teofilo (IRE)—Mazaaya (USA) (Cozzene (USA)) **S. Ali**
**49** B f 5/1 Cape Blanco (IRE)—Moon Giant (USA) (Giant's Causeway (USA)) (119047) **Mr V. I. Araci**
**50** B f 15/4 Royal Applause—Nahab (Selkirk (USA)) **S. Ali**
**51** Ch f 21/3 Shamardal (USA)—Neshla (Singspiel (IRE)) (45000) **S. Manana**
**52 NIDNOD,** b f 4/2 Myboycharlie (IRE)—
Littlemisstutti (IRE) (Noverre (USA)) (30000) **Anglia Bloodstock Syndicate VII**
**53** B c 25/4 Cockney Rebel (IRE)—Nine Red (Royal Applause) **R. C. Tooth**
**54 PERU,** b f 25/3 Motivator—Bolsena (USA) (Red Ransom (USA)) **W. J. and T. C. O. Gredley**
**55** B c 31/3 Poet's Voice—Poppo's Song (CAN) (Polish Navy (USA)) (45000) **De La Warr Racing**
**56** Ch c 27/2 Compton Place—Setting Forth (IRE) (Daggers Drawn (USA)) (35000)
**57 SHERIFF (IRE),** b c 14/4 Lawman (FR)—Dievotchkina (IRE) (Bluebird (USA)) (65000) **W. J. and T. C. O. Gredley**
**58** B c 3/4 Kodiac—Shobobb (Shamardal (USA)) (75000) **Dr A. Ridha**
**59** B br c 20/3 Elusive Pimpernel (USA)—Spiritville (IRE) (Invincible Spirit (IRE)) (39681)
**60** B c 21/3 Rock of Gibraltar (IRE)—Splashdown (Falbrav (IRE)) (85000) **Mr V. I. Araci**
**61** B f 30/3 Fast Company (IRE)—Sweet Home Alabama (IRE) (Desert Prince (IRE)) (27619) **Mr V. I. Araci**
**62 THE PARIS SHRUG,** b f 2/3 Manduro (GER)—
Miss Brown To You (IRE) (Fasliyev (USA)) **W. J. and T. C. O. Gredley**
**63** B c 9/4 Raven's Pass (USA)—Trading Places (Dansili) (20000) **Mr A. Al Mansoori**
**64** B f 9/5 Acclamation—Turning Light (GER) (Fantastic Light (USA)) (35000) **Seventh Lap Racing**
**65** B c 24/3 Sea The Stars (IRE)—Unity (IRE) (Sadler's Wells (USA)) (180000) **Mr V. I. Araci**
**66** B c 9/2 Kodiac—Zonic (Zafonic (USA)) (15000) **Seventh Lap Racing**

**Other Owners:** Mr D. A. Bovington, Mrs A. J. Brudenell, Mr C. G. A. Budgett, Mr C. Chisholm, Lord De La Warr, Countess De La Warr, The Duke of Devonshire, W. A. L. Duff Gordon, W. J. Gredley, T. C. O. Gredley, Mr P. Hernon, T. Hyde, Mr R. P. Jones, Mr R. P. Legh, Mr K. MacLennan, Mr M. V. Magnier, Miss P. E. Mains, Mr B. L. Mathieson, Mr M. J. McStay, Mr M. D. Moroney, Mrs V. H. Pakenham, Mr M. A. Ramsden, The Duke Of Roxburghe, Mrs L. M. Shanahan, Mr R. Smith, Mrs M. F. Taylor, Mr J. F. Taylor, Miss V. Webb.

**Apprentice:** Noel Garbutt.

---

## 474 MR H. A. PANTALL, Beaupreau

Postal: **Le Bois du Coin, Beaupreau 49600, France**
Contacts: **PHONE (0033) 241 636715 FAX (0033) 241 630530 MOBILE (0033) 607 450647**
**E-MAIL hapantall@wanadoo.fr WEBSITE www.ecuriepantall.fr**

**1 ANGELIC NEWS (FR),** 4, b f American Post—Angel Wing
**2 BONNOPTION,** 4, gr f Myboycharlie (IRE)—Slyta (FR)
**3 BONTONI (FR),** 5, ro g Silvano (GER)—Brictop (USA)
**4 CHORTLE,** 4, b f Dubawi (IRE)—Portmanteau
**5 DEUXIEME EMPIRE (FR),** 4, b c Naaqoos—Dentelle (FR)
**6 DIX NEUF SIX,** 4, b f Pyrus (USA)—Johanie Cara (FR)
**7 DOWNHILL ONLY,** 4, b g Montjeu (IRE)—Miss Emma May (IRE)
**8 EASTERBURG (FR),** 4, b c Sageburg (IRE)—Crazy Mask (IRE)
**9 GAMMARTH (FR),** 7, ch h Layman (USA)—Emouna Queen (IRE)
**10 GLOBAL JET (FR),** 4, ch g Kendargent (FR)—Norwegian Princess (IRE)
**11 HAZUMI (GER),** 4, b g Monsun (GER)—Hanami

## MR H. A. PANTALL - Continued

12 **IMPORTANT TIME (IRE),** 4, b f Oasis Dream—Satwa Queen (FR)
13 **JULIE CLARY (IRE),** 5, b m Dubai Destination (USA)—Queen of Naples
14 **KAMELLATA (FR),** 4, b f Pomellato (GER)—Kamakura (GER)
15 **LANDYM (FR),** 4, b c Lando (GER)—Ymlaen (IRE)
16 **LEXCEED (GER),** 4, ch c Exceed And Excel (AUS)—La Hermana
17 **LIVING DESERT,** 5, gr g Oasis Dream—Sell Out
18 **LOCAL LOVER (FR),** 5, b h Choisir (AUS)—La Victoria (IRE)
19 **LOVELY STORY (IRE),** 4, b f Cape Cross (IRE)—Hush Money (CHI)
20 **MATORIO (FR),** 5, b m Oratorio (IRE)—Matwan (FR)
21 **MI VIDA (FR),** 4, b c Meshaheer (USA)—Belle Suisse (FR)
22 **MOMAYYAZ (IRE),** 4, b f Elusive Quality (USA)—Surrealism
23 **MORENA (FR),** 4, b f Zafeen (FR)—Star Godess (FR)
24 **NAJMA,** 4, b f Cape Cross (IRE)—Silkwood
25 **NALOUDIA (IRE),** 4, ch f Piccolo—Fanciful Dancer
26 **NIJAH (IRE),** 4, b f Pivotal—Vista Bella
27 **ORAGE NOIR (FR),** 4, b c Astronomer Royal (USA)—Atlantic Crossing (GER)
28 **ORANGEFIELD (FR),** 4, b g Soave (GER)—Moon Serenade
29 **ORION BEST (FR),** 4, b f King's Best (USA)—Okocha (GER)
30 **PASSARINHO (IRE),** 6, ch h Ad Valorem (USA)—Semiramide (IRE)
31 **PRAIRIE SALSA (FR),** 4, b f Meshaheer (USA)—Prairie Scilla (GER)
32 **PRINCESS BAVAROISE (FR),** 4, b f Desert Prince (IRE)—Sascilaria
33 **PUPA DI SARONNO (ITY),** 4, b f Orpen (USA)—Olonella
34 **RANGALI,** 4, ch c Namid—Tejaara (USA)
35 **RISADA (FR),** 4, b f Desert Style (IRE)—Romanche (FR)
36 **SCHOLARLY,** 4, b f Authorized (IRE)—Historian (IRE)
37 **SEE YOU SOON (FR),** 4, b c Zafeen (FR)—Summer Dance (FR)
38 **SIBLING HONOUR,** 4, b f Bernardini (USA)—Porto Roca (AUS)
39 **SIR TOBY (FR),** 4, b g Linngari (IRE)—Woodcut (SAF)
40 **SNAPE MALTINGS (IRE),** 8, b g Sadler's Wells (USA)—Hanami
41 **SON CESIO (FR),** 4, b c Zafeen (FR)—Slitana (FR)
42 **SORRY WOMAN (FR),** 5, b m Ivan Denisovich (IRE)—Oppamattox (FR)
43 **SPLIT STEP,** 4, b c Bahamian Bounty—Nellie Gwyn
44 **TANGATCHEK (IRE),** 6, ch h Mr Greeley (USA)—Tivadare (FR)
45 **TRUE MATCH (IRE),** 4, b f Cape Cross (IRE)—West Wind
46 **VANISHING CUPID (SWI),** 5, b h Galileo (IRE)—Vanishing Prairie (USA)
47 **ZYLPHA (IRE),** 4, b f Elusive City (USA)—Zaltana (USA)

## THREE-YEAR-OLDS

48 **A MAGIC TIGER (IRE),** br c Naaqoos—Magic Sun (GER)
49 **ALMA MARCEAU (FR),** ch f Kendargent—Avenue Marceau
50 **ALPINKATZE (FR),** ch f Linngari (IRE)—Amerissage (USA)
51 **AMERICAN ART (FR),** b g Excellent Art—Tres American Girl
52 **ANA'S BEST (FR),** b f King's Best (USA)—Ana Marie (FR)
53 **ANGEL ROYAL (FR),** b c Astronomer Royal (USA)—Lady Angele (FR)
54 **ANOTHER DANCE (FR),** b f Zafeen (FR)—American Tune (IRE)
55 **ARCHANGE (FR),** b f Arcano (IRE)—Carinae (USA)
56 **ASOMOUD MISRATA,** b c Champs Elysees—Passata (FR)
57 **BARBARA (FR),** b f Samson Happy (JPN)—Ballet Girl (USA)
58 **BARTAVELLE,** b f Makfi—West of Saturn (USA)
59 **BATTIT (FR),** b c Evasive—Dill (IRE)
60 **BEAUPREAU,** b c Mr Sidney (USA)—Kathy's Rocket (USA)
61 **BIG BOWL,** ch c Shamardal (USA)—Flower Bowl (FR)
62 **BIG LETTERS (IRE),** b f Whipper (USA)—Big Monologue (IRE)
63 **BLUE SMOKE (FR),** b c Zafeen (FR)—Blue Roses (IRE)
64 **BOWL IMPERIOR,** ch c Raven's Pass (USA)—Turtle Point (USA)
65 **CARRY OUT (FR),** b c Air Chief Marshal (IRE)—Respite
66 **CAYAMBE (SWI),** b c Blue Canari (FR)—Copacabana (IRE)
67 **CHASING ICE (IRE),** b f Duke of Marmalade (IRE)—Ballerina Blue (IRE)
68 **CHERBOURG (FR),** b c Dunkerque (FR)—Seduisante (FR)
69 **CIBOULETTE (IRE),** ch f Pivotal—Cumin (USA)
70 **CRACCO BOY (FR),** b c Creachadoir (IRE)—Goldy Honor (FR)
71 **DANTESSA (FR),** b f Soldier of Fortune (IRE)—Alsu (IRE)
72 **DAWN PRAYER,** b c Acclamation—Nice Matin (USA)
73 **DIAMOND RED (FR),** b c Diamond Green (FR)—Massatixa (FR)
74 **DIPANKARA (FR),** gr f Aqlaam—La Barquera

## MR H. A. PANTALL - Continued

75 **EARNESTINE (GER),** b f New Approach (IRE)—Earthly Paradise (GER)
76 **EL SUIZO (FR),** b c Meshaheer (USA)—Belle Suisse (FR)
77 **EMIRATES REWARDS,** ch f Dubawi (IRE)—Asi Siempre (USA)
78 **FLASHEEN (FR),** ch g Zafeen—Rain Lily
79 **FOND WORDS (IRE),** b f Shamardal (USA)—Nashmiah (IRE)
80 **FRASQUITA,** b f Equiano (FR)—Fabulously Red
81 **GENERATION DISCO (FR),** bl f Early March—Lady Stapara (IRE)
82 **GOKEN (FR),** b c Kendargent (FR)—Gooseley Chope (FR)
83 **GREEN FANCY (FR),** b f Diamond Green (FR)—Fancy Diamond (GER)
84 **GWALCHAVED,** b c Silver Frost (IRE)—Good Hope (GER)
85 **HIGH LAW (FR),** b c Lawman (FR)—High Limits (IRE)
86 **IMPERIALISTA,** ch f Halling (USA)—Empress Maud (USA)
87 **JUDGEMENT OF PARIS (FR),** b f Cape Cross (IRE)—Golden Bottle (USA)
88 **KALQOOS (SWI),** b g Naaqoos—Kalti (FR)
89 **KATALEYA (FR),** b f Youmzain—Kamakura
90 **KENFREEZE (FR),** b c Kendargent (FR)—Damdam Freeze (FR)
91 **KENOUSKA (FR),** ch f Kendargent (FR)—Dame Anouska (IRE)
92 **KENSHA (FR),** b f Kendargent (FR)—Sabasha (FR)
93 **KENZINGO (FR),** gr c Kendargent—Blazing Beauty
94 **KHAREEF (IRE),** ch c Monsun (GER)—Hanami
95 **KINGPHIL,** ch c Notnowcato—Hot And Spicy
96 **LADY SYBIL (FR),** b f Siyouni (FR)—Arsila (IRE)
97 **LEADER WRITER (FR),** b c Pivotal—Miss Emma May (IRE)
98 **LINNWOOD (FR),** b g Linngari (IRE)—Woodcut (SAF)
99 **LOVEMEDO (FR),** ch f Zafeen (FR)—Suvretta Queen (IRE)
100 **LUTECE,** b f Cape Cross (IRE)—Loutka (FR)
101 **MANRICO,** b c Montjeu (IRE)—Majoune (FR)
102 **MAYBE RIVER (FR),** b f Stormy River—Maybe (GER)
103 **MIND STORY (FR),** b f Diamond Green (FR)—Mind Master (USA)
104 **MISS SOPHIE (FR),** b f Linngari (IRE)—Western Bowl (USA)
105 **MISTER IFF,** b c Iffraaj—Miss Sissy (FR)
106 **MUST BE THE ONE (FR),** b f Meshaheer (USA)—Silver Market (FR)
107 **MY COUNTRY (IRE),** b f Invincible Spirit (IRE)—National Day (IRE)
108 **MYLA ROSE (FR),** ch f Danehill Dancer (IRE)—Sunday Rose
109 **NACHT (FR),** b f Sabiango (GER)—Nonoalka (GER)
110 **NAVIGATRICE,** gr f Aussie Rules (USA)—Nightdance Sun (GER)
111 **NEW RECORD (IRE),** br c Dansili—Precocious Star (IRE)
112 **ORION KING (IRE),** b c King's Best (USA)—Okocha (GER)
113 **ORYM (FR),** b c Orpen (USA)—Ymlaen (IRE)
114 **PLAISIR D'AMOUR (FR),** b f Linngari (IRE)—Analfabeta (FR)
115 **POP CHART,** b f Dubawi (IRE)—Baila Me (GER)
116 **PRADARA (FR),** b f Aussie Rules (USA)—Vaillante (IRE)
117 **PROCESSIONAL (USA),** gr ro f Authorized (IRE)—Wedding March (IRE)
118 **RANDIUM (FR),** b f Sinndar—Retina (GER)
119 **REINE MAGIQUE,** ch f Mount Nelson—Reading Habit (USA)
120 **ROYAL GREEN (FR),** b f Myboycharlie (IRE)—October Winds (USA)
121 **SCALA DI MILANO,** b f Motivator—Serpina (IRE)
122 **SHANAKILLA (FR),** gr f Lord Shanakill (USA)—Carinamix (FR)
123 **SHINING BAY,** b f Makfi—Costa Brava (IRE)
124 **SILVER LAKE (FR),** b f Silver Frost (IRE)—Miss Loulou (FR)
125 **SOUND MONEY,** b c Zamindar (USA)—Alpensinfonie (IRE)
126 **SPINNING CLOUD (USA),** b f Street Cry (IRE)—Sky Song (IRE)
127 **SVELTEZZA (FR),** b f Soldier of Fortune (IRE)—Suerte Loca (IRE)
128 **TANDRAGEE (USA),** b f Bernardini (USA)—Abhisheka (IRE)
129 **TEJAHAA (FR),** ch f Haafhd—Tejaara (USA)
130 **TIMIZMIZ (FR),** b f Zebedee—La Ville Lumiere (USA)
131 **TOUBAX (FR),** b f Aqlaam—Bold Classic (USA)
132 **TRADE FLOW (FR),** b c Danehill Dancer (IRE)—Dubai Rose
133 **TRIESTE,** ch f Dubawi (IRE)—Porto Roca (AUS)
134 **TRIGGER TOUCH (FR),** b f Panis—Trigger Shot
135 **TRUE REFLECTION (IRE),** b f Mastercraftsman (IRE)—Glittering Prize (UAE)
136 **TRULLY ME (FR),** b f Cima de Triomphe (IRE)—Trully Belle (IRE)
137 **UNION SACREE (FR),** b f Naaqoos—Queen's Conquer
138 **VAL D'HIVER (FR),** bl f Zafeen (FR)—Verzasca (IRE)
139 **VANGAUG (FR),** b c Gentlewave (IRE)—Be Yourself (FR)

## MR H. A. PANTALL - Continued

**140 WOOMIE (IRE),** ch f Mastercraftsman (IRE)—Pom Pom Pom
**141 XAARINA (FR),** gr f Aussie Rules (USA)—Xaarienne
**142 ZARIYANO (FR),** ch c Linngari (IRE)—Zariyana (IRE)

## TWO-YEAR-OLDS

**143 ACCORD D'ARGENT (FR),** gr f 29/1 Kendargent—Accordia (Smart Strike)
**144** B c 1/1 Invincible Spirit (IRE)—Alpensinfonie (IRE) (Montjeu (IRE))
**145** B c 16/5 Royal Applause—Alsace (King's Best (USA)) (29365)
**146 AMERICAN STAR (FR),** b c 26/1 Kendargent (FR)—Tres American Girl (FR) (American Post)
**147 ANIELDARGENT (FR),** gr c 16/4 Kendargent—Augira (Sternkoenig)
**148 BEAMA (FR),** b f 6/2 Elusive City (USA)—High Will (FR) (High Chaparral (IRE)) (11111)
**149 BLONVILLE (FR),** bl f 13/4 Le Havre (IRE)—La Mouche (Dubawi (IRE)) (35714)
**150 BOMBAY NIGHT (FR),** b c 11/5 Wootton Bassett—Blue Roses (IRE) (Oratorio (IRE)) (9523)
**151 BRANCAIO (FR),** bl c 9/1 Denon (USA)—Brictop (USA) (Mizzen Mast (USA)) (15873)
**152 BRIGHT FACE (FR),** b f 14/3 Way of Light (USA)—Beriosova (FR) (Starborough) (7936)
**153 BROKEN CIRCLE (FR),** b c 22/4 Canford Cliffs—Baracoa (Llandaff)
**154 CLASSE POWER (FR),** b c 30/4 Soul City (IRE)—Avec Classe (FR) (Johann Quatz (FR)) (7142)
**155** B c 5/2 Exceed And Excel (AUS)—Clinet (IRE) (Docksider (USA)) (43650)
**156 DAMILA (FR),** b f 9/4 Milanais—Dawaes (Marchand De Sable)
**157 DHEVANAFUSHI,** gr c 18/2 Kendargent (FR)—Tejaara (USA) (Kingmambo (USA))
**158 EL COLOMBIANO (FR),** ch c 1/2 Way Of Light—Belle Suisse (Hamas)
**159 ETERNAL ARMY (FR),** ch c 22/3 American Post—Earth Affair (GER) (Acatenango (GER)) (6746)
**160** B c 1/1 New Approach (IRE)—Flower Bowl (FR) (Anabaa (USA))
**161** B c 5/4 Showcasing—Freedom Pass (USA) (Gulch (USA))
**162 IRISH LADY'S (IRE),** b f 13/1 Pour Moi (IRE)—Irish Queen (FR) (Speedmaster (GER))
**163 KAYDEE (FR),** b c 1/2 King's Best (USA)—Dragonessa (IRE) (Red Ransom (USA)) (19047)
**164 KENDALEE (FR),** gr f 20/3 Kendargent—Zandalee (Trempolino)
**165 KENLOVER (FR),** ch c 4/4 Kendargent—Nicole (FR) (Dashing Blade)
**166 LES PRADEAUX (FR),** b c 1/1 Acclamation—Pennegale (IRE) (Pennekamp (USA))
**167 MAGARI (FR),** b c 4/5 Denon (USA)—Shakila (Cadeaux Genereux) (11904)
**168 MAGIC TIME (FR),** b f 28/4 Kendargent (FR)—Magic Potion (FR) (Divine Light (JPN)) (47619)
**169** Gr f 1/1 Kendargent (FR)—Maya Dushka (IRE) (Dansili)
**170 MISS TOOTSY (FR),** b f 1/1 Authorized (IRE)—Miss Sissy (FR) (Sicyos (USA))
**171** B c 8/5 Cape Cross (IRE)—National Day (IRE) (Barathea (IRE))
**172** B f 9/2 Canford Cliffs (IRE)—Nellie Gwyn (King's Best (USA))
**173 OCTAVIA (FR),** ch f 28/2 Aqlaam—Orlena (USA) (Gone West (USA)) (19047)
**174 ONE WISH (FR),** b f 11/1 Meshaheer (USA)—Olive Green (USA) (Diesis) (7936)
**175 PARK SQUARE (FR),** b c 7/3 Myboycharlie (IRE)—Adeje Park (IRE) (Night Shift (USA))
**176 PASTRIDA (FR),** b f 8/3 Alexandros—Pearl Argyle (FR) (Oasis Dream)
**177** B f 15/2 Stormy River—Planete (Danehill Dancer)
**178** Ch c 25/3 Equiano (FR)—Queenly Bearing (Night Shift (USA)) (29365)
**179 RESTIANA (FR),** b f 18/2 Kendargent—Restia (FR) (Montjeu)
**180** B f 3/3 Le Havre (IRE)—Retiens La Nuit (USA) (Grand Slam (USA)) (9523)
**181 ROMANTIC DREAMS (FR),** ch f 3/2 Zafeen (FR)—Rocky Mixa (FR) (Rock of Gibraltar (IRE)) (23015)
**182** B c 14/4 Turtle Bowl (IRE)—Rosey de Megeve (Efisio) (19841)
**183** B f 12/4 Authorized (IRE)—Shining Sea (FR) (Anabaa Blue) (9523)
**184** B f 28/2 Myboycharlie (IRE)—Silver Market (FR) (Marchand de Sable (USA)) (14285)
**185 SKY BOLT (FR),** ch c 14/2 Denon—Suvretta Queen (Polish Precedent)
**186 SNOWMASTER (FR),** ch c 13/3 Linngari (IRE)—Indochine (BRZ) (Special Nash (IRE))
**187** Ch c 25/2 Pivotal—Soho Star (Smarty Jones (USA))
**188 SUPER RIDGE (FR),** b c 2/2 Linngari (IRE)—Superstition (FR) (Kutub (IRE)) (50793)
**189 TEXAS RANGER (FR),** b c 3/5 Bushranger (IRE)—Singapore Fairy (FR) (Sagacity (FR)) (7142)
**190 TRES ROCK GLORY (IRE),** b f 14/2 Fastnet Rock (AUS)—Tres Ravi (GER) (Monsun (GER))
**191** Gr f 16/3 Makfi—Trip To Glory (FR) (Where Or When (IRE))
**192** B c 1/1 Mawatheeq (USA)—Turtle Point (USA) (Giant's Causeway (USA)) (31746)
**193** B f 15/2 Way of Light (USA)—Verzasca (IRE) (Sadler's Wells (USA)) (13492)
**194 WINNER PRINCE (FR),** b c 1/1 Astronomer Royal—Crazy Mask
**195 ZALVADOS (FR),** ch c 1/1 Soldier Of Fortune—Zariyana
**196 ZAROSE (FR),** b c 1/1 Zafeen—Rose The One

**Assistant Trainer:** Ludovic Gadbin (0033) 685 070620

**Jockey (flat):** Fabrice Veron, Sebastien Martineau, Antoine Werle.

## 475 MR JOHN PANVERT, Tiverton

Postal: **Steart Farm Racing Stables, Stoodleigh, Tiverton, Devon, EX16 9QA**
Contacts: **MOBILE (07590) 120314**

1 **EDDY,** 6, b g Exit To Nowhere (USA)—Sharway Lady **J. F. Panvert**
2 **REBEL ISLAND (IRE),** 6, b m Heron Island (IRE)—Rebel Rebel (FR) **J. F. Panvert**
3 **TITCH STRIDER (IRE),** 10, b m Milan—Just Little **J. F. Panvert**
4 **WATCHMETAIL (IRE),** 9, b br g Amilynx (FR)—Ellie Anna (IRE) **J. F. Panvert**

**Jockey (flat):** Jim Crowley, Luke Morris. **Jockey (NH):** David England, Conor O'Farrell.

## 476 MRS HILARY PARROTT, Redmarley

Postal: **Chapel Farm, Chapel Lane, Redmarley, Gloucester, Gloucestershire, GL19 3JF**
Contacts: **PHONE (01452) 840139 FAX (01452) 840139 MOBILE (07972) 125030**
**E-MAIL hkparrott@btinternet.com**

1 **DAIZY (IRE),** 6, ch g Presenting—I Remember It Well (IRE) **Mr T. J. & Mrs H. Parrott**
2 **SIMPLY CHARLES (IRE),** 8, ch g Blueprint (IRE)—Stormy Sea (IRE) **Mr T. J. & Mrs H. Parrott**
3 **SPINNING SCOOTER,** 5, b g Sleeping Indian—Spinning Coin **T. J. Parrott**
4 **TINOS TANK (IRE),** 6, b g Flemensfirth (USA)—Tinopasa (FR) **T. J. Parrott**
5 **WAYWARD PRINCE,** 11, b g Alflora (IRE)—Bellino Spirit (IRE) **Mr T. J. & Mrs H. Parrott**

**Other Owners:** Mrs H. Parrott.

## 477 MR BEN PAULING, Bourton-On-The-Water

Postal: **Bourton Hill Farm, Bourton-On-The-Water, Gloucestershire, GL54 3BJ**
Contacts: **PHONE (01451) 821252 MOBILE (07825) 232888**
**E-MAIL ben@benpaulingracing.com WEBSITE www.benpaulingracing.com**

1 **ALWAYS LION (IRE),** 5, b g Let The Lion Roar—Addie's Choice (IRE) **Mr & Mrs Paul & Clare Rooney**
2 **ASSIREM (FR),** 5, b g Spirit One (FR)—Sweet Orientfawn (IRE) **Mr & Mrs Paul & Clare Rooney**
3 **BALLYHENRY (IRE),** 5, br g Presenting—Afarka (IRE) **The Vestey Family Partnership**
4 **BARTERS HILL (IRE),** 5, b g Kalanisi (IRE)—Circle The Wagons (IRE) **Circle Of Friends**
5 **BATHS WELL (IRE),** 5, br g Beat All (USA)—Bathsheba **Mr & Mrs Paul & Clare Rooney**
6 **BORN TO SUCCEED (IRE),** 5, b g Robin des Pres (FR)—Born To Win (IRE) **Mr & Mrs Paul & Clare Rooney**
7 **BURGUNDY BETTY (IRE),** 5, b m Presenting—Lady Meribel **Mrs B. M. Henley**
8 **CADEAU GEORGE,** 6, b g Relief Pitcher—Sovereign's Gift **Genesis Racing Partnership**
9 **CASSIE,** 5, b m Refuse To Bend (IRE)—Strictly Cool (USA) **Pump & Plant Services Ltd**
10 **CHARLIE BREEKIE (IRE),** 6, b g Alkaadhem—Highland Breeze (IRE) **The Harefield Racing Club**
11 **COSWAY SPIRIT (IRE),** 8, ch g Shantou (USA)—Annalisa (IRE) **Alan Marsh & Partners**
12 **DREAMISI (IRE),** 6, b g Kalanisi (IRE)—Marvellous Dream (FR) **Mr & Mrs Paul & Clare Rooney**
13 **EMPEROR COMMODOS,** 8, b g Midnight Legend—Theme Arena **R. Mathew**
14 **ERGO SUM,** 8, bl g Fair Mix (IRE)—Idiot's Lady **R. Mathew**
15 **EWINGS (IRE),** 5, b g Mahler—Fine Wings (IRE) **Mr & Mrs Paul & Clare Rooney**
16 **KELLYS BROW (IRE),** 8, b g Golan (IRE)—Eyebright (IRE) **Foxtrot Racing Heythrop Partnership**
17 **KINGUSSIE,** 7, b g Diktat—Highland Gait **The High T Party**
18 **LOCK TOWERS (IRE),** 6, b g Classic Cliche (IRE)—Katieella (IRE) **Mr T P Finch Mr M Lanz & Mr E Branston**
19 **MALIBU SUN,** 8, ch g Needwood Blade—Lambadora **Easy Going Racing**
20 **MIDNIGHT SAIL,** 12, b g Midnight Legend—Mayina **Mrs A. C. Houldsworth**
21 **NEWTON GERONIMO,** 6, b br g Brian Boru—Newton Commanche (IRE) **J. H. & N. J. Foxon**
22 **NEWTON MARTINI,** 6, b m Brian Boru—Wedidthat (IRE) **Warwick Members Racing Club**
23 **NEWTON THISTLE,** 8, b g Erhaab (USA)—Newton Venture **J. H. & N. J. Foxon**
24 **ONE LUCKY LORD,** 4, b g Lucky Story (USA)—One For Philip **S W Group Logistics Limited**
25 **PITHIVIER (FR),** 5, b g Poliglote—Kelbelange (FR) **Mr & Mrs Paul & Clare Rooney**
26 **RAVEN'S TOWER (USA),** 5, b g Raven's Pass (USA)—Tizdubai (USA) **Faithful Friends**
27 **RHAMNUS,** 5, b g Sakhee's Secret—Happy Lady (FR) **Rockcliffe Stud**
28 **RIDE ON TIME (IRE),** 5, b g Presenting—Polly Anthus **Whatalot**
29 **SHOWBOATER (IRE),** 6, b g Milan—Dazala (IRE) **Mr & Mrs Paul & Clare Rooney**
30 **SILVER SCOTCH (IRE),** 6, gr m Tikkanen (USA)—Wee Scotch (IRE) **Mr & Mrs Paul & Clare Rooney**
31 **SMART FREDDY,** 9, b g Groom Dancer (USA)—Smart Topsy **Mrs R. D. Sumpter**
32 **SMART STORY,** 8, b g Iktibas—Clever Nora (IRE) **Mrs R. Outhwaite**
33 **SPACE WALKER (IRE),** 4, b g Astronomer Royal (USA)—Hot Property (USA) **Mr & Mrs Paul & Clare Rooney**
34 **SPRING STEEL (IRE),** 6, b g Dushyantor (USA)—Fieldtown (IRE) **Tim Finch & Mike Lanz**

## MR BEN PAULING - Continued

**35 SUMMERTIME LADY,** 7, b m Desert King (IRE)—Shelayly (IRE) **The Milk Sheiks**
**36 URBAN STORM (IRE),** 5, b g Urban Ocean (FR)—Jessaway (IRE) **The Urban Partnership**
**37 WADSWICK HAROLD,** 5, b g Septieme Ciel (USA)—
Miss Flinders **Tim & Carolyn Barton Wadswick countrystore Ltd**
**38 WILLOUGHBY COURT (IRE),** 4, br g Court Cave (IRE)—Willoughby Sue (IRE) **Mr & Mrs Paul & Clare Rooney**

**Other Owners:** Mr D. Abraham, T. Barton, Mrs C. A. Barton, Mr G. Bennett, Mr E. Branston, Mrs L. M. Bugden, Mrs P. L. Capper, Mr R. J. Claydon, Mrs P. M. Colson, Mr J. Deacon, Mr N. C. Deacon, Mr P. M. Drewett, Mr T. P. Finch, Mr J. H. Foxon, Mrs N. J. Foxon, Mr R. Foxon, Mrs C. S. Heber-Percy, Mr R. S. Johnson, Mr S. L. Keswick, Mr B. W. Keswick, Mr M. E. Lanz, Mr S. M. P. Leahy, Mr K. D. Linsley, Mr A. R. W. Marsh, Mr P. McGrath, Mrs J. Pauling, Mr B. P. Pauling, Mr T. Robinson-Gamby, Mr P. A. Rooney, Mrs C. Rooney, Miss M. R. Stark, Mrs M. T. Stopford-Sackville, Mr N. E. Stumbles, Lord Vestey, Lady Vestey, Mr R. W. P. Weeks, Mr D. H Williams, Mr B. H. Wilson, Mr A. J. Windle.

**Assistant Trainer:** Mary Vestey

**Jockey (NH):** David Bass, James Davies, Felix De Giles, Jason Maguire. **Conditional:** Harrison Beswick, Nico De Boinville.

---

## 478 MR RAY PEACOCK, Tenbury Wells

Postal: **Elliott House Farm, Vine Lane, Kyre, Tenbury Wells, Worcestershire, WR15 8RL**
Contacts: **PHONE (01885) 410772 MOBILE (07748) 565574/ 07881440135**

**1 GIFTED HEIR (IRE),** 11, b g Princely Heir (IRE)—Inzar Lady (IRE) **R. E. Peacock**
**2 INTERCHOICE STAR,** 10, b g Josr Algarhoud (IRE)—Blakeshall Girl **Mr J. P. Evitt**
**3 RICH HARVEST (USA),** 10, b br g High Yield (USA)—Mangano (USA) **R. E. Peacock**
**4 SWORDS,** 13, b g Vettori (IRE)—Pomorie (IRE) **R. E. Peacock**

**Assistant Trainer:** Mrs C Peacock

**Jockey (flat):** David Probert. **Apprentice:** Charles Bishop. **Amateur:** Miss S. Peacock.

---

## 479 MRS LYDIA PEARCE, Newmarket

Postal: **Wroughton House, 37 Old Station Road, Newmarket, Suffolk, CB8 8DT**
Contacts: **PHONE (01638) 664669 MOBILE (07787) 517864**
**E-MAIL lsp_8@live.co.uk**

**1 BLACK ICEMAN,** 7, gr g Iceman—Slite **Mrs J. R. Marsh**
**2 DR FINLEY (IRE),** 8, ch g Dr Fong (USA)—Farrfesheena (USA) **Mr P. J. Stephenson**
**3 GHUFA (IRE),** 11, b g Sakhee (USA)—Hawriyah (USA) **Mr P. J. Stephenson**
**4 HATTA STREAM (IRE),** 9, b g Oasis Dream—Rubies From Burma (USA) **Mrs L. S. Pearce**
**5 MINSTREL LAD,** 7, ch g Where Or When (IRE)—Teal Flower **S & M Supplies (Aylsham) Ltd**
**6 OLNEY LASS,** 8, b m Lucky Story (USA)—Zalebe **Mrs L. J. Marsh**
**7 PICTURE DEALER,** 6, b g Royal Applause—Tychy **Killarney Glen**
**8 SEXY SECRET,** 4, b g Sakhee's Secret—Orange Walk (IRE) **Oceana Racing**
**9 SHAMALAD,** 5, b g Shamardal (USA)—Steam Cuisine **Killarney Glen**

### THREE-YEAR-OLDS

**10 CAPTAIN NAVARRE,** b g Excellent Art—Quantum (IRE) **Thoroughbred Racing Syndicate V**
**11 ROWELLIAN (IRE),** b g High Chaparral (IRE)—Steam Cuisine **Killarney Glen**
**12 TAILORMADE,** b g Josr Algarhoud (IRE)—Victoriana **Mr R. Devereux**

### TWO-YEAR-OLDS

**13 CYTRINGAN,** b f 3/5 Equiano (FR)—Scisciabubu (IRE) (Danehill (USA)) (15000) **Killarney Glen**

**Other Owners:** Mr Stuart Andrews, Mr Alexander Baker, Mr N. M. Hanger, Mr John Harrison, Mr Eric Jones, Mrs Jennifer Marsh, Mrs Louise Marsh, Mrs Lydia Pearce, Mr P. J. Stephenson, Thoroughbred Racing Limited, Mr R. G. Thurston.

**Assistant Trainer:** Jeff Pearce

**Jockey (flat):** Simon Pearce.

## 480 MR OLLIE PEARS, Malton

Postal: **The Office, Old Farmhouse, Beverley Road, Norton, Malton, North Yorkshire, YO17 9PJ**
Contacts: **PHONE (01653) 690746 MOBILE (07760) 197103**
**E-MAIL info@olliepearsracing.co.uk WEBSITE www.olliepearsracing.co.uk**

1 **AUGUSTA ADA,** 4, b f Byron—Preference **T. J. O'Gram**
2 **BREUGHEL (GER),** 4, b g Dutch Art—Bezzaaf **C. V. Wentworth**
3 **DIZOARD,** 5, b m Desideratum—Riviere **Dr R. G. Fairs**
4 **EXCLUSIVE CONTRACT (IRE),** 4, br f High Chaparral (IRE)—Birthday (IRE) **Richard Walker & Ollie Pears**
5 **HORATIO CARTER,** 10, b g Bahamian Bounty—Jitterbug (IRE)
6 **JACBEQUICK,** 4, b g Calcutta—Toking N' Joken (IRE) **Cherry Garth Racing**
7 **LEAN ON PETE (IRE),** 6, b g Oasis Dream—Superfonic (FR) **K. C. West**
8 **NAOISE (IRE),** 7, ch g Stormy Atlantic (USA)—Machinale (USA) **T. Elsey**
9 **NO LEAF CLOVER (IRE),** 4, b c Kodiac—Rajmahal (UAE) **C. V. Wentworth**
10 **NOODLES BLUE BOY,** 9, b g Makbul—Dee Dee Girl (IRE) **K. C. West**

### THREE-YEAR-OLDS

11 **BLACK PUDDING (IRE),** b g Baltic King—Top of The Ridge (IRE) **Mr A. Caygill**
12 B g Halling (USA)—Cape Dancer (IRE) **C. V. Wentworth**
13 **CHARLIE LAD,** b g Myboycharlie (IRE)—Night Owl **S. & A. Mares**
14 **DAD'S GIRL,** ch f Sakhee's Secret—China Cherub **Ownaracehorse Ltd**
15 **DEEP BLUE DIAMOND,** b f Sir Percy—Apple Blossom (IRE) **GG Bloodstock & Racing - Anne Gillespie**
16 **LITTLEMISSPARTON,** b f Sir Percy—Miss Prism **Ontoawinner & GG Bloodstock and Racing**
17 **MICHAEL DIVINE,** b g Calcutta—Divine Miss-P **Cherry Garth Racing**
18 **SECRET PATTERN,** b g Sakhee's Secret—Saddlers Bend (IRE) **David Scott & Co (Pattern Makers) Ltd**
19 **STUDIO STAR,** ch g Showcasing—Forrest Star **Ownaracehorse Ltd**
20 **UNNOTICED,** b g Observatory (USA)—Celestial Empire (USA) **Mr J. M. Worrall**
21 **WINN LILY,** b f Captain Gerrard (IRE)—Scisciabubu (IRE) **Mrs V. A. Pears**
22 **ZEBELINI (IRE),** gr f Zebedee—Ma Nikitia (IRE) **Mr T. L. Alcock**

### TWO-YEAR-OLDS

23 B f 1/4 Fast Company (IRE)—Aljafliyah (Halling (USA)) (21000) **S. & A. Mares**
24 B f 3/3 Amadeus Wolf—Ashover Amber (Green Desert (USA)) (3000) **Ownaracehorse Ltd**
25 **CITADEL,** ch c 11/4 Haafhd—Preference (Efisio)
26 **ROARING RORY,** ch c 4/3 Sakhee's Secret—Barbieri (IRE) (Encosta de Lago (AUS)) (3809) **Ownaracehorse Ltd**
27 **SECRETAN,** ch c 29/3 Monsieur Bond (IRE)—Real Diamond (Bertolini (USA)) (2095) **J. H. Sissons**
28 **SENSATIONAL SECRET,** ch f 25/4 Sakhee's Secret—Eolith (Pastoral Pursuits) (4761) **Ownaracehorse Ltd**
29 B f 15/4 Makfi—Triple Edition (USA) (Lear Fan (USA)) (10000) **Mr A. Caygill**

**Other Owners:** Miss V. Cartmel, Mr L. Gedge-Gibson, Dr A. J. F. Gillespie, Mr S. Mares, Mrs A. Mares, N. J. O'Brien, O. J. Pears, L. C. Sigsworth, Mr R. Wake, Mrs H. A. Wake, R. Walker.

**Assistant Trainer:** Vicky Pears

**Jockey (NH):** Brian Hughes.

## 481 MR DAVID PEARSON, High Peak

Postal: **Lower Fold Farm, Rowarth, High Peak, Derbyshire, SK22 1ED**
Contacts: **PHONE (01663) 741471 MOBILE (07775) 842009**

1 **BALLYCRACKEN (IRE),** 11, b g Flemensfirth (USA)—Cons Dual Sale (IRE) **D. Pearson**
2 **SHOOTERS WOOD (IRE),** 11, b g Needle Gun (IRE)—Talbot's Hollow (IRE) **D. Pearson**

**Assistant Trainer:** Eileen Pearson

## 482 MR GEORGE PECKHAM, Newmarket

Postal: **29 Tea Kettle Lane, Stetchworth, Newmarket, Suffolk, CB8 9TP**
Contacts: **PHONE (01638) 508194 FAX (01638) 508726 MOBILE (07823) 335013**
**E-MAIL george@aislabie.com WEBSITE www.aislabie.com**

1 **EMPERICAL,** 5, b g Oasis Dream—Kalima **F. Nass**
2 **KRYPTON FACTOR,** 7, b br g Kyllachy—Cool Question **F. Nass**
3 **YORK GLORY (USA),** 7, gr ro h Five Star Day (USA)—Minicolony (USA) **Salman Rashed**

## MR GEORGE PECKHAM - Continued

### THREE-YEAR-OLDS

4 **BIG BEAR (FR),** b g Thewayyouare (USA)—Alivera (FR) **F. Nass**
5 **BOMBALURINA (IRE),** ch f Rip Van Winkle (IRE)—Real Cat (USA) **F. Nass**
6 **DELTORA QUEST,** b g Compton Place—Maysarah (IRE) **F. Nass**
7 **HENRYTHEGHOST (USA),** gr ro c Henrythenavigator (USA)—Fonce De (FR) **F. Nass**
8 **JAARIH (IRE),** ch c Starspangledbanner (AUS)—Bridge Note (USA) **F. Nass**
9 **MAJROOH (IRE),** b c Acclamation—Neve Lieve (IRE) **F. Nass**
10 **MUHAZWARA (IRE),** b f Fastnet Rock (AUS)—Carn Lady (IRE) **F. Nass**
11 **RAAKID (IRE),** ch c Raven's Pass (USA)—Perfect Hedge **F. Nass**
12 **ROCK ROYALTY,** ch c Kyllachy—Mayaar (USA) **F. Nass**
13 **ROYAL BLESSING,** b g Royal Applause—Zuleika Dobson **F. Nass**

### TWO-YEAR-OLDS

14 **ESTRELLA ERIA (FR),** gr f 1/2 Mastercraftsman (IRE)—Madrid Beauty (FR) (Sendawar (IRE)) (39682) **F. Nass**
15 B f 26/2 Oasis Dream—Gakalina (IRE) (Galileo (IRE)) (80000) **F. Nass**
16 B g 7/3 Monsieur Bond (IRE)—Maysarah (IRE) (Green Desert (USA)) **F. Nass**
17 Ch c 7/5 Motivator—More Sirens (IRE) (Night Shift (USA)) **F. Nass**
18 B c 6/3 Giant's Causeway (USA)—Persist (USA) (Tiznow (USA)) (97532) **F. Nass**
19 B f 13/2 Acclamation—Pioneer Bride (USA) (Gone West (USA)) (130000) **F. Nass**
20 B g 3/5 Sir Percy—Play Bouzouki (Halling (USA)) (26000) **F. Nass**
21 B br c 30/3 Super Saver (USA)—Raise Fee (USA) (Menifee (USA)) (80321) **F. Nass**
22 B f 21/3 Acclamation—Silver Kestrel (USA) (Silver Hawk (USA)) (60000) **F. Nass**
23 **SUMMER DOVE (USA),** gr ro f 2/2 Super Saver (USA)—
No Foul Play (CAN) (Great Gladiator (USA)) (91795) **F. Nass**
24 B c 29/3 Unbridled's Song (USA)—The Best Day Ever (USA) (Brahms (USA)) (177854) **F. Nass**
25 B f 5/1 New Approach (IRE)—Tinaar (USA) (Giant's Causeway (USA)) (100000) **F. Nass**

**Other Owners:** Mohamed Khalifa.

---

## 483 MISS LINDA PERRATT, East Kilbride

Postal: **North Allerton Farm, East Kilbride, Glasgow, Lanarkshire, G75 8RR**
Contacts: **PHONE (01355) 303425 MOBILE (07931) 306147**
**E-MAIL linda.perratt@btinternet.com**

1 **ANITOPIA,** 10, gr g Alflora (IRE)—The Whirlie Weevil **Nil Sine Labore Partnership**
2 **BANNOCK TOWN,** 4, b g Denounce—Miss Pigalle **The Hon Miss H. Galbraith**
3 **BERBICE (IRE),** 10, gr g Acclamation—Pearl Bright (FR) **J. K. McGarrity**
4 **BUNCE (IRE),** 7, b g Good Reward (USA)—Bold Desire **Peter Tsim & Helen Perratt**
5 **DARK CRYSTAL,** 4, b f Multiplex—Glitz (IRE) **Nil Sine Labore Partnership**
6 **FINDOG,** 5, b g Pastoral Pursuits—Night Home (ITY) **J. K. McGarrity**
7 **GEANIE MAC (IRE),** 6, ch m Needwood Blade—Dixie Evans **J. K. McGarrity**
8 **JAMMY MOMENT,** 4, ch f Duke of Marmalade (IRE)—Special Moment (IRE) **J. K. McGarrity**
9 **JINKY,** 7, b g Noverre (USA)—Aries (GER) **Mr J. Murphy**
10 **MYSTICAL KING,** 5, b g Notnowcato—Mystical Ayr (IRE) **Jackton Racing Club**
11 **NEW COLOURS,** 4, gr g Verglas (IRE)—Briery (IRE) **J. K. McGarrity**
12 **PITT RIVERS,** 6, br g Vital Equine (IRE)—Silca Boo **Mrs H. F. Perratt**
13 **ROCK CANYON (IRE),** 6, b g Rock of Gibraltar (IRE)—Tuesday Morning **Mrs H. F. Perratt**
14 **SAXONETTE,** 7, b m Piccolo—Solmorin **Mr J. Murphy**
15 **SCHMOOZE (IRE),** 6, b m One Cool Cat (USA)—If Dubai (USA) **Jackton Racing Club**
16 **SILVER RIME (FR),** 10, gr g Verglas (IRE)—Severina **J. K. McGarrity**
17 **TADALAVIL,** 10, gr g Clodovil (IRE)—Blandish (USA) **J. K. McGarrity**

### THREE-YEAR-OLDS

18 **IT'S TIME FOR BED,** gr f Zebedee—Mystical Ayr (IRE) **Mrs H. F. Perratt**
19 **LITTLE BELTER (IRE),** gr c Dandy Man (IRE)—On Thin Ice (IRE) **J. K. McGarrity**

### TWO-YEAR-OLDS

20 B c 30/4 Fast Company (IRE)—Curie Express (IRE) (Fayruz) (13333) **Jordan Electrical**
21 **SNEAKIN'PETE,** b c 18/3 Frozen Power (IRE)—Jillolini (Bertolini (USA)) (11428) **John Murphy & Helen Perratt**

**Other Owners:** Mr B. Atkins, Mr T. Hughes, Mr J. J. Sheridan.

**Assistant Trainer:** Mr Ross Smith

## MISS LINDA PERRATT - Continued

**Jockey (flat):** Tom Eaves, Paul Hanagan, Graham Lee, Phillip Makin. **Jockey (NH):** Brian Hughes, Wilson Renwick. **Conditional:** Callum Whillans.

---

## 484 MRS AMANDA PERRETT, Pulborough

Postal: **Coombelands Racing Stables, Pulborough, West Sussex, RH20 1BP**
Contacts: **OFFICE (01798) 873011 HOME (01798) 874894 FAX (01798) 875163**
**MOBILE (07803) 088713**
**E-MAIL aperrett@coombelands-stables.com WEBSITE www.amandaperrett.com**

1 **A LEGACY OF LOVE (IRE),** 4, b f Sea The Stars (IRE)—Nashmiah (IRE) **Mrs B. A. Karn-Smith**
2 **APPROACHING (IRE),** 4, ch c New Approach (IRE)—Dust Dancer **Bluehills Racing Limited**
3 **ARCH VILLAIN (IRE),** 6, b g Arch (USA)—Barzah (IRE) **Mr & Mrs F Cotton,Mr & Mrs P Conway**
4 **ARTFUL ROGUE (IRE),** 4, b g Excellent Art—Szabo (IRE) **Mr & Mrs F Cotton,Mr & Mrs P Conway**
5 **ASTRONEREUS (IRE),** 4, ch c Sea The Stars (IRE)—Marie Rheinberg (GER) **John Connolly & Odile Griffith**
6 **BLACK SHADOW,** 4, b g New Approach (IRE)—Shadow Dancing **A. D. Spence**
7 **BLUE SURF,** 6, ch g Excellent Art—Wavy Up (IRE) **John Connolly And Partners**
8 **BRAMSHAW (USA),** 8, gr ro g Langfuhr (CAN)—Milagra (USA) **Mrs A. J. Perrett**
9 **BRAMSHILL LASS,** 6, ch m Notnowcato—Disco Ball **Mrs K. J. L. Hancock**
10 **BURANO (IRE),** 6, ch h Dalakhani (IRE)—Kalimanta (IRE) **Burano Partnership**
11 **CZECH IT OUT (IRE),** 5, b g Oratorio (IRE)—Naval Affair (IRE) **G. D. P. Materna**
12 **ELYSIAN FIELDS (GR),** 4, ch f Champs Elysees—Second of May **Mrs A. J. Chandris**
13 **EXTRASOLAR,** 5, b g Exceed And Excel (AUS)—Amicable Terms **Odile Griffith & John Connolly**
14 **EYE OF THE STORM (IRE),** 5, ch h Galileo (IRE)—Mohican Princess **G. D. P. Materna**
15 **LU'S BUDDY (GR),** 4, b g Reel Buddy (USA)—Papality **The LLC Partnership**
16 **NEW REACTION,** 4, b g New Approach (IRE)—Intaaj (IRE) **Mrs A. J. Chandris**
17 **PACK LEADER (IRE),** 4, b g Hurricane Run (IRE)—Bright Enough **G. D. P. Materna**
18 **PRESTO VOLANTE (IRE),** 7, b g Oratorio (IRE)—
Very Racy (USA) **Mrs S Conway Mr & Mrs M Swayne Mr A Brooke Mrs R Doel**
19 **SABORIDO (USA),** 9, gr g Dixie Union (USA)—Alexine (ARG) **Mrs A. J. Perrett**
20 **SAUCY MINX (IRE),** 5, b m Dylan Thomas (IRE)—Market Day **Mr & Mrs F Cotton,Mr & Mrs P Conway**
21 **SPACELAB,** 4, b f Champs Elysees—Shuttle Mission **K. Abdullah**
22 **SUNNY AGAIN,** 4, ch f Shirocco (GER)—Spotlight **Bluehills Racing Limited**
23 **TORRID,** 4, ch c Three Valleys (USA)—Western Appeal (USA) **K. Abdullah**

### THREE-YEAR-OLDS

24 **BECCABUDDYBLUES (GR),** ch f Reel Buddy (USA)—Second of May **Mr R. J. Steele**
25 **BOUNCING CZECH,** b g Dandy Man (IRE)—Correlandie (USA) **G. D. P. Materna**
26 **CRISSCROSSED,** b c Oasis Dream—Double Crossed **K. Abdullah**
27 **FLIGHTY FILIA (IRE),** gr f Raven's Pass (USA)—Coventina (IRE) **Cotton, Conway**
28 **FRONT FIVE (IRE),** b g Teofilo (IRE)—Samdaniya **G. D. P. Materna**
29 **GENTLE PERSUASION,** b f Rock of Gibraltar (IRE)—Play Bouzouki **A. D. Spence**
30 **GLORIFIED FORCE (GR),** ch c Apotheosis (USA)—Nephetriti Way (IRE) **Mrs A. J. Chandris**
31 **HARMONY BROWN (GR),** b f Harmonic Way—Papality **Mrs B. A. Karn-Smith**
32 **INCLUDED,** b f Champs Elysees—Cordoba **K. Abdullah**
33 **ISAMOL,** b c Intikhab (USA)—Uvinza **John Connolly & Odile Griffith**
34 **LIGHTNING CHARLIE,** b g Myboycharlie (IRE)—Lighted Way **Lightning Charlie Partnership**
35 **NEW REVIVE,** b g New Approach (IRE)—Dance Lively (USA) **Mrs A. J. Chandris**
36 **OPEN THE RED,** b g Lawman (FR)—Acquainted **G. D. P. Materna**
37 **POLARIZED,** b f Medicean—Razzle (USA) **K. Abdullah**
38 **PROCESS,** b c Nayef (USA)—Intense **K. Abdullah**
39 **PROVATO (IRE),** ch g Approve (IRE)—Sagemacca (IRE) **The Provato Partnership**
40 **PURPLE GENIE (GR),** ch f Tiantai (USA)—Purple Way (GR) **Mrs A. J. Chandris**
41 **REST EASY,** b f Rip Van Winkle (IRE)—Early Evening **Rest Easy Partnership**
42 **SEVERAL (USA),** b c Rock Hard Ten (USA)—Proud Fact (USA) **K. Abdullah**
43 **SHOWTIME BLUES,** b g Showcasing—Night Symphonie **A. D. Spence**
44 **SONIC RAINBOW (GR),** ch f Harmonic Way—Rainbow Way
45 **TOWNSVILLE,** b c Zamindar (USA)—Rule of Nature **K. Abdullah**

### TWO-YEAR-OLDS

46 **BALANCING TIME,** b c 19/5 Pivotal—Time On (Sadler's Wells (USA)) (140000) **John Connolly & Odile Griffith**
47 **CANFORD BELLE,** b f 12/2 Canford Cliffs (IRE)—
Ballyea (IRE) (Acclamation) (20000) **Coombelands Racing Syndicate 3**

## MRS AMANDA PERRETT - Continued

**48** B c 5/2 Zamindar (USA)—Disclose (Dansili) **K. Abdullah**
**49** B c 1/4 Sinndar (IRE)—Intense (Dansili) **K. Abdullah**
**50** Ch c 3/3 Frozen Power (IRE)—La Mere Germaine (IRE) (Indian Ridge) (52000) **A. D. Spence**
**51 LADY ROCKA,** ch f 25/3 Rock of Gibraltar (IRE)—Tap Dance Way (IRE) (Azamour (IRE)) (7500) **Coombelands Racing Syndicate**
**52** B f 14/2 Oasis Dream—Mirror Lake (Dubai Destination (USA)) **K. Abdullah**
**53 MISCHIEF MAISY (IRE),** gr f 10/4 Clodovil (IRE)—Maise and Blue (USA) (Distant View (USA)) (25000) **Cotton, Conway**
**54 NUTBOURNE LAD (IRE),** b c 2/3 Lilbourne Lad (IRE)—Cape Sydney (IRE) (Cape Cross (IRE)) (20000) **Coombelands Racing Syndicate 2**
**55** B c 17/2 Rail Link—Photographic (Oasis Dream) **K. Abdullah**
**56** B f 15/4 Rock Hard Ten (USA)—Proud Fact (USA) (Known Fact (USA)) **K. Abdullah**
**57** B f 31/3 Equiano (FR)—Rougette (Red Ransom (USA)) **D. M. James**
**58 ROYAL HERO,** b c 6/2 Royal Applause—Heronetta (Halling (USA)) (48000) **Harwoods Racing Club Limited**
**59 YOU'RE HIRED,** b g 8/4 Dalakhani (IRE)—Heaven Sent (Pivotal) (130000) **G. D. P. Materna**
**60 ZHUI FENG (IRE),** b c 5/2 Invincible Spirit (IRE)—Es Que (Inchinor) (340000) **John Connolly & Odile Griffith**

**Other Owners:** Mr S. W. Barnett, A. W. Brooke, J. P. Connolly, Mrs S. M. Conway, F. G. Cotton, Mrs S. H. Cotton, Mr P. A. Cuttill, Mrs R. J. Doel, Mr L. Esposito, Ms O. L. Griffith, Guy Harwood, Mr A. A. Lewer, Mr M. B. Swayne, Mrs A. J. Swayne.

**Assistant Trainer:** Mark Perrett

---

## 485 MR PAT PHELAN, Epsom

Postal: **Ermyn Lodge, Shepherds Walk, Epsom, Surrey, KT18 6DF**
Contacts: **PHONE (01372) 229014 FAX (01372) 229001 MOBILE (07917) 762781**
**E-MAIL pat.phelan@ermynlodge.com WEBSITE www.ermynlodge.com**

**1 COUP DE GRACE (IRE),** 6, b g Elusive City (USA)—No Way (IRE) **Mr J. F. Lang**
**2 DELLBUOY,** 6, b g Acclamation—Ruthie **Timesquare Ltd**
**3 EDE'S THE BUSINESS,** 4, ch f Halling (USA)—My Amalie (IRE) **Ede's (UK) Ltd**
**4 EPSOM FLYER,** 5, ch g Haafhd—River Cara (USA) **Celtic Contractors Limited**
**5 ERMYN LODGE,** 9, br g Singspiel (IRE)—Rosewood Belle (USA) **Ermyn Lodge Stud Limited**
**6 FLEETWOOD NIX,** 5, b m Acclamation—Antediluvian **I. W. Harfitt**
**7 ISABELLA BEETON,** 4, b f Archipenko (USA)—Famcred **Mr A. J. Smith**
**8 JAKEY (IRE),** 5, b g Cape Cross (IRE)—Off Message (IRE) **A. B. Pope**
**9 LEAH FREYA (IRE),** 4, b f Aussie Rules (USA)—A Woman In Love **Mr E. Gleeson**
**10 LUCKY DOTTIE,** 4, b br f Lucky Story (USA)—Auntie Dot Com **Mr A. J. Smith**
**11 REGGIE PERRIN,** 7, ch g Storming Home—Tecktal (FR) **Ermyn Lodge Stud Limited**
**12 REPRESENTINGCELTIC (IRE),** 10, ch g Presenting—Nobull (IRE) **Celtic Contractors Limited**
**13 RIGHT STEP,** 8, b g Xaar—Maid To Dance **A. B. Pope**
**14 RON WAVERLY (IRE),** 5, ch g Haatef (USA)—Mermaid Beach **I. W. Harfitt**
**15 SOFTLY SHE TREADS (IRE),** 4, b f Azamour (IRE)—Lady Lucre (IRE) **Mr B. P. Donovan**
**16 THE BIG MARE,** 6, b m Doyen (IRE)—Fizzy Lady **Ermyn Lodge Stud Limited**
**17 YOUNG DOTTIE,** 9, b m Desert Sun—Auntie Dot Com **Mr A. J. Smith**

### THREE-YEAR-OLDS

**18 ALFIE THE PUG,** b g Pastoral Pursuits—Kapsiliat (IRE) **The HP Partnership**
**19 BLACKADDER,** b g Myboycharlie (IRE)—Famcred **Epsom Racegoers 4**
**20 CELTIC AVA (IRE),** b f Peintre Celebre (USA)—Denices Desert **Celtic Contractors Limited**
**21 DEFTERA LAD (IRE),** b g Fast Company (IRE)—Speedbird (USA) **Mr Y. Mustafa**
**22 DOTTIES BOY,** ch g Kheleyf (USA)—Auntie Dot Com **Mr A. J. Smith**
**23 EPSOM POEMS,** b g Pastoral Pursuits—My Amalie (IRE) **Epsom Racegoers No.3**
**24** B f Myboycharlie (IRE)—Marah **Sutton Business Centre**
**25** B g Royal Applause—Ruthie **Ermyn Lodge Stud Limited**

**Other Owners:** Mr M. Hess, Ms L. M. Hess, Mr G. Maginn.

**Jockey (flat):** Fergus Sweeney. **Jockey (NH):** James Best, Josh Moore. **Conditional:** Paddy Bradley. **Apprentice:** Paddy Bradley. **Amateur:** Miss Laura Dempster.

## 486 MR ALAN PHILLIPS, Callow End

Postal: **Jennet Tree Farm, Kents Green, Callow End, Worcestershire, WR2 4UA**

1 **ARUMUN (IRE),** 14, b g Posidonas—Adwoa (IRE) **Mr S. P. Turford**
2 **BIG TIME BILLY (IRE),** 9, b m Definite Article—Zaratu (IRE) **Miss R. L. Bryan**
3 **CAPTAIN DEVIOUS,** 4, b c Captain Gerrard (IRE)—Aspen Ridge (IRE) **Wood Bank Racing**
4 **CONSULT,** 8, ch g Dr Fong (USA)—Merle
5 **MY STROPPY POPPY,** 6, b m Multiplex—Aspen Ridge (IRE) **Wood Bank Racing**
6 **NEEDWOOD RIDGE,** 8, ch g Needwood Blade—Aspen Ridge (IRE) **Wood Bank Racing**
7 **OPERATIC HEIGHTS (IRE),** 6, b g Golan (IRE)—Opera Lover (IRE) **Miss R. L. Edwards**
8 **SYDNEY OPERA (IRE),** 9, gr g Oscar (IRE)—Hallatte (USA) **B. M. Barrett**

**Other Owners:** Mrs J. Maund-Powell, Mr T. J. Maund-Powell, Miss S. B. Munrowd.

## 487 MR RICHARD PHILLIPS, Moreton-in-Marsh

Postal: **Adlestrop Stables, Adlestrop, Moreton-in-Marsh, Gloucestershire, GL56 0YN**
Contacts: **PHONE (01608) 658710 FAX (01608) 658713 MOBILE (07774) 832715**
**E-MAIL info@richardphillipsracing.com WEBSITE www.richardphillipsracing.com**

1 **ARCTIC CHIEF,** 5, b g Sleeping Indian—Neiges Eternelles (FR) **Too Many Chiefs**
2 **ATA BOY (IRE),** 9, br g Key of Luck (USA)—Atalina (FR) **The Adlestrop Club**
3 **BEAUTIFUL PEOPLE (FR),** 4, b br f Early March—Night Fever (FR) **Beautiful People**
4 **BERKELEY BARRON (IRE),** 7, b g Subtle Power (IRE)—Roseabel (IRE) **Mrs E. A. Prowting**
5 **BLUE COMET,** 4, b g Blueprint (IRE)—Be My Valentine (IRE) **Mrs J. A. Watts**
6 **BRAVE HELIOS,** 5, b g High Chaparral (IRE)—Renowned (IRE) **Mrs J. A. Watts**
7 **CALL ME EMMA (IRE),** 7, b m Beneficial—Clody Girl (IRE) **Upthorpe Racing**
8 **CATKIN COPSE,** 7, b m Alflora (IRE)—Run Tiger (IRE) **Mrs S. C. Welch**
9 **CRYSTAL SWING,** 8, b g Trade Fair—Due West **Enjoy The Journey**
10 **FIRE TOWER,** 7, ch m Firebreak—Lamper's Light **The Firebirds**
11 **FLEMENSBAY,** 7, b m Flemensfirth (USA)—Mandys Native (IRE) **Dozen Dreamers Partnership**
12 **IFITS A FIDDLE,** 6, b m Kalanisi (IRE)—Fiddling Again **Mrs E. C. Roberts**
13 **LISHEEN HILL (IRE),** 9, b g Witness Box (USA)—Lady Lamb (IRE) **The Aspirationals**
14 4, B g Craigsteel—Mahon Rose (IRE) **Mr M. R. Barnes**
15 **MASTER VINTAGE,** 7, b g Kayf Tara—What A Vintage (IRE) **The Summer Club**
16 **MIGHTY TARA,** 5, b m Kayf Tara—Tiger Moss **S. M. Smith, K. Hunter, P. J. Duffen**
17 **MISTER HYDE (IRE),** 10, b g Beneficial—Solar Quest (IRE) **Bensaranat Club & Mr W McLuskey**
18 **MISTER NEWBY (IRE),** 9, b g Oscar (IRE)—Sallie's Girl (IRE) **C. Pocock**
19 **MOTOU (FR),** 10, b g Astarabad (USA)—Picoletta (FR) **The Summer Club**
20 **MR TINGLE,** 11, br g Beat All (USA)—Dianthus (IRE) **Mr & Mrs W. Brogan-Higgins & Gryffindor**
21 **MUTHABIR (IRE),** 5, b g Nayef (USA)—Northern Melody (IRE) **Ms F. Baxter**
22 **ORGAN MORGAN,** 5, b g Dylan Thomas (IRE)—Abide (FR) **C Humber & SM Smith**
23 **OUR PROJECT (IRE),** 4, b g Mountain High (IRE)—House-of-Hearts (IRE) **The Irish Experience**
24 **PALOMA'S PRINCE (IRE),** 6, ch g Nayef (USA)—Ma Paloma (FR) **Serendipity Syndicate 2006**
25 **POWDERONTHEBONNET (IRE),** 7, b g Definite Article—Zuhal **Mr W. McLuskey**
26 **RAFAAF (IRE),** 7, b g Royal Applause—Sciunfona (IRE) **J. A. Gent**
27 **SAPPHIRE MOON,** 8, b m Alflora (IRE)—Be My Valentine (IRE) **Mrs J. A. Watts**
28 **SEAVIPER (IRE),** 6, b g Presenting—Priority Post (IRE) **The Irish Experience**
29 **SHEELBEWHATSHEELBE (IRE),** 5, b m Oscar (IRE)—Cheerymount (IRE) **B. J. Duckett**
30 **TEMLETT (IRE),** 11, b g Desert Prince (IRE)—Bering Down (USA) **Mrs J. A. Watts**
31 **THORNTON ALICE,** 10, b m Kayf Tara—Lindrick Lady (IRE) **The Listeners**
32 **TIME WISE,** 5, b m Kayf Tara—Ceoperk (IRE) **Hopeful Travellers**
33 **TRUCKERS FIRST,** 7, b m Kayf Tara—Cheeky Trucker **S. F. Benton**
34 **VINAIGRETTE,** 6, b m Kayf Tara—What A Vintage (IRE) **The Someday's Here Racing Partnership**
35 **VIVA RAFA (IRE),** 5, b g Scorpion (IRE)—Back To Stay (IRE) **Ms F. Baxter**
36 **WHAT A SCORE,** 5, gr g Rail Link—Karsiyaka (IRE) **Nut Club Partnership**
37 **WHAT A TEMPEST,** 5, b m Kayf Tara—What A Vintage (IRE) **The Someday's Here Racing Partnership**
38 **WHICHEVER,** 9, ch m Where Or When (IRE)—Pips Way (IRE) **Upthorpe Racing**

### THREE-YEAR-OLDS

39 **ORGANDI (FR),** bl f Early March—Creme Pralinee (FR) **Beautiful People**
40 **SUPER MOON,** b g Black Sam Bellamy (IRE)—Aussie Deal (IRE) **Mrs J. A. Watts**

## MR RICHARD PHILLIPS - Continued

**Other Owners:** Mr C. A. J. Allan, Ms K. M. Anderson, J. E. Barnes, Mr J. R. Brown, Mr E. G. Brown, Mr M. P. Chitty, Mr J. E. S. Colling, Mrs H. Colraine, Lady S. Davis, Mr P. J. Duffen, Mrs S. J. Harvey, Mr C. M. Humber, K. L. Hunter, Mrs H. M. Nixseaman, R. T. Phillips, M. T. Phillips, S. M. Smith, Dr E. D. Theodore, Mr M. Warren, Mrs S. J. Warren.

**Conditional:** Daniel Hiskett.

---

## 488 MISS IMOGEN PICKARD, Leominster

Postal: **The Granary, Sodgeley Farm, Kingsland, Leominster, Herefordshire, HR6 9PY**
Contacts: **MOBILE (07884) 437720**
**E-MAIL bundlepickardracing@yahoo.co.uk**

1 **BRING BACK CHARLIE,** 5, bl g Green Card (USA)—Nafertiti (IRE) **Mr D. D. Genner**
2 **MIDNIGHT ROCKER,** 8, b g Zafeen (FR)—Dafne **If Only Partnership**
3 **MISTER FIZZ,** 7, b g Sulamani (IRE)—Court Champagne **Mrs M. J. Wilson**
4 **PRIVATE JONES,** 6, br g Trade Fair—Dafne **Mr A. P. Rogers**
5 **REGAL PARK (IRE),** 8, b g Montjeu (IRE)—Classic Park **G. Byard**

### THREE-YEAR-OLDS

6 **KEEP 'R LIT,** b f Multiplex—Cashel Dancer **Mrs M. J. Wilson**

**Other Owners:** Miss S. Bather, Mr Glenn Provost.

---

## 489 MR DAVID PIPE, Wellington

Postal: **Pond House, Nicholashayne, Wellington, Somerset, TA21 9QY**
Contacts: **PHONE (01884) 840715 FAX (01884) 841343**
**E-MAIL david@davidpipe.com WEBSITE www.davidpipe.com**

1 **A HAIRY KOALA (FR),** 5, ch g Dom Alco (FR)—Kandy de Vonnas (FR) **Mr S. Quinlan**
2 **AINSI FIDELES (FR),** 5, ch g Dream Well (FR)—Loya Lescribaa (FR) **Mr Simon Munir & Mr Isaac Souede**
3 **ALEZANNA,** 6, ch m Halling (USA)—Denica (IRE) **Mr A. B. Phipps**
4 **ALL FORCE MAJEURE (FR),** 5, gr g Dom Alco (FR)—
Naiade du Moulin (FR) **Professor Caroline Tisdall & Bryan Drew**
5 **ALTERNATIF (FR),** 5, b g Shaanmer (IRE)—Katerinette (FR) **Prof C. Tisdall**
6 **AMIGO (FR),** 8, b g Ballingarry (IRE)—Allez Y (FR) **A. L. Cohen & Willsford Racing**
7 **BALGARRY (FR),** 8, ch g Ballingarry (IRE)—Marie de Motreff (FR) **Brocade Racing**
8 **BALLYNAGOUR (IRE),** 9, b g Shantou (USA)—Simply Deep (IRE) **A. Stennett**
9 **BALLYWILLIAM (IRE),** 5, b g Mahler—Henrietta Howard (IRE) **M. C. Pipe**
10 **BALTIMORE ROCK (IRE),** 6, b g Tiger Hill (IRE)—La Vita E Bella (IRE) **R. S. Brookhouse**
11 **BARAKA DE THAIX (FR),** 4, gr g Dom Alco (FR)—Jaka de Thaix (FR) **Mr Simon Munir & Mr Isaac Souede**
12 **BARNEBY (FR),** 4, ro g Dom Alco (FR)—Jimanji (FR) **Professor Caroline Tisdall & Bryan Drew**
13 **BATAVIR (FR),** 6, ch g Muhtathir—Elsie (GER) **The Angove Family**
14 **BELLA (FR),** 4, b br f Johann Quatz (FR)—Hasta Manana (FR) **Prof C. Tisdall**
15 **BENGALI (IRE),** 6, br m Beneficial—Kigali (IRE) **Somerset Racing**
16 **BIDOUREY (FR),** 4, b br g Voix du Nord (FR)—Love Wisky (FR) **Brocade Racing**
17 **BIG OCCASION (IRE),** 8, b g Sadler's Wells (USA)—Asnieres (USA) **The Old Betfairians**
18 **BLADOUN (FR),** 7, gr g Smadoun (FR)—Blabliramic (FR) **H. M. W. Clifford**
19 **BORDER BREAKER (IRE),** 6, br g Indian Danehill (IRE)—Flying Answer (IRE) **Jimmy Hack Racing Partners 1**
20 **BRENDA DE RONCERAY (FR),** 4, b f Al Namix (FR)—Landza de Ronceray (FR) **Rob & Ron Racing**
21 **BROADWAY BUFFALO (IRE),** 7, ch g Broadway Flyer (USA)—Benbradagh Vard (IRE) **Mrs J. Tracey**
22 **BROOK (FR),** 4, ch g Kandidate—Ninon de Re (FR) **Pipe - Dreaming Ladies**
23 **BYGONES SOVEREIGN (IRE),** 9, b g Old Vic—Miss Hollygrove (IRE) **Arnie & Alan Kaplan**
24 **CHAMPAGNE'N'CHIPS (FR),** 4, gr g Martaline—Ile de See (FR) **Prof C. Tisdall**
25 **CHIC THEATRE (IRE),** 5, gr g King's Theatre (IRE)—La Reine Chic (FR) **Mr B. J. C. Drew**
26 **CLASSICAL ART (IRE),** 4, ch g Excellent Art—Ask Carol (IRE) **Mr Simon Munir & Mr Isaac Souede**
27 **CLOUGHERNAGH BOY (IRE),** 7, ch g Flemensfirth (USA)—
Windy Bee (IRE) **Stuart & Simon Mercer & Peter Green**
28 **COURTLANDS PRINCE,** 6, b g Presenting—Bathwick Annie **Mrs S. Clifford**
29 **DELL' ARCA (IRE),** 6, b g Sholokhov (IRE)—Daisy Belle (GER) **Prof C. Tisdall**
30 **DIAMOND LIFE,** 9, b g Silver Patriarch (IRE)—Myrrh **M. C. Denmark**
31 **DOD (IRE),** 4, ch g Flemensfirth (USA)—Impudent (IRE) **Mr R. J. H. Geffen**
32 **DRAMA KING (IRE),** 4, b g King's Theatre (IRE)—Miss Arteea (IRE) **M. D. Poland**
33 **DYNASTE (FR),** 9, gr g Martaline—Bellissima de Mai (FR) **Mr A. J. White**

## MR DAVID PIPE - Continued

34 **EASTER METEOR,** 9, b g Midnight Legend—Easter Comet **Mr & Mrs S. C. Willes**
35 **FAMOUSANDFEARLESS (IRE),** 7, b g Presenting—Clandestine **The Bravo Partnership**
36 **FLABELLO (IRE),** 5, br g Publisher (USA)—Uptodate (IRE) **Mrs A. Buchanan**
37 **FOR 'N' AGAINST (IRE),** 6, br g Presenting—Cut 'n' Run (IRE) **Mr E. A. P. Scouller**
38 **GEORGE HERBERT,** 4, b g Yeats (IRE)—Colorado Dawn **Mr R. J. H. Geffen**
39 **GEVREY CHAMBERTIN (FR),** 7, gr g Dom Alco (FR)—Fee Magic (FR) **Roger Stanley & Yvonne Reynolds III**
40 **GOOD VALUE,** 4, ch g Champs Elysees—Change Course **W. F. Frewen**
41 **GREAT CHOICE (IRE),** 6, b g Westerner—Granuale (IRE) **Mrs J. Gerard-Pearse**
42 **HEATH HUNTER (IRE),** 8, b g Shantou (USA)—Deep Supreme (IRE) **The Heath Hunter Partnership**
43 **HERBERT PARK (IRE),** 5, b g Shantou (USA)—Traluide (FR) **Brocade Racing**
44 **HOME RUN (GER),** 7, ch g Motivator—Hold Off (IRE) **W. F. Frewen**
45 **HOUSTON DYNIMO (IRE),** 10, b g Rock of Gibraltar (IRE)—Quiet Mouse (USA) **Miss S. E. Hartnell**
46 **IT'LL BE GRAND,** 6, b g Beat All (USA)—Everything's Rosy **Mrs A. M. Varmen & R J D Varmen**
47 **KALIFOURCHON (FR),** 4, gr g Martaline—Kaly Flight (FR) **CHM Partnership**
48 **KATKEAU (FR),** 8, b g Kotky Bleu (FR)—Levine (FR) **Prof C Tisdall, Mr J A Gent, Mr R Wilkin**
49 **KEEP THE CASH (IRE),** 7, b g Oscar (IRE)—Waterloo Ball (IRE) **M. C. Pipe**
50 **KINGS PALACE (IRE),** 7, b g King's Theatre (IRE)—Sarahs Quay (IRE) **Drew, George & Johnson Family**
51 **KNIGHT OF NOIR (IRE),** 6, b g Winged Love (IRE)—At Dawn (IRE) **H. M. W. Clifford**
52 **LADY OF LONGSTONE (IRE),** 5, ch m Beneficial—Christdalo (IRE) **Miss S. E. Hartnell**
53 **LOLA GALLI,** 7, br m Old Vic—Tahoe (IRE) **M. B. Jones**
54 **LOOK WEST,** 6, b g Westerner—Uppermost **James & Jean Potter**
55 **LOW KEY (IRE),** 8, b g Pentire—La Capilla **G. D. Thompson**
56 4, B g Kalanisi (IRE)—Lucky Hand (IRE) **R J H Geffen & P Bennett-Jones**
57 **MARTABOT (FR),** 4, gr g Martaline—Reine de Sabot (FR) **Mrs S. J. Ling**
58 **MINISTER OF MAYHEM,** 5, ch g Sakhee's Secret—First Fantasy **Mr J. M. Wilson**
59 **MISS WILLIAMS,** 4, b f Kayf Tara—Wee Dinns (IRE) **The Earl Of Donoughmore**
60 **MOLO,** 5, b m Kalanisi (IRE)—Belle Magello (FR) **Mr R. J. H. Geffen**
61 **MONCARNO,** 5, b g Lucarno (USA)—Sparkling Jewel **David & Elaine Long**
62 **MONETAIRE (FR),** 9, b br g Anabaa (USA)—Monitrice (FR) **A. Stennett**
63 **MOON RACER (IRE),** 6, b g Saffron Walden (FR)—Angel's Folly **Professor Caroline Tisdall & Bryan Drew**
64 **MOUNT HAVEN (IRE),** 5, b g Mountain High (IRE)—Castlehaven (IRE) **The Angove Family**
65 **MOZO,** 4, b f Milan—Haudello (FR) **Mr R. J. H. Geffen**
66 **MULTIMEDIA,** 5, b g Multiplex—Sunday News'n'echo (USA) **A. Stennett**
67 **MY BROTHER SYLVEST,** 9, b g Bach (IRE)—Senna da Silva **Teddington Racing Club**
68 **NAVANMAN (IRE),** 6, b g Well Chosen—Teamplin (IRE) **Mrs Y. Fleet**
69 **NORTHERN BAY (GER),** 5, b g Desert Prince (IRE)—Nova Scotia (GER) **Mr F. G. Wilson**
70 **OBISTAR (FR),** 5, b g Astarabad (USA)—Vallee du Luy (FR) **Brocade Racing**
71 **OUR CHIEF (IRE),** 6, b g Old Vic—Torsha (IRE) **The Johnson Family**
72 **OUR FATHER (IRE),** 9, gr g Shantou (USA)—Rosepan (IRE) **The Ives & Johnson Families**
73 **PARTY GIRLS (FR),** 7, b m Astarabad (USA)—Canadiane (FR) **M. C. Pipe**
74 **PERSPICACE,** 4, b g Sir Percy—Cassique Lady (IRE) **M. C. Pipe**
75 **POOLE MASTER,** 10, ch g Fleetwood (IRE)—Juste Belle (FR) **G. D. Thompson**
76 **PRIDEOFTHECASTLE (IRE),** 8, b g Waky Nao—Park's Pet (IRE) **Mr B. J. C. Drew**
77 **PURPLE 'N GOLD (IRE),** 6, b g Strategic Prince—Golden Dew (IRE) **Mrs L. Webb**
78 **QALINAS (FR),** 8, gr g Malinas (GER)—Tabletiere (FR) **Middleham Park Racing XX & M C Pipe**
79 **RACE TO GLORY (FR),** 4, b g Montjeu (IRE)—Cawett (IRE) **T. Neill**
80 **RATHEALY (IRE),** 4, b g Baltic King—Baltic Belle (IRE) **The Goodman Partnership**
81 **RATHLIN ROSE (IRE),** 7, b g Bonbon Rose (FR)—A Plus Ma Puce (FR) **Stefanos Stefanou**
82 **RED SHERLOCK,** 6, ch g Shirocco (GER)—Lady Cricket (FR) **The Johnson Family**
83 **RINNCA FADA,** 4, b g Multiplex—Cashel Dancer **D. Mossop**
84 **SADLER'S GOLD (IRE),** 5, b g Gold Well—Mrs Quigley (IRE) **G. D. Thompson**
85 **SAIL BY THE SEA (IRE),** 7, b g Heron Island (IRE)—Trajectus **R. S. Brookhouse**
86 **SAINT JOHN HENRY (FR),** 5, b g Saint des Saints (FR)—Noceane (FR) **Mr B. J. C. Drew**
87 **SERIENSCHOCK (GER),** 7, br g Sholokhov (IRE)—Saldenehre (GER) **T. Neill**
88 **SHOEGAZER (IRE),** 10, b g Bach (IRE)—American Native (IRE) **H. M. W. Clifford**
89 **SHOTAVODKA (IRE),** 9, ch g Alderbrook—Another Vodka (IRE) **Mrs J. Gerard-Pearse**
90 **SINNDAR'S MAN,** 4, b g Sinndar (IRE)—Relish (IRE) **H. M. W. Clifford**
91 **SIR FRANK MORGAN (IRE),** 5, b g Montjeu (IRE)—Woodland Orchid (IRE) **P. Dean**
92 **SIVRON (IRE),** 7, b g Laveron—Maille Sissi (FR) **Prof C. Tisdall**
93 **SKYLANDER (IRE),** 6, b g Flemensfirth (USA)—Cat Burglar (IRE) **The Trap Team Partnership**
94 **SMILES FOR MILES (IRE),** 7, b g Oscar (IRE)—Native Kin (IRE) **Prof C. Tisdall**
95 **SOFTSONG (FR),** 7, b g Singspiel (IRE)—Soft Gold (USA) **Mr Andrew Cohen & Mr Alan Kaplan**
96 **SOLL,** 10, ch g Presenting—Montelfolene (IRE) **D. Mossop**
97 **STANDING OVATION (IRE),** 8, b g Presenting—Glittering Star (IRE) **The Bravo Partnership**
98 **STARS OVER THE SEA (USA),** 4, b g Sea The Stars (IRE)—Exciting Times (FR) **R. S. Brookhouse**

## MR DAVID PIPE - Continued

99 **STREET ENTERTAINER (IRE),** 8, br g Danehill Dancer (IRE)—Opera Ridge (FR) **M. C. Pipe**
100 **SUSIE SHEEP,** 5, ch m Robin des Champs (FR)—Haudello (FR) **Professor Caroline Tisdall & Bryan Drew**
101 **SWING BOWLER,** 8, b m Galileo (IRE)—Lady Cricket (FR) **Mr K. Alexander**
102 **TAJ BADALANDABAD (IRE),** 5, ch g Shantou (USA)—Last Chance Lady (IRE) **W. F. Frewen**
103 **THE DARLING BOY,** 10, b g Medicean—Silver Top Hat (USA) **The Hon Mrs D. Hulse**
104 **THE PACKAGE,** 12, br g Kayf Tara—Ardent Bride **The Johnson Family**
105 **TOO GENEROUS,** 7, b m Generous (IRE)—Little Feat **A. E. Frost**
106 **TOP WOOD (FR),** 8, ch g Kotky Bleu (FR)—Heure Bleu (FR) **Lady H. J. Clarke**
107 **TULLYESKER HILL (IRE),** 6, b g Shantou (USA)—Couture Daisy (IRE) **Mr B. J. C. Drew**
108 **TWENTYTWO'S TAKEN (IRE),** 7, b m King's Theatre (IRE)—Persian Desert (IRE) **Mr K. Alexander**
109 **UN TEMPS POUR TOUT (IRE),** 6, b g Robin des Champs (FR)—
Rougedespoir (FR) **Professor Caroline Tisdall & Bryan Drew**
110 **UNANIMITE (FR),** 4, ch g Kentucky Dynamite (USA)—
Dame Blanche (USA) **Mr Simon Munir & Mr Isaac Souede**
111 **UNIQUE DE COTTE (FR),** 7, b g Voix du Nord (FR)—Kadalka de Cotte (FR) **J. P. McManus**
112 **VAYLAND,** 6, ch g Generous (IRE)—Dotandadash (IRE) **Mr Simon Munir & Mr Isaac Souede**
113 **VAZARO DELAFAYETTE (FR),** 6, bl g Robin des Champs (FR)—Etoile du Merze (FR) **Mr B. J. C. Drew**
114 **VIEUX LION ROUGE (FR),** 6, ch g Sabiango (GER)—Indecise (FR) **Prof Caroline Tisdall & Mr John Gent**
115 **VIF ARGENT (FR),** 6, b g Dom Alco (FR)—Formosa (FR) **Stefanos Stefanou**
116 **VIRTUEL D'OUDON (FR),** 6, b g Network (GER)—La Belle Illusion (FR) **Mr S. Quinlan**
117 **VOLT FACE (FR),** 6, ch g Kapgarde (FR)—Jourenuit (FR) **R. S. Brookhouse**
118 **WEEKEND MILLIONAIR (IRE),** 8, ch g Arakan (USA)—Almi Ad (USA) **H. M. W. Clifford**
119 **WESTBROOKE WARRIOR (IRE),** 4, b g Robin des Champs (FR)—Tango Lady (IRE) **Mr B. J. C. Drew**
120 **WESTERN WARHORSE (IRE),** 7, b g Westerner—An Banog (IRE) **R. S. Brookhouse**
121 **WHAT A MOMENT (IRE),** 5, b g Milan—Cuiloge Lady (IRE) **Bryan Drew & Steve Roper**
122 **WILLEM (FR),** 5, b g Turtle Bowl (IRE)—Zita Blues (IRE) **Mrs P. Thompson**

**Other Owners:** Mr D. B. Angove, Mr S. J. Angove, J. Apiafi, Mr J. Attfield, Mr P. Bennett-Jones, Mr R. J. Brimage, Mrs R. C. V. Brook, Mr G. R. Broom, Mrs A. E. M. Broom, Mr S. W. Buckley, Mr J. T. Chalmers, A. L. Cohen, Mr S. F. Coton, Mrs C. Cruddace, Mr M. J. Cruddace, Mrs H. Danson, J. T. Ennis, Mrs L. A. Farquhar, J. A. Gent, Mr P. George, R. B. Gray, P. J. Green, J. J. Hathorn, Mrs F. K. Hathorn, Mr T. M. Hely-Hutchinson, Mr D. L. Ives, Mr K. R. Ives, Mrs D. A. Johnson, Mr S. D. Johnson, Mr R. Jones, Alan Kaplan, D. J. Long, Mrs E. Long, Mr W. J. Mackay, S. M. Mercer, Mr S. S. Mercer, S. E. Munir, T. S. Palin, Mr H. T. Pelham, J. E. Potter, Mrs M. J. Potter, M. Prince, D. J. Reid, Mrs Y. J. Reynolds, Mr S. R. Roper, Mr N. Ryan, Mrs B. P. Siddall, Mr I. Souede, R. K. Stanley, Mr C. R. R. Sweeting, Mr C. J. R. Sweeting, Mrs A. M. Varmen, Mr R. J. D. Varmen, Mr R. C. Wilkin, Mr S. C. Willes, Mrs M. Willes, Willsford Racing Ltd.

**Assistant Trainer:** Mr M. C. Pipe C.B.E.

**Jockey (NH):** Conor O'Farrell, Tom Scudamore. **Conditional:** Kieron Edgar, Michael Heard. **Amateur:** Mr Tom Greatrex, Mr David Noonan.

---

## 490 MR CHARLES POGSON, Newark

Postal: **Allamoor Farm, Mansfield Road, Farnsfield, Nottinghamshire, NG22 8HZ**
Contacts: **PHONE (01623) 882275 MOBILE (07977) 016155**

1 **ALL FOR LILY,** 6, b m Alflora (IRE)—Who Let The Foxout **C. T. Pogson**
2 **BALLYBOGEY (IRE),** 9, b g Definite Article—Beenaround (IRE) **James Callow Douglas Pryde Charles Pogson**
3 **BALLYCAMP (IRE),** 6, br g Kayf Tara—All Our Blessings (IRE) **Wordingham Plant Hire & Partner**
4 **BUSY LILLY,** 6, b m Bollin Eric—Princess Derry **C. T. Pogson**
5 **COUNTERSIGN,** 6, b g Authorized (IRE)—Circle of Love **C. T. Pogson**
6 **CUSHEEN BRIDGE (IRE),** 7, b h Oscar (IRE)—One Hell Ofa Woman (IRE) **Wordingham Plant Hire**
7 **HOPEAND,** 10, b m King's Theatre (IRE)—Land of Glory **C. T. Pogson**
8 **INSIDE KNOWLEDGE (USA),** 9, gr ro g Mizzen Mast (USA)—Kithira **C. T. Pogson**
9 **KAYFTON PETE,** 9, b g Kayf Tara—Jonchee (FR) **Wordingham Plant Hire & Partner**
10 **MINELLA FORFITNESS (IRE),** 8, b g Westerner—Ring of Water (USA) **Wordingham Plant Hire & Partner**
11 **MONDO CANE (IRE),** 8, b g Beneficial—La Vita E Bella (FR) **C. T. Pogson**
12 **NOBLE WITNESS (IRE),** 12, b g Witness Box (USA)—Jennas Pride (IRE) **Wordingham Plant Hire & Partner**
13 **NORTHERN OSCAR (IRE),** 7, b g Oscar (IRE)—Cailin's Princess (IRE) **Allott & Wordingham**
14 **WORDY'S BOY,** 10, b g Kayf Tara—Wordy's Wonder **Wordingham Plant Hire**

**Other Owners:** Mr J. Allott, J. R. Callow, D. G. Pryde, P. L. Wordingham, Mrs P. A. Wordingham.

**Assistant Trainer:** Adam Pogson

**Jockey (NH):** Adam Pogson.

## 491 MR KEITH POLLOCK, Carluke

Postal: **10 Lee Meadow Road, Braidwood, Carluke, Lanarkshire, ML8 5PJ**

1 **DESTINY AWAITS (IRE),** 6, b g Dubai Destination (USA)—Mellow Jazz **Mr Keith Pollock**
2 **GROUND TO GARDEN,** 5, b m Muhtathir—Tatbeeq (IRE) **Mr J. W. Farley**

## 492 MR NICHOLAS POMFRET, Tilton-on-the-Hill

Postal: **Red Lodge Farm, Marefield Lane, Tilton-on-the-Hill, Leicester, Leicestershire, LE7 9LJ**
Contacts: **PHONE (01162) 597537 MOBILE (07885) 598810**

1 6, Ch m Samraan (USA)—Araminta **R. P. Brett**
2 **BETTY BORGIA,** 9, ch m Killer Instinct—Bellefleur **N. J. Pomfret**

## 493 MR JONATHAN PORTMAN, Upper Lambourn

Postal: **Whitcoombe House Stables, Upper Lambourn, Hungerford, Berkshire, RG17 8RA**
Contacts: **PHONE (01488) 73894 FAX (01488) 72952 MOBILE (07798) 824513**
**E-MAIL jonathan@jonathanportmanracing.com WEBSITE www.jonathanportmanracing.com**

1 **AMOURITA (IRE),** 4, b f Azamour (IRE)—Akarita (IRE) **The SOHO Partnership**
2 **BALMORAL CASTLE,** 6, b g Royal Applause—Mimiteh (USA) **J. G. B. Portman**
3 **BENOORDENHOUT (IRE),** 4, br g Footstepsinthesand—Tara Too (IRE) **Prof C. D. Green**
4 **CLASSIC MISSION,** 4, ch g Bahamian Bounty—Triple Cee (IRE) **David & Gwyn Joseph**
5 **CONNAUGHT WATER (IRE),** 4, b g Aussie Rules (USA)—Chingford (IRE) **J. G. B. Portman**
6 **EVERYWISH,** 4, b f Quatre Saisons—Reine de Violette **Mr R. C. Chennells**
7 **FERNGROVE (USA),** 4, gr g Rockport Harbor (USA)—Lucky Pipit **Mr J. T. Habershon-Butcher**
8 **HALLINGHAM,** 5, b g Halling (USA)—In Luck **The Ladies Of The Manor Syndicate**
9 **JACK BEAR,** 4, b g Joe Bear (IRE)—Colins Lady (FR) **Joe Bear Racing**
10 **JOE PACKET,** 8, ch g Joe Bear (IRE)—Costa Packet (IRE) **J. G. B. Portman**
11 **MONSIEUR RIEUSSEC,** 5, bl g Halling (USA)—Muscovado (USA) **Mr J. T. Habershon-Butcher**
12 **NESHIKOT (IRE),** 4, gr g Oscar (IRE)—Winter Daydream (IRE) **Prof C. D. Green**
13 **NOW WHAT,** 8, ch m Where Or When (IRE)—Vallauris **Mrs S. J. Portman**
14 **PASAKA BOY,** 5, ch g Haafhd—Shesha Bear **RWH Partnership**
15 **RUSSIAN REMARQUE,** 4, b g Archipenko (USA)—Accede **The Traditionalists**
16 **UNCLE PETTIT (IRE),** 7, b br g Heron Island (IRE)—Special Ballot (IRE) **A. R. Boswood**
17 **ZINNOBAR,** 5, gr m Ishiguru (USA)—Demolition Jo **Prof C. D. Green**

### THREE-YEAR-OLDS

18 **ALBERT HERRING,** b g Tobougg (IRE)—Balsamita (FR) **A. R. Boswood**
19 **ALERT,** b f Zamindar (USA)—Tereshkina (IRE) **Mrs M. D. Stewart**
20 **AVAIL (IRE),** b g Moss Vale (IRE)—Mistress Bailey (IRE) **J. G. B. Portman**
21 **BOLLYWOOD DREAM,** b f Sleeping Indian—Act Three **Mrs G. Hamilton-Fairley**
22 **BUCKLEBERRY,** ch g Sakhee's Secret—Smart Hostess **Berkeley Racing**
23 **CLASSIC CAROLINE,** b f Monsieur Bond (IRE)—Kanisfluh **D. Joseph**
24 **EDGE OF HEAVEN,** b f Pastoral Pursuits—Halfwaytoparadise **Mascalls Stud**
25 **ENGELBERG (IRE),** gr f Zebedee—Chingford (IRE) **Prof C. D. Green**
26 **EPPING FOREST (IRE),** b f Bushranger (IRE)—Ringmoor Down **Prof C. D. Green**
27 **FASOLT,** b c Tobougg (IRE)—Mighty Splash **A. R. Boswood**
28 Ch g Double Trigger (IRE)—Galette **J. Hayden/J. Portman**
29 **HOUND MUSIC,** ch f Ashkalani (IRE)—Saffron Fox **Mrs E. Edwards-Heathcote**
30 **ICKYMASHO,** b f Multiplex—Icky Woo **C.R. Lambourne, M. Forbes, D. Losse**
31 **JO BIBIDIA,** ch f Joe Bear (IRE)—Veni Bidi Vici **M. Webley/S. McPhee**
32 **MADAME LAFITE,** b f Dutch Art—Poppo's Song (CAN) **Mr J. T. Habershon-Butcher**
33 **MAYBELATER,** b f Mount Nelson—Muscovado (USA) **Mrs J. Wigan**
34 **RAGTIME DANCER,** ch f Medicean—Honky Tonk Sally **Mrs H. Maitland-Jones**
35 **ROYAL RAZALMA (IRE),** ch f Lope de Vega (IRE)—Twiggy's Sister (IRE) **David & Gwyn Joseph**
36 **RUSSIAN RADIANCE,** ch f Paco Boy (IRE)—Russian Ruby (FR) **The Traditionalists**
37 **SECRET BAY (IRE),** ch f Arcano (IRE)—Caribbean Escape **R. Dollar & D. Powell**
38 **SPARKS (IRE),** b f Elusive City (USA)—Hambye **Pump & Plant Services Ltd**
39 **STARLIGHT GENIE,** b f Hellvelyn—Anneliina **Mrs J. A. Watts**

## MR JONATHAN PORTMAN - Continued

**40 STARLIGHT JUNE,** gr f Hellvelyn—Pelican Key (IRE) **P. Thorman**
**41 VAN HUYSEN (IRE),** br g Excellent Art—Tara Too (IRE) **Prof C. D. Green**

## TWO-YEAR-OLDS

**42** B f 1/4 Excellent Art—Accede (Acclamation) (11428)
**43** B f 6/3 Lawman (FR)—An Ghalanta (IRE) (Holy Roman Emperor (IRE)) (22000) **Tom Edwards & Partners**
**44 BELLOTTA,** ch f 12/2 Nayef (USA)—Ela Paparouna (Vettori (IRE)) (4761) **P. Afia**
**45** B f 19/2 Zebedee—Chingford (IRE) (Redback) **Prof C. D. Green**
**46** Gr f 22/4 Aussie Rules (USA)—Gower Diva (Sakhee (USA)) **David & Gwyn Joseph**
**47** B f 7/5 Holy Roman Emperor (IRE)—Hollow Quaill (IRE) (Entrepreneur) **David & Gwyn Joseph**
**48 INTIMATELY,** b c 20/3 Intense Focus (USA)—
Midnight Fling (Groom Dancer (USA)) (9523) **Whitcoombe Park Racing**
**49** Ch c 29/1 Paco Boy (IRE)—La Polka (Carnival Dancer) **D. Hunt**
**50** B c 8/3 Art Connoisseur (IRE)—Madhaaq (IRE) (Medicean) (2857) **Follow The Flag Partnership**
**51 MAYA ANGELOU (IRE),** b f 14/4 Big Bad Bob (IRE)—
Cosmic Breeze (IRE) (Fasliyev (USA)) (15000) **Berkeley Racing**
**52** B f 30/4 Approve (IRE)—Min Asl Wafi (IRE) (Octagonal (NZ)) (6000) **D. Powell & Partners**
**53 MISTER SHOWMAN,** b br c 17/3 Showcasing—Theatre Royal (Royal Applause) **Runs In The Family**
**54** B f 12/4 Roderic O'Connor (IRE)—Nutshell (Dubai Destination (USA)) (5000)
**55** Br f 17/2 Sir Percy—Overlook (Generous (IRE)) (11000)
**56** Ch f 13/4 Paco Boy (IRE)—Photographie (USA) (Trempolino (USA)) (7000) **Mrs H. Maitland-Jones**
**57** Ch f 24/3 Sakhee's Secret—Pin Cushion (Pivotal) (7000) **Follow The Flag Partnership**
**58 POP CULTURE,** ch f 14/3 Equiano (FR)—Naizak (Medicean) (10000) **Mr & Mrs L. J. Walker**
**59 RAVENSWOOD,** b c 30/3 Lawman (FR)—Whatami (Daylami (IRE)) (47000) **Mr J. T. Habershon-Butcher**
**60 RUSSIAN RANGER (IRE),** b g 10/4 Bushranger (IRE)—
Pink Sovietstaia (FR) (Soviet Star (USA)) (10317) **Graham Clark & Partners**
**61** B g 15/3 Approve (IRE)—Tentears (Cadeaux Genereux) (8571)
**62 TIZ HERSELF (IRE),** gr f 5/3 Dandy Man (IRE)—Pitullie (USA) (Rockport Harbor (USA)) (16190) **Berkeley Racing**
**63** Gr f 11/4 Intense Focus (USA)—Way To The Stars (Dansili) **Tom Edwards & Partners**
**64** B c 1/4 Royal Applause—Zarkavean (Medicean) (15000) **C. R. Lambourne, M. Forbes, D. Losse**

**Other Owners:** Mr J. Atkinson, Mr N. Austin, Mr I. Bath, Mr Jeremy Brownlee, Mr G. Clark, Mr Steve Dawes, R. C. Dollar, Mr Tom F. Edwards, Mr A. Elliot, Mr S. Emmet, Mr G. Gash, Mrs Susan Hearn, My Barry Hearn, Mr J. Hobson, Mrs L. Hobson, Mr J. Homan, Mr J. Homan, Mr D. M. Joseph, Mr D. G. Joseph, Mr S. McDonald, Mr Stuart McPhee, Mr D. Milton, Mr R. O'Callaghan, The Hon Mrs R. Pease, Mrs A. Plummer, Mr D. Popely, D. F. Powell, Mr M. A. Ransom, Mr S. M. Ransom, Mrs E. Scaddan, Mr H. Symonds, Mr P. Thorman, Mr M. Tye, Mr T. Weishler, Mr G. Wickens, Mr G. C. Wickens.

**Assistant Trainer:** Sophie Portman

**Apprentice:** Jack Budge, Ned Curtis. **Amateur:** Mr J. Harding.

---

## 494 MR JAMIE POULTON, Lewes

Postal: **White Cottage, Telscombe, Lewes, East Sussex, BN7 3HZ**
Contacts: **YARD (01273) 300515 HOME (01273) 300127 FAX (01273) 300915**
**MOBILE (07980) 596952**
**E-MAIL jamie@poulton8.orangehome.co.uk**

**1 BANGKOK PETE (IRE),** 10, b g Alflora (IRE)—Kinnegads Pride (IRE) **The Never Dropped Partnership**
**2 DOUBLE DEALITES,** 5, b m Double Trigger (IRE)—Linden Grace (USA) **Miss V. Markowiak**
**3 FARBREAGA (IRE),** 9, b g Shernazar—Gleann Alainn **Miss V. Markowiak**
**4 FEATHER DANCER,** 5, b m Norse Dancer (IRE)—Featherlight
**5 FIX UP LOOK SHARP,** 4, b c Sakhee (USA)—Featherlight **Miss V. Markowiak**
**6 GORHAMS GIFT,** 7, b g Double Trigger (IRE)—Linden Grace (USA) **The Never Dropped Partnership**
**7 NORMAN THE RED,** 5, ch g Tobougg (IRE)—Linden Lime **The Never Dropped Partnership**
**8 TISH BAY,** 9, ch g Karinga Bay—Tisho **J. R. Poulton**
**9 UP FOUR IT (IRE),** 7, b g Luso—Newgate Beauty (IRE) **Mr L. C. Best**

## THREE-YEAR-OLDS

**10 TANGO TURNER (IRE),** ch c Excellent Art—Kassyderia (IRE) **Tango Turner Partnership**

**Other Owners:** Mr I. C. Cusselle, Mr K. Farmer.

**Assistant Trainer:** Mrs C D Poulton

**Jockey (NH):** Mattie Batchelor.

## 495 MR BRENDAN POWELL, Upper Lambourn

Postal: **Newlands Stables, Upper Lambourn, Hungerford, Berkshire, RG17 8QX**
Contacts: **PHONE (01488) 73650 FAX (01488) 73650 MOBILE (07785) 390737**
**E-MAIL brendan.powell@btconnect.com WEBSITE www.brendanpowellracing.com**

1 **ALLA SVELTA (IRE),** 9, b g Milan—Miss Greinton (GER) **Mr P. Conway**
2 **AMAZING SCENES (IRE),** 6, b br g Desert King (IRE)—Lady Leila (IRE) **Let's Get Ready To Rumble Partnership**
3 **BENEFITS WELL (IRE),** 8, b g Beneficial—Farran Lady (IRE) **B. G. Powell**
4 **CANADIAN DIAMOND (IRE),** 8, ch g Halling (USA)—Six Nations (USA) **Nicholls Family**
5 **CHAPELLERIE (IRE),** 6, b m Acclamation—Castellane (FR) **Mr T. M. Clarke**
6 **DARK AMBER,** 5, b m Sakhee (USA)—Donna Vita **Mr C. McGuckin**
7 **DARK AND DANGEROUS (IRE),** 7, b g Cacique (IRE)—Gilah (IRE) **North South Alliance**
8 **DARK EMERALD (IRE),** 5, gr g Dark Angel (IRE)—Xema **Mr K. R. E. Rhatigan**
9 **DUNKELLY CASTLE (IRE),** 11, ch g Old Vic—Nanna's Joy (IRE) **Vetlab Supplies Ltd**
10 **ELEMENT QUARTET (IRE),** 6, b m Brian Boru—Glendante (IRE) **Ontoawinner, J Farmer & Partner**
11 **ELUSIVE ELLEN (IRE),** 5, b m Elusive City (USA)—Ellen's Girl (IRE) **C. F. Harrington**
12 **GANNICUS,** 4, b g Phoenix Reach (IRE)—Rasmani **Winterbeck Manor Stud Ltd**
13 **GRAFFITI ART,** 6, b m Kayf Tara—Art Affair (GER) **Mr R. L. Fanshawe**
14 **JACKPOT,** 5, b m Avonbridge—Strat's Quest **P. Banfield**
15 **JULIE PRINCE (IRE),** 9, b g Desert Prince (IRE)—Daniella Ridge (IRE) **L. Gilbert**
16 **KEYCHAIN (IRE),** 5, b g Key of Luck (USA)—Sarifa (IRE) **Chasing Gold Limited**
17 **LADY FROM GENEVA,** 8, ch m Generous (IRE)—Schizo-Phonic **Geneva Finance PLC**
18 **LETTHERIVERRUNDRY (IRE),** 5, br g Diamond Green (FR)—Dissitation (IRE) **J. P. McManus**
19 **LITTLE FLO,** 4, ch f Midnight Legend—Sweet Robinia (IRE) **P. H. Betts**
20 **MERCHANT OF MILAN,** 7, b g Milan—Repunzel **Mr & Mrs A. J. Mutch**
21 **MORESTEAD (IRE),** 10, ch g Traditionally (USA)—Itsy Bitsy Betsy (USA) **L. Gilbert**
22 **MORTHANALEGEND,** 6, b g Midnight Legend—Morwenna (IRE)
23 **PHANTOM PRINCE (IRE),** 6, b g Jeremy (USA)—Phantom Waters **C. F. Harrington**
24 **PRIM AND PROPER,** 4, b f Sleeping Indian—Quite Fantastic (IRE) **Mr & Mrs A. J. Mutch**
25 **PURPLE SAGE (IRE),** 9, b m Danehill Dancer (IRE)—Kylemore (IRE) **Mr R. J. Bandey**
26 **QUINLANDIO (IRE),** 5, b g Thousand Words—La Shalak (IRE) **Mr T. M. Clarke**
27 **RAKAAN (IRE),** 8, ch g Bahamian Bounty—Petite Spectre **ACC Syndicate**
28 **REACH THE BEACH,** 6, ch m Phoenix Reach (IRE)—Comtesse Noire (CAN) **Winterbeck Manor Stud Ltd**
29 **SONORAN SANDS (IRE),** 7, b g Footstepsinthesand—Atishoo (IRE) **C. F. Harrington**
30 **STOCK HILL FAIR,** 7, b g Sakhee (USA)—April Stock **Mrs M Fairbairn, E Gadsden & P Dean**
31 **SUN AND STARS,** 7, ch g Haafhd—Leading Role **J. H. Widdows**
32 **TELLOVOI (IRE),** 7, b h Indian Haven—Kloonlara (IRE) **Mr T. M. Clarke**
33 **TERRA FIRMA,** 5, b g Lucarno (USA)—Solid Land (FR) **P. L. Winkworth**
34 **THUNDERING CLOUD (IRE),** 4, b f Clodovil (IRE)—Porky Pie (IRE) **Mr K. R. E. Rhatigan**
35 **UNCLE DERMOT (IRE),** 7, b g Arakan (USA)—Cappadoce (IRE) **Mr K. R. E. Rhatigan**
36 **VIOLETS BOY (IRE),** 8, br g King's Theatre (IRE)—Sunshine Rays **H. Redknapp**

### THREE-YEAR-OLDS

37 **CARAMBA (IRE),** b f Lord Shanakill (USA)—Known Class (USA) **P. Banfield**
38 **HEAVENLYFRIENDSHIP,** b f Multiplex—Nut (IRE) **Falfairshank Partnership**

**Other Owners:** Mr S. Bridge, P. Dean, Mrs M. Fairbairn, Mr M. A. Fairhurst, Mrs J. Fallon, E. J. S. Gadsden, Mr C. McAvoy, Mr P. Morris, Mr J. Morris, Mr A. J. Mutch, Mrs S. Mutch, Mr R. Nicholls, Mrs E. Nicholls, N. J. O'Brien, Mr J. R. Peppiatt, A. J. Viall.

**Jockey (flat):** Seb Sanders. **Jockey (NH):** A P McCoy, Andrew Tinkler. **Conditional:** Brendan Powell. **Apprentice:** Matthew Lawson. **Amateur:** Miss Jenny Powell.

## 496 MR TED POWELL, Reigate

Postal: **Nutwood Farm, Gatton Park Road, Reigate, Surrey, RH2 0SX**
Contacts: **PHONE (01737) 765612**

1 **AJJAADD (USA),** 9, b g Elusive Quality (USA)—Millstream (USA) **Katy & Lol Pratt**
2 **SNOW KING (USA),** 5, ch g Elusive Quality (USA)—Cloudspin (USA) **Mr D. G. Acomb**

**Other Owners:** Mrs K. J. Pratt, L. C. Pratt.

## 497 SIR MARK PRESCOTT BT, Newmarket

Postal: **Heath House, Newmarket, Suffolk, CB8 8DU**
Contacts: **PHONE (01638) 662117 FAX (01638) 666572**

1 **ALCAEUS,** 5, b h Hernando (FR)—Alvarita **Ne'er Do Wells IV**
2 **ALWILDA,** 5, gr m Hernando (FR)—Albanova **Miss K. Rausing**
3 **BIG THUNDER,** 5, gr g Dalakhani (IRE)—Charlotte O Fraise (IRE) **John Brown & Megan Dennis**
4 **DEAUVILLE DANCER (IRE),** 4, b g Tamayuz—Mathool (IRE) **Suffolk Bloodstock**
5 **DON'T BE,** 5, b m Cape Cross (IRE)—Faslen (USA) **Mrs O. Hoare**
6 **HIGH SECRET (IRE),** 4, b g High Chaparral (IRE)—Secret Question (USA) **Charles C. Walker - Osborne House**
7 **JOLIE BLONDE,** 4, ch f Sir Percy—Affaire d'amour **Miss K. Rausing**
8 **LEGAL SHARK (IRE),** 4, b g Lawman (FR)—Sea Searcher (USA) **Tim Bunting - Osborne House II**
9 **MOSCATO,** 4, gr g Hernando (FR)—Alba Stella **The Green Door Partnership**
10 **PALLASATOR,** 6, b g Motivator—Ela Athena **Qatar Racing Ltd**
11 **SARPECH (IRE),** 4, b g Sea The Stars (IRE)—Sadima (IRE) **Qatar Racing Ltd**
12 **SEA PRIDE (IRE),** 4, b f Sea The Stars (IRE)—Claxon **Bluehills Racing Ltd**
13 **THE STEWARD (USA),** 4, b g Street Cry (IRE)—Candlelight (USA) **Donald R. Dizney**
14 **WILLIAM OF ORANGE,** 4, b g Duke of Marmalade (IRE)—Critical Acclaim **Nicholas Jones**

### THREE-YEAR-OLDS

15 **ALEATOR (USA),** b c Blame (USA)—Alma Mater **Miss K. Rausing**
16 **ALL FOR THE BEST (IRE),** b g Rip Van Winkle (IRE)—Alleluia **Mrs S. Rogers & Miss K. Rausing**
17 **AMOUR DE NUIT (IRE),** b g Azamour (IRE)—Umthoulah (IRE) **Mr L. A. Larratt - Osborne House**
18 **CELESTIAL PATH (IRE),** b c Footstepsinthesand—Miss Kittyhawk (IRE) **Gordon C. Woodall & Prof C. Tisdall**
19 **DARK SWAN (IRE),** b f Zamindar (USA)—
Brooklyn's Storm (USA) **The Prince of Wales & The Duchess of Cornwall**
20 **DEAUVILLE DAME,** b f Alflora (IRE)—Hispalis (IRE) **The With The Grain Partnership**
21 **KACHOU,** b f Excellent Art—Milwaukee (FR) **Lady Fairhaven & The Hon C & H Broughton**
22 **LIGHT BREAKS (IRE),** b g Dylan Thomas (IRE)—Anywaysmile (IRE) **Moyglare Stud**
23 **MEGARA,** ch g Medicean—Alicante **Bluehills Racing Ltd**
24 **MERRITT ISLAND,** b f Exceed And Excel (AUS)—Moon Crystal **Mr & Mrs J. Kelsey-Fry**
25 **MOLLY DOLLY (IRE),** b f Exceed And Excel (AUS)—Garra Molly (IRE) **Mrs J. Rooney**
26 **NIGHT GENERATION (GER),** ch g Sholokhov (IRE)—Night Woman (GER) **John Brown & Megan Dennis**
27 **POETIC LICENSE (IRE),** b g Dylan Thomas (IRE)—Bright Bank (IRE) **Mr & Mrs William Rucker**
28 **RAINBOW PRIDE (IRE),** gr g Clodovil (IRE)—Rahila (IRE) **Mr W. E. Sturt - Osborne House IV**
29 **SEA OF HEAVEN (IRE),** b g Sea The Stars (IRE)—Maid of Killeen (IRE) **Lady Bamford**
30 **SEYCHELLOISE,** b f Pivotal—Starlit Sands **Miss K. Rausing**
31 **SINGOALLA,** b f Arch (USA)—Songerie **Miss K. Rausing**
32 **TAFOLAU (IRE),** b f Dylan Thomas (IRE)—Sliding Scale **Mr & Mrs J. Kelsey-Fry**

### TWO-YEAR-OLDS

33 **ABBEYLEIX,** gr c 30/4 Sir Percy—Alvarita (Selkirk (USA)) (43650) **Mr T. J. Rooney**
34 **ALAKAZAM,** b c 20/4 Archipenko (USA)—Alakananda (Hernando (FR)) (45000) **Mr R. P. Fry - Osborne House**
35 **ALINSTANTE,** b f 22/4 Archipenko (USA)—Algarade (Green Desert (USA)) **Miss K. Rausing**
36 **ALSACIENNE,** gr f 1/3 Dalakhani (IRE)—Alabastrine (Green Desert (USA)) (27777) **Miss K. Rausing**
37 **BEAR FACED,** b c 16/1 Intikhab (USA)—
Hulcote Rose (IRE) (Rock of Gibraltar (IRE)) (40000) **The Barkers & Chris Jenkins**
38 **CARTWRIGHT,** b c 4/4 High Chaparral (IRE)—One So Marvellous (Nashwan (USA)) (160000) **Mr J. L. C. Pearce**
39 **CLINE,** ch f 5/4 Pivotal—Graduation (Lomitas) **Cheveley Park Stud**
40 **COLOMBE BLEU,** b f 12/3 Manduro (GER)—Blue Dream (IRE) (Cadeaux Genereux) **Mr J. B. Haggas**
41 **COTE D'AZUR,** ch c 25/2 Champs Elysees—Florentia (Medicean) **Mr N. Greig**
42 B f 15/2 Roderic O'Connor (IRE)—Dollar Bird (IRE) (Kris) (32000) **Biddestone Racing Partnership**
43 **DUSTY RAVEN,** ch c 30/4 Raven's Pass (USA)—Dust Dancer (Suave Dancer (USA)) **Bluehills Racing Ltd**
44 **DUTCH HEIRESS,** b f 7/2 Dutch Art—Regal Heiress (Pivotal) **Cheveley Park Stud**
45 **HER EMINENCE,** b f 1/4 Dubawi (IRE)—Intrigued (Darshaan) **Denford Stud**
46 Br f 24/2 Authorized (IRE)—Hydro Calido (USA) (Nureyev (USA)) **Lordship Stud**
47 B f 24/4 Cape Cross (IRE)—Lady Rockfield (IRE) (Rock of Gibraltar (IRE)) (30000) **Axom (LVII)**
48 **LUGANO,** b c 2/3 Galileo (IRE)—Swiss Lake (USA) (Indian Ridge) (250000) **Mr J. L. C. Pearce**
49 **MARSHA (IRE),** b f 16/3 Acclamation—Marlinka (Marju (IRE)) **Elite Racing**
50 **MEDDLESOME,** b c 5/3 Medicean—Meddle (Diktat) (20000) **Mr N. Greig - Osborne House**
51 **MISS MARINA BAY,** ch f 3/2 Galileo (IRE)—Miss Corniche (Hernando (FR)) **Mr J. L. C. Pearce**
52 **MOCKINBIRD (IRE),** b f 27/3 Makfi—Littlefeather (IRE) (Indian Ridge) (43650) **Sir Edmund Loder Bt**
53 **MONJENI,** b c 7/2 Montjeu (IRE)—
Polly's Mark (IRE) (Mark of Esteem (IRE)) (650000) **Fergus Anstock & Alice Mills**
54 **MOTIVATE,** b c 28/2 Motivator—Hispalis (IRE) (Barathea (IRE)) **Mr P. Bamford - Osborne House**

## SIR MARK PRESCOTT BT - Continued

55 **MYSTIQUE HEIGHTS,** b c 6/4 High Chaparral (IRE)—Musique Magique (IRE) (Mozart (IRE)) (85000) **Mr G. C. Woodall**
56 **PALISADE,** b c 12/4 Fastnet Rock (AUS)—Portal (Hernando (FR)) **Cheveley Park Stud**
57 **RED BOX,** b f 31/3 Exceed And Excel (AUS)—Confidential Lady (Singspiel (IRE)) **Cheveley Park Stud**
58 B f 14/2 Jeremy (USA)—Rising Wind (IRE) (Shirocco (GER)) **Lady O'Reilly**
59 **SILAS R (IRE),** b c 9/4 Pour Moi (IRE)—Playwithmyheart (Diktat) (67460) **Mr T. J. Rooney**
60 B c 14/5 Dylan Thomas (IRE)—Sliding Scale (Sadler's Wells (USA)) **Mr & Mrs Kelsey-Fry**
61 **SOUND OF THE SEA,** b f 4/3 Acclamation—Summer Night (Nashwan (USA)) **Miss K. Rausing**
62 **ST MICHEL,** b c 25/2 Sea The Stars (IRE)—Miss Provence (Hernando (FR)) **Mr J. L. C. Pearce**
63 **STATUS QUO (IRE),** br c 8/4 Thewayyouare (USA)—Again Royale (IRE) (Royal Academy (USA)) (22221) **Mr G. Moore - Osborne House II**
64 **TENZING NORGAY,** gr c 13/5 Aussie Rules (USA)—Miss Katmandu (IRE) (Rainbow Quest (USA)) **Mr J. L. C. Pearce**
65 **TIME WARP,** ch c 28/1 Archipenko (USA)—Here To Eternity (USA) (Stormy Atlantic (USA)) (29364) **Mr W. E. Sturt - Osborne House**
66 B c 4/3 More Than Ready (USA)—Tjinouska (USA) (Cozzene (USA)) (63109) **Mr Baxter, Mr Gregson, Mr Jenkins & Mr Warman**
67 B c 10/2 Galileo (IRE)—Turning Top (IRE) (Pivotal) **Michael Tabor**
68 **TYRANNICAL,** br c 5/4 Dansili—Queen of Mean (Pivotal) (110000) **Mr Bunting -Osborne House, Sir P. Vela, P. Stanley**

**Other Owners:** Mr E. A. Baxter, Mr B. D. Burnet, Mr Terry Corden, Mr Darren Ellis, Mr Phil Fry, Mr P. G. Goulandris, The Hon. Mrs G. Greenwood, Mrs Caroline Gregson, Mr Chris Jenkins, Mr L. A. Larratt, Mr Mike Rudd, Mr & Mrs Dennis Russell, Prince Faisal Salman, Mr Barry Taylor, Mrs J. Taylor, Mr Mark Tracey, The Hon. Lady Troubridge, Mrs S. L. Warman, Mr E. J. Williams.

**Assistant Trainer:** William Butler, **Pupil Assistant:** Robert McDowall

**Jockey (flat):** L. Morris, C. Catlin. **Apprentice:** R. Jessop, M. Fernandes.

---

## 498 MR ANDREW PRICE, Leominster

Postal: **Eaton Hall Farm, Leominster, Herefordshire, HR6 0NA**
Contacts: **PHONE (01568) 611137 FAX (01568) 611137 MOBILE (07729) 838660**
**E-MAIL helen@aepriceracing.plus.com**

1 **BERTIE LUGG,** 7, b g Beat All (USA)—Flakey Dove **Mr A Price & Mr A Bathurst**
2 5, B m Needwood Blade—Castanet
3 **CHESTERWOOD,** 6, b g Revoque (IRE)—Clover Dove **A. E. Price**
4 **FLORA LEA,** 8, b m Alflora (IRE)—Castanet **Mrs C. Davis**
5 **MIDNIGHT DOVE,** 10, ch g Karinga Bay—Flighty Dove **M. G. Racing**
6 **SPENCER LEA,** 7, b g Overbury (IRE)—Castanet **Mrs C. Davis**

**Other Owners:** A. G. Bathurst, Mr M. Jones, Mrs E. R. Kitt.

**Assistant Trainer:** Mrs H L Price

---

## 499 MR RICHARD PRICE, Hereford

Postal: **Criftage Farm, Ullingswick, Hereford, Herefordshire, HR1 3JG**
Contacts: **PHONE (01432) 820263 FAX (01432) 820785 MOBILE (07929) 200598**

1 **BONJOUR STEVE,** 4, b g Bahamian Bounty—Anthea **B. Veasey**
2 **CHEVETON,** 11, ch g Most Welcome—Attribute **Mrs K. E. Oseman**
3 **DISTANT HIGH,** 4, b f High Chaparral (IRE)—Distant Dreamer (USA) **My Left Foot Racing Syndicate**
4 **GRACCHUS (USA),** 9, b g Black Minnaloushe (USA)—Montessa (USA) **R. H. Harris**
5 **GREYEMKAY,** 7, gr g Fair Mix (IRE)—Magic Orb **Richard Price & Maria Slade**
6 **IGUACU,** 11, b g Desert Prince (IRE)—Gay Gallanta (USA) **Mr & Mrs D. C. Holder**
7 **ROWLESTONE LASS,** 5, b m Hernando (FR)—Charmante Femme **Ocean's Five**
8 **TAURUS TWINS,** 9, b g Deportivo—Intellibet One **G. E. Amey & G. D. Bailey**
9 **WATTS UP SON,** 7, b g Diktat—Local Fancy **Mrs V. J. Morse**
10 **ZARIA,** 4, b f Tomba—Princess Zara **Mrs K. E. Oseman**

**Other Owners:** G. E. Amey, Mr G. D. Bailey, Mr D. Boddy, A. J. Chance, P. J. Hoare, D. C. Holder, Mrs C. R. Holder, R. J. Price, Mrs L. M. Slade.

**Assistant Trainer:** Jane Price **Amateur:** Mr M. Price.

## 500 MR PETER PRITCHARD, Shipston-on-Stour

Postal: **The Gate House, Whatcote, Shipston-On-Stour, Warwickshire, CV36 5EF**
Contacts: **PHONE (01295) 680689**

1 5, B g Passing Glance—Earcomesannie (IRE) **Unregistered Partnership**
2 **EARCOMESTHEDREAM (IRE),** 12, b g Marignan (USA)—Play It By Ear (IRE) **Woodland Generators & Mr D R Pritchard**
3 **OVERTON LAD,** 14, gr g Overbury (IRE)—Safe Arrival (USA) **D. R. Pritchard**
4 **SHADESOFNAVY,** 9, ch g Fleetwood (IRE)—Safe Arrival (USA) **Whittington Racing Club**
5 **TIKKETORIDE,** 7, gr g Tikkanen (USA)—Safe Arrival (USA) **D. R. Pritchard**
6 **TISFREETDREAM (IRE),** 14, b g Oscar (IRE)—Gayley Gale (IRE) **Woodland Generators & Mr D R Pritchard**

**Other Owners:** Mr W. R. Evans, Woodlands (Worcestershire) Ltd.

**Assistant Trainer:** Mrs. E. Gardner

**Jockey (NH):** Jack Doyle, Jamie Moore.

## 501 MR PETER PURDY, Bridgwater

Postal: **Fyne Court Farm, Broomfield, Bridgwater, Somerset, TA5 2EQ**
Contacts: **PHONE (01823) 451632 FAX (01823) 451632 MOBILE (07860) 392786**
**E-MAIL purdy844@btinternet.com**

1 **COURT FINALE,** 14, ch g One Voice (USA)—Tudor Sunset **P. D. Purdy**
2 **MAY COURT,** 8, b g Groomsbridge May I—Tudor Sunset **P. D. Purdy**
3 **TENSION IN COURT,** 7, b g High Tension (USA)—Tudor Sunset **P. D. Purdy**
4 **THE BLONDE EMPEROR,** 10, ch g Emperor Fountain—Tudor Blonde **P. D. Purdy**
5 8, B g High Tension (USA)—Tudor Blonde **P. D. Purdy**
6 6, Ch m Mutazayid (IRE)—Tudor Blonde **P. D. Purdy**

**Jockey (NH):** Wayne Kavanagh.

## 502 MR NOEL QUINLAN, Newmarket

Postal: **Harraton Stables, Chapel Street, Exning, Newmarket, Suffolk, CB8 7HA**
Contacts: **PHONE (01638) 578674 FAX (01638) 577831 MOBILE (07815) 072946**
**E-MAIL noelquinlanracing@hotmail.co.uk**

1 **BOBOLI GARDENS,** 5, b g Medicean—Park Crystal (IRE) **Brookside Breeders Club**
2 **FIRE IN BABYLON (IRE),** 7, b g Montjeu (IRE)—Three Owls (IRE) **Mrs F. A. Shaw**
3 **GOLDEN SPEAR,** 4, ch c Kyllachy—Penmayne **Newtown Anner Stud Farm Ltd**
4 **NOTNOWSAM,** 4, ch g Notnowcato—First Fantasy **R. C. Tooth**
5 **POWERFUL PIERRE,** 8, ch g Compton Place—Alzianah **Newtown Anner Stud Farm Ltd**

### THREE-YEAR-OLDS

6 **DAT IL DO,** b f Bahamian Bounty—Broughtons Revival **Mr P. Hollingsworth**
7 **FREE RADICAL,** b c Iffraaj—La Jwaab **Newtown Anner Stud Farm Ltd**
8 **HYMN OF HOPE (IRE),** b c Acclamation—Musical Treat (IRE) **Mrs Catherine Cashman**
9 **MR MOROCCO,** b c Shirocco (GER)—Moxby **Mr G. Wilding**
10 **MR SUNDOWNER (USA),** b br g Scat Daddy (USA)—Bold Answer (USA) **Mr J. L. Head**
11 **NEBULLA,** ch c Iffraaj—Kelowna (IRE) **Newtown Anner Stud Farm Ltd**
12 **RIO FALLS (IRE),** b g Captain Rio—Swallow Falls (IRE) **Mr N. P. Quinlan**
13 **THREE GRACEZ,** b f Kyllachy—Three Ducks **Mr Neil Hormann**
14 **ZINGIBER,** ch g Manduro (GER)—Titoli di Coda (IRE) **Mr G. Wilding**

### TWO-YEAR-OLDS

15 B f 22/2 Equiano (FR)—Bible Box (IRE) (Bin Ajwaad (IRE)) **Mr G. Wilding**
16 B f 15/3 Jeremy (USA)—Causeway Coast (USA) (Giant's Causeway (USA)) **Mr David O'Rourke**
17 B br f 5/4 Kheleyf (USA)—Haiti Dancer (Josr Algarhoud (IRE)) **Brookside Breeders Club**
18 B f 21/4 Makfi—Hanella (IRE) (Galileo (IRE)) **Johayro Investments**
19 B c 14/4 Canford Cliffs (IRE)—Idle Chatter (IRE) (Galileo (IRE)) **J. Lynch**
20 B c 14/3 Kheleyf (USA)—It's The War (USA) (Consolidator (USA)) **Hamad Kadfoor**
21 B c 27/1 Sakhee's Secret—Lemon Rock (Green Desert (USA)) **Mr Tommy Cummins**
22 Ch f 24/1 Approve (IRE)—Mairead Anne (USA) (Elusive Quality (USA)) (16000) **Shane Long**

## MR NOEL QUINLAN - Continued

**23** Br f 29/3 Dark Angel (IRE)—Najaaba (USA) (Bahhare (USA)) (30000) **Mrs C. Cashman**
**24** Ch f 24/4 Frozen Power (IRE)—Sanfrancullinan (IRE) (Bluebird (USA)) (3809) **Mrs Debbie Black**
**25** B f 3/4 Frozen Power (IRE)—
Speckled Hen (IRE) (Titus Livius (FR)) (5500) **R. Morris, J. Russell, Doyle & Murphy**
**26** B f 11/5 Hellvelyn—Ziggy Zaggy (Diktat) **Mr N. P. Quinlan**

**Other Owners:** Mr Stephen Holmes, Mr John James, Mr R. Morris, Miss M. A. Quinlan, Mr S. Russell.

---

## 503 MR DENIS QUINN, Newmarket
Postal: **122 New Cheveley Road, Newmarket, Suffolk, CB8 8BY**
Contacts: **MOBILE (07435) 340008**

1 **CHERRY STREET,** 6, b g Alhaarth (IRE)—Weqaar (USA) **Mr A. Dal Pos**
2 **CLOCK ON TOM,** 5, b g Trade Fair—Night Owl **Mr J. T. Mangan**
3 **CRAFTYBIRD,** 4, ch f Mastercraftsman (IRE)—Tobaranama (IRE) **Mr J. T. Mangan**
4 **DIAMOND BACK (IRE),** 4, b c Diamond Green (FR)—Raqiqah **Mr M. McGovern**
5 **GIANTSTEPSAHEAD (IRE),** 6, br g Footstepsinthesand—Salty Air (IRE) **Mr K. R. Hills**
6 **HELAMIS,** 5, b m Shirocco (GER)—Alnoor (USA) **Mr J. T. Mangan**
7 **ICEMAN GEORGE,** 11, b g Beat Hollow—Diebiedale **Mr J. T. Mangan**
8 **LOUD,** 5, ch g Dutch Art—Applauding (IRE) **Mr Z. Chaudhry**
9 **NORMAN'S STAR,** 4, b g Tiger Hill (IRE)—Canis Star **Mrs S. Dwyer**
10 **SALBATORE,** 7, ch g Chineur (FR)—Au Contraire **Mr J. T. Mangan**
11 **VALE MENTOR (IRE),** 4, b c Moss Vale (IRE)—Sinamay (USA) **Mr J. A. Alsabah**

### THREE-YEAR-OLDS

12 **RED FLUTE,** ch g Piccolo—Fee Faw Fum (IRE) **Mr T. Al Nisf**

---

## 504 MR JOHN QUINN, Malton
Postal: **Bellwood Cottage Stables, Settrington, Malton, North Yorkshire, YO17 8NR**
Contacts: **PHONE (01944) 768370 MOBILE (07899) 873304**
**E-MAIL johnquinnracing@btconnect.com**

1 **ARTHURS SECRET,** 5, ch g Sakhee's Secret—Angry Bark (USA) **David Scott & Co (Pattern Makers) Ltd**
2 **AURORE D'ESTRUVAL (FR),** 5, ch m Nickname (FR)—Option d'estruval (FR) **Mr C. S. Hinchy**
3 **BOLD CAPTAIN (IRE),** 4, ch g Captain Rio—Indianaca (IRE) **Highfield Racing**
4 **CALCULATED RISK,** 6, ch g Motivator—Glen Rosie (IRE) **J. T. Warner**
5 **CAPTAIN WHOOSH (IRE),** 4, gr g Dandy Man (IRE)—Caerella (IRE) **Mr D. Ward**
6 **CHIEFTAIN'S CHOICE (IRE),** 6, b g King's Theatre (IRE)—Fairy Native (IRE) **Mr C. S. Hinchy**
7 **COSMIC TIGRESS,** 4, b f Tiger Hill (IRE)—Cosmic Case **The Cosmic Cases**
8 **DARLING BOYZ,** 4, ch g Auction House (USA)—Summertime Parkes **J. N. Blackburn**
9 **DISTIME (IRE),** 9, b g Flemensfirth (USA)—Technohead (IRE) **Middleham Park Racing & Cosyseal Racing**
10 **EL BEAU (IRE),** 4, ch g Camacho—River Beau (IRE) **Highfield Racing (Camacho)**
11 **EVANESCENT (IRE),** 6, b g Elusive City (USA)—Itsanothergirl **Mrs S. Quinn**
12 **FANTASY GLADIATOR,** 9, b g Ishiguru (USA)—Fancier Bit **The Fantasy Fellowship**
13 **FINAL COUNTDOWN,** 4, ch g Selkirk (USA)—Culture Queen **Estio Pinnacle Racing**
14 **FISHER,** 6, br g Jeremy (USA)—Elfin Laughter **Exors of the Late Mr D. W. Barker**
15 **FORCED FAMILY FUN,** 5, b g Refuse To Bend (IRE)—Juniper Girl (IRE) **The Top Silk Syndicate**
16 **GRAND MEISTER,** 4, gr g Mastercraftsman (IRE)—Wait It Out (USA) **Highfield Racing 4**
17 **GREAT HALL,** 5, b g Halling (USA)—L'affaire Monique **Mr C. S. Hinchy**
18 **HIDDEN JUSTICE (IRE),** 6, b g Lawman (FR)—Uncharted Haven **Highfield Racing 2**
19 **KASHMIR PEAK (IRE),** 6, b g Tiger Hill (IRE)—Elhareer (IRE) **Win Only SP Only Partnership**
20 **KASHSTAREE,** 4, b f Sakhee (USA)—Celestial Welcome **Star Alliance 5**
21 **KILAS GIRL (IRE),** 5, b m Millenary—Ballybeg Dusty (IRE) **Mr R. Harmon**
22 **L'AIGLE ROYAL (GER),** 4, b g Sholokhov (IRE)—Laren (GER) **J. T. Warner**
23 **LADY BEAUFORT,** 4, ch f Shirocco (GER)—Kadassa (IRE) **The Desperados**
24 **MOIDORE,** 6, b g Galileo (IRE)—Flash of Gold **Estio Pinnacle Racing**
25 **MR GALLIVANTER (IRE),** 4, ch g Heliostatic (IRE)—Purepleasureseeker (IRE) **Mr R. Harmon**
26 **NOBLE ASSET,** 4, ch g Compton Place—Chance For Romance **Caron & Paul Chapman**
27 **PARK PLACE,** 5, b g Beat Hollow—Blend **Crowe Partnership**
28 **PEARL CASTLE (IRE),** 5, b g Montjeu (IRE)—Ghurra (USA) **Cosy Seal Racing Limited**
29 **POETIC VERSE,** 5, gr m Byron—Nina Fontenail (FR) **J. N. Blackburn**

## MR JOHN QUINN - Continued

30 **RACING PULSE (IRE),** 6, b g Garuda (IRE)—Jacks Sister (IRE) **Mr C. S. Hinchy**
31 **RUTHERGLEN,** 5, b g Tiger Hill (IRE)—Hanella (IRE) **The Beer Swigging Strangers**
32 **SCOPPIO DEL CARRO,** 4, b g Medicean—Sadie Thompson (IRE) **Mr R. Harmon**
33 **SCRAFTON,** 4, b g Leporello (IRE)—Some Diva **Fletcher, Outhart, Moran & Maddison**
34 **SWNYMOR (IRE),** 6, b g Dylan Thomas (IRE)—Propaganda (IRE) **Mr C. S. Hinchy**
35 **TAHIRA (GER),** 5, ch m Doyen (IRE)—Tennessee Queen (GER) **Mr C. S. Hinchy**
36 **THINGS CHANGE (IRE),** 7, b g Old Vic—Northwood May **Mrs E. Wright**
37 **VILLORESI (IRE),** 6, b g Clodovil (IRE)—Villafranca (IRE) **Mr S. Burns**
38 **ZERMATT (IRE),** 6, ch g Strategic Prince—Await (IRE) **Mr R. L. Houlton**

### THREE-YEAR-OLDS

39 **ARTISTIC FLARE,** ch f Dutch Art—Pantile **Cosy Seal Racing Limited**
40 **FUWAIRT (IRE),** b g Arcano (IRE)—Safiya Song (IRE) **Al Shaqab Racing UK Limited**
41 **GEORDIE GEORGE (IRE),** b g Kodiac—Trika **Fletcher, Outhart, Moran & Maddison**
42 **HEADING HOME (FR),** b g Dutch Art—Nelly Dean **Mr M. Walker**
43 **HUBERTAS,** b g Lord of England (GER)—Western Eyes (IRE) **Chasemore Farm LLP**
44 **MOONLIGHTNAVIGATOR (USA),** b br c Henrythenavigator (USA)—Victorica (USA) **Mr M. Walker**
45 **OUR TIME WILL COME (IRE),** b f Rock of Gibraltar (IRE)—Signorina Cattiva (USA) **Mr R. Harmon**
46 **RACING ANGEL (IRE),** b f Dark Angel (IRE)—Roclette (USA) **Carl Hinchy & Danny Kearns**
47 **RACING KNIGHT (IRE),** b g Sir Percy—Salydora (FR) **Mr C. S. Hinchy**
48 **RACING SPIRIT,** ch g Sir Percy—Suertuda **Mr C. S. Hinchy**
49 **SALTARELLO (IRE),** b c Fast Company (IRE)—Step Dancing **Five Fleet Footed Fellas**
50 **SPEND A PENNY (IRE),** b g Acclamation—Coachhouse Lady (USA) **Mr M. Walker**
51 **THE WOW SIGNAL (IRE),** b c Starspangledbanner (AUS)—Muravka (IRE) **Al Shaqab Racing UK Limited**
52 **YOUONLYLIVEONCE (IRE),** b g Lawman (FR)—Caerlonore (IRE) **J. N. Blackburn**

### TWO-YEAR-OLDS

**53** B f 2/2 Fast Company (IRE)—Alltherightmoves (IRE) (Namid) (27777) **Racing Ventures 2014**
**54** **ANCIENT ASTRONAUT,** b c 23/4 Kodiac—Tatora (Selkirk (USA)) (80000) **Harlen Ltd**
**55** B f 26/3 Kodiac—Atishoo (IRE) (Revoque (IRE)) (40000) **Harlen Ltd**
**56** **CATASTROPHE,** b c 26/1 Intikhab (USA)—Mrs Snaffles (IRE) (Indian Danehill (IRE)) (13333) **J. N. Blackburn**
**57** B c 12/4 Compton Place—Church Melody (Oasis Dream) (57142) **Mr M. Walker**
**58** B c 30/3 Monsieur Bond (IRE)—Existentialist (Exceed And Excel (AUS)) (61904) **Racing Ventures 2014 1**
**59** **INDIAN PURSUIT (IRE),** gr c 29/3 Zebedee—Sampers (IRE) (Exceed And Excel (AUS)) (47619) **Mr M. Walker**
**60** B f 21/3 Zoffany (IRE)—Muravka (IRE) (High Chaparral (IRE)) (142857) **Chasemore Farm LLP**
**61** Br f 1/2 Kheleyf (USA)—Perino (IRE) (Speightstown (USA)) (31745) **Mr T. G. S. Wood**
**62** **SAFE VOYAGE (IRE),** b c 15/4 Fast Company (IRE)—Shishangaan (IRE) (Mujadil (USA)) (49523) **Mr R. Harmon**
**63** B c 7/4 Royal Applause—Semaphore (Zamindar (USA)) (66666) **Highclere Thoroughbred Racing (Applause)**
**64** B c 30/4 Lilbourne Lad (IRE)—Tagula Mon (IRE) (Tagula (IRE)) (23809) **Racing Ventures 2014 1**
**65** B c 9/4 Frozen Power (IRE)—Taqarub (IRE) (Marju (IRE)) (45714) **Racing Ventures 2014 1**
**66** B c 13/2 Fast Company (IRE)—Trentini (IRE) (Singspiel (IRE)) (45714) **Racing Ventures 2014 1**
**67** B f 5/3 Exceed And Excel (AUS)—Tropical Paradise (IRE) (Verglas (IRE)) (114285) **Al Shaqab Racing UK Limited**

**Other Owners:** Mr R. P. Armitage, Mr S. T. Avery, A. W. Black, Mrs J. E. Black, Mr R. Blades, A. M. Blewitt, I. T. Buchanan, M. A. Burrowes, P. Chapman, Mrs C. A. Chapman, P. Coll, Mr N. Fletcher, Mr P. R. Halkett, The Hon H. M. Herbert, Highclere Thoroughbred Racing Ltd, Mr S. A. Kaznowski, Mr D. Kearns, L. W. Lawson, N. E. F. Luck, Mr I. Marmion, Ms J. A. Moran, Mr J. Murphy, Mrs M. S. Nelson, A. J. Outhart, T. S. Palin, M. Prince, Mr S. A. T. Quinn, Mr A. P. Reed, Mr C. G. Simmonds, Mr G. S. Slater, Mr M. Thomas, R. E. Turner, Mr A. Worrall.

---

## 505 MR MICK QUINN, Newmarket

Postal: **Southgate Barn, Hamilton Road, Newmarket, Suffolk, CB8 0WY**
Contacts: **PHONE (01638) 660017 FAX (01638) 660017 MOBILE (07973) 260054**
**E-MAIL mick@quinn2562.fsnet.co.uk**

1 **MIAKORA,** 7, ch m Compton Place—Hickleton Lady (IRE) **M. Quinn**
2 **REFUSE COLETTE (IRE),** 6, ch m Refuse To Bend (IRE)—Roclette (USA) **YNWA Partnership**
3 **ROCKIE ROAD (IRE),** 4, b g Footstepsinthesand—Roclette (USA) **YNWA Partnership**
4 **WORLD RECORD (IRE),** 5, b g Choisir (AUS)—Dancing Debut **J. E. Quorn**

**Other Owners:** Mr D. Kearns.

**Assistant Trainer:** Miss Karen Davies

**Jockey (flat):** Franny Norton.

## 506 MR W. T. REED, Hexham

Postal: **Moss Kennels, Haydon Bridge, Hexham, Northumberland, NE47 6NL**
Contacts: **PHONE (01434) 344016 MOBILE (07703) 270408 / (07889) 111885**
**E-MAIL timreed8@aol.com**

1 **PRINCESS OF ROCK,** 6, ch m Rock of Gibraltar (IRE)—Principessa **Mr W. T. Reed**
2 **SILENT SNOW (IRE),** 10, ch g Moscow Society (USA)—Miss Ogan (IRE) **Mr W. T. Reed**
3 **SIMPLY LUCKY (IRE),** 6, b g Flemensfirth (USA)—Derrygowna Court (IRE) **Mr & Mrs Philip C. Smith**
4 **VIKING REBEL (IRE),** 13, b g Taipan (IRE)—Clodagh's Dream **Mr W. T. Reed**

**Other Owners:** Mr P. C. Smith, Mrs J. W. Smith.

**Assistant Trainer:** Mrs E J. Reed

**Jockey (NH):** Peter Buchanan. **Amateur:** Mr Harry Reed.

## 507 MR WILLIAM REED, Umberleigh

Postal: **Stowford Farm, East Stowford, Chittlehampton, Umberleigh, Devon, EX37 9RU**
Contacts: **PHONE (01769) 540292 MOBILE (07967) 130991**

1 **J R HAWK (IRE),** 7, b br g Hawk Wing (USA)—Miss Shivvy (IRE) **W. J. Reed**
2 **LITTLE WADHAM,** 10, b m Bandmaster (USA)—Sport of Fools (IRE) **W. J. Reed**
3 **WHAT A JOKE (IRE),** 8, b g Vinnie Roe (IRE)—Shaping **W. J. Reed**

## 508 MR DAVID REES, Haverfordwest

Postal: **The Grove Yard, Clarbeston Road, Haverfordwest, Pembrokeshire, SA63 4SP**
Contacts: **PHONE (01437) 731308 FAX (01437) 731551 MOBILE (07775) 662463**
**E-MAIL davidreesfencing@lineone.net**

1 **ACCORDINGTOPALM (IRE),** 9, ch g Great Palm (USA)—Supreme Accord (IRE) **A Farrier, A Fencer & Two Farmers**
2 **CAWDOR HOUSE BERT,** 8, b g Kayf Tara—Lady Shanan (IRE) **A. J. & Dai Rees**
3 **FISHING BRIDGE (IRE),** 10, ch g Definite Article—Rith Ar Aghaidh (IRE) **D. A. Rees**
4 **LUKES HILL (IRE),** 7, b g Bandari (IRE)—New Power (IRE) **Mr RJC Lewis/Mr P.A.T. Rice**
5 **LYDSTEP POINT,** 8, b g Beat All (USA)—Compton Chick (IRE) **Mrs J. Mathias**
6 **MACARTHUR,** 11, b g Montjeu (IRE)—Out West (USA) **Mr D. Rees & Mr B. Evans**
7 **PAY YOUR WAY (IRE),** 7, gr g Cloudings (IRE)—Supreme Bond (IRE) **D. A. Rees**
8 **PLATO (JPN),** 8, ch g Bago (FR)—Taygete (USA) **Mr E. W. Morris**
9 **ROMEO IS BLEEDING (IRE),** 9, b g Carroll House—Ean Eile (IRE) **D. A. Rees**
10 **SHANKSFORAMILLION,** 6, b g Needle Gun (IRE)—Cool Connie (IRE) **BW & RE Mansell**
11 **SINGH IS KING,** 7, br g Fair Mix (IRE)—Leading Lady **D. A. Rees**
12 **SIR MATTIE (IRE),** 10, b br g Moscow Society (USA)—Manhattan Catch (IRE) **Mr RJC Lewis/Mr P.A.T. Rice**

**Other Owners:** W. J. Evans, Mr R. J. C. Lewis, Mrs R. E. Mansell, Mr B. W. Mansell, Mr A. J. Rees, Mr P. A. T. Rice, Exors of the Late G. Roberts, Mr N. E. Youngman.

## 509 MRS HELEN REES, Dorchester

Postal: **Distant Hills, Chalmington, Dorchester, Dorset, DT2 0HB**
Contacts: **PHONE (01300) 320683 MOBILE (07715) 558289**
**E-MAIL helen-rees@live.co.uk**

1 **KAHDIAN (IRE),** 5, br g Rock of Gibraltar (IRE)—Katiykha (IRE) **Mrs H. E. Rees**
2 **RESIDENCE AND SPA (IRE),** 7, b g Dubai Destination (USA)—Toffee Nosed **Mrs H. E. Rees**

**Assistant Trainer:** Mr Rupert Rees

## 510 MR SEAN REGAN, Middleham

Postal: **Low Beck, Coverham, Middleham, Leyburn, North Yorkshire, DL8 4TJ**
Contacts: **MOBILE (07866) 437476**
**E-MAIL sean@seanreganracing.com WEBSITE www.seanreganracing.com**

1 **MOISSANITE,** 6, b m Danbird (AUS)—Nikita Sunrise (IRE) **Mrs L. Grasby**
2 **PTOLOMEOS,** 12, b g Kayf Tara—Lucy Tufty **Mrs C. D. Taylor**
3 **RED LEGACY,** 7, ch m Distant Music (USA)—Emma May **Mrs L. Grasby**
4 **SHEILA'S CASTLE,** 11, b m Karinga Bay—Candarela **S. Regan**
5 **TOURTIERE,** 7, b g Act One—Kindle **Mr G. Andrews**

## 511 MR ANDREW REID, Mill Hill, London

Postal: **Highwood Lodge, Highwood Hill, Mill Hill, London, NW7 4HB**
Contacts: **PHONE (07836) 214617 (07747) 751603 FAX (02089) 061255**
**E-MAIL cbithell2000@yahoo.co.uk**

1 **ATHLETIC,** 6, b g Doyen (IRE)—Gentle Irony **A. S. Reid**
2 **DIALOGUE,** 9, b g Singspiel (IRE)—Zonda **A. S. Reid**
3 **MODERN SOCIETY,** 5, pt h I Was Framed (USA)—Artzola (IRE) **A. S. Reid**
4 **NOTNOWDOCTOR,** 4, b g Notnowcato—Arantxa **A. S. Reid**
5 **TREASURE THE RIDGE (IRE),** 6, b g Galileo (IRE)—Treasure The Lady (IRE) **A. S. Reid**

### THREE-YEAR-OLDS

6 **EXIT EUROPE,** ch g Bahamian Bounty—Depressed **A. S. Reid**
7 **PURPLE SURPRISE,** b f Teofilio (IRE)—Manic **A. S. Reid**

### TWO-YEAR-OLDS

8 Ch f 15/3 Bahamian Bounty—Depressed (Most Welcome) **A. S. Reid**
9 Ch f 9/4 Bahamian Bounty—Pants (Pivotal) **A. S. Reid**
10 B br f 19/3 Bahamian Bounty—Rise (Polar Falcon (USA)) **A. S. Reid**

**Assistant Trainer:** Michael Keady

**Jockey (flat):** Jim Crowley. **Apprentice:** Alfie Warwick.

## 512 MRS JACQUELINE RETTER, Cullompton

Postal: **Dulford Cottage, Dulford, Cullompton, Devon, EX15 2DX**
Contacts: **PHONE/FAX (01884) 266078 MOBILE (07912) 889655**

1 **EXILES RETURN (IRE),** 13, b g Needle Gun (IRE)—Moores Girl (IRE) **Mrs J. G. Retter**

## 513 MR KEITH REVELEY, Saltburn

Postal: **Groundhill Farm, Lingdale, Saltburn-by-the-Sea, Cleveland, TS12 3HD**
Contacts: **OFFICE (01287) 650456 FAX (01287) 653095 MOBILE (07971) 784539**
**E-MAIL reveleyracing@yahoo.co.uk**

1 **BALMUSETTE,** 6, b m Halling (USA)—Tcherina (IRE) **Mr & Mrs W. J. Williams**
2 **BOOK AT BEDTIME,** 4, b f Midnight Legend—Northern Native (IRE) **Mrs S. A. Smith**
3 4, B f Alflora (IRE)—Brackenmoss (IRE) **Reveley Farms**
4 **BRAVE SPARTACUS (IRE),** 9, b g Spartacus (IRE)—Peaches Polly **R. Collins**
5 **BROCTUNE PAPA GIO,** 8, b g Tobougg (IRE)—Fairlie **D. Renton, C. Alessi, D. Young, Reveley Farms**
6 **CATEGORICAL,** 12, b g Diktat—Zibet **Rug, Grub & Pub Partnership**
7 **CORSAIR PRINCE,** 5, b g Black Sam Bellamy (IRE)—Nobratinetta (FR) **The Supreme Alliance & Reveley Farms**
8 **DANCE OF TIME,** 8, b g Presenting—Northern Native (IRE) **Mrs S. A. Smith**
9 **DELTA FORTY,** 7, b m Alflora (IRE)—Northern Native (IRE) **Mrs S. A. Smith**
10 **DONNA'S PRIDE,** 6, b m Beat All (USA)—Pennys Pride (IRE) **Sun King Partnership & Partner**
11 **HARVEY'S HOPE,** 9, b g Sinndar (IRE)—Ancara **The Home & Away Partnership**
12 **IVAN BORU (IRE),** 7, b g Brian Boru—Miranda's Lace (IRE) **Thwaites Furness & Zetland**
13 **MADRASA (IRE),** 7, b g High Chaparral (IRE)—Shir Dar (FR) **Mr M. W. Joyce**
14 **MIDNIGHT MONTY,** 5, ch g Midnight Legend—Marello **Mr & Mrs W. J. Williams**

## MR KEITH REVELEY - Continued

15 **MR BEATLE,** 6, br g Beat All (USA)—Northern Native (IRE) **Mrs I. C. Sellars & Major & Mrs P. Arkwright**
16 **MR SUPREME (IRE),** 10, b g Beneficial—Ardfallon (IRE) **Mrs S. P. Granger**
17 **MY TEESCOMPONENTS,** 5, b m Fair Mix (IRE)—Our Tees Component (IRE) **Tees Components Ltd**
18 **NIGHT IN MILAN (IRE),** 9, b g Milan—Chione (IRE) **R. Collins**
19 **PENNYS DOUBLE,** 5, ch m Double Trigger (IRE)—Pennys Pride (IRE) **Reveley Farms**
20 **REDKALANI (IRE),** 7, b g Ashkalani (IRE)—La Femme En Rouge **Christiana's Crew**
21 **RIO COBOLO (IRE),** 9, b g Captain Rio—Sofistication (IRE) **Mr P. Collins**
22 **ROBBIE,** 11, b g Robellino (USA)—Corn Lily **Mrs S. McDonald & Reveley Farms**
23 **SAMEDI SOIR,** 5, b m Black Sam Bellamy (IRE)—Bonne Anniversaire **Shade Oak Stud**
24 **SAMSASWINGER,** 4, b g Black Sam Bellamy (IRE)—Nobratinetta (FR) **The Lingdale Optimists**
25 **SHADRACK (IRE),** 11, gr g Tamayaz (CAN)—Alba Dancer **Mrs S. P. Granger**
26 **SOMME BOY (FR),** 4, b g Sulamani (IRE)—Heritage River (FR) **J. J. G. Good & C. Anderson**
27 **SPECIAL CATCH (IRE),** 8, b g Catcher In The Rye (IRE)—Top Quality **Mr Mike Browne & Mr William McKeown**
28 **SPICULAS (IRE),** 6, ch g Beneficial—Alicia's Charm (IRE) **R. Collins**
29 **VICTOR HEWGO,** 10, b g Old Vic—Pennys Pride (IRE) **Sir Ian Good**
30 **WALTZ DARLING (IRE),** 7, b g Iffraaj—Aljafliyah **Mrs M. B. Thwaites & Mr M. E. Foxton**
31 **WHICHWAYTOBOUGIE,** 6, b g Tobougg (IRE)—Whichway Girl **The Supreme Partnership**

### THREE-YEAR-OLDS

32 **HOOKERGATE GRAMMAR,** b g Yeats (IRE)—Oulianovsk (IRE) **Mr M. W. Joyce**
33 Ch f Sulamani (IRE)—Let It Be **Mr A. Frame**
34 **THE NAME'S BOND,** ch g Monsieur Bond (IRE)—Fairlie **The Phoenix Racing Partnership**

**Other Owners:** Mr C. Anderson, Mr Philip Arkwright, Mrs Philip Arkwright, Mr Doug Bauckham, Mrs Marilyn Bauckham, Mr D. E. Baxter, Mrs C. M. Baxter, Mr J. P. Bladen, Mr M. Bradley, Mr Mike Browne, Mrs M. Clark-Wright, Mr E. Coll, Mr A. E. Corbett, Mr M. Cressey, Mr Bernard Drinkall, Mr M. E. Foxton, Mrs J. W. Furness, Sir Ian Good, Mr Brian W. Goodall, Mr Jeff Goodall, Mr David A. Green, Mrs D. Greenhalgh, Mr Roger Hart, Mrs Emma Hockenhull, Mr P. D. Hockenhull, Mr Ron MacDonald, Mr W. McKeown, Mr Alistair Rae, Exors of the Late Mr John Renton, Mr Douglas Renton, Mr Graeme Renton, Reveley Farms, Mr D. M. D. Robinson, Mrs A. Rodgers, Mrs Ian Sellars, Mr D. W. E. Sowden, Mr Jim Struth, Mrs M. B. Thwaites, Mr W. J. Williams, Mrs M. Williams, Mr M. Wood, Lord Zetland.

**Assistant Trainer:** Fiona Reveley

**Jockey (NH):** James Reveley. **Conditional:** Colm McCormack.

---

## 514 MR DAVID RICHARDS, Abergavenny

Postal: **White House, Llantilio Crossenny, Abergavenny, Gwent, NP7 8SU**
Contacts: **PHONE (01600) 780235**

1 **ANOTHER KATE (IRE),** 11, gr m Norwich—Cracking Kate (IRE) **D. M. Richards**

**Jockey (NH):** Sam Thomas.

---

## 515 MRS LYDIA RICHARDS, Chichester

Postal: **Lynch Farm, Hares Lane, Funtington, Chichester, West Sussex, PO18 9LW**
Contacts: **YARD (01243) 574379 HOME (01243) 574882 MOBILE (07803) 199061**
**E-MAIL lydia.richards@sky.com**

1 **AALY,** 8, b g Milan—Leyaaly **Mrs Lydia Richards**
2 **BEEP,** 5, b m Beat Hollow—Dialing Tone (USA) **The Beep Partnership**
3 **HONG KONG JOE,** 5, b g Oasis Dream—Singed **The Demoiselle Bond Partnership**
4 **LEYLA'S GIFT,** 6, b m Milan—Leyaaly **Mrs Lydia Richards**
5 **MAIGH DARA (IRE),** 6, br g Cacique (IRE)—Dara Diva (IRE) **The Inner Steel Partnership**
6 **MIGHTY THOR,** 5, b g Norse Dancer (IRE)—Leyaaly **Mrs Lydia Richards**
7 **MYETTA,** 7, gr m Silver Patriarch (IRE)—Henrietta Holmes (IRE) **Mrs E. F. J. Seal**
8 **NOVEL DANCER,** 7, b g Dansili—Fictitious **Mrs Lydia Richards**
9 **ROYAL WARRIOR,** 4, b g Royal Applause—Tiana **Mrs Lydia Richards**
10 **SPIDER BAY,** 6, gr m Almaty (IRE)—Severance (USA) **Mrs Lydia Richards**
11 **VENETIAN LAD,** 10, ro g Midnight Legend—Henrietta Holmes (IRE) **The Venetian Lad Partnership**
12 **VOLIO VINCENTE (FR),** 8, b br g Corri Piano (FR)—Vollore (FR) **Mrs Lydia Richards**
13 **ZIGZAGA (IRE),** 9, b g Zagreb (USA)—Mrs McClintock (IRE) **The Zigzaga Partnership**

**Other Owners:** Mr H. B. Kinmond, Mr G. H. R. Musker, Mr M. E. Thompsett, E. T. Wright.

## 516 MR NICKY RICHARDS, Greystoke

Postal: **Rectory Farm, Greystoke, Penrith, Cumbria, CA11 0UJ**
Contacts: **OFFICE (01768) 483392 HOME (01768) 483160 FAX (01768) 483933**
**MOBILE (07771) 906609**
**E-MAIL n.g.richards@virgin.net WEBSITE www.nickyrichardsracing.com**

1 **AND THE MAN,** 9, ch g Generous (IRE)—Retro's Lady (IRE) **Jimmy Dudgeon & Partner**
2 **ANOTHER BILL (IRE),** 5, ch g Beneficial—Glacier Lilly (IRE) **Langdale Bloodstock**
3 **ARC WARRIOR (FR),** 11, b g Even Top (IRE)—What The Hell (IRE) **Mrs C. B. Paterson**
4 4, B g Gold Well—Arequipa (IRE) **Mr David Wesley Yates**
5 4, B g Presenting—Azalea (IRE) **David & Nicky Robinson**
6 **AZURE GLAMOUR (IRE),** 6, br g Golan (IRE)—Mirazur (IRE) **E. G. Tunstall**
7 **BAYWING (IRE),** 6, br g Winged Love (IRE)—Cerise de Totes (FR) **David & Nicky Robinson**
8 **BERNARDELLI (IRE),** 7, b g Golan (IRE)—Beautiful Blue (IRE) **Henriques & Lloyd-Bakers**
9 **BETAMECHE (FR),** 4, gr g Kapgarde (FR)—Kaldona (FR) **Langdale Bloodstock**
10 4, B g Morozov (USA)—Bubble Bann (IRE) **Tarzan Bloodstock**
11 **CAIUS MARCIUS (IRE),** 4, b g King's Theatre (IRE)—Ain't Misbehavin (IRE) **Mr Peter Norbury**
12 **CARINENA (IRE),** 6, b m Shantou (USA)—Dinny Kenn (IRE) **Mrs C. A. Torkington**
13 **CHIDSWELL (IRE),** 6, b g Gold Well—Manacured (IRE) **David & Nicky Robinson**
14 4, B g Scorpion (IRE)—Cooline Jana (IRE) **Tarzan Bloodstock**
15 4, B g Mahler—Corravilla (IRE) **Tarzan Bloodstock**
16 **CRINKLE CRAGS (IRE),** 5, ch g Trans Island—Ashanti Dancer (IRE) **D. Wesley-Yates**
17 **CULTRAM ABBEY,** 8, br g Fair Mix (IRE)—Kansas City (FR) **The Roper Family**
18 4, B g Stowaway—Dolphins View (IRE) **Tarzan Bloodstock**
19 **DUKE OF NAVAN (IRE),** 7, b br g Presenting—Greenfieldflyer (IRE) **David & Nicky Robinson**
20 **EDUARD (IRE),** 7, b g Morozov (USA)—Dinny Kenn (IRE) **Eddie Melville**
21 **GLINGERBURN (IRE),** 7, b g King's Theatre (IRE)—Wychnor Dawn (IRE) **James Westoll**
22 **GLINGERSIDE (IRE),** 4, b g Milan—Kettle 'n Cran (IRE) **James Westoll**
23 **GOLD FUTURES (IRE),** 6, b g Gold Well—Don't Discount Her (IRE) **Mrs C. A. Torkington**
24 **IMADA (IRE),** 5, br g Arcadio (GER)—Anck Su Namun (IRE) **Langdale Bloodstock**
25 5, B g Gold Well—Itsonlyraheen (IRE) **Tarzan Bloodstock**
26 **LOOKING WELL (IRE),** 6, b g Gold Well—Different Level (IRE) **D. Wesley-Yates**
27 4, B g Azamour (IRE)—Madam Gaffer **Arf Ltd**
28 **MALIN BAY (IRE),** 10, b g Milan—Mirror of Flowers **David & Nicky Robinson**
29 **MARDALE (IRE),** 5, b m Robin des Champs (FR)—Lizzy Langtry (IRE) **East To West Partnership**
30 **MISTER MARKER (IRE),** 11, ch g Beneficial—Bavards Girl (IRE) **J. A. Dudgeon**
31 5, B g Milan—Newcastlebeauty (IRE) **Tarzan Bloodstock**
32 5, B g Mahler—Niamh's Leader (IRE) **Langdale Bloodstock**
33 **NOBLE ALAN (GER),** 12, gr g King's Theatre (IRE)—Nirvavita (FR) **C. Bennett**
34 **ONE FOR HARRY (IRE),** 7, b g Generous (IRE)—Strawberry Fool (FR) **The Fife Boys + 1**
35 **ONE FOR HOCKY (IRE),** 7, b g Brian Boru—Wire Lady (IRE) **Kingdom Taverns Ltd**
36 **PARC DES PRINCES (USA),** 9, b br g Ten Most Wanted (USA)—Miss Orah **Miss J. R. Richards**
37 **PEACHEY MOMENT (USA),** 10, b br g Stormin Fever (USA)—Given Moment (USA) **Mrs J. Fortescue**
38 **SCARLET FIRE (IRE),** 8, b g Helissio (FR)—Ross Dana (IRE) **Miss J. R. Richards**
39 **SIMPLY NED (IRE),** 8, ch g Fruits of Love (USA)—Bishops Lass (IRE) **David & Nicky Robinson**
40 **SIR VINSKI (IRE),** 6, ch g Vinnie Roe (IRE)—Mill Emerald **The Northern Raiders**
41 **ST GREGORY (IRE),** 7, ch m Presenting—Ardrom **The Grafton Lounge Partnership**
42 **STREAMS OF WHISKEY (IRE),** 8, br g Spadoun (FR)—Cherry Tops (IRE) **Mr & Mrs R. G. Kelvin-Hughes**
43 **TEDDY TEE (IRE),** 6, b g Mountain High (IRE)—Knocksouna Lady (IRE) **David & Nicky Robinson**
44 **TOP BILLING,** 6, br g Monsun (GER)—La Gandilie (FR) **Doreen McGawn & Stewart Tate**
45 **TUTCHEC (FR),** 8, gr g Turgeon (USA)—Pocahontas (FR) **Club 4 Racing**
46 **UN NOBLE (FR),** 5, gr g Near Honor (GER)—Noble Gary (FR) **Mrs C. A. Torkington**
47 **WARRIORS TALE,** 6, b g Midnight Legend—Samandara (FR) **Straightline Construction Ltd**
48 **WESTERN RULES (IRE),** 5, b g Westerner—Ryehill Lady (IRE) **Bob Bennett & Jimmy Dudgeon**
49 5, B g Fruits of Love (USA)—Whenever Wherever (IRE) **Langdale Bloodstock**
50 **WICKED SPICE (IRE),** 6, b g Old Vic—Afdala (IRE) **Mrs Pat Sloan**
51 **WINTER ALCHEMY (IRE),** 10, b g Fruits of Love (USA)—Native Land **The Alchemy Partnership**

**Other Owners:** Mr Noel Anderson, Mr D. Burdon, Mr A. Clark, Mr Gerard Dowling, Mr Charlie Fortescue, Mr Nick Fortescue, Mr Kenny Haughey, Mr M. Henriques, Mr P. Laverty, Mr C. G. M. Lloyd-Baker, Mr H. M. A. Lloyd-Baker, Mrs A. Melville, Mr Walter Morris, Mr Ken Roper, Mrs Elinor M. Roper.

**Assistant Trainer:** Miss Joey Richards

**Jockey (NH):** Brian Harding. **Conditional:** Harry Challoner. **Amateur:** Miss J. R. Richards.

## 517 MR JOHN DAVID RICHES, Pilling

Postal: **Moss Side Farm, Off Lancaster Road, Scronkey, Pilling, Lancashire, PR3 6SR**

1 **FORZARZI (IRE),** 11, b g Forzando—Zarzi (IRE) **J. D. Riches**
2 **GAMBINO (IRE),** 5, b g Red Clubs (IRE)—Temptation Island (IRE) **J. D. Riches**
3 **IDAROSE (IRE),** 6, b m Scorpion (IRE)—Garra Princess (IRE) **J. D. Riches**
4 **INDIAN GIVER,** 7, b m Indesatchel (IRE)—Bint Baddi (FR) **J. D. Riches**
5 **LOVELY TOUCH (IRE),** 6, b g Humbel (USA)—My Touch (IRE) **Mr D. J. Eaton**
6 **MUBROOK (USA),** 10, b g Alhaarth (IRE)—Zomaradah **Gold Tooth Racing**
7 **SNOW DANCER (IRE),** 11, b m Desert Style (IRE)—Bella Vie (IRE) **Mrs L. Wohlers**
8 **SPOKEN WORDS,** 6, b m Fruits of Love (USA)—Jerre Jo Glanville (USA) **Mrs L. Wohlers**

**Other Owners:** Mr R. S. W. Purbrick, Mr G. J. Vallely.

## 518 MRS PATRICIA RIGBY, Llangollen

Postal: **Tower Cottage, Garth, Trevor, Llangollen, LL20 7YH**
Contacts: **PHONE (01978) 822198 MOBILE (07926) 961504**

1 **FFYNNON SARA (IRE),** 7, b m Luso—Sycamore House (IRE) **Mrs P. A. Rigby**
2 **WELSH WALLS,** 9, b g Beat All (USA)—Sharp Pet **Mrs P. A. Rigby**

**Assistant Trainer:** Keith Rigby

**Conditional:** Tom Messenger.

## 519 MR MARK RIMELL, Witney

Postal: **Fairspear Racing Stables, Fairspear Road, Leafield, Witney, Oxfordshire, OX29 9NT**
Contacts: **PHONE (01993) 878551 MOBILE (07778) 648303/(07973) 627054**
**E-MAIL rimell@rimellracing.com WEBSITE www.rimellracing.com**

1 **BHAKTI (IRE),** 8, b g Rakti—Royal Bossi (IRE) **M. G. Rimell**
2 **ROYAL ROO,** 6, b m Overbury (IRE)—Royal Roxy (IRE) **Mrs A. Rimell**
3 5, B m Black Sam Bellamy (IRE)—Royal Roxy (IRE)
4 **SAIL WITH SULTANA,** 4, ch f Black Sam Bellamy (IRE)—Strathtay **Mrs M. R. T. Rimell**
5 **SPIRAEA,** 5, ch m Bahamian Bounty—Salvia **M. G. Rimell**

### THREE-YEAR-OLDS

6 **OVERLORD,** b g Lawman (FR)—Hip
7 B f Kayf Tara—Royal Roxy (IRE)
8 Ch g Schiaparelli (GER)—Strathtay **Mrs M. R. T. Rimell**

### TWO-YEAR-OLDS

9 Ch f 24/5 Midnight Legend—Royal Roxy (IRE) (Exit To Nowhere (USA)) (6666)
10 Ch g 4/4 Midnight Legend—Vin Rose (Alflora (IRE))

**Assistant Trainer:** Anne Rimell

## 520 MISS BETH ROBERTS, Bridgend

Postal: **14 Pwllcarn Terrace, Pontycymmer, Bridgend, Mid-Glamorgan, CF32 8AS**
Contacts: **PHONE (01656) 870076**

1 **CHESNUT ANNIE (IRE),** 14, ch m Weld—Leaden Sky (IRE) **Miss H. E. Roberts**
2 **KIMS QUEST (IRE),** 7, b m Needle Gun (IRE)—Flyingagain (IRE) **Miss H. E. Roberts**

## 521 MR DAVE ROBERTS, Shrewsbury

Postal: **Leasowes Farm, Kenley, Shrewsbury, Shropshire, SY5 6NY**
Contacts: **PHONE (01746) 785255**

1 **COCKNEY CLASS (USA),** 8, gr ro g Speightstown (USA)—Snappy Little Cat (USA) **D. B. Roberts**
2 **SLEEPY SUNDAY,** 5, b m Revoque (IRE)—Cool Spring (IRE) **D. B. Roberts**
3 **SPIRIT RIVER (FR),** 10, b g Poliglote—Love River (FR) **D. B. Roberts**
4 **TANTALIZED,** 6, b m Authorized (IRE)—Tarabela (CHI) **D. B. Roberts**
5 **THE MOBB (IRE),** 7, b g Westerner—Marlogan (IRE) **D. B. Roberts**

### THREE-YEAR-OLDS

6 **NUMBER ONE HERMIT,** b c Sulamani (IRE)—Musical Chimes **J. Jones Racing Ltd**
7 **WHAT A SQUIRTLE,** b c What A Caper (IRE)—Squirtle (IRE) **J. Jones Racing Ltd**

## 522 MR MIKE ROBERTS, Hailsham

Postal: **Summertree Farm, Bodle Street Green, Hailsham, East Sussex, BN27 4QT**
Contacts: **PHONE (01435) 830231 FAX (01435) 830887 MOBILE (07774) 208040**
**E-MAIL mike@summertree-racing.com**

1 **BETSY BOO BOO,** 6, b m King's Theatre (IRE)—Quark Top (FR) **M. J. Roberts**
2 **BLACKJAX,** 5, b br m Black Sam Bellamy (IRE)—Jaxelle (FR) **M. J. Roberts**
3 **BRAVE CUPID,** 5, ch m Black Sam Bellamy (IRE)—Newport (FR) **M. J. Roberts**
4 **CUPID STAR,** 5, b m Fragrant Mix (IRE)—Esperanza IV (FR) **M. J. Roberts**
5 **I'M A RASCAL,** 6, ch g Erhaab (USA)—Mohican Pass **M. J. Roberts**
6 **SAUCYSIOUX,** 5, b m Tobougg (IRE)—Mohican Pass **M. J. Roberts**
7 **SNIPPETYDOODAH,** 7, b m King's Theatre (IRE)—Kimpour (FR) **M. J. Roberts**
8 **UNDERWOOD (FR),** 7, b g Assessor (IRE)—Attualita (FR) **M. J. Roberts**
9 **URANOX (FR),** 7, b br g Special Kaldoun (IRE)—Judelle (FR) **M. J. Roberts**
10 **UTALY (FR),** 7, b g Shaanmer (IRE)—Nataly (FR) **M. J. Roberts**

**Assistant Trainer:** Marie Martin

## 523 MISS SARAH ROBINSON, Bridgwater

Postal: **Newnham Farm, Shurton, Stogursey, Bridgwater, Somerset, TA5 1QG**
Contacts: **PHONE (01278) 732357 FAX (01278) 732357 MOBILE (07866) 435197 / (07518) 785291**
**E-MAIL info@sarahrobinsonracing.co.uk WEBSITE www.sarahrobinsonracing.co.uk**

1 **FIRST SPIRIT,** 9, ch m First Trump—Flaming Spirt **Mr N. S. Shaw**
2 **NEWNHAM FLYER (IRE),** 13, gr m Exit To Nowhere (USA)—Paper Flight **Mr B. Robinson**
3 **SHINING GRACE,** 6, gr m Proclamation (IRE)—Shining Oasis (IRE) **Mr B. Robinson**
4 **THEROADTOGOREY (IRE),** 9, b g Revoque (IRE)—Shannon Mor (IRE) **Mr N. S. Shaw**

**Assistant Trainer:** Mr B. Robinson

**Jockey (NH):** Ian Popham. **Conditional:** Kevin Jones. **Amateur:** Mr Luke Kilgarriff, Miss S. Robinson.

## 524 MISS PAULINE ROBSON, Capheaton

Postal: **Kidlaw Farm, Capheaton, Newcastle Upon Tyne, NE19 2AW**
Contacts: **PHONE (01830) 530241 MOBILE (07721) 887489 or (07814) 708725 (David)**
**E-MAIL pauline.robson@virgin.net**

1 **FULL JACK (FR),** 8, b g Kahyasi—Full Contact (FR) **Mr & Mrs Raymond Anderson Green**
2 **HABBIE SIMPSON,** 10, b g Elmaamul (USA)—Hamanaka (USA) **S. Love**
3 **MWANGAZA (FR),** 5, gr m Martaline—Saloria (FR) **Mr & Mrs Raymond Anderson Green**
4 **RIVAL D'ESTRUVAL (FR),** 10, b g Khalkevi (IRE)—Kermesse d'estruval (FR) **Mr & Mrs Raymond Anderson Green**
5 **SALFORD DREAM,** 6, ch g Halling (USA)—Spitting Image (IRE) **Hale Racing Limited**
6 **SCIMON TEMPLAR (FR),** 7, b br g Saint des Saints (FR)—Made In Law (FR) **Mr & Mrs Raymond Anderson Green**
7 **SHARP RISE (IRE),** 8, b g Croco Rouge (IRE)—Missusan (IRE) **I Couldn't Switch Club**
8 **TEO VIVO (FR),** 8, gr g Great Pretender (IRE)—Ifranne (FR) **It's a Bargain Syndicate**

## MISS PAULINE ROBSON - Continued

9 **TRAPRAIN (FR)**, 6, gr g Turgeon (USA)—Paola Pierji (FR) **Mr & Mrs Raymond Anderson Green**
10 **UPSILON BLEU (FR)**, 7, b g Panoramic—Glycine Bleue (FR) **Mr & Mrs Raymond Anderson Green**
11 **VISION DE LA VIE (FR)**, 5, ch g Sin Kiang (FR)—Vidahermosa (FR) **I Couldn't Switch Club**

**Other Owners:** Mrs J. M. Dodd, Mrs E. M. Fairbairn, Mr D. A. Green, Mrs Anita Green, Mr Raymond Anderson Green, Mr Matthew Jenkins.

**Assistant Trainer:** David Parker

---

## 525 MR FRANCOIS ROHAUT, Sauvagnon

Postal: **26 Rue du Bearn, 64230 Sauvagnon, France**
Contacts: **PHONE (0033) 55 9332486 FAX (0033) 55 9624652 MOBILE (0033) 6727 75619**
**E-MAIL ecurie.rohaut@wanadoo.fr**

1 **ACROSS THE SKY (IRE)**, 4, b f Cape Cross (IRE)—How High The Sky (IRE) **Mrs M. Bryant**
2 **AL MAFYAR (FR)**, 4, ch g New Approach (IRE)—Hexane (FR) **Al Shaqab Racing**
3 **AMORINE (IRE)**, 4, b f Montjeu (IRE)—Amorama (FR) **Haras de Saint Pair**
4 **BEST EXIT (FR)**, 4, b f King's Best (USA)—No Exit (FR) **Ahmed Mouknass**
5 **BEST FOUAD (FR)**, 4, b g King's Best (USA)—Raheefa (USA) **Mrs J. Rusu**
6 **BHAKTAPUR (FR)**, 4, b f Naaqoos—Queen Maeve **Safsaf Canarias**
7 **BORGO (FR)**, 7, b g Poliglote—Bengalie (FR) **Mr F. Rohaut**
8 **BORODINO (FR)**, 6, ch g Turtle Bowl (IRE)—Baie (FR) **Mr J. Calva**
9 **BREZENA (IRE)**, 4, b f Lawman (FR)—Winning Family (IRE) **Al Shaqab Racing**
10 **FARMAH (USA)**, 4, b f Speightstown (USA)—Torrestrella (IRE) **Hamdan Al Maktoum**
11 **HORPENSA (FR)**, 4, b f Orpen (USA)—Hortanse (FR) **Mrs Y. Seydoux de Clausonne**
12 **ILTEMAS (USA)**, 4, b f Galileo (IRE)—Arkadina (IRE) **Al Shaqab Racing**
13 **L'ESQUISSE (FR)**, 4, b f Naaqoos—Torte (IRE) **Jean-Jacques Taieb**
14 **LA GOHANNIERE (FR)**, 4, b f Le Havre (IRE)—Landskia (FR) **Mr G. Augustin Normand**
15 **LICTUS (FR)**, 5, b g Literato (FR)—Lunaba (FR) **Mr J. Calva**
16 **MONGOLIA (FR)**, 4, b f Gold Away (IRE)—Monava (FR) **Mr N. Elwes**
17 **PISTOLETTO (SPA)**, 4, b g Green Tune (USA)—Ishi Adiva **Mrs J. Rusu**
18 **PLAISANCIERE (FR)**, 4, ch f Astronomer Royal (USA)—Princesse Jasmine (FR) **Mr P. Sabban**
19 **PRETTY PANTHER (FR)**, 5, ch m Hurricane Run (IRE)—Princesse Jasmine (FR) **Mr P. Sabban**
20 **QUATORZE (FR)**, 5, b h Elusive City (USA)—Queseraisjesanstoi (FR) **Haras d'Etreham**
21 **ROERO (FR)**, 6, b g Acclamation—Ricine (IRE) **Haras de Saint Pair**
22 **ROYAL SUN (FR)**, 4, gr c Astronomer Royal (USA)—Princess Love (FR) **Jacques-Eric Strauss**
23 **SANTO SPIRITO**, 4, ch c Monsun (GER)—San Sicharia (IRE) **Haras de Saint Pair**
24 **SCALAMBRA**, 4, ch f Nayef (USA)—Seal Bay (IRE) **Mr M. Lagasse**
25 **SIGNS OF BLESSING (IRE)**, 4, b c Invincible Spirit (IRE)—Sun Bittern (USA) **Pandora Racing**
26 **VODKA REDBULLA (FR)**, 4, b f Turtle Bowl (IRE)—Melanzane **Mr M. Cordero**
27 **WAHSHI (IRE)**, 4, b g Invincible Spirit (IRE)—Apperella **Al Shaqab Racing**
28 **ZACK HALL (FR)**, 8, b g Muhtathir—Halawa (IRE) **Mr M. Offenstadt**

### THREE-YEAR-OLDS

29 **AL MAS (FR)**, b f King's Best (USA)—Ma Preference (FR) **Sheikh Abdullah Bin Khalifa Al Thani**
30 **AUDERVILLE (FR)**, b f Le Havre (IRE)—Artana (FR) **Mr G. Augustin Normand**
31 **BAROOD (FR)**, b g Soldier of Fortune (IRE)—Beau Fete (ARG) **Sheikh Abdullah Bin Khalifa Al Thani**
32 **BATINAH (FR)**, b f Naaqoos—Baie (FR) **Mr F. Rohaut**
33 **BOWL (FR)**, b c Turtle Bowl (IRE)—Baldamelle (FR) **Mr M. Offenstadt**
34 **CHEEKY LADY (FR)**, b f Siyouni (FR)—La Fresca **Mrs J. Rusu**
35 **CYNTHIANA (FR)**, ch f Siyouni (FR)—Fonage **Ecurie du Grand Chene**
36 **DONA SOLA (IRE)**, b f Iffraaj—Anna Pavlova **Haras de Saint Pair**
37 **EIGHT ANGELS (FR)**, b c Diamond Green (FR)—Eight Stars (IRE) **Mr G. Laboureau**
38 **ERHAAF (USA)**, b c Street Sense (USA)—Saraama (USA) **Hamdan Al Maktoum**
39 **GROWING GLORY (FR)**, b f Orpen (USA)—Trois Rivieres (IRE) **Safsaf Canarias**
40 **HADAYAANA**, ch f Shamardal (USA)—Bahja (USA) **Hamdan Al Maktoum**
41 **HAILSTORM**, gr f Verglas (IRE)—Hideaway (FR) **Skymarc Farm**
42 **HELISA (FR)**, b f Elusive City (USA)—Hortanse (FR) **Mrs Y. Seydoux de Clausonne**
43 **IROMEA (IRE)**, gr f Dansili—In The Mist **Haras de Saint Pair**
44 **KINGS LYN (FR)**, b g King's Best (USA)—Monava (FR) **Mr N. Elwes**
45 **KITKATIE (FR)**, f Dansili—Kitcat (GER) **Haras de Saint Pair**
46 **L'ECRIVAIN DORE (FR)**, b c Literato (FR)—Golden Lily (FR) **Pandora Racing**
47 **LADHEEDA (FR)**, b f Halling (USA)—Cadenza (FR) **Hamdan Al Maktoum**
48 **LANDIGOU (FR)**, b c Le Havre (IRE)—Landskia (FR) **Mr G. Augustin Normand**

## MR FRANCOIS ROHAUT - Continued

49 **LARMINA (FR),** b f Thewayyouare (USA)—Lilac Charm (IRE) **Haras de Beauvoir**
50 **LONGUEIL (FR),** b c Le Havre (IRE)—Love Queen (IRE) **Mr G. Augustin Normand**
51 **MAHIR (FR),** b c Makfi—Shifting Sands (FR) **Shiekh Abdullah Bin Khalifa Al Thani**
52 **MIZAAJ (FR),** b c Arcano (IRE)—Subilita (GER) **Hamdan Al Maktoum**
53 **MOONTATHIR (FR),** ch f Muhtathir—Mosogna Moon **Shiekh Abdullah Bin Khalifa Al Thani**
54 **MR. OWEN (USA),** b c Invincible Spirit (IRE)—Mrs Lindsay (USA) **Mr M. Offenstadt & Mrs B. Jenney**
55 **MURAFEJ (IRE),** ch c Halling (USA)—Mokaraba **Hamdan Al Maktoum**
56 **PEACE NEWS (GER),** b c Sholokhov (IRE)—Peaceful Love (GER) **Pandora Racing**
57 **TAGADIRT,** b c Aqlaam—Latent Lover (IRE) **Pandora Racing**
58 **TAKBEER (IRE),** b g Aqlaam—Precious Secret (IRE) **Hamdan Al Maktoum**
59 **THAKERAH (IRE),** ch f New Approach (IRE)—Tadris (USA) **Hamdan Al Maktoum**
60 **THE JINAD (IRE),** b c Dyhim Diamond (IRE)—Kyria **Faisal Al Rahmani**
61 **VIN CHAUD (FR),** b c Teofilo (IRE)—Mulled Wine (FR) **Mr K. Dasmal**
62 **WADYHATTA,** br f Cape Cross (IRE)—Thamarat **Hamdan Al Maktoum**
63 **WINOGRAFA,** b f Teofilo (IRE)—Winning Family (IRE) **Haras D'Etreham**
64 **ZALAT (FR),** b f American Post—Highness Royale (FR) **Mr P. Offenstadt**

## TWO-YEAR-OLDS

65 **ALWARD (IRE),** ch c 24/3 Aqlaam—Sharedah (IRE) (Pivotal) **Hamdan Al Maktoum**
66 B c 15/5 Shamardal (USA)—
Anna Pavlova (Danehill Dancer (IRE)) (119047) **Sheikh Abdullah Bin Khalifa Al Thani**
67 B c 15/3 Makfi—Baine (FR) (Country Reel (USA)) (111111) **Sheikh Abdullah Bin Kalifa Al Thani**
68 B f 11/2 Lope de Vega (IRE)—Black Dalhia (FR) (Sanglamore (USA)) **Al Shaqab Racing**
69 B c 1/3 Diamond Green (FR)—Carnet de Bal (Kingsalsa (USA)) (39682) **Mrs J. Rusu**
70 B f 22/1 Elusive City (USA)—Chantilly Creme (USA) (Johannesburg (USA)) (25396) **Mrs J. Rusu**
71 **COURBEPINE (FR),** b f 14/3 Samum (GER)—
Princesse Jasmine (FR) (Gold Away (IRE)) (23809) **Mr G. Augustin-Normand**
72 B f 4/5 Dream Ahead (USA)—Courchevel (IRE) (Whipper (USA)) (119047) **Skymarc Farm**
73 **CROIX MARE (FR),** b f 14/3 Diktat—Congostena (IRE) (Dr Devious (IRE)) (22222) **Mr G. Augustin-Normand**
74 **DAREESHA (IRE),** b f 21/4 Naaqoos—Cadenza (FR) (Dansili) **Hamdan Al Maktoum**
75 Ch f 19/3 Nayef (USA)—Divine Promesse (FR) (Verglas (IRE)) (35714) **Sheikh Abdullah Bin Khalifa Al Thani**
76 **DIVONA (FR),** b f 6/2 Le Havre (IRE)—Nostalchia (FR) (Genereux Genie) (103174) **Mr G. Augustin Normand**
77 B f 1/1 High Chaparral (IRE)—Everlasting Love (Pursuit of Love) (35714) **Skymarc Farm**
78 **FIRST NAME (FR),** b c 4/2 Kendargent (FR)—Daewoo Ling (GER) (Observatory (USA)) (11111) **Mr P. Sabban**
79 **GLOS (FR),** b f 4/3 Air Chief Marshal (IRE)—Fancy Dance (Rainbow Quest (USA)) **Mr G. Augustin Normand**
80 **GOLDEN FILLY (FR),** gr f 11/4 Dark Angel (IRE)—
Golden Digger (USA) (Mr Prospector (USA)) **Haras de Beauvoir**
81 **HAWWA (FR),** b f 17/2 Turtle Bowl (IRE)—
Grandes Illusions (FR) (Kendor (FR)) **Sheikh Abdullah Bin Khalifa Al Thani**
82 **LA BOUILLE,** b f 2/5 Le Havre (IRE)—Landskia (FR) (Lando (GER)) **Mr G. Augustin Normand**
83 **LAQUYOOD,** ch c 17/2 Medicean—Elmaam (Nayef (USA)) **Hamdan Al Maktoum**
84 **LISON (FR),** b c 12/3 Le Havre (IRE)—
Lazy Afternoon (IRE) (Hawk Wing (USA)) (39682) **Mr G. Augustin Normand**
85 **LOYALE (FR),** b f 12/2 Turtle Bowl (IRE)—Luminosity (Sillery (USA)) **Mr M. Lagasse**
86 B f 1/1 Intikhab (USA)—Lunassa (FR) (Groom Dancer (USA)) (107142) **Mrs J. Rusu**
87 **MAMNOON (IRE),** b c 9/4 Cape Cross (IRE)—Masaafat (Act One) **Hamdan Al Maktoum**
88 **MASHKOOR (IRE),** b c 17/5 Shamardal (USA)—Mokaraba (Unfuwain (USA)) **Hamdan Al Maktoum**
89 **MAWAWEEL (IRE),** b f 21/3 Authorized (IRE)—Perfect Plum (IRE) (Darshaan) **Hamdan Al Maktoum**
90 B f 6/5 Sinndar (IRE)—Monava (FR) (El Prado (IRE)) **Mr N. Elwes**
91 **MUQADRAT (USA),** b f 19/4 Medaglia d'Oro (USA)—
Jaish (USA) (Seeking The Gold (USA)) **Hamdan Al Maktoum**
92 B c 9/4 Acclamation—
Perfect Day (IRE) (Holy Roman Emperor (IRE)) (35714) **Sheikh Abdullah Bin Khalifa Al Thani**
93 **QURBAAN (USA),** ch c 22/1 Speightstown (USA)—Flip Flop (FR) (Zieten (USA)) **Hamdan Al Maktoum**
94 B f 27/1 Canford Cliffs (IRE)—Rainbow Crossing (Cape Cross (IRE)) (126984) **Al Shaqab Racing**
95 **SAAJID (IRE),** ch c 21/4 Tamayuz—Tomoohat (USA) (Danzig (USA)) **Hamdan Al Maktoum**
96 **SAINT NOM (FR),** b c 10/4 Turtle Bowl (IRE)—Princess Love (FR) (Verglas (IRE)) (30158) **Jacques-Eric Strauss**
97 **SEA SATIN (IRE),** b f 12/4 Elusive City (USA)—Seal Bay (IRE) (Hernando (FR)) (14285) **Mr P. Sabban**
98 **SWEAT DREAMS (FR),** b c 4/5 Dream Ahead (USA)—Santa Louisia (Highest Honor (FR)) (17460) **Mr K. Dasmal**
99 **TAMRAH (IRE),** b f 24/4 Sakhee (USA)—Wajaha (IRE) (Haafhd) **Hamdan Al Maktoum**
100 **THOMASTOWN (FR),** b c 17/1 Dream Ahead (USA)—Tarawa (FR) (Green Tune (USA)) (71428) **Mr K. Dasmal**
101 B f 19/3 Siyouni (FR)—Tres Froide (FR) (Bering) (39682) **Pandora Racing**
102 B c 1/2 Zamindar (USA)—Zainzana (FR) (Green Desert (USA)) (31746) **Sheikh Abdullah Bin Khalifa Al Thani**

**Jockey (flat):** Francois-Xavier Bertras, Sylvain Ruis. **Apprentice:** Florent Gavilan.

## 526 MR W. M. ROPER, Curragh

Postal: **French Furze, Maddenstown, The Curragh, Co. Kildare, Ireland**
Contacts: **PHONE (00353) 45 441821 MOBILE (00353) 86 823 4279**
**E-MAIL markroper1@eircom.net**

1 **CLARIOR EX OBSCURO (IRE),** 9, br g Morozov (USA)—Achates (IRE) **Mr W. M. Roper**
2 **COURTLY CONDUCT (IRE),** 10, b g Court Cave (IRE)—Regency Charm (IRE) **Mr P. E. I. Newell**
3 **THE MAGPIE MAN (IRE),** 4, b g Echo of Light—Inspectors Choice (IRE) **Piers Dennis**
4 **VAALWATER (IRE),** 10, b g Danehill Dancer (IRE)—Amaranthus (USA) **Mr W. M. Roper**
5 4, B f Echo of Light—Woodland Dancer (IRE) **M. H. Keogh**

### THREE-YEAR-OLDS

6 B c Dylan Thomas (IRE)—Roshanak (IRE) **M. H. Keogh**

**Assistant Trainer:** Barry Heffernan

---

## 527 MR BRIAN ROTHWELL, Malton

Postal: **Old Post Office, Oswaldkirk, York, North Yorkshire, YO62 5XT**
Contacts: **PHONE (01439) 788859 MOBILE (07969) 968241**
**E-MAIL brian.rothwell1@googlemail.com**

1 4, B f Azamour (IRE)—Aladiyna (IRE) **Mr A. J. Sparks**
2 **BERTHA BURNETT (IRE),** 4, gr f Verglas (IRE)—Starsazi **Mrs G. Sparks**
3 **DOUBLE HAPPINESS,** 5, ch m Sakhee (USA)—Fu Wa (USA) **B. S. Rothwell**
4 **PETERGATE,** 4, b g Alhaarth (IRE)—Shamayel **Mrs G. Sparks**
5 **QUEEN OF EPIRUS,** 7, ch m Kirkwall—Andromache **B. S. Rothwell**
6 **TAKEMYBREATHAWAY,** 4, b f Court Masterpiece—Corblets **Mrs M. Lingwood**
7 **TELL ME WHEN,** 4, b f Monsieur Bond (IRE)—Giffoine **Mrs M. Lingwood**
8 **TEMPLESHELIN (IRE),** 6, b g Olden Times—Reasoning **B. S. Rothwell**
9 **TINSELTOWN,** 9, b g Sadler's Wells (USA)—Peony **Mr A. F. Arnott**
10 **TORNESEL,** 4, b g Teofilo (IRE)—Bezant (IRE) **P. Moorhouse**
11 **YAWAIL,** 4, b br f Medicean—Al Tamooh (IRE) **Mr A. J. Sparks**

### THREE-YEAR-OLDS

12 **GOOD MOVE (IRE),** b f Aussie Rules (USA)—Lady Lafitte (USA) **Mrs June Jackson**

**Other Owners:** Mr Andrew Sparks.

---

## 528 MR RICHARD ROWE, Pulborough

Postal: **Ashleigh House Stables, Sullington Lane, Storrington, Pulborough, West Sussex, RH20 4AE**
Contacts: **PHONE (01903) 742871 MOBILE (07831) 345636**
**E-MAIL r.rowe.racing@virgin.net WEBSITE www.richardrowe-racing.co.uk**

1 **ALTERANTHELA (IRE),** 11, br g Alderbrook—Anthela (GER) **T. L. Clowes**
2 **FULL OF MISCHIEF (IRE),** 7, ch m Classic Cliche (IRE)—
Drama Chick **The Chicanery Partnership, Mr C. J. Baldwin, Mr C. B. Hatch**
3 **GRACE AND FORTUNE,** 8, b m Grape Tree Road—Nouveau Cheval **Richard Rowe Racing Partnership**
4 **L'ASSOMMOIR (FR),** 6, b br g Saint des Saints (FR)—Double Spring (FR) **T. Thompson**
5 **LIKE SULLY (IRE),** 7, b br g Presenting—Swing Into Action (IRE) **Winterfields Farm Ltd**
6 **PASTORAL DANCER,** 6, b g Pastoral Pursuits—Dancing Flame **B. H. Page**
7 **PASTORAL JET,** 7, b br h Pastoral Pursuits—Genteel (IRE) **R. Rowe**
8 **SIR HUBERT,** 5, b g Multiplex—Lacounsel (FR) **Capt Adrian Pratt & Friends**
9 **STRANGE BIRD (IRE),** 10, b m Revoque (IRE)—Ethel's Bay (IRE) **Richard Rowe Racing Partnership**
10 **TANG ROYAL (FR),** 8, ch g Epalo (GER)—Bea de Forme (FR) **R. Rowe**
11 **WHATAGOA (IRE),** 8, b m Bishop of Cashel—Gotta Goa (IRE) **Richard Rowe Racing Partnership**

**Other Owners:** Mr C. J. Baldwin, Mr D. M. Bradshaw, Mrs H. C. G. Butcher, Mrs J. Case, Mrs J. E. Debenham, Mr C. B. Hatch, Capt A. Pratt, T. W. Wellard.

## 529 MISS MANDY ROWLAND, Lower Blidworth

Postal: **Kirkfields, Calverton Road, Lower Blidworth, Nottingham, Nottinghamshire, NG21 0NW**
Contacts: **PHONE (01623) 794831 MOBILE (07768) 224666**
**E-MAIL kirkfieldsriding@hotmail.co.uk**

1 **ANNIES IDEA,** 6, ch m Yoshka—Danum Diva (IRE) **Miss M. E. Rowland**
2 **AUDACIOUS,** 7, b g Motivator—Flash of Gold **Miss M. E. Rowland**
3 **CHIEF EXECUTIVE (IRE),** 5, gr g Dalakhani (IRE)—Lucky (IRE) **Mr S. P. Giles**
4 **CHINA EXCELS,** 8, b g Exceed And Excel (AUS)—China Beauty **Miss M. E. Rowland**
5 **CLUBLAND (IRE),** 6, b g Red Clubs (IRE)—Racjilanemm **Mr L. P. Keane**
6 **HICKSTER (IRE),** 4, br g Intense Focus (USA)—Surrender To Me (USA) **Mr L. P. Keane**
7 **MR CHOCOLATE DROP (IRE),** 11, b g Danetime (IRE)—Forest Blade (IRE) **Miss M. E. Rowland**
8 **PIPERS PIPING (IRE),** 9, b g Noverre (USA)—Monarchy (IRE) **Miss M. E. Rowland**
9 **PROHIBITION (IRE),** 9, b g Danehill Dancer (IRE)—Crumpetsfortea (IRE) **Miss M. E. Rowland**
10 **ROXY MADAM,** 6, br m Generous (IRE)—Masouri Sana (IRE) **Miss M. E. Rowland**

### THREE-YEAR-OLDS

11 **COOL BEANS,** b g Kyllachy—Stellar Brilliant (USA) **Mr L. P. Keane**
12 **DOUGLAS BANK (IRE),** b g Dandy Man (IRE)—Balance The Books **Mr L. P. Keane**
13 **REASSERT,** b g Assertive—Zonta Zitkala **Mr L. P. Keane**

**Assistant Trainer:** Sarah Mitchel

**Jockey (flat):** Adam Kirby, Jimmy Quinn. **Jockey (NH):** Adam Pogson. **Apprentice:** Nathan Alison.

## 530 MR A. DE ROYER-DUPRE, Chantilly

Postal: **3 Chemin des Aigles, 60500 Chantilly, France**
Contacts: **PHONE (0033) 34458 0303 FAX (0033) 34457 3938 MOBILE (0033) 6702 32901**
**E-MAIL de-royer-dupre@wanadoo.fr**

1 **BRIONIYA,** 4, ch f Pivotal—Bahia Breeze **Andrey Milovanov, Kostyantyn Zgara, Viktor Timoshenko**
2 **CELTIC ROCK,** 6, ch h Rock of Gibraltar (IRE)—Luna Celtica (IRE) **Mme Maria de Los Angeles Maestre Torres**
3 **CLADOCERA (GER),** 4, b f Oasis Dream—Caesarine (FR) **Haras de la Perelle**
4 **CORESSOS (FR),** 4, b c Dalakhani (IRE)—Nearthyka (IRE) **San Paolo Agri-Stud SRL**
5 **DARDIZA (IRE),** 4, b f Street Cry (IRE)—Darkara (IRE) **Princess Z. P. Aga Khan**
6 **DAURAN (IRE),** 4, b c Manduro (GER)—Dawera (IRE) **S. A. Aga Khan**
7 **DEBUTANTE (FR),** 4, b f Gold Away (IRE)—Danedrop (IRE)
**Ecurie des Monceaux, Meridian International, Scuderia Waldeck SRL, Benoit Chalmel, Vincent Larnicol**
8 **DOLNIYA (FR),** 4, b f Azamour (IRE)—Daltama (IRE) **S. A. Aga Khan**
9 **DOURADA (FR),** 4, b f Invincible Spirit (IRE)—Dardania **S. A. Aga Khan**
10 **GENERALISSIME (FR),** 5, gr g Literato (FR)—Rotina (FR) **Mme Gilles Forien, Eduardo Fierro**
11 **GRACIOUSLY,** 4, b f Shamardal (USA)—Gracefully (IRE) **Mise de Moratalla**
12 **HAPPY VALENTINE (SAF),** 5, ch m Silvano (GER)—Happy Ever After (SAF) **Team Valor**
13 **HIDDEN COVE (IRE),** 5, b m Nayef (USA)—Pas d'heure (IRE) **Mise de Moratalla**
14 **KONRADS,** 4, b c Medaglia d'Oro (USA)—
Quetsche (USA) **Peter Maher, Ron Finemore, David Kobritz, Gerard Thomas Ryan**
15 **MARALIKA (FR),** 4, b f Dubawi (IRE)—Marasima (IRE) **S. A. Aga Khan**
16 **NAZMIA (IRE),** 4, b f Holy Roman Emperor (IRE)—Narmina (IRE) **S. A. Aga Khan**
17 **OAK HARBOUR,** 4, b c Sinndar (IRE)—Onega Lake (IRE) **Peter Baumgartner**
18 **REDBROOK (IRE),** 4, b c Raven's Pass (USA)—Nawal (FR) **Al Shaqab**
19 **SANDY'S CHOICE (FR),** 4, b f Footstepsinthesand—Zafonia (FR) **Mme Magalen Bryant**
20 **SARZANA (FR),** 4, b f Azamour (IRE)—Sarlisa (FR) **S. A. Aga Khan**
21 **SHEMYA (FR),** 4, gr f Dansili—Shemima **S. A. Aga Khan**
22 **SHIVANA (FR),** 4, b f Sinndar (IRE)—Shivera (FR) **S. A. Aga Khan**
23 **STRIKING CREATION (IRE),** 4, b f Smart Strike (CAN)—Anabaa's Creation (IRE) **Prestonwood Racing LLC**

### THREE-YEAR-OLDS

24 **AFSHEEN (FR),** b f Invincible Spirit (IRE)—Asharna (IRE) **S. A. Aga Khan**
25 **AKATEA (IRE),** ch f Shamardal (USA)—Altamira **Ecurie Wildenstein**
26 **ALMIYR (FR),** gr c Dubawi (IRE)—Alnamara (FR) **H. H. Aga Khan**
27 **AS ALWAYS,** ch f Kitten's Joy (USA)—Siempre Asi (USA) **Mme Africa Cuadra-Lores**
28 **ASHIRA (FR),** b f Rock of Gibraltar (IRE)—Ashalina (FR) **H. H. Aga Khan**
29 **ASHLAN (FR),** b c Dansili—Ashalanda (FR) **H. H. Aga Khan**
30 **BAKSAR (FR),** b c New Approach (IRE)—Balankiya (IRE) **S. A. Aga Khan**

## MR A. DE ROYER-DUPRE - Continued

31 **BEHNASA (FR),** b f Dansili—Behkara (IRE) **S. A. Aga Khan**
32 **BLUE KIMONO (IRE),** b f Invincible Spirit (IRE)—Bastet (IRE) **Ecurie Wildenstein**
33 **CANDARLIYA (FR),** gr f Dalakhani (IRE)—Candara (FR) **H. H. Aga Khan**
34 **COISA BOA (IRE),** b f Lawman (FR)—Ragazza Mio (IRE) **Haras de Vieux Pont**
35 **DARADIYNA (FR),** b f Sea The Stars (IRE)—Dardania **S. A. Aga Khan**
36 **DARANNDA (FR),** b f Invincible Spirit (IRE)—Darsha (FR) **S. A. Aga Khan**
37 **DARIYAN (FR),** b c Shamardal (USA)—Daryakana (FR) **S. A. Aga Khan**
38 **DHORSELL (IRE),** gr f Mastercraftsman (IRE)—Dacca **Zaro SRL, Mme Sandra Debernardi**
39 **DJIDANI (FR),** b c Oasis Dream—Darjina (FR) **Princess Z. P. Aga Khan**
40 **FEYZABAD,** br c Pivotal—Fraloga (IRE) **H. H. Aga Khan**
41 **GANGSTER OF LOVE (FR),** ch c Thewayyouare (USA)—Attilia (GER) **Rosemont Stud Pty Ltd**
42 **KARAKTAR (IRE),** b c High Chaparral (IRE)—Karawana (IRE) **S. A. Aga Khan**
43 **KASSIM (IRE),** b c Shamardal (USA)—Kastoria (IRE) **S. A. Aga Khan**
44 **KATANIYA (IRE),** b f Raven's Pass (USA)—Katiykha (IRE) **S. A. Aga Khan**
45 **KHEZERABAD (FR),** ch c Dalakhani (IRE)—Khelwa (FR) **S. A. Aga Khan**
46 **KIYRNA (FR),** f Manduro (GER)—Kadiana (IRE) **S. A. Aga Khan**
47 **LOULIYAN (FR),** b c Cape Cross (IRE)—Ludiana (FR) **H. H. Aga Khan**
48 **LOVE IS BLINDNESS (IRE),** b f Sir Percy—On Fair Stage (IRE) **Salinity Service AB**
49 **MANDHEERA (USA),** b f Bernardini (USA)—Mandesha (FR) **Princess Z. P. Aga Khan**
50 **MARUNOUCHI (IRE),** ch f Peintre Celebre (USA)—Morning Line (FR) **Ecurie Wildenstein**
51 **MINYA (FR),** b f Sinndar (IRE)—Minatlya (FR) **H. H. Aga Khan**
52 **MONISHA (FR),** b f Sinndar (IRE)—Mintly Fresh (USA) **H. H. Aga Khan**
53 **NABUNGA (FR),** b g Aussie Rules (USA)—Grantsville (GER) **Rosemont Stud Pty Ltd**
54 **PARADE MUSIC (USA),** b f Giant's Causeway (USA)—Parade Militaire (IRE) **Ecurie Wildenstein**
55 **PERLE RARE (USA),** ch f Distorted Humor (USA)—Peinture Rare (IRE) **Ecurie Wildenstein**
56 **PRUDENTE (FR),** b f Dansili—Platonic **Ecurie Skymarc Farm, Ecurie des Monceaux**
57 **REMAKE,** b f Dansili—Reggane **Haras de la Perelle**
58 **ROYANA (FR),** b f Sea The Stars (IRE)—Rosanara (FR) **H. H. Aga Khan**
59 **SACRIFICE MY SOUL (IRE),** b f Nayef (USA)—Via Saleria (IRE) **Salinity Service AB**
60 **SAGAMIYNA (FR),** b f Azamour (IRE)—Sagalina (IRE) **H. H. Aga Khan**
61 **SAINT KILDA (IRE),** b c Fastnet Rock (AUS)—
Thanks Again (IRE) **Peter Maher, Ron Finemore, David Moodie, Gerard Thomas Ryan**
62 **SAJID (FR),** b c Selkirk (USA)—Sadiyna (FR) **H. H. Aga Khan**
63 **SAMADRISA (IRE),** b f Oasis Dream—Sanariya (IRE) **S. A. Aga Khan**
64 **SANAM (USA),** gr ro c More Than Ready (USA)—Saliyna (FR) **H. H. Aga Khan**
65 **SANNKALA (FR),** b f Medicean—Sanaya (IRE) **S. A. Aga Khan**
66 **SAUSALITO (FR),** b g Dansili—Seal Bay (IRE) **Mme Magalen Bryant**
67 **SAYANA (FR),** b f Galileo (IRE)—Sichilla (IRE) **H. H. Aga Khan**
68 **SECRETARIAT HUMOR (USA),** ch f Distorted Humor (USA)—Secretariat's Soul (IRE) **Charles E. Fipke**
69 **SHAHNILA (FR),** b f Elusive City (USA)—Shamakiya (IRE) **S. A. Aga Khan**
70 **SHAYWAN (IRE),** b c Sinndar (IRE)—Shawara (IRE) **S. A. Aga Khan**
71 **SHENDINI (IRE),** b c Medicean—Shehira (FR) **S. A. Aga Khan**
72 **SHENSI (FR),** b c Invincible Spirit (IRE)—Shemiyla (FR) **S. A. Aga Khan**
73 **SHERINGA (FR),** gr f Oasis Dream—Shemima **S. A. Aga Khan**
74 **SULTANA GOLD,** b f Sea The Stars (IRE)—Sudarynya (IRE) **Viktor Timoshenko**
75 **SYLVANES (IRE),** b f Teofilo (IRE)—Sierra Slew **AB Ascot**
76 **TANIYAR (IRE),** b c Shamardal (USA)—Tanoura (IRE) **S. A. Aga Khan**
77 **TAYWARA (FR),** b f Elusive City (USA)—Tazmiyna (FR) **S. A. Aga Khan**
78 **THREESOME (FR),** b f Sinndar (IRE)—Gamma (FR) **Bloomsbury Stud**
79 **TORECILLAS (FR),** f Azamour (IRE)—Too Marvelous (FR) **Mise de Moratalla**
80 **VADARIYA,** b f Sea The Stars (IRE)—Vadapolina (FR) **H. H. Aga Khan**
81 **VAITAHU (FR),** b c Soldier of Fortune (IRE)—Verveine (USA) **Ecurie Wildenstein**
82 **VAZIRABAD (FR),** b c Manduro (GER)—Visorama (IRE) **H. H. Aga Khan**
83 **VEDOUMA (FR),** b f Dalakhani (IRE)—Vadawina (IRE) **H. H. Aga Khan**
84 **ZAHEER (FR),** b c Pivotal—Zaidiyna (FR) **S. A. Aga Khan**
85 **ZALZALI (FR),** c Dalakhani (IRE)—Zalaiyka (FR) **S. A. Aga Khan**
86 **ZARKAR (FR),** b c Galileo (IRE)—Zarkava (IRE) **S. A. Aga Khan**
87 **ZAZIYR (FR),** b c Cape Cross (IRE)—Zayanida (IRE) **S. A. Aga Khan**
88 **ZOURKHAN (IRE),** b c Shamardal (USA)—Zarkasha (IRE) **S. A. Aga Khan**
89 **ZUBAYR (IRE),** b c Authorized (IRE)—Zaziyra (IRE) **S. A. Aga Khan**

## TWO-YEAR-OLDS

90 **ANDREA MANTEGNA (USA),** ch c 24/3 Giant's Causeway (USA)—
Adventure Seeker (FR) (Bering) **Ecurie Wildenstein**
**91** B c 3/4 Tamayuz—Asharna (IRE) (Darshaan) **S. A. Aga Khan**

## MR A. DE ROYER-DUPRE - Continued

92 **ASTERINA,** ch f 9/4 Dalakhani (IRE)—Altamira (Peintre Celebre (USA)) **Ecurie Wildenstein**
93 **BARHANPOUR (FR),** b c 8/3 Raven's Pass (USA)—Balankiya (IRE) (Darshaan) **S. A. Aga Khan**
94 **BESHARA (FR),** b f 26/3 Cape Cross (IRE)—Behkara (IRE) (Kris) **S. A. Aga Khan**
95 **BOLD EMPEROR (IRE),** b c 15/4 Galileo (IRE)—Bastet (IRE) (Giant's Causeway (USA)) **Ecurie Wildenstein**
96 **CHARISMATIC MAN (IRE),** b c 2/5 Dalakhani (IRE)—On Fair Stage (IRE) (Sadler's Wells (USA)) (115079) **Salinity Service AB, AB Ascot, Gurners Bloodstock Company**
97 Ch c 26/1 New Approach (IRE)—Daltaiyma (IRE) (Doyoun) **S. A. Aga Khan**
98 B f 8/5 Authorized (IRE)—Daltaya (FR) (Anabaa (USA)) **S. A. Aga Khan**
99 Gr f 21/4 Exceed And Excel (AUS)—Dardania (Dalakhani (IRE)) **S. A. Aga Khan**
100 B c 8/4 Dansili—Daryakana (FR) (Selkirk (USA)) **S. A. Aga Khan**
101 **DOUNYAPOUR (FR),** ch c 21/4 Lope de Vega (IRE)—Diamond Tango (FR) (Acatenango (GER)) **H. H. Aga Khan**
102 **LACHARES (IRE),** ch c 27/1 Manduro (GER)—Louve Imperiale (USA) (Giant's Causeway (USA)) **Ecurie Wildenstein**
103 **MAN OF HONOR (IRE),** ch c 1/4 Raven's Pass (USA)—Pride (FR) (Peintre Celebre (USA)) **Fair Salinia Ltd**
104 B c 28/4 Azamour (IRE)—Mintly Fresh (USA) (Rubiano (USA)) **S. A. Aga Khan**
105 **PAINTER'S MUSE,** b f 9/2 Smart Strike (CAN)—Peinture Rare (IRE) (Sadler's Wells (USA)) **Ecurie Wildenstein**
106 **PANDORA'S STAR (IRE),** ch f 25/2 Smart Strike (CAN)—Parade Militaire (IRE) (Peintre Celebre (USA)) **Ecurie Wildenstein**
107 **PRAIRIE SONG (IRE),** b f 3/2 Montjeu (IRE)—Prairie Runner (IRE) (Arazi (USA)) **Ecurie Wildenstein**
108 **RASHKANI (FR),** b c 29/3 Pivotal—Radiyya (IRE) (Sinndar (IRE)) **H. H. Aga Khan**
109 **ROBIANO (IRE),** b c 28/3 Dubawi (IRE)—Reggane (Red Ransom (USA)) (277777) **Haras de la Perelle, San Paolo Agri-Stud SRL**
110 B f 23/3 Dansili—Rosanara (FR) (Sinndar (IRE)) **H. H. Aga Khan**
111 **SARZAMEEN (FR),** b f 18/2 Siyouni (FR)—Sarlisa (FR) (Rainbow Quest (USA)) **S. A. Aga Khan**
112 **SAYED (FR),** b br c 13/3 Stormy Atlantic (USA)—Saliyna (FR) (Linamix (FR)) **H. H. Aga Khan**
113 **SHAHMEEN (FR),** b f 15/3 Shamardal (USA)—Shamanova (IRE) (Danehill Dancer (IRE)) **S. A. Aga Khan**
114 **SHAMSHAD (FR),** b c 6/3 Sea The Stars (IRE)—Shamakiya (IRE) (Intikhab (USA)) **S. A. Aga Khan**
115 B f 26/4 Azamour (IRE)—Shemima (Dalakhani (IRE)) **S. A. Aga Khan**
116 B c 9/4 Acclamation—Shemiyla (FR) (Dalakhani (IRE)) **S. A. Aga Khan**
117 B c 21/3 Dalakhani (IRE)—Vadiya (FR) (Peintre Celebre (USA)) **S. A. Aga Khan**
118 Ch c 4/3 Rock of Gibraltar (IRE)—Valasyra (FR) (Sinndar (IRE)) **H. H. Aga Khan**
119 B c 1/3 Dubawi (IRE)—Zarkava (IRE) (Zamindar (USA)) **S. A. Aga Khan**
120 Ch f 26/2 Raven's Pass (USA)—Zayanida (IRE) (King's Best (USA)) **S. A. Aga Khan**

**Assistant Trainers:** Laurent Metais, Pierre Groualle

**Jockey (flat):** Antoine Hamelin, Christophe Soumillon. **Apprentice:** Mickael Berto.

---

## 531 MS LUCINDA RUSSELL, Kinross

Postal: **Arlary House Stables, Milnathort, Kinross, Tayside, KY13 9SJ**
Contacts: **PHONE (01577) 865512 FAX (01577) 861171 MOBILE (07970) 645261**
**E-MAIL lucinda@arlary.fsnet.co.uk WEBSITE www.lucindarussell.com**

1 **ALIZEE DE JANEIRO (FR),** 5, b m Network (GER)—Katana (GER) **Ms D. Thomson**
2 **AMORE MIO (GER),** 10, b g Trempolino (USA)—Amore (GER) **Team Kirkton**
3 **BACK TO BRACKA (IRE),** 8, b g Rudimentary (USA)—Martha's Glimpse (IRE) **Straightline Construction Ltd**
4 **BADGER FOOT (IRE),** 10, br g Beneficial—Droim Alton Gale (IRE) **P. J. S. Russell**
5 **BALLYBEN (IRE),** 7, ch g Beneficial—I'm Maggy (NZ) **Drew & Ailsa Russell**
6 **BALLYCOOL (IRE),** 8, b g Helissio (FR)—Carnoustie (USA) **Mr & Mrs T. P. Winnell**
7 **BEIDH TINE ANSEO (IRE),** 9, b g Rock of Gibraltar (IRE)—Siamsa (USA) **Mr I. D. Miller**
8 **BESCOT SPRINGS (IRE),** 10, b g Saddlers' Hall (IRE)—Silver Glen (IRE) **Kelso Lowflyers & Mr PJS Russell**
9 **BIG RIVER (IRE),** 5, b g Milan—Call Kate (IRE) **Two Black Labs**
10 **BIGGAR (IRE),** 7, b g Court Cave (IRE)—Native Success (IRE) **Mr A. McAllister**
11 **BLAZIN WHITE FACE (IRE),** 8, b m Noverre (USA)—Watch The Clock **Mr I. D. Miller**
12 **BLENHEIM BROOK (IRE),** 10, br g Alderbrook—Blenheim Blinder (IRE) **The County Set Three**
13 **BLUESIDE BOY (IRE),** 7, b g Blueprint (IRE)—Asidewager (IRE) **Mr G. F. Adam**
14 **BOLD SIR BRIAN (IRE),** 9, b g Brian Boru—Black Queen (IRE) **Major A. R. Trotter**
15 **CASTLELAWN (IRE),** 8, b g Runyon (IRE)—Pure Magic (IRE) **J. R. Adam**
16 **CATCHTHEMOONLIGHT,** 7, b m Generous (IRE)—Moon Catcher **Dig In Racing**
17 4, B f Yeats (IRE)—Classic Gale (USA) **Straightline Construction Ltd**
18 **CLIFF LANE (IRE),** 6, b g Scorpion (IRE)—Susan's Dream (IRE) **Lynne & Angus Maclennan**
19 **CLONDAW KNIGHT (IRE),** 7, b g Heron Island (IRE)—Sarah Supreme (IRE) **Mr A. N. Seymour**
20 **COBAJAYISLAND (IRE),** 7, b g Heron Island (IRE)—Shinora (IRE) **Mrs L. Maclennan**
21 **CRACKERJACK LAD (IRE),** 12, br g Exit To Nowhere (USA)—Crowther Homes **Mr I. D. Miller**

## MS LUCINDA RUSSELL - Continued

22 **DOTTIES DILEMA (IRE),** 7, b g Pierre—Tellarue (IRE) **Stewart Dempster Mitchell**
23 **DUN BAY CREEK,** 4, b g Dubai Destination (USA)—Over It **Mr J. J. Murray**
24 **FARRAGON (IRE),** 5, b g Marienbard (IRE)—Oath of Allegiance (IRE) **Mrs S Russell & A M Russell**
25 **FIFTEEN KINGS (IRE),** 5, b g King's Theatre (IRE)—Mistletoeandwine (IRE) **E. Bruce**
26 **FINAL ASSAULT (IRE),** 6, b br g Beneficial—Last Campaign (IRE) **Mrs S Russell & A M Russell**
27 4, B f Milan—Gaye Preskina (IRE) **J. R. Adam**
28 4, B f Alkaadhem—Go Franky (IRE) **Mr K. Alexander**
29 **GREEN FLAG (IRE),** 8, b g Milan—Erin Go Brea (IRE) **J. R. Adam**
30 **HALLMARK STAR,** 6, b g Nayef (USA)—Spring **The County Set (Two)**
31 **IMJOEKING (IRE),** 8, b g Amilynx (FR)—Go Franky (IRE) **Mr K. Alexander**
32 **INNOCENT GIRL (IRE),** 6, b m King's Theatre (IRE)—Belle Innocence (FR) **John J. Murray & Niall Farrell**
33 **ISLAND CONFUSION (IRE),** 7, b g Heron Island (IRE)—Anshan Gail (IRE) **Mrs A. E. Giles**
34 **ISLAND HEIGHTS (IRE),** 6, b g Heron Island (IRE)—La Reina (IRE) **Mr G. R. McGladery**
35 **IT'S HIGH TIME (IRE),** 7, b g Kalanisi (IRE)—Windsor Dancer (IRE) **Straightline Construction Ltd**
36 **ITSTIMEFORAPINT (IRE),** 7, b g Portrait Gallery (IRE)—Executive Pearl (IRE) **IMEJ Racing**
37 **JACK STEEL (IRE),** 5, b g Craigsteel—Wake Me Gently (IRE) **J. P. McManus**
38 **JUST CHILLY,** 6, b m Kayf Tara—Your Punishment (IRE) **Mrs V. J. McKie**
39 **JUST FOR PLEASURE (IRE),** 5, b m Kayf Tara—Heltornic (IRE) **Let's Live Racing**
40 **KAI BROON (IRE),** 8, b g Marju (IRE)—Restiv Star (FR) **John R. Adam & Sons Ltd**
41 **KATALYSTIC (IRE),** 4, br g Kalanisi (IRE)—Beltane Queen (IRE) **Mr R. B. H. Young**
42 4, B f King's Theatre (IRE)—Keys Pride (IRE) **Mr K. Alexander**
43 **KINGS FOLLY (IRE),** 7, b g Dushyantor (USA)—Beltane Queen (IRE) **Mrs M. C. Coltman**
44 **KINGSWELL THEATRE,** 6, b g King's Theatre (IRE)—Cresswell Native (IRE) **Mr J. J. Murray**
45 **KNOCKANDO,** 10, b g Milan—Cherry Lane **Distillery Racing Club**
46 **KUMBESHWAR,** 8, b g Doyen (IRE)—Camp Fire (IRE) **The Twentyfivers**
47 **LADY OF VERONA (IRE),** 8, b m Old Vic—Innovate (IRE) **Peter K. Dale Ltd**
48 **LONE FOOT LADDIE (IRE),** 6, b g Red Clubs (IRE)—Alexander Phantom (IRE) **Dr J. Wilson**
49 **MAKE IT HAPPEN (IRE),** 6, b g Saffron Walden (FR)—Kelpie (IRE) **Wright Mitchell Wilson**
50 **MARAWEH (IRE),** 5, b g Muhtathir—Itqaan (USA) **Tay Valley Chasers Racing Club**
51 **MARCUS ANTONIUS,** 8, b g Mark of Esteem (IRE)—Star of The Course (USA) **Mr K. J. Mackie**
52 **MISS HIGH TIME (IRE),** 4, b f Kalanisi (IRE)—Windsor Dancer (IRE) **Straightline Construction Ltd**
53 **MOMKINZAIN (USA),** 8, b g Rahy (USA)—Fait Accompli (USA) **P. J. S. Russell**
54 **MORNING TIME (IRE),** 9, b g Hawk Wing (USA)—Desert Trail (IRE) **Mr W. G. H. Forrester**
55 **MUMGOS DEBUT (IRE),** 7, b g Royal Anthem (USA)—Black Queen (IRE) **Mrs Suzy Brown & Mr Peter R Brown**
56 **MYSTEREE (IRE),** 7, b g Gold Well—Hillside Native (IRE) **Mrs L. Maclennan**
57 **NO DEAL (IRE),** 9, b g Revoque (IRE)—Noble Choice **Gilbert McClung (Kelso) Ltd**
58 **ONE FOR ARTHUR (IRE),** 6, b g Milan—Nonnetia (FR) **Two Golf Widows**
59 **ORIONINVERNESS (IRE),** 4, b g Brian Boru—Woodville Leader (IRE) **Tay Valley Chasers Racing Club**
60 **OUTLAW TOM (IRE),** 11, b g Luso—Timely Approach (IRE) **Milnathort Racing Club**
61 **PRESENT FLIGHT (IRE),** 6, ch g Presenting—Grangeclare Flight (IRE) **Kilco (International) Ltd**
62 **PRESENT LODGER (IRE),** 7, b g Presenting—Hannigan's Lodger (IRE) **Mr A. N. Seymour**
63 **PRESENTING REBEL (IRE),** 9, ch g Presenting—Random Bless (IRE) **Mr W. T. Scott**
64 **PROSECCO (IRE),** 13, b g Perpendicular—Bay Gale (IRE) **Tay Valley Chasers Racing Club**
65 **PULPITARIAN (USA),** 7, b g Pulpit (USA)—Bedanken (USA) **Two Black Labs**
66 **QUITO DU TRESOR (FR),** 11, b g Jeune Homme (USA)—Itiga (FR) **Kelso Lowflyers & Mr PJS Russell**
67 **REAPING THE REWARD (IRE),** 11, b g Sylvan Express—Zamaine (IRE) **Mr & Mrs Raymond Anderson Green**
68 **REVOCATION,** 7, b g Revoque (IRE)—Fenella **Mr Michael & Lady Jane Kaplan**
69 **RHYMERS STONE,** 7, b g Desideratum—Salu **Mr G. F. Adam**
70 5, B m Milan—Rockwell College (IRE) **John R. Adam & Sons Ltd**
71 **ROWDY ROCHER (IRE),** 9, br g Winged Love (IRE)—Madam Rocher (IRE) **Michelle And Dan Macdonald**
72 **RYTON RUNNER (IRE),** 7, b g Sadler's Wells (USA)—Love For Ever (IRE) **County Set Four**
73 **SAPHIR RIVER (FR),** 9, gr g Slickly (FR)—Miss Bio (FR) **Mr A. N. Seymour**
74 **SETTLEDOUTOFCOURT (IRE),** 9, b g Court Cave (IRE)—Ardagh Princess **Mr A. McAllister**
75 **SEVENBALLS OF FIRE (IRE),** 6, b g Milan—Leadamurraydance (IRE) **Mr A. M. Russell**
76 **SHINE A DIAMOND (IRE),** 7, gr g St Jovite (USA)—Mossy Grey (IRE) **Kilco (International) Ltd**
77 **SIMARTHUR,** 8, gr g Erhaab (USA)—Dusty Too **Hexham Racing Club**
78 **SKY KHAN,** 6, b g Cape Cross (IRE)—Starlit Sky **The Ormello Way**
79 **SPIRIT OSCAR (IRE),** 7, b m Oscar (IRE)—Grange Classic (IRE) **Ms D. Thomson**
80 **SPOILS OF WAR (IRE),** 6, b g Craigsteel—Mooreshill Lady (IRE) **Mr L. M. Wilde**
81 **STAR DATE (IRE),** 6, b g Galileo (IRE)—Play Misty For Me (IRE) **The County Set (Five)**
82 **STYLISH CHAP (IRE),** 5, b g New South Wales—Curragh Bawn Lass (IRE) **Mr Michael & Lady Jane Kaplan**
83 **SUPERIOR COMMAND (IRE),** 6, b g Lahib (USA)—Decent Dime (IRE) **P. J. S. Russell**
84 **TAKETHEPUNISHMENT,** 5, b g Revoque (IRE)—Your Punishment (IRE) **Mrs V. J. McKie**
85 **TANTAMOUNT,** 6, b g Observatory (USA)—Cantanta **Mutual Friends**
86 **TAP NIGHT (USA),** 8, ch g Pleasant Tap (USA)—Day Mate (USA) **J. P. McManus**

## MS LUCINDA RUSSELL - Continued

87 **THE COBBLER SWAYNE (IRE),** 6, b g Milan—Turtle Lamp (IRE) **Mrs R. A. Stobart**
88 **THE FRIARY (IRE),** 8, b g Kris Kin (USA)—Native Design (IRE) **Mrs S Russell & A M Russell**
89 **THE LADY MAGGI (FR),** 5, b m Robin des Champs (FR)—Miss Poutine (FR) **Mr A. N. Seymour**
90 **THE SQUINTY BRIDGE,** 7, b g Heron Island (IRE)—The Storm Bell (IRE) **Mrs J. Perratt**
91 **THE TOFT,** 6, b m Kayf Tara—Gretton **P. J. S. Russell**
92 **THE VILLAGE (IRE),** 6, b g Lahib (USA)—Melisande **Milnathort Racing Club**
93 **THIS THYNE JUDE,** 7, gr m Silver Patriarch (IRE)—This Thyne **G. S. Brown**
94 **THORPE (IRE),** 5, b g Danehill Dancer (IRE)—Minkova (IRE) **Mr G. Truscott**
95 **THROTHETHATCH (IRE),** 6, b g Beneficial—Castletownroche (IRE) **Mrs A. E. Giles**
96 **UISGE BEATHA (IRE),** 7, b g Alderbrook—Me Grannys Endoors (IRE) **Last Alders**
97 **ULTRA DU CHATELET (FR),** 7, b g Network (GER)—Grandeur Royale (FR) **Brahms & Liszt**
98 **URBAN KODE (IRE),** 7, b g Kodiac—Urbanize (USA) **Suzy Brown, John Baird, Tony Evans**
99 **VENGEUR DE GUYE (FR),** 6, b g Dom Alco (FR)—Mascotte de Guye (FR) **Brahms & Liszt**
100 **VOYAGE A NEW YORK (FR),** 6, b g Kapgarde (FR)—Pennsylvanie (FR) **Fyffees**

**Other Owners:** Mr W. Agnew, Mr J. A. Aitkenhead, Mr J. B. Baird, M. Ball, G. F. Bear, Mrs S. Brown, Mr P. R. Brown, Ms S. J. Burns, A. Cadger, Mr J. E. Chernouski, Mr A. B. Cuthill, Mr C. Dempster, Mr E. W. Dempster, Mr I. Dobson, Mr D. J. Eggie, Mr A. Evans, Mrs B. V. Evans, N. Farrell, L. R. Frampton, Mr J. Fyffe, Mr S. Fyffe, G. Godsman, E. Graham, Mrs I. M. Grant, R. A. Green, Mrs A. Green, Mr M. J. Guthrie, E. D. Haggart, Mrs M. Hamilton, Mr A. W. Henderson, Kelso Members Lowflyers Club, Mrs M Kennedy, Mrs C. J. Lamb, Mr J. S. Lessells, Ms F. E. MacInnes, Mrs M. Macdonald, Mr W. D. Macdonald, M. F. Mackay, Mr J. Mackenzie, Mr A. Maclennan, Mrs M. M. Macleod, Mr J. M. Mcintyre, Mr M. G. Mellor, Mr J. D. Miller, Mr J. Mitchell, Mr J. M. Murphy, Mrs J. M. Murray, Mr G. G. Ritchie, R. Robinson, Ms L. V. Russell, Mrs S. C. Russell, Mrs A. Russell, A. J. R. Russell, Mr A. M. Russell, Mr A. Savage, Mr G. Scott, Mr A. B. Shepherd, Mr B. T. E. Shrubsall, A. W. Sinclair, A. D. Stewart, Mr T. P. Winnell, Mrs M. Winnell, Mr D. J. Gordon Wright.

**Assistant Trainers:** Peter Scudamore, Jaimie Duff, Nick Orpwood

**Jockey (NH):** Peter Buchanan. **Conditional:** Grant Cockburn, Derek Fox, Craig Nichol, Ryan Nichol, Graham Watters. **Amateur:** Mr Ross Chapman, Mr Nick Orpwood, Mr Harry Reed.

---

## 532 MR JOHN RYALL, Yeovil

Postal: **Higher Farm, Rimpton, Yeovil, Somerset, BA22 8AD**
Contacts: **PHONE/FAX (01935) 850222 MOBILE (07592) 738848**
**E-MAIL bjmryall@btconnect.com**

1 **BIT OF A CHARLIE,** 6, b g Emperor Fountain—Win A Hand **B. J. M. Ryall**
2 **CYPRESS GROVE (IRE),** 12, b g Windsor Castle—Grecian Queen **B. J. M. Ryall**
3 **HI BRONCO,** 8, b g Emperor Fountain—Win A Hand **B. J. M. Ryall**
4 5, B m Apple Tree (FR)—Spring Grass **B. J. M. Ryall**
5 5, B g Franklins Gardens—Tin Symphony **B. J. M. Ryall**

**Assistant Trainer:** Mrs R C Ryall

---

## 533 MR JOHN RYAN, Newmarket

Postal: **Cadland Stables, Moulton Road, Newmarket, Suffolk, CB8 8DU**
Contacts: **PHONE (01638) 664172 MOBILE (07739) 801235**
**E-MAIL john.ryan@jryanracing.com WEBSITE www.jryanracing.com**

1 **APPLEJACK LAD,** 4, ch g Three Valleys (USA)—Fittonia (FR) **Mr G. R. McGladery**
2 **EVACUSAFE LADY,** 4, ch f Avonbridge—Snow Shoes **Mr J. B. Ryan**
3 **FOCAIL MEAR,** 4, b f Oratorio (IRE)—Glittering Image (IRE) **John Ryan Racing Partnership**
4 **OCEAN APPLAUSE,** 5, b g Royal Applause—Aldora **Mr W. McLuskey**
5 **OCEAN TEMPEST,** 6, gr g Act One—Ipsa Loquitur **Mr W. McLuskey & Mr C. Little**
6 **OPUS TOO (IRE),** 4, b g Lawman (FR)—Jerez (IRE) **Mr A. Dee**
7 **PLUCKY DIP,** 4, b g Nayef (USA)—Plucky **Mr Byron, Mr Lavallin & Mr Donnison**
8 **TENOR (IRE),** 5, b g Oratorio (IRE)—Cedar Sea (IRE) **Kilco (International) Ltd**
9 **THE GAY CAVALIER,** 4, b g Henrythenavigator (USA)—Dear Daughter **The Gay Cavaliers Partnership**
10 **THECORNISHCOWBOY,** 6, b g Haafhd—Oriental Dance **Mr C. Letcher & Mr J. Ryan**

### THREE-YEAR-OLDS

11 **BIG MCINTOSH (IRE),** b c Bushranger (IRE)—Three Decades (IRE) **Kilco (International) Ltd**
12 **CELESTINE ABBEY,** b f Authorized (IRE)—Billie Jean **Mr A. Dee**
13 **DUKE OF ROMANCE,** ch g Duke of Marmalade (IRE)—Chance For Romance **Coutts & Partners**

## MR JOHN RYAN - Continued

14 **EXCEEDWELL,** b f Exceed And Excel (AUS)—Muja Farewell **Masters Stud**
15 **HONCHO (IRE),** gr g Dark Angel (IRE)—Disco Lights **Mr G. R. McGladery**
16 **LORD REASON,** b c Sixties Icon—Luck Will Come (IRE) **Greenstead Hall Racing Ltd**
17 **MERCY ME,** b f Mawatheeq (USA)—Fantastic Santanyi **Mr G. F. Smith-Bernal**
18 **OCEAN CRYSTAL,** b f Stimulation (IRE)—Crystal Gale (IRE) **Mr W. McLuskey & Mr J. Ryan**
19 B g Humbel (USA)—Tamara Moon (IRE) **Mr W. McLuskey**
20 **THECORNISHBARRON (IRE),** b g Bushranger (IRE)—Tripudium (IRE) **Mr C. Letcher & Mr J. Ryan**

### TWO-YEAR-OLDS

21 B g 14/2 Equiano (FR)—Fittonia (FR) (Ashkalani (IRE)) (17000) **Mr W. McLuskey**
22 **LADY NAYEF,** b f 8/3 Nayef (USA)—Luck Will Come (IRE) (Desert Style (IRE))
23 B g 29/4 Captain Gerrard (IRE)—My Heart's On Fire (IRE) (Beat Hollow) (1500) **Mr J. B. Ryan**

**Other Owners:** Mr M. Byron, Miss L. M. Collins, Mrs K. L. Coutts, Mr P. J. Donnison, Mr J. Fyffe, Mr S. Fyffe, Mr D. A. Hill, Mr P. A. Howkins, Mr Simon Kerr, Mr W. R. Kingston, Mr S. Lavallin, Mr Christopher Letcher, Mr C. W. Little, S & M Supplies (Aylsham) Ltd, Mr G. Smith-Bernal, Mrs J. Williams.

---

## 534 MR KEVIN RYAN, Hambleton

Postal: **Hambleton Lodge, Hambleton, Thirsk, North Yorkshire, YO7 2HA**
Contacts: **PHONE Office (01845) 597010 / (01845) 597622 FAX (01845) 597622**
**MOBILE (07768) 016930**
**E-MAIL kevin.hambleton@virgin.net WEBSITE www.kevinryanracing.com**

1 **ARDMAY (IRE),** 6, b g Strategic Prince—Right After Moyne (IRE) **A. C. Henson**
2 **ASTAIRE (IRE),** 4, b c Intense Focus (USA)—Runway Dancer **Mrs A. Bailey**
3 **BLAINE,** 5, ch g Avonbridge—Lauren Louise **Matt & Lauren Morgan**
4 **BOGART,** 6, ch g Bahamian Bounty—Lauren Louise **Mrs A. Bailey**
5 **COMINO (IRE),** 4, b g Tagula (IRE)—Malta (USA) **Exors of the Late Mr D. W. Barker**
6 **DISTANT PAST,** 4, b g Pastoral Pursuits—Faraway Lass **Mr M. Wynne**
7 **GLORY AWAITS (IRE),** 5, ch h Choisir (AUS)—Sandbox Two (IRE) **Ahmad Abdulla Al Shaikh & Co**
8 **GREEN LIGHT (FR),** 4, b g Way of Light (USA)—Soma Bay (FR) **Ms Ineta Zingere**
9 **HOPES N DREAMS (IRE),** 7, b m Elusive City (USA)—Hope of Pekan (IRE) **J. C. G. Chua & C. K. Ong**
10 **HOT STREAK (IRE),** 4, ch c Iffraaj—Ashirah (USA) **Qatar Racing Ltd**
11 **KEEP TO THE BEAT,** 4, b f Beat Hollow—Cadeau Speciale **Hambleton Racing Ltd XXIX**
12 **KELINNI (IRE),** 7, b g Refuse To Bend (IRE)—Orinoco (IRE) **Amplitudo**
13 **LESHA (IRE),** 4, b g Amadeus Wolf—Dane Blue (IRE) **Mr Mubarak Al Naemi**
14 **LEXINGTON ABBEY,** 4, b g Sleeping Indian—Silvereine (FR) **Middleham Park Racing XIX**
15 **LIGHTNING CLOUD (IRE),** 7, gr g Sleeping Indian—Spree (IRE) **Hambleton Racing Ltd XVIII**
16 **MADAME MIRASOL (IRE),** 4, b f Sleeping Indian—Confidentiality (IRE) **Mrs M. Forsyth**
17 **MOONLIGHT VENTURE,** 4, ch g Tobougg (IRE)—Evening **Guy Reed Racing**
18 **MUKAYNIS (IRE),** 4, b c Tamayuz—Wild Ways **Mr Mubarak Al Naemi**
19 **ONLINE ALEXANDER (IRE),** 4, b f Acclamation—Dance Club (IRE) **Mr Noel O'Callaghan**
20 **PIAZON,** 4, br g Striking Ambition—Colonel's Daughter **Mr F. Gillespie**
21 **REALIZE,** 5, b g Zafeen (FR)—Relkida **Mr J. C. G. Chua**
22 **SEARCHLIGHT,** 4, b g Kyllachy—Baralinka (IRE) **Elite Racing Club**
23 **STRAITS OF MALACCA,** 4, ch g Compton Place—Cultural Role **J. C. G. Chua & C. K. Ong**
24 **THE GREY GATSBY (IRE),** 4, gr c Mastercraftsman (IRE)—Marie Vison (IRE) **Mr F. Gillespie**
25 **TRAIL BLAZE (IRE),** 6, b g Tagula (IRE)—Kingpin Delight **Mr & Mrs Julian & Rosie Richer**

### THREE-YEAR-OLDS

26 **AL GHAF (IRE),** gr c Zebedee—Baby Bunting **Mr Mubarak Al Naemi**
27 **AL GHEZLANIYA (IRE),** b f Dandy Man (IRE)—Gala Style (IRE) **Mr Mubarak Al Naemi**
28 **AL NEHAYY,** gr c Mastercraftsman (IRE)—Yacht Woman (USA) **Mr Mubarak Al Naemi**
29 **AL RAYYAN (IRE),** ch c Danehill Dancer (IRE)—Inca Trail (USA) **Mr Mubarak Al Naemi**
30 **ALHELLA,** b f Kyllachy—Maid In The Shade **Sheikh Abdullah Almalek Alsabah**
31 **AZYAAN (IRE),** gr f Mastercraftsman (IRE)—Hidden Heart (USA) **Sheikh Abdullah Almalek Alsabah**
32 **BACALL,** b f Paco Boy (IRE)—Xtrasensory **Mrs A. Bailey**
33 **BAPAK ASMARA (IRE),** ro g Zebedee—Sheba Five (USA) **Mr T. A. Rahman**
34 **BRANDO,** ch c Pivotal—Argent du Bois (USA) **Mrs A. Bailey**
35 **CALYPSO BEAT (USA),** b f Speightstown (USA)—African Skies **Cockerill Hillen & Graham**
36 **CAN YOU REVERSE,** b g Piccolo—Give Her A Whirl **Guy Reed Racing**
37 **CAPTAIN COLBY (USA),** b g Bernstein (USA)—Escape To Victory **Mrs R. G. Hillen**
38 B f Peintre Celebre (USA)—Card Games **Guy Reed Racing**

## MR KEVIN RYAN - Continued

39 **CHARLIE CROKER (IRE),** b c Fast Company (IRE)—Officious Madam (USA) **Mr Malih L. Al Basti**
40 **COOPER,** b c Sir Percy—Blossom **Guy Reed Racing**
41 **COUNT MONTECRISTO (FR),** b c Siyouni (FR)—Blackberry Pie (USA) **Middleham Park Racing XLVI**
42 **CRYSTAL WISH,** b f Exceed And Excel (AUS)—Crystal Mountain (USA) **Mrs A. Cantillon**
43 **CYRIL,** b g Rail Link—Nurse Gladys **Guy Reed Racing**
44 **ELEUTHERA,** ch g Bahamian Bounty—Cha Cha Cha **Guy Reed Racing**
45 **ERIK THE RED (FR),** b g Kendargent (FR)—Norwegian Princess (IRE) **Mr F. Gillespie**
46 **FAST ACT (IRE),** ch c Fast Company (IRE)—Nullarbor **Hambleton Racing Ltd XXXII**
47 **FIRGROVE BRIDGE (IRE),** ch g Dandy Man (IRE)—Over Rating **Mrs M. Forsyth**
48 **FLAMING SPEAR (IRE),** ch c Lope de Vega (IRE)—Elshamms **Qatar Racing & Essafinaat**
49 **GEOLOGY,** b g Rock of Gibraltar (IRE)—Baralinka (IRE) **Elite Racing Club**
50 **KYLACH ME IF U CAN,** b c Kyllachy—Raskutani **Geoff & Sandra Turnbull**
51 **LET'S TWIST,** ch g Piccolo—Takes Two To Tango **Guy Reed Racing**
52 **LIGHTNING SPREE (IRE),** gr g Jeremy (USA)—Spree (IRE) **Hambleton Racing Ltd XXXIV**
53 **MERCURY,** ch g Showcasing—Miss Rimex (IRE) **Mrs A. Bailey**
54 **MIGHTY ZIP (USA),** ch c City Zip (USA)—Incredulous (FR) **Qatar Racing Ltd**
55 **MOUNT TAHAN (IRE),** b c Lope de Vega (IRE)—Sorpresa (USA) **Mr T. A. Rahman**
56 **MOVING UPWARDS,** ch g Bahamian Bounty—Rainbow End **Matt & Lauren Morgan**
57 **NO BACKCHAT (IRE),** b c Dutch Art—Brilliana **Mr Khalid Mishref**
58 **ONLY JUST (IRE),** b g Bushranger (IRE)—Inter Madera (IRE)
59 **OUT OF ACES,** ch c Piccolo—Subtle Move (USA) **Mr J. Beard**
60 **PEACE LILLY (USA),** b br f Distorted Humor (USA)—Julia Tuttle (USA) **H H Stable**
61 **QATAR FALCON (IRE),** ch c Mastercraftsman (IRE)—Nouveau Riche (IRE) **Mr Mubarak Al Naemi**
62 **QATAR ROCK (IRE),** gr g Zebedee—Spinning Gold **Mr Mubarak Al Naemi**
63 **RED MAJESTY,** b c Acclamation—Red Shareef **Qatar Racing Ltd**
64 **RIVER OF DREAMS (IRE),** br g Big Bad Bob (IRE)—Toberanthawn (IRE) **Matt & Lauren Morgan 1**
65 **SALATEEN,** ch c Dutch Art—Amanda Carter **Sheikh Abdullah Almalek Alsabah**
66 **SERENADE,** b f Oratorio (IRE)—After You **Guy Reed Racing**
67 **SIGURD (GER),** ch g Sholokhov (IRE)—Sky News (GER) **Mr F. Gillespie**
68 **SIR DOMINO (FR),** b c Evasive—Domino Queen (IRE) **Hambleton Racing Ltd XXXV**
69 **SIR KEATING,** b g Sir Percy—Moiava (FR) **B. E. Holland**
70 **SOFT LOVE (IRE),** b f Kodiac—Appley Bridge (IRE) **Mr Hussain Alabbas Lootah**
71 **STENID,** ch g Exceed And Excel (AUS)—Indian Mystery (IRE) **Mr Khalid Mishref**
72 **SWIFT APPROVAL (IRE),** ch g Approve (IRE)—Tiltili (IRE) **Middleham Park Racing XLIX**
73 **TEMPTING CHARM,** ch c Kyllachy—Top Flight Queen **H H Stable**
74 **TERUNTUM STAR (FR),** ch c Dutch Art—Seralia **Mr T. A. Rahman**
75 **THE WEE BARRA (IRE),** b f Rock of Gibraltar (IRE)—Gamra (IRE) **Highbank Stud**
76 **THOWAR (USA),** gr ro g Exchange Rate (USA)—Elusive Fancy (USA) **Sheikh Abdullah Almalek Alsabah**
77 **UNDER SIEGE (IRE),** b g Invincible Spirit (IRE)—Interpose **Clipper Logistics**
78 **UPTIGHT (FR),** b c Zamindar (USA)—Terre d'espoir (FR) **Matt & Lauren Morgan**
79 **WELD AL EMARAT,** b c Dubawi (IRE)—Spirit of Dubai (IRE) **Mr Ahmad Abdulla Al Shaikh**

## TWO-YEAR-OLDS

80 **AHLAN BIL EMARATI (IRE),** ch c 12/4 Fast Company (IRE)—
Law Review (IRE) (Case Law) (57142) **Ahmad Abdulla Al Shaikh & Co**
81 B c 4/5 Piccolo—America Lontana (FR) (King's Theatre (IRE)) (19047) **Mr J. Hanson**
82 B g 10/4 Paco Boy (IRE)—Anosti (Act One) (15000) **Theobalds Stud**
83 Gr c 25/3 Equiano (FR)—Bandanna (Bandmaster (USA)) (33333) **Mr T. A. Rahman**
84 Ch f 15/4 Fast Company (IRE)—Changari (USA) (Gulch (USA)) (20952) **Hambleton Racing Ltd XLII**
85 Ch c 29/3 Pastoral Pursuits—Charlotte Vale (Pivotal) (14285) **Mr J. Nixon**
86 B c 30/3 Kheleyf (USA)—Choosey Girl (IRE) (Choisir (AUS)) (22857) **NAD Partnership**
87 **DODGY BOB,** b c 21/4 Royal Applause—Rustam (Dansili) (21000) **Jack Berry & John Nixon**
88 Ch c 8/2 Sir Percy—Ekhraaj (USA) (El Prado (IRE)) (28571) **The Better Together Partnership**
89 Gr c 24/3 Mastercraftsman (IRE)—Elisium (Proclamation (IRE)) (27777)
90 Ch c 6/4 Peintre Celebre (USA)—Evening (Mark of Esteem (IRE)) **Guy Reed Racing**
91 B c 23/3 Sleeping Indian—Ewenny (Warrshan (USA)) (16190) **Mr Kenneth MacPherson**
92 Ch c 12/3 Peintre Celebre (USA)—Fluffy (Efisio) **Guy Reed Racing**
93 **GLORIOUS TIMES (IRE),** b f 25/3 Galileo (IRE)—
Quiet Mouse (USA) (Quiet American (USA)) **Mr Ahmad Abdulla Al Shaikh**
94 **GOOD INTENT (USA),** b c 4/2 Scat Daddy (USA)—Liza Lu (USA) (Menifee (USA)) **H R Stable**
95 B c 5/4 Exceed And Excel (AUS)—Great Hope (IRE) (Halling (USA)) (297619) **Qatar Racing Ltd**
96 B c 9/5 Arcano (IRE)—Hidden Meaning (Cadeaux Genereux) (20000) **Mrs M. Forsyth**
97 **KAJAKI (IRE),** gr c 8/5 Mastercraftsman (IRE)—No Quest (IRE) (Rainbow Quest (USA)) (67460) **Mr F. Gillespie**
98 B c 14/4 Makfi—Liberty Chery (Statue of Liberty (USA)) (17142) **Hambleton Racing Ltd XXXVIII**

**MR KEVIN RYAN - Continued**

**99 MJNOON (IRE),** b c 6/4 Roderic O'Connor (IRE)—
Elshamms (Zafonic (USA)) (51586) **Mr Hussain Alabbas Lootah**
**100** Ch c 5/3 Poet's Voice—North East Bay (USA) (Prospect Bay (CAN)) (60000) **Mr Sultan Ali**
**101** Gr c 4/2 Bahamian Bounty—Palais Glide (Proclamation (IRE)) **Guy Reed Racing**
**102** B c 8/6 Dylan Thomas (IRE)—Polo (Warning) **Guy Reed Racing**
**103** B f 21/4 Sea The Stars (IRE)—Puteri Wentworth (Sadler's Wells (USA)) **Mr T. A. Rahman**
**104 SMOOTH LIKE SILK,** b f 6/5 Zoffany (IRE)—
Maggie Lou (IRE) (Red Ransom (USA)) (22000) **Mr Abdulla Ahmad Al Shaikh**
**105** B f 21/1 Canford Cliffs (IRE)—Stylish One (IRE) (Invincible Spirit (IRE)) (20952) **Hambleton Racing Ltd XXXVII**
**106** B c 17/4 Sakhee's Secret—Vodka Shot (USA) (Holy Bull (USA)) (11000)
**107** B c 28/2 Dick Turpin (IRE)—Whirly Dancer (Danehill Dancer (IRE)) (30476) **Mr T. A. Rahman**
**108** B c 18/3 Distorted Humor (USA)—Wile Cat (USA) (Storm Cat (USA)) (149168) **Qatar Racing Ltd**

**Other Owners:** Mr J. Airey, Mr J. E. Barnes, Mr J. Cannon, Mr R. Crosbie, Mrs A. Dawson, Mr Neil Dawson, Mrs Jane Dwyer, Mr Tony Hill, Mrs D. Hughes, Mr A. Kerr, Mr M. Mogg, Miss M. Noden, Mr T. Palin, Mr K. Panos, Mr G. K. Panos, Mr M. Prince, Mr N. Ridgway, Mr S. R. H. Turner, Mrs I. M. Wainwright, Mr M. Wainwright.

**Assistant Trainer:** Joe O'Gorman

**Jockey (flat):** Amy Ryan. **Apprentice:** Shane Gray, Kevin Stott.

---

## 535 MR AYTACH SADIK, Kidderminster

Postal: **Wolverley Court Coach House, Wolverley, Kidderminster, Worcestershire, DY10 3RP**
Contacts: **PHONE (01562) 852362 MOBILE (07803) 040344**

**1 FINCH FLYER (IRE),** 8, ch g Indian Ridge—Imelda (USA) **A. M. Sadik**
**2 FRAZIER (IRE),** 4, b g Teofilo (IRE)—Innclassic (IRE) **A. M. Sadik**
**3** 6, B g Robert Emmet (IRE)—Lough N Uisce (IRE) **A. M. Sadik**

---

## 536 MRS DEBORAH SANDERSON, Retford

Postal: **Poplar Cottage, Wheatley Road, Sturton-le-Steeple, Retford, Nottinghamshire, DN22 9HU**
Contacts: **PHONE (01427) 884692 FAX (01427) 884692 MOBILE (07968) 821074**
**E-MAIL debsando999@gmail.com**

**1 MUNAAWIB,** 7, b g Haafhd—Mouwadh (USA) **W. McKay**
**2 NINE BEFORE TEN (IRE),** 7, ch m Captain Rio—Sagaing **W. McKay**
**3 PRIGSNOV DANCER (IRE),** 10, ch g Namid—Brave Dance (IRE) **Mr J. M. Lacey**
**4 ROGER THORPE,** 6, b g Firebreak—Nunthorpe **Mr J. M. Lacey**

### THREE-YEAR-OLDS

**5 DIAMOND RUNNER (IRE),** b g Amadeus Wolf—Hawk Eyed Lady (IRE) **Bawtry Racing Club**

**Other Owners:** Mrs Amanda Barrett, Mr John Lacey, Mr Willie McKay, Mrs Debbie Sanderson.

**Assistant Trainer:** Mark Sanderson

---

## 537 MRS KATHLEEN SANDERSON, Calverleigh

Postal: **New Cottage, Rackenford Road, Calverleigh, Tiverton, Devon, EX16 8BE**
Contacts: **PHONE (01884) 254217**
**E-MAIL h9bas@live.co.uk**

**1 APPLAUSE FOR AMY (IRE),** 8, b m King's Theatre (IRE)—Amathea (FR) **Mrs K. M. Sanderson**
**2 BLINDING LIGHTS (IRE),** 10, b g Snurge—Tender Return (IRE) **Mrs K. M. Sanderson**
**3 CALVERLEIGH COURT (IRE),** 8, b m Presenting—Alexandra Parade (IRE) **Mrs K. M. Sanderson**
**4 PAULS CONN (IRE),** 6, ch g Whitmore's Conn (USA)—Toute Aplomb (IRE) **Mrs K. M. Sanderson**

**Conditional:** Micheal Nolan. **Amateur:** Mr Matthew Hampton.

## 538 MR JOSE SANTOS, Upper Lambourn

Postal: **The Croft, Upper Lambourn, Hungerford, Berkshire, RG17 8QH**

1 **BOLD RUNNER,** 4, ch g Mount Nelson—Music In Exile (USA) **R. Cooper Racing Ltd**
2 **GLENNTEN,** 6, b g Ishiguru (USA)—Uplifting **R. Cooper Racing Ltd**
3 **MISSTEMPER (IRE),** 4, b f Diamond Green (FR)—Legnani **R. Cooper Racing Ltd**
4 **OPERA BUFF,** 6, b g Oratorio (IRE)—Opera Glass **R. Cooper Racing Ltd**

### THREE-YEAR-OLDS

5 **DIPPINGANDDIVING (IRE),** ch f Captain Rio—Arabis **R. Cooper Racing Ltd**
6 **IDLE TALKER (IRE),** b c Dandy Man (IRE)—Special Pearl (IRE) **Mr J. M. Dos Santos**

## 539 MR MALCOLM SAUNDERS, Wells

Postal: **Blue Mountain Farm, Wells Hill Bottom, Haydon, Wells, Somerset, BA5 3EZ**
Contacts: **OFFICE/FAX (01749) 841011 MOBILE (07771) 601035**
**E-MAIL malcolm@malcolmsaunders.co.uk WEBSITE www.malcolmsaunders.co.uk**

1 **ALZARICA (IRE),** 4, b g Amadeus Wolf—Allegorica (IRE) **M. S. Saunders**
2 **BABYFACT,** 4, b f Piccolo—Pennyspider (IRE) **Mrs V. L. Nicholas**
3 **CAMELEY DAWN,** 4, b f Alhaarth (IRE)—Apply Dapply **Mr & Mrs J Harris**
4 **DANZ STAR (IRE),** 4, ch g Ad Valorem (USA)—Await (IRE) **Mr P. S. G. Nicholas**
5 **GINZAN,** 7, b m Desert Style (IRE)—Zyzania **Mr P. S. G. Nicholas**
6 **LADY BAYSIDE,** 7, ch m Ishiguru (USA)—Seldemosa **M. S. Saunders**
7 **LUCKY CLOVER,** 4, ch f Lucky Story (USA)—Willisa **Lockstone Business Services Ltd**
8 **SARANGOO,** 7, b m Piccolo—Craic Sa Ceili (IRE) **Lockstone Business Services Ltd**
9 **SILVERRICA (IRE),** 5, gr m Ad Valorem (USA)—Allegorica (IRE) **Mrs V. L. Nicholas**
10 **SUNNY FUTURE (IRE),** 9, b g Masterful (USA)—Be Magic **M. S. Saunders**

### THREE-YEAR-OLDS

11 **HENRIETTA DANCER,** ch f Sakhee's Secret—Craic Sa Ceili (IRE) **M. S. Saunders**
12 **LIBERTY RULES (IRE),** b c Aussie Rules (USA)—Polynesian Queen (IRE) **M. S. Saunders**
13 **PIXELEEN,** b f Pastoral Pursuits—Ballyalla **Biddestone Racing Partnership IX 1**
14 **SPIRIT IN TIME (IRE),** b f Vale of York (IRE)—Star Port **M. S. Saunders**
15 **TITUS SECRET,** ch g Sakhee's Secret—Crimson Fern (IRE) **Lockstone Business Services Ltd**

**Other Owners:** T. Al-Mazeedi, T. P. Bostwick, Mr J. E. Harris, Mrs P. A. Harris.

## 540 MRS DIANNE SAYER, Penrith

Postal: **Town End Farm, Hackthorpe, Penrith, Cumbria, CA10 2HX**
Contacts: **PHONE (01931) 712245 MOBILE (07980) 295316**

1 **BAILEYS CONCERTO (IRE),** 9, b g Bach (IRE)—None The Wiser (IRE) **United Five Racing & Mr Andrew Sayer**
2 **BELL WEIR,** 7, gr g Tobougg (IRE)—Belly Dancer (IRE) **SJD Racing & Dianne Sayer**
3 **BLUE JACKET (USA),** 4, ro f Mizzen Mast (USA)—Complex (USA) **J. A. Sayer**
4 **BORUMA (IRE),** 5, b g Brian Boru—Itlallendintears (IRE) **Tony Price & Mrs Linda White**
5 **BRIGHT ABBEY,** 7, ch g Halling (USA)—Bright Hope (IRE) **A. R. White**
6 **CALL OF DUTY (IRE),** 10, br g Storming Home—Blushing Barada (USA) **J. A. Sayer**
7 **COOL BARANCA (GER),** 9, b m Beat Hollow—Cool Storm (IRE) **Mr D. J. Coppola**
8 **DISCOVERIE,** 7, b g Runyon (IRE)—Sri (IRE) **Mr D. J. Coppola**
9 **ENDEAVOR,** 10, ch g Selkirk (USA)—Midnight Mambo (USA) **Mrs M. Coppola**
10 **GOLD CHAIN (IRE),** 5, b m Authorized (IRE)—Mountain Chain (USA) **Mrs M. Coppola**
11 **GREAT DEMEANOR (USA),** 5, b g Bernstein (USA)—Hangin Withmy Buds (USA) **Mr D. J. Coppola**
12 **HONEYCHILE RYDER,** 4, ch f Black Sam Bellamy (IRE)—Dusky Dante (IRE) **The Transatlantics & Diane Sayer**
13 **LANGLEY HOUSE (IRE),** 8, b m Milan—No Moore Bills **E. G. Tunstall**
14 **MIGHTY CLICHE (IRE),** 6, b g Classic Cliche (IRE)—Mighty Mandy (IRE) **Affordable Fun**
15 **NOBLE BELL,** 5, ch g Ad Valorem (USA)—Mindanao **Anna Noble & Andy Bell**
16 **OCTAGON,** 5, b g Overbury (IRE)—Dusky Dante (IRE) **Mr A. S. Ambler**
17 **OH RIGHT (IRE),** 11, b g Zagreb (USA)—Conna Bride Lady (IRE) **Tom Sayer & Andrew Sayer**
18 **SACKETT,** 4, b g Midnight Legend—Gloriana **Mr A. S. Ambler**
19 **SENDIYM (FR),** 8, b g Rainbow Quest (USA)—Seraya (FR) **United Five Racing & Mr Andrew Sayer**
20 **SERGEANT PINK (IRE),** 9, b g Fasliyev (USA)—Ring Pink (USA) **J. A. Sayer**

## MRS DIANNE SAYER - Continued

21 **SILVER SHUFFLE (IRE),** 8, ch g Big Shuffle (USA)—Silvetta **Sprayclad UK & CSS Group**
22 **SPIRIT OF KAYF,** 4, b g Kayf Tara—Over Sixty **Sprayclad UK & CSS Group**
23 **TURTLE CASK (IRE),** 6, b g Turtle Island (IRE)—Sayce (IRE) **Sprayclad UK & CSS Group**
24 **WEAPON OF CHOICE (IRE),** 7, b g Iffraaj—Tullawadgeen (IRE) **Mrs H. D. Sayer**

**Other Owners:** Mr L. G. Aldsworth, Mr A. Bell, Mr K. J. Burrow, Mr A. J. Burrow, Mr I. T. Conroy, Mr A. L. Ellison, Mrs C Fitzgerald, Mrs J. D. Howard, Mr D. Hunter, Mr P. Moorby, Mr K. E. Moorby, Mr S. Nicholson, Mrs A. M. Noble, Mr T. Noble, Mr D. A. Price, Mr T. Sayer, Mr D. Swindlehurst, Mrs L. White.

**Assistant Trainer:** Miss Joanna Sayer

**Conditional:** Emma Sayer. **Apprentice:** Emma Sayer. **Amateur:** Miss Liz Butterworth.

---

## 541 DR JON SCARGILL, Newmarket

Postal: **Red House Stables, Hamilton Road, Newmarket, Suffolk, CB8 0TE**
Contacts: **PHONE (01638) 667767 MOBILE (07785) 350705**
**E-MAIL scargill@redhousestables.freeserve.co.uk WEBSITE www.jonscargill.co.uk**

1 **ASIA MINOR (IRE),** 6, ch m Pivotal—Anka Britannia (USA) **Strawberry Fields Stud**
2 **IZZY TOO,** 5, b m Oratorio (IRE)—Quiet Counsel (IRE) **Kingree Bloodstock**
3 **MAN IN THE ARENA,** 5, b g Bertolini (USA)—Torver **Mrs S. M. Scargill**
4 **SCAFELL PIKE,** 4, b g Bertolini (USA)—Torver **J P T Partnership**
5 **THE GINGER BERRY,** 5, ch g First Trump—Dolly Coughdrop (IRE) **Strawberry Fields Stud & Stuart Howard**
6 **VENUS GRACE,** 4, b f Royal Applause—Basque Beauty **J P T Partnership**

### THREE-YEAR-OLDS

7 B c Sakhee (USA)—Chine **Strawberry Fields Stud**
8 **FIGHT KNIGHT,** ch g Sir Percy—Great White Hope (IRE) **Silent Partners**
9 **FRIDGE KID,** b f Kheleyf (USA)—Snow Shoes **Silent Partners**
10 **HAPPISBURGH MAN,** br g Footstepsinthesand—Contemplate **Silent Partners**
11 **LIPIKUM,** b f Multiplex—Lipica (IRE) **Kingree Bloodstock**
12 **PRIMA PAGINA,** ch f Showcasing—La Gazzetta (IRE) **Silent Partners**
13 **QUALIFICATION (USA),** b br f Afleet Alex (USA)—Dreamt **Theme Tune Partnership**

### TWO-YEAR-OLDS

14 B f 8/2 Iffraaj—Alybgood (CAN) (Alydeed (CAN)) (18000) **Mr D. Tunmore**
15 B f 1/3 Kheleyf (USA)—Torver (Lake Coniston (IRE)) **Susan Scargill**

**Other Owners:** C. Blundell, H. Bourchier, S. Brewster, G. Bridgford, M. Capon, M. Crookes, R. Dalton, P. Darlington, J. Dyer, P. Eacott, W. Eacott, P. Edwards, Mr S. J. Howard, L. Meadows, D. Meilton, P. Reis, R. Riccio, Mr G. F. L. Robinson, K. Ruttle, Mrs Susan Scargill, Mr P. J. Scargill, R. Smith, W. Smith, P. Stanton, D. Tunmore, S. Vance, B. Watson, R. Watson, Mr Basil White.

---

## 542 MR DERRICK SCOTT, Minehead

Postal: **East Lynch, Minehead, Somerset, TA24 8SS**
Contacts: **PHONE (01643) 702430 FAX (01643) 702430**

1 **LUPITA (IRE),** 11, ch m Intikhab (USA)—Sarah (IRE) **Mrs R. Scott**
2 **ROYBUOY,** 8, b g Royal Applause—Wavy Up (IRE) **Mrs R. Scott**

---

## 543 MR JEREMY SCOTT, Dulverton

Postal: **Higher Holworthy Farm, Brompton Regis, Dulverton, Somerset, TA22 9NY**
Contacts: **PHONE (01398) 371414 MOBILE (07709) 279483**
**E-MAIL holworthyfarm@yahoo.com**

1 **ADDICTION,** 10, b m Alflora (IRE)—Premier Princess **Gale Force Four**
2 **ALBEROBELLO (IRE),** 7, b g Old Vic—Tourist Attraction (IRE) **Bradley Partnership**
3 **BEST BOY BARNEY (IRE),** 9, b g Rashar (USA)—Graigue Lass (IRE) **Mr G. T. Lever**
4 **BLUE APRIL (FR),** 4, b g Blue Bresil (FR)—Royale Little (FR) **Mrs C. C. Scott**
5 **BOOGIE IN THE BARN (IRE),** 7, b g Milan—Presenting Mist (IRE) **Bradley Partnership**
6 **BRAVE DEED (IRE),** 9, b g Kadeed (IRE)—Merlins Return (IRE) **Gale Force Seven**

## MR JEREMY SCOTT - Continued

7 **DAINTY DIVA (IRE),** 7, b m Indian Danehill (IRE)—She's So Dainty (IRE) **Langleys**
8 **DASHAWAY (IRE),** 6, ch g Shantou (USA)—Backaway (IRE) **The Town & Country Partnership 2**
9 **DASHUL (IRE),** 6, b m Generous (IRE)—Midway (IRE) **On A Mission**
10 **DAVERON (IRE),** 7, b g Winged Love (IRE)—Double Doc (IRE) **Mr N. A. Holder**
11 **DECIMUS (IRE),** 8, b g Bienamado (USA)—Catch Me Dreaming (IRE) **The Ten 2 One Gang**
12 **DREAM DEAL,** 7, b g Presenting—Rowlands Dream (IRE) **Mrs Messer-Bennetts,Clarke Hall & Gilbert**
13 **EXMOOR CHALLENGE,** 6, b g Thank Heavens—Bullys Maid **Mrs D. Bullard**
14 **GETON XMOOR (IRE),** 8, b g Heron Island (IRE)—Get On With It (IRE) **Mr J. Winzer**
15 **GUNNA BE A DEVIL (IRE),** 11, b g Alflora (IRE)—Gunna Be Precious **Mr R. J. Lock**
16 **I'M OSCAR (IRE),** 5, b g Oscar (IRE)—I'm Maggy (NZ) **The Free Spirits Partnership**
17 **KILMURVY (IRE),** 7, b g Shantou (USA)—Spagna (IRE) **I. R. Murray**
18 **LANTA'S LEGACY,** 5, ch m Central Park (IRE)—Purple Patch **Mr G. T. Lever**
19 **MASTER BENJAMIN,** 8, b g Fair Mix (IRE)—Morning Flight (IRE) **The Master Partners 2**
20 **MELODIC RENDEZVOUS,** 9, ch g Where Or When (IRE)—Vic Melody (FR) **Cash For Honours**
21 **MIDNIGHT MINT,** 5, b m Midnight Legend—Calamintha **Mrs K. Holmes**
22 **MISS SERIOUS (IRE),** 5, br m Kalanisi (IRE)—Burnt Out (IRE) **Pillhead House Partners**
23 **MOORLANDS GEORGE,** 7, b g Grape Tree Road—Sandford Springs (USA) **Mrs L. M. Williams**
24 **MOORLANDS JACK,** 10, b g Cloudings (IRE)—Sandford Springs (USA) **Mrs L. M. Williams**
25 5, B g Crosspeace (IRE)—My Dancing Kin **Gale Force Four**
26 **MYSTIC APPEAL (IRE),** 9, br g Alderbrook—Piseog (IRE) **Gale Force Two**
27 **NOTARFBAD (IRE),** 9, b g Alderbrook—Angels Flame (IRE) **Govier & Brown**
28 **OH DEVEE,** 6, b g Grape Tree Road—Charm Offensive **Mr A P Helliar & Mr A J W Hill**
29 **ON THE BRIDGE (IRE),** 10, b g Milan—Bay Dove **Mr C. J. James**
30 **PAUPERS PRESENT (IRE),** 7, b m Presenting—Paumafi (IRE) **A. G. Selway**
31 **PEACEFUL GARDENS,** 6, b m Franklins Gardens—So Peaceful **Twelve Twelve Twelve**
32 **POPPING ALONG,** 6, ch m Volochine (IRE)—So Long **Mrs C. C. Scott**
33 **PORTERS WAR (IRE),** 13, ch g Flemensfirth (USA)—Grainne Geal **Sarah Waugh & Paul Porter**
34 **SHOOFLY MILLY (IRE),** 6, b m Milan—Jacksister (IRE) **Gale Force One**
35 **SPECIAL ACCOUNT (IRE),** 10, b g Luso—Thegirlfromslane (IRE) **Mrs J. M. Perry**
36 **SPILLERS DREAM (IRE),** 6, b g Shantou (USA)—Eibhlinarun (IRE) **Bradley Partnership**
37 **THAT'S GONNA STING (IRE),** 4, b g Scorpion (IRE)—Creme d'arblay (IRE) **Mr C. J. James**
38 **THE SNAPPY POET,** 6, ch g Byron—Runaway Star **Jeremy Scott Racing Club**
39 **WINGERS DIGGERS,** 7, ch g Pasternak—Song of Kenda **J Wingfield Digby & M Sechiari**

**Other Owners:** Mr M. P. Ansell, Mr J. Bagwell-Purefoy, Mr P. W. Brockman, G. S. Brown, Mrs C. Clarke-Hall, R. Coates, Mr C. Cole, Mrs M. A. Cole, D. J. Coles, Mr R. J. L. Flood, Mr A. P. Gale, Mrs A. G. Gale, Mrs K. Gilbert, Mrs G. D. Giles, Mr P. Govier, Mr P. F. Govier, M. D. Greatorex, Mr C. F. Hayes, A. P. Helliar, A. J. W. Hill, Mr W. M. Izaby-White, R. W. S. Jevon, Mr D. E. Langley, Mr S. J. Loosemore, Miss N. Martin, Mrs S. D. Messer-Bennetts, P. Porter, Mrs S. M. Ragg, Mr J. R. M. Scott, Mrs R. Scott, Mr M. J. Sechiari, Mr J. Simpson, Mr M. J. Swallow, Miss S. M. Waugh, Mrs J. B. Wingfield Digby.

**Assistant Trainer:** Camilla Scott

**Jockey (NH):** Nick Scholfield. **Conditional:** Matt Griffiths, David Pritchard. **Amateur:** Mr Tom Humphries, Miss Laura Scott, Miss V. Wade.

---

## 544 MR BERNARD SCRIVEN, Taunton

Postal: **Cogload Farm, Durston, Taunton, Somerset, TA3 5AW**
Contacts: **PHONE (01823) 490208**

1 **PUERTO AZUL (IRE),** 11, ch g Beneficial—Droichidin **B. Scriven**

**Assistant Trainer:** Miss Kay Scriven

---

## 545 MR MICHAEL SCUDAMORE, Bromsash

Postal: **Eccleswall Court, Bromsash, Nr. Ross-on-Wye, Herefordshire, HR9 7PP**
Contacts: **PHONE (01989) 750844 FAX (01989) 750281 MOBILE (07901) 853520**
**E-MAIL michael.scu@btconnect.com WEBSITE www.michaelscudamoreracing.co.uk**

1 **BENENDEN (IRE),** 7, b g Moscow Society (USA)—Ashanti Dancer (IRE) **Mr M. R. Blandford**
2 **CORNER CREEK (IRE),** 5, b g Presenting—No Moore Bills **Mr M. R. Blandford**
3 **DAN EMMETT (USA),** 5, ch g Flower Alley (USA)—Singing Dixie (USA) **Mrs L. Maclennan**
4 **DAWNIERIVER (IRE),** 5, br m Indian River (FR)—In Sin (IRE) **Don't Tell Ken**

## MR MICHAEL SCUDAMORE - Continued

5 **EASTERN DRAGON (IRE),** 5, b g Elnadim (USA)—Shulammite Woman (IRE) **JCG Chua & CK Ong**
6 **FAR FROM DEFEAT (IRE),** 5, b g Robin des Pres (FR)—Clonsingle Native (IRE) **M. Scudamore**
7 **FROMTHETOP (IRE),** 9, b g Windsor Castle—Rose of Solway **Mr M. R. Blandford**
8 **GRACE TARA,** 6, b m Kayf Tara—Fenney Spring **Mr R. A. Cocks**
9 **HYPNOTISM,** 5, ch g Pivotal—Hypnotize **C. G. J. Chua**
10 **KILCULLEN ARTICLE (IRE),** 7, b g Definite Article—Mood I'm In (GER) **C. G. J. Chua**
11 **LINE D'AOIS (IRE),** 7, b g Craigsteel—Old Line (IRE) **Mr S. M. Smith & Keith Hunter**
12 **MONBEG DUDE (IRE),** 10, b g Witness Box (USA)—Ten Dollar Bill (IRE) **Oydunow**
13 **NANGANNA,** 4, b g Cape Cross (IRE)—Miss Meltemi (IRE) **JCG Chua & CK Ong**
14 **NEXT SENSATION (IRE),** 8, b g Brian Boru—Road Trip (IRE) **Mr M. R. Blandford**
15 **NO THROUGH ROAD,** 8, b g Grape Tree Road—Pendil's Delight **A. P. Barwell**
16 **PRINCESSE FLEUR,** 7, b m Grape Tree Road—Princesse Grec (FR) **The Honfleur Syndicate**
17 **RED CURRENT,** 11, b m Soviet Star (USA)—Fleet Amour (USA) **Mr R. A. Cocks**
18 **RIPTIDE,** 9, b g Val Royal (FR)—Glittering Image (IRE) **Middletons**
19 **SHADES OF SILVER,** 5, b g Dansili—Silver Pivotal (IRE) **The Champion Family & Michael Scudamore**
20 **STEVENTON STAR,** 4, b g Pastoral Pursuits—Premiere Dance (IRE) **C. G. J. Chua**
21 **STREETS OF PROMISE (IRE),** 6, b m Westerner—Miracle Lady **Gempro**
22 **ZAYFIRE ARAMIS,** 6, ch g Zafeen (FR)—Kaylifa Aramis **Aramis Racing**

**Other Owners:** S. A. Baker, Mr N. C. Champion, Mrs A. P. Champion, Mr D. E. Coltman, Mr T. S. Hopkins, K. L. Hunter, Mr N. McGawley, A. D. Middleton, Mr F. Ong, Mrs I. Phipps Coltman, Dr S. M. Readings, Mr N. J. Robinson, Mr J. D. Simpson-Daniel, S. M. Smith.

---

## 546 MR IAN SEMPLE, Haddington

Postal: **61 Kirk Road, Carluke, Lanarkshire, ML8 5BP**
Contacts: **PHONE (01620) 830233 MOBILE (07950) 175207**
**E-MAIL ian.semple48@yahoo.com**

1 **CLABARE,** 4, b g Proclamation (IRE)—Choral Singer **Annie Mowbray & Rona Mowbray**
2 **L'AMI LOUIS (IRE),** 7, b g Elusive City (USA)—Princess Electra (IRE) **Kenny Robson,David Shaw,William Robinson**
3 **POLLY'S ROSE,** 6, b m Bahamian Bounty—Tiana **Mr K. Pollock**

### THREE-YEAR-OLDS

4 **KNOTTY JACK (IRE),** b g Zebedee—Half-Hitch (USA) **D. W. Shaw**

**Other Owners:** Mr Neil Anderson, Mr D. Arnott, Mr C. McGaffin, Miss Annie Mowbray, Ms Rona Mowbray, Mr Billy Robinson, Mr Kenny Robson, Mr D. W. Shaw.

**Assistant Trainer:** David Shaw **Pupil Assistant:** Annie Mowbray

**Jockey (flat):** Tom Eaves, Jason Hart. **Jockey (NH):** Dougie Costello.

---

## 547 MR DEREK SHAW, Sproxton

Postal: **The Sidings, Saltby Road, Sproxton, Melton Mowbray, Leicestershire, LE14 4RA**
Contacts: **PHONE (01476) 860578 FAX (01476) 860578 MOBILE (07721) 039645**
**E-MAIL mail@derekshawracing.com WEBSITE www.derekshawracing.com**

1 **AGE OF INNOCENCE,** 4, b g Invincible Spirit (IRE)—Elusive Legend (USA) **Mr B. Johnson**
2 **ARASHI,** 9, b g Fantastic Light (USA)—Arriving **Mr P. Derbyshire**
3 **ARGENT TOUCH,** 4, gr g Elnadim (USA)—The Manx Touch (IRE) **Mr B. Johnson**
4 **BOROUGH BOY (IRE),** 5, b g Jeremy (USA)—Ostrusa (AUT) **Mr B. Johnson**
5 **DANCINGTOTHESTARS,** 4, b f Tiger Hill (IRE)—Dancing Duo **Mrs L. J. Shaw**
6 **DARING DRAGON,** 5, gr g Intikhab (USA)—The Manx Touch (IRE) **Mr D. Shaw**
7 **DAY STAR LAD,** 4, b g Footstepsinthesand—Eurolink Mayfly **Mr B. Johnson**
8 **DIAMONDSINTHESKY (IRE),** 4, b f Dandy Man (IRE)—Colourpoint (USA) **Mr D. Shaw**
9 **DONT TELL NAN,** 4, b f Major Cadeaux—Charlie Girl **Mr B. Johnson**
10 **DYNAMO WALT (IRE),** 4, b g Acclamation—Cambara **Mr B. Johnson**
11 **EXTREME SUPREME,** 4, b g Piccolo—Kitty Kitty Cancan **Mrs L. J. Shaw**
12 **INVIGILATOR,** 7, b g Motivator—Midpoint (USA) **The Warren Partnership**
13 **LOYALTY,** 8, b g Medicean—Ecoutila (USA) **Mr B. Johnson**
14 **MAIZIN,** 8, b g Danroad (AUS)—Haunt The Zoo **Mrs L. J. Shaw**
15 **POLARBROOK (IRE),** 8, br g Alderbrook—Frozen Cello (IRE) **Mr J. R. Saville**

## MR DEREK SHAW - Continued

16 **RUN WITH PRIDE (IRE),** 5, b g Invincible Spirit (IRE)—Zibilene **The Whiteman Partnership**
17 **SAM SPADE (IRE),** 5, gr g Clodovil (IRE)—Red Empress **Mr J. R. Saville**
18 **SHAFT OF LIGHT,** 4, b g Exceed And Excel (AUS)—Injaaz **Mr D. Shaw**
19 **SHAWKANTANGO,** 8, b g Piccolo—Kitty Kitty Cancan **Shawthing Racing Partnership**
20 **STUN GUN,** 5, b g Medicean—Tapas En Bal (FR) **Mr J. R. Saville**
21 **TOP BOY,** 5, b g Exceed And Excel (AUS)—Injaaz **Mr B. Johnson**
22 **UNEX MODIGLIANI (IRE),** 6, ch g Hurricane Run (IRE)—Chronicle **Mr B. Johnson**
23 **WELLIESINTHEWATER (IRE),** 5, b g Footstepsinthesand—Shadow Ash (IRE) **The Whiteman Partnership**

## THREE-YEAR-OLDS

24 **AUNTIE DIF,** b f Equiano (FR)—Meditation **P. E. Barrett**
25 **DESERT APOSTLE (IRE),** b f Tagula (IRE)—Cambara **Mr B. Johnson**
26 **DEVILUTION (IRE),** b g Bluegrass Cat (USA)—Meniatarra (USA) **Mr B. Johnson**
27 **DIAMOND MAN,** b g Exceed And Excel (AUS)—Inaminute (IRE) **Mr B. Johnson**
28 **FREEDOM ROSE (IRE),** br f Alfred Nobel (IRE)—Colourpoint (USA) **Mr B. Johnson**
29 **INVECTUS HERO,** b g Paco Boy (IRE)—Blur **Mr B. Johnson**
30 **JUNIOR BEN,** b g Equiano (FR)—Pretty Girl (IRE) **Mr B. Johnson**
31 B c Piccolo—Kitty Kitty Cancan **Mrs L. J. Shaw**
32 **LA BRANA,** b g Exceed And Excel (AUS)—Oatcake **Mr B. Johnson**
33 **MAGIC DELIGHT (IRE),** ch f Exceed And Excel (AUS)—Stravella (IRE) **Mr B. Johnson**
34 **MIDNIGHT DESTINY (IRE),** ro f Dark Angel (IRE)—Cappella (IRE) **Mr B. Johnson**
35 **OLYMPIC CHARM,** b g Invincible Spirit (IRE)—Super Sleuth (IRE) **Mr B. Johnson**
36 **PRINCE ROFAN (IRE),** gr g Strategic Prince—Rofan (USA) **Mr B. Johnson**
37 **SPARKLE GIRL,** ch f Stimulation (IRE)—Seren Teg **Mr J. R. Saville**
38 B br f Medicean—Specific Dream **Mr B. Johnson**
39 **SUPREME BELLE (IRE),** b f Tamayuz—Final Opinion (IRE) **Mr B. Johnson**

## TWO-YEAR-OLDS

40 Ch c 20/3 Zebedee—Beth (Deportivo) (26666) **Mr B. Johnson**
41 B c 12/4 Canford Cliffs (IRE)—Blur (Oasis Dream) (50000) **Mr B. Johnson**
42 B c 8/1 Dream Ahead (USA)—Chinese Wall (IRE) (Aussie Rules (USA)) (41904) **Mr B. Johnson**
43 B f 14/4 Kodiac—Cool Tarifa (IRE) (One Cool Cat (USA)) (33333) **Mr B. Johnson**
44 B f 25/1 Dick Turpin (IRE)—Crinkle (IRE) (Distant Relative) (16000) **P. E. Barrett**
45 B f 11/3 Piccolo—Dancing Duo (Groom Dancer (USA)) **Mrs L. Shaw**
46 Br c 1/2 Rock of Gibraltar (IRE)—Emonoja (IRE) (Sadler's Wells (USA)) (19047) **Mr B. Johnson**
47 B c 27/2 Teofilo (IRE)—Endorsement (Warning) (55000) **Mr B. Johnson**
48 B f 1/4 Elnadim (USA)—Key Light (IRE) (Acclamation) (19047) **Mr B. Johnson**
49 Ch f 29/3 Poet's Voice—Lily Again (American Post) (50000) **Mr B. Johnson**
50 Ch f 25/3 Compton Place—Meditation (Inchinor) **P. E. Barrett**
51 Gr f 6/2 Sleeping Indian—Ming Meng (IRE) (Intikhab (USA)) **P. E. Barrett**
52 B f 3/4 Paco Boy (IRE)—Saktoon (USA) (El Prado (IRE)) (13333) **Mrs L. Shaw**
53 B f 14/4 Cockney Rebel (IRE)—Shaws Diamond (USA) (Ecton Park (USA)) **Mrs L. Shaw**
54 B c 20/4 Paco Boy (IRE)—Tartatartufata (Tagula (IRE)) **Mrs L. Shaw**
55 Gr f 10/3 Intikhab (USA)—The Manx Touch (IRE) (Petardia) **L. Shaw & B. Johnson**

**Other Owners:** Mrs H. Franklin, Mr S. Warren, S. A. Whiteman.

**Yard Sponsor:** Grosvenor Contracts Leasing Ltd

---

**548**

## MRS FIONA SHAW, Dorchester

Postal: **Skippet Cottage, Bradford Peverell, Dorchester, Dorset, DT2 9SE**
Contacts: **PHONE (01305) 889350 MOBILE (07970) 370444**
**E-MAIL fiona.shaw05@gmail.com**

1 **ACT CASUAL,** 5, b m Act One—Eatons **P. B. Shaw**
2 **BOUND HILL,** 6, b g Kayf Tara—Ardent Bride **John & Heather Snook**
3 5, B g Tobougg (IRE)—Let It Be **Mrs F. M. Shaw**
4 **PIMBURY (IRE),** 13, b g Pistolet Bleu (IRE)—Duchess of Kinsale (IRE) **Mrs F. M. Shaw**

## 549 MRS PATRICIA SHAW, Looe

Postal: **Kilminorth Park, Looe, Cornwall, PL13 2NE**

1 **ACADEMY GENERAL (IRE),** 9, b g Beneficial—Discerning Air **Mr D. C. Odgers**
2 6, Br m Weld—Bella Astra
3 **FIREWELD,** 8, b m Weld—Bella Astra **Mr D. C. Odgers**
4 **JOAACI (IRE),** 15, b g Presenting—Miss Sarajevo (IRE) **Mr D. C. Odgers**

## 550 MR MATT SHEPPARD, Ledbury

Postal: **Home Farm Cottage, Eastnor, Ledbury, Herefordshire, HR8 1RD**
Contacts: **FAX (01531) 634846 MOBILE (07770) 625061**
**E-MAIL matthew.sheppard@cmail.co.uk**

1 **ANOTHER FLUTTER (IRE),** 11, b g Lahib (USA)—Golden Fizz **Mr A. J. Scrivin**
2 **CANDELITA,** 8, b m Trade Fair—Gramada (IRE) **Mrs N. Sheppard**
3 **COOL BOB (IRE),** 12, b g Bob Back (USA)—Rosie Jaques **Mrs N. Sheppard**
4 **FAUSTINA PIUS (IRE),** 7, b m Antonius Pius (USA)—Out In The Sun (USA) **Lost In The Summer Wine**
5 **IKTIVIEW,** 7, ch g Iktibas—Eastview Princess **Matt Sheppard Racing Club**
6 **KERRYHEAD STORM (IRE),** 10, b g Glacial Storm (USA)—Kerryhead Girl (IRE) **S. J. D. Gegg**
7 **LOUGHALDER (IRE),** 9, ch g Alderbrook—Lough Lein Leader (IRE) **Mr Simon Gegg & Mr Tony Scrivin**
8 **MODELIGO (IRE),** 6, b g Indian Danehill (IRE)—Glens Lady (IRE) **S. J. D. Gegg**
9 **REGAL D'ESTRUVAL (FR),** 10, b g Panoramic—Haie d'estruval (FR) **Lost In The Summer Wine**
10 **ROCK ON ROCKY,** 7, b g Overbury (IRE)—Tachometer (IRE) **Jan Johnson & Terry Harman**

**Other Owners:** Mr C. M. Brookes, Mr T. A. Harman, Mrs J. M. Johnson, R. A. Kujawa, Mr P. R. W. Smith.

**Amateur:** Mr S. Sheppard.

## 551 MR OLIVER SHERWOOD, Upper Lambourn

Postal: **Rhonehurst House, Upper Lambourn, Hungerford, Berkshire, RG17 8RG**
Contacts: **PHONE (01488) 71411 FAX (01488) 72786 MOBILE (07979) 591867**
**E-MAIL oliver.sherwood@virgin.net WEBSITE www.oliversherwood.com**

1 4, Ch g Presenting—Aventia (IRE) **Diana Whateley & Tim Syder**
2 **BEFOREALL (IRE),** 7, b g Spadoun (FR)—Maggie Howard (IRE) **Beforeall Partnership**
3 **BERTIE'S DESIRE,** 7, b g King's Theatre (IRE)—Temptation (FR) **T. D. J. Syder**
4 **BLAMEITALONMYROOTS (IRE),** 5, b m Turtle Island (IRE)—Makingyourmindup (IRE) **T. D. J. Syder**
5 **BLU PASSIONE,** 4, gr f Halling (USA)—Dissolve **P. K. Gardner T/A Springcombe Park Stud**
6 4, Br g Scorpion (IRE)—Call Her Again (IRE) **Diana Whateley & Tim Syder**
7 **CARRY ON SYDNEY,** 5, ch g Notnowcato—River Fantasy (USA) **The Sydney Arms Partnership**
8 **CLOUDBURST,** 4, gr f Authorized (IRE)—Secret Night **P. K. Gardner T/A Springcombe Park Stud**
9 **COCO DES CHAMPS (IRE),** 5, br m Robin des Champs (FR)—American Chick (IRE) **Michael & Gerry Worcester**
10 **COLONY CLUB (IRE),** 6, b g Heron Island (IRE)—Whistful Suzie (IRE) **Michael & Gerry Worcester**
11 **COME ON LAURIE (IRE),** 7, b g Oscar (IRE)—Megan's Magic **Mr P. Mellett**
12 **DEPUTY DAN (IRE),** 7, b g Westerner—Louisas Dream (IRE) **T. D. J. Syder**
13 **EASTERN CALM,** 6, b m Kayf Tara—New Dawn **Mr M. A. Burton**
14 **EVENING STANLEY (IRE),** 5, b g Stowaway—Suzy Q (IRE) **M. St Quinton & Tim Syder**
15 **FINANCIAL CLIMATE (IRE),** 8, b g Exit To Nowhere (USA)—Claudia's Pearl **Sara Fillery & Friends**
16 **FURROWS,** 10, b g Alflora (IRE)—See More Furrows **Furrows Ltd**
17 **GLOBAL POWER (IRE),** 9, b g Subtle Power (IRE)—Bartelko (IRE) **It Wasn't Us**
18 **GOT THE NAC (IRE),** 6, br g Beneficial—Hey Jude (IRE) **Million in Mind Partnership**
19 **HORSEHILL (IRE),** 6, b g Flemensfirth (USA)—
Maid For Adventure (IRE) **Ian Barratt, Stephen Short & Adam Signy**
20 **ITS A STING (IRE),** 6, b g Scorpion (IRE)—Wyndham Sweetmarie (IRE) **Mr M. A. Burton**
21 **KASBADALI (FR),** 10, b g Kahyasi—Nikalie (FR) **T. D. J. Syder**
22 **KILGEEL HILL (IRE),** 5, b g Oscar (IRE)—Park Jewel (IRE) **Mr M. A. Burton**
23 **KNOCKALONGI,** 9, b g Fair Mix (IRE)—Understudy **The St Joseph Partnership**
24 **LEGEND LADY,** 4, b f Midnight Legend—Aoninch **Legend Lady Partnership**
25 4, B f Kayf Tara—Lemon's Mill (USA) **G. R. Waters**
26 **LEMONY BAY,** 6, b g Overbury (IRE)—Lemon's Mill (USA) **G. R. Waters**
27 **LIARS POKER (IRE),** 8, b g Beneficial—Strong Willed **Ian Barratt, Stephen Short & Adam Signy**
28 **MANY CLOUDS (IRE),** 8, br g Cloudings (IRE)—Bobbing Back (IRE) **T. J. Hemmings**

## MR OLIVER SHERWOOD - Continued

29 **MCKENZIE'S FRIEND (IRE),** 4, b g Flemensfirth (USA)—Escrea (IRE) **Jeremy Dougall & Will Watt**
30 **MISCHIEVOUS MILLY (IRE),** 7, b m Old Vic—Jennifers Diary (IRE) **A. Stewart & A. Taylor**
31 **MORNING REGGIE,** 6, gr g Turgeon (USA)—Nile Cristale (FR) **T. D. J. Syder**
32 **MOULIN DE LA CROIX,** 11, b m Muhtarram (USA)—Brambly Hedge **Luksonwood Partnership**
33 **MR CARDLE (IRE),** 6, b g Golan (IRE)—Leave Me Be (IRE) **Mr M. A. Burton**
34 **PITON PETE (IRE),** 4, b g Westerner—Glenair Lucy (IRE) **Mr P. Mellett**
35 **PUFFIN BILLY (IRE),** 7, b g Heron Island (IRE)—Downtown Train (IRE) **T. D. J. Syder**
36 **RAYVIN BLACK,** 6, b g Halling (USA)—Optimistic **V. J. Walsh**
37 **ROBINESSE (IRE),** 4, ch f Robin des Champs (FR)—Jennifers Diary (IRE) **Mr A Taylor & The Three Underwriters**
38 **ROBINSSON (IRE),** 5, b g Robin des Champs (FR)—Silver Proverb **A. Taylor**
39 **ROMULUS DU DONJON (IRE),** 4, gr g Stormy River (FR)—
Spring Stroll (USA) **Mr Simon Munir & Mr Isaac Souede**
40 **ROUGE ET BLANC (FR),** 10, ch g Mansonnien (FR)—Fidelety (FR) **O Sherwood & Tim Syder**
41 **ROYALRAISE (IRE),** 6, b g Royal Anthem (USA)—
Raise The Issue (IRE) **Ian Barratt, Stephen Short & Adam Signy**
42 **SANTA'S SECRET (IRE),** 7, b g Basanta (IRE)—Rivers Town Rosie (IRE) **Barratt, Gumienny, Johnsons & Signys**
43 **SURTEE DU BERLAIS (IRE),** 5, b m High Chaparral (IRE)—Marina du Berlais (FR) **Mrs S. Griffiths**
44 **TANIOKEY (IRE),** 5, b m Scorpion (IRE)—Creation (IRE) **Mr M. A. Burton**
45 **THE CONN (IRE),** 5, b g Milan—Grandy Invader (IRE) **T. J. Hemmings**
46 **WESTSTREET (IRE),** 5, b g Westerner—Klipperstreet (IRE) **Weststreet Partnership**
47 **WHAT A SCORCHER,** 4, b f Authorized (IRE)—Street Fire (IRE) **Mr & Mrs I Barratt**

**Other Owners:** Mr I. J. Barratt, Mrs C. J. Barratt, A. R. Bromley, Mr B. D. Carpenter, Mr H. W. Cox, J. M. Dougall, Mrs R. Duckworth, Mrs S. C. Fillery, Mrs C. M. Frewer, G. F. Goode, Mr M. S. Gumienny, Mr A. Holt, Mrs A. T. Lambert, Mrs J. K. Lukas, W. D. C. Minton, S. E. Munir, Mrs D. C. Nicholson, J. S. Palfreyman, H. M. J. Pope, Mrs M. Prowse, Mr T. J. Ramsden, Mr J. D. Robinson, Mr M. E. Sangster, The Hon Mrs L. J. Sherwood, O. M. C. Sherwood, Mr A. Signy, Mr I. Souede, M. G. St Quinton, Mr A. R. Stewart, Lady Thompson, D. P. Walsh, W. S. Watt, Mrs D. L. Whateley, Winterfields Farm Ltd, Mr M. G. Worcester, Mrs G. S. Worcester.

**Assistant Trainer:** Andy Llewellyn **Head Lad:** Stefan Namesansky **Secretary:** Emma Chugg

**Jockey (NH):** Leighton Aspell. **Conditional:** Ben Ffrench-Davis, Thomas Garner. **Amateur:** Mr Harry Cruickshank.

---

## 552 MR RAYMOND SHIELS, Jedburgh

Postal: **Thickside Farm, Jedburgh, Roxburghshire, TD8 6QY**
Contacts: **PHONE (01835) 864060 MOBILE (07790) 295645**

1 7, B m Overbury (IRE)—Cool Island (IRE) **R. Shiels**
2 **DAMSON GIN,** 8, b m Fair Mix (IRE)—Sing And Dance **R. Shiels**
3 **TIKKANDEMICKEY (IRE),** 9, gr g Tikkanen (USA)—Miss Vikki (IRE) **R. Shiels**

---

## 553 MISS LYNN SIDDALL, Tadcaster

Postal: **Stonebridge Farm, Colton, Tadcaster, North Yorkshire, LS24 8EP**
Contacts: **PHONE (01904) 744291 FAX (01904) 744291 MOBILE (07778) 216692/4**

1 **ALFIE'S BOW,** 8, ch g Alflora (IRE)—Long Shot **G. Kennington**
2 **ANNIE'S DAUGHTER,** 8, b m Danbird (AUS)—Moondance **Podso Racing**
3 **BLUE COVE,** 10, ch g Karinga Bay—Meadow Blue **G. Kennington**
4 **CADGERS HOLE,** 8, b g Helissio (FR)—Not So Prim **Mrs D. Ibbotson**
5 **DIRECT APPROACH (IRE),** 11, b g Tel Quel (FR)—Miss Telimar (IRE) **G. Kennington**
6 **FIRST OF NEVER (IRE),** 9, b g Systematic—Never Promise (FR) **Lynn Siddall Racing II**
7 **I KNOW THE CODE (IRE),** 10, b g Viking Ruler (AUS)—Gentle Papoose **Lynn Siddall Racing II**
8 **LISDONAGH HOUSE (IRE),** 13, b g Little Bighorn—Lifinsa Barina (IRE) **J. P. G. Cooke**
9 **PADDY'S ROCK (IRE),** 4, b g Whipper (USA)—Hedera (USA) **Mr J. A. Kay**
10 **RUBYMINX,** 9, b m Grape Tree Road—Windfola **Miss J. M. Slater**
11 **WESTWIRE TOBY (IRE),** 13, ch g Anshan—Ware It Well (IRE) **Stonebridge Racing II**
12 **YORKSHIREMAN (IRE),** 5, b g Red Clubs (IRE)—Ossiana (IRE) **Miss J. M. Slater**

**Other Owners:** Mrs P. J. Clark, Mrs E. W. Cooper, Mrs P. M. Hornby, Mrs K. M. Kennington, Miss L. C. Siddall, Miss S. E. Vinden.

**Assistant Trainer:** Stephen Hackney

**Jockey (NH):** Tom Siddall.

## 554 MR DAVID SIMCOCK, Newmarket

Postal: **The Office, Trillium Place, Birdcage Walk, Newmarket, Suffolk, CB8 0NE**
Contacts: **PHONE (01638) 662968 FAX (01638) 663888 MOBILE (07808) 954109**
**E-MAIL david@davidsimcock.co.uk WEBSITE www.davidsimcock.co.uk**

1 **BARYE,** 4, b g Archipenko (USA)—Oblige
2 **BRETON ROCK (IRE),** 5, b g Bahamian Bounty—Anna's Rock (IRE)
3 **CALLING OUT (FR),** 4, b br c Martaline—Exit The Straight (IRE)
4 **CAPTAIN MORLEY,** 4, b g Hernando (FR)—Oval Office
5 **CASPAR NETSCHER,** 6, b h Dutch Art—Bella Cantata
6 **CASTILO DEL DIABLO (IRE),** 6, br g Teofilo (IRE)—Hundred Year Flood (USA)
7 **CURBYOURENTHUSIASM (IRE),** 4, gr g Mastercraftsman (IRE)—Mohican Princess
8 **DOCTOR SARDONICUS,** 4, ch g Medicean—Never A Doubt
9 **FRACTAL,** 4, b g High Chaparral (IRE)—Clincher Club
10 **GLASS OFFICE,** 5, gr h Verglas (IRE)—Oval Office
11 **HALATION (IRE),** 4, b g Azamour (IRE)—Ghenwah (FR)
12 **HORSTED KEYNES (FR),** 5, ch g Giant's Causeway (USA)—Viking's Cove (USA)
13 **MADAME CHIANG,** 4, b f Archipenko (USA)—Robe Chinoise
14 **MOMENTUS (IRE),** 4, b f Montjeu (IRE)—Race For The Stars (USA)
15 **RELATED,** 5, b g Kheleyf (USA)—Balladonia
16 **SHEIKHZAYEDROAD,** 6, b g Dubawi (IRE)—Royal Secrets (IRE)
17 **SWAN LAKES (IRE),** 4, gr f Dalakhani (IRE)—Rock Salt
18 **THE CORSICAN (IRE),** 4, b c Galileo (IRE)—Walklikeanegyptian (IRE)
19 **TRADE STORM,** 7, b br h Trade Fair—Frisson

### THREE-YEAR-OLDS

20 **AINSLIE (IRE),** gr ro c Mastercraftsman (IRE)—Capriole
21 **ALLIANCE FRANCAISE,** ch f Archipenko (USA)—Affaire d'amour
22 **ANY GIVEN TIME (IRE),** ch c Fast Company (IRE)—Five of Wands
23 **BALIOS (IRE),** ch c Shamardal (USA)—Elle Galante (GER)
24 **BATEEL (IRE),** b f Dubawi (IRE)—Attractive Crown (USA)
25 **CALLAC,** b g Aqlaam—Fifty (IRE)
26 **CARTIER (IRE),** b f Montjeu (IRE)—Rosamixa (FR)
27 **CONSORTIUM (IRE),** b g Teofilo (IRE)—Wish List (IRE)
28 **CROWNED WITH STARS (IRE),** b g Sea The Stars (IRE)—Drifting (IRE)
29 **DESERT ENCOUNTER (IRE),** b c Halling (USA)—La Chicana (IRE)
30 **ENCORE L'AMOUR,** b f Azamour (IRE)—Centime
31 **ESCRICK (IRE),** b f Vale of York (IRE)—Dubai Power
32 **EVERY INSTINCT (IRE),** b c Danehill Dancer (IRE)—Phrase
33 **FALCON'S SONG (USA),** b br f U S Ranger (USA)—Saudia (USA)
34 **HAPPY DREAMS (IRE),** b c Fastnet Rock (AUS)—Timeless Dream
35 **HIGHLAND GAMES,** b c Cape Cross (IRE)—High Barn
36 **HOPE YOU DANCE (FR),** ch f Mastercraftsman (IRE)—Anna of Dubai (GER)
37 **INTRUDE,** b g Intikhab (USA)—Don't Tell Mum (IRE)
38 **LADY HARE (IRE),** b f Approve (IRE)—Peaceful Kingdom (USA)
39 **LAKE NONA,** b f Authorized (IRE)—Bellona (IRE)
40 **MADAM MIDNIGHT,** ch f Shamardal (USA)—Miss Marvellous (USA)
41 B f Mastercraftsman (IRE)—Market Day
42 **MAYBE TOMORROW,** b f Zamindar (USA)—Appointed One (USA)
43 **MIDLIGHT,** b g Elusive City (USA)—My Heart's Deelite (USA)
44 **NONIOS (IRE),** b g Oasis Dream—Young and Daring (USA)
45 **ORACOLO (IRE),** b g Cape Cross (IRE)—Illuminise (IRE)
46 **OUD METHA,** ch f Manduro (GER)—Royal Secrets (IRE)
47 **PADLOCK (IRE),** br c Key of Luck (USA)—Rumuz (IRE)
48 **PRINCESS TANSY,** b f Equiano (FR)—Tanasie
49 **RULER OF THE NILE,** b c Exceed And Excel (AUS)—Dinka Raja (USA)
50 **SHINOOK,** ch f Teofilo (IRE)—La Vida Loca (IRE)
51 **STATE SOVEREIGNTY,** b f Authorized (IRE)—Sovereign's Honour (USA)
52 **STRIDING OUT (IRE),** b f Cape Cross (IRE)—Honours Stride (IRE)
53 **TERROR (IRE),** b f Kodiac—Baltic Belle (IRE)
54 **THE CASHEL MAN (IRE),** b g High Chaparral (IRE)—Hadarama (IRE)
55 **VISERION,** ch c Tamayuz—Frivolity
56 **WAVELET,** b f Archipenko (USA)—Weather Report

## MR DAVID SIMCOCK - Continued

## TWO-YEAR-OLDS

**57** B f 10/2 Mastercraftsman (IRE)—Abbeyleix Lady (IRE) (Montjeu (IRE)) (41904)
**58** B f 2/3 Kodiac—Admire The View (IRE) (Dubawi (IRE)) (17142)
**59** Gr c 9/4 Archipenko (USA)—Albanova (Alzao (USA)) (140000)
**60** Gr f 20/4 Sir Percy—Altitude (Green Desert (USA)) (28000)
**61** B f 27/3 Sir Percy—Artistic Blue (USA) (Diesis) (52000)
**62** B f 8/2 Danehill Dancer (IRE)—Big Heart (Mr Greeley (USA))
**63** **CHINOISERIES,** b f 4/2 Archipenko (USA)—Robe Chinoise (Robellino (USA))
**64** B f 19/3 Invincible Spirit (IRE)—Convention (Encosta de Lago (AUS))
**65** B c 17/4 Teofilo (IRE)—Creese (Halling (USA))
**66** **CRY OF JOY,** ch c 15/2 Dream Ahead (USA)—Lamentation (Singspiel (IRE)) (95000)
**67** B c 17/3 Intikhab (USA)—Crystal Moments (Haafhd)
**68** B f 1/2 Aqlaam—Dhan Dhana (IRE) (Dubawi (IRE))
**69** B f 1/4 Dubawi (IRE)—Diary (IRE) (Green Desert (USA))
**70** B c 29/3 Vale of York (IRE)—Dubai Power (Cadeaux Genereux)
**71** Gr f 16/4 Mastercraftsman (IRE)—Duchess Dee (IRE) (Bachelor Duke (USA))
**72** **ELECTORAL (IRE),** b c 24/4 Rip Van Winkle (IRE)—Sumingasefa (Danehill (USA)) (222221)
**73** B f 20/3 Invincible Spirit (IRE)—Elle Galante (GER) (Galileo (IRE))
**74** Ch f 1/4 Iffraaj—Fascination (IRE) (Galileo (IRE)) (40000)
**75** Ch g 25/3 New Approach (IRE)—Frivolity (Pivotal)
**76** B f 27/1 Dutch Art—Ghenwah (FR) (Selkirk (USA))
**77** B f 18/2 Sea The Stars (IRE)—Hespera (Danehill (USA))
**78** **HIGH HOPES,** b f 12/3 Zamindar (USA)—Dixielake (IRE) (Lake Coniston (IRE))
**79** **HOLY BOY (IRE),** b c 1/4 Holy Roman Emperor (IRE)—Sister Golightly (Mtoto) (55555)
**80** Ch c 28/2 Medicean—Hymnsheet (Pivotal) (48000)
**81** B f 17/3 Authorized (IRE)—Kahalah (IRE) (Darshaan) (17000)
**82** B c 4/2 Bahamian Bounty—Kerrys Requiem (IRE) (King's Best (USA)) (70000)
**83** **KING OF DREAMS,** ch c 9/2 Dream Ahead (USA)—Complexion (Hurricane Run (IRE)) (240000)
**84** B c 17/4 Cape Cross (IRE)—La Felicita (Shareef Dancer (USA)) (19000)
**85** **LADY MARWAH (IRE),** b f 16/2 Iffraaj—Eyrecourt (IRE) (Efisio) (40000)
**86** **LESSON (FR),** b c 23/2 Lawman (FR)—Dissitation (IRE) (Spectrum (IRE)) (39682)
**87** B c 15/1 Galileo (IRE)—Looking Back (IRE) (Stravinsky (USA))
**88** B c 17/4 Galileo (IRE)—Looking Lovely (IRE) (Storm Cat (USA))
**89** **LOOSE ENDS,** b f 28/4 Authorized (IRE)—Crooked Wood (USA) (Woodman (USA))
**90** B f 29/1 Makfi—Marine Bleue (IRE) (Desert Prince (IRE))
**91** **MS GILLARD,** b f 31/1 Aussie Rules (USA)—Oval Office (Pursuit of Love)
**92** **NAMOOSE (USA),** b c 19/2 Blame (USA)—Petition the Lady (USA) (Petionville (USA)) (60240)
**93** B c 20/3 Shamardal (USA)—Nasheej (USA) (Swain (IRE))
**94** Ch c 14/2 Poet's Voice—O Fourlunda (Halling (USA)) (26000)
**95** B c 1/3 Excellent Art—Park Twilight (IRE) (Bertolini (USA)) (45000)
**96** B f 2/4 Shirocco (GER)—Pelagia (IRE) (Lycius (USA)) (45000)
**97** B f 25/3 Bushranger (IRE)—Piacenza (IRE) (Darshaan)
**98** Ch f 21/3 Roderic O'Connor (IRE)—Quick Return (Polish Precedent (USA))
**99** B c 12/3 Roderic O'Connor (IRE)—Red Vale (IRE) (Halling (USA)) (42000)
**100** Br f 18/3 Sea The Stars (IRE)—Riotous Applause (Royal Applause)
**101** Ch c 25/1 New Approach (IRE)—Sister Act (Marju (IRE)) (300000)
**102** B f 22/4 Poet's Voice—Starchy (Cadeaux Genereux) (85000)
**103** Gr c 6/2 Starspangledbanner (AUS)—Ultimate Best (King's Best (USA)) (219047)
**104** **VEENA (FR),** b f 19/2 Elusive City (USA)—Kensita (FR) (Soviet Star (USA)) (31746)

**Owners:** Abdullah Al Mansouri, Al Asayl Bloodstock Ltd, Ali Saeed, Alison Jackson, Andrew Stone, Andrew Whitlock, Andrew Whitlock Racing Ltd, Aru Sivananthan, Black Gold Partnership, Car Colston Hall Stud, Charles Wentworth, Charlie Wyatt, Chippenham Lodge Stud, City & Provincial Partnership, CJJR Partnership, Daniel Pittack, Dr Ali Ridha, Dukes Stud, Dunchurch Lodge Stud, Happy Valley Racing & Breeding Ltd, Highclere Thoroughbreds (Earl Grey), John Cook, Jonathan Barnett, Jos Rodesthenous, Khalifa Dasmal, Kirsten Rausing, Malcolm Caine, Malih Al Basti, Martin Collins, Mary Kennel, Matthew Gibbens, Michael Fitzpatrick, Michael Tabor, Millingbrook Racing, Mohammed Jaber, Mr D. Smith, Mrs Fitri Hay, Mrs J. Magnier, Mrs Julia Annable, Mrs Z. Wentworth, Nabil Mourad, Olly Brendon, Qatar Racing Ltd, Richard Starcezwski, Roger Allsop, Saeed Manana, Saeed Suhail, Sheikh Juma Dalmook Al Maktoum, Simon Hope, St Alban's Bloodstock Ltd, Stephen Barrow, Sultan Ali, The Eclipse Partnership, The Khat Partnership, Tick Tock Partnership, Tony Hogarth, Trillium Place Racing.

**Assistant Trainer:** Tom Clover

**Jockey (flat):** Martin Lane, Jim Crowley, Jamie Spencer. **Apprentice:** George Buckell, Sophie Killoran, Milly Naseb.

## 555 MR DAN SKELTON, Alcester

Postal: **Lodge Hill, Shelfield Green, Alcester, Warwickshire, B49 6JR**
Contacts: **PHONE (01789) 336339**
**E-MAIL office@danskeltonracing.com WEBSITE www.danskeltonracing.com**

1 **ADRAKHAN (FR),** 4, b g Martaline—Annee de La Femme (IRE) **R. C. Tooth**
2 **AGE OF DISCOVERY,** 4, b g Nayef (USA)—Magic Tree (UAE) **The LAM Partnership**
3 **AMROTH BAY,** 11, b g Alflora (IRE)—La Bella Villa **West Mercia Fork Trucks Ltd**
4 **ARMEMENT (FR),** 4, b g Smadoun (FR)—Apparemment (IRE) **Mr C. Buckingham**
5 **ARTHAMINT,** 7, b g Passing Glance—Araminta **Mrs A. J. Higgins**
6 **AT THE TOP (FR),** 5, b m Network (GER)—Quaiou (FR) **Nick Skelton & Judy Craymer**
7 **BALLYHACK BUCK (IRE),** 7, b g Shantou (USA)—L'argenterie (FR) **Massive**
8 **BEAUTIFUL GEM (FR),** 5, ch m Muhtathir—Hunorisk (FR)
9 **BEKKENSFIRTH,** 6, b g Flemensfirth (USA)—Bekkaria (FR) **Mrs P. M. Scott**
10 **BELLENOS (FR),** 7, b g Apsis—Palmeria (FR) **Mr & Mrs J. D. Cotton**
11 **BENISSIMO (IRE),** 5, b g Beneficial—Fennor Rose (IRE) **A Chandler,L Westwood,D Balchin,K Jones**
12 **BERTIMONT (FR),** 5, gr g Slickly (FR)—Bocanegra (FR) **Mr C. M. Giles**
13 **BILZIC (FR),** 4, b br g Axxos (GER)—Izellane (FR) **Donlon, Doyle & MacDonald**
14 **BLUE HERON (IRE),** 7, b g Heron Island (IRE)—American Chick (IRE) **Horwood Harriers Partnership**
15 **BLUE PRAIRIE,** 4, b g Tobougg (IRE)—Prairie Sun (GER) **Horwood Hunters**
16 **BON CHIC (IRE),** 6, b m Presenting—Homebird (IRE) **Coral Champions Club**
17 **BOSS DES MOTTES (FR),** 4, b g Califet (FR)—Puszta des Mottes (FR) **Mr C. A. Donlon**
18 **BUBBA N SQUEAK (FR),** 4, ch g Dom Alco (FR)—Naiade du Moulin (FR) **Mr C. A. Donlon**
19 **CATWALK BABE (IRE),** 5, br m Presenting—Supreme Dreamer (IRE) **Mr T. Spraggett**
20 **CHARLIE'S OSCAR (IRE),** 5, b g Oscar (IRE)—Blue Gallery (IRE) **Universal Recycling Company**
21 **CHOSEN DESTINY (IRE),** 5, b m Well Chosen—Despute (IRE) **Racegoers Club Owners Group**
22 **DRAGON DE LA TOUR (FR),** 4, b g Royal Dragon (USA)—Turga de La Tour (FR) **Three Celts**
23 **DUNLOUGH BAY (IRE),** 9, ch g Flemensfirth (USA)—Loch Lomond (IRE) **The Horwoods Partnership**
24 **DYNAMO (IRE),** 4, b g Galileo (IRE)—Trading Places **Ms B. J. Abt**
25 **EARL THE PEARL,** 5, b g Multiplex—Colorado Pearl (IRE) **J-P Lim & D Skelton**
26 **FAIRYTALE THEATRE (IRE),** 8, b m King's Theatre (IRE)—Bay Dove **Mr M. Fennessy**
27 **FASCINO RUSTICO,** 7, b g Milan—Rustic Charm (IRE) **Mr J. R. Hales**
28 **GAYE MEMORIES,** 7, b m Overbury (IRE)—Gaye Memory **Mrs J. S. Allen**
29 **GAYE TIME,** 5, b m Grape Tree Road—Persian Gaye (IRE) **Mr M. Fennessy**
30 **GO ODEE GO (IRE),** 7, b g Alkaadhem—Go Franky (IRE) **N. W. Lake**
31 **GUIDING GEORGE (IRE),** 7, b g Flemensfirth (USA)—Shatani (IRE) **Mr T. Crowe**
32 **HERONS HEIR (IRE),** 7, b g Heron Island (IRE)—Kyle Lamp (IRE) **Highclere Thoroughbred Racing - Herons Heir**
33 **HURRICANE HOLLOW,** 5, b g Beat Hollow—Veenwouden **Mr M. J. Rozenbroek**
34 **IF IT BE YOUR WILL,** 5, gr g Kadastrof (FR)—My Beautiful Loser (IRE) **Mr J. C. Clemmow**
35 **JUST A NORMAL DAY (IRE),** 5, b g High Chaparral (IRE)—Thats Luck (IRE) **Mr Howard Spooner**
36 **LATE NIGHT LILY,** 4, b f Midnight Legend—Ready To Crown (USA) **Braybrook Lodge Partnership**
37 **LAWSONS THORNS (IRE),** 6, b g Presenting—Ardnurcher (IRE) **Miss J. Craymer**
38 **LIKE MINDED,** 11, b g Kayf Tara—Sun Dante (IRE) **D. J. Coles**
39 **LOCHALSH (IRE),** 4, ch g Duke of Marmalade (IRE)—Kylemore (IRE) **Mr C. Buckingham**
40 **LYNDA'S BOY,** 4, b g Rainbow High—Braybrooke Lady (IRE) **The On The Bridle Partnership**
41 **MADAME TRIGGER,** 7, b m Double Trigger (IRE)—Marathea (FR) **The Wildmoor Racing Partnership**
42 **MANY STARS (IRE),** 7, b g Oscar (IRE)—Tempest Belle (IRE) **James Hughes,John Hughes,Charles Hughes**
43 **MASTERFUL ACT (USA),** 8, ch g Pleasantly Perfect (USA)—Catnip (USA) **Universal Recycling Company**
44 **MIDNIGHT TUESDAY (FR),** 10, b g Kapgarde (FR)—Deat Heat (FR) **A. C. Eaves**
45 **MISTER GREZ (FR),** 9, gr g Turgeon (USA)—Yoruba (FR) **Gilmans Point Racing Syndicate**
46 **MISTER KALANISI (IRE),** 6, b g Kalanisi (IRE)—Maxis Girl (IRE) **Paul & Linda Dixon & Mike Rozenbroek**
47 **MISTER MIYAGI (IRE),** 6, b g Zagreb (USA)—Muckle Flugga (IRE) **Ben Turner & Jay Tabb**
48 4, B g Kalanisi (IRE)—Nut Touluze (IRE) **D. J. Coles**
49 **OULAMAYO (FR),** 4, b g Solon (GER)—La Titie du Perche (FR) **D. J. Coles**
50 **POPAFLORA,** 9, gr g Alflora (IRE)—Poppet **The Punchestown Syndicate**
51 **PRIMOGENITURE (IRE),** 4, b g Glory of Dancer—Jacqueline (IND) **F. Gillespie**
52 **RASCAL (IRE),** 6, b g Milan—Montagues Lady (IRE) **The Really Wild Bunch**
53 **RENE'S GIRL (IRE),** 5, b m Presenting—Brogella (IRE) **Andy & Sharon Measham**
54 **ROCK CHICK SUPREMO (IRE),** 4, b f Scorpion (IRE)—Ballerina Queen (IRE) **Judy Craymer & Nick Skelton**
55 **ROCK OF LEON,** 4, b g Rock of Gibraltar (IRE)—Leonica **Andy Jansons & Dan Skelton**
56 **RUBICHAMPS,** 5, ch m Robin des Champs (FR)—Bekkaria (FR) **Mrs P. M. Scott**
57 **SANTO DE LUNE (FR),** 5, gr g Saint des Saints (FR)—Tikidoun (FR) **Donlon & MacDonald**
58 **SEA CURRENT (IRE),** 7, b g Pilsudski (IRE)—Nautical Lady (IRE) **N. W. Lake**
59 **SEA THE SPRINGS (FR),** 4, gr g Slickly (FR)—Cristal Springs (FR) **Mr K. Sumner**
60 **SHADY LANE,** 8, b m Alflora (IRE)—Stoney Path **Mrs S. C. Welch**

## MR DAN SKELTON - Continued

61 **SHELFORD (IRE),** 6, b g Galileo (IRE)—Lyrical **Mr C. Hodgson**
62 **SQUIRE TRELAWNEY,** 9, b g Domedriver (IRE)—Crockadore (USA) **P. J. Haycock**
63 **STAR LANE,** 6, b g Beat All (USA)—Czarina's Sister **Mr M. F. Barraclough**
64 **STEPHANIE FRANCES (IRE),** 7, b m King's Theatre (IRE)—Brownlow Castle (IRE) **Miss M. J. Hall**
65 **STEPHEN HERO (IRE),** 5, br g Celtic Swing—Albaiyda (IRE) **Three Celts**
66 **STORM OF SWORDS (IRE),** 7, ch g Beneficial—Crossbar Lady (IRE) **The McKilocon Syndicate**
67 5, B m Robin des Champs (FR)—Sugar Island (IRE) **Mr Howard Spooner**
68 **THE SHROPSHIRE LAD,** 5, gr g Fair Mix (IRE)—Shropshire Girl **Mrs C. M. Graves**
69 **THE WESTERN FORCE (IRE),** 5, b g Westerner—Park Belle (IRE) **Local Parking Security Limited**
70 **THREE MUSKETEERS (IRE),** 5, b g Flemensfirth (USA)—
Friendly Craic (IRE) **Mrs G. Widdowson & Mrs R. Kelvin-Hughes**
71 **TOBY LERONE (IRE),** 8, b g Old Vic—Dawn's Double (IRE) **G.Regan, A.Pettey & S.Morgan**
72 **TOMMY RAPPER (IRE),** 4, b g Milan—Supreme Evening (IRE) **Judy Craymer & Nick Skelton**
73 **TRAFALGAR (FR),** 8, b g Laveron—Dzaoudzie (FR) **Mr & Mrs Gordon Pink**
74 **TWO TAFFS (IRE),** 5, b g Flemensfirth (USA)—Richs Mermaid (IRE) **Walters Plant Hire & James & Jean Potter**
75 **VALUE AT RISK,** 6, b g Kayf Tara—Miss Orchestra (IRE) **D. M. Huglin**
76 **VERONAISE (FR),** 4, ch f Epalo (GER)—Duchesse Pierji (FR) **Mr C. A. Donlon**
77 **WALK ON AL (IRE),** 7, b g Alflora (IRE)—Wave Back (IRE) **Donlon, MacDonald & McGowan**
78 **WEE HOLIO (IRE),** 4, b g Tikkanen (USA)—Eskimo Kiss (IRE) **Mr C. Buckingham**
79 **WELSH SHADOW (IRE),** 5, b g Robin des Champs (FR)—What A Mewsment (IRE) **Walters Plant Hire Ltd**
80 **WHAT A GOOD NIGHT (IRE),** 7, br g Westerner—Southern Skies (IRE) **Mr & Mrs Gordon Pink**
81 **WHAT A WARRIOR (IRE),** 8, b g Westerner—Be Right (IRE) **Mr & Mrs Gordon Pink**
82 **WORK IN PROGRESS (IRE),** 5, b g Westerner—Parsons Term (IRE) **Donlon & Doyle**
83 **WORKBENCH (FR),** 7, b g Network (GER)—Danhelis (FR) **N. W. Lake**
84 **ZARIB (IRE),** 4, b g Azamour (IRE)—Zariziyna (IRE) **Notalotterry**

**Other Owners:** Mr D. Balchin, M. A. Bates, Mr H. F. Bowley, Mr A. Chandler, P. F. Charter, S. J. Clare, J. D. Cotton, Mrs B. Cotton, P. Cunningham, P. M. Cunningham, P. Dixon, Mrs L. J. Dixon, Mr A. Doyle, Mr D. J. Flynn, Dr M. F. Ford, Mr J. B. Gilruth, Miss L. J. Hales, Mr T. Hanrahan, The Hon H. M. Herbert, Highclere Thoroughbred Racing Ltd, Mr J. C. Hughes, Mr J. R. Hughes, Mr A. Jansons, N. R. Jennings, Mr K. D. Jones, Mrs E. A. Kelvin-Hughes, R. G. Kelvin-Hughes, Mr T. Kilroe, Ms L. Kraut, Mr J. P. Lim, Mr A. F. Lousada, Ms M. Machin-Jefferies, Mr A. N. McGowan, Mr A. R. Measham, Mrs S. M. Measham, Mr P. D. Moore, Mr S. Morgan, Mrs K. J. Morgan, Ms L. M. Mulcahy, Mr D. Noble, T. H. Northwood, Mr T. O'Connor, Mr G. K. G. Pink, Mrs K. M. Pink, Mr C. D. Platel, J. E. Potter, Mrs M. J. Potter, G. J. P. Regan, Mrs L. Scott-MacDonald, A. G. Sim, Mr N. Skelton, Mr D. N. Skelton, Mr J. A. Tabb, Mr J. Torrington, Mr B. H. Turner, Mr L. J. Westwood, Mrs B. A. Widdowson.

**Assistant Trainer:** Josh Guerriero

**Jockey (NH):** Harry Skelton, Anthony Freeman. **Amateur:** Miss Bridget Andrews.

---

## 556 MRS EVELYN SLACK, Appleby

Postal: **Stoneriggs, Hilton, Appleby, Cumbria, CA16 6LS**
Contacts: **PHONE (01768) 351354 MOBILE (07503) 161240**

1 **ALMOST GEMINI (IRE),** 6, gr g Dylan Thomas (IRE)—Streetcar (IRE) **A. Slack**
2 **GRAND VINTAGE (IRE),** 9, gr g Basanta (IRE)—Rivers Town Rosie (IRE) **A. Slack**
3 **MOUNT CHEIRON (USA),** 4, b g Henrythenavigator (USA)—Chalamont (IRE) **A. Slack**
4 **MY FRIEND GEORGE,** 9, ch g Alflora (IRE)—Snowgirl (IRE) **A. Slack**
5 **OMID,** 7, b g Dubawi (IRE)—Mille Couleurs (FR) **Mrs D. E. Slack**
6 **STAR FOR LIFE (USA),** 6, b g Giant's Causeway (USA)—Clerical Etoile (ARG) **Mrs D. E. Slack**
7 **VAN MILDERT (IRE),** 6, b m Observatory (USA)—Vanilla Delight (IRE) **Mrs D. E. Slack**

**Other Owners:** Mrs H. D. Sayer.

**Assistant Trainer:** K. A. A. Slack (01768) 351922 Or (07931) 137413

---

## 557 MRS PAM SLY, Peterborough

Postal: **Singlecote, Thorney, Peterborough, Cambridgeshire, PE6 0PB**
Contacts: **PHONE (01733) 270212 MOBILE (07850) 511267**
**E-MAIL pamslyracing@btconnect.com**

1 **ACERTAIN CIRCUS,** 5, ch g Definite Article—Circus Rose **G.A.Libson D.L.Bayliss G.Taylor P.M.Sly**
2 **ARKAIM,** 7, b g Oasis Dream—Habariya (IRE) **G.A.Libson D.L.Bayliss G.Taylor P.M.Sly**
3 **ASTEROIDEA,** 4, b f Sea The Stars (IRE)—Speciosa (IRE) **M. H. Sly, Dr T. Davies & Mrs P. Sly**

## MRS PAM SLY - Continued

4 **BOUGGIETOPIECES,** 5, b g Tobougg (IRE)—Bonnet's Pieces **Mrs P. M. Sly**
5 **BOUNTIFUL BESS,** 5, ch m Bahamian Bounty—Saida Lenasera (FR) **Mrs P. M. Sly**
6 **GHINIA (IRE),** 4, b f Mastercraftsman (IRE)—Jorghinia (FR) **D. L. Bayliss**
7 **KAYAAN,** 8, br g Marju (IRE)—Raheefa (USA) **D. L. Bayliss**
8 **STAND 'N' BOOGIE,** 5, ch m Tobougg (IRE)—Standing Bloom **The Stablemates**
9 **SYNCOPATE,** 6, b g Oratorio (IRE)—Millistar **Mrs P. M. Sly**
10 **TAWEYLA (IRE),** 4, b f Teofilo (IRE)—Qasirah (IRE) **Pam's People**
11 **VERMUYDEN,** 6, b g Oasis Dream—Speciosa (IRE)
12 **WU ZETIAN,** 4, b f Invincible Spirit (IRE)—China **D. L. Bayliss**

### THREE-YEAR-OLDS

13 **HANGON HARRIET,** b f Sir Percy—Black Salix (USA) **Mrs P. M. Sly**
14 **INDULGENCE,** b f Sir Percy—Kaloni (IRE) **Mrs P. M. Sly**
15 **ROXIE LOT,** b f Exceed And Excel (AUS)—Orlena (USA) **Mr G. A. Libson**

### TWO-YEAR-OLDS

16 B f 27/4 Aussie Rules (USA)—Black Salix (USA) (More Than Ready (USA)) **Mrs P. M. Sly**
17 B f 23/4 Teofilo (IRE)—Speciosa (IRE) (Danehill Dancer (IRE)) **M. H. Sly, Dr T. Davies, Mrs P. M. Sly**
18 Ch c 10/5 Dutch Art—Spinneret (Pivotal) **David L. Bourne**

**Other Owners:** Mr David L. Bayliss, Dr T. J. W. Davies, Mrs S. E. Godfrey, Mr G. A. Libson, Mr Michael H. Sly, Mrs P. M. Sly, Mr G. Taylor.

**Conditional:** Kielan Woods. **Amateur:** Miss Gina Andrews.

---

## 558 MR DAVID SMAGA, Lamorlaye

Postal: **17 Voie de la Grange des Pres, 60260 Lamorlaye, France**
Contacts: **PHONE (0033) 3442 15005 FAX (0033) 3442 15356**

1 **ALMERIA,** 4, b f Shamardal (USA)—Suedoise **Mr A. M. Haddad**
2 **ARABIAN LADY (FR),** 4, ch f Gentlewave (IRE)—Sometime (FR) **Mr R. Nahas**
3 **DON BOSCO (FR),** 8, ch h Barathea (IRE)—Perfidie (IRE) **Mr O. El Sharif**
4 **FAIR MOON (FR),** 5, b m Gold Away (IRE)—La Fee de Breizh (FR) **Mr A. Louis-Dreyfus**
5 **FEE DE LUNE (FR),** 4, gr f Kentucky Dynamite (USA)—La Fee de Breizh (FR) **Mr A. Louis-Dreyfus**
6 **FRED LALLOUPET,** 8, b h Elusive City (USA)—Firm Friend (IRE) **Mr M. Lagasse**
7 **FRIDA LA BLONDE (FR),** 4, b f Elusive City (USA)—Firm Friend (IRE) **Mr M. Lagasse**
8 **GATEAUX (URU),** 6, b m T H Approval (USA)—Yambol (ARG) **Mr B. Steinbruch**
9 **LARC (FR),** 4, b c Cape Cross (IRE)—Luminosity **Haras D'Etreham**
10 **MAGICIENMAKE MYDAY,** 4, b c Whipper (USA)—Whisper To Dream (USA) **Mr R. Nahas**
11 **MASTERMAMBO (IRE),** 4, b f Mastercraftsman (IRE)—Poltava (FR) **Mr D. Smaga**
12 **NOLLEVAL (FR),** 4, b c Gold Away (IRE)—Amazing Story (FR) **Mr G. Augustin-Normand**
13 **PRIMUS INCITATUS (IRE),** 4, ch c Mastercraftsman (IRE)—Chaibia (IRE) **Mr A. M. Haddad**
14 **RAFFINEE (FR),** 4, b f Air Eminem (IRE)—Gioconda Umbra (ITY) **Mme M. Fougy**
15 **ROYAL MANIFICO (IRE),** 5, b h Hannouma (IRE)—Poltava (FR) **Mr D. Smaga**
16 **SAPHIRSIDE (IRE),** 6, b g Elusive City (USA)—Silirisa (FR) **Mr G. Augustin-Normand**
17 **VICTORIOUS CHAMP (FR),** 4, b c New Approach (IRE)—Sasanuma (USA) **Mr R. Nahas**

### THREE-YEAR-OLDS

18 **ABLON (FR),** b c Medicean—Wadjeka (USA) **Mr G. Augustin-Normand**
19 **ADMIT,** ch c Beat Hollow—Disclose **K. Abdulla**
20 **BANADA (FR),** b c Elusive City (USA)—Sasanuma (USA) **Mr R. Nahas**
21 **BOMBA NOVA (FR),** b f Whipper (USA)—Larme (IRE) **Mr R. Nahas**
22 **BRAZILIAN CHAP (FR),** b c High Chaparral (IRE)—Vezara (IRE) **Mr R. Nahas**
23 **CLASSIFICATION,** b c Three Valleys (USA)—Striking Choice (USA) **K. Abdulla**
24 **DJIGUITE (FR),** b c Makfi—Envoutement (FR) **Mr A. Louis-Dreyfus**
25 **ENDIVE,** b f Champs Elysees—Plum Fairy **K. Abdulla**
26 **FROU FROU (FR),** b f Elusive City (USA)—Victoria College (FR) **Mr A. M. Haddad**
27 **GLORIFICATION,** b f Champs Elysees—Light Ballet **K. Abdulla**
28 **HABIBI HABIB (FR),** b c Elusive City (USA)—Stefer (USA) **Mr R. Nahas**
29 **I LOVE YOU (FR),** b f Aqlaam—Pyrana (USA) **Mr B. Steinbruch**
30 **IMMEDIATE,** b f Oasis Dream—Emergency **K. Abdulla**
31 **LANTERNFISH (USA),** b br f Mizzen Mast (USA)—Deep Feeling (USA) **K. Abdulla**
32 **MARCHAND CELEBRE (FR),** b f High Chaparral (IRE)—Anestasia (IRE) **Mr O. Thomas**

## MR DAVID SMAGA - Continued

**33 MEZZO MEZZO (FR),** ch f Mount Nelson—Ibizane (USA) **Mme M. Fougy**
**34 MISS DERNA (FR),** b f Air Chief Marshal (IRE)—Lamask (USA) **Mr A. Louis-Dreyfus**
**35 MOORING MAST (USA),** gr ro c Mizzen Mast (USA)—Arboreta (USA) **K. Abdulla**
**36 NIMBLE (IRE),** b f Excellent Art—Deira (USA) **Mr G. Augustin-Normand**
**37 OJALA (FR),** ch f Dunkerque (FR)—Gioconda Umbra (ITY) **Mr A. M. Haddad**
**38 PARATI (IRE),** b c Makfi—Patanegra (IRE) **Haras d'Etreham**
**39 PATRICIA'S CHARM,** b f Whipper (USA)—Spring Fun (FR) **Mr R. Nahas**
**40 PILANSBERG,** b c Rail Link—Posteritas (USA) **K. Abdulla**
**41 PROGRESSION,** b c Dansili—Pretty Face **K. Abdulla**
**42 RE EMPLOY (USA),** b br f Mizzen Mast (USA)—Gainful (USA) **K. Abdulla**
**43 RODEIO (FR),** b f King's Best (USA)—Arrow of Desire **Mr R. Nahas**
**44 SONHO NOVO (FR),** b f Makfi—Whisper To Dream (USA) **Mr R. Nahas**
**45 STRELKITA (FR),** b f Dr Fong (USA)—Olonella **Mr A. Louis-Dreyfus**
**46 SULA'S CHARM (FR),** ch f Makfi—Heaven's Cause (USA) **Mr R. Nahas**
**47 ZIGOTO (FR),** b c Whipper (USA)—Sometime (FR) **Mr R. Nahas**

### TWO-YEAR-OLDS

**48** B c 30/1 Rail Link—Arrow of Desire (Danehill Dancer (IRE)) **Mr R. Nahas**
**49** Gr ro c 11/2 Mizzen Mast (USA)—Deep Feeling (USA) (Empire Maker (USA)) **K. Abdulla**
**50** Ch f 20/2 Teofilo (IRE)—Emergency (Dr Fong (USA)) **K. Abdulla**
**51** B c 5/2 Makfi—Galipette (Green Desert (USA)) (17460) **Mr M. Lagasse**
**52** B f 22/2 Lonhro (AUS)—Gateway (USA) (A P Indy (USA)) **K. Abdulla**
**53** B f 17/3 First Defence (USA)—Introducing (USA) (Deputy Minister (CAN)) **K. Abdulla**
**54** B c 23/3 Fastnet Rock (AUS)—M'oubliez Pas (USA) (El Corredor (USA)) (41269) **Mr A. M. Haddad**
**55 MAD SPEED,** b c 19/3 Makfi—La Fee de Breizh (FR) (Verglas (IRE)) **Mr A. Louis-Dreyfus**
**56** B f 9/2 Dansili—Modern Look (Zamindar (USA)) **K. Abdulla**
**57 PLEASEMETOO (IRE),** b f 25/4 Vale of York (IRE)—Shakeyourbody (USA) (Giant's Causeway (USA)) (43650) **Mr J. E. Dubois**
**58** Ch f 5/5 Mastercraftsman (IRE)—Poltava (FR) (Victory Note (USA)) (27777) **Mr P. Talvard**
**59** B c 19/4 Oasis Dream—Pretty Face (Rainbow Quest (USA)) **K. Abdulla**
**60** B c 21/4 Makfi—Punta Rosa (USA) (War Chant (USA)) (17460) **Aleyrion Bloodstock**
**61** B c 23/3 Blame (USA)—Reflections (Sadler's Wells (USA)) **K. Abdulla**
**62** B c 9/5 Whipper (USA)—Sometime (FR) (Anabaa (USA)) **Mr R. Nahas**
**63** Ch c 21/4 Makfi—Stefer (USA) (Johannesburg (USA)) **Mr R. Nahas**
**64 THURGOVIA (IRE),** b f 3/2 Fastnet Rock (AUS)—T'as d'Beaux Yeux (Red Ransom (USA)) **Mr M. Lagasse**
**65** B f 31/3 Elusive City (USA)—Vezara (IRE) (Grand Lodge (USA)) **Mr R. Nahas**
**66** B c 3/3 Whipper (USA)—Victoria College (FR) (Rock of Gibraltar (IRE)) **Mr A. M. Haddad**
**67 VILARO (FR),** b c 9/3 Whipper (USA)—Envoutement (FR) (Vettori (IRE)) **Mr A. Louis-Dreyfus**
**68** B c 6/3 Champs Elysees—Winter Bloom (USA) (Aptitude (USA)) **K. Abdulla**

**Other Owners:** J. S. Moore, S. O'Sullivan.

---

## 559 MR BRYAN SMART, Hambleton

Postal: **Hambleton House, Sutton Bank, Thirsk, North Yorkshire, YO7 2HA**
Contacts: **PHONE (01845) 597481 FAX (01845) 597480 MOBILE (07748) 634797**
**E-MAIL office@bryansmart.plus.com WEBSITE www.bryansmart-racing.com**

**1 ALPHA DELPHINI,** 4, b g Captain Gerrard (IRE)—Easy To Imagine (USA) **The Alpha Delphini Partnership**
**2 ENDERBY SPIRIT (GR),** 9, gr g Invincible Spirit (IRE)—Arctic Ice (IRE) **Mrs P. M. Brown**
**3 FEEL THE HEAT,** 8, ch g Firebreak—Spindara (IRE) **B. Smart**
**4 ICHIMOKU,** 5, b g Indesatchel (IRE)—Mythicism **Crossfields Racing**
**5 LEXINGTON ROSE,** 4, b f Captain Gerrard (IRE)—Silca Destination **Middleham Park Racing VIII & Partners**
**6 LLANDANWG,** 4, b f Lawman (FR)—New Light **Dr J. A. E. Hobby**
**7 MAJOR ROWAN,** 4, b g Captain Gerrard (IRE)—Julie's Gift **David H. Cox**
**8 MANDY LAYLA (IRE),** 5, ch m Excellent Art—Chervil **Mrs V Smart & Miss C Derighetti**
**9 MEADWAY,** 4, b g Captain Gerrard (IRE)—Tibesti **Mr Michael Moses & Mr Terry Moses**
**10 MONTE CASSINO (IRE),** 10, ch g Choisir (AUS)—Saucy Maid (IRE) **Woodcock Electrical Limited**
**11 MOVIESTA (USA),** 5, b g Hard Spun (USA)—Miss Brickyard (USA) **Redknapp, Salthouse & Fiddes**
**12 NAMEITWHATYOULIKE,** 6, b g Trade Fair—Emma Peel **Simon Chappell & Ritchie Fiddes**
**13 ORWELLIAN,** 6, b g Bahamian Bounty—Trinny **B. Smart**
**14 PLAYTOTHEWHISTLE,** 4, b g Sakhee's Secret—Prima Ballerina **B. Smart**
**15 RED PIKE (IRE),** 4, ch g Kheleyf (USA)—Fancy Feathers (IRE) **Sir A Ferguson, P Deal & G Lowe**
**16 SECRET OASIS,** 4, b f Captain Gerrard (IRE)—Annellis (UAE) **The Smart Annellis Partnership**

## MR BRYAN SMART - Continued

17 **SMALLJOHN,** 9, ch g Needwood Blade—My Bonus **B. Smart**
18 **TANGERINE TREES,** 10, b g Mind Games—Easy To Imagine (USA) **Tangerine Trees Partnership**
19 **TINCHY RYDER,** 4, b g Dylan Thomas (IRE)—Keyaki (IRE) **M. Barber**

### THREE-YEAR-OLDS

20 **ARMS AROUND ME (IRE),** ch g Lope de Vega (IRE)—Mexican Milly (IRE) **Suzanne & Nigel Williams**
21 **CAPTAIN FUTURE,** b g Captain Gerrard (IRE)—Saorocain (IRE) **The Smart Saorocain Partnership**
22 **CHARLES MESSIER,** b g Acclamation—Praesepe **Ceffyl Racing**
23 **COMPTON RIVER,** b c Compton Place—Inagh River **The Smart Inagh River Partnership**
24 **CUMBRIANNA,** b f Hellvelyn—Positivity **The Smart Positivity Partnership**
25 **DUCHESS OF RIPON (IRE),** br f Lord Shanakill (USA)—Rakiza (IRE) **Mr R. S. Fiddes**
26 **EMBLAZE,** b f Showcasing—Chushka **Crossfields Racing**
27 **ESPECIAL,** b c Misu Bond (IRE)—Lady In The Bath **David H. Cox**
28 **EXCLUSIVE DIAMOND,** b f Iffraaj—Poppets Sweetlove **Mr R C Bond & Mr C S Bond**
29 **FENDALE,** b c Exceed And Excel (AUS)—Adorn **Mr R. S. Fiddes**
30 **GEORGE BAILEY (IRE),** b g Zebedee—Zuzu (IRE) **Ceffyl Racing**
31 **GERRARD'S SLIP,** b g Captain Gerrard (IRE)—Park's Girl **Middleham Park Racing LXXX & Partner**
32 **GREYBOOTER (IRE),** gr g Dark Angel (IRE)—Babacora (IRE) **R. Fiddes & S. Chappell**
33 **HELVIS,** br gr g Hellvelyn—Easy Mover (IRE) **Woodcock Electrical Limited**
34 **KI KI,** ch f Kheleyf (USA)—Peryllys **B. Smart**
35 **KYLLACH ME (IRE),** b g Kyllachy—Good For Her **The Smart Stoneacre Sarah Partnership**
36 **LEWIS VALENTINE (IRE),** b c Rip Van Winkle (IRE)—Full of Love (IRE) **Suzanne & Nigel Williams**
37 **MYTHMAKER,** b c Major Cadeaux—Mythicism **Crossfields Racing**
38 **SHOOTINGSTA (IRE),** b g Fast Company (IRE)—Kiva **Redknapp, Salthouse & Fiddes**
39 **STRAIGHTOTHEPOINT,** b g Kyllachy—Choisette **Crossfields Racing**
40 **WHAT COULD SHE BE (IRE),** b f Dark Angel (IRE)—Halliwell House **Mr R. S. Fiddes**
41 **YTHAN WATERS,** b g Hellvelyn—Primrose Queen **BEFG Partnership**

### TWO-YEAR-OLDS

42 **AYRESOME ANGEL,** ch f 19/3 Captain Gerrard (IRE)—Almunia (IRE) (Mujadil (USA)) (10000) **Mr D. S. Blake**
**43** Br f 25/2 Dark Angel (IRE)—Cheeky Weeky (Cadeaux Genereux) **Mr R. S. Fiddes**
**44** B c 21/4 Dream Ahead (USA)—Danaskaya (IRE) (Danehill (USA)) (33000) **Mr Michael Moses & Mr Terry Moses**
**45** B f 18/1 Roderic O'Connor (IRE)—Dawaama (IRE) (Dansili) (2777) **Barraston Racing**
**46** B f 18/5 Kodiac—Dispol Veleta (Makbul) (11428) **B. Smart & Mr A. Welch**
**47** B f 28/1 Equiano (FR)—Fame Is The Spur (Motivator) (23809) **Biddestone Stud**
**48** B c 17/2 Acclamation—Grand Slam Maria (FR) (Anabaa (USA)) (11904) **R. Fiddes & S. Chappell**
49 **JAY EM GEE (IRE),** gr c 7/4 Mastercraftsman (IRE)—
Pallas Athena (IRE) (Sadler's Wells (USA)) (31000) **Mr J. M. G. Glendinning**
**50** Br c 2/4 Rip Van Winkle (IRE)—Prealpina (IRE) (Indian Ridge) (7936) **R. Fiddes & S. Chappell**
**51** B c 4/3 Hellvelyn—Racina (Bluebird (USA)) (15238) **B. Smart**
**52** Ch f 17/3 Monsieur Bond (IRE)—
Satin Doll (Diktat) (761) **Middleham Park Racing, Mrs A. D. Bourne, Mr B. Smart**
**53** Ch f 5/2 Frozen Power (IRE)—Shadow Mountain (Selkirk (USA)) (17142) **Middleham Park Racing & The Barkers**
**54** Gr f 24/3 Dark Angel (IRE)—Staceymac (IRE) (Elnadim (USA)) (28571) **R. Fiddes & S. Chappell**
**55** B f 18/3 Kodiac—Zaynaba (IRE) (Traditionally (USA)) (15872) **R. Fiddes & S. Chappell**
**56** Br c 5/3 Dick Turpin (IRE)—Zietunzeen (IRE) (Zieten (USA)) (32380) **The Smart Zietunzeen Partnership**

**Other Owners:** Mr S. A. Barningham, Mr R. C. Bond, Mr C. S. Bond, Mr M. G. Bullock, Mrs Tina Bullock, Mr S. Chappell, Mr P. A. Deal, Miss Chanelle Derighetti, Mr Dave Elders, Sir Alex Ferguson, Mr Ritchie Fiddes, Mr Bill Fraser, Mr John M. Glendinning, Mrs A. C. Hudson, Mr R. Kent, Mr G. Lowe, Mrs B. A. Matthews, Mr J. McGrandles, Mrs W. McGrandles, Mr T. J. Moses, Mr M. Moses, Mr Richard Page, Mr T. S. Palin, Mr M. Prince, Mr Harry Redknapp, Mr W. J. Salthouse, Mrs V. R. Smart, Mr B. Smart, Mrs Suzanne Williams, Mr N. Williams.

**Assistant Trainers:** Mrs V. R. Smart, Mr K. Edmunds **Pupil Assistant:** Miss Beth Smart

**Jockey (flat):** Phil Makin, Paul Mulrennan. **Apprentice:** Adam Carter.

---

## MR CHARLES SMITH, Temple Bruer

Postal: **6-7 Thompsons Bottom, Temple Bruer, Lincoln, Lincolnshire, LN5 0DE**
Contacts: **PHONE/FAX (01526) 833245 MOBILE (07778) 149188**

1 **ALPHA TAURI (USA),** 9, b g Aldebaran (USA)—Seven Moons (JPN) **Mr J. R. Theaker**
2 **DAISIE RAYMOND,** 7, br m Kayf Tara—Santa Ana **Mr N. J. Baines**
3 **GENERAL TUFTO,** 10, b g Fantastic Light (USA)—Miss Pinkerton **Mr J. R. Theaker**

## MR CHARLES SMITH - Continued

4 **ROBBIAN,** 4, b c Bertolini (USA)—Crathes **R. J. Lewin**
5 **SAIRAAM (IRE),** 9, b m Marju (IRE)—Sayedati Eljamilah (USA) **J. Martin-Hoyes**

### TWO-YEAR-OLDS

6 **VOCALISE,** gr f 19/3 Hellvelyn—Church Hill Queen (Monsieur Bond (IRE)) **Mr N. J. Baines**

---

## 561 MR JULIAN SMITH, Tirley

Postal: **Tirley Court, Tirley, Gloucester**
Contacts: **PHONE (01452) 780461 FAX (01452) 780461 MOBILE (07748) 901175**
**E-MAIL nicola.smith9156@o2.co.uk**

1 **EMERALD ROSE,** 8, b m Sir Harry Lewis (USA)—Swiss Rose **Grand Jury Partnership**
2 **FORTUNA ROSE,** 9, b m Sir Harry Lewis (USA)—Swiss Rose **Grand Jury Partnership**
3 **HARRIET'S ARK,** 8, ch m Sir Harry Lewis (USA)—Brush The Ark **Exors of the Late Mr D. E. S. Smith**
4 **ILLUSIONARY STAR,** 7, b m Sir Harry Lewis (USA)—Tirley Pop Eye **Exors of the Late Mr D. E. S. Smith**
5 **IONA DAYS (IRE),** 10, br g Epistolaire (IRE)—Miss Best (FR) **Mrs J.A. Benson & Miss S.N. Benson**
6 **NO PRINCIPLES,** 12, b g Overbury (IRE)—Selective Rose **Exors of the Late Mr D. E. S. Smith**
7 **PASS ON THE MANTLE,** 7, b g Bollin Eric—Swiss Rose **Grand Jury Partnership**
8 **PENNIES AND POUNDS,** 8, b m Sir Harry Lewis (USA)—Sense of Value **Exors of the Late Mr D. E. S. Smith**
9 **PETIT FLEUR,** 13, b m Nomadic Way (USA)—Sense of Value **Exors of the Late Mr D. E. S. Smith**

**Other Owners:** Mrs J. A. Benson, Miss S. N. Benson, A. W. Brookes, R. Brookes.

**Assistant Trainer:** Mrs Nicky Smith

**Jockey (NH):** Mark Grant, Sam Twiston-Davies. **Amateur:** Mr J. M. Ridley.

---

## 562 MR MARTIN SMITH, Newmarket

Postal: **Stable Cottage, Calder Park, Hamilton Road, Newmarket, Suffolk, CB8 0NY**
Contacts: **MOBILE (07712) 493589**
**WEBSITE www.martinsmithracing.com**

1 **HILLBILLY BOY (IRE),** 5, b g Haafhd—Erreur (IRE) **Macguire's Bloodstock Ltd**
2 **KHELFAN,** 4, b f Kheleyf (USA)—Fanny's Fancy **Little Princess Racing I**
3 **NO REFUND (IRE),** 4, b g Invincible Spirit (IRE)—Evangeline **Macguire's Bloodstock Ltd**
4 **NOTEBOOK,** 4, b g Invincible Spirit (IRE)—Love Everlasting **Little Princess Racing**
5 **OSSIE'S DANCER,** 6, ch g Osorio (GER)—Nina Ballerina **Mrs V. Garner**

### THREE-YEAR-OLDS

6 **ALFIE BOY (BHR),** b c Bravemore (USA)—Aelfie's Way (USA)
7 Ch g Avonbridge—Ashantiana **SN Racing VI**
8 **INDOMITABLE SPIRIT,** b g Zebedee—Gayala (IRE) **Mrs M. E. Smith**
9 **LITTLEMISSPOSITIVE,** b f Pastoral Pursuits—Spirito Libro (USA) **Little Princess Racing II**

### TWO-YEAR-OLDS

10 Gr f 12/3 Sakhee's Secret—Actionplatinum (IRE) (Act One)
11 B c 25/2 Dick Turpin (IRE)—Fairy Slipper (Singspiel (IRE))
12 B f 1/3 Big Bad Bob (IRE)—Spring Will Come (IRE) (Desert Prince (IRE)) **Miss A. L. Mortlock**

**Other Owners:** Miss N. F. Davey, S. Nunn, Mr M. P. B. Smith.

---

## 563 MR MICHAEL SMITH, Newcastle Upon Tyne

Postal: **Toft Hall Farm, Kirkheaton, Newcastle Upon Tyne, Tyne and Wear, NE19 2DH**
Contacts: **PHONE (01830) 530044 MOBILE (07976) 903233**
**E-MAIL michaelsmithracing@hotmail.co.uk**

1 **BENEFIT IN KIND (IRE),** 7, b g Beneficial—She's So Beautiful (IRE) **Mrs S Smith, Mr E Cassie**
2 **BLACK INK,** 4, b g Black Sam Bellamy (IRE)—Incony **M. Smith**
3 **BLAST MARTHA (IRE),** 6, b m Definite Article—Calendula **Alderclad Ltd**
4 **BOP ALONG (IRE),** 8, b g Double Eclipse (IRE)—Bob Girl (IRE) **Mr E. Cassie**

## MR MICHAEL SMITH - Continued

5 **BRUNELLO,** 7, b g Leporello (IRE)—Lydia Maria **Ownaracehorse Ltd**
6 **CANGO (IRE),** 7, b g Presenting—Marble Desire (IRE) **D Gilbert, M Lawrence, A Bruce**
7 **DREAM FLYER (IRE),** 8, ch g Moscow Society (USA)—Bright Choice (IRE) **T. Alderson**
8 6, B g Blueprint (IRE)—Ebony Countess (IRE)
9 **KILGEFIN STAR (IRE),** 7, b g Saddlers' Hall (IRE)—
High Church Annie (IRE) **Mrs Sandra Smith & Mrs Christine Stephenson**
10 **MISTER SPINGSPRONG (IRE),** 8, b g Flemensfirth (USA)—Watts Hill (IRE) **D Gilbert, M Lawrence, A Bruce**
11 **MOST HONOURABLE,** 5, b g Halling (USA)—Her Ladyship **Simpson Blacklock & Smith**
12 **MR WITMORE (IRE),** 5, b g Whitmore's Conn (USA)—Bright Future (IRE) **Mr Ivor Fox Mrs S Smith**
13 **NATIVE SPA (IRE),** 7, b g Norwich—Thethirstyscholars (IRE) **Miss R. J. Smith**
14 5, B g Milan—One Swoop (IRE) **Mrs S. Smith**
15 **ORSIPPUS (USA),** 9, b br g Sunday Break (JPN)—Mirror Dancing (USA) **Mrs S. Smith**
16 **PETRE' ISLAND (IRE),** 6, b m Pierre—Bannow Island (IRE) **Mrs S Smith, Mr E Cassie**
17 **STARPLEX,** 5, b g Multiplex—Turtle Bay **G & J Park**
18 **TURTLEPLEX,** 4, b f Multiplex—Turtle Bay **G & J Park**

### TWO-YEAR-OLDS

19 **PADDYPLEX,** b c 17/3 Multiplex—Turtle Bay (Dr Fong (USA)) **G & J Park**

**Other Owners:** Mr I. M. Blacklock, Mr I. Fox, Mr D. R. Gilbert, Mr M. Lawrence, Mr G. Park, Miss J. Park, Mr I. Simpson, Mrs C. S. Stephenson.

**Assistant Trainer:** Sandra Smith

**Jockey (NH):** Danny Cook. **Conditional:** Adam Nicol. **Amateur:** Mr Brendan Wood.

---

## 564 MR R. MIKE SMITH, Galston

Postal: **West Loudoun Farm, Galston, Ayrshire, KA4 8PB**
Contacts: **PHONE (01563) 822062 MOBILE (07711) 692122**
**E-MAIL mike@mikesmithracing.co.uk WEBSITE www.mikesmithracing.co.uk**

1 **EILEAN MOR,** 7, ch g Ishiguru (USA)—Cheviot Heights **R. M. Smith**
2 **HAYMARKET,** 6, b g Singspiel (IRE)—Quickstyx **Mr A. M. Ross**
3 **HOPEFULL,** 5, br bl m Overbury (IRE)—Maryscross (IRE) **R. M. Smith**
4 **KATIES CHOICE (IRE),** 7, gr g Croco Rouge (IRE)—Rosetown Girl (IRE) **R. M. Smith**
5 **OSCAR DALLAS (IRE),** 8, b g Oscar (IRE)—Ring Mam (IRE) **Mrs A. D. Matheson**
6 **PETERS GREY (IRE),** 5, gr g Aussie Rules (USA)—Aliyshan (IRE) **P. Tsim**
7 **SCOTCH WARRIOR,** 11, ch g Karinga Bay—Tarda **R. M. Smith**
8 **U NAME IT (IRE),** 7, b g Gold Well—Bypharthebest (IRE) **Smith & Spittal**
9 **UR HONOUR (IRE),** 5, br g Double Eclipse (IRE)—Honor Love (FR) **R. M. Smith**
10 **WEST BRIT (IRE),** 7, b g High Chaparral (IRE)—Aldburgh **R. M. Smith**

**Other Owners:** Miss B. Spittal.

---

## 565 MR RALPH SMITH, Chipstead

Postal: **Stud Managers Cottage, Cheval Court Stud, High Road, Chipstead, Surrey, CR5 3SD**
Contacts: **PHONE (01737) 201693 FAX (01737) 201693 MOBILE (07795) 327003**
**E-MAIL rjsmith.racing@hotmail.com WEBSITE www.rjsmithracing.com**

1 **BEAVER CREEK,** 4, ch g Three Valleys (USA)—Delta **Homecroft Wealth & Cheval Court**
2 **BLACK VALE (IRE),** 4, b g Moss Vale (IRE)—Limit (IRE) **Homecroft Wealth & F.J.E. Willson**
3 **BLISTERING DANCER (IRE),** 5, b g Moss Vale (IRE)—Datura **Mrs Evelyn Madden**
4 **CALITXO (SPA),** 6, b g Diamond Green (FR)—Citadelle (CHI) **Maggie Brighton, Jean King**
5 **CAPERS ROYAL STAR (FR),** 4, b g What A Caper (IRE)—Arundhati (IRE) **J. P. Duffy**
6 **CHELLA THRILLER (SPA),** 6, b m Chevalier (IRE)—Arundhati (IRE) **The Saucy Horse Partnership**
7 **HURRICANE VOLTA (IRE),** 4, ch c Hurricane Run (IRE)—Haute Volta (FR)
8 **NEW LOOK (IRE),** 5, b g New Approach (IRE)—Lady Miletrian (IRE)
9 **ROYAL MIZAR (SPA),** 5, b g What A Caper (IRE)—Zahaadid (FR) **J. P. Duffy**
10 **THE CASH GENERATOR (IRE),** 7, b g Peintre Celebre (USA)—
Majestic Launch **Kevin Old & The Cash Generator Corp**
11 **TWO IN THE PINK (IRE),** 5, b m Clodovil (IRE)—Secret Circle **Homecroft Wealth Racing & Mr Kevin Old**
12 **VICTOR'S BET (SPA),** 6, b g Leadership—Marmaria (SPA) **Homecroft Wealth & Clear Racing**
13 **WATTABOUTSTEVE,** 4, b g Araafa (IRE)—Angel Kate (IRE) **The Wattever Partnership**

## MR RALPH SMITH - Continued

### THREE-YEAR-OLDS

14 **DREAM APPROACH (IRE),** b f New Approach (IRE)—Witch of Fife (USA) **Fishdance Ltd**
15 **DUCHESSOFMARMALADE,** b f Duke of Marmalade (IRE)—Helena Molony (IRE) **Fishdance Ltd**
16 **MISS BUCKAROO (IRE),** b f Acclamation—Pearl Trader (IRE) **Buckhurst Chevaliers**

**Other Owners:** Mike Baker, Maggie Brighton, Mr Steve Brown, Henry Bulteel, Clear Racing, Fishdance Ltd, Mr M. J. Foxton-Duffy, Mr Tony Hirschfeld, Jean King, Evelyn Madden, Mr K. P. McCarthy, Mr Kevin Old, Mr S. J. Piper, Mr Nick Pogmore, Mr S. Wilkinson, Mr F. Willson.

**Assistant Trainer:** Jayne Smith

**Amateur:** Miss Ella Smith.

---

## 566 MRS SUE SMITH, Bingley

Postal: **Craiglands Farm, High Eldwick, Bingley, West Yorkshire, BD16 3BE**
Contacts: **PHONE (01274) 564930 FAX (01274) 560626**
**E-MAIL craiglandsracing@yahoo.co.uk**

1 **ABSOLUTE (IRE),** 4, b g Danehill Dancer (IRE)—Beyond Belief (IRE) **Mrs S. J. Smith**
2 **ALBA KING (IRE),** 9, b g Beauchamp King—Alba Dancer **Mrs S. J. Smith**
3 **ALF THE AUDACIOUS,** 9, gr g Alflora (IRE)—Rua Ros (IRE) **Mr R. Preston**
4 **ALTA ROCK (IRE),** 10, b g Luso—Princess Lulu (IRE) **Mrs S. J. Smith**
5 5, B g Lucky Story (USA)—Alumisiyah (USA) **Mrs S. J. Smith**
6 **BALLYMOAT,** 8, b g Grape Tree Road—Frosty Mistress **Mr J. Goodrick**
7 **BE A DREAMER,** 7, ch g Dreams End—Miss Fahrenheit (IRE) **Mrs S. J. Smith**
8 **BENNYS WELL (IRE),** 9, b g Beneficial—Alure (IRE) **Mrs A. Ellis**
9 **BLAKE DEAN,** 7, b g Halling (USA)—Antediluvian **Widdop Wanderers**
10 **BLAKEMOUNT (IRE),** 7, br g Presenting—Smashing Leader (IRE) **Mrs J. Conroy**
11 **BROTHER SCOTT,** 8, b g Kirkwall—Crimson Shower **Mrs S. J. Smith**
12 **CLAN WILLIAM (IRE),** 7, b g Antonius Pius (USA)—Celebrated Smile (IRE) **Mr A. M. Phillips**
13 **CLOUDY TOO (IRE),** 9, b g Cloudings (IRE)—Curra Citizen (IRE) **Formulated Polymer Products Ltd**
14 **COMEBACK COLIN,** 7, b g Beat Hollow—Queen G (USA) **Beningtonbury Stud/Laundry Cottage Stud**
15 **DARTFORD WARBLER (IRE),** 8, b br g Overbury (IRE)—Stony View (IRE) **Mrs S. J. Smith**
16 **DE BOITRON (FR),** 11, b g Sassanian (USA)—Pondiki (FR) **Mrs J. Morgan & Mrs Lindsey J. Shaw**
17 **DE VOUS A MOI (FR),** 7, b g Sinndar (IRE)—Dzinigane (FR) **Mrs J. Morgan**
18 **EMRAL SILK,** 7, b g Revoque (IRE)—Silk Stockings (FR) **Mrs A. Ellis**
19 **FILL THE POWER (IRE),** 9, b g Subtle Power (IRE)—Our Alma (IRE) **McGoldrick Racing Syndicates**
20 **FLEMERINA (IRE),** 6, b m Flemensfirth (USA)—Ballerina Laura (IRE) **Mrs S. J. Smith**
21 **FOCAL POINT,** 5, ch g Pivotal—Centreofattention (AUS) **D G Pryde, J Beaumont & D Van Der Hoeven**
22 **FORWARD FLIGHT (IRE),** 9, b g Dilshaan—Too Advanced (USA) **J. P. McManus**
23 **FRIENDLY ROYAL (IRE),** 6, b g Royal Anthem (USA)—Friendly Girl (IRE) **Formulated Polymer Products Ltd**
24 **GLEN COUNTESS (IRE),** 8, b m Pilsudski (IRE)—Countessdee (IRE) **The Naughty Partnership**
25 **GRATE FELLA (IRE),** 7, b g King's Best (USA)—Moonlight Paradise (USA) **Mrs M. Ashby**
26 **GREEN WIZARD (IRE),** 9, b g Wizard King—Ajo Green (IRE) **Mrs S. J. Smith**
27 **GROOMED (IRE),** 7, b g Acclamation—Enamoured **Mrs S. J. Smith**
28 **HAINAN (FR),** 4, gr g Laveron—Honor Smytzer **Mrs J. Morgan & Mrs Lindsey J. Shaw**
29 **HERISING (IRE),** 7, b g Heron Island (IRE)—Lady Rising (IRE) **Mrs S. J. Smith**
30 **HIT THE TOP (IRE),** 8, b g Gold Well—Smooth Leader (IRE) **Mrs S. J. Smith**
31 **KARISMA KING,** 6, br g Supreme Sound—Hollybush (IRE) **Broadway Racing Club 15**
32 **KENT STREET (IRE),** 10, ch g Flemensfirth (USA)—Fernhill (IRE) **K. Nicholson**
33 **LACKAMON,** 10, b g Fleetwood (IRE)—Pearlossa **Mrs S. J. Smith**
34 **LAVELLA WELLS,** 7, b m Alflora (IRE)—Jazzy Refrain (IRE) **Mrs S. J. Smith**
35 **MARGRAY,** 5, b g Kayf Tara—Agnese **M. B. Scholey & R. H. Scholey**
36 **MAXED OUT KING (IRE),** 7, ch g Desert King (IRE)—Lady Max (IRE) **Mrs S. J. Smith**
37 **MINELLA FIVEO (IRE),** 7, b g Westerner—Autumn Sky (IRE) **Mrs S. J. Smith**
38 **MISTER JONES,** 7, b g Val Royal (FR)—Madame Jones (IRE) **Mrs S. J. Smith**
39 **MOSSEY LAKE,** 7, b g Overbury (IRE)—Phildante (IRE) **Mrs S. J. Smith**
40 **MR MOONSHINE (IRE),** 11, b g Double Eclipse (IRE)—Kinross **DG Pryde,J Beaumont,DP van der Hoeven 1**
41 **MR PEPPERPOT,** 6, b g Sir Harry Lewis (USA)—Parslin **The Trevor-McDonald Partnership**
42 **MWALESHI,** 10, b g Oscar (IRE)—Roxy River **Mrs S. J. Smith**
43 **NEXT HIGHT (IRE),** 8, b g High Chaparral (IRE)—Night Petticoat (GER) **Mrs S. J. Smith**
44 **NO PLANNING,** 8, b g Kayf Tara—Poor Celt **Mrs J. Conroy**
45 **NOT A BOTHER BOY (IRE),** 7, b g Flemensfirth (USA)—Cab In The Storm (IRE) **Mrs S. J. Smith**
46 **OORAYVIC (IRE),** 8, ch g Snurge—Miss Murtle (IRE) **Mrs S. J. Smith**

## MRS SUE SMITH - Continued

47 **OPTICAL HIGH,** 6, b g Rainbow High—Forsweets **Mrs S. J. Smith**
48 **PALM GREY (IRE),** 7, gr g Great Palm (USA)—Lucy Cooper (IRE) **Mrs S. J. Smith**
49 **PAPA CARUSO,** 11, b g Kayf Tara—Madonna da Rossi **Mrs S. J. Smith**
50 **PERSIAN HERALD,** 7, gr g Proclamation (IRE)—Persian Fortune **The Cartmel Syndicate**
51 **PINEROLO,** 9, b g Milan—Hollybush (IRE) **McGoldrick Racing Syndicates (2)**
52 **RATTLIN,** 7, b m Bollin Eric—Parslin **Broadband Partnership**
53 **RED DANAHER (IRE),** 8, ch g Shantou (USA)—Red Rover **Mrs S. J. Smith**
54 **SILVER SOPHFIRE,** 9, gr m Silver Patriarch (IRE)—Princess Timon **Mrs S. J. Smith**
55 **SILVER VOGUE,** 7, gr g Revoque (IRE)—Pusslin **Mrs S. J. Smith**
56 **SMOOTH STEPPER,** 6, b g Alflora (IRE)—Jazzy Refrain (IRE) **Mrs S. J. Smith**
57 **SPARKLING WINE (IRE),** 7, b g Kayf Tara—Sparkling Yasmin **Mrs S. J. Smith**
58 **SPECIAL WELLS,** 6, ch g Alflora (IRE)—Oso Special **Mr D. Sutherland**
59 **STRAIDNAHANNA (IRE),** 6, gr g Medaaly—Sue's Song **M. B. Scholey & R. H. Scholey**
60 **SWING HARD (IRE),** 7, br g Zagreb (USA)—Hurricane Jane (IRE) **DP van der Hoeven, DG Pryde & J Beaumont**
61 **TAHITI PEARL (IRE),** 11, b g Winged Love (IRE)—Clara's Dream (IRE) **M. B. Scholey & R. H. Scholey**
62 **TROOPER ROYAL,** 5, b g Zafeen (FR)—Faithful Beauty (IRE) **Mrs C. Steel**
63 **TWICE LUCKY,** 11, b g Mtoto—Foehn Gale (IRE) **Mrs S. J. Smith**
64 **VINTAGE CLOUDS (IRE),** 5, gr g Cloudings (IRE)—Rare Vintage (IRE) **T. J. Hemmings**
65 **VINTAGE STAR (IRE),** 9, b g Presenting—Rare Vintage (IRE) **T. J. Hemmings**
66 **WAKANDA (IRE),** 6, b g Westerner—Chanson Indienne (FR) **M. B. Scholey & R. H. Scholey**
67 **WAKHAN (IRE),** 7, b g Dalakhani (IRE)—Wrapitraise (USA) **Jim Beaumont & Douglas Pryde**
68 5, B g Scorpion (IRE)—Welsh Rhapsody (IRE) **John Regan & John Conroy**
69 **WHISKEY RIDGE (IRE),** 9, b g High-Rise (IRE)—Little Chartridge **Widdop Wanderers**
70 **YOU KNOW YOURSELF (IRE),** 12, b g Dr Massini (IRE)—Gift of The Gab (IRE) **Mrs S. J. Smith**

**Other Owners:** J. J. Beaumont, Mr R. S. Bebb, R. F. Broad, Mrs M. Bryce, Mr P. Butters, J. Conroy, Mrs E. M. Grundy, A. D. Hollinrake, W. S. D. Lamb, R. J. Longley, C. C. S. MacMillan, P. J. Martin, S. McDonald, D. Musgrave, D. G. Pryde, Mrs J. B. Pye, J. Regan, Mrs M. B. Scholey, R. H. Scholey, Mrs L. J. Shaw, Mrs E. Smith, S. P. Trevor, Mr D. P. van der Hoeven.

**Assistant Trainer:** Ryan Clavin

**Conditional:** Callum Bewley, Jonathan England.

---

## 567 MISS SUZY SMITH, Lewes

Postal: **County Stables, The Old Racecourse, Lewes, East Sussex, BN7 1UR**
Contacts: **PHONE (01273) 477173 FAX (01273) 477173 MOBILE (07970) 550828**
**E-MAIL suzy@suzysmithracing.co.uk WEBSITE www.suzysmithracing.co.uk**

1 **AZABITMOUR (FR),** 5, b g Azamour (IRE)—Brixa (FR) **Mr G Jones & Mr B Malt**
2 **BEAU LAKE (IRE),** 11, b br g Heron Island (IRE)—
Brennan For Audits (IRE) **Sergio Gordon-Watson & Graham Willetts**
3 **BOLD IMAGE (IRE),** 4, b f Milan—Golden Bay **S. Addington-Smith & D. Tribe**
4 **BRAVE DECISION,** 8, gr g With Approval (CAN)—Brave Vanessa (USA) **Mr R. I. Knight**
5 **GINNY'S TONIC (IRE),** 6, b m Oscar (IRE)—Golden Bay **S. Addington-Smith & D. Tribe**
6 **INVICTA LAKE (IRE),** 8, b g Dr Massini (IRE)—Classic Material **Bernard & Jan Wolford**
7 **JENNIFER ECCLES,** 5, b m Midnight Legend—Cherrygayle (IRE) **P Mercer & K W Allisat**
8 **KOOS (GER),** 7, b m Konigstiger (GER)—Kiss Me (GER) **Mr J. M. Hicks**
9 **LAUGHTON PARK,** 10, ch g Karinga Bay—Brass Castle (IRE) **The Sams Partnership**
10 **LITTLE BOY BORU (IRE),** 7, b g Brian Boru—How Is Things (IRE) **John Logan, David Harrison & Suzy Smith**
11 **MADAME EVELYN,** 4, gr f Beat All (USA)—Madam Blaze **Roger & Yvonne Allsop**
12 **MALIBU ROCK,** 7, b g Tiger Hill (IRE)—High Straits **Mr D. R. Jinks**
13 **MARIET,** 6, ch m Dr Fong (USA)—Medway (IRE) **Miss S. Smith**
14 **MIGHTY VIC (IRE),** 7, b g Old Vic—Mighty Marble (IRE) **Mr S. N. Riley**
15 **OURMANMASSINI (IRE),** 7, b g Dr Massini (IRE)—Aunty Dawn (IRE) **The Seagull Partnership**
16 4, B g Zagreb (USA)—Rapsan (IRE) **R. Allsop**
17 **RED DEVIL STAR (IRE),** 5, b g Beneficial—Gortbofearna (IRE) **Mrs V. Palmer**
18 **SHANTY TOWN (IRE),** 6, b g Zagreb (USA)—Rapsan (IRE) **Mrs E. C. Stewart**
19 **STORM PATROL,** 4, b f Shirocco (GER)—Material World **Storm Force Ten**
20 **TED SPREAD,** 8, b g Beat Hollow—Highbrook (USA) **False Nose 'n Glasses Partnership**

### THREE-YEAR-OLDS

21 **LEXI GRADY ALICE,** b f Royal Applause—Missoula (IRE) **Mr Steve Ashley & Mr Gary Pettit**

## MISS SUZY SMITH - Continued

### TWO-YEAR-OLDS

22 **RUMOR,** ch f 14/3 Malinas (GER)—Atabaas Allure (FR) (Alhaarth (IRE))

**Other Owners:** Mrs S. A. Addington-Smith, Mrs K. H. Allisat, Mrs Y. E. Allsop, Mr S. A. Ashley, Mr G. Barrett, S. Gordon-Watson, Mr D. J. Harrison, Mr M. Hess, Mr G. R. Jones, J. A. A. S. Logan, Mr R. C. Malt, P. J. Mercer, Mr G. Pettit, R. F. Smith, Mr D. R. Tribe, Mr G. J. Willetts, B. Wolford, Mrs J. Wolford, Mrs H. M. T. Woods.

**Assistant Trainer:** Mr S E Gordon-Watson

**Jockey (flat):** Luke Morris. **Jockey (NH):** Paddy Brennan. **Conditional:** Micheal Nolan. **Amateur:** Mr Harry Bannister.

---

## 568 MR GILES SMYLY, Broadway

Postal: **Garden Cottage, Wormington Grange, Broadway, Worcestershire, WR12 7NJ**
Contacts: **PHONE (01386) 584085 FAX (01386) 584085 MOBILE (07747) 035169**
**E-MAIL gilessmiler@aol.com WEBSITE www.smylyracing.co.uk**

1 **BADGER WOOD,** 6, b g Overbury (IRE)—Parlour Game **A. C. Ward-Thomas**
2 **DANNERS (IRE),** 9, b br g Old Vic—The Great O'malley (IRE) **Mark Hingley & David Doolittle**
3 **LETEMGO (IRE),** 7, b g Brian Boru—Leteminletemout (IRE) **A. C. Ward-Thomas**
4 **MAYBE PLENTY,** 6, b m Overbury (IRE)—Mays Delight (IRE) **Nick Sutton & Adam Waugh**
5 **STELLA'S FELLA,** 7, b g Septieme Ciel (USA)—Gaspaisie (FR) **A E Agnew & A Ward Thomas**
6 **TAIGAN (FR),** 8, b g Panoramic—Lazary (FR) **M. Burford**
7 **THE GUNNER BRADY (IRE),** 6, b g Heron Island (IRE)—Cooling Off (IRE) **N. R. A. Sutton**

**Other Owners:** Mr A. Agnew, D. W. Doolittle, M. Hingley, A. R. G. Waugh.

**Assistant Trainer:** Kim Smyly

**Jockey (NH):** David England, Liam Treadwell. **Conditional:** Ed Cookson.

---

## 569 MR JAMIE SNOWDEN, Lambourn

Postal: **Folly House, Upper Lambourn Road, Lambourn, Hungerford, Berkshire, RG17 8QG**
Contacts: **PHONE (01488) 72800 (office) Twitter: @jamiesnowden MOBILE (07779) 497563**
**E-MAIL info@jamiesnowdenracing.co.uk WEBSITE www.jamiesnowdenracing.co.uk**

1 **AGENOR (GER),** 4, b g Medicean—Acerba (GER) **Sir Chippendale Keswick**
2 **ALANJOU (FR),** 5, b g Maresca Sorrento (FR)—Partie Time (FR) **The Cherry Pickers**
3 **BELCANTO (IRE),** 5, b m Bach (IRE)—Love Divided (IRE) **Jamie Snowden Racing Club**
4 **BLACKDOWN HILLS,** 5, b m Presenting—Lady Prunella (IRE) **Mrs P. de W. Johnson**
5 **BORGUY (FR),** 5, b g Irish Wells (FR)—Bally Borg (FR) **Mrs S. F. Snowden**
6 **BREAKING BITS (IRE),** 8, br g Oscar (IRE)—Lantern Lark (IRE) **Colin Peake & John H. W. Finch**
7 4, B f Oscar (IRE)—Burrator
8 **CAMACHOICE (IRE),** 5, b g Camacho—Nouvelle Reve (GER) **Valerie Antell & Friends**
9 **CENTORIA (IRE),** 7, ch m Generous (IRE)—Cent Prime **The Wife Loves It Partnership**
10 **DARK LOVER (GER),** 10, b g Zinaad—Dark Lady (GER) **The Dark Lovers**
11 **DENBOY (IRE),** 5, b g King's Theatre (IRE)—Miss Denman (IRE) **Sir M. F. Broughton & Friends**
12 **DETROIT BLUES,** 5, ch g Tobougg (IRE)—Blue Missy (USA) **Ade & The Winettes**
13 **DINO MITE,** 4, b f Doctor Dino (FR)—Compose **ValueRacingClub.co.uk**
14 **ETHELRED (IRE),** 7, b g Alflora (IRE)—Navale (FR) **D. N. Hearson**
15 **FACT OF THE MATTER (IRE),** 5, b g Brian Boru—Womanofthemountain (IRE) **Batterby, Birchall, Cahalne**
16 **FREDERIC CHOPIN,** 4, ch g Tamayuz—Eliza Gilbert **Mr C. Buckingham**
17 **FUTURE GILDED (FR),** 6, b g Lost World (IRE)—Doree du Pin (FR) **Owners For Owners: Future Gilded**
18 **HERONRY (IRE),** 7, b g Heron Island (IRE)—In A Tizzy **Chalke Valley Racing**
19 **IDAMAY (IRE),** 4, br f Stowaway—Aguida (FR) **Mr Tony Bath & Kate Austin**
20 **IMPERIAL PLAN (IRE),** 5, b g Antonius Pius (USA)—White Paper (IRE) **The Imperial Plan Racing Partnership**
21 **JEAN FLEMING (IRE),** 8, b m Flemensfirth (USA)—Dromhale Lady (IRE) **Mrs K. Gunn**
22 **KAPGARDE KING (FR),** 4, ch g Kapgarde (FR)—Cybertina (FR) **The Konkerers**
23 **KASSIS,** 6, b m Kalanisi (IRE)—Gastina (FR) **Mrs Julia Thomas**
24 **LEY LADY GREY,** 5, gr m With Approval (CAN)—Prospectress (USA) **Fawley House Stud**
25 **LUNAR FLOW,** 4, b g With The Flow (USA)—Misty Move (IRE) **William Wallace**
26 **MAJOR MILBORNE,** 7, ch g Exit To Nowhere (USA)—Motown Melody (IRE) **Nowhere To Run Friends**
27 **MIDNIGHT SILVER,** 5, gr m Midnight Legend—Ruggtah **Foxtrot NH Racing Partnership IX**
28 **MONBEG THEATRE (IRE),** 6, b g King's Theatre (IRE)—Amberina (IRE) **Tim Dykes & Lynda Lovell**
29 **NIKI ROYAL (FR),** 10, b m Nikos—Balgarde (FR) **Jamie Snowden Racing Club**

## MR JAMIE SNOWDEN - Continued

30 **ORCHARD PARK (IRE),** 4, b g Milan—Tough As Leather (IRE) **Mr D. I. Ryder**
31 **OUR THREE SONS (IRE),** 4, b g Shantou (USA)—Ballyquinn (IRE) **A. J. & Mrs J. Ward**
32 **PRESENT VIEW,** 7, b g Presenting—Carry Me (IRE) **Sir Chippendale Keswick**
33 **RAVENOUS,** 4, b g Raven's Pass (USA)—Supereva (IRE) **The Duchess Of Cornwall & Sir Chips Keswick**
34 **REVES D'AMOUR (IRE),** 6, ch m Midnight Legend—Poppy Maroon **The TTF Partnership**
35 **RHYTHM STAR,** 5, b m Beat All (USA)—Star Award (IRE) **ValueRacingClub.co.uk**
36 **SILVER DJEBEL,** 4, gr f Tobougg (IRE)—Navale (FR) **The Folly Partnership**
37 **SIOBHANS BEAUTY (IRE),** 7, gr g Cloudings (IRE)—Farrangalway Lass (IRE) **The Encore Syndicate**
38 **SOURIYAN (FR),** 4, b g Alhaarth (IRE)—Serasana **The GD Partnership**
39 **STAGE TWENTY (IRE),** 5, b m King's Theatre (IRE)—Last Century (IRE) **Mr T. J. Dykes**
40 **STAR SOVEREIGN (IRE),** 4, b f Brian Boru—Bobs Star (IRE) **Richard Stone**
41 **TEA CADDY,** 9, b m Kadastrof (FR)—Little Tern (IRE) **R. T. S. Matthews**
42 **TO THE SKY (IRE),** 7, b g Saffron Walden (FR)—Tara Tara (IRE) **White Diamond Racing Partnership**
43 **VAL DE LAW (FR),** 6, b g Epalo (GER)—Law (FR) **Sir Chippendale Keswick**
44 **WHAT A LARK (IRE),** 4, b f Kalanisi (IRE)—Grangeclare Lark (IRE) **Mr C. Buckingham**
45 **ZAKTI (IRE),** 5, gr m Shirocco (GER)—Inner Strength (FR) **Mr T. J. Dykes**
46 **ZEPHYR,** 4, ch g Shirocco (GER)—Pelagia (IRE) **Mr Tim Dykes**

**Other Owners:** Mr D. Abraham, Mrs J. Abraham, Mr Ray Antell, Mr J. Anthony, Mr Oliver Battersby, Mr S. Beccle, Mr Phil Bell, Mr Glynn Berrington-Evans, Mr M. Bower-Dyke, Mr Paul Boyle, Mr L. H. Brewin, Mr Stephen Broughton, Mr A. P. Brown, Mr Scott Buchanan, Mr Tom Castle, Mr D. J. Coles, The Duchess of Cornwall, Mr James Couldwell, Mr Paul Couldwell, Mr Paul Donaldson, Mr Tim Dykes, Mr John H. W. Finch, Mr H. M. Glyn-Davies, Mrs Jane Glyn-Davies, Mr Mike Hammond, Mr M. Holman, Mr Jon Hughes, Mr Andrew J. Huntly, Mr P. Hurst, Sir Chips Keswick, Mr S. Lambert, Mr O. C. S. Lazenby, Mrs L. R. Lovell, Mr Brendan McManus, Mr A. Morley, Dr M. M. Ogilvy, Mr Darren Price, Mr Hugh Shapter, Mr W. G. Shaw, Mr B. D. Smith, Mr Dave Smithyes, Mrs L. Snowden, Mr J. E. Snowden, Mr Jeremy Sykes, Mr A. J. Ward, Mrs Janet Ward, Mr James D. G. Wright, Mr Jordan Wylie, Miss Anna Yorke.

**Assistant Trainer:** James Ward **Head Girl:** Kate Robinson

**Jockey (NH):** Daryl Jacob, Brendan Powell, Gavin Sheehan. **Conditional:** Will Featherstone, Micheal Nolan, Conor Shoemark.

---

## 570 MR MIKE SOWERSBY, York

Postal: **Southwold Farm, Goodmanham Wold, Market Weighton, York, East Yorkshire, YO43 3NA**
Contacts: **PHONE (01430) 810534 MOBILE (07855) 551056**

1 **AGENT LOUISE,** 7, b m Alflora (IRE)—Oso Special **M. E. Sowersby**
2 **AUTO MAC,** 7, b g Auction House (USA)—Charlottevalentina (IRE) **Mounted Gamess Assoc Syndicate**
3 **BASHURE,** 6, b g Tillerman—Blackburn Meadows **Mr G. Parkinson**
4 **CARMELA MARIA,** 10, b m Medicean—Carmela Owen **Mrs Janet Cooper & Mr M. E. Sowersby**
5 **FEAST OF FIRE (IRE),** 8, ch g St Jovite (USA)—Bellagrana **Mrs E. A. Verity**
6 **FROSTY DAWN,** 7, b m Desideratum—Frosty Petal **Mrs J. M. Plummer**
7 **ONEOFAPEAR (IRE),** 9, b g Pyrus (USA)—Whitegate Way **Mr B. W. Gibson**
8 **STRICTLY GLITZ (IRE),** 4, b f Kodiac—Dancing Steps **R. D. Seldon**
9 **TENNESSEE BIRD,** 7, b g Danbird (AUS)—Tennessee Star **Queens Head Racing Club**
10 **TREGARO (FR),** 9, b g Phantom Breeze—Touques (FR) **A. Lyons**

**Other Owners:** Mrs J. H. Cooper, Mr J. Heslop, Mr J. E. Scott, B. Valentine, Mrs J. Wiltschinsky, Mrs C. J. Zetter-Wells.

**Assistant Trainer:** Mary Sowersby

**Jockey (flat):** Tom Eaves, James Sullivan. **Jockey (NH):** Brian Hughes. **Conditional:** Adam Nichol, Gavin Sheehan. **Amateur:** Mr Russell Lindsay.

---

## 571 MR JOHN SPEARING, Kinnersley

Postal: **Kinnersley Racing Limited, Kinnersley Racing Stables, Kinnersley, Severn Stoke, Worcestershire, WR8 9JR**
Contacts: **PHONE (01905) 371054 FAX (01905) 371054 MOBILE (07801) 552922**
**E-MAIL jlspearing@aol.com**

1 **ASHPAN SAM,** 6, b g Firebreak—Sweet Patoopie **Advantage Chemicals Holdings Ltd**
2 **BARTON GIFT,** 8, b g Alflora (IRE)—Marina Bird **Mercy Rimell & Kate Ive**
3 **CLEAR SPRING (IRE),** 7, b h Chineur (FR)—Holly Springs **Mr H. James**
4 **EURATO (FR),** 5, ch g Medicean—Double Green (IRE) **Good Breed Limited**

## MR JOHN SPEARING - Continued

5 **HAWK MOTH (IRE),** 7, b g Hawk Wing (USA)—Sasimoto (USA) **Kinnersley Partnership**
6 **HOWZ THE FAMILY (IRE),** 4, b g Myboycharlie (IRE)—Lady Raj (USA) **Mr G. Barot**
7 **INSIGHT (IRE),** 4, b f Bushranger (IRE)—Ribbon Glade (UAE) **Mr G. Barot**
8 **OVER THE AIR,** 7, br m Overbury (IRE)—Moonlight Air **Mrs W. M. Badger**
9 **PEARLS LEGEND,** 8, b g Midnight Legend—Pearl's Choice (IRE) **The Corsairs**
10 **ROCK ON CANDY,** 6, b m Excellent Art—Rock Candy (IRE) **T. M. Hayes**
11 **SWEEPING ROCK (IRE),** 5, b g Rock of Gibraltar (IRE)—Sweeping Story (USA) **Kinnersley Partnership II**
12 **TABLE BLUFF (IRE),** 6, ch g Indian Haven—Double Deal **Advantage Chemicals Holdings Ltd**
13 **TUNDRIDGE,** 6, b g Authorized (IRE)—Salanka (IRE) **T. M. Hayes**
14 **WHITECREST,** 7, ch m Ishiguru (USA)—Risky Valentine **G. M. Eales**
15 **WITH HINDSIGHT (IRE),** 7, ch g Ad Valorem (USA)—Lady From Limerick (IRE) **Mr G. Barot**

### THREE-YEAR-OLDS

16 **DEAR BRUIN (IRE),** b f Kodiac—Namu **Advantage Chemicals Holdings Ltd**
17 **LADY AMPTHILL (IRE),** b f Strategic Prince—Pixie's Blue (IRE) **J. L. Spearing**
18 **OVERSTONE LASS (IRE),** b f Excellent Art—Clinging Vine (USA) **G. M. Eales**

**Other Owners:** Miss C. J. Ive, Mr H. C. M. Porter, Mrs M. Rimell.

**Assistant Trainer:** Miss C. Ive

---

## 572 MR MICHAEL SQUANCE, Newmarket

Postal: **36 Golden Miller Close, Newmarket, Suffolk, CB8 7RT**
Contacts: **PHONE (01638) 661824 MOBILE (07532) 372557**
**WEBSITE www.michaelsquanceracing.co.uk**

1 **DIPLOMATIC (IRE),** 10, b g Cape Cross (IRE)—Embassy **Miss K. L. Squance**
2 **GABRIAL'S WAWA,** 5, b g Dubai Destination (USA)—Celestial Welcome **R Morris J Russell O Doyle J Murphy**
3 **HARROGATE FAIR,** 5, b g Trade Fair—Starbeck (IRE) **Miss K. L. Squance**
4 **MUMARASAAT (USA),** 4, b f Elusive Quality (USA)—Reefaljamal (USA) **Miss M. Bishop-Peck**

### THREE-YEAR-OLDS

5 **MANOFMANYTALENTS,** b g Bertolini (USA)—Starbeck (IRE) **Miss K. L. Squance**
6 **MASIPA (IRE),** b f Lawman (FR)—Barconey (IRE) **Miss K. L. Squance**

### TWO-YEAR-OLDS

7 B f 12/4 Pastoral Pursuits—Lee Miller (IRE) (Danehill Dancer (IRE)) (761)
8 Br g 30/4 Bertolini (USA)—Music Maid (IRE) (Inzar (USA)) **K. D. Crabb**
9 B f 24/3 Bertolini (USA)—Starbeck (IRE) (Spectrum (IRE)) **K. D. Crabb**

**Other Owners:** Mr R. Morris, Mr S. Russell.

---

## 573 MR TOMMY STACK, Cashel

Postal: **Thomastown Castle Stud, Golden, Cashel, Co. Tipperary, Ireland**
**E-MAIL tommystack@eircom.net**

1 **BARBEQUE (IRE),** 5, b m Elusive City (USA)—Babberina (IRE)
2 **GRADATIM (IRE),** 4, b g High Chaparral (IRE)—Fear And Greed (IRE)
3 **ONENIGHTIDREAMED (IRE),** 4, ch g Footstepsinthesand—Pivotalia (IRE)
4 **OVERLAND EXPRESS (IRE),** 5, b m Dylan Thomas (IRE)—No Way (IRE)
5 **ROBIN'S CHOICE (IRE),** 4, b f Bushranger (IRE)—Creekhaven (IRE)

### THREE-YEAR-OLDS

6 **CURRENT STATE (IRE),** b f High Chaparral (IRE)—Thoughtful (IRE)
7 B c Duke of Marmalade (IRE)—Golden Mask (USA)
8 **HURRICANE CASS (IRE),** b c Hurricane Run (IRE)—Rahya Cass (IRE)
9 B f Montjeu (IRE)—Inkling (USA)
10 **K ROCK,** b c Rock of Gibraltar (IRE)—Asheyana (IRE)
11 **LANDALE,** ch f Raven's Pass (USA)—Fraulein
12 B f Myboycharlie (IRE)—Lauren Louise
13 **LOVE ROSIE (IRE),** b f Zebedee—Exponent (USA)

## MR TOMMY STACK - Continued

**14 UNCHANGED (IRE),** b br c Thewayyouare (USA)—Mini Dane (IRE)
**15** B g Zebedee—Unfortunate

## TWO-YEAR-OLDS

**16** B f 12/4 Cape Blanco (IRE)—Alabaq (USA) (Riverman (USA))
**17** B c 6/2 Arcano (IRE)—Blue Dahlia (IRE) (Shamardal (USA))
**18** B f 21/2 High Chaparral (IRE)—Chieftess (IRE) (Mr Greeley (USA))
**19 CIAVENNA (IRE),** b f 14/4 Canford Cliffs (IRE)—Chantarella (IRE) (Royal Academy (USA))
**20** B c 17/3 Cacique (IRE)—Elegant Beauty (Olden Times) (62000)
**21** B f 1/4 High Chaparral (IRE)—Fand (USA) (Kingmambo (USA))
**22** B f 2/3 Fastnet Rock (AUS)—Front House (IRE) (Sadler's Wells (USA))
**23** B f 17/5 Pour Moi (IRE)—Golden Mask (USA) (Seeking The Gold (USA))
**24** B f 18/4 Duke of Marmalade (IRE)—Heaven's Vault (IRE) (Hernando (FR))
**25** B f 3/3 Holy Roman Emperor (IRE)—Highindi (Montjeu (IRE)) (67460)
**26** B c 11/3 Holy Roman Emperor (IRE)—Ice Box (IRE) (Pivotal) (19047)
**27** B f 2/4 Arcano (IRE)—Lady of Kildare (IRE) (Mujadil (USA)) (31745)
**28** B c 6/2 Holy Roman Emperor (IRE)—Lisa Gherardini (IRE) (Barathea (IRE)) (44761)
**29** B f 9/2 Champs Elysees—Looby Loo (Kyllachy) (91269)
**30** B f 10/5 Holy Roman Emperor (IRE)—Medicean Star (IRE) (Galileo (IRE))
**31** B c 8/5 High Chaparral (IRE)—Miss Beatrix (IRE) (Danehill Dancer (IRE)) (111110)
**32** B c 20/5 Dylan Thomas (IRE)—Pure Greed (IRE) (Galileo (IRE))
**33** B c 18/2 Duke of Marmalade (IRE)—Queen Wasp (IRE) (Shamardal (USA)) (17460)
**34** B f 11/1 Fastnet Rock (AUS)—Question Times (Shamardal (USA)) (43650)
**35** B f 17/3 Duke of Marmalade (IRE)—Rahya Cass (IRE) (Rahy (USA))
**36** B c 20/4 Approve (IRE)—Reign of Fire (IRE) (Perugino (USA)) (42000)
**37** B c 11/4 Royal Applause—Rhapsilian (Dansili) (27777)
**38** B f 8/4 Danehill Dancer (IRE)—River Flow (USA) (Affirmed (USA)) (47619)
**39** B c 15/3 Dutch Art—Rotunda (Pivotal) (38095)
**40** B c 18/2 Arcano (IRE)—Sassy Gal (IRE) (King's Best (USA)) (60000)
**41** Br f 6/4 Rip Van Winkle (IRE)—Sheezalady (Zafonic (USA)) (65000)
**42** B f 31/3 Holy Roman Emperor (IRE)—Stellarina (IRE) (Night Shift (USA))
**43** B c 27/4 Henrythenavigator (USA)—Tashawak (IRE) (Night Shift (USA)) (41269)
**44** Ch f 4/4 Duke of Marmalade (IRE)—True Joy (IRE) (Zilzal (USA)) (28571)

**Owners:** Mr Michael Begley, Mr Sam Britt, Mr John Byrne, Mr Justin Caffrey, Mr Arunas Cicenas, Mr Terry Corden, Mr M. L. House, Mr T. Hyde Jnr, JSC Kasandros Grape, Mr D. Keoghan, Mrs J. Magnier, Mr Casey McLiney, Mr J. P. McManus, The New Pension Fund Syndicate, Newtownanner Stud, Mr B. Parker, Mr Peter Piller, G. A. Rupert, Mary Slack, Mr David Slater, Mr Michael Tabor, Ms Kinvara Vaughan.

**Jockey (flat):** Wayne Lordan. **Jockey (NH):** W. J. Lee.

---

## MR EUGENE STANFORD, Newmarket

Postal: **Lemberg Stables, Hamilton Road, Newmarket, Suffolk, CB8 7JQ**
Contacts: **PHONE (01638) 660142**

**1 GODWIT,** 7, b m Noverre (USA)—Hen Harrier **Mr E. V. Stanford**
**2 LADY OF YUE,** 5, b m Manduro (GER)—Desert Royalty (IRE) **Mrs J. M. Quy**
**3 THE HAPPY HAMMER (IRE),** 9, b g Acclamation—Emma's Star (ITY) **Newmarketracingclub.co.uk**
**4 UNTIL MIDNIGHT (IRE),** 5, b g Moss Vale (IRE)—Emma's Star (ITY) **Newmarketracingclub.co.uk**

## THREE-YEAR-OLDS

**5 CEREBELLUM,** b g Pivotal—Lovely Thought
**6 ISLAND AUTHORITY,** b f Authorized (IRE)—Island Odyssey **Mrs J. M. Quy**

**Other Owners:** New Sports Media Ltd, C. Woof.

## 575 MR DANIEL STEELE, Henfield

Postal: **Blacklands House, Wheatsheaf Road, Wineham, nr Henfield, West Sussex, BN5 9BE**
Contacts: **MOBILE (07500) 556398**
**E-MAIL danielsteele14@hotmail.co.uk**

1 **ACCORDING TO THEM (IRE),** 11, ch g Quws—Any Old Music (IRE) **Mr D. R. Steele**
2 **ACHEMENES (FR),** 6, gr g Bonbon Rose (FR)—Aimessa du Berlais (FR) **Mr D. R. Steele**
3 **FINTAN,** 12, ch g Generous (IRE)—Seeker **Mr D. R. Steele**
4 **HOLD THE BUCKS (USA),** 9, b g Hold That Tiger (USA)—Buck's Lady (USA) **Mr D. R. Steele**
5 **HUDIBRAS (IRE),** 11, b g Bluebird (USA)—Mannequin (IRE) **Mr D. R. Steele**
6 **PRESIDENTIAL LADY (IRE),** 6, b m Hurricane Run (IRE)—Sheer Glamour (IRE) **Mr D. R. Steele**
7 **SILVER CHAPERONE (IRE),** 8, gr g Alderbrook—Katie's Castle (IRE) **Mr D. R. Steele**
8 **THE SNEEZER (IRE),** 12, br g Topanoora—Bel Azur (IRE) **Mr D. R. Steele**

## 576 MRS JACKIE STEPHEN, Inverurie

Postal: **Conglass Farmhouse, Inverurie, Aberdeenshire, AB51 5DN**
Contacts: **PHONE (01467) 621267 FAX (01467) 620511 MOBILE (07980) 785924**
**E-MAIL jackieprovan123@hotmail.co.uk**

1 **AMILLIONTIMES (IRE),** 7, b g Olden Times—Miss Million (IRE) **Mr P. G. Stephen**
2 **MO ROUGE (IRE),** 7, b g Croco Rouge (IRE)—Just A Mo (IRE) **Mrs J. S. Stephen**
3 **PROBLEMA TIC (FR),** 9, b g Kapgarde (FR)—Atreide (FR) **Mrs J. S. Stephen**
4 **RELAND (FR),** 10, ch g Shaanmer (IRE)—Falkland III (FR) **Mr P. G. Stephen**
5 **WELCOME BEN (IRE),** 6, b g High Roller (IRE)—Bramble Cottage (IRE) **Mrs J. S. Stephen**

## 577 MR ROBERT STEPHENS, Caldicot

Postal: **The Knoll, St. Brides Netherwent, Caldicot, Gwent, NP26 3AT**
Contacts: **MOBILE (07717) 477177**
**E-MAIL robertdavidstephens@btinternet.com**

1 **ALDBOROUGH (IRE),** 5, b g Danehill Dancer (IRE)—Kitty O'shea
2 **AVERTOR,** 9, b g Oasis Dream—Avessia **D. J. Deer**
3 **BELTOR,** 4, b g Authorized (IRE)—Carahill (AUS) **Alison Mossop**
4 **DETANK (IRE),** 8, b g Oscar (IRE)—Ou La La (IRE) **Julia Oakey, P Bancroft, M Waddingham**
5 **MILE HOUSE (IRE),** 7, b g Close Conflict (USA)—Clogheen Lass (IRE) **Castle Farm Racing**
6 **MODUS,** 5, ch g Motivator—Alessandra **D. J. Deer**
7 **PICODEAN,** 7, b g Tikkanen (USA)—Gipsy Girl **Mr D. O. Stephens**
8 **QUEBEC,** 4, b g Dansili—Milford Sound **Mr R. D. Stephens**
9 **RENDL BEACH (IRE),** 8, b g Milan—Erins Emblem (IRE) **M Duthie & A Mossop**
10 **RIVER DREAMER (IRE),** 4, ch f Intense Focus (USA)—Guard Hill (USA) **Mr R. D. Stephens**
11 **SECONDO (FR),** 5, b g Sakhee's Secret—Royal Jade **D. J. Deer**
12 **SUPAPOWERS (IRE),** 9, ch m Subtle Power (IRE)—Hi Sheree (IRE) **Castle Farm Racing**
13 **TEMPLEBRADEN (IRE),** 8, b g Brian Boru—Baunfaun Run (IRE) **J. Mcgrath**
14 6, B g Motivator—Wild Academy (IRE) **D. J. Deer**
15 **WINTOUR LEAP,** 4, b f Nayef (USA)—Mountain Leap (IRE) **Mr P. M. Cooper**
16 **YES DADDY (IRE),** 7, b g Golan (IRE)—Hollygrove Samba (IRE) **Mr P. M. Cooper**

### THREE-YEAR-OLDS

17 **EQUITA,** b f Equiano (FR)—Oasis Jade **D. J. Deer**

**Other Owners:** Mr Patrick Bancroft, Mr M. Duthie, Alison Mossop, Miss Julia Oakey, Mr R. Stephens, Mr M. C. Waddingham.

**Assistant Trainer:** Rosie Stephens

**Jockey (flat):** Chris Catlin, Liam Jones. **Jockey (NH):** Tom O'Brien. **Apprentice:** Daniel Muscutt.

## 578 MR OLLY STEVENS, Chiddingfold

Postal: **Robins Farm Stables, Fisher Lane, Chiddingfold, Godalming, Surrey, GU8 4TB**
Contacts: **PHONE (01428) 682059 FAX (01428) 682466 MOBILE (07585) 123178**
**E-MAIL ostevens@robinsfarmracing.com WEBSITE www.robinsfarmracing.com**

1 **BURNING BLAZE,** 5, b g Danroad (AUS)—Demeter (USA) **Mr O. Stevens**
2 **EXTORTIONIST (IRE),** 4, b c Dandy Man (IRE)—Dream Date (IRE) **Sheikh S. A. K. H. Al Thani**
3 **GAMESOME (FR),** 4, b c Rock of Gibraltar (IRE)—Hot Coal (USA) **Qatar Racing & Essafinaat**
4 **GOLD RUN,** 4, b g Hurricane Run (IRE)—Trick (IRE) **Mrs J K Powell & Pearl Bloodstock Ltd**
5 **GREEN DOOR (IRE),** 4, b c Camacho—Inourhearts (IRE) **Pearl Bloodstock & Mrs John Redvers**
6 **HEISMAN (IRE),** 4, b c Teofilo (IRE)—Luminata (IRE) **Qatar Racing Limited**
7 **LADY BRIGID (IRE),** 4, b f Holy Roman Emperor (IRE)—Brigids Cross (IRE) **M. H. and Mrs G. Tourle**
8 **LIGHTNING SPEAR,** 4, ch c Pivotal—Atlantic Destiny (IRE) **Qatar Racing Limited**
9 **LIGHTNING THUNDER,** 4, b f Dutch Art—Sweet Coincidence **Mr Mohd Al Kubasi & Pearl Bloodstock Ltd**
10 **MICROWAVE (IRE),** 4, b f Fastnet Rock (AUS)—Chrisalice (GR) **Qatar Racing Limited**

### THREE-YEAR-OLDS

11 **AGE OF ELEGANCE (IRE),** b f Makfi—Elegant Pride **Isidore Carivalis & Pearl Bloodstock Ltd**
12 **CESCA (IRE),** b f Fastnet Rock (AUS)—Mark of An Angel (IRE) **Chasemore Farm LLP**
13 **DUTCHESS OF ART,** br f Dutch Art—Kind of Light **Reuben Foundation**
14 **GIN TRAP (USA),** b c Distorted Humor (USA)—Ticket to Seattle (USA) **Qatar Racing Limited**
15 **HERCULLIAN PRINCE,** b g Royal Applause—Thara'a (IRE) **Pearl Bloodstock Limited**
16 **HUNGERFORD,** b c Pastoral Pursuits—Truly Pink **Trinity Park Stud**
17 **LAMPS OF HEAVEN (IRE),** b f Invincible Spirit (IRE)—Star Studded **Pearl Bloodstock Ltd & Mr William Lemon**
18 **MAN FROM ATLANTIS,** b g Aqlaam—Showstar (IRE) **Mr C. P. Watson**
19 **NEXT GENERATION (IRE),** b f Royal Applause—Gazebo **QRL/Sheikh Suhaim Al Thani/M Al Kubaisi**
20 **PEACE AND WAR (USA),** b f War Front (USA)—More Oats Please (USA) **Qatar Racing Limited**
21 **QATAR SUCCESS,** b f Kyllachy—Cherokee Stream (IRE) **Chris Fahy, Jon Collins & R Williams**
22 **ROBINS PEARL (FR),** ch f Linngari (IRE)—Fire Sale (ARG) **Pearl Bloodstock Limited**
23 **ROYAL ALBERT HALL,** b g Royal Applause—Victoria Sponge (IRE) **Mrs M. U. B. Redvers**
24 **SHACKLED N DRAWN (USA),** b c Candy Ride (ARG)—Cajun Flash (USA) **Clipper Group Holdings Ltd**
25 **SPRING SERAPH (IRE),** gr g Dark Angel (IRE)—Saffron Crocus **Kennet Valley Thoroughbreds III**
26 **THE OLYMPUS MAN,** b g Paco Boy (IRE)—Blandish (USA) **Qatar Racing Limited**
27 **TOTAL DEMOLITION (IRE),** ch g Thewayyouare (USA)—Margaux Dancer (IRE) **Qatar Racing & Kareem Altaji**
28 **WAHKUNA,** ch f Footstepsinthesand—Atira (IRE)

### TWO-YEAR-OLDS

29 **CACCINI,** b c 26/4 Authorized (IRE)—Key Change (IRE) (Darshaan)
30 Ch f 14/3 Dutch Art—Carved Emerald (Pivotal) (107142) **Qatar Racing Limited**
31 B c 10/3 Drosselmeyer (USA)—Choice Play (USA) (Vindication (USA)) (47045) **Pearl Bloodstock Limited**
32 **GOLDENFIELD (IRE),** b c 24/1 Footstepsinthesand—Society Gal (IRE) (Galileo (IRE)) (55000) **Mr & Mrs W W Fleming**
33 B c 21/2 Dandy Man (IRE)—Masakira (IRE) (Royal Academy (USA)) (28571) **Qatar Racing Limited**
34 **MIMESIS,** ch f 29/4 Shirocco (GER)—Canouan (IRE) (Sadler's Wells (USA))
35 **SHOW AYA (IRE),** ch f 10/4 Showcasing—Mimiteh (USA) (Maria's Mon (USA)) (25714) **S. Al Ansari**
36 Ch c 12/4 Footstepsinthesand—St Edith (IRE) (Desert King (IRE)) (31428) **Qatar Racing Limited**
37 B f 27/3 Fast Company (IRE)—Tawaafur (Fantastic Light (USA)) (78095) **Qatar Racing Limited**
38 **WARRIOR SONG (USA),** b f 18/5 Harlan's Holiday (USA)—More Oats Please (USA) (Smart Strike (CAN)) (83189) **Qatar Racing Ltd & Sheikh Suhaim Al Thani**

**Other Owners:** Mr M. A. M. K. Al - Kubaisi, Sheikh M. B. K. Al Maktoum, Mr K. A. A. Altaji, A. W. Black, Mrs J. E. Black, Mr I. Carivalis, Mr J. A. Collins, Mr C. J. Fahy, Mr W. W. Fleming, Mrs S. A. M. Fleming, Mr R. S. Hoskins, W. R. Lemon, Mr P. O'Driscoll, Mrs J. K. Powell, Mr D. Redvers, Mr J. A. Reuben, N. J. F. Robinson, Mrs R. L. Tincknell, Mr R. Tincknell, Mr M. H. Tourle, Mrs G. O. Tourle, Mr R. E. Williams.

**Assistant Trainer:** Rachel Rodman

**Jockey (flat):** Andrea Atzeni, Oisin Murphy.

## 579 MISS ANN STOKELL, Southwell

Postal: **2 Chippendale Road, Lincoln, Lincolnshire, LN6 3PP**
Contacts: **MOBILE (07814) 579982**
**E-MAIL ann.stokell@gmail.com**

1 **ANJUNA BEACH (USA),** 5, b g Artie Schiller (USA)—Hidden Temper (USA) **Mr G. B. Pacey**

## MISS ANN STOKELL - Continued

2 **BAPAK BANGSAWAN,** 5, b g Pastoral Pursuits—Nsx **Mr G. B. Pacey**
3 **CROPLEY (IRE),** 6, gr g Galileo (IRE)—Niyla (IRE) **Mr G. B. Pacey**
4 **FAST FINIAN (IRE),** 6, gr g Clodovil (IRE)—Delphie Queen (IRE) **Mr M. C. Elvin**
5 7, Ch m Blue Dakota (IRE)—Fizzy Whizzy
6 **GEORGE FENTON,** 6, ch g Piccolo—Mashmoum **Mr G. B. Pacey**
7 **HOLD THE STAR,** 9, b m Red Ransom (USA)—Sydney Star **Mr G. B. Pacey**
8 **ISLAND EXPRESS (IRE),** 8, b g Chineur (FR)—Cayman Expresso (IRE) **Mr G. B. Pacey**
9 **MRS MEDLEY,** 9, b m Rambling Bear—Animal Cracker **Ms C. Stokell**
10 **SEA WHISPER,** 4, ch f Compton Place—Starfleet **Mrs J. A. Cornwell**
11 **SPEIGHTOWNS KID (USA),** 7, gr ro g Speightstown (USA)—Seize the Wind (USA) **Mr G. B. Pacey**
12 **STEEL CITY BOY (IRE),** 12, b g Bold Fact (USA)—Balgren (IRE) **Mr G. B. Pacey**

**Assistant Trainer:** Caron Stokell

---

## 580 MR WILLIAM STONE, West Wickham

Postal: **The Meadow, Streetly End, West Wickham, Cambridge, Cambridgeshire, CB21 4RP**
Contacts: **PHONE (01223) 894617 MOBILE (07788) 971094**
**E-MAIL williamstone1@hotmail.co.uk**

1 **CLOCK OPERA (IRE),** 5, b m Excellent Art—Moving Diamonds **Caroline Scott & Shane Fairweather**
2 **DIAMOND LADY,** 4, b f Multiplex—Ellen Mooney **The Going Great Guns Partnership**
3 **EVENING ATTIRE,** 4, b g Pastoral Pursuits—Markova's Dance **Miss C. M. Scott**
4 **IMJIN RIVER (IRE),** 8, b g Namid—Lady Nasrana (FR) **Miss C. M. Scott**
5 **OUTRAGEOUS REQUEST,** 9, ch g Rainbow Quest (USA)—La Sorrela (IRE) **Miss C. M. Scott**
6 **TOUCH THE CLOUDS,** 4, b g Sleeping Indian—Aptina (USA) **Miss C. M. Scott**
7 **WARDEN BOND,** 7, ch g Monsieur Bond (IRE)—Warden Rose **Mr J A Ross & Miss C Scott**

### TWO-YEAR-OLDS

8 B f 28/4 Bushranger (IRE)—Alexander Anapolis (IRE) (Spectrum (IRE)) (10000) **The Plenipo Partnership**

**Other Owners:** Mr S. A. Fairweather, Mr J. A. Ross.

---

## 581 MR BRIAN STOREY, Kirklinton

Postal: **Low Dubwath, Kirklinton, Carlisle, Cumbria, CA6 6EF**
Contacts: **PHONE (01228) 675168 FAX (01228) 675977 MOBILE (07950) 925576/ (07912) 898740**
**E-MAIL bstoreyracing@aol.com WEBSITE www.brianstoreyracing.co.uk**

1 **BALTIC PATHFINDER (IRE),** 11, b g Alflora (IRE)—Boro Bow (IRE) **Mrs E. M. Smith**
2 **COURT RISE (IRE),** 6, br g Court Cave (IRE)—Raise A Flag (IRE) **B. Storey**
3 **DIAMOND NATIVE (IRE),** 7, b g Alderbrook—Native Sylph (IRE) **B. Storey**

### THREE-YEAR-OLDS

4 Ch f And Beyond (IRE)—Enlisted (IRE) **Mr Peter Storey**

**Assistant Trainer:** Mrs Jackie Storey

**Jockey (flat):** P. J. McDonald. **Jockey (NH):** Brian Hughes, Richie McGrath. **Conditional:** Jamie Hamilton. **Amateur:** Miss Jackie Coward, Mr Tom Hamilton.

---

## 582 MR WILF STOREY, Consett

Postal: **Grange Farm & Stud, Muggleswick, Consett, Co. Durham, DH8 9DW**
Contacts: **PHONE (01207) 255259 FAX (01207) 255259 MOBILE (07860) 510441**
**E-MAIL wlstorey@metronet.co.uk WEBSITE www.wilfstorey.com**

1 **CARD HIGH (IRE),** 5, b g Red Clubs (IRE)—Think (FR) **Gremlin Racing**
2 **JAN SMUTS (IRE),** 7, b g Johannesburg (USA)—Choice House (USA) **H. S. Hutchinson & W. Storey**
3 **MONTHLY MEDAL,** 12, b g Danehill Dancer (IRE)—Sovereign Abbey (IRE) **Wilf Storey**
4 **NELSON'S BAY,** 6, b g Needwood Blade—In Good Faith (USA) **Wilf Storey & A. B. Bennett**
5 **NONAGON,** 4, b g Pastoral Pursuits—Nine Red **Geegeez.co.uk 1**

## MR WILF STOREY - Continued

### THREE-YEAR-OLDS

6 B f Sakhee (USA)—Cugina **Wilf Storey**

**Other Owners:** Mr A. B. Bennett, Mr M. Bisogno, Mr M. Burton, Mr D. D. Gillies, Mr H. S. Hutchinson, Mr D. McPharlane, Mr P. McVey, Mr S. Meikle, Mr A. Morrison, Mr A. Rugg, Mr W. Storey.

**Assistant Trainer:** Miss S. Storey

**Amateur:** Miss S. M. Doolan.

---

## 583 SIR MICHAEL STOUTE, Newmarket

Postal: **Freemason Lodge, Bury Road, Newmarket, Suffolk, CB8 7BY**
Contacts: **PHONE (01638) 663801 FAX (01638) 667276**

1 **ABSEIL (USA),** 5, b g First Defence (USA)—Intercontinental
2 **ALTAAYIL (IRE),** 4, br g Sea The Stars (IRE)—Alleluia
3 **ARAB SPRING (IRE),** 5, b h Monsun (GER)—Spring Symphony (IRE)
4 **ASYAD (IRE),** 4, b f New Approach (IRE)—Elle Danzig (GER)
5 **BRAGGING (USA),** 4, b br f Exchange Rate (USA)—Boasting (USA)
6 **CANNOCK CHASE (USA),** 4, b c Lemon Drop Kid (USA)—Lynnwood Chase (USA)
7 **GOSPEL CHOIR,** 6, ch g Galileo (IRE)—Chorist
8 **GOTHIC,** 4, b g Danehill Dancer (IRE)—Riberac
9 **HILLSTAR,** 5, b h Danehill Dancer (IRE)—Crystal Star
10 **INTEGRAL,** 5, b m Dalakhani (IRE)—Echelon
11 **MUNAASER,** 4, b g New Approach (IRE)—Safwa (IRE)
12 **PROVENANCE,** 4, b f Galileo (IRE)—Echelon
13 **SNOW SKY,** 4, b c Nayef (USA)—Winter Silence
14 **STOMACHION (IRE),** 5, b g Duke of Marmalade (IRE)—Insight (FR)
15 **TELESCOPE (IRE),** 5, b h Galileo (IRE)—Velouette
16 **TOP TUG (IRE),** 4, ch g Halling (USA)—Top Romance (IRE)

### THREE-YEAR-OLDS

17 **AL HAMLA (USA),** b br f Medaglia d'Oro (USA)—Genuine Devotion (IRE)
18 **ALLA BREVE,** b f Dansili—Allegretto (IRE)
19 **ALMONER,** b f Oasis Dream—Alumni
20 **ANGEL VISION (IRE),** b f Oasis Dream—Islington (IRE)
21 **APPROACHING SQUALL (IRE),** ch c New Approach (IRE)—Lady Miletrian (IRE)
22 **AREIOPAGOS (IRE),** br g Lawman (FR)—Athene (IRE)
23 **BERNHARD (IRE),** b c Bernardini (USA)—Nasheej (USA)
24 **BISHARA (USA),** ch f Dubawi (IRE)—Kaseema (USA)
25 **CALL OUT LOUD,** b c Aqlaam—Winner's Call
26 **CAPEL PATH (USA),** br c Street Cry (IRE)—Miss Lucifer (FR)
27 **CHAPEL CHOIR,** gr f Dalakhani (IRE)—Chorist
28 **CHRISTMAS HAMPER (IRE),** b c Dubawi (IRE)—Gift Range (IRE)
29 **CONFLICTING ADVICE (USA),** b c Iffraaj—Assertive Lass (AUS)
30 **CONSORT (IRE),** gr c Lope de Vega (IRE)—Mundus Novus (USA)
31 **CONVEY,** b c Dansili—Insinuate (USA)
32 **COORG (IRE),** ch c Teofilo (IRE)—Creese
33 **CRYPTONYM,** b f Dansili—Codename
34 **CRYSTAL ZVEZDA,** ch f Dubawi (IRE)—Crystal Star
35 **DANNYDAY,** b c Dansili—Dayrose
36 **DARK DEED,** b c Dansili—High Heeled (IRE)
37 **DARSHINI,** b c Sir Percy—Fairy Flight (USA)
38 **DARTMOUTH,** b c Dubawi (IRE)—Galatee (FR)
39 **DISEGNO (IRE),** b c Fastnet Rock (AUS)—Seven Magicians (USA)
40 **DISSOLUTION,** b c New Approach (IRE)—Portodora (USA)
41 **EBEN DUBAI (IRE),** b g New Approach (IRE)—Eldalil
42 **ENTITY,** ch f Shamardal (USA)—Echelon
43 **EXOSPHERE,** b c Beat Hollow—Bright And Clear
44 **GRAND INQUISITOR,** b c Dansili—Dusty Answer
45 **HAKKA,** b c Dansili—African Rose
46 **HOORAYFORHOLLYWOOD,** b f Oasis Dream—Dalisay (IRE)
47 **HORSESHOE BAY (IRE),** b c Arch (USA)—Sweepstake (IRE)
48 **I ZINGARI,** b c Dansili—Hi Calypso (IRE)

## SIR MICHAEL STOUTE - Continued

**49 INDELIBLE INK (IRE),** b g Invincible Spirit (IRE)—Serres (IRE)
**50 INDIAN MONSOON (IRE),** b c Monsun (GER)—Madhya (USA)
**51 INSHAA,** b c Dansili—Hidden Brief
**52 INTIMATION,** b f Dubawi (IRE)—Infallible
**53 KIP,** b f Rip Van Winkle (IRE)—Catopuma (USA)
**54 KISUMU,** b c High Chaparral (IRE)—Arum Lily (USA)
**55 MAKZON (USA),** b c Henrythenavigator (USA)—Fab's Melody (USA)
**56 MASHKOOR APPROACH,** ch c New Approach (IRE)—Winners Chant (IRE)
**57 MONASADA,** b f Nayef (USA)—Asawer (IRE)
**58 MOONLIGHT SONATA,** b f Galileo (IRE)—Blue Rhapsody
**59 MORUADH (IRE),** b f Fastnet Rock (AUS)—Olympienne (IRE)
**60 MUKHAYYAM,** b g Dark Angel (IRE)—Caster Sugar (USA)
**61 MUNTADAB (IRE),** b c Invincible Spirit (IRE)—Chibola (ARG)
**62 MUSIC AND DANCE,** b f Galileo (IRE)—Jamboretta (IRE)
**63 MUSICAL BEAT (IRE),** b f Acclamation—Musical Bar (IRE)
**64 MUSTAAQEEM (USA),** b c Dynaformer (USA)—Wasseema (USA)
**65 MUSTARD,** b c Motivator—Flash of Gold
**66 MUTAMAKKIN (USA),** br c War Front (USA)—La Laja (USA)
**67 ONDA DISTRICT (IRE),** b g Oasis Dream—Leocorno (IRE)
**68 PANDA SPIRIT (USA),** b f Invincible Spirit (IRE)—Towanda (USA)
**69 PERFECT GLANCE (USA),** br f Rock Hard Ten (USA)—Brief Look
**70 PETERHOF,** b c Dansili—Spinning Queen
**71 PETRUCCI (IRE),** b c Azamour (IRE)—Spring Symphony (IRE)
**72 PHANTASMAGORIC (IRE),** b f Dansili—Sacred Song (USA)
**73 PLANE SONG (IRE),** ch c Nayef (USA)—Kitty Hawk
**74 PLEIADES,** b c Galileo (IRE)—Angara
**75 PROFUSION,** b c Dansili—Red Bloom
**76 QUICK DEFENCE (USA),** b c First Defence (USA)—Quickfire
**77 RADDEH,** gr f Shamardal (USA)—Hathrah (IRE)
**78 RADHAADH (IRE),** b f Nayef (USA)—Safwa (IRE)
**79 RIB RESERVE (IRE),** b g Azamour (IRE)—Fringe Success (IRE)
**80 RUSSIAN HEROINE,** b f Invincible Spirit (IRE)—Russian Rhythm (USA)
**81 SANDY CAY (USA),** gr f Mizzen Mast (USA)—Camanoe (USA)
**82 SEA SCENT (USA),** ch f Mizzen Mast (USA)—July Jasmine (USA)
**83 SHOAL,** b f Oasis Dream—Midsummer
**84 STRAVAGANTE (IRE),** b c Rip Van Winkle (IRE)—Star Ruby (IRE)
**85 SUDDYAN (IRE),** b c Holy Roman Emperor (IRE)—Raydaniya (IRE)
**86 SURPRISE CALL,** ch c New Approach (IRE)—Calakanga
**87 SYMPATHY (USA),** b f Henrythenavigator (USA)—Sweet Temper (USA)
**88 TEALIGHT,** b f Teofilo (IRE)—Floodlit
**89 THREE BY THREE (IRE),** b f Invincible Spirit (IRE)—Threefold (USA)
**90 TRADEMARK (IRE),** b c Galileo (IRE)—Ice Queen (IRE)
**91 VOICE CONTROL (IRE),** gr g Dalakhani (IRE)—Scottish Stage (IRE)
**92 YARROW (IRE),** b f Sea The Stars (IRE)—Highland Gift (IRE)
**93 YET AGAIN,** b f Oasis Dream—Quiff

## TWO-YEAR-OLDS

**94 ALYDAY,** ch f 13/4 Kyllachy—Dayrose (Daylami (IRE))
**95** B c 28/2 High Chaparral (IRE)—Amathusia (Selkirk (USA))
**96 ARISTOCRATIC,** b f 18/2 Exceed And Excel (AUS)—Peeress (Pivotal)
**97 AUTOCRATIC,** b c 22/1 Dubawi (IRE)—Canda (USA) (Storm Cat (USA))
**98** B c 13/4 Dansili—Ballet Ballon (USA) (Rahy (USA)) (300000)
**99** B c 27/3 Acclamation—Belgique (IRE) (Compton Place) (75000)
**100** Gr ro f 19/2 Exchange Rate (USA)—Boasting (USA) (Kris S (USA))
**101 CANONBURY (IRE),** b br f 30/1 Oasis Dream—Islington (IRE) (Sadler's Wells (USA))
**102** B c 11/4 Shamardal (USA)—Cape Dollar (IRE) (Cape Cross (IRE))
**103 CARLO GOLDINI (IRE),** b c 8/4 Lawman (FR)—Eleanora Duse (IRE) (Azamour (IRE))
**104 CLEAR EVIDENCE,** b c 5/4 Cape Cross (IRE)—Rainbow's Edge (Rainbow Quest (USA))
**105 DIPLOMA,** b f 26/4 Dubawi (IRE)—Enticement (Montjeu (IRE))
**106 DIVINE QUICKSTEP (IRE),** b f 3/2 Dansili—La Divina (IRE) (Sadler's Wells (USA))
**107 DUBKA,** b f 16/3 Dubawi (IRE)—Rosika (Sakhee (USA))
**108 ENGAGE (IRE),** b f 28/4 Pour Moi (IRE)—Brooklyn's Storm (USA) (Storm Cat (USA)) (160000)
**109 ESTIDRAAK (IRE),** ch c 5/3 Iffraaj—Gold Hush (USA) (Seeking The Gold (USA)) (130000)
**110** B f 2/4 Dansili—Eva Luna (USA) (Alleged (USA))
**111** B c 23/1 Oasis Dream—Exemplify (Dansili)

## SIR MICHAEL STOUTE - Continued

**112 FIDAAWY,** ch c 9/2 New Approach (IRE)—Haymana (IRE) (Pivotal)
**113** Ch c 15/3 Poet's Voice—Floral Beauty (Shamardal (USA))
**114 GALVANIZE (USA),** b c 26/3 Medaglia d'Oro (USA)—Enthused (USA) (Seeking The Gold (USA))
**115** B f 27/1 Street Cry (IRE)—Giants Play (USA) (Giant's Causeway (USA))
**116 HAMMER GUN (USA),** b br c 6/2 Smart Strike (CAN)—Caraboss (Cape Cross (IRE))
**117 HAWKER HUNTER (IRE),** gr c 28/1 Dalakhani (IRE)—Kitty Hawk (Danehill Dancer (IRE))
**118** B c 18/2 Dubawi (IRE)—Heat Haze (Green Desert (USA))
**119 HEAVENLY NOTE,** ch f 28/3 Dutch Art—Heavenly Dawn (Pivotal)
**120 HEDGEROSE,** b f 8/3 Zamindar (USA)—Rosacara (Green Desert (USA))
**121** B c 23/3 Dansili—Hi Calypso (IRE) (In The Wings)
**122 IDYLLIC (IRE),** b f 24/4 Rip Van Winkle (IRE)—Cilium (IRE) (War Chant (USA)) (50000)
**123 INFATUATION,** b f 20/3 Invincible Spirit (IRE)—Fantasize (Groom Dancer (USA))
**124 JANTINA,** ch f 27/3 Dutch Art—Zykina (Pivotal)
**125 LABYRINTH (IRE)** B f 27/2 Lawman (FR)—Kerry Gal (IRE) (Galileo (IRE)) (260000)
**126** B c 25/2 Rip Van Winkle (IRE)—L'ancresse (IRE) (Darshaan)
**127** Ch c 11/3 Kyllachy—Laurentina (Cadeaux Genereux) (110000)
**128 LOLWAH,** ch f 20/3 Pivotal—Palace Affair (Pursuit of Love) (220000)
**129** B c 5/5 Galileo (IRE)—Mauralakana (FR) (Muhtathir) (510000)
**130 MAWAANY (IRE),** gr c 10/4 Teofilo (IRE)—Middle Persia (Dalakhani (IRE))
**131** B c 16/1 Galileo (IRE)—Midday (Oasis Dream)
**132** B f 29/4 Oasis Dream—Midsummer (Kingmambo (USA))
**133** B c 21/3 Dansili—Modesta (IRE) (Sadler's Wells (USA))
**134 MOKHALAD,** ch c 11/3 Dubawi (IRE)—Model Queen (USA) (Kingmambo (USA)) (500000)
**135 MUSTASHRY,** b br c 9/3 Tamayuz—Safwa (IRE) (Green Desert (USA))
**136 MYSTIC STORM,** ch f 7/5 Pivotal—Moon Goddess (Rainbow Quest (USA))
**137 PAVONINE,** b f 12/1 High Chaparral (IRE)—Pearl City (IRE) (Zamindar (USA))
**138** Ch c 15/4 Pivotal—Pediment (Desert Prince (IRE)) (90000)
**139 PELOPONNESE (FR),** b f 17/2 Montjeu (IRE)—Mimalia (USA) (Silver Hawk (USA))
**140 PERCY'S ROMANCE,** ch f 29/4 Sir Percy—Top Romance (IRE) (Entrepreneur)
**141** B c 30/4 War Front (USA)—Queen of The Night (Sadler's Wells (USA))
**142 QUEEN'S TRUST,** b f 4/3 Dansili—Queen's Best (King's Best (USA))
**143** B br f 20/3 Hat Trick (JPN)—Relaxed (USA) (Royal Academy (USA))
**144** B c 15/3 Hat Trick (JPN)—Rochitta (USA) (Arch (USA)) (85000)
**145** Ch c 9/2 Rip Van Winkle (IRE)—Satwa Pearl (Rock of Gibraltar (IRE))
**146 SCOTTISH SUMMIT (IRE),** b c 16/2 Shamardal (USA)—Scottish Stage (IRE) (Selkirk (USA))
**147** B f 25/1 Montjeu (IRE)—Sense of Style (USA) (Thunder Gulch (USA))
**148 SHABBAH (IRE),** br c 8/4 Sea The Stars (IRE)—Alizaya (IRE) (Highest Honor (FR)) (200000)
**149 SHALL WE (IRE),** b f 2/5 Dansili—Insight (FR) (Sadler's Wells (USA))
**150 SIDLE (IRE),** b f 14/3 Lawman (FR)—Slink (Selkirk (USA)) (170000)
**151** B c 26/2 Canford Cliffs (IRE)—Star Ruby (IRE) (Rock of Gibraltar (IRE))
**152 STATUESQUE,** b f 24/2 Sea The Stars (IRE)—Kahara (Sadler's Wells (USA)) (375000)
**153 STERLING WORK (IRE),** b c 8/2 Invincible Spirit (IRE)—Drama Class (IRE) (Caerleon (USA))
**154** B c 19/4 Poet's Voice—Street Star (USA) (Street Cry (IRE)) (85000)
**155 SUPERYACHT (IRE),** b c 13/3 Fastnet Rock (AUS)—Olympienne (IRE) (Sadler's Wells (USA))
**156** B c 15/4 Iffraaj—Sweet Nicole (Okawango (USA)) (75000)
**157 THETIS (IRE),** b f 10/2 Invincible Spirit (IRE)—Serres (IRE) (Daylami (IRE))
**158** B f 5/4 Arch (USA)—Tsar's Pride (Sadler's Wells (USA))
**159 ULYSSES (IRE),** ch c 20/3 Galileo (IRE)—Light Shift (USA) (Kingmambo (USA))
**160 UNDER ATTACK (IRE),** b c 10/2 Dubawi (IRE)—Ship's Biscuit (Tiger Hill (IRE))
**161** B c 28/3 Sea The Stars (IRE)—Victoria Cross (IRE) (Mark of Esteem (IRE)) (600000)
**162** B br f 4/4 Arch (USA)—Visit (Oasis Dream)
**163 VOLITION (IRE),** gr f 23/1 Dark Angel (IRE)—Warshah (IRE) (Shamardal (USA)) (300000)
**164** B c 5/4 Poet's Voice—Whirly Bird (Nashwan (USA)) (300000)
**165** B f 19/3 Shirocco (GER)—Winners Chant (IRE) (Dalakhani (IRE))

**Owners:** Her Majesty The Queen, Mr Khalid Abdullah, Mr Malih Al Basti, Mr Hamdan Al Maktoum, Mr Abdullah Saeed Al Naboodah, Al Shaqab Racing, Antoniades Family, Ballymacoll Stud, Bermuda Thoroughbred Racing Ltd, Cheveley Park Stud, Mr Athos Christodoulou, Mr Peter Done, Sir Alex Ferguson, Mrs Elizabeth Haynes, Highclere Thoroughbred Racing, Mr S. Lamprell, Mrs John Magnier, Newsells Park Stud, Mr Philip Newton, Mr Robert Ng, Niarchos Family, Qatar Racing, Sir Eveleyn de Rothschild, Lady Rothschild, Mr Derrick Smith, Mr George Strawbridge, Mr Saeed Suhail, Mrs Doreen Tabor, Mr Michael Tabor, Mrs Anita Wigan, Mr James Wigan.

## 584 MRS ALI STRONGE, Eastbury

Postal: **Castle Piece Racing Stables, Eastbury, Hungerford, Berkshire, RG17 7JR**
Contacts: **PHONE (01488) 72818 FAX (01488) 670378 MOBILE (07779) 285205**
**E-MAIL office@castlepiecestables.com WEBSITE www.castlepiecestables.com**

1 **ABRUZZI,** 7, b g Milan—Shannon Native (IRE) **Mrs A. J. Stronge**
2 **ALFRAAMSEY,** 7, b g Fraam—Evanesce **Tapestry Partnership**
3 **BAKU BAY (IRE),** 7, b g Flemensfirth (USA)—The Girlfriend (IRE) **Mr I. Kidger, Mr I. Mason & The Lanza Boys**
4 **BARENGER (IRE),** 8, b g Indian Danehill (IRE)—Build A Dream (USA) **Kings Of The Castle**
5 **CALL THE DETECTIVE (IRE),** 6, b g Winged Love (IRE)—Aneeza (IRE) **Mr J. J. King**
6 **CAPPIELOW PARK,** 6, b g Exceed And Excel (AUS)—Barakat **Mr Tim Dykes & Mr James Burley**
7 **HATTERS RIVER (IRE),** 8, b g Milan—Curzon Ridge (IRE) **Susan & Gerard Nock**
8 **KING SPIRIT (IRE),** 7, b g Fruits of Love (USA)—Tariana (IRE) **Mr J. J. King**
9 **KOLONEL KIRKUP,** 5, b g Dr Fong (USA)—Strawberry Lolly **Girls On Tour**
10 **MABDHOOL (IRE),** 4, b g Mount Nelson—Berry Baby (IRE) **Mrs B. V. Evans**
11 **MEETINGS MAN (IRE),** 8, gr g Footstepsinthesand—Missella (IRE) **Mrs B. V. Evans**
12 **MONEYMIX,** 8, gr g Fair Mix (IRE)—Sticky Money **Mrs A. J. Stronge**
13 4, B br g Milan—Presenting Shares (IRE) **Matthew Gibbens**
14 **PROUD TIMES (USA),** 9, b br g Proud Citizen (USA)—
Laura's Pistolette (USA) **Crowcombe Racing & Mrs Ali Stronge**
15 **ROYAL GUARDSMAN (IRE),** 8, b br g King's Theatre (IRE)—Lisa du Chenet (FR) **Camilla & Rosie Nock**
16 **SCARLETT LADY,** 7, b br m Kayf Tara—Frosty Mistress **Susan & Gerard Nock**
17 **SKINT,** 9, b g King's Theatre (IRE)—No More Money **Mrs B. V. Evans**
18 **SPECIAL MISS,** 4, b f Authorized (IRE)—Whatamiss (USA) **Mr T. J. Dykes**
19 **SURGING SEAS (IRE),** 6, b g Tiger Hill (IRE)—Musardiere **The Hot Hooves Syndicate**
20 **TONYTHETARMACKER (IRE),** 4, b g Westerner—Dianeme **Mr F. J. Walters**
21 **UNCLE MUF (USA),** 5, b g Curlin (USA)—Peak Maria's Way (USA) **Mr R. W. Tyrrell**
22 **UNIFY,** 5, b m Midnight Legend—Holy Smoke **Mr Nicholas John Jones**

**Other Owners:** Mr James Burley, Mrs Wendy Burley, Mr R. D. Conway, Mr Tim Dykes, Mr Ian Kidger, Mr J. J. King, Mr S. C. Leigh, Miss Jacques Malone, Mr I. P. Mason, Mrs Susan Nock, Miss R. Nock, Miss C. D. Nock, Mr Gerard Nock, Mr C. J. Orme, Mrs V. Peppiatt, Mr N. D. Peppiatt, Mrs Ali Stronge, Mr Freddie Tulloch.

**Assistant Trainer:** Sam Stronge

**Jockey (NH):** Aidan Coleman, Jack Doyle.

## 585 MISS KRISTIN STUBBS, Malton

Postal: **Beverley House, Beverley Road, Norton, Malton, North Yorkshire, YO17 9PJ**
Contacts: **PHONE (01653) 698731 FAX (01653) 698724 MOBILE (07932) 977279 / (07801) 167707**
**E-MAIL l.stubbs@btconnect.com**

1 **BOGSNOG (IRE),** 5, b g Moss Vale (IRE)—Lovers Kiss **Facts & Figures**
2 **BRONZE BEAU,** 8, ch g Compton Place—Bella Cantata **D. G. Arundale**
3 **GOLD BEAU (FR),** 5, b g Gold Away (IRE)—Theorie (FR) **Mr D Arundale & Mr N Lyons**
4 **KEENE'S POINTE,** 5, br g Avonbridge—Belle's Edge **Mr Paul Saxton**
5 **LYNNGALE,** 4, b f Myboycharlie (IRE)—Belle Annie (USA) **Mrs L. Gale**
6 **MAGNOLIA RIDGE (IRE),** 5, b g Galileo (IRE)—Treasure The Lady (IRE) **Mr D. R. Grieve**
7 **MEGAMUNCH (IRE),** 5, b g Camacho—Liscoa (IRE) **P & L Partners**
8 **PAGEANT BELLE,** 4, ch f Bahamian Bounty—Procession **Mr D. R. Grieve**
9 **RED PALADIN (IRE),** 5, b g Red Clubs (IRE)—Alexander Goldmine **Mr D. R. Grieve**
10 **REPETITION,** 5, b g Royal Applause—Uno **The B.P.J. Partnership**
11 **SILVERWARE (USA),** 7, b br g Eurosilver (USA)—Playing Footsie (USA) **Paul & Linda Dixon**
12 **YARD OF ALE,** 4, ch g Compton Place—Highly Liquid **O. J. Williams**

### THREE-YEAR-OLDS

13 **COMPETENT,** b g Compton Place—Pantita **Chester Racing Club Ltd**
14 **DANCRUISE (IRE),** b g Dandy Man (IRE)—Crua Mna **Chester Racing Club Ltd**
15 **MON GRIS (IRE),** gr c Falco (USA)—Turpitude **P & L Partners**
16 **PAFIYA,** b g Paco Boy (IRE)—Tafiya **Chester Racing Club Ltd**
17 **SOIE D'LEAU,** b g Monsieur Bond (IRE)—Silky Silence **F.A.T.J Partnership**
18 **SOMETHING LUCKY (IRE),** gr c Clodovil (IRE)—Lucky Leigh **Paul & Linda Dixon**
19 **WINK OLIVER,** b g Winker Watson—Nadinska **P & L Partners**

## MISS KRISTIN STUBBS - Continued

### TWO-YEAR-OLDS

**20** B f 2/4 Frozen Power (IRE)—Dark Albatross (USA) (Sheikh Albadou) **Mr D. R. Grieve**

**Other Owners:** Mr D. Arundale, Mr Paul W. H. Dixon, Mrs L. J. Dixon, Mr J. P. Hames, Mr F. Harrison, Mr A. Larkin, Mr Nigel Lyons, Mr Barry Midgley, Mr G. Pickering, Mrs Valerie Pittman, Mr T S Pople, Mr P. A. Saxton, Mr P. G. Shorrock, Miss K. Stubbs, Mr R. W. Stubbs, Mr John Wright.

**Jockey (flat):** Tom Eaves, Graham Gibbons. **Apprentice:** Jacob Butterfield, Shane Gray. **Amateur:** Mr Aaron James.

---

## 586 MR ROB SUMMERS, Solihull

Postal: **Summerhill Cottage, Danzey Green, Tanworth-in-Arden, Solihull, B94 5BJ**
Contacts: **PHONE (01564) 742667 MOBILE (07775) 898327**

1 **ARCTIC DIXIE,** 7, ch m Desideratum—Arctic Oats **R. P. D. T. Dineen**
2 **MASSACHUSETTS,** 8, ch g Singspiel (IRE)—Royal Passion **Miss G. L. Henderson**
3 **MR ROBINSON (FR),** 8, b g Robin des Pres (FR)—Alberade (FR) **Mrs G. M. Summers**
4 **PHOTOGENIQUE (FR),** 12, b m Cyborg (FR)—Colombia (FR) **Mrs G. M. Summers**
5 **QUINOLA DES OBEAUX (FR),** 11, b g Useful (FR)—Zaouia (FR) **O. P. J. Meli**
6 **RED ROSSO,** 10, ch g Executive Perk—Secret Whisper **Mrs G. M. Summers**
7 **RED WHISPER,** 11, ch g Midnight Legend—Secret Whisper **Mrs G. M. Summers**
8 **ROSE RED,** 8, ch m Weld—Secret Whisper **Mrs G. M. Summers**
9 **ROSEINI (IRE),** 9, b m Dr Massini (IRE)—Deise Rose (IRE) **Mrs G. M. Summers**

**Assistant Trainer:** Mrs G. M. Summers

---

## 587 MR ALAN SWINBANK, Richmond

Postal: **Western House Stables, East Road, Melsonby, Richmond, North Yorkshire, DL10 5NF**
Contacts: **PHONE (01325) 339964 FAX (01325) 377113 MOBILE (07860) 368365 / (07711) 488341**
**E-MAIL info@alanswinbank.com WEBSITE www.alanswinbank.com**

1 **ARAMIST (IRE),** 5, gr g Aussie Rules (USA)—Mistic Sun **Pam & Richard Ellis**
2 **ARYIZAD (IRE),** 6, b m Hurricane Run (IRE)—Daziyra (IRE) **Mrs J. Porter**
3 **BIG WATER (IRE),** 7, ch g Saffron Walden (FR)—Magic Feeling (IRE) **T. B. Tarn**
4 **BOBS LORD TARA,** 5, b g Kayf Tara—Bob Back's Lady (IRE) **J. R. Wills**
5 **CHEVALGRIS,** 5, gr g Verglas (IRE)—Danzelline **D. C. Young**
6 **DANCIN ALPHA,** 4, ch g Bahamian Bounty—Phoebe Woodstock (IRE) **Elm Row Racing Syndicate**
7 **DARK RULER (IRE),** 6, b g Dark Angel (IRE)—Gino Lady (IRE) **Mr K. Walters**
8 **DEEP RESOLVE (IRE),** 4, b g Intense Focus (USA)—I'll Be Waiting **Panther Racing Limited**
9 **DIVINE PORT (USA),** 5, b g Arch (USA)—Out of Reach **Mr C. G. Harrison**
10 **ENTIHAA,** 7, b g Tiger Hill (IRE)—Magic Tree (UAE) **Elsa Crankshaw & G. Allan**
11 **EUTROPIUS (IRE),** 6, b g Ad Valorem (USA)—Peps (IRE) **Mr A. J. Sparks**
12 **FLY HOME HARRY,** 6, b g Sir Harry Lewis (USA)—Fly Home **Mrs J. M. Penney**
13 **GOGEO (IRE),** 8, b g Val Royal (FR)—Steal 'em **Mrs J. Porter**
14 **HAIL BOLD CHIEF (USA),** 8, b g Dynaformer (USA)—Yanaseeni (USA)
15 **I'M SUPER TOO (IRE),** 8, b g Fasliyev (USA)—Congress (IRE) **D. C. Young**
16 **IN FOCUS (IRE),** 4, ch c Intense Focus (USA)—Reine de Neige **Mr G. H. Bell**
17 **JOHN DORY (IRE),** 4, b g Excellent Art—Elauyun (IRE) **The Trio Syndicate**
18 **KINEMA (IRE),** 4, b g Galileo (IRE)—Bon Nuit (IRE) **Mrs T. Blackett**
19 **LADY KASHAAN (IRE),** 6, b m Manduro (GER)—Lady's Secret (IRE) **Mr G. Brogan**
20 **LIBRAN (IRE),** 4, b g Lawman (FR)—True Crystal (IRE) **Mrs J. Porter**
21 **LIGHT OF ASIA (IRE),** 4, b g Oratorio (IRE)—Lucy Cavendish (USA) **Mrs B. V. Sangster**
22 **LOTHAIR (IRE),** 6, b g Holy Roman Emperor (IRE)—Crafty Example (USA) **Mrs J. Porter**
23 **MICKLEGATE RUN,** 4, b g Tiger Hill (IRE)—Mamoura (IRE) **Mr A. J. Sparks**
24 **MINIONETTE (IRE),** 4, b f Manduro (GER)—La Vita E Bella (IRE) **Elsa Crankshaw & G. Allan**
25 **MISS BURNETT (USA),** 4, ch f Mr Greeley (USA)—Tink So (USA) **Mrs G. Sparks**
26 **MITCHELL'S WAY,** 8, ch g Needwood Blade—Ghana (GER) **Ontoawinner 2**
27 **MOONSHINE RIDGE (IRE),** 4, b f Duke of Marmalade (IRE)—Dreams Come True (FR) **Elm Row Racing Syndicate**
28 **MOORSHOLM (IRE),** 4, b g High Chaparral (IRE)—Arctic Freedom (USA) **Mr & Mrs Melvyn Miller**
29 **MUJAAHER (IRE),** 4, ch g Nayef (USA)—Raaya (USA) **Elm Row Racing Syndicate**
30 **NATIVE FALLS (IRE),** 4, ch g Elnadim (USA)—Sagrada (GER) **Ms A. McCubbin**
31 **NORTHSIDE PRINCE (IRE),** 9, b g Desert Prince (IRE)—Spartan Girl (IRE) **Mrs J. M. Penney**

## MR ALAN SWINBANK - Continued

32 **NUSANTARA,** 4, b f New Approach (IRE)—Pentatonic **Elm Row Syndicate 2**
33 **ONE MORE GO (IRE),** 4, b g Papal Bull—Enchanted Wood (IRE) **B. Valentine**
34 **PHOENIX RETURNS (IRE),** 7, br g Phoenix Reach (IRE)—Oscar's Lady (IRE) **Mrs J. Porter**
35 **RALPHY LAD (IRE),** 4, b g Iffraaj—Hawattef (IRE) **The Trio Syndicate**
36 4, B f Byron—Skiddaw Wolf **J. R. Wills**
37 **STANARLEY PIC,** 4, b g Piccolo—Harlestone Lady **The Twopin Partnership**
38 **TEN TREES,** 5, b m Millkom—Island Path (IRE) **Mr J. Nelson**
39 **TINY DANCER (IRE),** 7, b g Darsi (FR)—Taipans Girl (IRE) **Ms A. J. McCubbin**

### THREE-YEAR-OLDS

40 B c Beat Hollow—Dombeya (IRE) **Mr G. McCann**
41 **GOLD PURSUIT,** b g Pastoral Pursuits—Goldeva **B. Valentine**
42 **LOPES DANCER (IRE),** b g Lope de Vega (IRE)—Ballet Dancer (IRE) **Mr C. G. Harrison**
43 B g Le Havre (IRE)—Mambo Mistress (USA) **Mr G. McCann**
44 B c Bushranger (IRE)—Prealpina (IRE) **B. Valentine**
45 B c Equiano (FR)—Sharplaw Venture **B. Valentine**

### TWO-YEAR-OLDS

46 B c 23/4 Arcano (IRE)—Bryanstown Girl (IRE) (Kalanisi (IRE)) (16000) **Iris Gibson**
47 B f 19/2 Pour Moi (IRE)—Garra Molly (IRE) (Nayef (USA)) (9523) **Mr B. Valentine**
48 Gr c 9/4 Strategic Prince—Golden Rose (GER) (Winged Love (IRE)) (10317) **The Trio Syndicate**
49 B f 27/3 Roderic O'Connor (IRE)—Halicardia (Halling (USA)) (18253) **Elm Row Racing Syndicate**
50 Gr c 15/1 Zebedee—La Bella Grande (IRE) (Giant's Causeway (USA)) (15872) **Mr B. Valentine**
51 B c 2/2 Aqlaam—Miss Cambridge (Dubawi (IRE)) (5000) **S. Haynes**
52 B c 2/5 Pour Moi (IRE)—Noble Pearl (GER) (Dashing Blade) (27777) **Mr G. McCann**
53 B c 13/4 Lawman (FR)—Second Act (Sadler's Wells (USA)) (27777) **Mrs J. Porter**
54 Ch c 9/3 Arcano (IRE)—Shulammite Woman (IRE) (Desert Sun) (22000) **S. Haynes**

**Other Owners:** Mr G. Allan, P. Blackett, S. Clark, Miss Elsa Crankshaw, R. Ellis, P. Ellis, Fantails Restaurant, Iris Gibson, S. Hall, Miss Sally R. Haynes, Mr Arnold Headdock, Mr K. Hogg, Mr K. Hogg, Mrs D. Jeromson, Mr N. J. O'Brien, Dr Roy Palmer, W. Perratt, D. Pitcher, P. Richards, Ben Sangster, Miss M. Swinbank, Mrs T. Tarn, Mr J. Tweddall.

**Assistant Trainers:** Mr W.W. Haigh, Miss Sally Haynes

**Jockey (flat):** David Allan, Ben Curtis, Robert Winston. **Jockey (NH):** Paddy Brennan, Paul Moloney.
**Conditional:** Jake Greenall. **Amateur:** Mr A. Bartlett, Mr O. R. J. Sangster.

---

## 588 MR TOM SYMONDS, Hentland

Postal: **Dason Court Cottage, Hentland, Ross-on-Wye, Herefordshire, HR9 6LW**
Contacts: **PHONE (01989) 730869 MOBILE (07823) 324649**
**E-MAIL dasoncourt@gmail.com WEBSITE www.thomassymonds.co.uk**

1 **ACCORDINGTOJODIE (IRE),** 9, b g Accordion—La Fiamma (FR) **Sir Peter & Lady Gibbings**
2 **ALBERTO'S DREAM,** 6, b g Fantastic Spain (USA)—Molly's Folly **Wallys Dream Syndicate**
3 **ARDEN DENIS (IRE),** 6, ch g Generous (IRE)—Christian Lady (IRE) **T. C. and A. Winter & Partners**
4 **BAR BOY (IRE),** 6, gr g Acambaro (GER)—Carminda Thyne (IRE) **Sir Peter & Lady Gibbings**
5 **BRIERY BLOSSOM,** 6, b m Norse Dancer (IRE)—Hong Kong Classic **Mrs H Plumbly J Trafford K Deane S Holme**
6 **BRIERY BUBBLES,** 7, br m Grape Tree Road—Hong Kong Classic **The Mumbo Jumbos**
7 **CARHUE PRINCESS (IRE),** 9, b m Desert Prince (IRE)—Carhue Journey (IRE) **The Ever Hopeful Partnership**
8 **DIXIE BULL (IRE),** 10, br g Milan—Calora (USA) **Bailey-Carvill Equine**
9 **DUKE OF MONMOUTH (IRE),** 8, b g Presenting—Hayley Cometh (IRE) **Bryan & Philippa Burrough**
10 **DUNMALLET BELLE,** 6, b m Kayf Tara—Magic Mistress **Brian J Griffiths & John Nicholson**
11 **EATON ROCK (IRE),** 6, b g Rocamadour—Duchess of Kinsale (IRE) **Mr K. J. Price**
12 **FALCONS FALL (IRE),** 4, ch g Vertical Speed (FR)—Ellie Park (IRE) **Mr T. R. Symonds**
13 **FOXCUB (IRE),** 7, b g Bahri (USA)—Foxglove **Celia & Michael Baker**
14 **FRANKLY SPEAKING,** 5, ch g Flemensfirth (USA)—No More Money **David Jenks & Celia & Michael Baker**
15 **HIDDEN LINK,** 5, b g Rail Link—Gloved Hand **Mr T. R. Symonds**
16 **HOME FOR TEA,** 6, b g Westerner—Wolnai **Mr Ian Low & Mr Peter Crawford**
17 **KAKI DE LA PREE (FR),** 8, b g Kapgarde (FR)—Kica (FR) **Sir Peter & Lady Gibbings**
18 **KATARRHINI,** 6, b m Kayf Tara—Dedrunknmunky (IRE) **Mrs K. Casini**
19 **KINGS APOLLO,** 6, b g King's Theatre (IRE)—Temple Dancer **G & M Roberts, Churchward, Frost, Green, W-Williams**
20 **LAST ECHO (IRE),** 4, b f Whipper (USA)—Priory Rock (IRE) **Wainwright, Hill, Cheshire & Rowlinson**

## MR TOM SYMONDS - Continued

21 **LEWIS,** 6, b g Kayf Tara—Island of Memories (IRE) **Celia & Michael Baker**
22 **LIME STREET (IRE),** 4, b g Presenting—Specifiedrisk (IRE) **Valda Burke & Bryan Burrough**
23 **MIDNIGHT BELLE,** 8, b m Midnight Legend—Cherry Alley (IRE) **Mrs P. E. Holtorp**
24 **MR OOOSH,** 5, b g Midnight Legend—Blackbriery Thyne (IRE) **T. C. and A. Winter & Partners**
25 **SNATCHITBACK,** 4, b g Overbury (IRE)—Talk The Talk **Mark & Jane Frieze**
26 **STRAITS OF MESSINA (IRE),** 6, b g Mountain High (IRE)—Scylla **Lost In Space**
27 **SUMMER SOUNDS (IRE),** 6, b br g Definite Article—Marble Sound (IRE) **Sir Peter & Lady Gibbings**
28 **TED DOLLY (IRE),** 11, b br g Bob's Return (IRE)—Little Pearl (IRE) **Mr T. R. Symonds**
29 **THEATREBAR,** 7, b g King's Theatre (IRE)—Ardenbar **Mrs C. A. Wyatt**
30 **TROJAN SUN,** 9, b br g Kayf Tara—Sun Dante (IRE) **I. A. Low**

**Other Owners:** Mr Alan Abbott, Mr Philip Andrews, Mr R. F. Bailey, Mrs Celia Baker, Mr Michael Baker, Mrs P. J. Buckler, Mrs Valda Burke, Mr B. R. H. Burrough, Mrs Philippa Burrough, Mr R. K. Carvill, Mr Peter Crawford, Mrs K. Deane, Mrs Jane Frieze, Mr Mark Frieze, Sir Peter Gibbings, Lady Gibbings, Mr F. M. Green, Mr Brian J. Griffiths, Mrs Gwen Griffiths, Mrs S. Holme, Mr David Jenks, Mr I. A. Low, Mr Jeremy Mason, Mr J. M. Nicholson, Mr Roy Ovel, Mrs Helen Plumbly, Mr R. T. R. Price, Mr G. A. Roberts, Mrs Jane Rowlinson, Mr Thomas R. Symonds, Mrs Jane Symonds, Mrs Jane Trafford, Mr Michael Wainwright, Mr T. Winter, Mr A. Winter, Mr C. Winter.

**Jockey (NH):** Felix De Giles. **Conditional:** Ben Poste. **Amateur:** Mr James Nixon.

---

## 589 MR JAMES TATE, Newmarket

Postal: **Jamesfield Place, Hamilton Road, Newmarket, Suffolk, CB8 7JQ**
Contacts: **PHONE (01638) 669861 FAX (01638) 676634 MOBILE (07703) 601283**
**E-MAIL james@jamestateracing.com WEBSITE www.jamestateracing.com**

1 **BLHADAWA (IRE),** 4, b f Iffraaj—Trois Heures Apres **Sheikh J. D. Al Maktoum**
2 **LAMAR (IRE),** 4, b f Cape Cross (IRE)—Deveron (USA) **S. Ali**
3 **RUWAIYAN (USA),** 6, b br h Cape Cross (IRE)—Maskunah (IRE) **S. Manana**
4 **RUWASI,** 4, b c Authorized (IRE)—Circle of Love **S. Manana**
5 **SBRAASE,** 4, ch c Sir Percy—Hermanita **S. Manana**
6 **URBAN CASTLE (USA),** 4, b f Street Cry (IRE)—Cloud Castle **S. Manana**

## THREE-YEAR-OLDS

7 **AL FAREEJ (IRE),** b f Iffraaj—Shining Hour (USA) **S. Ali**
8 **CEASELESS (IRE),** b f Iffraaj—Sheer Bliss (IRE) **Sheikh R. D. Al Maktoum**
9 **CLAMPDOWN,** ch g Kheleyf (USA)—Miss McGuire **S. Manana**
10 **DANSEUR NOBLE,** b c Kheleyf (USA)—Posy Fossil (USA) **S. Manana**
11 **DARKENING NIGHT,** b c Cape Cross (IRE)—Garanciere (FR) **Sheikh J. D. Al Maktoum**
12 B f Bahamian Bounty—Dream In Waiting **S. Ali**
13 Ch f Raven's Pass (USA)—Edetana (USA) **S. Manana**
14 **FARAAJH (IRE),** ch f Iffraaj—Neshla **S. Manana**
15 **FIT THE BILL (IRE),** b c Iffraaj—Najam **S. Manana**
16 **FREE ENTRY (IRE),** b f Approve (IRE)—Dear Catch (IRE) **Sheikh R. D. Al Maktoum**
17 **GOLD SANDS (IRE),** b f Cape Cross (IRE)—Lil's Jessy (IRE) **S. Manana**
18 **GROOR,** b c Archipenko (USA)—Alta Moda **Sheikh J. D. Al Maktoum**
19 B f Bahamian Bounty—Intermission (IRE) **S. Manana**
20 **JAIYANA,** b f Dansili—Jira **S. Manana**
21 Ch c Aqlaam—Kunda (IRE) **S. Manana**
22 **LADY MOSCOU (IRE),** b f Sir Percy—Place de Moscou (IRE) **S. Manana**
23 **LIGHT AND SHADE,** b f Aqlaam—Tara Moon **S. Manana**
24 **LIGHT WAVE (IRE),** b c Echo of Light—Meynell **S. Ali**
25 **MIDDLE EAST PEARL,** b f Equiano (FR)—Zia (GER) **S. Ali**
26 **NAMHROODAH (IRE),** br gr f Sea The Stars (IRE)—Independant **S. Manana**
27 **NEW SAABOOG,** b f New Approach (IRE)—Saabiq (USA) **S. Ali**
28 **NICE THOUGHTS (IRE),** b c Shamardal (USA)—Zacheta **S. Ali**
29 **OFFSHORE,** gr c Iffraaj—Ronaldsay **S. Manana**
30 **QUEST FOR WONDER,** b f Makfi—Sinndiya (IRE) **S. Ali**
31 B f Medaglia d'Oro (USA)—Rajeem **S. Manana**
32 **REVERENT (IRE),** b f Teofilo (IRE)—Wadaat **S. Manana**
33 **SECRET LIAISON (IRE),** b f Dandy Man (IRE)—Kiss And Don'tell (USA) **Sheikh R. D. Al Maktoum**
34 **SIREN'S COVE,** b f Sir Percy—Siren Sound **S. Ali**
35 **SLOVAK (IRE),** ch f Iffraaj—Bratislava **S. Manana**
36 **STAMP OF AUTHORITY (IRE),** b c Invincible Spirit (IRE)—Silver Bracelet **Sheikh J. D. Al Maktoum**
37 **SUNNY YORK (IRE),** b f Vale of York (IRE)—Alexander Ridge (IRE) **S. Ali**

## MR JAMES TATE - Continued

**38 SUPERLATIVE (IRE),** ch f Iffraaj—Slieve Mish (IRE) **S. Manana**
**39 TAAQAH (USA),** b br f Arch (USA)—Classic West (USA) **Sheikh J. D. Al Maktoum**
**40** Ch f Teofilo (IRE)—Zam Zoom (IRE) **S. Manana**

## TWO-YEAR-OLDS

**41** Ch c 25/3 Lope de Vega (IRE)—Aglow (Spinning World (USA)) (48000) **Sheikh J. D. Al Maktoum**
**42** B f 8/4 Dream Ahead (USA)—Ballymore Lady (USA) (War Chant (USA)) (47000) **S. Ali**
**43** B f 6/2 Arch (USA)—Banyan Street (USA) (Gone West (USA)) (86058) **Sheikh J. D. Al Maktoum**
**44** B c 15/4 Dubawi (IRE)—Casanga (IRE) (Rainbow Quest (USA)) (100000) **S. Ali**
**45 DUBAWI FIFTY,** b c 6/4 Dubawi (IRE)—Plethora (Sadler's Wells (USA)) (50000) **S. Ali**
**46** B f 14/2 Kyllachy—Eucharist (IRE) (Acclamation) (64761) **Sheikh R. D. Al Maktoum**
**47** Ch f 5/5 Exceed And Excel (AUS)—Fashionable (Nashwan (USA)) (119047) **Sheikh J. D. Al Maktoum**
**48** Ch f 28/1 Iffraaj—Funday (Daylami (IRE)) (27000) **S. Ali**
**49** Ch f 27/4 Equiano (FR)—Gay Romance (Singspiel (IRE)) (10000) **S. Manana**
**50** B c 30/4 Lilbourne Lad (IRE)—Gold Again (USA) (Touch Gold (USA)) (65000) **Sheikh R. D. Al Maktoum**
**51** Ch f 10/3 Raven's Pass (USA)—Guarantia (Selkirk (USA)) (16000) **S. Manana**
**52** B f 25/3 Dream Ahead (USA)—Jallaissine (IRE) (College Chapel) (21000) **S. Manana**
**53** B f 7/5 Dansili—Jira (Medicean) (65000) **S. Manana**
**54** Ch c 19/1 Stormy Atlantic (USA)—Kiswahili (Selkirk (USA)) (40000) **S. Ali**
**55** B f 12/3 Dream Ahead (USA)—Knapton Hill (Zamindar (USA)) (82000) **S. Ali**
**56** Ch f 23/3 Iffraaj—Lanzana (IRE) (Kalanisi (IRE)) (71428) **Sheikh R. D. Al Maktoum**
**57** B c 14/4 Dream Ahead (USA)—Leopard Creek (Weldnaas (USA)) (59523) **Sheikh R. D. Al Maktoum**
**58** B c 12/4 Motivator—Lindy Hop (IRE) (Danehill Dancer (IRE)) (15000) **S. Manana**
**59** B f 30/4 Sir Percy—Lyric Art (USA) (Red Ransom (USA)) (20000) **S. Ali**
**60** B f 22/1 Iffraaj—Lysandra (IRE) (Danehill (USA)) (28571) **Sheikh J. D. Al Maktoum**
**61** B c 16/2 Dark Angel (IRE)—Miss Windley (IRE) (Oratorio (IRE)) (50000) **S. Manana**
**62** Br f 16/2 Dick Turpin (IRE)—Misty Eyed (IRE) (Paris House) (32000) **S. Manana**
**63** B f 25/4 Iffraaj—Mitawa (IRE) (Alhaarth (IRE)) (22000) **Sheikh R. D. Al Maktoum**
**64** B c 1/3 Iffraaj—Musical Sands (Green Desert (USA)) (50000) **S. Ali**
**65** Br f 13/2 Diktat—Najraan (Cadeaux Genereux) **S. Manana**
**66** B c 5/2 Kyllachy—On Her Way (Medicean) (47000) **S. Ali**
**67** B f 31/1 Makfi—Party (IRE) (Cadeaux Genereux) (60000) **S. Ali**
**68** B f 29/3 Iffraaj—Peace Signal (USA) (Time For A Change (USA)) (70000) **Sheikh J. D. Al Maktoum**
**69** B c 24/3 Bushranger (IRE)—Rajmahal (UAE) (Indian Ridge) (18000) **Sheikh J. D. Al Maktoum**
**70** B c 26/4 Medicean—Red Camellia (Polar Falcon (USA)) (30000) **S. Manana**
**71** Gr c 11/4 Dandy Man (IRE)—Red Riddle (IRE) (Verglas (IRE)) (47619) **Sheikh R. D. Al Maktoum**
**72** B f 5/3 Pivotal—Saadiah (IRE) (Dubai Destination (USA)) (20000) **S. Manana**
**73** B c 8/5 Aqlaam—Sabaweeya (Street Cry (IRE)) **S. Ali**
**74** B f 21/2 Kodiac—Sheila Blige (Zamindar (USA)) (59047) **Sheikh J. D. Al Maktoum**
**75** B c 25/3 Arcano (IRE)—Spanish Pride (IRE) (Night Shift (USA)) (38000) **Sheikh R. D. Al Maktoum**
**76** B f 2/5 Cape Cross (IRE)—Sri Kandi (Pivotal) (20000) **S. Manana**
**77** Ch c 11/3 Medicean—Stagecoach Jade (IRE) (Peintre Celebre (USA)) (25000) **S. Manana**
**78** Br c 20/4 Cape Cross (IRE)—Stairway To Glory (IRE) (Kalanisi (IRE)) (23000) **S. Ali**
**79** B f 3/2 Teofilo (IRE)—Sunset Avenue (USA) (Street Cry (IRE)) (80000) **S. Ali**
**80** B f 18/2 Kheleyf (USA)—Takawiri (IRE) (Danehill (USA)) (12000) **S. Manana**
**81** Gr f 16/3 Dark Angel (IRE)—The Hermitage (IRE) (Kheleyf (USA)) (9000) **S. Manana**
**82** B c 20/3 Sir Percy—Whole Grain (Polish Precedent (USA)) (65000) **S. Manana**

**Assistant Trainer:** Mrs Lucinda Tate

---

## 590 MR TOM TATE, Tadcaster

Postal: **Castle Farm, Hazelwood, Tadcaster, North Yorkshire, LS24 9NJ**
Contacts: **PHONE (01937) 836036 FAX (01937) 530011 MOBILE (07970) 122818**
**E-MAIL tomtate@castlefarmstables.fsnet.co.uk WEBSITE www.tomtate.co.uk**

**1 AHOY THERE (IRE),** 4, ch g Captain Rio—Festivite (IRE) **Ms M. F. Cassidy & Mr T. P. Tate**
**2 EAGLE ROCK (IRE),** 7, b g High Chaparral (IRE)—Silk Fan (IRE) **The Ivy Syndicate**
**3 EMPRESS ALI (IRE),** 4, b f Holy Roman Emperor (IRE)—Almansa (IRE) **T T Racing**
**4 PRINCE OF JOHANNE (IRE),** 9, gr g Johannesburg (USA)—Paiute Princess (FR) **Mr D. Storey**

## MR TOM TATE - Continued

### THREE-YEAR-OLDS

5 **DOCTOR WATSON,** ch g Winker Watson—Cibenze **T T Racing**
6 **RED HARRY (IRE),** ch c Manduro (GER)—Iktidar **Mr Peter Harrison**
7 **SHEMAY,** b f Shirocco (GER)—Shemanikha (FR) **T T Racing**

### TWO-YEAR-OLDS

**8** B f 1/5 Royal Applause—Anthurium (GER) (Hector Protector (USA)) (10476) **T T Racing**
**9** B f 12/3 Stimulation (IRE)—Ellway Queen (USA) (Bahri (USA)) (5714) **T T Racing**
10 **LE ROI DU TEMPS (USA),** ch c 8/3 Leroidesanimaux (BRZ)—
Minute Limit (IRE) (Pivotal) (18095) **Mr Peter Harrison**
**11** B c 25/1 Dick Turpin (IRE)—Presto Levanter (Rock of Gibraltar (IRE)) (26666) **Ms M. F. Cassidy**

**Other Owners:** Ms Fionnuala Cassidy, Mr Peter Harrison, Mr D. M. W. Hodgkiss, Mrs S. Hodgkiss, Mr Peter Mina, Mr David Storey, Mrs Hazel Tate, Mr T. P. Tate.

**Assistant Trainer:** Hazel Tate

**Jockey (flat):** Andrew Elliott, James Sullivan. **Jockey (NH):** Dougie Costello.

---

## 591 MR COLIN TEAGUE, Wingate

Postal: **Bridgefield Farm, Trimdon Lane, Station Town, Wingate, Co. Durham, TS28 5NE**
Contacts: **PHONE (01429) 837087 MOBILE (07967) 330929**
**E-MAIL colin.teague@btopenworld.com**

1 **DURHAM EXPRESS (IRE),** 8, b g Acclamation—Edwina (IRE) **Mr J. C. Johnson**
2 **JALDARSHAAN (IRE),** 8, b m Fath (USA)—Jaldini (IRE) **T. B. Tarn**
3 **MONTE PATTINO (USA),** 11, ch g Rahy (USA)—Jood (USA) **A. Rice**
4 **ON THE HIGH TOPS (IRE),** 7, b g Kheleyf (USA)—Diplomats Daughter **A. Rice**
5 **RUBICON BAY (IRE),** 8, b m One Cool Cat (USA)—Mrs Moonlight **Collins Chauffeur Driven Executive Cars**

### THREE-YEAR-OLDS

6 **SATNAV STAN,** ch c Phoenix Reach (IRE)—Pink Supreme **A. Rice**

---

## 592 MR ROGER TEAL, Epsom

Postal: **Thirty Acre Barn Stables, Shepherds Walk, Epsom, Surrey, KT18 6BX**
Contacts: **PHONE (01372) 279535 FAX (01372) 271981 MOBILE (07710) 325521**
**E-MAIL rteal@thirtyacre.co.uk WEBSITE www.thirtyacrestables.co.uk**

1 **BERKELEY VALE,** 4, b g Three Valleys (USA)—Intriguing Glimpse **Mrs Muriel Forward & Dr G. C. Forward**
2 **JACK OF DIAMONDS (IRE),** 6, b g Red Clubs (IRE)—Sakkara Star (IRE) **Inside Track Racing Club**
3 **JOHNNY SPLASH (IRE),** 6, b g Dark Angel (IRE)—Ja Ganhou **Mr B. Kitcherside**
4 **LANGLEY VALE,** 6, b g Piccolo—Running Glimpse (IRE) **Mrs Muriel Forward & Dr G. C. Forward**
5 **MISS LILLIE,** 4, b f Exceed And Excel (AUS)—Never Lose **The Rat Racers**
6 **PUCON,** 6, b m Kyllachy—The Fugative **Mr J. A. Redmond**
7 **STORM RUN (IRE),** 4, ch f Hurricane Run (IRE)—Jabroot (IRE) **The Thirty Acre Racing Partnership**
8 **THE TICHBORNE (IRE),** 7, b g Shinko Forest (IRE)—Brunswick **Mr Chris Simpson & Mr Mick Waghorn**
9 **TIGERS TALE (IRE),** 6, b g Tiger Hill (IRE)—Vayenga (FR) **Mr B. Kitcherside & Big Cat Partnership**
10 **TILSTARR (IRE),** 5, b m Shamardal (USA)—Vampire Queen (IRE) **Homecroft Wealth Racing**

### THREE-YEAR-OLDS

**11** B c Cockney Rebel (IRE)—Intriguing Glimpse **A. J. Morton**
12 **ROSIE ROYALE (IRE),** gr f Verglas (IRE)—Fearn Royal (IRE) **The Idle B'S**
13 **VINAMAR (IRE),** b f Approve (IRE)—Shalev (GER) **Mr J. A. Redmond**

### TWO-YEAR-OLDS

**14** B f 15/5 Holy Roman Emperor (IRE)—Freedom (GER) (Second Empire (IRE)) (10000)
15 **ORMERING,** b f 27/2 Kyllachy—Lihou Island (Beveled (USA)) (25000) **The Idle B's 2**
16 **ROBERTO LOPEZ,** b g 5/4 Royal Applause—The Fugative (Nicholas (USA)) (15000) **Mr J. A. Redmond**
**17** Br c 17/5 Manduro (GER)—Saree (Barathea (IRE)) (8000) **Mr John Morton**

**Other Owners:** Mrs Emma Curley, Mr Barry Kitcherside, Mr R. Kolien, Mr John Morton, Mr S. J. Piper, Mrs R. Pott, Mr E. Sames, Mr Darren Waterer, Mr Martin Wynn.

## 593 MR HENRY TETT, Lambourn

Postal: **Wormstall, Wickham, Newbury, Berkshire, RG20 8HB**
Contacts: **MOBILE (07796) 098220**
**E-MAIL htett@hotmail.com WEBSITE www.henrytettracing.co.uk**

1 **BALLY GUNNER,** 10, br g Needle Gun (IRE)—Rich Pickings **The Bally Gunners**
2 **ELEGANT OLIVE,** 12, b m Alflora (IRE)—Strong Cloth (IRE) **Collective Dreamers**
3 **GYPSY RIDER,** 6, b g Ishiguru (USA)—Spaniola (IRE) **The Racing 4 Fun Partnership**
4 **LADY CLICHE,** 6, b m Kirkwall—Madam Cliche **The Maderson Blue Partnership**
5 **VICTORY RICH (IRE),** 4, b g Kheleyf (USA)—Imperial Graf (USA) **Mrs Victoria Tett**

**Other Owners:** R. Curtis, Mrs D. S. Gibbs, Mrs P. McCluskey, Mr H. G. M. Tett.

**Jockey (NH):** Hadden Frost. **Amateur:** Mr Fred Tett.

## 594 MR DAVID THOMPSON, Darlington

Postal: **South View Racing, Ashley Cottage, South View, Bolam, Darlington, Co. Durham, DL2 2UP**
Contacts: **PHONE (01388) 835806 (01388) 832658 FAX (01325) 835806 MOBILE (07795) 161657**
**E-MAIL dwthompson61@hotmail.co.uk WEBSITE www.dwthompson.co.uk**

1 **BALLYTHOMAS,** 8, b g Kayf Tara—Gregale **Mr Alan Moore & Mr Tony Livingston**
2 **BOWDLER'S MAGIC,** 8, b g Hernando (FR)—Slew The Moon (ARG) **Mr N. Park**
3 **IZBUSHKA (IRE),** 4, b g Bushranger (IRE)—Zaynaba (IRE) **J. A. Moore**
4 **LORD ROB,** 4, b g Rob Roy (USA)—First Grey **A. Suddes**
5 **TESTING (FR),** 4, gr f New Approach (IRE)—Testama (FR) **Mr A. Sayers**
6 **TROUBLED (IRE),** 8, b g Vinnie Roe (IRE)—Tart of Tipp (IRE) **Mr T. J. A. Thompson**
7 **WEYBRIDGE LIGHT,** 10, b g Fantastic Light (USA)—Nuryana **J. A. Moore**
8 **ZAMASTAR,** 4, b g Zamindar (USA)—Kissogram **Wildcard Racing Syndicate**
9 **ZRUDA,** 4, b f Observatory (USA)—Pagan Princess **Mr K. M. Everitt**

**Other Owners:** Mr A. J. Bonarius, Mr N. J. Bonarius, Mr A. J. Livingston.

**Assistant Trainer:** A Dickman

**Jockey (flat):** Andrew Elliott, Tony Hamilton.

## 595 MR VICTOR THOMPSON, Alnwick

Postal: **Link House Farm, Newton By The Sea, Embleton, Alnwick, Northumberland, NE66 3ED**
Contacts: **PHONE (01665) 576272 MOBILE (07739) 626248**

1 **CHANCEOFA LIFETIME (IRE),** 8, ch g Beneficial—Bounty Queen (IRE) **V. Thompson**
2 **CHOSEN KEYS (IRE),** 9, b m Well Chosen—Lost Keys (IRE) **V. Thompson**
3 **COBH NATIONAL (IRE),** 7, b g Millenary—Not A Bother Tohim (IRE) **V. Thompson**
4 **DUHALLOWCOUNTRY (IRE),** 9, b g Beneficial—Milltown Lass (IRE) **V. Thompson**
5 **GIN COBBLER,** 9, b g Beneficial—Cassia **V. Thompson**
6 **HAVE ONE FOR ME (IRE),** 8, b g Sonus (IRE)—Dunmanogue (IRE) **V. Thompson**
7 **INDIAN PRINT (IRE),** 11, ch g Blueprint (IRE)—Commanche Glen (IRE) **V. Thompson**
8 **KING OF THE DARK (IRE),** 8, b g Zagreb (USA)—Dark Bird (IRE) **V. Thompson**
9 **MONOGRAM,** 11, ch g Karinga Bay—Dusky Dante (IRE) **V. Thompson**
10 **MR SHAHADY (IRE),** 10, b g Xaar—Shunaire (USA) **V. Thompson**
11 **NELLY LA RUE (IRE),** 8, b m Flemensfirth (USA)—Desperately Hoping (IRE) **V. Thompson**
12 **SENOR ALCO (FR),** 9, gr g Dom Alco (FR)—Alconea (FR) **V. Thompson**
13 **SHARIVARRY (FR),** 9, ch g Ballingarry (IRE)—Sharsala (IRE) **V. Thompson**
14 **STONEY (IRE),** 8, b g Stowaway—Classical Rachel (IRE) **V. Thompson**
15 **TOMMYS LAD (IRE),** 9, br g Luso—Monalee Dream (IRE) **V. Thompson**
16 **TOMMYSTEEL (IRE),** 10, br g Craigsteel—Sarahs Music (IRE) **V. Thompson**
17 **TWO STROKE (IRE),** 9, b br g Turtle Island (IRE)—Bannockburn (IRE) **V. Thompson**
18 **WAR ON (IRE),** 8, br g Presenting—Alannico **V. Thompson**

**Assistant Trainer:** M Thompson

## 596 MR SANDY THOMSON, Greenlaw

Postal: **Lambden, Greenlaw, Duns, Berwickshire, TD10 6UN**
Contacts: **PHONE (01361) 810211 MOBILE (07876) 142787**
**E-MAIL sandy@lambdenfarm.co.uk WEBSITE www.lambdenracing.co.uk**

1 **ANY GIVEN MOMENT (IRE),** 9, b g Alhaarth (IRE)—Shastri (USA) **Mr & Mrs A. M. Thomson**
2 **BLUE KASCADE (IRE),** 8, ch g Kaieteur (USA)—Lydia Blue (IRE) **Mrs Q. R. Thomson**
3 **BUCKLED,** 5, b g Midnight Legend—Mulberry Wine **Matros Racing 2**
4 **CHAIN OF BEACONS,** 6, b g Midnight Legend—Millennium Girl **Mrs Q. R. Thomson**
5 **FLY VINNIE (IRE),** 6, b g Vinnie Roe (IRE)—Great Days (IRE) **Matros Racing 2**
6 **HARRY THE VIKING,** 10, ch g Sir Harry Lewis (USA)—
Viking Flame **Jim Beaumont, Douglas Pryde & Quona Thomson**
7 **IMPERIAL PRINCE (IRE),** 6, b g Subtle Power (IRE)—Satco Rose (IRE) **W Muir & Matros Racing 2**
8 **JUST AWAKE,** 8, b g Prince Daniel (USA)—Katinka **Mr & Mrs A. M. Thomson**
9 **KILQUIGGAN (IRE),** 7, gr g Vinnie Roe (IRE)—Irene's Call (IRE) **Mrs Q. R. Thomson**
10 **MOSSIES WELL (IRE),** 6, b g Morozov (USA)—Kidora (IRE) **Matros Racing**
11 **NEPTUNE EQUESTER,** 12, b g Sovereign Water (FR)—All Things Nice **J. J. Beaumont**
12 **NETMINDER (IRE),** 9, b g Insatiable (IRE)—
Princess Douglas **Quona Thomson, David Spratt, Kevin McMunigal**
13 **OSCAR LATEEN (IRE),** 7, b g Oscar (IRE)—Storm Call **Mr J. R. Adam**
14 **PRAIRIE LAD,** 7, b g Alflora (IRE)—An Bothar Dubh **Mr J. R. Adam**
15 **SEEYOUATMIDNIGHT,** 7, b g Midnight Legend—Morsky Baloo **Mrs Q. R. Thomson**
16 **SELDOM INN,** 7, ch g Double Trigger (IRE)—Portland Row (IRE) **W. A. Walker**
17 **SPUR O THE MOMENT,** 6, b m Kayf Tara—Portland Row (IRE) **W. A. Walker**
18 **THE SHRIMP (IRE),** 8, gr g Indian Danehill (IRE)—Rheban Lass (IRE) **Mrs Q. R. Thomson**

**Other Owners:** Mr Jim Beaumont, Mr Kevin McMunigal, Mr William Muir, Mr D. G. Pryde, Mr D. Spratt, Exors of the Late Mr J. Stephenson, Mr R. Thayne, Mrs A. M. Thomson, Mr A. M. Thomson, Mr M. Wright.

**Assistant Trainer:** Mrs A. M. Thomson

## 597 MR NIGEL TINKLER, Malton

**Trainer did not wish details of his string to appear**

## 598 MR COLIN TIZZARD, Sherborne

Postal: **Venn Farm, Milborne Port, Sherborne, Dorset, DT9 5RA**
Contacts: **PHONE (01963) 250598 FAX (01963) 250598 MOBILE (07976) 778656**
**E-MAIL info@colintizzard.co.uk WEBSITE www.colintizzard.co.uk**

1 **ALLCHILLEDOUT,** 6, b g Alflora (IRE)—Miss Chinchilla **Gale Force Six**
2 4, B g Kayf Tara—Ardrom
3 **BEARS RAILS,** 5, b g Flemensfirth (USA)—Clandestine **P. M. Warren**
4 **BILLY NO NAME (IRE),** 7, b g Westerner—Just Little **Mrs J. R. Bishop**
5 4, B g Kayf Tara—Blue Ride (IRE) **R. G. Tizzard**
6 **BOLD CUFFS,** 6, b g Dutch Art—Chambray (IRE) **Mr J. P. Romans**
7 **BRAMBLE BROOK,** 5, b g Kayf Tara—Briery Ann **Brocade Racing**
8 **BUCKHORN TIMOTHY,** 6, b g Tamure (IRE)—Waimea Bay **The Buckhorn Racing Team**
9 **BUCKHORN TOM,** 7, b g Tamure (IRE)—Waimea Bay **The Buckhorn Racing Team**
10 4, B g Apple Tree (FR)—Chipewyas (FR) **D. V. Stevens**
11 **COTSWOLD ROAD,** 5, b g Flemensfirth (USA)—Crystal Ballerina (IRE) **Chasing Gold Limited**
12 **CUE CARD,** 9, b g King's Theatre (IRE)—Wicked Crack (IRE) **Mrs J. R. Bishop**
13 **DARK DESIRE,** 6, br g Generous (IRE)—Diletia **Chasing Gold Limited**
14 **DEAR DARLING,** 5, b m Midnight Legend—Easibrook Jane **Wendy & Malcolm Hezel**
15 **DEFINITE JOKER,** 6, b g Definite Article—Sabi Sand **K S B, Mr M Doughty & Mrs Sarah Tizzard**
16 **DUSKY LARK,** 5, b g Nayef (USA)—Snow Goose **Mrs Sara Biggins & Mrs Celia Djivanovic**
17 **EAST HILL,** 5, b g Lucarno (USA)—Sunnyland **The Con Club**
18 **FLAMING CHARMER (IRE),** 7, ch g Flemensfirth (USA)—Kates Charm (IRE) **Tom Chadney & Peter Green**
19 **FOURTH ACT (IRE),** 6, b g King's Theatre (IRE)—Erintante (IRE) **Mrs J. R. Bishop**
20 **GENTLEMAN JON,** 7, b g Beat All (USA)—Sudden Spirit (FR) **Mr J. P. Romans**
21 **GOLDEN CHIEFTAIN (IRE),** 10, b g Tikkanen (USA)—Golden Flower (GER) **Brocade Racing**
22 **GRAND VISION (IRE),** 9, gr g Old Vic—West Hill Rose (IRE) **J. T. Warner**

## MR COLIN TIZZARD - Continued

23 **HANDY ANDY (IRE),** 9, b g Beneficial—Maslam (IRE) **Brocade Racing**
24 **HAWAIAN ROSE,** 5, b m Helissio (FR)—Waimea Bay **Wendy & Malcolm Hezel**
25 **HEY BIG SPENDER (IRE),** 12, b g Rudimentary (USA)—Jims Monkey **Brocade Racing**
26 **IVOR'S KING (IRE),** 8, b g King's Theatre (IRE)—Christelle (IRE) **W. I. M. Perry**
27 **JUMPS ROAD,** 8, b g Clerkenwell (USA)—Diletia **Chasing Gold Limited**
28 **JUSTATENNER,** 4, b g Northern Legend—Shelayly (IRE) **Mrs S. I. Tainton**
29 **KINGFISHER CREEK,** 5, b g Kayf Tara—Symbiosis **Brocade Racing**
30 **KINGS LAD (IRE),** 8, b g King's Theatre (IRE)—Festival Leader (IRE) **G. F. Gingell**
31 **KINGS WALK (IRE),** 4, b g King's Theatre (IRE)—Shuil Sionnach (IRE) **Mrs J. R. Bishop**
32 **KINGSCOURT NATIVE (IRE),** 7, b g King's Theatre (IRE)—
Freydis (IRE) **K S B, Mr M Doughty & Mrs Sarah Tizzard**
33 **MARDEN COURT (IRE),** 5, b g Tikkanen (USA)—Shilling Hill (IRE) **J K Farms**
34 **MASTERS HILL (IRE),** 9, gr g Tikkanen (USA)—Leitrim Bridge (IRE) **K S B, Mr M Doughty & Mrs Sarah Tizzard**
35 **MOORLANDS MIST,** 8, gr g Fair Mix (IRE)—Sandford Springs (USA) **J. T. Warner**
36 **MORELLO ROYALE (IRE),** 5, b m King's Theatre (IRE)—Mystic Cherry (IRE) **Ann & Tony Gale**
37 **MURRAYANA (IRE),** 5, b g King's Theatre (IRE)—Royalrova (FR) **Mrs S. I. Tainton**
38 **NATIVE RIVER (IRE),** 5, ch g Indian River (FR)—Native Mo (IRE) **Brocade Racing**
39 **NEVER LEARN (IRE),** 4, b g King's Theatre (IRE)—
Hamari Gold (IRE) **Brocade Racing J P Romans Terry Warner**
40 **OHIO GOLD (IRE),** 9, b g Flemensfirth (USA)—Kiniohio (FR) **P. M. Warren**
41 **OISEAU DE NUIT (FR),** 13, b g Evening World (FR)—Idylle du Marais (FR) **J. T. Warner**
42 **QUITE BY CHANCE,** 6, b g Midnight Legend—Hop Fair **T Hamlin,J M Dare,J W Snook,J T Warner**
43 **ROBINSFIRTH (IRE),** 6, b g Flemensfirth (USA)—Phardester (IRE) **Christine Knowles & Wendy Carter**
44 **ROYAL VACATION (IRE),** 5, b g King's Theatre (IRE)—Summer Break (IRE) **Mrs J. R. Bishop**
45 **SANDY BEACH,** 5, b g Notnowcato—Picacho (IRE) **Brocade Racing**
46 **SEW ON TARGET (IRE),** 10, b g Needle Gun (IRE)—Ballykea (IRE) **A. G. Selway**
47 **SPENDING TIME,** 6, b g King's Theatre (IRE)—Karello Bay **Brocade Racing**
48 4, B g King's Theatre (IRE)—Steel Grey Lady (IRE) **J. W. Snook**
49 4, B g Ashkalani (IRE)—Stylish Type (IRE)
50 **THE CIDER MAKER,** 5, b g Kayf Tara—Dame Fonteyn **Mrs C Djivanovic, Joanna Tizzard, KSB**
51 **THEATRE GUIDE (IRE),** 8, b g King's Theatre (IRE)—Erintante (IRE) **Mrs J. R. Bishop**
52 **THEATRICAL STAR,** 9, b g King's Theatre (IRE)—Lucy Glitters **Brocade Racing**
53 **THIRD ACT (IRE),** 6, b g King's Theatre (IRE)—Starry Lady (IRE) **Blackmore Vale Syndicate**
54 **THIRD INTENTION (IRE),** 8, b g Azamour (IRE)—Third Dimension (FR) **Mr & Mrs R. Tizzard**
55 **THISTLECRACK,** 7, b g Kayf Tara—Ardstown **John & Heather Snook**
56 **TIKKAPICK (IRE),** 5, b g Tikkanen (USA)—Takeanotherpick (IRE) **Mrs S. I. Tainton**
57 **ULTRAGOLD (FR),** 7, b br g Kapgarde (FR)—Hot d'or (FR) **Brocade Racing J P Romans Terry Warner**
58 **VIRGINIA ASH (IRE),** 7, ch g Definite Article—Peace Time Girl (IRE) **Mr J. P. Romans**
59 **WEST APPROACH,** 5, b g Westerner—Ardstown **John & Heather Snook**
60 **WESTEND PRINCE (IRE),** 4, gr g King's Theatre (IRE)—Caltra Princess (IRE) **The Steal Syndicate**
61 **WHEN BEN WHEN (IRE),** 6, b g Beneficial—Almnadia (IRE) **Mrs S. I. Tainton**
62 **WIZARDS BRIDGE,** 6, b g Alflora (IRE)—Island Hopper **The Butterwick Syndicate**
63 **XAARCET (IRE),** 8, b g Xaar—Anoukit **The Missiles**
64 **ZANSTRA (IRE),** 5, b g Morozov (USA)—Enistar (IRE) **Moonrakers**

**Other Owners:** Mrs S. J. Biggins, Mr K. W. Biggins, Mr G. R. Broom, Mrs A. E. M. Broom, G. S. Brown, Mrs W. Carter, T. H. Chadney, Mr C. Cole, Mr C. E. G. Collier, Mr J. M. Dare, Mrs C. J. Djivanovic, Mr M. Doughty, Mr A. P. Gale, Mrs A. G. Gale, Mr R. Goodfellow, Mr P. Govier, Mr P. F. Govier, Mr P. C. W. Green, T. Hamlin, Mrs W. M. Hezel, Mr M. W. Hezel, Mr K. F. Honeybun, Mrs J. Honeybun, M. M. Hooker, Mrs C. Knowles, Mr E. N. Liddiard, Mr D. A. Mayes, Mr C. D. Pritchard, Mrs H. A. Snook, Mr D. J. Stevens, P. A. Stranger, Mrs S. L. Tizzard, Miss J. Tizzard, Mr E. R. Vickery.

**Assistant Trainers:** Mrs K. Gingell, Joe Tizzard

**Jockey (NH):** Daryl Jacobs, Brendan Powell. **Conditional:** Paul O'Brien. **Amateur:** Mr M. Legg.

---

## 599 MR MARTIN TODHUNTER, Penrith

Postal: **The Park, Orton, Penrith, Cumbria, CA10 3SD**
Contacts: **PHONE (01539) 624314 FAX (01539) 624811 MOBILE (07976) 440082**
**WEBSITE www.martintodhunter.co.uk**

1 **ACORDINGTOSCRIPT (IRE),** 9, ch g Accordion—Jane Jones (IRE) **The Surf & Turf Partnership**
2 **ALLANARD (IRE),** 11, b g Oscar (IRE)—Allatrim (IRE) **Mrs K. Hall**
3 **BONZO BING (IRE),** 7, b g Gold Well—She's A Dreamer (IRE) **Leeds Plywood & Doors Ltd**
4 **CARLOS FANDANGO (IRE),** 9, gr g Silver Patriarch (IRE)—Elegant City **Murphy's Law Partnership**
5 **CLARAGH NATIVE (IRE),** 10, ch g Beneficial—Susy In The Summer (IRE) **Mrs S. J. Matthews**

## MR MARTIN TODHUNTER - Continued

6 **DE CHISSLER (IRE),** 8, b g Zagreb (USA)—Lady Lola (IRE) **Mr A. Bell**
7 **MARTIN CHUZZLEWIT (IRE),** 6, ch g Galileo (IRE)—Alta Anna (FR) **Mr L. Richards**
8 **MISS MACNAMARA (IRE),** 6, b m Dylan Thomas (IRE)—Kincob (USA) **Javas Charvers**
9 **MITCD (IRE),** 4, gr f Mastercraftsman (IRE)—Halicardia **Team Toddie**
10 **MONBEG RIVER (IRE),** 6, b br g Indian River (FR)—So Pretty (IRE) **V Vyner-Brookes & Bill Hazeldean**
11 **MORNING WITH IVAN (IRE),** 5, b m Ivan Denisovich (IRE)—Grinneas (IRE) **Mr L. Richards**
12 **OLYMPIAD (IRE),** 7, b g Galileo (IRE)—Caumshinaun (IRE) **Sir R. Ogden C.B.E., LLD**
13 **PLAYHARA (IRE),** 6, b m King's Theatre (IRE)—Harringay **Mr L. Richards**
14 **PRESENTING JUNIOR (IRE),** 8, b g Presenting—Dr Alice (IRE) **Mr W. & Mrs J. Garnett**
15 **QUESTION OF FAITH,** 4, b f Yeats (IRE)—Anastasia Storm **Mr K. Fitzsimons & Mr G. Fell**
16 **ROCKABILLY RIOT (IRE),** 5, br g Footstepsinthesand—Zawariq (IRE) **J. D. Gordon**
17 **UPLIFTED (IRE),** 4, b g Jeremy (USA)—Misty Peak (IRE) **Park Farms Racing Syndicate 1**

### THREE-YEAR-OLDS

18 **WILLIAM TYNDALE (IRE),** b g Duke of Marmalade (IRE)—Blessing (USA) **Sir R. Ogden C.B.E., LLD**

**Other Owners:** P. G. Airey, P. W. Clement, Mr P. M. Croan, W. Downs, Mr G. Fell, K. Fitzsimons, Mr J. W. Fryer-Spedding, Mr W. W. Garnett, Mrs J. M. Garnett, J. W. Hazeldean, Mr C. G. Snoddy, Mr J. I. A. Spedding, D. M. Todhunter, Mr V. R. Vyner-Brooks.

**Jockey (NH):** Wilson Renwick, Henry Brooke, Graham Watters.

---

## 600 MR JAMES TOLLER, Newmarket

Postal: **Eve Lodge Stables, Hamilton Road, Newmarket, Suffolk, CB8 0NY**
Contacts: **PHONE (01638) 668918 FAX (01638) 669384 MOBILE (07887) 942234**
**E-MAIL james.toller@btconnect.com / jamestoller@btconnect.com**

1 **SATURATION POINT,** 4, b f Beat Hollow—Query (USA) **P. Pearce & S. A. Herbert**

### THREE-YEAR-OLDS

2 **DEMONSTRATION (IRE),** b c Cape Cross (IRE)—Quiet Protest (USA) **P. C. J. Dalby & R. D. Schuster**
3 **TAKE NOTE (IRE),** b f Azamour (IRE)—Lolla's Spirit (IRE) **Take Note Partnership**
4 **WISEWIT,** b g Royal Applause—Loveleaves **P. C. J. Dalby & R. D. Schuster**
5 **ZAMSINA,** b f Zamindar (USA)—Bolsena (USA) **M. E. Wates**

### TWO-YEAR-OLDS

6 **COLD SNAP (IRE),** b c 6/3 Medicean—Shivering (Royal Applause) (62000) **P. C. J. Dalby & R. D. Schuster**
7 B f 5/2 Showcasing—Gala Rose (Selkirk (USA)) (22000) **G. B. Partnership**
8 **LULWORTH (IRE),** b c 30/4 Canford Cliffs (IRE)—
Aitch (IRE) (Alhaarth (IRE)) (22000) **P. C. J. Dalby & R. D. Schuster**
9 B f 28/2 Passing Glance—Violet's Walk (Dr Fong (USA)) **M. E. Wates**

**Other Owners:** Mr N. J. Charrington, Mr P. C. J. Dalby, Mr M. G. H. Heald, Mr Andrew Heald, Mr S. A. Herbert, Mrs Anna Pearce, Mr Philip Pearce, Mr Richard Schuster, Mr J. A. R. Toller.

**Jockey (flat):** Robert Havlin.

---

## 601 MR MARK TOMPKINS, Newmarket

Postal: **Exeter Ride, The Watercourse, Newmarket, Suffolk, CB8 8LW**
Contacts: **PHONE (01638) 661434 FAX (01638) 668107 MOBILE (07799) 663339**
**E-MAIL mht@marktompkins.co.uk WEBSITE www.marktompkins.co.uk**

1 **ASTROCAT,** 4, b f Zamindar (USA)—Mega (IRE) **Mystic Meg Limited**
2 **ASTROVIRTUE,** 4, b g Virtual—Astrolove (IRE) **Mystic Meg Limited**
3 **ASTROWOLF,** 4, b g Halling (USA)—Optimistic **Mystic Meg Limited**
4 **BLUE BOUNTY,** 4, ch g Bahamian Bounty—Laheen (IRE) **Raceworld**
5 **COMRADE BOND,** 7, ch g Monsieur Bond (IRE)—Eurolink Cafe **Raceworld**
6 **MY GUARDIAN ANGEL,** 6, b g Araafa (IRE)—Angels Guard You **Sarabex and Partners**
7 **SINGING HINNIE,** 4, b f Halling (USA)—Tawny Way **J. A. Reed**
8 **STAR COMMANDER,** 7, b g Desert Style (IRE)—Barakat **J. Brenchley**
9 **SWILKEN,** 4, ch g Halling (USA)—Azure Mist **Mr D. P. Noblett**
10 **TOPALING,** 4, ch f Halling (USA)—Topatori (IRE) **M. P. Bowring**

## MR MARK TOMPKINS - Continued

11 **TOPAMICHI,** 5, b g Beat Hollow—Topatori (IRE) **Roalco Ltd**
12 **TOPTEMPO,** 6, ch m Halling (USA)—Topatoo **Roalco Ltd**

### THREE-YEAR-OLDS

13 **ASTROMAJOR,** b g Royal Applause—Astromancer (USA) **Mystic Meg Limited**
14 **ASTROVALOUR,** ch g Shirocco (GER)—Mega (IRE) **Mystic Meg Limited**
15 **BRACKEN BRAE,** b f Champs Elysees—Azure Mist **Mr D. P. Noblett**
16 **HOLD FIRM,** b c Refuse To Bend (IRE)—Four Miracles **Raceworld**
17 **HUMPHRY REPTON,** b g Virtual—Qilin (IRE) **Dullingham Park**
18 **LEGAL ART,** ch f Dutch Art—Sosumi **Sakal Family**
19 **PEEPS,** ch f Halling (USA)—Twelfth Night (IRE) **Judi Dench & Bryan Agar**
20 **PRAYER TIME,** ch g Pastoral Pursuits—Nice Time (IRE) **Sarabex**
21 **SANT'ELIA,** b f Authorized (IRE)—Trew Class **Russell Trew Ltd**
22 **SMILE THAT SMILE,** b f Champs Elysees—Tenpence **Dahab Racing**
23 **TOPARALI,** b f Rail Link—Topatoo **Dullingham Park**

### TWO-YEAR-OLDS

24 B f 16/3 Equiano (FR)—Amanda Carter (Tobougg (IRE)) (45000) **Mrs Janis MacPherson**
25 Ch c 31/1 Medicean—Astrodonna (Carnival Dancer) (18000) **Kenneth MacPherson**
26 B f 22/3 Royal Applause—Astromancer (USA) (Silver Hawk (USA)) (2000) **Dahab Racing**
27 **ASTROSECRET,** b f 8/3 Halling (USA)—Optimistic (Reprimand) **Mystic Meg Limited**
28 **ASTROWIZARD,** ch c 4/5 Zamindar (USA)—Mega (IRE) (Petardia) **Mystic Meg Limited**
29 **CARELESS RAPTURE,** ch f 1/2 Champs Elysees—Cushat Law (IRE) (Montjeu (IRE)) **Mr A. Reed**
30 B f 13/4 Sir Percy—Four Miracles (Vettori (IRE)) **Mr Richard Farleigh**
31 **HEAVENSFIELD,** b f 27/1 Motivator—Astrodiva (Where Or When (IRE)) **Mr & Mrs Franklin**
32 B f 1/2 Lawman (FR)—Katajan (Halling (USA)) (25000) **Dahab Racing**
33 **MARKTIME,** b f 26/4 Royal Applause—Nice Time (IRE) (Tagula (IRE)) **Sarabex**
34 B f 13/2 Authorized (IRE)—Missouri (Charnwood Forest (IRE)) **J. Brenchley**
35 B c 14/3 Nayef (USA)—Seasonal Blossom (IRE) (Fairy King (USA)) **Dullingham Park**
36 **SWEEPING BEAUTY,** b f 5/2 Authorized (IRE)—Brushing (Medicean) **J. Brenchley**
37 B f 3/5 Motivator—Tenpence (Bob Back (USA)) **Dullingham Park**
38 **TOPALOVA,** ch f 11/2 Champs Elysees—Topatori (IRE) (Topanoora) **M. P. Bowring**

**Other Owners:** Dahab Racing, Mr Bryan Agar, Mr M. P. Bowring, Judi Dench, Mr R. D. E. Marriott, Mrs W. L. Marriott, Mrs P. M. Rickett, Mr P. A. Sakal, Mrs Fiona Sakal, Mr M. H. Tompkins, Mrs M. H. Tompkins, Mr David Tompkins.

**Assistant Trainer:** Steven Avery

---

## 602 MR KEVIN TORK, Leigh

Postal: **Westcoats Farm, Clayhill Road, Leigh, Reigate, Surrey, RH2 8PB**
Contacts: **PHONE (01306) 611616 MOBILE (07988) 206544**

1 **ETON DORNEY (USA),** 6, b g Medaglia d'Oro (USA)—Sweet and Firm (USA) **K. Tork**
2 **JUNE FRENCH (FR),** 7, b m Jimble (FR)—Sunbelt Broker **Brigadier Racing**
3 **POSH BOY (IRE),** 5, b g Duke of Marmalade (IRE)—Sauvage (FR) **K. Tork**
4 **UPTON MEAD (IRE),** 8, b g Jimble (FR)—Inchinnan **K. Tork**

**Other Owners:** D. J. Bussell, Mr R. J. Moore, Mrs L. G. Thomas.

**Assistant Trainer:** Mr Max Tork

**Amateur:** Mr F. Penford.

---

## 603 MR MARCUS TREGONING, Whitsbury

Postal: **Whitsbury Manor Racing Stables, Whitsbury, Fordingbridge, Hampshire, SP6 3QQ**
Contacts: **PHONE (01725) 518889 FAX (01725) 518042 MOBILE (07767) 888100**
**E-MAIL info@marcustregoningracing.co.uk WEBSITE www.marcustregoningracing.co.uk**

1 **ATALANTA BAY (IRE),** 5, b m Strategic Prince—Wood Sprite **Miss S. M. Sharp**
2 **BETWEEN WICKETS,** 4, b g Compton Place—Intermission (IRE) **R. C. C. Villers**
3 **BOOM AND BUST (IRE),** 8, b g Footstepsinthesand—Forest Call **Mr J. Singh**
4 **BOWSERS BOLD,** 4, gr g Firebreak—Cristal Clear (IRE) **Mrs J. R. A. Aldridge**
5 **BRONZE ANGEL (IRE),** 6, b g Dark Angel (IRE)—Rihana (IRE) **Lady Tennant**

## MR MARCUS TREGONING - Continued

6 **CASTLE COMBE (IRE),** 4, b g Dylan Thomas (IRE)—Mundus Novus (USA) **Gaskell, Wallis & Partners**
7 **CATARIA GIRL (USA),** 6, b m Discreet Cat (USA)—Elaflaak (USA) **Mr & Mrs A. E. Pakenham**
8 **CAVALEIRO (IRE),** 6, ch g Sir Percy—Khibraat **Mr G. C. B. Brook**
9 **CLOVELLY BAY (IRE),** 4, b g Bushranger (IRE)—Crystalline Stream (FR) **M. P. Tregoning**
10 **COBHAM'S CIRCUS (IRE),** 4, ch g Hernando (FR)—Protectorate **Lady N. F. Cobham**
11 **EMPEROR FERDINAND (IRE),** 4, b g Holy Roman Emperor (IRE)—Moon Flower (IRE) **M. P. Tregoning**
12 **FYRECRACKER (IRE),** 4, ch g Kheleyf (USA)—Spirit of Hope (IRE) **Mrs Lynn Turner & Mr Guy Brook**
13 **MONEYPENNIE,** 4, b f Captain Gerrard (IRE)—Snoozy **Miss S. M. Sharp**
14 **OSKAR DENARIUS (IRE),** 4, b g Authorized (IRE)—
Elizabethan Age (FR) **Hon David Howard & Mr Bruce Johnson**
15 **SECRET PURSUIT (IRE),** 4, b f Lawman (FR)—Secret Melody (FR) **Mr G. C. B. Brook**
16 **SERENA GRAE,** 4, gr f Arakan (USA)—Success Story **Mrs H. B. Raw**
17 **SIR PERCY BLAKENEY,** 4, b g Sir Percy—Sulitelma (USA) **M. P. Tregoning**
18 **SNOW TROUBLE (USA),** 4, gr c Tapit (USA)—Smara (USA) **Mr G. C. B. Brook**
19 **STILLA AFTON,** 4, b br f Nayef (USA)—Sourire **Miss K. Rausing**
20 **SWEET P,** 4, b f Sir Percy—Desert Run (IRE) **M. P. Tregoning**

### THREE-YEAR-OLDS

21 **AFRAAS (IRE),** b f Elnadim (USA)—Aadaat (USA) **Hamdan Al Maktoum**
22 **AIR OF MYSTERY,** ch f Sakhee's Secret—Belle des Airs (IRE) **Mrs H. I. Slade**
23 **BURMESE,** b g Sir Percy—Swan Queen **Sir Thomas Pilkington**
24 **CONCORD (IRE),** b g Mawatheeq (USA)—Amhooj **Park Walk Racing**
25 **DIAMOND BLAISE,** b f Iffraaj—See You Later **Mrs H. I. Slade**
26 **MAGICAL THOMAS,** ch c Dylan Thomas (IRE)—Magical Cliche (USA) **G. P. and Miss S. J. Hayes**
27 **MULAASEQ,** b c Showcasing—Lonely Heart **Hamdan Al Maktoum**
28 **PERCEUS,** b c Sir Percy—Lady Hestia (USA) **Mr & Mrs A. E. Pakenham**
29 **PERFECT ORANGE,** ch f Sir Percy—La Peinture (GER) **Marcus Tregoning Racing Club**
30 **PRIORS GATE (IRE),** b g Acclamation—Key Rose (IRE) **Lady Tennant**
31 **RIVER DART (IRE),** ch c Dutch Art—Sky Galaxy (USA) **Mr G. C. B. Brook**
32 **ROYAL ROSLEA,** b f Royal Applause—Roslea Lady (IRE) **G. P. and Miss S. J. Hayes**
33 **SAHAAYEF (IRE),** b f Mawatheeq (USA)—Nasheed (USA) **Hamdan Al Maktoum**
34 **SHAAKIS (IRE),** gr g Dark Angel (IRE)—Curious Lashes (IRE) **Hamdan Al Maktoum**
35 **SILVER LINING (IRE),** gr c Dark Angel (IRE)—Out of Woods (USA) **Mr G. C. B. Brook**
36 **TAZYEEN,** ch f Tamayuz—Shohrah (IRE) **Hamdan Al Maktoum**
37 **THAMES KNIGHT,** b c Sir Percy—Bermondsey Girl **R. C. C. Villers**

### TWO-YEAR-OLDS

38 **ALAMODE,** ch f 27/3 Sir Percy—Almamia (Hernando (FR)) **Miss K. Rausing**
39 B f 16/1 Medicean—Atyaab (Green Desert (USA)) **Wedgewood Estates**
40 **DANCE THE DREAM,** b f 26/4 Sir Percy—Shadow Dancing (Unfuwain (USA)) (70000) **Mrs M. A. Dalgety**
41 **DAWREYA (IRE),** b f 31/1 Acclamation—Darajaat (USA) (Elusive Quality (USA)) **Hamdan Al Maktoum**
42 B c 22/2 Sakhee's Secret—Dombeya (IRE) (Danehill (USA)) (13491)
43 B br f 23/1 Dream Ahead (USA)—Dream of The Hill (IRE) (Tiger Hill (IRE)) **Mr G. C. B. Brook**
44 **FAST GOLD (IRE),** b c 20/3 Fast Company (IRE)—
Gold Tobougg (Tobougg (IRE)) (19047) **G. P. and Miss S. J. Hayes**
45 B c 4/3 Aussie Rules (USA)—Giusina Mia (USA) (Diesis) (20000) **M. P. Tregoning**
46 **HYGROVE PERCY,** ch c 29/1 Sir Percy—
Hygrove Welshlady (IRE) (Langfuhr (CAN)) (15238) **G. P. and Miss S. J. Hayes**
47 B c 10/4 Lord Shanakill (USA)—Jillian (USA) (Royal Academy (USA)) (11904)
48 B f 11/3 Sir Percy—Lady Hestia (USA) (Belong To Me (USA)) **Mr & Mrs A. E. Pakenham**
49 B c 5/4 Iffraaj—Loose Julie (IRE) (Cape Cross (IRE)) **Mr G. C. B. Brook**
50 Ch g 20/3 Schiaparelli (GER)—Maid of Perth (Mark of Esteem (IRE)) **Mr J. A. Tabet**
51 **MISS BLONDELL,** ch f 12/4 Compton Place—Where's Broughton (Cadeaux Genereux) (7500) **Miss S. M. Sharp**
52 **MUROOR,** ch c 30/3 Nayef (USA)—Raaya (USA) (Giant's Causeway (USA)) **Hamdan Al Maktoum**
53 **MYSTIKANA,** ch f 21/3 Sir Percy—Peintre d'argent (IRE) (Peintre Celebre (USA)) (13000) **Mrs V. M. Brown**
54 **POET'S SONG (IRE),** b c 17/3 Poet's Voice—Bee Eater (IRE) (Green Desert (USA)) (103174) **Lady Tennant**
55 **SUMOU (IRE),** b c 27/3 Arcano (IRE)—Three Times (Bahamian Bounty) (66666) **Hamdan Al Maktoum**
56 **TAZAAYUD,** b c 27/4 Kodiac—Esteemed Lady (IRE) (Mark of Esteem (IRE)) (85714) **Hamdan Al Maktoum**
57 **THAQAFFA (IRE),** b c 17/4 Kodiac—Incense (Unfuwain (USA)) (80000) **Hamdan Al Maktoum**
58 **TUKHOOM (IRE),** b g 16/2 Acclamation—Carioca (IRE) (Rakti) (100000) **Hamdan Al Maktoum**
59 **WESTCHESTER,** b c 6/5 Sakhee (USA)—Burqa (Nashwan (USA)) **R. J. McCreery**
60 B c 17/4 Sea The Stars (IRE)—Zarara (USA) (Manila (USA)) **Mr G. C. B. Brook**

## MR MARCUS TREGONING - Continued

**Other Owners:** Dowager Viscountess Allendale, Mrs Nona Baker, Mr Adie Bamboye, Mr & Mrs Giles Blomfield, Mr Colin Chisolm, Mr R. F. U. Gaskell, Mr Patrick Hawes, Mrs Elizabeth Heaven, Mr Roland Hill, Mr Victor Hoare, Mr Mark Horne, Mrs Rose Marston, Mr Michael Moore, Mr Adrian Nurse, Mr Terry Pearce, Mrs Denise Reynolds, Mr J. R. Wallis, Mr Stephen Wallis, Mr John Wallis.

**Assistant Trainer:** Angie Kennedy

**Jockey (flat):** Martin Dwyer, Shane Kelly. **Amateur:** Mr George Tregoning.

---

## 604 MR EDWIN TUER, Northallerton

Postal: **Granary Barn, Birkby, Northallerton, North Yorkshire, DL7 0EF**
Contacts: **PHONE (01609) 881798 FAX (01609) 881798 MOBILE (07808) 330306**

1 **BLUE MAISEY,** 7, b m Monsieur Bond (IRE)—Blue Nile (IRE) **Ontoawinner**
2 **BULAS BELLE,** 5, b m Rob Roy (USA)—Bula Rose (IRE) **E. Tuer**
3 **EASY TERMS,** 8, b m Trade Fair—Effie **E. Tuer**
4 **FAZZA,** 8, ch g Sulamani (IRE)—Markievicz (IRE) **Ontoawinner**
5 **GOLD SHOW,** 6, gr m Sir Percy—Pearl Bright (FR) **Ontoawinner**
6 **MYSTICAL MOMENT,** 5, ch m Dutch Art—Tinnarinka **E. Tuer**
7 **PATAVIUM (IRE),** 12, b g Titus Livius (FR)—Arcevia (IRE) **Mr J. A. Nixon**
8 **SALLY FRIDAY (IRE),** 7, b m Footstepsinthesand—Salee (IRE) **Ontoawinner**
9 **SPRING BACK,** 7, b m Silver Patriarch (IRE)—Danceback (IRE) **E. Tuer**
10 **THE BLUE BANANA (IRE),** 6, b g Red Clubs (IRE)—Rinneen (IRE) **E. Tuer**
11 **THE RIGHT MIX (IRE),** 6, b m Fair Mix (IRE)—Areyouwithme **Mr P. King**
12 **WISKEE LIL,** 4, b f Rob Roy (USA)—Bula Rose (IRE) **E. Tuer**

### TWO-YEAR-OLDS

13 B f 2/3 Stimulation (IRE)—Demolition Jo (Petong) (2380) **E. Tuer**
14 B f 14/2 Bushranger (IRE)—Jawaaneb (USA) (Kingmambo (USA)) (2857) **E. Tuer**

**Other Owners:** N. J. O'Brien.

**Assistant Trainer:** Fergus King (07813) 153982

---

## 605 MR JOSEPH TUITE, Great Shefford

Postal: **Tailswins, Abingdon Road, East Ilsley, Newbury, Berkshire, RG20 7LZ**
Contacts: **MOBILE (07769) 977351**
**E-MAIL joe.tuite@tuiteracing.com WEBSITE www.tuiteracing.co.uk**

1 **BOHEMIAN RHAPSODY (IRE),** 6, b g Galileo (IRE)—Quiet Mouse (USA) **Mr A. A. Byrne**
2 **CINCUENTA PASOS (IRE),** 4, ch g Footstepsinthesand—Sweet Nicole **Mr Mark Wellbelove & Mr Peter Gleeson**
3 **DOZY JOE,** 7, b g Sleeping Indian—Surrey Down (USA) **P. E. Barrett**
4 **FLASHY QUEEN (IRE),** 4, ch f Bahamian Bounty—Somersault **B Woodward,P & A Burton & B & A Lampard**
5 **FOR AYMAN,** 4, b g Bertolini (USA)—Saharan Song (IRE) **Mr A. A. Byrne**
6 **HAMOODY (USA),** 11, ch g Johannesburg (USA)—Northern Gulch (USA) **Mr A. Liddiard**
7 4, B f Shirocco (GER)—Kohiba (IRE) **Withyslade**
8 **KOHUMA,** 5, ch m Halling (USA)—Kohiba (IRE) **Withyslade**
9 **LADY KATHIAN (IRE),** 4, gr f Verglas (IRE)—Nurama **I & K Prince**
10 **LADY SYLVIA,** 6, ch m Haafhd—Abide (FR) **Mr D. J. Keast**
11 **LITIGANT,** 7, b g Sinndar (IRE)—Jomana (IRE) **Mr A. A. Byrne**
12 **POSH BOUNTY,** 4, ch f Bahamian Bounty—Fission **The Lamb Inn - Pethy**
13 **PRESBURG (IRE),** 6, b g Balmont (USA)—Eschasse (USA) **www.isehove.com**
14 **THANE OF CAWDOR (IRE),** 6, b g Danehill Dancer (IRE)—Holy Nola (USA) **Alan & Christine Bright**
15 **TIME TO TANGO (IRE),** 4, b g Tiger Hill (IRE)—Bravo Dancer **Mr J. M. Tuite**

### THREE-YEAR-OLDS

16 **BELLE DORMANT (IRE),** b f Rip Van Winkle (IRE)—Lady Rockfield (IRE) **Mr A. A. Byrne**
17 **FAST DANCER (IRE),** b g Fast Company (IRE)—Tereed Elhawa **Mr & Mrs A Bright**
18 B c Approve (IRE)—Mashie **Mr M. Kurt**
19 **ONE BIG SURPRISE,** b f Kier Park (IRE)—Cloridja **Withyslade**
20 **PIKE CORNER CROSS (IRE),** b c Cape Cross (IRE)—Smart Coco (USA) **Mr A. A. Byrne**

## MR JOSEPH TUITE - Continued

**21 STEP INTO THE TIDE (IRE),** ch c Footstepsinthesand—Pivka **Ardent Tide Flyers**
**22 ZIPEDEEDODAH (IRE),** b c Zebedee—Beverley Macca **D.M Synergy & Mark Wellbelove**

### TWO-YEAR-OLDS

**23** B f 23/2 Dream Ahead (USA)—Almaviva (IRE) (Grand Lodge (USA)) (20000) **P. J. Gleeson**
**24 CHIEF SITTINGBULL,** ch c 22/3 Indian Haven—Saharan Song (IRE) (Singspiel (IRE)) (1142) **Mr A. A. Byrne**
**25 COOL ANGEL (IRE),** gr f 9/4 Zebedee—Malthouse Mistress (IRE) (Peintre Celebre (USA)) (19840) **Mr A. A. Byrne**
**26** B c 2/3 Pastoral Pursuits—Grand Design (Danzero (AUS)) (8333) **Shefford Valley Racing**
**27 JUST EMMA,** b f 19/3 Bertolini (USA)—Royal Obsession (IRE) (Val Royal (FR)) (1047) **Mr A. A. Byrne**
**28** B c 11/3 Tagula (IRE)—Trixiebelle (IRE) (Kheleyf (USA)) (12380) **Mr J. M. Tuite**
**29 WHITSTABLE PEARL (IRE),** b f 20/4 Kodiac—
Amber's Bluff (Mind Games) (14285) **Mr M Wellbelove & Mr B Woodward**

**Other Owners:** Mr David Bond, Mr A. D. Bright, Mrs C. Bright, Mrs P. C. Burton, Mr M. Chesney, Mr M. Clarke, Mr L. Eke, Mrs R. G. Hillen, Mrs A. Johnson, Mr R. J. Lampard, Mr D. Marsh, Miss H. Pease, Mr I. D. Prince, Mrs K. Prince, R. L. Squire, Mr M. J. Wellbelove, Mr B. Woodward.

---

## 606 MR ANDREW TURNELL, Swindon

Postal: **Elmcross House, Broad Hinton, Swindon, Wiltshire, SN4 9PF**
Contacts: **PHONE (01793) 731481 FAX (01793) 739001 MOBILE (07973) 933450**
**E-MAIL info@andyturnellracing.com WEBSITE www.andyturnellracing.com**

**1 ANGELENA BALLERINA (IRE),** 8, ch m Indian Haven—Nom Francais **Power Bloodstock Ltd**
**2 ARISTOCRACY,** 4, b g Royal Applause—Pure Speculation **The Not So Privileged**
**3 CANDIDE (IRE),** 8, ch g Albano (IRE)—Sweet Cicely (IRE) **The Three Nations Partnership**
**4** 4, B c Dubai Destination (USA)—Cutting Glance (USA) **Mrs B. Hardiman**
**5 EDGWARE ROAD,** 7, ch g Selkirk (USA)—Bayswater **Power Bloodstock Ltd**
**6 KILLIMORDALY (IRE),** 6, b br g Indian River (FR)—Bramblehill Fairy (IRE) **Mrs B. Hardiman**
**7 SOUTHERN CROSS,** 4, ch f Mount Nelson—Bread of Heaven **P Rich & V Askew**
**8 WADDINGTOWN HERO (IRE),** 8, b g Subtle Power (IRE)—Miss Liz (IRE) **L. M. Power**
**9 WELL PAINTED (IRE),** 6, ch g Excellent Art—Aoife (IRE) **Power Bloodstock Ltd**

**Other Owners:** V. Askew, Ms A. Baldwin, Mr G. A. Morgan, Mr R. S. Parker, P. M. Rich, Mr M. Walsh.

**Jockey (NH):** James Banks, Nick Scholfield, Gerard Tumelty.

---

## 607 MR BILL TURNER, Sherborne

Postal: **Sigwells Farm, Sigwells, Corton Denham, Sherborne, Dorset, DT9 4LN**
Contacts: **PHONE (01963) 220523 FAX (01963) 220046 MOBILE (07932) 100173**
**E-MAIL billturnerracing@gmail.com**

**1 BREAN SPLASH SUSIE,** 4, b f Tobougg (IRE)—Straight As A Die **Unity Farm Holiday Centre Ltd**
**2 EDLOMOND (IRE),** 9, gr g Great Palm (USA)—Samardana (IRE) **Mrs P. A. Turner**
**3 EL DUQUE,** 4, b g Byron—Royal Tavira Girl (IRE) **Ansells Of Watford**
**4 FLORAL SPINNER,** 8, b m Alflora (IRE)—Dawn Spinner **The Floral Farmers**
**5 FRECKLE FACE,** 8, br g Septieme Ciel (USA)—Wavet **Mrs C. M. Goldsmith**
**6 IT'S ONLY BUSINESS,** 5, ch g Haafhd—Noble Plum (IRE) **Ansells Of Watford**
**7 LORD OF THE STORM,** 7, b g Avonbridge—Just Run (IRE) **Mrs M. S. Teversham**
**8 LUCKY STARS,** 5, ch m Lucky Story (USA)—Cosmic Countess (IRE) **R. V. Young**
**9 MISTERAY,** 5, ch g Singspiel (IRE)—Hannda (IRE) **Ansells Of Watford**

### THREE-YEAR-OLDS

**10 BREAN GOLF BIRDIE,** br f Striking Ambition—Straight As A Die **Unity Farm Holiday Centre Ltd**
**11 HELL OF A LORD,** br c Hellvelyn—Miss Brookie **Mrs M. S. Teversham**
**12 MAGIC ROUND (IRE),** gr g Zebedee—Street Kitty (IRE) **Gongolfin**
**13 TURBO CHARGED (IRE),** b g Jeremy (USA)—House Rebel (IRE) **Mr E. A. Brook**

### TWO-YEAR-OLDS

**14** B c 13/2 Bushranger (IRE)—Auspicious (Shirley Heights) (2777) **The Three Fellas (Synd)**
**15 BLUE SMOKE,** gr f 1/2 Hellvelyn—Easy Mover (IRE) (Bluebird (USA)) **Tracy Turner**
**16 FABULOUS FLYER,** b f 10/2 Equiano (FR)—Lucky Flyer (Lucky Story (USA)) (9523) **Gracelands Stud**
**17** B g 23/2 Bushranger (IRE)—Fancy Feathers (IRE) (Redback) **Mr E. A. Brook**

## MR BILL TURNER - Continued

**18 FINAL WARNING,** b f 31/3 Piccolo—Karminskey Park (Sabrehill (USA)) (952) **Tracy Turner**
**19** B c 26/3 Avonbridge—First Among Equals (Primo Valentino (IRE)) **Catherine Dyer**
**20** B f 13/3 Avonbridge—Lady Killer (IRE) (Daggers Drawn (USA)) **Mrs M. S. Teversham**
**21** B g 11/3 Dandy Man (IRE)—Miss Sharapova (IRE) (Almutawakel) (5714) **Mr E. A. Brook**
**22 MUSTN'T GRUMBLE (IRE),** ch c 30/4 Intense Focus (USA)—Lough Mist (IRE) (Captain Rio) (11110) **Mr E. A. Brook**
**23** Ch f 23/2 Pastoral Pursuits—Pomponette (USA) (Rahy (USA)) **Mascalls Stud**
**24** B c 28/4 Hellvelyn—Shake Baby Shake (Reel Buddy (USA)) **Tracy Turner**
**25 THE TIME HAS COME (IRE),** gr c 18/2 Elusive Pimpernel (USA)—Sidecar (IRE) (Spectrum (IRE)) (4761) **Mr E. A. Brook**
**26 THEE AND ME (IRE),** b c 16/4 Canford Cliffs (IRE)—Lake Ladoga (Green Desert (USA)) (19840) **Mr E. A. Brook**
**27 THICK AS THEIVES,** b f 24/2 Dick Turpin (IRE)—Norse Dame (Halling (USA)) **Tracy Turner**

**Other Owners:** Mr B. C. Ansell, Mrs B. C. Ansell, Mrs Natasha Ansell, Mr R. L. Ansell, Mr R. A. Bracken, Mr Nick Conduit, Mr R. C. Dollar, Mr A. Morrish, Mr David F. Powell, Mr G. M. Tregaskes, Mr E. Vickery.

**Conditional:** Ryan While. **Apprentice:** Ryan While.

---

## 608 MR JAMES TURNER, Helperby

Postal: **Mayfield Farm, Norton-le-Clay, Helperby, York**
Contacts: **PHONE (01423) 322239 FAX (01423) 322239**

**1 BONDI BEACH BABE,** 5, b m Misu Bond (IRE)—Nice One **Mr G. R. Turner & Mr H. Turner**
**2 BONDI BEACH BOY,** 6, b g Misu Bond (IRE)—Nice One **Mr G. R. Turner & Mr H. Turner**
**3 ZAKETY ZAK,** 4, b g Overbury (IRE)—Jeanne d'arc **Mr D. M. Wordsworth**

**Other Owners:** Mr G. R. Turner, Mr H. Turner.

**Assistant Trainer:** Oliver J. Turner

---

## 609 MRS KAREN TUTTY, Northallerton

Postal: **Trenholme House Farm, Osmotherley, Northallerton, North Yorkshire, DL6 3QA**
Contacts: **PHONE (01609) 883624 FAX 01609 883624 MOBILE (07967) 837406**
**E-MAIL karentutty@btinternet.com WEBSITE www.karentuttyracing.co.uk**

**1 ELAND ALLY,** 7, b g Striking Ambition—Dream Rose (IRE) **Thoroughbred Homes Ltd**
**2 GAELIC WIZARD (IRE),** 7, b g Fasliyev (USA)—Fife (IRE) **Grange Park Racing**
**3 MERCERS ROW,** 8, b g Bahamian Bounty—Invincible **K. Fitzsimons**
**4 MOROCCO,** 6, b g Rock of Gibraltar (IRE)—Shanghai Lily (IRE) **Mr R. J. Smeaton**
**5 PERCY'S GAL,** 4, ch f Sir Percy—Galette **Arrand & Tutty**
**6 TALENT SCOUT (IRE),** 9, b g Exceed And Excel (AUS)—Taalluf (USA) **Thoroughbred Homes Ltd**
**7 UNDER APPROVAL,** 4, b g Captain Gerrard (IRE)—Dockside Strike **Grange Park Racing**

### THREE-YEAR-OLDS

**8 CROWN GREEN,** b f Royal Applause—Grasshoppergreen (IRE) **Thoroughbred Homes Ltd**
**9 JOHNNY SORRENTO,** b g Zamindar (USA)—Glorious Dreams (USA) **Thoroughbred Homes Ltd**
**10** B f Papal Bull—No Tippling (IRE)
**11 ORICANO,** ch f Arcano (IRE)—Dhuyoof (IRE) **Thoroughbred Homes Ltd**
**12 POLLY JACKSON,** b f Sir Percy—Fly In Style **Thoroughbred Homes Ltd**

### TWO-YEAR-OLDS

**13** B f 26/4 Sir Percy—Alizadora (Zilzal (USA)) (8500)

**Other Owners:** Mr C. G. Arrand, A. D. Crombie, Mr E. Surr, N. D. Tutty.

**Apprentice:** Gemma Tutty.

## 610 MR NIGEL TWISTON-DAVIES, Cheltenham

Postal: **T/a Grange Hill Farm Limited, Grange Hill Farm, Naunton, Cheltenham, Gloucestershire, GL54 3AY**
Contacts: **PHONE (01451) 850278 FAX (01451) 850101 MOBILE (07836) 664440**
**E-MAIL nigel@nigeltwistondavies.co.uk WEBSITE www.nigeltwistondavies.co.uk**

1 **A DOLL IN MILAN (IRE),** 5, b m Milan—Tawny Owl (IRE) **Mr Simon Munir & Mr Isaac Souede**
2 **ABIGAIL LYNCH (IRE),** 7, b m Oscar (IRE)—Tanit Lady (IRE) **Rose Tinted Racing**
3 **ALDEBURGH,** 6, b g Oasis Dream—Orford Ness **W. E. Sturt**
4 **ALGERNON PAZHAM (IRE),** 6, b g Milan—Kitty Star (IRE) **Graham & Alison Jelley**
5 **ALLTHEGEAR NO IDEA (IRE),** 8, b g Sayarshan (FR)—All The Gear (IRE) **The Yes No Wait Sorries**
6 **ARTHUR'S GIFT (IRE),** 4, b g Presenting—Uncertain Affair (IRE) **H. R. Mould**
7 **ARTHUR'S SECRET (FR),** 5, b br g Secret Singer (FR)—Luna Park (FR) **H. R. Mould**
8 **ASTRACAD (FR),** 9, br g Cadoudal (FR)—Astre Eria (FR) **H. R. Mould**
9 **BALLY BEAUFORT (IRE),** 7, b g Old Vic—Miss Compliance (IRE) **Mr R. J. Rexton**
10 **BALLY BRAES (IRE),** 7, b g Old Vic—Gaelic Stream (IRE) **Mr C. J. Haughey**
11 **BALLYBOLLEY (IRE),** 6, b g Kayf Tara—Gales Hill (IRE) **Mr Simon Munir & Mr Isaac Souede**
12 **BALLYKAN,** 5, b g Presenting—La Marianne **N. A. Twiston-Davies**
13 **BALLYRATH (IRE),** 5, b g Flemensfirth (USA)—Rose Wee (IRE) **The Stirling Partnership**
14 **BELMOUNT (IRE),** 6, b g Westerner—Artist's Jewel **N. A. Twiston-Davies**
15 **BENBENS (IRE),** 10, ch g Beneficial—Millicent Bridge (IRE) **S Such & CG Paletta**
16 **BENDOMINGO (IRE),** 4, b g Beneficial—Bobbies Storm (IRE) **DG Partners**
17 **BIG CASINO,** 9, b g Court Cave (IRE)—Migsy Malone **The Jukes Family**
18 **BLAKLION,** 6, b g Kayf Tara—Franciscaine (FR) **S Such & CG Paletta**
19 **BRISTOL DE MAI (FR),** 4, gr g Saddler Maker (IRE)—La Bole Night (FR) **Mr Simon Munir & Mr Isaac Souede**
20 **BROWNVILLE,** 6, b g Kayf Tara—Cool Spice **Mrs F. E. Griffin**
21 **BUDDY LOVE,** 8, gr m Silver Patriarch (IRE)—O My Love **Mr S. Cottrill**
22 **COGRY,** 6, b g King's Theatre (IRE)—Wyldello **Graham & Alison Jelley**
23 **COLIN'S BROTHER,** 5, b g Overbury (IRE)—Dd's Glenalla (IRE) **Mrs C. S. C. Beresford-Wylie**
24 **COUNT GUIDO DEIRO (IRE),** 8, b g Accordion—Ivy Lane (IRE) **R. Bevis**
25 **DAZZLING RITA,** 9, b m Midnight Legend—Pytchley Dawn **The Atkin Partnership**
26 **DEFINITLEY LOVELY,** 10, b m Definite Article—Fair Maid Marion (IRE) **N. A. Twiston-Davies**
27 **DEPUTY COMMANDER (IRE),** 6, b g Shantou (USA)—Artic Native (IRE) **Imperial Racing Partnership No.7**
28 **DOUBLE COURT (IRE),** 4, b g Court Cave (IRE)—Miss Top (IRE) **Synergy Racing**
29 **DOUBLE ROSS (IRE),** 9, ch g Double Eclipse (IRE)—Kinross **Options O Syndicate**
30 **EMPTY THE TANK (IRE),** 5, b g Lawman (FR)—Asian Alliance (IRE) **Asinus Verendus Syndicate**
31 **FALSE ACCUSATION (IRE),** 6, b g Artan (IRE)—Annadot (IRE) **N. A. Twiston-Davies**
32 **FIVE STAR WILSHAM (IRE),** 11, b g Bob's Return (IRE)—Riverpauper (IRE) **N. A. Twiston-Davies**
33 **FLORRIE BOY (IRE),** 4, b g Milan—Second Best (IRE) **Option O Syndicate**
34 **FOND MEMORY (IRE),** 7, b g Dr Massini (IRE)—Glacier Lilly (IRE) **The Stirling Partnership**
35 **FOXBRIDGE (IRE),** 9, b g King's Theatre (IRE)—Fairy Native (IRE) **Walters Plant Hire Spiers & Hartwell**
36 **FOXTAIL HILL (IRE),** 6, b g Dr Massini (IRE)—Flynn's Girl (IRE) **Options O Syndicate**
37 **FRONTIER SPIRIT (IRE),** 11, b g New Frontier (IRE)—Psalmist **Jump For Fun Racing**
38 **FRONTIER VIC,** 8, b g Old Vic—Right On Target (IRE) **Jump For Fun Racing**
39 **GINJO,** 5, b m Sakhee (USA)—Gulshan **N. A. Twiston-Davies**
40 **GLASGOW CENTRAL,** 4, b g Rail Link—Musical Key **Mrs J. K. Powell**
41 **GOAT CASTLE (IRE),** 11, b g Goldmark (USA)—Rolands Girl (IRE) **N. A. Twiston-Davies**
42 **GOLDEN JUBILEE (USA),** 6, b br g Zavata (USA)—Love Play (USA) **Mrs J. K. Powell**
43 **GOLDIE HORN,** 7, ch m Where Or When (IRE)—Gulshan **N. A. Twiston-Davies**
44 **GOODBYE DANCER (FR),** 4, b g Dragon Dancer—Maribia Bella (FR) **The Yes No Wait Sorries**
45 **GUITING POWER,** 4, b g Lucarno (USA)—Sparkling Jewel **David Langdon**
46 **HE'S THE DADDY,** 8, b g Generous (IRE)—Brambly Hedge **Mr A. Gillman**
47 **HERECOMESTHEHOLLOW (IRE),** 9, ch g Flemensfirth (USA)—Drumcay Polly (IRE) **The Hollow Partnership**
48 **HOLLOW BLUE SKY (FR),** 8, gr g Turgeon (USA)—Run For Laborie (FR) **The Hollow Partnership**
49 **I AM COLIN,** 6, b g Zafeen (FR)—Dd's Glenalla (IRE) **Mrs C. S. C. Beresford-Wylie**
50 **IMPERIAL LEADER (IRE),** 7, b g Flemensfirth (USA)—Glamorous Leader (IRE) **Imperial Racing Partnership No.2**
51 **JAUNTY JOURNEY,** 12, ch g Karinga Bay—Jaunty June **Mr C. Roberts**
52 **KILRONAN HIGH (IRE),** 6, b m Mountain High (IRE)—Broadcast **Mrs J. K. Powell**
53 **LISTEN BOY (IRE),** 9, ch g Presenting—Buckalong (IRE) **Bryan & Philippa Burrough**
54 **LITTLE JON,** 7, b g Pasternak—Jowoody **Mr R Frosell & Mrs L Taylor**
55 **LITTLE POP,** 7, b g Pasternak—Flagship Daisy May (IRE) **S Such & CG Paletta**
56 **MAJOR MALARKEY (IRE),** 12, b g Supreme Leader—Valley (IRE) **Baker Dodd & Cooke**
57 **MILLICENT SILVER,** 6, gr m Overbury (IRE)—Common Girl (IRE) **Mr J. Goodman**
58 **MINELLA RECEPTION (IRE),** 9, b g King's Theatre (IRE)—Cadourova (FR) **Options O Syndicate**
59 **MINI MUCK,** 9, b m Kayf Tara—Madam Muck **Jilly Scott & Sarah MacEchern**

## MR NIGEL TWISTON-DAVIES - Continued

60 **MUCKLE ROE (IRE),** 6, b g Westerner—Island Crest **Mrs V. J. Lane**
61 **NORTHANDSOUTH (IRE),** 5, ch g Spadoun (FR)—Ennel Lady (IRE) **Mills & Mason Partnership**
62 **OKAFRANCA (IRE),** 10, b g Okawango (USA)—Villafranca (IRE) **W. E. Sturt**
63 **PAPRADON,** 11, b g Tobougg (IRE)—Salvezza (IRE) **A. J. Cresser**
64 **PARADIS BLANC (FR),** 4, b g Early March—Mont Paradis (FR) **Fourway Flyers**
65 **PIGEON ISLAND,** 12, gr g Daylami (IRE)—Morina (USA) **H. R. Mould**
66 **PURE SCIENCE (IRE),** 7, ch g Galileo (IRE)—Rebelline (IRE) **H. R. Mould**
67 **RALLY,** 6, b g Rail Link—Waki Music (USA) **Walters Plant Hire Ltd**
68 **RANSOM NOTE,** 8, b g Red Ransom (USA)—Zacheta **H. R. Mould**
69 **RED ROUBLE (IRE),** 10, ch g Moscow Society (USA)—Chirouble (IRE) **N. A. Twiston-Davies**
70 **RIDDLEOFTHESANDS (IRE),** 11, b br g Oscar (IRE)—Flaxen Pride (IRE) **N. A. Twiston-Davies**
71 **ROSSONERI (IRE),** 8, b g Milan—Native Crystal (IRE) **Phil Dixon, Steve Jones & Davina Tanner**
72 **SCOMMETTITRICE (IRE),** 7, b m Le Vie Dei Colori—Hard To Lay (IRE) **N. A. Twiston-Davies**
73 **SEACON BEG (IRE),** 6, b g Generous (IRE)—Moon Storm (IRE) **N. A. Twiston-Davies**
74 **SPEED MASTER (IRE),** 9, b g King's Theatre (IRE)—Handy Lass **Spiers & Hartwell and N A Twiston-Davies**
75 **SPLASH OF GINGE,** 7, b g Oscar (IRE)—Land of Honour **Mr J. Neild**
76 **SUSQUEHANNA RIVER (IRE),** 8, b g Indian River (FR)—Calistoga (IRE) **The Wasting Assets**
77 **SWORD OF THE LORD,** 5, b g Kheleyf (USA)—Blue Echo **The Yes No Wait Sorries**
78 **SYBARITE (FR),** 9, b br g Dark Moondancer—Haida III (FR) **H. R. Mould**
79 **TARA MUCK,** 8, b m Kayf Tara—Madam Muck **N. A. Twiston-Davies**
80 **THE CAT,** 4, gr f Josr Algarhoud (IRE)—Animal Cracker **Mr S. P. Catton**
81 **THE MUSICAL GUY (IRE),** 9, b g Lahib (USA)—Orchestral Sport (IRE) **The Musical Guy's Girls**
82 **THE NEW ONE (IRE),** 7, b g King's Theatre (IRE)—Thuringe (FR) **S Such & CG Paletta**
83 **TOUR DES CHAMPS (FR),** 8, b br g Robin des Champs (FR)—Massada (FR) **H. R. Mould**
84 **TRIUMPH DAVIS (IRE),** 6, b m Flemensfirth (USA)—Bodhran Davis (FR) **Million in Mind Partnership**
85 **VALID POINT (IRE),** 9, b g Val Royal (FR)—Ricadonna **W. E. Sturt & C. Walker**
86 **WHAT AN OSCAR (IRE),** 10, b g Oscar (IRE)—Katie Buckers (IRE) **N. A. Twiston-Davies**
87 **WINGED CRUSADER (IRE),** 7, b g Winged Love (IRE)—Reine Berengere (FR) **Imperial Racing Partnership No.6**

**Other Owners:** Mr T. J. Atkin, Mr James A. Atkin, Mr A. P. Bridges, Mr A. R. Bromley, Mr B. R. H. Burrough, Mrs Philippa Burrough, Mr Chris Coley, Mr Paul J. Costello, Mr P. J. Dixon, Mr Robert Frosell, Mr A. B. Greenfield, Mr David Hussey, Mrs Christopher Jerram, Mr S. F. Jones, Mr R. Jukes, Mrs Margaret Jukes, Mr H. J. Kelly, Mr David Langdon, Mrs James Layton, Mrs S. A. MacEchern, Mr David Mason, Mr Martin Maxted, Mrs Susan Maxted, Mrs Lynne Merson, Mr F. J. Mills, Mr W. R. Mills, Mr D. Minton, Mr S. Munir, Mr C. G. Paletta, Mr Richard Pascoe, Mr G. J. Pascoe, Mr C. Pettigrew, Mrs Scilla Phillips, Mr G. M. Powell, Mr Ian A. Robinson, Mrs C. M. Scott, Mr R. I. Sims, Mr Tim Slade, Mr Isaac Souede, Spiers & Hartwell Ltd, Mrs Deborah Stoneham, Mr Steven Studley, Mrs S. Such, Mrs D. L. Tanner, Mrs L. C. Taylor, Mr Sam Thorp, Mr Nigel Twiston-Davies, Walters Plant Hire Ltd, Mr S. Wignall.

**Assistant Trainer:** Carl Llewellyn

**Jockey (flat):** William Twiston-Davies. **Jockey (NH):** Sam Twiston-Davies, David England.
**Conditional:** Jamie Bargary, Ryan Hatch.

---

## 611 MR JAMES UNETT, Oswestry

Postal: **Garden Cottage, Tedsmore, West Felton, Oswestry, Shropshire, SY11 4HD**
Contacts: **PHONE (01691) 610001 FAX (01691) 610001 MOBILE (07887) 534753**
**E-MAIL jamesunett1327@yahoo.co.uk WEBSITE www.jamesunettracing.com**

1 **BIG SMILE (IRE),** 7, b g Zagreb (USA)—Pretty Buckskin (IRE) **G. D. Kendrick**
2 **CLARATY,** 5, b m Firebreak—Claradotnet **G. D. Kendrick**
3 **CLARY (IRE),** 5, b m Clodovil (IRE)—Kibarague **J. W. Unett**
4 **DUTCH LADY ROSEANE,** 4, b f Dutch Art—Lady Rose Anne (IRE) **Mr S. M. Jones**
5 **HARRY BOSCH,** 5, b g Kyllachy—Fen Guest **Miss G. M. Kelleway**
6 **HEAT STORM (IRE),** 4, b g Lawman (FR)—Coconut Show **Northern Line Racing Ltd**
7 **MCCOOL RUNNINGS,** 4, b g Cockney Rebel (IRE)—Dances With Angels (IRE) **Mr M. A. Sheehy**
8 **THE FENLAND MAN,** 4, b g Rob Roy (USA)—Spark Up **Mr M. B. Hall**

### THREE-YEAR-OLDS

9 B g Manduro (GER)—Barley Bree (IRE)
10 **SKELL GILL,** b g Multiplex—Socceroo **Mr P. S. Sutherland**
11 **VIVRE LA REVE,** b f Assertive—Noor El Houdah (IRE) **Northern Line Racing Ltd**

**Assistant Trainer:** Miss C. H. Jones

## 612 MR JOHN UPSON, Towcester

Postal: **Glebe Stables, Blakesley Heath, Maidford, Towcester, Northamptonshire, NN12 8HN**
Contacts: **PHONE (01327) 860043 FAX (01327) 860238**

1 **BLACKWELL SYNERGY (FR),** 9, b g Antarctique (IRE)—Pyu (GER) **The Peter Partnership**
2 **CHAMPION VERSIONS (IRE),** 8, b g Presenting—Kelly Gales (IRE) **The Peter Partnership**
3 **GIANT O MURCHU (IRE),** 11, b g Carroll House—Centralspires Best **Miss Tracey Leeson**
4 **ISAAC'S WARRIOR (IRE),** 9, b g Pushkin (IRE)—Point The Finger (IRE) **Lord Nicholas Wilson**
5 **OAK WOOD (IRE),** 7, ch g Bienamado (USA)—Oakum (IRE) **Lord Nicholas Wilson**
6 **QUEL BRUERE (FR),** 11, gr g Sassanian (USA)—Housseliere (FR)
7 **STEEL GOLD (IRE),** 9, b g Craigsteel—It Time To Run (IRE) **Lord Nicholas Wilson**
8 **THEFRIENDLYGREMLIN,** 7, b g Vinnie Roe (IRE)—Queens Fantasy **The Nap Hand Partnership**
9 **WOOTSTEPS (IRE),** 7, ch g Shantou (USA)—Mandyslady (IRE) **The Marron Partnership**

**Other Owners:** M. H. Beesley, D. Deveney, Mr J. D. Horgan, Mrs J. M. Letts, Miss K. J. Letts, M. E. White.

## 613 MR MARK USHER, Lambourn

Postal: **Saxon House Stables, Upper Lambourn, Hungerford, Berkshire, RG17 8QH**
Contacts: **PHONE (01488) 72598 (01488) 73630 MOBILE (07831) 873531**
**E-MAIL markusherracing@btconnect.com WEBSITE www.markusherracing.co.uk**

1 **BAY FORTUNA,** 6, b g Old Vic—East Rose **The Ridgeway Partnership**
2 **BLACK TRUFFLE (FR),** 5, b g Kyllachy—Some Diva **Ushers Court**
3 **DANCING LAUREATE (IRE),** 7, b m Cadeaux Genereux—Persea (IRE) **The Dancing Laureate Partnership**
4 **HAATEFINA,** 5, b m Haatef (USA)—Felona **Ushers Court**
5 **KATMAI RIVER (IRE),** 8, b g Choisir (AUS)—Katavi (USA) **M. D. I. Usher**
6 **LADY PERCY (IRE),** 6, b m Sir Percy—Genuinely (IRE) **Ushers Court**
7 **LITTLECOTE LADY,** 6, b m Byron—Barefooted Flyer (USA) **Littlecote House Racing**
8 **REGINALD CLAUDE,** 7, b g Monsieur Bond (IRE)—Miller's Melody **High Five Racing**
9 **SPICE FAIR,** 8, ch g Trade Fair—Focosa (ITY) **Saxon House Racing**

### THREE-YEAR-OLDS

10 **BOUNTY BAH,** ch g Bahamian Bounty—Eternity Ring **High Five Racing**
11 **EVO CAMPO (IRE),** b f Approve (IRE)—Billie Bailey (USA) **Saxon House Racing**
12 **MISU PETE,** b c Misu Bond (IRE)—Smart Ass (IRE) **Saxon House Racing**
13 **SPINDLE (IRE),** b f Dubai Destination (USA)—Phantom Turtle (IRE) **Saxon House Racing**

### TWO-YEAR-OLDS

14 **ARLECCHINO'S ROCK,** ch c 6/3 Rock of Gibraltar (IRE)—Xtra Special (Xaar) (21000) **Mr Kevin Senior**
15 B c 5/5 Royal Applause—Caledonia Princess (Kyllachy) (2000) **Ushers Court**
16 **INDIGO,** gr f 9/2 Medicean—Jessica Ennis (USA) (English Channel (USA)) **Ushers Court**
17 **MISS FORTUNE,** ch f 23/1 Notnowcato—Rowan Flower (IRE) (Ashkalani (IRE)) (3500) **Mr Clark Fortune**
18 **ROSIE'S VISION,** b f 5/5 Passing Glance—Bold Rose (Bold Edge) **Ushers Court**
19 B c 23/4 Duke of Marmalade (IRE)—Shimoni (Mark of Esteem (IRE)) (14000) **Ushers Court**

**Other Owners:** Mr R. H. Brookes, Mr Paul Duffy, Mrs Jill Pellett, Mr Brian Rogan, Mr John Stansfield, Mr M. D. I. Usher.

**Jockey (flat):** Liam Keniry. **Jockey (NH):** David Crosse. **Apprentice:** Charlotte Jenner.

## 614 MR ROGER VARIAN, Newmarket

Postal: **Kremlin House Stables, Fordham Road, Newmarket, Suffolk, CB8 7AQ**
Contacts: **PHONE (01638) 661702 FAX (01638) 667018**
**E-MAIL office@varianstable.com WEBSITE www.varianstable.com**

1 **ALJAMAAHEER (IRE),** 6, ch h Dubawi (IRE)—Kelly Nicole (IRE) **Hamdan Al Maktoum**
2 **AYRAD (IRE),** 4, ch c Dalakhani (IRE)—Sweet Firebird (IRE) **Saleh Al Homaizi & Imad Al Sagar**
3 **BATTERSEA,** 4, b c Galileo (IRE)—Gino's Spirits **H.R.H. Sultan Ahmad Shah**
4 **BEST KEPT,** 4, ch g Sakhee's Secret—Ashlinn (IRE) **Michael Hill**
5 **CERTIFICATE,** 4, ch g Pivotal—Graduation **Cheveley Park Stud Limited**
6 **DOUBLE UP,** 4, b g Exceed And Excel (AUS)—My Love Thomas (IRE) **Mr A D Spence & Mr M B Spence**
7 **GO SAKHEE,** 4, br g Sakhee's Secret—Bling Bling (IRE) **K Allen G Moss R & S Marchant & G Jarvis**
8 **IDDER (IRE),** 4, br c Authorized (IRE)—Epiphany **Saleh Al Homaizi & Imad Al Sagar**
9 **IGIDER (IRE),** 4, b c Teofilo (IRE)—Changeable **Saleh Al Homaizi & Imad Al Sagar**

## MR ROGER VARIAN - Continued

10 **JUSTINEO,** 6, b h Oasis Dream—Loulwa (IRE) **Saleh Al Homaizi & Imad Al Sagar**
11 **KEEPER'S RING (USA),** 4, b f Street Cry (IRE)—Liffey Dancer (IRE) **Merry Fox Stud Limited**
12 **KHATIBA (IRE),** 4, b f Kheleyf (USA)—Tempete **Sheikh Ahmed Al Maktoum**
13 **KINGSTON HILL,** 4, gr ro c Mastercraftsman (IRE)—Audacieuse **Mr P. D. Smith**
14 **MINDUROWNBUSINESS (IRE),** 4, b c Cape Cross (IRE)—Whos Mindin Who (IRE) **A. D. Spence**
15 **PRINCESS LOULOU (IRE),** 5, ch m Pivotal—Aiming **Saleh Al Homaizi & Imad Al Sagar**
16 **REKDHAT (IRE),** 4, b br f Shamardal (USA)—Taarkod (IRE) **Sheikh Ahmed Al Maktoum**
17 **STAR JET (IRE),** 4, br gr f Teofilo (IRE)—Silver Shoon (IRE) **Ladas**
18 **STEPS (IRE),** 7, br g Verglas (IRE)—Killinallan **Michael Hill**
19 **STEVE ROGERS (IRE),** 4, b g Montjeu (IRE)—Three Owls (IRE) **N. Bizakov**
20 **TALMADA (USA),** 4, b f Cape Cross (IRE)—Aryaamm (IRE) **Sheikh Ahmed Al Maktoum**
21 **TOOFI (FR),** 4, b c Henrythenavigator (USA)—Silver Bark **Saleh Al Homaizi & Imad Al Sagar**

## THREE-YEAR-OLDS

22 **AJAADAT,** b f Shamardal (USA)—Taarkod (IRE) **Sheikh Ahmed Al Maktoum**
23 **ALMOHTASEB,** b c Oasis Dream—Cuis Ghaire (IRE) **Hamdan Al Maktoum**
24 **AMERICAN ARTIST (IRE),** ch c Danehill Dancer (IRE)—American Adventure (USA) **Thurloe Thoroughbreds XXXV**
25 **ANDRETTI,** b c Oasis Dream—Anna Amalia (IRE) **N. Bizakov**
26 **ATLETICO (IRE),** b c Kodiac—Queenofthefairies **A. D. Spence**
27 **BAADI,** b c Dansili—Dashing (IRE) **Saleh Al Homaizi & Imad Al Sagar**
28 **BELARDO (IRE),** b c Lope de Vega (IRE)—Danaskaya (IRE) **Godolphin & Prince A A Faisal**
29 **BELLA LULU,** b f Iffraaj—Loulwa (IRE) **Saleh Al Homaizi & Imad Al Sagar**
30 **CATSBURY (IRE),** b f Teofilo (IRE)—Chatham Islands (USA) **Qatar Racing Limited**
31 **CURSORY GLANCE (USA),** b f Distorted Humor (USA)—Time Control **Merry Fox Stud Limited**
32 **DASAATEER (IRE),** b c Mount Nelson—Trishuli **Hamdan Al Maktoum**
33 **DECORATED KNIGHT,** ch c Galileo (IRE)—Pearling (USA) **Saleh Al Homaizi & Imad Al Sagar**
34 **DELAIRE,** b g Sakhee's Secret—Moody Margaret **Ms Y. Ferguson**
35 **EFFECTUAL,** b f Exceed And Excel (AUS)—Our Faye **Cheveley Park Stud Limited**
36 **EL TEL,** ch c Sixties Icon—Chelsea (USA) **Ballymore Sterling Syndicate**
37 **ERSHAAD (IRE),** b g Acclamation—Emerald Peace (IRE) **Sheikh Ahmed Al Maktoum**
38 **ESTIKHRAAJ,** b c Dansili—Shimah (USA) **Hamdan Al Maktoum**
39 **FADDWA (IRE),** b f Arcano (IRE)—Heart's Desire (IRE) **Saleh Al Homaizi & Imad Al Sagar**
40 **FIRST DREAM (IRE),** b c Oasis Dream—First **N. Bizakov**
41 **FIVE OF DIAMONDS (FR),** b f Peintre Celebre (USA)—Give Me Five (GER) **A. D. Spence**
42 **GUILTY TWELVE (USA),** b f Giant's Causeway (USA)—Arkadina (IRE) **Merry Fox Stud Limited**
43 **HEAVENLY SCENT,** b f Galileo (IRE)—Flora Trevelyan **G. B. Partnership**
44 **HENRY HUDSON,** b c Rip Van Winkle (IRE)—Shanghai Lily (IRE) **Mr P Smith, Mrs D Tabor & Mrs J Magnier**
45 **IMTIYAAZ (IRE),** b f Starspangledbanner (AUS)—Endure (IRE) **Mr M. Al-Qatami & Mr K. M. Al-Mudhaf**
46 **INTILAAQ (USA),** b c Dynaformer (USA)—Torrestrella (IRE) **Hamdan Al Maktoum**
47 **ISTINFAAR (USA),** b c Street Cry (IRE)—Yaqeen **Hamdan Al Maktoum**
48 **JOSEPH JEFFERSON (IRE),** b c Rip Van Winkle (IRE)—Vas Y Carla (USA) **Mrs J Magnier, Mr P Smith & Mrs D Tabor**
49 **LADURELLI (IRE),** b c Mastercraftsman (IRE)—Chanter **Mrs F. H. Hay**
50 **LADY IN WHITE (IRE),** ro f Zebedee—Alexander Phantom (IRE) **Cheveley Park Stud Limited**
51 **LAYALEE (IRE),** b f Lawman (FR)—Red Feather (IRE) **Hamdan Al Maktoum**
52 **LUISA CALDERON,** b f Nayef (USA)—La Felicita **Miss K. Rausing**
53 **MALJAA,** ch g Paco Boy (IRE)—Kerry's Dream **Hamdan Al Maktoum**
54 **MANHATTAN PRINCESS,** ch f Pivotal—Fibou (USA) **Mr Simon Munir & Mr Isaac Souede**
55 **MARASIM,** ch c Exceed And Excel (AUS)—Muffled (USA) **Sheikh Ahmed Al Maktoum**
56 **MARKABAH (IRE),** b f Dubawi (IRE)—Ghaidaa (IRE) **Hamdan Al Maktoum**
57 **MASTER OF SPEED (IRE),** ch g Mastercraftsman (IRE)—Mango Groove (IRE) **Jon Collins, Chris Fahy & Mrs H. Varian**
58 **MEDIATION,** b f Azamour (IRE)—Macleya (GER) **Cheveley Park Stud Limited**
59 **MUDAMMERA (IRE),** b f Dubawi (IRE)—Fatanah (IRE) **Hamdan Al Maktoum**
60 **MUJASSAM,** ch c Kyllachy—Naizak **Hamdan Al Maktoum**
61 **MUQTASER (USA),** b c Distorted Humor (USA)—Life Well Lived (USA) **Hamdan Al Maktoum**
62 **MURAHANA (IRE),** b f Invincible Spirit (IRE)—By Request **Hamdan Al Maktoum**
63 **MUSAAID (IRE),** br c Lawman (FR)—Fonda (USA) **Saleh Al Homaizi & Imad Al Sagar**
64 **MUTANAAWAL,** ch g Intikhab (USA)—Pikaboo **Hamdan Al Maktoum**
65 **MUWALAAH (USA),** b br f Smart Strike (CAN)—Almoutezah (USA) **Hamdan Al Maktoum**
66 **PARISH (IRE),** b g Dark Angel (IRE)—Penicuik **HighclereThoroughbredRacing(Coronation)**
67 **PRIVILEGED (IRE),** b f Exceed And Excel (AUS)—Almaviva (IRE) **Cheveley Park Stud Limited**
68 **PROPEL (IRE),** ch f Dubawi (IRE)—Hit The Sky (IRE) **Mr J. M. Camilleri**
69 **QUEEN'S PEARL (IRE),** b f Exceed And Excel (AUS)—Gimasha **Z. A. Galadari**

## MR ROGER VARIAN - Continued

70 **RAISING SAND,** b c Oasis Dream—Balalaika **Castle Down Racing & Mrs H. Varian**
71 **RASHASH (IRE),** b c Kyllachy—Labisa (IRE) **Sheikh Ahmed Al Maktoum**
72 **RIFLE RANGE (IRE),** b g Shamardal (USA)—Ratukidul (FR) **Mr J. M. Camilleri**
73 **ROKBAAN,** b g Camacho—Salinia (IRE) **Sheikh Ahmed Al Maktoum**
74 **SADAARA (IRE),** b f Kheleyf (USA)—Tempete **Sheikh Ahmed Al Maktoum**
75 **SEARCHING (IRE),** ro c Mastercraftsman (IRE)—Miracolia (IRE) **A. D. Spence**
76 **SHASAG (IRE),** b f Arcano (IRE)—Popolo (IRE) **Z. A. Galadari**
77 **SILVER BID (USA),** gr c Exchange Rate (USA)—Micaela's Moon (USA) **Sheikh J. D. Al Maktoum**
78 **SNOW COVER,** gr f Verglas (IRE)—Cover Look (SAF) **K. A. Dasmal**
79 **SOLIANA,** ch f Dutch Art—Pink Stone (FR) **Sheikh Ahmed Al Maktoum**
80 **SPANGLED,** ch f Starspangledbanner (AUS)—Zykina **Cheveley Park Stud Limited**
81 **STOCKING,** gr f Acclamation—Red Boots (IRE) **Highclere T'Bred Racing(Prince Of Wales)**
82 **SYLVETTE,** ch f Selkirk (USA)—Souvenance **Miss K. Rausing**
83 **SYNOPSIS,** b f Azamour (IRE)—Censored **Cheveley Park Stud Limited**
84 **TAHKEEM (USA),** ch c Candy Ride (ARG)—Mini Sermon (USA) **Hamdan Al Maktoum**
85 **TAJBELL (IRE),** b f New Approach (IRE)—Ameerat **Sheikh Ahmed Al Maktoum**
86 **TARAZ,** b c Oasis Dream—Tamarind (IRE) **N. Bizakov**
87 **TAWAASHEEH (IRE),** b c New Approach (IRE)—Sana Abel (IRE) **Hamdan Al Maktoum**
88 **TAZFFIN (IRE),** b f Iffraaj—Tarfshi **Sheikh Ahmed Al Maktoum**
89 **TIGRILLA (IRE),** gr f Clodovil (IRE)—Lisieux Orchid (IRE) **Cheveley Park Stud Limited**
90 **TINGLEO,** ch f Galileo (IRE)—Tingling (USA) **N. Bizakov**
91 **TROPICANA BAY,** b f Oasis Dream—Ballet Ballon (USA) **Helena Springfield Ltd**
92 **VERT DE GRECE (IRE),** gr c Verglas (IRE)—Tiny Petal (IRE) **Britannia Thoroughbreds 1**
93 **VINNITSA,** b f Montjeu (IRE)—Rare Ransom **N. Bizakov**
94 **YA LATIF (IRE),** b f Iffraaj—Albahja **Sheikh Ahmed Al Maktoum**
95 **ZARI,** b f Azamour (IRE)—Epiphany **Saleh Al Homaizi & Imad Al Sagar**

## TWO-YEAR-OLDS

96 **AGHAANY,** gr f 26/4 Dubawi (IRE)—Hathrah (IRE) (Linamix (FR)) **Hamdan Al Maktoum**
97 **ALLE STELLE,** b f 1/2 Sea The Stars (IRE)—Alta Moda (Sadler's Wells (USA)) (50000) **Miss K. Rausing**
98 **ALQUFFAAL,** br c 2/4 Dansili—Cuis Ghaire (IRE) (Galileo (IRE)) **Hamdan Al Maktoum**
99 Ch c 4/3 Danehill Dancer (IRE)—Alsace Lorraine (IRE) (Giant's Causeway (USA)) (330000) **Mr P. D. Smith**
100 B c 14/5 Dream Ahead (USA)—Anna's Rock (IRE) (Rock of Gibraltar (IRE)) (70000) **Mr S. Rashid**
101 Ch c 30/1 Exceed And Excel (AUS)—Annabelle's Charm (IRE) (Indian Ridge) **Merry Fox Stud Limited**
102 B c 24/4 Street Cry (IRE)—
Arkadina (IRE) (Danehill (USA)) (200000) **China Horse Club (HK) Investment Holdings Limited**
103 B c 23/3 Showcasing—Avessia (Averti (IRE)) (75000) **Sheikh Ahmed Al Maktoum**
104 Gr c 28/2 Rip Van Winkle (IRE)—Bali Breeze (IRE) (Common Grounds) (80000) **A. D. Spence**
105 B c 6/4 Dark Angel (IRE)—Bowness (Efisio) (55000) **Sheikh R. D. Al Maktoum**
106 B f 3/4 Dark Angel (IRE)—Brazilian Flame (IRE) (Camacho) (30000) **Mr M. Al-Qatami & Mr K. M. Al-Mudhaf**
107 B c 21/4 Rip Van Winkle (IRE)—
Cawett (IRE) (Danehill Dancer (IRE)) (134920) **China Horse Club (HK) Investment Holdings Limited**
108 Gr c 1/4 Zebedee—Champion Tipster (Pursuit of Love) (90000) **Sheikh Ahmed Al Maktoum**
109 **COMPEL (FR),** ch f 31/3 Exceed And Excel (AUS)—
Good Hope (GER) (Seattle Dancer (USA)) (35714) **Miss Y. M. G. Jacques**
110 **CORINTHIAN,** b c 12/2 Sea The Stars (IRE)—
Contradictive (USA) (Kingmambo (USA)) (100000) **Highclere Thoroughbred Racing(Gladstone)**
111 **DALALAH,** b f 16/2 Exceed And Excel (AUS)—Bashasha (USA) (Kingmambo (USA)) **Hamdan Al Maktoum**
112 **DANCE BAND (IRE),** b f 16/4 Danehill Dancer (IRE)—
Maidin Maith (IRE) (Montjeu (IRE)) (119047) **Cheveley Park Stud Limited**
113 B f 31/1 Canford Cliffs (IRE)—
Decorative (IRE) (Danehill Dancer (IRE)) (171428) **Saleh Al Homaizi & Imad Al Sagar**
114 Ch c 9/3 Cape Blanco (IRE)—Desert Sky (IRE) (Green Desert (USA)) (78000) **Mr M. Almutairi**
115 B c 3/2 Cape Cross (IRE)—Emsiyah (USA) (Bernardini (USA)) (43650) **Jon Collins, Chris Fahy & Mrs H. Varian**
116 Ch c 1/3 Sea The Stars (IRE)—
Evensong (GER) (Waky Nao) (674602) **China Horse Club (HK) Investment Holdings Limited**
117 Ch c 26/4 Sea The Stars (IRE)—Fair Sailing (IRE) (Docksider (USA)) (100000) **H.R.H. Sultan Ahmad Shah**
118 B c 13/3 Teofilo (IRE)—Family (USA) (Danzig (USA)) (165000) **Al Shaqab Racing UK Limited**
119 Br c 3/4 Kheleyf (USA)—Fantastic Santanyi (Fantastic Light (USA)) (23000) **Compas Racing Columbus**
120 B f 25/2 Dubawi (IRE)—Ferdoos (Dansili) **Sheikh Ahmed Al Maktoum**
121 **FIRST RATE,** b c 13/4 Kyllachy—Hooray (Invincible Spirit (IRE)) **Cheveley Park Stud Limited**
122 **FOOL TO CRY (IRE),** ch f 25/3 Fast Company (IRE)—Islandagore (IRE) (Indian Ridge) (17000) **J. Shack**
123 **FORBIDDING (USA),** ch c 29/1 Kitten's Joy (USA)—
La Coruna (USA) (Thunder Gulch (USA)) (390000) **Prince A. A. Faisal**
124 Gr c 5/5 Mastercraftsman (IRE)—Gold Charm (GER) (Key of Luck (USA)) (100000) **Mr P. D. Smith**

## MR ROGER VARIAN - Continued

**125** B f 10/1 Invincible Spirit (IRE)—Golden Whip (GER) (Seattle Dancer (USA)) (60000)
**126** B c 26/2 Roderic O'Connor (IRE)—Harvest Joy (IRE) (Daggers Drawn (USA)) (41269)
**127 HEART SPRINKLED (IRE),** b f 15/4 Galileo (IRE)—Heart Shaped (USA) (Storm Cat (USA)) **T. Yoshida**
**128 IDEALIST,** b f 7/5 Rip Van Winkle (IRE)—Illusion (Anabaa (USA)) **Cheveley Park Stud Limited**
**129** B c 14/2 Equiano (FR)—Ile Deserte (Green Desert (USA)) (67460) **Newsells Park Stud Limited**
**130** B f 14/2 Exceed And Excel (AUS)—
Impressionism (IRE) (Elusive Quality (USA)) (420000) **Saleh Al Homaizi & Imad Al Sagar**
**131 ISTANBUL BEY,** ro c 6/2 Exceed And Excel (AUS)—
Starfala (Galileo (IRE)) (85000) **Mr Simon Munir & Mr Isaac Souede**
**132 KARAKOZ,** b f 31/1 Danehill Dancer (IRE)—Card Shop (USA) (Chester House (USA)) **N. Bizakov**
**133** B c 27/1 Cape Blanco (IRE)—Keepers Hill (IRE) (Danehill (USA)) (150000) **Mr P. D. Smith**
**134** Gr c 14/1 Galileo (IRE)—Laddies Poker Two (IRE) (Choisir (AUS)) **Mr P. D. Smith**
**135** B c 2/4 Hat Trick (JPN)—Lady Simpson (Yankee Victor (USA)) (27000) **S Hassiakos, M Mannaseh & H Varian**
**136** B c 11/3 Deep Impact (JPN)—Listen (IRE) (Sadler's Wells (USA)) **Qatar Racing Limited**
**137** B c 15/3 Sea The Stars (IRE)—Loulwa (IRE) (Montjeu (IRE)) **Saleh Al Homaizi & Imad Al Sagar**
**138 MAJDOOL (IRE),** b c 6/2 Acclamation—Maany (USA) (Mr Greeley (USA)) **Hamdan Al Maktoum**
**139 MORANDO (FR),** b c 28/2 Kendargent (FR)—
Moranda (FR) (Indian Rocket) (182539) **H.H. Sheikh Mohammed bin Khalifa Al-Thani**
**140 MUTARAJJIL (IRE),** b c 8/4 Acclamation—
Rouge Noir (USA) (Saint Ballado (CAN)) (105000) **Hamdan Al Maktoum**
**141** B f 25/1 Hard Spun (USA)—My Dubai (IRE) (Dubai Millennium) **Sheikh Ahmed Al Maktoum**
**142 MYSTIC IMAGE (USA),** b f 17/2 Distorted Humor (USA)—
Time Control (Sadler's Wells (USA)) **Merry Fox Stud Limited**
**143 NAASIK,** b c 8/5 Poet's Voice—Shemriyna (IRE) (King of Kings (IRE)) **Hamdan Al Maktoum**
**144** B f 28/1 Medaglia d'Oro (USA)—Nasmatt (Danehill (USA)) **Sheikh Ahmed Al Maktoum**
**145 NOTARY,** b f 27/3 Lawman (FR)—Purity (Pivotal) **Cheveley Park Stud Limited**
**146** B c 20/4 Equiano (FR)—Nouvelle Amie (GER) (Noverre (USA)) (16000)
**147** Ch c 16/4 Kyllachy—Our Faye (College Chapel) (38095) **Mrs H. Varian**
**148 PAPER FACES (USA),** ch f 1/2 Lemon Drop Kid (USA)—
Liffey Dancer (IRE) (Sadler's Wells (USA)) **Merry Fox Stud Limited**
**149** B c 4/3 Dubawi (IRE)—Pearling (USA) (Storm Cat (USA)) **Saleh Al Homaizi & Imad Al Sagar**
**150** B f 30/1 Dutch Art—Penang Cry (Barathea (IRE)) (58000) **Mr M. Al-Qatami & Mr K. M. Al-Mudhaf**
**151 PLANTATION (IRE),** b c 10/4 Invincible Spirit (IRE)—
Matula (IRE) (Halling (USA)) (87300) **Highclere Thoroughbred Racing (Rosebery)**
**152** B c 21/3 High Chaparral (IRE)—Plaza (USA) (Chester House (USA)) (150000) **H.R.H. Sultan Ahmad Shah**
**153** Ch c 23/1 Lope de Vega (IRE)—Quesada (IRE) (Peintre Celebre (USA)) (180000) **Sheikh Ahmed Al Maktoum**
**154 RASHAAQA,** b f 19/4 Oasis Dream—Shimah (USA) (Storm Cat (USA)) **Hamdan Al Maktoum**
**155** B c 18/4 Street Cry (IRE)—Red Dune (IRE) (Red Ransom (USA)) **Sheikh Ahmed Al Maktoum**
**156 REDEMPTION,** b f 20/2 Olden Times—Gentle On My Mind (IRE) (Sadler's Wells (USA)) **Prince A. A. Faisal**
**157** B f 21/2 Acclamation—
Roo (Rudimentary (USA)) (300000) **China Horse Club (HK) Investment Holdings Limited**
**158 RUSSIAN APPROACH (IRE),** b c 28/2 New Approach (IRE)—Velvet Flicker (IRE) (Fasliyev (USA)) (200000)
**159** B c 12/4 Paco Boy (IRE)—Russian Rhapsody (Cosmonaut) (32000) **Mrs H. Varian**
**160 SHANYRRAK,** b c 29/1 Medicean—Shabyt (Sadler's Wells (USA)) **N. Bizakov**
**161** Ch c 21/2 Le Havre (IRE)—She Is Zen (FR) (Zieten (USA)) (38000)
**162** B f 20/2 Lawman (FR)—Solar Event (Galileo (IRE)) **Qatar Racing Limited**
**163** B f 6/5 Iffraaj—Spiritual Air (Royal Applause) (74285) **Qatar Racing Limited**
**164** B c 10/2 Rip Van Winkle (IRE)—Superfonic (FR) (Zafonic (USA)) (85000) **Mr M. Almutairi**
**165** Ch f 10/2 Mastercraftsman (IRE)—
Sweet Firebird (IRE) (Sadler's Wells (USA)) (174602) **Saleh Al Homaizi & Imad Al Sagar**
**166 TALENT TO AMUSE (IRE),** b f 23/3 Manduro (GER)—
Burn Baby Burn (IRE) (King's Theatre (IRE)) (31000) **J. Shack**
**167 TARSEEKH,** b c 25/2 Kyllachy—Constitute (USA) (Gone West (USA)) (320000) **Hamdan Al Maktoum**
**168 TAWWAAQ (IRE),** gr f 24/3 Zebedee—Killinallan (Vettori (IRE)) (114285) **Hamdan Al Maktoum**
**169 TESTIMONY,** b f 10/2 Lawman (FR)—Macleya (GER) (Winged Love (IRE)) **Cheveley Park Stud Limited**
**170** B c 24/3 Canford Cliffs (IRE)—That's My Style (Dalakhani (IRE)) (61904) **Thurloe Thoroughbreds XXXVI**
**171 TIERCEL,** b c 14/4 Olden Times—Sharp Mode (USA) (Diesis) **Prince A. A. Faisal**
**172 TIFL,** ch c 15/2 Approve (IRE)—Isobel Rose (IRE) (Royal Applause) (36190) **Hamdan Al Maktoum**
**173** B c 5/4 Dream Ahead (USA)—
Tiger Spice (Royal Applause) (87300) **China Horse Club (HK) Investment Holdings Limited**
**174** B c 4/2 Dubawi (IRE)—Time Saved (Green Desert (USA)) (550000) **R. Barnett**
**175** B f 3/5 Fastnet Rock (AUS)—
Up At Dawn (Inchinor) (90000) **China Horse Club (HK) Investment Holdings Limited**
**176** B f 30/1 Montjeu (IRE)—Vital Statistics (Indian Ridge)

## MR ROGER VARIAN - Continued

**177 VIZIER,** b c 1/2 Pivotal—Rare Ransom (Oasis Dream) **N. Bizakov**
**178** B c 2/3 King's Best (USA)—Zayn Zen (Singspiel (IRE)) **Sheikh Ahmed Al Maktoum**

**Other Owners:** K. M. Al-Mudhaf, Mohammed Jasem Al-Qatami, I. J. Al-Sagar, Mr K. Allen, G. M. Barnard, Mr J. A. Collins, Mrs H. S. Ellingsen, Mr C. J. Fahy, Mr F. Frankland, Godolphin Management Company Ltd, Mr C. P. Gordon-Watson, S. Hassiakos, M. G. H. Heald, Mr A. M. H. Heald, The Hon H. M. Herbert, Highclere Thoroughbred Racing Ltd, Saleh Al Homaizi, Mrs G. A. S. Jarvis, Mr R. P. Legh, Mrs S. Magnier, M. Manasseh, Mr R. P. Marchant, Mr S. Marchant, Mr M. D. Moroney, Mr G. Moss, Mr C. Mullin, Mrs M. T. Mullin, S. E. Munir, Mr M. D. Orlandi, O. J. W. Pawle, Mr I. Souede, Mr M. B. Spence, Mr J. A. B. Stafford, Mrs D. A. Tabor, M. Weinfeld.

**Assistant Trainer:** Michael Marshall

**Apprentice:** Ross Atkinson.

---

## 615 MR ED VAUGHAN, Newmarket

Postal: **Machell Place Cottage, Old Station Road, Newmarket, Suffolk, CB8 8DW**
Contacts: **PHONE (01638) 667411 FAX (01638) 667452 MOBILE (07799) 144901**
**E-MAIL ed@efvaughan.com WEBSITE www.efvaughan.com**

1 **ADVENTURE SEEKER (IRE),** 4, gr c Dalakhani (IRE)—Adventure (USA)
2 **CLAIM THE ROSES (USA),** 4, b br c Speightstown (USA)—Reboot (USA)
3 **COSTA FILEY,** 4, b g Pastoral Pursuits—Cosmic Destiny (IRE)
4 **DANCE AND DANCE (IRE),** 9, b g Royal Applause—Caldy Dancer (IRE)
5 **FLAMBOROUGH BREEZE,** 6, ro m Ad Valorem (USA)—Lothian Lass (IRE)
6 **INTERCONNECTION,** 4, ch g Mount Nelson—Lacework
7 **OLIVERS MOUNT,** 5, ch g Mount Nelson—Phoebe Woodstock (IRE)
8 **REDVERS (IRE),** 7, br g Ishiguru (USA)—Cradle Brief (IRE)
9 **SI SENOR (IRE),** 4, b g Dansili—Kotsi (IRE)

### THREE-YEAR-OLDS

10 **ABSENT LADY (USA),** b f Lemon Drop Kid (USA)—Missing Miss (USA)
11 **BARTEL (IRE),** b c Aussie Rules (USA)—Kirunavaara (IRE)
12 **CAFE CAPRICE,** ch f Duke of Marmalade (IRE)—Midpoint (USA)
13 **CAYTON BAY,** br f Equiano (FR)—Hearsay
14 **MEHRONISSA,** ch f Iffraaj—Miss University (USA)
15 **PRIMROSE VALLEY,** b f Pastoral Pursuits—Cosmic Destiny (IRE)
16 **RHYTHM EXCEL,** b f Exceed And Excel (AUS)—Caldy Dancer (IRE)
17 **SIGNS AND SIGNALS (IRE),** b f Kodiac—Larrocha (IRE)
18 **SUFFOLK SKY,** b f Pastoral Pursuits—Charlevoix (IRE)

### TWO-YEAR-OLDS

19 **BONNEFIO,** b f 11/3 Teofilo (IRE)—Crimson Ribbon (USA) (Lemon Drop Kid (USA))
20 B f 21/1 Royal Applause—Caldy Dancer (IRE) (Soviet Star (USA))
21 B c 5/3 Vale of York (IRE)—Finnmark (Halling (USA))
22 B c 8/2 Aqlaam—Gretna (Groom Dancer (USA)) (3000)
23 B c 19/3 Acclamation—Hijab (King's Best (USA)) (52000)
24 B f 14/2 Equiano (FR)—Italian Connection (Cadeaux Genereux) (20000)
25 B f 26/3 Exceed And Excel (AUS)—Madam Ninette (Mark of Esteem (IRE)) (80000)
26 **MISS FRIDAYTHORPE,** b f 29/3 Pastoral Pursuits—Cosmic Destiny (IRE) (Soviet Star (USA))
27 **ROMAN HOLIDAY (IRE),** b f 9/5 Holy Roman Emperor (IRE)—Burn The Breeze (IRE) (Beat Hollow)
28 B f 8/3 Frozen Power (IRE)—Tuscania (USA) (Woodman (USA)) (7000)
29 B f 25/2 Exceed And Excel (AUS)—Wild Gardenia (Alhaarth (IRE)) (50000)

**Owners:** Sheikh Saoud Al Thani, Mr H. R. Bin Ghadayer, Bloomsbury Stud, Mr M. Hawkes, Mr E. J. C. Hawkes, Mr Rupert P. Legh, Mr Michael D. Moroney, A. M. Pickering, Qatar Racing Limited, Mr S. Rashid, Mr M. Rashid, Mrs Jill Sinclair, Mr M. Sinclair, Mr D. Thorpe.

---

## 616 MR TIM VAUGHAN, Cowbridge

Postal: **Pant Wilkin Stables, Llanquian Road, Aberthin, Cowbridge, South Glamorgan, CF71 7HE**
Contacts: **PHONE (01446) 771626 FAX (01446) 774371 MOBILE (07841) 800081**
**E-MAIL tim@timvaughanracing.com WEBSITE www.timvaughanracing.com**

1 **ACKERTAC (IRE),** 10, ch g Anshan—Clonsingle Native (IRE) **The Mount Fawcus Partnership**

## MR TIM VAUGHAN - Continued

2 **AKULA (IRE),** 8, ch g Soviet Star (USA)—Danielli (IRE) **Itsfuninit**
3 **ALPHABETICAL ORDER,** 7, b g Alflora (IRE)—Lady Turk (FR) **Great Northern Partnership**
4 **ASHFORD WOOD (IRE),** 7, b g Stowaway—Shambala (IRE) **David & Susan Luke**
5 **ASHKOUN (FR),** 4, b g Sinndar (IRE)—Ashalina (FR) **Galopp Syndicate Ltd**
6 **AWBEG MASSINI (IRE),** 9, b g Dr Massini (IRE)—Awbeg Flower (IRE) **Mr R. I. Clay**
7 **BALLYROCK (IRE),** 9, b g Milan—Ardent Love (IRE) **Pearn's Pharmacies Ltd**
8 4, B g Alflora (IRE)—Barton Flower **Four Leaf Clover Partnership**
9 **BASSARABAD (FR),** 4, b g Astarabad (USA)—Grivette (FR) **Pearn's Pharmacies Ltd**
10 **BE BOP BORU (IRE),** 8, b g Brian Boru—Henrietta Howard (IRE) **The Oak Syndicate**
11 **BEAT THE TIDE,** 5, b g Black Sam Bellamy (IRE)—Sablonne (USA) **Mrs Z. Wentworth**
12 **BELIZE,** 4, b g Rail Link—Costa Rica (IRE) **Mr D. R. Passant**
13 **BELLS OF AILSWORTH (IRE),** 5, b g Kayf Tara—Volverta (FR) **Mr S. Grys & Mr M. O'Boyle**
14 **BELLS OF CASTOR (IRE),** 5, ch g Golan (IRE)—Tocane (FR) **Mr S. Grys & Mr M. O'Boyle**
15 **BENABILITY (IRE),** 5, b g Beneficial—Whataliability (IRE) **Mrs L. Bowtell**
16 **BENNACHIE (IRE),** 6, b g Milan—Stormy Lady (IRE) **Oceans Racing**
17 **BLEU ET NOIR,** 4, b g Enrique—Gastina (FR) **A. E. Peterson**
18 **BO'S RETURN,** 5, b g Tobougg (IRE)—Lamp's Return **Bovian Racing**
19 **BONVILSTON BOY,** 4, b g Martaline—Lisa du Chenet (FR) **Mr N. Harris**
20 **BUCKING THE TREND,** 7, b g Kayf Tara—Macklette (IRE) **The Marinades**
21 **BUY BACK BOB (IRE),** 8, b g Big Bad Bob (IRE)—Abeyr **R P B Michaelson & Robin Clay**
22 **CAGE FIGHTER (IRE),** 4, b g Misternando—Native Mistress (IRE) **T. E. Vaughan**
23 **CANTON PRINCE (IRE),** 4, b g Shantou (USA)—Hasainm (IRE) **Tertia Racing**
24 **CASPIAN PIPER (IRE),** 8, b g Millenary—Pepsi Starlet (IRE) **Oceans Racing**
25 **CHAMPAGNE CHASER,** 5, b g Tobougg (IRE)—Champagne Lil **Mrs M. A. O'Sullivan**
26 4, B g King's Theatre (IRE)—Clairefontaine
27 **CREATEUR (IRE),** 4, b g Muhtathir—Cracovie **Oceans Racing**
28 **DADSINTROUBLE (IRE),** 5, b g Presenting—Gemini Lucy (IRE) **Mr J. P. M. Bowtell**
29 **DALAMAN (IRE),** 4, b g Duke of Marmalade (IRE)—Crimphill (IRE) **Diamond Racing Ltd**
30 **DEBECE,** 4, b g Kayf Tara—Dalamine (FR) **R. M. Kirkland**
31 **DESHAN (GER),** 4, b g Soldier Hollow—Desimona (GER) **Mr S. A. Clarke**
32 **DESTROYER DEPLOYED,** 9, b g Deploy—Supreme Cove **The Craftsmen**
33 **DOVILS DATE,** 6, gr g Clodovil (IRE)—Lucky Date (IRE) **Itsfuninit**
34 **DUBH EILE (IRE),** 7, br m Definite Article—Aine Dubh (IRE) **T. E. Vaughan**
35 **ESSTEEPEE,** 6, b g Double Trigger (IRE)—Lamper's Light **Shoot The Pot Racing**
36 **EXPERIMENTALIST,** 7, b g Monsieur Bond (IRE)—Floppie (FR) **Two Gents & An Orange Bloke Racing**
37 **EXPLAINED (IRE),** 8, b g Exit To Nowhere (USA)—All Told (IRE) **D N V Churton & Mrs C Wilson**
38 **FALCARRAGH (IRE),** 8, ch g Alderbrook—Magherareagh Lady (IRE) **Mr M. A. Stratford**
39 **FAYETTE COUNTY (IRE),** 8, b g Golden Lariat (USA)—Midsyn Lady (IRE) **J. P. McManus**
40 **FIELDS OF GLORY (FR),** 5, b g King's Best (USA)—Lavandou **Pearn's Pharmacies Ltd**
41 **FIGARO,** 7, ch g Medicean—Chorist **Pearn's Pharmacies Ltd**
42 **FIRST FANDANGO,** 8, b g Hernando (FR)—First Fantasy **WRB Racing 40 & Premier Chance Racing**
43 **GIFTED ISLAND (IRE),** 5, b g Turtle Island (IRE)—Life Support (IRE) **Oceans Racing**
44 **GOLAN WAY,** 11, b g Golan (IRE)—Silk Daisy **T. E. Vaughan**
45 **GOLDEN FEET,** 4, b g Dubawi (IRE)—One So Marvellous **Mr D. R. Passant**
46 **GORMAN (FR),** 4, b c King's Best (USA)—Gerone (FR) **Mr M. J. Haines**
47 **GRACIE B (IRE),** 6, b m Golan (IRE)—Me Grannys Endoors (IRE) **Diamond Racing Ltd**
48 **GREAT OAK (IRE),** 9, b m Dushyantor (USA)—Reginella (IRE) **Mrs M. A. O'Sullivan**
49 **HAWKHILL (IRE),** 9, b g Hawk Wing (USA)—Crimphill (IRE) **Mr L. Helps**
50 **HIDDEN IDENTITY (IRE),** 9, b m Beneficial—Swanbrook Leader (IRE) **Mr J. P. M. Bowtell**
51 **HONEY POUND (IRE),** 7, b g Big Bad Bob (IRE)—Moon Review (USA) **D&S Luke & Great Northern Partnership II**
52 **IFAN (IRE),** 7, b g Ivan Denisovich (IRE)—Montana Miss (IRE) **WRB Racing 61 & Derek & Jean Clee**
53 **JIMBILL (IRE),** 9, br g Flying Legend (USA)—Ah Gowan (IRE) **Brian Ead & Martin Moore**
54 **JIMMY SHAN (IRE),** 7, b g Milan—Divine Prospect (IRE) **Power Panels Electrical Systems Ltd**
55 **KALIMANTAN (IRE),** 5, b g Azamour (IRE)—Kalamba (IRE) **D. J. Wallis**
56 **KEY PEOPLE (IRE),** 8, b g Alderbrook—Diamond Forever **T. E. Vaughan**
57 **KING ROLFE (IRE),** 7, b g King's Theatre (IRE)—Lady Rolfe (IRE) **Four Corners Syndicate**
58 **KNIGHT'S REWARD,** 5, b g Sir Percy—Wardeh **The Mount Fawcus Partnership**
59 **KOULTAS KING (IRE),** 8, b g Exit To Nowhere (USA)—Carrigmoorna Style (IRE) **Pearn's Pharmacies Ltd**
60 **LAMOOL (GER),** 8, b g Mamool (IRE)—Linara (GER) **Mr J. H. Frost**
61 **LAWLESS ISLAND (IRE),** 6, b g Heron Island (IRE)—Nylon (GER) **Pearn's Pharmacies Ltd**
62 **LE FIN BOIS (FR),** 5, b g Poliglote—La Mache (FR) **Power Panels Electrical Systems Ltd**
63 **LIBERTY COURT (IRE),** 8, b g Court Cave (IRE)—Miss Vikki (IRE) **Passant & Butt**
64 **LORD BRANTWOOD,** 4, b g Sir Percy—Diddymu (IRE) **Mr & Mrs D. D. Clee**
65 **LORD LIR (IRE),** 9, b g Oscar Schindler (IRE)—Milford Woman (IRE) **Two Gents & An Orange Bloke Racing**

## MR TIM VAUGHAN - Continued

66 **LOVELY BUBBLY,** 4, b g Kayf Tara—Champagne Lil **R. M. Kirkland**
67 **MASSINI'S MAGUIRE (IRE),** 14, b g Dr Massini (IRE)—Molly Maguire (IRE) **A. E. Peterson**
68 **MASTER DANCER,** 4, gr g Mastercraftsman (IRE)—Isabella Glyn (IRE) **select-racing-club.co.uk & Mr C Davies**
69 **MASTER HIDE (IRE),** 5, b g Stowaway—Carrigeen Acer (IRE) **R. M. Kirkland**
70 **MESSERY (FR),** 4, b g Poliglote—Iris du Berlais (FR) **Mrs B. N. Ead**
71 **MISIRLOU (FR),** 5, b br g Limnos (JPN)—Other Salsa (FR) **The Misirlou Gang**
72 **MIST THE BOAT,** 7, b g Generous (IRE)—Baily Mist (IRE) **Craftsmen2**
73 **MURCHU (IRE),** 9, b g Oscar (IRE)—Bottle A Knock (IRE) **Oceans Racing**
74 **NASH POINT (IRE),** 6, ch g Kris Kin (USA)—Ten Dollar Bill (IRE) **Mr G Handley & Mr G Pesticcio**
75 **NATHANS PRIDE (IRE),** 7, ch g Definite Article—Tricias Pride (IRE) **Mr J. P. M. Bowtell**
76 **NELLIE THE ELEGANT,** 4, b f Mount Nelson—Mexican Hawk (USA) **W R B Racing 53**
77 **NINE IRON (IRE),** 5, gr g Verglas (IRE)—Sevi's Choice (USA) **Oceans Racing**
78 **NUMBER ONE LONDON (IRE),** 5, b g Invincible Spirit (IRE)—Vadorga **D. J. Wallis**
79 **OFFICER HOOLIHAN,** 5, b g Kayf Tara—Major Hoolihan **R. M. Kirkland**
80 **ONE LEADER (IRE),** 4, b g Oscar (IRE)—Be My Leader (IRE) **Tertia Racing**
81 **OSCARS DEN (IRE),** 7, b g Oscar (IRE)—Lyre Hill (IRE) **Mrs Z. Wentworth**
82 **OSKAR'S EVA (IRE),** 5, gr m Black Sam Bellamy (IRE)—Sardagna (FR) **Sally Morgan & Richard Prince**
83 **PARTING WAY (IRE),** 7, b g Golan (IRE)—Best Mother (IRE) **Brian Ead & Martin Moore**
84 **PRESENTING RED (IRE),** 5, b g Presenting—Bolly (IRE) **R. M. Kirkland**
85 **PURE ANTICIPATION (IRE),** 10, gr m Old Vic—Lady of Gortmerron (IRE) **Middleton Nevin Racing**
86 **RENFREW (IRE),** 5, b g Robin des Pres (FR)—Allstar Rose (IRE) **R. M. Kirkland**
87 **REV IT UP (IRE),** 9, b g Revoque (IRE)—Von Carty (IRE) **The Bill & Ben Partnership**
88 **ROCK DOCTOR (IRE),** 5, b g Flemensfirth (USA)—Often Quoted (IRE) **Oceans Racing**
89 **ROYALE DJANGO (IRE),** 6, b g Kayf Tara—Royale Boja (FR) **Mr J Durston & Mr N Harris**
90 **RUSTAMABAD (FR),** 5, ch g Dylan Thomas (IRE)—Rosawa (FR) **Mr D. R. Passant**
91 **RYE HOUSE (IRE),** 6, b g Dansili—Threefold (USA) **Oceans Racing**
92 **SACRED SUMMIT (IRE),** 4, ch g Mountain High (IRE)—D'ygrande (IRE) **Oceans Racing**
93 **SHARPASAKNIFE (IRE),** 5, b g Flemensfirth (USA)—Omas Lady (IRE) **The Mount Fawcus Partnership**
94 4, B g Brian Boru—Sheebadiva (IRE) **T. E. Vaughan**
95 **SHOUT IT ALOUD,** 6, b g Proclamation (IRE)—Party Charmer **The Mount Fawcus Partnership**
96 **SMOKER,** 5, b g Motivator—Request **T. E. Vaughan**
97 4, B g Double Trigger (IRE)—Soloism **T. E. Vaughan**
98 **TANIT RIVER (IRE),** 5, br g Indian River (FR)—Tanit Lady (IRE) **Brian Ead & Martin Moore**
99 **TEA IN TRANSVAAL (IRE),** 4, b f Teofilo (IRE)—Mpumalanga **Mr M. J. Haines**
100 **THE OMEN,** 9, b g Sir Harry Lewis (USA)—High Sturt **Oceans Racing**
101 **THE WALLACE LINE (IRE),** 4, b g Mastercraftsman (IRE)—Surval (IRE) **Diamond Racing Ltd**
102 **THELIGNY (FR),** 4, gr g Martaline—Romilly (FR) **Pearn's Pharmacies Ltd**
103 **TIDESTREAM,** 5, b g Galileo (IRE)—Sweet Stream (ITY) **Delamere Cottage Racing Partners (1996)**
104 **TIME AND AGAIN (FR),** 5, b g Sassanian (USA)—Petillante Royale (FR) **Oceans Racing**
105 **TIME ON YOUR HANDS (IRE),** 5, b g Beneficial—Zalda **Pearn's Pharmacies Ltd**
106 **TIPSY GYPSY (IRE),** 8, b g Milan—Montanara (IRE) **Mr J. P. M. Bowtell**
107 4, B c Passing Glance—Tizzy Blue (IRE) **T. E. Vaughan**
108 **TOBACCO ROAD (IRE),** 5, b g Westerner—Virginias Best **T. E. Vaughan**
109 **TOMSK (FR),** 5, ch g Priolo (USA)—Kauto Relstar (FR) **Oceans Racing**
110 **UNCLE TONE (IRE),** 6, b g Pelder (IRE)—Daisy A Day (IRE) **Kings Head Duffield Racing Partnership**
111 **UP THE JUNCTION,** 4, b g New Approach (IRE)—Hyabella **The Junction Partnership**
112 **VODKA ISLAND (IRE),** 6, b m Turtle Island (IRE)—Fromrussiawithlove **Folly Road Racing Partners (1996)**
113 **WARRIGAL (IRE),** 5, ch g Mount Nelson—Waldblume (GER) **Mr B. M. Jones**
114 **WINGS OF SMOKE (IRE),** 10, gr g King's Theatre (IRE)—Grey Mo (IRE) **Pearn's Pharmacies Ltd**
115 **WISTARI ROCKS (IRE),** 6, b g Heron Island (IRE)—Hi Honey (IRE) **Four Leaf Clover Partnership**

## THREE-YEAR-OLDS

116 **C'EST DU GATEAU (FR),** b g Laveron—Programmee (FR) **Pearn's Pharmacies Ltd**
117 B c Flemensfirth (USA)—In Our Intrest (IRE) **Pearn's Pharmacies Ltd**
118 B g Getaway (GER)—Knock Down (IRE) **Pearn's Pharmacies Ltd**
119 Ch gr g Presenting—Pink Mist (IRE) **Mr D. R. Passant**
120 **TANACANDO (FR),** b g Ballingarry (IRE)—Tamaziya (IRE) **Mr M. Trezise**
121 **WITHOUT FRONTIER (IRE),** b g Stowaway—Hollygrove Samba (IRE) **Mr J Durston & Mr N Harris**

## MR TIM VAUGHAN - Continued

**Other Owners:** Mr P. G. Amos, A. W. A. Bates, Mr N. Berrisford, Mr G. W. T. Butt, Mr R. J. Churches, Mr D. N. V. Churton, Mr A. Clarke, D. D. Clee, Mrs J. P. Clee, Mr M. J. Curtis, Mr C. Davies, Mr R. Denness, Mr J. Durston, Mr B. Ead, Mr P. C. Etty, Mrs M. W. Fawcus, Mr D. S. Fawcus, K. H. Foster, Mr M. Gear, Mr A. L. Gregg, Mr S. Grys, Miss M. Gut, Mr G. Handley, Mr S. R. Hartley, Mrs K. E. Hollingworth, Mr R. Jackson, D. M. Jenkins, Mr I. C. Jenkins, T. E. Kerfoot, J. K. S. Law, Mr G. T. Lever, Mrs S. Luke, Mr D. A. Luke, Dr C. H. Mason, Mr F. M. McGuinness, R. P. B. Michaelson, Mr R. Middleton, Mr S. Middleton, Mr M. E. Moore, Mr J. M. Mordecai, Mrs S. Morgan, Mr M. O'Boyle, Mr G. P. O'Shea, Mr J. C. Peak, Mr G. Pesticcio, Miss D. E. Pettle, Mr J. T. Phillips, Mr A. J. Pigott, Mr R. G. Price, R. J. Prince, Mr N. S. C. Proctor, Mr P. Pyatt, Mr P. Ragan, A. Robinson, Mr N. J. Robinson, Mr J. Sanders, The Select Racing Club Limited, D. A. Shinton, Mr A. Smallman, Wetherby Racing Bureau Ltd, Mr N. D. Whitham, Mrs C. S. Wilson.

**Assistant Trainer:** Jonathan Phillips

**Jockey (flat):** David Probert, Fergus Sweeney. **Jockey (NH):** Richard Johnson, Michael Byrne. **Conditional:** Alan Johns. **Amateur:** Mr Evan David, Mr Bradley Gibbs, Mr K. Hamner, Mr Jason Kiely.

---

## MR CHRISTIAN VON DER RECKE, Weilerswist

Postal: **Rennstall Recke, Hovener Hof, D-53919, Weilerswist, Germany**
Contacts: **PHONE (0049) 2254 84 53 14 FAX (0049) 2254 845315 MOBILE (0049) 171 542 50 50**
**E-MAIL recke@t-online.de WEBSITE www.rennstall-recke.de**

1 **AEGAEUS,** 6, b g Monsun (GER)—Ouija Board **MBA Racing**
2 **AL MAMZAR (IRE),** 6, b g Teofilo (IRE)—Avila **Andreas Hacker**
3 **AWAKAHN (GER),** 7, ch g Banyumanik (IRE)—Anna Suitor (GER) **Iris Blieschies**
4 **BANZAI (FR),** 4, b c Great Journey (JPN)—Machudi **van der Hulst Special**
5 **BASILARIS (GER),** 5, ch m Kalatos (GER)—Bromelia (GER) **Caroline Fuchs**
6 **CIOCCO SAM (GER),** 7, b h Samum (GER)—Cioccolata (GER) **Stall Blankenese**
7 **DREAMSPEED (IRE),** 8, b g Barathea (IRE)—Kapria (FR) **BMK Racing**
8 **EARL OF HEAVEN (GER),** 4, b c Areion (GER)—Evry (GER) **M. Haller**
9 **END OF WAR (FR),** 4, b c Air Eminem (IRE)—End Music (JPN) **van der Hulst Special**
10 **ERIC (GER),** 4, ch c Tertullian (USA)—Ericarrow (IRE) **Gabriele Gaul**
11 **FALSE ECONOMY (IRE),** 10, b g Orpen (USA)—Ashanti Dancer (IRE) **Gabriele Gaul**
12 **HOT BED (IRE),** 6, b g Dashing Blade—Mer de Corail (IRE) **Stall Chevalex**
13 **LIRO,** 5, b g Samum (GER)—La Donna **Stall Winterhude**
14 **LONESOME (GER),** 6, ch m Toylsome—Lady In Red (GER) **Birgit Houy**
15 **MAXIM GORKY (IRE),** 8, b g Montjeu (IRE)—Altruiste (USA) **MBA Racing**
16 **OSTARAKOV (GER),** 4, b f Sholokhov (IRE)—Orsina (IRE) **Stall Weiss-Blau**
17 **PARIGINO (FR),** 7, b g Panis (USA)—Loretta Gianni (FR) **MBA Racing**
18 **PERFECT CARE (SWI),** 4, b c Captain Rio—Perfectly Chilled (IRE) **Stall Klosters-Serneus**
19 **PHOENIX SHADOW (GER),** 4, b g Mamool (IRE)—Pawella (GER) **Stall Walcheren**
20 4, Ch f Literato (FR)—Queen's Diamond (GER) **Stall Quadriga GmbH**
21 **ROCK OF CASHEL (GER),** 4, b c Areion (GER)—Rocket Light (GER) **Zalim Bifov**
22 **SECRET EDGE,** 7, b g Tobougg (IRE)—Burton Ash **Gabriele Gaul**
23 4, B c Byron—Spinneret **C. von der Recke**
24 **TAQARROB (IRE),** 4, b g Bushranger (IRE)—Lucky Date (IRE) **Iris Blieschies**
25 **THE ART OF RACING (IRE),** 5, b g Acclamation—Divert (IRE) **MBA Racing**
26 **THEOLOGY,** 8, b g Galileo (IRE)—Biographie **Stall Saarbrucken**
27 **TIN SOLDIER (GER),** 6, ch h Martillo (GER)—Ta Sterna (GER) **Caroline Fuchs**
28 **TINLEY LODGE,** 6, b h Montjeu (IRE)—Shining Bright **Ulrike and Heiner Alck**
29 **TIREX (GER),** 4, b c Sabiango (GER)—Think Twice (GER) **Anne-Claire Bresges**
30 **TRACE OF SCENT (IRE),** 4, b f Acclamation—Red Blossom (USA) **Stall Karlshorst**
31 **ZAMPATA (IRE),** 4, b f Tagula (IRE)—Virevolle (FR) **Lester McGarrity**

### THREE-YEAR-OLDS

32 **CALL ME NUMBER ONE (GER),** b c Touch Down (GER)—Carrie Anne **H. H. Brand u.a.**
33 **EASTSITE ONE (GER),** b c Mamool (IRE)—Ericarrow (IRE) **Gabriele Gaul**
34 **JAMES COOK (GER),** b c Nicaron (GER)—Jalta (GER) **Stall Nizza**
35 **JUNGLEBOOGIE (GER),** b c Nicaron (GER)—Jive (GER) **Stall Nizza**
36 **PAR AVANT (GER),** b c Adlerflug (GER)—Pakama (GER) **Dirk von Mitzlaff**
37 **PETITE PARADISE (FR),** ch f Lord of England (GER)—Paradise Rain **Andreas Hacker**
38 **PIZ MORITZ (GER),** b f Mamool (IRE)—Pirquina (GER) **Stall Chevalex**
39 **SAMEER (IRE),** ch c Approve (IRE)—Brazilian Flame (IRE) **Stall Dein-Rennpferd.de**
40 **SAVELLETRI (IRE),** br c Cape Cross (IRE)—Elopa (GER) **Stall Gamshof**
41 **SHADOW SADNESS (GER),** b c Soldier Hollow—Shadow Queen (GER) **Stall Weiss-Blau**

## MR CHRISTIAN VON DER RECKE - Continued

### TWO-YEAR-OLDS

42 **CHANDOS BELLE (GER),** b f 1/1 Mamool—Chandos Rose **H. H. Brand u.a.**
43 **ERICA (GER),** b f 8/5 Mamool (IRE)—Ericarrow (IRE) (Bollin Eric) (15873) **Gabriele Gaul**
44 **IBIZA EMPRESS (IRE),** b f 2/4 Tertullian (USA)—Ibiza Dream (Night Shift (USA)) **MBA Racing**
45 **JAGUAR (GER),** b c 27/2 Nicaron (GER)—Juvena (GER) (Platini (GER)) **Stall Nizza**
46 **JOKER (GER),** b c 24/3 Nicaron (GER)—Jive (GER) (Montjeu (IRE)) **Stall Nizza**
47 **QUICK STEP (GER),** ch c 14/3 Distant Music (USA)—
Quadraga (GER) (Kornado) (2777) **Marquardt von Hodenberg**
48 **ZASADA (IRE),** gr f 25/2 Mastercraftsman (IRE)—Zagreb Flyer (Old Vic) (20634) **MBA Racing**

---

## 618 MR JOHN WADE, Sedgefield

Postal: **Howe Hills, Mordon, Sedgefield, Cleveland, TS21 2HG**
Contacts: **PHONE (01740) 630310 FAX (01740) 630310 MOBILE (07831) 686968**

1 **AIAAM AL NAMOOS,** 6, b g Teofilo (IRE)—Deveron (USA) **J. Wade**
2 **ALLEZ COOL (IRE),** 6, ch g Flemensfirth (USA)—La Fisarmonica (IRE) **J. Wade**
3 **ALWAYS RIGHT (IRE),** 13, ch g Right Win (IRE)—Kemal Brave (IRE) **J. Wade**
4 **APACHE BLUE (IRE),** 11, b g Presenting—La Eile (IRE) **J. Wade**
5 **BELLRINGER,** 5, b g Black Sam Bellamy (IRE)—Reamzafonic **J. Wade**
6 **CASUAL CAVALIER (IRE),** 7, br g Presenting—Asklynn (IRE) **J. Wade**
7 **CLUES AND ARROWS (IRE),** 7, b g Clerkenwell (USA)—Ballela Girl (IRE) **J. Wade**
8 **CORRELATE,** 5, ch g Zamindar (USA)—Snow Blossom **J. Wade**
9 **DEAN'S WALK (IRE),** 6, b g Craigsteel—Killashee (IRE) **J. Wade**
10 **DINGO BAY,** 9, b g Karinga Bay—Do It On Dani **Miss M. D. Myco**
11 **EXOTIC MAN (FR),** 10, ch g Arvico (FR)—Northine (FR) **J. Wade**
12 **FORTY CROWN (IRE),** 9, b g Court Cave (IRE)—Forty Quid (IRE) **Miss M. D. Myco**
13 **FOURTH ESTATE (IRE),** 9, b g Fantastic Light (USA)—Papering (IRE) **J. Wade**
14 **GHAFAAN (IRE),** 4, b g High Chaparral (IRE)—Nightdance Sun (GER) **J. Wade**
15 **GREEN PASTURES (IRE),** 7, b g Diamond Green (FR)—Continuous (IRE) **J. Wade**
16 **HARRIS HAWK,** 10, b g Karinga Bay—Harristown Lady **J. Wade**
17 **JAGO RIVER (IRE),** 9, b g Milan—Light And Airy **J. Wade**
18 **JOKERS AND ROGUES (IRE),** 7, b g Beneficial—Ashfield Girl (IRE) **J. Wade**
19 **JUKEBOX MELODY (IRE),** 9, b g Brian Boru—Carmels Cottage (IRE) **J. Wade**
20 **KINGS GREY (IRE),** 11, gr g King's Theatre (IRE)—Grey Mo (IRE) **J. Wade**
21 **MANNERED,** 10, b g Alflora (IRE)—Manettia (IRE) **J. Wade**
22 **MOON INDIGO,** 9, b g Sadler's Wells (USA)—Solo de Lune (IRE) **J. Wade**
23 **NEW ACADEMY,** 7, ch g Zamindar (USA)—New Abbey **J. Wade**
24 **NEWSPAGE (IRE),** 9, b g Blueprint (IRE)—Newlineview (IRE) **J. Wade**
25 **PEGASUS PRINCE (USA),** 11, b g Fusaichi Pegasus (USA)—Avian Eden (USA) **J. Wade**
26 **PIKARNIA,** 5, b g Authorized (IRE)—Kartuzy (JPN) **J. Wade**
27 **PUDSEY HOUSE,** 8, b g Double Trigger (IRE)—Dara's Pride (IRE) **J. Wade**
28 **RISKIER,** 10, gr g Kier Park (IRE)—Risky Girl **J. Wade**
29 **ROSEVILLE COTTAGE (IRE),** 8, b g Kris Kin (USA)—Johnny's Idea (IRE) **J. Wade**
30 **RUNSWICK DAYS (IRE),** 8, b g Presenting—Miss Lauren Dee (IRE) **J. Wade**
31 **RUNSWICK RELAX,** 9, ch g Generous (IRE)—Zany Lady **J. Wade**
32 **SHEPHERD STORM (IRE),** 5, b g September Storm (GER)—Clerhane Belle (IRE) **J. Wade**
33 **SPANISH FLEET,** 7, b g Cadeaux Genereux—Santisima Trinidad (IRE) **J. Wade**
34 **VANILLA RUN (IRE),** 4, b f Hurricane Run (IRE)—Vanilla Delight (IRE) **J. Wade**
35 **VIKING CHIEF (IRE),** 8, b g Westerner—Diamond Sal **J. Wade**
36 **WALSER (IRE),** 8, b g Milan—Brass Neck (IRE) **J. Wade**

**Assistant Trainer:** Miss Maria Myco (07798) 775932

**Jockey (NH):** Brian Hughes, Wilson Renwick, James Reveley. **Amateur:** Mr John Dawson, Mr C. M. O'Mahony.

---

## 619 MRS LUCY WADHAM, Newmarket

Postal: **The Trainer's House, Moulton Paddocks, Newmarket, Suffolk, CB8 7PJ**
Contacts: **PHONE (01638) 662411 FAX (01638) 668821 MOBILE (07980) 545776**
**E-MAIL lucy.wadham@virgin.net WEBSITE www.lucywadhamracing.co.uk**

1 **A BOY NAMED SUZI,** 7, b g Medecis—Classic Coral (USA) **ABS Partnership**
2 **ALIZEE JAVILEX (FR),** 5, b m Le Fou (IRE)—Etoile du Lion (FR) **J. J. W. Wadham**

## MRS LUCY WADHAM - Continued

3 **AMIDON (FR),** 5, b g Dom Alco (FR)—Immage (FR) **P. H. Betts**
4 **ARTIFICE SIVOLA (FR),** 5, gr g Dom Alco (FR)—Kerrana (FR) **R. B. Holt**
5 **ATTWAAL (IRE),** 6, b g Teofilo (IRE)—Qasirah (IRE) **Dr & Mrs Clive Layton**
6 **AVIADOR (GER),** 9, b g Paolini (GER)—Albarana (GER) **J. J. W. Wadham**
7 **BABY SHINE (IRE),** 9, b m King's Theatre (IRE)—Brambleshine (IRE) **P.A.Philipps,T.S.Redman & Mrs L. Redman**
8 **BARI (IRE),** 4, b f Cape Cross (IRE)—Genoa **Mr Mark Dixon & Luke Lillingston**
9 **CANUSPOTIT,** 8, b g Nomadic Way (USA)—Play Alone (IRE) **D. A. Wales & S. J. Wood**
10 **CHARPENTIERE,** 4, b f Shirocco (GER)—Lumiere d'espoir (FR) **Vogue Development Company (Kent) Ltd**
11 **DAWN TWISTER (GER),** 8, br g Monsun (GER)—Dawn Side (CAN) **Mr R. Davies**
12 **DOCTOR'S ORDERS (IRE),** 5, b g Mountain High (IRE)—Ballinaroone Girl (IRE) **Dr & Mrs Clive Layton**
13 **EL DANCER (GER),** 11, b g Seattle Dancer (USA)—Elea (GER) **Mr R. Davies**
14 **KENDAL MINT,** 4, b f Kyllachy—Windermere Island **Mrs J. Scott**
15 4, Gr g Montmartre (FR)—Kyria **Sceptre**
16 **LADY TIANA,** 4, b f Sir Percy—Cartoon **The FOPS**
17 **LANCEUR (FR),** 6, b g Rail Link—Lanciana (IRE) **P. H. Betts**
18 **LE REVE (IRE),** 7, br g Milan—Open Cry (IRE) **P. H. Betts**
19 **LETTER EXIT (IRE),** 5, b g Exit To Nowhere (USA)—Letterwoman (IRE) **Mr B. M. A. Hopkins**
20 **MINSTRELS GALLERY (IRE),** 6, ch g Refuse To Bend (IRE)—Lilakiya (IRE) **G. Pascoe & S. Brewer**
21 **MISS SPENT (IRE),** 5, b m Presenting—Cash And New (IRE) **The Wynn Partnership**
22 **MYSTIC SKY,** 4, b f Midnight Legend—Kentucky Sky **Mr T. R. Wood**
23 **NOBLE SILK,** 6, gr g Sir Percy—Tussah **The FOPS**
24 **RENDEZVOUS PEAK,** 6, b g High-Rise (IRE)—Jurado Park (IRE) **Tom Ford & Tony Regan**
25 **RISING TEAL,** 6, b m Phoenix Reach (IRE)—Tealby **The Dyball Partnership**
26 **ROAD TO FREEDOM,** 6, b g Revoque (IRE)—Go Classic **Mr R. S. Keeley**
27 **RUBY RAMBLER,** 5, b m Notnowcato—Arruhan (IRE) **Sara Dennis,J J W Wadham & J C S Wilson**
28 **SHANROE SANTOS (IRE),** 6, b g Definite Article—Jane Hall (IRE) **Mr J. Summers**
29 **SONGSMITH,** 7, b g Librettist (USA)—Venus Rising **Team Supreme**
30 **SUNSHINE CORNER (IRE),** 4, b f King's Theatre (IRE)—Coolgreaney (IRE) **P A Philipps & Mrs G J Redman**
31 **TEALISSIO,** 9, b g Helissio (FR)—Tealby **The Dyball Partnership**
32 **WATERED SILK,** 7, gr g Encosta de Lago (AUS)—Tussah **Mr & Mrs A. E. Pakenham**
33 **WHISPERING SPEED (IRE),** 5, ch g Vertical Speed (FR)—Midnight Lover **The A. T. Partnership**
34 **WIESENTRAUM (GER),** 9, ch g Next Desert (IRE)—Wiesenblute (GER) **G. Pascoe & S. Brewer**

### THREE-YEAR-OLDS

35 **ASHDOWN LASS,** b f Sir Percy—Antibes (IRE) **The FOPS**
36 **ATWIX,** br f Sakhee (USA)—Atwirl **The Calculated Speculators**
37 **COURTSIDER,** b f Kyllachy—Elhareer (IRE) **The Calculated Speculators**
38 **LADY VIOLA,** b f Sir Percy—String Quartet (IRE) **Mr & Mrs A. E. Pakenham**

### TWO-YEAR-OLDS

39 **PERNICKETY,** b f 14/2 Sir Percy—Nicola Bella (IRE) (Sadler's Wells (USA)) **Mr & Mrs A. E. Pakenham**
40 **TAFFETA LADY,** ch f 23/5 Sir Percy—Bombazine (IRE) (Generous (IRE)) **Mr & Mrs A. E. Pakenham**
41 **VICTRICE,** b f 20/2 Invincible Spirit (IRE)—Cassique Lady (IRE) (Langfuhr (CAN)) **Mr & Mrs A. E. Pakenham**

**Other Owners:** S. J. Brewer, J. J. Brummitt, Mrs S. Dennis, M. H. Dixon, D. J. S. Dyball, C. A. Dyball, T. E. Ford, Mr C. A. Hamilton, Mr S. J. High, Dr C. A. Layton, Mrs H. M. Layton, L. Lillingston, J. R. O'Leary, Mrs S. F. O'Leary, A. E. Pakenham, Mrs V. H. Pakenham, G. J. Pascoe, Mr M. Pendlebury, P. A. Philipps, T. S. Redman, Mrs G. J. Redman, Mrs L. E. Redman, A. W. Regan, A. H. Slone, Mr C. D. Smith, L. G. Straszewski, Mrs L. A. M. Wadham, Mr E. R. Wakelin, D. A. Wales, J. C. S. Wilson, Mr S. J. Wood.

**Jockey (NH):** Leighton Aspell. **Conditional:** Matt Crawley, Luke Ingram. **Amateur:** Mr Sam Davis.

---

## 620 MISS TRACY WAGGOTT, Spennymoor

Postal: **Awakening Stables, Merrington Lane, Spennymoor, Co. Durham, DL16 7HB**
Contacts: **PHONE (01388) 819012 MOBILE (07979) 434498**

1 **BORDER BANDIT (USA),** 7, b g Selkirk (USA)—Coretta (IRE) **Elsa Crankshaw Gordon Allan**
2 **BRIGHT APPLAUSE,** 7, b g Royal Applause—Sadaka (USA) **Littlethorpe Park Racing**
3 **CAPTAIN ROYALE (IRE),** 10, ch g Captain Rio—Paix Royale **H. Conlon**
4 **CAYJO,** 4, b g Josr Algarhoud (IRE)—Caysue **Mr D. Tate**
5 **COPT HILL,** 7, b g Avonbridge—Lalique (IRE) **H. Conlon**
6 **EXCLUSIVE WATERS (IRE),** 5, b g Elusive City (USA)—Pelican Waters (IRE) **Northumbria Leisure Ltd**
7 **GABRIAL'S HOPE (FR),** 6, b g Teofilo (IRE)—Wedding Night (FR) **Mr D. Tate**

## MISS TRACY WAGGOTT - Continued

8 **KING'S PROSPECT,** 4, b g Authorized (IRE)—Sovereign's Honour (USA) **H. Conlon**
9 **MISSION IMPOSSIBLE,** 10, gr g Kyllachy—Eastern Lyric **H. Conlon**
10 **SHADOWTIME,** 10, b g Singspiel (IRE)—Massomah (USA) **H. Conlon**
11 **SHEARIAN,** 5, b g Royal Applause—Regal Asset (USA) **Mr D. Tate**
12 **SOLAR SPIRIT (IRE),** 10, b g Invincible Spirit (IRE)—Misaayef (USA) **Elsa Crankshaw Gordon Allan**
13 **VALANTINO OYSTER (IRE),** 8, b g Pearl of Love (IRE)—Mishor **Mr S. Sawley**
14 **WHISPERED TIMES (USA),** 8, b br g More Than Ready (USA)—Lightning Show (USA) **J. J. Maguire**
15 **WINDFORPOWER (IRE),** 5, b g Red Clubs (IRE)—Dubai Princess (IRE) **Mr D. Tate**

### THREE-YEAR-OLDS

16 **BRIGHTSIDE,** b g Indesatchel (IRE)—Romantic Destiny **Mr D. Tate**
17 **MIGHTY BOND,** b g Misu Bond (IRE)—Mighty Flyer (IRE) **Mr D. Tate**
18 **MY SPECIALBRU,** b g Arabian Gleam—Carati **Mr D. Tate**
19 **QUESTO,** ch g Monsieur Bond (IRE)—Ex Gracia **J. J. Maguire**

### TWO-YEAR-OLDS

**20** B f 15/3 Medicean—Dand Nee (USA) (Kabool)

**Other Owners:** G. Allan, Miss E. Crankshaw, J. M. Hughes, Mr A. Stainton.

---

## 621 MR JOHN WAINWRIGHT, Malton

Postal: **Granary House, Beverley Road, Norton, Malton, North Yorkshire, YO17 9PJ**
Contacts: **PHONE (01653) 692993 MOBILE (07798) 778070**
**E-MAIL jswainwright@googlemail.com**

1 **ACQUAINT (IRE),** 4, gr f Verglas (IRE)—Azia (IRE) **FRT Racing Club**
2 **BLAZEOFENCHANTMENT (USA),** 5, b g Officer (USA)—Willow Rush (USA) **FRT Racing Club**
3 **EENY MAC (IRE),** 8, ch g Redback—Sally Green (IRE) **Chatterbox Racing Partnership**
4 **EXIT TO FREEDOM,** 9, ch g Exit To Nowhere (USA)—Bobanvi **I. J. Barran**
5 **KNOCKAMANY BENDS (IRE),** 5, b g Majestic Missile (IRE)—Sweet Compliance **D. R. & E. E. Brown**
6 **MEDECIS MOUNTAIN,** 6, b g Medecis—Moon Cat (IRE) **J. S. Wainwright**
7 **OBBOORR,** 6, b g Cape Cross (IRE)—Felawnah (USA) **Mr R. Kaye**
8 **ROSSINGTON,** 6, b g Gentleman's Deal (IRE)—Ettrbee (IRE) **Brian Robb. David Hoyes. Mark Phillips.**

### THREE-YEAR-OLDS

9 **EAST RIVER (IRE),** ch c Captain Rio—Eastern Blue (IRE) **Mr R. Kaye**
10 **FOREST MISSILE (IRE),** b g Majestic Missile (IRE)—Garnock Academy (USA) **P. W. Cooper**
11 **NORTH BAY LADY (IRE),** b f Fast Company (IRE)—Straight Sets (IRE) **Mr W Bavill, Mr A P Bluck, Mr D Bavill**
12 **ROCCO'S DELIGHT,** b g Multiplex—No Page (IRE) **P. W. Cooper**

**Other Owners:** Mr W. C. Bavill, Mr D. Bavill, Mr A. P. Bluck, D. R. Brown, Mrs E. E. Brown, Mr D. N. Hoyes, Mr J. Lamerton, Mr M. D. Phillips, Mr B. W. Robb, Mr P. R. Walker, Mr P. Walker.

**Assistant Trainer:** Mrs Fiona Wainwright

**Jockey (flat):** Tom Eaves, Paddy Aspell, Tony Hamilton. **Amateur:** Mr Alexander French, Mr Kaine Wood.

---

## 622 MR ROBERT WALEY-COHEN, Banbury

Postal: **Upton Viva, Banbury, Oxfordshire, OX15 6HT**
Contacts: **PHONE (02072) 446022 MOBILE (07831) 888778**
**E-MAIL rwc@uptonviva.co.uk WEBSITE www.uptonestate.co.uk**

1 **ATOMIC TANGERINE,** 5, ch m Midnight Legend—Perle de Puce (FR) **R. B. Waley-Cohen**
2 **FREE THINKING,** 7, b br m Hernando (FR)—Liberthine (FR) **R. B. Waley-Cohen**
3 **MAKADAMIA,** 6, b m Kahyasi—Makounji (FR) **R. B. Waley-Cohen**
4 **OSCAR TIME (IRE),** 14, b g Oscar (IRE)—Baywatch Star (IRE) **R. B. Waley-Cohen**
5 **RUMBAVU (IRE),** 9, br g Overbury (IRE)—Strong Swimmer (IRE) **R. B. Waley-Cohen**
6 **SING TO ME,** 5, ch m Presenting—Symphonique (FR) **R. B. Waley-Cohen**
7 **STORM LANTERN,** 6, b g King's Theatre (IRE)—Katoune (FR) **R. B. Waley-Cohen**
8 **THE MISSUS,** 4, b f Presenting—Violet Express (FR) **R. B. Waley-Cohen**

## MR ROBERT WALEY-COHEN - Continued

**Assistant Trainer:** Kate Mawle

**Amateur:** Mr S. Waley-Cohen.

---

## 623 MR MARK WALFORD, Sheriff Hutton

Postal: **Cornborough Manor, Sheriff Hutton, York, YO60 6QN**
Contacts: **PHONE (01347) 878382 FAX (01347) 878547 MOBILE (07734) 265689**
**E-MAIL g_walford@hotmail.com WEBSITE www.timwalford.co.uk**

1 **ADAM'S ALE,** 6, b g Ishiguru (USA)—Aqua **Mrs M. J. Hills**
2 **BARLEYCORN LADY (IRE),** 4, b f Nayef (USA)—Partly Sunny **G Mett Racing & Mr T Chadney**
3 **BIG SOUND,** 8, b g Supreme Sound—Tarbolton Moss **Hanson & Hamilton**
4 **CORNBOROUGH,** 4, ch g Sir Percy—Emirates First (IRE) **Cornborough Racing Club**
5 **CRAGGAKNOCK,** 4, b g Authorized (IRE)—Goodie Twosues **Mrs Mary & David Longstaff**
6 **EVERLASTING LIGHT,** 5, b m Authorized (IRE)—Blue Rocket (IRE) **Mrs G. B. Walford**
7 **FENTARA,** 10, b m Kayf Tara—Miss Fencote **Chasing Gold Limited**
8 4, B g Josr Algarhoud (IRE)—Festive Chimes (IRE)
9 **FLY BY KNIGHT,** 6, b g Desert King (IRE)—Lox Lane (IRE) **Mrs C. Townroe**
10 **HERE COMES ARTHUR (FR),** 5, b g Smadoun (FR)—Toulouzette (IRE) **Mr J Toes & Mr J O'Loan**
11 **HIGHLANDER TED,** 7, b g Midnight Legend—Half Each **Mrs Carol Watson**
12 **HOME FLYER (IRE),** 4, b g Tagula (IRE)—Lady Flyer (IRE) **Mrs J Collins,Mrs H Forman,Miss J Sawney**
13 **KING OF STRINGS (IRE),** 6, b g Desert King (IRE)—Lemon Cello (IRE) **F. M. & Mrs E. Holmes**
14 **KODICIL (IRE),** 7, b g Kodiac—Miss Caoimhe (IRE) **The Elephant Group**
15 **LILLY'S LEGEND,** 5, ch m Midnight Legend—Dalticia (FR) **Mr N. Skinner & Mr J. Grindal**
16 **LORIMER'S LOT (IRE),** 4, ch f Camacho—Alwiyda (USA) **Lorimer Walford**
17 **MISSY WELLS,** 5, b m Misu Bond (IRE)—Aqua **Mrs M. J. Hills**
18 **MR SNOOZY,** 6, b g Pursuit of Love—Hard To Follow **T. W. Heseltine**
19 **OLIVER'S GOLD,** 7, b g Danehill Dancer (IRE)—Gemini Gold (IRE) **Quench Racing Partnership**
20 **SHIMLA DAWN (IRE),** 7, b g Indian Danehill (IRE)—Tina Thyne (IRE) **Mrs M. Cooper**
21 **TARA'S ROCKET,** 4, b g Kayf Tara—Whizz Back (IRE) **Mrs R. Haggie**
22 **UNO VALOROSO (FR),** 7, b g Voix du Nord (FR)—Danse d'avril (FR) **Mr C. N. Herman**
23 **WITHOUT REGARD (IRE),** 7, ch m Millkom—Habla Me (IRE) **P. Maddison**
24 **WOODY BAY,** 5, b g New Approach (IRE)—Dublino (USA) **Mr P. C. Thompson**

### THREE-YEAR-OLDS

25 **CAPE HIDEAWAY,** b g Mount Nelson—Amiata **Cornborough Racing Club**
26 **REGAL MISSILE (IRE),** b c Royal Applause—Leenane (IRE) **Dickson, Hamilton, Smeaton & Skinner**
27 **SOUTHVIEW LADY,** b f Misu Bond (IRE)—Salalah **Cornborough Racing Club**
28 **VANILLA ROSE (IRE),** b f Bushranger (IRE)—Vanilla Loan (IRE) **Cornborough Racing Club**

### TWO-YEAR-OLDS

**29** B f 7/1 Sir Percy—Bruma (IRE) (Footstepsinthesand) (857)
**30** B g 16/3 Piccolo—Faithful Beauty (IRE) (Last Tycoon)
**31** Ch g 25/2 Monsieur Bond (IRE)—Silk (IRE) (Machiavellian (USA)) (7142)

**Other Owners:** Mr M. A. Blades, T. H. Chadney, Lady N. F. Cobham, Mr R. Colclough, Mrs J. Collins, D. J. Dickson, Mr B. Downard, Mrs H. Forman, C. J. Grindal, Mr K. Hamilton, Mr K. Hanson, F. M. Holmes, Mrs E. Holmes, Mr S. A. Jackson, Mrs M. Longstaff, Mr D. Longstaff, Mr P. P. Lorimer, S. N. Lorimer, Mr John O'Loan, Mr M. Preedy, Miss J. Sawney, N. Skinner, Mr R. J. Smeaton, Mr J. Toes, Mrs C. A. Watson.

**Assistant Trainer:** Tim Walford

**Jockey (flat):** Duran Fentiman, Graham Gibbons, Jason Hart.

---

## 624 MR ROBERT WALFORD, Blandford

Postal: **Heart of Oak Stables, Okeford Fitzpane, Blandford, Dorset, DT11 0LW**
Contacts: **MOBILE (07815) 116209**
**E-MAIL robertwalford1@gmail.com**

1 **ALBERT D'OLIVATE (FR),** 5, b br g Alberto Giacometti (IRE)—Komunion (FR) **Chris Pugsley & Nigel Skinner**
2 **ART DECO MARSAL (FR),** 5, b g Passing Sale (FR)—Guiguite du Pots (FR) **G. D. Thompson**
3 **ASTRE DE LA COUR (FR),** 5, b br g Khalkevi (IRE)—Gracieuse Delacour (FR) **The Front Runners Partnership**
4 **BRODY BLEU (FR),** 8, b g Kotky Bleu (FR)—Brodie Blue (FR) **Mr R. J. Brown**

## MR ROBERT WALFORD - Continued

5 **CAMPING GROUND (FR),** 5, b g Goldneyev (USA)—Camomille (GER) **G. L. Porter**
6 **CAROLE'S SPIRIT,** 7, b m Hernando (FR)—Carole's Crusader **P. Murphy**
7 **CASTARNIE,** 7, b g Alflora (IRE)—Just Jenny (IRE) **Sue & Clive Cole & Ann & Tony Gale**
8 **PILGREEN (FR),** 10, ch g Green Tune (USA)—Galinetta (FR) **Mrs S. De Wilde**
9 **REDANNA (IRE),** 6, b m Presenting—Ask June (IRE) **The White Hart Company**
10 **ROSA IMPERIALIS,** 6, ch m Imperial Dancer—Motcombe (IRE) **Lady N. F. Cobham**
11 **SAINT RAPH (FR),** 7, gr g Saint des Saints (FR)—Speed Padoline (FR) **Mrs C. M. Hinks**
12 **SUN WILD LIFE (FR),** 5, b g Antarctique (IRE)—Nidelia (FR) **The Keightley Lambert Partnership**
13 **SWINCOMBE STAR,** 6, b g With The Flow (USA)—Lady Felix **Yeo Racing Partnership**
14 **TRIBULATION (IRE),** 7, br g Diktat—Royal York **Mrs C. A. Lewis-Jones**
15 **UMBERTO D'OLIVATE (FR),** 7, b g Alberto Giacometti (IRE)—Komunion (FR) **Mrs S. De Wilde**

**Other Owners:** Mr C. Cole, Mrs S. S. Cole, Mr A. P. Gale, Mrs A. G. Gale, Mr P. Goodwin, Mr A. G. Ham, Mrs C. Keightley, Mr T P Lambert, K. B. W. Parkhouse, C. C. Pugsley, Mr S. Reed, N. Skinner, Mr E. W. White, Mrs K. D. Yeo.

**Jockey (NH):** Dougie Costello, Daryl Jacob, Felix De Gilles.

---

## MR ED WALKER, Newmarket

Postal: **The Bungalow, Warren Place, Newmarket, Suffolk, CB8 8QQ**
Contacts: **PHONE (01638) 660464 MOBILE (07787) 534145**
**E-MAIL ed@edwalkerracing.com WEBSITE www.edwalkerracing.com**

1 **BOLD PREDICTION (IRE),** 5, b g Kodiac—Alexander Eliott (IRE) **John Nicholls (Trading) & Matthew Cottis**
2 **BUSHCRAFT (IRE),** 4, b c Bushranger (IRE)—Lady Lucia (IRE) **L. A. Bellman**
3 **GLORIOUS PROTECTOR (IRE),** 5, b g Azamour (IRE)—Hasaiyda (IRE) **Mrs A. A. Lau Yap**
4 **GLORIOUS SUN,** 4, b g Medicean—Sweet Cando (IRE) **Ms Judy Yap & Ms Salina Yang**
5 **LIGHTNING MOON (IRE),** 4, b c Shamardal (USA)—Catch The Moon (IRE) **Mr M. Betamar**
6 **NICHOLASCOPERNICUS (IRE),** 6, ch g Medicean—Ascendancy **D. A. Halsall**
7 **PERSONA GRATA,** 4, b f Sir Percy—Kaldounya **Middleham Park Racing XLI**
8 **SMART SALUTE,** 4, b g Royal Applause—Naizak **Mr B. T. C. Liu**
9 **WILLIE WAG TAIL (USA),** 6, b g Theatrical—Night Risk (USA) **Qatar Racing Limited**

### THREE-YEAR-OLDS

10 B c Authorized (IRE)—Awwal Malika (USA) **N. Mourad**
11 **BUSHEPHALUS (IRE),** gr g Dark Angel (IRE)—White Daffodil (IRE) **Mr E. Bush**
12 **COLOURFILLY,** ch f Compton Place—Where's Broughton **L. A. Bellman**
13 **DARK EMPIRE (IRE),** b g Dark Angel (IRE)—Rose's Destination (IRE) **Mr C. U. F. Ma**
14 **DARK WAVE,** ch g Zebedee—Rule Britannia **Mr C. U. F. Ma**
15 **DOUBLE HEAVEN,** b g Dutch Art—Popocatepetl (FR) **Mr C. F. Ma**
16 **EDGE OF LOVE,** b f Kyllachy—Upskittled **Sheikh R. D. Al Maktoum**
17 **FILLOTHEWISP,** b f Teofilo (IRE)—Euroceleb (IRE) **Mrs O. Hoare**
18 **GLORIOUS ASSET,** b c Aqlaam—Regal Asset (USA) **Mrs A. A. Lau Yap**
19 **GLORIOUS DANCER,** br c Royal Applause—Provence **Mrs A. A. Lau Yap**
20 **GUN CASE,** b c Showcasing—Bassinet (USA) **Sheikh J. D. Al Maktoum**
21 **INVINCIBLE GOLD (IRE),** b c Invincible Spirit (IRE)—Urgele (FR) **Mr John Coleman & Mr Clarence Cheng**
22 **JUSTICE BELLE (IRE),** b f Montjeu (IRE)—Metaphor (USA) **Mr R. Ng**
23 **JUSTICE KNIGHT (IRE),** b g Raven's Pass (USA)—New Story (USA) **Mr R. Ng**
24 **LA MARCHESA (IRE),** b f Duke of Marmalade (IRE)—Brindisi **Mrs Olivia Hoare & Mark Dixon**
25 **LAAHIJ,** b c Arcano (IRE)—Acicula (IRE) **Khalifa Dasmal & Mr M Hareb**
26 **MILLPIKE (USA),** b br g Fastnet Rock (AUS)—Forever Beautiful (USA) **Reiko Baum & Michael Baum**
27 **NOUVEAU FORET,** b f Myboycharlie (IRE)—Forest Express (AUS) **Mr N. Bowden**
28 **RUSTIQUE,** ch f Pastoral Pursuits—Nihal (IRE) **Dubai Thoroughbred Racing**
29 **SHOWBIRD,** b f Showcasing—Dancing Feather **K. A. Dasmal**
30 **SINGLE LENSE (IRE),** b c Kodiac—Undulation **Sheikh R. D. Al Maktoum**
31 **TWICE CERTAIN (IRE),** b f Lawman (FR)—Leopard Hunt (USA) **R. A. Donworth**
32 **VANISHING,** b f Sir Percy—Valoria **Mr S. A. Stuckey**

### TWO-YEAR-OLDS

33 B c 26/4 Holy Roman Emperor (IRE)—Al Saqiya (USA) (Woodman (USA)) (67460) **L. A. Bellman**
34 **ATLANTEIA (IRE),** ch f 13/4 Duke of Marmalade (IRE)—Teide Lady (Nashwan (USA)) (20000) **Mr M. J. Cottis**
35 **CAPTAIN COURAGEOUS (IRE),** b c 1/3 Canford Cliffs (IRE)—Annacloy Pearl (IRE) (Mull of Kintyre (USA)) (50000) **E. C. D. Walker**
36 Ch f 17/2 Dream Ahead (USA)—Centreofattention (AUS) (Danehill (USA)) (45000) **Mrs D. A. Shah**
37 B f 19/4 Whipper (USA)—Coco (USA) (Storm Bird (CAN)) (22222) **L. A. Bellman**

## MR ED WALKER - Continued

**38** B c 28/4 Shamardal (USA)—Deveron (USA) (Cozzene (USA)) (100000) **Mr M. H. Lui**
**39 DREAM GLORY (IRE),** b c 5/2 Dream Ahead (USA)—
Do The Honours (IRE) (Highest Honor (FR)) (200000) **Ms A A Yap & Mr F Ma**
**40 EASY GOLD (IRE),** ch c 21/3 Mastercraftsman (IRE)—
Aiming Upwards (Blushing Flame (USA)) (65000) **Mr J. A. Coleman**
**41** B c 22/2 Pour Moi (IRE)—Endearing (Selkirk (USA)) (55000) **Mrs A. A. Lau Yap**
**42** B c 27/4 Kyllachy—Epistoliere (IRE) (Alzao (USA)) **L. A. Bellman**
**43 GALE SONG,** b f 10/2 Invincible Spirit (IRE)—Please Sing (Royal Applause) **Lordship Stud**
**44** B c 7/2 Iffraaj—Green Poppy (Green Desert (USA)) (115000) **Mr C. U. F. Ma**
**45** Br c 26/3 Lawman (FR)—Koniya (IRE) (Doyoun) (45000) **E. C. D. Walker**
**46** B c 24/3 Manduro (GER)—Qui Moi (CAN) (Swain (IRE)) (55000) **Mrs A. A. Lau Yap**
**47** B c 1/4 High Chaparral (IRE)—Ratukidul (FR) (Danehill (USA)) (50000) **Mr M. H. Lui**
**48** B c 16/5 Exceed And Excel (AUS)—Rayyana (IRE) (Rainbow Quest (USA)) (80000) **Mr M. H. Lui**
**49** B c 10/4 Arcano (IRE)—Red Blossom (USA) (Silver Hawk (USA)) (40000) **Mrs D. A. Shah**
**50** Ch c 19/2 Poet's Voice—Sky Wonder (Observatory (USA)) (85000) **Mrs A. A. Lau Yap**
**51** B f 8/2 Kyllachy—Time Crystal (IRE) (Sadler's Wells (USA)) (70000) **Ms A A Yap & Mr F Ma**
**52 TRIKINGDOM,** b c 11/2 Showcasing—Spritzeria (Bigstone (IRE)) (60000) **F Ma, R Cheung, S Tung**

**Other Owners:** Mr Michael Baum, Mrs Reiko Baum, Mr Laurence A. Bellman, Mr Richard Cheung, Mr J. A. Coleman, Mr Matthew Cottis, Mr Khalifa Dasmal, Mr M. H. Dixon, Mr Alastair Donald, Mr M. S. Hareb, Mr T. F. Harris, Mrs E. A. Harris, Mrs Olivia Hoare, John Nicholls (Trading) Ltd, Ms A. A. Yap, Mr F. Ma, Mr T. S. Palin, Mr M. Prince, Mr S. Tung, Mr E. C. D. Walker, Mr T. Walker, Mrs T. Walker, Ms Salina Yang.

**Assistant Trainer:** Jack Steels

---

## 626 MR CHRIS WALL, Newmarket

Postal: **Induna Stables, Fordham Road, Newmarket, Suffolk, CB8 7AQ**
Contacts: **OFFICE (01638) 661999 HOME (01638) 668896 FAX (01638) 667279**
**MOBILE (07764) 940255**
**E-MAIL christianwall@btconnect.com WEBSITE www.chriswallracing.co.uk**

**1 ELEUSIS,** 4, b f Elnadim (USA)—Demeter (USA) **Lady Juliet Tadgell**
**2 FEVER FEW,** 6, b m Pastoral Pursuits—Prairie Oyster **Mrs C A Wall & Mr R Wayman**
**3 FLIGHT FIGHT,** 4, b g Raven's Pass (USA)—Sunspear (IRE) **Ms A. Fustoq**
**4 JOHARA (IRE),** 4, b f Iffraaj—Hurricane Irene (IRE) **Mrs Claude Lilley**
**5 KATAWI,** 4, b f Dubawi (IRE)—Purring (USA) **Moyns Park Estate and Stud Ltd**
**6 MAY QUEEN,** 4, ch f Shamardal (USA)—Mango Lady **Ms A. Fustoq**
**7 MR WIN (IRE),** 4, b g Intikhab (USA)—Midnight Oasis **Mr D. M. Thurlby**
**8 OH SO SASSY,** 5, b m Pastoral Pursuits—Almasi (IRE) **The Eight of Diamonds**
**9 QANAN,** 6, b g Green Desert (USA)—Strings **Alan & Jill Smith**
**10 SILVALA DANCE,** 5, b m Kyllachy—Bride of The Sea **Mrs D. Lochhead**
**11 SOUVILLE,** 4, b f Dalakhani (IRE)—Royale Danehill (IRE) **Hughes & Scott**
**12 SYRIAN PEARL,** 4, gr f Clodovil (IRE)—Syrian Queen **The Clodhoppers**
**13 THE NEW PHARAOH (IRE),** 4, b g Montjeu (IRE)—Out West (USA) **Ms A. Fustoq**
**14 TRUCANINI,** 5, b m Mount Nelson—Jalissa **Dolly's Dream Syndicate**
**15 VENUS MARINA,** 4, b f Tiger Hill (IRE)—Danvers **Highgrounds Partnership**
**16 WINDY CITI,** 4, ch f Zamindar (USA)—Windy Britain **Scuderia Giocri Ltd**
**17 ZE KING,** 6, b g Manduro (GER)—Top Flight Queen **Ms A. Fustoq**

### THREE-YEAR-OLDS

**18 ACCIPITER,** ch f Showcasing—Mexican Hawk (USA) **Follow The Flag Partnership**
**19 BELVOIR DIVA,** br f Exceed And Excel (AUS)—Merry Diva **Mrs Barry Green & Partners**
**20** B f Shirocco (GER)—Cloud Hill **Strawberry Fields Stud**
**21 CLOUD SEVEN,** br c New Approach (IRE)—Regrette Rien (USA) **Ms A. Fustoq**
**22 COOLCALMCOLLECTED (IRE),** b f Acclamation—Jalissa **Mr D. M. Thurlby**
**23 ENCHANTED MOMENT,** b f Lawman (FR)—Gentle Thoughts **Mr D. S. Lee**
**24 KENOBE STAR (IRE),** b c Clodovil (IRE)—Maimana (IRE) **Mr J. Stewart**
**25 KRISTJANO (GER),** b g Nayef (USA)—Kalahari Dancer **B. R. Westley**
**26 LAURA B,** b f Acclamation—New Design (IRE) **Lady Juliet Tadgell**
**27 MULTISTAR,** b f Multiplex—Express Logic **Bringloe & Clarke**
**28 OASIS SPEAR,** b g Oasis Dream—Sunspear (IRE) **Ms A. Fustoq**
**29 POLLY GARTER,** b f Dylan Thomas (IRE)—Esteemed Lady (IRE) **D. Swinburn & P. Scott**
**30 ROYAL ALTITUDE,** b c Zamindar (USA)—Royal Assent **Follow The Flag Partnership**
**31 ROYAL RETTIE,** b f Royal Applause—Bended Knee **Bringloe & Clarke**

## MR CHRIS WALL - Continued

32 **SAHARA (IRE),** b f Clodovil (IRE)—Celtic Lynn (IRE) **Qatar Racing Limited**
33 **STAMP OF APPROVAL (IRE),** b f Approve (IRE)—Wassendale **Induna Racing Partners (Two)**
34 B g Dylan Thomas (IRE)—Tencarola (IRE) **Mr Simon Kwok**
35 **TTAINTED LOVE,** b f Mastercraftsman (IRE)—Eve **Mr D. S. Lee**
36 B c Rip Van Winkle (IRE)—Turning Light (GER) **Mr Simon Kwok**

## TWO-YEAR-OLDS

37 **ALL FOR LOVE,** b f 15/4 Giant's Causeway (USA)—Wallis (King's Best (USA)) (70000) **Ms A. Fustoq**
38 **ALWAYS A DREAM,** b f 19/1 Oasis Dream—Always Remembered (IRE) (Galileo (IRE)) **Ms A. Fustoq**
39 **CAMBODIA (IRE),** ch c 25/4 Fast Company (IRE)—
Remarkable Story (Mark of Esteem (IRE)) (45000) **Mr D. M. Thurlby**
40 B c 6/5 Royal Applause—Danvers (Cape Cross (IRE)) (15000) **Executive Bloodlines**
41 **EAGLE FALLS,** b c 26/1 Paco Boy (IRE)—
Miss Excel (Exceed And Excel (AUS)) (18000) **Follow The Flag Partnership**
42 **KILUNA,** b f 12/4 Mawatheeq (USA)—Shamara (IRE) (Spectrum (IRE)) (4500) **Lady Juliet Tadgell**
43 B f 17/3 Bahri (USA)—Lark In The Park (IRE) (Grand Lodge (USA)) **Mia Racing**
44 **LUDI LU (FR),** b f 31/3 New Approach (IRE)—Sunspear (IRE) (Montjeu (IRE)) **Ms A. Fustoq**
45 B c 19/3 Iffraaj—Maine Rose (Red Ransom (USA)) (80000) **Sheikh Rashid Dalmook Al Maktoum**
46 **MATILDA'S LAW,** b f 3/4 Aussie Rules (USA)—Oatey (Master Willie) (5500) **Archangels 2**
47 **MIX AND MINGLE (IRE),** ch f 25/2 Exceed And Excel (AUS)—
Mango Lady (Dalakhani (IRE)) (50000) **Ms A. Fustoq**
48 B f 12/2 Invincible Spirit (IRE)—Sauvage (FR) (Sri Pekan (USA)) (48000) **Mr D. M. Thurlby**
49 **SONG OF PARADISE,** ch f 19/2 Kyllachy—Merry Diva (Bahamian Bounty) (18000) **The Equema Partners**
50 Ch f 6/2 Medicean—Thymesthree (IRE) (Galileo (IRE)) (2857) **Mr P. Botham**

**Other Owners:** Mr M. Ayers, Mr T. Bater, Mr N. Belcher, Mr Hugh Bethell, Mr & Mrs Burrows, Mrs V. Carpenter, Mr D. Cherry, Mrs S. Cunningham, Mr & Mrs G. Davies, Mrs J. E. Dobie, Mr Stuart Feast, Mr R. Fraiser, Mrs Barry Green, Mr C. Harker, Mr P. Hitchcock, Mrs Jill Kerr-Smiley, Mr Richard Machin, Mrs M. Middleton, Mr B. Payne, Mr D. Popely, Mr R. A. Popely, Mr P. Proctor, Mr R. Rice, Mr D. Rice, Mrs T. Rigby, Pruedence Lady Salt, Sir Patrick & Lady Mary Salt, Mr A. Smith, Mr M. Stevens, Lady Stuttaford, Mr Richard Sutton, Mr Alan Tickle, Mrs Irene Tickle, Mr Mathew Tickle, Mrs C. J. Walker, Mrs E. Wass, Miss H. Wass, Mrs P. Williams.

**Assistant Trainer:** Richard Freeman

**Jockey (flat):** George Baker, Ted Durcan. **Apprentice:** Sam Clarke, Jess Sharp.

---

**627**

## MRS SARAH WALL, Dallington

Postal: **Little Pines, Bakers Lane, Dallington, Heathfield, East Sussex, TN21 9JS**
Contacts: **PHONE/FAX (01435) 831048 MOBILE (07783) 370856**
**E-MAIL sarah55french@btinternet.com**

1 **BACH TO FRONT (IRE),** 10, b m Bach (IRE)—Celtic Leader (IRE) **J. P. C. Wall**
2 **BALLINHASSIG (IRE),** 10, ch g Beneficial—Dear Polly (IRE) **Mrs S. Wall**

**Assistant Trainer:** Jeremy Wall

**Jockey (NH):** Marc Goldstein.

---

## MR TREVOR WALL, Craven Arms

Postal: **Hope Farm Stables, Twitchen, Clunbury, Craven Arms, Shropshire, SY7 0HN**
Contacts: **PHONE (01588) 660219 MOBILE (07972) 732080**

1 **FAIRY ALISHA,** 7, ch m Doyen (IRE)—Regal Fairy (IRE) **D. Pugh**
2 **FEMME D'ESPERE,** 9, b m Celts Espere—Drummer's Dream (IRE) **Ricochet Management Limited**
3 **HELMSLEY FLYER (IRE),** 5, b g Baltic King—Dorn Hill **The Wenlock Edge Optimists**
4 **HOT MADRAS (IRE),** 7, b m Milan—Hot Fudge (IRE) **T. R. Wall**
5 **MAXI MAC (IRE),** 5, ch g Thousand Words—Crimada (IRE) **D. Pugh**

**Other Owners:** Mr P. Cowell, Mr J. D. Evans.

**Assistant Trainer:** Mrs J. A. Wall

**Conditional:** Josh Wall.

## 629 MRS JANE WALTON, Otterburn

Postal: **Dunns Houses, Otterburn, Newcastle Upon Tyne, Tyne and Wear, NE19 1LB**
Contacts: **PHONE (01830) 520677 FAX (01830) 520677 MOBILE (07808) 592701**
**E-MAIL dunnshouses@hotmail.com WEBSITE www.janewaltonhorseracing.co.uk**

1 **ALWAYSRECOMMENDED (IRE),** 6, ch g Gamut (IRE)—Awbeg Beauty (IRE) **Highly Recommended Partnership 2**
2 **HAVE YOU HAD YOURS (IRE),** 9, br g Whitmore's Conn (USA)—Mandys Moynavely (IRE) **Highly Recommended Partnership**
3 **HEEZ A STEEL (IRE),** 14, b g Naheez (USA)—Ari's Fashion **Mrs J. M. Walton**
4 **MASTER MURPHY (IRE),** 10, b g Flemensfirth (USA)—Awbeg Beauty (IRE) **Mrs J. M. Walton**
5 **REVERSE THE CHARGE (IRE),** 8, b g Bishop of Cashel—Academy Jane (IRE) **Fresh Start Partnership**
6 **THEDFACTOR (IRE),** 6, b g Kalanisi (IRE)—Insan Magic (IRE) **Fresh Start Partnership**
7 **WESTEND THEATRE (IRE),** 6, b g Darsi (FR)—Ballyvelig Lady (IRE) **Mrs J. M. Walton**
8 **WILDEST DREAMS (IRE),** 6, b g Flemensfirth (USA)—Suspicious Minds **Joyce Rutherford Jane Walton**

**Other Owners:** Mrs L. Duncan, Mr John McCreanor, Mr David J. Parkins, Recommended Freight Ltd, Mrs M. Ridley, Miss J. Rutherford, Mrs J. M. Walton.

**Assistant Trainer:** Mrs Patricia Robson

**Jockey (NH):** Alistair Findlay.

## 630 MR JASON WALTON, Morpeth

Postal: **Flotterton Hall, Thropton, Morpeth, Northumberland, NE65 7LF**
Contacts: **PHONE (01669) 640253 FAX (01669) 640288 MOBILE (07808) 592701**

1 **BOSSY BECCY,** 6, b m And Beyond (IRE)—Merry Tina **Messrs F. T. Walton**
2 **CENTRAL FLAME,** 7, ch g Central Park (IRE)—More Flair **Messrs F. T. Walton**
3 **COQUET HEAD,** 9, br g Alflora (IRE)—Coquet Gold **Messrs F. T. Walton**
4 **DON'T POINT,** 6, ch m Double Trigger (IRE)—Posh Stick **Messrs F. T. Walton**
5 **HECKLEY HERBERT,** 8, b g Helissio (FR)—Heckley Spark **Messrs F. T. Walton**
6 **HIGHLAND CATHEDRAL,** 11, ch g Minster Son—Celtic Waters **Messrs F. T. Walton**
7 **PLAY PRACTICE,** 5, b m Josr Algarhoud (IRE)—More Flair **Messrs F. T. Walton**
8 **ROLL OF THUNDER,** 6, b g Antonius Pius (USA)—Ischia **Messrs F. T. Walton**
9 **RUPERT BEAR,** 9, b g Rambling Bear—Glittering Stone **Messrs F. T. Walton**
10 **SADDLE PACK (IRE),** 12, b g Saddlers' Hall (IRE)—Zuhal **Messrs F. T. Walton**
11 **STRATEGIC ISLAND (IRE),** 4, b f Strategic Prince—Island Music (IRE) **Messrs F. T. Walton**

**Other Owners:** J. B. Walton, F. A. Walton.

## 631 MRS SHEENA WALTON, Hexham

Postal: **Linacres, Wark, Hexham, Northumberland, NE48 3DP**
Contacts: **PHONE (01434) 230656 MOBILE (07752) 755184**
**E-MAIL linacres@btconnect.com**

1 **CUDDYS WELL,** 5, b g Gamut (IRE)—Elleena Rose (IRE) **Linacres Racing Partnership**
2 **DYSTONIA'S REVENGE (IRE),** 10, b g Woods of Windsor (USA)—Lady Isaac (IRE) **Mr J. L. Blacklock**
3 **ETHAN (IRE),** 6, b g Beneficial—Timissa (IRE) **R. H. & S. C. Walton**
4 **NATIVE OPTIMIST (IRE),** 8, b g Broadway Flyer (USA)—Native Orchid (IRE) **R. H. & S. C. Walton**
5 **WARKSBURN BOY,** 5, b g Kayf Tara—Bonchester Bridge **Rede Tyne Racing**

**Other Owners:** Mrs M. Rogerson, Mrs S. Walton, R. H. Walton.

**Assistant Trainer:** Mr R. H. Walton

**Amateur:** Miss C. Walton.

## 632 MR JASON WARD, Middleham

Postal: **The Dante Yard, Manor House Stables, Middleham, Leyburn, North Yorkshire, DL8 4QL**
Contacts: **PHONE (01969) 622730 MOBILE (07967) 357595**
**E-MAIL info@jasonwardracing.co.uk WEBSITE www.jasonwardracing.co.uk**

1 **BAHAMA DANCER,** 4, ch f Bahamian Bounty—Arlene Phillips **Andrew Catterall & Brian Harker**
2 **HEROSTATUS,** 8, ch g Dalakhani (IRE)—Desired **R. Naylor**
3 **HOPE FOR GLORY,** 6, b g Proclamation (IRE)—Aissa **Pear Tree Partnership**
4 **LONGSHADOW,** 5, ch g Monsun (GER)—La Felicita **David Robertson & J Ward**
5 **SOLID JUSTICE (IRE),** 4, b g Rock of Gibraltar (IRE)—Burnin' Memories (USA) **Roger Naylor & Nicholas Carr**
6 **YPRES,** 6, b g Byron—Esligier (IRE) **B Harker, M Walmsley, S Roebuck, J Teal**

### THREE-YEAR-OLDS

7 **PANCAKE DAY,** b c Mullionmileanhour (IRE)—Fangfoss Girls **Stuart Matheson & Jill Ward**

### TWO-YEAR-OLDS

**8** B c 6/4 Mullionmileanhour (IRE)—Fangfoss Girls (Monsieur Bond (IRE))

**Other Owners:** Mr N. H. Carr, A. W. Catterall, Mr B. Harker, Mr S. J. Matheson, Mr D. A. Robertson, Mr S. G. Roebuck, Mr J. Teal, Mr M. Walmsley.

**Assistant Trainer:** Tim Ward

**Jockey (flat):** Tom Eaves, P J McDonald. **Jockey (NH):** Brian Hughes. **Amateur:** Mr Ross Turner.

## 633 MISS TRACEY WATKINS, Kington

Postal: **Rose Villa, Holmes Marsh, Lyonshall, Kington, Herefordshire, HR5 3JS**
Contacts: **PHONE (01544) 340471 MOBILE (07812) 804758**
**E-MAIL traceyswatkins@googlemail.com**

1 **ONE COOL BOY (IRE),** 6, b br g One Cool Cat (USA)—Pipewell (IRE) **K. M. Parry**
2 **SANNDIYR (IRE),** 7, b g Red Ransom (USA)—Sinndiya (IRE) **K. M. Parry**

**Assistant Trainer:** Kevin Parry

**Jockey (NH):** Ben Poste. **Amateur:** Miss Brodie Hampson, Mr Tom McKeown.

## 634 MR FREDERICK WATSON, Sedgefield

Postal: **Beacon Hill, Sedgefield, Stockton-On-Tees, Cleveland, TS21 3HN**
Contacts: **PHONE (01740) 620582 MOBILE (07773) 321472**
**E-MAIL fredwatson@talktalk.net**

1 **ADDICTIVE DREAM (IRE),** 8, ch g Kheleyf (USA)—Nottambula (IRE) **Mr B Morton & Northumbria Leisure Ltd**
2 **BRETON BLUES,** 5, b g Street Cry (IRE)—Many Colours **F. Watson**
3 **DESTINATION AIM,** 8, b g Dubai Destination (USA)—Tessa Reef (IRE) **F. Watson**
4 **FREEWHEEL (IRE),** 5, br g Galileo (IRE)—La Chunga (USA) **B. Morton**
5 **JOYFUL STAR,** 5, b g Teofilo (IRE)—Extreme Beauty (USA) **F. Watson**
6 4, B g Misu Bond (IRE)—Mrs Quince **F. Watson**
7 **OPUS DEI,** 8, b g Oasis Dream—Grail (USA) **B. Morton**
8 **RODRIGO DE TORRES,** 8, ch g Bahamian Bounty—Leonica **B. Morton**
9 5, B m Misu Bond (IRE)—Shardda **F. Watson**
10 **SPOKESPERSON (USA),** 7, b g Henny Hughes (USA)—Verbal (USA) **F. Watson**

### THREE-YEAR-OLDS

11 **GYPSY MAJOR,** ch g Major Cadeaux—Romany Gypsy **Ms S. V. Hattersley**

**Other Owners:** Mr Brian Morton, Northumbria Leisure Ltd.

## 635 MRS SHARON WATT, Richmond

Postal: **Rosey Hill Farm, Scorton Road, Brompton on Swale, Richmond, North Yorkshire, DL10 7EQ**
Contacts: **PHONE (01748) 812064 FAX (01748) 812064 MOBILE (07970) 826046**
**E-MAIL wattfences@aol.com**

1 **CHAMPAGNE RULES,** 4, gr g Aussie Rules (USA)—Garabelle (IRE) **Rosey Hill Partnership**
2 **HARRISON'S CAVE,** 7, b g Galileo (IRE)—Sitara **Major E. J. Watt**
3 **MADAM LILIBET (IRE),** 6, b m Authorized (IRE)—Foxilla (IRE) **D. H. Montgomerie**
4 **RUBY VODKA,** 4, b f Oscar (IRE)—Auntie Kathleen **Major E. J. Watt**
5 **VODKA MOON,** 6, gr g Beat All (USA)—Auntie Kathleen **Rosey Hill Partnership**

### THREE-YEAR-OLDS

6 **SERAFFIMO,** ch g Monsieur Bond (IRE)—Hula Ballew **Rosey Hill Partnership**

### TWO-YEAR-OLDS

7 **CALPURNIA,** b f 21/3 Sleeping Indian—Africa's Star (IRE) (Johannesburg (USA))

**Other Owners:** F. C. Previtali.

**Jockey (NH):** Keith Mercer. **Conditional:** Joseph Palmowski.

## 636 MR SIMON WAUGH, Morpeth

Postal: **A G Waugh & Sons Limited, Molesden House, Molesden, Morpeth, Northumberland, NE61 3QF**
Contacts: **MOBILE (07860) 561445**
**E-MAIL swaugh@dircon.co.uk**

1 **ARABIAN SUNSET (IRE),** 4, b f Dubawi (IRE)—Summer Sunset (IRE) **Yacht London Racing Ltd**
2 **BIG GEORGE,** 8, b g Alflora (IRE)—Petrea **Mrs S. A. York**
3 **BORIC,** 7, b g Grape Tree Road—Petrea **Mrs S. A. York**
4 **CROW DOWN (IRE),** 6, b g Oratorio (IRE)—Louve Sereine (FR) **Northumberland Racing Club**
5 **MICK MELODY (IRE),** 7, b g Bach (IRE)—Roche Melody (IRE)
6 **MY ESCAPADE (IRE),** 4, ch f Tamayuz—Highly Respected (IRE) **Yacht London Racing Ltd**
7 **NEWYEARSRESOLUTION (IRE),** 11, b g Mr Combustible (IRE)—That's Magic (IRE) **Northumberland Racing Club**
8 **PADDY THE PLUMBER (IRE),** 9, b g Dr Massini (IRE)—Heather Ville (IRE) **S. G. Waugh**
9 **ROYAL FLUSH,** 4, b c Multiplex—Mystical Feelings (BEL) **S. G. Waugh**
10 **SECRET KODE (IRE),** 4, b f Kodiac—Finty (IRE) **Yacht London Racing Ltd**
11 **TOTAL ASSETS,** 7, b m Alflora (IRE)—Maid Equal **Northumberland Racing Club**

**Other Owners:** Mrs V. A. Y. Knox.

## 637 MISS AMY WEAVER, Lamorlaye

Postal: **6 Rue Charles Pratt, 60260 Lamorlaye, France**
Contacts: **MOBILE (07947) 442083**
**E-MAIL amy@amyweaverracing.com WEBSITE www.amyweaverracing.com**

1 **SILVER TREASURE (FR),** 4, gr g Clodovil (IRE)—Ardesia Si (FR)
2 **SUCH FUN (IRE),** 4, b f Whipper (USA)—Balamiyda (IRE)
3 **TUBEANIE (IRE),** 4, ch f Intense Focus (USA)—Ryalahna (IRE)

### THREE-YEAR-OLDS

4 **JUSTIFY,** b f Dalakhani (IRE)—Purity
5 **SPRING IN KENTUCKY,** b f Nayef (USA)—Red Blossom

### TWO-YEAR-OLDS

6 **FORCEFULL (IRE),** b f 18/2 Thousand Words—Littlepromisedland (IRE) (Titus Livius (FR)) (5555)
7 B c 31/1 Dark Angel (IRE)—Zalafira (FR) (Nashwan (USA)) (23015)

## 638 MR ROBERT WEBB-BOWEN, Wincanton

Postal: **Sycamore Farm, Stoke Trister, Wincanton, Somerset, BA9 9PE**
Contacts: **PHONE (01963) 31647 FAX (01963) 31647 MOBILE (07919) 884895**
**E-MAIL robert@webb-bowen.co.uk WEBSITE www.camrosestud.org.uk**

1 **VINMIX DE BESSY (FR),** 14, gr g River Bay (USA)—Hesse (FR) **Mrs D. J. Webb-Bowen**

**Assistant Trainer:** Mrs Dinah Webb-Bowen

## 639 MR PAUL WEBBER, Banbury

Postal: **Cropredy Lawn, Mollington, Banbury, Oxfordshire, OX17 1DR**
Contacts: **PHONE (01295) 750226 FAX (01295) 758482 MOBILE (07836) 232465**
**E-MAIL paul@paulwebberracing.com WEBSITE www.paulwebberracing.com**

1 **ALFIBOY,** 5, b g Alflora (IRE)—Cloudy Pearl **D. C. R. Allen**
2 **AMORUCCIO (FR),** 5, b g Le Fou (IRE)—Mandchou (FR) **Mr S. A. Al Helaissi**
3 **ARAMARA (IRE),** 5, b m Marju (IRE)—Atalina (FR) **Kenilworth House Stud**
4 **AUSTRALIA DAY (IRE),** 12, gr g Key of Luck (USA)—Atalina (FR) **Skippy & The Partners**
5 **BAYLEY'S DREAM,** 6, b g Presenting—Swaythe (USA) **The Sweep Stakes Partnership**
6 **BUFFLERS HOLT (IRE),** 6, b m Flemensfirth (USA)—Water Stratford (IRE) **C. W. Booth**
7 **BURMA (FR),** 4, b br f Charming Groom (FR)—Tadorna (FR) **The Smillie Watters Partnership**
8 **CANTLOW (IRE),** 10, b g Kayf Tara—Winnowing (IRE) **J. P. McManus**
9 4, B f Presenting—Chinatownqueen (IRE) **R. C. Moody**
10 **COPPERFACEJACK (IRE),** 5, b g Robin des Pres (FR)—Leone Des Pres (FR) **R. W. Barnett**
11 **COULDHAVEHADITALL (IRE),** 7, b g Milan—Night Leader (IRE) **D. C. R. Allen**
12 **DASHING OVER,** 7, b g Overbury (IRE)—Dashing Executive (IRE) **Fawley House Stud**
13 **DEVON DRUM,** 7, b g Beat Hollow—West Devon (USA) **Mr D. Carrington**
14 **FINGERS CROSSED (IRE),** 5, b g Bach (IRE)—Awesome Miracle (IRE) **D. C. R. Allen**
15 **FIRM ORDER (IRE),** 10, b g Winged Love (IRE)—Fairylodge Scarlet (IRE) **The Syndicators**
16 **HONOUR A PROMISE,** 7, b m Norse Dancer (IRE)—Motcombe (IRE) **Lady Cobham & Paul Webber**
17 **ICY COLT (ARG),** 9, br g Colonial Affair (USA)—Icy Desert (USA) **P. R. Webber**
18 **JUST A FEELING,** 5, ch m Flemensfirth (USA)—Precious Lady **Swanbridge Bloodstock Limited**
19 **KOOLALA (IRE),** 7, b m Kayf Tara—Squaw Talk (USA) **Lady Wellesley**
20 **LADY KATHLEEN,** 8, b m Hernando (FR)—Lady of Fortune (IRE) **R. C. Moody**
21 5, B m Multiplex—Lucy Glitters **Paul Webber Racing**
22 **MAETRUFEL ANNIE,** 6, b m Flemensfirth (USA)—Materiality **Jolly Wolf Racing**
23 **MISS TONGABEZI,** 6, b m Overbury (IRE)—Shiwa **Turf 2014 & Mrs D. J. Webber**
24 **MR BANKS (IRE),** 4, br g Kalanisi (IRE)—She's Supersonic (IRE) **Cropredy Lawn Racing**
25 **MR K (IRE),** 4, b g Kheleyf (USA)—Undertone (IRE) **C. M. Budgett**
26 **OBSTACLE,** 5, ch g Observatory (USA)—Stage Left **The Obstacle Coursers**
27 **PERFECT TIMING (FR),** 5, b m Sassanian (USA)—Royale Sulawesie (FR) **D. C. R. Allen**
28 **PINAMAR,** 5, ch m Shirocco (GER)—Highland Ceilidh (IRE) **C. Humphris**
29 **PRETTY MOBILE (FR),** 4, gr f Al Namix (FR)—Gobeline (FR) **Mrs A. W. Timpson**
30 **RED COSSACK (CAN),** 4, ch g Rebellion—Locata (USA) **Solario Racing (Banbury)**
31 **RHAPANDO,** 6, b g Hernando (FR)—Rhapsody Rose **D. C. R. Allen**
32 **ROYALRACKET (IRE),** 7, b g Royal Anthem (USA)—Allaracket (IRE) **David Allen**
33 **RUBBER SOLE (IRE),** 6, gr g Milan—Silver Sonus (IRE) **Mrs A. W. Timpson**
34 **RUN ON STERLING,** 6, b g Dr Fong (USA)—Dansara **Mr A. J. Rowland**
35 **SEPTEMBER BLAZE,** 8, b m Exit To Nowhere (USA)—Mid Day Chaser (IRE) **The Blaze Partnership**
36 **SIX ONE AWAY (IRE),** 6, gr g Tikkanen (USA)—Surfing France (FR) **Mrs A. W. Timpson**
37 **SIXTY SOMETHING (FR),** 9, gr g Dom Alco (FR)—Jaunas (FR) **Mrs A. W. Timpson**
38 **SUGAR TRAIN,** 5, b g Rail Link—Plum Fairy **Cropredy Lawn Racing**
39 **TAFIKA,** 11, b g Kayf Tara—Shiwa **The Tafika Partnership**
40 **THE VENERABLE BEDE (IRE),** 4, b g Kalanisi (IRE)—Feedthegoodmare (IRE) **Mrs A. W. Timpson**
41 **THECORRUPTOR (IRE),** 5, b br g Robin des Pres (FR)—Cappard View (IRE) **R. V. Shaw**
42 **THOM THUMB (IRE),** 9, ch g Flemensfirth (USA)—Ardlea Dawn (IRE) **Mr S. A. Al Helaissi**
43 **TINDARO (FR),** 8, gr g Kingsalsa (USA)—Star's Mixa (FR) **The Tindaro Partnership**
44 **TOO MUCH TOO SOON (IRE),** 6, b g Craigsteel—Zara Rose (IRE) **Dunton Racing Partnership**
45 **TURKEY CREEK (IRE),** 6, b g Scorpion (IRE)—Emesions Lady (IRE) **J. P. McManus**
46 **TWO SWALLOWS,** 5, b m Kayf Tara—One Gulp **Mr R. J. Mcalpine & Mrs C. A. Waters**
47 **UNSEEN (FR),** 7, gr g Dom Alco (FR)—Cathou (FR) **Mrs C. H. Covell**
48 **VERY LIVE (FR),** 6, b g Secret Singer (FR)—Iona Will (FR) **R. V. Shaw**
49 **VIKING QUEEN,** 4, b f Presenting—Swaythe (USA) **Higgy, Mette & Friends**

## MR PAUL WEBBER - Continued

### THREE-YEAR-OLDS

50 **DUNNSCOTIA,** b g Showcasing—Black And Amber **Mrs P. A. Scott-Dunn**
51 **GLENLYON,** b g Thewayyouare (USA)—Helena **Paul Webber**
52 **MICHAELA,** ch f Sholokhov (IRE)—La Capilla **John Nicholls (Trading) Ltd**

**Other Owners:** Mr Nigel Birch, Mr P. Bowden, Mr A. Brooks, Mr D. G. Carrington, Mr Simon K. I. Double, Mrs Sarah Drysdale, Mr Robert Frosell, Mrs Margaret Gardiner, Mr Peter Hewett, Mr D. W. Higgins, Mr P. S. Lewis, Sir I. Magee, Mr M. V. Magnier, Mr R. J. McAlpine, Mrs S. McGrath, Mr R. McGrath, Professor David Metcalf, Mr J. Neville, Mr Martin Pepper, Mr Philip Rocher, Mr Nicholas Sercombe, Mr James Smillie, Mrs C. A. Waters, Mr Iain Russell Watters, Mrs John Webber, Mr Paul Webber.

**Conditional:** Luke Watson.

---

## 640 MR D. K. WELD, The Curragh

Postal: **Rosewell House, Curragh, Co. Kildare, Ireland**
Contacts: **PHONE (00353) 4544 1273 / 441 476 FAX (00353) 4544 1119**
**E-MAIL dkweld@eircom.net**

1 **AFTERNOON SUNLIGHT (IRE),** 4, ch f Sea The Stars (IRE)—Lady Luck (IRE) **Moyglare Stud Farms Ltd**
2 **BEHESHT (FR),** 4, b c Sea The Stars (IRE)—Behkara (IRE) **Calumet Farm**
3 **BROOCH (USA),** 4, b f Empire Maker (USA)—Daring Diva **K. Abdullah**
4 **CARLA BIANCA (IRE),** 4, gr f Dansili—Majestic Silver (IRE) **Moyglare Stud Farms Ltd**
5 **FASCINATING ROCK (IRE),** 4, b c Fastnet Rock (AUS)—Miss Polaris **Newtown Anner Stud Farm Ltd**
6 **FORGOTTEN RULES (IRE),** 5, b g Nayef (USA)—Utterly Heaven (IRE) **Moyglare Stud Farms Ltd**
7 **FREE EAGLE (IRE),** 4, b c High Chaparral (IRE)—Polished Gem (IRE) **Moyglare Stud Farms Ltd**
8 **HISAABAAT (IRE),** 7, b g Dubawi (IRE)—Phariseek (IRE) **Mr Dominick Glennane**
9 **MANALAPAN (IRE),** 5, b g Six Sense (JPN)—Mia Mambo (USA) **Deus Bros Syndicate**
10 **MASSINGA (IRE),** 4, ch f Selkirk (USA)—Masiyma (IRE) **H. H. Aga Khan**
11 **MUSTAJEEB,** 4, ch c Nayef (USA)—Rifqah (USA) **Hamdan Al Maktoum**
12 **SHOW COURT (IRE),** 6, b g Vinnie Roe (IRE)—Sparkling Gem (IRE) **Mr K. Weld**
13 **SIERRA SUN (IRE),** 4, b f Hernando (FR)—Sierra Slew **Lady Chryss O'Reilly**
14 **SILVER CONCORDE,** 7, b g Dansili—Sacred Pearl (IRE) **Dr R. Lambe**
15 **TANDEM,** 6, b g Dansili—Light Ballet **The Bellamy Syndicate**
16 **TESTED,** 4, b f Selkirk (USA)—Prove **K. Abdullah**
17 **VIGIL (IRE),** 6, b g Dansili—Magnolia Lane (IRE) **M. F. Bourke/N. Furlong**
18 **VINTAGE NOUVEAU (IRE),** 4, b f Montjeu (IRE)—Utterly Heaven (IRE) **Moyglare Stud Farms Ltd**
19 **WINDSOR PARK (IRE),** 6, b g Galileo (IRE)—Blissful (USA) **Dr R. Lambe**

### THREE-YEAR-OLDS

20 **ALMELA (IRE),** b f Sea The Stars (IRE)—Aliya (IRE) **H. H. Aga Khan**
21 **ASHRAF (IRE),** b c Cape Cross (IRE)—Askeria (IRE) **H. H. Aga Khan**
22 **CHINESE LIGHT (IRE),** gr f Dalakhani (IRE)—Chiang Mai (IRE) **Lady Chryss O'Reilly**
23 **DON CAMILLO (USA),** b c Ghostzapper (USA)—Potra Clasica (ARG) **Stronach Stables**
24 **EDELPOUR (IRE),** gr c Mastercraftsman (IRE)—Ebadiyla (IRE) **H. H. Aga Khan**
25 **ESHERA (IRE),** b f Oratorio (IRE)—Eytarna (IRE) **H. H. Aga Khan**
26 **ESPRIT DE VIE (USA),** b f Street Cry (IRE)—Irresistible Jewel (IRE) **Moyglare Stud Farms Ltd**
27 **FASEEHA (IRE),** ch f Teofilo (IRE)—Turkana Girl **Hamdan Al Maktoum**
28 **GRIKO (IRE),** b g Iffraaj—Magna Graecia (IRE) **Godolphin**
29 **GULF OF POETS,** b c Oasis Dream—Sandglass **K. Abdullah**
30 **HAWRAA,** br f Dansili—Bethrah (IRE) **Hamdan Al Maktoum**
31 **INFINITE LOOP (USA),** br c Unusual Heat (USA)—Midnite Mama (USA) **Calumet Farm**
32 **INTRANSIVE,** b c Dansili—Imroz (USA) **K. Abdullah**
33 **JOAILLIERE (IRE),** b f Dubawi (IRE)—Majestic Silver (IRE) **Moyglare Stud Farms Ltd**
34 **KATIYMANN (IRE),** b c Shamardal (USA)—Katiyra (IRE) **H. H. Aga Khan**
35 **MARSALI (USA),** b br f More Than Ready (USA)—Milago (USA) **Calumet Farm**
36 **MORSELLE,** b f Showcasing—Mirthful (USA) **K. Abdullah**
37 **MULKEYYA (IRE),** b f Mawatheeq (USA)—Rifqah (USA) **Hamdan Al Maktoum**
38 **MUTADHAMEN,** ch g Arcano (IRE)—Janina **Hamdan Al Maktoum**
39 **NEW AGENDA,** b c New Approach (IRE)—Prove **K. Abdullah**
40 **PETIT ADAGIO (IRE),** b f Cape Cross (IRE)—Thoughtless Moment (IRE) **Moyglare Stud Farms Ltd**
41 **POSTULATION (USA),** b g Harlan's Holiday (USA)—Supposition **K. Abdullah**
42 **RADANPOUR (IRE),** b c Sea The Stars (IRE)—Rose Quartz **H. H. Aga Khan**
43 **RAVENS HEART (IRE),** b g Dansili—Hymn of Love (IRE) **Moyglare Stud Farms Ltd**
44 **SEREFELI (IRE),** b c Footstepsinthesand—Seraya (FR) **H. H. Aga Khan**

## MR D. K. WELD - Continued

**45 SIGHT HOUND (USA),** ch c English Channel (USA)—Fiji **Calumet Farm**
**46 STORMFLY (IRE),** gr f Dark Angel (IRE)—Intaglia (GER) **Deus Bros Syndicate**
**47 SUGGESTION,** gr c Dansili—Jibboom (USA) **K. Abdullah**
**48 SUMMAYA (IRE),** b f Azamour (IRE)—Simawa (IRE) **H. H. Aga Khan**
**49 TADAANY (IRE),** b c Acclamation—Park Haven (IRE) **Hamdan Al Maktoum**
**50 TIME TO INSPIRE (IRE),** ch c Galileo (IRE)—Utterly Heaven (IRE) **Moyglare Stud Farms Ltd**
**51 TOMBELAINE (USA),** b c First Defence (USA)—Kithira **K. Abdullah**
**52 TUK TUK,** b c Sinndar (IRE)—Shuttle Mission **K. Abdullah**
**53 VALAC (IRE),** gr c Dark Angel (IRE)—Polished Gem (IRE) **Moyglare Stud Farms Ltd**
**54 VARIABLE,** b f Sea The Stars (IRE)—Proportional **K. Abdullah**
**55 ZAFILANI (IRE),** b c Azamour (IRE)—Zafayra (IRE) **H. H. Aga Khan**
**56 ZANNDA (IRE),** b f Azamour (IRE)—Zanoubiya (IRE) **H. H. Aga Khan**
**57 ZARAND (USA),** b c Arch (USA)—Zaralanta (IRE) **H. H. Aga Khan**
**58 ZAWRAQ (IRE),** b c Shamardal (USA)—Sundus (USA) **Hamdan Al Maktoum**
**59 ZHUKOVA (IRE),** b f Fastnet Rock (AUS)—Nightime (IRE) **Mrs C. C. Regalado-Gonzalez**

## TWO-YEAR-OLDS

**60 A LIKELY STORY (IRE),** b c 10/4 Exceed And Excel (AUS)—Where We Left Off (Dr Devious (IRE)) **Moyglare Stud Farms Ltd**
**61 AASHEQ (IRE),** b c 18/2 Dubawi (IRE)—Beach Bunny (IRE) (High Chaparral (IRE)) **Hamdan Al Maktoum**
**62** B f 2/2 High Chaparral (IRE)—Agnetha (GER) (Big Shuffle (USA)) (210000) **Calumet Farm**
**63 ALALIYA (IRE),** ch f 12/2 Iffraaj—Aliyama (IRE) (Red Ransom (USA)) **H. H. Aga Khan**
**64 ALSINAAFY (IRE),** b c 23/1 Oasis Dream—Bethrah (IRE) (Marju (IRE)) **Hamdan Al Maktoum**
**65 ARAQEEL,** b c 7/3 Dutch Art—Alice Alleyne (IRE) (Oasis Dream) **Hamdan Al Maktoum**
**66** B f 9/2 Shamardal (USA)—Askeria (IRE) (Sadler's Wells (USA)) **H. H. Aga Khan**
**67 BEAUTIFUL LIGHT (USA),** br f 17/4 English Channel (USA)—Runup The Colors (USA) (A P Indy (USA)) **Calumet Farm**
**68** B c 14/3 Dark Angel (IRE)—Bogini (IRE) (Holy Roman Emperor (IRE)) (87300) **Dr R. Lambe**
**69** Ch c 14/4 Teofilo (IRE)—Bouvardia (Oasis Dream) **K. Abdullah**
**70 COLOUR BRIGHT (IRE),** b f 3/4 Dream Ahead (USA)—Flashing Green (Green Desert (USA)) (277777) **Moyglare Stud Farms Ltd**
**71 DELTA SIERRA (USA),** b br f 9/2 More Than Ready (USA)—Delta Rhythm (USA) (A P Indy (USA)) **Calumet Farm**
**72** B c 15/4 Raven's Pass (USA)—Ebadiyla (IRE) (Sadler's Wells (USA)) **H. H. Aga Khan**
**73** B c 19/3 Sea The Stars (IRE)—Ebaza (IRE) (Sinndar (IRE)) **H. H. Aga Khan**
**74** B c 20/3 Shamardal (USA)—Emiyna (USA) (Maria's Mon (USA)) **H. H. Aga Khan**
**75** B f 12/4 Dansili—Etoile Montante (USA) (Miswaki (USA)) **K. Abdullah**
**76 FOXTROT CHARLIE (USA),** ch c 4/4 English Channel (USA)—Flashy Four (USA) (Storm Cat (USA)) **Calumet Farm**
**77** B c 25/1 First Defence (USA)—Gainful (USA) (Gone West (USA)) **K. Abdullah**
**78** Ch f 18/3 More Than Ready (USA)—Gatherindy (USA) (A P Indy (USA)) **Calumet Farm**
**79** Ch c 19/2 Summer Bird (USA)—Golden Party (USA) (Seeking The Gold (USA)) (158729) **Hamdan Al Maktoum**
**80 HAQEEBA (IRE),** b f 11/4 Haatef (USA)—Katoom (IRE) (Soviet Star (USA)) **Hamdan Al Maktoum**
**81** Br c 6/3 Sea The Stars (IRE)—Hazariya (IRE) (Xaar) **H. H. Aga Khan**
**82 HEARTFUL (IRE),** b f 29/3 Shamardal (USA)—Mad About You (IRE) (Indian Ridge) **Moyglare Stud Farms Ltd**
**83 HOPPALA (IRE),** b c 9/2 Acclamation—She's Our Mark (Ishiguru (USA)) **Moyglare Stud Farms Ltd**
**84** B f 5/5 Oasis Dream—Jibboom (USA) (Mizzen Mast (USA)) **K. Abdullah**
**85 JULIETTE FAIR (IRE),** gr f 17/2 Dark Angel (IRE)—Capulet Monteque (IRE) (Camacho) (190476) **Moyglare Stud Farms Ltd**
**86** B f 17/2 Cape Cross (IRE)—Kalarouna (IRE) (Selkirk (USA)) **H. H. Aga Khan**
**87** Ch f 3/3 Sea The Stars (IRE)—Kalima (Kahyasi) **K. Abdullah**
**88** B c 20/2 Kitten's Joy (USA)—Kaloura (IRE) (Sinndar (IRE)) **H. H. Aga Khan**
**89 KARALARA (IRE),** b f 25/2 Shamardal (USA)—Karasiyra (IRE) (Alhaarth (IRE)) **H. H. Aga Khan**
**90** B c 15/2 Cape Cross (IRE)—Kasanka (IRE) (Galileo (IRE)) **H. H. Aga Khan**
**91** Ch f 27/3 Sea The Stars (IRE)—Katiyra (IRE) (Peintre Celebre (USA)) **H. H. Aga Khan**
**92 KENTUCKY GIANT (USA),** ch c 7/2 Giant's Causeway (USA)—Miss Du Bois (USA) (Mr Prospector (USA)) **Calumet Farm**
**93 KIDD MALIBU (USA),** ch c 20/1 Malibu Moon (USA)—Kiddari (USA) (Smarty Jones (USA)) (315547) **Hamdan Al Maktoum**
**94** B f 29/4 Galileo (IRE)—Lesson In Humility (IRE) (Mujadil (USA)) **Mrs J. Magnier**
**95 LONAROO (USA),** b c 29/3 Lonhro (AUS)—Milago (USA) (Danzig (USA)) **Calumet Farm**
**96 LONDON DRY GIN (USA),** ch c 26/1 English Channel (USA)—Greenapple Martini (CAN) (Medaglia d'Oro (USA)) **Calumet Farm**
**97 LOOK CLOSER (IRE),** ch c 10/2 Danehill Dancer (IRE)—Key Secure (IRE) (Sadler's Wells (USA)) **Moyglare Stud Farms Ltd**
**98 LOST STARS (IRE),** b f 14/2 Sea The Stars (IRE)—Moving Heart (IRE) (Anabaa (USA)) **Moyglare Stud Farms Ltd**

## MR D. K. WELD - Continued

**99 LOVE IN THE SUN (IRE),** b f 1/2 Kodiac—Summer Trysting (USA) (Alleged (USA)) **Moyglare Stud Farms Ltd**
**100 LUNE DE SABLE (IRE),** b f 24/1 Medicean—Token Gesture (IRE) (Alzao (USA)) **Moyglare Stud Farms Ltd**
**101 MALADH,** ch f 12/3 Tamayuz—Malakaat (USA) (Danzig (USA)) **Hamdan Al Maktoum**
**102 MASSAYAN (IRE),** ch c 4/3 Iffraaj—Masiyma (IRE) (Dalakhani (IRE)) **H. H. Aga Khan**
**103** Gr c 29/3 Shamardal (USA)—Midnight Angel (Machiavellian (USA)) (370000) **Hamdan Al Maktoum**
**104** Ch f 21/4 Raven's Pass (USA)—Mouramara (IRE) (Kahyasi) **H. H. Aga Khan**
**105 MUNAASHID (USA),** b br c 28/1 Lonhro (AUS)—
Freefourracing (USA) (French Deputy (USA)) (357142) **Hamdan Al Maktoum**
**106 NOBLE BEQUEST (USA),** b br c 13/3 Lonhro (AUS)—Supposition (Dansili) **K. Abdullah**
**107 ORANGEY RED (IRE),** b f 4/3 Lawman (FR)—Triple Try (IRE) (Sadler's Wells (USA)) **Moyglare Stud Farms Ltd**
**108 PIAZZINI (IRE),** b f 15/3 Kyllachy—Polite Reply (IRE) (Be My Guest (USA)) **Moyglare Stud Farms Ltd**
**109** B c 9/3 Zoffany (IRE)—Poinsettia (IRE) (Galileo (IRE)) (125000) **Dr R. Lambe**
**110 PROPRIANO (USA),** b c 27/1 More Than Ready (USA)—
Primadona (IRE) (Galileo (IRE)) **Moyglare Stud Farms Ltd**
**111** B c 27/2 Zamindar (USA)—Prove (Danehill (USA)) **K. Abdullah**
**112** B c 23/2 Cacique (IRE)—Pure Joy (Zamindar (USA)) **K. Abdullah**
**113 PURPLE VELVET (IRE),** b f 28/4 Dark Angel (IRE)—
Hidden Charm (IRE) (Big Shuffle (USA)) **Moyglare Stud Farms Ltd**
**114 RAJAPUR,** gr ro c 31/3 Dalakhani (IRE)—A Beautiful Mind (GER) (Winged Love (IRE)) **Calumet Farm**
**115 RAYMONDA (USA),** b f 11/2 Lonhro (AUS)—Daring Diva (Dansili) **K. Abdullah**
**116** Gr ro f 10/4 Exchange Rate (USA)—Red Herring (USA) (Empire Maker (USA)) **K. Abdullah**
**117 RESTLESS RAMBLER (USA),** b c 5/4 Ghostzapper (USA)—
Restless Song (USA) (Songandaprayer (USA)) **Calumet Farm**
**118 RICH JADE (USA),** b f 28/4 Henrythenavigator (USA)—
Endless Expanse (IRE) (Red Ransom (USA)) **Moyglare Stud Farms Ltd**
**119 RIXIANO (FR),** gr f 25/2 Equiano (FR)—Restless Rixa (FR) (Linamix (FR)) **Calumet Farm**
**120 ROSE DE PIERRE (IRE),** b f 17/3 Dubawi (IRE)—
Profound Beauty (IRE) (Danehill (USA)) **Moyglare Stud Farms Ltd**
**121 ROSE PINK (IRE),** br f 15/2 Big Bad Bob (IRE)—
Blackangelheart (IRE) (Danehill Dancer (IRE)) **Miss Chiara Bucher**
**122** B f 15/5 Harlan's Holiday (USA)—Sense of Joy (Dansili) **K. Abdullah**
**123** Ch f 26/4 Shamardal (USA)—Shamayel (Pivotal) (67460) **Mr D. K. Weld**
**124** B f 25/2 Dubawi (IRE)—Shareen (IRE) (Bahri (USA)) **H. H. Aga Khan**
**125** B c 24/4 Dr Fong (USA)—Sindiyma (IRE) (Kalanisi (IRE)) **H. H. Aga Khan**
**126 SMOKEY QUARTZ (IRE),** gr f 3/4 Dark Angel (IRE)—
Instant Sparkle (IRE) (Danehill (USA)) **Moyglare Stud Farms Ltd**
**127 SOCIAL TREASURE (IRE),** ch c 12/2 Galileo (IRE)—
Society Hostess (USA) (Seeking The Gold (USA)) **Moyglare Stud Farms Ltd**
**128 STAY TRUE TO YOU (IRE),** b f 21/3 Pour Moi (IRE)—Eva's Time (IRE) (Monsun (GER)) **Mr Mischa Bucher**
**129 SUNGLIDER (IRE),** b c 30/3 High Chaparral (IRE)—
Desert Ease (IRE) (Green Desert (USA)) **Moyglare Stud Farms Ltd**
**130** B f 14/3 Dansili—Take The Hint (Montjeu (IRE)) **K. Abdullah**
**131** B f 17/2 Dubawi (IRE)—Tanoura (IRE) (Dalakhani (IRE)) **H. H. Aga Khan**
**132** Ch c 22/3 Dutch Art—Tarakala (IRE) (Dr Fong (USA)) **H. H. Aga Khan**
**133 TARAYEF (IRE),** b f 25/2 Teofilo (IRE)—
Grecian Bride (IRE) (Groom Dancer (USA)) (753967) **Hamdan Al Maktoum**
**134** Ch c 30/3 Zamindar (USA)—Tates Creek (USA) (Rahy (USA)) **K. Abdullah**
**135** B c 13/3 Sea The Stars (IRE)—Timabiyra (IRE) (Linamix (FR)) **H. H. Aga Khan**
**136 TOPAZ CLEAR (IRE),** b f 2/5 Pivotal—Utterly Heaven (IRE) (Danehill (USA)) **Moyglare Stud Farms Ltd**
**137** B f 3/4 Oasis Dream—Trojan Queen (USA) (Empire Maker (USA)) **K. Abdullah**
**138 TRUE SOLITAIRE (IRE),** b c 21/4 Oasis Dream—Majestic Silver (IRE) (Linamix (FR)) **Moyglare Stud Farms Ltd**
**139 TURF TITAN (USA),** ch c 17/3 Kitten's Joy (USA)—Heavenly Ransom (USA) (Red Ransom (USA)) **Calumet Farm**
**140 VA PENSIERO (IRE),** b f 17/5 High Chaparral (IRE)—
Thoughtless Moment (IRE) (Pivotal) **Moyglare Stud Farms Ltd**
**141** B c 3/5 Sinndar (IRE)—Velandia (IRE) (Sadler's Wells (USA)) **H. H. Aga Khan**
**142 VITRUVIAN MAN (USA),** b c 3/5 Bernardini (USA)—Venatrix (USA) (Theatrical) **Calumet Farm**
**143 WADALANI,** ch c 1/2 Dalakhani (IRE)—Wilde Perle (Platini (GER)) (63492) **Calumet Farm**
**144 YASOOD (IRE),** b c 18/4 Acclamation—Lucina (Machiavellian (USA)) (300000) **Hamdan Al Maktoum**
**145** Ch f 14/3 Dutch Art—Zafayra (IRE) (Nayef (USA)) **H. H. Aga Khan**
**146** B c 15/3 Dutch Art—Zanoubiya (IRE) (Dalakhani (IRE)) **H. H. Aga Khan**
**147** B c 8/3 Canford Cliffs (IRE)—Zanzibar Girl (USA) (Johannesburg (USA)) (71428) **Calumet Farm**
**148 ZORAVAN (USA),** ch c 26/2 More Than Ready (USA)—Zaralanta (IRE) (Danehill Dancer (IRE)) **H. H. Aga Khan**
**149 ZULU ALPHA (USA),** b c 8/2 Street Cry (IRE)—Zori (USA) (A P Indy (USA)) **Calumet Farm**

**Jockey (flat):** P. J. Smullen. **Apprentice:** L. F. Roche.

## 641 MISS SHEENA WEST, Lewes

Postal: **5 Balmer Farm Cottages, Brighton Road, Lewes, East Sussex, BN7 3JN**
Contacts: **PHONE (01273) 621303 FAX (01273) 622189 MOBILE (07748) 181804**
**E-MAIL sheenawest11@aol.com WEBSITE www.sheenawest.com**

1 **BRILLIANT BARCA,** 7, b g Imperial Dancer—Fading Away **G. West**
2 **CANNON FODDER,** 8, b m Nomadic Way (USA)—Grace Dieu **The Cheapskates**
3 **CRASHING THEW LIFE,** 5, b g Tobougg (IRE)—Kalmina (USA) **G. West**
4 **FEB THIRTYFIRST,** 6, ch g Shirocco (GER)—My Mariam **M. Moriarty**
5 **HI NOTE,** 7, b m Acclamation—Top Tune **G. West**
6 **JUSTANOTHER MUDDLE,** 6, gr g Kayf Tara—Spatham Rose **Saloop**
7 **LEG IRON (IRE),** 10, b g Snurge—Southern Skies (IRE) **M. Moriarty**
8 **MR MUDDLE,** 8, gr g Imperial Dancer—Spatham Rose **Saloop**
9 **SCREAMING BRAVE,** 9, br g Hunting Lion (IRE)—Hana Dee **Tracey Walsom & Alex Woodger**
10 **SPANISH FORK (IRE),** 6, br g Trans Island—Wings Awarded **G. West**
11 4, B g Kayf Tara—Spatham Rose **Saloop**
12 **WARRANT OFFICER,** 5, gr g Misu Bond (IRE)—Kilmovee **M. Moriarty**
13 **YA HAFED,** 7, ch g Haafhd—Rule Britannia **G. West**

**Other Owners:** Mr L. T. Morris, Mrs C. S. Muddle, R. A. Muddle, Mrs E. Turner, Miss T. Walsom, Mr A. G. R. Woodger.

**Jockey (NH):** M. Goldstein.

## 642 MR SIMON WEST, Middleham

Postal: **14A St Alkeldas Road, Middleham, Leyburn, North Yorkshire, DL8 4PW**
Contacts: **MOBILE (07855) 924529**
**E-MAIL simonwest21@hotmail.co.uk WEBSITE www.mkmracing.co.uk**

1 **AFIENYA (IRE),** 5, gr m Tikkanen (USA)—Tullyfoyle (IRE) **Mr P. Hothersall**
2 **AMOOD (IRE),** 4, ch c Elnadim (USA)—Amanah (USA) **Mr C. R. Hirst**
3 **DANESIDE (IRE),** 8, b g Danehill Dancer (IRE)—Sidecar (IRE) **Mr P. Hothersall**
4 **FASTNET RED,** 4, b g Fastnet Rock (AUS)—Gyroscope **Mr C. R. Hirst**
5 **KUKURUDU (IRE),** 8, b g Tikkanen (USA)—Tullyfoyle (IRE) **Mr P. Hothersall**
6 **LADY BRIENNE (IRE),** 6, b m Flemensfirth (USA)—Spirit Rock (IRE) **Red Squares**
7 **MADAKHEEL (USA),** 4, b f Mr Greeley (USA)—Manaal (USA) **Miss K Milligan & Mr P Fowlie**
8 **NAM MA PROW,** 4, ch g Bahamian Bounty—Charlotte Vale **Mr C. R. Hirst**
9 **SLIM CHANCE (IRE),** 6, b m Clodovil (IRE)—Valluga (IRE) **Mrs B. Hothersall**
10 **SLIPPER SATIN (IRE),** 5, b m Excellent Art—In The Ribbons **Mrs J. M. L. Milligan**
11 **TAPAIDH FRANKIE (IRE),** 6, br m Waveney (UAE)—Corravilla (IRE) **Mr S. G. West**
12 **TARUMA (FR),** 7, gr g Martaline—Vie de Reine (FR) **J. D. Gordon**
13 **TURJUMAN (USA),** 10, ch g Swain (IRE)—Hachiyah (IRE) **Mr S. G. West**

### THREE-YEAR-OLDS

14 Ch f Monsieur Bond (IRE)—Meltwater (USA)

**Other Owners:** Mr K. Flint, Mr S. Flint, Mr P. Fowlie, Miss M. K. Milligan.

**Apprentice:** Paul Pickard.

## 643 MR DAVID WESTON, Marlborough

Postal: **C/o Flintstone Stud, West Overton, Marlborough, Wiltshire, SN8 4ER**
Contacts: **MOBILE (07966) 641001**
**E-MAIL flintstone007@icloud.com**

1 **AT FIRST LIGHT,** 6, b m Echo of Light—Bisaat (USA) **Miss E. Tanner**
2 **BEDROCK FRED,** 9, ch g Monsieur Bond (IRE)—Sea Mist (IRE) **Miss E. Tanner**
3 **LUCKSTER,** 5, b g Lucky Story (USA)—Bisaat (USA) **Miss E. Tanner**

## 644 MISS JESSICA WESTWOOD, Chulmleigh

Postal: **Molland Ridge Farm, Chulmleigh, Devon, EX18 7EF**
Contacts: **MOBILE (07536) 021449**
**E-MAIL Jesswestwoodracing@gmail.com WEBSITE www.jesswestwoodracing.com**

1 **BILLY BOY BEAMAN,** 4, b g Rocamadour—Icicles **Miss C. J. Beaman**
2 **BLESS ME JIM,** 5, ch g Babodana—Gambling Again **Miss J. J. Westwood**
3 **DONT CALL ME DORIS,** 5, b m Franklins Gardens—Grove Dancer **Holnicote Partnership**
4 **MONKERTY TUNKERTY,** 12, b g Silver Patriarch (IRE)—Orphan Annie **Miss J. J. Westwood**
5 **VINCESON (IRE),** 7, b g Vinnie Roe (IRE)—Velvet Huxley (IRE) **Holnicote Partnership**

**Other Owners:** Mr M. L. J. Fooks, Mr A. Westwood.

## 645 MR JOHN WEYMES, Middleham

Postal: **Ashgill, Coverham, Leyburn, North Yorkshire, DL8 4TJ**
Contacts: **PHONE (01969) 640420 FAX (01969) 640505 MOBILE (07753) 792516**
**E-MAIL kirsty@johnweymesracing.co.uk WEBSITE www.johnweymesracing.co.uk**

1 4, B g Grape Tree Road—Banoo (IRE)
2 **BIGINDIE (IRE),** 5, ch g Indian Haven—Graceful Air (IRE) **Mr R Lilley, Clarke, Highmoor Racing**
3 **BISCUIT,** 4, ch f Black Sam Bellamy (IRE)—Falcon's Gunner **Falcon's Line Ltd**
4 **BLACKCOMBE,** 5, b g Grape Tree Road—Banoo (IRE) **High Moor & Thoroughbred Partners**
5 **CELESTIAL DAWN,** 6, b m Echo of Light—Celestial Welcome **High Moor & Thoroughbred Partners**
6 **DREAM ALLY (IRE),** 5, b g Oasis Dream—Alexander Alliance (IRE) **Highmoor Racing 4 & Tag Racing**
7 **FALCON'S LEGEND,** 5, ch m Midnight Legend—Bling Noir (FR) **Falcon's Line Ltd**
8 **JUST FIVE (IRE),** 9, b g Olmodavor (USA)—Wildsplash (USA) **Highmoor Racing 4 & Tag Racing**
9 **PRINCESS ROSE,** 4, b f Royal Applause—Mystical Spirit (IRE) **T. A. Scothern**
10 4, B g Dr Massini (IRE)—Scarlet Target (IRE)
11 **TAKE THE LEAD,** 5, ch m Assertive—My Dancer (IRE) **Highmoor Racing 4 & Tag Racing**

### THREE-YEAR-OLDS

12 **RUBY HIND,** b f Firebreak—Linden's Lady **High Moor Racing 1**
13 **SPIRITUAL ACCLAIM (IRE),** b f Acclamation—Sister Clement (IRE) **T. A. Scothern**

### TWO-YEAR-OLDS

14 B g 15/2 Kheleyf (USA)—Burza (Bold Edge) (1500)
15 B c 24/2 Kyllachy—Steal The Curtain (Royal Applause) (952) **Mrs R. L. Heaton**

**Other Owners:** Mr P. D. Bickley, Miss K. Buckle, Mr P. R. Clarke, Mr R. Gayton, Mr A. J. R. Lilley, J. R. Weymes.

**Assistant Trainer:** Kirsty Buckle

**Jockey (flat):** Philip Makin. **Jockey (NH):** Dougie Costello, Keith Mercer.

## 646 MR ERIC WHEELER, Marlborough

Postal: **15 St Michaels Close, Lambourn, Hungerford, Berkshire, RG17 8FA**
Contacts: **PHONE (07795) 844185 (01672) 811423 MOBILE (07795) 844185**

1 **BEGGERS LUCK,** 5, b m Lucky Story (USA)—Dropitlikeit's Hot (IRE) **Mr G. W. Witheford**
2 **CENTRALIZED,** 4, ch g Central Park (IRE)—Millie The Filly **Ms L. Williams**
3 **EL LIBERTADOR (USA),** 9, b br g Giant's Causeway (USA)—Istikbal (USA) **Mr J. L. Day**
4 **MALIH,** 6, b g Echo of Light—Sultry Lass (USA) **Wedgewood Estates**

**Assistant Trainer:** Mr C Witheford

## 647 MR ALISTAIR WHILLANS, Hawick

Postal: **Esker House, Newmill-On-Slitrig, Hawick, Roxburghshire, TD9 9UQ**
Contacts: **PHONE (01450) 376642 FAX (01450) 376082 MOBILE (07771) 550555**
**E-MAIL acwracing@hotmail.com**

1 **ALEXANDRAKOLLONTAI (IRE),** 5, b m Amadeus Wolf—Story **Chris Spark & William Orr**
2 **APACHEE PRINCE (IRE),** 6, b g Indian Danehill (IRE)—Wheredidthemoneygo (IRE) **J. D. Wright**

## MR ALISTAIR WHILLANS - Continued

3 **CLAUDE CARTER,** 11, b g Elmaamul (USA)—Cruz Santa **Mrs L. M. Whillans**
4 **DECLAMATION (IRE),** 5, ch g Shamardal (USA)—Dignify (IRE) **A. C. Whillans**
5 **DIAMOND FIZZ (IRE),** 6, br g Scorpion (IRE)—Champagne Warrior (IRE) **I. Hamilton**
6 **FUNKY MUNKY,** 10, b g Talaash (IRE)—Chilibang Bang **The Twelve Munkys**
7 **GALILEE CHAPEL (IRE),** 6, b g Baltic King—Triple Zero (IRE) **A. C. Whillans**
8 **GLACIAL ROCK (IRE),** 9, b g Sonus (IRE)—Glacial Princess (IRE) **Mr M. Bell**
9 **GLEANN NA NDOCHAIS (IRE),** 9, b g Zagreb (USA)—Nissereen (USA) **Mr W J E Scott & Mrs M A Scott**
10 **LOVE MARMALADE (IRE),** 5, ch g Duke of Marmalade (IRE)—Green Castle (IRE) **Akela Construction Ltd**
11 **MAGIC MAISIE,** 4, b f Tiger Hill (IRE)—Silcasue **Mr F. Lowe**
12 **MARTHA MILAN,** 6, b m Milan—Martha Reilly (IRE) **C. Bird**
13 **MAYZE BELL,** 6, br m And Beyond (IRE)—Eleanor May **A. C. Whillans**
14 **MEADOWCROFT BOY,** 6, b g Kayf Tara—Blackbriery Thyne (IRE) **Mr W J E Scott & Mrs M A Scott**
15 **OPT OUT,** 5, ch g Pivotal—Easy Option (IRE) **Akela Construction Ltd**
16 **PIXIE CUT (IRE),** 5, b m Chineur (FR)—Fantastic Cee (IRE) **J Wilson, C Spark, W Orr**
17 **RALPHY BOY (IRE),** 6, b g Acclamation—Silcasue **Mr F. Lowe**
18 **RED STORY,** 4, b g Kayf Tara—Marabunta (SPA) **W. J. E. Scott**
19 **SAMSTOWN,** 8, b g Kingsalsa (USA)—Red Peony **Mrs E. B. Ferguson**
20 **SCRAPPER SMITH (IRE),** 9, b g Choisir (AUS)—Lady Ounavarra (IRE) **A. C. Whillans**
21 **VICKY VALENTINE,** 5, b m Rock of Gibraltar (IRE)—Silcasue **Mr F. Lowe**
22 **VITTACHI,** 8, b g Bertolini (USA)—Miss Lorilaw (FR) **Sutherland Five**
23 **W SIX TIMES,** 9, b m Double Trigger (IRE)—Be My Mot (IRE) **Mrs L. M. Whillans**
24 **WEE JOCK ELLIOT,** 5, b g Overbury (IRE)—Caitlin Ash **John & Liz Elliot**
25 **WHAT A STEEL (IRE),** 11, b g Craigsteel—Sonya's Pearl (IRE) **J. D. Wright**
26 **WYFIELD ROSE,** 6, b m Kayf Tara—Miniature Rose **John & Liz Elliot**

### THREE-YEAR-OLDS

27 **HIDDEN REBEL,** b f Cockney Rebel (IRE)—Medicea Sidera **J. D. Wright**
28 **MISTER ARCHIE,** b g Archipenko (USA)—Zooming (IRE) **J. D. Wright**

**Other Owners:** W. M. Ballantyne, J. J. Elliot, Mrs E. J. Elliot, Mr R. J. Goodfellow, Mr J. S. B. Harrold, Mrs S. Harrow, Mr B. Melrose, Mr W. Orr, Mrs M. A. Scott, Mr C. Spark, Mr J. R. L. Wilson, Mrs S. L. Wright.

---

## 648 MR DONALD WHILLANS, Hawick

Postal: **Dodlands Steading, Hawick, Roxburghshire, TD9 8LG**
Contacts: **BUSINESS (01450) 373128 HOME (01450) 379810 FAX (01450) 376082 MOBILE (07840) 997570**
**E-MAIL donaldwhillans@aol.com WEBSITE www.donaldwhillansracing.com**

1 **BOLLIN FIONA,** 11, ch m Silver Patriarch (IRE)—Bollin Nellie **C. N. Whillans**
2 **BOLLIN JULIE,** 8, b m Bollin Eric—Bollin Nellie **C. N. Whillans**
3 **CHAMPAGNE AGENT (IRE),** 9, b g Smadoun (FR)—Madame Jean (FR) **Star Racing**
4 **CHARLIE BUCKET,** 12, ch g Sugarfoot—Stoproveritate **D. W. Whillans**
5 **EGON SPENGLAR,** 7, b g River Falls—Wee Willow **D. W. Whillans**
6 **ELLISTRIN BELLE,** 7, b m Helissio (FR)—Hannah Park (IRE) **Mrs E. Smith**
7 **HARTFORTH,** 7, ch g Haafhd—St Edith (IRE) **The Brave Lads Partnership**
8 **NEARLY MAY,** 7, b m Winged Love (IRE)—Lindajane (IRE) **D. W. Whillans**
9 **NODDA HIGH KID,** 9, ch g Sir Harry Lewis (USA)—Lindajane (IRE) **D. W. Whillans**
10 **SHADES OF MIDNIGHT,** 5, b g Midnight Legend—Hannah Park (IRE) **The Potassium Partnership**
11 **SNAPPING TURTLE (IRE),** 10, b g Turtle Island (IRE)—Rachael's Dawn **D. W. Whillans**
12 **TOMAHAWK WOOD,** 6, ch g Courteous—Meda's Song **Mr G. Aitken**

**Other Owners:** Mr I. Aitcken, Mr Nick Bannerman, Mr H. G. Beeby, Mr A. Duncan, Mrs A. Rhind, Mr S. Taylor, Mrs H. M. Whillans, Mr D. W. Whillans.

**Assistant Trainer:** Garry Whillans

**Jockey (flat):** Garry Whillans. **Jockey (NH):** Callum Whillans.

## 649 MR RICHARD WHITAKER, Scarcroft

Postal: **Hellwood Racing Stables, Hellwood Lane, Scarcroft, Leeds, West Yorkshire, LS14 3BP**
Contacts: **PHONE (01132) 892265 FAX (01132) 893680 MOBILE (07831) 870454**
**E-MAIL rmwhitaker@btconnect.com WEBSITE www.richardwhitaker.org**

1 **AVON BREEZE,** 6, b m Avonbridge—African Breeze **Grange Park Racing II & Partner**
2 **ICY BLUE,** 7, b g Iceman—Bridal Path **Country Lane Partnership**
3 **LOVE ISLAND,** 6, b m Acclamation—Sally Traffic **J Barry Pemberton & R M Whitaker**
4 **MEY BLOSSOM,** 10, ch m Captain Rio—Petra Nova **Waz Developments Ltd**
5 **PIPERS NOTE,** 5, ch g Piccolo—Madam Valentine **Six Iron Partnership & Partner**
6 **RIO SANDS,** 10, b g Captain Rio—Sally Traffic **R. M. Whitaker**
7 **ROCKY'S PRIDE (IRE),** 9, b g Rock of Gibraltar (IRE)—L'animee **R. M. Whitaker**
8 **TUMBLEWIND,** 5, ch m Captain Rio—African Breeze **Nice Day Out Partnership**
9 **WOODACRE,** 8, b g Pyrus (USA)—Fairy Ring (IRE) **Mrs R. M. Whitaker**
10 **WOTALAD,** 5, b g Bertolini (USA)—Cosmic Song **Mrs J. M. Willows**

### THREE-YEAR-OLDS

11 **BOND MYSTERY,** b g Monsieur Bond (IRE)—Scooby Dooby Do **P. Davies**
12 **DESERT CHIEF,** b g Kheleyf (USA)—African Breeze **R. M. Whitaker**
13 **JUBILEE SONG,** b f Royal Applause—Cosmic Song **Mr D. A. Walker**
14 **MO HENRY,** b c Monsieur Bond (IRE)—Mo Mhuirnin (IRE) **Shevlin Whelan Syndicate**
15 **SPARKLING SAPPHIRE,** ro f Monsieur Bond (IRE)—Velvet Band **Nice Day Out Partnership**
16 **TOTALLY MAGIC (IRE),** b f Captain Rio—Hypocrisy **Mr James Marshall & Mr Chris Marshall**

### TWO-YEAR-OLDS

**17** B c 12/5 Royal Applause—African Breeze (Atraf)
**18** B f 5/4 Equiano (FR)—Cosmic Song (Cosmonaut) (5000)
**19** B c 9/5 Royal Applause—Luanshya (First Trump) **R. C. Dollar, T. Adams, G. F. Pemberton Trust**
**20** B f 22/5 Monsieur Bond (IRE)—Mo Mhuirnin (IRE) (Danetime (IRE)) (761) **Shevlin Whelan Syndicate**
**21** Ch f 17/3 Equiano (FR)—Rose Street (USA) (Street Cry (IRE)) (2857)
**22** **SEBASTIAN'S WISH (IRE),** b c 21/4 Aqlaam—Swish (GER) (Monsun (GER)) (40000) **R. Macgregor**
**23** B f 25/3 Misu Bond (IRE)—Velvet Band (Verglas (IRE)) (952)
**24** Ch c 23/1 Monsieur Bond (IRE)—Wotatomboy (Captain Rio) **Mrs J. M. Willows, R. M. Whitaker**

**Other Owners:** K. M. Brown, A. D. Crombie, Robert Macgregor, J. R. Marshall, Mr C. R. Marshall, Mr A. Norrington, J. B. Pemberton, G. Sanderson, Mr L. M. Shevlin, R. Whelan.

**Assistant Trainer:** Simon R Whitaker

## 650 MR ARTHUR WHITEHEAD, Craven Arms

Postal: **Lawn Farm, Beambridge, Aston on Clun, Craven Arms, Shropshire, SY7 0HA**
Contacts: **PHONE (01588) 660424**

1 **DELLA SUN (FR),** 9, b g Della Francesca (USA)—Algarve Sunrise (IRE) **A. J. Whitehead**
2 **JAWAHAL DU MATHAN (FR),** 7, b g Smadoun (FR)—Stone's Glow (USA) **A. J. Whitehead**
3 **ROYAL DEFENCE (IRE),** 9, b g Refuse To Bend (IRE)—Alessia (GER) **A. J. Whitehead**
4 **ZALGARRY (FR),** 8, b g Ballingarry (IRE)—Spleen (FR) **A. J. Whitehead**

**Other Owners:** P. M. Clarkson, Mr M. Watkinson.

**Conditional:** Josh Wall.

## 651 MR ARTHUR WHITING, Dursley

Postal: **38 Barrs Lane, North Nibley, Dursley, Gloucestershire, GL11 6DT**
Contacts: **PHONE (01453) 546375 MOBILE (07786) 152539**

1 **BARRS LANE,** 7, b m Sir Harry Lewis (USA)—Cashel Dancer **A. J. Whiting**
2 **BONNIE BLACK ROSE,** 5, b m Black Sam Bellamy (IRE)—Fragrant Rose **A. J. Whiting**
3 **CHARLIE RUFFLES (IRE),** 7, b g Milan—Rosie Ruffles (IRE) **A. J. Whiting**
4 **DRIVING WELL (IRE),** 7, b g Oscar (IRE)—Polly Anthus **A. J. Whiting**
5 **ITSUPTOYOU (IRE),** 11, b g Dr Massini (IRE)—I Blame Theparents **A. J. Whiting**
6 **THE WEE MIDGET,** 10, b g Mtoto—Fragrant Rose **A. J. Whiting**

## 652 MR CHARLES WHITTAKER, Frome

Postal: **West Forest Farm, Gare Hill, Frome, Somerset, BA11 5EZ**
Contacts: **PHONE (01373) 836500**

1 **BANCO DE LOGOS (FR),** 4, b g Laverock (IRE)—Funkia (FR) **C. R. Whittaker**
2 **CHINATOWN BOY (IRE),** 7, ch g Presenting—Asian Maze (IRE) **C. R. Whittaker**
3 **GUNSHYCOWBOY (IRE),** 6, b g Definite Article—Cebola (FR) **C. R. Whittaker**
4 **PERTINENT (FR),** 12, b g Sleeping Car (FR)—Jamais de La Vie (FR) **C. R. Whittaker**
5 **RUAPEHU (IRE),** 9, b g Presenting—Silver Prayer (IRE) **C. R. Whittaker**
6 **SOUTHFIELD FAIRY,** 4, b f Victory Note (USA)—Laureldean Belle (IRE) **Mrs A. B. Yeoman**

## 653 MR HARRY WHITTINGTON, Sparsholt

Postal: **Hill Barn, Sparsholt, Wantage, Oxfordshire, OX12 9XB**
Contacts: **PHONE (01235) 751869 MOBILE (07734) 388357**
**E-MAIL harry@harrywhittington.co.uk WEBSITE www.harrywhittington.co.uk**

1 **ARZAL (FR),** 5, b br g Vendangeur (IRE)—Ghostaline (FR) **The Hennessy Six**
2 **BISHOP WULSTAN (IRE),** 4, b c Oratorio (IRE)—Laurentine (USA) **Middleham Park Racing Bellman Trowbridge**
3 **DISTESO (IRE),** 4, b g Milan—Made Easy (IRE) **P. G. Jacobs**
4 **DRIFTER (IRE),** 4, b g Footstepsinthesand—Bright Bank (IRE) **L Bellman, D Lowe, K Trowbridge**
5 **FOUROVAKIND,** 10, b g Sir Harry Lewis (USA)—Four M's **Andrew F Sawyer,G W Hazell & C Bosley**
6 **HIGH LOVE (IRE),** 4, b f High Chaparral (IRE)—All Embracing (IRE) **Laurence Bellman & David Lowe**
7 **ISLA DI MILANO (IRE),** 4, b g Milan—Monagee Island (IRE) **Noted & Agreed**
8 **MOLLASSES,** 4, b f Authorized (IRE)—Muscovado (USA) **Atkin, Bullen-Smith, Gamon, Pelly**
9 **PINK PLAY (IRE),** 4, b f King's Theatre (IRE)—Strawberry Fool (FR) **P. G. Jacobs**
10 **POLSTAR (FR),** 6, b g Poliglote—Star Dancing **Dixon,Ellis,Lynds,Travers,Watkins**
11 **QASSER (IRE),** 6, b g Intikhab (USA)—Surrender To Me (USA) **Lead The Way Syndicate**
12 **TOMIBOLA (IRE),** 7, b g Definite Article—Cebola (FR) **Laurence Bellman & Harry Whittington**

**Other Owners:** Mrs C. J. Atkin, L. A. Bellman, C. M. Bosley, Mrs L. Bullen-Smith, Mr B. D. Carpenter, Mr D. G. Christian, Mr C. N. Clark, P. J. Dixon, Mr D. Ellis, Mrs A. M. Fitzgerald O'Connor, Mrs M. S. Gamon, M. G. Hazell, Mr G. W. Hazell, Mr A. Holt, Mr D. J. Lowe, Mr I. Macnabb, Mr J. Pak, T. S. Palin, Mrs S. E. Pelly, M. Prince, Mr J. D. Robinson, Mr A. F. Sawyer, A. Taylor, K. P. Trowbridge, C. H. O. Whittington, Mr S. Willis.

**Assistant Trainer:** Paul O'Brien

## 654 MR MICHAEL WIGHAM, Newmarket

Postal: **Hamilton Stables, Hamilton Road, Newmarket, Suffolk, CB8 7JQ**
Contacts: **PHONE (01638) 668806 FAX (01638) 668806 MOBILE (07831) 456426**
**E-MAIL michaelwigham@hotmail.co.uk WEBSITE www.michaelwighamracing.co.uk**

1 **ADAM FOREVER,** 4, b g Myboycharlie (IRE)—Dust **D. Hassan**
2 **BRYCEWISE,** 4, b g Firebreak—Jan Mayen **Palatinate Thoroughbred Racing, D Hassan**
3 **CHAIN OF EVENTS,** 8, ch g Nayef (USA)—Ermine (IRE) **Mr P. J. Edwards**
4 **DISTANT SHADOW,** 4, gr f Rock of Gibraltar (IRE)—Daheeya **Follow The Flag Partnership**
5 **FAIRWAY TO HEAVEN (IRE),** 6, b g Jeremy (USA)—Luggala (IRE) **Palatinate Thoroughbred Racing Limited**
6 **FOXY FOREVER (IRE),** 5, b g Kodiac—Northern Tara (IRE) **D. Hassan, J. Cullinan**
7 **GIN AND TONIC,** 5, ch g Phoenix Reach (IRE)—Arctic Queen **The Gin & Tonic Partnership**
8 **HAPPY JACK (IRE),** 4, b g Elusive City (USA)—Miss Pelling (IRE) **G Linder, B Green, D Hassan, S Osman**
9 **SHOTGUN START,** 5, b g Kyllachy—Fly In Style **Palatinate Thoroughbred Racing Limited**
10 **TEE IT UP TOMMO (IRE),** 6, gr g Clodovil (IRE)—Lamh Eile (IRE) **Palatinate Thoroughbred Racing Limited**
11 **TROJAN ROCKET (IRE),** 7, b g Elusive City (USA)—Tagula Bay (IRE) **G Linder, D Hassan, R Warner**

### THREE-YEAR-OLDS

12 **DEMBABA (IRE),** b c Moss Vale (IRE)—Wildsplash (USA) **Palatinate Thoroughbred Racing, D Hassan**
13 **ELIS ELIZ (IRE),** b f Lord Shanakill (USA)—Suailce (IRE) **T Akman & D Hassan**
14 **STAR ASSET,** b c Dutch Art—Black Belt Shopper (IRE) **Mr T. Akman**
15 **TOMBISH (FR),** ch c Three Valleys (USA)—Dalawala (IRE) **T Akman & D Hassan**

**MR MICHAEL WIGHAM - Continued**

**Other Owners:** Mr Tugay Akman, Mr Carl Appleton, Mr J. M. Cullinan, Mr Peter Edwards, Mr D. Hassan, Mr G. D. J. Linder, Mr Seyhan Osman, Palatinate Thoroughbred Racing Limited, Mr R. Warner, Mr Michael Wigham.

**Assistant Trainer:** Sharon Kenyon

---

## 655 MR MARTIN WILESMITH, Dymock

Postal: **Bellamys Farm, Dymock, Gloucestershire, GL18 2DX**
Contacts: **PHONE (01531) 890410 (01684) 561238 FAX (01684) 893428 MOBILE (07970) 411638**
**E-MAIL martin@mswilesmith.co.uk**

1 **AT YOUR PERIL,** 13, b g Alflora (IRE)—Teenero
2 6, B m Alflora (IRE)—Clouding Over **M. S. Wilesmith**
3 6, B g Midnight Legend—Flame O'frensi **M. S. Wilesmith**
4 **GREENWAY CROSS,** 8, b g Alflora (IRE)—Might Be **M. S. Wilesmith**
5 **LORD BELLAMY (IRE),** 13, b g Lord Americo—Paean Express (IRE) **M. S. Wilesmith**
6 6, Gr m Fair Mix (IRE)—Mrs White (IRE) **M. S. Wilesmith**
7 5, B m Black Sam Bellamy (IRE)—Mrs White (IRE) **M. S. Wilesmith**
8 **RED OATS,** 9, ch m Alflora (IRE)—Silk Oats **M. S. Wilesmith**
9 **SHE'SOLOVELY,** 11, b m Alflora (IRE)—Cashmere Lady **M. S. Wilesmith**
10 **SILK ROSE,** 11, gr m Terimon—Silk Oats **M. S. Wilesmith**
11 **THE HUMBEL BUTLER (IRE),** 14, b g Humbel (USA)—Butler's Lady **M. S. Wilesmith**

**Assistant Trainer:** Ms E. C. Wilesmith (07976 926906)

**Amateur:** Mr M. C. Wilesmith.

---

## 656 MR EVAN WILLIAMS, Llancarfan

Postal: **Aberogwrn Farm, Llancarfan, Nr Barry, Vale of Glamorgan**
Contacts: **PHONE (01446) 754069 FAX (01446) 754069 MOBILE (07950) 381227**
**E-MAIL cath@evanwilliams.co.uk**

1 **ABBEYGREY (IRE),** 6, b g Generous (IRE)—Garw Valley **R. E. R. Williams**
2 **ALLEZ VIC (IRE),** 9, b g Old Vic—Newgate Fairy **Mr R. J. Gambarini**
3 **AQUA DUDE (IRE),** 5, br g Flemensfirth (USA)—Miss Cozzene (FR) **Mr & Mrs William Rucker**
4 **ARMCHAIR THEATRE (IRE),** 5, b g King's Theatre (IRE)—Oh Susannah (FR) **Ms S. A. Howell**
5 **BALLYGLASHEEN (IRE),** 5, ch g Galileo (IRE)—Luas Line (IRE) **Mr R. J. Gambarini**
6 **BARRAKILLA (IRE),** 8, b g Milan—Kigali (IRE) **Mr & Mrs William Rucker**
7 **BLANDFORDS GUNNER,** 6, b g Needle Gun (IRE)—Miss Millbrook **Kevin & Anne Glastonbury**
8 **BLOOD BROTHER (IRE),** 5, b g Presenting—Mardi Roberta (IRE) **R. E. R. Williams**
9 4, B f Court Cave (IRE)—Bobazure (IRE)
10 **BONOBO (IRE),** 8, b g Quws—Better Folly (IRE) **Mary & Billy Evans**
11 **BRASSICK,** 8, b g Presenting—No More Money **Mr & Mrs William Rucker**
12 **BUCK MULLIGAN,** 10, b g Robellino (USA)—Music Park (IRE) **Mr T. L. Fell**
13 **BULLET STREET (IRE),** 7, ch g Arakan (USA)—Play A Tune (IRE) **Mrs Janet Davies & Mrs C Williams**
14 **BUYWISE (IRE),** 8, b g Tikkanen (USA)—Greenogue Princess (IRE) **T. H. Jones**
15 **CANICALLYOUBACK,** 7, b g Auction House (USA)—Island Colony (USA) **R. E. R. Williams**
16 **CAPE CASTER (IRE),** 4, br g Cape Cross (IRE)—Playboy Mansion (IRE) **D P Barrie & D Redhead**
17 **CAPILLA (IRE),** 7, gr g Beneficial—Cap The Rose (IRE) **Mrs J. Davies**
18 **CAPPA BLEU (IRE),** 13, b g Pistolet Bleu (IRE)—Cappagale (IRE) **Mr & Mrs William Rucker**
19 **CLYNE,** 5, b g Hernando (FR)—Lauderdale (GER) **Mr D. M. Williams**
20 **COPPER BIRCH (IRE),** 7, ch g Beneficial—Givehertime (IRE) **Mrs J. Davies**
21 **COURT MINSTREL (IRE),** 8, b g Court Cave (IRE)—Theatral **Mrs J. Davies**
22 **DANCING ECCO (IRE),** 6, b g Elnadim (USA)—Ecco Mi (IRE) **Mr James W. Barrett**
23 **DARK SPIRIT (IRE),** 7, b m Whipper (USA)—Dark Raider (IRE) **Richard Abbott & Mario Stavrou**
24 **DE FAOITHESDREAM (IRE),** 9, br g Balakheri (IRE)—Cutteen Lass (IRE) **Mr R Abbott & Mr M Stavrou**
25 **DEFINITE DREAM (IRE),** 8, b g Definite Article—Brooks Chariot (IRE) **Mr R. J. H. Geffen**
26 **DEIA SUNRISE (IRE),** 6, gr g Clodovil (IRE)—Hedera (USA) **R. E. R. Williams**
27 **DEVIL'S DYKE (USA),** 7, b br g Redoute's Choice (AUS)—Kotuku **Mr R Abbott & Mr M Stavrou**
28 **DYE OF A NEEDLE (IRE),** 5, ch g Lakeshore Road (USA)—Laskine (IRE) **A Turton & J Blackburn**
29 **FIREBIRD FLYER (IRE),** 8, b g Winged Love (IRE)—Kiora Lady (IRE) **R. E. R. Williams**
30 **FORGIVIENNE,** 8, b m Alflora (IRE)—Always Forgiving **Gwili Syndicate**
31 4, B g Darsi (FR)—Geray Lady (IRE)
32 **GOING CONCERN (IRE),** 8, b g Overbury (IRE)—Scorpio Girl **Mr P. M. Langford**

## MR EVAN WILLIAMS - Continued

33 **HANG 'EM HIGH (IRE),** 5, br g Westerner—Reticent Bride (IRE) **Mrs C. A. Williams**
34 **HO LEE MOSES (IRE),** 5, bl g Kalanisi (IRE)—Tipsy Miss (IRE) **Ms S. A. Howell**
35 **HOLD COURT (IRE),** 8, br g Court Cave (IRE)—Tipsy Miss (IRE) **Edwards & Howell**
36 **HUGHESIE (IRE),** 6, b g Indian Danehill (IRE)—Collatrim Choice (IRE) **Mr A. Turton & Mr P. Langford**
37 **IN ON THE ACT,** 5, b g Act One—Pequenita **R. E. R. Williams**
38 **IN THE HOLD (IRE),** 5, b g Stowaway—Carrigeen Kerria (IRE) **Mr & Mrs William Rucker**
39 **IT'S A STEAL (IRE),** 8, b g Craigsteel—Mimosa Rose (IRE) **Mr & Mrs William Rucker**
40 **JOHN CONSTABLE (IRE),** 4, b c Montjeu (IRE)—Dance Parade (USA) **Walters Plant Hire Ltd**
41 **KING MASSINI (IRE),** 9, b g Dr Massini (IRE)—King's Linnet (IRE) **Border Pointers**
42 **KING'S ODYSSEY (IRE),** 6, b g King's Theatre (IRE)—Ma Furie (FR) **Mr & Mrs William Rucker**
43 **KUDU COUNTRY (IRE),** 9, gr g Captain Rio—Nirvavita (FR) **W. J. Evans**
44 **LASER HAWK (IRE),** 8, b g Rashar (USA)—Alphablend (IRE) **W. J. Evans**
45 **LAVA LAMP (GER),** 8, b g Shamardal (USA)—La Felicita **Mrs J. Davies**
46 **MAC BERTIE,** 6, b g Beat All (USA)—Macnance (IRE) **Keith & Sue Lowry**
47 **MAC LE COUTEAU,** 7, b g Overbury (IRE)—Macnance (IRE) **Keith & Sue Lowry**
**48** 4, B g Multiplex—Macnance (IRE) **K. R. Lowry**
49 **MAKETHE MOSTOFNOW (IRE),** 10, b g Milan—Pass The Leader (IRE) **Mrs J. Davies**
50 **MAXANISI (IRE),** 5, br g Kalanisi (IRE)—Maxis Girl (IRE) **Mrs J. Davies**
51 **MILESTONE (IRE),** 5, b g Galileo (IRE)—Cassydora **Mr R. J. Gambarini**
52 **MR KIT CAT,** 5, ch g Lucarno (USA)—Makeabreak (IRE) **Mr & Mrs William Rucker**
53 **MR MOSS (IRE),** 10, b g Moscow Society (USA)—Yesterdays Gorby (IRE) **Mr & Mrs William Rucker**
**54** 4, B f Westerner—My Magic (IRE)
55 **NANSAROY,** 5, br g Indian River (FR)—Jurado Park (IRE) **T. H. Jones**
**56** 4, Br g Primary (USA)—Next Venture (IRE) **R. E. R. Williams**
57 **NORDICAL (IRE),** 5, b g Beneficial—Nordic Abu (IRE) **R. E. R. Williams**
58 **ON THE ROAD (IRE),** 5, b g Stowaway—B Greenhill **Mrs C. A. Williams**
59 **ON TOUR (IRE),** 7, b g Croco Rouge (IRE)—Galant Tour (IRE) **T. H. Jones**
60 **OSCAR HALFPENNY (IRE),** 5, b g Oscar (IRE)—Temporary Setback (IRE) **Geoff & Anne Price**
61 **OSCAR SUNSET (IRE),** 8, b g Oscar (IRE)—Derravarra Sunset (IRE) **Geoff & Anne Price**
62 **PADGE (IRE),** 6, b g Flemensfirth (USA)—Mona Vic (IRE) **Mr & Mrs William Rucker**
63 **PHARSPIRIT (IRE),** 4, b g Yeats (IRE)—Lovely Snoopy (IRE) **Mrs J. Davies**
64 **POBBLES BAY (IRE),** 5, b g Oscar (IRE)—Rose de Beaufai (FR) **Mr D. M. Williams**
65 **POULANASSY (IRE),** 5, b g Tikkanen (USA)—Winsome Mary (IRE) **Mr P. M. Langford**
66 **PRESENT TIMES (IRE),** 4, b g Kalanisi (IRE)—Beguiling (IRE) **Mrs C. A. Waters**
67 **PRIMA PORTA,** 9, b m American Post—Porta Marzia (CHI) **D.P.Barrie & H.A.F. Parshall**
68 **RICHARD RABBIT (IRE),** 5, b g Mahler—Aos Dana (IRE) **Mr & Mrs William Rucker**
**69** 4, B g Morozov (USA)—Saltee Great (IRE)
**70** 4, B g Gold Well—Shamriyna (IRE)
**71** 4, B g Marienbard (IRE)—Smashing Leader (IRE)
**72** 4, B f Robin des Champs (FR)—South Queen Lady (IRE)
73 **SPARKSFROMMYHEELS (IRE),** 5, b g Oscar (IRE)—Shesourpresent (IRE) **Ms S. A. Howell**
74 **STILL BELIEVING (IRE),** 7, ch m Blueprint (IRE)—Im A Believer (IRE) **R. E. R. Williams**
75 **SUBLIME TALENT (IRE),** 9, b g Sadler's Wells (USA)—Summer Trysting (USA) **Mrs C. A. Williams**
76 **TENANT FARMER (IRE),** 5, gr g Touch of Land (FR)—Miss McCormick (IRE) **R. E. R. Williams**
77 **THE GIPPER (IRE),** 5, b g King's Theatre (IRE)—Merrill Gaye (IRE) **R. E. R. Williams**
**78** 4, B g Brian Boru—The Rebel Lady (IRE)
79 **THINK ITS ALL OVER (USA),** 8, b g Tiznow (USA)—A P Petal (USA) **R. E. R. Williams**
80 **TIMESAWASTIN (IRE),** 9, b g Curtain Time (IRE)—Innocent Approach (IRE) **Mrs C. A. Waters**
81 **TORNADO IN MILAN (IRE),** 9, b g Milan—Julika (GER) **Mr & Mrs William Rucker**
82 **UPSANDDOWNS (IRE),** 7, b g Definite Article—Courtain (USA) **ARC**
83 **VINNIE RED (IRE),** 6, ch g Vinnie Roe (IRE)—Conzara (IRE) **Mr & Mrs William Rucker**
**84** 4, B g Oscar (IRE)—Voodoo Magic (GER)
85 **WABANAKI (IRE),** 5, b g Indian River (FR)—Treasure Island **Mrs C. A. Williams**
86 **WILD BILL (IRE),** 6, b g Westerner—Sarahall (IRE) **Mr & Mrs William Rucker**
87 **WILLIAM'S WISHES (IRE),** 10, b g Oscar (IRE)—Strong Wishes (IRE) **Mrs D. E. Cheshire**
88 **WYCHWOODS BROOK,** 9, b g Midnight Legend—Miss Millbrook **Kevin & Anne Glastonbury**
89 **ZAMA ZAMA,** 8, b g Sakhee (USA)—Insinuation (IRE) **Mr W. J. Eddy-Williams**
90 **ZARZAL (IRE),** 7, b g Dr Fong (USA)—Zarwala (IRE) **Mrs J. Davies**

## THREE-YEAR-OLDS

91 **SHOWCASTER,** b f Showcasing—Casterossa **Mr D. P. Barrie & Mr M. J. Rees**

## TWO-YEAR-OLDS

92 **CASTINMIXA,** b f 11/3 Fair Mix (IRE)—Casterossa (Rossini (USA)) **Mr D. P. Barrie & Mr M. J. Rees**

## MR EVAN WILLIAMS - Continued

**Other Owners:** R. J. Abbott, D. P. Barrie, J. N. Blackburn, J. R. Edwards, Mrs M. Evans, Mr D. C. Footman, K. J. Glastonbury, Mrs A. J. Glastonbury, Mr P. Griffiths, Mrs S. B. Lowry, W. J. G. Morse, Mr H. A. F. Parshall, Mr G. Price, Mrs A. C. Price, Mr D. P. Redhead, M. J. Rees, W. J. Rucker, Mrs A. Rucker, M. Stavrou, D. I. Thomas, Mr A. Turton, Mr S. Williams.

**Assistant Trainer:** Cath Williams

**Jockey (NH):** Paul Moloney, Adam Wedge. **Conditional:** Lewis Gordon, Conor Ring. **Amateur:** Mr Conor Orr, Mr Darach Skelly.

---

## 657 MR IAN WILLIAMS, Alvechurch

Postal: **Dominion Racing Stables, Seafield Lane, Alvechurch, Birmingham, B48 7HL**
Contacts: **PHONE (01564) 822392 FAX (01564) 829475 MOBILE (07976) 645384**
**E-MAIL info@ianwilliamsracing.com WEBSITE www.ianwilliamsracing.com**

1 **A TAIL OF INTRIGUE (IRE),** 7, b g Tillerman—Princess Commanche (IRE) **Mr Oscar Singh & Miss Priya Purewal**
2 **ADMAN SAM (IRE),** 4, b g Black Sam Bellamy (IRE)—Koral Bay (FR) **Mr P. A. Downing**
3 **AGHA DES MOTTES (FR),** 5, b g Mister Sacha (FR)—Java des Mottes (FR) **A. L. R. Morton**
4 **ALL REDDY,** 4, ch g Compton Place—Raphaela (FR) **Ms S. A. Howell**
5 **ALMANACK,** 5, b g Haatef (USA)—Openness **Mr P. Slater**
6 **ASCOTS MASCOT,** 7, b m Septieme Ciel (USA)—Red Dahlia **Macable Partnership**
7 **BALLYALTON (IRE),** 8, b g Pierre—Almilto (IRE) **Mr J. Westwood**
8 **BALLYFARSOON (IRE),** 4, ch g Medicean—Amzara (IRE) **P. Kelly**
9 4, Ch g Mahler—Bayloughbess (IRE)
10 **BOBCATBILLY (IRE),** 9, b g Overbury (IRE)—Cush Jewel (IRE) **P. J. Vogt**
11 **CASHPOINT,** 10, b g Fantastic Light (USA)—Cashew **Macable Partnership**
12 **COMMISSAR,** 6, b g Soviet Star (USA)—Sari **S. Hassiakos**
13 **CONRY (IRE),** 9, ch g Captain Rio—Altizaf **Mr & Mrs H. Parmar**
14 **COOL SKY,** 6, b g Millkom—Intersky High (USA) **Norte Sur Partnership**
15 **COTILLION,** 9, b g Sadler's Wells (USA)—Riberac **P. J. Vogt**
16 **DESTRUCT,** 5, b g Rail Link—Daring Miss **The Three Graces**
17 **DONAPOLLO,** 7, b g Kayf Tara—Star of Wonder (FR) **Mr J. P. D. Stead**
18 **DRUMLANG (IRE),** 9, b g Soviet Star (USA)—Sherekiya (IRE) **Mr M Roberts & Mr J Tredwell**
19 **EARLS QUARTER (IRE),** 9, b g Shantou (USA)—Par Street (IRE) **P. Kelly**
20 **ETANIA,** 7, b m King's Theatre (IRE)—Linnet (GER) **Mr & Mrs H. Parmar**
21 **FAITHFUL MOUNT,** 6, b h Shirocco (GER)—Lady Lindsay (IRE) **Macable Partnership**
22 **FERRYVIEW PLACE,** 6, b g Compton Place—Songsheet **Mr J. Rocke**
23 **FREDO (IRE),** 11, ch g Lomitas—Felina (GER) **Mrs J. S. Allen**
24 **FREEDOM FIGHTER (IRE),** 5, b h Danehill Dancer (IRE)—Rose of Petra (IRE) **Global Commodity Imports Ltd**
25 **FREUD (FR),** 5, b g Dalakhani (IRE)—Ailette **M. H. Watt**
26 **GAMBOL (FR),** 5, ch g New Approach (IRE)—Guardia (GER) **I. P. Williams**
27 **GENAX (IRE),** 4, b f Green Desert (USA)—Steam Cuisine **Ian Williams Racing Club**
28 **GHOST OF A SMILE (IRE),** 7, b g Oscar (IRE)—Dix Huit Brumaire (FR) **Mr S. Cox**
29 **GRAND GIGOLO (FR),** 6, b g Enrique—Belle D'ecajeul (FR) **Mr P. A. Downing**
30 **HENRYBROWNEYES (IRE),** 6, ch g Goldmark (USA)—The Vine Browne (IRE) **Mr P. R. Williams**
31 4, B g Westerner—Hill Fairy
32 **HOLLOW TREE,** 7, b g Beat Hollow—Hesperia **Brannon Dick Holden**
33 **HOWABOUTNEVER (IRE),** 7, b g Shantou (USA)—Sarah's Cottage (IRE) **Brannon, Dick, Hernon & Holden**
34 **HOWABOUTNOW (IRE),** 8, ch g Shantou (USA)—Sarah's Cottage (IRE) **Brannon, Dick, Hernon & Holden**
35 **IL PRESIDENTE (GER),** 8, ch g Royal Dragon (USA)—Independent Miss (GER) **P. J. Vogt**
36 **INDIAN CASTLE (IRE),** 7, b g Dr Massini (IRE)—Indian Legend (IRE) **Askew Dick Hernon Reynard**
37 **IOANNOU,** 6, b g Excellent Art—Sandtime (IRE) **A & P Skips Limited**
38 **KAPSTADT (FR),** 5, b br g Country Reel (USA)—King's Parody (IRE) **Mr P. Vogt**
39 **KONZERT (ITY),** 5, b g Hurricane Cat (USA)—Known Alibi (USA) **Ian Williams Racing Club**
40 **LEATH ACRA MOR (IRE),** 9, b g King's Theatre (IRE)—Happy Native (IRE) **I. P. Williams**
41 **LILY LITTLE LEGS (IRE),** 6, gr m Westerner—Silvers Promise (IRE) **J. P. Hanifin**
42 **MAC'S GREY (IRE),** 8, gr g Great Palm (USA)—Gypsy Kelly (IRE) **Macable Partnership**
43 **MANDY'S BOY (IRE),** 5, b g Kyllachy—African Queen (IRE) **Mr P. M. Mannion**
44 **MINGALABAR,** 4, b g Shirocco (GER)—Veenwouden **Wood Hall Stud Limited**
45 **MONALEEN (IRE),** 4, b br f High Chaparral (IRE)—Dawn Air (USA) **Farranamanagh**
46 **MOULIN ROUGE (DEN),** 4, ch f Zambezi Sun—Embattle (FR) **Mr Eric Brook & Mr Inge Knutsson**
47 4, B g Byron—Nursling (IRE)
48 **PARIS SNOW,** 5, b g Montjeu (IRE)—Snow Key (USA) **M. H. Watt**

## MR IAN WILLIAMS - Continued

**49 POKER SCHOOL (IRE),** 5, b g Gold Well—Broken Pockets (IRE) **Aniol Chandler PTR Ltd Turner Westwood**
**50 PORTWAY FLYER (IRE),** 7, br g King's Theatre (IRE)—Next Best Thing (IRE) **P. Kelly**
**51 PRINCE OSCAR (IRE),** 6, b g Oscar (IRE)—Athy Princess (IRE)
**52** 5, Ch g Indian River (FR)—Red Rover
**53 ROSSMORE'S PRIDE (IRE),** 7, br g Heron Island (IRE)—Parsons Supreme (IRE) **Mr D. H. Slater**
**54 SALOON DAY (GER),** 5, b h Dai Jin—Saloon Rum (GER) **M. H. Watt**
**55 SHADY MCCOY (USA),** 5, b g English Channel (USA)—Raw Gold (USA) **Allwins Stables**
**56 SIR MAXIMILIAN (IRE),** 6, b g Royal Applause—Nebraska Lady (IRE) **Mr P. E. Wildes**
**57 SOLIX (FR),** 9, b br g Al Namix (FR)—Solimade (FR) **Fromthestables.com Racing**
**58 SONOFAGUN (FR),** 9, b g Turgeon (USA)—Detonante (FR) **The Piranha Partnership**
**59 SUBLIMATION (IRE),** 5, ch g Manduro (GER)—Meon Mix **The Dream Team**
**60 SUPER DUTY (IRE),** 9, b g Shantou (USA)—Sarah's Cottage (IRE) **Brannon, Dick, Hernon & Holden**
**61 SWINTON DIAMOND (IRE),** 4, b g Dubai Destination (USA)—Absent Beauty (IRE) **Mr & Mrs I P Earnshaw**
**62 TAURIAN,** 4, b f Central Park (IRE)—Emma-Lyne **Macable Partnership**
**63 TEAK (IRE),** 8, b g Barathea (IRE)—Szabo (IRE) **Macable Partnership**
**64 THE FLYING COLUMN (IRE),** 9, b g Dr Massini (IRE)—Annie Cares (IRE) **Brannon, Dick, Hernon & Holden**
**65 THE PERFECT CRIME (IRE),** 6, b g Oscar (IRE)—Gimme Peace (IRE) **Mr S. Cox**
**66 TWOJAYSLAD,** 6, b g Kayf Tara—Fulwell Hill **J. Tredwell**
**67 VIRGIL EARP,** 8, b g Fasliyev (USA)—Karakorum (IRE)
**68 WATT BRODERICK (IRE),** 6, ch g Hawk Wing (USA)—Kingsridge (IRE) **P. Kelly**
**69 WILDES (IRE),** 4, b g Manduro (GER)—Balloura (USA) **Mr P. E. Wildes**
**70 ZAFRANAGAR (IRE),** 10, b g Cape Cross (IRE)—Zafaraniya (IRE) **Mr P. A. Downing**

### THREE-YEAR-OLDS

**71** B c Moss Vale (IRE)—Bois de Citron (USA) **Mr P. M. Mannion**
**72 BRASTED (IRE),** ch c Footstepsinthesand—Ellen (IRE) **Buxted Partnership**
**73 BROADSWORD (IRE),** ch f Dandy Man (IRE)—Petticoat Hill (UAE) **Mr P. Slater**
**74 CALCULATOR (FR),** b c Siyouni (FR)—Addition (FR) **Mr P. E. Wildes**
**75 CONVICTED (FR),** b c Lawman (FR)—Passiflore (FR) **Mr N. Martin**
**76 LADY TATIANA,** b f Sakhee (USA)—Telori **I. P. Williams**
**77 MIDTECH STAR (IRE),** b g Kodiac—Royal Rival (IRE) **Midtech**
**78 MR BISSTO,** b c High Chaparral (IRE)—Senta's Dream **S. & A. Mares & J. & L. Rawlings**
**79 PENSAX BOY,** b g Rail Link—Cyclone Connie **S. & A. Mares**
**80** B f Kalanisi (IRE)—Reseda (GER)
**81 ROMAN DE BRUT (IRE),** ch g Rock of Gibraltar (IRE)—Nesmeh (USA) **Mr P. Slater**
**82** B g Duke of Marmalade (IRE)—Thewaytosanjose (IRE)

### TWO-YEAR-OLDS

**83** Ch f 31/3 Excellent Art—Cutting Glance (USA) (Woodman (USA)) **Mr P. M. Mannion**
**84** B c 8/4 Ask—Reseda (GER) (Lavirco (GER))

**Other Owners:** Mr G. Anderson, Mr A. Aniol, E. A. Brook, Mr A. Chandler, Mr N. A. Coster, Mr A. D. Dick, Dr P. A. I. Doro, Mr I. P. Earnshaw, Mrs J. Earnshaw, T. Hart, Mr P. Holden, Mrs D. Hopkins, Mr I. Knutsson, Mr P. J. Legros, Mr S. Mackintosh, Mr F. W. Mackintosh, Mr C. R. Mander, Mr S. Mares, Mrs A. Mares, Mr I. G. Martin, Mr A. Miles, Mr M. Morrissey, Mrs A. Morrissey, Palatinate Thoroughbred Racing Limited, Mr H. Parmar, Mrs K. Parmar, Miss P. Purewal, Mrs L. Rawlings, Mr J. Rawlings, Mr J. A. Reynard, Mr M. G. Roberts, S. Rudolf, Mrs J. Ruthven, Mr A. Singh, Mr P. Thwaites, Mr S. W. Turner, Mr L. J. Westwood.

**Assistant Trainer:** Richard Ryan

**Jockey (NH):** Will Kennedy. **Conditional:** Robbie McCarth.

---

## 658 MR NICK WILLIAMS, South Molton

Postal: **Culverhill Farm, George Nympton, South Molton, Devon, EX36 4JE**
Contacts: **HOME (01769) 574174 MOBILE (07855) 450379**
**E-MAIL nandjwilliams@live.co.uk**

**1 ABRACADABRA SIVOLA (FR),** 5, b g Le Fou (IRE)—Pierrebrune (FR) **The Arthur White Partnership**
**2 AFTER EIGHT SIVOLA (FR),** 5, b g Shaanmer (IRE)—Eva de Chalamont (FR) **Larkhills Racing Partnership III**
**3 AGRAPART (FR),** 4, b br g Martaline—Afragha (IRE) **The Gascoigne Brookes Partnership III**
**4 ALFIE SPINNER (IRE),** 10, b g Alflora (IRE)—Little Red Spider **Alan Beard & Brian Beard**
**5 AMORE ALATO,** 6, b g Winged Love (IRE)—Sardagna (FR) **Mrs S. J. Faulks**
**6 AMOUR D'OR,** 4, b f Winged Love (IRE)—Diletia **French Gold**
**7 AUBUSSON (FR),** 6, b g Ballingarry (IRE)—Katioucha (FR) **Mrs J. R. Williams**

## MR NICK WILLIAMS - Continued

8 **BARRANCO VALLEY,** 4, b g Midnight Legend—Shali San (FR) **John White & Anne Underhill**
9 **BASILIC D'ALENE (FR),** 4, gr g Fragrant Mix (IRE)—Haifa du Noyer (FR) **John White & Anne Underhill**
10 **BENEFIQUE ROYALE,** 7, ch m Beneficial—Royale De Vassy (FR) **Len,Davies,Downes,Hewlett,White,Booth**
11 **BRISE COEUR (FR),** 4, b g Daramsar (FR)—Rose Bombon (FR) **French Gold**
12 **BRISE VENDEENNE (FR),** 4, gr f Dom Alco (FR)—Naiade Mag (FR) **B. Dunn**
13 **CORNAS (NZ),** 13, b g Prized (USA)—Duvessa (NZ) **The Gascoigne Brookes Partnership III**
14 **DOLORES DELIGHTFUL (FR),** 5, b m Saint des Saints (FR)—Us Et Coutumes (FR) **Miss E. Morgan**
15 **FOX NORTON (FR),** 5, b g Lando (GER)—Natt Musik (FR) **B. Dunn**
16 **GREYWELL BOY,** 8, gr g Fair Mix (IRE)—Rakajack **Chasing Gold Limited**
17 **HINT OF MINT,** 6, b g Passing Glance—Juno Mint **Sandie & David Newton**
18 **HORATIO HORNBLOWER (IRE),** 7, b br g Presenting—Countess Camilla **Huw & Richard Davies**
19 **LE ROCHER (FR),** 5, b g Saint des Saints (FR)—Belle du Roi (FR) **John White & Anne Underhill**
20 **LORD OF THE HOSTS,** 4, gr g Saint des Saints (FR)—Telmar Flyer **Mrs J. N. Humphreys**
21 **PINKNEYS PRINCE,** 8, b g Fair Mix (IRE)—Cool Run **Mr M. F. Stenning**
22 **QUEEN OF THE STAGE (IRE),** 5, b m King's Theatre (IRE)—Supreme du Casse (IRE) **Mrs Jane Williams**
23 **REVE DE SIVOLA (FR),** 10, b g Assessor (IRE)—Eva de Chalamont (FR) **Paul Duffy Diamond Partnership**
24 **RIO DE SIVOLA (FR),** 6, bl g Caballo Raptor (CAN)—Pierrebrune (FR) **Forty Winks Syndicate**
25 **RIVERSBRIDGE,** 6, b g Desert King (IRE)—Kinsford Water **Faulks, Sutton & Toller**
26 **SAINT LINO (FR),** 4, b br g Saint des Saints (FR)—Dona Rez (FR) **French Gold**
27 **TEA FOR TWO,** 6, b g Kayf Tara—One For Me **Mrs Jane Williams & Mr Len Jakeman**
28 **THE ITALIAN YOB (IRE),** 7, b g Milan—The Rebel Lady (IRE) **The Macaroni Beach Society**
29 **ULIS DE VASSY (FR),** 7, b g Voix du Nord (FR)—Helathou (FR) **Len&White,Hewlett,Robinson,Banyard&Booth**
30 **VEAUCE DE SIVOLA (FR),** 6, b g Assessor (IRE)—Eva de Chalamont (FR) **D. P. Duffy**
31 **WAYWARD FROLIC,** 9, br g Fair Mix (IRE)—Mighty Frolic **Mrs J. R. Williams**

### THREE-YEAR-OLDS

32 **COO STAR SIVOLA (FR),** b g Assessor (IRE)—Santorine (FR) **Babbit Racing**
33 **CULTURE DE SIVOLA (FR),** b f Assessor (IRE)—Neva de Sivola (FR) **Larkhills Racing Partnership**
34 **GRAND COUREUR (FR),** b br g Grand Couturier—Iris du Berlais (FR) **You Can Be Sure**
35 **ONE OF US,** b g Presenting—One Gulp **Forty Winks Syndicate**
36 **PINKIE BROWN (FR),** gr g Gentlewave (IRE)—Natt Musik (FR) **B. Dunn**
37 **SKY LINO (FR),** b g Martaline—Sky Dance (FR) **Mr K Alexander & Mr R Watts**
38 **THE COFFEE HUNTER (FR),** gr g Doctor Dino (FR)—
Mamamia (FR) **Allen, Dunn, Elliott, Hurst, Jones & Williams**

### TWO-YEAR-OLDS

39 **ADMIRAL BARRATRY (FR),** b g 25/4 Soldier of Fortune (IRE)—
Haskilclara (FR) (Green Tune (USA)) (12698) **Mr R. Forster**
40 **DAISY DE SIVOLA (FR),** b f 10/3 Assessor (IRE)—Kerrana (FR) (Cadoudal (FR)) **Mr K. Alexander**
41 **DENTLEY DE MEE (FR),** b g 26/3 Lauro (GER)—Natty Twigy (FR) (Video Rock (FR)) **Babbit Racing**

**Other Owners:** Mr D. R. Allen, Mr Kerry Barker, Mr Alan Beard, Mr B. Beard, Dr Martin Booth, Mr N. Brookes, Mr T. H. Chadney, Mrs V. J. Chadney, Mr Kevin Conlan, Mr Huw Davies, Mr R. L. Davies, Mr Paul Duffy, Mrs Sarah Faulks, Mr M. J. Freer, Mr Tony Gale, Mr C. Garner, Mr D. A. Gascoigne, Mr A. Holt, Mr Len Jakeman, Mr Joe Lawrence, Mrs Sarah Ling, Miss Eliisa Morgan, Mr David Morgan, Mr David Newton, Mrs Sandie Newton, Mr Ian Paye, Mr Martin Pepper, Mr G. C. Pratt, Mr J. Robinson, Mrs K. Salters, Miss Alice Simmons, Mr R. A. C. Toller, Mrs A. Underhill, Mr R. C. Watts, Mr A. J. White, Mrs Jane Williams.

**Assistant Trainer:** Mrs Jane Williams

**Conditional:** Lizzie Kelly.

---

## 659 MR NOEL WILLIAMS, Blewbury

Postal: **White Shoot, Woodway Road, Blewbury, Oxfordshire, OX11 9EY**
Contacts: **PHONE (01235) 850806 MOBILE (07887) 718678**
**E-MAIL noel@noelwilliamsracing.co.uk WEBSITE www.noelwilliamsracing.co.uk**

1 **AUTHORIZED TOO,** 4, b g Authorized (IRE)—Audaz **Miss Clare Ludlow**
2 **BINGO D'OLIVATE (FR),** 4, b g Laverock (IRE)—Ombrelle de L'orme (FR) **Didntt Partnership**
3 **BRIERY QUEEN,** 6, b m King's Theatre (IRE)—Briery Gale **Helen Plumbly & Kathryn Leadbeater**
4 **CHANCE TAKEN,** 7, b m Overbury (IRE)—New Dawn **Chance Takers**
5 **DAISY PICKER,** 5, b m Piccolo—Duly Noted (IRE) **Mrs W. A. Harrison-Allan**
6 **ENTER PARADISE (IRE),** 11, ch g Moscow Society (USA)—
Cappamore Girl (IRE) **The Four Minutes Of Madness Partnership**

## MR NOEL WILLIAMS - Continued

7 5, B m Kayf Tara—Fashion House **Mr S. Hind**
8 **FRIENDLY SOCIETY (IRE),** 10, ch g Moscow Society (USA)—Friendly Breeze **Whiteshoot Racing**
9 **GALIOTTO (IRE),** 9, b g Galileo (IRE)—Welsh Motto (USA) **Ian Payne & Kim Franklin**
10 **HOT WHISKEY N ICE (IRE),** 6, b g Milan—Fair Gina (IRE) **Whitehorsemen**
11 **KINCORA FORT (IRE),** 6, b g Brian Boru—Glenview Rose (IRE) **EPDS Racing Partnership 8**
12 **KING KAYF,** 6, b g Kayf Tara—Firecracker Lady (IRE) **J.C.Harrison Lee & T.Howard Partnership**
13 **KRACKATOA KING,** 7, b g Kayf Tara—Firecracker Lady (IRE) **J.C.Harrison Lee & T.Howard Partnership**
14 **MENACE,** 4, ch g Papal Bull—Wishfully Tropical (IRE) **Whiteshoot Racing**
15 **PATTARA,** 6, b m Kayf Tara—Fortunes Course (IRE) **J. E. Garrett**
16 **PRIMO BLUE,** 5, b g Primo Valentino (IRE)—Flintwood **Mr R. Skillen**

**Other Owners:** Mr David Bellamy, Mr R. Bullock, Mr A. Clark, Mr N. Clyne, Miss K. M. Franklin, Mrs W. Harrison-Allan, Ms J. C. Harrison-Lee, Mr R. C. Heginbotham, Mr S. Hind, Mr R. Horton, Miss T. Howard, Mr A. Keys, Mrs Kathryn Leadbeater, Miss Clare Ludlow, Mr I. Payne, Mrs Helen Plumbly, Mr John Powell, Mr R. Shorting, Mr Robert Skillen, Mrs Louise Skillen, Miss T. Sloan, Mr Simon Smith, Mr J. Thompson, Mr Matthew White, Mr Noel Williams.

**Jockey (NH):** James Banks, Wayne Hutchinson, Gerard Tumelty.

---

## 660 MR STUART WILLIAMS, Newmarket

Postal: **Diomed Stables, Hamilton Road, Newmarket, Suffolk, CB8 0PD**
Contacts: **STABLES/OFFICE (01638) 663984 HOME (01638) 560143 MOBILE (07730) 314102**
**E-MAIL stuart@stuartwilliamsracing.co.uk**
**WEBSITE www.stuartwilliamsracing.co.uk TWITTER: @Williamsstuart**

1 **BOOTS AND SPURS,** 6, b g Oasis Dream—Arctic Char **Mr S. E. Chappell**
2 **CORDIAL,** 4, b f Oasis Dream—Mirabilis (USA) **D. A. Shekells**
3 **CREW CUT (IRE),** 7, gr g Acclamation—Carabine (USA) **P. W. Stevens**
4 **DAISY BOY (IRE),** 4, b g Cape Cross (IRE)—Muluk (IRE) **Mr G. M. C. Johnson**
5 **DOCTOR PARKES,** 9, b g Diktat—Lucky Parkes **Mrs S Mason & Partners**
6 **EXAMINER (IRE),** 4, ch g Excellent Art—Therry Girl (IRE) **DJM Racing**
7 **HARWOODS STAR (IRE),** 5, b g Danehill Dancer (IRE)—Showbiz (IRE) **Mrs C. M. A. Seagroatt**
8 **HOLLEY SHIFTWELL,** 5, ch m Bahamian Bounty—Persario **J. W. Parry**
9 **LUNAR DEITY,** 6, b g Medicean—Luminda (IRE) **The Morley Family**
10 **MEZZOTINT (IRE),** 6, b g Diamond Green (FR)—Aquatint **Mr S. E. Chappell**
11 **MR SOPRANO,** 4, ch g Halling (USA)—Rima Baciata **Mr P. Kendall**
12 **PACTOLUS (IRE),** 4, b g Footstepsinthesand—Gold Marie (IRE) **T W Morley & Mrs J Morley**
13 **POUNCING TIGER,** 4, b f Tiger Hill (IRE)—Ipsa Loquitur **Alasdair Simpson**
14 **ROCK CHARM,** 4, b g Araafa (IRE)—Evening Charm (IRE) **P. J. Ransley**
15 **ROYAL BATTALION,** 4, b c Sea The Stars (IRE)—Yummy Mummy **Qatar Racing Limited**
16 **ROYAL BIRTH,** 4, b c Exceed And Excel (AUS)—Princess Georgina **The Morley Family**
17 **RUBAN (IRE),** 6, ch g Dubawi (IRE)—Piece Unique **S. C. Williams**
18 **SPINNING COBBLERS,** 4, b g Royal Applause—Tychy **Brian Piper & David Cobill**
19 **SUZI'S CONNOISSEUR,** 4, b g Art Connoisseur (IRE)—Suzi Spends (IRE) **Qatar Racing Limited**
20 **TETE ORANGE,** 4, ch f Pastoral Pursuits—Imperialistic (IRE) **J. W. Parry**
21 **TSARGLAS,** 4, gr g Verglas (IRE)—Russian Empress (IRE) **Essex Racing Club et al**
22 **TYCHAIOS,** 5, b g Green Desert (USA)—Tychy **Mr P. Ellinas**
23 **WELEASE BWIAN (IRE),** 6, b g Kheleyf (USA)—Urbanize (USA) **W. E. Enticknap**

### THREE-YEAR-OLDS

24 **AUTHORIZED SPIRIT,** b f Authorized (IRE)—World Spirit **Stapleford Racing Ltd**
25 **BEN MUIR,** b g Observatory (USA)—Chapel Corner (IRE) **Seize The Day Racing Partnership**
26 **BLACK NIGHT (IRE),** b c Excellent Art—Starfish (IRE) **Qatar Racing Limited**
27 **EXCELLENT GEORGE,** b c Exceed And Excel (AUS)—Princess Georgina **D. A. Shekells**
28 **HAPPY PURSUIT,** b f Pastoral Pursuits—Carollan (IRE) **Happy Valley Racing & Breeding Limited**
29 B c Lord Shanakill (USA)—Hollow Green (IRE) **Qatar Racing Limited**
30 **INVADE (IRE),** ch f Intense Focus (USA)—Spinning Well (IRE) **Happy Valley Racing & Breeding Limited**
31 **J'ASPIRE,** b f Zamindar (USA)—Ipsa Loquitur **Mr Alasdair Simpson**
32 **LITTLE LORD NELSON,** b g Mount Nelson—Cactus Curtsey **S. C. Williams**
33 **MONNA VALLEY,** ch g Exceed And Excel (AUS)—Monnavanna (IRE) **Happy Valley Racing & Breeding Limited**
34 **MY TRINGALING (IRE),** ch f Summer Bird (USA)—Lady Amira (USA) **J. W. Parry**
35 **OAKLEY GIRL,** b f Sir Percy—Pivotting **The Parry's**
36 **OHSOSECRET,** ch f Sakhee's Secret—Warden Rose **The Secretly Hopeful Partnership**
37 **RED HOUSE REBEL (IRE),** b c Cockney Rebel (IRE)—Avril Rose (IRE) **Mr B Piper & Mr B Ralph**

## MR STUART WILLIAMS - Continued

**38 SWEETLY DOES IT,** ch f Shirocco (GER)—Sweetness Herself **D. A. Shekells**
**39 SWIFT SUSIE,** b f Kheleyf (USA)—Overwing (IRE) **Mr K. R. Robinson**

## TWO-YEAR-OLDS

**40** B f 5/4 Canford Cliffs (IRE)—Flora Trevelyan (Cape Cross (IRE)) (60000) **J. W. Parry**
**41** B f 6/2 Royal Applause—George's Gift (Haafhd) (5000) **Mrs A. Shone**
**42** B f 10/4 Elusive City (USA)—Lady Stardust (Spinning World (USA)) (28000) **J. W. Parry**
**43** B f 9/2 Tamayuz—Lovers Peace (IRE) (Oratorio (IRE)) (85000) **J. W. Parry**
**44** B c 4/3 Kheleyf (USA)—Posy Fossil (USA) (Malibu Moon (USA)) (10000) **J. W. Parry**
**45** B f 27/2 Kheleyf (USA)—Pretty Kool (Inchinor) (6000) **D. A. Shekells**
**46** B f 31/3 Royal Applause—Victoria Sponge (IRE) (Marju (IRE)) (16000) **D. A. Shekells**

**Other Owners:** Mr David Cobill, Mrs H. J. Lewis, Mrs F. M. Midwood, Mr T. W. Morley, Mrs J. Morley, Mr Bernard Ralph, Mr Barry Root, Mrs Joan Root, Dr Paula Sells.

**Assistant Trainer:** Mr J W Parry

**Apprentice:** Aaron Jones.

---

## 661 MISS VENETIA WILLIAMS, Hereford

Postal: **Aramstone, Kings Caple, Hereford, Herefordshire, HR1 4TU**
Contacts: **PHONE (01432) 840646 MOBILE (07770) 627108**
**E-MAIL venetia.williams@virgin.net WEBSITE www.venetiawilliams.com**

**1 AACHEN,** 11, b g Rainbow Quest (USA)—Anna of Saxony **Mr A. G. Bloom**
**2 ABUNDANTLY,** 6, b m Sakhee (USA)—Composing (IRE) **Mrs Fay Kempe & Deborah North**
**3 ART PROFESSOR (IRE),** 11, b g In The Wings—Itab (USA) **J. P. Hancock**
**4 ARTHUR'S OAK,** 7, b g Kayf Tara—Myumi **Mrs J. K. Burt**
**5 ASO (FR),** 5, b br g Goldneyev (USA)—Odyssee du Cellier (FR) **The Bellamy Partnership**
**6 ASTIGOS (FR),** 8, b br g Trempolino (USA)—Astonishing (BRZ) **Mr A. L. Brooks**
**7 AZERT DE COEUR (FR),** 5, b g Tiger Groom—Eden de Coeur (FR) **Gay And Peter Hartley**
**8 BALLYOLIVER,** 11, b g Kayf Tara—Macklette (IRE) **Mr R. M. Britten-Long**
**9 BARADARI (IRE),** 5, br g Manduro (GER)—Behra (IRE) **Mr A. L. Brooks**
**10 BEACON LADY,** 6, ch m Haafhd—Oriental Lady (IRE) **The Pro-Claimers**
**11 BECAUSESHESAIDSO (IRE),** 7, b g Winged Love (IRE)—Huit de Coeur (FR) **Lady M. A. Bolton**
**12 BENNYS KING (IRE),** 4, b g Beneficial—Hellofafaithful (IRE) **Mezzone Family**
**13 BENNYS MIST (IRE),** 9, b g Beneficial—Dark Mist (IRE) **Mezzone Family**
**14 BOBBLE BORU (IRE),** 7, b m Brian Boru—Balreask Lady (IRE) **Mr T. Fawcett**
**15 BONNE QUESTION (FR),** 6, gr g Tagula (IRE)—Amonita (GER) **Falcon's Line Ltd**
**16 BOURTON STAR,** 5, b g Tiger Hill (IRE)—Fanfare **Mr A. O. Wiles**
**17 BRICK RED,** 8, ch g Dubawi (IRE)—Duchcov **Julian Taylor & Andrew Brooks**
**18 BROWNS BROOK (IRE),** 9, b g Bob Back (USA)—All Over Now (IRE) **Mrs V. A. Bingham**
**19 BURTONS WELL (IRE),** 6, b g Well Chosen—Despute (IRE) **T. J. Hemmings**
**20 CASH AND GO (IRE),** 8, b g Sulamani (IRE)—Calcida (GER) **Mrs C. G. Watson**
**21 CENTURIUS,** 5, ch g New Approach (IRE)—Questina (FR) **Andrew Brooks & Julian Taylor**
**22 CITIZENSHIP,** 9, b g Beat Hollow—Three More (USA) **The Fizz Fund**
**23 COLD MARCH (FR),** 5, b br g Early March—Tumultueuse (FR) **Mr A. L. Brooks**
**24 DARE ME (IRE),** 11, b g Bob Back (USA)—Gaye Chatelaine (IRE) **Shire Birds**
**25 DRUMSHAMBO (USA),** 9, b g Dynaformer (USA)—Gossamer (USA) **The Grouse Partnership**
**26 DRUMVIREDY (IRE),** 6, b m Flemensfirth (USA)—Leitrim Bridge (IRE) **The M. Shones**
**27 DUBAWI ISLAND (FR),** 6, b g Dubawi (IRE)—Housa Dancer (FR) **Andrew Brooks & Julian Taylor**
**28 EASTERN WITNESS (IRE),** 8, b g Witness Box (USA)—Eastertide (IRE) **Robert & Prudence Cooper**
**29 ECO WARRIOR,** 5, b g Echo of Light—Kryssa **Mrs Julian Blackwell**
**30 EMINENT POET,** 4, b g Montjeu (IRE)—Contare **B. C. Dice**
**31 EMPEROR'S CHOICE (IRE),** 8, b g Flemensfirth (USA)—House-of-Hearts (IRE) **The Bellamy Partnership**
**32 FINE LILY,** 6, gr m Fair Mix (IRE)—Lily Grey (FR) **Allen & Monica Powley**
**33 GARDEFORT (FR),** 6, b br g Agent Bleu (FR)—La Fresnaie (FR) **Mr A. L. Brooks**
**34 GORGEHOUS LLIEGE (FR),** 9, b g Lavirco (GER)—Charme d'estruval (FR) **Mr A. L. Brooks**
**35 GUANTOSHOL (IRE),** 4, ch c Sholokhov (IRE)—Glicine (GER) **John Nicholls (Trading) & John Moorhouse**
**36 HADA MEN (USA),** 10, b g Dynaformer (USA)—Catchy (USA) **Gay & Peter Hartley**
**37 HOUBLON DES OBEAUX (FR),** 8, b g Panoramic—Harkosa (FR) **Mrs J. Blackwell**
**38 HOWARD'S LEGACY (IRE),** 9, b g Generous (IRE)—Ismene (FR) **A. G. Parker**
**39 HUFF AND PUFF,** 8, b g Azamour (IRE)—Coyote **Gay & Peter Hartley**
**40 JEANPASCAL (FR),** 4, b g Muhaymin (USA)—Miss Karad (FR) **Dr M. A. Hamlin**

## MISS VENETIA WILLIAMS - Continued

41 **JOHN LOUIS,** 7, ch g Bertolini (USA)—Native Ring (FR) **Mr A. L. Brooks**
42 **JUPITER REX (FR),** 8, ch g Dano-Mast—Creme Pralinee (FR) **Mr P. G. Nathan & Mrs J. Young**
43 **KAP JAZZ (FR),** 5, b g Kapgarde (FR)—Jazz And Liquer (FR) **Brooks, Vando, Pummell, Martin & Armstrong**
44 **KATENKO (FR),** 9, b g Laveron—Katiana (FR) **Mr A. L. Brooks**
45 **KING OF GLORY,** 7, b g Kayf Tara—Glory Be **Mrs B. M. Willcocks**
46 **KINGCORA (FR),** 7, b g King's Theatre (IRE)—Coralisse Royale (FR) **Mrs J. Blackwell**
47 **KINGS RIVER (FR),** 6, b br g Lost World (IRE)—Si Parfaite (FR) **Mrs J. Blackwell**
48 **LANDSCAPE (FR),** 7, b g Lando (GER)—Universelle (USA) **Mr A. L. Brooks**
49 **LAST SHOT (FR),** 8, b g Le Fou (IRE)—Lucky Shot (FR) **Mr Basil Richards & Lady Bolton**
50 **LEVIATHAN,** 8, b g Dubawi (IRE)—Gipsy Moth **H. E. Ansell**
51 **LOWER HOPE DANDY,** 8, gr g Karinga Bay—Cheeky Mare **Mr W. S. C. Richards**
52 **MIRACLE CURE (IRE),** 6, b g Whipper (USA)—Bring Back Matron (IRE) **R. J. Cadoret**
53 **MIXCHIEVOUS,** 4, gr g Fair Mix (IRE)—Cheeky Mare **Tolostley Partnership**
54 **MOUJIK BORGET (FR),** 7, ch g Layman (USA)—Fancy Tune (FR) **Sunday Lunch Partnership**
55 **MR STEEL (IRE),** 8, b g Alamshar (IRE)—Wigwam Mam (IRE) **T. J. Hemmings**
56 **MUDITA MOMENT (IRE),** 10, b g Heron Island (IRE)—
Woodville Leader (IRE) **John Moorhouse & John Nicholls (Trading)**
57 **NICEONEFRANKIE,** 9, b g Ishiguru (USA)—Chesnut Ripple **Old Carthusian Racing Society**
58 **OTAGO TRAIL (IRE),** 7, b g Heron Island (IRE)—Cool Chic (IRE) **Mrs M. L. Shone**
59 **PANAMA PETRUS (IRE),** 7, b g Alflora (IRE)—Pride 'n' Joy (IRE) **Andrew Brooks & Julian Taylor**
60 **PEPITE ROSE (FR),** 8, b br m Bonbon Rose (FR)—Sambre (FR) **Falcon's Line Ltd**
61 **PINK TARA,** 4, b f Kayf Tara—Red And White (IRE) **F. M. P. Mahon**
62 **POLO (GER),** 5, ch g Sholokhov (IRE)—Poule d'essai (GER) **Mrs J. Blackwell**
63 **RELAX (FR),** 10, b g Fragrant Mix (IRE)—Magik (FR) **The Bellamy Partnership**
64 **RENARD (FR),** 10, b br g Discover d'auteuil (FR)—Kirmelia (FR) **ROA Arkle Partnership**
65 **RICHMOND (FR),** 10, b g Assessor (IRE)—Hirondel de Serley (FR) **Hills of Ledbury Ltd**
66 **RIGADIN DE BEAUCHENE (FR),** 10, b br g Visionary (FR)—Chipie d'angron (FR) **Mr A. O. Wiles**
67 **ROSA FLEET (IRE),** 7, b m Alflora (IRE)—Crimond (IRE) **Mezzone Family**
68 **ROYAL PALLADIUM (FR),** 7, gr g King's Theatre (IRE)—Dent Sucree (FR) **Mrs A. W. Timpson**
69 **RUSSBOROUGH (FR),** 6, b g Turgeon (USA)—Heritage River (FR) **Lady M. A. Bolton**
70 **RYDALIS (FR),** 10, b m Kapgarde (FR)—Fleurissa (FR) **Mrs V. A. Bingham**
71 **SAROQUE (IRE),** 8, b g Revoque (IRE)—Sarakin (IRE) **Mr A. L. Brooks**
72 **SEA CLARIA (FR),** 5, b m Sinndar (IRE)—Triclaria (GER) **Kate & Andrew Brooks**
73 **SHANGANI (USA),** 9, b g Giant's Causeway (USA)—Tanzania (IRE) **The Bellamy Partnership**
74 **SHATTERED DREAM (IRE),** 7, ch g Flemensfirth (USA)—Suspicious Minds **Mr A. L. Brooks**
75 **SMART MONEY (IRE),** 8, br g Spadoun (FR)—Victoria Day **Mrs Peter Andrews & Mrs Louise Jones**
76 **SOMEMOTHERSDOHAVEM,** 6, ch g Avonbridge—Show Off **The Neighbours Partnership**
77 **STONE LIGHT (FR),** 7, ch m Ballingarry (IRE)—Yellow Light (FR) **Kate & Andrew Brooks**
78 **SUMMERY JUSTICE (IRE),** 11, b g Witness Box (USA)—Kinsellas Rose (IRE) **Mrs P. Brown**
79 **SUPER SAM,** 6, gr g Overbury (IRE)—Gaye Sophie **Mrs A. W. Timpson**
80 **TAKE THE MICK,** 8, b g Ishiguru (USA)—Michaelmas Daizy **Sir Geoffrey & Lady Vos**
81 **TANGO DE JUILLEY (FR),** 7, b g Lesotho (USA)—Lasalsa de Juilley (FR) **Mr M. N. Khan**
82 **TARRACO (FR),** 8, b g Sassanian (USA)—Marie Esther (FR) **Mrs V. A. Bingham**
83 **TENOR NIVERNAIS (FR),** 8, b g Shaanmer (IRE)—Hosanna II (FR) **Mr M. N. Khan**
84 **THE CLOCK LEARY (IRE),** 7, b g Helissio (FR)—Kiwi Babe **Brooks, Vando, Pummell, Martin & Armstrong**
85 **TOUBEERA,** 9, b m Tobougg (IRE)—Efizia **Mr R. M. Britten-Long**
86 **TRIUMVIRATE,** 5, b m Rail Link—Strike Lightly **Lady M. A. Bolton**
87 **TWELVE STRINGS (IRE),** 6, b g Iffraaj—Favoritely (USA) **Mezzone Family**
88 **UHLAN BUTE (FR),** 7, ch g Brier Creek (USA)—Jonquiere (FR) **R Elliott & N Coe**
89 **UNION JACK D'YCY (FR),** 7, b g Bonnet Rouge (FR)—Jacady (FR) **Mr I. R. P. Josephs**
90 **UPEPITO (FR),** 7, b g Khalkevi (IRE)—Friandise II (FR) **Mr A. L. Brooks**
91 **URANIUM (FR),** 7, ch g Dear Doctor (FR)—Kalgary (FR) **P & T Brooks & A Brooks**
92 **VIVACCIO (FR),** 6, b g Antarctique (IRE)—Cybelle (FR) **Boultbee Brooks Ltd**
93 **WALDORF SALAD,** 7, b g Millenary—Ismene (FR) **A. G. Parker**
94 **WING MIRA (IRE),** 7, b g Winged Love (IRE)—Miraflores (IRE) **You Can Be Sure**
95 **YALA ENKI (FR),** 5, b g Nickname (FR)—Cadiane (FR) **Hills of Ledbury Ltd**
96 **ZAMDY MAN,** 6, b g Authorized (IRE)—Lauderdale (GER) **Mr M. N. Khan**

**Other Owners:** Mrs P. Armstrong, Mr Edward Beckley, Mrs C. Belloc Lowndes, Mr A. Black, Dr Martin Booth, Mrs C. Boultbee-Brooks, Mrs Kate Brazier, Mr P. L. Brooks, Mrs E. T. L. Brooks, Mrs Pat Churchward, Mr T. H. G. Cooper, Dr Chris Cowell, Mr J. S. Dale, Mr P. Davies, Mr Michael J. Davies, Mr P. A. Deal, Mrs W. Dice, Mrs Sadie Evans, Mrs Lisa Fellows, Miss H. Frankham, Mrs Jeremy Hancock, Mr Christopher James, Mr B. H. Lenaghan, Mr S. A. Martin, Mr Graham Mezzone, Mr M. A. R. Pummell, Mr Maurice Ryan, Mrs Marie Shone, Ms Melissa Shone, Mr Michael Shone, Mr M. Stone, Mr James Richard Terry, Mr Julian Tolhurst, Mr Lee Vanderson.

## MISS VENETIA WILLIAMS - Continued

**Jockey (NH):** Aidan Coleman, Liam Treadwell. **Conditional:** Jamie Hamilton, Callum Whillans. **Amateur:** Mr Joe Knox, Miss Lucy Turner.

---

## 662 MRS LISA WILLIAMSON, Chester

Postal: **Saighton Hall, Saighton, Chester, Cheshire, CH3 6EE**
Contacts: **PHONE (01244) 314254 FAX (01244) 314254 (please ring before sending) MOBILE (07970) 437679**
**E-MAIL info@lisawilliamson.co.uk WEBSITE www.lisawilliamson.co.uk**

1 **BERTIE BLU BOY,** 7, b g Central Park (IRE)—Shaymee's Girl **B & B Hygiene Limited**
2 **CHESTER DEELYTE (IRE),** 7, b m Desert Style (IRE)—Bakewell Tart (IRE) **Hindford Oak Racing**
3 7, B g Pursuit of Love—Classic Quartet **Mrs L. V. Williamson**
4 **GARDE VILLE (FR),** 5, ch g Kapgarde (FR)—Ville Eagle (FR) **Mrs Y. Fleet**
5 **GO CHARLIE,** 4, b g Myboycharlie (IRE)—Branston Gem **Miss H. J. Roberts**
6 **MISTY SECRET (IRE),** 5, b m Clodovil (IRE)—Villafranca (IRE) **Simon&Jeanette Pierpoint&Paul Salisbury**
7 **MUSICAL BRIDGE,** 9, b g Night Shift (USA)—Carrie Pooter **Mr A. J. Conway**
8 **MY SONNY BOY,** 4, b g Imperial Dancer—Lily of Tagula (IRE) **Tregarth Racing**
9 **ODD BALL (IRE),** 8, b g Redback—Luceball (IRE) **Mr A. T Sykes**
10 **RAT CATCHER (IRE),** 5, b g One Cool Cat (USA)—Molly Marie (IRE) **Mr R. Jones**
11 **ROUGHLYN,** 6, ch g Haafhd—Dime Bag **Mrs L. V. Williamson**
12 **RYAN STYLE (IRE),** 9, b g Desert Style (IRE)—Westlife (IRE) **Heath House Racing**
13 **SENORA LOBO (IRE),** 5, b m Amadeus Wolf—Valencia (FR) **Mr G. H. Briers**
14 **SERAPHIMA,** 5, b m Fusaichi Pegasus (USA)—Millestan (IRE) **Heath House Racing**
15 **YOUR GIFTED (IRE),** 8, b m Trans Island—Dame Laura (IRE) **Mr A. T Sykes**

### THREE-YEAR-OLDS

16 **ARTHUR'S WAY (IRE),** b g Royal Applause—Chantilly Pearl (USA) **Heath House Racing**
17 **HARPS OF BRETAGNE,** b f Monsieur Bond (IRE)—Lavernock Lady **Mr J. Levenson**

**Other Owners:** Mrs E. L. Berry, Mr H. Hall, Exors of the Late M. S. Heath, Miss C. L. Howard, Mr S. Jennings, Mr J. H. Martin, Mr S. W. Pierpoint, Mr M. L. Rush, Mr P. J. Salisbury, Mr R. L. Williams.

**Assistant Trainer:** Mark Williamson

**Jockey (NH):** Brian Hughes. **Conditional:** Harry Challoner. **Amateur:** Mr C. Ellingham, Mr Alexander French.

---

## 663 MR ANDREW WILSON, Greystoke

Postal: **Silver Howe, Orton, Penrith, Cumbria, CA10 3RQ**
Contacts: **PHONE (01539) 624071 MOBILE (07813) 846768**

1 **REXMEHEAD (IRE),** 14, b g Fort Morgan (USA)—Moon Rose (IRE) **Mrs H. J. Wilson**
2 **SO BAZAAR (IRE),** 8, b g Xaar—Nature Girl (USA) **Mrs H. J. Wilson**
3 **TARA DEE (IRE),** 6, b m Golan (IRE)—Liberwoman (IRE) **Mrs H. J. Wilson**
4 **ZABALEE (IRE),** 5, b m Robin des Pres (FR)—Ballinapierce Lady (IRE) **Mrs H. J. Wilson**

---

## 664 MR CHRISTOPHER WILSON, Darlington

Postal: **Manor Farm, Manfield, Darlington, Co. Durham, DL2 2RW**
Contacts: **PHONE (01325) 374595 FAX (01325) 374595 MOBILE (07815) 952306/(07721) 379277**
**E-MAIL wilsonracing@aol.com**

1 **ESME RIDES A GAINE,** 13, gr m Doubletour (USA)—Silver Penny **Mrs J. Wilson**
2 **INGENTI,** 7, ch m Blue Dakota (IRE)—Kungfu Kerry **D. A. J. Bartlett**
3 **LATEST FASHION (IRE),** 9, ch m Ashkalani (IRE)—Musical Bramble (IRE) **Mrs J. Wilson**
4 **NICEONEMYSON,** 6, b g Misu Bond (IRE)—Kungfu Kerry **D. A. J. Bartlett**
5 **NO TIME TO CRY,** 6, b m Josr Algarhoud (IRE)—Autumn Bloom (IRE) **Mrs J. Wilson**
6 **SHARP SHOES,** 8, br g Needwood Blade—Mary Jane **Mrs J. Wilson**
7 **VALSESIA (IRE),** 8, b m Milan—Ballinapierce Lady (IRE) **Mrs J. Wilson**

**Assistant Trainer:** Julie Wilson

**Jockey (flat):** Paddy Aspell, Silvestre De Sousa. **Jockey (NH):** Keith Mercer, Ewan Whillans. **Apprentice:** Julie Burke.

## 665 MR JIM WILSON, Cheltenham

Postal: **Glenfall Stables, Ham, Charlton Kings, Cheltenham, Gloucestershire, GL52 6NH**
Contacts: **PHONE (01242) 244713 FAX (01242) 226319 MOBILE (07932) 157243**
**E-MAIL ajwglenfall@aol.com**

1 **RUBY VALENTINE (FR),** 12, b m Kayf Tara—A Ma Valentine (FR) **The Winbledon Partnership**
2 **SEYMOUR LEGEND,** 9, b g Midnight Legend—Rosehall **Mrs M. J. Wilson**
3 **VITARRA,** 6, b m Kayf Tara—Vivante (IRE) **Mrs M. J. Wilson**
4 5, B g Midnight Legend—Vivante (IRE)

**Other Owners:** H. H. J. Fentum.

## 666 MR NOEL WILSON, Middleham

Postal: **Caphall Lodge, Coverham, Middleham, Leyburn, North Yorkshire, DL8 4TL**
Contacts: **PHONE (01969) 622780 FAX (01969) 622780 MOBILE (07718) 613206**
**E-MAIL nlwilson69@live.com**

1 5, Gr g Iffraaj—Alphilda **Mrs J. Bartley**
2 **CROCKETT,** 4, b g Rail Link—Tarocchi (USA) **John Blair & Lloyd Martell**
3 **GREAT ROAR (USA),** 7, b g Thunder Gulch (USA)—Boasting (USA) **T. Alderson**
4 **PAVERS BOUNTY,** 4, ch g Bahamian Bounty—Pride of Kinloch **Mrs C. K. Paver**
5 **PAVERS STAR,** 6, ch g Pastoral Pursuits—Pride of Kinloch **Mrs C. K. Paver**

### THREE-YEAR-OLDS

6 **CABBIES LOU,** b f Sakhee's Secret—Regal Run (USA) **Mr G. Budden**
7 **GHOSTLY ARC (IRE),** b g Arcano (IRE)—Cheyenne's Spirit (IRE) **G. J. Paver**
8 **KINLOCH PRIDE,** ch f Kyllachy—Pride of Kinloch **Mrs C. K. Paver**
9 **LAZY DAYS IN LOULE (IRE),** b f Approve (IRE)—Lazy Lady **Pow Partnership**
10 **LILY MORETON (IRE),** b f Kodiac—Hollow Haze (USA) **D. J. Emsley**
11 **MR CHRISTOPHER (IRE),** b g Bahamian Bounty—Embassy Pearl (IRE) **Mrs M. C. Antrobus**
12 **PENCAITLAND,** b f Champs Elysees—Anthea **Hurn Racing Club & Gary Kennedy**
13 **THE FULWELL END,** b g Amadeus Wolf—Green Silk (IRE) **Junco Partners 2**
14 **UBEDIZZY (IRE),** b c Captain Rio—Karenka (IRE)

**Other Owners:** Mr J. J. Blair, Mr P. A. Burgess, Mrs I. M. Jessop, Mr G. Kennedy, Mr L. Martell, J. R. Owen, Mr S. Roberts, P. M. Watson.

**Assistant Trainer:** Miss Alex Porritt

**Jockey (flat):** Duran Fentiman, Daniel Tudhope. **Jockey (NH):** Wilson Renwick. **Apprentice:** Neil Farley, Joey Haynes.

## 667 MR KEN WINGROVE, Bridgnorth

Postal: **6 Netherton Farm Barns, Netherton Lane, Highley, Bridgnorth, Shropshire, WV16 6NJ**
Contacts: **HOME (01746) 861534 MOBILE (07974) 411267**
**E-MAIL kenwingrove@btinternet.com**

1 **ANTOELLA (IRE),** 8, gr m Antonius Pius (USA)—Bella Estella (GER)
2 **ARTY FARMER,** 11, b g Karinga Bay—One of Those Days
3 6, B m Oscar (IRE)—Bryan's Pet (IRE)
4 **COPPICE LAD,** 6, b g Thethingaboutitis (USA)—Coppice Lane
5 **FERNANDO (IRE),** 11, b g Fruits of Love (USA)—Dancing Venus
6 **FEROCIOUS FRAN (IRE),** 7, b m Footstepsinthesand—Tipsy Lady
7 **GRAND FELLA (IRE),** 10, ch g Raise A Grand (IRE)—Mummys Best
8 **KWANTO,** 5, b m Piccolo—Craic Sa Ceili (IRE)
9 **REINVIGORATE (IRE),** 5, b m Invincible Spirit (IRE)—Miss Serendipity (IRE)
10 **STREELE (USA),** 5, gr m Thunder Gulch (USA)—Crown Capers (USA)
11 **WEET IN NERJA,** 9, b g Captain Rio—Persian Fortune
12 **WINROB,** 9, b g Exceed And Excel (AUS)—High Standard
13 **WOR JOSIE (IRE),** 7, br m Zagreb (USA)—Garw Valley

**Assistant Trainer:** Isobel Willer

## 668 MR PETER WINKS, Barnsley

Postal: **Homefield Racing Stables, Rotherham Road, Little Houghton, Barnsley, South Yorkshire, S72 0HA**
Contacts: **MOBILE (07846) 899993**

1 **CHESTNUT BEN (IRE),** 10, ch g Ridgewood Ben—Betseale (IRE) **Mr P. Winks**
2 **DASHING GEORGE (IRE),** 13, ch g Beneficial—Here It Is **Mr P. Winks**
3 **HARTSIDE (GER),** 6, b g Montjeu (IRE)—Helvellyn (USA) **Mr P. Winks**
4 **RULER OF ALL (IRE),** 9, b g Sadler's Wells (USA)—Shabby Chic (USA) **Mr P. Winks**
5 **SOLSTICE DAWN,** 7, b m Lyphento (USA)—Ryders Hill **Mr P. Winks**

**Assistant Trainer:** Ryan Winks

**Amateur:** Mr Ryan Winks.

## 669 MR ADRIAN WINTLE, Westbury-On-Severn

Postal: **Yew Tree Stables, Rodley, Westbury-On-Severn, Gloucestershire, GL14 1QZ**
Contacts: **MOBILE (07767) 351144**

1 **ASPECIALPRESENT (IRE),** 5, br g Presenting—Escrea (IRE) **Search For Stars**
2 **BILLY CONGO (IRE),** 8, b br g Zagreb (USA)—Delicate Child (IRE) **Mr N. R. Hopkins**
3 **HALLINGS COMET,** 6, ch g Halling (USA)—Landinium (ITY) **Lord J. Blyth**
4 **MILLY MALONE (IRE),** 9, b m Milan—Sharp Single (IRE) **Mr S. R. Whistance**
5 **NOBLE PERK,** 10, ch g Executive Perk—Far From Perfect (IRE) **A. J. Williams**
6 **RESTRAINT,** 4, b g Kheleyf (USA)—Inhibition **Mr S R Whistance & Mr A J Williams**
7 **STAR BENEFIT (IRE),** 5, b g Beneficial—Beautiful Night (FR) **Search For Stars**
8 **TINCTORIA,** 5, b m Oratorio (IRE)—Blue Indigo (FR) **A. A. Wintle**
9 **TODOISTODARE,** 5, b m Tobougg (IRE)—Misrepresented (IRE) **T. G. Warren**
10 **WORTHY SPIRIT (GER),** 4, b g Shirocco (GER)—Wakytara (GER) **Search For Stars**

**Other Owners:** Mr R. G. Owens, Mr R. J. Williams.

## 670 MR STEVE WOODMAN, Chichester

Postal: **Parkers Barn Stables, Pook Lane, East Lavant, Chichester, West Sussex, PO18 0AU**
Contacts: **OFFICE (01243) 527136 FAX (01243) 527136 MOBILE (07889) 188519**
**E-MAIL stevewoodman83@msn.com**

1 **CHEVISE (IRE),** 7, b m Holy Roman Emperor (IRE)—Lipica (IRE) **The Chevise Partnership**
2 **CROWNING STAR (IRE),** 6, b g Royal Applause—Dossier **Countrywide Classics Ltd**
3 **GOING TWICE,** 10, b g Josr Algarhoud (IRE)—Its Your Bid **Mrs S. B. Woodman**
4 **HIGHLY LIKELY (IRE),** 6, b g Elnadim (USA)—Height of Fantasy (IRE) **Mrs S. B. Woodman**

### THREE-YEAR-OLDS

5 **SOLVEIG'S SONG,** b f Norse Dancer (IRE)—Ivory Lace **Sally Woodman & D. Mortimer**

**Other Owners:** Mr D. Mortimer, Mrs P. M. Tyler.

## 671 MR GARRY WOODWARD, Newark

Postal: **21 Camden Grove, Maltby, Rotherham, South Yorkshire, S66 8GE**
Contacts: **HOME (01709) 813431 MOBILE (07739) 382052**
**E-MAIL gwoodwardracing@aol.com WEBSITE www.garrywoodward.co.uk**

1 **PRINCEOFTHEDESERT,** 9, b g Nayef (USA)—Twilight Sonnet **Mrs E. Cash**
2 **RISING RAINBOW,** 4, b g Rainbow High—Lord Conyers (IRE) **The Lord Conyers Racing Partnership**
3 **SELF EMPLOYED,** 8, b g Sakhee (USA)—Twilight Sonnet **J. Pownall**

### THREE-YEAR-OLDS

**4** B g Denounce—Lord Conyers (IRE) **The Lord Conyers Racing Partnership**

### TWO-YEAR-OLDS

**5** B g 28/2 Native Ruler—Lord Conyers (IRE) (Inzar (USA)) **The Lord Conyers Racing Partnership**

## MR GARRY WOODWARD - Continued

**Other Owners:** Mr D. R. Cope, Mrs R. Cope.

**Jockey (flat):** Graham Lee, Luke Morris.

---

## 672 MR RICHARD WOOLLACOTT, South Molton

Postal: **Nethercott Manor, Rose Ash, South Molton, Devon, EX36 4RE**
Contacts: **PHONE (01769) 550483 MOBILE (07780) 006995**
**E-MAIL info@richardwoollacottracing.co.uk WEBSITE www.richardwoollacottracing.co.uk**

1 **BANG ON TIME (IRE),** 9, b g Chevalier (IRE)—Dysart Lady **Taunton Racecourse Owners Group**
2 **CASH INJECTION,** 6, b g Halling (USA)—Cape Siren **Eight Ball Partnership**
3 **DARSI'S DREAM (IRE),** 5, b g Darsi (FR)—Lady Farina (IRE) **Ann & Tony Gale**
4 **FLORESCO (GER),** 5, ch g Santiago (GER)—Fiori (GER) **D. G. Staddon**
5 **KUDU SHINE,** 9, b g Karinga Bay—Flora Bright **Mr D. Stevens & Mr G. Jewell**
6 **LADY GARVAGH,** 5, b m Lucarno (USA)—Dedrunknmunky (IRE) **Mrs J. Bloomfield**
7 **LIBERTY ONE (IRE),** 9, b g Milan—Same Old Story (IRE) **D. G. Staddon**
8 **LOCAL SHOW (IRE),** 7, br g Oscar (IRE)—Loughaderra Rose (IRE) **Nicholas Piper & Claire E. Phillipson**
9 **MILLANISI BOY,** 6, b g Kalanisi (IRE)—Millennium Rose (IRE) **Mr D. Stevens & Mrs S. Stevens**
10 **POSITIVE VIBES,** 6, ch g Nayef (USA)—Steeple **Mr M. Watkinson**
11 **SHEER POETRY (IRE),** 4, b f Yeats (IRE)—Sassari (IRE) **R. J. Weeks**
12 **SILVERGROVE,** 7, b g Old Vic—Classic Gale (USA) **Nicholas Piper & Claire E. Phillipson**
13 **THEIONLADY (IRE),** 5, gr m Presenting—Valleya (FR) **Mrs H. Broggio**

**Other Owners:** Mr M. Bevan, Mr G. J. Evans, Mr Tony Gale, Mrs Ann Gale, Mr J. Heal, Mr G. D. C. Jewell, Miss C. Phillipson, Mr N. Piper, Mr Martin Rhoades, Mr D. J. Stevens, Mrs S. E. Stevens.

**Assistant Trainer:** Mrs Kayley Woollacott

---

## 673 MR RAYMOND YORK, Cobham

Postal: **Newmarsh Farm, Horsley Road, Cobham, Surrey, KT11 3JX**
Contacts: **PHONE (01932) 863594 MOBILE (07808) 344131**
**E-MAIL ray.york@virgin.net**

1 **CRAIGS DREAM (IRE),** 9, b g Craigsteel—Sinead's Dream (IRE) **R. H. York**
2 **ENCANTADORA,** 8, ch m Generous (IRE)—Sninfia (IRE) **R. H. York**
3 **HARRY'S CHOICE,** 7, b g Sir Harry Lewis (USA)—Chosen (IRE) **R. H. York**
4 7, Gr g Terimon—Kilshey **R. H. York**
5 **QUEEN'S PAWN (IRE),** 8, br g Strategic Choice (USA)—Curragh Queen (IRE) **F. D. Camis**
6 6, B g Bollin Eric—Woodford Consult **R. H. York**

**Amateur:** Mr P. York.

---

## 674 MRS LAURA YOUNG, Bridgwater

Postal: **Rooks Castle Stables, Broomfield, Bridgwater, Somerset, TA5 2EW**
Contacts: **PHONE (01278) 664595 FAX (01278) 661555 MOBILE (07766) 514414**
**E-MAIL ljyracing@hotmail.com WEBSITE www.laurayoungracing.com**

1 **ADMIRAL BLAKE,** 8, b g Witness Box (USA)—Brenda Bella (FR) **Mrs L. J. Young**
2 **BILIDN,** 7, b m Tiger Hill (IRE)—Brightest Star **Total Plumbing Supporters Club**
3 **BORDER STATION (IRE),** 9, b g Shantou (USA)—Telemania (IRE) **Total Plumbing Supporters Club**
4 **BUCKBORU (IRE),** 7, b m Brian Boru—Buckland Filleigh (IRE) **Mrs L. J. Young**
5 **CASTLETOWN (IRE),** 7, b g Oscar (IRE)—Closing Thyne (IRE) **The Isle Of Frogs Partnership**
6 **CREATIVE BORU (IRE),** 7, b g Brian Boru—Ruths Rhapsody (IRE) **The Isle Of Frogs Partnership**
7 **GILMER (IRE),** 4, b g Exceed And Excel (AUS)—Cherokee Rose (IRE) **Total Plumbing Supporters Club**
8 **HALEO,** 4, ch g Halling (USA)—Oatey **Total Plumbing Supporters Club**
9 **JIGSAW FINANCIAL (IRE),** 9, b g Brian Boru—Ardcolm Cailin (IRE) **Mrs L. J. Young**
10 **KAP WEST (FR),** 10, b g Kapgarde (FR)—Themis Eria (FR) **Mrs S. A. White**
11 **MONSIEUR DARSI (IRE),** 5, b g Darsi (FR)—Durgams Delight (IRE) **Mrs S. A. White**
12 **MY DIAMOND (IRE),** 4, b g Brian Boru—Our Idol (IRE) **The Isle Of Frogs Partnership**
13 **ON ALBERTS HEAD (IRE),** 5, b g Mountain High (IRE)—Dear Money (IRE) **Mrs S. A. White**
14 **SUFFICE (IRE),** 6, b g Iffraaj—Shallat (IRE) **Mrs L. J. Young**

**MRS LAURA YOUNG - Continued**

15 **TWYFORD,** 8, b g Bach (IRE)—Commanche Token (IRE) **Total Plumbing Supporters Club**
16 **WHISKEY JOHN,** 5, b g Westerner—Cherry Lane **The Isle Of Frogs Partnership**
17 **WOLFTRAP (IRE),** 6, b g Mountain High (IRE)—Dear Money (IRE) **Mrs S. A. White**

**Other Owners:** C. E. Handford, Mr I. D. Moses, Mr G. C. Vining, Mr C. V. Vining.

**Assistant Trainer:** James Young

**Jockey (NH):** Dougie Costello, Robert Dunne.

---

## 675 MR WILLIAM YOUNG, Carluke

Postal: **Watchknowe Lodge, Crossford, Carluke, Lanarkshire, ML8 5QT**
Contacts: **PHONE (01555) 860856 (01555) 860226 FAX (01555) 860137 MOBILE (07900) 408210**
**E-MAIL watchknowe@talktalk.net**

1 **MILAN OF HOPE (IRE),** 8, b g Milan—Miss Bertaine (IRE) **W. G. Young**
2 **MILANS WELL (IRE),** 9, b g Milan—Panoora Queen (IRE) **W. G. Young**
3 **RAIFTEIRI (IRE),** 8, b g Galileo (IRE)—Naziriya (FR) **W. G. Young**

**Assistant Trainer:** William G Young Snr

# INDEX TO HORSES

**The Figure before** the name of the horse refers to the number of the team in which it appears and **The Figure after** the horse supplies a ready reference to each animal. Horses are indexed strictly alphabetically, e.g. THE NEW PHARAOH appears in the T's, MR FICKLE in the MR's, ST DOMINICK in the ST's etc.

459 **DEPORTATION** (GB) 2
268 **DEPORTMENT** (GB) C 76
511 **DEPRESSED** (GB) F 8
460 **DEPTH CHARGE** (IRE) 19
610 **DEPUTY COMMANDER** (IRE) 27
551 **DEPUTY DAN** (IRE) 12
187 **DERBYSHIRE** (IRE) 24
294 **DERKSEN** (IRE) 37
13 **DERRINTOGHER BLISS** (IRE) 12
405 **DERRYDOON** (GB) 6
146 **DERRYOGUE** (IRE) 7
190 **DERULO** (IRE) 3
136 **DERVAL** (IRE) F 50
460 **DESAFINADO** (IRE) 20
469 **DESCARO** (USA) 3
160 **DESERT ACE** (IRE) 3
547 **DESERT APOSTLE** (IRE) 25
649 **DESERT CHIEF** (GB) 12
17 **DESERT COMMAND** (GB) 9
399 **DESERT CRY** (IRE) 39
554 **DESERT ENCOUNTER** (IRE) 29
53 **DESERT FORTUNE** (FR) 22
22 **DESERT ISLAND DUSK** (GB) 5
354 **DESERT JOE** (IRE) 23
150 **DESERT LOCATION** (GB) C 27
87 **DESERT NOVA** (IRE) 2
471 **DESERT RECLUSE** (IRE) 5
354 **DESERT ROBE** (GB) 24
465 **DESERT ROYALTY** (IRE) C 15
614 **DESERT SKY** (IRE) C 114
46 **DESERT SNOW** (GB) 8
162 **DESERT STRIKE** (GB) 5
187 **DESERTMORE STREAM** (IRE) 25
616 **DESHAN** (GER) 31
249 **DESIGN PERFECTION** (USA) F 124
196 **DESILVANO** (GB) 2
432 **DESIRABLE** (GB) 56
201 **DESIRE** (GB) 89
399 **DESOTO COUNTY** (GB) 40
297 **DESPERADO DANCER** (GB) 2
342 **DESSERTOFLIFE** (IRE) 120
292 **DESTIN** (FR) 15
634 **DESTINATION AIM** (GB) 3
491 **DESTINY AWAITS** (IRE) 1
224 **DESTINY BLUE** (IRE) 3
16 **DESTINY'S GOLD** (IRE) 9
16 **DESTINY'S SHADOW** (IRE) 45
616 **DESTROYER DEPLOYED** (GB) 32
657 **DESTRUCT** (GB) 16
577 **DETANK** (IRE) 4
569 **DETROIT BLUES** (GB) 12
300 **DETROIT RED** (GB) 4
249 **DEUCE AGAIN** (GB) 5
474 **DEUXIEME EMPIRE** (FR) 5
405 **DEVENISH ISLAND** (GB) 7
625 **DEVERON** (USA) C 38
354 **DEVIL TO PAY** (GB) 25
656 **DEVIL'S DYKE** (USA) 27
207 **DEVILMENT** (GB) 10
6 **DEVILMENT** (GB) 11
440 **DEVILS BRIDE** (IRE) 50
547 **DEVILUTION** (IRE) 26
201 **DEVIOUS SPIRIT** (IRE) 90
639 **DEVON DRUM** (GB) 13
416 **DEVONIAN** (GB) 18
106 **DEVONSHIRE PLACE** (IRE) 28
461 **DEVOTED TO YOU** (IRE) C 130
181 **DEW POND** (GB) 51
7 **DEWALA** (GB) 14
152 **DEWBERRY** (GB) 3
238 **DEXCITE** (FR) 18
239 **DEXTER BENJAMIN** (IRE) 4
106 **DEXTEROUS** (GB) 29
554 **DHAN DHANA** (IRE) F 68
249 **DHAROOS** (IRE) 125
276 **DHARWA** (GB) 40
243 **DHAULAR DHAR** (IRE) 13
474 **DHEVANAFUSHI** (GB) 157
530 **DHORSELL** (IRE) 38
366 **DI KAPRIO** (FR) 2
440 **DIAKALI** (FR) 51
285 **DIAKTOROS** (IRE) 3
160 **DIAL A LOG** (GB) 53
249 **DIALAFARA** (FR) F 126
362 **DIALECTIC** (IRE) 19
511 **DIALOGUE** (GB) 2
416 **DIAM QUEEN** (GER) C 33
334 **DIAMANTE** (GB) 16
503 **DIAMOND BACK** (IRE) 4
461 **DIAMOND BANGLE** (IRE) 42
603 **DIAMOND BLAISE** (GB) 25
164 **DIAMOND CHARLIE** (IRE) 5
43 **DIAMOND D'AMOUR** (IRE) 7
647 **DIAMOND FIZZ** (IRE) 5
463 **DIAMOND GESTURE** (IRE) 8
100 **DIAMOND JOEL** (GB) 60
399 **DIAMOND KING** (IRE) 41
580 **DIAMOND LADY** (GB) 2
489 **DIAMOND LIFE** (GB) 30
466 **DIAMOND LIGHT** (USA) G 66
32 **DIAMOND LIGHT** (USA) F 91
547 **DIAMOND MAN** (GB) 27
82 **DIAMOND MINE** (GB) 6
581 **DIAMOND NATIVE** (IRE) 3
474 **DIAMOND RED** (FR) 73
471 **DIAMOND ROCK** (GB) 6
390 **DIAMOND RUN** (GB) C 22
536 **DIAMOND RUNNER** (IRE) 5
358 **DIAMOND SAM** (GB) 20
282 **DIAMOND VINE** (IRE) 7
262 **DIAMONDS A DANCING** (GB) 1
461 **DIAMONDSANDRUBIES** (IRE) 43
547 **DIAMONDSINTHESKY** (IRE) 8
554 **DIARY** (IRE) F 69
139 **DIATOMIC** (IRE) 26
357 **DIBBLE BRIDGE** (GB) 14
190 **DIBIYA** (IRE) F 34
461 **DICK WHITTINGTON** (IRE) 44
159 **DICKY SHORE** (GB) 1
440 **DICOSIMO** (FR) 52
274 **DIDDY ERIC** (GB) 13
168 **DIDDYPURPTOON** (GB) 2
31 **DIEGO SUAREZ** (FR) 7
86 **DIESCENTRIC** (USA) 2
294 **DIFFERENT GRAVEY** (IRE) 38
69 **DIFFERENT SCENARIO** (GB) 4
440 **DIGEANTA** (IRE) 53
77 **DIGGER'S MATE** (GB) 2
425 **DIGNIFY** (IRE) F 134
292 **DIHNA** (FR) 16
377 **DILETTA TOMMASA** (IRE) 5
359 **DILGURA** (GB) 2
359 **DILYS** (GB) G 22
302 **DIMAKYA** (USA) F 123
281 **DIMINUTIVE** (IRE) 7
204 **DIMITAR** (USA) 6
251 **DIMPLE** (FR) 11
100 **DING DING** (GB) 11
255 **DINGAAN** (IRE) 2
618 **DINGO BAY** (GB) 10
89 **DINKUM DIAMOND** (IRE) 5
32 **DINNERATMIDNIGHT** (GB) 5
569 **DINO MITE** (GB) 13
399 **DIOCLES** (IRE) 42
474 **DIPANKARA** (FR) 74
56 **DIPITY DOO DAH** (GB) 11
583 **DIPLOMA** (GB) 105
572 **DIPLOMATIC** (IRE) 1
538 **DIPPINGANDDIVING** (IRE) 5
371 **DIRACAN** (IRE) 11
355 **DIRE STRAITS** (IRE) 6
553 **DIRECT APPROACH** (IRE) 5
103 **DIRECT TIMES** (IRE) 3
6 **DIRECTIONAL** (GB) 69
266 **DIRECTOR** (IRE) 34
99 **DIRECTORSHIP** (GB) 5
342 **DISAVOW** (GB) 41
65 **DISC PLAY** (GB) 15
452 **DISCAY** (GB) 9
484 **DISCLOSE** (GB) C 48
200 **DISCLOSURE** (GB) 3
201 **DISCO DALE** (IRE) 11
377 **DISCO DAVE** (IRE) 6
540 **DISCOVERIE** (GB) 8
443 **DISCUSSIONTOFOLLOW** (IRE) 6
583 **DISEGNO** (IRE) 39
51 **DISHY GURU** (GB) 3
409 **DISKO** (FR) 22
559 **DISPOL VELETA** (GB) F 46
399 **DISPOUR** (IRE) 43
172 **DISPUTE** (USA) F 21
241 **DISSENT** (IRE) 3
292 **DISSERTATION** (GB) 17
583 **DISSOLUTION** (GB) 40
263 **DISTANT DREAMER** (USA) F 40
499 **DISTANT HIGH** (GB) 3
534 **DISTANT PAST** (GB) 6
654 **DISTANT SHADOW** (GB) 4
276 **DISTANT SKIES** (GB) F 137
653 **DISTESO** (IRE) 3
504 **DISTIME** (IRE) 9
361 **DISTINCTIVE** (GB) F 19
362 **DISTINGO** (IRE) 50
202 **DISTRICT ATTORNEY** (IRE) 2
136 **DISUSHE STAR** (GB) 39
57 **DIVERTIMENTI** (IRE) 4
100 **DIVINE** (IRE) 12
432 **DIVINE AUTHORITY** (IRE) F 57
60 **DIVINE CALL** (GB) 2
6 **DIVINE DIXIE** (USA) F 168
55 **DIVINE JOY** (GB) 90
276 **DIVINE LAW** (GB) 41
587 **DIVINE PORT** (USA) 9
525 **DIVINE PROMESSE** (FR) F 75
583 **DIVINE QUICKSTEP** (IRE) 106
423 **DIVINE RULE** (IRE) 3
184 **DIVINE TOUCH** (GB) 18
110 **DIVINISSIME** (USA) 48
525 **DIVONA** (FR) 76
474 **DIX NEUF SIX** (GB) 6
588 **DIXIE BULL** (IRE) 8
333 **DIXIE'S DREAM** (IRE) 2
266 **DIXIELAND KISS** (USA) F 109
480 **DIZOARD** (GB) 3

187 **NATIONAL SERVICE** (USA) 52
46 **NATIVE BLUE** (GB) C 131
294 **NATIVE DISPLAY** (IRE) 92
389 **NATIVE EXPLORER** (GB) 20
587 **NATIVE FALLS** (IRE) 30
151 **NATIVE GALLERY** (IRE) 2
463 **NATIVE MOUNTAIN** (IRE) 19
298 **NATIVE NICKEL** (IRE) C 16
631 **NATIVE OPTIMIST** (IRE) 4
185 **NATIVE PRINCESS** (GB) 10
598 **NATIVE RIVER** (IRE) 38
563 **NATIVE SPA** (IRE) 13
408 **NATURAL FLAIR** (USA) F 46
334 **NAUTICAL TWILIGHT** (GB) 34
332 **NAVAJO CHIEF** (GB) 10
7 **NAVAJO DREAM** (GB) 35
489 **NAVANMAN** (IRE) 68
408 **NAVIGATE** (IRE) 26
474 **NAVIGATRICE** (GB) 110
302 **NAWAASY** (USA) 74
46 **NAWAIET** (USA) F 132
55 **NAYEF DREAM** (GB) 105
276 **NAYEL** (IRE) 71
411 **NAZIBA** (IRE) 8
266 **NAZLI** (IRE) 61
530 **NAZMIA** (IRE) 16
37 **NEAR WILD HEAVEN** (GB) 5
432 **NEARLY CAUGHT** (IRE) 14
648 **NEARLY MAY** (GB) 8
120 **NEAT SHILLING** (IRE) C 12
434 **NEATH ABBEY** (GB) 33
425 **NEBULA STORM** (IRE) 77
502 **NEBULLA** (GB) 11
304 **NECK OR NOTHING** (GER) 68
409 **NED BUNTLINE** (GB) 47
354 **NED STARK** (IRE) 79
100 **NEDWA** (GB) F 131
100 **NEEDLESS SHOUTING** (IRE) 35
124 **NEEDWOOD PARK** (GB) 3
486 **NEEDWOOD RIDGE** (GB) 6
72 **NEFETARI** (GB) 17
399 **NEFYN BAY** (GB) 106
39 **NEISSA** (USA) C 30
474 **NELLIE GWYN** (GB) F 172
408 **NELLIE NOLAN** (USA) C 47
616 **NELLIE THE ELEGANT** (GB) 76
595 **NELLY LA RUE** (IRE) 11
404 **NELSON DU RONCERAY** (FR) 4
234 **NELSON QUAY** (IRE) 12
582 **NELSON'S BAY** (GB) 4
149 **NELSON'S HILL** (GB) 3
326 **NELSON'S PRIDE** (GB) 8
416 **NELSONS TRICK** (GB) 26
596 **NEPTUNE EQUESTER** (GB) 11
39 **NEPTUNE'S GIRL** (IRE) C 31
89 **NEQAAWI** (GB) C 56
464 **NERANO** (IRE) 19
463 **NERVOUS NINETIES** (GB) 20
493 **NESHIKOT** (IRE) 12
473 **NESHLA** (GB) F 51
294 **NESTERENKO** (GER) 93
440 **NET D'ECOSSE** (FR) 100
13 **NET WORK ROUGE** (FR) 30
425 **NETHERBY** (GB) 78
596 **NETMINDER** (IRE) 12
139 **NEUTRON BOMB** (IRE) 34
276 **NEVADA PRINCESS** (IRE) C 189
302 **NEVER A DOUBT** (GB) C 154
46 **NEVER CHANGE** (IRE) 82
201 **NEVER EASY** (IRE) 122
243 **NEVER FOREVER** (GB) 40
191 **NEVER FORGET POPPY** (IRE) 7
598 **NEVER LEARN** (IRE) 39
358 **NEVER LET YOU DOWN** (IRE) C 47
74 **NEVER LOSE** (GB) F 36
350 **NEVER LOST** (GB) F 15
46 **NEVER MISS** (GB) 83
399 **NEVER NEVER** (IRE) 107
145 **NEVER PERFECT** (IRE) 4
466 **NEVER TO BE** (USA) 37
452 **NEVEROWNUP** (IRE) 19
280 **NEVERUSHACON** (IRE) 32
304 **NEVILLE** (GB) 69
242 **NEVILLE WOODS** (GB) 3
351 **NEW ABBEY ANGEL** (IRE) 24
351 **NEW ABBEY DANCER** (IRE) 15
618 **NEW ACADEMY** (GB) 23
640 **NEW AGENDA** (GB) 39
465 **NEW BIDDER** (GB) 4
425 **NEW CODE** (GB) 79
483 **NEW COLOURS** (GB) 11
74 **NEW DEAL** (GB) F 37
60 **NEW DECADE** (GB) 6
52 **NEW DIRECTION** (IRE) 40
126 **NEW HAPPINESS** (IRE) 34
294 **NEW HORIZONS** (IRE) 94
112 **NEW IDENTITY** (IRE) 9
234 **NEW LEYF** (IRE) 13
565 **NEW LOOK** (IRE) 8
294 **NEW MEMBER** (IRE) 95
6 **NEW MUSIC** (IRE) 106
294 **NEW PROVIDENCE** (FR) 96
473 **NEW PROVIDENCE** (GB) 15
484 **NEW REACTION** (GB) 16
474 **NEW RECORD** (IRE) 111
484 **NEW REVIVE** (GB) 35
339 **NEW RICH** (GB) 8
589 **NEW SAABOOG** (GB) 28
422 **NEW STORY** (GB) 7
46 **NEW STRATEGY** (IRE) 84
68 **NEW STREAM** (IRE) 19
38 **NEW STREET** (IRE) 16
46 **NEW STYLE** (USA) 85
94 **NEW TARABELA** (GB) 29
207 **NEW YEAR'S EVE** (GB) 21
6 **NEW YEAR'S NIGHT** (IRE) 32
458 **NEW YOUMZAIN** (FR) 14
280 **NEWBERRY NEW** (IRE) 72
516 **NEWCASTLEBEAUTY** (IRE) G 31
139 **NEWERA** (GB) 35
78 **NEWFORGE HOUSE** (IRE) 6
123 **NEWGATE QUEEN** (GB) 14
6 **NEWMARCH** (GB) 107
523 **NEWNHAM FLYER** (IRE) 2
407 **NEWORLD** (FR) 27
52 **NEWS AT SIX** (IRE) 7
618 **NEWSPAGE** (IRE) 24
6 **NEWSPEAK** (IRE) 108
25 **NEWSTEAD ABBEY** (GB) 19
294 **NEWSWORTHY** (IRE) 97
477 **NEWTON GERONIMO** (GB) 21
477 **NEWTON MARTINI** (GB) 22
477 **NEWTON THISTLE** (GB) 23
223 **NEWTOWN CROSS** (IRE) 6
636 **NEWYEARSRESOLUTION** (IRE) 7
136 **NEXIUS** (IRE) 19
249 **NEXT APPROACH** (GB) 69
357 **NEXT EDITION** (IRE) 37
578 **NEXT GENERATION** (IRE) 19
566 **NEXT HIGHT** (IRE) 43
545 **NEXT SENSATION** (IRE) 14
454 **NEXT STOP** (GB) 20
120 **NEXT TO THE TOP** (GB) C 63
193 **NEXT TRAIN'S GONE** (GB) 21
656 **NEXT VENTURE** (IRE) G 56
33 **NEYMAR** (GB) 36
111 **NEZAMI** (IRE) 2
82 **NEZAR** (IRE) 10
436 **NI SIN E MO AINM** (IRE) 43
516 **NIAMH'S LEADER** (IRE) G 32
33 **NIBLAWI** (IRE) 37
589 **NICE THOUGHTS** (IRE) 29
368 **NICENE CREED** (GB) 12
32 **NICEOFYOUTOTELLME** (GB) 15
360 **NICEONECENTURION** (GB) 41
661 **NICEONEFRANKIE** (GB) 57
664 **NICEONEMYSON** (GB) 4
625 **NICHOLASCOPERNICUS** (IRE) 6
440 **NICHOLS CANYON** (GB) 101
440 **NICKNAME EXIT** (FR) 102
469 **NICKY NUTJOB** (GER) 6
294 **NICOLAS CHAUVIN** (IRE) 98
473 **NIDNOD** (GB) 52
402 **NIFTY KIER** (GB) 6
249 **NIGEL** (GB) 70
460 **NIGEL'S DESTINY** (USA) 6
497 **NIGHT GENERATION** (GER) 26
513 **NIGHT IN MILAN** (IRE) 18
27 **NIGHT OF LIGHT** (IRE) 38
276 **NIGHT OF THUNDER** (IRE) 12
122 **NIGHT PREMIERE** (IRE) C 80
282 **NIGHT TRADE** (IRE) 17
78 **NIGHT'S WATCH** (GB) 7
137 **NIGHTFLY** (GB) 23
249 **NIGHTIME** (IRE) C 160
137 **NIGHTLINE** (GB) 24
292 **NIGWAH** (FR) 30
474 **NIJAH** (IRE) 26
569 **NIKI ROYAL** (FR) 29
558 **NIMBLE** (IRE) 36
193 **NIMBLE KIMBLE** (GB) 7
302 **NIMBOO** (USA) F 155
389 **NIMBUS GALE** (IRE) 21
362 **NIMPHEAS** (USA) 60
416 **NINA FONTENAIL** (FR) F 37
273 **NINE ALTARS** (IRE) 4
536 **NINE BEFORE TEN** (IRE) 2
616 **NINE IRON** (IRE) 77
473 **NINE RED** (GB) C 53
469 **NINEPOINTSIXTHREE** (GB) 7
169 **NINETTA** (IRE) 48
39 **NINETY MINUTES** (IRE) 9
379 **NINGXAI** (IRE) 48
276 **NINJAGO** (GB) 13
4 **NIQNAAQPAADIWAAQ** (GB) 14
379 **NISRIYNA** (IRE) C 72
229 **NITROGEN** (IRE) 34
46 **NITYA** (FR) F 133
534 **NO BACKCHAT** (IRE) 57
389 **NO BAD NEWS** (GB) 22
66 **NO BUTS** (GB) 24
227 **NO CEILING** (IRE) 11
531 **NO DEAL** (IRE) 57
6 **NO DELUSION** (USA) 109

94 **OEIL DE TIGRE** (FR) 32
332 **OETZI** (GB) 11
240 **OFCOURSEWECAN** (USA) 12
181 **OFF ART** (GB) 30
132 **OFF DUTY** (IRE) 35
399 **OFF THE CUFF** (GB) 108
365 **OFF THE GROUND** (IRE) 40
380 **OFF THE PULSE** (GB) 13
189 **OFF THE SCALE** (IRE) 102
187 **OFFICER CADET** (GB) 55
38 **OFFICER DRIVEL** (IRE) 17
616 **OFFICER HOOLIHAN** (GB) 79
82 **OFFICER IN COMMAND** (USA) 12
409 **OFFICIEUX** (FR) 49
589 **OFFSHORE** (GB) 30
461 **OFTEN** (IRE) 80
267 **OGARITMO** (GB) 11
302 **OGBOURNE DOWNS** (GB) 14
543 **OH DEVEE** (GB) 28
355 **OH LAND ABLOOM** (IRE) 18
540 **OH RIGHT** (IRE) 17
425 **OH SO FRUITY** (GB) 80
626 **OH SO SASSY** (GB) 8
136 **OH SO SAUCY** (GB) C 59
276 **OH THIS IS US** (IRE) 190
598 **OHIO GOLD** (IRE) 40
660 **OHSOSECRET** (GB) 36
5 **OIL BURNER** (GB) 6
180 **OIL STRIKE** (GB) 25
598 **OISEAU DE NUIT** (FR) 41
128 **OISHIN** (GB) 13
558 **OJALA** (FR) 37
294 **OK CORRAL** (IRE) 100
610 **OKAFRANCA** (IRE) 62
362 **OKANA** (GB) 62
461 **OKLAHOMA CITY** (GB) 22
391 **OKOTOKS** (IRE) 40
461 **OL' MAN RIVER** (IRE) 81
362 **OLANTHIA** (IRE) 26
7 **OLD FASHION** (GB) 60
455 **OLD GUARD** (GB) 73
368 **OLD MAGIC** (IRE) 13
180 **OLD MAN CLEGG** (GB) 26
170 **OLD PHOBIE** (IRE) 6
398 **OLD TOWN BOY** (GB) 5
94 **OLEANA** (IRE) F 33
106 **OLIMPIC GIRL** (IRE) F 75
161 **OLINDERA** (GER) G 11
623 **OLIVER'S GOLD** (GB) 19
299 **OLIVER'S HILL** (IRE) 11
615 **OLIVERS MOUNT** (GB) 7
251 **OLLIE G** (GB) 26
171 **OLLISU LAD** (IRE) 6
479 **OLNEY LASS** (GB) 6
238 **OLOFI** (FR) 41
357 **OLY'ROCCS** (IRE) 38
184 **OLYMNIA** (GB) 7
599 **OLYMPIAD** (IRE) 12
368 **OLYMPIAN BOY** (IRE) 14
547 **OLYMPIC CHARM** (GB) 35
276 **OLYMPIC MEDAL** (GB) C 191
466 **OMANOME** (IRE) 39
556 **OMID** (GB) 5
141 **OMMADAWN** (IRE) G 8
67 **OMOTESANDO** (GB) 6
461 **ON A PEDESTAL** (IRE) 82
342 **ON A SOAPBOX** (USA) C 166
377 **ON A WHIM** (GB) 26
674 **ON ALBERTS HEAD** (IRE) 13
95 **ON BUDGET** (IRE) 16
307 **ON DEMAND** (GB) 5
41 **ON FIRE** (GB) 26
589 **ON HER WAY** (GB) C 67
440 **ON HIS OWN** (IRE) 104
543 **ON THE BRIDGE** (IRE) 29
158 **ON THE BUCKLE** (GB) 17
238 **ON THE CASE** (GB) 42
591 **ON THE HIGH TOPS** (IRE) 4
33 **ON THE HUH** (GB) 38
366 **ON THE RIGHT PATH** (GB) 9
656 **ON THE ROAD** (IRE) 58
74 **ON THE TILES** (GB) 22
566 **ON THE VINE** (GB) 46
656 **ON TOUR** (IRE) 59
239 **ON TREND** (IRE) 14
17 **ONCE OVER** (GB) F 153
335 **ONCE REMOVED** (GB) C 43
583 **ONDA DISTRICT** (IRE) 67
365 **ONDERUN** (IRE) 41
605 **ONE BIG SURPRISE** (GB) 19
160 **ONE BOY** (IRE) 16
82 **ONE CHANCE** (IRE) 13
633 **ONE COOL BOY** (IRE) 1
424 **ONE COOL POET** (IRE) 18
531 **ONE FOR ARTHUR** (IRE) 58
516 **ONE FOR HARRY** (IRE) 34
516 **ONE FOR HOCKY** (IRE) 35
78 **ONE FOR THE BOSS** (IRE) 8
294 **ONE FOR THE GUV'NR** (IRE) 101
127 **ONE IN A ROW** (IRE) 13
306 **ONE LAST DREAM** (GB) 6
616 **ONE LEADER** (IRE) 80
371 **ONE LIFE LIVE IT** (GB) 13
294 **ONE LUCKY LADY** (GB) 102
477 **ONE LUCKY LORD** (GB) 24
33 **ONE MAN ARMY** (GB) 39
120 **ONE MOMENT** (GB) 37
461 **ONE MOMENT IN TIME** (IRE) C 154
587 **ONE MORE GO** (IRE) 33
231 **ONE MORE PUSEY** (GB) 16
295 **ONE MORE TUNE** (IRE) 20
658 **ONE OF US** (GB) 35
107 **ONE SWOOP** (IRE) F 5
563 **ONE SWOOP** (IRE) G 14
132 **ONE TERM** (IRE) 36
256 **ONE TRACK MIND** (IRE) 55
474 **ONE WISH** (FR) 174
181 **ONE WORD MORE** (IRE) 31
304 **ONEFITZALL** (IRE) 70
358 **ONELASTFLING** (GB) 30
573 **ONENIGHTIDREAMED** (IRE) 3
304 **ONENIGHTINVIENNA** (IRE) 71
570 **ONEOFAPEAR** (IRE) 7
55 **ONESIE** (IRE) 107
534 **ONLINE ALEXANDER** (IRE) 19
294 **ONLY FOR LOVE** (GB) 103
72 **ONLY FOR YOU** (GB) 11
473 **ONLY JOKING** (GB) 17
534 **ONLY JUST** (IRE) 58
274 **ONLY ORSENFOOLSIES** (GB) 30
335 **ONLY TEN PER CENT** (IRE) 21
59 **ONLY TIME'LL TELL** (IRE) 13
58 **ONORINA** (IRE) 13
468 **ONTHEWESTERNFRONT** (IRE) 58
424 **ONTOPOFTHEWORLD** (IRE) 12
467 **ONURBIKE** (GB) 3
333 **ONWARDSANDUPWARDS** 25
455 **ONWITHTHEPARTY** (GB) 74
247 **ONWITHTHEPARTY** (GB) 17
362 **ONYX** (FR) 27
362 **OOGLI** (GB) 28
386 **OOJAR** (GB) 1
566 **OORAYVIC** (IRE) 47
106 **OOTY HILL** (GB) 44
66 **OPECHEE** (IRE) 26
440 **OPEN EAGLE** (IRE) 105
294 **OPEN HEARTED** (GB) 104
52 **OPEN HOUSE** (IRE) 94
27 **OPEN MIND** (FR) 82
484 **OPEN THE RED** (GB) 36
229 **OPENING BATSMAN** (IRE) 35
296 **OPENING CEREMONY** (USA) C 14
538 **OPERA BUFF** (GB) 4
249 **OPERA COMIQUE** (FR) F 161
358 **OPERA DANCER** (GB) C 49
17 **OPERA GLASS** (GB) F 154
17 **OPERA LAD** (IRE) 89
285 **OPERATEUR** (IRE) 11
486 **OPERATIC HEIGHTS** (IRE) 7
399 **OPERATING** (IRE) 109
434 **OPHIR** (GB) 9
55 **OPINIONATED** (IRE) C 108
302 **OPITO BAY** (IRE) 75
181 **OPOPMIL** (IRE) C 103
139 **OPPORTUNA** (GB) 36
172 **OPPOSITION** (GB) 78
647 **OPT OUT** (GB) 15
566 **OPTICAL HIGH** (GB) 48
129 **OPTIMA PETAMUS** (GB) 50
468 **OPTIMISTIC BIAS** (IRE) 59
17 **OPTIMYSTIC** (IRE) 90
634 **OPUS DEI** (GB) 7
533 **OPUS TOO** (IRE) 6
1 **OR DE GRUGY** (FR) 28
304 **ORABORA** (GB) 72
434 **ORACLE BOY** (GB) 10
554 **ORACOLO** (IRE) 45
474 **ORAGE NOIR** (FR) 27
33 **ORANGE BLOOM** (GB) 40
376 **ORANGE NASSAU** (FR) 39
276 **ORANGE PIP** (GB) C 192
17 **ORANGE WALK** (USA) 91
97 **ORANGEADAY** (GB) 23
474 **ORANGEFIELD** (FR) 28
392 **ORANGER** (FR) 3
640 **ORANGEY RED** (IRE) 107
472 **ORATORIO'S JOY** (IRE) 7
160 **ORBIT THE MOON** (IRE) 17
17 **ORBITAL ORCHID** (GB) C 155
376 **ORBY'S MAN** (IRE) 40
569 **ORCHARD PARK** (IRE) 30
140 **ORCHARD ROAD** (USA) 4
464 **ORCHESTRAL RUN** (IRE) 20
358 **ORCRAIG** (GB) 15
165 **ORDENSRITTER** (GER) 16
243 **ORDER OF SERVICE** (GB) 41
461 **ORDER OF ST GEORGE** (IRE) 83
206 **ORDERS FROM ROME** (IRE) 6
354 **ORDO AB CHAO** (IRE) 81
342 **OREGON GIFT** (GB) 65
27 **ORELLE** (GB) 39
27 **ORFORD NESS** (GB) F 83
487 **ORGAN MORGAN** (GB) 22
333 **ORGAN SCHOLAR** (GB) 26

205 **THE DUCKING STOOL** (GB) 15
241 **THE DUKKERER** (IRE) 12
455 **THE EAGLEHASLANDED** (IRE) 113
432 **THE FAIRIES DID IT** (USA) F 75
611 **THE FENLAND MAN** (GB) 8
449 **THE FINGER POST** (IRE) 8
377 **THE FIRM** (IRE) 18
1 **THE FLAMING MATRON** (IRE) 36
657 **THE FLYING COLUMN** (IRE) 64
531 **THE FRIARY** (IRE) 88
376 **THE FUGITIVE** (IRE) 59
666 **THE FULWELL END** (GB) 13
425 **THE GAME IS A FOOT** (IRE) 101
533 **THE GAY CAVALIER** (GB) 9
315 **THE GEEGEEZ GEEGEE** (IRE) 30
66 **THE GIANT BOLSTER** (GB) 37
541 **THE GINGER BERRY** (GB) 5
656 **THE GIPPER** (IRE) 77
463 **THE GOVANESS** (GB) 33
14 **THE GOVERNOR** (IRE) 3
17 **THE GRADUATE** (IRE) 173
425 **THE GREEN OGRE** (GB) 102
534 **THE GREY GATSBY** (IRE) 24
189 **THE GREY TAYLOR** (IRE) 76
568 **THE GUNNER BRADY** (IRE) 7
574 **THE HAPPY HAMMER** (IRE) 3
461 **THE HAPPY PRINCE** (IRE) 102
77 **THE HAPPY WARRIOR** (GB) 6
409 **THE HERDS GARDEN** (GB) 72
589 **THE HERMITAGE** (IRE) F 82
128 **THE HOLYMAN** (IRE) 10
100 **THE HON MACKINLAY** (IRE) 47
126 **THE HOODED CLAW** (IRE) 8
655 **THE HUMBEL BUTLER** (IRE) 11
379 **THE ICE MEISTER** (IRE) 55
439 **THE INFORMANT** (GB) 41
461 **THE ISLANDER** (IRE) 26
658 **THE ITALIAN YOB** (IRE) 28
525 **THE JINAD** (IRE) 60
360 **THE JUGGLER** (GB) 45
119 **THE JUGOPOLIST** (IRE) 4
169 **THE KURATOR** (IRE) 27
349 **THE KVILLEKEN** (GB) 32
531 **THE LADY MAGGI** (FR) 89
80 **THE LAMPO GENIE** (GB) 51
341 **THE LAST BRIDGE** (GB) 3
100 **THE LAST CAVALIER** (IRE) 48
365 **THE LAST EURO** (IRE) 54
405 **THE LAST LEG** (IRE) 13
371 **THE LAST MELON** (GB) 14
399 **THE LAST SAMURI** (IRE) 152
137 **THE LATE SHIFT** (GB) 36
154 **THE LION MAN** (IRE) 24
7 **THE LOCK MASTER** (IRE) 54
526 **THE MAGPIE MAN** (IRE) 3
33 **THE MAJOR** (GB) 78
547 **THE MANX TOUCH** (IRE) F 55
249 **THE MIGHTY EAGLE** (GB) 88
622 **THE MISSUS** (GB) 8
521 **THE MOBB** (IRE) 5
170 **THE MOUSE DOCTOR** (IRE) 25
354 **THE MUMPER** (IRE) 107
41 **THE MUNSHI** (GB) 18
610 **THE MUSICAL GUY** (IRE) 81
9 **THE NAB** (USA) 27
193 **THE NAME IS JAMES** (GB) 26
513 **THE NAME'S BOND** (GB) 34
290 **THE NAMES HARRY** (GB) 6
468 **THE NEPHEW** (IRE) 81
190 **THE NEW MASTER** (GB) 44
610 **THE NEW ONE** (IRE) 82
626 **THE NEW PHARAOH** (IRE) 13
578 **THE OLYMPUS MAN** (GB) 26
616 **THE OMEN** (GB) 100
376 **THE OPPIDAN** (IRE) 60
1 **THE ORANGE ROGUE** (IRE) 37
141 **THE OSTEOPATH** (IRE) 4
238 **THE OULD LAD** (IRE) 56
455 **THE OUTLAW** (IRE) 114
489 **THE PACKAGE** (GB) 104
334 **THE PANAMA KID** (IRE) 47
440 **THE PAPARRAZI KID** (IRE) 152
473 **THE PARIS SHRUG** (GB) 62
274 **THE PEAKY BLINDER** (GB) 43
657 **THE PERFECT CRIME** (IRE) 65
354 **THE PIRATE'S QUEEN** (IRE) 108
13 **THE PLAYFUL PRIEST** (IRE) 37
100 **THE POCKET DOT** (GB) 49
432 **THE POODLE FAKER** (GB) 19
31 **THE PURCHASER** (IRE) 18
274 **THE RAMBLIN KID** (GB) 44
300 **THE RATTLER OBRIEN** (IRE) 15
656 **THE REBEL LADY** (IRE) G 78
176 **THE RECTIFIER** (USA) 12
99 **THE REEL WAY** (GR) 14
604 **THE RIGHT MIX** (IRE) 11
94 **THE RIGHT TIME** (GB) 57
56 **THE ROAD AHEAD** (GB) 37
132 **THE ROMFORD PELE** (IRE) 47
468 **THE SAINT JAMES** (FR) 82
13 **THE SCARLETT WOMAN** (GB) 38
187 **THE SCOURGE** (IRE) 77
100 **THE SCREAMER** (IRE) F 146
596 **THE SHRIMP** (IRE) 18
555 **THE SHROPSHIRE LAD** (GB) 68
304 **THE SKYFARMER** (GB) 104
543 **THE SNAPPY POET** (GB) 39
575 **THE SNEEZER** (IRE) 8
101 **THE SOCIETY MAN** (IRE) 14
342 **THE SPECIAL HOUSE** (IRE) 80
122 **THE SPECIAL ONE** (IRE) 91
531 **THE SQUINTY BRIDGE** (GB) 90
497 **THE STEWARD** (USA) 13
187 **THE STORYTELLER** (IRE) 78
592 **THE TICHBORNE** (IRE) 8
607 **THE TIME HAS COME** (IRE) 25
203 **THE TIN MAN** (GB) 49
531 **THE TOFT** (GB) 91
354 **THE TOURARD MAN** (IRE) 109
424 **THE TRACTOR MAN** (IRE) 16
302 **THE TWISLER** (GB) 93
354 **THE UNIT** (IRE) 110
639 **THE VENERABLE BEDE** (IRE) 40
531 **THE VILLAGE** (IRE) 92
616 **THE WALLACE LINE** (IRE) 101
461 **THE WARRIOR** (IRE) 103
422 **THE WAY YOU DANCE** (IRE) 22
534 **THE WEE BARRA** (IRE) 75
223 **THE WEE CHIEF** (IRE) 7
651 **THE WEE MIDGET** (GB) 6
464 **THE WEST'S AWAKE** (IRE) 31
442 **THE WESTENER BOY** (IRE) 9
555 **THE WESTERN FORCE** (IRE) 69
349 **THE WEXFORDIAN** (IRE) 33
353 **THE WHITE DUKE** (IRE) 14
407 **THE WINKING PRAWN** (IRE) 35
110 **THE WISE LADY** (FR) C 70
120 **THE WISPE** (GB) 46
266 **THE WORLD** (GB) F 167
504 **THE WOW SIGNAL** (IRE) 52
94 **THE YANK** (GB) 58
436 **THE YOUNG MASTER** (GB) 61
237 **THEA'S DANCE** (GB) 9
251 **THEATRE ACT** (GB) 32
598 **THEATRE GUIDE** (IRE) 51
588 **THEATREBAR** (GB) 29
598 **THEATRICAL STAR** (GB) 52
399 **THEATRICAL STYLE** (IRE) 153
533 **THECORNISHBARRON** (IRE) 20
533 **THECORNISHCOWBOY** (GB) 10
639 **THECORRUPTOR** (IRE) 41
629 **THEDFACTOR** (IRE) 6
13 **THEDRINKYMEISTER** (IRE) 39
607 **THEE AND ME** (IRE) 26
612 **THEFRIENDLYGREMLIN** (GB) 8
38 **THEHILL OFTHE ROCK** (IRE) 27
404 **THEHOODLUM** (GB) 6
294 **THEINVAL** (FR) 138
672 **THEIONLADY** (IRE) 13
616 **THELIGNY** (FR) 102
146 **THELORDBEWITHYOU** (IRE) 22
33 **THEM AND US** (IRE) 52
97 **THEMANFROM MINELLA** (IRE) 33
27 **THEME ASTRAL** (FR) 13
239 **THEO'S CHARM** (IRE) 21
52 **THEODORICO** (IRE) 109
617 **THEOLOGY** (GB) 26
266 **THEORY OF LAW** (GB) F 168
468 **THERE IS NO POINT** (IRE) 83
172 **THERE WITH ME** (USA) C 96
280 **THERE YOU GO** (IRE) 49
455 **THERE'S NO PANIC** (IRE) 115
306 **THERE'S TWO** (IRE) F 7
471 **THEREGOESTHETRUTH** (IRE) 17
399 **THEREORTHEREABOUTS** (IRE) 154
242 **THEREVEREND CLOVER** (GB) 4
201 **THERMAL COLUMN** (IRE) 145
523 **THEROADTOGOREY** (IRE) 4
271 **THESPIS OF ICARIA** (IRE) 7
583 **THETIS** (IRE) 157
287 **THEUNNAMEDSOLDIER** (GB) 31
657 **THEWAYTOSANJOSE** (IRE) G 82
297 **THEWESTWALIAN** (USA) 11
104 **THEYDON BOIS** (GB) 7
104 **THEYDON THUNDER** (GB) 8
607 **THICK AS THEIVES** (GB) 27
27 **THINDY** (FR) 50
94 **THINGER LICHT** (FR) 59
504 **THINGS CHANGE** (IRE) 37
435 **THINK** (GB) 5
656 **THINK ITS ALL OVER** (USA) 79
342 **THINK SNOW** (USA) 81
598 **THIRD ACT** (IRE) 53
136 **THIRD DIMENSION** (FR) G 65
379 **THIRD DIMENSION** (GB) 15
598 **THIRD INTENTION** (IRE) 54
425 **THIRD STRIKE** (GB) 103
201 **THIRD TIME LUCKY** (IRE) 146
379 **THIRTEEN DIAMONDS** (IRE) 16
91 **THIS IS ME** (GB) 6
11 **THIS IS TOO** (IRE) 20
531 **THIS THYNE JUDE** (GB) 93
598 **THISTLECRACK** (GB) 55
639 **THOM THUMB** (IRE) 42

# LATE ENTRIES

## MR RICHARD BRABAZON, Curragh

Postal: **Rangers Lodge, The Curragh, Co. Kildare, Ireland**
Contacts: **PHONE 00353 (0) 45 441259 FAX 00353 (0) 45 441906 MOBILE 00353 (0) 87 2515626**
**E-MAIL richardbrabazon@eircom.net WEBSITE www.richardbrabazon.ie**

1 **FLOWING AIR (IRE),** 5, b m Authorized (IRE)—Al Kamah (USA) **Mrs Alice Perry & Richard Brabazon**
2 **KORBOUS (IRE),** 6, ch g Choisir (AUS)—Puppet Play (IRE) **Mrs F. D. McAuley**
3 **PLACERE (IRE),** 7, ch m Noverre (USA)—Puppet Play (IRE) **Mrs F. D. McAuley**

### THREE-YEAR-OLDS

4 B g Archipenko (USA)—Flor Y Nata (USA) **Richard Brabazon**
5 B g Duke of Marmalade (IRE)—Quest For Eternity (IRE) **David Moran**

### TWO-YEAR-OLDS

6 Ch g 13/4 Archipenko (USA)—Nadeszhda (Nashwan (USA)) (5555) **Richard Brabazon**

## MR J. C. ROUGET, Pau

Postal: **Chemin de la Foret Bastard, Domaine de l'Aragnon, 64000 Pau, France**
Contacts: **PHONE (0033) 5593 32790 FAX (0033) 5593 32930 MOBILE (0033) 6102 70335**
**E-MAIL ste.rouget@orange.fr**

1 **AVENIR CERTAIN (FR),** 4, b f Le Havre (IRE)—Puggy (IRE) **A. Caro & G. Augustin-Normand**
2 **BAINO HOPE (FR),** 4, b f Jeremy (USA)—Baino Ridge (FR) **Ecurie I.M. Fares**
3 **CHANCELIER (FR),** 5, b g Peer Gynt (JPN)—Particuliere **G. Augustin-Normand & J.-C. Rouget (S)**
4 **ELUSIVE KAY (FR),** 4, b f Elusive City (USA)—Lunashkaya **A. Jathiere**
5 **ESPERO (FR),** 6, gr g Verglas (IRE)—Queen's Conquer **G. Augustin-Normand & J-C Rouget (S)**
6 **ETALONDES (FR),** 5, b h Royal Applause—Fancy Dance **G. Augustin-Normand**
7 **FREE WALK (FR),** 5, b h Librettist (USA)—River Ballade (USA) **J. F. Gribomont**
8 **GRACE OF LOVE (IRE),** 4, b f Lawman (FR)—Rampoldina **P. Augier & J-C Rouget (S)**
9 **HONEYMOON COCKTAIL (FR),** 4, gr c Martaline—Caipirinia (FR) **D-Y Treves**
10 **KENDEMAI (FR),** 4, b c Carlotamix (FR)—Kendorya (FR) **B. Belinguier & J-C Rouget (S)**
11 **L'ARDENT (FR),** 4, ch c Soldier of Fortune (IRE)—Princesse de Viane (FR) **B. Magrez Horses**
12 **LORESHO (FR),** 4, b c Halling (USA)—Luna Gulch (FR) **H. H. Aga Khan**
13 **LUANNAN (IRE),** 4, b c Zamindar (USA)—Laxlova (FR) **H. H. Aga Khan**
14 **PASSION BLANCHE,** 4, b f Dutch Art—Siren Sound **B. Magrez Horses & J-C Roget**
15 **PRINCE GIBRALTAR (FR),** 4, ch c Rock of Gibraltar (IRE)—
Princess Sofia (UAE) **Gribomont, Ecurie du Loup & Ecurie La Vallee Martigny**
16 **SAANE (FR),** 4, b g Le Havre (IRE)—Salamon **G Augustin-Normand**
17 **SAINT GREGOIRE (FR),** 4, b c Le Havre (IRE)—Scapegrace (IRE) **G Augustin-Normand**
18 **SILAS MARNER (FR),** 8, b h Muhtathir—Street Kendra (FR) **A. Jathiere**
19 **SPEED ROAD (FR),** 4, ch c King's Best (USA)—Life On The Road (IRE) **L. Dassault**
20 **SUNNY (FR),** 6, ch g Muhtathir—Vol Sauvage (FR) **B. Margrez Horses & J-C Rouget**
21 **TRADER OF FORTUNE (FR),** 4, b c Soldier of Fortune (IRE)—
Back The Winner (IRE) **Ecurie J-L Tepper & F. McNulty**
22 **WIRELESS (FR),** 4, ch c Kentucky Dynamite (USA)—Sachet (USA) **Ecurie I M Fares**
23 **ZLATAN IN PARIS (FR),** 4, b c Slickly (FR)—Tossup (USA) **Ecurie J-L Tepper & F. McNulty**

### THREE-YEAR-OLDS

24 **ADARA (FR),** ch f Charge d'affaires—Malinday (FR) **O. Carli & M. G. Augustin-Normand**
25 **AIMLESS LADY,** b f Peer Gynt (JPN)—Poet's Studio (USA) **Ecurie M. Sardou / J.-C. Rouget (s)**
26 **AL ALNOOD (IRE),** ch f New Approach (IRE)—Tierra Luna (IRE) **Al Shaqab Racing**
27 **AL ANQA,** b f Galileo (IRE)—Zaneton (FR) **Al Shaqab Racing**
28 **AL DWEHA (IRE),** b f Invincible Spirit (IRE)—Romie's Kastett (GER) **Al Shaqab Racing**
29 **ALCOY,** b c Aussie Rules (USA)—Breath of Love (USA) **Ecurie A. Caro**
30 **ANNOUVILLE (FR),** b f Air Chief Marshal (IRE)—Langrune (IRE) **G. Augustin-Normand**
31 **ANTOGNONI,** b c Nayef (USA)—Tanguista (FR) **Mme M. Hervet & J.-C. Rouget (s)**
32 **AUCUN DOUTE (IRE),** b f Elusive City (USA)—Corrozal (GER) **B. Magrez Horses**

## MR J. C. ROUGET—continued

33 **BLUEGRASS (FR),** ch c Kentucky Dynamite (USA)—Little Jaw **Ecurie I M Fares**
34 **BROADWAY BOOGIE (IRE),** b c Distorted Humor (USA)—Grande Melody (IRE) **J. Allen**
35 **CARLO BAY,** b c Diktat—Lady Cree (IRE) **Mme M. Hervet**
36 **CAYIRLI (FR),** b g Medicean—Clarinda (FR) **H. H. Aga Khan**
37 **CHEREK (FR),** b c Paco Boy (IRE)—Cherryxma (FR) **H. H. Aga Khan**
38 **CLISHET,** b c Sinndar (IRE)—Sachet (USA) **Ecurie I. M. Fares**
39 **CLOSER TO HOME (IRE),** b c Soldier of Fortune (IRE)—
Maid For Music (IRE) **Ecurie M. Sardou / J.-C. Rouget (S)**
40 **CROSSTHEWIRE (IRE),** b c Cape Cross (IRE)—Lady Elgar (IRE) **Ecurie I.M. Fares**
41 **DACHENKA,** b f Dansili—Blaze of Colour **Caudra Montalban**
42 **DANCE ON THE HILL (IRE),** br f Danehill Dancer (IRE)—Hitra (USA) **Ecurie J.-L. Tepper**
43 **DELIVRANCE,** b f Makfi—Mrs Ting (USA) **Ecurie La Vallee Martigny / Lachaud / De Villeneuve**
44 **DESIRE TO WIN (IRE),** b f Lawman (FR)—Perfidie (IRE) **Qatar Racing Limited**
45 **DUKE OF DUNDEE (FR),** b g Duke of Marmalade (IRE)—Santa Louisia **Ecurie J. - L. Tepper**
46 **EASY FEELING,** b f Elusive Quality (USA)—Wonder Woman (USA) **J. Allen**
47 **EDILISA (IRE),** b f Azamour (IRE)—Elbasana (IRE) **S. A. Aga Khan**
48 **ELKA (IRE),** b f Elusive City (USA)—Lunashkaya **A. Jathiere**
49 **ELUSIVE PARTICLE,** b g Elusive City (USA)—From This Day On (USA) **K. M. Al Attiyah**
50 **ERVEDYA (FR),** b f Siyouni (FR)—Elva (IRE) **S. A. Aga Khan**
51 **FEE D'ARTOIS (FR),** b f Palace Episode (USA)—Vallabelle (FR) **O. Carli**
52 **GHARBEYA (USA),** gr ro f More Than Ready (USA)—Muhaawara (USA) **Hamdan Al Maktoum**
53 **GOJICI,** b c Whipper (USA)—Life On The Road (IRE) **Ecurie Lafeu**
54 **HARPY (IRE),** b f Makfi—Miss Wind (FR) **Qatar Racing & Al Shaqab Racing**
55 **HENRI'S DELIGHT,** b f Henrythenavigator (USA)—Belle Turquoise (FR) **Ecurie I. M. Fares**
56 **HONORARY DEGREE,** b g Elusive City (USA)—Heliocentric (FR) **M. Schwartz**
57 **ILIOUSHKA (IRE),** b f Iffraaj—Pearlescence (USA) **A. Jathiere**
58 **INTO THE MYSTIC (IRE),** ch f Galileo (IRE)—Tamazirte (IRE) **R. C. Porter**
59 **JAY GATSBY,** b c Giant's Causeway (USA)—Starry Dreamer (USA) **J. Allen**
60 **KARENINE,** b f High Chaparral (IRE)—Louvain (IRE) **A. Jathiere & E. Puerari**
61 **KENCHAROVA (FR),** b f Kendargent (FR)—Kirona **A. Jathiere**
62 **KERMAN (FR),** b c Invincible Spirit (IRE)—Kerasha (FR) **S. A. Aga Khan**
63 **KEZAH (FR),** ch f Zamindar (USA)—Sanada (IRE) **Ecurie des Monceaux / Qatar Racing Limited**
64 **KHAYRAWANI (FR),** b c Oratorio (IRE)—Khazina (FR) **S. A. Aga Khan**
65 **LA CORNICHE,** b f Naaqoos—Mademoisellechichi (FR) **Augier, Rouget, Tepper**
66 **LA RENAISSANCE,** b f Astronomer Royal (USA)—America Nova (FR) **Ecurie La Boetie / Boetie Racing**
67 **LARVOTTO,** b c Astronomer Royal (USA)—Senderlea (IRE) **Mme M. Hervet**
68 **LE DEPUTE (FR),** ch c Literato (FR)—
Hamida (USA) **La Vallee Martigny/ C-A. du Buisson de Courson/P. Vigier/ J. L. Dupont**
69 **LE VAGABOND (FR),** bl c Footstepsinthesand—Miryale (FR) **B. Margrez Horses**
70 **LIGHT IN PARIS (IRE),** b f Aussie Rules (USA)—Grande Rousse (FR) **Ecurie J.-L. Tepper & G. Ben Lassin**
71 **LOUCELLES (FR),** gr f Le Havre (IRE)—Love In Paradise **G. Augustin Normand**
72 **LUCELLE (IRE),** b f High Chaparral (IRE)—Larceny (IRE) **Ecurie des Charmes / Haras de la Morsangliere**
73 **MAFAAHIM,** ch c Arcano (IRE)—Mawaakeb (USA) **Hamdan Al Maktoum**
74 **MALVASIA,** b f Hannouma (IRE)—
Charmer Sweet (USA) **Chauvigny Global Equine SAS, S. Brogi & J.-C. Rouget**
75 **MANAASEK (IRE),** b c Raven's Pass (USA)—Thaahira (USA) **Hamdan Al Maktoum**
76 **MANCORA (FR),** ch f Iffraaj—Mantadive (FR) **P. Segalot**
77 **MAPATONICK (FR),** b c Peer Gynt (JPN)—Symphonie Bere (FR) **Seche, Vallee Lambert & Rouget**
78 **MARTINENGO (ITY),** b c Red Rocks (IRE)—Queen Cheap **M. B. Weill & M. D.-Y. Treves**
79 **MASTERBLASTER (FR),** b c Sunday Break (JPN)—Monatora (FR) **D.-Y. Treves / H. Parkes / SNC Regnier**
80 **MEAN STREET,** b g Hannouma (IRE)—Spark Sept (FR) **D.-Y. Treves**
81 **MISTY LOVE (FR),** b c Duke of Marmalade (IRE)—Misty Heights **Scuderia Aleali SRL**
82 **MONSIEUR CAB (FR),** b c Mastercraftsman (IRE)—Oakcabin (IRE) **Scuderia Aleali SRL**
83 **MOONLIGHT IN PARIS (FR),** b f Literato (FR)—Isalou (FR) **Ecurie J-L Tepper**
84 **MY YEAR IS A DAY,** b f King's Best (USA)—Aliyeska (IRE) **D.-Y. Treves**
85 **NEVERTALK IN PARIS (IRE),** b c Azamour (IRE)—Top Toss (IRE) **Ecurie J.-L. Tepper**
86 **NIGHT RUN (FR),** gr c Martaline—Spring Morning (FR) **D.-Y Treves**
87 **PENEBSCOT (IRE),** b c Lawman (FR)—Curgell (FR) **D.-Y. Treves**
88 **PEPPY MILLER (FR),** ch f Iffraaj—Shining Vale (USA) **D.-Y. Treves**
89 **PINARUH,** b br f Iffraaj—Banyu Dewi (GER) **Qatar Racing Limited**
90 **PITORE (IRE),** b c Bernardini (USA)—Peinture Rose (USA) **A. Jathiere / J. P. J. Dubois**
91 **PLUMETOT (FR),** ch c Le Havre (IRE)—Polysheba (FR) **G. Augustin-Normand**
92 **POLITICAL ACT,** b f Political Force (USA)—Rare Blend (USA) **J. Allen**
93 **PONTORSON (FR),** ch c Le Havre (IRE)—Pennedepie **G. Augustin-Normand**
94 **QAWAAREB (IRE),** ch c Teofilo (IRE)—Masaafat **Hamdan Al Maktoum**
95 **RAFAADAH,** br f Oasis Dream—Joanna (IRE) **Hamdan Al Maktoum**

## MR J. C. ROUGET—continued

96 **RAT PACK (IRE),** gr c Verglas (IRE)—How High The Sky (IRE) **D.-Y. Treves & G. Augustin-Normand**
97 **RIFJAH (IRE),** b f Dubawi (IRE)—Mohafazaat (IRE) **Hamdan Al Maktoum**
98 **ROMEO LIMA,** b c Medaglia d'Oro (USA)—Storybook (UAE) **J. Allen**
99 **SALAD MOOD (USA),** ch f Malibu Moon (USA)—Miss Salsa (USA) **Ecurie I.M. Fares**
100 **SENORA DE LA PLATA (FR),** b f Evasive—Quellaffaire (FR) **M. Chartier**
101 **SLON HE,** b g Danehill Dancer (IRE)—Key Figure **Zerolo, McNulty, Puerari & Gravereaux**
102 **STAY THE NIGHT (USA),** b f Arch (USA)—Louve Royale (IRE) **J. Allen**
103 **STON (IRE),** gr c Lope de Vega (IRE)—Lady Raj (USA) **P. Beziat/J.-C. Rouget (S)/S. Lauray/P. Moreno**
104 **SUPER SISTER (ITY),** b f Orpen (USA)—Torrian (IRE) **D.-Y. Treves**
105 **TANIYAR (IRE),** b c Shamardal (USA)—Tanoura (IRE) **S. A. Aga Khan**
106 **TEAM COLORS,** b c Street Cry (IRE)—Teammate (USA) **J. Allen**
107 **VELANNDA (FR),** b f Sea The Stars (IRE)—Valima (FR) **H. H. Aga Khan**
108 **VISOLIYA (FR),** gr f Nayef (USA)—Visionnaire (FR) **H. H. Aga Khan**
109 **VIYANA (IRE),** b f Azamour (IRE)—Virana (IRE) **S. A. Aga Khan**
110 **WAR DISPATCH,** b c War Front (USA)—Photograph (USA) **J. Allen**
111 **WEEKELA,** b f Hurricane Run (IRE)—Moonrise (GER) **D.-Y. Treves**
112 **WELCOME IN PARIS,** b f Azamour (IRE)—Caipirinia (FR) **Ecurie J.-L. Tepper & Mme G. Forien**
113 **ZAFIRO (FR),** b c Sageburg (IRE)—La Romagne (FR) **A. Caro**
114 **ZARIDIYA (IRE),** b f Duke of Marmalade (IRE)—Zarkalia (IRE) **S. A. Aga Khan**
115 **ZUMA BEACH,** b f Showcasing—Bandanna **D.-Y. Treves**
116 **ZVARKHOVA (FR),** ch f Makfi—Varsity **A. Jathiere**
117 **ZVETKA (IRE),** b f Lawman (FR)—Shepton Mallet (FR) **A. Jathiere**
118 **ZYRJANN (IRE),** ch c Rock of Gibraltar (IRE)—Zariziyna (IRE) **S. A. Aga Khan**

## TWO-YEAR-OLDS

119 **A SONG FOR YOU,** b f 30/3 Makfi—Isabella Glyn (IRE) (Sadler's Wells (USA)) (40000) **D.-Y. Treves**
120 **ABOULIE (IRE),** b f 14/2 Exceed And Excel (AUS)—
Anja (IRE) (Indian Ridge) **Haras d'Etreham / M. Lagasse / Riviera Equine**
121 **ACADEMIC (IRE),** ch c 29/4 Zamindar (USA)—Heliocentric (FR) (Galileo (IRE)) **M. Schwartz**
122 **AFSANE (FR),** b f 21/5 Siyouni (FR)—La Barquera (Nayef (USA)) (43650) **D.-Y. Treves**
123 Ch c 21/2 Sea The Stars (IRE)—Aiglonne (USA) (Silver Hawk (USA)) (238095) **Al Shaqab Racing**
124 **AJOU (FR),** b f 18/3 Siyouni (FR)—Azucar (IRE) (Desert Prince (IRE)) (55555) **G. Augustin-Normand**
125 **ALCYONE (FR),** b c 12/1 Air Chief Marshal (IRE)—
Golding Star (FR) (Gold Away (IRE)) **G. Augustin-Normand / Mme E. Vidal**
126 **ALDABA (FR),** b f 11/3 Loup Breton (IRE)—Mille Etoiles (USA) (Malibu Moon (USA)) **Ecurie A. Caro**
127 **ALLIED COMMAND (USA),** b c 1/1 War Front (USA)—Louve Royale (IRE) (Peintre Celebre (USA)) **J. Allen**
128 **ALMANZOR (FR),** b c 11/3 Wootton Bassett—
Darkova (FR) (Maria's Mon (USA)) (79365) **Ecurie A. Caro / G. Augustin-Normand**
129 **ALNAJMAH,** br f 13/2 Dansili—Joanna (IRE) (High Chaparral (IRE)) **Hamdan Al Maktoum**
130 **AMAZING LADY (GER),** b f 27/2 Lord of England (GER)—
Audrey (GER) (Sholokhov (IRE)) (7936) **P. Beziat / S. Lauray**
131 **AMERICAN WHIPPER (FR),** b c 20/2 Whipper (USA)—
Abondante (USA) (Thunder Gulch (USA)) (21428) **P. Augier / Ecurie du Loup**
132 B f 16/4 Turtle Bowl (IRE)—Ashalina (FR) (Linamix (FR)) **H. H. Aga Khan**
133 B f 1/1 Holy Roman Emperor (IRE)—Baino Ridge (FR) (Highest Honor (FR)) (59523) **Ecurie I. M. Fares**
134 **BAROU (FR),** b c 21/4 Le Havre (IRE)—Salamon (Montjeu (IRE)) **G. Augustin-Normand**
135 B c 23/3 Muhtathir—Benzolina (IRE) (Second Empire (IRE)) (41269) **Ecurie La Boetie**
136 **BEYCHEVELLE (USA),** b f 20/4 War Front (USA)—La Conseillante (USA) (Elusive Quality (USA)) **J. Allen**
137 **BEYNOSTORM (FR),** ch c 24/4 Stormy River (FR)—Beynotown (Authorized (IRE)) **Ecurie I.M. Fares**
138 B f 16/2 Exceed And Excel (AUS)—Bikini Babe (IRE) (Montjeu (IRE)) (285714) **Al Shaqab Racing**
139 **BILLIONNAIRE (IRE),** gr c 6/3 Acclamation—Marie Rossa (Testa Rossa (AUS)) (51587) **C & L Marzocco**
140 **CAMP COURAGE (USA),** b c 4/4 War Front (USA)—Storybook (UAE) (Halling (USA)) **J. Allen**
141 **CANDLE IN THE WIND (FR),** b f 24/2 Lope de Vega (IRE)—
Talon Bleu (FR) (Anabaa Blue) (47619) **Ecurie J.-L. Tepper**
142 B f 1/3 Invincible Spirit (IRE)—Causa Proxima (FR) (Kendor (FR)) (158730) **Al Shaqab Racing**
143 B c 28/4 Azamour (IRE)—Cherryxma (FR) (Linamix (FR)) **H. H. Aga Khan**
144 **CLAIRE DE LUNE (IRE),** ch f 3/5 Galileo (IRE)—Solo de Lune (IRE) (Law Society (USA)) **J. Allen**
145 B c 1/1 Azamour (IRE)—Clarinda (FR) (Montjeu (IRE)) **H. H. Aga Khan**
146 **CLEON (FR),** ch c 11/1 Zafeen (FR)—
Santa Christiana (FR) (Danehill Dancer (IRE)) (19047) **G. Augustin-Normand / Mme E. Vidal**
147 **COUDREE (FR),** b f 17/4 King's Best (USA)—Resafe (FR) (Poliglote) (22222) **D.-Y. Treves**
148 **CROSS TIE WALKER (IRE),** gr c 6/3 Cape Cross (IRE)—
Netrebko (IRE) (Linamix (FR)) (25000) **Ecurie J.-L. Tepper / J.-C. Rouget**
149 **DARICE (IRE),** b f 11/4 Cape Cross (IRE)—Darakiyla (IRE) (Last Tycoon) **Razza Pallorsi SNC**
150 **DAYANA (FR),** ch f 1/1 Iffraaj—Decouverte (IRE) (Rainbow Quest (USA)) (55555) **Ecurie J.-L. Tepper**

## MR J. C. ROUGET—continued

**151** Gr c 4/3 Azamour (IRE)—Diasilixa (FR) (Linamix (FR)) **H. H. Aga Khan**
**152** Ch c 15/1 Sea The Stars (IRE)—Don't Hurry Me (IRE) (Hurricane Run (IRE)) (206349) **Al Shaqab Racing**
**153 DREAM OF ARC (FR),** b f 23/2 Hurricane Cat (USA)—Kunoichi (USA) (Vindication (USA)) (30158) **J.-F. Gribomont**
**154 DUC DES LOGES (FR),** ch c 30/4 Le Havre (IRE)—Birdy Namnam (USA) (Langfuhr (CAN)) **Le Clerc, Ecurie du Loup, Ecurie La Vallee Martigny, Prouveur**
**155 ECHAUFFOUR (FR),** b c 1/4 Le Havre (IRE)—Langrune (IRE) (Fasliyev (USA)) **G. Augustin-Normand**
**156** Ch f 26/4 Exceed And Excel (AUS)—Elva (IRE) (King's Best (USA)) **S. A. Aga Khan**
**157 ET TOI ET MOI (FR),** b f 1/1 Footstepsinthesand—En Vitesse (Peintre Celebre (USA)) (79365) **Riviera Equine**
**158 ETERNITE (IRE),** b f 4/3 Mastercraftsman (IRE)—Time Pressure (Montjeu (IRE)) (71428) **Ecurie La Vallee Martigny, Ecurie des Charmes, Skymarc Farm**
**159** B c 18/3 Acclamation—Frangy (Sadler's Wells (USA)) (87301) **Ecurie des Monceaux**
**160 FRANKO FOLIE (FR),** b f 27/4 Kendargent (FR)—Atlantic Festival (USA) (Theatrical) (25396) **D.-Y. Treves**
**161 FRESH AIR (IRE),** b f 16/2 Montjeu (IRE)—Silver Star (Zafonic (USA)) **J. Allen**
**162 FRONT PAGE STORY (USA),** b f 1/1 War Front (USA)—Tempo West (USA) (Rahy (USA)) **J. Allen**
**163 GARBOE (IRE),** b f 20/1 Montjeu (IRE)—Kasora (IRE) (Darshaan) **J. Allen**
**164 GEORGE PATTON (USA),** gr ro c 21/2 War Front (USA)—Photograph (USA) (Unbridled's Song (USA)) **J. Allen**
**165 GETBACK IN PARIS (IRE),** ch c 24/1 Galileo (IRE)—Elusive Wave (IRE) (Elusive City (USA)) **Tepper, Magnier, Smith, Tabor**
**166 GHAALY,** b c 30/3 Tamayuz—Ghizlaan (USA) (Seeking The Gold (USA)) **Hamdan Al Maktoum**
**167 GOONA CHOPE (FR),** b f 8/2 Namid—Gooseley Lane (Pyramus (USA)) (39682) **A. Chopard / F. Nicolle / J.-C. Rouget (S)**
**168 GREGORACI (FR),** bl f 10/4 Poet's Voice—Gaudera (GER) (Big Shuffle (USA)) (31746) **C. & L. Marzocco**
**169** B c 11/3 Tale of The Cat (USA)—Gypsy Hollow (USA) (Dixieland Band (USA)) (71428) **Al Shaqab Racing**
**170 HATTAAB,** b c 1/5 Intikhab (USA)—Sundus (USA) (Sadler's Wells (USA)) **Hamdan Al Maktoum**
**171 HEAR AND NOW (IRE),** b f 21/4 Galileo (IRE)—Absolutelyfabulous (IRE) (Mozart (IRE)) **J. Allen**
**172 HIGH SCHOOL DAYS (USA),** ch f 30/4 Elusive Quality (USA)—Baroness Richter (IRE) (Montjeu (IRE)) **J. Allen**
**173 HIGHWAY MARY (USA),** b f 26/4 U S Ranger (USA)—Wandering Star (USA) (Red Ransom (USA)) **J. Allen**
**174 HOUSE OF DIXIE (USA),** b f 24/5 War Front (USA)—Homebound (USA) (Dixie Union (USA)) **J. Allen**
**175 HURRICANE (FR),** b c 1/1 Hurricane Cat (USA)—Monatora (FR) (Hector Protector (USA)) (14285) **D.-Y. Treves**
**176 IMAGINE IN PARIS (FR),** b f 23/1 Myboycharlie (IRE)—Adamantina (FR) (Muhtathir) (59523) **Ecurie J.-L. Tepper**
**177 IN A GADDA DA VIDA (FR),** b f 30/1 Tamayuz—Sahara Lady (IRE) (Lomitas) (15873) **Ecurie M. Sardou / J.-C. Rouget (S)**
**178 JAZZ IN MONTREUX (FR),** b c 1/1 Rip Van Winkle (IRE)—Back The Winner (IRE) (Entrepreneur) (55555) **D.-Y. Treves**
**179 JUST DANCE,** b f 11/4 Equiano (FR)—Mutoon (IRE) (Erhaab (USA)) (21428) **Kubla Racing/B. Benaych/Mme K. Byrne/S. Brogi**
**180 JUSTWANTACONTACT (IRE),** ch c 23/2 Rock of Gibraltar (IRE)—Just Little (FR) (Grand Slam (USA)) (79365) **Ecurie La Vallee Martigny/Ecurie J.-L. Tepper/N. Saltiel**
**181** B f 19/2 Danehill Dancer (IRE)—Kartica (Rainbow Quest (USA)) (158730) **Al Shaqab Racing**
**182 KERILA (FR),** b f 25/4 Makfi—Kerasha (FR) (Daylami (IRE)) **S. A. Aga Khan**
**183 KHAMRY,** b c 6/2 Poet's Voice—Poppets Sweetlove (Foxhound (USA)) (525000) **Hamdan Al Maktoum**
**184 KINGLIGHT (FR),** b c 7/4 Kendargent (FR)—Vespona (FR) (Vespone (IRE)) (31746) **G. Ben Lassin / Ecurie J.-L. Tepper**
**185 KIPANGA (FR),** b f 1/1 Lawman (FR)—Avventura (USA) (Johannesburg (USA)) (17460) **C. & L. Marzocco**
**186 KLIMTH (FR),** b c 8/2 Peintre Celebre (USA)—Inca Wood (UAE) (Timber Country (USA)) (26984) **D.-Y. Treves**
**187 KOMODO (FR),** b c 8/4 Le Havre (IRE)—Kinlochrannoch (Kyllachy) **G. Augustin-Normand / Mme E. Vidal**
**188 KOTAMA (FR),** b f 27/4 Siyouni (FR)—Kozaka (FR) (Mark of Esteem (IRE)) **S. A. Aga Khan**
**189 L'ENCHANTEUR (FR),** b c 14/3 Caradak (IRE)—Golden Section (USA) (Royal Academy (USA)) (21428) **L. Dassault**
**190 LA CRESSONNIERE (FR),** b f 5/4 Le Havre (IRE)—Absolute Lady (IRE) (Galileo (IRE)) **Ecurie A. Caro / G. Augustin-Normand**
**191 LAKALAS (FR),** b f 13/3 Turtle Bowl (IRE)—Nazlia (FR) (Polish Precedent (USA)) (71428) **Ecurie J.-L. Tepper/ Ecurie des Charmes**
**192 LAKOTA TREATY (IRE),** b f 3/3 Sageburg (IRE)—Peace Talk (FR) (Sadler's Wells (USA)) **M. Zerolo / Mme A. Gravereaux / E. Puerari**
**193 LASSON (FR),** ch c 24/3 Sea The Stars (IRE)—Lady Meydan (FR) (American Post) **G. Augustin-Normand**
**194** B f 27/3 Nayef (USA)—Lemon Twist (IRE) (Marju (IRE)) (57142) **Al Shaqab Racing**
**195 LET IT BE IN PARIS (FR),** b c 12/3 Dark Angel (IRE)—Guiana (GER) (Tiger Hill (IRE)) (63492) **Ecurie J.-L. Tepper / Ecurie La Vallee Martigny / N. Saltiel**
**196 LITTLE GHETTO BOY,** b c 3/3 Lawman (FR)—Ahea (USA) (Giant's Causeway (USA)) (20000) **Ecurie M. Sardou**
**197 LOUP ROYAL (IRE),** b c 9/2 Astronomer Royal (USA)—Lia Waltz (FR) (Linamix (FR)) **Ecurie du Loup/Ecurie La Vallee Martigny/B. Patou/Mme M. Romano**
**198 MAGNOLEA (IRE),** b f 16/3 Acclamation—Carcassonne (IRE) (Montjeu (IRE)) (119047) **F. Salman**
**199 MAIZE AND BLUE (IRE),** b c 26/4 Danehill Dancer (IRE)—Grande Melody (IRE) (Grand Lodge (USA)) **J. Allen**

## MR J. C. ROUGET—continued

**200 MASHKA (IRE),** ch f 4/2 Exceed And Excel (AUS)—
Mambia (Aldebaran (USA)) (126984) **A. Jathiere / G. Laboureau**
**201 MASLOOL (IRE),** b c 19/4 Dream Ahead (USA)—Love And Laughter (IRE) (Theatrical) **Hamdan Al Maktoum**
**202 MESONERA (FR),** b f 17/3 Sunday Break (JPN)—Niska (USA) (Smart Strike (CAN)) (17460) **Ecurie A. Caro**
**203 MEZIDON (FR),** gr c 8/2 Le Havre (IRE)—Belliflore (FR) (Verglas (IRE)) **G. Augustin-Normand / Mme E. Vidal**
**204** B f 15/3 Lawman (FR)—Militante (IRE) (Johannesburg (USA)) (91269) **Qatar Racing Limited**
**205 MILLEPASSI (IRE),** b c 19/3 Holy Roman Emperor (IRE)—Gaselee (USA) (Toccet (USA)) **D.-Y. Treves**
**206** B c 23/2 Halling (USA)—Miss Spinamix (IRE) (Verglas (IRE)) (67460) **Ecurie La Boetie**
**207 MOISVILLE,** br f 14/2 Hat Trick (JPN)—Mixed Intention (IRE) (Elusive City (USA)) **G. Augustin-Normand**
**208** B c 8/5 Galileo (IRE)—Moments of Joy (Darshaan) **Mrs S. Magnier / D. Smith / M. Tabor**
**209 MORE THAN A DREAM (IRE),** b c 19/2 Halling (USA)—Chabelle (Shirocco (GER)) (32000) **D.-Y. Treves**
**210** B f 28/2 Include (USA)—Mouraniya (IRE) (Azamour (IRE)) **S. A. Aga Khan**
**211 MUSHAWWEQ,** b br c 22/2 Dubawi (IRE)—Mudaaraah (Cape Cross (IRE)) **Hamdan Al Maktoum**
**212 MUTAMADED (IRE),** b c 14/2 Arcano (IRE)—Sahaayeb (IRE) (Indian Haven) **Hamdan Al Maktoum**
**213** B f 3/5 Galileo (IRE)—Naissance Royale (IRE) (Giant's Causeway (USA)) (492063) **Al Shaqab Racing**
**214** Ch f 4/3 Lope de Vega (IRE)—Nawal (FR) (Homme de Loi (IRE)) (79365) **Al Shaqab Racing**
**215 NAWARAT,** b f 17/4 Street Sense (USA)—Taseel (USA) (Danzig (USA)) **Hamdan Al Maktoum**
**216 NOINTOT,** b c 1/1 Zamindar (USA)—Zamid (FR) (Namid) (103174) **G. Augustin-Normand / Mme E. Vidal**
**217** B c 1/1 Sea The Stars (IRE)—Olga Prekrasa (USA) (Kingmambo (USA)) (142857) **Al Shaqab Racing**
**218 OMAR BRADLEY (USA),** b c 21/4 War Front (USA)—
Louve des Reves (IRE) (Sadler's Wells (USA)) **Mrs S. Magnier / D. Smith / M. Tabor**
**219 OUEZY (IRE),** br f 22/2 Le Havre (IRE)—Merville (FR) (Montjeu (IRE)) **G. Augustin-Normand**
**220** Ch f 7/4 Zoffany (IRE)—Out of Honour (IRE) (Highest Honor (FR)) (58730) **Qatar Racing Limited**
**221 PASSADOBLE (IRE),** b f 12/2 Dream Ahead (USA)—
Pertinence (IRE) (Fasliyev (USA)) (214285) **Riviera Equine / Haras d'Etreham**
**222** B f 1/1 Rock of Gibraltar (IRE)—Pegase Hurry (USA) (Fusaichi Pegasus (USA)) (23809) **J.-F. Gribomont**
**223 PHENICEAN (IRE),** b c 20/3 Rock of Gibraltar (IRE)—
Public Ransom (IRE) (Red Ransom (USA)) (31746) **E. Puerari / Mme D. Ades-Hazan / M. Henochsberg**
**224 POSITIVE VIBRATION (IRE),** br f 25/4 Canford Cliffs (IRE)—
Midnight Partner (IRE) (Marju (IRE)) (12000) **Ecurie M. Sardou**
**225 PRINCESS DUTCH,** ch f 2/2 Dutch Art—Almahroosa (FR) (Green Tune (USA)) (59523) **S. Boucheron**
**226 RED KITTEN,** b c 31/3 Kitten's Joy (USA)—Red Diadem (Pivotal) **Ecurie I. M. Fares**
**227 RELY ON ME (FR),** b c 7/2 Diamond Green (FR)—
Tirissa (FR) (Country Reel (USA)) (15873) **J. Seche / J.P. Vallee-Lambert**
**228 ROCHENKA,** bl f 1/1 Rock of Gibraltar (IRE)—Lunashkaya (Muhtathir) **A.Jathiere**
**229 ROMAZZINO,** b c 18/2 Rip Van Winkle (IRE)—
Doctors Nurse (USA) (Kingmambo (USA)) (55555) **C. & L. Marzocco**
**230 ROSAY (IRE),** b f 21/2 Raven's Pass (USA)—
Petit Calva (FR) (Desert King (IRE)) (60000) **G. Augustin-Normand / Mme E. Vidal**
**231 SADIA (FR),** b f 17/3 Teofilo (IRE)—Sadiyna (FR) (Sinndar (IRE)) **H. H. Aga Khan**
**232 SAINT SIMEON (IRE),** b c 20/4 Le Havre (IRE)—
Sahara Sonnet (USA) (Stravinsky (USA)) (61904) **G. Augustin-Normand / Mme E. Vidal**
**233 SAVE THE NATION,** ch c 8/5 Sea The Stars (IRE)—
Sefroua (USA) (Kingmambo (USA)) **Riviera Equine Sarl / Haras d'Etreham**
**234** Ch c 1/1 Dubawi (IRE)—Seeharn (IRE) (Pivotal) **Al Shaqab Racing**
**235** Gr c 11/4 Iffraaj—Serasana (Red Ransom (USA)) **S. A. Aga Khan**
**236** B c 12/2 High Chaparral (IRE)—Shamalana (IRE) (Sinndar (IRE)) **S. A. Aga Khan**
**237** B f 8/3 Dark Angel (IRE)—Shamsa (FR) (Selkirk (USA)) **S. A. Aga Khan**
**238** B c 26/3 Rock of Gibraltar (IRE)—Shepton Mallet (FR) (Ocean of Wisdom (USA)) (11904) **M. Zerolo / E. Puerari**
**239 SOME ROMANCE (IRE),** b f 20/4 Galileo (IRE)—Withorwithoutyou (IRE) (Danehill (USA)) **J. Allen**
**240 SOTTEVILLE (FR),** b f 14/2 Le Havre (IRE)—Sandsnow (IRE) (Verglas (IRE)) **G. Augustin-Normand**
**241 STICKY FINGERS (FR),** b c 1/3 Peer Gynt (JPN)—
Honeymoon Suite (FR) (Double Bed (FR)) (20634) **J.-M. Lapoujade / F. Nicolle / J.-C. Rouget (S)**
**242 TAAREEF (USA),** ch c 14/3 Kitten's Joy (USA)—
Sacred Feather (USA) (Carson City (USA)) (387263) **Hamdan Al Maktoum**
**243** B c 7/3 Manduro (GER)—Takaniya (IRE) (Rainbow Quest (USA)) **S. A. Aga Khan**
**244 TAMASHEQ,** b f 1/1 Manduro (GER)—
Tamazirte (IRE) (Danehill Dancer (IRE)) **Ecurie La Vallee Martigny / Ecurie du Loup**
**245 TAMBOURINE MAN (IRE),** br c 11/2 Equiano (FR)—Babycakes (IRE) (Marju (IRE)) (71428) **D.-Y. Treves**
**246 TELL ME NOW (IRE),** b f 12/3 Galileo (IRE)—Sing Softly (USA) (Hennessy (USA)) **J. Allen**
**247 THE TURNING POINT (FR),** b c 18/3 Hurricane Cat (USA)—
L'ete (CHI) (Hussonet (USA)) (18253) **J.P. Barjon/Ec. La Vallee Martigny/J. Seche/J.-C. Rouget (S)**
**248** B c 23/2 Red Rocks (IRE)—Tina Donizetti (IRE) (Monsun (GER)) **D.-Y. Treves**
**249** B f 1/3 Acclamation—Valima (FR) (Linamix (FR)) **H. H. Aga Khan**
**250 VIA ALPINA (IRE),** ch f 25/1 Arakan (USA)—Quela (GER) (Acatenango (GER)) (11904) **D.-Y. Treves**
**251 VOLKHOV (IRE),** gr c 6/3 Kendargent (FR)—Blue Blue Sea (Galileo (IRE)) (103174) **A. Jathiere / G. Laboureau**

## MR J. C. ROUGET—continued

**252** Ch c 17/2 Makfi—Wait And See (FR) (Montjeu (IRE)) (71428) **Qatar Racing Limited**
**253 WAR FLAG (USA),** b f 3/5 War Front (USA)—Black Speck (USA) (Arch (USA)) **J. Allen**
**254 WESTADORA (IRE),** b f 17/3 Le Havre (IRE)—Stranded (Montjeu (IRE)) **Ecurie du Grand Chene**
**255 WIN ON SUNDAY (FR),** ch c 10/3 Never On Sunday (FR)—Go To Win (FR) (Coroner (IRE)) (12698) **D.-Y. Treves**
**256 WINTER COUNT,** gr ro f 20/4 Mizzen Mast (USA)—Louvakhova (USA) (Maria's Mon (USA)) **M. Zerolo / Mme A. Gravereaux**
**257 ZALAMEA (IRE),** b c 14/3 Lope de Vega (IRE)—Tanzania (IRE) (Alzao (USA)) **M. Zerolo / E. Puerari**
**258** B c 13/3 Pivotal—Zaneton (FR) (Mtoto) **E. Puerari / M. Zerolo**
**259 ZGHORTA DANCE (FR),** ch f 28/3 Le Havre (IRE)—Ana Zghorta (Anabaa (USA)) **Ecurie I. M. Fares**
**260 ZVALINSKA,** b f 1/1 Sea The Stars (IRE)—Peinture Rose (USA) (Storm Cat (USA)) (253968) **A. Jathiere**

**Assistant Trainer:** Jean Bernard Roth, Jean Rene Dubosq

**Jockey (flat):** Jean-Bernard Eyquem, Matthias Lauron, Ioritz Mendizabal, Christophe Soumillon.
**Apprentice:** Jefferson Smith, Sofiane Saadi.

# STOP PRESS Additional horses

## MR NOEL WILSON, Middleham

The following horses were received after the trainer's list had been compiled

1 **BACKFORCE,** 7, b g Jelani (IRE)—Scoffera **Mrs J. M. Wandless**
2 **GALVANIZE,** 4, b g Bahamian Bounty—Xtrasensory **NWJB Racing Ltd**

### TWO-YEAR-OLDS

3 Ch f 17/1 Bahamian Bounty—Feabhas (IRE) (Spectrum (IRE)) (3800) **NWJB Racing Ltd**
4 Ch f 10/3 Motivator—New Design (IRE) (Bluebird (USA)) (6000) **NWJB Racing Ltd**
5 B f 30/4 Monsieur Bond (IRE)—Priti Fabulous (IRE) (Invincible Spirit (IRE)) (3500) **NWJB Racing Ltd**
6 Ch c 29/4 Compton Place—Show Off (Efisio) (10000) **NWJB Racing Ltd**
7 **THE NAME'S PAVER,** ch c 21/4 Monsieur Bond (IRE)—Pride of Kinloch (Dr Devious (IRE)) **Mrs C. K. Paver**
8 B f 27/2 Kheleyf (USA)—Tripti (IRE) (Sesaro (USA)) (3500) **NWJB Racing Ltd**
9 Ch f 12/2 Monsieur Bond (IRE)—Zamindari (Zamindar (USA)) (4500) **NWJB Racing Ltd**
10 **ZEPHYR BREEZE,** b c 9/4 Piccolo—Bold Love (Bold Edge) (22000) **Glyn Budden & Roy Phillips**

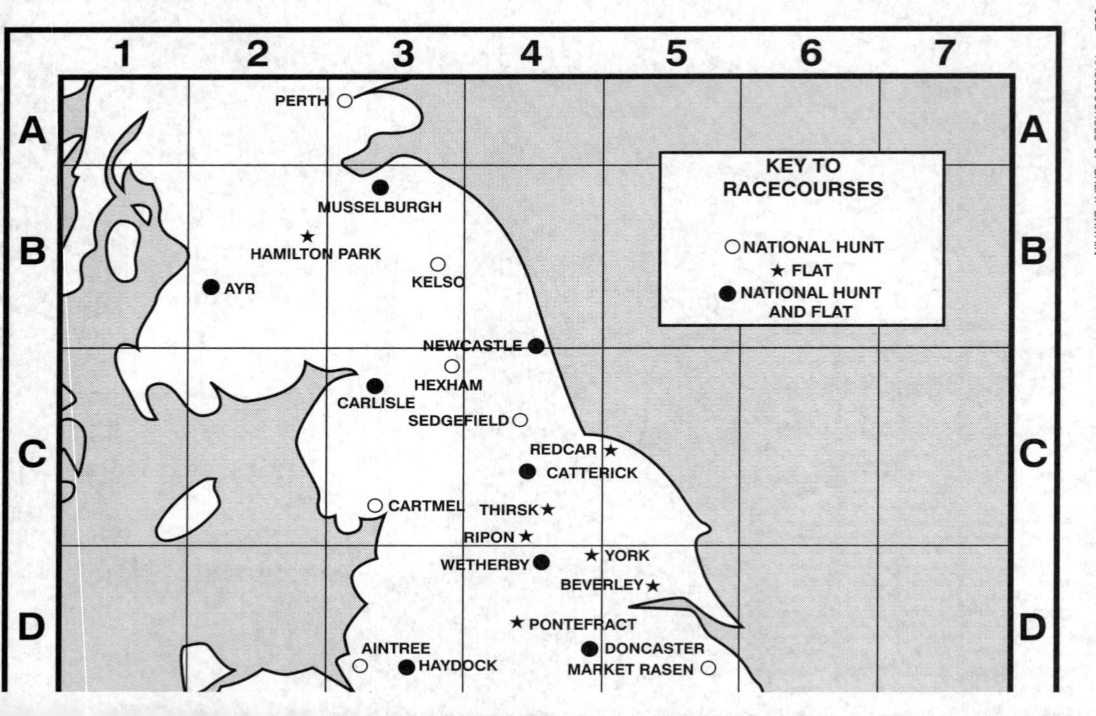
1
2
3
4
5
6
7
A
B
C
D
KEY TO RACECOURSES
NATIONAL HUNT
FLAT
NATIONAL HUNT AND FLAT
PERTH
MUSSELBURGH
HAMILTON PARK
AYR
KELSO
NEWCASTLE
HEXHAM
CARLISLE
SEDGEFIELD
REDCAR
CATTERICK
CARTMEL
THIRSK
RIPON
YORK
WETHERBY
BEVERLEY
PONTEFRACT
AINTREE
DONCASTER
HAYDOCK
MARKET RASEN

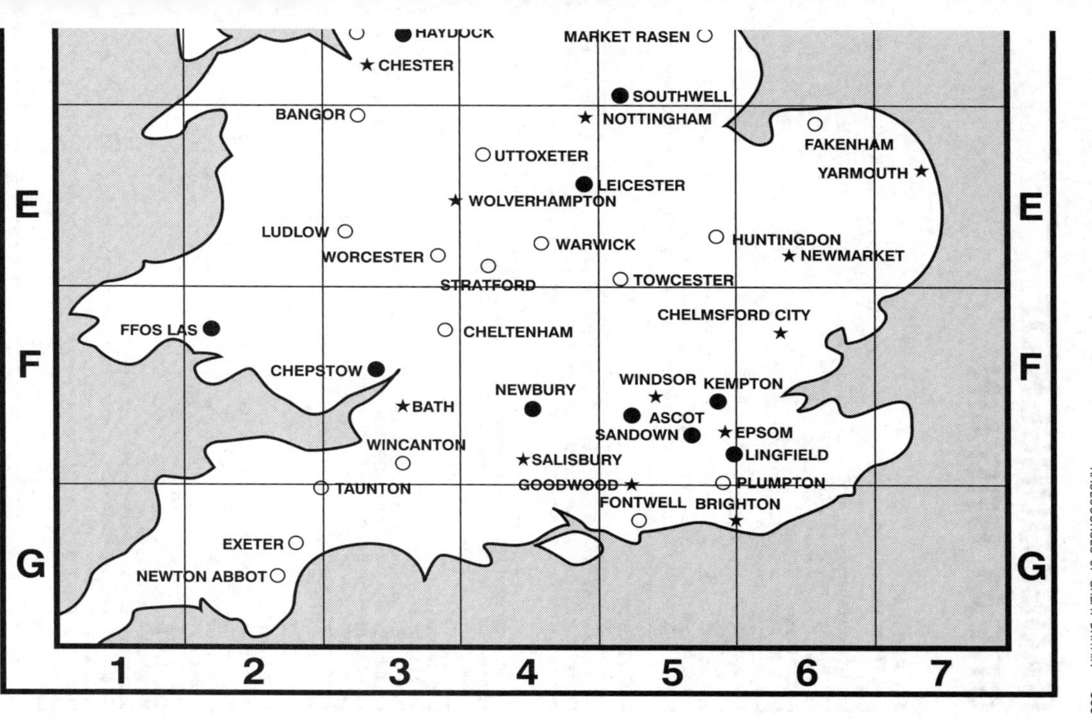
HAYDOCK
MARKET RASEN
CHESTER
SOUTHWELL
BANGOR
NOTTINGHAM
FAKENHAM
UTTOXETER
YARMOUTH
LEICESTER
WOLVERHAMPTON
E
LUDLOW
WORCESTER
WARWICK
HUNTINGDON
NEWMARKET
STRATFORD
TOWCESTER
CHELMSFORD CITY
FFOS LAS
CHELTENHAM
F
CHEPSTOW
WINDSOR
KEMPTON
NEWBURY
BATH
ASCOT
SANDOWN
EPSOM
WINCANTON
LINGFIELD
SALISBURY
GOODWOOD
PLUMPTON
TAUNTON
FONTWELL
BRIGHTON
EXETER
G
NEWTON ABBOT
1
2
3
4
5
6
7

# RACECOURSES OF GREAT BRITAIN

## AINTREE (L.H)

**Grand National Course:** Triangular, 2m 2f (16) 494y run-in with elbow. Perfectly flat. A severe test for both horse and rider, putting a premium on jumping ability, fitness and courage.
**Mildmay Course:** Rectangular, 1m 4f (8) 260y run-in. A very fast, flat course with sharp bends.
**Address:** Aintree Racecourse, Ormskirk Road, Aintree, Liverpool, L9 5AS Tel: 0151 523 2600
Fax: 01515 222920 Website: www.aintree.co.uk
**Regional Director:** John Baker
**Clerk of the Course:** Andrew Tulloch 07831 315104
**Going Reports:** 01515 232600.
**Stabling:** Boxes allocated in strict rotation. Facilities are available on the course for up to 100 stable staff. 01515 222937.
**By Road:** North of the City, near the junction of the M57 and M58 with the A59 (Preston).
**By Rail:** Aintree Station is adjacent to the Stands, from Liverpool Central.
**By Air:** Liverpool (John Lennon) Airport is 10 miles. Helicopter landing facility by prior arrangement.

---

## ASCOT (R.H)

**Flat:** Right-handed triangular track just under 1m 6f in length. The Round course descends from the 1m 4f start into Swinley Bottom, the lowest part of the track. It then turns right-handed and joins the Old Mile Course, which starts on a separate chute. The course then rises to the right-handed home turn over an underpass to join the straight mile course. The run-in is about 3f, rising slightly to the winning post. The whole course is of a galloping nature with easy turns.
**N.H.** Triangular, 1m 6f (10) 240y run-in mostly uphill. A galloping course with an uphill finish, Ascot provides a real test of stamina. The fences are stiff and sound jumping is essential, especially for novices.
**Address:** Ascot Racecourse, Ascot, Berkshire SL5 7JX Tel: 08707 271234 Fax: 08704 601250
Website: www.ascot.co.uk
**Clerk of the Course:** Chris Stickels 01344 878502 / 07970 621440
**Chief Executive:** Guy Henderson
**Going Reports:** Day: 01344 878502
**Stabling:** 175 boxes. Free, with shavings, straw or paper provided. Tel: 01344 878454 Fax: 08704 214755
**By Road:** West of the town on the A329. Easy access from the M3 (Junction 3) and the M4 (Junction 6). Car parking adjoining the course and Ascot Heath.
**By Rail:** Regular service from Waterloo to Ascot (500y from the racecourse).
**By Air:** Helicopter landing facility at the course. London (Heathrow) Airport 15 miles, White Waltham Airfield 12 miles (01427) 718800.

---

## AYR (L.H)

**Flat:** A left-handed, galloping, flat oval track of 1m 4f with a 4f run-in. The straight 6f is essentially flat.
**N.H.** Oval, 1m 4f (9) 210y run-in. Relatively flat and one of the fastest tracks in Great Britain. It is a well-drained course and the ground rarely becomes testing. Suits the long-striding galloper.
**Address:** Ayr Racecourse, Whitletts Road, Ayr KA8 0JE Tel: 01292 264179 Fax: 01292 610140
Website: www.ayr-racecourse.co.uk
**Clerk of the Course:** Emma Marley 07881 908702
**Managing Director:** David Brown
**Going Reports:** Contact Clerk of the Course as above.
**Stabling:** 175 boxes. Free stabling and accommodation for lads and lasses. Tel: 01292 264179 ext 141.
**By Road:** East of the town on the A758. Free parking for buses and cars.
**By Rail:** Ayr Station (trains on the half hour from Glasgow Central). Journey time 55 minutes. Buses and taxis also to the course.
**By Air:** Prestwick International Airport (10 minutes), Glasgow Airport (1 hour).

---

## BANGOR-ON-DEE (L.H)

**N.H.** Circular, 1m 4f (9) 325y run-in. Apart from some 'ridge and furrow', this is a flat course notable for three sharp bends, especially the paddock turn. Suits handy, speedy sorts.
**Address:** Bangor-On-Dee Racecourse, Overton Road, Bangor-On-Dee, Wrexham. LL13 0DA
Tel: 01978 782081, Fax: 01978 780985 Website: www.bangorondeeraces.co.uk
**Racecourse Manager & Clerk of the Course:** Andrew Morris
**Chief Executive:** Richard Thomas
**General Manager:** Jeannie Chantler
**Going Reports:** Contact Clerk of the Course as above.
**Stabling:** 85 stables, allotted on arrival. Shavings (straw on request). Applications to the Manager. Tel: 01978 782081.
**By Road:** 5 miles southeast of Wrexham, off the B5069.
**By Rail:** Wrexham Station (bus or taxi to the course).
**By Air:** Helicopters may land by prior arrangement with Clerk of the Course at entirely their own risk.

---

## BATH (L.H)

**Flat:** Galloping, left-handed, level oval of 1m 4f 25y, with long, stiff run-in of about 4f which bends to the left. An extended chute provides for sprint races.
**Address:** The Racecourse, Lansdown, Bath BA1 9BU. Tel: 01225 424609 Fax: 01225 444415.
Website: www.bath-racecourse.co.uk
**Clerk of the Course:** Jo Hall
**Clerk of the Course:** Katie Stephens
**Going Reports:** Contact Clerk of the Course as above.
**Stabling:** 120 boxes. Free stabling and accommodation for lads and lasses. Tel: 01225 424609
**By Road:** 2 miles northwest of the City (M4 Junction 18) at Lansdown. Unlimited free car and coach parking space immediately behind the stands. Special bus services operate from Bath to the racecourse.
**By Rail:** Bath Station (from Paddington).
**By Air:** Bristol or Colerne Airports. Helicopter landing facilities available by prior arrangement.

---

## BEVERLEY (R.H)

**Flat:** A right-handed oval of 1m 3f, generally galloping, with an uphill run-in of two and a half furlongs. The 5f course is very stiff.
**Address:** Beverley Race Co. Ltd., York Road, Beverley, Yorkshire HU17 9QZ
Tel: 01482 867488 / 882645.Website: www.beverley-racecourse.co.uk
**General Manager:** Sally Iggulden 07850 458605
**Clerk of the Course:** John Morley
**Going Reports:** Tel: 01482 867488 / 882645
**Stabling:** 111 boxes. Free stabling. Accommodation available for lads and lasses
Tel: 01482 867488 / 882645.
**By Road:** 7 miles from the M62 (Junction 38) off the A1035. Free car parking opposite the course. Owners and trainers use a separate enclosure.
**By Rail:** Beverley Station (Hull-Scarborough line). Occasional bus service to the course (1 mile).

---

## BRIGHTON (L.H)

**Flat:** Left-handed, 1m 4f horseshoe with easy turns and a run-in of three and a half furlongs. Undulating and sharp, the track suits handy types.
**Address:** Brighton Racecourse, Brighton, East Sussex BN2 2XZ Tel: 01273 603580 Fax: 01273 673267
Website: www.brighton-racecourse.co.uk
**Clerk of the Course:** Edward Arkell 07977 587713
**General Manager:** Davina Wells
**Going Reports:** Available on www.brighton-racecourse.co.uk or contact main office/Clerk of the Course as above
**Stabling:** 102 boxes. Stabling & accommodation: Tel: 01273 603580, available on request.
**By Road:** East of the city on the A27 (Lewes Road). Car park adjoins the course.
**By Rail:** Brighton Station (from Victoria on the hour, London Bridge or Portsmouth). Special bus service to the course from the station (approx 2 miles).
**By Air:** Helicopters may land by prior arrangement.

---

## CARLISLE (R.H)

**Flat:** Right-handed, 1m 4f pear-shaped track. Galloping and undulating with easy turns and a stiff uphill run-in of three and a half furlongs. The 6f course begins on an extended chute.
**N.H.** Pear-shaped, 1m 5f (9) 300y run-in uphill. Undulating and a stiff test of stamina, ideally suited to the long-striding thorough stayer. Three-mile chases start on a chute, and the first fence is only jumped once.
**Address:** Carlisle Racecourse, Durdar Road, Carlisle CA2 4TS Tel: 01228 554700 Fax: 01228 554747
Website: www.carlisle-races.co.uk
**Regional Director:** John Baker
**Clerk of the Course:** Andrew Tulloch 07831 315104
**General Manager:** Geraldine McKay
**Going Reports:** 01228 554700 recorded or contact Clerk of the Course above
**Stabling:** 98 boxes. Stabling and accommodation available on request. Please phone Head Groundsman on 07889 987542, or Fax Stable Office on 01228 554747 by 1pm day before racing.
**By Road:** 2 miles south of the city (Durdar Road). Easy access from the M6 (Junction 42). The car park is free (adjacent to the course).
**By Rail:** Carlisle Station (2 miles from the course).
**By Air:** Helicopter landing facility by prior arrangement.

---

## CARTMEL (L.H)

**N.H.:** Oval, 1m 1f (6) 800y run-in. Almost perfectly flat but very sharp, with the longest run-in in the country, approximately half a mile. The fences are stiff but fair.
**Address:** Cartmel Racecourse, Cartmel, nr Grange-Over-Sands, Cumbria LA11 6QF Tel: 01539 536340. Out of season: 01539 533335 Fax: 01539 536004 Website: www.cartmel-racecourse.co.uk
**Managing Director:** Jonathan Garratt
**Clerk of the Course:** Anthea Morshead 07837 559861
**Going Reports:** 01539 536340 or contact Clerk of the Course as above.
**Stabling:** 75 boxes. Boxes and accommodation for lads and lasses is limited. Prior booking is required by 12 noon the day before racing 01539 534609.
**By Road:** 1 mile west of the town, 2 miles off the B5277 (Grange-Haverthwaite road). M6 (Junction 36).
**By Rail:** Cark-in-Cartmel Station (2 miles) (Carnforth-Barrow line). Raceday bus service.
**By Air:** Light aircraft facilities available at Cark Airport (4 miles from the course). Helicopter landing facility at the course, by prior arrangement only.

---

## CATTERICK (L.H)

**Flat:** A sharp, left-handed, undulating oval of 1m 180y with a downhill run-in of 3f.
**N.H.** Oval, 1m 1f (9) 240y run-in. Undulating, sharp track that favours the handy, front-running sort, rather than the long-striding galloper.
**Address:** The Racecourse, Catterick Bridge, Richmond, North Yorkshire DL10 7PE Tel: 01748 811478
Fax: 01748 811082 Website: www.catterickbridge.co.uk
**General Manager & Clerk of the Course:** Fiona Needham 07831 688625
**Going Reports:** Contact Clerk of the Course as above
**Stabling:** 116 Boxes. Allotted on arrival.
**By Road:** The course is adjacent to the A1, 1 mile northwest of the town on the A6136. There is a free car park.
**By Rail:** Darlington Station (special buses to course - 14 mile journey).
**By Air:** Helicopters can land by prior arrangement. Fixed wing planes contact RAF Leeming Tel: 01677 423041

---

## CHELMSFORD CITY (L.H)

**Flat:** A left-handed, Polytrack oval of 1m with sweeping bends and a 2f home straight. Races over 7f and 1m start from separate chutes.
**Address:** Chelmsford City Racecourse, Great Leighs, Essex, CM3 1QP Tel: 01245 362412
Fax: 01245 361850
**Website:** www.chelmsfordcityracecourse.com
**Manager:** Phil Siers
**Clerk of the Course:** Andy Waitt
**By Road:** At Great Leighs, five miles north of Chelmsford on the A31
**By Rail:** Chelmsford station (from Liverpool Street)
**By Air:** Stansted Airport (17 miles)

---

## CHELTENHAM (L.H)

**Old Course:** Oval, 1m 4f (9) 350y run-in. A testing, undulating track with stiff fences. The ability to stay is essential.
**New Course:** Oval, 1m 5f (10) 220y run-in. Undulating, stiff fences, testing course, uphill for the final half-mile.
**Address:** Cheltenham Racecourse, Prestbury Park, Cheltenham, Gloucestershire GL50 4SH
Tel: 01242 513014 Fax: 01242 224227
**Website:** www.cheltenham.co.uk
**Regional Director:** Ian Renton
**Director of Racing & Clerk of the Course:** Simon Claisse 07785 293966
**Going Reports:** Available from six days before racing 01242 513014 (option 2, then 6)
**Stabling:** 299 boxes. Ample stabling and accommodation for lads.
Apply to the Stable Manager 01242 537602 or 521950.
**By Road:** 1.5 miles north of the town on the A435. M5 (Junction 10 or 11).
**By Rail:** Cheltenham Spa Station. Buses and taxis to course.
**By Air:** Helicopter landing site to the northeast of the stands.

---

## CHEPSTOW (L.H)

**Flat:** A left-handed, undulating oval of about 2m, with easy turns, and a straight run-in of 5f. There is a straight track of 1m 14y.
**N.H.** Oval, 2m (11) 240y run-in. Many changing gradients, five fences in the home straight. Favours the long-striding front-runner, but stamina is important.
**Address:** Chepstow Racecourse, Chepstow, Monmouthshire NP16 6BE Tel: 01291 622260
Fax: 01291 627061 Website: www.chepstow-racecourse.co.uk
**Clerk of the Course:** Keith Ottesen 07813 043453
**Executive Director:** Phil Bell
**Going Reports:** Contact Clerk of the Course as above.
**Stabling:** 106 boxes, allotted on arrival. Limited accommodation for lads and lasses. Apply: 01291 622260.
**By Road:** 1 mile North-West of the town on the A466. (1 mile from Junction 22 of the M4 (Severn Bridge) or M48 Junction 2. There is a free public car park opposite the entrance.
**By Rail:** Chepstow Station (from Paddington, change at Gloucester or Newport). The course is a mile from the station.
**By Air:** Helicopter landing facility in the centre of the course.

---

## CHESTER (L.H)

**Flat:** A level, sharp, left-handed, circular course of 1m 73y, with a short run-in of 230y.
Chester is a specialists' track which generally suits the sharp-actioned horse.
**Address:** The Racecourse, Chester CH1 2LY Tel: 01244 304600 Fax: 01244 304648
Website: www.chester-races.co.uk
**Racecourse Manager & Clerk of the Course:** Andrew Morris
**Chief Executive:** Richard Thomas
**Going Reports:** Contact Main Office 01244 304600
**Stabling:** 138 boxes and accommodation. Tel: 01244 324880 or 01244 304610
**By Road:** The course is near the centre of the city on the A548 (Queensferry Road). The Owners' and Trainers' car park is adjacent to the Leverhulme Stand. There is a public car park in the centre of the course.
**By Rail:** Chester Station (¾ mile from the course). Services from Euston, Paddington and Northgate.
**By Air:** Hawarden Airport (2 miles). Helicopters are allowed to land on the racecourse by prior arrangement only.

---

## DONCASTER (L.H)

**Flat:** A left-handed, flat, galloping course of 1m 7f 110y, with a long run-in which extends to a straight mile.
**N.H.** Conical, 2m (11) 247y run-in. A very fair, flat track ideally suited to the long-striding galloper.
**Address:** Doncaster Racecourse, Leger Way, Doncaster DN2 6BB Tel: 01302 304200, Fax: 01302 323271
**Email:** info@doncaster-racecourse.co.uk Website: www.doncaster-racecourse.co.uk
**Clerk of the Course:** Roderick Duncan 07772 958685
**Managing Director:** Mark Spincer
**Going Reports:** Contact Clerk of the Course as above or Estate Manager 07831 260373.

**Stabling:** 147 boxes. Free stabling and accommodation. Tel: 01302 304200
**By Road:** East of the town, off the A638 (M18 Junctions 3 & 4). Club members' car park reserved. Large public car park free and adjacent to the course.
**By Rail:** Doncaster Central Station (from King's Cross). Special bus service from the station (1 mile).
**By Air:** Helicopter landing facility by prior arrangement only. Doncaster Robin Hood Airport is 15 minutes from the racecourse.

---

## EPSOM (L.H)

**Flat:** Left-handed and undulating with easy turns, and a run-in of just under 4f. The straight 5f course is also undulating and downhill all the way, making it the fastest 5f in the world.
**Address:** The Racecourse, Epsom Downs, Surrey, KT18 5LQ. Tel: 01372 726311, Fax: 01372 748253 Website: www.epsomderby.co.uk
**Regional Director:** Rupert Trevelyan
**Clerk of the Course:** Andrew Cooper. Tel: 01372 726311, Mobile: 07774 230850
**General Manager:** Simon Durrant
**Going Reports:** Contact Clerk of the Course as above.
**Stabling:** 108 boxes. Free stabling and accommodation. Tel: 01372 460454
**By Road:** Two miles south of the town on the B290 (M25 Junctions 8 & 9). For full car park particulars apply to: The Club Secretary, Epsom Grandstand, Epsom Downs, Surrey KT18 5LQ. Tel: 01372 726311.
**By Rail:** Epsom, Epsom Downs or Tattenham Corner Stations (trains from London Bridge, Waterloo, Victoria). Regular bus services run to the course from Epsom and Morden Underground Station.
**By Air:** London (Heathrow) and London (Gatwick) are both within 30 miles of the course. Heliport (Derby Meeting only) apply to Hascombe Aviation. Tel: 01279 680291.

---

## EXETER (R.H)

**N.H.:** Oval, 2m (11) 300y run-in uphill. Undulating with a home straight of half a mile. A good test of stamina, suiting the handy, well-balanced sort.
**Address:** Exeter Racecourse, Kennford, Exeter, Devon EX6 7XS Tel: 01392 832599 Fax: 01392 833454 Email: Exeter@thejockeyclub.co.uk Website: www.exeter-racecourse.co.uk
**Regional Director:** Ian Renton
**Clerk of the Course:** Barry Johnson 07976 791578
**General Manager:** Tim Darby
**Going Reports:** Contact Clerk of the Course as above.
**Stabling:** 90 loose boxes at the course. Sleeping accommodation and canteen for both lads and lasses by prior arrangement. Apply to Racecourse Office. Tel: 01392 832599 by 12 noon on day before racing.
**By Road:** The course is at Haldon, 5 miles southwest of Exeter on the A38 (Plymouth) road, 2 miles east of Chudleigh.
**By Rail:** Exeter (St Davids) Station. Free bus service to course.
**By Air:** Helicopters can land by prior arrangement.

---

## FAKENHAM (L.H)

**N.H.** Square, 1m (6) 200y run-in. On the turn almost throughout and undulating, suiting the handy front-runner. The going rarely becomes heavy.
**Address:** The Racecourse, Fakenham, Norfolk NR21 7NY Tel: 01328 862388 Fax: 01328 855908 email: info@fakenhamracecourse.co.uk Website: www.fakenhamracecourse.co.uk
**Clerk of the Course & Chief Executive:** David Hunter Tel: 01328 862388 Mobile: 07767 802206.
**Going Reports:** Contact Clerk of the Course as above.
**Stabling:** 70 boxes available. Tel: 01328 862388 Fax: 01328 855908.
**By Road:** A mile south of the town on the B1146 (East Dereham) road.
**By Rail:** Norwich Station (26 miles) (Liverpool Street line), King's Lynn (22 miles) (Liverpool Street/Kings Cross).
**By Air:** Helicopter landing facility in the centre of the course by prior arrangement only.

---

## FFOS LAS (L.H)

**Flat & N.H.:** The track is a 60m wide, basically flat, 1m4f oval with sweeping bends. Races over 5f and 6f start on a chute.
**Address:** Ffos Las Racecourse, Trimsaran, Carmarthenshire, SA17 4DE Tel: 01554 811092 Fax: 01554 811037 Website: www.ffoslasracecourse.com
**Clerk of the Course:** Keith Ottesen 07813 043453
**Going Reports:** Contact Clerk of the Course as above.

**Stabling:** 120 box stable yard.
**By Road:** From the east take J48 from the M4 and join the A4138 to Llanelli, then follow the brown tourist signs to the racecourse. From the west take the A48 to Carmarthen then the A484 to Kidwelly before following the brown signs.
**By Air:** The course has the facilities to land helicopters on race days.

---

## FOLKESTONE (R.H)

**No 2015 fixtures scheduled by owners Arena Racing Company**

---

## FONTWELL PARK (Fig. 8)

**N.H.** 2m (7) 230y run-in with left-hand bend close home. The figure-of-eight chase course suits handy types and is something of a specialists' track. The left-handed hurdle course is oval, one mile round with nine hurdles per two and a quarter miles.
**Address:** Fontwell Park Racecourse, nr Arundel, West Sussex BN18 0SX Tel: 01243 543335
Fax: 01243 543904 Website: www.fontwellpark.co.uk
**Clerk of the Course:** Edward Arkell 07977 587713
**General Manager:** Simon Williams
**Going Reports:** 01243 543335 during office hours.
**Stabling:** 90 boxes. Limited accommodation. If arriving the day before the meeting, contact:
Tel: 01243 543335.
**By Road:** South of village at the junction of the A29 (Bognor) and A27 (Brighton-Chichester) roads.
**By Rail:** Barnham Station (2 miles). Brighton-Portsmouth line (access via London Victoria).
**By Air:** Helicopter landing facility by prior arrangement with the Clerk of the Course.

---

## GOODWOOD (R.H)

**Flat:** A sharp, undulating, essentially right-handed track with a long run-in. There is also a straight 6f course.
**Address:** Goodwood Racecourse Ltd., Goodwood, Chichester, West Sussex PO18 0PX
Tel: 01243 755022, Fax: 01243 755025 Website: www.goodwood.co.uk
**Managing Director:** Adam Waterworth
**Clerk of the Course:** Seamus Buckley 07774 100223
**Going Reports:** 01243 755022 (recorded message) or Clerk of the Course.
**Stabling:** Free stabling and accommodation for runners (130 well equipped boxes at Goodwood House). Please book in advance. Subsidised canteen and recreational facilities. Tel: 01243 755022 / 755036.
**By Road:** 6 miles north of Chichester between the A286 & A285. There is a car park adjacent to the course. Ample free car and coach parking.
**By Rail:** Chichester Station (from Victoria or London Bridge). Regular bus service to the course (6 miles).
**By Air:** Helicopter landing facility by prior arrangement 01243 755030. Goodwood Airport 2 miles (taxi to the course).

---

## HAMILTON PARK (R.H)

**Flat:** Sharp, undulating, right-handed course of 1m 5f with a five and a half-furlong, uphill run-in. There is a straight track of 6f.
**Address:** Hamilton Park Racecourse, Bothwell Road, Hamilton, Lanarkshire ML3 0DW Tel: 01698 283806
Fax: 01698 286621 Website: www.hamilton-park.co.uk
**Racing Manager & Clerk of the Course:** Hazel Peplinski 01698 283806 (raceday). Mobile: 07774 116733.
Fax: 01698 286621
**Chief Executive:** Vivien Kyles 01698 283806
**Going Reports:** Track Manager: 07736 101130 or Clerk of the Course.
**Stabling:** Free stabling (102 boxes) and accommodation on request. Tel: 01698 284892 or Office.
**By Road:** Off the A72 on the B7071 (Hamilton-Bothwell road). (M74 Junction 5). Free parking for cars and buses.
**By Rail:** Hamilton West Station (1 mile).
**By Air:** Glasgow Airport (20 miles).

---

## HAYDOCK PARK (L.H)

**Flat:** A galloping, almost flat, oval track, 1m 5f round, with a run-in of four and a half furlongs and a straight six-furlong course.
**N.H.** Oval, 1m 5f (10) 440y run-in. Flat, galloping chase course. The hurdle track, which is sharp, is inside the chase course and has some tight bends.
**Address:** Haydock Park Racecourse, Newton-le-Willows, Merseyside WA12 0HQ Tel: 01942 402609 Fax: 01942 270879 Website: www.haydock-park.co.uk
**Regional Director:** John Baker
**General Manager:** Jason Fildes
**Clerk of the Course:** Kirkland Tellwright 01942 725963 or 07748 181595
**Going Reports:** Contact Clerk of the Course as above or Head Groundsman 07831 849298
**Stabling:** 124 boxes. Applications to be made to the Racecourse for stabling and accommodation. Tel: 01942 725963 or 01942 402615 (racedays).
**By Road:** The course is on the A49 near Junction 23 of the M6.
**By Rail:** Newton-le-Willows Station (Manchester-Liverpool line) is 2.5 miles from the course. Earlstown 3 miles from the course. Warrington Bank Quay and Wigan are on the London to Carlisle/Glasgow line.
**By Air:** Landing facilities in the centre of the course for helicopters and planes not exceeding 10,000lbs laden weight. Apply to the Sales Office.

## HEREFORD (R.H)

**No 2015 fixtures scheduled by leaseholders Arena Racing Company**

## HEXHAM (L.H)

**N.H.** Oval, 1m 4f (10) 220y run-in. An undulating course that becomes very testing when the ground is soft, it has easy fences and a stiff uphill climb to the finishing straight, which is on a separate spur.
**Address:** Hexham Racecourse, The Riding, Hexham, Northumberland NE46 2JP Tel: 01434 606881 Fax: 01434 605814, Racedays: 01434 603738. Email: admin@hexham-racecourse.co.uk Website: www.hexham-racecourse.co.uk
**Chief Executive:** Charles Enderby
**Clerk of the Course:** James Armstrong 01434 606881 or 07801 166820
**Going Reports:** Contact Clerk of the Course as above
**Stabling:** 93 Boxes allocated in rotation. Please book stabling and accommodation the day before by Fax: 01434 605814.
**By Road:** 1.5 miles southwest of the town off the B6305.
**By Rail:** Hexham Station (Newcastle-Carlisle line). Free bus to the course.
**By Air:** Helicopter landing facility in centre of course (by special arrangement only).

## HUNTINGDON (R.H)

**N.H.** Oval, 1m 4f (9) 200y run-in. Perfectly flat, galloping track with a tricky open ditch in front of the stands. The two fences in the home straight can cause problems for novice chasers. Suits front runners.
**Address:** The Racecourse, Brampton, Huntingdon, Cambridgeshire PE28 4NL Tel: 01480 453373 Fax: 01480 455275 Website: www.huntingdon-racecourse.co.uk
**Regional Director:** Amy Starkey
**Clerk of the Course:** Sulekha Varma
**Managing Director:** Nadia Gollings
**Going Reports:** Tel: 01480 453373 or 07990 774295
**Stabling:** 100 boxes available. Allotted on arrival. Telephone Racecourse Office.
**By Road:** The course is situated at Brampton, 2 miles west of Huntingdon on the A14. Easy access from the A1 (½ mile from the course).
**By Rail:** Huntingdon Station. Buses and taxis to course.
**By Air:** Helicopter landing facility by prior arrangement.

## KELSO (L.H)

**N.H.** Oval, 1m 3f (8), uphill run-in of just over a furlong. Rather undulating with two downhill fences opposite the stands, it suits the nippy, front-running sort, though the uphill finish helps the true stayer. The hurdle course is smaller and very sharp with a tight turn away from the stands.
**Address:** Kelso Racecourse, Kelso, Roxburghshire TD5 7SX Tel: 01668 280800 Website: www.kelso-races.co.uk
**Clerk of the Course:** Hazel Peplinski 07774 116733
**Managing Director:** Richard Landale
**Going Reports:** Racecourse: 01573 224822 Groundsman Tel: 07774 172527

**Stabling:** 94 boxes allotted in rotation. Reservations for stabling and accommodation for lads and lasses at the racecourse, please phone Head Groundsman Tel: 01573 224767 or Racecourse stables: 01573 224822 from 3pm the day before racing.
**By Road:** 1 mile north of the town, off the B6461.
**By Rail:** Berwick-upon-Tweed Station. 23-mile bus journey to Kelso.
**By Air:** Helicopters can land at course by arrangement, fixed wing aircraft Winfield, regular aircraft Edinburgh.

---

## KEMPTON PARK (R.H)

**Flat:** A floodlit Polytrack circuit. A 1m 2f outer track accommodates races over 6f, 7f, 1m, 1m 3f, 1m 4f and 2m. The 1m inner track caters for races over 5f and 1m 2f.
**N.H.** Triangular, 1m 5f (10) 175y run-in. Practically flat; sharp course where the long run between the last obstacle on the far side and the first in the home straight switches the emphasis from jumping to speed. The hurdles track is on the outside of the chase track. The course crosses the Polytrack at two points on each circuit.
**Address:** Kempton Park Racecourse, Sunbury-on-Thames, Middlesex TW16 5AQ Tel: 01932 782292 Fax: 01932 782044 Raceday Fax: 01932 779525 Website: www.kempton.co.uk Email: kempton@rht.net
**Regional Director:** Rupert Trevelyan
**Clerk of the Course & Director of Racing:** Brian Clifford 07880 784484
**General Manager:** Phil White
**Going Reports:** 01932 782292 if unavailable contact Clerk of the Course as above
**Stabling:** 117 boxes. Allocated on arrival. Prior booking required for overnight stay. Tel: 01932 782292
**By Road:** On the A308 near Junction 1 of the M3.
**By Rail:** Kempton Park Station (from Waterloo).
**By Air:** London (Heathrow) Airport 6 miles.

---

## LEICESTER (R.H)

**Flat:** Stiff, galloping, right-handed oval of 1m 5f, with a 5f run-in. There is a straight course of seven furlongs.
**N.H.** Rectangular, 1m 6f (10) 250y run-in uphill. An undulating course with an elbow 150y from the finish, it can demand a high degree of stamina, for the going can become extremely heavy and the last three furlongs are uphill.
**Address:** Leicester Racecourse, Oadby, Leicester LE2 4AL. Tel: 01162 716515 Fax: 01162 711746 Website:www.leicester-racecourse.co.uk
**Clerk of the Course:** Jimmy Stevenson 01162 712115 or 07774 497281
**General Manager:** Rob Bracken
**Going Reports:** Recorded message 01162 710875 or contact Clerk of the Course as above.
**Stabling:** 108 boxes. Allocated on arrival. Canteen opens at 7.30a.m. Tel: 01162 712115.
**By Road:** The course is 2.5 miles southeast of the City on the A6 (M1, Junction 21). The car park is free.
**By Rail:** Leicester Station (from St Pancras) is 2.5 miles.
**By Air:** Helicopter landing facility in the centre of the course.

---

## LINGFIELD PARK (L.H)

**Flat, Turf:** A sharp, undulating left-handed circuit, with a 7f 140y straight course.
**Flat, Polytrack:** The left-handed Polytrack is 1m 2f round, with an extended chute to provide a 1m 5f start. It is a sharp, level track with a short run-in.
**N.H.** Conical, 1m 5f (10) 200y run-in. Severely undulating with a tight downhill turn into the straight, the chase course suits front runners and those of doubtful resolution.
**Address:** Lingfield Park Racecourse, Lingfield, Surrey RH7 6PQ Tel: 01342 834800 Fax: 01342 832833 Website: www.lingfield-racecourse.co.uk
**Clerk of the Course:** Emma Dyer
**Executive Manager:** Andrew Perkins
**Going Reports:** Contact Clerk of the Course as above.
**Stabling:** 106 boxes. For details of accommodation Tel: 01342 831718. Advance notice for overnight accommodation required before 12 noon on the day before racing.
**By Road:** Southeast of the town off the A22 M25 (Junction 6). Ample free parking.
**By Rail:** Lingfield Station (regular services from London Bridge and Victoria). ½ mile walk to the course.
**By Air:** London (Gatwick) Airport 10 miles. Helicopter landing facility south of wind-sock.

---

## LUDLOW (R.H)

**N.H.** Oval, 1m 4f (9) 185y run-in. The chase course is flat and has quite sharp bends into and out of the home straight, although long-striding horses never seem to have any difficulties. The hurdle course is on the outside of the chase track and is not so sharp.
**Address:** Ludlow Race Club Ltd, The Racecourse, Bromfield, Ludlow, Shropshire SY8 2BT
Tel: 01584 856221 (Racedays) or see below. Website:www.ludlowracecourse.co.uk
**Clerk of the Course:** Simon Sherwood
**General Manager:** Bob Davies. Tel: 01584 856221, Mobile 07970 861533, Fax: 01584 856217
Email: bobdavies@ludlowracecourse.co.uk
**Going Reports:** Contact Clerk of the Course as above or Groundsman Tel: 01584 856289 or 07970 668353
**Stabling:** Free and allocated on arrival. 100 stables, mainly cardboard with a limited number of shavings and straw. Tel: 01584 856221.
**By Road:** The course is situated at Bromfield, 2 miles north of Ludlow on the A49.
**By Rail:** Ludlow Station (Hereford-Shrewsbury line) 2 miles.
**By Air:** Helicopter landing facility in the centre of the course by arrangement with the Clerk of the Course and entirely at own risk.

---

## MARKET RASEN (R.H)

**N.H.** Oval, 1m 2f (8) 250y run-in. A sharp, undulating course with a long run to the straight, it favours the handy, front-running type.
**Address:** Market Rasen Racecourse, Legsby Road, Market Rasen, Lincolnshire LN8 3EA
Tel: 01673 843434 Fax: 01673 844532 Website: www.marketrasenraces.co.uk
**Regional Director:** Amy Starkey
**Clerk of the Course:** Jane Hedley
**General Manager:** Nadia Gollings
**Going Reports:** Contact Clerk of the Course as above.
**Stabling:** 86 boxes at the course, allocated on arrival. Accommodation for lads and lasses is by reservation only. Tel: 01673 842307 (racedays only)
**By Road:** The town is just off the A46, and the racecourse is one mile east of the town on the A631. Free car parks.
**By Rail:** Market Rasen Station 1 mile (King's Cross - Cleethorpes line).
**By Air:** Helicopter landing facility by prior arrangement only.

---

## MUSSELBURGH (R.H)

**Flat:** A sharp, level, right-handed oval of 1m 2f, with a run-in of 4f. There is an additional 5f straight course.
**N.H.** Rectangular, 1m 3f (8) 150y run-in (variable). A virtually flat track with sharp turns, suiting the handy, front-running sort. Drains well.
**Address:** Musselburgh Racecourse, Linkfield Road, Musselburgh, East Lothian EH21 7RG
Tel: 01316 652859 (Racecourse) Fax: 01316 532083 Website:www.musselburgh-racecourse.co.uk
**Clerk of the Course:** Harriet Graham 07843 380401
**General Manager:** Bill Farnsworth 07710 536134
**Going Reports:** Contact main office as above or Clerk of the Course.
**Stabling:** 101 boxes. Free stabling. Accommodation provided. Tel: 07773 048638, Stables (racedays): 01316 652796.
**By Road:** The course is situated at Musselburgh, 5 miles east of Edinburgh on the A1. Car park, adjoining course, free for buses and cars.
**By Rail:** Waverley Station (Edinburgh). Local Rail service to Musselburgh.
**By Air:** Edinburgh (Turnhouse) Airport 30 minutes

---

## NEWBURY (L.H)

**Flat:** Left-handed, oval track of about 1m 7f, with a slightly undulating straight mile. The round course is level and galloping with a four and a half furlong run-in. Races over the round mile start on the adjoining chute.
**N.H.** Oval, 1m 6f (11) 255y run-in. Slightly undulating, wide and galloping in nature. The fences are stiff and sound jumping is essential. One of the fairest tracks in the country.
**Address:** Newbury Racecourse, Newbury, Berkshire RG14 7NZ Tel: 01635 40015 Fax: 01635 528354
Website: www.newbury-racecourse.co.uk
**Chief Executive:** Julian Thick
**Raceday Clerk:** Richard Osgood 07977 426947
**Going Reports:** Clerk of the Course as above.
**Stabling:** 164 boxes. Free stabling and accommodation for lads and lasses. Tel: 01635 40015.

**By Road:** East of the town off the A34 (M4, Junction 12 or 13). Car park, adjoining enclosures, free.
**By Rail:** Newbury Racecourse Station adjoins the course.
**By Air:** Light Aircraft landing strip East/West. 830 metres by 30 metres wide. Helicopter landing facilities.

---

## NEWCASTLE (L.H)

**Flat:** Galloping, easy, left-handed oval of 1m 6f, with an uphill 4f run-in. There is a straight course of 1m 3y.
**N.H.** Oval, 1m 6f (11) 220y run-in. A gradually rising home straight of four furlongs makes this galloping track a true test of stamina, especially as the ground can become very heavy.
**Address:** High Gosforth Park, Newcastle-Upon-Tyne NE3 5HP Tel: 01912 362020 Fax: 01912 367761 Website: www.newcastle-racecourse.co.uk
**Clerk of the Course:** James Armstrong 07801 166820
**Executive Director:** David Williamson
**Stabling:** 135 boxes. Stabling Free. It is essential to book accommodation in advance. Apply via the Racecourse Office.
**Going Reports:** Contact Clerk of the Course as above or Head Groundsman 07860 274289.
**By Road:** 4 miles north of the city on the A6125 (near the A1). Car and coach park free.
**By Rail:** Newcastle Central Station (from King's Cross). A free bus service operates from South Gosforth and Regent Centre Metro Station.
**By Air:** Helicopter landing facility by prior arrangement. The Airport is 4 miles from the course.

---

## NEWMARKET (R.H)

**Rowley Mile Course:** There is a straight ten-furlong course, which is wide and galloping. Races over 1m 4f or more are right-handed. The Rowley Mile course has a long run-in and a stiff finish.
**July Course:** Races up to a mile are run on the Bunbury course, which is straight. Races over 1m 2f or more are right-handed, with a 7f run-in. Like the Rowley Mile course, the July Course track is stiff.
**Address:** Newmarket Racecourse, Newmarket, Suffolk CB8 0TG Tel: 01638 663482 (Main Office), 01638 663762 (Rowley), 01638 675416 (July) Fax: Rowley 01638 675340. Fax: July 01638 675410 Website: www.newmarketracecourses.co.uk
**Clerk of the Course:** Michael Prosser, Westfield House, The Links, Newmarket. Tel: 01638 675504 or 07802 844578
**Regional Director:** Amy Starkey
**Going Reports:** Contact main office or Clerk of the Course as above
**Stabling:** 100 boxes. Free accommodation available at the Links Stables. Tel: 01638 662200 or 07747 766614
**By Road:** Southwest of the town on the A1304 London Road (M11 Junction 9). Free car parking at the rear of the enclosure. Annual Badge Holders' car park free all days. Free courtesy bus service from Newmarket Station, Bus Station and High Street, commencing 90 minutes prior to the first race, and return trips up to 60 minutes after the last race.
**By Rail:** Infrequent rail service to Newmarket Station from Cambridge (Liverpool Street) or direct bus service from Cambridge (13-mile journey).
**By Air:** Landing facilities for light aircraft and helicopters on racedays at both racecourses. See Flight Guide. Cambridge Airport 11 miles.

---

## NEWTON ABBOT (L.H)

**N.H.** Oval, 1m 2f (7) 300y run-in. Flat with two tight bends and a water jump situated three fences from home. The nippy, agile sort is favoured. The run-in can be very short on the hurdle course.
**Address:** Newton Abbot Races Ltd., Kingsteignton Road, Newton Abbot, Devon TQ12 3AF
Tel: 01626 353235 Fax: 01626 336972 Website: www.newtonabbotracing.com
**Clerk of the Course:** Jason Loosemore 07766 228109
**Managing Director:** Pat Masterson. Tel: 01626 353235 Fax: 01626 336972 Mobile: 07917 830144.
**Going reports:** Clerk of the Course as above.
**Stabling:** 80 boxes, allocated on arrival. Tel: 07766 202938
**By Road:** North of the town on the A380. Torquay 6 miles, Exeter 17 miles.
**By Rail:** Newton Abbot Station (from Paddington) ¾ mile. Buses and taxis operate to and from the course.
**By Air:** Helicopter landing pad in the centre of the course.

---

## NOTTINGHAM (L.H)

**Flat:** Left-handed, galloping, oval of about 1m 4f, and a run-in of four and a half furlongs. Flat with easy turns.
**Address:** Nottingham Racecourse, Colwick Park, Nottingham NG2 4BE Tel: 0870 8507634
Fax: 01159 584515 Website: www.nottinghamracecourse.co.uk
**Regional Director:** Amy Starkey
**Clerk of the Course:** Jane Hedley
**Managing Director:** James Knox
**Going Reports:** Contact main office as above or Clerk of the Course.
**Stabling:** 122 boxes allotted on arrival. Hostel for lads and lasses. Tel: 08708 507634
**By Road:** 2 miles east of the city on the B686.
**By Rail:** Nottingham (Midland) Station. Regular bus service to course (2 miles).
**By Air:** Helicopter landing facility in the centre of the course.

---

## PERTH (R.H)

**N.H.** Rectangular, 1m 2f (8) 283y run-in. A flat, easy track with sweeping turns. Not a course for the long-striding galloper. An efficient watering system ensures that the ground rarely gets hard.
**Address:** Perth Racecourse, Scone Palace Park, Perth PH2 6BB Tel: 01738 551597 Fax: 01738 553021 Website: www.perth-races.co.uk
**Clerk of the Course:** Harriet Graham 07843 380401
**General Manager:** Sam Morshead Tel: 01738 551597 Mobile: 07768 868848
**Going Reports:** Groundsman: 07899 034012 or contact Clerk of the Course as above.
**Stabling:** 96 boxes and accommodation for lads and lasses Tel: 01738 551597. Stables Tel: 01738 621604 (racedays only).
**By Road:** 4 miles north of the town off the A93.
**By Rail:** Perth Station (from Dundee) 4 miles. There are buses to the course.
**By Air:** Scone Airport (3.75 miles). Edinburgh Airport 45 minutes.

---

## PLUMPTON (L.H)

**N.H.** Oval, 1m 1f (7) 200y run-in uphill. A tight, undulating circuit with an uphill finish, Plumpton favours the handy, fast jumper. The ground often gets heavy, as the course is based on clay soil.
**Address:** Plumpton Racecourse, Plumpton, East Sussex, BN7 3AL Tel: 01273 890383 Fax: 01273 891557 Website: www.plumptonracecourse.co.uk
**Clerk of the Course:** Mark Cornford 07759 151617
**Chief Executive:** Michael Moloney
**Going Reports:** Tel: 01273 890383 / 07759 151617.
**Stabling:** 76 boxes. Advance notice required for overnight arrival. Tel: 07759 151617
**By Road:** 2 miles north of the village off the B2116.
**By Rail:** Plumpton Station (from Victoria) adjoins course.
**By Air:** Helicopter landing facility by prior arrangement with the Clerk of the Course.

---

## PONTEFRACT (L.H)

**Flat:** Left-handed oval, undulating course of 2m 133y, with a short run-in of 2f. It is a particularly stiff track with the last 3f uphill.
**Address:** Pontefract Park Race Co. Ltd., The Park, Pontefract, West Yorkshire Tel: 01977 781307 (Racedays) Fax: 01977 781850 Website: www.pontefract-races.co.uk
**Managing Director & Clerk of the Course:** Norman Gundill 01977 781307
**Assistant Manager & Clerk of the Course:** Richard Hamill
**Going Reports:** Contact Office as above, or Clerk of the Course
**Stabling:** 113 boxes. Stabling and accommodation must be reserved. They will be allocated on a first come-first served basis. Tel: 01977 702323
**By Road:** 1 mile north of the town on the A639. Junction 32 of M62. Free car park adjacent to the course.
**By Rail:** Pontefract Station (Tanshelf, every hour to Wakefield), 1½ miles from the course. Regular bus service from Leeds.
**By Air:** Helicopters by arrangement only. (Nearest Airfields: Robin Hood (Doncaster), Sherburn-in-Elmet, Yeadon (Leeds Bradford).

---

## REDCAR (L.H)

**Flat:** Left-handed, level, galloping, oval course of 1m 6f with a straight run-in of 5f. There is also a straight mile.
**Address:** Redcar Racecourse, Redcar, Cleveland TS10 2BY Tel: 01642 484068 Fax: 01642 488272 Website: www.redcarracing.com
**Clerk of the Course:** Jonjo Sanderson Tel: 01642 484068 Mobile: 07766 022893
**General Manager:** Amy Fair
**Going Reports:** Contact main office as above or Clerk of the Course.
**Stabling:** 144 Boxes available. Tel: Stables 01642 484068 or racedays only 01642 484254.
**By Road:** In town off the A1085. Free parking adjoining the course for buses and cars.
**By Rail:** Redcar Station (¼ mile from the course).
**By Air:** Landing facilities at Turners Arms Farm (600yds runway) Yearby, Cleveland. Two miles south of the racecourse - transport available. Durham Tees Valley airport (18 miles west of Redcar).

---

## RIPON (R.H)

**Flat:** A sharp, undulating, right-handed oval of 1m 5f, with a 5f run-in. There is also a 6f straight course.
**Address:** Ripon Racecourse, Boroughbridge Road, Ripon, North Yorkshire HG4 1UG Tel: 01765 530530 Fax: 01765 698900 E-mail: info@ripon-races.co.uk Website: www.ripon-races.co.uk
**Clerk of the Course & Managing Director:** James Hutchinson
**Going Reports:** Tel: 01765 603696 or Head Groundsman 07976 960177
**Stabling:** Trainers requiring stabling (103 boxes available) are requested to contact the Stable Manager prior to 12 noon the day before racing. Tel: 01765 604135
**By Road:** The course is situated 2 miles southeast of the city, on the B6265. There is ample free parking for cars and coaches. For reservations apply to the Secretary.
**By Rail:** Harrogate Station (11 miles), or Thirsk (15 miles). Bus services to Ripon.
**By Air:** Helicopters only on the course. Otherwise Leeds/Bradford airport.

---

## SALISBURY (R.H)

**Flat:** Right-handed and level, with a run-in of 4f. There is a straight mile track. The last half-mile is uphill, providing a stiff test of stamina.
**Address:** Salisbury Racecourse, Netherhampton, Salisbury, Wiltshire SP2 8PN Tel: 01722 326461 Fax: 01722 412710 Website: www.salisburyracecourse.co.uk
**Clerk of the Course & General Manager:** Jeremy Martin 07880 744999
**Going Reports:** Contact Clerk of the Course as above
**Stabling:** Free stabling (114 boxes) and accommodation for lads and lasses, apply to the Stabling Manager 01722 327327.
**By Road:** 3 miles southwest of the city on the A3094 at Netherhampton. Free car park adjoins the course.
**By Rail:** Salisbury Station is 3.5 miles (from London Waterloo). Bus service to the course.
**By Air:** Helicopter landing facility near the 1m 2f start.

---

## SANDOWN PARK (R.H)

**Flat:** An easy right-handed oval course of 1m 5f with a stiff straight uphill run-in of 4f. Separate straight 5f track is also uphill. Galloping.
**N.H.** Oval, 1m 5f (11) 220y run-in uphill. Features seven fences on the back straight; the last three (the Railway Fences) are very close together and can often decide the outcome of races. The stiff climb to the finish puts the emphasis very much on stamina, but accurate-jumping, free-running sorts are also favoured. Hurdle races are run on the Flat course.
**Address:** Sandown Park Racecourse, Esher, Surrey KT10 9AJ Tel: 01372 464348 Fax: 01372 470427 Website: www.sandown.co.uk
**Regional Director:** Rupert Trevelyan
**Clerk of the Course:** Andrew Cooper, Sandown Park, Esher, Surrey. Tel: 01372 461213 Mobile: 07774 230850.
**Going Reports:** 01372 461212.
**Stabling:** 110 boxes. Free stabling and accommodation for lads and lasses. Tel: 01372 463511.
**By Road:** Four miles southwest of Kingston-on-Thames, on the A307 (M25 Junction 10).
**By Rail:** Esher Station (from Waterloo) adjoins the course.
**By Air:** London (Heathrow) Airport 12 miles.

---

## SEDGEFIELD (L.H)

**N.H.** Oval, 1m 2f (8) 200y run-in: Hurdles 200y run-in. Undulating with fairly tight turns, it doesn't suit big, long-striding horses.
**Address:** Sedgefield Racecourse, Sedgefield, Stockton-on-Tees, Cleveland TS21 2HW Tel: 01740 621925 Office Fax: 01740 620663 Website: www.sedgefield-racecourse.co.uk
**Clerk of the Course:** Sophie Barton
**General Manager:** Jill Williamson
**Going Reports:** Tel: 01740 621925 or contact Clerk of the Course as above
**Stabling:** 116 boxes filled in rotation. No forage. Accommodation for horse attendants: Tel: 01740 621925
**By Road:** ¾ mile southwest of the town, near the junction of the A689 (Bishop Auckland) and the A177 (Durham) roads. The car park is free.
**By Rail:** Darlington Station (9 miles). Durham Station (12 miles).
**By Air:** Helicopter landing facility in car park area by prior arrangement only.

---

## SOUTHWELL (L.H)

**Flat, Turf:** Tight left-handed track.
**Flat, Fibresand:** Left-handed oval, Fibresand course of 1m 2f with a 3f run-in. There is a straight 5f. Sharp and level, Southwell suits front-runners.
**N.H.** Oval, 1m 1f (7) 220y run-in. A tight, flat track with a short run-in, suits front-runners.
**Address:** Southwell Racecourse, Rolleston, Newark, Nottinghamshire NG25 0TS Tel: 01636 814481 Fax: 01636 812271 Website: www.southwell-racecourse.co.uk
**Managing Director:** Dave Roberts
**Clerk of the Course:** Roderick Duncan 07772 958685
**General Manager:** Amanda Boby
**Going Reports:** Contact Clerk of the Course as above.
**Stabling:** 113 boxes at the course. Applications for staff and horse accommodation to be booked by noon the day before racing on 01636 814481.
**By Road:** The course is situated at Rolleston, 3 miles south of Southwell, 5 miles from Newark.
**By Rail:** Rolleston Station (Nottingham-Newark line) adjoins the course.
**By Air:** Helicopters can land by prior arrangement.

---

## STRATFORD-ON-AVON (L.H)

**N.H.** Triangular, 1m 2f (8) 200y run-in. Virtually flat with two tight bends, and quite a short home straight. A sharp and turning course, Stratford-on-Avon suits the well-balanced, handy sort.
**Address:** Stratford Racecourse, Luddington Road, Stratford-upon-Avon, Warwickshire CV37 9SE Tel: 01789 267949 Fax: 01789 415850 Website: www.stratfordracecourse.net
**Managing Director:** Ilona Barnett
**Clerk of the Course:** Nessie Lambert
**Going reports:** Contact main office as above or Head Groundsman Tel: 07770 623366.
**Stabling:** 89 boxes allotted on arrival. Advance notice must be given for overnight stays. Tel: 01789 267949.
**By Road:** A mile from the town centre, off the A429 (Evesham road).
**By Rail:** Stratford-on-Avon Station (from Birmingham New Street or Leamington Spa) 1 mile.
**By Air:** Helicopter landing facility by prior arrangement.

---

## TAUNTON (R.H)

**N.H.** Elongated oval, 1m 2f (8) 150y run-in uphill. Sharp turns, especially after the winning post, with a steady climb from the home bend. Suits the handy sort.
**Address:** Taunton Racecourse, Orchard Portman, Taunton, Somerset TA3 7BL Tel: 01823 337172 Office Fax: 01823 325881 Website: www.tauntonracecourse.co.uk
**Clerk of the Course:** Jason Loosemore
**General Manager:** Bob Young
**Going reports:** Contact Clerk of the Course as above, or Head Groundsman (after 4.30pm) 07971 695132.
**Stabling:** 90 boxes allotted on arrival. Advance bookings for long journeys. Apply to the Stable Manager, 01823 337172
**By Road:** Two miles south of the town on the B3170 (Honiton) road (M5 Junction 25).
**By Rail:** Taunton Station 2 miles. There are buses and taxis to course.
**By Air:** Helicopter landing facility by prior arrangement.

---

## THIRSK (L.H)

**Flat:** Left-handed, oval of 1m 2f with sharp turns and an undulating run-in of 4f. There is a straight 6f track.
**Address:** The Racecourse, Station Road, Thirsk, North Yorkshire YO7 1QL Tel: 01845 522276
Fax: 01845 525353. Website: www.thirskracecourse.net
**Clerk of the Course & Managing Director:** James Sanderson
**Going reports:** Contact main office or Clerk of the Course as above
**Stabling:** 110 boxes. For stabling and accommodation apply to the Racecourse Tel: 01845 522096
**By Road:** West of the town on the A61. Free car park adjacent to the course for buses and cars.
**By Rail:** Thirsk Station (from King's Cross). ½ mile from the course.
**By Air:** Helicopters can land by prior arrangement. Tel: Racecourse 01845 522276. Fixed wing aircraft can land at RAF Leeming. Tel: 01677 423041. Light aircraft at Bagby. Tel: 01845 597385 or 01845 537555.

---

## TOWCESTER (R.H)

**N.H.** Square, 1m 6f (10) 200y run-in uphill. The final six furlongs are uphill. One of the most testing tracks in the country with the emphasis purely on stamina.
**Address:** The Racecourse, Easton Neston, Towcester, Northants NN12 7HS Tel: 01327 353414
Fax: 01327 358534 Website: www.towcester-racecourse.co.uk
**Clerk of the Course:** Robert Bellamy 07836 241458
**General Manager:** Kevin Ackerman.
**Going Reports:** Tel: 01327 353414 or contact Clerk of the Course as above.
**Stabling:** 101 stables in a new block. Allocated on arrival. Please contact racecourse in advance for overnight stabling / accommodation 01327 350200.
**By Road:** 1 mile southeast of the town on the A5 (Milton Keynes road). M1 (Junction 15a).
**By Rail:** Northampton Station (Euston) 9 miles, buses to Towcester; or Milton Keynes (Euston) 12 miles, taxis available.
**By Air:** Helicopters can land by prior arrangement with the Racecourse Manager.

---

## UTTOXETER (L.H)

**N.H.** Oval, 1m 2f (8) 170y run-in. A few undulations, easy bends and fences and a flat home straight of over half a mile. Suits front-runners, especially on the 2m hurdle course.
**Address:** The Racecourse, Wood Lane, Uttoxeter, Staffordshire ST14 8BD Tel: 01889 562561
Fax: 01889 562786 Website: www.uttoxeter-racecourse.co.uk
**Clerk of the Course:** Charlie Moore 07764 255500
**General Manager:** David MacDonald
**Going Reports:** Contact main office or Clerk of the Course as above.
**Stabling:** 102 boxes, allotted on arrival. Tel: 01889 562561. Overnight and Accommodation requirements must be notified in advance as no hostel at course.
**By Road:** South-East of the town off the B5017 (Marchington Road).
**By Rail:** Uttoxeter Station (Crewe-Derby line) adjoins the course.
**By Air:** Helicopters can land by prior arrangement with the raceday office.

---

## WARWICK (L.H)

**Flat:** Discontinued after 2014.
**N.H.** Circular, 1m 6f (10) 240y run-in. Undulating with tight bends, five quick fences in the back straight and a short home straight, Warwick favours handiness and speed rather than stamina.
**Address:** Warwick Racecourse, Hampton Street, Warwick CV34 6HN Tel: 01926 491553
Fax: 01926 403223 Website: www.warwickracecourse.co.uk
**Regional Director:** Ian Renton
**Clerk of the Course:** Sulekha Varma
**Managing Director:** Huw Williams
**Going Reports:** Contact main office or Clerk of the Course as above.
**Stabling:** 117 boxes allocated on arrival or by reservation 01926 491553.
**By Road:** West of the town on the B4095 adjacent to Junction 15 of the M40.
**By Rail:** Warwick or Warwick Parkway Stations.
**By Air:** Helicopters can land by prior arrangement with the Clerk of the Course.

---

## WETHERBY (L.H)

**Flat** To be staged for the first time in 2015
**N.H.** Oval, 1m 4f (9) 200y run-in slightly uphill. A flat, very fair course which suits the long-striding galloper.
**Address:** The Racecourse, York Road, Wetherby, LS22 5EJ Tel: 01937 582035 Fax: 01937 588021
Website: www.wetherbyracing.co.uk
**Clerk of the Course & Chief Executive:** Jonjo Sanderson 07831 437453
**Going reports:** Tel: 01937 582035, or Head Groundsman: 07880 722586
**Stabling:** 91 boxes allocated on arrival. Accommodation available. Tel: 01937 582035 or from 2pm the day before racing 01937 582074.
**By Road:** East of the town off the B1224 (York Road). Adjacent to the A1. Excellent bus and coach facilities. Car park free.
**By Rail:** Leeds Station 12 miles. Buses to Wetherby.
**By Air:** Helicopters can land by prior arrangement

---

## WINCANTON (R.H)

**N.H.** Rectangular, 1m 3f (9) 200y run-in. Good galloping course where the going rarely becomes heavy. The home straight is mainly downhill.
**Address:** Wincanton Racecourse, Wincanton, Somerset BA9 8BJ Tel: 01963 32344 Fax: (01963) 34668
Website: www.wincantonracecourse.co.uk
**Regional Director:** Ian Renton
**Clerk of the Course:** Barry Johnson 07976 791578
**General Manager:** Steve Parlett
**Going Reports:** Contact Racecourse Office as above.
**Stabling:** 94 boxes allocated on arrival, overnight accommodation must be booked in advance. Apply to the Stable Manager, Wincanton Racecourse. Tel: 01963 32344.
**By Road:** 1 mile north of the town on the B3081.
**By Rail:** Gillingham Station (from Waterloo) or Castle Cary Station (from Paddington). Buses and taxis to the course.
**By Air:** Helicopter landing area is situated in the centre of the course.

---

## WINDSOR (Fig. 8)

**Flat:** Figure of eight track of 1m 4f 110y. The course is level and sharp with a long run-in. The 6f course is essentially straight.
**Address:** Royal Windsor Racecourse, Maidenhead Road, Windsor, Berkshire SL4 5JJ Tel: 01753 498400
Fax: 01753 830156. Website: www.windsor-racecourse.co.uk
**Clerk of the Course:** Jeff Green
**Executive Director:** Stuart Dorn
**Going Reports:** Contact Clerk of the Course as above.
**Stabling:** 114 boxes available. Reservation required for overnight stay and accommodation only.
Tel: 07825 603236 or 01753 498405 (racedays).
**By Road:** North of the town on the A308 (M4 Junction 6).
**By Rail:** Windsor Central Station (from Paddington) or Windsor & Eton Riverside Station (from Waterloo).
**By Air:** London (Heathrow) Airport 15 minutes. Also White Waltham Airport (West London Aero Club) 15 minutes.
**River Bus:** Seven minutes from Barry Avenue promenade at Windsor.

---

## WOLVERHAMPTON (L.H)

**Flat:** Left-handed oval Polytrack of 1m, with a run-in of 380y. A level track with sharp bends.
**Address:** Wolverhampton Racecourse, Dunstall Park, Gorsebrook Road, Wolverhampton WV6 0PE
Tel: 01902 390000 Fax: 01902 421621 Website: www.wolverhampton-racecourse.co.uk
**Clerk of the Course:** Fergus Cameron 07971 531162
**General Manager:** Dave Roberts
**Going Reports:** Contact Main Office as above
**Stabling:** 103 boxes allotted on arrival. Applications for lads and lasses, and overnight stables must be made to Racecourse by noon on the day before racing. Tel: 07971 531162. Fax: 01902 421621.
**By Road:** 1 mile north of the city on the A449 (M54 Junction 2 or M6 Junction 12). Car parking free of charge.
**By Rail:** Wolverhampton Station (from Euston) 1 mile.
**By Air:** Halfpenny Green Airport 8 miles.

---

## WORCESTER (L.H)

**N.H.** Elongated oval, 1m 5f (9) 220y run-in. Flat with easy turns, Worcester is a very fair, galloping track.
**Address:** Worcester Racecourse, Pitchcroft, Worcester WR1 3EJ Tel: 01905 25364 Fax: 01905 617563 Website: www.worcester-racecourse.co.uk
**Clerk of the Course:** Keith Ottesen
**Managing Director:** Dave Roberts 01905 25364.
**Going Reports:** Contact Clerk of the Course as above, or 01905 25364 (racedays).
**Stabling:** 97 boxes allotted on arrival. Overnight accommodation for lads and lasses in Worcester. Tel: 01905 25364 Fax: 01905 617563.
**By Road:** West of the city off the A449 (Kidderminster road) (M5 Junction 8).
**By Rail:** Foregate Street Station, Worcester (from Paddington) ¾ mile.
**By Air:** Helicopter landing facility in the centre of the course, by prior arrangement only.

---

## YARMOUTH (L.H)

**Flat:** Left-handed, level circuit of 1m 4f, with a run-in of 5f. The straight course is 1m long.
**Address:** The Racecourse, Jellicoe Road, Great Yarmouth, Norfolk NR30 4AU Tel: 01493 842527 Fax: 01493 843254 Website: www.greatyarmouth-racecourse.co.uk
**Clerk of the Course:** Richard Aldous 07738 507643
**General Manager:** Glenn Tubby
**Going Reports:** Contact Main Office or Clerk of the Course as above
**Stabling:** 127 boxes available. Allocated on arrival. Tel: 01493 855651 (racedays only) or racecourse office.
**By Road:** 1 mile east of town centre (well signposted from A47 & A12).
**By Rail:** Great Yarmouth Station (1 mile). Bus service to the course.
**By Air:** Helicopter landing available by prior arrangement with Racecourse Office

---

## YORK (L.H)

**Flat:** Left-handed, level, galloping track, with a straight 6f. There is also an adjoining course of 6f 214y.
**Address:** The Racecourse, York YO23 1EX Tel: 01904 683932 Fax: 01904 611071 Website: www.yorkracecourse.co.uk
**Clerk of the Course & Chief Executive:** William Derby 07812 961176
**Assistant Clerk of the Course:** Anthea Morshead
**Going Reports:** Contact 01904 683932 or Clerk of the Course as above.
**Stabling:** 177 boxes available Tel: 01904 706317 (Racedays) or 07712 676434.
**By Road:** 1 mile southeast of the city on the A1036.
**By Rail:** 1½ miles York Station (from King's Cross). Special bus service from station to the course.
**By Air:** Light aircraft and helicopter landing facilities available at Rufforth aerodrome (5,000ft tarmac runway). £20 landing fee - transport arranged to course. Leeds Bradford airport (25 miles).

---

# THE INVESTEC DERBY STAKES (GROUP 1), EPSOM DOWNS SATURDAY 6TH JUNE 2015

## SECOND ENTRIES BY NOON APRIL 7TH; SUPPLEMENTARY ENTRIES BY NOON JUNE 1ST.

| HORSE | TRAINER |
|---|---|
| **AARED (IRE)** | K. Prendergast, Ireland |
| **ABLAN (IRE)** | |
| **AD DABARAN (GER)** | Charlie Appleby |
| **AKWAAN** | |
| **AL NEHAYY** | Kevin Ryan |
| **ALEATOR (USA)** | Sir Mark Prescott Bt |
| **ALGAITH (USA)** | B. W. Hills |
| **ALGHAAZ** | William Haggas |
| **ALGONQUIN** | J. S. Bolger, Ireland |
| **ALMODOVAR (IRE)** | David Lanigan |
| **ALMOHTASEB** | Roger Varian |
| **ALNASHAMA** | Charles Hills |
| **ALOFT (IRE)** | Aidan O'Brien, Ireland |
| **ALQUDS (IRE)** | F. Head, France |
| **ALTERNO (IRE)** | J. S. Bolger, Ireland |
| **ALTITUDES (JPN)** | J. E. Pease, France |
| **ANTIQUARIUM (IRE)** | Charlie Appleby |
| **APPROACHING DAWN** | John Gosden |
| **AQDAAR** | Mark Johnston |
| **ARABIAN LEADER** | |
| **ARABIAN OASIS** | Charlie Appleby |
| **ARCHANGEL RAPHAEL (IRE)** | Aidan O'Brien, Ireland |
| **ARCHERY PEAK** | Luca Cumani |
| **ARGUS (IRE)** | Ralph Beckett |
| **ASHDAQ (USA)** | William Haggas |
| **ASHLAN (FR)** | A. de Royer Dupre, France |
| **ASHRAF (IRE)** | D. K. Weld, Ireland |
| **ASPEN COLORADO (IRE)** | Aidan O'Brien, Ireland |
| **BAADI** | Roger Varian |
| **BAKSAR (FR)** | A. de Royer Dupre, France |
| **BALLYNANTY (IRE)** | Andrew Balding |
| **BANTRY BAY (IRE)** | Aidan O'Brien, Ireland |
| **BARBAROUS (IRE)** | |
| **BAREFOOT DANCER** | Michael Bell |
| **BARNACLE BILL (IRE)** | Mrs Jessie Harrington, Ireland |
| **BARREESH (IRE)** | Richard Hannon |
| **BASATEEN (IRE)** | Richard Hannon |
| **BAYOU (IRE)** | Aidan O'Brien, Ireland |
| **BEAU KNIGHT** | William Jarvis |
| **BENJAMIN DISRAELI (IRE)** | John Best |
| **BERMONDSEY** | Luca Cumani |
| **BEST OF TIMES** | Saeed bin Suroor |
| **BLENHEIM WARRIOR** | William Haggas |
| **BNEDEL (IRE)** | Richard Hannon |
| **BONDI BEACH (IRE)** | Aidan O'Brien, Ireland |
| **BONJOUR (IRE)** | Aidan O'Brien, Ireland |
| **BRIGHTLY SHINING (IRE)** | J. S. Bolger, Ireland |
| **BURNER (IRE)** | Lady Cecil |
| **CELESTIAL PATH (IRE)** | Sir Mark Prescott Bt |
| **CHEMICAL CHARGE (IRE)** | Ralph Beckett |
| **CHINA CLUB (IRE)** | John Gosden |
| **CHORUS OF LIES** | Charlie Appleby |
| **CHRISTMAS HAMPER (IRE)** | Sir Michael Stoute |
| **CHRISTOPHERMARLOWE (USA)** | John Gosden |
| **CIRCADIAN (FR)** | J. E. Pease, France |
| **CLASSIC COLLECTION** | Saeed bin Suroor |
| **CODESHARE** | Lady Cecil |
| **CONSORT (IRE)** | Sir Michael Stoute |
| **COSMO BIOS (JPN)** | Y. Suzuki, Japan |
| **COSMO REGULUS (USA)** | H. Shimizu, Japan |
| **CROCODILE ROCK (IRE)** | Aidan O'Brien, Ireland |
| **DANNYDAY** | Sir Michael Stoute |
| **DARIYAN (FR)** | A. de Royer Dupre, France |
| **DARK DEED** | Sir Michael Stoute |
| **DARTMOUTH** | Sir Michael Stoute |
| **DASAATEER (IRE)** | Roger Varian |
| **DAWN MIRAGE** | David Wachman, Ireland |
| **DAZZLING TIMES (USA)** | Charlie Appleby |
| **DECORATED KNIGHT** | Roger Varian |
| **DEEP CHALLENGER (IRE)** | Ger Lyons, Ireland |
| **DEERFIELD** | Charlie Appleby |
| **DESERT ENCOUNTER (IRE)** | David Simcock |
| **DIGITAL REBELLION (IRE)** | |
| **DISEGNO (IRE)** | Sir Michael Stoute |
| **DISSOLUTION** | Sir Michael Stoute |
| **EAST INDIA** | Aidan O'Brien, Ireland |
| **EASTERN APPROACH (IRE)** | J. S. Bolger, Ireland |
| **EDELPOUR (IRE)** | D. K. Weld, Ireland |
| **EGMONT** | George Moore |
| **EMIRATES SKYWARDS (IRE)** | Charlie Appleby |
| **ERUPT (IRE)** | F-H Graffard, France |
| **ESTIKHRAAJ** | Roger Varian |
| **ETIBAAR (USA)** | Brian Meehan |
| **EXCELLENT TEAM** | Saeed bin Suroor |
| **EXTERNALITY (USA)** | F-H Graffard, France |
| **FATHER CHRISTMAS (IRE)** | Aidan O'Brien, Ireland |
| **FESTIVE FARE** | Charlie Appleby |
| **FIELDS OF ATHENRY (IRE)** | Aidan O'Brien, Ireland |
| **FIESOLE** | Luca Cumani |
| **FUTURE EMPIRE** | Saeed bin Suroor |
| **GAME SET DASH (USA)** | G. M. Lyons, Ireland |
| **GAME SHOW** | Charlie Appleby |
| **GAYATH (GER)** | Richard Hannon |
| **GIANT REDWOOD (IRE)** | Aidan O'Brien, Ireland |
| **GIBB'S BEACH (IRE)** | Aidan O'Brien, Ireland |
| **GIBEON (IRE)** | Richard Hannon |
| **GIOVANNI CANALETTO (IRE)** | Aidan O'Brien, Ireland |
| **GIUSEPPE PIAZZI (IRE)** | Aidan O'Brien, Ireland |
| **GLOBALIST (GER)** | John Gosden |
| **GOLDEN BULLET** | Saeed bin Suroor |
| **GOLDEN INK (IRE)** | J. S. Bolger, Ireland |
| **GOOD JUDGE (USA)** | Saeed bin Suroor |
| **GOODWILL (IRE)** | Aidan O'Brien, Ireland |
| **GRAN PARADISO (IRE)** | Aidan O'Brien, Ireland |
| **GRAND INQUISITOR** | Sir Michael Stoute |
| **GREAT GLEN** | Ralph Beckett |
| **HAIL THE HERO (IRE)** | David O'Meara |
| **HALL OF FAME (IRE)** | J. S. Bolger, Ireland |
| **HALLMARK (IRE)** | Aidan O'Brien, Ireland |
| **HANOVER STREET (IRE)** | Aidan O'Brien, Ireland |
| **HANS HOLBEIN** | Aidan O'Brien, Ireland |
| **HARLEM** | A. Fabre, France |
| **HAVISHAM** | Andrew Balding |
| **HENRY HUDSON** | Roger Varian |
| **HEREDITY (FR)** | A. Fabre, France |
| **HIGH ADMIRAL** | Andrew Balding |
| **HIGHLAND REEL (IRE)** | Aidan O'Brien, Ireland |
| **HIPPARCHUS** | A. Fabre, France |

| HORSE | TRAINER |
|---|---|
| **HOBART (IRE)** | Aidan O'Brien, Ireland |
| **HOMELAND (IRE)** | Aidan O'Brien, Ireland |
| **HORSESHOE BAY (IRE)** | Sir Michael Stoute |
| **HUSHED TONES (IRE)** | David Wachman, Ireland |
| **I WANT TO FLY** | John Gosden |
| **I ZINGARI** | Sir Michael Stoute |
| **I'LL FIND MY WAY** | Mrs Jessie Harrington, Ireland |
| **IMPERIAL PALACE (IRE)** | Aidan O'Brien, Ireland |
| **IMPORTANT MESSAGE** | Saeed bin Suroor |
| **IN MY POCKET (IRE)** | John M. Oxx, Ireland |
| **INDIAN MONSOON (IRE)** | Sir Michael Stoute |
| **INSHAA** | Sir Michael Stoute |
| **INTILAAQ (USA)** | Roger Varian |
| **IRISH HAWKE (IRE)** | Luca Cumani |
| **IVANOVICH GORBATOV (IRE)** | Aidan O'Brien, Ireland |
| **JACK HOBBS** | John Gosden |
| **JACOBEAN (IRE)** | Aidan O'Brien, Ireland |
| **JAMAICA (IRE)** | Aidan O'Brien, Ireland |
| **JINSHA LAKE (IRE)** | Aidan O'Brien, Ireland |
| **JOHN F KENNEDY (IRE)** | Aidan O'Brien, Ireland |
| **JOSEPH JEFFERSON (IRE)** | Roger Varian |
| **KALAWAR (USA)** | D. K. Weld, Ireland |
| **KARAKTAR (IRE)** | A. de Royer Dupre, France |
| **KASSIM (IRE)** | A. de Royer Dupre, France |
| **KATIYMANN (IRE)** | D. K. Weld, Ireland |
| **KEBLE (IRE)** | John Gosden |
| **KERRYMERRY (IRE)** | Ismail Mohammed |
| **KILIMANJARO (IRE)** | Aidan O'Brien, Ireland |
| **KING OF ARAGON (IRE)** | Aidan O'Brien, Ireland |
| **KING OF COUNTRY** | Charlie Appleby |
| **KISUMU** | Sir Michael Stoute |
| **KYRENIA CASTLE (GER)** | David Nicholls |
| **LANATHEER** | F. Head, France |
| **LATIN QUARTER (IRE)** | Aidan O'Brien, Ireland |
| **LAUNCHED (IRE)** | P. Bary, France |
| **LE CIRQUE (IRE)** | Aidan O'Brien, Ireland |
| **LEGEND'S GATE (IRE)** | Charlie Appleby |
| **LIBRISA BREEZE** | Jeremy Noseda |
| **LORD BEN STACK (IRE)** | K. R. Burke |
| **LOS BARBADOS (IRE)** | Aidan O'Brien, Ireland |
| **MAGNETICJIM (IRE)** | P. Bary, France |
| **MALAF (USA)** | John Gosden |
| **MANAASEK (IRE)** | Jean Claude Rouget, France |
| **MARMION** | John Gosden |
| **MAWJOOD** | William Haggas |
| **MEDINA SIDONIA (IRE)** | Aidan O'Brien, Ireland |
| **MILKY WAY (IRE)** | Gary Moore |
| **MISHGHAR** | |
| **MISTER UNIVERSE** | Mark Johnston |
| **MOAYADD (USA)** | |
| **MOHATEM (USA)** | B. W. Hills |
| **MONEIN (USA)** | Charlie Appleby |
| **MONT D'ARGENT** | Mark Johnston |
| **MORNING MIX (IRE)** | J. S. Bolger, Ireland |
| **MR BISSTO** | Ian Williams |
| **MR QUICKSILVER** | Andrew Balding |
| **MR SINGH** | John Gosden |
| **MUFFARREH (USA)** | B. W. Hills |
| **MUFRAD (IRE)** | K. Prendergast, Ireland |
| **MUHTADIM (IRE)** | William Haggas |
| **MULZAMM (IRE)** | Charlie Appleby |
| **MUQTASER (USA)** | Roger Varian |
| **MURGAN** | Peter Chapple-Hyam |
| **MUSHTARAK** | J. E. Hammond, France |
| **MUSTAQQIL (IRE)** | John Gosden |

| HORSE | TRAINER |
|---|---|
| **MUTAMID** | Ismail Mohammed |
| **NAFAQA (IRE)** | B. W. Hills |
| **NEW AGENDA** | D. K. Weld, Ireland |
| **NEW DIRECTION (IRE)** | J. S. Bolger, Ireland |
| **NEWERA** | Tom Dascombe |
| **NEWMARCH** | Charlie Appleby |
| **NEWSPEAK (IRE)** | Charlie Appleby |
| **NORTH AMERICA** | Charlie Appleby |
| **NOVA (IRE)** | David Wachman, Ireland |
| **NOVIS ADVENTUS (IRE)** | J. S. Bolger, Ireland |
| **NUCIFERA (USA)** | J. E. Pease, France |
| **OCEANOGRAPHER** | Charlie Appleby |
| **OL' MAN RIVER (IRE)** | Aidan O'Brien, Ireland |
| **ORDER OF ST GEORGE (IRE)** | Aidan O'Brien, Ireland |
| **PATHWAY TO HONOUR** | Charlie Appleby |
| **PENANG PAPARAJA (IRE)** | Michael Bell |
| **PERCHE** | Charlie Appleby |
| **PETERHOF** | Sir Michael Stoute |
| **PETRUCCI (IRE)** | Sir Michael Stoute |
| **PICTOGRAM** | |
| **PIETRANGELO (IRE)** | David Lanigan |
| **PLANE SONG (IRE)** | Sir Michael Stoute |
| **PLAYMAKER (IRE)** | Charlie Appleby |
| **PLEIADES** | Sir Michael Stoute |
| **PORT** | Richard Hannon |
| **PORTAMENTO (IRE)** | Charlie Appleby |
| **POWER GAME** | Saeed bin Suroor |
| **PREDOMINANCE (IRE)** | William Haggas |
| **PRINCE GAGARIN (IRE)** | Ed Dunlop |
| **PROPOSED** | Richard Hannon |
| **PROSPECTOR (USA)** | Aidan O'Brien, Ireland |
| **PUERTO PADRE (IRE)** | Charlie Appleby |
| **PURPLE ROCK (IRE)** | Charles Hills |
| **PYTHON** | P. Bary, France |
| **QAWAAREB (IRE)** | Jean Claude Rouget, France |
| **RAAKID (IRE)** | George Peckham |
| **RACING HISTORY (IRE)** | Saeed bin Suroor |
| **RADANPOUR (IRE)** | D. K. Weld, Ireland |
| **RAFEEQ (FR)** | Ed Dunlop |
| **RARE RHYTHM** | Charlie Appleby |
| **RAW IMPULSE** | Clive Cox |
| **RED CARDINAL (IRE)** | Aidan O'Brien, Ireland |
| **RICHARD OF YORKE** | Luca Cumani |
| **RINGMASTER (IRE)** | Aidan O'Brien, Ireland |
| **ROCKET PUNCH (IRE)** | Andrew Balding |
| **ROCKY RIDER** | Andrew Balding |
| **ROGUE RUNNER (GER)** | Andreas Wohler, Germany |
| **ROOM KEY** | Eve Johnson Houghton |
| **SAHAAFY (USA)** | B. W. Hills |
| **SAMBA STORM (IRE)** | Michael Figge, Germany |
| **SANDRO BOTTICELLI (IRE)** | Aidan O'Brien, Ireland |
| **SECOND WAVE (IRE)** | Charlie Appleby |
| **SEYFERT GALAXY** | P. Bary, France |
| **SHALIYAN (FR)** | M. Delzangles, France |
| **SHARK ISLAND (IRE)** | Aidan O'Brien, Ireland |
| **SHAYWAN (IRE)** | A. de Royer Dupre, France |
| **SHERLOCK HOLMES (IRE)** | Aidan O'Brien, Ireland |
| **SIGHT HOUND (USA)** | D. K. Weld, Ireland |
| **SIGNED SEALED (USA)** | John Gosden |
| **SILK KNIGHT** | W. Jarvis |
| **SIR GEORGE AIRY (IRE)** | Aidan O'Brien, Ireland |
| **SIR ISAAC NEWTON** | Aidan O'Brien, Ireland |
| **SIRHEED (IRE)** | Richard Hannon |
| **SKY CAPE** | Charlie Appleby |
| **SKYGAZER (IRE)** | Ali Rashid Al Raihe, U.A.E. |

| HORSE | TRAINER |
|---|---|
| **SLEEP EASY** | Hughie Morrison |
| **SLEIGHT OF HAND (IRE)** | Jamie Osborne |
| **SNEAKING BUDGE** | David Lanigan |
| **SNOANO** | John Gosden |
| **SPACE AGE (IRE)** | Charlie Appleby |
| **SPANISH SQUEEZE (IRE)** | Hugo Palmer |
| **SPEEDY MOVE (IRE)** | Ismail Mohammed |
| **SPERRIN (IRE)** | Charlie Appleby |
| **ST PATRICK'S DAY (IRE)** | Aidan O'Brien, Ireland |
| **ST SAVIOUR** | Andrew Balding |
| **STORM CHECK** | |
| **SUBCONTINENT (IRE)** | Charlie Appleby |
| **SUMMER PARADISE (FR)** | J. Hirschberger, Germany |
| **SURPRISE CALL** | Sir Michael Stoute |
| **SYMBOLIC STAR (IRE)** | Charlie Appleby |
| **SYNODIC (USA)** | David Lanigan |
| **TALE OF LIFE (JPN)** | P. Bary, France |
| **TAMARIND COVE (IRE)** | Aidan O'Brien, Ireland |
| **TANIYAR (IRE)** | A. de Royer Dupre, France |
| **TAQASEEM** | K. Prendergast, Ireland |
| **TASHAAR (IRE)** | |
| **TATAWU (IRE)** | Brian Meehan |
| **TAWAASHEEH (IRE)** | Roger Varian |
| **THAHAB (IRE)** | Richard Hannon |
| **THE GREAT MAGOO (USA)** | |
| **TIME TEST** | Roger Charlton |
| **TIME TO INSPIRE (IRE)** | D. K. Weld, Ireland |
| **TIRYAM (IRE)** | D. K. Weld, Ireland |
| **TOCCATA (IRE)** | Aidan O'Brien, Ireland |
| **TORREY PINES (IRE)** | Aidan O'Brien, Ireland |
| **TOSCANELLI (IRE)** | Aidan O'Brien, Ireland |
| **TRACT (IRE)** | P. Bary, France |
| **TREVISANI (IRE)** | David Lanigan |
| **TUK TUK** | D. K. Weld, Ireland |
| **TWELFTH DAN** | Jim Allen |
| **UNYIELDING** | Mrs Jessie Harrington, Ireland |
| **USTINOV** | Brian Meehan |
| **VAZIRABAD (FR)** | A. de Royer Dupre, France |
| **VISANDI (FR)** | |
| **VOCALISER (IRE)** | J. S. Bolger, Ireland |
| **WARDELL** | David Wachman, Ireland |
| **WATHAAB (IRE)** | Jean Claude Rouget, France |
| **WELD AL EMARAT** | Kevin Ryan |
| **WELL OFF (GER)** | Saeed bin Suroor |
| **WEMYSS POINT** | |
| **WHAT SAY YOU (IRE)** | Rae Guest |
| **WHO DARES WINS (IRE)** | Richard Hannon |
| **WISDEN (IRE)** | |
| **YA HADE YE DELIL** | Richard Hannon |
| **YUKON GOLD** | Abdulla bin Huzaim, U.A.E. |
| **ZAIN GALILEO (IRE)** | Robert Cowell |
| **ZAINISH (IRE)** | D. K. Weld, Ireland |
| **ZARAND (USA)** | D. K. Weld, Ireland |
| **ZARKAR (FR)** | A. de Royer Dupre, France |
| **ZAWRAQ (IRE)** | D. K. Weld, Ireland |
| **ZOURKHAN (IRE)** | A. de Royer Dupre, France |
| **ZYRJANN (IRE)** | Jean Claude Rouget, France |
| **EX CEILIDH BAND** | Brian Barr |
| **EX CIRCLE OF LIFE (USA)** | Aidan O'Brien, Ireland |
| **EX RAGS TO RICHES (USA)** | Aidan O'Brien, Ireland |
| **EX SHAMARA (IRE)** | |

# THE CSP EUROPEAN FREE HANDICAP

## NEWMARKET CRAVEN MEETING 2015 (ON THE ROWLEY MILE COURSE) WEDNESDAY APRIL 15TH

The CSP European Free Handicap (Class 1) (Listed race) with total prize fund of £37,000 for two-year-olds only of 2014 which are included in the European 2-y-o Thoroughbred Rankings or which, in 2014, either ran in Great Britain or ran for a trainer who at the time was licensed by the British Horseracing Authority, and are Rated 100 or above; lowest weight 8st; highest weight 9st 7lbs.

Penalty for a winner after December 31st 2014, 5 lbs. Seven furlongs.

| Rating | | st | lb |
|---|---|---|---|
| 119 | **BELARDO** (IRE) | 9 | 7 |
| 118 | **CHARMING THOUGHT** (GB) | 9 | 6 |
| 117 | **ELM PARK** (GB) | 9 | 5 |
| 117 | **FOUND** (IRE) | 9 | 5 |
| 117 | **IVAWOOD** (IRE) | 9 | 5 |
| 117 | **TIGGY WIGGY** (IRE) | 9 | 5 |
| 116 | **GLENEAGLES** (IRE) | 9 | 4 |
| 116 | **RICHARD PANKHURST** (GB) | 9 | 4 |
| 116 | **THE WOW SIGNAL** (IRE) | 9 | 4 |
| 115 | **DICK WHITTINGTON** (IRE) | 9 | 3 |
| 115 | **ESTIDHKAAR** (IRE) | 9 | 3 |
| 115 | **HOOTENANNY** (USA) | 9 | 3 |
| 115 | **KODI BEAR** (IRE) | 9 | 3 |
| 115 | **LIMATO** (IRE) | 9 | 3 |
| 115 | **VERT DE GRECE** (IRE) | 9 | 3 |
| 114 | **ANTHEM ALEXANDER** (IRE) | 9 | 2 |
| 114 | **FULL MAST** (USA) | 9 | 2 |
| 114 | **JOHN F KENNEDY** (IRE) | 9 | 2 |
| 114 | **MUHAARAR** (GB) | 9 | 2 |
| 114 | **OL' MAN RIVER** (IRE) | 9 | 2 |
| 114 | **TERRITORIES** (IRE) | 9 | 2 |
| 113 | **CAPPELLA SANSEVERO** (GB) | 9 | 1 |
| 113 | **EPICURIS** (GB) | 9 | 1 |
| 113 | **KOOL KOMPANY** (IRE) | 9 | 1 |
| 113 | **TOOCOOLFORSCHOOL** (IRE) | 9 | 1 |
| 113 | **TOSCANINI** (IRE) | 9 | 1 |
| 112 | **BURNT SUGAR** (IRE) | 9 | 0 |
| 112 | **CURSORY GLANCE** (USA) | 9 | 0 |
| 112 | **ERVEDYA** (FR) | 9 | 0 |
| 112 | **MAFTOOL** (USA) | 9 | 0 |
| 112 | **PEACE AND WAR** (USA) | 9 | 0 |
| 111 | **ALOFT** (IRE) | 8 | 13 |
| 111 | **COTAI GLORY** (GB) | 8 | 13 |
| 111 | **DUTCH CONNECTION** (GB) | 8 | 13 |
| 111 | **HIGH CELEBRITY** (FR) | 8 | 13 |
| 111 | **LUCIDA** (IRE) | 8 | 13 |
| 111 | **MATTMU** (GB) | 8 | 13 |
| 111 | **SUNSET GLOW** (USA) | 8 | 13 |
| 111 | **WAR ENVOY** (USA) | 8 | 13 |
| 110 | **ALEA LACTA** (GB) | 8 | 12 |
| 110 | **BRISANTO** (GB) | 8 | 12 |
| 110 | **CELESTIAL PATH** (IRE) | 8 | 12 |
| 110 | **EVASIVE'S FIRST** (FR) | 8 | 12 |
| 110 | **FAITHFUL CREEK** (IRE) | 8 | 12 |
| 110 | **HERO LOOK** (IRE) | 8 | 12 |
| 110 | **JUNGLE CAT** (IRE) | 8 | 12 |
| 110 | **MEDLEY CHIC** (IRE) | 8 | 12 |
| 110 | **RAPID APPLAUSE** (GB) | 8 | 12 |
| 110 | **RAYDARA** (IRE) | 8 | 12 |
| 110 | **SMUGGLER'S COVE** (IRE) | 8 | 12 |
| 110 | **TOGETHER FOREVER** (IRE) | 8 | 12 |
| 109 | **AGNES STEWART** (IRE) | 8 | 11 |
| 109 | **AHLAN EMARATI** (IRE) | 8 | 11 |
| 109 | **COMMEMORATIVE** (GB) | 8 | 11 |
| 109 | **HIGHLAND REEL** (IRE) | 8 | 11 |
| 109 | **JUSTICE GOOD** (IRE) | 8 | 11 |
| 109 | **MALABAR** (GB) | 8 | 11 |
| 109 | **NAFAQA** (IRE) | 8 | 11 |
| 109 | **OSAILA** (IRE) | 8 | 11 |
| 109 | **WINTER'S MOON** (IRE) | 8 | 11 |
| 108 | **ACES** (IRE) | 8 | 10 |
| 108 | **AKTABANTAY** (GB) | 8 | 10 |
| 108 | **ANGELIC LORD** (IRE) | 8 | 10 |
| 108 | **BAITHA ALGA** (IRE) | 8 | 10 |
| 108 | **FADHAYYIL** (IRE) | 8 | 10 |
| 107 | **BEACON** (GB) | 8 | 9 |
| 107 | **GLENALMOND** (IRE) | 8 | 9 |
| 107 | **JOHNNY BARNES** (IRE) | 8 | 9 |
| 107 | **LIKELY** (GER) | 8 | 9 |
| 107 | **MARKAZ** (IRE) | 8 | 9 |
| 107 | **STRATH BURN** (GB) | 8 | 9 |
| 107 | **TENDU** (GB) | 8 | 9 |
| 107 | **TERROR** (IRE) | 8 | 9 |
| 107 | **THE GREAT WAR** (USA) | 8 | 9 |
| 106 | **DISEGNO** (IRE) | 8 | 8 |
| 106 | **PEACOCK** (GB) | 8 | 8 |
| 106 | **PRIZE EXHIBIT** (GB) | 8 | 8 |
| 106 | **THE WARRIOR** (IRE) | 8 | 8 |
| 105 | **ADAAY** (IRE) | 8 | 7 |
| 105 | **ELYSIAN FLYER** (IRE) | 8 | 7 |
| 105 | **FAST ACT** (IRE) | 8 | 7 |
| 105 | **MARSH HAWK** (GB) | 8 | 7 |
| 104 | **ASTROPHYSICS** (GB) | 8 | 6 |
| 104 | **BASATEEN** (IRE) | 8 | 6 |
| 104 | **CALYPSO BEAT** (USA) | 8 | 6 |
| 104 | **CRAFTY CHOICE** (GB) | 8 | 6 |
| 104 | **HAWKESBURY** (GB) | 8 | 6 |
| 104 | **MURAAQABA** (GB) | 8 | 6 |
| 104 | **NEW PROVIDENCE** (GB) | 8 | 6 |
| 104 | **PORTAMENTO** (IRE) | 8 | 6 |

| Rating | | st | lb |
|---|---|---|---|
| 104 | **SECRET BRIEF** (IRE) | 8 | 6 |
| 104 | **WET SAIL** (USA) | 8 | 6 |
| 104 | **WHITE LAKE** (GB) | 8 | 6 |
| 103 | **BRONZE MAQUETTE** (IRE) | 8 | 5 |
| 103 | **ROOM KEY** (GB) | 8 | 5 |
| 103 | **SMAIH** (GER) | 8 | 5 |
| 103 | **TIGRILLA** (IRE) | 8 | 5 |
| 102 | **ACCEPTED** (IRE) | 8 | 4 |
| 102 | **CODE RED** (GB) | 8 | 4 |
| 102 | **ELITE GARDENS** (USA) | 8 | 4 |
| 102 | **FAYDHAN** (USA) | 8 | 4 |
| 102 | **HEARTBREAK HERO** (GB) | 8 | 4 |
| 102 | **HOME OF THE BRAVE** (IRE) | 8 | 4 |
| 102 | **IZZTHATRIGHT** (IRE) | 8 | 4 |
| 102 | **JAMAICA** (GB) | 8 | 4 |
| 102 | **LOUIE DE PALMA** (GB) | 8 | 4 |
| 102 | **MIND OF MADNESS** (IRE) | 8 | 4 |
| 102 | **MUBTAGHAA** (IRE) | 8 | 4 |
| 102 | **NEWSLETTER** (IRE) | 8 | 4 |
| 102 | **OUTLAW COUNTRY** (IRE) | 8 | 4 |
| 102 | **ROYAL RAZALMA** (IRE) | 8 | 4 |
| 102 | **RUSSIAN PUNCH** (GB) | 8 | 4 |

| Rating | | st | lb |
|---|---|---|---|
| 102 | **STROLL PATROL** (GB) | 8 | 4 |
| 101 | **ARABIAN QUEEN** (IRE) | 8 | 3 |
| 101 | **AZMAAM** (IRE) | 8 | 3 |
| 101 | **BOSSY GUEST** (IRE) | 8 | 3 |
| 101 | **DARK RECKONING** (GB) | 8 | 3 |
| 101 | **FOX TROTTER** (IRE) | 8 | 3 |
| 101 | **JACOBEAN** (IRE) | 8 | 3 |
| 101 | **SALATEEN** (GB) | 8 | 3 |
| 101 | **SHAGAH** (IRE) | 8 | 3 |
| 100 | **ALGAITH** (USA) | 8 | 2 |
| 100 | **BALLYMORE CASTLE** (IRE) | 8 | 2 |
| 100 | **COCK OF THE NORTH** (GB) | 8 | 2 |
| 100 | **DIAZ** (IRE) | 8 | 2 |
| 100 | **FUTURE EMPIRE** (GB) | 8 | 2 |
| 100 | **MEDRANO** (GB) | 8 | 2 |
| 100 | **PARSLEY** (IRE) | 8 | 2 |
| 100 | **PATIENCE ALEXANDER** (IRE) | 8 | 2 |
| 100 | **RESTORER** (GB) | 8 | 2 |
| 100 | **SNOANO** (GB) | 8 | 2 |
| 100 | **SQUATS** (IRE) | 8 | 2 |
| 100 | **TUPI** (IRE) | 8 | 2 |
| 100 | **VOLATILE** (SWE) | 8 | 2 |

# LONGINES WORLD'S BEST RACEHORSE RANKINGS AND EUROPEAN THOROUGHBRED RANKINGS 2014

for three-year-olds rated 115 or greater by the IFHA World's Best Racehorse Rankings Conference. Horses rated 114-110 by the European Thoroughbred Rankings Conference do not constitute a part of the World's Best Racehorse Rankings. Those ratings were compiled on behalf of the European Pattern Committee.

| Rating | | Trained |
|---|---|---|
| 127 | **AUSTRALIA** (GB) | IRE |
| 127 | **KINGMAN** (GB) | GB |
| 127 | **THE GREY GATSBY** (IRE) | GB |
| 125 | **BAYERN** (USA) | USA |
| 125 | **SEA THE MOON** (GER) | GER |
| 124 | **CALIFORNIA CHROME** (USA) | USA |
| 124 | **TOAST OF NEW YORK** (USA) | GB |
| 123 | **SHARED BELIEF** (USA) | USA |
| 123 | **TAGHROODA** (GB) | GB |
| 122 | **CHARM SPIRIT** (IRE) | FR |
| 121 | **NIGHT OF THUNDER** (IRE) | GB |
| 120 | **ADELAIDE** (IRE) | IRE |
| 120 | **FREE EAGLE** (IRE) | IRE |
| 120 | **KARAKONTIE** (JPN) | FR |
| 120 | **KINGSTON HILL** (GB) | GB |
| 120 | **PRIORE PHILIP** (ITY) | ITY |
| 120 | **TAPESTRY** (IRE) | IRE |
| 120 | **TO THE WORLD** (JPN) | JPN |
| 120 | **TONALIST** (USA) | USA |
| 119 | **EAGLE TOP** (GB) | GB |
| 119 | **ONE AND ONLY** (JPN) | JPN |
| 119 | **RIDE ON CURLIN** (USA) | USA |
| 119 | **TOORMORE** (IRE) | GB |
| 119 | **UNTAPABLE** (USA) | USA |
| 118 | **COMMANDING CURVE** (USA) | USA |
| 118 | **G FORCE** (IRE) | GB |
| 118 | **GAILO CHOP** (FR) | FR |
| 118 | **IL CAMPIONE** (CHI) | CHI |
| 118 | **LUCKY LION** (GB) | GER |
| 118 | **OUTSTRIP** (GB) | GB |
| 118 | **TOHO JACKAL** (JPN) | JPN |
| 118 | **V E DAY** (USA) | USA |
| 118 | **WICKED STRONG** (USA) | USA |
| 117 | **ACT OF WAR** (SAF) | SAF |
| 117 | **DANZA** (USA) | USA |
| 117 | **ECTOT** (GB) | FR |
| 117 | **HARP STAR** (JPN) | JPN |
| 117 | **HOPPERTUNITY** (USA) | USA |
| 117 | **ISLA BONITA** (JPN) | JPN |
| 117 | **MUSTAJEEB** (GB) | IRE |
| 117 | **PENIAPHOBIA** (IRE) | HK |
| 117 | **PRINCE GIBRALTAR** (FR) | FR |
| 117 | **SIR FEVER** (URU) | URU |
| 117 | **SOUNDS OF EARTH** (JPN) | JPN |
| 117 | **TAPITURE** (USA) | USA |
| 117 | **WAR COMMAND** (USA) | IRE |
| 116 | **AVENIR CERTAIN** (FR) | FR |
| 116 | **BOBBY'S KITTEN** (USA) | USA |
| 116 | **COMMISSIONER** (USA) | USA |
| 116 | **DOLNIYA** (FR) | FR |
| 116 | **DUE DILIGENCE** (USA) | IRE |
| 116 | **DYLAN MOUTH** (IRE) | ITY |
| 116 | **GALLANTE** (IRE) | FR |
| 116 | **MARVELLOUS** (IRE) | IRE |
| 116 | **NOOZHOH CANARIAS** (SPA) | FR |
| 116 | **PAINT NAIF** (BRZ) | BRZ |
| 116 | **POSTPONED** (IRE) | GB |
| 116 | **PRESTIGE VENDOME** (FR) | FR |
| 116 | **RANGALI** (GB) | FR |
| 116 | **RICH ENUFF** (AUS) | AUS |
| 116 | **SHOOTING TO WIN** (AUS) | AUS |
| 116 | **YUFTEN** (GB) | GB |
| 115 | **ALEX ROSSI** (ARG) | PER |
| 115 | **ARTEMIS AGROTERA** (USA) | USA |
| 115 | **BLUES TRAVELER** (ARG) | ARG |
| 115 | **BONAPARTE** (BRZ) | BRZ |
| 115 | **BOW CREEK** (IRE) | GB |
| 115 | **BRAZEN BEAU** (AUS) | AUS |
| 115 | **CAIRO PRINCE** (USA) | USA |
| 115 | **CANDY BOY** (USA) | USA |
| 115 | **CONSTITUTION** (USA) | USA |
| 115 | **DANZENO** (GB) | GB |
| 115 | **EL MOISES** (ARG) | ARG |
| 115 | **HALLOWED CROWN** (AUS) | AUS |
| 115 | **HAMPTON COURT** (AUS) | AUS |
| 115 | **IL FORNAIO** (ARG) | ARG |
| 115 | **LIBERAL** (PER) | PER |
| 115 | **MEINER FROST** (JPN) | JPN |
| 115 | **MISS FRANCE** (IRE) | FR |
| 115 | **MR SPEAKER** (USA) | USA |
| 115 | **OUTPLAY** (BRZ) | BRZ |
| 115 | **PREFERMENT** (NZ) | AUS |
| 115 | **PROTONICO** (USA) | USA |
| 115 | **ROMSDAL** (GB) | GB |
| 115 | **RUBICK** (AUS) | AUS |
| 115 | **SHIFTING POWER** (GB) | GB |
| 115 | **TARIS** (USA) | USA |
| 115 | **VICAR'S IN TROUBLE** (USA) | USA |
| 115 | **WE ARE** (IRE) | FR |
| 114 | **EURO CHARLINE** (GB) | GB |
| 114 | **FINTRY** (IRE) | FR |
| 114 | **HOT STREAK** (IRE) | GB |
| 114 | **MANATEE** (GB) | FR |
| 114 | **SIRIUS** (GER) | GER |
| 114 | **SOMEWHAT** (USA) | GB |
| 114 | **WESTERN HYMN** (GB) | GB |
| 113 | **BAWINA** (IRE) | FR |
| 113 | **EXTORTIONIST** (IRE) | GB |
| 113 | **HADAATHA** (IRE) | GB |
| 113 | **MADAME CHIANG** (GB) | GB |
| 113 | **SAVANNE** (IRE) | FR |
| 113 | **SHAMKIYR** (FR) | FR |
| 113 | **SIGNS OF BLESSING** (IRE) | FR |
| 113 | **SNOW SKY** (GB) | GB |

| Rating | | Trained |
|---|---|---|
| 113 | **TARFASHA** (IRE) | IRE |
| 113 | **TELETEXT** (USA) | FR |
| 113 | **VEDA** (FR) | FR |
| 112 | **AMOUR A PAPA** (FR) | FR |
| 112 | **BERKSHIRE** (IRE) | GB |
| 112 | **BODHI** (FR) | FR |
| 112 | **BRACELET** (IRE) | IRE |
| 112 | **COUGAR MOUNTAIN** (IRE) | IRE |
| 112 | **FEODORA** (GER) | GER |
| 112 | **FREE PORT LUX** (GB) | FR |
| 112 | **LAVENDER LANE** (IRE) | FR |
| 112 | **LIGHTNING MOON** (IRE) | GB |
| 112 | **MAGIC ARTIST** (IRE) | GER |
| 112 | **MUWAARY** (GB) | GB |
| 112 | **PORNICHET** (FR) | FR |
| 112 | **RIZEENA** (IRE) | GB |
| 112 | **SHAMKALA** (FR) | FR |
| 112 | **TRUE STORY** (GB) | GB |
| 112 | **VORDA** (FR) | FR |
| 112 | **WILD CHIEF** (GER) | GER |
| 112 | **WINDSHEAR** (GB) | GB |
| 112 | **XCELLENCE** (FR) | FR |
| 111 | **AJAXANA** (GER) | GER |
| 111 | **ANJAAL** (GB) | GB |
| 111 | **ASTAIRE** (IRE) | GB |
| 111 | **BALL DANCING** (USA) | USA |
| 111 | **CANNOCK CHASE** (USA) | GB |
| 111 | **EBANORAN** (IRE) | IRE |
| 111 | **ERIC** (GER) | GER |
| 111 | **FASCINATING ROCK** (IRE) | IRE |
| 111 | **FINAL SCORE** (IRE) | ITY |
| 111 | **GONNA RUN** (FR) | FR |
| 111 | **INDIAN RAINBOW** (IRE) | GER |
| 111 | **KINGFISHER** (IRE) | IRE |
| 111 | **LIGHTNING THUNDER** (GB) | GB |
| 111 | **MEKONG RIVER** (IRE) | IRE |
| 111 | **MUTAKAYYEF** (GB) | GB |
| 111 | **ORCHESTRA** (IRE) | IRE |
| 111 | **VOLUME** (GB) | GB |
| 110 | **AROD** (IRE) | GB |
| 110 | **BIG ORANGE** (GB) | GB |
| 110 | **CLEO FAN** (ITY) | ITY |
| 110 | **CRISOLLES** (FR) | FR |
| 110 | **ELLIPTIQUE** (IRE) | FR |
| 110 | **FARMAH** (USA) | FR |
| 110 | **FOREVER NOW** (GB) | GB |
| 110 | **GALIWAY** (GB) | FR |
| 110 | **GEOFFREY CHAUCER** (USA) | IRE |
| 110 | **GIANT'S CAULDRON** (GER) | GER |
| 110 | **GUARDINI** (FR) | GER |
| 110 | **HAKEEM** (USA) | TUR |
| 110 | **HARTNELL** (GB) | GB |
| 110 | **IHTIMAL** (IRE) | GB |
| 110 | **INCHILA** (GB) | GB |
| 110 | **INDONESIENNE** (IRE) | FR |
| 110 | **KIYOSHI** (GB) | GB |
| 110 | **LA HOGUETTE** (FR) | FR |
| 110 | **LACY** (GER) | GER |
| 110 | **LESSTALK IN PARIS** (IRE) | FR |
| 110 | **MARZOCCO** (USA) | GB |
| 110 | **MECCA'S ANGEL** (IRE) | GB |
| 110 | **NORDICO** (GER) | GER |
| 110 | **PANAMA HAT** (GB) | IRE |
| 110 | **PLANETAIRE** (GB) | FR |
| 110 | **PRINCE OF ALL** (GB) | IRE |
| 110 | **SON CESIO** (FR) | FR |
| 110 | **TESTED** (GB) | IRE |
| 110 | **WANNABE YOURS** (IRE) | GB |

# OLDER HORSES 2014

for four-year-olds and up rated 115 or greater by the IFHA World's Best Racehorse Rankings Conference. Horses rated 114-110 by the European Thoroughbred Rankings Conference do not constitute a part of the World's Best Racehorse Rankings. Those ratings were compiled on behalf of the European Pattern Committee.

| Rating | Horse | Age | Trained |
|---|---|---|---|
| 130 | **JUST A WAY** (JPN) | 5 | JPN |
| 129 | **EPIPHANEIA** (JPN) | 4 | JPN |
| 127 | **ABLE FRIEND** (AUS) | 5 | HK |
| 127 | **VARIETY CLUB** (SAF) | 6 | UAE |
| 126 | **TREVE** (FR) | 4 | FR |
| 124 | **GAME ON DUDE** (USA) | 7 | USA |
| 124 | **GOLD SHIP** (JPN) | 5 | JPN |
| 124 | **MAIN SEQUENCE** (USA) | 5 | USA |
| 124 | **THE FUGUE** (GB) | 5 | GB |
| 124 | **WISE DAN** (USA) | 7 | USA |
| 123 | **AFRICAN STORY** (GB) | 7 | GB |
| 123 | **CIRRUS DES AIGLES** (FR) | 8 | FR |
| 123 | **DESIGNS ON ROME** (IRE) | 4 | HK |
| 123 | **FLINTSHIRE** (GB) | 4 | FR |
| 123 | **LANKAN RUPEE** (AUS) | 5 | AUS |
| 123 | **MAGICIAN** (IRE) | 4 | IRE |
| 123 | **PALACE MALICE** (USA) | 4 | USA |
| 123 | **RAVE** (IRE) / **MILITARY ATTACK** (IRE) | 6 | HK |
| 123 | **TERRAVISTA** (AUS) | 5 | AUS |
| 122 | **AKEED MOFEED** (GB) | 5 | HK |
| 122 | **CHAUTAUQUA** (AUS) | 4 | AUS |
| 122 | **DUNDEEL** (NZ) | 5 | NZ |
| 122 | **GOLD-FUN** (IRE) | 5 | HK |
| 122 | **NOBLE MISSION** (GB) | 5 | GB |
| 122 | **OLYMPIC GLORY** (IRE) | 4 | GB |
| 122 | **TELESCOPE** (IRE) | 4 | GB |
| 121 | **ADMIRE RAKTI** (JPN) | 6 | JPN |
| 121 | **AL KAZEEM** (GB) | 6 | GB |
| 121 | **BLAZING SPEED** (GB) | 5 | HK |
| 121 | **DISSIDENT** (AUS) | 4 | AUS |
| 121 | **KIZUNA** (JPN) | 4 | JPN |
| 121 | **MUKHADRAM** (GB) | 5 | GB |
| 121 | **TORONADO** (IRE) | 4 | GB |
| 121 | **WILL TAKE CHARGE** (USA) | 4 | USA |
| 120 | **BAL A BALI** (BRZ) | 4 | BRZ |
| 120 | **GOLDENCENTS** (USA) | 4 | USA |
| 120 | **IVANHOWE** (GER) | 4 | GER |
| 120 | **LUCKY NINE** (IRE) | 7 | HK |
| 120 | **OBVIOUSLY** (IRE) | 6 | USA |
| 120 | **PROTECTIONIST** (GER) | 4 | GER |
| 120 | **SACRED FALLS** (NZ) | 5 | AUS |
| 120 | **SPIELBERG** (JPN) | 5 | JPN |
| 119 | **CARLTON HOUSE** (USA) | 6 | AUS |
| 119 | **DUNBOYNE EXPRESS** (IRE) | 6 | HK |
| 119 | **HOKKO TARUMAE** (JPN) | 5 | JPN |
| 119 | **LEA** (USA) | 5 | USA |
| 119 | **PRIVATE ZONE** (CAN) | 5 | USA |
| 119 | **RULER OF THE WORLD** (IRE) | 4 | IRE |
| 119 | **SLADE POWER** (IRE) | 5 | IRE |
| 119 | **TWILIGHT ECLIPSE** (USA) | 5 | USA |
| 119 | **VERRAZANO** (USA) | 4 | IRE |
| 119 | **WAR AFFAIR** (NZ) | 4 | SIN |
| 119 | **YORKER** (SAF) | 5 | SAF |
| 118 | **AEROVELOCITY** (NZ) | 6 | HK |
| 118 | **ANODIN** (IRE) | 4 | FR |
| 118 | **BOBAN** (AUS) | 5 | AUS |
| 118 | **BROWN PANTHER** (GB) | 6 | GB |
| 118 | **FAWKNER** (AUS) | 7 | AUS |
| 118 | **GENTILDONNA** (JPN) | 5 | JPN |
| 118 | **GRAND PRIX BOSS** (JPN) | 6 | JPN |
| 118 | **HARDEST CORE** (USA) | 4 | USA |
| 118 | **IDOLO PORTENO** (ARG) | 4 | ARG |
| 118 | **LAST IMPACT** (JPN) | 4 | JPN |
| 118 | **SAHARA SKY** (USA) | 6 | USA |
| 118 | **SIR WINSALOT** (ARG) | 4 | ARG |
| 118 | **SOLE POWER** (GB) | 7 | IRE |
| 118 | **SPALATO** (NZ) | 5 | SIN |
| 118 | **STERLING CITY** (AUS) | 6 | HK |
| 118 | **TRADING LEATHER** (IRE) | 4 | IRE |
| 118 | **TULLIUS** (IRE) | 6 | GB |
| 118 | **VERCINGETORIX** (SAF) | 5 | SAF |
| 117 | **AL REP** (IRE) / **PACKING WHIZ** (IRE). | 6 | HK |
| 117 | **AMBER SKY** (AUS) | 5 | HK |
| 117 | **AMBITIOUS DRAGON** (NZ) | 8 | HK |
| 117 | **ARASIN** (IRE) / **HELENE SPIRIT** (IRE) | 7 | HK |
| 117 | **BEHOLDER** (USA) | 4 | USA |
| 117 | **BUFFERING** (AUS) | 7 | AUS |
| 117 | **CLOSE HATCHES** (USA) | 4 | USA |
| 117 | **COPANO RICHARD** (JPN) | 4 | JPN |
| 117 | **COPANO RICKEY** (JPN) | 4 | JPN |
| 117 | **CRITERION** (NZ) | 4 | AUS |
| 117 | **CUSTOM CUT** (IRE) | 5 | GB |
| 117 | **DANON SHARK** (JPN) | 6 | JPN |
| 117 | **DOMINANT** (IRE) | 6 | HK |
| 117 | **ENDOWING** (IRE) | 5 | HK |
| 117 | **ESOTERIQUE** (IRE) | 4 | FR |
| 117 | **FENOMENO** (JPN) | 5 | JPN |
| 117 | **FIORENTE** (IRE) | 6 | AUS |
| 117 | **HAPPY TRAILS** (AUS) | 7 | AUS |
| 117 | **HILLSTAR** (GB) | 4 | GB |
| 117 | **INTEGRAL** (GB) | 4 | GB |
| 117 | **IOTAPA** (USA) | 4 | USA |
| 117 | **LEADING LIGHT** (IRE) | 4 | IRE |
| 117 | **LEGISLATE** (SAF) | 4 | SAF |
| 117 | **MOONSHINE MULLIN** (USA) | 6 | USA |
| 117 | **MORENO** (USA) | 4 | USA |
| 117 | **MYSTERY TRAIN** (ARG) | 4 | ARG |
| 117 | **REAL SOLUTION** (USA) | 5 | USA |
| 117 | **SILENT ACHIEVER** (NZ) | 6 | NZ |
| 117 | **SOLOW** (GB) | 4 | FR |
| 117 | **TAC DE BOISTRON** (FR) | 7 | GB |
| 117 | **WORK ALL WEEK** (USA) | 5 | USA |
| 116 | **AHTOUG** (GB) | 6 | UAE |
| 116 | **AMRALAH** (IRE) | 4 | GB |
| 116 | **APPEARANCE** (AUS) | 6 | AUS |
| 116 | **BALTIC BARONESS** (GER) | 4 | FR |
| 116 | **CAPTAIN OF ALL** (SAF) | 4 | SAF |
| 116 | **CAZALS** (IRE) / **WILLIE CAZALS** (IRE) . | 6 | HK |
| 116 | **CURREN MIROTIC** (JPN) | 6 | JPN |
| 116 | **FIERO** (JPN) | 5 | JPN |
| 116 | **FORETELLER** (GB) | 7 | AUS |
| 116 | **GLORIOUS DAYS** (AUS) | 7 | HK |
| 116 | **GORDON LORD BYRON** (IRE) | 6 | IRE |
| 116 | **HERE COMES WHEN** (IRE) | 4 | GB |
| 116 | **HOKKO BRAVE** (JPN) | 6 | JPN |
| 116 | **I'M YOUR MAN** (FR) | 5 | AUS |

| Rating | Horse | Age | Trained |
|---|---|---|---|
| 116 | **IMAGINING** (USA) | 6 | USA |
| 116 | **ITSMYLUCKYDAY** (USA) | 4 | USA |
| 116 | **KAIGUN** (CAN) | 4 | CAN |
| 116 | **KING OF PAIN** (SAF) | 5 | SAF |
| 116 | **LIVINGSTONE** (ARG) | 4 | ARG |
| 116 | **LOCHTE** (USA) | 4 | USA |
| 116 | **LOUIS THE KING** (SAF) | 4 | SAF |
| 116 | **MASTER OF MY FATE** (SAF) | 5 | SAF |
| 116 | **MOMENT OF CHANGE** (AUS) | 6 | AUS |
| 116 | **NASHVILLE** (NZ) | 6 | NZ |
| 116 | **PRINCE BISHOP** (IRE) | 7 | GB |
| 116 | **PRINCESS OF SYLMAR** (USA) | 4 | USA |
| 116 | **REBEL DANE** (AUS) | 5 | AUS |
| 116 | **RICH TAPESTRY** (IRE) | 6 | HK |
| 116 | **SEEK AGAIN** (USA) | 4 | USA |
| 116 | **SHAMUS AWARD** (AUS) | 4 | AUS |
| 116 | **SHEA SHEA** (SAF) | 7 | SAF |
| 116 | **SIDE GLANCE** (GB) | 7 | GB |
| 116 | **THISTLE BIRD** (GB) | 6 | GB |
| 116 | **TRUST IN A GUST** (AUS) | 4 | AUS |
| 116 | **VAGABOND SHOES** (IRE) | 7 | USA |
| 116 | **WIN VARIATION** (JPN) | 6 | JPN |
| 116 | **WORLD ACE** (JPN) | 5 | JPN |
| 115 | **ALJAMAAHEER** (IRE) | 5 | GB |
| 115 | **ANSGAR** (IRE) | 6 | IRE |
| 115 | **BELLE GALLANTEY** (USA) | 5 | USA |
| 115 | **BIG BLUE KITTEN** (USA) | 6 | USA |
| 115 | **BIG MACHER** (USA) | 4 | USA |
| 115 | **CAPETOWN NOIR** (SAF) | 5 | SAF |
| 115 | **CAVALRYMAN** (GB) | 8 | GB |
| 115 | **CHARLES THE GREAT** (IRE) | 5 | HK |
| 115 | **CLEARLY NOW** (USA) | 4 | USA |
| 115 | **COPPER PARADE** (SAF) | 7 | SAF |
| 115 | **DADS CAPS** (USA) | 4 | USA |
| 115 | **DAYATTHESPA** (USA) | 5 | USA |
| 115 | **DESPERADO** (JPN) | 6 | JPN |
| 115 | **DIBAYANI** (IRE) | 4 | HK |
| 115 | **DON'T TELL SOPHIA** (USA) | 6 | USA |
| 115 | **EMPOLI** (GER) | 4 | GER |
| 115 | **ERNEST HEMINGWAY** (IRE) | 5 | IRE |
| 115 | **EUROZONE** (AUS) | 4 | AUS |
| 115 | **FAMOUS SEAMUS** (NZ) | 6 | AUS |
| 115 | **FARRAAJ** (IRE) | 5 | GB |
| 115 | **FLAMINGO STAR** (GER) | 4 | GER |
| 115 | **FRENCH NAVY** (GB) | 6 | GB |
| 115 | **FUTURA** (SAF) | 4 | SAF |
| 115 | **GARSWOOD** (GB) | 4 | GB |
| 115 | **GOSPEL CHOIR** (GB) | 5 | GB |
| 115 | **GREEN MOON** (IRE) | 7 | AUS |
| 115 | **GREGORIAN** (IRE) | 5 | GB |
| 115 | **GROUPIE DOLL** (USA) | 6 | USA |
| 115 | **GUEST OF HONOUR** (IRE) | 5 | GB |
| 115 | **HANGOVER KID** (USA) | 6 | USA |
| 115 | **HAWKSPUR** (AUS) | 5 | AUS |
| 115 | **HILL FIFTY FOUR** (SAF) | 6 | SAF |
| 115 | **HIT THE TARGET** (JPN) | 6 | JPN |
| 115 | **IMPERATIVE** (USA) | 4 | USA |
| 115 | **IP MAN** (NZ) | 6 | SIN |
| 115 | **JUDY THE BEAUTY** (CAN) | 5 | USA |
| 115 | **JUNOOB** (GB) | 6 | AUS |
| 115 | **L'AMOUR DE MA VIE** (USA) | 5 | FR |
| 115 | **LACHESIS** (JPN) | 4 | JPN |
| 115 | **LENOVO** (ARG) | 4 | ARG |
| 115 | **LIDERIS** (USA) | 4 | PER |
| 115 | **LINES OF BATTLE** (USA) | 4 | HK |
| 115 | **LONG JOHN** (AUS) | 4 | UAE |
| 115 | **LOVE IS BOO SHET** (JPN) | 5 | JPN |
| 115 | **MAJESTIC HARBOR** (USA) | 6 | USA |
| 115 | **MARCHMAN** (USA) | 4 | USA |
| 115 | **MIDNIGHT LUCKY** (USA) | 4 | USA |
| 115 | **MSHAWISH** (USA) | 4 | FR |
| 115 | **MUSIC VAN** (ARG) | 5 | ARG |
| 115 | **NAMURA VICTOR** (JPN) | 5 | JPN |
| 115 | **NOT LISTENIN'TOME** (AUS) | 4 | AUS |
| 115 | **OFFER** (IRE) | 5 | AUS |
| 115 | **PALACE** (USA) | 5 | USA |
| 115 | **POMOLOGY** (USA) | 4 | GB |
| 115 | **PUCCINI** (NZ) | 4 | NZ |
| 115 | **PUISSANCE DE LUNE** (IRE) | 6 | AUS |
| 115 | **RED CADEAUX** (GB) | 8 | GB |
| 115 | **RED TRACER** (AUS) | 7 | AUS |
| 115 | **ROYAL DESCENT** (AUS) | 5 | AUS |
| 115 | **SECRET CIRCLE** (USA) | 5 | USA |
| 115 | **SERTORIUS** (AUS) | 7 | AUS |
| 115 | **SHAKIN IT UP** (USA) | 4 | USA |
| 115 | **SHAMEXPRESS** (NZ) | 5 | AUS |
| 115 | **SHUKA** (NZ) | 6 | NZ |
| 115 | **SHURUQ** (USA) | 4 | UAE |
| 115 | **SKY HUNTER** (GB) | 4 | GB |
| 115 | **SMOKING SUN** (USA) | 5 | FR |
| 115 | **SNOW DRAGON** (JPN) | 6 | JPN |
| 115 | **SOMMERABEND** (GB) | 7 | GER |
| 115 | **SPEEDINESS** (AUS) | 7 | AUS |
| 115 | **SPIRIT OF BOOM** (AUS) | 7 | AUS |
| 115 | **STEEN** (URU) | 4 | URU |
| 115 | **STEINBECK** (IRE) | 7 | NZ |
| 115 | **SUMMER FRONT** (USA) | 5 | USA |
| 115 | **TODO UN AMIGUITO** (ARG) | 6 | ARG |
| 115 | **TOM'S TRIBUTE** (USA) | 4 | USA |
| 115 | **TOSEN RA** (JPN) | 6 | JPN |
| 115 | **TRADE STORM** (GB) | 6 | GB |
| 115 | **TROPICS** (USA) | 6 | GB |
| 115 | **UP WITH THE BIRDS** (CAN) | 4 | CAN |
| 115 | **WONDER ACUTE** (JPN) | 8 | JPN |
| 115 | **WYLIE HALL** (AUS) | 5 | SAF |
| 115 | **ZAC SPIRIT** (AUS) | 5 | SIN |
| 115 | **ZIVO** (USA) | 5 | USA |
| 114 | **ALMANDIN** (GER) | 4 | GER |
| 114 | **ALTANO** (GER) | 8 | GER |
| 114 | **CHICQUITA** (IRE) | 4 | IRE |
| 114 | **DARWIN** (USA) | 4 | IRE |
| 114 | **EARL OF TINSDAL** (GER) | 6 | GER |
| 114 | **ES QUE LOVE** (IRE) | 5 | GB |
| 114 | **MULL OF KILLOUGH** (IRE) | 8 | GB |
| 114 | **NORSE KING** (FR) | 5 | FR |
| 114 | **OCEAN TEMPEST** (GB) | 5 | GB |
| 114 | **RIBBONS** (GB) | 4 | GB |
| 114 | **STEPPER POINT** (GB) | 5 | GB |
| 114 | **TERRUBI** (IRE) | 4 | FR |
| 114 | **UNDRAFTED** (USA) | 4 | USA |
| 114 | **VERDETTO FINALE** (GB) | 4 | ITY |
| 113 | **AHZEEMAH** (IRE) | 5 | GB |
| 113 | **BRETON ROCK** (IRE) | 4 | GB |
| 113 | **CAPTAIN CAT** (IRE) | 5 | GB |
| 113 | **CATCALL** (FR) | 5 | FR |
| 113 | **FEUERBLITZ** (GER) | 5 | GER |
| 113 | **FIESOLANA** (IRE) | 5 | IRE |
| 113 | **FORGOTTEN RULES** (IRE) | 4 | IRE |
| 113 | **GATEWOOD** (GB) | 6 | GB |
| 113 | **GRANDEUR** (IRE) | 5 | GB |
| 113 | **GRAPHIC** (IRE) | 5 | GB |
| 113 | **LUCKY SPEED** (IRE) | 4 | GER |
| 113 | **MAAREK** (GB) | 7 | IRE |
| 113 | **MISSUNITED** (IRE) | 7 | IRE |

| Rating | | Age | Trained |
|---|---|---|---|
| 113 | **MOVE IN TIME** (GB) | 6 | GB |
| 113 | **PENITENT** (GB) | 8 | GB |
| 113 | **PETHER'S MOON** (IRE) | 4 | GB |
| 113 | **RED DUBAWI** (IRE) | 6 | GER |
| 113 | **SHEIKHZAYEDROAD** (GB) | 5 | GB |
| 113 | **SILJAN'S SAGA** (FR) | 4 | FR |
| 113 | **SOFT FALLING RAIN** (SAF) | 5 | SAF |
| 113 | **SPIRITJIM** (FR) | 4 | FR |
| 113 | **SULTANINA** (GB) | 4 | GB |
| 113 | **TAKE COVER** (GB) | 7 | GB |
| 113 | **WAKE FOREST** (GER) | 4 | GER |
| 112 | **AMARON** (GB) | 5 | GER |
| 112 | **AMBIVALENT** (IRE) | 5 | GB |
| 112 | **CERTERACH** (IRE) | 6 | IRE |
| 112 | **CHOPIN** (GER) | 4 | GER |
| 112 | **CUBANITA** (GB) | 5 | GB |
| 112 | **FRACTIONAL** (IRE) | 5 | FR |
| 112 | **GOING SOMEWHERE** (BRZ) | 5 | FR |
| 112 | **HIGH JINX** (IRE) | 6 | GB |
| 112 | **MOUNT ATHOS** (IRE) | 7 | GB |
| 112 | **MOVIESTA** (USA) | 4 | GB |
| 112 | **MUSIC MASTER** (GB) | 4 | GB |
| 112 | **NIGHT WISH** (GER) | 4 | GER |
| 112 | **NOW WE CAN** (GB) | 5 | FR |
| 112 | **PARISH HALL** (IRE) | 5 | IRE |
| 112 | **PEARL SECRET** (GB) | 5 | GB |
| 112 | **PINTURICCHIO** (IRE) | 6 | FR |
| 112 | **RUSSIAN SOUL** (IRE) | 6 | IRE |
| 112 | **SEISMOS** (IRE) | 6 | GB |
| 112 | **SINGING** (FR) | 4 | GER |
| 112 | **TIGER CLIFF** (IRE) | 5 | GB |
| 111 | **AIR PILOT** (GB) | 5 | GB |
| 111 | **ARAB SPRING** (IRE) | 4 | GB |
| 111 | **BATHYRHON** (GER) | 4 | FR |
| 111 | **BRENDAN BRACKAN** (IRE) | 5 | IRE |
| 111 | **BRONZE ANGEL** (IRE) | 5 | GB |
| 111 | **CAT O'MOUNTAIN** (USA) | 4 | GB |
| 111 | **CHIL THE KITE** (GB) | 5 | GB |
| 111 | **COCKTAIL QUEEN** (IRE) | 4 | FR |
| 111 | **DANK** (GB) | 5 | GB |
| 111 | **DARTAGNAN D'AZUR** (FR) | 5 | GER |
| 111 | **DUCA DI MANTOVA** (GB) | 5 | ITY |
| 111 | **JACK DEXTER** (GB) | 5 | GB |
| 111 | **JUST THE JUDGE** (IRE) | 4 | GB |
| 111 | **KINGSGATE NATIVE** (IRE) | 9 | GB |
| 111 | **MEDICEAN MAN** (GB) | 8 | GB |
| 111 | **MUTUAL REGARD** (IRE) | 5 | IRE |
| 111 | **NARROW HILL** (GER) | 6 | FR |
| 111 | **NEATICO** (GER) | 7 | GER |
| 111 | **SIMENON** (IRE) | 7 | IRE |
| 111 | **SPIRIT QUARTZ** (IRE) | 6 | FR |
| 111 | **SRUTHAN** (IRE) | 4 | IRE |

| Rating | | Age | Trained |
|---|---|---|---|
| 111 | **STAR LAHIB** (IRE) | 5 | GER |
| 111 | **TOP NOTCH TONTO** (IRE) | 4 | GB |
| 111 | **TRIPLE THREAT** (FR) | 4 | FR |
| 111 | **WILLING FOE** (USA) | 7 | GB |
| 111 | **WINDHOEK** (GB) | 4 | GB |
| 110 | **AMARILLO** (IRE) | 5 | GER |
| 110 | **AMERICAN DEVIL** (FR) | 5 | FR |
| 110 | **AU REVOIR** (GB) | 4 | FR |
| 110 | **BANK OF BURDEN** (USA) | 7 | NOR |
| 110 | **BENVENUE** (IRE) | 5 | ITY |
| 110 | **BIOGRAPHER** (GB) | 5 | GB |
| 110 | **ENCKE** (USA) | 5 | GB |
| 110 | **ENTREE** (GB) | 4 | FR |
| 110 | **EUPHRASIA** (IRE) | 5 | IRE |
| 110 | **FENCING** (USA) | 5 | GB |
| 110 | **FLY WITH ME** (FR) | 4 | FR |
| 110 | **HALL OF MIRRORS** (IRE) | 4 | IRE |
| 110 | **HEERAAT** (IRE) | 5 | GB |
| 110 | **INIS MEAIN** (USA) | 7 | IRE |
| 110 | **INTRANSIGENT** (GB) | 5 | GB |
| 110 | **JOSHUA TREE** (IRE) | 7 | GB |
| 110 | **KENHOPE** (FR) | 4 | FR |
| 110 | **KOKALTASH** (FR) | 4 | FR |
| 110 | **LOUIS THE PIOUS** (GB) | 6 | GB |
| 110 | **MELEAGROS** (IRE) | 5 | FR |
| 110 | **MIRZA** (GB) | 7 | GB |
| 110 | **MONTCLAIR** (IRE) | 4 | FR |
| 110 | **MY OLD HUSBAND** (FR) | 6 | FR |
| 110 | **NARNIYN** (IRE) | 4 | FR |
| 110 | **NAUSICA TIME** (GER) | 4 | GER |
| 110 | **ORSINO** (GER) | 7 | GER |
| 110 | **PALLASATOR** (GB) | 5 | GB |
| 110 | **PEACE AT LAST** (IRE) | 4 | FR |
| 110 | **PEACE BURG** (FR) | 4 | IRE |
| 110 | **POLLYANA** (IRE) | 5 | FR |
| 110 | **PRINCESS LOULOU** (IRE) | 4 | GB |
| 110 | **PRODUCER** (GB) | 5 | GB |
| 110 | **ROERO** (FR) | 5 | FR |
| 110 | **ROYAL DIAMOND** (IRE) | 8 | IRE |
| 110 | **SEAL OF APPROVAL** (GB) | 5 | GB |
| 110 | **SECRET GESTURE** (GB) | 4 | GB |
| 110 | **SHARESTAN** (IRE) | 6 | GB |
| 110 | **SILK SARI** (GB) | 4 | GB |
| 110 | **SKY LANTERN** (IRE) | 4 | GB |
| 110 | **SPOIL THE FUN** (FR) | 5 | FR |
| 110 | **STEPS** (IRE) | 6 | GB |
| 110 | **TENOR** (IRE) | 4 | GB |
| 110 | **THAWAANY** (IRE) | 4 | FR |
| 110 | **VENUS DE MILO** (IRE) | 4 | IRE |
| 110 | **VIF MONSIEUR** (GER) | 4 | GER |
| 110 | **VILLAGE WIND** (TUR) | 4 | TUR |
| 110 | **WITHOUT FEAR** (FR) | 6 | NOR |

# RACEFORM CHAMPIONS 2014

**ONLY HORSES TRAINED IN EUROPE ARE INCLUDED.**

## FOUR-YEAR-OLDS AND UP

| Horse | Rating |
|---|---|
| TREVE | 127 |
| CIRRUS DES AIGLES | 126 |
| THE FUGUE | 125 |
| FLINTSHIRE | 125 |
| OLYMPIC GLORY | 125 |
| TELESCOPE | 125 |
| MAGICIAN | 124 |
| TORONADO | 124 |

## THREE-YEAR-OLD COLT

| Horse | Rating |
|---|---|
| AUSTRALIA | 129 |
| KINGMAN | 128 |
| THE GREY GATSBY | 126 |
| CHARM SPIRIT | 124 |
| NIGHT OF THUNDER | 124 |

## THREE-YEAR-OLD FILLY

| Horse | Rating |
|---|---|
| TAGHROODA | 125 |
| TAPESTRY | 121 |
| AVENIR CERTAIN | 118 |
| DOLNIYA | 117 |
| MARVELLOUS | 117 |
| MISS FRANCE | 117 |

## SPRINTER

| Horse | Rating |
|---|---|
| SLADE POWER | 123 |
| G FORCE | 121 |
| GORDON LORD BYRON | 121 |
| SOLE POWER | 120 |
| MAAREK | 118 |
| RANGALI | 118 |

## STAYER

| Horse | Rating |
|---|---|
| LEADING LIGHT | 121 |
| BROWN PANTHER | 119 |
| KINGSTON HILL | 119 |
| TAC DE BOISTRON | 119 |
| CAVALRYMAN | 118 |

## TWO-YEAR-OLD COLT

| Horse | Rating |
|---|---|
| BELARDO | 119 |
| ELM PARK | 118 |
| CHARMING THOUGHT | 117 |
| IVAWOOD | 117 |
| ESTIDHKAAR | 116 |
| GLENEAGLES | 116 |
| THE WOW SIGNAL | 116 |

## TWO-YEAR-OLD FILLY

| Horse | Rating |
|---|---|
| TIGGY WIGGY | 117 |
| FOUND | 116 |
| ANTHEM ALEXANDER | 115 |
| CURSORY GLANCE | 112 |
| HIGH CELEBRITY | 111 |
| LUCIDIA | 111 |

# MEDIAN TIMES 2014

The following Raceform median times are used in the calculation of the Split Second speed figures. They represent a true average time for the distance, which has been arrived at after looking at the winning times for all races over each distance within the past five years, except for those restricted to two or three-year-olds.

Some current race distances have been omitted as they have not yet had a sufficient number of races run over them to produce a reliable average time.

## ASCOT

| Distance | Time |
|---|---|
| 5f | 1m 0.50 |
| 6f | 1m 14.50 |
| 7f | 1m 27.60 |
| 1m Round | 1m 40.70 |
| 1m Straight | 1m 40.80 |
| 1m 2f | 2m 7.40 |
| 1m 4f | 2m 32.50 |
| 1m 6f | 3m 1.00 |
| 2m | 3m 29.00 |
| 2m 4f | 4m 24.80 |
| 2m 5f 159y | 4m 49.40 |

## AYR

| Distance | Time |
|---|---|
| 5f | 59.40 |
| 6f | 1m 12.40 |
| 7f 50y | 1m 33.40 |
| 1m | 1m 43.80 |
| 1m 1f 20y | 1m 57.50 |
| 1m 2f | 2m 12.00 |
| 1m 5f 13y | 2m 54.00 |
| 1m 7f | 3m 20.40 |
| 2m 1f 105y | 3m 55.00 |

## BATH

| Distance | Time |
|---|---|
| 5f 11y | 1m 2.50 |
| 5f 161y | 1m 11.20 |
| 1m 5y | 1m 40.80 |
| 1m 2f 46y | 2m 11.00 |
| 1m 3f 144y | 2m 30.60 |
| 1m 5f 22y | 2m 52.00 |
| 2m 1f 34y | 3m 51.90 |

## BEVERLEY

| Distance | Time |
|---|---|
| 5f | 1m 3.50 |
| 7f 100y | 1m 33.80 |
| 1m 100y | 1m 47.60 |
| 1m 1f 207y | 2m 7.00 |
| 1m 4f 16y | 2m 39.80 |
| 2m 35y | 3m 39.80 |

## BRIGHTON

| Distance | Time |
|---|---|
| 5f 59y | 1m 2.30 |
| 5f 213y | 1m 10.20 |
| 6f 209y | 1m 23.10 |
| 7f 214y | 1m 36.00 |
| 1m 1f 209y | 2m 3.60 |
| 1m 3f 196y | 2m 32.70 |

## CARLISLE

| Distance | Time |
|---|---|
| 5f | 1m 0.80 |
| 5f 193y | 1m 13.70 |
| 6f 192y | 1m 27.10 |
| 7f 200y | 1m 40.00 |
| 1m 1f 61y | 1m 57.60 |
| 1m 3f 107y | 2m 23.10 |
| 1m 6f 32y | 3m 7.50 |
| 2m 1f 52y | 3m 53.00 |

## CATTERICK

| Distance | Time |
|---|---|
| 5f | 59.80 |
| 5f 212y | 1m 13.60 |
| 7f | 1m 27.00 |
| 1m 3f 214y | 2m 38.90 |
| 1m 5f 175y | 3m 3.60 |
| 1m 7f 177y | 3m 32.00 |

## CHEPSTOW

| Distance | Time |
|---|---|
| 5f 16y | 59.30 |
| 6f 16y | 1m 12.00 |
| 7f 16y | 1m 23.20 |
| 1m 14y | 1m 36.20 |
| 1m 2f 36y | 2m 10.60 |
| 1m 4f 23y | 2m 39.00 |
| 2m 49y | 3m 38.90 |
| 2m 2f | 4m 3.60 |

## CHESTER

| Distance | Time |
|---|---|
| 5f 16y | 1m 1.00 |
| 5f 110y | 1m 6.20 |
| 6f 18y | 1m 13.80 |
| 7f 2y | 1m 26.50 |
| 7f 122y | 1m 33.80 |
| 1m 2f 75y | 2m 11.20 |
| 1m 3f 79y | 2m 24.80 |
| 1m 4f 66y | 2m 38.50 |
| 1m 5f 89y | 2m 52.70 |
| 1m 6f 91y | 3m 7.00 |
| 1m 7f 195y | 3m 28.00 |
| 2m 2f 147y | 4m 4.80 |

## DONCASTER

| Distance | Time |
|---|---|
| 5f | 1m 0.50 |
| 5f 140y | 1m 8.80 |
| 6f | 1m 13.60 |
| 6f 110y | 1m 19.90 |
| 7f | 1m 26.30 |
| 1m Straight | 1m 39.30 |
| 1m Round | 1m 39.70 |
| 1m 2f 60y | 2m 9.40 |
| 1m 4f | 2m 34.90 |
| 1m 6f 132y | 3m 7.40 |
| 2m 110y | 3m 40.40 |
| 2m 2f | 3m 55.00 |

## EPSOM

5f........ 55.70
6f........ 1m 9.40
7f........ 1m 23.30
1m 114y........ 1m 46.10
1m 2f 18y........ 2m 9.70
1m 4f 10y........ 2m 38.90

## FFOS LAS

5f........ 58.30
6f........ 1m 10.00
1m........ 1m 41.00
1m 2f........ 2m 9.40
1m 4f........ 2m 37.40
1m 6f........ 3m 3.80
2m........ 3m 30.00

## GOODWOOD

5f........ 1m 0.20
6f........ 1m 12.20
7f........ 1m 27.00
1m........ 1m 39.90
1m 1f........ 1m 56.30
1m 1f 192y........ 2m 8.10
1m 3f........ 2m 26.50
1m 4f........ 2m 38.40
1m 6f........ 3m 3.60
2m........ 3m 29.00
2m 5f........ 4m 31.00

## HAMILTON

5f 4y........ 1m 0.00
6f 5y........ 1m 12.20
1m 65y........ 1m 48.40
1m 1f 36y........ 1m 59.70
1m 3f 16y........ 2m 25.60
1m 4f 17y........ 2m 38.60
1m 5f 9y........ 2m 53.90

## HAYDOCK

5f........ 1m 0.80
5fI........ 1m 0.80
6f........ 1m 13.80
6fI........ 1m 13.80
7f........ 1m 30.70
1m........ 1m 43.70
1m 2f 95y........ 2m 15.50
1m 3f 200y........ 2m 33.80
1m 6f........ 3m 2.00
2m 45y........ 3m 34.30

## KEMPTON (A.W)

5f........ 1m 0.50
6f........ 1m 13.10
7f........ 1m 26.00
1m........ 1m 39.80
1m 2f........ 2m 8.00
1m 3f........ 2m 21.90
1m 4f........ 2m 34.50
2m........ 3m 30.10

## LEICESTER

5f 2y........ 1m 0.00
5f 218y........ 1m 13.00
7f 9y........ 1m 26.20
1m 60y........ 1m 45.10
1m 1f 218y........ 2m 7.90
1m 3f 183y........ 2m 33.90

## LINGFIELD

5f........ 58.20
6f........ 1m 11.20
7f........ 1m 23.30
7f 140y........ 1m 32.30
1m 1f........ 1m 56.60
1m 2f........ 2m 10.50
1m 3f 106y........ 2m 31.50
1m 6f........ 3m 10.00

## LINGFIELD (A.W)

5f 6y........ 58.80
6f 1y........ 1m 11.90
7f 1y........ 1m 24.80
1m 1y........ 1m 38.20
1m 2f........ 2m 6.60
1m 4f........ 2m 33.00
1m 5f........ 2m 46.00
1m 7f 169y........ 3m 25.70

## MUSSELBURGH

5f........ 1m 0.40
7f 30y........ 1m 29.00
1m........ 1m 41.20
1m 1f........ 1m 53.90
1m 4f 100y........ 2m 42.00
1m 5f........ 2m 52.00
1m 6f........ 3m 5.30
2m........ 3m 33.50

## NEWBURY

5f 34y........ 1m 1.40
6f 8y........ 1m 13.00
6f 110y........ 1m 19.30
7f Straight........ 1m 25.70
1m Straight........ 1m 39.70
1m 7y Round........ 1m 38.70
1m 1f........ 1m 55.50
1m 2f 6y........ 2m 8.80
1m 3f 5y........ 2m 21.20
1m 4f 5y........ 2m 35.50
1m 5f 61y........ 2m 52.00
2m........ 3m 32.00

## NEWCASTLE

5f........ 1m 1.10
6f........ 1m 14.60
7f........ 1m 27.80
1m Round........ 1m 45.30
1m 3y Straight........ 1m 43.40
1m 2f 32y........ 2m 11.90
1m 4f 93y........ 2m 45.60
1m 6f 97y........ 3m 11.30
2m 19y........ 3m 39.40

## NEWMARKET (ROWLEY MILE)

| Distance | Time |
|---|---|
| 5f | 59.10 |
| 6f | 1m 12.20 |
| 7f | 1m 25.40 |
| 1m | 1m 38.60 |
| 1m 1f | 1m 51.70 |
| 1m 2f | 2m 5.80 |
| 1m 4f | 2m 32.00 |
| 1m 6f | 2m 57.00 |
| 2m | 3m 30.50 |
| 2m 2f | 3m 52.00 |

## NEWMARKET (JULY COURSE)

| Distance | Time |
|---|---|
| 5f | 59.10 |
| 6f | 1m 12.50 |
| 7f | 1m 25.70 |
| 1m | 1m 40.00 |
| 1m 2f | 2m 5.50 |
| 1m 4f | 2m 32.90 |
| 1m 5f | 2m 44.00 |
| 1m 6f 175y | 3m 8.40 |
| 2m 24y | 3m 27.00 |

## NOTTINGHAM

| Distance | Time |
|---|---|
| 5f 13y | 1m 1.50 |
| 5f 13y Inner | 1m 1.50 |
| 6f 15y | 1m 14.70 |
| 1m 75y | 1m 49.00 |
| 1m 75y Inner | 1m 49.00 |
| 1m 1f | 1m 57.60 |
| 1m 2f 50y | 2m 14.30 |
| 1m 2f 50y Inner | 2m 14.30 |
| 1m 6f 15y | 3m 7.00 |
| 1m 6f 15y Inner | 3m 7.00 |
| 2m 9y | 3m 34.50 |

## PONTEFRACT

| Distance | Time |
|---|---|
| 5f | 1m 3.30 |
| 6f | 1m 16.90 |
| 1m 4y | 1m 45.90 |
| 1m 2f 6y | 2m 13.70 |
| 1m 4f 8y | 2m 40.80 |
| 2m 1f 22y | 3m 44.60 |
| 2m 1f 216y | 3m 56.20 |
| 2m 5f 122y | 4m 51.00 |

## REDCAR

| Distance | Time |
|---|---|
| 5f | 58.60 |
| 6f | 1m 11.80 |
| 7f | 1m 24.50 |
| 1m | 1m 36.60 |
| 1m 1f | 1m 53.00 |
| 1m 2f | 2m 7.10 |
| 1m 6f 19y | 3m 4.70 |
| 2m 4y | 3m 31.40 |

## RIPON

| Distance | Time |
|---|---|
| 5f | 1m 0.00 |
| 6f | 1m 13.00 |
| 1m | 1m 41.40 |
| 1m 1f | 1m 54.70 |
| 1m 1f 170y | 2m 5.40 |
| 1m 4f 10y | 2m 36.70 |
| 2m | 3m 31.80 |

## SALISBURY

| Distance | Time |
|---|---|
| 5f | 1m 1.00 |
| 6f | 1m 14.80 |
| 6f 212y | 1m 28.60 |
| 1m | 1m 43.50 |
| 1m 1f 198y | 2m 9.90 |
| 1m 4f | 2m 38.00 |
| 1m 6f 21y | 3m 7.40 |

## SANDOWN

| Distance | Time |
|---|---|
| 5f 6y | 1m 1.60 |
| 7f 16y | 1m 29.50 |
| 1m 14y | 1m 43.30 |
| 1m 1f | 1m 55.70 |
| 1m 2f 7y | 2m 10.50 |
| 1m 6f | 3m 4.50 |
| 2m 78y | 3m 38.70 |

## SOUTHWELL (A.W)

| Distance | Time |
|---|---|
| 5f | 59.70 |
| 6f | 1m 16.50 |
| 7f | 1m 30.30 |
| 1m | 1m 43.70 |
| 1m 3f | 2m 28.00 |
| 1m 4f | 2m 41.00 |
| 1m 6f | 3m 8.30 |
| 2m | 3m 45.50 |

## THIRSK

| Distance | Time |
|---|---|
| 5f | 59.60 |
| 6f | 1m 12.70 |
| 7f | 1m 27.20 |
| 1m | 1m 40.10 |
| 1m 4f | 2m 36.20 |
| 2m | 3m 28.30 |

## WINDSOR

| Distance | Time |
|---|---|
| 5f 10y | 1m 0.30 |
| 6f | 1m 13.00 |
| 1m 67y | 1m 44.70 |
| 1m 2f 7y | 2m 8.70 |
| 1m 3f 135y | 2m 29.50 |

## WOLVERHAMPTON (A.W)

| Distance | Time |
|---|---|
| 5f 20y | 1m 1.90 |
| 5f 216y | 1m 14.50 |
| 7f 32y | 1m 28.80 |
| 1m 141y | 1m 50.10 |
| 1m 1f 103y | 2m 0.80 |
| 1m 4f 50y | 2m 40.80 |
| 1m 5f 194y | 3m 4.80 |
| 2m 119y | 3m 43.70 |

**YARMOUTH**

| | | | | | |
|---|---|---|---|---|---|
| 5f 43y | 1m 2.70 | 1m 3y | 1m 40.60 | 1m 3f 101y | 2m 28.70 |
| 6f 3y | 1m 14.40 | 1m 1f | 1m 55.80 | 1m 6f 17y | 3m 7.60 |
| 7f 3y | 1m 26.60 | 1m 2f 21y | 2m 10.50 | 2m | 3m 32.40 |

**YORK**

| | | | | | |
|---|---|---|---|---|---|
| 5f | 59.30 | 1m | 1m 39.00 | 1m 4f | 2m 33.20 |
| 5f 89y | 1m 4.10 | 1m 110y | 1m 45.90 | 1m 6f | 3m 0.20 |
| 6f | 1m 11.90 | 1m 208y | 1m 52.00 | 2m 88y | 3m 34.50 |
| 7f | 1m 25.30 | 1m 2f 88y | 2m 12.50 | 2m 2f | 3m 55.40 |

# RACEFORM RECORD TIMES (FLAT)

## ASCOT

| DISTANCE | TIME | AGE | WEIGHT | GOING | HORSE | DATE | | |
|---|---|---|---|---|---|---|---|---|
| 5f | 58.80 secs | 2 | 9-1 | Good To Firm | **NO NAY NEVER** | Jun | 20 | 2013 |
| 5f | 57.44 secs | 6 | 9-1 | Good To Firm | **MISS ANDRETTI** | Jun | 19 | 2007 |
| 6f | 1m 12.46 | 2 | 9-1 | Good To Firm | **HENRYTHENAVIGATOR** | Jun | 19 | 2007 |
| 6f | 1m 11.50 | 3 | 9-10 | Good To Firm | **MINCE** | Aug | 11 | 2012 |
| 7f | 1m 26.55 | 2 | 9-0 | Good To Firm | **MALABAR** | July | 25 | 2014 |
| 7f | 1m 24.28 | 4 | 8-11 | Good To Firm | **GALICIAN** | July | 27 | 2013 |
| 1m (Rnd) | 1m 39.55 | 2 | 8-12 | Good | **JOSHUA TREE** | Sep | 26 | 2009 |
| 1m (Rnd) | 1m 38.32 | 3 | 9-0 | Good To Firm | **GHANAATI** | Jun | 19 | 2009 |
| 1m (Str) | 1m 37.09 | 4 | 9-0 | Good To Firm | **INTEGRAL** | Jun | 18 | 2014 |
| 1m 2f | 2m 01.90 | 5 | 8-11 | Good To Firm | **THE FUGUE** | Jun | 18 | 2014 |
| 1m 4f | 2m 24.60 | 4 | 9-7 | Good | **NOVELLIST** | July | 27 | 2013 |
| 2m | 3m 24.13 | 3 | 9-1 | Good To Firm | **HOLBERG** | May | 2 | 2007 |
| 2m 4f | 4m 16.92 | 6 | 9-2 | Good To Firm | **RITE OF PASSAGE** | Jun | 17 | 2010 |
| 2m 5f 159y | 4m 47.79 | 7 | 9-2 | Good To Firm | **BERGO** | Jun | 19 | 2010 |

## AYR

| DISTANCE | TIME | AGE | WEIGHT | GOING | HORSE | DATE | | |
|---|---|---|---|---|---|---|---|---|
| 5f | 56.9 secs | 2 | 8-11 | Good | **BOOGIE STREET** | Sep | 18 | 2003 |
| 5f | 55.68 secs | 3 | 8-11 | Good To Firm | **LOOK BUSY** | Jun | 21 | 2008 |
| 6f | 1m 09.7 | 2 | 7-10 | Good | **SIR BERT** | Sep | 17 | 1969 |
| 6f | 1m 08.37 | 5 | 8-6 | Good To Firm | **MAISON DIEU** | Jun | 21 | 2008 |
| 7f 50y | 1m 28.9 | 2 | 9-0 | Good | **TAFAAHUM** | Sep | 19 | 2003 |
| 7f 50y | 1m 28.07 | 5 | 9-0 | Good To Firm | **GINGER JACK** | May | 30 | 2012 |
| 1m | 1m 39.18 | 2 | 9-7 | Good | **MOONLIGHTNAVIGATOR** | Sep | 18 | 2014 |
| 1m | 1m 36.0 | 4 | 7-13 | Firm | **SUFI** | Sep | 16 | 1959 |
| 1m 1f 20y | 1m 50.3 | 4 | 9-3 | Good | **RETIREMENT** | Sep | 19 | 2003 |
| 1m 2f | 2m 04.0 | 4 | 9-9 | Good To Firm | **ENDLESS HALL** | July | 17 | 2000 |
| 1m 5f 13y | 2m 45.8 | 4 | 9-7 | Good To Firm | **EDEN'S CLOSE** | Sep | 18 | 1993 |
| 1m 7f | 3m 13.1 | 3 | 9-4 | Good | **ROMANY RYE** | Sep | 19 | 1991 |
| 2m 1f 105y | 3m 45.0 | 4 | 6-13 | Good | **CURRY** | Sep | 16 | 1955 |

## BATH

| DISTANCE | TIME | AGE | WEIGHT | GOING | HORSE | DATE | | |
|---|---|---|---|---|---|---|---|---|
| 5f 11y | 59.50 secs | 2 | 9-2 | Firm | **AMOUR PROPRE** | July | 24 | 2008 |
| 5f 11y | 58.75 secs | 3 | 8-12 | Firm | **ENTICING** | May | 1 | 2007 |
| 5f 161y | 1m 08.7 | 2 | 8-12 | Firm | **QALAHARI** | July | 24 | 2008 |
| 5f 161y | 1m 08.1 | 6 | 9-0 | Firm | **MADRACO** | May | 22 | 1989 |
| 1m 5y | 1m 39.51 | 2 | 9-2 | Firm | **NATURAL CHARM** | Sep | 14 | 2014 |
| 1m 5y | 1m 37.2 | 5 | 8-12 | Good To Firm | **ADOBE** | Jun | 17 | 2000 |
| 1m 5y | 1m 37.2 | 3 | 8-7 | Firm | **ALASHA** | Aug | 18 | 2012 |
| 1m 2f 46y | 2m 05.6 | 3 | 9-0 | Good To Firm | **CONNOISSEUR BAY** | May | 29 | 1998 |
| 1m 3f 144y | 2m 25.74 | 3 | 9-0 | Hard | **TOP OF THE CHARTS** | Sep | 8 | 2005 |
| 1m 5f 22y | 2m 47.2 | 4 | 10-0 | Firm | **FLOWN** | Aug | 13 | 1991 |
| 2m 1f 34y | 3m 43.4 | 6 | 7-9 | Firm | **YAHESKA** | Jun | 14 | 2003 |

## BEVERLEY

| DISTANCE | TIME | AGE | WEIGHT | GOING | HORSE | DATE | | |
|---|---|---|---|---|---|---|---|---|
| 5f | 1m 00.89 | 2 | 8-12 | Good To Firm | **LANGAVAT** | Jun | 8 | 2013 |
| 5f | 1m 00.1 | 4 | 9-5 | Firm | **PIC UP STICKS** | Apr | 16 | 2003 |
| 7f 100y | 1m 31.1 | 2 | 9-0 | Firm | **MAJAL** | July | 30 | 1991 |
| 7f 100y | 1m 31.1 | 2 | 9-7 | Good To Firm | **CHAMPAGNE PRINCE** | Aug | 10 | 1995 |
| 7f 100y | 1m 29.5 | 3 | 7-8 | Firm | **WHO'S TEF** | July | 30 | 1991 |
| 1m 100y | 1m 43.3 | 2 | 9-0 | Firm | **ARDEN** | Sep | 24 | 1986 |
| 1m 100y | 1m 42.2 | 3 | 8-4 | Firm | **LEGAL CASE** | Jun | 14 | 1989 |
| 1m 1f 207y | 2m 01.00 | 3 | 9-7 | Good To Firm | **EASTERN ARIA** | Aug | 29 | 2009 |
| 1m 4f 16y | 2m 34.75 | 3 | 8-13 | Good To Firm | **LEADERENE** | Sep | 17 | 2014 |
| 2m 35y | 3m 29.5 | 4 | 9-2 | Good To Firm | **RUSHEN RAIDER** | Aug | 14 | 1996 |

## BRIGHTON

| DISTANCE | TIME | AGE | WEIGHT | GOING | HORSE | DATE | | |
|---|---|---|---|---|---|---|---|---|
| 5f 59y | 1m.00.1 | 2 | 9-0 | Firm | **BID FOR BLUE** | May | 6 | 1993 |
| 5f 59y | 59.3 secs | 3 | 8-9 | Firm | **PLAY HEVER GOLF** | May | 26 | 1993 |
| 5f 213y | 1m 08.1 | 2 | 8-9 | Firm | **SONG MIST** | July | 16 | 1996 |
| 5f 213y | 1m 07.3 | 3 | 8-9 | Firm | **THIRD PARTY** | Jun | 3 | 1997 |
| 5f 213y | 1m 07.3 | 5 | 9-1 | Good To Firm | **BLUNDELL LANE** | May | 4 | 2000 |
| 7f 214y | 1m 32.8 | 2 | 9-7 | Firm | **ASIAN PETE** | Oct | 3 | 1989 |
| 7f 214y | 1m 30.5 | 5 | 8-11 | Firm | **MYSTIC RIDGE** | May | 27 | 1999 |
| 1m 1f 209y | 2m 04.7 | 2 | 9-0 | Good To Soft | **ESTEEMED MASTER** | Nov | 2 | 2001 |
| 1m 1f 209y | 1m 57.2 | 3 | 9-0 | Firm | **GET THE MESSAGE** | Apr | 30 | 1984 |
| 1m 3f 196y | 2m 25.8 | 4 | 8-2 | Firm | **NEW ZEALAND** | July | 4 | 1985 |

## CARLISLE

| DISTANCE | TIME | AGE | WEIGHT | GOING | HORSE | DATE | | |
|---|---|---|---|---|---|---|---|---|
| 5f | 1m 00.1 | 2 | 8-5 | Firm | **LA TORTUGA** | Aug | 2 | 1999 |
| 5f | 58.8 secs | 3 | 9-8 | Good To Firm | **ESATTO** | Aug | 21 | 2002 |
| 5f 193y | 1m 12.45 | 2 | 9-6 | Good To Firm | **MUSICAL GUEST** | Sep | 11 | 2005 |
| 5f 193y | 1m 10.83 | 4 | 9-0 | Good To Firm | **BO MCGINTY** | Sep | 11 | 2005 |
| 6f 192y | 1m 24.3 | 3 | 8-9 | Good To Firm | **MARJURITA** | Aug | 21 | 2002 |
| 7f 200y | 1m 37.34 | 5 | 9-7 | Good To Firm | **HULA BALLEW** | Aug | 17 | 2005 |
| 1m 1f 61y | 1m 53.8 | 3 | 9-0 | Firm | **LITTLE JIMBOB** | Jun | 14 | 2004 |
| 1m 3f 107y | 2m 22.00 | 7 | 9-5 | Good To Firm | **TARTAN GIGHA** | Jun | 4 | 2012 |
| 1m 3f 206y | 2m 29.13 | 5 | 9-8 | Good To Firm | **TEMPSFORD** | Sep | 19 | 2005 |
| 1m 6f 32y | 3m 02.2 | 6 | 8-10 | Firm | **EXPLOSIVE SPEED** | May | 26 | 1994 |

## CATTERICK

| DISTANCE | TIME | AGE | WEIGHT | GOING | HORSE | DATE | | |
|---|---|---|---|---|---|---|---|---|
| 5f | 57.6 secs | 2 | 9-0 | Firm | **H HARRISON** | Oct | 8 | 2002 |
| 5f | 57.1 secs | 4 | 8-7 | Firm | **KABCAST** | July | 7 | 1989 |
| 5f 212y | 1m 11.4 | 2 | 9-4 | Firm | **CAPTAIN NICK** | July | 11 | 1978 |
| 5f 212y | 1m 09.8 | 9 | 8-13 | Good To Firm | **SHARP HAT** | May | 30 | 2003 |
| 7f | 1m 24.1 | 2 | 8-11 | Firm | **LINDA'S FANTASY** | Sep | 18 | 1982 |
| 7f | 1m 22.5 | 6 | 8-7 | Firm | **DIFFERENTIAL** | May | 31 | 2003 |
| 1m 3f 214y | 2m 30.5 | 3 | 8-8 | Good To Firm | **RAHAF** | May | 30 | 2003 |
| 1m 5f 175y | 2m 54.8 | 3 | 8-5 | Firm | **GERYON** | May | 31 | 1984 |
| 1m 7f 177y | 3m 20.8 | 4 | 7-11 | Firm | **BEAN BOY** | July | 8 | 1982 |

## CHEPSTOW

| DISTANCE | TIME | AGE | WEIGHT | GOING | HORSE | DATE | | |
|---|---|---|---|---|---|---|---|---|
| 5f 16y | 57.6 secs | 2 | 8-11 | Firm | **MICRO LOVE** | July | 8 | 1986 |
| 5f 16y | 56.8 secs | 3 | 8-4 | Firm | **TORBAY EXPRESS** | Sep | 15 | 1979 |
| 6f 16y | 1m 08.5 | 2 | 9-2 | Firm | **NINJAGO** | July | 27 | 2012 |
| 6f 16y | 1m 08.1 | 3 | 9-7 | Firm | **AMERICA CALLING** | Sep | 18 | 2001 |
| 7f 16y | 1m 20.8 | 2 | 9-0 | Good To Firm | **ROYAL AMARETTO** | Sep | 12 | 1996 |
| 7f 16y | 1m 19.3 | 3 | 9-0 | Firm | **TARANAKI** | Sep | 18 | 2001 |
| 1m 14y | 1m 33.1 | 2 | 8-11 | Good To Firm | **SKI ACADEMY** | Aug | 28 | 1995 |
| 1m 14y | 1m 31.6 | 3 | 8-13 | Firm | **STOLI** | Sep | 18 | 2001 |
| 1m 2f 36y | 2m 04.1 | 5 | 8-9 | Hard | **LEONIDAS** | July | 5 | 1983 |
| 1m 2f 36y | 2m 04.1 | 5 | 7-8 | Good To Firm | **IT'S VARADAN** | Sep | 9 | 1989 |
| 1m 2f 36y | 2m 04.1 | 3 | 8-5 | Good To Firm | **ELA ATHENA** | July | 23 | 1999 |
| 1m 4f 23y | 2m 31.0 | 3 | 8-9 | Good To Firm | **SPRITSAIL** | July | 13 | 1989 |
| 2m 49y | 3m 27.7 | 4 | 9-0 | Good To Firm | **WIZZARD ARTIST** | July | 1 | 1989 |
| 2m 2f | 3m 56.4 | 5 | 8-7 | Good To Firm | **LAFFAH** | July | 8 | 2000 |

## CHELMSFORD CITY (A.W)

| DISTANCE | TIME | AGE | WEIGHT | GOING | HORSE | DATE | | |
|---|---|---|---|---|---|---|---|---|
| 5f | 1m 0.26 | 2 | 9-4 | Standard | **RAINBOW SEEKER** | Dec | 6 | 2008 |
| 5f | 58.80 secs | 3 | 8-6 | Standard | **THE GAME** | Dec | 18 | 2008 |
| 6f | 1m 12.94 | 2 | 9-4 | Standard | **JOE CASTER** | Nov | 27 | 2008 |
| 6f | 1m 11.52 | 6 | 9-1 | Standard | **NOTA BENE** | May | 29 | 2008 |
| 1m | 1m 39.24 | 2 | 9-0 | Standard | **SHAMPAGNE** | Sept | 27 | 2008 |
| 1m | 1m 37.16 | 3 | 8-8 | Standard | **ROARING FORTE** | Sept | 27 | 2008 |
| 1m 2f | 2m 05.2 | 4 | 8-12 | Standard | **MUTAJAREED** | May | 28 | 2008 |
| 1m 5f 66y | 2m 48.87 | 5 | 9-7 | Standard | **RED GALA** | Sept | 27 | 2008 |
| 1m 6f | 3m 0.73 | 3 | 9-7 | Standard | **DETONATOR** | Sept | 14 | 2008 |
| 2my | 3m 28.69 | 4 | 9-1 | Standard | **WHAXAAR** | April | 30 | 2008 |

## CHESTER

| DISTANCE | TIME | AGE | WEIGHT | GOING | HORSE | DATE | | |
|---|---|---|---|---|---|---|---|---|
| 5f 16y | 59.94 secs | 2 | 9-2 | Good To Firm | **LEIBA LEIBA** | Jun | 26 | 2010 |
| 5f 16y | 58.88 secs | 3 | 8-7 | Good To Firm | **PETERKIN** | July | 11 | 2014 |
| 5f 110y | 1m 6.39 | 2 | 8-7 | Good To Firm | **KINEMATIC** | Sep | 11 | 2014 |
| 5f 110y | 1m 5.28 | 3 | 9-1 | Good To Firm | **MAPPIN TIME** | Aug | 20 | 2011 |
| 6f 18y | 1m 12.85 | 2 | 8-11 | Good To Firm | **FLYING EXPRESS** | Aug | 31 | 2002 |
| 6f 18y | 1m 12.78 | 3 | 8-3 | Good To Firm | **PLAY HEVER GOLF** | May | 4 | 1993 |
| 6f 18y | 1m 12.78 | 6 | 9-2 | Good | **STACK ROCK** | Jun | 23 | 1993 |
| 7f 2y | 1m 25.29 | 2 | 9-0 | Good To Firm | **DUE RESPECT** | Sep | 25 | 2002 |
| 7f 2y | 1m 23.75 | 5 | 8-13 | Good To Firm | **THREE GRACES** | July | 9 | 2005 |
| 7f 122y | 1m 32.29 | 2 | 9-0 | Good To Firm | **BIG BAD BOB** | Sep | 25 | 2002 |
| 7f 122y | 1m 30.91 | 3 | 8-12 | Good To Firm | **CUPID'S GLORY** | Aug | 18 | 2005 |
| 1m 2f 75y | 2m 7.15 | 3 | 8-8 | Good To Firm | **STOTSFOLD** | Sep | 23 | 2006 |
| 1m 3f 79y | 2m 22.17 | 3 | 8-12 | Good To Firm | **PERFECT TRUTH** | May | 6 | 2009 |
| 1m 4f 66y | 2m 33.7 | 3 | 8-10 | Good To Firm | **FIGHT YOUR CORNER** | May | 7 | 2002 |
| 1m 5f 89y | 2m 45.4 | 5 | 8-11 | Firm | **RAKAPOSHI KING** | May | 7 | 1987 |
| 1m 7f 195y | 3m 20.33 | 4 | 9-0 | Good To Firm | **GRAND FROMAGE** | July | 13 | 2002 |
| 2m 2f 147y | 3m 58.59 | 7 | 9-2 | Good To Firm | **GREENWICH MEANTIME** | May | 9 | 2007 |

## DONCASTER

| DISTANCE | TIME | AGE | WEIGHT | GOING | HORSE | DATE | | |
|---|---|---|---|---|---|---|---|---|
| 5f | 58.1 secs | 2 | 9-5 | Good To Firm | **SAND VIXEN** | Sep | 11 | 2009 |
| 5f | 57.2 secs | 6 | 9-12 | Good To Firm | **CELTIC MILL** | Sep | 9 | 2004 |
| 5f 140y | 1m 07.26 | 2 | 9-0 | Good To Firm | **CARTOGRAPHY** | Jun | 29 | 2003 |
| 5f 140y | 1m 05.38 | 4 | 9-7 | Good | **MUTHMIR** | Sep | 13 | 2014 |
| 6f | 1m 09.6 | 2 | 8-11 | Good | **CAESAR BEWARE** | Sep | 8 | 2004 |
| 6f | 1m 09.56 | 3 | 8-10 | Good To Firm | **PROCLAIM** | May | 30 | 2009 |
| 6f 110y | 1m 17.22 | 2 | 8-3 | Good To Firm | **SWILLY FERRY** | Sep | 10 | 2009 |
| 7f | 1m 22.6 | 2 | 9-1 | Good To Firm | **LIBRETTIST** | Sep | 8 | 2004 |
| 7f | 1m 21.6 | 3 | 9-4 | Good To Firm | **PASTORAL PURSUITS** | Sep | 9 | 2004 |
| 1m Str | 1m 36.5 | 2 | 8-6 | Good To Firm | **SINGHALESE** | Sep | 9 | 2004 |
| 1m Rnd | 1m 35.4 | 2 | 9-0 | Good To Firm | **PLAYFUL ACT** | Sep | 9 | 2004 |
| 1m Str | 1m 34.95 | 6 | 8-9 | Firm | **QUICK WIT** | July | 18 | 2013 |
| 1m Rnd | 1m 34.46 | 4 | 8-12 | Good To Firm | **STAYING ON** | Apr | 18 | 2009 |
| 1m 2f 60y | 2m 13.4 | 2 | 8-8 | Good | **YARD BIRD** | Nov | 6 | 1981 |
| 1m 2f 60y | 2m 04.81 | 4 | 8-13 | Good To Firm | **RED GALA** | Sep | 12 | 2007 |
| 1m 4f | 2m 27.48 | 3 | 8-4 | Good To Firm | **SWIFT ALHAARTH** | Sep | 10 | 2011 |
| 1m 6f 132y | 3m 00.44 | 3 | 9-0 | Good To Firm | **MASKED MARVEL** | Sep | 10 | 2011 |
| 2m 110y | 3m 34.4 | 4 | 9-12 | Good To Firm | **FARSI** | Jun | 12 | 1992 |
| 2m 2f | 3m 48.41 | 4 | 9-4 | Good To Firm | **SEPTIMUS** | Sep | 14 | 2007 |

## EPSOM

| DISTANCE | TIME | AGE | WEIGHT | GOING | HORSE | DATE | | |
|---|---|---|---|---|---|---|---|---|
| 5f | 55.0 secs | 2 | 8-9 | Good To Firm | **PRINCE ASLIA** | Jun | 9 | 1995 |
| 5f | 53.6 secs | 4 | 9-5 | Firm | **INDIGENOUS** | Jun | 2 | 1960 |
| 6f | 1m 07.8 | 2 | 8-11 | Good To Firm | **SHOWBROOK** | Jun | 5 | 1991 |
| 6f | 1m 07.21 | 5 | 9-13 | Good To Firm | **MAC GILLE EOIN** | July | 2 | 2009 |
| 7f | 1m 21.3 | 2 | 8-9 | Good To Firm | **RED PEONY** | July | 29 | 2004 |
| 7f | 1m 20.1 | 4 | 8-7 | Firm | **CAPISTRANO** | Jun | 7 | 1972 |
| 1m 114y | 1m 42.8 | 2 | 8-5 | Good To Firm | **NIGHTSTALKER** | Aug | 30 | 1988 |
| 1m 114y | 1m 40.7 | 3 | 8-6 | Good To Firm | **SYLVA HONDA** | Jun | 5 | 1991 |
| 1m 2f 18y | 2m 03.5 | 5 | 7-13 | Good | **CROSSBOW** | Jun | 7 | 1967 |
| 1m 4f 10y | 2m 31.3 | 3 | 9-0 | Good To Firm | **WORKFORCE** | Jun | 5 | 2010 |

## FFOS LAS

| DISTANCE | TIME | AGE | WEIGHT | GOING | HORSE | DATE | | |
|---|---|---|---|---|---|---|---|---|
| 5f | 57.06 secs | 2 | 9-3 | Good To Firm | **MR MAJEIKA** | May | 5 | 2011 |
| 5f | 56.35 secs | 5 | 8-8 | Good | **HAAJES** | Sep | 12 | 2009 |
| 6f | 1m 9.00 | 2 | 9-5 | Good To Firm | **WONDER OF QATAR** | Sep | 14 | 2014 |
| 6f | 1m 7.80 | 8 | 8-4 | Good To Firm | **THE JAILER** | May | 5 | 2011 |
| 1m | 1m 39.36 | 2 | 9-2 | Good To Firm | **HALA HALA** | Sep | 2 | 2013 |
| 1m | 1m 37.12 | 5 | 9-0 | Good To Firm | **ZEBRANO** | May | 5 | 2011 |
| 1m 2f | 2m 04.85 | 8 | 8-12 | Good To Firm | **PELHAM CRESCENT** | May | 5 | 2011 |
| 1m 4f | 2m 31.58 | 4 | 8-9 | Good To Firm | **MEN DON'T CRY** | July | 23 | 2013 |
| 1m 6f | 2m 58.61 | 4 | 9-7 | Good To Firm | **LADY ECLAIR** | July | 12 | 2010 |
| 2m | 3m 29.58 | 4 | 8-9 | Good To Firm | **ANNALUNA** | July | 1 | 2013 |

## GOODWOOD

| DISTANCE | TIME | AGE | WEIGHT | GOING | HORSE | DATE | | |
|---|---|---|---|---|---|---|---|---|
| 5f | 57.30 secs | 2 | 9-1 | Good To Firm | **COTAI GLORY** | July | 29 | 2014 |
| 5f | 56.0 secs | 5 | 9-0 | Good To Firm | **RUDI'S PET** | July | 27 | 1999 |
| 6f | 1m 09.8 | 2 | 8-11 | Good To Firm | **BACHIR** | July | 28 | 1999 |
| 6f | 1m 09.1 | 6 | 9-0 | Good To Firm | **TAMAGIN** | Sep | 12 | 2009 |
| 7f | 1m 24.9 | 2 | 8-11 | Good To Firm | **EKRAAR** | July | 29 | 1999 |
| 7f | 1m 23.8 | 3 | 8-7 | Firm | **BRIEF GLIMPSE** | July | 25 | 1995 |
| 1m | 1m 37.21 | 2 | 9-0 | Good | **CALDRA** | Sep | 9 | 2006 |
| 1m | 1m 35.61 | 4 | 8-9 | Good To Firm | **SPECTAIT** | Aug | 4 | 2006 |
| 1m 1f | 1m 56.27 | 2 | 9-3 | Good To Firm | **DORDOGNE** | Sep | 22 | 2010 |
| 1m 1f | 1m 52.8 | 3 | 9-6 | Good | **VENA** | July | 27 | 1995 |
| 1m 1f 192y | 2m 02.81 | 3 | 9-3 | Good To Firm | **ROAD TO LOVE** | Aug | 3 | 2006 |
| 1m 3f | 2m 23.0 | 3 | 8-8 | Good To Firm | **ASIAN HEIGHTS** | May | 22 | 2001 |
| 1m 4f | 2m 31.5 | 3 | 8-10 | Firm | **PRESENTING** | July | 25 | 1995 |
| 1m 6f | 2m 57.61 | 4 | 9-6 | Good To Firm | **MEEZNAH** | July | 28 | 2011 |
| 2m | 3m 21.55 | 5 | 9-10 | Good To Firm | **YEATS** | Aug | 3 | 2006 |
| 2m 4f | 4m 11.7 | 3 | 7-10 | Firm | **LUCKY MOON** | Sep | 2 | 1990 |

## HAMILTON

| DISTANCE | TIME | AGE | WEIGHT | GOING | HORSE | DATE | | |
|---|---|---|---|---|---|---|---|---|
| 5f 4y | 57.95 secs | 2 | 8-8 | Good To Firm | **ROSE BLOSSOM** | May | 29 | 2009 |
| 6f 5y | 1m 10.0 | 2 | 8-12 | Good To Firm | **BREAK THE CODE** | Aug | 24 | 1999 |
| 6f 5y | 1m 09.3 | 4 | 8-7 | Firm | **MARCUS GAME** | July | 11 | 1974 |
| 1m 65y | 1m 45.8 | 2 | 8-11 | Firm | **HOPEFUL SUBJECT** | Sep | 24 | 1973 |
| 1m 65y | 1m 42.7 | 6 | 7-7 | Firm | **CRANLEY** | Sep | 25 | 1972 |
| 1m 1f 36y | 1m 53.6 | 5 | 9-6 | Good To Firm | **REGENT'S SECRET** | Aug | 10 | 2005 |
| 1m 3f 16y | 2m 19.32 | 3 | 8-1 | Good To Firm | **CAPTAIN WEBB** | May | 16 | 2008 |
| 1m 4f 17y | 2m 30.52 | 5 | 9-10 | Good To Firm | **RECORD BREAKER** | Jun | 10 | 2009 |
| 1m 5f 9y | 2m 45.1 | 6 | 9-6 | Firm | **MENTALASANYTHIN** | Jun | 14 | 1995 |

## HAYDOCK

| DISTANCE | TIME | AGE | WEIGHT | GOING | HORSE | DATE | | |
|---|---|---|---|---|---|---|---|---|
| 5f | 58.56 secs | 2 | 8-2 | Good To Firm | **BARRACUDA BOY** | Aug | 11 | 2012 |
| 5f | 56.39 secs | 5 | 9-4 | Firm | **BATED BREATH** | May | 26 | 2012 |
| 5f (Inner) | 59.66 secs | 2 | 8-12 | Good | **DEEDS NOT WORDS** | Sep | 27 | 2013 |
| 5f (Inner) | 57.67 secs | 4 | 9-4 | Good To Firm | **SOLE POWER** | May | 21 | 2011 |
| 6f (Inner) | 1m 10.72 | 2 | 9-2 | Good To Firm | **EASY TICKET** | Sep | 27 | 2013 |
| 6f | 1m 09.9 | 4 | 9-0 | Good To Firm | **IKTAMAL** | Sep | 7 | 1996 |
| 6f | 1m 10.98 | 4 | 9-9 | Good To Firm | **WOLFHOUND** | Sep | 4 | 1993 |
| 6f (Inner) | 1m 09.40 | 7 | 9-3 | Good To Firm | **MARKAB** | Sep | 4 | 2010 |
| 7f | 1m 27.62 | 2 | 9-4 | Good | **TICKLE TIME** | Aug | 10 | 2012 |
| 7f | 1m 25.95 | 7 | 9-9 | Good To Firm | **SET THE TREND** | Jul | 20 | 2013 |
| 1m | 1m 39.02 | 3 | 8-11 | Good | **LADY MACDUFF** | Aug | 10 | 2012 |
| 1m 2f 95y | 2m 08.25 | 3 | 9-0 | Good To Firm | **PRUSSIAN** | Sep | 7 | 2012 |
| 1m 3f 200y | 2m 25.53 | 4 | 8-12 | Good To Firm | **NUMBER THEORY** | May | 24 | 2012 |
| 1m 6f | 2m 55.20 | 5 | 9-9 | Good To Firm | **HUFF AND PUFF** | Sep | 7 | 2012 |
| 2m 45y | 3m 26.98 | 5 | 8-13 | Good To Firm | **DE RIGUEUR** | Jun | 8 | 2013 |

## KEMPTON (A.W)

| DISTANCE | TIME | AGE | WEIGHT | GOING | HORSE | DATE | | |
|---|---|---|---|---|---|---|---|---|
| 5f | 58.96 | 2 | 8-6 | Standard | **GLAMOROUS SPIRIT** | Nov | 28 | 2008 |
| 5f | 58.33 | 3 | 9-1 | Standard | **EXCEEDANCE** | May | 7 | 2012 |
| 6f | 1m 11.36 | 2 | 9-0 | Standard | **TENDU** | Sep | 3 | 2014 |
| 6f | 1m 9.76 | 4 | 8-11 | Standard | **TRINITYELITEDOTCOM** | Mar | 29 | 2014 |
| 7f | 1m 23.95 | 2 | 8-10 | Standard | **TAMARKUZ** | Oct | 10 | 2012 |
| 7f | 1m 23.10 | 6 | 9-9 | Standard | **SIRIUS PROSPECT** | Nov | 20 | 2014 |
| 1m | 1m 37.50 | 2 | 9-4 | Standard | **I'M BACK** | Oct | 3 | 2012 |
| 1m | 1m 35.73 | 3 | 8-9 | Standard | **WESTERN ARISTOCRAT** | Sep | 5 | 2011 |
| 1m 2f | 2m 2.97 | 5 | 9-0 | Standard | **REBELLIOUS GUEST** | Mar | 5 | 2014 |
| 1m 3f | 2m 16.09 | 4 | 8-7 | Standard | **SALUTATION** | Mar | 29 | 2014 |
| 1m 4f | 2m 28.99 | 6 | 9-3 | Standard | **SPRING OF FAME** | Nov | 7 | 2012 |
| 2m | 3m 21.50 | 4 | 8-12 | Standard | **COLOUR VISION** | May | 2 | 2012 |

## LEICESTER

| DISTANCE | TIME | AGE | WEIGHT | GOING | HORSE | DATE | | |
|---|---|---|---|---|---|---|---|---|
| 5f 2y | 58.4 secs | 2 | 9-0 | Firm | **CUTTING BLADE** | Jun | 9 | 1986 |
| 5f 2y | 57.85 secs | 5 | 9-5 | Good To Firm | **THE JOBBER** | Sep | 18 | 2006 |
| 5f 218y | 1m 09.99 | 2 | 9-0 | Good | **EL MANATI** | Aug | 1 | 2012 |
| 5f 218y | 1m 09.12 | 6 | 8-12 | Good To Firm | **PETER ISLAND** | Apr | 25 | 2009 |
| 7f 9y | 1m 22.6 | 2 | 9-0 | Good To Firm | **MARIE DE MEDICI** | Oct | 6 | 2009 |
| 7f 9y | 1m 20.8 | 3 | 8-7 | Firm | **FLOWER BOWL** | Jun | 9 | 1986 |
| 1m 60y | 1m 44.05 | 2 | 8-11 | Good To Firm | **CONGRESSIONAL** | Sep | 6 | 2005 |
| 1m 60y | 1m 41.89 | 5 | 9-7 | Good To Firm | **VAINGLORY** | Jun | 18 | 2009 |
| 1m 1f 218y | 2m 05.3 | 2 | 9-1 | Good To Firm | **WINDSOR CASTLE** | Oct | 14 | 1996 |
| 1m 1f 218y | 2m 02.4 | 3 | 8-11 | Firm | **EFFIGY** | Nov | 4 | 1985 |
| 1m 1f 218y | 2m 02.4 | 4 | 9-6 | Good To Firm | **LADY ANGHARAD** | Jun | 18 | 2000 |
| 1m 3f 183y | 2m 27.1 | 5 | 8-12 | Good To Firm | **MURGHEM** | Jun | 18 | 2000 |

## LINGFIELD (TURF)

| DISTANCE | TIME | AGE | WEIGHT | GOING | HORSE | DATE | | |
|---|---|---|---|---|---|---|---|---|
| 5f | 57.07 secs | 2 | 9-0 | Good To Firm | **QUITE A THING** | Jun | 11 | 2011 |
| 5f | 56.09 secs | 3 | 9-4 | Good To Firm | **WHITECREST** | Sep | 16 | 2011 |
| 6f | 1m 08.36 | 2 | 8-12 | Good To Firm | **FOLLY BRIDGE** | Sep | 8 | 2009 |
| 6f | 1m 08.13 | 6 | 9-8 | Firm | **CLEAR PRAISE** | Aug | 10 | 2013 |
| 7f | 1m 20.55 | 2 | 8-11 | Good To Firm | **HIKING** | Aug | 17 | 2013 |
| 7f | 1m 20.05 | 3 | 8-5 | Good To Firm | **PERFECT TRIBUTE** | May | 7 | 2011 |
| 7f 140y | 1m 29.32 | 2 | 9-3 | Good To Firm | **DUNDONNELL** | Aug | 4 | 2012 |
| 7f 140y | 1m 26.7 | 3 | 8-6 | Good To Firm | **HIAAM** | Jul | 11 | 1987 |
| 1m 1f | 1m 52.4 | 4 | 9-2 | Good To Firm | **QUANDARY** | July | 15 | 1995 |
| 1m 2f | 2m 04.6 | 3 | 9-3 | Firm | **USRAN** | July | 15 | 1989 |
| 1m 3f 106y | 2m 23.9 | 3 | 8-5 | Firm | **NIGHT-SHIRT** | July | 14 | 1990 |
| 1m 6f | 2m 59.1 | 5 | 9-5 | Firm | **IBN BEY** | July | 1 | 1989 |
| 2m | 3m 23.7 | 3 | 9-5 | Good To Firm | **LAURIES CRUSADOR** | Aug | 13 | 1988 |

## LINGFIELD (A.W)

| DISTANCE | TIME | AGE | WEIGHT | GOING | HORSE | DATE | | |
|---|---|---|---|---|---|---|---|---|
| 5f 6y | 58.11 secs | 2 | 9-5 | Standard | **IVORS REBEL** | Sep | 23 | 2014 |
| 5f 6y | 56.67 secs | 5 | 8-12 | Standard | **LADIES ARE FOREVER** | Mar | 16 | 2013 |
| 6f 1y | 1m 09.99 | 2 | 8-12 | Standard | **SWISS DIVA** | Nov | 19 | 2008 |
| 6f 1y | 1m 08.75 | 7 | 9-2 | Standard | **TAROOQ** | Dec | 18 | 2013 |
| 7f 1y | 1m 22.67 | 2 | 9-3 | Standard | **COMPLICIT** | Nov | 23 | 2013 |
| 7f 1y | 1m 21.92 | 5 | 9-6 | Standard | **GREY MIRAGE** | Feb | 21 | 2014 |
| 1m 1y | 1m 36.33 | 2 | 9-7 | Standard | **YARROOM** | Dec | 5 | 2012 |
| 1m 1y | 1m 34.51 | 5 | 9-5 | Standard | **CAPTAIN CAT** | Apr | 18 | 2014 |
| 1m 2f | 2m 00.99 | 5 | 9-0 | Standard | **FARRAAJ** | Mar | 16 | 2013 |
| 1m 4f | 2m 27.97 | 4 | 9-3 | Standard | **MIDSUMMER SUN** | Apr | 14 | 2012 |
| 1m 5f | 2m 39.70 | 3 | 8-10 | Standard | **HIDDEN GOLD** | Oct | 30 | 2014 |
| 1m 7f 169y | 3m 16.73 | 5 | 9-2 | Standard | **ARCH VILLAIN** | Jan | 22 | 2014 |

## MUSSELBURGH

| DISTANCE | TIME | AGE | WEIGHT | GOING | HORSE | DATE | | |
|---|---|---|---|---|---|---|---|---|
| 5f | 57.7 secs | 2 | 8-2 | Firm | **ARASONG** | May | 16 | 1994 |
| 5f | 57.3 secs | 3 | 8-12 | Firm | **CORUNNA** | Jun | 3 | 2000 |
| 7f 30y | 1m 27.46 | 2 | 8-8 | Good | **DURHAM REFLECTION** | Sep | 14 | 2009 |
| 7f 30y | 1m 26.30 | 3 | 9-5 | Firm | **WALTZING WIZARD** | Aug | 22 | 2002 |
| 1m | 1m 40.3 | 2 | 8-12 | Good To Firm | **SUCCESSION** | Sep | 26 | 2004 |
| 1m | 1m 36.83 | 3 | 9-5 | Good To Firm | **GINGER JACK** | July | 13 | 2010 |
| 1m 1f | 1m 50.42 | 8 | 8-11 | Good To Firm | **DHAULAR DHAR** | Sep | 3 | 2010 |
| 1m 4f 100y | 2m 36.80 | 3 | 8-3 | Good To Firm | **HARRIS TWEED** | Jun | 5 | 2010 |
| 1m 5f | 2m 46.41 | 3 | 9-5 | Good To Firm | **ALCAEUS** | Sep | 29 | 2013 |
| 1m 6f | 2m 57.98 | 7 | 8-5 | Good To Firm | **JONNY DELTA** | Apr | 18 | 2014 |
| 2m | 3m 26.23 | 9 | 9-7 | Good To Firm | **LA BACOUETTEUSE** | July | 22 | 2014 |

## NEWBURY

| DISTANCE | TIME | AGE | WEIGHT | GOING | HORSE | DATE | | |
|---|---|---|---|---|---|---|---|---|
| 5f 34y | 59.1 secs | 2 | 8-6 | Good To Firm | **SUPERSTAR LEO** | July | 22 | 2000 |
| 5f 34y | 59.2 secs | 3 | 9-5 | Good To Firm | **THE TRADER** | Aug | 18 | 2001 |
| 6f 8y | 1m 11.07 | 2 | 8-4 | Good To Firm | **BAHATI** | May | 30 | 2009 |
| 6f 8y | 1m 09.42 | 3 | 8-11 | Good To Firm | **NOTA BENE** | May | 13 | 2005 |
| 7f | 1m 24.1 | 2 | 8-11 | Good To Firm | **HAAFHD** | Aug | 15 | 2003 |
| 7f | 1m 21.5 | 3 | 8-4 | Good To Firm | **THREE POINTS** | July | 21 | 2000 |
| 1m | 1m 37.5 | 2 | 9-1 | Good To Firm | **WINGED CUPID** | Sep | 16 | 2005 |
| 1m | 1m 33.59 | 6 | 9-0 | Firm | **RAKTI** | May | 14 | 2005 |
| 1m 1f | 1m 49.6 | 3 | 8-0 | Good To Firm | **HOLTYE** | May | 21 | 1995 |
| 1m 2f 6y | 2m 1.2 | 3 | 8-7 | Good To Firm | **WALL STREET** | July | 20 | 1996 |
| 1m 3f 5y | 2m 16.5 | 3 | 8-9 | Good To Firm | **GRANDERA** | Sep | 22 | 2001 |
| 1m 4f 5y | 2m 28.26 | 4 | 9-7 | Good To Firm | **AZAMOUR** | July | 23 | 2005 |
| 1m 5f 61y | 2m 44.9 | 5 | 10-0 | Good To Firm | **MYSTIC HILL** | July | 20 | 1996 |
| 2m | 3m 25.4 | 8 | 9-12 | Good To Firm | **MOONLIGHT QUEST** | July | 19 | 1996 |

## NEWCASTLE

| DISTANCE | TIME | AGE | WEIGHT | GOING | HORSE | DATE | | |
|---|---|---|---|---|---|---|---|---|
| 5f | 58.8 secs | 2 | 9-0 | Firm | **ATLANTIC VIKING** | Jun | 4 | 1997 |
| 5f | 57.81 secs | 3 | 9-3 | Good | **G FORCE** | Apr | 24 | 2014 |
| 6f | 1m 11.98 | 2 | 9-3 | Good | **PEARL ARCH** | Sep | 6 | 2010 |
| 6f | 1m 10.58 | 4 | 9-9 | Good To Firm | **JONNY MUDBALL** | Jun | 26 | 2010 |
| 7f | 1m 24.2 | 2 | 9-0 | Good To Firm | **ISCAN** | Aug | 31 | 1998 |
| 7f | 1m 23.3 | 4 | 9-2 | Good To Firm | **QUIET VENTURE** | Aug | 31 | 1998 |
| 1m 3y | 1m 37.1 | 2 | 8-3 | Good To Firm | **HOH STEAMER** | Aug | 31 | 1998 |
| 1m 3y | 1m 37.3 | 3 | 8-8 | Good To Firm | **IT'S MAGIC** | May | 27 | 1999 |
| 1m 1f 9y | 2m 03.2 | 2 | 8-13 | Soft | **RESPONSE** | Oct | 30 | 1993 |
| 1m 1f 9y | 1m 58.4 | 3 | 8-8 | Good To Firm | **INTRODUCING** | Aug | 6 | 2003 |
| 1m 2f 32y | 2m 06.5 | 3 | 8-11 | Firm | **MISSIONARY RIDGE** | July | 29 | 1990 |
| 1m 4f 93y | 2m 36.9 | 4 | 9-3 | Good To Firm | **LIVIA'S DREAM** | Jul | 27 | 2013 |
| 1m 6f 97y | 3m 06.4 | 3 | 9-6 | Good To Firm | **ONE OFF** | Aug | 6 | 2003 |
| 2m 19y | 3m 24.3 | 4 | 8-10 | Good | **FAR CRY** | Jun | 26 | 1999 |

## NEWMARKET (ROWLEY MILE)

| DISTANCE | TIME | AGE | WEIGHT | GOING | HORSE | DATE | | |
|---|---|---|---|---|---|---|---|---|
| 5f | 58.76 secs | 2 | 8-5 | Good To Firm | **VALIANT ROMEO** | Oct | 3 | 2002 |
| 5f | 56.8 secs | 6 | 9-2 | Good To Firm | **LOCHSONG** | Apr | 30 | 1994 |
| 6f | 1m 09.56 | 2 | 8-12 | Good To Firm | **BUSHRANGER** | Oct | 3 | 2008 |
| 7f | 1m 22.39 | 2 | 8-12 | Good To Firm | **ASHRAM** | Oct | 2 | 2008 |
| 7f | 1m 22.18 | 3 | 9-0 | Good To Firm | **CODEMASTER** | May | 14 | 2011 |
| 1m | 1m 35.67 | 2 | 8-12 | Good | **STEELER** | Sep | 29 | 2012 |
| 1m | 1m 34.07 | 4 | 9-0 | Good To Firm | **EAGLE MOUNTAIN** | Oct | 3 | 2008 |
| 1m 1f | 1m 47.26 | 5 | 8-12 | Good To Firm | **MANDURO** | Apr | 19 | 2007 |
| 1m 2f | 2m 04.6 | 2 | 9-4 | Good | **HIGHLAND CHIEFTAIN** | Nov | 2 | 1985 |
| 1m 2f | 2m 00.13 | 3 | 8-12 | Good | **NEW APPROACH** | Oct | 18 | 2008 |
| 1m 4f | 2m 26.07 | 3 | 8-9 | Good To Firm | **MOHEDIAN LADY** | Sep | 22 | 2011 |
| 1m 6f | 2m 51.59 | 3 | 8-7 | Good | **ART EYES** | Sep | 29 | 2005 |
| 2m | 3m 18.64 | 5 | 9-6 | Good To Firm | **TIMES UP** | Sep | 22 | 2011 |
| 2m 2f | 3m 47.5 | 3 | 7-12 | Hard | **WHITEWAY** | Oct | 15 | 1947 |

## NEWMARKET (JULY COURSE)

| DISTANCE | TIME | AGE | WEIGHT | GOING | HORSE | DATE | | |
|---|---|---|---|---|---|---|---|---|
| 5f | 58.5 secs | 2 | 8-10 | Good | **SEDUCTRESS** | July | 10 | 1990 |
| 5f | 56.09 secs | 6 | 9-11 | Good | **BORDERLESCOTT** | Aug | 22 | 2008 |
| 6f | 1m 10.35 | 2 | 8-11 | Good | **ELNAWIN** | Aug | 22 | 2008 |
| 6f | 1m 09.11 | 4 | 9-5 | Good To Firm | **LETHAL FORCE** | July | 13 | 2013 |
| 7f | 1m 23.57 | 2 | 9-5 | Good To Firm | **LIGHT UP MY LIFE** | Aug | 18 | 2012 |
| 7f | 1m 22.5 | 3 | 9-7 | Firm | **HO LENG** | July | 9 | 1998 |
| 1m | 1m 37.47 | 2 | 8-13 | Good | **WHIPPERS LOVE** | Aug | 28 | 2009 |
| 1m | 1m 35.5 | 3 | 8-6 | Good To Firm | **LOVERS KNOT** | July | 8 | 1998 |
| 1m 2f | 2m 00.91 | 3 | 9-5 | Good To Firm | **MAPUTO** | July | 11 | 2013 |
| 1m 4f | 2m 25.11 | 3 | 8-11 | Good | **LUSH LASHES** | Aug | 22 | 2008 |
| 1m 5f | 2m 42.01 | 3 | 9-0 | Good | **KITE WOOD** | July | 9 | 2009 |
| 1m 6f 175y | 3m 04.2 | 3 | 8-5 | Good | **ARRIVE** | July | 11 | 2001 |
| 2m 24y | 3m 20.2 | 7 | 9-10 | Good | **YORKSHIRE** | July | 11 | 2001 |

## NOTTINGHAM

| DISTANCE | TIME | AGE | WEIGHT | GOING | HORSE | DATE | | |
|---|---|---|---|---|---|---|---|---|
| 5f 13y (Inner) | 59.43 secs | 2 | 9-5 | Good To Firm | **BURTONWOOD** | Apr | 19 | 2014 |
| 5f 13y (Inner) | 58.49 secs | 4 | 9-2 | Good To Soft | **IT MUST BE FAITH** | Oct | 29 | 2014 |
| 5f 13y | 57.9 secs | 2 | 8-9 | Firm | **HOH MAGIC** | May | 13 | 1994 |
| 5f 13y | 57.71secs | 4 | 8-11 | Good To Firm | **DINKUM DIAMOND** | Aug | 14 | 2002 |
| 6f 15y | 1m 11.4 | 2 | 8-11 | Firm | **JAMEELAPI** | Aug | 8 | 1983 |
| 6f 15y | 1m 10.0 | 4 | 9-2 | Firm | **AJANAC** | Aug | 8 | 1988 |
| 1m 75y | 1m 45.23 | 2 | 9-0 | Good To Firm | **TACTFULLY** | Sep | 28 | 2011 |
| 1m 75y | 1m 42.25 | 5 | 9-1 | Good To Firm | **RIO DE LA PLATA** | Jun | 2 | 2010 |
| 1m 2f 50y | 2m 07.13 | 5 | 9-8 | Good To Firm | **VASILY** | July | 19 | 2013 |
| 1m 2f 50y (Inner) | 2m 06.66 | 2 | 9-3 | Soft | **LETHAL GLAZE** | Oct | 1 | 2008 |
| 1m 2f 50y (Inner) | 2m 09.4 | 3 | 9-5 | Good | **CENTURIUS** | Apr | 20 | 2013 |
| 1m 6f 15y | 2m 57.8 | 3 | 8-10 | Firm | **BUSTER JO** | Oct | 1 | 1985 |
| 2m 9y | 3m 25.25 | 3 | 9-5 | Good | **BULWARK** | Sep | 27 | 2005 |
| 2m 97y (Inner) | 3m 34.39 | 3 | 8-0 | Good | **BENOZZO GOZZOLI** | Oct | 28 | 2009 |

## PONTEFRACT

| DISTANCE | TIME | AGE | WEIGHT | GOING | HORSE | DATE | | |
|---|---|---|---|---|---|---|---|---|
| 5f | 1m 01.1 | 2 | 9-0 | Firm | **GOLDEN BOUNTY** | Sep | 20 | 2001 |
| 5f | 1m 00.8 | 4 | 8-9 | Firm | **BLUE MAEVE** | Sep | 29 | 2004 |
| 6f | 1m 14.0 | 2 | 9-3 | Firm | **FAWZI** | Sep | 6 | 1983 |
| 6f | 1m 12.6 | 3 | 7-13 | Firm | **MERRY ONE** | Aug | 29 | 1970 |
| 1m 4y | 1m 42.8 | 2 | 9-13 | Firm | **STAR SPRAY** | Sep | 6 | 1970 |
| 1m 4y | 1m 42.80 | 2 | 9-0 | Firm | **ALASIL** | Sep | 26 | 2002 |
| 1m 4y | 1m 40.6 | 4 | 9-10 | Good To Firm | **ISLAND LIGHT** | Apr | 13 | 2002 |
| 1m 2f 6y | 2m 10.10 | 2 | 9-0 | Firm | **SHANTY STAR** | Oct | 7 | 2002 |
| 1m 2f 6y | 2m 08.2 | 4 | 7-8 | Hard | **HAPPY HECTOR** | July | 9 | 1979 |
| 1m 4f 8y | 2m 33.72 | 3 | 8-7 | Firm | **AJAAN** | Aug | 8 | 2007 |
| 2m 1f 22y | 3m 40.67 | 4 | 8-7 | Good To Firm | **PARADISE FLIGHT** | Jun | 6 | 2005 |
| 2m 1f 216y | 3m 51.1 | 3 | 8-8 | Firm | **KUDZ** | Sep | 9 | 1986 |
| 2m 5f 122y | 4m 47.8 | 4 | 8-4 | Firm | **PHYSICAL** | May | 14 | 1984 |

## REDCAR

| DISTANCE | TIME | AGE | WEIGHT | GOING | HORSE | DATE | | |
|---|---|---|---|---|---|---|---|---|
| 5f | 56.88 secs | 2 | 9-7 | Good To Soft | **WOLFOFWALLSTREET** | Oct | 27 | 2014 |
| 5f | 56.01 secs | 10 | 9-3 | Firm | **HENRY HALL** | Sep | 20 | 2006 |
| 6f | 1m 08.8 | 2 | 8-3 | Good To Firm | **OBE GOLD** | Oct | 2 | 2004 |
| 6f | 1m 08.6 | 3 | 9-2 | Good To Firm | **SIZZLING SAGA** | Jun | 21 | 1991 |
| 7f | 1m 21.28 | 2 | 9-3 | Firm | **KAROO BLUE** | Sep | 20 | 2006 |
| 7f | 1m 21.0 | 3 | 9-1 | Firm | **EMPTY QUARTER** | Oct | 3 | 1995 |
| 1m | 1m 34.37 | 2 | 9-0 | Firm | **MASTERSHIP** | Sep | 20 | 2006 |
| 1m | 1m 32.42 | 4 | 10-0 | Firm | **NANTON** | Sep | 20 | 2006 |
| 1m 1f | 1m 52.4 | 2 | 9-0 | Firm | **SPEAR** | Sep | 13 | 2004 |
| 1m 1f | 1m 48.5 | 5 | 8-12 | Firm | **MELLOTTIE** | July | 25 | 1990 |
| 1m 2f | 2m 10.1 | 2 | 8-11 | Good | **ADDING** | Nov | 10 | 1989 |
| 1m 2f | 2m 01.4 | 5 | 9-2 | Firm | **ERADICATE** | May | 28 | 1990 |
| 1m 3f | 2m 17.2 | 3 | 8-9 | Firm | **PHOTO CALL** | Aug | 7 | 1990 |
| 1m 6f 19y | 2m 59.81 | 4 | 9-1 | Good To Firm | **ESPRIT DE CORPS** | Sep | 11 | 2006 |
| 2m 4y | 3m 24.9 | 3 | 9-3 | Good To Firm | **SUBSONIC** | Oct | 8 | 1991 |

## RIPON

| DISTANCE | TIME | AGE | WEIGHT | GOING | HORSE | DATE | | |
|---|---|---|---|---|---|---|---|---|
| 5f | 57.8 secs | 2 | 8-8 | Firm | **SUPER ROCKY** | July | 5 | 1991 |
| 5f | 57.6 secs | 5 | 8-5 | Good | **BROADSTAIRS BEAUTY** | May | 21 | 1995 |
| 6f | 1m 10.9 | 2 | 9-2 | Good | **CUMBRIAN VENTURE** | Aug | 17 | 2002 |
| 6f | 1m 09.72 | 4 | 8-9 | Good | **BACCARAT** | Aug | 17 | 2013 |
| 1m | 1m 38.77 | 2 | 9-4 | Good | **GREED IS GOOD** | Sep | 28 | 2013 |
| 1m | 1m 36.62 | 4 | 8-11 | Good To Firm | **GRANSTON** | Aug | 29 | 2005 |
| 1m 1f | 1m 49.97 | 6 | 9-3 | Good To Firm | **GINGER JACK** | Jun | 20 | 2013 |
| 1m 2f | 2m 02.6 | 3 | 9-4 | Firm | **SWIFT SWORD** | July | 20 | 1990 |
| 1m 4f 10y | 2m 31.40 | 4 | 8-8 | Good To Firm | **DANDINO** | Apr | 16 | 2011 |
| 2m | 3m 27.07 | 5 | 9-12 | Good To Firm | **GREENWICH MEANTIME** | Aug | 30 | 2005 |

## SALISBURY

| DISTANCE | TIME | AGE | WEIGHT | GOING | HORSE | DATE | | |
|---|---|---|---|---|---|---|---|---|
| 5f | 59.3 secs | 2 | 9-0 | Good To Firm | **AJIGOLO** | May | 12 | 2005 |
| 6f | 1m 12.1 | 2 | 8-0 | Good To Firm | **PARISIAN LADY** | Jun | 10 | 1997 |
| 6f | 1m 11.09 | 3 | 9-0 | Firm | **L'AMI LOUIS** | May | 1 | 2011 |
| 6f 212y | 1m 25.9 | 2 | 9-0 | Firm | **MORE ROYAL** | Jun | 29 | 1995 |
| 6f 212y | 1m 24.91 | 3 | 9-4 | Firm | **CHILWORTH LAD** | May | 1 | 2011 |
| 1m | 1m 40.48 | 2 | 8-13 | Firm | **CHOIR MASTER** | Sep | 17 | 2002 |
| 1m | 1m 38.29 | 3 | 8-7 | Good To Firm | **LAYMAN** | Aug | 11 | 2005 |
| 1m 1f 198y | 2m 04.81 | 3 | 8-5 | Good To Firm | **PRIMEVERE** | Aug | 10 | 2011 |
| 1m 4f | 2m 31.6 | 3 | 9-5 | Good To Firm | **ARRIVE** | Jun | 27 | 2001 |
| 1m 6f 21y | 3m 0.84 | 8 | 8-12 | Firm | **KANGAROO COURT** | May | 24 | 2012 |

## SANDOWN

| DISTANCE | TIME | AGE | WEIGHT | GOING | HORSE | DATE | | |
|---|---|---|---|---|---|---|---|---|
| 5f 6y | 59.4 secs | 2 | 9-3 | Firm | **TIMES TIME** | July | 22 | 1982 |
| 5f 6y | 58.8 secs | 6 | 8-9 | Good To Firm | **PALACEGATE TOUCH** | Sep | 17 | 1996 |
| 7f 16y | 1m 26.56 | 2 | 9-0 | Good To Firm | **RAVEN'S PASS** | Sep | 1 | 2007 |
| 7f 16y | 1m 26.3 | 3 | 9-0 | Firm | **MAWSUFF** | Jun | 14 | 1983 |
| 1m 14y | 1m 41.1 | 2 | 8-11 | Firm | **REFERENCE POINT** | Sep | 23 | 1986 |
| 1m 14y | 1m 38.87 | 7 | 9-10 | Good To Firm | **PRINCE OF JOHANNE** | July | 6 | 2013 |
| 1m 1f | 1m 54.6 | 2 | 8-8 | Good To Firm | **FRENCH PRETENDER** | Sep | 20 | 1988 |
| 1m 1f | 1m 52.4 | 7 | 9-3 | Good To Firm | **BOURGAINVILLE** | Aug | 11 | 2005 |
| 1m 2f 7y | 2m 02.1 | 4 | 8-11 | Firm | **KALAGLOW** | May | 31 | 1982 |
| 1m 6f | 2m 56.9 | 4 | 8-7 | Good To Firm | **LADY ROSANNA** | July | 19 | 1989 |
| 2m 78y | 3m 29.38 | 6 | 9-0 | Good To Firm | **CAUCUS** | July | 6 | 2013 |

## SOUTHWELL (A.W)

| DISTANCE | TIME | AGE | WEIGHT | GOING | HORSE | DATE | | |
|---|---|---|---|---|---|---|---|---|
| 5f | 57.85 secs | 2 | 9-3 | Standard | **ARCTIC FEELING** | Mar | 31 | 2010 |
| 5f | 56.80 secs | 5 | 9-7 | Standard | **GHOSTWING** | Jan | 3 | 2012 |
| 6f | 1m 14.0 | 2 | 8-5 | Standard | **PANALO** | Nov | 8 | 1989 |
| 6f | 1m 13.3 | 3 | 9-2 | Standard | **RAMBO EXPRESS** | Dec | 18 | 1990 |
| 7f | 1m 27.1 | 2 | 8-12 | Standard | **WINGED ICARUS** | Aug | 28 | 2012 |
| 7f | 1m 26.8 | 5 | 8-4 | Standard | **AMENABLE** | Dec | 13 | 1990 |
| 1m | 1m 38.0 | 2 | 8-9 | Standard | **ALPHA RASCAL** | Nov | 13 | 1990 |
| 1m | 1m 38.0 | 2 | 8-10 | Standard | **ANDREW'S FIRST** | Dec | 30 | 1989 |
| 1m | 1m 37.2 | 3 | 8-6 | Standard | **VALIRA** | Nov | 3 | 1990 |
| 1m 3f | 2m 21.5 | 4 | 9-7 | Standard | **TEMPERING** | Dec | 5 | 1990 |
| 1m 4f | 2m 33.9 | 4 | 9-12 | Standard | **FAST CHICK** | Nov | 8 | 1989 |
| 1m 6f | 3m 01.6 | 3 | 7-7 | Standard | **QUALITAIR AVIATOR** | Dec | 1 | 1989 |
| 1m 6f | 3m 01.6 | 3 | 7-8 | Standard | **EREVNON** | Dec | 29 | 1990 |
| 2m | 3m 37.6 | 9 | 8-12 | Standard | **OLD HUBERT** | Dec | 5 | 1990 |

## THIRSK

| DISTANCE | TIME | AGE | WEIGHT | GOING | HORSE | DATE | | |
|---|---|---|---|---|---|---|---|---|
| 5f | 57.2 secs | 2 | 9-7 | Good To Firm | **PROUD BOAST** | Aug | 5 | 2000 |
| 5f | 56.1 secs | 7 | 8-0 | Firm | **SIR SANDROVITCH** | Jun | 26 | 2003 |
| 6f | 1m 09.2 | 2 | 9-6 | Good To Firm | **WESTCOURT MAGIC** | Aug | 25 | 1995 |
| 6f | 1m 08.8 | 6 | 9-4 | Firm | **JOHAYRO** | July | 23 | 1999 |
| 7f | 1m 23.7 | 2 | 8-9 | Firm | **COURTING** | July | 23 | 1999 |
| 7f | 1m 22.8 | 4 | 8-5 | Firm | **SILVER HAZE** | May | 21 | 1988 |
| 1m | 1m 37.9 | 2 | 9-0 | Good To Firm | **SUNDAY SYMPHONY** | Sep | 4 | 2004 |
| 1m | 1m 34.8 | 4 | 8-13 | Firm | **YEARSLEY** | May | 5 | 1990 |
| 1m 4f | 2m 29.9 | 5 | 9-12 | Firm | **GALLERY GOD** | Jun | 4 | 2001 |
| 2m | 3m 22.3 | 3 | 8-10 | Firm | **TOMASCHEK** | Aug | 1 | 1964 |

## WINDSOR

| DISTANCE | TIME | AGE | WEIGHT | GOING | HORSE | DATE | | |
|---|---|---|---|---|---|---|---|---|
| 5f 10y | 58.69 secs | 2 | 9-0 | Good To Firm | **CHARLES THE GREAT** | May | 23 | 2011 |
| 5f 10y | 58.08 secs | 5 | 8-13 | Good To Firm | **TAURUS TWINS** | Apr | 4 | 2011 |
| 6f | 1m 10.5 | 2 | 9-5 | Good To Firm | **CUBISM** | Aug | 17 | 1998 |
| 6f | 1m 09.89 | 4 | 9-0 | Good To Firm | **BATED BREATH** | May | 23 | 2011 |
| 1m 67y | 1m 42.46 | 2 | 8-9 | Good To Firm | **TIGER CUB** | Oct | 10 | 2011 |
| 1m 67y | 1m 39.81 | 5 | 9-7 | Good | **FRENCH NAVY** | Jun | 29 | 2013 |
| 1m 2f 7y | 2m 01.62 | 6 | 9-1 | Good | **AL KAZEEM** | Aug | 23 | 2014 |
| 1m 3f 135y | 2m 21.5 | 3 | 9-2 | Firm | **DOUBLE FLORIN** | May | 19 | 1980 |

## WOLVERHAMPTON (A.W)

Only records on Tapeta surface are included

| DISTANCE | TIME | AGE | WEIGHT | GOING | HORSE | DATE | | |
|---|---|---|---|---|---|---|---|---|
| 5f 20y | 1m 00.50 | 2 | 9-0 | Standard | **PORTAMENTO** | Dec | 6 | 2014 |
| 5f 20y | 1m 00.25 | 3 | 8-12 | Standard | **BOOM THE GROOM** | Nov | 22 | 2014 |
| 5f 216y | 1m 13.24 | 2 | 9-5 | Standard | **ENCORE D'OR** | Oct | 11 | 2014 |
| 5f 216y | 1m 11.84 | 3 | 8-6 | Standard | **PRETEND** | Dec | 19 | 2014 |
| 7f 32y | 1m 27.79 | 2 | 9-0 | Standard | **SPERRY** | Nov | 15 | 2014 |
| 7f 32y | 1m 26.44 | 4 | 9-6 | Standard | **CAPO ROSSO** | Oct | 25 | 2014 |
| 1m 141y | 1m 47.38 | 2 | 9-5 | Standard | **JACK HOBBS** | Dec | 27 | 2014 |
| 1m 141y | 1m 46.44 | 6 | 9-8 | Standard | **GRAPHIC** | Feb | 2 | 2015 |
| 1m 1f 103y | 1m 57.15 | 5 | 8-5 | Standard | **DOCS LEGACY** | Nov | 6 | 2014 |
| 1m 4f 50y | 2m 37.01 | 5 | 9-10 | Standard | **GABRIAL'S STAR** | Nov | 2 | 2014 |
| 1m 5f 194y | 2m 57.55 | 6 | 9-7 | Standard | **ENTIHAA** | Dec | 6 | 2014 |
| 2m 119y | 3m 33.40 | 6 | 9-5 | Standard | **JOHN REEL** | Feb | 2 | 2015 |

## YARMOUTH

| DISTANCE | TIME | AGE | WEIGHT | GOING | HORSE | DATE | | |
|---|---|---|---|---|---|---|---|---|
| 5f 43y | 1m 00.4 | 2 | 8-6 | Good To Firm | **EBBA** | July | 26 | 1999 |
| 5f 43y | 59.80 secs | 4 | 8-13 | Good To Firm | **ROXANNE MILL** | Aug | 25 | 2002 |
| 6f 3y | 1m 10.4 | 2 | 9-0 | Firm | **LANCHESTER** | Aug | 15 | 1988 |
| 6f 3y | 1m 9.90 | 4 | 8-9 | Firm | **MALHUB** | Jun | 13 | 2002 |
| 7f 3y | 1m 22.2 | 2 | 9-0 | Good To Firm | **WARRSHAN** | Sep | 14 | 1988 |
| 7f 3y | 1m 22.12 | 4 | 9-4 | Good To Firm | **GLENBUCK** | Apr | 26 | 2007 |
| 1m 3y | 1m 36.3 | 2 | 8-2 | Good To Firm | **OUT RUN** | Sep | 15 | 1988 |
| 1m 3y | 1m 33.9 | 3 | 8-8 | Firm | **BONNE ETOILE** | Jun | 27 | 1995 |
| 1m 1f | 1m 52.00 | 3 | 9-5 | Good To Firm | **TOUCH GOLD** | July | 5 | 2012 |
| 1m 2f 21y | 2m 02.83 | 3 | 8-9 | Firm | **REUNITE** | July | 18 | 2006 |
| 1m 3f 101y | 2m 23.1 | 3 | 8-9 | Firm | **RAHIL** | July | 1 | 1993 |
| 1m 6f 17y | 2m 57.8 | 3 | 8-2 | Good To Firm | **BARAKAT** | July | 24 | 1990 |
| 2m | 3m 26.7 | 4 | 8-2 | Good To Firm | **ALHESN** | July | 26 | 1999 |

## YORK

| DISTANCE | TIME | AGE | WEIGHT | GOING | HORSE | DATE | | |
|---|---|---|---|---|---|---|---|---|
| 5f 3y | 58.47 secs | 2 | 8-11 | Good To Firm | **HOWICK FALLS** | Aug | 20 | 2003 |
| 5f 3y | 56.20 secs | 3 | 9-9 | Good To Firm | **OASIS DREAM** | Aug | 21 | 2003 |
| 5f 89y | 1m 3.20 | 2 | 9-3 | Good To Firm | **THE ART OF RACING** | Sep | 12 | 2012 |
| 5f 89y | 1m 1.72 | 4 | 9-7 | Good To Firm | **BOGART** | Aug | 21 | 2013 |
| 6f | 1m 8.90 | 2 | 9-0 | Good | **TIGGY WIGGY** | Aug | 21 | 2014 |
| 6f | 1m 08.23 | 3 | 8-11 | Good To Firm | **MINCE** | Sep | t9 | 2012 |
| 7f | 1m 22.32 | 2 | 9-1 | Good To Firm | **DUTCH CONNECTION** | Aug | 20 | 2014 |
| 7f | 1m 21.83 | 4 | 9-8 | Good To Firm | **DIMENSION** | July | 28 | 2012 |
| 1m | 1m 39.20 | 2 | 8-1 | Good To Firm | **MISSOULA** | Aug | 31 | 2005 |
| 1m | 1m 35.14 | 6 | 9-11 | Good To Firm | **THE RECTIFIER** | Jul | 13 | 2013 |
| 1m 205y | 1m 52.4 | 2 | 8-1 | Good To Firm | **ORAL EVIDENCE** | Oct | 6 | 1988 |
| 1m 208y | 1m 46.76 | 5 | 9-8 | Good To Firm | **ECHO OF LIGHT** | Sep | 5 | 2007 |
| 1m 2f 88y | 2m 05.29 | 3 | 8-11 | Good To Firm | **SEA THE STARS** | Aug | 18 | 2009 |
| 1m 3f 198y | 2m 27.4 | 4 | 9-4 | Good To Firm | **ISLINGTON** | Aug | 20 | 2003 |
| 1m 6f | 2m 54.96 | 4 | 9-0 | Good To Firm | **TACTIC** | May | 22 | 2010 |
| 1m 7f 195y | 3m 18.4 | 3 | 8-0 | Good To Firm | **DAM BUSTERS** | Aug | 16 | 1988 |
| 2m 88y | 3m 28.97 | 5 | 9-5 | Good To Firm | **GABRIAL'S KING** | July | 12 | 2014 |

# TOP FLAT JOCKEYS IN BRITAIN 2014

## (JANUARY 1ST - DECEMBER 31ST)

| W-R | % | JOCKEY | 2ND | 3RD | TOTAL PRIZE | WIN PRIZE |
|---|---|---|---|---|---|---|
| 192-1200 | 16% | ADAM KIRBY | 165 | 145 | 2,014,052 | 1,422,476 |
| 189-1524 | 12% | LUKE MORRIS | 212 | 191 | 1,431,796 | 902,171 |
| 168-1177 | 14% | JOE FANNING | 156 | 146 | 2,133,747 | 1,523,541 |
| 166-941 | 18% | RICHARD HUGHES | 153 | 107 | 3,754,311 | 2,007,418 |
| 162-775 | 21% | RYAN MOORE | 120 | 84 | 4,378,553 | 2,740,777 |
| 162-826 | 20% | GEORGE BAKER | 102 | 110 | 1,640,680 | 927,028 |
| 159-1071 | 15% | GRAHAM LEE | 133 | 108 | 1,551,962 | 1,068,837 |
| 125-692 | 18% | WILLIAM BUICK | 97 | 94 | 2,963,260 | 1,673,562 |
| 125-704 | 18% | ANDREA ATZENI | 95 | 100 | 3,460,459 | 2,142,927 |
| 121-683 | 18% | JAMES DOYLE | 131 | 70 | 3,281,017 | 2,354,840 |
| 115-873 | 13% | JIM CROWLEY | 101 | 98 | 1,810,527 | 1,214,475 |
| 110-666 | 17% | DANIEL TUDHOPE | 73 | 102 | 1,428,400 | 1,000,132 |
| 107-584 | 18% | PAUL HANAGAN | 76 | 60 | 3,134,625 | 2,314,408 |
| 107-867 | 12% | DAVID PROBERT | 80 | 96 | 1,103,208 | 664,801 |
| 102-674 | 15% | SILVESTRE DE SOUSA | 89 | 82 | 1,451,192 | 891,883 |
| 102-753 | 14% | PAUL MULRENNAN | 80 | 80 | 782,666 | 516,537 |
| 87-586 | 15% | RICHARD KINGSCOTE | 71 | 80 | 960,363 | 603,943 |
| 84-634 | 13% | ROBERT WINSTON | 88 | 71 | 790,130 | 329,506 |
| 81-758 | 11% | TOM QUEALLY | 72 | 74 | 846,810 | 557,033 |
| 79-579 | 14% | MARTIN HARLEY | 87 | 76 | 922,743 | 514,364 |
| 79-635 | 12% | GRAHAM GIBBONS | 70 | 52 | 687,345 | 477,550 |
| 77-530 | 15% | FREDERIK TYLICKI | 73 | 73 | 722,312 | 448,904 |
| 76-633 | 12% | OISIN MURPHY | 92 | 68 | 1,047,812 | 699,008 |
| 74-565 | 13% | JAMIE SPENCER | 83 | 57 | 1,495,824 | 598,852 |
| 67-749 | 9% | LIAM KENIRY | 71 | 80 | 410,439 | 221,195 |
| 66-852 | 8% | TOM EAVES | 79 | 78 | 528,167 | 289,938 |
| 65-548 | 12% | TONY HAMILTON | 79 | 67 | 566,027 | 342,215 |
| 64-642 | 10% | SHANE KELLY | 75 | 93 | 569,061 | 343,796 |
| 62-478 | 13% | KIEREN FALLON | 43 | 56 | 1,242,500 | 798,099 |
| 62-496 | 13% | DANE O'NEILL | 59 | 72 | 719,908 | 342,163 |
| 61-474 | 13% | MARTIN DWYER | 47 | 54 | 596,903 | 272,889 |
| 61-508 | 12% | CONNOR BEASLEY | 64 | 59 | 467,343 | 284,603 |
| 59-588 | 10% | CAM HARDIE | 76 | 64 | 584,068 | 385,972 |
| 56-495 | 11% | BEN CURTIS | 51 | 55 | 403,698 | 238,632 |
| 54-458 | 12% | PHILLIP MAKIN | 49 | 66 | 431,385 | 264,348 |
| 54-478 | 11% | ANDREW MULLEN | 56 | 52 | 454,245 | 292,922 |
| 54-483 | 11% | SEAN LEVEY | 67 | 53 | 509,207 | 273,333 |
| 54-556 | 10% | FERGUS SWEENEY | 43 | 58 | 434,999 | 297,075 |
| 54-577 | 9% | ROBERT HAVLIN | 74 | 71 | 490,446 | 225,412 |
| 54-629 | 9% | P J MCDONALD | 65 | 80 | 448,340 | 256,986 |
| 52-493 | 11% | DAVID ALLAN | 57 | 61 | 544,093 | 313,439 |
| 51-605 | 8% | WILLIAM CARSON | 66 | 65 | 284,048 | 150,964 |
| 50-353 | 14% | TED DURCAN | 51 | 40 | 383,833 | 243,528 |
| 50-419 | 12% | GEORGE CHALONER | 59 | 40 | 586,490 | 410,823 |
| 49-459 | 11% | PAT COSGRAVE | 41 | 54 | 281,912 | 155,684 |
| 49-461 | 11% | MARTIN LANE | 65 | 52 | 516,447 | 310,343 |
| 48-450 | 11% | FRANNY NORTON | 59 | 72 | 592,368 | 280,584 |
| 48-477 | 10% | CHRIS CATLIN | 38 | 46 | 215,216 | 130,651 |
| 48-484 | 10% | JASON HART | 51 | 40 | 299,003 | 193,180 |
| 45-429 | 10% | DALE SWIFT | 51 | 51 | 310,237 | 178,375 |

# TOP FLAT TRAINERS IN BRITAIN 2014

## (JANUARY 1st - DECEMBER 31st)

| TRAINER | LEADING HORSE | W-R | 2ND | 3RD | 4TH | TOTAL PRIZE | WIN PRIZE |
|---|---|---|---|---|---|---|---|
| RICHARD HANNON | Night Of Thunder | 206-1404 | 199 | 195 | 158 | 4,749,469 | 2,729,648 |
| JOHN GOSDEN | Taghrooda | 132-613 | 95 | 81 | 68 | 4,241,990 | 2,876,012 |
| MARK JOHNSTON | Secret Brief | 207-1344 | 177 | 189 | 131 | 2,992,111 | 1,985,940 |
| RICHARD FAHEY | Bond's Girl | 192-1502 | 207 | 179 | 159 | 2,882,652 | 1,882,767 |
| A P O'BRIEN | Australia | 11-81 | 8 | 9 | 5 | 2,882,212 | 2,025,979 |
| WILLIAM HAGGAS | Mukhadram | 113-520 | 68 | 72 | 52 | 2,281,869 | 1,478,038 |
| ROGER VARIAN | Kingston Hill | 78-471 | 82 | 70 | 46 | 2,252,219 | 1,374,851 |
| SIR MICHAEL STOUTE | Telescope | 81-461 | 75 | 49 | 57 | 2,211,794 | 1,293,230 |
| ANDREW BALDING | Elm Park | 119-659 | 82 | 88 | 76 | 2,035,497 | 1,335,198 |
| DAVID O'MEARA | G Force | 112-830 | 87 | 109 | 76 | 1,772,806 | 1,257,328 |
| MARCO BOTTI | De Rigueur | 80-579 | 83 | 75 | 83 | 1,580,093 | 859,912 |
| SAEED BIN SUROOR | Cavalryman | 93-405 | 69 | 45 | 45 | 1,575,124 | 957,720 |
| CHARLIE APPLEBY | Sudden Wonder | 102-549 | 84 | 82 | 43 | 1,493,782 | 924,235 |
| DAVID SIMCOCK | Madame Chiang | 78-474 | 68 | 55 | 47 | 1,295,345 | 973,543 |
| EDWARD LYNAM | Slade Power | 7-15 | 3 | 1 | 1 | 1,219,176 | 1,083,161 |
| KEVIN RYAN | The Grey Gatsby | 78-634 | 69 | 68 | 68 | 1,189,547 | 597,660 |
| LUCA CUMANI | Silk Sari | 54-297 | 47 | 49 | 25 | 1,082,606 | 597,912 |
| LADY CECIL | Noble Mission | 19-149 | 27 | 24 | 21 | 1,076,350 | 962,177 |
| ROGER CHARLTON | Al Kazeem | 52-295 | 44 | 37 | 30 | 1,043,272 | 511,222 |
| MICK CHANNON | Bossy Guest | 81-711 | 107 | 101 | 78 | 970,874 | 539,831 |
| CHARLES HILLS | Muhaarar | 68-541 | 67 | 63 | 53 | 950,292 | 574,627 |
| RALPH BECKETT | Air Pilot | 80-453 | 73 | 46 | 56 | 839,361 | 514,051 |
| TIM EASTERBY | Mattmu | 53-769 | 85 | 82 | 86 | 740,473 | 346,857 |
| CLIVE COX | Es Que Love | 62-385 | 59 | 49 | 42 | 723,392 | 377,914 |
| K R BURKE | Toocoolforschool | 67-441 | 67 | 76 | 39 | 723,372 | 398,095 |
| MICHAEL APPLEBY | Demora | 89-565 | 73 | 69 | 62 | 693,483 | 472,340 |
| TOM DASCOMBE | Brown Panther | 62-487 | 56 | 73 | 56 | 693,228 | 407,632 |
| F HEAD | Charm Spirit | 1-3 | 0 | 1 | 0 | 688,061 | 632,344 |
| BRIAN ELLISON | Balty Boys | 56-570 | 61 | 53 | 60 | 639,584 | 398,216 |
| D K WELD | Forgotten Rules | 3-8 | 1 | 1 | 0 | 565,310 | 306,234 |
| DAVID BARRON | Pearl Secret | 47-352 | 40 | 28 | 37 | 546,458 | 346,631 |
| HENRY CANDY | Limato | 38-269 | 21 | 30 | 34 | 537,537 | 378,054 |
| A FABRE | Miss France | 3-11 | 3 | 2 | 1 | 518,097 | 320,340 |
| ED DUNLOP | Red Avenger | 27-318 | 38 | 31 | 43 | 507,508 | 266,432 |
| ROBERT COWELL | Intrinsic | 37-287 | 50 | 39 | 37 | 504,986 | 288,349 |
| MICHAEL DODS | Spinatrix | 38-292 | 43 | 32 | 38 | 444,046 | 295,646 |
| PETER CHAPPLE-HYAM | Arod | 22-188 | 26 | 22 | 25 | 436,767 | 153,935 |
| MARCUS TREGONING | Bronze Angel | 27-195 | 26 | 28 | 24 | 435,055 | 356,101 |
| JAMES FANSHAWE | Hors De Combat | 40-300 | 42 | 39 | 44 | 433,858 | 210,078 |
| WILLIAM MUIR | Stepper Point | 40-291 | 36 | 37 | 37 | 433,283 | 188,388 |
| HUGHIE MORRISON | Vent De Force | 44-313 | 45 | 32 | 31 | 418,702 | 251,090 |
| HUGO PALMER | New Providence | 24-148 | 25 | 14 | 11 | 417,357 | 216,515 |
| KEITH DALGLEISH | Chookie Royale | 67-542 | 59 | 60 | 52 | 416,732 | 271,183 |
| DAVID EVANS | Forest Edge | 66-682 | 83 | 98 | 85 | 410,317 | 245,339 |
| DEAN IVORY | Tropics | 23-254 | 25 | 17 | 27 | 404,899 | 135,340 |
| BRIAN MEEHAN | J Wonder | 36-289 | 35 | 29 | 33 | 403,446 | 243,353 |
| JEREMY NOSEDA | Grandeur | 34-190 | 35 | 19 | 17 | 398,632 | 336,021 |
| CLIVE BRITTAIN | Rizeena | 11-177 | 16 | 20 | 24 | 388,393 | 266,355 |
| JIM GOLDIE | Jack Dexter | 46-467 | 49 | 42 | 65 | 379,542 | 210,303 |
| JOHN QUINN | The Wow Signal | 33-310 | 36 | 42 | 30 | 377,178 | 235,726 |

# TOP FLAT OWNERS IN BRITAIN IN 2014

| OWNER | LEADING HORSE | W-R | 2ND | 3RD | 4TH | TOTAL PRIZE | WIN PRIZE |
|---|---|---|---|---|---|---|---|
| HAMDAN AL MAKTOUM | TAGHROODA | 136-670 | 114 | 72 | 61 | 3,653,740 | 2,521,147 |
| GODOLPHIN | SUDDEN WONDER | 196-960 | 155 | 128 | 88 | 3,286,101 | 1,943,770 |
| K ABDULLAH | NOBLE MISSION | 64-317 | 52 | 29 | 36 | 2,243,731 | 1,725,498 |
| SHEIKH HAMDAN BIN MOHAMMED AL MAKTOUM | SECRET BRIEF | 114-633 | 81 | 82 | 62 | 1,772,059 | 1,297,697 |
| D SMITH/MRS J MAGNIER/M TABOR/T AH KHING | AUSTRALIA | 2-3 | 0 | 1 | 0 | 1,284,698 | 1,236,278 |
| AL SHAQAB RACING | TORONADO | 26-119 | 17 | 24 | 11 | 1,107,482 | 869,121 |
| CHEVELEY PARK STUD | INTEGRAL | 46-314 | 41 | 42 | 39 | 1,091,488 | 764,781 |
| MRS S POWER | SLADE POWER | 5-8 | 1 | 0 | 1 | 1,011,491 | 986,754 |
| QATAR RACING LIMITED | AROD | 38-286 | 32 | 33 | 31 | 943,190 | 412,454 |
| SAEED MANANA | NIGHT OF THUNDER | 31-323 | 48 | 40 | 33 | 908,767 | 388,377 |
| DR MARWAN KOUKASH | ANGEL GABRIAL | 50-401 | 61 | 49 | 40 | 847,733 | 520,129 |
| HRH PRINCESS HAYA OF JORDAN | ROMSDAL | 18-117 | 17 | 16 | 11 | 731,827 | 179,752 |
| PAUL SMITH | KINGSTON HILL | 1-4 | 1 | 0 | 1 | 689,435 | 368,615 |
| H H SHEIKH ABDULLA BIN KHALIFA AL THANI | CHARM SPIRIT | 1-2 | 0 | 0 | 0 | 644,449 | 632,344 |
| DERRICK SMITH & MRS JOHN MAGNIER & MICHAEL TABOR | LEADING LIGHT | 5-21 | 2 | 3 | 0 | 599,401 | 339,764 |
| MISS K RAUSING | MADAME CHIANG | 17-88 | 8 | 12 | 10 | 503,561 | 466,522 |
| F GILLESPIE | THE GREY GATSBY | 6-22 | 3 | 1 | 0 | 492,170 | 285,771 |
| HIGHCLERE THOROUGHBRED RACING -WAVERTREE | TELESCOPE | 1-5 | 3 | 1 | 0 | 462,354 | 120,962 |
| SHEIKH MOHAMMED OBAID AL MAKTOUM | POSTPONED | 23-94 | 16 | 12 | 4 | 431,526 | 305,309 |
| SHEIKH RASHID DALMOOK AL MAKTOUM | RIZEENA | 13-75 | 13 | 11 | 11 | 415,678 | 293,039 |
| D J DEER | AL KAZEEM | 11-75 | 11 | 11 | 6 | 404,896 | 88,530 |
| MICHAEL TABOR & DERRICK SMITH & MRS JOHN MAGNIER | MAGICIAN | 2-19 | 2 | 1 | 0 | 385,602 | 121,019 |
| PRINCE A A FAISAL | BELARDO | 9-33 | 3 | 3 | 6 | 380,436 | 349,574 |
| POTENSIS LTD/C GILES/MERRIEBELLE STABLES | TIGGY WIGGY | 3-4 | 1 | 0 | 0 | 347,163 | 325,663 |
| HER MAJESTY THE QUEEN | ESTIMATE | 23-117 | 17 | 18 | 8 | 344,661 | 219,002 |
| MRS JOHN MAGNIER & MICHAEL TABOR & DERRICK SMITH | TOGETHER FOREVER | 2-20 | 2 | 2 | 3 | 340,339 | 175,801 |
| SEASONS HOLIDAYS | CAPTAIN CAT | 7-46 | 9 | 4 | 2 | 332,401 | 205,004 |
| MOYGLARE STUD FARM | FORGOTTEN RULES | 1-5 | 0 | 1 | 0 | 324,838 | 178,636 |
| J C SMITH | HEARTBREAK HERO | 15-141 | 18 | 9 | 18 | 318,957 | 106,370 |
| CROWN SELECT | BOND'S GIRL | 4-9 | 1 | 1 | 1 | 315,811 | 291,001 |
| LORD LLOYD-WEBBER | THE FUGUE | 2-10 | 2 | 1 | 1 | 310,109 | 301,479 |
| MRS FITRI HAY | HERE COMES WHEN | 19-141 | 11 | 18 | 18 | 306,810 | 178,882 |
| SHEIKH AHMED AL MAKTOUM | FARRAAJ | 21-97 | 16 | 19 | 14 | 305,200 | 240,260 |
| GEORGE STRAWBRIDGE | BORN IN BOMBAY | 19-70 | 15 | 9 | 7 | 296,165 | 206,674 |
| H R H SULTAN AHMAD SHAH | BATTERSEA | 12-72 | 12 | 12 | 6 | 290,412 | 232,870 |
| NORMANDIE STUD LTD | SULTANINA | 12-41 | 11 | 6 | 1 | 289,679 | 238,681 |
| BALLYMORE THOROUGHBRED LTD | MISS FRANCE | 1-6 | 1 | 0 | 0 | 289,617 | 246,617 |
| LADY TENNANT | BRONZE ANGEL | 3-12 | 1 | 1 | 2 | 289,278 | 271,397 |
| SALEH AL HOMAIZI & IMAD AL SAGAR | GWAFA | 18-131 | 24 | 18 | 19 | 274,567 | 95,501 |
| N A JACKSON | DE RIGUEUR | 6-18 | 3 | 4 | 0 | 268,663 | 213,877 |
| DR CYRUS POONAWALLA & MORGAN J CAHALAN | GORDON LORD BYRON | 1-3 | 1 | 0 | 0 | 266,551 | 207,856 |
| KINGSCLERE RACING CLUB | INTRANSIGENT | 14-49 | 2 | 11 | 4 | 265,303 | 230,993 |
| LADY BAMFORD | EAGLE TOP | 10-45 | 4 | 7 | 7 | 256,246 | 167,200 |
| JEAN-CLAUDE-ALAIN DUPOUY | CIRRUS DES AIGLES | 1-2 | 0 | 0 | 0 | 255,450 | 218,900 |
| J K SHANNON & M A SCAIFE | ALBEN STAR | 4-27 | 2 | 2 | 5 | 240,917 | 177,455 |
| SHEIKH JUMA DALMOOK AL MAKTOUM | BATTALION | 22-151 | 15 | 17 | 15 | 227,784 | 129,894 |
| ANDREW TINKLER | MUTUAL REGARD | 4-37 | 7 | 3 | 6 | 224,915 | 195,630 |
| LADY ROTHSCHILD | THISTLE BIRD | 17-83 | 18 | 7 | 16 | 219,304 | 138,968 |
| DEAN IVORY | TROPICS | 1-10 | 2 | 0 | 1 | 216,637 | 22,684 |
| MISS YVONNE JACQUES | GRANDEUR | 7-45 | 8 | 5 | 2 | 209,164 | 197,164 |

# TOP FLAT HORSES IN BRITAIN 2014

| HORSE (AGE) | WIN & PLACE £ | W-R | TRAINER | OWNER | BREEDER |
|---|---|---|---|---|---|
| **AUSTRALIA** (3) | 1,284,698 | 2-3 | A P O'Brien | D Smith/Mrs J Magnier/ M Tabor/T Ah Khing | Stanley Estate And Stud Co |
| **TAGHROODA** (3) | 995,323 | 3-4 | John Gosden | Hamdan Al Maktoum | Shadwell Estate Company Limited |
| **NOBLE MISSION** (5) | 852,916 | 3-4 | Lady Cecil | K Abdullah | Juddmonte Farms Ltd |
| **KINGSTON HILL** (3) | 689,435 | 1-4 | Roger Varian | Paul Smith | Ridgecourt Stud |
| **CHARM SPIRIT** (3) | 644,449 | 1-2 | F Head | H H Sheikh Abdulla Bin Khalifa Al Thani | Ecurie Des Monceaux |
| **NIGHT OF THUNDER** (3) | 588,455 | 1-5 | Richard Hannon | Saeed Manana | Frank Dunne |
| **SLADE POWER** (5) | 586,948 | 2-2 | Edward Lynam | Mrs S Power | Mrs S Power |
| **KINGMAN** (3) | 513,568 | 3-4 | John Gosden | K Abdullah | Juddmonte Farms Ltd |
| **TELESCOPE** (4) | 462,354 | 1-5 | Sir Michael Stoute | Highclere Thoroughbred Racing -Wavertree | Barronstown Stud |
| **MUKHADRAM** (5) | 440,809 | 1-4 | William Haggas | Hamdan Al Maktoum | Wardall Bloodstock |
| **SOLE POWER** (7) | 414,438 | 3-4 | Edward Lynam | Mrs S Power | G Russell |
| **MADAME CHIANG** (3) | 389,881 | 2-3 | David Simcock | Miss K Rausing | Miss K Rausing |
| **TIGGY WIGGY** (2) | 381,181 | 6-8 | Richard Hannon | Potensis Ltd C Giles Merriebelle Stables | CBS Bloodstock |
| **SECRET BRIEF** (2) | 354,940 | 3-7 | Mark Johnston | Sheikh Hamdan bin Mohammed Al Maktoum | Airlie Stud |
| **AL KAZEEM** (6) | 328,140 | 1-3 | Roger Charlton | D J Deer | D J And Mrs Deer |
| **INTEGRAL** (4) | 323,696 | 3-5 | Sir Michael Stoute | Cheveley Park Stud | Cheveley Park Stud Ltd |
| **BOND'S GIRL** (2) | 312,515 | 3-6 | Richard Fahey | Crown Select | David Holgate |
| **ROMSDAL** (3) | 306,784 | 1-6 | John Gosden | HRH Princess Haya Of Jordan | W And R Barnett Ltd |
| **THE FUGUE** (5) | 303,802 | 1-2 | John Gosden | Lord Lloyd-Webber | Watership Down Stud |
| **TORONADO** (4) | 294,354 | 1-2 | Richard Hannon | Al Shaqab Racing | Paul Nataf |
| **MISS FRANCE** (3) | 289,617 | 1-2 | A Fabre | Ballymore Thoroughbred Ltd | Dayton Investments Ltd |
| **BRONZE ANGEL** (5) | 289,278 | 3-11 | Marcus Tregoning | Lady Tennant | Rihana Partnership |
| **BELARDO** (2) | 281,765 | 3-5 | Roger Varian | Godolphin & Prince A A Faisal | Ballylinch Stud |
| **THE GREY GATSBY** (3) | 271,040 | 1-4 | Kevin Ryan | F Gillespie | M Parrish |
| **GORDON LORD BYRON** (6) | 266,551 | 1-3 | T Hogan | Dr Cyrus Poonawalla & Morgan J Cahalan | Roland H Alder |
| **RIZEENA** (3) | 255,662 | 1-3 | Clive Brittain | Sheikh Rashid Dalmook Al Maktoum | Roundhill Stud |
| **CIRRUS DES AIGLES** (8) | 255,450 | 1-2 | Mme C Barande-Barbe | Jean-Claude-Alain Dupouy | M Yvon Lelimouzin & M Benoit Deschamps |
| **CAPTAIN CAT** (5) | 241,626 | 3-8 | Roger Charlton | Seasons Holidays | Azienda Agricola Mediterranea |
| **SILK SARI** (4) | 218,791 | 3-6 | Luca Cumani | Michael Watt, IJF, Racing Welfare | Fittocks Stud Ltd & Arrow Farm Stud |
| **SNOW SKY** (3) | 217,818 | 2-6 | Sir Michael Stoute | K Abdullah | Juddmonte Farms Ltd |
| **TROPICS** (6) | 216,637 | 1-10 | Dean Ivory | Dean Ivory | D Konecny, S Branch & A Branch |
| **LEADING LIGHT** (4) | 212,662 | 1-2 | A P O'Brien | Derrick Smith & Mrs John Magnier & Michael Tabor | Lynch-Bages Ltd |
| **ELM PARK** (2) | 212,040 | 4-5 | Andrew Balding | Qatar Racing Limited | Kingsclere Stud |
| **OSAILA** (2) | 205,868 | 3-5 | Richard Hannon | Al Shaqab Racing | Mennetou Syndicate |
| **TULLIUS** (6) | 205,858 | 1-6 | Andrew Balding | Kennet Valley Thoroughbreds VI | Sc Archi Romani |
| **TOORMORE** (3) | 194,153 | 1-5 | Richard Hannon | Middleham Park Racing IX & James Pak | BEC Bloodstock |
| **TAPESTRY** (3) | 192,205 | 1-3 | A P O'Brien | Mrs Magnier/Tabor/Smith/ Flaxman Stables | Orpendale And The Niarchos Family |
| **G FORCE** (3) | 189,192 | 3-8 | David O'Meara | Middleham Park Racing XVIII | Kildaragh Stud Twelve Oaks Stud Est |
| **LOUIS THE PIOUS** (6) | 179,309 | 2-10 | David O'Meara | F Gillespie | Ashbrittle Stud |
| **FORGOTTEN RULES** (4) | 178,636 | 1-1 | D K Weld | Moyglare Stud Farm | Moyglare Stud Farm Ltd |

# TOP NH JOCKEYS IN BRITAIN 2013/14

| W-R | % | JOCKEY | 2ND | 3RD | TOTAL PRIZE |
|---|---|---|---|---|---|
| 218-903 | 24% | A P MCCOY | 150 | 118 | 2,248,650 |
| 155-831 | 19% | RICHARD JOHNSON | 126 | 119 | 1,880,985 |
| 130-662 | 20% | JASON MAGUIRE | 108 | 86 | 897,083 |
| 127-596 | 21% | NOEL FEHILY | 73 | 79 | 1,315,413 |
| 115-774 | 15% | SAM TWISTON-DAVIES | 112 | 99 | 1,549,696 |
| 100-629 | 16% | TOM SCUDAMORE | 91 | 68 | 1,587,003 |
| 97-647 | 15% | AIDAN COLEMAN | 97 | 80 | 1,111,238 |
| 86-617 | 14% | BRIAN HUGHES | 97 | 99 | 678,359 |
| 77-527 | 15% | PADDY BRENNAN | 77 | 60 | 636,526 |
| 74-528 | 14% | TOM O'BRIEN | 75 | 53 | 723,083 |
| 70-361 | 19% | DARYL JACOB | 67 | 41 | 1,179,133 |
| 65-402 | 16% | LEIGHTON ASPELL | 61 | 41 | 1,176,513 |
| 64-445 | 14% | DENIS O'REGAN | 62 | 54 | 481,465 |
| 60-480 | 13% | JAMIE MOORE | 67 | 69 | 1,030,321 |
| 60-530 | 11% | NICK SCHOLFIELD | 55 | 55 | 662,829 |
| 57-238 | 24% | BARRY GERAGHTY | 32 | 31 | 1,671,482 |
| 54-325 | 17% | WAYNE HUTCHINSON | 31 | 35 | 533,622 |
| 53-339 | 16% | RYAN MANIA | 46 | 38 | 533,043 |
| 52-515 | 10% | PAUL MOLONEY | 51 | 63 | 606,150 |
| 50-325 | 15% | GAVIN SHEEHAN | 44 | 41 | 323,099 |
| 47-345 | 14% | PETER BUCHANAN | 43 | 47 | 392,687 |
| 46-369 | 12% | WILSON RENWICK | 46 | 49 | 343,785 |
| 42-292 | 14% | LIAM TREADWELL | 26 | 37 | 374,637 |
| 41-254 | 16% | JAMES REVELEY | 35 | 56 | 343,026 |
| 41-390 | 11% | BRENDAN POWELL | 33 | 44 | 406,383 |
| 37-295 | 13% | ROBERT THORNTON | 47 | 32 | 557,878 |
| 36-337 | 11% | BRIAN HARDING | 35 | 31 | 308,639 |
| 34-248 | 14% | MICHAEL BYRNE | 23 | 19 | 182,265 |
| 32-431 | 7% | DOUGIE COSTELLO | 45 | 53 | 268,665 |
| 30-247 | 12% | FELIX DE GILES | 31 | 21 | 206,356 |
| 29-188 | 15% | TREVOR WHELAN | 23 | 28 | 151,128 |
| 29-233 | 12% | ANDREW TINKLER | 34 | 23 | 250,228 |
| 29-281 | 10% | HENRY BROOKE | 25 | 29 | 198,431 |
| 27-151 | 18% | NICO DE BOINVILLE | 12 | 16 | 226,675 |
| 27-260 | 10% | ADAM WEDGE | 25 | 34 | 245,894 |
| 26-198 | 13% | HARRY SKELTON | 28 | 28 | 326,444 |
| 26-209 | 12% | CONOR SHOEMARK | 32 | 21 | 162,050 |
| 26-213 | 12% | DAVID BASS | 19 | 18 | 197,268 |
| 25-241 | 10% | JAMES BEST | 23 | 23 | 188,050 |
| 25-364 | 7% | TOM CANNON | 42 | 44 | 241,219 |
| 24-164 | 15% | DONAL DEVEREUX | 9 | 10 | 168,530 |
| 24-220 | 11% | JAKE GREENALL | 22 | 26 | 166,589 |
| 24-281 | 9% | IAN POPHAM | 35 | 23 | 308,650 |
| 23-194 | 12% | KIELAN WOODS | 22 | 30 | 137,265 |
| 23-221 | 10% | JOSHUA MOORE | 27 | 35 | 261,858 |
| 23-299 | 8% | RICHIE MCLERNON | 29 | 32 | 426,434 |
| 23-350 | 7% | ANDREW THORNTON | 36 | 37 | 214,427 |
| 22-165 | 13% | CRAIG NICHOL | 24 | 30 | 129,503 |
| 22-179 | 12% | TONY KELLY | 19 | 34 | 109,997 |
| 22-196 | 11% | JONATHAN ENGLAND | 24 | 20 | 199,751 |

# TOP NH TRAINERS IN BRITAIN 2013/14

| TRAINER | LEADING HORSE | W-R | 2ND | 3RD | 4TH | TOTAL PRIZE | WIN PRIZE |
|---|---|---|---|---|---|---|---|
| PAUL NICHOLLS | SILVINIACO CONTI | 118-587 | 107 | 70 | 59 | 2,469,893 | 1,383,758 |
| NICKY HENDERSON | MY TENT OR YOURS | 124-514 | 77 | 56 | 48 | 2,019,936 | 1,357,750 |
| PHILIP HOBBS | BALTHAZAR KING | 106-542 | 74 | 52 | 52 | 1,583,307 | 977,475 |
| JONJO O'NEILL | MORE OF THAT | 134-800 | 105 | 91 | 75 | 1,567,990 | 1,146,912 |
| DAVID PIPE | DYNASTE | 90-589 | 64 | 57 | 64 | 1,432,879 | 1,019,595 |
| NIGEL TWISTON-DAVIES | THE NEW ONE | 77-559 | 82 | 71 | 49 | 1,165,772 | 702,180 |
| ALAN KING | BALDER SUCCES | 75-436 | 63 | 48 | 52 | 1,111,142 | 645,228 |
| VENETIA WILLIAMS | HOUBLON DES OBEAUX | 86-573 | 73 | 72 | 49 | 1,110,493 | 739,012 |
| DONALD MCCAIN | DESERT CRY | 141-768 | 116 | 109 | 77 | 960,847 | 662,256 |
| DR RICHARD NEWLAND | PINEAU DE RE | 38-167 | 22 | 24 | 9 | 929,129 | 821,178 |
| W P MULLINS | ANNIE POWER | 11-68 | 8 | 8 | 8 | 855,395 | 452,542 |
| GARY MOORE | SIRE DE GRUGY | 45-309 | 35 | 46 | 29 | 824,665 | 677,658 |
| PETER BOWEN | AL CO | 69-356 | 62 | 36 | 49 | 598,397 | 441,890 |
| SUE SMITH | CLOUDY TOO | 61-395 | 57 | 45 | 38 | 598,180 | 378,550 |
| EVAN WILLIAMS | BUYWISE | 55-415 | 52 | 59 | 53 | 595,998 | 383,280 |
| COLIN TIZZARD | CUE CARD | 26-308 | 30 | 43 | 37 | 564,335 | 270,447 |
| EMMA LAVELLE | SHOTGUN PADDY | 40-228 | 36 | 39 | 19 | 515,156 | 303,638 |
| LUCINDA RUSSELL | GREEN FLAG | 66-521 | 65 | 84 | 59 | 503,244 | 296,799 |
| CHARLIE LONGSDON | ELY BROWN | 77-382 | 48 | 52 | 35 | 489,458 | 337,034 |
| TOM GEORGE | MODULE | 40-288 | 47 | 25 | 36 | 448,343 | 270,627 |
| TIM VAUGHAN | HIDDEN IDENTITY | 59-496 | 76 | 54 | 59 | 419,878 | 244,614 |
| REBECCA CURTIS | O'FAOLAINS BOY | 38-236 | 39 | 37 | 24 | 413,100 | 231,806 |
| J H CULLOTY | LORD WINDERMERE | 2-7 | 0 | 0 | 0 | 367,669 | 363,301 |
| JOHN FERGUSON | SEA LORD | 50-218 | 35 | 22 | 23 | 365,546 | 247,346 |
| FERGAL O'BRIEN | ALVARADO | 47-311 | 34 | 37 | 48 | 357,296 | 221,454 |
| KIM BAILEY | HARRY TOPPER | 34-260 | 25 | 33 | 35 | 340,548 | 244,990 |
| DAN SKELTON | WILLOW'S SAVIOUR | 27-170 | 26 | 22 | 20 | 327,271 | 230,525 |
| NICK WILLIAMS | REVE DE SIVOLA | 23-129 | 19 | 10 | 17 | 309,874 | 200,998 |
| DAVID BRIDGWATER | THE GIANT BOLSTER | 21-210 | 28 | 28 | 27 | 300,295 | 175,031 |
| OLIVER SHERWOOD | DEPUTY DAN | 34-185 | 35 | 29 | 24 | 297,964 | 167,395 |
| HARRY FRY | ROCK ON RUBY | 32-113 | 17 | 9 | 8 | 295,773 | 210,866 |
| GORDON ELLIOTT | TIGER ROLL | 19-79 | 19 | 8 | 6 | 293,271 | 148,749 |
| BRIAN ELLISON | YORKIST | 37-274 | 42 | 40 | 28 | 280,085 | 166,752 |
| NICKY RICHARDS | SIMPLY NED | 25-166 | 25 | 18 | 17 | 253,353 | 173,251 |
| MRS JESSICA HARRINGTON | JEZKI | 1-7 | 1 | 0 | 1 | 248,672 | 238,051 |
| JEREMY SCOTT | MELODIC RENDEZVOUS | 23-200 | 18 | 27 | 18 | 248,172 | 186,347 |
| HENRY DALY | MICKIE | 35-180 | 30 | 21 | 12 | 245,714 | 154,904 |
| MICK CHANNON | SOMERSBY | 10-61 | 10 | 13 | 8 | 241,135 | 68,128 |
| WARREN GREATREX | COLE HARDEN | 40-176 | 25 | 25 | 17 | 239,962 | 152,628 |
| MARTIN KEIGHLEY | ANNACOTTY | 21-206 | 33 | 17 | 10 | 234,497 | 132,193 |
| RICHARD LEE | MOUNTAINOUS | 17-155 | 28 | 29 | 12 | 233,564 | 137,248 |
| IAN WILLIAMS | BALLYALTON | 29-192 | 28 | 22 | 16 | 229,558 | 133,302 |
| MALCOLM JEFFERSON | KING OF THE WOLDS | 30-187 | 25 | 29 | 17 | 227,453 | 128,588 |
| PAUL WEBBER | CANTLOW | 15-205 | 31 | 21 | 26 | 222,348 | 116,177 |
| KEITH REVELEY | NIGHT IN MILAN | 19-134 | 18 | 34 | 9 | 187,318 | 134,065 |
| JOHN QUINN | COCKNEY SPARROW | 18-85 | 12 | 15 | 5 | 177,644 | 117,082 |
| SEAMUS MULLINS | FERGALL | 24-213 | 25 | 24 | 28 | 176,575 | 114,265 |
| TIM EASTERBY | HAWK HIGH | 13-101 | 17 | 12 | 10 | 169,655 | 111,191 |
| N W ALEXANDER | JET MASTER | 24-181 | 22 | 25 | 15 | 166,183 | 110,714 |
| NEIL MULHOLLAND | CAROLE'S DESTRIER | 31-246 | 26 | 27 | 23 | 161,971 | 115,881 |

# TOP NH OWNERS IN BRITAIN IN 2013/14

| OWNER | LEADING HORSE | W-R | 2ND | 3RD | 4TH | TOTAL PRIZE | WIN PRIZE |
|---|---|---|---|---|---|---|---|
| JOHN P MCMANUS | Jezki | 121-610 | 91 | 73 | 52 | 2,052,076 | 1,294,384 |
| J A PROVAN | Pineau De Re | 5-18 | 2 | 2 | 0 | 596,828 | 579,085 |
| THE PRESTON FAMILY & FRIENDS LTD. | Sire De Grugy | 6-7 | 1 | 0 | 0 | 483,572 | 468,613 |
| DR R LAMBE | Lord Windermere | 3-7 | 0 | 0 | 0 | 401,839 | 397,471 |
| ANDREA & GRAHAM WYLIE | On His Own | 8-55 | 8 | 5 | 9 | 397,015 | 173,452 |
| R S BROOKHOUSE | Western Warhorse | 29-93 | 10 | 8 | 14 | 377,261 | 318,341 |
| BLOOMFIELDS | Sea Lord | 49-213 | 34 | 21 | 22 | 360,141 | 245,397 |
| POTENSIS BLOODSTOCK LTD & CHRIS GILES | Silviniaco Conti | 5-13 | 4 | 1 | 3 | 352,606 | 213,744 |
| GIGGINSTOWN HOUSE STUD | Tiger Roll | 4-31 | 4 | 2 | 4 | 330,360 | 219,215 |
| MRS DIANA L WHATELEY | Captain Chris | 25-68 | 9 | 7 | 7 | 328,615 | 265,073 |
| MRS S RICCI | Annie Power | 5-16 | 2 | 0 | 2 | 326,000 | 225,584 |
| THE BRUSHMAKERS | Balthazar King | 4-9 | 1 | 1 | 0 | 303,682 | 90,712 |
| MRS S SUCH | The New One | 7-14 | 4 | 1 | 0 | 292,382 | 220,875 |
| TREVOR HEMMINGS | Hawk High | 17-135 | 25 | 10 | 19 | 248,220 | 123,134 |
| A J WHITE | Dynaste | 1-4 | 2 | 0 | 0 | 236,805 | 156,612 |
| WALTERS PLANT HIRE LTD | Whisper | 9-45 | 6 | 7 | 4 | 235,180 | 192,337 |
| MRS T P RADFORD | Somersby | 9-39 | 10 | 8 | 3 | 224,672 | 64,229 |
| MRS GAY SMITH | Holywell | 15-80 | 10 | 5 | 8 | 207,431 | 179,536 |
| MRS JEAN R BISHOP | Cue Card | 3-19 | 3 | 5 | 3 | 200,397 | 117,185 |
| THE STEWART FAMILY | Saphir Du Rheu | 8-41 | 4 | 4 | 7 | 192,938 | 134,830 |
| SIMON MUNIR | Ma Filleule | 5-28 | 6 | 4 | 1 | 189,738 | 114,364 |
| MR & MRS R KELVIN-HUGHES | Hadrian's Approach | 8-24 | 1 | 2 | 2 | 171,699 | 154,588 |
| F LLOYD | Al Co | 6-37 | 6 | 5 | 6 | 154,678 | 140,281 |
| P J MARTIN | Conquisto | 14-86 | 19 | 12 | 10 | 153,204 | 91,597 |
| MASTERSON HOLDINGS LIMITED | Balder Succes | 10-34 | 2 | 2 | 5 | 147,610 | 137,542 |
| PAUL & CLARE ROONEY | Dispour | 24-102 | 22 | 11 | 11 | 140,638 | 100,666 |
| MRS S SMITH | Coverholder | 19-161 | 17 | 24 | 12 | 139,917 | 89,757 |
| MR & MRS WILLIAM RUCKER | Alvarado | 7-52 | 5 | 10 | 10 | 132,501 | 56,127 |
| OPTIONS O SYNDICATE | Double Ross | 4-16 | 3 | 3 | 0 | 131,932 | 96,974 |
| N A TWISTON-DAVIES | Baby Run | 19-107 | 17 | 11 | 12 | 131,089 | 65,681 |
| CHRISTOPHER W T JOHNSTON | Johns Spirit | 2-5 | 0 | 0 | 1 | 129,877 | 122,400 |
| POTENSIS LIMITED | Lac Fontana | 5-10 | 1 | 0 | 1 | 129,771 | 125,924 |
| MR & MRS SANDY ORR | Triolo D'Alene | 2-8 | 0 | 2 | 0 | 124,806 | 113,738 |
| THE JOHNSON & STEWART FAMILIES | Rocky Creek | 1-15 | 5 | 0 | 1 | 124,671 | 4,106 |
| FAVOURITES RACING | Godsmejudge | 10-68 | 10 | 9 | 4 | 121,772 | 40,318 |
| SIMON MUNIR & ISAAC SOUEDE | Kentucky Hyden | 7-37 | 6 | 2 | 6 | 120,942 | 46,994 |
| SIMON HUNT & GARY LAMBTON | The Giant Bolster | 1-2 | 0 | 1 | 0 | 118,449 | 56,950 |
| J HALES | Al Ferof | 3-21 | 3 | 4 | 1 | 118,401 | 52,518 |
| MRS P SLOAN | Guitar Pete | 1-19 | 1 | 6 | 3 | 116,681 | 56,270 |
| T G LESLIE | Franciscan | 22-93 | 14 | 12 | 12 | 116,227 | 81,639 |
| J D NEILD | Splash Of Ginge | 2-9 | 2 | 2 | 2 | 115,571 | 92,047 |
| CASH FOR HONOURS | Melodic Rendezvous | 3-6 | 0 | 0 | 0 | 114,705 | 111,253 |
| THE BELLAMY PARTNERSHIP | Relax | 5-26 | 3 | 3 | 0 | 114,589 | 88,492 |
| R J H GEFFEN | Wonderful Charm | 10-33 | 3 | 3 | 0 | 114,454 | 63,802 |
| MARTIN BROUGHTON & FRIENDS 1 | Taquin Du Seuil | 4-6 | 1 | 1 | 0 | 114,430 | 103,312 |
| TIM SYDER | Deputy Dan | 11-37 | 9 | 4 | 1 | 113,967 | 71,688 |
| MR AND MRS J D COTTON | Sametegal | 7-26 | 6 | 4 | 0 | 112,712 | 57,265 |
| TREMBATH, HYDE, OUTHART & HILL | O'Faolains Boy | 2-5 | 1 | 0 | 0 | 110,915 | 103,516 |
| MRS JANET DAVIES | Court Minstrel | 8-63 | 4 | 12 | 8 | 109,603 | 65,917 |
| PROF CAROLINE TISDALL | Dell' Arca | 2-18 | 2 | 4 | 2 | 109,057 | 60,848 |

# TOP NH HORSES IN BRITAIN 2013/14

| HORSE (AGE) | WIN & PLACE £ | W-R | TRAINER | OWNER | BREEDER |
|---|---|---|---|---|---|
| **PINEAU DE RE** (11) | 590,616 | 2-11 | Dr Richard Newland | J A Provan | Michel Hardy |
| **SIRE DE GRUGY** (8) | 483,572 | 6-7 | Gary Moore | The Preston Family & Friends Ltd | La Grugerie |
| **LORD WINDERMERE** (8) | 327,325 | 1-2 | J H Culloty | Dr R Lambe | Edmond Coleman |
| **BALTHAZAR KING** (10) | 289,300 | 3-4 | Philip Hobbs | The Brushmakers | Sunnyhill Stud |
| **THE NEW ONE** (6) | 266,908 | 3-5 | Nigel Twiston-Davies | Mrs S Such | R Brown & Ballylinch Stud |
| **SILVINIACO CONTI** (8) | 250,792 | 2-4 | Paul Nicholls | Potensis Bloodstock Ltd & Chris Giles | Patrick Joubert |
| **JEZKI** (6) | 238,051 | 1-1 | Mrs J Harrington | John P McManus | Gerard M McGrath |
| **DYNASTE** (8) | 236,805 | 1-4 | David Pipe | A J White | Paul Chartier |
| **MY TENT OR YOURS** (7) | 210,036 | 2-4 | Nicky Henderson | John P McManus | F Dunne |
| **MORE OF THAT** (6) | 209,608 | 4-4 | Jonjo O'Neill | John P McManus | Mrs Eleanor Hadden |
| **CUE CARD** (8) | 162,600 | 1-3 | Colin Tizzard | Mrs Jean R Bishop | R T Crellin |
| **ANNIE POWER** (6) | 147,671 | 3-4 | W P Mullins | Mrs S Ricci | Eamon Cleary |
| **SOMERSBY** (10) | 139,238 | 1-4 | Mick Channon | Mrs T P Radford | Miss Nicola Ann Adams |
| **WHISPER** (6) | 137,593 | 3-6 | Nicky Henderson | Walters Plant Hire Ltd | Hubert & Sandra Hosselet |
| **AL CO** (9) | 137,113 | 2-7 | Peter Bowen | F Lloyd | Jacky Rauch & Mme Colette Rauch |
| **JOHNS SPIRIT** (7) | 129,877 | 2-5 | Jonjo O'Neill | Christopher W T Johnston | Arctic Tack Stud & Crossogue Stud |
| **DOUBLE ROSS** (8) | 125,744 | 3-9 | Nigel Twiston-Davies | Options O Syndicate | T McIlhagga |
| **ON HIS OWN** (10) | 124,821 | 0-2 | W P Mullins | Andrea & Graham Wylie | Ms Margaret Treacy |
| **TRIOLO D'ALENE** (7) | 124,348 | 2-5 | Nicky Henderson | Mr & Mrs Sandy Orr | Louis Couteaudier |
| **BALDER SUCCES** (6) | 123,344 | 5-7 | Alan King | Masterson Holdings Limited | Damien Bellanger Et Al |
| **THE GIANT BOLSTER** (9) | 120,374 | 1-5 | David Bridgwater | Simon Hunt & Gary Lambton | Gestut Fahrhof |
| **BOSTON BOB** (9) | 117,029 | 1-3 | W P Mullins | Andrea & Graham Wylie | Burgage Stud |
| **SPLASH OF GINGE** (6) | 115,571 | 2-9 | Nigel Twiston-Davies | J D Neild | Stewart Pike |
| **MELODIC RENDEZVOUS** (8) | 114,705 | 3-6 | Jeremy Scott | Cash For Honours | Mrs N A Ward |
| **MA FILLEULE** (6) | 114,623 | 2-5 | Nicky Henderson | Simon Munir | Serge Dubois |
| **TAQUIN DU SEUIL** (7) | 114,430 | 4-6 | Jonjo O'Neill | Martin Broughton & Friends 1 | Marc Boudot |
| **HOLYWELL** (7) | 112,616 | 4-7 | Jonjo O'Neill | Mrs Gay Smith | Patrick Doyle |
| **LAC FONTANA** (5) | 111,862 | 4-5 | Paul Nicholls | Potensis Limited | S C A La Perrigne |
| **O'FAOLAINS BOY** (7) | 110,915 | 2-5 | Rebecca Curtis | Trembath, Hyde, Outhart & Hill | Tom And P Phelan |
| **CAPTAIN CHRIS** (10) | 108,461 | 2-3 | Philip Hobbs | Mrs Diana L Whateley | Mrs Noreen Walsh |
| **DOUBLE SEVEN** (8) | 105,500 | 0-1 | Martin Brassil | John P McManus | M Doran |
| **WESTERN WARHORSE** (6) | 103,852 | 2-5 | David Pipe | R S Brookhouse | Harry Kavanagh |
| **WILLOW'S SAVIOUR** (7) | 103,031 | 3-3 | Dan Skelton | Triple F Partnership | Mrs M Cuff |
| **HADRIAN'S APPROACH** (7) | 101,257 | 2-5 | Nicky Henderson | Mr & Mrs R Kelvin-Hughes | Marie Gavin |
| **HARRY TOPPER** (7) | 99,938 | 2-5 | Kim Bailey | D J Keyte | The Round Oak Partnership |
| **CHANCE DU ROY** (10) | 99,737 | 1-4 | Philip Hobbs | Miss I D Du Pre | Jean, Raymond And Jean-Claude Campos |
| **DELL' ARCA** (5) | 99,640 | 1-5 | David Pipe | Prof Caroline Tisdall | Bernhard & Brigitta Matusche |
| **HIDDEN CYCLONE** (9) | 98,263 | 0-3 | John J Hanlon | Mrs A F Mee & David Mee | Ronald O'Neill |
| **HOUBLON DES OBEAUX** (7) | 94,745 | 2-8 | Venetia Williams | Mrs Julian Blackwell | Mme Marie Devilder & Benjamin Devilder |
| **UXIZANDRE** (6) | 91,600 | 3-5 | Alan King | John P McManus | Frederic Aimez |
| **BALLY LEGEND** (9) | 87,228 | 3-9 | Caroline Keevil | Brian Derrick | V Thorne, B Derrick And P R Rodford |
| **ZARKANDAR** (7) | 86,910 | 0-6 | Paul Nicholls | Potensis Bloodstock Ltd & Chris Giles | His Highness The Aga Khan's Studs S C |
| **ROCKY CREEK** (8) | 85,267 | 0-3 | Paul Nicholls | The Johnson & Stewart Families | Colm Griffin |
| **MODULE** (7) | 82,479 | 1-4 | Tom George | Simon W Clarke | David Lumet & Jean-Marie Baradeau |

# LEADING SIRES OF 2014 IN GREAT BRITAIN AND IRELAND

| STALLION | BREEDING | RNRS | WNRS | WINS | WIN MONEY | PLACES | PLACE MONEY | TOTAL |
|---|---|---|---|---|---|---|---|---|
| **GALILEO (IRE)** | by Sadler's Wells (USA) | 222 | 104 | 146 | 5275754 | 330 | 1954450 | 7230204 |
| **INVINCIBLE SPIRIT (IRE)** | by Green Desert (USA) | 219 | 103 | 158 | 2317688 | 459 | 890837 | 3208526 |
| **SHAMARDAL (USA)** | by Giant's Causeway (USA) | 166 | 84 | 134 | 1867581 | 330 | 876314 | 2743895 |
| **DUBAWI (IRE)** | by Dubai Millennium (GB) | 151 | 72 | 110 | 1251103 | 239 | 1243081 | 2494184 |
| **TEOFILO (IRE)** | by Galileo (IRE) | 167 | 62 | 87 | 955084 | 260 | 1050372 | 2005457 |
| **OASIS DREAM (GB)** | by Green Desert (USA) | 169 | 83 | 123 | 1332801 | 337 | 617204 | 1950005 |
| **MASTERCRAFTSMAN (IRE)** | by Danehill Dancer (IRE) | 108 | 38 | 54 | 1221737 | 163 | 723201 | 1944937 |
| **DUTCH ART (GB)** | by Medicean (GB) | 128 | 51 | 78 | 1153095 | 232 | 508070 | 1661165 |
| **MONTJEU (IRE)** | by Sadler's Wells (USA) | 92 | 28 | 52 | 1137262 | 121 | 435269 | 1572531 |
| **DANSILI (GB)** | by Danehill (USA) | 131 | 61 | 86 | 1116116 | 210 | 448093 | 1564209 |
| **DARK ANGEL (IRE)** | by Acclamation (GB) | 124 | 56 | 92 | 1020506 | 280 | 505914 | 1526420 |
| **SEA THE STARS (IRE)** | by Cape Cross (IRE) | 71 | 34 | 45 | 1200492 | 112 | 320364 | 1520856 |
| **CAPE CROSS (IRE)** | by Green Desert (USA) | 170 | 81 | 120 | 902908 | 336 | 612743 | 1515651 |
| **ACCLAMATION (GB)** | by Royal Applause (GB) | 209 | 90 | 128 | 991965 | 427 | 504472 | 1496438 |
| **KODIAC (GB)** | by Danehill (USA) | 154 | 73 | 107 | 951990 | 301 | 538392 | 1490381 |
| **KYLLACHY (GB)** | by Pivotal (GB) | 145 | 65 | 96 | 887042 | 307 | 432367 | 1319409 |
| **EXCEED AND EXCEL (AUS)** | by Danehill (USA) | 179 | 78 | 118 | 732474 | 347 | 581578 | 1314052 |
| **PIVOTAL (GB)** | by Polar Falcon (USA) | 143 | 69 | 106 | 818001 | 283 | 413973 | 1231974 |
| **HIGH CHAPARRAL (IRE)** | by Sadler's Wells (USA) | 128 | 38 | 59 | 615516 | 215 | 545141 | 1160656 |
| **IFFRAAJ (GB)** | by Zafonic (USA) | 133 | 58 | 90 | 639113 | 250 | 490657 | 1129769 |
| **NEW APPROACH (IRE)** | by Galileo (IRE) | 115 | 50 | 76 | 728079 | 168 | 361548 | 1089627 |
| **DANEHILL DANCER (IRE)** | by Danehill (USA) | 127 | 47 | 69 | 700700 | 229 | 384849 | 1085549 |
| **DALAKHANI (IRE)** | by Darshaan | 88 | 38 | 52 | 669527 | 129 | 342250 | 1011777 |
| **FOOTSTEPSINTHESAND (GB)** | by Giant's Causeway (USA) | 132 | 63 | 91 | 597333 | 290 | 356738 | 954071 |
| **VERGLAS (IRE)** | by Highest Honor (FR) | 110 | 52 | 79 | 678224 | 204 | 244083 | 922307 |

# LEADING SIRES OF 2014 (GREAT BRITAIN, IRELAND AND OVERSEAS)

| STALLION | BREEDING | DOMESTIC | | WIN | OVERSEAS | | WIN | TOTAL |
|---|---|---|---|---|---|---|---|---|
| | | WNRS | WINS | MONEY | WNRS | WINS | MONEY | |
| **GALILEO (IRE)** | by Sadler's Wells (USA) | 104 | 146 | 5275754 | 51 | 73 | 2775138 | 8050892 |
| **HOLY ROMAN EMPEROR (IRE)** | by Danehill (USA) | 41 | 59 | 545695 | 93 | 165 | 4699384 | 5245079 |
| **PIVOTAL (GB)** | by Polar Falcon (USA) | 69 | 106 | 818001 | 54 | 86 | 4361722 | 5179723 |
| **SHAMARDAL (USA)** | by Giant's Causeway (USA) | 84 | 134 | 1867581 | 75 | 155 | 2807142 | 4674723 |
| **INVINCIBLE SPIRIT (IRE)** | by Green Desert (USA) | 103 | 158 | 2317688 | 55 | 89 | 1782781 | 4100470 |
| **DUBAWI (IRE)** | by Dubai Millennium (GB) | 72 | 110 | 1251103 | 69 | 121 | 2706563 | 3957666 |
| **DANSILI (GB)** | by Danehill (USA) | 61 | 86 | 1116116 | 58 | 89 | 2257271 | 3373388 |
| **MOTIVATOR (GB)** | by Montjeu (IRE) | 14 | 19 | 224788 | 19 | 37 | 2853040 | 3077827 |
| **DYLAN THOMAS (IRE)** | by Danehill (USA) | 34 | 54 | 568288 | 53 | 88 | 2468277 | 3036565 |
| **MONTJEU (IRE)** | by Sadler's Wells (USA) | 28 | 52 | 1137262 | 41 | 66 | 1437791 | 2575053 |
| **OASIS DREAM (GB)** | by Green Desert (USA) | 83 | 123 | 1332801 | 62 | 110 | 1203922 | 2536722 |
| **EXCEED AND EXCEL (AUS)** | by Danehill (USA) | 78 | 118 | 732474 | 54 | 106 | 1792689 | 2525163 |
| **MASTERCRAFTSMAN (IRE)** | by Danehill Dancer (IRE) | 38 | 54 | 1221737 | 32 | 38 | 1112853 | 2334590 |
| **FOOTSTEPSINTHESAND (GB)** | by Giant's Causeway (USA) | 63 | 91 | 597333 | 79 | 144 | 1731935 | 2329268 |
| **DUTCH ART (GB)** | by Medicean (GB) | 51 | 78 | 1153095 | 42 | 87 | 1112441 | 2265536 |
| **SEA THE STARS (IRE)** | by Cape Cross (IRE) | 34 | 45 | 1200492 | 22 | 37 | 956229 | 2156721 |
| **CAPE CROSS (IRE)** | by Green Desert (USA) | 81 | 120 | 902908 | 39 | 63 | 1153227 | 2056135 |
| **HIGH CHAPARRAL (IRE)** | by Sadler's Wells (USA) | 38 | 59 | 615516 | 58 | 101 | 1298040 | 1913556 |
| **TEOFILO (IRE)** | by Galileo (IRE) | 62 | 87 | 955084 | 36 | 67 | 901715 | 1856799 |
| **DANEHILL DANCER (IRE)** | by Danehill (USA) | 47 | 69 | 700700 | 43 | 62 | 1139337 | 1840037 |
| **ACCLAMATION (GB)** | by Royal Applause (GB) | 90 | 128 | 991965 | 42 | 82 | 721908 | 1713874 |
| **ORATORIO (IRE)** | by Danehill (USA) | 43 | 70 | 381393 | 75 | 129 | 1270472 | 1651865 |
| **VERGLAS (IRE)** | by Highest Honor (FR) | 52 | 79 | 678224 | 70 | 145 | 919756 | 1597980 |
| **AUTHORIZED (IRE)** | by Montjeu (IRE) | 41 | 60 | 549114 | 36 | 54 | 1003130 | 1552244 |
| **HALLING (USA)** | by by Diesis | 33 | 44 | 293805 | 40 | 68 | 1090910 | 1384715 |

# LEADING TWO-YEAR-OLD SIRES OF 2014 IN GREAT BRITAIN AND IRELAND

| STALLION | BREEDING | RNRS | WNRS | WINS | WIN MONEY | PLACES | PLACE MONEY | TOTAL |
|---|---|---|---|---|---|---|---|---|
| **KODIAC (GB)** | by Danehill (USA) | 80 | 36 | 55 | 659734 | 140 | 318308 | 978042 |
| **GALILEO (IRE)** | by Sadler's Wells (USA) | 54 | 24 | 31 | 650355 | 54 | 160884 | 811239 |
| **SHAMARDAL (USA)** | by Giant's Causeway (USA) | 53 | 20 | 29 | 546082 | 79 | 246963 | 793046 |
| **LOPE DE VEGA (IRE)** | by Shamardal (USA) | 36 | 13 | 17 | 416643 | 49 | 77430 | 494073 |
| **SHOWCASING (GB)** | by Oasis Dream (GB) | 48 | 26 | 41 | 310616 | 92 | 166161 | 476777 |
| **OASIS DREAM (GB)** | by Green Desert (USA) | 42 | 15 | 20 | 335060 | 49 | 128369 | 463428 |
| **DARK ANGEL (IRE)** | by Acclamation (GB) | 58 | 23 | 32 | 235682 | 97 | 203271 | 438953 |
| **ACCLAMATION (GB)** | by Royal Applause (GB) | 75 | 24 | 32 | 299147 | 105 | 126292 | 425439 |
| **MONSIEUR BOND (IRE)** | by Danehill Dancer (IRE) | 45 | 8 | 14 | 346121 | 55 | 60899 | 407020 |
| **ZEBEDEE (GB)** | by Invincible Spirit (IRE) | 72 | 26 | 39 | 228281 | 114 | 166593 | 394874 |
| **INVINCIBLE SPIRIT (IRE)** | by Green Desert (USA) | 57 | 23 | 30 | 205538 | 85 | 187708 | 393247 |
| **EQUIANO (FR)** | by Acclamation (GB) | 56 | 16 | 21 | 175681 | 91 | 158276 | 333957 |
| **RIP VAN WINKLE (IRE)** | by Galileo (IRE) | 42 | 13 | 19 | 270086 | 31 | 43169 | 313255 |
| **IFFRAAJ (GB)** | by Zafonic (USA) | 60 | 22 | 27 | 114302 | 82 | 180601 | 294903 |
| **FAST COMPANY (IRE)** | by Danehill Dancer (IRE) | 58 | 22 | 30 | 180122 | 100 | 113788 | 293909 |
| **EXCEED AND EXCEL (AUS)** | by Danehill (USA) | 59 | 22 | 26 | 119665 | 66 | 171095 | 290760 |
| **PACO BOY (IRE)** | by Desert Style (IRE) | 50 | 19 | 28 | 181264 | 78 | 109434 | 290698 |
| **DUBAWI (IRE)** | by Dubai Millennium (GB) | 60 | 21 | 30 | 205566 | 61 | 84844 | 290410 |
| **STARSPANGLEDBANNER (AUS)** | by Choisir (AUS) | 17 | 10 | 14 | 175292 | 25 | 92705 | 267996 |
| **TEOFILO (IRE)** | by Galileo (IRE) | 44 | 9 | 10 | 65048 | 40 | 193439 | 258487 |
| **DANEHILL DANCER (IRE)** | by Danehill (USA) | 24 | 5 | 7 | 221567 | 26 | 35093 | 256660 |
| **DISTORTED HUMOR (USA)** | by Forty Niner (USA) | 7 | 5 | 7 | 201193 | 5 | 34703 | 235896 |
| **PHOENIX REACH (IRE)** | by Alhaarth (IRE) | 5 | 3 | 6 | 216962 | 5 | 2862 | 219824 |
| **BAHAMIAN BOUNTY (GB)** | by Cadeaux Genereux | 33 | 9 | 14 | 99021 | 40 | 120091 | 219112 |
| **FASTNET ROCK (AUS)** | by Danehill (USA) | 35 | 9 | 11 | 105468 | 29 | 113172 | 218640 |

# LEADING FIRST CROP SIRES OF 2014 IN GREAT BRITAIN AND IRELAND

| STALLION | BREEDING | RNRS | WNRS | WINS | WIN MONEY | PLACES | PLACE MONEY | TOTAL |
|---|---|---|---|---|---|---|---|---|
| **LOPE DE VEGA (IRE)** | by Shamardal (USA) | 36 | 13 | 17 | 416643 | 49 | 77430 | 494073 |
| **SHOWCASING (GB)** | by Oasis Dream (GB) | 48 | 26 | 41 | 310616 | 92 | 166161 | 476777 |
| **ZEBEDEE (GB)** | by Invincible Spirit (IRE) | 72 | 26 | 39 | 228281 | 114 | 166593 | 394874 |
| **EQUIANO (FR)** | by Acclamation (GB) | 56 | 16 | 21 | 175681 | 91 | 158276 | 333957 |
| **RIP VAN WINKLE (IRE)** | by Galileo (IRE) | 42 | 13 | 19 | 270086 | 31 | 43169 | 313255 |
| **FAST COMPANY (IRE)** | by Danehill Dancer (IRE) | 58 | 22 | 30 | 180122 | 100 | 113788 | 293909 |
| **PACO BOY (IRE)** | by Desert Style (IRE) | 50 | 19 | 28 | 181264 | 78 | 109434 | 290698 |
| **STARSPANGLEDBANNER (AUS)** | by Choisir (AUS) | 17 | 10 | 14 | 175292 | 25 | 92705 | 267996 |
| **APPROVE (IRE)** | by Oasis Dream (GB) | 49 | 23 | 27 | 118351 | 76 | 73817 | 192168 |
| **ARCANO (IRE)** | by Oasis Dream (GB) | 45 | 12 | 16 | 87123 | 54 | 102920 | 190044 |
| **VALE OF YORK (IRE)** | by Invincible Spirit (IRE) | 35 | 12 | 15 | 53436 | 49 | 84368 | 137804 |
| **MAKFI (GB)** | by Dubawi (IRE) | 32 | 10 | 11 | 57012 | 40 | 39805 | 96817 |
| **ALFRED NOBEL (IRE)** | by Danehill Dancer (IRE) | 22 | 6 | 7 | 31452 | 32 | 64267 | 95720 |
| **LORD SHANAKILL (USA)** | by Speightstown (USA) | 26 | 9 | 11 | 74942 | 25 | 19150 | 94092 |
| **HELLVELYN (GB)** | by Ishiguru (USA) | 21 | 6 | 8 | 21995 | 38 | 42603 | 64598 |
| **STIMULATION (IRE)** | by Choisir (AUS) | 30 | 6 | 6 | 16173 | 39 | 45907 | 62079 |
| **VOCALISED (USA)** | by Vindication (USA) | 10 | 3 | 3 | 46588 | 8 | 8867 | 55454 |
| **QUALITY ROAD (USA)** | by Elusive Quality (USA) | 1 | 1 | 1 | 34026 | 0 | 0 | 34026 |
| **SIYOUNI (FR)** | by Pivotal (GB) | 4 | 1 | 3 | 25144 | 1 | 289 | 25433 |
| **MUNNINGS (USA)** | by Speightstown (USA) | 1 | 1 | 1 | 2911 | 5 | 21507 | 24418 |
| **LOOKIN AT LUCKY (USA)** | by Smart Strike (CAN) | 3 | 1 | 2 | 7763 | 4 | 2743 | 10506 |
| **ARABIAN GLEAM (GB)** | by Kyllachy (GB) | 8 | 1 | 2 | 7439 | 4 | 1299 | 8738 |
| **LE CADRE NOIR (IRE)** | by Danetime (IRE) | 4 | 1 | 1 | 5750 | 2 | 886 | 6636 |
| **SILVER FROST (IRE)** | by Verglas (IRE) | 5 | 1 | 1 | 2727 | 7 | 3464 | 6191 |
| **EVASIVE (GB)** | by Elusive Quality (USA) | 1 | 1 | 1 | 4852 | 1 | 963 | 5814 |

# LEADING MATERNAL GRANDSIRES OF 2014 IN GREAT BRITAIN AND IRELAND

| STALLION | BREEDING | RNRS | WNRS | WINS | WIN MONEY | PLACES | PLACE MONEY | TOTAL |
|---|---|---|---|---|---|---|---|---|
| **DANEHILL (USA)** | by Danzig (USA) | 249 | 124 | 196 | 3989669 | 446 | 1212415 | 5202084 |
| **SADLER'S WELLS (USA)** | by Northern Dancer | 377 | 133 | 190 | 2860601 | 641 | 1097221 | 3957822 |
| **DARSHAAN** | by Shirley Heights | 174 | 64 | 93 | 1352138 | 288 | 1306967 | 2659106 |
| **CAPE CROSS (IRE)** | by Green Desert (USA) | 79 | 31 | 51 | 2121403 | 121 | 404435 | 2525838 |
| **RAINBOW QUEST (USA)** | by Blushing Groom (FR) | 164 | 67 | 109 | 1134390 | 317 | 961382 | 2095772 |
| **PIVOTAL (GB)** | by Polar Falcon (USA) | 203 | 93 | 155 | 1236368 | 365 | 545447 | 1781816 |
| **INDIAN RIDGE** | by Ahonoora | 175 | 66 | 99 | 917438 | 332 | 625452 | 1542890 |
| **GALILEO (IRE)** | by Sadler's Wells (USA) | 109 | 46 | 58 | 728063 | 181 | 668487 | 1396551 |
| **GREEN DESERT (USA)** | by Danzig (USA) | 192 | 76 | 116 | 848958 | 343 | 484012 | 1332970 |
| **SELKIRK (USA)** | by Sharpen Up | 166 | 58 | 87 | 663857 | 306 | 537011 | 1200868 |
| **MONTJEU (IRE)** | by Sadler's Wells (USA) | 83 | 36 | 49 | 943139 | 147 | 256301 | 1199441 |
| **ENTREPRENEUR (GB)** | by Sadler's Wells (USA) | 42 | 13 | 22 | 845111 | 56 | 253649 | 1098760 |
| **SINGSPIEL (IRE)** | by In The Wings | 123 | 45 | 63 | 498669 | 207 | 517307 | 1015977 |
| **MARK OF ESTEEM (IRE)** | by Darshaan | 95 | 45 | 64 | 438385 | 179 | 452182 | 890567 |
| **IN THE WINGS** | by Sadler's Wells (USA) | 88 | 41 | 61 | 587365 | 159 | 280047 | 867412 |
| **CADEAUX GENEREUX** | by Young Generation | 131 | 49 | 74 | 482311 | 221 | 384791 | 867102 |
| **BARATHEA (IRE)** | by Sadler's Wells (USA) | 146 | 52 | 86 | 565647 | 264 | 288794 | 854441 |
| **DANSILI (GB)** | by Danehill (USA) | 88 | 33 | 50 | 398741 | 146 | 442426 | 841167 |
| **EFISIO** | by Formidable (USA) | 87 | 41 | 62 | 490023 | 180 | 322471 | 812494 |
| **ROYAL APPLAUSE (GB)** | by Waajib | 120 | 56 | 83 | 457879 | 239 | 330868 | 788748 |
| **STORM CAT (USA)** | by Storm Bird (CAN) | 58 | 17 | 22 | 535864 | 87 | 219696 | 755561 |
| **GIANT'S CAUSEWAY (USA)** | by Storm Cat (USA) | 56 | 25 | 40 | 356418 | 140 | 396169 | 752587 |
| **ZAMINDAR (USA)** | by Gone West (USA) | 30 | 10 | 17 | 620211 | 49 | 128714 | 748925 |
| **NIGHT SHIFT (USA)** | by Northern Dancer | 129 | 49 | 71 | 400207 | 236 | 327180 | 727387 |
| **ZAFONIC (USA)** | by Gone West (USA) | 98 | 41 | 66 | 487917 | 179 | 224015 | 711932 |

# FLAT STALLIONS' EARNINGS FOR 2014

(includes every stallion who sired a winner on the Flat in Great Britain and Ireland in 2014)

| STALLIONS | RNRS | STARTS | WNRS | WINS | PLACES | TOTAL (£) |
|---|---|---|---|---|---|---|
| ACCLAMATION (GB) | 209 | 1200 | 90 | 128 | 427 | 1496437.52 |
| ACT ONE (GB) | 13 | 59 | 2 | 5 | 23 | 154124.40 |
| ADMIRALOFTHEFLEET (USA) | 1 | 12 | 1 | 1 | 9 | 14378.60 |
| AD VALOREM (USA) | 32 | 186 | 11 | 18 | 52 | 127238.46 |
| AGENT BLEU (FR) | 1 | 1 | 1 | 1 | 0 | 10833.33 |
| AGNES GOLD (JPN) | 3 | 12 | 1 | 1 | 8 | 39461.35 |
| ALDEBARAN (USA) | 1 | 8 | 1 | 1 | 5 | 5330.50 |
| ALDERBROOK (GB) | 1 | 6 | 1 | 1 | 0 | 9487.50 |
| ALFRED NOBEL (IRE) | 22 | 90 | 6 | 7 | 32 | 95719.55 |
| ALHAARTH (IRE) | 29 | 152 | 8 | 10 | 35 | 72563.38 |
| ALKAADHEM (GB) | 1 | 9 | 1 | 1 | 2 | 5187.50 |
| AMADEUS WOLF (GB) | 64 | 366 | 17 | 35 | 93 | 290266.79 |
| AMERICAN POST (GB) | 5 | 37 | 3 | 5 | 11 | 54381.69 |
| ANABAA (USA) | 12 | 44 | 2 | 2 | 8 | 59128.14 |
| AND BEYOND (IRE) | 3 | 21 | 1 | 1 | 10 | 5867.25 |
| ANTONIUS PIUS (USA) | 33 | 202 | 10 | 16 | 61 | 114800.64 |
| APPROVE (IRE) | 49 | 217 | 23 | 27 | 76 | 192168.04 |
| AQLAAM (GB) | 36 | 154 | 12 | 17 | 61 | 170367.38 |
| ARAAFA (IRE) | 17 | 95 | 6 | 9 | 38 | 73674.45 |
| ARABIAN GLEAM (GB) | 8 | 25 | 1 | 2 | 4 | 8738.37 |
| ARAKAN (USA) | 27 | 129 | 9 | 15 | 33 | 321942.84 |
| ARCANO (IRE) | 45 | 171 | 12 | 16 | 54 | 190043.64 |
| ARCH (USA) | 29 | 118 | 13 | 17 | 49 | 308074.85 |
| ARCHIPENKO (USA) | 34 | 160 | 17 | 24 | 49 | 601547.06 |
| AREION (GER) | 5 | 13 | 1 | 1 | 5 | 11527.50 |
| ARTAN (IRE) | 1 | 8 | 1 | 1 | 1 | 5743.75 |
| ART CONNOISSEUR (IRE) | 28 | 123 | 4 | 8 | 38 | 102813.87 |
| ARTIE SCHILLER (USA) | 2 | 17 | 1 | 2 | 2 | 4699.45 |
| ASSERTIVE (GB) | 33 | 223 | 15 | 22 | 72 | 182952.21 |
| ASTRONOMER ROYAL (USA) | 11 | 48 | 5 | 6 | 20 | 27141.13 |
| ATRAF (GB) | 6 | 18 | 2 | 2 | 5 | 8131.70 |
| AUCTION HOUSE (USA) | 12 | 54 | 4 | 6 | 7 | 27248.45 |
| AUSSIE RULES (USA) | 62 | 349 | 22 | 33 | 126 | 471757.89 |
| AUTHORIZED (IRE) | 107 | 499 | 41 | 60 | 178 | 866862.99 |
| AVONBRIDGE (GB) | 62 | 397 | 18 | 26 | 118 | 201832.01 |
| AZAMOUR (IRE) | 100 | 433 | 36 | 47 | 169 | 500868.98 |
| BACHELOR DUKE (USA) | 19 | 110 | 6 | 8 | 34 | 58396.25 |
| BAHAMIAN BOUNTY (GB) | 137 | 808 | 49 | 81 | 257 | 824056.31 |
| BAHHARE (USA) | 2 | 7 | 1 | 1 | 3 | 3240.00 |
| BAHRI (USA) | 11 | 41 | 1 | 1 | 7 | 8474.30 |
| BALLET MASTER (USA) | 4 | 36 | 3 | 6 | 13 | 21553.27 |
| BALMONT (USA) | 8 | 47 | 3 | 4 | 15 | 44414.55 |
| BALTIC KING (GB) | 26 | 203 | 15 | 29 | 85 | 208226.97 |
| BARATHEA (IRE) | 17 | 100 | 3 | 5 | 36 | 84579.94 |
| BEAT ALL (USA) | 6 | 28 | 2 | 3 | 13 | 30261.17 |
| BEAT HOLLOW (GB) | 43 | 226 | 16 | 20 | 72 | 220916.60 |
| BELLAMY ROAD (USA) | 1 | 7 | 1 | 1 | 4 | 5027.85 |
| BENEFICIAL (GB) | 6 | 8 | 1 | 1 | 0 | 5750.00 |
| BERING | 1 | 5 | 1 | 1 | 3 | 2854.60 |
| BERNARDINI (USA) | 10 | 48 | 3 | 5 | 15 | 37311.43 |
| BERNSTEIN (USA) | 9 | 54 | 5 | 8 | 18 | 87008.77 |
| BERTOLINI (USA) | 63 | 422 | 21 | 42 | 112 | 231247.18 |
| BIG BAD BOB (IRE) | 52 | 225 | 20 | 24 | 66 | 263782.27 |
| BIG BROWN (USA) | 3 | 9 | 2 | 2 | 2 | 70921.67 |
| BIRDSTONE (USA) | 4 | 15 | 1 | 1 | 8 | 15053.97 |
| BLACK SAM BELLAMY (IRE) | 12 | 59 | 4 | 9 | 16 | 48136.63 |
| BLUE DAKOTA (IRE) | 2 | 15 | 1 | 1 | 2 | 2746.70 |
| BLUEGRASS CAT (USA) | 3 | 13 | 1 | 2 | 5 | 10187.75 |

| STALLIONS | RNRS | STARTS | WNRS | WINS | PLACES | TOTAL (£) |
|---|---|---|---|---|---|---|
| BOLD EDGE (GB) | 1 | 16 | 1 | 1 | 5 | 3809.05 |
| BROKEN VOW (USA) | 3 | 16 | 1 | 1 | 8 | 4960.49 |
| BUSHRANGER (IRE) | 107 | 567 | 31 | 47 | 153 | 315622.49 |
| BYRON (GB) | 78 | 479 | 28 | 47 | 157 | 634882.86 |
| CACIQUE (IRE) | 2 | 28 | 1 | 2 | 10 | 7644.45 |
| CADEAUX GENEREUX | 18 | 96 | 7 | 10 | 41 | 76639.82 |
| CALCUTTA (GB) | 2 | 10 | 1 | 3 | 3 | 15295.50 |
| CAMACHO (GB) | 61 | 373 | 21 | 30 | 116 | 269949.36 |
| CANDY RIDE (ARG) | 6 | 25 | 3 | 6 | 10 | 49299.36 |
| CAPE CROSS (IRE) | 170 | 836 | 81 | 120 | 336 | 1515651.06 |
| CAPTAIN GERRARD (IRE) | 55 | 338 | 16 | 28 | 115 | 210418.42 |
| CAPTAIN MARVELOUS (IRE) | 16 | 82 | 4 | 4 | 21 | 38675.79 |
| CAPTAIN RIO (GB) | 81 | 547 | 39 | 66 | 166 | 472473.45 |
| THE CARBON UNIT (USA) | 12 | 55 | 4 | 4 | 25 | 45534.68 |
| CARLOTAMIX (FR) | 1 | 16 | 1 | 3 | 5 | 10333.78 |
| CATCHER IN THE RYE (IRE) | 9 | 32 | 2 | 5 | 11 | 37933.32 |
| CELTIC SWING (GB) | 16 | 105 | 6 | 11 | 32 | 191853.31 |
| CENTRAL PARK (IRE) | 3 | 33 | 2 | 5 | 9 | 19318.21 |
| CHAMPS ELYSEES (GB) | 62 | 280 | 26 | 34 | 93 | 438174.69 |
| CHEVALIER (IRE) | 12 | 74 | 6 | 10 | 31 | 70017.17 |
| CHINEUR (FR) | 22 | 177 | 9 | 13 | 65 | 133602.41 |
| CHOISIR (AUS) | 44 | 293 | 18 | 24 | 84 | 374163.99 |
| CITY ON A HILL (USA) | 3 | 17 | 2 | 3 | 5 | 10883.42 |
| CITY ZIP (USA) | 6 | 18 | 1 | 2 | 6 | 14094.52 |
| CLODOVIL (IRE) | 89 | 536 | 41 | 68 | 173 | 901878.87 |
| COCKNEY REBEL (IRE) | 45 | 213 | 15 | 23 | 69 | 197158.71 |
| COMMANDS (AUS) | 3 | 10 | 1 | 1 | 3 | 9694.45 |
| COMPTON PLACE (GB) | 95 | 602 | 33 | 58 | 189 | 482880.86 |
| COUNTRY REEL (USA) | 4 | 26 | 1 | 1 | 8 | 5245.58 |
| COURT CAVE (IRE) | 5 | 17 | 1 | 1 | 2 | 6358.33 |
| CRAIGSTEEL (GB) | 1 | 12 | 1 | 1 | 4 | 7574.99 |
| CREACHADOIR (IRE) | 2 | 7 | 1 | 2 | 1 | 49949.50 |
| DAAHER (CAN) | 5 | 11 | 2 | 2 | 3 | 13849.57 |
| DAI JIN (GB) | 2 | 7 | 1 | 2 | 4 | 9203.95 |
| DALAKHANI (IRE) | 88 | 390 | 38 | 52 | 129 | 1011777.13 |
| DANBIRD (AUS) | 10 | 65 | 5 | 8 | 16 | 31377.27 |
| DANCING SPREE (USA) | 2 | 13 | 1 | 2 | 6 | 9615.08 |
| DANDY MAN (IRE) | 68 | 403 | 25 | 41 | 158 | 506108.73 |
| DANEHILL (USA) | 2 | 10 | 1 | 4 | 4 | 12040.83 |
| DANEHILL DANCER (IRE) | 127 | 655 | 47 | 69 | 229 | 1085549.27 |
| DANETIME (IRE) | 8 | 69 | 2 | 2 | 11 | 16770.74 |
| DANROAD (AUS) | 7 | 46 | 3 | 4 | 16 | 39165.24 |
| DANSILI (GB) | 131 | 576 | 61 | 86 | 210 | 1564209.30 |
| DARK ANGEL (IRE) | 124 | 741 | 56 | 92 | 280 | 1526420.38 |
| DASHING BLADE | 1 | 5 | 1 | 1 | 2 | 4547.30 |
| DAYLAMI (IRE) | 5 | 25 | 1 | 2 | 3 | 9148.03 |
| DELLA FRANCESCA (USA) | 1 | 10 | 1 | 1 | 2 | 2889.45 |
| DELTA DANCER (GB) | 3 | 14 | 1 | 3 | 3 | 6917.40 |
| DENOUNCE (GB) | 4 | 26 | 2 | 3 | 8 | 71292.25 |
| DEPORTIVO (GB) | 6 | 33 | 4 | 8 | 12 | 114336.25 |
| DESERT MILLENNIUM (IRE) | 4 | 16 | 1 | 2 | 3 | 6929.20 |
| DESERT PRINCE (IRE) | 8 | 41 | 2 | 2 | 16 | 20840.60 |
| DESERT STYLE (IRE) | 13 | 86 | 4 | 5 | 28 | 37289.55 |
| DESERT SUN (GB) | 1 | 7 | 1 | 1 | 1 | 2421.70 |
| DESIDERATUM (GB) | 4 | 12 | 1 | 1 | 6 | 5832.20 |
| DIAMOND GREEN (FR) | 40 | 216 | 6 | 9 | 64 | 115279.11 |
| DIKTAT (GB) | 18 | 118 | 7 | 12 | 37 | 157738.84 |
| DISCREET CAT (USA) | 3 | 21 | 2 | 5 | 7 | 14583.65 |
| DISTANT MUSIC (USA) | 4 | 17 | 1 | 1 | 2 | 3453.40 |
| DISTORTED HUMOR (USA) | 20 | 79 | 10 | 14 | 29 | 330199.38 |
| DIXIE UNION (USA) | 6 | 35 | 4 | 5 | 14 | 24525.97 |
| DOCTOR DINO (FR) | 1 | 4 | 1 | 1 | 1 | 2543.75 |
| DOMEDRIVER (IRE) | 2 | 10 | 1 | 1 | 1 | 2408.45 |

| STALLIONS | RNRS | STARTS | WNRS | WINS | PLACES | TOTAL (£) |
|---|---|---|---|---|---|---|
| DONERAILE COURT (USA) | 1 | 13 | 1 | 1 | 4 | 5116.65 |
| DOYEN (IRE) | 16 | 84 | 3 | 6 | 35 | 91867.68 |
| DR FONG (USA) | 27 | 139 | 4 | 5 | 55 | 99828.94 |
| DR MASSINI (IRE) | 4 | 15 | 1 | 2 | 1 | 11683.33 |
| DUBAI DESTINATION (USA) | 39 | 204 | 15 | 22 | 78 | 251029.37 |
| DUBAWI (IRE) | 151 | 583 | 72 | 110 | 239 | 2494183.54 |
| DUKE OF MARMALADE (IRE) | 106 | 476 | 37 | 53 | 159 | 653722.08 |
| DUTCH ART (GB) | 128 | 644 | 51 | 78 | 232 | 1661165.38 |
| D'WILDCAT (USA) | 1 | 4 | 1 | 1 | 2 | 6753.25 |
| DYLAN THOMAS (IRE) | 89 | 475 | 34 | 54 | 162 | 918330.85 |
| DYNAFORMER (USA) | 24 | 99 | 6 | 8 | 44 | 186982.23 |
| ECHO OF LIGHT (GB) | 43 | 202 | 11 | 17 | 56 | 135413.79 |
| E DUBAI (USA) | 2 | 13 | 1 | 1 | 4 | 6664.80 |
| EFISIO | 3 | 24 | 1 | 1 | 7 | 11576.65 |
| EL CORREDOR (USA) | 1 | 4 | 1 | 1 | 3 | 5338.40 |
| ELNADIM (USA) | 43 | 275 | 21 | 31 | 96 | 207323.53 |
| EL PRADO (IRE) | 3 | 26 | 1 | 2 | 8 | 8328.09 |
| ELUSIVE CITY (USA) | 63 | 424 | 31 | 48 | 138 | 518215.39 |
| ELUSIVE QUALITY (USA) | 45 | 242 | 16 | 22 | 69 | 292070.26 |
| EMPIRE MAKER (USA) | 10 | 34 | 2 | 4 | 15 | 85469.71 |
| ENCOSTA DE LAGO (AUS) | 1 | 5 | 1 | 1 | 3 | 3287.85 |
| ENGLISH CHANNEL (USA) | 9 | 50 | 3 | 5 | 16 | 71851.62 |
| EQUIANO (FR) | 56 | 232 | 16 | 21 | 91 | 333956.60 |
| EREWHON (USA) | 9 | 49 | 1 | 1 | 10 | 10627.57 |
| EUROSILVER (USA) | 1 | 9 | 1 | 1 | 3 | 8701.35 |
| EVASIVE (GB) | 1 | 2 | 1 | 1 | 1 | 5814.25 |
| EVEN TOP (IRE) | 1 | 2 | 1 | 1 | 1 | 255450.98 |
| EXCEED AND EXCEL (AUS) | 179 | 980 | 78 | 118 | 347 | 1314051.81 |
| EXCELLENT ART (GB) | 119 | 639 | 44 | 68 | 225 | 674148.33 |
| EXCHANGE RATE (USA) | 7 | 21 | 2 | 4 | 10 | 92844.43 |
| FAIR MIX (IRE) | 6 | 23 | 1 | 2 | 9 | 7861.70 |
| FALBRAV (IRE) | 3 | 25 | 3 | 4 | 5 | 13423.70 |
| FALCO (USA) | 3 | 19 | 1 | 1 | 10 | 65836.76 |
| FANTASTIC LIGHT (USA) | 15 | 142 | 9 | 12 | 65 | 102067.91 |
| FASLIYEV (USA) | 22 | 189 | 7 | 13 | 63 | 92411.41 |
| FAST COMPANY (IRE) | 58 | 262 | 22 | 30 | 100 | 293909.26 |
| FASTNET ROCK (AUS) | 61 | 230 | 22 | 33 | 84 | 587811.80 |
| FATH (USA) | 10 | 83 | 4 | 8 | 18 | 61116.45 |
| FAYRUZ | 1 | 14 | 1 | 1 | 4 | 16209.45 |
| FIREBREAK (GB) | 43 | 256 | 18 | 28 | 78 | 235762.42 |
| FIRST DEFENCE (USA) | 14 | 52 | 7 | 9 | 17 | 105470.54 |
| FIRST SAMURAI (USA) | 4 | 11 | 1 | 1 | 3 | 10131.65 |
| FIRST TRUMP (GB) | 2 | 9 | 1 | 2 | 2 | 4861.70 |
| FLOWER ALLEY (USA) | 1 | 6 | 1 | 1 | 2 | 3315.20 |
| FOOTSTEPSINTHESAND (GB) | 132 | 777 | 63 | 91 | 290 | 954070.71 |
| FOREST DANGER (USA) | 1 | 8 | 1 | 2 | 3 | 10779.17 |
| FOXHOUND (USA) | 2 | 20 | 1 | 1 | 2 | 3285.05 |
| FRUITS OF LOVE (USA) | 7 | 32 | 3 | 4 | 5 | 15981.25 |
| GALILEO (IRE) | 222 | 848 | 104 | 146 | 330 | 7230203.92 |
| GENTLEMAN'S DEAL (IRE) | 6 | 33 | 4 | 7 | 15 | 31118.70 |
| GENTLEWAVE (IRE) | 5 | 24 | 3 | 4 | 5 | 16698.45 |
| GHOSTZAPPER (USA) | 2 | 6 | 1 | 2 | 2 | 20208.33 |
| GIANT'S CAUSEWAY (USA) | 23 | 124 | 14 | 20 | 41 | 157806.32 |
| GLORY OF DANCER (GB) | 2 | 8 | 1 | 1 | 5 | 12987.50 |
| GOLAN (IRE) | 7 | 21 | 1 | 2 | 3 | 144354.50 |
| GOLD AWAY (IRE) | 7 | 44 | 3 | 4 | 16 | 69772.92 |
| GOLDEN SNAKE (USA) | 3 | 20 | 1 | 2 | 8 | 27346.50 |
| GONE WEST (USA) | 2 | 12 | 1 | 1 | 5 | 26401.30 |
| GOOD REWARD (USA) | 1 | 20 | 1 | 3 | 3 | 16665.20 |
| GREAT EXHIBITION (USA) | 5 | 13 | 2 | 2 | 3 | 8990.75 |
| GREEN DESERT (USA) | 29 | 185 | 13 | 18 | 61 | 144742.29 |
| GREEN TUNE (USA) | 5 | 23 | 1 | 2 | 10 | 11106.92 |
| HAAFHD (GB) | 46 | 302 | 26 | 46 | 105 | 315083.82 |

| STALLIONS | RNRS | STARTS | WNRS | WINS | PLACES | TOTAL (£) |
|---|---|---|---|---|---|---|
| HAATEF (USA) | 32 | 195 | 14 | 16 | 77 | 140864.90 |
| HALLING (USA) | 103 | 498 | 33 | 44 | 160 | 767925.65 |
| HAMAIRI (IRE) | 1 | 6 | 1 | 3 | 2 | 7790.80 |
| HARD SPUN (USA) | 24 | 139 | 13 | 24 | 44 | 222918.47 |
| HARLAN'S HOLIDAY (USA) | 4 | 9 | 2 | 2 | 3 | 12073.50 |
| HAT TRICK (JPN) | 2 | 14 | 1 | 1 | 4 | 3707.45 |
| HAWK WING (USA) | 26 | 146 | 9 | 12 | 40 | 87973.92 |
| HELIOSTATIC (IRE) | 7 | 22 | 1 | 2 | 8 | 18023.10 |
| HELISSIO (FR) | 3 | 10 | 2 | 2 | 2 | 16787.50 |
| HELLVELYN (GB) | 21 | 96 | 6 | 8 | 38 | 64597.71 |
| HENNY HUGHES (USA) | 4 | 32 | 3 | 5 | 12 | 38577.20 |
| HENRYTHENAVIGATOR (USA) | 55 | 280 | 17 | 20 | 95 | 257039.69 |
| HERNANDO (FR) | 28 | 148 | 13 | 23 | 75 | 458114.80 |
| HIGH CHAPARRAL (IRE) | 128 | 564 | 38 | 59 | 215 | 1160656.45 |
| HIGHEST HONOR (FR) | 2 | 3 | 1 | 1 | 1 | 2518.20 |
| HOLY ROMAN EMPEROR (IRE) | 111 | 620 | 41 | 59 | 209 | 846422.74 |
| HOLZMEISTER (USA) | 1 | 5 | 1 | 1 | 3 | 9801.85 |
| HOMME D'HONNEUR (FR) | 1 | 8 | 1 | 2 | 4 | 25669.40 |
| HURRICANE RUN (IRE) | 43 | 206 | 15 | 21 | 87 | 545234.52 |
| ICEMAN (GB) | 25 | 183 | 7 | 11 | 65 | 103861.37 |
| IFFRAAJ (GB) | 133 | 673 | 58 | 90 | 250 | 1129769.41 |
| IMPERIAL DANCER (GB) | 5 | 44 | 2 | 6 | 15 | 31733.26 |
| INCHINOR (GB) | 3 | 17 | 1 | 1 | 5 | 29944.30 |
| INDESATCHEL (IRE) | 33 | 198 | 12 | 20 | 47 | 269550.18 |
| INDIAN CHARLIE (USA) | 1 | 2 | 1 | 1 | 1 | 2972.40 |
| INDIAN DANEHILL (IRE) | 3 | 14 | 1 | 2 | 4 | 6262.05 |
| INDIAN HAVEN (GB) | 19 | 121 | 9 | 14 | 38 | 108905.38 |
| INDIAN RIDGE | 11 | 96 | 4 | 8 | 26 | 45674.24 |
| INTENSE FOCUS (USA) | 76 | 432 | 28 | 42 | 160 | 484334.19 |
| INTIKHAB (USA) | 59 | 283 | 22 | 31 | 93 | 217932.55 |
| INVASOR (ARG) | 5 | 27 | 3 | 4 | 9 | 18013.96 |
| INVINCIBLE SPIRIT (IRE) | 219 | 1173 | 103 | 158 | 459 | 3208525.79 |
| ISHIGURU (USA) | 36 | 353 | 23 | 48 | 109 | 351050.26 |
| IVAN DENISOVICH (IRE) | 11 | 91 | 6 | 11 | 31 | 59239.08 |
| JADE ROBBERY (USA) | 2 | 10 | 1 | 1 | 3 | 4310.30 |
| JAZIL (USA) | 4 | 12 | 1 | 1 | 1 | 3659.77 |
| JEREMY (USA) | 71 | 344 | 24 | 33 | 97 | 437522.51 |
| JOHANNESBURG (USA) | 11 | 82 | 4 | 7 | 24 | 45772.80 |
| JOSR ALGARHOUD (IRE) | 7 | 33 | 2 | 6 | 6 | 15834.17 |
| KAHYASI | 4 | 5 | 1 | 2 | 0 | 10637.50 |
| KALANISI (IRE) | 11 | 38 | 3 | 5 | 11 | 86343.14 |
| KARINGA BAY | 3 | 12 | 1 | 3 | 2 | 17066.67 |
| KAVAFI (IRE) | 2 | 12 | 2 | 4 | 4 | 33481.10 |
| KEY OF LUCK (USA) | 7 | 43 | 3 | 5 | 11 | 53998.69 |
| KHELEYF (USA) | 129 | 856 | 53 | 96 | 299 | 791159.02 |
| KIER PARK (IRE) | 3 | 33 | 2 | 5 | 2 | 12256.25 |
| KING CHARLEMAGNE (USA) | 3 | 10 | 1 | 1 | 2 | 2333.70 |
| KINGSALSA (USA) | 5 | 26 | 2 | 2 | 6 | 18865.20 |
| KING'S BEST (USA) | 45 | 223 | 14 | 24 | 86 | 213987.66 |
| KING'S THEATRE (IRE) | 9 | 28 | 3 | 3 | 8 | 35325.02 |
| KIRKWALL (GB) | 2 | 12 | 2 | 3 | 4 | 18137.32 |
| KITTEN'S JOY (USA) | 11 | 33 | 1 | 1 | 14 | 68943.24 |
| KODIAC (GB) | 154 | 864 | 73 | 107 | 301 | 1490381.27 |
| KONIGSTIGER (GER) | 3 | 6 | 1 | 1 | 2 | 5140.05 |
| KYLLACHY (GB) | 145 | 919 | 65 | 96 | 307 | 1319408.92 |
| LAHIB (USA) | 3 | 13 | 1 | 1 | 5 | 7763.43 |
| LANDO (GER) | 7 | 29 | 3 | 7 | 9 | 26685.09 |
| LANGFUHR (CAN) | 6 | 23 | 3 | 5 | 5 | 62180.40 |
| LATENT HEAT (USA) | 2 | 16 | 1 | 1 | 8 | 6594.75 |
| LAWMAN (FR) | 103 | 486 | 38 | 52 | 171 | 558879.84 |
| LEADERSHIP (GB) | 1 | 4 | 1 | 2 | 1 | 8990.64 |
| LE CADRE NOIR (IRE) | 4 | 13 | 1 | 1 | 2 | 6636.36 |
| LE HAVRE (IRE) | 6 | 17 | 1 | 1 | 5 | 3991.25 |

| STALLIONS | RNRS | STARTS | WNRS | WINS | PLACES | TOTAL (£) |
|---|---|---|---|---|---|---|
| LEMON DROP KID (USA) | 10 | 36 | 2 | 4 | 12 | 100943.02 |
| LEPORELLO (IRE) | 4 | 13 | 1 | 2 | 6 | 12272.50 |
| LE VIE DEI COLORI (GB) | 11 | 84 | 6 | 11 | 36 | 264116.48 |
| LIBRETTIST (USA) | 12 | 72 | 6 | 10 | 22 | 33839.76 |
| LIMNOS (JPN) | 1 | 13 | 1 | 3 | 6 | 7855.80 |
| LINAMIX (FR) | 2 | 7 | 1 | 1 | 2 | 24400.00 |
| LINNGARI (IRE) | 3 | 14 | 2 | 3 | 2 | 19102.80 |
| LION HEART (USA) | 4 | 22 | 1 | 2 | 4 | 30637.50 |
| LITERATO (FR) | 3 | 14 | 1 | 1 | 12 | 9534.35 |
| LOMITAS (GB) | 5 | 32 | 2 | 3 | 12 | 46956.43 |
| LOOKIN AT LUCKY (USA) | 3 | 10 | 1 | 2 | 4 | 10505.80 |
| LOPE DE VEGA (IRE) | 36 | 108 | 13 | 17 | 49 | 494072.94 |
| LORD OF ENGLAND (GER) | 3 | 4 | 1 | 1 | 0 | 2911.05 |
| LORD SHANAKILL (USA) | 26 | 85 | 9 | 11 | 25 | 94092.00 |
| LUCKY STORY (USA) | 46 | 295 | 16 | 19 | 73 | 98170.61 |
| LUJAIN (USA) | 7 | 68 | 4 | 7 | 22 | 37639.85 |
| MACHIAVELLIAN (USA) | 4 | 17 | 1 | 2 | 3 | 12991.66 |
| MAJESTIC MISSILE (IRE) | 29 | 166 | 8 | 14 | 55 | 126275.02 |
| MAJOR CADEAUX (GB) | 38 | 200 | 16 | 20 | 66 | 137459.78 |
| MAKBUL | 4 | 28 | 3 | 3 | 6 | 16948.10 |
| MAKFI (GB) | 32 | 102 | 10 | 11 | 40 | 96817.04 |
| MALIBU MOON (USA) | 2 | 5 | 1 | 2 | 0 | 9056.60 |
| MANDURO (GER) | 63 | 266 | 16 | 19 | 77 | 362935.29 |
| MARJU (IRE) | 34 | 189 | 12 | 16 | 64 | 151527.95 |
| MARK OF ESTEEM (IRE) | 8 | 39 | 2 | 2 | 11 | 12393.98 |
| MARQUETRY (USA) | 1 | 4 | 1 | 2 | 1 | 5685.90 |
| MARTALINE (GB) | 1 | 2 | 1 | 1 | 1 | 38183.33 |
| MARTINO ALONSO (IRE) | 1 | 11 | 1 | 1 | 4 | 21849.70 |
| MASTERCRAFTSMAN (IRE) | 108 | 444 | 38 | 54 | 163 | 1944937.47 |
| MASTERFUL (USA) | 1 | 7 | 1 | 3 | 1 | 12992.72 |
| MEDAGLIA D'ORO (USA) | 23 | 87 | 9 | 13 | 25 | 111314.69 |
| MEDECIS (GB) | 7 | 32 | 3 | 5 | 4 | 24414.48 |
| MEDICEAN (GB) | 100 | 577 | 37 | 57 | 211 | 640023.21 |
| MIDNIGHT LEGEND (GB) | 4 | 22 | 2 | 3 | 7 | 10217.10 |
| MIESQUE'S SON (USA) | 1 | 11 | 1 | 2 | 4 | 8278.00 |
| MILK IT MICK (GB) | 16 | 115 | 6 | 12 | 25 | 54728.75 |
| MILLKOM (GB) | 3 | 23 | 1 | 1 | 9 | 9327.80 |
| MIND GAMES (GB) | 6 | 35 | 2 | 2 | 7 | 18873.01 |
| MISU BOND (IRE) | 24 | 166 | 7 | 15 | 53 | 109029.59 |
| MIZZEN MAST (USA) | 27 | 132 | 9 | 14 | 34 | 86641.34 |
| MODIGLIANI (USA) | 5 | 12 | 2 | 3 | 4 | 92124.00 |
| MONSIEUR BOND (IRE) | 76 | 394 | 21 | 36 | 121 | 791817.93 |
| MONSUN (GER) | 23 | 84 | 9 | 15 | 34 | 344330.21 |
| MONTJEU (IRE) | 92 | 366 | 28 | 52 | 121 | 1572530.58 |
| MONTJOY (USA) | 1 | 5 | 1 | 1 | 0 | 6469.00 |
| MORE THAN READY (USA) | 18 | 76 | 6 | 6 | 30 | 157323.84 |
| MOSS VALE (IRE) | 51 | 293 | 17 | 24 | 89 | 229717.44 |
| MOTIVATOR (GB) | 47 | 198 | 14 | 19 | 78 | 473760.30 |
| MOUNT NELSON (GB) | 67 | 357 | 31 | 39 | 136 | 567633.66 |
| MR GREELEY (USA) | 16 | 69 | 3 | 3 | 33 | 51860.90 |
| MTOTO | 1 | 6 | 1 | 1 | 3 | 3371.20 |
| MUHTATHIR (GB) | 8 | 62 | 2 | 3 | 16 | 19487.97 |
| MUJADIL (USA) | 18 | 146 | 5 | 7 | 53 | 90545.39 |
| MUJAHID (USA) | 7 | 56 | 3 | 4 | 24 | 37682.32 |
| MULLIONMILEANHOUR (IRE) | 6 | 27 | 1 | 1 | 5 | 3993.30 |
| MULL OF KINTYRE (USA) | 5 | 32 | 3 | 6 | 10 | 92016.80 |
| MULTIPLEX (GB) | 54 | 329 | 15 | 29 | 92 | 152497.83 |
| MUNNINGS (USA) | 1 | 7 | 1 | 1 | 5 | 24417.69 |
| MUSTAMEET (USA) | 1 | 8 | 1 | 2 | 2 | 20825.00 |
| MYBOYCHARLIE (IRE) | 45 | 237 | 14 | 20 | 88 | 221654.85 |
| NAAQOOS (GB) | 11 | 37 | 4 | 6 | 15 | 29607.83 |
| NAMID (GB) | 21 | 178 | 6 | 11 | 60 | 72406.25 |
| NAYEF (USA) | 88 | 395 | 28 | 44 | 158 | 893747.64 |

| STALLIONS | RNRS | STARTS | WNRS | WINS | PLACES | TOTAL (£) |
|---|---|---|---|---|---|---|
| NEEDWOOD BLADE (GB) | 23 | 179 | 13 | 18 | 71 | 105355.92 |
| NEW APPROACH (IRE) | 115 | 398 | 50 | 76 | 168 | 1089627.07 |
| NIGHT SHIFT (USA) | 5 | 69 | 4 | 8 | 24 | 64699.70 |
| NORSE DANCER (IRE) | 19 | 92 | 6 | 11 | 25 | 54021.40 |
| NOTNOWCATO (GB) | 38 | 179 | 12 | 18 | 58 | 376919.13 |
| NOVERRE (USA) | 20 | 154 | 7 | 13 | 62 | 86501.64 |
| OASIS DREAM (GB) | 169 | 885 | 83 | 123 | 337 | 1950004.90 |
| OBSERVATORY (USA) | 17 | 79 | 7 | 11 | 26 | 64123.87 |
| OFFICER (USA) | 3 | 25 | 1 | 1 | 6 | 6888.00 |
| OKAWANGO (USA) | 1 | 4 | 1 | 1 | 2 | 3659.55 |
| OLD VIC | 2 | 3 | 1 | 1 | 0 | 5606.25 |
| OLMODAVOR (USA) | 1 | 6 | 1 | 1 | 2 | 3082.10 |
| ONE COOL CAT (USA) | 23 | 160 | 9 | 14 | 47 | 80988.34 |
| ORATORIO (IRE) | 98 | 590 | 43 | 70 | 226 | 615432.34 |
| ORIENTATE (USA) | 2 | 17 | 2 | 3 | 9 | 28355.92 |
| ORIENTOR (GB) | 9 | 63 | 4 | 11 | 23 | 91716.87 |
| ORPEN (USA) | 10 | 31 | 2 | 2 | 6 | 9187.20 |
| OSORIO (GER) | 3 | 29 | 2 | 3 | 10 | 10221.80 |
| OVERBURY (IRE) | 1 | 5 | 1 | 3 | 1 | 60333.33 |
| PACO BOY (IRE) | 50 | 205 | 19 | 28 | 78 | 290698.47 |
| PAIRUMANI STAR (IRE) | 1 | 22 | 1 | 2 | 7 | 19122.91 |
| PANIS (USA) | 3 | 10 | 1 | 1 | 4 | 10887.00 |
| PAOLINI (GER) | 1 | 3 | 1 | 1 | 0 | 2264.15 |
| PAPAL BULL (GB) | 25 | 100 | 3 | 4 | 22 | 35456.36 |
| PARIS HOUSE (GB) | 6 | 27 | 1 | 1 | 5 | 9525.10 |
| PASSING GLANCE (GB) | 10 | 36 | 3 | 6 | 13 | 36889.29 |
| PASTORAL PURSUITS (GB) | 123 | 668 | 52 | 69 | 218 | 513915.33 |
| PEARL OF LOVE (IRE) | 2 | 13 | 1 | 3 | 4 | 12843.20 |
| PEER GYNT (JPN) | 3 | 16 | 2 | 3 | 9 | 19840.30 |
| PEINTRE CELEBRE (USA) | 30 | 111 | 7 | 8 | 34 | 135279.64 |
| PENTIRE (GB) | 2 | 11 | 2 | 3 | 3 | 8323.00 |
| PETARDIA (GB) | 1 | 9 | 1 | 2 | 5 | 6337.20 |
| PETIONVILLE (USA) | 1 | 14 | 1 | 1 | 7 | 4333.00 |
| PHOENIX REACH (IRE) | 19 | 115 | 11 | 22 | 38 | 396217.69 |
| PICCOLO (GB) | 71 | 500 | 27 | 40 | 167 | 331796.77 |
| PIVOTAL (GB) | 143 | 776 | 69 | 106 | 283 | 1231974.43 |
| PLEASANTLY PERFECT (USA) | 1 | 6 | 1 | 2 | 1 | 21614.70 |
| PLEASANT TAP (USA) | 2 | 4 | 1 | 1 | 1 | 2456.55 |
| PRIMARY (USA) | 3 | 11 | 1 | 1 | 2 | 2533.65 |
| PRIMO VALENTINO (IRE) | 8 | 51 | 3 | 6 | 15 | 58340.67 |
| PROCLAMATION (IRE) | 30 | 160 | 8 | 13 | 52 | 85384.73 |
| PROUD CITIZEN (USA) | 6 | 40 | 1 | 4 | 11 | 42474.12 |
| PULPIT (USA) | 2 | 9 | 1 | 1 | 5 | 9029.58 |
| PUSHKIN (IRE) | 1 | 3 | 1 | 2 | 1 | 14091.67 |
| PYRUS (USA) | 12 | 80 | 5 | 7 | 38 | 71572.02 |
| QUALITY ROAD (USA) | 1 | 1 | 1 | 1 | 0 | 34026.00 |
| RAHY (USA) | 5 | 19 | 2 | 2 | 9 | 35039.82 |
| RAIL LINK (GB) | 44 | 202 | 17 | 20 | 83 | 194306.77 |
| RAKTI (GB) | 10 | 66 | 5 | 7 | 23 | 51872.18 |
| RAMONTI (FR) | 6 | 32 | 1 | 1 | 8 | 25204.80 |
| RANSOM O'WAR (USA) | 1 | 2 | 1 | 1 | 1 | 164945.00 |
| RAVEN'S PASS (USA) | 51 | 181 | 21 | 29 | 73 | 334391.28 |
| REDBACK (GB) | 21 | 111 | 7 | 11 | 25 | 79054.03 |
| RED CLUBS (IRE) | 44 | 362 | 20 | 35 | 104 | 277340.30 |
| REDOUTE'S CHOICE (AUS) | 4 | 11 | 2 | 2 | 4 | 9223.40 |
| RED RANSOM (USA) | 11 | 68 | 2 | 3 | 19 | 22407.46 |
| REEL BUDDY (USA) | 7 | 38 | 2 | 3 | 17 | 15182.70 |
| REFUSE TO BEND (IRE) | 58 | 318 | 19 | 32 | 90 | 161126.48 |
| REPENT (USA) | 1 | 9 | 1 | 1 | 1 | 6620.83 |
| RESET (AUS) | 5 | 40 | 3 | 3 | 13 | 16661.30 |
| RESPLENDENT GLORY (IRE) | 8 | 63 | 2 | 4 | 16 | 18179.08 |
| REVOQUE (IRE) | 3 | 10 | 1 | 1 | 1 | 7250.00 |
| RIP VAN WINKLE (IRE) | 42 | 120 | 13 | 19 | 31 | 313254.96 |

| STALLIONS | RNRS | STARTS | WNRS | WINS | PLACES | TOTAL (£) |
|---|---|---|---|---|---|---|
| ROB ROY (USA) | 4 | 16 | 1 | 1 | 4 | 4771.55 |
| ROCAMADOUR (GB) | 1 | 5 | 1 | 2 | 2 | 13073.24 |
| ROCK OF GIBRALTAR (IRE) | 126 | 635 | 44 | 62 | 240 | 741194.40 |
| ROMAN RULER (USA) | 3 | 26 | 1 | 1 | 5 | 4283.48 |
| ROYAL APPLAUSE (GB) | 156 | 868 | 54 | 85 | 255 | 791305.16 |
| SADLER'S WELLS (USA) | 13 | 49 | 3 | 3 | 13 | 16299.84 |
| SAFFRON WALDEN (FR) | 6 | 17 | 1 | 1 | 4 | 7662.00 |
| SAHM (USA) | 1 | 2 | 1 | 1 | 0 | 4312.50 |
| SAKHEE (USA) | 43 | 248 | 15 | 21 | 81 | 163094.60 |
| SAKHEE'S SECRET (GB) | 92 | 458 | 31 | 47 | 134 | 303245.94 |
| SAMPOWER STAR (GB) | 2 | 18 | 1 | 2 | 7 | 28087.40 |
| SAMUM (GER) | 6 | 32 | 3 | 3 | 11 | 14412.50 |
| SCORPION (IRE) | 4 | 8 | 1 | 2 | 0 | 6145.55 |
| SEA THE STARS (IRE) | 71 | 250 | 34 | 45 | 112 | 1520855.66 |
| SELKIRK (USA) | 54 | 282 | 24 | 45 | 104 | 618278.59 |
| SEPTIEME CIEL (USA) | 2 | 23 | 2 | 3 | 8 | 10029.50 |
| SHAMARDAL (USA) | 166 | 809 | 84 | 134 | 330 | 2743894.79 |
| SHANTOU (USA) | 2 | 10 | 1 | 3 | 7 | 124011.45 |
| SHINKO FOREST (IRE) | 3 | 22 | 1 | 2 | 7 | 10436.77 |
| SHIROCCO (GER) | 43 | 187 | 13 | 23 | 55 | 424889.58 |
| SHOLOKHOV (IRE) | 6 | 21 | 1 | 1 | 4 | 5817.55 |
| SHOWCASING (GB) | 48 | 214 | 26 | 41 | 92 | 476777.22 |
| SILVER FROST (IRE) | 5 | 20 | 1 | 1 | 7 | 6191.10 |
| SILVER PATRIARCH (IRE) | 7 | 18 | 1 | 1 | 1 | 4082.25 |
| SINGSPIEL (IRE) | 50 | 210 | 16 | 25 | 81 | 398501.22 |
| SINNDAR (IRE) | 11 | 37 | 4 | 6 | 13 | 140489.66 |
| SINTARAJAN (IRE) | 1 | 11 | 1 | 4 | 0 | 13081.40 |
| SIR PERCY (GB) | 100 | 428 | 35 | 49 | 171 | 581679.17 |
| SIX SENSE (JPN) | 1 | 4 | 1 | 1 | 2 | 18166.66 |
| SIXTIES ICON (GB) | 25 | 166 | 13 | 14 | 71 | 127713.11 |
| SIYOUNI (FR) | 4 | 10 | 1 | 3 | 1 | 25432.60 |
| SKY MESA (USA) | 2 | 10 | 1 | 1 | 6 | 4128.08 |
| SLEEPING INDIAN (GB) | 72 | 497 | 25 | 46 | 165 | 292600.71 |
| SLICKLY (FR) | 1 | 2 | 1 | 1 | 0 | 8625.00 |
| SMART STRIKE (CAN) | 15 | 49 | 2 | 2 | 27 | 32151.56 |
| SOLDIER OF FORTUNE (IRE) | 4 | 25 | 1 | 3 | 16 | 65864.72 |
| SONGANDAPRAYER (USA) | 1 | 15 | 1 | 1 | 5 | 4610.08 |
| SOVIET STAR (USA) | 20 | 142 | 9 | 11 | 40 | 71310.52 |
| SPARTACUS (IRE) | 5 | 25 | 1 | 1 | 6 | 7980.70 |
| SPEIGHTSTOWN (USA) | 26 | 126 | 10 | 24 | 37 | 397088.21 |
| SPINNING WORLD (USA) | 3 | 19 | 2 | 3 | 5 | 14255.67 |
| STARCRAFT (NZ) | 3 | 23 | 2 | 2 | 3 | 8455.15 |
| STARDAN (IRE) | 1 | 4 | 1 | 1 | 1 | 5312.50 |
| STARSPANGLEDBANNER (AUS) | 17 | 67 | 10 | 14 | 25 | 267996.45 |
| STATUE OF LIBERTY (USA) | 11 | 58 | 2 | 4 | 13 | 26640.81 |
| STIMULATION (IRE) | 30 | 162 | 6 | 6 | 39 | 62079.18 |
| STORMING HOME (GB) | 12 | 68 | 4 | 4 | 31 | 100052.51 |
| STORMY ATLANTIC (USA) | 8 | 65 | 6 | 11 | 13 | 48417.18 |
| STRATEGIC PRINCE (GB) | 49 | 335 | 19 | 34 | 120 | 249624.16 |
| STREET BOSS (USA) | 3 | 14 | 1 | 1 | 10 | 11173.15 |
| STREET CRY (IRE) | 67 | 307 | 24 | 44 | 104 | 427950.69 |
| STREET SENSE (USA) | 9 | 34 | 3 | 4 | 11 | 15148.75 |
| STRIKING AMBITION (GB) | 14 | 81 | 4 | 6 | 22 | 53038.60 |
| SUCCESSFUL APPEAL (USA) | 3 | 16 | 1 | 2 | 2 | 11101.35 |
| SUGARFOOT (GB) | 2 | 14 | 1 | 3 | 4 | 18358.60 |
| SULAMANI (IRE) | 14 | 93 | 6 | 7 | 26 | 64897.58 |
| SUPERIOR PREMIUM (GB) | 6 | 34 | 2 | 3 | 8 | 31866.20 |
| SUPREME LEADER | 1 | 6 | 1 | 1 | 0 | 1940.70 |
| TAGULA (IRE) | 60 | 335 | 23 | 40 | 82 | 366772.46 |
| TAJRAASI (USA) | 2 | 5 | 1 | 1 | 1 | 6216.67 |
| TAKE RISKS (FR) | 1 | 2 | 1 | 1 | 1 | 64126.00 |
| TALE OF THE CAT (USA) | 8 | 42 | 2 | 2 | 16 | 50452.74 |
| TAMAYUZ (GB) | 61 | 337 | 30 | 51 | 136 | 552702.61 |

| STALLIONS | RNRS | STARTS | WNRS | WINS | PLACES | TOTAL (£) |
|---|---|---|---|---|---|---|
| TAPIT (USA) | 3 | 8 | 1 | 2 | 4 | 18817.66 |
| TEOFILO (IRE) | 167 | 687 | 62 | 87 | 260 | 2005456.66 |
| THEATRICAL | 3 | 8 | 2 | 4 | 2 | 21553.85 |
| THEWAYYOUARE (USA) | 36 | 125 | 9 | 9 | 21 | 40427.78 |
| THOUSAND WORDS (GB) | 21 | 102 | 4 | 5 | 38 | 79962.64 |
| THREE VALLEYS (USA) | 36 | 170 | 11 | 19 | 57 | 138664.02 |
| TIGER HILL (IRE) | 60 | 313 | 19 | 27 | 113 | 287141.08 |
| TILLERMAN (GB) | 2 | 13 | 2 | 2 | 6 | 7641.10 |
| TITUS LIVIUS (FR) | 11 | 56 | 4 | 5 | 17 | 33405.02 |
| TIZNOW (USA) | 5 | 13 | 1 | 3 | 1 | 11012.07 |
| TOBOUGG (IRE) | 49 | 245 | 13 | 21 | 74 | 140520.01 |
| TOMBA (GB) | 5 | 20 | 1 | 1 | 6 | 10544.60 |
| TORRENTIAL (USA) | 1 | 7 | 1 | 1 | 5 | 43699.80 |
| TRADE FAIR (GB) | 27 | 168 | 10 | 15 | 42 | 131404.21 |
| TRADITIONALLY (USA) | 7 | 20 | 2 | 2 | 6 | 8216.38 |
| TRANS ISLAND (GB) | 9 | 83 | 2 | 5 | 32 | 160999.65 |
| TUMBLEBRUTUS (USA) | 1 | 14 | 1 | 2 | 4 | 5341.97 |
| URGENT REQUEST (IRE) | 3 | 15 | 2 | 2 | 7 | 13199.40 |
| U S RANGER (USA) | 6 | 36 | 1 | 1 | 18 | 14898.22 |
| VALE OF YORK (IRE) | 35 | 152 | 12 | 15 | 49 | 137804.11 |
| VAL ROYAL (FR) | 17 | 75 | 7 | 13 | 14 | 69111.60 |
| VAN NISTELROOY (USA) | 2 | 19 | 2 | 5 | 7 | 27969.61 |
| VERGLAS (IRE) | 110 | 618 | 52 | 79 | 204 | 922306.63 |
| VETTORI (IRE) | 6 | 27 | 2 | 2 | 8 | 31751.66 |
| VINDICATION (USA) | 1 | 25 | 1 | 2 | 7 | 10966.66 |
| VIRTUAL (GB) | 21 | 78 | 3 | 4 | 25 | 26329.91 |
| VISION OF NIGHT (GB) | 1 | 9 | 1 | 1 | 0 | 5175.20 |
| VITAL EQUINE (IRE) | 4 | 28 | 3 | 3 | 9 | 21157.40 |
| VITA ROSA (JPN) | 2 | 16 | 1 | 2 | 3 | 7766.87 |
| VITUS (GB) | 1 | 18 | 1 | 2 | 9 | 7896.30 |
| VOCALISED (USA) | 10 | 33 | 3 | 3 | 8 | 55454.17 |
| WAR CHANT (USA) | 9 | 60 | 4 | 6 | 21 | 65939.98 |
| WAR FRONT (USA) | 31 | 103 | 17 | 23 | 47 | 534328.34 |
| WELSH LION (IRE) | 1 | 4 | 1 | 1 | 1 | 5379.17 |
| WESTERNER (GB) | 7 | 36 | 4 | 6 | 8 | 39887.00 |
| WHERE OR WHEN (IRE) | 5 | 39 | 3 | 4 | 19 | 22471.75 |
| WHIPPER (USA) | 35 | 196 | 13 | 21 | 72 | 273901.17 |
| WINDSOR KNOT (IRE) | 19 | 86 | 4 | 8 | 22 | 80143.84 |
| WINKER WATSON (GB) | 19 | 94 | 3 | 4 | 38 | 35778.14 |
| WISEMAN'S FERRY (USA) | 2 | 15 | 1 | 1 | 5 | 11115.85 |
| WITH APPROVAL (CAN) | 3 | 16 | 1 | 1 | 7 | 5556.35 |
| XAAR (GB) | 4 | 27 | 1 | 2 | 5 | 12474.99 |
| YANKEE GENTLEMAN (USA) | 2 | 11 | 1 | 1 | 4 | 14496.58 |
| YEATS (IRE) | 18 | 61 | 5 | 9 | 14 | 82655.70 |
| YOUNG ERN (GB) | 2 | 12 | 1 | 1 | 3 | 2988.65 |
| ZAFEEN (FR) | 14 | 59 | 5 | 7 | 10 | 37434.97 |
| ZAMBEZI SUN (GB) | 1 | 4 | 1 | 2 | 1 | 4555.15 |
| ZAMINDAR (USA) | 59 | 302 | 21 | 32 | 100 | 443839.34 |
| ZAVATA (USA) | 1 | 9 | 1 | 1 | 6 | 6653.15 |
| ZEBEDEE (GB) | 72 | 330 | 26 | 39 | 114 | 394873.69 |

*BY KIND PERMISSION OF WEATHERBYS*

# NH STALLIONS' EARNINGS FOR 2013/14

(includes every stallion who sired a winner over jumps in Great Britain and Ireland in 2013/14)

| STALLIONS | RNRS | STARTS | WNRS | WINS | PLACES | TOTAL (£) |
|---|---|---|---|---|---|---|
| ABOO HOM (GB) | 9 | 39 | 2 | 3 | 10 | 18808.21 |
| ACCESS SKI | 1 | 8 | 1 | 1 | 3 | 6113.16 |
| ACCLAMATION (GB) | 18 | 65 | 3 | 4 | 23 | 40769.80 |
| ACCORDION | 58 | 217 | 12 | 15 | 75 | 360775.98 |
| ACTION THIS DAY (USA) | 1 | 2 | 1 | 1 | 0 | 2053.20 |
| ACT ONE (GB) | 19 | 50 | 4 | 4 | 16 | 24143.46 |
| AD VALOREM (USA) | 10 | 24 | 3 | 3 | 2 | 8926.80 |
| AGENT BLEU (FR) | 4 | 28 | 3 | 11 | 9 | 151116.35 |
| AKBAR (IRE) | 3 | 18 | 1 | 2 | 6 | 35418.72 |
| ALBERTO GIACOMETTI (IRE) | 5 | 24 | 3 | 8 | 5 | 82567.97 |
| ALDERBROOK (GB) | 81 | 348 | 24 | 38 | 129 | 340629.40 |
| ALEXIUS (IRE) | 3 | 21 | 3 | 3 | 9 | 22582.65 |
| ALFLORA (IRE) | 149 | 600 | 40 | 58 | 202 | 497929.62 |
| ALHAARTH (IRE) | 35 | 131 | 9 | 12 | 46 | 122936.89 |
| ALKALDE (GER) | 2 | 7 | 2 | 3 | 4 | 43221.36 |
| AL NAMIX (FR) | 11 | 39 | 4 | 8 | 16 | 134698.16 |
| ALWUHUSH (USA) | 2 | 16 | 1 | 1 | 6 | 9017.68 |
| AMADEUS WOLF (GB) | 6 | 13 | 1 | 1 | 1 | 3535.20 |
| AMERICAN POST (GB) | 3 | 18 | 1 | 1 | 9 | 20192.70 |
| AMILYNX (FR) | 14 | 63 | 4 | 4 | 19 | 28922.76 |
| ANABAA (USA) | 9 | 46 | 2 | 2 | 15 | 29770.77 |
| ANABAA BLUE (GB) | 5 | 11 | 1 | 1 | 4 | 2916.14 |
| AND BEYOND (IRE) | 13 | 73 | 3 | 8 | 15 | 44929.56 |
| ANGE GABRIEL (FR) | 1 | 5 | 1 | 3 | 1 | 15865.85 |
| ANSHAN | 92 | 410 | 27 | 36 | 122 | 549689.93 |
| ANTARCTIQUE (IRE) | 10 | 42 | 2 | 3 | 15 | 41577.73 |
| ANTONIUS PIUS (USA) | 28 | 105 | 4 | 5 | 41 | 62618.54 |
| ANZILLERO (GER) | 3 | 14 | 1 | 3 | 1 | 48819.11 |
| APRIL NIGHT (FR) | 10 | 48 | 8 | 11 | 17 | 71336.46 |
| APSIS (GB) | 2 | 10 | 2 | 3 | 6 | 30654.80 |
| ARAAFA (IRE) | 11 | 44 | 6 | 6 | 14 | 28315.43 |
| ARAKAN (USA) | 11 | 51 | 3 | 5 | 20 | 49272.29 |
| ARCADIO (GER) | 14 | 29 | 2 | 3 | 7 | 21611.23 |
| ARCTIC LORD | 3 | 15 | 1 | 2 | 3 | 20009.20 |
| ARKADIAN HERO (USA) | 5 | 15 | 1 | 1 | 6 | 7949.55 |
| ARTAN (IRE) | 9 | 21 | 2 | 3 | 1 | 14083.94 |
| ARVICO (FR) | 2 | 7 | 1 | 4 | 2 | 116459.79 |
| ASSESSOR (IRE) | 9 | 37 | 5 | 6 | 13 | 109595.00 |
| ASTARABAD (USA) | 15 | 74 | 5 | 8 | 18 | 182792.67 |
| ATRAF (GB) | 10 | 53 | 1 | 1 | 12 | 15554.36 |
| AUCTION HOUSE (USA) | 6 | 27 | 2 | 7 | 6 | 26580.24 |
| AUSSIE RULES (USA) | 11 | 55 | 4 | 7 | 17 | 42417.85 |
| AUTHORIZED (IRE) | 22 | 71 | 9 | 12 | 23 | 172045.95 |
| AVONBRIDGE (GB) | 10 | 42 | 1 | 1 | 11 | 12836.13 |
| AZAMOUR (IRE) | 28 | 122 | 11 | 23 | 41 | 272093.07 |
| BABY TURK | 3 | 10 | 1 | 1 | 6 | 36805.30 |
| BACH (IRE) | 68 | 256 | 13 | 26 | 61 | 146365.12 |
| BACHELOR DUKE (USA) | 13 | 42 | 2 | 4 | 8 | 27232.75 |
| BADOLATO (USA) | 1 | 3 | 1 | 1 | 1 | 2693.71 |
| BAHHARE (USA) | 6 | 30 | 2 | 7 | 8 | 46400.57 |
| BAHRI (USA) | 9 | 46 | 2 | 4 | 19 | 25828.51 |
| BALAKHERI (IRE) | 5 | 27 | 3 | 4 | 9 | 31787.16 |
| BAL HARBOUR (GB) | 4 | 21 | 1 | 2 | 9 | 10923.85 |
| BALKO (FR) | 4 | 17 | 3 | 5 | 8 | 64263.68 |
| BALLA COVE | 2 | 5 | 1 | 1 | 1 | 1133.10 |
| BALLINGARRY (IRE) | 18 | 72 | 4 | 9 | 30 | 95754.51 |
| BALTIC KING (GB) | 1 | 3 | 1 | 1 | 1 | 4033.62 |
| BANDARI (IRE) | 9 | 15 | 1 | 1 | 3 | 3089.26 |
| BANYUMANIK (IRE) | 2 | 3 | 1 | 1 | 1 | 15416.00 |
| BARATHEA (IRE) | 25 | 90 | 6 | 6 | 26 | 35509.69 |

| STALLIONS | RNRS | STARTS | WNRS | WINS | PLACES | TOTAL (£) |
|---|---|---|---|---|---|---|
| BARYSHNIKOV (AUS) | 14 | 48 | 3 | 5 | 12 | 24243.89 |
| BASANTA (IRE) | 8 | 38 | 2 | 3 | 13 | 37650.50 |
| BEAT ALL (USA) | 69 | 219 | 12 | 14 | 46 | 82592.51 |
| BEAT HOLLOW (GB) | 45 | 170 | 18 | 26 | 57 | 205850.69 |
| BEAT OF DRUMS (GB) | 1 | 10 | 1 | 2 | 6 | 15000.90 |
| BEAUCHAMP KING (GB) | 7 | 24 | 2 | 2 | 4 | 4589.00 |
| BENEFICIAL (GB) | 365 | 1628 | 117 | 176 | 505 | 2088273.12 |
| BERING | 6 | 28 | 3 | 5 | 13 | 51229.16 |
| BERNEBEAU (FR) | 4 | 19 | 2 | 3 | 9 | 28074.52 |
| BERNSTEIN (USA) | 3 | 14 | 2 | 2 | 4 | 15636.73 |
| BERTOLINI (USA) | 21 | 73 | 4 | 6 | 22 | 52281.04 |
| BEST OF THE BESTS (IRE) | 7 | 35 | 2 | 2 | 8 | 16646.92 |
| BIENAMADO (USA) | 16 | 66 | 5 | 9 | 11 | 53298.20 |
| BIG BAD BOB (IRE) | 8 | 29 | 1 | 2 | 12 | 18871.34 |
| BISHOP OF CASHEL (GB) | 17 | 77 | 4 | 5 | 14 | 43668.74 |
| BLACK SAM BELLAMY (IRE) | 16 | 71 | 6 | 8 | 27 | 181023.21 |
| BLUE OCEAN (USA) | 2 | 12 | 1 | 2 | 7 | 81224.11 |
| BLUEPRINT (IRE) | 42 | 219 | 12 | 19 | 71 | 152888.42 |
| BLUSHING FLAME (USA) | 1 | 8 | 1 | 1 | 1 | 2655.90 |
| BOB BACK (USA) | 60 | 264 | 20 | 32 | 74 | 669831.76 |
| BOB'S RETURN (IRE) | 39 | 181 | 10 | 13 | 61 | 118039.16 |
| BOLLIN ERIC (GB) | 34 | 150 | 10 | 22 | 44 | 111458.17 |
| BONBON ROSE (FR) | 4 | 28 | 3 | 5 | 11 | 74602.71 |
| BONNET ROUGE (FR) | 2 | 8 | 1 | 1 | 1 | 4852.80 |
| BORREGO (USA) | 2 | 8 | 1 | 2 | 3 | 8387.79 |
| BRIAN BORU (GB) | 86 | 409 | 28 | 44 | 136 | 381848.23 |
| BRIER CREEK (USA) | 10 | 50 | 7 | 10 | 16 | 53865.06 |
| BROADWAY FLYER (USA) | 19 | 98 | 4 | 6 | 34 | 53573.09 |
| BROKEN HEARTED | 5 | 18 | 2 | 2 | 9 | 60763.99 |
| BUSTER KING | 3 | 14 | 1 | 1 | 3 | 3056.58 |
| BUSY FLIGHT (GB) | 5 | 28 | 1 | 1 | 7 | 7822.24 |
| BYZANTIUM (FR) | 1 | 2 | 1 | 1 | 1 | 4722.84 |
| CABALLO RAPTOR (CAN) | 6 | 30 | 2 | 3 | 11 | 26634.93 |
| CACHET NOIR (USA) | 1 | 10 | 1 | 1 | 5 | 6272.35 |
| CACIQUE (IRE) | 2 | 11 | 2 | 2 | 2 | 11874.43 |
| CADOUBEL (FR) | 1 | 9 | 1 | 2 | 6 | 10740.31 |
| CADOUDAL (FR) | 7 | 24 | 1 | 1 | 15 | 102724.84 |
| CALIFET (FR) | 9 | 33 | 4 | 6 | 16 | 103390.85 |
| CAPE CROSS (IRE) | 37 | 137 | 13 | 22 | 42 | 202944.67 |
| CAPTAIN MARVELOUS (IRE) | 2 | 10 | 1 | 2 | 3 | 15873.50 |
| CAPTAIN RIO (GB) | 12 | 27 | 2 | 3 | 9 | 35238.51 |
| CARNIVAL DANCER (GB) | 2 | 9 | 1 | 1 | 3 | 3154.62 |
| CARROLL HOUSE | 18 | 62 | 3 | 4 | 20 | 35299.64 |
| CATCHER IN THE RYE (IRE) | 58 | 200 | 10 | 17 | 35 | 128522.50 |
| CELTIC SWING (GB) | 20 | 76 | 7 | 7 | 32 | 56668.72 |
| CENTRAL PARK (IRE) | 25 | 83 | 5 | 9 | 29 | 53125.05 |
| CHARMING GROOM (FR) | 3 | 14 | 1 | 1 | 4 | 4707.00 |
| CHEVALIER (IRE) | 17 | 59 | 4 | 6 | 15 | 47937.36 |
| CHINOOK ECLIPSE (USA) | 2 | 17 | 2 | 2 | 4 | 12443.19 |
| CHOCOLAT DE MEGURO (USA) | 1 | 10 | 1 | 1 | 5 | 7912.62 |
| CHOISIR (AUS) | 16 | 43 | 2 | 4 | 10 | 41541.24 |
| CHRISTOPHENE (USA) | 1 | 6 | 1 | 1 | 0 | 4284.55 |
| CITY HONOURS (USA) | 19 | 84 | 4 | 5 | 21 | 58005.35 |
| CLASSIC CLICHE (IRE) | 49 | 185 | 12 | 19 | 42 | 106516.21 |
| CLERKENWELL (USA) | 6 | 24 | 2 | 4 | 5 | 45426.14 |
| CLODOVIL (IRE) | 9 | 25 | 2 | 4 | 8 | 19674.39 |
| CLOSE CONFLICT (USA) | 15 | 47 | 2 | 2 | 15 | 23703.58 |
| CLOUDINGS (IRE) | 80 | 381 | 29 | 51 | 109 | 397881.09 |
| COCKNEY REBEL (IRE) | 5 | 21 | 2 | 3 | 10 | 84584.32 |
| COLONEL COLLINS (USA) | 3 | 13 | 1 | 2 | 2 | 40245.29 |
| COMMANCHE RUN | 3 | 16 | 1 | 2 | 8 | 14471.91 |
| COMMANDER COLLINS (IRE) | 3 | 13 | 1 | 1 | 5 | 6750.18 |
| COMPTON PLACE (GB) | 5 | 14 | 2 | 2 | 5 | 9764.05 |
| CONILLON (GER) | 1 | 3 | 1 | 1 | 1 | 6831.90 |

| STALLIONS | RNRS | STARTS | WNRS | WINS | PLACES | TOTAL (£) |
|---|---|---|---|---|---|---|
| CONVINCED | 2 | 5 | 1 | 1 | 1 | 1190.50 |
| CORRI PIANO (FR) | 2 | 15 | 2 | 3 | 6 | 18004.82 |
| COUNTRY REEL (USA) | 2 | 4 | 1 | 1 | 2 | 4824.84 |
| COURT CAVE (IRE) | 66 | 316 | 22 | 33 | 96 | 269215.62 |
| COZZENE (USA) | 1 | 7 | 1 | 2 | 2 | 12016.25 |
| CRAIGSTEEL (GB) | 73 | 267 | 14 | 22 | 77 | 175830.63 |
| CROCO ROUGE (IRE) | 20 | 82 | 4 | 8 | 27 | 67411.92 |
| CURTAIN TIME (IRE) | 6 | 18 | 1 | 1 | 8 | 39573.84 |
| CYBORG (FR) | 3 | 15 | 1 | 2 | 4 | 11257.63 |
| DADARISSIME (FR) | 2 | 10 | 1 | 1 | 7 | 10946.02 |
| DALAKHANI (IRE) | 31 | 147 | 6 | 10 | 47 | 73190.87 |
| DALIAPOUR (IRE) | 6 | 36 | 4 | 7 | 14 | 66321.09 |
| DANCING SPREE (USA) | 2 | 7 | 1 | 1 | 2 | 4871.88 |
| DANEHILL DANCER (IRE) | 42 | 168 | 11 | 17 | 48 | 138526.50 |
| DANSILI (GB) | 29 | 123 | 7 | 10 | 36 | 119721.12 |
| DARK ANGEL (IRE) | 11 | 38 | 4 | 9 | 12 | 179500.53 |
| DARK MOONDANCER (GB) | 9 | 44 | 4 | 5 | 12 | 37795.96 |
| DARNAY (GB) | 3 | 17 | 1 | 1 | 4 | 3171.85 |
| DARSI (FR) | 21 | 85 | 5 | 7 | 25 | 42048.45 |
| DASHING BLADE | 2 | 6 | 1 | 1 | 0 | 2183.65 |
| DAYLAMI (IRE) | 24 | 85 | 5 | 5 | 34 | 52976.22 |
| DEFINITE ARTICLE (GB) | 167 | 599 | 43 | 58 | 181 | 480532.29 |
| DELLA FRANCESCA (USA) | 4 | 27 | 1 | 2 | 10 | 19367.71 |
| DENHAM RED (FR) | 1 | 3 | 1 | 3 | 0 | 41195.12 |
| DEPLOY | 21 | 75 | 3 | 4 | 16 | 32389.28 |
| DESERT KING (IRE) | 30 | 98 | 5 | 7 | 34 | 44709.82 |
| DESERT PRINCE (IRE) | 16 | 74 | 6 | 10 | 19 | 273274.16 |
| DESERT STYLE (IRE) | 8 | 47 | 4 | 6 | 15 | 46716.19 |
| DESIDERATUM (GB) | 6 | 26 | 1 | 2 | 10 | 12261.60 |
| DIAMOND GREEN (FR) | 16 | 48 | 5 | 7 | 12 | 30729.59 |
| DIESIS | 5 | 16 | 2 | 2 | 5 | 19694.08 |
| DIKTAT (GB) | 13 | 59 | 3 | 4 | 17 | 34279.57 |
| DILSHAAN (GB) | 15 | 56 | 3 | 5 | 9 | 22458.70 |
| DISCOVER D'AUTEUIL (FR) | 7 | 38 | 4 | 9 | 9 | 89424.58 |
| DOM ALCO (FR) | 33 | 138 | 17 | 22 | 51 | 733282.91 |
| DOUBLE ECLIPSE (IRE) | 11 | 44 | 3 | 6 | 13 | 191076.73 |
| DOUBLETOUR (USA) | 2 | 21 | 1 | 1 | 12 | 8265.48 |
| DOUBLE TRIGGER (IRE) | 32 | 86 | 7 | 7 | 22 | 32705.86 |
| DOVER PATROL (IRE) | 1 | 5 | 1 | 1 | 1 | 2697.66 |
| DOYEN (IRE) | 32 | 132 | 7 | 10 | 54 | 144003.20 |
| DREAM WELL (FR) | 7 | 24 | 1 | 1 | 11 | 14236.85 |
| DR FONG (USA) | 23 | 100 | 7 | 9 | 44 | 70643.49 |
| DR MASSINI (IRE) | 114 | 484 | 29 | 47 | 149 | 506956.60 |
| DUBAI DESTINATION (USA) | 43 | 162 | 9 | 11 | 58 | 109708.16 |
| DUBAWI (IRE) | 21 | 92 | 12 | 22 | 34 | 187112.88 |
| DUSHYANTOR (USA) | 59 | 263 | 14 | 18 | 70 | 144480.05 |
| D'WILDCAT (USA) | 1 | 8 | 1 | 2 | 3 | 17927.55 |
| DYLAN THOMAS (IRE) | 30 | 111 | 8 | 12 | 46 | 100972.73 |
| DYNAFORMER (USA) | 15 | 84 | 7 | 10 | 30 | 135188.83 |
| EARLY MARCH (GB) | 2 | 13 | 2 | 2 | 6 | 15710.25 |
| ECHO OF LIGHT (GB) | 10 | 37 | 3 | 5 | 5 | 16200.26 |
| ELMAAMUL (USA) | 4 | 25 | 2 | 3 | 12 | 13299.65 |
| ELNADIM (USA) | 4 | 17 | 1 | 1 | 1 | 5575.00 |
| ELUSIVE CITY (USA) | 8 | 18 | 1 | 1 | 5 | 7859.28 |
| ELUSIVE QUALITY (USA) | 5 | 12 | 1 | 1 | 2 | 9064.30 |
| EMPEROR FOUNTAIN | 6 | 17 | 1 | 1 | 3 | 4961.89 |
| ENDOLI (USA) | 6 | 25 | 1 | 1 | 7 | 29396.97 |
| ENRIQUE (GB) | 11 | 50 | 4 | 6 | 19 | 49874.48 |
| EPALO (GER) | 10 | 30 | 2 | 4 | 6 | 133750.80 |
| ERHAAB (USA) | 20 | 64 | 6 | 8 | 21 | 62216.26 |
| EVEN TOP (IRE) | 3 | 9 | 1 | 2 | 2 | 7182.94 |
| EXCEED AND EXCEL (AUS) | 7 | 22 | 2 | 2 | 9 | 20527.11 |
| EXCELLENT ART (GB) | 9 | 40 | 3 | 3 | 9 | 29350.50 |
| EXECUTIVE PERK | 7 | 24 | 2 | 3 | 6 | 19216.16 |

| STALLIONS | RNRS | STARTS | WNRS | WINS | PLACES | TOTAL (£) |
|---|---|---|---|---|---|---|
| EXIT TO NOWHERE (USA) | 80 | 276 | 17 | 27 | 80 | 257227.90 |
| EXPELLED (USA) | 4 | 15 | 1 | 1 | 2 | 9538.51 |
| FAIR MIX (IRE) | 61 | 197 | 9 | 11 | 52 | 82833.93 |
| FANTASTIC LIGHT (USA) | 14 | 76 | 7 | 11 | 24 | 59189.53 |
| FASLIYEV (USA) | 7 | 52 | 4 | 10 | 15 | 59781.90 |
| FATH (USA) | 9 | 40 | 2 | 5 | 6 | 35087.76 |
| FIREBREAK (GB) | 5 | 12 | 1 | 1 | 3 | 3224.10 |
| FIRST TRUMP (GB) | 6 | 16 | 1 | 1 | 4 | 6154.92 |
| FLEETWOOD (IRE) | 10 | 28 | 1 | 2 | 5 | 31253.10 |
| FLEMENSFIRTH (USA) | 333 | 1235 | 87 | 127 | 414 | 1322488.21 |
| FLYING LEGEND (USA) | 12 | 38 | 3 | 5 | 7 | 21402.03 |
| FOOTSTEPSINTHESAND (GB) | 11 | 35 | 5 | 8 | 11 | 45775.99 |
| FOURSTARS ALLSTAR (USA) | 6 | 23 | 1 | 2 | 6 | 9624.62 |
| FRAAM (GB) | 12 | 52 | 5 | 6 | 14 | 33553.87 |
| FRAGRANT MIX (IRE) | 11 | 36 | 4 | 7 | 9 | 141002.48 |
| FREDDIE'S STAR | 1 | 5 | 1 | 1 | 1 | 3037.50 |
| FRUITS OF LOVE (USA) | 68 | 220 | 18 | 24 | 80 | 209118.76 |
| FUNNY BABY (FR) | 1 | 3 | 1 | 1 | 1 | 3525.66 |
| GALILEO (IRE) | 73 | 254 | 18 | 24 | 91 | 229680.76 |
| GAMUT (IRE) | 42 | 143 | 11 | 13 | 40 | 116141.71 |
| GARUDA (IRE) | 8 | 24 | 3 | 6 | 4 | 44151.34 |
| GENEROUS (IRE) | 88 | 329 | 24 | 31 | 109 | 206058.14 |
| GENTLEMAN'S DEAL (IRE) | 10 | 27 | 1 | 2 | 4 | 6739.20 |
| GENTLEWAVE (IRE) | 1 | 3 | 1 | 1 | 1 | 6075.20 |
| GERMANY (USA) | 13 | 62 | 6 | 11 | 22 | 258079.16 |
| GIANT'S CAUSEWAY (USA) | 13 | 45 | 3 | 4 | 17 | 76689.52 |
| GILDORAN | 2 | 5 | 1 | 1 | 1 | 3816.00 |
| GLACIAL STORM (USA) | 4 | 22 | 1 | 1 | 8 | 9059.93 |
| GOLAN (IRE) | 91 | 305 | 19 | 26 | 76 | 281636.20 |
| GOLD AWAY (IRE) | 4 | 12 | 2 | 2 | 3 | 7377.58 |
| GOLDEN LARIAT (USA) | 1 | 3 | 1 | 2 | 1 | 7986.89 |
| GOLDEN TORNADO (IRE) | 12 | 38 | 4 | 8 | 11 | 53474.99 |
| GOLDMARK (USA) | 15 | 60 | 7 | 9 | 19 | 191626.06 |
| GOLDNEYEV (USA) | 4 | 26 | 2 | 7 | 12 | 229970.31 |
| GOLD WELL (GB) | 58 | 262 | 24 | 46 | 93 | 550473.76 |
| GONE WEST (USA) | 2 | 10 | 1 | 1 | 3 | 5514.66 |
| GRAND LODGE (USA) | 4 | 19 | 1 | 1 | 5 | 5471.82 |
| GRAND SEIGNEUR (FR) | 1 | 4 | 1 | 1 | 2 | 8071.80 |
| GRAND TRESOR (FR) | 4 | 12 | 1 | 1 | 3 | 2817.61 |
| GRAPE TREE ROAD (GB) | 54 | 174 | 7 | 7 | 57 | 44283.11 |
| GREAT EXHIBITION (USA) | 5 | 14 | 1 | 1 | 2 | 9278.33 |
| GREAT PALM (USA) | 43 | 180 | 13 | 14 | 62 | 121335.21 |
| GREAT PRETENDER (IRE) | 6 | 21 | 2 | 3 | 10 | 103133.02 |
| GREEN TUNE (USA) | 6 | 29 | 6 | 9 | 10 | 47053.36 |
| GREY RISK (FR) | 3 | 11 | 2 | 2 | 5 | 56928.02 |
| GROOM DANCER (USA) | 9 | 34 | 3 | 3 | 12 | 22271.97 |
| HAAFHD (GB) | 22 | 88 | 10 | 17 | 32 | 100810.77 |
| HALLING (USA) | 32 | 155 | 15 | 21 | 65 | 151660.53 |
| HAMAIRI (IRE) | 3 | 14 | 1 | 1 | 5 | 6626.97 |
| HAMAS (IRE) | 1 | 9 | 1 | 1 | 4 | 9728.88 |
| HANNOUMA (IRE) | 1 | 8 | 1 | 2 | 5 | 10470.24 |
| HAWK WING (USA) | 42 | 150 | 8 | 17 | 42 | 112346.37 |
| HELISSIO (FR) | 40 | 165 | 10 | 14 | 36 | 81649.81 |
| HERNANDO (FR) | 35 | 138 | 13 | 22 | 59 | 217647.06 |
| HERON ISLAND (IRE) | 118 | 386 | 31 | 47 | 129 | 390779.62 |
| HIGH CHAPARRAL (IRE) | 70 | 251 | 20 | 24 | 66 | 276382.00 |
| HIGHEST HONOR (FR) | 7 | 30 | 2 | 2 | 10 | 15139.25 |
| HIGH-RISE (IRE) | 19 | 80 | 2 | 4 | 17 | 23917.63 |
| HIGH ROLLER (IRE) | 3 | 12 | 1 | 1 | 6 | 4788.89 |
| HOLD THAT TIGER (USA) | 2 | 16 | 1 | 2 | 3 | 8582.72 |
| HOLY ROMAN EMPEROR (IRE) | 14 | 56 | 2 | 2 | 15 | 18836.65 |
| HOUMAYOUN (FR) | 1 | 4 | 1 | 1 | 2 | 5027.50 |
| HOUSE OF CARDS | 2 | 13 | 1 | 2 | 3 | 13195.53 |
| HUBBLY BUBBLY (USA) | 7 | 18 | 1 | 1 | 7 | 8113.45 |

| STALLIONS | RNRS | STARTS | WNRS | WINS | PLACES | TOTAL (£) |
|---|---|---|---|---|---|---|
| HUNTING LION (IRE) | 1 | 4 | 1 | 1 | 1 | 2187.90 |
| HURRICANE RUN (IRE) | 34 | 103 | 9 | 12 | 31 | 110381.32 |
| ICEMAN (GB) | 9 | 38 | 1 | 1 | 17 | 16391.35 |
| IDRIS (IRE) | 1 | 8 | 1 | 1 | 4 | 4864.86 |
| IFFRAAJ (GB) | 15 | 42 | 3 | 4 | 11 | 17006.70 |
| IKTIBAS (GB) | 4 | 21 | 2 | 3 | 5 | 8203.75 |
| IMPERIAL BALLET (IRE) | 9 | 45 | 4 | 6 | 14 | 66610.84 |
| IMPERIAL DANCER (GB) | 11 | 46 | 3 | 5 | 20 | 58168.32 |
| IN COMMAND (IRE) | 1 | 4 | 1 | 1 | 0 | 3249.00 |
| INDESATCHEL (IRE) | 5 | 22 | 1 | 3 | 6 | 30811.57 |
| INDIAN CREEK (GB) | 2 | 15 | 1 | 1 | 7 | 6464.02 |
| INDIAN DANEHILL (IRE) | 51 | 204 | 10 | 13 | 62 | 122010.83 |
| INDIAN HAVEN (GB) | 16 | 63 | 5 | 8 | 26 | 55219.26 |
| INDIAN RIDGE | 11 | 50 | 4 | 4 | 18 | 18448.60 |
| INDIAN RIVER (FR) | 23 | 80 | 5 | 9 | 19 | 42866.64 |
| INSAN (USA) | 5 | 27 | 1 | 2 | 11 | 8576.91 |
| INSATIABLE (IRE) | 11 | 45 | 1 | 1 | 18 | 15768.41 |
| IN THE WINGS | 10 | 36 | 2 | 2 | 9 | 27301.11 |
| INTIKHAB (USA) | 14 | 60 | 5 | 5 | 17 | 30280.86 |
| INVINCIBLE SPIRIT (IRE) | 18 | 65 | 3 | 4 | 23 | 54461.39 |
| IRISH WELLS (FR) | 4 | 12 | 2 | 2 | 3 | 24444.67 |
| ISHIGURU (USA) | 10 | 38 | 3 | 4 | 19 | 37886.27 |
| ISLAND HOUSE (IRE) | 1 | 5 | 1 | 1 | 3 | 24447.70 |
| IVAN DENISOVICH (IRE) | 15 | 38 | 4 | 5 | 8 | 20270.18 |
| JAMMAAL (GB) | 3 | 17 | 2 | 4 | 8 | 84489.64 |
| JAVA GOLD (USA) | 1 | 10 | 1 | 2 | 2 | 5913.37 |
| JEREMY (USA) | 30 | 104 | 10 | 14 | 37 | 132540.31 |
| JEUNE HOMME (USA) | 1 | 10 | 1 | 1 | 6 | 17181.80 |
| JIMBLE (FR) | 10 | 63 | 4 | 5 | 26 | 36244.55 |
| JOHANNESBURG (USA) | 7 | 23 | 1 | 2 | 7 | 8077.29 |
| JOSR ALGARHOUD (IRE) | 10 | 30 | 1 | 1 | 6 | 4391.10 |
| KADALKO (FR) | 2 | 7 | 1 | 1 | 3 | 10151.20 |
| KADASTROF (FR) | 10 | 46 | 3 | 3 | 11 | 20240.49 |
| KAHYASI | 26 | 108 | 8 | 9 | 33 | 133681.69 |
| KAIETEUR (USA) | 3 | 9 | 1 | 1 | 2 | 4012.20 |
| KALANISI (IRE) | 73 | 201 | 13 | 22 | 57 | 141885.23 |
| KAPGARDE (FR) | 34 | 151 | 14 | 24 | 69 | 187763.00 |
| KARINGA BAY | 98 | 416 | 32 | 54 | 121 | 427850.24 |
| KAYF TARA (GB) | 236 | 784 | 81 | 123 | 288 | 1052895.30 |
| KELTOS (FR) | 1 | 5 | 1 | 1 | 4 | 13145.20 |
| KENDOR (FR) | 2 | 7 | 1 | 1 | 0 | 19494.00 |
| KENTUCKY DYNAMITE (USA) | 2 | 7 | 1 | 1 | 4 | 49728.50 |
| KEY OF LUCK (USA) | 14 | 59 | 4 | 4 | 28 | 25823.89 |
| KHALKEVI (IRE) | 6 | 21 | 3 | 4 | 8 | 24604.77 |
| KHELEYF (USA) | 13 | 48 | 1 | 1 | 11 | 12503.67 |
| KIER PARK (IRE) | 4 | 15 | 2 | 4 | 5 | 12533.88 |
| KING CHARLEMAGNE (USA) | 6 | 29 | 1 | 1 | 10 | 6428.78 |
| KINGSALSA (USA) | 5 | 25 | 3 | 6 | 13 | 85293.91 |
| KING'S BEST (USA) | 41 | 173 | 9 | 12 | 57 | 104841.54 |
| KING'S THEATRE (IRE) | 268 | 1217 | 118 | 191 | 421 | 2673170.49 |
| KIRKWALL (GB) | 9 | 45 | 2 | 3 | 16 | 16565.27 |
| KITTEN'S JOY (USA) | 3 | 9 | 1 | 2 | 3 | 19756.68 |
| KODIAC (GB) | 7 | 34 | 2 | 2 | 15 | 12426.37 |
| KOTASHAAN (FR) | 4 | 19 | 2 | 2 | 3 | 14785.68 |
| KOTKY BLEU (FR) | 2 | 10 | 2 | 3 | 4 | 25131.69 |
| KRIS KIN (USA) | 29 | 92 | 4 | 6 | 27 | 55891.22 |
| KUTUB (IRE) | 14 | 43 | 2 | 3 | 15 | 20053.89 |
| KYLLACHY (GB) | 17 | 70 | 3 | 5 | 25 | 37135.83 |
| LAHIB (USA) | 40 | 146 | 8 | 10 | 37 | 89806.64 |
| LAHINT (USA) | 1 | 2 | 1 | 1 | 0 | 2560.14 |
| LANDO (GER) | 10 | 31 | 2 | 2 | 11 | 37184.80 |
| LANGFUHR (CAN) | 2 | 5 | 1 | 1 | 3 | 3462.64 |
| LAVEROCK (IRE) | 1 | 4 | 1 | 2 | 2 | 20475.00 |
| LAVERON (GB) | 21 | 65 | 6 | 7 | 23 | 62773.85 |

| STALLIONS | RNRS | STARTS | WNRS | WINS | PLACES | TOTAL (£) |
|---|---|---|---|---|---|---|
| LAVIRCO (GER) | 22 | 108 | 13 | 20 | 39 | 239024.40 |
| LAWMAN (FR) | 6 | 17 | 2 | 2 | 5 | 22982.84 |
| LAYMAN (USA) | 3 | 16 | 1 | 1 | 4 | 15018.48 |
| LEADING COUNSEL (USA) | 7 | 28 | 2 | 3 | 6 | 65899.83 |
| LE BALAFRE (FR) | 5 | 20 | 2 | 3 | 8 | 29640.18 |
| LE FOU (IRE) | 8 | 42 | 4 | 5 | 23 | 91954.87 |
| LEMON DROP KID (USA) | 12 | 56 | 4 | 5 | 17 | 45103.11 |
| LEND A HAND (GB) | 6 | 31 | 2 | 3 | 7 | 28358.45 |
| LET THE LION ROAR (GB) | 2 | 6 | 1 | 1 | 2 | 3086.42 |
| LIBRETTIST (USA) | 12 | 23 | 1 | 1 | 5 | 10454.40 |
| LIMNOS (JPN) | 4 | 13 | 1 | 1 | 4 | 7760.59 |
| LINAMIX (FR) | 10 | 41 | 1 | 2 | 16 | 19538.74 |
| LION HEART (USA) | 1 | 8 | 1 | 2 | 3 | 15955.38 |
| LOMITAS (GB) | 12 | 55 | 1 | 1 | 25 | 41426.85 |
| LORD AMERICO | 28 | 108 | 9 | 10 | 20 | 112021.40 |
| LORD DU SUD (FR) | 2 | 5 | 1 | 1 | 3 | 18750.75 |
| LORD OF APPEAL (GB) | 16 | 68 | 5 | 6 | 15 | 37409.98 |
| LORD OF ENGLAND (GER) | 2 | 10 | 1 | 2 | 8 | 23027.10 |
| LOST SOLDIER (USA) | 1 | 11 | 1 | 1 | 7 | 8921.40 |
| LOST WORLD (IRE) | 13 | 72 | 5 | 6 | 32 | 76648.27 |
| LOUP SAUVAGE (USA) | 13 | 26 | 2 | 2 | 4 | 4693.04 |
| LOUP SOLITAIRE (USA) | 4 | 12 | 1 | 3 | 5 | 33004.59 |
| LOXIAS (FR) | 1 | 9 | 1 | 2 | 6 | 17961.28 |
| LUCKY OWNERS (NZ) | 4 | 18 | 1 | 1 | 5 | 7659.59 |
| LUCKY STORY (USA) | 9 | 28 | 1 | 2 | 9 | 16730.15 |
| LUSO (GB) | 85 | 348 | 16 | 21 | 88 | 149438.70 |
| LUTE ANTIQUE (FR) | 2 | 3 | 1 | 1 | 0 | 1949.40 |
| MACHIAVELLIAN TSAR (FR) | 1 | 6 | 1 | 1 | 4 | 6145.84 |
| MAILLE PISTOL (FR) | 2 | 11 | 1 | 2 | 2 | 6381.48 |
| MAKBUL | 5 | 23 | 1 | 4 | 3 | 25276.86 |
| MALINAS (GER) | 8 | 28 | 4 | 8 | 10 | 118706.42 |
| MAMOOL (IRE) | 3 | 11 | 2 | 4 | 2 | 31601.40 |
| MANDURO (GER) | 15 | 39 | 4 | 6 | 11 | 34125.98 |
| MANSONNIEN (FR) | 7 | 37 | 2 | 2 | 17 | 20812.16 |
| MARATHON (USA) | 3 | 28 | 2 | 2 | 8 | 13498.72 |
| MARESCA SORRENTO (FR) | 7 | 26 | 2 | 3 | 11 | 602114.06 |
| MARIGNAN (USA) | 18 | 79 | 3 | 3 | 17 | 44762.22 |
| MARJU (IRE) | 14 | 63 | 5 | 10 | 25 | 89105.18 |
| MARK OF ESTEEM (IRE) | 12 | 63 | 3 | 3 | 22 | 29905.67 |
| MARTALINE (GB) | 22 | 99 | 9 | 15 | 49 | 445098.55 |
| MEDAALY (GB) | 6 | 21 | 1 | 3 | 9 | 33705.82 |
| MEDICEAN (GB) | 44 | 204 | 17 | 21 | 68 | 151154.93 |
| MIDNIGHT LEGEND (GB) | 122 | 489 | 40 | 70 | 150 | 570368.79 |
| MILAN (GB) | 326 | 1341 | 114 | 170 | 429 | 2253715.00 |
| MILLENARY (GB) | 40 | 127 | 7 | 12 | 26 | 73499.73 |
| MILLKOM (GB) | 4 | 16 | 1 | 1 | 5 | 6002.37 |
| MINASHKI (IRE) | 1 | 6 | 1 | 1 | 2 | 8897.60 |
| MINSTER SON | 6 | 21 | 2 | 2 | 12 | 13200.59 |
| MISSED FLIGHT (GB) | 2 | 10 | 1 | 1 | 7 | 7722.18 |
| MISTERNANDO (GB) | 6 | 14 | 1 | 1 | 1 | 5481.54 |
| MISTER SACHA (FR) | 3 | 8 | 1 | 1 | 6 | 22143.91 |
| MIZZEN MAST (USA) | 8 | 31 | 1 | 1 | 7 | 4312.58 |
| MONASHEE MOUNTAIN (USA) | 5 | 12 | 1 | 1 | 0 | 3926.83 |
| MONSIEUR BOND (IRE) | 5 | 30 | 3 | 5 | 17 | 38966.17 |
| MONSUN (GER) | 14 | 63 | 5 | 7 | 24 | 75553.88 |
| MONTJEU (IRE) | 64 | 306 | 18 | 27 | 107 | 504491.24 |
| MONTJOY (USA) | 1 | 3 | 1 | 1 | 1 | 14705.40 |
| MOONAX (IRE) | 7 | 22 | 3 | 3 | 6 | 15431.68 |
| MORESPEED | 1 | 4 | 1 | 1 | 2 | 99737.00 |
| MORE THAN READY (USA) | 4 | 14 | 1 | 2 | 1 | 14577.24 |
| MOROZOV (USA) | 24 | 80 | 6 | 12 | 28 | 99435.56 |
| MORPETH (GB) | 9 | 23 | 2 | 2 | 4 | 7450.43 |
| MOSCOW SOCIETY (USA) | 69 | 260 | 21 | 30 | 85 | 242956.00 |
| MOTIVATOR (GB) | 34 | 141 | 12 | 20 | 42 | 142600.30 |

| STALLIONS | RNRS | STARTS | WNRS | WINS | PLACES | TOTAL (£) |
|---|---|---|---|---|---|---|
| MOUNTAIN HIGH (IRE) | 21 | 61 | 6 | 7 | 16 | 30467.69 |
| MOUNTING SPENDENT (GB) | 1 | 2 | 1 | 1 | 0 | 2495.60 |
| MR COMBUSTIBLE (IRE) | 22 | 100 | 5 | 6 | 24 | 86612.13 |
| MR DINOS (IRE) | 6 | 24 | 1 | 2 | 3 | 15062.60 |
| MR GREELEY (USA) | 7 | 20 | 2 | 2 | 9 | 11258.84 |
| MTOTO | 7 | 33 | 1 | 1 | 11 | 8985.69 |
| MUHTARRAM (USA) | 14 | 59 | 4 | 9 | 27 | 69465.20 |
| MUHTATHIR (GB) | 11 | 43 | 4 | 6 | 17 | 82816.86 |
| MUJADIL (USA) | 4 | 28 | 2 | 2 | 9 | 12508.76 |
| MUJAHID (USA) | 6 | 29 | 2 | 3 | 7 | 14979.72 |
| MULL OF KINTYRE (USA) | 11 | 51 | 2 | 3 | 15 | 29409.04 |
| MULTIPLEX (GB) | 25 | 92 | 3 | 3 | 32 | 30098.07 |
| MURMURE (FR) | 1 | 4 | 1 | 2 | 0 | 4055.35 |
| MY RISK (FR) | 2 | 10 | 1 | 6 | 2 | 486027.40 |
| NAHEEZ (USA) | 6 | 34 | 2 | 3 | 10 | 16917.65 |
| NAYEF (USA) | 33 | 108 | 7 | 11 | 35 | 69743.79 |
| NEEDLE GUN (IRE) | 21 | 77 | 4 | 4 | 14 | 50138.75 |
| NEEDWOOD BLADE (GB) | 24 | 93 | 4 | 8 | 32 | 55178.45 |
| NETWORK (GER) | 30 | 112 | 6 | 9 | 38 | 168225.52 |
| NEW FRONTIER (IRE) | 16 | 75 | 4 | 7 | 28 | 63703.59 |
| NEXT DESERT (IRE) | 4 | 12 | 1 | 2 | 2 | 23756.85 |
| NICARON (GER) | 2 | 8 | 1 | 1 | 4 | 4841.15 |
| NICKNAME (FR) | 2 | 5 | 2 | 2 | 2 | 10518.12 |
| NIGHT TANGO (GER) | 1 | 4 | 1 | 2 | 1 | 11670.74 |
| NOMADIC WAY (USA) | 18 | 81 | 3 | 4 | 29 | 45992.86 |
| NONONITO (FR) | 4 | 13 | 1 | 1 | 5 | 7648.12 |
| NOROIT (GER) | 1 | 10 | 1 | 2 | 6 | 10368.99 |
| NORSE DANCER (IRE) | 16 | 37 | 4 | 5 | 13 | 21372.33 |
| NORTHERN PARK (USA) | 1 | 6 | 1 | 2 | 2 | 13848.60 |
| NORTH LIGHT (IRE) | 2 | 11 | 1 | 1 | 2 | 7245.43 |
| NORWICH | 35 | 151 | 10 | 16 | 50 | 190644.86 |
| NOTNOWCATO (GB) | 12 | 32 | 2 | 2 | 8 | 10505.07 |
| NOVERRE (USA) | 15 | 54 | 3 | 4 | 14 | 24724.40 |
| NUMEROUS (USA) | 2 | 10 | 1 | 1 | 3 | 3888.30 |
| OASIS DREAM (GB) | 13 | 48 | 2 | 5 | 11 | 27716.68 |
| OBSERVATORY (USA) | 14 | 83 | 4 | 8 | 34 | 61344.39 |
| OFFICIEL (FR) | 1 | 3 | 1 | 3 | 0 | 10396.80 |
| OKAWANGO (USA) | 2 | 12 | 2 | 2 | 4 | 27692.30 |
| OLD VIC | 223 | 902 | 68 | 99 | 318 | 1125714.83 |
| ONE COOL CAT (USA) | 14 | 56 | 3 | 7 | 10 | 60039.38 |
| ONE MORE TIGER (GB) | 1 | 7 | 1 | 1 | 2 | 2794.92 |
| ORATORIO (IRE) | 26 | 88 | 4 | 6 | 23 | 35573.08 |
| ORPEN (USA) | 7 | 39 | 2 | 2 | 13 | 23385.42 |
| OSCAR (IRE) | 358 | 1464 | 119 | 177 | 465 | 2508119.00 |
| OSCAR SCHINDLER (IRE) | 22 | 81 | 3 | 4 | 28 | 53164.78 |
| OSORIO (GER) | 2 | 10 | 1 | 1 | 6 | 6740.64 |
| OVERBURY (IRE) | 120 | 397 | 26 | 35 | 119 | 320714.27 |
| PANORAMIC | 7 | 46 | 6 | 8 | 27 | 226164.94 |
| PAOLINI (GER) | 2 | 8 | 1 | 1 | 3 | 9729.00 |
| PASSING GLANCE (GB) | 22 | 77 | 4 | 7 | 26 | 75716.08 |
| PASSING SALE (FR) | 9 | 40 | 1 | 1 | 22 | 18854.18 |
| PASTERNAK (GB) | 19 | 67 | 2 | 3 | 19 | 71569.50 |
| PEINTRE CELEBRE (USA) | 8 | 17 | 2 | 2 | 6 | 9857.97 |
| PELDER (IRE) | 5 | 22 | 4 | 4 | 10 | 36064.69 |
| PENTIRE (GB) | 4 | 18 | 2 | 2 | 6 | 8022.61 |
| PERPENDICULAR (GB) | 1 | 5 | 1 | 1 | 2 | 5359.50 |
| PERUGINO (USA) | 6 | 13 | 1 | 1 | 3 | 5364.63 |
| PHANTOM BREEZE | 1 | 11 | 1 | 1 | 2 | 4811.82 |
| PHOENIX REACH (IRE) | 13 | 45 | 2 | 2 | 18 | 18342.43 |
| PIERRE (GB) | 27 | 94 | 8 | 13 | 22 | 152817.71 |
| PILSUDSKI (IRE) | 21 | 89 | 4 | 9 | 28 | 55520.83 |
| PISTOLET BLEU (IRE) | 16 | 34 | 2 | 5 | 11 | 200383.53 |
| PIVOTAL (GB) | 27 | 85 | 8 | 12 | 21 | 68792.77 |
| POLIGLOTE (GB) | 18 | 78 | 6 | 12 | 35 | 229062.42 |

| STALLIONS | RNRS | STARTS | WNRS | WINS | PLACES | TOTAL (£) |
|---|---|---|---|---|---|---|
| POLISH PRECEDENT (USA) | 5 | 27 | 1 | 2 | 8 | 32463.43 |
| POLISH SUMMER (GB) | 4 | 38 | 2 | 7 | 13 | 133868.73 |
| POLTARF (USA) | 1 | 5 | 1 | 1 | 1 | 6883.33 |
| PORT LYAUTEY (FR) | 2 | 11 | 1 | 1 | 2 | 5185.90 |
| PORTRAIT GALLERY (IRE) | 33 | 141 | 12 | 16 | 30 | 94982.26 |
| PRESENTING (GB) | 394 | 1517 | 118 | 177 | 504 | 1905570.91 |
| PRIMITIVE RISING (USA) | 3 | 10 | 1 | 1 | 3 | 4233.70 |
| PRIMO VALENTINO (IRE) | 7 | 22 | 2 | 5 | 7 | 54210.12 |
| PRINCE DANIEL (USA) | 7 | 21 | 1 | 1 | 3 | 2390.85 |
| PROCLAMATION (IRE) | 25 | 82 | 1 | 4 | 26 | 48184.85 |
| PROTEKTOR (GER) | 3 | 8 | 1 | 1 | 3 | 5685.30 |
| PROUD CITIZEN (USA) | 1 | 9 | 1 | 4 | 2 | 12069.96 |
| PURSUIT OF LOVE (GB) | 6 | 23 | 3 | 3 | 9 | 10720.67 |
| PUSHKIN (IRE) | 7 | 33 | 2 | 2 | 11 | 19707.43 |
| PUTRA SANDHURST (IRE) | 1 | 5 | 1 | 1 | 2 | 11336.38 |
| PYRUS (USA) | 15 | 50 | 3 | 4 | 17 | 30197.42 |
| QUEST FOR FAME | 1 | 4 | 1 | 1 | 3 | 3255.24 |
| QUWS (GB) | 17 | 84 | 4 | 5 | 18 | 34483.94 |
| RAGMAR (FR) | 6 | 30 | 2 | 2 | 13 | 18107.00 |
| RAHY (USA) | 4 | 14 | 1 | 2 | 6 | 11780.82 |
| RAIL LINK (GB) | 14 | 40 | 3 | 6 | 9 | 32994.95 |
| RAINBOW HIGH (GB) | 11 | 56 | 3 | 5 | 14 | 67042.11 |
| RAINBOW QUEST (USA) | 12 | 60 | 6 | 10 | 16 | 68048.90 |
| RAISE A GRAND (IRE) | 6 | 35 | 2 | 2 | 15 | 42535.98 |
| RAKAPOSHI KING | 7 | 33 | 5 | 8 | 11 | 40616.84 |
| RAKTI (GB) | 13 | 58 | 4 | 5 | 14 | 26717.64 |
| RASHAR (USA) | 19 | 71 | 4 | 4 | 17 | 26893.29 |
| RAVEN'S PASS (USA) | 4 | 18 | 2 | 5 | 6 | 29137.80 |
| REDBACK (GB) | 9 | 30 | 1 | 1 | 1 | 10995.51 |
| RED CLUBS (IRE) | 16 | 68 | 6 | 7 | 20 | 47679.25 |
| RED RANSOM (USA) | 18 | 61 | 4 | 4 | 21 | 86828.95 |
| RED SUNSET | 1 | 1 | 1 | 1 | 0 | 2053.20 |
| REEFSCAPE (GB) | 2 | 7 | 1 | 1 | 5 | 35015.40 |
| REFUSE TO BEND (IRE) | 31 | 115 | 9 | 14 | 32 | 92682.89 |
| RELIEF PITCHER | 8 | 30 | 2 | 2 | 8 | 13405.76 |
| RELIGIOUSLY (USA) | 4 | 15 | 1 | 1 | 5 | 9146.33 |
| RESET (AUS) | 7 | 20 | 1 | 1 | 0 | 1949.40 |
| RESPLENDENT GLORY (IRE) | 1 | 4 | 1 | 1 | 2 | 4263.84 |
| REVOQUE (IRE) | 65 | 268 | 18 | 24 | 81 | 220657.44 |
| RIDGEWOOD BEN (GB) | 3 | 21 | 1 | 2 | 9 | 13914.76 |
| RIVERHEAD (USA) | 1 | 6 | 1 | 1 | 3 | 8755.60 |
| ROBELLINO (USA) | 4 | 27 | 1 | 2 | 14 | 29804.37 |
| ROBIN DES CHAMPS (FR) | 26 | 77 | 8 | 14 | 26 | 383162.78 |
| ROCAMADOUR (GB) | 3 | 8 | 1 | 1 | 1 | 2196.90 |
| ROCK HOPPER | 6 | 20 | 2 | 2 | 6 | 100061.25 |
| ROCK OF GIBRALTAR (IRE) | 35 | 123 | 6 | 8 | 33 | 117976.27 |
| ROI DE ROME (USA) | 5 | 19 | 1 | 1 | 10 | 18656.77 |
| ROMAN SADDLE (IRE) | 1 | 7 | 1 | 1 | 3 | 12146.34 |
| ROSSINI (USA) | 2 | 11 | 1 | 2 | 2 | 15574.40 |
| ROYAL ANTHEM (USA) | 32 | 102 | 5 | 5 | 19 | 27164.75 |
| ROYAL APPLAUSE (GB) | 22 | 81 | 3 | 5 | 21 | 32860.74 |
| RUDIMENTARY (USA) | 33 | 173 | 16 | 24 | 52 | 183791.86 |
| RUNYON (IRE) | 8 | 34 | 1 | 2 | 11 | 14649.10 |
| SABIANGO (GER) | 3 | 8 | 1 | 3 | 3 | 14975.88 |
| SADDLERS' HALL (IRE) | 66 | 302 | 16 | 22 | 96 | 274157.66 |
| SADLER'S WELLS (USA) | 41 | 165 | 13 | 15 | 62 | 141557.11 |
| SAFFRON WALDEN (FR) | 23 | 112 | 11 | 12 | 39 | 137563.97 |
| SAGACITY (FR) | 10 | 38 | 2 | 3 | 4 | 10463.94 |
| SAGAMIX (FR) | 5 | 16 | 1 | 1 | 8 | 22947.46 |
| SAINT CYRIEN (FR) | 1 | 6 | 1 | 1 | 2 | 5495.58 |
| SAINT DES SAINTS (FR) | 29 | 104 | 10 | 12 | 38 | 233721.91 |
| SAKHEE (USA) | 27 | 116 | 7 | 9 | 46 | 105546.54 |
| SAKHEE'S SECRET (GB) | 7 | 17 | 2 | 4 | 3 | 14590.50 |
| SALFORD EXPRESS (IRE) | 4 | 18 | 2 | 5 | 5 | 24098.28 |

| STALLIONS | RNRS | STARTS | WNRS | WINS | PLACES | TOTAL (£) |
|---|---|---|---|---|---|---|
| SAMRAAN (USA) | 6 | 17 | 1 | 1 | 7 | 9510.60 |
| SAMUM (GER) | 2 | 2 | 1 | 1 | 0 | 5393.34 |
| SASSANIAN (USA) | 12 | 48 | 3 | 6 | 17 | 52419.79 |
| SATRI (IRE) | 1 | 5 | 1 | 2 | 1 | 9936.12 |
| SAUMAREZ | 1 | 4 | 1 | 1 | 2 | 5581.44 |
| SCORPION (IRE) | 43 | 117 | 10 | 10 | 28 | 119637.84 |
| SCRIBANO (GB) | 2 | 19 | 1 | 1 | 6 | 12909.62 |
| SEA FREEDOM (GB) | 2 | 9 | 1 | 1 | 3 | 3737.18 |
| SEA RAVEN (IRE) | 5 | 16 | 1 | 1 | 2 | 17238.30 |
| SECOND EMPIRE (IRE) | 5 | 20 | 2 | 2 | 8 | 150846.16 |
| SECRET SINGER (FR) | 5 | 11 | 1 | 3 | 5 | 30679.78 |
| SELKIRK (USA) | 27 | 104 | 6 | 11 | 35 | 57651.72 |
| SEPTIEME CIEL (USA) | 11 | 35 | 2 | 6 | 8 | 121666.62 |
| SESARO (USA) | 1 | 4 | 1 | 1 | 2 | 3568.93 |
| SHAMARDAL (USA) | 9 | 48 | 4 | 6 | 15 | 43033.80 |
| SHAMBO | 3 | 15 | 1 | 2 | 7 | 9081.75 |
| SHANTOU (USA) | 90 | 380 | 34 | 50 | 121 | 592847.61 |
| SHERNAZAR | 16 | 70 | 6 | 8 | 26 | 46183.70 |
| SHEYRANN | 1 | 3 | 1 | 1 | 2 | 5440.50 |
| SHIROCCO (GER) | 29 | 87 | 12 | 23 | 22 | 412926.69 |
| SHOLOKHOV (IRE) | 11 | 36 | 4 | 7 | 16 | 210313.19 |
| SILVER PATRIARCH (IRE) | 62 | 216 | 13 | 16 | 62 | 126560.54 |
| SINGSPIEL (IRE) | 22 | 69 | 5 | 9 | 26 | 92878.99 |
| SINNDAR (IRE) | 11 | 42 | 3 | 3 | 16 | 71698.85 |
| SIR HARRY LEWIS (USA) | 72 | 317 | 24 | 34 | 110 | 326846.30 |
| SIR PERCY (GB) | 8 | 33 | 3 | 4 | 5 | 19546.80 |
| SIXTIES ICON (GB) | 4 | 15 | 2 | 2 | 6 | 10464.70 |
| SLEEPING CAR (FR) | 18 | 81 | 5 | 7 | 31 | 44353.73 |
| SLICKLY (FR) | 3 | 8 | 1 | 1 | 1 | 5708.90 |
| SLIP ANCHOR | 4 | 14 | 1 | 1 | 5 | 6312.72 |
| SMADOUN (FR) | 14 | 52 | 7 | 10 | 14 | 151640.58 |
| SMART STRIKE (CAN) | 4 | 23 | 1 | 1 | 8 | 6696.63 |
| SNURGE | 40 | 204 | 8 | 14 | 65 | 151154.76 |
| SOLDIER HOLLOW (GB) | 2 | 12 | 2 | 4 | 7 | 58174.26 |
| SONUS (IRE) | 8 | 26 | 2 | 3 | 5 | 19990.99 |
| SOVEREIGN WATER (FR) | 2 | 9 | 1 | 1 | 5 | 11873.73 |
| SOVIET STAR (USA) | 16 | 75 | 2 | 3 | 19 | 25505.36 |
| SPADOUN (FR) | 24 | 105 | 9 | 19 | 40 | 128072.53 |
| SPARTACUS (IRE) | 15 | 61 | 3 | 4 | 22 | 28517.36 |
| STARBOROUGH (GB) | 4 | 16 | 2 | 2 | 6 | 15124.39 |
| STARDAN (IRE) | 2 | 14 | 1 | 1 | 2 | 9623.57 |
| STATUE OF LIBERTY (USA) | 9 | 41 | 3 | 3 | 17 | 54591.42 |
| ST JOVITE (USA) | 12 | 42 | 1 | 1 | 8 | 7587.33 |
| STORMING HOME (GB) | 15 | 62 | 5 | 7 | 26 | 49137.81 |
| STORMY RIVER (FR) | 5 | 16 | 2 | 3 | 5 | 49008.53 |
| STOWAWAY (GB) | 46 | 207 | 13 | 19 | 71 | 312357.17 |
| STRATEGIC CHOICE (USA) | 7 | 29 | 3 | 3 | 9 | 55319.18 |
| STRATEGIC PRINCE (GB) | 12 | 42 | 2 | 2 | 15 | 16210.49 |
| STREET CRY (IRE) | 17 | 62 | 6 | 8 | 17 | 71786.12 |
| STREET SENSE (USA) | 1 | 2 | 1 | 1 | 1 | 4393.80 |
| SUBTLE POWER (IRE) | 19 | 72 | 7 | 8 | 21 | 88605.74 |
| SUGARFOOT (GB) | 3 | 5 | 1 | 1 | 1 | 2220.15 |
| SULAMANI (IRE) | 26 | 105 | 10 | 12 | 46 | 138646.37 |
| SUNSHINE STREET (USA) | 7 | 25 | 2 | 5 | 8 | 51732.85 |
| SUPREME LEADER | 17 | 81 | 3 | 4 | 27 | 64912.83 |
| SUPREME SOUND (GB) | 10 | 33 | 2 | 2 | 6 | 16533.88 |
| SWIFT GULLIVER (IRE) | 3 | 11 | 1 | 2 | 1 | 6003.94 |
| SYLVAN EXPRESS | 1 | 6 | 1 | 1 | 2 | 7500.90 |
| SYSTEMATIC (GB) | 4 | 19 | 1 | 1 | 6 | 3975.40 |
| TAGULA (IRE) | 8 | 21 | 1 | 1 | 4 | 7080.04 |
| TAIPAN (IRE) | 8 | 25 | 4 | 5 | 4 | 21162.01 |
| TAJRAASI (USA) | 4 | 18 | 1 | 1 | 4 | 14918.70 |
| TAKE RISKS (FR) | 5 | 28 | 1 | 1 | 10 | 15752.80 |
| TALAASH (IRE) | 1 | 7 | 1 | 1 | 2 | 5027.04 |

| STALLIONS | RNRS | STARTS | WNRS | WINS | PLACES | TOTAL (£) |
|---|---|---|---|---|---|---|
| TALKIN MAN (CAN) | 14 | 31 | 2 | 3 | 9 | 32849.50 |
| TAMAYAZ (CAN) | 27 | 112 | 7 | 9 | 28 | 65137.29 |
| TAMURE (IRE) | 29 | 113 | 5 | 7 | 41 | 78202.97 |
| TEL QUEL (FR) | 6 | 25 | 2 | 2 | 4 | 6061.36 |
| TENDULKAR (USA) | 3 | 12 | 1 | 1 | 5 | 5528.73 |
| TEOFILO (IRE) | 13 | 34 | 6 | 7 | 11 | 37680.27 |
| TERIMON | 11 | 49 | 6 | 7 | 16 | 50726.70 |
| TERTULLIAN (USA) | 3 | 10 | 1 | 1 | 4 | 3689.72 |
| THEATRICAL | 5 | 14 | 2 | 3 | 5 | 18584.76 |
| THEATRICAL CHARMER | 1 | 3 | 1 | 1 | 1 | 14420.00 |
| TIGER HILL (IRE) | 48 | 133 | 5 | 9 | 46 | 116367.20 |
| TIKKANEN (USA) | 44 | 202 | 14 | 23 | 57 | 233832.24 |
| TILLERMAN (GB) | 10 | 43 | 1 | 2 | 17 | 24407.16 |
| TIRAAZ (USA) | 2 | 8 | 1 | 1 | 5 | 20333.75 |
| TIRWANAKO (FR) | 1 | 7 | 1 | 3 | 4 | 18557.40 |
| TITUS LIVIUS (FR) | 6 | 25 | 2 | 3 | 12 | 20710.86 |
| TOBOUGG (IRE) | 55 | 173 | 10 | 17 | 36 | 123166.36 |
| TOCCET (USA) | 2 | 8 | 1 | 1 | 2 | 6569.10 |
| TOMBA (GB) | 3 | 12 | 1 | 1 | 4 | 7893.74 |
| TOPANOORA | 7 | 25 | 1 | 1 | 4 | 6391.82 |
| TOT OU TARD (IRE) | 1 | 6 | 1 | 2 | 3 | 15221.40 |
| TRADE FAIR (GB) | 22 | 80 | 4 | 4 | 28 | 30581.25 |
| TRADITIONALLY (USA) | 8 | 48 | 2 | 2 | 20 | 38755.48 |
| TRANS ISLAND (GB) | 23 | 73 | 4 | 6 | 23 | 54697.98 |
| TREMPOLINO (USA) | 11 | 65 | 6 | 7 | 31 | 89553.72 |
| TURGEON (USA) | 35 | 147 | 14 | 25 | 56 | 311181.30 |
| TURTLE BOWL (IRE) | 2 | 7 | 2 | 3 | 2 | 30077.65 |
| TURTLE ISLAND (IRE) | 61 | 260 | 9 | 10 | 86 | 118748.82 |
| ULTIMATELY LUCKY (IRE) | 2 | 13 | 1 | 2 | 5 | 31261.30 |
| UMISTIM (GB) | 3 | 13 | 1 | 1 | 3 | 3721.11 |
| UNGARO (GER) | 9 | 33 | 3 | 4 | 9 | 34503.58 |
| UNTIL SUNDOWN (USA) | 2 | 10 | 1 | 3 | 2 | 24392.94 |
| URBAN OCEAN (FR) | 11 | 34 | 4 | 7 | 7 | 41552.61 |
| USEFUL (FR) | 6 | 29 | 2 | 3 | 10 | 14679.81 |
| VAL ROYAL (FR) | 20 | 51 | 3 | 3 | 13 | 13420.94 |
| VALSEUR (USA) | 1 | 6 | 1 | 1 | 2 | 9557.10 |
| VANGELIS (USA) | 2 | 8 | 1 | 2 | 3 | 12408.12 |
| VARESE (FR) | 3 | 9 | 1 | 1 | 1 | 2278.74 |
| VERGLAS (IRE) | 27 | 86 | 4 | 4 | 23 | 30549.41 |
| VERTICAL SPEED (FR) | 11 | 31 | 3 | 6 | 8 | 37262.21 |
| VETTORI (IRE) | 7 | 23 | 1 | 2 | 6 | 7633.05 |
| VIDEO ROCK (FR) | 7 | 42 | 2 | 7 | 14 | 33238.57 |
| VIKING RULER (AUS) | 10 | 43 | 2 | 3 | 16 | 24058.35 |
| VINNIE ROE (IRE) | 90 | 362 | 23 | 34 | 105 | 297564.04 |
| VISIONARY (FR) | 5 | 17 | 2 | 2 | 1 | 45129.90 |
| VOIX DU NORD (FR) | 14 | 48 | 6 | 11 | 18 | 193466.58 |
| WAKY NAO (GB) | 13 | 36 | 3 | 5 | 5 | 38855.23 |
| WALK IN THE PARK (IRE) | 2 | 8 | 1 | 1 | 3 | 3599.92 |
| WAREED (IRE) | 25 | 70 | 3 | 3 | 18 | 26287.77 |
| WAVENEY (UAE) | 3 | 13 | 1 | 1 | 2 | 4525.05 |
| WELL CHOSEN (GB) | 13 | 52 | 3 | 9 | 13 | 70861.75 |
| WESTERNER (GB) | 149 | 594 | 49 | 72 | 187 | 777195.10 |
| WHERE OR WHEN (IRE) | 12 | 38 | 2 | 5 | 8 | 124094.12 |
| WHIPPER (USA) | 17 | 64 | 8 | 13 | 23 | 102114.53 |
| WHITMORE'S CONN (USA) | 14 | 58 | 3 | 5 | 16 | 120999.61 |
| WHYWHYWHY (USA) | 2 | 4 | 1 | 1 | 0 | 4914.63 |
| WINDSOR CASTLE (GB) | 13 | 33 | 2 | 2 | 11 | 10617.09 |
| WINDSOR KNOT (IRE) | 7 | 33 | 2 | 2 | 12 | 100958.58 |
| WINGED LOVE (IRE) | 84 | 353 | 26 | 40 | 117 | 453273.59 |
| WITH APPROVAL (CAN) | 8 | 26 | 1 | 3 | 7 | 35858.74 |
| WITHOUT CONNEXION (IRE) | 1 | 7 | 1 | 1 | 4 | 5199.53 |
| WITNESS BOX (USA) | 58 | 289 | 19 | 25 | 107 | 351740.20 |
| WIZARD KING (GB) | 14 | 60 | 2 | 4 | 7 | 21176.87 |
| WOLFE TONE (IRE) | 3 | 9 | 1 | 1 | 1 | 4454.64 |

| STALLIONS | RNRS | STARTS | WNRS | WINS | PLACES | TOTAL (£) |
|---|---|---|---|---|---|---|
| **WOODS OF WINDSOR (USA)** | 4 | 14 | 1 | 1 | 7 | 27197.81 |
| **XAAR (GB)** | 11 | 49 | 1 | 1 | 18 | 24718.04 |
| **ZAFFARAN (USA)** | 7 | 19 | 1 | 1 | 9 | 9201.96 |
| **ZAGREB (USA)** | 56 | 212 | 15 | 21 | 69 | 158074.58 |
| **ZAMINDAR (USA)** | 10 | 28 | 1 | 1 | 2 | 5281.06 |
| **ZINAAD (GB)** | 2 | 7 | 1 | 1 | 4 | 17697.53 |

***BY KIND PERMISSION OF WEATHERBYS***

# HIGH-PRICED YEARLINGS OF 2014 AT TATTERSALLS SALES

**The following yearlings realised 82,000 Guineas and over at Tattersalls Sales in 2014:-**

| Name and Breeding | Purchaser | Guineas |
|---|---|---|
| B C GALILEO (IRE) - PENANG PEARL (FR) | MV MAGNIER | 2600000 |
| BR C SHAMARDAL (USA) - CASSANDRA GO (IRE) | JOHN FERGUSON BS | 1700000 |
| B C DUBAWI (IRE) - CRYSTAL MUSIC (USA) | JOHN FERGUSON BS | 1600000 |
| B C DUBAWI (IRE) - COMIC (IRE) | JOHN FERGUSON BS | 1400000 |
| **WHITE HOT (IRE)** B F GALILEO (IRE) - GWYNN (IRE) | J DELAHOOKE | 1250000 |
| B C STREET CRY (IRE) - MEEZNAH (USA) | JOHN FERGUSON BS | 1000000 |
| B F WAR FRONT (USA) - ICON PROJECT (USA) | JOHN FERGUSON BS | 950000 |
| CH C GALILEO (IRE) - ANOTHER STORM (USA) | CHINA HORSE CLUB | 875000 |
| CH C DUBAWI (IRE) - DASH TO THE FRONT (GB) | JOHN FERGUSON BS | 800000 |
| B C OASIS DREAM (GB) - TITIVATION (GB) | JOHN FERGUSON BS | 775000 |
| B C GALILEO (IRE) - FLIRTATION (GB) | MV MAGNIER | 750000 |
| CH F DUBAWI (IRE) - MISHEER (GB) | JOHN FERGUSON BS | 750000 |
| B C GALILEO (IRE) - HVEGER (AUS) | MV MAGNIER | 750000 |
| B C DUBAWI (IRE) - COSMODROME (USA) | JOHN FERGUSON BS | 725000 |
| **PERFECT VOICE (GB)** B F POET'S VOICE (GB) - PERFECT SPIRIT (IRE) | AL SHAQAB RACING | 700000 |
| B F DANSILI (GB) - TYRANNY (GB) | SOLIS/LITT | 700000 |
| B C INVINCIBLE SPIRIT (IRE) - BRUSCA (USA) | J WARREN BS | 680000 |
| B C MONTJEU (IRE) - HONORLINA (FR) | MV MAGNIER | 675000 |
| **UAE PRINCE (IRE)** B C SEA THE STARS (IRE) - BY REQUEST (GB) | C GORDON-WATSON BS | 650000 |
| **BEAUTIFUL MORNING (GB)** B F GALILEO (IRE) - DATE WITH DESTINY (IRE) | MCCALMONT BS | 650000 |
| **MONJENI (GB)** B C MONTJEU (IRE) - POLLY'S MARK (IRE) | SIR MARK PRESCOTT BT | 650000 |
| B C LOPE DE VEGA (IRE) - DAZZLE DANCER (IRE) | JOHN FERGUSON BS | 650000 |
| B C OASIS DREAM (GB) - ZEE ZEE TOP (GB) | JOHN FERGUSON BS | 625000 |
| B F GALILEO (IRE) - JACQUELINE QUEST (IRE) | MV MAGNIER | 625000 |
| B C NEW APPROACH (IRE) - AHLA WASAHL (GB) | JOHN FERGUSON BS | 600000 |
| B F SEA THE STARS (IRE) - OUR QUEEN OF KINGS (GB) | BERTRAND LE METAYER BS | 600000 |
| B C SEA THE STARS (IRE) - VICTORIA CROSS (IRE) | C GORDON-WATSON BS | 600000 |
| B/GR C GALILEO (IRE) - FAMOUS (IRE) | BLANDFORD BS | 600000 |
| B C MONTJEU (IRE) - SPLENDID (IRE) | MV MAGNIER | 575000 |
| B C SHAMARDAL (USA) - MULTICOLOUR WAVE (IRE) | PETER ROSS DOYLE BS | 550000 |
| **MATERIALISTIC (GB)** B F OASIS DREAM (GB) - PONGEE (GB) | VENDOR | 550000 |
| CH F GALILEO (IRE) - ALEAGUEOFTHEIROWN (IRE) | MV MAGNIER | 550000 |
| B C OASIS DREAM (GB) - WARLING (IRE) | C GORDON-WATSON BS | 550000 |
| B C DUBAWI (IRE) - TIME SAVED (GB) | VENDOR | 550000 |
| **KHAMRY (GB)** B C POET'S VOICE (GB) - POPPETS SWEETLOVE (GB) | SHADWELL ESTATE COMPANY | 525000 |
| B C GALILEO (IRE) - MAURALAKANA (FR) | MICK FLANAGAN | 510000 |
| **MOKHALAD (GB)** CH C DUBAWI (IRE) - MODEL QUEEN (USA) | SHADWELL ESTATE COMPANY | 500000 |
| B F SEA THE STARS (IRE) - OUT WEST (USA) | K MCMANUS | 500000 |
| B F OASIS DREAM (GB) - LADY OF EVEREST (IRE) | TONY NERSES | 500000 |
| B C SEA THE STARS (IRE) - LIDAKIYA (IRE) | RABBAH BS | 500000 |
| B C DUBAWI (IRE) - LONGING TO DANCE (GB) | JOHN FERGUSON BS | 500000 |
| B F GALILEO (IRE) - DIALAFARA (FR) | J WARREN BS | 480000 |
| B C POET'S VOICE (GB) - PAST THE POST (USA) | AL SHAQAB RACING | 475000 |
| B C ZOFFANY (IRE) - MOUNT CRYSTAL (IRE) | J WARREN BS | 475000 |
| **THRILLED (IRE)** B F KODIAC (GB) - FUERTA VENTURA (IRE) | FLAXMAN STABLES IRELAND | 460000 |
| **MULK (GB)** CH C NEW APPROACH (IRE) - NANNINA (GB) | SHADWELL ESTATE COMPANY | 450000 |
| B C OASIS DREAM (GB) - SETA (GB) | JOHN FERGUSON BS | 425000 |
| BR F NEW APPROACH (IRE) - ENSEMBLE (FR) | BERTRAND LE METAYER BS | 420000 |
| B F GALILEO (IRE) - LANDMARK (USA) | DAVID REDVERS BS | 420000 |
| B F EXCEED AND EXCEL (AUS) - IMPRESSIONISM (IRE) | ROGER P VARIAN | 420000 |
| **ESTIKMAAL (IRE)** B C OASIS DREAM (GB) - ROSIE'S POSY (IRE) | SHADWELL ESTATE COMPANY | 400000 |
| **CLOTH OF STARS (IRE)** B C SEA THE STARS (IRE) - STRAWBERRY FLEDGE (USA) | JOHN FERGUSON BS | 400000 |
| B C GALILEO (IRE) - LADY ICARUS (GB) | C GORDON-WATSON BS | 400000 |
| B C GALILEO (IRE) - CARESSOR (USA) | SHAWN DUGAN, AGENT | 400000 |
| B F DREAM AHEAD (USA) - FLANDERS (IRE) | KERN/LILLINGSTON ASSOCIATION | 400000 |
| **TAQDEES (IRE)** CH F SEA THE STARS (IRE) - AQUARELLE BLEUE (GB) | SHADWELL ESTATE COMPANY | 400000 |
| **POINT OF VIEW (IRE)** B C NEW APPROACH (IRE) - ARTISTI (GB) | J WARREN BS | 400000 |
| **JABBAAR (GB)** CH C MEDICEAN (GB) - ECHELON (GB) | SHADWELL ESTATE COMPANY | 400000 |
| CH C SHAMARDAL (USA) - NIGHTIME (IRE) | J WARREN BS | 400000 |
| B F GALILEO (IRE) - LIKE A DAME (GB) | C GORDON-WATSON BS | 400000 |
| BR C HOLY ROMAN EMPEROR (IRE) - MISSKINTA (IRE) | K MCMANUS | 390000 |
| **FORBIDDING (USA)** CH C KITTEN'S JOY (USA) - LA CORUNA (USA) | NAWARA STUD COMPANY | 390000 |
| **MANSHOOD (IRE)** B C IFFRAAJ (GB) - THAWRAH (IRE) | SHADWELL ESTATE COMPANY | 380000 |
| CH C PIVOTAL (GB) - MAIL THE DESERT (IRE) | J WARREN BS | 380000 |
| B C SHAMARDAL (USA) - HYPNOLOGY (USA) | JOHN FERGUSON BS | 380000 |
| **STATUESQUE (GB)** B F SEA THE STARS (IRE) - KAHARA (GB) | CHEVELEY PARK STUD | 375000 |
| B F SHAMARDAL (USA) - IDILIC CALM (IRE) | VENDOR | 370000 |
| CH C SHAMARDAL (USA) - VIA MILANO (FR) | JOHN FERGUSON BS | 370000 |

| Name and Breeding | Purchaser | Guineas |
|---|---|---|
| GR C SHAMARDAL (USA) - MIDNIGHT ANGEL (GB) | SHADWELL ESTATE COMPANY | 370000 |
| **PREQUEL (IRE)** B F DARK ANGEL (IRE) - MISS INDIGO (GB) | C GORDON-WATSON BS | 360000 |
| **SUN LOVER (GB)** B C OASIS DREAM (GB) - COME TOUCH THE SUN (IRE) | J WARREN BS | 360000 |
| B C SEA THE STARS (IRE) - LOCKUP (IRE) | FORM BS | 350000 |
| B C INVINCIBLE SPIRIT (IRE) - WINNING SEQUENCE (FR) | C GORDON-WATSON BS | 350000 |
| B F POUR MOI (IRE) - SISTINE (GB) | J WARREN BS | 350000 |
| B C ZOFFANY (IRE) - MISS CHILDREY (IRE) | PETER ROSS DOYLE BS | 350000 |
| **ROCKERY (IRE)** B F FASTNET ROCK (AUS) - RAIN FLOWER (IRE) | BBA IRELAND | 350000 |
| CH C DUTCH ART (GB) - KELOWNA (IRE) | AL MIRQAB RACING | 340000 |
| B F IFFRAAJ (GB) - LOGICA (IRE) | JOHN FERGUSON BS | 340000 |
| **SIR GEORGE SOMERS (USA)** CH C CAPE BLANCO (IRE) - SENSE OF CLASS (USA) | J WARREN BS | 340000 |
| **ZHUI FENG (IRE)** B C INVINCIBLE SPIRIT (IRE) - ES QUE (GB) | PETER ROSS DOYLE BS | 340000 |
| GR C TEOFILO (IRE) - WATER FOUNTAIN (GB) | JOHN FERGUSON BS | 340000 |
| CH C DANEHILL DANCER (IRE) - ALSACE LORRAINE (IRE) | PAUL SMITH | 330000 |
| B F OASIS DREAM (GB) - LADEENA (IRE) | SHAWN DUGAN, AGENT | 330000 |
| CH F GIANT'S CAUSEWAY (USA) - DYNAFORCE (USA) | RB RACING | 325000 |
| **ZABEEL PRINCE (IRE)** CH C LOPE DE VEGA (IRE) - PRINCESS SERENA (USA) | C GORDON-WATSON BS | 325000 |
| B C CHAMPS ELYSEES (GB) - DAHAMA (GB) | J WARREN BS | 320000 |
| **TARSEEKH (GB)** B C KYLLACHY (GB) - CONSTITUTE (USA) | SHADWELL ESTATE COMPANY | 320000 |
| B F DANEHILL DANCER (IRE) - GILDED VANITY (IRE) | PETER ROSS DOYLE BS | 320000 |
| B F SEA THE STARS (IRE) - PURSUIT OF LIFE (GB) | AL MIRQAB RACING | 320000 |
| B F FASTNET ROCK (AUS) - MASSEERA (IRE) | SHAWN DUGAN, AGENT | 320000 |
| CH C GALILEO (IRE) - GLINTING DESERT (IRE) | DAVID REDVERS BS | 310000 |
| B F ACCLAMATION (GB) - ROO (GB) | CHINA HORSE CLUB | 300000 |
| B F IFFRAAJ (GB) - PITRIZZA (IRE) | RABBAH BS | 300000 |
| B C DANSILI (GB) - BALLET BALLON (USA) | C GORDON-WATSON BS | 300000 |
| **GOLD VIBE (IRE)** CH C DREAM AHEAD (USA) - WHISPER DANCE (USA) | PAN SUTONG | 300000 |
| **RATTLE ON (GB)** CH C PIVOTAL (GB) - SABREON (GB) | J WARREN BS | 300000 |
| B C POET'S VOICE (GB) - WHIRLY BIRD (GB) | C GORDON-WATSON BS | 300000 |
| CH C NEW APPROACH (IRE) - SISTER ACT (GB) | DAVID REDVERS BS | 300000 |
| **VOLITION (IRE)** GR F DARK ANGEL (IRE) - WARSHAH (IRE) | CHEVELEY PARK STUD | 300000 |
| **URBAN BEAUTY (IRE)** CH F SEA THE STARS (IRE) - ONE DAY IN SPAIN (GB) | VENDOR | 300000 |
| **YASOOD (IRE)** B C ACCLAMATION (GB) - LUCINA (GB) | SHADWELL ESTATE COMPANY | 300000 |
| B F IFFRAAJ (GB) - EVENING TIME (IRE) | PETER ROSS DOYLE BS | 300000 |
| B F SEA THE STARS (IRE) - LAHALEEB (IRE) | VENDOR | 300000 |
| B C DUBAWI (IRE) - PEARLY SHELLS (GB) | VENDOR | 295000 |
| B C KYLLACHY (GB) - JUST DEVINE (IRE) | WILLIAM R MUIR | 280000 |
| B C KODIAC (GB) - TYMORA (USA) | PETER ROSS DOYLE BS | 280000 |
| **AMANAAT (IRE)** B C EXCEED AND EXCEL (AUS) - PIETRA DURA (GB) | SHADWELL ESTATE COMPANY | 280000 |
| B F SEA THE STARS (IRE) - SOMETHING MON (USA) | PETER ROSS DOYLE BS | 280000 |
| **MANSOOB (GB)** CH C PACO BOY (IRE) - DESCRIPTIVE (IRE) | SHADWELL ESTATE COMPANY | 280000 |
| B C OASIS DREAM (GB) - KIRINDA (IRE) | JOHN FERGUSON BS | 280000 |
| B F CAPE CROSS (IRE) - ALLELUIA (GB) | KERN/LILLINGSTON ASSOCIATION | 280000 |
| **CANYON CITY (GB)** B C AUTHORIZED (IRE) - COLORADO DAWN (GB) | JOHN FERGUSON BS | 275000 |
| B C CANFORD CLIFFS (IRE) - BRIGHT SAPPHIRE (IRE) | MRS A SKIFFINGTON | 270000 |
| **NATHRA (IRE)** B F IFFRAAJ (GB) - RADA (IRE) | J WARREN BS | 270000 |
| B F GALILEO (IRE) - BEWITCHED (IRE) | SHAWN DUGAN, AGENT | 270000 |
| B F ZOFFANY (IRE) - SIODUIL (IRE) | BLANDFORD BS | 260000 |
| B C STARSPANGLEDBANNER (AUS) - SZABO (IRE) | PETER ROSS DOYLE BS | 260000 |
| B C HIGH CHAPARRAL (IRE) - WURFKLINGE (GER) | BLANDFORD BS | 260000 |
| CH F SEA THE STARS (IRE) - ALTESSE IMPERIALE (IRE) | HUGO MERRY BS | 260000 |
| B C RIP VAN WINKLE (IRE) - CHEHALIS SUNSET (GB) | BLANDFORD BS | 260000 |
| B F LAWMAN (FR) - KERRY GAL (IRE) | J WARREN BS | 260000 |
| B F FASTNET ROCK (AUS) - STARFISH (IRE) | J WARREN BS | 260000 |
| B C DANSILI (GB) - SALINIA (IRE) | C GORDON-WATSON BS | 260000 |
| B C OASIS DREAM (GB) - BRIOLETTE (IRE) | C GORDON-WATSON BS | 250000 |
| B F POUR MOI (IRE) - AWAIT (IRE) | BERTRAND LE METAYER BS | 250000 |
| **EL VIP (IRE)** B C PIVOTAL (GB) - ELLE DANZIG (GER) | C GORDON-WATSON BS | 250000 |
| B F KODIAC (GB) - BARRACADE (IRE) | HUGO LASCELLES BS | 250000 |
| B C KODIAC (GB) - REDSTONE DANCER (IRE) | JOHN FERGUSON BS | 250000 |
| **LUGANO (GB)** B C GALILEO (IRE) - SWISS LAKE (USA) | JEREMY BRUMMITT | 250000 |
| CH C DUTCH ART (GB) - HELEN GLAZ (IRE) | JOHN FERGUSON BS | 250000 |
| B C OASIS DREAM (GB) - INDEPENDENCE (GB) | VENDOR | 250000 |
| GR C EXCEED AND EXCEL (AUS) - COMEBACK QUEEN (GB) | J WARREN BS | 240000 |
| B C SEA THE STARS (IRE) - ALSHAHBAA (IRE) | PETER ROSS DOYLE BS | 240000 |
| **KING OF DREAMS (GB)** CH C DREAM AHEAD (USA) - COMPLEXION (GB) | MARK CROSSMAN | 240000 |
| B C HIGH CHAPARRAL (IRE) - WALKAMIA (FR) | DEMI O'BYRNE | 240000 |
| B F GALILEO (IRE) - CRYSTAL VALKYRIE (IRE) | AL SHAQAB RACING | 230000 |
| B F ACCLAMATION (GB) - REBELLINE (IRE) | C GORDON-WATSON BS | 230000 |
| B C EXCEED AND EXCEL (AUS) - RUSE (GB) | PETER ROSS DOYLE BS | 230000 |
| B C FASTNET ROCK (AUS) - MOUNT KLINOVEC (IRE) | STEPHEN HILLEN BS | 220000 |

| Name and Breeding | Purchaser | Guineas |
|---|---|---|
| **CIENAGA (IRE)** B C OASIS DREAM (GB) - TUPELO HONEY (IRE) | C GORDON-WATSON BS | 220000 |
| **LOLWAH (GB)** CH F PIVOTAL (GB) - PALACE AFFAIR (GB) | J WARREN BS | 220000 |
| **PIACERE (IRE)** B F NEW APPROACH (IRE) - ANEEDAH (IRE) | VENDOR | 220000 |
| B C PIVOTAL (GB) - FORGOTTEN DREAMS (IRE) | JOHN FERGUSON BS | 220000 |
| **MASARZAIN (IRE)** BR C KODIAC (GB) - CACHE CREEK (IRE) | SHADWELL ESTATE COMPANY | 220000 |
| B C KYLLACHY (GB) - REGENCY ROSE (GB) | TONY NERSES | 220000 |
| **DAAFIK (GB)** B C SHAMARDAL (USA) - PRINCESS DANAH (IRE) | SHADWELL ESTATE COMPANY | 220000 |
| **GALAPIAT (GB)** B C GALILEO (IRE) - LADY JANE DIGBY (GB) | VENDOR | 220000 |
| **JOULES (GB)** B C OASIS DREAM (GB) - FRAPPE (IRE) | STEPHEN HILLEN BS | 215000 |
| **PACIFIC SALT (IRE)** GR C ZEBEDEE (GB) - VILLA NOVA (IRE) | HARRIET JELLETT ANGLIA BS | 210000 |
| B C POET'S VOICE (GB) - RIVER MOUNTAIN (GB) | JOHN FERGUSON BS | 210000 |
| **DHEYAA (IRE)** B F DREAM AHEAD (USA) - LADY LIVIUS (IRE) | SHADWELL ESTATE COMPANY | 210000 |
| B C POUR MOI (IRE) - MARJALINA (IRE) | MV MAGNIER | 210000 |
| **PARTY FOR EVER (IRE)** B F IFFRAAJ (GB) - MISS PARTY LINE (USA) | BBA IRELAND | 210000 |
| GR F MASTERCRAFTSMAN (IRE) - BALLET MOVE (GB) | J O'BYRNE | 210000 |
| **ZANJABEEL (GB)** B C AUSSIE RULES (USA) - GRAIN ONLY (GB) | SHADWELL ESTATE COMPANY | 210000 |
| **RAAFID (GB)** B C SHAMARDAL (USA) - TIME AWAY (IRE) | SHADWELL ESTATE COMPANY | 210000 |
| B F HIGH CHAPARRAL (IRE) - AGNETHA (GER) | ARMANDO DUARTE | 210000 |
| CH C EXCEED AND EXCEL (AUS) - INDIAN LOVE BIRD (GB) | OLIVER ST LAWRENCE BS | 200000 |
| B F PIVOTAL (GB) - WHAZZAT (GB) | J WARREN BS | 200000 |
| B C ACCLAMATION (GB) - RED BLOOM (GB) | JOHN FERGUSON BS | 200000 |
| **DREAM GLORY (IRE)** B C DREAM AHEAD (USA) - DO THE HONOURS (IRE) | SACKVILLEDONALD | 200000 |
| B C HIGH CHAPARRAL (IRE) - URSULA MINOR (IRE) | PETER ROSS DOYLE BS | 200000 |
| B F SEA THE STARS (IRE) - BITOOH (GB) | JOHN FERGUSON BS | 200000 |
| B F TEOFILO (IRE) - MORINQUA (IRE) | JOHN FERGUSON BS | 200000 |
| B C SHAMARDAL (USA) - RIBERAC (GB) | J WARREN BS | 200000 |
| **GOLDEN CHAPTER (GB)** B F DANEHILL DANCER (IRE) - FARFALA (FR) | PAN SUTONG | 200000 |
| **CASTLE HARBOUR (GB)** B C KYLLACHY (GB) - GYPSY CARNIVAL (GB) | J WARREN BS | 200000 |
| B F NEW APPROACH (IRE) - DANEHILL DREAMER (USA) | JOHN FERGUSON BS | 200000 |
| **SHABBAH (IRE)** BR C SEA THE STARS (IRE) - ALIZAYA (IRE) | J WARREN BS | 200000 |
| B C APPROVE (IRE) - ASHTOWN GIRL (IRE) | THE HONG KONG JOCKEY CLUB | 200000 |
| B C POET'S VOICE (GB) - KELLY NICOLE (IRE) | JOHN FERGUSON BS | 200000 |
| **RUSSIAN APPROACH (IRE)** B C NEW APPROACH (IRE) - VELVET FLICKER (IRE) | DERMOT FARRINGTON | 200000 |
| B/BR F ARCH (USA) - PRINCESS KRIS (GB) | MRS A SKIFFINGTON | 200000 |
| B C STREET CRY (IRE) - ARKADINA (IRE) | CHINA HORSE CLUB | 200000 |
| B F SEA THE STARS (IRE) - PLEASANTRY (GB) | JOHN FERGUSON BS | 200000 |
| **EX LOVER (GB)** CH C MONSUN (GER) - TU ERES MI AMORE (IRE) | C GORDON-WATSON BS | 200000 |
| B C OASIS DREAM (GB) - PERFECT TOUCH (USA) | BLANDFORD BS | 200000 |
| **GOLD FAITH (IRE)** GR C DARK ANGEL (IRE) - LIVADREAM (IRE) | PAN SUTONG | 200000 |
| B F SEA THE STARS (IRE) - ARDBRAE LADY (GB) | DERMOT FARRINGTON (P.S.) | 200000 |
| B F OASIS DREAM (GB) - RAINBOW SPRINGS (GB) | HUGO MERRY BS | 200000 |
| **WAJEEZ (IRE)** CH C LOPE DE VEGA (IRE) - CHANTER (GB) | SHADWELL ESTATE COMPANY | 190000 |
| **COMMODITY (IRE)** CH C DUTCH ART (GB) - ROYALE DANEHILL (IRE) | J WARREN BS | 190000 |
| B C IFFRAAJ (GB) - CHEAL ROSE (IRE) | RABBAH BS | 185000 |
| B C OASIS DREAM (GB) - GENEROUS LADY (GB) | C GORDON-WATSON BS | 185000 |
| B F ZOFFANY (IRE) - VANITY (IRE) | J O'BYRNE | 185000 |
| B C FASTNET ROCK (AUS) - TASHZARA (IRE) | THE HONG KONG JOCKEY CLUB | 180000 |
| B C SEA THE STARS (IRE) - UNITY (IRE) | BBA IRELAND | 180000 |
| **EXIST (GB)** B F EXCEED AND EXCEL (AUS) - HARRYANA (GB) | CHEVELEY PARK STUD | 180000 |
| CH C LOPE DE VEGA (IRE) - QUESADA (IRE) | SHADWELL ESTATE COMPANY | 180000 |
| B C AUTHORIZED (IRE) - HONKY TONK SALLY (GB) | JOHN FERGUSON BS | 180000 |
| **TANASOQ (IRE)** B C ACCLAMATION (GB) - ALEXANDER YOUTH (IRE) | SHADWELL ESTATE COMPANY | 180000 |
| B C DUTCH ART (GB) - CZARNA ROZA (GB) | VENDOR | 175000 |
| **ALPHONSUS (GB)** B C INVINCIBLE SPIRIT (IRE) - ELA ATHENA (GB) | BBA IRELAND | 175000 |
| B C CACIQUE (IRE) - KINNAIRD (IRE) | C GORDON-WATSON BS | 175000 |
| B C SEA THE STARS (IRE) - JUMOOH (GB) | PETER ROSS DOYLE BS | 175000 |
| B F INVINCIBLE SPIRIT (IRE) - CHIRKOVA (USA) | STEVE PARKIN | 170000 |
| B C HOLY ROMAN EMPEROR (IRE) - DAHLIA'S KRISSY (USA) | JEREMY BRUMMITT | 170000 |
| B C INVINCIBLE SPIRIT (IRE) - GHURRA (USA) | C GORDON-WATSON BS | 170000 |
| **MALAKKY (IRE)** B C TAMAYUZ (GB) - SAFIYA SONG (IRE) | SHADWELL ESTATE COMPANY | 170000 |
| CH C RODERIC O'CONNOR (IRE) - LUCKY PIPIT (GB) | SHADWELL ESTATE COMPANY | 170000 |
| B C RIP VAN WINKLE (IRE) - JABROOT (IRE) | STEPHEN HILLEN BS | 170000 |
| **MUATADEL (GB)** B C EXCEED AND EXCEL (AUS) - ROSE BLOSSOM (GB) | SHADWELL ESTATE COMPANY | 170000 |
| **SIDLE (IRE)** B F LAWMAN (FR) - SLINK (GB) | CHEVELEY PARK STUD | 170000 |
| B C TEOFILO (IRE) - FAMILY (USA) | C GORDON-WATSON BS | 165000 |
| **ROCKAWAY VALLEY (IRE)** B C HOLY ROMAN EMPEROR (IRE) - SHARAPOVA (IRE) | BBA IRELAND | 165000 |
| B F SEA THE STARS (IRE) - MEETYOUTHERE (IRE) | KERN/LILLINGSTON ASSOCIATION | 165000 |
| **QEYAADAH (IRE)** B C ACCLAMATION (GB) - EFFERVESCE (IRE) | SHADWELL ESTATE COMPANY | 160000 |
| B C EXCEED AND EXCEL (AUS) - MAGIC NYMPH (IRE) | JOHN FERGUSON BS | 160000 |
| **COOL SILK GIRL (GB)** BR F MOTIVATOR (GB) - CAPTAIN'S PARADISE (IRE) | A STROUD BS | 160000 |
| **SAHREEJ (IRE)** B C ZEBEDEE (GB) - PETITE BOULANGERE (IRE) | SHADWELL ESTATE COMPANY | 160000 |

| Name and Breeding | Purchaser | Guineas |
|---|---|---|
| **ETIDAAL (IRE)** B C DARK ANGEL (IRE) - ELLASHA (GB) | SHADWELL ESTATE COMPANY | 160000 |
| B C KODIAC (GB) - DEPORTMENT (GB) | JOHN FERGUSON BS | 160000 |
| **RAASMAAL (GB)** B C POET'S VOICE (GB) - LUMINDA (IRE) | SHADWELL ESTATE COMPANY | 160000 |
| **FREESIA (IRE)** B F DANSILI (GB) - FIELD OF HOPE (IRE) | GRUNDY BS | 160000 |
| B C NEW APPROACH (IRE) - UNDER THE RAINBOW (GB) | JOHN FERGUSON BS | 160000 |
| B C DUTCH ART (GB) - KATIMONT (IRE) | VENDOR | 160000 |
| **CARTWRIGHT (GB)** B C HIGH CHAPARRAL (IRE) - ONE SO MARVELLOUS (GB) | SIR MARK PRESCOTT BT | 160000 |
| B F CACIQUE (IRE) - MOONLIGHT MYSTERY (GB) | C GORDON-WATSON BS | 160000 |
| B C FASTNET ROCK (AUS) - RUBY ROCKET (IRE) | BLANDFORD BS | 160000 |
| **ENGAGE (IRE)** B F POUR MOI (IRE) - BROOKLYN'S STORM (USA) | J WARREN BS | 160000 |
| CH C MASTERCRAFTSMAN (IRE) - GIFT OF SPRING (USA) | STEPHEN HILLEN BS | 160000 |
| **TORMENT (GB)** BL/GR C DARK ANGEL (IRE) - SELKIRK SKY (GB) | J WARREN BS | 160000 |
| GR F DARK ANGEL (IRE) - KELSEY ROSE (GB) | GILL RICHARDSON BS | 155000 |
| B F POUR MOI (IRE) - ONEREUSE (GB) | BLANDFORD BS | 155000 |
| B C PIVOTAL (GB) - TURMALIN (IRE) | JOHN FERGUSON BS | 150000 |
| B C INVINCIBLE SPIRIT (IRE) - NESSINA (USA) | VENDOR | 150000 |
| **HOUSE OF COMMONS (IRE)** B C SEA THE STARS (IRE) - REALITY (FR) | HUGO MERRY BS | 150000 |
| B C NEW APPROACH (IRE) - DAVIE'S LURE (USA) | OLIVER ST LAWRENCE BS | 150000 |
| CH C NEW APPROACH (IRE) - WADAAT (GB) | J WARREN BS | 150000 |
| B C HIGH CHAPARRAL (IRE) - PLAZA (USA) | C GORDON-WATSON BS | 150000 |
| B C CANFORD CLIFFS (IRE) - WELSH DIVA (GB) | MV MAGNIER | 150000 |
| B F OASIS DREAM (GB) - APPLAUDED (IRE) | BLANDFORD BS | 150000 |
| **BEDROCK (GB)** B C FASTNET ROCK (AUS) - GEMSTONE (IRE) | J WARREN BS | 150000 |
| B F DUTCH ART (GB) - SECRET HISTORY (USA) | KATSUMI YOSHIDA | 150000 |
| **COSMICA SIDERA (IRE)** B F GALILEO (IRE) - BYWAYOFTHESTARS (GB) | MARGARET O'TOOLE (P.S.) | 150000 |
| **RAVENS QUEST (GB)** CH C RAVEN'S PASS (USA) - SERADIM (GB) | VENDOR | 150000 |
| B C LOPE DE VEGA (IRE) - DANIELLI (IRE) | ROB SPEERS | 150000 |
| B F DANSILI (GB) - SELINKA (GB) | BLANDFORD BS (P.S.) | 150000 |
| B C CAPE BLANCO (IRE) - KEEPERS HILL (IRE) | C GORDON-WATSON BS | 150000 |
| CH F DREAM AHEAD (USA) - LADY ALEXANDER (IRE) | JOE FOLEY | 150000 |
| B C GALILEO (IRE) - BELESTA (GB) | BLANDFORD BS | 150000 |
| B F OASIS DREAM (GB) - DASHING (IRE) | RABBAH BS | 145000 |
| GR C ARCHIPENKO (USA) - ALBANOVA (GB) | BBA IRELAND | 140000 |
| **ATTITUDE ROCKS (GB)** B C DANSILI (GB) - DORELIA (IRE) | CLIVE COX RACING | 140000 |
| BR C SHAMARDAL (USA) - ANGELS STORY (IRE) | C GORDON-WATSON (P.S.) | 140000 |
| B C SHAMARDAL (USA) - ARTHUR'S GIRL (GB) | SHADWELL ESTATE COMPANY | 140000 |
| CH C POET'S VOICE (GB) - ISLA AZUL (IRE) | SHADWELL ESTATE COMPANY | 140000 |
| B C ACCLAMATION (GB) - GAY MIRAGE (GER) | BECKHAMPTON STABLES | 140000 |
| **TASKEEN (IRE)** B C LILBOURNE LAD (IRE) - LOLA ROSA (IRE) | PETER ROSS DOYLE BS | 140000 |
| B C INVINCIBLE SPIRIT (IRE) - WIMPLE (USA) | BLANDFORD BS | 140000 |
| B C SHOWCASING (GB) - ROODEYE (GB) | THE HONG KONG JOCKEY CLUB | 140000 |
| **BALANCING TIME (GB)** B C PIVOTAL (GB) - TIME ON (GB) | PETER ROSS DOYLE BS | 140000 |
| B F FASTNET ROCK (AUS) - KUSHNARENKOVO (GB) | RB RACING | 140000 |
| GR F DALAKHANI (IRE) - SPECIFICALLY (USA) | VENDOR | 140000 |
| **TAQWAA (IRE)** CH C IFFRAAJ (GB) - HALLOWED PARK (IRE) | PETER ROSS DOYLE BS | 140000 |
| **SWEET DRAGON FLY (GB)** B F OASIS DREAM (GB) - SWEET CECILY (IRE) | STEPHEN HILLEN BS (P.S.) | 140000 |
| B F SEA THE STARS (IRE) - NIGHT FAIRY (IRE) | HUGO MERRY BS | 140000 |
| **ENACTING (USA)** B C HENRYTHENAVIGATOR (USA) - RANDOM CHANCE (USA) | SUZANNE ROBERTS | 135000 |
| B F GALILEO (IRE) - KITE MARK (GB) | TINA RAU BS (P.S.) | 135000 |
| **MULLIGATAWNY (IRE)** B C LOPE DE VEGA (IRE) - WILD WHIM (IRE) | BBA IRELAND | 135000 |
| B C POUR MOI (IRE) - ISLAND DREAMS (USA) | JAMIE LLOYD | 135000 |
| B F POUR MOI (IRE) - WANNA (IRE) | VENDOR | 130000 |
| **YOU'RE HIRED (GB)** B G DALAKHANI (IRE) - HEAVEN SENT (GB) | PETER ROSS DOYLE BS | 130000 |
| B C SEA THE STARS (IRE) - RHADEGUNDA (GB) | JOHN FERGUSON BS | 130000 |
| B F MONTJEU (IRE) - CHARROUX (IRE) | EUROWEST BS | 130000 |
| B C LILBOURNE LAD (IRE) - RED PLANET (GB) | C GORDON-WATSON BS | 130000 |
| B F LILBOURNE LAD (IRE) - GENUINE CHARM (IRE) | JEREMY NOSEDA RACING | 130000 |
| B C ACCLAMATION (GB) - CARPET LADY (IRE) | VENDOR | 130000 |
| B C ZOFFANY (IRE) - ROHAIN (IRE) | STEPHEN HILLEN BS | 130000 |
| B C RAVEN'S PASS (USA) - RED INTRIGUE (IRE) | JOHN FERGUSON BS | 130000 |
| GR F DARK ANGEL (IRE) - JASMINE FLOWER (GB) | BLANDFORD BS | 130000 |
| B C KYLLACHY (GB) - CARDRONA (GB) | SHADWELL ESTATE COMPANY | 130000 |
| **NOBLE STAR (IRE)** B C ACCLAMATION (GB) - WRONG ANSWER (GB) | SACKVILLEDONALD | 130000 |
| **ESTIDRAAK (IRE)** CH C IFFRAAJ (GB) - GOLD HUSH (USA) | SHADWELL ESTATE COMPANY | 130000 |
| B F IFFRAAJ (GB) - POWDER BLUE (GB) | JOHN FERGUSON BS | 130000 |
| B F ACCLAMATION (GB) - OASIS SUNSET (IRE) | PETER ROSS DOYLE BS | 130000 |
| **ANGIE'S GIRL (GB)** B F EXCEED AND EXCEL (AUS) - EXPEDIENCE (USA) | CLIVE COX RACING | 130000 |
| B F ACCLAMATION (GB) - PIONEER BRIDE (USA) | OLIVER ST LAWRENCE BS | 130000 |
| B C DUTCH ART (GB) - CZARNA ROZA (GB) | SUZANNE ROBERTS | 130000 |
| B F EXCEED AND EXCEL (AUS) - AKHMATOVA (GB) | J WARREN BS | 125000 |
| B C RIP VAN WINKLE (IRE) - ANNE TUDOR (IRE) | C GORDON-WATSON BS | 125000 |

| Name and Breeding | Purchaser | Guineas |
|---|---|---|
| B/GR C CAPE CROSS (IRE) - VANISHING GREY (IRE) | JOHN FERGUSON BS | 125000 |
| B C ZOFFANY (IRE) - POINSETTIA (IRE) | AIDAN O'RYAN/D K WELD | 125000 |
| **STRAWBERRY SORBET (GB)** B F STREET CRY (IRE) - STRAWBERRYDAIQUIRI (GB) | AIRLIE STUD | 125000 |
| BR C NEW APPROACH (IRE) - MAMBO HALO (USA) | RABBAH BS | 120000 |
| **RUE RIVOLI (IRE)** B C CHAMPS ELYSEES (GB) - RONDO ALLA TURCA (IRE) | BARBERINI BS | 120000 |
| **OPPOSITION (GB)** GR C DALAKHANI (IRE) - CENSORED (GB) | J WARREN BS | 120000 |
| B C IFFRAAJ (GB) - SOLVA (GB) | NORRIS/HUNTINGDON | 120000 |
| **EMTIDAAD (IRE)** CH C KYLLACHY (GB) - HANA DEE (GB) | J WARREN BS | 120000 |
| **BIGMOUTH STRIKES (IRE)** CH C RAVEN'S PASS (USA) - CHIOSINA (IRE) | HARROWGATE BS LTD | 120000 |
| **MARBOOH (IRE)** B C DARK ANGEL (IRE) - MULUK (IRE) | SHADWELL ESTATE COMPANY | 120000 |
| B F MASTERCRAFTSMAN (IRE) - ZACCHERA (GB) | J WARREN BS | 120000 |
| **STEEL OF MADRID (IRE)** B C LOPE DE VEGA (IRE) - BIBURY (GB) | PETER ROSS DOYLE BS | 120000 |
| **CATALAN (IRE)** B F DUKE OF MARMALADE (IRE) - TWICE THE EASE (GB) | AIRLIE STUD | 120000 |
| B C IFFRAAJ (GB) - THROUGH THE FOREST (USA) | PETER ROSS DOYLE BS | 120000 |
| B F ELUSIVE QUALITY (USA) - SCHAUNCIE (USA) | FORM BS | 120000 |
| B C PIVOTAL (GB) - FRIGID (GB) | R O'GORMAN BS | 120000 |
| CH C RAVEN'S PASS (USA) - BEAUTIFUL FILLY (GB) | JOHN FERGUSON BS | 120000 |
| GR C INVINCIBLE SPIRIT (IRE) - LADY SPRINGBANK (IRE) | JAMIE LLOYD | 120000 |
| B F POET'S VOICE (GB) - LUNDA (IRE) | MERIDIAN INTERNATIONAL | 120000 |
| **TIGERWOLF (IRE)** BR C DREAM AHEAD (USA) - SINGING FIELD (IRE) | GILL RICHARDSON BS | 120000 |
| B C DUBAWI (IRE) - KILTUBBER (IRE) | RABBAH BS | 120000 |
| B F PIVOTAL (GB) - FINE THREADS (GB) | JOHN FERGUSON BS | 120000 |
| **LORD KELVIN (IRE)** B C IFFRAAJ (GB) - EASTERN APPEAL (IRE) | HUGO MERRY BS | 120000 |
| B F CANFORD CLIFFS (IRE) - SAPHIRA'S FIRE (IRE) | DERMOT FARRINGTON | 120000 |
| **CAPABILITY BAY (GB)** B C EQUIANO (FR) - FABULOUSLY FAST (USA) | SAM SANGSTER | 120000 |
| **GIRL WITH A PEARL (IRE)** CH F DUTCH ART (GB) - POINTED ARCH (IRE) | KERN/LILLINGSTON (P.S.) | 120000 |
| **TOWERLANDS PARK (IRE)** B C DANEHILL DANCER (IRE) - STRATEGY (GB) | WJ GREDLEY | 120000 |
| B F SEA THE STARS (IRE) - BRISEIDA (GB) | TINA RAU BS | 115000 |
| B C IFFRAAJ (GB) - GREEN POPPY (GB) | SACKVILLEDONALD | 115000 |
| BR F POET'S VOICE (GB) - LUCKY TOKEN (IRE) | SACKVILLEDONALD | 115000 |
| CH C NEW APPROACH (IRE) - ZACHETA (GB) | VENDOR | 115000 |
| B C ACCLAMATION (GB) - FIRST TURN (GB) | SURBIRINDER SINGH SIDHU | 115000 |
| B C AUTHORIZED (IRE) - ALAMANNI (USA) | PETER ROSS DOYLE BS | 110000 |
| CH C CHAMPS ELYSEES (GB) - DALVINA (GB) | VENDOR | 110000 |
| B F RAVEN'S PASS (USA) - HAVE FAITH (IRE) | VENDOR | 110000 |
| **ENMESHING (GB)** CH C MASTERCRAFTSMAN (IRE) - YACHT CLUB (USA) | SUZANNE ROBERTS | 110000 |
| **WRAPPED (GB)** CH F IFFRAAJ (GB) - MUFFLED (USA) | CHEVELEY PARK STUD | 110000 |
| B C IFFRAAJ (GB) - QUAICH (GB) | SHADWELL ESTATE COMPANY | 110000 |
| B F KODIAC (GB) - REKINDLED CROSS (IRE) | JOHN FERGUSON BS | 110000 |
| CH F NEW APPROACH (IRE) - CLASSIC REMARK (IRE) | VENDOR | 110000 |
| **TYRANNICAL (GB)** BR C DANSILI (GB) - QUEEN OF MEAN (GB) | SIR MARK PRESCOTT BT | 110000 |
| CH C FROZEN POWER (IRE) - PENNY ROUGE (IRE) | RABBAH BS | 110000 |
| **CHELSEA'S BOY (IRE)** GR C RIP VAN WINKLE (IRE) - ST ROCH (IRE) | CLIVE COX RACING | 110000 |
| CH C KYLLACHY (GB) - LAURENTINA (GB) | J WARREN BS | 110000 |
| **POINT OF WOODS (GB)** B C SHOWCASING (GB) - ROMANTIC MYTH (GB) | BBA IRELAND | 110000 |
| CH F SEA THE STARS (IRE) - PICKLE (GB) | VENDOR | 110000 |
| B C STARSPANGLEDBANNER (AUS) - DONNA GIOVANNA (GB) | BLANDFORD BS | 105000 |
| **KHAWANEEJ (GB)** B C AZAMOUR (IRE) - DANCE EAST (GB) | J WARREN BS | 105000 |
| **MUTARAJJIL (IRE)** B C ACCLAMATION (GB) - ROUGE NOIR (USA) | SHADWELL ESTATE COMPANY | 105000 |
| B F FASTNET ROCK (AUS) - QUIET PROTEST (USA) | VENDOR | 105000 |
| B F MONTJEU (IRE) - FESTOSO (IRE) | STEVE PARKIN | 105000 |
| B F KYLLACHY (GB) - ALBAVILLA (GB) | J WARREN BS | 105000 |
| GR C CACIQUE (IRE) - STRAWBERRY MORN (CAN) | OLIVER ST LAWRENCE BS | 105000 |
| **ICE GALLEY (IRE)** B C GALILEO (IRE) - ICE QUEEN (IRE) | PHILIP KIRBY | 105000 |
| B F NEW APPROACH (IRE) - INTRUM MORSHAAN (IRE) | VENDOR | 100000 |
| B C SHAMARDAL (USA) - DEVERON (USA) | SACKVILLEDONALD | 100000 |
| B F OASIS DREAM (GB) - MASKUNAH (IRE) | VENDOR | 100000 |
| CH F EXCEED AND EXCEL (AUS) - SNOW CRYSTAL (IRE) | BBA IRELAND | 100000 |
| **CORINTHIAN (GB)** B C SEA THE STARS (IRE) - CONTRADICTIVE (USA) | J WARREN BS | 100000 |
| B C AUTHORIZED (IRE) - ELAN (GB) | JOHN FERGUSON BS | 100000 |
| **IONA ISLAND (GB)** B F DUTCH ART (GB) - STILL SMALL VOICE (GB) | BBA IRELAND | 100000 |
| **HIGH SHIELDS (IRE)** B C SHAMARDAL (USA) - MARINE CITY (JPN) | AMANDA SKIFFINGTON | 100000 |
| B C ZOFFANY (IRE) - TAN TAN (GB) | GRANGEBARRY | 100000 |
| **BATTAILES (GB)** B C ACCLAMATION (GB) - ADA RIVER (GB) | ANTHONY STROUD BS | 100000 |
| **HORTENSIO (IRE)** B C POUR MOI (IRE) - O' BELLA BALLERINA (USA) | SAM SANGSTER BS | 100000 |
| B F MOTIVATOR (GB) - SPICEBIRD (IRE) | J WARREN BS | 100000 |
| B C INVINCIBLE SPIRIT (IRE) - SAHAFH (USA) | THE HONG KONG JOCKEY CLUB | 100000 |
| **IN THE CITY (GB)** CH C EXCEED AND EXCEL (AUS) - SOFT MORNING (GB) | HIGHFLYER BS | 100000 |
| **LEE BAY (GB)** B C CACIQUE (IRE) - BANTU (GB) | BLANDFORD BS | 100000 |
| B C INVINCIBLE SPIRIT (IRE) - ZANZIBAR (IRE) | SC WILLIAMS | 100000 |
| **TOUMAR (GB)** CH F SEA THE STARS (IRE) - TINGLING (USA) | VENDOR | 100000 |

| Name and Breeding | Purchaser | Guineas |
|---|---|---|
| B F NEW APPROACH (IRE) - TINAAR (USA) | VENDOR | 100000 |
| CH C STREET CRY (IRE) - SAY NO NOW (IRE) | JOHN FERGUSON BS | 100000 |
| B F AQLAAM (GB) - TAMZIN (GB) | FIONA SHAW | 100000 |
| B C DUBAWI (IRE) - CASANGA (IRE) | RABBAH BS | 100000 |
| B F OASIS DREAM (GB) - QUAN YIN (IRE) | RABBAH BS | 100000 |
| CH C SEA THE STARS (IRE) - FAIR SAILING (IRE) | C GORDON-WATSON BS | 100000 |
| **RIDE THE LIGHTNING (GB)** B C DALAKHANI (IRE) - BRIGHT HALO (IRE) | C DE MOUBRAY | 100000 |
| **ALTARSHEED (IRE)** B C LILBOURNE LAD (IRE) - LILAKIYA (IRE) | PETER ROSS DOYLE BS | 100000 |
| CH C RAVEN'S PASS (USA) - SISTER RED (IRE) | VENDOR | 100000 |
| **SHAWAAHID (IRE)** B C ELNADIM (USA) - VEXATIOUS (IRE) | PETER ROSS DOYLE BS | 100000 |
| **GAWDAWPALIN (IRE)** B C HOLY ROMAN EMPEROR (IRE) - DIRTYBIRDIE (GB) | PETER ROSS DOYLE BS | 100000 |
| **RAUCOUS (GB)** B C DREAM AHEAD (USA) - SHYRL (GB) | J WARREN BS | 100000 |
| GR C FASTNET ROCK (AUS) - HOTELGENIE DOT COM (GB) | HOWSON / HOLDSWORTH BS | 100000 |
| GR C MASTERCRAFTSMAN (IRE) - GOLD CHARM (GER) | ROGER P VARIAN | 100000 |
| B C SHOWCASING (GB) - NEVER LET YOU DOWN (IRE) | S KIRK | 100000 |
| **SHARARA (GB)** CH C DUTCH ART (GB) - TAFAWUT (GB) | SHADWELL ESTATE COMPANY | 100000 |
| **TUKHOOM (IRE)** B G ACCLAMATION (GB) - CARIOCA (IRE) | SHADWELL ESTATE COMPANY | 100000 |
| B F KODIAC (GB) - AGUILAS PERLA (IRE) | ROBERT MH COWELL | 100000 |
| **MENAI (IRE)** B C DARK ANGEL (IRE) - GLISTEN (GB) | BW HILLS | 100000 |
| **TARBOOSH (GB)** B C BAHAMIAN BOUNTY (GB) - MULLEIN (GB) | SHADWELL ESTATE COMPANY | 100000 |
| BR F BIG BAD BOB (IRE) - GALISTIC (IRE) | VENDOR | 100000 |
| **THE GRADUATE (IRE)** BR C MASTERCRAFTSMAN (IRE) - BALLYVARRA (IRE) | ANDREW BALDING | 100000 |
| **DREAM DANA (IRE)** B F DREAM AHEAD (USA) - LIDANNA (GB) | FEDERICO BARBERINI, AGENT | 100000 |
| CH C LOPE DE VEGA (IRE) - KEEP DANCING (IRE) | RABBAH BS | 95000 |
| BR C IFFRAAJ (GB) - CLASSIC VISION (GB) | RICKY PF YIU | 95000 |
| **CRY OF JOY (GB)** CH C DREAM AHEAD (USA) - LAMENTATION (GB) | MARK CROSSMAN | 95000 |
| **GIRL OF THE HOUR (GB)** B F MAKFI (GB) - AMERICAN SPIRIT (IRE) | VENDOR | 90000 |
| B F FASTNET ROCK (AUS) - UP AT DAWN (GB) | CHINA HORSE CLUB | 90000 |
| CH C DANEHILL DANCER (IRE) - ALTHEA ROSE (IRE) | HUGO MERRY BS | 90000 |
| **SIMPLY ME (GB)** B F NEW APPROACH (IRE) - EGO (GB) | SACKVILLEDONALD (P.S.) | 90000 |
| **LIMONATA (IRE)** B F BUSHRANGER (IRE) - COME APRIL (GB) | H CANDY | 90000 |
| B F FASTNET ROCK (AUS) - TREASURE THE LADY (IRE) | CHINA HORSE CLUB | 90000 |
| B F ELUSIVE QUALITY (USA) - ATTRACTIVE (IRE) | JOHN FERGUSON BS | 90000 |
| B C INVINCIBLE SPIRIT (IRE) - MALAISIENNE (FR) | THE CHANNEL CONSIGNMENT | 90000 |
| B C MEDICEAN (GB) - ADELE BLANC SEC (FR) | SHADWELL ESTATE COMPANY | 90000 |
| CH C PIVOTAL (GB) - PEDIMENT (GB) | J WARREN BS | 90000 |
| **KESSELRING (GB)** CH C NEW APPROACH (IRE) - ANNA OLEANDA (IRE) | VENDOR | 90000 |
| GR C ZEBEDEE (GB) - CHAMPION TIPSTER (GB) | ROGER P VARIAN | 90000 |
| **VISCOUNT BARFIELD (GB)** B C RAVEN'S PASS (USA) - MADONNA DELL'ORTO (GB) | ANDREW BALDING (P.S.) | 90000 |
| CH C SHOWCASING (GB) - MALELANE (IRE) | R O'RYAN / R FAHEY | 90000 |
| B C ROCK OF GIBRALTAR (IRE) - AMAYA (USA) | C GORDON-WATSON BS | 90000 |
| CH F EXCEED AND EXCEL (AUS) - MY LOVE THOMAS (IRE) | BBA IRELAND | 90000 |
| B C SMART STRIKE (CAN) - EXCITING TIMES (FR) | C GORDON-WATSON BS | 90000 |
| CH C DUTCH ART (GB) - PINK FLAMES (IRE) | RABBAH BS | 90000 |
| **BLUES SISTER (GB)** B F COMPTON PLACE (GB) - PERSARIO (GB) | ANTHONY STROUD BS | 88000 |
| B C RIP VAN WINKLE (IRE) - SUPERFONIC (FR) | ROGER P VARIAN | 85000 |
| B F TAMAYUZ (GB) - LOVERS PEACE (IRE) | SC WILLIAMS | 85000 |
| **HUNGARIAN RHAPSODY (GB)** B C SHOWCASING (GB) - ROCKBURST (GB) | JAMIE OSBORNE | 85000 |
| **LORD ASLAN (IRE)** B C THEWAYYOUARE (USA) - LUNAR LUSTRE (IRE) | JEREMY BRUMMITT | 85000 |
| CH C RIP VAN WINKLE (IRE) - APACHE DREAM (IRE) | JAMIE LLOYD | 85000 |
| **CARPE DIEM LADY (IRE)** B F ACCLAMATION (GB) - GREENISLAND (IRE) | CLIVE COX RACING | 85000 |
| B C POET'S VOICE (GB) - STREET STAR (USA) | J WARREN BS | 85000 |
| **ALEEF (IRE)** B C KODIAC (GB) - OKBA (USA) | SHADWELL ESTATE COMPANY | 85000 |
| B F KODIAC (GB) - DIXIELAND KISS (USA) | RABBAH BS | 85000 |
| B F INVINCIBLE SPIRIT (IRE) - WHITE AND RED (IRE) | MARK JOHNSTON RACING | 85000 |
| B C ROCK OF GIBRALTAR (IRE) - SPLASHDOWN (GB) | ROB SPEERS | 85000 |
| **MYSTIQUE HEIGHTS (GB)** B C HIGH CHAPARRAL (IRE) - MUSIQUE MAGIQUE (IRE) | JEREMY BRUMMITT | 85000 |
| B C IFFRAAJ (GB) - PELLINORE (USA) | A AND E BS | 85000 |
| B C HAT TRICK (JPN) - ROCHITTA (USA) | J WARREN BS | 85000 |
| B F IFFRAAJ (GB) - SEMINOLE LASS (USA) | ANTHONY STROUD BS | 85000 |
| CH C POET'S VOICE (GB) - SKY WONDER (GB) | SACKVILLEDONALD | 85000 |
| CH F EXCEED AND EXCEL (AUS) - MISS HONORINE (IRE) | J WARREN BS | 85000 |
| B C HOLY ROMAN EMPEROR (IRE) - ROMIE'S KASTETT (GER) | BBA IRELAND | 85000 |
| B F POET'S VOICE (GB) - STARCHY (GB) | BLANDFORD BS | 85000 |
| **WAVE REVIEWS (GB)** B C FASTNET ROCK (AUS) - CRITICAL ACCLAIM (GB) | VENDOR | 85000 |
| **ISTANBUL BEY (GB)** RO C EXCEED AND EXCEL (AUS) - STARFALA (GB) | HIGHFLYER BS | 85000 |
| **OCTOBER STORM (GB)** BR C SHIROCCO (GER) - CYBER STAR (GB) | GILL RICHARDSON BS | 85000 |
| B F DREAM AHEAD (USA) - KNAPTON HILL (GB) | RABBAH BS | 82000 |
| B F ZEBEDEE (GB) - BAILEYS CREAM (GB) | BLANDFORD BS | 82000 |

# HIGH-PRICED YEARLINGS OF 2014 AT GOFFS

**The following yearlings realised 67,000 euros and over at Goffs Sales in 2014:-**

| Name and Breeding | Purchaser | Euros |
|---|---|---|
| B C GALILEO (IRE) - SCRIBONIA (IRE) | M V MAGNIER | 1500000 |
| **SIGNE (IRE)** B F SEA THE STARS (IRE) - GREEN ROOM (USA) | A SKIFFINGTON | 1100000 |
| **SPLIT DECISION (IRE)** B F TEOFILO (IRE) - NIGHT VISIT (GB) | JOHN MCCORMACK BS | 950000 |
| B F TEOFILO (IRE) - GRECIAN BRIDE (IRE) | SHADWELL ESTATE CO | 950000 |
| CH C SEA THE STARS (IRE) - EVENSONG (GER) | M WALLACE BS | 850000 |
| B F INVINCIBLE SPIRIT (IRE) - PROPAGANDA (IRE) | SHADWELL ESTATE CO | 720000 |
| B F LAWMAN (FR) - ROSE DE FRANCE (IRE) | T NERSES | 520000 |
| **MUNAASHID (USA)** B/BR C LONHRO (AUS) - FREEFOURRACING (USA) | SHADWELL ESTATE CO | 450000 |
| B C FASTNET ROCK (AUS) - PERIHELION (IRE) | BLANDFORD BS | 400000 |
| **IJLAAL (IRE)** B C EXCEED AND EXCEL (AUS) - SPECIAL DANCER (GB) | SHADWELL ESTATE CO | 400000 |
| B/BR C TIZNOW (USA) - MOUSSE AU CHOCOLAT (USA) | M PLAYER | 380000 |
| B C EXCEED AND EXCEL (AUS) - GREAT HOPE (IRE) | D REDVERS | 375000 |
| CH F GALILEO (IRE) - LA SYLVIA (IRE) | JAPAN HEALTH SUMMIT | 375000 |
| **COLOUR BRIGHT (IRE)** B F DREAM AHEAD (USA) - FLASHING GREEN (GB) | MOYGLARE STUD | 350000 |
| **JAZZ CAT (IRE)** CH F TAMAYUZ (GB) - CHELSEA ROSE (IRE) | S HILLEN | 350000 |
| B C ZOFFANY (IRE) - HOW'S SHE CUTTIN' (IRE) | BBA (IRELAND) | 340000 |
| **MANAAFIDH (IRE)** B C ZEBEDEE (GB) - STARRING (FR) | PETER ROSS DOYLE BS | 330000 |
| **BASMA (GB)** B F EXCEED AND EXCEL (AUS) - MISS CHICANE (GB) | SHADWELL ESTATE CO | 325000 |
| B C KODIAC (GB) - CALL LATER (USA) | HONG KONG JOCKEY CLUB | 325000 |
| B F GALILEO (IRE) - HEALING MUSIC (FR) | FORM BS | 320000 |
| BR F SEA THE STARS (IRE) - PHOTOPHORE (IRE) | SUNDERLAND HOLDING | 300000 |
| B F INVINCIBLE SPIRIT (IRE) - BRATISLAVA (GB) | S PARKIN | 300000 |
| **PLENARY (USA)** CH C KITTEN'S JOY (USA) - SOUTHERN ALIBI (USA) | F SHAW | 300000 |
| **CLEAR CUT (GB)** B C ACCLAMATION (GB) - CLAIOMH SOLAIS (IRE) | BBA (IRELAND) | 300000 |
| B C GALILEO (IRE) - INCA PRINCESS (IRE) | BBA (IRELAND) | 300000 |
| B C SEA THE STARS (IRE) - KINCOB (USA) | J FERGUSON | 290000 |
| **ELECTORAL (IRE)** B C RIP VAN WINKLE (IRE) - SUMINGASEFA (GB) | S HILLEN | 280000 |
| B C SCAT DADDY (USA) - OUI SAY OUI (IRE) | F SHAW | 280000 |
| CH F PIVOTAL (GB) - TRISKEL (GB) | FORM BS | 260000 |
| B C SHAMARDAL (USA) - TIME HONOURED (GB) | J FERGUSON | 260000 |
| B/BR F NEW APPROACH (IRE) - CHANGEABLE (GB) | FORM BS | 250000 |
| **JULIETTE FAIR (IRE)** GR F DARK ANGEL (IRE) - CAPULET MONTEQUE (IRE) | MOYGLARE STUD | 240000 |
| **MUNSHID (IRE)** B C DUTCH ART (GB) - LIGHTWOOD LADY (IRE) | SHADWELL ESTATE CO | 240000 |
| **MZYOON (IRE)** B F GALILEO (IRE) - HIGH SOCIETY (IRE) | S HILLEN | 240000 |
| **ARCHIMEDES (IRE)** B C INVINCIBLE SPIRIT (IRE) - WAVEBAND (GB) | HUGO MERRY BS | 240000 |
| CH F MASTERCRAFTSMAN (IRE) - SWEET FIREBIRD (IRE) | T NERSES | 220000 |
| B F DREAM AHEAD (USA) - ZEITING (IRE) | ANTHONY STROUD BS | 220000 |
| B C CACIQUE (IRE) - MONICALEW (GB) | BBA (IRELAND) | 215000 |
| B C RIP VAN WINKLE (IRE) - GRECIAN DANCER (GB) | BADGERS BS | 215000 |
| CH C SUMMER BIRD (USA) - GOLDEN PARTY (USA) | SHADWELL ESTATE CO | 200000 |
| GR F DARK ANGEL (IRE) - COVER GIRL (IRE) | M V MAGNIER | 200000 |
| B C CANFORD CLIFFS (IRE) - LULAWIN (GB) | M V MAGNIER | 200000 |
| B C POUR MOI (IRE) - MADEIRA MIST (IRE) | BADGERS BS | 200000 |
| B C CANFORD CLIFFS (IRE) - AWJILA (GB) | D WACHMAN | 190000 |
| **MATRON OF HONOUR (IRE)** B F TEOFILO (IRE) - WEDDING GIFT (FR) | A TINKLER (P.S.) | 190000 |
| **FOUNDATION (IRE)** CH C ZOFFANY (IRE) - ROYSTONEA (GB) | J WARREN BS | 190000 |
| B F GALILEO (IRE) - DONNADANE (AUS) | JAPAN HEALTH SUMMIT | 190000 |
| B C FASTNET ROCK (AUS) - AMENIXA (FR) | HONG KONG JOCKEY CLUB | 180000 |
| **KASSIA (IRE)** B F ACCLAMATION (GB) - SPEEDY SONATA (USA) | GILL RICHARDSON BS | 180000 |
| **PERSUASIVE (IRE)** GR F DARK ANGEL (IRE) - CHOOSE ME (IRE) | CHEVELEY PARK STUD | 180000 |
| BR C FOOTSTEPSINTHESAND (GB) - CAPRIOLE (GB) | HONG KONG JOCKEY CLUB | 180000 |
| B F HIGH CHAPARRAL (IRE) - INCH PERFECT (USA) | FORM BS | 180000 |
| **DANCING YEARS (IRE)** CH F IFFRAAJ (GB) - DAGANYA (IRE) | CHEVELEY PARK STUD | 175000 |
| B C RIP VAN WINKLE (IRE) - CAWETT (IRE) | M WALLACE BS | 170000 |
| **REHEARSE (IRE)** B C BIG BAD BOB (IRE) - AND AGAIN (USA) | J WARREN BS | 170000 |
| CH F EXCEED AND EXCEL (AUS) - LANDELA (GB) | RABBAH BS | 165000 |
| B F SCAT DADDY (USA) - EXCELENTE (IRE) | SACKVILLEDONALD | 160000 |
| B C CANFORD CLIFFS (IRE) - TARASCON (IRE) | M V MAGNIER | 160000 |
| **MISS GILLIAN (IRE)** B F CANFORD CLIFFS (IRE) - BELLA BELLA (IRE) | FLAXMAN STABLES | 160000 |
| B F MONTJEU (IRE) - NECKLACE (GB) | VENDOR | 150000 |
| B C RIP VAN WINKLE (IRE) - AMHOOJ (GB) | PETER ROSS DOYLE BS | 150000 |
| CH F EXCEED AND EXCEL (AUS) - FASHIONABLE (GB) | RABBAH BS | 150000 |
| **DANCE BAND (IRE)** B F DANEHILL DANCER (IRE) - MAIDIN MAITH (IRE) | CHEVELEY PARK STUD | 150000 |
| CH F CHAMPS ELYSEES (GB) - FLECHE D'OR (GB) | S PARKIN | 150000 |
| B C MAKFI (GB) - UNDULANT WAY (GB) | VENDOR | 150000 |
| CH F DUTCH ART (GB) - TENDER IS THENIGHT (IRE) | VENDOR | 150000 |
| B C LAWMAN (FR) - MILLAY (GB) | D REDVERS | 140000 |
| B C SEA THE STARS (IRE) - FOUR ROSES (IRE) | J FERGUSON | 140000 |

| Name and Breeding | Purchaser | Euros |
|---|---|---|
| B C HIGH CHAPARRAL (IRE) - MISS BEATRIX (IRE) | CORMAC MCCORMACK BS | 140000 |
| B F IFFRAAJ (GB) - ENCOURAGEMENT (GB) | J FERGUSON | 140000 |
| B F MASTERCRAFTSMAN (IRE) - LUCY CAVENDISH (USA) | D WACHMAN | 140000 |
| CH F DUTCH ART (GB) - CARVED EMERALD (GB) | D REDVERS | 135000 |
| **POET'S SONG (IRE)** B C POET'S VOICE (GB) - BEE EATER (IRE) | PETER ROSS DOYLE BS | 130000 |
| B C FAST COMPANY (IRE) - CAPPUCCINO (IRE) | J FERGUSON | 130000 |
| B C ACCLAMATION (GB) - ARIS (IRE) | S HILLEN | 130000 |
| B F DARK ANGEL (IRE) - KATE THE GREAT (GB) | BBA (IRELAND) | 130000 |
| B C CANFORD CLIFFS (IRE) - MOWAADAH (IRE) | D REDVERS | 125000 |
| **THE TULIP (IRE)** B F LAWMAN (FR) - LADY SLIPPERS (IRE) | H MORRISON | 125000 |
| **TAFTEESH (IRE)** B C KODIAC (GB) - MUDALALAH (IRE) | SHADWELL ESTATE CO | 120000 |
| **RISING SUNSHINE (IRE)** B C DARK ANGEL (IRE) - LITTLE AUDIO (IRE) | PETER ROSS DOYLE BS | 120000 |
| B C HIGH CHAPARRAL (IRE) - LYRA'S DAEMON (GB) | J OSBORNE | 120000 |
| B C HIGH CHAPARRAL (IRE) - CIVILITY CAT (USA) | BBA (IRELAND) | 115000 |
| **WAR WHISPER (IRE)** B C ROYAL APPLAUSE (GB) - FEATHERWEIGHT (IRE) | PETER ROSS DOYLE BS | 115000 |
| **GOLDEN STUNNER (IRE)** CH F DREAM AHEAD (USA) - PINA COLADA (GB) | P SUTONG | 115000 |
| **EJAAZAH (IRE)** B F ACCLAMATION (GB) - ENGLISH BALLET (IRE) | PETER ROSS DOYLE BS | 115000 |
| **VENTURA FALCON (IRE)** B F EXCELLENT ART (GB) - DANISH GEM (GB) | PETER ROSS DOYLE BS | 115000 |
| **SHANGHAI GLORY (IRE)** CH C EXCEED AND EXCEL (AUS) - HECUBA (GB) | SACKVILLEDONALD | 115000 |
| B F HIGH CHAPARRAL (IRE) - UNCHARTED HAVEN (GB) | J OSBORNE | 110000 |
| **KIRI SUNRISE (IRE)** B F IFFRAAJ (GB) - LUCKY FLIRT (USA) | R F RACING | 110000 |
| **PIXEL (IRE)** B F RIP VAN WINKLE (IRE) - HADARAMA (IRE) | F SHAW | 110000 |
| B C POUR MOI (IRE) - BOUNCE (FR) | BBA (IRELAND) | 110000 |
| B F INVINCIBLE SPIRIT (IRE) - ANKLET (IRE) | VENDOR | 110000 |
| **GARTER (IRE)** B F FASTNET ROCK (AUS) - PRINCESS IRIS (IRE) | J WARREN BS | 110000 |
| **OH THIS IS US (IRE)** B C ACCLAMATION (GB) - SHAMWARI LODGE (IRE) | PETER ROSS DOYLE BS | 110000 |
| **PLANTATION (IRE)** B C INVINCIBLE SPIRIT (IRE) - MATULA (IRE) | J WARREN BS | 110000 |
| B C DREAM AHEAD (USA) - TIGER SPICE (GB) | M WALLACE BS | 110000 |
| B F EXCEED AND EXCEL (AUS) - TAARKOD (IRE) | EMERALD BS | 110000 |
| **LONG JOHN SILVER (IRE)** B C CANFORD CLIFFS (IRE) - BILLET (IRE) | F BARBERINI | 105000 |
| **SEVILLE STAR (IRE)** CH C LOPE DE VEGA (IRE) - AL BASAR (USA) | J S BOLGER | 105000 |
| B C IFFRAAJ (GB) - MUJARAH (IRE) | HIGHFIELD FARM | 105000 |
| B C CANFORD CLIFFS (IRE) - SNIPPETS (IRE) | B O'RYAN | 105000 |
| **MEISTER (IRE)** B C MASTERCRAFTSMAN (IRE) - DASH BACK (USA) | M DODS | 105000 |
| **JERSEY BREEZE (IRE)** GR F DARK ANGEL (IRE) - SIXFIELDS FLYER (IRE) | GILL RICHARDSON BS | 105000 |
| **REGAL RESPONSE (IRE)** B C ACCLAMATION (GB) - QALAHARI (IRE) | M DODS | 105000 |
| B C FASTNET ROCK (AUS) - ECOUTILA (USA) | BBA (IRELAND) | 100000 |
| **SERRADURA (IRE)** B F ACCLAMATION (GB) - DAYS OF SUMMER (IRE) | SACKVILLEDONALD | 100000 |
| **CHARTREUSE (IRE)** B F LAWMAN (FR) - BUFERA (IRE) | J WARREN BS | 100000 |
| B F IFFRAAJ (GB) - BURREN ROSE (USA) | D REDVERS | 100000 |
| **WAFI STAR (IRE)** B C SHOWCASING (GB) - OPHELIA'S SONG (GB) | VENDOR | 100000 |
| B F DANEHILL DANCER (IRE) - BARZAH (IRE) | FORM BS | 100000 |
| B C IFFRAAJ (GB) - HOMEGROWN (IRE) | HONG KONG JOCKEY CLUB | 100000 |
| **SEA COMMANDER (IRE)** B C SEA THE STARS (IRE) - MYRINE (IRE) | F CASTRO | 100000 |
| B/BR C DISTORTED HUMOR (USA) - STUPENDOUS MISS (USA) | JOHN FERGUSON BS (P.S.) | 100000 |
| **SIR ROGER MOORE (IRE)** B C KODIAC (GB) - TRULY MAGNIFICENT (USA) | BBA (IRELAND) | 100000 |
| B F CANFORD CLIFFS (IRE) - REVEUSE DE JOUR (IRE) | JAPAN HEALTH SUMMIT | 100000 |
| B C STARSPANGLEDBANNER (AUS) - SHAANBAR (IRE) | PETER ROSS DOYLE BS | 100000 |
| B F POET'S VOICE (GB) - SESMEN (GB) | J FERGUSON | 100000 |
| B F KYLLACHY (GB) - POETICAL (IRE) | ANTHONY STROUD BS | 100000 |
| B C DANEHILL DANCER (IRE) - MOON FLOWER (IRE) | D WACHMAN | 100000 |
| B C FASTNET ROCK (AUS) - MYTH (USA) | FORM BS | 100000 |
| B F RAVEN'S PASS (USA) - LUCKY NORWEGIAN (IRE) | GILL RICHARDSON BS | 95000 |
| **GOLDEN TEMPO (IRE)** B F CANFORD CLIFFS (IRE) - HAUTE VOLTA (FR) | P SUTONG | 95000 |
| B F LILBOURNE LAD (IRE) - MONA EM (IRE) | TINA RAU BS | 95000 |
| B F RAVEN'S PASS (USA) - VASSIANA (FR) | VENDOR | 95000 |
| B G ARCANO (IRE) - THIRD DIMENSION (FR) | T MALONE | 92000 |
| B F CANFORD CLIFFS (IRE) - RENASHAAN (FR) | BBA (IRELAND) | 90000 |
| B C CANFORD CLIFFS (IRE) - ZANZIBAR GIRL (USA) | D K WELD MRCVS | 90000 |
| **RAS AL MAL (IRE)** CH C TAMAYUZ (GB) - MIDNIGHT GLIMMER (IRE) | C GORDON-WATSON BS | 90000 |
| B C HOLY ROMAN EMPEROR (IRE) - LOVE THIRTY (GB) | R COWELL | 90000 |
| B F MOTIVATOR (GB) - BRIDAL PATH (GB) | E LYNAM | 90000 |
| B C HOLY ROMAN EMPEROR (IRE) - REINE VIOLETTE (FR) | GILL RICHARDSON BS | 90000 |
| B F CAPE CROSS (IRE) - CATCH THE SEA (IRE) | FORM BS | 90000 |
| **WAYFARING STRANGER (IRE)** B C LOPE DE VEGA (IRE) - PORTELET (GB) | F BARBERINI | 90000 |
| CH F IFFRAAJ (GB) - LANZANA (IRE) | RABBAH BS | 90000 |
| B C BIG BAD BOB (IRE) - SHINE SILENTLY (IRE) | TRICKLEDOWN STUD | 90000 |
| CH F DUTCH ART (GB) - CLYTHA (GB) | F BARBERINI | 87000 |
| BR C BIG BAD BOB (IRE) - FIRE UP (GB) | A SKIFFINGTON | 87000 |
| CH F SHAMARDAL (USA) - SHAMAYEL (GB) | B O'RYAN | 85000 |
| **SILAS R (IRE)** B C POUR MOI (IRE) - PLAYWITHMYHEART (GB) | J BRUMMITT | 85000 |

| Name and Breeding | Purchaser | Euros |
|---|---|---|
| B C HOLY ROMAN EMPEROR (IRE) - AL SAQIYA (USA) | SACKVILLEDONALD | 85000 |
| **PAPA LUIGI (IRE)** B C ZOFFANY (IRE) - NAMAADHEJ (USA) | PETER ROSS DOYLE BS | 85000 |
| B F DANEHILL DANCER (IRE) - SHAANARA (IRE) | R COWELL | 85000 |
| B F HOLY ROMAN EMPEROR (IRE) - HIGHINDI (GB) | CORMAC MCCORMACK BS | 85000 |
| **HYLAND HEATHER (IRE)** B F LILBOURNE LAD (IRE) - MAIDSERVANT (USA) | R O'RYAN | 85000 |
| B C THEWAYYOUARE (USA) - STORMY LARISSA (IRE) | NARVICK INTERNATIONAL | 85000 |
| **SURBETT (IRE)** B C ROCK OF GIBRALTAR (IRE) - CAUSEWAY QUEEN (IRE) | J LLOYD | 85000 |
| B C SHOWCASING (GB) - NIGHT SYMPHONIE (GB) | M O'TOOLE | 82000 |
| B F HOLY ROMAN EMPEROR (IRE) - FOLLE BLANCHE (USA) | PETER ROSS DOYLE BS | 80000 |
| B F DUKE OF MARMALADE (IRE) - TAKING LIBERTIES (IRE) | J WARREN BS | 80000 |
| B F HIGH CHAPARRAL (IRE) - CRYSTAL CROSSING (IRE) | KERR CO | 80000 |
| B C CANFORD CLIFFS (IRE) - FIRECROSS (IRE) | R HAUGEN (P.S.) | 80000 |
| GR F MASTERCRAFTSMAN (IRE) - GOLDEN LEGACY (IRE) | G DEVLIN | 80000 |
| B C BIG BAD BOB (IRE) - SHINE SILENTLY (IRE) | G LYONS | 80000 |
| B F INVINCIBLE SPIRIT (IRE) - SKIPHALL (GB) | K BURKE | 80000 |
| B C CANFORD CLIFFS (IRE) - DANEHILL'S DREAM (IRE) | NORRIS/HUNTINGDON | 80000 |
| **LUSITANE (IRE)** B F BIG BAD BOB (IRE) - LUNATHEA (IRE) | CANIROLA BS | 80000 |
| **OUR ELTON (USA)** CH C SPEIGHTSTOWN (USA) - WARSAW BALLET (CAN) | SACKVILLEDONALD | 80000 |
| B F NEW APPROACH (IRE) - USHINDI (IRE) | VENDOR | 80000 |
| B C BIG BAD BOB (IRE) - ALL DAY (CHI) | B O'RYAN | 80000 |
| B C POUR MOI (IRE) - AHDAAB (USA) | R HAUGEN | 80000 |
| **SWILLY SUNSET (GB)** B C KYLLACHY (GB) - SPANISH SPRINGS (IRE) | BBA (IRELAND) | 80000 |
| **SANDAHL (IRE)** B C FOOTSTEPSINTHESAND (GB) - LITTLE SCOTLAND (GB) | BBA (IRELAND) | 80000 |
| **ANOTHER TOUCH (GB)** B C ARCANO (IRE) - ALSALWA (IRE) | O RYAN | 80000 |
| B F TEOFILO (IRE) - POSTERITY (IRE) | J KELLY | 80000 |
| B F POUR MOI (IRE) - TRULY MINE (IRE) | CRAMPSCASTLE BS | 80000 |
| **GO AHEAD (IRE)** CH C DREAM AHEAD (USA) - GLADSTONE STREET (IRE) | M CROSSMAN | 75000 |
| CH C LOPE DE VEGA (IRE) - SUPER SUPREME (IND) | G LYONS | 75000 |
| B F LOPE DE VEGA (IRE) - MARIE OSORIO (GB) | PETER ROSS DOYLE BS | 75000 |
| **ARD SAN AER (IRE)** B C ACCLAMATION (GB) - ALLANNAH ABU (GB) | J S BOLGER | 75000 |
| B C DREAM AHEAD (USA) - LEOPARD CREEK (GB) | RABBAH BS | 75000 |
| **HEARTY (IRE)** B C BIG BAD BOB (IRE) - ULANOVA (IRE) | BRIAN GRASSICK BS | 75000 |
| CH F BEAT HOLLOW (GB) - ATIZA (IRE) | CLEMENT/RAU | 75000 |
| **INJAM (IRE)** B C POUR MOI (IRE) - SNIFFLE (IRE) | O ST LAWRENCE | 75000 |
| B C HOLY ROMAN EMPEROR (IRE) - OPEN BOOK (GB) | J CHAN | 75000 |
| BR C BIG BAD BOB (IRE) - CAUSEWAY CHARM (USA) | BADGERS BS | 75000 |
| B C INVINCIBLE SPIRIT (IRE) - HOT TICKET (IRE) | CHURCH FARM | 75000 |
| B F LILBOURNE LAD (IRE) - KHATELA (IRE) | PETER ROSS DOYLE BS | 75000 |
| B C LILBOURNE LAD (IRE) - NISRIYNA (IRE) | G LYONS | 75000 |
| B C KODIAC (GB) - SUPREME SEDUCTRESS (IRE) | D REDVERS | 75000 |
| **AHLAN BIL EMARATI (IRE)** CH C FAST COMPANY (IRE) - LAW REVIEW (IRE) | S HILLEN | 72000 |
| **ACADEMY HOUSE (IRE)** B C KODIAC (GB) - JOYFULLNESS (USA) | A C ELLIOTT BS | 72000 |
| CH C EXCEED AND EXCEL (AUS) - LIXIROVA (FR) | N B BS | 72000 |
| B C PACO BOY (IRE) - SHEER INDULGENCE (FR) | SACKVILLEDONALD | 72000 |
| CH C RAVEN'S PASS (USA) - TURKANA GIRL (GB) | J FERGUSON | 70000 |
| FALCON ANNIE (IRE) B F KODIAC (GB) - FROSTED (GB) | SACKVILLEDONALD | 70000 |
| B F ACCLAMATION (GB) - INTERACTION (GB) | A O'RYAN | 70000 |
| **KOMEDY (IRE)** B F KODIAC (GB) - DANCING JEST (IRE) | BBA (IRELAND) | 70000 |
| **BINT KODIAC (IRE)** B F KODIAC (GB) - MAGNIFICENT BELL (IRE) | RABBAH BS | 70000 |
| B C JEREMY (USA) - STEP WITH STYLE (USA) | B O'RYAN | 70000 |
| B C KODIAC (GB) - BECUILLE (IRE) | G LYONS | 70000 |
| B C DARK ANGEL (IRE) - HEADBOROUGH LASS (IRE) | B O'RYAN | 70000 |
| B F ZOFFANY (IRE) - TROIS GRACES (USA) | P REED | 70000 |
| B C ACCLAMATION (GB) - GOLD BUBBLES (USA) | MARK JOHNSTON RACING | 70000 |
| B F ACCLAMATION (GB) - DIVINE AUTHORITY (IRE) | SACKVILLEDONALD | 70000 |
| B C ACCLAMATION (GB) - WINGED HARRIET (IRE) | J FERGUSON | 70000 |
| B F INVINCIBLE SPIRIT (IRE) - SLIP DANCE (IRE) | VENDOR | 70000 |
| **HOLY BOY (IRE)** B C HOLY ROMAN EMPEROR (IRE) - SISTER GOLIGHTLY (GB) | BLANDFORD BS | 70000 |
| **ZIPPITY DO DA (IRE)** B F MAKFI (GB) - POLISH ROMANCE (USA) | W MCCREERY | 68000 |
| **ZHANNA (IRE)** B F HOLY ROMAN EMPEROR (IRE) - PORTENTOUS (GB) | KERN/LILLINGSTON ASS | 68000 |
| **SPECTRE (IRE)** B C DREAM AHEAD (USA) - LIDANSKI (IRE) | F CASTRO | 67000 |

# HIGH-PRICED YEARLINGS OF 2014 AT DONCASTER

**The following yearlings realised 39,047 Guineas and over at Doncaster Sales in 2014:-**

| Name and Breeding | Purchaser | Guineas |
|---|---|---|
| GR C STARSPANGLEDBANNER (AUS) - ULTIMATE BEST (GB) | D REDVERS | 219047 |
| B F CANFORD CLIFFS (IRE) - DECORATIVE (IRE) | T NERSES | 171428 |
| **TABARRAK (IRE)** B C ACCLAMATION (GB) - BAHATI (IRE) | PETER ROSS DOYLE BS | 171428 |
| B F ZOFFANY (IRE) - MURAVKA (IRE) | CHASEMORE FARM | 142857 |
| **TASHWEEQ (IRE)** B C BIG BAD BOB (IRE) - DANCE HALL GIRL (IRE) | SHADWELL ESTATE CO | 142857 |
| **TAQDEER (IRE)** CH C FAST COMPANY (IRE) - BRIGANTIA (GB) | SHADWELL ESTATE CO | 133333 |
| B C ZEBEDEE (GB) - KIVA (GB) | A SKIFFINGTON | 133333 |
| B C CANFORD CLIFFS (IRE) - CHILD BRIDE (USA) | T NERSES | 133333 |
| **TARAABUT (IRE)** B C LILBOURNE LAD (IRE) - CUILAPHUCA (IRE) | PETER ROSS DOYLE BS | 123809 |
| B C DREAM AHEAD (USA) - POPPY SEED (GB) | T NERSES | 123809 |
| **TAWWAAQ (IRE)** GR F ZEBEDEE (GB) - KILLINALLAN (GB) | SHADWELL ESTATE CO | 114285 |
| **AHDAATH (IRE)** B F KODIAC (GB) - SONNY SUNSHINE (GB) | SHADWELL ESTATE CO | 114285 |
| B C ZOFFANY (IRE) - CHAMELEON (GB) | A SKIFFINGTON | 114285 |
| B C ACCLAMATION (GB) - CLASSIC LEGEND (GB) | R O'GORMAN | 114285 |
| B F EXCEED AND EXCEL (AUS) - TROPICAL PARADISE (IRE) | MANDORE INTERNATIONAL | 114285 |
| CH F DUTCH ART (GB) - AGONY AND ECSTASY (GB) | F BARBERINI | 109523 |
| B C RIP VAN WINKLE (IRE) - I HEARYOU KNOCKING (IRE) | D REDVERS | 104761 |
| **ALBARAAHA (IRE)** B F IFFRAAJ (GB) - TOLZEY (USA) | SHADWELL ESTATE CO | 104761 |
| B C CANFORD CLIFFS (IRE) - YANDINA (IRE) | D WACHMAN | 100000 |
| CH C COMPTON PLACE (GB) - HELIOGRAPH (GB) | HKJC | 100000 |
| B F ZOFFANY (IRE) - PROMISE OF LOVE (GB) | PETER ROSS DOYLE BS | 95238 |
| B C DARK ANGEL (IRE) - WHITE DAFFODIL (IRE) | PETER ROSS DOYLE BS | 90476 |
| CH C ZOFFANY (IRE) - TROPICAL LADY (IRE) | BLANDFORD BS | 90476 |
| **ILLUMINATE (IRE)** B F ZOFFANY (IRE) - QUEEN OF STARS (USA) | PETER ROSS DOYLE BS | 90476 |
| **TAWDHEEF (IRE)** BR C ZEBEDEE (GB) - DUCHESS OF FOXLAND (IRE) | SHADWELL ESTATE CO | 87619 |
| **TAZAAYUD (GB)** B C KODIAC (GB) - ESTEEMED LADY (IRE) | SHADWELL ESTATE CO | 85714 |
| B C SHOWCASING (GB) - CHEEKY GIRL (GB) | CRAMPSCASTLE BS | 85714 |
| **PROJECTION (GB)** B C ACCLAMATION (GB) - SPOTLIGHT (GB) | J J WARREN | 85714 |
| B C EXCELLENT ART (GB) - CHEAP THRILLS (GB) | RICHARDS | 85714 |
| CH C EXCEED AND EXCEL (AUS) - HILL WELCOME (GB) | SACKVILLEDONALD | 80952 |
| B F BAHAMIAN BOUNTY (GB) - LAUREN LOUISE (GB) | D REDVERS | 80952 |
| B C FAST COMPANY (IRE) - ANN'S ANNIE (IRE) | BBA (IRELAND) | 80952 |
| B C KODIAC (GB) - SEEKING THE FUN (USA) | S HILLEN | 80952 |
| GR C DARK ANGEL (IRE) - OBAMA RULE (IRE) | VENDOR | 80952 |
| **TADAAWOL (GB)** B C KYLLACHY (GB) - BRIGHT EDGE (GB) | PETER ROSS DOYLE BS | 78095 |
| B F HIGH CHAPARRAL (IRE) - TEDDY BEARS PICNIC (GB) | S LYNAM | 78095 |
| B F FAST COMPANY (IRE) - TAWAAFUR (GB) | D REDVERS | 78095 |
| B C ACCLAMATION (GB) - PHOTO FLASH (IRE) | J J WARREN | 78095 |
| **ZEBEDAIOS (IRE)** B C ZEBEDEE (GB) - REFUSE TO GIVE UP (IRE) | P MARTIN | 76190 |
| B F IFFRAAJ (GB) - SPIRITUAL AIR (GB) | D REDVERS | 74285 |
| **SKY OF STARS (IRE)** B C FROZEN POWER (IRE) - SO SO LUCKY (IRE) | PETER ROSS DOYLE BS | 71428 |
| **VIBRANT CHORDS (GB)** B C POET'S VOICE (GB) - LOVELY THOUGHT (GB) | H CANDY | 71428 |
| **SPEY SECRET (IRE)** BR C KYLLACHY (GB) - CHIAREZZA (AUS) | SACKVILLEDONALD | 71428 |
| B C ELNADIM (USA) - DUQUESA (IRE) | HIGHFIELD FARM | 69523 |
| **A MOMENTOFMADNESS (GB)** B C ELNADIM (USA) - ROYAL BLUSH (GB) | GEOFFREY HOWSON BS | 68571 |
| **SENSE OF SNOW (IRE)** CH C KYLLACHY (GB) - MISS SMILLA (GB) | W MUIR | 68571 |
| **TAWAKKOL (GB)** B C FIREBREAK (GB) - DAYVILLE (USA) | SHADWELL ESTATE CO | 66666 |
| **MOGAZ (GB)** GR C SAKHEE'S SECRET (GB) - TINA'S SPIRIT (IRE) | SHADWELL ESTATE CO | 66666 |
| B C ROYAL APPLAUSE (GB) - SEMAPHORE (GB) | J J WARREN | 66666 |
| CH C STARSPANGLEDBANNER (AUS) - MILTON OF CAMPSIE (GB) | VENDOR | 66666 |
| B C POET'S VOICE (GB) - MISS LACEY (IRE) | R O'GORMAN | 66666 |
| **SUMOU (IRE)** B C ARCANO (IRE) - THREE TIMES (GB) | SHADWELL ESTATE CO | 66666 |
| **AUXILIARY (GB)** B C FAST COMPANY (IRE) - LADY XARA (IRE) | J J WARREN | 66666 |
| **QAREEN (GB)** B C KYLLACHY (GB) - VIRGINIA HALL (GB) | SHADWELL ESTATE CO | 66666 |
| B C DANDY MAN (IRE) - LA BATAILLE (USA) | SACKVILLEDONALD | 66666 |
| B C SHOWCASING (GB) - CARSULAE (IRE) | BBA (IRELAND) | 66666 |
| **PHOENIX BEAT (GB)** B F PHOENIX REACH (IRE) - BEAT SEVEN (GB) | G KELLEWAY | 66666 |
| **JAWAAYIZ (GB)** B F KODIAC (GB) - SILKENVEIL (IRE) | SHADWELL ESTATE CO | 64761 |
| B F KYLLACHY (GB) - EUCHARIST (IRE) | RABBAH BS | 64761 |
| B C CANFORD CLIFFS (IRE) - THAT'S MY STYLE (GB) | WILL EDMEADES BS | 61904 |
| B C MONSIEUR BOND (IRE) - EXISTENTIALIST (GB) | RICHARD KNIGHT BS | 61904 |
| **RANTAN (IRE)** B C KODIAC (GB) - PEACE TALKS (GB) | H D ATKINSON | 61904 |
| **TURAATHY (IRE)** B F LILBOURNE LAD (IRE) - KEY GIRL (IRE) | SHADWELL ESTATE CO | 61904 |
| B F KODIAC (GB) - SHEILA BLIGE (GB) | RABBAH BS | 59047 |
| B C DANDY MAN (IRE) - ROMARCA (IRE) | HIGHFIELD FARM | 59047 |
| **RYAN THE GIANT (GB)** B C FASTNET ROCK (AUS) - COMERAINCOMESHINE (IRE) | PETER ROSS DOYLE BS | 59047 |
| **GREAT COMPANY (IRE)** B C FAST COMPANY (IRE) - SUNLIT SILENCE (IRE) | M CROSSMAN | 57142 |

| Name and Breeding | Purchaser | Guineas |
|---|---|---|
| CH F LE HAVRE (IRE) - OCCITANE (GB) | ANTHONY STROUD BS | 57142 |
| B C COMPTON PLACE (GB) - CHURCH MELODY (GB) | RICHARD KNIGHT BS | 57142 |
| **SHARRIS (IRE)** B C ZEBEDEE (GB) - ALSHIMAAL (IRE) | SHADWELL ESTATE CO | 57142 |
| **GIRLS IN A BENTLEY (GB)** B F ACCLAMATION (GB) - LAURELEI (IRE) | A STROUD | 57142 |
| B C DANDY MAN (IRE) - ROSKEEN (IRE) | T NERSES | 57142 |
| **PRESS GANG (GB)** B C MOUNT NELSON (GB) - RUTBA (GB) | A SKIFFINGTON | 57142 |
| **ASHJAN (GB)** B C MEDICEAN (GB) - VIOLET (IRE) | GILL RICHARDSON BS | 55238 |
| **SOMERS LAD (IRE)** B C LILBOURNE LAD (IRE) - SOMAGGIA (IRE) | PETER ROSS DOYLE BS | 55238 |
| **LEMBIT AND BUTLER (IRE)** B C LILBOURNE LAD (IRE) - FATHOMING (USA) | SACKVILLEDONALD | 55238 |
| B F COMPTON PLACE (GB) - CANUKEEPASECRET (GB) | HIGHFIELD FARM | 55238 |
| BR C BUSHRANGER (IRE) - DREAM DATE (IRE) | BBA (IRELAND) | 54285 |
| B C LILBOURNE LAD (IRE) - MONTEFINO (IRE) | A DUFFIELD | 53333 |
| **HIDDEN TREASURES (GB)** CH F ZOFFANY (IRE) - SWYNFORD PLEASURE (GB) | F BARBERINI | 53333 |
| **MADRINHO (IRE)** CH C FROZEN POWER (IRE) - PERFECTLY CLEAR (USA) | PETER ROSS DOYLE BS | 52380 |
| CH C ZEBEDEE (GB) - OUR SHEILA (GB) | GROVE STUD | 52380 |
| B F FAST COMPANY (IRE) - LUCKY LEIGH (GB) | T MALONE | 52380 |
| **SEARCH FOR ED (GB)** B C MONSIEUR BOND (IRE) - SPONTANEITY (IRE) | A STROUD | 52380 |
| **SPACE MOUNTAIN (GB)** B C SEA THE STARS (IRE) - RIPPLES MAID (GB) | MARK JOHNSTON RACING | 52380 |
| **MISTY LORD (IRE)** B C LILBOURNE LAD (IRE) - MISTY NIGHT (IRE) | J LLOYD | 51428 |
| **ATLANTIC SUN (GB)** B C RODERIC O'CONNOR (IRE) - ROBEMA (GB) | PETER ROSS DOYLE BS | 49523 |
| CH F DUTCH ART (GB) - MY GIRL JODE (GB) | ANTHONY STROUD BS | 49523 |
| **SAFE VOYAGE (IRE)** B C FAST COMPANY (IRE) - SHISHANGAAN (IRE) | RICHARD KNIGHT BS | 49523 |
| **SIR DUDLEY (IRE)** B C ARCANO (IRE) - ROSY DUDLEY (IRE) | A STROUD | 49523 |
| **TASLEET (GB)** B C SHOWCASING (GB) - BIRD KEY (GB) | SHADWELL ESTATE CO | 49523 |
| B C KYLLACHY (GB) - DUBAI BOUNTY (GB) | SACKVILLEDONALD | 49523 |
| **SIGN OF THE KODIAC (IRE)** B C KODIAC (GB) - SUMMER MAGIC (IRE) | A STROUD | 47619 |
| **DUBAI ME DIAMONDS (IRE)** B C ACCLAMATION (GB) - HEN NIGHT (IRE) | BRIAN ELLISON RACING | 47619 |
| GR C DANDY MAN (IRE) - RED RIDDLE (IRE) | RABBAH BS | 47619 |
| B F ACCLAMATION (GB) - MAID TO ORDER (IRE) | HIGHFIELD FARM | 47619 |
| **ZLATAN (IRE)** B C DARK ANGEL (IRE) - GUARD HILL (USA) | SACKVILLEDONALD | 47619 |
| **SIR RODERIC (IRE)** B C RODERIC O'CONNOR (IRE) - BEGIN THE BEGUINE (IRE) | GEOFFREY HOWSON BS | 47619 |
| B C SIYOUNI (FR) - EMULATE (GB) | M O'TOOLE | 47619 |
| **ARCTIC ANGEL (IRE)** B C DARK ANGEL (IRE) - CHARLENE LACY (IRE) | PETER ROSS DOYLE BS | 47619 |
| CH C ZOFFANY (IRE) - FRABJOUS (GB) | BBA (IRELAND) | 47619 |
| B F DANEHILL DANCER (IRE) - RIVER FLOW (USA) | F STACK | 47619 |
| CH C COMPTON PLACE (GB) - DANCE AWAY (GB) | C C BARRIERS | 47619 |
| B C MAKFI (GB) - PRESENT DANGER (GB) | D REDVERS | 47619 |
| B C INTENSE FOCUS (USA) - ROYAL ESTEEM (GB) | GILL RICHARDSON BS | 45714 |
| GR/RO C ZEBEDEE (GB) - BREAK OF DAWN (USA) | JILL LAMB BS | 45714 |
| B F DARK ANGEL (IRE) - JO BO BO (IRE) | R KENT | 45714 |
| B C FAST COMPANY (IRE) - TRENTINI (IRE) | RICHARD KNIGHT BS | 45714 |
| B C FROZEN POWER (IRE) - TAQARUB (IRE) | RICHARD KNIGHT BS | 45714 |
| **DEGAS BRONZE (GB)** B F SHOWCASING (GB) - LOCAL FANCY (GB) | B O'RYAN | 45714 |
| B C HOLY ROMAN EMPEROR (IRE) - LISA GHERARDINI (IRE) | M O'TOOLE | 44761 |
| B F KODIAC (GB) - BALM (GB) | S LYNAM | 43809 |
| **PHANTOM FLIPPER (GB)** CH C BAHAMIAN BOUNTY (GB) - ARTISTIC LICENSE (IRE) | PETER ROSS DOYLE BS | 43809 |
| **REGAL GAIT (IRE)** B C TAGULA (IRE) - BABYLONIAN (GB) | H CANDY | 42857 |
| B C JEREMY (USA) - SWIZZLE STICK (IRE) | S LYNAM | 42857 |
| CH C RAVEN'S PASS (USA) - HOLLY'S KID (USA) | VENDOR | 42857 |
| **REFLEKTOR (IRE)** CH C BAHAMIAN BOUNTY (GB) - BABY BUNTING (GB) | SACKVILLEDONALD | 42857 |
| **REBEL RAISER (GB)** B C KHELEYF (USA) - TRUMP STREET (GB) | P CUNNINGHAM | 42857 |
| B F KYLLACHY (GB) - LUCY LIMELITES (GB) | J CULLINAN | 42857 |
| **PETRONAS (GB)** CH C PASTORAL PURSUITS (GB) - GILT LINKED (GB) | SACKVILLEDONALD | 41904 |
| **LOADING (IRE)** B C ARCANO (IRE) - SALLY WOOD (CAN) | MANDORE INTERNATIONAL | 41904 |
| B F MASTERCRAFTSMAN (IRE) - ABBEYLEIX LADY (IRE) | BLANDFORD BS | 41904 |
| B C DREAM AHEAD (USA) - CHINESE WALL (IRE) | DEREK SHAW RACING | 41904 |
| CH C CAPE BLANCO (IRE) - A MIND OF HER OWN (IRE) | O COLE | 40952 |
| CH C ARCANO (IRE) - BOND DEAL (IRE) | SACKVILLEDONALD | 40000 |
| B C KODIAC (GB) - SHE'S A MINX (IRE) | VENDOR | 40000 |
| **ROCK ON (IRE)** CH C ROCK OF GIBRALTAR (IRE) - SPECTACULAR SHOW (IRE) | S HILLEN | 40000 |
| B F KODIAC (GB) - PEARLY BROOKS (GB) | MCCALMONT BS | 40000 |
| **LONDON REBEL (IRE)** CH F ARCANO (IRE) - PICCADILLY FILLY (IRE) | P CUNNINGHAM | 40000 |
| B F KODIAC (GB) - ATISHOO (IRE) | RICHARD KNIGHT BS | 40000 |
| B C JEREMY (USA) - POULKOVO (IRE) | BBA (IRELAND) | 40000 |
| B C SHOWCASING (GB) - BE DECISIVE (GB) | J FRETWELL | 39047 |

# HIGH-PRICED YEARLINGS OF 2014 AT TATTERSALLS IRELAND SALES

**The following yearlings realised 26,000 euros and over at Tattersalls Ireland Sales in 2014:-**

| Name and Breeding | Purchaser | Euros |
|---|---|---|
| **VIREN'S ARMY (IRE)** B C TWIRLING CANDY (USA) - BLUE ANGEL (IRE) | PETER ROSS DOYLE BS | 115000 |
| B C DARK ANGEL (IRE) - BOGINI (IRE) | B O'RYAN | 110000 |
| B C KODIAC (GB) - FIKRAH (GB) | R GORELL | 85000 |
| **KAJAKI (IRE)** GR C MASTERCRAFTSMAN (IRE) - NO QUEST (IRE) | HILLEN RYAN | 85000 |
| B F AZAMOUR (IRE) - BRIDAL DANCE (IRE) | A SKIFFINGTON | 80000 |
| B F ACCLAMATION (GB) - NEW DEAL (GB) | D REDVERS | 67000 |
| **MODELLO (IRE)** B F INTIKHAB (USA) - PRECIOUS CITIZEN (USA) | GARY MOORE RACING | 65000 |
| B C PRESENTING (GB) - POMME TIEPY (FR) | A MURPHY | 65000 |
| B C FLEMENSFIRTH (USA) - DABAYA (IRE) | JOHN O'BYRNE | 62000 |
| **INDIAN PURSUIT (IRE)** GR C ZEBEDEE (GB) - SAMPERS (IRE) | RICHARD KNIGHT BS | 60000 |
| B G ROBIN DES CHAMPS (FR) - ROLI FLIGHT (IRE) | ALAN HARTE BS | 60000 |
| B F FROZEN POWER (IRE) - SPRING SURPRISE (GB) | BALLYHANE STUD | 56000 |
| B C ACCLAMATION (GB) - PRETTY DEMANDING (IRE) | C MARNANE | 52000 |
| B F ZEBEDEE (GB) - BREEDJ (IRE) | E LYNAM | 52000 |
| BR G KAYF TARA (GB) - KERADA (FR) | HIGHFLYER BS | 50000 |
| B/BR C ELUSIVE PIMPERNEL (USA) - SPIRITVILLE (IRE) | A SKIFFINGTON | 50000 |
| B C KODIAC (GB) - RIGHT AFTER MOYNE (IRE) | R NG | 50000 |
| **MAJESTIQUE (IRE)** BR F HIGH CHAPARRAL (IRE) - GERMANE (GB) | BRIAN GRASSICK BS | 49000 |
| B C CAPTAIN RIO (GB) - INOURTHOUGHTS (IRE) | SACKVILLEDONALD | 48000 |
| B C INVINCIBLE SPIRIT (IRE) - RUSSIAN ROUBLES (IRE) | C MARNANE | 48000 |
| B F KODIAC (GB) - RED REMANSO (IRE) | PETER ROSS DOYLE BS | 48000 |
| GR F MARTALINE (GB) - MISS POUTINE (FR) | VENDOR | 48000 |
| GR C ALFRED NOBEL (IRE) - MY GIRL LISA (USA) | KARL BURKE RACING | 47000 |
| BR F POET'S VOICE (GB) - HEAR MY CRY (USA) | J LLOYD | 47000 |
| **STYLISH BOY (GB)** B C PACO BOY (IRE) - BLACK BARONESS (GB) | MIDDLEHAM PARK RACING | 47000 |
| CH C EQUIANO (FR) - PULSATE (GB) | BBA (IRELAND) | 46000 |
| B F DARK ANGEL (IRE) - TIMBRE (GB) | KERN/LILLINGSTON ASS | 45000 |
| B C ZEBEDEE (GB) - ZARA'S GIRL (IRE) | B O'RYAN | 45000 |
| GR C ZEBEDEE (GB) - VIGOROUS (IRE) | CHURCH FARM STABLES | 45000 |
| **COMPEL (FR)** CH F EXCEED AND EXCEL (AUS) - GOOD HOPE (GER) | BRIAN GRASSICK BS | 45000 |
| **WHISPERING SOUL (IRE)** B F MAJESTIC MISSILE (IRE) - BELLE OF THE BLUES (IRE) | ANN DUFFIELD BS | 45000 |
| **SILVER STREAK (IRE)** GR C DARK ANGEL (IRE) - HAPPY TALK (IRE) | ANN DUFFIELD BS | 45000 |
| B C FLEMENSFIRTH (USA) - ROAMING (IRE) | BOBBY O'RYAN | 45000 |
| GR C SIR PERCY (GB) - CONCILIATORY (GB) | J M OXX | 44000 |
| B F RIP VAN WINKLE (IRE) - CHRONICLE (GB) | VENDOR | 44000 |
| B/RO F ZEBEDEE (GB) - SHAUNA'S PRINCESS (IRE) | BBA (IRELAND) | 43000 |
| B G BENEFICIAL (GB) - FASHION'S WORTH (IRE) | JOHN O'BYRNE | 43000 |
| CH F STOWAWAY (GB) - GUIGONE (FR) | VENDOR | 42000 |
| CH C SHOLOKHOV (IRE) - KARUMA (GER) | H KIRK | 42000 |
| **CRAFTED JEWEL (IRE)** GR F MASTERCRAFTSMAN (IRE) - ADORING (IRE) | CHINOOK FARM | 41000 |
| CH C DUKE OF MARMALADE (IRE) - EMBARK (GB) | BBA (IRELAND) | 41000 |
| B/BR G BENEFICIAL (GB) - TANIT LADY (IRE) | MARGARET O'TOOLE | 40000 |
| CH G PRESENTING (GB) - NATIVE MONK (IRE) | HIGHFLYER BS | 40000 |
| B C LILBOURNE LAD (IRE) - BREACH OF PEACE (USA) | A O'RYAN | 40000 |
| BR F BIG BAD BOB (IRE) - MONTBRETIA (GB) | BRIAN ELLISON RACING | 40000 |
| **G'DAY AUSSIE (GB)** B C AUSSIE RULES (USA) - MOI AUSSI (USA) | BRIAN ELLISON RACING | 40000 |
| B C ELNADIM (USA) - ELIZA DOOLITTLE (GB) | PETER ROSS DOYLE BS | 40000 |
| B C DARK ANGEL (IRE) - NINA BLINI (GB) | YEOMANSTOWN STUD | 40000 |
| BR F KHELEYF (USA) - PERINO (IRE) | RICHARD KNIGHT BS | 40000 |
| B F ACCLAMATION (GB) - COME WHAT MAY (GB) | A BALDING | 40000 |
| BR F BIG BAD BOB (IRE) - DESERT ALCHEMY (IRE) | J BRUMMITT | 40000 |
| CH G STOWAWAY (GB) - FAIRY DAWN (IRE) | T LACEY | 40000 |
| **STORMY ART (IRE)** B C EXCELLENT ART (GB) - MAYBE GRACE (IRE) | M DODS | 39000 |
| B C CANFORD CLIFFS (IRE) - ALENTEJA (IRE) | F BARBERINI | 39000 |
| B F WHIPPER (USA) - SPY EYE (USA) | A LYNAM | 38000 |
| **SACRED ROCK (IRE)** B G ROCK OF GIBRALTAR (IRE) - SNOWPALM (GB) | RAFFLES RACING | 38000 |
| **DYNAMIC TRIO (FR)** B/BR G VOIX DU NORD (FR) - LADY JANNINA (GB) | BROWN ISLAND STABLES | 38000 |
| B C SHOLOKHOV (IRE) - SUNSHINE STORY (IRE) | ALAN HARTE BS | 37000 |
| **PRINCESS DJEYNA (IRE)** CH F DANEHILL DANCER (IRE) - SUSTAIN (GB) | D WACHMAN | 37000 |
| GR F MASTERCRAFTSMAN (IRE) - GRETA D'ARGENT (IRE) | M JOHNSTON | 37000 |
| **NUCKY THOMPSON (GB)** B C COCKNEY REBEL (IRE) - VINO VERITAS (USA) | P CUNNINGHAM | 37000 |
| **TIME WARP (GB)** CH C ARCHIPENKO (USA) - HERE TO ETERNITY (USA) | J BRUMMITT | 37000 |
| CH F DUKE OF MARMALADE (IRE) - TRUE JOY (IRE) | C GORDON WATSON | 36000 |
| B C KODIAC (GB) - ANTHYLLIS (IRE) | KILRONAN STUD | 36000 |
| **GREAT PAGE (IRE)** B F RODERIC O'CONNOR (IRE) - AREEDA (IRE) | PETER ROSS DOYLE BS | 35000 |
| B F SHOWCASING (GB) - UNASUMING (IRE) | JC BS | 35000 |
| **INFORMATEUR (FR)** B C MARESCA SORRENTO (FR) - ISARELLA (GER) | NIALL HANNITY | 35000 |

| Name and Breeding | Purchaser | Euros |
|---|---|---|
| B F FAST COMPANY (IRE) - ALLTHERIGHTMOVES (IRE) | RICHARD KNIGHT BS | 35000 |
| GR F MASTERCRAFTSMAN (IRE) - LA CHASSOTTE (FR) | F BARBERINI | 35000 |
| B F FROZEN POWER (IRE) - SAGA CELEBRE (FR) | A STROUD BS | 35000 |
| B C KODIAC (GB) - RINNEEN (IRE) | A O'RYAN | 35000 |
| B C EXCELLENT ART (GB) - ENDLESS PEACE (IRE) | A O'RYAN | 35000 |
| **GIN IN THE INN (IRE)** B C ALFRED NOBEL (IRE) - NOSE ONE'S WAY (IRE) | O'RYAN/FAHEY | 35000 |
| B C THEWAYYOUARE (USA) - TRESPASS (GB) | R NG | 35000 |
| GR F DARK ANGEL (IRE) - ISLAND SUNSET (IRE) | A O'RYAN | 35000 |
| B G BEAT HOLLOW (GB) - SAMBRE (FR) | MARGARET O'TOOLE | 35000 |
| B F KODIAC (GB) - SENSASSE (IRE) | GAY BROOK LODGE | 35000 |
| CH G MIDNIGHT LEGEND (GB) - LADY SAMANTHA (GB) | FABRICATED PRODUCTS LTD | 35000 |
| CH F SHOWCASING (GB) - MANSIYA (GB) | GRANGEBARRY | 34000 |
| B G FLEMENSFIRTH (USA) - DENWOMAN (IRE) | FABRICATED PRODUCTS LTD | 34000 |
| **RIAL (IRE)** B F DARK ANGEL (IRE) - COIN BOX (GB) | J LLOYD | 33000 |
| B G OSCAR (IRE) - SUPREME VON PRES (IRE) | ALAN HARTE BS | 33000 |
| CH C PACO BOY (IRE) - GALICUIX (GB) | A SKIFFINGTON | 33000 |
| B G KHELEYF (USA) - CROZON (GB) | BRIAN ELLISON RACING | 33000 |
| B G FLEMENSFIRTH (USA) - LADY PETIT (IRE) | VENDOR | 33000 |
| B G MILAN (GB) - ROCK ME GENTLY (GB) | JAMES MERNAGH | 33000 |
| B G SHANTOU (USA) - KNOCKARA ONE (IRE) | WESTWINDS STABLES | 32000 |
| B F FASTNET ROCK (AUS) - JAZZ BABY (IRE) | BBA (IRELAND) | 32000 |
| B C VALE OF YORK (IRE) - LIVADIYA (IRE) | M JOHNSTON | 32000 |
| B G MAHLER (GB) - MELODY THYME (IRE) | CALLUNA HOUSE STABLES | 32000 |
| B/BR F BIG BAD BOB (IRE) - FASHIONISTA (IRE) | VENDOR | 32000 |
| **SOMETHING NEW (IRE)** CH C ROCK OF GIBRALTAR (IRE) - PASSIONFORFASHION (IRE) | A BOTTI | 31000 |
| B C TAMAYUZ (GB) - CANNIKIN (IRE) | D FARRINGTON | 31000 |
| B G FLEMENSFIRTH (USA) - LABOC (GB) | ALAN HARTE BS | 30000 |
| B F ZEBEDEE (GB) - PURE FOLLY (IRE) | CHURCH FARM STABLES | 30000 |
| **CALDER PRINCE (IRE)** BR C DARK ANGEL (IRE) - FLAME OF IRELAND (IRE) | SACKVILLEDONALD | 30000 |
| GR C RODERIC O'CONNOR (IRE) - INDUS RIDGE (IRE) | VENDOR | 30000 |
| B G STOWAWAY (GB) - SHARPS EXPRESS (IRE) | JIM PAYNE | 30000 |
| B G BEAT HOLLOW (GB) - MISS DENMAN (IRE) | VENDOR | 30000 |
| B C KODIAC (GB) - CABOPINO (IRE) | SACKVILLEDONALD | 30000 |
| B G SHANTOU (USA) - CHALICE WELLS (GB) | KEVIN ROSS BS | 30000 |
| B C NOTNOWCATO (GB) - HOPE ISLAND (IRE) | GILL RICHARDSON BS | 30000 |
| CH F LOPE DE VEGA (IRE) - SALPIGLOSSIS (GER) | T MALONE | 30000 |
| B F YEATS (IRE) - BLEU CIEL ET BLANC (FR) | VENDOR | 30000 |
| B C AQLAAM (GB) - MEAON (IRE) | C MARNANE | 29000 |
| **TEKAP (FR)** CH G KAPGARDE (FR) - TEXTUELLE (FR) | MOUNT EATON STUD | 28000 |
| CH G BENEFICIAL (GB) - GIVEHERTIME (IRE) | HERE TO WIN SYNDICATE | 28000 |
| B C FOOTSTEPSINTHESAND (GB) - ZAWARIQ (IRE) | C GORDON WATSON BS | 28000 |
| B C YEATS (IRE) - ELAYOON (USA) | RICHARD KNIGHT BS | 28000 |
| **ARCTIC ROYAL (IRE)** CH F FROZEN POWER (IRE) - BRONZE QUEEN (IRE) | ANN DUFFIELD BS | 28000 |
| GR C ZEBEDEE (GB) - JAYARBEE (IRE) | BELIAR BS | 28000 |
| BR C ALFRED NOBEL (IRE) - TALLASSEE (GB) | K BURKE | 28000 |
| B C LILBOURNE LAD (IRE) - MOOCHING ALONG (IRE) | C GORDON WATSON BS | 28000 |
| B C FROZEN POWER (IRE) - SPRINGFORT (IRE) | BBA (IRELAND) | 28000 |
| **ICE DREAM (IRE)** B F FROZEN POWER (IRE) - MIKES BABY (IRE) | SACKVILLEDONALD | 28000 |
| B C COMPTON PLACE (GB) - TRUMPET LILY (GB) | A O'RYAN | 28000 |
| B C MOUNT NELSON (GB) - APPLE SAUCE (GB) | PETER ROSS DOYLE BS | 27000 |
| B F RIP VAN WINKLE (IRE) - HURRY HOME HYDEE (USA) | JANDA BS | 27000 |
| **BALTIC RAIDER (IRE)** B G BALTIC KING (GB) - FRIPPET (IRE) | M DODS | 27000 |
| CH C CAPTAIN RIO (GB) - ANKLESOCKS (IRE) | M DODS | 27000 |
| B C ZEBEDEE (GB) - BOBBY JANE (GB) | G LYONS | 27000 |
| BR C MILAN (GB) - DERRAVARAGH NATIVE (IRE) | PETER ROSS DOYLE BS | 27000 |
| B C ELNADIM (USA) - DA'S WISH (IRE) | BBA (IRELAND) | 26000 |
| GR C DARK ANGEL (IRE) - BINT AL HAMMOUR (IRE) | B O'RYAN | 26000 |
| B C ZEBEDEE (GB) - ARTEMIS CULTURE (USA) | CLIVE COX RACING | 26000 |
| B F FOOTSTEPSINTHESAND (GB) - FILLTHEGOBLETAGAIN (IRE) | C GORDON WATSON BS | 26000 |
| B C JEREMY (USA) - COILL CRI (IRE) | M DODS | 26000 |
| B C LORD SHANAKILL (USA) - CHERRY CREEK (IRE) | VENDOR | 26000 |
| CH C STOWAWAY (GB) - GLEANNTAN (IRE) | BARLEY BS | 26000 |
| BR F BIG BAD BOB (IRE) - KRISTAL XENIA (IRE) | B O'RYAN | 26000 |
| B C MILAN (GB) - BLESSINGINDISGUISE (IRE) | ORMOND BS | 26000 |
| **KENDARLYSA (FR)** B F KENDARGENT (FR) - ARSILA (IRE) | CHURCH FARM | 26000 |
| B F KODIAC (GB) - THAISY (USA) | P D EVANS | 26000 |
| B C GOLD WELL (GB) - STATEABLE CASE (IRE) | A MURPHY | 26000 |

## 2000 GUINEAS STAKES (3y) Newmarket-1 mile

| Year | Owner | Winner and Price | Jockey | Trainer | Second | Third | Ran | Time |
|---|---|---|---|---|---|---|---|---|
| 1973 | Mrs B Davis's | **MON FILS** (50/1) | F Durr | R Hannon | Noble Decree | Sharp Edge | 18 | 1 42.97 |
| 1974 | Mme M Berger's | **NONOALCO** (19/2) | Y Saint Martin | F Boutin | Giacometti | Apalachee | 12 | 1 39.53 |
| 1975 | C d'Alessio's | **BOLKONSKI** (33/1) | G Dettori | H Cecil | Grundy | Dominion | 24 | 1 39.53 |
| 1976 | C d'Alessio's | **WOLLOW** (evens) | G Dettori | H Cecil | Vitiges | Thieving Demon | 17 | 1 38.09 |
| 1977 | N Schibbye's | **NEBBIOLO** (20/1) | G Curran | K Prendergast | Tachypous | The Minstrel | 18 | 1 38.54 |
| 1978 | J Hayter's | **ROLAND GARDENS** (28/1) | F Durr | D Sasse | Remainder Man | Weth Nan | 19 | 1 47.33 |
| 1979 | A Shead's | **TAP ON WOOD** (20/1) | S Cauthen | B Hills | Kris | Young Generation | 20 | 1 43.60 |
| 1980 | K Abdulla's | **KNOWN FACT** (14/1) | W Carson | J Tree | Posse | Night Alert | 14 | 1 40.46 |
| | (Nureyev finished first but was disqualified) | | | | | | | |
| 1981 | Mrs A Muinos's | **TO-AGORI-MOU** (5/2) | G Starkey | G Harwood | Mattaboy | Bel Bolide | 19 | 1 41.43 |
| 1982 | G Oldham's | **ZINO** (8/1) | F Head | F Boutin | Wind and Wuthering | Tender King | 26 | 1 37.13 |
| 1983 | R Sangster's | **LOMOND** (9/1) | Pat Eddery | V O'Brien | Tolomeo | Muscatite | 16 | 1 43.87 |
| 1984 | R Sangster's | **EL GRAN SENOR** (15/8) | Pat Eddery | V O'Brien | Chief Singer | Lear Fan | 9 | 1 37.41 |
| 1985 | Maktoum Al Maktoum's | **SHADEED** (4/5) | L Piggott | M Stoute | Bairn | Supreme Leader | 14 | 1 37.41 |
| 1986 | K Abdulla's | **DANCING BRAVE** (15/8) | G Starkey | G Harwood | Green Desert | Huntingdale | 15 | 1 40.00 |
| 1987 | J Horgan's | **DON'T FORGET ME** (9/1) | W Carson | R Hannon | Bellotto | Midyan | 13 | 1 36.74 |
| 1988 | H H Aga Khan's | **DOYOUN** (4/5) | W R Swinburn | M Stoute | Charmer | Bellefella | 9 | 1 41.73 |
| 1989 | Hamdan Al-Maktoum's | **NASHWAN** (3/1) | W Carson | R Hern | Exbourne | Danehill | 14 | 1 36.44 |
| 1990 | John Horgan's | **TIROL** (9/1) | M Kinane | R Hannon | Machiavellian | Anshan | 14 | 1 35.84 |
| 1991 | Lady Beaverbrook's | **MYSTIKO** (13/2) | M Roberts | C Brittain | Lycius | Ganges | 14 | 1 37.83 |
| 1992 | R Sangster's | **RODRIGO DE TRIANO** (6/1) | L Piggott | P Chapple-Hyam | Lucky Lindy | Pursuit of Love | 16 | 1 38.37 |
| 1993 | K Abdulla's | **ZAFONIC** (5/6) | Pat Eddery | A Fabre | Barathea | Bin Ajwaad | 14 | 1 35.32 |
| 1994 | G R Bailey Ltd's | **MISTER BAILEYS** (16/1) | J Weaver | M Johnston | Grand Lodge | Colonel Collins | 23 | 1 35.08 |
| 1995 | Sheikh Mohammed's | **PENNEKAMP** (9/2) | T Jarnet | A Fabre | Celtic Swing | Bahri | 11 | 1 35.16 |
| 1996 | Godolphin's | **MARK OF ESTEEM** (8/1) | L Dettori | S bin Suroor | Even Top | Bijou D'Inde | 13 | 1 37.59 |
| 1997 | M Tabor & Mrs J Magnier's | **ENTREPRENEUR** (11/2) | M Kinane | M Stoute | Revoque | Poteen | 16 | 1 35.64 |
| 1998 | M Tabor & Mrs J Magnier's | **KING OF KINGS** (7/2) | M Kinane | A O'Brien | Lend A Hand | Border Arrow | 18 | 1 39.25 |
| 1999 | Godolphin's | **ISLAND SANDS** (10/1) | L Dettori | S Bin Suroor | Enrique | Mujahid | 16 | 1 37.14 |
| | (Run on July Course) | | | | | | | |
| 2000 | Saeed Suhail's | **KING'S BEST** (13/2) | K Fallon | Sir M Stoute | Giant's Causeway | Barathea Guest | 27 | 1 37.77 |
| 2001 | Lord Weinstock's | **GOLAN** (11/1) | K Fallon | Sir M Stoute | Tamburlaine | Frenchmans Bay | 18 | 1 37.48 |
| 2002 | Sir A Ferguson & Mrs J Magnier's | **ROCK OF GIBRALTAR** (9/1) | J Murtagh | A O'Brien | Hawk Wing | Redback | 22 | 1 36.50 |
| 2003 | Moyglare Stud Farm's | **REFUSE TO BEND** (9/2) | P J Smullen | D Weld | Zafeen | Norse Dancer | 20 | 1 37.98 |
| 2004 | Hamdan Al Maktoum's | **HAAFHD** (11/2) | R Hills | B Hills | Snow Ridge | Azamour | 14 | 1 36.60 |
| 2005 | Mr M Tabor & Mrs John Magnier's | **FOOTSTEPSINTHESAND** (13/2) | K Fallon | A O'Brien | Rebel Rebel | Kandidate | 19 | 1 36.10 |
| 2006 | Mrs J Magnier, Mr M Tabor & Mr D Smith's | **GEORGE WASHINGTON** (6/4) | K Fallon | A O'Brien | Sir Percy | Olympian Odyssey | 14 | 1 36.80 |
| 2007 | P Cunningham's | **COCKNEY REBEL** (25/1) | O Peslier | G Huffer | Vital Equine | Dutch Art | 24 | 1 35.28 |
| 2008 | Mrs J. Magnier's | **HENRYTHENAVIGATOR** (11/1) | J Murtagh | A O'Brien | New Approach | Stubbs Art | 15 | 1 39.14 |
| 2009 | C Tsui's | **SEA THE STARS** (8/1) | M Kinane | J Oxx | Delegator | Gan Amhras | 15 | 1 35.88 |
| 2010 | M Offenstadt's | **MAKFI** (33/1) | C Lemaire | M Delzangles | Dick Turpin | Canford Cliffs | 19 | 1 36.35 |
| 2011 | K Abdulla's | **FRANKEL** (1/2) | T Queally | H Cecil | Dubawi Gold | Native Khan | 13 | 1 37.30 |
| 2012 | D Smith, Mrs J Magnier & M Tabor's | **CAMELOT** (15/8) | J O'Brien | A O'Brien | French Fifteen | Hermival | 18 | 1 42.46 |
| 2014 | Saeed Manana's | **NIGHT OF THUNDER** (40/1) | K Fallon | R Hannon jnr | Kingman | Australia | 14 | 1 36.61 |

## 1000 GUINEAS STAKES (3y fillies) Newmarket-1 mile

| Year | Owner | Winner and Price | Jockey | Trainer | Second | Third | Ran | Time |
|---|---|---|---|---|---|---|---|---|
| 1972 | Mrs R Stanley's | **WATERLOO** (8/1) | E Hide | J W Watts | Marisela | Rose Dubarry | 18 | 1 39.49 |
| 1973 | G Pope's | **MYSTERIOUS** (11/1) | G Lewis | N Murless | Jacinth | Shellshock | 14 | 1 42.12 |
| 1974 | The Queen's | **HIGHCLERE** (12/1) | J Mercer | R Hern | Polygamy | Mrs Twiggywinkle | 15 | 1 40.32 |
| 1975 | Mrs D O' Kelly's | **NOCTURNAL SPREE** (14/1) | J Roe | S Murless | Girl Friend | Joking Apart | 16 | 1 41.65 |
| 1976 | D Wildenstein's | **FLYING WATER** (2/1) | Y Saint Martin | A Penna | Konafa | Kesar Queen | 25 | 1 37.83 |
| 1977 | Mrs E Kettlewell's | **MRS MCARDY** (16/1) | E Hide | M W Easterby | Freeze the Secret | Sanedtki | 18 | 1 40.07 |
| 1978 | R Bonnycastle's | **ENSTONE SPARK** (35/1) | E Johnson | B Hills | Fair Salinia | Seraphima | 16 | 1 41.56 |
| 1979 | Helena Springfield Ltd's | **ONE IN A MILLION** (evens) | J Mercer | H Cecil | Abbeydale | Yanuka | 17 | 1 43.06 |
| 1980 | O Phipps's | **QUICK AS LIGHTNING** (12/1) | B Rouse | J Dunlop | Our Home | Mrs Penny | 23 | 1 41.89 |
| 1981 | H Joel's | **FAIRY FOOTSTEPS** (6/4) | L Piggott | H Cecil | Tolmi | Go Leasing | 14 | 1 40.43 |
| 1982 | Sir P Oppenheimer's | **ON THE HOUSE** (33/1) | J Reid | H Wragg | Time Charter | Dione | 15 | 1 40.45 |
| 1983 | Maktoum Al-Maktoum's | **MA BICHE** (5/2) | F Head | Mme C Head | Favoridge | Habibti | 18 | 1 41.71 |
| 1984 | M Lemos's | **PEBBLES** (8/1) | P Robinson | C Brittain | Meis El-Reem | Desirable | 15 | 1 38.18 |
| 1985 | Sheikh Mohammed's | **OH SO SHARP** (2/1) | S Cauthen | H Cecil | Al Bahathri | Bella Colora | 17 | 1 36.85 |
| 1986 | H Ranier's | **MIDWAY LADY** (10/1) | R Cochrane | B Hanbury | Maysoon | Sonic Lady | 15 | 1 41.54 |
| 1987 | S Niarchos's | **MIESQUE** (15/8) | F Head | F Boutin | Milligram | Interval | 14 | 1 38.48 |
| 1988 | E Aland's | **RAVINELLA** (4/5) | G W Moore | Mme C Head | Dabaweyaa | Diminuendo | 12 | 1 40.88 |
| 1989 | Sheikh Mohammed's | **MUSICAL BLISS** (7/2) | W R Swinburn | M Stoute | Kerrera | Aldbourne | 7 | 1 42.69 |
| 1990 | Hamdan Al-Maktoum's | **SALSABIL** (6/4) | W Carson | J Dunlop | Heart of Joy | Negligent | 10 | 1 38.06 |
| 1991 | Hamdan Al-Maktoum's | **SHADAYID** (4/6) | W Carson | J Dunlop | Kooyonga | Crystal Gazing | 14 | 1 38.18 |
| 1992 | Maktoum Al-Maktoum's | **HATOOF** (5/1) | W R Swinburn | Mme C Head | Marling | Kenbu | 14 | 1 39.45 |
| 1993 | Mohamed Obaida's | **SAYYEDATI** (4/1) | W R Swinburn | C Brittain | Niche | Ajfan | 12 | 1 37.34 |
| 1994 | R Sangster's | **LAS MENINAS** (12/1) | J Reid | T Stack | Balanchine | Coup de Genie | 15 | 1 36.71 |
| 1995 | Hamdan Al-Maktoum's | **HARAYIR** (5/1) | R Hills | Major W R Hern | Aqaarid | Moonshell | 14 | 1 36.72 |
| 1996 | Wafic Said's | **BOSRA SHAM** (10/11) | Pat Eddery | H Cecil | Matiya | Bint Shadayid | 13 | 1 37.75 |
| 1997 | Greenbay Stables Ltd's | **SLEEPYTIME** (5/1) | K Fallon | H Cecil | Oh Nellie | Dazzle | 15 | 1 37.66 |
| 1998 | Godolphin's | **CAPE VERDI** (100/30) | L Dettori | S Bin Suroor | Shahtoush | Exclusive | 16 | 1 37.86 |
| 1999 | K Abdulla's (Run on July Course) | **WINCE** (4/1) | K Fallon | H Cecil | Wannabe Grand | Valentine Waltz | 22 | 1 37.91 |
| 2000 | Hamdan Al-Maktoum's | **LAHAN** (14/1) | R Hills | J Gosden | Princess Ellen | Petrushka | 18 | 1 36.38 |
| 2001 | Sheikh Ahmed Al Maktoum's | **AMEERAT** (11/1) | P Robinson | M Jarvis | Muwakleh | Toroca | 15 | 1 38.36 |
| 2002 | Godolphin's | **KAZZIA** (14/1) | L Dettori | S Bin Suroor | Snowfire | Alasha | 17 | 1 37.85 |
| 2003 | Cheveley Park Stud's | **RUSSIAN RHYTHM** (12/1) | K Fallon | Sir M Stoute | Six Perfections | Intercontinental | 19 | 1 38.43 |
| 2004 | Duke of Roxburghe's | **ATTRACTION** (11/2) | K Darley | M Johnston | Sundrop | Hathrah | 16 | 1 36.70 |
| 2005 | Mrs John Magnier & Mr M Tabor's | **VIRGINIA WATERS** (12/1) | K Fallon | A O'Brien | Maids Causeway | Vista Bella | 20 | 1 36.50 |
| 2006 | M Sly, Dr Davies & Mrs P Sly's | **SPECIOSA** (10/1) | M Fenton | Mrs P Sly | Confidential Lady | Nasheej | 13 | 1 40.50 |
| 2007 | M Ryan's | **FINSCEAL BEO** (5/4) | K Manning | J Bolger | Arch Swing | Simply Perfect | 21 | 1 34.94 |
| 2008 | S. Friborg's | **NATAGORA** (11/4) | C Lemaire | P Bary | Spacious | Saoirse Abu | 15 | 1 38.99 |
| 2009 | Hamdan Al-Maktoum's | **GHANAATI** (20/1) | R Hills | B Hills | Cuis Ghaire | Super Sleuth | 14 | 1 34.22 |
| 2010 | K Abdulla's (The first two placings were reversed by the Stewards) | **SPECIAL DUTY** (9/2) | S. Pasquier | Mme C Head-Maarek | Jacqueline Quest | Gile Na Greine | 17 | 1 39.66 |
| 2011 | Godolphin's | **BLUE BUNTING** (16/1) | L Dettori | M Al Zarooni | Together | Maqaasid | 18 | 1 39.27 |
| 2012 | Mrs John Magnier, M Tabor & D Smith's | **HOMECOMING QUEEN** (25/1) | R Moore | A O'Brien | Starscope | Maybe | 17 | 1 40.45 |
| 2013 | B Keswick's | **SKY LANTERN** (9/1) | R Hughes | R Hannon | Just The Judge | Moth | 15 | 1 36.38 |
| 2014 | Ballymore Thoroughbred Ltd's | **MISS FRANCE** (7/1) | M Guyon | A Fabre | Lightning Thunder | Ihtimal | 17 | 1 37.40 |

# OAKS STAKES (3y fillies) Epsom-1 mile 4 furlongs 10 yards

| Year | Owner | Winner and Price | Jockey | Trainer | Second | Third | Ran | Time |
|---|---|---|---|---|---|---|---|---|
| 1976 | D Wildenstein's | **PAWNEESE** (6/5) | Y Saint Martin | A Penna | Roses for the Star | African Dancer | 14 | 2 35.25 |
| 1977 | The Queen's | **DUNFERMLINE** (6/1) | W Carson | R Hern | Freeze the Secret | Vaguely Deb | 13 | 2 36.53 |
| 1978 | S Hanson's | **FAIR SALINIA** (8/1) | G Starkey | M Stoute | Dancing Maid | Suni | 15 | 2 36.82 |
| 1979 | J Morrison's | **SCINTILLATE** (20/1) | Pat Eddery | J Tree | Bonnie Isle | Britannia's Rule | 14 | 2 43.74 |
| 1980 | R Hollingsworth's | **BIREME** (9/2) | W Carson | R Hern | Vielle | The Dancer | 11 | 2 34.33 |
| 1981 | Mrs B Firestone's | **BLUE WIND** (3/1) | L Piggott | D Weld | Madam Gay | Leap Lively | 12 | 2 40.93 |
| 1982 | R Barnett's | **TIME CHARTER** (12/1) | W Newnes | H Candy | Slightly Dangerous | Last Feather | 13 | 2 34.21 |
| 1983 | Sir M Sobell's | **SUN PRINCESS** (6/1) | W Carson | R Hern | Acclimatise | New Coins | 15 | 2 40.98 |
| 1984 | Sir R McAlpine's | **CIRCUS PLUME** (4/1) | L Piggott | J Dunlop | Media Luna | Poquito Queen | 15 | 2 38.97 |
| 1985 | Sheikh Mohammed's | **OH SO SHARP** (6/4) | S Cauthen | H Cecil | Triptych | Dubian | 12 | 2 41.37 |
| 1986 | H Ranier's | **MIDWAY LADY** (15/8) | R Cochrane | B Hanbury | Untold | Maysoon | 15 | 2 35.60 |
| 1987 | Sheikh Mohammed's | **UNITE** (11/1) | W R Swinburn | M Stoute | Bourbon Girl | Three Tails | 11 | 2 38.17 |
| 1988 | Sheikh Mohammed's | **DIMINUENDO** (7/4) | S Cauthen | H Cecil | Sudden Love | Animatrice | 11 | 2 35.02 |
| 1989 | Saeed Maktoum Al Maktoum's | **SNOW BRIDE** (13/2) | S Cauthen | H Cecil | Roseate Tern | Mamaluna | 9 | 2 34.22 |
| | (Aliysa finished first but was disqualified) | | | | | | | |
| 1990 | Hamdan Al-Maktoum's | **SALSABIL** (2/1) | W Carson | J Dunlop | Game Plan | Knight's Baroness | 8 | 2 38.70 |
| 1991 | Maktoum Al-Maktoum's | **JET SKI LADY** (50/1) | C Roche | J Bolger | Shamshir | Shadayid | 9 | 2 37.30 |
| 1992 | W J Gredley's | **USER FRIENDLY** (5/1) | G Duffield | C Brittain | All At Sea | Pearl Angel | 7 | 2 39.77 |
| 1993 | Sheikh Mohammed's | **INTREPIDITY** (5/1) | M Roberts | A Fabre | Royal Ballerina | Oakmead | 14 | 2 34.19 |
| 1994 | Godolphin's | **BALANCHINE** (6/1) | L Dettori | H Ibrahim | Wind In Her Hair | Hawajiss | 10 | 2 40.37 |
| 1995 | Maktoum Al Maktoum/ Godolphin's | **MOONSHELL** (3/1) | L Dettori | S Bin Suroor | Dance A Dream | Pure Grain | 10 | 2 35.44 |
| 1996 | Wafic Said's | **LADY CARLA** (100/30) | Pat Eddery | H Cecil | Pricket | Mezzogiorno | 11 | 2 35.55 |
| 1997 | K Abdulla's | **REAMS OF VERSE** (5/6) | K Fallon | H Cecil | Gazelle Royale | Crown of Light | 12 | 2 35.59 |
| 1998 | Mrs D Nagle & Mrs J Magnier's | **SHAHTOUSH** (12/1) | M Kinane | A O'Brien | Bahr | Midnight Line | 8 | 2 38.23 |
| 1999 | F Salman's | **RAMRUMA** (3/1) | K Fallon | H Cecil | Noushkey | Zahrat Dubai | 10 | 2 38.72 |
| 2000 | Lordship Stud's | **LOVE DIVINE** (9/4) | T Quinn | H Cecil | Kalypso Katie | Melikah | 16 | 2 43.11 |
| 2001 | Mrs D. Nagle & Mrs J Magnier's | **IMAGINE** (3/1) | M Kinane | A O'Brien | Flight Of Fancy | Relish The Thought | 14 | 2 36.70 |
| 2002 | Godolphin's | **KAZZIA** (100/30) | L Dettori | S Bin Suroor | Quarter Moon | Shadow Dancing | 14 | 2 44.52 |
| 2003 | W S Farish III's | **CASUAL LOOK** (10/1) | M Dwyer | A Balding | Yesterday | Summitville | 15 | 2 38.07 |
| 2004 | Lord Derby's | **OUIJA BOARD** (7/2) | K Fallon | E Dunlop | All Too Beautiful | Punctilious | 7 | 2 35.40 |
| 2005 | Hamdan Al Maktoum's | **ESWARAH** (11/4) | R Hills | M Jarvis | Something Exciting | Pictavia | 12 | 2 39.00 |
| 2006 | Mrs J Magnier, Mr M Tabor & Mr D Smith's | **ALEXANDROVA** (9/4) | K Fallon | A O'Brien | Rising Cross | Short Skirt | 10 | 2 37.70 |
| 2007 | Niarchos Family's | **LIGHT SHIFT** (13/2) | T Durcan | H Cecil | Peeping Fawn | All My Loving | 14 | 2 40.38 |
| 2008 | J H Richmond-Watson's | **LOOK HERE** (33/1) | S Sanders | R Beckett | Moonstone | Katiyra | 16 | 2 36.89 |
| 2009 | Lady Bamford's | **SARISKA** (9/4) | J Spencer | M Bell | Midday | High Heeled | 10 | 2 35.28 |
| 2010 | Anamoine Ltd's | **SNOW FAIRY** (9/1) | R Moore | E Dunlop | Remember When | Rumoush | 15 | 2 35.77 |
| | (Meeznah finished second but was disqualified) | | | | | | | |
| 2011 | M J & L A Taylor's | **DANCING RAIN** (20/1) | J Murtagh | W Haggas | Wonder of Wonders | Izzi Top | 13 | 2 41.73 |
| 2012 | D Smith, Mrs J Magnier & M Tabor's | **WAS** (20/1) | S Hefferman | A O'Brien | Shirocco Star | The Fugue | 12 | 2 38.68 |
| 2013 | J L Rowsell & M H Dixon's | **TALENT** (20/1) | R Hughes | R Beckett | Secret Gesture | The Lark | 11 | 2 42.00 |
| 2014 | Hamdan Al Maktoum's | **TAGHROODA** (5/1) | P Hanagan | J Gosden | Tarfasha | Volume | 17 | 2 34.89 |

# DERBY STAKES (3y) Epsom-1 mile 4 furlongs 10 yards

| Year | Owner | Winner and Price | Jockey | Trainer | Second | Third | Ran | Time |
|---|---|---|---|---|---|---|---|---|
| 1977 | R Sangster's | **THE MINSTREL** (5/1) | L Piggott | V O'Brien | Hot Grove | Blushing Groom | 22 | 2 36.44 |
| 1978 | Lord Halifax's | **SHIRLEY HEIGHTS** (8/1) | G Starkey | J Dunlop | Hawaiian Sound | Remainder Man | 25 | 2 35.30 |
| 1979 | Sir M Sobell's | **TROY** (6/1) | W Carson | R Hern | Dickens Hill | Northern Baby | 23 | 2 36.59 |
| 1980 | Mrs A Plesch's | **HENBIT** (7/1) | W Carson | R Hern | Master Willie | Rankin | 24 | 2 34.77 |
| 1981 | H H Aga Khan's | **SHERGAR** (10/11) | W Swinburn | M Stoute | Glint of Gold | Scintillating Air | 18 | 2 44.21 |
| 1982 | R Sangster's | **GOLDEN FLEECE** (3/1) | Pat Eddery | V O'Brien | Touching Wood | Silver Hawk | 18 | 2 34.27 |
| 1983 | E Moller's | **TEENOSO** (9/2) | L Piggott | G Wragg | Carlingford Castle | Shearwalk | 21 | 2 49.07 |
| 1984 | L Miglitti's | **SECRETO** (14/1) | C Roche | D O'Brien | El Gran Senor | Mighty Flutter | 17 | 2 39.12 |
| 1985 | Lord H. de Walden's | **SLIP ANCHOR** (9/4) | S Cauthen | H Cecil | Law Society | Damister | 14 | 2 36.23 |
| 1986 | H H Aga Khan's | **SHAHRASTANI** (11/2) | W Swinburn | M Stoute | Dancing Brave | Mashkour | 17 | 2 37.13 |
| 1987 | L Freedman's | **REFERENCE POINT** (6/4) | S Cauthen | H Cecil | Most Welcome | Bellotto | 19 | 2 33.90 |
| 1988 | H H Aga Khan's | **KAHYASI** (11/1) | R Cochrane | L Cumani | Glacial Storm | Doyoun | 14 | 2 33.84 |
| 1989 | Hamdan Al-Maktoum's | **NASHWAN** (5/4) | W Carson | R Hern | Terimon | Cacoethes | 12 | 2 34.90 |
| 1990 | K Abdulla's | **QUEST FOR FAME** (7/1) | Pat Eddery | R Charlton | Blue Stag | Elmaamul | 18 | 2 37.26 |
| 1991 | F Salman's | **GENEROUS** (9/1) | A Munro | P Cole | Marju | Star of Gdansk | 13 | 2 34.00 |
| 1992 | Sidney H Craig's | **DR DEVIOUS** (8/1) | J Reid | P Chapple-Hyam | St Jovite | Silver Wisp | 18 | 2 36.19 |
| 1993 | K Abdulla's | **COMMANDER IN CHIEF** (15/2) | M Kinane | H Cecil | Blue Judge | Blues Traveller | 16 | 2 34.51 |
| 1994 | Hamdan Al-Maktoum's | **ERHAAB** (7/2) | W Carson | J Dunlop | King's Theatre | Colonel Collins | 25 | 2 34.16 |
| 1995 | Saeed Maktoum Al Maktoum's | **LAMMTARRA** (14/1) | W Swinburn | S Bin Suroor | Tamure | Presenting | 15 | 2 32.31 |
| 1996 | K Dasmal's | **SHAAMIT** (12/1) | M Hills | W Haggas | Dushyantor | Shantou | 20 | 2 35.05 |
| 1997 | L Knight's | **BENNY THE DIP** (11/1) | W Ryan | J Gosden | Silver Patriarch | Romanov | 13 | 2 35.77 |
| 1998 | Sheikh Mohammed Obaid Al Maktoum's | **HIGH-RISE** (20/1) | O Peslier | L Cumani | City Honours | Border Arrow | 15 | 2 33.88 |
| 1999 | The Thoroughbred Corporation's | **OATH** (13/2) | K Fallon | H Cecil | Daliapour | Beat All | 16 | 2 37.43 |
| 2000 | H H Aga Khan's | **SINNDAR** (7/1) | J Murtagh | J Oxx | Sakhee | Beat Hollow | 15 | 2 36.75 |
| 2001 | M Tabor & Mrs J Magnier's | **GALILEO** (11/4) | M Kinane | A O'Brien | Golan | Tobougg | 12 | 2 33.27 |
| 2002 | M Tabor & Mrs J Magnier's | **HIGH CHAPARRAL** (7/2) | J Murtagh | A O'Brien | Hawk Wing | Moon Ballad | 12 | 2 39.45 |
| 2003 | Saeed Suhail's | **KRIS KIN** (6/1) | K Fallon | Sir M Stoute | The Great Gatsby | Alamshar | 20 | 2 33.35 |
| 2004 | Ballymacoll Stud's | **NORTH LIGHT** (7/2) | K Fallon | Sir M Stoute | Rule Of Law | Let The Lion Roar | 14 | 2 33.70 |
| 2005 | The Royal Ascot Racing Club's | **MOTIVATOR** (3/1) | J Murtagh | M Bell | Walk In The Park | Dubawi | 13 | 2 35.60 |
| 2006 | A E Pakenham's | **SIR PERCY** (6/1) | M Dwyer | M Tregoning | Dragon Dancer | Dylan Thomas | 18 | 2 35.20 |
| 2007 | Saleh Al Homaizi & Imad Al Sagar's | **AUTHORIZED** (5/4) | L Dettori | P Chapple-Hyam | Eagle Mountain | Aqaleem | 17 | 2 34.77 |
| 2008 | HRH Princess Haya of Jordan's | **NEW APPROACH** (5/1) | K. Manning | J Bolger | Tartan Bearer | Casual Conquest | 16 | 2 36.50 |
| 2009 | C Tsui's | **SEA THE STARS** (11/4) | M Kinane | J Oxx | Fame And Glory | Mastercofthehorse | 12 | 2 36.74 |
| 2010 | K Abdulla's | **WORKFORCE** (6/1) | R Moore | Sir M Stoute | At First Sight | Rewilding | 12 | 2 31.33 |
| 2011 | Mrs John Magnier, M Tabor & D Smith's | **POUR MOI** (4/1) | M Barzalona | A Fabre | Treasure Beach | Carlton House | 13 | 2 34.54 |
| 2012 | D Smith, Mrs J Magnier & M Tabor's | **CAMELOT** (8/13) | J O'Brien | A O'Brien | Main Sequence | Astrology | 9 | 2 33.90 |
| 2013 | Mrs John Magnier, Michael Tabor & Derrick Smith's | **RULER OF THE WORLD** (7/1) | R Moore | A O'Brien | Libertarian | Galileo Rock | 12 | 2 39.06 |
| 2014 | D Smith, Mrs J Magnier, M Tabor & T Ah Khing's | **AUSTRALIA** (11/8) | J O'Brien | A O'Brien | Kingston Hill | Romsdal | 16 | 2 33.63 |

# ST LEGER STAKES (3y) Doncaster-1 mile 6 furlongs 132 yards

| Year | Owner | Winner and Price | Jockey | Trainer | Second | Third | Ran | Time |
|---|---|---|---|---|---|---|---|---|
| 1973 | W Behrens's | **PELEID** (28/1) | F Durr | W Elsey | Buoy | Duke of Ragusa | 13 | 3 8.21 |
| 1974 | Lady Beaverbrook's | **BUSTINO** (11/10) | J Mercer | R Hern | Giacometti | Riboson | 10 | 3 9.02 |
| 1975 | C St George's | **BRUNI** (9/1) | A Murray | R Price | King Pellinore | Libra's Rib | 12 | 3 9.02 |
| 1976 | D Wildenstein's | **CROW** (6/1) | Y Saint-Martin | A Penna | Secret Man | Scallywag | 15 | 3 13.17 |
| 1977 | The Queen's | **DUNFERMLINE** (10/1) | W Carson | R Hern | Alleged | Classic Example | 13 | 3 5.17 |
| 1978 | M Lemos's | **JULIO MARINER** (28/1) | E Hide | C Brittain | Le Moss | M-Lolshan | 14 | 3 4.94 |
| 1979 | A Rolland's | **SON OF LOVE** (20/1) | A Lequeux | R Collet | Soleil Noir | Niniski | 17 | 3 9.02 |
| 1980 | H Joel's | **LIGHT CAVALRY** (3/1) | J Mercer | H Cecil | Water Mill | World Leader | 7 | 3 11.48 |
| 1981 | Sir J Astor's | **CUT ABOVE** (28/1) | J Mercer | R Hern | Glint of Gold | Bustomi | 7 | 3 11.60 |
| 1982 | Maktoum Al Maktoum's | **TOUCHING WOOD** (7/1) | P Cook | H T Jones | Zilos | Diamond Shoal | 15 | 3 3.53 |
| 1983 | Sir M Sobell's | **SUN PRINCESS** (11/8) | W Carson | R Hern | Esprit du Nord | Carlingford Castle | 10 | 3 16.65 |
| 1984 | I Allan's | **COMMANCHE RUN** (7/4) | L Piggott | L Cumani | Baynoun | Alphabatim | 11 | 3 9.93 |
| 1985 | Sheikh Mohammed's | **OH SO SHARP** (8/11) | S Cauthen | H Cecil | Phardante | Lanfranco | 6 | 3 7.13 |
| 1986 | Duchess of Norfolk's | **MOON MADNESS** (9/2) | Pat Eddery | J Dunlop | Celestial Storm | Untold | 8 | 3 5.03 |
| 1987 | L Freedman's | **REFERENCE POINT** (4/11) | S Cauthen | H Cecil | Mountain Kingdom | Dry Dock | 7 | 3 5.91 |
| 1988 | Lady Beaverbrook's | **MINSTER SON** (15/2) | W Carson | N A Graham | Diminuendo | Sheriff's Star | 6 | 3 6.80 |
| 1989 | C St George's (Run at Ayr) | **MICHELOZZO** (6/4) | S Cauthen | H Cecil | Sapience | Roseate Tern | 8 | 3 20.72 |
| 1990 | M Arbib's | **SNURGE** (7/2) | T Quinn | P Cole | Hellenic | River God | 8 | 3 8.78 |
| 1991 | K Abdulla's | **TOULON** (5/2) | Pat Eddery | A Fabre | Saddlers' Hall | Micheletti | 10 | 3 3.12 |
| 1992 | W J Gredley's | **USER FRIENDLY** (7/4) | G Duffield | C Brittain | Sonus | Bonny Scot | 7 | 3 5.48 |
| 1993 | Mrs G A E Smith's | **BOB'S RETURN** (3/1) | P Robinson | M Tompkins | Armiger | Edbaysaan | 9 | 3 7.85 |
| 1994 | Sheikh Mohammed's | **MOONAX** (40/1) | Pat Eddery | B Hills | Broadway Flyer | Double Trigger | 8 | 3 4.19 |
| 1995 | Godolphin's | **CLASSIC CLICHE** (100/30) | L Dettori | S Bin Suroor | Minds Music | Istidaad | 10 | 3 9.74 |
| 1996 | Sheikh Mohammed's | **SHANTOU** (8/1) | L Dettori | J Gosden | Dushyantor | Samraan | 11 | 3 5.10 |
| 1997 | P Winfield's | **SILVER PATRIARCH** (5/4) | Pat Eddery | J Dunlop | Vertical Speed | The Fly | 10 | 3 6.92 |
| 1998 | Godolphin's | **NEDAWI** (5/2) | J Reid | S Bin Suroor | High and Low | Sunshine Street | 9 | 3 5.61 |
| 1999 | Godolphin's | **MUTAFAWEQ** (11/2) | R Hills | S Bin Suroor | Ramruma | Adair | 9 | 3 2.75 |
| 2000 | N Jones' | **MILLENARY** (11/4) | T Quinn | J Dunlop | Air Marshall | Chimes At Midnight | 11 | 3 2.58 |
| 2001 | M Tabor & Mrs J Magnier's | **MILAN** (13/8) | M Kinane | A O'Brien | Demophilos | Mr Combustible | 10 | 3 5.16 |
| 2002 | Sir Neil Westbrook's | **BOLLIN ERIC** (7/1) | K Darley | T Easterby | Highest | Bandari | 8 | 3 2.92 |
| 2003 | Mrs J Magnier's | **BRIAN BORU** (5/4) | J P Spencer | A O'Brien | High Accolade | Phoenix Reach | 12 | 3 4.64 |
| 2004 | Godolphin's | **RULE OF LAW** (3/1) | K McEvoy | S Bin Suroor | Quiff | Tycoon | 9 | 3 6.20 |
| 2005 | Mrs J Magnier & M Tabor's | **SCORPION** (10/11) | L Dettori | A O'Brien | The Geezer | Tawqeet | 6 | 3 19.00 |
| 2006 | Mrs S Roy's (Run at York) | **SIXTIES ICON** (11/8) | L Dettori | J Noseda | The Last Drop | Red Rocks | 11 | 2 57.20 |
| 2007 | G Strawbridge's | **LUCARNO** (7/2) | J Fortune | J Gosden | Mahler | Honolulu | 10 | 3 1.90 |
| 2008 | Ballymacoll Stud's | **CONDUIT** (8/1) | L Dettori | Sir M Stoute | Unsung Heroine | Look Here | 14 | 3 7.92 |
| 2009 | Godolphin's | **MASTERY** (14/1) | T Durcan | S Bin Suroor | Kite Wood | Monitor Closely | 8 | 3 4.81 |
| 2010 | Ms R Hood & R Geffen's | **ARCTIC COSMOS** (12/1) | W Buick | J Gosden | Midas Touch | Corsica | 10 | 3 3.12 |
| 2011 | B Nielsen's | **MASKED MARVEL** (15/2) | W Buick | J Gosden | Brown Panther | Sea Moon | 9 | 3 0.44 |
| 2012 | Godolphin's | **ENCKE** (25/1) | M Barzalona | M Al Zarooni | Camelot | Michelangelo | 9 | 3 3.81 |
| 2013 | Derrick Smith & Mrs John Magnier & Michael Tabor's | **LEADING LIGHT** (7/2) | J O'Brien | A O'Brien | Talent | Galileo Rock | 11 | 3 9.20 |
| 2014 | Paul Smith's | **KINGSTON HILL** (9/4) | A Atzeni | R Varian | Romsdal | Snow Sky | 12 | 3 5.42 |

# KING GEORGE VI AND QUEEN ELIZABETH STAKES Ascot-1 mile 4 furlongs

| Year | Owner | Winner and Price | Jockey | Trainer | Second | Third | Ran | Time |
|---|---|---|---|---|---|---|---|---|
| 1975 | Dr C Vittadini's | **GRUNDY** 3-8-7 (4/5) | P Eddery | P Walwyn | Bustino | Dahlia | 11 | 2 26.98 |
| 1976 | D Wildenstein's | **PAWNEESE** 3-8-5 (9/4) | Y Saint Martin | A Penna | Bruni | Orange Bay | 10 | 2 29.36 |
| 1977 | R Sangster's | **THE MINSTREL** 3-8-8 (7/4) | L Piggott | V O'Brien | Orange Bay | Exceller | 11 | 2 30.48 |
| 1978 | D McCall's | **ILE DE BOURBON** 3-8-8 (12/1) | J Reid | F Houghton | Hawaiian Sound | Montcontour | 14 | 2 30.53 |
| 1979 | Sir M Sobell's | **TROY** 3-8-8 (2/5) | W Carson | R Hern | Gay Mecene | Ela-Mana-Mou | 7 | 2 33.75 |
| 1980 | S Weinstock's | **ELA-MANA-MOU** 4-9-7 (11/4) | W Carson | R Hern | Mrs Penny | Gregorian | 10 | 2 35.39 |
| 1981 | H H Aga Khan's | **SHERGAR** 3-8-8 (2/5) | W Swinburn | M Stoute | Madam Gay | Fingals Cave | 7 | 2 35.40 |
| 1982 | A Ward's | **KALAGLOW** 4-9-7 (13-2) | G Starkey | G Harwood | Assert | Glint of Gold | 9 | 2 31.58 |
| 1983 | R Barnett's | **TIME CHARTER** 4-9-4 (5/1) | J Mercer | H Candy | Diamond Shoal | Sun Princess | 9 | 2 30.78 |
| 1984 | E Moller's | **TEENOSO** 4-9-7 (13/2) | L Piggott | G Wragg | Sadler's Wells | Tolomeo | 13 | 2 27.95 |
| 1985 | Lady Beaverbrook's | **PETOSKI** 3-8-8 (12/1) | W Carson | R Hern | Oh So Sharp | Rainbow Quest | 12 | 2 27.61 |
| 1986 | K Abdulla's | **DANCING BRAVE** 3-8-8 (6/4) | Pat Eddery | G Harwood | Shardari | Triptych | 9 | 2 29.49 |
| 1987 | L Freedman's | **REFERENCE POINT** 3-8-8 (11/10) | S Cauthen | H Cecil | Celestial Storm | Triptych | 9 | 2 34.63 |
| 1988 | Sheikh Ahmed Al Maktoum | **MTOTO** 5-9-7 (4/1) | M Roberts | A C Stewart | Unfuwain | Tony Bin | 10 | 2 37.33 |
| 1989 | Hamdan Al-Maktoum's | **NASHWAN** 3-8-8 (2/9) | W Carson | R Hern | Cacoethes | Top Class | 7 | 2 32.27 |
| 1990 | Sheikh Mohammed's | **BELMEZ** 3-8-9 (15/2) | M Kinane | H Cecil | Old Vic | Assatis | 11 | 2 30.76 |
| 1991 | F Salman's | **GENEROUS** 3-8-9 (4/6) | A Munro | P Cole | Sanglamore | Rock Hopper | 9 | 2 28.99 |
| 1992 | Mrs V K Payson's | **ST JOVITE** 3-8-9 (4/5) | S Craine | J Bolger | Saddlers' Hall | Opera House | 8 | 2 30.85 |
| 1993 | Sheikh Mohammed's | **OPERA HOUSE** 5-9-7 (8/1) | M Roberts | M Stoute | White Muzzle | Commander in Chief | 10 | 2 33.94 |
| 1994 | Sheikh Mohammed's | **KING'S THEATRE** 3-8-9 (12/1) | M Kinane | H Cecil | White Muzzle | Wagon Master | 12 | 2 28.92 |
| 1995 | Saeed Maktoum Al Maktoum's | **LAMMTARRA** 3-8-9 (9/4) | L Dettori | S Bin Suroor | Pentire | Strategic Choice | 7 | 2 31.01 |
| 1996 | Mollers Racing's | **PENTIRE** 4-9-7 (100/30) | M Hills | G Wragg | Classic Cliche | Shaamit | 8 | 2 28.11 |
| 1997 | Godolphin's | **SWAIN** 5-9-7 (16/1) | J Reid | S Bin Suroor | Pilsudski | Helissio | 8 | 2 36.45 |
| 1998 | Godolphin's | **SWAIN** 6-9-7 (11/2) | L Dettori | S Bin Suroor | High-Rise | Royal Anthem | 8 | 2 29.06 |
| 1999 | Godolphin's | **DAYLAMI** 5-9-7 (3/1) | L Dettori | S Bin Suroor | Nedawi | Fruits Of Love | 8 | 2 29.35 |
| 2000 | M Tabor's | **MONTJEU** 4-9-7 (1/3) | M Kinane | J Hammond | Fantastic Light | Daliapour | 7 | 2 29.98 |
| 2001 | Mrs J Magnier & M Tabor's | **GALILEO** 3-8-9 (1/2) | M Kinane | A O'Brien | Fantastic Light | Hightori | 12 | 2 27.71 |
| 2002 | Exors of the late Lord Weinstock's | **GOLAN** 4-9-7 (11/2) | K Fallon | Sir M Stoute | Nayef | Zindabad | 9 | 2 29.70 |
| 2003 | H H Aga Khan | **ALAMSHAR** 3-8-9 (13/2) | J Murtagh | J Oxx | Sulamani | Kris Kin | 12 | 2 33.26 |
| 2004 | Godolphin's | **DOYEN** 4-9-7 (11/10) | L Dettori | S Bin Suroor | Hard Buck | Sulamani | 11 | 2 33.10 |
| 2005 | H H Aga Khan's (Run at Newbury) | **AZAMOUR** 4-9-7 (5/2) | M Kinane | J Oxx | Norse Dancer | Bago | 12 | 2 28.20 |
| 2006 | M Tabor's | **HURRICANE RUN** 4-9-7 (5/6) | C Soumillon | A Fabre | Electrocutionist | Heart's Cry | 6 | 2 30.20 |
| 2007 | Mrs J Magnier & M Tabor's | **DYLAN THOMAS** 4-9-7 (5/4) | J Murtagh | A O'Brien | Youmzain | Maraahel | 7 | 2 31.10 |
| 2008 | Mrs J Magnier & M Tabor's | **DUKE OF MARMALADE** 4-9-7 (4/6) | J Murtagh | A O'Brien | Papal Bull | Youmzain | 8 | 2 27.91 |
| 2009 | Ballymacoll Stud's | **CONDUIT** 4-9-7 (13/8) | R Moore | Sir M Stoute | Tartan Bearer | Ask | 9 | 2 28.73 |
| 2010 | Highclere Thoroughbred Racing (Adm. Rous)'s | **HARBINGER** 4-9-7 (4/1) | O Peslier | Sir M Stoute | Cape Blanco | Youmzain | 6 | 2 26.78 |
| 2011 | Lady Rothschild's | **NATHANIEL** 3-8-9 (11/2) | W Buick | J Gosden | Workforce | St Nicholas Abbey | 5 | 2 35.07 |
| 2012 | Gestut Burg Eberstein & Teruya Yoshida's | **DANEDREAM** 4-9-4 (9/1) | A Starke | P Schiergen | Nathaniel | St Nicholas Abbey | 10 | 2 31.62 |
| 2013 | Dr Christophe Berglar's | **NOVELLIST** 4-9-7 (13/2) | J Murtagh | A Wohler | Trading Leather | Hillstar | 8 | 2 24.60 |
| 2014 | Hamdan Al Maktoum's | **TAGHROODA** 3-8-6 (7/2) | P Hanagan | J Gosden | Telescope | Mukhadram | 8 | 2 28.13 |

# PRIX DE L'ARC DE TRIOMPHE Longchamp-1 mile 4 furlongs

| Year | Owner | Winner and Price | Jockey | Trainer | Second | Third | Ran | Time |
|---|---|---|---|---|---|---|---|---|
| 1974 | D Wildenstein's | **ALLEZ FRANCE** 4-9-3 (1/2) | Y Saint Martin | A Penna | Comtesse de Loir | Margouillat | 20 | 2 36.90 |
| 1975 | W Zeitelhack's | **STAR APPEAL** 5-9-6 (119/1) | G Starkey | T Grieper | On My Way | Comtesse de Loir | 24 | 2 33.60 |
| 1976 | J Wertheimer's | **IVANJICA** 4-9-1 (71/10) | F Head | A Head | Crow | Youth | 20 | 2 39.40 |
| 1977 | R Sangster's | **ALLEGED** 3-8-11 (38/10) | L Piggott | V O'Brien | Balmerino | Crystal Palace | 26 | 2 30.60 |
| 1978 | R Sangster's | **ALLEGED** 4-9-4 (7/5) | L Piggott | V O'Brien | Trillion | Dancing Maid | 18 | 2 36.10 |
| 1979 | Mme G Head's | **THREE TROIKAS** 3-8-8 (88/10) | F Head | Mme C Head | Le Marmot | Troy | 22 | 2 28.90 |
| 1980 | R Sangster's | **DETROIT** 3-8-8 (67/10) | Pat Eddery | O Douieb | Argument | Ela-Mana-Mou | 20 | 2 28.00 |
| 1981 | J Wertheimer's | **GOLD RIVER** 4-9-1 (53/1) | G W Moore | A Head | Bikala | April Run | 24 | 2 35.20 |
| 1982 | H H Aga Khan's | **AKIYDA** 3-8-8 (43/4) | Y Saint Martin | F. Mathet | Ardross | Awaasif | 17 | 2 37.00 |
| 1983 | D Wildenstein's | **ALL ALONG** 4-9-1 (173/10) | W Swinburn | P Biancone | Sun Princess | Luth Enchantee | 26 | 2 28.10 |
| 1984 | D Wildenstein's | **SAGACE** 4-9-4 (29/10) | Y Saint Martin | P Biancone | Northern Trick | All Along | 22 | 2 39.10 |
| 1985 | K Abdulla's | **RAINBOW QUEST** 4-9-4 (71/10) | Pat Eddery | J Tree | Sagace | Kozana | 15 | 2 29.50 |
| | (The first two placings were reversed by the Stewards) | | | | | | | |
| 1986 | K Abdulla's | **DANCING BRAVE** 3-8-11 (11/10) | Pat Eddery | G Harwood | Bering | Triptych | 15 | 2 27.70 |
| 1987 | P de Moussac's | **TREMPOLINO** 3-8-11 (20/1) | Pat Eddery | A Fabre | Tony Bin | Triptych | 11 | 2 26.30 |
| 1988 | Mrs V Gaucci del Bono's | **TONY BIN** 5-9-4 (14/1) | J Reid | L Camici | Mtoto | Boyatino | 24 | 2 27.30 |
| 1989 | A Balzarini's | **CARROLL HOUSE** 4-9-4 (19/1) | M Kinane | M Jarvis | Behera | Saint Andrews | 19 | 2 30.80 |
| 1990 | B McNall's | **SAUMAREZ** 3-8-11 (15/1) | G Mosse | N Clement | Epervier Bleu | Snurge | 21 | 2 29.80 |
| 1991 | H Chalhoub's | **SUAVE DANCER** 3-8-11 (37/10) | C Asmussen | J Hammond | Magic Night | Pistolet Bleu | 14 | 2 31.40 |
| 1992 | O Lecerf's | **SUBOTICA** 4-9-4 (88/10) | T Jarnet | A Fabre | User Friendly | Vert Amande | 18 | 2 39.00 |
| 1993 | D Tsui's | **URBAN SEA** 4-9-1 (37/1) | E Saint Martin | J Lesbordes | White Muzzle | Opera House | 23 | 2 37.90 |
| 1994 | Sheikh Mohammed's | **CARNEGIE** 3-8-11 (3/1) | T Jarnet | A Fabre | Hernando | Apple Tree | 20 | 2 31.10 |
| 1995 | Saeed Maktoum Al Maktoum's | **LAMMTARRA** 3-8-11 (2/1) | L Dettori | S Bin Suroor | Freedom Cry | Swain | 16 | 2 31.80 |
| 1996 | E Sarasola's | **HELISSIO** 3-8-11 (18/10) | O Peslier | E Lellouche | Pilsudski | Oscar Schindler | 16 | 2 29.90 |
| 1997 | D Wildenstein's | **PEINTRE CELEBRE** 3-8-11 (22/10) | O Peslier | A Fabre | Pilsudski | Borgia | 18 | 2 24.60 |
| 1998 | J-L Lagardere's | **SAGAMIX** 3-8-11 (5/2) | O Peslier | A Fabre | Leggera | Tiger Hill | 14 | 2 34.50 |
| 1999 | M Tabor's | **MONTJEU** 3-8-11 (6/4) | M Kinane | J Hammond | El Condor Pasa | Croco Rouge | 14 | 2 38.50 |
| 2000 | H H Aga Khan's | **SINNDAR** 3-8-11 (6/4) | J Murtagh | J Oxx | Egyptband | Volvoreta | 10 | 2 25.80 |
| 2001 | Godolphin's | **SAKHEE** 4-9-5 (22/10) | L Dettori | S Bin Suroor | Aquarelliste | Sagacity | 17 | 2 36.10 |
| 2002 | Godolphin's | **MARIENBARD** 5-9-5 (158/10) | L Dettori | S Bin Suroor | Sulamani | High Chaparral | 16 | 2 26.70 |
| 2003 | H H Aga Khan's | **DALAKHANI** 3-8-11 (9/4) | C Soumillon | A De Royer-Dupre | Mubtaker | High Chaparral | 13 | 2 32.30 |
| 2004 | Niarchos Family's | **BAGO** 3-8-11 (10/1) | T Gillet | J E Pease | Cherry Mix | Ouija Board | 13 | 2 25.00 |
| 2005 | M Tabor's | **HURRICANE RUN** 3-8-11 (11/4) | K Fallon | A Fabre | Westerner | Bago | 15 | 2 27.40 |
| 2006 | K Abdulla's | **RAIL LINK** 3-8-11 (8/1) | S Pasquier | A Fabre | Pride | Hurrricane Run | 8 | 2 26.30 |
| | (Deep Impact disqualified from third place) | | | | | | | |
| 2007 | Mrs J Magnier & M Tabor's | **DYLAN THOMAS** 4-9-5 (11/2) | K Fallon | A O'Brien | Youmzain | Sagara | 12 | 2 28.50 |
| 2008 | H H Aga Khan's | **ZARKAVA** 3-8-8 (13/8) | C Soumillon | A De Royer-Dupre | Youmzain | Soldier of Fortune/It's Gino | 16 | 2 28.80 |
| 2009 | C Tsui's | **SEA THE STARS** 3-8-11 (4/6) | M Kinane | J Oxx | Youmzain | Cavalryman | 19 | 2 26.30 |
| 2010 | K Abdulla's | **WORKFORCE** 3-8-11 (6/1) | R Moore | Sir M Stoute | Nakayama Festa | Sarafina | 18 | 2 35.30 |
| 2011 | Gestut Burg Eberstein & T Yoshida's | **DANEDREAM** 3-8-8 (20/1) | A Starke | P Schiergen | Shareta | Snow Fairy | 16 | 2 24.49 |
| 2012 | Wertheimer & Frere's | **SOLEMIA** 4-9-2 (33/1) | O Peslier | C Laffon-Parias | Orfevre | Masterstroke | 18 | 2 37.68 |
| 2013 | H E Sheikh Joaan Bin Hamad Al Thani's | **TREVE** 3-8-8 (9/2) | T Jarnet | Mme C Head-Maarek | Orfevre | Intello | 17 | 2 32.04 |
| 2014 | Al Shaqab Racing's | **TREVE** 4-9-2 (11/1) | T Jarnet | Mme C Head-Maarek | Flintshire | Taghrooda | 20 | 2 26.05 |

# GRAND NATIONAL STEEPLECHASE Aintree-4m 3f 110y (4m 4f before 2013)

| Year | Winner and Price | Age & Weight | Jockey | Second | Third | Ran | Time |
|---|---|---|---|---|---|---|---|
| 1969 | **HIGHLAND WEDDING** (100/9) | 12 10 4 | E Harty | Steel Bridge | Rondetto | 30 | 9 30.80 |
| 1970 | **GAY TRIP** (15/1) | 8 11 5 | P Taaffe | Vulture | Miss Hunter | 28 | 9 38.00 |
| 1971 | **SPECIFY** (28/1) | 9 10 13 | J Cook | Black Secret | Astbury | 38 | 9 34.20 |
| 1972 | **WELL TO DO** (14/1) | 9 10 1 | G Thorner | Gay Trip | Black Secret/General Symons | 42 | 10 08.40 |
| 1973 | **RED RUM** (9/1) | 8 10 5 | B Fletcher | Crisp | L'Escargot | 38 | 9 01.90 |
| 1974 | **RED RUM** (11/1) | 9 12 0 | B Fletcher | L'Escargot | Charles Dickens | 42 | 9 20.30 |
| 1975 | **L'ESCARGOT** (13/2) | 12 11 3 | T Carberry | Red Rum | Spanish Steps | 31 | 9 31.10 |
| 1976 | **RAG TRADE** (14/1) | 10 10 12 | J Burke | Red Rum | Eyecatcher | 32 | 9 20.90 |
| 1977 | **RED RUM** (9/1) | 12 11 8 | T Stack | Churchtown Boy | Eyecatcher | 42 | 9 30.30 |
| 1978 | **LUCIUS** (14/1) | 9 10 9 | B R Davies | Sebastian V | Drumroan | 37 | 9 33.90 |
| 1979 | **RUBSTIC** (25/1) | 10 10 0 | M Barnes | Zongalero | Rough and Tumble | 34 | 9 52.90 |
| 1980 | **BEN NEVIS** (40/1) | 12 10 12 | Mr C Fenwick | Rough and Tumble | The Pilgarlic | 30 | 10 17.40 |
| 1981 | **ALDANITI** (10/1) | 11 10 13 | R Champion | Spartan Missile | Royal Mail | 39 | 9 47.20 |
| 1982 | **GRITTAR** (7/1) | 9 11 5 | E Saunders | Hard Outlook | Loving Words | 39 | 9 12.60 |
| 1983 | **CORBIERE** (13/1) | 8 11 4 | B de Haan | Greasepaint | Yer Man | 41 | 9 47.04 |
| 1984 | **HALLO DANDY** (13/1) | 10 10 2 | N Doughty | Greasepaint | Corbiere | 40 | 9 21.04 |
| 1985 | **LAST SUSPECT** (50/1) | 11 10 5 | H Davies | Mr Snugfit | Corbiere | 40 | 9 42.70 |
| 1986 | **WEST TIP** (15/2) | 9 10 11 | R Dunwoody | Young Driver | Classified | 40 | 9 33.00 |
| 1987 | **MAORI VENTURE** (28/1) | 11 10 13 | S C Knight | The Tsarevich | Lean Ar Aghaidh | 40 | 9 19.30 |
| 1988 | **RHYME 'N' REASON** (10/1) | 9 11 0 | B Powell | Durham Edition | Monanore | 40 | 9 53.50 |
| 1989 | **LITTLE POLVEIR** (28/1) | 12 10 3 | J Frost | West Tip | The Thinker | 40 | 10 06.80 |
| 1990 | **MR FRISK** (16/1) | 11 10 6 | Mr M Armytage | Durham Edition | Rinus | 38 | 8 47.80 |
| 1991 | **SEAGRAM** (12/1) | 11 10 6 | N Hawke | Garrison Savannah | Auntie Dot | 40 | 9 29.90 |
| 1992 | **PARTY POLITICS** (14/1) | 8 10 7 | C Llewellyn | Romany King | Laura's Beau | 40 | 9 06.30 |
| 1993 | Race Void - false start | | | | | | |
| 1994 | **MIINNEHOMA** (16/1) | 11 10 8 | R Dunwoody | Just So | Moorcroft Boy | 36 | 10 18.80 |
| 1995 | **ROYAL ATHLETE** (40/1) | 12 10 6 | J Titley | Party Politics | Over The Deel | 35 | 9 04.00 |
| 1996 | **ROUGH QUEST** (7/1) | 10 10 7 | M Fitzgerald | Encore Un Peu | Superior Finish | 27 | 9 00.80 |
| 1997 | **LORD GYLLENE** (14/1) | 9 10 0 | A Dobbin | Suny Bay | Camelot Knight | 36 | 9 05.80 |
| 1998 | **EARTH SUMMIT** (7/1) | 10 10 5 | C Llewellyn | Suny Bay | Samlee | 37 | 10 51.40 |
| 1999 | **BOBBYJO** (10/1) | 9 10 0 | P Carberry | Blue Charm | Call It A Day | 32 | 9 14.00 |
| 2000 | **PAPILLON** (10/1) | 9 10 12 | R Walsh | Mely Moss | Niki Dee | 40 | 9 09.70 |
| 2001 | **RED MARAUDER** (33/1) | 11 10 11 | R Guest | Smarty | Blowing Wind | 40 | 11 00.10 |
| 2002 | **BINDAREE** (20/1) | 8 10 4 | J Culloty | What's Up Boys | Blowing Wind | 40 | 9 09.00 |
| 2003 | **MONTY'S PASS** (16/1) | 10 10 7 | B J Geraghty | Supreme Glory | Amberleigh House | 40 | 9 21.70 |
| 2004 | **AMBERLEIGH HOUSE** (16/1) | 12 10 10 | G Lee | Clan Royal | Lord Atterbury | 39 | 9 20.30 |
| 2005 | **HEDGEHUNTER** (7/1) | 9 11 1 | R Walsh | Royal Auclair | Simply Gifted | 40 | 9 20.80 |
| 2006 | **NUMBERSIXVALVERDE** (11/1) | 10 10 8 | N Madden | Hedgehunter | Clan Royal | 40 | 9 41.00 |
| 2007 | **SILVER BIRCH** (33/1) | 10 10 6 | R M Power | McKelvey | Slim Pickings | 40 | 9 13.60 |
| 2008 | **COMPLY OR DIE** (7/1) | 9 10 9 | T Murphy | King Johns Castle | Snowy Morning | 40 | 9 16.60 |
| 2009 | **MON MOME** (100/1) | 9 11 0 | L Treadwell | Comply Or Die | My Will | 40 | 9 32.90 |
| 2010 | **DON'T PUSH IT** (10/1) | 10 11 0 | A P McCoy | Black Apalachi | State Of Play | 40 | 9 04.60 |
| 2011 | **BALLABRIGGS** (14/1) | 10 11 0 | J Maguire | Oscar Time | Don't Push It | 40 | 9 01.20 |
| 2012 | **NEPTUNE COLLONGES** (33/1) | 11 11 6 | D Jacob | Sunnyhillboy | Seabass | 40 | 9 05.10 |
| 2013 | **AURORAS ENCORE** (66/1) | 11 10 3 | R Mania | Cappa Bleu | Teaforthree | 40 | 9 12.00 |
| 2014 | **PINEAU DE RE** (25/1) | 11 10 6 | L Aspell | Balthazar King | Double Seven | 40 | 9 9.90 |

# WINNERS OF GREAT RACES

## LINCOLN HANDICAP
Doncaster-1m

2005 **STREAM OF GOLD** 4-9-10 ....22
*2006 **BLYTHE KNIGHT** 6-8-10 ....30
**2007 **VERY WISE** 5-8-11 ....20
2008 **SMOKEY OAKEY** 4-8-9 ....21
2009 **EXPRESSO STAR** 4-8-12 ....20
2010 **PENITENT** 4-9-2 ....21
2011 **SWEET LIGHTNING** 6-9-4 ....21
2012 **BRAE HILL** 6-9-1 ....22
2013 **LEVITATE** 5-8-4 ....22
2014 **OCEAN TEMPEST** 5-9-3 ....17

*Run at Redcar
**Run at Newcastle

## GREENHAM STAKES (3y)
Newbury-7f

2005 **INDESATCHEL** 9-0 ....9
2006 **RED CLUBS** 9-0 ....5
2007 **MAJOR CADEAUX** 9-0 ....6
2008 **PACO BOY** 9-0 ....8
2009 **VOCALISED** 9-0 ....8
2010 **DICK TURPIN** 9-0 ....5
2011 **FRANKEL** 9-0 ....6
2012 **CASPAR NETSCHER** 9-0 ....5
2013 **OLYMPIC GLORY** 9-0 ....5
2014 **KINGMAN** 9-0 ....10

## EUROPEAN FREE HANDICAP (3y)
Newmarket-7f

2005 **KAMAKIRI** 8-10 ....8
2006 **MISU BOND** 8-13 ....8
2007 **PRIME DEFENDER** 9-5 ....7
2008 **STIMULATION** 9-3 ....11
2009 **OUQBA** 8-9 ....10
2010 **RED JAZZ** 9-6 ....7
2011 **PAUSANIAS** 8-12 ....6
2012 **TELWAAR** 8-11 ....7
2013 **GARSWOOD** 9-0 ....10
2014 **SHIFTING POWER** 9-1 ....6

## CRAVEN STAKES (3y)
Newmarket-1m

2005 **DEMOCRATIC DEFICIT** 8-12 ....8
2006 **KILLYBEGS** 8-12 ....9
2007 **ADAGIO** 8-12 ....8
2008 **TWICE OVER** 8-12 ....10
2009 **DELEGATOR** 8-12 ....7
2010 **ELUSIVE PIMPERNEL** 8-12 ....9
2011 **NATIVE KHAN** 8-12 ....6
2012 **TRUMPET MAJOR** 9-1 ....12
2013 **TORONADO** 9-1 ....4
2014 **TOORMORE** 9-3 ....6

## JOCKEY CLUB STAKES
Newmarket-1m 4f

2005 **ALKAASED** 5-8-9 ....5
2006 **SHIROCCO** 5-9-3 ....7
2007 **SIXTIES ICON** 4-9-3 ....5
2008 **GETAWAY** 5-9-1 ....10
2009 **BRONZE CANNON** 4-8-12 ....3
2010 **JUKEBOX JURY** 4-9-3 ....5
2011 **DANDINO** 4-8-11 ....6
2012 **AL KAZEEM** 4-8-12 ....8
2013 **UNIVERSAL** 4-8-12 ....4
2014 **GOSPEL CHOIR** 5-9-0 ....8

## SANDOWN MILE
Sandown-1m

2005 **HURRICANE ALAN** 5-9-0 ....8
2006 **ROB ROY** 4-9-0 ....8
2007 **JEREMY** 4-9-0 ....9
2008 **MAJOR CADEAUX** 4-9-0 ....8
2009 **PACO BOY** 4-9-6 ....7
2010 **PACO BOY** 5-9-0 ....9
2011 **DICK TURPIN** 4-9-0 ....5
2012 **PENITENT** 6-9-0 ....6
2013 **TRUMPET MAJOR** 4-9-0 ....7
2014 **TULLIUS** 6-9-1 ....6

## CHESTER VASE (3y)
Chester-1m 4f 66yds

2005 **HATTAN** 8-10 ....5
2006 **PAPAL BULL** 8-12 ....5
2007 **SOLDIER OF FORTUNE** 9-2 ....4
2008 **DOCTOR FREMANTLE** 8-12 ....8
2009 **GOLDEN SWORD** 8-12 ....8
2010 **TED SPREAD** 8-12 ....7
2011 **TREASURE BEACH** 8-12 ....5
2012 **MICKDAAM** 8-12 ....5
2013 **RULER OF THE WORLD** 8-12 ....4
2014 **ORCHESTRA** 9-0 ....8

## CHESTER CUP
Chester-2m 2f 147yds

2005 **ANAK PEKAN** 5-9-6 ....17
2006 **ADMIRAL** 5-8-1 ....17
2007 **GREENWICH MEANTIME** 7-9-2 ....17
2008 **BULWARK** 6-9-4 ....17
2009 **DARAAHEM** 4-9-0 ....17
2010 **MAMLOOK** 6-8-12 ....17
2011 **OVERTURN** 7-8-13 ....17
2012 **ILE DE RE** 6-8-11 ....16
2013 **ADDRESS UNKNOWN** 6-9-0 ....17
2014 **SUEGIOO** 5-9-4 ....17

## OAKS TRIAL (3y fillies)
Lingfield-1m 3f 106yds

2005 **CASSYDORA** 8-10 ....6
2006 **SINDIRANA** 8-10 ....10
2007 **KAYAH** 8-12 ....7
2008 **MIRACLE SEEKER** 8-12 ....6
2009 **MIDDAY** 8-12 ....9
2010 **DYNA WALTZ** 8-12 ....5
2011 **ZAIN AL BOLDAN** 8-12 ....9
*2012 **VOW** 8-12 ....8
2013 **SECRET GESTURE** 8-12 ....7
2014 **HONOR BOUND** 9-0 ....10

*Run over 1m4f on Polytrack

## DERBY TRIAL (3y)
Lingfield-1m 3f 106yds

2005 **KONG** 8-10 ....6
2006 **LINDA'S LAD** 9-3 ....5
2007 **AQALEEM** 8-12 ....7

2008 **ALESSANDRO VOLTA** 8-12 ............ 5
2009 **AGE OF AQUARIUS** 8-12 ............ 5
2010 **BULLET TRAIN** 8-12 ............ 7
2011 **DORDOGNE** 8-12 ............ 6
*2012 **MAIN SEQUENCE** 8-12 ............ 8
2013 **NEVIS** 8-12 ............ 4
2014 **SNOW SKY** 9-0 ............ 9
*Run over 1m4f on Polytrack

## MUSIDORA STAKES (3y fillies)
York-1m 2f 88yds
2005 **SECRET HISTORY** 8-10 ............ 6
2006 **SHORT SKIRT** 8-12 ............ 6
2007 **PASSAGE OF TIME** 9-1 ............ 5
2008 **LUSH LASHES** 8-12 ............ 8
2009 **SARISKA** 8-12 ............ 6
2010 **AVIATE** 8-12 ............ 8
2011 **JOVIALITY** 8-12 ............ 5
2012 **THE FUGUE** 8-12 ............ 6
2013 **LIBER NAUTICUS** 8-12 ............ 6
2014 **MADAME CHIANG** 9-0 ............ 9

## DANTE STAKES (3y)
York-1m 2f 88yds
2005 **MOTIVATOR** 8-11 ............ 6
2006 **SEPTIMUS** 9-0 ............ 6
2007 **AUTHORIZED** 9-0 ............ 6
2008 **TARTAN BEARER** 9-0 ............ 6
2009 **BLACK BEAR ISLAND** 9-0 ............ 10
2010 **CAPE BLANCO** 9-0 ............ 5
2011 **CARLTON HOUSE** 9-0 ............ 6
2012 **BONFIRE** 9-0 ............ 7
2013 **LIBERTARIAN** 9-0 ............ 8
2014 **THE GREY GATSBY** 9-0 ............ 6

## MIDDLETON STAKES (fillies and mares)
York-1m 2f 88yds
2005 **ALL TOO BEAUTIFUL** 4-8-9 ............ 5
2006 **STRAWBERRY DALE** 4-8-12 ............ 7
2007 **TOPATOO** 5-8-12 ............ 7
2008 **PROMISING LEAD** 4-8-12 ............ 5
2009 **CRYSTAL CAPELLA** 4-9-2 ............ 5
2010 **SARISKA** 4-8-12 ............ 4
2011 **MIDDAY** 5-9-3 ............ 8
2012 **IZZI TOP** 4-8-12 ............ 9
2013 **DALKALA** 4-9-0 ............ 8
2014 **AMBIVALENT** 5-9-0 ............ 8

## YORKSHIRE CUP
York-1m 6f (1m 5f 194yds before 2007)
2005 **FRANKLINS GARDENS** 5-8-10 ............ 9
2006 **PERCUSSIONIST** 5-8-12 ............ 7
2007 **SERGEANT CECIL** 8-9-3 ............ 10
2008 **GEORDIELAND** 7-8-12 ............ 5
2009 **ASK** 6-8-13 ............ 8
2010 **MANIFEST** 4-8-12 ............ 5
2011 **DUNCAN** 6-9-2 ............ 8
2012 **RED CADEAUX** 6-9-0 ............ 8
2013 **GLEN'S DIAMOND** 5-9-0 ............ 8
2014 **GOSPEL CHOIR** 5-9-0 ............ 12

## DUKE OF YORK STAKES
York-6f
2005 **THE KIDDYKID** 5-9-2 ............ 11
2006 **STEENBERG** 7-9-2 ............ 16
2007 **AMADEUS WOLF** 4-9-2 ............ 17
2008 **ASSERTIVE** 5-9-7 ............ 17
2009 **UTMOST RESPECT** 5-9-7 ............ 16
2010 **PRIME DEFENDER** 6-9-7 ............ 12
2011 **DELEGATOR** 5-9-7 ............ 14
2012 **TIDDLIWINKS** 6-9-7 ............ 13
2013 **SOCIETY ROCK** 6-9-13 ............ 17
2014 **MAAREK** 7-9-13 ............ 13

## LOCKINGE STAKES
Newbury-1m
2005 **RAKTI** 6-9-0 ............ 8
2006 **PEERESS** 5-8-11 ............ 9
2007 **RED EVIE** 4-8-11 ............ 8
2008 **CREACHADOIR** 4-9-0 ............ 11
2009 **VIRTUAL** 4-9-0 ............ 11
2010 **PACO BOY** 5-9-0 ............ 9
2011 **CANFORD CLIFFS** 4-9-0 ............ 7
2012 **FRANKEL** 4-9-0 ............ 6
2013 **FARHH** 5-9-0 ............ 12
2014 **OLYMPIC GLORY** 4-9-0 ............ 8

## HENRY II STAKES
Sandown-2m 78yds
2005 **FIGHT YOUR CORNER** 6-9-0 ............ 16
2006 **TUNGSTEN STRIKE** 5-9-2 ............ 7
2007 **ALLEGRETTO** 4-9-0 ............ 7
2008 **FINALMENTE** 6-9-2 ............ 8
2009 **GEORDIELAND** 8-9-2 ............ 7
2010 **AKMAL** 4-9-0 ............ 9
2011 **BLUE BAJAN** 9-9-2 ............ 8
2012 **OPINION POLL** 6-9-4 ............ 10
2013 **GLOOMY SUNDAY** 4-8-11 ............ 10
2014 **BROWN PANTHER** 6-9-4 ............ 11

## TEMPLE STAKES
Haydock-5f
(Run at Sandown before 2008)
2005 **CELTIC MILL** 7-9-4 ............ 13
2006 **REVERENCE** 5-9-4 ............ 12
2007 **SIERRA VISTA** 7-9-1 ............ 8
2008 **FLEETING SPIRIT** 3-8-11 ............ 12
2009 **LOOK BUSY** 4-9-1 ............ 9
2010 **KINGSGATE NATIVE** 5-9-4 ............ 9
2011 **SOLE POWER** 4-9-4 ............ 12
2012 **BATED BREATH** 5-9-4 ............ 12
2013 **KINGSGATE NATIVE** 8-9-4 ............ 10
2014 **HOT STREAK** 3-8-10 ............ 9

## BRIGADIER GERARD STAKES
Sandown-1m 2f 7yds
2005 **NEW MORNING** 4-8-7 ............ 5
2006 **NOTNOWCATO** 4-9-3 ............ 6
2007 **TAKE A BOW** 6-9-0 ............ 7
2008 **SMOKEY OAKEY** 4-9-0 ............ 14
2009 **CIMA DE TRIOMPHE** 4-9-0 ............ 12
2010 **STOTSFOLD** 7-9-0 ............ 8
2011 **WORKFORCE** 4-9-7 ............ 8
2012 **CARLTON HOUSE** 4-9-0 ............ 6
2013 **MUKHADRAM** 4-9-0 ............ 5
2014 **SHARESTAN** 6-9-0 ............ 3

## CORONATION CUP
Epsom-1m 4f 10yds
2005 **YEATS** 4-9-0 ............ 7
2006 **SHIROCCO** 5-9-0 ............ 6
2007 **SCORPION** 5-9-0 ............ 7
2008 **SOLDIER OF FORTUNE** 4-9-0 ............ 11
2009 **ASK** 6-9-0 ............ 8
2010 **FAME AND GLORY** 4-9-0 ............ 9
2011 **ST NICHOLAS ABBEY** 4-9-0 ............ 5

2012 **ST NICHOLAS ABBEY** 5-9-0 ....6
2013 **ST NICHOLAS ABBEY** 6-9-0 ....5
2014 **CIRRUS DES AIGLES** 8-9-0 ....7

## CHARITY SPRINT HANDICAP (3y)
York-6f
2005 **TAX FREE** 8-9 ....20
2006 **PRINCE TAMINO** 8-13 ....18
2007 ABANDONED
2008 **BRAVE PROSPECTOR** 9-0 ....19
2009 **SWISS DIVA** 9-1 ....20
2010 **VICTOIRE DE LYPHAR** 8-7 ....20
2011 **LEXI'S HERO** 8-11 ....20
2012 **SHOLAAN** 8-9 ....17
2013 **BODY AND SOUL** 8-11 ....19
2014 **SEE THE SUN** 8-7 ....20

## QUEEN ANNE STAKES
Ascot-1m (st)
*2005 **VALIXIR** 4-9-0 ....7
2006 **AD VALOREM** 4-9-0 ....7
2007 **RAMONTI** 5-9-0 ....8
2008 **HARADASUN** 5-9-0 ....11
2009 **PACO BOY** 4-9-0 ....9
2010 **GOLDIKOVA** 5-8-11 ....10
2011 **CANFORD CLIFFS** 4-9-0 ....7
2012 **FRANKEL** 4-9-0 ....11
2013 **DECLARATION OF WAR** 4-9-0 ....13
2014 **TORONADO** 4-9-0 ....10
*Run at York

## PRINCE OF WALES'S STAKES
Ascot-1m 2f
*2005 **AZAMOUR** 4-9-0 ....8
2006 **OUIJA BOARD** 5-8-11 ....7
2007 **MANDURO** 5-9-0 ....6
2008 **DUKE OF MARMALADE** 4-9-0 ....12
2009 **VISION D'ETAT** 4-9-0 ....8
2010 **BYWORD** 4-9-0 ....12
2011 **REWILDING** 4-9-0 ....7
2012 **SO YOU THINK** 6-9-0 ....11
2013 **AL KAZEEM** 5-9-0 ....11
2014 **THE FUGUE** 5-8-11 ....8
*Run at York

## ST JAMES'S PALACE STAKES (3y)
Ascot-1m (rnd)
*2005 **SHAMARDAL** 9-0 ....8
2006 **ARAAFA** 9-0 ....11
2007 **EXCELLENT ART** 9-0 ....8
2008 **HENRYTHENAVIGATOR** 9-0 ....8
2009 **MASTERCRAFTSMAN** 9-0 ....10
2010 **CANFORD CLIFFS** 9-0 ....9
2011 **FRANKEL** 9-0 ....9
2012 **MOST IMPROVED** 9-0 ....16
2013 **DAWN APPROACH** 9-0 ....9
2014 **KINGMAN** 9-0 ....7
*Run at York

## COVENTRY STAKES (2y)
Ascot-6f
*2005 **RED CLUBS** 8-12 ....14
2006 **HELLVELYN** 9-1 ....21
2007 **HENRYTHENAVIGATOR** 9-1 ....20
2008 **ART CONNOISSEUR** 9-1 ....18
2009 **CANFORD CLIFFS** 9-1 ....13
2010 **STRONG SUIT** 9-1 ....13
2011 **POWER** 9-1 ....23
2012 **DAWN APPROACH** 9-1 ....22
2013 **WAR COMMAND** 9-1 ....15
2014 **THE WOW SIGNAL** 9-1 ....15
*Run at York

## KING EDWARD VII STAKES (3y)
Ascot-1m 4f
*2005 **PLEA BARGAIN** 8-11 ....5
2006 **PAPAL BULL** 8-12 ....9
2007 **BOSCOBEL** 8-12 ....9
2008 **CAMPANOLOGIST** 8-12 ....9
2009 **FATHER TIME** 8-12 ....12
2010 **MONTEROSSO** 8-12 ....8
2011 **NATHANIEL** 8-12 ....10
2012 **THOMAS CHIPPENDALE** 8-12 ....5
2013 **HILLSTAR** 8-12 ....8
2014 **EAGLE TOP** 9-0 ....9
*Run at York

## JERSEY STAKES (3y)
Ascot-7f
*2005 **PROCLAMATION** 8-13 ....21
2006 **JEREMY** 9-1 ....14
2007 **TARIQ** 9-1 ....15
2008 **AQLAAM** 9-1 ....16
2009 **OUQBA** 9-1 ....16
2010 **RAINFALL** 8-12 ....13
2011 **STRONG SUIT** 9-6 ....9
2012 **ISHVANA** 8-12 ....22
2013 **GALE FORCE TEN** 9-1 ....21
2014 **MUSTAJEEB** 9-4 ....23
*Run at York

## DUKE OF CAMBRIDGE STAKES (fillies & mares)
Ascot-1m (st)
(Windsor Forest Stakes before 2013)
*2005 **PEERESS** 4-8-9 ....8
2006 **SOVIET SONG** 6-8-12 ....10
2007 **NANNINA** 4-8-12 ....9
2008 **SABANA PERDIDA** 5-8-12 ....13
2009 **SPACIOUS** 4-8-12 ....9
2010 **STRAWBERRYDAIQUIRI** 4-8-12 ....10
2011 **LOLLY FOR DOLLY** 4-8-12 ....13
2012 **JOVIALITY** 4-8-12 ....13
2013 **DUNTLE** 4-8-12 ....9
2014 **INTEGRAL** 4-9-0 ....14
*Run at York

## QUEEN MARY STAKES (2y fillies)
Ascot-5f
*2005 **FLASHY WINGS** 8-10 ....17
2006 **GILDED** 8-12 ....15
2007 **ELLETELLE** 8-12 ....21
2008 **LANGS LASH** 8-12 ....17
2009 **JEALOUS AGAIN** 8-12 ....13
2010 **MAQAASID** 8-12 ....18
2011 **BEST TERMS** 8-12 ....14
2012 **CEILING KITTY** 8-12 ....27
2013 **RIZEENA** 8-12 ....23
2014 **ANTHEM ALEXANDER** 9-0 ....21
*Run at York

## CORONATION STAKES (3y fillies)
Ascot-1m (rnd)
*2005 **MAIDS CAUSEWAY** 9-0 ....10
2006 **NANNINA** 9-0 ....15
2007 **INDIAN INK** 9-0 ....13

2008 **LUSH LASHES** 9-0 ........ 11
2009 **GHANAATI** 9-0 ........ 10
2010 **LILLIE LANGTRY** 9-0 ........ 13
2011 **IMMORTAL VERSE** 9-0 ........ 12
2012 **FALLEN FOR YOU** 9-0 ........ 10
2013 **SKY LANTERN** 9-0 ........ 17
2014 **RIZEENA** 9-0 ........ 12
*Run at York

## ROYAL HUNT CUP

Ascot-1m (st)
*2005 **NEW SEEKER** 5-9-0 ........ 22
2006 **CESARE** 5-8-8 ........ 30
2007 **ROYAL OATH** 4-9-0 ........ 26
2008 **MR AVIATOR** 4-9-5 ........ 29
2009 **FORGOTTEN VOICE** 4-9-1 ........ 25
2010 **INVISIBLE MAN** 4-8-9 ........ 29
2011 **JULIENAS** 4-8-8 ........ 28
2012 **PRINCE OF JOHANNE** 6-9-3 ........ 30
2013 **BELGIAN BILL** 5-8-11 ........ 28
2014 **FIELD OF DREAM** 7-9-1 ........ 28
*Run at York

## QUEEN'S VASE (3y)

Ascot-2m
*2005 **MELROSE AVENUE** 8-11 ........ 10
2006 **SOAPY DANGER** 9-1 ........ 11
2007 **MAHLER** 9-1 ........ 15
2008 **PATKAI** 9-1 ........ 12
2009 **HOLBERG** 9-1 ........ 14
2010 **MIKHAIL GLINKA** 9-1 ........ 12
2011 **NAMIBIAN** 9-1 ........ 11
2012 **ESTIMATE** 8-12 ........ 10
2013 **LEADING LIGHT** 9-4 ........ 15
2014 **HARTNELL** 9-3 ........ 10
*Run at York

## DIAMOND JUBILEE STAKES

Ascot-6f
(Golden Jubilee Stakes before 2012)
*2005 **CAPE OF GOOD HOPE** 7-9-4 ........ 15
2006 **LES ARCS** 6-9-4 ........ 18
2007 **SOLDIER'S TALE** 6-9-4 ........ 21
2008 **KINGSGATE NATIVE** 3-8-11 ........ 17
2009 **ART CONNOISSEUR** 3-8-11 ........ 14
2010 **STARSPANGLEDBANNER** 4-9-4 ........ 24
2011 **SOCIETY ROCK** 4-9-4 ........ 16
2012 **BLACK CAVIAR** 6-9-1 ........ 14
2013 **LETHAL FORCE** 4-9-4 ........ 18
2014 **SLADE POWER** 5-9-4 ........ 14
*Run at York

## NORFOLK STAKES (2y)

Ascot-5f
*2005 **MASTA PLASTA** 8-12 ........ 12
2006 **DUTCH ART** 9-1 ........ 11
2007 **WINKER WATSON** 9-1 ........ 11
2008 **SOUTH CENTRAL** 9-1 ........ 11
2009 **RADIOHEAD** 9-1 ........ 11
2010 **APPROVE** 9-1 ........ 12
2011 **BAPAK CHINTA** 9-1 ........ 15
2012 **RECKLESS ABANDON** 9-1 ........ 11
2013 **NO NAY NEVER** 9-1 ........ 14
2014 **BAITHA ALGA** 9-1 ........ 9
*Run at York

## GOLD CUP

Ascot-2m 4f
*2005 **WESTERNER** 6-9-2 ........ 17
2006 **YEATS** 5-9-2 ........ 12
2007 **YEATS** 6-9-2 ........ 14
2008 **YEATS** 7-9-2 ........ 10
2009 **YEATS** 8-9-2 ........ 9
2010 **RITE OF PASSAGE** 6-9-2 ........ 12
2011 **FAME AND GLORY** 5-9-2 ........ 15
2012 **COLOUR VISION** 4-9-0 ........ 9
2013 **ESTIMATE** 4-8-11 ........ 14
2014 **LEADING LIGHT** 4-9-0 ........ 12
*Run at York

## RIBBLESDALE STAKES (3y fillies)

Ascot-1m 4f
*2005 **THAKAFAAT** 8-11 ........ 9
2006 **MONT ETOILE** 8-12 ........ 11
2007 **SILKWOOD** 8-12 ........ 12
2008 **MICHITA** 8-12 ........ 9
2009 **FLYING CLOUD** 8-12 ........ 10
2010 **HIBAAYEB** 8-12 ........ 11
2011 **BANIMPIRE** 8-12 ........ 12
2012 **PRINCESS HIGHWAY** 8-12 ........ 14
2013 **RIPOSTE** 8-12 ........ 9
2014 **BRACELET** 9-0 ........ 12
*Run at York

## HARDWICKE STAKES

Ascot-1m 4f
*2005 **BANDARI** 6-8-9 ........ 6
2006 **MARAAHEL** 5-9-0 ........ 8
2007 **MARAAHEL** 6-9-0 ........ 7
2008 **MACARTHUR** 4-9-0 ........ 9
2009 **BRONZE CANNON** 4-9-3 ........ 9
2010 **HARBINGER** 4-9-0 ........ 11
2011 **AWAIT THE DAWN** 4-9-0 ........ 9
2012 **SEA MOON** 4-9-0 ........ 12
2013 **THOMAS CHIPPENDALE** 4-9-0 ........ 8
2014 **TELESCOPE** 4-9-1 ........ 10
*Run at York

## WOKINGHAM STAKES

Ascot-6f
*2005 **IFFRAAJ** 4-9-6 ........ 17
2006 **BALTIC KING** 6-9-10 ........ 28
2007 **DARK MISSILE** 4-8-6 ........ 26
2008 **BIG TIMER** 4-9-2 ........ 27
2009 **HIGH STANDING** 4-8-12 ........ 26
2010 **LADDIES POKER TWO** 5-8-11 ........ 27
2011 **DEACON BLUES** 4-8-13 ........ 25
2012 **DANDY BOY** 6-9-8 ........ 28
2013 **YORK GLORY** 5-9-2 ........ 26
2014 **BACCARAT** 5-9-2 ........ 28
*Run at York

## KING'S STAND STAKES

Ascot-5f
*2005 **CHINEUR** 4-9-2 ........ 16
2006 **TAKEOVER TARGET** 7-9-7 ........ 28
2007 **MISS ANDRETTI** 6-9-1 ........ 20
2008 **EQUIANO** 3-8-12 ........ 13
2009 **SCENIC BLAST** 5-9-4 ........ 15
2010 **EQUIANO** 5-9-4 ........ 12
2011 **PROHIBIT** 6-9-4 ........ 19
2012 **LITTLE BRIDGE** 6-9-4 ........ 22

2013 **SOLE POWER** 6-9-4 ........................................19
2014 **SOLE POWER** 7-9-4 ........................................16
*Run at York

## NORTHUMBERLAND PLATE

Newcastle-2m 19yds
2005 **SERGEANT CECIL** 6-8-8 ...............................20
2006 **TOLDO** 4-8-2 ...................................................20
2007 **JUNIPER GIRL** 4-8-11 .....................................20
2008 **ARC BLEU** 7-8-2 ...............................................18
2009 **SOM TALA** 6-8-8 ...............................................17
2010 **OVERTURN** 6-8-7 ..............................................19
2011 **TOMINATOR** 4-8-5 ............................................19
2012 **ILE DE RE** 6-9-3 ...............................................16
2013 **TOMINATOR** 6-9-10 ..........................................18
2014 **ANGEL GABRIAL** 5-8-12 ...................................19

## ECLIPSE STAKES

Sandown-1m 2f 7yds
2005 **ORATORIO** 3-8-10 ...............................................7
2006 **DAVID JUNIOR** 4-9-7 ..........................................9
2007 **NOTNOWCATO** 5-9-7 ...........................................8
2008 **MOUNT NELSON** 4-9-7 .........................................8
2009 **SEA THE STARS** 3-8-10 ......................................10
2010 **TWICE OVER** 5-9-7 ...............................................5
2011 **SO YOU THINK** 5-9-7 ............................................5
2012 **NATHANIEL** 4-9-7 ..................................................9
2013 **AL KAZEEM** 5-9-7 .................................................7
2014 **MUKHADRAM** 5-9-7 ................................................9

## LANCASHIRE OAKS (fillies and mares)

Haydock-1m 3f 200yds
2005 **PLAYFUL ACT** 3-8-5 ...............................................8
2006 **ALLEGRETTO** 3-8-6 ................................................8
*2007 **TURBO LINN** 4-9-5 ..............................................12
2008 **ANNA PAVLOVA** 5-9-8 ...........................................9
2009 **BARSHIBA** 5-9-5 .....................................................8
2010 **BARSHIBA** 6-9-5 ...................................................10
2011 **GERTRUDE BELL** 4-9-5 ...........................................7
2012 **GREAT HEAVENS** 3-8-6 ...........................................9
2013 **EMIRATES QUEEN** 4-9-5 .........................................8
2014 **POMOLOGY** 4-9-5 ....................................................9
*Run at Newmarket

## DUCHESS OF CAMBRIDGE STAKES (2y fillies)

Newmarket-6f
(Cherry Hinton Stakes before 2013)
2005 **DONNA BLINI** 8-9 .......................................................8
2006 **SANDER CAMILLO** 8-12 .............................................10
2007 **YOU'RESOTHRILLING** 8-12 .........................................14
2008 **PLEASE SING** 8-12 .......................................................8
2009 **MISHEER** 8-12 ............................................................10
2010 **MEMORY** 8-12 ...............................................................7
2011 **GAMILATI** 8-12 ............................................................11
2012 **SENDMYLOVETOROSE** 8-12 ........................................10
2013 **LUCKY KRISTALE** 8-12 ...................................................8
2014 **ARABIAN QUEEN** 9-0 ......................................................5

## BUNBURY CUP

(Run as 32Red Trophy in 2010)
Newmarket-7f
2005 **MINE** 7-9-9 .................................................................18
2006 **MINE** 8-9-10 ...............................................................19
2007 **GIGANTICUS** 4-8-8 ......................................................18
2008 **LITTLE WHITE LIE** 4-9-0 ...........................................18
2009 **PLUM PUDDING** 6-9-10 .................................................19
2010 **ST MORITZ** 4-9-1 ..........................................................19
2011 **BRAE HILL** 5-9-1 ..........................................................20
2012 **BONNIE BRAE** 5-9-9 ......................................................15
2013 **FIELD OF DREAM** 6-9-7 ................................................19
2014 **HEAVEN'S GUEST** 4-9-3 ................................................13

## PRINCESS OF WALES'S STAKES

Newmarket-1m 4f
2005 **GAMUT** 6-9-2 ..................................................................5
2006 **SOAPY DANGER** 3-8-3 .....................................................4
2007 **PAPAL BULL** 4-9-2 ..........................................................12
2008 **LUCARNO** 4-9-7 .................................................................6
2009 **DOCTOR FREMANTLE** 4-9-2 ...........................................9
2010 **SANS FRONTIERES** 4-9-2 .................................................8
2011 **CRYSTAL CAPELLA** 6-8-13 ................................................8
2012 **FIORENTE** 4-9-2 ...............................................................7
2013 **AL KAZEEM** 4-9-5 ...............................................................6
2014 **CAVALRYMAN** 8-9-2 ...........................................................6

## JULY STAKES (2y)

Newmarket-6f
2005 **IVAN DENISOVICH** 8-10 ................................................11
2006 **STRATEGIC PRINCE** 8-12 .................................................9
2007 **WINKER WATSON** 9-1 ......................................................13
2008 **CLASSIC BLADE** 8-12 .........................................................7
2009 **ARCANO** 8-12 ....................................................................11
2010 **LIBRANNO** 8-12 ....................................................................5
2011 **FREDERICK ENGELS** 8-12 ..................................................7
2012 **ALHEBAYEB** 8-12 .................................................................7
2013 **ANJAAL** 8-12 ......................................................................11
2014 **IVAWOOD** 9-0 .......................................................................12

## FALMOUTH STAKES (fillies & mares)

Newmarket-1m
2005 **SOVIET SONG** 5-9-1 ..............................................................7
2006 **RAJEEM** 3-8-10 ........................................................................7
2007 **SIMPLY PERFECT** 3-8-10 .........................................................7
2008 **NAHOODH** 3-8-10 ....................................................................11
2009 **GOLDIKOVA** 4-9-5 ....................................................................8
2010 **MUSIC SHOW** 3-8-10 ..................................................................8
2011 **TIMEPIECE** 4-9-5 ......................................................................11
2012 **GIOFRA** 4-9-5 ...........................................................................10
2013 **ELUSIVE KATE** 4-9-5 ..................................................................4
2014 **INTEGRAL** 4-9-7 ...........................................................................7

## SUPERLATIVE STAKES (2y)

Newmarket-7f
2005 **HORATIO NELSON** 8-11 .........................................................11
2006 **HALICARNASSUS** 8-11 ..............................................................7
2007 **HATTA FORT** 9-0 .......................................................................10
2008 **FIRTH OF FIFTH** 9-0 ....................................................................9
2009 **SILVER GRECIAN** 9-0 ...................................................................8
2010 **KING TORUS** 9-0 ...........................................................................6
2011 **RED DUKE** 9-0 .............................................................................11
2012 **OLYMPIC GLORY** 9-0 ......................................................................9
2013 **GOOD OLD BOY LUKEY** 9-0 ...........................................................8
2014 **ESTIDHKAAR** 9-1 ...........................................................................8

## JULY CUP

Newmarket-6f
2005 **PASTORAL PURSUITS** 4-9-5 ......................................................19
2006 **LES ARCS** 6-9-5 ........................................................................15
2007 **SAKHEE'S SECRET** 3-8-13 .........................................................18
2008 **MARCHAND D'OR** 5-9-5 .............................................................13
2009 **FLEETING SPIRIT** 4-9-2 ..............................................................13
2010 **STARSPANGLEDBANNER** 4-9-5 ......................................................14
2011 **DREAM AHEAD** 3-8-13 .................................................................16
2012 **MAYSON** 4-9-5 ...............................................................................12

2013 **LETHAL FORCE** 4-9-5 ........ 11
2014 **SLADE POWER** 5-9-6 ........ 13

## WEATHERBYS SUPER SPRINT (2y)

Newbury-5f 34 yds
2005 **LADY LIVIUS** 8-5 ........ 25
2006 **ELHAMRI** 9-4 ........ 23
2007 ABANDONED
2008 **JARGELLE** 8-6 ........ 23
2009 **MONSIEUR CHEVALIER** 8-12 ........ 20
2010 **TEMPLE MEADS** 8-6 ........ 24
2011 **CHARLES THE GREAT** 8-11 ........ 25
2012 **BODY AND SOUL** 7-12 ........ 22
2013 **PENIAPHOBIA** 8-8 ........ 24
2014 **TIGGY WIGGY** 9-1 ........ 24

## SUMMER MILE

Ascot-1m (rnd)
2007 **CESARE** 6-9-1 ........ 9
2008 **ARCHIPENKO** 4-9-6 ........ 7
2009 **AQLAAM** 4-9-1 ........ 7
2010 **PREMIO LOCO** 6-9-1 ........ 8
2011 **DICK TURPIN** 4-9-4 ........ 5
2012 **FANUNALTER** 6-9-1 ........ 8
2013 **ALJAMAAHEER** 4-9-1 ........ 11
2014 **GUEST OF HONOUR** 5-9-1 ........ 9

## PRINCESS MARGARET STAKES (2y fillies)

Ascot-6f
*2005 **MIXED BLESSING** 8-9 ........ 12
2006 **SCARLET RUNNER** 8-12 ........ 10
2007 **VISIT** 8-12 ........ 13
2008 **AFRICAN SKIES** 8-12 ........ 16
2009 **LADY OF THE DESERT** 8-12 ........ 9
2010 **SORAAYA** 8-12 ........ 11
2011 **ANGELS WILL FALL** 8-12 ........ 7
2012 **MAUREEN** 8-12 ........ 6
2013 **PRINCESS NOOR** 8-12 ........ 10
2014 **OSAILA** 9-0 ........ 8
*Run at Newbury

## LENNOX STAKES

Goodwood-7f
2005 **COURT MASTERPIECE** 5-9-0 ........ 14
2006 **IFFRAAJ** 5-9-4 ........ 10
2007 **TARIQ** 3-8-9 ........ 13
2008 **PACO BOY** 3-8-9 ........ 9
2009 **FINJAAN** 3-8-9 ........ 8
2010 **LORD SHANAKILL** 4-9-2 ........ 12
2011 **STRONG SUIT** 3-8-9 ........ 9
2012 **CHACHAMAIDEE** 5-8-13 ........ 7
2013 **GARSWOOD** 3-8-9 ........ 10
2014 **ES QUE LOVE** 5-9-3 ........ 7

## STEWARDS' CUP

Goodwood-6f
2005 **GIFT HORSE** 5-9-7 ........ 27
2006 **BORDERLESCOTT** 4-9-5 ........ 27
2007 **ZIDANE** 5-9-1 ........ 27
2008 **CONQUEST** 4-8-9 ........ 27
2009 **GENKI** 5-9-1 ........ 26
2010 **EVENS AND ODDS** 6-8-10 ........ 28
2011 **HOOF IT** 4-10-0 ........ 27
2012 **HAWKEYETHENOO** 6-9-9 ........ 27
2013 **REX IMPERATOR** 4-9-4 ........ 27
*2014 **INTRINSIC** 4-8-11 ........ 24
*Run as 32Red Cup in 2014

## GORDON STAKES (3y)

Goodwood-1m 4f
2005 **THE GEEZER** 8-10 ........ 5
2006 **SIXTIES ICON** 9-0 ........ 7
2007 **YELLOWSTONE** 9-0 ........ 9
2008 **CONDUIT** 9-0 ........ 6
2009 **HARBINGER** 9-0 ........ 9
2010 **REBEL SOLDIER** 9-0 ........ 10
2011 **NAMIBIAN** 9-3 ........ 10
2012 **NOBLE MISSION** 9-0 ........ 7
2013 **CAP O'RUSHES** 9-0 ........ 7
2014 **SNOW SKY** 9-1 ........ 7

## VINTAGE STAKES (2y)

Goodwood-7f
2005 **SIR PERCY** 8-11 ........ 7
2006 **STRATEGIC PRINCE** 9-3 ........ 10
2007 **RIO DE LA PLATA** 9-0 ........ 7
2008 **ORIZABA** 9-0 ........ 9
2009 **XTENSION** 9-0 ........ 10
2010 **KING TORUS** 9-3 ........ 7
2011 **CHANDLERY** 9-0 ........ 7
2012 **OLYMPIC GLORY** 9-3 ........ 10
2013 **TOORMORE** 9-0 ........ 12
2014 **HIGHLAND REEL** 9-1 ........ 8

## SUSSEX STAKES

Goodwood-1m
2005 **PROCLAMATION** 3-8-13 ........ 12
2006 **COURT MASTERPIECE** 6-9-7 ........ 7
2007 **RAMONTI** 5-9-7 ........ 8
2008 **HENRYTHENAVIGATOR** 3-8-13 ........ 6
2009 **RIP VAN WINKLE** 3-8-13 ........ 8
2010 **CANFORD CLIFFS** 3-8-13 ........ 7
2011 **FRANKEL** 3-8-13 ........ 4
2012 **FRANKEL** 4-9-7 ........ 4
2013 **TORONADO** 3-8-13 ........ 7
2014 **KINGMAN** 3-9-0 ........ 4

## RICHMOND STAKES (2y)

Goodwood-6f
2005 **ALWAYS HOPEFUL** 8-11 ........ 6
2006 **HAMOODY** 9-0 ........ 7
2007 **STRIKE THE DEAL** 9-0 ........ 9
2008 **PROLIFIC** 9-0 ........ 12
2009 **DICK TURPIN** 9-0 ........ 9
2010 **LIBRANNO** 9-3 ........ 6
2011 **HARBOUR WATCH** 9-0 ........ 10
2012 **HEAVY METAL** 9-0 ........ 8
2013 **SAAYERR** 9-0 ........ 10
2014 **IVAWOOD** 9-3 ........ 8

## KING GEORGE STAKES

Goodwood-5f
2005 **FIRE UP THE BAND** 6-9-0 ........ 12
2006 **LA CUCARACHA** 5-8-11 ........ 18
2007 **MOORHOUSE LAD** 4-9-0 ........ 17
2008 **ENTICING** 4-8-11 ........ 12
2009 **KINGSGATE NATIVE** 4-9-0 ........ 17
2010 **BORDERLESCOTT** 8-9-0 ........ 15
2011 **MASAMAH** 5-9-0 ........ 11
2012 **ORTENSIA** 7-9-5 ........ 17
2013 **MOVIESTA** 3-8-12 ........ 17
2014 **TAKE COVER** 7-9-1 ........ 15

## GOODWOOD CUP
Goodwood-2m
2005 **DISTINCTION** 6-9-5 ......10
2006 **YEATS** 5-9-10 ......15
2007 **ALLEGRETTO** 4-9-5 ......15
2008 **YEATS** 7-9-12 ......8
2009 **SCHIAPARELLI** 6-9-7 ......10
2010 **ILLUSTRIOUS BLUE** 7-9-7 ......10
2011 **OPINION POLL** 5-9-7 ......15
2012 **SADDLER'S ROCK** 4-9-7 ......10
2013 **BROWN PANTHER** 5-9-7 ......14
2014 **CAVALRYMAN** 8-9-8 ......8

## MOLECOMB STAKES (2y)
Goodwood-5f
2005 **STRIKE UP THE BAND** 9-1 ......15
2006 **ENTICING** 8-11 ......13
2007 **FLEETING SPIRIT** 8-11 ......16
2008 **FINJAAN** 9-0 ......11
2009 **MONSIEUR CHEVALIER** 9-0 ......11
2010 **ZEBEDEE** 9-0 ......12
2011 **REQUINTO** 9-0 ......13
2012 **BUNGLE INTHEJUNGLE** 9-0 ......10
2013 **BROWN SUGAR** 9-0 ......8
2014 **COTAI GLORY** 9-1 ......8

## NASSAU STAKES (fillies and mares)
Goodwood-1m 1f 192yds
2005 **ALEXANDER GOLDRUN** 4-9-3 ......11
2006 **OUIJA BOARD** 5-9-5 ......7
2007 **PEEPING FAWN** 3-8-10 ......8
2008 **HALFWAY TO HEAVEN** 3-8-10 ......9
2009 **MIDDAY** 3-8-10 ......10
2010 **MIDDAY** 4-9-6 ......7
2011 **MIDDAY** 5-9-6 ......6
2012 **THE FUGUE** 3-8-11 ......8
2013 **WINSILI** 3-8-11 ......14
2014 **SULTANINA** 4-9-7 ......6

## HUNGERFORD STAKES
Newbury-7f
2005 **SLEEPING INDIAN** 4-9-0 ......9
2006 **WELSH EMPEROR** 7-9-3 ......7
2007 **RED EVIE** 4-9-4 ......10
2008 **PACO BOY** 3-9-0 ......9
2009 **BALTHAZAAR'S GIFT** 6-9-3 ......9
2010 **SHAKESPEAREAN** 3-8-11 ......7
2011 **EXCELEBRATION** 3-8-13 ......9
2012 **LETHAL FORCE** 3-8-12 ......9
2013 **GREGORIAN** 4-9-3 ......5
2014 **BRETON ROCK** 4-9-5 ......6

## GEOFFREY FREER STAKES
Newbury-1m 5f 61yds
2005 **LOCHBUIE** 4-9-3 ......5
2006 **ADMIRAL'S CRUISE** 4-9-3 ......5
2007 **PAPAL BULL** 4-9-7 ......5
2008 **SIXTIES ICON** 5-9-5 ......10
2009 **KITE WOOD** 3-8-8 ......8
2010 **SANS FRONTIERES** 4-9-8 ......8
2011 **CENSUS** 3-8-6 ......10
2012 **MOUNT ATHOS** 5-9-4 ......6
2013 **ROYAL EMPIRE** 4-9-4 ......10
2014 **SEISMOS** 6-9-4 ......11

## INTERNATIONAL STAKES
York-1m 2f 88yds
2005 **ELECTROCUTIONIST** 4-9-5 ......7
2006 **NOTNOWCATO** 4-9-5 ......7
2007 **AUTHORIZED** 3-8-11 ......7
*2008 **DUKE OF MARMALADE** 4-9-5 ......9
2009 **SEA THE STARS** 3-8-11 ......4
2010 **RIP VAN WINKLE** 4-9-5 ......9
2011 **TWICE OVER** 6-9-5 ......5
2012 **FRANKEL** 4-9-5 ......9
2013 **DECLARATION OF WAR** 4-9-5 ......6
2014 **AUSTRALIA** 3-8-12 ......6
*Run at Newmarket (July) over 1m 2f

## GREAT VOLTIGEUR STAKES (3y)
York-1m 4f
2005 **HARD TOP** 8-9 ......6
2006 **YOUMZAIN** 8-12 ......10
2007 **LUCARNO** 8-12 ......9
*2008 **CENTENNIAL** 8-12 ......5
2009 **MONITOR CLOSELY** 8-12 ......7
2010 **REWILDING** 8-12 ......10
2011 **SEA MOON** 8-12 ......8
2012 **THOUGHT WORTHY** 8-12 ......6
2013 **TELESCOPE** 8-12 ......7
2014 **POSTPONED** 9-0 ......9
*Run at Goodwood

## LOWTHER STAKES (2y fillies)
York-6f
2005 **FLASHY WINGS** 9-2 ......6
2006 **SILK BLOSSOM** 8-12 ......7
2007 **NAHOODH** 8-12 ......10
*2008 **INFAMOUS ANGEL** 8-12 ......7
2009 **LADY OF THE DESERT** 8-12 ......12
2010 **HOORAY** 8-12 ......8
2011 **BEST TERMS** 9-1 ......11
2012 **ROSDHU QUEEN** 8-12 ......10
2013 **LUCKY KRISTALE** 9-1 ......9
2014 **TIGGY WIGGY** 9-0 ......9
*Run at Newmarket (July)

## YORKSHIRE OAKS (fillies and mares)
York-1m 4f
2005 **PUNCTILIOUS** 4-9-4 ......11
2006 **ALEXANDROVA** 3-8-11 ......6
2007 **PEEPING FAWN** 3-8-11 ......7
*2008 **LUSH LASHES** 3-8-11 ......6
2009 **DAR RE MI** 4-9-7 ......6
2010 **MIDDAY** 4-9-7 ......8
2011 **BLUE BUNTING** 3-8-11 ......8
2012 **SHARETA** 4-9-7 ......6
2013 **THE FUGUE** 4-9-7 ......7
2014 **TAPESTRY** 3-8-11 ......7
*Run at Newmarket (July)

## EBOR HANDICAP
York-1m 6f (1m 5f 194yds before 2007)
2005 **SERGEANT CECIL** 6-8-12 ......20
2006 **MUDAWIN** 5-8-4 ......19
2007 **PURPLE MOON** 4-9-4 ......19
*2008 **ALL THE GOOD** 5-9-0 ......20
2009 **SESENTA** 5-8-8 ......19
2010 **DIRAR** 5-9-1 ......20
2011 **MOYENNE CORNICHE** 6-8-10 ......20
2012 **WILLING FOE** 5-9-2 ......19

2013 **TIGER CLIFF** 4-9-0 ........ 14
2014 **MUTUAL REGARD** 5-9-4 ........ 19
*Run as Newburgh Handicap at Newbury over 1m 5f 61yds

## GIMCRACK STAKES (2y)

York-6f
2005 **AMADEUS WOLF** 8-11 ........ 13
2006 **CONQUEST** 8-12 ........ 6
2007 **SIR GERRY** 8-12 ........ 8
*2008 **SHAWEEL** 8-12 ........ 12
2009 **SHOWCASING** 8-12 ........ 6
2010 **APPROVE** 9-1 ........ 11
2011 **CASPAR NETSCHER** 8-12 ........ 9
2012 **BLAINE** 8-12 ........ 8
2013 **ASTAIRE** 8-12 ........ 7
2014 **MUHAARAR** 9-0 ........ 9
*Run at Newbury

## NUNTHORPE STAKES

York-5f
2005 **LA CUCARACHA** 4-9-8 ........ 16
2006 **REVERENCE** 5-9-11 ........ 14
2007 **KINGSGATE NATIVE** 2-8-1 ........ 16
*2008 **BORDERLESCOTT** 6-9-11 ........ 14
2009 **BORDERLESCOTT** 7-9-11 ........ 16
2010 **SOLE POWER** 3-9-9 ........ 12
2011 **MARGOT DID** 3-9-6 ........ 15
2012 **ORTENSIA** 7-9-8 ........ 19
2013 **JWALA** 4-9–8 ........ 17
2014 **SOLE POWER** 7-9-11 ........ 13
*Run at Newmarket (July)

## LONSDALE CUP

York-2m 88y (1m 7f 198y before 2006)
2005 **MILLENARY** 8 9-4 ........ 8
2006 **SERGEANT CECIL** 7 9-1 ........ 11
2007 **SEPTIMUS** 4 9-1 ........ 9
2008 ABANDONED
2009 **ASKAR TAU** 4 9-1 ........ 5
2010 **OPINION POLL** 4 9-1 ........ 8
2011 **OPINION POLL** 5 9-4 ........ 10
2012 **TIMES UP** 6 9-1 ........ 11
2013 **AHZEEMAH** 4 9-3 ........ 7
2014 **PALE MIMOSA** 5-9-0 ........ 7

## PRESTIGE STAKES (2y fillies)

Goodwood-7f
2005 **NANNINA** 8-9 ........ 9
2006 **SESMEN** 9-0 ........ 10
2007 **SENSE OF JOY** 9-0 ........ 7
2008 **FANTASIA** 9-0 ........ 10
2009 **SENT FROM HEAVEN** 9-0 ........ 8
2010 **THEYSKENS' THEORY** 9-0 ........ 7
2011 **REGAL REALM** 9-0 ........ 6
2012 **OLLIE OLGA** 9-0 ........ 8
2013 **AMAZING MARIA** 9-0 ........ 7
2014 **MALABAR** 9-0 ........ 8

## CELEBRATION MILE

Goodwood-1m
2005 **CHIC** 5-8-12 ........ 8
2006 **CARADAK** 5-9-1 ........ 6
2007 **ECHELON** 5-8-12 ........ 8
2008 **RAVEN'S PASS** 3-8-9 ........ 5
2009 **DELEGATOR** 3-8-9 ........ 7
2010 **POET'S VOICE** 3-8-9 ........ 4
2011 **DUBAWI GOLD** 3-8-9 ........ 7
2012 **PREMIO LOCO** 8-9-1 ........ 5
2013 **AFSARE** 6-9-1 ........ 8
2014 **BOW CREEK** 3-8-12 ........ 8

## SOLARIO STAKES (2y)

Sandown-7f 16yds
2005 **OPERA CAPE** 8-11 ........ 7
2006 **DRUMFIRE** 9-0 ........ 8
2007 **RAVEN'S PASS** 9-0 ........ 9
2008 **SRI PUTRA** 9-0 ........ 11
2009 **SHAKESPEAREAN** 9-0 ........ 8
2010 **NATIVE KHAN** 9-0 ........ 6
2011 **TALWAR** 9-0 ........ 4
2012 **FANTASTIC MOON** 9-0 ........ 7
2013 **KINGMAN** 9-0 ........ 4
2014 **AKTABANTAY** 9-1 ........ 5

## SPRINT CUP

Haydock-6f
2005 **GOODRICKE** 3-8-12 ........ 17
2006 **REVERENCE** 5-9-3 ........ 11
2007 **RED CLUBS** 4-9-3 ........ 14
*2008 **AFRICAN ROSE** 3-8-12 ........ 15
2009 **REGAL PARADE** 5-9-3 ........ 14
2010 **MARKAB** 7-9-3 ........ 13
2011 **DREAM AHEAD** 3-9-1 ........ 16
2012 **SOCIETY ROCK** 5-9-3 ........ 13
2013 **GORDON LORD BYRON** 5-9-3 ........ 13
2014 **G FORCE** 3-9-1 ........ 17
*Run at Doncaster

## SEPTEMBER STAKES

Kempton-1m 4f Polytrack
*2005 **IMPERIAL STRIDE** 4-9-8 ........ 6
2006 **KANDIDATE** 4-9-4 ........ 6
2007 **STEPPE DANCER** 4-9-4 ........ 7
2008 **HATTAN** 6-9-7 ........ 12
2009 **KIRKLEES** 5-9-9 ........ 10
2010 **LAAHEB** 4-9-4 ........ 9
2011 **MODUN** 4-9-4 ........ 7
2012 **DANDINO** 5-9-4 ........ 9
2013 **PRINCE BISHOP** 6-9-4 ........ 10
2014 **PRINCE BISHOP** 7-9-12 ........ 7
*Run at Newmarket (July)

## MAY HILL STAKES (2y fillies)

Doncaster-1m
2005 **NASHEEJ** 8-13 ........ 8
*2006 **SIMPLY PERFECT** 8-12 ........ 9
2007 **SPACIOUS** 8-12 ........ 12
2008 **RAINBOW VIEW** 9-1 ........ 7
2009 **POLLENATOR** 8-12 ........ 7
2010 **WHITE MOONSTONE** 8-12 ........ 7
2011 **LYRIC OF LIGHT** 8-12 ........ 8
2012 **CERTIFY** 8-12 ........ 7
2013 **IHTIMAL** 8-12 ........ 7
2014 **AGNES STEWART** 9-0 ........ 8
*Run at York

## PORTLAND HANDICAP

Doncaster-5f 140yds
2005 **OUT AFTER DARK** 4-8-12 ........ 21
*2006 **FANTASY BELIEVER** 8-8-13 ........ 19
2007 **FULLANDBY** 5-8-13 ........ 21
2008 **HOGMANEIGH** 5-9-6 ........ 21
2009 **SANTO PADRE** 5-9-1 ........ 22
2010 **POET'S PLACE** 5-9-4 ........ 22
2011 **NOCTURNAL AFFAIR** 5-9-5 ........ 21

2012 **DOC HAY** 5-8-11 ....... 20
2013 **ANGELS WILL FALL** 4-9-2 ....... 21
2014 **MUTHMIR** 4-9-7 ....... 20
*Run at York over 5f 89yds

## PARK HILL STAKES (fillies and mares)
Doncaster-1m 6f 132yds
2005 **SWEET STREAM** 5-9-3 ....... 11
*2006 **RISING CROSS** 3-8-7 ....... 7
2007 **HI CALYPSO** 3-8-7 ....... 14
2008 **ALLEGRETTO** 5-9-4 ....... 8
2009 **THE MINIVER ROSE** 3-8-6 ....... 9
2010 **EASTERN ARIA** 4-9-4 ....... 12
2011 **MEEZNAH** 4-9-4 ....... 7
2012 **WILD COCO** 4-9-4 ....... 9
2013 **THE LARK** 3-8–6 ....... 9
2014 **SILK SARI** 4-9-5 ....... 13
*Run at York

## DONCASTER CUP
Doncaster-2m 2f
2005 **MILLENARY** 8-9-4 ....... 7
*2006 **SERGEANT CECIL** 7-9-4 ....... 8
2007 **SEPTIMUS** 4-9-4 ....... 8
2008 **HONOLULU** 4-9-1 ....... 9
2009 **ASKAR TAU** 4-9-4 ....... 5
2010 **SAMUEL** 6-9-1 ....... 10
2011 **SADDLER'S ROCK** 3-8-1 ....... 7
2012 **TIMES UP** 6-9-1 ....... 10
2013 **TIMES UP** 7-9-3 ....... 7
2014 **ESTIMATE** 5-9-0 ....... 12
*Run at York

## CHAMPAGNE STAKES (2y)
Doncaster-7f
2005 **CLOSE TO YOU** 8-10 dead heated with
**SILENT TIMES** 8-10 ....... 7
*2006 **VITAL EQUINE** 8-12 ....... 8
2007 **MCCARTNEY** 8-12 ....... 10
2008 **WESTPHALIA** 8-12 ....... 7
2009 **POET'S VOICE** 8-12 ....... 7
2010 **SAAMIDD** 8-12 ....... 6
2011 **TRUMPET MAJOR** 8-12 ....... 5
2012 **TORONADO** 8-12 ....... 5
2013 **OUTSTRIP** 8-12 ....... 4
2014 **ESTIDHKAAR** 9-3 ....... 6
*Run at York

## PARK STAKES
Doncaster-7f
2005 **IFFRAAJ** 4-9-0 ....... 11
2006 **IFFRAAJ** 5-9-6 ....... 9
2007 **ARABIAN GLEAM** 3-8-12 ....... 6
2008 **ARABIAN GLEAM** 4-9-4 ....... 9
2009 **DUFF** 6-9-4 ....... 6
2010 **BALTHAZAR'S GIFT** 7-9-4 ....... 12
2011 **PREMIO LOCO** 7-9-4 ....... 5
2012 **LIBRANNO** 4-9-4 ....... 8
2013 **VIZTORIA** 3-8-11 ....... 9
2014 **ANSGAR** 6-9-4 ....... 7

## FLYING CHILDERS STAKES (2y)
Doncaster-5f
2005 **GODFREY STREET** 8-12 ....... 9
*2006 **WI DUD** 9-0 ....... 9
2007 **FLEETING SPIRIT** 8-11 ....... 8
2008 **MADAME TROP VITE** 8-11 ....... 12
2009 **SAND VIXEN** 8-11 ....... 10
2010 **ZEBEDEE** 9-0 ....... 12
2011 **REQUINTO** 9-0 ....... 10
2012 **SIR PRANCEALOT** 9-0 ....... 9
2013 **GREEN DOOR** 9-0 ....... 7
2014 **BEACON** 9-1 ....... 14
*Run at York

## AYR GOLD CUP
Ayr-6f
2005 **PRESTO SHINKO** 4-9-2 ....... 27
2006 **FONTHILL ROAD** 6-9-2 ....... 23
2007 **ADVANCED** 4-9-9 ....... 28
2008 **REGAL PARADE** 4-8-10 ....... 27
2009 **JIMMY STYLES** 5-9-2 ....... 26
2010 **REDFORD** 5-9-2 ....... 26
2011 **OUR JONATHAN** 4-9-6 ....... 26
2012 **CAPTAIN RAMIUS** 6-9-0 ....... 26
2013 **HIGHLAND COLORI** 5-8-13 ....... 26
2014 **LOUIS THE PIOUS** 6-9-4 ....... 27

## MILL REEF STAKES (2y)
Newbury-6f 8yds
2005 **COOL CREEK** 8-12 ....... 13
2006 **EXCELLENT ART** 9-1 ....... 6
2007 **DARK ANGEL** 9-1 ....... 6
2008 **LORD SHANAKILL** 9-1 ....... 9
2009 **AWZAAN** 9-1 ....... 7
2010 **TEMPLE MEADS** 9-1 ....... 7
2011 **CASPAR NETSCHER** 9-4 ....... 9
2012 **MOOHAAJIM** 9-1 ....... 8
2013 **SUPPLICANT** 9-1 ....... 7
2014 **TOOCOOLFORSCHOOL** 9-1 ....... 6

## ROYAL LODGE STAKES (2y)
Newmarket-1m (run at Ascot before 2011)
*2005 **LEO** 8-11 ....... 8
2006 **ADMIRALOFTHEFLEET** 8-12 ....... 7
2007 **CITY LEADER** 8-12 ....... 11
2008 **JUKEBOX JURY** 8-12 ....... 8
2009 **JOSHUA TREE** 8-12 ....... 10
2010 **FRANKEL** 8-12 ....... 5
2011 **DADDY LONG LEGS** 8-12 ....... 6
2012 **STEELER** 8-12 ....... 8
2013 **BERKSHIRE** 8-12 ....... 5
2014 **ELM PARK** 9-0 ....... 6
*Run at Newmarket

## CHEVELEY PARK STAKES (2y fillies)
Newmarket-6f
2005 **DONNA BLINI** 8-11 ....... 10
2006 **INDIAN INK** 8-12 ....... 11
2007 **NATAGORA** 8-12 ....... 14
2008 **SERIOUS ATTITUDE** 8-12 ....... 16
2009 **SPECIAL DUTY** 8-12 ....... 8
2010 **HOORAY** 8-12 ....... 11
2011 **LIGHTENING PEARL** 8-12 ....... 9
2012 **ROSDHU QUEEN** 8-12 ....... 11
2013 **VORDA** 8-12 ....... 7
2014 **TIGGY WIGGY** 9-0 ....... 9

## SUN CHARIOT STAKES (fillies and mares)
Newmarket-1m
2005 **PEERESS** 4-9-0 ....... 10
2006 **SPINNING QUEEN** 3-8-12 ....... 5
2007 **MAJESTIC ROI** 3-8-13 ....... 9
2008 **HALFWAY TO HEAVEN** 3-8-13 ....... 10
2009 **SAHPRESA** 4-9-2 ....... 8
2010 **SAHPRESA** 5-9-2 ....... 11

2011 **SAHPRESA** 6-9-3 .......... 8
2012 **SIYOUMA** 4-9-3 .......... 8
2013 **SKY LANTERN** 3-8-13 .......... 7
2014 **INTEGRAL** 4-9-3 .......... 7

## CAMBRIDGESHIRE

Newmarket-1m 1f
2005 **BLUE MONDAY** 4-9-3 .......... 30
2006 **FORMAL DECREE** 3-8-9 .......... 33
2007 **PIPEDREAMER** 3-8-12 .......... 34
2008 **TAZEEZ** 4-9-2 .......... 28
2009 **SUPASEUS** 6-9-1 .......... 32
2010 **CREDIT SWAP** 5-8-7 .......... 35
2011 **PRINCE OF JOHANNE** 5-8-9 .......... 32
2012 **BRONZE ANGEL** 3-8-8 .......... 33
2013 **EDUCATE** 4-9-9 .......... 31
2014 **BRONZE ANGEL** 5-8-8 .......... 31

## CUMBERLAND LODGE STAKES

Ascot-1m 4f
*2005 **MUBTAKER** 8-9-0 .......... 6
2006 **YOUNG MICK** 4-9-0 .......... 8
2007 **ASK** 4-9-3 .......... 8
2008 **SIXTIES ICON** 5-9-3 .......... 5
2009 **MAWATHEEQ** 4-9-0 .......... 12
2010 **LAAHEB** 4-9-3 .......... 6
2011 **QUEST FOR PEACE** 3-8-7 .......... 7
2012 **HAWAAFEZ** 4-8-11 .......... 6
2013 **SECRET NUMBER** 3-8-7 .......... 7
2014 **PETHER'S MOON** 4-9-6 .......... 5
*Run at Newmarket

## FILLIES' MILE (2y fillies)

Newmarket-1m (run at Ascot before 2011)
*2005 **NANNINA** 8-10 .......... 6
2006 **SIMPLY PERFECT** 8-12 .......... 8
2007 **LISTEN** 8-12 .......... 7
2008 **RAINBOW VIEW** 8-12 .......... 8
2009 **HIBAAYEB** 8-12 .......... 9
2010 **WHITE MOONSTONE** 8-12 .......... 5
2011 **LYRIC OF LIGHT** 8-12 .......... 8
2012 **CERTIFY** 8-12 .......... 6
2013 **CHRISELLIAM** 8-12 .......... 8
2014 **TOGETHER FOREVER** 9-0 .......... 7
*Run at Newmarket (Rowley Mile)

## MIDDLE PARK STAKES (2y)

Newmarket-6f
2005 **AMADEUS WOLF** 8-11 .......... 6
2006 **DUTCH ART** 8-12 .......... 6
2007 **DARK ANGEL** 8-12 .......... 9
2008 **BUSHRANGER** 8-12 .......... 9
2009 **AWZAAN** 8-12 .......... 5
2010 **DREAM AHEAD** 8-12 .......... 8
2011 **CRUSADE** 8-12 .......... 16
2012 **RECKLESS ABANDON** 8-12 .......... 10
2013 **ASTAIRE** 9-0 .......... 10
2014 **CHARMING THOUGHT** 9-0 .......... 6

## CHALLENGE STAKES

Newmarket-7f
2005 **LE VIE DEI COLORI** 5-9-0 .......... 15
2006 **SLEEPING INDIAN** 5-9-3 .......... 16
2007 **MISS LUCIFER** 3-8-12 .......... 15
2008 **STIMULATION** 3-9-1 .......... 15
2009 **ARABIAN GLEAM** 5-9-3 .......... 9
2010 **RED JAZZ** 3-9-1 .......... 14
2011 **STRONG SUIT** 3-9-5 .......... 8
2012 **FULBRIGHT** 3-9-1 .......... 11
2013 **FIESOLANA** 4-9-0 .......... 9
2014 **HERE COMES WHEN** 4-9-7 .......... 13

## DEWHURST STAKES (2y)

Newmarket-7f
2005 **SIR PERCY** 9-0 .......... 8
2006 **TEOFILO** 9-1 .......... 15
2007 **NEW APPROACH** 9-1 .......... 10
2008 **INTENSE FOCUS** 9-1 .......... 13
2009 **BEETHOVEN** 9-1 .......... 15
2010 **FRANKEL** 9-1 .......... 6
2011 **PARISH HALL** 9-1 .......... 9
2012 **DAWN APPROACH** 9-1 .......... 6
2013 **WAR COMMAND** 9-1 .......... 6
2014 **BELARDO** 9-1 .......... 6

## CESAREWITCH

Newmarket-2m 2f
2005 **SERGEANT CECIL** 6-9-8 .......... 34
2006 **DETROIT CITY** 4-9-1 .......... 31
2007 **LEG SPINNER** 6-8-11 .......... 33
2008 **CARACCIOLA** 11-9-6 .......... 32
2009 **DARLEY SUN** 3-8-6 .......... 32
2010 **AAIM TO PROSPER** 6-7-13 .......... 32
2011 **NEVER CAN TELL** 4-8-11 .......... 33
2012 **AAIM TO PROSPER** 8-9-10 .......... 34
2013 **SCATTER DICE** 4-8-8 .......... 33
2014 **BIG EASY** 7-8-7 .......... 33

## ROCKFEL STAKES (2y fillies)

Newmarket-7f
2005 **SPECIOSA** 8-9 .......... 14
2006 **FINSCEAL BEO** 9-2 .......... 14
2007 **KITTY MATCHAM** 8-12 .......... 10
2008 **LAHALEEB** 8-12 .......... 15
2009 **MUSIC SHOW** 8-12 .......... 11
2010 **CAPE DOLLAR** 8-12 .......... 10
2011 **WADING** 8-12 .......... 9
2012 **JUST THE JUDGE** 8-12 .......... 11
2013 **AL THAKHIRA** 8-12 .......... 8
2014 **LUCIDA** 9-0 .......... 9

## QIPCO BRITISH CHAMPIONS SPRINT STAKES

Ascot-6f
(run as Diadem Stakes before 2011)
2011 **DEACON BLUES** 4-9-0 .......... 16
2012 **MAAREK** 5-9-0 .......... 15
2013 **SLADE POWER** 4-9-0 .......... 14
2014 **GORDON LORD BYRON** 6-9-2 .......... 15

## QUEEN ELIZABETH II STAKES (BRITISH CHAMPIONS MILE)

Ascot-1m (st - rnd before 2011)
*2005 **STARCRAFT** 5-9-1 .......... 6
2006 **GEORGE WASHINGTON** 3-8-13 .......... 8
2007 **RAMONTI** 5-9-3 .......... 7
2008 **RAVEN'S PASS** 3-8-13 .......... 7
2009 **RIP VAN WINKLE** 3-8-13 .......... 4
2010 **POET'S VOICE** 3-8-13 .......... 8
2011 **FRANKEL** 3-9-0 .......... 8
2012 **EXCELEBRATION** 4-9-3 .......... 8
2013 **OLYMPIC GLORY** 3-9-0 .......... 12
2014 **CHARM SPIRIT** 3-9-1 .......... 11
*Run at Newmarket

## QIPCO BRITISH CHAMPIONS LONG DISTANCE CUP

(formerly Jockey Club Cup, run at Newmarket before 2011)
Ascot-2m

2011 **FAME AND GLORY** 5-9-0 .......... 10
2012 **RITE OF PASSAGE** 8-9-7 .......... 9
2013 **ROYAL DIAMOND** 7-9-7 .......... 12
2014 **FORGOTTEN RULES** 4-9-7 .......... 9

## QIPCO BRITISH CHAMPIONS FILLIES' AND MARES' STAKES

(formerly Pride Stakes, run at Newmarket before 2011)
Ascot-1m 4f

2011 **DANCING RAIN** 3-8-10 .......... 10
2012 **SAPPHIRE** 4-9-3 .......... 10
2013 **SEAL OF APPROVAL** 4-9-3 .......... 8
2014 **MADAME CHIANG** 3-8-12 .......... 10

## QIPCO CHAMPION STAKES (BRITISH CHAMPIONS MIDDLE DISTANCE)

Ascot-1m 2f
(run at Newmarket before 2011)

2005 **DAVID JUNIOR** 3-8-11 .......... 15
2006 **PRIDE** 6-9-0 .......... 8
2007 **LITERATO** 3-8-12 .......... 12
2008 **NEW APPROACH** 3-8-12 .......... 11
2009 **TWICE OVER** 4-9-3 .......... 14
2010 **TWICE OVER** 5-9-3 .......... 10
2011 **CIRRUS DES AIGLES** 5-9-3 .......... 12
2012 **FRANKEL** 4-9-3 .......... 6
2013 **FARHH** 5-9-3 .......... 10
2014 **NOBLE MISSION** 5-9-5 .......... 9

## CORNWALLIS STAKES (2y)

Ascot-5f

*2005 **HUNTER STREET** 8-12 .......... 12
2006 **ALZERRA** 8-1 .......... 10
2007 **CAPTAIN GERRARD** 9-0 .......... 12
2008 **AMOUR PROPRE** 9-0 .......... 19
2009 **OUR JONATHAN** 9-0 .......... 17
2010 **ELECTRIC WAVES** 8-11 .......... 14
2011 **PONTY ACCLAIM** 8-11 .......... 16
2012 **BUNGLE INTHEJUNGLE** 9-3 .......... 6
2013 **HOT STREAK** 9-0 .......... 12
2014 **ROYAL RAZALMA** 8-12 .......... 12

*Run at Salisbury

## TWO-YEAR-OLD TROPHY (2y)

Redcar-6f

2005 **MISU BOND** 9-0 .......... 24
2006 **DANUM DANCER** 8-3 .......... 24
2007 **DUBAI DYNAMO** 9-2 .......... 23
2008 **TOTAL GALLERY** 8-9 .......... 22
2009 **LUCKY LIKE** 8-6 .......... 22
2010 **LADIES ARE FOREVER** 7-12 .......... 22
2011 **BOGART** 8-12 .......... 22
2012 **BODY AND SOUL** 8-1 .......... 21
2013 **VENTURA MIST** 8-7 .......... 23
2014 **LIMATO** 8-12 .......... 23

## HORRIS HILL STAKES (2y)

Newbury-7f

2005 **HURRICANE CAT** 8-9 .......... 13
2006 **DIJEERR** 8-12 .......... 10
2007 **BEACON LODGE** 8-12 .......... 11
2008 **EVASIVE** 8-12 .......... 13
2009 **CARNABY STREET** 8-12 .......... 14
2010 **KLAMMER** 8-12 .......... 10
2011 **TELL DAD** 8-12 .......... 14
2012 **TAWHID** 8-12 .......... 8
2013 **PIPING ROCK** 8-12 .......... 11
2014 **SMAIH** 9-0 .......... 6

## RACING POST TROPHY (2y)

Doncaster-1m

2005 **PALACE EPISODE** 9-0 .......... 7
*2006 **AUTHORIZED** 9-0 .......... 14
2007 **IBN KHALDUN** 9-0 .......... 12
2008 **CROWDED HOUSE** 9-0 .......... 15
2009 **ST NICHOLAS ABBEY** 9-0 .......... 11
2010 **CASAMENTO** 9-0 .......... 10
2011 **CAMELOT** 9-0 .......... 5
2012 **KINGSBARNS** 9-0 .......... 7
2013 **KINGSTON HILL** 9-0 .......... 11
2014 **ELM PARK** 9-1 .......... 8

*Run at Newbury

## NOVEMBER HANDICAP

Doncaster-1m 4f

2005 **COME ON JONNY** 3-8-0 .......... 21
*2006 **GROUP CAPTAIN** 4-9-5 .......... 20
2007 **MALT OR MASH** 3-8-10 .......... 21
2008 **TROPICAL STRAIT** 5-8-13 .......... 21
2009 **CHARM SCHOOL** 4-8-12 .......... 23
2010 **TIMES UP** 4-8-13 .......... 22
2011 **ZUIDER ZEE** 4-8-13 .......... 23
2012 **ART SCHOLAR** 5-8-7 .......... 23
2013 **CONDUCT** 6-9-2 .......... 23
2014 **OPEN EAGLE** 5-8-12 .......... 23

*Run at Windsor

# WINNERS OF PRINCIPAL RACES IN IRELAND

## IRISH 2000 GUINEAS (3y)
The Curragh-1m
2005 **DUBAWI** 9-0....8
2006 **ARAAFA** 9-0....11
2007 **COCKNEY REBEL** 9-0....12
2008 **HENRYTHENAVIGATOR** 9-0....5
2009 **MASTERCRAFTSMAN** 9-0....9
2010 **CANFORD CLIFFS** 9-0....13
2011 **RODERIC O'CONNOR** 9-0....8
2012 **POWER** 9-0....10
2013 **MAGICIAN** 9-0....10
2014 **KINGMAN** 9-0....11

## TATTERSALLS GOLD CUP
The Curragh-1m 2f 110yds
2005 **GREY SWALLOW** 4-9-0....6
2006 **HURRICANE RUN** 4-9-0....3
2007 **NOTNOWCATO** 5-9-0....9
2008 **DUKE OF MARMALADE** 4-9-0....6
2009 **CASUAL CONQUEST** 4-9-0....5
2010 **FAME AND GLORY** 4-9-0....6
2011 **SO YOU THINK** 5-9-1....5
2012 **SO YOU THINK** 6-9-1....5
2013 **AL KAZEEM** 5-9-3....4
2014 **NOBLE MISSION** 5-9-3....5

## IRISH 1000 GUINEAS (3y fillies)
The Curragh-1m
2005 **SAOIRE** 9-0....18
2006 **NIGHTIME** 9-0....15
2007 **FINSCEAL BEO** 9-0....11
2008 **HALFWAY TO HEAVEN** 9-0....13
2009 **AGAIN** 9-0....16
2010 **BETHRAH** 9-0....19
2011 **MISTY FOR ME** 9-0....15
2012 **SAMITAR** 9-0....8
2013 **JUST THE JUDGE** 9-0....15
2014 **MARVELLOUS** 9-0....11

## IRISH DERBY (3y)
The Curragh-1m 4f
2005 **HURRICANE RUN** 9-0....9
2006 **DYLAN THOMAS** 9-0....8
2007 **SOLDIER OF FORTUNE** 9-0....11
2008 **FROZEN FIRE** 9-0....11
2009 **FAME AND GLORY** 9-0....11
2010 **CAPE BLANCO** 9-0....10
2011 **TREASURE BEACH** 9-0....8
2012 **CAMELOT** 9-0....5
2013 **TRADING LEATHER** 9-0....9
2014 **AUSTRALIA** 9-0....5

## PRETTY POLLY STAKES (fillies and mares)
Curragh-1m 2f
2005 **ALEXANDER GOLDRUN**4-9-7....10
2006 **ALEXANDER GOLDRUN** 5-9-8....7
2007 **PEEPING FAWN** 3-8-11....9
2008 **PROMISING LEAD** 4-9-9....9
2009 **DAR RE MI** 4-9-9....7
2010 **CHINESE WHITE** 5-9-9....9
2011 **MISTY FOR ME** 3-8-12....7
2012 **IZZI TOP** 4-9-9....4
2013 **AMBIVALENT** 4-9-10....9
2014 **THISTLE BIRD** 6-9-10....8

## IRISH OAKS (3y fillies)
The Curragh-1m 4f
2005 **SHAWANDA** 9-0....13
2006 **ALEXANDROVA** 9-0....6
2007 **PEEPING FAWN** 9-0....12
2008 **MOONSTONE** 9-0....14
2009 **SARISKA** 9-0....10
2010 **SNOW FAIRY** 9-0....15
2011 **BLUE BUNTING** 9-0....9
2012 **GREAT HEAVENS** 9-0....7
2013 **CHICQUITA** 9-0....7
2014 **BRACELET** 9–0....10

## PHOENIX STAKES (2y)
The Curragh-6f
2005 **GEORGE WASHINGTON** 9-0....7
2006 **HOLY ROMAN EMPEROR** 9-1....7
2007 **SAOIRSE ABU** 8-12....6
2008 **MASTERCRAFTSMAN** 9-1....5
2009 **ALFRED NOBEL** 9-1....8
2010 **ZOFFANY** 9-1....7
2011 **LA COLLINA** 8-12....9
2012 **PEDRO THE GREAT** 9-3....6
2013 **SUDIRMAN** 9-3....5
2014 **DICK WHITTINGTON** 9-3....6

## MATRON STAKES (fillies and mares)
Leopardstown-1m
2005 **ATTRACTION** 4-9-2....9
2006 **RED EVIE** 3-8-12....8
2007 **ECHELON** 5-9-3....9
2008 **LUSH LASHES** 3-8-12....10
2009 **RAINBOW VIEW** 3-8-12....7
2010 **LILLIE LANGTRY** 3-8-12....6
2011 **EMULOUS** 4-9-5....8
*2012 **CHACHAMAIDEE** 5-9-5....11
2013 **LA COLLINA** 4-9-5....12
2014 **FIESOLANA** 5-9-5....10
*Duntle disqualified from first place

## IRISH CHAMPION STAKES
Leopardstown-1m 2f
2005 **ORATORIO** 3-8-11....10
2006 **DYLAN THOMAS** 3-9-0....5
2007 **DYLAN THOMAS** 4-9-7....6
2008 **NEW APPROACH** 3-9-0....8
2009 **SEA THE STARS** 3-9-0....9
2010 **CAPE BLANCO** 3-9-0....6
2011 **SO YOU THINK** 5-9-7....6
2012 **SNOW FAIRY** 5-9-4....6
2013 **THE FUGUE** 4-9-4....6
2014 **THE GREY GATSBY** 3-9-0....7

## IRISH CAMBRIDGESHIRE

The Curragh-1m
2005 **KESTREL CROSS** 3-9-1 ........ 20
2006 **QUINMASTER** 4-10-1 ........ 22
2007 **JALMIRA** 6-8-13 ........ 24
2008 **TIS MIGHTY** 5-8-1 ........ 21
2009 **POET** 4-9-9 ........ 27
2010 **HUJAYLEA** 7-8-3 ........ 25
2011 **CASTLE BAR SLING** 6-8-11 ........ 21
2012 **PUNCH YOUR WEIGHT** 3-8-6 ........ 18
2013 **MORAN GRA** 6-8-13 ........ 20
2014 **SRETAW** 5-8-8 ........ 21

## MOYGLARE STUD STAKES (2y fillies)

The Curragh-7f
2005 **RUMPLESTILTSKIN** 8-11 ........ 9
2006 **MISS BEATRIX** 8-12 ........ 12
2007 **SAOIRSE ABU** 8-12 ........ 9
2008 **AGAIN** 8-12 ........ 12
2009 **TERMAGANT** 8-12 ........ 7
2010 **MISTY FOR ME** 8-12 ........ 12
2011 **MAYBE** 9-1 ........ 8
2012 **SKY LANTERN** 9-0 ........ 13
2013 **RIZEENA** 9-0 ........ 7
2014 **CURSORY GLANCE** 9-0 ........ 10

## VINCENT O'BRIEN (NATIONAL) STAKES (2y)

The Curragh-7f
2005 **GEORGE WASHINGTON** 9-0 ........ 7
2006 **TEOFILO** 9-1 ........ 6
2007 **NEW APPROACH** 9-1 ........ 9
2008 **MASTERCRAFTSMAN** 9-1 ........ 7
2009 **KINGSFORT** 9-1 ........ 6
2010 **PATHFORK** 9-1 ........ 9
2011 **POWER** 9-1 ........ 9
2012 **DAWN APPROACH** 9-3 ........ 7
2013 **TOORMORE** 9-3 ........ 5
2014 **GLENEAGLES** 9-3 ........ 5

## IRISH ST LEGER

The Curragh-1m 6f
2005 **COLLIER HILL** 7-9-8 ........ 9
2006 **KASTORIA** 5-9-7 ........ 8
2007 **YEATS** 6-9-11 ........ 9
2008 **SEPTIMUS** 5-9-11 ........ 9
2009 **ALANDI** 4-9-11 ........ 8
2010 **SANS FRONTIERES** 4-9-11 ........ 8
2011 **DUNCAN** 6-9-11 dead heated with ........ 6
**JUKEBOX JURY** 5-9-11 ........ 6
2012 **ROYAL DIAMOND** 6-9-11 ........ 9
2013 **VOLEUSE DE COEURS** 4-9-8 ........ 10
2014 **BROWN PANTHER** 6-9-11 ........ 11

## IRISH CESAREWITCH

The Curragh-2m
2005 **CLARA ALLEN** 7-8-0 ........ 17
2006 **IKTITAF** 5-8-8 ........ 16
2007 **SANDYMOUNT EARL** 4-9-3 ........ 21
2008 **SUAILCE** 3-8-1 ........ 28
2009 **DANI CALIFORNIA** 5-8-0 ........ 29
2010 **BRIGHT HORIZON** 3-8-7 ........ 23
2011 **MINSK** 3-8-9 ........ 19
2012 **VOLEUSE DE COEURS** 3-9-1 ........ 27
2013 **MONTEFELTRO** 5-9-4 ........ 30
2014 **EL SALVADOR** 5-9-5 ........ 21

## BOYLESPORTS HURDLE

Leopardstown-2m
(Pierse Hurdle 2006-9, MCR Hurdle in 2010-11)
2006 **STUDMASTER** 6-10-3 ........ 27
2007 **SPRING THE QUE** 8-10-3 ........ 30
2008 **BARKER** 7-10-6 ........ 28
2009 **PENNY'S BILL** 7-9-9 ........ 29
2010 **PUYOL** 8-10-10 ........ 30
2011 **FINAL APPROACH** 5-10-9 ........ 26
2012 **CITIZENSHIP** 6-10-3 ........ 30
2013 **ABBEY LANE** 8-10-8 ........ 28
2014 **GILGAMBOA** 6-10-9 ........ 24
2015 **KATIE T** 6-10-9 ........ 24

## IRISH CHAMPION HURDLE

Leopardstown-2m
2006 **BRAVE INCA** 8-11-10 ........ 7
2007 **HARDY EUSTACE** 10-11-10 ........ 8
2008 **SIZING EUROPE** 6-11-10 ........ 6
2009 **BRAVE INCA** 11-11-10 ........ 9
2010 **SOLWHIT** 6-11-10 ........ 7
2011 **HURRICANE FLY** 7-11-10 ........ 5
2012 **HURRICANE FLY** 8-11-10 ........ 5
2013 **HURRICANE FLY** 9-11-10 ........ 5
2014 **HURRICANE FLY** 10-11-10 ........ 4
2015 **HURRICANE FLY** 11-11-10 ........ 6

## HENNESSY GOLD CUP

Leopardstown-3m
2006 **BEEF OR SALMON** 10-11-12 ........ 7
2007 **BEEF OR SALMON** 11-11-12 ........ 5
2008 **THE LISTENER** 9-11-10 ........ 8
2009 **NEPTUNE COLLONGES** 8-11-10 ........ 6
2010 **JONCOL** 7-11-10 ........ 7
2011 **KEMPES** 8-11-10 ........ 9
2012 **QUEL ESPRIT** 8-11-10 ........ 7
2013 **SIR DES CHAMPS** 7-11-10 ........ 4
2014 **LAST INSTALMENT** 9-11-10 ........ 7
2015 **CARLINGFORD LOUGH** 9-11-10 ........ 8

## IRISH GRAND NATIONAL

Fairyhouse-3m 5f
2005 **NUMBERSIXVALVERDE** 9-10-1 ........ 26
2006 **POINT BARROW** 8-10-8 ........ 26
2007 **BUTLER'S CABIN** 7-10-4 ........ 29
2008 **HEAR THE ECHO** 7-10-0 ........ 23
2009 **NICHE MARKET** 8-10-5 ........ 30
2010 **BLUESEA CRACKER** 8-10-4 ........ 26
2011 **ORGANISEDCONFUSION** 6-9-13 ........ 25
2012 **LION NA BEARNAI** 10-10-5 ........ 29
2013 **LIBERTY COUNSEL** 10-9-5 ........ 28
2014 **SHUTTHEFRONTDOOR** 7-10-13 ........ 26

# WINNERS OF PRINCIPAL RACES IN FRANCE

## PRIX GANAY

Longchamp-1m 2f 110yds

2005 **BAGO** 4-9-2 ............ 9
2006 **CORRE CAMINOS** 4-9-2 ............ 7
2007 **DYLAN THOMAS** 4-9-2 ............ 8
2008 **DUKE OF MARMALADE** 4-9-2 ............ 6
2009 **VISION D'ETAT** 4-9-2 ............ 8
2010 **CUTLASS BAY** 4-9-2 ............ 9
2011 **PLANTEUR** 4-9-2 ............ 7
2012 **CIRRUS DES AIGLES** 6-9-2 ............ 6
2013 **PASTORIUS** 4-9-2 ............ 9
2014 **CIRRUS DES AIGLES** 8-9-2 ............ 8

## POULE D'ESSAI DES POULAINS (3y)

Longchamp-1m

2005 **SHAMARDAL** 9-2 ............ 15
2006 **AUSSIE RULES** 9-2 ............ 11
2007 **ASTRONOMER ROYAL** 9-2 ............ 14
2008 **FALCO** 9-2 ............ 19
2009 **SILVER FROST** 9-2 ............ 6
2010 **LOPE DE VEGA** 9-2 ............ 15
2011 **TIN HORSE** 9-2 ............ 14
2012 **LUCAYAN** 9-2 ............ 12
2013 **STYLE VENDOME** 9-2 ............ 18
2014 **KARAKONTIE** 9-2 ............ 12

## POULE D'ESSAI DES POULICHES (3y fillies)

Longchamp-1m

2005 **DIVINE PROPORTIONS** 9-0 ............ 8
*2006 **TIE BLACK** 9-0 ............ 13
2007 **DARJINA** 9-0 ............ 13
2008 **ZARKAVA** 9-0 ............ 14
2009 **ELUSIVE WAVE** 9-0 ............ 11
**2010 **SPECIAL DUTY** 9-0 ............ 10
2011 **GOLDEN LILAC** 9-0 ............ 16
2012 **BEAUTY PARLOUR** 9-0 ............ 13
2013 **FLOTILLA** 9-0 ............ 20
2014 **AVENIR CERTAIN** 9-0 ............ 16

*Price Tag disqualified from first place
**Lilside disqualified from first place

## PRIX SAINT-ALARY (3y fillies)

Longchamp-1m 2f

2005 **VADAWINA** 9-0 ............ 8
2006 **GERMANCE** 9-0 ............ 8
2007 **COQUERELLE** 9-0 ............ 6
2008 **BELLE ET CELEBRE** 9-0 ............ 7
2009 **STACELITA** 9-0 ............ 7
2010 **SARAFINA** 9-0 ............ 9
2011 **WAVERING** 9-0 ............ 12
2012 **SAGAWARA** 9-0 ............ 8
2013 **SILASOL** 9-0 ............ 8
*2014 **VAZIRA** 9-0 ............ 8

* We Are disqualified from first place

## PRIX JEAN PRAT (3y)

Chantilly-1m (1m 1f before 2005)

2005 **TURTLE BOWL** 9-2 ............ 8
2006 **STORMY RIVER** 9-2 ............ 11
2007 **LAWMAN** 9-2 ............ 7
2008 **TAMAYUZ** 9-2 ............ 16
2009 **LORD SHANAKILL** 9-2 ............ 9
2010 **DICK TURPIN** 9-2 ............ 8
2011 **MUTUAL TRUST** 9-2 ............ 7
2012 **AESOP'S FABLES** 9-2 ............ 8
2013 **HAVANA GOLD** 9-2 ............ 12
2014 **CHARM SPIRIT** 9-2 ............ 7

## PRIX D'ISPAHAN

Longchamp-1m 1f 55yds

2005 **VALIXIR** 4-9-2 ............ 8
2006 **LAVEROCK** 4-9-2 ............ 11
2007 **MANDURO** 5-9-2 ............ 5
2008 **SAGEBURG** 4-9-2 ............ 6
2009 **NEVER ON SUNDAY** 4-9-2 ............ 9
2010 **GOLDIKOVA** 5-8-13 ............ 8
2011 **GOLDIKOVA** 6-8-13 ............ 9
2012 **GOLDEN LILAC** 4-8-13 ............ 8
2013 **MAXIOS** 5-9-2 ............ 7
2014 **CIRRUS DES AIGLES** 8-9-2 ............ 6

## PRIX DU JOCKEY CLUB (3y)

Chantilly-1m 2f 110yds (1m 4f before 2005)

2005 **SHAMARDAL** 9-2 ............ 17
2006 **DARSI** 9-2 ............ 15
2007 **LAWMAN** 9-2 ............ 20
2008 **VISION D'ETAT** 9-2 ............ 20
2009 **LE HAVRE** 9-2 ............ 17
2010 **LOPE DE VEGA** 9-2 ............ 22
2011 **RELIABLE MAN** 9-2 ............ 16
2012 **SAONOIS** 9-2 ............ 20
2013 **INTELLO** 9-2 ............ 19
2014 **THE GREY GATSBY** 9-2 ............ 16

## PRIX DE DIANE (3y fillies)

Chantilly-1m 2f 110yds

2005 **DIVINE PROPORTIONS** 9-0 ............ 10
2006 **CONFIDENTIAL LADY** 9-0 ............ 16
2007 **WEST WIND** 9-0 ............ 14
2008 **ZARKAVA** 9-0 ............ 13
2009 **STACELITA** 9-0 ............ 12
2010 **SARAFINA** 9-0 ............ 9
2011 **GOLDEN LILAC** 9-0 ............ 9
2012 **VALYRA** 9-0 ............ 12
2013 **TREVE** 9-0 ............ 11
2014 **AVENIR CERTAIN** 9-0 ............ 12

## GRAND PRIX DE PARIS (3y)

Longchamp-1m 4f

2005 **SCORPION** 9-2 ............ 9
2006 **RAIL LINK** 9-2 ............ 9
2007 **ZAMBEZI SUN** 9-2 ............ 7
2008 **MONTMARTRE** 9-2 ............ 13
2009 **CAVALRYMAN** 9-2 ............ 8
2010 **BEHKABAD** 9-2 ............ 9
2011 **MEANDRE** 9-2 ............ 7
2012 **IMPERIAL MONARCH** 9-2 ............ 9
2013 **FLINTSHIRE** 9-2 ............ 8
2014 **GALLANTE** 9-2 ............ 11

## GRAND PRIX DE SAINT-CLOUD
Saint-Cloud-1m 4f
2005 **ALKAASED** 5-9-2 ....11
2006 **PRIDE** 6-8-13 ....6
2007 **MOUNTAIN HIGH** 5-9-2 ....6
2008 **YOUMZAIN** 5-9-2 ....9
2009 **SPANISH MOON** 5-9-2 ....10
2010 **PLUMANIA** 4-8-13 ....7
2011 **SARAFINA** 4-8-13 ....5
2012 **MEANDRE** 4-9-2 ....4
2013 **NOVELLIST** 4-9-2 ....11
*2014 **NOBLE MISSION** 5-9-2 ....7
*Spiritjim disqualified from first place

## PRIX MAURICE DE GHEEST
Deauville-6f 110yds
2005 **WHIPPER** 4-9-2 ....13
2006 **MARCHAND D'OR** 3-8-11 ....17
2007 **MARCHAND D'OR** 4-9-2 ....13
2008 **MARCHAND D'OR** 5-9-2 ....16
2009 **KING'S APOSTLE** 5-9-2 ....12
2010 **REGAL PARADE** 6-9-2 ....15
2011 **MOONLIGHT CLOUD** 3-8-8 ....13
2012 **MOONLIGHT CLOUD** 4-8-13 ....9
2013 **MOONLIGHT CLOUD** 5-8-13 ....14
2014 **GARSWOOD** 4-9-2 ....14

## PRIX JACQUES LE MAROIS
Deauville-1m
2005 **DUBAWI** 3-8-11 ....6
2006 **LIBRETTIST** 4-9-4 ....10
2007 **MANDURO** 5-9-4 ....6
2008 **TAMAYUZ** 3-8-11 ....8
2009 **GOLDIKOVA** 4-9-0 ....9
2010 **MAKFI** 3-8-11 ....8
2011 **IMMORTAL VERSE** 3-8-8 ....12
2012 **EXCELEBRATION** 4-9-4 ....11
2013 **MOONLIGHT CLOUD** 5-9-1 ....13
2014 **KINGMAN** 3-8-13 ....5

## PRIX MORNY (2y)
Deauville-6f
2005 **SILCA'S SISTER** 8-11 ....7
2006 **DUTCH ART** 9-0 ....7
2007 **MYBOYCHARLIE** 8-13 ....6
2008 **BUSHRANGER** 9-0 ....14
2009 **ARCANO** 9-0 ....5
2010 **DREAM AHEAD** 9-0 ....11
2011 **DABIRSIM** 9-0 ....7
2012 **RECKLESS ABANDON** 9-0 ....11
2013 **NO NAY NEVER** 9-0 ....10
2014 **THE WOW SIGNAL** 9-0 ....9

## PRIX DU MOULIN DE LONGCHAMP
Longchamp-1m
2005 **STARCRAFT** 5-9-2 ....9
2006 **LIBRETTIST** 4-9-2 ....8
2007 **DARJINA** 3-8-8 ....9
2008 **GOLDIKOVA** 3-8-8 ....11
2009 **AQLAAM** 4-9-2 ....9
2010 **FUISSE** 4-9-2 ....6
2011 **EXCELEBRATION** 3-8-11 ....8
2012 **MOONLIGHT CLOUD** 4-8-13 ....4
2013 **MAXIOS** 5-9-2 ....7
2014 **CHARM SPIRIT** 3-8-11 ....10

## CRITERIUM INTERNATIONAL (2y)
Saint-Cloud-1m
2005 **CARLOTAMIX** 9-0 ....6
2006 **MOUNT NELSON** 9-0 ....10
2007 **THEWAYYOUARE** 9-0 ....6
2008 **ZAFISIO** 9-0 ....11
2009 **JAN VERMEER** 9-0 ....7
2010 **RODERIC O'CONNOR** 9-0 ....10
2011 **FRENCH FIFTEEN** 9-0 ....11
2012 **LOCH GARMAN** 9-0 ....6
2013 **ECTOT** 9-0 ....4
2014 **VERT DE GRACE** 9-0 ....9

## PRIX VERMEILLE (fillies and mares)
Longchamp-1m 4f
2005 **SHAWANDA** 3-8-7 ....6
2006 **MANDESHA** 3-8-7 ....11
2007 **MRS LINDSAY** 3-8-9 ....10
2008 **ZARKAVA** 3-8-8 ....12
*2009 **STACELITA** 3-8-8 ....12
2010 **MIDDAY** 4-9-3 ....12
2011 **GALIKOVA** 3-8-8 ....6
2012 **SHARETA** 4-9-2 ....13
2013 **TREVE** 3-8-8 ....10
2014 **BALTIC BARONESS** 4-9-3 ....9
*Dar Re Mi disqualified from first place

## PRIX DU CADRAN
Longchamp-2m 4f
2005 **REEFSCAPE** 4-9-2 ....10
2006 **SERGEANT CECIL** 7-9-2 ....7
2007 **LE MIRACLE** 6-9-2 ....6
2008 **BANNABY** 5-9-2 ....11
2009 **ALANDI** 4-9-2 ....12
2010 **GENTOO** 6-9-2 ....8
2011 **KASBAH BLISS** 9-9-2 ....10
2012 **MOLLY MALONE** 4-8-13 ....10
2013 **ALTANO** 7-9-2 ....10
2014 **HIGH JINX** 6-9-2 ....8

## PRIX DE L'ABBAYE DE LONGCHAMP
Longchamp-5f
2005 **AVONBRIDGE** 5-9-11 ....17
2006 **DESERT LORD** 6-9-11 ....14
2007 **BENBAUN** 6-9-11 ....17
*2008 **MARCHAND D'OR** 5-9-11 ....17
2009 **TOTAL GALLERY** 3-9-11 ....16
2010 **GILT EDGE GIRL** 4-9-7 ....21
2011 **TANGERINE TREES** 6-9-11 ....15
2012 **WIZZ KID** 4-9-7 ....18
2013 **MAAREK** 6-9-11 ....20
2014 **MOVE IN TIME** 6-9-11 ....18
* re-run; Overdose won void first running

## PRIX MARCEL BOUSSAC (2y fillies)
Longchamp-1m
2005 **RUMPLESTILTSKIN** 8-11 ....15
2006 **FINSCEAL BEO** 8-11 ....13
2007 **ZARKAVA** 8-11 ....10
2008 **PROPORTIONAL** 8-11 ....16
2009 **ROSANARA** 8-11 ....11
2010 **MISTY FOR ME** 8-11 ....8
2011 **ELUSIVE KATE** 8-11 ....5
2012 **SILASOL** 8-11 ....9
2013 **INDONESIENNE** 8-11 ....12
2014 **FOUND** 8-11 ....12

### PRIX JEAN-LUC LAGARDERE (2y)
Longchamp-7f
2005 **HORATIO NELSON** 9-0 ....................6
2006 **HOLY ROMAN EMPEROR** 9-0 ....................9
2007 **RIO DE LA PLATA** 9-0 ....................8
2008 **NAAQOOS** 9-0 ....................7
2009 **SIYOUNI** 9-0 ....................7
2010 **WOOTTON BASSETT** 9-0 ....................9
2011 **DABIRSIM** 9-0 ....................7
2012 **OLYMPIC GLORY** 9-0 ....................8
2013 **KARAKONTIE** 9-0 ....................8
*2014 **FULL MAST** 9-0 ....................9
*Gleneagles disqualified from first place

### PRIX DE LA FORET
Longchamp-7f
2005 **COURT MASTERPIECE** 5-9-2 ....................8
2006 **CARADAK** 5-9-3 ....................14
2007 **TOYLSOME** 8-9-2 ....................13
2008 **PACO BOY** 3-9-0 ....................8
2009 **VARENAR** 3-9-0 ....................14
2010 **GOLDIKOVA** 5-8-13 ....................10
2011 **DREAM AHEAD** 3-9-0 ....................8
2012 **GORDON LORD BYRON** 4-9-2 ....................11
2013 **MOONLIGHT CLOUD** 5-8-13 ....................11
2014 **OLYMPIC GLORY** 4-9-2 ....................14

### PRIX ROYAL-OAK
Longchamp-1m 7f 110yds
2005 **ALCAZAR** 10-9-4 ....................11
2006 **MONTARE** 4-9-1 ....................10
2007 **ALLEGRETTO** 4-9-1 ....................11
2008 **YEATS** 7-9-4 ....................11
2009 **ASK** 6-9-4 ....................9
2010 **GENTOO** 6-9-4 ....................10
2011 **BE FABULOUS** 4-9-1 ....................14
2012 **LES BEAUFS** 3-8-9 ....................9
2013 **TAC DE BOISTRON** 6-9-4 ....................15
2014 **TAC DE BOISTRON** 7-9-4 ....................13

### CRITERIUM DE SAINT-CLOUD (2y)
Saint-Cloud-1m 2f
2005 **LINDA'S LAD** 9-0 ....................5
2006 **PASSAGE OF TIME** 8-11 ....................13
2007 **FULL OF GOLD** 9-0 ....................6
2008 **FAME AND GLORY** 9-0 ....................11
2009 **PASSION FOR GOLD** 9-0 ....................9
2010 **RECITAL** 9-0 ....................10
2011 **MANDAEAN** 9-0 ....................8
2012 **MORANDI** 9-0 ....................8
2013 **PRINCE GIBRALTAR** 9-0 ....................12
2014 **EPICURIS** 9-0 ....................6

# WINNERS OF OTHER OVERSEAS RACES

### DUBAI WORLD CUP
Meydan-1m 2f Tapeta
(Run at Nad Al Sheba on dirt before 2010)
2005 **ROSES IN MAY** 5-9-0 ....................12
2006 **ELECTROCUTIONIST** 5-9-0 ....................11
2007 **INVASOR** 5-9-0 ....................7
2008 **CURLIN** 4-9-0 ....................12
2009 **WELL ARMED** 6-9-0 ....................14
2010 **GLORIA DE CAMPEAO** 7-9-0 ....................14
2011 **VICTOIRE PISA** 4-9-0 ....................14
2012 **MONTEROSSO** 5-9-0 ....................13
2013 **ANIMAL KINGDOM** 5-9-0 ....................13
2014 **AFRICAN STORY** 7-9-0 ....................16

### KENTUCKY DERBY
Churchill Downs-1m 2f dirt
2005 **GIACOMO** 9-0 ....................20
2006 **BARBARO** 9-0 ....................20
2007 **STREET SENSE** 9-0 ....................20
2008 **BIG BROWN** 9-0 ....................20
2009 **MINE THAT BIRD** 9-0 ....................19
2010 **SUPER SAVER** 9-0 ....................20
2011 **ANIMAL KINGDOM** 9-0 ....................19
2012 **I'LL HAVE ANOTHER** 9-0 ....................20
2013 **ORB** 9-0 ....................19
2014 **CALIFORNIA CHROME** 9-0 ....................19

### BREEDERS' CUP TURF
Various courses-1m 4f
2005 **SHIROCCO** 4-9-0 ....................13
2006 **RED ROCKS** 3-8-10 ....................11
2007 **ENGLISH CHANNEL** 5-9-0 ....................8
2008 **CONDUIT** 3-8-9 ....................11
2009 **CONDUIT** 4-9-0 ....................7
2010 **DANGEROUS MIDGE** 4-9-0 ....................7
2011 **ST NICHOLAS ABBEY** 4-9-0 ....................9
2012 **LITTLE MIKE** 5-9-0 ....................12
2013 **MAGICIAN** 3-8-10 ....................12
2014 **MAIN SEQUENCE** 5-9-0 ....................12

### BREEDERS' CUP CLASSIC
Various courses-1m 2f dirt/pro-ride
2005 **SAINT LIAM** 5-9-0 ....................13
2006 **INVASOR** 4-9-0 ....................13
2007 **CURLIN** 3-8-9 ....................9
2008 **RAVEN'S PASS** 3-8-9 ....................12
2009 **ZENYATTA** 5-8-11 ....................12
2010 **BLAME** 4-9-0 ....................12
2011 **DROSSELMEYER** 4-9-0 ....................12
2012 **FORT LARNED** 4-9-0 ....................12
2013 **MUCHO MACHO MAN** 5-9-0 ....................11
2014 **BAYERN** 3-8-10 ....................14

### MELBOURNE CUP
Flemington-2m
2005 **MAKYBE DIVA** 6-9-2 ....................24
2006 **DELTA BLUES** 5-8-11 ....................23
2007 **EFFICIENT** 4-8-8 ....................21
2008 **VIEWED** 5-8-5 ....................24
2009 **SHOCKING** 4-8-0 ....................23
2010 **AMERICAIN** 5-8-8 ....................23
2011 **DUNADEN** 5-8-8 ....................23
2012 **GREEN MOON** 5-8-6 ....................24
2013 **FIORENTE** 5-8-9 ....................24
2014 **PROTECTIONIST** 4-8-13 ....................22

### JAPAN CUP
Tokyo-1m 4f

2005 **ALKAASED** 5-9-0 ........ 18
2006 **DEEP IMPACT** 4-9-0 ........ 11
2007 **ADMIRE MOON** 4-9-0 ........ 18
2008 **SCREEN HERO** 4-9-0 ........ 17
2009 **VODKA** 5-8-10 ........ 18
*2010 **ROSE KINGDOM** 3-8-9 ........ 18
2011 **BUENA VISTA** 5-8-9 ........ 16
2012 **GENTILDONNA** 3-8-5 ........ 17
2013 **GENTILDONNA** 4-8-9 ........ 17
2014 **EPIPHANEIA** 4-9-0 ........ 18
*Buena Vista disqualified from first place

# WINNERS OF PRINCIPAL NATIONAL HUNT RACES

### PADDY POWER GOLD CUP (HANDICAP CHASE)
Cheltenham-2m 4f 110yds

2005 **OUR VIC** 7-11-7 ........ 18
2006 **EXOTIC DANCER** 6-11-2 ........ 16
2007 **L'ANTARTIQUE** 7-10-13 ........ 20
2008 **IMPERIAL COMMANDER** 7-10-7 ........ 19
2009 **TRANQUIL SEA** 7-10-13 ........ 16
2010 **LITTLE JOSH** 8-10-5 ........ 18
2011 **GREAT ENDEAVOUR** 7-10-3 ........ 20
2012 **AL FEROF** 7-11-8 ........ 18
2013 **JOHNS SPIRIT** 6-10-2 ........ 20
2014 **CAID DU BERLAIS** 5-10-13 ........ 18

### BETFAIR CHASE
Haydock-3m

2006 **KAUTO STAR** 6-11-8 ........ 6
2007 **KAUTO STAR** 7-11-7 ........ 7
2008 **SNOOPY LOOPY** 10-11-7 ........ 6
2009 **KAUTO STAR** 9-11-7 ........ 7
2010 **IMPERIAL COMMANDER** 9-11-7 ........ 7
2011 **KAUTO STAR** 11-11-7 ........ 6
2012 **SILVINIACO CONTI** 6-11-7 ........ 5
2013 **CUE CARD** 7-11-7 ........ 8
2014 **SILVINIACO CONTI** 8-11-7 ........ 9

### HENNESSY GOLD CUP HANDICAP CHASE
Newbury-3m 2f 110yds

2005 **TRABOLGAN** 7-11-12 ........ 19
2006 **STATE OF PLAY** 6-11-4 ........ 16
2007 **DENMAN** 7-11-12 ........ 18
2008 **MADISON DU BERLAIS** 7-11-4 ........ 15
2009 **DENMAN** 9-11-12 ........ 19
2010 **DIAMOND HARRY** 7-10-0 ........ 20
2011 **CARRUTHERS** 8-10-4 ........ 18
2012 **BOBS WORTH** 7-11-6 ........ 19
2013 **TRIOLO D'ALENE** 6-11-1 ........ 21
2014 **MANY CLOUDS** 7-11-6 ........ 19

### TINGLE CREEK CHASE
Sandown-2m

2005 **KAUTO STAR** 5-11-7 ........ 7
2006 **KAUTO STAR** 6-11-7 ........ 7
2007 **TWIST MAGIC** 5-11-7 ........ 8
2008 **MASTER MINDED** 5-11-7 ........ 7
2009 **TWIST MAGIC** 7-11-7 ........ 5
*2010 **MASTER MINDED** 7-11-7 ........ 9
2011 **SIZING EUROPE** 9-11-7 ........ 7
2012 **SPRINTER SACRE** 6-11-7 ........ 7
2013 **SIRE DE GRUGY** 7-11-7 ........ 9
2014 **DODGING BULLETS** 6-11-7 ........ 10
*Run at Cheltenham over 2m 110yds

### CHRISTMAS HURDLE
Kempton-2m

*2005 **FEATHARD LADY** 5-11-0 ........ 7
2006 **JAZZ MESSENGER** 6-11-7 ........ 7
2007 **STRAW BEAR** 6-11-7 ........ 6
2008 **HARCHIBALD** 9-11-7 ........ 7
2009 **GO NATIVE** 6-11-7 ........ 7
**2010 **BINOCULAR** 7-11-7 ........ 6
2011 **BINOCULAR** 7-11-7 ........ 5
2012 **DARLAN** 5-11-7 ........ 7
2013 **MY TENT OR YOURS** 6-11-7 ........ 6
2014 **FAUGHEEN** 6-11-7 ........ 6
*Run at Sandown
**Run in January 2011

### KING GEORGE VI CHASE
Kempton-3m

*2005 **KICKING KING** 7-11-10 ........ 9
2006 **KAUTO STAR** 6-11-10 ........ 9
2007 **KAUTO STAR** 7-11-10 ........ 7
2008 **KAUTO STAR** 8-11-10 ........ 10
2009 **KAUTO STAR** 9-11-10 ........ 13
**2010 **LONG RUN** 6-11-10 ........ 9
2011 **KAUTO STAR** 11-11-10 ........ 7
2012 **LONG RUN** 7-11-10 ........ 9
2013 **SILVINIACO CONTI** 7-11-10 ........ 9
2014 **SILVINIACO CONTI** 8-11-10 ........ 10
*Run at Sandown
**Run in January 2011

### WELSH GRAND NATIONAL (HANDICAP CHASE)
Chepstow-3m 5f 110yds

2005 **L'AVENTURE** 6-10-4 ........ 18
2006 **HALCON GENELARDAIS** 6-11-3 ........ 18
2007 **MIKO DE BEAUCHENE** 7-10-5 ........ 18
2008 **NOTRE PERE** 7-11-0 ........ 20
2009 **DREAM ALLIANCE** 8-10-8 ........ 18
*2010 **SYNCHRONISED** 8-11-6 ........ 18
2011 **LE BEAU BAI** 8-10-1 ........ 20
**2012 **MONBEG DUDE** 8-10-1 ........ 17
2013 **MOUNTAINOUS** 8-10-0 ........ 20
2014 **EMPEROR'S CHOICE** 7-10-8 ........ 19
*Run in January 2011
**Run in January 2013

## CLARENCE HOUSE CHASE
(Victor Chandler Chase before 2014)
(Handicap before 2008)
Ascot-2m 1f

*2006 **TYSOU** 9-11-2 .... 10
2007 ABANDONED
2008 **TAMARINBLEU** 8-11-7 .... 7
2009 **MASTER MINDED** 6-11-7 .... 5
2010 **TWIST MAGIC** 8-11-7 .... 7
2011 **MASTER MINDED** 8-11-7 .... 9
2012 **SOMERSBY** 8-11-7 .... 8
**2013 **SPRINTER SACRE** 7-11-7 .... 7
2014 **SIRE DE GRUGY** 8-11-7 .... 7
2015 **DODGING BULLETS** 7-11-7 .... 5

*Run at Sandown over 2m
**Run at Cheltenham over 2m 110 yds

## BETFAIR H'CAP HURDLE
Newbury-2m 110yds
(Totesport Trophy 2006-2011)

2006 ABANDONED
2007 **HEATHCOTE** 5-10-6 .... 20
2008 **WINGMAN** 6-10-0 .... 24
2009 ABANDONED
2010 **GET ME OUT OF HERE** 6-10-6 .... 23
2011 **RECESSION PROOF** 5-10-8 .... 15
2012 **ZARKANDAR** 5-11-1 .... 20
2013 **MY TENT OR YOURS** 6-11-2 .... 21
2014 **SPLASH OF GINGE** 6-10-3 .... 20
2015 **VIOLET DANCER** 5-10-9 .... 23

## SUPREME NOVICES' HURDLE
Cheltenham-2m 110yds

2005 **ARCALIS** 5-11-7 .... 20
2006 **NOLAND** 5-11-7 .... 20
2007 **EBAZIYAN** 6-11-7 .... 22
2008 **CAPTAIN CEE BEE** 7-11-7 .... 22
2009 **GO NATIVE** 6-11-7 .... 20
2010 **MENORAH** 5-11-7 .... 18
2011 **AL FEROF** 6-11-7 .... 15
2012 **CINDERS AND ASHES** 5-11-7 .... 19
2013 **CHAMPAGNE FEVER** 6-11-7 .... 12
2014 **VAUTOUR** 5-11-7 .... 18

## ARKLE CHALLENGE TROPHY (NOVICES' CHASE)
Cheltenham-2m

2005 **CONTRABAND** 7-11-7 .... 19
2006 **VOY POR USTEDES** 5-11-2 .... 14
2007 **MY WAY DE SOLZEN** 7-11-7 .... 13
2008 **TIDAL BAY** 7-11-7 .... 14
2009 **FORPADYDEPLASTERER** 7-11-7 .... 17
2010 **SIZING EUROPE** 8-11-7 .... 12
2011 **CAPTAIN CHRIS** 7-11-7 .... 10
2012 **SPRINTER SACRE** 6-11-7 .... 6
2013 **SIMONSIG** 7-11-7 .... 7
2014 **WESTERN WARHORSE** 6-11-4 .... 9

## CHAMPION HURDLE
Cheltenham-2m 110yds

2005 **HARDY EUSTACE** 8-11-10 .... 14
2006 **BRAVE INCA** 8-11-10 .... 18
2007 **SUBLIMITY** 7-11-10 .... 10
2008 **KATCHIT** 5-11-10 .... 15
2009 **PUNJABI** 6-11-10 .... 23
2010 **BINOCULAR** 6-11-10 .... 12
2011 **HURRICANE FLY** 7-11-10 .... 11
2012 **ROCK ON RUBY** 7-11-10 .... 10
2013 **HURRICANE FLY** 9-11-10 .... 9
2014 **JEZKI** 6-11-10 .... 9

## QUEEN MOTHER CHAMPION CHASE
Cheltenham-2m

2005 **MOSCOW FLYER** 11-11-10 .... 8
2006 **NEWMILL** 8-11-10 .... 12
2007 **VOY POR USTEDES** 6-11-10 .... 10
2008 **MASTER MINDED** 5-11-10 .... 8
2009 **MASTER MINDED** 6-11-10 .... 12
2010 **BIG ZEB** 9-11-10 .... 9
2011 **SIZING EUROPE** 9-11-10 .... 11
2012 **FINIAN'S RAINBOW** 9-11-10 .... 8
2013 **SPRINTER SACRE** 7-11-10 .... 7
2014 **SIRE DE GRUGY** 8-11-10 .... 11

## NEPTUNE INVESTMENT MANAGEMENT NOVICES' HURDLE
(Royal & SunAlliance Hurdle until 2007,
Ballymore Hurdle 2008-9)
Cheltenham-2m 5f

2005 **NO REFUGE** 5-11-7 .... 20
2006 **NICANOR** 5-11-7 .... 17
2007 **MASSINI'S MAGUIRE** 6-11-7 .... 15
2008 **FIVEFORTHREE** 6-11-7 .... 15
2009 **MIKAEL D'HAGUENET** 5-11-7 .... 14
2010 **PEDDLERS CROSS** 5-11-7 .... 17
2011 **FIRST LIEUTENANT** 6-11-7 .... 12
2012 **SIMONSIG** 6-11-7 .... 17
2013 **THE NEW ONE** 5-11-7 .... 8
2014 **FAUGHEEN** 6-11-7 .... 15

## RSA CHASE
(Royal & SunAlliance Chase before 2009)
(Cheltenham-3m

2005 **TRABOLGAN** 7-11-4 .... 9
2006 **STAR DE MOHAISON** 5-10-8 .... 15
2007 **DENMAN** 7-11-4 .... 17
2008 **ALBERTAS RUN** 7-11-4 .... 11
2009 **COOLDINE** 7-11-4 .... 15
2010 **WEAPON'S AMNESTY** 7-11-4 .... 9
2011 **BOSTONS ANGEL** 7-11-4 .... 12
2012 **BOBS WORTH** 7-11-4 .... 9
2013 **LORD WINDERMERE** 7-11-4 .... 11
2014 **O'FAOLAINS BOY** 7-11-4 .... 15

## WORLD HURDLE
Cheltenham-3m

2005 **INGLIS DREVER** 6-11-10 .... 12
2006 **MY WAY DE SOLZEN** 6-11-10 .... 20
2007 **INGLIS DREVER** 8-11-10 .... 14
2008 **INGLIS DREVER** 9-11-10 .... 17
2009 **BIG BUCK'S** 6-11-10 .... 14
2010 **BIG BUCK'S** 7-11-10 .... 14
2011 **BIG BUCK'S** 8-11-10 .... 13
2012 **BIG BUCK'S** 9-11-10 .... 11
2013 **SOLWHIT** 9-11-10 .... 13
2014 **MORE OF THAT** 6-11-10 .... 10

## TRIUMPH HURDLE (4y)
Cheltenham-2m 1f

2005 **PENZANCE** 11-0 .... 23
2006 **DETROIT CITY** 11-0 .... 17
2007 **KATCHIT** 11-0 .... 23
2008 **CELESTIAL HALO** 11-0 .... 14
2009 **ZAYNAR** 11-0 .... 18
2010 **SOLDATINO** 11-0 .... 17
2011 **ZARKANDAR** 11-0 .... 23
2012 **COUNTRYWIDE FLAME** 11-0 .... 20

2013 **OUR CONOR** 11-0 ........ 17
2014 **TIGER ROLL** 11-0 ........ 15

## CHELTENHAM GOLD CUP

Cheltenham-3m 2f 110yds
2005 **KICKING KING** 7-11-10 ........ 15
2006 **WAR OF ATTRITION** 7-11-10 ........ 22
2007 **KAUTO STAR** 7-11-10 ........ 18
2008 **DENMAN** 8-11-10 ........ 12
2009 **KAUTO STAR** 9-11-10 ........ 16
2010 **IMPERIAL COMMANDER** 9-11-10 ........ 11
2011 **LONG RUN** 6-11-0 ........ 13
2012 **SYNCHRONISED** 9-11-10 ........ 14
2013 **BOBS WORTH** 8-11-10 ........ 9
2014 **LORD WINDERMERE** 8-11-10 ........ 13

## RYANAIR CHASE (FESTIVAL TROPHY)

Cheltenham-2m 5f
2005 **THISTHATANDTOTHER** 9-11-3 ........ 12
2006 **FONDMORT** 10-11-0 ........ 11
2007 **TARANIS** 6-11-0 ........ 9
2008 **OUR VIC** 10-11-10 ........ 9
2009 **IMPERIAL COMMANDER** 8-11-10 ........ 10
2010 **ALBERTAS RUN** 9-11-10 ........ 13
2011 **ALBERTAS RUN** 10-11-10 ........ 11
2012 **RIVERSIDE THEATRE** 8-11-10 ........ 12
2013 **CUE CARD** 7-11-10 ........ 8
2014 **DYNASTE** 8-11-10 ........ 11

## BETFRED BOWL CHASE

(Betfair Bowl Chase 2005-8)
(Totesport Bowl Chase 2009-11)
Aintree-3m 1f
2005 **GREY ABBEY** 11-11-12 ........ 8
2006 **CELESTIAL GOLD** 8-11-8 ........ 9
2007 **EXOTIC DANCER** 7-11-12 ........ 5
2008 **OUR VIC** 10-11-10 ........ 5
2009 **MADISON DU BERLAIS** 8-11-10 ........ 10
2010 **WHAT A FRIEND** 7-11-7 ........ 5
2011 **NACARAT** 10-11-7 ........ 6
2012 **FOLLOW THE PLAN** 9-11-7 ........ 11
2013 **FIRST LIEUTENANT** 8-11-7 ........ 8
2014 **SILVINIACO CONTI** 8-11-7 ........ 6

## MELLING CHASE

Aintree-2m 4f
2005 **MOSCOW FLYER** 11-11-10 ........ 6
2006 **HI CLOY** 9-11-10 ........ 11
2007 **MONET'S GARDEN** 9-11-10 ........ 6
2008 **VOY POR USTEDES** 7-11-10 ........ 6
2009 **VOY POR USTEDES** 8-11-10 ........ 10
2010 **ALBERTAS RUN** 9-11-10 ........ 11
2011 **MASTER MINDED** 8-11-10 ........ 10
2012 **FINIAN'S RAINBOW** 9-11-10 ........ 8
2013 **SPRINTER SACRE** 7-11-10 ........ 6
2014 **BOSTON BOB** 9-11-10 ........ 10

## AINTREE HURDLE

Aintree-2m 4f
2005 **AL EILE** 5-11-7 ........ 9
2006 **ASIAN MAZE** 7-11-0 ........ 9
2007 **AL EILE** 7-11-7 ........ 11
2008 **AL EILE** 8-11-7 ........ 9
2009 **SOLWHIT** 5-11-7 ........ 16
2010 **KHYBER KIM** 8-11-7 ........ 7
2011 **OSCAR WHISKY** 6-11-7 ........ 8
2012 **OSCAR WHISKY** 7-11-7 ........ 5
2013 **ZARKANDAR** 6-11-7 ........ 9
2014 **THE NEW ONE** 6-11-7 ........ 7

## SCOTTISH GRAND NATIONAL (H'CAP CHASE)

Ayr-4m 110 yds (4m 1f before 2007)
2005 **JOES EDGE** 8-9-11 ........ 20
2006 **RUN FOR PADDY** 10-10-2 ........ 30
2007 **HOT WELD** 8-9-9 ........ 23
2008 **IRIS DE BALME** 8-9-7 ........ 24
2009 **HELLO BUD** 11-10-9 ........ 17
2010 **MERIGO** 9-10-0 ........ 30
2011 **BESHABAR** 9-10-4 ........ 28
2012 **MERIGO** 11-10-2 ........ 24
2013 **GODSMEJUDGE** 7-11-3 ........ 24
2014 **AL CO** 9-10-0 ........ 29

## BET365 GOLD CUP (H'CAP CHASE)

(Betfred Gold Cup 2005-7)
Sandown-3m 5f 110yds
2005 **JACK HIGH** 10-10-0 ........ 19
2006 **LACDOUDAL** 7-11-5 ........ 18
2007 **HOT WELD** 8-10-0 ........ 10
2008 **MONKERHOSTIN** 11-10-13 ........ 19
2009 **HENNESSY** 8-10-7 ........ 14
2010 **CHURCH ISLAND** 11-10-5 ........ 19
2011 **POKER DE SIVOLA** 8-10-12 ........ 18
2012 **TIDAL BAY** 11-11-12 ........ 19
2013 **QUENTIN COLLONGES** 9-10-12 ........ 19
2014 **HADRIAN'S APPROACH** 7-11-0 ........ 19

## DISTANCE CONVERSION

| | | | | | | | |
|---|---|---|---|---|---|---|---|
| 5f | 1,000m | 10f | 2,000m | 15f | 3,000m | 20f | 4,000m |
| 6f | 1,200m | 11f | 2,200m | 16f | 3,200m | 21f | 4,200m |
| 7f | 1,400m | 12f | 2,400m | 17f | 3,400m | 22f | 4,400m |
| 8f | 1,600m | 13f | 2,600m | 18f | 3,600m | | |
| 9f | 1,800m | 14f | 2,800m | 19f | 3,800m | | |

# LEADING TRAINERS ON THE FLAT: 1898-2014

1898 R Marsh
1899 J Porter
1900 R Marsh
1901 J Huggins
1902 R S Sievier
1903 G Blackwell
1904 P P Gilpin
1905 W T Robinson
1906 Hon G Lambton
1907 A Taylor
1908 C Morton
1909 A Taylor
1910 A Taylor
1911 Hon G Lambton
1912 Hon G Lambton
1913 R Wootton
1914 A Taylor
1915 P P Gilpin
1916 R C Dawson
1917 A Taylor
1918 A Taylor
1919 A Taylor
1920 A Taylor
1921 A Taylor
1922 A Taylor
1923 A Taylor
1924 R C Dawson
1925 A Taylor
1926 F Darling
1927 Frank Butters
1928 Frank Butters
1929 R C Dawson
1930 H S Persse
1931 J Lawson
1932 Frank Butters
1933 F Darling
1934 Frank Butters
1935 Frank Butters
1936 J Lawson
1937 C Boyd-Rochfort
1938 C Boyd-Rochfort
1939 J L Jarvis
1940 F Darling
1941 F Darling
1942 F Darling
1943 W Nightingall
1944 Frank Butters
1945 W Earl
1946 Frank Butters
1947 F Darling
1948 C F N Murless
1949 Frank Butters
1950 C H Semblat
1951 J L Jarvis
1952 M Marsh
1953 J L Jarvis
1954 C Boyd-Rochfort
1955 C Boyd-Rochfort
1956 C F Elsey
1957 C F N Murless
1958 C Boyd-Rochfort
1959 C F N Murless
1960 C F N Murless
1961 C F N Murless
1962 W Hern
1963 P Prendergast
1964 P Prendergast
1965 P Prendergast
1966 M V O'Brien
1967 C F N Murless
1968 C F N Murless
1969 A M Budgett
1970 C F N Murless
1971 I Balding
1972 W Hern
1973 C F N Murless
1974 P Walwyn
1975 P Walwyn
1976 H Cecil
1977 M V O'Brien
1978 H Cecil
1979 H Cecil
1980 W Hern
1981 M Stoute
1982 H Cecil
1983 W Hern
1984 H Cecil
1985 H Cecil
1986 M Stoute
1987 H Cecil
1988 H Cecil
1989 M Stoute
1990 H Cecil
1991 P Cole
1992 R Hannon Snr
1993 H Cecil
1994 M Stoute
1995 J Dunlop
1996 Saeed bin Suroor
1997 M Stoute
1998 Saeed bin Suroor
1999 Saeed bin Suroor
2000 Sir M Stoute
2001 A O'Brien
2002 A O'Brien
2003 Sir M Stoute
2004 Saeed bin Suroor
2005 Sir M Stoute
2006 Sir M Stoute
2007 A O'Brien
2008 A O'Brien
2009 Sir M Stoute
2010 R Hannon Snr
2011 R Hannon Snr
2012 J Gosden
2013 R Hannon Snr
2014 R Hannon Jnr

# CHAMPION JOCKEYS ON THE FLAT: 1897-2014

1897 M Cannon ........ 145
1898 O Madden ........ 161
1899 S Loates ........ 160
1900 L Reiff ........ 143
1901 O Madden ........ 130
1902 W Lane ........ 170
1903 O Madden ........ 154
1904 O Madden ........ 161
1905 E Wheatley ........ 124
1906 W Higgs ........ 149
1907 W Higgs ........ 146
1908 D Maher ........ 139
1909 F Wootton ........ 165
1910 F Wootton ........ 137
1911 F Wootton ........ 187
1912 F Wootton ........ 118
1913 D Maher ........ 115
1914 S Donoghue ........ 129
1915 S Donoghue ........ 62
1916 S Donoghue ........ 43
1917 S Donoghue ........ 42
1918 S Donoghue ........ 66
1919 S Donoghue ........ 129
1920 S Donoghue ........ 143
1921 S Donoghue ........ 141
1922 S Donoghue ........ 102
1923 S Donoghue ........ 89
C Elliott ........ 89
1924 C Elliott ........ 106
1925 G Richards ........ 118
1926 T Weston ........ 95
1927 G Richards ........ 164
1928 G Richards ........ 148
1929 G Richards ........ 135
1930 F Fox ........ 129
1931 G Richards ........ 145
1932 G Richards ........ 190
1933 G Richards ........ 259
1934 G Richards ........ 212
1935 G Richards ........ 217
1936 G Richards ........ 174
1937 G Richards ........ 216
1938 G Richards ........ 206
1939 G Richards ........ 155
1940 G Richards ........ 68
1941 H Wragg ........ 71
1942 G Richards ........ 67
1943 G Richards ........ 65
1944 G Richards ........ 88
1945 G Richards ........ 104
1946 G Richards ........ 212
1947 G Richards ........ 269
1948 G Richards ........ 224
1949 G Richards ........ 261
1950 G Richards ........ 201
1951 G Richards ........ 227
1952 G Richards ........ 231
1953 Sir G Richards ........ 191
1954 D Smith ........ 129
1955 D Smith ........ 168
1956 D Smith ........ 155
1957 A Breasley ........ 173
1958 D Smith ........ 165
1959 D Smith ........ 157
1960 L Piggott ........ 170
1961 A Breasley ........ 171

| Year | Jockey | Wins |
|---|---|---|
| 1962 | A Breasley | 179 |
| 1963 | A Breasley | 176 |
| 1964 | L Piggott | 140 |
| 1965 | L Piggott | 160 |
| 1966 | L Piggott | 191 |
| 1967 | L Piggott | 117 |
| 1968 | L Piggott | 139 |
| 1969 | L Piggott | 163 |
| 1970 | L Piggott | 162 |
| 1971 | L Piggott | 162 |
| 1972 | W Carson | 132 |
| 1973 | W Carson | 164 |
| 1974 | Pat Eddery | 148 |
| 1975 | Pat Eddery | 164 |
| 1976 | Pat Eddery | 162 |
| 1977 | Pat Eddery | 176 |
| 1978 | W Carson | 182 |
| 1979 | J Mercer | 164 |
| 1980 | W Carson | 166 |
| 1981 | L Piggott | 179 |
| 1982 | L Piggott | 188 |
| 1983 | W Carson | 159 |
| 1984 | S Cauthen | 130 |
| 1985 | S Cauthen | 195 |
| 1986 | Pat Eddery | 176 |
| 1987 | S Cauthen | 197 |
| 1988 | Pat Eddery | 183 |
| 1989 | Pat Eddery | 171 |
| 1990 | Pat Eddery | 209 |
| 1991 | Pat Eddery | 165 |
| 1992 | M Roberts | 206 |
| 1993 | Pat Eddery | 169 |
| 1994 | L Dettori | 233 |
| 1995 | L Dettori | 211 |
| 1996 | Pat Eddery | 186 |
| 1997 | K Fallon | 196 |
| 1998 | K Fallon | 185 |
| 1999 | K Fallon | 200 |
| 2000 | K Darley | 152 |
| 2001 | K Fallon | 166 |
| 2002 | K Fallon | 144 |
| 2003 | K Fallon | 208 |
| 2004 | L Dettori | 192 |
| 2005 | J Spencer | 163 |
| 2006 | R Moore | 180 |
| 2007 | S Sanders | 190 |
| | J Spencer | 190 |
| 2008 | R Moore | 186 |
| 2009 | R Moore | 174 |
| 2010 | P Hanagan | 191 |
| 2011 | P Hanagan | 165 |
| 2012 | R Hughes | 172 |
| 2013 | R Hughes | 203 |
| 2014 | R Hughes | 161 |

# CHAMPION APPRENTICES ON THE FLAT 1980-2014

| Year | Apprentice | Wins |
|---|---|---|
| 1980 | P Robinson | 59 |
| 1981 | B Crossley | 45 |
| 1982 | W Newnes | 57 |
| 1983 | M Hills | 39 |
| 1984 | T Quinn | 62 |
| 1985 | G Carter | 37 |
| | W Ryan | 37 |
| 1986 | G Carter | 34 |
| 1987 | G Bardwell | 27 |
| 1988 | G Bardwell | 39 |
| 1989 | L Dettori | 71 |
| 1990 | J Fortune | 46 |
| 1991 | D Holland | 79 |
| 1992 | D Harrison | 56 |
| 1993 | D Harrison | 40 |
| 1994 | S Davies | 45 |
| 1995 | S Sanders | 61 |
| 1996 | D O'Neill | 79 |
| 1997 | R Ffrench | 77 |
| 1998 | C Lowther | 72 |
| 1999 | R Winston | 49 |
| 2000 | L Newman | 87 |
| 2001 | C Catlin | 71 |
| 2002 | P Hanagan | 81 |
| 2003 | R Moore | 52 |
| 2004 | T Queally | 59 |
| 2005 | S Golam | 44 |
| | H Turner | 44 |
| 2006 | S Donohoe | 44 |
| 2007 | G Fairley | 65 |
| 2008 | W Buick | 50 |
| | D Probert | 50 |
| 2009 | F Tylicki | 60 |
| 2010 | M Lane | 41 |
| 2011 | M Harley | 57 |
| 2012 | A Ryan | 40 |
| 2013 | J Hart | 51 |
| 2014 | O Murphy | 74 |

# LEADING OWNERS ON THE FLAT: 1895-2014

|  |  |
|---|---|
| 1895 | Ld de Rothschild |
| 1896 | Ld de Rothschild |
| 1897 | Mr J Gubbins |
| 1898 | Ld de Rothschild |
| 1899 | Duke of Westminster |
| 1900 | H.R.H. The Prince of Wales |
| 1901 | Sir G Blundell Maple |
| 1902 | Mr R S Sievier |
| 1903 | Sir James Miller |
| 1904 | Sir James Miller |
| 1905 | Col W Hall Walker |
| 1906 | Ld Derby (late) |
| 1907 | Col W Hall Walker |
| 1908 | Mr J B Joel |
| 1909 | Mr "Fairie" |
| 1910 | Mr "Fairie" |
| 1911 | Ld Derby |
| 1912 | Mr T Pilkington |
| 1913 | Mr J B Joel |
| 1914 | Mr J B Joel |
| 1915 | Mr L Neumann |
| 1916 | Mr E Hulton |
| 1917 | Mr "Fairie" |
| 1918 | Lady James Douglas |
| 1919 | Ld Glanely |
| 1920 | Sir Robert Jardine |
| 1921 | Mr S B Joel |
| 1922 | Ld Woolavington |
| 1923 | Ld Derby |
| 1924 | H.H. Aga Khan |
| 1925 | Ld Astor |
| 1926 | Ld Woolavington |
| 1927 | Ld Derby |
| 1928 | Ld Derby |
| 1929 | H.H. Aga Khan |
| 1930 | H.H. Aga Khan |
| 1931 | Mr J A Dewar |
| 1932 | H.H. Aga Khan |
| 1933 | Ld Derby |
| 1934 | H.H. Aga Khan |
| 1935 | H.H. Aga Khan |
| 1936 | Ld Astor |
| 1937 | H.H. Aga Khan |
| 1938 | Ld Derby |
| 1939 | Ld Rosebery |
| 1940 | Lord Rothermere |
| 1941 | Ld Glanely |
| 1942 | His Majesty |
| 1943 | Miss D Paget |
| 1944 | H.H. Aga Khan |
| 1945 | Ld Derby |
| 1946 | H.H. Aga Khan |
| 1947 | H.H. Aga Khan |
| 1948 | H.H. Aga Khan |
| 1949 | H.H. Aga Khan |
| 1950 | M M Boussac |
| 1951 | M M Boussac |
| 1952 | H.H. Aga Khan |
| 1953 | Sir Victor Sassoon |
| 1954 | Her Majesty |
| 1955 | Lady Zia Wernner |
| 1956 | Maj L B Holliday |
| 1957 | Her Majesty |
| 1958 | Mr J McShain |
| 1959 | Prince Aly Khan |
| 1960 | Sir Victor Sassoon |
| 1961 | Maj L B Holliday |
| 1962 | Maj L B Holliday |
| 1963 | Mr J R Mullion |
| 1964 | Mrs H E Jackson |
| 1965 | M J Ternynck |
| 1966 | Lady Zia Wernher |
| 1967 | Mr H J Joel |
| 1968 | Mr Raymond R Guest |
| 1969 | Mr D Robinson |
| 1970 | Mr C Engelhard |
| 1971 | Mr P Mellon |
| 1972 | Mrs J Hislop |
| 1973 | Mr N B Hunt |
| 1974 | Mr N B Hunt |
| 1975 | Dr C Vittadini |
| 1976 | Mr D Wildenstein |
| 1977 | Mr R Sangster |
| 1978 | Mr R Sangster |
| 1979 | Sir M Sobell |
| 1980 | S Weinstock |
| 1981 | H.H. Aga Khan |

1982 Mr R Sangster
1983 Mr R Sangster
1984 Mr R Sangster
1985 Sheikh Mohammed
1986 Sheikh Mohammed
1987 Sheikh Mohammed
1988 Sheikh Mohammed
1989 Sheikh Mohammed
1990 Mr Hamdan Al-Maktoum
1991 Sheikh Mohammed
1992 Sheikh Mohammed
1993 Sheikh Mohammed
1994 Mr Hamdan Al-Maktoum
1995 Mr Hamdan Al-Maktoum
1996 Godolphin
1997 Sheikh Mohammed
1998 Godolphin
1999 Godolphin
2000 H.H. Aga Khan
2001 Godolphin
2002 Mr Hamdan Al-Maktoum
2003 K Abdullah
2004 Godolphin
2005 Mr Hamdan Al-Maktoum
2006 Godolphin
2007 Godolphin
2008 HRH Princess Haya of Jordan
2009 Mr Hamdan Al-Maktoum
2010 K Abdullah
2011 K Abdullah
2012 Godolphin
2013 Godolphin
2014 Mr Hamdan Al-Maktoum

# LEADING SIRES ON THE FLAT: 1895-2014

1895 St Simon
1896 St Simon
1897 Kendal
1898 Galopin
1899 Orme
1900 St Simon
1901 St Simon
1902 Persimmon
1903 St Frusquin
1904 Gallinule
1905 Gallinule
1906 Persimmon
1907 St Frusquin
1908 Persimmon
1909 Cyllene
1910 Cyllene
1911 Sundridge
1912 Persimmon
1913 Desmond
1914 Polymelus
1915 Polymelus
1916 Polymelus
1917 Bayardo
1918 Bayardo
1919 The Tetrarch
1920 Polymelus
1921 Polymelus
1922 Lemberg
1923 Swynford
1924 Son-in-Law
1925 Phalaris
1926 Hurry On
1927 Buchan
1928 Phalaris
1929 Tetratema
1930 Son-in-Law
1931 Pharos
1932 Gainsborough
1933 Gainsborough
1934 Blandford
1935 Blandford
1936 Fairway
1937 Solario
1938 Blandford
1939 Fairway
1940 Hyperion
1941 Hyperion
1942 Hyperion
1943 Fairway
1944 Fairway
1945 Hyperion
1946 Hyperion
1947 Nearco
1948 Big Game
1949 Nearco
1950 Fair Trial
1951 Nasrullah
1952 Tehran
1953 Chanteur II
1954 Hyperion
1955 Alycidon
1956 Court Martial
1957 Court Martial
1958 Mossborough
1959 Petition
1960 Aureole
1961 Aureole
1962 Never Say Die
1963 Ribot
1964 Chamossaire
1965 Court Harwell
1966 Charlottesville
1967 Ribot
1968 Ribot
1969 Crepello
1970 Northern Dancer
1971 Never Bend
1972 Queen's Hussar
1973 Vaguely Noble
1974 Vaguely Noble
1975 Great Nephew
1976 Wolver Hollow
1977 Northern Dancer
1978 Mill Reef (USA)
1979 Petingo
1980 Pitcairn
1981 Great Nephew
1982 Be My Guest (USA)
1983 Northern Dancer
1984 Northern Dancer
1985 Kris
1986 Nijinsky (CAN)
1987 Mill Reef (USA)
1988 Caerleon (USA)
1989 Blushing Groom (FR)
1990 Sadler's Wells (USA)
1991 Caerleon (USA)
1992 Sadler's Wells (USA)
1993 Sadler's Wells (USA)
1994 Sadler's Wells (USA)
1995 Sadler's Wells (USA)
1996 Sadler's Wells (USA)
1997 Sadler's Wells (USA)
1998 Sadler's Wells (USA)
1999 Sadler's Wells (USA)
2000 Sadler's Wells (USA)
2001 Sadler's Wells (USA)
2002 Sadler's Wells (USA)
2003 Sadler's Wells (USA)
2004 Sadler's Wells (USA)
2005 Danehill (USA)
2006 Danehill (USA)
2007 Danehill (USA)
2008 Galileo (IRE)
2009 Danehill Dancer (IRE)
2010 Galileo (IRE)
2011 Galileo (IRE)
2012 Galileo (IRE)
2013 Galileo (IRE)
2014 Galileo (IRE)

# LEADING BREEDERS ON THE FLAT: 1911-2014

1911 Ld Derby (late)
1912 Col. W Hall Walker
1913 Mr J B Joel
1914 Mr J B Joel
1915 Mr L Neumann
1916 Mr E Hulton
1917 Mr "Fairie"
1918 Lady James Douglas
1919 Ld Derby
1920 Ld Derby
1921 Mr S B Joel
1922 Ld Derby
1923 Ld Derby
1924 Lady Sykes
1925 Ld Astor
1926 Ld Woolavington
1927 Ld Derby
1928 Ld Derby
1929 Ld Derby
1930 Ld Derby
1931 Ld Dewar
1932 H.H. Aga Khan
1933 Sir Alec Black
1934 H.H. Aga Khan

1935 H.H. Aga Khan
1936 Ld Astor
1937 H.H. Aga Khan
1938 Ld Derby
1939 Ld Rosebery
1940 Mr H E Morriss
1941 Ld Glanely
1942 National Stud
1943 Miss D Paget
1944 Ld Rosebery
1945 Ld Derby
1946 Lt- Col H Boyd-Rochfort
1947 H.H. Aga Khan
1948 H.H. Aga Khan
1949 H.H. Aga Khan
1950 M M Boussac
1951 M M Boussac
1952 H. H. Aga Khan
1953 Mr F Darling
1954 Maj L B Holliday
1955 Someries Stud
1956 Maj L B Holliday
1957 Eve Stud
1958 Mr R Ball
1959 Prince Aly Khan and the late H.H. Aga Khan
1960 Eve Stud Ltd
1961 Eve Stud Ltd
1962 Maj L B Holliday
1963 Mr H F Guggenheim
1964 Bull Run Stud
1965 Mr J Ternynck
1966 Someries Stud
1967 Mr H J Joel
1968 Mill Ridge Farm
1969 Lord Rosebery
1970 Mr E P Taylor
1971 Mr P Mellon
1972 Mr J Hislop
1973 Claiborne Farm
1974 Mr N B Hunt
1975 Overbury Stud
1976 Dayton Ltd
1977 Mr E P Taylor
1978 Cragwood Estates Inc
1979 Ballymacoll Stud
1980 P Clarke
1981 H.H. Aga Khan
1982 Someries Stud
1983 White Lodge Stud
1984 Mr E P Taylor
1985 Dalham Stud Farms
1986 H.H. Aga Khan
1987 Cliveden Stud
1988 H. H. Aga Khan
1989 Mr Hamdan Al-Maktoum
1990 Capt. Macdonald- Buchanan
1991 Barronstown Stud
1992 Swettenham Stud
1993 Juddmonte Farms
1994 Shadwell Farm & Estate Ltd
1995 Shadwell Farm & Estate Ltd
1996 Sheikh Mohammed
1997 Sheikh Mohammed
1998 Sheikh Mohammed
1999 H. H. The Aga Khan's Studs
2000 H. H. The Aga Khan's Studs
2001 Shadwell Farm & Estate Ltd
2002 Gainsborough Stud
2003 Juddmonte
2004 Juddmonte
2005 Shadwell Farm & Estate Ltd
2006 Darley
2007 Darley
2008 Darley
2009 Darley
2010 Juddmonte
2011 Juddmonte
2012 Juddmonte
2013 Darley
2014 Darley

# LEADING TRAINERS OVER JUMPS: 1946-2013

1946-47 F T T Walwyn
1947-48 F T T Walwyn
1948-49 F T T Walwyn
1949-50 P V F Cazalet
1950-51 T F Rimell
1951-52 N Crump
1952-53 M V O'Brien
1953-54 M V O'Brien
1954-55 H R Price
1955-56 W Hall
1956-57 N Crump
1957-58 F T T Walwyn
1958-59 H R Price
1959-60 P V F Cazalet
1960-61 T F Rimell
1961-62 H R Price
1962-63 K Piggott
1963-64 F T T Walwyn
1964-65 P V F Cazalet
1965-66 H R Price
1966-67 H R Price
1967-68 Denys Smith
1968-69 T F Rimell
1969-70 T F Rimell
1970-71 F T Winter
1971-72 F T Winter
1972-73 F T Winter
1973-74 F T Winter
1974-75 F T Winter
1975-76 T F Rimell
1976-77 F T Winter
1977-78 F T Winter
1978-79 M H Easterby
1979-80 M H Easterby
1980-81 M H Easterby
1981-82 M W Dickinson
1982-83 M W Dickinson
1983-84 M W Dickinson
1984-85 F T Winter
1985-86 N J Henderson
1986-87 N J Henderson
1987-88 D R C Elsworth
1988-89 M C Pipe
1989-90 M C Pipe
1990-91 M C Pipe
1991-92 M C Pipe
1992-93 M C Pipe
1993-94 D Nicholson
1994-95 D Nicholson
1995-96 M C Pipe
1996-97 M C Pipe
1997-98 M C Pipe
1998-99 M C Pipe
1999-00 M C Pipe
2000-01 M C Pipe
2001-02 M C Pipe
2002-03 M C Pipe
2003-04 M C Pipe
2004-05 M C Pipe
2005-06 P F Nicholls
2006-07 P F Nicholls
2007-08 P F Nicholls
2008-09 P F Nicholls
2009-10 P F Nicholls
2010-11 P F Nicholls
2010-11 P F Nicholls
2011-12 P F Nicholls
2012-13 N J Henderson
2013-14 P F Nicholls

# CHAMPION JOCKEYS OVER JUMPS: 1901-2014

Prior to the 1925-26 season the figure relates to racing between January and December

| Year | Jockey | Wins |
|---|---|---|
| 1901 | F Mason | 58 |
| 1902 | F Mason | 67 |
| 1903 | P Woodland | 54 |
| 1904 | F Mason | 59 |
| 1905 | F Mason | 73 |
| 1906 | F Mason | 58 |
| 1907 | F Mason | 59 |
| 1908 | P Cowley | 65 |
| 1909 | R Gordon | 45 |
| 1910 | E Piggott | 67 |
| 1911 | W Payne | 76 |
| 1912 | I Anthony | 78 |
| 1913 | E Piggott | 60 |
| 1914 | Mr J R Anthony | 60 |
| 1915 | E Piggott | 44 |
| 1916 | C Hawkins | 17 |
| 1917 | W Smith | 15 |
| 1918 | G Duller | 17 |
| 1919 | Mr H Brown | 48 |
| 1920 | F B Rees | 64 |
| 1921 | F B Rees | 65 |

1922 J Anthony 78
1923 F B Rees 64
1924 F B Rees 108
1925 E Foster 76
1925-26 T Leader 61
1926-27 F B Rees 59
1927-28 W Stott 88
1928-29 W Stott 65
1929-30 W Stott 77
1930-31 W Stott 81
1931-32 W Stott 77
1932-33 G Wilson 61
1933-34 G Wilson 56
1934-35 G Wilson 73
1935-36 G Wilson 57
1936-37 G Wilson 45
1937-38 G Wilson 59
1938-39 T F Rimell 61
1939-40 T F Rimell 24
1940-41 G Wilson 22
1941-42 R Smyth 12
1942-43 No racing
1943-44 No racing
1944-45 H Nicholson 15
T F Rimell 15
1945-46 T F Rimell 54
1946-47 J Dowdeswell 58
1947-48 B Marshall 66
1948-49 T Moloney 60
1949-50 T Moloney 95
1950-51 T Moloney 83
1951-52 T Moloney 99
1952-53 F Winter 121
1953-54 R Francis 76
1954-55 T Moloney 67
1955-56 F Winter 74
1956-57 F Winter 80
1957-58 F Winter 82
1958-59 T Brookshaw 83
1959-60 S Mellor 68
1960-61 S Mellor 118
1961-62 S Mellor 80
1962-63 J Gifford 70
1963-64 J Gifford 94
1964-65 T Biddlecombe 114
1965-66 T Biddlecombe 102
1966-67 J Gifford 122
1967-68 J Gifford 82
1968-69 B R Davies 77
T Biddlecombe 77
1969-70 B R Davies 91
1970-71 G Thorner 74
1971-72 B R Davies 89
1972-73 R Barry 125
1973-74 R Barry 94
1974-75 T Stack 82
1975-76 J Francome 96
1976-77 T Stack 97
1977-78 J J O'Neill 149
1978-79 J Francome 95
1979-80 J J O'Neill 117
1980-81 J Francome 105
1981-82 J Francome 120
P Scudamore 120
1982-83 J Francome 106
1983-84 J Francome 131
1984-85 J Francome 101
1985-86 P Scudamore 91
1986-87 P Scudamore 123
1987-88 P Scudamore 132
1988-89 P Scudamore 221
1989-90 P Scudamore 170
1990-91 P Scudamore 141
1991-92 P Scudamore 175
1992-93 R Dunwoody 173
1993-94 R Dunwoody 197
1994-95 R Dunwoody 160
1995-96 A P McCoy 175
1996-97 A P McCoy 190
1997-98 A P McCoy 253
1998-99 A P McCoy 186
1999-00 A P McCoy 245
2000-01 A P McCoy 191
2001-02 A P McCoy 289
2002-03 A P McCoy 256
2003-04 A P McCoy 209
2004-05 A P McCoy 200
2005-06 A P McCoy 178
2006-07 A P McCoy 184
2007-08 A P McCoy 140
2008-09 A P McCoy 186
2009-10 A P McCoy 195
2010-11 A P McCoy 218
2011-12 A P McCoy 199
2012-13 A P McCoy 185
2013-14 A P McCoy 218

# LEADING OWNERS OVER JUMPS: 1946-2014

(Please note that prior to the 1994-95 season the leading owner was determined by win prizemoney only)

1946-47 Mr J J McDowell
1947-48 Mr J Proctor
1948-49 Mr W F Williamson
1949-50 Mrs L Brotherton
1950-51 Mr J Royle
1951-52 Miss D Paget
1952-53 Mr J H Griffin
1953-54 Mr J H Griffin
1954-55 Mrs W H E Welman
1955-56 Mrs L Carver
1956-57 Mrs Geoffrey Kohn
1957-58 Mr D J Coughlan
1958-59 Mr J E Bigg
1959-60 Miss W H Wallace
1960-61 Mr C Vaughan
1961-62 Mr N Cohen
1962-63 Mr P B Raymond
1963-64 Mr J K Goodman
1964-65 Mrs M Stephenson
1965-66 Duchess of Westminster
1966-67 Mr C P T Watkins
1967-68 Mr H S Alper
1968-69 Mr B P Jenks
1969-70 Mr E R Courage
1970-71 Mr F Pontin
1971-72 Capt T A Forster
1972-73 Mr N H Le Mare
1973-74 Mr N H Le Mare
1974-75 Mr R Guest
1975-76 Mr P B Raymond
1976-77 Mr N H Le Mare
1977-78 Mrs O Jackson
1978-79 Snailwell Stud Co Ltd
1979-80 Mr H J Joel
1980-81 Mr R J Wilson
1981-82 Sheikh Ali Abu Khamsin
1982-83 Sheikh Ali Abu Khamsin
1983-84 Sheikh Ali Abu Khamsin
1984-85 T Kilroe and Son Ltd
1985-86 Sheikh Ali Abu Khamsin
1986-87 Mr H J Joel
1987-88 Miss Juliet E Reed
1988-89 Mr R Burridge
1989-90 Mrs Harry J Duffey
1990-91 Mr P Piller
1991-92 Whitcombe Manor Racing Stables Ltd
1992-93 Mrs J Mould
1993-94 Pell-Mell Partners
1994-95 Roach Foods Limited
1995-96 Mr A T A Wates
1996-97 Mr R Ogden
1997-98 Mr D A Johnson
1998-99 Mr J P McManus
1999-00 Mr R Ogden
2000-01 Sir R Ogden
2001-02 Mr D A Johnson
2002-03 Mr D A Johnson
2003-04 Mr D A Johnson
2004-05 Mr D A Johnson
2005-06 Mr J P McManus
2006-07 Mr J P McManus
2007-08 Mr D A Johnson
2008-09 Mr J P McManus
2009-10 Mr J P McManus
2010-11 Mr T Hemmings
2011-12 Mr J P McManus
2012-13 Mr J P McManus
2013-14 Mr J P McManus

# LEADING AMATEUR RIDERS OVER JUMPS: 1947-2014

1947-48 Ld Mildmay 22
1948-49 Ld Mildmay 30
1949-50 Ld Mildmay 38
1950-51 Mr P Chisman 13
1951-52 Mr C Straker 19
1952-53 Mr A H Moralee 22
1953-54 Mr A H Moralee 22
1954-55 Mr A H Moralee 16
1955-56 Mr R McCreery 13
Mr A H Moralee 13
1956-57 Mr R McCreery 23
1957-58 Mr J Lawrence 18

1958-59 Mr J Sutcliffe ........ 18
1959-60 Mr G Kindersley ........ 22
1960-61 Sir W Pigott-Brown ........ 28
1961-62 Mr A Biddlecombe ........ 30
1962-63 Sir W Pigott-Brown ........ 20
1963-64 Mr S Davenport ........ 32
1964-65 Mr M Gifford ........ 15
1965-66 Mr C Collins ........ 24
1966-67 Mr C Collins ........ 33
1967-68 Mr R Tate ........ 30
1968-69 Mr R Tate ........ 17
1969-70 Mr M Dickinson ........ 23
1970-71 Mr J Lawrence ........ 17
1971-72 Mr W Foulkes ........ 26
1972-73 Mr R Smith ........ 56
1973-74 Mr A Webber ........ 21
1974-75 Mr R Lamb ........ 22
1975-76 Mr P Greenall ........ 25
Mr G Jones ........ 25
1976-77 Mr P Greenall ........ 27
1977-78 Mr G Sloan ........ 23
1978-79 Mr T G Dun ........ 26
1979-80 Mr O Sherwood ........ 29
1980-81 Mr P Webber ........ 32
1981-82 Mr D Browne ........ 28
1982-83 Mr D Browne ........ 33
1983-84 Mr S Sherwood ........ 28
1984-85 Mr S Sherwood ........ 30
1985-86 Mr T Thomson Jones ........ 25
1986-87 Mr T Thomson Jones ........ 19
1987-88 Mr T Thomson Jones ........ 15
1988-89 Mr P Fenton ........ 18
1989-90 Mr P McMahon ........ 15
1990-91 Mr K Johnson ........ 24
1991-92 Mr M P Hourigan ........ 24
1992-93 Mr A Thornton ........ 26
1993-94 Mr J Greenall ........ 21
1994-95 Mr D Parker ........ 16
1995-96 Mr J Culloty ........ 40
1996-97 Mr R Thornton ........ 30
1997-98 Mr S Durack ........ 41
1998-99 Mr A Dempsey ........ 47
1999-00 Mr P Flynn ........ 41
2000-01 Mr T Scudamore ........ 24
2001-02 Mr D Crosse ........ 19
2002-03 Mr C Williams ........ 23
2003-04 Mr O Nelmes ........ 14
2004-05 Mr T Greenall ........ 31
2005-06 Mr T O'Brien ........ 32
2006-07 Mr T Greenall ........ 31
2007-08 Mr T Greenall ........ 23
2008-09 Mr O Greenall ........ 23
2009-10 Mr O Greenall ........ 41
2010-11 Mr R Mahon ........ 19
2011-12 Miss E Sayer ........ 11
2012-13 Mr N de Boinville ........ 16
2013-14 Mr H Bannister ........ 11

## LEADING SIRES OVER JUMPS: 1986-2013

1986 Deep Run
1987 Deep Run
1988 Deep Run
1989 Deep Run
1989-90 Deep Run
1990-91 Deep Run
1991-92 Deep Run
1992-93 Deep Run
1993-94 Strong Gale
1994-95 Strong Gale
1995-96 Strong Gale
1996-97 Strong Gale
1997-98 Strong Gale
1998-99 Strong Gale
1999-00 Strong Gale
2000-01 Be My Native (USA)
2001-02 Be My Native (USA)
2002-03 Be My Native (USA)
2003-04 Be My Native (USA)
2004-05 Supreme Leader
2005-06 Supreme Leader
2006-07 Presenting
2007-08 Old Vic
2008-09 Presenting
2009-10 Presenting
2010-11 Presenting
2011-12 King's Theatre
2012-13 Beneficial
2013-14 King's Theatre

# JOCKEYS' AGENTS

## Jockeys' Agents and their Contact Details

| Agent | Telephone | Mobile/Email | Fax |
|---|---|---|---|
| **NICKY ADAMS** | 01488 72004/72964 | 07796 547659<br>nickadams2594@hotmail.com | |
| **NEIL ALLAN** | 01243 543870 | 07985 311141/07825 549081 | |
| **NIGEL BAXTER** | 01942 269972 | 07973 561521<br>nigelbaxter@blueyonder.co.uk | |
| **NICK BELL** | 07557 941366 | bellnick70@googlemail.com | |
| **PAUL BRIERLEY** | 01434 608212 | 07824 828750<br>bbjockeys@hotmail.co.uk | |
| **CHRIS BROAD** | 01452 760482/447 | 07836 622858<br>chrisd.broad@yahoo.co.uk | 01452 760394 |
| **ANTHONY BURKE** | 01638 602208 | 07825 330392<br>anyprice2001@yahoo.com | |
| **GLORIA CHARNOCK** | 01653 695004 | 07951 576912<br>gloriacharnock@hotmail.com | |
| **PAUL CLARKE** | 01638 660804 | 07885 914306<br>paul.clarke79@btinternet.com | |
| **RAY COCHRANE** | 01223 812008 | 07798 651247<br>ray@raysagency.co.uk | |
| **SIMON DODDS** | 01509 852344/852254 | 07974 924735<br>simon.dodds@btinternet.com | |
| **JACQUI DOYLE** | 01488 72788 | 07831 880678<br>doyleracing@yahoo.co.uk | |

| Agent | Telephone | Mobile/Email | Fax |
|---|---|---|---|
| **SHIPPY ELLIS** | 01638 668484 | 07860 864864<br>shippysjockeys@btconnect.com | 01638 660946 |
| **JOHN W FORD** | 01954 261122 | 07830 294210<br>john.ford47@btinternet.com | |
| **MARK FURNASS** | 01347 824633 | 07474 242332<br>jockeysagent@gmail.com | |
| **LUKE GEDGE-GIBSON** | 01842 756322 | 07580 948206<br>lukegedge08@hotmail.com | |
| **MICHAEL HAGGAS** | 01638 660811 | 07740 624550<br>mhaggas@ntlworld.com | |
| **RICHARD HALE** | 01768 88699 | 07909 520542<br>richardhale77@hotmail.co.uk | |
| **NIALL HANNITY** | 01677 423363 | 07710 141084<br>niallhannity@yahoo.co.uk | |
| **DAVID HARRISON** | 01614 087888 | 07592 767206<br>davidpharrison@hotmail.com | |
| **ALAN HARRISON** | 01969 625006 | 07846 187991<br>ahjockagent60@yahoo.co.uk | 0560 2729293 |
| **TONY HIND** | 01638 724997 | 07807 908599<br>tonyhind@jockeysagent.com | |
| **GAVIN HORNE** | 01392 423352 | 07914 897170<br>gavin.horne@hotmail.co.uk | |
| **JO HUGHES** | 01488 71103 | 07900 680189<br>johughes3@aol.co.uk | 01488 71444 |
| **RUSS JAMES** | 01653 699466 | 07947 414001<br>russjames2006@btinternet.com | 01653 699581 |

| Agent | Telephone | Mobile/Email | Fax |
|---|---|---|---|
| **BRUCE JEFFREY** | 01750 21521 | 07747 854684<br>brucejeffrey@live.co.uk | |
| **GUY JEWELL** | 01672 861231 | 07765 248859<br>guyjewell@btconnect.com | 01672 861231 |
| **ANDREW LEWIS** | 01908 473812 | 07838 506594<br>andrew.lewis11@sky.com | |
| **SARA-LOUISE METCALFE** | 01635 269647 | 07918 525354<br>troopersjockeys@hotmail.co.uk | |
| **LOUISE MILLMAN** | 01884 266620 | 07740 932791<br>rod.millman@ic24.net | |
| **PHILIP MITCHELL** | 01367 820299 | 07836 231462<br>philipmitchell48@gmail.com | |
| **LEE NEWTON** | 01302 376370 | 07710 422437<br>newton808@btinternet.com | |
| **CLARE NICHOLLS** | 07525 159431 | trotandsweets@hotmail.com | |
| **GARETH OWEN** | 01603 569390 | 07958 335206<br>gareth@willowracing.com | |
| **SHASHI RIGHTON** | 01353 688594 | 07825 381350<br>slasher74@aol.com | |
| **DAVE ROBERTS** | 01737 221368/222876 | 07860 234342<br>daveroberts.racing@nhworld.com | |
| **PHILIP SHEA** | 07585 120297 | pucklad2@hotmail.com | |
| **SAM STRONGE** | 01488 72818 | 07775 727778<br>sam.stronge@virgin.net | 01488 670378 |
| **GARY THOMSON** | 01642 873152 | 07986 607014<br>garythomson73@me.com | |

| Agent | Telephone | Mobile/Email | Fax |
| --- | --- | --- | --- |
| **JENNIFER WALSH** | 00353 45883704 | 00353 872528025<br>jennifer@ruby-walsh.com | 00353 45871929 |
| **IAN WARDLE** | 01793 688858 | 07831 865974<br>ian.wardlex@googlemail.com | |
| **LAURA WAY** | 01704 834488 | 07775 777494<br>laura.way@btconnect.com | |
| **IAN WOOD** | 01488 72324 | 07733 156380<br>ianwood@chase3c.com | |

# FLAT JOCKEYS

## Riding weights and contact details

An index of agents appears on page 707

| Jockey | Weight | Contact |
|---|---|---|
| AHMED AJTEBI | 8 - 8 | Mr G. R. Owen |
| LUCY ALEXANDER | 9 - 0 | Mr R. A. Hale |
| DAVID ALLAN | 8 - 9 | Mrs G. S. Charnock |
| DONNA ASPELL | 7 - 10 | M. Furnass |
| PADDY ASPELL | 8 - 9 | M. Furnass |
| ANDREA ATZENI | 8 - 2 | Mr Paul Clarke |
| GEORGE BAKER | 9 - 0 | Mr G. D. Jewell |
| GARY BARTLEY | 9 - 0 | Mr R. A. Hale |
| DECLAN BATES | 8 - 5 | Mr L. R. James |
| HARRY BENTLEY | 8 - 4 | Mr G. R. Owen |
| ADAM BESCHIZZA | 8 - 4 | Mr John W. Ford |
| IAN BRENNAN | 7 - 13 | Mr R. A. Hale |
| WILLIAM BUICK | 8 - 6 | Mr M. R. Haggas |
| WILLIAM CARSON | 8 - 2 | Mr Neil Allan |
| ADAM CARTER | 8 - 8 | 07787415289 |
| CHRIS CATLIN | 8 - 4 | Mr N. M. Adams |
| PAT COSGRAVE | 8 - 8 | Mr N. M. Adams |
| MATTHEW COSHAM | 8 - 5 | 07875601737 |
| DOUGIE COSTELLO | 8 - 10 | Mr Dave Roberts\ Mr G. D. Jewell |
| MARK COUMBE | 8 - 4 | 01372 745 880 |
| STEPHEN CRAINE | 8 - 12 | Mr S. T. Dodds |
| BILLY CRAY | 8 - 3 | Mr S. M. Righton |
| JIM CROWLEY | 8 - 7 | Mr G. D. Jewell |
| BEN CURTIS | 8 - 4 | Mr S. T. Dodds |
| DUILIO DA SILVA | 8 - 5 | Mr Alan Harrison |
| RAUL DA SILVA | 8 - 0 | Mr Paul Brierley |
| SILVESTRE DE SOUSA | 8 - 0 | Mr G. R. Owen |
| LEMOS DE SOUZA | 8 - 6 | P. C. Shea |
| FRANKIE DETTORI | 8 - 9 | Mr R. Cochrane |
| PAT DOBBS | 8 - 7 | Mr Tony Hind |
| PATRICK DONAGHY | 8 - 6 | Mr N. A. Baxter |
| STEVIE DONOHOE | 8 - 6 | Mr L. R. James |
| JAMES DOYLE | 8 - 7 | Mr M. R. Haggas |
| STEVE DROWNE | 8 - 7 | Mr I. P. Wardle |
| TED DURCAN | 8 - 6 | Mr David Harrison\ Mrs L. H. Way |
| MARTIN DWYER | 8 - 3 | Mr S. T. Dodds |
| NATASHA EATON | 7 - 10 | 07572 463 483 |
| TOM EAVES | 8 - 7 | Mr R. A. Hale |
| J. F. EGAN | 8 - 3 | Mr N. Hannity |
| ANDREW ELLIOTT | 8 - 4 | Mr S. M. Righton |
| MIKEY ENNIS | 9 - 2 | Mr L. R. James |
| KIEREN FALLON | 8 - 6 | Mr S. T. Dodds |
| JOE FANNING | 8 - 2 | Mr N. Hannity |
| DURAN FENTIMAN | 8 - 2 | Mr Alan Harrison |
| JENNIFER FERGUSON | 8 - 0 | 01622 880 767 |
| ROYSTON FFRENCH | 8 - 4 | M. Furnass |
| ROBBIE FITZPATRICK | 8 - 6 | 07961 782399 |
| JIMMY FORTUNE | 8 - 9 | Mr Tony Hind |
| KIEREN FOX | 8 - 2 | M. Furnass |
| ANTONIO FRESU | 8 - 2 | Mr A. D. Burke |
| NATALIA GEMELOVA | 7 - 9 | 07966910511 |
| GRAHAM GIBBONS | 8 - 5 | Mrs L. H. Way |
| SALEEM GOLAM | 8 - 5 | Mr Paul Clarke |
| IRINEU GONCALVES | 8 - 2 | Mr A. D. Lewis |
| J-P. GUILLAMBERT | 8 - 9 | Mr S. M. Righton |
| TONY HAMILTON | 8 - 7 | Mr N. Hannity |

| Jockey | Weight | Contact |
|---|---|---|
| PAUL HANAGAN | 8 - 3 | Mr R. A. Hale |
| MARTIN HARLEY | 8 - 9 | Mr Neil Allan |
| JASON HART | 8 - 4 | Mr Alan Harrison |
| ROBERT HAVLIN | 8 - 6 | Mr I. P. Wardle |
| SAM HITCHCOTT | 8 - 5 | Mr N. M. Adams |
| BRIAN HUGHES | 9 - 7 | Mr R. A. Hale |
| RICHARD HUGHES | 8 - 7 | Mr Tony Hind |
| LIAM JONES | 8 - 2 | Mr Paul Clarke |
| SHANE KELLY | 8 - 7 | Mrs L. H. Way |
| LIAM KENIRY | 8 - 7 | Mr N. M. Adams |
| RUSS KENNEMORE | 8 - 7 | Mr L. R. James |
| RICHARD KINGSCOTE | 8 - 6 | Mr G. D. Jewell |
| ADAM KIRBY | 9 - 0 | Mr N. M. Adams |
| RACHEAL KNELLER | 8 - 0 | M. Furnass |
| MARTIN LANE | 8 - 0 | Mr S. T. Dodds |
| GRAHAM LEE | 8 - 9 | Mr R. A. Hale |
| SEAN LEVEY | 8 - 10 | Mr Tony Hind |
| NORA LOOBY | 7 - 6 | 07592768090 |
| FERGAL LYNCH | 8 - 6 | Mr R. A. Hale |
| NICKY MACKAY | 8 - 0 | Mr Paul Clarke |
| PHILLIP MAKIN | 8 - 11 | Mr R. A. Hale |
| JEMMA MARSHALL | 8 - 0 | 01273 620405 |
| PATRICK MATHERS | 8 - 2 | M. Furnass |
| FRANKIE MCDONALD | 7 - 13 | Mr N. M. Adams |
| P. J. MCDONALD | 8 - 4 | Mr R. A. Hale |
| BARRY MCHUGH | 8 - 3 | Mr R. A. Hale |
| JACK MITCHELL | 8 - 8 | Mr Paul Clarke |
| RYAN MOORE | 8 - 7 | Mr Tony Hind |
| LUKE MORRIS | 8 - 0 | Mr Neil Allan |
| ANDREW MULLEN | 8 - 0 | Mr S. M. Righton |
| PAUL MULRENNAN | 8 - 7 | Mr R. A. Hale |
| OISIN MURPHY | 8 - 3 | Miss S. L. Metcalfe |
| ADRIAN NICHOLLS | 8 - 3 | Mrs Clare Nicholls |
| DAVID NOLAN | 8 - 13 | Mr R. A. Hale |
| FRANNY NORTON | 8 - 0 | Mr I. P. Wardle |
| CONOR O'FARRELL | 9 - 10 | Mr Dave Roberts |
| SLADE O'HARA | 8 - 8 | 0777 300 9787 |
| DANE O'NEILL | 8 - 6 | Mr N. M. Adams |
| KIERAN O'NEILL | 8 - 0 | Mr G. D. Jewell |
| OSCAR PEREIRA | 8 - 7 | 07766658392 |
| PAUL PICKARD | 8 - 6 | Mr A. D. Lewis |
| HARRY POULTON | 8 - 9 | Mr Ian Wood |
| BRENDAN POWELL | 9 - 0 | Mr Dave Roberts |
| RYAN POWELL | 8 - 0 | Mr N. M. Adams |
| DAVID PROBERT | 8 - 0 | Miss S. L. Metcalfe |
| TOM QUEALLY | 8 - 8 | Mr S. T. Dodds |
| AMIR QUINN | 8 - 11 | 07989 184308 |
| JIMMY QUINN | 8 - 0 | Mr Paul Clarke |
| PAUL QUINN | 8 - 0 | Mr S. M. Righton |
| JAMES ROGERS | 8 - 8 | 07784543729 |
| AMY RYAN | 8 - 2 | Mr R. A. Hale |
| SEB SANDERS | 8 - 7 | P. C. Shea |
| VICTOR SANTOS | 7 - 12 | 07506 218446 |
| AMY SCOTT | 7 - 13 | M. Furnass |
| PAOLO SIRIGU | 8 - 0 | Mr S. M. Righton |
| RENATO SOUZA | 8 - 11 | Mr Ian Wood |
| JAMIE SPENCER | 8 - 7 | Mr David Harrison |
| MICHAEL STAINTON | 8 - 10 | Mr John W. Ford |

| Jockey | Weight | Contact |
|---|---|---|
| **ANN STOKELL** | 8 - 7 | 07814 579982 |
| **JAMES SULLIVAN** | 8 - 0 | Mr R. A. Hale |
| **FERGUS SWEENEY** | 8 - 9 | Mr G. D. Jewell |
| **DALE SWIFT** | 8 - 9 | Mr R. A. Hale |
| **F. TAHIR** | 8 - 12 | 07833707587 |
| **ROBERT TART** | 8 - 7 | M. Furnass |
| **LEE TOPLISS** | 8 - 10 | 07944 634532 |
| **DANIEL TUDHOPE** | 8 - 9 | Mrs L. H. Way |
| **HAYLEY TURNER** | 8 - 2 | Mr G. D. Jewell |
| **WILLIAM TWISTON-DAVIES** | 8 - 7 | Mr Neil Allan |
| **FREDERIK TYLICKI** | 8 - 6 | Mrs L. H. Way |
| **GARRY WHILLANS** | 8 - 9 | Mr J. B. Jeffrey |
| **ROBERT WINSTON** | 8 - 7 | Mr L. Newton |

Are your contact details missing or incorrect?
If so please update us by email:
richard.lowther@racingpost.co.uk

# APPRENTICES

## Riding weights and contact details

An index of agents appears on page 707

| Apprentice | Weight | Contact |
|---|---|---|
| **NATHAN ALISON** (William Haggas) | 8 - 0 | Mr A. D. Lewis |
| **AHMAD AL SUBOUSI** (Saeed bin Suroor) | 8 - 1 | Mr N. Hannity |
| **ROSS ATKINSON** (Roger Varian) | 8 - 4 | Mr N. M. Adams |
| **TOBY ATKINSON** (Noel Quinlan) | 8 - 6 | P. C. Shea |
| **LEAH-ANNE AVERY** (Harry Dunlop) | 8 - 1 | c/o 01488 73584 |
| **LAMORNA BARDWELL** (Seamus Mullins) | 7 - 7 | c/o 07702 559634 |
| **CONNOR BEASLEY** (Michael Dods) | 8 - 2 | Mr R. A. Hale |
| **SAMANTHA BELL** (Richard Fahey) | 7 - 9 | Mr R. A. Hale |
| **CHARLIE BENNETT** (Hughie Morrison) | 8 - 2 | P. C. Shea |
| **SHELLEY BIRKETT** (Julia Feilden) | 8 - 0 | Mr John W. Ford |
| **CHARLES BISHOP** (Olly Stevens) | 8 - 6 | Mr A. D. Lewis |
| **PAUL BOOTH** (Dean Ivory) | 8 - 0 | Mr L. R. James |
| **PADDY BRADLEY** (Pat Phelan) | 8 - 11 | Mr A. D. Lewis |
| **BECKY BRISBOURNE** (Mark Brisbourne) | 8 - 5 | c/o 07803 019651 |
| **DANNY BROCK** (Philip McBride) | 8 - 0 | Mr Ian Wood |
| **THOMAS BROWN** (Andrew Balding) | 8 - 7 | Miss S. L. Metcalfe |
| **GEORGE BUCKELL** (David Simcock) | 8 - 5 | Mr G. D. Jewell |
| **JACK BUDGE** (Jonathan Portman) | 8 - 5 | P. C. Shea |
| **HARRY BURNS** (David Evans) | 8 - 2 | Mr S. M. Righton |
| **JACOB BUTTERFIELD** (Ollie Pears) | 8 - 5 | Mr L. Newton |
| **MEGAN CARBERRY** (Brian Ellison) | 8 - 5 | Mr R. A. Hale |
| **GEORGE CHALONER** (Richard Fahey) | 8 - 2 | Mr R. A. Hale |
| **TIM CLARK** (Alan Bailey) | 8 - 2 | Mr N. M. Adams |
| **SAMUEL CLARKE** (Chris Wall) | 8 - 2 | c/o 01638 661999 |
| **PAUL COOLEY** (Jim Best) | 8 - 4 | c/o 01435 882073 |
| **GEORGIA COX** (William Haggas) | 8 - 3 | c/o 07860 282281 |
| **DANIEL CREMIN** (Mick Channon) | 8 - 0 | Mr I. P. Wardle |
| **HECTOR CROUCH** (Gary Moore) | 7 - 8 | Mr John W. Ford |
| **NED CURTIS** (Jonathan Portman) | 8 - 9 | Mr L. R. James |
| **ALFIE DAVIES** (George Baker) | 8 - 3 | c/o 01672 515493 |
| **LOUISE DAY** (Daniel Loughnane) | 8 - 3 | c/o 07805 531021 |
| **PHIL DENNIS** (Michael Dods) | 8 - 2 | Mr R. A. Hale |
| **JACK DINSMORE** (Sylvester Kirk) | 8 - 0 | c/o 07768 855261 |
| **ROBERT DODSWORTH** (Ollie Pears) | 7 - 10 | c/o 01653 690746 |
| **GEORGE DOWNING** (Tony Carroll) | 8 - 7 | Mr L. R. James |
| **JOE DOYLE** (John Quinn) | 7 - 7 | Mr R. A. Hale |
| **JOSH DOYLE** (David O'Meara) | 8 - 0 | Mr R. A. Hale |
| **JACK DUERN** (Andrew Hollinshead) | 8 - 4 | Mr L. Newton |
| **JANE ELLIOTT** (Michael Appleby) | 8 - 0 | Mr S. M. Righton |
| **NEIL FARLEY** (Declan Carroll) | 8 - 4 | Mr Alan Harrison |
| **MANUEL FERNANDES** (Sir Mark Prescott Bt) | 8 - 3 | c/o 01638 662117 |
| **KRISTY FRENCH** (Clive Cox) | 7 - 6 | c/o 01488 73072 |
| **NOEL GARBUTT** (Hugo Palmer) | 7 - 1 | Mr L. R. James |
| **THOMAS GARNER** (Oliver Sherwood) | 9 - 0 | Mr Dave Roberts |
| **JACK GARRITTY** (Richard Fahey) | 7 - 9 | Mr R. A. Hale |
| **JOSEPHINE GORDON** (J. S. Moore) | 8 - 0 | Mr L. R. James |
| **SHANE GRAY** (Kevin Ryan) | 8 - 0 | Mr S. T. Dodds |
| **NICOLA GRUNDY** (Richard Ford) | 7 - 12 | c/o 01995 605790 |
| **CAM HARDIE** (Richard Hannon) | 7 - 9 | Mr Tony Hind |
| **TOMAS HARRIGAN** (Simon Dow) | 8 - 4 | P. C. Shea |
| **RUSSELL HARRIS** (Scott Dixon) | 8 - 0 | c/o 01777 869300 Emma Gavigan |
| **JOEY HAYNES** (K. R. Burke) | 8 - 0 | Mr N. Hannity |
| **THOMAS HEMSLEY** (Chris Dwyer) | 8 - 3 | c/o 07831 579844 |
| **ANNA HESKETH** (David Nicholls) | 7 - 12 | M. Furnass |
| **RYAN HOLLEY** (David Elsworth) | 7 - 12 | c/o 01638 665511 |
| **RYAN HOLMES** (Barry Leavy) | 8 - 0 | c/o 07540 806915 |
| **ROB HORNBY** (Andrew Balding) | 8 - 0 | Mr N. M. Adams |
| **RHIAIN INGRAM** (Roger Ingram) | 7 - 10 | c/o 07715 993911 |

**SAM JAMES** (David O'Meara) .......... 8 - 6 Mr R. A. Hale
**CHARLOTTE JENNER** (Mark Usher) .......... 8 - 0 M. Furnass
**ROSIE JESSOP** (Sir Mark Prescott Bt) .......... 7 - 12 Mr G. R. Owen\Mr N. A. Baxter
**STEPHANIE JOANNIDES** (William Haggas) .......... 7 - 10 c/o 07860 282281
**AARON JONES** (Stuart Williams) .......... 8 - 0 Mr John W. Ford
**MICHAEL KENNEALLY** (Michael Bell) .......... 8 - 0 Mr Nick Bell
**SOPHIE KILLORAN** (David Simcock) .......... 7 - 5 M. Furnass
**ABIE KNOWLES** (Ronald Harris) .......... 7 - 9 c/o 07831 770899
**MATTHEW LAWSON** (Saeed bin Suroor) .......... 8 - 5 c/o 01638 569956
**LUKE LEADBITTER** (Declan Carroll) .......... 8 - 5 Mr Alan Harrison
**CLIFFORD LEE** (Ed Walker) .......... 8 - 8 c/o 01638 660464
**KEVIN LUNDIE** (Shaun Harris) .......... 8 - 3 Mr A. D. Lewis
**GARY MAHON** (Richard Hannon) .......... 8 - 0 Mr S. M. Righton
**GABRIELE MALUNE** (Luca Cumani) .......... 7 - 12 c/o 01638 665432
**TOM MARQUAND** (Richard Hannon) .......... 7 - 9 Mr S. M. Righton
**EILISH MCCALL** (John Gallagher) .......... 7 - 6 Mr A. D. Lewis
**PAUL MCGIFF** (David Barron) .......... 8 - 5 c/o 01845 587435
**CIARAN MCKEE** (John O'Shea) .......... 9 - 4 Mr L. R. James
**CHRIS MEEHAN** (George Baker) .......... 9 - 0 Mr S. M. Righton
**PAT MILLMAN** (Rod Millman) .......... 8 - 10 Mr Ian Wood
**DANIELLE MOONEY** (Michael Easterby) .......... 8 - 0 Mr S. M. Righton
**RYAN M. MOORE** (Julia Feilden) .......... 7 - 6 c/o 07974 817694
**ASHLEY MORGAN** (Chris Wall) .......... 8 - 6 Mr L. R. James
**PAULA MUIR** (Mark Johnston) .......... 7 - 12 c/o 01969 622237
**MICHAEL J. M. MURPHY** (Mark Johnston) .......... 8 - 2 Mr S. T. Dodds
**CLAIRE MURRAY** (David Brown) .......... 8 - 4 c/o 07889 132931
**DANIEL MUSCUTT** (Marco Botti) .......... 8 - 0 Miss S. L. Metcalfe
**MILLY NASEB** (David Simcock) .......... 7 - 11 c/o 07808 954109
**JORDAN NASON** (Marjorie Fife) .......... 8 - 3 M. Furnass
**JASON NUTTALL** (Gary Moore) .......... 9 - 0 Mr John W. Ford
**TOMMY O'CONNOR** (B. W. Hills) .......... 8 - 0 c/o 01488 73144
**PATRICK O'DONNELL** (Ralph Beckett) .......... 8 - 2 Mr S. T. Dodds
**DAVID PARKES** (Jeremy Gask) .......... 8 - 6 Miss S. L. Metcalfe
**PADDY PILLEY** (Mick Channon) .......... 7 - 7 P. C. Shea
**BEN POSTE** (Tom Symonds) .......... 9 - 2 Mr Dave Roberts
**JENNY POWELL** (Tom Dascombe) .......... 7 - 10 Mr G. D. Jewell
**PHILIP PRINCE** (Liam Corcoran) .......... 8 - 0 Mr S. M. Righton
**JOSH QUINN** (Richard Hannon) .......... 8 - 4 Mrs G. S. Charnock
**ALISTAIR RAWLINSON** (Michael Appleby) .......... 8 - 5 Mr S. M. Righton
**RACHEL RICHARDSON** (Tim Easterby) .......... 7 - 12 Mr Alan Harrison
**LUKE ROWE** (Richard Rowe) .......... 8 - 2 P. C. Shea
**TYLER SAUNDERS** (B. W. Hills) .......... 8 - 0 c/o 01488 73144
**EMMA SAYER** (Dianne Sayer) .......... 8 - 9 Mr R. A. Hale
**KIERAN SCHOFIELD** (George Moore) .......... 7 - 11 c/o 07711 321117
**ROWAN SCOTT** (Ann Duffield) .......... 8 - 0 Mr R. A. Hale
**CALLUM SHEPHERD** (William Knight) .......... 7 - 12 Miss S. L. Metcalfe
**KIERAN SHOEMARK** (Andrew Balding) .......... 7 - 13 Mr Tony Hind
**KIRSTEN SMITH** (Jamie Osborne) .......... 8 - 2 Mr L. O. Gedge-Gibson
**LULU STANFORD** (Michael Bell) .......... 7 - 7 c/o 01638 666567
**LOUIS STEWARD** (Michael Bell) .......... 8 - 4 Mr Paul Clarke
**MATHEW STILL** (Mel Brittain) .......... 8 - 0 c/o 01759 371472
**LEWIS STONES** (Michael Mullineaux) .......... 8 - 7 c/o 07753 650263
**KEVIN STOTT** (Kevin Ryan) .......... 8 - 4 Mr R. A. Hale
**JORDAN SWARBRICK** (Brian Baugh) .......... 7 - 13 c/o 07771 693666
**PETER SWORD** (K. R. Burke) .......... 8 - 9 Mr Alan Harrison
**RYAN TATE** (Clive Cox) .......... 8 - 4 Mr G. D. Jewell
**MELISSA THOMPSON** (Richard Guest) .......... 8 - 2 c/o 01937 587552
**GEMMA TUTTY** (Karen Tutty) .......... 7 - 12 Mr S. M. Righton
**JORDAN VAUGHAN** (K. R. Burke) .......... 8 - 0 Mr R. A. Hale
**PATRICK VAUGHAN** (Tom Dascombe) .......... 8 - 4 c/o 01948 820485 Alex
**EOIN WALSH** (Daniel Loughnane) .......... 8 - 4 Mr N. M. Adams
**ALFIE WARWICK** (Andrew Reid) .......... 8 - 5 Mr A. D. Lewis
**RYAN WHILE** (Bill Turner) .......... 8 - 4 Mr Ian Wood\Mr S. M. Righton
**ROBERT WILLIAMS** (Bernard Llewellyn) .......... 9 - 2 c/o 07971 233473
**DANIEL WRIGHT** (Andrew Balding) .......... 8 - 0 c/o 01635 298210

# JUMP JOCKEYS

## Riding weights and contact details

An index of agents appears on page 707

| Jockey | Weight | Contact |
|---|---|---|
| LUCY ALEXANDER | 9 - 7 | Mr R. A. Hale |
| LEIGHTON ASPELL | 10 - 0 | Mr Dave Roberts |
| JAMES BANKS | 10 - 0 | Mr L. R. James |
| DAVID BASS | 10 - 5 | Mr Dave Roberts |
| MATTIE BATCHELOR | 9 - 7 | Mr Dave Roberts |
| DECLAN BATES | 8 - 10 | Mr L. R. James |
| JONATHON BEWLEY | 9 - 12 | 01450860651 |
| COLIN BOLGER | 10 - 0 | 01273 306105 |
| PADDY BRENNAN | 9 - 12 | Mr Dave Roberts |
| HENRY BROOKE | 10 - 0 | Mr R. A. Hale |
| PETER BUCHANAN | 10 - 0 | Mr Paul Brierley |
| MICHAEL BYRNE | 10 - 2 | Mr S. Stronge |
| TOM CANNON | 10 - 0 | Mr Dave Roberts |
| ALAIN CAWLEY | 9 - 10 | Mr Dave Roberts |
| AIDAN COLEMAN | 9 - 10 | Mr S. Stronge |
| AODHAGAN CONLON | 10 - 0 | Mr Dave Roberts |
| DANNY COOK | 10 - 5 | Mr J. B. Jeffrey |
| ED COOKSON | 9 - 13 | Mr C. D. Broad |
| DOUGIE COSTELLO | 10 - 0 | Mr Dave Roberts\ Mr G. D. Jewell |
| STEPHEN CRAINE | 10 - 0 | Mr S. T. Dodds |
| DAVE CROSSE | 10 - 0 | Mr C. D. Broad |
| JAMES DAVIES | 10 - 0 | Mr L. R. James |
| FELIX DE GILES | 10 - 0 | Mr S. Stronge |
| GARY DERWIN | 9 - 7 | Mr Dave Roberts |
| DONAL DEVEREUX | 10 - 0 | Mr Dave Roberts |
| JACK DOYLE | 10 - 4 | Mr S. Stronge |
| SAMANTHA DRAKE | 9 - 9 | 07921 003155 |
| ROBERT DUNNE | 10 - 0 | Mr Dave Roberts |
| LEE EDWARDS | 10 - 0 | Mr C. D. Broad |
| DOMINIC ELSWORTH | 10 - 0 | 07776 255736 |
| DAVID ENGLAND | 10 - 0 | Mr L. R. James |
| MIKEY ENNIS | 9 - 7 | Mr L. R. James |
| NOEL FEHILY | 10 - 4 | Mr C. D. Broad |
| ALISTAIR FINDLAY | 10 - 0 | Mr Paul Brierley |
| RHYS FLINT | 10 - 7 | Mr Dave Roberts |
| ANTHONY FREEMAN | 9 - 9 | 07795143759 |
| HADDEN FROST | 10 - 12 | Mr Dave Roberts |
| LUCY GARDNER | 9 - 12 | 07814 979 699 |
| OLLIE GARNER | 9 - 7 | Mr L. R. James |
| BARRY GERAGHTY | 10 - 6 | Mr Dave Roberts |
| MARC GOLDSTEIN | 9 - 9 | Mr Dave Roberts |
| GEMMA GRACEY-DAVISON | 9 - 7 | 07727 190834 |
| MARK GRANT | 10 - 0 | Mr C. D. Broad |
| RACHAEL GREEN | 9 - 7 | 01300 068272 |
| JAKE GREENALL | 10 - 0 | Mr Dave Roberts |
| BRIAN HARDING | 10 - 0 | Mr R. A. Hale |
| HARRY HAYNES | 10 - 0 | Mr Dave Roberts |
| LIAM HEARD | 10 - 2 | Mr L. R. James |
| BRIAN HUGHES | 9 - 7 | Mr R. A. Hale |
| WAYNE HUTCHINSON | 10 - 0 | Mr C. D. Broad |
| DARYL JACOB | 10 - 2 | Mr C. D. Broad |
| KYLE JAMES | 9 - 11 | Mr L. R. James |
| KENNY JOHNSON | 10 - 5 | 07774 131121 |
| RICHARD JOHNSON | 10 - 0 | Mr Dave Roberts |
| KEVIN JONES | 10 - 4 | Mr L. R. James |
| SAM JONES | 10 - 0 | Mr L. R. James |
| WAYNE KAVANAGH | 9 - 7 | Mr Dave Roberts |
| WILL KENNEDY | 10 - 0 | Mr S. Stronge\ Mr Dave Roberts |
| JOHN KINGTON | 9 - 11 | Mr J. B. Jeffrey |
| ADRIAN LANE | 10 - 0 | Mr G. J. Thomson |
| JASON MAGUIRE | 10 - 6 | Mr C. D. Broad |
| RYAN MAHON | 10 - 0 | Mr Dave Roberts |
| MICHAEL MCALISTER | 10 - 0 | Mr Paul Brierley |
| ROB MCCARTH | 9 - 12 | Mr C. D. Broad |
| A. P. MCCOY | 10 - 4 | Mr Dave Roberts |
| RICHIE MCLERNON | 9 - 10 | Mr Dave Roberts |
| TOM MESSENGER | 10 - 0 | Mr J. B. Jeffrey |
| PAUL MOLONEY | 10 - 0 | Mr Dave Roberts |
| JAMIE MOORE | 10 - 0 | Mr Dave Roberts |
| JOSHUA MOORE | 10 - 0 | Mr Dave Roberts |
| RAYMOND O'BRIEN | 9 - 10 | |
| TOM O'BRIEN | 10 - 0 | Mr Dave Roberts |
| CONOR O'FARRELL | 9 - 12 | Mr Dave Roberts |
| DENIS O'REGAN | 10 - 2 | Mr S. Stronge |
| TOMMY PHELAN | 9 - 13 | Mr Dave Roberts |
| ADAM POGSON | 10 - 0 | 07977016155 |
| IAN POPHAM | 10 - 0 | Mr Dave Roberts |
| CHARLIE POSTE | 10 - 0 | Mr Dave Roberts |
| BRENDAN POWELL | 8 - 10 | Mr Dave Roberts |
| JACK QUINLAN | 9 - 10 | Mr Dave Roberts |
| MARK QUINLAN | 9 - 9 | Mr C. D. Broad |
| SEAN QUINLAN | 10 - 0 | Mr C. D. Broad |
| WILSON RENWICK | 10 - 0 | Mr R. A. Hale |
| JAMES REVELEY | 10 - 5 | Mr J. B. Jeffrey |
| GARY RUTHERFORD | 9 - 2 | Mr J. B. Jeffrey |
| NICK SCHOLFIELD | 10 - 0 | Mr Dave Roberts |
| TOM SCUDAMORE | 10 - 0 | Mr Dave Roberts |
| GAVIN SHEEHAN | 10 - 0 | Mr C. D. Broad |
| TOM SIDDALL | 10 - 0 | Mr Dave Roberts |
| HARRY SKELTON | 10 - 0 | Mr Dave Roberts |
| J. W. STEVENSON | 9 - 7 | 07933 440810 |
| SAM THOMAS | 10 - 4 | Mr S. Stronge |
| ANDREW THORNTON | 10 - 4 | Mr Dave Roberts |
| ANDREW TINKLER | 10 - 0 | Mr Dave Roberts |
| LIAM TREADWELL | 10 - 0 | Mr Dave Roberts |
| GERARD TUMELTY | 10 - 0 | Mr L. R. James |
| SAM TWISTON-DAVIES | 10 - 0 | Mr C. D. Broad |
| R. WALSH | 10 - 1 | Miss J. Walsh |
| ADAM WEDGE | 9 - 11 | Mr Dave Roberts |
| KIELAN WOODS | 10 - 0 | Mr C. D. Broad |

# CONDITIONALS

## Their employer and contact details

An index of agents appears on page 707

| Jockey (Employer) | Weight | Contact |
|---|---|---|
| **JAMIE BARGARY** (Nigel Twiston-Davies) | 9 - 5 | Mr C. D. Broad |
| **TOM BELLAMY** (Alan King) | 10 - 0 | Mr Dave Roberts |
| **JAMES BEST** (Philip Hobbs) | 10 - 0 | Mr Dave Roberts |
| **HARRISON BESWICK** (Ben Pauling) | 9 - 7 | Mr C. D. Broad |
| **CALLUM BEWLEY** (Sue Smith) | 9 - 7 | Mr J. B. Jeffrey |
| **DARAGH BOURKE** (James Ewart) | 10 - 4 | Mr J. B. Jeffrey |
| **SEAN BOWEN** (Paul Nicholls) | 9 - 0 | Mr Dave Roberts |
| **PADDY BRADLEY** (Pat Phelan) | 9 - 0 | Mr A. D. Lewis |
| **CONOR BRASSIL** (Harry Fry) | 9 - 12 | Mr Dave Roberts |
| **BLAIR CAMPBELL** (N. W. Alexander) | 9 - 7 | c/o 07831 488210 |
| **PETER CARBERRY** (Nicky Henderson) | 9 - 6 | Mr Dave Roberts |
| **HARRY CHALLONER** (Nicky Richards) | 9 - 9 | Mr R. A. Hale |
| **THOMAS CHEESMAN** (Philip Hobbs) | 9 - 7 | Mr Dave Roberts |
| **GRANT COCKBURN** (Lucinda Russell) | 10 - 0 | Mr Paul Brierley\Mr J. B. Jeffrey |
| **KEITH COGLEY** (Rebecca Curtis) | 10 - 0 | c/o 07970 710690 |
| **JOE COLLIVER** (Micky Hammond) | 9 - 9 | Mr R. A. Hale |
| **JAMES CORBETT** (Susan Corbett) | 9 - 4 | c/o 07713 651215 |
| **JOE CORNWALL** (John Cornwall) | 8 - 12 | c/o 07939 557091 |
| **JAMES COWLEY** (Donald McCain) | 9 - 7 | Mr R. A. Hale |
| **PATRICK COWLEY** (Jonjo O'Neill) | 9 - 5 | c/o 01386 584209 |
| **BEN FFRENCH DAVIS** (Oliver Sherwood) | 10 - 0 | Mr C. D. Broad |
| **RYAN DAY** (Lisa Harrison) | 9 - 7 | Mr R. A. Hale |
| **NICO DE BOINVILLE** (Nicky Henderson) | 9 - 9 | Mr Dave Roberts |
| **CHARLIE DEUTSCH** (Charlie Longsdon) | 9 - 7 | Mr Dave Roberts |
| **TOMMY DOWLING** (Charlie Mann) | 9 - 6 | Mr C. D. Broad |
| **KIERON EDGAR** (David Pipe) | 9 - 7 | Mr Dave Roberts |
| **JONATHAN ENGLAND** (Sue Smith) | 9 - 7 | Mr J. B. Jeffrey |
| **WILLIAM FEATHERSTONE** (Jamie Snowden) | 10 - 0 | Mr L. R. James |
| **DEREK FOX** (Lucinda Russell) | 10 - 0 | Mr J. B. Jeffrey |
| **STEVEN FOX** (Sandy Thomson) | 10 - 4 | Mr J. B. Jeffrey |
| **CRAIG GALLAGHER** (Brian Ellison) | 9 - 6 | Mr R. A. Hale |
| **THOMAS GARNER** (Oliver Sherwood) | 9 - 5 | Mr Dave Roberts |
| **LEWIS GORDON** (Evan Williams) | 9 - 10 | c/o 01446 754069 |
| **GEORGE GORMAN** (Gary Moore) | 9 - 12 | Mr Dave Roberts |
| **MATT GRIFFITHS** (Jeremy Scott) | 10 - 2 | Mr Dave Roberts |
| **MIKEY HAMILL** (Neil Mulholland) | 9 - 10 | Mr Dave Roberts |
| **JAMIE HAMILTON** (Venetia Williams) | 9 - 0 | Mr C. D. Broad |
| **RYAN HATCH** (Nigel Twiston-Davies) | 10 - 0 | Mr C. D. Broad |
| **GILES HAWKINS** (Victor Dartnall) | 10 - 3 | Mr L. R. James |
| **MICHAEL HEARD** (David Pipe) | 9 - 7 | Mr L. R. James |
| **DANIEL HISKETT** (Richard Phillips) | 9 - 7 | Mr Dave Roberts |
| **JAKE HODSON** (David Bridgwater) | 9 - 12 | Mr Dave Roberts |
| **LUKE INGRAM** (Lucy Wadham) | 8 - 12 | c/o 07980 545776 |
| **JAMIE INSOLE** (Alan King) | 10 - 0 | Mr L. R. James |
| **DALE IRVING** (James Ewart) | 9 - 10 | Mr J. B. Jeffrey |
| **ALAN JOHNS** (Tim Vaughan) | 10 - 0 | Mr Dave Roberts |
| **TONY KELLY** (Rebecca Menzies) | 10 - 0 | Mr R. A. Hale |
| **LIZZIE KELLY** (Neil King) | 10 - 2 | Mr Dave Roberts |
| **GARRY LAVERY** (Brian Ellison) | 9 - 7 | Mr J. B. Jeffrey |
| **MAURICE LINEHAN** (Jonjo O'Neill) | 9 - 7 | Mr C. D. Broad |
| **COLM MCCORMACK** (Keith Reveley) | 10 - 0 | Mr R. A. Hale |
| **DYLAN MCDONAGH** (Micky Hammond) | 9 - 4 | c/o 07808 572777 |
| **JEREMIAH MCGRATH** (Nicky Henderson) | 10 - 2 | Mr Dave Roberts |
| **MARTIN MCINTYRE** (Neil Mulholland) | 9 - 10 | Mr C. D. Broad |
| **CIARAN MCKEE** (John O'Shea) | 9 - 4 | Mr L. R. James |
| **CHRIS MEEHAN** (George Baker) | 9 - 7 | Mr S. M. Righton |
| **FREDDIE MITCHELL** (Nicky Henderson) | 9 - 7 | Mr Philip Mitchell\Mr Dave Roberts |
| **KILLIAN MOORE** (Sophie Leech) | 9 - 11 | Mr Dave Roberts |

| | | |
|---|---|---|
| **NATHAN MOSCROP** (Brian Ellison) | 10 - 6 | Mr J. B. Jeffrey |
| **STEPHEN MULQUEEN** (Maurice Barnes) | 9 - 10 | Mr G. J. Thomson |
| **CRAIG NICHOL** (Lucinda Russell) | 10 - 0 | Mr R. A. Hale |
| **RYAN NICHOL** (Lucinda Russell) | 10 - 0 | Mr Paul Brierley |
| **ADAM NICOL** (Philip Kirby) | 9 - 7 | Mr R. A. Hale |
| **MICHEAL NOLAN** (Philip Hobbs) | 10 - 2 | Mr Dave Roberts |
| **JASON NUTTALL** (Gary Moore) | 9 - 0 | Mr John W. Ford |
| **PAUL O'BRIEN** (Colin Tizzard) | 10 - 0 | Mr S. Stronge |
| **PAUL N. O'BRIEN** (Harry Whittington) | 8 - 9 | c/o 01235 751869 |
| **RICHIE O'DEA** (Emma Lavelle) | 10 - 0 | c/o 01264 735412 |
| **DIARMUID O'REGAN** (Chris Grant) | 9 - 4 | Mr R. A. Hale |
| **FINIAN O'TOOLE** (Malcolm Jefferson) | 10 - 2 | Mr J. B. Jeffrey |
| **JOSEPH PALMOWSKI** (Robin Dickin) | 9 - 4 | c/o 07979 518593 |
| **BEN POSTE** (Tom Symonds) | 9 - 7 | Mr Dave Roberts |
| **DEAN PRATT** (John Quinn) | 10 - 0 | Mr Paul Brierley |
| **DAVID PRICHARD** (Jeremy Scott) | 9 - 0 | Mr L. R. James |
| **SHANE QUINLAN** (David Dennis) | 9 - 4 | c/o 07867 974880 |
| **CONOR RING** (Evan Williams) | 9 - 10 | Mr C. D. Broad |
| **TREVOR RYAN** (Steve Gollings) | 9 - 12 | c/o 01507 343204 |
| **JACK SAVAGE** (Jonjo O'Neill) | 9 - 9 | c/o 01386 584209 |
| **EMMA SAYER** (Dianne Sayer) | 9 - 0 | Mr R. A. Hale |
| **JACK SHERWOOD** (Paul Nicholls) | 9 - 7 | Mr Dave Roberts |
| **CONOR SHOEMARK** (Fergal O'Brien) | 10 - 0 | Mr Dave Roberts |
| **NICK SLATTER** (Donald McCain) | 9 - 7 | Mr R. A. Hale |
| **CONOR SMITH** (Philip Hobbs) | 10 - 2 | Mr Dave Roberts |
| **BENJAMIN STEPHENS** (George Bewley) | 9 - 4 | c/o 07704 924783 |
| **LEWIS STONES** (Michael Mullineaux) | 8 - 7 | c/o 07753 650263 |
| **JOHN STOREY** (Jim Best) | 9 - 7 | c/o 01435 882073 Leon Best |
| **JOSH WALL** (Trevor Wall) | 9 - 10 | Mr L. R. James |
| **CONOR WALSH** (Warren Greatrex) | 9 - 5 | Mr C. D. Broad |
| **CHRISTOPHER WARD** (Dr Richard Newland) | 9 - 9 | Mr L. R. James |
| **GRAHAM WATTERS** (Lucinda Russell) | 10 - 0 | Mr R. A. Hale |
| **TREVOR WHELAN** (Neil King) | 9 - 7 | Mr Dave Roberts |
| **RYAN WHILE** (Bill Turner) | 9 - 0 | Mr Ian Wood\Mr S. M. Righton |
| **CALLUM WHILLANS** (Venetia Williams) | 9 - 7 | Mr Dave Roberts |
| **ROBERT WILLIAMS** (Bernard Llewellyn) | 9 - 12 | c/o 07971 233473 |

Are your contact details missing or incorrect?
If so please update us by email:
richard.lowther@racingpost.co.uk

# AMATEUR RIDERS

## Riding weights and contact details

An index of agents appears on page 707

**PAHLMAN, J. V.** 9 - 0 ............ 07712714226
**SPENCER, M. E.** 9 - 0 ............ 07568 513984
**BASTYAN, M. S.** 9 - 10 ............ 07783455114
**AKEHURST, J.** 10 - 6 ............ Mr Paul Brierley
**AKINCI, L.** 9 - 7 ............ 07868 136085
**ALEXANDER, C.** 9 - 10 ............ 07799 191093
**ALLAN, V. L.** 9 - 2 ............ 07703355878
**ALONSO, A. J.** 9 - 4 ............ 078310 16765
**ANDREWS, B. E.** 9 - 0 ............ 07921 394107
**ANDREWS, D. I. J.** 10 - 7 ............ 07817 322974
**ANDREWS, G.** 9 - 12 ............ Mr C. D. Broad
**ASQUITH, R.** 9 - 8 ............ 07592 990461
**AYRES, K.** 8 - 7 ............ 07805 190978
**BAILEY, J.** 10 - 9 ............ 07813 994 980
**BAKER, Z. C. N.** 10 - 0 ............ Mr C. D. Broad
**BAMENT, J. J.** 9 - 10 ............ 07964 587682
**BANNISTER, H. A. A.** 9 - 1 ............ Mr C. D. Broad
**BARBER, C. R.** 9 - 0 ............ 07747 021313
**BARBER, M.** 10 - 4 ............ 07974 619012
**BARFOOT-SAUNT, G. C.** 10 - 9 ............ 01684 833227
**BARRETT, E.** 10 - 0 ............ 07805 683189
**BARTLETT, D.** 10 - 1 ............ 01388 835596
**BARTLEY, C. A.** 8 - 10 ............ 07734 303862
**BEAUMONT, G.** 10 - 0 ............ 07535 501654
**BEGLEY, K. F.** 8 - 4 ............ 01544 267672
**BELLAMY, A.** 9 - 7 ............ 07979256894
**BETHELL, H.** 9 - 10 ............ 07733424242
**BIDDICK, W. E. T.** 11 - 0 ............ 07976 556823
**BIRKETT, R. A.** 10 - 0 ............ Mr S. T. Dodds
**BISHOP-PECK, M.** 8 - 2 ............ 07775 564080
**BLAGG, P.** 11 - 3 ............ 079466 05987
**BLAKEMORE, A.** 8 - 10 ............ 07581 576739
**BOXALL, C. E.** 9 - 5 ............ Mr L. R. James
**BRAITHWAITE, A. J.** 10 - 12 ............ 01638 675903
**BRIDGE, E. L.** 10 - 2 ............ 01980 845 921
**BRIDGWATER, P. K.** 8 - 10 ............ 07824470324
**BROOKE, L.** 9 - 4 ............ 07786 962 911
**BROOME, A.** 9 - 10 ............ 01584 890028
**BROTHERTON, S.** 8 - 12 ............ 07740 257 110
**BROUDER, K.** 9 - 10 ............
**BROUGHTON, T. P.** 9 - 4 ............ 07769311769
**BRYANT, M. P.** 9 - 8 ............ 07976 217542
**BUCK, J. M.** 9 - 9 ............ 01984 667 229
**BULLOCK, E.** 7 - 11 ............ 07593 951904
**BURCHELL, D. G.** 10 - 7 ............ 07824332899
**BURKE, T.** 9 - 7 ............ Mr A. D. Burke
**BURTON, D. J.** 10 - 0 ............ Mr L. R. James
**BUSHBY, S.** 8 - 5 ............ 07866001090
**BUSHE, E.** 9 - 0 ............ 07903364953
**CAMPBELL, F. D.** 11 - 5 ............ 07760 573666
**CARROLL, C. E.** 10 - 6 ............ 01386 861020
**CARSON, G.** 9 - 10 ............ 07525 370078
**CARTER, N.** 11 - 0 ............ 07900 808272
**CATTON, B. S. E.** 10 - 0 ............ 07944538157
**CHANIN, T.** 10 - 12 ............ 07815 431533
**CHAPMAN, R.** 9 - 7 ............ Mr Paul Brierley
**CHASTON, E.** 8 - 4 ............ 07753 441571
**CHENERY, M.** 11 - 0 ............ 07967911360
**CHESHIRE, N. P. T.** 9 - 12 ............ 07531 002966
**CLARKE, W. R.** 10 - 3 ............ 07540723993
**COATES, J.** 8 - 2 ............ 07710170568
**COCHRANE, G. H.** 9 - 0 ............ 07741253461
**COLL, S. A.** 10 - 0 ............ 07912 604950
**COLLINGTON, P. P. M.** 9 - 3 ............ Mr Paul Clarke
**COLLINS, P.** 11 - 5 ............ 07779 794684
**COLLINSON, R. E.** 10 - 3 ............ 077037 88722
**COLTHERD, S. W.** 9 - 5 ............ Mr J. B. Jeffrey
**COOPER, C.** 9 - 7 ............ 07969 668909
**CORNOCK, H. R. L.** 10 - 0 ............ 07581 675899
**COTTLE, D. G. G.** 9 - 7 ............ 01653 698915
**COULSON, J. T.** 10 - 7 ............ 07460471492
**CRATE, G. D.** 9 - 7 ............ Mr G. J. Horne
**CROW, G. M.** 10 - 12 ............ 01928 740555
**CRUICKSHANK, H. J. F.** 10 - 4 ............ Mr L. R. James
**CUTHBERT, H. E.** 9 - 0 ............ 01228 560700
**DAGGE, R.** 10 - 0 ............ 07772 136378
**DALTON, A.** 9 - 12 ............ 07787 501331
**DAVID, E.** 10 - 5 ............ 07500 383138
**DAVID, T. R.** 10 - 4 ............ 07866 775562
**DAVIES, V. G.** 9 - 4 ............ 07786 925 756
**DAVIES, Y.** 7 - 10 ............
**DAVIES-THOMAS, S.** 11 - 0 ............ 07769 337473
**DAWSON, C. T.** 11 - 7 ............ 07796 530 084
**DAWSON, J. A.** 10 - 0 ............ Mr Paul Brierley
**DEBENHAM, I.** 7 - 0 ............ 07867 917568
**DEFAGO, R. P.** 10 - 0 ............ 07515 390341
**DEGNAN, W.** 10 - 0 ............ 07400 626696
**DENIEL, A.** 8 - 10 ............ 01302 861 000
**DISNEY, G. F.** 11 - 0 ............ 07816 847947
**DIXON, J.** 9 - 7 ............ 07761 998988
**DOE, J. M.** 9 - 8 ............ 07904 407258
**DOWSON, T. J.** 9 - 7 ............ 07807695195
**DRINKWATER, J.** 9 - 0 ............ 07765 258976
**DRINKWATER, S. W.** 10 - 7 ............ 07747 444633
**DROWNE, L.** 10 - 0 ............ 07506 871171
**DUKES, H. R.** 9 - 2 ............ 077585 18358
**DUNKLEY, E.** 9 - 4 ............ 07795148927
**DUNN, A.** 9 - 0 ............ 07738 512 924
**DUNSDON, D.** 10 - 7 ............ 07885 110 826
**EASTERBY, W. H.** 9 - 2 ............ 07772 216 507
**EDDEN, M. L.** 9 - 0 ............ 07773 420078
**EDMUNDS, L.** 8 - 3 ............ 07815 030133
**EDWARDS, A. W.** 10 - 0 ............ 07590 683295
**EDWARDS, D. M.** 11 - 0 ............ 07811 898 002
**ELEY, T. J.** 9 - 0 ............ 07807 742049
**ELLIS, J. B.** 8 - 5 ............ 07827 316360
**ELLIS, T.** 10 - 10 ............ 01926 632770
**ENNIS, M. C.** 8 - 7 ............ 07733601642
**FELD, P.** 8 - 7 ............ 07718 175095
**FERGUSON, A. R. D.** 8 - 9 ............ 07788 876161
**FERGUSON, J.** 10 - 4 ............ 0782 5563 773
**FERGUSON, L.** 9 - 7 ............ 0776851064
**FOULARD, L.** 8 - 7 ............ 07557774693
**FRENCH, A.** 9 - 0 ............ 07776 306588
**FRISWELL, G.** 8 - 5 ............ 07807 959636
**FROST, B.** 9 - 7 ............ 078618 14643

**FULLER, M. P. F.** 8 - 10 .......... 07876 473926
**GANNON, D. C.** 9 - 4 .......... P. C. Shea
**GERETY, P. H.** 10 - 10 .......... 00353 852160097
**GETHINGS, C.** 9 - 13 .......... Mr Dave Roberts
**GIBBS, B.** 10 - 10 .......... 07818 407883
**GIBSON, W.** 8 - 7 .......... 01759 372932
**GILLAM, J.** 9 - 3 .......... 07847607391
**GILLARD, T.** 9 - 0 .......... 07824 772444
**GLASSONBURY, E.** 10 - 12 .......... 07917 167236
**GORDON, W.** 9 - 0 .......... 07796 230473
**GOSCHEN, A.** 10 - 7 .......... 07719 611 301
**GOWING, K.** 9 - 7 .......... 07501474589
**GRANT, C.** 10 - 3 .......... 07415 896552
**GREATREX, T.** 9 - 7 .......... 07918852348
**GREENALL, O. C.** 11 - 0 .......... 07771 571 000
**GREENWAY, C. A.** 9 - 5 .......... 07526 923647
**GREENWOOD, T. O. M.** 9 - 7 .......... Mr J. B. Jeffrey
**GUERRIERO, J. T.** 11 - 7 .......... 07778541714
**GUERRINI, A.** 9 - 10 .......... 07746 428431
**HADDOCK, M.** 9 - 7 .......... 077737 13794
**HALL, L.** 9 - 12 .......... 07972 136644
**HALL, P. G.** 11 - 7 .......... 01892 553160
**HAMILTON, T.** 9 - 3 .......... Mr J. B. Jeffrey
**HAMMOND, C.** 9 - 0 .......... 07508492020
**HAMPSON, B.** 9 - 0 .......... 07557056551
**HAMPTON, M. L.** 10 - 7 .......... 01722 334797
**HANNAFORD, D.** 8 - 7 .......... 07837 118919
**HANSON, S. P.** 9 - 12 .......... 07817 275107
**HARBOUR, E.** 9 - 12 .......... 07814 646 230
**HARDING, J.** 9 - 6 .......... 07858 783909
**HARDY, P.** 9 - 2 .......... 07949198410
**HARPER, H.** 9 - 3 .......... 07765 494447
**HART, C. V.** 9 - 10 .......... 07808511705
**HAWKER, C. R.** 8 - 7 .......... 07825 210749
**HAWKER, R.** 10 - 5 .......... Mr Dave Roberts
**HEAL, H.** 8 - 0 .......... 07890 260919
**HENDERSON, G. L.** 8 - 1 .......... 07864 036893
**HENDERSON, R. G.** 10 - 0 .......... 07789 332185
**HICKMAN, F. J.** 9 - 0 .......... 07972 186098
**HILL, J. P.** 11 - 7 .......... 07584 373313
**HILL, R. L.** 9 - 0 .......... 0755753940
**HOGG, R. C.** 10 - 0 .......... 07548 934272
**HOGG, W. S.** 9 - 12 .......... 07876 778372
**HOLLAND, P. A.** 9 - 10 .......... 07775892315
**HOLMES, D. T. R.** 12 - 0 .......... 01912847093
**HOOPER, R.** 9 - 12 .......... 0784957211
**HORNE, R. J.** 9 - 5 .......... 07808 898709
**HOULIHAN, S. M.** 9 - 7 .......... 07714820838
**HUGHES, J.** 9 - 7 .......... 07884 432672
**HUGHES, J.** 9 - 7 .......... Mrs Joanna Hughes
**HUMPHRIES, T. M.** 10 - 0 .......... 07787408321
**HUNT, H.** 8 - 0 .......... 07585 895632
**JACK, E. L.** 8 - 10 .......... 07800 908951
**JAMES, A. M.** 9 - 7 .......... 07932 479035
**JAY, B.** 10 - 0 .......... 07581 116245
**JEAVONS, J.** 9 - 5 .......... 07972 871876
**JEFFREY, P.** 9 - 0 .......... 07591 478991
**JENKINS, L. L.** 9 - 0 .......... 07557041595
**JOHNSON, M.** 10 - 10 .......... 07788 138634
**JOHNSON, M. S.** 9 - 3 .......... 07816609314
**JONES, A.** 9 - 3 .......... 07950 456397
**JONES, E. J.** 9 - 2 .......... 07775 846925
**JONES, L. J.** 10 - 0 .......... 07973 689040
**JORDAN, J.** 11 - 0 .......... 07725 913220
**KEIGHLEY, A. M.** 9 - 0 .......... 07961 723010
**KELK, S. F.** 9 - 7 .......... 07554 173519
**KEMP, D. J.** 11 - 7 .......... 07771 857 493
**KENDRICK, M. J. P.** 9 - 7 .......... Mr C. D. Broad
**KIELY, J.** 10 - 2 .......... 07715621602
**KILGARRIFF, L.** 9 - 7 .......... Mr A. D. Lewis
**KING, A. M.** 9 - 0 .......... 07710 406834
**KING, J.** 9 - 9 .......... 07929 831484
**KING, M.** 8 - 7 .......... 07815 793736
**KITCHMAN, W.** 10 - 7 .......... 07454 264727
**KLUG, S.** 10 - 0 .......... 07787 820577
**KNOX, J. S.** 10 - 7 .......... 07792 196146
**LAUNCHBURY, J.** 10 - 10 .......... 07920 118627
**LEGG, M. D.** 9 - 7 .......... Mr Dave Roberts
**LEVEY, D.** 9 - 13 .......... 078100 16073
**LEWIS, H. M.** 9 - 2 .......... 07899 649644
**LEYSHON, R.** 8 - 10 .......... 07977545239
**LINDSAY, R. W.** 10 - 0 .......... 07709 366404
**LOCKING, K. P.** 9 - 0 .......... 07835 360125
**LYONS, K.** 9 - 10 .......... Mr L. R. James
**LYTTLE, J.** 10 - 8 .......... 07774060675
**MABON, K.** 8 - 7 .......... 07565 331808
**MAHOT, J. H. M.** 10 - 10 .......... 07779 797079
**MANN, P. R.** 11 - 7 .......... 07929 535608
**MANSELL, D.** 11 - 0 .......... 07912974653
**MARGARSON, K. L.** 9 - 0 .......... Mr Paul Brierley
**MARSHALL, C.** 9 - 6 .......... 07516 296716
**MARTIN, C. J.** 9 - 12 .......... Mr Ian Wood
**MARTIN, J. I.** 10 - 3 .......... 07815698359
**MASON, J. L.** 8 - 12 .......... Mr N. Hannity
**MASON, P. W.** 11 - 2 .......... 07921 707292
**MATHIAS, J. F.** 11 - 3 .......... 01437 731308
**MAXWELL, D.** 11 - 7 .......... 0207 529 2323
**MCCORMICK, A. K.** 8 - 0 .......... Mr A. D. Lewis
**MCDONALD, R. M.** 9 - 5 .......... 07713 113393
**MCGREGOR, A. L.** 9 - 7 .......... 0780 3525449
**MCKEOWN, T. L.** 9 - 7 .......... 07975536617
**MCLERNON, J.** 9 - 0 .......... 07875 532791
**MEEK, N.** 9 - 2 .......... 0787 650 5442
**MICHAEL, A. H. L.** 11 - 0 .......... 01980 842537
**MILLER, C.** 10 - 0 .......... 07817 455592
**MILLER, H. G.** 9 - 13 .......... 07825 750836
**MILLS, A.** 8 - 10 .......... Mr L. R. James
**MOORCROFT, B.** 10 - 0 .......... 07971 806968
**MOORE, H. J.** 9 - 0 .......... 07736 149 669
**MORRIS, J.** 9 - 11 .......... 07825 599426
**MORSHEAD, H.** 9 - 10 .......... 07983 855286
**MULLINEAUX, M.** 8 - 7 .......... 01829 261440
**MURPHY, C.** 10 - 5 ..........
**MURPHY, M. J. J.** 9 - 7 .......... 07956 040477
**MURTAGH, L. A.** 8 - 7 .......... Mr R. A. Hale
**MUSPRATT, L.** 10 - 0 .......... 07585 772198
**NEWMAN, J.** 9 - 7 .......... Mr S. Stronge
**NICHOLLS, M.** 8 - 5 .......... Mr C. D. Broad
**NIMMO, F.** 8 - 6 .......... 07786 985034
**NIXON, J.** 10 - 2 .......... 07456600103
**NOONAN, D. G.** 9 - 9 .......... Mr L. R. James
**NUGENT, H. F.** 9 - 7 .......... 07868 146696
**O'BRIEN, T. M.** 10 - 2 .......... 01386 584209
**O'MAHONY, C. M.** 10 - 1 .......... 07770182102
**O'NEILL, J. J.** 10 - 0 .......... 07557038016
**O'REILLY, R.** 10 - 2 .......... 07934778414
**O'SULLIVAN, J. P.** 9 - 4 .......... 07966438987
**ORPWOOD, N.** 10 - 12 .......... 07831 836 626
**ORR, C. J.** 9 - 4 .......... 07477 093106
**PAINTING, S. W.** 10 - 0 .......... 07919 454844
**PARIS-CROFTS, B.** 9 - 4 .......... 07557475301
**PARKER, N. L.** 9 - 5 .......... 07877 151521
**PATRICK, R. P.** 9 - 5 .......... Mr L. R. James
**PEACOCK, S.** 9 - 2 .......... 07775 791153
**PEARCE, J.** 9 - 5 .......... 07538 110484
**PENFORD, F.** 9 - 10 .......... 07927 371882

**PETTIS, W.** 9 - 7 .......... 07908 572141
**PIMLOTT, O.** 10 - 0 .......... 07969216409
**POOLES, R. L.** 10 - 7 .......... 07766 244716
**PRICHARD, C.** 9 - 7 .......... 07870291498
**RANDALL, K. A.** 8 - 7 .......... 07951 952650
**REDDEN, T.** 8 - 13 .......... 07946155966
**REDDINGTON, J. J.** 11 - 8 .......... 07766767464
**REED, W. H. R.** 9 - 0 .......... Mr Paul Brierley
**REYNOLDS, E.** 9 - 2 .......... 07816 531845
**RICHARDS, J. R.** 9 - 0 .......... Mr G. J. Thomson
**RIDLEY, J. M.** 10 - 7 .......... 0755 787 9646
**ROBERTS, ANNABEL** 9 - 0 .......... 07709 430667
**ROBERTS, M.** 9 - 9 .......... 01305 782 218
**ROBINSON, I. P. B.** 9 - 2 .......... 07581 361986
**ROBINSON, M.** 10 - 0 .......... 077155 63038
**ROBINSON, S. C.** 12 - 0 .......... 01424 204190
**ROWNTREE, K.** 10 - 0 .......... 07714474640
**RUSSELL, J. J.** 11 - 4 .......... 07710482300
**RUSSELL, W.** 10 - 2 .......... 01273 274 733
**SANDERS, L.** 9 - 7 .......... 07791244494
**SANGSTER, O. R. J.** 9 - 10 .......... 07787 745046
**SANSOM, D.** 9 - 7 .......... 07821520829
**SCOTT, L.** 10 - 0 .......... 07443597049
**SHEPPARD, S.** 9 - 4 .......... 07712166115
**SIBBICK, E.** 9 - 7 .......... 07957 241945
**SKELLY, D.** 11 - 0 ..........
**SKINNER, R. C.** 11 - 7 .......... 01392 493 096
**SMITH, E. J.** 9 - 7 .......... 07790 507410
**SMITH, G. R.** 10 - 4 .......... 07748064384
**SMITH, J.** 9 - 7 .......... 07562 137956
**SMITH, R.** 8 - 12 .......... 07716 919975
**SNOWDEN, J. E.** 9 - 12 .......... 01488 72800
**SOLE, J. D.** 10 - 1 .......... 07968 947091
**SPEKE, T.** 10 - 3 .......... 07870 813256
**SPENCER, R. G. R.** 10 - 0 .......... 07976 958440
**SQUIRE, T. D.** 10 - 0 .......... 07990 964850
**STIRLING, A. E.** 10 - 0 .......... Mr Dave Roberts
**STOCK, H.** 9 - 7 .......... Mr R. A. Hale
**SUTHERLAND, T.** 9 - 10 .......... 07920 090156
**SUTTON, D.** 9 - 10 .......... 07850 106068
**SWAFFIELD, C.** 9 - 2 .......... 077950 36047
**SWAN, G.** 9 - 7 .......... 07966 801736
**TAYLOR, R. M.** 9 - 4 .......... 07973 774660
**TEAL, H.** 10 - 0 .......... 07949240199
**TEAL, J.** 10 - 9 .......... 07984 649070
**TETT, F.** 9 - 0 .......... 077863 14587
**THOMAS, P. J.** 9 - 7 .......... 01789 298346
**TICKLE, L.** 9 - 12 .......... 07769 183447
**TIMBY, R.** 9 - 0 .......... 07792 118563
**TODD, E. L.** 9 - 3 .......... Mr Paul Brierley
**TREACY, G.** 10 - 7 .......... 07901199386
**TURNER, D. I.** 9 - 0 .......... 07768 094 908
**TURNER, L. M.** 10 - 0 .......... 07984 531836
**TURNER, R.** 8 - 13 .......... 07943564194
**WADE, V. L.** 9 - 8 .......... 07772 925721
**WAILES, J.** 9 - 0 .......... 07712 416170
**WALEY-COHEN, S. B.** 10 - 0 .......... 07887848425
**WALKER, K.** 9 - 4 .......... 07875 738696
**WALKER, S. A.** 9 - 7 .......... Mr S. T. Dodds
**WALL, M.** 8 - 10 .......... Mr L. O. Gedge-Gibson
**WALL, M. J.** 10 - 7 .......... 07990 995 053
**WALLACE, A.** 9 - 0 .......... 07867 923 642
**WALLACE, H. A. R.** 11 - 0 .......... 07974 360 462
**WALTERS, G.** 8 - 7 .......... 07794652944
**WALTON, C. M.** 9 - 2 .......... Mr J. B. Jeffrey
**WALTON, J.** 9 - 0 .......... 07955 260 235
**WALTON, M.** 10 - 10 .......... 07717 024223
**WATLING, C.** 8 - 5 .......... 07826842985
**WATSON, H.** 9 - 0 .......... 07974 442 856
**WAUGH, A.** 8 - 5 .......... 07761040963
**WEDMORE, O. Z. F.** 9 - 10 .......... 07806 517766
**WELCH, H. J.** 9 - 2 .......... 07968 839899
**WEST, L. L.** 9 - 4 .......... 07894 733035
**WESTON, T. H.** 10 - 7 .......... 07752 313 698
**WHEELER, G. F.** 11 - 3 .......... 07778 157 245
**WHEELER, T. W.** 9 - 7 .......... 07432 095447
**WILD, O. C.** 9 - 1 .......... 07780 705385
**WILKINSON, D. S.** 8 - 0 .......... 01969 640223
**WILLEY, J. P.** 9 - 4 .......... Mr A. D. Lewis
**WILLIAMS, C.** 10 - 5 .......... 07849 833672
**WILLIAMS, J. C.** 9 - 2 .......... 07841 576 651
**WILLIAMS, J. P.** 8 - 9 .......... 07554 886584
**WILLIAMS, L.** 8 - 8 .......... 07871 448437
**WILLIAMS, S. R.** 10 - 12 .......... 07590 208675
**WILLMOTT, A.** 8 - 11 .......... 07530 278100
**WILSON, A.** 10 - 0 .......... 07816 669962
**WILSON, L. J.** 8 - 10 .......... 07411 902747
**WILSON, R.** 9 - 12 .......... 07943 237205
**WILSON, R. E.** 9 - 0 .......... 07770732007
**WINKS, R. P.** 9 - 7 .......... 01226 340011
**WOOD, B.** 10 - 0 .......... 07873 792060
**WOOD, K.** 9 - 10 .......... 07429 078066
**WOODS, C. M. E.** 10 - 7 .......... 07775 517 129
**WOODWARD, M. J.** 10 - 4 .......... 07790647315
**WORSLEY, T.** 9 - 12 .......... 07825 067820
**WRIGHT, A.** 10 - 10 .......... 07515373070
**WRIGHT, J.** 10 - 0 .......... 07787 365500
**YORK, P.** 10 - 7 .......... 07774 962168
**YOUNG, K.** 8 - 7 .......... 07784 942377

Are your contact details missing or incorrect?
If so please update us by email:
richard.lowther@racingpost.co.uk